Global Development Finance

1997

Global Development Finance

1997

VOLUME 2

COUNTRY TABLES

The World Bank
Washington, D.C.

Manufactured in the United States of America
First printing March 1997

Global Development Finance was formerly published under the title *World Debt Tables.*

This publication has been compiled by the staff of the Financial Data (FIN) Team, part of the Development Data Group and the International Finance Division of the World Bank's International Economics Department. The World Bank does not accept responsibility for the accuracy or completeness of this publication. Any judgments expressed are those of World Bank staff or consultants and do not necessarily reflect the views of the Board of Executive Directors or the governments they represent.

ISSN 1020-5454

ISBN 0-8213-3788-2 (vol. 1)
ISBN 0-8213-3789-0 (two-volume set)

Contents

Preface

Global Development Finance was formerly published as the *World Debt Tables*. The new name reflects the report's expanded scope and greater coverage of private financial flows.

Global Development Finance consists of two volumes. Volume 1 contains analysis and commentary on recent developments in international finance for developing countries, together with summary statistical tables for selected regional and analytical groups comprising 150 developing countries.

Volume 2 contains statistical tables on the external debt of the 136 countries that report public and publicly guaranteed debt under the Debtor Reporting System (DRS). New to Volume 2 are tables of selected debt and resource flow statistics for individual reporting countries as well as summary tables for regional and income groups. Reported for the first time are the IBRD and IMF obligations and short-term debt of Bosnia and Herzegovina. The Republic of Korea is now classified as a high-income country.

For the convenience of readers, charts on pages xx to xxii summarize graphically the relation between the debt stock and its components; the computation of net flows, aggregate net resource flows, and aggregate net transfers; and the relation between net resource flows and the balance of payments. Exact definitions of these and other terms used in *Global Development Finance* are found in the Sources and Definitions section.

The economic aggregates presented in the tables are prepared for the convenience of users. Although debt indicators can give useful information about developments in debt-servicing capacity, conclusions drawn from them will not be valid unless accompanied by careful economic evaluation. The macroeconomic information provided is from standard sources, but many of them are subject to considerable margins of error, and the usual care must be taken in interpreting the indicators. This is particularly true for the most recent year or two, when figures are preliminary and subject to revision.

This volume was prepared by the Financial Data Team of the Development Data Group, led by Punam Chuhan and comprising Alma Conty, Mahyar Eshragh-Tabary, Nevin Fahmy, Shelley Fu, Weili Gu, Young Kim, Ibrahim Levent, Mohey Ragab, and Gloria Reyes. The team was assisted by John Herring, Ye Hong, Tony Nadora, Perlita Peret, Endang Setyowati, and Graciela Soria. Robin Lynch and Jong-goo Park provided the macroeconomic data. Many others inside the World Bank provided helpful input, especially Paul Armington, Sarwar Lateef, the staff of the International Finance Division, and the country economists who reviewed the data. Meta de Coquereaumont was the principal editor. The volume was laid out by Mark Bock and Glenn McGrath. The work was carried out under the management of Shaida Badiee and under the general direction of Masood Ahmed.

Acronyms and abbreviations

BIS	Bank for International Settlements
CRS	Creditor Reporting System (of the OECD)
DAC	Development Assistance Committee (of the OECD)
DRS	Debtor Reporting System (of the World Bank)
GNP	Gross national product
IBRD	International Bank for Reconstruction and Development/World Bank
IDA	International Development Association (of the World Bank)
IECDD	Development Data Group of the International Economics Department (of the World Bank)
IMF	International Monetary Fund
LIBOR	London interbank offer rate
MYRA	Multiyear rescheduling agreement
OECD	Organization for Economic Cooperation and Development
OPEC	Organization of Petroleum Exporting Countries
RXD	Revised external debt
SDR	Special drawing right (of the IMF)

Methodology

The World Bank is the sole repository for statistics on the external debt of developing countries on a loan-by-loan basis. The Debtor Reporting System (DRS), set up in 1951 to monitor these statistics, is maintained by the staff of the Financial Data Team (FIN), part of the Development Data Group of the International Economics Department (IECDD).

Methodology for aggregating data

Using the DRS data, in combination with information obtained from creditors through the debt data collection systems of other agencies such as the Bank for International Settlements (BIS) and the Organization for Economic Cooperation and Development (OECD), the staff of the IECDD estimate the total external indebtedness of developing countries. The data are also supplemented by estimates made by country economists of the World Bank and desk officers of the International Monetary Fund (IMF).

Converting to a common currency

Since debt data are normally reported to the World Bank in the currency of repayment, they have to be converted into a common currency (usually U.S. dollars) to produce summary tables. Stock figures (such as the amount of debt outstanding) are converted using end-period exchange rates, as published in the IMF's *International Financial Statistics* (line ae). Flow figures are converted at annual average exchange rates (line rf). Projected debt service is converted using end-period exchange rates. Debt repayable in multiple currencies, goods, or services and debt with a provision for maintenance of value of the currency of repayment are shown at book value. Because flow data are converted at annual average exchange rates and stock data at year-end exchange rates, year-to-year changes in debt outstanding and disbursed are sometimes not equal to net flows (disbursements less principal repayments); similarly, changes in debt outstanding including undisbursed debt differ from commitments less repayments. Discrepancies are particularly significant when exchange rates have moved sharply during the year; cancellations and reschedulings of other liabilities into long-term public debt also contribute to the differences.

Public and publicly guaranteed debt

All data related to public and publicly guaranteed debt are from debtors except for lending by some multilateral agencies, in which case data are taken from the creditors' records. These creditors include the African Development Bank, the Asian Development Bank, the Central Bank for Economic Integration, the IMF, the Inter-American Development Bank, and the International Bank for Reconstruction and Development (IBRD) and International Development Association (IDA). (The IBRD and IDA are components of the World Bank.)

Starting with the 1988–89 edition of *World Debt Tables* (as this book was previously titled), all data pertaining to World Bank loans from 1985 onward are recorded at their current market value. Starting with the 1991–92 edition, all data pertaining to Asian Development Bank loans from 1989 onward are recorded at their current market value as well.

Private nonguaranteed debt

The DRS was expanded in 1970 to incorporate private nonguaranteed long-term debt. Reports, submitted annually, contain aggregate data for disbursed and outstanding debt, disbursements, principal repayments, interest payments, principal and interest rescheduled for the reporting year, and projected payments of principal and interest. Data are usually presented in dollars and currency conversion is not necessary. A few reporting countries choose to provide data on their private nonguaranteed debt in the loan-by-loan format used for reporting public and publicly guaranteed debt. In those cases the currency conversion and projection methodology just described is used.

Although the reporting countries fully recognize the importance of collecting data on private nonguaranteed debt when it constitutes a significant portion of total external debt, detailed data are available only in countries that have registration requirements covering private debt, most commonly in connection with exchange controls. Where formal registration of foreign borrowing is not mandatory, compilers must rely on balance of payments data and financial surveys.

Thirty-one countries report their private nonguaranteed debt to the DRS. Estimates are made for twenty-nine others that do not report but for which this type of debt is known to be significant.

For private nonguaranteed debt that is not reported, the standard estimation approach starts from a calculation of the stock of debt outstanding, using data available from creditors. Figures on guaranteed export credits, obtained from the OECD's Creditor Reporting System (CRS), are supplemented by loan-by-loan information on official lending to private borrowers and by information on noninsured commercial bank lending to the private sector.

Disbursements and debt service payments for private nonguaranteed debt are more difficult to estimate. Amortization is estimated by making an assumption regarding the proportion of debt repaid each year and then applying these ratios to generate a first approximation of annual principal repayments. Disbursements are then estimated as a residual between net flows (equal to the change in the stock of debt) and estimated amortization. Interest payments are estimated by applying an assumed average interest rate to the stock of debt outstanding.

Data on the balance of payments flows provide useful guidelines in the process of building a time series because private nonguaranteed debt can be treated as a residual between total net long-term borrowing and net long-term borrowing recorded in the DRS for public and publicly guaranteed debt.

Short-term debt

The World Bank regards the individual reporting country as the authoritative source of information on its own external liabilities. But for short-term debt, defined as debt with an original maturity of one year or less, accurate information is not widely available from debtors. By its nature, short-term debt is difficult to monitor; loan-by-loan registration is normally impractical, and most reporting arrangements involve periodic returns to a country's central bank from its banking sector. Since 1982 the quality of such reporting has improved, but only a few developing countries have figures available for short-term debt.

Where information from debtors is not available, data from creditors can indicate the magnitude of a country's short-term debt. The most important source is the BIS's semiannual series showing the maturity distribution of commercial banks' claims on developing countries. Those data are reported residually. However, an estimate of short-term liabilities by original maturity can be calculated by deducting from claims due in one year those that had a maturity of between one and two years twelve months earlier.

There are several problems with this method. Valuation adjustments caused by exchange rate movements will affect the calculations, as will prepayment and refinancing of long-term maturities falling due. Moreover, not all countries' commercial banks report in a way that allows the full maturity distribution to be determined, and the BIS data include liabilities only to banks within the reporting area. Nevertheless, combining these estimates with data on officially guaranteed short-term suppliers' credits compiled by the OECD gives what may be thought of as a lower-bound estimate of a country's short-term debt. Even on this basis, however, the results need to be interpreted with caution. Where short-term debt has been rescheduled, the effect of lags in reporting and differences in the treatment of the rescheduled debt by debtors and creditors may result in double counting if short-term debt derived from creditor sources is added to long-term debt reported by the country to obtain total external liabilities.

Some of the short-term debt estimates published are drawn from debtor and creditor sources, but most are from creditor sources. Only for a few countries can the data be regarded as authoritative, but they offer a guide to the size of a country's short-term (and, hence, its total) external debt. The quality of these data is likely to improve.

Use of IMF credit

Data related to the operations of the IMF come from the IMF Treasurer's Department and are converted from special drawing rights (SDRs) into dollars using end-of-period exchange rates for stocks and average over the period exchange rates for converting flows, as described earlier. IMF trust fund loans and operations under the structural adjustment and enhanced structural adjustment facilities are presented together with all of the Fund's special facilities (the buffer stock, compensatory financing, extended fund, and oil facilities).

Treatment of arrears

The DRS collects information on arrears in both principal and interest. Principal in arrears is included and identified in the amount of long-term debt outstanding. Interest in arrears of long-term debt and the use of IMF credit is included and identified in the amount of short-term debt outstanding. If and when interest in arrears is capitalized under a debt reorganization agreement, the amount of interest capitalized will be added to the amount of long-term debt outstanding and the corresponding deduction made from the amount of short-term debt outstanding.

Treatment of debt restructurings

The DRS attempts to capture accurately the effects of the different kinds of restructurings on both debt stocks and debt flows, consistent with the circumstances under which the restructuring takes place. Whether a flow has taken place is sometimes difficult to determine.

In compiling and presenting the debt data, a distinction is made between cash flows and imputed flows. Based on this criterion, rescheduled service payments and the shift in liabilities from one financial instrument to another as a result of rescheduling are considered to be imputed flows.

The imputed flows are recorded separately in the Revised External Debt (RXD) system, but these debt restructuring transactions are not evident in the main body of the debt data—only the resulting effect of these transactions is reflected.

Changes in creditor and debtor status that can result from debt restructuring are also reflected. For example, when insured commercial credits are rescheduled, the creditor classification shifts from private sources to official sources (bilateral). This reflects the assumption of the assets by the official credit insurance agencies of the creditor countries. The debts to the original creditors are reduced by the amounts rescheduled, and a new obligation to the official creditor agencies is created. This shift also applies to private nonguaranteed debt that is reduced by the amounts rescheduled, which in turn are included in the public and publicly guaranteed debt owed to official creditors. On the debtor side, when a government accepts responsibility for the payment of rescheduled debt previously owed by private enterprises, the DRS registers a change in debtor categories in the DRS. Similarly, when short-term debt is included in a restructuring agreement, the rescheduled amount is shifted from short-term to long-term debt.

Methodology for projecting data

An important feature of the RXD system of the DRS is its ability to project future disbursements of unutilized commitments and future debt service payments.

Undisbursed debt

Projections of disbursements help underpin future capital requirements in the implementation of externally financed projects. In addition, they help determine the interest portion of projected debt service. Future interest payments are based on projected debt outstanding that is itself determined by projected disbursements and repayments. The underlying assumptions of these projections are that loan commitments will be fully utilized and that the debtor country will repay all sums due. Future disbursements and debt service refer only to existing debt and do not reflect any assumptions on future borrowing.

Disbursement projections use two methods:

- *Specific schedules.* Debtor countries are requested to submit a calendar of future disbursements, if available, at the time individual loans are first reported. Country authorities are in a better position to provide estimated disbursement schedules when there is a solid public sector investment program in place.
- *Standard schedules.* In the absence of specific schedules, the RXD system projects disbursements by applying a set of profiles to the last actual undisbursed balance of individual loans. The profiles are derived under the assumption that specific sources of funds have some common characteristics that cause them to disburse, in the aggregate, in some observable pattern. Accordingly, some thirty profiles have been derived that roughly correspond to creditor type. Profiles exist for concessional and nonconcessional loans from official creditors. For bilateral lending, profiles have been developed for the Development Assistance Committee, the Organization of Petroleum-Exporting Countries (OPEC), and other creditor groupings. For multilateral lending, specific profiles are available for major international organizations. An estimating equation for each profile is derived by applying regression analysis techniques to a body of data that contains actual disbursement information for more than 100,000 loans. Although these standard profiles are reestimated from time to time, under the best scenario they can only approximate the disbursement pattern of any single loan.

Future debt service payments

Most projections of future debt service payments generated by the RXD system are based on the repayment terms of the loans. Principal repayments (amortization) are based on the amount of loan commitments, and the amortization profile of most loans follows a set pattern. Using the first and final payment dates and the frequency of the payments, the system calculates the stream of principal payments due. If future payments are irregular, the RXD system requires a schedule.

Projected future interest payments are calculated similarly. Interest is based on the amount of debt disbursed and outstanding at the beginning of the period. Again, using the first and final interest payment dates and the frequency of payments, the system calculates the stream of interest payments due. If interest payments are irregular, the RXD system requires a schedule.

The published figures for projected debt service obligations are converted into U.S. dollars using the end-December 1995 exchange rates. Likewise the projection routine for variable interest rate debt, such as commercial bank debt based on the London interbank offer rate (LIBOR), assumes that the rate prevailing at the end of December 1995 will be effective throughout.

Sources and definitions

This edition of *Global Development Finance* presents reported or estimated data on the total external debt of all low- and middle-income countries.

Format

Volume 2 has been expanded to include summary tables along with the standard country tables for the 136 individual countries that report to the World Bank's Debtor Reporting System (DRS). Summary tables present selected debt and resource flow statistics for the individual reporting countries and external debt data for regional and income groups. Regional and income group totals in the summary tables include estimates for the fourteen low- and middle-income countries that do not report to the DRS. Because these estimates are not shown separately in the tables, most group totals are larger than the sum of the DRS figures shown. The format of the regional and income group tables draws on the individual country table format and includes graphic presentations.

For the 136 individual countries that report to the World Bank's DRS, tables are presented in a four-page layout containing ten sections.

SECTION 1 summarizes the external debt of the country.

Total debt stocks (EDT) consist of public and publicly guaranteed long-term debt, private nonguaranteed long-term debt (whether reported or estimated by the staff of the World Bank), the use of IMF credit, and estimated short-term debt. Interest in arrears on long-term debt and the use of IMF credit are added to the short-term debt estimates and shown as separate lines. Arrears of principal and of interest have been disaggregated to show the arrears owed to official creditors and those owed to private creditors. Export credits and principal in arrears on long-term debt are shown as memorandum items.

Total debt flows are consolidated data on disbursements, principal repayments, and interest payments for total long-term debt and transactions with the IMF.

Net flows on debt are disbursements on long-term debt and IMF purchases minus principal repayments on long-term debt and IMF repurchases up to 1984. Beginning in 1985 this line includes the change in stock of short-term debt (including interest arrears for long-term debt). Thus if the change in stock is positive, a disbursement is assumed to have taken place; if negative, a repayment is assumed to have taken place.

Total debt service (TDS) shows the debt service payments on total long-term debt (public and publicly guaranteed and private nonguaranteed), use of IMF credit, and interest on short-term debt.

SECTION 2 provides data series for aggregate net resource flows and net transfers (long term).

Net resource flows (long term) are the sum of net resource flows on long-term debt (excluding IMF) plus net foreign direct investment, portfolio equity flows, and official grants (excluding technical cooperation). Grants for technical cooperation are shown as a memorandum item.

Net transfers (long term) are equal to net long-term resource flows minus interest payments on long-term loans and foreign direct investment profits.

SECTION 3 provides data series for major economic aggregates. The gross national product (GNP) series uses yearly average exchange rates in converting GNP from local currency into U.S. dollars. The economic aggregates are prepared for the convenience of users; the usual caution should be exercised in using them for economic analysis.

SECTION 4 provides debt indicators: ratios of debt and debt service to some of the economic aggregates.

SECTION 5 provides detailed information on stocks and flows of long-term debt and its various components. Data on bonds issued by private entities without public guarantee, compiled for major borrowers, are included in private nonguaranteed debt. IBRD loans and IDA credits are shown as memorandum items.

SECTION 6 provides information on the currency composition of long-term debt. The six major currencies in which the external debt of low- and middle-income countries is contracted are separately identified, as is debt denominated in special drawing rights and debt repayable in multiple currencies.

SECTION 7 provides information on restructurings of long-term debt starting in 1985. It shows both the stock and flows rescheduled each year. In addition, the amount of debt forgiven (interest forgiven is shown as a memorandum item) and the amount of debt stock reduction (including debt buyback) are also shown separately. (See the Methodology section for a detailed explanation of restructuring data.)

SECTION 8 reconciles the stock and flow data on total external debt for each year, beginning with 1989. This section is designed to illustrate the changes in stock that have taken place due to five factors: the net flow on debt, the net change in interest arrears, the capitalization of interest, the reduction in debt resulting from debt forgiveness or other debt reduction mechanisms, and the cross-currency valuation effects. The residual difference—the change in stock not explained by any of the factors identified above—is also presented. The residual is calculated as the sum of identified accounts minus the change in stock. Where the residual is large it can, in some cases, serve as an illustration of the inconsistencies in the reported data. More often, however, it can be explained by specific borrowing phenomena in individual countries. These are explained in the Country Notes section.

SECTION 9 provides information on the average terms of new commitments on public and publicly guaranteed debt and information on the level of commitments from official and private sources.

SECTION 10 provides anticipated disbursements and contractual obligations on long-term debt contracted up to December 1995.

Sources

The principal sources of information for the tables in these two volumes are reports to the World Bank through the DRS from member countries that have received either IBRD loans or IDA credits. Additional information has been drawn from the files of the World Bank and the IMF.

Reporting countries submit detailed (loan-by-loan) reports through the DRS on the annual status, transactions, and terms of the long-term external debt of public agencies and that of private ones guaranteed by a public agency in the debtor country. This information forms the basis for the tables in these volumes.

Aggregate data on private debt without public guarantee are compiled and published as reliable reported and estimated information becomes available. This edition includes data on private nonguaranteed debt reported by thirty-one developing countries and complete or partial estimates for an additional twenty-nine countries.

The short-term debt data are as reported by the debtor countries or are estimates derived from creditor sources. The principal creditor sources are the semiannual series of commercial banks' claims on developing countries, published by the Bank for International Settlements (BIS), and data on officially guaranteed suppliers' credits compiled by the Organization for Economic Cooperation and Development (OECD). For some countries, estimates were prepared by pooling creditor and debtor information.

Interest in arrears on long-term debt and the use of IMF credit are added to the short-term debt estimates and shown as separate lines in section 1. Arrears of interest and of principal owed to official and to private creditors are identified separately.

Export credits are shown as a memorandum item in section 1. They include official export credits, and suppliers' credits and bank credits officially guaranteed or insured by an export credit agency. Both long-term and short-term export credits are included. The source for this information is the Creditor Reporting System (CRS) of the OECD.

Data on long-term debt reported by member countries are checked against, and supplemented by, data from several other sources. Among these are the statements and reports of several regional development banks and government lending agencies, as well as the reports received by the World Bank under the CRS from the members of the Development Assistance Committee (DAC) of the OECD.

Every effort has been made to ensure the accuracy and completeness of the debt statistics. Nevertheless, quality and coverage vary among debtors and may also vary for the same debtor from year to year. Coverage has been improved through the efforts of the reporting agencies and the work of World Bank missions, which visit member countries to gather data and to provide technical assistance on debt issues.

Definitions

For all regional, income, and individual country tables, data definitions are presented below or footnoted where appropriate. Data definitions for other summary tables are, likewise, consistent with those below.

Summary debt data

TOTAL DEBT STOCKS are defined as the sum of public and publicly guaranteed long-term debt, private nonguaranteed long-term debt, the use of IMF credit, and short-term debt. The relation between total debt stock and its components is illustrated on page xx.

Long-term external debt is defined as debt that has an original or extended maturity of more than one year and that is owed to nonresidents and repayable in foreign currency, goods, or services. Long-term debt has three components:

- *Public debt,* which is an external obligation of a public debtor, including the national government, a political subdivision (or an agency of either), and autonomous public bodies
- *Publicly guaranteed debt,* which is an external obligation of a private debtor that is guaranteed for repayment by a public entity
- *Private nonguaranteed external debt,* which is an external obligation of a private debtor that is not guaranteed for repayment by a public entity.

In the tables, public and publicly guaranteed long-term debt are aggregated.

Short-term external debt is defined as debt that has an original maturity of one year or less. Available data permit no distinction between public and private nonguaranteed short-term debt.

Interest in arrears on long-term debt is defined as interest payment due but not paid, on a cumulative basis.

Principal in arrears on long-term debt is defined as principal repayment due but not paid, on a cumulative basis.

The memorandum item *export credits* includes official export credits, suppliers' credits, and bank credits officially guaranteed or insured by an export credit agency. Both long-term and short-term credits are included here.

Use of IMF credit denotes repurchase obligations to the IMF with respect to all uses of IMF resources (excluding those resulting from drawings in the reserve tranche) shown for the end of the year specified. Use of IMF credit comprises purchases outstanding under the credit tranches, including enlarged access resources and all special facilities (the buffer stock, compensatory financing, extended fund, and oil facilities), trust fund loans, and operations under the structural adjustment and enhanced structural adjustment facilities. Data are from the Treasurer's Department of the IMF.

- *IMF purchases* are total drawings on the general resources account of the IMF during the year specified, excluding drawings in the reserve tranche.
- *IMF repurchases* are total repayments of outstanding drawings from the general resources account during the year specified, excluding repayments due in the reserve tranche.

To maintain comparability between data on transactions with the IMF and data on long-term debt, use of IMF credit outstanding at year end (stock) is converted to dollars at the SDR exchange rate in effect at the end of the year. Purchases and repurchases (flows) are converted at the average SDR exchange rate for the year in which transactions take place.

Net purchases will usually not reconcile changes in the use of IMF credit from year to year. Valuation effects from the use of different exchange rates frequently explain much of the difference, but not all. Other factors are increases in quotas (which expand a country's reserve tranche and can thereby lower the use of IMF credit as defined here), approved purchases of a country's currency by another member country drawing on the general resources account, and various administrative uses of a country's currency by the IMF.

Total debt flows include disbursements, principal repayments, net flows and transfers on debt, and interest payments.

Disbursements are drawings on loan commitments during the year specified.

Principal repayments are the amounts of principal (amortization) paid in foreign currency, goods, or services in the year specified.

Net flows on debts (or net lending or net disbursements) are disbursements minus principal repayments.

Interest payments are the amounts of interest paid in foreign currency, goods, or services in the year specified.

Net transfers on debt are net flows minus interest payments (or disbursements minus total debt service payments).

The concepts of net flows on debt, net transfers on debt, and aggregate net flows and net transfers are illustrated on pages xxi and xxii.

Total debt service paid (TDS) is debt service payments on total long-term debt (public and publicly guaranteed and private nonguaranteed), use of IMF credit, and interest on short-term debt.

Aggregate net resource flows and transfers

Net resource flows (long term) are the sum of net resource flows on long-term debt (excluding IMF) plus non-debt-creating flows.

Non-debt-creating flows are net foreign direct investment, portfolio equity flows, and official grants (excluding technical cooperation). Net foreign direct investment and portfolio equity flows are treated as private source flows. Grants for technical cooperation are shown as a memorandum item.

Foreign direct investment (FDI) is defined as investment that is made to acquire a lasting management interest (usually 10 percent of voting stock) in an enterprise operating in a country other than that of the investor (defined according to residency), the investor's purpose being an effective voice in the management of the enterprise. It is the sum of equity capital, reinvestment of earnings, other long-term capital, and short-term capital as shown in the balance of payments.

Portfolio equity flows are the sum of country funds, depository receipts (American or global), and direct purchases of shares by foreign investors.

Grants are defined as legally binding commitments that obligate a specific value of funds available for disbursement for which there is no repayment requirement.

The memo item *technical cooperation grants* includes free-standing technical cooperation grants, which are intended to finance the transfer of technical and managerial skills or of technology for the purpose of building up general national capacity without reference to any specific investment projects; and investment-related technical cooperation grants, which are provided to strengthen the capacity to execute specific investment projects.

Profit remittances on foreign direct investment are the sum of reinvested earnings on direct investment and other direct investment income and are part of net transfers.

Major economic aggregates

Five economic aggregates are provided for the reporting economies.

Gross national product (GNP) is the measure of the total domestic and foreign output claimed by residents of an economy, less the domestic output claimed by nonresidents. GNP does not include deductions for depreciation. Data on GNP are from the Macroeconomic Indicators Team of the Development Data Group of the World Bank's International Economics Department.

Exports of goods and services (XGS) are the total value of goods and services exported as well as income and worker remittances received.

Imports of goods and services (MGS) are the total value of goods and services imported and income paid.

International reserves (RES) are the sum of a country's monetary authority's holdings of special drawing rights (SDRs), its reserve position in the IMF, its holdings of foreign exchange, and its holdings of gold (valued at year-end London prices).

Current account balance is the sum of the credits less the debits arising from international transactions in goods, services, income, and current transfers. It represents the transactions that add to or subtract from an economy's stock of foreign financial items.

Data on exports and imports (on a balance of payments basis), international reserves, and current account balances are drawn mainly from the files of the IMF, complemented by World Bank staff estimates. Balance of payments data are presented according to the fifth edition of the IMF's *Balance of Payments Manual,* which made several adjustments to its presentation of trade statistics. Coverage of goods was expanded to include in imports the value of goods received for processing and repair (on a gross basis). Their subsequent re-export is recorded in exports (also on a gross basis). This approach will cause a country's imports and exports to increase without affecting the balance of goods. In addition, all capital transfers, which were included with current transfers in the fourth edition of the *Balance of Payments Manual,* are now shown in a separate capital (as opposed to financial) account, and so do not contribute to the current account balance.

Debt indicators

The macroeconomic aggregates and debt data provided in the tables are used to generate ratios that analysts use to assess the external situations of developing countries. Different analysts give different weights to these indicators, but no single indicator or set of indicators can substitute for a thorough analysis of the overall situation of an economy. The advantage of the indicators in *Global Development Finance* is that they are calculated from standardized data series that are compiled on a consistent basis by the World Bank and the IMF. The ratios offer various measures of the cost of, or capacity for, servicing debt in terms of the foreign exchange or output forgone. The following ratios are provided based on total external debt:

EDT/XGS is total external debt to exports of goods and services (including workers' remittances).

EDT/GNP is total external debt to gross national product.

TDS/XGS, also called the debt service ratio, is total debt service to exports of goods and services (including workers' remittances).

INT/XGS, also called the interest service ratio, is total interest payments to exports of goods and services (including workers' remittances).

INT/GNP is total interest payments to gross national product.

RES/EDT is international reserves to total external debt.

RES/MGS is international reserves to imports of goods and services.

Short-term/EDT is short-term debt to total external debt.

Concessional/EDT is concessional debt to total external debt.

Multilateral/EDT is multilateral debt to total external debt.

Long-term debt

Data on long-term debt include eight main elements:

DEBT OUTSTANDING AND DISBURSED is the total outstanding debt at year end.

DISBURSEMENTS are drawings on loan commitments by the borrower during the year.

PRINCIPAL REPAYMENTS are amounts paid by the borrower during the year.

NET FLOWS received by the borrower during the year are disbursements minus principal repayments.

INTEREST PAYMENTS are amounts paid by the borrower during the year.

NET TRANSFERS are net flows minus interest payments during the year; negative transfers show net transfers made by the borrower to the creditor during the year.

DEBT SERVICE (LTDS) is the sum of principal repayments and interest payments actually made.

UNDISBURSED DEBT is total debt undrawn at year end; data for private nonguaranteed debt are not available.

Data from individual reporters are aggregated by type of creditor. *Official creditors* includes multilateral and bilateral debt.

- *Loans from multilateral organizations* are loans and credits from the World Bank, regional development banks, and other multilateral and intergovernmental agencies. Excluded are loans from funds administered by an international organization on behalf of a single donor government; these are classified as loans from governments.
- *Bilateral loans* are loans from governments and their agencies (including central banks), loans from autonomous bodies, and direct loans from official export credit agencies.

Private creditors include bonds, commercial banks, and other private creditors. Commercial banks and other private creditors comprise bank and trade-related lending.

- *Bonds* include publicly issued or privately placed bonds.
- *Commercial banks* are loans from private banks and other private financial institutions.
- *Other private* includes credits from manufacturers, exporters, and other suppliers of goods, and bank credits covered by a guarantee of an export credit agency.

Four characteristics of a country's debt are given as memorandum items for long-term debt outstanding and disbursed (LDOD).

Concessional LDOD conveys information about the borrower's receipt of aid from official lenders at concessional terms as defined by the DAC, that is, loans with an original grant element of 25 percent or more.

Variable interest rate LDOD is long-term debt with interest rates that float with movements in a key market rate such as the London interbank offer rate (LIBOR) or the U.S. prime rate. This item conveys information about the borrower's exposure to changes in international interest rates.

Public sector LDOD and private sector LDOD convey information about the distribution of long-term debt by type of debtor (central government, state and local government, central bank; private bank, private debt).

Currency composition of long-term debt

The six major currencies in which the external debt of low- and middle-income countries is contracted are separately identified, as is debt denominated in special drawing rights and debt repayable in multiple currencies.

Debt restructurings

Debt restructurings include restructurings in the context of the Paris Club, commercial banks, debt-equity swaps, buybacks, and bond exchanges. Debt restructuring data capture the noncash or inferred flows associated with rescheduling and restructuring. These are presented to complement the cash-basis transactions recorded in the main body of the data.

Debt stock rescheduled is the amount of debt outstanding rescheduled in any given year.

Principal rescheduled is the amount of principal due or in arrears that was rescheduled in any given year.

Interest rescheduled is the amount of interest due or in arrears that was rescheduled in any given year.

Debt forgiven is the amount of principal due or in arrears that was written off or forgiven in any given year.

Interest forgiven is the amount of interest due or in arrears that was written off or forgiven in any given year.

Debt stock reduction is the amount that has been netted out of the stock of debt using debt conversion schemes such as buybacks and equity swaps or the discounted value of long-term bonds that were issued in exchange for outstanding debt.

Debt stock–flow reconciliation

Stock and flow data on total external debt are reconciled for each year, beginning with 1989. The data show the changes in stock that have taken place due to the net flow on debt, the net change in interest arrears, the capitalization of interest, the reduction in debt resulting from debt forgiveness or other debt reduction mechanisms, and the cross-currency valuation effects. The residual difference—the change in stock not explained by any of these factors—is also presented, calculated as the sum of identified accounts minus the change in stock.

Average terms of new commitments

The average terms of borrowing on public and publicly guaranteed debt are given for all new loans contracted during the year and separately for loans from official and private creditors. To obtain averages, the interest rates, maturities, and grace periods in each category have been weighted by the amounts of the loans. The grant equivalent of a loan is its commitment (present) value, less the discounted present value of its contractual debt service; conventionally, future service payments are discounted at 10 percent. The grant element of a loan is the grant equivalent expressed as a percentage of the amount committed. It is used as a measure of the overall cost of borrowing. Loans with an original grant element of 25 percent or more are defined as concessional. The average grant element has been weighted by the amounts of the loans.

Commitments cover the total amount of loans for which contracts were signed in the year specified; data for private nonguaranteed debt are not available.

Projections on existing pipeline

Projected *debt service* payments are estimates of payments due on existing debt outstanding, including undisbursed. They do not include service payments that may become due as a result of new loans contracted in subsequent years. Nor do they allow for effects on service payments of changes in repayment patterns owing to prepayment of loans or to rescheduling or refinancing, including repayment of outstanding arrears, that occurred after the last year of reported data.

Projected *disbursements* are estimates of drawings of unutilized balances. The projections do not take into account future borrowing by the debtor country. See Methodology section for a detailed explanation of the methods of projecting undisbursed balances.

Exchange rates

Data received by the World Bank from its members are expressed in the currencies in which the debts are repayable or in which the transactions took place. For aggregation, the Bank converts these amounts to U.S. dollars using the IMF par values or central rates, or the current market rates where appropriate. Service payments, commitments, and disbursements (flows) are converted to U.S. dollars at the average rate for the year. Debt outstanding and disbursed at the end of a given year (a stock) is converted at the rate in effect at the end of that year. Projected debt service, however, is converted to U.S. dollars at rates in effect at end-December 1995. Debt repayable in multiple currencies, goods, or services and debt with a provision for maintenance of value of the currency of repayment are shown at book value.

Adjustments

Year-to-year changes in debt outstanding and disbursed are sometimes not equal to net flows; similarly, changes in debt outstanding, including undisbursed, differ from commitments less repayments. The reasons for these differences are cancellations, adjustments caused by the use of different exchange rates, and the rescheduling of other liabilities into long-term public debt.

Symbols

The following symbols have been used throughout:
0.0 indicates that a datum exists, but is negligible, or is a true zero.
.. indicates that a datum is not available.
Dollars are current U.S. dollars unless otherwise specified.

Debt stock and its components

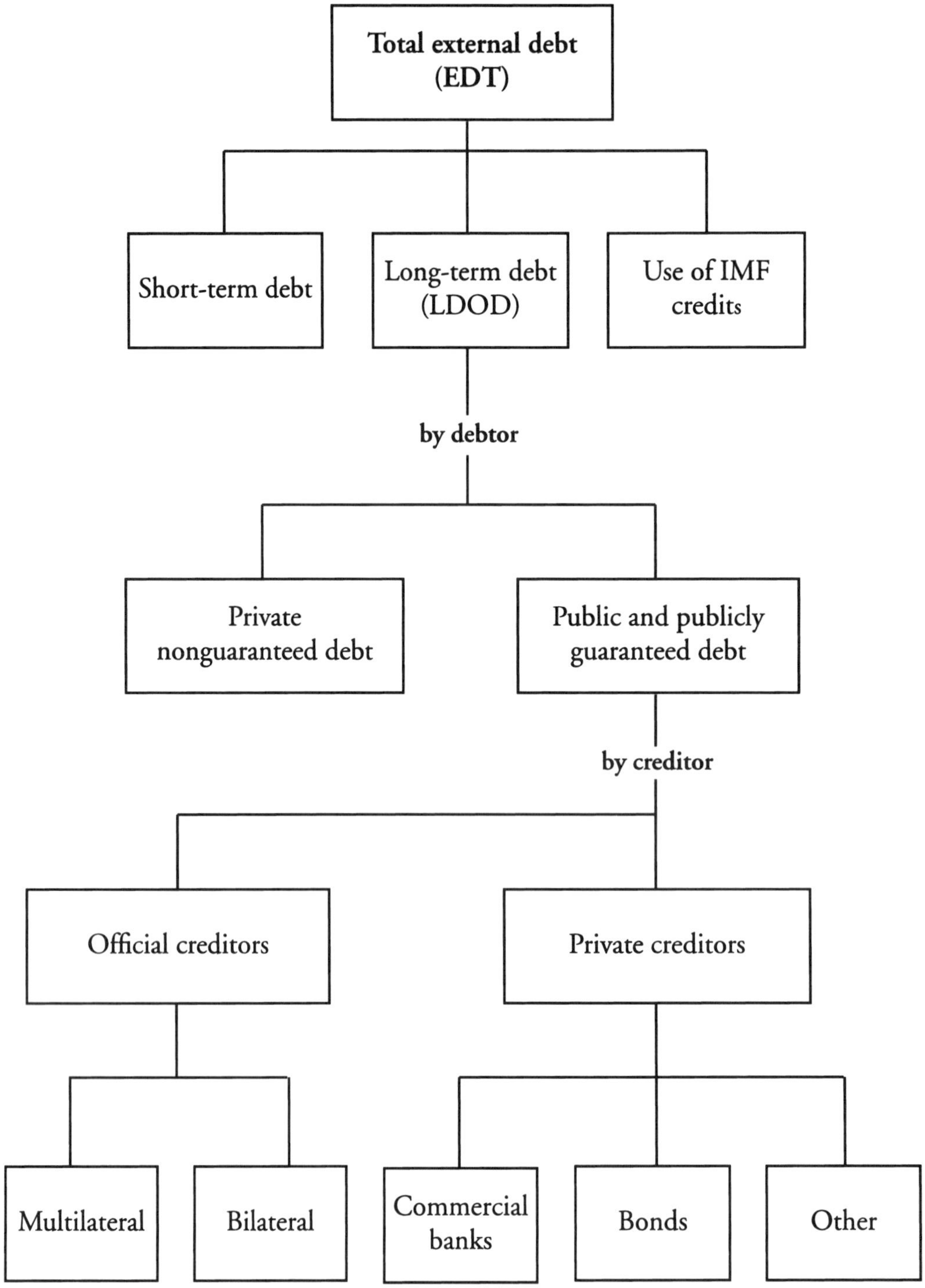

Aggregate net resource flows and net transfers (long-term) to developing countries

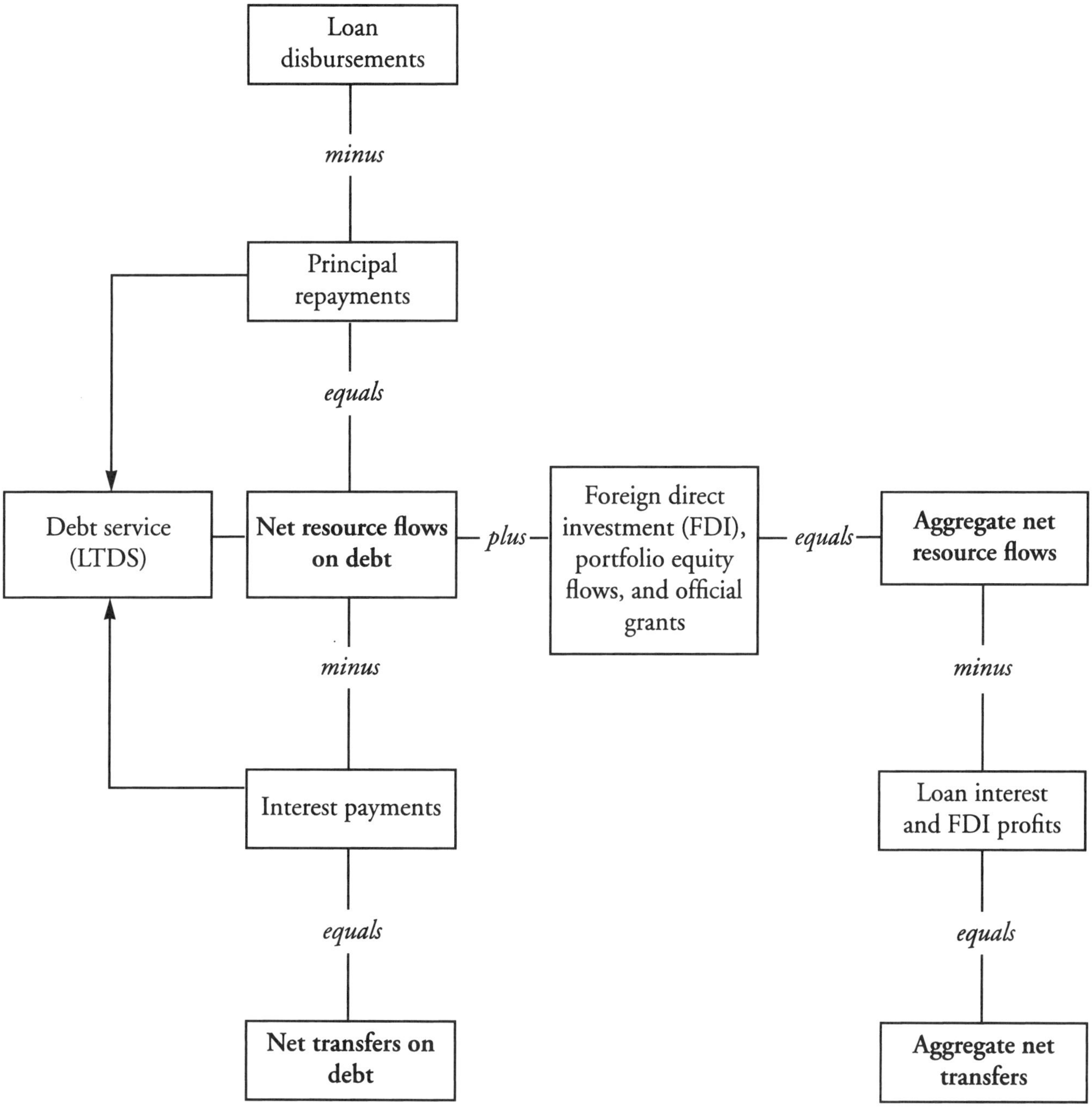

Note: Includes only loans with an original maturity of more than one year (long-term loans). Excludes IMF transactions.

Aggregate net resource flows (long-term) and the balance of payments

	Credits	*Debits*
Current account	• Exports of goods and services • Income received • Current transfers Including workers' remittances and private grants	• Imports of goods and services • Income paid • Current transfers
	• Official unrequited transfers (by foreign governments)	• Official unrequited transfers (by national government)
Capital and financial account	• Official unrequited transfers (by foreign governments) • Foreign direct investment (by nonresidents) (disinvestment shown as negative)	• Official unrequited transfers (by national government) • Foreign direct investment (by residents) (disinvestment shown as negative)
	• Portfolio investment (by nonresidents) (amortizations shown as negative) • Other long-term capital inflows (by nonresidents) (amortizations shown as negative)	• Portfolio investment (abroad by residents) (amortizations shown as negative) • Other long-term capital outflow (by residents) (amortizations shown as negative)
	• Short-term capital inflow	• Short-term capital outflow
Reserve account	Net changes in reserves	

Aggregate net resource flows

Net resource flows on debt (long-term)

Country groups

East Asia and the Pacific

Cambodia (P)
China (P)
Fiji (A)
Indonesia (P)
Lao PDR (P)
Malaysia (P)
Mongolia (A)
Myanmar (A)
Papua New Guinea (A)
Philippines (P)
Solomon Islands (A)
Thailand (P)
Tonga (A)
Vanuatu (A)
Vietnam (P)
Western Samoa (A)
Kiribati
Korea, Dem. Rep.

Europe and Central Asia

Albania (A)
Armenia (P)
Azerbaijan (P)
Belarus (A)
Bosnia and Herzegovina[a]
Bulgaria (A)
Croatia (A)
Czech Republic (P)
Estonia (A)
Georgia (A)
Hungary (A)
Kazakstan (A)
Kyrgyz Republic (A)
Latvia (P)
Lithuania (A)
Macedonia, FYR (A)
Malta (A)
Moldova (A)
Poland (A)
Romania (A)
Russian Federation[b] (P)
Slovak Republic (P)
Slovenia (A)
Tajikistan (E)
Turkey (A)
Turkmenistan (A)
Ukraine (A)
Uzbekistan (A)
Yugoslavia, former[a] (E)
Gibraltar
Greece

Latin America and the Caribbean

Argentina (A)
Barbados (A)
Belize (A)
Bolivia (A)
Brazil (P)
Chile (A)
Colombia (A)
Costa Rica (A)
Dominica (A)
Dominican Republic (A)
Ecuador (A)
El Salvador (A)
Grenada (A)
Guatemala (P)
Guyana (A)
Haiti (P)
Honduras (A)
Jamaica (P)
Mexico (A)
Nicaragua (P)
Panama (A)
Paraguay (A)
Peru (A)
St. Kitts and Nevis (A)
St. Lucia (A)
St.Vincent and the Grenadines (A)
Trinidad and Tobago (A)
Uruguay (A)
Venezuela (E)
Antigua and Barbuda
Cuba
Suriname

Middle East and North Africa

Algeria (A)
Egypt, Arab Rep. (A)
Iran, Islamic Rep. (E)
Jordan (A)
Lebanon (A)
Morocco (P)
Oman (A)
Syrian Arab Republic (E)
Tunisia (P)
Yemen, Rep. (A)
Bahrain
Iraq
Libya
Saudi Arabia

South Asia

Bangladesh (A)
Bhutan (A)
India (A)
Maldives (A)
Nepal (A)
Pakistan (A)
Sri Lanka (A)
Afghanistan

Sub-Saharan Africa

Angola (A)
Benin (P)
Botswana (A)
Burkina Faso (A)
Burundi (A)
Cameroon (A)
Cape Verde (A)
Central African Republic (A)
Chad (P)
Comoros (A)
Congo (A)
Côte d'Ivoire (A)
Djibouti (E)
Equatorial Guinea (E)
Ethiopia[c] (A)
Gabon (A)
Gambia, The (E)
Ghana (A)
Guinea (P)
Guinea-Bissau (P)
Kenya (A)
Lesotho (A)
Liberia (E)
Madagascar (A)
Malawi (P)
Mali (P)
Mauritania (P)
Mauritius (A)
Mozambique (A)
Niger (A)
Nigeria (E)
Rwanda (E)
São Tomé and Principe (A)
Senegal (A)
Seychelles (E)
Sierra Leone (A)
Somalia (E)
Sudan (E)
Swaziland (P)
Tanzania (A)
Togo (A)
Uganda (P)
Zaire (E)
Zambia (P)
Zimbabwe (A)
Namibia
South Africa

Note: Countries printed in normal type are reporters to the Debtor Reporting System (DRS); those printed in italics are non-DRS countries. Letters in parenthesis indicate DRS reporters' status: (A) as reported, (P) preliminary, and (E) estimated. The status "as reported" indicates that the country was fully current in its reporting under the (DRS) and that World Bank staff are satisfied that the reported data give an adequate and fair representation of the country's total public debt. "Preliminary" data are based on reported or collected information but, because of incompleteness or other reasons, include an element of staff estimation. "Estimated" data indicate that countries are not current in their reporting and that a significant element of staff estimation has been necessary in producing the data tables.

a. For Bosnia and Herzegovina total debt, excluding IBRD and IMF obligations and short-term debt, is included under Yugoslavia, former.
b. Includes the debt of the former Soviet Union on the assumption that 100 percent of all outstanding external debt as of December 1991 has become a liability of the Russian Federation.
c. Debt data for 1995 include $24.3 million of IDA credit for Eritrea.

Income groups

Low-income countries

Afghanistan
Albania
Angola
Armenia
Azerbaijan
Bangladesh
Benin
Bhutan
Bosnia and Herzegovina
Burkina Faso
Burundi
Cambodia
Cameroon
Central African Republic
Chad
China
Comoros
Congo
Côte d'Ivoire
Equatorial Guinea
Eritrea
Ethiopia
Gambia, The
Georgia
Ghana
Guinea
Guinea-Bissau
Guyana
Haiti
Honduras
India
Kenya
Kyrgyz Republic
Lao PDR
Liberia
Madagascar
Malawi
Mali
Mauritania
Mongolia
Mozambique
Myanmar
Nepal
Nicaragua
Niger
Nigeria
Pakistan
Rwanda
São Tomé and Principe
Senegal
Sierra Leone
Somalia
Sri Lanka
Sudan
Tajikistan
Tanzania
Togo
Uganda
Vietnam
Yemen, Rep.
Zaire
Zambia
Zimbabwe

Middle-income countries

Algeria
American Samoa
Antigua and Barbuda
Argentina
Bahrain
Barbados
Belarus
Belize
Bolivia
Botswana
Brazil
Bulgaria
Cape Verde
Chile
Colombia
Costa Rica
Croatia
Cuba
Czech Republic
Djibouti
Dominica
Dominican Republic
Ecuador
Egypt, Arab Rep.
El Salvador
Estonia
Fiji
Gabon
Gibraltar
Guadeloupe
Greece
Grenada
Guatemala
Hungary
Indonesia
Iran, Islamic Rep.
Iraq
Isle of Man
Jamaica
Jordan
Kazakstan
Kiribati
Korea, Dem. Rep.
Latvia
Lebanon
Lesotho
Libya
Lithuania
Macedonia, FYR
Malaysia
Maldives
Malta
Marshall Islands
Mauritius
Mayotte
Mexico
Micronesia, Fed. Sts.
Moldova
Morocco
Namibia
Oman
Panama
Papua New Guinea
Paraguay
Peru
Philippines
Poland
Puerto Rico
Romania
Russian Federation
Saudi Arabia
Seychelles
Slovak Republic
Slovenia
Solomon Islands
South Africa
St. Kitts and Nevis
St. Lucia
St. Vincent and the Grenadines
Suriname
Swaziland
Syrian Arab Republic
Thailand
Tonga
Trinidad and Tobago
Tunisia
Turkey
Turkmenistan
Ukraine
Uruguay
Uzbekistan
Vanuatu
Venezuela
West Bank and Gaza
Western Samoa
Yugoslavia, Fed. Rep. (Serbia and Montenegro)

Note: Low-income countries are those in which 1995 GNP per capita (calculated using the *World Bank Atlas* method) was no more than $765; middle-income countries are those in which GNP per capita was between $766 and $3,035.

Debt tables

Note to users

Long-term public and publicly guaranteed debt data are as reported for eighty-nine countries; for forty-seven other countries the data are preliminary (that is, substantially based on reported data) or estimated by World Bank staff (the status of each country is given in the Country Groups section).

For twenty-three of the thirty-one countries reporting private nonguaranteed debt, data for 1995 are as reported. The data for the other eight countries are preliminary or estimates by World Bank staff.

Data for exports, imports, and international reserves are standard series drawn from the International Monetary Fund (IMF) and maintained in the data files of the World Bank. Data for gross national product denominated in U.S. dollars are drawn directly from the files of the Macroeconomic Data Team of the Development Data Group of the World Bank. Data for direct foreign investment are drawn from the IMF, and data for grants are drawn from the OECD and supplemented by estimates by World Bank staff. The charts on pages xx to xxii are intended to help the reader interpret the debt stocks and flows reported in the tables.

For the period 1991–95 all ruble debt owed to the former Soviet Union is converted at a rate of one ruble = $1.795, except in cases where a bilateral agreement specifying a different conversion rate is in place. This valuation method does not constitute an endorsement by World Bank staff of the appropriateness or validity of this method or the exchange rate used. The appropriate valuation is a matter to be resolved bilaterally between the Russian Federation and its debtor countries.

Debt data for 1995 include $24.3 million of IDA credit for Eritrea.

The following abbreviations are used in the principal ratios and indicator charts:

EDT	Total external debt, including short-term and use of IMF credit
LDOD	Total long-term debt outstanding and disbursed
INT	Total interest payments on long-term and short-term debt, including IMF charges
TDS	Total debt service on long-term debt and short-term (interest only), including IMF credits
FDI	Foreign direct investment
GNP	Gross national product
XGS	Exports of goods and services
MGS	Imports of goods and services
RES	International reserves

Summary tables

AGGREGATE NET RESOURCE FLOWS (LONG-TERM)

(US$ million, unless otherwise indicated)

Group and country	Aggregate net resource flows (excl. IMF) Annual average 1990-94	1995	Private flows: Foreign direct investment Annual average 1990-94	1995	Portfolio equity Annual average 1990-94	1995	Bonds Annual average 1990-94	1995	Bank and trade - related lending Annual average 1990-94	1995	Official flows (including grants) Annual average 1990-94	1995
Low-Income Countries	**59,238**	**81,782**	**19,325**	**41,570**	**3,875**	**5,612**	**1,405**	**483**	**6,603**	**5,783**	**28,029**	**28,334**
Severely indebted	**17,762**	**17,222**	**2,400**	**3,560**	**198**	**446**	**30**	**-13**	**-9**	**-463**	**15,143**	**13,692**
Angola	894	891	254	400	0	0	0	0	375	123	265	368
Burundi	213	257	1	2	0	0	0	0	-3	-1	215	256
Cambodia	144	544	31	151	0	0	0	0	0	13	112	380
Cameroon	586	206	2	102	0	0	0	0	1	-53	583	157
Central African Republic	148	139	-4	3	0	0	0	0	0	0	153	136
Congo	121	20	0	1	0	0	0	0	-12	-50	132	69
Cote d'Ivoire	722	680	-12	19	1	3	0	0	-19	14	752	644
Equatorial Guinea	53	18	24	1	0	0	0	0	0	0	29	17
Ethiopia	963	627	6	7	0	0	0	0	35	-49	921	669
Ghana	840	1,078	83	230	111	267	0	0	27	29	618	553
Guinea	333	325	22	35	0	0	0	0	-9	-15	320	304
Guinea-Bissau	75	65	1	1	0	0	0	0	0	0	74	64
Guyana	107	19	1	3	0	0	0	0	-12	-10	119	26
Honduras	474	228	41	50	0	0	30	-13	0	28	403	163
Kenya	660	500	18	32	0	0	0	0	10	-74	632	542
Liberia	90	107	0	0	0	0	0	0	0	0	90	107
Madagascar	352	230	16	10	0	0	0	0	-10	-6	347	226
Malawi	349	319	0	1	0	0	0	0	-7	-15	356	333
Mali	289	334	3	1	0	0	0	0	-1	0	288	333
Mauritania	190	181	7	3	0	0	0	0	-1	0	184	178
Mozambique	901	1,001	24	36	0	0	0	0	1	28	877	937
Myanmar	113	95	3	10	6	16	0	0	6	36	97	34
Nicaragua	569	524	19	70	0	0	0	0	1	-77	549	531
Niger	268	161	0	1	0	0	0	0	-23	-24	290	184
Nigeria	826	312	1,100	650	3	6	0	0	-392	-203	114	-141
Rwanda	317	608	4	1	0	0	0	0	-1	0	314	607
Sao Tome and Principe	44	30	0	0	0	0	0	0	0	0	44	30
Sierra Leone	125	135	5	1	0	0	0	0	1	-29	119	163
Somalia	487	150	2	1	0	0	0	0	0	0	485	149
Sudan	479	184	0	0	0	0	0	0	0	0	479	184
Tanzania	887	747	16	150	0	0	0	0	0	-13	871	610
Togo	123	138	0	0	0	0	0	0	0	0	123	138
Uganda	534	682	29	121	0	0	0	0	-9	-10	514	570
Vietnam	423	881	39	150	76	155	0	0	14	-67	294	643
Yemen,Rep. of	640	145	418	0	0	0	0	0	44	-2	178	147
Zaire	379	161	1	1	0	0	0	0	-6	0	384	160
Zambia	701	482	80	66	0	0	0	0	-27	-36	648	452
Moderately indebted	**12,387**	**10,123**	**707**	**1,862**	**1,739**	**2,297**	**358**	**180**	**1,441**	**890**	**8,142**	**4,894**
Bangladesh	1,470	906	7	2	10	33	0	0	16	-25	1,438	896
Benin	220	218	7	1	0	0	0	0	0	0	213	217
Burkina Faso	305	322	0	0	0	0	0	0	0	0	305	322
Chad	211	181	6	7	0	0	0	0	-1	0	206	174
Comoros	32	29	1	2	0	0	0	0	0	0	31	27
Gambia, The	63	34	7	10	0	0	0	0	-5	0	60	24
Haiti	216	587	8	2	0	0	0	0	0	0	208	585
India	5,867	3,282	269	1,300	1,383	1,517	353	210	1,217	566	2,645	-311
Lao PDR	184	292	40	88	0	0	0	0	0	0	144	205
Pakistan	2,235	2,511	320	409	336	729	39	0	216	305	1,324	1,068

AGGREGATE NET RESOURCE FLOWS (LONG-TERM)

(US$ million, unless otherwise indicated)

Group and country	Aggregate net resource flows (excl. IMF) Annual average 1990-94	Aggregate net resource flows (excl. IMF) 1995	Private flows: Foreign direct investment Annual average 1990-94	Foreign direct investment 1995	Portfolio equity Annual average 1990-94	Portfolio equity 1995	Bonds Annual average 1990-94	Bonds 1995	Bank and trade - related lending Annual average 1990-94	Bank and trade - related lending 1995	Official flows (including grants) Annual average 1990-94	Official flows (including grants) 1995
Senegal	515	394	27	1	0	0	0	0	-18	-25	506	419
Zimbabwe	479	450	14	40	10	18	-34	-30	17	71	472	351
Other selected countries												
Albania	256	206	26	70	0	0	0	0	14	0	216	136
Armenia	*208*	200	*0*	8	*0*	0	*0*	0	*0*	0	*208*	192
Azerbaijan	*112*	270	*0*	110	*0*	0	*0*	0	*0*	0	*112*	160
Bhutan	35	38	0	0	0	0	0	0	-2	-2	37	41
China	27,226	51,870	16,062	35,849	1,916	2,807	1,017	317	5,176	5,366	3,054	7,531
Georgia	*243*	169	*0*	0	*0*	0	*0*	0	*1*	0	*243*	169
Kyrgyz Republic	*172*	187	*5*	15	*0*	0	*0*	0	*0*	0	*167*	172
Mongolia	*114*	151	*9*	10	*0*	0	*0*	0	*-2*	-14	*108*	155
Nepal	289	287	5	8	0	0	0	0	-12	-10	297	289
Sri Lanka	612	631	115	63	22	61	0	0	-22	16	497	491
Tajikistan	*172*	106	*5*	15	*0*	0	*0*	0	*0*	0	*167*	91
Middle-Income Countries	**97,971**	**155,416**	**31,195**	**53,919**	**15,533**	**26,476**	**16,102**	**28,025**	**7,584**	**22,322**	**27,557**	**24,674**
Severely indebted	**33,874**	**58,664**	**10,760**	**16,243**	**10,527**	**7,184**	**7,722**	**11,870**	**354**	**9,361**	**4,510**	**14,005**
Argentina	6,639	8,650	2,183	1,319	1,512	211	1,960	4,906	6	768	979	1,447
Bolivia	505	748	23	150	0	0	0	0	-8	41	490	557
Brazil	7,349	17,783	1,703	4,859	2,624	4,411	2,285	2,637	1,825	7,190	-1,088	-1,314
Bulgaria	410	455	52	135	80	400	-29	-6	-47	-41	353	-34
Ecuador	389	867	293	470	1	1	0	1	-32	90	127	306
Gabon	108	170	-14	-50	0	0	0	0	-10	-75	133	295
Jamaica	243	188	122	167	0	0	14	13	-37	8	145	0
Jordan	456	546	7	43	0	11	-9	0	-51	-197	509	690
Mexico	15,396	23,443	5,409	6,963	5,830	520	3,490	4,321	-490	1,265	1,157	10,374
Panama	141	221	134	220	41	20	-1	-1	-12	-12	-20	-7
Peru	1,758	4,119	740	1,895	441	1,611	12	0	87	26	479	587
Syrian Arab Republic	422	285	104	65	0	0	0	0	-43	-22	361	242
Moderately indebted	**42,976**	**53,944**	**11,348**	**25,122**	**3,097**	**10,071**	**7,149**	**9,916**	**3,207**	**1,736**	**18,175**	**7,099**
Algeria	298	1,005	11	5	1	1	-251	-278	-42	401	579	876
Chile	2,319	2,481	879	1,695	383	274	66	489	917	1,772	74	-1,749
Colombia	687	3,342	862	2,501	98	131	120	855	-132	254	-262	-399
Egypt, Arab Rep.	3,252	1,210	639	598	2	2	0	0	-289	-306	2,900	916
Hungary	2,336	7,628	1,287	4,519	107	483	1,724	2,094	-1,250	746	468	-213
Indonesia	6,802	12,999	1,693	4,348	1,311	4,873	213	2,248	780	180	2,805	1,350
Macedonia, FYR	*-19*	58	*0*	0	*0*	0	*0*	0	*-8*	0	*-11*	58
Morocco	1,139	388	389	290	13	150	0	0	46	132	691	-184
Papua New Guinea	440	931	129	453	0	450	-3	-32	-22	-293	336	353
Philippines	2,812	4,234	826	1,478	637	1,961	435	1,060	-239	106	1,154	-371
Poland	2,416	8,375	930	3,659	81	921	28	250	-92	228	1,470	3,318
Russia Federation	8,064	2,121	407	2,017	54	141	55	-810	3,427	-232	4,120	1,006
St. Vincent and Grenadines	34	74	24	31	0	0	0	0	1	0	9	43
Trinidad and Tobago	176	330	270	299	0	0	-28	97	-112	-126	46	59
Tunisia	717	907	344	264	0	0	-12	588	-94	-102	478	157
Turkey	3,667	1,249	716	885	326	630	1,607	616	650	-131	368	-751
Uruguay	216	241	52	124	5	4	129	62	-113	26	144	24
Venezuela	1,575	634	836	900	69	7	509	-328	-488	-110	648	165
Western Samoa	41	28	5	3	0	0	0	0	0	0	37	25

AGGREGATE NET RESOURCE FLOWS (LONG-TERM)

(US$ million, unless otherwise indicated)

Group and country	Aggregate net resource flows (excl. IMF) Annual average 1990-94	1995	Private flows: Foreign direct investment Annual average 1990-94	1995	Portfolio equity Annual average 1990-94	1995	Bonds Annual average 1990-94	1995	Bank and trade - related lending Annual average 1990-94	1995	Official flows (including grants) Annual average 1990-94	1995
Other selected countries												
Barbados	-7	10	10	12	0	0	-17	35	-2	-32	2	-5
Belarus	*420*	287	*13*	20	*0*	0	*0*	0	*103*	83	*305*	183
Belize	34	33	14	21	0	0	0	0	2	-4	18	16
Botswana	28	100	-43	70	0	0	0	0	1	-6	70	36
Cape Verde	77	79	1	10	0	0	0	0	0	0	76	69
Costa Rica	238	275	222	396	1	1	-15	-4	-40	-9	70	-109
Croatia	*81*	340	*86*	81	*0*	0	*0*	0	*56*	265	*-60*	-6
Czech Republic	1,365	5,675	548	2,568	37	82	139	38	385	2,908	256	79
Djibouti	86	61	2	4	0	0	0	0	0	0	84	57
Dominica	25	39	17	12	0	0	0	0	0	0	8	27
Dominican Republic	154	281	156	271	0	0	0	0	-37	-34	35	44
El Salvador	365	170	16	38	0	0	0	0	-10	-30	359	161
Estonia	*247*	291	*188*	201	*5*	7	*0*	0	*-6*	-1	*60*	84
Fiji	34	51	48	67	0	0	0	0	-7	-21	-7	5
Grenada	31	30	18	24	0	0	0	0	2	-2	11	8
Guatemala	194	169	88	75	0	0	4	46	5	-35	98	83
Iran, Islamic Rep. of	201	..	-111	17	0	0	0	..	762	..	-450	..
Kazakstan	*592*	1,000	*168*	284	*0*	0	*0*	0	*157*	216	*268*	500
Latvia	*235*	269	*130*	180	*0*	0	*0*	43	*10*	1	*96*	44
Lebanon	90	1,317	5	35	0	34	0	750	0	333	84	165
Lesotho	115	123	12	23	0	0	0	0	-3	9	106	91
Lithuania	*161*	307	*22*	73	*0*	4	*0*	60	*17*	56	*122*	113
Malaysia	6,528	11,856	4,174	5,800	1,139	2,299	52	2,240	1,061	1,585	103	-69
Maldives	33	60	7	9	0	0	0	0	1	2	25	50
Malta	94	104	68	98	0	0	0	0	0	22	26	-17
Mauritius	103	309	22	15	6	4	0	150	44	135	31	5
Moldova	*142*	197	*13*	64	*0*	0	*0*	0	*0*	15	*129*	118
Oman	104	136	121	150	5	5	0	0	-97	-28	74	10
Paraguay	32	343	118	200	0	0	0	0	-63	-26	-22	169
Romania	827	1,415	110	419	0	1	0	0	135	267	581	728
Seychelles	38	44	28	40	0	0	0	0	-2	-2	12	6
Slovak Republic	389	855	80	183	0	60	110	0	47	410	151	202
Slovenia	*271*	778	*121*	176	*0*	0	*0*	0	*197*	662	*-46*	-59
Solomon Islands	29	40	14	17	0	0	0	0	-2	2	17	22
St. Kitts and Nevis	27	21	22	20	0	0	0	0	1	-1	4	2
St. Lucia	60	111	42	63	0	0	0	0	-1	0	19	48
Swaziland	82	74	68	58	0	0	0	0	-2	0	15	16
Thailand	5,378	9,753	1,948	2,068	615	2,154	1,240	2,023	1,280	2,898	295	610
Tonga	16	24	1	2	0	0	0	0	0	0	15	22
Turkmenistan	*159*	28	*0*	0	*0*	0	*0*	0	*46*	19	*113*	9
Ukraine	*800*	710	*180*	267	*0*	0	*0*	0	*251*	-20	*370*	463
Uzbekistan	*342*	488	*48*	115	*0*	0	*0*	0	*76*	120	*219*	254
Vanuatu	44	54	24	31	0	0	0	0	0	0	20	23
Yugoslavia, former	363	1,412	72	0	0	0	0	0	-387	0	678	1,412
All Developing Countries	**157,625**	**237,197**	**50,520**	**95,489**	**19,824**	**32,087**	**17,507**	**28,508**	**14,188**	**28,105**	**55,586**	**53,008**

Note: Individual country data are shown for Debtor Reporting System countries only. Data for Bosnia and Herzegovina are not shown separately. Totals include estimates for countries not part of the DRS. A country is classified as severely indebted if for 1993-95 the average ratio of the present value of total debt service due to GNP is higher than 80 percent or the average ratio of the present value of total debt service due to exports is higher than 220 percent. A country is classified as moderately indebted if for 1993-95 the average ratio of the present value of total debt service due to GNP is less than 80 percent but higher than 48 percent or the average ratio of the present value of total debt service due to exports is less than 220 percent but higher than 132 percent. Figures in italics are for years other than those specified.

NET FLOWS AND TRANSFERS ON DEBT

(US$ million, unless otherwise indicated)

Group and country	Net flows on debt		Net transfers on debt		Net flows on debt / GNP (%)		Net flows on long-term debt: Total		Net flows on long-term debt: Official (excl.IMF)		Net flows on long-term debt: Private	
	Annual average 1990-94	1995	Annual average 1990-94	1995	Annual average 1990-94	1995	Annual average 1990-94	1995	Annual average 1990-94	1995	Annual average 1990-94	1995
Low-Income Countries	**22,228**	**24,249**	**7,997**	**7,760**	**2.2**	**1.8**	**20,152**	**17,681**	**12,143**	**11,415**	**8,009**	**6,266**
Severely indebted	**4,288**	**3,471**	**-180**	**-335**	**2.5**	**1.6**	**4,203**	**2,024**	**4,182**	**2,500**	**21**	**-476**
Angola	542	-144	427	-274	12.0	-3.5	433	164	57	40	375	123
Burundi	60	26	47	15	5.7	2.5	61	27	63	28	-3	-1
Cambodia	15	106	1	103	0.7	3.8	12	81	12	68	0	13
Cameroon	315	66	110	-145	3.3	0.9	340	-101	340	-48	1	-53
Central African Republic	65	25	56	19	5.4	..	65	30	65	30	0	0
Congo	37	166	-89	69	2.1	10.1	48	-67	59	-17	-12	-50
Cote d'Ivoire	420	935	-147	514	3.7	12.4	412	205	432	190	-19	14
Equatorial Guinea	12	-8	11	-9	9.2	-5.4	8	2	8	2	0	0
Ethiopia	257	138	212	75	4.0	2.6	262	145	227	194	35	-49
Ghana	378	348	262	251	5.9	5.6	329	343	302	315	27	29
Guinea	139	104	95	57	4.8	2.9	152	55	160	70	-9	-15
Guinea-Bissau	29	14	24	8	12.0	5.3	30	13	30	13	0	0
Guyana	79	-8	19	-43	30.2	-1.4	34	-5	45	5	-12	-10
Honduras	233	105	65	-112	7.6	2.9	213	56	183	41	31	15
Kenya	166	193	-134	-64	2.1	2.6	167	226	157	300	10	-74
Liberia	-4	0	-7	-2	..	..	-2	0	-2	0	0	0
Madagascar	89	48	35	21	3.2	1.6	102	55	111	61	-10	-6
Malawi	95	93	59	53	5.5	7.2	101	59	108	74	-7	-15
Mali	93	187	72	162	3.9	8.1	85	126	86	126	-1	0
Mauritania	56	69	16	31	6.0	6.8	63	43	64	43	-1	0
Mozambique	153	192	101	109	13.2	14.7	154	195	153	168	1	28
Myanmar	46	-74	-14	-144	..	..	45	-95	39	-130	6	36
Nicaragua	126	-55	39	-142	12.2	-3.5	191	46	190	123	1	-77
Niger	21	-12	-6	-27	1.0	-0.7	41	-6	63	18	-23	-24
Nigeria	-218	-450	-1,848	-1,212	-0.7	-1.8	-371	-376	21	-173	-392	-203
Rwanda	47	53	37	44	2.1	4.7	50	43	51	43	-1	0
Sao Tome and Principe	20	13	19	11	44.8	31.2	22	12	22	12	0	0
Sierra Leone	92	-147	69	-168	13.5	-19.1	56	47	55	76	1	-29
Somalia	14	0	13	-1	..	..	11	0	11	0	0	0
Sudan	132	0	118	-16	..	..	96	36	96	36	0	0
Tanzania	194	106	120	20	5.3	3.0	185	147	185	159	0	-13
Togo	15	38	-7	26	1.3	3.1	36	18	36	18	0	0
Uganda	230	185	191	146	6.7	3.3	207	161	217	171	-9	-10
Vietnam	194	639	106	471	..	3.1	122	231	108	298	14	-67
Yemen, Rep. of	-21	36	-83	-1	-2.2	0.9	101	53	57	55	44	-2
Zaire	9	61	-54	38	0.0	1.2	128	0	134	0	-6	0
Zambia	50	379	-123	-170	1.6	10.6	108	55	135	91	-27	-36
Moderately indebted	**5,987**	**2,467**	**151**	**-3,948**	**1.6**	**0.6**	**6,252**	**1,760**	**4,454**	**691**	**1,799**	**1,070**
Bangladesh	623	131	431	-55	2.6	0.5	625	193	609	218	16	-25
Benin	90	96	74	72	5.0	4.7	83	68	83	68	0	0
Burkina Faso	106	124	88	104	4.2	5.4	102	83	102	83	0	0
Chad	88	59	81	54	7.5	5.3	87	53	87	53	-1	0
Comoros	5	11	4	11	2.1	4.9	5	9	5	9	0	0
Gambia, The	13	-9	5	-14	3.9	..	12	6	17	6	-5	0
Haiti	1	79	-7	47	-0.4	3.9	13	73	13	73	0	0
India	3,437	-1,025	-957	-5,649	1.3	-0.3	3,664	-91	2,094	-867	1,570	775
Lao PDR	88	90	84	83	8.3	5.2	79	75	79	75	0	0
Pakistan	1,158	2,510	266	1,313	2.5	4.1	1,276	1,186	1,021	881	255	305

NET FLOWS AND TRANSFERS ON DEBT

(US$ million, unless otherwise indicated)

Group and country	Net flows on debt: Annual average 1990-94	Net flows on debt: 1995	Net transfers on debt: Annual average 1990-94	Net transfers on debt: 1995	Net flows on debt / GNP (%): Annual average 1990-94	Net flows on debt / GNP (%): 1995	Net flows on long-term debt — Total: Annual average 1990-94	Total: 1995	Official (excl.IMF): Annual average 1990-94	Official (excl.IMF): 1995	Private: Annual average 1990-94	Private: 1995
Senegal	71	52	-15	-22	1.2	1.1	86	23	105	48	-18	-25
Zimbabwe	306	350	98	110	5.5	5.7	222	84	239	43	-17	41
Other selected countries												
Albania	167	-109	164	-115	12.8	-4.9	48	60	34	60	14	0
Armenia	*82*	149	*79*	140	*4.4*	7.0	*74*	102	*74*	102	*0*	0
Azerbaijan	*37*	207	*37*	197	*0.9*	6.0	*34*	102	*34*	102	*0*	0
Bhutan	2	-1	0	-3	0.6	-0.3	2	-1	5	1	-2	-2
China	10,890	17,728	7,167	11,732	2.5	2.6	8,963	12,885	2,769	7,202	6,194	5,683
Georgia	*365*	-285	*359*	-305	*15.1*	-12.4	*110*	85	*110*	85	*1*	0
Kyrgyz Republic	*137*	166	*128*	143	*4.0*	5.5	*99*	118	*99*	118	*0*	0
Mongolia	*75*	66	*65*	57	*10.6*	7.9	*62*	67	*64*	81	*-2*	-14
Nepal	141	60	111	27	3.7	1.3	132	108	145	118	-12	-10
Sri Lanka	360	293	204	133	3.8	2.3	296	333	318	317	-22	16
Tajikistan	*130*	38	*129*	38	*5.5*	2.0	*130*	38	*130*	38	*0*	0
Middle-Income Countries	**60,490**	**108,770**	**1,306**	**29,302**	**1.8**	**2.8**	**35,171**	**59,340**	**11,485**	**8,993**	**23,686**	**50,347**
Severely indebted	**21,678**	**50,965**	**2,868**	**18,886**	**1.9**	**3.5**	**10,389**	**33,097**	**2,313**	**11,865**	**8,076**	**21,232**
Argentina	4,054	11,966	878	6,594	1.5	4.4	2,917	7,085	951	1,411	1,966	5,674
Bolivia	194	333	54	160	3.8	5.7	185	313	193	272	-8	41
Brazil	5,542	8,041	1,405	-3,136	1.3	1.2	2,971	8,449	-1,139	-1,378	4,110	9,827
Bulgaria	290	-233	14	-828	2.9	-2.0	207	-100	282	-54	-75	-46
Ecuador	300	-152	-159	-818	2.1	-0.9	44	328	75	238	-32	90
Gabon	6	90	-166	-136	0.1	2.4	63	133	73	208	-10	-75
Jamaica	-35	-114	-261	-347	-1.0	-3.6	-36	-43	-13	-64	-23	21
Jordan	118	477	-202	206	4.6	7.6	139	273	200	471	-60	-197
Mexico	9,890	26,051	1,817	14,924	3.4	11.0	4,114	15,929	1,114	10,343	3,000	5,586
Panama	-145	-11	-376	-212	-2.6	-0.1	-116	-33	-103	-21	-14	-12
Peru	518	3,132	-65	2,469	1.3	5.5	352	343	253	317	99	26
Syrian Arab Republic	341	460	163	259	2.7	2.9	114	149	157	172	-43	-22
Moderately indebted	**24,304**	**25,404**	**-4,481**	**-8,765**	**1.9**	**1.9**	**18,622**	**9,277**	**8,266**	**-2,375**	**10,356**	**11,652**
Algeria	67	1,287	-1,819	-544	0.4	3.3	216	929	509	806	-294	123
Chile	1,461	673	51	-814	3.5	1.1	982	459	-1	-1,802	983	2,261
Colombia	300	1,120	-998	-260	0.4	1.5	-335	637	-324	-472	-11	1,109
Egypt, Arab Rep.	-309	-53	-1,513	-1,453	-0.9	-0.1	205	-396	494	-90	-289	-306
Hungary	780	2,613	-907	503	2.0	6.1	845	2,600	371	-239	473	2,839
Indonesia	5,241	8,770	566	2,551	4.2	4.6	3,542	3,529	2,549	1,101	993	2,428
Macedonia, FYR	*-5*	77	*-25*	66	*-0.3*	4.2	*-19*	58	*-11*	58	*-8*	0
Morocco	266	-205	-1,130	-1,582	1.0	-0.7	375	-151	329	-284	46	132
Papua New Guinea	33	-227	-128	-341	2.2	-5.0	45	-240	70	84	-26	-325
Philippines	1,373	-281	-460	-2,608	2.5	-0.4	1,066	519	871	-648	195	1,166
Poland	313	-1,637	-506	-3,426	0.5	-1.4	166	394	230	-84	-64	478
Russian Federation	4,425	4,619	2,323	1,591	1.0	1.4	5,633	-944	2,150	98	3,483	-1,043
St. Vincent and the Grenadines	16	63	14	57	7.3	25.7	6	-2	5	-2	1	0
Trinidad and Tobago	-89	303	-268	122	-2.0	6.4	-101	21	39	49	-140	-28
Tunisia	346	366	-129	-176	2.5	2.1	252	586	358	99	-106	487
Turkey	3,186	4,028	-527	-416	1.6	2.4	2,016	-705	-242	-1,190	2,257	485
Uruguay	132	191	-170	-188	0.9	1.2	149	97	133	9	16	88
Venezuela	1,175	-1,401	-1,242	-3,804	2.2	-1.9	663	-291	642	147	21	-438
Western Samoa	14	6	12	4	9.6	3.0	14	4	14	4	0	0

NET FLOWS AND TRANSFERS ON DEBT

(US$ million, unless otherwise indicated)

Group and country	Net flows on debt		Net transfers on debt		Net flows on debt / GNP (%)		Net flows on long-term debt					
							Total		Official (excl.IMF)		Private	
	Annual average 1990-94	1995	Annual average 1990-94	1995	Annual average 1990-94	1995	Annual average 1990-94	1995	Annual average 1990-94	1995	Annual average 1990-94	1995
Other selected countries												
Barbados	-6	-22	-50	-63	-0.4	-1.3	-22	-4	-3	-6	-19	3
Belarus	*361*	349	*340*	277	*1.4*	1.7	*285*	131	*182*	47	*103*	83
Belize	12	26	5	15	2.8	4.7	11	5	9	9	2	-4
Botswana	15	2	-20	-26	0.4	0.0	15	2	14	8	1	-6
Cape Verde	11	33	9	30	3.5	8.5	10	14	10	14	0	0
Costa Rica	-22	-152	-244	-402	-0.2	-1.7	-34	-150	21	-137	-55	-13
Croatia	*121*	601	*-4*	448	*0.8*	3.3	*-5*	259	*-60*	-6	*56*	265
Czech Republic	699	5,136	209	4,221	2.5	11.5	728	2,980	204	34	524	2,946
Djibouti	13	9	8	3	..	..	15	8	15	8	0	0
Dominica	2	2	0	-1	1.4	0.8	2	3	2	3	0	0
Dominican Republic	-21	79	-163	-114	-0.2	0.7	-32	-30	4	4	-37	-34
El Salvador	108	368	14	245	1.6	3.8	109	31	119	61	-10	-30
Estonia	*61*	118	*52*	104	*1.7*	2.6	*33*	66	*39*	67	*-6*	-1
Fiji	-31	-37	-56	-53	-2.0	-2.1	-31	-36	-24	-16	-7	-21
Grenada	8	-3	5	-5	3.4	-0.9	7	-2	5	0	2	-2
Guatemala	56	142	-72	-6	0.5	1.0	25	-11	16	-21	8	10
Iran, Islamic Rep. of	3,489	..	2,622	..	..	..	249	..	-513	..	762	..
Kazakstan	*605*	939	*579*	800	*3.1*	6.0	*406*	705	*249*	489	*157*	216
Latvia	*149*	90	*137*	65	*2.6*	1.5	*86*	67	*76*	23	*10*	44
Lebanon	123	1,230	37	1,089	3.5	10.6	-15	1,204	-15	120	0	1,083
Lesotho	51	39	40	24	4.3	2.6	45	42	48	33	-3	9
Lithuania	*211*	298	*193*	267	*2.9*	3.7	*116*	215	*99*	98	*17*	116
Malaysia	1,952	4,831	746	3,240	3.2	6.0	1,169	3,746	57	-80	1,112	3,825
Maldives	10	30	8	26	5.8	11.7	12	28	11	26	1	2
Malta	78	146	42	104	..	..	14	-7	14	-29	0	22
Mauritius	96	326	42	253	3.1	8.3	59	268	15	-17	44	285
Moldova	*184*	188	*179*	158	*4.3*	4.8	*104*	123	*104*	108	*0*	15
Oman	-29	29	-218	-176	-0.3	0.3	-55	-34	42	-6	-97	-28
Paraguay	-28	305	-153	176	-0.6	3.9	-107	109	-44	136	-63	-26
Romania	850	986	707	695	3.1	2.9	583	965	448	698	135	267
Seychelles	-1	-13	-9	-20	-0.1	-2.7	1	-3	3	-1	-2	-2
Slovak Republic	530	878	339	608	4.3	5.1	280	601	123	191	158	410
Slovenia	*357*	615	*223*	424	*2.6*	3.3	*151*	602	*-46*	-59	*197*	662
Solomon Islands	-2	3	-5	2	-0.2	0.9	-2	4	0	2	-2	2
St. Kitts and Nevis	4	0	3	-2	2.6	-0.1	4	1	3	2	1	-1
St. Lucia	10	12	5	7	2.2	2.3	8	5	9	5	-1	0
Swaziland	-9	4	-18	-2	-1.0	0.4	-6	0	-5	0	-2	0
Thailand	4,201	9,707	1,707	6,876	4.0	6.0	2,672	5,432	152	511	2,520	4,921
Tonga	2	4	2	3	1.9	2.4	2	4	2	4	0	0
Turkmenistan	*186*	-45	*172*	-69	*3.6*	-1.1	*146*	27	*100*	8	*46*	19
Ukraine	*692*	1,552	*620*	1,051	*0.7*	2.0	*453*	380	*203*	400	*251*	-20
Uzbekistan	*430*	442	*412*	368	*2.0*	2.0	*284*	360	*208*	241	*76*	120
Vanuatu	4	1	3	0	2.5	0.3	5	1	5	1	0	0
Yugoslavia, former	-787	120	-1,552	120	..	..	-648	0	-261	0	-387	0
All Developing Countries	**82,718**	**133,019**	**9,303**	**37,063**	**1.9**	**2.5**	**55,323**	**77,021**	**23,628**	**20,408**	**31,695**	**56,613**

Note: Individual country data are shown for Debtor Reporting System countries only. Data for Bosnia and Herzegovina are not shown separately. Totals include estimates for countries not part of the DRS. A country is classified as severely indebted if for 1993-95 the average ratio of the present value of total debt service due to GNP is higher than 80 percent or the average ratio of the present value of total debt service due to exports is higher than 220 percent. A country is classified as moderately indebted if for 1993-95 the average ratio of the present value of total debt service due to GNP is less than 80 percent but higher than 48 percent or the average ratio of the present value of total debt service due to exports is less than 220 percent but higher than 132 percent. Figures in italics are for years other than those specified.

EXTERNAL DEBT

(US$ million, unless otherwise indicated)

Group and country	Total debt stock		Total debt / GNP(%)		Long-term debt/total debt (%)		Distribution of long-term debt (%): Multilateral		Bilateral		Private	
	1990	1995	1990	1995	1990	1995	1990	1995	1990	1995	1990	1995
Low-Income Countries	**405,622**	**534,794**	**42**	**39**	**85**	**85**	**25**	**30**	**45**	**42**	**29**	**28**
Severely indebted	**212,280**	**245,167**	**135**	**112**	**86**	**83**	**21**	**27**	**55**	**56**	**24**	**17**
Angola	8,443	11,482	115	275	89	83	1	2	24	22	75	76
Burundi	907	1,157	81	110	94	95	78	85	21	15	1	0
Cambodia	1,854	2,031	166	74	91	96	0	6	100	93	0	1
Cameroon	6,679	9,350	63	124	84	88	24	20	46	66	31	14
Central African Republic	699	944	55	..	89	90	73	75	24	24	4	2
Congo	4,953	6,032	231	366	85	82	14	14	59	67	28	19
Cote d'Ivoire	17,259	18,952	196	252	77	77	27	27	31	37	42	37
Equatorial Guinea	241	293	191	196	87	78	32	44	59	49	9	7
Ethiopia	3,809	5,221	45	100	96	95	35	48	55	44	10	8
Ghana	3,873	5,874	63	95	73	78	66	65	25	25	9	10
Guinea	2,476	3,242	95	91	91	92	30	49	65	48	5	3
Guinea-Bissau	712	894	287	354	91	95	41	59	54	41	5	0
Guyana	1,945	2,105	708	377	90	85	27	36	65	61	8	4
Honduras	3,724	4,567	134	125	94	90	45	53	40	36	15	11
Kenya	7,056	7,381	87	98	80	86	44	46	22	36	34	18
Liberia	1,849	2,127	..	..	60	55	39	39	44	43	17	18
Madagascar	3,720	4,302	127	142	90	86	37	46	59	52	4	2
Malawi	1,579	2,140	87	167	89	92	77	85	19	14	5	1
Mali	2,502	3,066	102	132	95	93	39	49	60	51	1	0
Mauritania	2,141	2,467	223	243	85	89	36	42	59	58	5	0
Mozambique	4,665	5,781	380	444	91	92	11	25	73	73	16	2
Myanmar	4,695	5,771	..	..	95	93	28	25	67	68	6	7
Nicaragua	10,692	9,287	1,081	590	77	86	12	19	71	69	18	12
Niger	1,793	1,633	74	91	87	92	45	58	31	34	24	9
Nigeria	33,440	35,005	115	141	96	83	12	17	42	54	47	29
Rwanda	711	1,008	28	89	93	94	82	85	18	15	1	0
Sao Tome and Principe	153	277	312	693	89	94	56	70	44	30	1	0
Sierra Leone	1,206	1,226	154	160	54	79	28	43	58	56	15	0
Somalia	2,370	2,678	284	..	81	73	39	40	59	58	2	2
Sudan	14,762	17,623	169	..	65	58	18	21	60	56	22	23
Tanzania	6,286	7,333	171	207	90	84	36	47	56	47	9	7
Togo	1,286	1,486	80	121	85	87	52	56	43	40	5	4
Uganda	2,583	3,564	61	64	84	86	59	72	26	25	16	3
Vietnam	22,253	26,495	..	130	93	87	1	1	94	95	5	4
Yemen, Rep. of	6,345	6,212	100	155	81	89	20	23	48	46	32	31
Zaire	10,270	13,137	126	255	88	73	21	25	69	66	10	9
Zambia	7,265	6,853	242	191	67	74	29	43	61	54	10	3
Moderately indebted	**130,080**	**156,442**	**34**	**35**	**86**	**90**	**35**	**42**	**41**	**34**	**24**	**24**
Bangladesh	12,757	16,370	57	56	94	95	55	63	43	36	2	2
Benin	1,245	1,646	69	82	95	92	46	57	52	43	2	0
Burkina Faso	834	1,267	30	55	90	90	75	87	20	13	5	0
Chad	530	908	45	81	89	92	70	79	28	21	2	0
Comoros	185	203	74	89	93	92	66	82	34	19	0	0
Gambia, The	369	426	116	..	84	90	66	84	28	16	6	0
Haiti	889	807	30	40	84	93	65	81	29	19	6	0
India	83,862	93,766	28	28	87	92	30	35	37	31	34	34
Lao PDR	1,768	2,165	204	125	99	97	15	30	85	70	0	0
Pakistan	20,663	30,152	50	50	81	84	41	48	54	41	5	11

EXTERNAL DEBT

(US$ million, unless otherwise indicated)

Group and country	Total debt stock		Total debt / GNP(%)		Long-term debt/total debt (%)		Distribution of long-term debt (%): Multilateral		Bilateral		Private	
	1990	1995	1990	1995	1990	1995	1990	1995	1990	1995	1990	1995
Senegal	3,731	3,845	68	82	80	84	46	58	47	39	8	4
Zimbabwe	3,247	4,885	50	79	82	77	24	43	33	31	43	26
Other selected countries												
Albania	349	709	17	32	10	79	0	20	6	26	94	55
Armenia	*134*	374	*7*	18	*100*	80	*45*	69	*55*	31	*0*	0
Azerbaijan	*36*	321	*1*	9	*100*	64	*0*	48	*100*	52	*0*	0
Bhutan	84	87	29	29	96	99	52	79	25	13	23	8
China	55,301	118,090	16	17	82	81	13	17	19	21	68	62
Georgia	*559*	1,189	*20*	52	*100*	83	*17*	24	*70*	65	*13*	11
Kyrgyz Republic	*294*	610	*7*	20	*80*	78	*21*	39	*79*	62	*0*	0
Mongolia	*350*	512	*48*	62	*78*	88	*21*	38	*39*	45	*40*	17
Nepal	1,640	2,398	45	53	96	97	81	84	12	14	7	2
Sri Lanka	5,864	8,230	74	64	86	86	32	40	54	51	14	9
Tajikistan	*382*	665	*13*	35	*100*	92	*16*	12	*84*	88	*0*	0
Middle-Income Countries	**1,074,548**	**1,530,883**	**33**	**40**	**78**	**77**	**15**	**14**	**27**	**32**	**58**	**54**
Severely indebted	**427,223**	**578,582**	**45**	**40**	**79**	**76**	**12**	**12**	**28**	**29**	**60**	**59**
Argentina	62,233	89,747	46	33	78	82	10	13	13	16	77	71
Bolivia	4,275	5,266	101	91	90	89	41	55	46	38	13	7
Brazil	119,643	159,130	28	24	79	81	12	7	19	15	69	78
Bulgaria	10,890	10,887	57	92	90	88	6	19	11	18	83	63
Ecuador	12,109	13,957	123	84	83	89	21	24	19	18	60	58
Gabon	3,984	4,492	82	122	79	91	10	16	67	79	23	5
Jamaica	4,671	4,270	125	135	85	83	29	34	56	53	14	13
Jordan	8,184	7,944	226	126	86	87	13	17	39	55	49	28
Mexico	104,442	165,743	44	70	78	68	18	17	10	18	72	66
Panama	6,679	7,180	145	101	60	54	26	16	12	17	62	68
Peru	20,064	30,831	63	54	70	66	16	18	31	52	53	30
Syrian Arab Republic	17,068	21,318	148	135	87	79	6	6	86	87	8	7
Moderately indebted	**495,383**	**679,844**	**38**	**50**	**81**	**81**	**16**	**15**	**28**	**35**	**56**	**50**
Algeria	27,896	32,610	48	83	95	93	8	12	14	38	78	49
Chile	19,227	25,562	67	43	76	73	28	15	7	4	65	81
Colombia	17,232	20,760	45	28	92	75	39	34	15	11	46	55
Egypt, Arab Rep.	33,402	34,116	97	73	86	93	12	13	61	80	27	6
Hungary	21,277	31,248	67	73	85	89	14	12	1	3	85	85
Indonesia	69,872	107,831	64	57	83	79	25	23	32	37	43	40
Macedonia, FYR	*972*	1,213	*59*	66	*87*	88	*27*	27	*27*	31	*47*	42
Morocco	23,527	22,147	95	71	95	98	21	32	52	42	27	27
Papua New Guinea	2,576	2,431	83	53	95	95	31	40	12	23	57	37
Philippines	30,615	39,445	69	52	83	85	25	25	36	41	39	33
Poland	49,366	42,291	89	36	80	100	1	5	70	72	29	23
Russia Federation	59,817	120,461	10	38	80	83	1	2	12	55	87	43
St. Vincent and the Grenadines	59	206	32	84	96	42	83	64	17	30	0	6
Trinidad and Tobago	2,512	2,556	54	54	82	72	5	29	26	23	69	49
Tunisia	7,691	9,938	65	57	90	91	32	41	44	39	24	20
Turkey	49,238	73,592	32	44	81	78	24	16	21	15	54	70
Uruguay	4,415	5,307	55	32	71	74	22	32	6	9	71	60
Venezuela	33,170	35,842	70	49	85	85	6	11	1	5	93	84
Western Samoa	92	162	61	82	99	99	89	93	9	7	2	0

EXTERNAL DEBT

(US$ million, unless otherwise indicated)

	Total debt stock		Total debt / GNP(%)		Long-term debt/total debt (%)		Distribution of long-term debt (%)					
							Multilateral		Bilateral		Private	
Group and country	**1990**	**1995**	**1990**	**1995**	**1990**	**1995**	**1990**	**1995**	**1990**	**1995**	**1990**	**1995**
Other selected countries												
Barbados	683	597	40	36	74	62	36	44	13	7	51	49
Belarus	*969*	1,648	*4*	8	*89*	76	*13*	15	*56*	46	*32*	39
Belize	154	261	39	47	96	85	39	41	41	39	20	20
Botswana	563	699	19	16	99	98	70	70	25	24	5	7
Cape Verde	135	216	50	56	97	86	67	80	32	19	2	1
Costa Rica	3,756	3,800	68	43	90	88	34	40	36	34	30	26
Croatia	*2,523*	3,662	*22*	20	*95*	81	*23*	18	*36*	33	*41*	49
Czech Republic	6,383	16,576	20	37	62	69	5	9	2	4	94	88
Djibouti	206	260	..	..	76	84	57	63	43	37	0	0
Dominica	82	93	51	43	91	91	70	62	30	38	0	0
Dominican Republic	4,372	4,259	63	37	81	84	24	29	43	53	32	19
El Salvador	2,147	2,583	46	27	90	80	41	66	50	29	10	5
Estonia	*154*	309	*4*	7	*62*	61	*47*	70	*15*	17	*38*	13
Fiji	413	253	31	14	97	94	50	64	19	8	30	29
Grenada	103	113	49	42	88	87	43	47	55	46	3	7
Guatemala	2,840	3,275	38	22	83	81	42	36	36	42	22	22
Iran, Islamic Rep. of	9,021	21,935	8	..	20	79	6	..	6	..	88	..
Kazakstan	*1,724*	3,712	*6*	24	*94*	78	*2*	14	*86*	65	*12*	21
Latvia	*236*	462	*4*	8	*52*	59	*54*	52	*33*	23	*13*	26
Lebanon	1,779	2,966	50	26	20	54	24	12	29	14	47	73
Lesotho	395	659	38	45	96	93	77	75	14	20	9	5
Lithuania	*330*	802	*4*	10	*61*	61	*49*	34	*18*	31	*33*	35
Malaysia	16,421	34,352	40	43	88	79	13	6	16	12	71	82
Maldives	78	155	60	62	82	98	51	60	43	34	6	6
Malta	601	955	24	..	21	16	19	23	81	64	0	13
Mauritius	995	1,801	39	46	93	81	34	19	38	29	29	53
Moldova	*285*	691	*5*	18	*69*	66	*29*	48	*71*	49	*0*	3
Oman	2,736	3,107	29	30	88	83	5	7	8	16	86	77
Paraguay	2,106	2,288	39	29	82	66	42	52	27	40	31	8
Romania	1,140	6,653	3	20	20	65	0	39	95	30	5	31
Seychelles	195	164	55	34	76	92	31	42	50	44	19	15
Slovak Republic	2,008	5,827	13	34	75	63	6	26	2	11	92	64
Slovenia	*1,909*	3,489	*15*	19	*93*	85	*26*	18	*15*	6	*59*	76
Solomon Islands	121	158	58	45	86	94	60	53	27	11	14	37
St. Kitts and Nevis	45	56	30	27	98	95	45	55	49	35	6	10
St. Lucia	80	128	22	24	91	87	59	71	38	29	4	0
Swaziland	262	251	29	24	98	94	47	52	51	48	3	0
Thailand	28,088	56,789	33	35	70	68	19	8	23	20	59	71
Tonga	54	70	46	41	83	98	51	61	49	24	0	15
Turkmenistan	*276*	393	*5*	10	*100*	96	*9*	16	*44*	42	*47*	43
Ukraine	*3,713*	8,434	*3*	11	*96*	79	*4*	9	*78*	56	*18*	35
Uzbekistan	*1,032*	1,630	*5*	8	*91*	77	*0*	20	*84*	59	*16*	22
Vanuatu	40	48	25	23	76	90	55	74	41	25	5	1
Yugoslavia, former	17,837	13,839	20	..	94	83	18	11	26	29	55	60
All Developing Countries	**1,480,170**	**2,065,676**	**35**	**40**	**80**	**79**	**18**	**18**	**33**	**35**	**50**	**47**

Note: Individual country data are shown for Debtor Reporting System countries only. Data for Bosnia and Herzegovina are not shown separately. Totals include estimates for countries not part of the DRS. A country is classified as severely indebted if for 1993-95 the average ratio of the present value of total debt service due to GNP is higher than 80 percent or the average ratio of the present value of total debt service due to exports is higher than 220 percent. A country is classified as moderately indebted if for 1993-95 the average ratio of the present value of total debt service due to GNP is less than 80 percent but higher than 48 percent or the average ratio of the present value of total debt service due to exports is less than 220 percent but higher than 132 percent. Figures in italics are for years other than those specified.

ALL DEVELOPING COUNTRIES

(US$ million, unless otherwise indicated)

	1970	1980	1989	1990	1991	1992	1993	1994	1995	*Preliminary* 1996
1. SUMMARY DEBT DATA										
TOTAL DEBT STOCKS (EDT)	..	**615,711**	**1,374,182**	**1,480,170**	**1,562,942**	**1,636,186**	**1,783,661**	**1,926,941**	**2,065,676**	**2,177,047**
Long-term debt (LDOD)	**59,174**	**452,289**	**1,114,862**	**1,184,455**	**1,244,401**	**1,284,250**	**1,408,266**	**1,538,260**	**1,626,376**	**1,708,391**
Public and publicly guaranteed	43,972	384,021	1,065,596	1,123,854	1,170,730	1,192,077	1,291,880	1,393,290	1,448,646	1,486,001
Private nonguaranteed	15,202	68,268	49,266	60,601	73,672	92,173	116,386	144,971	177,731	222,390
Use of IMF credit	**756**	**11,564**	**32,076**	**34,652**	**38,129**	**38,264**	**39,897**	**44,151**	**61,105**	**60,192**
Short-term debt	..	**151,859**	**227,244**	**261,063**	**280,412**	**313,671**	**335,498**	**344,530**	**378,195**	**408,463**
of which interest arrears on LDOD	..	1,023	36,663	52,258	53,095	46,776	45,642	42,862	43,631	34,548
Official creditors	..	582	18,590	19,861	16,940	18,029	20,168	22,833	25,358	..
Private creditors	..	442	18,074	32,397	36,154	28,746	25,475	20,030	18,272	..
Memo: principal arrears on LDOD	..	1,966	47,563	58,855	62,447	76,126	80,773	92,915	108,692	97,902
Official creditors	..	718	23,799	27,071	29,694	34,439	38,822	48,169	58,994	..
Private creditors	..	1,248	23,763	31,784	32,753	41,687	41,951	44,746	49,698	..
Memo: export credits	..	..	263,584	299,939	330,193	320,784	326,073	386,073	403,973	..
TOTAL DEBT FLOWS										
Disbursements	**12,764**	**114,475**	**119,331**	**134,273**	**136,759**	**158,222**	**179,560**	**179,781**	**229,151**	**242,108**
Long-term debt	12,432	109,084	113,651	126,029	127,096	151,165	172,559	171,380	201,237	233,723
IMF purchases	332	5,392	5,680	8,244	9,663	7,057	7,001	8,401	27,914	8,385
Principal repayments	**6,528**	**43,401**	**84,959**	**90,540**	**89,117**	**97,320**	**107,361**	**120,073**	**135,350**	**143,428**
Long-term debt	5,797	41,338	76,950	82,351	82,604	91,415	101,999	113,245	124,216	135,664
IMF repurchases	730	2,063	8,010	8,189	6,513	5,905	5,361	6,828	11,134	7,764
Net flows on debt	**14,985**	**114,449**	**53,777**	**62,372**	**66,366**	**100,480**	**101,379**	**82,991**	**133,019**	**138,015**
of which short-term debt	..	..	19,405	18,639	18,724	39,578	29,180	23,284	39,217	39,335
Interest payments (INT)	..	**49,084**	**74,420**	**73,107**	**74,735**	**70,720**	**70,548**	**77,963**	**95,956**	**101,195**
Long-term debt	2,281	32,923	56,779	56,000	55,952	54,720	52,785	59,505	74,501	78,706
IMF charges	0	455	2,382	2,504	2,494	2,442	2,348	1,808	2,738	2,457
Short-term debt	..	15,706	15,259	14,602	16,289	13,558	15,415	16,650	18,717	20,032
Net transfers on debt	..	**65,365**	**-20,643**	**-10,735**	**-8,369**	**29,761**	**30,831**	**5,028**	**37,063**	**36,820**
Total debt service (TDS)	..	**92,485**	**159,379**	**163,647**	**163,852**	**168,040**	**177,909**	**198,037**	**231,306**	**244,623**
Long-term debt	8,078	74,261	133,729	138,351	138,556	146,135	154,784	172,751	198,717	214,370
IMF repurchases and charges	730	2,517	10,392	10,693	9,007	8,347	7,709	8,636	13,872	10,221
Short-term debt (interest only)	..	15,706	15,259	14,602	16,289	13,558	15,415	16,650	18,717	20,032
2. AGGREGATE NET RESOURCE FLOWS AND NET TRANSFERS (LONG-TERM)										
NET RESOURCE FLOWS	**10,930**	**86,051**	**82,602**	**100,629**	**122,514**	**145,971**	**212,028**	**206,982**	**237,197**	**284,575**
Net flow of long-term debt (ex. IMF)	6,635	67,746	36,701	43,678	44,492	59,750	70,560	58,134	77,021	98,059
Foreign direct investment (net)	2,202	5,092	23,168	24,549	33,478	43,644	67,214	83,716	95,489	109,514
Portfolio equity flows	0	0	3,372	3,225	7,207	11,012	44,987	32,688	32,087	45,700
Grants (excluding technical coop.)	2,093	13,213	19,360	29,177	37,337	31,565	29,267	32,443	32,600	31,302
Memo: technical coop. grants	1,733	6,313	12,136	14,162	15,721	17,878	18,526	17,359	20,677	20,000
NET TRANSFERS	**2,184**	**29,411**	**8,875**	**27,232**	**48,419**	**70,419**	**136,450**	**122,667**	**136,323**	**175,614**
Interest on long-term debt	2,281	32,923	56,779	56,000	55,952	54,720	52,785	59,505	74,501	78,706
Profit remittances on FDI	6,466	23,717	16,949	17,397	18,143	20,833	22,793	24,810	26,373	30,255
3. MAJOR ECONOMIC AGGREGATES										
Gross national product (GNP)	796,862	2,927,241	3,949,058	4,250,544	4,164,381	4,289,868	4,400,861	4,728,643	5,221,362	5,881,167
Exports of goods & services (XGS)	94,406	712,132	802,114	896,484	893,000	934,714	992,144	1,131,779	1,364,543	1,488,725
of which workers' remittances	2,056	20,580	23,518	25,834	26,651	31,470	32,164	35,745	39,374	35,842
Imports of goods & services (MGS)	99,052	696,566	859,069	945,975	976,015	1,037,591	1,134,451	1,228,269	1,481,716	1,629,379
International reserves (RES)	27,570	232,081	207,196	239,311	287,542	298,112	368,175	434,014	538,368	..
Current account balance	5,844	25,964	-47,341	-40,860	-71,626	-85,026	-131,837	-84,560	-101,036	-123,186
4. DEBT INDICATORS										
EDT / XGS (%)	..	86.5	171.3	165.1	175.0	175.0	179.8	170.3	151.4	146.2
EDT / GNP (%)	..	21.0	34.8	34.8	37.5	38.1	40.5	40.8	39.6	37.0
TDS / XGS (%)	..	13.0	19.9	18.3	18.3	18.0	17.9	17.5	17.0	16.4
INT / XGS (%)	..	6.9	9.3	8.2	8.4	7.6	7.1	6.9	7.0	6.8
INT / GNP (%)	..	1.7	1.9	1.7	1.8	1.6	1.6	1.6	1.8	1.7
RES / EDT (%)	..	37.7	15.1	16.2	18.4	18.2	20.6	22.5	26.1	..
RES / MGS (months)	3.3	4.0	2.9	3.0	3.5	3.4	3.9	4.2	4.4	..
Short-term / EDT (%)	..	24.7	16.5	17.6	17.9	19.2	18.8	17.9	18.3	18.8
Concessional / EDT (%)	..	17.8	20.4	20.8	21.0	21.3	22.5	22.4	21.1	19.9
Multilateral / EDT (%)	..	7.6	13.2	14.2	14.6	14.3	14.2	14.5	14.3	14.2

ALL DEVELOPING COUNTRIES

(US$ million, unless otherwise indicated)

	1970	*1980*	*1989*	*1990*	*1991*	*1992*	*1993*	*1994*	*1995*	*Preliminary 1996*
5. LONG-TERM DEBT										
DEBT OUTSTANDING (LDOD)	**59,174**	**452,289**	**1,114,862**	**1,184,455**	**1,244,401**	**1,284,250**	**1,408,266**	**1,538,260**	**1,626,376**	**1,708,391**
Public and publicly guaranteed	**43,972**	**384,021**	**1,065,596**	**1,123,854**	**1,170,730**	**1,192,077**	**1,291,880**	**1,393,290**	**1,448,646**	**1,486,001**
Official creditors	31,688	171,142	536,152	596,243	645,397	669,053	754,603	828,603	860,932	860,259
Multilateral	7,288	46,836	181,770	209,515	227,565	234,539	252,855	279,600	294,915	309,312
Concessional	5,570	21,229	64,701	73,414	80,756	85,936	93,257	105,934	114,770	..
Bilateral	24,400	124,306	354,382	386,729	417,832	434,514	501,748	549,003	566,018	550,947
Concessional	20,922	88,481	215,229	234,769	246,747	262,454	307,756	325,755	320,232	..
Private creditors	12,284	212,879	529,444	527,611	525,332	523,024	537,277	564,687	587,714	625,743
Bonds	1,805	18,780	51,432	111,947	121,199	133,118	172,750	246,628	267,670	..
Commercial banks	3,622	130,972	344,748	269,327	260,537	246,448	221,924	173,399	178,234	..
Other private	6,857	63,128	133,264	146,336	143,596	143,458	142,604	144,661	141,810	..
Private nonguaranteed	**15,202**	**68,268**	**49,266**	**60,601**	**73,672**	**92,173**	**116,386**	**144,971**	**177,731**	**222,390**
Bonds	..	..	49	347	1,974	9,304	27,242	42,149	53,221	..
Commerical banks	..	..	49,217	60,255	71,698	82,869	89,145	102,822	124,509	..
Memo:										
IBRD	4,382	20,432	80,996	92,333	97,155	95,301	100,323	107,894	111,893	..
IDA	1,806	11,775	39,263	45,005	49,660	53,514	58,221	66,419	71,549	..
DISBURSEMENTS	**12,432**	**109,084**	**113,651**	**126,029**	**127,096**	**151,165**	**172,559**	**171,380**	**201,237**	**233,723**
Public and publicly guaranteed	**8,307**	**88,181**	**102,471**	**108,704**	**109,525**	**117,914**	**129,157**	**122,595**	**140,009**	**159,763**
Official creditors	4,757	28,178	44,660	52,084	54,867	51,930	54,446	50,497	65,795	55,997
Multilateral	1,194	9,049	22,454	27,672	28,983	28,004	31,546	29,204	32,358	33,856
Concessional	574	3,112	6,156	7,319	8,320	8,904	8,727	10,171	10,047	..
Bilatarel	3,563	19,128	22,206	24,412	25,884	23,926	22,900	21,293	33,438	22,141
Concessional	2,815	10,925	14,451	14,392	14,038	12,364	12,709	13,048	13,611	..
Private creditors	3,550	60,004	57,811	56,620	54,658	65,984	74,711	72,098	74,213	103,766
Bonds	146	3,103	7,408	6,863	11,106	12,489	29,192	22,890	29,746	..
Commercial banks	1,286	35,303	24,548	17,523	15,188	19,771	17,589	22,004	22,869	..
Other private	2,117	21,597	25,855	32,234	28,364	33,724	27,930	27,204	21,599	..
Private nonguaranteed	**4,126**	**20,903**	**11,180**	**17,325**	**17,571**	**33,251**	**43,402**	**48,785**	**61,228**	**73,960**
Bonds	..	..	47	291	1,626	7,515	18,228	16,774	14,607	..
Commercial banks	..	..	11,133	17,034	15,945	25,736	25,174	32,011	46,621	..
Memo:										
IBRD	672	4,224	10,565	13,442	11,926	10,218	12,884	11,339	13,139	..
IDA	173	1,587	3,591	4,378	4,604	5,143	4,862	6,065	5,474	..
PRINCIPAL REPAYMENTS	**5,797**	**41,338**	**76,950**	**82,351**	**82,604**	**91,415**	**101,999**	**113,245**	**124,216**	**135,664**
Public and publicly guaranteed	**3,350**	**29,651**	**66,244**	**75,086**	**73,566**	**77,856**	**77,542**	**88,321**	**96,540**	**106,240**
Official creditors	1,496	7,042	22,623	24,995	26,568	28,080	28,754	37,288	45,387	46,514
Multilateral	387	1,593	10,592	12,187	13,941	15,473	16,192	18,882	21,307	18,818
Concessional	230	385	1,018	1,222	1,571	1,740	1,813	1,860	2,198	..
Bilateral	1,110	5,449	12,031	12,808	12,627	12,607	12,562	18,405	24,080	27,696
Concessional	614	2,444	4,455	5,737	4,843	4,955	5,442	7,062	8,862	..
Private creditors	1,853	22,609	43,621	50,091	46,998	49,776	48,788	51,033	51,152	59,726
Bonds	143	502	3,453	4,832	2,641	9,946	11,206	8,364	11,804	..
Commercial banks	675	13,711	22,765	24,278	19,318	19,596	18,872	20,086	19,400	..
Other private	1,035	8,396	17,403	20,981	25,039	20,234	18,710	22,584	19,948	..
Private nonguaranteed	**2,448**	**11,687**	**10,705**	**7,265**	**9,038**	**13,559**	**24,458**	**24,925**	**27,676**	**29,424**
Bonds	..	..	0	0	0	165	289	1,997	4,042	..
Commerical banks	..	..	10,705	7,265	9,038	13,394	24,169	22,928	23,635	..
Memo:										
IBRD	249	997	7,237	7,941	8,990	9,886	9,945	11,335	11,705	..
IDA	0	30	207	248	305	343	394	455	542	..
NET FLOWS ON DEBT	**6,635**	**67,746**	**36,701**	**43,678**	**44,492**	**59,750**	**70,560**	**58,134**	**77,021**	**98,059**
Public and publicly guaranteed	**4,957**	**58,530**	**36,226**	**33,618**	**35,959**	**40,058**	**51,616**	**34,274**	**43,469**	**53,523**
Official creditors	3,261	21,136	22,037	27,089	28,299	23,850	25,692	13,210	20,408	9,483
Multilateral	807	7,456	11,862	15,486	15,042	12,531	15,354	10,322	11,050	15,038
Concessional	344	2,727	5,138	6,096	6,748	7,164	6,914	8,311	7,850	..
Bilateral	2,453	13,680	10,175	11,604	13,258	11,319	10,339	2,888	9,358	-5,555
Concessional	2,201	8,481	9,996	8,655	9,195	7,409	7,267	5,986	4,750	..
Private creditors	1,696	37,394	14,190	6,529	7,660	16,208	25,923	21,065	23,061	44,040
Bonds	3	2,601	3,955	2,032	8,465	2,543	17,986	14,526	17,942	..
Commercial banks	611	21,593	1,783	-6,756	-4,130	174	-1,283	1,918	3,469	..
Other private	1,082	13,201	8,452	11,253	3,324	13,491	9,219	4,620	1,650	..
Private nonguaranteed	**1,678**	**9,216**	**475**	**10,060**	**8,533**	**19,692**	**18,944**	**23,860**	**33,552**	**44,536**
Bonds	..	..	47	291	1,626	7,350	17,939	14,778	10,566	..
Commerical banks	..	..	428	9,769	6,907	12,342	1,006	9,083	22,986	..
Memo:										
IBRD	423	3,227	3,328	5,502	2,937	332	2,940	4	1,434	..
IDA	172	1,556	3,383	4,130	4,299	4,801	4,469	5,611	4,932	..

ALL DEVELOPING COUNTRIES

(US$ million, unless otherwise indicated)

	1970	*1980*	*1989*	*1990*	*1991*	*1992*	*1993*	*1994*	*1995*	*Preliminary 1996*
INTEREST PAYMENTS (LINT)	**2,281**	**32,923**	**56,779**	**56,000**	**55,952**	**54,720**	**52,785**	**59,505**	**74,501**	**78,706**
Public and publicly guaranteed	**1,528**	**26,238**	**52,028**	**51,601**	**50,963**	**49,282**	**46,529**	**51,972**	**64,044**	**66,645**
Official creditors	854	5,867	17,175	20,068	21,357	22,280	23,702	25,878	30,578	30,650
Multilateral	308	2,434	9,455	10,919	12,470	12,580	13,189	13,472	14,158	15,075
Concessional	214	398	757	861	1,021	1,087	1,166	1,268	1,425	..
Bilateral	546	3,433	7,721	9,150	8,887	9,700	10,512	12,406	16,420	15,575
Concessional	378	1,752	3,290	4,202	3,929	4,893	5,481	6,128	6,426	..
Private creditors	674	20,372	34,853	31,533	29,606	27,002	22,827	26,094	33,467	35,995
Bonds	97	1,457	3,183	4,840	7,994	7,678	8,521	11,303	17,136	..
Commercial banks	252	14,519	24,420	19,392	13,856	13,036	8,697	8,239	9,421	..
Other private	325	4,396	7,250	7,300	7,756	6,288	5,609	6,552	6,909	..
Private nonguaranteed	**753**	**6,685**	**4,751**	**4,399**	**4,990**	**5,438**	**6,256**	**7,534**	**10,457**	**12,061**
Bonds	..	..	0	3	47	225	925	2,233	3,315	..
Commerical banks	..	..	4,751	4,396	4,943	5,212	5,332	5,301	7,142	..
Memo:										
IBRD	243	1,669	6,067	6,869	7,701	7,571	7,822	7,829	7,986	..
IDA	12	79	268	302	348	372	395	432	503	..
NET TRANSFERS ON DEBT	**4,354**	**34,822**	**-20,078**	**-12,322**	**-11,460**	**5,030**	**17,775**	**-1,371**	**2,520**	**19,354**
Public and publicly guaranteed	**3,429**	**32,292**	**-15,802**	**-17,983**	**-15,004**	**-9,225**	**5,087**	**-17,698**	**-20,575**	**-13,122**
Official creditors	2,407	15,269	4,861	7,021	6,943	1,570	1,991	-12,669	-10,170	-21,167
Multilateral	499	5,023	2,407	4,567	2,572	-49	2,165	-3,150	-3,108	-37
Concessional	130	2,329	4,381	5,235	5,727	6,077	5,748	7,044	6,425	..
Bilateral	1,908	10,247	2,454	2,454	4,371	1,619	-174	-9,518	-7,062	-21,130
Concessional	1,823	6,729	6,706	4,453	5,266	2,516	1,786	-142	-1,677	..
Private creditors	1,022	17,023	-20,663	-25,004	-21,946	-10,795	3,096	-5,029	-10,406	8,045
Bonds	-95	1,144	772	-2,809	471	-5,135	9,465	3,223	806	..
Commercial banks	359	7,074	-22,637	-26,148	-17,985	-12,862	-9,980	-6,320	-5,952	..
Other private	757	8,805	1,202	3,953	-4,432	7,202	3,611	-1,932	-5,259	..
Private nonguaranteed	**925**	**2,530**	**-4,276**	**5,660**	**3,544**	**14,255**	**12,688**	**16,327**	**23,095**	**32,475**
Bonds	..	..	47	288	1,580	7,125	17,014	12,545	7,251	..
Commerical banks	..	..	-4,323	5,372	1,964	7,130	-4,326	3,782	15,845	..
Memo:										
IBRD	180	1,557	-2,739	-1,368	-4,764	-7,239	-4,883	-7,825	-6,552	..
IDA	161	1,478	3,116	3,828	3,951	4,429	4,074	5,178	4,428	..
DEBT SERVICE (LTDS)	**8,078**	**74,261**	**133,729**	**138,351**	**138,556**	**146,135**	**154,784**	**172,751**	**198,717**	**214,370**
Public and publicly guaranteed	**4,878**	**55,889**	**118,273**	**126,687**	**124,529**	**127,139**	**124,070**	**140,293**	**160,584**	**172,885**
Official creditors	2,350	12,908	39,799	45,063	47,924	50,360	52,456	63,166	75,965	77,164
Multilateral	694	4,027	20,047	23,105	26,411	28,053	29,382	32,354	35,465	33,893
Concessional	444	783	1,775	2,084	2,592	2,827	2,979	3,128	3,622	..
Bilateral	1,656	8,882	19,752	21,958	21,514	22,307	23,074	30,812	40,500	43,271
Concessional	991	4,195	7,745	9,939	8,772	9,848	10,923	13,190	15,288	..
Private creditors	2,528	42,981	78,474	81,623	76,605	76,778	71,615	77,127	84,619	95,721
Bonds	241	1,959	6,637	9,672	10,635	17,624	19,727	19,666	28,940	..
Commercial banks	927	28,230	47,185	43,671	33,174	32,633	27,569	28,325	28,821	..
Other private	1,360	12,792	24,653	28,281	32,796	26,522	24,319	29,136	26,857	..
Private nonguaranteed	**3,200**	**18,372**	**15,456**	**11,665**	**14,028**	**18,996**	**30,714**	**32,458**	**38,133**	**41,485**
Bonds	..	..	0	3	47	390	1,214	4,229	7,357	..
Commerical banks	..	..	15,456	11,662	13,981	18,606	29,500	28,229	30,776	..
Memo:										
IBRD	492	2,666	13,304	14,810	16,690	17,457	17,767	19,164	19,691	..
IDA	12	109	475	550	653	714	788	887	1,045	..
UNDISBURSED DEBT	**16,165**	**135,155**	**197,635**	**214,843**	**233,430**	**241,103**	**249,973**	**246,933**	**239,239**	**..**
Official creditors	12,823	87,438	149,208	162,806	179,313	185,014	187,882	194,885	190,056	..
Private creditors	3,342	47,718	48,427	52,038	54,117	56,089	62,092	52,047	49,183	..
Memorandum items										
Concessional LDOD	26,491	109,710	279,930	308,183	327,502	348,390	401,012	431,688	435,002	432,464
Variable rate LDOD	15,964	184,834	447,981	433,312	461,341	481,915	537,426	583,405	645,572	..
Public sector LDOD	42,707	329,470	970,546	1,027,748	1,067,708	1,083,763	1,185,109	1,279,462	1,333,426	..
Private sector LDOD	16,467	75,907	54,515	66,721	79,525	98,492	121,055	148,370	178,953	..

6. CURRENCY COMPOSITION OF LONG-TERM DEBT (PERCENT)

	1970	*1980*	*1989*	*1990*	*1991*	*1992*	*1993*	*1994*	*1995*	*Preliminary 1996*
Deutsche mark	8.6	6.4	7.3	8.6	8.9	8.5	7.6	7.3	7.3	..
French franc	5.3	5.3	4.8	5.4	5.5	5.1	4.4	4.4	4.5	..
Japanese yen	2.2	5.8	9.8	9.9	10.7	10.9	11.4	12.1	11.6	..
Pound sterling	11.6	3.3	2.2	2.2	2.2	1.7	1.6	1.5	1.4	..
Swiss franc	1.1	1.5	1.7	1.8	1.6	1.3	1.2	0.9	1.0	..
U.S. dollars	45.6	47.2	43.5	40.3	38.9	40.1	43.4	43.5	44.3	..
Multiple currency	12.1	10.3	13.2	14.3	14.4	14.8	14.1	14.2	14.2	..
Special drawing rights	0.0	0.0	0.2	0.2	0.3	0.2	0.2	0.3	0.3	..
All other currencies	13.5	8.1	9.0	9.3	9.2	8.8	8.2	7.9	7.8	..

ALL DEVELOPING COUNTRIES

(US$ million, unless otherwise indicated)

	1970	1980	1989	1990	1991	1992	1993	1994	1995	*Preliminary* 1996
7. DEBT RESTRUCTURINGS										
Total amount rescheduled	..	..	35,659	79,110	46,254	58,105	64,680	91,237	32,509	..
Debt stock rescheduled	..	..	14,571	61,910	14,955	26,949	23,999	54,140	9,049	..
Principal rescheduled	..	..	14,315	10,361	20,110	15,101	18,097	15,154	15,137	..
Official	..	..	4,862	5,881	12,849	8,820	7,029	4,577	7,034	..
Private	..	..	9,453	4,481	7,261	6,281	11,067	10,576	8,103	..
Interest rescheduled	..	..	5,816	5,855	10,897	13,746	16,088	15,059	5,186	..
Official	..	..	4,049	4,648	8,748	4,458	3,973	3,398	2,178	..
Private	..	..	1,767	1,207	2,149	9,288	12,115	11,661	3,009	..
Principal forgiven	..	..	6,907	12,633	5,964	2,367	2,451	7,271	2,070	..
Memo: interest forgiven	..	..	226	2,890	582	291	309	698	969	..
Debt stock reduction	..	..	16,022	25,196	5,314	16,482	6,708	13,314	4,125	..
of which debt buyback	..	..	2,457	4,360	897	7,607	606	1,709	162	..
8. DEBT STOCK-FLOW RECONCILIATION										
Total change in debt stocks	..	..	73,683	105,988	82,772	73,244	147,475	143,281	138,735	111,370
Net flows on debt	..	..	53,777	62,372	66,366	100,480	101,379	82,991	133,019	138,015
Net change in interest arrears	..	..	11,523	15,594	837	-6,319	-1,133	-2,780	768	-9,083
Interest capitalized	..	..	5,816	5,855	10,897	13,746	16,088	15,059	5,186	..
Debt forgiveness or reduction	..	..	-20,472	-33,470	-10,381	-11,241	-8,553	-18,876	-6,033	..
Cross-currency valuation	..	..	-12,896	51,521	6,373	-23,354	1,711	57,748	11,558	..
Residual	..	..	35,935	4,116	8,681	-68	37,983	9,139	-5,764	..
9. AVERAGE TERMS OF NEW COMMITMENTS										
ALL CREDITORS										
Interest (%)	5	9.1	6.8	7	6.4	6	5.6	5.5	6.3	..
Maturity (years)	21.2	15.7	16.2	18.1	16	15.5	14.6	16.2	13.5	..
Grace period (years)	6.4	4.8	5.1	5.6	5	4.7	4.9	5.2	4.5	..
Grant element (%)	34.7	10	21.1	20.1	21.7	22.6	23.8	26.6	20.2	..
Official creditors										
Interest (%)	3.6	5.4	5.2	5.6	5.5	5.2	4.7	4.9	6	..
Maturity (years)	28.5	24	22.3	22.2	20.6	21.1	21.3	22.5	18.8	..
Grace period (years)	8.9	6.3	6.4	6.6	6.1	6	6.1	6.4	5.2	..
Grant element (%)	49.2	34.9	34.5	32.7	31	32.4	35.8	36.7	27.3	..
Private creditors										
Interest (%)	7.2	11.9	8.5	8.5	7.8	6.7	6.3	6.3	6.6	..
Maturity (years)	9.5	9.6	9.5	13.7	9.6	9.6	9.2	8.3	7.5	..
Grace period (years)	2.4	3.7	3.7	4.5	3.5	3.3	4	3.7	3.8	..
Grant element (%)	11.7	-8.5	6.2	6.7	8.6	12.3	14.1	14	12.3	..
Memorandum items										
Commitments	11,227	93,657	106,917	120,386	128,960	133,391	139,036	105,856	132,103	..
Official creditors	6,891	39,908	56,125	62,052	75,301	68,508	62,028	58,724	69,862	..
Private creditors	4,336	53,749	50,792	58,334	53,659	64,884	77,008	47,132	62,242	..

10. RESOURCE FLOW CHARTS

(US$ million)

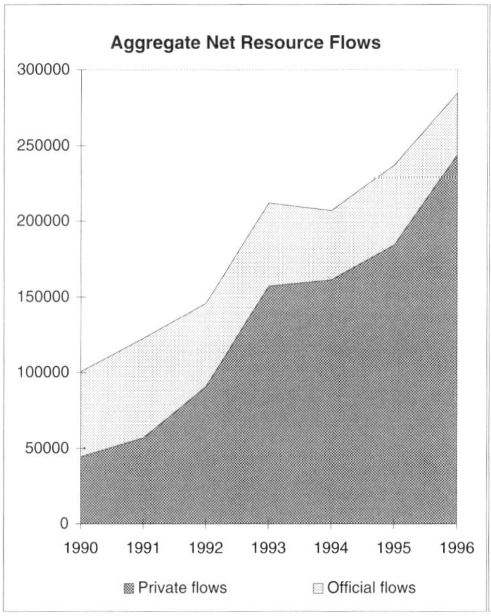

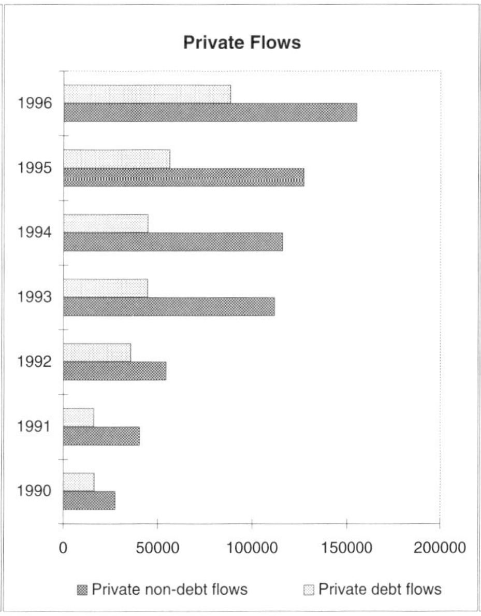

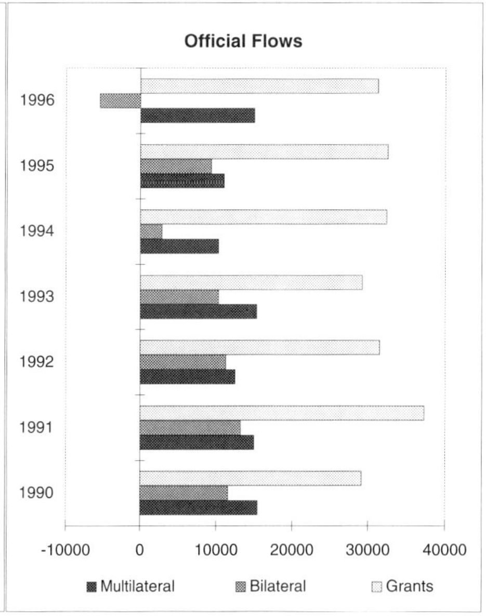

EAST ASIA AND PACIFIC

(US$ million, unless otherwise indicated)

	1970	1980	1989	1990	1991	1992	1993	1994	1995	*Preliminary* 1996
1. SUMMARY DEBT DATA										
TOTAL DEBT STOCKS (EDT)	..	**64,600**	**207,233**	**239,099**	**268,462**	**299,874**	**326,518**	**362,325**	**404,458**	**451,847**
Long-term debt (LDOD)	**5,997**	**48,438**	**174,791**	**199,054**	**219,345**	**238,780**	**262,102**	**295,809**	**322,568**	**355,056**
Public and publicly guaranteed	3,992	39,688	160,108	177,419	189,326	201,679	223,508	249,014	264,542	268,084
Private nonguaranteed	2,004	8,751	14,683	21,635	30,019	37,101	38,595	46,794	58,026	86,972
Use of IMF credit	**224**	**1,551**	**3,114**	**2,085**	**1,479**	**1,319**	**1,430**	**1,493**	**1,337**	**1,270**
Short-term debt	..	**14,611**	**29,328**	**37,960**	**47,638**	**59,775**	**62,987**	**65,023**	**80,552**	**95,521**
of which interest arrears on LDOD	..	2	885	1,474	1,823	2,105	2,270	2,624	2,753	2,987
Official creditors	..	1	714	1,182	1,468	1,823	1,842	2,163	2,265	..
Private creditors	..	1	171	292	355	282	428	461	488	..
Memo: principal arrears on LDOD	..	5	1,495	2,266	4,129	6,647	7,002	9,266	11,257	13,321
Official creditors	..	1	948	1,410	3,162	5,871	6,412	8,595	10,437	..
Private creditors	..	4	547	856	966	776	590	670	820	..
Memo: export credits	..	..	25,239	28,751	33,552	41,633	48,681	63,425	71,449	..
TOTAL DEBT FLOWS										
Disbursements	**1,582**	**12,795**	**26,587**	**30,019**	**31,695**	**44,099**	**45,809**	**52,034**	**58,966**	**73,067**
Long-term debt	1,517	12,271	26,277	29,961	31,211	43,874	45,502	51,759	58,764	72,783
IMF purchases	66	524	310	58	484	224	308	275	203	284
Principal repayments	**616**	**4,271**	**16,104**	**18,037**	**18,145**	**23,866**	**27,524**	**29,406**	**32,949**	**33,800**
Long-term debt	611	4,066	15,439	16,751	17,071	23,537	27,330	29,105	32,559	33,485
IMF repurchases	6	205	666	1,286	1,075	329	194	301	390	315
Net flows on debt	**2,225**	**11,906**	**12,298**	**20,026**	**22,878**	**32,088**	**21,332**	**24,311**	**41,418**	**54,004**
of which short-term debt	..	..	1,816	8,044	9,329	11,855	3,047	1,682	15,400	14,737
Interest payments (INT)	..	**4,814**	**12,598**	**12,659**	**14,225**	**13,768**	**14,930**	**16,880**	**19,594**	**21,828**
Long-term debt	162	3,000	10,120	10,259	11,287	11,047	11,727	13,114	15,205	16,910
IMF charges	0	60	250	245	156	94	127	73	69	43
Short-term debt	..	1,754	2,227	2,155	2,782	2,627	3,076	3,694	4,320	4,875
Net transfers on debt	..	**7,092**	**-299**	**7,367**	**8,654**	**18,321**	**6,402**	**7,431**	**21,824**	**32,176**
Total debt service (TDS)	..	**9,085**	**28,702**	**30,696**	**32,370**	**37,633**	**42,453**	**46,286**	**52,543**	**55,628**
Long-term debt	772	7,066	25,559	27,010	28,357	34,584	39,057	42,219	47,764	50,395
IMF repurchases and charges	6	265	915	1,531	1,231	423	321	373	459	358
Short-term debt (interest only)	..	1,754	2,227	2,155	2,782	2,627	3,076	3,694	4,320	4,875
2. AGGREGATE NET RESOURCE FLOWS AND NET TRANSFERS (LONG-TERM)										
NET RESOURCE FLOWS	**1,798**	**10,666**	**24,004**	**27,250**	**29,497**	**45,478**	**72,990**	**79,571**	**95,764**	**116,079**
Net flow of long-term debt (ex. IMF)	906	8,206	10,838	13,210	14,140	20,338	18,172	22,654	26,205	39,298
Foreign direct investment (net)	201	1,312	8,330	10,179	12,706	20,923	38,128	44,105	51,776	61,120
Portfolio equity flows	0	0	2,623	1,750	704	2,057	14,619	10,088	14,715	12,900
Grants (excluding technical coop.)	690	1,149	2,213	2,112	1,947	2,160	2,071	2,724	3,069	2,761
Memo: technical coop. grants	384	1,003	2,041	2,434	2,630	3,007	3,099	3,037	3,318	3,017
NET TRANSFERS	**1,288**	**2,758**	**9,548**	**12,148**	**13,172**	**28,118**	**54,347**	**58,808**	**71,686**	**88,548**
Interest on long-term debt	162	3,000	10,120	10,259	11,287	11,047	11,727	13,114	15,205	16,910
Profit remittances on FDI	349	4,909	4,336	4,844	5,038	6,312	6,915	7,649	8,873	10,621
3. MAJOR ECONOMIC AGGREGATES										
Gross national product (GNP)	127,119	372,504	599,050	644,162	706,173	789,246	844,268	1,009,477	1,228,132	1,465,370
Exports of goods & services (XGS)	9,649	78,930	149,707	175,726	202,414	238,575	265,789	333,174	411,550	456,759
of which workers' remittances	24	881	675	636	736	850	832	1,361	1,640	1,604
Imports of goods & services (MGS)	11,679	86,616	163,147	181,124	209,534	248,179	295,832	348,589	447,302	516,831
International reserves (RES)	2,220	30,780	52,560	71,376	94,243	82,069	100,536	136,204	166,516	..
Current account balance	-1,939	-6,431	-11,431	-3,576	-4,728	-6,353	-27,226	-12,714	-25,439	-43,345
4. DEBT INDICATORS										
EDT / XGS (%)	..	81.8	138.4	136.1	132.6	125.7	122.8	108.7	98.3	98.9
EDT / GNP (%)	..	17.3	34.6	37.1	38.0	38.0	38.7	35.9	32.9	30.8
TDS / XGS (%)	..	11.5	19.2	17.5	16.0	15.8	16.0	13.9	12.8	12.2
INT / XGS (%)	..	6.1	8.4	7.2	7.0	5.8	5.6	5.1	4.8	4.8
INT / GNP (%)	..	1.3	2.1	2.0	2.0	1.7	1.8	1.7	1.6	1.5
RES / EDT (%)	..	47.6	25.4	29.9	35.1	27.4	30.8	37.6	41.2	..
RES / MGS (months)	2.3	4.3	3.9	4.7	5.4	4.0	4.1	4.7	4.5	..
Short-term / EDT (%)	..	22.6	14.2	15.9	17.7	19.9	19.3	17.9	19.9	21.1
Concessional / EDT (%)	..	23.1	30.2	30.6	29.5	27.5	28.0	28.0	25.5	22.7
Multilateral / EDT (%)	..	8.4	13.9	14.6	14.4	13.3	13.5	13.7	13.3	12.5

EAST ASIA AND PACIFIC

(US$ million, unless otherwise indicated)

5. LONG-TERM DEBT

	1970	1980	1989	1990	1991	1992	1993	1994	1995	*Preliminary* 1996
DEBT OUTSTANDING (LDOD)	**5,997**	**48,438**	**174,791**	**199,054**	**219,345**	**238,780**	**262,102**	**295,809**	**322,568**	**355,056**
Public and publicly guaranteed	**3,992**	**39,688**	**160,108**	**177,419**	**189,326**	**201,679**	**223,508**	**249,014**	**264,542**	**268,084**
Official creditors	3,129	21,017	92,551	107,803	119,002	126,689	141,920	157,364	165,455	165,319
Multilateral	451	5,457	28,712	34,980	38,765	39,856	44,065	49,696	53,607	56,344
Concessional	370	1,594	6,686	8,590	9,947	11,001	12,607	14,688	16,040	..
Bilateral	2,678	15,560	63,839	72,823	80,237	86,833	97,855	107,668	111,847	108,975
Concessional	2,303	13,326	55,983	64,635	69,238	71,382	78,677	86,816	87,176	..
Private creditors	864	18,671	67,557	69,616	70,324	74,989	81,588	91,650	99,088	102,765
Bonds	125	1,655	12,112	12,683	13,078	15,071	17,544	21,712	23,455	..
Commercial banks	303	9,677	35,834	34,851	34,226	32,375	35,116	36,338	38,974	..
Other private	436	7,339	19,612	22,081	23,021	27,543	28,928	33,600	36,660	..
Private nonguaranteed	**2,004**	**8,751**	**14,683**	**21,635**	**30,019**	**37,101**	**38,595**	**46,794**	**58,026**	**86,972**
Bonds	..	..	33	160	571	1,281	4,090	10,502	16,524	..
Commerical banks	..	..	14,650	21,476	29,448	35,820	34,505	36,292	41,502	..
Memo:										
IBRD	434	3,229	17,857	20,176	22,072	21,858	23,748	26,017	27,912	..
IDA	6	848	4,310	5,130	5,866	6,577	7,482	8,682	9,692	..
DISBURSEMENTS	**1,517**	**12,271**	**26,277**	**29,961**	**31,211**	**43,874**	**45,502**	**51,759**	**58,764**	**72,783**
Public and publicly guaranteed	**753**	**9,360**	**20,593**	**20,120**	**20,911**	**31,075**	**35,716**	**34,494**	**37,960**	**33,591**
Official creditors	546	3,041	10,532	10,283	11,278	12,386	14,591	13,596	16,785	12,462
Multilateral	68	1,231	4,479	4,711	5,068	4,726	5,839	5,943	6,123	6,092
Concessional	40	212	931	1,209	1,336	1,437	1,578	1,461	1,554	..
Bilatarel	478	1,810	6,054	5,572	6,210	7,660	8,752	7,652	10,663	6,370
Concessional	424	1,201	5,379	4,831	3,852	4,368	4,889	5,390	5,189	..
Private creditors	207	6,319	10,061	9,838	9,633	18,689	21,125	20,899	21,174	21,129
Bonds	0	235	952	1,052	713	1,194	4,697	5,028	3,999	..
Commercial banks	87	3,067	4,977	4,093	4,203	7,214	8,557	5,746	8,107	..
Other private	120	3,016	4,132	4,692	4,717	10,280	7,871	10,125	9,068	..
Private nonguaranteed	**764**	**2,911**	**5,684**	**9,841**	**10,300**	**12,800**	**9,785**	**17,265**	**20,804**	**39,192**
Bonds	..	..	31	120	410	721	2,791	6,329	6,081	..
Commercial banks	..	..	5,653	9,721	9,889	12,079	6,994	10,936	14,723	..
Memo:										
IBRD	57	793	2,681	2,532	2,825	2,444	3,193	3,163	3,168	..
IDA	4	92	608	604	704	904	922	904	934	..
PRINCIPAL REPAYMENTS	**611**	**4,066**	**15,439**	**16,751**	**17,071**	**23,537**	**27,330**	**29,105**	**32,559**	**33,485**
Public and publicly guaranteed	**227**	**2,184**	**12,502**	**14,183**	**13,216**	**18,030**	**19,618**	**20,118**	**22,162**	**23,239**
Official creditors	79	659	3,835	4,467	4,548	5,940	6,088	7,786	8,226	7,888
Multilateral	22	157	1,662	2,032	2,103	2,701	2,748	3,651	3,095	3,342
Concessional	17	39	96	136	141	160	194	225	233	..
Bilateral	57	502	2,173	2,435	2,445	3,239	3,340	4,136	5,132	4,546
Concessional	37	260	931	1,316	1,456	2,006	1,914	2,540	3,108	..
Private creditors	148	1,526	8,667	9,716	8,668	12,090	13,530	12,332	13,936	15,351
Bonds	32	41	990	1,098	533	2,414	2,637	1,607	2,104	..
Commercial banks	40	493	4,466	5,395	4,675	5,975	6,403	5,234	5,617	..
Other private	76	991	3,210	3,223	3,460	3,701	4,490	5,491	6,215	..
Private nonguaranteed	**384**	**1,881**	**2,937**	**2,569**	**3,854**	**5,506**	**7,712**	**8,987**	**10,397**	**10,246**
Bonds	..	..	0	0	0	0	0	0	120	..
Commerical banks	..	..	2,937	2,569	3,854	5,506	7,712	8,987	10,277	..
Memo:										
IBRD	22	118	1,380	1,462	1,444	2,065	1,744	2,549	2,152	..
IDA	0	2	14	19	23	27	31	44	50	..
NET FLOWS ON DEBT	**906**	**8,206**	**10,838**	**13,210**	**14,140**	**20,338**	**18,172**	**22,654**	**26,205**	**39,298**
Public and publicly guaranteed	**527**	**7,175**	**8,091**	**5,938**	**7,695**	**13,044**	**16,098**	**14,377**	**15,798**	**10,352**
Official creditors	467	2,383	6,697	5,816	6,730	6,446	8,503	5,809	8,559	4,574
Multilateral	46	1,074	2,816	2,679	2,965	2,025	3,091	2,293	3,028	2,750
Concessional	23	173	835	1,073	1,195	1,277	1,384	1,237	1,321	..
Bilateral	421	1,309	3,881	3,137	3,765	4,421	5,412	3,517	5,532	1,824
Concessional	387	941	4,448	3,516	2,396	2,363	2,975	2,850	2,080	..
Private creditors	60	4,793	1,394	122	965	6,599	7,595	8,567	7,239	5,778
Bonds	-32	194	-38	-45	180	-1,220	2,059	3,421	1,895	..
Commercial banks	47	2,574	511	-1,302	-472	1,239	2,155	512	2,490	..
Other private	44	2,025	921	1,469	1,257	6,579	3,381	4,635	2,853	..
Private nonguaranteed	**380**	**1,030**	**2,747**	**7,272**	**6,446**	**7,294**	**2,073**	**8,278**	**10,408**	**28,946**
Bonds	..	..	31	120	410	721	2,791	6,329	5,961	..
Commerical banks	..	..	2,716	7,152	6,035	6,573	-718	1,949	4,447	..
Memo:										
IBRD	35	675	1,301	1,070	1,380	380	1,449	613	1,016	..
IDA	4	90	595	585	682	877	891	861	884	..

EAST ASIA AND PACIFIC

(US$ million, unless otherwise indicated)

	1970	1980	1989	1990	1991	1992	1993	1994	1995	*Preliminary* 1996
INTEREST PAYMENTS (LINT)	**162**	**3,000**	**10,120**	**10,259**	**11,287**	**11,047**	**11,727**	**13,114**	**15,205**	**16,910**
Public and publicly guaranteed	**94**	**2,124**	**9,003**	**8,969**	**9,217**	**8,919**	**9,447**	**10,633**	**12,313**	**12,755**
Official creditors	61	710	3,282	3,768	4,131	4,521	5,310	5,950	6,481	6,065
Multilateral	25	354	1,841	2,147	2,343	2,481	2,626	2,856	3,054	3,161
Concessional	21	45	115	149	175	210	245	276	317	..
Bilateral	37	356	1,441	1,621	1,788	2,039	2,684	3,094	3,428	2,904
Concessional	28	208	889	1,094	1,314	1,424	1,789	1,970	2,149	..
Private creditors	32	1,414	5,721	5,201	5,087	4,398	4,137	4,683	5,832	6,690
Bonds	9	88	924	911	868	775	825	933	1,243	..
Commercial banks	12	824	3,271	2,800	2,590	1,964	1,874	1,777	2,427	..
Other private	10	501	1,526	1,489	1,629	1,660	1,439	1,973	2,162	..
Private nonguaranteed	**68**	**876**	**1,118**	**1,290**	**2,069**	**2,128**	**2,280**	**2,480**	**2,892**	**4,155**
Bonds	..	..	0	2	15	35	65	222	584	..
Commerical banks	..	..	1,118	1,289	2,054	2,094	2,215	2,259	2,308	..
Memo:										
IBRD	25	261	1,390	1,521	1,641	1,700	1,749	1,890	2,000	..
IDA	0	6	28	34	39	45	48	59	69	..
NET TRANSFERS ON DEBT	**745**	**5,206**	**718**	**2,951**	**2,853**	**9,291**	**6,444**	**9,541**	**11,000**	**22,388**
Public and publicly guaranteed	**433**	**5,052**	**-911**	**-3,031**	**-1,523**	**4,125**	**6,651**	**3,743**	**3,485**	**-2,403**
Official creditors	406	1,673	3,415	2,048	2,599	1,925	3,193	-141	2,078	-1,491
Multilateral	21	720	976	532	622	-456	465	-563	-26	-411
Concessional	2	128	720	924	1,020	1,067	1,139	961	1,004	..
Bilateral	385	953	2,440	1,516	1,977	2,381	2,728	423	2,104	-1,080
Concessional	359	733	3,559	2,422	1,082	939	1,186	880	-69	..
Private creditors	28	3,379	-4,326	-5,079	-4,122	2,200	3,458	3,884	1,407	-912
Bonds	-41	106	-963	-957	-688	-1,994	1,235	2,488	652	..
Commercial banks	35	1,750	-2,759	-4,102	-3,062	-725	281	-1,266	63	..
Other private	34	1,524	-604	-20	-372	4,919	1,943	2,662	691	..
Private nonguaranteed	**312**	**154**	**1,629**	**5,982**	**4,376**	**5,165**	**-207**	**5,797**	**7,515**	**24,791**
Bonds	..	..	31	118	395	686	2,726	6,107	5,377	..
Commerical banks	..	..	1,598	5,864	3,981	4,479	-2,933	-310	2,138	..
Memo:										
IBRD	11	414	-90	-451	-261	-1,320	-301	-1,277	-984	..
IDA	4	84	566	551	643	832	843	801	815	..
DEBT SERVICE (LTDS)	**772**	**7,066**	**25,559**	**27,010**	**28,357**	**34,584**	**39,057**	**42,219**	**47,764**	**50,395**
Public and publicly guaranteed	**320**	**4,308**	**21,504**	**23,151**	**22,434**	**26,949**	**29,065**	**30,751**	**34,475**	**35,994**
Official creditors	140	1,369	7,117	8,235	8,679	10,461	11,398	13,736	14,708	13,953
Multilateral	47	512	3,503	4,179	4,446	5,182	5,374	6,507	6,148	6,503
Concessional	38	85	210	285	316	370	439	501	549	..
Bilateral	94	857	3,614	4,056	4,233	5,278	6,024	7,230	8,559	7,450
Concessional	65	468	1,820	2,409	2,770	3,429	3,703	4,509	5,257	..
Private creditors	180	2,940	14,387	14,916	13,755	16,489	17,667	17,015	19,768	22,041
Bonds	41	130	1,915	2,009	1,401	3,188	3,462	2,540	3,347	..
Commercial banks	53	1,317	7,737	8,195	7,265	7,939	8,277	7,011	8,043	..
Other private	86	1,492	4,736	4,712	5,089	5,361	5,929	7,464	8,377	..
Private nonguaranteed	**452**	**2,757**	**4,055**	**3,859**	**5,924**	**7,635**	**9,992**	**11,467**	**13,289**	**14,401**
Bonds	..	..	0	2	15	35	65	222	704	..
Commerical banks	..	..	4,055	3,858	5,908	7,600	9,927	11,246	12,585	..
Memo:										
IBRD	46	379	2,771	2,983	3,085	3,764	3,493	4,439	4,151	..
IDA	0	8	42	53	61	73	79	103	119	..
UNDISBURSED DEBT	**1,209**	**23,264**	**40,442**	**44,405**	**45,067**	**46,768**	**56,940**	**59,337**	**62,656**	**..**
Official creditors	1,112	17,265	30,223	32,804	36,464	37,321	42,518	48,832	50,917	..
Private creditors	98	5,999	10,218	11,601	8,603	9,447	14,422	10,506	11,740	..
Memorandum items										
Concessional LDOD	2,673	14,920	62,669	73,225	79,185	82,382	91,284	101,505	103,216	102,551
Variable rate LDOD	2,009	18,637	63,993	72,792	82,855	87,341	92,454	106,223	124,174	..
Public sector LDOD	3,978	36,308	155,778	173,037	184,189	195,582	216,260	241,661	256,804	..
Private sector LDOD	2,019	8,774	15,175	22,102	30,379	37,382	38,997	47,644	59,219	..
6. CURRENCY COMPOSITION OF LONG-TERM DEBT (PERCENT)										
Deutsche mark	7.0	5.5	4.1	4.0	3.8	2.9	2.3	2.7	2.7	..
French franc	2.9	3.6	1.5	1.7	1.6	1.5	1.3	1.3	1.4	..
Japanese yen	8.3	18.6	29.0	28.4	29.0	28.0	28.6	30.0	27.1	..
Pound sterling	6.2	1.0	0.8	0.9	0.9	0.7	0.7	0.5	0.4	..
Swiss franc	1.0	0.7	0.8	0.8	0.7	0.5	0.5	0.6	0.5	..
U.S. dollars	36.0	35.8	25.6	23.0	24.1	28.4	30.5	31.4	35.4	..
Multiple currency	11.1	18.1	19.8	22.5	22.0	20.8	20.1	19.2	18.9	..
Special drawing rights	0.0	0.0	0.1	0.1	0.1	0.1	0.1	0.1	0.2	..
All other currencies	27.5	8.3	15.8	16.3	15.3	14.2	12.8	11.6	11.0	..

EAST ASIA AND PACIFIC

(US$ million, unless otherwise indicated)

	1970	1980	1989	1990	1991	1992	1993	1994	1995	Preliminary 1996
7. DEBT RESTRUCTURINGS										
Total amount rescheduled	..	..	1,968	1,068	3,691	4,416	1,078	0	235	..
Debt stock rescheduled	..	..	0	0	1,262	2,261	258	0	0	..
Principal rescheduled	..	..	1,657	882	2,273	748	532	0	109	..
Official	..	..	236	196	1,676	503	279	0	108	..
Private	..	..	1,422	686	597	245	254	0	0	..
Interest rescheduled	..	..	311	186	156	235	231	0	103	..
Official	..	..	180	117	119	199	119	0	103	..
Private	..	..	131	69	37	37	112	0	0	..
Principal forgiven	..	..	0	0	113	7	37	0	12	..
Memo: interest forgiven	..	..	0	0	5	4	20	0	7	..
Debt stock reduction	..	..	493	1,803	245	2,259	0	0	0	..
of which debt buyback	..	..	0	721	94	1,175	0	0	0	..
8. DEBT STOCK-FLOW RECONCILIATION										
Total change in debt stocks	..	..	27,779	31,866	29,363	31,412	26,644	35,806	42,133	..
Net flows on debt	..	..	12,298	20,026	22,878	32,088	21,332	24,311	41,418	..
Net change in interest arrears	..	..	661	589	349	282	165	354	130	..
Interest capitalized	..	..	311	186	156	235	231	0	103	..
Debt forgiveness or reduction	..	..	-493	-1,082	-264	-1,091	-37	0	-12	..
Cross-currency valuation	..	..	-6,927	8,440	4,980	-2,196	8,675	15,857	-1,106	..
Residual	..	..	21,929	3,707	1,264	2,094	-3,722	-4,715	1,600	..
9. AVERAGE TERMS OF NEW COMMITMENTS										
ALL CREDITORS										
Interest (%)	4.5	9.1	6.6	6.6	5.8	5.9	5.1	5.1	5.9	..
Maturity (years)	25.5	16.4	18.6	19.3	19.2	17.3	15.7	17.7	15	..
Grace period (years)	6.7	5	5.6	5.4	5.5	4.4	4.5	5.2	4.6	..
Grant element (%)	40.5	10.7	22.9	23.7	27.7	23.6	26.5	30	22.5	..
Official creditors										
Interest (%)	4	5.5	5.5	5	5.1	5.1	4.4	4.7	5.5	..
Maturity (years)	28.7	22.9	23.1	24.4	22.7	21.9	21.9	23.3	21.1	..
Grace period (years)	7.3	6.9	6.8	7	6.6	6	6	6.4	5.4	..
Grant element (%)	46.4	33	32.5	38	34.6	34	38.3	38.1	30.6	..
Private creditors										
Interest (%)	6.9	12.7	8.1	8.4	6.9	6.6	5.6	5.5	6.3	..
Maturity (years)	10.6	9.7	12.2	13.6	13	13.4	11.2	11.5	9.7	..
Grace period (years)	4	3.1	3.9	3.6	3.4	3	3.5	4	3.9	..
Grant element (%)	12.6	-12.1	8.9	7.6	15.1	14.8	18.1	21.1	15.4	..
Memorandum items										
Commitments	1,038	14,814	21,584	23,458	23,703	33,431	45,617	35,151	43,359	..
Official creditors	856	7,482	12,795	12,450	15,227	15,258	18,973	18,446	20,197	..
Private creditors	182	7,332	8,789	11,007	8,475	18,174	26,644	16,704	23,162	..

10. RESOURCE FLOW CHARTS

(US$ million)

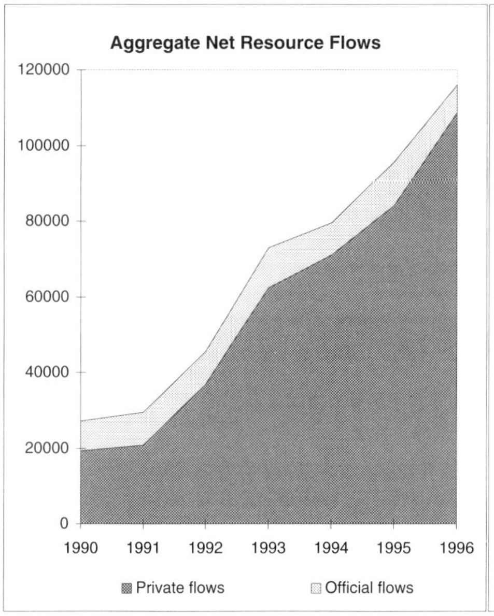

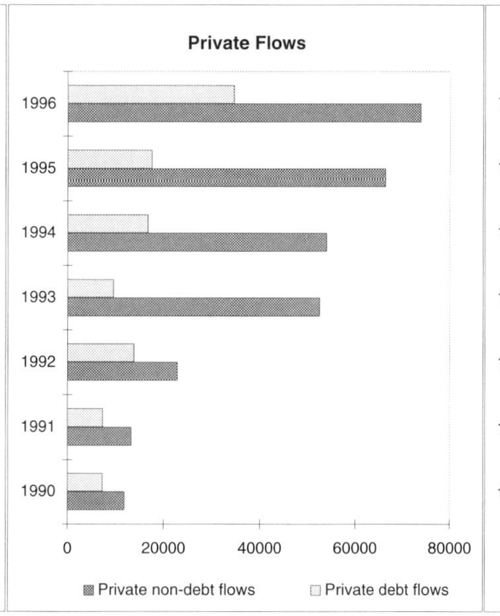

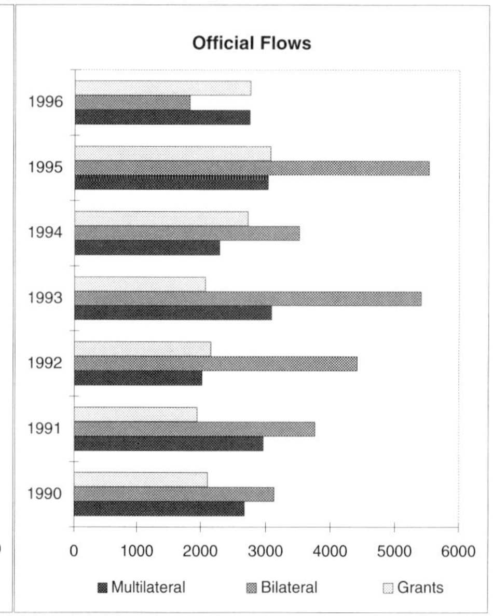

EUROPE AND CENTRAL ASIA

(US$ million, unless otherwise indicated)

	1970	1980	1989	1990	1991	1992	1993	1994	1995	Preliminary 1996
1. SUMMARY DEBT DATA										
TOTAL DEBT STOCKS (EDT)	..	**87,919**	**236,228**	**262,306**	**283,978**	**303,138**	**366,679**	**396,480**	**425,319**	**451,432**
Long-term debt (LDOD)	**3,990**	**63,299**	**174,738**	**199,407**	**219,497**	**232,604**	**292,012**	**317,752**	**330,224**	**346,051**
Public and publicly guaranteed	3,094	51,759	170,463	194,487	212,829	223,863	279,392	302,338	309,715	323,877
Private nonguaranteed	896	11,540	4,276	4,921	6,668	8,741	12,620	15,414	20,509	22,174
Use of IMF credit	**74**	**2,143**	**1,190**	**1,305**	**4,956**	**6,456**	**8,460**	**11,732**	**16,946**	**20,109**
Short-term debt	..	**22,477**	**60,299**	**61,594**	**59,525**	**64,079**	**66,207**	**66,996**	**78,149**	**85,272**
of which interest arrears on LDOD	..	312	7,830	13,041	11,809	9,329	7,118	7,317	8,679	4,893
Official creditors	..	13	6,100	6,573	3,677	2,506	1,170	2,112	2,691	..
Private creditors	..	299	1,730	6,468	8,132	6,823	5,947	5,205	5,988	..
Memo: principal arrears on LDOD	..	56	4,996	6,326	7,232	15,497	17,255	22,211	32,564	22,415
Official creditors	..	21	3,292	4,584	4,577	3,810	3,534	5,697	9,202	..
Private creditors	..	35	1,704	1,742	2,655	11,687	13,721	16,514	23,362	..
Memo: export credits	..	..	57,932	72,323	84,889	70,329	61,381	85,283	96,161	..
TOTAL DEBT FLOWS										
Disbursements	**1,082**	**22,741**	**26,556**	**32,248**	**34,414**	**35,560**	**37,470**	**37,945**	**43,427**	**40,639**
Long-term debt	1,007	21,503	26,492	31,501	30,697	33,201	35,182	33,359	35,272	35,622
IMF purchases	75	1,238	64	748	3,717	2,359	2,288	4,586	8,155	5,017
Principal repayments	**585**	**7,543**	**20,609**	**21,197**	**21,376**	**14,747**	**15,376**	**25,212**	**26,865**	**21,783**
Long-term debt	513	7,214	19,431	20,465	21,145	14,121	15,133	23,314	23,815	20,466
IMF repurchases	72	329	1,177	732	231	626	243	1,898	3,051	1,317
Net flows on debt	**1,486**	**24,483**	**14,555**	**7,135**	**12,243**	**27,846**	**29,199**	**13,523**	**27,153**	**29,697**
of which short-term debt	..	..	8,608	-3,917	-795	7,033	7,105	790	10,592	10,841
Interest payments (INT)	..	**6,270**	**14,776**	**15,353**	**15,305**	**12,457**	**12,196**	**12,907**	**17,963**	**18,764**
Long-term debt	150	3,980	10,829	11,264	11,278	9,222	8,982	9,581	13,986	14,239
IMF charges	0	103	168	128	254	376	419	500	711	907
Short-term debt	..	2,187	3,779	3,961	3,773	2,858	2,796	2,825	3,266	3,618
Net transfers on debt	..	**18,214**	**-221**	**-8,218**	**-3,062**	**15,389**	**17,003**	**617**	**9,190**	**10,933**
Total debt service (TDS)	..	**13,813**	**35,384**	**36,550**	**36,681**	**27,204**	**27,573**	**38,119**	**44,828**	**40,547**
Long-term debt	663	11,193	30,260	31,729	32,423	23,344	24,115	32,896	37,801	34,705
IMF repurchases and charges	72	432	1,346	860	485	1,002	662	2,398	3,762	2,224
Short-term debt (interest only)	..	2,187	3,779	3,961	3,773	2,858	2,796	2,825	3,266	3,618
2. AGGREGATE NET RESOURCE FLOWS AND NET TRANSFERS (LONG-TERM)										
NET RESOURCE FLOWS	**699**	**15,313**	**9,110**	**15,091**	**24,024**	**34,430**	**38,605**	**28,776**	**40,570**	**45,349**
Net flow of long-term debt (ex. IMF)	494	14,289	7,061	11,036	9,552	19,079	20,049	10,045	11,457	15,156
Foreign direct investment (net)	120	727	1,744	2,102	4,390	6,313	8,399	8,071	17,215	14,997
Portfolio equity flows	0	0	71	235	0	65	984	2,253	2,772	6,700
Grants (excluding technical coop.)	85	298	235	1,719	10,082	8,973	9,173	8,407	9,126	8,496
Memo: technical coop. grants	47	159	282	359	1,016	2,056	2,748	2,697	4,682	4,519
NET TRANSFERS	**508**	**11,230**	**-1,930**	**3,499**	**12,319**	**24,381**	**28,667**	**18,148**	**25,501**	**29,685**
Interest on long-term debt	150	3,980	10,829	11,264	11,278	9,222	8,982	9,581	13,986	14,239
Profit remittances on FDI	41	104	211	328	427	828	956	1,046	1,083	1,425
3. MAJOR ECONOMIC AGGREGATES										
Gross national product (GNP)	329,490	889,014	1,399,908	1,452,452	1,282,274	1,172,036	1,118,028	975,912	1,066,846	1,301,489
Exports of goods & services (XGS)	34,807	186,608	259,730	254,986	222,669	205,364	230,979	258,230	325,392	357,566
of which workers' remittances	661	3,198	4,469	5,097	4,988	5,565	5,599	5,592	6,823	6,536
Imports of goods & services (MGS)	31,758	180,187	262,434	280,297	233,798	222,409	258,684	264,775	346,289	387,668
International reserves (RES)	10,897	23,252	37,891	35,205	34,144	35,155	51,876	67,545	110,018	..
Current account balance	11,172	7,454	6,412	-18,490	912	-7,191	-18,800	2,886	-10,632	-23,291
4. DEBT INDICATORS										
EDT / XGS (%)	..	47.1	91.0	102.9	127.5	147.6	158.7	153.5	130.7	126.3
EDT / GNP (%)	..	9.9	16.9	18.1	22.1	25.9	32.8	40.6	39.9	34.7
TDS / XGS (%)	..	7.4	13.6	14.3	16.5	13.2	11.9	14.8	13.8	11.3
INT / XGS (%)	..	3.4	5.7	6.0	6.9	6.1	5.3	5.0	5.5	5.2
INT / GNP (%)	..	0.7	1.1	1.1	1.2	1.1	1.1	1.3	1.7	1.4
RES / EDT (%)	..	26.4	16.0	13.4	12.0	11.6	14.1	17.0	25.9	..
RES / MGS (months)	4.1	1.5	1.7	1.5	1.8	1.9	2.4	3.1	3.8	..
Short-term / EDT (%)	..	25.6	25.5	23.5	21.0	21.1	18.1	16.9	18.4	18.9
Concessional / EDT (%)	..	8.9	5.3	5.4	5.2	8.1	15.6	14.1	11.3	10.3
Multilateral / EDT (%)	..	5.4	8.5	8.4	8.7	8.5	7.7	8.0	7.9	7.9

EUROPE AND CENTRAL ASIA

(US$ million, unless otherwise indicated)

	1970	1980	1989	1990	1991	1992	1993	1994	1995	*Preliminary* 1996
5. LONG-TERM DEBT										
DEBT OUTSTANDING (LDOD)	**3,990**	**63,299**	**174,738**	**199,407**	**219,497**	**232,604**	**292,012**	**317,752**	**330,224**	**346,051**
Public and publicly guaranteed	**3,094**	**51,759**	**170,463**	**194,487**	**212,829**	**223,863**	**279,392**	**302,338**	**309,715**	**323,877**
Official creditors	2,672	19,098	59,181	70,149	82,235	83,229	135,119	147,969	145,816	152,457
Multilateral	639	4,707	19,996	22,104	24,666	25,650	28,148	31,682	33,596	35,633
Concessional	470	1,031	2,058	2,186	2,398	2,498	2,725	3,175	4,085	..
Bilateral	2,033	14,391	39,185	48,045	57,568	57,578	106,971	116,287	112,220	116,824
Concessional	1,746	6,791	10,456	11,930	12,311	22,060	54,503	52,830	43,894	..
Private creditors	422	32,661	111,282	124,338	130,595	140,634	144,273	154,369	163,899	171,420
Bonds	41	264	12,360	16,210	21,010	26,536	38,511	59,051	62,997	..
Commercial banks	10	21,048	74,368	76,372	72,519	69,801	63,731	54,541	60,603	..
Other private	371	11,348	24,554	31,756	37,066	44,298	42,031	40,776	40,299	..
Private nonguaranteed	**896**	**11,540**	**4,276**	**4,921**	**6,668**	**8,741**	**12,620**	**15,414**	**20,509**	**22,174**
Bonds	..	..	16	16	16	66	50	149	188	..
Commerical banks	..	..	4,260	4,905	6,652	8,675	12,570	15,265	20,321	..
Memo:										
IBRD	302	3,323	9,539	10,272	10,836	10,945	11,915	14,243	16,244	..
IDA	83	189	162	157	153	150	192	310	669	..
DISBURSEMENTS	**1,007**	**21,503**	**26,492**	**31,501**	**30,697**	**33,201**	**35,182**	**33,359**	**35,272**	**35,622**
Public and publicly guaranteed	**540**	**18,205**	**25,223**	**29,740**	**29,611**	**29,858**	**30,274**	**29,146**	**27,467**	**31,007**
Official creditors	480	4,875	2,779	7,392	9,625	7,195	7,250	6,980	7,161	10,304
Multilateral	163	1,055	1,512	2,595	3,969	3,686	4,729	3,919	4,800	5,175
Concessional	52	35	51	20	356	318	498	530	879	..
Bilatarel	317	3,820	1,267	4,797	5,656	3,509	2,521	3,062	2,361	5,129
Concessional	271	1,646	490	1,116	1,200	1,075	954	1,179	1,010	..
Private creditors	61	13,330	22,444	22,348	19,986	22,662	23,025	22,166	20,307	20,703
Bonds	0	30	4,812	3,446	4,931	7,560	13,600	8,021	9,646	..
Commercial banks	0	6,564	10,801	4,194	2,885	3,747	2,413	7,311	5,662	..
Other private	61	6,736	6,832	14,708	12,170	11,356	7,011	6,834	4,999	..
Private nonguaranteed	**466**	**3,298**	**1,269**	**1,761**	**1,086**	**3,343**	**4,908**	**4,213**	**7,805**	**4,615**
Bonds	..	..	16	0	0	50	0	99	36	..
Commercial banks	..	..	1,253	1,761	1,086	3,293	4,908	4,114	7,769	..
Memo:										
IBRD	55	833	770	1,218	1,561	1,433	1,709	2,659	2,741	..
IDA	7	0	0	0	0	2	49	117	370	..
PRINCIPAL REPAYMENTS	**513**	**7,214**	**19,431**	**20,465**	**21,145**	**14,121**	**15,133**	**23,314**	**23,815**	**20,466**
Public and publicly guaranteed	**305**	**5,172**	**18,492**	**18,968**	**19,476**	**12,501**	**13,739**	**20,684**	**20,613**	**17,514**
Official creditors	190	1,733	4,636	3,533	3,583	3,510	3,379	3,834	5,776	4,678
Multilateral	81	190	2,279	1,705	1,689	1,914	2,096	2,415	3,528	2,493
Concessional	35	34	104	86	67	101	265	239	374	..
Bilateral	108	1,543	2,357	1,828	1,895	1,596	1,283	1,419	2,247	2,185
Concessional	47	483	507	490	814	588	602	547	517	..
Private creditors	116	3,440	13,856	15,435	15,893	8,992	10,360	16,850	14,838	12,836
Bonds	2	3	188	357	368	1,599	1,672	2,733	4,391	..
Commercial banks	2	1,617	9,111	9,508	7,818	4,673	5,692	7,484	5,827	..
Other private	112	1,820	4,557	5,571	7,707	2,720	2,997	6,633	4,619	..
Private nonguaranteed	**208**	**2,041**	**939**	**1,497**	**1,669**	**1,620**	**1,395**	**2,631**	**3,201**	**2,952**
Bonds	..	..	0	0	0	0	16	0	0	..
Commerical banks	..	..	939	1,497	1,669	1,620	1,379	2,631	3,201	..
Memo:										
IBRD	13	133	1,659	1,133	1,218	1,006	967	1,165	1,222	..
IDA	0	1	5	4	4	5	6	6	6	..
NET FLOWS ON DEBT	**494**	**14,289**	**7,061**	**11,036**	**9,552**	**19,079**	**20,049**	**10,045**	**11,457**	**15,156**
Public and publicly guaranteed	**235**	**13,032**	**6,731**	**10,772**	**10,135**	**17,356**	**16,536**	**8,462**	**6,854**	**13,493**
Official creditors	290	3,142	-1,857	3,859	6,042	3,686	3,871	3,146	1,385	5,626
Multilateral	82	865	-767	890	2,280	1,772	2,633	1,503	1,271	2,682
Concessional	17	1	-53	-66	289	217	233	291	505	..
Bilateral	208	2,277	-1,090	2,970	3,761	1,914	1,239	1,643	114	2,944
Concessional	224	1,164	-17	626	387	487	351	632	493	..
Private creditors	-55	9,891	8,588	6,913	4,093	13,671	12,665	5,316	5,469	7,867
Bonds	-2	27	4,624	3,089	4,564	5,961	11,929	5,289	5,254	..
Commercial banks	-2	4,947	1,689	-5,314	-4,933	-927	-3,278	-174	-165	..
Other private	-51	4,917	2,276	9,137	4,463	8,636	4,014	201	380	..
Private nonguaranteed	**259**	**1,257**	**329**	**264**	**-583**	**1,723**	**3,513**	**1,583**	**4,603**	**1,663**
Bonds	..	..	16	0	0	50	-16	99	36	..
Commerical banks	..	..	313	264	-583	1,673	3,529	1,483	4,568	..
Memo:										
IBRD	42	700	-889	85	342	427	741	1,494	1,519	..
IDA	7	-1	-5	-4	-4	-3	43	111	364	..

EUROPE AND CENTRAL ASIA

(US$ million, unless otherwise indicated)	*1970*	*1980*	*1989*	*1990*	*1991*	*1992*	*1993*	*1994*	*1995*	*Preliminary 1996*
INTEREST PAYMENTS (LINT)	**150**	**3,980**	**10,829**	**11,264**	**11,278**	**9,222**	**8,982**	**9,581**	**13,986**	**14,239**
Public and publicly guaranteed	**116**	**3,131**	**10,530**	**10,823**	**10,896**	**8,547**	**8,626**	**9,055**	**13,041**	**13,447**
Official creditors	76	878	2,468	2,657	2,776	2,932	3,027	3,106	5,347	5,240
Multilateral	25	373	1,541	1,592	1,669	1,700	1,749	1,567	1,937	2,143
Concessional	19	54	98	91	97	116	107	125	158	..
Bilateral	51	505	928	1,065	1,107	1,232	1,278	1,539	3,410	3,097
Concessional	35	158	339	251	228	413	657	620	936	..
Private creditors	41	2,253	8,062	8,166	8,121	5,615	5,599	5,949	7,694	8,207
Bonds	1	27	562	925	1,125	1,435	1,736	2,305	3,518	..
Commercial banks	1	1,476	5,923	5,636	4,971	3,381	2,917	2,310	2,640	..
Other private	38	750	1,577	1,605	2,025	799	946	1,334	1,537	..
Private nonguaranteed	**34**	**849**	**299**	**442**	**382**	**675**	**356**	**527**	**945**	**792**
Bonds	..	..	0	1	1	2	2	2	13	..
Commerical banks	..	..	299	440	380	673	353	525	932	..
Memo:										
IBRD	16	257	835	809	825	744	745	855	949	..
IDA	1	1	1	1	1	1	1	2	3	..
NET TRANSFERS ON DEBT	**344**	**10,310**	**-3,768**	**-228**	**-1,726**	**9,857**	**11,067**	**464**	**-2,529**	**917**
Public and publicly guaranteed	**119**	**9,901**	**-3,799**	**-51**	**-761**	**8,810**	**7,909**	**-593**	**-6,187**	**46**
Official creditors	214	2,263	-4,325	1,202	3,266	753	844	40	-3,961	386
Multilateral	57	492	-2,308	-702	612	72	884	-63	-665	539
Concessional	-2	-53	-151	-156	192	101	125	166	347	..
Bilateral	157	1,771	-2,018	1,905	2,655	681	-40	103	-3,296	-153
Concessional	189	1,005	-356	376	158	74	-306	13	-443	..
Private creditors	-95	7,638	527	-1,253	-4,027	8,056	7,065	-632	-2,225	-340
Bonds	-4	-1	4,061	2,164	3,439	4,526	10,192	2,984	1,736	..
Commercial banks	-3	3,472	-4,234	-10,949	-9,904	-4,307	-6,196	-2,483	-2,805	..
Other private	-89	4,167	699	7,532	2,437	7,838	3,069	-1,133	-1,157	..
Private nonguaranteed	**225**	**408**	**30**	**-178**	**-965**	**1,048**	**3,158**	**1,056**	**3,658**	**871**
Bonds	..	..	16	-1	-1	48	-18	98	23	..
Commerical banks	..	..	14	-176	-964	1,000	3,176	959	3,635	..
Memo:										
IBRD	26	443	-1,724	-724	-483	-318	-3	639	570	..
IDA	7	-2	-6	-5	-6	-4	42	110	361	..
DEBT SERVICE (LTDS)	**663**	**11,193**	**30,260**	**31,729**	**32,423**	**23,344**	**24,115**	**32,896**	**37,801**	**34,705**
Public and publicly guaranteed	**421**	**8,304**	**29,022**	**29,790**	**30,372**	**21,048**	**22,365**	**29,739**	**33,654**	**30,961**
Official creditors	266	2,611	7,104	6,190	6,359	6,442	6,405	6,940	11,122	9,918
Multilateral	106	563	3,819	3,297	3,358	3,614	3,845	3,982	5,465	4,636
Concessional	53	87	202	176	164	217	372	364	532	..
Bilateral	160	2,049	3,285	2,893	3,001	2,828	2,561	2,959	5,657	5,282
Concessional	82	641	845	740	1,042	1,001	1,259	1,166	1,453	..
Private creditors	156	5,692	21,918	23,601	24,013	14,606	15,959	22,798	22,532	21,043
Bonds	4	31	750	1,281	1,492	3,034	3,408	5,037	7,909	..
Commercial banks	3	3,092	15,034	15,143	12,789	8,054	8,609	9,794	8,467	..
Other private	150	2,570	6,133	7,176	9,732	3,518	3,943	7,967	6,156	..
Private nonguaranteed	**241**	**2,890**	**1,238**	**1,939**	**2,051**	**2,296**	**1,751**	**3,157**	**4,147**	**3,744**
Bonds	..	..	0	1	1	2	18	2	13	..
Commerical banks	..	..	1,238	1,937	2,049	2,294	1,732	3,155	4,134	..
Memo:										
IBRD	29	390	2,493	1,943	2,043	1,751	1,712	2,020	2,172	..
IDA	1	3	6	5	6	6	7	8	9	..
UNDISBURSED DEBT	**1,842**	**13,821**	**14,695**	**17,124**	**24,821**	**30,443**	**31,239**	**29,697**	**30,434**	**..**
Official creditors	1,619	6,325	6,938	9,211	14,515	17,700	18,592	18,705	18,403	..
Private creditors	222	7,496	7,757	7,913	10,306	12,743	12,647	10,992	12,030	..
Memorandum items										
Concessional LDOD	2,216	7,821	12,515	14,116	14,709	24,558	57,227	56,005	47,979	46,700
Variable rate LDOD	952	25,866	77,857	89,369	105,173	113,725	137,828	137,728	146,165	..
Public sector LDOD	2,868	43,878	148,943	171,601	186,317	194,908	248,443	264,569	270,943	..
Private sector LDOD	1,122	12,379	5,203	5,982	7,756	10,016	13,673	16,355	21,418	..
6. CURRENCY COMPOSITION OF LONG-TERM DEBT (PERCENT)										
Deutsche mark	15.9	9.6	19.2	22.3	23.8	23.4	18.5	16.4	15.9	..
French franc	2.7	8.0	3.7	4.4	4.3	4.2	2.9	2.7	2.8	..
Japanese yen	0.1	2.1	6.8	6.7	7.4	7.6	7.7	8.0	8.4	..
Pound sterling	5.5	2.3	1.4	1.6	1.3	1.0	1.3	1.0	0.9	..
Swiss franc	1.4	3.9	5.5	5.8	4.8	3.5	2.7	1.7	1.9	..
U.S. dollars	44.3	36.2	29.1	28.5	27.5	29.9	40.0	41.2	39.9	..
Multiple currency	15.2	18.7	12.0	9.4	8.6	8.3	7.2	8.4	10.0	..
Special drawing rights	0.0	0.0	0.0	0.0	0.0	0.0	0.0	0.0	0.0	..
All other currencies	14.9	5.6	10.2	10.1	10.3	9.8	8.9	8.4	8.0	..

EUROPE AND CENTRAL ASIA

(US$ million, unless otherwise indicated)

	1970	1980	1989	1990	1991	1992	1993	1994	1995	Preliminary 1996
7. DEBT RESTRUCTURINGS										
Total amount rescheduled	..	..	12,270	3,559	9,455	28,511	28,070	21,981	10,363	..
Debt stock rescheduled	..	..	6,821	0	29	22,488	2,259	6,903	225	..
Principal rescheduled	..	..	3,514	1,391	4,707	3,489	13,095	5,884	7,383	..
Official	..	..	1,149	746	4,260	2,927	3,723	499	4,075	..
Private	..	..	2,365	645	447	562	9,372	5,386	3,309	..
Interest rescheduled	..	..	1,934	2,168	4,662	2,534	6,381	4,150	1,354	..
Official	..	..	1,777	1,998	4,558	1,899	2,343	812	738	..
Private	..	..	157	170	104	635	4,038	3,338	615	..
Principal forgiven	..	..	2	233	7	1,001	664	3,800	3	..
Memo: interest forgiven	..	..	0	61	0	0	0	0	0	..
Debt stock reduction	..	..	619	1,779	554	1,092	1,674	7,680	146	..
of which debt buyback	..	..	365	883	327	0	0	1,379	30	..
8. DEBT STOCK-FLOW RECONCILIATION										
Total change in debt stocks	..	..	16,566	26,079	21,672	19,160	63,541	29,801	28,839	..
Net flows on debt	..	..	14,555	7,135	12,243	27,846	29,199	13,523	27,153	..
Net change in interest arrears	..	..	730	5,211	-1,233	-2,480	-2,211	199	1,362	..
Interest capitalized	..	..	1,934	2,168	4,662	2,534	6,381	4,150	1,354	..
Debt forgiveness or reduction	..	..	-255	-1,130	-235	-2,093	-2,338	-10,101	-119	..
Cross-currency valuation	..	..	-711	13,473	-486	-7,280	-5,916	10,995	6,374	..
Residual	..	..	313	-778	6,721	633	38,425	11,035	-7,285	..
9. AVERAGE TERMS OF NEW COMMITMENTS										
ALL CREDITORS										
Interest (%)	4.2	10.3	8.3	8.4	7.4	6.6	6	6.6	6.4	..
Maturity (years)	19.3	12.4	8.8	16.7	10.9	8.6	9.7	11.7	11	..
Grace period (years)	6.7	4.3	3.9	5.5	4.1	3.4	4.8	4.8	4.7	..
Grant element (%)	37	1.7	7.5	8	11	12.4	16.6	16.3	17	..
Official creditors										
Interest (%)	3.9	7.6	6.4	8	6.5	6	5.4	6.3	5.8	..
Maturity (years)	20.2	16.7	15.3	13.6	11.7	12	14.9	15.3	16.6	..
Grace period (years)	7.2	5.1	5.3	5.9	4.7	4.5	4.9	4.9	5.1	..
Grant element (%)	39.9	18.7	21.9	11.2	16.5	18.2	25.1	21.1	25.3	..
Private creditors										
Interest (%)	6.3	11.2	8.5	8.6	8.1	6.9	6.3	6.9	6.7	..
Maturity (years)	13.4	10.9	8	18	10.4	6.9	7.3	8.6	8.2	..
Grace period (years)	3.6	4	3.7	5.3	3.7	2.9	4.7	4.7	4.5	..
Grant element (%)	18.2	-4.4	5.7	6.6	6.9	9.6	12.7	12.3	12.9	..
Memorandum items										
Commitments	766	12,622	22,435	30,286	33,615	33,084	28,807	17,126	21,884	..
Official creditors	662	3,346	2,489	9,255	14,530	10,943	9,126	7,830	7,292	..
Private creditors	105	9,275	19,945	21,031	19,085	22,141	19,681	9,296	14,592	..

10. RESOURCE FLOW CHARTS

(US$ million)

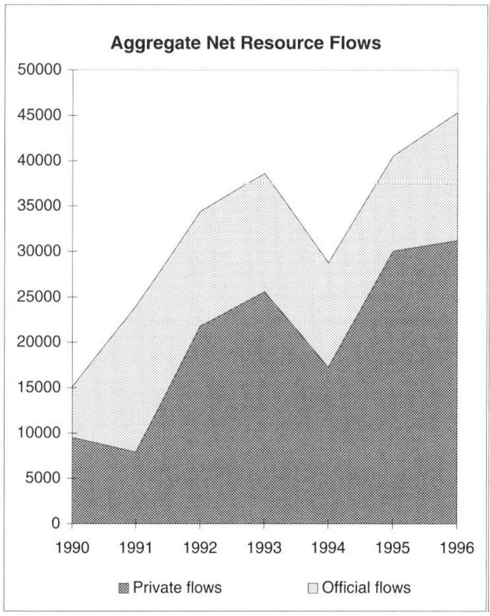

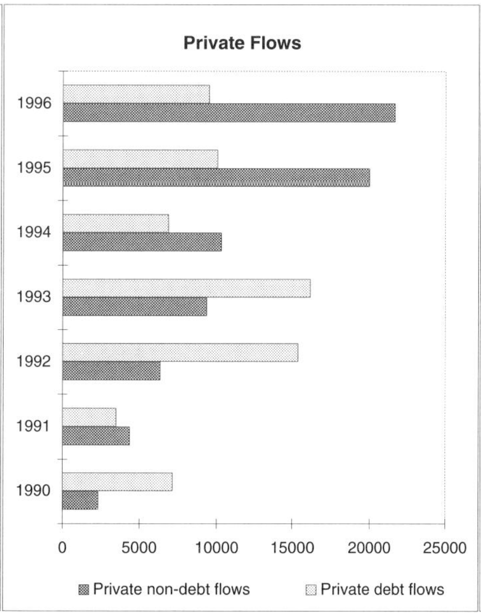

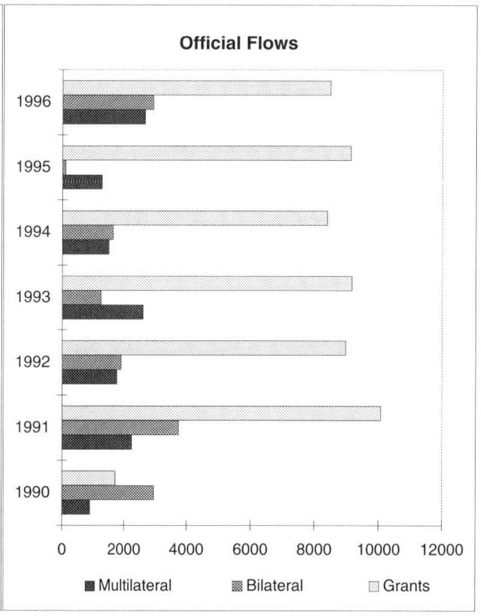

LATIN AMERICA AND THE CARIBBEAN

(US$ million, unless otherwise indicated)

1. SUMMARY DEBT DATA

	1970	1980	1989	1990	1991	1992	1993	1994	1995	*Preliminary* 1996
TOTAL DEBT STOCKS (EDT)	..	**257,266**	**452,794**	**474,892**	**491,720**	**508,849**	**550,841**	**585,674**	**636,594**	**656,543**
Long-term debt (LDOD)	**27,637**	**187,256**	**377,461**	**379,179**	**387,441**	**398,653**	**426,453**	**454,022**	**490,344**	**510,688**
Public and publicly guaranteed	15,764	144,798	355,960	354,118	359,254	360,617	370,167	386,739	409,830	424,732
Private nonguaranteed	11,873	42,458	21,501	25,061	28,187	38,036	56,286	67,283	80,514	85,956
Use of IMF credit	**128**	**1,413**	**15,759**	**18,298**	**17,357**	**15,140**	**14,255**	**13,849**	**26,719**	**23,825**
Short-term debt	..	**68,597**	**59,574**	**77,415**	**86,922**	**95,056**	**110,133**	**117,804**	**119,531**	**122,030**
of which interest arrears on LDOD	..	60	16,521	25,586	26,917	20,879	17,822	12,363	9,139	2,513
Official creditors	..	22	3,278	4,062	3,100	2,798	3,016	2,788	2,496	..
Private creditors	..	38	13,243	21,524	23,817	18,082	14,806	9,576	6,643	..
Memo: principal arrears on LDOD	..	606	18,221	24,616	24,124	23,934	20,242	20,124	16,231	9,379
Official creditors	..	93	6,139	7,614	6,991	5,964	5,278	6,361	5,978	..
Private creditors	..	513	12,082	17,002	17,133	17,970	14,964	13,763	10,253	..
Memo: export credits	..	..	61,532	72,068	82,629	87,054	92,602	99,131	94,338	..
TOTAL DEBT FLOWS										
Disbursements	**6,494**	**44,786**	**22,228**	**33,978**	**28,379**	**37,415**	**57,216**	**48,979**	**87,659**	**80,556**
Long-term debt	6,370	44,371	19,367	29,142	25,958	35,634	54,546	47,813	71,887	79,388
IMF purchases	124	415	2,862	4,836	2,421	1,781	2,671	1,166	15,772	1,168
Principal repayments	**3,736**	**21,703**	**24,031**	**22,795**	**21,704**	**30,052**	**37,113**	**35,379**	**41,259**	**59,069**
Long-term debt	3,438	21,210	20,921	19,140	18,290	26,685	33,560	32,937	38,366	55,583
IMF repurchases	298	492	3,110	3,655	3,414	3,367	3,553	2,442	2,894	3,486
Net flows on debt	**7,545**	**46,072**	**951**	**20,295**	**15,017**	**21,535**	**38,872**	**26,729**	**51,352**	**30,613**
of which short-term debt	..	..	2,753	9,113	8,342	14,172	18,769	13,129	4,952	9,126
Interest payments (INT)	..	**24,601**	**25,744**	**22,563**	**23,984**	**22,894**	**24,114**	**28,267**	**37,225**	**38,192**
Long-term debt	1,393	17,567	20,507	18,565	18,250	18,288	18,191	21,705	29,502	30,185
IMF charges	0	95	1,235	1,459	1,420	1,307	1,241	723	1,055	1,147
Short-term debt	..	6,939	4,002	2,539	4,315	3,299	4,683	5,840	6,669	6,861
Net transfers on debt	..	**21,471**	**-24,794**	**-2,268**	**-8,967**	**-1,359**	**14,757**	**-1,538**	**14,127**	**-7,579**
Total debt service (TDS)	..	**46,304**	**49,775**	**45,358**	**45,688**	**52,946**	**61,228**	**63,646**	**78,485**	**97,261**
Long-term debt	4,831	38,777	41,428	37,706	36,539	44,973	51,751	54,642	67,867	85,768
IMF repurchases and charges	298	588	4,345	5,114	4,834	4,674	4,794	3,165	3,949	4,633
Short-term debt (interest only)	..	6,939	4,002	2,539	4,315	3,299	4,683	5,840	6,669	6,861

2. AGGREGATE NET RESOURCE FLOWS AND NET TRANSFERS (LONG-TERM)

	1970	1980	1989	1990	1991	1992	1993	1994	1995	1996
NET RESOURCE FLOWS	**4,193**	**29,899**	**9,370**	**21,596**	**30,556**	**32,524**	**65,128**	**54,915**	**66,884**	**69,159**
Net flow of long-term debt (ex. IMF)	2,932	23,161	-1,555	10,001	7,668	8,949	20,986	14,876	33,522	23,805
Foreign direct investment (net)	1,091	6,148	8,138	8,121	12,504	12,740	14,066	24,238	22,897	25,925
Portfolio equity flows	0	0	434	1,099	6,228	8,229	27,185	13,160	7,190	16,500
Grants (excluding technical coop.)	170	591	2,352	2,374	4,156	2,606	2,891	2,641	3,276	2,929
Memo: technical coop. grants	258	775	1,803	2,047	2,393	2,658	2,793	2,941	3,292	3,077
NET TRANSFERS	**771**	**7,456**	**-18,421**	**-3,327**	**5,099**	**6,763**	**37,948**	**23,303**	**26,800**	**26,563**
Interest on long-term debt	1,393	17,567	20,507	18,565	18,250	18,288	18,191	21,705	29,502	30,185
Profit remittances on FDI	2,029	4,876	7,284	6,358	7,208	7,473	8,989	9,907	10,583	12,411

3. MAJOR ECONOMIC AGGREGATES

	1970	1980	1989	1990	1991	1992	1993	1994	1995	1996
Gross national product (GNP)	154,807	714,492	907,175	1,020,887	1,079,666	1,195,386	1,330,032	1,518,413	1,553,765	1,587,656
Exports of goods & services (XGS)	19,201	127,486	165,816	185,609	188,306	201,242	215,737	250,899	300,214	323,728
of which workers' remittances	99	1,206	3,824	4,776	5,831	7,288	7,071	8,400	9,851	9,580
Imports of goods & services (MGS)	22,691	158,858	177,937	193,448	211,473	241,067	264,539	303,971	337,283	354,806
International reserves (RES)	5,481	57,382	43,392	58,341	74,143	96,377	117,829	113,786	139,037	..
Current account balance	1,327	-30,468	-9,361	-2,763	-18,178	-34,859	-45,159	-49,179	-33,257	-27,813

4. DEBT INDICATORS

	1970	1980	1989	1990	1991	1992	1993	1994	1995	1996
EDT / XGS (%)	..	201.8	273.1	255.9	261.1	252.9	255.3	233.4	212.0	202.8
EDT / GNP (%)	..	36.0	49.9	46.5	45.5	42.6	41.4	38.6	41.0	41.4
TDS / XGS (%)	..	36.3	30.0	24.4	24.3	26.3	28.4	25.4	26.1	30.0
INT / XGS (%)	..	19.3	15.5	12.2	12.7	11.4	11.2	11.3	12.4	11.8
INT / GNP (%)	..	3.4	2.8	2.2	2.2	1.9	1.8	1.9	2.4	2.4
RES / EDT (%)	..	22.3	9.6	12.3	15.1	18.9	21.4	19.4	21.8	..
RES / MGS (months)	2.9	4.3	2.9	3.6	4.2	4.8	5.3	4.5	4.9	..
Short-term / EDT (%)	..	26.7	13.2	16.3	17.7	18.7	20.0	20.1	18.8	18.6
Concessional / EDT (%)	..	9.6	10.2	10.3	10.4	10.4	9.9	9.8	9.3	9.0
Multilateral / EDT (%)	..	5.5	11.5	12.6	12.7	12.1	11.8	11.7	11.4	11.5

LATIN AMERICA AND THE CARIBBEAN

(US$ million, unless otherwise indicated)

	1970	1980	1989	1990	1991	1992	1993	1994	1995	Preliminary 1996
5. LONG-TERM DEBT										
DEBT OUTSTANDING (LDOD)	**27,637**	**187,256**	**377,461**	**379,179**	**387,441**	**398,653**	**426,453**	**454,022**	**490,344**	**510,688**
Public and publicly guaranteed	**15,764**	**144,798**	**355,960**	**354,118**	**359,254**	**360,617**	**370,167**	**386,739**	**409,830**	**424,732**
Official creditors	8,124	45,017	130,359	146,508	157,621	164,506	168,787	175,850	189,156	177,385
Multilateral	2,951	14,125	52,120	60,013	62,413	61,792	65,224	68,753	72,697	75,217
Concessional	1,983	3,268	6,089	6,445	6,708	6,932	7,219	7,658	8,340	..
Bilateral	5,173	30,893	78,238	86,494	95,208	102,715	103,563	107,097	116,458	102,169
Concessional	3,920	21,553	40,111	42,447	44,542	46,067	47,473	49,540	51,008	..
Private creditors	7,640	99,781	225,602	207,610	201,633	196,111	201,380	210,889	220,674	247,347
Bonds	1,234	9,599	19,141	75,976	79,129	81,798	108,890	157,044	171,699	..
Commercial banks	3,072	77,007	178,471	102,428	97,205	94,538	75,090	38,000	34,013	..
Other private	3,334	13,176	27,990	29,206	25,299	19,775	17,401	15,845	14,963	..
Private nonguaranteed	**11,873**	**42,458**	**21,501**	**25,061**	**28,187**	**38,036**	**56,286**	**67,283**	**80,514**	**85,956**
Bonds	..	..	0	171	1,387	7,957	22,308	30,295	34,886	..
Commerical banks	..	..	21,501	24,890	26,800	30,078	33,979	36,988	45,628	..
Memo:										
IBRD	2,067	7,706	29,655	34,760	35,668	33,553	34,558	35,419	36,390	..
IDA	112	427	963	1,117	1,317	1,475	1,646	1,900	2,186	..
DISBURSEMENTS	**6,370**	**44,371**	**19,367**	**29,142**	**25,958**	**35,634**	**54,546**	**47,813**	**71,887**	**79,388**
Public and publicly guaranteed	**3,610**	**31,410**	**16,252**	**24,440**	**20,817**	**19,924**	**27,940**	**24,356**	**44,212**	**59,262**
Official creditors	1,340	6,849	9,653	13,731	11,765	10,724	12,365	10,138	24,088	12,712
Multilateral	583	2,964	6,199	8,980	7,466	7,377	9,067	6,687	9,942	9,238
Concessional	255	515	459	483	705	743	670	692	938	..
Bilatarel	757	3,885	3,454	4,751	4,299	3,347	3,298	3,451	14,146	3,474
Concessional	434	1,118	1,470	2,433	1,326	1,033	1,574	1,167	2,090	..
Private creditors	2,270	24,562	6,599	10,709	9,052	9,200	15,576	14,218	20,124	46,550
Bonds	129	1,219	619	1,938	3,842	3,596	10,880	7,968	14,013	..
Commercial banks	1,150	19,889	2,203	5,618	2,860	3,234	2,934	4,462	4,507	..
Other private	991	3,453	3,777	3,153	2,350	2,371	1,761	1,788	1,604	..
Private nonguaranteed	**2,760**	**12,960**	**3,114**	**4,702**	**5,141**	**15,709**	**26,605**	**23,457**	**27,675**	**20,126**
Bonds	..	..	0	171	1,216	6,745	14,642	9,934	7,413	..
Commercial banks	..	..	3,114	4,531	3,925	8,964	11,963	13,524	20,263	..
Memo:										
IBRD	354	1,586	3,423	6,139	4,067	3,213	4,803	3,052	4,642	..
IDA	9	60	94	119	205	198	167	208	277	..
PRINCIPAL REPAYMENTS	**3,438**	**21,210**	**20,921**	**19,140**	**18,290**	**26,685**	**33,560**	**32,937**	**38,366**	**55,583**
Public and publicly guaranteed	**1,667**	**14,250**	**15,077**	**16,943**	**15,842**	**21,486**	**19,549**	**20,851**	**25,225**	**40,898**
Official creditors	506	2,130	5,392	6,993	8,301	9,475	9,918	11,450	14,740	20,925
Multilateral	171	712	3,796	4,748	5,872	6,400	6,646	7,169	8,334	6,705
Concessional	105	167	185	225	431	442	382	304	330	..
Bilateral	336	1,418	1,596	2,245	2,429	3,075	3,272	4,281	6,406	14,220
Concessional	119	368	286	726	273	283	428	664	943	..
Private creditors	1,160	12,120	9,685	9,950	7,541	12,011	9,631	9,401	10,485	19,973
Bonds	77	401	1,848	2,008	926	5,438	4,325	3,013	4,390	..
Commercial banks	609	9,371	5,695	5,201	2,942	3,043	1,932	2,183	3,141	..
Other private	475	2,348	2,142	2,741	3,673	3,530	3,375	4,205	2,954	..
Private nonguaranteed	**1,771**	**6,960**	**5,844**	**2,198**	**2,448**	**5,199**	**14,011**	**12,086**	**13,141**	**14,685**
Bonds	..	..	0	0	0	165	273	1,997	3,922	..
Commerical banks	..	..	5,844	2,198	2,448	5,034	13,738	10,089	9,220	..
Memo:										
IBRD	105	395	2,502	3,310	3,866	4,285	4,496	4,531	4,984	
IDA	0	2	7	9	13	9	10	10	21	..
NET FLOWS ON DEBT	**2,932**	**23,161**	**-1,555**	**10,001**	**7,668**	**8,949**	**20,986**	**14,876**	**33,522**	**23,805**
Public and publicly guaranteed	**1,944**	**17,161**	**1,175**	**7,497**	**4,975**	**-1,561**	**8,391**	**3,505**	**18,987**	**18,364**
Official creditors	834	4,719	4,261	6,738	3,463	1,249	2,447	-1,312	9,348	-8,213
Multilateral	412	2,252	2,403	4,232	1,593	977	2,421	-482	1,609	2,533
Concessional	150	347	275	258	274	301	289	388	609	..
Bilateral	422	2,467	1,858	2,506	1,870	272	26	-830	7,739	-10,746
Concessional	316	750	1,184	1,706	1,053	750	1,146	503	1,147	..
Private creditors	1,110	12,442	-3,086	759	1,512	-2,811	5,944	4,817	9,639	26,577
Bonds	52	819	-1,229	-70	2,917	-1,842	6,556	4,955	9,623	..
Commercial banks	541	10,518	-3,492	418	-82	191	1,003	2,279	1,366	..
Other private	517	1,105	1,636	412	-1,322	-1,159	-1,614	-2,417	-1,350	..
Private nonguaranteed	**989**	**6,000**	**-2,730**	**2,504**	**2,693**	**10,510**	**12,594**	**11,371**	**14,534**	**5,441**
Bonds	..	..	0	171	1,216	6,580	14,369	7,937	3,491	..
Commerical banks	..	..	-2,730	2,333	1,477	3,930	-1,775	3,435	11,043	..
Memo:										
IBRD	249	1,192	921	2,829	201	-1,072	307	-1,479	-342	..
IDA	9	59	87	110	193	189	157	198	257	..

LATIN AMERICA AND THE CARIBBEAN

(US$ million, unless otherwise indicated)

	1970	*1980*	*1989*	*1990*	*1991*	*1992*	*1993*	*1994*	*1995*	*Preliminary 1996*
INTEREST PAYMENTS (LINT)	**1,393**	**17,567**	**20,507**	**18,565**	**18,250**	**18,288**	**18,191**	**21,705**	**29,502**	**30,185**
Public and publicly guaranteed	**765**	**13,138**	**17,808**	**16,521**	**16,264**	**16,183**	**15,101**	**17,999**	**23,898**	**24,310**
Official creditors	302	1,980	4,773	6,137	7,072	7,415	7,928	8,216	9,544	9,201
Multilateral	157	1,000	3,435	4,125	4,828	4,751	5,020	4,789	4,883	5,158
Concessional	101	130	105	135	185	158	185	157	173	..
Bilateral	144	980	1,338	2,011	2,245	2,665	2,908	3,426	4,661	4,043
Concessional	75	401	384	772	701	809	737	796	747	..
Private creditors	463	11,158	13,035	10,384	9,192	8,767	7,173	9,783	14,355	15,109
Bonds	72	727	1,077	2,398	5,458	4,950	5,342	7,560	11,807	..
Commercial banks	227	9,443	10,658	6,680	2,525	2,869	1,054	1,481	1,677	..
Other private	164	988	1,300	1,306	1,209	949	777	742	871	..
Private nonguaranteed	**628**	**4,429**	**2,699**	**2,045**	**1,985**	**2,106**	**3,090**	**3,707**	**5,603**	**5,875**
Bonds	..	..	0	0	30	189	857	1,988	2,660	..
Commerical banks	..	..	2,699	2,045	1,955	1,917	2,234	1,718	2,943	..
Memo:										
IBRD	114	633	2,070	2,538	2,847	2,883	3,040	2,654	2,658	..
IDA	1	3	6	8	12	7	9	10	23	..
NET TRANSFERS ON DEBT	**1,539**	**5,593**	**-22,061**	**-8,564**	**-10,581**	**-9,340**	**2,795**	**-6,829**	**4,020**	**-6,380**
Public and publicly guaranteed	**1,179**	**4,022**	**-16,632**	**-9,023**	**-11,289**	**-17,744**	**-6,709**	**-14,494**	**-4,911**	**-5,946**
Official creditors	532	2,739	-512	602	-3,609	-6,166	-5,481	-9,528	-196	-17,414
Multilateral	255	1,252	-1,032	107	-3,234	-3,773	-2,599	-5,272	-3,275	-2,625
Concessional	49	218	170	123	90	143	104	231	436	..
Bilateral	278	1,487	520	495	-375	-2,393	-2,882	-4,256	3,079	-14,789
Concessional	241	350	800	935	351	-59	409	-292	400	..
Private creditors	646	1,283	-16,121	-9,625	-7,680	-11,578	-1,228	-4,966	-4,715	11,468
Bonds	-20	92	-2,306	-2,468	-2,541	-6,792	1,214	-2,605	-2,184	..
Commercial banks	313	1,075	-14,150	-6,263	-2,607	-2,679	-51	798	-311	..
Other private	353	117	335	-894	-2,531	-2,108	-2,391	-3,159	-2,220	..
Private nonguaranteed	**360**	**1,571**	**-5,429**	**459**	**708**	**8,404**	**9,504**	**7,665**	**8,931**	**-434**
Bonds	..	..	0	171	1,186	6,391	13,513	5,949	831	..
Commerical banks	..	..	-5,429	288	-478	2,013	-4,009	1,716	8,100	..
Memo:										
IBRD	135	559	-1,150	291	-2,646	-3,955	-2,733	-4,133	-3,000	..
IDA	8	55	81	102	181	182	148	187	234	..
DEBT SERVICE (LTDS)	**4,831**	**38,777**	**41,428**	**37,706**	**36,539**	**44,973**	**51,751**	**54,642**	**67,867**	**85,768**
Public and publicly guaranteed	**2,431**	**27,388**	**32,885**	**33,463**	**32,106**	**37,668**	**34,649**	**38,849**	**49,123**	**65,208**
Official creditors	808	4,110	10,165	13,129	15,374	16,890	17,845	19,665	24,284	30,126
Multilateral	328	1,712	7,231	8,873	10,700	11,150	11,666	11,958	13,217	11,863
Concessional	206	297	290	360	615	600	567	461	502	..
Bilateral	480	2,398	2,934	4,256	4,674	5,740	6,180	7,707	11,067	18,263
Concessional	193	768	671	1,498	975	1,092	1,165	1,459	1,690	..
Private creditors	1,623	23,278	22,720	20,334	16,732	20,778	16,804	19,184	24,839	35,082
Bonds	149	1,128	2,925	4,406	6,384	10,387	9,667	10,573	16,197	..
Commercial banks	836	18,815	16,353	11,881	5,467	5,912	2,986	3,664	4,818	..
Other private	638	3,336	3,442	4,047	4,882	4,479	4,152	4,947	3,824	..
Private nonguaranteed	**2,400**	**11,389**	**8,543**	**4,243**	**4,433**	**7,305**	**17,101**	**15,792**	**18,744**	**20,560**
Bonds	..	..	0	0	30	354	1,130	3,985	6,582	..
Commerical banks	..	..	8,543	4,243	4,403	6,952	15,971	11,807	12,162	..
Memo:										
IBRD	219	1,028	4,573	5,848	6,713	7,168	7,536	7,185	7,642	..
IDA	1	5	13	17	24	16	19	21	44	..
UNDISBURSED DEBT	**5,041**	**34,997**	**44,838**	**45,859**	**51,155**	**54,088**	**55,197**	**59,004**	**57,567**	**..**
Official creditors	3,226	20,564	31,859	32,691	37,374	41,964	39,985	43,502	43,107	..
Private creditors	1,815	14,432	12,980	13,168	13,780	12,124	15,213	15,502	14,460	..
Memorandum items										
Concessional LDOD	5,903	24,821	46,200	48,893	51,250	52,999	54,692	57,199	59,348	59,382
Variable rate LDOD	12,501	117,248	236,802	196,337	198,074	208,854	228,106	238,274	266,762	..
Public sector LDOD	15,267	124,643	327,363	323,921	326,378	323,732	336,023	353,324	376,230	..
Private sector LDOD	12,370	48,219	24,199	28,477	31,389	41,513	58,084	69,011	82,231	..

6. CURRENCY COMPOSITION OF LONG-TERM DEBT (PERCENT)

	1970	*1980*	*1989*	*1990*	*1991*	*1992*	*1993*	*1994*	*1995*	*Preliminary 1996*
Deutsche mark	7.8	5.5	5.0	5.9	5.7	5.0	4.5	4.4	4.9	..
French franc	2.3	1.8	3.3	3.6	3.6	3.0	2.6	2.5	2.5	..
Japanese yen	0.1	4.4	6.2	5.7	6.2	6.1	6.1	6.3	6.7	..
Pound sterling	4.5	1.4	1.6	1.4	1.5	1.1	0.9	0.9	0.7	..
Swiss franc	1.9	1.2	0.7	0.9	0.8	0.7	0.5	0.5	0.5	..
U.S. dollars	63.0	63.1	57.7	55.0	53.3	53.4	56.6	57.4	58.2	..
Multiple currency	16.9	9.4	15.3	17.4	17.9	19.1	18.0	17.7	16.6	..
Special drawing rights	0.0	0.0	0.0	0.0	0.0	0.0	0.0	0.0	0.0	..
All other currencies	3.6	3.4	2.9	2.5	2.7	2.4	2.1	2.1	2.0	..

LATIN AMERICA AND THE CARIBBEAN

(US$ million, unless otherwise indicated)

	1970	1980	1989	1990	1991	1992	1993	1994	1995	Preliminary 1996
7. DEBT RESTRUCTURINGS										
Total amount rescheduled	..	..	6,201	63,742	11,536	16,639	30,148	47,151	7,755	..
Debt stock rescheduled	..	..	1,803	59,087	2,102	141	18,489	36,263	3,350	..
Principal rescheduled	..	..	3,359	3,035	6,624	7,044	2,758	1,914	966	..
Official	..	..	1,214	1,546	3,823	3,271	2,449	1,445	800	..
Private	..	..	2,145	1,489	2,800	3,773	308	469	166	..
Interest rescheduled	..	..	833	1,507	3,138	9,388	8,835	8,050	2,435	..
Official	..	..	472	967	2,072	1,461	1,233	572	559	..
Private	..	..	360	540	1,066	7,926	7,603	7,478	1,876	..
Principal forgiven	..	..	809	180	1,684	228	723	86	525	..
Memo: interest forgiven	..	..	95	259	244	38	8	185	733	..
Debt stock reduction	..	..	14,663	21,302	3,771	9,065	4,766	5,158	3,704	..
of which debt buyback	..	..	2,092	2,756	445	5,098	589	323	102	..
8. DEBT STOCK-FLOW RECONCILIATION										
Total change in debt stocks	..	..	-3,258	22,098	16,828	17,129	41,993	34,833	50,919	..
Net flows on debt	..	..	950	20,295	15,017	21,535	38,872	26,729	51,352	..
Net change in interest arrears	..	..	7,917	9,065	1,331	-6,038	-3,057	-5,459	-3,225	..
Interest capitalized	..	..	833	1,507	3,138	9,388	8,835	8,050	2,435	..
Debt forgiveness or reduction	..	..	-13,380	-18,726	-5,009	-4,195	-4,900	-4,921	-4,127	..
Cross-currency valuation	..	..	-3,217	11,297	819	-5,987	-155	9,802	2,940	..
Residual	..	..	3,639	-1,341	1,531	2,426	2,398	631	1,544	..
9. AVERAGE TERMS OF NEW COMMITMENTS										
ALL CREDITORS										
Interest (%)	7	11.5	8	7.9	7.4	7.3	6.8	6.6	7.4	..
Maturity (years)	14.4	11.2	14	14.8	14.7	15.1	12.2	11.5	10.1	..
Grace period (years)	3.6	4.2	4.4	5	4.7	4.5	4.9	4.2	3.6	..
Grant element (%)	16.6	-5.7	11.2	11.9	14.9	14.5	15.8	15.9	12.1	..
Official creditors										
Interest (%)	6	7.8	7	7.1	6.9	7.1	6.3	6.2	7.6	..
Maturity (years)	23.4	16.8	16.8	18	18.5	19	17.9	18.5	14.1	..
Grace period (years)	5.5	4.5	5	5	5.1	5.1	5	5.2	4	..
Grant element (%)	27.4	14.5	17.8	18.2	19.3	18.4	22.3	24.1	15.4	..
Private creditors										
Interest (%)	7.7	13	9.6	9	8.2	7.7	7.2	6.9	7.1	..
Maturity (years)	8.9	8.9	9.6	10.6	8.1	6.9	8.2	4.9	4.5	..
Grace period (years)	2.4	4.1	3.3	5	3.9	3.4	4.8	3.3	3.1	..
Grant element (%)	10	-14.1	0.9	3.9	7.3	6.3	11.3	8.2	7.4	..
Memorandum items										
Commitments	4,375	33,302	16,178	26,202	27,371	24,816	31,073	29,564	46,647	..
Official creditors	1,648	9,755	9,853	14,745	17,250	16,849	12,828	14,278	27,605	..
Private creditors	2,728	23,548	6,324	11,457	10,121	7,967	18,245	15,286	19,042	..

10. RESOURCE FLOW CHARTS

(US$ million)

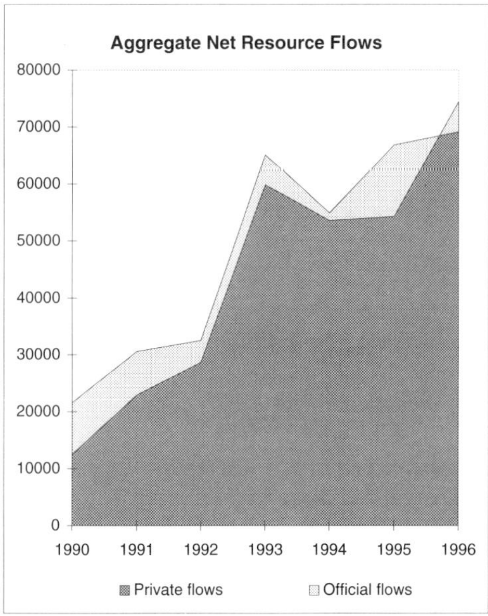

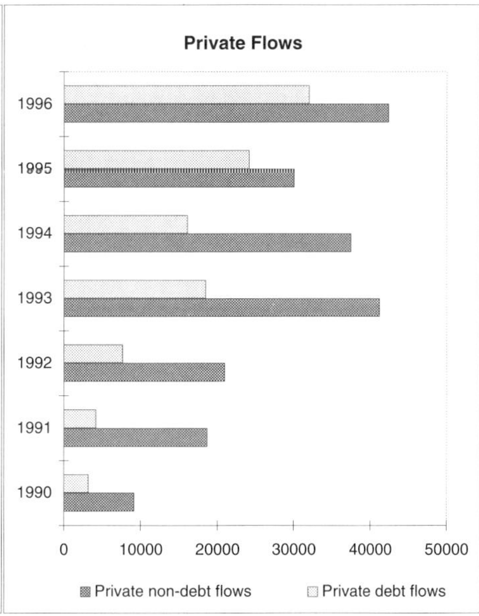

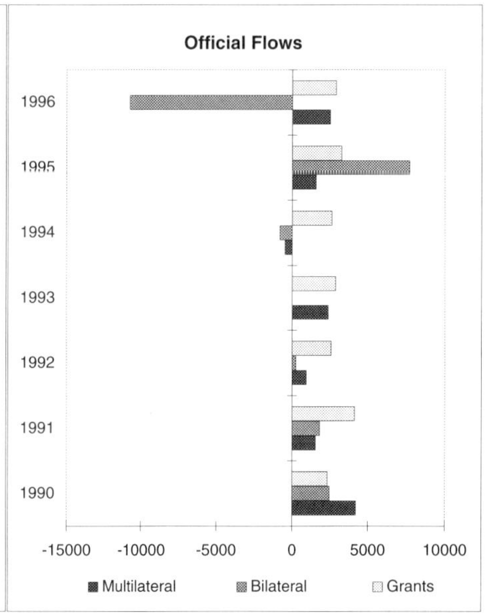

MIDDLE EAST AND NORTH AFRICA

(US$ million, unless otherwise indicated)

	1970	1980	1989	1990	1991	1992	1993	1994	1995	*Preliminary* 1996
1. SUMMARY DEBT DATA										
TOTAL DEBT STOCKS (EDT)	..	83,793	189,005	182,548	186,811	187,987	193,654	210,168	216,046	220,801
Long-term debt (LDOD)	4,166	61,734	143,413	136,955	138,479	133,922	138,231	157,705	165,089	167,791
Public and publicly guaranteed	4,151	61,139	141,399	134,975	137,151	132,864	137,348	155,484	161,825	163,199
Private nonguaranteed	15	595	2,015	1,981	1,328	1,058	882	2,221	3,263	4,592
Use of IMF credit	100	916	1,998	1,815	2,050	1,838	1,324	1,946	2,177	2,576
Short-term debt	..	21,144	43,594	43,778	46,282	52,227	54,100	50,517	48,780	50,434
of which interest arrears on LDOD	..	391	4,291	2,816	1,798	1,444	1,643	1,932	2,219	2,423
Official creditors	..	391	3,319	1,588	994	1,139	1,388	1,647	1,909	..
Private creditors	..	0	972	1,228	804	304	255	285	310	..
Memo: principal arrears on LDOD	..	114	8,941	8,089	5,929	5,200	5,767	7,122	8,729	9,765
Official creditors	..	108	4,781	3,515	2,421	3,162	4,180	5,275	6,630	..
Private creditors	..	6	4,160	4,574	3,508	2,039	1,587	1,846	2,099	..
Memo: export credits	..	..	60,799	62,505	63,963	59,628	60,957	70,199	73,590	..
TOTAL DEBT FLOWS										
Disbursements	890	12,318	20,308	14,600	19,551	17,512	16,163	16,467	14,046	16,121
Long-term debt	852	11,968	19,440	14,535	18,948	17,259	16,148	15,532	13,457	15,317
IMF purchases	38	350	868	65	603	253	16	935	590	804
Principal repayments	413	5,060	13,366	15,722	16,456	16,212	14,009	14,596	14,488	10,424
Long-term debt	382	4,827	13,039	15,325	16,068	15,824	13,472	14,190	14,098	10,087
IMF repurchases	31	233	327	397	388	388	537	406	390	337
Net flows on debt	1,029	8,655	11,348	537	6,617	7,599	6,627	8,900	2,866	7,146
of which short-term debt	..	..	4,406	1,659	3,523	6,299	4,473	7,029	3,308	1,449
Interest payments (INT)	..	6,454	9,176	8,624	8,043	9,723	8,843	8,720	9,722	10,604
Long-term debt	100	3,934	6,184	5,244	4,925	6,673	5,568	5,940	6,784	7,590
IMF charges	0	33	130	181	158	154	108	74	112	113
Short-term debt	..	2,488	2,863	3,199	2,960	2,896	3,167	2,706	2,826	2,901
Net transfers on debt	..	2,201	2,172	-8,087	-1,426	-2,124	-2,216	180	-6,856	-3,458
Total debt service (TDS)	..	11,514	22,543	24,346	24,499	25,935	22,852	23,316	24,210	21,028
Long-term debt	482	8,761	19,223	20,569	20,993	22,497	19,040	20,130	20,882	17,677
IMF repurchases and charges	31	265	457	578	546	542	645	480	502	450
Short-term debt (interest only)	..	2,488	2,863	3,199	2,960	2,896	3,167	2,706	2,826	2,901
2. AGGREGATE NET RESOURCE FLOWS AND NET TRANSFERS (LONG-TERM)										
NET RESOURCE FLOWS	1,185	8,525	10,023	10,206	11,308	7,609	9,462	8,557	2,420	10,884
Net flow of long-term debt (ex. IMF)	469	7,141	6,401	-790	2,880	1,435	2,675	1,342	-641	5,230
Foreign direct investment (net)	294	-3,313	1,966	2,757	1,825	2,228	4,187	2,958	-347	2,229
Portfolio equity flows	0	0	0	0	0	0	0	106	203	650
Grants (excluding technical coop.)	422	4,696	1,657	8,239	6,603	3,946	2,600	4,151	3,206	2,775
Memo: technical coop. grants	269	990	1,882	2,566	2,734	2,581	2,751	2,302	2,636	2,643
NET TRANSFERS	-1,859	-5,260	2,730	3,679	4,890	-626	2,608	1,352	-5,618	1,909
Interest on long-term debt	100	3,934	6,184	5,244	4,925	6,673	5,568	5,940	6,784	7,590
Profit remittances on FDI	2,944	9,850	1,109	1,284	1,493	1,561	1,286	1,265	1,253	1,385
3. MAJOR ECONOMIC AGGREGATES										
Gross national product (GNP)	45,037	457,151	436,944	473,473	459,308	472,108	448,906	514,437	579,839	649,236
Exports of goods & services (XGS)	12,851	203,732	117,699	154,718	154,379	162,687	148,094	148,284	161,974	174,160
of which workers' remittances	1,035	9,657	8,271	9,234	8,515	11,167	10,559	10,720	11,107	9,796
Imports of goods & services (MGS)	11,330	148,694	123,443	142,538	175,638	175,960	162,339	145,176	156,614	164,125
International reserves (RES)	4,477	82,281	50,204	49,899	54,941	55,211	60,406	64,170	70,499	..
Current account balance	-1,302	58,843	-17,651	-1,837	-40,095	-25,622	-29,049	-11,659	-10,596	-6,132
4. DEBT INDICATORS										
EDT / XGS (%)	..	41.1	160.6	118.0	121.0	115.6	130.8	141.7	133.4	126.8
EDT / GNP (%)	..	18.3	43.3	38.6	40.7	39.8	43.1	40.9	37.3	34.0
TDS / XGS (%)	..	5.7	19.2	15.7	15.9	15.9	15.4	15.7	14.9	12.1
INT / XGS (%)	..	3.2	7.8	5.6	5.2	6.0	6.0	5.9	6.0	6.1
INT / GNP (%)	..	1.4	2.1	1.8	1.8	2.1	2.0	1.7	1.7	1.6
RES / EDT (%)	..	98.2	26.6	27.3	29.4	29.4	31.2	30.5	32.6	..
RES / MGS (months)	4.7	6.6	4.9	4.2	3.8	3.8	4.5	5.3	5.4	..
Short-term / EDT (%)	..	25.2	23.1	24.0	24.8	27.8	27.9	24.0	22.6	22.8
Concessional / EDT (%)	..	21.6	23.6	23.7	25.2	25.2	25.3	25.1	26.0	25.6
Multilateral / EDT (%)	..	6.7	8.1	8.6	9.2	9.4	9.8	10.1	10.6	11.0

MIDDLE EAST AND NORTH AFRICA

(US$ million, unless otherwise indicated)

	1970	1980	1989	1990	1991	1992	1993	1994	1995	*Preliminary* 1996
5. LONG-TERM DEBT										
DEBT OUTSTANDING (LDOD)	**4,166**	**61,734**	**143,413**	**136,955**	**138,479**	**133,922**	**138,231**	**157,705**	**165,089**	**167,791**
Public and publicly guaranteed	**4,151**	**61,139**	**141,399**	**134,975**	**137,151**	**132,864**	**137,348**	**155,484**	**161,825**	**163,199**
Official creditors	3,042	31,456	85,960	80,212	84,080	85,886	91,887	108,790	117,717	119,237
Multilateral	172	5,603	15,391	15,783	17,191	17,663	19,053	21,185	22,852	24,254
Concessional	91	2,673	5,061	3,931	4,012	4,070	4,392	4,916	5,686	..
Bilateral	2,870	25,853	70,569	64,428	66,889	68,223	72,834	87,605	94,865	94,983
Concessional	2,465	15,446	39,581	39,321	43,066	43,325	44,668	47,924	50,543	..
Private creditors	1,109	29,682	55,439	54,763	53,072	46,979	45,461	46,694	44,109	43,962
Bonds	38	720	2,301	2,234	2,142	1,814	1,663	1,301	2,036	..
Commercial banks	56	10,327	19,908	18,131	20,235	19,125	16,386	17,221	16,592	..
Other private	1,014	18,636	33,230	34,398	30,695	26,040	27,412	28,172	25,481	..
Private nonguaranteed	**15**	**595**	**2,015**	**1,981**	**1,328**	**1,058**	**882**	**2,221**	**3,263**	**4,592**
Bonds	..	..	0	0	0	0	0	0	50	..
Commerical banks	..	..	2,015	1,981	1,328	1,058	882	2,221	3,213	..
Memo:										
IBRD	139	2,384	7,328	8,301	8,765	8,942	9,308	9,978	10,671	..
IDA	32	669	1,676	1,743	1,782	1,799	1,845	1,942	2,059	..
DISBURSEMENTS	**852**	**11,968**	**19,440**	**14,535**	**18,948**	**17,259**	**16,148**	**15,532**	**13,457**	**15,317**
Public and publicly guaranteed	**844**	**11,714**	**19,260**	**14,396**	**18,871**	**17,197**	**15,965**	**14,000**	**12,281**	**13,877**
Official creditors	419	5,778	7,725	6,416	7,583	7,262	6,783	5,495	5,645	6,078
Multilateral	32	703	2,124	2,400	2,755	2,839	2,876	2,817	3,223	3,544
Concessional	12	194	324	328	313	515	511	623	934	..
Bilatarel	387	5,075	5,602	4,016	4,829	4,422	3,908	2,678	2,423	2,534
Concessional	255	3,447	2,645	1,855	3,622	1,775	1,669	1,812	1,944	..
Private creditors	425	5,937	11,535	7,979	11,288	9,935	9,182	8,505	6,636	7,799
Bonds	5	66	320	0	1	0	15	272	1,288	..
Commercial banks	17	1,626	2,621	807	4,026	2,706	997	2,171	1,199	..
Other private	403	4,244	8,594	7,172	7,261	7,229	8,170	6,062	4,148	..
Private nonguaranteed	**8**	**254**	**180**	**139**	**77**	**62**	**183**	**1,532**	**1,175**	**1,440**
Bonds	..	..	0	0	0	0	0	0	50	..
Commerical banks	..	..	180	139	77	62	183	1,532	1,125	..
Memo:										
IBRD	23	421	996	1,164	1,154	1,349	1,099	1,018	1,455	..
IDA	8	82	57	35	52	61	66	87	125	..
PRINCIPAL REPAYMENTS	**382**	**4,827**	**13,039**	**15,325**	**16,068**	**15,824**	**13,472**	**14,190**	**14,098**	**10,087**
Public and publicly guaranteed	**380**	**4,714**	**12,799**	**15,148**	**15,816**	**15,461**	**13,246**	**13,959**	**13,910**	**9,857**
Official creditors	228	910	4,856	5,059	5,071	4,107	3,790	6,922	7,846	4,886
Multilateral	16	202	1,033	1,338	1,607	1,706	1,572	1,794	2,106	2,084
Concessional	3	21	102	162	250	321	187	202	240	..
Bilateral	212	708	3,822	3,721	3,464	2,402	2,218	5,128	5,739	2,802
Concessional	137	386	1,244	1,629	713	425	677	729	695	..
Private creditors	152	3,804	7,944	10,090	10,745	11,354	9,457	7,037	6,064	4,971
Bonds	3	33	151	148	114	238	663	445	278	..
Commercial banks	2	1,465	1,749	2,119	2,203	2,711	2,683	2,199	1,659	..
Other private	146	2,307	6,044	7,822	8,429	8,405	6,111	4,394	4,127	..
Private nonguaranteed	**3**	**114**	**240**	**177**	**252**	**363**	**226**	**231**	**188**	**230**
Bonds	..	..	0	0	0	0	0	0	0	..
Commerical banks	..	..	240	177	252	363	226	231	188	..
Memo:										
IBRD	16	140	653	761	855	897	899	1,008	1,118	..
IDA	0	1	10	14	18	19	22	24	27	..
NET FLOWS ON DEBT	**469**	**7,141**	**6,401**	**-790**	**2,880**	**1,435**	**2,675**	**1,342**	**-641**	**5,230**
Public and publicly guaranteed	**464**	**7,001**	**6,461**	**-752**	**3,055**	**1,736**	**2,718**	**41**	**-1,628**	**4,020**
Official creditors	191	4,868	2,870	1,358	2,512	3,155	2,994	-1,427	-2,200	1,192
Multilateral	16	501	1,091	1,062	1,148	1,134	1,304	1,023	1,116	1,460
Concessional	10	174	222	166	63	194	325	421	695	..
Bilateral	175	4,367	1,779	296	1,365	2,021	1,690	-2,451	-3,316	-268
Concessional	118	3,061	1,401	226	2,909	1,351	992	1,083	1,249	..
Private creditors	273	2,133	3,591	-2,110	543	-1,419	-275	1,468	572	2,828
Bonds	2	34	170	-148	-113	-238	-648	-173	1,010	..
Commercial banks	15	162	872	-1,312	1,823	-5	-1,686	-28	-460	..
Other private	257	1,937	2,550	-650	-1,167	-1,175	2,059	1,668	22	..
Private nonguaranteed	**5**	**140**	**-60**	**-38**	**-175**	**-301**	**-43**	**1,301**	**987**	**1,210**
Bonds	..	..	0	0	0	0	0	0	50	..
Commerical banks	..	..	-60	-38	-175	-301	-43	1,301	937	..
Memo:										
IBRD	8	281	342	403	299	452	200	10	337	..
IDA	8	81	46	21	34	42	44	62	98	..

MIDDLE EAST AND NORTH AFRICA

(US$ million, unless otherwise indicated)

	1970	1980	1989	1990	1991	1992	1993	1994	1995	Preliminary 1996
INTEREST PAYMENTS (LINT)	**100**	**3,934**	**6,184**	**5,244**	**4,925**	**6,673**	**5,568**	**5,940**	**6,784**	**7,590**
Public and publicly guaranteed	**99**	**3,884**	**6,025**	**5,100**	**4,833**	**6,613**	**5,514**	**5,867**	**6,681**	**7,428**
Official creditors	65	953	2,734	2,480	2,093	2,614	2,826	3,224	3,985	4,768
Multilateral	9	239	743	870	1,010	1,096	1,152	1,302	1,401	1,487
Concessional	3	28	67	71	90	89	93	110	135	..
Bilateral	56	714	1,991	1,610	1,083	1,517	1,673	1,923	2,584	3,281
Concessional	42	333	466	445	314	600	717	787	971	..
Private creditors	34	2,931	3,291	2,619	2,740	4,000	2,688	2,642	2,696	2,660
Bonds	2	71	147	158	157	115	70	80	108	..
Commercial banks	0	1,488	1,386	942	1,032	2,271	1,107	1,160	1,206	..
Other private	32	1,372	1,758	1,519	1,551	1,615	1,511	1,402	1,382	..
Private nonguaranteed	**1**	**50**	**159**	**144**	**92**	**60**	**54**	**74**	**104**	**162**
Bonds	..	..	0	0	0	0	0	0	0	..
Commerical banks	..	..	159	144	92	60	54	74	104	..
Memo:										
IBRD	9	198	522	598	657	675	685	756	750	..
IDA	0	5	12	12	13	13	13	14	15	..
NET TRANSFERS ON DEBT	**369**	**3,207**	**217**	**-6,034**	**-2,046**	**-5,238**	**-2,893**	**-4,598**	**-7,426**	**-2,360**
Public and publicly guaranteed	**365**	**3,117**	**436**	**-5,852**	**-1,778**	**-4,877**	**-2,795**	**-5,826**	**-8,309**	**-3,408**
Official creditors	126	3,915	136	-1,122	419	541	168	-4,652	-6,185	-3,576
Multilateral	7	262	347	192	138	38	151	-279	-284	-27
Concessional	6	146	155	95	-27	105	232	311	559	..
Bilateral	119	3,653	-212	-1,314	282	503	17	-4,373	-5,900	-3,549
Concessional	76	2,728	935	-220	2,595	751	275	296	277	..
Private creditors	239	-799	301	-4,730	-2,198	-5,418	-2,963	-1,174	-2,124	168
Bonds	-1	-38	23	-307	-270	-353	-718	-252	902	..
Commercial banks	14	-1,326	-514	-2,255	790	-2,276	-2,793	-1,188	-1,666	..
Other private	225	565	792	-2,169	-2,718	-2,790	548	266	-1,360	..
Private nonguaranteed	**4**	**90**	**-219**	**-182**	**-267**	**-361**	**-98**	**1,227**	**884**	**1,048**
Bonds	..	..	0	0	0	0	0	0	50	..
Commerical banks	..	..	-219	-182	-267	-361	-98	1,227	834	..
Memo:										
IBRD	-1	83	-180	-195	-358	-223	-485	-746	-413	..
IDA	8	76	34	9	21	29	31	48	83	..
DEBT SERVICE (LTDS)	**482**	**8,761**	**19,223**	**20,569**	**20,993**	**22,497**	**19,040**	**20,130**	**20,882**	**17,677**
Public and publicly guaranteed	**479**	**8,598**	**18,824**	**20,248**	**20,649**	**22,074**	**18,760**	**19,825**	**20,590**	**17,285**
Official creditors	293	1,862	7,590	7,539	7,164	6,721	6,615	10,146	11,830	9,654
Multilateral	25	441	1,776	2,208	2,617	2,802	2,724	3,096	3,507	3,571
Concessional	6	48	169	233	340	410	279	311	375	..
Bilateral	268	1,421	5,813	5,331	4,547	3,919	3,891	7,051	8,323	6,083
Concessional	179	719	1,710	2,075	1,028	1,025	1,394	1,516	1,667	..
Private creditors	186	6,735	11,234	12,709	13,485	15,354	12,145	9,679	8,760	7,631
Bonds	6	104	298	307	270	353	733	524	386	..
Commercial banks	3	2,952	3,135	3,062	3,235	4,982	3,790	3,359	2,865	..
Other private	178	3,679	7,802	9,341	9,980	10,019	7,622	5,796	5,509	..
Private nonguaranteed	**3**	**164**	**399**	**321**	**344**	**423**	**280**	**305**	**292**	**392**
Bonds	..	..	0	0	0	0	0	0	0	..
Commerical banks	..	..	399	321	344	423	280	305	292	..
Memo:										
IBRD	24	338	1,175	1,359	1,513	1,572	1,584	1,764	1,868	..
IDA	0	6	23	26	31	32	35	39	42	..
UNDISBURSED DEBT	**1,916**	**28,043**	**29,259**	**31,561**	**36,849**	**37,525**	**35,777**	**29,921**	**26,466**	**..**
Official creditors	1,543	16,056	17,636	19,016	21,653	22,331	23,635	20,978	20,158	..
Private creditors	374	11,987	11,623	12,545	15,196	15,194	12,142	8,943	6,308	..
Memorandum items										
Concessional LDOD	2,556	18,120	44,642	43,252	47,078	47,395	49,060	52,840	56,229	56,520
Variable rate LDOD	41	10,209	29,083	30,633	28,932	29,321	33,141	47,265	51,865	..
Public sector LDOD	4,128	53,408	118,907	114,194	115,823	113,461	116,980	134,815	141,972	..
Private sector LDOD	37	741	2,090	2,055	1,418	1,244	1,144	1,515	1,540	..
6. CURRENCY COMPOSITION OF LONG-TERM DEBT (PERCENT)										
Deutsche mark	7.7	6.4	5.5	6.7	6.7	7.2	6.8	7.2	7.2	..
French franc	18.5	9.3	8.3	10.7	11.5	11.3	10.3	10.4	11.1	..
Japanese yen	0.0	5.7	5.5	6.3	7.6	8.1	8.7	8.8	8.5	..
Pound sterling	4.1	1.3	1.2	1.5	1.4	1.3	1.3	1.2	1.1	..
Swiss franc	1.1	1.3	0.8	0.9	0.8	0.7	0.7	0.7	0.8	..
U.S. dollars	33.0	46.3	45.3	38.3	36.1	36.3	37.2	38.5	38.4	..
Multiple currency	3.1	4.7	6.3	7.6	8.1	8.6	9.0	8.7	8.9	..
Special drawing rights	0.0	0.0	0.3	0.4	0.6	0.1	0.1	0.1	0.2	..
All other currencies	32.6	12.5	10.9	12.3	11.9	11.9	11.3	11.2	11.9	..

MIDDLE EAST AND NORTH AFRICA

(US$ million, unless otherwise indicated)

	1970	*1980*	*1989*	*1990*	*1991*	*1992*	*1993*	*1994*	*1995*	*Preliminary 1996*
7. DEBT RESTRUCTURINGS										
Total amount rescheduled	..	..	1,223	4,537	17,260	2,607	4,410	15,943	10,927	..
Debt stock rescheduled	..	..	19	2,732	11,523	0	2,993	10,900	5,332	..
Principal rescheduled	..	..	814	1,039	3,851	1,728	1,142	4,279	4,963	..
Official	..	..	492	693	1,859	798	194	822	801	..
Private	..	..	323	346	1,992	930	948	3,457	4,162	..
Interest rescheduled	..	..	361	219	1,706	502	356	632	538	..
Official	..	..	208	152	1,080	219	58	179	135	..
Private	..	..	153	67	626	282	298	452	402	..
Principal forgiven	..	..	2,759	10,614	3,095	444	215	325	356	..
Memo: interest forgiven	..	..	0	2,481	169	150	142	80	4	..
Debt stock reduction	..	..	0	0	406	530	97	0	0	..
of which debt buyback	..	..	0	0	0	0	0	0	0	..
8. DEBT STOCK-FLOW RECONCILIATION										
Total change in debt stocks	..	..	9,688	-6,457	4,263	1,176	5,667	16,514	5,878	..
Net flows on debt	..	..	11,348	537	6,617	7,599	6,627	8,900	2,866	..
Net change in interest arrears	..	..	996	-1,475	-1,018	-354	200	289	287	..
Interest capitalized	..	..	361	219	1,706	502	356	632	538	..
Debt forgiveness or reduction	..	..	-2,759	-10,614	-3,501	-974	-312	-325	-356	..
Cross-currency valuation	..	..	-451	6,125	338	-3,251	-766	6,485	2,593	..
Residual	..	..	194	-1,248	121	-2,345	-438	533	-50	..
9. AVERAGE TERMS OF NEW COMMITMENTS										
ALL CREDITORS										
Interest (%)	4.7	6.5	7.1	7.5	6.3	5.7	5.6	5.8	5.9	..
Maturity (years)	17.1	17.8	13.8	13.4	14.2	12.6	14.8	13.8	14.6	..
Grace period (years)	5.5	4.7	3.8	4	4.4	4.6	4.6	3.9	4.4	..
Grant element (%)	32.3	23.5	16.7	15.4	21.4	21.5	22.9	20.9	21.3	..
Official creditors										
Interest (%)	3.7	4.8	5.8	5.6	5.2	5.5	5.5	5.5	5.1	..
Maturity (years)	21.6	24	19	21.2	21.2	16.9	19.5	20.9	18.4	..
Grace period (years)	7.4	6.1	5.5	6.1	6.4	5.6	5.8	5.9	4.7	..
Grant element (%)	42.5	38.1	27.8	31.3	34.7	27.3	29.1	30	27.4	..
Private creditors										
Interest (%)	6.3	8.6	8.3	8.9	7.2	5.9	5.7	6.1	7.4	..
Maturity (years)	9.4	10.1	8.8	7.4	7.8	9.7	8.6	6.7	7.6	..
Grace period (years)	2	2.9	2.1	2.4	2.7	3.9	3.1	1.9	3.7	..
Grant element (%)	14.7	5.4	6.2	3.3	9.3	17.5	14.6	11.8	10.1	..
Memorandum items										
Commitments	1,156	11,393	18,334	15,228	23,133	18,910	13,059	7,581	7,924	..
Official creditors	734	6,295	8,930	6,603	11,040	7,763	7,458	3,784	5,141	..
Private creditors	423	5,099	9,405	8,625	12,093	11,147	5,600	3,797	2,783	..

10. RESOURCE FLOW CHARTS

(US$ million)

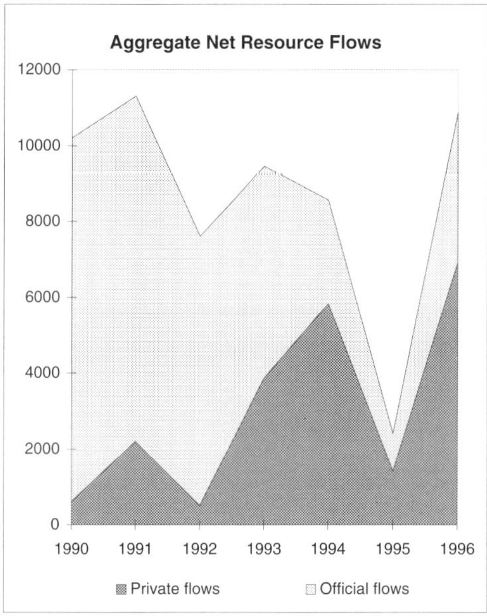

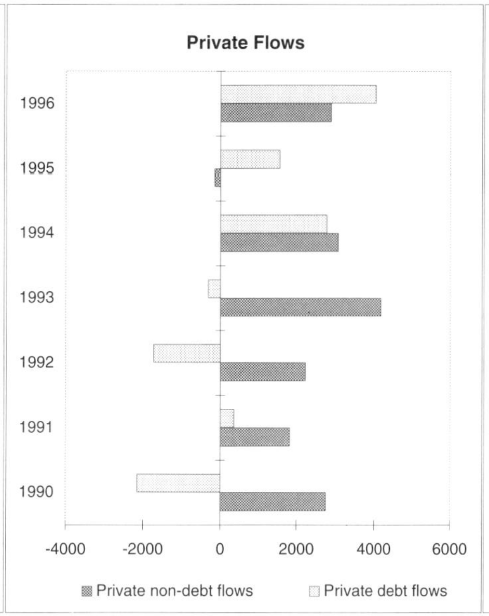

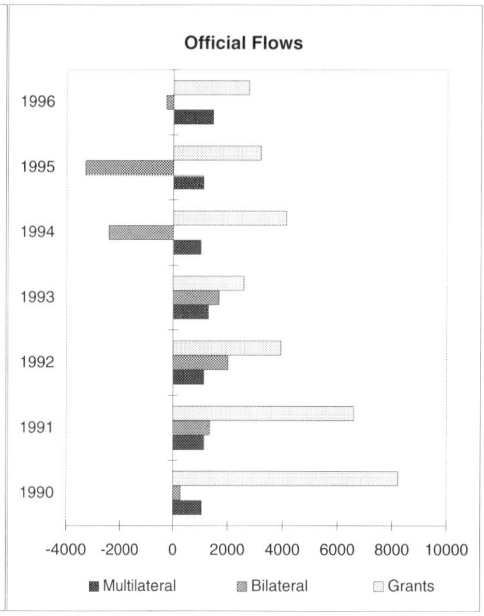

SOUTH ASIA

(US$ million, unless otherwise indicated)

1. SUMMARY DEBT DATA

	1970	1980	1989	1990	1991	1992	1993	1994	1995	Preliminary 1996
TOTAL DEBT STOCKS (EDT)	..	**38,014**	**116,770**	**130,034**	**136,174**	**142,770**	**147,581**	**161,073**	**156,778**	**160,999**
Long-term debt (LDOD)	**11,329**	**33,053**	**102,323**	**113,125**	**118,591**	**124,323**	**134,115**	**146,851**	**142,435**	**146,820**
Public and publicly guaranteed	11,224	32,695	100,502	111,398	116,522	122,185	131,198	139,164	134,134	137,041
Private nonguaranteed	105	357	1,821	1,727	2,069	2,138	2,917	7,687	8,301	9,779
Use of IMF credit	**124**	**2,508**	**3,636**	**4,537**	**5,685**	**7,166**	**7,410**	**7,211**	**5,252**	**3,728**
Short-term debt	..	**2,454**	**10,811**	**12,371**	**11,898**	**11,281**	**6,056**	**7,011**	**9,090**	**10,451**
of which interest arrears on LDOD	..	0	12	17	22	26	34	47	59	59
Official creditors	..	0	6	7	6	7	9	15	21	..
Private creditors	..	0	7	11	16	19	26	33	38	..
Memo: principal arrears on LDOD	..	0	32	34	33	37	46	67	104	90
Official creditors	..	0	32	34	27	29	33	39	45	..
Private creditors	..	0	0	1	5	8	12	28	58	..
Memo: export credits	..	..	7,758	9,370	9,819	10,434	11,061	13,167	14,706	..
TOTAL DEBT FLOWS										
Disbursements	**1,475**	**6,357**	**11,651**	**12,253**	**13,061**	**13,599**	**13,262**	**12,826**	**11,276**	**16,644**
Long-term debt	1,466	4,710	10,937	10,378	11,203	11,686	12,690	12,306	11,074	16,287
IMF purchases	10	1,647	714	1,875	1,859	1,912	573	520	202	357
Principal repayments	**721**	**1,553**	**4,754**	**5,336**	**5,202**	**5,885**	**6,394**	**9,196**	**11,316**	**11,547**
Long-term debt	461	1,226	3,328	4,168	4,410	5,219	6,014	7,882	9,320	9,791
IMF repurchases	260	326	1,425	1,168	792	666	380	1,314	1,996	1,756
Net flows on debt	**1,179**	**5,850**	**8,227**	**8,472**	**7,381**	**7,093**	**1,637**	**4,572**	**2,027**	**6,456**
of which short-term debt	..	..	1,330	1,555	-478	-621	-5,232	942	2,067	1,359
Interest payments (INT)	..	**1,217**	**5,257**	**6,204**	**5,942**	**5,471**	**5,498**	**5,721**	**6,294**	**6,289**
Long-term debt	282	864	4,085	4,747	4,563	4,533	4,715	5,001	5,435	5,484
IMF charges	0	61	307	253	278	325	316	269	233	127
Short-term debt	..	292	864	1,204	1,101	614	467	451	627	678
Net transfers on debt	..	**4,632**	**2,970**	**2,268**	**1,439**	**1,622**	**-3,861**	**-1,149**	**-4,267**	**167**
Total debt service (TDS)	..	**2,770**	**10,011**	**11,540**	**11,144**	**11,356**	**11,891**	**14,917**	**17,610**	**17,836**
Long-term debt	743	2,090	7,414	8,915	8,973	9,752	10,729	12,883	14,755	15,275
IMF repurchases and charges	260	387	1,733	1,420	1,070	991	695	1,584	2,229	1,883
Short-term debt (interest only)	..	292	864	1,204	1,101	614	467	451	627	678

2. AGGREGATE NET RESOURCE FLOWS AND NET TRANSFERS (LONG-TERM)

	1970	1980	1989	1990	1991	1992	1993	1994	1995	1996
NET RESOURCE FLOWS	**1,357**	**6,488**	**11,530**	**9,223**	**10,714**	**9,997**	**11,765**	**14,438**	**8,405**	**17,035**
Net flow of long-term debt (ex. IMF)	1,005	3,484	7,609	6,210	6,793	6,467	6,676	4,424	1,754	6,496
Foreign direct investment (net)	69	185	487	464	456	624	841	1,231	1,791	2,632
Portfolio equity flows	0	0	168	105	23	380	2,025	6,223	2,340	5,400
Grants (excluding technical coop.)	283	2,820	3,266	2,444	3,443	2,525	2,223	2,560	2,519	2,507
Memo: technical coop. grants	138	690	1,554	1,588	1,648	1,849	1,702	1,524	1,574	1,667
NET TRANSFERS	**1,061**	**5,603**	**7,366**	**4,383**	**6,074**	**5,360**	**6,938**	**9,308**	**2,818**	**11,357**
Interest on long-term debt	282	864	4,085	4,747	4,563	4,533	4,715	5,001	5,435	5,484
Profit remittances on FDI	14	22	78	92	77	104	113	129	152	194

3. MAJOR ECONOMIC AGGREGATES

	1970	1980	1989	1990	1991	1992	1993	1994	1995	1996
Gross national product (GNP)	79,037	218,950	357,479	390,609	372,648	390,404	398,972	453,534	514,207	568,476
Exports of goods & services (XGS)	4,270	23,679	37,108	41,020	43,546	44,858	51,953	60,676	71,696	77,121
of which workers' remittances	169	4,883	5,276	5,112	5,660	5,424	6,284	8,297	8,335	6,771
Imports of goods & services (MGS)	5,949	30,482	50,096	56,319	51,571	54,135	60,044	69,789	83,777	89,618
International reserves (RES)	1,404	15,431	11,179	8,893	12,018	14,833	21,965	34,471	31,104	..
Current account balance	-1,494	-5,596	-11,427	-13,604	-5,093	-5,946	-5,409	-5,372	-9,677	-11,142

4. DEBT INDICATORS

	1970	1980	1989	1990	1991	1992	1993	1994	1995	1996
EDT / XGS (%)	..	160.5	314.7	317.0	312.7	318.3	284.1	265.5	218.7	208.8
EDT / GNP (%)	..	17.4	32.7	33.3	36.5	36.6	37.0	35.5	30.5	28.3
TDS / XGS (%)	..	11.7	27.0	28.1	25.6	25.3	22.9	24.6	24.6	23.1
INT / XGS (%)	..	5.1	14.2	15.1	13.6	12.2	10.6	9.4	8.8	8.2
INT / GNP (%)	..	0.6	1.5	1.6	1.6	1.4	1.4	1.3	1.2	1.1
RES / EDT (%)	..	40.6	9.6	6.8	8.8	10.4	14.9	21.4	19.8	..
RES / MGS (months)	2.8	6.1	2.7	1.9	2.8	3.3	4.4	5.9	4.5	..
Short-term / EDT (%)	..	6.5	9.3	9.5	8.7	7.9	4.1	4.4	5.8	6.5
Concessional / EDT (%)	..	75.3	57.1	56.5	55.3	55.0	56.0	56.6	57.1	53.3
Multilateral / EDT (%)	..	24.6	28.1	29.4	31.4	32.3	33.9	35.4	36.4	37.3

SOUTH ASIA

(US$ million, unless otherwise indicated)

	1970	1980	1989	1990	1991	1992	1993	1994	1995	Preliminary 1996
5. LONG-TERM DEBT										
DEBT OUTSTANDING (LDOD)	**11,329**	**33,053**	**102,323**	**113,125**	**118,591**	**124,323**	**134,115**	**146,851**	**142,435**	**146,820**
Public and publicly guaranteed	**11,224**	**32,695**	**100,502**	**111,398**	**116,522**	**122,185**	**131,198**	**139,164**	**134,134**	**137,041**
Official creditors	10,544	30,288	77,533	86,832	90,808	95,564	101,285	112,511	109,559	111,639
Multilateral	2,205	9,345	32,871	38,287	42,753	46,161	50,024	56,958	57,058	60,002
Concessional	1,972	8,191	23,846	27,266	29,829	31,877	34,120	38,677	39,904	..
Bilateral	8,338	20,943	44,663	48,545	48,056	49,404	51,260	55,553	52,502	51,637
Concessional	7,545	20,430	42,802	46,221	45,491	46,706	48,463	52,517	49,602	..
Private creditors	680	2,407	22,969	24,566	25,714	26,620	29,913	26,654	24,575	25,402
Bonds	14	2	2,479	2,707	4,169	4,088	3,903	4,003	3,429	..
Commercial banks	54	1,679	15,435	16,841	16,671	17,728	19,765	15,187	14,239	..
Other private	612	726	5,055	5,018	4,875	4,804	6,245	7,464	6,907	..
Private nonguaranteed	**105**	**357**	**1,821**	**1,727**	**2,069**	**2,138**	**2,917**	**7,687**	**8,301**	**9,779**
Bonds	..	..	0	0	0	0	794	1,203	1,065	..
Commerical banks	..	..	1,821	1,727	2,069	2,138	2,123	6,484	7,236	..
Memo:										
IBRD	852	1,242	8,187	9,646	10,780	11,576	12,609	14,165	13,035	..
IDA	1,347	7,065	19,172	21,071	22,683	24,230	25,582	28,421	29,001	..
DISBURSEMENTS	**1,466**	**4,710**	**10,937**	**10,378**	**11,203**	**11,686**	**12,690**	**12,306**	**11,074**	**16,287**
Public and publicly guaranteed	**1,438**	**4,413**	**10,620**	**10,125**	**10,742**	**10,893**	**11,235**	**11,008**	**9,140**	**14,084**
Official creditors	1,317	3,371	6,892	7,036	7,965	7,567	6,965	7,826	6,371	8,272
Multilateral	198	1,417	4,171	4,439	5,060	4,603	4,379	4,860	3,903	4,747
Concessional	117	1,211	1,886	2,397	2,551	2,712	2,188	2,974	2,254	..
Bilatarel	1,119	1,955	2,722	2,597	2,905	2,963	2,586	2,966	2,468	3,525
Concessional	1,002	1,803	2,007	2,034	2,418	2,408	1,996	2,408	2,079	..
Private creditors	121	1,042	3,728	3,089	2,777	3,327	4,270	3,182	2,769	5,812
Bonds	0	0	705	427	1,619	0	0	150	0	..
Commercial banks	16	797	2,760	2,067	607	2,496	2,078	1,037	1,389	..
Other private	105	245	263	595	552	830	2,193	1,995	1,380	..
Private nonguaranteed	**28**	**297**	**317**	**253**	**461**	**793**	**1,455**	**1,298**	**1,934**	**2,203**
Bonds	..	..	0	0	0	0	794	412	520	..
Commercial banks	..	..	317	253	461	793	661	885	1,414	..
Memo:										
IBRD	108	190	1,862	1,576	1,644	1,239	1,566	1,055	860	..
IDA	84	928	1,135	1,583	1,658	1,893	1,427	1,860	1,372	..
PRINCIPAL REPAYMENTS	**461**	**1,226**	**3,328**	**4,168**	**4,410**	**5,219**	**6,014**	**7,882**	**9,320**	**9,791**
Public and publicly guaranteed	**435**	**1,128**	**2,972**	**3,809**	**4,064**	**4,779**	**5,344**	**7,490**	**8,824**	**9,065**
Official creditors	322	940	2,092	2,409	2,637	3,012	3,384	4,399	5,677	4,422
Multilateral	64	135	713	1,011	1,075	1,251	1,534	1,869	2,226	1,983
Concessional	47	64	239	280	317	338	377	417	497	..
Bilateral	259	805	1,379	1,398	1,562	1,761	1,850	2,531	3,450	2,439
Concessional	166	732	1,152	1,262	1,291	1,378	1,403	2,024	3,022	..
Private creditors	113	188	880	1,400	1,427	1,767	1,960	3,091	3,147	4,643
Bonds	3	0	27	280	239	206	338	381	310	..
Commercial banks	12	44	409	390	459	687	814	1,620	1,853	..
Other private	98	144	444	729	729	874	808	1,090	985	..
Private nonguaranteed	**26**	**98**	**356**	**359**	**346**	**440**	**670**	**391**	**496**	**726**
Bonds	..	..	0	0	0	0	0	0	0	..
Commerical banks	..	..	356	359	346	440	670	391	496	..
Memo:										
IBRD	64	99	424	553	638	771	926	1,019	1,173	..
IDA	0	19	129	151	186	208	239	269	318	..
NET FLOWS ON DEBT	**1,005**	**3,484**	**7,609**	**6,210**	**6,793**	**6,467**	**6,676**	**4,424**	**1,754**	**6,496**
Public and publicly guaranteed	**1,003**	**3,285**	**7,648**	**6,317**	**6,678**	**6,114**	**5,892**	**3,518**	**316**	**5,019**
Official creditors	995	2,431	4,800	4,627	5,328	4,555	3,581	3,427	695	3,850
Multilateral	134	1,281	3,457	3,428	3,984	3,353	2,845	2,991	1,677	2,764
Concessional	70	1,147	1,648	2,117	2,235	2,375	1,811	2,558	1,757	..
Bilateral	860	1,150	1,343	1,199	1,344	1,202	736	435	-982	1,086
Concessional	836	1,072	856	773	1,127	1,030	593	384	-943	..
Private creditors	8	854	2,848	1,690	1,350	1,559	2,310	91	-379	1,169
Bonds	-3	0	678	147	1,380	-206	-338	-231	-310	..
Commercial banks	4	753	2,351	1,677	148	1,809	1,264	-583	-464	..
Other private	8	101	-182	-134	-178	-44	1,384	906	395	..
Private nonguaranteed	**2**	**199**	**-39**	**-107**	**115**	**353**	**784**	**906**	**1,438**	**1,477**
Bonds	..	..	0	0	0	0	794	412	520	..
Commerical banks	..	..	-39	-107	115	353	-10	494	918	..
Memo:										
IBRD	44	91	1,438	1,023	1,006	467	640	37	-314	..
IDA	84	909	1,007	1,433	1,472	1,685	1,189	1,591	1,054	..

SOUTH ASIA

(US$ million, unless otherwise indicated)

	1970	1980	1989	1990	1991	1992	1993	1994	1995	Preliminary 1996
INTEREST PAYMENTS (LINT)	**282**	**864**	**4,085**	**4,747**	**4,563**	**4,533**	**4,715**	**5,001**	**5,435**	**5,484**
Public and publicly guaranteed	**276**	**832**	**3,935**	**4,599**	**4,416**	**4,369**	**4,510**	**4,519**	**4,773**	**4,885**
Official creditors	236	653	1,993	2,309	2,401	2,569	2,679	2,906	3,035	2,992
Multilateral	57	181	906	1,072	1,180	1,336	1,437	1,565	1,644	1,707
Concessional	44	83	200	222	240	266	292	320	350	..
Bilateral	179	472	1,087	1,237	1,220	1,234	1,243	1,342	1,391	1,285
Concessional	137	443	961	1,076	1,047	1,056	1,052	1,148	1,119	..
Private creditors	40	179	1,942	2,290	2,016	1,800	1,830	1,612	1,738	1,893
Bonds	1	0	147	187	200	234	342	214	204	..
Commercial banks	3	123	1,581	1,809	1,483	1,250	1,182	934	1,035	..
Other private	36	56	215	294	332	316	306	465	499	..
Private nonguaranteed	**6**	**32**	**150**	**148**	**147**	**164**	**206**	**483**	**662**	**599**
Bonds	..	..	0	0	0	0	1	21	58	..
Commerical banks	..	..	150	148	147	164	205	462	604	..
Memo:										
IBRD	48	104	640	753	806	889	918	979	995	..
IDA	9	47	136	150	159	172	185	198	215	..
NET TRANSFERS ON DEBT	**723**	**2,620**	**3,524**	**1,463**	**2,230**	**1,935**	**1,961**	**-577**	**-3,680**	**1,012**
Public and publicly guaranteed	**727**	**2,453**	**3,713**	**1,717**	**2,262**	**1,745**	**1,382**	**-1,001**	**-4,457**	**134**
Official creditors	759	1,778	2,807	2,318	2,927	1,986	902	520	-2,340	858
Multilateral	77	1,100	2,552	2,356	2,804	2,017	1,409	1,427	33	1,057
Concessional	26	1,064	1,448	1,896	1,994	2,108	1,519	2,237	1,408	..
Bilateral	682	678	256	-38	123	-32	-507	-907	-2,373	-199
Concessional	699	629	-105	-304	80	-27	-459	-764	-2,061	..
Private creditors	-32	675	906	-600	-666	-240	480	-1,521	-2,116	-724
Bonds	-4	0	532	-40	1,180	-440	-680	-445	-514	..
Commercial banks	1	630	771	-133	-1,336	560	82	-1,516	-1,498	..
Other private	-28	45	-397	-428	-510	-360	1,079	440	-104	..
Private nonguaranteed	**-4**	**167**	**-190**	**-255**	**-32**	**189**	**579**	**424**	**776**	**878**
Bonds	..	..	0	0	0	0	793	392	462	..
Commerical banks	..	..	-190	-255	-32	189	-215	32	315	..
Memo:										
IBRD	-4	-13	798	270	200	-422	-278	-942	-1,309	..
IDA	75	862	870	1,282	1,313	1,512	1,004	1,393	839	..
DEBT SERVICE (LTDS)	**743**	**2,090**	**7,414**	**8,915**	**8,973**	**9,752**	**10,729**	**12,883**	**14,755**	**15,275**
Public and publicly guaranteed	**711**	**1,960**	**6,907**	**8,408**	**8,480**	**9,148**	**9,853**	**12,009**	**13,597**	**13,950**
Official creditors	559	1,594	4,085	4,718	5,038	5,581	6,063	7,306	8,712	7,414
Multilateral	121	316	1,619	2,083	2,256	2,586	2,971	3,433	3,870	3,690
Concessional	92	147	439	501	557	604	670	737	847	..
Bilateral	438	1,277	2,466	2,635	2,782	2,995	3,092	3,872	4,841	3,724
Concessional	302	1,175	2,112	2,338	2,338	2,435	2,456	3,172	4,140	..
Private creditors	152	367	2,822	3,690	3,443	3,567	3,790	4,703	4,885	6,536
Bonds	4	0	174	467	439	440	680	595	514	..
Commercial banks	15	167	1,990	2,200	1,942	1,937	1,996	2,553	2,887	..
Other private	134	200	659	1,024	1,062	1,190	1,114	1,555	1,484	..
Private nonguaranteed	**32**	**130**	**507**	**507**	**493**	**604**	**876**	**874**	**1,158**	**1,325**
Bonds	..	..	0	0	0	0	1	21	58	..
Commerical banks	..	..	507	507	493	604	875	853	1,100	..
Memo:										
IBRD	112	203	1,064	1,306	1,444	1,660	1,843	1,998	2,169	..
IDA	10	66	265	301	345	380	424	466	533	..
UNDISBURSED DEBT	**3,421**	**14,183**	**37,629**	**41,605**	**41,221**	**39,046**	**39,260**	**38,561**	**33,813**	**..**
Official creditors	3,043	12,836	35,923	38,783	38,449	35,246	34,348	35,294	32,113	..
Private creditors	379	1,347	1,706	2,822	2,772	3,801	4,912	3,267	1,700	..
Memorandum items										
Concessional LDOD	9,517	28,621	66,649	73,487	75,320	78,583	82,583	91,194	89,506	85,846
Variable rate LDOD	105	1,009	13,018	14,702	16,606	18,306	21,318	27,372	27,444	..
Public sector LDOD	10,779	31,006	94,685	105,582	110,500	116,106	125,091	132,846	127,890	..
Private sector LDOD	550	852	2,618	2,497	2,822	2,865	3,642	8,428	8,965	..

6. CURRENCY COMPOSITION OF LONG-TERM DEBT (PERCENT)

	1970	1980	1989	1990	1991	1992	1993	1994	1995	Preliminary 1996
Deutsche mark	9.7	8.3	5.9	5.9	6.0	5.8	5.2	5.8	5.7	..
French franc	1.5	2.3	1.7	1.7	1.8	1.8	1.6	1.9	2.0	..
Japanese yen	5.5	8.8	11.2	11.9	13.0	13.7	15.0	16.6	15.4	..
Pound sterling	22.5	17.7	5.4	4.9	4.8	4.3	3.8	3.5	3.5	..
Swiss franc	0.4	0.3	0.6	0.6	0.5	0.5	0.5	0.6	0.6	..
U.S. dollars	42.0	41.9	52.6	51.6	48.8	48.2	48.3	44.2	44.9	..
Multiple currency	8.5	7.3	11.8	13.6	15.4	16.2	17.0	19.0	19.2	..
Special drawing rights	0.0	0.0	0.6	0.8	0.8	0.8	0.8	1.0	1.2	..
All other currencies	9.9	9.6	5.1	4.6	4.4	4.2	3.6	3.4	3.4	..

SOUTH ASIA

(US$ million, unless otherwise indicated)

	1970	1980	1989	1990	1991	1992	1993	1994	1995	Preliminary 1996
7. DEBT RESTRUCTURINGS										
Total amount rescheduled	..	..	0	0	0	0	0	0	0	..
Debt stock rescheduled	..	..	0	0	0	0	0	0	0	..
Principal rescheduled	..	..	0	0	0	0	0	0	0	..
Official	..	..	0	0	0	0	0	0	0	..
Private	..	..	0	0	0	0	0	0	0	..
Interest rescheduled	..	..	0	0	0	0	0	0	0	..
Official	..	..	0	0	0	0	0	0	0	..
Private	..	..	0	0	0	0	0	0	0	..
Principal forgiven	..	..	0	0	310	2	2	2	7	..
Memo: interest forgiven	..	..	0	0	0	0	0	0	0	..
Debt stock reduction	..	..	0	0	0	0	0	0	0	..
of which debt buyback	..	..	0	0	0	0	0	0	0	..
8. DEBT STOCK-FLOW RECONCILIATION										
Total change in debt stocks	..	..	16,786	13,264	6,140	6,596	4,811	13,492	-4,296	..
Net flows on debt	..	..	8,227	8,472	7,381	7,093	1,637	4,572	2,027	..
Net change in interest arrears	..	..	6	5	5	4	8	13	12	..
Interest capitalized	..	..	0	0	0	0	0	0	0	..
Debt forgiveness or reduction	..	..	0	0	-310	-2	-2	-2	-7	..
Cross-currency valuation	..	..	-1,032	2,551	1,290	586	2,122	7,980	-3,620	..
Residual	..	..	9,585	2,236	-2,226	-1,085	1,047	929	-2,708	..
9. AVERAGE TERMS OF NEW COMMITMENTS										
ALL CREDITORS										
Interest (%)	2.6	4.7	5.2	4.6	5.2	4.3	5	3.4	3.8	..
Maturity (years)	32.6	32.5	21.7	24.6	22.5	24	20.2	25.5	22.4	..
Grace period (years)	9.8	7.5	6.7	7.7	6.9	7.2	5.8	7.6	7.1	..
Grant element (%)	59.5	48	34.9	41.7	37.6	41.6	34.4	49.5	43.2	..
Official creditors										
Interest (%)	2.3	2.2	4.1	3.6	3.9	3.2	3.2	3	3.9	..
Maturity (years)	34.9	39.3	25.3	28.9	27	29.1	27.2	28.2	26.1	..
Grace period (years)	10.6	8.7	6.5	8.1	7.5	7.6	7.7	8.3	7.4	..
Grant element (%)	64.2	66.4	44.4	51.6	48	54	52.4	54.9	46.1	..
Private creditors										
Interest (%)	5.9	12.8	8.1	6.7	9.2	6.9	7.4	5.9	3.3	..
Maturity (years)	11.6	10.9	12.5	14.9	7.7	13.1	10.5	7.8	8	..
Grace period (years)	2.6	3.6	7.3	6.8	5	6.2	3	3.1	5.8	..
Grant element (%)	17.9	-10.7	10.5	19.4	3.2	14.8	9.2	14.1	31.7	..
Memorandum items										
Commitments	2,002	8,182	16,116	13,711	11,733	13,811	12,979	10,254	6,747	..
Official creditors	1,798	6,227	11,606	9,524	9,009	9,420	7,558	8,902	5,370	..
Private creditors	204	1,956	4,510	4,187	2,724	4,391	5,421	1,352	1,377	..

10. RESOURCE FLOW CHARTS

(US$ million)

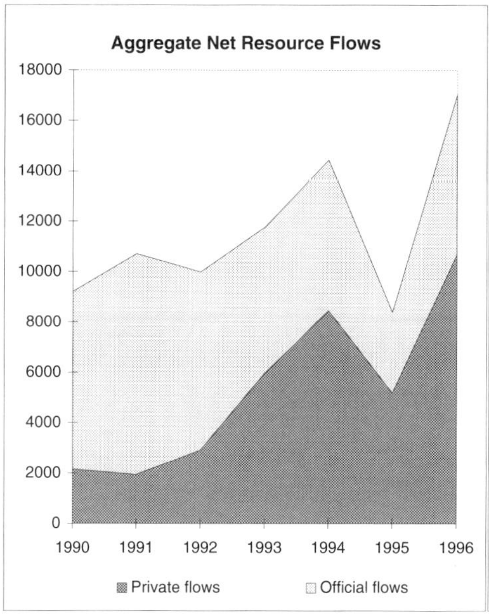

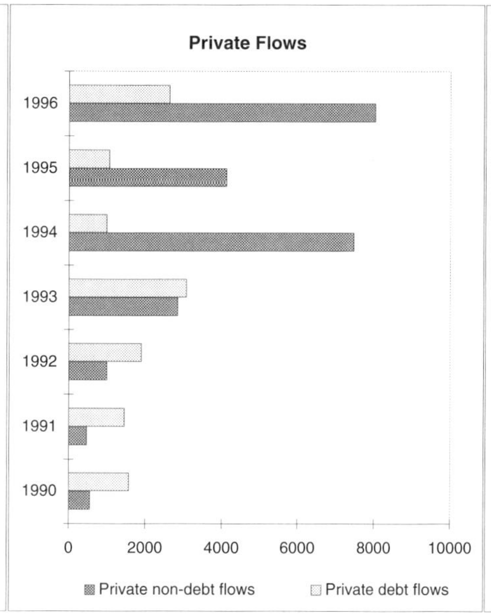

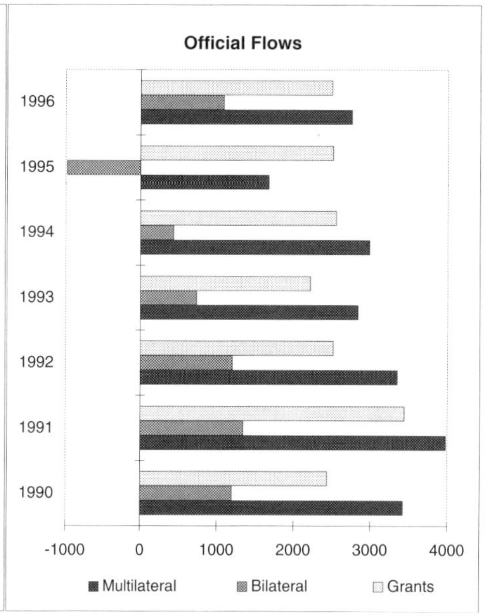

SUB-SAHARAN AFRICA

(US$ million, unless otherwise indicated)

	1970	1980	1989	1990	1991	1992	1993	1994	1995	*Preliminary* 1996
1. SUMMARY DEBT DATA										
TOTAL DEBT STOCKS (EDT)	..	**84,119**	**172,153**	**191,291**	**195,798**	**193,567**	**198,387**	**211,221**	**226,483**	**235,425**
Long-term debt (LDOD)	**6,057**	**58,509**	**142,135**	**156,735**	**161,048**	**155,969**	**155,354**	**166,122**	**175,717**	**181,986**
Public and publicly guaranteed	5,748	53,942	137,164	151,459	155,646	150,870	150,268	160,550	168,600	169,069
Private nonguaranteed	309	4,567	4,971	5,276	5,402	5,099	5,086	5,572	7,117	12,917
Use of IMF credit	**106**	**3,033**	**6,380**	**6,612**	**6,603**	**6,345**	**7,019**	**7,920**	**8,673**	**8,684**
Short-term debt	..	**22,577**	**23,638**	**27,944**	**28,147**	**31,254**	**36,015**	**37,179**	**42,093**	**44,755**
of which interest arrears on LDOD	..	259	7,124	9,323	10,726	12,993	16,756	18,579	20,783	21,673
Official creditors	..	155	5,173	6,449	7,695	9,757	12,743	14,108	15,977	..
Private creditors	..	104	1,951	2,874	3,031	3,236	4,013	4,471	4,806	..
Memo: principal arrears on LDOD	..	1,184	13,878	17,524	21,001	24,810	30,460	34,126	39,808	42,932
Official creditors	..	495	8,608	9,915	12,515	15,603	19,383	22,201	26,702	..
Private creditors	..	690	5,270	7,610	8,485	9,207	11,077	11,925	13,106	..
Memo: export credits	..	..	50,324	54,922	55,341	51,706	51,391	54,868	53,729	..
TOTAL DEBT FLOWS										
Disbursements	**1,241**	**15,478**	**12,001**	**11,175**	**9,660**	**10,039**	**9,639**	**11,529**	**13,777**	**15,081**
Long-term debt	1,222	14,261	11,138	10,513	9,081	9,511	8,492	10,611	10,783	14,326
IMF purchases	19	1,217	862	662	579	527	1,146	918	2,994	755
Principal repayments	**457**	**3,272**	**6,096**	**7,453**	**6,234**	**6,559**	**6,945**	**6,285**	**8,473**	**6,805**
Long-term debt	394	2,795	4,791	6,501	5,621	6,029	6,490	5,818	6,059	6,252
IMF repurchases	63	477	1,304	952	614	530	455	467	2,413	553
Net flows on debt	**1,521**	**17,484**	**6,398**	**5,908**	**2,229**	**4,320**	**3,713**	**4,956**	**8,202**	**10,099**
of which short-term debt	..	..	493	2,186	-1,197	840	1,019	-288	2,898	1,823
Interest payments (INT)	..	**5,729**	**6,869**	**7,705**	**7,236**	**6,408**	**4,967**	**5,469**	**5,157**	**5,517**
Long-term debt	194	3,580	5,054	5,922	5,650	4,957	3,602	4,164	3,589	4,298
IMF charges	0	103	292	238	228	186	138	170	559	120
Short-term debt	..	2,046	1,523	1,545	1,359	1,266	1,227	1,135	1,009	1,099
Net transfers on debt	..	**11,755**	**-471**	**-1,797**	**-5,007**	**-2,088**	**-1,254**	**-513**	**3,046**	**4,581**
Total debt service (TDS)	..	**9,001**	**12,965**	**15,158**	**13,471**	**12,967**	**11,912**	**11,754**	**13,629**	**12,322**
Long-term debt	587	6,374	9,845	12,423	11,270	10,985	10,092	9,982	9,649	10,550
IMF repurchases and charges	63	581	1,596	1,190	841	716	592	636	2,972	673
Short-term debt (interest only)	..	2,046	1,523	1,545	1,359	1,266	1,227	1,135	1,009	1,099
2. AGGREGATE NET RESOURCE FLOWS AND NET TRANSFERS (LONG-TERM)										
NET RESOURCE FLOWS	**1,698**	**15,159**	**18,488**	**17,227**	**16,163**	**15,798**	**14,079**	**20,726**	**23,154**	**26,069**
Net flow of long-term debt (ex. IMF)	828	11,466	6,347	4,012	3,460	3,483	2,002	4,793	4,723	8,074
Foreign direct investment (net)	428	33	2,504	926	1,597	816	1,593	3,113	2,157	2,611
Portfolio equity flows	0	0	0	0	0	144	174	860	4,868	3,550
Grants (excluding technical coop.)	442	3,659	9,637	12,289	11,106	11,355	10,310	11,960	11,405	11,834
Memo: technical coop. grants	637	2,696	4,573	5,168	5,300	5,728	5,432	4,858	5,175	5,077
NET TRANSFERS	**415**	**7,623**	**9,504**	**6,815**	**6,613**	**6,287**	**5,942**	**11,748**	**15,135**	**17,552**
Interest on long-term debt	194	3,580	5,054	5,922	5,650	4,957	3,602	4,164	3,589	4,298
Profit remittances on FDI	1,090	3,956	3,931	4,490	3,900	4,554	4,535	4,814	4,430	4,219
3. MAJOR ECONOMIC AGGREGATES										
Gross national product (GNP)	61,373	275,130	248,503	268,961	264,312	270,689	260,654	256,870	278,574	308,940
Exports of goods & services (XGS)	13,627	91,698	72,055	84,425	81,686	81,988	79,591	80,516	93,717	99,391
of which workers' remittances	67	756	1,004	979	921	1,176	1,819	1,376	1,617	1,554
Imports of goods & services (MGS)	15,644	91,729	82,012	92,249	94,001	95,841	93,013	95,969	110,451	116,332
International reserves (RES)	3,091	22,956	11,969	15,597	18,054	14,467	15,563	17,839	21,195	..
Current account balance	-1,921	2,161	-3,883	-591	-4,445	-5,055	-6,193	-8,521	-11,436	-11,464
4. DEBT INDICATORS										
EDT / XGS (%)	..	91.7	238.9	226.6	239.7	236.1	249.3	262.3	241.7	236.9
EDT / GNP (%)	..	30.6	69.3	71.1	74.1	71.5	76.1	82.2	81.3	76.2
TDS / XGS (%)	..	9.8	18.0	18.0	16.5	15.8	15.0	14.6	14.5	12.4
INT / XGS (%)	..	6.2	9.5	9.1	8.9	7.8	6.2	6.8	5.5	5.6
INT / GNP (%)	..	2.1	2.8	2.9	2.7	2.4	1.9	2.1	1.9	1.8
RES / EDT (%)	..	27.3	7.0	8.2	9.2	7.5	7.8	8.4	9.4	..
RES / MGS (months)	2.4	3.0	1.8	2.0	2.3	1.8	2.0	2.2	2.3	..
Short-term / EDT (%)	..	26.8	13.7	14.6	14.4	16.1	18.2	17.6	18.6	19.0
Concessional / EDT (%)	..	18.3	27.5	28.9	30.6	32.3	33.4	34.5	34.8	34.6
Multilateral / EDT (%)	..	9.0	19.0	20.0	21.3	22.4	23.4	24.3	24.3	24.6

SUB-SAHARAN AFRICA

(US$ million, unless otherwise indicated)

	1970	1980	1989	1990	1991	1992	1993	1994	1995	Preliminary 1996
5. LONG-TERM DEBT										
DEBT OUTSTANDING (LDOD)	**6,057**	**58,509**	**142,135**	**156,735**	**161,048**	**155,969**	**155,354**	**166,122**	**175,717**	**181,986**
Public and publicly guaranteed	**5,748**	**53,942**	**137,164**	**151,459**	**155,646**	**150,870**	**150,268**	**160,550**	**168,600**	**169,069**
Official creditors	4,177	24,266	90,568	104,740	111,651	113,179	115,606	126,119	133,230	134,222
Multilateral	869	7,599	32,681	38,347	41,777	43,418	46,341	51,326	55,104	57,863
Concessional	684	4,473	20,961	24,995	27,863	29,559	32,194	36,819	40,716	..
Bilateral	3,308	16,667	57,888	66,393	69,874	69,762	69,265	74,793	78,126	76,359
Concessional	2,943	10,934	26,295	30,215	32,099	32,914	33,973	36,127	38,008	..
Private creditors	1,571	29,677	46,595	46,719	43,995	37,691	34,662	34,431	35,370	34,847
Bonds	352	6,540	3,039	2,137	1,673	3,811	2,239	3,517	4,055	..
Commercial banks	128	11,234	20,733	20,705	19,682	12,881	11,836	12,112	13,814	..
Other private	1,090	11,904	22,823	23,877	22,640	20,999	20,588	18,803	17,501	..
Private nonguaranteed	**309**	**4,567**	**4,971**	**5,276**	**5,402**	**5,099**	**5,086**	**5,572**	**7,117**	**12,917**
Bonds	..	..	0	0	0	0	0	0	508	..
Commerical banks	..	..	4,971	5,276	5,402	5,099	5,086	5,572	6,609	..
Memo:										
IBRD	587	2,548	8,430	9,179	9,033	8,427	8,185	8,072	7,641	..
IDA	226	2,578	12,981	15,787	17,860	19,284	21,474	25,164	27,942	..
DISBURSEMENTS	**1,222**	**14,261**	**11,138**	**10,513**	**9,081**	**9,511**	**8,492**	**10,611**	**10,783**	**14,326**
Public and publicly guaranteed	**1,121**	**13,078**	**10,522**	**9,883**	**8,573**	**8,968**	**8,027**	**9,591**	**8,948**	**7,942**
Official creditors	655	4,264	7,078	7,226	6,651	6,797	6,493	6,464	5,745	6,169
Multilateral	150	1,680	3,970	4,548	4,666	4,772	4,657	4,979	4,367	5,060
Concessional	97	945	2,504	2,882	3,059	3,179	3,282	3,891	3,488	..
Bilatarel	505	2,584	3,108	2,679	1,985	2,025	1,836	1,485	1,377	1,109
Concessional	429	1,710	2,459	2,123	1,620	1,704	1,627	1,093	1,300	..
Private creditors	466	8,814	3,444	2,657	1,923	2,171	1,534	3,127	3,204	1,773
Bonds	13	1,552	0	0	0	140	0	1,450	800	..
Commercial banks	16	3,360	1,186	743	608	374	610	1,278	2,005	..
Other private	437	3,902	2,258	1,914	1,314	1,657	924	399	399	..
Private nonguaranteed	**101**	**1,183**	**616**	**630**	**507**	**544**	**466**	**1,020**	**1,835**	**6,384**
Bonds	..	..	0	0	0	0	0	0	508	..
Commerical banks	..	..	616	630	507	544	466	1,020	1,327	..
Memo:										
IBRD	75	400	835	813	676	540	516	392	274	..
IDA	61	424	1,696	2,037	1,984	2,085	2,231	2,889	2,395	..
PRINCIPAL REPAYMENTS	**394**	**2,795**	**4,791**	**6,501**	**5,621**	**6,029**	**6,490**	**5,818**	**6,059**	**6,252**
Public and publicly guaranteed	**337**	**2,202**	**4,403**	**6,036**	**5,151**	**5,599**	**6,047**	**5,219**	**5,807**	**5,667**
Official creditors	171	671	1,812	2,534	2,427	2,036	2,197	2,896	3,123	3,715
Multilateral	33	198	1,108	1,353	1,594	1,502	1,596	1,986	2,018	2,211
Concessional	23	60	293	335	367	379	409	474	525	..
Bilateral	138	473	704	1,182	832	535	600	910	1,106	1,504
Concessional	109	216	335	314	296	275	418	559	577	..
Private creditors	166	1,532	2,590	3,501	2,725	3,562	3,850	2,323	2,683	1,952
Bonds	27	24	249	941	462	52	1,571	185	330	..
Commercial banks	10	721	1,335	1,665	1,221	2,507	1,349	1,366	1,304	..
Other private	129	787	1,006	895	1,042	1,004	930	772	1,050	..
Private nonguaranteed	**57**	**592**	**389**	**466**	**469**	**430**	**444**	**599**	**253**	**585**
Bonds	..	..	0	0	0	0	0	0	0	..
Commerical banks	..	..	389	466	469	430	444	599	253	..
Memo:										
IBRD	29	111	618	721	968	862	913	1,063	1,056	..
IDA	0	5	43	51	62	74	86	102	120	..
NET FLOWS ON DEBT	**828**	**11,466**	**6,347**	**4,012**	**3,460**	**3,483**	**2,002**	**4,793**	**4,723**	**8,074**
Public and publicly guaranteed	**784**	**10,876**	**6,119**	**3,847**	**3,422**	**3,369**	**1,980**	**4,372**	**3,142**	**2,275**
Official creditors	484	3,593	5,266	4,692	4,224	4,761	4,297	3,567	2,621	2,454
Multilateral	117	1,482	2,862	3,195	3,071	3,270	3,061	2,993	2,350	2,849
Concessional	74	885	2,212	2,547	2,692	2,800	2,873	3,417	2,963	..
Bilateral	367	2,111	2,404	1,497	1,153	1,491	1,236	574	272	-395
Concessional	320	1,493	2,125	1,808	1,325	1,429	1,209	534	723	..
Private creditors	300	7,283	853	-844	-802	-1,392	-2,316	805	521	-179
Bonds	-14	1,528	-249	-941	-462	88	-1,571	1,265	470	..
Commercial banks	6	2,639	-149	-922	-612	-2,133	-739	-88	701	..
Other private	308	3,116	1,251	1,019	273	654	-6	-372	-651	..
Private nonguaranteed	**44**	**590**	**228**	**165**	**38**	**114**	**22**	**421**	**1,582**	**5,799**
Bonds	..	..	0	0	0	0	0	0	508	..
Commerical banks	..	..	228	165	38	114	22	421	1,074	..
Memo:										
IBRD	46	289	216	92	-292	-322	-397	-671	-782	..
IDA	61	419	1,653	1,986	1,922	2,011	2,145	2,788	2,275	..

SUB-SAHARAN AFRICA

(US$ million, unless otherwise indicated)

	1970	1980	1989	1990	1991	1992	1993	1994	1995	Preliminary 1996
INTEREST PAYMENTS (LINT)	**194**	**3,580**	**5,054**	**5,922**	**5,650**	**4,957**	**3,602**	**4,164**	**3,589**	**4,298**
Public and publicly guaranteed	**178**	**3,129**	**4,728**	**5,591**	**5,336**	**4,652**	**3,331**	**3,900**	**3,338**	**3,820**
Official creditors	114	692	1,926	2,718	2,884	2,230	1,932	2,476	2,187	2,384
Multilateral	35	286	990	1,112	1,440	1,216	1,206	1,393	1,240	1,419
Concessional	26	59	172	193	234	248	244	279	292	..
Bilateral	79	406	936	1,606	1,444	1,014	726	1,083	947	965
Concessional	61	208	252	564	324	591	529	808	504	..
Private creditors	65	2,437	2,803	2,873	2,452	2,423	1,399	1,424	1,152	1,436
Bonds	12	543	326	261	187	169	206	212	256	..
Commercial banks	8	1,166	1,602	1,525	1,254	1,302	563	577	438	..
Other private	45	728	874	1,087	1,010	951	630	636	458	..
Private nonguaranteed	**16**	**451**	**326**	**331**	**314**	**304**	**271**	**264**	**251**	**478**
Bonds	..	..	0	0	0	0	0	0	0	..
Commerical banks	..	..	326	331	314	304	271	264	251	..
Memo:										
IBRD	32	217	610	651	925	680	686	695	633	..
IDA	1	16	83	97	124	132	139	149	179	..
NET TRANSFERS ON DEBT	**635**	**7,887**	**1,293**	**-1,910**	**-2,190**	**-1,474**	**-1,600**	**629**	**1,134**	**3,776**
Public and publicly guaranteed	**606**	**7,747**	**1,391**	**-1,743**	**-1,914**	**-1,283**	**-1,351**	**472**	**-197**	**-1,545**
Official creditors	370	2,901	3,340	1,974	1,340	2,531	2,365	1,091	435	70
Multilateral	83	1,197	1,872	2,083	1,632	2,054	1,855	1,600	1,110	1,430
Concessional	48	826	2,040	2,354	2,458	2,553	2,629	3,137	2,671	..
Bilateral	288	1,704	1,468	-109	-291	477	511	-508	-675	-1,360
Concessional	259	1,285	1,873	1,244	1,001	838	681	-274	218	..
Private creditors	236	4,846	-1,949	-3,717	-3,254	-3,814	-3,716	-620	-631	-1,615
Bonds	-26	985	-575	-1,202	-650	-81	-1,777	1,054	214	..
Commercial banks	-2	1,474	-1,751	-2,447	-1,867	-3,435	-1,302	-665	264	..
Other private	263	2,387	377	-68	-738	-298	-637	-1,008	-1,108	..
Private nonguaranteed	**28**	**140**	**-98**	**-166**	**-276**	**-191**	**-249**	**157**	**1,331**	**5,321**
Bonds	..	..	0	0	0	0	0	0	508	..
Commerical banks	..	..	-98	-166	-276	-191	-249	157	823	..
Memo:										
IBRD	14	72	-394	-559	-1,216	-1,002	-1,084	-1,366	-1,415	..
IDA	60	403	1,570	1,889	1,799	1,879	2,007	2,639	2,096	..
DEBT SERVICE (LTDS)	**587**	**6,374**	**9,845**	**12,423**	**11,270**	**10,985**	**10,092**	**9,982**	**9,649**	**10,550**
Public and publicly guaranteed	**515**	**5,331**	**9,131**	**11,626**	**10,487**	**10,251**	**9,378**	**9,119**	**9,145**	**9,487**
Official creditors	285	1,363	3,738	5,252	5,311	4,266	4,128	5,372	5,310	6,099
Multilateral	68	484	2,098	2,465	3,034	2,718	2,803	3,379	3,257	3,630
Concessional	49	119	465	528	601	627	653	753	817	..
Bilateral	217	879	1,640	2,788	2,276	1,548	1,326	1,993	2,053	2,469
Concessional	170	424	586	879	620	866	946	1,367	1,081	..
Private creditors	230	3,968	5,393	6,374	5,176	5,985	5,249	3,747	3,835	3,388
Bonds	38	567	575	1,202	650	221	1,777	397	586	..
Commercial banks	18	1,886	2,937	3,190	2,475	3,809	1,912	1,943	1,741	..
Other private	174	1,515	1,881	1,982	2,052	1,955	1,560	1,408	1,507	..
Private nonguaranteed	**72**	**1,043**	**714**	**797**	**784**	**734**	**714**	**863**	**504**	**1,063**
Bonds	..	..	0	0	0	0	0	0	0	..
Commerical banks	..	..	714	797	784	734	714	863	504	..
Memo:										
IBRD	61	328	1,228	1,372	1,892	1,542	1,599	1,758	1,689	..
IDA	1	22	127	148	186	206	225	251	299	..
UNDISBURSED DEBT	**2,736**	**20,848**	**30,774**	**34,289**	**34,317**	**33,232**	**31,561**	**30,413**	**28,303**	**..**
Official creditors	2,281	14,391	26,630	30,301	30,858	30,452	28,804	27,575	25,359	..
Private creditors	455	6,457	4,143	3,989	3,459	2,780	2,756	2,838	2,945	..
Memorandum items										
Concessional LDOD	3,627	15,407	47,256	55,210	59,961	62,473	66,167	72,946	78,724	81,466
Variable rate LDOD	356	11,866	27,228	29,480	29,700	24,369	24,579	26,543	29,162	..
Public sector LDOD	5,687	40,228	124,871	139,413	144,502	139,974	142,311	152,247	159,587	..
Private sector LDOD	370	4,943	5,231	5,609	5,761	5,472	5,516	5,416	5,579	..
6. CURRENCY COMPOSITION OF LONG-TERM DEBT (PERCENT)										
Deutsche mark	6.6	5.4	5.3	6.1	6.1	5.4	5.1	5.5	5.6	..
French franc	14.5	10.8	12.7	13.4	13.7	13.8	13.3	13.2	13.4	..
Japanese yen	0.1	1.6	3.6	3.7	4.3	4.5	5.1	5.4	5.2	..
Pound sterling	22.6	4.5	4.8	5.2	5.2	4.2	4.0	4.0	3.7	..
Swiss franc	0.3	1.3	1.9	2.0	2.0	1.9	1.8	1.7	1.8	..
U.S. dollars	21.5	27.6	36.6	34.7	34.6	35.5	37.6	37.6	37.8	..
Multiple currency	11.2	6.9	9.5	9.9	10.1	10.4	10.7	10.5	10.1	..
Special drawing rights	0.0	0.0	0.6	0.6	0.7	0.8	0.9	1.0	1.0	..
All other currencies	23.2	17.1	16.1	16.5	16.5	16.7	16.4	16.2	16.4	..

SUB-SAHARAN AFRICA

(US$ million, unless otherwise indicated)

	1970	1980	1989	1990	1991	1992	1993	1994	1995	Preliminary 1996
7. DEBT RESTRUCTURINGS										
Total amount rescheduled	..	..	13,998	6,203	4,311	5,933	975	6,162	3,229	..
Debt stock rescheduled	..	..	5,928	91	40	2,059	1	74	142	..
Principal rescheduled	..	..	4,971	4,014	2,656	2,092	570	3,076	1,716	..
Official	..	..	1,772	2,700	1,231	1,320	385	1,811	1,250	..
Private	..	..	3,199	1,315	1,425	771	185	1,265	466	..
Interest rescheduled	..	..	2,377	1,774	1,234	1,087	285	2,227	757	..
Official	..	..	1,412	1,413	918	679	220	1,834	642	..
Private	..	..	965	361	316	408	64	393	115	..
Principal forgiven	..	..	3,337	1,606	754	685	810	3,059	1,167	..
Memo: interest forgiven	..	..	130	88	164	99	138	432	224	..
Debt stock reduction	..	..	247	312	339	3,536	172	476	275	..
of which debt buyback	..	..	0	0	31	1,335	17	8	29	..
8. DEBT STOCK-FLOW RECONCILIATION										
Total change in debt stocks	..	..	6,123	19,138	4,507	-2,231	4,820	12,834	15,262	..
Net flows on debt	..	..	6,398	5,908	2,229	4,320	3,713	4,956	8,202	..
Net change in interest arrears	..	..	1,214	2,199	1,403	2,267	3,763	1,824	2,203	..
Interest capitalized	..	..	2,377	1,774	1,234	1,087	285	2,227	757	..
Debt forgiveness or reduction	..	..	-3,584	-1,918	-1,062	-2,886	-964	-3,527	-1,413	..
Cross-currency valuation	..	..	-557	9,636	-568	-5,227	-2,248	6,630	4,378	..
Residual	..	..	275	1,540	1,270	-1,791	272	725	1,135	..
9. AVERAGE TERMS OF NEW COMMITMENTS										
ALL CREDITORS										
Interest (%)	3.7	7	4.2	4.3	4.1	3.4	3.3	2.9	3	..
Maturity (years)	25.7	17.2	24.9	25.1	26.7	28	26.9	29.4	27.4	..
Grace period (years)	9.4	5	7	6.9	7	7.5	7.6	7.7	7.3	..
Grant element (%)	47.7	21.8	44.2	43.5	45.5	51.2	51.3	55.8	54.1	..
Official creditors										
Interest (%)	2	4.1	3.5	3.5	3.6	2.9	2.6	2.4	1.7	..
Maturity (years)	34.8	24.8	27.8	28	29.2	30.9	31.4	32.1	33.4	..
Grace period (years)	13.8	6.7	7.9	7.7	7.8	8.2	8.9	8.5	9	..
Grant element (%)	67.7	42.6	50.6	51.1	50.9	56.9	60.3	61.7	67.6	..
Private creditors										
Interest (%)	6.6	10	7.9	8.1	7.7	7.4	6	6.7	7.1	..
Maturity (years)	10.2	9.4	8.4	11.6	8.9	5.8	7.8	8.1	7.5	..
Grace period (years)	1.8	3.3	2.3	2.8	1.7	1.6	2.2	1.6	1.8	..
Grant element (%)	13.3	0.1	7.6	7.7	7.3	6.4	12.7	9.4	9.2	..
Memorandum items										
Commitments	1,890	13,344	12,271	11,502	9,406	9,339	7,503	6,181	5,543	..
Official creditors	1,194	6,804	10,452	9,475	8,244	8,275	6,085	5,485	4,257	..
Private creditors	696	6,540	1,819	2,027	1,162	1,065	1,418	697	1,286	..

10. RESOURCE FLOW CHARTS

(US$ million)

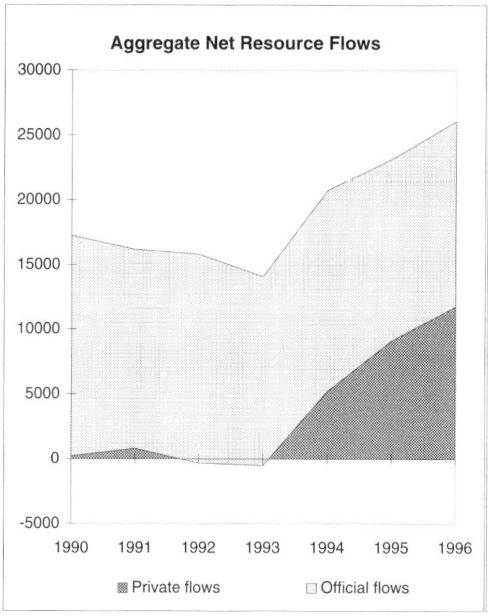

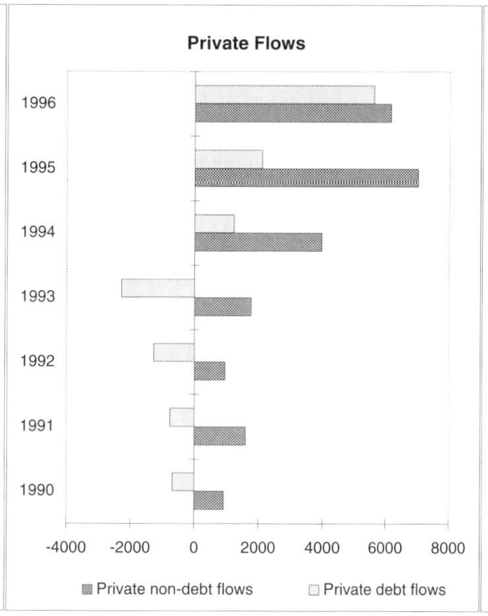

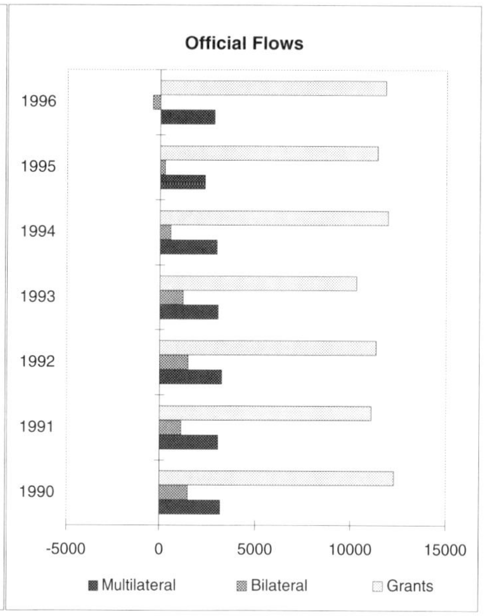

LOW-INCOME COUNTRIES

(US$ million, unless otherwise indicated)

	1970	1980	1989	1990	1991	1992	1993	1994	1995	*Preliminary* 1996
1. SUMMARY DEBT DATA										
TOTAL DEBT STOCKS (EDT)	..	**106,209**	**356,880**	**405,622**	**422,853**	**443,456**	**470,564**	**512,185**	**534,794**	**548,282**
Long-term debt (LDOD)	**17,723**	**87,521**	**307,364**	**346,047**	**360,994**	**372,983**	**400,622**	**437,496**	**452,108**	**461,328**
Public and publicly guaranteed	17,290	82,430	300,595	339,124	353,621	365,650	392,142	424,425	437,814	441,694
Private nonguaranteed	433	5,091	6,770	6,922	7,373	7,333	8,480	13,071	14,294	19,634
Use of IMF credit	**258**	**5,797**	**11,042**	**11,771**	**12,555**	**13,918**	**14,151**	**15,118**	**14,299**	**13,193**
Short-term debt	..	**12,891**	**38,474**	**47,805**	**49,304**	**56,555**	**55,791**	**59,571**	**68,387**	**73,761**
of which interest arrears on LDOD	..	281	9,734	12,702	13,792	16,673	20,561	23,608	25,564	25,690
Official creditors	..	171	6,929	8,858	9,796	12,416	15,332	17,787	20,010	..
Private creditors	..	110	2,805	3,844	3,996	4,257	5,229	5,821	5,554	..
Memo: principal arrears on LDOD	..	1,265	18,438	23,268	28,478	35,846	42,249	50,044	57,041	60,545
Official creditors	..	559	11,354	13,453	17,682	24,280	28,881	35,299	41,851	..
Private creditors	..	706	7,084	9,815	10,796	11,566	13,369	14,745	15,190	..
Memo: export credits	..	..	62,003	68,172	70,446	70,187	73,533	86,386	90,133	..
TOTAL DEBT FLOWS										
Disbursements	**2,826**	**22,088**	**32,640**	**33,681**	**31,829**	**40,922**	**43,302**	**39,042**	**45,150**	**46,746**
Long-term debt	2,783	19,133	31,053	31,018	29,308	38,358	42,220	37,309	41,462	45,050
IMF purchases	43	2,955	1,587	2,663	2,521	2,564	1,082	1,733	3,688	1,696
Principal repayments	**1,223**	**5,361**	**12,451**	**15,077**	**15,130**	**17,005**	**17,610**	**21,063**	**28,288**	**29,713**
Long-term debt	891	4,598	9,639	12,364	13,300	15,835	16,690	19,266	23,781	27,313
IMF repurchases	332	762	2,813	2,713	1,830	1,170	920	1,798	4,507	2,400
Net flows on debt	**2,805**	**19,816**	**20,226**	**25,365**	**17,278**	**28,288**	**21,125**	**19,083**	**24,249**	**22,364**
of which short-term debt	..	..	38	6,761	579	4,371	-4,567	1,105	7,388	5,331
Interest payments (INT)	..	**5,115**	**13,200**	**15,033**	**15,221**	**13,491**	**12,644**	**14,765**	**16,489**	**17,451**
Long-term debt	486	3,611	10,339	11,815	12,206	11,072	10,308	12,540	13,280	14,595
IMF charges	0	173	656	588	527	518	513	420	780	242
Short-term debt	..	1,331	2,205	2,630	2,487	1,901	1,823	1,805	2,429	2,614
Net transfers on debt	..	**14,701**	**7,026**	**10,332**	**2,057**	**14,797**	**8,481**	**4,318**	**7,760**	**4,913**
Total debt service (TDS)	..	**10,476**	**25,651**	**30,110**	**30,351**	**30,496**	**30,254**	**35,828**	**44,777**	**47,164**
Long-term debt	1,377	8,209	19,978	24,180	25,506	26,907	26,998	31,806	37,061	41,908
IMF repurchases and charges	332	936	3,469	3,300	2,358	1,688	1,433	2,217	5,287	2,642
Short-term debt (interest only)	..	1,331	2,205	2,630	2,487	1,901	1,823	1,805	2,429	2,614
2. AGGREGATE NET RESOURCE FLOWS AND NET TRANSFERS (LONG-TERM)										
NET RESOURCE FLOWS	**3,114**	**21,836**	**41,559**	**38,888**	**40,853**	**53,426**	**77,401**	**85,623**	**81,782**	**93,876**
Net flow of long-term debt (ex. IMF)	1,892	14,535	21,414	18,654	16,008	22,523	25,530	18,043	17,681	17,737
Foreign direct investment (net)	196	106	6,289	4,509	7,132	13,870	31,995	39,120	41,570	49,492
Portfolio equity flows	0	0	168	105	686	1,574	5,930	11,081	5,612	9,087
Grants (excluding technical coop.)	1,027	7,195	13,688	15,620	17,027	15,459	13,946	17,380	16,920	17,560
Memo: technical coop. grants	1,011	3,719	6,797	7,650	7,878	8,658	8,215	7,541	8,310	8,206
NET TRANSFERS	**1,825**	**15,588**	**30,244**	**25,781**	**27,554**	**41,134**	**65,494**	**71,285**	**66,428**	**76,326**
Interest on long-term debt	486	3,611	10,339	11,815	12,206	11,072	10,308	12,540	13,280	14,595
Profit remittances on FDI	803	2,637	976	1,291	1,092	1,220	1,598	1,799	2,074	2,955
3. MAJOR ECONOMIC AGGREGATES										
Gross national product (GNP)	233,801	650,489	909,828	957,257	949,941	988,650	1,002,813	1,159,297	1,381,532	1,651,962
Exports of goods & services (XGS)	18,113	109,665	136,924	159,549	167,934	182,222	195,018	240,703	290,882	315,231
of which workers' remittances	340	9,528	7,471	7,783	7,860	8,063	9,670	11,527	12,059	10,300
Imports of goods & services (MGS)	21,781	124,492	171,092	176,424	181,116	204,444	235,830	261,895	321,390	361,270
International reserves (RES)	3,638	40,523	41,667	52,804	71,151	47,051	57,561	102,375	124,351	..
Current account balance	-3,903	-13,323	-26,457	-7,884	-1,158	-9,183	-29,177	-9,925	-19,509	-33,919
4. DEBT INDICATORS										
EDT / XGS (%)	..	96.8	260.6	254.2	251.8	243.4	241.3	212.8	183.9	173.9
EDT / GNP (%)	..	16.3	39.2	42.4	44.5	44.9	46.9	44.2	38.7	33.2
TDS / XGS (%)	..	9.6	18.7	18.9	18.1	16.7	15.5	14.9	15.4	15.0
INT / XGS (%)	..	4.7	9.6	9.4	9.1	7.4	6.5	6.1	5.7	5.5
INT / GNP (%)	..	0.8	1.5	1.6	1.6	1.4	1.3	1.3	1.2	1.1
RES / EDT (%)	..	38.2	11.7	13.0	16.8	10.6	12.2	20.0	23.3	..
RES / MGS (months)	2.0	3.9	2.9	3.6	4.7	2.8	2.9	4.7	4.6	..
Short-term / EDT (%)	..	12.1	10.8	11.8	11.7	12.8	11.9	11.6	12.8	13.5
Concessional / EDT (%)	..	44.7	42.7	42.6	42.6	42.4	42.4	42.8	42.0	41.1
Multilateral / EDT (%)	..	17.2	20.8	21.5	22.9	23.3	24.0	25.1	25.5	26.3

LOW-INCOME COUNTRIES

(US$ million, unless otherwise indicated)

	1970	1980	1989	1990	1991	1992	1993	1994	1995	Preliminary 1996
5. LONG-TERM DEBT										
DEBT OUTSTANDING (LDOD)	**17,723**	**87,521**	**307,364**	**346,047**	**360,994**	**372,983**	**400,622**	**437,496**	**452,108**	**461,328**
Public and publicly guaranteed	**17,290**	**82,430**	**300,595**	**339,124**	**353,621**	**365,650**	**392,142**	**424,425**	**437,814**	**441,694**
Official creditors	14,981	58,975	214,222	244,334	257,363	267,459	284,395	312,589	323,905	326,331
Multilateral	3,147	18,296	74,382	87,221	96,754	103,256	113,098	128,795	136,141	144,083
Concessional	2,711	13,665	50,297	58,883	65,277	70,018	76,142	86,991	93,832	..
Bilateral	11,834	40,679	139,840	157,112	160,609	164,203	171,298	183,794	187,763	182,248
Concessional	10,661	33,810	102,046	114,103	115,038	117,940	123,542	132,214	130,970	..
Private creditors	2,309	23,455	86,373	94,791	96,258	98,191	107,747	111,836	113,909	115,363
Bonds	368	699	8,072	8,434	10,624	12,330	14,533	17,975	17,180	..
Commercial banks	203	11,232	42,613	47,240	47,030	44,997	49,826	46,329	47,700	..
Other private	1,738	11,524	35,688	39,117	38,604	40,864	43,388	47,531	49,029	..
Private nonguaranteed	**433**	**5,091**	**6,770**	**6,922**	**7,373**	**7,333**	**8,480**	**13,071**	**14,294**	**19,634**
Bonds	..	..	0	0	0	200	1,350	1,786	2,155	..
Commerical banks	..	..	6,770	6,922	7,373	7,133	7,130	11,285	12,139	..
Memo:										
IBRD	1,470	3,949	19,336	22,103	23,599	23,996	25,962	28,765	28,480	..
IDA	1,579	10,055	36,083	41,729	46,298	50,117	54,740	62,743	67,633	..
DISBURSEMENTS	**2,783**	**19,133**	**31,053**	**31,018**	**29,308**	**38,358**	**42,220**	**37,309**	**41,462**	**45,050**
Public and publicly guaranteed	**2,645**	**17,577**	**30,147**	**30,185**	**28,373**	**36,834**	**39,979**	**35,625**	**38,589**	**38,421**
Official creditors	2,038	9,012	17,891	17,914	17,923	18,698	20,359	19,809	21,911	19,486
Multilateral	376	3,400	9,440	10,520	11,557	11,376	11,957	13,174	12,123	13,273
Concessional	232	2,395	5,095	6,097	6,601	7,101	6,740	8,202	7,557	..
Bilatarel	1,662	5,612	8,451	7,394	6,366	7,322	8,403	6,635	9,788	6,213
Concessional	1,461	4,258	6,728	5,634	4,394	5,082	5,158	4,930	4,626	..
Private creditors	607	8,565	12,256	12,272	10,450	18,136	19,620	15,816	16,678	18,935
Bonds	6	102	1,155	704	1,879	894	2,889	3,487	1,224	..
Commercial banks	44	3,259	5,554	5,698	3,624	7,970	8,270	3,845	6,993	..
Other private	557	5,205	5,547	5,870	4,946	9,273	8,461	8,484	8,461	..
Private nonguaranteed	**138**	**1,556**	**906**	**833**	**936**	**1,524**	**2,240**	**1,684**	**2,873**	**6,629**
Bonds	..	..	0	0	0	198	1,126	412	1,064	..
Commercial banks	..	..	906	833	936	1,326	1,114	1,272	1,809	..
Memo:										
IBRD	196	610	3,245	3,038	2,989	2,308	3,027	2,775	2,574	..
IDA	146	1,455	3,469	4,296	4,483	5,007	4,746	5,867	5,198	..
PRINCIPAL REPAYMENTS	**891**	**4,598**	**9,639**	**12,364**	**13,300**	**15,835**	**16,690**	**19,266**	**23,781**	**27,313**
Public and publicly guaranteed	**805**	**3,864**	**8,892**	**11,531**	**12,501**	**14,966**	**15,572**	**18,282**	**23,054**	**26,022**
Official creditors	503	1,739	4,629	6,061	6,212	6,169	6,878	8,667	10,496	10,300
Multilateral	100	360	1,868	2,714	3,063	3,083	3,569	4,390	4,884	4,932
Concessional	73	130	562	673	788	797	879	1,013	1,169	..
Bilateral	403	1,379	2,761	3,347	3,149	3,086	3,309	4,277	5,613	5,368
Concessional	280	995	1,636	1,862	1,830	2,062	2,195	2,948	4,067	..
Private creditors	302	2,125	4,263	5,470	6,289	8,797	8,694	9,615	12,557	15,722
Bonds	30	24	110	637	503	1,353	1,199	872	1,805	..
Commercial banks	31	788	1,964	2,203	2,980	4,440	4,053	3,889	5,047	..
Other private	242	1,313	2,189	2,630	2,806	3,005	3,442	4,854	5,705	..
Private nonguaranteed	**86**	**735**	**747**	**834**	**799**	**868**	**1,118**	**984**	**728**	**1,291**
Bonds	..	..	0	0	0	0	0	0	0	..
Commerical banks	..	..	747	834	799	868	1,118	984	728	..
Memo:										
IBRD	94	210	1,071	1,559	1,853	1,847	2,105	2,413	2,595	..
IDA	0	25	177	211	261	295	340	396	480	..
NET FLOWS ON DEBT	**1,892**	**14,535**	**21,414**	**18,654**	**16,008**	**22,523**	**25,530**	**18,043**	**17,681**	**17,737**
Public and publicly guaranteed	**1,839**	**13,713**	**21,255**	**18,655**	**15,872**	**21,868**	**24,407**	**17,343**	**15,535**	**12,399**
Official creditors	1,535	7,273	13,262	11,853	11,711	12,529	13,481	11,142	11,415	9,186
Multilateral	276	3,040	7,573	7,806	8,494	8,294	8,387	8,784	7,239	8,341
Concessional	159	2,265	4,533	5,424	5,814	6,304	5,861	7,189	6,387	..
Bilateral	1,258	4,233	5,690	4,047	3,217	4,235	5,094	2,358	4,175	845
Concessional	1,181	3,263	5,091	3,772	2,564	3,020	2,964	1,982	559	..
Private creditors	304	6,440	7,993	6,802	4,161	9,339	10,927	6,201	4,121	3,213
Bonds	-24	79	1,045	67	1,377	-459	1,690	2,615	-581	..
Commercial banks	13	2,470	3,590	3,495	644	3,530	4,217	-44	1,946	..
Other private	315	3,891	3,358	3,240	2,140	6,268	5,019	3,630	2,756	..
Private nonguaranteed	**53**	**822**	**158**	**-1**	**137**	**655**	**1,122**	**701**	**2,145**	**5,338**
Bonds	..	..	0	0	0	198	1,126	412	1,064	..
Commerical banks	..	..	158	-1	137	458	-4	288	1,081	..
Memo:										
IBRD	102	400	2,174	1,479	1,136	461	923	362	-21	..
IDA	146	1,430	3,291	4,086	4,222	4,712	4,406	5,471	4,719	..

LOW-INCOME COUNTRIES

(US$ million, unless otherwise indicated)

	1970	1980	1989	1990	1991	1992	1993	1994	1995	Preliminary 1996
INTEREST PAYMENTS (LINT)	**486**	**3,611**	**10,339**	**11,815**	**12,206**	**11,072**	**10,308**	**12,540**	**13,280**	**14,595**
Public and publicly guaranteed	**464**	**3,107**	**9,863**	**11,341**	**11,746**	**10,608**	**9,824**	**11,792**	**12,384**	**13,567**
Official creditors	356	1,436	4,418	5,713	6,221	5,469	5,699	6,846	6,766	7,175
Multilateral	95	519	2,063	2,559	3,137	2,965	3,128	3,569	3,650	4,025
Concessional	72	162	412	475	564	587	621	716	782	..
Bilateral	261	917	2,355	3,154	3,084	2,505	2,571	3,278	3,116	3,150
Concessional	199	679	1,421	1,867	1,693	1,942	2,013	2,466	2,091	..
Private creditors	108	1,671	5,445	5,629	5,525	5,139	4,126	4,946	5,618	6,392
Bonds	12	16	511	567	567	581	750	715	971	..
Commercial banks	13	1,066	3,421	3,387	3,129	2,710	1,999	2,107	2,523	..
Other private	82	589	1,514	1,675	1,829	1,848	1,377	2,124	2,124	..
Private nonguaranteed	**23**	**504**	**476**	**474**	**460**	**464**	**484**	**748**	**896**	**1,028**
Bonds	..	..	0	0	0	0	13	47	92	..
Commerical banks	..	..	476	474	460	464	472	701	804	..
Memo:										
IBRD	82	336	1,380	1,694	2,111	1,856	1,926	2,055	2,103	..
IDA	10	66	244	278	323	347	369	406	475	..
NET TRANSFERS ON DEBT	**1,405**	**10,924**	**11,075**	**6,839**	**3,802**	**11,451**	**15,222**	**5,503**	**4,401**	**3,142**
Public and publicly guaranteed	**1,376**	**10,607**	**11,392**	**7,314**	**4,125**	**11,260**	**14,583**	**5,550**	**3,151**	**-1,168**
Official creditors	1,179	5,838	8,845	6,140	5,490	7,060	7,782	4,295	4,649	2,011
Multilateral	181	2,521	5,510	5,247	5,357	5,329	5,260	5,215	3,589	4,316
Concessional	87	2,103	4,121	4,948	5,250	5,718	5,241	6,473	5,605	..
Bilateral	998	3,316	3,335	893	133	1,730	2,523	-919	1,059	-2,305
Concessional	982	2,585	3,671	1,904	871	1,079	951	-484	-1,532	..
Private creditors	196	4,769	2,548	1,174	-1,364	4,200	6,801	1,255	-1,497	-3,179
Bonds	-36	63	534	-500	809	-1,040	940	1,900	-1,552	..
Commercial banks	-1	1,404	169	108	-2,485	820	2,219	-2,151	-578	..
Other private	233	3,302	1,845	1,565	311	4,420	3,642	1,506	633	..
Private nonguaranteed	**30**	**317**	**-318**	**-475**	**-324**	**191**	**638**	**-47**	**1,249**	**4,310**
Bonds	..	..	0	0	0	198	1,114	365	972	..
Commerical banks	..	..	-318	-475	-324	-7	-475	-412	277	..
Memo:										
IBRD	20	64	794	-215	-975	-1,395	-1,004	-1,692	-2,124	..
IDA	135	1,364	3,047	3,808	3,899	4,366	4,037	5,065	4,243	..
DEBT SERVICE (LTDS)	**1,377**	**8,209**	**19,978**	**24,180**	**25,506**	**26,907**	**26,998**	**31,806**	**37,061**	**41,908**
Public and publicly guaranteed	**1,269**	**6,971**	**18,755**	**22,872**	**24,247**	**25,575**	**25,396**	**30,075**	**35,438**	**39,589**
Official creditors	859	3,174	9,046	11,774	12,433	11,638	12,577	15,514	17,262	17,475
Multilateral	195	878	3,931	5,273	6,200	6,047	6,697	7,959	8,533	8,957
Concessional	145	292	974	1,149	1,351	1,383	1,500	1,728	1,951	..
Bilateral	664	2,296	5,116	6,500	6,233	5,591	5,880	7,555	8,729	8,518
Concessional	479	1,673	3,057	3,729	3,523	4,003	4,207	5,414	6,158	..
Private creditors	410	3,796	9,709	11,098	11,814	13,936	12,819	14,561	18,176	22,114
Bonds	42	40	621	1,203	1,070	1,934	1,949	1,588	2,776	..
Commercial banks	44	1,854	5,385	5,590	6,109	7,150	6,051	5,996	7,571	..
Other private	324	1,902	3,702	4,305	4,635	4,852	4,819	6,978	7,829	..
Private nonguaranteed	**108**	**1,239**	**1,223**	**1,308**	**1,259**	**1,332**	**1,602**	**1,731**	**1,624**	**2,319**
Bonds	..	..	0	0	0	0	13	47	92	..
Commerical banks	..	..	1,223	1,308	1,259	1,332	1,590	1,684	1,532	..
Memo:										
IBRD	176	547	2,450	3,253	3,963	3,703	4,031	4,467	4,698	..
IDA	11	91	422	489	584	642	709	802	955	..
UNDISBURSED DEBT	**6,485**	**41,646**	**80,873**	**88,895**	**87,828**	**86,779**	**90,946**	**91,433**	**85,081**	**..**
Official creditors	5,622	31,816	71,024	77,527	79,456	77,472	77,464	82,079	77,506	..
Private creditors	862	9,831	9,849	11,367	8,371	9,307	13,482	9,354	7,574	..
Memorandum items										
Concessional LDOD	13,371	47,475	152,344	172,987	180,314	187,958	199,685	219,205	224,802	225,261
Variable rate LDOD	479	16,244	56,763	63,445	66,146	63,011	70,822	80,778	86,127	..
Public sector LDOD	16,801	80,235	294,339	332,800	347,084	359,084	385,367	416,937	429,910	..
Private sector LDOD	922	6,092	8,005	8,201	8,640	8,548	9,874	14,982	16,618	..

6. CURRENCY COMPOSITION OF LONG-TERM DEBT (PERCENT)

	1970	1980	1989	1990	1991	1992	1993	1994	1995	1996
Deutsche mark	8.6	7.5	5.1	5.4	5.3	4.7	4.2	4.6	4.6	..
French franc	5.5	7.5	6.1	6.2	6.2	6.0	5.4	5.4	5.5	..
Japanese yen	3.6	6.0	10.4	10.5	11.1	11.3	12.0	13.3	12.4	..
Pound sterling	22.3	10.0	4.1	4.0	4.0	3.2	2.9	2.7	2.5	..
Swiss franc	0.4	1.0	1.1	1.1	1.1	1.0	0.9	0.9	0.9	..
U.S. dollars	35.8	38.3	41.8	40.1	40.0	42.1	43.9	42.7	44.2	..
Multiple currency	9.5	11.3	12.5	13.8	14.0	14.1	14.2	14.6	14.2	..
Special drawing rights	0.0	0.0	0.5	0.6	0.6	0.6	0.7	0.8	0.8	..
All other currencies	14.3	17.0	16.8	16.7	16.2	15.5	14.5	13.7	13.6	..

LOW-INCOME COUNTRIES

(US$ million, unless otherwise indicated)

	1970	1980	1989	1990	1991	1992	1993	1994	1995	Preliminary 1996
7. DEBT RESTRUCTURINGS										
Total amount rescheduled	..	..	14,418	6,844	8,934	6,182	2,959	5,279	3,727	..
Debt stock rescheduled	..	..	6,144	411	1,979	2,060	261	201	367	..
Principal rescheduled	..	..	5,078	4,166	4,757	2,249	1,077	2,360	1,811	..
Official	..	..	1,976	2,925	3,295	1,449	567	1,443	1,250	..
Private	..	..	3,103	1,241	1,462	799	510	917	561	..
Interest rescheduled	..	..	2,411	1,905	1,802	1,173	560	1,816	850	..
Official	..	..	1,480	1,532	1,452	747	377	1,486	712	..
Private	..	..	931	372	351	426	184	330	138	..
Principal forgiven	..	..	3,307	1,635	2,095	731	826	2,889	1,587	..
Memo: interest forgiven	..	..	136	99	391	106	162	435	957	..
Debt stock reduction	..	..	305	353	546	3,632	172	485	1,620	..
of which debt buyback	..	..	0	0	190	1,344	17	8	149	..
8. DEBT STOCK-FLOW RECONCILIATION										
Total change in debt stocks	..	..	47,190	48,743	17,230	20,604	27,108	41,621	22,609	..
Net flows on debt	..	..	20,226	25,365	17,278	28,288	21,125	19,083	24,249	..
Net change in interest arrears	..	..	2,319	2,969	1,090	2,881	3,889	3,047	1,956	..
Interest capitalized	..	..	2,411	1,905	1,802	1,173	560	1,816	850	..
Debt forgiveness or reduction	..	..	-3,611	-1,988	-2,450	-3,019	-981	-3,366	-3,059	..
Cross-currency valuation	..	..	-3,465	14,217	1,968	-4,547	2,024	18,365	-106	..
Residual	..	..	29,310	6,276	-2,458	-4,172	490	2,677	-1,282	..
9. AVERAGE TERMS OF NEW COMMITMENTS										
ALL CREDITORS										
Interest (%)	3.2	6.5	5.3	5.2	4.9	4.7	4.7	4.1	5.2	..
Maturity (years)	28.9	21.7	21.9	22.6	22.7	21.2	18.2	22.2	17.5	..
Grace period (years)	9.6	5.7	6.4	6.4	6.4	5.7	5.1	6.5	4.8	..
Grant element (%)	53.4	29.4	34.2	35.3	37.5	35.5	32.4	41.3	29.6	..
Official creditors										
Interest (%)	2.2	3.3	4	3.6	3.8	3.4	3.3	3.4	4.5	..
Maturity (years)	34.3	30.5	26.2	28.3	27	28	25.9	27.4	25.3	..
Grace period (years)	11.8	7.7	7.1	7.9	7.5	7.4	7.2	7.7	6.5	..
Grant element (%)	64.9	52.7	45.4	51.1	47.4	50.9	49.9	51.1	41.5	..
Private creditors										
Interest (%)	6.5	11	8.2	8	7.9	6.5	6	5.6	6.1	..
Maturity (years)	10.3	9.4	12.1	13.5	10.3	12	11	10.9	7.5	..
Grace period (years)	1.9	2.9	4.6	3.9	3.3	3.5	3.2	3.9	2.6	..
Grant element (%)	14.1	-3	8.6	10.1	8.9	14.7	15.8	20.1	14.3	..
Memorandum items										
Commitments	4,008	27,394	37,139	36,547	30,988	42,074	47,419	36,036	36,349	..
Official creditors	3,099	15,947	25,861	22,493	22,975	24,161	23,037	24,693	20,429	..
Private creditors	909	11,447	11,278	14,054	8,013	17,913	24,382	11,343	15,921	..

10. RESOURCE FLOW CHARTS

(US$ million)

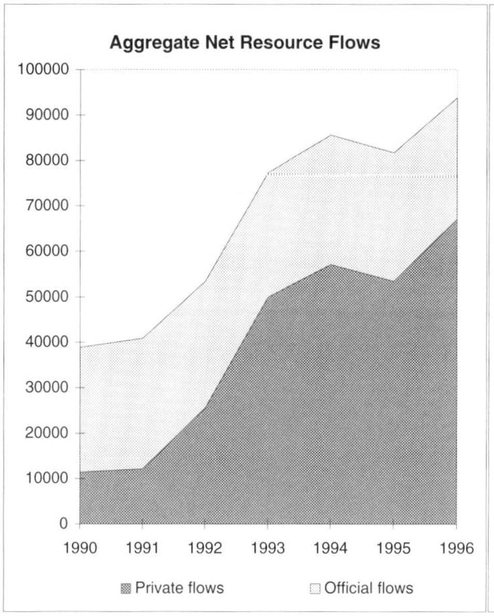

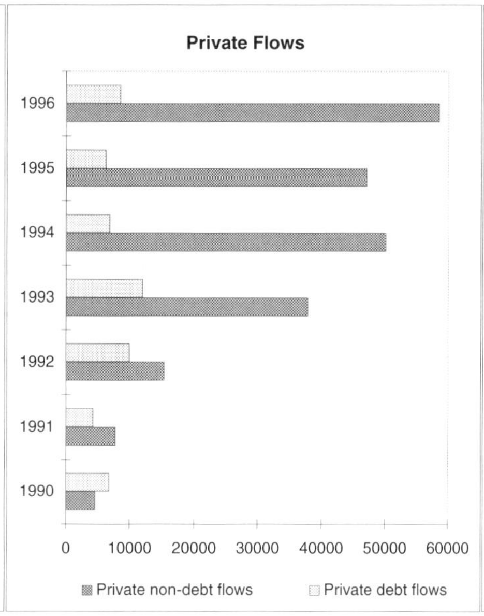

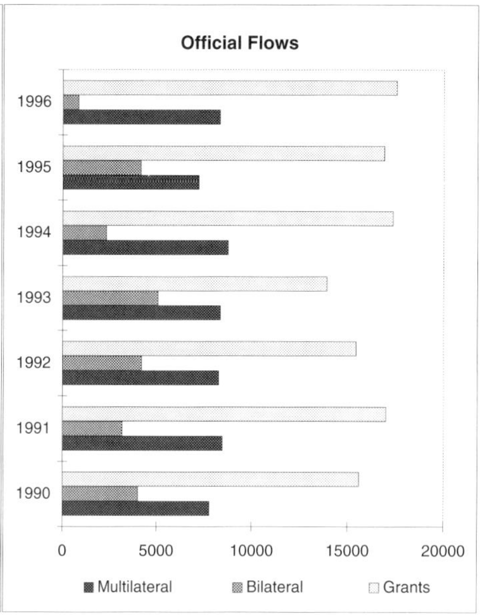

MIDDLE-INCOME COUNTRIES

(US$ million, unless otherwise indicated)

	1970	1980	1989	1990	1991	1992	1993	1994	1995	Preliminary 1996
1. SUMMARY DEBT DATA										
TOTAL DEBT STOCKS (EDT)	..	**509,503**	**1,017,302**	**1,074,548**	**1,140,090**	**1,192,729**	**1,313,097**	**1,414,756**	**1,530,883**	**1,628,765**
Long-term debt (LDOD)	**41,451**	**364,768**	**807,497**	**838,409**	**883,408**	**911,267**	**1,007,644**	**1,100,764**	**1,174,269**	**1,247,063**
Public and publicly guaranteed	26,682	301,591	765,001	784,730	817,109	826,427	899,738	968,865	1,010,832	1,044,307
Private nonguaranteed	14,769	63,176	42,496	53,679	66,299	84,840	107,906	131,900	163,437	202,756
Use of IMF credit	**498**	**5,767**	**21,035**	**22,881**	**25,574**	**24,347**	**25,746**	**29,033**	**46,806**	**46,999**
Short-term debt	..	**138,968**	**188,770**	**213,258**	**231,108**	**257,116**	**279,707**	**284,959**	**309,809**	**334,702**
of which interest arrears on LDOD	..	743	26,930	39,555	39,303	30,103	25,081	19,254	18,066	8,858
Official creditors	..	411	11,661	11,003	7,144	5,613	4,836	5,046	5,348	..
Private creditors	..	332	15,269	28,553	32,158	24,490	20,245	14,209	12,719	..
Memo: principal arrears on LDOD	..	701	29,124	35,587	33,968	40,279	38,523	42,871	51,651	37,357
Official creditors	..	159	12,445	13,618	12,012	10,159	9,941	12,870	17,143	..
Private creditors	..	542	16,679	21,969	21,957	30,121	28,582	30,001	34,508	..
Memo: export credits	..	..	201,581	231,767	259,747	250,597	252,540	299,687	313,840	..
TOTAL DEBT FLOWS										
Disbursements	**9,938**	**92,387**	**86,691**	**100,592**	**104,930**	**117,301**	**136,258**	**140,739**	**184,001**	**195,362**
Long-term debt	9,650	89,951	82,598	95,011	97,788	112,808	130,339	134,071	159,775	188,673
IMF purchases	288	2,437	4,093	5,581	7,142	4,493	5,919	6,668	24,227	6,689
Principal repayments	**5,305**	**38,040**	**72,508**	**75,463**	**73,987**	**80,315**	**89,751**	**99,010**	**107,061**	**113,715**
Long-term debt	4,906	36,740	67,311	69,987	69,304	75,580	85,309	93,980	100,434	108,351
IMF repurchases	398	1,300	5,197	5,477	4,682	4,735	4,442	5,030	6,627	5,364
Net flows on debt	**12,180**	**94,633**	**33,551**	**37,008**	**49,088**	**72,193**	**80,254**	**63,908**	**108,770**	**115,651**
of which short-term debt	..	..	19,368	11,879	18,144	35,207	33,747	22,179	31,830	34,004
Interest payments (INT)	..	**43,969**	**61,220**	**58,074**	**59,514**	**57,229**	**57,904**	**63,198**	**79,467**	**83,744**
Long-term debt	1,794	29,312	46,440	44,185	43,746	43,648	42,477	46,965	61,221	64,111
IMF charges	0	282	1,726	1,917	1,967	1,924	1,835	1,388	1,959	2,215
Short-term debt	..	14,375	13,054	11,972	13,802	11,657	13,592	14,845	16,288	17,419
Net transfers on debt	..	**50,664**	**-27,669**	**-21,066**	**-10,426**	**14,964**	**22,350**	**709**	**29,302**	**31,907**
Total debt service (TDS)	..	**82,009**	**133,728**	**133,538**	**133,501**	**137,544**	**147,655**	**162,209**	**186,529**	**197,459**
Long-term debt	6,701	66,052	113,751	114,172	113,050	119,228	127,786	140,945	161,655	172,462
IMF repurchases and charges	398	1,582	6,923	7,393	6,649	6,659	6,277	6,418	8,586	7,579
Short-term debt (interest only)	..	14,375	13,054	11,972	13,802	11,657	13,592	14,845	16,288	17,419
2. AGGREGATE NET RESOURCE FLOWS AND NET TRANSFERS (LONG-TERM)										
NET RESOURCE FLOWS	**7,816**	**64,215**	**40,215**	**60,756**	**80,908**	**92,205**	**134,627**	**121,359**	**155,416**	**190,699**
Net flow of long-term debt (ex. IMF)	4,743	53,211	15,288	25,024	28,484	37,227	45,030	40,091	59,340	80,322
Foreign direct investment (net)	2,007	4,986	16,879	20,040	26,346	29,774	35,219	44,596	53,919	60,022
Portfolio equity flows	0	0	2,377	2,134	5,768	9,098	39,057	21,608	26,476	36,613
Grants (excluding technical coop.)	1,066	6,018	5,672	13,557	20,310	16,106	15,321	15,064	15,681	13,742
Memo: technical coop. grants	723	2,594	5,339	6,512	7,843	9,220	10,310	9,818	12,367	11,794
NET TRANSFERS	**359**	**13,823**	**-22,197**	**465**	**20,112**	**28,945**	**70,956**	**51,382**	**69,895**	**99,288**
Interest on long-term debt	1,794	29,312	46,440	44,185	43,746	43,648	42,477	46,965	61,221	64,111
Profit remittances on FDI	5,663	21,079	15,973	16,106	17,051	19,613	21,195	23,011	24,300	27,300
3. MAJOR ECONOMIC AGGREGATES										
Gross national product (GNP)	563,062	2,276,752	3,039,230	3,293,287	3,214,440	3,301,218	3,398,048	3,569,346	3,839,831	4,229,205
Exports of goods & services (XGS)	76,292	602,468	665,190	736,935	725,066	752,492	797,125	891,076	1,073,661	1,173,494
of which workers' remittances	1,715	11,053	16,047	18,051	18,791	23,407	22,493	24,219	27,314	25,542
Imports of goods & services (MGS)	77,271	572,074	687,976	769,551	794,900	833,147	898,621	966,374	1,160,326	1,268,108
International reserves (RES)	23,931	191,558	165,528	186,507	216,391	251,061	310,614	331,640	414,017	..
Current account balance	9,747	39,287	-20,884	-32,976	-70,468	-75,843	-102,660	-74,635	-81,528	-89,268
4. DEBT INDICATORS										
EDT / XGS (%)	..	84.6	152.9	145.8	157.2	158.5	164.7	158.8	142.6	138.8
EDT / GNP (%)	..	22.4	33.5	32.6	35.5	36.1	38.6	39.6	39.9	38.5
TDS / XGS (%)	..	13.6	20.1	18.1	18.4	18.3	18.5	18.2	17.4	16.8
INT / XGS (%)	..	7.3	9.2	7.9	8.2	7.6	7.3	7.1	7.4	7.1
INT / GNP (%)	..	1.9	2.0	1.8	1.9	1.7	1.7	1.8	2.1	2.0
RES / EDT (%)	..	37.6	16.3	17.4	19.0	21.0	23.7	23.4	27.0	..
RES / MGS (months)	3.7	4.0	2.9	2.9	3.3	3.6	4.1	4.1	4.3	..
Short-term / EDT (%)	..	27.3	18.6	19.8	20.3	21.6	21.3	20.1	20.2	20.5
Concessional / EDT (%)	..	12.2	12.5	12.6	12.9	13.5	15.3	15.0	13.7	12.7
Multilateral / EDT (%)	..	5.6	10.6	11.4	11.5	11.0	10.6	10.7	10.4	10.1

MIDDLE-INCOME COUNTRIES

(US$ million, unless otherwise indicated)

5. LONG-TERM DEBT

	1970	1980	1989	1990	1991	1992	1993	1994	1995	*Preliminary* 1996
DEBT OUTSTANDING (LDOD)	**41,451**	**364,768**	**807,497**	**838,409**	**883,408**	**911,267**	**1,007,644**	**1,100,764**	**1,174,269**	**1,247,063**
Public and publicly guaranteed	**26,682**	**301,591**	**765,001**	**784,730**	**817,109**	**826,427**	**899,738**	**968,865**	**1,010,832**	**1,044,307**
Official creditors	16,707	112,167	321,931	351,910	388,034	401,594	470,208	516,013	537,027	533,928
Multilateral	4,141	28,540	107,388	122,293	130,811	131,283	139,757	150,805	158,773	165,229
Concessional	2,859	7,564	14,404	14,531	15,479	15,918	17,115	18,943	20,939	..
Bilateral	12,566	83,627	214,543	229,616	257,223	270,311	330,451	365,209	378,254	368,699
Concessional	10,261	54,671	113,183	120,666	131,709	144,514	184,213	193,541	189,262	..
Private creditors	9,975	189,424	443,071	432,820	429,075	424,833	429,530	452,851	473,804	510,380
Bonds	1,436	18,081	43,360	103,514	110,575	120,788	158,217	228,652	250,490	..
Commercial banks	3,420	119,740	302,135	222,087	213,507	201,451	172,098	127,070	130,534	..
Other private	5,119	51,604	97,575	107,219	104,992	102,594	99,215	97,129	92,780	..
Private nonguaranteed	**14,769**	**63,176**	**42,496**	**53,679**	**66,299**	**84,840**	**107,906**	**131,900**	**163,437**	**202,756**
Bonds	..	..	49	347	1,974	9,104	25,892	40,363	51,066	..
Commerical banks	..	..	42,447	53,332	64,325	75,736	82,014	91,537	112,370	..
Memo:										
IBRD	2,912	16,483	61,660	70,230	73,556	71,305	74,361	79,129	83,412	..
IDA	227	1,720	3,180	3,276	3,362	3,398	3,481	3,676	3,916	..
DISBURSEMENTS	**9,650**	**89,951**	**82,598**	**95,011**	**97,788**	**112,808**	**130,339**	**134,071**	**159,775**	**188,673**
Public and publicly guaranteed	**5,662**	**70,604**	**72,324**	**78,519**	**81,153**	**81,080**	**89,178**	**86,970**	**101,420**	**121,342**
Official creditors	2,719	19,166	26,769	34,171	36,944	33,232	34,087	30,688	43,884	36,511
Multilateral	818	5,650	13,014	17,152	17,426	16,628	19,590	16,030	20,235	20,583
Concessional	342	717	1,061	1,221	1,718	1,803	1,987	1,970	2,491	..
Bilatarel	1,902	13,516	13,755	17,018	19,518	16,605	14,498	14,658	23,650	15,928
Concessional	1,354	6,667	7,723	8,758	9,644	7,282	7,550	8,118	8,985	..
Private creditors	2,943	51,438	45,555	44,348	44,209	47,848	55,091	56,282	57,535	84,831
Bonds	140	3,001	6,253	6,159	9,227	11,595	26,303	19,403	28,522	..
Commercial banks	1,242	32,045	18,994	11,825	11,564	11,801	9,319	18,160	15,876	..
Other private	1,560	16,392	20,308	26,363	23,417	24,452	19,468	18,720	13,137	..
Private nonguaranteed	**3,987**	**19,347**	**10,275**	**16,492**	**16,636**	**31,728**	**41,161**	**47,101**	**58,355**	**67,331**
Bonds	..	..	47	291	1,626	7,318	17,101	16,362	13,543	..
Commercial banks	..	..	10,227	16,201	15,009	24,410	24,060	30,739	44,812	..
Memo:										
IBRD	476	3,613	7,321	10,405	8,938	7,910	9,857	8,564	10,565	..
IDA	27	132	122	82	121	136	117	198	275	..
PRINCIPAL REPAYMENTS	**4,906**	**36,740**	**67,311**	**69,987**	**69,304**	**75,580**	**85,309**	**93,980**	**100,434**	**108,351**
Public and publicly guaranteed	**2,544**	**25,788**	**57,353**	**63,555**	**61,065**	**62,890**	**61,970**	**70,039**	**73,486**	**80,218**
Official creditors	994	5,303	17,995	18,934	20,356	21,911	21,876	28,620	34,891	36,214
Multilateral	287	1,234	8,725	9,472	10,878	12,390	12,623	14,493	16,424	13,886
Concessional	157	255	455	549	784	943	934	848	1,028	..
Bilateral	707	4,070	9,270	9,462	9,478	9,521	9,253	14,128	18,467	22,328
Concessional	334	1,449	2,818	3,875	3,014	2,893	3,247	4,114	4,795	..
Private creditors	1,551	20,484	39,358	44,621	40,710	40,979	40,094	41,418	38,595	44,004
Bonds	114	479	3,343	4,195	2,139	8,593	10,007	7,492	10,000	..
Commercial banks	644	12,923	20,801	22,075	16,338	15,157	14,819	16,197	14,353	..
Other private	793	7,083	15,214	18,351	22,233	17,229	15,268	17,730	14,243	..
Private nonguaranteed	**2,362**	**10,953**	**9,958**	**6,432**	**8,239**	**12,690**	**23,340**	**23,941**	**26,948**	**28,133**
Bonds	..	..	0	0	0	165	289	1,997	4,042	..
Commerical banks	..	..	9,958	6,432	8,239	12,525	23,050	21,944	22,907	..
Memo:										
IBRD	155	787	6,167	6,382	7,137	8,039	7,840	8,922	9,110	..
IDA	0	6	30	37	44	48	54	59	62	..
NET FLOWS ON DEBT	**4,743**	**53,211**	**15,288**	**25,024**	**28,484**	**37,227**	**45,030**	**40,091**	**59,340**	**80,322**
Public and publicly guaranteed	**3,118**	**44,817**	**14,971**	**14,964**	**20,088**	**18,190**	**27,208**	**16,932**	**27,934**	**41,124**
Official creditors	1,726	13,863	8,774	15,237	16,588	11,321	12,211	2,068	8,993	297
Multilateral	531	4,416	4,290	7,680	6,548	4,237	6,966	1,538	3,811	6,697
Concessional	186	462	606	673	935	860	1,053	1,122	1,463	..
Bilateral	1,195	9,447	4,485	7,557	10,040	7,084	5,245	530	5,183	-6,400
Concessional	1,020	5,218	4,905	4,883	6,631	4,389	4,303	4,004	4,190	..
Private creditors	1,392	30,954	6,197	-273	3,499	6,869	14,997	14,864	18,940	40,827
Bonds	26	2,522	2,910	1,964	7,089	3,002	16,297	11,911	18,523	..
Commercial banks	599	19,122	-1,807	-10,250	-4,774	-3,356	-5,500	1,962	1,523	..
Other private	767	9,309	5,094	8,013	1,184	7,223	4,200	991	-1,106	..
Private nonguaranteed	**1,625**	**8,394**	**316**	**10,061**	**8,396**	**19,037**	**17,822**	**23,160**	**31,407**	**39,198**
Bonds	..	..	47	291	1,626	7,153	16,812	14,365	9,502	..
Commerical banks	..	..	269	9,770	6,770	11,884	1,009	8,794	21,905	..
Memo:										
IBRD	321	2,827	1,154	4,023	1,800	-129	2,017	-359	1,455	..
IDA	27	126	92	45	77	88	63	139	213	..

MIDDLE-INCOME COUNTRIES

(US$ million, unless otherwise indicated)

	1970	1980	1989	1990	1991	1992	1993	1994	1995	*Preliminary* 1996
INTEREST PAYMENTS (LINT)	**1,794**	**29,312**	**46,440**	**44,185**	**43,746**	**43,648**	**42,477**	**46,965**	**61,221**	**64,111**
Public and publicly guaranteed	**1,064**	**23,131**	**42,165**	**40,260**	**39,216**	**38,674**	**36,704**	**40,179**	**51,660**	**53,078**
Official creditors	498	4,431	12,758	14,356	15,135	16,811	18,003	19,032	23,812	23,475
Multilateral	213	1,915	7,392	8,360	9,333	9,615	10,062	9,903	10,508	11,050
Concessional	142	236	345	386	457	501	546	552	643	..
Bilateral	285	2,516	5,366	5,996	5,803	7,196	7,941	9,129	13,304	12,425
Concessional	178	1,073	1,870	2,334	2,236	2,952	3,469	3,661	4,335	..
Private creditors	566	18,700	29,407	25,904	24,081	21,864	18,701	21,148	27,848	29,603
Bonds	85	1,441	2,673	4,274	7,427	7,097	7,772	10,587	16,165	..
Commercial banks	239	13,453	20,998	16,005	10,727	10,326	6,699	6,132	6,898	..
Other private	242	3,806	5,736	5,625	5,928	4,441	4,231	4,429	4,786	..
Private nonguaranteed	**730**	**6,181**	**4,275**	**3,925**	**4,529**	**4,974**	**5,772**	**6,786**	**9,561**	**11,033**
Bonds	..	..	0	3	47	225	912	2,186	3,224	..
Commerical banks	..	..	4,275	3,922	4,483	4,748	4,860	4,601	6,338	..
Memo:										
IBRD	161	1,333	4,687	5,175	5,590	5,715	5,896	5,774	5,883	..
IDA	2	12	23	24	25	25	26	26	28	..
NET TRANSFERS ON DEBT	**2,949**	**23,899**	**-31,152**	**-19,161**	**-15,262**	**-6,421**	**2,553**	**-6,874**	**-1,881**	**16,212**
Public and publicly guaranteed	**2,053**	**21,686**	**-27,194**	**-25,296**	**-19,129**	**-20,484**	**-9,496**	**-23,248**	**-23,726**	**-11,954**
Official creditors	1,228	9,432	-3,983	881	1,453	-5,490	-5,792	-16,964	-14,818	-23,178
Multilateral	318	2,501	-3,102	-680	-2,785	-5,378	-3,095	-8,365	-6,697	-4,353
Concessional	44	226	260	287	478	359	507	570	820	..
Bilateral	910	6,930	-881	1,561	4,238	-112	-2,696	-8,599	-8,122	-18,825
Concessional	842	4,144	3,036	2,549	4,395	1,438	835	343	-145	..
Private creditors	826	12,254	-23,211	-26,177	-20,582	-14,995	-3,705	-6,284	-8,908	11,224
Bonds	-59	1,082	237	-2,309	-338	-4,095	8,525	1,324	2,358	..
Commercial banks	360	5,669	-22,806	-26,255	-15,501	-13,682	-12,198	-4,169	-5,375	..
Other private	524	5,503	-642	2,388	-4,743	2,782	-31	-3,438	-5,891	..
Private nonguaranteed	**895**	**2,213**	**-3,958**	**6,136**	**3,867**	**14,064**	**12,050**	**16,374**	**21,846**	**28,165**
Bonds	..	..	47	288	1,580	6,928	15,900	12,180	6,278	..
Commerical banks	..	..	-4,006	5,848	2,288	7,136	-3,851	4,194	15,567	..
Memo:										
IBRD	160	1,494	-3,533	-1,152	-3,790	-5,844	-3,879	-6,133	-4,428	..
IDA	25	114	69	20	53	63	37	113	185	..
DEBT SERVICE (LTDS)	**6,701**	**66,052**	**113,751**	**114,172**	**113,050**	**119,228**	**127,786**	**140,945**	**161,655**	**172,462**
Public and publicly guaranteed	**3,609**	**48,919**	**99,518**	**103,815**	**100,282**	**101,564**	**98,674**	**110,218**	**125,146**	**133,296**
Official creditors	1,492	9,734	30,752	33,290	35,491	38,722	39,879	47,652	58,703	59,689
Multilateral	500	3,149	16,117	17,832	20,210	22,006	22,685	24,396	26,932	24,936
Concessional	299	491	801	935	1,241	1,444	1,480	1,400	1,671	..
Bilateral	992	6,586	14,636	15,458	15,281	16,716	17,194	23,257	31,771	34,753
Concessional	512	2,522	4,688	6,209	5,249	5,845	6,716	7,775	9,130	..
Private creditors	2,117	39,184	68,766	70,525	64,791	62,842	58,795	62,566	66,443	73,607
Bonds	199	1,919	6,016	8,469	9,565	15,690	17,778	18,079	26,164	..
Commercial banks	882	26,375	41,800	38,081	27,065	25,483	21,518	22,329	21,251	..
Other private	1,036	10,889	20,950	23,976	28,161	21,670	19,500	22,158	19,028	..
Private nonguaranteed	**3,092**	**17,134**	**14,233**	**10,357**	**12,769**	**17,664**	**29,112**	**30,727**	**36,509**	**39,166**
Bonds	..	..	0	3	47	390	1,201	4,182	7,265	..
Commerical banks	..	..	14,233	10,354	12,722	17,274	27,910	26,545	29,244	..
Memo:										
IBRD	316	2,120	10,854	11,557	12,727	13,754	13,736	14,696	14,993	..
IDA	2	18	53	62	69	73	80	85	90	..
UNDISBURSED DEBT	**9,681**	**93,509**	**116,762**	**125,948**	**145,602**	**154,324**	**159,027**	**155,500**	**154,158**	**..**
Official creditors	7,201	55,622	78,184	85,278	99,857	107,542	110,418	112,806	112,550	..
Private creditors	2,480	37,887	38,578	40,670	45,745	46,782	48,609	42,694	41,609	..
Memorandum items										
Concessional LDOD	13,120	62,235	127,587	135,196	147,188	160,432	201,328	212,484	210,200	207,203
Variable rate LDOD	15,486	168,590	391,219	369,867	395,195	418,904	466,604	502,627	559,444	..
Public sector LDOD	25,905	249,235	676,208	694,947	720,624	724,679	799,742	862,526	903,516	..
Private sector LDOD	15,546	69,815	46,510	58,520	70,885	89,944	111,181	133,388	162,335	..

6. CURRENCY COMPOSITION OF LONG-TERM DEBT (PERCENT)

	1970	1980	1989	1990	1991	1992	1993	1994	1995	1996
Deutsche mark	8.6	6.1	8.2	9.9	10.4	10.2	9.0	8.5	8.4	..
French franc	5.1	4.7	4.3	5.1	5.2	4.8	4.0	4.0	4.1	..
Japanese yen	1.3	5.7	9.5	9.6	10.5	10.7	11.1	11.6	11.3	..
Pound sterling	4.8	1.4	1.5	1.5	1.4	1.1	1.1	0.9	0.8	..
Swiss franc	1.6	1.6	1.9	2.1	1.9	1.5	1.3	1.0	1.0	..
U.S. dollars	52.0	49.6	44.1	40.4	38.5	39.1	43.2	43.9	44.4	..
Multiple currency	13.7	10.0	13.4	14.4	14.6	15.1	14.1	14.1	14.2	..
Special drawing rights	0.0	0.0	0.1	0.1	0.1	0.0	0.0	0.0	0.0	..
All other currencies	12.9	5.6	5.9	6.0	6.2	5.8	5.5	5.4	5.3	..

MIDDLE-INCOME COUNTRIES

(US$ million, unless otherwise indicated)

	1970	1980	1989	1990	1991	1992	1993	1994	1995	Preliminary 1996
7. DEBT RESTRUCTURINGS										
Total amount rescheduled	..	..	21,241	72,265	37,320	51,923	61,721	85,957	28,781	..
Debt stock rescheduled	..	..	8,427	61,499	12,976	24,889	23,738	53,939	8,682	..
Principal rescheduled	..	..	9,237	6,196	15,353	12,852	17,020	12,794	13,326	..
Official	..	..	2,886	2,956	9,553	7,371	6,462	3,135	5,784	..
Private	..	..	6,350	3,240	5,799	5,481	10,558	9,659	7,542	..
Interest rescheduled	..	..	3,405	3,950	9,094	12,573	15,528	13,243	4,336	..
Official	..	..	2,569	3,116	7,296	3,711	3,596	1,912	1,466	..
Private	..	..	836	834	1,798	8,861	11,932	11,331	2,870	..
Principal forgiven	..	..	3,601	10,998	3,869	1,635	1,624	4,382	483	..
Memo: interest forgiven	..	..	90	2,792	191	185	147	263	12	..
Debt stock reduction	..	..	15,718	24,843	4,769	12,850	6,537	12,829	2,505	..
of which debt buyback	..	..	2,457	4,360	706	6,263	589	1,702	13	..
8. DEBT STOCK-FLOW RECONCILIATION										
Total change in debt stocks	..	..	26,494	57,245	65,542	52,640	120,367	101,660	116,126	..
Net flows on debt	..	..	33,551	37,008	49,088	72,193	80,254	63,908	108,770	..
Net change in interest arrears	..	..	9,204	12,626	-253	-9,200	-5,022	-5,827	-1,188	..
Interest capitalized	..	..	3,405	3,950	9,094	12,573	15,528	13,243	4,336	..
Debt forgiveness or reduction	..	..	-16,861	-31,482	-7,931	-8,222	-7,572	-15,510	-2,974	..
Cross-currency valuation	..	..	-9,431	37,304	4,405	-18,808	-313	39,383	11,664	..
Residual	..	..	6,625	-2,160	11,140	4,104	37,492	6,463	-4,481	..
9. AVERAGE TERMS OF NEW COMMITMENTS										
ALL CREDITORS										
Interest (%)	6	10.2	7.5	7.8	6.9	6.5	6.1	6.2	6.7	..
Maturity (years)	16.9	13.2	13.2	16.1	14	12.9	12.8	13	12	..
Grace period (years)	4.6	4.5	4.4	5.2	4.6	4.2	4.8	4.5	4.4	..
Grant element (%)	24.3	2	14.1	13.5	16.7	16.7	19.4	19	16.7	..
Official creditors										
Interest (%)	4.8	6.8	6.2	6.7	6.2	6.2	5.6	5.9	6.6	..
Maturity (years)	23.8	19.6	19	18.7	17.8	17.4	18.7	18.9	16.1	..
Grace period (years)	6.5	5.4	5.7	5.8	5.5	5.2	5.4	5.4	4.6	..
Grant element (%)	36.3	23.1	25.2	22.2	23.8	22.3	27.5	26.2	21.4	..
Private creditors										
Interest (%)	7.4	12.1	8.6	8.7	7.8	6.8	6.5	6.5	6.8	..
Maturity (years)	9.2	9.6	8.7	13.8	9.5	8.7	8.4	7.4	7.6	..
Grace period (years)	2.5	3.9	3.4	4.7	3.5	3.3	4.4	3.6	4.2	..
Grant element (%)	11.1	-10	5.6	5.7	8.6	11.4	13.4	12.1	11.7	..
Memorandum items										
Commitments	7,219	66,263	69,779	83,839	97,972	91,318	91,617	69,820	95,754	..
Official creditors	3,792	23,962	30,264	39,559	52,326	44,347	38,991	34,031	49,433	..
Private creditors	3,427	42,302	39,514	44,280	45,646	46,971	52,626	35,789	46,321	..

10. RESOURCE FLOW CHARTS

(US$ million)

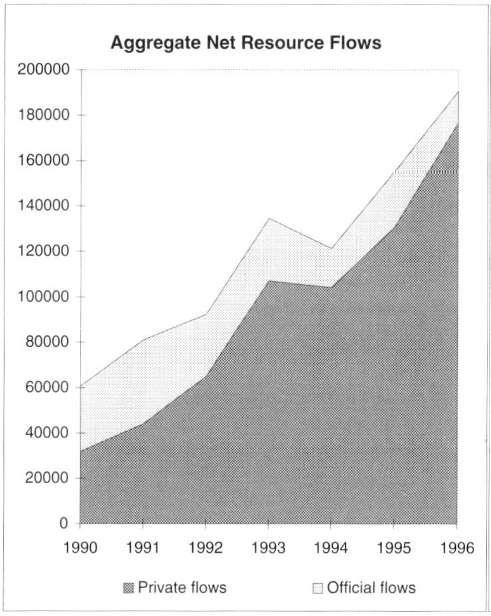

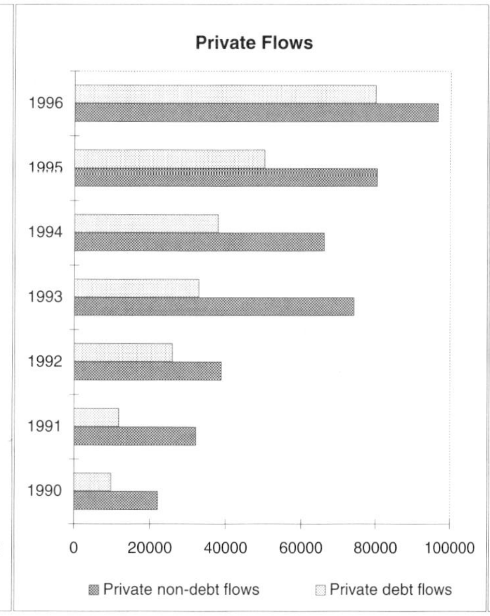

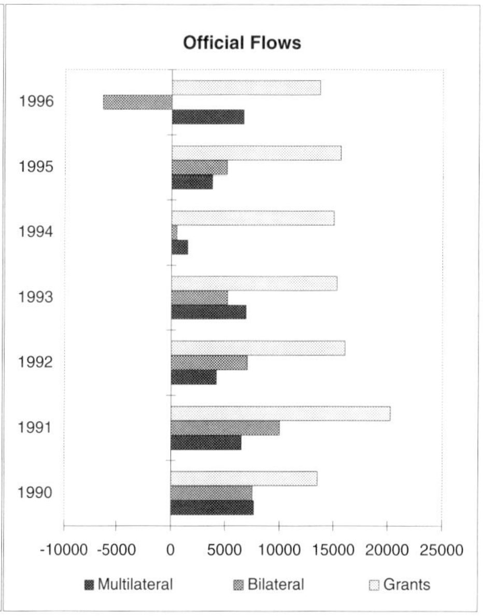

Country tables

ALBANIA

(US$ million, unless otherwise indicated)

	1970	1980	1988	1989	1990	1991	1992	1993	1994	1995
1. SUMMARY DEBT DATA										
TOTAL DEBT STOCKS (EDT)	..	..	..	**74.4**	**348.6**	**511.5**	**638.8**	**830.8**	**922.5**	**708.7**
Long-term debt (LDOD)	..	..	..	**0.0**	**35.7**	**86.2**	**126.9**	**215.2**	**263.5**	**556.7**
Public and publicly guaranteed	..	..	..	0.0	35.7	86.2	126.9	215.2	263.5	556.7
Private nonguaranteed	0.0	0.0	0.0	0.0	0.0	0.0	0.0	0.0	0.0	0.0
Use of IMF credit	**0.0**	**0.0**	**0.0**	**0.0**	**0.0**	**0.0**	**13.3**	**29.7**	**54.2**	**64.5**
Short-term debt	..	..	..	**74.4**	**312.9**	**425.3**	**498.6**	**585.9**	**604.8**	**87.5**
of which interest arrears on LDOD	..	..	..	0.0	0.0	5.3	9.0	9.4	25.1	26.8
Official creditors	..	..	..	0.0	0.0	0.0	0.0	0.3	1.4	1.7
Private creditors	..	..	..	0.0	0.0	5.3	9.0	9.1	23.6	25.2
Memo: principal arrears on LDOD	..	..	..	0.0	0.0	1.5	23.4	38.6	83.5	89.6
Official creditors	..	..	..	0.0	0.0	0.0	4.0	5.5	17.2	17.2
Private creditors	..	..	..	0.0	0.0	1.5	19.4	33.1	66.3	72.4
Memo: export credits	..	..	16.0	13.0	16.0	29.0	24.0	30.0	29.0	34.0
TOTAL DEBT FLOWS										
Disbursements	..	..	..	**0.0**	**33.1**	**48.8**	**66.2**	**81.2**	**74.3**	**70.2**
Long-term debt	..	..	..	0.0	33.1	48.8	52.6	64.6	52.0	59.5
IMF purchases	0.0	0.0	0.0	0.0	0.0	0.0	13.6	16.6	22.2	10.7
Principal repayments	..	..	..	**0.0**	**0.0**	**0.8**	**0.0**	**0.0**	**8.2**	**1.2**
Long-term debt	..	..	..	0.0	0.0	0.8	0.0	0.0	8.2	0.0
IMF repurchases	0.0	0.0	0.0	0.0	0.0	0.0	0.0	0.0	0.0	1.2
Net flows on debt	..	..	..	**74.4**	**271.6**	**155.1**	**135.8**	**203.3**	**69.3**	**-109.0**
of which short-term debt	..	..	..	74.4	238.5	107.1	69.6	122.1	3.2	-178.0
Interest payments (INT)	..	..	..	**0.0**	**3.1**	**2.8**	**2.0**	**1.2**	**4.0**	**6.0**
Long-term debt	..	..	..	0.0	3.1	2.8	1.9	0.3	2.9	1.8
IMF charges	0.0	0.0	0.0	0.0	0.0	0.0	0.1	0.9	1.1	1.3
Short-term debt	..	..	..	0.0	0.0	0.0	0.0	0.0	0.0	3.0
Net transfers on debt	..	..	..	**74.4**	**268.5**	**152.4**	**133.8**	**202.1**	**65.3**	**-115.0**
Total debt service paid (TDS)	..	..	..	**0.0**	**3.1**	**3.6**	**2.0**	**1.2**	**12.2**	**7.2**
Long-term debt	..	..	..	0.0	3.1	3.6	1.9	0.3	11.1	1.8
IMF repurchases and charges	0.0	0.0	0.0	0.0	0.0	0.0	0.1	0.9	1.1	2.5
Short-term debt (interest only)	..	..	..	0.0	0.0	0.0	0.0	0.0	0.0	3.0
2. AGGREGATE NET RESOURCE FLOWS AND NET TRANSFERS (LONG-TERM)										
NET RESOURCE FLOWS	..	..	..	**0.1**	**35.0**	**368.3**	**406.2**	**306.0**	**165.2**	**206.0**
Net flow of long-term debt (ex. IMF)	0.0	0.0	0.0	0.0	33.1	48.0	52.6	64.6	43.8	59.5
Foreign direct investment (net)	0.0	0.0	0.0	0.0	0.0	0.0	20.0	58.0	53.0	70.0
Portfolio equity flows	..	..	..	0.0	0.0	0.0	0.0	0.0	0.0	0.0
Grants (excluding technical coop.)	0.0	0.0	0.0	0.1	1.9	320.3	333.6	183.4	68.4	76.5
Memo: technical coop. grants	0.0	0.0	5.5	8.7	9.2	4.0	11.5	24.5	27.3	32.3
NET TRANSFERS	..	..	..	**0.1**	**31.9**	**365.6**	**404.2**	**305.7**	**162.3**	**204.2**
Interest on long-term debt	..	..	..	0.0	3.1	2.8	1.9	0.3	2.9	1.8
Profit remittances on FDI	0.0	0.0	0.0	0.0	0.0	0.0	0.0	0.0	0.0	0.0
3. MAJOR ECONOMIC AGGREGATES										
Gross national product (GNP)	..	..	..	..	2,105.6	1,103.8	640.3	1,661.0	1,807.9	2,245.1
Exports of goods & services (XGS)	..	385.5	375.1	434.3	353.6	83.0	242.9	528.9	540.2	760.3
of which workers remittances	..	0.0	0.0	0.0	0.0	0.0	150.0	274.8	264.7	384.6
Imports of goods & services (MGS)	..	375.3	409.2	484.2	486.9	340.3	667.3	794.4	774.8	864.7
International reserves (RES)	..	..	..	..	..	..	..	166.5	223.6	265.3
Current account balance	..	16.0	-27.1	-39.3	-118.3	-168.0	-50.7	14.9	-157.3	-11.6
4. DEBT INDICATORS										
EDT / XGS (%)	..	..	..	17.1	98.6	616.2	263.0	157.1	170.8	93.2
EDT / GNP (%)	..	..	..	..	16.6	46.3	99.8	50.0	51.0	31.6
TDS / XGS (%)	..	..	..	0.0	0.9	4.3	0.8	0.2	2.3	0.9
INT / XGS (%)	..	..	..	0.0	0.9	3.3	0.8	0.2	0.7	0.8
INT / GNP (%)	..	..	..	..	0.1	0.3	0.3	0.1	0.2	0.3
RES / EDT (%)	..	..	..	..	..	..	..	20.0	24.2	37.4
RES / MGS (months)	..	..	..	..	..	..	..	2.5	3.5	3.7
Short-term / EDT (%)	..	..	..	100.0	89.8	83.1	78.1	70.5	65.6	12.4
Concessional / EDT (%)	..	..	..	0.0	0.6	1.6	7.8	10.6	14.9	28.3
Multilateral / EDT (%)	..	..	..	0.0	0.0	0.0	0.3	3.3	7.1	15.6

ALBANIA

(US$ million, unless otherwise indicated)

	1970	1980	1988	1989	1990	1991	1992	1993	1994	1995
5. LONG-TERM DEBT										
DEBT OUTSTANDING (LDOD)	..	..	..	**0.0**	**35.7**	**86.2**	**126.9**	**215.2**	**263.5**	**556.7**
Public and publicly guaranteed	..	..	..	**0.0**	**35.7**	**86.2**	**126.9**	**215.2**	**263.5**	**556.7**
Official creditors	..	..	..	0.0	2.0	22.1	63.5	139.9	190.0	253.4
Multilateral	..	..	..	0.0	0.0	0.0	2.0	27.6	65.7	110.2
Concessional	..	..	..	0.0	0.0	0.0	2.0	27.6	65.5	109.8
Bilateral	..	..	..	0.0	2.0	22.1	61.5	112.2	124.2	143.2
Concessional	..	..	..	0.0	2.0	8.2	47.6	60.1	71.9	90.9
Private creditors	..	..	..	0.0	33.7	64.1	63.3	75.4	73.6	303.3
Bonds	..	..	..	0.0	0.0	0.0	0.0	0.0	0.0	225.0
Commercial banks	..	..	..	0.0	0.0	26.4	24.8	23.2	25.8	27.9
Other private	..	..	..	0.0	33.7	37.7	38.5	52.2	47.8	50.4
Private nonguaranteed	**0.0**	**0.0**	**0.0**	**0.0**	**0.0**	**0.0**	**0.0**	**0.0**	**0.0**	**0.0**
Bonds	..	..	..	0.0	0.0	0.0	0.0	0.0	0.0	0.0
Commercial banks	..	..	..	0.0	0.0	0.0	0.0	0.0	0.0	0.0
Memo:										
IBRD	0.0	0.0	0.0	0.0	0.0	0.0	0.0	0.0	0.0	0.0
IDA	0.0	0.0	0.0	0.0	0.0	0.0	2.0	27.6	64.7	109.0
DISBURSEMENTS	..	..	..	**0.0**	**33.1**	**48.8**	**52.6**	**64.6**	**52.0**	**59.5**
Public and publicly guaranteed	..	..	..	**0.0**	**33.1**	**48.8**	**52.6**	**64.6**	**52.0**	**59.5**
Official creditors	..	..	..	0.0	1.9	19.7	49.4	48.4	52.0	59.5
Multilateral	..	..	..	0.0	0.0	0.0	2.1	25.8	36.0	43.6
Concessional	..	..	..	0.0	0.0	0.0	2.1	25.8	35.8	43.3
Bilateral	..	..	..	0.0	1.9	19.7	47.3	22.6	16.1	15.9
Concessional	..	..	..	0.0	1.9	5.8	47.3	19.4	15.9	15.9
Private creditors	..	..	..	0.0	31.2	29.2	3.2	16.2	0.0	0.0
Bonds	..	..	..	0.0	0.0	0.0	0.0	0.0	0.0	0.0
Commercial banks	..	..	..	0.0	0.0	25.0	0.0	0.0	0.0	0.0
Other private	..	..	..	0.0	31.2	4.2	3.2	16.2	0.0	0.0
Private nonguaranteed	**0.0**	**0.0**	**0.0**	**0.0**	**0.0**	**0.0**	**0.0**	**0.0**	**0.0**	**0.0**
Bonds	..	..	..	0.0	0.0	0.0	0.0	0.0	0.0	0.0
Commercial banks	..	..	..	0.0	0.0	0.0	0.0	0.0	0.0	0.0
Memo:										
IBRD	0.0	0.0	0.0	0.0	0.0	0.0	0.0	0.0	0.0	0.0
IDA	0.0	0.0	0.0	0.0	0.0	0.0	2.1	25.8	35.0	43.3
PRINCIPAL REPAYMENTS	..	..	..	**0.0**	**0.0**	**0.8**	**0.0**	**0.0**	**8.2**	**0.0**
Public and publicly guaranteed	..	..	..	**0.0**	**0.0**	**0.8**	**0.0**	**0.0**	**8.2**	**0.0**
Official creditors	..	..	..	0.0	0.0	0.0	0.0	0.0	0.0	0.0
Multilateral	..	..	..	0.0	0.0	0.0	0.0	0.0	0.0	0.0
Concessional	..	..	..	0.0	0.0	0.0	0.0	0.0	0.0	0.0
Bilateral	..	..	..	0.0	0.0	0.0	0.0	0.0	0.0	0.0
Concessional	..	..	..	0.0	0.0	0.0	0.0	0.0	0.0	0.0
Private creditors	..	..	..	0.0	0.0	0.8	0.0	0.0	8.2	0.0
Bonds	..	..	..	0.0	0.0	0.0	0.0	0.0	0.0	0.0
Commercial banks	..	..	..	0.0	0.0	0.8	0.0	0.0	0.0	0.0
Other private	..	..	..	0.0	0.0	0.0	0.0	0.0	8.2	0.0
Private nonguaranteed	**0.0**	**0.0**	**0.0**	**0.0**	**0.0**	**0.0**	**0.0**	**0.0**	**0.0**	**0.0**
Bonds	..	..	..	0.0	0.0	0.0	0.0	0.0	0.0	0.0
Commercial banks	..	..	..	0.0	0.0	0.0	0.0	0.0	0.0	0.0
Memo:										
IBRD	0.0	0.0	0.0	0.0	0.0	0.0	0.0	0.0	0.0	0.0
IDA	0.0	0.0	0.0	0.0	0.0	0.0	0.0	0.0	0.0	0.0
NET FLOWS ON DEBT	..	..	..	**0.0**	**33.1**	**48.0**	**52.6**	**64.6**	**43.8**	**59.5**
Public and publicly guaranteed	..	..	..	**0.0**	**33.1**	**48.0**	**52.6**	**64.6**	**43.8**	**59.5**
Official creditors	..	..	..	0.0	1.9	19.7	49.4	48.4	52.0	59.5
Multilateral	..	..	..	0.0	0.0	0.0	2.1	25.8	36.0	43.6
Concessional	..	..	..	0.0	0.0	0.0	2.1	25.8	35.8	43.3
Bilateral	..	..	..	0.0	1.9	19.7	47.3	22.6	16.1	15.9
Concessional	..	..	..	0.0	1.9	5.8	47.3	19.4	15.9	15.9
Private creditors	..	..	..	0.0	31.2	28.4	3.2	16.2	-8.2	0.0
Bonds	..	..	..	0.0	0.0	0.0	0.0	0.0	0.0	0.0
Commercial banks	..	..	..	0.0	0.0	24.2	0.0	0.0	0.0	0.0
Other private	..	..	..	0.0	31.2	4.2	3.2	16.2	-8.2	0.0
Private nonguaranteed	**0.0**	**0.0**	**0.0**	**0.0**	**0.0**	**0.0**	**0.0**	**0.0**	**0.0**	**0.0**
Bonds	..	..	..	0.0	0.0	0.0	0.0	0.0	0.0	0.0
Commercial banks	..	..	..	0.0	0.0	0.0	0.0	0.0	0.0	0.0
Memo:										
IBRD	0.0	0.0	0.0	0.0	0.0	0.0	0.0	0.0	0.0	0.0
IDA	0.0	0.0	0.0	0.0	0.0	0.0	2.1	25.8	35.0	43.3

ALBANIA

(US$ million, unless otherwise indicated)

	1970	1980	1988	1989	1990	1991	1992	1993	1994	1995
INTEREST PAYMENTS (LINT)	..	..	..	**0.0**	**3.1**	**2.8**	**1.9**	**0.3**	**2.9**	**1.8**
Public and publicly guaranteed	..	..	..	**0.0**	**3.1**	**2.8**	**1.9**	**0.3**	**2.9**	**1.8**
Official creditors	..	..	..	0.0	0.0	0.2	0.3	0.3	1.3	1.4
Multilateral	..	..	..	0.0	0.0	0.0	0.0	0.0	0.2	0.6
Concessional	..	..	..	0.0	0.0	0.0	0.0	0.0	0.2	0.6
Bilateral	..	..	..	0.0	0.0	0.2	0.3	0.3	1.0	0.9
Concessional	..	..	..	0.0	0.0	0.0	0.1	0.3	1.0	0.9
Private creditors	..	..	..	0.0	3.1	2.5	1.6	0.0	1.6	0.3
Bonds	..	..	..	0.0	0.0	0.0	0.0	0.0	0.0	0.0
Commercial banks	..	..	..	0.0	0.0	1.0	0.0	0.0	0.0	0.0
Other private	..	..	..	0.0	3.1	1.5	1.6	0.0	1.6	0.3
Private nonguaranteed	**0.0**	**0.0**	**0.0**	**0.0**	**0.0**	**0.0**	**0.0**	**0.0**	**0.0**	**0.0**
Bonds	..	..	..	0.0	0.0	0.0	0.0	0.0	0.0	0.0
Commercial banks	..	..	..	0.0	0.0	0.0	0.0	0.0	0.0	0.0
Memo:										
IBRD	0.0	0.0	0.0	0.0	0.0	0.0	0.0	0.0	0.0	0.0
IDA	0.0	0.0	0.0	0.0	0.0	0.0	0.0	0.0	0.2	0.6
NET TRANSFERS ON DEBT	..	..	..	**0.0**	**30.0**	**45.3**	**50.6**	**64.3**	**40.9**	**57.7**
Public and publicly guaranteed	..	..	..	**0.0**	**30.0**	**45.3**	**50.6**	**64.3**	**40.9**	**57.7**
Official creditors	..	..	..	0.0	1.9	19.4	49.1	48.1	50.8	58.1
Multilateral	..	..	..	0.0	0.0	0.0	2.1	25.8	35.7	43.0
Concessional	..	..	..	0.0	0.0	0.0	2.1	25.8	35.6	42.8
Bilateral	..	..	..	0.0	1.9	19.4	47.0	22.3	15.0	15.1
Concessional	..	..	..	0.0	1.9	5.8	47.2	19.1	14.9	15.1
Private creditors	..	..	..	0.0	28.1	25.8	1.6	16.2	-9.9	-0.3
Bonds	..	..	..	0.0	0.0	0.0	0.0	0.0	0.0	0.0
Commercial banks	..	..	..	0.0	0.0	23.2	0.0	0.0	0.0	0.0
Other private	..	..	..	0.0	28.1	2.7	1.6	16.2	-9.9	-0.3
Private nonguaranteed	**0.0**	**0.0**	**0.0**	**0.0**	**0.0**	**0.0**	**0.0**	**0.0**	**0.0**	**0.0**
Bonds	..	..	..	0.0	0.0	0.0	0.0	0.0	0.0	0.0
Commercial banks	..	..	..	0.0	0.0	0.0	0.0	0.0	0.0	0.0
Memo:										
IBRD	0.0	0.0	0.0	0.0	0.0	0.0	0.0	0.0	0.0	0.0
IDA	0.0	0.0	0.0	0.0	0.0	0.0	2.1	25.8	34.8	42.8
DEBT SERVICE (LTDS)	..	..	..	**0.0**	**3.1**	**3.6**	**1.9**	**0.3**	**11.1**	**1.8**
Public and publicly guaranteed	..	..	..	**0.0**	**3.1**	**3.6**	**1.9**	**0.3**	**11.1**	**1.8**
Official creditors	..	..	..	0.0	0.0	0.2	0.3	0.3	1.3	1.4
Multilateral	..	..	..	0.0	0.0	0.0	0.0	0.0	0.2	0.6
Concessional	..	..	..	0.0	0.0	0.0	0.0	0.0	0.2	0.6
Bilateral	..	..	..	0.0	0.0	0.2	0.3	0.3	1.0	0.9
Concessional	..	..	..	0.0	0.0	0.0	0.1	0.3	1.0	0.9
Private creditors	..	..	..	0.0	3.1	3.3	1.6	0.0	9.9	0.3
Bonds	..	..	..	0.0	0.0	0.0	0.0	0.0	0.0	0.0
Commercial banks	..	..	..	0.0	0.0	1.8	0.0	0.0	0.0	0.0
Other private	..	..	..	0.0	3.1	1.5	1.6	0.0	9.9	0.3
Private nonguaranteed	**0.0**	**0.0**	**0.0**	**0.0**	**0.0**	**0.0**	**0.0**	**0.0**	**0.0**	**0.0**
Bonds	..	..	..	0.0	0.0	0.0	0.0	0.0	0.0	0.0
Commercial banks	..	..	..	0.0	0.0	0.0	0.0	0.0	0.0	0.0
Memo:										
IBRD	0.0	0.0	0.0	0.0	0.0	0.0	0.0	0.0	0.0	0.0
IDA	0.0	0.0	0.0	0.0	0.0	0.0	0.0	0.0	0.2	0.6
UNDISBURSED DEBT	..	..	..	**1.8**	**20.1**	**86.5**	**104.5**	**133.7**	**210.0**	**285.4**
Official creditors	..	..	..	1.8	0.0	51.3	69.9	116.0	191.1	272.4
Private creditors	..	..	..	0.0	20.1	35.2	34.6	17.7	19.0	13.1
Memorandum items										
Concessional LDOD	..	..	..	0.0	2.0	8.2	49.7	87.7	137.5	200.7
Variable rate LDOD	..	..	..	0.0	33.7	78.0	77.2	103.3	101.9	331.8
Public sector LDOD	..	..	..	0.0	35.7	86.2	126.9	215.2	263.5	556.7
Private sector LDOD	..	..	..	0.0	0.0	0.0	0.0	0.0	0.0	0.0

6. CURRENCY COMPOSITION OF LONG-TERM DEBT (PERCENT)

	1970	1980	1988	1989	1990	1991	1992	1993	1994	1995
Deutsche mark	..	..	..	0.0	100.0	76.7	56.4	33.1	29.9	15.6
French franc	..	..	..	0.0	0.0	0.0	0.0	0.0	0.0	0.0
Japanese yen	..	..	..	0.0	0.0	0.0	0.0	0.0	3.2	1.5
Pound sterling	..	..	..	0.0	0.0	0.0	0.0	0.0	0.0	0.0
Swiss franc	..	..	..	0.0	0.0	0.0	0.0	0.0	0.0	0.0
U.S.dollars	..	..	..	0.0	0.0	16.1	12.9	43.3	49.4	72.1
Multiple currency	..	..	..	0.0	0.0	0.0	0.0	0.0	0.0	0.0
Special drawing rights	..	..	..	0.0	0.0	0.0	0.0	0.0	0.0	0.0
All other currencies	..	..	..	0.0	0.0	7.2	30.7	23.6	17.5	10.9

ALBANIA

(US$ million, unless otherwise indicated)

	1970	1980	1988	1989	1990	1991	1992	1993	1994	1995
7. DEBT RESTRUCTURINGS										
Total amount rescheduled	0.0	0.0	0.0	0.0	0.0	0.0	0.0	35.1	1.1	225.0
Debt stock rescheduled	0.0	0.0	0.0	0.0	0.0	0.0	0.0	0.0	0.0	225.0
Principal rescheduled	0.0	0.0	0.0	0.0	0.0	0.0	0.0	35.2	0.0	0.0
Official	0.0	0.0	0.0	0.0	0.0	0.0	0.0	0.0	0.0	0.0
Private	0.0	0.0	0.0	0.0	0.0	0.0	0.0	35.2	0.0	0.0
Interest rescheduled	0.0	0.0	0.0	0.0	0.0	0.0	0.0	0.1	0.0	0.0
Official	0.0	0.0	0.0	0.0	0.0	0.0	0.0	0.1	0.0	0.0
Private	0.0	0.0	0.0	0.0	0.0	0.0	0.0	0.0	0.0	0.0
Debt forgiven	..	..	0.0	0.0	0.0	0.0	0.0	0.0	8.4	0.0
Memo: interest forgiven	..	..	0.0	0.0	0.0	0.0	0.0	0.0	0.0	0.0
Debt stock reduction	0.0	0.0	0.0	0.0	0.0	0.0	0.0	0.0	0.0	146.0
of which debt buyback	0.0	0.0	0.0	0.0	0.0	0.0	0.0	0.0	0.0	30.0
8. DEBT STOCK-FLOW RECONCILIATION										
Total change in debt stocks	..	..	..	74.4	274.2	162.9	127.3	192.0	91.7	-213.8
Net flows on debt	..	..	..	74.4	271.6	155.1	135.8	203.3	69.3	-109.0
Net change in interest arrears	..	..	..	0.0	0.0	5.3	3.8	0.4	15.6	1.8
Interest capitalized	..	..	..	0.0	0.0	0.0	0.0	0.1	0.0	0.0
Debt forgiveness or reduction	..	..	..	0.0	0.0	0.0	0.0	0.0	-8.4	-116.0
Cross-currency valuation	..	..	..	0.0	4.9	-1.1	-12.2	-10.9	12.2	8.5
Residual	..	..	..	0.0	-2.3	3.6	0.0	-0.9	3.0	0.9
9. AVERAGE TERMS OF NEW COMMITMENTS										
ALL CREDITORS										
Interest (%)	..	..	..	0.7	10.0	4.7	1.8	0.9	1.7	2.5
Maturity (years)	..	..	..	39.8	4.7	10.9	31.5	36.0	34.6	27.4
Grace period (years)	..	..	..	10.2	2.8	5.1	9.0	9.6	9.2	8.2
Grant element (%)	..	..	..	80.6	-0.4	31.2	65.4	76.3	69.5	58.4
Official creditors										
Interest (%)	..	..	..	0.7	0.0	3.0	1.6	0.9	1.7	2.5
Maturity (years)	..	..	..	39.8	0.0	15.9	32.8	36.0	34.6	27.7
Grace period (years)	..	..	..	10.2	0.0	8.0	9.3	9.6	9.2	8.1
Grant element (%)	..	..	..	80.6	0.0	48.2	67.9	76.3	69.5	58.5
Private creditors										
Interest (%)	..	..	..	0.0	10.0	7.1	5.8	0.0	0.0	3.0
Maturity (years)	..	..	..	0.0	4.7	3.3	5.0	0.0	0.0	22.7
Grace period (years)	..	..	..	0.0	2.8	0.8	1.5	0.0	0.0	11.7
Grant element (%)	..	..	..	0.0	-0.4	5.6	10.8	0.0	0.0	55.9
Memorandum items										
Commitments	..	..	..	1.6	49.8	112.8	76.5	96.3	120.3	143.5
Official creditors	..	..	..	1.6	0.0	67.8	73.1	96.3	120.3	137.3
Private creditors	..	..	..	0.0	49.8	45.0	3.4	0.0	0.0	6.2

10. CONTRACTUAL OBLIGATIONS ON OUTSTANDING LONG-TERM DEBT

	1996	1997	1998	1999	2000	2001	2002	2003	2004	2005
TOTAL										
Disbursements	83.5	83.4	55.9	33.5	16.4	6.2	2.6	0.9	0.5	0.0
Principal	17.0	6.4	8.5	12.4	16.9	7.7	16.6	15.0	17.6	22.0
Interest	19.3	33.7	34.8	35.1	34.8	34.2	33.8	33.2	32.7	32.2
Official creditors										
Disbursements	73.7	81.3	55.1	33.1	16.4	6.2	2.6	0.9	0.5	0.0
Principal	4.3	6.4	8.5	12.4	16.9	7.7	16.6	15.0	17.6	22.0
Interest	5.2	6.9	8.0	8.3	8.0	7.4	7.0	6.5	6.0	5.4
Bilateral creditors										
Disbursements	21.8	20.2	12.7	7.6	3.9	2.0	0.9	0.2	0.0	0.0
Principal	3.5	5.6	7.6	9.7	12.1	1.6	10.0	7.3	8.5	11.0
Interest	3.6	3.7	3.6	3.2	2.7	2.3	2.3	2.1	2.0	1.8
Multilateral creditors										
Disbursements	51.9	61.1	42.4	25.5	12.5	4.2	1.7	0.7	0.5	0.0
Principal	0.8	0.8	0.8	2.7	4.8	6.2	6.6	7.7	9.1	11.0
Interest	1.6	3.2	4.4	5.1	5.3	5.1	4.8	4.4	4.0	3.6
Private creditors										
Disbursements	9.8	2.1	0.8	0.4	0.0	0.0	0.0	0.0	0.0	0.0
Principal	12.7	0.0	0.0	0.0	0.0	0.0	0.0	0.0	0.0	0.0
Interest	14.1	26.7	26.8	26.8	26.8	26.8	26.8	26.8	26.8	26.8
Commercial banks										
Disbursements	3.0	2.1	0.8	0.4	0.0	0.0	0.0	0.0	0.0	0.0
Principal	0.0	0.0	0.0	0.0	0.0	0.0	0.0	0.0	0.0	0.0
Interest	0.1	0.1	0.2	0.2	0.2	0.2	0.2	0.2	0.2	0.2
Other private										
Disbursements	6.8	0.0	0.0	0.0	0.0	0.0	0.0	0.0	0.0	0.0
Principal	12.7	0.0	0.0	0.0	0.0	0.0	0.0	0.0	0.0	0.0
Interest	14.0	26.6	26.6	26.6	26.6	26.6	26.6	26.6	26.6	26.6

ALGERIA

(US$ million, unless otherwise indicated)

	1970	1980	1988	1989	1990	1991	1992	1993	1994	1995
1. SUMMARY DEBT DATA										
TOTAL DEBT STOCKS (EDT)	..	**19,365**	**26,041**	**27,087**	**27,896**	**28,216**	**27,062**	**26,033**	**30,167**	**32,610**
Long-term debt (LDOD)	**940**	**17,040**	**24,421**	**24,629**	**26,435**	**25,981**	**25,473**	**24,861**	**28,371**	**30,442**
Public and publicly guaranteed	940	17,040	24,421	24,629	26,435	25,981	25,473	24,861	28,371	30,442
Private nonguaranteed	0	0	0	0	0	0	0	0	0	0
Use of IMF credit	**0**	**0**	**0**	**619**	**670**	**995**	**795**	**471**	**1,159**	**1,478**
Short-term debt	..	**2,325**	**1,621**	**1,840**	**791**	**1,239**	**794**	**702**	**637**	**690**
of which interest arrears on LDOD	..	0	0	0	0	0	1	2	1	0
Official creditors	..	0	0	0	0	0	0	1	0	0
Private creditors	..	0	0	0	0	0	1	1	1	0
Memo: principal arrears on LDOD	..	2	0	0	1	0	6	8	1	0
Official creditors	..	0	0	0	0	0	1	2	0	0
Private creditors	..	2	0	0	0	0	5	6	1	0
Memo: export credits	..	..	11,150	12,166	13,220	13,538	13,386	14,091	16,882	18,250
TOTAL DEBT FLOWS										
Disbursements	**313**	**3,398**	**6,174**	**6,165**	**6,939**	**6,834**	**7,521**	**6,501**	**5,825**	**3,781**
Long-term debt	313	3,398	6,174	5,561	6,939	6,526	7,521	6,501	4,983	3,307
IMF purchases	0	0	0	604	0	308	0	0	841	475
Principal repayments	**35**	**2,529**	**4,587**	**5,114**	**6,781**	**7,223**	**7,237**	**7,252**	**3,588**	**2,548**
Long-term debt	35	2,529	4,587	5,114	6,781	7,223	7,071	6,923	3,393	2,378
IMF repurchases	0	0	0	0	0	0	166	329	195	171
Net flows on debt	**279**	**869**	**1,892**	**1,270**	**-891**	**58**	**-163**	**-844**	**2,172**	**1,287**
of which short-term debt	..	..	305	219	-1,049	448	-446	-93	-64	54
Interest payments (INT)	..	**1,556**	**1,954**	**1,888**	**2,025**	**1,947**	**2,084**	**1,777**	**1,594**	**1,831**
Long-term debt	10	1,440	1,682	1,740	1,784	1,789	1,815	1,700	1,530	1,734
IMF charges	0	0	0	22	62	59	70	42	31	69
Short-term debt	..	116	272	126	179	100	200	36	33	28
Net transfers on debt	..	**-686**	**-62**	**-618**	**-2,915**	**-1,889**	**-2,247**	**-2,621**	**578**	**-544**
Total debt service paid (TDS)	..	**4,084**	**6,541**	**7,002**	**8,805**	**9,170**	**9,321**	**9,029**	**5,183**	**4,380**
Long-term debt	45	3,968	6,269	6,853	8,564	9,012	8,886	8,623	4,923	4,112
IMF repurchases and charges	0	0	0	22	62	59	235	371	226	240
Short-term debt (interest only)	..	116	272	126	179	100	200	36	33	28
2. AGGREGATE NET RESOURCE FLOWS AND NET TRANSFERS (LONG-TERM)										
NET RESOURCE FLOWS	**381**	**1,295**	**1,656**	**528**	**203**	**-612**	**532**	**-314**	**1,681**	**1,005**
Net flow of long-term debt (ex. IMF)	279	869	1,587	448	158	-698	450	-422	1,591	929
Foreign direct investment (net)	47	349	13	12	0	12	12	15	18	5
Portfolio equity flows	0	0	0	0	0	0	0	0	5	1
Grants (excluding technical coop.)	56	77	56	68	45	73	71	93	67	70
Memo: technical coop. grants	44	96	69	63	107	115	110	123	97	101
NET TRANSFERS	**221**	**-831**	**-513**	**-1,365**	**-1,732**	**-2,732**	**-1,483**	**-2,164**	**21**	**-874**
Interest on long-term debt	10	1,440	1,682	1,740	1,784	1,789	1,815	1,700	1,530	1,734
Profit remittances on FDI	150	687	487	153	152	332	200	150	130	145
3. MAJOR ECONOMIC AGGREGATES										
Gross national product (GNP)	4,760	41,147	56,773	53,043	57,814	43,458	45,709	48,015	40,343	39,265
Exports of goods & services (XGS)	..	14,906	8,541	10,486	13,887	13,026	12,548	12,456	11,272	12,345
of which workers remittances	..	406	379	345	352	233	380	350	310	350
Imports of goods & services (MGS)	..	14,552	10,592	11,762	12,448	10,643	11,418	10,564	11,788	13,580
International reserves (RES)	352	7,064	3,191	3,086	2,704	3,460	3,318	3,656	4,814	4,164
Current account balance	..	249	-2,040	-1,081	1,420	2,367	1,020	802	-1,821	-2,310
4. DEBT INDICATORS										
EDT / XGS (%)	..	129.9	304.9	258.3	200.9	216.6	215.7	209.0	267.6	264.2
EDT / GNP (%)	..	47.1	45.9	51.1	48.3	64.9	59.2	54.2	74.8	83.1
TDS / XGS (%)	..	27.4	76.6	66.8	63.4	70.4	74.3	72.5	46.0	35.5
INT / XGS (%)	..	10.4	22.9	18.0	14.6	14.9	16.6	14.3	14.1	14.8
INT / GNP (%)	..	3.8	3.4	3.6	3.5	4.5	4.6	3.7	4.0	4.7
RES / EDT (%)	..	36.5	12.3	11.4	9.7	12.3	12.3	14.0	16.0	12.8
RES / MGS (months)	..	5.8	3.6	3.1	2.6	3.9	3.5	4.2	4.9	3.7
Short-term / EDT (%)	..	12.0	6.2	6.8	2.8	4.4	2.9	2.7	2.1	2.1
Concessional / EDT (%)	..	6.5	2.3	2.2	3.0	3.3	3.8	4.6	6.8	9.4
Multilateral / EDT (%)	..	1.5	5.3	5.9	7.3	9.5	10.2	11.1	11.1	11.6

ALGERIA

(US$ million, unless otherwise indicated)

	1970	1980	1988	1989	1990	1991	1992	1993	1994	1995
5. LONG-TERM DEBT										
DEBT OUTSTANDING (LDOD)	**940**	**17,040**	**24,421**	**24,629**	**26,435**	**25,981**	**25,473**	**24,861**	**28,371**	**30,442**
Public and publicly guaranteed	**940**	**17,040**	**24,421**	**24,629**	**26,435**	**25,981**	**25,473**	**24,861**	**28,371**	**30,442**
Official creditors	485	3,495	4,698	4,730	5,715	6,469	6,452	6,478	11,001	15,454
Multilateral	16	284	1,391	1,610	2,038	2,668	2,761	2,886	3,344	3,787
Concessional	4	14	49	70	94	116	125	160	172	220
Bilateral	470	3,211	3,306	3,120	3,677	3,802	3,690	3,592	7,657	11,667
Concessional	470	1,239	547	513	734	804	894	1,026	1,889	2,841
Private creditors	454	13,545	19,723	19,899	20,719	19,512	19,022	18,383	17,371	14,988
Bonds	5	410	1,169	1,347	1,420	1,436	1,281	645	261	0
Commercial banks	20	5,503	7,580	6,764	6,052	5,024	5,320	4,878	4,912	4,714
Other private	430	7,632	10,974	11,787	13,247	13,052	12,421	12,859	12,198	10,274
Private nonguaranteed	**0**	**0**	**0**	**0**	**0**	**0**	**0**	**0**	**0**	**0**
Bonds	0	0	0	0	0	0	0	0	0	0
Commercial banks	0	0	0	0	0	0	0	0	0	0
Memo:										
IBRD	16	253	895	960	1,208	1,413	1,474	1,512	1,709	2,049
IDA	0	0	0	0	0	0	0	0	0	0
DISBURSEMENTS	**313**	**3,398**	**6,174**	**5,561**	**6,939**	**6,526**	**7,521**	**6,501**	**4,983**	**3,307**
Public and publicly guaranteed	**313**	**3,398**	**6,174**	**5,561**	**6,939**	**6,526**	**7,521**	**6,501**	**4,983**	**3,307**
Official creditors	45	566	769	1,138	1,855	1,829	1,475	1,310	1,781	1,480
Multilateral	0	54	468	459	613	955	553	473	700	797
Concessional	0	1	9	27	24	29	29	43	15	56
Bilateral	45	512	300	679	1,241	874	922	837	1,081	683
Concessional	45	73	35	53	268	132	196	221	508	403
Private creditors	268	2,832	5,406	4,423	5,084	4,696	6,046	5,191	3,202	1,827
Bonds	5	30	448	232	0	1	0	0	0	0
Commercial banks	17	891	1,394	355	406	170	1,256	459	117	241
Other private	246	1,911	3,565	3,836	4,678	4,525	4,791	4,732	3,085	1,585
Private nonguaranteed	**0**	**0**	**0**	**0**	**0**	**0**	**0**	**0**	**0**	**0**
Bonds	0	0	0	0	0	0	0	0	0	0
Commercial banks	0	0	0	0	0	0	0	0	0	0
Memo:										
IBRD	0	39	170	204	300	347	268	176	300	554
IDA	0	0	0	0	0	0	0	0	0	0
PRINCIPAL REPAYMENTS	**35**	**2,529**	**4,587**	**5,114**	**6,781**	**7,223**	**7,071**	**6,923**	**3,393**	**2,378**
Public and publicly guaranteed	**35**	**2,529**	**4,587**	**5,114**	**6,781**	**7,223**	**7,071**	**6,923**	**3,393**	**2,378**
Official creditors	13	244	966	1,011	1,204	1,292	1,244	1,263	701	674
Multilateral	3	42	208	214	314	392	343	358	439	455
Concessional	1	1	4	6	6	8	11	11	11	12
Bilateral	10	203	758	797	890	900	900	904	262	220
Concessional	10	72	94	85	97	77	77	76	42	27
Private creditors	22	2,284	3,621	4,103	5,577	5,931	5,827	5,661	2,692	1,703
Bonds	0	15	98	40	16	5	129	663	445	278
Commercial banks	2	918	704	905	1,330	1,326	938	1,107	383	218
Other private	19	1,352	2,819	3,158	4,231	4,601	4,760	3,891	1,865	1,208
Private nonguaranteed	**0**	**0**	**0**	**0**	**0**	**0**	**0**	**0**	**0**	**0**
Bonds	0	0	0	0	0	0	0	0	0	0
Commercial banks	0	0	0	0	0	0	0	0	0	0
Memo:										
IBRD	3	13	112	112	130	176	166	170	208	260
IDA	0	0	0	0	0	0	0	0	0	0
NET FLOWS ON DEBT	**279**	**869**	**1,587**	**448**	**158**	**-698**	**450**	**-422**	**1,591**	**929**
Public and publicly guaranteed	**279**	**869**	**1,587**	**448**	**158**	**-698**	**450**	**-422**	**1,591**	**929**
Official creditors	32	322	-198	127	651	538	231	47	1,080	806
Multilateral	-3	13	260	245	299	563	210	115	261	342
Concessional	-1	0	5	21	18	21	18	32	4	43
Bilateral	35	309	-458	-118	351	-26	21	-68	820	464
Concessional	35	1	-59	-32	171	56	119	145	465	376
Private creditors	247	548	1,785	320	-493	-1,235	219	-470	510	123
Bonds	5	15	350	192	-16	-4	-129	-663	-445	-278
Commercial banks	15	-27	689	-550	-924	-1,155	318	-648	-265	24
Other private	227	559	746	678	447	-76	30	841	1,220	378
Private nonguaranteed	**0**	**0**	**0**	**0**	**0**	**0**	**0**	**0**	**0**	**0**
Bonds	0	0	0	0	0	0	0	0	0	0
Commercial banks	0	0	0	0	0	0	0	0	0	0
Memo:										
IBRD	-3	26	58	92	170	171	101	6	92	294
IDA	0	0	0	0	0	0	0	0	0	0

ALGERIA

(US$ million, unless otherwise indicated)

	1970	1980	1988	1989	1990	1991	1992	1993	1994	1995
INTEREST PAYMENTS (LINT)	**10**	**1,440**	**1,682**	**1,740**	**1,784**	**1,789**	**1,815**	**1,700**	**1,530**	**1,734**
Public and publicly guaranteed	**10**	**1,440**	**1,682**	**1,740**	**1,784**	**1,789**	**1,815**	**1,700**	**1,530**	**1,734**
Official creditors	4	159	329	307	317	356	391	383	393	812
Multilateral	1	29	93	97	117	154	197	206	206	256
Concessional	0	1	3	5	5	6	7	7	8	9
Bilateral	3	130	236	210	201	203	194	177	188	556
Concessional	3	32	16	12	14	17	19	20	31	84
Private creditors	6	1,280	1,353	1,433	1,466	1,432	1,424	1,316	1,137	922
Bonds	0	45	63	91	105	98	90	68	49	13
Commercial banks	0	672	529	564	526	446	358	355	343	253
Other private	6	563	760	779	836	889	976	893	745	657
Private nonguaranteed	**0**	**0**	**0**	**0**	**0**	**0**	**0**	**0**	**0**	**0**
Bonds	0	0	0	0	0	0	0	0	0	0
Commercial banks	0	0	0	0	0	0	0	0	0	0
Memo:										
IBRD	1	25	72	70	73	107	112	113	119	137
IDA	0	0	0	0	0	0	0	0	0	0
NET TRANSFERS ON DEBT	**269**	**-570**	**-95**	**-1,292**	**-1,626**	**-2,486**	**-1,365**	**-2,122**	**61**	**-805**
Public and publicly guaranteed	**269**	**-570**	**-95**	**-1,292**	**-1,626**	**-2,486**	**-1,365**	**-2,122**	**61**	**-805**
Official creditors	28	162	-527	-180	333	181	-160	-336	687	-6
Multilateral	-4	-17	167	149	183	410	13	-92	55	86
Concessional	-1	-1	2	16	13	15	11	25	-4	34
Bilateral	32	179	-694	-328	151	-228	-173	-245	632	-92
Concessional	32	-31	-75	-44	156	39	100	125	434	292
Private creditors	240	-732	432	-1,113	-1,959	-2,667	-1,206	-1,786	-626	-799
Bonds	5	-30	286	101	-120	-102	-220	-731	-493	-291
Commercial banks	14	-699	161	-1,113	-1,450	-1,601	-40	-1,003	-608	-229
Other private	221	-4	-15	-101	-389	-964	-946	-52	475	-279
Private nonguaranteed	**0**	**0**	**0**	**0**	**0**	**0**	**0**	**0**	**0**	**0**
Bonds	0	0	0	0	0	0	0	0	0	0
Commercial banks	0	0	0	0	0	0	0	0	0	0
Memo:										
IBRD	-4	0	-14	21	97	64	-11	-107	-27	157
IDA	0	0	0	0	0	0	0	0	0	0
DEBT SERVICE (LTDS)	**45**	**3,968**	**6,269**	**6,853**	**8,564**	**9,012**	**8,886**	**8,623**	**4,923**	**4,112**
Public and publicly guaranteed	**45**	**3,968**	**6,269**	**6,853**	**8,564**	**9,012**	**8,886**	**8,623**	**4,923**	**4,112**
Official creditors	17	404	1,296	1,317	1,521	1,648	1,634	1,646	1,094	1,486
Multilateral	4	71	302	310	431	545	540	565	645	711
Concessional	1	2	7	11	11	14	18	18	19	22
Bilateral	13	333	994	1,007	1,091	1,103	1,094	1,081	449	775
Concessional	13	104	109	97	112	94	96	97	73	111
Private creditors	28	3,564	4,973	5,536	7,043	7,364	7,252	6,977	3,829	2,626
Bonds	0	60	161	131	120	103	220	731	493	291
Commercial banks	3	1,590	1,233	1,468	1,856	1,771	1,296	1,462	725	470
Other private	25	1,915	3,579	3,937	5,067	5,490	5,736	4,784	2,610	1,865
Private nonguaranteed	**0**	**0**	**0**	**0**	**0**	**0**	**0**	**0**	**0**	**0**
Bonds	0	0	0	0	0	0	0	0	0	0
Commercial banks	0	0	0	0	0	0	0	0	0	0
Memo:										
IBRD	4	39	184	183	203	283	278	282	327	397
IDA	0	0	0	0	0	0	0	0	0	0
UNDISBURSED DEBT	**738**	**11,717**	**8,531**	**11,612**	**12,721**	**14,727**	**14,411**	**13,916**	**10,139**	**8,274**
Official creditors	579	4,169	3,230	5,166	5,347	5,986	5,631	6,438	5,020	4,474
Private creditors	159	7,548	5,301	6,446	7,374	8,741	8,780	7,478	5,119	3,800
Memorandum items										
Concessional LDOD	473	1,252	597	583	828	920	1,019	1,186	2,062	3,061
Variable rate LDOD	26	4,265	9,228	9,955	10,721	10,614	11,906	12,442	14,791	16,428
Public sector LDOD	940	17,040	24,413	24,594	26,354	25,885	25,354	24,756	28,276	30,353
Private sector LDOD	0	0	8	35	80	97	120	105	95	89

6. CURRENCY COMPOSITION OF LONG-TERM DEBT (PERCENT)

	1970	1980	1988	1989	1990	1991	1992	1993	1994	1995
Deutsche mark	1.9	9.9	6.8	9.0	10.5	10.1	8.3	6.5	6.2	7.2
French franc	36.0	10.9	14.6	14.8	16.8	15.8	13.1	12.0	13.7	16.0
Japanese yen	0.0	13.4	19.1	15.7	15.2	15.8	15.4	15.7	15.0	13.0
Pound sterling	8.3	2.2	2.0	1.6	1.5	1.4	1.1	0.9	1.0	0.9
Swiss franc	0.2	2.7	1.3	1.2	0.8	0.6	0.6	0.6	0.7	0.8
U.S.dollars	37.0	41.5	37.2	37.5	33.9	34.0	39.8	43.4	41.6	39.1
Multiple currency	1.7	3.4	3.7	4.0	4.9	6.3	6.9	7.4	7.4	8.1
Special drawing rights	0.0	0.0	0.0	0.0	0.0	0.0	0.0	0.0	0.0	0.0
All other currencies	15.1	16.0	15.4	16.2	16.4	16.1	14.9	13.5	14.5	14.8

ALGERIA

(US$ million, unless otherwise indicated)

	1970	1980	1988	1989	1990	1991	1992	1993	1994	1995
7. DEBT RESTRUCTURINGS										
Total amount rescheduled	0	0	0	0	0	0	0	0	4,251	4,838
Debt stock rescheduled	0	0	0	0	0	0	0	0	0	0
Principal rescheduled	0	0	0	0	0	0	0	0	3,720	4,427
Official	0	0	0	0	0	0	0	0	639	629
Private	0	0	0	0	0	0	0	0	3,082	3,798
Interest rescheduled	0	0	0	0	0	0	0	0	428	387
Official	0	0	0	0	0	0	0	0	88	71
Private	0	0	0	0	0	0	0	0	340	316
Debt forgiven	..	..	0	0	0	0	0	0	0	0
Memo: interest forgiven	..	..	0	0	0	0	0	0	0	0
Debt stock reduction	0	0	0	0	0	0	0	0	0	0
of which debt buyback	0	0	0	0	0	0	0	0	0	0
8. DEBT STOCK-FLOW RECONCILIATION										
Total change in debt stocks	..	..	..	1,046	808	320	-1,154	-1,029	4,133	2,443
Net flows on debt	..	..	..	1,270	-891	58	-163	-844	2,172	1,287
Net change in interest arrears	..	..	..	0	0	0	1	0	-1	-1
Interest capitalized	..	..	..	0	0	0	0	0	428	387
Debt forgiveness or reduction	..	..	..	0	0	0	0	0	0	0
Cross-currency valuation	..	..	..	-168	1,827	183	-860	-137	1,535	820
Residual	..	..	..	-56	-128	79	-132	-48	-2	-50
9. AVERAGE TERMS OF NEW COMMITMENTS										
ALL CREDITORS										
Interest (%)	5.7	8.1	7.4	7.7	8.4	7.4	5.7	5.6	6.0	6.3
Maturity (years)	12.7	12.3	7.3	10.9	8.9	9.3	10.7	9.7	8.6	7.7
Grace period (years)	3.6	3.5	2.7	3.3	2.5	3.5	4.7	4.3	2.6	2.4
Grant element (%)	23.1	8.3	8.4	10.1	6.9	10.2	19.8	17.4	12.0	10.6
Official creditors										
Interest (%)	2.8	7.7	6.2	7.5	7.1	7.8	6.0	5.5	7.3	5.5
Maturity (years)	23.9	17.6	8.8	14.7	16.4	14.8	15.0	13.2	15.1	8.9
Grace period (years)	9.2	5.1	3.4	5.5	3.9	6.6	6.8	6.3	5.2	2.6
Grant element (%)	54.4	13.5	15.1	13.9	18.4	13.4	24.4	23.1	13.1	13.0
Private creditors										
Interest (%)	6.4	8.4	7.7	7.9	8.9	7.2	5.7	5.6	5.5	7.3
Maturity (years)	9.8	9.3	7.0	8.8	6.3	7.6	9.8	8.0	6.0	5.8
Grace period (years)	2.1	2.6	2.6	2.1	2.1	2.5	4.3	3.2	1.6	2.0
Grant element (%)	14.9	5.4	7.2	8.0	2.8	9.2	18.9	14.5	11.6	7.0
Memorandum items										
Commitments	378	3,538	9,546	9,839	8,057	10,747	9,995	6,505	2,765	1,759
Official creditors	79	1,258	1,393	3,478	2,119	2,585	1,685	2,156	782	1,049
Private creditors	299	2,279	8,153	6,361	5,938	8,163	8,311	4,348	1,983	710

10. CONTRACTUAL OBLIGATIONS ON OUTSTANDING LONG-TERM DEBT

	1996	1997	1998	1999	2000	2001	2002	2003	2004	2005
TOTAL										
Disbursements	4,105	1,920	933	444	232	124	62	35	24	11
Principal	2,362	1,686	2,846	2,839	2,609	2,338	2,101	2,064	1,982	1,995
Interest	2,084	2,354	2,193	2,002	1,832	1,666	1,515	1,374	1,237	1,106
Official creditors										
Disbursements	1,566	1,119	662	386	219	124	62	35	24	11
Principal	785	874	1,005	1,170	1,320	1,288	1,235	1,299	1,361	1,473
Interest	1,175	1,416	1,450	1,404	1,339	1,258	1,177	1,095	1,010	919
Bilateral creditors										
Disbursements	1,089	618	313	134	56	26	9	5	3	0
Principal	263	281	472	649	802	784	831	933	1,040	1,198
Interest	878	1,124	1,172	1,146	1,107	1,057	1,007	952	890	820
Multilateral creditors										
Disbursements	477	502	350	252	164	98	54	30	21	11
Principal	521	592	533	521	518	505	404	367	321	275
Interest	296	292	278	258	232	201	170	144	120	99
Private creditors										
Disbursements	2,539	801	271	58	12	0	0	0	0	0
Principal	1,577	813	1,841	1,670	1,289	1,050	866	765	620	522
Interest	909	938	743	598	494	408	338	279	228	187
Commercial banks										
Disbursements	232	89	29	4	0	0	0	0	0	0
Principal	243	226	514	408	456	535	467	443	366	313
Interest	346	332	303	274	248	214	180	149	120	98
Other private										
Disbursements	2,307	712	242	54	12	0	0	0	0	0
Principal	1,334	587	1,326	1,262	833	515	400	322	254	210
Interest	564	606	440	324	245	194	158	130	107	89

ANGOLA

(US$ million, unless otherwise indicated)

	1970	1980	1988	1989	1990	1991	1992	1993	1994	1995
1. SUMMARY DEBT DATA										
TOTAL DEBT STOCKS (EDT)	..	..	**6,290**	**7,205**	**8,443**	**8,874**	**9,940**	**10,486**	**11,293**	**11,482**
Long-term debt (LDOD)	..	..	**5,901**	**6,591**	**7,483**	**7,605**	**8,015**	**8,591**	**9,133**	**9,533**
Public and publicly guaranteed	..	..	5,901	6,591	7,483	7,605	8,015	8,591	9,133	9,533
Private nonguaranteed	0	0	0	0	0	0	0	0	0	0
Use of IMF credit	**0**	**0**	**0**	**0**	**0**	**0**	**0**	**0**	**0**	**0**
Short-term debt	..	..	**388**	**613**	**959**	**1,270**	**1,925**	**1,895**	**2,160**	**1,949**
of which interest arrears on LDOD	..	..	81	74	174	354	605	904	1,127	1,224
Official creditors	..	..	18	11	51	106	147	201	240	264
Private creditors	..	..	63	64	123	248	458	702	887	959
Memo: principal arrears on LDOD	..	..	236	268	502	1,194	1,938	3,114	3,716	4,291
Official creditors	..	..	41	48	96	361	586	861	921	1,190
Private creditors	..	..	195	219	406	833	1,352	2,253	2,795	3,101
Memo: export credits	..	..	1,067	1,302	1,639	1,596	1,870	2,147	2,124	2,108
TOTAL DEBT FLOWS										
Disbursements	..	..	**718**	**503**	**806**	**327**	**643**	**692**	**427**	**493**
Long-term debt	..	..	718	503	806	327	643	692	427	493
IMF purchases	0	0	0	0	0	0	0	0	0	0
Principal repayments	..	..	**97**	**128**	**176**	**199**	**150**	**60**	**146**	**329**
Long-term debt	..	..	97	128	176	199	150	60	146	329
IMF repurchases	0	0	0	0	0	0	0	0	0	0
Net flows on debt	..	..	**800**	**797**	**927**	**259**	**897**	**303**	**322**	**-144**
of which short-term debt	..	..	180	422	298	131	404	-329	42	-308
Interest payments (INT)	..	..	**136**	**124**	**144**	**137**	**100**	**90**	**104**	**130**
Long-term debt	..	..	105	99	101	84	46	24	49	77
IMF charges	0	0	0	0	0	0	0	0	0	0
Short-term debt	..	..	31	25	43	53	54	66	55	53
Net transfers on debt	..	..	**664**	**674**	**784**	**123**	**797**	**212**	**218**	**-274**
Total debt service paid (TDS)	..	..	**233**	**252**	**320**	**336**	**250**	**150**	**250**	**458**
Long-term debt	..	..	202	227	277	283	196	84	195	406
IMF repurchases and charges	0	0	0	0	0	0	0	0	0	0
Short-term debt (interest only)	..	..	31	25	43	53	54	66	55	53
2. AGGREGATE NET RESOURCE FLOWS AND NET TRANSFERS (LONG-TERM)										
NET RESOURCE FLOWS	..	..	**849**	**679**	**487**	**982**	**966**	**1,104**	**931**	**891**
Net flow of long-term debt (ex. IMF)	..	43	620	375	629	128	493	632	280	164
Foreign direct investment (net)	0	0	131	200	-335	665	288	302	350	400
Portfolio equity flows	..	..	0	0	0	0	0	0	0	0
Grants (excluding technical coop.)	0	32	97	103	192	189	186	170	301	327
Memo: technical coop. grants	0	16	43	50	36	57	94	76	73	80
NET TRANSFERS	..	..	**559**	**277**	**72**	**585**	**558**	**679**	**472**	**364**
Interest on long-term debt	..	..	105	99	101	84	46	24	49	77
Profit remittances on FDI	0	0	185	303	314	313	362	400	410	450
3. MAJOR ECONOMIC AGGREGATES										
Gross national product (GNP)	..	..	6,633	7,783	7,330	3,689	4,066	2,995	4,104	4,176
Exports of goods & services (XGS)	..	..	2,620	3,164	4,003	3,636	3,991	3,017	3,121	3,653
of which workers remittances	..	..	0	0	0	0	0	0	0	0
Imports of goods & services (MGS)	..	..	3,121	3,292	4,161	4,243	4,828	3,615	3,906	4,260
International reserves (RES)	..	..	..	..	..	..	..	..	..	..
Current account balance	..	..	-469	-132	-236	-580	-735	-500	-780	-527
4. DEBT INDICATORS										
EDT / XGS (%)	..	..	240.1	227.7	210.9	244.1	249.0	347.6	361.8	314.3
EDT / GNP (%)	..	..	94.8	92.6	115.2	240.6	244.5	350.1	275.2	274.9
TDS / XGS (%)	..	..	8.9	8.0	8.0	9.2	6.3	5.0	8.0	12.5
INT / XGS (%)	..	..	5.2	3.9	3.6	3.8	2.5	3.0	3.3	3.5
INT / GNP (%)	..	..	2.1	1.6	2.0	3.7	2.5	3.0	2.5	3.1
RES / EDT (%)	..	..	..	..	..	..	..	..	..	..
RES / MGS (months)	..	..	..	..	..	..	..	..	..	..
Short-term / EDT (%)	..	..	6.2	8.5	11.4	14.3	19.4	18.1	19.1	17.0
Concessional / EDT (%)	..	..	10.0	12.5	14.3	14.3	13.0	12.6	12.5	13.0
Multilateral / EDT (%)	..	..	0.8	0.8	0.7	1.1	1.1	1.2	1.4	1.7

ANGOLA

(US$ million, unless otherwise indicated)

	1970	1980	1988	1989	1990	1991	1992	1993	1994	1995
5. LONG-TERM DEBT										
DEBT OUTSTANDING (LDOD)	..	..	**5,901**	**6,591**	**7,483**	**7,605**	**8,015**	**8,591**	**9,133**	**9,533**
Public and publicly guaranteed	..	..	**5,901**	**6,591**	**7,483**	**7,605**	**8,015**	**8,591**	**9,133**	**9,533**
Official creditors	..	..	1,179	1,499	1,878	1,941	1,959	1,971	2,220	2,306
Multilateral	..	..	51	55	59	96	112	125	163	195
Concessional	..	..	11	16	22	38	43	53	89	121
Bilateral	..	..	1,128	1,444	1,819	1,845	1,847	1,846	2,057	2,112
Concessional	..	..	620	886	1,183	1,230	1,254	1,264	1,321	1,371
Private creditors	..	..	4,722	5,093	5,605	5,664	6,056	6,620	6,913	7,227
Bonds	..	..	0	0	0	0	0	0	0	0
Commercial banks	..	..	183	197	193	201	212	227	610	1,307
Other private	..	..	4,539	4,896	5,412	5,463	5,843	6,392	6,303	5,920
Private nonguaranteed	**0**	**0**	**0**	**0**	**0**	**0**	**0**	**0**	**0**	**0**
Bonds	..	..	0	0	0	0	0	0	0	0
Commercial banks	..	..	0	0	0	0	0	0	0	0
Memo:										
IBRD	0	0	0	0	0	0	0	0	0	0
IDA	0	0	0	0	0	0	6	15	50	81
DISBURSEMENTS	..	..	**718**	**503**	**806**	**327**	**643**	**692**	**427**	**493**
Public and publicly guaranteed	..	..	**718**	**503**	**806**	**327**	**643**	**692**	**427**	**493**
Official creditors	..	..	69	111	163	125	101	59	72	69
Multilateral	..	..	10	8	5	37	19	14	33	30
Concessional	..	..	7	5	5	16	6	10	33	30
Bilateral	..	..	59	103	158	88	81	45	39	38
Concessional	..	..	21	19	44	51	39	28	39	32
Private creditors	..	..	649	393	643	202	542	633	354	424
Bonds	..	..	0	0	0	0	0	0	0	0
Commercial banks	..	..	9	17	16	15	22	16	299	396
Other private	..	..	640	376	627	187	521	616	55	28
Private nonguaranteed	**0**	**0**	**0**	**0**	**0**	**0**	**0**	**0**	**0**	**0**
Bonds	..	..	0	0	0	0	0	0	0	0
Commercial banks	..	..	0	0	0	0	0	0	0	0
Memo:										
IBRD	0	0	0	0	0	0	0	0	0	0
IDA	0	0	0	0	0	0	6	10	33	30
PRINCIPAL REPAYMENTS	..	..	**97**	**128**	**176**	**199**	**150**	**60**	**146**	**329**
Public and publicly guaranteed	..	..	**97**	**128**	**176**	**199**	**150**	**60**	**146**	**329**
Official creditors	..	..	39	62	63	61	44	25	42	28
Multilateral	..	..	4	4	4	2	0	0	0	1
Concessional	..	..	0	0	0	0	0	0	0	0
Bilateral	..	..	35	58	59	59	44	25	42	27
Concessional	..	..	1	0	2	4	2	2	7	5
Private creditors	..	..	58	66	113	138	106	35	105	300
Bonds	..	..	0	0	0	0	0	0	0	0
Commercial banks	..	..	6	21	24	7	6	1	48	107
Other private	..	..	52	44	90	131	101	35	57	193
Private nonguaranteed	**0**	**0**	**0**	**0**	**0**	**0**	**0**	**0**	**0**	**0**
Bonds	..	..	0	0	0	0	0	0	0	0
Commercial banks	..	..	0	0	0	0	0	0	0	0
Memo:										
IBRD	0	0	0	0	0	0	0	0	0	0
IDA	0	0	0	0	0	0	0	0	0	0
NET FLOWS ON DEBT	..	..	**620**	**375**	**629**	**128**	**493**	**632**	**280**	**164**
Public and publicly guaranteed	..	..	**620**	**375**	**629**	**128**	**493**	**632**	**280**	**164**
Official creditors	..	..	29	48	100	65	57	34	31	40
Multilateral	..	..	6	4	1	36	19	14	33	29
Concessional	..	..	6	5	5	16	6	10	33	30
Bilateral	..	..	24	44	99	29	38	20	-3	11
Concessional	..	..	20	19	42	47	37	26	32	28
Private creditors	..	..	591	327	530	64	436	598	250	123
Bonds	..	..	0	0	0	0	0	0	0	0
Commercial banks	..	..	2	-5	-8	8	16	16	252	289
Other private	..	..	589	332	537	56	420	582	-2	-166
Private nonguaranteed	**0**	**0**	**0**	**0**	**0**	**0**	**0**	**0**	**0**	**0**
Bonds	..	..	0	0	0	0	0	0	0	0
Commercial banks	..	..	0	0	0	0	0	0	0	0
Memo:										
IBRD	0	0	0	0	0	0	0	0	0	0
IDA	0	0	0	0	0	0	6	10	33	30

ANGOLA

(US$ million, unless otherwise indicated)

	1970	1980	1988	1989	1990	1991	1992	1993	1994	1995
INTEREST PAYMENTS (LINT)	..	..	**105**	**99**	**101**	**84**	**46**	**24**	**49**	**77**
Public and publicly guaranteed	..	..	**105**	**99**	**101**	**84**	**46**	**24**	**49**	**77**
Official creditors	..	..	33	23	26	22	15	8	10	13
Multilateral	..	..	2	2	2	3	5	0	0	1
Concessional	..	..	0	0	0	0	0	0	0	0
Bilateral	..	..	31	21	24	19	10	8	10	12
Concessional	..	..	3	2	1	3	2	3	6	7
Private creditors	..	..	72	76	74	62	31	16	39	64
Bonds	..	..	0	0	0	0	0	0	0	0
Commercial banks	..	..	8	12	8	5	5	3	11	31
Other private	..	..	64	64	67	57	27	14	28	34
Private nonguaranteed	**0**	**0**	**0**	**0**	**0**	**0**	**0**	**0**	**0**	**0**
Bonds	..	..	0	0	0	0	0	0	0	0
Commercial banks	..	..	0	0	0	0	0	0	0	0
Memo:										
IBRD	0	0	0	0	0	0	0	0	0	0
IDA	0	0	0	0	0	0	0	0	0	0
NET TRANSFERS ON DEBT	..	..	**515**	**276**	**529**	**45**	**447**	**607**	**231**	**87**
Public and publicly guaranteed	..	..	**515**	**276**	**529**	**45**	**447**	**607**	**231**	**87**
Official creditors	..	..	-3	25	74	43	42	26	20	28
Multilateral	..	..	4	2	-2	33	14	14	33	28
Concessional	..	..	6	5	4	15	6	10	33	30
Bilateral	..	..	-7	24	75	10	28	12	-13	-1
Concessional	..	..	17	17	41	44	35	23	26	21
Private creditors	..	..	519	251	455	2	405	581	211	59
Bonds	..	..	0	0	0	0	0	0	0	0
Commercial banks	..	..	-6	-16	-15	2	11	13	241	258
Other private	..	..	525	267	471	-1	393	568	-30	-199
Private nonguaranteed	**0**	**0**	**0**	**0**	**0**	**0**	**0**	**0**	**0**	**0**
Bonds	..	..	0	0	0	0	0	0	0	0
Commercial banks	..	..	0	0	0	0	0	0	0	0
Memo:										
IBRD	0	0	0	0	0	0	0	0	0	0
IDA	0	0	0	0	0	0	6	10	33	30
DEBT SERVICE (LTDS)	..	..	**202**	**227**	**277**	**283**	**196**	**84**	**195**	**406**
Public and publicly guaranteed	..	..	**202**	**227**	**277**	**283**	**196**	**84**	**195**	**406**
Official creditors	..	..	72	85	89	82	59	33	52	41
Multilateral	..	..	6	7	6	5	5	0	0	2
Concessional	..	..	0	0	0	0	0	0	0	0
Bilateral	..	..	66	79	83	77	53	33	52	39
Concessional	..	..	4	2	3	7	3	5	13	12
Private creditors	..	..	130	142	188	201	138	51	143	364
Bonds	..	..	0	0	0	0	0	0	0	0
Commercial banks	..	..	15	33	31	13	10	3	58	138
Other private	..	..	116	109	156	188	127	48	85	227
Private nonguaranteed	**0**	**0**	**0**	**0**	**0**	**0**	**0**	**0**	**0**	**0**
Bonds	..	..	0	0	0	0	0	0	0	0
Commercial banks	..	..	0	0	0	0	0	0	0	0
Memo:										
IBRD	0	0	0	0	0	0	0	0	0	0
IDA	0	0	0	0	0	0	0	0	0	0
UNDISBURSED DEBT	..	..	**1,754**	**1,650**	**1,393**	**1,461**	**1,585**	**1,297**	**1,135**	**1,073**
Official creditors	..	..	358	403	481	589	777	692	655	554
Private creditors	..	..	1,396	1,246	912	873	808	605	480	519
Memorandum items										
Concessional LDOD	..	..	631	902	1,205	1,268	1,296	1,317	1,410	1,492
Variable rate LDOD	..	..	239	402	440	420	368	372	554	797
Public sector LDOD	..	..	5,889	6,585	7,478	7,600	8,008	8,584	9,104	9,504
Private sector LDOD	..	..	12	6	5	5	7	7	30	30

6. CURRENCY COMPOSITION OF LONG-TERM DEBT (PERCENT)

	1970	1980	1988	1989	1990	1991	1992	1993	1994	1995
Deutsche mark	..	..	0.2	0.4	0.3	0.3	0.2	0.2	0.2	0.2
French franc	..	..	2.8	3.7	3.6	3.8	3.6	3.6	4.0	4.4
Japanese yen	..	..	0.4	0.4	0.3	0.4	0.4	0.4	0.4	0.4
Pound sterling	..	..	1.2	1.1	1.5	1.4	1.0	0.9	0.9	0.9
Swiss franc	..	..	0.3	0.2	0.7	0.4	0.2	0.1	0.1	0.1
U.S.dollars	..	..	80.9	80.9	80.3	80.3	81.7	82.5	80.9	80.3
Multiple currency	..	..	0.5	0.5	0.5	1.0	1.1	1.1	1.0	1.0
Special drawing rights	..	..	0.0	0.0	0.0	0.0	0.0	0.1	0.3	0.5
All other currencies	..	..	13.6	12.8	12.7	12.6	11.8	11.2	12.1	12.1

ANGOLA

(US$ million, unless otherwise indicated)

	1970	1980	1988	1989	1990	1991	1992	1993	1994	1995
7. DEBT RESTRUCTURINGS										
Total amount rescheduled	0	0	467	600	262	0	0	0	365	437
Debt stock rescheduled	0	0	262	195	53	0	0	0	0	0
Principal rescheduled	0	0	148	286	155	0	0	0	206	293
Official	0	0	22	36	16	0	0	0	39	0
Private	0	0	126	250	139	0	0	0	167	293
Interest rescheduled	0	0	40	116	40	0	0	0	44	70
Official	0	0	10	28	6	0	0	0	8	0
Private	0	0	30	88	34	0	0	0	36	70
Debt forgiven	..	..	0	0	0	0	0	0	0	0
Memo: interest forgiven	..	..	0	0	0	0	0	0	0	0
Debt stock reduction	0	0	0	0	0	0	0	0	0	0
of which debt buyback	0	0	0	0	0	0	0	0	0	0
8. DEBT STOCK-FLOW RECONCILIATION										
Total change in debt stocks	..	..	..	915	1,238	432	1,065	546	807	189
Net flows on debt	..	..	..	797	927	259	897	303	322	-144
Net change in interest arrears	..	..	..	-7	100	179	251	299	223	97
Interest capitalized	..	..	..	116	40	0	0	0	44	70
Debt forgiveness or reduction	..	..	..	0	0	0	0	0	0	0
Cross-currency valuation	..	..	..	14	181	-8	-70	-56	115	96
Residual	..	..	..	-5	-10	1	-12	1	102	70
9. AVERAGE TERMS OF NEW COMMITMENTS										
ALL CREDITORS										
Interest (%)	..	..	6.3	6.5	6.9	5.0	5.6	6.5	6.1	8.1
Maturity (years)	..	..	13.7	8.2	11.3	17.5	13.0	6.1	3.7	8.7
Grace period (years)	..	..	3.3	3.0	2.6	4.6	3.1	1.3	0.6	0.4
Grant element (%)	..	..	19.7	15.6	14.4	31.3	22.8	9.6	6.7	5.5
Official creditors										
Interest (%)	..	..	6.4	7.4	5.8	3.4	3.3	0.7	3.0	8.1
Maturity (years)	..	..	16.9	8.9	16.7	26.1	28.7	39.8	30.3	9.9
Grace period (years)	..	..	3.6	2.6	3.7	6.4	7.0	10.3	2.3	0.4
Grant element (%)	..	..	22.2	12.8	22.1	49.8	51.9	80.6	50.1	6.4
Private creditors										
Interest (%)	..	..	6.2	6.0	7.7	7.1	6.9	6.8	6.2	8.1
Maturity (years)	..	..	11.1	7.8	7.4	6.3	4.0	4.6	3.0	8.7
Grace period (years)	..	..	3.1	3.2	1.8	2.2	0.9	0.9	0.6	0.4
Grant element (%)	..	..	17.7	17.4	9.1	7.2	6.0	6.4	5.6	5.5
Memorandum items										
Commitments	..	..	350	402	525	404	862	459	280	476
Official creditors	..	..	157	156	216	229	315	20	7	6
Private creditors	..	..	193	246	309	175	548	439	273	470

10. CONTRACTUAL OBLIGATIONS ON OUTSTANDING LONG-TERM DEBT

	1996	1997	1998	1999	2000	2001	2002	2003	2004	2005
TOTAL										
Disbursements	220	103	54	32	15	6	4	1	0	0
Principal	1,239	879	581	671	407	328	293	254	246	171
Interest	292	227	173	142	107	84	66	51	37	24
Official creditors										
Disbursements	101	76	50	30	15	6	4	1	0	0
Principal	310	119	120	112	88	72	72	41	33	32
Interest	47	38	31	25	19	15	12	9	8	7
Bilateral creditors										
Disbursements	41	21	10	6	2	2	1	1	0	0
Principal	299	113	113	105	82	64	62	31	25	23
Interest	42	32	26	20	15	11	8	6	5	4
Multilateral creditors										
Disbursements	60	55	40	24	13	5	3	0	0	0
Principal	11	7	7	7	7	8	9	10	8	8
Interest	6	6	5	5	5	4	4	4	3	3
Private creditors										
Disbursements	119	27	5	2	0	0	0	0	0	0
Principal	929	760	461	559	319	256	222	213	213	139
Interest	245	189	142	117	88	69	54	42	29	18
Commercial banks										
Disbursements	37	11	4	2	0	0	0	0	0	0
Principal	219	178	117	99	92	90	90	90	90	56
Interest	81	70	58	51	44	37	31	24	18	12
Other private										
Disbursements	82	16	0	0	0	0	0	0	0	0
Principal	710	582	345	460	227	166	132	123	123	83
Interest	164	119	84	67	44	32	24	18	12	6

ARGENTINA

(US$ million, unless otherwise indicated)

	1970	1980	1988	1989	1990	1991	1992	1993	1994	1995
1. SUMMARY DEBT DATA										
TOTAL DEBT STOCKS (EDT)	..	**27,157**	**58,741**	**65,257**	**62,233**	**65,403**	**68,345**	**70,576**	**77,434**	**89,747**
Long-term debt (LDOD)	**5,171**	**16,774**	**49,346**	**53,632**	**48,705**	**49,374**	**49,855**	**58,403**	**66,052**	**73,446**
Public and publicly guaranteed	1,880	10,181	47,546	51,832	46,905	47,574	47,611	52,034	55,832	62,181
Private nonguaranteed	3,291	6,593	1,800	1,800	1,800	1,800	2,244	6,369	10,220	11,265
Use of IMF credit	**0**	**0**	**3,678**	**3,100**	**3,083**	**2,483**	**2,314**	**3,520**	**4,211**	**6,131**
Short-term debt	..	**10,383**	**5,717**	**8,525**	**10,445**	**13,546**	**16,176**	**8,653**	**7,171**	**10,170**
of which interest arrears on LDOD	..	0	2,131	5,642	7,562	8,625	9,076	1	1	0
Official creditors	..	0	68	213	132	259	627	0	0	0
Private creditors	..	0	2,063	5,428	7,429	8,366	8,450	1	1	0
Memo: principal arrears on LDOD	..	0	1,986	2,364	4,369	4,982	5,782	0	0	0
Official creditors	..	0	383	273	224	331	430	0	0	0
Private creditors	..	0	1,603	2,091	4,145	4,652	5,352	0	0	0
Memo: export credits	..	..	7,299	8,164	8,964	9,608	9,579	11,408	12,631	12,740
TOTAL DEBT FLOWS										
Disbursements	**907**	**4,708**	**2,438**	**1,442**	**1,587**	**2,844**	**3,433**	**11,964**	**9,599**	**13,326**
Long-term debt	907	4,708	1,902	1,206	1,150	2,443	2,609	10,352	8,722	10,960
IMF purchases	0	0	536	236	437	400	824	1,613	876	2,365
Principal repayments	**772**	**1,853**	**1,920**	**2,228**	**3,444**	**2,618**	**2,178**	**3,255**	**2,582**	**4,360**
Long-term debt	772	1,853	1,406	1,513	2,747	1,627	1,279	2,871	2,168	3,875
IMF repurchases	0	0	513	716	697	991	898	384	415	484
Net flows on debt	**135**	**2,855**	**925**	**-1,489**	**-1,857**	**2,264**	**3,434**	**10,895**	**5,534**	**11,966**
of which short-term debt	..	..	406	-703	0	2,038	2,179	2,186	-1,482	3,000
Interest payments (INT)	..	**2,329**	**3,104**	**2,129**	**2,717**	**2,927**	**2,826**	**3,301**	**4,110**	**5,372**
Long-term debt	338	1,337	2,733	1,520	2,209	2,377	2,401	2,527	3,406	4,577
IMF charges	0	0	248	276	277	237	178	206	203	275
Short-term debt	..	992	123	333	231	312	246	568	502	520
Net transfers on debt	..	**526**	**-2,179**	**-3,619**	**-4,574**	**-663**	**609**	**7,594**	**1,424**	**6,594**
Total debt service paid (TDS)	..	**4,182**	**5,023**	**4,357**	**6,161**	**5,545**	**5,003**	**6,556**	**6,693**	**9,732**
Long-term debt	1,110	3,190	4,139	3,032	4,956	4,005	3,681	5,399	5,573	8,452
IMF repurchases and charges	0	0	761	992	975	1,228	1,077	590	618	759
Short-term debt (interest only)	..	992	123	333	231	312	246	568	502	520

	1970	1980	1988	1989	1990	1991	1992	1993	1994	1995
2. AGGREGATE NET RESOURCE FLOWS AND NET TRANSFERS (LONG-TERM)										
NET RESOURCE FLOWS	**143**	**3,535**	**1,664**	**783**	**273**	**3,717**	**4,303**	**16,523**	**8,378**	**8,650**
Net flow of long-term debt (ex. IMF)	135	2,855	496	-307	-1,597	816	1,330	7,480	6,555	7,085
Foreign direct investment (net)	11	678	1,147	1,028	1,836	2,439	2,555	3,482	603	1,319
Portfolio equity flows	0	0	0	8	13	420	392	5,529	1,205	211
Grants (excluding technical coop.)	..	2	21	53	21	42	27	32	16	36
Memo: technical coop. grants	12	35	82	80	84	101	112	138	159	166
NET TRANSFERS	**-268**	**1,593**	**-1,729**	**-1,412**	**-2,573**	**533**	**1,057**	**13,050**	**3,853**	**2,773**
Interest on long-term debt	338	1,337	2,733	1,520	2,209	2,377	2,401	2,527	3,406	4,577
Profit remittances on FDI	73	605	660	675	637	807	845	946	1,120	1,300

	1970	1980	1988	1989	1990	1991	1992	1993	1994	1995
3. MAJOR ECONOMIC AGGREGATES										
Gross national product (GNP)	30,396	76,287	120,716	70,220	135,150	183,857	224,522	254,917	277,959	271,408
Exports of goods & services (XGS)	..	11,202	11,360	12,042	16,654	16,132	16,551	17,781	21,440	28,027
of which workers remittances	..	0	0	0	0	0	0	0	0	0
Imports of goods & services (MGS)	..	15,999	12,932	13,355	13,100	17,572	22,616	25,240	31,125	30,856
International reserves (RES)	682	9,297	5,158	3,217	6,222	7,463	11,447	15,499	16,003	15,979
Current account balance	..	-4,774	-1,572	-1,305	4,552	-647	-5,403	-7,047	-9,366	-2,399

	1970	1980	1988	1989	1990	1991	1992	1993	1994	1995
4. DEBT INDICATORS										
EDT / XGS (%)	..	242.4	517.1	541.9	373.7	405.4	412.9	396.9	361.2	320.2
EDT / GNP (%)	..	35.6	48.7	92.9	46.0	35.6	30.4	27.7	27.9	33.1
TDS / XGS (%)	..	37.3	44.2	36.2	37.0	34.4	30.2	36.9	31.2	34.7
INT / XGS (%)	..	20.8	27.3	17.7	16.3	18.1	17.1	18.6	19.2	19.2
INT / GNP (%)	..	3.1	2.6	3.0	2.0	1.6	1.3	1.3	1.5	2.0
RES / EDT (%)	..	34.2	8.8	4.9	10.0	11.4	16.7	22.0	20.7	17.8
RES / MGS (months)	..	7.0	4.8	2.9	5.7	5.1	6.1	7.4	6.2	6.2
Short-term / EDT (%)	..	38.2	9.7	13.1	16.8	20.7	23.7	12.3	9.3	11.3
Concessional / EDT (%)	..	1.8	0.4	0.9	1.0	0.9	1.7	2.7	2.9	3.1
Multilateral / EDT (%)	..	4.0	6.9	6.7	8.0	8.3	7.4	10.1	10.0	10.5

ARGENTINA

(US$ million, unless otherwise indicated)

	1970	1980	1988	1989	1990	1991	1992	1993	1994	1995
5. LONG-TERM DEBT										
DEBT OUTSTANDING (LDOD)	**5,171**	**16,774**	**49,346**	**53,632**	**48,705**	**49,374**	**49,855**	**58,403**	**66,052**	**73,446**
Public and publicly guaranteed	**1,880**	**10,181**	**47,546**	**51,832**	**46,905**	**47,574**	**47,611**	**52,034**	**55,832**	**62,181**
Official creditors	637	1,903	8,739	9,607	11,226	12,576	13,166	16,834	18,830	21,123
Multilateral	281	1,087	4,029	4,361	5,007	5,419	5,037	7,112	7,748	9,414
Concessional	108	154	118	110	102	89	70	32	17	11
Bilateral	356	816	4,710	5,246	6,219	7,157	8,130	9,722	11,082	11,709
Concessional	166	329	114	492	498	531	1,105	1,882	2,251	2,737
Private creditors	1,243	8,278	38,808	42,226	35,679	34,998	34,445	35,200	37,002	41,058
Bonds	386	832	9,117	9,824	11,514	11,661	11,620	33,974	35,628	39,441
Commercial banks	121	6,065	27,943	30,869	22,661	22,019	21,618	804	916	1,207
Other private	735	1,381	1,748	1,533	1,504	1,318	1,207	422	459	410
Private nonguaranteed	**3,291**	**6,593**	**1,800**	**1,800**	**1,800**	**1,800**	**2,244**	**6,369**	**10,220**	**11,265**
Bonds	0	0	0	0	21	286	1,671	5,225	7,366	7,582
Commercial banks	3,291	6,593	1,800	1,800	1,779	1,514	573	1,144	2,854	3,683
Memo:										
IBRD	181	404	2,265	2,281	2,609	2,790	2,505	3,739	4,109	4,913
IDA	0	0	0	0	0	0	0	0	0	0
DISBURSEMENTS	**907**	**4,708**	**1,902**	**1,206**	**1,150**	**2,443**	**2,609**	**10,352**	**8,722**	**10,960**
Public and publicly guaranteed	**482**	**2,839**	**1,742**	**1,136**	**1,129**	**2,178**	**1,209**	**6,747**	**4,383**	**8,610**
Official creditors	162	276	952	864	910	1,537	906	3,315	1,469	2,803
Multilateral	64	208	718	820	736	951	504	2,540	787	1,936
Concessional	14	9	16	9	14	142	152	0	0	0
Bilateral	98	69	235	43	174	586	402	775	683	867
Concessional	46	13	0	0	149	10	2	575	238	630
Private creditors	321	2,563	790	272	219	641	304	3,431	2,914	5,808
Bonds	119	136	0	0	0	500	250	3,291	2,726	5,623
Commercial banks	53	2,173	714	215	183	134	33	91	110	119
Other private	149	253	76	57	36	7	21	49	77	66
Private nonguaranteed	**424**	**1,869**	**160**	**70**	**21**	**265**	**1,400**	**3,605**	**4,339**	**2,350**
Bonds	0	0	0	0	21	265	1,400	3,605	2,430	834
Commercial banks	424	1,869	160	70	0	0	0	0	1,910	1,516
Memo:										
IBRD	32	71	487	316	405	460	171	1,507	548	941
IDA	0	0	0	0	0	0	0	0	0	0
PRINCIPAL REPAYMENTS	**772**	**1,853**	**1,406**	**1,513**	**2,747**	**1,627**	**1,279**	**2,871**	**2,168**	**3,875**
Public and publicly guaranteed	**344**	**1,146**	**1,256**	**1,444**	**2,747**	**1,627**	**1,044**	**2,821**	**1,678**	**2,610**
Official creditors	110	218	510	438	454	759	788	643	738	1,392
Multilateral	16	121	365	402	405	660	718	564	665	512
Concessional	4	17	26	27	26	140	152	27	16	5
Bilateral	94	97	144	36	49	98	71	79	74	880
Concessional	11	34	2	0	0	0	0	13	20	58
Private creditors	234	928	747	1,006	2,293	869	256	2,178	939	1,219
Bonds	20	178	611	892	878	349	219	2,077	810	920
Commercial banks	69	481	18	27	1,343	417	14	49	63	173
Other private	145	268	118	87	72	103	24	52	67	125
Private nonguaranteed	**428**	**707**	**150**	**69**	**0**	**0**	**235**	**50**	**490**	**1,265**
Bonds	0	0	0	0	0	0	15	50	290	631
Commercial banks	428	707	150	69	0	0	220	0	200	634
Memo:										
IBRD	5	34	188	221	233	351	383	334	425	259
IDA	0	0	0	0	0	0	0	0	0	0
NET FLOWS ON DEBT	**135**	**2,855**	**496**	**-307**	**-1,597**	**816**	**1,330**	**7,480**	**6,555**	**7,085**
Public and publicly guaranteed	**139**	**1,693**	**486**	**-308**	**-1,618**	**551**	**165**	**3,925**	**2,705**	**6,000**
Official creditors	52	58	443	426	456	778	118	2,672	731	1,411
Multilateral	47	86	353	419	332	290	-214	1,976	122	1,424
Concessional	10	-8	-10	-19	-11	2	0	-27	-16	-5
Bilateral	5	-29	91	7	125	488	332	696	609	-13
Concessional	35	-20	-2	0	149	10	2	562	219	572
Private creditors	87	1,635	43	-733	-2,074	-227	47	1,253	1,974	4,589
Bonds	99	-42	-611	-892	-878	151	31	1,214	1,916	4,703
Commercial banks	-16	1,692	696	189	-1,160	-283	19	42	48	-54
Other private	4	-16	-42	-30	-36	-96	-3	-3	10	-60
Private nonguaranteed	**-4**	**1,162**	**10**	**1**	**21**	**265**	**1,165**	**3,555**	**3,849**	**1,085**
Bonds	0	0	0	0	21	265	1,385	3,555	2,140	203
Commercial banks	-4	1,162	10	1	0	0	-220	0	1,710	882
Memo:										
IBRD	27	37	299	96	172	109	-211	1,173	123	682
IDA	0	0	0	0	0	0	0	0	0	0

ARGENTINA

(US$ million, unless otherwise indicated)

	1970	1980	1988	1989	1990	1991	1992	1993	1994	1995
INTEREST PAYMENTS (LINT)	**338**	**1,337**	**2,733**	**1,520**	**2,209**	**2,377**	**2,401**	**2,527**	**3,406**	**4,577**
Public and publicly guaranteed	**121**	**841**	**2,490**	**1,320**	**2,065**	**2,244**	**2,275**	**2,310**	**2,845**	**3,692**
Official creditors	33	146	410	428	456	604	721	944	1,185	1,415
Multilateral	18	98	315	369	375	441	456	476	588	617
Concessional	7	12	8	7	6	19	19	3	2	1
Bilateral	16	49	94	59	81	163	265	469	597	798
Concessional	4	15	0	0	0	0	0	43	73	114
Private creditors	88	695	2,080	892	1,609	1,641	1,554	1,366	1,661	2,278
Bonds	23	80	348	224	973	882	812	1,310	1,594	2,176
Commercial banks	9	504	1,685	648	623	726	736	28	42	72
Other private	56	111	47	21	14	33	6	28	25	30
Private nonguaranteed	**217**	**496**	**243**	**200**	**144**	**133**	**126**	**217**	**560**	**885**
Bonds	0	0	0	0	0	2	38	172	469	641
Commercial banks	217	496	243	200	144	131	89	46	92	244
Memo:										
IBRD	11	37	159	196	182	216	228	233	284	306
IDA	0	0	0	0	0	0	0	0	0	0
NET TRANSFERS ON DEBT	**-203**	**1,518**	**-2,237**	**-1,827**	**-3,806**	**-1,562**	**-1,071**	**4,953**	**3,149**	**2,508**
Public and publicly guaranteed	**18**	**852**	**-2,004**	**-1,628**	**-3,683**	**-1,694**	**-2,110**	**1,615**	**-140**	**2,308**
Official creditors	18	-88	33	-2	0	175	-604	1,728	-454	-4
Multilateral	30	-11	37	49	-44	-151	-670	1,500	-466	807
Concessional	3	-20	-18	-26	-17	-17	-19	-30	-18	-6
Bilateral	-11	-77	-4	-52	44	325	66	228	12	-810
Concessional	31	-35	-2	0	149	10	2	519	145	458
Private creditors	0	940	-2,037	-1,625	-3,683	-1,868	-1,506	-113	314	2,312
Bonds	77	-122	-959	-1,116	-1,851	-731	-781	-95	322	2,527
Commercial banks	-25	1,189	-989	-459	-1,782	-1,009	-718	14	6	-126
Other private	-52	-127	-89	-51	-50	-128	-8	-31	-14	-89
Private nonguaranteed	**-221**	**666**	**-233**	**-199**	**-123**	**132**	**1,039**	**3,338**	**3,289**	**200**
Bonds	0	0	0	0	21	263	1,347	3,384	1,671	-438
Commercial banks	-221	666	-233	-199	-144	-131	-309	-46	1,618	638
Memo:										
IBRD	16	0	140	-101	-10	-107	-439	940	-161	376
IDA	0	0	0	0	0	0	0	0	0	0
DEBT SERVICE (LTDS)	**1,110**	**3,190**	**4,139**	**3,032**	**4,956**	**4,005**	**3,681**	**5,399**	**5,573**	**8,452**
Public and publicly guaranteed	**464**	**1,987**	**3,746**	**2,763**	**4,812**	**3,872**	**3,320**	**5,131**	**4,523**	**6,302**
Official creditors	143	364	919	866	910	1,362	1,510	1,587	1,923	2,806
Multilateral	34	219	681	771	780	1,101	1,174	1,040	1,252	1,129
Concessional	11	29	34	34	31	159	171	30	18	6
Bilateral	109	146	239	95	130	261	336	548	671	1,677
Concessional	15	48	2	0	0	0	0	56	93	171
Private creditors	321	1,623	2,827	1,898	3,902	2,509	1,810	3,544	2,600	3,496
Bonds	42	258	959	1,116	1,851	1,231	1,031	3,387	2,404	3,096
Commercial banks	78	985	1,703	674	1,966	1,143	751	77	105	245
Other private	201	380	165	108	86	136	29	80	92	155
Private nonguaranteed	**646**	**1,203**	**393**	**269**	**144**	**133**	**361**	**267**	**1,050**	**2,150**
Bonds	0	0	0	0	0	2	53	222	759	1,272
Commercial banks	646	1,203	393	269	144	131	309	46	292	878
Memo:										
IBRD	16	71	347	417	414	567	611	567	709	565
IDA	0	0	0	0	0	0	0	0	0	0
UNDISBURSED DEBT	**577**	**2,176**	**5,643**	**4,797**	**4,315**	**4,977**	**5,762**	**3,958**	**4,759**	**6,592**
Official creditors	325	1,122	4,951	4,276	3,897	4,576	5,363	3,488	4,152	6,098
Private creditors	252	1,054	691	521	419	401	399	470	607	494
Memorandum items										
Concessional LDOD	274	483	232	602	600	620	1,175	1,915	2,268	2,748
Variable rate LDOD	3,291	12,417	41,281	33,931	28,187	27,899	27,559	31,377	35,583	38,450
Public sector LDOD	1,780	7,979	46,736	50,262	44,737	45,451	45,551	52,011	55,817	62,159
Private sector LDOD	3,390	8,795	2,610	3,370	3,969	3,924	4,304	6,393	10,236	11,287

6. CURRENCY COMPOSITION OF LONG-TERM DEBT (PERCENT)

	1970	1980	1988	1989	1990	1991	1992	1993	1994	1995
Deutsche mark	15.7	9.5	6.8	7.1	10.4	9.5	9.0	7.2	8.5	10.4
French franc	1.8	1.2	0.9	1.0	1.5	1.4	1.3	0.9	0.9	1.2
Japanese yen	0.2	5.8	8.0	6.5	6.7	6.7	6.6	4.0	5.9	8.3
Pound sterling	2.9	1.6	0.8	0.6	1.1	1.0	0.8	0.2	0.2	0.2
Swiss franc	1.9	3.4	2.0	1.5	2.2	1.9	1.8	1.0	1.1	1.4
U.S.dollars	47.7	64.5	60.5	63.4	54.5	54.3	55.9	72.2	68.2	63.4
Multiple currency	17.7	10.3	17.2	16.4	19.5	21.2	21.0	11.9	11.8	11.7
Special drawing rights	0.0	0.0	0.0	0.0	0.0	0.0	0.0	0.0	0.0	0.0
All other currencies	12.0	3.6	3.8	3.5	4.2	3.9	3.5	2.6	3.4	3.4

ARGENTINA

(US$ million, unless otherwise indicated)

	1970	1980	1988	1989	1990	1991	1992	1993	1994	1995
7. DEBT RESTRUCTURINGS										
Total amount rescheduled	0	0	0	559	932	860	631	26,503	847	248
Debt stock rescheduled	0	0	0	0	0	0	0	18,036	0	0
Principal rescheduled	0	0	0	477	512	620	523	973	844	198
Official	0	0	0	326	381	543	456	963	834	158
Private	0	0	0	151	131	77	67	10	10	40
Interest rescheduled	0	0	0	82	420	237	107	7,495	3	50
Official	0	0	0	23	382	212	88	88	3	22
Private	0	0	0	59	38	25	19	7,407	0	29
Debt forgiven	..	..	0	0	0	0	0	0	0	0
Memo: interest forgiven	..	..	0	0	0	0	0	0	0	0
Debt stock reduction	0	0	1,354	1,508	7,202	698	661	3,265	399	863
of which debt buyback	0	0	0	0	1,232	0	0	0	0	0
8. DEBT STOCK-FLOW RECONCILIATION										
Total change in debt stocks	..	..	..	6,516	-3,023	3,170	2,942	2,231	6,859	12,313
Net flows on debt	..	..	..	-1,489	-1,857	2,264	3,434	10,895	5,534	11,966
Net change in interest arrears	..	..	..	3,511	1,920	1,063	452	-9,076	0	-1
Interest capitalized	..	..	..	82	420	237	107	7,495	3	50
Debt forgiveness or reduction	..	..	..	-1,508	-5,970	-698	-661	-3,265	-399	-863
Cross-currency valuation	..	..	..	-328	1,688	132	-770	-170	1,684	912
Residual	..	..	..	6,248	775	172	380	-3,648	35	248
9. AVERAGE TERMS OF NEW COMMITMENTS										
ALL CREDITORS										
Interest (%)	7.3	13.7	7.7	8.1	6.4	7.9	8.1	7.1	7.3	7.1
Maturity (years)	11.9	8.6	15.1	13.1	17.0	17.9	17.9	11.8	9.5	10.3
Grace period (years)	2.9	4.5	4.2	3.5	3.5	5.4	5.4	6.0	3.9	4.2
Grant element (%)	12.6	-17.5	11.6	8.8	19.3	12.3	10.6	15.0	12.3	12.8
Official creditors										
Interest (%)	7.5	6.1	7.6	7.9	6.5	7.8	8.2	6.5	5.8	6.4
Maturity (years)	16.7	14.5	16.4	16.0	19.1	20.8	19.5	15.3	16.6	16.3
Grace period (years)	3.4	5.2	4.5	4.5	4.0	5.5	5.4	4.8	4.8	4.7
Grant element (%)	11.4	20.2	12.8	10.7	20.6	13.8	11.1	19.8	24.5	20.0
Private creditors										
Interest (%)	7.3	14.3	8.5	8.6	6.0	8.4	8.1	7.8	8.3	7.7
Maturity (years)	10.6	8.2	7.7	6.0	8.4	6.6	6.5	8.0	4.4	5.3
Grace period (years)	2.7	4.4	2.4	1.1	1.4	5.0	5.0	7.3	3.2	3.8
Grant element (%)	13.0	-20.5	4.5	4.2	14.1	6.2	7.2	9.6	3.3	6.9
Memorandum items										
Commitments	494	3,062	2,947	361	572	3,030	2,437	5,270	5,269	10,353
Official creditors	105	225	2,494	255	460	2,408	2,134	2,770	2,216	4,675
Private creditors	389	2,837	453	105	113	623	304	2,500	3,053	5,678

10. CONTRACTUAL OBLIGATIONS ON OUTSTANDING LONG-TERM DEBT

	1996	1997	1998	1999	2000	2001	2002	2003	2004	2005
TOTAL										
Disbursements	2,064	1,679	966	660	460	284	208	131	91	50
Principal	9,268	8,597	7,925	7,492	6,834	3,820	4,592	4,292	2,807	2,020
Interest	4,440	4,189	3,640	3,535	2,725	2,323	2,137	1,864	1,606	1,459
Official creditors										
Disbursements	1,765	1,545	911	653	460	284	208	131	91	50
Principal	2,184	2,498	2,422	2,722	2,442	2,137	1,875	1,607	1,541	1,505
Interest	1,506	1,457	1,364	1,227	1,072	929	801	690	591	494
Bilateral creditors										
Disbursements	417	317	171	95	46	23	13	4	2	0
Principal	1,522	1,783	1,546	1,697	1,355	935	741	584	583	556
Interest	746	654	562	457	349	270	213	174	140	106
Multilateral creditors										
Disbursements	1,349	1,229	740	557	414	260	195	127	89	50
Principal	662	714	876	1,024	1,088	1,201	1,134	1,023	959	949
Interest	760	803	802	771	722	659	587	516	452	388
Private creditors										
Disbursements	299	133	55	7	0	0	0	0	0	0
Principal	7,084	6,099	5,503	4,770	4,392	1,684	2,717	2,685	1,266	515
Interest	2,934	2,733	2,276	2,307	1,654	1,394	1,336	1,174	1,015	966
Commercial banks										
Disbursements	298	133	55	7	0	0	0	0	0	0
Principal	240	224	191	170	151	139	132	99	82	73
Interest	98	92	84	72	60	53	43	33	26	20
Other private										
Disbursements	1	0	0	0	0	0	0	0	0	0
Principal	6,844	5,875	5,313	4,600	4,241	1,544	2,585	2,586	1,184	442
Interest	2,836	2,640	2,192	2,236	1,593	1,341	1,293	1,140	989	946

ARMENIA

(US$ million, unless otherwise indicated)

	1970	1980	1988	1989	1990	1991	1992	1993	1994	1995
1. SUMMARY DEBT DATA										
TOTAL DEBT STOCKS (EDT)	..	..	..	..	..	..	**40.9**	**133.9**	**214.3**	**373.5**
Long-term debt (LDOD)	..	..	..	..	..	..	**2.9**	**133.9**	**188.6**	**300.4**
Public and publicly guaranteed	..	..	..	..	..	..	2.9	133.9	188.6	300.4
Private nonguaranteed	0.0	0.0	0.0	0.0	0.0	0.0	0.0	0.0	0.0	0.0
Use of IMF credit	**0.0**	**0.0**	**0.0**	**0.0**	**0.0**	**0.0**	**0.0**	**0.0**	**24.6**	**70.2**
Short-term debt	..	..	..	..	..	..	**38.0**	**0.0**	**1.1**	**2.9**
of which interest arrears on LDOD	..	..	..	..	..	..	0.0	0.0	1.1	1.9
Official creditors	..	..	..	..	..	..	0.0	0.0	1.1	1.9
Private creditors	..	..	..	..	..	..	0.0	0.0	0.0	0.0
Memo: principal arrears on LDOD	..	..	..	..	..	..	0.0	0.0	31.2	79.4
Official creditors	..	..	..	..	..	..	0.0	0.0	31.2	79.4
Private creditors	..	..	..	..	..	..	0.0	0.0	0.0	0.0
Memo: export credits	..	..	0.0	0.0	0.0	0.0	7.0	0.0	0.0	0.0
TOTAL DEBT FLOWS										
Disbursements	..	..	..	..	..	..	**3.4**	**87.3**	**84.7**	**148.5**
Long-term debt	..	..	..	..	..	..	3.4	87.3	60.5	102.4
IMF purchases	0.0	0.0	0.0	0.0	0.0	0.0	0.0	0.0	24.2	46.1
Principal repayments	..	..	..	..	..	..	**0.0**	**0.6**	**0.0**	**0.7**
Long-term debt	..	..	..	..	..	..	0.0	0.6	0.0	0.7
IMF repurchases	0.0	0.0	0.0	0.0	0.0	0.0	0.0	0.0	0.0	0.0
Net flows on debt	..	..	..	..	..	..	**41.4**	**79.6**	**84.7**	**148.8**
of which short-term debt	..	..	..	..	..	..	38.0	-7.2	0.0	1.0
Interest payments (INT)	..	..	..	..	..	..	**0.0**	**1.4**	**4.4**	**8.4**
Long-term debt	..	..	..	..	..	..	0.0	1.4	4.4	6.7
IMF charges	0.0	0.0	0.0	0.0	0.0	0.0	0.0	0.0	0.0	1.7
Short-term debt	..	..	..	..	..	..	0.0	0.0	0.0	0.0
Net transfers on debt	..	..	..	..	..	..	**41.4**	**78.1**	**80.3**	**140.4**
Total debt service paid (TDS)	..	..	..	..	..	..	**0.0**	**2.0**	**4.4**	**9.1**
Long-term debt	..	..	..	..	..	..	0.0	2.0	4.4	7.3
IMF repurchases and charges	0.0	0.0	0.0	0.0	0.0	0.0	0.0	0.0	0.0	1.7
Short-term debt (interest only)	..	..	..	..	..	..	0.0	0.0	0.0	0.0
2. AGGREGATE NET RESOURCE FLOWS AND NET TRANSFERS (LONG-TERM)										
NET RESOURCE FLOWS	..	..	..	..	..	..	**22.1**	**183.6**	**231.5**	**200.3**
Net flow of long-term debt (ex. IMF)	..	..	..	..	..	..	3.4	86.8	60.5	101.7
Foreign direct investment (net)	..	..	..	..	..	..	0.0	0.0	0.0	8.0
Portfolio equity flows	..	..	..	..	..	..	0.0	0.0	0.0	0.0
Grants (excluding technical coop.)	..	..	..	..	..	..	18.7	96.8	171.0	90.6
Memo: technical coop. grants	..	..	..	..	..	..	3.1	12.7	14.8	38.6
NET TRANSFERS	..	..	..	..	..	..	**22.1**	**182.2**	**227.1**	**193.6**
Interest on long-term debt	..	..	..	..	..	..	0.0	1.4	4.4	6.7
Profit remittances on FDI	..	..	..	..	..	..	0.0	0.0	0.0	0.0
3. MAJOR ECONOMIC AGGREGATES										
Gross national product (GNP)	..	..	..	..	..	..	1,978.6	1,821.1	1,926.3	2,122.3
Exports of goods & services (XGS)	..	..	..	..	..	..	..	173.5	251.2	313.5
of which workers remittances	..	..	..	..	..	..	..	0.0	0.0	12.4
Imports of goods & services (MGS)	..	..	..	..	..	..	..	295.5	463.0	740.8
International reserves (RES)	..	..	..	..	..	..	..	..	32.3	86.0
Current account balance	..	..	..	..	..	..	..	-66.8	-106.2	-279.4
4. DEBT INDICATORS										
EDT / XGS (%)	..	..	..	..	..	..	..	77.2	85.3	119.1
EDT / GNP (%)	..	..	..	..	..	..	2.1	7.4	11.1	17.6
TDS / XGS (%)	..	..	..	..	..	..	..	1.2	1.8	2.9
INT / XGS (%)	..	..	..	..	..	..	..	0.8	1.8	2.7
INT / GNP (%)	..	..	..	..	..	..	0.0	0.1	0.2	0.4
RES / EDT (%)	..	..	..	..	..	..	..	..	15.1	23.0
RES / MGS (months)	..	..	..	..	..	..	..	..	0.8	1.4
Short-term / EDT (%)	..	..	..	..	..	..	93.0	0.0	0.5	0.8
Concessional / EDT (%)	..	..	..	..	..	..	5.5	14.3	21.9	38.2
Multilateral / EDT (%)	..	..	..	..	..	..	0.0	45.3	48.6	55.7

ARMENIA

(US$ million, unless otherwise indicated)

	1970	1980	1988	1989	1990	1991	1992	1993	1994	1995
5. LONG-TERM DEBT										
DEBT OUTSTANDING (LDOD)	..	..	..	..	..	..	**2.9**	**133.9**	**188.6**	**300.4**
Public and publicly guaranteed	..	..	..	..	..	..	**2.9**	**133.9**	**188.6**	**300.4**
Official creditors	..	..	..	..	..	..	2.9	133.9	188.6	300.4
Multilateral	..	..	..	..	..	..	0.0	60.7	104.1	208.0
Concessional	..	..	..	..	..	..	0.0	2.6	31.9	127.8
Bilateral	..	..	..	..	..	..	2.9	73.2	84.6	92.4
Concessional	..	..	..	..	..	..	2.3	16.6	15.1	14.9
Private creditors	..	..	..	..	..	..	0.0	0.0	0.0	0.0
Bonds	..	..	..	..	..	..	0.0	0.0	0.0	0.0
Commercial banks	..	..	..	..	..	..	0.0	0.0	0.0	0.0
Other private	..	..	..	..	..	..	0.0	0.0	0.0	0.0
Private nonguaranteed	**0.0**	**0.0**	**0.0**	**0.0**	**0.0**	**0.0**	**0.0**	**0.0**	**0.0**	**0.0**
Bonds	..	..	..	..	..	..	0.0	0.0	0.0	0.0
Commercial banks	..	..	..	..	..	..	0.0	0.0	0.0	0.0
Memo:										
IBRD	0.0	0.0	0.0	0.0	0.0	0.0	0.0	0.5	1.6	4.8
IDA	0.0	0.0	0.0	0.0	0.0	0.0	0.0	0.0	5.6	90.9
DISBURSEMENTS	..	..	..	..	..	..	**3.4**	**87.3**	**60.5**	**102.4**
Public and publicly guaranteed	..	..	..	..	..	..	**3.4**	**87.3**	**60.5**	**102.4**
Official creditors	..	..	..	..	..	..	3.4	87.3	60.5	102.4
Multilateral	..	..	..	..	..	..	0.0	63.4	37.3	102.4
Concessional	..	..	..	..	..	..	0.0	2.6	29.2	99.0
Bilateral	..	..	..	..	..	..	3.4	24.0	23.2	0.0
Concessional	..	..	..	..	..	..	2.8	2.3	0.0	0.0
Private creditors	..	..	..	..	..	..	0.0	0.0	0.0	0.0
Bonds	..	..	..	..	..	..	0.0	0.0	0.0	0.0
Commercial banks	..	..	..	..	..	..	0.0	0.0	0.0	0.0
Other private	..	..	..	..	..	..	0.0	0.0	0.0	0.0
Private nonguaranteed	**0.0**	**0.0**	**0.0**	**0.0**	**0.0**	**0.0**	**0.0**	**0.0**	**0.0**	**0.0**
Bonds	..	..	..	..	..	..	0.0	0.0	0.0	0.0
Commercial banks	..	..	..	..	..	..	0.0	0.0	0.0	0.0
Memo:										
IBRD	0.0	0.0	0.0	0.0	0.0	0.0	0.0	0.5	1.0	3.4
IDA	0.0	0.0	0.0	0.0	0.0	0.0	0.0	0.0	5.5	88.5
PRINCIPAL REPAYMENTS	..	..	..	..	..	..	**0.0**	**0.6**	**0.0**	**0.7**
Public and publicly guaranteed	..	..	..	..	..	..	**0.0**	**0.6**	**0.0**	**0.7**
Official creditors	..	..	..	..	..	..	0.0	0.6	0.0	0.7
Multilateral	..	..	..	..	..	..	0.0	0.0	0.0	0.0
Concessional	..	..	..	..	..	..	0.0	0.0	0.0	0.0
Bilateral	..	..	..	..	..	..	0.0	0.6	0.0	0.7
Concessional	..	..	..	..	..	..	0.0	0.0	0.0	0.0
Private creditors	..	..	..	..	..	..	0.0	0.0	0.0	0.0
Bonds	..	..	..	..	..	..	0.0	0.0	0.0	0.0
Commercial banks	..	..	..	..	..	..	0.0	0.0	0.0	0.0
Other private	..	..	..	..	..	..	0.0	0.0	0.0	0.0
Private nonguaranteed	**0.0**	**0.0**	**0.0**	**0.0**	**0.0**	**0.0**	**0.0**	**0.0**	**0.0**	**0.0**
Bonds	..	..	..	..	..	..	0.0	0.0	0.0	0.0
Commercial banks	..	..	..	..	..	..	0.0	0.0	0.0	0.0
Memo:										
IBRD	0.0	0.0	0.0	0.0	0.0	0.0	0.0	0.0	0.0	0.0
IDA	0.0	0.0	0.0	0.0	0.0	0.0	0.0	0.0	0.0	0.0
NET FLOWS ON DEBT	..	..	..	..	..	..	**3.4**	**86.8**	**60.5**	**101.7**
Public and publicly guaranteed	..	..	..	..	..	..	**3.4**	**86.8**	**60.5**	**101.7**
Official creditors	..	..	..	..	..	..	3.4	86.8	60.5	101.7
Multilateral	..	..	..	..	..	..	0.0	63.4	37.3	102.4
Concessional	..	..	..	..	..	..	0.0	2.6	29.2	99.0
Bilateral	..	..	..	..	..	..	3.4	23.4	23.2	-0.7
Concessional	..	..	..	..	..	..	2.8	2.3	0.0	0.0
Private creditors	..	..	..	..	..	..	0.0	0.0	0.0	0.0
Bonds	..	..	..	..	..	..	0.0	0.0	0.0	0.0
Commercial banks	..	..	..	..	..	..	0.0	0.0	0.0	0.0
Other private	..	..	..	..	..	..	0.0	0.0	0.0	0.0
Private nonguaranteed	**0.0**	**0.0**	**0.0**	**0.0**	**0.0**	**0.0**	**0.0**	**0.0**	**0.0**	**0.0**
Bonds	..	..	..	..	..	..	0.0	0.0	0.0	0.0
Commercial banks	..	..	..	..	..	..	0.0	0.0	0.0	0.0
Memo:										
IBRD	0.0	0.0	0.0	0.0	0.0	0.0	0.0	0.5	1.0	3.4
IDA	0.0	0.0	0.0	0.0	0.0	0.0	0.0	0.0	5.5	88.5

ARMENIA

(US$ million, unless otherwise indicated)

	1970	1980	1988	1989	1990	1991	1992	1993	1994	1995
INTEREST PAYMENTS (LINT)	..	..	..	..	..	..	**0.0**	**1.4**	**4.4**	**6.7**
Public and publicly guaranteed	..	..	..	..	..	..	**0.0**	**1.4**	**4.4**	**6.7**
Official creditors	..	..	..	..	..	..	0.0	1.4	4.4	6.7
Multilateral	..	..	..	..	..	..	0.0	1.3	4.4	6.7
Concessional	..	..	..	..	..	..	0.0	0.1	0.5	2.1
Bilateral	..	..	..	..	..	..	0.0	0.0	0.0	0.0
Concessional	..	..	..	..	..	..	0.0	0.0	0.0	0.0
Private creditors	..	..	..	..	..	..	0.0	0.0	0.0	0.0
Bonds	..	..	..	..	..	..	0.0	0.0	0.0	0.0
Commercial banks	..	..	..	..	..	..	0.0	0.0	0.0	0.0
Other private	..	..	..	..	..	..	0.0	0.0	0.0	0.0
Private nonguaranteed	**0.0**	**0.0**	**0.0**	**0.0**	**0.0**	**0.0**	**0.0**	**0.0**	**0.0**	**0.0**
Bonds	..	..	..	..	..	..	0.0	0.0	0.0	0.0
Commercial banks	..	..	..	..	..	..	0.0	0.0	0.0	0.0
Memo:										
IBRD	0.0	0.0	0.0	0.0	0.0	0.0	0.0	0.0	0.1	0.2
IDA	0.0	0.0	0.0	0.0	0.0	0.0	0.0	0.0	0.0	0.2
NET TRANSFERS ON DEBT	..	..	..	..	..	..	**3.4**	**85.4**	**56.1**	**95.0**
Public and publicly guaranteed	..	..	..	..	..	..	**3.4**	**85.4**	**56.1**	**95.0**
Official creditors	..	..	..	..	..	..	3.4	85.4	56.1	95.0
Multilateral	..	..	..	..	..	..	0.0	62.0	32.9	95.7
Concessional	..	..	..	..	..	..	0.0	2.4	28.7	96.9
Bilateral	..	..	..	..	..	..	3.4	23.4	23.2	-0.7
Concessional	..	..	..	..	..	..	2.8	2.3	0.0	0.0
Private creditors	..	..	..	..	..	..	0.0	0.0	0.0	0.0
Bonds	..	..	..	..	..	..	0.0	0.0	0.0	0.0
Commercial banks	..	..	..	..	..	..	0.0	0.0	0.0	0.0
Other private	..	..	..	..	..	..	0.0	0.0	0.0	0.0
Private nonguaranteed	**0.0**	**0.0**	**0.0**	**0.0**	**0.0**	**0.0**	**0.0**	**0.0**	**0.0**	**0.0**
Bonds	..	..	..	..	..	..	0.0	0.0	0.0	0.0
Commercial banks	..	..	..	..	..	..	0.0	0.0	0.0	0.0
Memo:										
IBRD	0.0	0.0	0.0	0.0	0.0	0.0	0.0	0.5	0.9	3.2
IDA	0.0	0.0	0.0	0.0	0.0	0.0	0.0	0.0	5.5	88.3
DEBT SERVICE (LTDS)	..	..	..	..	..	..	**0.0**	**2.0**	**4.4**	**7.3**
Public and publicly guaranteed	..	..	..	..	..	..	**0.0**	**2.0**	**4.4**	**7.3**
Official creditors	..	..	..	..	..	..	0.0	2.0	4.4	7.3
Multilateral	..	..	..	..	..	..	0.0	1.3	4.4	6.7
Concessional	..	..	..	..	..	..	0.0	0.1	0.5	2.1
Bilateral	..	..	..	..	..	..	0.0	0.6	0.0	0.7
Concessional	..	..	..	..	..	..	0.0	0.0	0.0	0.0
Private creditors	..	..	..	..	..	..	0.0	0.0	0.0	0.0
Bonds	..	..	..	..	..	..	0.0	0.0	0.0	0.0
Commercial banks	..	..	..	..	..	..	0.0	0.0	0.0	0.0
Other private	..	..	..	..	..	..	0.0	0.0	0.0	0.0
Private nonguaranteed	**0.0**	**0.0**	**0.0**	**0.0**	**0.0**	**0.0**	**0.0**	**0.0**	**0.0**	**0.0**
Bonds	..	..	..	..	..	..	0.0	0.0	0.0	0.0
Commercial banks	..	..	..	..	..	..	0.0	0.0	0.0	0.0
Memo:										
IBRD	0.0	0.0	0.0	0.0	0.0	0.0	0.0	0.0	0.1	0.2
IDA	0.0	0.0	0.0	0.0	0.0	0.0	0.0	0.0	0.0	0.2
UNDISBURSED DEBT	..	..	..	..	..	..	**50.1**	**80.9**	**171.2**	**188.9**
Official creditors	..	..	..	..	..	..	50.1	80.9	171.2	188.9
Private creditors	..	..	..	..	..	..	0.0	0.0	0.0	0.0
Memorandum items										
Concessional LDOD	..	..	..	..	..	..	2.3	19.2	47.0	142.7
Variable rate LDOD	..	..	..	..	..	..	0.6	113.1	163.8	190.6
Public sector LDOD	..	..	..	..	..	..	2.9	133.9	188.6	300.4
Private sector LDOD	..	..	..	..	..	..	0.0	0.0	0.0	0.0

6. CURRENCY COMPOSITION OF LONG-TERM DEBT (PERCENT)

	1970	1980	1988	1989	1990	1991	1992	1993	1994	1995
Deutsche mark	..	..	..	..	..	..	0.0	0.0	0.0	0.0
French franc	..	..	..	..	..	..	0.0	0.0	0.0	0.0
Japanese yen	..	..	..	..	..	..	0.0	0.0	0.0	0.0
Pound sterling	..	..	..	..	..	..	0.0	0.0	0.0	0.0
Swiss franc	..	..	..	..	..	..	0.0	0.0	0.0	0.0
U.S.dollars	..	..	..	..	..	..	21.0	31.9	42.0	62.8
Multiple currency	..	..	..	..	..	..	0.0	0.4	0.8	1.6
Special drawing rights	..	..	..	..	..	..	0.0	0.0	0.0	0.0
All other currencies	..	..	..	..	..	..	79.0	67.7	57.2	35.6

ARMENIA

(US$ million, unless otherwise indicated)

	1970	1980	1988	1989	1990	1991	1992	1993	1994	1995
7. DEBT RESTRUCTURINGS										
Total amount rescheduled	0.0	0.0	0.0	0.0	0.0	0.0	0.0	45.1	0.0	0.0
Debt stock rescheduled	0.0	0.0	0.0	0.0	0.0	0.0	0.0	0.0	0.0	0.0
Principal rescheduled	0.0	0.0	0.0	0.0	0.0	0.0	0.0	30.8	0.0	0.0
Official	0.0	0.0	0.0	0.0	0.0	0.0	0.0	0.0	0.0	0.0
Private	0.0	0.0	0.0	0.0	0.0	0.0	0.0	30.8	0.0	0.0
Interest rescheduled	0.0	0.0	0.0	0.0	0.0	0.0	0.0	0.0	0.0	0.0
Official	0.0	0.0	0.0	0.0	0.0	0.0	0.0	0.0	0.0	0.0
Private	0.0	0.0	0.0	0.0	0.0	0.0	0.0	0.0	0.0	0.0
Debt forgiven	..	..	0.0	0.0	0.0	0.0	0.0	0.0	0.0	0.0
Memo: interest forgiven	..	..	0.0	0.0	0.0	0.0	0.0	0.0	0.0	0.0
Debt stock reduction	0.0	0.0	0.0	0.0	0.0	0.0	0.0	0.0	0.0	0.0
of which debt buyback	0.0	0.0	0.0	0.0	0.0	0.0	0.0	0.0	0.0	0.0
8. DEBT STOCK-FLOW RECONCILIATION										
Total change in debt stocks	..	..	..	..	..	..	40.0	93.0	80.4	159.2
Net flows on debt	..	..	..	..	..	..	41.4	79.6	84.7	148.8
Net change in interest arrears	..	..	..	..	..	..	0.0	0.0	1.1	0.8
Interest capitalized	..	..	..	..	..	..	0.0	0.0	0.0	0.0
Debt forgiveness or reduction	..	..	..	..	..	..	0.0	0.0	0.0	0.0
Cross-currency valuation	..	..	..	..	..	..	0.1	-26.9	-17.2	-1.8
Residual	..	..	..	..	..	..	-1.5	40.4	11.8	11.4
9. AVERAGE TERMS OF NEW COMMITMENTS										
ALL CREDITORS										
Interest (%)	..	..	..	..	..	..	3.5	4.4	3.2	1.4
Maturity (years)	..	..	..	..	..	..	3.3	10.9	20.7	32.6
Grace period (years)	..	..	..	..	..	..	3.1	3.4	6.0	9.2
Grant element (%)	..	..	..	..	..	..	17.1	23.8	46.6	71.7
Official creditors										
Interest (%)	..	..	..	..	..	..	3.5	4.4	3.2	1.4
Maturity (years)	..	..	..	..	..	..	3.3	10.9	20.7	32.6
Grace period (years)	..	..	..	..	..	..	3.1	3.4	6.0	9.2
Grant element (%)	..	..	..	..	..	..	17.1	23.8	46.6	71.7
Private creditors										
Interest (%)	..	..	..	..	..	..	0.0	0.0	0.0	0.0
Maturity (years)	..	..	..	..	..	..	0.0	0.0	0.0	0.0
Grace period (years)	..	..	..	..	..	..	0.0	0.0	0.0	0.0
Grant element (%)	..	..	..	..	..	..	0.0	0.0	0.0	0.0
Memorandum items										
Commitments	..	..	..	..	..	..	56.8	124.0	172.8	131.1
Official creditors	..	..	..	..	..	..	56.8	124.0	172.8	131.1
Private creditors	..	..	..	..	..	..	0.0	0.0	0.0	0.0

10. CONTRACTUAL OBLIGATIONS ON OUTSTANDING LONG-TERM DEBT

	1996	1997	1998	1999	2000	2001	2002	2003	2004	2005
TOTAL										
Disbursements	46.2	52.6	37.8	25.0	15.6	6.9	3.5	0.6	0.6	0.0
Principal	23.0	28.3	32.2	32.6	15.4	9.6	9.6	10.2	10.9	13.3
Interest	10.5	10.5	9.7	8.3	6.9	6.3	5.8	5.2	4.6	3.9
Official creditors										
Disbursements	46.2	52.6	37.8	25.0	15.6	6.9	3.5	0.6	0.6	0.0
Principal	23.0	28.3	32.2	32.6	15.4	9.6	9.6	10.2	10.9	13.3
Interest	10.5	10.5	9.7	8.3	6.9	6.3	5.8	5.2	4.6	3.9
Bilateral creditors										
Disbursements	9.8	8.6	5.2	3.3	1.6	0.8	0.4	0.0	0.0	0.0
Principal	23.0	23.1	23.1	23.1	5.8	0.0	0.0	0.6	0.6	0.6
Interest	5.8	4.6	3.2	1.8	0.7	0.5	0.5	0.5	0.5	0.4
Multilateral creditors										
Disbursements	36.4	44.0	32.6	21.7	14.0	6.1	3.1	0.6	0.6	0.0
Principal	0.0	5.2	9.2	9.6	9.6	9.6	9.6	9.6	10.3	12.6
Interest	4.7	5.9	6.4	6.5	6.2	5.8	5.3	4.7	4.1	3.5
Private creditors										
Disbursements	0.0	0.0	0.0	0.0	0.0	0.0	0.0	0.0	0.0	0.0
Principal	0.0	0.0	0.0	0.0	0.0	0.0	0.0	0.0	0.0	0.0
Interest	0.0	0.0	0.0	0.0	0.0	0.0	0.0	0.0	0.0	0.0
Commercial banks										
Disbursements	0.0	0.0	0.0	0.0	0.0	0.0	0.0	0.0	0.0	0.0
Principal	0.0	0.0	0.0	0.0	0.0	0.0	0.0	0.0	0.0	0.0
Interest	0.0	0.0	0.0	0.0	0.0	0.0	0.0	0.0	0.0	0.0
Other private										
Disbursements	0.0	0.0	0.0	0.0	0.0	0.0	0.0	0.0	0.0	0.0
Principal	0.0	0.0	0.0	0.0	0.0	0.0	0.0	0.0	0.0	0.0
Interest	0.0	0.0	0.0	0.0	0.0	0.0	0.0	0.0	0.0	0.0

AZERBAIJAN

(US$ million, unless otherwise indicated)

1. SUMMARY DEBT DATA	1970	1980	1988	1989	1990	1991	1992	1993	1994	1995
TOTAL DEBT STOCKS (EDT)	..	..	..	..	..	..	..	**35.5**	**112.8**	**321.0**
Long-term debt (LDOD)	..	..	..	..	..	..	..	**35.5**	**103.2**	**206.1**
Public and publicly guaranteed	..	..	..	..	..	..	..	35.5	103.2	206.1
Private nonguaranteed	0.0	0.0	0.0	0.0	0.0	0.0	0.0	0.0	0.0	0.0
Use of IMF credit	**0.0**	**0.0**	**0.0**	**0.0**	**0.0**	**0.0**	**0.0**	**0.0**	**0.0**	**100.9**
Short-term debt	..	..	..	..	..	..	..	**0.0**	**9.6**	**14.0**
of which interest arrears on LDOD	..	..	..	..	..	..	..	0.0	3.6	6.0
Official creditors	..	..	..	..	..	..	..	0.0	3.6	6.0
Private creditors	..	..	..	..	..	..	..	0.0	0.0	0.0
Memo: principal arrears on LDOD	..	..	..	..	..	..	..	0.0	20.3	35.5
Official creditors	..	..	..	..	..	..	..	0.0	20.3	35.5
Private creditors	..	..	..	..	..	..	..	0.0	0.0	0.0
Memo: export credits	..	..	0.0	0.0	0.0	0.0	0.0	0.0	0.0	0.0
TOTAL DEBT FLOWS										
Disbursements	..	..	..	..	..	..	..	**0.0**	**67.4**	**205.0**
Long-term debt	..	..	..	..	..	..	..	0.0	67.4	102.1
IMF purchases	0.0	0.0	0.0	0.0	0.0	0.0	0.0	0.0	0.0	103.0
Principal repayments	..	..	..	..	..	..	..	**0.0**	**0.0**	**0.0**
Long-term debt	..	..	..	..	..	..	..	0.0	0.0	0.0
IMF repurchases	0.0	0.0	0.0	0.0	0.0	0.0	0.0	0.0	0.0	0.0
Net flows on debt	..	..	..	..	..	..	..	**0.0**	**73.4**	**207.0**
of which short-term debt	..	..	..	..	..	..	..	0.0	6.0	2.0
Interest payments (INT)	..	..	..	..	..	..	..	**0.0**	**0.3**	**10.1**
Long-term debt	..	..	..	..	..	..	..	0.0	0.0	8.7
IMF charges	0.0	0.0	0.0	0.0	0.0	0.0	0.0	0.0	0.0	1.1
Short-term debt	..	..	..	..	..	..	..	0.0	0.3	0.3
Net transfers on debt	..	..	..	..	..	..	..	**0.0**	**73.1**	**196.9**
Total debt service paid (TDS)	..	..	..	..	..	..	..	**0.0**	**0.3**	**10.1**
Long-term debt	..	..	..	..	..	..	..	0.0	0.0	8.7
IMF repurchases and charges	0.0	0.0	0.0	0.0	0.0	0.0	0.0	0.0	0.0	1.1
Short-term debt (interest only)	..	..	..	..	..	..	..	0.0	0.3	0.3

2. AGGREGATE NET RESOURCE FLOWS AND NET TRANSFERS (LONG-TERM)	1970	1980	1988	1989	1990	1991	1992	1993	1994	1995
NET RESOURCE FLOWS	..	..	..	..	..	..	..	**12.6**	**211.5**	**270.0**
Net flow of long-term debt (ex. IMF)	..	..	..	..	..	..	..	0.0	67.4	102.1
Foreign direct investment (net)	..	..	..	..	..	..	..	0.0	0.0	110.0
Portfolio equity flows	..	..	..	..	..	..	..	0.0	0.0	0.0
Grants (excluding technical coop.)	..	..	..	..	..	..	..	12.6	144.1	57.9
Memo: technical coop. grants	..	..	..	..	..	..	..	9.3	3.3	20.8
NET TRANSFERS	..	..	..	..	..	..	..	**12.6**	**211.5**	**261.3**
Interest on long-term debt	..	..	..	..	..	..	..	0.0	0.0	8.7
Profit remittances on FDI	..	..	..	..	..	..	..	0.0	0.0	0.0

3. MAJOR ECONOMIC AGGREGATES	1970	1980	1988	1989	1990	1991	1992	1993	1994	1995
Gross national product (GNP)	..	..	..	..	..	..	..	4,729.6	3,891.7	3,474.7
Exports of goods & services (XGS)	..	..	..	..	..	..	..	..	..	..
of which workers remittances	..	..	..	..	..	..	..	..	..	..
Imports of goods & services (MGS)	..	..	..	..	..	..	..	..	..	..
International reserves (RES)	..	..	..	..	..	..	..	0.6	2.0	83.9
Current account balance	..	..	..	..	..	..	..	..	..	..

4. DEBT INDICATORS	1970	1980	1988	1989	1990	1991	1992	1993	1994	1995
EDT / XGS (%)	..	..	..	..	..	..	..	..	..	..
EDT / GNP (%)	..	..	..	..	..	..	..	0.8	2.9	9.2
TDS / XGS (%)	..	..	..	..	..	..	..	..	..	..
INT / XGS (%)	..	..	..	..	..	..	..	..	..	..
INT / GNP (%)	..	..	..	..	..	..	..	0.0	0.0	0.3
RES / EDT (%)	..	..	..	..	..	..	..	1.7	1.8	26.1
RES / MGS (months)	..	..	..	..	..	..	..	..	..	..
Short-term / EDT (%)	..	..	..	..	..	..	..	0.1	8.5	4.4
Concessional / EDT (%)	..	..	..	..	..	..	..	0.0	0.0	9.4
Multilateral / EDT (%)	..	..	..	..	..	..	..	0.0	7.5	30.8

AZERBAIJAN

(US$ million, unless otherwise indicated)

	1970	1980	1988	1989	1990	1991	1992	1993	1994	1995
5. LONG-TERM DEBT										
DEBT OUTSTANDING (LDOD)	..	..	..	..	..	..	..	**35.5**	**103.2**	**206.1**
Public and publicly guaranteed	..	..	..	..	..	..	..	**35.5**	**103.2**	**206.1**
Official creditors	..	..	..	..	..	..	..	35.5	103.2	206.1
Multilateral	..	..	..	..	..	..	..	0.0	8.4	98.8
Concessional	..	..	..	..	..	..	..	0.0	0.0	30.2
Bilateral	..	..	..	..	..	..	..	35.5	94.8	107.3
Concessional	..	..	..	..	..	..	..	0.0	0.0	0.0
Private creditors	..	..	..	..	..	..	..	0.0	0.0	0.0
Bonds	..	..	..	..	..	..	..	0.0	0.0	0.0
Commercial banks	..	..	..	..	..	..	..	0.0	0.0	0.0
Other private	..	..	..	..	..	..	..	0.0	0.0	0.0
Private nonguaranteed	**0.0**	**0.0**	**0.0**	**0.0**	**0.0**	**0.0**	**0.0**	**0.0**	**0.0**	**0.0**
Bonds	..	..	..	..	..	..	..	0.0	0.0	0.0
Commercial banks	..	..	..	..	..	..	..	0.0	0.0	0.0
Memo:										
IBRD	0.0	0.0	0.0	0.0	0.0	0.0	0.0	0.0	0.0	0.0
IDA	0.0	0.0	0.0	0.0	0.0	0.0	0.0	0.0	0.0	30.2
DISBURSEMENTS	..	..	..	..	..	..	..	**0.0**	**67.4**	**102.1**
Public and publicly guaranteed	..	..	..	..	..	..	..	**0.0**	**67.4**	**102.1**
Official creditors	..	..	..	..	..	..	..	0.0	67.4	102.1
Multilateral	..	..	..	..	..	..	..	0.0	8.2	89.5
Concessional	..	..	..	..	..	..	..	0.0	0.0	30.2
Bilateral	..	..	..	..	..	..	..	0.0	59.3	12.5
Concessional	..	..	..	..	..	..	..	0.0	0.0	0.0
Private creditors	..	..	..	..	..	..	..	0.0	0.0	0.0
Bonds	..	..	..	..	..	..	..	0.0	0.0	0.0
Commercial banks	..	..	..	..	..	..	..	0.0	0.0	0.0
Other private	..	..	..	..	..	..	..	0.0	0.0	0.0
Private nonguaranteed	**0.0**	**0.0**	**0.0**	**0.0**	**0.0**	**0.0**	**0.0**	**0.0**	**0.0**	**0.0**
Bonds	..	..	..	..	..	..	..	0.0	0.0	0.0
Commercial banks	..	..	..	..	..	..	..	0.0	0.0	0.0
Memo:										
IBRD	0.0	0.0	0.0	0.0	0.0	0.0	0.0	0.0	0.0	0.0
IDA	0.0	0.0	0.0	0.0	0.0	0.0	0.0	0.0	0.0	30.2
PRINCIPAL REPAYMENTS	..	..	..	..	..	..	..	**0.0**	**0.0**	**0.0**
Public and publicly guaranteed	..	..	..	..	..	..	..	**0.0**	**0.0**	**0.0**
Official creditors	..	..	..	..	..	..	..	0.0	0.0	0.0
Multilateral	..	..	..	..	..	..	..	0.0	0.0	0.0
Concessional	..	..	..	..	..	..	..	0.0	0.0	0.0
Bilateral	..	..	..	..	..	..	..	0.0	0.0	0.0
Concessional	..	..	..	..	..	..	..	0.0	0.0	0.0
Private creditors	..	..	..	..	..	..	..	0.0	0.0	0.0
Bonds	..	..	..	..	..	..	..	0.0	0.0	0.0
Commercial banks	..	..	..	..	..	..	..	0.0	0.0	0.0
Other private	..	..	..	..	..	..	..	0.0	0.0	0.0
Private nonguaranteed	**0.0**	**0.0**	**0.0**	**0.0**	**0.0**	**0.0**	**0.0**	**0.0**	**0.0**	**0.0**
Bonds	..	..	..	..	..	..	..	0.0	0.0	0.0
Commercial banks	..	..	..	..	..	..	..	0.0	0.0	0.0
Memo:										
IBRD	0.0	0.0	0.0	0.0	0.0	0.0	0.0	0.0	0.0	0.0
IDA	0.0	0.0	0.0	0.0	0.0	0.0	0.0	0.0	0.0	0.0
NET FLOWS ON DEBT	..	..	..	..	..	..	..	**0.0**	**67.4**	**102.1**
Public and publicly guaranteed	..	..	..	..	..	..	..	**0.0**	**67.4**	**102.1**
Official creditors	..	..	..	..	..	..	..	0.0	67.4	102.1
Multilateral	..	..	..	..	..	..	..	0.0	8.2	89.5
Concessional	..	..	..	..	..	..	..	0.0	0.0	30.2
Bilateral	..	..	..	..	..	..	..	0.0	59.3	12.5
Concessional	..	..	..	..	..	..	..	0.0	0.0	0.0
Private creditors	..	..	..	..	..	..	..	0.0	0.0	0.0
Bonds	..	..	..	..	..	..	..	0.0	0.0	0.0
Commercial banks	..	..	..	..	..	..	..	0.0	0.0	0.0
Other private	..	..	..	..	..	..	..	0.0	0.0	0.0
Private nonguaranteed	**0.0**	**0.0**	**0.0**	**0.0**	**0.0**	**0.0**	**0.0**	**0.0**	**0.0**	**0.0**
Bonds	..	..	..	..	..	..	..	0.0	0.0	0.0
Commercial banks	..	..	..	..	..	..	..	0.0	0.0	0.0
Memo:										
IBRD	0.0	0.0	0.0	0.0	0.0	0.0	0.0	0.0	0.0	0.0
IDA	0.0	0.0	0.0	0.0	0.0	0.0	0.0	0.0	0.0	30.2

AZERBAIJAN

(US$ million, unless otherwise indicated)

	1970	1980	1988	1989	1990	1991	1992	1993	1994	1995
INTEREST PAYMENTS (LINT)	..	..	..	..	..	..	..	**0.0**	**0.0**	**8.7**
Public and publicly guaranteed	..	..	..	..	..	..	..	**0.0**	**0.0**	**8.7**
Official creditors	..	..	..	..	..	..	..	0.0	0.0	8.7
Multilateral	..	..	..	..	..	..	..	0.0	0.0	1.9
Concessional	..	..	..	..	..	..	..	0.0	0.0	0.0
Bilateral	..	..	..	..	..	..	..	0.0	0.0	6.8
Concessional	..	..	..	..	..	..	..	0.0	0.0	0.0
Private creditors	..	..	..	..	..	..	..	0.0	0.0	0.0
Bonds	..	..	..	..	..	..	..	0.0	0.0	0.0
Commercial banks	..	..	..	..	..	..	..	0.0	0.0	0.0
Other private	..	..	..	..	..	..	..	0.0	0.0	0.0
Private nonguaranteed	**0.0**	**0.0**	**0.0**	**0.0**	**0.0**	**0.0**	**0.0**	**0.0**	**0.0**	**0.0**
Bonds	..	..	..	..	..	..	..	0.0	0.0	0.0
Commercial banks	..	..	..	..	..	..	..	0.0	0.0	0.0
Memo:										
IBRD	0.0	0.0	0.0	0.0	0.0	0.0	0.0	0.0	0.0	0.0
IDA	0.0	0.0	0.0	0.0	0.0	0.0	0.0	0.0	0.0	0.0
NET TRANSFERS ON DEBT	..	..	..	..	..	..	..	**0.0**	**67.4**	**93.4**
Public and publicly guaranteed	..	..	..	..	..	..	..	**0.0**	**67.4**	**93.4**
Official creditors	..	..	..	..	..	..	..	0.0	67.4	93.4
Multilateral	..	..	..	..	..	..	..	0.0	8.2	87.6
Concessional	..	..	..	..	..	..	..	0.0	0.0	30.2
Bilateral	..	..	..	..	..	..	..	0.0	59.3	5.7
Concessional	..	..	..	..	..	..	..	0.0	0.0	0.0
Private creditors	..	..	..	..	..	..	..	0.0	0.0	0.0
Bonds	..	..	..	..	..	..	..	0.0	0.0	0.0
Commercial banks	..	..	..	..	..	..	..	0.0	0.0	0.0
Other private	..	..	..	..	..	..	..	0.0	0.0	0.0
Private nonguaranteed	**0.0**	**0.0**	**0.0**	**0.0**	**0.0**	**0.0**	**0.0**	**0.0**	**0.0**	**0.0**
Bonds	..	..	..	..	..	..	..	0.0	0.0	0.0
Commercial banks	..	..	..	..	..	..	..	0.0	0.0	0.0
Memo:										
IBRD	0.0	0.0	0.0	0.0	0.0	0.0	0.0	0.0	0.0	0.0
IDA	0.0	0.0	0.0	0.0	0.0	0.0	0.0	0.0	0.0	30.2
DEBT SERVICE (LTDS)	..	..	..	..	..	..	..	**0.0**	**0.0**	**8.7**
Public and publicly guaranteed	..	..	..	..	..	..	..	**0.0**	**0.0**	**8.7**
Official creditors	..	..	..	..	..	..	..	0.0	0.0	8.7
Multilateral	..	..	..	..	..	..	..	0.0	0.0	1.9
Concessional	..	..	..	..	..	..	..	0.0	0.0	0.0
Bilateral	..	..	..	..	..	..	..	0.0	0.0	6.8
Concessional	..	..	..	..	..	..	..	0.0	0.0	0.0
Private creditors	..	..	..	..	..	..	..	0.0	0.0	0.0
Bonds	..	..	..	..	..	..	..	0.0	0.0	0.0
Commercial banks	..	..	..	..	..	..	..	0.0	0.0	0.0
Other private	..	..	..	..	..	..	..	0.0	0.0	0.0
Private nonguaranteed	**0.0**	**0.0**	**0.0**	**0.0**	**0.0**	**0.0**	**0.0**	**0.0**	**0.0**	**0.0**
Bonds	..	..	..	..	..	..	..	0.0	0.0	0.0
Commercial banks	..	..	..	..	..	..	..	0.0	0.0	0.0
Memo:										
IBRD	0.0	0.0	0.0	0.0	0.0	0.0	0.0	0.0	0.0	0.0
IDA	0.0	0.0	0.0	0.0	0.0	0.0	0.0	0.0	0.0	0.0
UNDISBURSED DEBT	..	..	..	..	..	..	..	**250.0**	**329.4**	**413.3**
Official creditors	..	..	..	..	..	..	..	250.0	329.4	413.3
Private creditors	..	..	..	..	..	..	..	0.0	0.0	0.0
Memorandum items										
Concessional LDOD	..	..	..	..	..	..	..	0.0	0.0	30.2
Variable rate LDOD	..	..	..	..	..	..	..	35.5	103.2	175.9
Public sector LDOD	..	..	..	..	..	..	..	35.5	103.2	206.1
Private sector LDOD	..	..	..	..	..	..	..	0.0	0.0	0.0

6. CURRENCY COMPOSITION OF LONG-TERM DEBT (PERCENT)

	1970	1980	1988	1989	1990	1991	1992	1993	1994	1995
Deutsche mark	..	..	..	..	..	..	..	0.0	0.0	0.0
French franc	..	..	..	..	..	..	..	0.0	0.0	0.0
Japanese yen	..	..	..	..	..	..	..	0.0	0.0	0.0
Pound sterling	..	..	..	..	..	..	..	0.0	0.0	0.0
Swiss franc	..	..	..	..	..	..	..	0.0	0.0	0.0
U.S.dollars	..	..	..	..	..	..	..	0.0	57.5	51.4
Multiple currency	..	..	..	..	..	..	..	0.0	0.0	0.0
Special drawing rights	..	..	..	..	..	..	..	0.0	0.0	0.0
All other currencies	..	..	..	..	..	..	..	100.0	42.5	48.6

AZERBAIJAN

(US$ million, unless otherwise indicated)

	1970	1980	1988	1989	1990	1991	1992	1993	1994	1995
7. DEBT RESTRUCTURINGS										
Total amount rescheduled	0.0	0.0	0.0	0.0	0.0	0.0	0.0	35.5	0.0	0.0
Debt stock rescheduled	0.0	0.0	0.0	0.0	0.0	0.0	0.0	0.0	0.0	0.0
Principal rescheduled	0.0	0.0	0.0	0.0	0.0	0.0	0.0	0.0	0.0	0.0
Official	0.0	0.0	0.0	0.0	0.0	0.0	0.0	0.0	0.0	0.0
Private	0.0	0.0	0.0	0.0	0.0	0.0	0.0	0.0	0.0	0.0
Interest rescheduled	0.0	0.0	0.0	0.0	0.0	0.0	0.0	0.0	0.0	0.0
Official	0.0	0.0	0.0	0.0	0.0	0.0	0.0	0.0	0.0	0.0
Private	0.0	0.0	0.0	0.0	0.0	0.0	0.0	0.0	0.0	0.0
Debt forgiven	..	..	0.0	0.0	0.0	0.0	0.0	0.0	0.0	0.0
Memo: interest forgiven	..	..	0.0	0.0	0.0	0.0	0.0	0.0	0.0	0.0
Debt stock reduction	0.0	0.0	0.0	0.0	0.0	0.0	0.0	0.0	0.0	0.0
of which debt buyback	0.0	0.0	0.0	0.0	0.0	0.0	0.0	0.0	0.0	0.0
8. DEBT STOCK-FLOW RECONCILIATION										
Total change in debt stocks	..	..	..	..	..	..	..	36.0	77.3	208.2
Net flows on debt	..	..	..	..	..	..	..	0.0	73.4	207.0
Net change in interest arrears	..	..	..	..	..	..	..	0.0	3.6	2.4
Interest capitalized	..	..	..	..	..	..	..	0.0	0.0	0.0
Debt forgiveness or reduction	..	..	..	..	..	..	..	0.0	0.0	0.0
Cross-currency valuation	..	..	..	..	..	..	..	-24.2	-22.2	-3.3
Residual	..	..	..	..	..	..	..	60.0	22.4	2.0
9. AVERAGE TERMS OF NEW COMMITMENTS										
ALL CREDITORS										
Interest (%)	..	..	..	..	..	..	..	3.0	6.8	1.4
Maturity (years)	..	..	..	..	..	..	..	5.3	7.8	32.2
Grace period (years)	..	..	..	..	..	..	..	1.8	3.4	9.4
Grant element (%)	..	..	..	..	..	..	..	19.6	11.3	71.8
Official creditors										
Interest (%)	..	..	..	..	..	..	..	3.0	6.8	1.4
Maturity (years)	..	..	..	..	..	..	..	5.3	7.8	32.2
Grace period (years)	..	..	..	..	..	..	..	1.8	3.4	9.4
Grant element (%)	..	..	..	..	..	..	..	19.6	11.3	71.8
Private creditors										
Interest (%)	..	..	..	..	..	..	..	0.0	0.0	0.0
Maturity (years)	..	..	..	..	..	..	..	0.0	0.0	0.0
Grace period (years)	..	..	..	..	..	..	..	0.0	0.0	0.0
Grant element (%)	..	..	..	..	..	..	..	0.0	0.0	0.0
Memorandum items										
Commitments	..	..	..	..	..	..	..	250.0	144.1	187.8
Official creditors	..	..	..	..	..	..	..	250.0	144.1	187.8
Private creditors	..	..	..	..	..	..	..	0.0	0.0	0.0

10. CONTRACTUAL OBLIGATIONS ON OUTSTANDING LONG-TERM DEBT

	1996	1997	1998	1999	2000	2001	2002	2003	2004	2005
TOTAL										
Disbursements	198.5	116.4	59.1	22.3	12.3	3.3	1.3	0.0	0.0	0.0
Principal	84.6	174.0	84.6	7.2	8.2	8.2	8.2	8.2	6.9	9.2
Interest	16.4	16.9	7.1	5.7	5.5	5.1	4.6	4.1	3.6	3.2
Official creditors										
Disbursements	198.5	116.4	59.1	22.3	12.3	3.3	1.3	0.0	0.0	0.0
Principal	84.6	174.0	84.6	7.2	8.2	8.2	8.2	8.2	6.9	9.2
Interest	16.4	16.9	7.1	5.7	5.5	5.1	4.6	4.1	3.6	3.2
Bilateral creditors										
Disbursements	111.7	47.9	18.6	0.0	0.0	0.0	0.0	0.0	0.0	0.0
Principal	83.3	83.3	83.3	0.0	0.0	0.0	0.0	0.0	0.0	0.0
Interest	10.9	10.3	5.6	0.0	0.0	0.0	0.0	0.0	0.0	0.0
Multilateral creditors										
Disbursements	86.8	68.5	40.5	22.3	12.3	3.3	1.3	0.0	0.0	0.0
Principal	1.3	90.7	1.3	7.2	8.2	8.2	8.2	8.2	6.9	9.2
Interest	5.5	6.6	1.5	5.7	5.5	5.1	4.6	4.1	3.6	3.2
Private creditors										
Disbursements	0.0	0.0	0.0	0.0	0.0	0.0	0.0	0.0	0.0	0.0
Principal	0.0	0.0	0.0	0.0	0.0	0.0	0.0	0.0	0.0	0.0
Interest	0.0	0.0	0.0	0.0	0.0	0.0	0.0	0.0	0.0	0.0
Commercial banks										
Disbursements	0.0	0.0	0.0	0.0	0.0	0.0	0.0	0.0	0.0	0.0
Principal	0.0	0.0	0.0	0.0	0.0	0.0	0.0	0.0	0.0	0.0
Interest	0.0	0.0	0.0	0.0	0.0	0.0	0.0	0.0	0.0	0.0
Other private										
Disbursements	0.0	0.0	0.0	0.0	0.0	0.0	0.0	0.0	0.0	0.0
Principal	0.0	0.0	0.0	0.0	0.0	0.0	0.0	0.0	0.0	0.0
Interest	0.0	0.0	0.0	0.0	0.0	0.0	0.0	0.0	0.0	0.0

BANGLADESH

(US$ million, unless otherwise indicated)

	1970	1980	1988	1989	1990	1991	1992	1993	1994	1995
1. SUMMARY DEBT DATA										
TOTAL DEBT STOCKS (EDT)	..	4,230	10,693	11,119	12,757	13,470	13,898	14,619	16,223	16,370
Long-term debt (LDOD)	0	3,594	9,804	10,333	11,976	12,525	12,932	13,784	15,356	15,543
Public and publicly guaranteed	0	3,594	9,804	10,333	11,976	12,525	12,932	13,784	15,356	15,543
Private nonguaranteed	0	0	0	0	0	0	0	0	0	0
Use of IMF credit	0	424	840	719	626	727	732	682	669	622
Short-term debt	..	212	50	68	156	219	233	154	198	206
of which interest arrears on LDOD	..	0	0	1	1	1	3	6	13	22
Official creditors	..	0	0	1	1	1	3	5	12	19
Private creditors	..	0	0	0	0	1	0	0	0	3
Memo: principal arrears on LDOD	..	0	9	9	11	14	23	30	53	60
Official creditors	..	0	9	9	11	9	18	26	35	39
Private creditors	..	0	0	0	0	5	4	5	18	21
Memo: export credits	..	..	291	324	329	345	741	957	913	450
TOTAL DEBT FLOWS										
Disbursements	0	970	1,125	1,174	1,357	1,057	1,064	707	1,017	675
Long-term debt	0	743	979	1,150	1,296	823	941	667	1,017	675
IMF purchases	0	227	146	24	61	234	123	40	0	0
Principal repayments	0	199	320	323	573	433	402	391	406	543
Long-term debt	0	65	215	201	363	292	314	301	350	482
IMF repurchases	0	134	105	122	211	141	88	91	56	61
Net flows on debt	0	770	781	868	871	687	675	234	648	131
of which short-term debt	..	..	-24	17	88	63	13	-82	37	-1
Interest payments (INT)	..	79	185	201	218	197	172	176	197	186
Long-term debt	0	50	146	147	167	163	153	163	187	174
IMF charges	0	13	34	45	42	22	10	6	4	3
Short-term debt	..	16	5	9	9	12	9	7	7	10
Net transfers on debt	..	692	596	667	654	490	503	58	451	-55
Total debt service paid (TDS)	..	278	505	524	791	630	574	567	603	729
Long-term debt	0	115	362	348	529	455	466	464	537	656
IMF repurchases and charges	0	147	139	167	253	163	99	96	60	64
Short-term debt (interest only)	..	16	5	9	9	12	9	7	7	10
2. AGGREGATE NET RESOURCE FLOWS AND NET TRANSFERS (LONG-TERM)										
NET RESOURCE FLOWS	0	1,679	1,417	1,721	1,708	1,684	1,440	1,030	1,485	906
Net flow of long-term debt (ex. IMF)	0	678	764	949	934	531	627	366	667	193
Foreign direct investment (net)	0	0	2	0	3	1	4	14	11	2
Portfolio equity flows	0	0	0	0	0	0	0	0	48	33
Grants (excluding technical coop.)	0	1,001	651	772	772	1,153	809	650	760	678
Memo: technical coop. grants	0	159	199	214	239	263	314	303	300	294
NET TRANSFERS	0	1,629	1,271	1,574	1,542	1,522	1,287	867	1,298	733
Interest on long-term debt	0	50	146	147	167	163	153	163	187	174
Profit remittances on FDI	0	0	0	0	0	0	0	0	0	0
3. MAJOR ECONOMIC AGGREGATES										
Gross national product (GNP)	6,722	12,964	18,978	20,412	22,275	23,292	23,672	24,140	25,725	29,069
Exports of goods & services (XGS)	526	1,174	2,278	2,448	2,731	2,942	3,406	3,944	4,294	5,490
of which workers remittances	0	197	737	771	761	764	848	944	1,089	1,198
Imports of goods & services (MGS)	770	2,622	3,440	3,888	4,313	3,956	4,049	4,702	4,871	6,748
International reserves (RES)	..	331	1,077	532	660	1,308	1,854	2,447	3,175	2,376
Current account balance	-114	-844	-287	-703	-775	-101	301	-121	-70	-1,030
4. DEBT INDICATORS										
EDT / XGS (%)	..	360.4	469.4	454.2	467.1	457.9	408.1	370.7	377.8	298.2
EDT / GNP (%)	..	32.6	56.3	54.5	57.3	57.8	58.7	60.6	63.1	56.3
TDS / XGS (%)	..	23.7	22.2	21.4	29.0	21.4	16.9	14.4	14.1	13.3
INT / XGS (%)	..	6.7	8.1	8.2	8.0	6.7	5.1	4.4	4.6	3.4
INT / GNP (%)	..	0.6	1.0	1.0	1.0	0.8	0.7	0.7	0.8	0.6
RES / EDT (%)	..	7.8	10.1	4.8	5.2	9.7	13.3	16.7	19.6	14.5
RES / MGS (months)	..	1.5	3.8	1.6	1.8	4.0	5.5	6.2	7.8	4.2
Short-term / EDT (%)	..	5.0	0.5	0.6	1.2	1.6	1.7	1.1	1.2	1.3
Concessional / EDT (%)	..	83.1	88.8	90.0	90.7	89.9	90.2	91.8	92.6	93.2
Multilateral / EDT (%)	..	30.2	44.0	47.2	51.2	52.8	53.9	55.4	57.2	59.7

BANGLADESH

(US$ million, unless otherwise indicated)

	1970	1980	1988	1989	1990	1991	1992	1993	1994	1995
5. LONG-TERM DEBT										
DEBT OUTSTANDING (LDOD)	**0**	**3,594**	**9,804**	**10,333**	**11,976**	**12,525**	**12,932**	**13,784**	**15,356**	**15,543**
Public and publicly guaranteed	**0**	**3,594**	**9,804**	**10,333**	**11,976**	**12,525**	**12,932**	**13,784**	**15,356**	**15,543**
Official creditors	0	3,538	9,589	10,144	11,714	12,229	12,627	13,487	15,087	15,299
Multilateral	0	1,276	4,702	5,247	6,529	7,113	7,495	8,097	9,284	9,766
Concessional	0	1,269	4,683	5,228	6,496	7,100	7,494	8,096	9,283	9,765
Bilateral	0	2,263	4,887	4,897	5,185	5,116	5,132	5,391	5,803	5,533
Concessional	0	2,248	4,811	4,776	5,075	5,014	5,043	5,320	5,746	5,492
Private creditors	0	56	215	189	262	295	305	296	269	244
Bonds	0	0	0	0	0	0	0	0	0	0
Commercial banks	0	0	14	14	34	31	29	26	28	32
Other private	0	56	201	175	228	264	277	271	241	212
Private nonguaranteed	**0**	**0**	**0**	**0**	**0**	**0**	**0**	**0**	**0**	**0**
Bonds	0	0	0	0	0	0	0	0	0	0
Commercial banks	0	0	0	0	0	0	0	0	0	0
Memo:										
IBRD	0	55	66	62	64	65	60	58	58	55
IDA	0	926	3,188	3,441	4,095	4,360	4,534	4,824	5,378	5,638
DISBURSEMENTS	**0**	**743**	**979**	**1,150**	**1,296**	**823**	**941**	**667**	**1,017**	**675**
Public and publicly guaranteed	**0**	**743**	**979**	**1,150**	**1,296**	**823**	**941**	**667**	**1,017**	**675**
Official creditors	0	726	967	1,141	1,194	752	889	632	996	663
Multilateral	0	307	559	639	849	546	661	553	816	492
Concessional	0	306	556	633	819	546	661	553	816	492
Bilateral	0	419	408	502	345	206	228	79	181	171
Concessional	0	419	394	439	345	193	226	78	181	171
Private creditors	0	17	12	9	102	71	52	36	21	12
Bonds	0	0	0	0	0	0	0	0	0	0
Commercial banks	0	0	0	0	22	0	0	0	6	6
Other private	0	17	12	9	80	71	52	36	14	6
Private nonguaranteed	**0**	**0**	**0**	**0**	**0**	**0**	**0**	**0**	**0**	**0**
Bonds	0	0	0	0	0	0	0	0	0	0
Commercial banks	0	0	0	0	0	0	0	0	0	0
Memo:										
IBRD	0	0	0	0	0	0	0	0	0	0
IDA	0	156	291	299	484	253	327	306	412	197
PRINCIPAL REPAYMENTS	**0**	**65**	**215**	**201**	**363**	**292**	**314**	**301**	**350**	**482**
Public and publicly guaranteed	**0**	**65**	**215**	**201**	**363**	**292**	**314**	**301**	**350**	**482**
Official creditors	0	59	182	167	327	256	274	258	301	445
Multilateral	0	1	39	48	63	71	72	72	81	105
Concessional	0	1	37	42	47	51	60	72	81	105
Bilateral	0	58	143	119	264	185	202	186	219	340
Concessional	0	54	132	103	251	172	188	171	204	324
Private creditors	0	6	34	34	35	36	40	43	49	37
Bonds	0	0	0	0	0	0	0	0	0	0
Commercial banks	0	0	2	1	2	3	3	3	4	2
Other private	0	6	32	34	33	33	37	40	45	35
Private nonguaranteed	**0**	**0**	**0**	**0**	**0**	**0**	**0**	**0**	**0**	**0**
Bonds	0	0	0	0	0	0	0	0	0	0
Commercial banks	0	0	0	0	0	0	0	0	0	0
Memo:										
IBRD	0	0	1	2	2	1	3	4	4	5
IDA	0	0	9	11	13	16	20	28	33	41
NET FLOWS ON DEBT	**0**	**678**	**764**	**949**	**934**	**531**	**627**	**366**	**667**	**193**
Public and publicly guaranteed	**0**	**678**	**764**	**949**	**934**	**531**	**627**	**366**	**667**	**193**
Official creditors	0	667	785	974	867	496	614	374	696	218
Multilateral	0	306	520	590	786	475	589	481	735	387
Concessional	0	306	518	591	772	495	601	481	735	387
Bilateral	0	361	265	384	80	21	25	-108	-39	-169
Concessional	0	365	262	336	94	22	38	-93	-24	-153
Private creditors	0	11	-21	-25	67	35	13	-7	-29	-25
Bonds	0	0	0	0	0	0	0	0	0	0
Commercial banks	0	0	-2	-1	20	-3	-3	-3	2	4
Other private	0	11	-19	-25	47	38	16	-5	-31	-29
Private nonguaranteed	**0**	**0**	**0**	**0**	**0**	**0**	**0**	**0**	**0**	**0**
Bonds	0	0	0	0	0	0	0	0	0	0
Commercial banks	0	0	0	0	0	0	0	0	0	0
Memo:										
IBRD	0	0	-1	-2	-2	-1	-3	-4	-4	-5
IDA	0	156	282	288	472	237	307	278	380	155

BANGLADESH

(US$ million, unless otherwise indicated)

	1970	1980	1988	1989	1990	1991	1992	1993	1994	1995
INTEREST PAYMENTS (LINT)	**0**	**50**	**146**	**147**	**167**	**163**	**153**	**163**	**187**	**174**
Public and publicly guaranteed	**0**	**50**	**146**	**147**	**167**	**163**	**153**	**163**	**187**	**174**
Official creditors	0	48	135	139	155	152	143	152	176	167
Multilateral	0	11	44	42	53	59	64	71	78	87
Concessional	0	11	43	42	52	57	63	71	78	87
Bilateral	0	37	91	96	102	94	79	81	98	80
Concessional	0	36	85	88	92	84	70	74	90	75
Private creditors	0	2	11	9	11	10	10	10	11	6
Bonds	0	0	0	0	0	0	0	0	0	0
Commercial banks	0	0	1	0	1	2	1	1	1	0
Other private	0	2	11	9	11	9	9	10	10	6
Private nonguaranteed	**0**	**0**	**0**	**0**	**0**	**0**	**0**	**0**	**0**	**0**
Bonds	0	0	0	0	0	0	0	0	0	0
Commercial banks	0	0	0	0	0	0	0	0	0	0
Memo:										
IBRD	0	3	4	4	4	4	4	4	4	4
IDA	0	6	27	24	28	30	32	36	39	42
NET TRANSFERS ON DEBT	**0**	**628**	**618**	**801**	**767**	**368**	**475**	**204**	**480**	**19**
Public and publicly guaranteed	**0**	**628**	**618**	**801**	**767**	**368**	**475**	**204**	**480**	**19**
Official creditors	0	620	650	835	711	343	472	221	520	51
Multilateral	0	295	476	548	733	416	525	410	656	300
Concessional	0	295	475	549	721	438	538	410	657	300
Bilateral	0	325	174	287	-22	-73	-54	-189	-136	-249
Concessional	0	329	178	247	2	-63	-33	-167	-114	-228
Private creditors	0	8	-33	-34	56	25	3	-18	-40	-31
Bonds	0	0	0	0	0	0	0	0	0	0
Commercial banks	0	0	-2	-1	20	-4	-4	-3	2	3
Other private	0	8	-30	-33	36	29	7	-14	-41	-34
Private nonguaranteed	**0**	**0**	**0**	**0**	**0**	**0**	**0**	**0**	**0**	**0**
Bonds	0	0	0	0	0	0	0	0	0	0
Commercial banks	0	0	0	0	0	0	0	0	0	0
Memo:										
IBRD	0	-3	-6	-6	-5	-5	-7	-7	-7	-8
IDA	0	150	255	264	443	207	275	242	341	114
DEBT SERVICE (LTDS)	**0**	**115**	**362**	**348**	**529**	**455**	**466**	**464**	**537**	**656**
Public and publicly guaranteed	**0**	**115**	**362**	**348**	**529**	**455**	**466**	**464**	**537**	**656**
Official creditors	0	107	317	306	483	408	417	410	476	612
Multilateral	0	12	83	90	116	130	136	143	159	192
Concessional	0	11	81	84	98	108	123	143	159	192
Bilateral	0	94	234	215	367	278	281	267	317	420
Concessional	0	90	217	191	343	256	258	245	294	399
Private creditors	0	8	45	43	47	46	49	53	60	44
Bonds	0	0	0	0	0	0	0	0	0	0
Commercial banks	0	0	2	1	2	4	4	3	5	3
Other private	0	8	42	42	44	42	46	50	56	41
Private nonguaranteed	**0**	**0**	**0**	**0**	**0**	**0**	**0**	**0**	**0**	**0**
Bonds	0	0	0	0	0	0	0	0	0	0
Commercial banks	0	0	0	0	0	0	0	0	0	0
Memo:										
IBRD	0	3	6	6	5	5	7	7	7	8
IDA	0	6	36	35	41	47	52	64	71	83
UNDISBURSED DEBT	**0**	**2,113**	**4,112**	**3,853**	**4,141**	**4,151**	**4,137**	**4,089**	**4,197**	**4,105**
Official creditors	0	2,059	4,019	3,758	3,990	4,077	4,045	4,027	4,046	3,966
Private creditors	0	54	93	96	151	74	92	62	151	139
Memorandum items										
Concessional LDOD	0	3,517	9,494	10,004	11,571	12,114	12,537	13,415	15,029	15,257
Variable rate LDOD	0	5	16	14	34	31	62	64	60	53
Public sector LDOD	0	3,592	9,801	10,330	11,973	12,522	12,930	13,782	15,355	15,543
Private sector LDOD	0	2	3	2	3	3	2	1	1	0

6. CURRENCY COMPOSITION OF LONG-TERM DEBT (PERCENT)

	1970	1980	1988	1989	1990	1991	1992	1993	1994	1995
Deutsche mark	0.0	0.2	0.2	0.2	0.2	0.2	0.1	0.1	0.1	0.1
French franc	0.0	1.2	1.3	1.4	1.5	1.4	1.2	1.0	1.1	0.7
Japanese yen	0.0	21.6	28.5	25.5	24.1	25.2	25.3	25.9	26.0	24.9
Pound sterling	0.0	17.4	6.3	5.8	5.1	4.7	4.5	4.1	3.6	3.5
Swiss franc	0.0	0.2	0.1	0.1	0.1	0.0	0.0	0.0	0.0	0.0
U.S.dollars	0.0	42.6	45.6	47.7	48.7	46.9	46.5	45.3	43.2	43.3
Multiple currency	0.0	7.4	10.8	13.0	15.0	16.7	18.0	19.1	21.0	22.2
Special drawing rights	0.0	0.2	0.9	0.9	0.9	0.9	1.0	1.6	2.6	3.1
All other currencies	0.0	9.4	6.2	5.4	4.5	3.9	3.3	2.9	2.4	2.1

BANGLADESH

(US$ million, unless otherwise indicated)

	1970	1980	1988	1989	1990	1991	1992	1993	1994	1995
7. DEBT RESTRUCTURINGS										
Total amount rescheduled	0	0	0	0	0	0	0	0	0	0
Debt stock rescheduled	0	0	0	0	0	0	0	0	0	0
Principal rescheduled	0	0	0	0	0	0	0	0	0	0
Official	0	0	0	0	0	0	0	0	0	0
Private	0	0	0	0	0	0	0	0	0	0
Interest rescheduled	0	0	0	0	0	0	0	0	0	0
Official	0	0	0	0	0	0	0	0	0	0
Private	0	0	0	0	0	0	0	0	0	0
Debt forgiven	..	..	0	0	0	297	0	2	2	0
Memo: interest forgiven	..	..	0	0	0	0	0	0	0	0
Debt stock reduction	0	0	0	0	0	0	0	0	0	0
of which debt buyback	0	0	0	0	0	0	0	0	0	0
8. DEBT STOCK-FLOW RECONCILIATION										
Total change in debt stocks	..	..	..	426	1,638	713	427	722	1,603	147
Net flows on debt	..	..	..	868	871	687	675	234	648	131
Net change in interest arrears	..	..	..	1	1	0	2	3	7	9
Interest capitalized	..	..	..	0	0	0	0	0	0	0
Debt forgiveness or reduction	..	..	..	0	0	-297	0	-2	-2	0
Cross-currency valuation	..	..	..	-399	366	208	-130	383	568	-94
Residual	..	..	..	-44	400	116	-119	104	382	101
9. AVERAGE TERMS OF NEW COMMITMENTS										
ALL CREDITORS										
Interest (%)	0.0	1.7	2.0	1.1	1.9	1.0	1.1	1.1	1.3	1.9
Maturity (years)	0.0	36.0	32.2	36.2	33.6	38.3	35.8	35.2	33.3	37.8
Grace period (years)	0.0	8.9	9.2	9.8	9.3	9.7	9.7	9.7	9.0	10.0
Grant element (%)	0.0	68.5	66.6	74.8	67.6	77.2	74.7	75.0	70.8	69.0
Official creditors										
Interest (%)	0.0	1.5	1.9	1.1	1.3	1.0	0.9	1.1	1.0	1.9
Maturity (years)	0.0	36.8	32.3	36.6	36.3	38.3	37.4	35.2	35.1	37.8
Grace period (years)	0.0	9.1	9.2	9.9	10.0	9.7	10.1	9.7	9.3	10.0
Grant element (%)	0.0	70.3	67.0	75.4	73.8	77.2	77.6	74.9	74.6	69.0
Private creditors										
Interest (%)	0.0	7.5	7.1	2.4	6.7	0.0	4.0	0.8	5.0	0.0
Maturity (years)	0.0	10.7	9.7	10.5	11.3	0.0	13.8	38.4	12.2	0.0
Grace period (years)	0.0	2.4	2.0	2.7	3.1	0.0	4.3	8.9	4.2	0.0
Grant element (%)	0.0	11.3	10.5	34.2	16.5	0.0	33.2	79.0	25.9	0.0
Memorandum items										
Commitments	0	1,036	1,052	1,112	1,447	902	1,177	717	1,421	687
Official creditors	0	1,004	1,045	1,096	1,290	902	1,101	712	1,311	687
Private creditors	0	32	7	16	157	0	76	6	109	0

10. CONTRACTUAL OBLIGATIONS ON OUTSTANDING LONG-TERM DEBT

	1996	1997	1998	1999	2000	2001	2002	2003	2004	2005
TOTAL										
Disbursements	1,206	1,092	753	481	262	122	71	21	8	3
Principal	404	429	460	506	540	550	576	594	627	644
Interest	197	205	205	202	196	188	180	172	163	154
Official creditors										
Disbursements	1,148	1,065	745	477	262	122	71	21	8	3
Principal	357	392	416	464	504	524	549	577	611	628
Interest	185	193	194	193	189	183	177	169	161	153
Bilateral creditors										
Disbursements	275	260	168	107	62	38	19	9	6	3
Principal	248	268	277	301	321	318	325	328	336	327
Interest	92	94	91	87	82	77	71	66	61	56
Multilateral creditors										
Disbursements	873	805	577	370	200	84	52	12	1	0
Principal	109	124	139	163	182	206	225	249	275	301
Interest	92	99	103	106	107	107	105	103	101	98
Private creditors										
Disbursements	58	27	9	4	0	0	0	0	0	0
Principal	48	37	44	42	36	27	26	17	17	17
Interest	13	12	11	9	7	5	4	3	2	1
Commercial banks										
Disbursements	0	0	0	0	0	0	0	0	0	0
Principal	6	6	1	0	0	0	0	0	0	0
Interest	1	1	0	0	0	0	0	0	0	0
Other private										
Disbursements	58	27	9	4	0	0	0	0	0	0
Principal	42	31	43	42	36	27	26	16	16	16
Interest	12	12	10	9	7	5	4	3	2	1

BARBADOS

(US$ million, unless otherwise indicated)

	1970	1980	1988	1989	1990	1991	1992	1993	1994	1995
1. SUMMARY DEBT DATA										
TOTAL DEBT STOCKS (EDT)	..	**165.7**	**702.9**	**643.6**	**683.0**	**652.1**	**609.6**	**569.9**	**614.7**	**597.0**
Long-term debt (LDOD)	**12.9**	**97.8**	**529.0**	**480.0**	**504.1**	**482.8**	**400.6**	**348.0**	**370.6**	**369.6**
Public and publicly guaranteed	12.9	97.8	529.0	480.0	504.1	482.8	400.6	348.0	370.6	369.6
Private nonguaranteed	0.0	0.0	0.0	0.0	0.0	0.0	0.0	0.0	0.0	0.0
Use of IMF credit	**0.0**	**2.9**	**10.4**	**4.3**	**0.7**	**0.0**	**50.7**	**50.6**	**53.8**	**37.1**
Short-term debt	..	**65.0**	**163.4**	**159.3**	**178.1**	**169.4**	**158.4**	**171.3**	**190.3**	**190.3**
of which interest arrears on LDOD	..	0.0	6.4	1.8	0.2	0.4	0.4	0.3	0.3	0.3
Official creditors	..	0.0	0.3	0.6	0.2	0.4	0.4	0.3	0.3	0.3
Private creditors	..	0.0	6.1	1.2	0.0	0.0	0.0	0.0	0.0	0.0
Memo: principal arrears on LDOD	..	0.0	17.1	4.9	0.7	0.9	1.2	1.0	1.3	1.3
Official creditors	..	0.0	2.2	2.4	0.7	0.9	1.2	1.0	1.3	1.3
Private creditors	..	0.0	14.9	2.5	0.0	0.0	0.0	0.0	0.0	0.0
Memo: export credits	..	..	104.0	94.0	99.0	89.0	84.0	71.0	89.0	120.0
TOTAL DEBT FLOWS										
Disbursements	**0.0**	**38.4**	**126.3**	**25.2**	**90.6**	**69.1**	**65.5**	**14.4**	**62.2**	**55.4**
Long-term debt	0.0	38.4	126.3	25.2	90.6	69.1	13.6	14.4	62.2	55.4
IMF purchases	0.0	0.0	0.0	0.0	0.0	0.0	51.9	0.0	0.0	0.0
Principal repayments	**0.0**	**14.2**	**49.1**	**53.9**	**92.2**	**94.1**	**58.9**	**72.0**	**48.3**	**77.1**
Long-term debt	0.0	8.7	38.6	48.2	88.4	93.4	58.9	72.0	48.3	59.0
IMF repurchases	0.0	5.5	10.6	5.7	3.7	0.7	0.0	0.0	0.0	18.0
Net flows on debt	**0.0**	**24.2**	**136.2**	**-28.2**	**18.8**	**-33.9**	**-4.4**	**-44.6**	**32.8**	**-21.7**
of which short-term debt	..	..	59.0	0.5	20.4	-8.9	-11.0	13.0	19.0	0.0
Interest payments (INT)	..	**11.1**	**44.9**	**48.0**	**48.6**	**46.0**	**42.6**	**40.8**	**40.7**	**41.6**
Long-term debt	0.8	5.8	38.4	40.1	39.3	37.5	32.2	28.3	27.0	27.4
IMF charges	0.0	0.3	1.3	0.7	0.4	0.1	2.4	3.0	2.7	2.8
Short-term debt	..	5.0	5.2	7.2	8.9	8.4	8.1	9.5	10.9	11.4
Net transfers on debt	..	**13.1**	**91.3**	**-76.2**	**-29.8**	**-79.9**	**-47.0**	**-85.5**	**-7.8**	**-63.3**
Total debt service paid (TDS)	..	**25.2**	**94.0**	**101.9**	**140.7**	**140.1**	**101.6**	**112.9**	**89.0**	**118.7**
Long-term debt	0.8	14.5	77.0	88.3	127.7	130.9	91.1	100.4	75.4	86.5
IMF repurchases and charges	0.0	5.8	11.9	6.4	4.1	0.8	2.4	3.0	2.7	20.9
Short-term debt (interest only)	..	5.0	5.2	7.2	8.9	8.4	8.1	9.5	10.9	11.4
2. AGGREGATE NET RESOURCE FLOWS AND NET TRANSFERS (LONG-TERM)										
NET RESOURCE FLOWS	**9.5**	**33.2**	**102.2**	**-13.4**	**14.4**	**-16.0**	**-31.5**	**-29.0**	**26.0**	**9.5**
Net flow of long-term debt (ex. IMF)	0.0	29.7	87.8	-23.0	2.1	-24.3	-45.3	-57.6	13.8	-3.6
Foreign direct investment (net)	8.7	2.8	11.5	8.3	11.0	7.0	14.0	9.0	10.0	12.0
Portfolio equity flows	0.0	0.0	0.0	0.0	0.0	0.0	0.0	0.0	0.0	0.0
Grants (excluding technical coop.)	0.8	0.7	2.9	1.3	1.3	1.3	-0.2	19.6	2.2	1.1
Memo: technical coop. grants	0.6	2.6	2.5	2.0	2.4	3.5	3.0	2.4	2.1	2.1
NET TRANSFERS	**4.5**	**22.6**	**59.9**	**-60.5**	**-34.0**	**-61.2**	**-72.7**	**-65.4**	**-1.0**	**-21.9**
Interest on long-term debt	0.8	5.8	38.4	40.1	39.3	37.5	32.2	28.3	27.0	27.4
Profit remittances on FDI	4.2	4.8	3.8	7.0	9.1	7.7	9.0	8.0	0.0	4.0
3. MAJOR ECONOMIC AGGREGATES										
Gross national product (GNP)	180.8	836.9	1,495.2	1,668.8	1,700.0	1,630.9	1,539.6	1,574.6	1,670.7	1,683.2
Exports of goods & services (XGS)	101.7	572.7	782.9	887.8	836.4	832.1	822.4	877.6	..	..
of which workers remittances	0.0	0.0	0.0	0.0	0.0	0.0	0.0	0.0	..	..
Imports of goods & services (MGS)	148.7	619.8	756.9	868.9	895.2	890.2	718.8	839.1	..	..
International reserves (RES)	16.6	80.6	138.0	111.9	117.5	87.3	140.0	150.5	195.8	219.1
Current account balance	-41.8	-25.7	42.5	23.7	-16.4	-25.1	143.8	64.3	..	..
4. DEBT INDICATORS										
EDT / XGS (%)	..	28.9	89.8	72.5	81.7	78.4	74.1	64.9	..	..
EDT / GNP (%)	..	19.8	47.0	38.6	40.2	40.0	39.6	36.2	36.8	35.5
TDS / XGS (%)	..	4.4	12.0	11.5	16.8	16.8	12.3	12.9	..	..
INT / XGS (%)	..	1.9	5.7	5.4	5.8	5.5	5.2	4.7	..	..
INT / GNP (%)	..	1.3	3.0	2.9	2.9	2.8	2.8	2.6	2.4	2.5
RES / EDT (%)	..	48.6	19.6	17.4	17.2	13.4	23.0	26.4	31.9	36.7
RES / MGS (months)	1.3	1.6	2.2	1.5	1.6	1.2	2.3	2.2	..	..
Short-term / EDT (%)	..	39.2	23.3	24.8	26.1	26.0	26.0	30.1	31.0	31.9
Concessional / EDT (%)	..	22.3	13.4	14.3	13.6	14.3	11.8	12.2	10.5	10.0
Multilateral / EDT (%)	..	20.4	23.7	25.7	26.5	27.5	28.2	28.8	26.5	27.4

BARBADOS

(US$ million, unless otherwise indicated)

	1970	1980	1988	1989	1990	1991	1992	1993	1994	1995
5. LONG-TERM DEBT										
DEBT OUTSTANDING (LDOD)	**12.9**	**97.8**	**529.0**	**480.0**	**504.1**	**482.8**	**400.6**	**348.0**	**370.6**	**369.6**
Public and publicly guaranteed	**12.9**	**97.8**	**529.0**	**480.0**	**504.1**	**482.8**	**400.6**	**348.0**	**370.6**	**369.6**
Official creditors	0.0	60.6	221.7	222.4	246.0	241.8	209.0	199.8	192.2	189.6
Multilateral	0.0	33.7	166.9	165.1	180.9	179.3	171.7	164.0	163.1	163.6
Concessional	0.0	20.8	56.9	57.4	56.8	56.4	56.7	54.6	52.5	49.0
Bilateral	0.0	26.8	54.8	57.2	65.1	62.5	37.3	35.8	29.1	26.0
Concessional	0.0	16.2	37.5	34.5	35.9	37.1	15.5	14.9	11.8	10.5
Private creditors	12.9	37.2	307.3	257.6	258.2	240.9	191.6	148.2	178.4	180.1
Bonds	12.9	16.7	123.0	109.1	69.2	39.9	40.1	44.7	40.1	74.0
Commercial banks	0.0	20.5	148.2	116.4	163.1	179.5	134.8	91.6	131.2	103.6
Other private	0.0	0.1	36.0	32.1	25.9	21.5	16.7	12.0	7.2	2.4
Private nonguaranteed	**0.0**	**0.0**	**0.0**	**0.0**	**0.0**	**0.0**	**0.0**	**0.0**	**0.0**	**0.0**
Bonds	0.0	0.0	0.0	0.0	0.0	0.0	0.0	0.0	0.0	0.0
Commercial banks	0.0	0.0	0.0	0.0	0.0	0.0	0.0	0.0	0.0	0.0
Memo:										
IBRD	0.0	0.9	40.6	35.2	36.0	32.5	26.7	22.0	19.6	19.3
IDA	0.0	0.0	0.0	0.0	0.0	0.0	0.0	0.0	0.0	0.0
DISBURSEMENTS	**0.0**	**38.4**	**126.3**	**25.2**	**90.6**	**69.1**	**13.6**	**14.4**	**62.2**	**55.4**
Public and publicly guaranteed	**0.0**	**38.4**	**126.3**	**25.2**	**90.6**	**69.1**	**13.6**	**14.4**	**62.2**	**55.4**
Official creditors	0.0	16.6	24.2	23.1	33.9	15.7	13.6	13.2	12.2	15.4
Multilateral	0.0	12.3	23.0	14.4	21.9	12.4	12.2	9.1	11.0	13.7
Concessional	0.0	10.4	2.6	2.6	1.7	2.1	3.5	1.8	0.9	0.6
Bilateral	0.0	4.4	1.2	8.7	12.1	3.3	1.4	4.1	1.2	1.7
Concessional	0.0	1.1	0.0	0.2	2.5	2.9	1.1	0.8	0.3	0.4
Private creditors	0.0	21.7	102.2	2.1	56.6	53.5	0.0	1.2	50.0	40.0
Bonds	0.0	16.7	39.1	0.0	0.0	0.0	0.0	0.0	0.0	40.0
Commercial banks	0.0	5.1	63.1	2.1	56.6	53.5	0.0	1.2	50.0	0.0
Other private	0.0	0.0	0.0	0.0	0.0	0.0	0.0	0.0	0.0	0.0
Private nonguaranteed	**0.0**	**0.0**	**0.0**	**0.0**	**0.0**	**0.0**	**0.0**	**0.0**	**0.0**	**0.0**
Bonds	0.0	0.0	0.0	0.0	0.0	0.0	0.0	0.0	0.0	0.0
Commercial banks	0.0	0.0	0.0	0.0	0.0	0.0	0.0	0.0	0.0	0.0
Memo:										
IBRD	0.0	0.8	3.6	2.5	5.4	3.3	2.8	2.4	2.6	3.5
IDA	0.0	0.0	0.0	0.0	0.0	0.0	0.0	0.0	0.0	0.0
PRINCIPAL REPAYMENTS	**0.0**	**8.7**	**38.6**	**48.2**	**88.4**	**93.4**	**58.9**	**72.0**	**48.3**	**59.0**
Public and publicly guaranteed	**0.0**	**8.7**	**38.6**	**48.2**	**88.4**	**93.4**	**58.9**	**72.0**	**48.3**	**59.0**
Official creditors	0.0	3.0	18.6	16.8	17.8	20.5	21.6	24.0	20.7	21.8
Multilateral	0.0	0.6	11.8	12.3	13.2	15.1	16.8	18.6	14.9	16.9
Concessional	0.0	0.1	2.1	2.0	2.2	2.6	3.0	3.6	3.4	4.3
Bilateral	0.0	2.4	6.8	4.4	4.6	5.4	4.8	5.4	5.8	4.9
Concessional	0.0	0.3	1.5	1.6	0.9	1.4	1.0	1.3	1.4	1.6
Private creditors	0.0	5.7	20.0	31.4	70.6	72.9	37.3	48.1	27.6	37.3
Bonds	0.0	0.0	0.0	0.0	44.1	32.0	0.0	0.0	9.8	5.3
Commercial banks	0.0	5.4	14.6	27.6	20.2	36.5	32.5	43.3	13.1	27.1
Other private	0.0	0.3	5.3	3.8	6.2	4.4	4.8	4.8	4.8	4.8
Private nonguaranteed	**0.0**	**0.0**	**0.0**	**0.0**	**0.0**	**0.0**	**0.0**	**0.0**	**0.0**	**0.0**
Bonds	0.0	0.0	0.0	0.0	0.0	0.0	0.0	0.0	0.0	0.0
Commercial banks	0.0	0.0	0.0	0.0	0.0	0.0	0.0	0.0	0.0	0.0
Memo:										
IBRD	0.0	0.0	6.6	5.9	7.1	7.5	7.7	7.9	6.5	4.7
IDA	0.0	0.0	0.0	0.0	0.0	0.0	0.0	0.0	0.0	0.0
NET FLOWS ON DEBT	**0.0**	**29.7**	**87.8**	**-23.0**	**2.1**	**-24.3**	**-45.3**	**-57.6**	**13.8**	**-3.6**
Public and publicly guaranteed	**0.0**	**29.7**	**87.8**	**-23.0**	**2.1**	**-24.3**	**-45.3**	**-57.6**	**13.8**	**-3.6**
Official creditors	0.0	13.7	5.6	6.4	16.1	-4.8	-8.0	-10.7	-8.5	-6.4
Multilateral	0.0	11.7	11.2	2.1	8.6	-2.7	-4.6	-9.5	-3.9	-3.2
Concessional	0.0	10.4	0.5	0.5	-0.5	-0.6	0.5	-1.8	-2.5	-3.7
Bilateral	0.0	2.0	-5.6	4.2	7.5	-2.2	-3.4	-1.3	-4.6	-3.2
Concessional	0.0	0.8	-1.5	-1.4	1.6	1.5	0.1	-0.5	-1.1	-1.3
Private creditors	0.0	16.0	82.2	-29.3	-14.0	-19.5	-37.3	-46.9	22.4	2.7
Bonds	0.0	16.7	39.1	0.0	-44.1	-32.0	0.0	0.0	-9.8	34.7
Commercial banks	0.0	-0.4	48.5	-25.5	36.4	16.9	-32.5	-42.1	36.9	-27.1
Other private	0.0	-0.3	-5.3	-3.8	-6.2	-4.4	-4.8	-4.8	-4.8	-4.8
Private nonguaranteed	**0.0**	**0.0**	**0.0**	**0.0**	**0.0**	**0.0**	**0.0**	**0.0**	**0.0**	**0.0**
Bonds	0.0	0.0	0.0	0.0	0.0	0.0	0.0	0.0	0.0	0.0
Commercial banks	0.0	0.0	0.0	0.0	0.0	0.0	0.0	0.0	0.0	0.0
Memo:										
IBRD	0.0	0.8	-3.0	-3.5	-1.7	-4.2	-4.9	-5.5	-3.9	-1.2
IDA	0.0	0.0	0.0	0.0	0.0	0.0	0.0	0.0	0.0	0.0

BARBADOS

(US$ million, unless otherwise indicated)

	1970	1980	1988	1989	1990	1991	1992	1993	1994	1995
INTEREST PAYMENTS (LINT)	**0.8**	**5.8**	**38.4**	**40.1**	**39.3**	**37.5**	**32.2**	**28.3**	**27.0**	**27.4**
Public and publicly guaranteed	**0.8**	**5.8**	**38.4**	**40.1**	**39.3**	**37.5**	**32.2**	**28.3**	**27.0**	**27.4**
Official creditors	0.0	2.6	15.2	13.4	14.4	14.0	14.1	13.7	14.3	12.6
Multilateral	0.0	1.6	10.7	10.5	11.5	11.4	11.1	11.3	12.3	10.6
Concessional	0.0	0.5	1.6	1.5	1.6	1.7	1.7	1.6	1.8	1.6
Bilateral	0.0	1.1	4.5	2.9	2.9	2.6	3.0	2.4	2.0	1.9
Concessional	0.0	0.4	0.9	0.6	0.4	0.5	0.4	0.4	0.3	0.3
Private creditors	0.8	3.2	23.2	26.7	24.9	23.5	18.1	14.7	12.7	14.8
Bonds	0.8	0.0	8.9	8.4	8.1	4.7	2.7	3.1	3.2	3.1
Commercial banks	0.0	3.1	12.4	15.7	15.5	16.9	13.9	10.4	8.8	11.3
Other private	0.0	0.1	1.9	2.6	1.3	1.9	1.5	1.2	0.8	0.5
Private nonguaranteed	**0.0**	**0.0**	**0.0**	**0.0**	**0.0**	**0.0**	**0.0**	**0.0**	**0.0**	**0.0**
Bonds	0.0	0.0	0.0	0.0	0.0	0.0	0.0	0.0	0.0	0.0
Commercial banks	0.0	0.0	0.0	0.0	0.0	0.0	0.0	0.0	0.0	0.0
Memo:										
IBRD	0.0	0.2	3.6	3.1	2.9	2.7	2.4	2.1	1.7	1.6
IDA	0.0	0.0	0.0	0.0	0.0	0.0	0.0	0.0	0.0	0.0
NET TRANSFERS ON DEBT	**-0.8**	**23.9**	**49.3**	**-63.1**	**-37.2**	**-61.8**	**-77.5**	**-86.0**	**-13.2**	**-31.0**
Public and publicly guaranteed	**-0.8**	**23.9**	**49.3**	**-63.1**	**-37.2**	**-61.8**	**-77.5**	**-86.0**	**-13.2**	**-31.0**
Official creditors	0.0	11.1	-9.6	-7.0	1.7	-18.8	-22.0	-24.4	-22.8	-18.9
Multilateral	0.0	10.2	0.5	-8.4	-2.9	-14.1	-15.7	-20.8	-16.2	-13.8
Concessional	0.0	9.8	-1.1	-1.0	-2.1	-2.2	-1.2	-3.4	-4.3	-5.3
Bilateral	0.0	0.9	-10.1	1.4	4.5	-4.7	-6.3	-3.6	-6.6	-5.1
Concessional	0.0	0.4	-2.4	-2.0	1.2	1.0	-0.3	-0.9	-1.4	-1.5
Private creditors	-0.8	12.8	58.9	-56.0	-38.8	-42.9	-55.4	-61.6	9.6	-12.1
Bonds	-0.8	16.7	30.1	-8.4	-52.2	-36.7	-2.7	-3.1	-13.0	31.6
Commercial banks	0.0	-3.5	36.0	-41.2	20.9	0.1	-46.4	-52.5	28.2	-38.4
Other private	0.0	-0.4	-7.2	-6.5	-7.5	-6.3	-6.3	-6.0	-5.6	-5.2
Private nonguaranteed	**0.0**	**0.0**	**0.0**	**0.0**	**0.0**	**0.0**	**0.0**	**0.0**	**0.0**	**0.0**
Bonds	0.0	0.0	0.0	0.0	0.0	0.0	0.0	0.0	0.0	0.0
Commercial banks	0.0	0.0	0.0	0.0	0.0	0.0	0.0	0.0	0.0	0.0
Memo:										
IBRD	0.0	0.7	-6.6	-6.6	-4.7	-6.9	-7.4	-7.6	-5.6	-2.8
IDA	0.0	0.0	0.0	0.0	0.0	0.0	0.0	0.0	0.0	0.0
DEBT SERVICE (LTDS)	**0.8**	**14.5**	**77.0**	**88.3**	**127.7**	**130.9**	**91.1**	**100.4**	**75.4**	**86.5**
Public and publicly guaranteed	**0.8**	**14.5**	**77.0**	**88.3**	**127.7**	**130.9**	**91.1**	**100.4**	**75.4**	**86.5**
Official creditors	0.0	5.6	33.8	30.2	32.2	34.5	35.7	37.6	35.0	34.3
Multilateral	0.0	2.1	22.5	22.8	24.7	26.5	27.9	29.9	27.2	27.5
Concessional	0.0	0.6	3.7	3.5	3.8	4.3	4.7	5.2	5.2	5.9
Bilateral	0.0	3.4	11.3	7.3	7.5	8.0	7.8	7.8	7.8	6.8
Concessional	0.0	0.7	2.4	2.2	1.3	1.8	1.4	1.7	1.7	1.9
Private creditors	0.8	8.9	43.2	58.1	95.5	96.4	55.4	62.8	40.4	52.1
Bonds	0.8	0.0	8.9	8.4	52.2	36.7	2.7	3.1	13.0	8.4
Commercial banks	0.0	8.5	27.1	43.3	35.8	53.4	46.4	53.7	21.8	38.4
Other private	0.0	0.4	7.2	6.5	7.5	6.3	6.3	6.0	5.6	5.2
Private nonguaranteed	**0.0**	**0.0**	**0.0**	**0.0**	**0.0**	**0.0**	**0.0**	**0.0**	**0.0**	**0.0**
Bonds	0.0	0.0	0.0	0.0	0.0	0.0	0.0	0.0	0.0	0.0
Commercial banks	0.0	0.0	0.0	0.0	0.0	0.0	0.0	0.0	0.0	0.0
Memo:										
IBRD	0.0	0.2	10.2	9.0	10.0	10.3	10.1	10.0	8.2	6.3
IDA	0.0	0.0	0.0	0.0	0.0	0.0	0.0	0.0	0.0	0.0
UNDISBURSED DEBT	**2.8**	**78.4**	**91.0**	**98.9**	**110.1**	**44.8**	**49.5**	**130.8**	**139.8**	**127.8**
Official creditors	2.8	70.8	81.1	70.1	63.6	43.5	48.3	130.8	139.8	127.8
Private creditors	0.0	7.6	9.8	28.8	46.4	1.3	1.2	0.0	0.0	0.0
Memorandum items										
Concessional LDOD	0.0	37.0	94.4	91.9	92.6	93.6	72.2	69.5	64.3	59.5
Variable rate LDOD	0.0	15.9	134.4	113.9	155.8	119.3	81.5	56.8	49.4	29.8
Public sector LDOD	12.9	97.8	518.8	473.0	499.5	478.8	398.1	346.7	370.1	369.5
Private sector LDOD	0.0	0.0	10.2	7.0	4.6	3.9	2.6	1.3	0.6	0.2

6. CURRENCY COMPOSITION OF LONG-TERM DEBT (PERCENT)

	1970	1980	1988	1989	1990	1991	1992	1993	1994	1995
Deutsche mark	0.0	0.0	0.0	0.7	0.6	0.4	0.3	0.1	0.0	0.0
French franc	0.0	0.0	0.0	0.0	0.0	0.0	0.0	0.0	0.0	0.0
Japanese yen	0.0	0.0	21.5	20.8	13.7	8.3	10.0	12.8	10.8	9.2
Pound sterling	100.0	6.4	11.2	10.4	13.6	19.3	15.8	14.6	12.8	12.7
Swiss franc	0.0	0.0	0.0	0.0	0.0	0.0	0.0	0.0	0.0	0.0
U.S.dollars	0.0	30.7	33.2	31.2	35.3	33.4	32.9	27.2	34.9	36.9
Multiple currency	0.0	30.5	27.1	30.1	31.9	33.2	38.5	42.7	39.9	39.5
Special drawing rights	0.0	0.0	0.0	0.0	0.0	0.0	0.0	0.0	0.0	0.0
All other currencies	0.0	32.4	7.0	6.8	4.9	5.4	2.4	2.5	1.6	1.7

BARBADOS

(US$ million, unless otherwise indicated)

	1970	1980	1988	1989	1990	1991	1992	1993	1994	1995
7. DEBT RESTRUCTURINGS										
Total amount rescheduled	0.0	0.0	0.0	0.0	0.0	0.0	0.0	0.0	0.0	0.0
Debt stock rescheduled	0.0	0.0	0.0	0.0	0.0	0.0	0.0	0.0	0.0	0.0
Principal rescheduled	0.0	0.0	0.0	0.0	0.0	0.0	0.0	0.0	0.0	0.0
Official	0.0	0.0	0.0	0.0	0.0	0.0	0.0	0.0	0.0	0.0
Private	0.0	0.0	0.0	0.0	0.0	0.0	0.0	0.0	0.0	0.0
Interest rescheduled	0.0	0.0	0.0	0.0	0.0	0.0	0.0	0.0	0.0	0.0
Official	0.0	0.0	0.0	0.0	0.0	0.0	0.0	0.0	0.0	0.0
Private	0.0	0.0	0.0	0.0	0.0	0.0	0.0	0.0	0.0	0.0
Debt forgiven	..	..	0.0	0.0	0.0	0.0	20.4	0.0	0.0	0.0
Memo: interest forgiven	..	..	0.0	0.0	0.0	0.0	0.0	0.0	0.0	0.0
Debt stock reduction	0.0	0.0	0.0	0.0	0.0	0.0	0.0	0.0	0.0	0.0
of which debt buyback	0.0	0.0	0.0	0.0	0.0	0.0	0.0	0.0	0.0	0.0
8. DEBT STOCK-FLOW RECONCILIATION										
Total change in debt stocks	..	..	..	-59.3	39.4	-30.9	-42.5	-39.7	44.8	-17.7
Net flows on debt	..	..	..	-28.2	18.8	-33.9	-4.4	-44.6	32.8	-21.7
Net change in interest arrears	..	..	..	-4.6	-1.6	0.1	0.0	-0.1	0.0	0.0
Interest capitalized	..	..	..	0.0	0.0	0.0	0.0	0.0	0.0	0.0
Debt forgiveness or reduction	..	..	..	0.0	0.0	0.0	-20.4	0.0	0.0	0.0
Cross-currency valuation	..	..	..	-20.9	20.0	-1.3	-15.7	2.4	5.5	-1.9
Residual	..	..	..	-5.6	2.2	4.2	-2.0	2.6	6.5	5.9
9. AVERAGE TERMS OF NEW COMMITMENTS										
ALL CREDITORS										
Interest (%)	3.0	7.1	7.0	8.5	10.2	10.5	7.6	6.9	10.1	10.1
Maturity (years)	29.6	15.5	9.1	9.9	18.6	2.7	14.8	21.8	8.7	10.8
Grace period (years)	7.1	5.8	4.5	4.1	15.3	1.5	5.3	5.7	4.3	6.3
Grant element (%)	54.6	18.3	13.6	8.4	-5.5	-0.7	13.5	20.0	1.2	-1.6
Official creditors										
Interest (%)	3.0	6.1	8.0	5.3	6.5	9.1	7.6	6.9	7.2	6.6
Maturity (years)	29.6	19.9	6.0	15.1	15.4	23.1	14.8	21.8	20.3	20.0
Grace period (years)	7.1	5.2	1.4	4.2	4.9	4.8	5.3	5.7	4.4	4.0
Grant element (%)	54.6	26.6	5.0	27.1	21.7	4.7	13.5	20.0	17.3	21.0
Private creditors										
Interest (%)	0.0	8.3	6.8	10.3	11.7	10.5	0.0	0.0	11.2	10.4
Maturity (years)	0.0	10.3	9.5	7.0	19.8	2.4	0.0	0.0	4.2	10.0
Grace period (years)	0.0	6.6	4.9	4.0	19.3	1.4	0.0	0.0	4.2	6.5
Grant element (%)	0.0	8.7	14.6	-2.0	-16.1	-0.8	0.0	0.0	-5.1	-3.6
Memorandum items										
Commitments	2.5	61.9	60.5	39.0	102.0	12.2	21.2	96.1	69.6	43.6
Official creditors	2.5	33.3	6.4	14.0	28.5	0.2	21.2	96.1	19.6	3.6
Private creditors	0.0	28.6	54.1	25.0	73.5	12.0	0.0	0.0	50.0	40.0

10. CONTRACTUAL OBLIGATIONS ON OUTSTANDING LONG-TERM DEBT

	1996	1997	1998	1999	2000	2001	2002	2003	2004	2005
TOTAL										
Disbursements	28.8	32.0	24.2	18.7	12.2	6.4	3.2	1.0	0.4	0.2
Principal	43.1	55.1	36.3	56.2	26.1	23.2	30.1	27.4	26.6	24.8
Interest	33.1	31.0	28.9	27.6	23.0	21.6	20.0	17.7	15.5	13.5
Official creditors										
Disbursements	28.8	32.0	24.2	18.7	12.2	6.4	3.2	1.0	0.4	0.2
Principal	22.2	23.8	25.0	26.2	26.1	23.2	20.1	17.4	16.6	14.8
Interest	14.9	15.1	14.8	14.1	13.0	11.6	10.3	9.0	7.9	6.9
Bilateral creditors										
Disbursements	1.3	1.3	0.6	0.3	0.1	0.1	0.0	0.0	0.0	0.0
Principal	5.0	4.4	3.2	2.9	2.5	1.2	0.8	0.8	0.8	0.8
Interest	1.6	1.3	1.1	0.9	0.7	0.6	0.6	0.5	0.5	0.4
Multilateral creditors										
Disbursements	27.5	30.8	23.5	18.4	12.1	6.3	3.2	1.0	0.4	0.2
Principal	17.2	19.4	21.8	23.3	23.6	22.0	19.2	16.6	15.9	14.0
Interest	13.3	13.8	13.7	13.2	12.2	11.0	9.7	8.5	7.5	6.5
Private creditors										
Disbursements	0.0	0.0	0.0	0.0	0.0	0.0	0.0	0.0	0.0	0.0
Principal	20.9	31.3	11.4	30.0	0.0	0.0	10.0	10.0	10.0	10.0
Interest	18.1	15.9	14.0	13.5	10.0	10.0	9.7	8.7	7.6	6.6
Commercial banks										
Disbursements	0.0	0.0	0.0	0.0	0.0	0.0	0.0	0.0	0.0	0.0
Principal	7.1	20.0	0.0	30.0	0.0	0.0	0.0	0.0	0.0	0.0
Interest	11.8	10.4	9.3	9.3	5.8	5.8	5.8	5.8	5.8	5.8
Other private										
Disbursements	0.0	0.0	0.0	0.0	0.0	0.0	0.0	0.0	0.0	0.0
Principal	13.7	11.3	11.4	0.0	0.0	0.0	10.0	10.0	10.0	10.0
Interest	6.4	5.5	4.7	4.2	4.2	4.2	3.9	2.9	1.8	0.8

BELARUS

(US$ million, unless otherwise indicated)

	1970	1980	1988	1989	1990	1991	1992	1993	1994	1995
1. SUMMARY DEBT DATA										
TOTAL DEBT STOCKS (EDT)	..	..	..	..	..	..	**189**	**969**	**1,273**	**1,648**
Long-term debt (LDOD)	..	..	..	..	..	..	**189**	**866**	**1,100**	**1,256**
Public and publicly guaranteed	..	..	..	..	..	..	189	865	1,100	1,255
Private nonguaranteed	0	0	0	0	0	0	0	1	1	0
Use of IMF credit	**0**	**0**	**0**	**0**	**0**	**0**	**0**	**96**	**102**	**283**
Short-term debt	..	..	..	..	..	..	**0**	**7**	**70**	**110**
of which interest arrears on LDOD	..	..	..	..	..	..	0	7	15	18
Official creditors	..	..	..	..	..	..	0	0	0	0
Private creditors	..	..	..	..	..	..	0	7	15	18
Memo: principal arrears on LDOD	..	..	..	..	..	..	0	0	135	140
Official creditors	..	..	..	..	..	..	0	0	0	0
Private creditors	..	..	..	..	..	..	0	0	135	140
Memo: export credits	..	..	0	0	0	0	40	211	101	398
TOTAL DEBT FLOWS										
Disbursements	..	..	..	..	..	..	**190**	**429**	**329**	**421**
Long-term debt	..	..	..	..	..	..	190	331	329	239
IMF purchases	0	0	0	0	0	0	0	98	0	182
Principal repayments	..	..	..	..	..	..	**0**	**3**	**88**	**108**
Long-term debt	..	..	..	..	..	..	0	3	88	108
IMF repurchases	0	0	0	0	0	0	0	0	0	0
Net flows on debt	..	..	..	..	..	..	**190**	**426**	**296**	**349**
of which short-term debt	..	..	..	..	..	..	0	0	55	36
Interest payments (INT)	..	..	..	..	..	..	**1**	**12**	**31**	**72**
Long-term debt	..	..	..	..	..	..	1	11	22	58
IMF charges	0	0	0	0	0	0	0	1	5	10
Short-term debt	..	..	..	..	..	..	0	0	4	4
Net transfers on debt	..	..	..	..	..	..	**189**	**414**	**265**	**277**
Total debt service paid (TDS)	..	..	..	..	..	..	**1**	**15**	**119**	**180**
Long-term debt	..	..	..	..	..	..	1	13	110	166
IMF repurchases and charges	0	0	0	0	0	0	0	1	5	10
Short-term debt (interest only)	..	..	..	..	..	..	0	0	4	4

	1970	1980	1988	1989	1990	1991	1992	1993	1994	1995
2. AGGREGATE NET RESOURCE FLOWS AND NET TRANSFERS (LONG-TERM)										
NET RESOURCE FLOWS	..	..	..	..	..	..	**445**	**504**	**335**	**287**
Net flow of long-term debt (ex. IMF)	..	..	..	..	..	..	190	328	241	131
Foreign direct investment (net)	..	..	..	..	..	..	7	10	15	20
Portfolio equity flows	..	..	..	..	..	..	0	0	0	0
Grants (excluding technical coop.)	..	..	..	..	..	..	248	167	79	136
Memo: technical coop. grants	..	..	..	..	..	..	3	12	13	27
NET TRANSFERS	..	..	..	..	..	..	**444**	**494**	**313**	**229**
Interest on long-term debt	..	..	..	..	..	..	1	11	22	58
Profit remittances on FDI	..	..	..	..	..	..	0	0	0	0

	1970	1980	1988	1989	1990	1991	1992	1993	1994	1995
3. MAJOR ECONOMIC AGGREGATES										
Gross national product (GNP)	..	..	..	..	..	..	31,088	27,046	22,739	20,803
Exports of goods & services (XGS)	..	..	..	..	..	..	3,661	3,005	2,770	4,946
of which workers remittances	..	..	..	..	..	..	0	0	0	0
Imports of goods & services (MGS)	..	..	..	..	..	..	3,558	3,411	3,345	5,140
International reserves (RES)	..	..	..	..	..	..	..	..	101	377
Current account balance	..	..	..	..	..	..	182	-336	-505	-84

	1970	1980	1988	1989	1990	1991	1992	1993	1994	1995
4. DEBT INDICATORS										
EDT / XGS (%)	..	..	..	..	..	..	5.2	32.3	45.9	33.3
EDT / GNP (%)	..	..	..	..	..	..	0.6	3.6	5.6	7.9
TDS / XGS (%)	..	..	..	..	..	..	0.0	0.5	4.3	3.6
INT / XGS (%)	..	..	..	..	..	..	0.0	0.4	1.1	1.5
INT / GNP (%)	..	..	..	..	..	..	0.0	0.0	0.1	0.3
RES / EDT (%)	..	..	..	..	..	..	..	..	7.9	22.9
RES / MGS (months)	..	..	..	..	..	..	..	..	0.4	0.9
Short-term / EDT (%)	..	..	..	..	..	..	0.0	0.7	5.5	6.6
Concessional / EDT (%)	..	..	..	..	..	..	12.4	48.1	36.2	28.9
Multilateral / EDT (%)	..	..	..	..	..	..	0.5	11.5	13.6	11.4

BELARUS

(US$ million, unless otherwise indicated)

	1970	1980	1988	1989	1990	1991	1992	1993	1994	1995
5. LONG-TERM DEBT										
DEBT OUTSTANDING (LDOD)	..	..	..	..	..	..	**189**	**866**	**1,100**	**1,256**
Public and publicly guaranteed	..	..	..	..	..	..	**189**	**865**	**1,100**	**1,255**
Official creditors	..	..	..	..	..	..	24	593	718	769
Multilateral	..	..	..	..	..	..	1	112	173	188
Concessional	..	..	..	..	..	..	0	0	0	0
Bilateral	..	..	..	..	..	..	23	481	545	582
Concessional	..	..	..	..	..	..	23	467	461	477
Private creditors	..	..	..	..	..	..	164	272	382	486
Bonds	..	..	..	..	..	..	0	0	0	0
Commercial banks	..	..	..	..	..	..	0	0	0	2
Other private	..	..	..	..	..	..	164	272	382	483
Private nonguaranteed	**0**	**0**	**0**	**0**	**0**	**0**	**0**	**1**	**1**	**0**
Bonds	..	..	..	..	..	..	0	0	0	0
Commercial banks	..	..	..	..	..	..	0	1	1	0
Memo:										
IBRD	0	0	0	0	0	0	0	0	101	116
IDA	0	0	0	0	0	0	0	0	0	0
DISBURSEMENTS	..	..	..	..	..	..	**190**	**331**	**329**	**239**
Public and publicly guaranteed	..	..	..	..	..	..	**190**	**329**	**329**	**239**
Official creditors	..	..	..	..	..	..	24	212	211	131
Multilateral	..	..	..	..	..	..	1	116	111	77
Concessional	..	..	..	..	..	..	0	0	0	0
Bilateral	..	..	..	..	..	..	23	96	100	54
Concessional	..	..	..	..	..	..	23	81	30	20
Private creditors	..	..	..	..	..	..	166	117	117	107
Bonds	..	..	..	..	..	..	0	0	0	0
Commercial banks	..	..	..	..	..	..	0	0	0	3
Other private	..	..	..	..	..	..	166	117	117	105
Private nonguaranteed	**0**	**0**	**0**	**0**	**0**	**0**	**0**	**2**	**0**	**0**
Bonds	..	..	..	..	..	..	0	0	0	0
Commercial banks	..	..	..	..	..	..	0	2	0	0
Memo:										
IBRD	0	0	0	0	0	0	0	0	100	11
IDA	0	0	0	0	0	0	0	0	0	0
PRINCIPAL REPAYMENTS	..	..	..	..	..	..	**0**	**3**	**88**	**108**
Public and publicly guaranteed	..	..	..	..	..	..	**0**	**2**	**87**	**108**
Official creditors	..	..	..	..	..	..	0	0	60	84
Multilateral	..	..	..	..	..	..	0	0	60	70
Concessional	..	..	..	..	..	..	0	0	0	0
Bilateral	..	..	..	..	..	..	0	0	0	15
Concessional	..	..	..	..	..	..	0	0	0	0
Private creditors	..	..	..	..	..	..	0	2	27	24
Bonds	..	..	..	..	..	..	0	0	0	0
Commercial banks	..	..	..	..	..	..	0	0	0	0
Other private	..	..	..	..	..	..	0	2	27	24
Private nonguaranteed	**0**	**0**	**0**	**0**	**0**	**0**	**0**	**1**	**1**	**0**
Bonds	..	..	..	..	..	..	0	0	0	0
Commercial banks	..	..	..	..	..	..	0	1	1	0
Memo:										
IBRD	0	0	0	0	0	0	0	0	0	0
IDA	0	0	0	0	0	0	0	0	0	0
NET FLOWS ON DEBT	..	..	..	..	..	..	**190**	**328**	**241**	**131**
Public and publicly guaranteed	..	..	..	..	..	..	**190**	**327**	**242**	**131**
Official creditors	..	..	..	..	..	..	24	212	152	47
Multilateral	..	..	..	..	..	..	1	116	51	8
Concessional	..	..	..	..	..	..	0	0	0	0
Bilateral	..	..	..	..	..	..	23	96	100	40
Concessional	..	..	..	..	..	..	23	81	30	20
Private creditors	..	..	..	..	..	..	166	115	90	83
Bonds	..	..	..	..	..	..	0	0	0	0
Commercial banks	..	..	..	..	..	..	0	0	0	2
Other private	..	..	..	..	..	..	166	115	90	81
Private nonguaranteed	**0**	**0**	**0**	**0**	**0**	**0**	**0**	**1**	**-1**	**0**
Bonds	..	..	..	..	..	..	0	0	0	0
Commercial banks	..	..	..	..	..	..	0	1	-1	0
Memo:										
IBRD	0	0	0	0	0	0	0	0	100	11
IDA	0	0	0	0	0	0	0	0	0	0

BELARUS

(US$ million, unless otherwise indicated)

	1970	1980	1988	1989	1990	1991	1992	1993	1994	1995
INTEREST PAYMENTS (LINT)	..	..	..	..	..	..	**1**	**11**	**22**	**58**
Public and publicly guaranteed	..	..	..	..	..	..	**1**	**11**	**22**	**57**
Official creditors	..	..	..	..	..	..	0	5	7	32
Multilateral	..	..	..	..	..	..	0	5	6	23
Concessional	..	..	..	..	..	..	0	0	0	0
Bilateral	..	..	..	..	..	..	0	0	2	10
Concessional	..	..	..	..	..	..	0	0	1	1
Private creditors	..	..	..	..	..	..	1	5	15	25
Bonds	..	..	..	..	..	..	0	0	0	0
Commercial banks	..	..	..	..	..	..	0	0	0	0
Other private	..	..	..	..	..	..	1	5	15	25
Private nonguaranteed	**0**	**0**	**0**	**0**	**0**	**0**	**0**	**0**	**0**	**0**
Bonds	..	..	..	..	..	..	0	0	0	0
Commercial banks	..	..	..	..	..	..	0	0	0	0
Memo:										
IBRD	0	0	0	0	0	0	0	0	2	8
IDA	0	0	0	0	0	0	0	0	0	0
NET TRANSFERS ON DEBT	..	..	..	..	..	..	**189**	**317**	**219**	**73**
Public and publicly guaranteed	..	..	..	..	..	..	**189**	**316**	**220**	**73**
Official creditors	..	..	..	..	..	..	24	207	144	15
Multilateral	..	..	..	..	..	..	1	111	46	-15
Concessional	..	..	..	..	..	..	0	0	0	0
Bilateral	..	..	..	..	..	..	23	96	98	30
Concessional	..	..	..	..	..	..	23	81	29	19
Private creditors	..	..	..	..	..	..	165	110	75	58
Bonds	..	..	..	..	..	..	0	0	0	0
Commercial banks	..	..	..	..	..	..	0	0	0	2
Other private	..	..	..	..	..	..	165	110	75	56
Private nonguaranteed	**0**	**0**	**0**	**0**	**0**	**0**	**0**	**1**	**-1**	**0**
Bonds	..	..	..	..	..	..	0	0	0	0
Commercial banks	..	..	..	..	..	..	0	1	-1	0
Memo:										
IBRD	0	0	0	0	0	0	0	0	98	4
IDA	0	0	0	0	0	0	0	0	0	0
DEBT SERVICE (LTDS)	..	..	..	..	..	..	**1**	**13**	**110**	**166**
Public and publicly guaranteed	..	..	..	..	..	..	**1**	**13**	**109**	**165**
Official creditors	..	..	..	..	..	..	0	5	67	117
Multilateral	..	..	..	..	..	..	0	5	65	92
Concessional	..	..	..	..	..	..	0	0	0	0
Bilateral	..	..	..	..	..	..	0	0	2	24
Concessional	..	..	..	..	..	..	0	0	1	1
Private creditors	..	..	..	..	..	..	1	7	42	49
Bonds	..	..	..	..	..	..	0	0	0	0
Commercial banks	..	..	..	..	..	..	0	0	0	0
Other private	..	..	..	..	..	..	1	7	42	49
Private nonguaranteed	**0**	**0**	**0**	**0**	**0**	**0**	**0**	**1**	**1**	**0**
Bonds	..	..	..	..	..	..	0	0	0	0
Commercial banks	..	..	..	..	..	..	0	1	1	0
Memo:										
IBRD	0	0	0	0	0	0	0	0	2	8
IDA	0	0	0	0	0	0	0	0	0	0
UNDISBURSED DEBT	..	..	..	..	..	..	**380**	**498**	**383**	**266**
Official creditors	..	..	..	..	..	..	202	302	280	261
Private creditors	..	..	..	..	..	..	178	195	103	5
Memorandum items										
Concessional LDOD	..	..	..	..	..	..	23	467	461	477
Variable rate LDOD	..	..	..	..	..	..	165	452	578	670
Public sector LDOD	..	..	..	..	..	..	189	865	1,100	1,255
Private sector LDOD	..	..	..	..	..	..	0	1	1	0

6. CURRENCY COMPOSITION OF LONG-TERM DEBT (PERCENT)

	1970	1980	1988	1989	1990	1991	1992	1993	1994	1995
Deutsche mark	..	..	..	..	..	..	15.7	17.6	23.2	26.4
French franc	..	..	..	..	..	..	0.0	0.0	0.0	0.0
Japanese yen	..	..	..	..	..	..	0.0	0.0	2.9	2.4
Pound sterling	..	..	..	..	..	..	0.0	0.0	0.0	0.0
Swiss franc	..	..	..	..	..	..	0.0	0.0	0.0	0.7
U.S.dollars	..	..	..	..	..	..	83.8	63.9	55.5	52.7
Multiple currency	..	..	..	..	..	..	0.0	0.0	9.4	11.2
Special drawing rights	..	..	..	..	..	..	0.0	0.0	0.0	0.0
All other currencies	..	..	..	..	..	..	0.5	18.5	9.0	6.6

BELARUS

(US$ million, unless otherwise indicated)

	1970	1980	1988	1989	1990	1991	1992	1993	1994	1995
7. DEBT RESTRUCTURINGS										
Total amount rescheduled	0	0	0	0	0	0	0	385	0	0
Debt stock rescheduled	0	0	0	0	0	0	0	0	0	0
Principal rescheduled	0	0	0	0	0	0	0	0	0	0
Official	0	0	0	0	0	0	0	0	0	0
Private	0	0	0	0	0	0	0	0	0	0
Interest rescheduled	0	0	0	0	0	0	0	0	0	0
Official	0	0	0	0	0	0	0	0	0	0
Private	0	0	0	0	0	0	0	0	0	0
Debt forgiven	..	..	0	0	0	0	0	0	0	0
Memo: interest forgiven	..	..	0	0	0	0	0	0	0	0
Debt stock reduction	0	0	0	0	0	0	0	0	0	0
of which debt buyback	0	0	0	0	0	0	0	0	0	0
8. DEBT STOCK-FLOW RECONCILIATION										
Total change in debt stocks	..	..	..	..	..	..	189	781	303	375
Net flows on debt	..	..	..	..	..	..	190	426	296	349
Net change in interest arrears	..	..	..	..	..	..	0	7	8	3
Interest capitalized	..	..	..	..	..	..	0	0	0	0
Debt forgiveness or reduction	..	..	..	..	..	..	0	0	0	0
Cross-currency valuation	..	..	..	..	..	..	-2	-54	29	33
Residual	..	..	..	..	..	..	1	402	-30	-10
9. AVERAGE TERMS OF NEW COMMITMENTS										
ALL CREDITORS										
Interest (%)	..	..	..	..	..	..	6.2	7.2	6.7	5.7
Maturity (years)	..	..	..	..	..	..	6.8	12.4	12.2	14.0
Grace period (years)	..	..	..	..	..	..	2.8	4.6	3.7	4.9
Grant element (%)	..	..	..	..	..	..	11.5	4.2	16.3	25.6
Official creditors										
Interest (%)	..	..	..	..	..	..	4.6	6.9	6.9	5.2
Maturity (years)	..	..	..	..	..	..	7.8	13.9	13.0	16.0
Grace period (years)	..	..	..	..	..	..	2.6	5.2	4.0	5.6
Grant element (%)	..	..	..	..	..	..	17.2	2.2	16.9	29.9
Private creditors										
Interest (%)	..	..	..	..	..	..	7.3	7.8	5.9	8.7
Maturity (years)	..	..	..	..	..	..	6.2	9.3	6.8	3.4
Grace period (years)	..	..	..	..	..	..	3.0	3.4	1.7	1.2
Grant element (%)	..	..	..	..	..	..	7.7	8.6	12.6	3.6
Memorandum items										
Commitments	..	..	..	..	..	..	586	468	260	140
Official creditors	..	..	..	..	..	..	236	321	226	117
Private creditors	..	..	..	..	..	..	350	147	34	23

10. CONTRACTUAL OBLIGATIONS ON OUTSTANDING LONG-TERM DEBT

	1996	1997	1998	1999	2000	2001	2002	2003	2004	2005
TOTAL										
Disbursements	119	69	33	20	11	6	4	3	2	2
Principal	74	99	93	102	146	141	143	123	111	103
Interest	42	43	42	39	34	29	24	19	15	11
Official creditors										
Disbursements	114	68	33	20	11	6	4	3	2	2
Principal	21	37	43	52	103	106	112	108	102	99
Interest	30	34	34	33	30	26	22	18	14	11
Bilateral creditors										
Disbursements	10	7	4	2	1	0	0	0	0	0
Principal	16	24	24	16	65	59	61	61	54	54
Interest	10	10	8	7	6	5	5	4	3	3
Multilateral creditors										
Disbursements	104	62	29	17	10	5	3	3	2	2
Principal	6	13	19	35	38	47	51	48	48	45
Interest	20	25	26	26	24	21	18	14	11	8
Private creditors										
Disbursements	5	0	0	0	0	0	0	0	0	0
Principal	52	62	50	50	43	35	31	14	9	5
Interest	12	9	8	6	4	3	2	1	0	0
Commercial banks										
Disbursements	1	0	0	0	0	0	0	0	0	0
Principal	1	1	1	1	0	0	0	0	0	0
Interest	0	0	0	0	0	0	0	0	0	0
Other private										
Disbursements	4	0	0	0	0	0	0	0	0	0
Principal	51	62	49	49	43	35	31	14	9	5
Interest	11	9	8	6	4	3	2	1	0	0

BELIZE

(US$ million, unless otherwise indicated)

	1970	1980	1988	1989	1990	1991	1992	1993	1994	1995
1. SUMMARY DEBT DATA										
TOTAL DEBT STOCKS (EDT)	..	**62.9**	**140.3**	**145.0**	**154.2**	**170.8**	**187.6**	**198.7**	**200.7**	**260.5**
Long-term debt (LDOD)	**4.1**	**46.9**	**127.0**	**136.6**	**147.7**	**160.0**	**176.6**	**179.5**	**184.2**	**220.3**
Public and publicly guaranteed	4.1	46.9	119.2	128.9	136.6	151.1	170.2	175.9	182.7	220.3
Private nonguaranteed	0.0	0.0	7.8	7.7	11.1	8.9	6.4	3.6	1.5	0.0
Use of IMF credit	**0.0**	**0.0**	**7.8**	**3.3**	**0.4**	**0.0**	**0.0**	**0.0**	**0.0**	**0.0**
Short-term debt	..	**16.0**	**5.5**	**5.1**	**6.1**	**10.8**	**11.0**	**19.1**	**16.5**	**40.2**
of which interest arrears on LDOD	..	0.0	1.0	0.6	0.9	0.6	0.9	2.1	2.5	5.1
Official creditors	..	0.0	0.4	0.3	0.4	0.6	0.8	1.0	1.3	2.6
Private creditors	..	0.0	0.6	0.3	0.5	0.0	0.1	1.1	1.2	2.4
Memo: principal arrears on LDOD	..	0.0	2.5	2.0	2.0	1.2	2.2	2.8	6.1	11.4
Official creditors	..	0.0	1.5	1.0	0.8	1.2	2.2	2.3	3.9	5.1
Private creditors	..	0.0	1.1	1.0	1.2	0.0	0.1	0.5	2.1	6.4
Memo: export credits	..	..	31.0	26.0	30.0	45.0	31.0	34.0	47.0	45.0
TOTAL DEBT FLOWS										
Disbursements	**4.3**	**13.7**	**17.5**	**19.6**	**22.3**	**25.3**	**38.0**	**18.5**	**19.3**	**31.2**
Long-term debt	4.3	13.7	17.5	19.6	22.3	25.3	38.0	18.5	19.3	31.2
IMF purchases	0.0	0.0	0.0	0.0	0.0	0.0	0.0	0.0	0.0	0.0
Principal repayments	**0.0**	**0.6**	**11.3**	**10.8**	**12.9**	**13.2**	**12.8**	**14.3**	**18.8**	**26.2**
Long-term debt	0.0	0.6	8.3	6.6	9.9	12.8	12.8	14.3	18.8	26.2
IMF repurchases	0.0	0.0	3.0	4.2	3.0	0.4	0.0	0.0	0.0	0.0
Net flows on debt	**4.3**	**13.1**	**-3.4**	**8.8**	**10.2**	**17.1**	**25.2**	**11.0**	**-2.5**	**26.2**
of which short-term debt	..	..	-9.6	0.0	0.8	5.0	0.0	6.8	-3.0	21.2
Interest payments (INT)	..	**3.1**	**5.4**	**7.2**	**7.2**	**6.4**	**6.5**	**7.0**	**8.3**	**11.3**
Long-term debt	0.0	0.9	4.0	6.3	6.6	5.9	6.1	6.2	7.3	9.9
IMF charges	0.0	0.0	0.6	0.5	0.2	0.0	0.0	0.0	0.0	0.0
Short-term debt	..	2.2	0.8	0.4	0.4	0.5	0.4	0.8	0.9	1.4
Net transfers on debt	..	**10.0**	**-8.8**	**1.6**	**3.0**	**10.7**	**18.7**	**4.0**	**-10.8**	**14.9**
Total debt service paid (TDS)	..	**3.6**	**16.7**	**18.0**	**20.1**	**19.6**	**19.3**	**21.4**	**27.1**	**37.5**
Long-term debt	0.0	1.5	12.3	12.9	16.5	18.7	18.9	20.5	26.1	36.1
IMF repurchases and charges	0.0	0.0	3.6	4.7	3.2	0.4	0.0	0.0	0.0	0.0
Short-term debt (interest only)	..	2.2	0.8	0.4	0.4	0.5	0.4	0.8	0.9	1.4
2. AGGREGATE NET RESOURCE FLOWS AND NET TRANSFERS (LONG-TERM)										
NET RESOURCE FLOWS	**6.0**	**21.9**	**29.4**	**35.6**	**33.8**	**29.7**	**47.5**	**30.9**	**28.5**	**33.0**
Net flow of long-term debt (ex. IMF)	4.3	13.1	9.2	13.0	12.4	12.5	25.2	4.2	0.5	5.0
Foreign direct investment (net)	0.0	0.0	14.0	18.7	17.0	14.0	16.0	9.0	15.0	21.0
Portfolio equity flows	0.0	0.0	0.0	0.0	0.0	0.0	0.0	0.0	0.0	0.0
Grants (excluding technical coop.)	1.7	8.8	6.2	3.9	4.4	3.2	6.3	17.7	13.0	7.0
Memo: technical coop. grants	1.0	2.4	12.9	13.0	13.0	15.0	14.0	16.3	9.8	12.6
NET TRANSFERS	**6.0**	**21.0**	**20.6**	**24.4**	**19.7**	**14.9**	**29.0**	**12.3**	**8.3**	**10.1**
Interest on long-term debt	0.0	0.9	4.0	6.3	6.6	5.9	6.1	6.2	7.3	9.9
Profit remittances on FDI	0.0	0.0	4.8	4.8	7.5	8.9	12.4	12.4	12.8	13.0
3. MAJOR ECONOMIC AGGREGATES										
Gross national product (GNP)	51.6	192.8	306.0	350.7	396.1	421.9	459.8	504.8	530.5	555.0
Exports of goods & services (XGS)	..	..	214.8	237.9	268.9	269.4	306.1	301.5	293.5	302.1
of which workers remittances	..	..	12.9	17.9	13.7	12.3	16.2	13.1	13.0	13.9
Imports of goods & services (MGS)	..	..	230.3	270.1	269.2	310.9	348.9	366.4	348.0	351.5
International reserves (RES)	..	12.7	51.7	59.9	69.8	53.0	52.9	38.8	34.5	37.6
Current account balance	..	..	-2.6	-19.1	15.4	-25.8	-28.6	-48.5	-40.1	-30.4
4. DEBT INDICATORS										
EDT / XGS (%)	..	..	65.3	61.0	57.3	63.4	61.3	65.9	68.4	86.2
EDT / GNP (%)	..	32.6	45.8	41.3	38.9	40.5	40.8	39.4	37.8	46.9
TDS / XGS (%)	..	..	7.8	7.6	7.5	7.3	6.3	7.1	9.2	12.4
INT / XGS (%)	..	..	2.5	3.0	2.7	2.4	2.1	2.3	2.8	3.7
INT / GNP (%)	..	1.6	1.8	2.1	1.8	1.5	1.4	1.4	1.6	2.0
RES / EDT (%)	..	20.2	36.9	41.3	45.3	31.0	28.2	19.5	17.2	14.4
RES / MGS (months)	..	..	2.7	2.7	3.1	2.0	1.8	1.3	1.2	1.3
Short-term / EDT (%)	..	25.4	3.9	3.5	4.0	6.3	5.9	9.6	8.2	15.4
Concessional / EDT (%)	..	48.7	53.0	57.1	54.0	50.4	47.5	43.2	43.1	36.9
Multilateral / EDT (%)	..	35.7	29.6	35.8	37.4	35.6	34.0	31.7	35.4	34.4

BELIZE

(US$ million, unless otherwise indicated)

	1970	1980	1988	1989	1990	1991	1992	1993	1994	1995
5. LONG-TERM DEBT										
DEBT OUTSTANDING (LDOD)	**4.1**	**46.9**	**127.0**	**136.6**	**147.7**	**160.0**	**176.6**	**179.5**	**184.2**	**220.3**
Public and publicly guaranteed	**4.1**	**46.9**	**119.2**	**128.9**	**136.6**	**151.1**	**170.2**	**175.9**	**182.7**	**220.3**
Official creditors	4.1	39.9	102.6	113.0	118.3	127.7	143.1	144.4	151.4	175.8
Multilateral	0.0	22.5	41.5	51.9	57.7	60.8	63.9	63.0	71.0	89.7
Concessional	0.0	19.6	23.8	30.0	32.3	34.8	37.6	36.4	37.6	46.1
Bilateral	4.1	17.4	61.1	61.1	60.6	66.9	79.2	81.4	80.4	86.1
Concessional	0.0	11.1	50.6	52.7	50.9	51.3	51.5	49.3	48.9	49.9
Private creditors	0.0	7.1	16.6	15.9	18.2	23.4	27.1	31.6	31.3	44.5
Bonds	0.0	0.0	0.0	0.0	0.0	0.0	0.0	0.0	0.0	0.0
Commercial banks	0.0	0.0	14.3	14.1	16.4	18.9	23.4	22.0	24.3	38.7
Other private	0.0	7.1	2.4	1.9	1.8	4.5	3.7	9.6	7.0	5.8
Private nonguaranteed	**0.0**	**0.0**	**7.8**	**7.7**	**11.1**	**8.9**	**6.4**	**3.6**	**1.5**	**0.0**
Bonds	0.0	0.0	0.0	0.0	0.0	0.0	0.0	0.0	0.0	0.0
Commercial banks	0.0	0.0	7.8	7.7	11.1	8.9	6.4	3.6	1.5	0.0
Memo:										
IBRD	0.0	0.0	9.2	13.7	17.5	18.6	19.2	20.1	25.6	29.5
IDA	0.0	0.0	0.0	0.0	0.0	0.0	0.0	0.0	0.0	0.0
DISBURSEMENTS	**4.3**	**13.7**	**17.5**	**19.6**	**22.3**	**25.3**	**38.0**	**18.5**	**19.3**	**31.2**
Public and publicly guaranteed	**4.3**	**13.7**	**17.5**	**19.4**	**18.0**	**25.3**	**38.0**	**18.5**	**19.3**	**31.2**
Official creditors	4.3	7.8	8.4	18.4	13.3	16.4	31.0	11.8	14.7	25.8
Multilateral	0.0	4.6	3.9	13.6	5.9	6.2	8.9	4.2	10.6	12.4
Concessional	0.0	3.2	1.7	8.0	2.3	4.3	6.1	1.9	2.1	3.4
Bilateral	4.3	3.3	4.5	4.7	7.5	10.1	22.1	7.6	4.1	13.4
Concessional	0.0	0.7	4.2	4.5	4.6	2.6	7.0	0.0	0.0	3.5
Private creditors	0.0	5.8	9.1	1.0	4.6	8.9	7.0	6.7	4.6	5.3
Bonds	0.0	0.0	0.0	0.0	0.0	0.0	0.0	0.0	0.0	0.0
Commercial banks	0.0	0.0	8.5	1.0	4.6	4.8	6.3	0.0	4.6	4.8
Other private	0.0	5.8	0.6	0.0	0.0	4.2	0.8	6.7	0.0	0.5
Private nonguaranteed	**0.0**	**0.0**	**0.0**	**0.1**	**4.3**	**0.0**	**0.0**	**0.0**	**0.0**	**0.0**
Bonds	0.0	0.0	0.0	0.0	0.0	0.0	0.0	0.0	0.0	0.0
Commercial banks	0.0	0.0	0.0	0.1	4.3	0.0	0.0	0.0	0.0	0.0
Memo:										
IBRD	0.0	0.0	1.1	5.4	3.4	1.9	2.4	2.1	6.4	5.6
IDA	0.0	0.0	0.0	0.0	0.0	0.0	0.0	0.0	0.0	0.0
PRINCIPAL REPAYMENTS	**0.0**	**0.6**	**8.3**	**6.6**	**9.9**	**12.8**	**12.8**	**14.3**	**18.8**	**26.2**
Public and publicly guaranteed	**0.0**	**0.6**	**8.3**	**6.3**	**9.0**	**10.6**	**10.3**	**11.5**	**16.7**	**24.7**
Official creditors	0.0	0.5	5.4	4.7	6.6	6.7	7.6	9.3	11.8	17.1
Multilateral	0.0	0.4	2.3	2.9	2.7	3.8	4.1	4.7	5.3	7.2
Concessional	0.0	0.3	1.2	1.7	1.5	2.0	2.1	2.3	2.2	3.5
Bilateral	0.0	0.1	3.1	1.8	3.9	2.8	3.5	4.7	6.5	10.0
Concessional	0.0	0.1	0.3	0.3	1.1	1.5	1.6	1.5	1.6	2.6
Private creditors	0.0	0.1	2.9	1.6	2.4	3.9	2.7	2.2	4.9	7.6
Bonds	0.0	0.0	0.0	0.0	0.0	0.0	0.0	0.0	0.0	0.0
Commercial banks	0.0	0.0	0.8	1.3	2.3	2.2	1.8	1.5	2.3	4.7
Other private	0.0	0.1	2.1	0.3	0.1	1.7	0.9	0.7	2.7	2.9
Private nonguaranteed	**0.0**	**0.0**	**0.0**	**0.3**	**0.9**	**2.2**	**2.5**	**2.8**	**2.1**	**1.5**
Bonds	0.0	0.0	0.0	0.0	0.0	0.0	0.0	0.0	0.0	0.0
Commercial banks	0.0	0.0	0.0	0.3	0.9	2.2	2.5	2.8	2.1	1.5
Memo:										
IBRD	0.0	0.0	0.6	0.6	0.6	1.2	1.3	1.6	2.3	2.5
IDA	0.0	0.0	0.0	0.0	0.0	0.0	0.0	0.0	0.0	0.0
NET FLOWS ON DEBT	**4.3**	**13.1**	**9.2**	**13.0**	**12.4**	**12.5**	**25.2**	**4.2**	**0.5**	**5.0**
Public and publicly guaranteed	**4.3**	**13.1**	**9.2**	**13.1**	**8.9**	**14.7**	**27.7**	**7.0**	**2.6**	**6.5**
Official creditors	4.3	7.3	2.9	13.7	6.7	9.7	23.4	2.5	2.9	8.7
Multilateral	0.0	4.2	1.5	10.7	3.1	2.4	4.8	-0.4	5.3	5.2
Concessional	0.0	2.8	0.6	6.3	0.8	2.3	3.9	-0.4	-0.1	-0.1
Bilateral	4.3	3.1	1.4	3.0	3.6	7.3	18.6	2.9	-2.4	3.5
Concessional	0.0	0.7	3.8	4.2	3.5	1.1	5.4	-1.5	-1.6	0.9
Private creditors	0.0	5.8	6.3	-0.5	2.2	5.0	4.3	4.5	-0.4	-2.2
Bonds	0.0	0.0	0.0	0.0	0.0	0.0	0.0	0.0	0.0	0.0
Commercial banks	0.0	0.0	7.8	-0.2	2.3	2.5	4.5	-1.5	2.3	0.2
Other private	0.0	5.8	-1.5	-0.3	-0.1	2.5	-0.2	6.0	-2.7	-2.4
Private nonguaranteed	**0.0**	**0.0**	**0.0**	**-0.1**	**3.4**	**-2.2**	**-2.5**	**-2.8**	**-2.1**	**-1.5**
Bonds	0.0	0.0	0.0	0.0	0.0	0.0	0.0	0.0	0.0	0.0
Commercial banks	0.0	0.0	0.0	-0.1	3.4	-2.2	-2.5	-2.8	-2.1	-1.5
Memo:										
IBRD	0.0	0.0	0.5	4.8	2.8	0.7	1.1	0.5	4.1	3.1
IDA	0.0	0.0	0.0	0.0	0.0	0.0	0.0	0.0	0.0	0.0

BELIZE

(US$ million, unless otherwise indicated)

	1970	1980	1988	1989	1990	1991	1992	1993	1994	1995
INTEREST PAYMENTS (LINT)	**0.0**	**0.9**	**4.0**	**6.3**	**6.6**	**5.9**	**6.1**	**6.2**	**7.3**	**9.9**
Public and publicly guaranteed	**0.0**	**0.9**	**4.0**	**5.9**	**5.6**	**4.9**	**5.4**	**5.8**	**7.2**	**9.8**
Official creditors	0.0	0.9	3.5	3.8	4.2	4.0	4.6	5.2	5.4	7.6
Multilateral	0.0	0.6	2.1	2.4	2.7	2.8	2.8	2.8	2.8	4.0
Concessional	0.0	0.5	0.8	0.9	1.1	1.0	1.0	0.9	0.9	1.2
Bilateral	0.0	0.3	1.4	1.4	1.5	1.2	1.7	2.5	2.6	3.7
Concessional	0.0	0.0	0.5	0.5	0.6	0.5	0.5	0.6	0.6	0.8
Private creditors	0.0	0.0	0.6	2.1	1.4	0.9	0.9	0.6	1.8	2.2
Bonds	0.0	0.0	0.0	0.0	0.0	0.0	0.0	0.0	0.0	0.0
Commercial banks	0.0	0.0	0.4	1.6	1.4	0.8	0.5	0.3	1.2	1.6
Other private	0.0	0.0	0.1	0.6	0.0	0.1	0.4	0.2	0.6	0.6
Private nonguaranteed	**0.0**	**0.0**	**0.0**	**0.4**	**0.9**	**1.0**	**0.7**	**0.4**	**0.1**	**0.1**
Bonds	0.0	0.0	0.0	0.0	0.0	0.0	0.0	0.0	0.0	0.0
Commercial banks	0.0	0.0	0.0	0.4	0.9	1.0	0.7	0.4	0.1	0.1
Memo:										
IBRD	0.0	0.0	0.7	0.8	1.1	1.3	1.4	1.4	1.5	1.9
IDA	0.0	0.0	0.0	0.0	0.0	0.0	0.0	0.0	0.0	0.0
NET TRANSFERS ON DEBT	**4.3**	**12.2**	**5.2**	**6.6**	**5.8**	**6.6**	**19.1**	**-2.0**	**-6.9**	**-4.9**
Public and publicly guaranteed	**4.3**	**12.2**	**5.2**	**7.2**	**3.3**	**9.8**	**22.3**	**1.2**	**-4.6**	**-3.4**
Official creditors	4.3	6.4	-0.5	9.9	2.5	5.7	18.8	-2.7	-2.5	1.1
Multilateral	0.0	3.6	-0.5	8.3	0.4	-0.3	1.9	-3.2	2.5	1.2
Concessional	0.0	2.3	-0.3	5.4	-0.3	1.3	3.0	-1.3	-1.0	-1.3
Bilateral	4.3	2.9	0.0	1.6	2.1	6.1	16.9	0.4	-5.0	-0.2
Concessional	0.0	0.7	3.4	3.7	3.0	0.6	4.8	-2.1	-2.2	0.0
Private creditors	0.0	5.8	5.7	-2.7	0.8	4.1	3.5	4.0	-2.2	-4.4
Bonds	0.0	0.0	0.0	0.0	0.0	0.0	0.0	0.0	0.0	0.0
Commercial banks	0.0	0.0	7.3	-1.8	1.0	1.7	4.0	-1.8	1.1	-1.5
Other private	0.0	5.8	-1.6	-0.9	-0.2	2.4	-0.5	5.8	-3.3	-3.0
Private nonguaranteed	**0.0**	**0.0**	**0.0**	**-0.5**	**2.5**	**-3.2**	**-3.2**	**-3.2**	**-2.2**	**-1.6**
Bonds	0.0	0.0	0.0	0.0	0.0	0.0	0.0	0.0	0.0	0.0
Commercial banks	0.0	0.0	0.0	-0.5	2.5	-3.2	-3.2	-3.2	-2.2	-1.6
Memo:										
IBRD	0.0	0.0	-0.2	3.9	1.7	-0.6	-0.3	-0.9	2.6	1.2
IDA	0.0	0.0	0.0	0.0	0.0	0.0	0.0	0.0	0.0	0.0
DEBT SERVICE (LTDS)	**0.0**	**1.5**	**12.3**	**12.9**	**16.5**	**18.7**	**18.9**	**20.5**	**26.1**	**36.1**
Public and publicly guaranteed	**0.0**	**1.5**	**12.3**	**12.2**	**14.7**	**15.5**	**15.7**	**17.3**	**23.9**	**34.5**
Official creditors	0.0	1.4	8.9	8.5	10.8	10.7	12.2	14.6	17.2	24.8
Multilateral	0.0	1.0	4.4	5.3	5.4	6.6	6.9	7.4	8.1	11.2
Concessional	0.0	0.9	2.0	2.6	2.6	3.0	3.1	3.2	3.1	4.7
Bilateral	0.0	0.4	4.5	3.2	5.4	4.1	5.3	7.1	9.1	13.6
Concessional	0.0	0.1	0.8	0.8	1.6	2.0	2.1	2.1	2.2	3.5
Private creditors	0.0	0.1	3.4	3.7	3.8	4.8	3.6	2.7	6.7	9.8
Bonds	0.0	0.0	0.0	0.0	0.0	0.0	0.0	0.0	0.0	0.0
Commercial banks	0.0	0.0	1.2	2.8	3.7	3.1	2.3	1.8	3.4	6.3
Other private	0.0	0.1	2.2	0.9	0.2	1.8	1.3	0.9	3.3	3.5
Private nonguaranteed	**0.0**	**0.0**	**0.0**	**0.7**	**1.8**	**3.2**	**3.2**	**3.2**	**2.2**	**1.6**
Bonds	0.0	0.0	0.0	0.0	0.0	0.0	0.0	0.0	0.0	0.0
Commercial banks	0.0	0.0	0.0	0.7	1.8	3.2	3.2	3.2	2.2	1.6
Memo:										
IBRD	0.0	0.0	1.3	1.4	1.8	2.5	2.7	3.1	3.8	4.4
IDA	0.0	0.0	0.0	0.0	0.0	0.0	0.0	0.0	0.0	0.0
UNDISBURSED DEBT	**0.0**	**22.7**	**62.8**	**78.1**	**61.6**	**50.9**	**53.3**	**99.7**	**93.1**	**97.4**
Official creditors	0.0	17.9	61.5	55.9	50.5	44.6	52.0	74.3	78.1	85.6
Private creditors	0.0	4.8	1.3	22.2	11.1	6.3	1.2	25.4	15.0	11.8
Memorandum items										
Concessional LDOD	0.0	30.7	74.4	82.7	83.2	86.1	89.1	85.8	86.5	96.1
Variable rate LDOD	0.0	0.0	23.8	29.0	38.6	41.2	42.8	39.9	42.8	56.6
Public sector LDOD	4.1	46.9	119.2	128.9	136.6	151.1	170.2	175.9	182.7	220.3
Private sector LDOD	0.0	0.0	7.8	7.7	11.1	8.9	6.4	3.6	1.5	0.0

6. CURRENCY COMPOSITION OF LONG-TERM DEBT (PERCENT)

	1970	1980	1988	1989	1990	1991	1992	1993	1994	1995
Deutsche mark	0.0	0.9	1.0	0.9	0.7	0.5	0.4	0.3	0.3	0.2
French franc	0.0	0.0	0.0	0.0	0.0	0.0	0.0	0.0	0.0	0.0
Japanese yen	0.0	0.0	0.0	0.0	0.0	0.0	0.0	0.0	0.0	0.0
Pound sterling	100.0	15.3	23.7	20.0	23.6	23.0	16.7	14.4	13.0	10.3
Swiss franc	0.0	0.0	0.0	0.0	0.0	0.0	0.0	0.0	0.0	0.0
U.S.dollars	0.0	29.4	40.2	43.4	45.2	46.3	52.4	56.4	55.8	62.4
Multiple currency	0.0	23.4	21.2	22.6	23.4	21.5	19.0	18.3	20.0	17.6
Special drawing rights	0.0	0.0	0.3	0.5	0.5	0.4	0.2	0.7	0.8	0.6
All other currencies	0.0	31.1	13.5	12.6	6.7	8.2	11.2	9.9	10.3	8.9

BELIZE

(US$ million, unless otherwise indicated)

	1970	1980	1988	1989	1990	1991	1992	1993	1994	1995
7. DEBT RESTRUCTURINGS										
Total amount rescheduled	0.0	0.0	0.0	0.0	0.0	0.0	7.3	0.0	0.0	0.0
Debt stock rescheduled	0.0	0.0	0.0	0.0	0.0	0.0	7.3	0.0	0.0	0.0
Principal rescheduled	0.0	0.0	0.0	0.0	0.0	0.0	0.0	0.0	0.0	0.0
Official	0.0	0.0	0.0	0.0	0.0	0.0	0.0	0.0	0.0	0.0
Private	0.0	0.0	0.0	0.0	0.0	0.0	0.0	0.0	0.0	0.0
Interest rescheduled	0.0	0.0	0.0	0.0	0.0	0.0	0.0	0.0	0.0	0.0
Official	0.0	0.0	0.0	0.0	0.0	0.0	0.0	0.0	0.0	0.0
Private	0.0	0.0	0.0	0.0	0.0	0.0	0.0	0.0	0.0	0.0
Debt forgiven	..	..	0.0	0.0	9.1	0.0	0.0	0.0	0.0	0.0
Memo: interest forgiven	..	..	0.0	0.0	0.0	0.0	0.0	0.0	0.0	0.0
Debt stock reduction	0.0	0.0	0.0	0.0	0.0	0.0	0.0	0.0	0.0	0.0
of which debt buyback	0.0	0.0	0.0	0.0	0.0	0.0	0.0	0.0	0.0	0.0
8. DEBT STOCK-FLOW RECONCILIATION										
Total change in debt stocks	..	..	..	4.7	9.2	16.6	16.8	11.0	2.0	59.8
Net flows on debt	..	..	..	8.8	10.2	17.1	25.2	11.0	-2.5	26.2
Net change in interest arrears	..	..	..	-0.4	0.3	-0.3	0.3	1.3	0.3	2.6
Interest capitalized	..	..	..	0.0	0.0	0.0	0.0	0.0	0.0	0.0
Debt forgiveness or reduction	..	..	..	0.0	-9.1	0.0	0.0	0.0	0.0	0.0
Cross-currency valuation	..	..	..	-3.2	8.9	-1.0	-8.2	-1.5	4.0	1.1
Residual	..	..	..	-0.5	-1.0	0.8	-0.5	0.3	0.2	30.0
9. AVERAGE TERMS OF NEW COMMITMENTS										
ALL CREDITORS										
Interest (%)	7.0	5.6	7.1	5.7	5.0	7.7	6.2	6.2	5.8	6.0
Maturity (years)	26.0	18.0	17.1	22.4	10.0	12.0	18.3	11.8	14.7	17.6
Grace period (years)	3.0	4.7	4.5	5.5	2.5	2.3	2.7	3.1	4.2	3.9
Grant element (%)	20.7	29.0	21.7	33.6	21.2	10.3	21.5	15.9	22.5	23.0
Official creditors										
Interest (%)	7.0	4.4	5.4	0.4	5.0	7.1	6.2	6.4	5.8	5.9
Maturity (years)	26.0	25.0	21.0	38.4	10.0	13.7	19.0	16.0	17.6	17.9
Grace period (years)	3.0	6.7	6.1	7.3	2.5	2.6	2.8	4.4	5.2	3.9
Grant element (%)	20.7	43.0	32.0	80.2	21.2	13.2	22.3	19.6	26.4	23.3
Private creditors										
Interest (%)	0.0	7.2	11.1	9.2	0.0	9.9	7.1	6.0	5.9	8.6
Maturity (years)	0.0	7.7	7.7	11.8	0.0	5.4	5.9	6.6	5.5	4.8
Grace period (years)	0.0	1.7	0.7	4.3	0.0	1.0	1.4	1.6	1.0	0.3
Grant element (%)	0.0	8.6	-3.6	3.0	0.0	-0.5	7.9	11.4	10.0	2.7
Memorandum items										
Commitments	4.3	11.6	33.9	36.3	5.0	20.0	43.8	68.4	23.5	29.2
Official creditors	4.3	6.9	24.1	14.4	5.0	15.8	41.4	37.5	17.8	28.7
Private creditors	0.0	4.7	9.8	21.9	0.0	4.2	2.4	30.9	5.6	0.5

10. CONTRACTUAL OBLIGATIONS ON OUTSTANDING LONG-TERM DEBT

	1996	1997	1998	1999	2000	2001	2002	2003	2004	2005
TOTAL										
Disbursements	32.1	26.5	16.6	9.7	5.7	3.9	2.2	0.5	0.0	0.0
Principal	28.5	26.1	27.4	25.0	25.1	23.4	19.2	16.9	15.5	12.8
Interest	11.1	11.3	10.8	10.0	8.9	7.8	6.8	5.9	5.1	4.2
Official creditors										
Disbursements	23.6	24.3	15.6	9.7	5.7	3.9	2.2	0.5	0.0	0.0
Principal	18.1	17.7	19.2	18.5	19.3	18.1	17.8	15.5	14.1	12.7
Interest	8.5	9.0	8.9	8.5	7.9	7.1	6.4	5.6	4.9	4.1
Bilateral creditors										
Disbursements	9.8	8.4	5.0	2.4	1.4	0.8	0.4	0.2	0.0	0.0
Principal	10.9	10.5	10.9	8.9	8.1	7.6	7.3	6.9	6.2	5.2
Interest	3.6	3.5	3.2	2.9	2.6	2.3	2.0	1.8	1.5	1.3
Multilateral creditors										
Disbursements	13.7	15.9	10.6	7.3	4.3	3.1	1.8	0.3	0.0	0.0
Principal	7.2	7.2	8.3	9.6	11.3	10.5	10.5	8.6	7.9	7.6
Interest	4.9	5.5	5.7	5.7	5.3	4.8	4.4	3.8	3.3	2.9
Private creditors										
Disbursements	8.6	2.2	1.0	0.0	0.0	0.0	0.0	0.0	0.0	0.0
Principal	10.4	8.4	8.2	6.6	5.8	5.3	1.4	1.4	1.4	0.1
Interest	2.6	2.3	1.9	1.5	1.0	0.6	0.4	0.3	0.2	0.1
Commercial banks										
Disbursements	8.6	2.2	1.0	0.0	0.0	0.0	0.0	0.0	0.0	0.0
Principal	7.6	6.9	6.9	6.5	5.8	5.3	1.4	1.4	1.4	0.1
Interest	2.2	2.2	1.8	1.5	1.0	0.6	0.4	0.3	0.2	0.1
Other private										
Disbursements	0.0	0.0	0.0	0.0	0.0	0.0	0.0	0.0	0.0	0.0
Principal	2.8	1.5	1.3	0.1	0.1	0.0	0.0	0.0	0.0	0.0
Interest	0.3	0.2	0.1	0.0	0.0	0.0	0.0	0.0	0.0	0.0

BENIN

(US$ million, unless otherwise indicated)

	1970	1980	1988	1989	1990	1991	1992	1993	1994	1995
1. SUMMARY DEBT DATA										
TOTAL DEBT STOCKS (EDT)	..	**424**	**1,065**	**1,203**	**1,245**	**1,364**	**1,407**	**1,479**	**1,636**	**1,646**
Long-term debt (LDOD)	**41**	**334**	**914**	**1,127**	**1,177**	**1,284**	**1,358**	**1,401**	**1,532**	**1,514**
Public and publicly guaranteed	41	334	914	1,127	1,177	1,284	1,358	1,401	1,532	1,514
Private nonguaranteed	0	0	0	0	0	0	0	0	0	0
Use of IMF credit	**0**	**16**	**4**	**10**	**18**	**22**	**22**	**43**	**71**	**84**
Short-term debt	..	**73**	**147**	**66**	**50**	**57**	**27**	**35**	**33**	**48**
of which interest arrears on LDOD	..	5	88	23	15	12	9	15	10	9
Official creditors	..	0	12	8	13	11	8	14	9	9
Private creditors	..	5	75	15	2	1	1	1	1	0
Memo: principal arrears on LDOD	..	14	321	77	40	24	21	23	25	20
Official creditors	..	1	34	34	28	16	18	20	21	20
Private creditors	..	13	287	43	12	8	4	4	4	0
Memo: export credits	..	..	156	209	303	258	223	203	168	227
TOTAL DEBT FLOWS										
Disbursements	**2**	**71**	**57**	**141**	**120**	**112**	**104**	**100**	**125**	**105**
Long-term debt	2	62	57	133	120	99	104	78	99	92
IMF purchases	0	10	0	8	0	13	0	22	26	14
Principal repayments	**1**	**6**	**13**	**9**	**21**	**16**	**15**	**18**	**21**	**26**
Long-term debt	1	6	10	7	19	16	15	18	20	24
IMF repurchases	0	0	3	2	2	0	0	0	1	2
Net flows on debt	**1**	**66**	**-21**	**116**	**92**	**106**	**62**	**84**	**107**	**96**
of which short-term debt	..	..	-65	-17	-8	10	-27	2	3	16
Interest payments (INT)	..	**14**	**15**	**17**	**18**	**15**	**13**	**14**	**20**	**23**
Long-term debt	0	3	8	12	14	12	11	12	19	21
IMF charges	0	0	0	0	0	0	0	0	0	0
Short-term debt	..	11	7	5	4	3	2	1	1	2
Net transfers on debt	..	**51**	**-36**	**99**	**74**	**91**	**49**	**71**	**87**	**72**
Total debt service paid (TDS)	..	**20**	**28**	**26**	**38**	**31**	**28**	**32**	**41**	**49**
Long-term debt	2	9	18	19	33	28	26	30	38	45
IMF repurchases and charges	0	0	3	2	2	0	0	0	1	2
Short-term debt (interest only)	..	11	7	5	4	3	2	1	1	2
2. AGGREGATE NET RESOURCE FLOWS AND NET TRANSFERS (LONG-TERM)										
NET RESOURCE FLOWS	**17**	**101**	**120**	**243**	**213**	**231**	**262**	**204**	**192**	**218**
Net flow of long-term debt (ex. IMF)	1	56	46	126	102	84	89	60	79	68
Foreign direct investment (net)	7	4	0	1	1	13	7	10	5	1
Portfolio equity flows	0	0	0	0	0	0	0	0	0	0
Grants (excluding technical coop.)	9	41	73	116	110	134	166	134	108	149
Memo: technical coop. grants	6	26	46	48	50	60	56	58	54	63
NET TRANSFERS	**13**	**96**	**112**	**231**	**199**	**218**	**251**	**192**	**173**	**197**
Interest on long-term debt	0	3	8	12	14	12	11	12	19	21
Profit remittances on FDI	4	3	0	0	0	0	0	0	0	0
3. MAJOR ECONOMIC AGGREGATES										
Gross national product (GNP)	330	1,402	1,602	1,464	1,806	1,867	2,095	2,085	1,481	2,013
Exports of goods & services (XGS)	..	318	537	387	499	556	623	589	478	577
of which workers remittances	..	77	61	84	97	96	109	111	73	88
Imports of goods & services (MGS)	..	428	682	467	602	652	781	731	518	769
International reserves (RES)	16	15	9	8	69	196	249	248	263	202
Current account balance	..	-36	-52	82	19	-7	-39	-14	36	-203
4. DEBT INDICATORS										
EDT / XGS (%)	..	133.1	198.2	311.1	249.4	245.5	225.8	251.0	342.6	285.6
EDT / GNP (%)	..	30.2	66.5	82.2	68.9	73.0	67.2	70.9	110.5	81.8
TDS / XGS (%)	..	6.3	5.3	6.7	7.6	5.5	4.4	5.4	8.5	8.5
INT / XGS (%)	..	4.5	2.8	4.4	3.5	2.7	2.0	2.3	4.2	4.0
INT / GNP (%)	..	1.0	0.9	1.2	1.0	0.8	0.6	0.7	1.3	1.1
RES / EDT (%)	..	3.5	0.8	0.7	5.6	14.3	17.7	16.8	16.0	12.3
RES / MGS (months)	..	0.4	0.2	0.2	1.4	3.6	3.8	4.1	6.1	3.2
Short-term / EDT (%)	..	17.3	13.8	5.5	4.0	4.2	1.9	2.4	2.0	2.9
Concessional / EDT (%)	..	39.2	45.8	72.1	77.4	77.9	79.8	79.5	79.3	77.1
Multilateral / EDT (%)	..	24.5	35.7	35.9	43.1	43.6	44.8	46.2	48.0	52.3

BENIN

(US$ million, unless otherwise indicated)

	1970	1980	1988	1989	1990	1991	1992	1993	1994	1995
5. LONG-TERM DEBT										
DEBT OUTSTANDING (LDOD)	**41**	**334**	**914**	**1,127**	**1,177**	**1,284**	**1,358**	**1,401**	**1,532**	**1,514**
Public and publicly guaranteed	**41**	**334**	**914**	**1,127**	**1,177**	**1,284**	**1,358**	**1,401**	**1,532**	**1,514**
Official creditors	29	217	552	1,050	1,154	1,272	1,353	1,397	1,528	1,510
Multilateral	0	104	381	432	537	594	631	683	785	861
Concessional	0	84	341	394	498	557	596	653	762	837
Bilateral	29	113	171	618	617	678	723	714	743	649
Concessional	29	82	147	474	465	506	527	522	536	433
Private creditors	11	118	362	77	23	12	5	4	4	4
Bonds	0	0	0	0	0	0	0	0	0	0
Commercial banks	0	0	1	1	0	0	0	0	0	0
Other private	11	118	362	76	23	12	5	3	4	4
Private nonguaranteed	**0**	**0**	**0**	**0**	**0**	**0**	**0**	**0**	**0**	**0**
Bonds	0	0	0	0	0	0	0	0	0	0
Commercial banks	0	0	0	0	0	0	0	0	0	0
Memo:										
IBRD	0	0	0	0	0	0	0	0	0	0
IDA	0	52	209	253	326	370	389	418	464	498
DISBURSEMENTS	**2**	**62**	**57**	**133**	**120**	**99**	**104**	**78**	**99**	**92**
Public and publicly guaranteed	**2**	**62**	**57**	**133**	**120**	**99**	**104**	**78**	**99**	**92**
Official creditors	2	58	56	133	120	99	104	78	99	92
Multilateral	0	24	41	61	91	81	71	70	90	77
Concessional	0	19	36	59	82	76	67	68	87	72
Bilateral	1	35	15	72	29	18	32	8	8	14
Concessional	1	16	15	62	29	18	8	8	8	14
Private creditors	1	4	1	0	0	0	0	0	0	0
Bonds	0	0	0	0	0	0	0	0	0	0
Commercial banks	0	0	1	0	0	0	0	0	0	0
Other private	1	4	0	0	0	0	0	0	0	0
Private nonguaranteed	**0**	**0**	**0**	**0**	**0**	**0**	**0**	**0**	**0**	**0**
Bonds	0	0	0	0	0	0	0	0	0	0
Commercial banks	0	0	0	0	0	0	0	0	0	0
Memo:										
IBRD	0	0	0	0	0	0	0	0	0	0
IDA	0	12	22	48	56	42	33	30	29	31
PRINCIPAL REPAYMENTS	**1**	**6**	**10**	**7**	**19**	**16**	**15**	**18**	**20**	**24**
Public and publicly guaranteed	**1**	**6**	**10**	**7**	**19**	**16**	**15**	**18**	**20**	**24**
Official creditors	1	2	10	7	18	16	15	18	20	24
Multilateral	0	1	6	6	18	12	13	16	13	16
Concessional	0	0	3	2	7	6	6	10	9	12
Bilateral	1	2	4	1	0	3	2	2	6	7
Concessional	1	1	3	1	0	3	2	2	3	3
Private creditors	0	3	0	0	0	0	0	0	0	0
Bonds	0	0	0	0	0	0	0	0	0	0
Commercial banks	0	0	0	0	0	0	0	0	0	0
Other private	0	3	0	0	0	0	0	0	0	0
Private nonguaranteed	**0**	**0**	**0**	**0**	**0**	**0**	**0**	**0**	**0**	**0**
Bonds	0	0	0	0	0	0	0	0	0	0
Commercial banks	0	0	0	0	0	0	0	0	0	0
Memo:										
IBRD	0	0	0	0	0	0	0	0	0	0
IDA	0	0	1	1	1	1	2	2	3	3
NET FLOWS ON DEBT	**1**	**56**	**46**	**126**	**102**	**84**	**89**	**60**	**79**	**68**
Public and publicly guaranteed	**1**	**56**	**46**	**126**	**102**	**84**	**89**	**60**	**79**	**68**
Official creditors	0	56	46	126	102	84	89	60	79	68
Multilateral	0	23	35	55	73	69	59	55	77	61
Concessional	0	19	34	57	74	70	60	58	78	61
Bilateral	0	33	11	71	29	15	30	6	2	7
Concessional	0	15	12	61	29	15	6	6	6	12
Private creditors	1	0	0	0	0	0	0	0	0	0
Bonds	0	0	0	0	0	0	0	0	0	0
Commercial banks	0	0	1	0	0	0	0	0	0	0
Other private	1	0	0	0	0	0	0	0	0	0
Private nonguaranteed	**0**	**0**	**0**	**0**	**0**	**0**	**0**	**0**	**0**	**0**
Bonds	0	0	0	0	0	0	0	0	0	0
Commercial banks	0	0	0	0	0	0	0	0	0	0
Memo:										
IBRD	0	0	0	0	0	0	0	0	0	0
IDA	0	12	22	47	55	41	31	28	26	28

BENIN

(US$ million, unless otherwise indicated)

	1970	1980	1988	1989	1990	1991	1992	1993	1994	1995
INTEREST PAYMENTS (LINT)	**0**	**3**	**8**	**12**	**14**	**12**	**11**	**12**	**19**	**21**
Public and publicly guaranteed	**0**	**3**	**8**	**12**	**14**	**12**	**11**	**12**	**19**	**21**
Official creditors	0	2	8	6	14	12	11	12	19	21
Multilateral	0	1	5	5	13	10	8	9	8	9
Concessional	0	1	3	3	6	6	5	6	6	7
Bilateral	0	1	3	1	1	3	2	4	11	12
Concessional	0	0	2	1	1	3	2	3	3	4
Private creditors	0	1	0	6	0	0	0	0	0	0
Bonds	0	0	0	0	0	0	0	0	0	0
Commercial banks	0	0	0	0	0	0	0	0	0	0
Other private	0	1	0	6	0	0	0	0	0	0
Private nonguaranteed	**0**	**0**	**0**	**0**	**0**	**0**	**0**	**0**	**0**	**0**
Bonds	0	0	0	0	0	0	0	0	0	0
Commercial banks	0	0	0	0	0	0	0	0	0	0
Memo:										
IBRD	0	0	0	0	0	0	0	0	0	0
IDA	0	0	2	2	2	2	3	3	3	4
NET TRANSFERS ON DEBT	**1**	**53**	**39**	**114**	**88**	**71**	**78**	**48**	**61**	**47**
Public and publicly guaranteed	**1**	**53**	**39**	**114**	**88**	**71**	**78**	**48**	**61**	**47**
Official creditors	0	54	39	120	88	71	78	48	61	47
Multilateral	0	21	31	50	60	59	50	46	69	52
Concessional	0	18	31	54	69	64	55	52	71	54
Bilateral	0	33	8	70	28	12	28	2	-9	-5
Concessional	0	15	10	60	28	12	4	3	3	7
Private creditors	1	-1	0	-6	0	0	0	0	0	0
Bonds	0	0	0	0	0	0	0	0	0	0
Commercial banks	0	0	1	0	0	0	0	0	0	0
Other private	1	-1	0	-6	0	0	0	0	0	0
Private nonguaranteed	**0**	**0**	**0**	**0**	**0**	**0**	**0**	**0**	**0**	**0**
Bonds	0	0	0	0	0	0	0	0	0	0
Commercial banks	0	0	0	0	0	0	0	0	0	0
Memo:										
IBRD	0	0	0	0	0	0	0	0	0	0
IDA	0	12	20	45	53	38	29	25	23	24
DEBT SERVICE (LTDS)	**2**	**9**	**18**	**19**	**33**	**28**	**26**	**30**	**38**	**45**
Public and publicly guaranteed	**2**	**9**	**18**	**19**	**33**	**28**	**26**	**30**	**38**	**45**
Official creditors	2	4	18	13	32	28	26	30	38	45
Multilateral	0	2	11	11	31	22	21	24	21	25
Concessional	0	1	6	5	13	12	11	16	15	19
Bilateral	2	2	7	2	1	6	5	6	17	20
Concessional	2	1	5	2	1	6	4	5	5	7
Private creditors	0	4	0	6	0	0	0	0	0	0
Bonds	0	0	0	0	0	0	0	0	0	0
Commercial banks	0	0	0	0	0	0	0	0	0	0
Other private	0	4	0	6	0	0	0	0	0	0
Private nonguaranteed	**0**	**0**	**0**	**0**	**0**	**0**	**0**	**0**	**0**	**0**
Bonds	0	0	0	0	0	0	0	0	0	0
Commercial banks	0	0	0	0	0	0	0	0	0	0
Memo:										
IBRD	0	0	0	0	0	0	0	0	0	0
IDA	0	0	2	3	3	4	4	5	6	7
UNDISBURSED DEBT	**15**	**532**	**453**	**457**	**439**	**496**	**473**	**370**	**324**	**344**
Official creditors	15	154	429	457	439	496	473	370	324	344
Private creditors	0	379	23	0	0	0	0	0	0	0
Memorandum items										
Concessional LDOD	29	166	488	868	963	1,062	1,123	1,175	1,298	1,269
Variable rate LDOD	0	2	35	23	26	63	104	102	109	120
Public sector LDOD	41	334	914	1,127	1,177	1,284	1,358	1,401	1,532	1,514
Private sector LDOD	0	0	0	0	0	0	0	0	0	0

6. CURRENCY COMPOSITION OF LONG-TERM DEBT (PERCENT)

	1970	1980	1988	1989	1990	1991	1992	1993	1994	1995
Deutsche mark	5.2	0.3	0.2	0.1	0.3	0.2	0.2	0.2	0.2	0.3
French franc	16.8	27.2	21.7	22.9	19.4	20.6	20.6	19.9	19.3	12.8
Japanese yen	0.0	0.0	0.0	0.0	0.0	0.0	0.0	0.0	0.0	0.0
Pound sterling	0.0	0.0	1.1	0.8	0.9	0.5	0.8	0.8	0.8	0.8
Swiss franc	0.0	0.1	0.0	0.0	0.0	0.0	0.0	0.0	0.0	0.0
U.S.dollars	6.7	18.9	32.0	47.5	52.6	51.0	51.0	51.5	50.2	53.4
Multiple currency	0.0	6.7	8.3	6.4	7.6	8.8	9.6	10.2	11.1	12.6
Special drawing rights	0.0	0.0	2.2	1.9	1.9	1.8	1.8	1.8	1.8	1.9
All other currencies	71.6	46.9	34.5	20.4	17.4	17.1	16.0	15.7	16.5	18.3

BENIN

(US$ million, unless otherwise indicated)

	1970	1980	1988	1989	1990	1991	1992	1993	1994	1995
7. DEBT RESTRUCTURINGS										
Total amount rescheduled	0	0	0	404	22	58	49	12	8	8
Debt stock rescheduled	0	0	0	0	0	0	0	0	0	0
Principal rescheduled	0	0	0	279	21	7	6	2	2	0
Official	0	0	0	9	4	2	3	2	2	0
Private	0	0	0	270	17	5	3	0	0	0
Interest rescheduled	0	0	0	99	2	11	16	7	6	8
Official	0	0	0	6	0	10	16	7	6	8
Private	0	0	0	93	1	1	0	0	0	0
Debt forgiven	..	..	2	35	122	31	4	1	2	137
Memo: interest forgiven	..	..	0	5	3	9	2	5	4	5
Debt stock reduction	0	0	0	0	0	0	0	0	0	0
of which debt buyback	0	0	0	0	0	0	0	0	0	0
8. DEBT STOCK-FLOW RECONCILIATION										
Total change in debt stocks	..	..	..	138	41	119	43	72	158	10
Net flows on debt	..	..	..	116	92	106	62	84	107	96
Net change in interest arrears	..	..	..	-64	-8	-3	-3	6	-5	-1
Interest capitalized	..	..	..	99	2	11	16	7	6	8
Debt forgiveness or reduction	..	..	..	-35	-122	-31	-4	-1	-2	-137
Cross-currency valuation	..	..	..	8	51	-6	-38	-30	34	34
Residual	..	..	..	14	27	41	11	7	17	11
9. AVERAGE TERMS OF NEW COMMITMENTS										
ALL CREDITORS										
Interest (%)	1.8	8.3	2.5	2.0	1.3	1.1	1.2	0.1	0.8	1.3
Maturity (years)	32.0	11.7	31.7	32.3	39.3	37.1	39.9	28.8	35.8	33.2
Grace period (years)	7.0	3.7	8.0	9.0	8.3	9.4	9.5	9.5	10.1	8.6
Grant element (%)	59.9	8.9	59.6	65.5	71.9	74.6	76.1	79.1	78.3	70.6
Official creditors										
Interest (%)	1.1	4.4	2.5	2.0	1.3	1.1	1.2	0.1	0.8	1.3
Maturity (years)	36.0	26.0	31.7	32.3	39.3	37.1	39.9	28.8	35.8	33.2
Grace period (years)	8.0	5.3	8.0	9.0	8.3	9.4	9.5	9.5	10.1	8.6
Grant element (%)	67.7	40.7	59.6	65.5	71.9	74.6	76.1	79.1	78.3	70.6
Private creditors										
Interest (%)	6.0	8.8	0.0	0.0	0.0	0.0	0.0	0.0	0.0	0.0
Maturity (years)	7.5	9.9	0.0	0.0	0.0	0.0	0.0	0.0	0.0	0.0
Grace period (years)	0.5	3.5	0.0	0.0	0.0	0.0	0.0	0.0	0.0	0.0
Grant element (%)	11.7	4.8	0.0	0.0	0.0	0.0	0.0	0.0	0.0	0.0
Memorandum items										
Commitments	7	448	162	191	85	157	108	22	53	108
Official creditors	6	51	162	191	85	157	108	22	53	108
Private creditors	1	397	0	0	0	0	0	0	0	0

10. CONTRACTUAL OBLIGATIONS ON OUTSTANDING LONG-TERM DEBT

	1996	1997	1998	1999	2000	2001	2002	2003	2004	2005
TOTAL										
Disbursements	96	92	65	44	26	13	7	1	1	0
Principal	37	58	64	66	65	64	68	81	68	71
Interest	35	35	33	30	27	24	22	19	17	16
Official creditors										
Disbursements	96	92	65	44	26	13	7	1	1	0
Principal	37	58	64	66	65	64	68	81	68	71
Interest	35	35	33	30	27	24	22	19	17	16
Bilateral creditors										
Disbursements	6	6	4	3	2	1	1	1	0	0
Principal	15	34	39	41	40	38	40	53	39	39
Interest	26	25	23	20	18	15	13	11	9	8
Multilateral creditors										
Disbursements	90	85	61	41	24	12	6	1	1	0
Principal	22	24	25	25	25	26	28	28	29	31
Interest	10	10	10	10	9	9	9	8	8	8
Private creditors										
Disbursements	0	0	0	0	0	0	0	0	0	0
Principal	0	0	0	0	0	0	0	0	0	0
Interest	0	0	0	0	0	0	0	0	0	0
Commercial banks										
Disbursements	0	0	0	0	0	0	0	0	0	0
Principal	0	0	0	0	0	0	0	0	0	0
Interest	0	0	0	0	0	0	0	0	0	0
Other private										
Disbursements	0	0	0	0	0	0	0	0	0	0
Principal	0	0	0	0	0	0	0	0	0	0
Interest	0	0	0	0	0	0	0	0	0	0

BHUTAN

(US$ million, unless otherwise indicated)

	1970	1980	1988	1989	1990	1991	1992	1993	1994	1995
1. SUMMARY DEBT DATA										
TOTAL DEBT STOCKS (EDT)	..	0.0	67.1	73.9	83.5	86.3	83.6	85.0	87.4	87.2
Long-term debt (LDOD)	0.0	0.0	67.1	71.8	80.3	84.8	82.7	83.3	86.7	86.6
Public and publicly guaranteed	0.0	0.0	67.1	71.8	80.3	84.8	82.7	83.3	86.7	86.6
Private nonguaranteed	0.0	0.0	0.0	0.0	0.0	0.0	0.0	0.0	0.0	0.0
Use of IMF credit	0.0	0.0	0.0	0.0	0.0	0.0	0.0	0.0	0.0	0.0
Short-term debt	..	0.0	0.0	2.0	3.3	1.5	0.9	1.7	0.7	0.6
of which interest arrears on LDOD	..	0.0	0.0	0.0	0.3	0.5	0.6	0.7	0.7	0.6
Official creditors	..	0.0	0.0	0.0	0.3	0.5	0.6	0.7	0.7	0.6
Private creditors	..	0.0	0.0	0.0	0.0	0.0	0.0	0.0	0.0	0.0
Memo: principal arrears on LDOD	..	0.0	0.0	0.0	1.5	3.0	2.9	2.1	1.3	0.2
Official creditors	..	0.0	0.0	0.0	1.5	3.0	2.9	2.1	1.3	0.2
Private creditors	..	0.0	0.0	0.0	0.0	0.0	0.0	0.0	0.0	0.0
Memo: export credits	..	..	17.0	17.0	17.0	16.0	14.0	20.0	17.0	25.0
TOTAL DEBT FLOWS										
Disbursements	0.0	0.0	29.4	9.9	8.4	9.3	5.0	4.7	5.3	6.2
Long-term debt	0.0	0.0	29.4	9.9	8.4	9.3	5.0	4.7	5.3	6.2
IMF purchases	0.0	0.0	0.0	0.0	0.0	0.0	0.0	0.0	0.0	0.0
Principal repayments	0.0	0.0	0.6	4.1	2.9	5.2	4.1	4.6	5.1	7.2
Long-term debt	0.0	0.0	0.6	4.1	2.9	5.2	4.1	4.6	5.1	7.2
IMF repurchases	0.0	0.0	0.0	0.0	0.0	0.0	0.0	0.0	0.0	0.0
Net flows on debt	0.0	0.0	28.8	7.8	6.5	2.1	0.2	0.7	-0.8	-1.0
of which short-term debt	..	..	0.0	2.0	1.0	-2.0	-0.7	0.7	-1.0	0.0
Interest payments (INT)	..	0.0	0.7	2.5	2.3	2.0	1.8	2.0	1.7	1.7
Long-term debt	0.0	0.0	0.7	2.3	2.0	1.9	1.8	1.9	1.7	1.7
IMF charges	0.0	0.0	0.0	0.0	0.0	0.0	0.0	0.0	0.0	0.0
Short-term debt	..	0.0	0.0	0.2	0.2	0.1	0.0	0.1	0.0	0.0
Net transfers on debt	..	0.0	28.1	5.3	4.2	0.1	-1.6	-1.3	-2.5	-2.7
Total debt service paid (TDS)	..	0.0	1.3	6.5	5.2	7.2	5.9	6.7	6.8	8.9
Long-term debt	0.0	0.0	1.3	6.4	5.0	7.2	5.9	6.6	6.8	8.9
IMF repurchases and charges	0.0	0.0	0.0	0.0	0.0	0.0	0.0	0.0	0.0	0.0
Short-term debt (interest only)	..	0.0	0.0	0.2	0.2	0.1	0.0	0.1	0.0	0.0
2. AGGREGATE NET RESOURCE FLOWS AND NET TRANSFERS (LONG-TERM)										
NET RESOURCE FLOWS	0.2	2.3	44.3	24.0	22.4	41.4	33.1	34.9	42.7	38.2
Net flow of long-term debt (ex. IMF)	0.0	0.0	28.8	5.8	5.5	4.1	0.9	0.0	0.2	-1.0
Foreign direct investment (net)	0.0	0.0	0.0	0.0	0.0	0.0	0.0	0.0	0.0	0.0
Portfolio equity flows	0.0	0.0	0.0	0.0	0.0	0.0	0.0	0.0	0.0	0.0
Grants (excluding technical coop.)	0.2	2.3	15.5	18.2	16.9	37.3	32.2	34.9	42.5	39.2
Memo: technical coop. grants	0.0	6.0	17.5	19.1	24.7	20.8	22.2	27.1	29.5	29.3
NET TRANSFERS	0.2	2.3	43.6	21.7	20.4	39.4	31.4	33.0	41.0	36.5
Interest on long-term debt	0.0	0.0	0.7	2.3	2.0	1.9	1.8	1.9	1.7	1.7
Profit remittances on FDI	0.0	0.0	0.0	0.0	0.0	0.0	0.0	0.0	0.0	0.0
3. MAJOR ECONOMIC AGGREGATES										
Gross national product (GNP)	..	116.1	265.0	276.8	290.0	243.3	246.6	233.6	272.0	297.3
Exports of goods & services (XGS)	..	..	75.4	92.8	94.9	94.5	85.3	..	..	..
of which workers remittances	..	..	0.0	0.0	0.0	0.0	0.0	..	..	..
Imports of goods & services (MGS)	..	..	149.4	163.5	122.9	111.2	110.4	..	..	..
International reserves (RES)	..	..	94.1	98.5	86.0	98.9	77.9	..	115.2	124.3
Current account balance	..	..	..	..	..	..	..	..	..	..
4. DEBT INDICATORS										
EDT / XGS (%)	..	..	89.0	79.6	88.0	91.4	98.0	..	..	..
EDT / GNP (%)	..	0.0	25.3	26.7	28.8	35.5	33.9	36.4	32.1	29.3
TDS / XGS (%)	..	..	1.7	7.0	5.5	7.7	6.9	..	..	..
INT / XGS (%)	..	..	0.9	2.6	2.4	2.1	2.1	..	..	..
INT / GNP (%)	..	0.0	0.3	0.9	0.8	0.8	0.7	0.9	0.6	0.6
RES / EDT (%)	..	0.0	140.3	133.4	102.9	114.5	93.2	..	131.7	142.6
RES / MGS (months)	..	..	7.6	7.2	8.4	10.7	8.5	..	..	..
Short-term / EDT (%)	..	0.0	0.0	2.7	3.9	1.7	1.1	2.0	0.8	0.7
Concessional / EDT (%)	..	0.0	65.8	68.7	74.0	79.8	82.7	84.7	88.9	91.6
Multilateral / EDT (%)	..	0.0	37.6	42.9	50.1	56.0	60.4	64.3	71.1	78.2

BHUTAN

(US$ million, unless otherwise indicated)

	1970	1980	1988	1989	1990	1991	1992	1993	1994	1995
5. LONG-TERM DEBT										
DEBT OUTSTANDING (LDOD)	**0.0**	**0.0**	**67.1**	**71.8**	**80.3**	**84.8**	**82.7**	**83.3**	**86.7**	**86.6**
Public and publicly guaranteed	**0.0**	**0.0**	**67.1**	**71.8**	**80.3**	**84.8**	**82.7**	**83.3**	**86.7**	**86.6**
Official creditors	0.0	0.0	44.2	50.8	61.8	68.9	69.1	72.0	77.7	79.8
Multilateral	0.0	0.0	25.2	31.7	41.9	48.3	50.5	54.7	62.2	68.2
Concessional	0.0	0.0	25.2	31.7	41.9	48.3	50.5	54.7	62.2	68.2
Bilateral	0.0	0.0	18.9	19.0	19.9	20.6	18.6	17.3	15.5	11.6
Concessional	0.0	0.0	18.9	19.0	19.9	20.6	18.6	17.3	15.5	11.6
Private creditors	0.0	0.0	22.9	21.1	18.5	15.9	13.6	11.3	9.0	6.8
Bonds	0.0	0.0	0.0	0.0	0.0	0.0	0.0	0.0	0.0	0.0
Commercial banks	0.0	0.0	0.0	0.0	0.0	0.0	0.0	0.0	0.0	0.0
Other private	0.0	0.0	22.9	21.1	18.5	15.9	13.6	11.3	9.0	6.8
Private nonguaranteed	**0.0**	**0.0**	**0.0**	**0.0**	**0.0**	**0.0**	**0.0**	**0.0**	**0.0**	**0.0**
Bonds	0.0	0.0	0.0	0.0	0.0	0.0	0.0	0.0	0.0	0.0
Commercial banks	0.0	0.0	0.0	0.0	0.0	0.0	0.0	0.0	0.0	0.0
Memo:										
IBRD	0.0	0.0	0.0	0.0	0.0	0.0	0.0	0.0	0.0	0.0
IDA	0.0	0.0	10.2	13.0	16.1	17.8	17.7	18.6	20.9	22.5
DISBURSEMENTS	**0.0**	**0.0**	**29.4**	**9.9**	**8.4**	**9.3**	**5.0**	**4.7**	**5.3**	**6.2**
Public and publicly guaranteed	**0.0**	**0.0**	**29.4**	**9.9**	**8.4**	**9.3**	**5.0**	**4.7**	**5.3**	**6.2**
Official creditors	0.0	0.0	6.5	9.4	8.4	9.3	5.0	4.7	5.3	6.2
Multilateral	0.0	0.0	5.9	6.9	7.2	8.7	4.2	4.0	4.8	5.8
Concessional	0.0	0.0	5.9	6.9	7.2	8.7	4.2	4.0	4.8	5.8
Bilateral	0.0	0.0	0.7	2.5	1.2	0.6	0.8	0.7	0.5	0.4
Concessional	0.0	0.0	0.7	2.5	1.2	0.6	0.8	0.7	0.5	0.4
Private creditors	0.0	0.0	22.9	0.5	0.0	0.0	0.0	0.0	0.0	0.0
Bonds	0.0	0.0	0.0	0.0	0.0	0.0	0.0	0.0	0.0	0.0
Commercial banks	0.0	0.0	0.0	0.0	0.0	0.0	0.0	0.0	0.0	0.0
Other private	0.0	0.0	22.9	0.5	0.0	0.0	0.0	0.0	0.0	0.0
Private nonguaranteed	**0.0**	**0.0**	**0.0**	**0.0**	**0.0**	**0.0**	**0.0**	**0.0**	**0.0**	**0.0**
Bonds	0.0	0.0	0.0	0.0	0.0	0.0	0.0	0.0	0.0	0.0
Commercial banks	0.0	0.0	0.0	0.0	0.0	0.0	0.0	0.0	0.0	0.0
Memo:										
IBRD	0.0	0.0	0.0	0.0	0.0	0.0	0.0	0.0	0.0	0.0
IDA	0.0	0.0	2.1	2.9	2.0	1.5	0.6	0.9	1.3	1.2
PRINCIPAL REPAYMENTS	**0.0**	**0.0**	**0.6**	**4.1**	**2.9**	**5.2**	**4.1**	**4.6**	**5.1**	**7.2**
Public and publicly guaranteed	**0.0**	**0.0**	**0.6**	**4.1**	**2.9**	**5.2**	**4.1**	**4.6**	**5.1**	**7.2**
Official creditors	0.0	0.0	0.6	1.8	0.3	2.7	1.7	2.4	2.8	4.9
Multilateral	0.0	0.0	0.0	0.0	0.0	2.2	0.1	0.2	0.6	0.6
Concessional	0.0	0.0	0.0	0.0	0.0	2.2	0.1	0.2	0.6	0.6
Bilateral	0.0	0.0	0.6	1.8	0.3	0.6	1.6	2.2	2.2	4.3
Concessional	0.0	0.0	0.6	1.8	0.3	0.6	1.6	2.2	2.2	4.3
Private creditors	0.0	0.0	0.0	2.3	2.6	2.5	2.4	2.3	2.3	2.3
Bonds	0.0	0.0	0.0	0.0	0.0	0.0	0.0	0.0	0.0	0.0
Commercial banks	0.0	0.0	0.0	0.0	0.0	0.0	0.0	0.0	0.0	0.0
Other private	0.0	0.0	0.0	2.3	2.6	2.5	2.4	2.3	2.3	2.3
Private nonguaranteed	**0.0**	**0.0**	**0.0**	**0.0**	**0.0**	**0.0**	**0.0**	**0.0**	**0.0**	**0.0**
Bonds	0.0	0.0	0.0	0.0	0.0	0.0	0.0	0.0	0.0	0.0
Commercial banks	0.0	0.0	0.0	0.0	0.0	0.0	0.0	0.0	0.0	0.0
Memo:										
IBRD	0.0	0.0	0.0	0.0	0.0	0.0	0.0	0.0	0.0	0.0
IDA	0.0	0.0	0.0	0.0	0.0	0.0	0.0	0.0	0.1	0.1
NET FLOWS ON DEBT	**0.0**	**0.0**	**28.8**	**5.8**	**5.5**	**4.1**	**0.9**	**0.0**	**0.2**	**-1.0**
Public and publicly guaranteed	**0.0**	**0.0**	**28.8**	**5.8**	**5.5**	**4.1**	**0.9**	**0.0**	**0.2**	**-1.0**
Official creditors	0.0	0.0	5.9	7.6	8.1	6.6	3.3	2.3	2.5	1.3
Multilateral	0.0	0.0	5.9	6.9	7.2	6.5	4.1	3.8	4.2	5.3
Concessional	0.0	0.0	5.9	6.9	7.2	6.5	4.1	3.8	4.2	5.3
Bilateral	0.0	0.0	0.0	0.7	0.9	0.1	-0.8	-1.5	-1.7	-4.0
Concessional	0.0	0.0	0.0	0.7	0.9	0.1	-0.8	-1.5	-1.7	-4.0
Private creditors	0.0	0.0	22.9	-1.8	-2.6	-2.5	-2.4	-2.3	-2.3	-2.3
Bonds	0.0	0.0	0.0	0.0	0.0	0.0	0.0	0.0	0.0	0.0
Commercial banks	0.0	0.0	0.0	0.0	0.0	0.0	0.0	0.0	0.0	0.0
Other private	0.0	0.0	22.9	-1.8	-2.6	-2.5	-2.4	-2.3	-2.3	-2.3
Private nonguaranteed	**0.0**	**0.0**	**0.0**	**0.0**	**0.0**	**0.0**	**0.0**	**0.0**	**0.0**	**0.0**
Bonds	0.0	0.0	0.0	0.0	0.0	0.0	0.0	0.0	0.0	0.0
Commercial banks	0.0	0.0	0.0	0.0	0.0	0.0	0.0	0.0	0.0	0.0
Memo:										
IBRD	0.0	0.0	0.0	0.0	0.0	0.0	0.0	0.0	0.0	0.0
IDA	0.0	0.0	2.1	2.9	2.0	1.5	0.6	0.9	1.3	1.1

BHUTAN

(US$ million, unless otherwise indicated)

	1970	1980	1988	1989	1990	1991	1992	1993	1994	1995
INTEREST PAYMENTS (LINT)	**0.0**	**0.0**	**0.7**	**2.3**	**2.0**	**1.9**	**1.8**	**1.9**	**1.7**	**1.7**
Public and publicly guaranteed	**0.0**	**0.0**	**0.7**	**2.3**	**2.0**	**1.9**	**1.8**	**1.9**	**1.7**	**1.7**
Official creditors	0.0	0.0	0.7	0.7	0.4	0.6	0.6	0.9	0.9	1.1
Multilateral	0.0	0.0	0.3	0.3	0.3	0.4	0.4	0.5	0.5	0.6
Concessional	0.0	0.0	0.3	0.3	0.3	0.4	0.4	0.5	0.5	0.6
Bilateral	0.0	0.0	0.4	0.4	0.1	0.2	0.2	0.4	0.4	0.5
Concessional	0.0	0.0	0.4	0.4	0.1	0.2	0.2	0.4	0.4	0.5
Private creditors	0.0	0.0	0.0	1.6	1.6	1.3	1.2	1.1	0.8	0.6
Bonds	0.0	0.0	0.0	0.0	0.0	0.0	0.0	0.0	0.0	0.0
Commercial banks	0.0	0.0	0.0	0.0	0.0	0.0	0.0	0.0	0.0	0.0
Other private	0.0	0.0	0.0	1.6	1.6	1.3	1.2	1.1	0.8	0.6
Private nonguaranteed	**0.0**	**0.0**	**0.0**	**0.0**	**0.0**	**0.0**	**0.0**	**0.0**	**0.0**	**0.0**
Bonds	0.0	0.0	0.0	0.0	0.0	0.0	0.0	0.0	0.0	0.0
Commercial banks	0.0	0.0	0.0	0.0	0.0	0.0	0.0	0.0	0.0	0.0
Memo:										
IBRD	0.0	0.0	0.0	0.0	0.0	0.0	0.0	0.0	0.0	0.0
IDA	0.0	0.0	0.1	0.1	0.1	0.1	0.1	0.1	0.1	0.2
NET TRANSFERS ON DEBT	**0.0**	**0.0**	**28.1**	**3.5**	**3.5**	**2.1**	**-0.8**	**-1.9**	**-1.5**	**-2.7**
Public and publicly guaranteed	**0.0**	**0.0**	**28.1**	**3.5**	**3.5**	**2.1**	**-0.8**	**-1.9**	**-1.5**	**-2.7**
Official creditors	0.0	0.0	5.2	6.9	7.7	6.0	2.7	1.4	1.6	0.2
Multilateral	0.0	0.0	5.6	6.6	6.9	6.1	3.6	3.3	3.7	4.7
Concessional	0.0	0.0	5.6	6.6	6.9	6.1	3.6	3.3	3.7	4.7
Bilateral	0.0	0.0	-0.4	0.3	0.8	-0.1	-0.9	-1.9	-2.1	-4.4
Concessional	0.0	0.0	-0.4	0.3	0.8	-0.1	-0.9	-1.9	-2.1	-4.4
Private creditors	0.0	0.0	22.9	-3.4	-4.2	-3.8	-3.5	-3.3	-3.1	-2.9
Bonds	0.0	0.0	0.0	0.0	0.0	0.0	0.0	0.0	0.0	0.0
Commercial banks	0.0	0.0	0.0	0.0	0.0	0.0	0.0	0.0	0.0	0.0
Other private	0.0	0.0	22.9	-3.4	-4.2	-3.8	-3.5	-3.3	-3.1	-2.9
Private nonguaranteed	**0.0**	**0.0**	**0.0**	**0.0**	**0.0**	**0.0**	**0.0**	**0.0**	**0.0**	**0.0**
Bonds	0.0	0.0	0.0	0.0	0.0	0.0	0.0	0.0	0.0	0.0
Commercial banks	0.0	0.0	0.0	0.0	0.0	0.0	0.0	0.0	0.0	0.0
Memo:										
IBRD	0.0	0.0	0.0	0.0	0.0	0.0	0.0	0.0	0.0	0.0
IDA	0.0	0.0	2.0	2.8	1.9	1.4	0.5	0.8	1.1	0.9
DEBT SERVICE (LTDS)	**0.0**	**0.0**	**1.3**	**6.4**	**5.0**	**7.2**	**5.9**	**6.6**	**6.8**	**8.9**
Public and publicly guaranteed	**0.0**	**0.0**	**1.3**	**6.4**	**5.0**	**7.2**	**5.9**	**6.6**	**6.8**	**8.9**
Official creditors	0.0	0.0	1.3	2.4	0.7	3.3	2.3	3.3	3.7	6.0
Multilateral	0.0	0.0	0.3	0.3	0.3	2.5	0.6	0.7	1.1	1.2
Concessional	0.0	0.0	0.3	0.3	0.3	2.5	0.6	0.7	1.1	1.2
Bilateral	0.0	0.0	1.0	2.1	0.4	0.8	1.7	2.6	2.6	4.8
Concessional	0.0	0.0	1.0	2.1	0.4	0.8	1.7	2.6	2.6	4.8
Private creditors	0.0	0.0	0.0	3.9	4.2	3.8	3.5	3.3	3.1	2.9
Bonds	0.0	0.0	0.0	0.0	0.0	0.0	0.0	0.0	0.0	0.0
Commercial banks	0.0	0.0	0.0	0.0	0.0	0.0	0.0	0.0	0.0	0.0
Other private	0.0	0.0	0.0	3.9	4.2	3.8	3.5	3.3	3.1	2.9
Private nonguaranteed	**0.0**	**0.0**	**0.0**	**0.0**	**0.0**	**0.0**	**0.0**	**0.0**	**0.0**	**0.0**
Bonds	0.0	0.0	0.0	0.0	0.0	0.0	0.0	0.0	0.0	0.0
Commercial banks	0.0	0.0	0.0	0.0	0.0	0.0	0.0	0.0	0.0	0.0
Memo:										
IBRD	0.0	0.0	0.0	0.0	0.0	0.0	0.0	0.0	0.0	0.0
IDA	0.0	0.0	0.1	0.1	0.1	0.1	0.1	0.1	0.2	0.3
UNDISBURSED DEBT	**0.0**	**14.0**	**63.8**	**53.6**	**48.4**	**36.5**	**33.0**	**29.5**	**30.6**	**31.4**
Official creditors	0.0	14.0	63.3	53.6	48.4	36.5	33.0	29.5	30.6	31.4
Private creditors	0.0	0.0	0.5	0.0	0.0	0.0	0.0	0.0	0.0	0.0
Memorandum items										
Concessional LDOD	0.0	0.0	44.2	50.8	61.8	68.9	69.1	72.0	77.7	79.8
Variable rate LDOD	0.0	0.0	0.0	0.0	0.0	0.0	0.0	0.0	0.0	0.0
Public sector LDOD	0.0	0.0	67.1	71.8	80.3	84.8	82.7	83.3	86.7	86.6
Private sector LDOD	0.0	0.0	0.0	0.0	0.0	0.0	0.0	0.0	0.0	0.0

6. CURRENCY COMPOSITION OF LONG-TERM DEBT (PERCENT)

	1970	1980	1988	1989	1990	1991	1992	1993	1994	1995
Deutsche mark	0.0	0.0	0.0	0.0	0.0	0.0	0.0	0.0	0.0	0.0
French franc	0.0	0.0	0.0	0.0	0.0	0.0	0.0	0.0	0.0	0.0
Japanese yen	0.0	0.0	0.0	0.0	0.0	0.0	0.0	0.0	0.0	0.0
Pound sterling	0.0	0.0	0.0	0.0	0.0	0.0	0.0	0.0	0.0	0.0
Swiss franc	0.0	0.0	0.0	0.0	0.0	0.0	0.0	0.0	0.0	0.0
U.S.dollars	0.0	0.0	49.3	47.5	43.1	39.7	38.7	36.8	35.4	34.7
Multiple currency	0.0	0.0	15.2	18.7	22.8	26.3	28.9	31.0	34.4	38.2
Special drawing rights	0.0	0.0	7.3	7.5	9.3	9.7	10.9	12.2	13.3	14.7
All other currencies	0.0	0.0	28.2	26.4	24.8	24.3	21.5	19.8	16.9	12.5

BHUTAN

(US$ million, unless otherwise indicated)

	1970	1980	1988	1989	1990	1991	1992	1993	1994	1995
7. DEBT RESTRUCTURINGS										
Total amount rescheduled	0.0	0.0	0.0	0.0	0.0	0.0	0.0	0.0	0.0	0.0
Debt stock rescheduled	0.0	0.0	0.0	0.0	0.0	0.0	0.0	0.0	0.0	0.0
Principal rescheduled	0.0	0.0	0.0	0.0	0.0	0.0	0.0	0.0	0.0	0.0
Official	0.0	0.0	0.0	0.0	0.0	0.0	0.0	0.0	0.0	0.0
Private	0.0	0.0	0.0	0.0	0.0	0.0	0.0	0.0	0.0	0.0
Interest rescheduled	0.0	0.0	0.0	0.0	0.0	0.0	0.0	0.0	0.0	0.0
Official	0.0	0.0	0.0	0.0	0.0	0.0	0.0	0.0	0.0	0.0
Private	0.0	0.0	0.0	0.0	0.0	0.0	0.0	0.0	0.0	0.0
Debt forgiven	..	..	0.0	0.0	0.0	0.0	0.0	0.0	0.0	0.0
Memo: interest forgiven	..	..	0.0	0.0	0.0	0.0	0.0	0.0	0.0	0.0
Debt stock reduction	0.0	0.0	0.0	0.0	0.0	0.0	0.0	0.0	0.0	0.0
of which debt buyback	0.0	0.0	0.0	0.0	0.0	0.0	0.0	0.0	0.0	0.0
8. DEBT STOCK-FLOW RECONCILIATION										
Total change in debt stocks	..	..	..	6.8	9.7	2.8	-2.8	1.5	2.4	-0.3
Net flows on debt	..	..	..	7.8	6.5	2.1	0.2	0.7	-0.8	-1.0
Net change in interest arrears	..	..	..	0.0	0.3	0.2	0.1	0.1	0.0	-0.1
Interest capitalized	..	..	..	0.0	0.0	0.0	0.0	0.0	0.0	0.0
Debt forgiveness or reduction	..	..	..	0.0	0.0	0.0	0.0	0.0	0.0	0.0
Cross-currency valuation	..	..	..	-0.7	0.6	0.0	-1.4	0.2	0.6	0.3
Residual	..	..	..	-0.3	2.3	0.5	-1.7	0.4	2.6	0.5
9. AVERAGE TERMS OF NEW COMMITMENTS										
ALL CREDITORS										
Interest (%)	0.0	1.0	5.5	1.0	0.0	1.0	1.9	0.7	1.0	4.4
Maturity (years)	0.0	50.0	19.0	39.5	0.0	39.2	29.7	39.9	39.6	39.7
Grace period (years)	0.0	10.5	3.3	10.0	0.0	9.7	7.0	10.4	10.1	10.3
Grant element (%)	0.0	81.1	29.0	78.1	0.0	77.7	59.4	80.8	78.2	48.0
Official creditors										
Interest (%)	0.0	1.0	0.9	1.0	0.0	1.0	1.9	0.7	1.0	4.4
Maturity (years)	0.0	50.0	42.7	39.5	0.0	39.2	29.7	39.9	39.6	39.7
Grace period (years)	0.0	10.5	10.2	10.0	0.0	9.7	7.0	10.4	10.1	10.3
Grant element (%)	0.0	81.1	80.4	78.1	0.0	77.7	59.4	80.8	78.2	48.0
Private creditors										
Interest (%)	0.0	0.0	7.3	0.0	0.0	0.0	0.0	0.0	0.0	0.0
Maturity (years)	0.0	0.0	9.8	0.0	0.0	0.0	0.0	0.0	0.0	0.0
Grace period (years)	0.0	0.0	0.5	0.0	0.0	0.0	0.0	0.0	0.0	0.0
Grant element (%)	0.0	0.0	9.0	0.0	0.0	0.0	0.0	0.0	0.0	0.0
Memorandum items										
Commitments	0.0	14.2	32.5	2.4	0.0	7.4	10.0	5.4	5.4	7.1
Official creditors	0.0	14.2	9.1	2.4	0.0	7.4	10.0	5.4	5.4	7.1
Private creditors	0.0	0.0	23.4	0.0	0.0	0.0	0.0	0.0	0.0	0.0

10. CONTRACTUAL OBLIGATIONS ON OUTSTANDING LONG-TERM DEBT

	1996	1997	1998	1999	2000	2001	2002	2003	2004	2005
TOTAL										
Disbursements	7.7	7.6	6.1	4.5	3.0	1.5	0.8	0.2	0.0	0.0
Principal	4.2	4.8	4.9	2.8	2.8	3.0	3.0	3.0	2.8	2.6
Interest	1.4	1.3	1.2	1.1	1.1	1.1	1.0	1.0	1.0	0.9
Official creditors										
Disbursements	7.7	7.6	6.1	4.5	3.0	1.5	0.8	0.2	0.0	0.0
Principal	1.9	2.6	2.7	2.8	2.8	3.0	3.0	3.0	2.8	2.6
Interest	1.0	1.0	1.1	1.1	1.1	1.1	1.0	1.0	1.0	0.9
Bilateral creditors										
Disbursements	1.3	0.9	0.6	0.3	0.2	0.1	0.0	0.0	0.0	0.0
Principal	1.1	1.6	1.6	1.6	1.6	1.6	1.6	1.6	0.9	0.5
Interest	0.3	0.3	0.3	0.2	0.2	0.2	0.1	0.1	0.1	0.0
Multilateral creditors										
Disbursements	6.4	6.7	5.5	4.2	2.8	1.4	0.8	0.2	0.0	0.0
Principal	0.8	1.0	1.1	1.2	1.2	1.4	1.4	1.5	1.8	2.1
Interest	0.7	0.8	0.8	0.9	0.9	0.9	0.9	0.9	0.9	0.9
Private creditors										
Disbursements	0.0	0.0	0.0	0.0	0.0	0.0	0.0	0.0	0.0	0.0
Principal	2.3	2.3	2.3	0.0	0.0	0.0	0.0	0.0	0.0	0.0
Interest	0.5	0.3	0.1	0.0	0.0	0.0	0.0	0.0	0.0	0.0
Commercial banks										
Disbursements	0.0	0.0	0.0	0.0	0.0	0.0	0.0	0.0	0.0	0.0
Principal	0.0	0.0	0.0	0.0	0.0	0.0	0.0	0.0	0.0	0.0
Interest	0.0	0.0	0.0	0.0	0.0	0.0	0.0	0.0	0.0	0.0
Other private										
Disbursements	0.0	0.0	0.0	0.0	0.0	0.0	0.0	0.0	0.0	0.0
Principal	2.3	2.3	2.3	0.0	0.0	0.0	0.0	0.0	0.0	0.0
Interest	0.5	0.3	0.1	0.0	0.0	0.0	0.0	0.0	0.0	0.0

BOLIVIA

(US$ million, unless otherwise indicated)

	1970	1980	1988	1989	1990	1991	1992	1993	1994	1995
1. SUMMARY DEBT DATA										
TOTAL DEBT STOCKS (EDT)	..	**2,702**	**4,901**	**4,132**	**4,275**	**4,061**	**4,235**	**4,307**	**4,871**	**5,266**
Long-term debt (LDOD)	**491**	**2,274**	**4,339**	**3,626**	**3,864**	**3,672**	**3,810**	**3,879**	**4,307**	**4,692**
Public and publicly guaranteed	480	2,182	4,139	3,426	3,687	3,530	3,669	3,695	4,117	4,452
Private nonguaranteed	11	92	200	200	177	142	140	184	191	239
Use of IMF credit	**6**	**126**	**209**	**252**	**257**	**245**	**249**	**221**	**264**	**268**
Short-term debt	..	**303**	**353**	**255**	**154**	**145**	**176**	**207**	**300**	**307**
of which interest arrears on LDOD	..	3	108	50	6	15	11	14	34	20
Official creditors	..	2	101	45	2	5	2	3	21	7
Private creditors	..	1	7	5	4	10	9	11	13	13
Memo: principal arrears on LDOD	..	22	135	82	31	22	18	39	103	40
Official creditors	..	15	84	58	9	10	8	20	82	21
Private creditors	..	7	51	24	22	12	10	19	20	19
Memo: export credits	..	..	642	663	794	818	723	606	523	542
TOTAL DEBT FLOWS										
Disbursements	**58**	**553**	**424**	**437**	**331**	**316**	**445**	**369**	**431**	**511**
Long-term debt	58	457	333	379	300	285	394	369	388	486
IMF purchases	0	96	91	58	31	31	51	0	44	26
Principal repayments	**19**	**145**	**251**	**166**	**241**	**192**	**167**	**195**	**188**	**199**
Long-term debt	19	145	192	154	196	148	130	166	173	173
IMF repurchases	0	0	59	12	46	44	37	29	15	26
Net flows on debt	**39**	**408**	**2**	**231**	**32**	**107**	**313**	**203**	**316**	**333**
of which short-term debt	..	..	-171	-40	-57	-18	35	28	73	20
Interest payments (INT)	..	**220**	**121**	**126**	**144**	**138**	**121**	**139**	**160**	**173**
Long-term debt	7	173	97	93	117	118	109	127	148	155
IMF charges	0	3	9	12	13	9	4	2	1	1
Short-term debt	..	45	16	20	14	10	7	10	11	17
Net transfers on debt	..	**188**	**-119**	**105**	**-112**	**-31**	**192**	**64**	**156**	**160**
Total debt service paid (TDS)	..	**366**	**372**	**292**	**385**	**330**	**288**	**334**	**348**	**372**
Long-term debt	26	319	289	248	313	266	239	293	321	328
IMF repurchases and charges	0	3	67	24	59	54	41	31	16	28
Short-term debt (interest only)	..	45	16	20	14	10	7	10	11	17
2. AGGREGATE NET RESOURCE FLOWS AND NET TRANSFERS (LONG-TERM)										
NET RESOURCE FLOWS	**-34**	**407**	**287**	**378**	**317**	**724**	**563**	**404**	**516**	**748**
Net flow of long-term debt (ex. IMF)	39	312	140	225	104	137	264	203	215	313
Foreign direct investment (net)	-76	47	-10	-24	11	25	35	25	20	150
Portfolio equity flows	0	0	0	0	0	0	0	0	0	0
Grants (excluding technical coop.)	3	48	157	178	202	562	264	175	281	285
Memo: technical coop. grants	9	41	85	93	115	163	179	202	200	237
NET TRANSFERS	**-58**	**214**	**186**	**269**	**183**	**588**	**434**	**250**	**338**	**560**
Interest on long-term debt	7	173	97	93	117	118	109	127	148	155
Profit remittances on FDI	17	19	5	15	17	18	20	26	30	33
3. MAJOR ECONOMIC AGGREGATES										
Gross national product (GNP)	996	2,893	4,163	4,231	4,245	4,747	5,060	5,177	5,318	5,810
Exports of goods & services (XGS)	..	1,046	690	892	998	943	792	907	1,227	1,284
of which workers remittances	..	0	1	1	2	1	1	1	1	1
Imports of goods & services (MGS)	..	1,112	1,129	1,311	1,354	1,387	1,567	1,649	1,670	1,795
International reserves (RES)	46	553	473	563	511	422	480	572	793	1,006
Current account balance	..	-6	-304	-270	-199	-263	-534	-506	-218	-489
4. DEBT INDICATORS										
EDT / XGS (%)	..	258.4	710.5	463.5	428.6	430.9	535.0	474.9	396.9	410.1
EDT / GNP (%)	..	93.4	117.7	97.7	100.7	85.5	83.7	83.2	91.6	90.6
TDS / XGS (%)	..	35.0	54.0	32.7	38.6	35.0	36.4	36.8	28.3	28.9
INT / XGS (%)	..	21.1	17.6	14.1	14.4	14.6	15.3	15.4	13.0	13.5
INT / GNP (%)	..	7.6	2.9	3.0	3.4	2.9	2.4	2.7	3.0	3.0
RES / EDT (%)	..	20.5	9.6	13.6	12.0	10.4	11.3	13.3	16.3	19.1
RES / MGS (months)	..	6.0	5.0	5.2	4.5	3.7	3.7	4.2	5.7	6.7
Short-term / EDT (%)	..	11.2	7.2	6.2	3.6	3.6	4.2	4.8	6.2	5.8
Concessional / EDT (%)	..	24.8	31.6	40.2	45.1	43.2	45.7	50.9	50.6	52.1
Multilateral / EDT (%)	..	16.5	26.3	34.8	37.2	42.2	43.2	46.4	46.7	48.9

BOLIVIA

(US$ million, unless otherwise indicated)

	1970	1980	1988	1989	1990	1991	1992	1993	1994	1995
5. LONG-TERM DEBT										
DEBT OUTSTANDING (LDOD)	**491**	**2,274**	**4,339**	**3,626**	**3,864**	**3,672**	**3,810**	**3,879**	**4,307**	**4,692**
Public and publicly guaranteed	**480**	**2,182**	**4,139**	**3,426**	**3,687**	**3,530**	**3,669**	**3,695**	**4,117**	**4,452**
Official creditors	275	1,110	3,609	3,075	3,362	3,225	3,393	3,611	4,034	4,380
Multilateral	26	447	1,291	1,437	1,589	1,715	1,828	1,998	2,275	2,578
Concessional	26	182	669	808	922	1,004	1,034	1,139	1,272	1,433
Bilateral	249	663	2,319	1,638	1,773	1,510	1,565	1,613	1,759	1,802
Concessional	239	487	879	855	1,006	752	903	1,052	1,192	1,312
Private creditors	205	1,072	530	350	325	305	276	84	83	73
Bonds	67	73	35	35	35	35	35	18	17	17
Commercial banks	2	603	392	234	213	210	190	19	22	19
Other private	136	395	103	82	77	60	51	47	43	37
Private nonguaranteed	**11**	**92**	**200**	**200**	**177**	**142**	**140**	**184**	**191**	**239**
Bonds	0	0	0	0	0	0	0	0	0	0
Commercial banks	11	92	200	200	177	142	140	184	191	239
Memo:										
IBRD	0	175	228	199	194	172	146	129	116	95
IDA	18	64	249	325	393	443	464	547	648	770
DISBURSEMENTS	**58**	**457**	**333**	**379**	**300**	**285**	**394**	**369**	**388**	**486**
Public and publicly guaranteed	**55**	**441**	**333**	**379**	**300**	**285**	**391**	**319**	**363**	**419**
Official creditors	45	198	333	374	291	271	388	317	354	419
Multilateral	2	108	257	274	204	197	249	228	300	384
Concessional	2	29	142	152	103	93	82	105	129	174
Bilateral	43	91	76	100	86	74	139	89	55	35
Concessional	33	31	76	100	85	73	110	86	52	35
Private creditors	10	242	0	5	9	15	4	2	8	0
Bonds	0	0	0	0	0	0	0	0	0	0
Commercial banks	0	55	0	0	0	7	1	2	8	0
Other private	10	187	0	5	9	8	2	0	0	0
Private nonguaranteed	**3**	**16**	**0**	**0**	**0**	**0**	**2**	**51**	**25**	**67**
Bonds	0	0	0	0	0	0	0	0	0	0
Commercial banks	3	16	0	0	0	0	2	51	25	67
Memo:										
IBRD	0	73	0	0	0	0	0	0	0	0
IDA	2	2	112	79	49	48	55	66	80	113
PRINCIPAL REPAYMENTS	**19**	**145**	**192**	**154**	**196**	**148**	**130**	**166**	**173**	**173**
Public and publicly guaranteed	**17**	**126**	**192**	**154**	**172**	**114**	**126**	**160**	**154**	**155**
Official creditors	9	43	128	132	163	106	116	125	145	147
Multilateral	2	7	71	110	117	81	87	99	110	120
Concessional	2	1	9	11	14	15	17	21	24	27
Bilateral	7	36	56	22	46	25	29	26	35	27
Concessional	5	15	42	10	9	6	4	3	9	3
Private creditors	8	84	65	23	9	8	10	35	9	8
Bonds	0	1	1	0	0	0	0	0	0	0
Commercial banks	1	49	59	16	4	1	3	30	5	4
Other private	7	33	5	7	6	7	7	5	4	4
Private nonguaranteed	**2**	**19**	**0**	**0**	**24**	**35**	**4**	**7**	**19**	**18**
Bonds	0	0	0	0	0	0	0	0	0	0
Commercial banks	2	19	0	0	24	35	4	7	19	18
Memo:										
IBRD	0	3	23	19	21	25	22	23	24	27
IDA	0	0	1	1	2	2	2	2	2	2
NET FLOWS ON DEBT	**39**	**312**	**140**	**225**	**104**	**137**	**264**	**203**	**215**	**313**
Public and publicly guaranteed	**38**	**315**	**140**	**225**	**128**	**172**	**266**	**159**	**209**	**265**
Official creditors	36	156	205	242	128	165	272	192	209	272
Multilateral	0	101	185	164	87	116	162	129	190	264
Concessional	0	29	133	141	89	78	65	85	104	148
Bilateral	36	55	20	78	41	49	110	63	19	8
Concessional	28	17	34	89	76	67	106	83	43	32
Private creditors	2	159	-65	-18	0	7	-6	-33	0	-8
Bonds	0	-1	-1	0	0	0	0	0	0	0
Commercial banks	-1	6	-59	-16	-4	6	-2	-28	3	-4
Other private	3	154	-5	-2	3	1	-4	-5	-4	-4
Private nonguaranteed	**1**	**-3**	**0**	**0**	**-24**	**-35**	**-2**	**44**	**6**	**49**
Bonds	0	0	0	0	0	0	0	0	0	0
Commercial banks	1	-3	0	0	-24	-35	-2	44	6	49
Memo:										
IBRD	0	70	-23	-19	-21	-25	-22	-23	-24	-27
IDA	2	2	110	77	47	46	54	64	77	111

BOLIVIA

(US$ million, unless otherwise indicated)

	1970	1980	1988	1989	1990	1991	1992	1993	1994	1995
INTEREST PAYMENTS (LINT)	**7**	**173**	**97**	**93**	**117**	**118**	**109**	**127**	**148**	**155**
Public and publicly guaranteed	**7**	**164**	**97**	**93**	**103**	**107**	**98**	**112**	**132**	**137**
Official creditors	4	43	92	88	101	105	95	109	130	133
Multilateral	1	21	61	68	69	75	78	86	90	100
Concessional	1	3	9	11	13	15	16	17	19	20
Bilateral	3	21	31	21	32	30	17	24	40	33
Concessional	3	11	12	3	6	7	9	13	22	24
Private creditors	3	121	5	5	2	2	3	3	3	4
Bonds	1	3	2	0	0	0	0	0	0	0
Commercial banks	0	96	2	0	1	0	1	1	1	1
Other private	2	22	1	5	2	2	2	2	2	3
Private nonguaranteed	**1**	**9**	**0**	**0**	**14**	**12**	**12**	**15**	**16**	**19**
Bonds	0	0	0	0	0	0	0	0	0	0
Commercial banks	1	9	0	0	14	12	12	15	16	19
Memo:										
IBRD	0	10	20	18	15	16	14	12	11	9
IDA	0	1	2	2	3	3	3	4	4	6
NET TRANSFERS ON DEBT	**32**	**138**	**44**	**131**	**-13**	**19**	**155**	**76**	**67**	**158**
Public and publicly guaranteed	**31**	**151**	**44**	**131**	**25**	**65**	**168**	**47**	**76**	**128**
Official creditors	33	113	113	154	28	60	177	83	80	139
Multilateral	0	79	124	97	18	41	85	43	100	164
Concessional	0	26	125	131	76	63	49	68	85	128
Bilateral	33	34	-11	57	9	19	92	39	-21	-25
Concessional	26	6	22	87	71	59	97	70	22	9
Private creditors	-1	38	-70	-23	-3	5	-9	-35	-3	-11
Bonds	-1	-4	-3	0	0	0	0	0	0	0
Commercial banks	-1	-90	-60	-16	-4	5	-3	-29	2	-5
Other private	1	132	-7	-7	2	0	-6	-7	-6	-7
Private nonguaranteed	**0**	**-12**	**0**	**0**	**-38**	**-46**	**-13**	**29**	**-10**	**30**
Bonds	0	0	0	0	0	0	0	0	0	0
Commercial banks	0	-12	0	0	-38	-46	-13	29	-10	30
Memo:										
IBRD	0	60	-43	-37	-36	-42	-35	-35	-35	-36
IDA	2	1	109	75	45	43	50	60	73	105
DEBT SERVICE (LTDS)	**26**	**319**	**289**	**248**	**313**	**266**	**239**	**293**	**321**	**328**
Public and publicly guaranteed	**23**	**290**	**289**	**248**	**275**	**220**	**224**	**272**	**286**	**291**
Official creditors	13	85	219	220	263	210	211	234	275	280
Multilateral	3	28	132	178	186	156	165	185	200	220
Concessional	3	3	17	21	27	30	33	37	43	47
Bilateral	10	57	87	42	77	55	46	49	75	60
Concessional	7	25	54	13	14	14	13	16	31	27
Private creditors	11	205	70	28	12	10	13	38	12	11
Bonds	1	4	3	0	0	0	0	0	0	0
Commercial banks	1	145	60	16	4	1	4	31	6	5
Other private	8	56	7	12	8	8	9	7	6	7
Private nonguaranteed	**3**	**28**	**0**	**0**	**38**	**46**	**16**	**22**	**34**	**37**
Bonds	0	0	0	0	0	0	0	0	0	0
Commercial banks	3	28	0	0	38	46	16	22	34	37
Memo:										
IBRD	0	13	43	37	36	42	35	35	35	36
IDA	0	1	3	3	4	5	5	6	7	8
UNDISBURSED DEBT	**72**	**954**	**867**	**858**	**1,123**	**1,285**	**1,182**	**991**	**1,149**	**1,414**
Official creditors	66	804	823	840	1,107	1,270	1,172	983	1,149	1,408
Private creditors	6	150	45	19	16	15	11	8	0	6
Memorandum items										
Concessional LDOD	265	669	1,547	1,663	1,928	1,756	1,937	2,191	2,464	2,746
Variable rate LDOD	11	719	1,095	969	918	887	810	656	734	851
Public sector LDOD	467	2,166	4,139	3,426	3,687	3,530	3,669	3,695	4,117	4,452
Private sector LDOD	24	107	200	200	177	142	140	184	191	239

6. CURRENCY COMPOSITION OF LONG-TERM DEBT (PERCENT)

	1970	1980	1988	1989	1990	1991	1992	1993	1994	1995
Deutsche mark	2.3	6.8	3.6	5.7	7.0	8.8	8.9	9.2	9.6	10.0
French franc	0.1	0.8	1.4	2.0	2.2	2.4	2.3	2.2	2.2	2.1
Japanese yen	0.0	1.7	6.6	8.6	10.0	11.6	11.8	14.0	14.0	13.2
Pound sterling	0.0	2.0	0.6	0.7	0.9	1.0	0.7	0.7	0.6	0.7
Swiss franc	0.0	0.3	0.6	0.6	0.7	0.8	0.8	0.1	0.1	0.0
U.S.dollars	85.9	65.1	58.6	45.7	41.3	33.8	33.2	30.6	31.0	32.7
Multiple currency	11.7	18.1	22.5	29.0	29.4	32.2	33.4	35.1	34.5	33.7
Special drawing rights	0.0	0.0	0.0	0.0	0.0	0.0	0.0	0.0	0.0	0.1
All other currencies	0.0	5.3	6.0	7.7	8.6	9.4	8.9	8.1	7.9	7.6

BOLIVIA

(US$ million, unless otherwise indicated)

	1970	1980	1988	1989	1990	1991	1992	1993	1994	1995
7. DEBT RESTRUCTURINGS										
Total amount rescheduled	0	0	138	94	153	138	125	115	0	194
Debt stock rescheduled	0	0	0	0	0	8	0	0	0	0
Principal rescheduled	0	0	90	39	81	75	70	71	0	138
Official	0	0	42	25	69	64	62	70	0	137
Private	0	0	48	14	12	11	8	1	0	1
Interest rescheduled	0	0	39	52	63	54	54	40	0	46
Official	0	0	29	48	59	51	52	39	0	46
Private	0	0	10	4	4	2	2	1	0	1
Debt forgiven	..	..	1	696	92	403	60	55	17	74
Memo: interest forgiven	..	..	332	89	60	9	6	1	0	8
Debt stock reduction	0	0	305	169	20	19	20	171	0	0
of which debt buyback	0	0	34	16	4	2	2	27	0	0
8. DEBT STOCK-FLOW RECONCILIATION										
Total change in debt stocks	..	..	..	-769	143	-214	174	72	564	395
Net flows on debt	..	..	..	231	32	107	313	203	316	333
Net change in interest arrears	..	..	..	-58	-44	9	-4	3	20	-14
Interest capitalized	..	..	..	52	63	54	54	40	0	46
Debt forgiveness or reduction	..	..	..	-849	-109	-420	-77	-198	-17	-74
Cross-currency valuation	..	..	..	-28	143	18	-65	9	176	52
Residual	..	..	..	-116	57	20	-48	15	68	51
9. AVERAGE TERMS OF NEW COMMITMENTS										
ALL CREDITORS										
Interest (%)	1.9	8.4	4.1	4.1	4.2	4.9	3.1	3.1	3.5	3.9
Maturity (years)	47.7	15.5	30.0	27.5	29.1	25.3	31.2	27.0	28.3	28.5
Grace period (years)	4.0	4.5	8.0	7.4	7.9	6.6	8.9	7.6	7.3	7.6
Grant element (%)	66.6	13.0	47.4	46.8	47.8	39.0	56.6	53.4	51.1	49.1
Official creditors										
Interest (%)	1.8	8.1	4.1	4.0	4.1	4.7	3.1	3.1	3.5	3.8
Maturity (years)	48.2	21.5	30.0	28.1	29.4	25.7	31.2	27.0	28.3	28.7
Grace period (years)	4.0	5.3	8.0	7.5	7.9	6.6	8.9	7.6	7.3	7.7
Grant element (%)	67.4	20.4	47.4	47.9	48.3	40.2	56.6	53.4	51.1	49.5
Private creditors										
Interest (%)	12.0	8.7	0.0	7.5	9.4	8.5	0.0	0.0	0.0	6.7
Maturity (years)	5.5	10.1	0.0	7.3	5.8	13.4	0.0	0.0	0.0	5.4
Grace period (years)	3.5	3.9	0.0	3.3	1.5	4.1	0.0	0.0	0.0	1.0
Grant element (%)	-6.9	6.4	0.0	9.1	1.0	3.8	0.0	0.0	0.0	8.0
Memorandum items										
Commitments	24	370	409	417	549	451	389	129	497	684
Official creditors	24	176	409	405	542	436	389	129	497	678
Private creditors	0	194	0	12	7	15	0	0	0	6

10. CONTRACTUAL OBLIGATIONS ON OUTSTANDING LONG-TERM DEBT

	1996	1997	1998	1999	2000	2001	2002	2003	2004	2005
TOTAL										
Disbursements	452	394	261	167	88	33	16	2	1	0
Principal	221	222	302	302	272	260	274	269	247	243
Interest	181	181	198	186	172	157	143	129	115	104
Official creditors										
Disbursements	450	392	260	167	88	33	16	2	1	0
Principal	190	194	274	275	246	234	249	244	222	218
Interest	159	162	180	170	159	146	134	122	110	100
Bilateral creditors										
Disbursements	42	38	23	14	8	4	2	1	0	0
Principal	28	18	92	87	66	73	79	83	78	78
Interest	41	44	65	62	61	58	56	54	51	48
Multilateral creditors										
Disbursements	408	354	237	153	80	29	14	2	0	0
Principal	162	176	182	188	180	162	169	160	144	139
Interest	118	118	115	108	98	87	77	68	59	52
Private creditors										
Disbursements	2	2	1	0	0	0	0	0	0	0
Principal	31	28	28	27	26	26	25	25	25	25
Interest	22	20	18	16	14	12	10	8	6	4
Commercial banks										
Disbursements	0	0	0	0	0	0	0	0	0	0
Principal	4	2	2	0	0	0	0	0	0	0
Interest	1	0	0	0	0	0	0	0	0	0
Other private										
Disbursements	2	2	1	0	0	0	0	0	0	0
Principal	27	26	27	27	26	25	25	25	25	25
Interest	21	19	18	16	14	12	10	8	6	4

BOSNIA AND HERZEGOVINA

(US$ million, unless otherwise indicated)

	1970	1980	1988	1989	1990	1991	1992	1993	1994	1995
1. SUMMARY DEBT DATA										
TOTAL DEBT STOCKS (EDT)	..	..	..	..	..	..	..	..	..	..
Long-term debt (LDOD)	..	..	..	..	..	..	..	..	..	..
Public and publicly guaranteed	..	..	..	..	..	..	..	..	..	..
Private nonguaranteed	..	..	..	..	..	..	..	..	..	..
Use of IMF credit	**0.0**	**0.0**	**0.0**	**0.0**	**0.0**	**0.0**	**0.0**	**28.2**	**30.0**	**48.3**
Short-term debt	..	..	..	..	..	..	..	**1.9**	**38.5**	**31.1**
of which interest arrears on LDOD	..	..	..	..	..	..	..	..	..	..
Official creditors	..	..	..	..	..	..	..	..	..	..
Private creditors	..	..	..	..	..	..	..	..	..	..
Memo: principal arrears on LDOD	..	..	..	..	..	..	..	..	..	..
Official creditors	..	..	..	..	..	..	..	..	..	..
Private creditors	..	..	..	..	..	..	..	..	..	..
Memo: export credits	..	..	0.0	0.0	0.0	0.0	128.0	91.0	166.0	170.0
TOTAL DEBT FLOWS										
Disbursements	..	..	..	..	..	..	..	..	..	..
Long-term debt	..	..	..	..	..	..	..	..	..	..
IMF purchases	0.0	0.0	0.0	0.0	0.0	0.0	0.0	0.0	0.0	46.0
Principal repayments	..	..	..	..	..	..	..	..	..	..
Long-term debt	..	..	..	..	..	..	..	..	..	..
IMF repurchases	0.0	0.0	0.0	0.0	0.0	0.0	0.0	0.0	0.0	27.9
Net flows on debt	..	..	..	..	..	..	..	..	..	..
of which short-term debt	..	..	..	..	..	..	..	0.0	35.0	-3.9
Interest payments (INT)	..	..	..	..	..	..	..	..	..	..
Long-term debt	..	..	..	..	..	..	..	..	..	..
IMF charges	0.0	0.0	0.0	0.0	0.0	0.0	0.0	0.3	0.0	5.3
Short-term debt	..	..	..	..	..	..	..	0.0	0.0	0.0
Net transfers on debt	..	..	..	..	..	..	..	..	..	..
Total debt service paid (TDS)	..	..	..	..	..	..	..	..	..	..
Long-term debt	..	..	..	..	..	..	..	..	..	..
IMF repurchases and charges	0.0	0.0	0.0	0.0	0.0	0.0	0.0	0.3	0.0	33.2
Short-term debt (interest only)	..	..	..	..	..	..	..	0.0	0.0	0.0
2. AGGREGATE NET RESOURCE FLOWS AND NET TRANSFERS (LONG-TERM)										
NET RESOURCE FLOWS	..	..	..	..	..	..	..	..	..	..
Net flow of long-term debt (ex. IMF)	..	..	..	..	..	..	..	..	..	..
Foreign direct investment (net)	..	..	..	..	..	..	..	..	..	..
Portfolio equity flows	..	..	..	..	..	..	..	..	..	..
Grants (excluding technical coop.)	..	..	..	..	..	..	..	600.0	650.0	550.0
Memo: technical coop. grants	..	..	..	..	..	..	..	..	..	..
NET TRANSFERS	..	..	..	..	..	..	..	..	..	..
Interest on long-term debt	..	..	..	..	..	..	..	..	..	..
Profit remittances on FDI	..	..	..	..	..	..	..	..	..	..
3. MAJOR ECONOMIC AGGREGATES										
Gross national product (GNP)	..	..	..	..	..	..	..	..	2,100.0	2,323.0
Exports of goods & services (XGS)	..	..	..	..	..	..	..	..	194.0	381.0
of which workers remittances	..	..	..	..	..	..	..	..	0.0	0.0
Imports of goods & services (MGS)	..	..	..	..	..	..	..	..	1,250.0	1,511.0
International reserves (RES)	..	..	..	..	..	..	..	..	47.0	159.0
Current account balance	..	..	..	..	..	..	..	..	-177.0	-128.0
4. DEBT INDICATORS										
EDT / XGS (%)	..	..	..	..	..	..	..	..	..	..
EDT / GNP (%)	..	..	..	..	..	..	..	..	..	..
TDS / XGS (%)	..	..	..	..	..	..	..	..	..	..
INT / XGS (%)	..	..	..	..	..	..	..	..	..	..
INT / GNP (%)	..	..	..	..	..	..	..	..	..	..
RES / EDT (%)	..	..	..	..	..	..	..	..	..	..
RES / MGS (months)	..	..	..	..	..	..	..	..	0.5	1.[illegible]
Short-term / EDT (%)	..	..	..	..	..	..	..	..	..	..
Concessional / EDT (%)	..	..	..	..	..	..	..	..	..	..
Multilateral / EDT (%)	..	..	..	..	..	..	..	..	..	..

BOSNIA AND HERZEGOVINA

(US$ million, unless otherwise indicated)

	1970	1980	1988	1989	1990	1991	1992	1993	1994	1995
5. LONG-TERM DEBT										
DEBT OUTSTANDING (LDOD)	..	..	..	..	..	..	..	..	..	..
Public and publicly guaranteed	..	..	..	..	..	..	..	..	..	..
Official creditors	..	..	..	..	..	..	..	..	..	..
Multilateral	..	..	..	..	..	..	..	..	..	..
Concessional	..	..	..	..	..	..	..	..	..	..
Bilateral	..	..	..	..	..	..	..	..	..	..
Concessional	..	..	..	..	..	..	..	..	..	..
Private creditors	..	..	..	..	..	..	..	..	..	..
Bonds	..	..	..	..	..	..	..	..	..	..
Commercial banks	..	..	..	..	..	..	..	..	..	..
Other private	..	..	..	..	..	..	..	..	..	..
Private nonguaranteed	**0.0**	**0.0**	**0.0**	**0.0**	**0.0**	**0.0**	**0.0**	**0.0**	**0.0**	**0.0**
Bonds	..	..	..	..	..	..	..	..	..	..
Commercial banks	..	..	..	..	..	..	..	..	..	..
Memo:										
IBRD	0.0	0.0	0.0	0.0	0.0	0.0	0.0	424.2	452.2	472.4
IDA	0.0	0.0	0.0	0.0	0.0	0.0	0.0	0.0	0.0	0.0
DISBURSEMENTS	..	..	..	..	..	..	..	..	..	..
Public and publicly guaranteed	..	..	..	..	..	..	..	..	..	..
Official creditors	..	..	..	..	..	..	..	..	..	..
Multilateral	..	..	..	..	..	..	..	..	..	..
Concessional	..	..	..	..	..	..	..	..	..	..
Bilateral	..	..	..	..	..	..	..	..	..	..
Concessional	..	..	..	..	..	..	..	..	..	..
Private creditors	..	..	..	..	..	..	..	..	..	..
Bonds	..	..	..	..	..	..	..	..	..	..
Commercial banks	..	..	..	..	..	..	..	..	..	..
Other private	..	..	..	..	..	..	..	..	..	..
Private nonguaranteed	**0.0**	**0.0**	**0.0**	**0.0**	**0.0**	**0.0**	**0.0**	**0.0**	**0.0**	**0.0**
Bonds	..	..	..	..	..	..	..	..	..	..
Commercial banks	..	..	..	..	..	..	..	..	..	..
Memo:										
IBRD	0.0	0.0	0.0	0.0	0.0	0.0	0.0	0.0	0.0	0.0
IDA	0.0	0.0	0.0	0.0	0.0	0.0	0.0	0.0	0.0	0.0
PRINCIPAL REPAYMENTS	..	..	..	..	..	..	..	..	..	..
Public and publicly guaranteed	..	..	..	..	..	..	..	..	..	..
Official creditors	..	..	..	..	..	..	..	..	..	..
Multilateral	..	..	..	..	..	..	..	..	..	..
Concessional	..	..	..	..	..	..	..	..	..	..
Bilateral	..	..	..	..	..	..	..	..	..	..
Concessional	..	..	..	..	..	..	..	..	..	..
Private creditors	..	..	..	..	..	..	..	..	..	..
Bonds	..	..	..	..	..	..	..	..	..	..
Commercial banks	..	..	..	..	..	..	..	..	..	..
Other private	..	..	..	..	..	..	..	..	..	..
Private nonguaranteed	**0.0**	**0.0**	**0.0**	**0.0**	**0.0**	**0.0**	**0.0**	**0.0**	**0.0**	**0.0**
Bonds	..	..	..	..	..	..	..	..	..	..
Commercial banks	..	..	..	..	..	..	..	..	..	..
Memo:										
IBRD	0.0	0.0	0.0	0.0	0.0	0.0	0.0	0.0	0.0	0.0
IDA	0.0	0.0	0.0	0.0	0.0	0.0	0.0	0.0	0.0	0.0
NET FLOWS ON DEBT	..	..	..	..	..	..	..	..	..	..
Public and publicly guaranteed	..	..	..	..	..	..	..	..	..	..
Official creditors	..	..	..	..	..	..	..	..	..	..
Multilateral	..	..	..	..	..	..	..	..	..	..
Concessional	..	..	..	..	..	..	..	..	..	..
Bilateral	..	..	..	..	..	..	..	..	..	..
Concessional	..	..	..	..	..	..	..	..	..	..
Private creditors	..	..	..	..	..	..	..	..	..	..
Bonds	..	..	..	..	..	..	..	..	..	..
Commercial banks	..	..	..	..	..	..	..	..	..	..
Other private	..	..	..	..	..	..	..	..	..	..
Private nonguaranteed	**0.0**	**0.0**	**0.0**	**0.0**	**0.0**	**0.0**	**0.0**	**0.0**	**0.0**	**0.0**
Bonds	..	..	..	..	..	..	..	..	..	..
Commercial banks	..	..	..	..	..	..	..	..	..	..
Memo:										
IBRD	0.0	0.0	0.0	0.0	0.0	0.0	0.0	0.0	0.0	0.0
IDA	0.0	0.0	0.0	0.0	0.0	0.0	0.0	0.0	0.0	0.0

BOSNIA AND HERZEGOVINA

(US$ million, unless otherwise indicated)

	1970	1980	1988	1989	1990	1991	1992	1993	1994	1995
INTEREST PAYMENTS (LINT)	..	..	..	..	..	..	..	..	..	..
Public and publicly guaranteed	..	..	..	..	..	..	..	..	..	..
Official creditors	..	..	..	..	..	..	..	..	..	..
Multilateral	..	..	..	..	..	..	..	..	..	..
Concessional	..	..	..	..	..	..	..	..	..	..
Bilateral	..	..	..	..	..	..	..	..	..	..
Concessional	..	..	..	..	..	..	..	..	..	..
Private creditors	..	..	..	..	..	..	..	..	..	..
Bonds	..	..	..	..	..	..	..	..	..	..
Commercial banks	..	..	..	..	..	..	..	..	..	..
Other private	..	..	..	..	..	..	..	..	..	..
Private nonguaranteed	**0.0**	**0.0**	**0.0**	**0.0**	**0.0**	**0.0**	**0.0**	**0.0**	**0.0**	**0.0**
Bonds	..	..	..	..	..	..	..	..	..	..
Commercial banks	..	..	..	..	..	..	..	..	..	..
Memo:										
IBRD	0.0	0.0	0.0	0.0	0.0	0.0	0.0	0.0	0.0	0.0
IDA	0.0	0.0	0.0	0.0	0.0	0.0	0.0	0.0	0.0	0.0
NET TRANSFERS ON DEBT	..	..	..	..	..	..	..	..	..	..
Public and publicly guaranteed	..	..	..	..	..	..	..	..	..	..
Official creditors	..	..	..	..	..	..	..	..	..	..
Multilateral	..	..	..	..	..	..	..	..	..	..
Concessional	..	..	..	..	..	..	..	..	..	..
Bilateral	..	..	..	..	..	..	..	..	..	..
Concessional	..	..	..	..	..	..	..	..	..	..
Private creditors	..	..	..	..	..	..	..	..	..	..
Bonds	..	..	..	..	..	..	..	..	..	..
Commercial banks	..	..	..	..	..	..	..	..	..	..
Other private	..	..	..	..	..	..	..	..	..	..
Private nonguaranteed	**0.0**	**0.0**	**0.0**	**0.0**	**0.0**	**0.0**	**0.0**	**0.0**	**0.0**	**0.0**
Bonds	..	..	..	..	..	..	..	..	..	..
Commercial banks	..	..	..	..	..	..	..	..	..	..
Memo:										
IBRD	0.0	0.0	0.0	0.0	0.0	0.0	0.0	0.0	0.0	0.0
IDA	0.0	0.0	0.0	0.0	0.0	0.0	0.0	0.0	0.0	0.0
DEBT SERVICE (LTDS)	..	..	..	..	..	..	..	..	..	..
Public and publicly guaranteed	..	..	..	..	..	..	..	..	..	..
Official creditors	..	..	..	..	..	..	..	..	..	..
Multilateral	..	..	..	..	..	..	..	..	..	..
Concessional	..	..	..	..	..	..	..	..	..	..
Bilateral	..	..	..	..	..	..	..	..	..	..
Concessional	..	..	..	..	..	..	..	..	..	..
Private creditors	..	..	..	..	..	..	..	..	..	..
Bonds	..	..	..	..	..	..	..	..	..	..
Commercial banks	..	..	..	..	..	..	..	..	..	..
Other private	..	..	..	..	..	..	..	..	..	..
Private nonguaranteed	**0.0**	**0.0**	**0.0**	**0.0**	**0.0**	**0.0**	**0.0**	**0.0**	**0.0**	**0.0**
Bonds	..	..	..	..	..	..	..	..	..	..
Commercial banks	..	..	..	..	..	..	..	..	..	..
Memo:										
IBRD	0.0	0.0	0.0	0.0	0.0	0.0	0.0	0.0	0.0	0.0
IDA	0.0	0.0	0.0	0.0	0.0	0.0	0.0	0.0	0.0	0.0
UNDISBURSED DEBT	..	..	..	..	..	..	..	..	..	..
Official creditors	..	..	..	..	..	..	..	..	..	..
Private creditors	..	..	..	..	..	..	..	..	..	..
Memorandum items										
Concessional LDOD	..	..	..	..	..	..	..	..	..	..
Variable rate LDOD	..	..	..	..	..	..	..	..	..	..
Public sector LDOD	..	..	..	..	..	..	..	..	..	..
Private sector LDOD	..	..	..	..	..	..	..	..	..	..

6. CURRENCY COMPOSITION OF LONG-TERM DEBT (PERCENT)

	1970	1980	1988	1989	1990	1991	1992	1993	1994	1995
Deutsche mark	..	..	..	..	..	..	..	..	..	..
French franc	..	..	..	..	..	..	..	..	..	..
Japanese yen	..	..	..	..	..	..	..	..	..	..
Pound sterling	..	..	..	..	..	..	..	..	..	..
Swiss franc	..	..	..	..	..	..	..	..	..	..
U.S.dollars	..	..	..	..	..	..	..	..	..	..
Multiple currency	..	..	..	..	..	..	..	..	..	..
Special drawing rights	..	..	..	..	..	..	..	..	..	..
All other currencies	..	..	..	..	..	..	..	..	..	..

BOSNIA AND HERZEGOVINA

(US$ million, unless otherwise indicated)

	1970	1980	1988	1989	1990	1991	1992	1993	1994	1995
7. DEBT RESTRUCTURINGS										
Total amount rescheduled	0.0	0.0	0.0	0.0	0.0	0.0	0.0	0.0	0.0	0.0
Debt stock rescheduled	0.0	0.0	0.0	0.0	0.0	0.0	0.0	0.0	0.0	0.0
Principal rescheduled	0.0	0.0	0.0	0.0	0.0	0.0	0.0	0.0	0.0	0.0
Official	0.0	0.0	0.0	0.0	0.0	0.0	0.0	0.0	0.0	0.0
Private	0.0	0.0	0.0	0.0	0.0	0.0	0.0	0.0	0.0	0.0
Interest rescheduled	0.0	0.0	0.0	0.0	0.0	0.0	0.0	0.0	0.0	0.0
Official	0.0	0.0	0.0	0.0	0.0	0.0	0.0	0.0	0.0	0.0
Private	0.0	0.0	0.0	0.0	0.0	0.0	0.0	0.0	0.0	0.0
Debt forgiven	..	..	0.0	0.0	0.0	0.0	0.0	0.0	0.0	0.0
Memo: interest forgiven	..	..	0.0	0.0	0.0	0.0	0.0	0.0	0.0	0.0
Debt stock reduction	0.0	0.0	0.0	0.0	0.0	0.0	0.0	0.0	0.0	0.0
of which debt buyback	0.0	0.0	0.0	0.0	0.0	0.0	0.0	0.0	0.0	0.0
8. DEBT STOCK-FLOW RECONCILIATION										
Total change in debt stocks	..	..	..	..	..	..	..	..	..	..
Net flows on debt	..	..	..	..	..	..	..	..	..	..
Net change in interest arrears	..	..	..	..	..	..	..	..	..	..
Interest capitalized	..	..	..	..	..	..	..	..	..	..
Debt forgiveness or reduction	..	..	..	..	..	..	..	..	..	..
Cross-currency valuation	..	..	..	..	..	..	..	..	..	..
Residual	..	..	..	..	..	..	..	..	..	..
9. AVERAGE TERMS OF NEW COMMITMENTS										
ALL CREDITORS										
Interest (%)	..	..	..	..	..	..	..	..	..	..
Maturity (years)	..	..	..	..	..	..	..	..	..	..
Grace period (years)	..	..	..	..	..	..	..	..	..	..
Grant element (%)	..	..	..	..	..	..	..	..	..	..
Official creditors										
Interest (%)	..	..	..	..	..	..	..	..	..	..
Maturity (years)	..	..	..	..	..	..	..	..	..	..
Grace period (years)	..	..	..	..	..	..	..	..	..	..
Grant element (%)	..	..	..	..	..	..	..	..	..	..
Private creditors										
Interest (%)	..	..	..	..	..	..	..	..	..	..
Maturity (years)	..	..	..	..	..	..	..	..	..	..
Grace period (years)	..	..	..	..	..	..	..	..	..	..
Grant element (%)	..	..	..	..	..	..	..	..	..	..
Memorandum items										
Commitments	..	..	..	..	..	..	..	..	..	..
Official creditors	..	..	..	..	..	..	..	..	..	..
Private creditors	..	..	..	..	..	..	..	..	..	..

10. CONTRACTUAL OBLIGATIONS ON OUTSTANDING LONG-TERM DEBT

	1996	1997	1998	1999	2000	2001	2002	2003	2004	2005
TOTAL										
Disbursements	..	..	..	..	..	..	..	..	..	..
Principal	..	..	..	..	..	..	..	..	..	..
Interest	..	..	..	..	..	..	..	..	..	..
Official creditors										
Disbursements	..	..	..	..	..	..	..	..	..	..
Principal	..	..	..	..	..	..	..	..	..	..
Interest	..	..	..	..	..	..	..	..	..	..
Bilateral creditors										
Disbursements	..	..	..	..	..	..	..	..	..	..
Principal	..	..	..	..	..	..	..	..	..	..
Interest	..	..	..	..	..	..	..	..	..	..
Multilateral creditors										
Disbursements	0.0	0.0	0.0	0.0	0.0	0.0	0.0	0.0	0.0	0.0
Principal	113.3	100.4	78.9	55.7	38.8	11.2	0.0	0.0	0.0	0.0
Interest	30.5	20.8	13.3	7.6	3.0	0.5	0.0	0.0	0.0	0.0
Private creditors										
Disbursements	..	..	..	..	..	..	..	..	..	..
Principal	..	..	..	..	..	..	..	..	..	..
Interest	..	..	..	..	..	..	..	..	..	..
Commercial banks										
Disbursements	..	..	..	..	..	..	..	..	..	..
Principal	..	..	..	..	..	..	..	..	..	..
Interest	..	..	..	..	..	..	..	..	..	..
Other private										
Disbursements	..	..	..	..	..	..	..	..	..	..
Principal	..	..	..	..	..	..	..	..	..	..
Interest	..	..	..	..	..	..	..	..	..	..

BOTSWANA

(US$ million, unless otherwise indicated)

1. SUMMARY DEBT DATA

	1970	1980	1988	1989	1990	1991	1992	1993	1994	1995
TOTAL DEBT STOCKS (EDT)	**..**	**146.7**	**538.5**	**554.9**	**563.1**	**619.9**	**611.9**	**659.5**	**675.8**	**698.9**
Long-term debt (LDOD)	**17.4**	**142.7**	**534.7**	**551.3**	**557.3**	**613.3**	**605.6**	**651.8**	**664.6**	**682.1**
Public and publicly guaranteed	17.4	142.7	534.7	551.3	557.3	613.3	605.6	651.8	664.6	682.1
Private nonguaranteed	0.0	0.0	0.0	0.0	0.0	0.0	0.0	0.0	0.0	0.0
Use of IMF credit	**0.0**	**0.0**	**0.0**	**0.0**	**0.0**	**0.0**	**0.0**	**0.0**	**0.0**	**0.0**
Short-term debt	**..**	**4.0**	**3.8**	**3.6**	**5.8**	**6.6**	**6.3**	**7.7**	**11.2**	**16.8**
of which interest arrears on LDOD	..	0.0	0.6	0.5	2.6	3.4	3.1	4.5	7.8	12.8
Official creditors	..	0.0	0.6	0.5	1.3	1.7	1.0	1.6	2.3	6.8
Private creditors	..	0.0	0.0	0.0	1.3	1.7	2.1	3.0	5.5	6.0
Memo: principal arrears on LDOD	..	0.0	0.4	0.3	2.7	3.7	7.7	7.4	12.5	19.3
Official creditors	..	0.0	0.2	0.1	0.9	2.5	6.6	6.2	6.6	13.3
Private creditors	..	0.0	0.3	0.2	1.8	1.2	1.1	1.2	5.9	6.0
Memo: export credits	..	..	252.0	114.0	128.0	119.0	110.0	99.0	102.0	78.0
TOTAL DEBT FLOWS										
Disbursements	**5.7**	**27.5**	**58.2**	**71.3**	**29.7**	**103.0**	**84.4**	**101.9**	**56.1**	**65.9**
Long-term debt	5.7	27.5	58.2	71.3	29.7	103.0	84.4	101.9	56.1	65.9
IMF purchases	0.0	0.0	0.0	0.0	0.0	0.0	0.0	0.0	0.0	0.0
Principal repayments	**0.2**	**6.4**	**40.4**	**37.6**	**67.0**	**54.1**	**62.0**	**56.8**	**61.3**	**64.5**
Long-term debt	0.2	6.4	40.4	37.6	67.0	54.1	62.0	56.8	61.3	64.5
IMF repurchases	0.0	0.0	0.0	0.0	0.0	0.0	0.0	0.0	0.0	0.0
Net flows on debt	**5.6**	**21.1**	**17.8**	**33.5**	**-37.2**	**48.9**	**22.4**	**45.1**	**-5.0**	**2.1**
of which short-term debt	..	..	0.0	-0.1	0.1	0.0	0.0	0.0	0.2	0.6
Interest payments (INT)	**..**	**9.1**	**36.8**	**35.7**	**39.4**	**35.5**	**35.9**	**33.3**	**30.9**	**27.7**
Long-term debt	0.4	7.6	36.6	35.5	39.2	35.3	35.7	33.1	30.7	27.5
IMF charges	0.0	0.0	0.0	0.0	0.0	0.0	0.0	0.0	0.0	0.0
Short-term debt	..	1.5	0.2	0.2	0.2	0.2	0.2	0.2	0.2	0.2
Net transfers on debt	**..**	**12.0**	**-18.9**	**-2.2**	**-76.6**	**13.4**	**-13.5**	**11.8**	**-35.9**	**-25.7**
Total debt service paid (TDS)	**..**	**15.4**	**77.2**	**73.3**	**106.4**	**89.6**	**97.9**	**90.1**	**92.2**	**92.2**
Long-term debt	0.6	13.9	77.0	73.1	106.2	89.4	97.7	89.9	92.0	92.0
IMF repurchases and charges	0.0	0.0	0.0	0.0	0.0	0.0	0.0	0.0	0.0	0.0
Short-term debt (interest only)	..	1.5	0.2	0.2	0.2	0.2	0.2	0.2	0.2	0.2

2. AGGREGATE NET RESOURCE FLOWS AND NET TRANSFERS (LONG-TERM)

	1970	1980	1988	1989	1990	1991	1992	1993	1994	1995
NET RESOURCE FLOWS	**14.9**	**183.5**	**122.2**	**149.2**	**136.1**	**104.8**	**73.0**	**-189.7**	**14.0**	**99.9**
Net flow of long-term debt (ex. IMF)	5.6	21.1	17.8	33.6	-37.3	48.9	22.4	45.1	-5.2	1.5
Foreign direct investment (net)	0.0	111.6	39.9	42.2	95.0	-8.0	-2.0	-287.0	-14.0	70.0
Portfolio equity flows	0.0	0.0	0.0	0.0	0.0	0.0	0.0	0.0	0.1	0.0
Grants (excluding technical coop.)	9.3	50.8	64.5	73.4	78.4	63.9	52.6	52.2	33.1	28.4
Memo: technical coop. grants	2.5	47.5	65.2	58.4	60.7	59.6	59.1	60.5	48.3	53.9
NET TRANSFERS	**14.4**	**68.4**	**-160.0**	**-209.8**	**-200.8**	**-230.5**	**-247.7**	**-472.8**	**-296.7**	**-227.7**
Interest on long-term debt	0.4	7.6	36.6	35.5	39.2	35.3	35.7	33.1	30.7	27.5
Profit remittances on FDI	0.0	107.5	245.7	323.5	297.7	300.0	285.0	250.0	280.0	300.0

3. MAJOR ECONOMIC AGGREGATES

	1970	1980	1988	1989	1990	1991	1992	1993	1994	1995
Gross national product (GNP)	81.8	902.2	1,964.3	2,457.6	2,987.5	3,555.7	3,782.5	3,772.3	3,968.0	4,278.0
Exports of goods & services (XGS)	..	747.5	1,799.4	2,174.9	2,421.1	2,564.1	2,475.3	2,468.0	2,295.3	2,907.9
of which workers remittances	..	0.0	0.0	0.0	0.0	0.0	0.0	0.0	0.0	0.0
Imports of goods & services (MGS)	..	953.5	1,772.5	1,896.6	2,508.9	2,406.7	2,346.4	2,041.9	2,126.9	2,538.6
International reserves (RES)	..	343.7	2,258.1	2,841.1	3,385.3	3,772.4	3,844.6	4,153.1	4,462.4	4,764.4
Current account balance	..	-151.1	193.9	491.9	42.0	336.9	244.3	503.3	243.3	342.1

4. DEBT INDICATORS

	1970	1980	1988	1989	1990	1991	1992	1993	1994	1995
EDT / XGS (%)	..	19.6	29.9	25.5	23.3	24.2	24.7	26.7	29.4	24.0
EDT / GNP (%)	..	16.3	27.4	22.6	18.8	17.4	16.2	17.5	17.0	16.3
TDS / XGS (%)	..	2.1	4.3	3.4	4.4	3.5	4.0	3.7	4.0	3.2
INT / XGS (%)	..	1.2	2.0	1.6	1.6	1.4	1.5	1.3	1.3	1.0
INT / GNP (%)	..	1.0	1.9	1.5	1.3	1.0	0.9	0.9	0.8	0.6
RES / EDT (%)	..	234.2	419.4	512.0	601.2	608.5	628.3	629.7	660.3	681.7
RES / MGS (months)	..	4.3	15.3	18.0	16.2	18.8	19.7	24.4	25.2	22.5
Short-term / EDT (%)	..	2.7	0.7	0.6	1.0	1.1	1.0	1.2	1.7	2.4
Concessional / EDT (%)	..	42.3	25.6	30.3	33.5	37.6	38.8	41.2	44.8	50.2
Multilateral / EDT (%)	..	57.4	65.2	67.7	69.6	73.1	75.7	72.0	71.7	68.0

BOTSWANA

(US$ million, unless otherwise indicated)

	1970	1980	1988	1989	1990	1991	1992	1993	1994	1995
5. LONG-TERM DEBT										
DEBT OUTSTANDING (LDOD)	**17.4**	**142.7**	**534.7**	**551.3**	**557.3**	**613.3**	**605.6**	**651.8**	**664.6**	**682.1**
Public and publicly guaranteed	**17.4**	**142.7**	**534.7**	**551.3**	**557.3**	**613.3**	**605.6**	**651.8**	**664.6**	**682.1**
Official creditors	14.2	134.9	486.8	508.9	529.9	588.7	584.8	603.9	614.6	635.2
Multilateral	5.2	84.3	351.2	375.6	391.7	452.9	463.3	475.0	484.4	475.0
Concessional	5.2	34.2	71.5	98.1	116.9	152.9	157.0	177.8	203.7	217.2
Bilateral	8.9	50.6	135.7	133.3	138.2	135.8	121.6	128.9	130.2	160.2
Concessional	6.0	27.9	66.3	70.0	71.9	79.9	80.3	93.6	98.8	133.7
Private creditors	3.2	7.8	47.9	42.4	27.4	24.6	20.8	47.9	50.0	47.0
Bonds	2.6	2.5	0.0	0.0	0.0	0.0	0.0	0.0	0.0	0.0
Commercial banks	0.0	0.0	9.7	10.3	10.5	10.3	10.0	38.6	42.0	40.3
Other private	0.6	5.3	38.1	32.1	16.9	14.3	10.8	9.3	8.0	6.7
Private nonguaranteed	**0.0**	**0.0**	**0.0**	**0.0**	**0.0**	**0.0**	**0.0**	**0.0**	**0.0**	**0.0**
Bonds	0.0	0.0	0.0	0.0	0.0	0.0	0.0	0.0	0.0	0.0
Commercial banks	0.0	0.0	0.0	0.0	0.0	0.0	0.0	0.0	0.0	0.0
Memo:										
IBRD	0.0	50.0	163.0	155.2	155.2	150.0	129.3	124.7	113.6	96.3
IDA	5.2	15.6	14.2	13.9	13.6	13.3	12.9	12.4	12.0	11.5
DISBURSEMENTS	**5.7**	**27.5**	**58.2**	**71.3**	**29.7**	**103.0**	**84.4**	**101.9**	**56.1**	**65.9**
Public and publicly guaranteed	**5.7**	**27.5**	**58.2**	**71.3**	**29.7**	**103.0**	**84.4**	**101.9**	**56.1**	**65.9**
Official creditors	2.8	24.7	54.8	70.5	29.7	103.0	84.4	71.5	56.1	65.9
Multilateral	1.6	15.5	36.6	55.6	23.2	92.6	79.3	57.1	49.8	21.9
Concessional	1.6	6.7	7.7	28.6	14.4	37.9	16.5	29.8	29.6	15.9
Bilateral	1.2	9.2	18.2	15.0	6.5	10.4	5.1	14.4	6.3	44.0
Concessional	1.2	2.7	14.4	9.4	3.9	8.9	4.8	14.1	6.1	44.0
Private creditors	2.9	2.8	3.4	0.7	0.0	0.0	0.0	30.4	0.0	0.0
Bonds	2.6	0.0	0.0	0.0	0.0	0.0	0.0	0.0	0.0	0.0
Commercial banks	0.0	0.0	1.7	0.6	0.0	0.0	0.0	30.4	0.0	0.0
Other private	0.3	2.8	1.8	0.1	0.0	0.0	0.0	0.0	0.0	0.0
Private nonguaranteed	**0.0**	**0.0**	**0.0**	**0.0**	**0.0**	**0.0**	**0.0**	**0.0**	**0.0**	**0.0**
Bonds	0.0	0.0	0.0	0.0	0.0	0.0	0.0	0.0	0.0	0.0
Commercial banks	0.0	0.0	0.0	0.0	0.0	0.0	0.0	0.0	0.0	0.0
Memo:										
IBRD	0.0	9.7	13.7	10.3	7.0	11.9	4.8	12.4	1.1	0.6
IDA	1.6	0.0	0.0	0.0	0.0	0.0	0.0	0.0	0.0	0.0
PRINCIPAL REPAYMENTS	**0.2**	**6.4**	**40.4**	**37.6**	**67.0**	**54.1**	**62.0**	**56.8**	**61.3**	**64.5**
Public and publicly guaranteed	**0.2**	**6.4**	**40.4**	**37.6**	**67.0**	**54.1**	**62.0**	**56.8**	**61.3**	**64.5**
Official creditors	0.1	6.4	35.8	33.7	48.6	51.5	59.3	55.7	59.3	58.2
Multilateral	0.0	5.7	26.0	24.7	36.9	37.8	49.1	45.5	49.5	48.6
Concessional	0.0	0.1	2.7	2.5	2.8	3.3	5.6	8.0	10.4	8.1
Bilateral	0.1	0.7	9.8	9.0	11.7	13.7	10.2	10.3	9.9	9.7
Concessional	0.0	0.0	3.8	2.8	3.4	3.5	3.7	4.9	4.5	4.6
Private creditors	0.0	0.0	4.6	4.0	18.5	2.6	2.7	1.1	2.0	6.2
Bonds	0.0	0.0	0.8	0.0	0.0	0.0	0.0	0.0	0.0	0.0
Commercial banks	0.0	0.0	0.1	0.1	0.2	0.2	0.2	0.2	0.2	4.5
Other private	0.0	0.0	3.6	3.8	18.3	2.5	2.5	0.9	1.8	1.7
Private nonguaranteed	**0.0**	**0.0**	**0.0**	**0.0**	**0.0**	**0.0**	**0.0**	**0.0**	**0.0**	**0.0**
Bonds	0.0	0.0	0.0	0.0	0.0	0.0	0.0	0.0	0.0	0.0
Commercial banks	0.0	0.0	0.0	0.0	0.0	0.0	0.0	0.0	0.0	0.0
Memo:										
IBRD	0.0	5.4	15.1	12.3	19.0	19.2	20.6	19.8	21.0	23.7
IDA	0.0	0.1	0.2	0.3	0.3	0.3	0.4	0.4	0.4	0.5
NET FLOWS ON DEBT	**5.6**	**21.1**	**17.8**	**33.6**	**-37.3**	**48.9**	**22.4**	**45.1**	**-5.2**	**1.5**
Public and publicly guaranteed	**5.6**	**21.1**	**17.8**	**33.6**	**-37.3**	**48.9**	**22.4**	**45.1**	**-5.2**	**1.5**
Official creditors	2.7	18.3	19.0	36.8	-18.9	51.5	25.1	15.8	-3.3	7.7
Multilateral	1.6	9.8	10.6	30.9	-13.7	54.9	30.2	11.6	0.3	-26.7
Concessional	1.6	6.6	5.0	26.1	11.6	34.6	10.9	21.8	19.2	7.8
Bilateral	1.1	8.5	8.4	6.0	-5.2	-3.4	-5.1	4.1	-3.6	34.4
Concessional	1.2	2.7	10.6	6.6	0.5	5.4	1.1	9.3	1.7	39.4
Private creditors	2.9	2.8	-1.2	-3.2	-18.5	-2.6	-2.7	29.3	-2.0	-6.2
Bonds	2.6	0.0	-0.8	0.0	0.0	0.0	0.0	0.0	0.0	0.0
Commercial banks	0.0	0.0	1.5	0.5	-0.2	-0.2	-0.2	30.2	-0.2	-4.5
Other private	0.3	2.8	-1.8	-3.7	-18.3	-2.5	-2.5	-0.9	-1.8	-1.7
Private nonguaranteed	**0.0**	**0.0**	**0.0**	**0.0**	**0.0**	**0.0**	**0.0**	**0.0**	**0.0**	**0.0**
Bonds	0.0	0.0	0.0	0.0	0.0	0.0	0.0	0.0	0.0	0.0
Commercial banks	0.0	0.0	0.0	0.0	0.0	0.0	0.0	0.0	0.0	0.0
Memo:										
IBRD	0.0	4.3	-1.4	-2.0	-11.9	-7.3	-15.8	-7.5	-19.9	-23.1
IDA	1.6	0.0	-0.2	-0.3	-0.3	-0.3	-0.4	-0.4	-0.4	-0.5

BOTSWANA

(US$ million, unless otherwise indicated)

	1970	1980	1988	1989	1990	1991	1992	1993	1994	1995
INTEREST PAYMENTS (LINT)	**0.4**	**7.6**	**36.6**	**35.5**	**39.2**	**35.3**	**35.7**	**33.1**	**30.7**	**27.5**
Public and publicly guaranteed	**0.4**	**7.6**	**36.6**	**35.5**	**39.2**	**35.3**	**35.7**	**33.1**	**30.7**	**27.5**
Official creditors	0.4	6.6	33.0	31.9	36.2	32.9	33.5	32.0	29.5	24.5
Multilateral	0.0	4.7	25.0	23.6	27.9	24.6	25.9	24.8	24.9	21.0
Concessional	0.0	0.3	1.1	1.3	2.6	2.9	3.0	2.8	2.4	1.9
Bilateral	0.4	1.9	8.0	8.3	8.3	8.2	7.6	7.3	4.7	3.5
Concessional	0.2	0.5	1.3	1.9	1.8	2.3	2.4	3.0	1.5	1.0
Private creditors	0.0	1.0	3.5	3.6	3.0	2.5	2.2	1.1	1.2	3.0
Bonds	0.0	0.2	0.0	0.0	0.0	0.0	0.0	0.0	0.0	0.0
Commercial banks	0.0	0.5	0.8	1.0	0.1	0.9	0.9	0.3	0.3	2.7
Other private	0.0	0.3	2.7	2.6	3.0	1.5	1.3	0.7	0.8	0.3
Private nonguaranteed	**0.0**	**0.0**	**0.0**	**0.0**	**0.0**	**0.0**	**0.0**	**0.0**	**0.0**	**0.0**
Bonds	0.0	0.0	0.0	0.0	0.0	0.0	0.0	0.0	0.0	0.0
Commercial banks	0.0	0.0	0.0	0.0	0.0	0.0	0.0	0.0	0.0	0.0
Memo:										
IBRD	0.0	4.4	13.9	11.4	14.2	11.7	11.4	9.9	9.3	8.6
IDA	0.0	0.1	0.1	0.1	0.1	0.1	0.1	0.1	0.1	0.1
NET TRANSFERS ON DEBT	**5.1**	**13.5**	**-18.7**	**-1.9**	**-76.5**	**13.6**	**-13.3**	**12.0**	**-35.9**	**-26.1**
Public and publicly guaranteed	**5.1**	**13.5**	**-18.7**	**-1.9**	**-76.5**	**13.6**	**-13.3**	**12.0**	**-35.9**	**-26.1**
Official creditors	2.2	11.7	-14.0	5.0	-55.1	18.7	-8.5	-16.3	-32.8	-16.8
Multilateral	1.6	5.1	-14.4	7.3	-41.6	30.2	4.3	-13.1	-24.5	-47.7
Concessional	1.6	6.3	3.9	24.8	9.0	31.7	8.0	19.1	16.8	5.9
Bilateral	0.6	6.6	0.4	-2.4	-13.5	-11.6	-12.7	-3.1	-8.3	30.9
Concessional	1.0	2.1	9.3	4.6	-1.4	3.1	-1.3	6.3	0.2	38.4
Private creditors	2.9	1.9	-4.7	-6.8	-21.5	-5.1	-4.9	28.3	-3.1	-9.3
Bonds	2.6	-0.2	-0.9	0.0	0.0	0.0	0.0	0.0	0.0	0.0
Commercial banks	0.0	-0.5	0.7	-0.5	-0.2	-1.1	-1.1	29.9	-0.5	-7.2
Other private	0.2	2.5	-4.6	-6.3	-21.3	-4.0	-3.8	-1.7	-2.6	-2.0
Private nonguaranteed	**0.0**	**0.0**	**0.0**	**0.0**	**0.0**	**0.0**	**0.0**	**0.0**	**0.0**	**0.0**
Bonds	0.0	0.0	0.0	0.0	0.0	0.0	0.0	0.0	0.0	0.0
Commercial banks	0.0	0.0	0.0	0.0	0.0	0.0	0.0	0.0	0.0	0.0
Memo:										
IBRD	0.0	-0.1	-15.3	-13.5	-26.1	-19.0	-27.2	-17.4	-29.2	-31.7
IDA	1.6	-0.2	-0.4	-0.4	-0.4	-0.4	-0.5	-0.5	-0.5	-0.6
DEBT SERVICE (LTDS)	**0.6**	**13.9**	**77.0**	**73.1**	**106.2**	**89.4**	**97.7**	**89.9**	**92.0**	**92.0**
Public and publicly guaranteed	**0.6**	**13.9**	**77.0**	**73.1**	**106.2**	**89.4**	**97.7**	**89.9**	**92.0**	**92.0**
Official creditors	0.6	13.0	68.8	65.6	84.7	84.3	92.8	87.8	88.9	82.7
Multilateral	0.0	10.4	51.0	48.3	64.8	62.4	75.0	70.2	74.3	69.6
Concessional	0.0	0.4	3.8	3.8	5.4	6.3	8.5	10.8	12.8	10.0
Bilateral	0.5	2.6	17.8	17.3	20.0	22.0	17.9	17.5	14.5	13.1
Concessional	0.2	0.5	5.2	4.8	5.2	5.8	6.2	7.9	5.9	5.6
Private creditors	0.1	1.0	8.1	7.6	21.5	5.1	4.9	2.1	3.1	9.3
Bonds	0.0	0.2	0.9	0.0	0.0	0.0	0.0	0.0	0.0	0.0
Commercial banks	0.0	0.5	0.9	1.1	0.2	1.1	1.1	0.5	0.5	7.2
Other private	0.1	0.3	6.3	6.5	21.3	4.0	3.8	1.7	2.6	2.0
Private nonguaranteed	**0.0**	**0.0**	**0.0**	**0.0**	**0.0**	**0.0**	**0.0**	**0.0**	**0.0**	**0.0**
Bonds	0.0	0.0	0.0	0.0	0.0	0.0	0.0	0.0	0.0	0.0
Commercial banks	0.0	0.0	0.0	0.0	0.0	0.0	0.0	0.0	0.0	0.0
Memo:										
IBRD	0.0	9.7	29.0	23.7	33.1	30.9	32.0	29.8	30.3	32.3
IDA	0.0	0.2	0.4	0.4	0.4	0.4	0.5	0.5	0.5	0.6
UNDISBURSED DEBT	**31.1**	**159.6**	**342.1**	**337.7**	**410.3**	**360.6**	**313.1**	**240.7**	**204.1**	**114.9**
Official creditors	31.1	118.1	338.2	334.5	373.1	324.1	278.2	237.6	200.7	114.9
Private creditors	0.0	41.6	3.9	3.3	37.2	36.5	34.9	3.1	3.4	0.0
Memorandum items										
Concessional LDOD	11.2	62.1	137.9	168.1	188.8	232.8	237.2	271.4	302.5	350.9
Variable rate LDOD	0.0	0.0	67.4	70.3	73.1	77.5	71.4	105.4	110.3	105.8
Public sector LDOD	17.4	142.7	533.8	550.8	557.3	613.3	605.6	622.8	632.4	651.6
Private sector LDOD	0.0	0.0	0.9	0.5	0.0	0.0	0.0	29.0	32.3	30.5

6. CURRENCY COMPOSITION OF LONG-TERM DEBT (PERCENT)

	1970	1980	1988	1989	1990	1991	1992	1993	1994	1995
Deutsche mark	0.0	0.0	0.3	0.3	0.3	0.2	0.2	4.6	5.0	4.6
French franc	0.0	0.0	1.5	1.5	1.6	1.4	1.2	1.0	1.1	1.0
Japanese yen	0.0	0.0	2.3	3.6	4.3	5.7	5.8	6.0	6.6	11.4
Pound sterling	81.8	27.3	16.2	13.1	10.9	8.8	6.9	5.7	5.1	4.3
Swiss franc	0.0	0.0	0.0	0.0	0.0	0.0	0.0	0.0	0.0	0.0
U.S.dollars	0.0	23.8	12.2	11.9	11.7	10.8	10.8	10.5	10.8	11.3
Multiple currency	0.0	44.1	52.9	52.7	54.4	56.3	57.6	53.5	52.4	48.2
Special drawing rights	0.0	0.0	0.0	0.0	0.0	0.0	0.2	0.2	1.4	1.4
All other currencies	18.4	4.8	14.7	16.9	16.8	16.8	17.3	18.6	17.5	17.8

BOTSWANA

(US$ million, unless otherwise indicated)

	1970	1980	1988	1989	1990	1991	1992	1993	1994	1995
7. DEBT RESTRUCTURINGS										
Total amount rescheduled	0.0	0.0	0.0	0.0	0.0	0.0	0.0	0.0	0.0	0.0
Debt stock rescheduled	0.0	0.0	0.0	0.0	0.0	0.0	0.0	0.0	0.0	0.0
Principal rescheduled	0.0	0.0	0.0	0.0	0.0	0.0	0.0	0.0	0.0	0.0
Official	0.0	0.0	0.0	0.0	0.0	0.0	0.0	0.0	0.0	0.0
Private	0.0	0.0	0.0	0.0	0.0	0.0	0.0	0.0	0.0	0.0
Interest rescheduled	0.0	0.0	0.0	0.0	0.0	0.0	0.0	0.0	0.0	0.0
Official	0.0	0.0	0.0	0.0	0.0	0.0	0.0	0.0	0.0	0.0
Private	0.0	0.0	0.0	0.0	0.0	0.0	0.0	0.0	0.0	0.0
Debt forgiven	..	..	0.0	0.0	0.0	0.0	0.0	0.0	0.0	0.0
Memo: interest forgiven	..	..	0.0	0.0	0.0	0.0	0.0	0.0	0.0	0.0
Debt stock reduction	0.0	0.0	0.0	0.0	0.0	0.0	0.0	0.0	0.0	0.0
of which debt buyback	0.0	0.0	0.0	0.0	0.0	0.0	0.0	0.0	0.0	0.0
8. DEBT STOCK-FLOW RECONCILIATION										
Total change in debt stocks	..	..	..	16.4	8.3	56.8	-8.0	47.6	16.3	23.1
Net flows on debt	..	..	..	33.5	-37.2	48.9	22.4	45.1	-5.0	2.1
Net change in interest arrears	..	..	..	-0.1	2.1	0.9	-0.3	1.4	3.3	5.0
Interest capitalized	..	..	..	0.0	0.0	0.0	0.0	0.0	0.0	0.0
Debt forgiveness or reduction	..	..	..	0.0	0.0	0.0	0.0	0.0	0.0	0.0
Cross-currency valuation	..	..	..	-18.0	29.0	-1.8	-24.6	-4.0	19.8	1.6
Residual	..	..	..	1.0	14.4	8.9	-5.5	5.1	-1.7	14.4
9. AVERAGE TERMS OF NEW COMMITMENTS										
ALL CREDITORS										
Interest (%)	0.6	6.0	3.6	5.0	6.9	1.3	5.3	3.7	3.6	0.0
Maturity (years)	38.9	18.4	29.2	23.2	14.8	31.7	25.1	25.1	11.8	0.0
Grace period (years)	10.0	4.0	6.8	5.7	4.3	7.7	5.8	7.0	4.0	0.0
Grant element (%)	79.7	24.2	45.6	34.8	17.1	66.5	30.5	47.4	32.7	0.0
Official creditors										
Interest (%)	0.1	6.0	3.6	5.0	5.7	1.3	5.4	3.7	3.6	0.0
Maturity (years)	40.7	18.4	29.2	23.2	16.9	31.7	25.4	25.1	11.8	0.0
Grace period (years)	9.4	4.0	6.8	5.7	4.4	7.7	6.2	7.0	4.0	0.0
Grant element (%)	84.9	24.2	45.6	34.8	25.0	66.5	30.2	47.4	32.7	0.0
Private creditors										
Interest (%)	7.3	0.0	0.0	0.0	8.9	0.0	4.1	0.0	0.0	0.0
Maturity (years)	16.9	0.0	0.0	0.0	11.6	0.0	20.6	0.0	0.0	0.0
Grace period (years)	16.3	0.0	0.0	0.0	4.1	0.0	0.6	0.0	0.0	0.0
Grant element (%)	19.6	0.0	0.0	0.0	4.6	0.0	34.6	0.0	0.0	0.0
Memorandum items										
Commitments	37.6	69.3	122.1	76.7	79.4	61.5	79.8	50.0	6.2	0.0
Official creditors	34.7	69.3	122.1	76.7	48.4	61.5	73.8	50.0	6.2	0.0
Private creditors	2.9	0.0	0.0	0.0	31.0	0.0	6.1	0.0	0.0	0.0

10. CONTRACTUAL OBLIGATIONS ON OUTSTANDING LONG-TERM DEBT

	1996	1997	1998	1999	2000	2001	2002	2003	2004	2005
TOTAL										
Disbursements	37.5	27.9	20.3	12.2	7.8	2.0	0.1	0.0	0.0	0.0
Principal	67.0	66.6	63.8	60.1	54.2	46.6	36.8	32.8	30.5	27.2
Interest	32.2	29.3	26.2	23.0	20.0	17.2	14.8	13.0	11.5	10.1
Official creditors										
Disbursements	37.5	27.9	20.3	12.2	7.8	2.0	0.1	0.0	0.0	0.0
Principal	59.6	61.5	58.6	54.9	49.0	41.4	36.0	32.0	29.7	26.4
Interest	29.4	26.9	24.1	21.3	18.6	16.2	14.1	12.3	10.9	9.6
Bilateral creditors										
Disbursements	2.4	1.5	1.0	0.9	0.5	0.2	0.1	0.0	0.0	0.0
Principal	11.9	11.1	10.9	11.2	10.9	10.5	8.9	7.8	7.4	7.3
Interest	5.6	4.9	4.4	3.9	3.5	3.0	2.6	2.4	2.2	1.9
Multilateral creditors										
Disbursements	35.1	26.4	19.3	11.3	7.2	1.7	0.0	0.0	0.0	0.0
Principal	47.8	50.5	47.7	43.7	38.1	30.9	27.1	24.2	22.4	19.0
Interest	23.9	22.0	19.7	17.4	15.2	13.1	11.4	10.0	8.8	7.7
Private creditors										
Disbursements	0.0	0.0	0.0	0.0	0.0	0.0	0.0	0.0	0.0	0.0
Principal	7.3	5.1	5.2	5.2	5.2	5.2	0.8	0.8	0.8	0.8
Interest	2.8	2.4	2.1	1.7	1.4	1.0	0.8	0.7	0.6	0.5
Commercial banks										
Disbursements	0.0	0.0	0.0	0.0	0.0	0.0	0.0	0.0	0.0	0.0
Principal	4.5	4.5	5.0	5.0	5.0	5.0	0.7	0.7	0.7	0.7
Interest	2.5	2.2	1.9	1.6	1.3	0.9	0.7	0.6	0.5	0.5
Other private										
Disbursements	0.0	0.0	0.0	0.0	0.0	0.0	0.0	0.0	0.0	0.0
Principal	2.8	0.5	0.1	0.1	0.1	0.1	0.1	0.1	0.1	0.1
Interest	0.3	0.2	0.2	0.1	0.1	0.1	0.1	0.1	0.1	0.1

BRAZIL

(US$ million, unless otherwise indicated)

	1970	1980	1988	1989	1990	1991	1992	1993	1994	1995
1. SUMMARY DEBT DATA										
TOTAL DEBT STOCKS (EDT)	..	**71,520**	**117,183**	**114,330**	**119,643**	**120,702**	**128,749**	**143,765**	**151,595**	**159,130**
Long-term debt (LDOD)	**5,020**	**57,981**	**103,358**	**93,893**	**94,107**	**93,150**	**103,836**	**112,817**	**120,009**	**128,495**
Public and publicly guaranteed	3,314	41,375	91,843	87,885	87,436	85,313	90,656	91,901	95,309	96,609
Private nonguaranteed	1,706	16,605	11,514	6,008	6,671	7,837	13,180	20,916	24,701	31,887
Use of IMF credit	**0**	**0**	**3,333**	**2,423**	**1,821**	**1,238**	**799**	**304**	**186**	**142**
Short-term debt	..	**13,540**	**10,492**	**18,014**	**23,716**	**26,314**	**24,114**	**30,645**	**31,400**	**30,494**
of which interest arrears on LDOD	..	14	170	3,188	8,791	10,519	4,316	7,242	1,349	802
Official creditors	..	0	84	269	332	751	350	1,394	854	433
Private creditors	..	13	85	2,920	8,458	9,768	3,966	5,848	495	369
Memo: principal arrears on LDOD	..	432	1,000	1,596	3,712	4,853	4,033	5,233	3,526	4,246
Official creditors	..	3	464	533	789	1,678	781	868	861	826
Private creditors	..	429	536	1,063	2,923	3,175	3,253	4,365	2,665	3,419
Memo: export credits	..	..	17,906	20,512	23,906	26,464	27,651	27,937	28,519	25,673
TOTAL DEBT FLOWS										
Disbursements	**1,783**	**11,418**	**6,871**	**4,592**	**4,036**	**4,879**	**9,409**	**14,613**	**11,396**	**19,551**
Long-term debt	1,783	11,418	6,380	4,592	4,036	4,879	9,229	14,613	11,396	19,551
IMF purchases	0	0	491	0	0	0	180	0	0	0
Principal repayments	**531**	**6,848**	**4,213**	**8,907**	**5,924**	**4,810**	**4,742**	**6,803**	**9,572**	**11,150**
Long-term debt	456	6,848	3,283	8,095	5,158	4,242	4,162	6,300	9,438	11,101
IMF repurchases	75	0	929	812	765	567	579	503	134	49
Net flows on debt	**1,252**	**4,570**	**2,751**	**188**	**-1,788**	**940**	**8,670**	**11,415**	**8,473**	**8,041**
of which short-term debt	..	..	93	4,503	99	870	4,003	3,605	6,648	-359
Interest payments (INT)	..	**7,909**	**12,630**	**5,215**	**2,256**	**3,528**	**3,829**	**4,431**	**6,639**	**11,177**
Long-term debt	221	6,384	11,446	3,858	2,025	2,034	2,947	3,222	5,123	9,375
IMF charges	0	0	250	257	231	150	90	39	14	10
Short-term debt	..	1,525	934	1,100	0	1,344	792	1,170	1,503	1,792
Net transfers on debt	..	**-3,340**	**-9,879**	**-5,028**	**-4,045**	**-2,588**	**4,842**	**6,984**	**1,834**	**-3,136**
Total debt service paid (TDS)	..	**14,757**	**16,843**	**14,122**	**8,180**	**8,337**	**8,570**	**11,234**	**16,211**	**22,328**
Long-term debt	677	13,232	14,729	11,953	7,184	6,276	7,109	9,522	14,560	20,477
IMF repurchases and charges	75	0	1,180	1,069	996	718	669	542	148	59
Short-term debt (interest only)	..	1,525	934	1,100	0	1,344	792	1,170	1,503	1,792
2. AGGREGATE NET RESOURCE FLOWS AND NET TRANSFERS (LONG-TERM)										
NET RESOURCE FLOWS	**1,777**	**6,494**	**6,262**	**-2,193**	**-92**	**2,593**	**8,900**	**15,165**	**10,182**	**17,783**
Net flow of long-term debt (ex. IMF)	1,327	4,570	3,097	-3,504	-1,122	637	5,067	8,314	1,959	8,449
Foreign direct investment (net)	421	1,911	2,969	1,267	989	1,103	2,061	1,292	3,072	4,859
Portfolio equity flows	0	0	150	0	0	803	1,734	5,500	5,082	4,411
Grants (excluding technical coop.)	28	14	46	44	41	50	38	59	69	64
Memo: technical coop. grants	32	83	140	139	157	179	199	223	279	334
NET TRANSFERS	**1,169**	**-845**	**-7,439**	**-8,966**	**-4,010**	**-494**	**5,119**	**9,803**	**2,609**	**5,808**
Interest on long-term debt	221	6,384	11,446	3,858	2,025	2,034	2,947	3,222	5,123	9,375
Profit remittances on FDI	387	955	2,255	2,915	1,892	1,053	834	2,139	2,450	2,600
3. MAJOR ECONOMIC AGGREGATES										
Gross national product (GNP)	34,830	229,206	316,713	435,226	425,862	375,252	368,494	424,273	545,800	663,589
Exports of goods & services (XGS)	..	23,331	36,842	38,905	36,854	36,899	42,718	46,026	53,046	58,989
of which workers remittances	..	56	19	88	527	1,057	1,719	1,123	1,834	2,891
Imports of goods & services (MGS)	..	36,250	32,758	38,036	40,949	38,806	37,099	46,486	54,788	77,855
International reserves (RES)	1,190	6,875	8,090	8,729	9,200	8,749	23,265	31,747	38,492	51,477
Current account balance	..	-12,831	4,156	1,002	-3,823	-1,450	6,089	20	-1,153	-18,136
4. DEBT INDICATORS										
EDT / XGS (%)	..	306.5	318.1	293.9	324.6	327.1	301.4	312.4	285.8	269.8
EDT / GNP (%)	..	31.2	37.0	26.3	28.1	32.2	34.9	33.9	27.8	24.0
TDS / XGS (%)	..	63.3	45.7	36.3	22.2	22.6	20.1	24.4	30.6	37.9
INT / XGS (%)	..	33.9	34.3	13.4	6.1	9.6	9.0	9.6	12.5	18.9
INT / GNP (%)	..	3.5	4.0	1.2	0.5	0.9	1.0	1.0	1.2	1.7
RES / EDT (%)	..	9.6	6.9	7.6	7.7	7.2	18.1	22.1	25.4	32.3
RES / MGS (months)	..	2.3	3.0	2.8	2.7	2.7	7.5	8.2	8.4	7.9
Short-term / EDT (%)	..	18.9	9.0	15.8	19.8	21.8	18.7	21.3	20.7	19.2
Concessional / EDT (%)	..	2.6	2.5	2.5	2.5	2.4	2.0	1.8	1.7	1.8
Multilateral / EDT (%)	..	4.3	9.7	9.7	9.5	9.2	7.8	6.6	6.2	5.9

BRAZIL

(US$ million, unless otherwise indicated)

	1970	1980	1988	1989	1990	1991	1992	1993	1994	1995
5. LONG-TERM DEBT										
DEBT OUTSTANDING (LDOD)	**5,020**	**57,981**	**103,358**	**93,893**	**94,107**	**93,150**	**103,836**	**112,817**	**120,009**	**128,495**
Public and publicly guaranteed	**3,314**	**41,375**	**91,843**	**87,885**	**87,436**	**85,313**	**90,656**	**91,901**	**95,309**	**96,609**
Official creditors	1,779	7,306	25,520	26,547	29,279	28,702	30,335	30,088	29,536	28,817
Multilateral	376	3,092	11,408	11,084	11,391	11,074	10,067	9,479	9,375	9,366
Concessional	196	202	150	131	114	92	79	105	69	64
Bilateral	1,403	4,214	14,112	15,463	17,888	17,628	20,267	20,610	20,161	19,451
Concessional	1,308	1,678	2,753	2,699	2,863	2,862	2,509	2,514	2,491	2,864
Private creditors	1,535	34,069	66,323	61,339	58,157	56,611	60,321	61,813	65,772	67,791
Bonds	0	3,233	1,546	2,183	2,339	3,147	10,766	11,604	54,020	54,664
Commercial banks	748	24,251	55,800	50,077	46,290	44,226	43,545	44,837	6,560	8,404
Other private	787	6,585	8,978	9,079	9,528	9,239	6,011	5,372	5,193	4,724
Private nonguaranteed	**1,706**	**16,605**	**11,514**	**6,008**	**6,671**	**7,837**	**13,180**	**20,916**	**24,701**	**31,887**
Bonds	0	0	0	0	0	398	2,803	7,366	9,391	12,346
Commercial banks	1,706	16,605	11,514	6,008	6,671	7,439	10,377	13,550	15,310	19,541
Memo:										
IBRD	206	2,035	8,611	8,311	8,427	8,165	7,238	6,575	6,311	6,038
IDA	0	0	0	0	0	0	0	0	0	0
DISBURSEMENTS	**1,783**	**11,418**	**6,380**	**4,592**	**4,036**	**4,879**	**9,229**	**14,613**	**11,396**	**19,551**
Public and publicly guaranteed	**883**	**8,226**	**6,210**	**3,742**	**3,161**	**3,853**	**2,282**	**3,585**	**3,028**	**7,455**
Official creditors	260	1,343	1,553	1,551	1,316	1,343	911	877	1,104	2,463
Multilateral	108	535	1,291	1,073	1,001	1,079	883	865	950	1,257
Concessional	48	3	13	6	0	0	0	82	0	0
Bilateral	152	809	262	478	315	264	28	13	155	1,206
Concessional	96	46	11	49	80	33	5	9	3	744
Private creditors	623	6,883	4,658	2,191	1,845	2,509	1,371	2,708	1,924	4,992
Bonds	0	378	675	0	200	1,037	820	1,320	402	1,661
Commercial banks	333	4,826	2,956	812	765	772	302	1,257	1,209	2,961
Other private	290	1,679	1,027	1,379	880	700	249	131	313	370
Private nonguaranteed	**900**	**3,192**	**170**	**850**	**875**	**1,027**	**6,947**	**11,028**	**8,368**	**12,096**
Bonds	0	0	0	0	0	398	2,405	4,761	3,516	4,563
Commercial banks	900	3,192	170	850	875	628	4,542	6,267	4,853	7,533
Memo:										
IBRD	61	343	994	819	782	840	581	471	640	838
IDA	0	0	0	0	0	0	0	0	0	0
PRINCIPAL REPAYMENTS	**456**	**6,848**	**3,283**	**8,095**	**5,158**	**4,242**	**4,162**	**6,300**	**9,438**	**11,101**
Public and publicly guaranteed	**256**	**3,878**	**2,627**	**6,338**	**4,150**	**3,490**	**2,834**	**3,094**	**4,915**	**6,622**
Official creditors	76	518	1,491	1,328	1,954	2,402	1,829	1,881	3,182	3,841
Multilateral	32	164	1,194	1,096	1,518	1,536	1,568	1,652	1,674	1,683
Concessional	15	18	22	21	26	22	11	58	7	7
Bilateral	45	354	298	232	436	866	262	229	1,508	2,157
Concessional	40	97	5	10	21	62	21	31	200	357
Private creditors	180	3,360	1,135	5,010	2,196	1,089	1,005	1,213	1,733	2,781
Bonds	0	32	566	384	71	248	302	502	604	919
Commercial banks	137	2,430	21	4,179	1,595	100	57	102	319	973
Other private	43	898	549	447	531	740	646	609	810	890
Private nonguaranteed	**200**	**2,970**	**657**	**1,757**	**1,008**	**752**	**1,328**	**3,206**	**4,523**	**4,480**
Bonds	0	0	0	0	0	0	0	198	1,507	2,670
Commercial banks	200	2,970	657	1,757	1,008	752	1,328	3,008	3,016	1,810
Memo:										
IBRD	14	98	970	871	1,251	1,248	1,266	1,279	1,346	1,377
IDA	0	0	0	0	0	0	0	0	0	0
NET FLOWS ON DEBT	**1,327**	**4,570**	**3,097**	**-3,504**	**-1,122**	**637**	**5,067**	**8,314**	**1,959**	**8,449**
Public and publicly guaranteed	**627**	**4,348**	**3,584**	**-2,596**	**-989**	**362**	**-552**	**491**	**-1,887**	**833**
Official creditors	184	825	61	223	-638	-1,058	-918	-1,004	-2,078	-1,378
Multilateral	76	371	97	-23	-517	-457	-685	-787	-725	-426
Concessional	33	-15	-9	-15	-26	-22	-11	25	-7	-7
Bilateral	108	454	-36	246	-121	-601	-234	-217	-1,353	-952
Concessional	57	-50	7	39	59	-29	-16	-22	-197	387
Private creditors	444	3,523	3,522	-2,819	-351	1,421	366	1,495	191	2,211
Bonds	0	346	109	-384	129	789	518	817	-202	743
Commercial banks	196	2,397	2,936	-3,366	-829	672	245	1,155	890	1,988
Other private	247	780	478	932	349	-40	-397	-478	-498	-520
Private nonguaranteed	**700**	**222**	**-487**	**-908**	**-133**	**275**	**5,619**	**7,822**	**3,845**	**7,616**
Bonds	0	0	0	0	0	398	2,405	4,563	2,009	1,894
Commercial banks	700	222	-487	-908	-133	-124	3,214	3,259	1,836	5,722
Memo:										
IBRD	47	245	24	-52	-469	-408	-685	-808	-706	-539
IDA	0	0	0	0	0	0	0	0	0	0

BRAZIL

(US$ million, unless otherwise indicated)

	1970	1980	1988	1989	1990	1991	1992	1993	1994	1995
INTEREST PAYMENTS (LINT)	**221**	**6,384**	**11,446**	**3,858**	**2,025**	**2,034**	**2,947**	**3,222**	**5,123**	**9,375**
Public and publicly guaranteed	**132**	**4,253**	**9,877**	**3,111**	**1,566**	**1,696**	**2,397**	**2,172**	**3,974**	**7,216**
Official creditors	51	444	1,202	922	1,270	1,255	1,137	1,420	1,748	1,826
Multilateral	21	255	929	817	966	916	887	868	781	750
Concessional	11	15	10	10	9	8	7	32	6	6
Bilateral	30	189	273	105	304	338	250	553	967	1,075
Concessional	28	48	31	11	9	13	12	11	19	91
Private creditors	81	3,809	8,675	2,189	296	442	1,259	752	2,226	5,391
Bonds	0	234	89	100	14	39	125	435	1,744	4,779
Commercial banks	45	3,124	8,091	1,843	22	52	876	129	275	350
Other private	36	450	495	246	260	351	259	188	208	263
Private nonguaranteed	**89**	**2,132**	**1,568**	**747**	**460**	**338**	**551**	**1,050**	**1,149**	**2,159**
Bonds	0	0	0	0	0	0	85	313	656	900
Commercial banks	89	2,132	1,568	747	460	338	466	737	493	1,258
Memo:										
IBRD	11	177	744	604	725	669	647	579	537	491
IDA	0	0	0	0	0	0	0	0	0	0
NET TRANSFERS ON DEBT	**1,106**	**-1,815**	**-8,349**	**-7,362**	**-3,147**	**-1,397**	**2,120**	**5,092**	**-3,164**	**-926**
Public and publicly guaranteed	**495**	**95**	**-6,294**	**-5,707**	**-2,555**	**-1,334**	**-2,949**	**-1,681**	**-5,860**	**-6,384**
Official creditors	132	381	-1,141	-699	-1,908	-2,313	-2,056	-2,424	-3,825	-3,203
Multilateral	55	116	-832	-840	-1,483	-1,373	-1,572	-1,654	-1,505	-1,176
Concessional	23	-30	-19	-25	-35	-30	-18	-8	-13	-13
Bilateral	78	265	-309	141	-425	-940	-484	-770	-2,320	-2,027
Concessional	29	-98	-24	28	50	-42	-28	-33	-216	296
Private creditors	363	-286	-5,153	-5,008	-647	979	-893	743	-2,035	-3,180
Bonds	0	112	20	-484	115	750	393	383	-1,946	-4,036
Commercial banks	151	-728	-5,155	-5,209	-851	620	-630	1,027	615	1,639
Other private	212	330	-18	686	89	-391	-656	-666	-705	-783
Private nonguaranteed	**611**	**-1,910**	**-2,055**	**-1,655**	**-593**	**-63**	**5,068**	**6,772**	**2,696**	**5,458**
Bonds	0	0	0	0	0	398	2,320	4,250	1,353	994
Commercial banks	611	-1,910	-2,055	-1,655	-593	-461	2,748	2,522	1,343	4,464
Memo:										
IBRD	36	68	-720	-656	-1,193	-1,078	-1,332	-1,387	-1,242	-1,031
IDA	0	0	0	0	0	0	0	0	0	0
DEBT SERVICE (LTDS)	**677**	**13,232**	**14,729**	**11,953**	**7,184**	**6,276**	**7,109**	**9,522**	**14,560**	**20,477**
Public and publicly guaranteed	**388**	**8,131**	**12,504**	**9,449**	**5,716**	**5,186**	**5,230**	**5,266**	**8,888**	**13,838**
Official creditors	127	962	2,693	2,250	3,224	3,656	2,966	3,301	4,929	5,666
Multilateral	53	419	2,122	1,913	2,484	2,452	2,455	2,519	2,455	2,434
Concessional	25	33	32	31	35	30	18	90	13	13
Bilateral	75	543	571	337	740	1,204	512	782	2,475	3,233
Concessional	68	144	35	21	30	75	33	42	219	449
Private creditors	261	7,169	9,811	7,199	2,492	1,530	2,264	1,965	3,959	8,172
Bonds	0	266	655	484	85	287	427	937	2,347	5,697
Commercial banks	182	5,554	8,111	6,022	1,617	152	933	231	594	1,322
Other private	79	1,349	1,044	693	791	1,091	905	797	1,018	1,152
Private nonguaranteed	**289**	**5,102**	**2,225**	**2,504**	**1,468**	**1,089**	**1,879**	**4,256**	**5,672**	**6,639**
Bonds	0	0	0	0	0	0	85	511	2,163	3,570
Commercial banks	289	5,102	2,225	2,504	1,468	1,089	1,794	3,745	3,509	3,069
Memo:										
IBRD	25	275	1,714	1,475	1,975	1,917	1,913	1,858	1,883	1,868
IDA	0	0	0	0	0	0	0	0	0	0
UNDISBURSED DEBT	**1,480**	**14,052**	**14,346**	**13,458**	**13,184**	**13,410**	**14,601**	**14,688**	**17,005**	**14,498**
Official creditors	792	6,346	7,238	6,788	6,823	7,692	9,073	9,185	10,517	8,668
Private creditors	688	7,706	7,108	6,671	6,361	5,718	5,528	5,503	6,488	5,830
Memorandum items										
Concessional LDOD	1,504	1,880	2,903	2,831	2,977	2,954	2,588	2,619	2,560	2,927
Variable rate LDOD	2,111	41,557	78,389	68,744	66,642	66,324	76,654	84,410	82,950	90,802
Public sector LDOD	3,206	39,296	91,223	87,221	86,798	84,738	90,138	91,412	94,861	95,978
Private sector LDOD	1,814	18,685	12,134	6,671	7,309	8,412	13,698	21,405	25,148	32,517

6. CURRENCY COMPOSITION OF LONG-TERM DEBT (PERCENT)

	1970	1980	1988	1989	1990	1991	1992	1993	1994	1995
Deutsche mark	7.3	8.1	6.2	8.0	8.9	9.3	6.9	5.9	4.4	4.4
French franc	0.2	2.5	5.7	6.3	6.6	6.7	5.0	4.0	3.3	3.2
Japanese yen	0.0	8.5	6.7	5.6	7.4	7.5	6.1	6.4	5.0	6.9
Pound sterling	7.6	2.5	1.8	1.7	1.8	1.9	1.1	1.0	0.9	0.7
Swiss franc	2.2	1.3	0.6	0.7	1.0	1.0	0.8	0.7	0.3	0.3
U.S.dollars	72.1	67.8	65.6	63.9	60.3	59.3	61.8	63.1	68.7	67.5
Multiple currency	9.6	7.2	12.2	12.4	12.8	12.8	17.3	18.1	17.2	16.7
Special drawing rights	0.0	0.0	0.0	0.0	0.0	0.0	0.0	0.0	0.0	0.0
All other currencies	1.1	2.1	1.4	1.4	1.3	1.3	1.0	0.8	0.3	0.2

BRAZIL

(US$ million, unless otherwise indicated)

	1970	1980	1988	1989	1990	1991	1992	1993	1994	1995
7. DEBT RESTRUCTURINGS										
Total amount rescheduled	0	0	53,563	2,499	1,316	0	12,850	1,425	43,904	0
Debt stock rescheduled	0	0	51,647	1,100	0	0	0	0	35,758	0
Principal rescheduled	0	0	1,582	1,154	1,042	304	4,478	920	76	0
Official	0	0	281	232	212	94	1,978	792	0	0
Private	0	0	1,301	922	830	209	2,500	128	76	0
Interest rescheduled	0	0	334	245	274	114	8,341	502	7,273	0
Official	0	0	32	82	69	28	960	397	0	0
Private	0	0	301	164	205	86	7,382	105	7,273	0
Debt forgiven	..	..	0	0	0	0	0	0	0	0
Memo: interest forgiven	..	..	0	0	0	0	0	0	0	0
Debt stock reduction	0	0	5,115	6,800	1,259	690	257	0	4,104	0
of which debt buyback	0	0	0	2,076	776	0	0	0	204	0
8. DEBT STOCK-FLOW RECONCILIATION										
Total change in debt stocks	..	..	..	-2,853	5,314	1,058	8,047	15,016	7,830	7,535
Net flows on debt	..	..	..	188	-1,788	940	8,670	11,415	8,473	8,041
Net change in interest arrears	..	..	..	3,019	5,602	1,729	-6,203	2,926	-5,893	-547
Interest capitalized	..	..	..	245	274	114	8,341	502	7,273	0
Debt forgiveness or reduction	..	..	..	-4,724	-483	-690	-257	0	-3,900	0
Cross-currency valuation	..	..	..	-576	3,347	99	-1,667	-153	2,046	530
Residual	..	..	..	-1,005	-1,639	-1,133	-837	326	-169	-490
9. AVERAGE TERMS OF NEW COMMITMENTS										
ALL CREDITORS										
Interest (%)	7.0	12.1	9.4	8.8	8.2	7.4	7.7	8.2	8.2	6.3
Maturity (years)	14.0	10.7	11.4	11.5	11.5	11.5	12.4	8.0	10.3	8.0
Grace period (years)	3.3	4.0	4.0	3.5	3.7	3.9	4.0	4.0	3.7	2.9
Grant element (%)	17.2	-9.5	2.0	5.2	9.0	12.3	11.1	7.3	9.4	12.4
Official creditors										
Interest (%)	5.8	9.5	7.4	7.8	7.4	7.1	7.3	7.1	6.7	5.5
Maturity (years)	24.8	13.6	15.4	14.1	15.2	16.1	17.2	17.7	18.9	20.5
Grace period (years)	5.8	3.7	4.4	4.4	4.1	4.6	4.5	5.0	5.2	5.1
Grant element (%)	29.1	4.1	13.7	10.9	14.9	16.7	15.3	17.6	20.3	27.2
Private creditors										
Interest (%)	7.5	12.9	9.9	9.5	9.0	7.7	8.4	8.6	9.3	6.6
Maturity (years)	9.4	9.8	10.4	9.7	7.5	5.7	4.4	4.0	4.0	2.7
Grace period (years)	2.2	4.1	3.9	2.8	3.2	2.9	3.2	3.6	2.5	2.0
Grant element (%)	12.0	-13.5	-0.8	1.3	2.5	6.8	4.2	3.0	1.4	6.0
Memorandum items										
Commitments	1,439	10,093	5,194	3,131	2,966	4,747	4,215	3,971	5,712	6,205
Official creditors	431	2,303	1,007	1,285	1,555	2,657	2,620	1,162	2,430	1,868
Private creditors	1,008	7,789	4,188	1,846	1,411	2,090	1,595	2,809	3,282	4,336

10. CONTRACTUAL OBLIGATIONS ON OUTSTANDING LONG-TERM DEBT

	1996	1997	1998	1999	2000	2001	2002	2003	2004	2005
TOTAL										
Disbursements	3,554	2,376	1,534	1,046	657	406	245	149	81	38
Principal	20,979	22,865	14,014	12,881	3,973	4,252	4,728	4,569	5,271	5,093
Interest	7,840	6,725	5,528	4,693	4,024	3,794	3,244	2,939	2,901	2,558
Official creditors										
Disbursements	2,108	1,864	1,420	1,002	656	406	245	149	81	38
Principal	4,860	4,815	4,787	4,073	2,251	2,201	2,098	1,966	1,902	1,864
Interest	1,989	1,770	1,524	1,269	1,076	953	822	692	565	438
Bilateral creditors										
Disbursements	571	416	234	115	54	27	10	0	0	0
Principal	3,239	3,224	3,206	2,585	832	885	965	957	1,044	1,109
Interest	1,211	1,024	823	624	495	442	384	322	257	186
Multilateral creditors										
Disbursements	1,537	1,449	1,186	887	603	379	235	149	81	38
Principal	1,621	1,592	1,581	1,488	1,420	1,316	1,133	1,010	858	755
Interest	778	747	701	646	581	511	438	370	308	253
Private creditors										
Disbursements	1,446	512	114	44	1	0	0	0	0	0
Principal	16,120	18,049	9,227	8,809	1,721	2,051	2,630	2,603	3,369	3,229
Interest	5,851	4,955	4,004	3,423	2,947	2,841	2,422	2,247	2,337	2,120
Commercial banks										
Disbursements	1,133	412	87	39	0	0	0	0	0	0
Principal	2,531	2,645	1,782	2,006	448	55	45	31	16	6
Interest	599	460	307	174	32	12	7	4	1	0
Other private										
Disbursements	313	100	27	5	1	0	0	0	0	0
Principal	13,588	15,404	7,445	6,803	1,273	1,996	2,585	2,572	3,353	3,223
Interest	5,252	4,495	3,697	3,249	2,915	2,829	2,414	2,243	2,335	2,120

BULGARIA

(US$ million, unless otherwise indicated)

	1970	1980	1988	1989	1990	1991	1992	1993	1994	1995
1. SUMMARY DEBT DATA										
TOTAL DEBT STOCKS (EDT)	..	..	**8,944**	**10,137**	**10,890**	**12,055**	**12,388**	**12,886**	**11,087**	**10,887**
Long-term debt (LDOD)	..	..	**8,315**	**9,283**	**9,834**	**10,071**	**10,192**	**10,380**	**9,644**	**9,574**
Public and publicly guaranteed	..	..	8,315	9,283	9,834	10,071	10,192	10,380	9,644	9,574
Private nonguaranteed	0	0	0	0	0	0	0	0	0	0
Use of IMF credit	**0**	**0**	**0**	**0**	**0**	**414**	**590**	**632**	**941**	**717**
Short-term debt	..	..	**629**	**854**	**1,056**	**1,571**	**1,607**	**1,874**	**503**	**596**
of which interest arrears on LDOD	..	..	0	0	226	768	1,537	1,836	177	157
Official creditors	..	..	0	0	5	27	42	87	69	75
Private creditors	..	..	0	0	221	741	1,495	1,749	107	82
Memo: principal arrears on LDOD	..	..	0	3	356	1,456	5,037	5,997	680	777
Official creditors	..	..	0	0	1	145	214	352	404	438
Private creditors	..	..	0	3	354	1,311	4,823	5,645	277	339
Memo: export credits	..	..	1,723	1,243	4,798	3,786	1,974	1,225	1,376	1,462
TOTAL DEBT FLOWS										
Disbursements	..	..	**2,675**	**2,773**	**876**	**787**	**731**	**463**	**761**	**315**
Long-term debt	..	..	2,675	2,773	876	391	448	420	428	315
IMF purchases	0	0	0	0	0	396	282	43	333	0
Principal repayments	..	..	**1,856**	**1,904**	**865**	**109**	**167**	**42**	**499**	**662**
Long-term debt	..	..	1,856	1,904	865	109	82	42	430	415
IMF repurchases	0	0	0	0	0	0	85	0	69	246
Net flows on debt	..	..	**1,098**	**1,094**	**-14**	**692**	**-170**	**390**	**549**	**-233**
of which short-term debt	..	..	278	225	-24	15	-733	-32	288	113
Interest payments (INT)	..	..	**483**	**676**	**510**	**159**	**249**	**253**	**207**	**594**
Long-term debt	..	..	456	624	452	104	183	197	151	521
IMF charges	0	0	0	0	0	6	36	37	40	50
Short-term debt	..	..	28	52	58	49	30	19	16	24
Net transfers on debt	..	..	**615**	**418**	**-523**	**533**	**-418**	**136**	**342**	**-828**
Total debt service paid (TDS)	..	..	**2,339**	**2,580**	**1,375**	**268**	**416**	**295**	**706**	**1,256**
Long-term debt	..	..	2,311	2,528	1,317	213	265	239	581	936
IMF repurchases and charges	0	0	0	0	0	6	121	37	109	296
Short-term debt (interest only)	..	..	28	52	58	49	30	19	16	24
2. AGGREGATE NET RESOURCE FLOWS AND NET TRANSFERS (LONG-TERM)										
NET RESOURCE FLOWS	..	..	**820**	**869**	**19**	**458**	**490**	**480**	**606**	**455**
Net flow of long-term debt (ex. IMF)	0	0	820	869	11	282	367	378	-2	-100
Foreign direct investment (net)	0	0	0	0	4	56	42	55	105	135
Portfolio equity flows	..	..	0	0	0	0	0	0	400	400
Grants (excluding technical coop.)	0	0	0	0	4	120	81	47	103	19
Memo: technical coop. grants	0	0	0	0	0	7	47	33	43	92
NET TRANSFERS	..	..	**364**	**245**	**-433**	**354**	**307**	**283**	**453**	**-69**
Interest on long-term debt	..	..	456	624	452	104	183	197	151	521
Profit remittances on FDI	0	0	0	0	0	0	0	0	2	3
3. MAJOR ECONOMIC AGGREGATES										
Gross national product (GNP)	..	19,723	22,573	21,117	19,083	9,637	10,289	10,623	9,988	11,790
Exports of goods & services (XGS)	..	9,443	10,551	9,618	7,070	4,193	5,151	4,991	5,277	6,680
of which workers remittances	..	0	0	0	0	0	0	0	0	0
Imports of goods & services (MGS)	..	8,547	11,056	10,464	8,905	4,339	5,555	6,126	5,475	6,478
International reserves (RES)	..	..	394	385	393	361	340	265	360	400
Current account balance	..	954	-402	-769	-1,710	-77	-360	-1,098	-32	334
4. DEBT INDICATORS										
EDT / XGS (%)	..	..	84.8	105.4	154.0	287.5	240.5	258.2	210.1	163.0
EDT / GNP (%)	..	..	39.6	48.0	57.1	125.1	120.4	121.3	111.0	92.3
TDS / XGS (%)	..	..	22.2	26.8	19.4	6.4	8.1	5.9	13.4	18.8
INT / XGS (%)	..	..	4.6	7.0	7.2	3.8	4.8	5.1	3.9	8.9
INT / GNP (%)	..	..	2.1	3.2	2.7	1.6	2.4	2.4	2.1	5.0
RES / EDT (%)	..	..	4.4	3.8	3.6	3.0	2.7	2.1	3.2	3.7
RES / MGS (months)	..	..	0.4	0.4	0.5	1.0	0.7	0.5	0.8	0.7
Short-term / EDT (%)	..	..	7.0	8.4	9.7	13.0	13.0	14.5	4.5	5.5
Concessional / EDT (%)	..	..	0.0	0.0	0.0	0.0	0.2	1.6	2.2	2.6
Multilateral / EDT (%)	..	..	6.2	5.8	5.7	7.2	9.2	10.9	16.6	16.8

BULGARIA

(US$ million, unless otherwise indicated)

	1970	1980	1988	1989	1990	1991	1992	1993	1994	1995
5. LONG-TERM DEBT										
DEBT OUTSTANDING (LDOD)	**..**	**..**	**8,315**	**9,283**	**9,834**	**10,071**	**10,192**	**10,380**	**9,644**	**9,574**
Public and publicly guaranteed	**..**	**..**	**8,315**	**9,283**	**9,834**	**10,071**	**10,192**	**10,380**	**9,644**	**9,574**
Official creditors	..	..	1,464	1,504	1,669	2,083	2,368	2,760	3,478	3,538
Multilateral	..	..	551	591	624	865	1,136	1,404	1,845	1,829
Concessional	..	..	0	0	0	0	0	33	51	58
Bilateral	..	..	912	914	1,046	1,218	1,232	1,356	1,634	1,710
Concessional	..	..	0	0	0	0	31	170	189	221
Private creditors	..	..	6,851	7,779	8,165	7,988	7,823	7,620	6,166	6,036
Bonds	..	..	0	238	327	340	332	348	5,411	5,412
Commercial banks	..	..	5,079	6,209	7,002	7,395	7,263	7,072	606	495
Other private	..	..	1,772	1,332	836	253	228	200	148	129
Private nonguaranteed	**0**	**0**	**0**	**0**	**0**	**0**	**0**	**0**	**0**	**0**
Bonds	..	..	0	0	0	0	0	0	0	0
Commercial banks	..	..	0	0	0	0	0	0	0	0
Memo:										
IBRD	0	0	0	0	0	61	152	158	415	444
IDA	0	0	0	0	0	0	0	0	0	0
DISBURSEMENTS	**..**	**..**	**2,675**	**2,773**	**876**	**391**	**448**	**420**	**428**	**315**
Public and publicly guaranteed	**..**	**..**	**2,675**	**2,773**	**876**	**391**	**448**	**420**	**428**	**315**
Official creditors	..	..	430	96	80	272	311	420	411	186
Multilateral	..	..	185	67	44	261	275	276	400	95
Concessional	..	..	0	0	0	0	0	35	14	4
Bilateral	..	..	245	29	36	10	36	144	10	92
Concessional	..	..	0	0	0	0	33	144	0	32
Private creditors	..	..	2,246	2,677	796	120	137	0	17	129
Bonds	..	..	0	240	65	0	0	0	16	33
Commercial banks	..	..	1,322	1,802	576	106	126	0	2	96
Other private	..	..	924	635	155	14	12	0	0	0
Private nonguaranteed	**0**	**0**	**0**	**0**	**0**	**0**	**0**	**0**	**0**	**0**
Bonds	..	..	0	0	0	0	0	0	0	0
Commercial banks	..	..	0	0	0	0	0	0	0	0
Memo:										
IBRD	0	0	0	0	0	58	92	3	246	15
IDA	0	0	0	0	0	0	0	0	0	0
PRINCIPAL REPAYMENTS	**..**	**..**	**1,856**	**1,904**	**865**	**109**	**82**	**42**	**430**	**415**
Public and publicly guaranteed	**..**	**..**	**1,856**	**1,904**	**865**	**109**	**82**	**42**	**430**	**415**
Official creditors	..	..	52	35	23	20	24	8	7	240
Multilateral	..	..	19	25	22	19	0	0	1	160
Concessional	..	..	0	0	0	0	0	0	0	0
Bilateral	..	..	33	10	1	1	24	8	7	80
Concessional	..	..	0	0	0	0	0	0	0	0
Private creditors	..	..	1,804	1,869	842	89	58	34	423	176
Bonds	..	..	0	0	0	0	0	0	223	39
Commercial banks	..	..	875	800	241	19	34	16	200	114
Other private	..	..	929	1,069	601	70	24	18	0	23
Private nonguaranteed	**0**	**0**	**0**	**0**	**0**	**0**	**0**	**0**	**0**	**0**
Bonds	..	..	0	0	0	0	0	0	0	0
Commercial banks	..	..	0	0	0	0	0	0	0	0
Memo:										
IBRD	0	0	0	0	0	0	0	0	0	0
IDA	0	0	0	0	0	0	0	0	0	0
NET FLOWS ON DEBT	**..**	**..**	**820**	**869**	**11**	**282**	**367**	**378**	**-2**	**-100**
Public and publicly guaranteed	**..**	**..**	**820**	**869**	**11**	**282**	**367**	**378**	**-2**	**-100**
Official creditors	..	..	378	61	57	252	287	412	404	-54
Multilateral	..	..	166	42	21	242	275	276	400	-66
Concessional	..	..	0	0	0	0	0	35	14	4
Bilateral	..	..	212	19	36	10	12	136	4	12
Concessional	..	..	0	0	0	0	33	144	0	32
Private creditors	..	..	442	808	-46	30	79	-34	-406	-46
Bonds	..	..	0	240	65	0	0	0	-207	-6
Commercial banks	..	..	447	1,002	335	87	91	-16	-199	-18
Other private	..	..	-5	-434	-446	-57	-12	-18	0	-23
Private nonguaranteed	**0**	**0**	**0**	**0**	**0**	**0**	**0**	**0**	**0**	**0**
Bonds	..	..	0	0	0	0	0	0	0	0
Commercial banks	..	..	0	0	0	0	0	0	0	0
Memo:										
IBRD	0	0	0	0	0	58	92	3	246	15
IDA	0	0	0	0	0	0	0	0	0	0

BULGARIA

(US$ million, unless otherwise indicated)

	1970	1980	1988	1989	1990	1991	1992	1993	1994	1995
INTEREST PAYMENTS (LINT)	..	..	**456**	**624**	**452**	**104**	**183**	**197**	**151**	**521**
Public and publicly guaranteed	..	..	**456**	**624**	**452**	**104**	**183**	**197**	**151**	**521**
Official creditors	..	..	14	17	14	50	108	115	115	194
Multilateral	..	..	12	16	13	49	60	56	65	71
Concessional	..	..	0	0	0	0	0	0	1	3
Bilateral	..	..	2	2	0	1	48	59	49	123
Concessional	..	..	0	0	0	0	0	0	1	4
Private creditors	..	..	442	607	438	54	75	82	36	327
Bonds	..	..	0	0	16	10	16	24	36	315
Commercial banks	..	..	278	420	337	25	50	53	0	8
Other private	..	..	164	186	85	19	10	6	0	4
Private nonguaranteed	**0**	**0**	**0**	**0**	**0**	**0**	**0**	**0**	**0**	**0**
Bonds	..	..	0	0	0	0	0	0	0	0
Commercial banks	..	..	0	0	0	0	0	0	0	0
Memo:										
IBRD	0	0	0	0	0	0	7	12	15	31
IDA	0	0	0	0	0	0	0	0	0	0
NET TRANSFERS ON DEBT	..	..	**364**	**245**	**-441**	**178**	**184**	**181**	**-153**	**-621**
Public and publicly guaranteed	..	..	**364**	**245**	**-441**	**178**	**184**	**181**	**-153**	**-621**
Official creditors	..	..	364	44	44	202	180	297	289	-247
Multilateral	..	..	155	26	8	193	216	221	335	-136
Concessional	..	..	0	0	0	0	0	35	13	1
Bilateral	..	..	209	18	35	9	-36	77	-46	-111
Concessional	..	..	0	0	0	0	33	143	-1	28
Private creditors	..	..	0	201	-484	-24	4	-116	-442	-373
Bonds	..	..	0	240	49	-10	-16	-24	-243	-321
Commercial banks	..	..	169	582	-2	62	41	-69	-199	-26
Other private	..	..	-169	-620	-531	-76	-22	-24	0	-27
Private nonguaranteed	**0**	**0**	**0**	**0**	**0**	**0**	**0**	**0**	**0**	**0**
Bonds	..	..	0	0	0	0	0	0	0	0
Commercial banks	..	..	0	0	0	0	0	0	0	0
Memo:										
IBRD	0	0	0	0	0	58	85	-9	230	-16
IDA	0	0	0	0	0	0	0	0	0	0
DEBT SERVICE (LTDS)	..	..	**2,311**	**2,528**	**1,317**	**213**	**265**	**239**	**581**	**936**
Public and publicly guaranteed	..	..	**2,311**	**2,528**	**1,317**	**213**	**265**	**239**	**581**	**936**
Official creditors	..	..	65	53	37	70	132	123	122	433
Multilateral	..	..	30	41	36	69	60	56	66	231
Concessional	..	..	0	0	0	0	0	0	1	3
Bilateral	..	..	35	12	1	1	72	67	56	202
Concessional	..	..	0	0	0	0	0	0	1	4
Private creditors	..	..	2,246	2,476	1,280	143	133	116	459	503
Bonds	..	..	0	0	16	10	16	24	259	354
Commercial banks	..	..	1,153	1,220	578	44	84	69	200	122
Other private	..	..	1,093	1,255	686	89	33	24	0	27
Private nonguaranteed	**0**	**0**	**0**	**0**	**0**	**0**	**0**	**0**	**0**	**0**
Bonds	..	..	0	0	0	0	0	0	0	0
Commercial banks	..	..	0	0	0	0	0	0	0	0
Memo:										
IBRD	0	0	0	0	0	0	7	12	15	31
IDA	0	0	0	0	0	0	0	0	0	0
UNDISBURSED DEBT	..	..	**1,911**	**702**	**271**	**425**	**332**	**344**	**274**	**483**
Official creditors	..	..	86	49	25	394	320	336	243	483
Private creditors	..	..	1,825	652	246	31	12	8	31	0
Memorandum items										
Concessional LDOD	..	..	0	0	0	0	31	203	240	279
Variable rate LDOD	..	..	6,353	7,334	7,714	7,834	7,929	7,985	7,358	7,302
Public sector LDOD	..	..	8,315	9,283	9,834	10,071	10,192	10,380	9,644	9,574
Private sector LDOD	..	..	0	0	0	0	0	0	0	0

6. CURRENCY COMPOSITION OF LONG-TERM DEBT (PERCENT)

	1970	1980	1988	1989	1990	1991	1992	1993	1994	1995
Deutsche mark	..	..	25.9	29.7	33.9	33.3	30.6	28.3	6.9	7.8
French franc	..	..	0.5	0.5	0.5	0.5	0.4	0.4	0.4	0.4
Japanese yen	..	..	5.9	6.5	6.6	6.7	6.5	8.1	8.1	7.8
Pound sterling	..	..	0.4	0.3	0.3	0.2	0.2	0.2	0.2	0.2
Swiss franc	..	..	7.1	7.1	7.7	7.2	6.4	6.1	1.2	1.3
U.S.dollars	..	..	45.6	44.7	42.1	44.5	47.9	47.8	72.5	67.2
Multiple currency	..	..	8.5	5.3	2.5	0.7	1.6	1.6	4.4	4.7
Special drawing rights	..	..	0.0	0.0	0.0	0.0	0.0	0.0	0.0	0.0
All other currencies	..	..	6.1	6.0	6.3	6.9	6.5	7.5	6.4	10.6

BULGARIA

(US$ million, unless otherwise indicated)

	1970	1980	1988	1989	1990	1991	1992	1993	1994	1995
7. DEBT RESTRUCTURINGS										
Total amount rescheduled	0	0	0	0	0	480	276	31	5,306	54
Debt stock rescheduled	0	0	0	0	0	0	0	0	3,395	0
Principal rescheduled	0	0	0	0	0	377	219	29	230	44
Official	0	0	0	0	0	336	219	29	161	39
Private	0	0	0	0	0	41	0	0	69	5
Interest rescheduled	0	0	0	0	0	45	57	1	71	10
Official	0	0	0	0	0	42	57	1	57	9
Private	0	0	0	0	0	3	0	0	13	1
Debt forgiven	..	..	0	0	0	0	0	0	0	0
Memo: interest forgiven	..	..	0	0	0	0	0	0	0	0
Debt stock reduction	0	0	0	0	0	0	0	0	2,871	0
of which debt buyback	0	0	0	0	0	0	0	0	423	0
8. DEBT STOCK-FLOW RECONCILIATION										
Total change in debt stocks	..	..	..	1,193	753	1,166	333	497	-1,799	-201
Net flows on debt	..	..	..	1,094	-14	692	-170	390	549	-233
Net change in interest arrears	..	..	..	0	226	542	769	299	-1,659	-20
Interest capitalized	..	..	..	0	0	45	57	1	71	10
Debt forgiveness or reduction	..	..	..	0	0	0	0	0	-2,448	0
Cross-currency valuation	..	..	..	74	728	-33	-280	-157	262	149
Residual	..	..	..	26	-188	-80	-43	-36	1,427	-106
9. AVERAGE TERMS OF NEW COMMITMENTS										
ALL CREDITORS										
Interest (%)	..	..	8.5	9.3	9.1	8.2	5.5	5.8	6.7	6.1
Maturity (years)	..	..	5.4	5.1	3.4	11.6	12.5	14.7	13.3	12.9
Grace period (years)	..	..	3.5	3.3	2.3	6.2	5.1	4.0	5.0	4.1
Grant element (%)	..	..	5.2	2.6	2.3	9.1	24.7	22.6	16.5	17.3
Official creditors										
Interest (%)	..	..	8.3	9.4	9.3	8.2	4.9	5.8	6.7	6.7
Maturity (years)	..	..	9.0	4.2	6.1	11.7	13.9	14.7	14.5	15.0
Grace period (years)	..	..	4.1	2.2	3.0	6.3	5.7	4.0	5.7	4.3
Grant element (%)	..	..	8.0	1.8	2.6	9.2	29.7	22.6	17.8	16.8
Private creditors										
Interest (%)	..	..	8.5	9.3	9.1	7.0	6.7	0.0	6.6	3.5
Maturity (years)	..	..	5.2	5.1	3.1	2.8	9.5	0.0	4.8	3.8
Grace period (years)	..	..	3.5	3.3	2.3	0.9	3.9	0.0	0.7	3.3
Grant element (%)	..	..	5.0	2.7	2.3	4.8	14.5	0.0	7.0	19.5
Memorandum items										
Commitments	..	..	2,479	1,716	563	655	368	443	367	520
Official creditors	..	..	118	60	52	642	248	443	321	424
Private creditors	..	..	2,361	1,657	511	13	120	0	46	97

10. CONTRACTUAL OBLIGATIONS ON OUTSTANDING LONG-TERM DEBT

	1996	1997	1998	1999	2000	2001	2002	2003	2004	2005
TOTAL										
Disbursements	47	84	82	72	65	45	33	23	19	14
Principal	420	449	588	423	360	619	444	421	432	373
Interest	508	491	463	441	421	399	397	368	344	318
Official creditors										
Disbursements	47	84	82	72	65	45	33	23	19	14
Principal	146	319	415	349	336	586	338	242	221	129
Interest	204	203	183	166	146	122	86	68	54	42
Bilateral creditors										
Disbursements	3	1	0	0	0	0	0	0	0	0
Principal	110	92	156	263	228	379	223	126	105	14
Interest	108	103	97	86	68	48	24	12	5	0
Multilateral creditors										
Disbursements	44	83	82	72	65	45	33	23	19	14
Principal	36	226	259	86	109	207	115	115	115	115
Interest	96	101	86	80	78	74	62	56	49	42
Private creditors										
Disbursements	0	0	0	0	0	0	0	0	0	0
Principal	274	130	173	74	24	33	106	179	212	244
Interest	305	288	280	276	275	278	311	300	290	276
Commercial banks										
Disbursements	0	0	0	0	0	0	0	0	0	0
Principal	32	33	97	25	17	17	0	0	0	0
Interest	13	10	8	4	3	1	0	0	0	0
Other private										
Disbursements	0	0	0	0	0	0	0	0	0	0
Principal	242	98	76	49	7	16	106	179	212	244
Interest	292	297	272	271	273	277	311	300	290	276

BURKINA FASO

(US$ million, unless otherwise indicated)

1. SUMMARY DEBT DATA

	1970	1980	1988	1989	1990	1991	1992	1993	1994	1995
TOTAL DEBT STOCKS (EDT)	..	**330**	**845**	**717**	**834**	**967**	**1,040**	**1,117**	**1,128**	**1,267**
Long-term debt (LDOD)	**21**	**281**	**767**	**648**	**750**	**883**	**979**	**1,066**	**1,040**	**1,136**
Public and publicly guaranteed	21	281	767	648	750	883	979	1,066	1,040	1,136
Private nonguaranteed	0	0	0	0	0	0	0	0	0	0
Use of IMF credit	**0**	**15**	**3**	**1**	**0**	**9**	**9**	**21**	**48**	**75**
Short-term debt	..	**35**	**75**	**69**	**84**	**76**	**52**	**30**	**41**	**57**
of which interest arrears on LDOD	..	0	16	15	21	12	12	12	11	13
Official creditors	..	0	11	10	14	11	11	11	10	11
Private creditors	..	0	5	6	7	0	1	1	1	1
Memo: principal arrears on LDOD	..	0	45	52	64	25	28	35	36	38
Official creditors	..	0	23	27	34	25	26	34	34	35
Private creditors	..	0	22	25	30	1	2	1	2	3
Memo: export credits	..	..	112	115	200	125	148	79	68	103
TOTAL DEBT FLOWS										
Disbursements	**2**	**70**	**94**	**98**	**79**	**155**	**143**	**151**	**132**	**139**
Long-term debt	2	65	94	98	79	146	143	138	107	112
IMF purchases	1	4	0	0	0	9	0	12	25	27
Principal repayments	**2**	**11**	**24**	**18**	**19**	**25**	**15**	**20**	**27**	**29**
Long-term debt	2	11	21	16	18	25	15	20	27	29
IMF repurchases	0	0	3	2	1	0	0	0	0	0
Net flows on debt	**1**	**59**	**62**	**74**	**70**	**131**	**105**	**109**	**117**	**124**
of which short-term debt	..	..	-8	-6	10	1	-24	-22	12	14
Interest payments (INT)	..	**12**	**18**	**21**	**16**	**21**	**19**	**18**	**17**	**20**
Long-term debt	0	6	14	16	10	15	14	16	15	17
IMF charges	0	0	0	0	0	0	0	0	0	0
Short-term debt	..	5	5	5	6	6	5	2	2	2
Net transfers on debt	..	**48**	**44**	**53**	**54**	**110**	**86**	**91**	**100**	**104**
Total debt service paid (TDS)	..	**22**	**43**	**39**	**34**	**46**	**33**	**38**	**44**	**48**
Long-term debt	2	17	35	32	28	40	29	36	42	46
IMF repurchases and charges	0	0	3	2	1	0	0	0	0	0
Short-term debt (interest only)	..	5	5	5	6	6	5	2	2	2

2. AGGREGATE NET RESOURCE FLOWS AND NET TRANSFERS (LONG-TERM)

	1970	1980	1988	1989	1990	1991	1992	1993	1994	1995
NET RESOURCE FLOWS	**13**	**142**	**215**	**198**	**218**	**336**	**332**	**345**	**293**	**322**
Net flow of long-term debt (ex. IMF)	0	55	73	82	61	121	128	119	80	83
Foreign direct investment (net)	0	0	0	0	0	0	0	0	1	0
Portfolio equity flows	0	0	0	0	0	0	0	0	0	0
Grants (excluding technical coop.)	13	88	142	116	158	214	204	227	212	239
Memo: technical coop. grants	8	73	100	95	117	105	142	139	114	124
NET TRANSFERS	**11**	**128**	**201**	**182**	**209**	**321**	**318**	**329**	**278**	**304**
Interest on long-term debt	0	6	14	16	10	15	14	16	15	17
Profit remittances on FDI	2	9	0	0	0	0	0	0	0	0

3. MAJOR ECONOMIC AGGREGATES

	1970	1980	1988	1989	1990	1991	1992	1993	1994	1995
Gross national product (GNP)	421	1,698	2,366	2,351	2,758	2,780	2,978	2,798	1,842	2,305
Exports of goods & services (XGS)	..	376	500	409	507	467	489	460	306	366
of which workers remittances	..	150	187	155	140	113	129	117	80	80
Imports of goods & services (MGS)	..	596	747	652	785	773	934	933	472	591
International reserves (RES)	36	75	325	270	305	350	345	387	242	352
Current account balance	..	-49	-47	99	-86	-103	-97	-118	9	-243

4. DEBT INDICATORS

	1970	1980	1988	1989	1990	1991	1992	1993	1994	1995
EDT / XGS (%)	..	88.0	169.1	175.3	164.7	207.2	212.6	242.8	368.3	346.1
EDT / GNP (%)	..	19.5	35.7	30.5	30.2	34.8	34.9	39.9	61.3	55.0
TDS / XGS (%)	..	5.9	8.5	9.4	6.8	9.9	6.8	8.3	14.2	13.2
INT / XGS (%)	..	3.1	3.7	5.1	3.1	4.5	3.8	3.9	5.4	5.3
INT / GNP (%)	..	0.7	0.8	0.9	0.6	0.8	0.6	0.6	0.9	0.8
RES / EDT (%)	..	22.6	38.5	37.6	36.5	36.2	33.2	34.6	21.4	27.8
RES / MGS (months)	..	1.5	5.2	5.0	4.7	5.4	4.4	5.0	6.1	7.1
Short-term / EDT (%)	..	10.6	8.9	9.6	10.1	7.8	5.0	2.7	3.6	4.5
Concessional / EDT (%)	..	67.0	73.0	74.2	74.6	77.3	80.9	83.7	82.3	80.9
Multilateral / EDT (%)	..	42.8	54.7	69.4	67.7	66.1	68.5	70.9	78.1	77.6

BURKINA FASO

(US$ million, unless otherwise indicated)

	1970	1980	1988	1989	1990	1991	1992	1993	1994	1995
5. LONG-TERM DEBT										
DEBT OUTSTANDING (LDOD)	**21**	**281**	**767**	**648**	**750**	**883**	**979**	**1,066**	**1,040**	**1,136**
Public and publicly guaranteed	**21**	**281**	**767**	**648**	**750**	**883**	**979**	**1,066**	**1,040**	**1,136**
Official creditors	21	261	737	614	712	877	973	1,062	1,035	1,131
Multilateral	0	142	463	498	565	640	712	792	881	984
Concessional	0	133	402	431	484	561	636	723	833	939
Bilateral	21	119	275	116	147	237	262	270	154	147
Concessional	18	89	215	101	138	187	205	213	96	86
Private creditors	0	20	30	34	38	6	5	4	4	5
Bonds	0	0	0	0	0	0	0	0	0	0
Commercial banks	0	1	1	1	1	0	0	0	0	0
Other private	0	19	30	34	38	6	5	4	4	5
Private nonguaranteed	**0**	**0**	**0**	**0**	**0**	**0**	**0**	**0**	**0**	**0**
Bonds	0	0	0	0	0	0	0	0	0	0
Commercial banks	0	0	0	0	0	0	0	0	0	0
Memo:										
IBRD	0	0	0	0	0	0	0	0	0	0
IDA	0	77	234	255	282	326	364	425	518	608
DISBURSEMENTS	**2**	**65**	**94**	**98**	**79**	**146**	**143**	**138**	**107**	**112**
Public and publicly guaranteed	**2**	**65**	**94**	**98**	**79**	**146**	**143**	**138**	**107**	**112**
Official creditors	2	59	94	94	79	146	143	138	107	112
Multilateral	0	26	55	50	45	99	110	118	100	106
Concessional	0	22	42	41	36	91	104	115	100	106
Bilateral	2	33	39	44	34	47	33	21	7	6
Concessional	1	19	38	44	34	47	29	19	7	6
Private creditors	0	6	0	4	0	0	0	0	0	0
Bonds	0	0	0	0	0	0	0	0	0	0
Commercial banks	0	0	0	0	0	0	0	0	0	0
Other private	0	6	0	4	0	0	0	0	0	0
Private nonguaranteed	**0**	**0**	**0**	**0**	**0**	**0**	**0**	**0**	**0**	**0**
Bonds	0	0	0	0	0	0	0	0	0	0
Commercial banks	0	0	0	0	0	0	0	0	0	0
Memo:										
IBRD	0	0	0	0	0	0	0	0	0	0
IDA	0	12	20	25	15	42	50	64	79	85
PRINCIPAL REPAYMENTS	**2**	**11**	**21**	**16**	**18**	**25**	**15**	**20**	**27**	**29**
Public and publicly guaranteed	**2**	**11**	**21**	**16**	**18**	**25**	**15**	**20**	**27**	**29**
Official creditors	2	8	19	15	18	25	15	20	27	29
Multilateral	0	3	14	12	13	23	14	18	25	24
Concessional	0	2	12	9	10	13	9	11	18	18
Bilateral	2	5	6	3	4	2	1	2	2	5
Concessional	1	3	2	2	3	1	1	1	1	4
Private creditors	0	2	2	1	0	1	0	0	0	0
Bonds	0	0	0	0	0	0	0	0	0	0
Commercial banks	0	0	0	0	0	1	0	0	0	0
Other private	0	2	1	1	0	0	0	0	0	0
Private nonguaranteed	**0**	**0**	**0**	**0**	**0**	**0**	**0**	**0**	**0**	**0**
Bonds	0	0	0	0	0	0	0	0	0	0
Commercial banks	0	0	0	0	0	0	0	0	0	0
Memo:										
IBRD	0	0	0	0	0	0	0	0	0	0
IDA	0	0	1	1	1	2	2	3	3	4
NET FLOWS ON DEBT	**0**	**55**	**73**	**82**	**61**	**121**	**128**	**119**	**80**	**83**
Public and publicly guaranteed	**0**	**55**	**73**	**82**	**61**	**121**	**128**	**119**	**80**	**83**
Official creditors	0	51	75	79	61	122	128	119	80	83
Multilateral	0	23	41	38	32	77	96	100	75	82
Concessional	0	21	31	32	26	77	95	104	81	87
Bilateral	0	28	34	42	29	45	32	19	5	1
Concessional	1	16	36	42	31	46	29	18	6	2
Private creditors	0	4	-2	3	0	-1	0	0	0	0
Bonds	0	0	0	0	0	0	0	0	0	0
Commercial banks	0	0	0	0	0	-1	0	0	0	0
Other private	0	4	-1	3	0	0	0	0	0	0
Private nonguaranteed	**0**	**0**	**0**	**0**	**0**	**0**	**0**	**0**	**0**	**0**
Bonds	0	0	0	0	0	0	0	0	0	0
Commercial banks	0	0	0	0	0	0	0	0	0	0
Memo:										
IBRD	0	0	0	0	0	0	0	0	0	0
IDA	0	12	18	24	14	41	48	61	76	81

BURKINA FASO

(US$ million, unless otherwise indicated)

	1970	1980	1988	1989	1990	1991	1992	1993	1994	1995
INTEREST PAYMENTS (LINT)	**0**	**6**	**14**	**16**	**10**	**15**	**14**	**16**	**15**	**17**
Public and publicly guaranteed	**0**	**6**	**14**	**16**	**10**	**15**	**14**	**16**	**15**	**17**
Official creditors	0	4	13	16	10	15	14	16	15	17
Multilateral	0	2	8	8	7	14	9	11	11	11
Concessional	0	1	5	4	4	5	5	6	7	8
Bilateral	0	2	5	7	3	1	5	5	4	6
Concessional	0	1	3	4	3	1	1	1	1	1
Private creditors	0	3	0	0	0	0	0	0	0	0
Bonds	0	0	0	0	0	0	0	0	0	0
Commercial banks	0	0	0	0	0	0	0	0	0	0
Other private	0	2	0	0	0	0	0	0	0	0
Private nonguaranteed	**0**	**0**	**0**	**0**	**0**	**0**	**0**	**0**	**0**	**0**
Bonds	0	0	0	0	0	0	0	0	0	0
Commercial banks	0	0	0	0	0	0	0	0	0	0
Memo:										
IBRD	0	0	0	0	0	0	0	0	0	0
IDA	0	1	3	2	2	2	3	3	3	4
NET TRANSFERS ON DEBT	**-1**	**49**	**59**	**66**	**51**	**106**	**114**	**103**	**65**	**66**
Public and publicly guaranteed	**-1**	**49**	**59**	**66**	**51**	**106**	**114**	**103**	**65**	**66**
Official creditors	0	47	62	64	51	107	114	103	65	66
Multilateral	0	22	33	29	25	62	87	88	64	71
Concessional	0	20	26	28	21	72	91	98	75	79
Bilateral	0	26	29	34	27	44	27	14	1	-5
Concessional	0	16	33	38	28	45	27	17	5	1
Private creditors	0	1	-2	3	0	-1	0	0	0	0
Bonds	0	0	0	0	0	0	0	0	0	0
Commercial banks	0	0	-1	0	0	-1	0	0	0	0
Other private	0	2	-2	3	0	0	0	0	0	0
Private nonguaranteed	**0**	**0**	**0**	**0**	**0**	**0**	**0**	**0**	**0**	**0**
Bonds	0	0	0	0	0	0	0	0	0	0
Commercial banks	0	0	0	0	0	0	0	0	0	0
Memo:										
IBRD	0	0	0	0	0	0	0	0	0	0
IDA	0	11	16	22	12	38	45	58	73	77
DEBT SERVICE (LTDS)	**2**	**17**	**35**	**32**	**28**	**40**	**29**	**36**	**42**	**46**
Public and publicly guaranteed	**2**	**17**	**35**	**32**	**28**	**40**	**29**	**36**	**42**	**46**
Official creditors	2	12	33	31	28	40	29	36	42	46
Multilateral	0	5	22	21	21	37	23	30	36	35
Concessional	0	3	17	13	15	19	13	17	25	26
Bilateral	2	7	11	10	7	3	6	6	5	11
Concessional	1	3	5	6	6	2	2	2	1	5
Private creditors	0	5	2	1	0	1	0	0	0	0
Bonds	0	0	0	0	0	0	0	0	0	0
Commercial banks	0	0	1	0	0	1	0	0	0	0
Other private	0	5	2	1	0	0	0	0	0	0
Private nonguaranteed	**0**	**0**	**0**	**0**	**0**	**0**	**0**	**0**	**0**	**0**
Bonds	0	0	0	0	0	0	0	0	0	0
Commercial banks	0	0	0	0	0	0	0	0	0	0
Memo:										
IBRD	0	0	0	0	0	0	0	0	0	0
IDA	0	1	4	3	3	4	5	6	6	8
UNDISBURSED DEBT	**10**	**218**	**376**	**496**	**540**	**580**	**582**	**549**	**540**	**463**
Official creditors	9	214	360	483	525	566	568	536	525	448
Private creditors	1	4	16	13	15	15	14	13	14	16
Memorandum items										
Concessional LDOD	18	221	617	532	622	748	841	935	929	1,025
Variable rate LDOD	0	12	2	2	2	7	6	6	6	7
Public sector LDOD	21	276	766	647	749	882	979	1,066	1,040	1,136
Private sector LDOD	0	5	1	1	1	1	0	0	0	0

6. CURRENCY COMPOSITION OF LONG-TERM DEBT (PERCENT)

	1970	1980	1988	1989	1990	1991	1992	1993	1994	1995
Deutsche mark	10.1	12.1	0.0	0.0	0.0	0.1	0.1	0.1	0.1	0.1
French franc	32.7	31.3	32.7	14.5	16.6	18.8	18.3	16.9	7.0	6.5
Japanese yen	0.0	0.0	0.0	0.0	0.0	0.0	0.0	0.0	0.0	0.0
Pound sterling	20.2	0.7	0.5	0.5	0.5	0.5	0.4	0.3	0.4	0.3
Swiss franc	0.0	0.0	0.0	0.0	0.0	0.0	0.0	0.0	0.0	0.0
U.S.dollars	0.0	28.8	31.1	39.6	39.2	38.6	40.0	42.9	52.8	56.0
Multiple currency	0.0	8.9	12.3	16.0	15.3	15.7	16.9	17.4	19.2	18.9
Special drawing rights	0.0	0.0	1.6	2.1	2.1	2.8	2.5	2.3	2.3	2.2
All other currencies	37.0	18.2	21.7	27.2	26.2	23.6	21.7	20.1	18.2	16.2

BURKINA FASO

(US$ million, unless otherwise indicated)

	1970	1980	1988	1989	1990	1991	1992	1993	1994	1995
7. DEBT RESTRUCTURINGS										
Total amount rescheduled	0	0	0	0	0	43	14	6	0	0
Debt stock rescheduled	0	0	0	0	0	0	0	0	0	0
Principal rescheduled	0	0	0	0	0	27	8	3	0	0
Official	0	0	0	0	0	2	7	3	0	0
Private	0	0	0	0	0	25	0	1	0	0
Interest rescheduled	0	0	0	0	0	8	5	2	0	0
Official	0	0	0	0	0	2	5	2	0	0
Private	0	0	0	0	0	6	0	0	0	0
Debt forgiven	..	..	0	189	5	10	0	2	123	15
Memo: interest forgiven	..	..	0	0	0	2	0	2	0	0
Debt stock reduction	0	0	0	0	0	0	0	0	0	0
of which debt buyback	0	0	0	0	0	0	0	0	0	0
8. DEBT STOCK-FLOW RECONCILIATION										
Total change in debt stocks	..	..	..	-128	117	134	72	77	11	139
Net flows on debt	..	..	..	74	70	131	105	109	117	124
Net change in interest arrears	..	..	..	-1	6	-9	0	0	-1	2
Interest capitalized	..	..	..	0	0	8	5	2	0	0
Debt forgiveness or reduction	..	..	..	-189	-5	-10	0	-2	-123	-15
Cross-currency valuation	..	..	..	7	37	-3	-23	-20	4	15
Residual	..	..	..	-20	9	18	-14	-13	14	13
9. AVERAGE TERMS OF NEW COMMITMENTS										
ALL CREDITORS										
Interest (%)	2.3	4.3	2.6	1.7	2.5	1.0	0.8	1.2	0.9	0.8
Maturity (years)	36.3	21.5	30.5	31.4	27.5	37.9	41.7	33.0	38.0	39.9
Grace period (years)	8.1	6.5	8.0	8.3	8.7	9.5	10.0	7.9	9.8	10.4
Grant element (%)	61.9	37.8	55.7	65.7	59.0	76.4	80.6	69.3	78.4	80.8
Official creditors										
Interest (%)	1.7	4.0	1.8	1.7	2.5	1.0	0.8	1.2	0.9	0.8
Maturity (years)	40.6	23.0	34.2	31.4	27.5	37.9	41.7	33.0	38.0	39.9
Grace period (years)	8.9	7.0	8.9	8.3	8.7	9.5	10.0	7.9	9.8	10.4
Grant element (%)	69.4	40.9	63.5	65.7	59.0	76.4	80.6	69.3	78.4	80.8
Private creditors										
Interest (%)	6.8	7.3	7.0	0.0	0.0	0.0	0.0	0.0	0.0	0.0
Maturity (years)	7.2	5.6	10.0	0.0	0.0	0.0	0.0	0.0	0.0	0.0
Grace period (years)	2.8	1.1	3.0	0.0	0.0	0.0	0.0	0.0	0.0	0.0
Grant element (%)	11.3	6.6	13.5	0.0	0.0	0.0	0.0	0.0	0.0	0.0
Memorandum items										
Commitments	9	115	108	246	90	185	169	105	100	37
Official creditors	8	104	92	246	90	185	169	105	100	37
Private creditors	1	10	17	0	0	0	0	0	0	0

10. CONTRACTUAL OBLIGATIONS ON OUTSTANDING LONG-TERM DEBT

	1996	1997	1998	1999	2000	2001	2002	2003	2004	2005
TOTAL										
Disbursements	126	117	83	53	29	14	9	2	1	0
Principal	36	37	36	36	47	48	51	52	51	51
Interest	18	19	19	18	18	16	14	13	11	10
Official creditors										
Disbursements	126	117	83	53	29	14	9	2	1	0
Principal	35	36	36	36	47	48	51	52	51	51
Interest	18	19	19	18	18	16	14	13	11	10
Bilateral creditors										
Disbursements	10	12	8	5	3	2	1	1	0	0
Principal	8	8	8	6	16	15	15	15	14	15
Interest	6	6	6	6	6	5	4	3	2	1
Multilateral creditors										
Disbursements	116	106	75	48	26	13	8	2	0	0
Principal	27	28	28	30	32	33	36	36	37	37
Interest	12	12	12	12	12	11	10	10	9	9
Private creditors										
Disbursements	0	0	0	0	0	0	0	0	0	0
Principal	1	1	1	0	0	0	0	0	0	0
Interest	0	0	0	0	0	0	0	0	0	0
Commercial banks										
Disbursements	0	0	0	0	0	0	0	0	0	0
Principal	0	0	0	0	0	0	0	0	0	0
Interest	0	0	0	0	0	0	0	0	0	0
Other private										
Disbursements	0	0	0	0	0	0	0	0	0	0
Principal	1	1	1	0	0	0	0	0	0	0
Interest	0	0	0	0	0	0	0	0	0	0

BURUNDI

(US$ million, unless otherwise indicated)

	1970	1980	1988	1989	1990	1991	1992	1993	1994	1995
1. SUMMARY DEBT DATA										
TOTAL DEBT STOCKS (EDT)	..	**166**	**801**	**889**	**907**	**964**	**1,022**	**1,061**	**1,123**	**1,157**
Long-term debt (LDOD)	**7**	**118**	**756**	**832**	**851**	**901**	**947**	**998**	**1,062**	**1,095**
Public and publicly guaranteed	7	118	756	832	851	901	947	998	1,062	1,095
Private nonguaranteed	0	0	0	0	0	0	0	0	0	0
Use of IMF credit	**8**	**36**	**33**	**40**	**43**	**49**	**62**	**58**	**56**	**48**
Short-term debt	..	**12**	**13**	**16**	**13**	**13**	**13**	**5**	**6**	**14**
of which interest arrears on LDOD	..	0	1	1	0	0	1	1	1	1
Official creditors	..	0	1	1	0	0	1	1	1	1
Private creditors	..	0	0	0	0	0	0	0	0	0
Memo: principal arrears on LDOD	..	0	1	1	0	0	6	12	12	4
Official creditors	..	0	1	1	0	0	6	12	12	4
Private creditors	..	0	0	0	0	0	0	0	0	0
Memo: export credits	..	..	21	21	15	16	15	5	5	2
TOTAL DEBT FLOWS										
Disbursements	**4**	**45**	**121**	**120**	**96**	**91**	**126**	**77**	**53**	**45**
Long-term debt	1	39	104	109	96	85	107	77	53	45
IMF purchases	3	6	17	11	0	6	18	0	0	0
Principal repayments	**1**	**4**	**28**	**26**	**28**	**25**	**24**	**23**	**28**	**27**
Long-term debt	0	4	24	24	28	25	22	19	22	18
IMF repurchases	0	0	4	3	1	0	2	4	6	9
Net flows on debt	**3**	**41**	**68**	**97**	**65**	**66**	**101**	**45**	**25**	**26**
of which short-term debt	..	..	-25	4	-3	0	-1	-8	1	8
Interest payments (INT)	..	**4**	**19**	**16**	**14**	**14**	**16**	**13**	**13**	**12**
Long-term debt	0	2	17	15	12	12	14	12	12	11
IMF charges	0	1	0	0	0	0	0	0	0	0
Short-term debt	..	2	2	1	2	1	1	1	1	1
Net transfers on debt	..	**37**	**49**	**81**	**51**	**52**	**85**	**32**	**12**	**15**
Total debt service paid (TDS)	..	**9**	**46**	**43**	**42**	**39**	**40**	**36**	**41**	**39**
Long-term debt	1	6	40	39	40	38	36	31	34	29
IMF repurchases and charges	0	1	4	3	1	0	3	5	6	9
Short-term debt (interest only)	..	2	2	1	2	1	1	1	1	1

	1970	1980	1988	1989	1990	1991	1992	1993	1994	1995
2. AGGREGATE NET RESOURCE FLOWS AND NET TRANSFERS (LONG-TERM)										
NET RESOURCE FLOWS	**8**	**74**	**132**	**160**	**205**	**178**	**238**	**169**	**274**	**257**
Net flow of long-term debt (ex. IMF)	1	35	80	85	69	60	86	58	31	27
Foreign direct investment (net)	0	0	1	1	1	1	1	0	0	2
Portfolio equity flows	0	0	0	0	0	0	0	0	0	0
Grants (excluding technical coop.)	7	39	51	75	135	117	151	112	243	228
Memo: technical coop. grants	10	45	54	52	61	73	80	59	50	45
NET TRANSFERS	**8**	**72**	**113**	**143**	**189**	**164**	**220**	**154**	**259**	**243**
Interest on long-term debt	0	2	17	15	12	12	14	12	12	11
Profit remittances on FDI	0	0	2	3	3	2	4	3	3	3

	1970	1980	1988	1989	1990	1991	1992	1993	1994	1995
3. MAJOR ECONOMIC AGGREGATES										
Gross national product (GNP)	235	913	1,060	1,096	1,117	1,156	1,073	929	989	1,051
Exports of goods & services (XGS)	..	..	139	118	98	128	108	99	103	140
of which workers remittances	..	..	0	0	0	0	0	0	0	0
Imports of goods & services (MGS)	..	..	307	271	341	358	347	311	287	297
International reserves (RES)	15	105	77	107	112	148	180	170	211	216
Current account balance	..	..	-70	-12	-69	-33	-60	-29	-18	-7

	1970	1980	1988	1989	1990	1991	1992	1993	1994	1995
4. DEBT INDICATORS										
EDT / XGS (%)	..	..	575.2	756.5	928.7	751.0	943.2	1,068.9	1,086.1	829.3
EDT / GNP (%)	..	18.2	75.6	81.1	81.2	83.3	95.2	114.2	113.6	110.1
TDS / XGS (%)	..	..	33.3	36.4	43.4	30.6	36.6	36.4	39.6	27.7
INT / XGS (%)	..	..	13.3	14.0	14.4	10.8	14.5	13.1	12.7	8.5
INT / GNP (%)	..	0.5	1.8	1.5	1.3	1.2	1.5	1.4	1.3	1.1
RES / EDT (%)	..	63.2	9.6	12.0	12.3	15.3	17.6	16.0	18.8	18.7
RES / MGS (months)	..	..	3.0	4.7	3.9	4.9	6.2	6.6	8.8	8.7
Short-term / EDT (%)	..	7.2	1.6	1.8	1.5	1.4	1.3	0.5	0.5	1.2
Concessional / EDT (%)	..	62.6	85.3	86.4	87.4	88.3	88.5	90.4	91.4	91.8
Multilateral / EDT (%)	..	35.7	64.6	63.8	72.8	74.7	74.6	77.0	78.4	80.1

BURUNDI

(US$ million, unless otherwise indicated)

	1970	1980	1988	1989	1990	1991	1992	1993	1994	1995
5. LONG-TERM DEBT										
DEBT OUTSTANDING (LDOD)	**7**	**118**	**756**	**832**	**851**	**901**	**947**	**998**	**1,062**	**1,095**
Public and publicly guaranteed	**7**	**118**	**756**	**832**	**851**	**901**	**947**	**998**	**1,062**	**1,095**
Official creditors	6	110	736	819	842	895	943	995	1,059	1,093
Multilateral	5	59	518	567	660	719	763	817	881	926
Concessional	4	55	466	518	612	675	725	781	848	895
Bilateral	1	51	219	251	182	176	180	178	179	167
Concessional	1	49	217	250	182	176	180	178	179	167
Private creditors	2	8	19	14	9	6	4	3	2	2
Bonds	0	0	0	0	0	0	0	0	0	0
Commercial banks	0	5	11	6	1	0	0	0	0	0
Other private	1	4	9	8	8	6	4	3	2	2
Private nonguaranteed	**0**	**0**	**0**	**0**	**0**	**0**	**0**	**0**	**0**	**0**
Bonds	0	0	0	0	0	0	0	0	0	0
Commercial banks	0	0	0	0	0	0	0	0	0	0
Memo:										
IBRD	3	0	0	0	0	0	0	0	0	0
IDA	1	37	288	328	398	440	473	509	556	591
DISBURSEMENTS	**1**	**39**	**104**	**109**	**96**	**85**	**107**	**77**	**53**	**45**
Public and publicly guaranteed	**1**	**39**	**104**	**109**	**96**	**85**	**107**	**77**	**53**	**45**
Official creditors	1	39	98	108	94	85	107	77	53	45
Multilateral	1	21	74	63	64	67	85	69	48	41
Concessional	0	20	69	61	62	66	84	69	48	40
Bilateral	0	18	24	44	30	18	23	7	5	4
Concessional	0	18	24	44	30	18	23	7	5	4
Private creditors	0	0	6	1	2	0	0	0	0	0
Bonds	0	0	0	0	0	0	0	0	0	0
Commercial banks	0	0	0	0	0	0	0	0	0	0
Other private	0	0	6	1	2	0	0	0	0	0
Private nonguaranteed	**0**	**0**	**0**	**0**	**0**	**0**	**0**	**0**	**0**	**0**
Bonds	0	0	0	0	0	0	0	0	0	0
Commercial banks	0	0	0	0	0	0	0	0	0	0
Memo:										
IBRD	0	0	0	0	0	0	0	0	0	0
IDA	0	12	44	45	49	40	49	36	28	27
PRINCIPAL REPAYMENTS	**0**	**4**	**24**	**24**	**28**	**25**	**22**	**19**	**22**	**18**
Public and publicly guaranteed	**0**	**4**	**24**	**24**	**28**	**25**	**22**	**19**	**22**	**18**
Official creditors	0	1	17	17	19	23	20	18	21	17
Multilateral	0	0	6	8	11	12	13	11	15	12
Concessional	0	0	4	5	6	7	8	9	11	9
Bilateral	0	1	10	9	8	10	6	7	6	5
Concessional	0	1	9	9	8	10	6	7	6	5
Private creditors	0	3	7	7	8	3	2	1	1	1
Bonds	0	0	0	0	0	0	0	0	0	0
Commercial banks	0	2	6	5	5	1	0	0	0	0
Other private	0	1	1	2	3	1	2	1	1	1
Private nonguaranteed	**0**	**0**	**0**	**0**	**0**	**0**	**0**	**0**	**0**	**0**
Bonds	0	0	0	0	0	0	0	0	0	0
Commercial banks	0	0	0	0	0	0	0	0	0	0
Memo:										
IBRD	0	0	0	0	0	0	0	0	0	0
IDA	0	0	1	1	1	1	2	2	2	3
NET FLOWS ON DEBT	**1**	**35**	**80**	**85**	**69**	**60**	**86**	**58**	**31**	**27**
Public and publicly guaranteed	**1**	**35**	**80**	**85**	**69**	**60**	**86**	**58**	**31**	**27**
Official creditors	1	38	81	91	75	63	88	59	32	28
Multilateral	1	20	68	55	53	55	71	58	33	29
Concessional	0	20	65	57	56	59	76	61	37	32
Bilateral	0	17	13	35	22	8	17	1	-1	-1
Concessional	0	17	15	35	22	8	17	1	-1	-1
Private creditors	0	-3	-1	-6	-6	-3	-2	-1	-1	-1
Bonds	0	0	0	0	0	0	0	0	0	0
Commercial banks	0	-1	-6	-5	-5	-1	0	0	0	0
Other private	0	-1	5	-1	-1	-1	-2	-1	-1	-1
Private nonguaranteed	**0**	**0**	**0**	**0**	**0**	**0**	**0**	**0**	**0**	**0**
Bonds	0	0	0	0	0	0	0	0	0	0
Commercial banks	0	0	0	0	0	0	0	0	0	0
Memo:										
IBRD	0	0	0	0	0	0	0	0	0	0
IDA	0	12	44	44	48	38	48	35	26	24

BURUNDI

(US$ million, unless otherwise indicated)

	1970	1980	1988	1989	1990	1991	1992	1993	1994	1995
INTEREST PAYMENTS (LINT)	**0**	**2**	**17**	**15**	**12**	**12**	**14**	**12**	**12**	**11**
Public and publicly guaranteed	**0**	**2**	**17**	**15**	**12**	**12**	**14**	**12**	**12**	**11**
Official creditors	0	1	15	14	11	12	14	12	12	11
Multilateral	0	1	8	9	9	9	11	9	9	9
Concessional	0	0	4	5	5	5	6	6	7	6
Bilateral	0	0	7	5	2	3	3	3	3	2
Concessional	0	0	6	5	2	3	3	3	3	2
Private creditors	0	1	2	2	1	1	0	0	0	0
Bonds	0	0	0	0	0	0	0	0	0	0
Commercial banks	0	1	2	1	1	0	0	0	0	0
Other private	0	0	0	1	1	0	0	0	0	0
Private nonguaranteed	**0**	**0**	**0**	**0**	**0**	**0**	**0**	**0**	**0**	**0**
Bonds	0	0	0	0	0	0	0	0	0	0
Commercial banks	0	0	0	0	0	0	0	0	0	0
Memo:										
IBRD	0	0	0	0	0	0	0	0	0	0
IDA	0	0	2	2	3	3	3	3	4	5
NET TRANSFERS ON DEBT	**1**	**33**	**63**	**70**	**56**	**48**	**72**	**46**	**19**	**16**
Public and publicly guaranteed	**1**	**33**	**63**	**70**	**56**	**48**	**72**	**46**	**19**	**16**
Official creditors	1	37	66	77	64	51	74	47	19	17
Multilateral	1	20	59	46	44	45	61	50	24	20
Concessional	0	20	61	52	51	53	70	55	30	25
Bilateral	0	17	7	31	20	6	13	-3	-5	-3
Concessional	0	17	8	31	20	6	13	-3	-5	-3
Private creditors	0	-4	-3	-7	-7	-3	-2	-1	-1	-1
Bonds	0	0	0	0	0	0	0	0	0	0
Commercial banks	0	-2	-7	-6	-6	-1	0	0	0	0
Other private	0	-2	4	-2	-1	-2	-2	-1	-1	-1
Private nonguaranteed	**0**	**0**	**0**	**0**	**0**	**0**	**0**	**0**	**0**	**0**
Bonds	0	0	0	0	0	0	0	0	0	0
Commercial banks	0	0	0	0	0	0	0	0	0	0
Memo:										
IBRD	0	0	0	0	0	0	0	0	0	0
IDA	0	11	42	42	45	35	44	31	21	20
DEBT SERVICE (LTDS)	**1**	**6**	**40**	**39**	**40**	**38**	**36**	**31**	**34**	**29**
Public and publicly guaranteed	**1**	**6**	**40**	**39**	**40**	**38**	**36**	**31**	**34**	**29**
Official creditors	1	2	32	31	30	35	33	30	33	28
Multilateral	1	1	15	17	20	22	24	20	24	20
Concessional	1	0	8	10	11	13	14	14	17	15
Bilateral	0	1	17	14	10	13	10	10	9	8
Concessional	0	1	15	13	10	13	10	10	9	8
Private creditors	0	4	9	8	9	3	2	1	1	1
Bonds	0	0	0	0	0	0	0	0	0	0
Commercial banks	0	2	7	6	6	1	0	0	0	0
Other private	0	2	2	3	4	2	2	1	1	1
Private nonguaranteed	**0**	**0**	**0**	**0**	**0**	**0**	**0**	**0**	**0**	**0**
Bonds	0	0	0	0	0	0	0	0	0	0
Commercial banks	0	0	0	0	0	0	0	0	0	0
Memo:										
IBRD	0	0	0	0	0	0	0	0	0	0
IDA	0	0	3	3	4	4	5	5	6	8
UNDISBURSED DEBT	**2**	**184**	**401**	**401**	**459**	**476**	**426**	**410**	**369**	**312**
Official creditors	2	184	398	399	459	476	426	410	369	312
Private creditors	0	0	3	2	0	0	0	0	0	0
Memorandum items										
Concessional LDOD	5	104	683	768	793	850	905	960	1,026	1,062
Variable rate LDOD	0	0	3	2	0	0	0	0	0	0
Public sector LDOD	6	117	756	831	850	900	946	998	1,062	1,095
Private sector LDOD	2	1	0	1	2	2	2	0	0	0

6. CURRENCY COMPOSITION OF LONG-TERM DEBT (PERCENT)

	1970	1980	1988	1989	1990	1991	1992	1993	1994	1995
Deutsche mark	17.8	1.8	0.2	0.2	0.5	0.4	0.2	0.1	0.1	0.1
French franc	0.0	1.1	13.6	14.5	4.4	5.6	5.8	5.5	5.8	6.1
Japanese yen	0.0	0.0	0.3	1.6	2.0	2.4	2.8	3.0	3.1	2.9
Pound sterling	0.0	0.0	0.0	0.0	0.0	0.0	0.0	0.0	0.0	0.0
Swiss franc	0.0	0.0	0.3	0.2	0.0	0.0	0.0	0.0	0.0	0.0
U.S.dollars	15.1	34.4	42.1	43.1	50.3	51.8	52.4	52.9	53.5	54.9
Multiple currency	34.2	16.1	22.4	20.8	21.6	22.0	21.0	21.5	22.0	22.4
Special drawing rights	0.0	0.0	2.3	2.0	2.8	2.8	2.5	2.3	2.3	2.0
All other currencies	31.5	46.6	18.7	17.5	18.4	14.9	15.3	14.8	13.2	11.6

BURUNDI

(US$ million, unless otherwise indicated)

	1970	1980	1988	1989	1990	1991	1992	1993	1994	1995
7. DEBT RESTRUCTURINGS										
Total amount rescheduled	0	0	13	13	0	0	0	0	0	0
Debt stock rescheduled	0	0	4	13	0	0	0	0	0	0
Principal rescheduled	0	0	9	0	0	0	0	0	0	0
Official	0	0	9	0	0	0	0	0	0	0
Private	0	0	0	0	0	0	0	0	0	0
Interest rescheduled	0	0	0	0	0	0	0	0	0	0
Official	0	0	0	0	0	0	0	0	0	0
Private	0	0	0	0	0	0	0	0	0	0
Debt forgiven	..	..	0	0	105	15	5	0	0	16
Memo: interest forgiven	..	..	0	0	1	0	0	0	0	1
Debt stock reduction	0	0	0	0	0	0	0	0	0	0
of which debt buyback	0	0	0	0	0	0	0	0	0	0
8. DEBT STOCK-FLOW RECONCILIATION										
Total change in debt stocks	..	..	..	88	19	56	59	39	62	34
Net flows on debt	..	..	..	97	65	66	101	45	25	26
Net change in interest arrears	..	..	..	0	-1	0	1	1	0	0
Interest capitalized	..	..	..	0	0	0	0	0	0	0
Debt forgiveness or reduction	..	..	..	0	-105	-15	-5	0	0	-16
Cross-currency valuation	..	..	..	-2	16	0	-12	-4	12	11
Residual	..	..	..	-7	43	5	-26	-3	24	12
9. AVERAGE TERMS OF NEW COMMITMENTS										
ALL CREDITORS										
Interest (%)	2.9	1.3	1.1	1.0	0.9	1.2	0.7	1.1	0.8	0.8
Maturity (years)	4.7	41.9	37.1	35.0	40.1	40.3	40.9	28.0	21.0	38.0
Grace period (years)	2.2	9.0	10.1	9.9	10.3	10.1	10.1	10.1	11.0	9.8
Grant element (%)	20.3	73.6	76.0	74.8	78.7	77.0	80.5	71.0	71.4	78.4
Official creditors										
Interest (%)	2.3	1.3	1.0	1.0	0.9	1.2	0.7	1.1	0.8	0.8
Maturity (years)	4.8	41.9	37.6	35.0	40.1	40.3	40.9	28.0	21.0	38.0
Grace period (years)	2.5	9.0	10.3	9.9	10.3	10.1	10.1	10.1	11.0	9.8
Grant element (%)	22.5	73.6	77.1	74.8	78.7	77.0	80.5	71.0	71.4	78.4
Private creditors										
Interest (%)	7.6	0.0	7.5	0.0	0.0	0.0	0.0	0.0	0.0	0.0
Maturity (years)	3.6	0.0	5.7	0.0	0.0	0.0	0.0	0.0	0.0	0.0
Grace period (years)	0.1	0.0	0.7	0.0	0.0	0.0	0.0	0.0	0.0	0.0
Grant element (%)	3.8	0.0	5.8	0.0	0.0	0.0	0.0	0.0	0.0	0.0
Memorandum items										
Commitments	1	102	201	120	126	101	82	71	7	39
Official creditors	1	102	198	120	126	101	82	71	7	39
Private creditors	0	0	3	0	0	0	0	0	0	0

10. CONTRACTUAL OBLIGATIONS ON OUTSTANDING LONG-TERM DEBT

	1996	1997	1998	1999	2000	2001	2002	2003	2004	2005
TOTAL										
Disbursements	90	81	56	33	19	11	7	2	0	0
Principal	32	31	33	36	36	37	37	36	39	39
Interest	13	13	13	12	12	11	11	10	9	9
Official creditors										
Disbursements	90	81	56	33	19	11	7	2	0	0
Principal	31	31	33	36	36	37	37	36	39	39
Interest	13	13	13	12	12	11	11	10	9	9
Bilateral creditors										
Disbursements	14	10	6	3	2	1	1	1	0	0
Principal	12	11	11	14	13	13	12	10	10	8
Interest	3	3	3	3	3	3	2	2	2	2
Multilateral creditors										
Disbursements	76	71	51	30	17	10	7	2	0	0
Principal	19	20	21	22	23	25	25	26	29	30
Interest	10	10	10	9	9	9	8	8	8	8
Private creditors										
Disbursements	0	0	0	0	0	0	0	0	0	0
Principal	1	0	0	0	0	0	0	0	0	0
Interest	0	0	0	0	0	0	0	0	0	0
Commercial banks										
Disbursements	0	0	0	0	0	0	0	0	0	0
Principal	0	0	0	0	0	0	0	0	0	0
Interest	0	0	0	0	0	0	0	0	0	0
Other private										
Disbursements	0	0	0	0	0	0	0	0	0	0
Principal	1	0	0	0	0	0	0	0	0	0
Interest	0	0	0	0	0	0	0	0	0	0

CAMBODIA

(US$ million, unless otherwise indicated)

1. SUMMARY DEBT DATA

	1970	1980	1988	1989	1990	1991	1992	1993	1994	1995
TOTAL DEBT STOCKS (EDT)	..	..	..	**1,687**	**1,854**	**1,862**	**1,840**	**1,829**	**1,915**	**2,031**
Long-term debt (LDOD)	..	..	..	**1,549**	**1,688**	**1,689**	**1,680**	**1,685**	**1,745**	**1,942**
Public and publicly guaranteed	..	..	..	1,549	1,688	1,689	1,680	1,685	1,745	1,942
Private nonguaranteed	0	0	0	0	0	0	0	0	0	0
Use of IMF credit	**0**	**0**	**25**	**25**	**27**	**27**	**15**	**9**	**30**	**72**
Short-term debt	..	..	..	**114**	**140**	**146**	**145**	**135**	**140**	**17**
of which interest arrears on LDOD	..	..	..	96	107	114	113	104	110	5
Official creditors	..	..	..	96	106	114	113	103	110	5
Private creditors	..	..	..	0	0	0	0	0	0	0
Memo: principal arrears on LDOD	..	..	..	85	393	223	328	447	577	588
Official creditors	..	..	..	85	393	222	328	447	577	588
Private creditors	..	..	..	0	0	0	0	0	0	0
Memo: export credits	..	..	7	1	8	8	8	13	22	17
TOTAL DEBT FLOWS										
Disbursements	..	..	..	**0**	**0**	**0**	**0**	**14**	**75**	**128**
Long-term debt	..	..	..	0	0	0	0	5	55	85
IMF purchases	0	0	0	0	0	0	0	9	20	43
Principal repayments	..	..	..	**0**	**0**	**0**	**11**	**15**	**0**	**4**
Long-term debt	..	..	..	0	0	0	0	0	0	4
IMF repurchases	0	0	0	0	0	0	11	15	0	0
Net flows on debt	..	..	..	**5**	**15**	**-1**	**-11**	**-1**	**73**	**106**
of which short-term debt	..	..	..	5	15	-1	0	0	-2	-18
Interest payments (INT)	..	..	..	**12**	**30**	**16**	**2**	**19**	**2**	**2**
Long-term debt	..	..	..	11	29	15	1	0	0	1
IMF charges	0	0	0	0	0	0	0	18	1	1
Short-term debt	..	..	..	1	1	1	1	1	1	1
Net transfers on debt	..	..	..	**-7**	**-15**	**-17**	**-13**	**-21**	**71**	**103**
Total debt service paid (TDS)	..	..	..	**12**	**30**	**16**	**13**	**34**	**2**	**6**
Long-term debt	..	..	..	11	29	15	1	0	0	5
IMF repurchases and charges	0	0	0	0	0	0	11	33	1	1
Short-term debt (interest only)	..	..	..	1	1	1	1	1	1	1

2. AGGREGATE NET RESOURCE FLOWS AND NET TRANSFERS (LONG-TERM)

	1970	1980	1988	1989	1990	1991	1992	1993	1994	1995
NET RESOURCE FLOWS	..	..	..	**13**	**23**	**41**	**132**	**235**	**287**	**544**
Net flow of long-term debt (ex. IMF)	0	0	0	0	0	0	0	5	55	81
Foreign direct investment (net)	0	0	0	0	0	0	33	54	69	151
Portfolio equity flows	..	..	..	0	0	0	0	0	0	0
Grants (excluding technical coop.)	7	123	10	13	23	41	99	176	163	312
Memo: technical coop. grants	7	158	9	18	19	50	108	135	129	154
NET TRANSFERS	..	..	..	**2**	**-6**	**26**	**132**	**234**	**284**	**541**
Interest on long-term debt	..	..	..	11	29	15	1	0	0	1
Profit remittances on FDI	0	0	0	0	0	0	0	2	2	2

3. MAJOR ECONOMIC AGGREGATES

	1970	1980	1988	1989	1990	1991	1992	1993	1994	1995
Gross national product (GNP)	..	..	..	1,076	1,115	1,633	1,977	2,235	2,367	2,762
Exports of goods & services (XGS)	..	..	..	..	..	..	323	357	557	989
of which workers remittances	..	..	..	..	..	..	9	9	10	10
Imports of goods & services (MGS)	..	..	..	..	..	..	528	608	933	1,442
International reserves (RES)	..	..	..	..	..	..	..	24	119	192
Current account balance	..	..	..	..	..	..	-93	-104	-157	-186

4. DEBT INDICATORS

	1970	1980	1988	1989	1990	1991	1992	1993	1994	1995
EDT / XGS (%)	..	..	..	..	..	..	569.2	512.2	344.1	205.4
EDT / GNP (%)	..	..	..	156.9	166.4	114.0	93.1	81.8	80.9	73.5
TDS / XGS (%)	..	..	..	..	..	..	4.0	9.6	0.3	0.6
INT / XGS (%)	..	..	..	..	..	..	0.6	5.4	0.3	0.2
INT / GNP (%)	..	..	..	1.1	2.7	1.0	0.1	0.9	0.1	0.1
RES / EDT (%)	..	..	..	..	..	..	..	1.3	6.2	9.5
RES / MGS (months)	..	..	..	..	..	..	..	0.5	1.5	1.6
Short-term / EDT (%)	..	..	..	6.7	7.5	7.9	7.9	7.4	7.3	0.9
Concessional / EDT (%)	..	..	..	91.8	91.0	90.7	91.3	92.1	90.9	93.3
Multilateral / EDT (%)	..	..	..	0.1	0.1	0.1	0.0	0.3	3.0	5.8

CAMBODIA

(US$ million, unless otherwise indicated)

	1970	1980	1988	1989	1990	1991	1992	1993	1994	1995
5. LONG-TERM DEBT										
DEBT OUTSTANDING (LDOD)	..	..	..	**1,549**	**1,688**	**1,689**	**1,680**	**1,685**	**1,745**	**1,942**
Public and publicly guaranteed	..	..	..	**1,549**	**1,688**	**1,689**	**1,680**	**1,685**	**1,745**	**1,942**
Official creditors	..	..	..	1,548	1,688	1,688	1,680	1,685	1,745	1,929
Multilateral	..	..	..	1	1	1	0	5	58	118
Concessional	..	..	..	1	1	1	0	5	58	118
Bilateral	..	..	..	1,547	1,686	1,687	1,680	1,680	1,687	1,811
Concessional	..	..	..	1,547	1,686	1,687	1,680	1,680	1,683	1,777
Private creditors	..	..	..	0	0	0	0	0	0	13
Bonds	..	..	..	0	0	0	0	0	0	0
Commercial banks	..	..	..	0	0	0	0	0	0	0
Other private	..	..	..	0	0	0	0	0	0	13
Private nonguaranteed	**0**	**0**	**0**	**0**	**0**	**0**	**0**	**0**	**0**	**0**
Bonds	..	..	..	0	0	0	0	0	0	0
Commercial banks	..	..	..	0	0	0	0	0	0	0
Memo:										
IBRD	0	0	0	0	0	0	0	0	0	0
IDA	0	0	0	0	0	0	0	0	39	65
DISBURSEMENTS	..	..	..	**0**	**0**	**0**	**0**	**5**	**55**	**85**
Public and publicly guaranteed	..	..	..	**0**	**0**	**0**	**0**	**5**	**55**	**85**
Official creditors	..	..	..	0	0	0	0	5	55	69
Multilateral	..	..	..	0	0	0	0	5	50	61
Concessional	..	..	..	0	0	0	0	5	50	61
Bilateral	..	..	..	0	0	0	0	0	4	9
Concessional	..	..	..	0	0	0	0	0	0	9
Private creditors	..	..	..	0	0	0	0	0	0	16
Bonds	..	..	..	0	0	0	0	0	0	0
Commercial banks	..	..	..	0	0	0	0	0	0	0
Other private	..	..	..	0	0	0	0	0	0	16
Private nonguaranteed	**0**	**0**	**0**	**0**	**0**	**0**	**0**	**0**	**0**	**0**
Bonds	..	..	..	0	0	0	0	0	0	0
Commercial banks	..	..	..	0	0	0	0	0	0	0
Memo:										
IBRD	0	0	0	0	0	0	0	0	0	0
IDA	0	0	0	0	0	0	0	0	38	25
PRINCIPAL REPAYMENTS	..	..	..	**0**	**0**	**0**	**0**	**0**	**0**	**4**
Public and publicly guaranteed	..	..	..	**0**	**0**	**0**	**0**	**0**	**0**	**4**
Official creditors	..	..	..	0	0	0	0	0	0	1
Multilateral	..	..	..	0	0	0	0	0	0	0
Concessional	..	..	..	0	0	0	0	0	0	0
Bilateral	..	..	..	0	0	0	0	0	0	1
Concessional	..	..	..	0	0	0	0	0	0	0
Private creditors	..	..	..	0	0	0	0	0	0	3
Bonds	..	..	..	0	0	0	0	0	0	0
Commercial banks	..	..	..	0	0	0	0	0	0	0
Other private	..	..	..	0	0	0	0	0	0	3
Private nonguaranteed	**0**	**0**	**0**	**0**	**0**	**0**	**0**	**0**	**0**	**0**
Bonds	..	..	..	0	0	0	0	0	0	0
Commercial banks	..	..	..	0	0	0	0	0	0	0
Memo:										
IBRD	0	0	0	0	0	0	0	0	0	0
IDA	0	0	0	0	0	0	0	0	0	0
NET FLOWS ON DEBT	..	..	..	**0**	**0**	**0**	**0**	**5**	**55**	**81**
Public and publicly guaranteed	..	..	..	**0**	**0**	**0**	**0**	**5**	**55**	**81**
Official creditors	..	..	..	0	0	0	0	5	55	68
Multilateral	..	..	..	0	0	0	0	5	50	61
Concessional	..	..	..	0	0	0	0	5	50	61
Bilateral	..	..	..	0	0	0	0	0	4	8
Concessional	..	..	..	0	0	0	0	0	0	9
Private creditors	..	..	..	0	0	0	0	0	0	13
Bonds	..	..	..	0	0	0	0	0	0	0
Commercial banks	..	..	..	0	0	0	0	0	0	0
Other private	..	..	..	0	0	0	0	0	0	13
Private nonguaranteed	**0**	**0**	**0**	**0**	**0**	**0**	**0**	**0**	**0**	**0**
Bonds	..	..	..	0	0	0	0	0	0	0
Commercial banks	..	..	..	0	0	0	0	0	0	0
Memo:										
IBRD	0	0	0	0	0	0	0	0	0	0
IDA	0	0	0	0	0	0	0	0	38	25

CAMBODIA

(US$ million, unless otherwise indicated)

	1970	1980	1988	1989	1990	1991	1992	1993	1994	1995
INTEREST PAYMENTS (LINT)	..	..	..	**11**	**29**	**15**	**1**	**0**	**0**	**1**
Public and publicly guaranteed	..	..	..	**11**	**29**	**15**	**1**	**0**	**0**	**1**
Official creditors	..	..	..	11	29	15	1	0	0	1
Multilateral	..	..	..	0	0	0	1	0	0	1
Concessional	..	..	..	0	0	0	1	0	0	1
Bilateral	..	..	..	11	29	15	0	0	0	0
Concessional	..	..	..	11	29	15	0	0	0	0
Private creditors	..	..	..	0	0	0	0	0	0	0
Bonds	..	..	..	0	0	0	0	0	0	0
Commercial banks	..	..	..	0	0	0	0	0	0	0
Other private	..	..	..	0	0	0	0	0	0	0
Private nonguaranteed	**0**	**0**	**0**	**0**	**0**	**0**	**0**	**0**	**0**	**0**
Bonds	..	..	..	0	0	0	0	0	0	0
Commercial banks	..	..	..	0	0	0	0	0	0	0
Memo:										
IBRD	0	0	0	0	0	0	0	0	0	0
IDA	0	0	0	0	0	0	0	0	0	0
NET TRANSFERS ON DEBT	..	..	..	**-11**	**-29**	**-15**	**-1**	**5**	**54**	**80**
Public and publicly guaranteed	..	..	..	**-11**	**-29**	**-15**	**-1**	**5**	**54**	**80**
Official creditors	..	..	..	-11	-29	-15	-1	5	54	67
Multilateral	..	..	..	0	0	0	-1	5	50	60
Concessional	..	..	..	0	0	0	-1	5	50	60
Bilateral	..	..	..	-11	-29	-15	0	0	4	8
Concessional	..	..	..	-11	-29	-15	0	0	0	9
Private creditors	..	..	..	0	0	0	0	0	0	13
Bonds	..	..	..	0	0	0	0	0	0	0
Commercial banks	..	..	..	0	0	0	0	0	0	0
Other private	..	..	..	0	0	0	0	0	0	13
Private nonguaranteed	**0**	**0**	**0**	**0**	**0**	**0**	**0**	**0**	**0**	**0**
Bonds	..	..	..	0	0	0	0	0	0	0
Commercial banks	..	..	..	0	0	0	0	0	0	0
Memo:										
IBRD	0	0	0	0	0	0	0	0	0	0
IDA	0	0	0	0	0	0	0	0	38	24
DEBT SERVICE (LTDS)	..	..	..	**11**	**29**	**15**	**1**	**0**	**0**	**5**
Public and publicly guaranteed	..	..	..	**11**	**29**	**15**	**1**	**0**	**0**	**5**
Official creditors	..	..	..	11	29	15	1	0	0	2
Multilateral	..	..	..	0	0	0	1	0	0	1
Concessional	..	..	..	0	0	0	1	0	0	1
Bilateral	..	..	..	11	29	15	0	0	0	1
Concessional	..	..	..	11	29	15	0	0	0	0
Private creditors	..	..	..	0	0	0	0	0	0	3
Bonds	..	..	..	0	0	0	0	0	0	0
Commercial banks	..	..	..	0	0	0	0	0	0	0
Other private	..	..	..	0	0	0	0	0	0	3
Private nonguaranteed	**0**	**0**	**0**	**0**	**0**	**0**	**0**	**0**	**0**	**0**
Bonds	..	..	..	0	0	0	0	0	0	0
Commercial banks	..	..	..	0	0	0	0	0	0	0
Memo:										
IBRD	0	0	0	0	0	0	0	0	0	0
IDA	0	0	0	0	0	0	0	0	0	0
UNDISBURSED DEBT	..	..	..	**590**	**651**	**16**	**7**	**128**	**131**	**201**
Official creditors	..	..	..	590	651	16	7	128	115	201
Private creditors	..	..	..	0	0	0	0	0	16	0
Memorandum items										
Concessional LDOD	..	..	..	1,548	1,688	1,688	1,680	1,685	1,741	1,895
Variable rate LDOD	..	..	..	0	0	0	0	0	0	0
Public sector LDOD	..	..	..	1,549	1,688	1,689	1,680	1,685	1,745	1,942
Private sector LDOD	..	..	..	0	0	0	0	0	0	0
6. CURRENCY COMPOSITION OF LONG-TERM DEBT (PERCENT)										
Deutsche mark	..	..	..	0.4	0.4	0.4	0.0	0.0	0.0	0.1
French franc	..	..	..	0.5	0.5	0.5	0.4	0.4	0.4	1.4
Japanese yen	..	..	..	0.6	0.6	0.6	0.6	0.7	0.7	0.8
Pound sterling	..	..	..	0.0	0.0	0.0	0.0	0.0	0.0	0.0
Swiss franc	..	..	..	0.0	0.0	0.0	0.0	0.0	0.0	0.0
U.S.dollars	..	..	..	13.7	12.6	12.6	12.6	12.5	14.6	20.2
Multiple currency	..	..	..	0.0	0.0	0.0	0.0	0.3	1.1	2.7
Special drawing rights	..	..	..	0.0	0.0	0.0	0.0	0.0	0.0	0.0
All other currencies	..	..	..	84.9	86.0	86.0	86.4	86.1	83.2	74.8

CAMBODIA

(US$ million, unless otherwise indicated)

	1970	1980	1988	1989	1990	1991	1992	1993	1994	1995
7. DEBT RESTRUCTURINGS										
Total amount rescheduled	0	0	0	0	0	1,363	0	0	0	235
Debt stock rescheduled	0	0	0	0	0	0	0	0	0	0
Principal rescheduled	0	0	0	0	0	1,363	0	0	0	109
Official	0	0	0	0	0	1,363	0	0	0	108
Private	0	0	0	0	0	0	0	0	0	0
Interest rescheduled	0	0	0	0	0	0	0	0	0	103
Official	0	0	0	0	0	0	0	0	0	103
Private	0	0	0	0	0	0	0	0	0	0
Debt forgiven	..	..	0	0	0	0	7	0	0	6
Memo: interest forgiven	..	..	0	0	0	0	4	0	0	7
Debt stock reduction	0	0	0	0	0	0	0	0	0	0
of which debt buyback	0	0	0	0	0	0	0	0	0	0
8. DEBT STOCK-FLOW RECONCILIATION										
Total change in debt stocks	..	..	..	..	167	7	-22	-11	86	116
Net flows on debt	..	..	..	..	15	-1	-11	-1	73	106
Net change in interest arrears	..	..	..	..	11	8	-1	-10	7	-105
Interest capitalized	..	..	..	..	0	0	0	0	0	103
Debt forgiveness or reduction	..	..	..	..	0	0	-7	0	0	-6
Cross-currency valuation	..	..	..	..	3	0	-1	1	3	3
Residual	..	..	..	..	138	0	-2	0	3	15
9. AVERAGE TERMS OF NEW COMMITMENTS										
ALL CREDITORS										
Interest (%)	..	..	..	0.0	0.0	0.0	0.0	0.9	0.7	1.8
Maturity (years)	..	..	..	0.0	0.0	0.0	0.0	39.9	25.0	37.5
Grace period (years)	..	..	..	0.0	0.0	0.0	0.0	10.4	6.7	9.7
Grant element (%)	..	..	..	0.0	0.0	0.0	0.0	79.6	58.5	69.8
Official creditors										
Interest (%)	..	..	..	0.0	0.0	0.0	0.0	0.9	1.1	1.8
Maturity (years)	..	..	..	0.0	0.0	0.0	0.0	39.9	33.6	37.5
Grace period (years)	..	..	..	0.0	0.0	0.0	0.0	10.4	9.2	9.7
Grant element (%)	..	..	..	0.0	0.0	0.0	0.0	79.6	73.2	69.8
Private creditors										
Interest (%)	..	..	..	0.0	0.0	0.0	0.0	0.0	0.0	0.0
Maturity (years)	..	..	..	0.0	0.0	0.0	0.0	0.0	5.0	0.0
Grace period (years)	..	..	..	0.0	0.0	0.0	0.0	0.0	1.0	0.0
Grant element (%)	..	..	..	0.0	0.0	0.0	0.0	0.0	24.3	0.0
Memorandum items										
Commitments	..	..	..	0	0	0	0	127	53	161
Official creditors	..	..	..	0	0	0	0	127	37	161
Private creditors	..	..	..	0	0	0	0	0	16	0

10. CONTRACTUAL OBLIGATIONS ON OUTSTANDING LONG-TERM DEBT

	1996	1997	1998	1999	2000	2001	2002	2003	2004	2005
TOTAL										
Disbursements	37	47	36	30	23	15	10	2	1	0
Principal	125	128	131	130	127	39	41	42	44	47
Interest	4	6	8	8	8	8	8	8	7	8
Official creditors										
Disbursements	37	47	36	30	23	15	10	2	1	0
Principal	121	125	128	127	127	39	41	42	44	47
Interest	4	6	8	8	8	8	8	8	7	8
Bilateral creditors										
Disbursements	4	6	4	3	2	1	1	1	1	0
Principal	121	125	128	127	127	39	41	41	42	42
Interest	3	4	6	6	6	5	5	5	4	4
Multilateral creditors										
Disbursements	34	42	31	27	21	14	9	1	0	0
Principal	0	0	0	0	0	0	0	1	3	5
Interest	1	2	2	2	3	3	3	3	3	4
Private creditors										
Disbursements	0	0	0	0	0	0	0	0	0	0
Principal	3	3	3	3	0	0	0	0	0	0
Interest	0	0	0	0	0	0	0	0	0	0
Commercial banks										
Disbursements	0	0	0	0	0	0	0	0	0	0
Principal	0	0	0	0	0	0	0	0	0	0
Interest	0	0	0	0	0	0	0	0	0	0
Other private										
Disbursements	0	0	0	0	0	0	0	0	0	0
Principal	3	3	3	3	0	0	0	0	0	0
Interest	0	0	0	0	0	0	0	0	0	0

CAMEROON

(US$ million, unless otherwise indicated)

	1970	1980	1988	1989	1990	1991	1992	1993	1994	1995
1. SUMMARY DEBT DATA										
TOTAL DEBT STOCKS (EDT)	**..**	**2,588**	**4,778**	**5,440**	**6,679**	**6,898**	**7,349**	**7,452**	**8,254**	**9,350**
Long-term debt (LDOD)	**145**	**2,251**	**3,856**	**4,719**	**5,598**	**5,782**	**6,456**	**6,488**	**7,463**	**8,258**
Public and publicly guaranteed	136	2,073	3,429	4,341	5,368	5,597	6,202	6,219	7,230	8,061
Private nonguaranteed	9	178	427	378	230	184	254	269	233	197
Use of IMF credit	**0**	**59**	**100**	**113**	**121**	**121**	**63**	**16**	**44**	**51**
Short-term debt	**..**	**278**	**822**	**608**	**960**	**996**	**830**	**948**	**747**	**1,041**
of which interest arrears on LDOD	..	9	132	76	191	376	296	497	266	400
Official creditors	..	3	47	17	87	209	188	376	138	253
Private creditors	..	6	85	60	105	166	108	120	128	147
Memo: principal arrears on LDOD	..	7	296	102	350	600	448	641	536	623
Official creditors	..	2	72	26	103	228	126	251	199	247
Private creditors	..	5	224	76	247	372	322	391	336	376
Memo: export credits	..	..	1,632	1,773	2,193	2,221	2,204	2,219	2,616	2,889
TOTAL DEBT FLOWS										
Disbursements	**40**	**626**	**716**	**887**	**718**	**433**	**669**	**499**	**478**	**118**
Long-term debt	40	614	623	867	718	422	669	499	447	105
IMF purchases	0	12	94	20	0	11	0	0	31	13
Principal repayments	**6**	**131**	**388**	**208**	**270**	**214**	**203**	**282**	**204**	**212**
Long-term debt	6	114	380	203	269	202	149	235	198	206
IMF repurchases	0	17	8	5	1	12	54	47	6	6
Net flows on debt	**33**	**495**	**329**	**520**	**685**	**70**	**380**	**134**	**304**	**66**
of which short-term debt	..	..	1	-158	237	-148	-86	-83	30	160
Interest payments (INT)	**..**	**149**	**287**	**198**	**252**	**213**	**191**	**189**	**181**	**211**
Long-term debt	5	119	213	134	198	170	152	156	155	170
IMF charges	0	2	1	8	11	10	8	3	2	2
Short-term debt	..	28	74	57	43	33	31	30	24	39
Net transfers on debt	**..**	**346**	**42**	**323**	**433**	**-143**	**189**	**-55**	**123**	**-145**
Total debt service paid (TDS)	**..**	**280**	**676**	**406**	**522**	**427**	**393**	**471**	**385**	**423**
Long-term debt	11	233	592	337	467	372	300	391	354	376
IMF repurchases and charges	0	19	9	13	13	22	62	50	7	9
Short-term debt (interest only)	..	28	74	57	43	33	31	30	24	39
2. AGGREGATE NET RESOURCE FLOWS AND NET TRANSFERS (LONG-TERM)										
NET RESOURCE FLOWS	**70**	**659**	**371**	**802**	**649**	**464**	**753**	**379**	**687**	**206**
Net flow of long-term debt (ex. IMF)	33	500	243	664	449	220	520	264	249	-101
Foreign direct investment (net)	16	130	67	-87	-113	-15	29	5	105	102
Portfolio equity flows	0	0	0	0	0	0	0	0	0	0
Grants (excluding technical coop.)	21	29	61	225	313	259	204	110	333	205
Memo: technical coop. grants	17	85	118	107	128	123	134	122	101	124
NET TRANSFERS	**61**	**425**	**26**	**669**	**451**	**294**	**601**	**223**	**531**	**36**
Interest on long-term debt	5	119	213	134	198	170	152	156	155	170
Profit remittances on FDI	4	115	133	0	0	0	0	0	0	0
3. MAJOR ECONOMIC AGGREGATES										
Gross national product (GNP)	1,111	6,823	11,843	10,517	10,557	11,508	10,539	10,355	6,800	7,516
Exports of goods & services (XGS)	279	1,839	2,068	2,328	2,307	2,604	2,392	2,222	2,261	2,764
of which workers remittances	0	11	0	0	19	4	19	55	52	59
Imports of goods & services (MGS)	319	2,226	3,031	2,867	3,192	3,168	2,990	2,851	2,485	2,914
International reserves (RES)	81	206	188	92	37	54	30	14	14	15
Current account balance	-47	-478	-1,153	-655	-809	-499	-295	-623	-192	-215
4. DEBT INDICATORS										
EDT / XGS (%)	..	140.7	231.1	233.7	289.5	264.8	307.2	335.4	365.0	338.3
EDT / GNP (%)	..	37.9	40.3	51.7	63.3	59.9	69.7	72.0	121.4	124.4
TDS / XGS (%)	..	15.2	32.7	17.4	22.6	16.4	16.4	21.2	17.0	15.3
INT / XGS (%)	..	8.1	13.9	8.5	10.9	8.2	8.0	8.5	8.0	7.6
INT / GNP (%)	..	2.2	2.4	1.9	2.4	1.9	1.8	1.8	2.7	2.8
RES / EDT (%)	..	8.0	3.9	1.7	0.6	0.8	0.4	0.2	0.2	0.2
RES / MGS (months)	3.0	1.1	0.7	0.4	0.1	0.2	0.1	0.1	0.1	0.1
Short-term / EDT (%)	..	10.8	17.2	11.2	14.4	14.4	11.3	12.7	9.0	11.1
Concessional / EDT (%)	..	35.0	28.9	30.1	27.9	27.4	31.5	33.6	41.5	45.0
Multilateral / EDT (%)	..	16.7	22.0	20.3	19.7	20.9	19.8	19.2	20.2	17.9

CAMEROON

(US$ million, unless otherwise indicated)

	1970	1980	1988	1989	1990	1991	1992	1993	1994	1995
5. LONG-TERM DEBT										
DEBT OUTSTANDING (LDOD)	**145**	**2,251**	**3,856**	**4,719**	**5,598**	**5,782**	**6,456**	**6,488**	**7,463**	**8,258**
Public and publicly guaranteed	**136**	**2,073**	**3,429**	**4,341**	**5,368**	**5,597**	**6,202**	**6,219**	**7,230**	**8,061**
Official creditors	124	1,237	2,331	3,039	3,885	4,065	4,931	5,044	6,243	7,142
Multilateral	20	432	1,049	1,106	1,317	1,440	1,458	1,429	1,664	1,675
Concessional	13	243	373	370	373	368	362	356	577	651
Bilateral	104	805	1,282	1,933	2,568	2,625	3,473	3,615	4,579	5,467
Concessional	95	663	1,005	1,267	1,488	1,526	1,955	2,147	2,852	3,556
Private creditors	12	836	1,098	1,302	1,484	1,532	1,271	1,175	987	919
Bonds	0	0	0	0	0	0	0	0	0	0
Commercial banks	0	229	286	492	521	511	460	426	436	421
Other private	12	607	812	810	963	1,022	811	749	551	498
Private nonguaranteed	**9**	**178**	**427**	**378**	**230**	**184**	**254**	**269**	**233**	**197**
Bonds	0	0	0	0	0	0	0	0	0	0
Commercial banks	9	178	427	378	230	184	254	269	233	197
Memo:										
IBRD	3	152	508	572	651	724	723	707	695	639
IDA	9	146	240	239	238	235	232	227	406	443
DISBURSEMENTS	**40**	**614**	**623**	**867**	**718**	**422**	**669**	**499**	**447**	**105**
Public and publicly guaranteed	**29**	**564**	**507**	**786**	**665**	**393**	**542**	**419**	**440**	**105**
Official creditors	27	250	208	393	559	318	528	411	440	105
Multilateral	10	72	81	122	200	195	130	72	280	79
Concessional	7	28	6	4	2	4	14	9	217	62
Bilateral	18	178	128	272	359	123	398	339	159	26
Concessional	15	120	96	188	106	87	366	302	154	26
Private creditors	1	314	299	392	107	74	14	8	0	0
Bonds	0	0	0	0	0	0	0	0	0	0
Commercial banks	0	138	113	192	11	1	0	3	0	0
Other private	1	176	186	200	97	74	14	5	0	0
Private nonguaranteed	**11**	**50**	**115**	**82**	**53**	**29**	**127**	**80**	**7**	**0**
Bonds	0	0	0	0	0	0	0	0	0	0
Commercial banks	11	50	115	82	53	29	127	80	7	0
Memo:										
IBRD	3	28	48	107	75	123	54	59	22	6
IDA	4	19	4	1	0	0	0	0	180	35
PRINCIPAL REPAYMENTS	**6**	**114**	**380**	**203**	**269**	**202**	**149**	**235**	**198**	**206**
Public and publicly guaranteed	**5**	**82**	**152**	**73**	**139**	**127**	**91**	**170**	**156**	**183**
Official creditors	4	29	88	56	97	109	81	137	131	153
Multilateral	0	10	55	55	68	85	60	102	119	131
Concessional	0	3	7	7	9	9	11	11	12	13
Bilateral	4	19	33	2	29	23	21	35	12	23
Concessional	3	12	19	1	17	17	13	29	4	3
Private creditors	0	53	64	16	41	18	10	33	24	30
Bonds	0	0	0	0	0	0	0	0	0	0
Commercial banks	0	18	14	0	28	6	0	16	23	26
Other private	0	35	51	16	14	12	10	17	1	3
Private nonguaranteed	**2**	**32**	**228**	**131**	**130**	**75**	**57**	**65**	**43**	**23**
Bonds	0	0	0	0	0	0	0	0	0	0
Commercial banks	2	32	228	131	130	75	57	65	43	23
Memo:										
IBRD	0	4	36	36	42	63	30	87	82	92
IDA	0	1	2	2	3	4	2	5	4	4
NET FLOWS ON DEBT	**33**	**500**	**243**	**664**	**449**	**220**	**520**	**264**	**249**	**-101**
Public and publicly guaranteed	**24**	**482**	**355**	**713**	**527**	**266**	**451**	**249**	**284**	**-78**
Official creditors	23	221	120	337	461	209	447	273	308	-48
Multilateral	9	63	25	67	131	110	70	-30	161	-52
Concessional	7	25	-1	-2	-7	-5	3	-2	206	49
Bilateral	14	159	95	270	330	100	377	304	147	4
Concessional	12	109	76	187	89	70	353	273	150	24
Private creditors	1	261	235	376	66	57	4	-25	-24	-30
Bonds	0	0	0	0	0	0	0	0	0	0
Commercial banks	0	120	100	192	-17	-5	0	-13	-23	-26
Other private	1	141	135	184	83	62	4	-12	-1	-3
Private nonguaranteed	**9**	**18**	**-112**	**-49**	**-77**	**-46**	**69**	**15**	**-35**	**-23**
Bonds	0	0	0	0	0	0	0	0	0	0
Commercial banks	9	18	-112	-49	-77	-46	69	15	-35	-23
Memo:										
IBRD	3	24	12	72	33	60	24	-28	-60	-85
IDA	4	19	2	-1	-3	-4	-2	-5	176	31

CAMEROON

(US$ million, unless otherwise indicated)

	1970	1980	1988	1989	1990	1991	1992	1993	1994	1995
INTEREST PAYMENTS (LINT)	**5**	**119**	**213**	**134**	**198**	**170**	**152**	**156**	**155**	**170**
Public and publicly guaranteed	**4**	**104**	**121**	**95**	**181**	**152**	**114**	**136**	**141**	**163**
Official creditors	4	42	85	72	125	129	87	130	134	156
Multilateral	1	18	59	60	73	97	65	96	112	81
Concessional	0	4	6	5	5	6	5	4	5	7
Bilateral	3	24	26	12	52	33	22	34	23	75
Concessional	2	13	15	8	28	25	13	21	15	48
Private creditors	1	62	37	23	56	23	27	6	6	7
Bonds	0	0	0	0	0	0	0	0	0	0
Commercial banks	0	24	5	3	40	10	25	2	6	6
Other private	1	38	32	21	16	13	2	4	1	1
Private nonguaranteed	**1**	**15**	**91**	**39**	**17**	**18**	**38**	**20**	**15**	**7**
Bonds	0	0	0	0	0	0	0	0	0	0
Commercial banks	1	15	91	39	17	18	38	20	15	7
Memo:										
IBRD	0	13	45	45	49	64	33	87	58	56
IDA	0	1	2	2	2	2	1	3	2	3
NET TRANSFERS ON DEBT	**28**	**381**	**30**	**530**	**252**	**50**	**368**	**108**	**93**	**-271**
Public and publicly guaranteed	**19**	**378**	**234**	**618**	**346**	**114**	**337**	**113**	**143**	**-240**
Official creditors	19	180	35	265	336	80	360	144	174	-204
Multilateral	9	45	-34	7	59	13	5	-126	49	-132
Concessional	7	21	-7	-7	-12	-10	-1	-6	201	42
Bilateral	11	135	69	258	277	67	355	270	125	-72
Concessional	10	96	62	179	61	45	340	252	136	-24
Private creditors	0	199	198	353	10	34	-23	-31	-31	-37
Bonds	0	0	0	0	0	0	0	0	0	0
Commercial banks	0	96	95	190	-57	-15	-25	-15	-29	-33
Other private	0	103	103	163	66	49	2	-16	-2	-4
Private nonguaranteed	**9**	**3**	**-204**	**-88**	**-94**	**-65**	**32**	**-5**	**-50**	**-30**
Bonds	0	0	0	0	0	0	0	0	0	0
Commercial banks	9	3	-204	-88	-94	-65	32	-5	-50	-30
Memo:										
IBRD	3	12	-33	27	-16	-4	-9	-114	-119	-142
IDA	4	18	1	-3	-4	-6	-3	-8	174	28
DEBT SERVICE (LTDS)	**11**	**233**	**592**	**337**	**467**	**372**	**300**	**391**	**354**	**376**
Public and publicly guaranteed	**9**	**186**	**274**	**168**	**320**	**278**	**205**	**306**	**296**	**346**
Official creditors	8	71	173	128	222	238	168	267	266	309
Multilateral	1	28	114	115	141	182	126	198	231	211
Concessional	0	7	12	11	15	14	16	15	17	20
Bilateral	7	43	59	14	81	56	43	70	35	98
Concessional	6	25	34	9	46	42	26	50	19	50
Private creditors	1	115	101	39	98	41	37	39	31	37
Bonds	0	0	0	0	0	0	0	0	0	0
Commercial banks	0	42	18	3	67	16	25	17	29	33
Other private	1	73	83	37	30	25	12	21	2	4
Private nonguaranteed	**2**	**47**	**319**	**169**	**147**	**94**	**95**	**85**	**58**	**30**
Bonds	0	0	0	0	0	0	0	0	0	0
Commercial banks	2	47	319	169	147	94	95	85	58	30
Memo:										
IBRD	0	17	82	80	91	127	63	173	140	148
IDA	0	2	4	4	4	6	3	8	6	8
UNDISBURSED DEBT	**104**	**619**	**1,955**	**1,995**	**1,844**	**1,937**	**1,586**	**1,446**	**1,338**	**1,121**
Official creditors	103	545	1,299	1,520	1,526	1,683	1,359	1,240	1,122	1,026
Private creditors	1	74	656	475	318	254	227	206	216	95
Memorandum items										
Concessional LDOD	109	906	1,378	1,637	1,861	1,893	2,317	2,503	3,429	4,207
Variable rate LDOD	9	499	704	822	854	923	1,196	1,234	1,276	1,206
Public sector LDOD	128	2,006	3,380	4,240	5,245	5,477	6,095	6,122	7,159	7,984
Private sector LDOD	17	245	476	479	353	305	361	366	304	274

6. CURRENCY COMPOSITION OF LONG-TERM DEBT (PERCENT)

	1970	1980	1988	1989	1990	1991	1992	1993	1994	1995
Deutsche mark	10.7	8.6	11.7	16.0	16.9	17.2	16.5	15.6	16.9	15.6
French franc	15.8	36.8	25.5	28.6	31.4	31.9	35.6	37.3	34.4	32.8
Japanese yen	0.0	0.0	0.4	0.3	0.3	0.3	0.3	0.3	0.4	0.3
Pound sterling	2.8	2.0	2.8	2.1	2.3	2.2	1.6	1.5	1.2	1.0
Swiss franc	0.0	0.0	1.2	1.2	1.1	1.0	1.0	1.0	1.1	1.1
U.S.dollars	22.7	19.2	15.1	14.0	11.0	10.1	9.4	10.1	12.2	16.6
Multiple currency	4.9	10.5	19.5	16.7	16.5	18.1	16.8	16.5	14.7	12.5
Special drawing rights	0.0	0.0	0.0	0.0	0.0	0.0	0.0	0.1	0.1	0.2
All other currencies	43.1	22.9	23.8	21.1	20.4	19.2	18.8	17.5	19.1	20.0

CAMEROON

(US$ million, unless otherwise indicated)

	1970	1980	1988	1989	1990	1991	1992	1993	1994	1995
7. DEBT RESTRUCTURINGS										
Total amount rescheduled	0	0	0	435	75	0	922	66	1,242	739
Debt stock rescheduled	0	0	0	0	0	0	0	0	0	0
Principal rescheduled	0	0	0	220	26	0	408	16	489	308
Official	0	0	0	118	7	0	215	8	240	202
Private	0	0	0	102	19	0	193	8	249	105
Interest rescheduled	0	0	0	108	22	0	389	19	505	158
Official	0	0	0	74	6	0	102	2	391	130
Private	0	0	0	34	16	0	287	18	114	28
Debt forgiven	..	..	21	7	10	22	30	0	534	0
Memo: interest forgiven	..	..	0	0	0	0	0	0	13	0
Debt stock reduction	0	0	0	0	0	0	0	0	0	0
of which debt buyback	0	0	0	0	0	0	0	0	0	0
8. DEBT STOCK-FLOW RECONCILIATION										
Total change in debt stocks	..	..	..	662	1,239	219	451	104	801	1,096
Net flows on debt	..	..	..	520	685	70	380	134	304	66
Net change in interest arrears	..	..	..	-56	115	184	-80	201	-231	134
Interest capitalized	..	..	..	108	22	0	389	19	505	158
Debt forgiveness or reduction	..	..	..	-7	-10	-22	-30	0	-534	0
Cross-currency valuation	..	..	..	96	554	-48	-337	-305	581	498
Residual	..	..	..	1	-128	35	129	55	177	240
9. AVERAGE TERMS OF NEW COMMITMENTS										
ALL CREDITORS										
Interest (%)	4.7	6.9	5.2	6.7	6.6	6.1	4.5	4.9	2.3	2.1
Maturity (years)	28.4	23.3	14.3	15.8	15.5	19.7	19.5	18.1	31.9	28.4
Grace period (years)	8.0	5.9	3.9	5.0	5.3	5.4	7.1	10.2	9.4	8.7
Grant element (%)	39.9	25.9	26.5	19.8	21.3	25.5	37.7	36.3	63.7	61.7
Official creditors										
Interest (%)	4.6	6.1	5.9	6.7	6.6	6.0	4.5	4.9	2.3	2.1
Maturity (years)	28.8	24.8	17.5	18.6	15.5	20.2	19.5	18.1	31.9	28.4
Grace period (years)	8.1	6.3	5.3	5.8	5.3	5.6	7.1	10.2	9.4	8.7
Grant element (%)	40.4	30.6	25.5	21.2	21.4	26.7	37.7	36.3	63.7	61.7
Private creditors										
Interest (%)	6.0	14.7	4.5	6.8	7.0	9.5	0.0	0.0	0.0	0.0
Maturity (years)	7.2	8.2	10.9	7.1	13.2	7.1	0.0	0.0	0.0	0.0
Grace period (years)	1.7	2.4	2.4	2.7	2.7	0.6	0.0	0.0	0.0	0.0
Grant element (%)	13.0	-21.2	27.5	15.4	14.4	0.8	0.0	0.0	0.0	0.0
Memorandum items										
Commitments	42	170	1,078	860	479	580	272	347	403	116
Official creditors	41	155	546	654	473	554	272	347	403	116
Private creditors	1	15	532	206	6	25	0	0	0	0

10. CONTRACTUAL OBLIGATIONS ON OUTSTANDING LONG-TERM DEBT

	1996	1997	1998	1999	2000	2001	2002	2003	2004	2005
TOTAL										
Disbursements	325	303	208	132	78	44	21	3	1	0
Principal	474	684	590	572	494	474	513	531	553	553
Interest	308	379	348	318	290	264	238	208	179	150
Official creditors										
Disbursements	268	282	198	132	78	44	21	3	1	0
Principal	322	491	455	487	420	429	477	523	546	546
Interest	283	353	332	308	283	260	235	207	179	150
Bilateral creditors										
Disbursements	134	105	63	35	17	8	4	1	1	0
Principal	163	326	294	335	276	281	336	401	433	441
Interest	197	269	252	233	215	199	183	163	142	120
Multilateral creditors										
Disbursements	134	177	135	97	61	36	17	2	1	0
Principal	159	165	161	153	144	148	140	122	112	105
Interest	86	84	81	75	69	61	52	44	36	30
Private creditors										
Disbursements	58	22	10	0	0	0	0	0	0	0
Principal	152	193	135	85	74	45	36	7	7	7
Interest	25	26	16	10	7	5	3	1	1	1
Commercial banks										
Disbursements	55	22	10	0	0	0	0	0	0	0
Principal	81	81	30	1	0	0	0	0	0	0
Interest	8	4	0	0	0	0	0	0	0	0
Other private										
Disbursements	3	0	0	0	0	0	0	0	0	0
Principal	72	112	105	83	74	45	36	7	7	7
Interest	17	22	15	10	7	5	3	1	1	1

CAPE VERDE

(US$ million, unless otherwise indicated)

	1970	1980	1988	1989	1990	1991	1992	1993	1994	1995
1. SUMMARY DEBT DATA										
TOTAL DEBT STOCKS (EDT)	..	**20.8**	**126.5**	**127.7**	**135.3**	**135.0**	**142.1**	**149.4**	**179.7**	**216.3**
Long-term debt (LDOD)	..	**20.8**	**122.0**	**125.3**	**130.6**	**130.3**	**136.1**	**141.6**	**168.6**	**185.2**
Public and publicly guaranteed	..	20.8	122.0	125.3	130.6	130.3	136.1	141.6	168.6	185.2
Private nonguaranteed	0.0	0.0	0.0	0.0	0.0	0.0	0.0	0.0	0.0	0.0
Use of IMF credit	**0.0**	**0.0**	**0.0**	**0.0**	**0.0**	**0.0**	**0.0**	**0.0**	**0.0**	**0.0**
Short-term debt	..	**0.0**	**4.5**	**2.4**	**4.7**	**4.7**	**6.0**	**7.8**	**11.1**	**31.1**
of which interest arrears on LDOD	..	0.0	1.7	2.4	2.3	2.3	2.0	3.8	5.1	6.4
Official creditors	..	0.0	1.4	2.1	1.9	1.9	1.6	3.4	4.6	5.9
Private creditors	..	0.0	0.3	0.4	0.4	0.4	0.4	0.4	0.5	0.5
Memo: principal arrears on LDOD	..	0.0	5.0	7.7	11.1	10.4	10.6	16.9	21.2	25.9
Official creditors	..	0.0	4.5	7.1	10.4	9.9	9.8	15.8	19.9	24.3
Private creditors	..	0.0	0.5	0.6	0.7	0.5	0.8	1.1	1.3	1.6
Memo: export credits	..	..	12.0	12.0	11.0	13.0	13.0	13.0	13.0	19.0
TOTAL DEBT FLOWS										
Disbursements	..	**3.3**	**9.8**	**10.9**	**12.1**	**5.3**	**18.2**	**10.3**	**28.5**	**17.1**
Long-term debt	..	3.3	9.8	10.9	12.1	5.3	18.2	10.3	28.5	17.1
IMF purchases	0.0	0.0	0.0	0.0	0.0	0.0	0.0	0.0	0.0	0.0
Principal repayments	..	**0.1**	**4.2**	**4.1**	**3.7**	**5.9**	**8.1**	**3.7**	**4.6**	**3.3**
Long-term debt	..	0.1	4.2	4.1	3.7	5.9	8.1	3.7	4.6	3.3
IMF repurchases	0.0	0.0	0.0	0.0	0.0	0.0	0.0	0.0	0.0	0.0
Net flows on debt	..	**3.2**	**0.1**	**4.0**	**10.7**	**-0.6**	**11.6**	**6.6**	**26.0**	**32.6**
of which short-term debt	..	..	-5.5	-2.8	2.4	0.0	1.6	0.0	2.0	18.7
Interest payments (INT)	..	**0.2**	**4.0**	**2.5**	**2.0**	**2.8**	**3.1**	**1.8**	**1.9**	**2.6**
Long-term debt	..	0.1	3.6	2.3	1.9	2.7	2.9	1.6	1.7	1.8
IMF charges	0.0	0.0	0.0	0.0	0.0	0.0	0.0	0.0	0.0	0.0
Short-term debt	..	0.1	0.4	0.1	0.1	0.1	0.1	0.1	0.2	0.8
Net transfers on debt	..	**3.0**	**-3.9**	**1.5**	**8.7**	**-3.4**	**8.6**	**4.8**	**24.1**	**30.0**
Total debt service paid (TDS)	..	**0.3**	**8.2**	**6.6**	**5.7**	**8.7**	**11.2**	**5.5**	**6.4**	**5.8**
Long-term debt	..	0.2	7.8	6.5	5.6	8.6	11.1	5.3	6.2	5.1
IMF repurchases and charges	0.0	0.0	0.0	0.0	0.0	0.0	0.0	0.0	0.0	0.0
Short-term debt (interest only)	..	0.1	0.4	0.1	0.1	0.1	0.1	0.1	0.2	0.8
2. AGGREGATE NET RESOURCE FLOWS AND NET TRANSFERS (LONG-TERM)										
NET RESOURCE FLOWS	..	**43.2**	**64.7**	**70.5**	**86.5**	**69.2**	**72.2**	**67.4**	**88.8**	**79.3**
Net flow of long-term debt (ex. IMF)	0.0	3.2	5.6	6.8	8.3	-0.6	10.0	6.6	24.0	13.9
Foreign direct investment (net)	0.0	0.0	0.4	-0.6	0.0	1.0	-1.0	3.0	2.0	10.0
Portfolio equity flows	..	0.0	0.0	0.0	0.0	0.0	0.0	0.0	0.0	0.0
Grants (excluding technical coop.)	0.0	40.0	58.7	64.3	78.2	68.8	63.2	57.8	62.8	55.4
Memo: technical coop. grants	0.0	11.9	25.5	18.5	20.4	36.0	50.5	44.7	38.1	41.0
NET TRANSFERS	..	**43.1**	**61.1**	**68.2**	**84.7**	**66.5**	**69.3**	**65.8**	**87.1**	**77.5**
Interest on long-term debt	..	0.1	3.6	2.3	1.9	2.7	2.9	1.6	1.7	1.8
Profit remittances on FDI	0.0	0.0	0.0	0.0	0.0	0.0	0.0	0.0	0.0	0.0
3. MAJOR ECONOMIC AGGREGATES										
Gross national product (GNP)	37.4	110.1	208.9	201.5	271.4	289.9	333.8	306.0	319.8	383.4
Exports of goods & services (XGS)	..	62.8	84.0	104.2	113.3	111.4	125.0	116.6	141.8	182.7
of which workers remittances	..	40.1	35.7	40.2	46.4	53.0	61.4	63.3	76.7	95.9
Imports of goods & services (MGS)	..	87.5	126.0	139.4	156.4	155.4	204.4	188.1	235.0	294.1
International reserves (RES)	..	42.4	81.3	74.7	77.0	65.1	75.8	57.7	42.1	57.3
Current account balance	..	4.3	0.5	-4.6	-11.9	-7.9	-3.6	-10.6	-29.2	-38.8
4. DEBT INDICATORS										
EDT / XGS (%)	..	33.1	150.6	122.6	119.4	121.1	113.7	128.1	126.8	118.4
EDT / GNP (%)	..	18.9	60.6	63.4	49.8	46.6	42.6	48.8	56.2	56.4
TDS / XGS (%)	..	0.4	9.8	6.3	5.1	7.8	9.0	4.7	4.5	3.2
INT / XGS (%)	..	0.3	4.8	2.4	1.8	2.5	2.5	1.5	1.3	1.4
INT / GNP (%)	..	0.2	1.9	1.2	0.7	1.0	0.9	0.6	0.6	0.7
RES / EDT (%)	..	204.0	64.3	58.5	56.9	48.2	53.3	38.6	23.4	26.5
RES / MGS (months)	..	5.8	7.7	6.4	5.9	5.0	4.5	3.7	2.1	2.3
Short-term / EDT (%)	..	0.0	3.6	1.9	3.4	3.5	4.2	5.2	6.2	14.4
Concessional / EDT (%)	..	97.7	74.3	78.3	74.8	76.9	79.2	80.2	82.8	77.1
Multilateral / EDT (%)	..	82.6	59.0	61.6	64.3	65.4	68.2	69.4	74.3	68.6

CAPE VERDE

(US$ million, unless otherwise indicated)

	1970	1980	1988	1989	1990	1991	1992	1993	1994	1995
5. LONG-TERM DEBT										
DEBT OUTSTANDING (LDOD)	..	**20.8**	**122.0**	**125.3**	**130.6**	**130.3**	**136.1**	**141.6**	**168.6**	**185.2**
Public and publicly guaranteed	..	**20.8**	**122.0**	**125.3**	**130.6**	**130.3**	**136.1**	**141.6**	**168.6**	**185.2**
Official creditors	..	20.8	119.2	122.7	128.1	128.0	133.9	139.4	166.5	183.0
Multilateral	..	17.2	74.6	78.7	87.0	88.3	96.9	103.6	133.6	148.4
Concessional	..	17.2	60.5	65.9	74.2	77.2	87.1	95.1	126.4	142.2
Bilateral	..	3.6	44.6	43.9	41.2	39.7	37.0	35.8	32.9	34.6
Concessional	..	3.1	33.5	34.1	27.0	26.5	25.4	24.7	22.3	24.5
Private creditors	..	0.0	2.8	2.6	2.5	2.3	2.2	2.2	2.2	2.2
Bonds	..	0.0	0.0	0.0	0.0	0.0	0.0	0.0	0.0	0.0
Commercial banks	..	0.0	0.0	0.0	0.0	0.0	0.0	0.0	0.0	0.0
Other private	..	0.0	2.8	2.6	2.5	2.3	2.2	2.2	2.2	2.2
Private nonguaranteed	**0.0**	**0.0**	**0.0**	**0.0**	**0.0**	**0.0**	**0.0**	**0.0**	**0.0**	**0.0**
Bonds	..	0.0	0.0	0.0	0.0	0.0	0.0	0.0	0.0	0.0
Commercial banks	..	0.0	0.0	0.0	0.0	0.0	0.0	0.0	0.0	0.0
Memo:										
IBRD	0.0	0.0	0.0	0.0	0.0	0.0	0.0	0.0	0.0	0.0
IDA	0.0	0.0	7.3	10.7	13.6	16.6	17.1	20.6	26.6	33.0
DISBURSEMENTS	..	**3.3**	**9.8**	**10.9**	**12.1**	**5.3**	**18.2**	**10.3**	**28.5**	**17.1**
Public and publicly guaranteed	..	**3.3**	**9.8**	**10.9**	**12.1**	**5.3**	**18.2**	**10.3**	**28.5**	**17.1**
Official creditors	..	3.3	9.8	10.9	12.1	5.3	18.2	10.3	28.5	17.1
Multilateral	..	3.2	7.5	7.8	6.0	4.8	17.0	10.3	28.0	14.9
Concessional	..	3.2	7.5	7.8	6.0	4.8	17.0	10.3	28.0	14.9
Bilateral	..	0.0	2.3	3.1	6.1	0.5	1.2	0.0	0.6	2.2
Concessional	..	0.0	2.3	3.1	0.7	0.5	1.2	0.0	0.6	2.2
Private creditors	..	0.0	0.0	0.0	0.0	0.0	0.0	0.0	0.0	0.0
Bonds	..	0.0	0.0	0.0	0.0	0.0	0.0	0.0	0.0	0.0
Commercial banks	..	0.0	0.0	0.0	0.0	0.0	0.0	0.0	0.0	0.0
Other private	..	0.0	0.0	0.0	0.0	0.0	0.0	0.0	0.0	0.0
Private nonguaranteed	**0.0**	**0.0**	**0.0**	**0.0**	**0.0**	**0.0**	**0.0**	**0.0**	**0.0**	**0.0**
Bonds	..	0.0	0.0	0.0	0.0	0.0	0.0	0.0	0.0	0.0
Commercial banks	..	0.0	0.0	0.0	0.0	0.0	0.0	0.0	0.0	0.0
Memo:										
IBRD	0.0	0.0	0.0	0.0	0.0	0.0	0.0	0.0	0.0	0.0
IDA	0.0	0.0	1.3	3.5	2.0	2.7	1.2	3.5	5.0	6.0
PRINCIPAL REPAYMENTS	..	**0.1**	**4.2**	**4.1**	**3.7**	**5.9**	**8.1**	**3.7**	**4.6**	**3.3**
Public and publicly guaranteed	..	**0.1**	**4.2**	**4.1**	**3.7**	**5.9**	**8.1**	**3.7**	**4.6**	**3.3**
Official creditors	..	0.1	4.1	4.0	3.6	5.7	8.0	3.7	4.6	3.3
Multilateral	..	0.0	2.8	3.0	2.5	4.2	5.1	2.8	3.8	2.6
Concessional	..	0.0	1.8	1.9	1.4	2.5	4.2	1.6	1.9	1.5
Bilateral	..	0.1	1.2	1.1	1.1	1.5	2.9	0.9	0.7	0.7
Concessional	..	0.0	0.2	0.1	0.2	0.8	1.6	0.5	0.3	0.2
Private creditors	..	0.0	0.1	0.1	0.1	0.2	0.1	0.0	0.0	0.0
Bonds	..	0.0	0.0	0.0	0.0	0.0	0.0	0.0	0.0	0.0
Commercial banks	..	0.0	0.0	0.0	0.0	0.0	0.0	0.0	0.0	0.0
Other private	..	0.0	0.1	0.1	0.1	0.2	0.1	0.0	0.0	0.0
Private nonguaranteed	**0.0**	**0.0**	**0.0**	**0.0**	**0.0**	**0.0**	**0.0**	**0.0**	**0.0**	**0.0**
Bonds	..	0.0	0.0	0.0	0.0	0.0	0.0	0.0	0.0	0.0
Commercial banks	..	0.0	0.0	0.0	0.0	0.0	0.0	0.0	0.0	0.0
Memo:										
IBRD	0.0	0.0	0.0	0.0	0.0	0.0	0.0	0.0	0.0	0.0
IDA	0.0	0.0	0.0	0.0	0.0	0.0	0.0	0.1	0.1	0.1
NET FLOWS ON DEBT	..	**3.2**	**5.6**	**6.8**	**8.3**	**-0.6**	**10.0**	**6.6**	**24.0**	**13.9**
Public and publicly guaranteed	..	**3.2**	**5.6**	**6.8**	**8.3**	**-0.6**	**10.0**	**6.6**	**24.0**	**13.9**
Official creditors	..	3.2	5.7	6.9	8.5	-0.4	10.2	6.6	24.0	13.9
Multilateral	..	3.2	4.7	4.8	3.5	0.6	11.9	7.5	24.2	12.3
Concessional	..	3.2	5.7	5.8	4.6	2.3	12.7	8.8	26.1	13.4
Bilateral	..	0.0	1.1	2.1	4.9	-1.0	-1.7	-0.9	-0.2	1.6
Concessional	..	0.0	2.1	3.1	0.6	-0.3	-0.4	-0.5	0.2	2.0
Private creditors	..	0.0	-0.1	-0.1	-0.1	-0.2	-0.1	0.0	0.0	0.0
Bonds	..	0.0	0.0	0.0	0.0	0.0	0.0	0.0	0.0	0.0
Commercial banks	..	0.0	0.0	0.0	0.0	0.0	0.0	0.0	0.0	0.0
Other private	..	0.0	-0.1	-0.1	-0.1	-0.2	-0.1	0.0	0.0	0.0
Private nonguaranteed	**0.0**	**0.0**	**0.0**	**0.0**	**0.0**	**0.0**	**0.0**	**0.0**	**0.0**	**0.0**
Bonds	..	0.0	0.0	0.0	0.0	0.0	0.0	0.0	0.0	0.0
Commercial banks	..	0.0	0.0	0.0	0.0	0.0	0.0	0.0	0.0	0.0
Memo:										
IBRD	0.0	0.0	0.0	0.0	0.0	0.0	0.0	0.0	0.0	0.0
IDA	0.0	0.0	1.3	3.5	2.0	2.7	1.2	3.4	4.9	5.9

CAPE VERDE

(US$ million, unless otherwise indicated)

	1970	1980	1988	1989	1990	1991	1992	1993	1994	1995
INTEREST PAYMENTS (LINT)	..	**0.1**	**3.6**	**2.3**	**1.9**	**2.7**	**2.9**	**1.6**	**1.7**	**1.8**
Public and publicly guaranteed	..	**0.1**	**3.6**	**2.3**	**1.9**	**2.7**	**2.9**	**1.6**	**1.7**	**1.8**
Official creditors	..	0.1	3.6	2.3	1.9	2.6	2.9	1.6	1.7	1.8
Multilateral	..	0.0	2.3	1.3	1.2	2.0	1.9	1.4	1.5	1.7
Concessional	..	0.0	0.8	0.7	0.6	1.1	1.0	0.5	0.9	1.2
Bilateral	..	0.1	1.2	1.0	0.7	0.6	1.0	0.2	0.2	0.1
Concessional	..	0.0	0.3	0.3	0.0	0.0	0.1	0.1	0.1	0.1
Private creditors	..	0.0	0.0	0.0	0.0	0.1	0.1	0.0	0.0	0.0
Bonds	..	0.0	0.0	0.0	0.0	0.0	0.0	0.0	0.0	0.0
Commercial banks	..	0.0	0.0	0.0	0.0	0.0	0.0	0.0	0.0	0.0
Other private	..	0.0	0.0	0.0	0.0	0.1	0.1	0.0	0.0	0.0
Private nonguaranteed	**0.0**	**0.0**	**0.0**	**0.0**	**0.0**	**0.0**	**0.0**	**0.0**	**0.0**	**0.0**
Bonds	..	0.0	0.0	0.0	0.0	0.0	0.0	0.0	0.0	0.0
Commercial banks	..	0.0	0.0	0.0	0.0	0.0	0.0	0.0	0.0	0.0
Memo:										
IBRD	0.0	0.0	0.0	0.0	0.0	0.0	0.0	0.0	0.0	0.0
IDA	0.0	0.0	0.1	0.1	0.1	0.1	0.1	0.1	0.2	0.2
NET TRANSFERS ON DEBT	..	**3.1**	**2.0**	**4.5**	**6.5**	**-3.3**	**7.1**	**5.0**	**22.3**	**12.1**
Public and publicly guaranteed	..	**3.1**	**2.0**	**4.5**	**6.5**	**-3.3**	**7.1**	**5.0**	**22.3**	**12.1**
Official creditors	..	3.1	2.2	4.6	6.6	-3.0	7.3	5.0	22.3	12.1
Multilateral	..	3.2	2.3	3.5	2.3	-1.3	10.0	6.1	22.7	10.6
Concessional	..	3.2	4.9	5.1	4.0	1.2	11.8	8.2	25.2	12.1
Bilateral	..	-0.1	-0.2	1.1	4.3	-1.6	-2.7	-1.1	-0.3	1.5
Concessional	..	0.0	1.8	2.8	0.6	-0.3	-0.5	-0.6	0.1	2.0
Private creditors	..	0.0	-0.2	-0.1	-0.1	-0.3	-0.2	0.0	0.0	0.0
Bonds	..	0.0	0.0	0.0	0.0	0.0	0.0	0.0	0.0	0.0
Commercial banks	..	0.0	0.0	0.0	0.0	0.0	0.0	0.0	0.0	0.0
Other private	..	0.0	-0.2	-0.1	-0.1	-0.3	-0.2	0.0	0.0	0.0
Private nonguaranteed	**0.0**	**0.0**	**0.0**	**0.0**	**0.0**	**0.0**	**0.0**	**0.0**	**0.0**	**0.0**
Bonds	..	0.0	0.0	0.0	0.0	0.0	0.0	0.0	0.0	0.0
Commercial banks	..	0.0	0.0	0.0	0.0	0.0	0.0	0.0	0.0	0.0
Memo:										
IBRD	0.0	0.0	0.0	0.0	0.0	0.0	0.0	0.0	0.0	0.0
IDA	0.0	0.0	1.3	3.4	1.9	2.6	1.1	3.3	4.7	5.7
DEBT SERVICE (LTDS)	..	**0.2**	**7.8**	**6.5**	**5.6**	**8.6**	**11.1**	**5.3**	**6.2**	**5.1**
Public and publicly guaranteed	..	**0.2**	**7.8**	**6.5**	**5.6**	**8.6**	**11.1**	**5.3**	**6.2**	**5.1**
Official creditors	..	0.2	7.6	6.3	5.5	8.3	10.9	5.3	6.2	5.1
Multilateral	..	0.0	5.2	4.2	3.7	6.2	7.0	4.2	5.3	4.3
Concessional	..	0.0	2.6	2.6	2.0	3.6	5.2	2.1	2.8	2.8
Bilateral	..	0.1	2.4	2.1	1.8	2.1	3.9	1.1	0.9	0.7
Concessional	..	0.0	0.5	0.4	0.2	0.8	1.7	0.6	0.4	0.3
Private creditors	..	0.0	0.2	0.1	0.1	0.3	0.2	0.0	0.0	0.0
Bonds	..	0.0	0.0	0.0	0.0	0.0	0.0	0.0	0.0	0.0
Commercial banks	..	0.0	0.0	0.0	0.0	0.0	0.0	0.0	0.0	0.0
Other private	..	0.0	0.2	0.1	0.1	0.3	0.2	0.0	0.0	0.0
Private nonguaranteed	**0.0**	**0.0**	**0.0**	**0.0**	**0.0**	**0.0**	**0.0**	**0.0**	**0.0**	**0.0**
Bonds	..	0.0	0.0	0.0	0.0	0.0	0.0	0.0	0.0	0.0
Commercial banks	..	0.0	0.0	0.0	0.0	0.0	0.0	0.0	0.0	0.0
Memo:										
IBRD	0.0	0.0	0.0	0.0	0.0	0.0	0.0	0.0	0.0	0.0
IDA	0.0	0.0	0.1	0.1	0.1	0.1	0.1	0.2	0.2	0.4
UNDISBURSED DEBT	..	**60.7**	**68.0**	**69.8**	**99.9**	**106.1**	**124.2**	**161.3**	**175.8**	**172.9**
Official creditors	..	60.7	68.0	69.8	99.9	106.1	124.2	161.3	163.8	160.9
Private creditors	..	0.0	0.0	0.0	0.0	0.0	0.0	0.0	12.0	12.0
Memorandum items										
Concessional LDOD	..	20.3	94.0	100.0	101.3	103.7	112.5	119.8	148.8	166.7
Variable rate LDOD	..	0.0	0.0	0.0	0.0	0.0	0.0	0.0	0.0	0.0
Public sector LDOD	..	20.8	122.0	125.3	130.6	130.3	136.1	141.6	168.6	185.2
Private sector LDOD	..	0.0	0.0	0.0	0.0	0.0	0.0	0.0	0.0	0.0

6. CURRENCY COMPOSITION OF LONG-TERM DEBT (PERCENT)

	1970	1980	1988	1989	1990	1991	1992	1993	1994	1995
Deutsche mark	..	0.0	0.0	0.0	0.0	0.0	0.0	0.0	0.0	0.0
French franc	..	0.0	5.8	5.9	0.0	0.0	0.0	0.0	0.0	0.0
Japanese yen	..	0.0	0.0	0.0	0.0	0.0	0.0	0.0	0.0	0.0
Pound sterling	..	0.0	0.0	0.0	0.0	0.0	0.0	0.0	0.0	0.0
Swiss franc	..	0.0	0.0	0.0	0.0	0.0	0.0	0.0	0.0	0.0
U.S.dollars	..	77.5	34.3	35.0	38.1	38.5	35.1	35.9	34.0	35.5
Multiple currency	..	0.5	17.5	16.2	15.9	14.6	12.7	11.3	8.8	7.6
Special drawing rights	..	0.0	0.0	0.0	0.1	0.6	0.8	1.8	3.3	3.7
All other currencies	..	21.7	42.5	42.9	45.9	46.3	51.4	51.0	53.8	53.2

CAPE VERDE

(US$ million, unless otherwise indicated)

	1970	1980	1988	1989	1990	1991	1992	1993	1994	1995
7. DEBT RESTRUCTURINGS										
Total amount rescheduled	0.0	0.0	0.0	0.0	0.0	0.0	0.0	0.0	0.0	0.0
Debt stock rescheduled	0.0	0.0	0.0	0.0	0.0	0.0	0.0	0.0	0.0	0.0
Principal rescheduled	0.0	0.0	0.0	0.0	0.0	0.0	0.0	0.0	0.0	0.0
Official	0.0	0.0	0.0	0.0	0.0	0.0	0.0	0.0	0.0	0.0
Private	0.0	0.0	0.0	0.0	0.0	0.0	0.0	0.0	0.0	0.0
Interest rescheduled	0.0	0.0	0.0	0.0	0.0	0.0	0.0	0.0	0.0	0.0
Official	0.0	0.0	0.0	0.0	0.0	0.0	0.0	0.0	0.0	0.0
Private	0.0	0.0	0.0	0.0	0.0	0.0	0.0	0.0	0.0	0.0
Debt forgiven	..	..	0.0	0.0	8.2	0.0	0.0	0.0	0.0	0.0
Memo: interest forgiven	..	..	0.0	0.0	0.8	0.0	0.0	0.0	0.0	0.0
Debt stock reduction	0.0	0.0	0.0	0.0	0.0	0.0	0.0	0.0	0.0	0.0
of which debt buyback	0.0	0.0	0.0	0.0	0.0	0.0	0.0	0.0	0.0	0.0
8. DEBT STOCK-FLOW RECONCILIATION										
Total change in debt stocks	..	..	..	1.2	7.6	-0.3	7.2	7.2	30.4	36.5
Net flows on debt	..	..	..	4.0	10.7	-0.6	11.6	6.6	26.0	32.6
Net change in interest arrears	..	..	..	0.7	-0.2	0.1	-0.3	1.8	1.3	1.3
Interest capitalized	..	..	..	0.0	0.0	0.0	0.0	0.0	0.0	0.0
Debt forgiveness or reduction	..	..	..	0.0	-8.2	0.0	0.0	0.0	0.0	0.0
Cross-currency valuation	..	..	..	-0.7	3.9	-0.2	-2.8	-1.1	4.5	2.4
Residual	..	..	..	-2.8	1.3	0.5	-1.4	0.0	-1.4	0.2
9. AVERAGE TERMS OF NEW COMMITMENTS										
ALL CREDITORS										
Interest (%)	..	3.1	1.8	1.0	1.5	0.5	2.0	2.0	3.2	0.8
Maturity (years)	..	17.8	29.4	45.6	35.6	34.7	29.4	31.0	21.8	39.8
Grace period (years)	..	5.3	7.0	9.4	8.7	10.2	7.0	8.0	5.0	10.3
Grant element (%)	..	45.2	60.1	77.4	70.9	78.0	61.7	62.4	45.2	80.6
Official creditors										
Interest (%)	..	3.1	1.8	1.0	1.5	0.5	2.0	2.0	2.5	0.8
Maturity (years)	..	17.8	29.4	45.6	35.6	34.7	29.4	31.0	25.9	39.8
Grace period (years)	..	5.3	7.0	9.4	8.7	10.2	7.0	8.0	6.1	10.3
Grant element (%)	..	45.2	60.1	77.4	70.9	78.0	61.7	62.4	54.2	80.6
Private creditors										
Interest (%)	..	0.0	0.0	0.0	0.0	0.0	0.0	0.0	5.0	0.0
Maturity (years)	..	0.0	0.0	0.0	0.0	0.0	0.0	0.0	12.0	0.0
Grace period (years)	..	0.0	0.0	0.0	0.0	0.0	0.0	0.0	2.5	0.0
Grant element (%)	..	0.0	0.0	0.0	0.0	0.0	0.0	0.0	23.4	0.0
Memorandum items										
Commitments	..	43.8	20.7	14.6	35.9	11.2	49.0	48.6	41.3	11.5
Official creditors	..	43.8	20.7	14.6	35.9	11.2	49.0	48.6	29.3	11.5
Private creditors	..	0.0	0.0	0.0	0.0	0.0	0.0	0.0	12.0	0.0

10. CONTRACTUAL OBLIGATIONS ON OUTSTANDING LONG-TERM DEBT

	1996	1997	1998	1999	2000	2001	2002	2003	2004	2005
TOTAL										
Disbursements	37.7	45.5	33.2	22.7	14.6	8.8	6.2	1.9	0.6	0.0
Principal	8.2	11.7	13.3	14.5	12.9	13.2	11.9	12.3	12.7	12.8
Interest	3.0	3.6	3.8	3.9	3.7	3.6	3.4	3.2	3.0	2.7
Official creditors										
Disbursements	33.6	40.9	31.0	22.0	14.3	8.8	6.2	1.9	0.6	0.0
Principal	7.9	10.2	11.9	13.3	11.7	12.0	10.7	11.1	11.5	11.6
Interest	2.8	3.1	3.4	3.4	3.3	3.3	3.2	3.0	2.8	2.6
Bilateral creditors										
Disbursements	5.2	4.9	3.2	1.9	1.1	0.8	0.6	0.2	0.0	0.0
Principal	3.1	3.8	3.8	3.8	2.2	2.0	1.4	1.8	1.8	1.8
Interest	0.7	0.7	0.6	0.6	0.5	0.5	0.5	0.5	0.4	0.4
Multilateral creditors										
Disbursements	28.4	36.0	27.8	20.1	13.2	8.0	5.6	1.6	0.6	0.0
Principal	4.8	6.4	8.1	9.5	9.6	10.0	9.3	9.3	9.8	9.8
Interest	2.1	2.4	2.7	2.8	2.8	2.8	2.7	2.5	2.4	2.2
Private creditors										
Disbursements	4.1	4.6	2.3	0.7	0.4	0.0	0.0	0.0	0.0	0.0
Principal	0.2	1.4	1.3	1.2	1.2	1.2	1.2	1.2	1.2	1.2
Interest	0.2	0.4	0.5	0.4	0.4	0.3	0.3	0.2	0.2	0.1
Commercial banks										
Disbursements	0.0	0.0	0.0	0.0	0.0	0.0	0.0	0.0	0.0	0.0
Principal	0.0	0.0	0.0	0.0	0.0	0.0	0.0	0.0	0.0	0.0
Interest	0.0	0.0	0.0	0.0	0.0	0.0	0.0	0.0	0.0	0.0
Other private										
Disbursements	4.1	4.6	2.3	0.7	0.4	0.0	0.0	0.0	0.0	0.0
Principal	0.2	1.4	1.3	1.2	1.2	1.2	1.2	1.2	1.2	1.2
Interest	0.2	0.4	0.5	0.4	0.4	0.3	0.3	0.2	0.2	0.1

CENTRAL AFRICAN REPUBLIC

(US$ million, unless otherwise indicated)

	1970	1980	1988	1989	1990	1991	1992	1993	1994	1995
1. SUMMARY DEBT DATA										
TOTAL DEBT STOCKS (EDT)	**..**	**194.7**	**668.8**	**693.5**	**698.5**	**794.2**	**813.9**	**872.6**	**884.3**	**943.9**
Long-term debt (LDOD)	**24.1**	**146.5**	**580.1**	**621.4**	**624.1**	**716.9**	**729.6**	**770.6**	**798.5**	**852.0**
Public and publicly guaranteed	24.1	146.5	580.1	621.4	624.1	716.9	729.6	770.6	798.5	852.0
Private nonguaranteed	0.0	0.0	0.0	0.0	0.0	0.0	0.0	0.0	0.0	0.0
Use of IMF credit	**0.0**	**23.5**	**50.3**	**35.3**	**36.7**	**33.3**	**30.4**	**28.8**	**41.4**	**34.9**
Short-term debt	**..**	**24.6**	**38.4**	**36.8**	**37.7**	**44.0**	**53.9**	**73.1**	**44.5**	**57.1**
of which interest arrears on LDOD	..	10.6	12.6	17.0	15.0	18.3	27.9	39.1	25.5	35.7
Official creditors	..	1.7	11.6	15.6	13.1	16.4	24.6	35.3	24.0	31.7
Private creditors	..	8.8	1.0	1.3	1.9	1.9	3.3	3.7	1.5	3.9
Memo: principal arrears on LDOD	..	43.5	8.3	13.8	23.2	35.7	50.7	69.3	56.5	72.6
Official creditors	..	16.9	6.0	11.2	19.6	29.9	43.4	60.2	51.3	60.7
Private creditors	..	26.7	2.4	2.6	3.6	5.7	7.3	9.1	5.2	11.9
Memo: export credits	..	..	59.0	57.0	63.0	51.0	50.0	51.0	39.0	35.0
TOTAL DEBT FLOWS										
Disbursements	**1.7**	**39.8**	**102.5**	**63.8**	**121.1**	**97.5**	**45.9**	**48.7**	**58.7**	**32.6**
Long-term debt	1.7	25.2	90.2	63.8	112.8	97.5	45.9	48.7	43.3	32.6
IMF purchases	0.0	14.7	12.3	0.0	8.3	0.0	0.0	0.0	15.3	0.0
Principal repayments	**2.4**	**6.7**	**16.1**	**21.6**	**17.4**	**6.9**	**6.8**	**3.3**	**12.5**	**10.2**
Long-term debt	2.4	1.0	4.8	8.2	7.6	3.5	5.1	1.7	7.7	2.8
IMF repurchases	0.0	5.7	11.2	13.4	9.8	3.4	1.7	1.6	4.8	7.4
Net flows on debt	**-0.7**	**33.1**	**89.7**	**36.2**	**106.6**	**93.6**	**39.4**	**53.4**	**31.2**	**24.8**
of which short-term debt	..	..	3.3	-6.0	2.9	3.0	0.3	8.0	-15.0	2.4
Interest payments (INT)	**..**	**3.3**	**11.0**	**12.0**	**11.8**	**8.2**	**8.7**	**5.9**	**10.8**	**5.7**
Long-term debt	0.7	0.4	7.7	7.9	9.0	5.9	6.6	3.5	8.1	3.4
IMF charges	0.0	0.8	1.4	1.9	1.2	0.7	0.3	0.2	0.7	1.0
Short-term debt	..	2.1	1.9	2.1	1.6	1.6	1.8	2.2	2.0	1.2
Net transfers on debt	**..**	**29.8**	**78.8**	**24.2**	**94.9**	**85.4**	**30.7**	**47.5**	**20.4**	**19.2**
Total debt service paid (TDS)	**..**	**10.0**	**27.0**	**33.6**	**29.1**	**15.1**	**15.5**	**9.2**	**23.3**	**15.8**
Long-term debt	3.1	1.4	12.5	16.1	16.6	9.4	11.7	5.3	15.9	6.2
IMF repurchases and charges	0.0	6.5	12.6	15.4	11.0	4.1	1.9	1.8	5.4	8.4
Short-term debt (interest only)	..	2.1	1.9	2.1	1.6	1.6	1.8	2.2	2.0	1.2
2. AGGREGATE NET RESOURCE FLOWS AND NET TRANSFERS (LONG-TERM)										
NET RESOURCE FLOWS	**6.9**	**85.2**	**161.5**	**134.3**	**192.4**	**162.1**	**121.5**	**127.5**	**137.1**	**139.4**
Net flow of long-term debt (ex. IMF)	-0.7	24.1	85.4	55.6	105.2	94.0	40.8	47.0	35.6	29.8
Foreign direct investment (net)	1.2	5.3	-3.8	1.3	1.0	-5.0	-11.0	-10.0	4.0	3.0
Portfolio equity flows	0.0	0.0	0.0	0.0	0.0	0.0	0.0	0.0	0.0	0.0
Grants (excluding technical coop.)	6.4	55.8	79.9	77.4	86.2	73.1	91.7	90.5	97.5	106.6
Memo: technical coop. grants	8.1	34.2	53.1	49.5	56.9	54.8	54.0	54.0	43.8	48.5
NET TRANSFERS	**4.8**	**84.9**	**153.9**	**124.5**	**181.4**	**154.8**	**114.9**	**124.0**	**128.4**	**135.4**
Interest on long-term debt	0.7	0.4	7.7	7.9	9.0	5.9	6.6	3.5	8.1	3.4
Profit remittances on FDI	1.4	0.0	0.0	1.9	2.1	1.5	0.0	0.0	0.5	0.6
3. MAJOR ECONOMIC AGGREGATES										
Gross national product (GNP)	178.6	799.4	1,080.4	1,133.5	1,278.9	1,253.8	1,310.6	1,210.2	856.3	..
Exports of goods & services (XGS)	..	205.4	196.0	214.3	220.4	181.6	167.4	186.2	179.0	233.7
of which workers remittances	..	0.0	0.0	0.0	0.0	0.0	0.0	0.0	0.0	0.0
Imports of goods & services (MGS)	..	329.2	351.3	351.9	432.5	334.3	363.9	313.2	267.1	318.8
International reserves (RES)	1.4	61.7	113.0	117.5	122.9	106.9	103.8	116.3	214.3	237.9
Current account balance	..	-43.1	-34.6	-33.4	-89.1	-61.8	-83.1	-13.0	-24.7	-25.0
4. DEBT INDICATORS										
EDT / XGS (%)	..	94.8	341.2	323.6	316.9	437.3	486.2	468.6	494.0	403.9
EDT / GNP (%)	..	24.4	61.9	61.2	54.6	63.3	62.1	72.1	103.3	..
TDS / XGS (%)	..	4.9	13.8	15.7	13.2	8.3	9.3	5.0	13.0	6.8
INT / XGS (%)	..	1.6	5.6	5.6	5.3	4.5	5.2	3.2	6.0	2.4
INT / GNP (%)	..	0.4	1.0	1.1	0.9	0.7	0.7	0.5	1.3	..
RES / EDT (%)	..	31.7	16.9	16.9	17.6	13.5	12.8	13.3	24.2	25.2
RES / MGS (months)	..	2.2	3.9	4.0	3.4	3.8	3.4	4.5	9.6	9.0
Short-term / EDT (%)	..	12.6	5.7	5.3	5.4	5.5	6.6	8.4	5.0	6.0
Concessional / EDT (%)	..	30.1	66.1	71.2	73.1	76.7	77.2	77.2	81.4	80.7
Multilateral / EDT (%)	..	27.4	43.2	48.2	65.2	62.6	62.1	61.2	66.8	67.2

CENTRAL AFRICAN REPUBLIC

(US$ million, unless otherwise indicated)

	1970	1980	1988	1989	1990	1991	1992	1993	1994	1995
5. LONG-TERM DEBT										
DEBT OUTSTANDING (LDOD)	**24.1**	**146.5**	**580.1**	**621.4**	**624.1**	**716.9**	**729.6**	**770.6**	**798.5**	**852.0**
Public and publicly guaranteed	**24.1**	**146.5**	**580.1**	**621.4**	**624.1**	**716.9**	**729.6**	**770.6**	**798.5**	**852.0**
Official creditors	17.9	98.3	557.1	600.2	602.6	695.8	709.4	751.0	782.3	835.2
Multilateral	0.2	53.3	288.9	334.5	455.5	497.2	505.4	533.9	590.6	634.7
Concessional	0.2	41.6	262.8	310.6	429.4	474.8	485.6	514.6	577.4	619.4
Bilateral	17.7	44.9	268.3	265.7	147.0	198.6	204.0	217.1	191.7	200.5
Concessional	14.8	17.0	179.4	183.3	81.5	134.2	142.9	158.6	142.6	142.7
Private creditors	6.1	48.3	23.0	21.2	21.6	21.2	20.2	19.7	16.2	16.8
Bonds	0.0	0.0	0.0	0.0	0.0	0.0	0.0	0.0	0.0	0.0
Commercial banks	0.0	0.0	0.0	0.0	0.0	0.0	0.0	0.0	0.0	0.0
Other private	6.1	48.3	23.0	21.2	21.6	21.2	20.2	19.7	16.2	16.8
Private nonguaranteed	**0.0**	**0.0**	**0.0**	**0.0**	**0.0**	**0.0**	**0.0**	**0.0**	**0.0**	**0.0**
Bonds	0.0	0.0	0.0	0.0	0.0	0.0	0.0	0.0	0.0	0.0
Commercial banks	0.0	0.0	0.0	0.0	0.0	0.0	0.0	0.0	0.0	0.0
Memo:										
IBRD	0.0	0.0	0.0	0.0	0.0	0.0	0.0	0.0	0.0	0.0
IDA	0.2	28.8	160.3	179.5	265.1	290.3	299.5	323.2	377.2	414.0
DISBURSEMENTS	**1.7**	**25.2**	**90.2**	**63.8**	**112.8**	**97.5**	**45.9**	**48.7**	**43.3**	**32.6**
Public and publicly guaranteed	**1.7**	**25.2**	**90.2**	**63.8**	**112.8**	**97.5**	**45.9**	**48.7**	**43.3**	**32.6**
Official creditors	1.5	25.2	89.0	63.8	112.8	97.5	45.9	48.7	43.3	32.6
Multilateral	0.2	13.7	52.5	52.9	95.2	44.7	32.6	30.6	43.3	32.6
Concessional	0.2	13.5	50.3	52.3	93.6	42.3	32.1	30.6	43.3	32.0
Bilateral	1.3	11.5	36.6	10.9	17.6	52.9	13.3	18.1	0.0	0.0
Concessional	1.0	5.5	28.2	10.9	16.1	52.9	13.3	18.1	0.0	0.0
Private creditors	0.2	0.0	1.2	0.0	0.0	0.0	0.0	0.0	0.0	0.0
Bonds	0.0	0.0	0.0	0.0	0.0	0.0	0.0	0.0	0.0	0.0
Commercial banks	0.0	0.0	0.0	0.0	0.0	0.0	0.0	0.0	0.0	0.0
Other private	0.2	0.0	1.2	0.0	0.0	0.0	0.0	0.0	0.0	0.0
Private nonguaranteed	**0.0**	**0.0**	**0.0**	**0.0**	**0.0**	**0.0**	**0.0**	**0.0**	**0.0**	**0.0**
Bonds	0.0	0.0	0.0	0.0	0.0	0.0	0.0	0.0	0.0	0.0
Commercial banks	0.0	0.0	0.0	0.0	0.0	0.0	0.0	0.0	0.0	0.0
Memo:										
IBRD	0.0	0.0	0.0	0.0	0.0	0.0	0.0	0.0	0.0	0.0
IDA	0.2	10.3	39.4	22.0	70.4	23.3	20.7	23.7	40.1	29.8
PRINCIPAL REPAYMENTS	**2.4**	**1.0**	**4.8**	**8.2**	**7.6**	**3.5**	**5.1**	**1.7**	**7.7**	**2.8**
Public and publicly guaranteed	**2.4**	**1.0**	**4.8**	**8.2**	**7.6**	**3.5**	**5.1**	**1.7**	**7.7**	**2.8**
Official creditors	1.1	0.1	4.1	6.5	7.0	3.3	4.5	1.7	7.5	2.8
Multilateral	0.0	0.1	2.1	3.9	3.2	3.0	4.3	1.7	6.5	2.8
Concessional	0.0	0.1	1.0	1.4	1.8	1.7	2.1	1.2	4.4	2.4
Bilateral	1.1	0.0	2.0	2.6	3.8	0.2	0.2	0.0	1.0	0.0
Concessional	0.5	0.0	1.3	0.5	0.9	0.2	0.2	0.0	1.0	0.0
Private creditors	1.4	0.9	0.7	1.7	0.6	0.3	0.6	0.0	0.2	0.0
Bonds	0.0	0.0	0.0	0.0	0.0	0.0	0.0	0.0	0.0	0.0
Commercial banks	0.0	0.0	0.0	0.0	0.0	0.0	0.0	0.0	0.0	0.0
Other private	1.4	0.9	0.7	1.7	0.6	0.3	0.6	0.0	0.2	0.0
Private nonguaranteed	**0.0**	**0.0**	**0.0**	**0.0**	**0.0**	**0.0**	**0.0**	**0.0**	**0.0**	**0.0**
Bonds	0.0	0.0	0.0	0.0	0.0	0.0	0.0	0.0	0.0	0.0
Commercial banks	0.0	0.0	0.0	0.0	0.0	0.0	0.0	0.0	0.0	0.0
Memo:										
IBRD	0.0	0.0	0.0	0.0	0.0	0.0	0.0	0.0	0.0	0.0
IDA	0.0	0.1	0.2	0.3	0.5	0.5	0.8	1.0	1.2	1.3
NET FLOWS ON DEBT	**-0.7**	**24.1**	**85.4**	**55.6**	**105.2**	**94.0**	**40.8**	**47.0**	**35.6**	**29.8**
Public and publicly guaranteed	**-0.7**	**24.1**	**85.4**	**55.6**	**105.2**	**94.0**	**40.8**	**47.0**	**35.6**	**29.8**
Official creditors	0.4	25.0	85.0	57.3	105.8	94.3	41.4	47.0	35.8	29.8
Multilateral	0.2	13.6	50.4	49.0	92.0	41.6	28.3	28.9	36.8	29.8
Concessional	0.2	13.4	49.3	51.0	91.8	40.7	30.0	29.4	38.9	29.6
Bilateral	0.2	11.4	34.6	8.3	13.8	52.6	13.0	18.1	-1.0	0.0
Concessional	0.5	5.5	26.9	10.4	15.2	52.7	13.1	18.1	-1.0	0.0
Private creditors	-1.2	-0.9	0.5	-1.7	-0.6	-0.3	-0.6	0.0	-0.2	0.0
Bonds	0.0	0.0	0.0	0.0	0.0	0.0	0.0	0.0	0.0	0.0
Commercial banks	0.0	0.0	0.0	0.0	0.0	0.0	0.0	0.0	0.0	0.0
Other private	-1.2	-0.9	0.5	-1.7	-0.6	-0.3	-0.6	0.0	-0.2	0.0
Private nonguaranteed	**0.0**	**0.0**	**0.0**	**0.0**	**0.0**	**0.0**	**0.0**	**0.0**	**0.0**	**0.0**
Bonds	0.0	0.0	0.0	0.0	0.0	0.0	0.0	0.0	0.0	0.0
Commercial banks	0.0	0.0	0.0	0.0	0.0	0.0	0.0	0.0	0.0	0.0
Memo:										
IBRD	0.0	0.0	0.0	0.0	0.0	0.0	0.0	0.0	0.0	0.0
IDA	0.2	10.2	39.2	21.7	69.9	22.8	19.9	22.7	38.9	28.5

CENTRAL AFRICAN REPUBLIC

(US$ million, unless otherwise indicated)

	1970	1980	1988	1989	1990	1991	1992	1993	1994	1995
INTEREST PAYMENTS (LINT)	**0.7**	**0.4**	**7.7**	**7.9**	**9.0**	**5.9**	**6.6**	**3.5**	**8.1**	**3.4**
Public and publicly guaranteed	**0.7**	**0.4**	**7.7**	**7.9**	**9.0**	**5.9**	**6.6**	**3.5**	**8.1**	**3.4**
Official creditors	0.3	0.3	7.5	7.9	8.1	5.3	6.6	3.5	8.0	3.4
Multilateral	0.0	0.3	3.6	4.2	5.1	4.9	3.7	3.4	7.9	3.4
Concessional	0.0	0.2	1.8	2.2	2.8	3.0	2.9	2.4	6.3	3.3
Bilateral	0.3	0.0	4.0	3.7	3.1	0.3	2.9	0.1	0.1	0.0
Concessional	0.2	0.0	3.5	1.1	1.9	0.3	2.7	0.0	0.1	0.0
Private creditors	0.4	0.1	0.1	0.0	0.8	0.6	0.0	0.0	0.1	0.0
Bonds	0.0	0.0	0.0	0.0	0.0	0.0	0.0	0.0	0.0	0.0
Commercial banks	0.0	0.0	0.0	0.0	0.0	0.0	0.0	0.0	0.0	0.0
Other private	0.4	0.1	0.1	0.0	0.8	0.6	0.0	0.0	0.1	0.0
Private nonguaranteed	**0.0**	**0.0**	**0.0**	**0.0**	**0.0**	**0.0**	**0.0**	**0.0**	**0.0**	**0.0**
Bonds	0.0	0.0	0.0	0.0	0.0	0.0	0.0	0.0	0.0	0.0
Commercial banks	0.0	0.0	0.0	0.0	0.0	0.0	0.0	0.0	0.0	0.0
Memo:										
IBRD	0.0	0.0	0.0	0.0	0.0	0.0	0.0	0.0	0.0	0.0
IDA	0.0	0.2	1.1	1.2	1.5	2.0	2.1	2.1	2.8	2.9
NET TRANSFERS ON DEBT	**-1.4**	**23.8**	**77.8**	**47.7**	**96.3**	**88.2**	**34.2**	**43.5**	**27.4**	**26.4**
Public and publicly guaranteed	**-1.4**	**23.8**	**77.8**	**47.7**	**96.3**	**88.2**	**34.2**	**43.5**	**27.4**	**26.4**
Official creditors	0.1	24.7	77.4	49.3	97.6	89.0	34.8	43.5	27.8	26.4
Multilateral	0.2	13.3	46.8	44.7	86.9	36.7	24.6	25.5	28.9	26.4
Concessional	0.2	13.2	47.4	48.8	88.9	37.7	27.1	26.9	32.6	26.3
Bilateral	-0.1	11.4	30.6	4.6	10.7	52.3	10.2	18.0	-1.1	0.0
Concessional	0.3	5.5	23.4	9.3	13.4	52.4	10.4	18.1	-1.1	0.0
Private creditors	-1.6	-0.9	0.3	-1.7	-1.4	-0.9	-0.6	0.0	-0.4	0.0
Bonds	0.0	0.0	0.0	0.0	0.0	0.0	0.0	0.0	0.0	0.0
Commercial banks	0.0	0.0	0.0	0.0	0.0	0.0	0.0	0.0	0.0	0.0
Other private	-1.6	-0.9	0.3	-1.7	-1.4	-0.9	-0.6	0.0	-0.4	0.0
Private nonguaranteed	**0.0**	**0.0**	**0.0**	**0.0**	**0.0**	**0.0**	**0.0**	**0.0**	**0.0**	**0.0**
Bonds	0.0	0.0	0.0	0.0	0.0	0.0	0.0	0.0	0.0	0.0
Commercial banks	0.0	0.0	0.0	0.0	0.0	0.0	0.0	0.0	0.0	0.0
Memo:										
IBRD	0.0	0.0	0.0	0.0	0.0	0.0	0.0	0.0	0.0	0.0
IDA	0.2	10.0	38.1	20.5	68.4	20.9	17.8	20.6	36.1	25.6
DEBT SERVICE (LTDS)	**3.1**	**1.4**	**12.5**	**16.1**	**16.6**	**9.4**	**11.7**	**5.3**	**15.9**	**6.2**
Public and publicly guaranteed	**3.1**	**1.4**	**12.5**	**16.1**	**16.6**	**9.4**	**11.7**	**5.3**	**15.9**	**6.2**
Official creditors	1.4	0.5	11.6	14.4	15.2	8.5	11.2	5.3	15.5	6.2
Multilateral	0.0	0.4	5.7	8.2	8.3	8.0	8.0	5.1	14.4	6.2
Concessional	0.0	0.3	2.8	3.5	4.6	4.7	4.9	3.6	10.7	5.7
Bilateral	1.4	0.1	5.9	6.3	6.9	0.5	3.1	0.1	1.1	0.0
Concessional	0.6	0.0	4.8	1.6	2.7	0.5	2.9	0.0	1.1	0.0
Private creditors	1.8	0.9	0.9	1.7	1.4	0.9	0.6	0.0	0.4	0.0
Bonds	0.0	0.0	0.0	0.0	0.0	0.0	0.0	0.0	0.0	0.0
Commercial banks	0.0	0.0	0.0	0.0	0.0	0.0	0.0	0.0	0.0	0.0
Other private	1.8	0.9	0.9	1.7	1.4	0.9	0.6	0.0	0.4	0.0
Private nonguaranteed	**0.0**	**0.0**	**0.0**	**0.0**	**0.0**	**0.0**	**0.0**	**0.0**	**0.0**	**0.0**
Bonds	0.0	0.0	0.0	0.0	0.0	0.0	0.0	0.0	0.0	0.0
Commercial banks	0.0	0.0	0.0	0.0	0.0	0.0	0.0	0.0	0.0	0.0
Memo:										
IBRD	0.0	0.0	0.0	0.0	0.0	0.0	0.0	0.0	0.0	0.0
IDA	0.0	0.3	1.3	1.6	2.0	2.5	2.9	3.1	4.0	4.2
UNDISBURSED DEBT	**12.6**	**60.7**	**116.9**	**159.8**	**235.8**	**234.4**	**221.2**	**176.8**	**123.1**	**108.9**
Official creditors	10.8	60.7	116.9	159.8	235.8	234.4	221.2	176.8	123.1	108.9
Private creditors	1.7	0.0	0.0	0.0	0.0	0.0	0.0	0.0	0.0	0.0
Memorandum items										
Concessional LDOD	15.1	58.6	442.3	493.9	510.9	608.9	628.5	673.3	720.0	762.1
Variable rate LDOD	0.0	2.8	0.0	0.0	0.0	0.0	0.0	0.0	5.2	6.3
Public sector LDOD	24.1	146.5	579.2	620.4	624.1	716.6	729.1	770.2	798.2	851.7
Private sector LDOD	0.0	0.0	1.0	1.0	0.0	0.3	0.5	0.5	0.2	0.3

6. CURRENCY COMPOSITION OF LONG-TERM DEBT (PERCENT)

	1970	1980	1988	1989	1990	1991	1992	1993	1994	1995
Deutsche mark	19.5	1.2	0.7	0.6	0.7	0.6	0.5	0.5	0.4	0.4
French franc	39.9	16.9	33.9	31.5	11.0	10.5	10.2	10.1	5.3	5.2
Japanese yen	0.0	0.0	0.3	0.6	0.7	0.7	0.7	0.7	0.8	0.7
Pound sterling	0.4	0.8	0.1	0.1	0.1	0.1	0.1	0.1	0.1	0.0
Swiss franc	0.0	7.5	2.2	2.0	2.6	2.1	1.9	1.8	2.6	2.8
U.S.dollars	1.7	35.8	30.0	30.6	43.6	47.1	49.0	50.8	55.6	56.4
Multiple currency	0.0	7.5	13.8	16.8	21.5	20.3	20.0	19.1	19.3	18.5
Special drawing rights	0.0	0.0	6.6	6.8	7.6	7.0	6.8	6.7	7.0	6.7
All other currencies	37.8	30.4	12.4	11.0	12.2	11.6	10.8	10.3	9.0	9.2

CENTRAL AFRICAN REPUBLIC

(US$ million, unless otherwise indicated)

	1970	1980	1988	1989	1990	1991	1992	1993	1994	1995
7. DEBT RESTRUCTURINGS										
Total amount rescheduled	0.0	..	12.7	21.9	4.4	0.0	0.0	0.0	38.9	8.3
Debt stock rescheduled	0.0	..	0.0	14.5	0.0	0.0	0.0	0.0	0.0	0.0
Principal rescheduled	0.0	..	12.3	6.8	2.6	0.0	0.0	0.0	21.3	4.9
Official	0.0	..	12.3	6.8	2.6	0.0	0.0	0.0	13.0	4.9
Private	0.0	..	0.0	0.0	0.0	0.0	0.0	0.0	8.4	0.0
Interest rescheduled	0.0	..	0.2	0.2	0.3	0.0	0.0	0.0	12.9	0.9
Official	0.0	..	0.2	0.2	0.3	0.0	0.0	0.0	11.4	0.9
Private	0.0	..	0.0	0.0	0.0	0.0	0.0	0.0	1.5	0.0
Debt forgiven	..	..	2.0	16.7	153.1	4.6	0.0	0.0	49.2	1.0
Memo: interest forgiven	..	..	0.5	0.7	4.4	0.0	0.0	0.0	4.5	0.2
Debt stock reduction	0.0	..	0.0	0.0	0.0	0.0	0.0	0.0	0.0	0.0
of which debt buyback	0.0	..	0.0	0.0	0.0	0.0	0.0	0.0	0.0	0.0
8. DEBT STOCK-FLOW RECONCILIATION										
Total change in debt stocks	..	..	..	24.7	5.0	95.7	19.7	58.7	11.8	59.6
Net flows on debt	..	..	..	36.2	106.6	93.6	39.4	53.4	31.2	24.8
Net change in interest arrears	..	..	..	4.4	-1.9	3.2	9.6	11.2	-13.6	10.2
Interest capitalized	..	..	..	0.2	0.3	0.0	0.0	0.0	12.9	0.9
Debt forgiveness or reduction	..	..	..	-16.7	-153.1	-4.6	0.0	0.0	-49.2	-1.0
Cross-currency valuation	..	..	..	6.5	20.9	-2.0	-11.8	-7.6	7.4	11.4
Residual	..	..	..	-5.9	32.2	5.5	-17.5	1.7	23.1	13.3
9. AVERAGE TERMS OF NEW COMMITMENTS										
ALL CREDITORS										
Interest (%)	2.0	0.6	0.9	1.1	1.0	3.4	2.1	0.7	0.0	0.8
Maturity (years)	35.8	12.5	36.1	36.5	37.6	27.8	34.0	49.6	0.0	39.7
Grace period (years)	7.9	4.3	9.7	9.4	10.2	7.8	8.7	10.5	0.0	10.2
Grant element (%)	62.8	39.0	76.4	74.3	77.0	48.7	65.5	83.2	0.0	80.5
Official creditors										
Interest (%)	1.0	0.6	0.9	1.1	1.0	3.4	2.1	0.7	0.0	0.8
Maturity (years)	47.5	12.5	36.1	36.5	37.6	27.8	34.0	49.6	0.0	39.7
Grace period (years)	9.9	4.3	9.7	9.4	10.2	7.8	8.7	10.5	0.0	10.2
Grant element (%)	79.6	39.0	76.4	74.3	77.0	48.7	65.5	83.2	0.0	80.5
Private creditors										
Interest (%)	4.6	0.0	0.0	0.0	0.0	0.0	0.0	0.0	0.0	0.0
Maturity (years)	8.0	0.0	0.0	0.0	0.0	0.0	0.0	0.0	0.0	0.0
Grace period (years)	3.4	0.0	0.0	0.0	0.0	0.0	0.0	0.0	0.0	0.0
Grant element (%)	23.0	0.0	0.0	0.0	0.0	0.0	0.0	0.0	0.0	0.0
Memorandum items										
Commitments	6.5	38.4	74.4	111.9	174.9	96.6	42.6	12.0	0.0	16.6
Official creditors	4.6	38.4	74.4	111.9	174.9	96.6	42.6	12.0	0.0	16.6
Private creditors	1.9	0.0	0.0	0.0	0.0	0.0	0.0	0.0	0.0	0.0

10. CONTRACTUAL OBLIGATIONS ON OUTSTANDING LONG-TERM DEBT

	1996	1997	1998	1999	2000	2001	2002	2003	2004	2005
TOTAL										
Disbursements	39.8	31.0	17.0	10.7	4.9	2.5	1.9	0.7	0.1	0.0
Principal	24.9	21.7	24.1	24.5	27.7	27.5	26.1	24.8	24.8	24.1
Interest	11.6	11.1	10.7	10.0	9.3	8.6	8.0	7.4	6.9	6.3
Official creditors										
Disbursements	39.8	31.0	17.0	10.7	4.9	2.5	1.9	0.7	0.1	0.0
Principal	20.0	21.7	24.1	24.5	27.7	27.5	26.1	24.8	24.8	24.1
Interest	11.3	11.1	10.7	10.0	9.3	8.6	8.0	7.4	6.9	6.3
Bilateral creditors										
Disbursements	2.0	1.5	1.1	0.8	0.5	0.5	0.4	0.3	0.0	0.0
Principal	9.3	10.2	11.8	12.1	13.9	12.8	12.1	11.1	10.2	8.8
Interest	5.6	5.3	4.8	4.4	3.9	3.4	3.0	2.5	2.1	1.7
Multilateral creditors										
Disbursements	37.8	29.5	15.9	9.9	4.4	2.0	1.4	0.4	0.1	0.0
Principal	10.7	11.4	12.3	12.3	13.8	14.6	14.0	13.8	14.6	15.2
Interest	5.8	5.8	5.8	5.6	5.4	5.2	5.0	4.9	4.8	4.6
Private creditors										
Disbursements	0.0	0.0	0.0	0.0	0.0	0.0	0.0	0.0	0.0	0.0
Principal	4.9	0.0	0.0	0.0	0.0	0.0	0.0	0.0	0.0	0.0
Interest	0.2	0.0	0.0	0.0	0.0	0.0	0.0	0.0	0.0	0.0
Commercial banks										
Disbursements	0.0	0.0	0.0	0.0	0.0	0.0	0.0	0.0	0.0	0.0
Principal	0.0	0.0	0.0	0.0	0.0	0.0	0.0	0.0	0.0	0.0
Interest	0.0	0.0	0.0	0.0	0.0	0.0	0.0	0.0	0.0	0.0
Other private										
Disbursements	0.0	0.0	0.0	0.0	0.0	0.0	0.0	0.0	0.0	0.0
Principal	4.9	0.0	0.0	0.0	0.0	0.0	0.0	0.0	0.0	0.0
Interest	0.2	0.0	0.0	0.0	0.0	0.0	0.0	0.0	0.0	0.0

CHAD

(US$ million, unless otherwise indicated)

	1970	1980	1988	1989	1990	1991	1992	1993	1994	1995
1. SUMMARY DEBT DATA										
TOTAL DEBT STOCKS (EDT)	..	**285.3**	**392.1**	**398.5**	**530.0**	**634.2**	**727.9**	**771.3**	**824.8**	**908.4**
Long-term debt (LDOD)	**32.5**	**260.0**	**337.8**	**346.8**	**469.7**	**565.1**	**676.0**	**717.2**	**755.1**	**839.6**
Public and publicly guaranteed	32.5	260.0	337.8	346.8	469.7	565.1	676.0	717.2	755.1	839.6
Private nonguaranteed	0.0	0.0	0.0	0.0	0.0	0.0	0.0	0.0	0.0	0.0
Use of IMF credit	**2.5**	**13.8**	**16.5**	**23.6**	**30.5**	**30.6**	**29.5**	**27.7**	**42.8**	**49.0**
Short-term debt	..	**11.5**	**37.8**	**28.2**	**29.8**	**38.5**	**22.4**	**26.3**	**26.8**	**19.9**
of which interest arrears on LDOD	..	6.5	26.6	6.9	6.2	9.5	13.0	15.9	18.8	11.4
Official creditors	..	4.5	12.8	5.3	4.4	7.7	11.3	14.2	17.1	11.2
Private creditors	..	2.0	13.8	1.6	1.8	1.8	1.7	1.6	1.8	0.2
Memo: principal arrears on LDOD	..	31.7	59.6	18.8	15.7	20.0	25.3	26.3	31.7	32.6
Official creditors	..	12.0	26.7	16.3	13.1	17.0	21.9	23.5	28.4	32.6
Private creditors	..	19.7	32.8	2.4	2.7	3.1	3.4	2.8	3.3	0.1
Memo: export credits	..	..	40.0	40.0	52.0	53.0	49.0	30.0	39.0	45.0
TOTAL DEBT FLOWS										
Disbursements	**9.6**	**5.2**	**60.8**	**92.8**	**112.4**	**92.2**	**143.2**	**57.4**	**76.1**	**68.8**
Long-term debt	5.8	5.2	60.8	81.1	104.1	92.2	143.2	57.4	61.4	56.3
IMF purchases	3.8	0.0	0.0	11.8	8.3	0.0	0.0	0.0	14.8	12.5
Principal repayments	**2.5**	**5.4**	**5.4**	**8.2**	**6.8**	**4.4**	**4.0**	**8.0**	**9.5**	**10.2**
Long-term debt	2.5	2.6	3.1	3.7	3.2	4.4	4.0	6.3	7.7	3.2
IMF repurchases	0.0	2.8	2.3	4.5	3.6	0.0	0.0	1.7	1.8	7.0
Net flows on debt	**7.0**	**-0.3**	**56.9**	**94.8**	**107.9**	**97.0**	**119.7**	**50.4**	**64.3**	**59.1**
of which short-term debt	..	..	1.5	10.1	2.3	9.2	-19.5	1.0	-2.4	0.5
Interest payments (INT)	..	**0.6**	**4.2**	**3.8**	**5.3**	**6.5**	**7.0**	**9.2**	**8.7**	**5.5**
Long-term debt	0.4	0.0	3.6	1.7	3.3	4.7	5.7	8.1	7.7	4.1
IMF charges	0.0	0.5	0.6	0.6	0.3	0.2	0.2	0.1	0.5	1.0
Short-term debt	..	0.0	0.0	1.5	1.6	1.6	1.1	1.0	0.4	0.5
Net transfers on debt	..	**-0.8**	**52.7**	**91.0**	**102.6**	**90.5**	**112.7**	**41.2**	**55.6**	**53.6**
Total debt service paid (TDS)	..	**6.0**	**9.6**	**12.0**	**12.1**	**10.9**	**10.9**	**17.2**	**18.1**	**15.7**
Long-term debt	2.9	2.7	6.7	5.4	6.6	9.1	9.7	14.4	15.4	7.3
IMF repurchases and charges	0.0	3.3	2.9	5.1	3.9	0.2	0.2	1.9	2.3	7.9
Short-term debt (interest only)	..	0.0	0.0	1.5	1.6	1.6	1.1	1.0	0.4	0.5
2. AGGREGATE NET RESOURCE FLOWS AND NET TRANSFERS (LONG-TERM)										
NET RESOURCE FLOWS	**15.3**	**24.1**	**210.4**	**223.2**	**247.6**	**204.5**	**253.2**	**172.1**	**175.2**	**180.8**
Net flow of long-term debt (ex. IMF)	3.3	2.5	57.7	77.4	100.9	87.8	139.2	51.1	53.6	53.1
Foreign direct investment (net)	0.6	0.0	1.3	18.7	0.0	4.0	2.0	15.0	7.0	7.0
Portfolio equity flows	0.0	0.0	0.0	0.0	0.0	0.0	0.0	0.0	0.0	0.0
Grants (excluding technical coop.)	11.4	21.6	151.4	127.1	146.7	112.7	112.0	106.0	114.6	120.7
Memo: technical coop. grants	10.0	11.8	54.5	51.8	61.0	66.5	69.5	73.6	51.0	66.3
NET TRANSFERS	**13.2**	**24.1**	**206.8**	**221.5**	**244.3**	**199.8**	**258.7**	**164.1**	**167.5**	**176.7**
Interest on long-term debt	0.4	0.0	3.6	1.7	3.3	4.7	5.7	8.1	7.7	4.1
Profit remittances on FDI	1.7	0.0	0.0	0.0	0.0	0.0	-11.2	0.0	0.0	0.0
3. MAJOR ECONOMIC AGGREGATES										
Gross national product (GNP)	328.8	723.0	816.2	962.0	1,167.6	1,258.5	1,298.1	1,180.4	897.0	1,116.5
Exports of goods & services (XGS)	..	71.4	227.2	199.8	274.2	233.4	226.8	204.4	195.7	268.0
of which workers remittances	..	0.0	0.4	0.8	0.0	0.0	0.2	1.4	0.7	1.0
Imports of goods & services (MGS)	..	83.2	461.8	461.0	511.5	469.1	482.1	464.7	424.0	525.0
International reserves (RES)	2.3	11.8	67.6	116.2	132.1	123.7	84.2	43.3	80.3	146.8
Current account balance	..	8.6	25.5	-55.9	-45.6	-65.6	-85.7	-117.0	-38.0	-180.0
4. DEBT INDICATORS										
EDT / XGS (%)	..	399.6	172.6	199.5	193.3	271.7	321.0	377.3	421.4	339.0
EDT / GNP (%)	..	39.5	48.0	41.4	45.4	50.4	56.1	65.3	91.9	81.4
TDS / XGS (%)	..	8.4	4.2	6.0	4.4	4.6	4.8	8.4	9.3	5.9
INT / XGS (%)	..	0.8	1.8	1.9	1.9	2.8	3.1	4.5	4.4	2.1
INT / GNP (%)	..	0.1	0.5	0.4	0.5	0.5	0.5	0.8	1.0	0.5
RES / EDT (%)	..	4.1	17.2	29.2	24.9	19.5	11.6	5.6	9.7	16.2
RES / MGS (months)	..	1.7	1.8	3.0	3.1	3.2	2.1	1.1	2.3	3.4
Short-term / EDT (%)	..	4.0	9.6	7.1	5.6	6.1	3.1	3.4	3.3	2.2
Concessional / EDT (%)	..	60.0	69.4	75.6	77.3	79.3	75.1	77.7	81.8	81.8
Multilateral / EDT (%)	..	26.1	46.2	59.9	62.4	62.8	69.5	71.7	72.5	73.0

CHAD

(US$ million, unless otherwise indicated)

	1970	1980	1988	1989	1990	1991	1992	1993	1994	1995
5. LONG-TERM DEBT										
DEBT OUTSTANDING (LDOD)	**32.5**	**260.0**	**337.8**	**346.8**	**469.7**	**565.1**	**676.0**	**717.2**	**755.1**	**839.6**
Public and publicly guaranteed	**32.5**	**260.0**	**337.8**	**346.8**	**469.7**	**565.1**	**676.0**	**717.2**	**755.1**	**839.6**
Official creditors	24.7	206.3	298.4	338.5	461.1	557.1	668.8	711.5	749.2	837.4
Multilateral	1.5	74.5	181.3	238.9	330.9	398.3	506.2	552.9	598.1	663.3
Concessional	1.5	74.5	178.6	235.8	323.8	391.5	428.9	483.9	560.1	621.8
Bilateral	23.1	131.7	117.1	99.6	130.2	158.8	162.6	158.6	151.1	174.1
Concessional	22.6	96.6	93.6	65.5	86.1	111.4	117.4	115.2	114.8	121.4
Private creditors	7.9	53.7	39.4	8.3	8.6	8.0	7.2	5.7	5.9	2.2
Bonds	0.0	0.0	0.0	0.0	0.0	0.0	0.0	0.0	0.0	0.0
Commercial banks	0.6	0.5	0.0	0.0	0.0	0.0	0.0	0.0	0.0	0.0
Other private	7.3	53.3	39.4	8.3	8.6	8.0	7.2	5.7	5.9	2.2
Private nonguaranteed	**0.0**	**0.0**	**0.0**	**0.0**	**0.0**	**0.0**	**0.0**	**0.0**	**0.0**	**0.0**
Bonds	0.0	0.0	0.0	0.0	0.0	0.0	0.0	0.0	0.0	0.0
Commercial banks	0.0	0.0	0.0	0.0	0.0	0.0	0.0	0.0	0.0	0.0
Memo:										
IBRD	0.0	0.0	0.0	0.0	0.0	0.0	0.0	0.0	0.0	0.0
IDA	0.3	36.1	97.6	129.9	186.4	234.9	259.1	284.0	332.0	378.8
DISBURSEMENTS	**5.8**	**5.2**	**60.8**	**81.1**	**104.1**	**92.2**	**143.2**	**57.4**	**61.4**	**56.3**
Public and publicly guaranteed	**5.8**	**5.2**	**60.8**	**81.1**	**104.1**	**92.2**	**143.2**	**57.4**	**61.4**	**56.3**
Official creditors	2.7	5.2	59.8	81.1	104.1	92.2	143.2	57.4	61.4	56.3
Multilateral	0.2	5.2	41.1	60.5	71.5	66.9	130.0	54.8	60.0	55.9
Concessional	0.2	5.2	40.9	60.1	70.8	66.7	56.1	54.8	60.0	55.9
Bilateral	2.5	0.0	18.7	20.6	32.6	25.3	13.2	2.7	1.3	0.4
Concessional	1.9	0.0	18.2	19.8	25.5	25.2	13.2	2.7	1.3	0.4
Private creditors	3.1	0.0	1.1	0.0	0.0	0.0	0.0	0.0	0.0	0.0
Bonds	0.0	0.0	0.0	0.0	0.0	0.0	0.0	0.0	0.0	0.0
Commercial banks	0.1	0.0	0.0	0.0	0.0	0.0	0.0	0.0	0.0	0.0
Other private	3.0	0.0	1.1	0.0	0.0	0.0	0.0	0.0	0.0	0.0
Private nonguaranteed	**0.0**	**0.0**	**0.0**	**0.0**	**0.0**	**0.0**	**0.0**	**0.0**	**0.0**	**0.0**
Bonds	0.0	0.0	0.0	0.0	0.0	0.0	0.0	0.0	0.0	0.0
Commercial banks	0.0	0.0	0.0	0.0	0.0	0.0	0.0	0.0	0.0	0.0
Memo:										
IBRD	0.0	0.0	0.0	0.0	0.0	0.0	0.0	0.0	0.0	0.0
IDA	0.2	0.4	37.5	34.2	48.2	46.4	33.2	24.5	37.7	41.7
PRINCIPAL REPAYMENTS	**2.5**	**2.6**	**3.1**	**3.7**	**3.2**	**4.4**	**4.0**	**6.3**	**7.7**	**3.2**
Public and publicly guaranteed	**2.5**	**2.6**	**3.1**	**3.7**	**3.2**	**4.4**	**4.0**	**6.3**	**7.7**	**3.2**
Official creditors	1.4	2.6	2.8	3.1	2.7	3.9	3.6	5.1	7.4	3.2
Multilateral	0.0	2.0	2.2	3.0	2.6	3.3	3.0	4.6	5.9	2.5
Concessional	0.0	2.0	2.0	2.9	2.2	2.8	2.8	1.2	5.9	2.5
Bilateral	1.4	0.6	0.6	0.1	0.1	0.6	0.7	0.5	1.5	0.7
Concessional	1.4	0.6	0.0	0.0	0.0	0.0	0.1	0.0	0.0	0.0
Private creditors	1.1	0.0	0.3	0.6	0.6	0.5	0.4	1.2	0.3	0.0
Bonds	0.0	0.0	0.0	0.0	0.0	0.0	0.0	0.0	0.0	0.0
Commercial banks	0.1	0.0	0.0	0.0	0.0	0.0	0.0	0.0	0.0	0.0
Other private	1.0	0.0	0.3	0.6	0.6	0.5	0.4	1.2	0.3	0.0
Private nonguaranteed	**0.0**	**0.0**	**0.0**	**0.0**	**0.0**	**0.0**	**0.0**	**0.0**	**0.0**	**0.0**
Bonds	0.0	0.0	0.0	0.0	0.0	0.0	0.0	0.0	0.0	0.0
Commercial banks	0.0	0.0	0.0	0.0	0.0	0.0	0.0	0.0	0.0	0.0
Memo:										
IBRD	0.0	0.0	0.0	0.0	0.0	0.0	0.0	0.0	0.0	0.0
IDA	0.0	0.0	0.6	1.6	0.7	0.7	0.8	0.4	1.6	1.2
NET FLOWS ON DEBT	**3.3**	**2.5**	**57.7**	**77.4**	**100.9**	**87.8**	**139.2**	**51.1**	**53.6**	**53.1**
Public and publicly guaranteed	**3.3**	**2.5**	**57.7**	**77.4**	**100.9**	**87.8**	**139.2**	**51.1**	**53.6**	**53.1**
Official creditors	1.2	2.5	57.0	78.0	101.5	88.3	139.6	52.3	53.9	53.1
Multilateral	0.2	3.1	38.8	57.5	68.9	63.6	127.1	50.2	54.1	53.4
Concessional	0.2	3.1	39.0	57.2	68.5	64.0	53.4	53.5	54.1	53.4
Bilateral	1.1	-0.6	18.1	20.5	32.5	24.6	12.5	2.2	-0.2	-0.3
Concessional	0.6	-0.6	18.2	19.8	25.5	25.2	13.1	2.7	1.3	0.4
Private creditors	2.0	0.0	0.7	-0.6	-0.6	-0.5	-0.4	-1.2	-0.3	0.0
Bonds	0.0	0.0	0.0	0.0	0.0	0.0	0.0	0.0	0.0	0.0
Commercial banks	0.0	0.0	0.0	0.0	0.0	0.0	0.0	0.0	0.0	0.0
Other private	2.0	0.0	0.7	-0.6	-0.6	-0.5	-0.4	-1.2	-0.3	0.0
Private nonguaranteed	**0.0**	**0.0**	**0.0**	**0.0**	**0.0**	**0.0**	**0.0**	**0.0**	**0.0**	**0.0**
Bonds	0.0	0.0	0.0	0.0	0.0	0.0	0.0	0.0	0.0	0.0
Commercial banks	0.0	0.0	0.0	0.0	0.0	0.0	0.0	0.0	0.0	0.0
Memo:										
IBRD	0.0	0.0	0.0	0.0	0.0	0.0	0.0	0.0	0.0	0.0
IDA	0.2	0.4	36.9	32.6	47.6	45.7	32.4	24.1	36.1	40.5

CHAD

(US$ million, unless otherwise indicated)

	1970	1980	1988	1989	1990	1991	1992	1993	1994	1995
INTEREST PAYMENTS (LINT)	**0.4**	**0.0**	**3.6**	**1.7**	**3.3**	**4.7**	**5.7**	**8.1**	**7.7**	**4.1**
Public and publicly guaranteed	**0.4**	**0.0**	**3.6**	**1.7**	**3.3**	**4.7**	**5.7**	**8.1**	**7.7**	**4.1**
Official creditors	0.3	0.0	3.5	1.5	3.1	4.5	5.6	7.9	7.6	4.0
Multilateral	0.0	0.0	1.4	1.5	2.2	2.7	4.0	5.9	5.8	3.8
Concessional	0.0	0.0	1.3	1.3	1.9	2.5	2.8	2.7	3.9	3.3
Bilateral	0.3	0.0	2.1	0.0	1.0	1.8	1.6	2.0	1.8	0.2
Concessional	0.2	0.0	1.8	0.0	0.8	1.3	1.2	1.7	1.5	0.0
Private creditors	0.1	0.0	0.1	0.2	0.2	0.2	0.1	0.1	0.1	0.0
Bonds	0.0	0.0	0.0	0.0	0.0	0.0	0.0	0.0	0.0	0.0
Commercial banks	0.0	0.0	0.0	0.0	0.0	0.0	0.0	0.0	0.0	0.0
Other private	0.1	0.0	0.1	0.2	0.2	0.2	0.1	0.1	0.1	0.0
Private nonguaranteed	**0.0**	**0.0**	**0.0**	**0.0**	**0.0**	**0.0**	**0.0**	**0.0**	**0.0**	**0.0**
Bonds	0.0	0.0	0.0	0.0	0.0	0.0	0.0	0.0	0.0	0.0
Commercial banks	0.0	0.0	0.0	0.0	0.0	0.0	0.0	0.0	0.0	0.0
Memo:										
IBRD	0.0	0.0	0.0	0.0	0.0	0.0	0.0	0.0	0.0	0.0
IDA	0.0	0.0	0.7	0.7	1.1	1.4	1.8	1.7	2.5	2.8
NET TRANSFERS ON DEBT	**2.9**	**2.5**	**54.1**	**75.7**	**97.6**	**83.1**	**133.5**	**43.1**	**45.9**	**49.0**
Public and publicly guaranteed	**2.9**	**2.5**	**54.1**	**75.7**	**97.6**	**83.1**	**133.5**	**43.1**	**45.9**	**49.0**
Official creditors	1.0	2.5	53.5	76.5	98.3	83.7	134.0	44.4	46.3	49.1
Multilateral	0.2	3.1	37.4	55.9	66.8	60.9	123.1	44.3	48.2	49.6
Concessional	0.2	3.1	37.6	55.9	66.7	61.5	50.6	50.8	50.2	50.1
Bilateral	0.8	-0.6	16.0	20.5	31.6	22.8	10.9	0.1	-1.9	-0.5
Concessional	0.3	-0.6	16.4	19.8	24.7	24.0	11.9	0.9	-0.1	0.4
Private creditors	1.9	0.0	0.7	-0.8	-0.8	-0.6	-0.5	-1.4	-0.4	0.0
Bonds	0.0	0.0	0.0	0.0	0.0	0.0	0.0	0.0	0.0	0.0
Commercial banks	0.0	0.0	0.0	0.0	0.0	0.0	0.0	0.0	0.0	0.0
Other private	1.9	0.0	0.7	-0.8	-0.8	-0.6	-0.5	-1.4	-0.4	0.0
Private nonguaranteed	**0.0**	**0.0**	**0.0**	**0.0**	**0.0**	**0.0**	**0.0**	**0.0**	**0.0**	**0.0**
Bonds	0.0	0.0	0.0	0.0	0.0	0.0	0.0	0.0	0.0	0.0
Commercial banks	0.0	0.0	0.0	0.0	0.0	0.0	0.0	0.0	0.0	0.0
Memo:										
IBRD	0.0	0.0	0.0	0.0	0.0	0.0	0.0	0.0	0.0	0.0
IDA	0.2	0.3	36.2	31.9	46.5	44.3	30.6	22.4	33.6	37.7
DEBT SERVICE (LTDS)	**2.9**	**2.7**	**6.7**	**5.4**	**6.6**	**9.1**	**9.7**	**14.4**	**15.4**	**7.3**
Public and publicly guaranteed	**2.9**	**2.7**	**6.7**	**5.4**	**6.6**	**9.1**	**9.7**	**14.4**	**15.4**	**7.3**
Official creditors	1.7	2.7	6.3	4.6	5.8	8.4	9.2	13.0	15.0	7.2
Multilateral	0.0	2.1	3.6	4.5	4.8	6.0	7.0	10.5	11.8	6.3
Concessional	0.0	2.1	3.3	4.2	4.1	5.2	5.6	4.0	9.8	5.8
Bilateral	1.7	0.6	2.7	0.1	1.0	2.5	2.2	2.5	3.3	0.9
Concessional	1.6	0.6	1.8	0.0	0.8	1.3	1.3	1.7	1.5	0.0
Private creditors	1.2	0.0	0.4	0.8	0.8	0.6	0.5	1.4	0.4	0.0
Bonds	0.0	0.0	0.0	0.0	0.0	0.0	0.0	0.0	0.0	0.0
Commercial banks	0.1	0.0	0.0	0.0	0.0	0.0	0.0	0.0	0.0	0.0
Other private	1.1	0.0	0.4	0.8	0.8	0.6	0.5	1.4	0.4	0.0
Private nonguaranteed	**0.0**	**0.0**	**0.0**	**0.0**	**0.0**	**0.0**	**0.0**	**0.0**	**0.0**	**0.0**
Bonds	0.0	0.0	0.0	0.0	0.0	0.0	0.0	0.0	0.0	0.0
Commercial banks	0.0	0.0	0.0	0.0	0.0	0.0	0.0	0.0	0.0	0.0
Memo:										
IBRD	0.0	0.0	0.0	0.0	0.0	0.0	0.0	0.0	0.0	0.0
IDA	0.0	0.0	1.3	2.3	1.8	2.2	2.5	2.1	4.1	4.0
UNDISBURSED DEBT	**17.8**	**93.9**	**269.6**	**369.0**	**360.6**	**344.2**	**296.6**	**276.3**	**287.0**	**338.9**
Official creditors	10.8	75.5	269.6	369.0	360.6	344.2	296.6	276.3	287.0	338.9
Private creditors	7.0	18.3	0.0	0.0	0.0	0.0	0.0	0.0	0.0	0.0
Memorandum items										
Concessional LDOD	24.1	171.1	272.2	301.3	409.9	502.9	546.3	599.1	674.9	743.3
Variable rate LDOD	0.0	0.5	0.0	0.0	0.0	0.0	0.0	0.0	0.0	0.0
Public sector LDOD	32.5	260.0	331.9	346.2	469.2	564.6	675.6	716.9	754.8	839.3
Private sector LDOD	0.0	0.0	5.9	0.6	0.6	0.5	0.4	0.3	0.3	0.2

6. CURRENCY COMPOSITION OF LONG-TERM DEBT (PERCENT)

	1970	1980	1988	1989	1990	1991	1992	1993	1994	1995
Deutsche mark	10.8	2.7	2.0	1.9	1.5	1.1	0.8	0.7	0.7	0.1
French franc	35.1	14.4	20.8	6.2	10.3	10.0	9.5	8.7	9.3	11.1
Japanese yen	0.0	0.0	0.0	0.0	0.0	0.0	0.0	0.0	0.0	0.0
Pound sterling	1.2	0.2	0.1	0.1	0.1	0.1	0.0	0.0	0.0	0.0
Swiss franc	0.0	0.0	0.0	0.0	0.0	0.0	0.0	0.0	0.0	0.0
U.S.dollars	4.0	18.8	33.0	47.9	48.2	48.5	44.4	45.0	49.2	49.7
Multiple currency	3.7	9.6	18.2	25.2	25.4	25.5	22.7	24.1	26.7	26.1
Special drawing rights	0.0	0.0	0.0	0.0	0.0	0.0	0.0	0.0	0.1	0.2
All other currencies	44.9	54.2	25.9	18.8	14.6	14.9	22.5	21.5	14.1	12.8

CHAD

(US$ million, unless otherwise indicated)

	1970	1980	1988	1989	1990	1991	1992	1993	1994	1995
7. DEBT RESTRUCTURINGS										
Total amount rescheduled	0.0	0.0	0.0	40.2	7.8	3.9	0.0	0.0	0.0	17.6
Debt stock rescheduled	0.0	0.0	0.0	0.0	0.0	3.8	0.0	0.0	0.0	0.0
Principal rescheduled	0.0	0.0	0.0	34.2	3.1	0.0	0.0	0.0	0.0	2.2
Official	0.0	0.0	0.0	11.5	2.5	0.0	0.0	0.0	0.0	0.8
Private	0.0	0.0	0.0	22.8	0.6	0.0	0.0	0.0	0.0	1.4
Interest rescheduled	0.0	0.0	0.0	5.6	1.4	0.0	0.0	0.0	0.0	7.7
Official	0.0	0.0	0.0	0.0	1.3	0.0	0.0	0.0	0.0	7.1
Private	0.0	0.0	0.0	5.6	0.1	0.0	0.0	0.0	0.0	0.6
Debt forgiven	..	..	0.0	66.7	7.0	0.0	0.0	0.0	0.0	4.4
Memo: interest forgiven	..	..	0.0	13.7	0.0	0.0	0.0	0.0	0.0	8.3
Debt stock reduction	0.0	0.0	0.0	0.0	0.0	0.0	0.0	0.0	0.0	0.0
of which debt buyback	0.0	0.0	0.0	0.0	0.0	0.0	0.0	0.0	0.0	0.0
8. DEBT STOCK-FLOW RECONCILIATION										
Total change in debt stocks	..	..	..	6.4	131.5	104.2	93.7	43.3	53.5	83.7
Net flows on debt	..	..	..	94.8	107.9	97.0	119.7	50.4	64.3	59.1
Net change in interest arrears	..	..	..	-19.7	-0.7	3.3	3.5	2.9	3.0	-7.5
Interest capitalized	..	..	..	5.6	1.4	0.0	0.0	0.0	0.0	7.7
Debt forgiveness or reduction	..	..	..	-66.7	-7.0	0.0	0.0	0.0	0.0	-4.4
Cross-currency valuation	..	..	..	-3.3	9.2	-2.1	-13.1	-10.7	-17.7	13.8
Residual	..	..	..	-4.3	20.6	6.0	-16.4	0.8	3.9	14.9
9. AVERAGE TERMS OF NEW COMMITMENTS										
ALL CREDITORS										
Interest (%)	5.7	0.0	0.9	1.3	1.4	0.8	4.5	0.8	0.8	0.8
Maturity (years)	8.3	0.0	40.8	39.7	32.3	49.6	27.9	42.5	39.8	42.3
Grace period (years)	1.0	0.0	10.1	9.9	9.6	10.1	6.8	13.7	10.3	15.4
Grant element (%)	14.3	0.0	79.0	75.1	70.8	83.0	38.3	81.3	80.7	82.5
Official creditors										
Interest (%)	3.7	0.0	0.9	1.3	1.4	0.8	4.5	0.8	0.8	0.8
Maturity (years)	10.0	0.0	40.8	39.7	32.3	49.6	27.9	42.5	39.8	42.3
Grace period (years)	1.8	0.0	10.1	9.9	9.6	10.1	6.8	13.7	10.3	15.4
Grant element (%)	25.5	0.0	79.0	75.1	70.8	83.0	38.3	81.3	80.7	82.5
Private creditors										
Interest (%)	6.3	0.0	0.0	0.0	0.0	0.0	0.0	0.0	0.0	0.0
Maturity (years)	7.8	0.0	0.0	0.0	0.0	0.0	0.0	0.0	0.0	0.0
Grace period (years)	0.7	0.0	0.0	0.0	0.0	0.0	0.0	0.0	0.0	0.0
Grant element (%)	11.1	0.0	0.0	0.0	0.0	0.0	0.0	0.0	0.0	0.0
Memorandum items										
Commitments	9.8	0.0	175.9	182.5	73.2	73.2	117.3	75.0	55.9	96.2
Official creditors	2.2	0.0	175.9	182.5	73.2	73.2	117.3	75.0	55.9	96.2
Private creditors	7.6	0.0	0.0	0.0	0.0	0.0	0.0	0.0	0.0	0.0

10. CONTRACTUAL OBLIGATIONS ON OUTSTANDING LONG-TERM DEBT

	1996	1997	1998	1999	2000	2001	2002	2003	2004	2005
TOTAL										
Disbursements	65.8	93.4	70.4	50.6	33.6	17.1	7.6	0.6	0.0	0.0
Principal	11.7	15.1	20.2	24.0	25.4	27.7	29.1	29.2	27.2	28.1
Interest	12.7	13.0	13.0	12.7	12.1	11.5	10.8	10.7	10.6	10.0
Official creditors										
Disbursements	65.8	93.4	70.4	50.6	33.6	17.1	7.6	0.6	0.0	0.0
Principal	10.8	14.8	20.0	23.8	25.1	27.6	29.1	29.2	27.2	28.1
Interest	12.6	13.0	13.0	12.7	12.1	11.5	10.8	10.7	10.6	10.0
Bilateral creditors										
Disbursements	0.2	0.1	0.0	0.0	0.0	0.0	0.0	0.0	0.0	0.0
Principal	4.0	5.8	7.7	9.7	9.8	11.0	11.0	11.1	7.7	7.5
Interest	4.6	4.5	4.2	3.8	3.3	3.0	2.5	2.8	3.1	2.9
Multilateral creditors										
Disbursements	65.6	93.3	70.4	50.6	33.6	17.1	7.6	0.6	0.0	0.0
Principal	6.9	9.0	12.3	14.1	15.3	16.6	18.1	18.1	19.5	20.6
Interest	8.0	8.5	8.8	8.9	8.8	8.6	8.3	7.9	7.5	7.1
Private creditors										
Disbursements	0.0	0.0	0.0	0.0	0.0	0.0	0.0	0.0	0.0	0.0
Principal	0.8	0.2	0.2	0.2	0.2	0.1	0.0	0.0	0.0	0.0
Interest	0.1	0.0	0.0	0.0	0.0	0.0	0.0	0.0	0.0	0.0
Commercial banks										
Disbursements	0.0	0.0	0.0	0.0	0.0	0.0	0.0	0.0	0.0	0.0
Principal	0.0	0.0	0.0	0.0	0.0	0.0	0.0	0.0	0.0	0.0
Interest	0.0	0.0	0.0	0.0	0.0	0.0	0.0	0.0	0.0	0.0
Other private										
Disbursements	0.0	0.0	0.0	0.0	0.0	0.0	0.0	0.0	0.0	0.0
Principal	0.8	0.2	0.2	0.2	0.2	0.1	0.0	0.0	0.0	0.0
Interest	0.1	0.0	0.0	0.0	0.0	0.0	0.0	0.0	0.0	0.0

CHILE

(US$ million, unless otherwise indicated)

	1970	1980	1988	1989	1990	1991	1992	1993	1994	1995
1. SUMMARY DEBT DATA										
TOTAL DEBT STOCKS (EDT)	**..**	**12,081**	**19,582**	**18,032**	**19,227**	**17,947**	**19,134**	**20,637**	**24,722**	**25,562**
Long-term debt (LDOD)	**2,568**	**9,399**	**16,058**	**13,789**	**14,689**	**14,790**	**15,181**	**16,031**	**17,993**	**18,607**
Public and publicly guaranteed	2,067	4,705	13,696	10,866	10,426	10,071	9,578	8,868	8,989	7,178
Private nonguaranteed	501	4,693	2,361	2,924	4,263	4,720	5,603	7,164	9,004	11,429
Use of IMF credit	**2**	**123**	**1,322**	**1,270**	**1,157**	**958**	**722**	**476**	**291**	**0**
Short-term debt	**..**	**2,560**	**2,202**	**2,973**	**3,382**	**2,199**	**3,231**	**4,130**	**6,438**	**6,955**
of which interest arrears on LDOD	..	0	0	0	0	0	0	0	0	0
Official creditors	..	0	0	0	0	0	0	0	0	0
Private creditors	..	0	0	0	0	0	0	0	0	0
Memo: principal arrears on LDOD	..	0	0	0	0	0	0	0	0	0
Official creditors	..	0	0	0	0	0	0	0	0	0
Private creditors	..	0	0	0	0	0	0	0	0	0
Memo: export credits	..	..	1,598	1,782	2,062	2,145	2,064	2,242	2,585	2,637
TOTAL DEBT FLOWS										
Disbursements	**655**	**3,551**	**1,761**	**1,682**	**2,253**	**1,645**	**1,736**	**2,183**	**2,922**	**3,819**
Long-term debt	655	3,551	1,560	1,504	2,253	1,645	1,736	2,183	2,922	3,819
IMF purchases	0	0	202	178	0	0	0	0	0	0
Principal repayments	**254**	**1,513**	**885**	**1,032**	**980**	**1,144**	**1,353**	**1,722**	**1,699**	**3,663**
Long-term debt	207	1,462	617	833	771	947	1,150	1,472	1,488	3,360
IMF repurchases	47	52	269	199	209	196	203	249	211	303
Net flows on debt	**401**	**2,038**	**1,061**	**1,422**	**1,682**	**-682**	**1,415**	**1,360**	**3,532**	**673**
of which short-term debt	..	..	185	771	409	-1,183	1,032	899	2,308	517
Interest payments (INT)	**..**	**1,193**	**1,262**	**1,636**	**1,792**	**1,556**	**1,340**	**1,121**	**1,241**	**1,487**
Long-term debt	104	918	1,007	1,286	1,364	1,249	1,135	933	929	1,114
IMF charges	0	12	92	104	118	97	70	43	22	13
Short-term debt	..	262	163	246	310	209	136	145	290	360
Net transfers on debt	**..**	**845**	**-201**	**-215**	**-110**	**-2,238**	**74**	**239**	**2,291**	**-814**
Total debt service paid (TDS)	**..**	**2,706**	**2,147**	**2,668**	**2,772**	**2,700**	**2,693**	**2,842**	**2,940**	**5,150**
Long-term debt	312	2,380	1,624	2,119	2,135	2,197	2,285	2,405	2,417	4,475
IMF repurchases and charges	47	64	360	303	327	294	273	292	232	316
Short-term debt (interest only)	..	262	163	246	310	209	136	145	290	360
2. AGGREGATE NET RESOURCE FLOWS AND NET TRANSFERS (LONG-TERM)										
NET RESOURCE FLOWS	**381**	**2,312**	**1,136**	**2,232**	**2,465**	**1,317**	**1,664**	**2,008**	**4,141**	**2,481**
Net flow of long-term debt (ex. IMF)	448	2,089	943	671	1,481	698	586	710	1,434	459
Foreign direct investment (net)	-79	213	141	1,289	590	523	699	809	1,773	1,695
Portfolio equity flows	0	0	26	230	320	0	323	405	867	274
Grants (excluding technical coop.)	12	9	26	42	73	96	56	84	67	53
Memo: technical coop. grants	19	37	52	50	71	84	94	99	94	100
NET TRANSFERS	**173**	**1,307**	**-178**	**561**	**766**	**-576**	**-368**	**277**	**2,262**	**367**
Interest on long-term debt	104	918	1,007	1,286	1,364	1,249	1,135	933	929	1,114
Profit remittances on FDI	104	86	307	385	335	644	897	798	950	1,000
3. MAJOR ECONOMIC AGGREGATES										
Gross national product (GNP)	7,987	26,544	22,172	26,195	28,523	32,545	40,839	44,081	50,346	59,059
Exports of goods & services (XGS)	..	6,276	8,327	9,816	10,641	11,582	12,880	12,298	14,947	20,014
of which workers remittances	..	0	0	0	0	0	0	0	0	0
Imports of goods & services (MGS)	..	8,360	8,743	10,736	11,377	11,814	14,014	14,741	15,947	20,214
International reserves (RES)	392	4,128	3,909	4,331	6,784	7,700	9,790	10,369	13,802	14,860
Current account balance	..	-1,971	-234	-705	-536	109	-703	-2,073	-646	157
4. DEBT INDICATORS										
EDT / XGS (%)	..	192.5	235.2	183.7	180.7	155.0	148.6	167.8	165.4	127.7
EDT / GNP (%)	..	45.5	88.3	68.8	67.4	55.1	46.9	46.8	49.1	43.3
TDS / XGS (%)	..	43.1	25.8	27.2	26.0	23.3	20.9	23.1	19.7	25.7
INT / XGS (%)	..	19.0	15.2	16.7	16.8	13.4	10.4	9.1	8.3	7.4
INT / GNP (%)	..	4.5	5.7	6.2	6.3	4.8	3.3	2.5	2.5	2.5
RES / EDT (%)	..	34.2	20.0	24.0	35.3	42.9	51.2	50.2	55.8	58.1
RES / MGS (months)	..	5.9	5.4	4.8	7.2	7.8	8.4	8.4	10.4	8.8
Short-term / EDT (%)	..	21.2	11.2	16.5	17.6	12.3	16.9	20.0	26.0	27.2
Concessional / EDT (%)	..	6.2	2.7	2.8	2.3	2.1	1.7	1.5	1.4	1.4
Multilateral / EDT (%)	..	2.9	17.3	19.7	21.5	24.0	22.6	21.0	17.7	11.2

CHILE

(US$ million, unless otherwise indicated)

	1970	1980	1988	1989	1990	1991	1992	1993	1994	1995
5. LONG-TERM DEBT										
DEBT OUTSTANDING (LDOD)	**2,568**	**9,399**	**16,058**	**13,789**	**14,689**	**14,790**	**15,181**	**16,031**	**17,993**	**18,607**
Public and publicly guaranteed	**2,067**	**4,705**	**13,696**	**10,866**	**10,426**	**10,071**	**9,578**	**8,868**	**8,989**	**7,178**
Official creditors	1,180	1,360	4,467	4,592	5,182	5,280	5,187	5,104	5,150	3,584
Multilateral	177	351	3,391	3,550	4,143	4,315	4,333	4,327	4,374	2,871
Concessional	132	116	114	105	100	91	78	67	57	44
Bilateral	1,003	1,009	1,076	1,042	1,039	964	855	777	776	713
Concessional	658	628	419	394	338	281	253	250	281	311
Private creditors	887	3,345	9,229	6,274	5,244	4,791	4,390	3,764	3,839	3,595
Bonds	60	106	57	43	39	200	320	0	0	0
Commercial banks	291	2,420	8,417	5,679	4,748	4,230	3,799	3,554	3,728	3,508
Other private	536	818	755	551	457	361	271	210	111	87
Private nonguaranteed	**501**	**4,693**	**2,361**	**2,924**	**4,263**	**4,720**	**5,603**	**7,164**	**9,004**	**11,429**
Bonds	0	0	0	0	0	0	0	286	377	866
Commercial banks	501	4,693	2,361	2,924	4,263	4,720	5,603	6,878	8,627	10,563
Memo:										
IBRD	111	163	1,566	1,618	1,860	1,947	1,928	1,902	1,919	1,372
IDA	19	21	16	15	14	13	13	12	11	11
DISBURSEMENTS	**655**	**3,551**	**1,560**	**1,504**	**2,253**	**1,645**	**1,736**	**2,183**	**2,922**	**3,819**
Public and publicly guaranteed	**408**	**857**	**890**	**658**	**708**	**702**	**670**	**293**	**463**	**339**
Official creditors	131	62	756	541	650	468	549	270	351	195
Multilateral	34	46	511	481	583	420	480	247	292	146
Concessional	24	3	0	0	0	0	0	0	0	0
Bilateral	97	15	244	60	67	48	69	24	59	49
Concessional	44	3	32	7	0	1	13	24	59	49
Private creditors	277	796	135	117	58	234	121	23	113	145
Bonds	0	55	0	0	0	199	120	0	0	0
Commercial banks	119	568	18	15	37	18	0	23	113	138
Other private	158	172	117	102	21	18	0	0	0	7
Private nonguaranteed	**247**	**2,694**	**669**	**846**	**1,545**	**943**	**1,066**	**1,889**	**2,459**	**3,479**
Bonds	0	0	0	0	0	0	0	286	91	500
Commercial banks	247	2,694	669	846	1,545	943	1,066	1,603	2,368	2,979
Memo:										
IBRD	27	14	268	205	251	182	200	107	81	83
IDA	0	0	0	0	0	0	0	0	0	0
PRINCIPAL REPAYMENTS	**207**	**1,462**	**617**	**833**	**771**	**947**	**1,150**	**1,472**	**1,488**	**3,360**
Public and publicly guaranteed	**166**	**891**	**408**	**563**	**500**	**620**	**632**	**881**	**653**	**2,268**
Official creditors	76	207	128	316	356	419	495	480	545	1,997
Multilateral	15	15	117	225	263	298	349	353	430	1,884
Concessional	9	6	7	7	10	11	12	12	13	16
Bilateral	61	191	12	91	93	120	146	126	115	113
Concessional	21	69	3	29	33	26	24	25	31	23
Private creditors	90	685	280	247	144	202	137	401	107	271
Bonds	5	4	8	7	7	37	0	320	0	0
Commercial banks	32	464	170	114	32	55	61	22	4	238
Other private	54	217	102	125	105	110	76	60	104	33
Private nonguaranteed	**41**	**571**	**209**	**270**	**271**	**327**	**518**	**592**	**835**	**1,092**
Bonds	0	0	0	0	0	0	0	0	0	11
Commercial banks	41	571	209	270	271	327	518	592	835	1,081
Memo:										
IBRD	10	9	56	107	119	138	168	172	192	704
IDA	0	0	1	1	1	1	1	1	1	1
NET FLOWS ON DEBT	**448**	**2,089**	**943**	**671**	**1,481**	**698**	**586**	**710**	**1,434**	**459**
Public and publicly guaranteed	**242**	**-34**	**482**	**95**	**208**	**82**	**38**	**-587**	**-190**	**-1,929**
Official creditors	55	-145	627	225	294	49	54	-209	-195	-1,802
Multilateral	20	31	395	255	319	121	131	-107	-138	-1,739
Concessional	14	-3	-7	-7	-10	-11	-12	-12	-13	-16
Bilateral	36	-176	233	-31	-25	-72	-77	-103	-57	-64
Concessional	23	-66	29	-22	-33	-25	-11	-1	27	26
Private creditors	187	111	-145	-130	-86	32	-16	-378	5	-127
Bonds	-5	52	-8	-7	-7	161	120	-320	0	0
Commercial banks	87	104	-152	-99	5	-37	-60	2	109	-100
Other private	105	-45	15	-23	-85	-92	-76	-60	-104	-26
Private nonguaranteed	**206**	**2,123**	**461**	**576**	**1,274**	**616**	**548**	**1,297**	**1,624**	**2,387**
Bonds	0	0	0	0	0	0	0	286	91	489
Commercial banks	206	2,123	461	576	1,274	616	548	1,012	1,533	1,898
Memo:										
IBRD	18	5	212	97	132	44	32	-65	-111	-621
IDA	0	0	-1	-1	-1	-1	-1	-1	-1	-1

CHILE

(US$ million, unless otherwise indicated)

	1970	1980	1988	1989	1990	1991	1992	1993	1994	1995
INTEREST PAYMENTS (LINT)	**104**	**918**	**1,007**	**1,286**	**1,364**	**1,249**	**1,135**	**933**	**929**	**1,114**
Public and publicly guaranteed	**78**	**483**	**857**	**1,080**	**1,112**	**957**	**806**	**652**	**565**	**653**
Official creditors	40	80	276	335	384	403	396	383	379	387
Multilateral	9	26	249	269	313	343	345	341	353	348
Concessional	7	7	6	5	5	4	4	3	3	2
Bilateral	31	54	27	66	71	60	51	43	27	39
Concessional	12	22	9	9	10	7	6	6	6	7
Private creditors	39	403	581	745	729	554	410	269	186	266
Bonds	2	5	4	4	2	1	18	15	0	0
Commercial banks	19	325	512	695	688	513	369	238	175	258
Other private	17	73	64	46	39	40	24	16	11	8
Private nonguaranteed	**26**	**435**	**150**	**207**	**252**	**292**	**329**	**280**	**365**	**461**
Bonds	0	0	0	0	0	0	0	4	13	26
Commercial banks	26	435	150	207	252	292	329	277	352	435
Memo:										
IBRD	6	16	110	116	130	143	144	142	140	137
IDA	0	0	0	0	0	0	0	0	0	0
NET TRANSFERS ON DEBT	**344**	**1,171**	**-64**	**-615**	**117**	**-552**	**-549**	**-222**	**505**	**-656**
Public and publicly guaranteed	**164**	**-517**	**-375**	**-984**	**-905**	**-876**	**-768**	**-1,240**	**-754**	**-2,582**
Official creditors	16	-225	351	-110	-90	-354	-342	-593	-574	-2,190
Multilateral	10	5	146	-14	7	-221	-214	-447	-490	-2,087
Concessional	8	-11	-13	-12	-15	-15	-16	-15	-16	-18
Bilateral	5	-230	206	-97	-96	-132	-127	-146	-83	-103
Concessional	11	-88	20	-31	-42	-32	-17	-8	22	19
Private creditors	148	-292	-726	-874	-815	-522	-426	-647	-180	-392
Bonds	-7	47	-12	-11	-9	160	103	-335	0	0
Commercial banks	68	-221	-665	-794	-683	-550	-430	-236	-66	-358
Other private	87	-118	-49	-70	-123	-132	-99	-76	-114	-34
Private nonguaranteed	**180**	**1,688**	**310**	**369**	**1,022**	**324**	**219**	**1,017**	**1,259**	**1,926**
Bonds	0	0	0	0	0	0	0	282	78	463
Commercial banks	180	1,688	310	369	1,022	324	219	735	1,181	1,463
Memo:										
IBRD	12	-11	102	-19	2	-99	-112	-207	-251	-758
IDA	0	0	-1	-1	-1	-1	-1	-1	-1	-1
DEBT SERVICE (LTDS)	**312**	**2,380**	**1,624**	**2,119**	**2,135**	**2,197**	**2,285**	**2,405**	**2,417**	**4,475**
Public and publicly guaranteed	**244**	**1,375**	**1,265**	**1,642**	**1,612**	**1,578**	**1,438**	**1,533**	**1,217**	**2,921**
Official creditors	115	287	404	651	740	821	891	863	924	2,385
Multilateral	24	42	366	495	576	641	695	694	782	2,233
Concessional	16	14	13	12	15	15	16	15	16	18
Bilateral	91	245	39	157	164	180	196	169	142	152
Concessional	33	90	12	38	42	32	29	31	37	30
Private creditors	129	1,088	861	991	873	756	547	670	293	537
Bonds	7	8	12	11	9	39	18	335	0	0
Commercial banks	51	789	682	809	720	568	430	259	179	496
Other private	71	290	166	171	144	150	100	76	114	41
Private nonguaranteed	**67**	**1,006**	**359**	**477**	**523**	**619**	**847**	**872**	**1,200**	**1,553**
Bonds	0	0	0	0	0	0	0	4	13	37
Commercial banks	67	1,006	359	477	523	619	847	868	1,187	1,516
Memo:										
IBRD	16	25	166	224	249	281	312	314	332	841
IDA	0	0	1	1	1	1	1	1	1	1
UNDISBURSED DEBT	**469**	**432**	**1,321**	**1,340**	**1,550**	**1,989**	**1,847**	**1,800**	**1,277**	**1,198**
Official creditors	181	186	1,085	1,152	1,364	1,729	1,758	1,572	1,078	1,101
Private creditors	289	246	236	188	186	260	89	228	199	97
Memorandum items										
Concessional LDOD	790	744	534	499	438	372	331	317	338	354
Variable rate LDOD	501	7,104	12,706	10,481	11,126	11,343	11,894	12,856	14,903	16,459
Public sector LDOD	1,980	4,587	13,688	10,859	10,422	10,068	9,576	8,867	8,989	7,178
Private sector LDOD	589	4,811	2,370	2,930	4,267	4,722	5,605	7,164	9,004	11,429

6. CURRENCY COMPOSITION OF LONG-TERM DEBT (PERCENT)

	1970	1980	1988	1989	1990	1991	1992	1993	1994	1995
Deutsche mark	5.6	5.9	3.9	4.7	4.7	4.2	3.7	3.3	3.7	4.5
French franc	2.1	6.3	1.3	1.4	1.1	0.9	0.7	0.7	0.6	0.7
Japanese yen	0.0	1.8	8.2	7.8	8.2	8.5	8.2	8.4	8.8	9.5
Pound sterling	7.4	1.0	3.1	2.9	3.4	3.3	2.7	2.7	2.8	2.9
Swiss franc	0.9	0.4	1.0	0.8	0.6	0.5	0.5	0.6	0.7	0.9
U.S.dollars	75.1	74.6	55.7	47.7	40.2	37.9	37.7	34.9	34.9	42.3
Multiple currency	6.7	7.0	24.1	32.1	39.4	42.6	44.9	48.1	47.5	38.0
Special drawing rights	0.0	0.0	0.0	0.0	0.0	0.0	0.0	0.0	0.0	0.0
All other currencies	2.2	3.2	2.7	2.5	2.4	2.0	1.5	1.2	1.1	1.1

CHILE

(US$ million, unless otherwise indicated)

	1970	1980	1988	1989	1990	1991	1992	1993	1994	1995
7. DEBT RESTRUCTURINGS										
Total amount rescheduled	0	0	1,231	0	4,173	24	133	0	0	0
Debt stock rescheduled	0	0	1,050	0	4,170	24	132	0	0	0
Principal rescheduled	0	0	135	0	0	0	0	0	0	0
Official	0	0	6	0	0	0	0	0	0	0
Private	0	0	128	0	0	0	0	0	0	0
Interest rescheduled	0	0	0	0	0	0	0	0	0	0
Official	0	0	0	0	0	0	0	0	0	0
Private	0	0	0	0	0	0	0	0	0	0
Debt forgiven	..	..	0	0	0	16	15	0	0	0
Memo: interest forgiven	..	..	0	0	0	0	0	0	0	0
Debt stock reduction	0	0	3,063	2,754	1,101	496	279	264	32	145
of which debt buyback	0	0	164	0	0	0	0	0	0	0
8. DEBT STOCK-FLOW RECONCILIATION										
Total change in debt stocks	..	..	..	-1,549	1,195	-1,280	1,187	1,503	4,085	840
Net flows on debt	..	..	..	1,422	1,682	-682	1,415	1,360	3,532	673
Net change in interest arrears	..	..	..	0	0	0	0	0	0	0
Interest capitalized	..	..	..	0	0	0	0	0	0	0
Debt forgiveness or reduction	..	..	..	-2,754	-1,101	-512	-294	-264	-32	-145
Cross-currency valuation	..	..	..	-203	507	92	-293	112	569	-57
Residual	..	..	..	-14	107	-178	359	295	17	369
9. AVERAGE TERMS OF NEW COMMITMENTS										
ALL CREDITORS										
Interest (%)	6.8	13.9	6.8	7.9	7.8	7.0	6.8	3.1	7.5	6.2
Maturity (years)	12.4	8.4	13.1	16.3	17.6	14.9	20.1	11.4	13.3	18.2
Grace period (years)	3.5	3.7	3.6	5.2	4.2	4.0	5.6	4.2	6.0	5.5
Grant element (%)	15.6	-18.0	16.7	11.7	12.0	15.8	21.3	31.5	13.9	24.5
Official creditors										
Interest (%)	6.4	8.7	5.7	7.8	7.7	6.6	6.8	1.9	6.3	6.1
Maturity (years)	20.9	15.0	15.7	17.5	18.4	19.1	20.3	15.8	22.1	19.5
Grace period (years)	6.7	3.5	4.2	5.5	4.3	4.8	5.6	3.7	5.0	5.8
Grant element (%)	24.4	6.0	24.0	12.6	12.8	20.2	21.4	43.0	22.6	26.2
Private creditors										
Interest (%)	6.9	14.4	8.6	8.7	9.3	8.0	5.1	4.2	8.3	6.7
Maturity (years)	11.1	7.7	8.7	6.5	7.6	5.4	5.8	7.5	7.7	9.3
Grace period (years)	3.0	3.7	2.6	3.1	2.3	2.1	3.1	4.7	6.7	3.1
Grant element (%)	14.3	-20.4	4.1	4.4	1.7	5.8	16.1	21.1	8.3	14.1
Memorandum items										
Commitments	361	835	652	736	1,049	1,205	655	317	181	306
Official creditors	47	74	411	655	967	835	646	151	70	265
Private creditors	314	761	241	81	82	371	9	166	111	41

10. CONTRACTUAL OBLIGATIONS ON OUTSTANDING LONG-TERM DEBT

	1996	1997	1998	1999	2000	2001	2002	2003	2004	2005
TOTAL										
Disbursements	370	295	198	134	89	54	32	14	9	4
Principal	2,504	2,675	2,375	2,205	1,750	1,685	1,196	1,354	971	799
Interest	1,217	1,089	914	775	631	512	417	308	323	156
Official creditors										
Disbursements	310	270	189	132	89	54	32	14	9	4
Principal	399	393	396	405	400	375	372	338	300	262
Interest	241	231	218	201	181	161	141	119	98	79
Bilateral creditors										
Disbursements	126	117	69	42	23	12	6	1	1	0
Principal	123	113	101	108	105	103	102	68	30	20
Interest	24	23	22	19	17	14	12	9	7	6
Multilateral creditors										
Disbursements	185	153	120	90	66	42	26	13	8	3
Principal	276	281	295	297	296	273	270	270	270	241
Interest	217	208	196	181	164	147	129	110	91	72
Private creditors										
Disbursements	60	26	9	2	0	0	0	0	0	0
Principal	2,105	2,282	1,980	1,800	1,350	1,310	824	1,016	671	538
Interest	977	859	696	575	450	351	276	189	224	77
Commercial banks										
Disbursements	58	25	9	2	0	0	0	0	0	0
Principal	435	600	526	442	270	365	262	219	223	220
Interest	241	206	163	130	103	85	59	43	28	14
Other private										
Disbursements	2	1	0	0	0	0	0	0	0	0
Principal	1,670	1,682	1,454	1,358	1,081	945	562	798	448	317
Interest	735	653	534	445	347	266	217	146	196	64

CHINA

(US$ million, unless otherwise indicated)

1. SUMMARY DEBT DATA

	1970	1980	1988	1989	1990	1991	1992	1993	1994	1995
TOTAL DEBT STOCKS (EDT)	..	**4,504**	**42,439**	**44,933**	**55,301**	**60,259**	**72,428**	**85,928**	**100,457**	**118,090**
Long-term debt (LDOD)	..	**4,504**	**32,620**	**37,118**	**45,515**	**49,479**	**58,663**	**70,632**	**82,974**	**95,764**
Public and publicly guaranteed	..	4,504	32,620	37,118	45,515	49,479	58,463	70,076	82,391	94,675
Private nonguaranteed	0	0	0	0	0	0	200	556	583	1,090
Use of IMF credit	**0**	**0**	**1,013**	**908**	**469**	**0**	**0**	**0**	**0**	**0**
Short-term debt	..	**0**	**8,806**	**6,907**	**9,317**	**10,780**	**13,765**	**15,296**	**17,483**	**22,325**
of which interest arrears on LDOD	..	0	0	0	0	0	0	0	0	0
Official creditors	..	0	0	0	0	0	0	0	0	0
Private creditors	..	0	0	0	0	0	0	0	0	0
Memo: principal arrears on LDOD	..	0	0	0	0	0	0	0	0	0
Official creditors	..	0	0	0	0	0	0	0	0	0
Private creditors	..	0	0	0	0	0	0	0	0	0
Memo: export credits	..	..	7,861	7,344	8,076	10,108	12,790	15,851	23,370	26,154
TOTAL DEBT FLOWS										
Disbursements	..	**2,539**	**9,065**	**8,442**	**9,665**	**8,659**	**16,505**	**19,561**	**16,151**	**21,955**
Long-term debt	..	2,539	9,065	8,442	9,665	8,659	16,505	19,561	16,151	21,955
IMF purchases	0	0	0	0	0	0	0	0	0	0
Principal repayments	..	**613**	**2,368**	**2,444**	**3,809**	**4,574**	**5,213**	**6,729**	**6,343**	**9,070**
Long-term debt	..	613	2,285	2,365	3,319	4,123	5,213	6,729	6,343	9,070
IMF repurchases	0	0	83	79	490	451	0	0	0	0
Net flows on debt	..	**1,927**	**7,282**	**4,099**	**8,267**	**5,548**	**14,277**	**14,363**	**11,995**	**17,728**
of which short-term debt	..	..	585	-1,899	2,410	1,463	2,985	1,531	2,187	4,842
Interest payments (INT)	..	**318**	**2,197**	**3,206**	**3,248**	**3,731**	**3,405**	**3,439**	**4,792**	**5,996**
Long-term debt	..	318	1,611	2,511	2,534	2,954	2,708	2,630	3,844	4,657
IMF charges	0	0	51	67	66	24	0	0	0	0
Short-term debt	..	0	534	628	649	754	697	809	948	1,340
Net transfers on debt	..	**1,609**	**5,086**	**893**	**5,018**	**1,817**	**10,872**	**10,924**	**7,203**	**11,732**
Total debt service paid (TDS)	..	**930**	**4,565**	**5,650**	**7,057**	**8,305**	**8,618**	**10,168**	**11,135**	**15,066**
Long-term debt	..	930	3,896	4,876	5,853	7,076	7,921	9,359	10,187	13,726
IMF repurchases and charges	0	0	134	147	555	475	0	0	0	0
Short-term debt (interest only)	..	0	534	628	649	754	697	809	948	1,340

2. AGGREGATE NET RESOURCE FLOWS AND NET TRANSFERS (LONG-TERM)

	1970	1980	1988	1989	1990	1991	1992	1993	1994	1995
NET RESOURCE FLOWS	..	**1,934**	**10,279**	**9,715**	**10,082**	**9,797**	**23,969**	**44,437**	**47,847**	**51,870**
Net flow of long-term debt (ex. IMF)	0	1,927	6,780	6,078	6,346	4,536	11,292	12,832	9,808	12,885
Foreign direct investment (net)	0	0	3,194	3,393	3,487	4,366	11,156	27,515	33,787	35,849
Portfolio equity flows	..	0	0	0	0	653	1,194	3,818	3,915	2,807
Grants (excluding technical coop.)	0	7	304	245	249	242	327	272	337	329
Memo: technical coop. grants	0	48	329	314	393	401	456	500	497	569
NET TRANSFERS	..	**1,616**	**8,660**	**7,197**	**7,502**	**6,834**	**21,239**	**41,457**	**43,503**	**46,463**
Interest on long-term debt	..	318	1,611	2,511	2,534	2,954	2,708	2,630	3,844	4,657
Profit remittances on FDI	0	0	8	7	46	10	22	350	500	750

3. MAJOR ECONOMIC AGGREGATES

	1970	1980	1988	1989	1990	1991	1992	1993	1994	1995
Gross national product (GNP)	93,242	201,688	307,043	342,466	355,610	377,396	418,397	430,859	539,888	685,874
Exports of goods & services (XGS)	..	..	47,510	49,793	60,515	69,824	84,640	91,350	125,313	152,781
of which workers remittances	..	..	129	76	124	207	228	108	395	350
Imports of goods & services (MGS)	..	..	51,602	54,415	48,668	57,176	79,166	104,023	118,345	152,248
International reserves (RES)	..	10,091	23,752	23,053	34,476	48,165	24,853	27,348	57,781	80,288
Current account balance	..	..	-3,802	-4,317	11,997	13,272	6,401	-11,609	6,908	1,618

4. DEBT INDICATORS

	1970	1980	1988	1989	1990	1991	1992	1993	1994	1995
EDT / XGS (%)	..	..	89.3	90.2	91.4	86.3	85.6	94.1	80.2	77.3
EDT / GNP (%)	..	2.2	13.8	13.1	15.6	16.0	17.3	19.9	18.6	17.2
TDS / XGS (%)	..	..	9.6	11.3	11.7	11.9	10.2	11.1	8.9	9.9
INT / XGS (%)	..	..	4.6	6.4	5.4	5.3	4.0	3.8	3.8	3.9
INT / GNP (%)	..	0.2	0.7	0.9	0.9	1.0	0.8	0.8	0.9	0.9
RES / EDT (%)	..	224.1	56.0	51.3	62.3	79.9	34.3	31.8	57.5	68.0
RES / MGS (months)	..	..	5.5	5.1	8.5	10.1	3.8	3.2	5.9	6.3
Short-term / EDT (%)	..	0.0	20.7	15.4	16.8	17.9	19.0	17.8	17.4	18.9
Concessional / EDT (%)	..	0.5	14.9	17.5	17.6	17.9	15.8	15.7	15.9	14.7
Multilateral / EDT (%)	..	0.0	8.8	10.6	11.1	12.6	11.9	12.4	13.5	13.8

CHINA

(US$ million, unless otherwise indicated)

	1970	1980	1988	1989	1990	1991	1992	1993	1994	1995
5. LONG-TERM DEBT										
DEBT OUTSTANDING (LDOD)	..	**4,504**	**32,620**	**37,118**	**45,515**	**49,479**	**58,663**	**70,632**	**82,974**	**95,764**
Public and publicly guaranteed	..	**4,504**	**32,620**	**37,118**	**45,515**	**49,479**	**58,463**	**70,076**	**82,391**	**94,675**
Official creditors	..	447	10,536	12,039	14,514	17,073	19,105	24,339	28,973	36,282
Multilateral	..	0	3,753	4,783	6,111	7,576	8,614	10,690	13,588	16,302
Concessional	..	0	1,906	2,387	3,119	3,775	4,391	5,299	6,263	7,228
Bilateral	..	447	6,783	7,257	8,403	9,497	10,491	13,650	15,385	19,980
Concessional	..	24	4,399	5,460	6,599	6,990	7,041	8,165	9,729	10,155
Private creditors	..	4,057	22,085	25,079	31,001	32,406	39,358	45,737	53,418	58,393
Bonds	..	50	5,182	5,228	5,426	5,660	5,449	7,715	11,087	10,684
Commercial banks	..	1,514	10,393	11,432	14,520	14,963	17,913	20,678	21,475	23,869
Other private	..	2,492	6,510	8,419	11,055	11,783	15,996	17,344	20,856	23,840
Private nonguaranteed	**0**	**0**	**0**	**0**	**0**	**0**	**200**	**556**	**583**	**1,090**
Bonds	..	0	0	0	0	0	200	556	583	1,090
Commercial banks	..	0	0	0	0	0	0	0	0	0
Memo:										
IBRD	0	0	1,832	2,330	2,865	3,494	3,752	4,549	5,933	7,209
IDA	0	0	1,819	2,296	3,016	3,672	4,286	5,160	6,097	7,038
DISBURSEMENTS	..	**2,539**	**9,065**	**8,442**	**9,665**	**8,659**	**16,505**	**19,561**	**16,151**	**21,955**
Public and publicly guaranteed	..	**2,539**	**9,065**	**8,442**	**9,665**	**8,659**	**16,308**	**19,229**	**16,151**	**21,411**
Official creditors	..	245	1,848	2,761	2,578	2,649	3,103	5,501	4,200	8,373
Multilateral	..	0	1,124	1,169	1,158	1,455	1,523	2,252	2,559	2,838
Concessional	..	0	568	514	511	614	788	907	704	838
Bilateral	..	245	724	1,592	1,420	1,194	1,580	3,249	1,642	5,535
Concessional	..	23	593	1,514	1,022	184	223	923	1,171	902
Private creditors	..	2,294	7,218	5,681	7,088	6,010	13,204	13,729	11,951	13,038
Bonds	..	50	782	450	277	260	894	2,737	3,337	1,224
Commercial banks	..	159	4,470	2,017	3,247	2,623	5,062	5,624	2,380	4,977
Other private	..	2,085	1,967	3,215	3,564	3,127	7,248	5,367	6,234	6,837
Private nonguaranteed	**0**	**0**	**0**	**0**	**0**	**0**	**198**	**332**	**0**	**544**
Bonds	..	0	0	0	0	0	198	332	0	544
Commercial banks	..	0	0	0	0	0	0	0	0	0
Memo:										
IBRD	0	0	553	604	591	668	553	977	1,380	1,457
IDA	0	0	557	507	507	612	778	869	680	812
PRINCIPAL REPAYMENTS	..	**613**	**2,285**	**2,365**	**3,319**	**4,123**	**5,213**	**6,729**	**6,343**	**9,070**
Public and publicly guaranteed	..	**613**	**2,285**	**2,365**	**3,319**	**4,123**	**5,213**	**6,729**	**6,343**	**9,070**
Official creditors	..	50	492	485	851	605	760	886	1,083	1,171
Multilateral	..	0	41	63	220	141	215	272	359	420
Concessional	..	0	0	0	0	4	5	7	12	19
Bilateral	..	50	451	421	631	464	545	614	725	751
Concessional	..	0	8	11	145	65	142	204	276	315
Private creditors	..	563	1,793	1,880	2,468	3,517	4,453	5,843	5,260	7,899
Bonds	..	0	11	33	325	237	1,095	831	461	1,451
Commercial banks	..	161	754	867	808	2,010	2,046	2,895	1,803	2,645
Other private	..	401	1,028	980	1,335	1,271	1,312	2,117	2,997	3,803
Private nonguaranteed	**0**	**0**	**0**	**0**	**0**	**0**	**0**	**0**	**0**	**0**
Bonds	..	0	0	0	0	0	0	0	0	0
Commercial banks	..	0	0	0	0	0	0	0	0	0
Memo:										
IBRD	0	0	39	62	216	130	196	245	315	350
IDA	0	0	0	0	0	1	2	4	9	14
NET FLOWS ON DEBT	..	**1,927**	**6,780**	**6,078**	**6,346**	**4,536**	**11,292**	**12,832**	**9,808**	**12,885**
Public and publicly guaranteed	..	**1,927**	**6,780**	**6,078**	**6,346**	**4,536**	**11,095**	**12,500**	**9,808**	**12,342**
Official creditors	..	195	1,355	2,277	1,727	2,044	2,343	4,615	3,117	7,202
Multilateral	..	0	1,083	1,106	938	1,314	1,308	1,980	2,200	2,418
Concessional	..	0	568	514	511	610	782	899	692	819
Bilateral	..	195	273	1,171	789	730	1,035	2,635	917	4,784
Concessional	..	23	586	1,503	877	119	81	720	895	587
Private creditors	..	1,731	5,425	3,801	4,620	2,493	8,751	7,885	6,691	5,139
Bonds	..	50	771	417	-48	24	-201	1,906	2,876	-227
Commercial banks	..	-3	3,715	1,150	2,439	613	3,016	2,729	577	2,332
Other private	..	1,684	939	2,235	2,229	1,856	5,936	3,250	3,237	3,034
Private nonguaranteed	**0**	**0**	**0**	**0**	**0**	**0**	**198**	**332**	**0**	**544**
Bonds	..	0	0	0	0	0	198	332	0	544
Commercial banks	..	0	0	0	0	0	0	0	0	0
Memo:										
IBRD	0	0	514	542	376	538	357	732	1,066	1,107
IDA	0	0	557	507	507	611	777	865	671	798

CHINA

(US$ million, unless otherwise indicated)

	1970	1980	1988	1989	1990	1991	1992	1993	1994	1995
INTEREST PAYMENTS (LINT)	..	**318**	**1,611**	**2,511**	**2,534**	**2,954**	**2,708**	**2,630**	**3,844**	**4,657**
Public and publicly guaranteed	..	**318**	**1,611**	**2,511**	**2,534**	**2,954**	**2,708**	**2,618**	**3,818**	**4,624**
Official creditors	..	17	434	457	531	635	678	827	1,131	1,288
Multilateral	..	0	143	179	226	263	319	377	480	619
Concessional	..	0	17	16	20	25	31	36	45	55
Bilateral	..	17	291	278	305	372	358	450	651	669
Concessional	..	0	119	137	193	273	281	305	330	324
Private creditors	..	301	1,178	2,055	2,003	2,319	2,031	1,792	2,687	3,336
Bonds	..	3	289	347	367	356	337	286	363	594
Commercial banks	..	140	457	1,062	959	1,071	776	738	1,034	1,333
Other private	..	158	432	646	677	892	917	767	1,290	1,409
Private nonguaranteed	**0**	**0**	**0**	**0**	**0**	**0**	**0**	**12**	**26**	**33**
Bonds	..	0	0	0	0	0	0	12	26	33
Commercial banks	..	0	0	0	0	0	0	0	0	0
Memo:										
IBRD	0	0	126	161	200	227	264	299	364	460
IDA	0	0	15	14	19	23	29	34	41	49
NET TRANSFERS ON DEBT	..	**1,609**	**5,169**	**3,567**	**3,813**	**1,583**	**8,584**	**10,202**	**5,964**	**8,229**
Public and publicly guaranteed	..	**1,609**	**5,169**	**3,567**	**3,813**	**1,583**	**8,386**	**9,882**	**5,990**	**7,718**
Official creditors	..	178	922	1,820	1,196	1,409	1,665	3,788	1,986	5,914
Multilateral	..	0	940	927	712	1,052	988	1,604	1,720	1,799
Concessional	..	0	551	498	491	586	752	863	647	764
Bilateral	..	178	-18	893	484	357	677	2,184	266	4,116
Concessional	..	23	467	1,366	684	-153	-200	415	565	263
Private creditors	..	1,431	4,247	1,747	2,617	174	6,721	6,094	4,004	1,804
Bonds	..	47	482	70	-415	-332	-538	1,620	2,513	-821
Commercial banks	..	-142	3,259	88	1,480	-458	2,240	1,991	-457	999
Other private	..	1,526	507	1,589	1,551	964	5,019	2,483	1,948	1,626
Private nonguaranteed	**0**	**0**	**0**	**0**	**0**	**0**	**198**	**320**	**-26**	**511**
Bonds	..	0	0	0	0	0	198	320	-26	511
Commercial banks	..	0	0	0	0	0	0	0	0	0
Memo:										
IBRD	0	0	388	381	176	311	92	433	701	648
IDA	0	0	542	493	488	589	748	831	630	749
DEBT SERVICE (LTDS)	..	**930**	**3,896**	**4,876**	**5,853**	**7,076**	**7,921**	**9,359**	**10,187**	**13,726**
Public and publicly guaranteed	..	**930**	**3,896**	**4,876**	**5,853**	**7,076**	**7,921**	**9,348**	**10,161**	**13,693**
Official creditors	..	67	926	941	1,383	1,240	1,438	1,713	2,214	2,459
Multilateral	..	0	184	242	446	404	534	648	838	1,039
Concessional	..	0	17	16	20	29	36	44	57	74
Bilateral	..	67	742	699	937	837	903	1,064	1,376	1,419
Concessional	..	0	127	148	338	338	423	508	607	639
Private creditors	..	863	2,971	3,935	4,470	5,836	6,483	7,635	7,947	11,234
Bonds	..	3	300	380	692	593	1,432	1,117	824	2,045
Commercial banks	..	301	1,211	1,929	1,767	3,080	2,822	3,633	2,837	3,978
Other private	..	559	1,460	1,625	2,012	2,163	2,229	2,885	4,286	5,212
Private nonguaranteed	**0**	**0**	**0**	**0**	**0**	**0**	**0**	**12**	**26**	**33**
Bonds	..	0	0	0	0	0	0	12	26	33
Commercial banks	..	0	0	0	0	0	0	0	0	0
Memo:										
IBRD	0	0	165	223	415	357	460	543	679	810
IDA	0	0	15	14	19	23	30	38	50	63
UNDISBURSED DEBT	..	**2,430**	**8,896**	**8,800**	**9,298**	**8,973**	**10,948**	**16,156**	**16,235**	**16,028**
Official creditors	..	940	4,892	5,449	5,280	6,931	8,168	10,321	13,149	13,172
Private creditors	..	1,490	4,004	3,351	4,019	2,042	2,780	5,835	3,086	2,856
Memorandum items										
Concessional LDOD	..	24	6,306	7,847	9,718	10,765	11,432	13,464	15,992	17,382
Variable rate LDOD	..	2,649	12,528	13,901	16,491	16,809	17,289	20,624	23,272	28,370
Public sector LDOD	..	4,504	32,620	37,071	45,449	49,405	58,413	69,864	81,709	93,573
Private sector LDOD	..	0	0	47	66	74	250	767	1,265	2,192

6. CURRENCY COMPOSITION OF LONG-TERM DEBT (PERCENT)

	1970	1980	1988	1989	1990	1991	1992	1993	1994	1995
Deutsche mark	..	7.4	3.4	3.2	3.1	2.7	1.6	1.0	1.7	1.7
French franc	..	1.0	0.3	0.2	0.4	0.4	0.4	0.3	0.3	0.3
Japanese yen	..	12.8	40.8	33.2	30.4	28.4	22.6	21.0	23.2	20.7
Pound sterling	..	0.1	0.1	0.3	0.7	0.6	0.4	0.3	0.3	0.2
Swiss franc	..	0.1	0.2	0.2	0.2	0.1	0.0	0.0	0.1	0.0
U.S.dollars	..	15.4	31.4	30.4	29.1	36.3	48.2	54.2	53.5	57.9
Multiple currency	..	56.5	19.2	27.9	31.2	27.0	23.3	20.5	18.9	17.2
Special drawing rights	..	0.0	0.3	0.3	0.3	0.3	0.3	0.2	0.2	0.2
All other currencies	..	6.8	4.2	4.2	4.7	4.2	3.2	2.4	2.0	1.8

CHINA

(US$ million, unless otherwise indicated)

	1970	1980	1988	1989	1990	1991	1992	1993	1994	1995
7. DEBT RESTRUCTURINGS										
Total amount rescheduled	0	0	0	0	0	0	0	0	0	0
Debt stock rescheduled	0	0	0	0	0	0	0	0	0	0
Principal rescheduled	0	0	0	0	0	0	0	0	0	0
Official	0	0	0	0	0	0	0	0	0	0
Private	0	0	0	0	0	0	0	0	0	0
Interest rescheduled	0	0	0	0	0	0	0	0	0	0
Official	0	0	0	0	0	0	0	0	0	0
Private	0	0	0	0	0	0	0	0	0	0
Debt forgiven	..	..	0	0	0	0	0	0	0	0
Memo: interest forgiven	..	..	0	0	0	0	0	0	0	0
Debt stock reduction	0	0	0	0	0	0	0	0	0	0
of which debt buyback	0	0	0	0	0	0	0	0	0	0
8. DEBT STOCK-FLOW RECONCILIATION										
Total change in debt stocks	..	..	..	2,494	10,369	4,958	12,169	13,500	14,529	17,633
Net flows on debt	..	..	..	4,099	8,267	5,548	14,277	14,363	11,995	17,728
Net change in interest arrears	..	..	..	0	0	0	0	0	0	0
Interest capitalized	..	..	..	0	0	0	0	0	0	0
Debt forgiveness or reduction	..	..	..	0	0	0	0	0	0	0
Cross-currency valuation	..	..	..	-1,483	1,486	1,065	-297	1,608	2,931	-226
Residual	..	..	..	-123	617	-1,655	-1,812	-2,472	-397	131
9. AVERAGE TERMS OF NEW COMMITMENTS										
ALL CREDITORS										
Interest (%)	..	10.3	7.2	7.3	7.5	6.1	6.2	5.2	5.5	6.5
Maturity (years)	..	11.0	14.9	18.0	16.6	18.4	14.9	14.0	15.6	11.4
Grace period (years)	..	3.3	3.7	4.6	3.9	4.8	3.5	3.9	5.0	2.9
Grant element (%)	..	4.4	15.5	17.2	15.6	25.1	19.3	23.5	25.5	14.7
Official creditors										
Interest (%)	..	4.9	5.0	5.8	3.7	5.2	5.5	4.4	5.6	7.0
Maturity (years)	..	18.8	24.1	24.9	27.9	23.6	22.2	19.7	21.1	17.9
Grace period (years)	..	7.7	7.1	6.8	7.9	6.7	5.7	5.3	6.0	3.7
Grant element (%)	..	35.3	37.5	31.6	49.2	36.4	31.1	36.4	30.5	17.8
Private creditors										
Interest (%)	..	12.4	7.9	8.4	8.6	7.2	6.5	5.6	5.4	6.3
Maturity (years)	..	8.0	12.0	13.2	13.3	12.8	12.3	11.4	11.6	7.3
Grace period (years)	..	1.6	2.7	3.0	2.7	2.7	2.7	3.3	4.2	2.4
Grant element (%)	..	-7.7	8.7	7.2	5.7	13.0	15.0	17.8	21.7	12.9
Memorandum items										
Commitments	..	3,826	10,150	8,354	9,988	8,287	16,831	24,930	15,945	21,814
Official creditors	..	1,070	2,402	3,433	2,288	4,284	4,451	7,629	6,809	8,297
Private creditors	..	2,757	7,748	4,921	7,701	4,002	12,379	17,301	9,135	13,517

10. CONTRACTUAL OBLIGATIONS ON OUTSTANDING LONG-TERM DEBT

	1996	1997	1998	1999	2000	2001	2002	2003	2004	2005
TOTAL										
Disbursements	4,887	3,755	2,627	1,836	1,252	739	504	258	128	42
Principal	10,921	10,281	11,151	9,823	9,964	8,210	7,202	5,442	6,285	4,333
Interest	4,889	4,782	4,470	3,978	3,467	2,940	2,485	2,129	1,782	1,451
Official creditors										
Disbursements	3,360	2,869	2,313	1,726	1,235	738	503	258	128	42
Principal	1,501	1,919	2,299	2,539	2,793	2,991	3,023	2,954	2,931	2,718
Interest	1,448	1,807	1,860	1,843	1,789	1,676	1,539	1,389	1,232	1,076
Bilateral creditors										
Disbursements	867	479	239	87	40	9	1	1	0	0
Principal	1,001	1,323	1,559	1,625	1,681	1,671	1,625	1,562	1,549	1,334
Interest	639	918	905	848	785	699	614	532	453	377
Multilateral creditors										
Disbursements	2,494	2,390	2,074	1,639	1,195	729	503	257	128	42
Principal	500	596	740	914	1,113	1,320	1,398	1,392	1,382	1,384
Interest	810	889	954	994	1,004	978	926	856	779	699
Private creditors										
Disbursements	1,527	886	314	110	17	1	1	0	0	0
Principal	9,420	8,363	8,852	7,284	7,171	5,219	4,179	2,489	3,354	1,616
Interest	3,441	2,976	2,610	2,135	1,678	1,263	946	741	549	375
Commercial banks										
Disbursements	924	514	170	73	2	0	0	0	0	0
Principal	4,156	3,992	4,239	2,799	2,783	2,255	1,428	702	635	607
Interest	1,384	1,180	1,005	785	600	429	298	234	194	158
Other private										
Disbursements	603	372	144	37	15	1	1	0	0	0
Principal	5,264	4,371	4,613	4,485	4,388	2,963	2,752	1,787	2,719	1,008
Interest	2,057	1,796	1,606	1,350	1,078	834	648	507	355	217

COLOMBIA

(US$ million, unless otherwise indicated)

	1970	1980	1988	1989	1990	1991	1992	1993	1994	1995
1. SUMMARY DEBT DATA										
TOTAL DEBT STOCKS (EDT)	..	**6,941**	**16,995**	**16,878**	**17,232**	**17,334**	**17,196**	**17,156**	**19,429**	**20,760**
Long-term debt (LDOD)	**1,580**	**4,604**	**15,384**	**15,261**	**15,793**	**15,583**	**14,360**	**13,923**	**14,628**	**15,486**
Public and publicly guaranteed	1,297	4,089	13,846	13,989	14,671	14,469	13,237	12,844	13,617	12,983
Private nonguaranteed	283	515	1,538	1,272	1,123	1,114	1,123	1,079	1,012	2,503
Use of IMF credit	**55**	**0**	**0**	**0**	**0**	**0**	**0**	**0**	**0**	**0**
Short-term debt	..	**2,337**	**1,610**	**1,617**	**1,438**	**1,751**	**2,836**	**3,233**	**4,801**	**5,274**
of which interest arrears on LDOD	..	0	1	3	28	20	11	15	11	2
Official creditors	..	0	0	0	17	10	10	11	8	0
Private creditors	..	0	1	3	11	10	1	4	3	2
Memo: principal arrears on LDOD	..	0	436	335	409	253	145	192	230	224
Official creditors	..	0	5	1	42	58	90	119	138	125
Private creditors	..	0	431	334	367	195	55	73	92	99
Memo: export credits	..	..	3,692	3,534	3,908	3,846	3,172	3,090	3,235	3,402
TOTAL DEBT FLOWS										
Disbursements	**282**	**1,071**	**2,344**	**2,257**	**1,993**	**1,919**	**1,572**	**1,695**	**2,652**	**3,035**
Long-term debt	253	1,071	2,344	2,257	1,993	1,919	1,572	1,695	2,652	3,035
IMF purchases	29	0	0	0	0	0	0	0	0	0
Principal repayments	**210**	**263**	**1,725**	**2,151**	**2,171**	**2,215**	**2,497**	**2,097**	**2,529**	**2,398**
Long-term debt	137	263	1,725	2,151	2,171	2,215	2,497	2,097	2,529	2,398
IMF repurchases	73	0	0	0	0	0	0	0	0	0
Net flows on debt	**72**	**808**	**574**	**111**	**-381**	**25**	**168**	**-9**	**1,695**	**1,120**
of which short-term debt	..	..	-45	5	-204	322	1,093	393	1,572	483
Interest payments (INT)	..	**688**	**1,374**	**1,568**	**1,484**	**1,431**	**1,266**	**1,085**	**1,224**	**1,380**
Long-term debt	59	310	1,213	1,384	1,341	1,281	1,150	934	1,016	1,068
IMF charges	0	0	0	0	0	0	0	0	0	0
Short-term debt	..	378	161	184	143	149	116	151	208	312
Net transfers on debt	..	**120**	**-801**	**-1,457**	**-1,865**	**-1,405**	**-1,098**	**-1,093**	**471**	**-260**
Total debt service paid (TDS)	..	**951**	**3,099**	**3,719**	**3,654**	**3,645**	**3,763**	**3,181**	**3,753**	**3,778**
Long-term debt	197	573	2,938	3,535	3,511	3,496	3,647	3,030	3,545	3,466
IMF repurchases and charges	73	0	0	0	0	0	0	0	0	0
Short-term debt (interest only)	..	378	161	184	143	149	116	151	208	312

	1970	1980	1988	1989	1990	1991	1992	1993	1994	1995
2. AGGREGATE NET RESOURCE FLOWS AND NET TRANSFERS (LONG-TERM)										
NET RESOURCE FLOWS	**181**	**974**	**858**	**719**	**357**	**228**	**-107**	**803**	**2,154**	**3,342**
Net flow of long-term debt (ex. IMF)	115	808	619	106	-177	-296	-925	-401	123	637
Foreign direct investment (net)	43	157	203	576	500	457	729	959	1,667	2,501
Portfolio equity flows	0	0	0	0	0	0	0	169	320	131
Grants (excluding technical coop.)	23	8	36	37	35	68	89	76	45	73
Memo: technical coop. grants	14	46	76	73	85	97	101	100	136	159
NET TRANSFERS	**28**	**553**	**-948**	**-1,648**	**-1,947**	**-1,937**	**-2,300**	**-1,331**	**-261**	**774**
Interest on long-term debt	59	310	1,213	1,384	1,341	1,281	1,150	934	1,016	1,068
Profit remittances on FDI	94	110	592	983	964	884	1,043	1,200	1,400	1,500

	1970	1980	1988	1989	1990	1991	1992	1993	1994	1995
3. MAJOR ECONOMIC AGGREGATES										
Gross national product (GNP)	7,019	33,154	37,471	37,348	37,977	39,620	46,832	53,972	65,645	73,705
Exports of goods & services (XGS)	1,025	5,928	7,456	8,068	9,514	10,356	10,325	10,964	12,946	14,966
of which workers remittances	6	68	448	459	488	866	630	455	211	172
Imports of goods & services (MGS)	1,348	6,231	8,188	8,708	9,510	8,840	10,528	13,750	16,816	19,588
International reserves (RES)	207	6,474	3,700	3,862	4,453	6,335	7,551	7,670	7,862	8,205
Current account balance	-293	-206	-216	-201	542	2,349	901	-2,102	-3,219	-4,116

	1970	1980	1988	1989	1990	1991	1992	1993	1994	1995
4. DEBT INDICATORS										
EDT / XGS (%)	..	117.1	227.9	209.2	181.1	167.4	166.5	156.5	150.1	138.7
EDT / GNP (%)	..	20.9	45.4	45.2	45.4	43.8	36.7	31.8	29.6	28.2
TDS / XGS (%)	..	16.0	41.6	46.1	38.4	35.2	36.4	29.0	29.0	25.2
INT / XGS (%)	..	11.6	18.4	19.4	15.6	13.8	12.3	9.9	9.5	9.2
INT / GNP (%)	..	2.1	3.7	4.2	3.9	3.6	2.7	2.0	1.9	1.9
RES / EDT (%)	..	93.3	21.8	22.9	25.8	36.5	43.9	44.7	40.5	39.5
RES / MGS (months)	1.8	12.5	5.4	5.3	5.6	8.6	8.6	6.7	5.6	5.0
Short-term / EDT (%)	..	33.7	9.5	9.6	8.3	10.1	16.5	18.8	24.7	25.4
Concessional / EDT (%)	..	16.3	6.2	6.0	6.0	5.6	5.4	4.5	5.0	4.8
Multilateral / EDT (%)	..	19.5	33.0	33.5	35.4	35.5	34.2	33.0	27.8	25.6

COLOMBIA

(US$ million, unless otherwise indicated)

	1970	1980	1988	1989	1990	1991	1992	1993	1994	1995
5. LONG-TERM DEBT										
DEBT OUTSTANDING (LDOD)	**1,580**	**4,604**	**15,384**	**15,261**	**15,793**	**15,583**	**14,360**	**13,923**	**14,628**	**15,486**
Public and publicly guaranteed	**1,297**	**4,089**	**13,846**	**13,989**	**14,671**	**14,469**	**13,237**	**12,844**	**13,617**	**12,983**
Official creditors	1,112	2,393	8,124	8,033	8,540	8,471	7,816	7,221	7,277	7,017
Multilateral	445	1,350	5,613	5,651	6,103	6,158	5,874	5,657	5,392	5,320
Concessional	328	231	282	276	264	242	220	202	195	181
Bilateral	667	1,043	2,512	2,382	2,437	2,313	1,941	1,563	1,886	1,698
Concessional	604	899	769	745	769	735	717	577	773	814
Private creditors	185	1,696	5,722	5,956	6,131	5,998	5,421	5,623	6,339	5,965
Bonds	21	31	104	277	275	359	419	875	767	1,015
Commercial banks	24	1,371	4,257	4,146	4,208	4,137	3,828	3,724	4,623	4,163
Other private	140	294	1,361	1,533	1,648	1,502	1,175	1,023	949	788
Private nonguaranteed	**283**	**515**	**1,538**	**1,272**	**1,123**	**1,114**	**1,123**	**1,079**	**1,012**	**2,503**
Bonds	0	0	0	0	0	0	0	0	125	717
Commercial banks	283	515	1,538	1,272	1,123	1,114	1,123	1,079	887	1,786
Memo:										
IBRD	354	991	3,899	3,809	3,859	3,728	3,195	2,969	2,629	2,548
IDA	20	21	16	15	15	14	13	12	12	11
DISBURSEMENTS	**253**	**1,071**	**2,344**	**2,257**	**1,993**	**1,919**	**1,572**	**1,695**	**2,652**	**3,035**
Public and publicly guaranteed	**253**	**1,016**	**2,232**	**2,080**	**1,847**	**1,621**	**1,441**	**1,546**	**2,527**	**1,345**
Official creditors	194	413	915	741	698	713	838	715	1,158	638
Multilateral	74	303	717	615	559	590	681	629	602	397
Concessional	33	37	6	9	4	0	0	0	9	2
Bilateral	120	111	199	126	139	123	157	86	555	241
Concessional	101	9	27	7	26	11	40	15	205	70
Private creditors	59	603	1,317	1,339	1,150	908	604	830	1,369	708
Bonds	0	0	0	185	0	100	100	475	0	382
Commercial banks	8	500	1,088	704	874	617	401	260	1,223	257
Other private	50	103	229	450	275	191	103	95	146	69
Private nonguaranteed	**0**	**55**	**112**	**177**	**146**	**298**	**131**	**150**	**125**	**1,690**
Bonds	0	0	0	0	0	0	0	0	125	592
Commercial banks	0	55	112	177	146	298	131	150	0	1,098
Memo:										
IBRD	58	218	485	361	213	301	262	301	310	238
IDA	0	0	0	0	0	0	0	0	0	0
PRINCIPAL REPAYMENTS	**137**	**263**	**1,725**	**2,151**	**2,171**	**2,215**	**2,497**	**2,097**	**2,529**	**2,398**
Public and publicly guaranteed	**78**	**250**	**1,627**	**1,708**	**1,875**	**1,908**	**2,375**	**1,904**	**2,336**	**2,200**
Official creditors	39	136	581	639	737	863	1,251	1,266	1,625	1,110
Multilateral	22	80	424	420	527	602	794	915	1,299	647
Concessional	16	22	17	16	20	22	21	18	17	18
Bilateral	17	57	157	218	210	261	457	352	326	463
Concessional	7	30	35	39	36	44	35	47	24	39
Private creditors	40	114	1,046	1,069	1,138	1,045	1,124	638	711	1,090
Bonds	3	3	2	6	4	19	41	22	113	120
Commercial banks	12	52	784	798	849	687	683	366	334	723
Other private	25	59	261	265	284	339	401	249	265	248
Private nonguaranteed	**59**	**13**	**98**	**443**	**296**	**307**	**122**	**193**	**193**	**199**
Bonds	0	0	0	0	0	0	0	0	0	0
Commercial banks	59	13	98	443	296	307	122	193	193	199
Memo:										
IBRD	17	65	339	332	434	492	681	596	836	414
IDA	0	0	1	1	1	1	1	1	1	1
NET FLOWS ON DEBT	**115**	**808**	**619**	**106**	**-177**	**-296**	**-925**	**-401**	**123**	**637**
Public and publicly guaranteed	**174**	**766**	**605**	**372**	**-28**	**-288**	**-934**	**-358**	**190**	**-854**
Official creditors	155	277	334	102	-40	-150	-413	-551	-467	-472
Multilateral	52	223	293	195	32	-12	-113	-286	-697	-250
Concessional	17	16	-11	-7	-16	-22	-21	-18	-7	-16
Bilateral	104	54	42	-92	-72	-138	-300	-265	230	-222
Concessional	94	-21	-8	-32	-10	-32	5	-32	181	31
Private creditors	19	489	271	270	12	-138	-520	192	658	-382
Bonds	-3	-3	-2	179	-4	81	60	453	-113	263
Commercial banks	-4	449	304	-94	25	-71	-282	-106	889	-466
Other private	26	44	-32	185	-9	-148	-298	-154	-119	-179
Private nonguaranteed	**-59**	**42**	**14**	**-266**	**-149**	**-9**	**8**	**-43**	**-68**	**1,492**
Bonds	0	0	0	0	0	0	0	0	125	592
Commercial banks	-59	42	14	-266	-149	-9	8	-43	-193	900
Memo:										
IBRD	41	152	146	29	-221	-191	-419	-294	-526	-176
IDA	0	0	-1	-1	-1	-1	-1	-1	-1	-1

COLOMBIA

(US$ million, unless otherwise indicated)

	1970	1980	1988	1989	1990	1991	1992	1993	1994	1995
INTEREST PAYMENTS (LINT)	**59**	**310**	**1,213**	**1,384**	**1,341**	**1,281**	**1,150**	**934**	**1,016**	**1,068**
Public and publicly guaranteed	**44**	**279**	**1,135**	**1,197**	**1,240**	**1,183**	**1,077**	**871**	**963**	**946**
Official creditors	36	128	639	641	627	669	648	579	515	505
Multilateral	25	102	468	453	476	491	474	457	424	388
Concessional	18	15	8	7	9	6	6	5	6	5
Bilateral	12	26	171	187	150	177	174	122	91	117
Concessional	8	21	21	20	19	29	14	21	18	25
Private creditors	8	151	496	556	613	514	429	292	448	441
Bonds	1	2	8	19	27	25	23	25	57	58
Commercial banks	2	128	375	414	461	365	286	179	305	310
Other private	5	21	113	124	124	124	121	88	85	73
Private nonguaranteed	**15**	**31**	**79**	**187**	**101**	**99**	**73**	**63**	**53**	**122**
Bonds	0	0	0	0	0	0	0	0	0	15
Commercial banks	15	31	79	187	101	99	73	63	53	107
Memo:										
IBRD	20	79	326	308	318	307	278	242	218	191
IDA	0	0	0	0	0	0	0	0	0	0
NET TRANSFERS ON DEBT	**56**	**498**	**-595**	**-1,278**	**-1,518**	**-1,578**	**-2,075**	**-1,335**	**-893**	**-431**
Public and publicly guaranteed	**130**	**487**	**-530**	**-824**	**-1,268**	**-1,470**	**-2,011**	**-1,229**	**-772**	**-1,800**
Official creditors	119	149	-305	-538	-666	-819	-1,061	-1,129	-982	-977
Multilateral	27	121	-176	-259	-445	-503	-587	-742	-1,121	-638
Concessional	-1	1	-19	-15	-25	-28	-27	-23	-13	-21
Bilateral	92	28	-129	-280	-222	-316	-474	-387	139	-339
Concessional	86	-42	-29	-52	-29	-62	-9	-53	163	6
Private creditors	11	338	-225	-286	-601	-652	-950	-100	210	-823
Bonds	-3	-5	-9	160	-32	56	36	428	-170	204
Commercial banks	-7	321	-71	-508	-436	-436	-567	-285	584	-776
Other private	21	22	-145	61	-133	-272	-419	-242	-204	-252
Private nonguaranteed	**-74**	**11**	**-65**	**-453**	**-250**	**-107**	**-65**	**-106**	**-121**	**1,369**
Bonds	0	0	0	0	0	0	0	0	125	577
Commercial banks	-74	11	-65	-453	-250	-107	-65	-106	-246	793
Memo:										
IBRD	21	74	-180	-279	-538	-497	-697	-537	-744	-367
IDA	0	0	-1	-1	-1	-1	-1	-1	-1	-1
DEBT SERVICE (LTDS)	**197**	**573**	**2,938**	**3,535**	**3,511**	**3,496**	**3,647**	**3,030**	**3,545**	**3,466**
Public and publicly guaranteed	**123**	**529**	**2,762**	**2,905**	**3,115**	**3,091**	**3,452**	**2,774**	**3,299**	**3,145**
Official creditors	75	264	1,220	1,279	1,364	1,531	1,898	1,845	2,140	1,615
Multilateral	47	181	892	873	1,003	1,093	1,268	1,371	1,723	1,035
Concessional	34	36	25	23	29	28	27	23	23	23
Bilateral	28	83	328	406	361	439	631	473	417	580
Concessional	15	51	55	59	55	73	49	68	42	64
Private creditors	47	265	1,542	1,625	1,751	1,559	1,554	930	1,159	1,531
Bonds	3	5	9	25	32	44	64	47	170	178
Commercial banks	15	179	1,159	1,212	1,311	1,052	969	545	639	1,032
Other private	29	80	373	389	409	463	521	337	350	320
Private nonguaranteed	**74**	**44**	**177**	**630**	**397**	**405**	**195**	**256**	**246**	**321**
Bonds	0	0	0	0	0	0	0	0	0	15
Commercial banks	74	44	177	630	397	405	195	256	246	306
Memo:										
IBRD	37	144	665	640	751	798	959	838	1,054	604
IDA	0	0	1	1	1	1	1	1	1	1
UNDISBURSED DEBT	**576**	**2,455**	**4,465**	**4,594**	**4,034**	**4,651**	**3,895**	**3,915**	**2,791**	**2,757**
Official creditors	424	1,781	3,215	3,229	3,468	2,975	2,865	2,948	2,675	2,435
Private creditors	153	674	1,250	1,366	567	1,676	1,029	967	116	322
Memorandum items										
Concessional LDOD	932	1,130	1,051	1,021	1,033	976	937	779	968	995
Variable rate LDOD	283	1,877	7,764	7,713	7,788	7,910	7,604	7,462	7,577	8,610
Public sector LDOD	1,224	4,045	13,779	13,938	14,630	14,467	13,235	12,842	13,613	12,978
Private sector LDOD	356	559	1,606	1,323	1,163	1,116	1,125	1,081	1,015	2,508

6. CURRENCY COMPOSITION OF LONG-TERM DEBT (PERCENT)

	1970	1980	1988	1989	1990	1991	1992	1993	1994	1995
Deutsche mark	1.3	3.8	4.9	5.6	6.0	5.4	5.0	4.6	4.5	5.4
French franc	0.4	1.9	0.5	0.4	0.3	0.3	0.3	0.3	0.4	0.5
Japanese yen	0.0	0.1	7.4	5.4	4.9	4.7	4.3	4.0	4.3	6.1
Pound sterling	0.2	0.4	0.2	0.2	0.3	0.2	0.2	0.2	0.1	0.1
Swiss franc	0.3	0.0	0.2	0.2	0.3	0.2	0.2	0.2	0.2	0.2
U.S.dollars	66.1	60.4	44.2	45.4	44.0	44.2	44.6	46.6	52.4	49.9
Multiple currency	29.8	31.3	40.0	39.9	41.2	42.2	43.2	42.6	36.6	36.8
Special drawing rights	0.0	0.0	0.0	0.0	0.0	0.0	0.0	0.0	0.0	0.0
All other currencies	1.9	2.1	2.6	2.9	3.0	2.8	2.1	1.6	1.4	1.1

COLOMBIA

(US$ million, unless otherwise indicated)

	1970	1980	1988	1989	1990	1991	1992	1993	1994	1995
7. DEBT RESTRUCTURINGS										
Total amount rescheduled	0	0	0	0	0	0	0	254	0	0
Debt stock rescheduled	0	0	0	0	0	0	0	254	0	0
Principal rescheduled	0	0	0	0	0	0	0	0	0	0
Official	0	0	0	0	0	0	0	0	0	0
Private	0	0	0	0	0	0	0	0	0	0
Interest rescheduled	0	0	0	0	0	0	0	0	0	0
Official	0	0	0	0	0	0	0	0	0	0
Private	0	0	0	0	0	0	0	0	0	0
Debt forgiven	..	..	0	0	2	0	1	37	0	0
Memo: interest forgiven	..	..	0	0	0	0	0	0	0	0
Debt stock reduction	0	0	0	0	0	0	24	54	0	0
of which debt buyback	0	0	0	0	0	0	0	0	0	0
8. DEBT STOCK-FLOW RECONCILIATION										
Total change in debt stocks	..	..	..	-117	354	102	-138	-40	2,273	1,332
Net flows on debt	..	..	..	111	-381	25	168	-9	1,695	1,120
Net change in interest arrears	..	..	..	1	26	-9	-9	4	-5	-9
Interest capitalized	..	..	..	0	0	0	0	0	0	0
Debt forgiveness or reduction	..	..	..	0	-2	0	-25	-91	0	0
Cross-currency valuation	..	..	..	-223	429	-27	-384	-100	192	31
Residual	..	..	..	-6	283	113	111	156	391	189
9. AVERAGE TERMS OF NEW COMMITMENTS										
ALL CREDITORS										
Interest (%)	6.0	12.9	8.1	9.0	8.1	7.3	7.8	6.9	6.9	6.2
Maturity (years)	21.2	15.5	13.2	13.5	16.4	12.0	17.9	11.9	14.9	12.0
Grace period (years)	4.8	4.4	4.4	5.3	4.6	6.0	4.5	3.7	5.5	4.2
Grant element (%)	25.8	-20.4	9.3	4.8	11.0	14.4	12.6	13.7	17.6	18.5
Official creditors										
Interest (%)	5.2	8.9	7.8	7.3	7.8	6.8	7.8	7.2	6.5	6.2
Maturity (years)	29.8	18.0	17.8	17.2	18.6	18.7	17.9	17.3	19.3	20.5
Grace period (years)	7.2	4.3	4.7	5.1	5.4	5.4	4.5	4.2	5.2	4.8
Grant element (%)	36.9	6.5	12.2	15.5	13.9	20.1	12.7	16.1	21.8	24.4
Private creditors										
Interest (%)	7.2	15.4	8.3	9.9	9.3	7.4	11.1	6.7	7.5	6.2
Maturity (years)	7.2	13.9	10.6	11.5	9.9	10.9	12.4	6.0	8.4	6.0
Grace period (years)	1.0	4.5	4.3	5.4	2.2	6.1	3.8	3.1	6.1	3.8
Grant element (%)	7.9	-37.2	7.7	-1.1	2.3	13.5	-7.9	11.0	11.4	14.2
Memorandum items										
Commitments	363	1,566	2,439	2,894	1,269	2,343	836	1,625	1,561	1,567
Official creditors	224	602	875	1,026	951	319	831	849	933	656
Private creditors	139	964	1,564	1,868	318	2,025	5	776	627	911

10. CONTRACTUAL OBLIGATIONS ON OUTSTANDING LONG-TERM DEBT

	1996	1997	1998	1999	2000	2001	2002	2003	2004	2005
TOTAL										
Disbursements	874	707	453	314	191	93	59	28	23	16
Principal	2,102	1,894	2,304	1,920	2,023	1,348	1,206	1,264	942	439
Interest	1,057	958	858	711	604	485	405	334	229	189
Official creditors										
Disbursements	699	598	426	303	190	93	59	28	23	16
Principal	953	953	955	763	712	680	587	509	474	425
Interest	522	488	443	393	350	307	264	228	195	165
Bilateral creditors										
Disbursements	228	112	50	17	8	5	2	2	2	1
Principal	302	255	255	127	93	94	92	88	74	58
Interest	101	86	70	54	47	41	36	30	26	23
Multilateral creditors										
Disbursements	471	486	377	286	182	88	57	26	21	15
Principal	652	698	701	636	619	587	495	421	400	367
Interest	421	402	373	339	304	266	229	197	169	142
Private creditors										
Disbursements	175	109	27	11	1	0	0	0	0	0
Principal	1,149	941	1,349	1,157	1,311	668	619	754	468	14
Interest	535	470	415	319	253	178	141	106	34	24
Commercial banks										
Disbursements	72	48	19	8	0	0	0	0	0	0
Principal	509	493	624	756	582	441	284	258	259	6
Interest	260	236	213	164	117	79	53	34	12	3
Other private										
Disbursements	103	62	8	3	1	0	0	0	0	0
Principal	640	448	725	401	729	227	336	496	210	8
Interest	276	234	202	154	136	99	87	72	22	21

COMOROS

(US$ million, unless otherwise indicated)

1. SUMMARY DEBT DATA

	1970	1980	1988	1989	1990	1991	1992	1993	1994	1995
TOTAL DEBT STOCKS (EDT)	..	44.0	198.7	173.7	185.0	179.9	188.0	184.4	188.7	203.3
Long-term debt (LDOD)	1.2	43.0	187.7	161.0	172.6	166.1	174.9	169.2	175.5	186.7
Public and publicly guaranteed	1.2	43.0	187.7	161.0	172.6	166.1	174.9	169.2	175.5	186.7
Private nonguaranteed	0.0	0.0	0.0	0.0	0.0	0.0	0.0	0.0	0.0	0.0
Use of IMF credit	0.0	0.0	0.0	0.0	0.0	1.3	1.2	1.2	3.3	3.3
Short-term debt	..	1.0	11.0	12.7	12.5	12.5	11.8	14.0	9.8	13.2
of which interest arrears on LDOD	..	0.0	8.0	9.5	12.3	12.4	11.7	13.0	9.8	11.2
Official creditors	..	0.0	7.9	9.5	12.3	12.4	11.7	13.0	9.8	11.2
Private creditors	..	0.0	0.1	0.0	0.0	0.0	0.0	0.0	0.0	0.0
Memo: principal arrears on LDOD	..	0.0	14.3	19.4	25.5	17.3	19.4	18.8	17.7	23.2
Official creditors	..	0.0	14.1	19.4	25.5	17.3	19.4	18.8	17.7	23.2
Private creditors	..	0.0	0.2	0.0	0.0	0.0	0.0	0.0	0.0	0.0
Memo: export credits	..	..	3.0	3.0	2.0	1.0	1.0	1.0	4.0	4.0
TOTAL DEBT FLOWS										
Disbursements	0.0	13.0	8.3	4.1	5.4	4.4	17.5	5.3	9.6	9.6
Long-term debt	0.0	13.0	8.3	4.1	5.4	3.1	17.5	5.3	7.6	9.6
IMF purchases	0.0	0.0	0.0	0.0	0.0	1.2	0.0	0.0	1.9	0.0
Principal repayments	0.0	0.0	0.1	0.2	0.2	5.8	3.3	1.7	2.0	0.4
Long-term debt	0.0	0.0	0.1	0.2	0.2	5.8	3.3	1.7	2.0	0.4
IMF repurchases	0.0	0.0	0.0	0.0	0.0	0.0	0.0	0.0	0.0	0.0
Net flows on debt	0.0	13.0	1.1	4.3	2.2	-1.5	14.2	4.5	6.6	11.2
of which short-term debt	..	..	-7.1	0.3	-3.0	-0.1	0.0	0.9	-1.0	2.0
Interest payments (INT)	..	0.4	0.9	1.4	0.7	2.4	2.5	0.6	0.8	0.6
Long-term debt	0.0	0.3	0.4	0.8	0.6	2.3	2.5	0.6	0.7	0.5
IMF charges	0.0	0.0	0.0	0.0	0.0	0.0	0.0	0.0	0.0	0.0
Short-term debt	..	0.1	0.5	0.6	0.1	0.0	0.0	0.0	0.0	0.1
Net transfers on debt	..	12.6	0.2	2.9	1.4	-3.9	11.7	3.9	5.8	10.6
Total debt service paid (TDS)	..	0.4	1.0	1.5	1.0	8.2	5.8	2.3	2.8	1.0
Long-term debt	0.1	0.3	0.5	0.9	0.8	8.1	5.8	2.2	2.7	0.9
IMF repurchases and charges	0.0	0.0	0.0	0.0	0.0	0.0	0.0	0.0	0.0	0.0
Short-term debt (interest only)	..	0.1	0.5	0.6	0.1	0.0	0.0	0.0	0.0	0.1

2. AGGREGATE NET RESOURCE FLOWS AND NET TRANSFERS (LONG-TERM)

	1970	1980	1988	1989	1990	1991	1992	1993	1994	1995
NET RESOURCE FLOWS	3.1	30.9	38.1	26.9	31.9	33.0	38.0	33.4	24.1	28.7
Net flow of long-term debt (ex. IMF)	0.0	13.0	8.2	4.0	5.2	-2.7	14.2	3.6	5.6	9.2
Foreign direct investment (net)	0.0	0.0	3.8	3.3	-1.0	3.0	1.0	2.0	2.0	2.0
Portfolio equity flows	0.0	0.0	0.0	0.0	0.0	0.0	0.0	0.0	0.0	0.0
Grants (excluding technical coop.)	3.1	17.9	26.1	19.6	27.7	32.7	22.8	27.8	16.5	17.5
Memo: technical coop. grants	4.8	6.8	17.2	17.0	16.8	18.3	19.5	18.5	15.5	16.4
NET TRANSFERS	3.0	30.6	37.7	26.1	30.7	29.9	35.5	32.9	23.4	28.2
Interest on long-term debt	0.0	0.3	0.4	0.8	0.6	2.3	2.5	0.6	0.7	0.5
Profit remittances on FDI	0.0	0.0	0.0	0.0	0.6	0.8	0.0	0.0	0.0	0.0

3. MAJOR ECONOMIC AGGREGATES

	1970	1980	1988	1989	1990	1991	1992	1993	1994	1995
Gross national product (GNP)	24.7	124.0	205.2	200.0	249.3	246.3	267.8	281.6	201.0	227.8
Exports of goods & services (XGS)	..	15.7	47.5	47.8	48.1	73.3	93.4	125.6	89.0	106.2
of which workers remittances	..	1.6	7.4	7.9	9.9	10.2	8.2	11.0	7.8	9.3
Imports of goods & services (MGS)	..	34.3	90.5	78.2	92.2	104.7	114.9	127.7	112.8	133.3
International reserves (RES)	..	6.4	23.8	31.0	29.9	29.4	27.3	38.6	44.0	44.5
Current account balance	..	-8.9	-6.5	5.4	-9.3	-18.0	-26.9	-5.3	-26.3	-31.0

4. DEBT INDICATORS

	1970	1980	1988	1989	1990	1991	1992	1993	1994	1995
EDT / XGS (%)	..	280.1	418.3	363.4	384.7	245.4	201.3	146.8	212.0	191.4
EDT / GNP (%)	..	35.5	96.8	86.8	74.2	73.0	70.2	65.5	93.9	89.2
TDS / XGS (%)	..	2.6	2.2	3.2	2.1	11.1	6.2	1.8	3.1	0.9
INT / XGS (%)	..	2.6	1.9	2.8	1.5	3.2	2.6	0.5	0.9	0.5
INT / GNP (%)	..	0.3	0.4	0.7	0.3	1.0	0.9	0.2	0.4	0.2
RES / EDT (%)	..	14.6	12.0	17.8	16.2	16.3	14.5	20.9	23.3	21.9
RES / MGS (months)	..	2.2	3.2	4.8	3.9	3.4	2.9	3.6	4.7	4.0
Short-term / EDT (%)	..	2.3	5.5	7.3	6.8	7.0	6.3	7.6	5.2	6.5
Concessional / EDT (%)	..	96.8	87.2	85.3	85.8	87.6	89.3	87.9	89.0	88.1
Multilateral / EDT (%)	..	48.2	53.7	61.5	61.6	62.2	65.2	69.5	74.7	74.9

COMOROS

(US$ million, unless otherwise indicated)

	1970	1980	1988	1989	1990	1991	1992	1993	1994	1995
5. LONG-TERM DEBT										
DEBT OUTSTANDING (LDOD)	**1.2**	**43.0**	**187.7**	**161.0**	**172.6**	**166.1**	**174.9**	**169.2**	**175.5**	**186.7**
Public and publicly guaranteed	**1.2**	**43.0**	**187.7**	**161.0**	**172.6**	**166.1**	**174.9**	**169.2**	**175.5**	**186.7**
Official creditors	1.2	42.6	187.5	161.0	172.6	166.1	174.9	169.2	175.5	186.7
Multilateral	0.0	21.2	106.7	106.8	113.9	111.9	122.7	128.2	140.9	152.2
Concessional	0.0	21.2	93.7	94.1	100.2	103.4	115.6	121.1	133.3	144.6
Bilateral	1.2	21.4	80.9	54.2	58.6	54.1	52.3	41.0	34.7	34.5
Concessional	1.2	21.4	79.7	54.2	58.6	54.1	52.3	41.0	34.7	34.5
Private creditors	0.0	0.4	0.2	0.0	0.0	0.0	0.0	0.0	0.0	0.0
Bonds	0.0	0.0	0.0	0.0	0.0	0.0	0.0	0.0	0.0	0.0
Commercial banks	0.0	0.0	0.0	0.0	0.0	0.0	0.0	0.0	0.0	0.0
Other private	0.0	0.4	0.2	0.0	0.0	0.0	0.0	0.0	0.0	0.0
Private nonguaranteed	**0.0**	**0.0**	**0.0**	**0.0**	**0.0**	**0.0**	**0.0**	**0.0**	**0.0**	**0.0**
Bonds	0.0	0.0	0.0	0.0	0.0	0.0	0.0	0.0	0.0	0.0
Commercial banks	0.0	0.0	0.0	0.0	0.0	0.0	0.0	0.0	0.0	0.0
Memo:										
IBRD	0.0	0.0	0.0	0.0	0.0	0.0	0.0	0.0	0.0	0.0
IDA	0.0	4.2	33.9	34.8	37.5	39.0	40.1	44.8	53.9	64.1
DISBURSEMENTS	**0.0**	**13.0**	**8.3**	**4.1**	**5.4**	**3.1**	**17.5**	**5.3**	**7.6**	**9.6**
Public and publicly guaranteed	**0.0**	**13.0**	**8.3**	**4.1**	**5.4**	**3.1**	**17.5**	**5.3**	**7.6**	**9.6**
Official creditors	0.0	12.6	8.3	4.1	5.4	3.1	17.5	5.3	7.6	9.6
Multilateral	0.0	6.1	2.2	2.0	1.3	3.1	17.2	5.3	7.6	9.6
Concessional	0.0	6.1	2.2	2.0	1.3	3.1	17.2	5.3	7.6	9.6
Bilateral	0.0	6.5	6.1	2.2	4.2	0.0	0.2	0.0	0.0	0.0
Concessional	0.0	6.5	6.1	2.2	4.2	0.0	0.2	0.0	0.0	0.0
Private creditors	0.0	0.4	0.0	0.0	0.0	0.0	0.0	0.0	0.0	0.0
Bonds	0.0	0.0	0.0	0.0	0.0	0.0	0.0	0.0	0.0	0.0
Commercial banks	0.0	0.0	0.0	0.0	0.0	0.0	0.0	0.0	0.0	0.0
Other private	0.0	0.4	0.0	0.0	0.0	0.0	0.0	0.0	0.0	0.0
Private nonguaranteed	**0.0**	**0.0**	**0.0**	**0.0**	**0.0**	**0.0**	**0.0**	**0.0**	**0.0**	**0.0**
Bonds	0.0	0.0	0.0	0.0	0.0	0.0	0.0	0.0	0.0	0.0
Commercial banks	0.0	0.0	0.0	0.0	0.0	0.0	0.0	0.0	0.0	0.0
Memo:										
IBRD	0.0	0.0	0.0	0.0	0.0	0.0	0.0	0.0	0.0	0.0
IDA	0.0	1.8	2.0	1.5	0.7	1.4	2.6	4.9	7.6	9.6
PRINCIPAL REPAYMENTS	**0.0**	**0.0**	**0.1**	**0.2**	**0.2**	**5.8**	**3.3**	**1.7**	**2.0**	**0.4**
Public and publicly guaranteed	**0.0**	**0.0**	**0.1**	**0.2**	**0.2**	**5.8**	**3.3**	**1.7**	**2.0**	**0.4**
Official creditors	0.0	0.0	0.1	0.2	0.2	5.8	3.3	1.7	2.0	0.4
Multilateral	0.0	0.0	0.1	0.2	0.2	5.5	3.1	1.7	0.7	0.4
Concessional	0.0	0.0	0.1	0.2	0.2	0.4	2.0	1.7	0.7	0.4
Bilateral	0.0	0.0	0.0	0.0	0.0	0.3	0.2	0.0	1.3	0.0
Concessional	0.0	0.0	0.0	0.0	0.0	0.3	0.2	0.0	1.3	0.0
Private creditors	0.0	0.0	0.0	0.0	0.0	0.0	0.0	0.0	0.0	0.0
Bonds	0.0	0.0	0.0	0.0	0.0	0.0	0.0	0.0	0.0	0.0
Commercial banks	0.0	0.0	0.0	0.0	0.0	0.0	0.0	0.0	0.0	0.0
Other private	0.0	0.0	0.0	0.0	0.0	0.0	0.0	0.0	0.0	0.0
Private nonguaranteed	**0.0**	**0.0**	**0.0**	**0.0**	**0.0**	**0.0**	**0.0**	**0.0**	**0.0**	**0.0**
Bonds	0.0	0.0	0.0	0.0	0.0	0.0	0.0	0.0	0.0	0.0
Commercial banks	0.0	0.0	0.0	0.0	0.0	0.0	0.0	0.0	0.0	0.0
Memo:										
IBRD	0.0	0.0	0.0	0.0	0.0	0.0	0.0	0.0	0.0	0.0
IDA	0.0	0.0	0.0	0.0	0.1	0.1	0.2	0.2	0.3	0.4
NET FLOWS ON DEBT	**0.0**	**13.0**	**8.2**	**4.0**	**5.2**	**-2.7**	**14.2**	**3.6**	**5.6**	**9.2**
Public and publicly guaranteed	**0.0**	**13.0**	**8.2**	**4.0**	**5.2**	**-2.7**	**14.2**	**3.6**	**5.6**	**9.2**
Official creditors	0.0	12.6	8.2	4.0	5.2	-2.7	14.2	3.6	5.6	9.2
Multilateral	0.0	6.1	2.1	1.8	1.0	-2.4	14.1	3.6	7.0	9.2
Concessional	0.0	6.1	2.1	1.8	1.0	2.8	15.2	3.6	7.0	9.2
Bilateral	0.0	6.5	6.1	2.2	4.1	-0.3	0.1	0.0	-1.3	0.0
Concessional	0.0	6.5	6.1	2.2	4.1	-0.3	0.1	0.0	-1.3	0.0
Private creditors	0.0	0.4	0.0	0.0	0.0	0.0	0.0	0.0	0.0	0.0
Bonds	0.0	0.0	0.0	0.0	0.0	0.0	0.0	0.0	0.0	0.0
Commercial banks	0.0	0.0	0.0	0.0	0.0	0.0	0.0	0.0	0.0	0.0
Other private	0.0	0.4	0.0	0.0	0.0	0.0	0.0	0.0	0.0	0.0
Private nonguaranteed	**0.0**	**0.0**	**0.0**	**0.0**	**0.0**	**0.0**	**0.0**	**0.0**	**0.0**	**0.0**
Bonds	0.0	0.0	0.0	0.0	0.0	0.0	0.0	0.0	0.0	0.0
Commercial banks	0.0	0.0	0.0	0.0	0.0	0.0	0.0	0.0	0.0	0.0
Memo:										
IBRD	0.0	0.0	0.0	0.0	0.0	0.0	0.0	0.0	0.0	0.0
IDA	0.0	1.8	2.0	1.4	0.6	1.3	2.3	4.6	7.3	9.2

COMOROS

(US$ million, unless otherwise indicated)

	1970	1980	1988	1989	1990	1991	1992	1993	1994	1995
INTEREST PAYMENTS (LINT)	**0.0**	**0.3**	**0.4**	**0.8**	**0.6**	**2.3**	**2.5**	**0.6**	**0.7**	**0.5**
Public and publicly guaranteed	**0.0**	**0.3**	**0.4**	**0.8**	**0.6**	**2.3**	**2.5**	**0.6**	**0.7**	**0.5**
Official creditors	0.0	0.3	0.4	0.8	0.6	2.3	2.5	0.6	0.7	0.5
Multilateral	0.0	0.0	0.3	0.3	0.3	1.9	2.0	0.5	0.7	0.5
Concessional	0.0	0.0	0.3	0.3	0.3	1.3	1.0	0.5	0.7	0.5
Bilateral	0.0	0.3	0.1	0.5	0.3	0.4	0.4	0.0	0.0	0.0
Concessional	0.0	0.3	0.1	0.5	0.3	0.4	0.4	0.0	0.0	0.0
Private creditors	0.0	0.0	0.0	0.0	0.0	0.0	0.0	0.0	0.0	0.0
Bonds	0.0	0.0	0.0	0.0	0.0	0.0	0.0	0.0	0.0	0.0
Commercial banks	0.0	0.0	0.0	0.0	0.0	0.0	0.0	0.0	0.0	0.0
Other private	0.0	0.0	0.0	0.0	0.0	0.0	0.0	0.0	0.0	0.0
Private nonguaranteed	**0.0**	**0.0**	**0.0**	**0.0**	**0.0**	**0.0**	**0.0**	**0.0**	**0.0**	**0.0**
Bonds	0.0	0.0	0.0	0.0	0.0	0.0	0.0	0.0	0.0	0.0
Commercial banks	0.0	0.0	0.0	0.0	0.0	0.0	0.0	0.0	0.0	0.0
Memo:										
IBRD	0.0	0.0	0.0	0.0	0.0	0.0	0.0	0.0	0.0	0.0
IDA	0.0	0.0	0.3	0.2	0.3	0.3	0.3	0.3	0.3	0.4
NET TRANSFERS ON DEBT	**-0.1**	**12.7**	**7.8**	**3.2**	**4.6**	**-5.0**	**11.7**	**3.1**	**4.9**	**8.7**
Public and publicly guaranteed	**-0.1**	**12.7**	**7.8**	**3.2**	**4.6**	**-5.0**	**11.7**	**3.1**	**4.9**	**8.7**
Official creditors	-0.1	12.3	7.8	3.2	4.6	-5.0	11.7	3.1	4.9	8.7
Multilateral	0.0	6.1	1.8	1.5	0.7	-4.3	12.1	3.1	6.3	8.7
Concessional	0.0	6.1	1.8	1.5	0.7	1.5	14.2	3.1	6.3	8.7
Bilateral	-0.1	6.2	6.0	1.7	3.9	-0.7	-0.3	0.0	-1.3	0.0
Concessional	-0.1	6.2	6.0	1.7	3.9	-0.7	-0.3	0.0	-1.3	0.0
Private creditors	0.0	0.4	0.0	0.0	0.0	0.0	0.0	0.0	0.0	0.0
Bonds	0.0	0.0	0.0	0.0	0.0	0.0	0.0	0.0	0.0	0.0
Commercial banks	0.0	0.0	0.0	0.0	0.0	0.0	0.0	0.0	0.0	0.0
Other private	0.0	0.4	0.0	0.0	0.0	0.0	0.0	0.0	0.0	0.0
Private nonguaranteed	**0.0**	**0.0**	**0.0**	**0.0**	**0.0**	**0.0**	**0.0**	**0.0**	**0.0**	**0.0**
Bonds	0.0	0.0	0.0	0.0	0.0	0.0	0.0	0.0	0.0	0.0
Commercial banks	0.0	0.0	0.0	0.0	0.0	0.0	0.0	0.0	0.0	0.0
Memo:										
IBRD	0.0	0.0	0.0	0.0	0.0	0.0	0.0	0.0	0.0	0.0
IDA	0.0	1.7	1.7	1.2	0.3	0.9	2.0	4.3	7.0	8.7
DEBT SERVICE (LTDS)	**0.1**	**0.3**	**0.5**	**0.9**	**0.8**	**8.1**	**5.8**	**2.2**	**2.7**	**0.9**
Public and publicly guaranteed	**0.1**	**0.3**	**0.5**	**0.9**	**0.8**	**8.1**	**5.8**	**2.2**	**2.7**	**0.9**
Official creditors	0.1	0.3	0.5	0.9	0.8	8.1	5.8	2.2	2.7	0.9
Multilateral	0.0	0.0	0.4	0.4	0.5	7.4	5.2	2.2	1.4	0.9
Concessional	0.0	0.0	0.4	0.4	0.5	1.7	3.0	2.2	1.4	0.9
Bilateral	0.1	0.3	0.1	0.5	0.3	0.7	0.6	0.0	1.3	0.0
Concessional	0.1	0.3	0.1	0.5	0.3	0.7	0.6	0.0	1.3	0.0
Private creditors	0.0	0.0	0.0	0.0	0.0	0.0	0.0	0.0	0.0	0.0
Bonds	0.0	0.0	0.0	0.0	0.0	0.0	0.0	0.0	0.0	0.0
Commercial banks	0.0	0.0	0.0	0.0	0.0	0.0	0.0	0.0	0.0	0.0
Other private	0.0	0.0	0.0	0.0	0.0	0.0	0.0	0.0	0.0	0.0
Private nonguaranteed	**0.0**	**0.0**	**0.0**	**0.0**	**0.0**	**0.0**	**0.0**	**0.0**	**0.0**	**0.0**
Bonds	0.0	0.0	0.0	0.0	0.0	0.0	0.0	0.0	0.0	0.0
Commercial banks	0.0	0.0	0.0	0.0	0.0	0.0	0.0	0.0	0.0	0.0
Memo:										
IBRD	0.0	0.0	0.0	0.0	0.0	0.0	0.0	0.0	0.0	0.0
IDA	0.0	0.0	0.3	0.3	0.3	0.4	0.5	0.5	0.6	0.8
UNDISBURSED DEBT	**0.0**	**49.8**	**58.3**	**57.7**	**56.8**	**79.3**	**53.4**	**29.7**	**33.5**	**24.9**
Official creditors	0.0	48.8	58.3	57.7	56.8	79.3	53.4	29.7	33.5	24.9
Private creditors	0.0	1.0	0.0	0.0	0.0	0.0	0.0	0.0	0.0	0.0
Memorandum items										
Concessional LDOD	1.2	42.6	173.3	148.2	158.8	157.6	167.8	162.1	168.0	179.0
Variable rate LDOD	0.0	0.0	0.0	0.0	0.0	0.0	0.0	0.0	0.0	0.0
Public sector LDOD	1.2	43.0	187.7	161.0	172.6	166.1	174.9	169.2	175.5	186.7
Private sector LDOD	0.0	0.0	0.0	0.0	0.0	0.0	0.0	0.0	0.0	0.0

6. CURRENCY COMPOSITION OF LONG-TERM DEBT (PERCENT)

	1970	1980	1988	1989	1990	1991	1992	1993	1994	1995
Deutsche mark	0.0	0.0	0.0	0.0	0.0	0.0	0.0	0.0	0.0	0.0
French franc	100.0	2.8	32.6	22.4	23.8	22.5	20.7	21.1	19.9	18.9
Japanese yen	0.0	0.0	0.0	0.0	0.0	0.0	0.0	0.0	0.0	0.0
Pound sterling	0.0	0.0	0.0	0.0	0.0	0.0	0.0	0.0	0.0	0.0
Swiss franc	0.0	0.0	0.0	0.0	0.0	0.0	0.0	0.0	0.0	0.0
U.S.dollars	0.0	38.4	15.1	18.1	17.3	18.6	18.9	22.3	26.0	29.7
Multiple currency	0.0	10.2	7.2	8.2	8.1	8.4	7.0	6.1	5.4	4.9
Special drawing rights	0.0	0.0	0.0	0.0	0.0	0.0	0.0	0.0	0.0	0.0
All other currencies	0.0	48.6	45.1	51.2	50.8	50.5	53.4	50.6	48.8	46.5

COMOROS

(US$ million, unless otherwise indicated)

	1970	1980	1988	1989	1990	1991	1992	1993	1994	1995
7. DEBT RESTRUCTURINGS										
Total amount rescheduled	0.0	0.0	0.0	0.0	0.0	0.0	0.0	4.9	5.6	1.9
Debt stock rescheduled	0.0	0.0	0.0	0.0	0.0	0.0	0.0	0.0	0.0	0.0
Principal rescheduled	0.0	0.0	0.0	0.0	0.0	0.0	0.0	4.6	4.7	1.8
Official	0.0	0.0	0.0	0.0	0.0	0.0	0.0	4.6	4.7	1.8
Private	0.0	0.0	0.0	0.0	0.0	0.0	0.0	0.0	0.0	0.0
Interest rescheduled	0.0	0.0	0.0	0.0	0.0	0.0	0.0	0.3	0.9	0.1
Official	0.0	0.0	0.0	0.0	0.0	0.0	0.0	0.3	0.9	0.1
Private	0.0	0.0	0.0	0.0	0.0	0.0	0.0	0.0	0.0	0.0
Debt forgiven	..	..	0.0	26.1	0.1	4.2	0.0	11.3	4.6	0.4
Memo: interest forgiven	..	..	0.0	0.1	0.0	0.2	0.0	0.0	3.5	0.1
Debt stock reduction	0.0	0.0	0.0	0.0	0.0	0.0	0.0	0.0	0.0	0.0
of which debt buyback	0.0	0.0	0.0	0.0	0.0	0.0	0.0	0.0	0.0	0.0
8. DEBT STOCK-FLOW RECONCILIATION										
Total change in debt stocks	..	..	..	-25.0	11.3	-5.1	8.1	-3.6	4.3	14.6
Net flows on debt	..	..	..	4.3	2.2	-1.5	14.2	4.5	6.6	11.2
Net change in interest arrears	..	..	..	1.5	2.8	0.1	-0.7	1.3	-3.1	1.4
Interest capitalized	..	..	..	0.0	0.0	0.0	0.0	0.3	0.9	0.1
Debt forgiveness or reduction	..	..	..	-26.1	-0.1	-4.2	0.0	-11.3	-4.6	-0.4
Cross-currency valuation	..	..	..	-0.7	8.6	-0.4	-5.4	-2.4	6.4	4.3
Residual	..	..	..	-4.0	-2.1	0.9	0.0	4.0	-1.9	-1.9
9. AVERAGE TERMS OF NEW COMMITMENTS										
ALL CREDITORS										
Interest (%)	0.0	1.3	1.9	0.8	2.0	0.8	0.0	0.0	0.8	0.0
Maturity (years)	0.0	43.1	25.5	30.1	29.8	37.4	0.0	0.0	39.6	0.0
Grace period (years)	0.0	9.0	9.5	7.4	10.3	9.2	0.0	0.0	10.1	0.0
Grant element (%)	0.0	74.5	62.8	73.2	65.9	76.8	0.0	0.0	80.4	0.0
Official creditors										
Interest (%)	0.0	0.8	1.9	0.8	2.0	0.8	0.0	0.0	0.8	0.0
Maturity (years)	0.0	45.6	25.5	30.1	29.8	37.4	0.0	0.0	39.6	0.0
Grace period (years)	0.0	9.5	9.5	7.4	10.3	9.2	0.0	0.0	10.1	0.0
Grant element (%)	0.0	79.1	62.8	73.2	65.9	76.8	0.0	0.0	80.4	0.0
Private creditors										
Interest (%)	0.0	7.6	0.0	0.0	0.0	0.0	0.0	0.0	0.0	0.0
Maturity (years)	0.0	5.2	0.0	0.0	0.0	0.0	0.0	0.0	0.0	0.0
Grace period (years)	0.0	1.5	0.0	0.0	0.0	0.0	0.0	0.0	0.0	0.0
Grant element (%)	0.0	5.6	0.0	0.0	0.0	0.0	0.0	0.0	0.0	0.0
Memorandum items										
Commitments	0.0	23.4	5.6	8.8	0.9	27.2	0.0	0.0	18.1	0.0
Official creditors	0.0	21.9	5.6	8.8	0.9	27.2	0.0	0.0	18.1	0.0
Private creditors	0.0	1.4	0.0	0.0	0.0	0.0	0.0	0.0	0.0	0.0

10. CONTRACTUAL OBLIGATIONS ON OUTSTANDING LONG-TERM DEBT

	1996	1997	1998	1999	2000	2001	2002	2003	2004	2005
TOTAL										
Disbursements	7.7	5.6	3.6	2.6	1.4	0.2	0.0	0.0	0.0	0.0
Principal	6.6	7.5	7.7	8.2	8.5	6.2	5.6	5.0	4.4	4.5
Interest	1.6	1.6	1.5	1.4	1.3	1.2	1.1	1.0	1.0	1.0
Official creditors										
Disbursements	7.7	5.6	3.6	2.6	1.4	0.2	0.0	0.0	0.0	0.0
Principal	6.6	7.5	7.7	8.2	8.5	6.2	5.6	5.0	4.4	4.5
Interest	1.6	1.6	1.5	1.4	1.3	1.2	1.1	1.0	1.0	1.0
Bilateral creditors										
Disbursements	0.0	0.0	0.0	0.0	0.0	0.0	0.0	0.0	0.0	0.0
Principal	2.5	3.1	3.3	3.5	3.6	1.0	1.0	0.8	0.8	0.8
Interest	0.2	0.2	0.2	0.2	0.2	0.1	0.1	0.1	0.1	0.1
Multilateral creditors										
Disbursements	7.7	5.6	3.6	2.6	1.4	0.2	0.0	0.0	0.0	0.0
Principal	4.0	4.4	4.4	4.7	4.9	5.2	4.7	4.2	3.6	3.8
Interest	1.4	1.4	1.3	1.2	1.1	1.0	0.9	0.9	0.9	0.9
Private creditors										
Disbursements	0.0	0.0	0.0	0.0	0.0	0.0	0.0	0.0	0.0	0.0
Principal	0.0	0.0	0.0	0.0	0.0	0.0	0.0	0.0	0.0	0.0
Interest	0.0	0.0	0.0	0.0	0.0	0.0	0.0	0.0	0.0	0.0
Commercial banks										
Disbursements	0.0	0.0	0.0	0.0	0.0	0.0	0.0	0.0	0.0	0.0
Principal	0.0	0.0	0.0	0.0	0.0	0.0	0.0	0.0	0.0	0.0
Interest	0.0	0.0	0.0	0.0	0.0	0.0	0.0	0.0	0.0	0.0
Other private										
Disbursements	0.0	0.0	0.0	0.0	0.0	0.0	0.0	0.0	0.0	0.0
Principal	0.0	0.0	0.0	0.0	0.0	0.0	0.0	0.0	0.0	0.0
Interest	0.0	0.0	0.0	0.0	0.0	0.0	0.0	0.0	0.0	0.0

CONGO

(US$ million, unless otherwise indicated)

	1970	1980	1988	1989	1990	1991	1992	1993	1994	1995
1. SUMMARY DEBT DATA										
TOTAL DEBT STOCKS (EDT)	..	**1,526**	**4,090**	**4,279**	**4,953**	**4,832**	**4,770**	**5,081**	**5,422**	**6,032**
Long-term debt (LDOD)	**119**	**1,257**	**3,485**	**3,502**	**4,206**	**4,041**	**3,876**	**4,114**	**4,774**	**4,955**
Public and publicly guaranteed	119	1,257	3,485	3,502	4,206	4,041	3,876	4,114	4,774	4,955
Private nonguaranteed	0	0	0	0	0	0	0	0	0	0
Use of IMF credit	**0**	**22**	**15**	**12**	**11**	**6**	**6**	**5**	**20**	**19**
Short-term debt	..	**247**	**590**	**765**	**736**	**785**	**889**	**962**	**628**	**1,058**
of which interest arrears on LDOD	..	4	219	348	181	324	496	643	274	468
Official creditors	..	2	132	216	77	204	369	507	178	357
Private creditors	..	2	87	131	104	121	126	135	96	111
Memo: principal arrears on LDOD	..	10	450	681	572	757	1,029	1,255	801	1,043
Official creditors	..	5	99	156	126	256	483	697	400	604
Private creditors	..	5	352	526	445	501	545	558	400	439
Memo: export credits	..	..	1,486	1,511	1,877	1,331	1,551	1,616	1,945	2,562
TOTAL DEBT FLOWS										
Disbursements	**18**	**526**	**610**	**185**	**319**	**38**	**132**	**459**	**350**	**15**
Long-term debt	18	522	610	185	314	38	132	459	332	15
IMF purchases	0	4	0	0	5	0	0	0	18	0
Principal repayments	**6**	**41**	**294**	**203**	**362**	**209**	**98**	**77**	**305**	**84**
Long-term debt	6	34	291	199	355	204	98	76	302	82
IMF repurchases	0	7	3	3	7	5	0	1	3	2
Net flows on debt	**13**	**485**	**-96**	**29**	**95**	**-266**	**-35**	**310**	**79**	**166**
of which short-term debt	..	..	-412	47	138	-94	-68	-73	34	236
Interest payments (INT)	..	**68**	**128**	**138**	**169**	**91**	**64**	**51**	**252**	**97**
Long-term debt	3	37	81	91	120	50	29	21	232	61
IMF charges	0	1	1	1	1	1	0	0	1	1
Short-term debt	..	31	46	46	48	40	35	30	20	35
Net transfers on debt	..	**417**	**-224**	**-109**	**-74**	**-357**	**-99**	**258**	**-173**	**69**
Total debt service paid (TDS)	..	**109**	**422**	**341**	**531**	**300**	**162**	**128**	**557**	**181**
Long-term debt	9	71	372	290	475	255	127	97	533	142
IMF repurchases and charges	0	8	4	4	8	6	0	1	4	3
Short-term debt (interest only)	..	31	46	46	48	40	35	30	20	35
2. AGGREGATE NET RESOURCE FLOWS AND NET TRANSFERS (LONG-TERM)										
NET RESOURCE FLOWS	**18**	**548**	**347**	**13**	**8**	**-139**	**70**	**453**	**211**	**20**
Net flow of long-term debt (ex. IMF)	13	488	319	-15	-42	-167	33	383	30	-67
Foreign direct investment (net)	0	40	9	0	0	0	0	0	0	1
Portfolio equity flows	0	0	0	0	0	0	0	0	0	0
Grants (excluding technical coop.)	5	20	19	27	50	28	36	70	181	86
Memo: technical coop. grants	10	37	39	37	51	46	48	46	38	42
NET TRANSFERS	**15**	**505**	**203**	**-79**	**-112**	**-189**	**39**	**427**	**-25**	**-43**
Interest on long-term debt	3	37	81	91	120	50	29	21	232	61
Profit remittances on FDI	0	6	63	0	0	0	2	5	4	3
3. MAJOR ECONOMIC AGGREGATES										
Gross national product (GNP)	267	1,541	1,907	2,072	2,146	2,138	2,645	2,200	1,388	1,649
Exports of goods & services (XGS)	..	1,030	943	1,258	1,503	1,226	1,257	1,187	1,028	1,252
of which workers remittances	..	1	0	0	0	0	0	0	0	0
Imports of goods & services (MGS)	..	1,195	1,396	1,389	1,757	1,683	1,555	1,731	1,900	1,825
International reserves (RES)	9	93	9	11	10	9	8	6	55	64
Current account balance	..	-167	-446	-85	-251	-462	-317	-553	-793	-570
4. DEBT INDICATORS										
EDT / XGS (%)	..	148.2	433.8	340.1	329.6	394.2	379.4	428.2	527.5	481.8
EDT / GNP (%)	..	99.0	214.5	206.5	230.8	226.1	180.4	231.0	390.7	365.8
TDS / XGS (%)	..	10.6	44.7	27.1	35.3	24.5	12.9	10.8	54.2	14.4
INT / XGS (%)	..	6.6	13.6	11.0	11.2	7.4	5.1	4.3	24.5	7.7
INT / GNP (%)	..	4.4	6.7	6.7	7.9	4.3	2.4	2.3	18.2	5.9
RES / EDT (%)	..	6.1	0.2	0.2	0.2	0.2	0.2	0.1	1.0	1.1
RES / MGS (months)	..	0.9	0.1	0.1	0.1	0.1	0.1	0.0	0.3	0.4
Short-term / EDT (%)	..	16.2	14.4	17.9	14.9	16.2	18.6	18.9	11.6	17.5
Concessional / EDT (%)	..	26.5	24.5	24.3	35.3	37.8	37.0	33.4	36.7	34.7
Multilateral / EDT (%)	..	7.7	13.6	12.6	11.5	11.8	11.3	10.5	12.9	11.7

CONGO

(US$ million, unless otherwise indicated)

	1970	1980	1988	1989	1990	1991	1992	1993	1994	1995
5. LONG-TERM DEBT										
DEBT OUTSTANDING (LDOD)	**119**	**1,257**	**3,485**	**3,502**	**4,206**	**4,041**	**3,876**	**4,114**	**4,774**	**4,955**
Public and publicly guaranteed	**119**	**1,257**	**3,485**	**3,502**	**4,206**	**4,041**	**3,876**	**4,114**	**4,774**	**4,955**
Official creditors	104	605	2,048	2,082	3,052	3,141	2,985	2,874	3,825	4,035
Multilateral	29	118	555	538	570	571	537	534	702	703
Concessional	0	50	146	156	168	170	165	161	371	380
Bilateral	75	487	1,493	1,544	2,482	2,571	2,448	2,341	3,123	3,332
Concessional	75	355	855	885	1,582	1,657	1,601	1,537	1,621	1,715
Private creditors	14	653	1,437	1,421	1,155	900	891	1,240	949	920
Bonds	0	0	0	0	0	0	0	0	0	0
Commercial banks	0	282	768	752	726	527	548	916	814	784
Other private	14	371	670	668	429	373	343	324	135	136
Private nonguaranteed	**0**	**0**	**0**	**0**	**0**	**0**	**0**	**0**	**0**	**0**
Bonds	0	0	0	0	0	0	0	0	0	0
Commercial banks	0	0	0	0	0	0	0	0	0	0
Memo:										
IBRD	29	39	154	156	164	165	160	162	116	105
IDA	0	22	74	74	75	75	74	74	172	174
DISBURSEMENTS	**18**	**522**	**610**	**185**	**314**	**38**	**132**	**459**	**332**	**15**
Public and publicly guaranteed	**18**	**522**	**610**	**185**	**314**	**38**	**132**	**459**	**332**	**15**
Official creditors	16	109	164	58	128	32	17	8	331	15
Multilateral	0	23	104	23	11	4	2	1	247	1
Concessional	0	10	3	10	5	3	2	1	208	0
Bilateral	16	87	59	35	118	28	15	7	84	14
Concessional	16	39	55	30	115	28	15	7	84	14
Private creditors	2	412	446	127	185	6	114	451	1	0
Bonds	0	0	0	0	0	0	0	0	0	0
Commercial banks	0	277	310	109	174	0	95	449	0	0
Other private	2	135	136	18	11	6	19	2	1	0
Private nonguaranteed	**0**	**0**	**0**	**0**	**0**	**0**	**0**	**0**	**0**	**0**
Bonds	0	0	0	0	0	0	0	0	0	0
Commercial banks	0	0	0	0	0	0	0	0	0	0
Memo:										
IBRD	0	2	54	12	2	1	0	0	0	1
IDA	0	1	1	1	0	0	0	0	101	0
PRINCIPAL REPAYMENTS	**6**	**34**	**291**	**199**	**355**	**204**	**98**	**76**	**302**	**82**
Public and publicly guaranteed	**6**	**34**	**291**	**199**	**355**	**204**	**98**	**76**	**302**	**82**
Official creditors	2	21	22	25	70	4	1	1	145	32
Multilateral	1	6	20	22	30	2	0	0	106	19
Concessional	0	0	1	1	2	0	0	0	6	1
Bilateral	2	16	2	3	40	2	1	1	39	13
Concessional	1	11	1	1	1	0	0	1	2	5
Private creditors	4	12	270	174	285	200	97	75	157	50
Bonds	0	0	0	0	0	0	0	0	0	0
Commercial banks	0	0	231	144	257	182	56	68	117	46
Other private	4	12	39	30	28	18	41	7	40	4
Private nonguaranteed	**0**	**0**	**0**	**0**	**0**	**0**	**0**	**0**	**0**	**0**
Bonds	0	0	0	0	0	0	0	0	0	0
Commercial banks	0	0	0	0	0	0	0	0	0	0
Memo:										
IBRD	1	4	7	7	6	2	0	0	57	18
IDA	0	0	0	0	0	0	0	0	4	1
NET FLOWS ON DEBT	**13**	**488**	**319**	**-15**	**-42**	**-167**	**33**	**383**	**30**	**-67**
Public and publicly guaranteed	**13**	**488**	**319**	**-15**	**-42**	**-167**	**33**	**383**	**30**	**-67**
Official creditors	14	88	142	33	58	28	16	7	186	-17
Multilateral	-1	17	85	1	-19	2	2	1	142	-19
Concessional	0	10	2	9	3	3	2	1	202	-1
Bilateral	15	71	58	32	77	26	14	6	45	1
Concessional	14	28	54	29	114	28	15	6	82	9
Private creditors	-1	400	177	-47	-100	-195	17	376	-156	-50
Bonds	0	0	0	0	0	0	0	0	0	0
Commercial banks	0	277	79	-35	-83	-182	39	381	-117	-46
Other private	-1	123	97	-12	-17	-13	-22	-5	-39	-4
Private nonguaranteed	**0**	**0**	**0**	**0**	**0**	**0**	**0**	**0**	**0**	**0**
Bonds	0	0	0	0	0	0	0	0	0	0
Commercial banks	0	0	0	0	0	0	0	0	0	0
Memo:										
IBRD	-1	-2	47	6	-4	-1	0	0	-57	-17
IDA	0	1	1	0	0	0	0	0	97	-1

CONGO

(US$ million, unless otherwise indicated)

	1970	1980	1988	1989	1990	1991	1992	1993	1994	1995
INTEREST PAYMENTS (LINT)	**3**	**37**	**81**	**91**	**120**	**50**	**29**	**21**	**232**	**61**
Public and publicly guaranteed	**3**	**37**	**81**	**91**	**120**	**50**	**29**	**21**	**232**	**61**
Official creditors	3	25	34	37	68	14	7	4	182	20
Multilateral	2	6	21	31	30	5	0	0	65	11
Concessional	0	1	2	1	1	0	0	0	3	1
Bilateral	1	19	13	7	38	9	6	4	117	10
Concessional	1	11	10	5	28	8	5	4	90	8
Private creditors	1	13	48	54	52	36	22	17	50	40
Bonds	0	0	0	0	0	0	0	0	0	0
Commercial banks	0	2	41	45	44	27	13	16	37	39
Other private	1	11	7	8	8	9	10	1	13	2
Private nonguaranteed	**0**	**0**	**0**	**0**	**0**	**0**	**0**	**0**	**0**	**0**
Bonds	0	0	0	0	0	0	0	0	0	0
Commercial banks	0	0	0	0	0	0	0	0	0	0
Memo:										
IBRD	2	4	10	11	12	5	0	0	53	10
IDA	0	0	1	1	1	0	0	0	2	1
NET TRANSFERS ON DEBT	**10**	**451**	**237**	**-106**	**-162**	**-217**	**5**	**362**	**-202**	**-127**
Public and publicly guaranteed	**10**	**451**	**237**	**-106**	**-162**	**-217**	**5**	**362**	**-202**	**-127**
Official creditors	11	64	108	-5	-10	14	10	3	5	-37
Multilateral	-3	12	64	-30	-50	-4	2	1	77	-29
Concessional	0	10	0	8	1	3	2	1	198	-3
Bilateral	14	52	45	25	39	17	8	2	-72	-8
Concessional	14	17	44	24	86	20	10	2	-8	1
Private creditors	-2	388	129	-101	-151	-231	-5	360	-206	-90
Bonds	0	0	0	0	0	0	0	0	0	0
Commercial banks	0	275	39	-80	-127	-209	27	366	-153	-84
Other private	-2	112	90	-21	-24	-22	-32	-6	-53	-6
Private nonguaranteed	**0**	**0**	**0**	**0**	**0**	**0**	**0**	**0**	**0**	**0**
Bonds	0	0	0	0	0	0	0	0	0	0
Commercial banks	0	0	0	0	0	0	0	0	0	0
Memo:										
IBRD	-3	-6	37	-5	-16	-6	0	0	-110	-27
IDA	0	1	0	0	-1	0	0	0	95	-3
DEBT SERVICE (LTDS)	**9**	**71**	**372**	**290**	**475**	**255**	**127**	**97**	**533**	**142**
Public and publicly guaranteed	**9**	**71**	**372**	**290**	**475**	**255**	**127**	**97**	**533**	**142**
Official creditors	5	46	55	63	139	18	8	6	327	52
Multilateral	3	11	41	53	60	7	0	0	170	30
Concessional	0	1	3	2	3	0	0	0	10	3
Bilateral	2	35	15	10	78	11	7	6	156	22
Concessional	2	22	11	6	29	8	5	5	92	13
Private creditors	4	25	317	228	337	236	119	91	207	90
Bonds	0	0	0	0	0	0	0	0	0	0
Commercial banks	0	2	272	189	301	209	69	84	153	84
Other private	4	23	45	39	36	27	51	8	54	6
Private nonguaranteed	**0**	**0**	**0**	**0**	**0**	**0**	**0**	**0**	**0**	**0**
Bonds	0	0	0	0	0	0	0	0	0	0
Commercial banks	0	0	0	0	0	0	0	0	0	0
Memo:										
IBRD	3	8	17	17	18	7	0	0	110	27
IDA	0	0	1	1	1	0	0	0	6	3
UNDISBURSED DEBT	**42**	**735**	**1,243**	**856**	**404**	**298**	**336**	**439**	**309**	**340**
Official creditors	36	221	319	308	341	272	314	282	157	176
Private creditors	7	514	924	548	63	26	22	157	152	165
Memorandum items										
Concessional LDOD	75	405	1,001	1,041	1,750	1,827	1,765	1,698	1,992	2,095
Variable rate LDOD	0	82	732	703	885	822	814	1,183	1,187	1,155
Public sector LDOD	119	1,257	3,485	3,502	4,206	4,041	3,876	4,114	4,774	4,955
Private sector LDOD	0	0	0	0	0	0	0	0	0	0

6. CURRENCY COMPOSITION OF LONG-TERM DEBT (PERCENT)

	1970	1980	1988	1989	1990	1991	1992	1993	1994	1995
Deutsche mark	5.1	1.1	2.4	2.7	2.4	2.7	2.8	2.6	2.7	2.8
French franc	14.1	31.0	46.9	48.4	51.1	49.8	48.7	42.6	45.2	47.1
Japanese yen	0.0	0.0	0.2	0.2	0.2	0.2	0.2	0.2	0.2	0.2
Pound sterling	0.6	0.0	6.1	5.3	5.7	5.8	4.9	4.5	5.0	4.9
Swiss franc	0.0	2.1	0.4	0.4	0.4	0.4	0.5	0.4	0.4	0.5
U.S.dollars	2.4	25.1	18.8	17.9	16.5	16.3	18.5	27.0	25.1	23.7
Multiple currency	24.7	3.1	4.4	4.4	3.9	4.1	4.1	3.9	2.4	2.1
Special drawing rights	0.0	0.0	0.7	0.7	0.6	0.6	0.7	0.6	0.5	0.5
All other currencies	53.1	37.5	20.2	20.0	19.2	20.1	19.7	18.2	18.4	18.2

CONGO

(US$ million, unless otherwise indicated)

	1970	1980	1988	1989	1990	1991	1992	1993	1994	1995
7. DEBT RESTRUCTURINGS										
Total amount rescheduled	0	0	79	44	780	146	15	2	1,044	108
Debt stock rescheduled	0	0	0	0	0	0	0	0	0	0
Principal rescheduled	0	0	56	32	386	97	8	2	505	65
Official	0	0	28	25	101	55	2	2	355	60
Private	0	0	28	7	285	42	5	0	150	5
Interest rescheduled	0	0	20	9	370	50	4	0	436	42
Official	0	0	9	8	248	42	0	0	398	41
Private	0	0	11	1	121	8	4	0	38	1
Debt forgiven	..	..	0	6	0	11	0	3	126	24
Memo: interest forgiven	..	..	0	0	0	0	0	0	8	0
Debt stock reduction	0	0	0	0	0	0	0	0	0	0
of which debt buyback	0	0	0	0	0	0	0	0	0	0
8. DEBT STOCK-FLOW RECONCILIATION										
Total change in debt stocks	..	..	..	189	675	-121	-63	312	341	610
Net flows on debt	..	..	..	29	95	-266	-35	310	79	166
Net change in interest arrears	..	..	..	128	-167	143	171	147	-369	194
Interest capitalized	..	..	..	9	370	50	4	0	436	42
Debt forgiveness or reduction	..	..	..	-6	0	-11	0	-3	-126	-24
Cross-currency valuation	..	..	..	51	427	-31	-188	-140	270	249
Residual	..	..	..	-21	-51	-6	-15	-2	50	-18
9. AVERAGE TERMS OF NEW COMMITMENTS										
ALL CREDITORS										
Interest (%)	2.8	7.6	7.8	8.4	5.1	0.0	5.9	5.1	0.8	2.2
Maturity (years)	18.3	11.1	9.6	10.5	16.3	0.0	10.6	7.8	32.1	31.8
Grace period (years)	6.5	3.2	2.3	4.1	6.8	0.0	5.6	2.2	7.5	8.9
Grant element (%)	49.5	13.1	12.4	13.5	32.6	0.0	20.9	17.7	71.2	63.7
Official creditors										
Interest (%)	2.3	3.5	4.0	3.9	4.3	0.0	5.0	0.0	0.8	2.2
Maturity (years)	19.6	25.3	21.0	19.5	17.6	0.0	17.2	0.0	32.1	31.8
Grace period (years)	6.6	6.7	4.9	7.5	7.2	0.0	9.6	0.0	7.5	8.9
Grant element (%)	53.6	46.5	40.5	41.8	38.0	0.0	34.8	0.0	71.2	63.7
Private creditors										
Interest (%)	4.2	8.5	9.4	11.1	9.9	0.0	6.5	5.1	0.0	0.0
Maturity (years)	14.9	8.1	4.7	5.0	8.3	0.0	5.7	7.8	0.0	0.0
Grace period (years)	6.1	2.4	1.2	2.0	4.1	0.0	2.7	2.2	0.0	0.0
Grant element (%)	38.9	6.2	0.4	-3.8	-0.5	0.0	10.5	17.7	0.0	0.0
Memorandum items										
Commitments	31	966	270	169	192	0	199	593	250	31
Official creditors	23	165	81	64	165	0	85	0	250	31
Private creditors	9	801	189	105	27	0	114	593	0	0

10. CONTRACTUAL OBLIGATIONS ON OUTSTANDING LONG-TERM DEBT

	1996	1997	1998	1999	2000	2001	2002	2003	2004	2005
TOTAL										
Disbursements	101	103	53	24	13	5	2	1	0	0
Principal	475	447	417	348	327	312	253	252	224	223
Interest	200	178	157	137	118	101	85	73	61	50
Official creditors										
Disbursements	46	41	22	14	8	5	2	1	0	0
Principal	351	325	297	252	256	241	233	231	224	223
Interest	165	149	135	121	108	95	84	72	61	50
Bilateral creditors										
Disbursements	24	18	11	6	4	2	1	1	0	0
Principal	313	287	259	217	215	209	200	200	198	200
Interest	144	130	119	108	97	86	76	66	56	46
Multilateral creditors										
Disbursements	22	23	11	8	5	3	1	0	0	0
Principal	38	38	38	35	41	32	32	31	26	23
Interest	21	18	16	13	11	9	7	6	5	4
Private creditors										
Disbursements	56	62	31	10	5	0	0	0	0	0
Principal	125	122	120	96	71	71	21	21	0	0
Interest	35	29	23	15	10	6	2	1	0	0
Commercial banks										
Disbursements	0	0	0	0	0	0	0	0	0	0
Principal	94	94	94	74	50	50	0	0	0	0
Interest	32	25	18	11	6	3	0	0	0	0
Other private										
Disbursements	56	62	31	10	5	0	0	0	0	0
Principal	30	27	26	23	21	21	21	21	0	0
Interest	3	5	5	5	4	3	2	1	0	0

COSTA RICA

(US$ million, unless otherwise indicated)

	1970	1980	1988	1989	1990	1991	1992	1993	1994	1995
1. SUMMARY DEBT DATA										
TOTAL DEBT STOCKS (EDT)	..	**2,744**	**4,530**	**4,589**	**3,756**	**4,027**	**3,938**	**3,867**	**3,911**	**3,800**
Long-term debt (LDOD)	**246**	**2,112**	**3,863**	**3,849**	**3,367**	**3,601**	**3,514**	**3,415**	**3,451**	**3,346**
Public and publicly guaranteed	134	1,700	3,547	3,545	3,063	3,297	3,180	3,135	3,223	3,132
Private nonguaranteed	112	412	317	304	304	304	334	280	228	214
Use of IMF credit	**0**	**57**	**71**	**35**	**11**	**83**	**82**	**81**	**66**	**24**
Short-term debt	..	**575**	**596**	**705**	**377**	**343**	**343**	**371**	**393**	**429**
of which interest arrears on LDOD	..	0	280	385	77	68	27	32	38	31
Official creditors	..	0	66	22	76	59	22	28	34	27
Private creditors	..	0	214	363	1	9	5	5	4	4
Memo: principal arrears on LDOD	..	2	739	879	173	147	94	99	132	116
Official creditors	..	0	149	106	168	128	82	93	129	114
Private creditors	..	2	590	773	4	19	12	6	3	3
Memo: export credits	..	..	350	404	297	471	356	391	295	253
TOTAL DEBT FLOWS										
Disbursements	**62**	**556**	**167**	**126**	**207**	**398**	**251**	**211**	**199**	**201**
Long-term debt	60	536	167	126	207	322	245	211	199	201
IMF purchases	2	20	0	0	0	76	6	0	0	0
Principal repayments	**45**	**176**	**174**	**176**	**295**	**184**	**303**	**343**	**288**	**395**
Long-term debt	41	164	120	142	269	177	299	343	268	351
IMF repurchases	4	12	54	34	26	7	4	0	20	44
Net flows on debt	**17**	**380**	**-8**	**-46**	**-109**	**188**	**-11**	**-108**	**-72**	**-152**
of which short-term debt	..	..	-1	4	-20	-26	41	23	17	42
Interest payments (INT)	..	**179**	**229**	**170**	**206**	**234**	**242**	**209**	**215**	**250**
Long-term debt	14	171	189	133	171	199	216	185	193	224
IMF charges	0	4	8	5	3	5	6	5	4	3
Short-term debt	..	4	32	32	32	30	19	20	18	23
Net transfers on debt	..	**202**	**-236**	**-216**	**-315**	**-45**	**-253**	**-318**	**-287**	**-402**
Total debt service paid (TDS)	..	**354**	**402**	**345**	**501**	**418**	**545**	**552**	**504**	**646**
Long-term debt	55	335	309	275	440	376	515	527	462	575
IMF repurchases and charges	4	16	62	39	29	12	10	5	24	47
Short-term debt (interest only)	..	4	32	32	32	30	19	20	18	23
2. AGGREGATE NET RESOURCE FLOWS AND NET TRANSFERS (LONG-TERM)										
NET RESOURCE FLOWS	**48**	**425**	**284**	**224**	**210**	**373**	**194**	**146**	**267**	**275**
Net flow of long-term debt (ex. IMF)	19	373	47	-17	-63	145	-54	-132	-69	-150
Foreign direct investment (net)	26	53	122	101	163	178	226	247	298	396
Portfolio equity flows	0	0	0	0	0	0	0	0	4	1
Grants (excluding technical coop.)	3	0	114	139	110	50	22	31	35	28
Memo: technical coop. grants	4	14	58	66	74	83	92	88	63	81
NET TRANSFERS	**30**	**234**	**61**	**36**	**-21**	**109**	**-93**	**-104**	**-1**	**-29**
Interest on long-term debt	14	171	189	133	171	199	216	185	193	224
Profit remittances on FDI	4	20	34	55	60	65	70	65	75	80
3. MAJOR ECONOMIC AGGREGATES										
Gross national product (GNP)	971	4,600	4,304	4,921	5,512	5,402	6,469	7,332	8,046	8,930
Exports of goods & services (XGS)	..	1,219	1,659	1,951	2,094	2,301	2,693	3,017	3,472	3,945
of which workers remittances	..	0	0	0	0	0	0	0	0	0
Imports of goods & services (MGS)	..	1,897	2,093	2,558	2,709	2,518	3,237	3,781	3,871	4,241
International reserves (RES)	16	197	677	746	525	931	1,032	1,038	906	1,060
Current account balance	..	-664	-304	-480	-494	-99	-380	-620	-244	-143
4. DEBT INDICATORS										
EDT / XGS (%)	..	225.2	273.1	235.2	179.4	175.0	146.2	128.2	112.6	96.3
EDT / GNP (%)	..	59.7	105.3	93.3	68.1	74.5	60.9	52.7	48.6	42.5
TDS / XGS (%)	..	29.1	24.3	17.7	23.9	18.2	20.2	18.3	14.5	16.4
INT / XGS (%)	..	14.7	13.8	8.7	9.9	10.2	9.0	6.9	6.2	6.3
INT / GNP (%)	..	3.9	5.3	3.4	3.7	4.3	3.7	2.9	2.7	2.8
RES / EDT (%)	..	7.2	14.9	16.3	14.0	23.1	26.2	26.8	23.2	27.9
RES / MGS (months)	..	1.2	3.9	3.5	2.3	4.4	3.8	3.3	2.8	3.0
Short-term / EDT (%)	..	21.0	13.2	15.4	10.0	8.5	8.7	9.6	10.1	11.3
Concessional / EDT (%)	..	9.5	18.0	17.1	23.2	23.0	24.3	24.3	24.2	23.9
Multilateral / EDT (%)	..	16.4	23.1	23.4	30.4	29.4	29.9	31.5	33.6	35.5

COSTA RICA

(US$ million, unless otherwise indicated)

	1970	1980	1988	1989	1990	1991	1992	1993	1994	1995
5. LONG-TERM DEBT										
DEBT OUTSTANDING (LDOD)	**246**	**2,112**	**3,863**	**3,849**	**3,367**	**3,601**	**3,514**	**3,415**	**3,451**	**3,346**
Public and publicly guaranteed	**134**	**1,700**	**3,547**	**3,545**	**3,063**	**3,297**	**3,180**	**3,135**	**3,223**	**3,132**
Official creditors	96	791	2,122	2,188	2,361	2,629	2,541	2,488	2,583	2,491
Multilateral	57	450	1,048	1,074	1,141	1,184	1,178	1,219	1,313	1,347
Concessional	39	133	247	244	246	236	226	215	206	199
Bilateral	39	341	1,074	1,115	1,220	1,446	1,363	1,269	1,271	1,144
Concessional	36	128	569	543	626	691	730	726	742	710
Private creditors	38	909	1,424	1,357	702	668	639	647	640	641
Bonds	1	141	57	41	609	599	582	577	576	572
Commercial banks	20	712	1,312	1,262	41	17	11	26	24	33
Other private	17	55	55	54	52	51	46	44	40	36
Private nonguaranteed	**112**	**412**	**317**	**304**	**304**	**304**	**334**	**280**	**228**	**214**
Bonds	0	0	0	0	0	0	0	0	0	0
Commercial banks	112	412	317	304	304	304	334	280	228	214
Memo:										
IBRD	36	178	418	415	409	404	372	344	323	300
IDA	5	5	4	4	4	3	3	3	3	3
DISBURSEMENTS	**60**	**536**	**167**	**126**	**207**	**322**	**245**	**211**	**199**	**201**
Public and publicly guaranteed	**30**	**435**	**137**	**126**	**202**	**314**	**201**	**209**	**199**	**191**
Official creditors	19	200	136	122	170	303	199	165	197	180
Multilateral	13	97	87	82	89	139	123	133	150	167
Concessional	4	42	14	10	13	1	0	0	3	6
Bilateral	7	103	50	40	81	164	76	32	47	13
Concessional	7	20	26	5	76	62	76	18	18	12
Private creditors	10	235	1	4	32	11	2	44	2	11
Bonds	0	97	0	0	0	0	0	0	0	0
Commercial banks	6	120	0	0	30	5	1	43	1	11
Other private	4	17	1	4	1	6	1	2	1	0
Private nonguaranteed	**30**	**102**	**30**	**0**	**5**	**8**	**44**	**2**	**0**	**10**
Bonds	0	0	0	0	0	0	0	0	0	0
Commercial banks	30	102	30	0	5	8	44	2	0	10
Memo:										
IBRD	5	29	5	43	5	41	28	11	11	16
IDA	0	0	0	0	0	0	0	0	0	0
PRINCIPAL REPAYMENTS	**41**	**164**	**120**	**142**	**269**	**177**	**299**	**343**	**268**	**351**
Public and publicly guaranteed	**21**	**76**	**104**	**142**	**263**	**168**	**285**	**287**	**216**	**327**
Official creditors	7	23	85	113	92	126	254	251	206	317
Multilateral	3	15	74	86	79	97	105	100	120	176
Concessional	1	4	10	8	10	11	11	11	12	14
Bilateral	4	7	11	27	14	29	149	151	86	141
Concessional	3	3	1	3	3	4	28	31	31	43
Private creditors	14	53	19	30	171	42	31	36	11	10
Bonds	1	0	8	16	42	10	17	5	1	4
Commercial banks	12	41	8	11	124	29	8	27	4	2
Other private	1	12	4	3	5	4	6	3	6	4
Private nonguaranteed	**20**	**88**	**16**	**0**	**6**	**9**	**14**	**56**	**52**	**24**
Bonds	0	0	0	0	0	0	0	0	0	0
Commercial banks	20	88	16	0	6	9	14	56	52	24
Memo:										
IBRD	2	7	38	34	45	53	46	48	56	55
IDA	0	0	0	0	0	0	0	0	0	0
NET FLOWS ON DEBT	**19**	**373**	**47**	**-17**	**-63**	**145**	**-54**	**-132**	**-69**	**-150**
Public and publicly guaranteed	**9**	**359**	**33**	**-17**	**-62**	**146**	**-84**	**-78**	**-17**	**-136**
Official creditors	12	178	52	9	78	177	-55	-86	-9	-137
Multilateral	10	82	13	-4	11	42	18	32	30	-9
Concessional	2	38	4	2	4	-10	-11	-11	-9	-7
Bilateral	3	96	39	13	67	135	-74	-119	-38	-128
Concessional	4	17	26	2	73	57	48	-13	-13	-31
Private creditors	-3	182	-19	-26	-139	-32	-29	9	-9	1
Bonds	-1	97	-8	-16	-42	-10	-17	-5	-1	-4
Commercial banks	-5	79	-8	-11	-94	-24	-8	16	-2	9
Other private	3	5	-3	1	-4	2	-4	-2	-5	-4
Private nonguaranteed	**10**	**14**	**15**	**0**	**-1**	**0**	**30**	**-54**	**-52**	**-14**
Bonds	0	0	0	0	0	0	0	0	0	0
Commercial banks	10	14	15	0	-1	0	30	-54	-52	-14
Memo:										
IBRD	3	23	-33	9	-40	-13	-18	-37	-45	-39
IDA	0	0	0	0	0	0	0	0	0	0

COSTA RICA

(US$ million, unless otherwise indicated)

	1970	1980	1988	1989	1990	1991	1992	1993	1994	1995
INTEREST PAYMENTS (LINT)	**14**	**171**	**189**	**133**	**171**	**199**	**216**	**185**	**193**	**224**
Public and publicly guaranteed	**7**	**130**	**164**	**133**	**169**	**173**	**191**	**159**	**171**	**204**
Official creditors	4	42	103	105	104	125	150	120	132	162
Multilateral	3	27	67	69	77	82	81	79	90	96
Concessional	2	4	5	5	5	5	5	4	4	5
Bilateral	1	15	36	36	27	43	69	41	41	67
Concessional	1	3	2	12	9	10	26	17	23	30
Private creditors	3	88	61	28	65	48	41	39	40	41
Bonds	0	6	6	6	24	40	36	34	35	37
Commercial banks	2	78	52	18	36	3	0	0	1	0
Other private	1	4	4	4	5	5	5	4	4	4
Private nonguaranteed	**7**	**41**	**25**	**0**	**2**	**26**	**26**	**26**	**22**	**21**
Bonds	0	0	0	0	0	0	0	0	0	0
Commercial banks	7	41	25	0	2	26	26	26	22	21
Memo:										
IBRD	2	15	36	33	33	36	31	29	27	27
IDA	0	0	0	0	0	0	0	0	0	0
NET TRANSFERS ON DEBT	**5**	**202**	**-142**	**-149**	**-234**	**-54**	**-270**	**-316**	**-263**	**-374**
Public and publicly guaranteed	**2**	**229**	**-131**	**-149**	**-231**	**-28**	**-275**	**-236**	**-189**	**-340**
Official creditors	8	135	-51	-96	-27	52	-205	-206	-140	-299
Multilateral	6	54	-54	-73	-67	-40	-63	-47	-61	-105
Concessional	0	34	-1	-3	-1	-15	-15	-15	-13	-12
Bilateral	2	81	3	-23	40	92	-142	-160	-80	-195
Concessional	3	14	24	-10	64	48	22	-30	-35	-61
Private creditors	-6	94	-80	-54	-204	-80	-70	-30	-48	-40
Bonds	-1	91	-14	-21	-66	-50	-53	-39	-36	-41
Commercial banks	-7	2	-59	-29	-130	-26	-8	15	-3	9
Other private	2	1	-7	-3	-9	-3	-9	-6	-9	-8
Private nonguaranteed	**3**	**-28**	**-11**	**0**	**-3**	**-26**	**5**	**-80**	**-74**	**-35**
Bonds	0	0	0	0	0	0	0	0	0	0
Commercial banks	3	-28	-11	0	-3	-26	5	-80	-74	-35
Memo:										
IBRD	1	8	-69	-24	-73	-48	-50	-66	-72	-66
IDA	0	0	0	0	0	0	0	0	0	0
DEBT SERVICE (LTDS)	**55**	**335**	**309**	**275**	**440**	**376**	**515**	**527**	**462**	**575**
Public and publicly guaranteed	**28**	**206**	**268**	**275**	**432**	**342**	**475**	**445**	**388**	**531**
Official creditors	11	65	187	218	197	252	404	371	337	479
Multilateral	6	43	141	155	156	180	186	180	210	271
Concessional	3	8	15	12	15	17	16	16	16	19
Bilateral	5	22	46	62	40	72	218	192	127	208
Concessional	4	6	2	16	12	14	54	48	54	73
Private creditors	17	141	81	57	236	90	72	74	51	52
Bonds	1	6	14	21	66	50	53	39	36	41
Commercial banks	14	119	59	29	160	31	9	28	5	2
Other private	2	17	7	7	10	9	11	8	10	9
Private nonguaranteed	**28**	**129**	**41**	**0**	**8**	**34**	**40**	**82**	**74**	**45**
Bonds	0	0	0	0	0	0	0	0	0	0
Commercial banks	28	129	41	0	8	34	40	82	74	45
Memo:										
IBRD	4	21	74	67	79	89	77	76	83	81
IDA	0	0	0	0	0	0	0	0	0	0
UNDISBURSED DEBT	**95**	**793**	**765**	**995**	**993**	**845**	**764**	**1,228**	**1,347**	**1,065**
Official creditors	93	618	734	962	981	839	761	1,208	1,330	1,058
Private creditors	2	174	31	33	12	6	3	20	18	6
Memorandum items										
Concessional LDOD	75	262	816	786	872	927	955	940	948	909
Variable rate LDOD	122	1,203	2,065	2,136	1,061	1,192	1,129	1,005	961	984
Public sector LDOD	130	1,655	3,541	3,541	3,059	3,294	3,177	3,132	3,221	3,130
Private sector LDOD	116	457	322	308	308	307	337	283	230	216

6. CURRENCY COMPOSITION OF LONG-TERM DEBT (PERCENT)

	1970	1980	1988	1989	1990	1991	1992	1993	1994	1995
Deutsche mark	2.0	3.1	1.1	2.0	2.6	2.6	2.4	2.2	2.2	2.0
French franc	0.0	0.2	0.7	0.8	1.0	0.9	0.7	0.6	0.5	0.4
Japanese yen	0.0	0.5	0.9	1.6	3.0	5.0	7.0	8.0	8.9	8.1
Pound sterling	2.8	0.5	1.3	0.2	0.2	0.4	0.3	0.3	0.3	0.1
Swiss franc	0.0	0.7	0.0	0.0	0.0	0.0	0.0	0.0	0.0	0.0
U.S.dollars	67.1	69.2	67.3	66.7	58.2	57.0	55.3	53.9	52.1	52.1
Multiple currency	28.2	18.2	25.5	25.6	31.4	30.6	31.8	32.9	34.1	35.6
Special drawing rights	0.0	0.0	0.2	0.1	0.2	0.1	0.1	0.1	0.1	0.1
All other currencies	0.0	7.6	3.0	3.0	3.4	3.3	2.3	2.0	1.8	1.5

COSTA RICA

(US$ million, unless otherwise indicated)

	1970	1980	1988	1989	1990	1991	1992	1993	1994	1995
7. DEBT RESTRUCTURINGS										
Total amount rescheduled	0	0	150	189	641	225	42	29	0	0
Debt stock rescheduled	0	0	149	0	469	0	0	0	0	0
Principal rescheduled	0	0	0	110	20	146	34	17	0	0
Official	0	0	0	95	20	144	31	17	0	0
Private	0	0	0	15	0	2	3	0	0	0
Interest rescheduled	0	0	0	79	151	75	8	8	0	0
Official	0	0	0	44	10	73	6	7	0	0
Private	0	0	0	35	141	2	2	0	0	0
Debt forgiven	..	..	0	0	0	9	0	1	3	3
Memo: interest forgiven	..	..	0	0	187	1	1	0	0	0
Debt stock reduction	0	0	189	46	668	0	1	0	0	0
of which debt buyback	0	0	0	0	0	0	0	0	0	0
8. DEBT STOCK-FLOW RECONCILIATION										
Total change in debt stocks	..	..	..	59	-834	271	-89	-71	43	-111
Net flows on debt	..	..	..	-46	-109	188	-11	-108	-72	-152
Net change in interest arrears	..	..	..	105	-308	-9	-41	5	5	-7
Interest capitalized	..	..	..	79	151	75	8	8	0	0
Debt forgiveness or reduction	..	..	..	-46	-668	-9	-1	-1	-3	-3
Cross-currency valuation	..	..	..	-26	57	2	-46	10	61	-2
Residual	..	..	..	-6	42	24	3	16	52	52
9. AVERAGE TERMS OF NEW COMMITMENTS										
ALL CREDITORS										
Interest (%)	5.6	11.2	8.4	6.5	6.9	7.1	7.3	6.2	6.9	2.9
Maturity (years)	27.7	13.2	20.0	18.2	15.2	6.4	19.6	16.7	17.9	12.4
Grace period (years)	6.3	5.0	5.2	2.9	4.3	2.8	4.7	4.3	5.6	2.3
Grant element (%)	33.6	-1.3	7.1	19.9	17.9	7.7	15.6	19.9	19.8	20.7
Official creditors										
Interest (%)	5.3	7.2	8.4	6.6	6.4	7.0	7.3	6.1	6.9	2.9
Maturity (years)	29.8	18.3	20.1	18.3	17.6	6.5	19.6	17.5	17.9	12.4
Grace period (years)	7.2	6.3	5.2	2.9	5.0	2.9	4.7	4.5	5.6	2.3
Grant element (%)	37.3	19.6	7.1	19.9	20.9	8.0	15.6	20.9	19.8	20.7
Private creditors										
Interest (%)	7.1	15.8	9.4	5.8	9.5	10.0	0.0	7.1	0.0	0.0
Maturity (years)	14.9	7.6	5.8	10.3	3.2	1.1	0.0	8.0	0.0	0.0
Grace period (years)	0.9	3.6	2.8	4.3	1.1	0.8	0.0	2.1	0.0	0.0
Grant element (%)	12.2	-24.4	1.3	23.3	2.2	-0.3	0.0	9.6	0.0	0.0
Memorandum items										
Commitments	58	621	378	386	220	179	160	667	393	30
Official creditors	49	326	377	382	185	174	160	606	393	30
Private creditors	8	295	2	4	36	5	0	61	0	0

10. CONTRACTUAL OBLIGATIONS ON OUTSTANDING LONG-TERM DEBT

	1996	1997	1998	1999	2000	2001	2002	2003	2004	2005
TOTAL										
Disbursements	287	290	207	141	78	40	14	4	2	2
Principal	375	343	334	336	322	310	284	258	238	206
Interest	211	205	198	186	171	153	135	117	101	88
Official creditors										
Disbursements	282	288	207	141	78	40	14	4	2	2
Principal	335	303	294	295	268	244	217	192	174	161
Interest	149	147	144	135	124	111	98	86	75	64
Bilateral creditors										
Disbursements	26	32	20	8	3	2	1	0	0	0
Principal	188	149	126	114	93	87	69	56	42	34
Interest	44	36	30	25	20	16	13	10	8	7
Multilateral creditors										
Disbursements	256	257	188	132	75	38	13	4	2	2
Principal	146	154	168	181	175	156	147	136	132	127
Interest	105	111	113	111	104	95	85	76	66	57
Private creditors										
Disbursements	5	2	0	0	0	0	0	0	0	0
Principal	41	40	40	41	53	66	67	66	65	45
Interest	62	58	55	51	47	42	37	32	27	24
Commercial banks										
Disbursements	5	2	0	0	0	0	0	0	0	0
Principal	6	5	5	5	5	5	5	2	0	0
Interest	3	3	3	2	2	1	1	0	0	0
Other private										
Disbursements	0	0	0	0	0	0	0	0	0	0
Principal	35	34	35	36	49	62	62	64	65	45
Interest	58	55	52	49	46	41	36	32	27	24

COTE D'IVOIRE

(US$ million, unless otherwise indicated)

1. SUMMARY DEBT DATA

	1970	1980	1988	1989	1990	1991	1992	1993	1994	1995
TOTAL DEBT STOCKS (EDT)	**..**	**7,462**	**13,342**	**14,821**	**17,259**	**18,174**	**18,547**	**19,071**	**17,395**	**18,952**
Long-term debt (LDOD)	**267**	**6,339**	**10,947**	**11,555**	**13,223**	**13,868**	**13,860**	**13,727**	**13,852**	**14,559**
Public and publicly guaranteed	256	4,327	8,610	9,068	10,666	11,265	11,244	11,111	11,240	11,899
Private nonguaranteed	11	2,012	2,338	2,487	2,558	2,603	2,616	2,617	2,611	2,660
Use of IMF credit	**0**	**65**	**509**	**370**	**431**	**372**	**267**	**219**	**328**	**427**
Short-term debt	**..**	**1,059**	**1,887**	**2,897**	**3,604**	**3,935**	**4,420**	**5,125**	**3,215**	**3,966**
of which interest arrears on LDOD	..	0	456	758	827	926	1,043	1,251	961	1,076
Official creditors	..	0	58	175	73	78	166	379	45	90
Private creditors	..	0	398	583	753	848	877	872	915	986
Memo: principal arrears on LDOD	..	0	761	1,458	1,727	2,058	2,351	2,632	2,505	2,687
Official creditors	..	0	26	191	16	27	122	327	13	34
Private creditors	..	0	735	1,268	1,710	2,031	2,229	2,305	2,492	2,653
Memo: export credits	..	..	2,611	2,975	3,560	3,525	3,578	3,563	3,464	3,846
TOTAL DEBT FLOWS										
Disbursements	**82**	**1,777**	**648**	**712**	**1,172**	**948**	**853**	**813**	**1,405**	**924**
Long-term debt	82	1,739	527	674	1,019	903	853	813	1,235	743
IMF purchases	0	38	121	38	153	45	0	0	171	181
Principal repayments	**31**	**722**	**586**	**496**	**621**	**618**	**594**	**585**	**787**	**625**
Long-term debt	31	722	401	334	498	513	502	535	711	539
IMF repurchases	0	0	185	161	123	105	92	49	77	86
Net flows on debt	**51**	**1,055**	**227**	**924**	**1,189**	**561**	**627**	**726**	**-1,002**	**935**
of which short-term debt	..	..	165	709	639	231	368	497	-1,620	636
Interest payments (INT)	**..**	**685**	**489**	**581**	**641**	**662**	**565**	**509**	**457**	**421**
Long-term debt	12	590	367	400	443	491	410	382	426	390
IMF charges	0	0	43	39	31	33	26	18	11	8
Short-term debt	..	95	79	142	167	138	130	110	20	23
Net transfers on debt	**..**	**370**	**-261**	**344**	**548**	**-101**	**61**	**217**	**-1,459**	**514**
Total debt service paid (TDS)	**..**	**1,407**	**1,075**	**1,076**	**1,262**	**1,280**	**1,160**	**1,094**	**1,244**	**1,046**
Long-term debt	43	1,312	768	734	941	1,004	912	917	1,137	929
IMF repurchases and charges	0	0	228	200	155	137	118	67	87	94
Short-term debt (interest only)	..	95	79	142	167	138	130	110	20	23

2. AGGREGATE NET RESOURCE FLOWS AND NET TRANSFERS (LONG-TERM)

	1970	1980	1988	1989	1990	1991	1992	1993	1994	1995
NET RESOURCE FLOWS	**94**	**1,139**	**410**	**534**	**855**	**633**	**312**	**577**	**1,231**	**680**
Net flow of long-term debt (ex. IMF)	51	1,017	126	340	521	389	351	278	524	205
Foreign direct investment (net)	31	95	52	19	48	16	-231	88	17	19
Portfolio equity flows	0	0	0	0	0	0	0	0	7	3
Grants (excluding technical coop.)	12	27	232	176	287	228	192	211	683	454
Memo: technical coop. grants	21	99	65	100	131	139	131	125	115	122
NET TRANSFERS	**33**	**361**	**-98**	**79**	**349**	**80**	**-164**	**134**	**740**	**227**
Interest on long-term debt	12	590	367	400	443	491	410	382	426	390
Profit remittances on FDI	49	188	141	55	64	62	66	61	65	63

3. MAJOR ECONOMIC AGGREGATES

	1970	1980	1988	1989	1990	1991	1992	1993	1994	1995
Gross national product (GNP)	1,369	9,684	9,394	8,451	8,819	8,082	8,625	7,850	5,445	7,530
Exports of goods & services (XGS)	..	3,640	3,319	3,239	3,561	3,380	3,615	3,293	3,377	4,527
of which workers remittances	..	0	0	0	0	0	0	0	0	0
Imports of goods & services (MGS)	..	4,761	4,104	4,003	4,594	4,347	4,529	3,990	3,312	4,503
International reserves (RES)	119	46	29	33	21	29	22	20	221	546
Current account balance	..	-1,827	-1,241	-967	-1,214	-1,074	-1,013	-892	55	-269

4. DEBT INDICATORS

	1970	1980	1988	1989	1990	1991	1992	1993	1994	1995
EDT / XGS (%)	..	205.0	402.0	457.6	484.7	537.8	513.1	579.2	515.1	418.6
EDT / GNP (%)	..	77.1	142.0	175.4	195.7	224.9	215.0	242.9	319.5	251.7
TDS / XGS (%)	..	38.7	32.4	33.2	35.4	37.9	32.1	33.2	36.8	23.1
INT / XGS (%)	..	18.8	14.7	17.9	18.0	19.6	15.6	15.5	13.5	9.3
INT / GNP (%)	..	7.1	5.2	6.9	7.3	8.2	6.6	6.5	8.4	5.6
RES / EDT (%)	..	0.6	0.2	0.2	0.1	0.2	0.1	0.1	1.3	2.9
RES / MGS (months)	..	0.1	0.1	0.1	0.1	0.1	0.1	0.1	0.8	1.5
Short-term / EDT (%)	..	14.2	14.1	19.5	20.9	21.6	23.8	26.9	18.5	20.9
Concessional / EDT (%)	..	6.2	14.9	14.8	18.1	19.1	19.4	19.8	22.8	24.7
Multilateral / EDT (%)	..	7.0	22.9	20.7	20.8	20.8	20.1	18.7	21.4	20.6

COTE D'IVOIRE

(US$ million, unless otherwise indicated)

	1970	1980	1988	1989	1990	1991	1992	1993	1994	1995
5. LONG-TERM DEBT										
DEBT OUTSTANDING (LDOD)	**267**	**6,339**	**10,947**	**11,555**	**13,223**	**13,868**	**13,860**	**13,727**	**13,852**	**14,559**
Public and publicly guaranteed	**256**	**4,327**	**8,610**	**9,068**	**10,666**	**11,265**	**11,244**	**11,111**	**11,240**	**11,899**
Official creditors	143	1,247	5,609	6,065	7,686	8,432	8,596	8,602	8,641	9,214
Multilateral	14	523	3,058	3,061	3,585	3,787	3,727	3,557	3,715	3,897
Concessional	8	96	1,112	1,101	1,186	1,170	1,133	1,012	1,129	1,403
Bilateral	129	724	2,552	3,004	4,101	4,646	4,870	5,045	4,927	5,317
Concessional	114	369	877	1,093	1,946	2,298	2,464	2,767	2,844	3,284
Private creditors	112	3,080	3,000	3,003	2,980	2,832	2,648	2,509	2,599	2,685
Bonds	21	15	1	1	0	0	0	0	0	0
Commercial banks	32	1,611	2,449	2,491	2,640	2,614	2,518	2,393	2,514	2,630
Other private	59	1,454	550	511	340	218	129	116	85	55
Private nonguaranteed	**11**	**2,012**	**2,338**	**2,487**	**2,558**	**2,603**	**2,616**	**2,617**	**2,611**	**2,660**
Bonds	0	0	0	0	0	0	0	0	0	0
Commercial banks	11	2,012	2,338	2,487	2,558	2,603	2,616	2,617	2,611	2,660
Memo:										
IBRD	5	306	1,695	1,654	1,913	1,986	1,875	1,752	1,691	1,573
IDA	0	8	7	7	7	38	110	113	576	813
DISBURSEMENTS	**82**	**1,739**	**527**	**674**	**1,019**	**903**	**853**	**813**	**1,235**	**743**
Public and publicly guaranteed	**78**	**1,414**	**324**	**397**	**769**	**673**	**653**	**623**	**927**	**670**
Official creditors	43	231	289	395	758	666	651	623	918	669
Multilateral	12	136	234	197	460	428	365	137	582	340
Concessional	8	24	8	4	23	72	120	14	457	279
Bilateral	31	95	55	198	298	238	286	487	336	329
Concessional	25	34	35	184	283	192	279	455	314	309
Private creditors	35	1,183	35	2	11	6	2	0	9	1
Bonds	6	0	0	0	0	0	0	0	0	0
Commercial banks	7	634	16	0	2	0	0	0	0	1
Other private	22	550	19	2	9	6	2	0	9	0
Private nonguaranteed	**4**	**325**	**203**	**277**	**250**	**230**	**200**	**190**	**308**	**73**
Bonds	0	0	0	0	0	0	0	0	0	0
Commercial banks	4	325	203	277	250	230	200	190	308	73
Memo:										
IBRD	3	86	112	124	261	189	105	22	21	19
IDA	0	0	0	0	0	30	74	3	448	226
PRINCIPAL REPAYMENTS	**31**	**722**	**401**	**334**	**498**	**513**	**502**	**535**	**711**	**539**
Public and publicly guaranteed	**29**	**517**	**251**	**206**	**319**	**329**	**315**	**346**	**397**	**514**
Official creditors	9	55	207	184	247	273	290	294	355	478
Multilateral	0	17	203	183	230	258	268	278	291	285
Concessional	0	2	55	57	74	74	86	73	48	53
Bilateral	9	38	4	1	16	15	22	16	64	193
Concessional	6	16	1	0	5	8	9	7	13	19
Private creditors	20	462	44	22	72	56	25	53	42	36
Bonds	2	1	1	1	1	0	0	0	0	0
Commercial banks	2	301	23	9	25	11	10	44	5	5
Other private	15	161	21	13	46	45	14	8	37	30
Private nonguaranteed	**2**	**205**	**150**	**128**	**179**	**184**	**188**	**189**	**314**	**25**
Bonds	0	0	0	0	0	0	0	0	0	0
Commercial banks	2	205	150	128	179	184	188	189	314	25
Memo:										
IBRD	0	7	132	115	125	154	159	183	196	199
IDA	0	0	0	0	0	0	0	0	0	0
NET FLOWS ON DEBT	**51**	**1,017**	**126**	**340**	**521**	**389**	**351**	**278**	**524**	**205**
Public and publicly guaranteed	**49**	**897**	**74**	**191**	**450**	**344**	**338**	**277**	**529**	**156**
Official creditors	34	176	82	211	511	393	361	330	563	190
Multilateral	12	120	31	14	229	170	97	-141	291	55
Concessional	8	22	-48	-52	-51	-2	34	-59	408	226
Bilateral	22	57	51	197	282	223	264	471	272	136
Concessional	19	18	34	184	278	184	271	448	300	290
Private creditors	15	721	-9	-21	-62	-50	-23	-53	-34	-34
Bonds	4	-1	-1	-1	-1	0	0	0	0	0
Commercial banks	5	333	-7	-9	-23	-11	-10	-44	-5	-4
Other private	7	389	-1	-11	-38	-39	-12	-8	-29	-30
Private nonguaranteed	**2**	**120**	**53**	**149**	**71**	**46**	**12**	**1**	**-5**	**49**
Bonds	0	0	0	0	0	0	0	0	0	0
Commercial banks	2	120	53	149	71	46	12	1	-5	49
Memo:										
IBRD	3	78	-20	9	136	35	-54	-161	-175	-180
IDA	0	0	0	0	0	30	74	3	448	226

COTE D'IVOIRE

(US$ million, unless otherwise indicated)

	1970	1980	1988	1989	1990	1991	1992	1993	1994	1995
INTEREST PAYMENTS (LINT)	**12**	**590**	**367**	**400**	**443**	**491**	**410**	**382**	**426**	**390**
Public and publicly guaranteed	**12**	**353**	**206**	**190**	**205**	**289**	**244**	**225**	**296**	**257**
Official creditors	4	77	183	167	187	272	239	218	267	253
Multilateral	0	32	171	151	176	211	208	181	228	172
Concessional	0	2	3	2	4	6	10	8	10	11
Bilateral	4	45	12	17	12	61	31	38	39	81
Concessional	3	13	4	6	2	48	22	25	28	40
Private creditors	7	275	23	23	18	18	5	7	28	5
Bonds	1	1	0	0	0	0	0	0	0	0
Commercial banks	3	176	9	7	7	4	2	5	2	1
Other private	4	98	14	16	12	14	3	1	27	3
Private nonguaranteed	**0**	**237**	**161**	**210**	**237**	**202**	**166**	**157**	**131**	**133**
Bonds	0	0	0	0	0	0	0	0	0	0
Commercial banks	0	237	161	210	237	202	166	157	131	133
Memo:										
IBRD	0	22	156	136	141	169	159	155	144	135
IDA	0	0	0	0	0	0	1	1	2	5
NET TRANSFERS ON DEBT	**39**	**427**	**-240**	**-60**	**78**	**-102**	**-60**	**-104**	**98**	**-185**
Public and publicly guaranteed	**38**	**544**	**-133**	**1**	**245**	**54**	**94**	**52**	**234**	**-101**
Official creditors	30	99	-101	44	324	122	122	112	296	-62
Multilateral	11	87	-140	-136	54	-41	-111	-321	63	-117
Concessional	8	20	-50	-55	-55	-8	24	-67	399	215
Bilateral	18	11	39	180	271	163	232	433	233	55
Concessional	15	5	30	177	276	136	249	423	272	250
Private creditors	8	446	-32	-43	-80	-67	-28	-59	-62	-39
Bonds	3	-2	-1	-1	-1	0	0	0	0	0
Commercial banks	2	156	-16	-16	-30	-14	-13	-50	-7	-5
Other private	3	291	-15	-27	-49	-53	-15	-10	-55	-33
Private nonguaranteed	**2**	**-117**	**-108**	**-61**	**-167**	**-156**	**-153**	**-156**	**-136**	**-84**
Bonds	0	0	0	0	0	0	0	0	0	0
Commercial banks	2	-117	-108	-61	-167	-156	-153	-156	-136	-84
Memo:										
IBRD	3	56	-176	-127	-5	-135	-213	-316	-319	-315
IDA	0	0	0	0	0	30	73	2	446	222
DEBT SERVICE (LTDS)	**43**	**1,312**	**768**	**734**	**941**	**1,004**	**912**	**917**	**1,137**	**929**
Public and publicly guaranteed	**40**	**870**	**457**	**396**	**524**	**618**	**559**	**571**	**693**	**771**
Official creditors	13	133	390	351	434	545	529	512	622	731
Multilateral	1	49	374	334	406	469	476	458	519	457
Concessional	0	4	58	59	79	79	96	81	58	64
Bilateral	13	84	16	18	28	75	53	54	103	274
Concessional	9	29	5	7	7	56	31	32	41	59
Private creditors	27	738	67	45	90	73	30	59	71	40
Bonds	3	2	1	1	1	0	0	0	0	0
Commercial banks	5	477	32	16	32	14	13	50	7	7
Other private	19	259	35	29	58	59	17	10	64	33
Private nonguaranteed	**2**	**442**	**311**	**338**	**417**	**386**	**353**	**346**	**444**	**158**
Bonds	0	0	0	0	0	0	0	0	0	0
Commercial banks	2	442	311	338	417	386	353	346	444	158
Memo:										
IBRD	0	29	288	251	266	324	318	338	340	334
IDA	0	0	0	0	0	0	1	1	2	5
UNDISBURSED DEBT	**169**	**1,723**	**1,186**	**1,148**	**1,230**	**1,203**	**1,347**	**1,165**	**909**	**895**
Official creditors	108	747	1,061	1,033	1,131	1,181	1,328	1,147	897	886
Private creditors	61	976	126	115	99	22	19	19	11	9
Memorandum items										
Concessional LDOD	121	465	1,989	2,194	3,132	3,468	3,597	3,779	3,973	4,687
Variable rate LDOD	34	3,601	6,284	6,748	7,400	7,901	8,002	7,798	7,808	7,940
Public sector LDOD	255	4,277	8,606	9,065	10,663	11,263	11,243	11,109	11,239	11,898
Private sector LDOD	11	2,061	2,341	2,490	2,560	2,605	2,617	2,618	2,613	2,661

6. CURRENCY COMPOSITION OF LONG-TERM DEBT (PERCENT)

	1970	1980	1988	1989	1990	1991	1992	1993	1994	1995
Deutsche mark	10.5	4.5	3.5	3.7	3.9	3.8	3.7	3.6	4.1	4.4
French franc	47.7	34.6	33.1	36.2	38.1	38.1	38.5	39.5	38.8	39.1
Japanese yen	0.0	0.6	0.7	0.7	0.9	1.1	1.2	1.3	1.5	1.4
Pound sterling	0.0	1.4	1.2	1.2	1.3	1.2	1.0	1.1	1.0	0.9
Swiss franc	0.0	6.3	2.6	2.4	2.3	2.0	2.0	2.1	0.4	0.5
U.S.dollars	25.4	31.5	18.7	17.7	15.5	15.6	16.6	17.0	21.0	22.0
Multiple currency	2.1	9.9	23.2	21.9	22.7	23.1	22.5	22.3	22.3	20.1
Special drawing rights	0.0	0.0	0.5	0.4	0.4	0.4	0.6	0.6	0.6	0.6
All other currencies	14.3	11.2	16.6	15.7	14.9	14.7	13.9	12.6	10.4	11.1

COTE D'IVOIRE

(US$ million, unless otherwise indicated)

	1970	1980	1988	1989	1990	1991	1992	1993	1994	1995
7. DEBT RESTRUCTURINGS										
Total amount rescheduled	0	0	398	212	930	568	399	0	645	381
Debt stock rescheduled	0	0	0	0	0	0	0	0	0	0
Principal rescheduled	0	0	218	71	590	316	213	0	266	192
Official	0	0	118	34	407	245	150	0	257	189
Private	0	0	100	37	183	71	64	0	9	4
Interest rescheduled	0	0	133	57	287	130	84	0	306	131
Official	0	0	101	45	257	119	79	0	302	129
Private	0	0	32	12	29	11	5	0	4	1
Debt forgiven	..	..	5	29	50	0	0	0	1,352	292
Memo: interest forgiven	..	..	0	0	0	0	0	0	228	30
Debt stock reduction	0	0	0	0	0	0	0	0	0	0
of which debt buyback	0	0	0	0	0	0	0	0	0	0
8. DEBT STOCK-FLOW RECONCILIATION										
Total change in debt stocks	..	..	..	1,478	2,438	916	373	524	-1,676	1,557
Net flows on debt	..	..	..	924	1,189	561	627	726	-1,002	935
Net change in interest arrears	..	..	..	301	69	99	117	208	-290	115
Interest capitalized	..	..	..	57	287	130	84	0	306	131
Debt forgiveness or reduction	..	..	..	-29	-50	0	0	0	-1,352	-292
Cross-currency valuation	..	..	..	200	1,225	-92	-664	-533	648	725
Residual	..	..	..	24	-281	218	209	123	14	-57
9. AVERAGE TERMS OF NEW COMMITMENTS										
ALL CREDITORS										
Interest (%)	5.8	11.4	5.6	6.9	5.9	5.5	5.3	4.6	2.1	1.9
Maturity (years)	18.6	10.3	15.8	19.2	19.9	21.7	19.0	19.2	29.8	29.8
Grace period (years)	5.4	4.5	4.7	5.8	6.3	6.4	5.8	8.0	8.6	8.4
Grant element (%)	26.1	-5.6	20.2	19.1	27.4	31.5	30.6	38.5	64.0	63.7
Official creditors										
Interest (%)	4.9	6.2	5.4	6.8	5.9	5.5	5.3	4.6	2.0	1.9
Maturity (years)	22.5	18.8	15.9	19.4	19.9	21.7	19.0	19.2	29.9	29.8
Grace period (years)	7.4	5.7	4.8	5.9	6.3	6.4	5.8	8.0	8.6	8.5
Grant element (%)	35.3	25.4	21.3	19.5	27.4	31.5	30.6	38.5	64.6	63.8
Private creditors										
Interest (%)	7.4	11.9	10.1	9.6	0.0	0.0	0.0	0.0	11.4	14.4
Maturity (years)	12.1	9.5	12.6	8.3	0.0	0.0	0.0	0.0	12.0	19.6
Grace period (years)	2.1	4.4	3.1	0.8	0.0	0.0	0.0	0.0	2.5	0.1
Grant element (%)	10.9	-8.5	-1.4	0.4	0.0	0.0	0.0	0.0	-7.8	-10.0
Memorandum items										
Commitments	71	1,688	630	526	764	801	850	498	907	716
Official creditors	44	144	599	514	764	801	850	498	900	715
Private creditors	27	1,544	31	12	0	0	0	0	7	1

10. CONTRACTUAL OBLIGATIONS ON OUTSTANDING LONG-TERM DEBT

	1996	1997	1998	1999	2000	2001	2002	2003	2004	2005
TOTAL										
Disbursements	300	242	163	96	44	19	9	2	1	0
Principal	839	829	953	957	963	968	1,003	941	936	613
Interest	471	527	561	528	491	453	480	437	396	358
Official creditors										
Disbursements	293	241	162	96	44	19	9	2	1	0
Principal	539	529	654	661	667	669	716	692	687	493
Interest	338	394	428	396	360	322	349	306	266	227
Bilateral creditors										
Disbursements	91	61	36	18	9	6	3	1	1	0
Principal	224	189	335	353	385	425	470	455	457	277
Interest	137	208	260	246	227	205	246	218	191	167
Multilateral creditors										
Disbursements	203	179	126	78	35	13	6	1	0	0
Principal	315	340	319	308	282	243	246	238	231	216
Interest	201	187	168	150	133	117	103	88	74	60
Private creditors										
Disbursements	6	2	1	0	0	0	0	0	0	0
Principal	301	300	299	296	296	299	288	249	248	120
Interest	133	133	132	132	131	131	131	131	131	131
Commercial banks										
Disbursements	0	0	0	0	0	0	0	0	0	0
Principal	3	3	3	0	0	0	0	0	0	0
Interest	1	1	1	0	0	0	0	0	0	0
Other private										
Disbursements	6	2	1	0	0	0	0	0	0	0
Principal	297	297	297	296	296	299	288	249	248	120
Interest	132	132	132	131	131	131	131	131	131	131

CROATIA

(US$ million, unless otherwise indicated)

1. SUMMARY DEBT DATA

	1970	1980	1988	1989	1990	1991	1992	1993	1994	1995
TOTAL DEBT STOCKS (EDT)	..	..	..	..	..	..	..	**2,523**	**2,955**	**3,662**
Long-term debt (LDOD)	..	..	..	..	..	..	..	**2,396**	**2,587**	**2,950**
Public and publicly guaranteed	..	..	..	..	..	..	..	1,511	1,545	1,693
Private nonguaranteed	0	0	0	0	0	0	0	886	1,042	1,257
Use of IMF credit	**0**	**0**	**0**	**0**	**0**	**0**	**0**	**20**	**127**	**221**
Short-term debt	..	..	..	..	..	..	..	**107**	**242**	**492**
of which interest arrears on LDOD	..	..	..	..	..	..	..	52	70	71
Official creditors	..	..	..	..	..	..	..	4	2	1
Private creditors	..	..	..	..	..	..	..	48	68	70
Memo: principal arrears on LDOD	..	..	..	..	..	..	..	1,113	1,170	547
Official creditors	..	..	..	..	..	..	..	654	678	1
Private creditors	..	..	..	..	..	..	..	459	491	546
Memo: export credits	..	..	0	0	0	0	266	277	396	544
TOTAL DEBT FLOWS										
Disbursements	..	..	..	..	..	..	..	**158**	**331**	**618**
Long-term debt	..	..	..	..	..	..	..	158	219	518
IMF purchases	0	0	0	0	0	0	0	0	112	99
Principal repayments	..	..	..	..	..	..	..	**241**	**178**	**265**
Long-term debt	..	..	..	..	..	..	..	217	169	259
IMF repurchases	0	0	0	0	0	0	0	24	9	6
Net flows on debt	..	..	..	..	..	..	..	**-29**	**271**	**601**
of which short-term debt	..	..	..	..	..	..	..	55	117	249
Interest payments (INT)	..	..	..	..	..	..	..	**134**	**115**	**153**
Long-term debt	..	..	..	..	..	..	..	128	107	126
IMF charges	0	0	0	0	0	0	0	4	1	10
Short-term debt	..	..	..	..	..	..	..	3	7	18
Net transfers on debt	..	..	..	..	..	..	..	**-163**	**156**	**448**
Total debt service paid (TDS)	..	..	..	..	..	..	..	**376**	**293**	**419**
Long-term debt	..	..	..	..	..	..	..	345	276	385
IMF repurchases and charges	0	0	0	0	0	0	0	28	10	16
Short-term debt (interest only)	..	..	..	..	..	..	..	3	7	18

2. AGGREGATE NET RESOURCE FLOWS AND NET TRANSFERS (LONG-TERM)

	1970	1980	1988	1989	1990	1991	1992	1993	1994	1995
NET RESOURCE FLOWS	..	..	..	..	..	..	..	**14**	**148**	**340**
Net flow of long-term debt (ex. IMF)	..	..	..	..	..	..	..	-60	50	259
Foreign direct investment (net)	..	..	..	..	..	..	..	74	98	81
Portfolio equity flows	..	..	..	..	..	..	..	0	0	0
Grants (excluding technical coop.)	..	..	..	..	..	..	..	0	0	0
Memo: technical coop. grants	..	..	..	..	..	..	..	0	0	0
NET TRANSFERS	..	..	..	..	..	..	..	**-114**	**41**	**214**
Interest on long-term debt	..	..	..	..	..	..	..	128	107	126
Profit remittances on FDI	..	..	..	..	..	..	..	0	0	0

3. MAJOR ECONOMIC AGGREGATES

	1970	1980	1988	1989	1990	1991	1992	1993	1994	1995
Gross national product (GNP)	..	..	..	..	..	..	..	11,552	14,102	17,998
Exports of goods & services (XGS)	..	..	..	..	..	..	..	5,822	6,654	7,375
of which workers remittances	..	..	..	..	..	..	..	0	0	0
Imports of goods & services (MGS)	..	..	..	..	..	..	..	6,094	7,010	9,733
International reserves (RES)	..	..	..	..	..	..	..	617	1,410	2,036
Current account balance	..	..	..	..	..	..	..	104	103	-1,712

4. DEBT INDICATORS

	1970	1980	1988	1989	1990	1991	1992	1993	1994	1995
EDT / XGS (%)	..	..	..	..	..	..	..	43.3	44.4	49.7
EDT / GNP (%)	..	..	..	..	..	..	..	21.8	21.0	20.3
TDS / XGS (%)	..	..	..	..	..	..	..	6.5	4.4	5.7
INT / XGS (%)	..	..	..	..	..	..	..	2.3	1.7	2.1
INT / GNP (%)	..	..	..	..	..	..	..	1.2	0.8	0.9
RES / EDT (%)	..	..	..	..	..	..	..	24.5	47.7	55.6
RES / MGS (months)	..	..	..	..	..	..	..	1.2	2.4	2.5
Short-term / EDT (%)	..	..	..	..	..	..	..	4.2	8.2	13.4
Concessional / EDT (%)	..	..	..	..	..	..	..	0.8	1.0	21.4
Multilateral / EDT (%)	..	..	..	..	..	..	..	22.3	17.9	14.4

CROATIA

(US$ million, unless otherwise indicated)

	1970	1980	1988	1989	1990	1991	1992	1993	1994	1995
5. LONG-TERM DEBT										
DEBT OUTSTANDING (LDOD)	..	..	..	..	..	..	..	**2,396**	**2,587**	**2,950**
Public and publicly guaranteed	..	..	..	..	..	..	..	**1,511**	**1,545**	**1,693**
Official creditors	..	..	..	..	..	..	..	1,416	1,434	1,503
Multilateral	..	..	..	..	..	..	..	562	529	528
Concessional	..	..	..	..	..	..	..	21	21	11
Bilateral	..	..	..	..	..	..	..	854	905	975
Concessional	..	..	..	..	..	..	..	0	9	774
Private creditors	..	..	..	..	..	..	..	95	111	190
Bonds	..	..	..	..	..	..	..	0	0	0
Commercial banks	..	..	..	..	..	..	..	45	47	127
Other private	..	..	..	..	..	..	..	50	64	63
Private nonguaranteed	**0**	**0**	**0**	**0**	**0**	**0**	**0**	**886**	**1,042**	**1,257**
Bonds	..	..	..	..	..	..	..	0	0	0
Commercial banks	..	..	..	..	..	..	..	886	1,042	1,257
Memo:										
IBRD	0	0	0	0	0	0	0	104	84	117
IDA	0	0	0	0	0	0	0	0	0	0
DISBURSEMENTS	..	..	..	..	..	..	..	**158**	**219**	**518**
Public and publicly guaranteed	..	..	..	..	..	..	..	**34**	**51**	**203**
Official creditors	..	..	..	..	..	..	..	8	27	72
Multilateral	..	..	..	..	..	..	..	8	2	60
Concessional	..	..	..	..	..	..	..	0	0	0
Bilateral	..	..	..	..	..	..	..	0	25	12
Concessional	..	..	..	..	..	..	..	0	9	6
Private creditors	..	..	..	..	..	..	..	26	24	131
Bonds	..	..	..	..	..	..	..	0	0	0
Commercial banks	..	..	..	..	..	..	..	0	0	100
Other private	..	..	..	..	..	..	..	26	24	31
Private nonguaranteed	**0**	**0**	**0**	**0**	**0**	**0**	**0**	**124**	**168**	**316**
Bonds	..	..	..	..	..	..	..	0	0	0
Commercial banks	..	..	..	..	..	..	..	124	168	316
Memo:										
IBRD	0	0	0	0	0	0	0	1	1	50
IDA	0	0	0	0	0	0	0	0	0	0
PRINCIPAL REPAYMENTS	..	..	..	..	..	..	..	**217**	**169**	**259**
Public and publicly guaranteed	..	..	..	..	..	..	..	**91**	**89**	**98**
Official creditors	..	..	..	..	..	..	..	80	75	78
Multilateral	..	..	..	..	..	..	..	80	75	78
Concessional	..	..	..	..	..	..	..	4	2	12
Bilateral	..	..	..	..	..	..	..	0	0	0
Concessional	..	..	..	..	..	..	..	0	0	0
Private creditors	..	..	..	..	..	..	..	11	14	21
Bonds	..	..	..	..	..	..	..	0	0	0
Commercial banks	..	..	..	..	..	..	..	2	0	0
Other private	..	..	..	..	..	..	..	9	14	21
Private nonguaranteed	**0**	**0**	**0**	**0**	**0**	**0**	**0**	**127**	**79**	**161**
Bonds	..	..	..	..	..	..	..	0	0	0
Commercial banks	..	..	..	..	..	..	..	127	79	161
Memo:										
IBRD	0	0	0	0	0	0	0	33	29	20
IDA	0	0	0	0	0	0	0	0	0	0
NET FLOWS ON DEBT	..	..	..	..	..	..	..	**-60**	**50**	**259**
Public and publicly guaranteed	..	..	..	..	..	..	..	**-57**	**-39**	**105**
Official creditors	..	..	..	..	..	..	..	-72	-48	-6
Multilateral	..	..	..	..	..	..	..	-72	-74	-18
Concessional	..	..	..	..	..	..	..	-4	-2	-12
Bilateral	..	..	..	..	..	..	..	0	25	12
Concessional	..	..	..	..	..	..	..	0	9	6
Private creditors	..	..	..	..	..	..	..	15	10	111
Bonds	..	..	..	..	..	..	..	0	0	0
Commercial banks	..	..	..	..	..	..	..	-2	0	100
Other private	..	..	..	..	..	..	..	17	10	11
Private nonguaranteed	**0**	**0**	**0**	**0**	**0**	**0**	**0**	**-3**	**89**	**154**
Bonds	..	..	..	..	..	..	..	0	0	0
Commercial banks	..	..	..	..	..	..	..	-3	89	154
Memo:										
IBRD	0	0	0	0	0	0	0	-33	-28	29
IDA	0	0	0	0	0	0	0	0	0	0

CROATIA

(US$ million, unless otherwise indicated)

	1970	*1980*	*1988*	*1989*	*1990*	*1991*	*1992*	*1993*	*1994*	*1995*
INTEREST PAYMENTS (LINT)	**..**	**..**	**..**	**..**	**..**	**..**	**..**	**128**	**107**	**126**
Public and publicly guaranteed	**..**	**..**	**..**	**..**	**..**	**..**	**..**	**79**	**72**	**60**
Official creditors	..	..	..	..	..	..	..	70	63	54
Multilateral	..	..	..	..	..	..	..	59	54	52
Concessional	..	..	..	..	..	..	..	1	1	1
Bilateral	..	..	..	..	..	..	..	11	9	2
Concessional	..	..	..	..	..	..	..	0	0	0
Private creditors	..	..	..	..	..	..	..	9	9	5
Bonds	..	..	..	..	..	..	..	0	0	0
Commercial banks	..	..	..	..	..	..	..	6	4	0
Other private	..	..	..	..	..	..	..	4	4	5
Private nonguaranteed	**0**	**0**	**0**	**0**	**0**	**0**	**0**	**49**	**35**	**66**
Bonds	..	..	..	..	..	..	..	0	0	0
Commercial banks	..	..	..	..	..	..	..	49	35	66
Memo:										
IBRD	0	0	0	0	0	0	0	9	8	7
IDA	0	0	0	0	0	0	0	0	0	0
NET TRANSFERS ON DEBT	**..**	**..**	**..**	**..**	**..**	**..**	**..**	**-188**	**-57**	**133**
Public and publicly guaranteed	**..**	**..**	**..**	**..**	**..**	**..**	**..**	**-136**	**-111**	**45**
Official creditors	..	..	..	..	..	..	..	-141	-112	-60
Multilateral	..	..	..	..	..	..	..	-131	-128	-70
Concessional	..	..	..	..	..	..	..	-5	-3	-14
Bilateral	..	..	..	..	..	..	..	-11	16	10
Concessional	..	..	..	..	..	..	..	0	9	6
Private creditors	..	..	..	..	..	..	..	6	1	105
Bonds	..	..	..	..	..	..	..	0	0	0
Commercial banks	..	..	..	..	..	..	..	-8	-4	100
Other private	..	..	..	..	..	..	..	14	5	5
Private nonguaranteed	**0**	**0**	**0**	**0**	**0**	**0**	**0**	**-52**	**54**	**88**
Bonds	..	..	..	..	..	..	..	0	0	0
Commercial banks	..	..	..	..	..	..	..	-52	54	88
Memo:										
IBRD	0	0	0	0	0	0	0	-42	-36	22
IDA	0	0	0	0	0	0	0	0	0	0
DEBT SERVICE (LTDS)	**..**	**..**	**..**	**..**	**..**	**..**	**..**	**345**	**276**	**385**
Public and publicly guaranteed	**..**	**..**	**..**	**..**	**..**	**..**	**..**	**170**	**161**	**158**
Official creditors	..	..	..	..	..	..	..	150	139	132
Multilateral	..	..	..	..	..	..	..	139	129	130
Concessional	..	..	..	..	..	..	..	5	3	14
Bilateral	..	..	..	..	..	..	..	11	9	2
Concessional	..	..	..	..	..	..	..	0	0	0
Private creditors	..	..	..	..	..	..	..	20	23	26
Bonds	..	..	..	..	..	..	..	0	0	0
Commercial banks	..	..	..	..	..	..	..	8	4	0
Other private	..	..	..	..	..	..	..	13	19	26
Private nonguaranteed	**0**	**0**	**0**	**0**	**0**	**0**	**0**	**176**	**114**	**227**
Bonds	..	..	..	..	..	..	..	0	0	0
Commercial banks	..	..	..	..	..	..	..	176	114	227
Memo:										
IBRD	0	0	0	0	0	0	0	43	37	28
IDA	0	0	0	0	0	0	0	0	0	0
UNDISBURSED DEBT	**..**	**..**	**..**	**..**	**..**	**..**	**..**	**114**	**223**	**387**
Official creditors	..	..	..	..	..	..	..	90	161	307
Private creditors	..	..	..	..	..	..	..	25	62	81
Memorandum items										
Concessional LDOD	..	..	..	..	..	..	..	21	30	785
Variable rate LDOD	..	..	..	..	..	..	..	1,141	1,303	1,440
Public sector LDOD	..	..	..	..	..	..	..	1,496	1,531	1,681
Private sector LDOD	..	..	..	..	..	..	..	900	1,055	1,269

6. CURRENCY COMPOSITION OF LONG-TERM DEBT (PERCENT)

	1970	*1980*	*1988*	*1989*	*1990*	*1991*	*1992*	*1993*	*1994*	*1995*
Deutsche mark	..	..	..	..	..	..	..	2.8	3.1	4.0
French franc	..	..	..	..	..	..	..	1.1	1.0	0.4
Japanese yen	..	..	..	..	..	..	..	0.4	0.4	0.0
Pound sterling	..	..	..	..	..	..	..	17.4	16.5	13.4
Swiss franc	..	..	..	..	..	..	..	1.4	1.1	0.8
U.S.dollars	..	..	..	..	..	..	..	52.6	52.6	61.0
Multiple currency	..	..	..	..	..	..	..	6.9	5.4	6.9
Special drawing rights	..	..	..	..	..	..	..	0.0	0.0	0.0
All other currencies	..	..	..	..	..	..	..	17.3	19.8	13.4

CROATIA

(US$ million, unless otherwise indicated)

	1970	1980	1988	1989	1990	1991	1992	1993	1994	1995
7. DEBT RESTRUCTURINGS										
Total amount rescheduled	0	0	0	0	0	0	0	0	16	861
Debt stock rescheduled	0	0	0	0	0	0	0	0	0	0
Principal rescheduled	0	0	0	0	0	0	0	0	13	848
Official	0	0	0	0	0	0	0	0	0	810
Private	0	0	0	0	0	0	0	0	13	38
Interest rescheduled	0	0	0	0	0	0	0	0	3	13
Official	0	0	0	0	0	0	0	0	0	8
Private	0	0	0	0	0	0	0	0	3	5
Debt forgiven	..	..	0	0	0	0	0	0	0	0
Memo: interest forgiven	..	..	0	0	0	0	0	0	0	0
Debt stock reduction	0	0	0	0	0	0	0	0	0	0
of which debt buyback	0	0	0	0	0	0	0	0	0	0
8. DEBT STOCK-FLOW RECONCILIATION										
Total change in debt stocks	..	..	..	..	..	..	..	2,523	432	707
Net flows on debt	..	..	..	..	..	..	..	-29	271	601
Net change in interest arrears	..	..	..	..	..	..	..	52	18	1
Interest capitalized	..	..	..	..	..	..	..	0	3	13
Debt forgiveness or reduction	..	..	..	..	..	..	..	0	0	0
Cross-currency valuation	..	..	..	..	..	..	..	-37	91	39
Residual	..	..	..	..	..	..	..	2,538	49	53
9. AVERAGE TERMS OF NEW COMMITMENTS										
ALL CREDITORS										
Interest (%)	..	..	..	..	..	..	..	5.9	7.0	6.1
Maturity (years)	..	..	..	..	..	..	..	6.4	13.5	8.3
Grace period (years)	..	..	..	..	..	..	..	1.5	4.5	2.5
Grant element (%)	..	..	..	..	..	..	..	12.5	16.0	12.1
Official creditors										
Interest (%)	..	..	..	..	..	..	..	6.9	7.0	6.0
Maturity (years)	..	..	..	..	..	..	..	9.3	16.4	12.7
Grace period (years)	..	..	..	..	..	..	..	2.0	4.2	3.5
Grant element (%)	..	..	..	..	..	..	..	12.4	17.0	17.4
Private creditors										
Interest (%)	..	..	..	..	..	..	..	5.3	6.9	6.2
Maturity (years)	..	..	..	..	..	..	..	4.8	6.3	1.6
Grace period (years)	..	..	..	..	..	..	..	1.2	5.2	1.0
Grant element (%)	..	..	..	..	..	..	..	12.6	13.4	4.1
Memorandum items										
Commitments	..	..	..	..	..	..	..	43	213	360
Official creditors	..	..	..	..	..	..	..	16	151	217
Private creditors	..	..	..	..	..	..	..	28	62	144

10. CONTRACTUAL OBLIGATIONS ON OUTSTANDING LONG-TERM DEBT

	1996	1997	1998	1999	2000	2001	2002	2003	2004	2005
TOTAL										
Disbursements	96	104	67	43	29	18	12	8	6	5
Principal	402	262	290	240	243	215	122	116	140	113
Interest	107	99	90	79	69	59	56	52	46	38
Official creditors										
Disbursements	62	73	54	41	28	18	12	8	6	5
Principal	105	117	166	155	175	153	93	95	99	99
Interest	95	90	84	74	65	54	45	40	35	30
Bilateral creditors										
Disbursements	5	3	1	0	0	0	0	0	0	0
Principal	35	44	69	59	66	55	50	55	64	73
Interest	42	40	37	33	31	28	26	24	21	19
Multilateral creditors										
Disbursements	57	70	53	40	28	18	12	8	6	5
Principal	70	73	97	96	109	98	43	40	36	26
Interest	52	50	47	41	34	26	19	16	13	11
Private creditors										
Disbursements	34	31	13	2	1	0	0	0	0	0
Principal	297	145	125	85	68	62	29	21	40	14
Interest	13	9	6	5	5	5	12	12	11	8
Commercial banks										
Disbursements	0	0	0	0	0	0	0	0	0	0
Principal	109	9	9	0	0	0	0	0	0	0
Interest	7	1	0	0	0	0	0	0	0	0
Other private										
Disbursements	34	31	13	2	1	0	0	0	0	0
Principal	188	136	116	85	68	62	29	21	40	14
Interest	5	9	6	5	5	5	12	12	11	8

CZECH REPUBLIC

(US$ million, unless otherwise indicated)

1. SUMMARY DEBT DATA

	1970	1980	1988	1989	1990	1991	1992	1993	1994	1995
TOTAL DEBT STOCKS (EDT)	..	..	**5,642**	**6,217**	**6,383**	**8,032**	**7,572**	**9,174**	**10,695**	**16,576**
Long-term debt (LDOD)	..	..	**2,806**	**3,224**	**3,983**	**4,975**	**4,701**	**6,099**	**7,806**	**11,504**
Public and publicly guaranteed	..	..	2,806	3,224	3,983	4,973	4,690	5,888	7,038	9,610
Private nonguaranteed	0	0	0	0	0	2	11	212	768	1,894
Use of IMF credit	**0**	**0**	**0**	**0**	**0**	**914**	**1,073**	**1,072**	**0**	**0**
Short-term debt	..	..	**2,835**	**2,993**	**2,400**	**2,143**	**1,798**	**2,002**	**2,889**	**5,072**
of which interest arrears on LDOD	..	..	0	0	0	0	0	0	1	28
Official creditors	..	..	0	0	0	0	0	0	1	0
Private creditors	..	..	0	0	0	0	0	0	0	28
Memo: principal arrears on LDOD	..	..	0	0	0	0	0	0	0	105
Official creditors	..	..	0	0	0	0	0	0	0	0
Private creditors	..	..	0	0	0	0	0	0	0	105
Memo: export credits	..	..	1,081	1,052	1,693	2,297	1,562	1,519	2,836	3,101
TOTAL DEBT FLOWS										
Disbursements	..	..	**1,032**	**1,021**	**1,149**	**2,523**	**1,208**	**2,383**	**1,556**	**4,634**
Long-term debt	..	..	1,032	1,021	1,149	1,648	974	2,383	1,556	4,634
IMF purchases	0	0	0	0	0	875	234	0	0	0
Principal repayments	..	..	**790**	**820**	**537**	**668**	**1,097**	**919**	**2,000**	**1,654**
Long-term debt	..	..	790	820	537	668	1,063	919	882	1,654
IMF repurchases	0	0	0	0	0	0	34	0	1,118	0
Net flows on debt	..	..	**518**	**359**	**19**	**1,598**	**-235**	**1,668**	**442**	**5,136**
of which short-term debt	..	..	276	158	-593	-257	-346	205	886	2,156
Interest payments (INT)	..	..	**395**	**401**	**497**	**402**	**571**	**477**	**502**	**915**
Long-term debt	..	..	190	213	196	223	312	288	321	677
IMF charges	0	0	0	0	0	37	73	73	34	0
Short-term debt	..	..	206	188	301	142	185	116	147	238
Net transfers on debt	..	..	**123**	**-42**	**-478**	**1,196**	**-805**	**1,191**	**-60**	**4,221**
Total debt service paid (TDS)	..	..	**1,185**	**1,220**	**1,035**	**1,070**	**1,668**	**1,396**	**2,502**	**2,569**
Long-term debt	..	..	980	1,032	734	891	1,375	1,207	1,204	2,331
IMF repurchases and charges	0	0	0	0	0	37	108	73	1,152	0
Short-term debt (interest only)	..	..	206	188	301	142	185	116	147	238

2. AGGREGATE NET RESOURCE FLOWS AND NET TRANSFERS (LONG-TERM)

	1970	1980	1988	1989	1990	1991	1992	1993	1994	1995
NET RESOURCE FLOWS	..	..	**242**	**458**	**819**	**1,434**	**596**	**2,206**	**1,769**	**5,675**
Net flow of long-term debt (ex. IMF)	0	0	242	201	612	980	-89	1,463	674	2,980
Foreign direct investment (net)	0	0	0	257	207	400	600	654	878	2,568
Portfolio equity flows	..	..	0	0	0	0	31	38	114	82
Grants (excluding technical coop.)	0	0	0	0	0	54	54	50	103	45
Memo: technical coop. grants	0	0	0	0	0	24	75	50	40	98
NET TRANSFERS	..	..	**52**	**246**	**623**	**1,209**	**283**	**1,817**	**1,318**	**4,857**
Interest on long-term debt	..	..	190	213	196	223	312	288	321	677
Profit remittances on FDI	0	0	0	0	0	2	0	100	130	140

3. MAJOR ECONOMIC AGGREGATES

	1970	1980	1988	1989	1990	1991	1992	1993	1994	1995
Gross national product (GNP)	..	29,123	35,742	34,848	31,599	24,324	27,987	31,069	35,983	44,750
Exports of goods & services (XGS)	..	..	..	..	..	..	..	18,271	19,729	24,579
of which workers remittances	..	..	..	..	..	..	..	0	0	0
Imports of goods & services (MGS)	..	..	..	..	..	..	..	17,677	19,937	27,078
International reserves (RES)	..	..	..	..	..	..	..	4,551	6,949	14,613
Current account balance	..	..	..	..	..	..	..	681	-81	-1,906

4. DEBT INDICATORS

	1970	1980	1988	1989	1990	1991	1992	1993	1994	1995
EDT / XGS (%)	..	..	..	..	..	..	..	50.2	54.2	67.4
EDT / GNP (%)	..	..	15.8	17.8	20.2	33.0	27.1	29.5	29.7	37.0
TDS / XGS (%)	..	..	..	..	..	..	..	7.6	12.7	10.5
INT / XGS (%)	..	..	..	..	..	..	..	2.6	2.5	3.7
INT / GNP (%)	..	..	1.1	1.1	1.6	1.7	2.0	1.5	1.4	2.0
RES / EDT (%)	..	..	..	..	..	..	..	49.6	65.0	88.2
RES / MGS (months)	..	..	..	..	..	..	..	3.1	4.2	6.5
Short-term / EDT (%)	..	..	50.3	48.1	37.6	26.7	23.7	21.8	27.0	30.6
Concessional / EDT (%)	..	..	0.0	0.0	0.0	0.0	0.4	0.6	0.8	0.8
Multilateral / EDT (%)	..	..	3.2	2.9	2.8	6.8	9.9	9.0	8.6	6.1

CZECH REPUBLIC

(US$ million, unless otherwise indicated)

	1970	1980	1988	1989	1990	1991	1992	1993	1994	1995
5. LONG-TERM DEBT										
DEBT OUTSTANDING (LDOD)	..	..	2,806	3,224	3,983	4,975	4,701	6,099	7,806	11,504
Public and publicly guaranteed	..	..	2,806	3,224	3,983	4,973	4,690	5,888	7,038	9,610
Official creditors	..	..	280	263	252	649	1,061	1,218	1,351	1,433
Multilateral	..	..	179	179	179	543	748	822	925	1,007
Concessional	..	..	0	0	0	0	0	23	57	100
Bilateral	..	..	101	84	73	105	312	396	426	426
Concessional	..	..	0	0	0	0	29	28	30	33
Private creditors	..	..	2,526	2,961	3,732	4,324	3,630	4,670	5,687	8,177
Bonds	..	..	0	47	50	240	244	943	870	860
Commercial banks	..	..	1,209	1,546	1,970	2,677	2,423	2,423	3,678	6,444
Other private	..	..	1,317	1,369	1,712	1,407	963	1,304	1,138	873
Private nonguaranteed	0	0	0	0	0	2	11	212	768	1,894
Bonds	..	..	0	0	0	0	0	0	0	39
Commercial banks	..	..	0	0	0	2	11	212	768	1,855
Memo:										
IBRD	0	0	0	0	0	139	220	315	367	434
IDA	0	0	0	0	0	0	0	0	0	0
DISBURSEMENTS	..	..	1,032	1,021	1,149	1,648	974	2,383	1,556	4,634
Public and publicly guaranteed	..	..	1,032	1,021	1,149	1,648	966	2,238	1,368	3,261
Official creditors	..	..	16	8	19	408	525	232	105	139
Multilateral	..	..	3	0	5	349	281	132	79	114
Concessional	..	..	0	0	0	0	0	24	30	38
Bilateral	..	..	13	8	14	60	244	100	26	25
Concessional	..	..	0	0	0	0	30	0	0	0
Private creditors	..	..	1,016	1,013	1,130	1,240	441	2,006	1,263	3,122
Bonds	..	..	0	48	0	183	42	747	0	20
Commercial banks	..	..	432	585	435	726	159	668	907	2,915
Other private	..	..	585	379	696	331	239	592	356	187
Private nonguaranteed	0	0	0	0	0	0	9	145	189	1,373
Bonds	..	..	0	0	0	0	0	0	0	36
Commercial banks	..	..	0	0	0	0	9	145	189	1,338
Memo:										
IBRD	0	0	0	0	0	133	87	93	30	57
IDA	0	0	0	0	0	0	0	0	0	0
PRINCIPAL REPAYMENTS	..	..	790	820	537	668	1,063	919	882	1,654
Public and publicly guaranteed	..	..	790	820	537	668	1,063	912	859	1,407
Official creditors	..	..	26	34	43	28	77	59	62	105
Multilateral	..	..	0	8	5	3	43	35	32	71
Concessional	..	..	0	0	0	0	0	0	0	0
Bilateral	..	..	26	27	38	26	34	24	30	34
Concessional	..	..	0	0	0	0	0	0	0	0
Private creditors	..	..	764	785	494	640	986	853	796	1,303
Bonds	..	..	0	0	0	0	38	114	126	18
Commercial banks	..	..	296	263	20	40	333	227	355	810
Other private	..	..	469	522	474	600	614	512	316	475
Private nonguaranteed	0	0	0	0	0	0	0	7	24	247
Bonds	..	..	0	0	0	0	0	0	0	0
Commercial banks	..	..	0	0	0	0	0	7	24	247
Memo:										
IBRD	0	0	0	0	0	0	0	0	0	0
IDA	0	0	0	0	0	0	0	0	0	0
NET FLOWS ON DEBT	..	..	242	201	612	980	-89	1,463	674	2,980
Public and publicly guaranteed	..	..	242	201	612	980	-97	1,326	509	1,853
Official creditors	..	..	-10	-27	-24	380	448	173	43	34
Multilateral	..	..	3	-8	0	346	238	97	47	43
Concessional	..	..	0	0	0	0	0	24	30	38
Bilateral	..	..	-13	-19	-24	34	210	76	-5	-9
Concessional	..	..	0	0	0	0	30	0	0	0
Private creditors	..	..	252	228	636	600	-545	1,153	466	1,819
Bonds	..	..	0	48	0	183	5	633	-126	3
Commercial banks	..	..	136	322	414	686	-174	441	552	2,105
Other private	..	..	116	-143	222	-269	-375	80	40	-288
Private nonguaranteed	0	0	0	0	0	0	8	138	165	1,127
Bonds	..	..	0	0	0	0	0	0	0	36
Commercial banks	..	..	0	0	0	0	8	138	165	1,091
Memo:										
IBRD	0	0	0	0	0	133	87	93	30	57
IDA	0	0	0	0	0	0	0	0	0	0

CZECH REPUBLIC

(US$ million, unless otherwise indicated)

	1970	1980	1988	1989	1990	1991	1992	1993	1994	1995
INTEREST PAYMENTS (LINT)	..	..	**190**	**213**	**196**	**223**	**312**	**288**	**321**	**677**
Public and publicly guaranteed	..	..	**190**	**213**	**196**	**223**	**312**	**287**	**307**	**456**
Official creditors	..	..	22	25	24	18	58	74	82	97
Multilateral	..	..	14	18	18	14	48	59	55	68
Concessional	..	..	0	0	0	0	0	0	2	7
Bilateral	..	..	9	7	7	5	10	15	26	28
Concessional	..	..	0	0	0	0	2	0	2	1
Private creditors	..	..	167	188	172	205	254	213	225	359
Bonds	..	..	0	1	2	3	18	20	69	117
Commercial banks	..	..	75	90	91	125	160	140	120	141
Other private	..	..	92	97	79	77	76	53	36	101
Private nonguaranteed	**0**	**0**	**0**	**0**	**0**	**0**	**0**	**2**	**14**	**222**
Bonds	..	..	0	0	0	0	0	0	0	0
Commercial banks	..	..	0	0	0	0	0	2	14	222
Memo:										
IBRD	0	0	0	0	0	0	10	19	25	28
IDA	0	0	0	0	0	0	0	0	0	0
NET TRANSFERS ON DEBT	..	..	**53**	**-12**	**416**	**757**	**-401**	**1,175**	**353**	**2,303**
Public and publicly guaranteed	..	..	**53**	**-12**	**416**	**757**	**-409**	**1,039**	**202**	**1,398**
Official creditors	..	..	-32	-51	-48	362	390	99	-39	-63
Multilateral	..	..	-10	-25	-18	333	190	38	-8	-26
Concessional	..	..	0	0	0	0	0	24	28	31
Bilateral	..	..	-22	-26	-31	30	200	62	-31	-37
Concessional	..	..	0	0	0	0	29	0	-2	-1
Private creditors	..	..	85	40	464	395	-799	940	241	1,460
Bonds	..	..	0	47	-2	180	-14	613	-195	-114
Commercial banks	..	..	61	232	323	561	-334	300	432	1,964
Other private	..	..	24	-239	143	-346	-451	27	5	-389
Private nonguaranteed	**0**	**0**	**0**	**0**	**0**	**0**	**8**	**136**	**151**	**905**
Bonds	..	..	0	0	0	0	0	0	0	36
Commercial banks	..	..	0	0	0	0	8	136	151	869
Memo:										
IBRD	0	0	0	0	0	133	77	74	5	29
IDA	0	0	0	0	0	0	0	0	0	0
DEBT SERVICE (LTDS)	..	..	**980**	**1,032**	**734**	**891**	**1,375**	**1,207**	**1,204**	**2,331**
Public and publicly guaranteed	..	..	**980**	**1,032**	**734**	**891**	**1,375**	**1,199**	**1,166**	**1,863**
Official creditors	..	..	48	59	67	46	135	133	144	202
Multilateral	..	..	14	25	23	16	91	94	87	139
Concessional	..	..	0	0	0	0	0	0	2	7
Bilateral	..	..	35	34	45	30	44	39	57	62
Concessional	..	..	0	0	0	0	2	0	2	1
Private creditors	..	..	932	973	666	845	1,240	1,066	1,022	1,661
Bonds	..	..	0	1	2	3	56	134	195	134
Commercial banks	..	..	371	353	111	166	493	367	475	951
Other private	..	..	561	619	553	677	690	565	351	576
Private nonguaranteed	**0**	**0**	**0**	**0**	**0**	**0**	**0**	**9**	**38**	**468**
Bonds	..	..	0	0	0	0	0	0	0	0
Commercial banks	..	..	0	0	0	0	0	9	38	468
Memo:										
IBRD	0	0	0	0	0	0	10	19	25	28
IDA	0	0	0	0	0	0	0	0	0	0
UNDISBURSED DEBT	..	..	**1,433**	**1,510**	**447**	**757**	**702**	**808**	**650**	**534**
Official creditors	..	..	41	40	14	381	519	544	425	335
Private creditors	..	..	1,391	1,470	433	376	183	264	225	199
Memorandum items										
Concessional LDOD	..	..	0	0	0	0	29	51	87	133
Variable rate LDOD	..	..	908	1,144	1,192	2,049	2,394	3,275	3,992	5,480
Public sector LDOD	..	..	2,806	3,088	3,725	4,716	4,457	5,625	6,746	9,210
Private sector LDOD	..	..	0	137	258	259	244	475	1,061	2,293

6. CURRENCY COMPOSITION OF LONG-TERM DEBT (PERCENT)

	1970	1980	1988	1989	1990	1991	1992	1993	1994	1995
Deutsche mark	..	..	17.2	18.2	33.5	28.3	25.3	16.6	14.6	5.4
French franc	..	..	1.2	1.5	1.4	1.1	1.5	0.8	0.5	0.2
Japanese yen	..	..	6.6	7.2	9.0	10.4	10.7	14.1	12.1	8.2
Pound sterling	..	..	0.3	0.5	0.6	0.4	0.3	0.2	0.1	0.0
Swiss franc	..	..	6.6	10.0	13.8	9.8	7.4	4.8	3.9	3.1
U.S.dollars	..	..	24.9	30.5	26.6	32.3	33.5	32.8	24.3	19.7
Multiple currency	..	..	31.4	17.1	0.0	2.8	4.7	20.0	36.6	57.4
Special drawing rights	..	..	0.0	0.0	0.0	0.0	0.0	0.0	0.0	0.0
All other currencies	..	..	11.8	15.0	15.2	14.8	16.6	10.6	7.9	5.9

CZECH REPUBLIC

(US$ million, unless otherwise indicated)

	1970	1980	1988	1989	1990	1991	1992	1993	1994	1995
7. DEBT RESTRUCTURINGS										
Total amount rescheduled	0	0	0	0	0	0	0	0	0	0
Debt stock rescheduled	0	0	0	0	0	0	0	0	0	0
Principal rescheduled	0	0	0	0	0	0	0	0	0	0
Official	0	0	0	0	0	0	0	0	0	0
Private	0	0	0	0	0	0	0	0	0	0
Interest rescheduled	0	0	0	0	0	0	0	0	0	0
Official	0	0	0	0	0	0	0	0	0	0
Private	0	0	0	0	0	0	0	0	0	0
Debt forgiven	..	..	0	0	0	0	0	2	1	3
Memo: interest forgiven	..	..	0	0	0	0	0	0	0	0
Debt stock reduction	0	0	0	0	0	0	0	0	0	0
of which debt buyback	0	0	0	0	0	0	0	0	0	0
8. DEBT STOCK-FLOW RECONCILIATION										
Total change in debt stocks	..	..	..	575	166	1,649	-460	1,602	1,521	5,881
Net flows on debt	..	..	..	359	19	1,598	-235	1,668	442	5,136
Net change in interest arrears	..	..	..	0	0	0	0	0	1	27
Interest capitalized	..	..	..	0	0	0	0	0	0	0
Debt forgiveness or reduction	..	..	..	0	0	0	0	-2	-1	-3
Cross-currency valuation	..	..	..	20	390	-3	-167	-18	389	167
Residual	..	..	..	197	-243	54	-59	-46	690	553
9. AVERAGE TERMS OF NEW COMMITMENTS										
ALL CREDITORS										
Interest (%)	..	..	4.0	6.8	8.2	7.8	6.9	7.0	7.6	7.7
Maturity (years)	..	..	7.8	6.7	5.1	8.7	10.0	9.3	12.1	12.3
Grace period (years)	..	..	3.4	3.7	3.1	4.9	4.7	3.5	2.4	2.7
Grant element (%)	..	..	23.7	10.1	4.3	10.0	14.4	11.3	6.9	5.9
Official creditors										
Interest (%)	..	..	5.8	6.6	9.6	7.2	6.8	6.1	0.0	5.8
Maturity (years)	..	..	6.6	5.2	10.8	12.0	10.9	13.5	0.0	13.7
Grace period (years)	..	..	1.9	0.7	5.2	5.6	5.1	4.5	0.0	4.3
Grant element (%)	..	..	13.4	7.7	0.6	14.5	15.3	20.8	0.0	22.5
Private creditors										
Interest (%)	..	..	4.0	6.8	8.1	8.1	7.2	7.1	7.6	7.8
Maturity (years)	..	..	7.8	6.7	5.0	6.7	7.5	8.8	12.1	12.2
Grace period (years)	..	..	3.4	3.7	3.1	4.4	3.8	3.3	2.4	2.7
Grant element (%)	..	..	23.9	10.1	4.4	7.2	12.1	10.1	6.9	5.6
Memorandum items										
Commitments	..	..	1,383	953	785	2,003	935	2,367	1,212	2,861
Official creditors	..	..	20	5	18	761	672	265	0	40
Private creditors	..	..	1,363	947	767	1,242	263	2,102	1,212	2,820

10. CONTRACTUAL OBLIGATIONS ON OUTSTANDING LONG-TERM DEBT

	1996	1997	1998	1999	2000	2001	2002	2003	2004	2005
TOTAL										
Disbursements	240	145	63	41	25	12	4	1	0	0
Principal	1,691	1,927	1,452	1,087	1,830	646	585	515	543	488
Interest	788	685	558	466	393	289	245	204	169	121
Official creditors										
Disbursements	105	88	61	40	25	12	4	1	0	0
Principal	86	293	336	161	128	122	117	113	110	108
Interest	94	94	75	61	53	46	39	32	24	18
Bilateral creditors										
Disbursements	3	1	0	0	0	0	0	0	0	0
Principal	35	51	100	75	38	33	26	21	19	17
Interest	22	19	16	9	6	4	3	2	1	1
Multilateral creditors										
Disbursements	102	87	61	40	25	12	4	1	0	0
Principal	51	242	237	87	90	89	92	92	92	92
Interest	73	75	59	52	47	42	36	30	23	17
Private creditors										
Disbursements	135	58	3	1	0	0	0	0	0	0
Principal	1,605	1,634	1,116	926	1,702	524	467	402	433	379
Interest	693	591	483	406	339	242	206	173	144	103
Commercial banks										
Disbursements	127	53	1	0	0	0	0	0	0	0
Principal	564	1,122	890	565	608	400	387	379	379	378
Interest	464	439	361	308	271	228	196	164	133	102
Other private										
Disbursements	8	5	2	1	0	0	0	0	0	0
Principal	1,042	512	226	361	1,094	124	81	23	55	1
Interest	230	152	121	98	68	14	11	9	12	2

DJIBOUTI

(US$ million, unless otherwise indicated)

	1970	1980	1988	1989	1990	1991	1992	1993	1994	1995
1. SUMMARY DEBT DATA										
TOTAL DEBT STOCKS (EDT)	..	**31.8**	**184.5**	**178.6**	**206.3**	**192.2**	**192.4**	**225.3**	**246.9**	**260.2**
Long-term debt (LDOD)	**2.6**	**25.8**	**158.3**	**131.4**	**156.2**	**171.0**	**176.8**	**192.7**	**206.9**	**218.0**
Public and publicly guaranteed	2.6	25.8	158.3	131.4	156.2	171.0	176.8	192.7	206.9	218.0
Private nonguaranteed	0.0	0.0	0.0	0.0	0.0	0.0	0.0	0.0	0.0	0.0
Use of IMF credit	**0.0**	**0.0**	**0.0**	**0.0**	**0.0**	**0.0**	**0.0**	**0.0**	**0.0**	**0.0**
Short-term debt	..	**6.0**	**26.3**	**47.2**	**50.1**	**21.2**	**15.6**	**32.7**	**40.0**	**42.3**
of which interest arrears on LDOD	..	0.0	0.0	0.0	0.1	0.2	0.2	0.8	2.0	3.3
Official creditors	..	0.0	0.0	0.0	0.1	0.2	0.2	0.8	2.0	3.2
Private creditors	..	0.0	0.0	0.0	0.0	0.0	0.0	0.0	0.0	0.0
Memo: principal arrears on LDOD	..	0.0	0.0	0.3	1.5	3.1	6.4	11.9	17.8	23.9
Official creditors	..	0.0	0.0	0.3	1.5	3.0	6.2	11.7	17.6	23.7
Private creditors	..	0.0	0.0	0.0	0.1	0.1	0.2	0.2	0.2	0.2
Memo: export credits	..	..	31.0	28.0	27.0	25.0	21.0	16.0	10.0	8.0
TOTAL DEBT FLOWS										
Disbursements	**1.4**	**10.2**	**21.7**	**11.8**	**27.4**	**20.9**	**24.1**	**23.4**	**13.3**	**12.5**
Long-term debt	1.4	10.2	21.7	11.8	27.4	20.9	24.1	23.4	13.3	12.5
IMF purchases	0.0	0.0	0.0	0.0	0.0	0.0	0.0	0.0	0.0	0.0
Principal repayments	**0.1**	**2.2**	**9.5**	**9.1**	**8.4**	**7.9**	**7.0**	**5.3**	**4.6**	**4.8**
Long-term debt	0.1	2.2	9.5	9.1	8.4	7.9	7.0	5.3	4.6	4.8
IMF repurchases	0.0	0.0	0.0	0.0	0.0	0.0	0.0	0.0	0.0	0.0
Net flows on debt	**1.3**	**8.0**	**9.5**	**23.6**	**21.8**	**-15.9**	**11.4**	**34.6**	**14.8**	**8.7**
of which short-term debt	..	..	-2.7	20.9	2.8	-29.0	-5.6	16.5	6.1	1.0
Interest payments (INT)	..	**1.7**	**6.1**	**5.8**	**6.0**	**5.7**	**4.2**	**4.4**	**4.9**	**5.4**
Long-term debt	0.0	0.9	3.9	2.4	2.1	2.2	2.4	2.0	1.4	1.4
IMF charges	0.0	0.0	0.0	0.0	0.0	0.0	0.0	0.0	0.0	0.0
Short-term debt	..	0.8	2.2	3.4	3.9	3.5	1.8	2.4	3.5	4.0
Net transfers on debt	..	**6.3**	**3.3**	**17.8**	**15.8**	**-21.6**	**7.2**	**30.2**	**9.9**	**3.3**
Total debt service paid (TDS)	..	**3.9**	**15.7**	**14.9**	**14.5**	**13.6**	**11.2**	**9.7**	**9.5**	**10.3**
Long-term debt	0.1	3.1	13.5	11.5	10.6	10.1	9.4	7.3	5.9	6.3
IMF repurchases and charges	0.0	0.0	0.0	0.0	0.0	0.0	0.0	0.0	0.0	0.0
Short-term debt (interest only)	..	0.8	2.2	3.4	3.9	3.5	1.8	2.4	3.5	4.0

	1970	1980	1988	1989	1990	1991	1992	1993	1994	1995
2. AGGREGATE NET RESOURCE FLOWS AND NET TRANSFERS (LONG-TERM)										
NET RESOURCE FLOWS	**5.6**	**37.6**	**51.7**	**34.6**	**149.7**	**64.7**	**75.6**	**73.7**	**66.0**	**60.5**
Net flow of long-term debt (ex. IMF)	1.3	8.0	12.2	2.7	19.0	13.1	17.0	18.1	8.7	7.7
Foreign direct investment (net)	0.0	0.0	0.0	0.0	0.0	0.0	2.0	3.0	3.0	4.0
Portfolio equity flows	0.0	0.0	0.0	0.0	0.0	0.0	0.0	0.0	0.0	0.0
Grants (excluding technical coop.)	4.3	29.6	39.5	31.9	130.7	51.6	56.6	52.6	54.3	48.8
Memo: technical coop. grants	6.2	27.6	39.3	34.0	44.6	43.4	44.2	44.5	51.1	46.7
NET TRANSFERS	**5.6**	**36.7**	**47.7**	**32.2**	**147.6**	**62.5**	**69.9**	**69.2**	**61.7**	**56.1**
Interest on long-term debt	0.0	0.9	3.9	2.4	2.1	2.2	2.4	2.0	1.4	1.4
Profit remittances on FDI	0.0	0.0	0.0	0.0	0.0	0.0	3.3	2.5	3.0	3.0

	1970	1980	1988	1989	1990	1991	1992	1993	1994	1995
3. MAJOR ECONOMIC AGGREGATES										
Gross national product (GNP)	..	..	..	..	..	..	484.0	481.0	..	..
Exports of goods & services (XGS)	..	..	..	..	..	..	229.1	259.8	233.9	211.8
of which workers remittances	..	..	..	..	..	..	1.5	1.5	1.5	1.0
Imports of goods & services (MGS)	..	..	..	..	..	..	389.6	373.1	333.8	300.8
International reserves (RES)	..	..	64.4	59.2	93.6	100.0	83.4	75.1	73.8	72.2
Current account balance	..	..	..	..	..	..	-87.5	-34.3	-46.1	-23.0

	1970	1980	1988	1989	1990	1991	1992	1993	1994	1995
4. DEBT INDICATORS										
EDT / XGS (%)	..	..	..	..	..	..	84.0	86.7	105.6	122.9
EDT / GNP (%)	..	..	..	..	..	..	39.8	46.8	..	..
TDS / XGS (%)	..	..	..	..	..	..	4.9	3.7	4.0	4.8
INT / XGS (%)	..	..	..	..	..	..	1.8	1.7	2.1	2.6
INT / GNP (%)	..	..	..	..	..	..	0.9	0.9	..	..
RES / EDT (%)	..	..	34.9	33.1	45.4	52.0	43.3	33.3	29.9	27.7
RES / MGS (months)	..	..	..	..	..	..	2.6	2.4	2.7	2.9
Short-term / EDT (%)	..	18.9	14.2	26.4	24.3	11.0	8.1	14.5	16.2	16.2
Concessional / EDT (%)	..	49.8	83.5	73.1	75.5	88.7	91.7	85.3	83.7	83.6
Multilateral / EDT (%)	..	7.3	43.2	44.4	43.4	51.3	53.1	50.2	51.8	53.0

DJIBOUTI

(US$ million, unless otherwise indicated)

	1970	1980	1988	1989	1990	1991	1992	1993	1994	1995
5. LONG-TERM DEBT										
DEBT OUTSTANDING (LDOD)	**2.6**	**25.8**	**158.3**	**131.4**	**156.2**	**171.0**	**176.8**	**192.7**	**206.9**	**218.0**
Public and publicly guaranteed	**2.6**	**25.8**	**158.3**	**131.4**	**156.2**	**171.0**	**176.8**	**192.7**	**206.9**	**218.0**
Official creditors	2.6	21.2	157.0	130.8	156.0	170.8	176.6	192.5	206.7	217.7
Multilateral	0.0	2.3	79.7	79.4	89.6	98.6	102.3	113.2	128.0	138.0
Concessional	0.0	2.3	79.7	79.4	89.6	98.6	102.3	113.2	128.0	138.0
Bilateral	2.6	18.9	77.3	51.4	66.4	72.1	74.4	79.3	78.7	79.7
Concessional	2.6	13.5	74.5	51.1	66.1	71.9	74.2	79.1	78.6	79.6
Private creditors	0.0	4.7	1.3	0.6	0.2	0.2	0.2	0.2	0.2	0.2
Bonds	0.0	0.0	0.0	0.0	0.0	0.0	0.0	0.0	0.0	0.0
Commercial banks	0.0	4.7	1.3	0.6	0.2	0.2	0.2	0.2	0.2	0.2
Other private	0.0	0.0	0.0	0.0	0.0	0.0	0.0	0.0	0.0	0.0
Private nonguaranteed	**0.0**	**0.0**	**0.0**	**0.0**	**0.0**	**0.0**	**0.0**	**0.0**	**0.0**	**0.0**
Bonds	0.0	0.0	0.0	0.0	0.0	0.0	0.0	0.0	0.0	0.0
Commercial banks	0.0	0.0	0.0	0.0	0.0	0.0	0.0	0.0	0.0	0.0
Memo:										
IBRD	0.0	0.0	0.0	0.0	0.0	0.0	0.0	0.0	0.0	0.0
IDA	0.0	0.0	25.0	26.3	31.1	34.3	36.0	39.6	42.8	46.2
DISBURSEMENTS	**1.4**	**10.2**	**21.7**	**11.8**	**27.4**	**20.9**	**24.1**	**23.4**	**13.3**	**12.5**
Public and publicly guaranteed	**1.4**	**10.2**	**21.7**	**11.8**	**27.4**	**20.9**	**24.1**	**23.4**	**13.3**	**12.5**
Official creditors	1.4	5.3	21.7	11.8	27.4	20.9	24.1	23.4	13.3	12.5
Multilateral	0.0	2.4	12.1	5.5	8.9	11.3	11.9	13.7	11.6	10.4
Concessional	0.0	2.4	12.1	5.5	8.9	11.3	11.9	13.7	11.6	10.4
Bilateral	1.4	2.9	9.6	6.4	18.5	9.6	12.1	9.7	1.7	2.1
Concessional	1.4	0.0	9.6	6.4	18.5	9.6	12.1	9.7	1.7	2.1
Private creditors	0.0	5.0	0.0	0.0	0.0	0.0	0.0	0.0	0.0	0.0
Bonds	0.0	0.0	0.0	0.0	0.0	0.0	0.0	0.0	0.0	0.0
Commercial banks	0.0	5.0	0.0	0.0	0.0	0.0	0.0	0.0	0.0	0.0
Other private	0.0	0.0	0.0	0.0	0.0	0.0	0.0	0.0	0.0	0.0
Private nonguaranteed	**0.0**	**0.0**	**0.0**	**0.0**	**0.0**	**0.0**	**0.0**	**0.0**	**0.0**	**0.0**
Bonds	0.0	0.0	0.0	0.0	0.0	0.0	0.0	0.0	0.0	0.0
Commercial banks	0.0	0.0	0.0	0.0	0.0	0.0	0.0	0.0	0.0	0.0
Memo:										
IBRD	0.0	0.0	0.0	0.0	0.0	0.0	0.0	0.0	0.0	0.0
IDA	0.0	0.0	5.3	1.9	2.5	2.9	3.2	3.5	1.3	2.8
PRINCIPAL REPAYMENTS	**0.1**	**2.2**	**9.5**	**9.1**	**8.4**	**7.9**	**7.0**	**5.3**	**4.6**	**4.8**
Public and publicly guaranteed	**0.1**	**2.2**	**9.5**	**9.1**	**8.4**	**7.9**	**7.0**	**5.3**	**4.6**	**4.8**
Official creditors	0.1	2.2	7.8	8.4	8.1	7.9	7.0	5.3	4.6	4.8
Multilateral	0.0	0.0	4.0	4.0	3.6	3.5	3.7	2.9	2.5	2.7
Concessional	0.0	0.0	4.0	4.0	3.6	3.5	3.7	2.9	2.5	2.7
Bilateral	0.1	2.2	3.8	4.4	4.4	4.4	3.3	2.5	2.1	2.1
Concessional	0.1	1.7	3.5	4.4	4.4	4.3	3.2	2.4	2.0	2.1
Private creditors	0.0	0.0	1.7	0.7	0.4	0.0	0.0	0.0	0.0	0.0
Bonds	0.0	0.0	0.0	0.0	0.0	0.0	0.0	0.0	0.0	0.0
Commercial banks	0.0	0.0	1.4	0.7	0.4	0.0	0.0	0.0	0.0	0.0
Other private	0.0	0.0	0.2	0.0	0.0	0.0	0.0	0.0	0.0	0.0
Private nonguaranteed	**0.0**	**0.0**	**0.0**	**0.0**	**0.0**	**0.0**	**0.0**	**0.0**	**0.0**	**0.0**
Bonds	0.0	0.0	0.0	0.0	0.0	0.0	0.0	0.0	0.0	0.0
Commercial banks	0.0	0.0	0.0	0.0	0.0	0.0	0.0	0.0	0.0	0.0
Memo:										
IBRD	0.0	0.0	0.0	0.0	0.0	0.0	0.0	0.0	0.0	0.0
IDA	0.0	0.0	0.0	0.0	0.0	0.0	0.0	0.1	0.1	0.3
NET FLOWS ON DEBT	**1.3**	**8.0**	**12.2**	**2.7**	**19.0**	**13.1**	**17.0**	**18.1**	**8.7**	**7.7**
Public and publicly guaranteed	**1.3**	**8.0**	**12.2**	**2.7**	**19.0**	**13.1**	**17.0**	**18.1**	**8.7**	**7.7**
Official creditors	1.3	3.0	13.9	3.4	19.4	13.1	17.0	18.1	8.7	7.7
Multilateral	0.0	2.4	8.1	1.5	5.3	7.8	8.2	10.8	9.2	7.7
Concessional	0.0	2.4	8.1	1.5	5.3	7.8	8.2	10.8	9.2	7.7
Bilateral	1.3	0.6	5.8	2.0	14.1	5.3	8.8	7.3	-0.4	0.0
Concessional	1.3	-1.7	6.0	2.0	14.1	5.3	8.9	7.3	-0.4	0.1
Private creditors	0.0	5.0	-1.7	-0.7	-0.4	0.0	0.0	0.0	0.0	0.0
Bonds	0.0	0.0	0.0	0.0	0.0	0.0	0.0	0.0	0.0	0.0
Commercial banks	0.0	5.0	-1.4	-0.7	-0.4	0.0	0.0	0.0	0.0	0.0
Other private	0.0	0.0	-0.2	0.0	0.0	0.0	0.0	0.0	0.0	0.0
Private nonguaranteed	**0.0**	**0.0**	**0.0**	**0.0**	**0.0**	**0.0**	**0.0**	**0.0**	**0.0**	**0.0**
Bonds	0.0	0.0	0.0	0.0	0.0	0.0	0.0	0.0	0.0	0.0
Commercial banks	0.0	0.0	0.0	0.0	0.0	0.0	0.0	0.0	0.0	0.0
Memo:										
IBRD	0.0	0.0	0.0	0.0	0.0	0.0	0.0	0.0	0.0	0.0
IDA	0.0	0.0	5.3	1.9	2.5	2.9	3.2	3.4	1.2	2.4

DJIBOUTI

(US$ million, unless otherwise indicated)

	1970	1980	1988	1989	1990	1991	1992	1993	1994	1995
INTEREST PAYMENTS (LINT)	**0.0**	**0.9**	**3.9**	**2.4**	**2.1**	**2.2**	**2.4**	**2.0**	**1.4**	**1.4**
Public and publicly guaranteed	**0.0**	**0.9**	**3.9**	**2.4**	**2.1**	**2.2**	**2.4**	**2.0**	**1.4**	**1.4**
Official creditors	0.0	0.9	3.7	2.3	2.1	2.2	2.4	2.0	1.4	1.4
Multilateral	0.0	0.0	1.6	1.5	1.4	1.2	1.4	1.2	0.7	0.8
Concessional	0.0	0.0	1.6	1.5	1.4	1.2	1.4	1.2	0.7	0.8
Bilateral	0.0	0.9	2.1	0.8	0.7	1.0	1.0	0.7	0.7	0.6
Concessional	0.0	0.7	1.9	0.8	0.7	1.0	1.0	0.7	0.6	0.6
Private creditors	0.0	0.0	0.3	0.1	0.0	0.0	0.0	0.0	0.0	0.0
Bonds	0.0	0.0	0.0	0.0	0.0	0.0	0.0	0.0	0.0	0.0
Commercial banks	0.0	0.0	0.3	0.1	0.0	0.0	0.0	0.0	0.0	0.0
Other private	0.0	0.0	0.0	0.0	0.0	0.0	0.0	0.0	0.0	0.0
Private nonguaranteed	**0.0**	**0.0**	**0.0**	**0.0**	**0.0**	**0.0**	**0.0**	**0.0**	**0.0**	**0.0**
Bonds	0.0	0.0	0.0	0.0	0.0	0.0	0.0	0.0	0.0	0.0
Commercial banks	0.0	0.0	0.0	0.0	0.0	0.0	0.0	0.0	0.0	0.0
Memo:										
IBRD	0.0	0.0	0.0	0.0	0.0	0.0	0.0	0.0	0.0	0.0
IDA	0.0	0.0	0.2	0.2	0.2	0.2	0.3	0.3	0.2	0.3
NET TRANSFERS ON DEBT	**1.3**	**7.1**	**8.2**	**0.3**	**16.9**	**10.9**	**14.6**	**16.1**	**7.4**	**6.3**
Public and publicly guaranteed	**1.3**	**7.1**	**8.2**	**0.3**	**16.9**	**10.9**	**14.6**	**16.1**	**7.4**	**6.3**
Official creditors	1.3	2.1	10.2	1.2	17.3	10.9	14.6	16.1	7.4	6.3
Multilateral	0.0	2.4	6.5	0.0	3.9	6.6	6.8	9.5	8.5	6.9
Concessional	0.0	2.4	6.5	0.0	3.9	6.6	6.8	9.5	8.5	6.9
Bilateral	1.3	-0.3	3.7	1.2	13.4	4.3	7.8	6.5	-1.1	-0.6
Concessional	1.3	-2.4	4.1	1.2	13.4	4.3	7.9	6.6	-1.0	-0.6
Private creditors	0.0	5.0	-1.9	-0.9	-0.4	0.0	0.0	0.0	0.0	0.0
Bonds	0.0	0.0	0.0	0.0	0.0	0.0	0.0	0.0	0.0	0.0
Commercial banks	0.0	5.0	-1.7	-0.9	-0.4	0.0	0.0	0.0	0.0	0.0
Other private	0.0	0.0	-0.2	0.0	0.0	0.0	0.0	0.0	0.0	0.0
Private nonguaranteed	**0.0**	**0.0**	**0.0**	**0.0**	**0.0**	**0.0**	**0.0**	**0.0**	**0.0**	**0.0**
Bonds	0.0	0.0	0.0	0.0	0.0	0.0	0.0	0.0	0.0	0.0
Commercial banks	0.0	0.0	0.0	0.0	0.0	0.0	0.0	0.0	0.0	0.0
Memo:										
IBRD	0.0	0.0	0.0	0.0	0.0	0.0	0.0	0.0	0.0	0.0
IDA	0.0	0.0	5.1	1.7	2.3	2.7	2.9	3.1	0.9	2.1
DEBT SERVICE (LTDS)	**0.1**	**3.1**	**13.5**	**11.5**	**10.6**	**10.1**	**9.4**	**7.3**	**5.9**	**6.3**
Public and publicly guaranteed	**0.1**	**3.1**	**13.5**	**11.5**	**10.6**	**10.1**	**9.4**	**7.3**	**5.9**	**6.3**
Official creditors	0.1	3.1	11.5	10.7	10.1	10.1	9.4	7.3	5.9	6.3
Multilateral	0.0	0.0	5.6	5.5	5.0	4.7	5.1	4.1	3.2	3.5
Concessional	0.0	0.0	5.6	5.5	5.0	4.7	5.1	4.1	3.2	3.5
Bilateral	0.1	3.1	5.9	5.2	5.1	5.4	4.3	3.2	2.8	2.8
Concessional	0.1	2.4	5.4	5.1	5.1	5.3	4.3	3.1	2.7	2.7
Private creditors	0.0	0.0	1.9	0.9	0.4	0.0	0.0	0.0	0.0	0.0
Bonds	0.0	0.0	0.0	0.0	0.0	0.0	0.0	0.0	0.0	0.0
Commercial banks	0.0	0.0	1.7	0.9	0.4	0.0	0.0	0.0	0.0	0.0
Other private	0.0	0.0	0.2	0.0	0.0	0.0	0.0	0.0	0.0	0.0
Private nonguaranteed	**0.0**	**0.0**	**0.0**	**0.0**	**0.0**	**0.0**	**0.0**	**0.0**	**0.0**	**0.0**
Bonds	0.0	0.0	0.0	0.0	0.0	0.0	0.0	0.0	0.0	0.0
Commercial banks	0.0	0.0	0.0	0.0	0.0	0.0	0.0	0.0	0.0	0.0
Memo:										
IBRD	0.0	0.0	0.0	0.0	0.0	0.0	0.0	0.0	0.0	0.0
IDA	0.0	0.0	0.2	0.2	0.2	0.2	0.3	0.4	0.4	0.7
UNDISBURSED DEBT	**0.0**	**23.4**	**119.4**	**173.6**	**158.8**	**149.0**	**131.6**	**117.4**	**99.2**	**85.4**
Official creditors	0.0	23.4	119.4	173.6	158.8	149.0	131.6	117.4	99.2	85.4
Private creditors	0.0	0.0	0.0	0.0	0.0	0.0	0.0	0.0	0.0	0.0
Memorandum items										
Concessional LDOD	2.6	15.9	154.2	130.5	155.7	170.5	176.4	192.3	206.6	217.7
Variable rate LDOD	0.0	0.0	0.0	0.0	0.0	0.0	0.0	0.0	0.0	0.0
Public sector LDOD	2.6	25.8	158.3	131.4	156.2	171.0	176.8	192.7	206.9	218.0
Private sector LDOD	0.0	0.0	0.0	0.0	0.0	0.0	0.0	0.0	0.0	0.0

6. CURRENCY COMPOSITION OF LONG-TERM DEBT (PERCENT)

	1970	1980	1988	1989	1990	1991	1992	1993	1994	1995
Deutsche mark	0.0	0.0	0.0	0.0	0.0	0.0	0.0	0.0	0.0	0.0
French franc	100.0	91.0	17.1	2.8	2.7	2.4	2.4	2.1	2.1	2.3
Japanese yen	0.0	0.0	0.0	0.0	0.0	0.0	0.0	0.0	0.0	0.0
Pound sterling	0.0	0.0	0.0	0.0	0.0	0.0	0.0	0.0	0.0	0.0
Swiss franc	0.0	0.0	0.0	0.0	0.0	0.0	0.0	0.0	0.0	0.0
U.S.dollars	0.0	3.1	13.8	15.8	13.8	13.2	13.9	14.5	14.6	15.2
Multiple currency	0.0	0.8	11.1	14.2	16.7	19.4	22.1	25.0	29.1	28.9
Special drawing rights	0.0	0.4	5.5	8.1	8.8	9.1	8.5	7.8	7.9	7.7
All other currencies	0.0	5.0	52.4	59.2	58.0	56.0	53.1	50.6	46.3	45.8

DJIBOUTI

(US$ million, unless otherwise indicated)

	1970	1980	1988	1989	1990	1991	1992	1993	1994	1995
7. DEBT RESTRUCTURINGS										
Total amount rescheduled	0.0	0.0	0.0	0.0	0.0	0.0	0.0	0.0	0.0	0.0
Debt stock rescheduled	0.0	0.0	0.0	0.0	0.0	0.0	0.0	0.0	0.0	0.0
Principal rescheduled	0.0	0.0	0.0	0.0	0.0	0.0	0.0	0.0	0.0	0.0
Official	0.0	0.0	0.0	0.0	0.0	0.0	0.0	0.0	0.0	0.0
Private	0.0	0.0	0.0	0.0	0.0	0.0	0.0	0.0	0.0	0.0
Interest rescheduled	0.0	0.0	0.0	0.0	0.0	0.0	0.0	0.0	0.0	0.0
Official	0.0	0.0	0.0	0.0	0.0	0.0	0.0	0.0	0.0	0.0
Private	0.0	0.0	0.0	0.0	0.0	0.0	0.0	0.0	0.0	0.0
Debt forgiven	..	..	0.0	24.9	0.0	0.0	0.0	0.0	0.0	0.0
Memo: interest forgiven	..	..	0.0	0.6	0.0	0.0	0.0	0.0	0.0	0.0
Debt stock reduction	0.0	0.0	0.0	0.0	0.0	0.0	0.0	0.0	0.0	0.0
of which debt buyback	0.0	0.0	0.0	0.0	0.0	0.0	0.0	0.0	0.0	0.0
8. DEBT STOCK-FLOW RECONCILIATION										
Total change in debt stocks	..	..	..	-5.9	27.7	-14.1	0.2	32.9	21.6	13.3
Net flows on debt	..	..	..	23.6	21.8	-15.9	11.4	34.6	14.8	8.7
Net change in interest arrears	..	..	..	0.0	0.1	0.1	0.1	0.6	1.2	1.2
Interest capitalized	..	..	..	0.0	0.0	0.0	0.0	0.0	0.0	0.0
Debt forgiveness or reduction	..	..	..	-24.9	0.0	0.0	0.0	0.0	0.0	0.0
Cross-currency valuation	..	..	..	-2.4	4.2	-0.5	-7.5	-2.0	1.7	1.7
Residual	..	..	..	-2.2	1.6	2.2	-3.8	-0.2	3.9	1.6
9. AVERAGE TERMS OF NEW COMMITMENTS										
ALL CREDITORS										
Interest (%)	3.3	2.0	3.4	1.2	0.7	0.7	0.8	0.7	0.0	0.0
Maturity (years)	19.5	18.4	25.7	34.0	39.7	39.6	40.0	38.8	0.0	0.0
Grace period (years)	1.0	7.4	7.7	9.4	10.2	10.1	10.0	8.8	0.0	0.0
Grant element (%)	38.0	56.0	50.8	72.7	80.5	80.4	80.5	79.1	0.0	0.0
Official creditors										
Interest (%)	3.3	0.8	3.4	1.2	0.7	0.7	0.8	0.7	0.0	0.0
Maturity (years)	19.5	20.7	25.7	34.0	39.7	39.6	40.0	38.8	0.0	0.0
Grace period (years)	1.0	8.6	7.7	9.4	10.2	10.1	10.0	8.8	0.0	0.0
Grant element (%)	38.0	65.7	50.8	72.7	80.5	80.4	80.5	79.1	0.0	0.0
Private creditors										
Interest (%)	0.0	7.5	0.0	0.0	0.0	0.0	0.0	0.0	0.0	0.0
Maturity (years)	0.0	7.5	0.0	0.0	0.0	0.0	0.0	0.0	0.0	0.0
Grace period (years)	0.0	2.0	0.0	0.0	0.0	0.0	0.0	0.0	0.0	0.0
Grant element (%)	0.0	8.2	0.0	0.0	0.0	0.0	0.0	0.0	0.0	0.0
Memorandum items										
Commitments	0.2	29.5	19.1	67.9	6.2	10.7	33.6	10.5	0.0	0.0
Official creditors	0.2	24.6	19.1	67.9	6.2	10.7	33.6	10.5	0.0	0.0
Private creditors	0.0	5.0	0.0	0.0	0.0	0.0	0.0	0.0	0.0	0.0

10. CONTRACTUAL OBLIGATIONS ON OUTSTANDING LONG-TERM DEBT

	1996	1997	1998	1999	2000	2001	2002	2003	2004	2005
TOTAL										
Disbursements	19.6	20.3	15.0	10.5	7.6	5.1	2.9	0.6	0.0	0.0
Principal	12.3	12.4	12.2	12.7	12.8	12.1	11.3	8.9	8.2	8.4
Interest	2.6	2.6	2.5	2.5	2.3	2.2	2.1	1.9	1.7	1.6
Official creditors										
Disbursements	19.6	20.3	15.0	10.5	7.6	5.1	2.9	0.6	0.0	0.0
Principal	12.3	12.4	12.2	12.7	12.8	12.1	11.3	8.9	8.2	8.4
Interest	2.6	2.6	2.5	2.5	2.3	2.2	2.1	1.9	1.7	1.6
Bilateral creditors										
Disbursements	9.0	6.9	4.3	3.2	2.6	1.9	0.3	0.0	0.0	0.0
Principal	7.9	7.8	7.8	8.0	8.9	8.8	6.9	4.7	3.9	3.9
Interest	1.3	1.3	1.2	1.2	1.1	1.0	0.9	0.7	0.6	0.5
Multilateral creditors										
Disbursements	10.6	13.4	10.7	7.3	5.0	3.2	2.6	0.6	0.0	0.0
Principal	4.4	4.6	4.4	4.6	4.0	3.2	4.4	4.1	4.2	4.5
Interest	1.3	1.3	1.3	1.3	1.2	1.2	1.2	1.2	1.1	1.1
Private creditors										
Disbursements	0.0	0.0	0.0	0.0	0.0	0.0	0.0	0.0	0.0	0.0
Principal	0.0	0.0	0.0	0.0	0.0	0.0	0.0	0.0	0.0	0.0
Interest	0.0	0.0	0.0	0.0	0.0	0.0	0.0	0.0	0.0	0.0
Commercial banks										
Disbursements	0.0	0.0	0.0	0.0	0.0	0.0	0.0	0.0	0.0	0.0
Principal	0.0	0.0	0.0	0.0	0.0	0.0	0.0	0.0	0.0	0.0
Interest	0.0	0.0	0.0	0.0	0.0	0.0	0.0	0.0	0.0	0.0
Other private										
Disbursements	0.0	0.0	0.0	0.0	0.0	0.0	0.0	0.0	0.0	0.0
Principal	0.0	0.0	0.0	0.0	0.0	0.0	0.0	0.0	0.0	0.0
Interest	0.0	0.0	0.0	0.0	0.0	0.0	0.0	0.0	0.0	0.0

DOMINICA

(US$ million, unless otherwise indicated)

	1970	1980	1988	1989	1990	1991	1992	1993	1994	1995
1. SUMMARY DEBT DATA										
TOTAL DEBT STOCKS (EDT)	..	..	**70.4**	**74.4**	**81.9**	**84.2**	**81.6**	**80.0**	**90.4**	**93.0**
Long-term debt (LDOD)	..	..	**58.9**	**66.0**	**74.2**	**76.4**	**74.7**	**76.0**	**80.9**	**84.6**
Public and publicly guaranteed	..	..	58.9	66.0	74.2	76.4	74.7	76.0	80.9	84.6
Private nonguaranteed	0.0	0.0	0.0	0.0	0.0	0.0	0.0	0.0	0.0	0.0
Use of IMF credit	**0.0**	**0.0**	**8.8**	**6.6**	**5.7**	**4.8**	**3.8**	**3.1**	**2.5**	**1.7**
Short-term debt	..	..	**2.6**	**1.9**	**2.0**	**3.0**	**3.1**	**0.9**	**7.0**	**6.7**
of which interest arrears on LDOD	..	..	0.0	0.0	0.0	0.0	0.1	0.0	0.0	0.2
Official creditors	..	..	0.0	0.0	0.0	0.0	0.1	0.0	0.0	0.2
Private creditors	..	..	0.0	0.0	0.0	0.0	0.0	0.0	0.0	0.0
Memo: principal arrears on LDOD	..	..	0.0	0.0	0.2	0.1	0.8	0.1	0.0	1.5
Official creditors	..	..	0.0	0.0	0.2	0.1	0.8	0.1	0.0	1.5
Private creditors	..	..	0.0	0.0	0.1	0.0	0.0	0.0	0.0	0.0
Memo: export credits	..	..	7.0	8.0	8.0	8.0	6.0	6.0	6.0	5.0
TOTAL DEBT FLOWS										
Disbursements	..	..	**6.0**	**10.8**	**8.5**	**4.9**	**6.1**	**3.5**	**3.4**	**6.9**
Long-term debt	..	..	5.3	10.4	8.5	4.9	6.1	3.5	3.4	6.9
IMF purchases	0.0	0.0	0.7	0.3	0.0	0.0	0.0	0.0	0.0	0.0
Principal repayments	..	..	**4.6**	**4.8**	**3.6**	**3.4**	**3.3**	**4.6**	**4.8**	**4.7**
Long-term debt	..	..	1.7	2.4	2.3	2.4	2.5	3.9	4.0	3.8
IMF repurchases	0.0	0.0	2.9	2.4	1.4	0.9	0.8	0.8	0.8	0.8
Net flows on debt	..	..	**4.0**	**5.2**	**4.9**	**2.5**	**2.8**	**-3.2**	**4.7**	**1.7**
of which short-term debt	..	..	2.6	-0.8	0.1	1.0	0.0	-2.1	6.1	-0.5
Interest payments (INT)	..	..	**1.7**	**1.7**	**1.9**	**1.9**	**1.9**	**1.8**	**1.9**	**2.2**
Long-term debt	..	..	1.4	1.3	1.5	1.6	1.6	1.6	1.7	1.8
IMF charges	0.0	0.0	0.4	0.2	0.2	0.1	0.1	0.0	0.0	0.0
Short-term debt	..	..	0.0	0.2	0.1	0.2	0.2	0.1	0.2	0.4
Net transfers on debt	..	..	**2.2**	**3.5**	**3.1**	**0.6**	**0.9**	**-5.0**	**2.8**	**-0.5**
Total debt service paid (TDS)	..	..	**6.4**	**6.4**	**5.5**	**5.3**	**5.2**	**6.4**	**6.7**	**6.8**
Long-term debt	..	..	3.0	3.7	3.8	4.1	4.2	5.5	5.7	5.6
IMF repurchases and charges	0.0	0.0	3.3	2.5	1.6	1.1	0.8	0.8	0.8	0.9
Short-term debt (interest only)	..	..	0.0	0.2	0.1	0.2	0.2	0.1	0.2	0.4
2. AGGREGATE NET RESOURCE FLOWS AND NET TRANSFERS (LONG-TERM)										
NET RESOURCE FLOWS	..	..	**19.7**	**23.5**	**22.3**	**20.2**	**30.0**	**18.0**	**33.4**	**38.5**
Net flow of long-term debt (ex. IMF)	0.0	0.0	3.6	8.0	6.2	2.4	3.5	-0.3	-0.6	3.0
Foreign direct investment (net)	0.0	0.0	6.9	8.1	13.0	15.0	21.0	13.0	22.0	12.0
Portfolio equity flows	..	..	0.0	0.0	0.0	0.0	0.0	0.0	0.0	0.0
Grants (excluding technical coop.)	0.0	13.7	9.2	7.4	3.1	2.8	5.5	5.3	12.0	23.5
Memo: technical coop. grants	0.0	2.7	3.2	3.1	3.1	3.1	2.5	2.4	4.1	3.6
NET TRANSFERS	..	..	**15.3**	**18.2**	**15.3**	**12.1**	**22.1**	**10.8**	**25.7**	**29.8**
Interest on long-term debt	..	..	1.4	1.3	1.5	1.6	1.6	1.6	1.7	1.8
Profit remittances on FDI	0.0	0.0	3.0	4.0	5.5	6.5	6.3	5.5	6.0	7.0
3. MAJOR ECONOMIC AGGREGATES										
Gross national product (GNP)	20.2	58.7	138.1	148.6	159.9	171.3	183.7	193.2	198.0	217.6
Exports of goods & services (XGS)	..	24.9	95.2	84.2	102.9	103.9	110.0	106.8	108.9	112.1
of which workers remittances	..	8.6	12.9	9.3	9.4	8.3	8.2	9.6	10.3	10.6
Imports of goods & services (MGS)	..	55.0	104.8	127.9	142.9	136.6	135.1	134.0	142.8	148.6
International reserves (RES)	..	5.1	14.1	11.7	14.5	17.8	20.4	19.9	15.4	22.1
Current account balance	..	-14.3	-12.3	-45.5	-43.5	-33.6	-25.7	-28.2	-35.7	-37.6
4. DEBT INDICATORS										
EDT / XGS (%)	..	..	74.0	88.4	79.6	81.0	74.2	74.9	83.1	83.0
EDT / GNP (%)	..	..	51.0	50.1	51.2	49.1	44.4	41.4	45.7	42.7
TDS / XGS (%)	..	..	6.7	7.7	5.3	5.1	4.7	6.0	6.1	6.1
INT / XGS (%)	..	..	1.8	2.0	1.8	1.9	1.7	1.7	1.8	1.9
INT / GNP (%)	..	..	1.3	1.1	1.2	1.1	1.0	0.9	1.0	1.0
RES / EDT (%)	..	..	20.0	15.7	17.7	21.1	25.0	24.9	17.0	23.8
RES / MGS (months)	..	1.1	1.6	1.1	1.2	1.6	1.8	1.8	1.3	1.8
Short-term / EDT (%)	..	..	3.7	2.5	2.5	3.6	3.8	1.1	7.7	7.2
Concessional / EDT (%)	..	..	83.4	88.5	90.5	90.7	91.5	95.0	89.5	90.0
Multilateral / EDT (%)	..	..	57.3	61.9	63.2	63.6	62.8	61.8	54.9	56.5

DOMINICA

(US$ million, unless otherwise indicated)

	1970	1980	1988	1989	1990	1991	1992	1993	1994	1995
5. LONG-TERM DEBT										
DEBT OUTSTANDING (LDOD)	..	..	**58.9**	**66.0**	**74.2**	**76.4**	**74.7**	**76.0**	**80.9**	**84.6**
Public and publicly guaranteed	..	..	**58.9**	**66.0**	**74.2**	**76.4**	**74.7**	**76.0**	**80.9**	**84.6**
Official creditors	..	..	58.7	65.8	74.2	76.4	74.7	76.0	80.9	84.6
Multilateral	..	..	40.3	46.1	51.8	53.5	51.3	49.4	49.7	52.5
Concessional	..	..	40.3	46.0	51.8	53.5	51.3	49.4	49.7	51.7
Bilateral	..	..	18.4	19.8	22.4	22.8	23.4	26.6	31.3	32.0
Concessional	..	..	18.4	19.8	22.4	22.8	23.4	26.6	31.3	32.0
Private creditors	..	..	0.2	0.1	0.1	0.0	0.0	0.0	0.0	0.0
Bonds	..	..	0.0	0.0	0.0	0.0	0.0	0.0	0.0	0.0
Commercial banks	..	..	0.2	0.1	0.1	0.0	0.0	0.0	0.0	0.0
Other private	..	..	0.0	0.0	0.0	0.0	0.0	0.0	0.0	0.0
Private nonguaranteed	**0.0**	**0.0**	**0.0**	**0.0**	**0.0**	**0.0**	**0.0**	**0.0**	**0.0**	**0.0**
Bonds	..	..	0.0	0.0	0.0	0.0	0.0	0.0	0.0	0.0
Commercial banks	..	..	0.0	0.0	0.0	0.0	0.0	0.0	0.0	0.0
Memo:										
IBRD	0.0	0.0	0.0	0.0	0.0	0.0	0.0	0.0	0.0	0.0
IDA	0.0	0.0	7.2	8.7	10.4	11.1	11.0	11.1	11.8	12.2
DISBURSEMENTS	..	..	**5.3**	**10.4**	**8.5**	**4.9**	**6.1**	**3.5**	**3.4**	**6.9**
Public and publicly guaranteed	..	..	**5.3**	**10.4**	**8.5**	**4.9**	**6.1**	**3.5**	**3.4**	**6.9**
Official creditors	..	..	5.3	10.4	8.5	4.9	6.1	3.5	3.4	6.9
Multilateral	..	..	3.0	7.6	5.3	3.5	1.7	1.4	0.9	2.3
Concessional	..	..	3.0	7.6	5.3	3.5	1.7	1.4	0.9	1.7
Bilateral	..	..	2.2	2.9	3.2	1.4	4.4	2.1	2.5	4.6
Concessional	..	..	2.2	2.9	3.2	1.4	4.4	2.1	2.5	4.6
Private creditors	..	..	0.0	0.0	0.0	0.0	0.0	0.0	0.0	0.0
Bonds	..	..	0.0	0.0	0.0	0.0	0.0	0.0	0.0	0.0
Commercial banks	..	..	0.0	0.0	0.0	0.0	0.0	0.0	0.0	0.0
Other private	..	..	0.0	0.0	0.0	0.0	0.0	0.0	0.0	0.0
Private nonguaranteed	**0.0**	**0.0**	**0.0**	**0.0**	**0.0**	**0.0**	**0.0**	**0.0**	**0.0**	**0.0**
Bonds	..	..	0.0	0.0	0.0	0.0	0.0	0.0	0.0	0.0
Commercial banks	..	..	0.0	0.0	0.0	0.0	0.0	0.0	0.0	0.0
Memo:										
IBRD	0.0	0.0	0.0	0.0	0.0	0.0	0.0	0.0	0.0	0.0
IDA	0.0	0.0	0.4	1.7	0.9	0.6	0.4	0.1	0.3	0.1
PRINCIPAL REPAYMENTS	..	..	**1.7**	**2.4**	**2.3**	**2.4**	**2.5**	**3.9**	**4.0**	**3.8**
Public and publicly guaranteed	..	..	**1.7**	**2.4**	**2.3**	**2.4**	**2.5**	**3.9**	**4.0**	**3.8**
Official creditors	..	..	1.6	2.3	2.2	2.4	2.5	3.9	4.0	3.8
Multilateral	..	..	1.3	2.0	1.9	1.8	2.2	2.4	2.5	2.1
Concessional	..	..	1.3	2.0	1.9	1.8	2.2	2.4	2.5	2.1
Bilateral	..	..	0.3	0.3	0.3	0.6	0.4	1.4	1.5	1.7
Concessional	..	..	0.3	0.3	0.3	0.6	0.4	1.4	1.5	1.7
Private creditors	..	..	0.1	0.1	0.1	0.1	0.0	0.0	0.0	0.0
Bonds	..	..	0.0	0.0	0.0	0.0	0.0	0.0	0.0	0.0
Commercial banks	..	..	0.1	0.1	0.1	0.1	0.0	0.0	0.0	0.0
Other private	..	..	0.0	0.0	0.0	0.0	0.0	0.0	0.0	0.0
Private nonguaranteed	**0.0**	**0.0**	**0.0**	**0.0**	**0.0**	**0.0**	**0.0**	**0.0**	**0.0**	**0.0**
Bonds	..	..	0.0	0.0	0.0	0.0	0.0	0.0	0.0	0.0
Commercial banks	..	..	0.0	0.0	0.0	0.0	0.0	0.0	0.0	0.0
Memo:										
IBRD	0.0	0.0	0.0	0.0	0.0	0.0	0.0	0.0	0.0	0.0
IDA	0.0	0.0	0.0	0.0	0.0	0.0	0.0	0.1	0.1	0.1
NET FLOWS ON DEBT	..	..	**3.6**	**8.0**	**6.2**	**2.4**	**3.5**	**-0.3**	**-0.6**	**3.0**
Public and publicly guaranteed	..	..	**3.6**	**8.0**	**6.2**	**2.4**	**3.5**	**-0.3**	**-0.6**	**3.0**
Official creditors	..	..	3.7	8.1	6.3	2.5	3.5	-0.3	-0.6	3.0
Multilateral	..	..	1.7	5.5	3.4	1.7	-0.5	-1.0	-1.6	0.1
Concessional	..	..	1.7	5.5	3.4	1.7	-0.5	-1.0	-1.6	-0.5
Bilateral	..	..	2.0	2.6	2.9	0.8	4.0	0.7	1.1	2.9
Concessional	..	..	2.0	2.6	2.9	0.8	4.0	0.7	1.1	2.9
Private creditors	..	..	-0.1	-0.1	-0.1	-0.1	0.0	0.0	0.0	0.0
Bonds	..	..	0.0	0.0	0.0	0.0	0.0	0.0	0.0	0.0
Commercial banks	..	..	-0.1	-0.1	-0.1	-0.1	0.0	0.0	0.0	0.0
Other private	..	..	0.0	0.0	0.0	0.0	0.0	0.0	0.0	0.0
Private nonguaranteed	**0.0**	**0.0**	**0.0**	**0.0**	**0.0**	**0.0**	**0.0**	**0.0**	**0.0**	**0.0**
Bonds	..	..	0.0	0.0	0.0	0.0	0.0	0.0	0.0	0.0
Commercial banks	..	..	0.0	0.0	0.0	0.0	0.0	0.0	0.0	0.0
Memo:										
IBRD	0.0	0.0	0.0	0.0	0.0	0.0	0.0	0.0	0.0	0.0
IDA	0.0	0.0	0.4	1.7	0.9	0.6	0.4	0.0	0.2	0.0

DOMINICA

(US$ million, unless otherwise indicated)

	1970	1980	1988	1989	1990	1991	1992	1993	1994	1995
INTEREST PAYMENTS (LINT)	..	..	**1.4**	**1.3**	**1.5**	**1.6**	**1.6**	**1.6**	**1.7**	**1.8**
Public and publicly guaranteed	..	..	**1.4**	**1.3**	**1.5**	**1.6**	**1.6**	**1.6**	**1.7**	**1.8**
Official creditors	..	..	1.4	1.3	1.5	1.6	1.6	1.6	1.7	1.8
Multilateral	..	..	1.1	1.1	1.3	1.3	1.3	1.3	1.2	1.3
Concessional	..	..	1.1	1.1	1.3	1.3	1.3	1.3	1.2	1.3
Bilateral	..	..	0.2	0.2	0.2	0.3	0.3	0.3	0.4	0.5
Concessional	..	..	0.2	0.2	0.2	0.3	0.3	0.3	0.4	0.5
Private creditors	..	..	0.0	0.0	0.0	0.0	0.0	0.0	0.0	0.0
Bonds	..	..	0.0	0.0	0.0	0.0	0.0	0.0	0.0	0.0
Commercial banks	..	..	0.0	0.0	0.0	0.0	0.0	0.0	0.0	0.0
Other private	..	..	0.0	0.0	0.0	0.0	0.0	0.0	0.0	0.0
Private nonguaranteed	**0.0**	**0.0**	**0.0**	**0.0**	**0.0**	**0.0**	**0.0**	**0.0**	**0.0**	**0.0**
Bonds	..	..	0.0	0.0	0.0	0.0	0.0	0.0	0.0	0.0
Commercial banks	..	..	0.0	0.0	0.0	0.0	0.0	0.0	0.0	0.0
Memo:										
IBRD	0.0	0.0	0.0	0.0	0.0	0.0	0.0	0.0	0.0	0.0
IDA	0.0	0.0	0.1	0.1	0.1	0.1	0.1	0.1	0.1	0.1
NET TRANSFERS ON DEBT	..	..	**2.2**	**6.7**	**4.7**	**0.8**	**1.9**	**-2.0**	**-2.3**	**1.3**
Public and publicly guaranteed	..	..	**2.2**	**6.7**	**4.7**	**0.8**	**1.9**	**-2.0**	**-2.3**	**1.3**
Official creditors	..	..	2.3	6.8	4.8	0.9	1.9	-2.0	-2.3	1.3
Multilateral	..	..	0.6	4.4	2.1	0.4	-1.8	-2.3	-2.9	-1.1
Concessional	..	..	0.6	4.4	2.1	0.4	-1.8	-2.3	-2.9	-1.7
Bilateral	..	..	1.7	2.4	2.6	0.5	3.7	0.3	0.6	2.4
Concessional	..	..	1.7	2.4	2.6	0.5	3.7	0.3	0.6	2.4
Private creditors	..	..	-0.1	-0.1	-0.1	-0.1	0.0	0.0	0.0	0.0
Bonds	..	..	0.0	0.0	0.0	0.0	0.0	0.0	0.0	0.0
Commercial banks	..	..	-0.1	-0.1	-0.1	-0.1	0.0	0.0	0.0	0.0
Other private	..	..	0.0	0.0	0.0	0.0	0.0	0.0	0.0	0.0
Private nonguaranteed	**0.0**	**0.0**	**0.0**	**0.0**	**0.0**	**0.0**	**0.0**	**0.0**	**0.0**	**0.0**
Bonds	..	..	0.0	0.0	0.0	0.0	0.0	0.0	0.0	0.0
Commercial banks	..	..	0.0	0.0	0.0	0.0	0.0	0.0	0.0	0.0
Memo:										
IBRD	0.0	0.0	0.0	0.0	0.0	0.0	0.0	0.0	0.0	0.0
IDA	0.0	0.0	0.3	1.6	0.8	0.5	0.3	-0.1	0.2	-0.1
DEBT SERVICE (LTDS)	..	..	**3.0**	**3.7**	**3.8**	**4.1**	**4.2**	**5.5**	**5.7**	**5.6**
Public and publicly guaranteed	..	..	**3.0**	**3.7**	**3.8**	**4.1**	**4.2**	**5.5**	**5.7**	**5.6**
Official creditors	..	..	3.0	3.6	3.7	4.0	4.2	5.5	5.7	5.6
Multilateral	..	..	2.5	3.2	3.2	3.1	3.5	3.8	3.8	3.4
Concessional	..	..	2.5	3.2	3.2	3.1	3.5	3.8	3.7	3.4
Bilateral	..	..	0.5	0.5	0.6	0.9	0.7	1.7	1.9	2.1
Concessional	..	..	0.5	0.5	0.6	0.9	0.7	1.7	1.9	2.1
Private creditors	..	..	0.1	0.1	0.1	0.1	0.0	0.0	0.0	0.0
Bonds	..	..	0.0	0.0	0.0	0.0	0.0	0.0	0.0	0.0
Commercial banks	..	..	0.1	0.1	0.1	0.1	0.0	0.0	0.0	0.0
Other private	..	..	0.0	0.0	0.0	0.0	0.0	0.0	0.0	0.0
Private nonguaranteed	**0.0**	**0.0**	**0.0**	**0.0**	**0.0**	**0.0**	**0.0**	**0.0**	**0.0**	**0.0**
Bonds	..	..	0.0	0.0	0.0	0.0	0.0	0.0	0.0	0.0
Commercial banks	..	..	0.0	0.0	0.0	0.0	0.0	0.0	0.0	0.0
Memo:										
IBRD	0.0	0.0	0.0	0.0	0.0	0.0	0.0	0.0	0.0	0.0
IDA	0.0	0.0	0.1	0.1	0.1	0.1	0.1	0.1	0.1	0.2
UNDISBURSED DEBT	..	..	**30.3**	**22.1**	**17.6**	**14.3**	**11.0**	**15.9**	**11.6**	**20.8**
Official creditors	..	..	30.3	22.1	17.6	14.3	11.0	15.9	11.6	20.8
Private creditors	..	..	0.0	0.0	0.0	0.0	0.0	0.0	0.0	0.0
Memorandum items										
Concessional LDOD	..	..	58.7	65.8	74.1	76.4	74.7	76.0	80.9	83.7
Variable rate LDOD	..	..	0.0	0.0	0.0	0.0	0.0	0.0	0.0	0.0
Public sector LDOD	..	..	58.9	66.0	74.2	76.4	74.7	76.0	80.9	84.6
Private sector LDOD	..	..	0.0	0.0	0.0	0.0	0.0	0.0	0.0	0.0
6. CURRENCY COMPOSITION OF LONG-TERM DEBT (PERCENT)										
Deutsche mark	..	..	9.7	9.5	9.4	8.4	7.5	6.3	5.9	3.9
French franc	..	..	2.9	6.1	10.5	11.4	11.5	16.0	18.5	12.5
Japanese yen	..	..	0.3	0.3	0.3	0.3	0.3	0.1	0.1	0.1
Pound sterling	..	..	23.2	19.3	17.8	16.6	17.8	17.0	16.2	15.0
Swiss franc	..	..	0.0	0.0	0.0	0.0	0.0	0.0	0.0	0.0
U.S.dollars	..	..	47.3	49.1	48.4	47.9	47.8	45.8	44.5	54.1
Multiple currency	..	..	0.0	0.0	0.0	0.0	0.0	0.0	0.0	0.0
Special drawing rights	..	..	6.1	6.4	6.5	6.9	6.7	6.4	6.3	4.8
All other currencies	..	..	10.2	9.4	7.3	8.5	8.6	8.3	8.4	9.6

DOMINICA

(US$ million, unless otherwise indicated)

	1970	1980	1988	1989	1990	1991	1992	1993	1994	1995
7. DEBT RESTRUCTURINGS										
Total amount rescheduled	0.0	0.0	0.0	0.0	0.0	0.0	0.0	0.0	0.0	0.0
Debt stock rescheduled	0.0	0.0	0.0	0.0	0.0	0.0	0.0	0.0	0.0	0.0
Principal rescheduled	0.0	0.0	0.0	0.0	0.0	0.0	0.0	0.0	0.0	0.0
Official	0.0	0.0	0.0	0.0	0.0	0.0	0.0	0.0	0.0	0.0
Private	0.0	0.0	0.0	0.0	0.0	0.0	0.0	0.0	0.0	0.0
Interest rescheduled	0.0	0.0	0.0	0.0	0.0	0.0	0.0	0.0	0.0	0.0
Official	0.0	0.0	0.0	0.0	0.0	0.0	0.0	0.0	0.0	0.0
Private	0.0	0.0	0.0	0.0	0.0	0.0	0.0	0.0	0.0	0.0
Debt forgiven	..	..	0.0	0.0	3.3	0.0	0.0	0.0	0.0	0.0
Memo: interest forgiven	..	..	0.0	0.0	0.0	0.0	0.0	0.0	0.0	0.0
Debt stock reduction	0.0	0.0	0.0	0.0	0.0	0.0	0.0	0.0	0.0	0.0
of which debt buyback	0.0	0.0	0.0	0.0	0.0	0.0	0.0	0.0	0.0	0.0
8. DEBT STOCK-FLOW RECONCILIATION										
Total change in debt stocks	..	..	..	4.0	7.5	2.2	-2.5	-1.6	10.4	2.6
Net flows on debt	..	..	..	5.2	4.9	2.5	2.8	-3.2	4.7	1.7
Net change in interest arrears	..	..	..	0.0	0.0	0.0	0.1	-0.1	0.0	0.2
Interest capitalized	..	..	..	0.0	0.0	0.0	0.0	0.0	0.0	0.0
Debt forgiveness or reduction	..	..	..	0.0	-3.3	0.0	0.0	0.0	0.0	0.0
Cross-currency valuation	..	..	..	-0.9	5.4	-0.6	-4.2	-1.9	3.7	1.7
Residual	..	..	..	-0.3	0.5	0.3	-1.1	3.6	2.0	-1.0
9. AVERAGE TERMS OF NEW COMMITMENTS										
ALL CREDITORS										
Interest (%)	..	..	2.0	3.8	3.8	4.6	2.0	3.7	0.0	2.6
Maturity (years)	..	..	40.6	20.7	21.0	18.8	26.6	20.3	0.0	26.4
Grace period (years)	..	..	9.5	6.2	6.5	7.8	8.5	12.8	0.0	8.8
Grant element (%)	..	..	68.5	42.9	43.5	36.5	58.4	48.5	0.0	56.5
Official creditors										
Interest (%)	..	..	2.0	3.8	3.8	4.6	2.0	3.7	0.0	2.6
Maturity (years)	..	..	40.6	20.7	21.0	18.8	26.6	20.3	0.0	26.4
Grace period (years)	..	..	9.5	6.2	6.5	7.8	8.5	12.8	0.0	8.8
Grant element (%)	..	..	68.5	42.9	43.5	36.5	58.4	48.5	0.0	56.5
Private creditors										
Interest (%)	..	..	0.0	0.0	0.0	0.0	0.0	0.0	0.0	0.0
Maturity (years)	..	..	0.0	0.0	0.0	0.0	0.0	0.0	0.0	0.0
Grace period (years)	..	..	0.0	0.0	0.0	0.0	0.0	0.0	0.0	0.0
Grant element (%)	..	..	0.0	0.0	0.0	0.0	0.0	0.0	0.0	0.0
Memorandum items										
Commitments	..	..	5.3	3.1	1.7	2.0	4.8	8.8	0.0	5.1
Official creditors	..	..	5.3	3.1	1.7	2.0	4.8	8.8	0.0	5.1
Private creditors	..	..	0.0	0.0	0.0	0.0	0.0	0.0	0.0	0.0

10. CONTRACTUAL OBLIGATIONS ON OUTSTANDING LONG-TERM DEBT

	1996	1997	1998	1999	2000	2001	2002	2003	2004	2005
TOTAL										
Disbursements	5.9	5.5	3.7	2.6	1.5	0.8	0.5	0.2	0.1	0.0
Principal	4.3	4.4	5.1	5.3	5.3	5.4	5.2	4.9	4.8	4.9
Interest	1.9	1.9	1.9	1.8	1.7	1.6	1.5	1.3	1.2	1.1
Official creditors										
Disbursements	5.9	5.5	3.7	2.6	1.5	0.8	0.5	0.2	0.1	0.0
Principal	4.3	4.4	5.1	5.3	5.3	5.4	5.2	4.9	4.8	4.9
Interest	1.9	1.9	1.9	1.8	1.7	1.6	1.5	1.3	1.2	1.1
Bilateral creditors										
Disbursements	1.7	0.9	0.4	0.2	0.1	0.0	0.0	0.0	0.0	0.0
Principal	1.7	1.8	1.8	1.9	1.9	1.9	1.8	1.8	1.7	1.9
Interest	0.7	0.7	0.7	0.7	0.7	0.6	0.6	0.6	0.5	0.5
Multilateral creditors										
Disbursements	4.2	4.5	3.3	2.3	1.4	0.8	0.5	0.2	0.1	0.0
Principal	2.6	2.6	3.3	3.4	3.4	3.4	3.3	3.2	3.1	3.0
Interest	1.2	1.2	1.1	1.1	1.0	1.0	0.9	0.8	0.7	0.6
Private creditors										
Disbursements	0.0	0.0	0.0	0.0	0.0	0.0	0.0	0.0	0.0	0.0
Principal	0.0	0.0	0.0	0.0	0.0	0.0	0.0	0.0	0.0	0.0
Interest	0.0	0.0	0.0	0.0	0.0	0.0	0.0	0.0	0.0	0.0
Commercial banks										
Disbursements	0.0	0.0	0.0	0.0	0.0	0.0	0.0	0.0	0.0	0.0
Principal	0.0	0.0	0.0	0.0	0.0	0.0	0.0	0.0	0.0	0.0
Interest	0.0	0.0	0.0	0.0	0.0	0.0	0.0	0.0	0.0	0.0
Other private										
Disbursements	0.0	0.0	0.0	0.0	0.0	0.0	0.0	0.0	0.0	0.0
Principal	0.0	0.0	0.0	0.0	0.0	0.0	0.0	0.0	0.0	0.0
Interest	0.0	0.0	0.0	0.0	0.0	0.0	0.0	0.0	0.0	0.0

DOMINICAN REPUBLIC

(US$ million, unless otherwise indicated)

	1970	1980	1988	1989	1990	1991	1992	1993	1994	1995
1. SUMMARY DEBT DATA										
TOTAL DEBT STOCKS (EDT)	..	**2,002**	**3,970**	**4,039**	**4,372**	**4,491**	**4,613**	**4,860**	**4,153**	**4,259**
Long-term debt (LDOD)	**353**	**1,473**	**3,379**	**3,424**	**3,518**	**3,840**	**3,803**	**3,845**	**3,579**	**3,570**
Public and publicly guaranteed	212	1,220	3,261	3,320	3,420	3,757	3,737	3,794	3,543	3,550
Private nonguaranteed	141	254	118	105	99	83	66	51	35	19
Use of IMF credit	**7**	**49**	**218**	**123**	**72**	**89**	**123**	**186**	**190**	**160**
Short-term debt	..	**480**	**373**	**492**	**782**	**562**	**687**	**830**	**385**	**529**
of which interest arrears on LDOD	..	7	213	239	506	288	343	531	127	128
Official creditors	..	3	151	163	304	65	62	61	74	70
Private creditors	..	4	63	76	202	223	281	470	54	57
Memo: principal arrears on LDOD	..	13	276	361	614	408	479	574	294	321
Official creditors	..	4	227	276	444	195	168	217	249	262
Private creditors	..	8	49	85	169	213	310	357	45	59
Memo: export credits	..	..	940	905	967	778	691	875	943	968
TOTAL DEBT FLOWS										
Disbursements	**60**	**482**	**187**	**220**	**139**	**181**	**207**	**203**	**140**	**171**
Long-term debt	60	482	187	220	139	119	154	129	140	171
IMF purchases	0	0	0	0	0	61	53	74	0	0
Principal repayments	**32**	**200**	**158**	**201**	**146**	**158**	**197**	**183**	**294**	**235**
Long-term debt	27	135	107	114	88	113	182	173	286	201
IMF repurchases	5	65	51	88	58	45	15	10	8	34
Net flows on debt	**28**	**282**	**58**	**111**	**15**	**20**	**80**	**-25**	**-196**	**79**
of which short-term debt	..	..	28	93	23	-2	70	-45	-41	143
Interest payments (INT)	..	**179**	**182**	**121**	**86**	**106**	**149**	**147**	**221**	**193**
Long-term debt	13	121	150	92	59	84	126	119	195	163
IMF charges	0	5	17	16	9	7	6	8	10	10
Short-term debt	..	54	16	13	19	15	16	21	17	20
Net transfers on debt	..	**103**	**-124**	**-10**	**-71**	**-85**	**-69**	**-172**	**-417**	**-114**
Total debt service paid (TDS)	..	**379**	**340**	**322**	**232**	**264**	**346**	**330**	**516**	**428**
Long-term debt	39	256	256	206	147	197	309	292	481	364
IMF repurchases and charges	5	69	68	104	67	52	21	18	18	44
Short-term debt (interest only)	..	54	16	13	19	15	16	21	17	20
2. AGGREGATE NET RESOURCE FLOWS AND NET TRANSFERS (LONG-TERM)										
NET RESOURCE FLOWS	**114**	**454**	**245**	**250**	**213**	**169**	**174**	**191**	**25**	**281**
Net flow of long-term debt (ex. IMF)	33	346	81	106	51	6	-28	-44	-147	-30
Foreign direct investment (net)	72	93	106	110	133	145	180	191	132	271
Portfolio equity flows	0	0	0	0	0	0	0	0	0	0
Grants (excluding technical coop.)	9	14	58	34	29	18	23	44	39	40
Memo: technical coop. grants	5	16	36	37	44	51	55	59	54	59
NET TRANSFERS	**101**	**267**	**95**	**33**	**64**	**-36**	**-51**	**-37**	**-199**	**83**
Interest on long-term debt	13	121	150	92	59	84	126	119	195	163
Profit remittances on FDI	0	66	0	124	90	120	99	108	29	35
3. MAJOR ECONOMIC AGGREGATES										
Gross national product (GNP)	1,476	6,421	4,317	6,351	6,956	7,988	8,568	9,307	10,366	11,657
Exports of goods & services (XGS)	284	1,496	2,200	2,373	2,233	2,274	2,312	2,840	3,314	3,315
of which workers remittances	25	183	289	301	315	330	347	362	380	400
Imports of goods & services (MGS)	392	2,238	2,284	2,784	2,568	2,488	3,106	3,290	3,390	3,450
International reserves (RES)	32	279	261	171	69	448	506	658	259	373
Current account balance	-102	-720	-19	-327	-280	-157	-708	-447	-68	-125
4. DEBT INDICATORS										
EDT / XGS (%)	..	133.8	180.4	170.2	195.8	197.5	199.5	171.1	125.3	128.5
EDT / GNP (%)	..	31.2	92.0	63.6	62.9	56.2	53.8	52.2	40.1	36.5
TDS / XGS (%)	..	25.3	15.4	13.6	10.4	11.6	15.0	11.6	15.6	12.9
INT / XGS (%)	..	12.0	8.3	5.1	3.9	4.7	6.4	5.2	6.7	5.8
INT / GNP (%)	..	2.8	4.2	1.9	1.2	1.3	1.7	1.6	2.1	1.7
RES / EDT (%)	..	13.9	6.6	4.2	1.6	10.0	11.0	13.5	6.2	8.7
RES / MGS (months)	1.0	1.5	1.4	0.7	0.3	2.2	2.0	2.4	0.9	1.3
Short-term / EDT (%)	..	24.0	9.4	12.2	17.9	12.5	14.9	17.1	9.3	12.4
Concessional / EDT (%)	..	20.5	27.7	28.9	27.7	40.3	40.7	41.1	48.0	46.2
Multilateral / EDT (%)	..	10.2	18.7	19.3	19.6	19.6	18.8	18.3	22.5	24.0

DOMINICAN REPUBLIC

(US$ million, unless otherwise indicated)

	1970	1980	1988	1989	1990	1991	1992	1993	1994	1995
5. LONG-TERM DEBT										
DEBT OUTSTANDING (LDOD)	**353**	**1,473**	**3,379**	**3,424**	**3,518**	**3,840**	**3,803**	**3,845**	**3,579**	**3,570**
Public and publicly guaranteed	**212**	**1,220**	**3,261**	**3,320**	**3,420**	**3,757**	**3,737**	**3,794**	**3,543**	**3,550**
Official creditors	202	786	2,218	2,289	2,383	2,754	2,750	2,856	2,873	2,899
Multilateral	14	205	744	781	858	881	869	888	936	1,022
Concessional	0	146	409	424	439	430	417	413	418	430
Bilateral	188	581	1,473	1,507	1,525	1,874	1,881	1,967	1,937	1,877
Concessional	167	264	689	744	772	1,381	1,459	1,587	1,574	1,539
Private creditors	10	434	1,044	1,031	1,036	1,003	986	939	670	652
Bonds	0	0	0	0	0	0	0	0	520	520
Commercial banks	0	386	794	782	775	776	791	796	27	30
Other private	9	48	250	249	262	227	195	143	124	102
Private nonguaranteed	**141**	**254**	**118**	**105**	**99**	**83**	**66**	**51**	**35**	**19**
Bonds	0	0	0	0	0	0	0	0	0	0
Commercial banks	141	254	118	105	99	83	66	51	35	19
Memo:										
IBRD	11	66	194	201	238	254	255	261	276	283
IDA	0	18	21	20	20	20	19	19	18	17
DISBURSEMENTS	**60**	**482**	**187**	**220**	**139**	**119**	**154**	**129**	**140**	**171**
Public and publicly guaranteed	**38**	**415**	**187**	**220**	**139**	**119**	**154**	**129**	**140**	**171**
Official creditors	36	319	131	204	136	119	135	119	132	166
Multilateral	11	90	53	82	84	81	58	70	81	145
Concessional	0	52	19	21	21	10	2	16	22	32
Bilateral	25	229	78	122	53	38	77	50	51	21
Concessional	24	42	49	78	20	34	25	23	25	8
Private creditors	2	96	57	15	2	1	19	9	8	5
Bonds	0	0	0	0	0	0	0	0	0	0
Commercial banks	0	72	0	0	0	1	18	7	8	5
Other private	2	24	57	15	2	0	1	2	0	0
Private nonguaranteed	**22**	**67**	**0**	**0**	**0**	**0**	**0**	**0**	**0**	**0**
Bonds	0	0	0	0	0	0	0	0	0	0
Commercial banks	22	67	0	0	0	0	0	0	0	0
Memo:										
IBRD	11	39	16	32	39	42	35	26	33	36
IDA	0	0	0	0	0	0	0	0	0	0
PRINCIPAL REPAYMENTS	**27**	**135**	**107**	**114**	**88**	**113**	**182**	**173**	**286**	**201**
Public and publicly guaranteed	**7**	**62**	**97**	**99**	**83**	**97**	**166**	**157**	**271**	**185**
Official creditors	6	30	90	89	83	97	145	135	162	162
Multilateral	0	3	31	38	38	63	57	58	70	79
Concessional	0	0	9	6	7	18	16	18	18	21
Bilateral	6	27	59	51	44	35	88	78	92	83
Concessional	3	9	11	10	8	9	15	27	51	47
Private creditors	1	32	6	10	0	0	21	22	109	24
Bonds	0	0	0	0	0	0	0	0	0	0
Commercial banks	0	30	5	9	0	0	2	3	79	4
Other private	1	2	2	1	0	0	19	19	30	20
Private nonguaranteed	**20**	**74**	**10**	**15**	**5**	**16**	**17**	**16**	**15**	**16**
Bonds	0	0	0	0	0	0	0	0	0	0
Commercial banks	20	74	10	15	5	16	17	16	15	16
Memo:										
IBRD	0	2	23	20	19	31	25	25	36	40
IDA	0	0	0	0	0	1	0	1	1	1
NET FLOWS ON DEBT	**33**	**346**	**81**	**106**	**51**	**6**	**-28**	**-44**	**-147**	**-30**
Public and publicly guaranteed	**31**	**353**	**91**	**121**	**56**	**22**	**-12**	**-28**	**-131**	**-14**
Official creditors	30	289	40	116	54	22	-9	-16	-30	4
Multilateral	11	87	22	44	46	18	1	12	11	66
Concessional	0	52	9	15	15	-9	-14	-2	4	11
Bilateral	19	202	19	72	8	3	-10	-28	-41	-61
Concessional	22	33	39	68	11	25	11	-3	-26	-39
Private creditors	1	64	50	5	2	1	-2	-12	-101	-18
Bonds	0	0	0	0	0	0	0	0	0	0
Commercial banks	0	42	-5	-9	0	1	15	5	-72	2
Other private	1	22	55	15	2	0	-18	-17	-30	-20
Private nonguaranteed	**2**	**-7**	**-10**	**-15**	**-5**	**-16**	**-17**	**-16**	**-15**	**-16**
Bonds	0	0	0	0	0	0	0	0	0	0
Commercial banks	2	-7	-10	-15	-5	-16	-17	-16	-15	-16
Memo:										
IBRD	11	37	-6	12	20	12	10	1	-3	-4
IDA	0	0	0	0	0	-1	0	-1	-1	-1

DOMINICAN REPUBLIC

(US$ million, unless otherwise indicated)

	1970	1980	1988	1989	1990	1991	1992	1993	1994	1995
INTEREST PAYMENTS (LINT)	**13**	**121**	**150**	**92**	**59**	**84**	**126**	**119**	**195**	**163**
Public and publicly guaranteed	**4**	**92**	**143**	**83**	**56**	**77**	**120**	**114**	**191**	**161**
Official creditors	4	26	66	62	55	76	103	106	116	138
Multilateral	1	5	35	34	32	51	44	45	47	51
Concessional	0	2	7	6	4	11	9	9	9	10
Bilateral	4	21	31	29	24	25	58	62	69	87
Concessional	2	6	11	11	7	11	41	50	60	80
Private creditors	0	66	76	20	1	1	18	8	75	23
Bonds	0	0	0	0	0	0	0	0	5	13
Commercial banks	0	64	75	20	0	0	2	2	63	3
Other private	0	3	1	0	1	1	16	6	7	7
Private nonguaranteed	**8**	**29**	**7**	**9**	**3**	**7**	**6**	**5**	**4**	**2**
Bonds	0	0	0	0	0	0	0	0	0	0
Commercial banks	8	29	7	9	3	7	6	5	4	2
Memo:										
IBRD	0	3	17	16	14	23	19	20	20	21
IDA	0	0	0	0	0	0	0	0	0	0
NET TRANSFERS ON DEBT	**21**	**226**	**-69**	**14**	**-9**	**-78**	**-155**	**-163**	**-341**	**-193**
Public and publicly guaranteed	**27**	**261**	**-52**	**38**	**0**	**-55**	**-132**	**-143**	**-322**	**-175**
Official creditors	26	264	-26	53	-1	-54	-112	-122	-146	-134
Multilateral	10	83	-14	11	14	-32	-44	-33	-36	14
Concessional	0	51	2	9	10	-20	-23	-11	-5	1
Bilateral	16	181	-13	43	-15	-22	-69	-90	-110	-148
Concessional	20	27	28	58	4	14	-30	-53	-86	-119
Private creditors	1	-3	-26	-15	1	0	-20	-21	-176	-42
Bonds	0	0	0	0	0	0	0	0	-5	-13
Commercial banks	0	-22	-80	-30	0	1	13	3	-135	-2
Other private	1	20	53	15	1	-1	-33	-24	-36	-27
Private nonguaranteed	**-6**	**-35**	**-17**	**-25**	**-8**	**-23**	**-23**	**-20**	**-19**	**-18**
Bonds	0	0	0	0	0	0	0	0	0	0
Commercial banks	-6	-35	-17	-25	-8	-23	-23	-20	-19	-18
Memo:										
IBRD	10	34	-23	-4	6	-11	-9	-19	-23	-25
IDA	0	0	0	0	0	-1	-1	-1	-1	-1
DEBT SERVICE (LTDS)	**39**	**256**	**256**	**206**	**147**	**197**	**309**	**292**	**481**	**364**
Public and publicly guaranteed	**12**	**154**	**239**	**181**	**139**	**174**	**286**	**272**	**462**	**346**
Official creditors	10	56	157	151	138	173	247	242	278	300
Multilateral	1	7	66	71	70	113	101	102	118	130
Concessional	0	2	17	12	11	29	25	27	27	31
Bilateral	10	48	90	80	68	59	146	139	161	169
Concessional	4	15	22	20	15	20	56	77	111	127
Private creditors	1	98	83	30	1	1	39	30	184	47
Bonds	0	0	0	0	0	0	0	0	5	13
Commercial banks	0	94	80	30	0	0	4	4	143	7
Other private	1	4	3	1	1	1	35	26	36	27
Private nonguaranteed	**28**	**102**	**17**	**25**	**8**	**23**	**23**	**20**	**19**	**18**
Bonds	0	0	0	0	0	0	0	0	0	0
Commercial banks	28	102	17	25	8	23	23	20	19	18
Memo:										
IBRD	0	5	39	36	33	54	44	45	56	60
IDA	0	0	0	0	0	1	1	1	1	1
UNDISBURSED DEBT	**64**	**632**	**558**	**452**	**510**	**508**	**457**	**426**	**512**	**484**
Official creditors	42	537	516	426	483	459	429	408	501	472
Private creditors	22	94	42	26	27	48	28	18	11	12
Memorandum items										
Concessional LDOD	167	410	1,098	1,167	1,210	1,811	1,876	1,999	1,992	1,969
Variable rate LDOD	141	695	1,135	1,104	1,104	1,629	1,646	1,813	1,577	1,642
Public sector LDOD	197	1,185	3,232	3,291	3,391	3,729	3,705	3,765	3,515	3,524
Private sector LDOD	156	289	146	134	128	111	97	80	63	46

6. CURRENCY COMPOSITION OF LONG-TERM DEBT (PERCENT)

	1970	1980	1988	1989	1990	1991	1992	1993	1994	1995
Deutsche mark	0.0	0.6	1.7	1.8	2.0	1.6	1.4	0.9	1.0	1.0
French franc	0.0	0.0	0.4	0.5	0.5	0.2	0.2	0.4	0.6	0.8
Japanese yen	0.0	0.0	6.5	6.0	6.4	5.9	5.3	4.3	4.6	4.0
Pound sterling	0.0	0.0	0.0	0.0	0.0	0.0	0.0	0.0	0.0	0.0
Swiss franc	0.0	0.0	0.0	0.0	0.0	0.0	0.0	0.0	0.0	0.0
U.S.dollars	93.5	81.8	70.2	70.7	68.4	71.0	71.9	72.9	69.4	68.8
Multiple currency	6.6	11.5	19.3	20.1	21.8	20.5	20.4	20.8	23.7	24.8
Special drawing rights	0.0	0.0	0.1	0.2	0.2	0.2	0.1	0.1	0.1	0.1
All other currencies	0.0	6.0	1.8	0.8	0.7	0.6	0.6	0.6	0.5	0.5

DOMINICAN REPUBLIC

(US$ million, unless otherwise indicated)

	1970	1980	1988	1989	1990	1991	1992	1993	1994	1995
7. DEBT RESTRUCTURINGS										
Total amount rescheduled	0	0	261	31	8	624	91	162	520	0
Debt stock rescheduled	0	0	99	0	0	0	0	0	506	0
Principal rescheduled	0	0	155	31	1	325	67	104	6	0
Official	0	0	37	0	1	282	54	56	0	0
Private	0	0	119	31	0	43	13	49	6	0
Interest rescheduled	0	0	2	0	2	299	23	57	3	0
Official	0	0	2	0	2	256	19	11	0	0
Private	0	0	0	0	0	43	5	46	3	0
Debt forgiven	..	..	0	3	7	0	6	1	0	0
Memo: interest forgiven	..	..	0	0	0	0	0	0	180	0
Debt stock reduction	0	0	0	0	0	0	0	0	291	0
of which debt buyback	0	0	0	0	0	0	0	0	68	0
8. DEBT STOCK-FLOW RECONCILIATION										
Total change in debt stocks	..	..	..	69	334	119	122	248	-707	105
Net flows on debt	..	..	..	111	15	20	80	-25	-196	79
Net change in interest arrears	..	..	..	25	267	-218	55	188	-404	1
Interest capitalized	..	..	..	0	2	299	23	57	3	0
Debt forgiveness or reduction	..	..	..	-3	-7	0	-6	-1	-223	0
Cross-currency valuation	..	..	..	-38	40	11	-21	12	36	2
Residual	..	..	..	-27	16	6	-9	16	75	24
9. AVERAGE TERMS OF NEW COMMITMENTS										
ALL CREDITORS										
Interest (%)	2.4	8.9	6.7	5.2	5.9	5.0	7.3	3.9	3.3	6.9
Maturity (years)	28.4	12.3	14.6	13.7	24.4	19.2	16.8	22.7	29.1	19.8
Grace period (years)	4.8	4.0	4.1	5.9	6.4	5.6	4.1	5.7	8.3	5.3
Grant element (%)	53.4	10.2	16.8	29.3	31.2	33.8	14.3	41.4	52.4	19.7
Official creditors										
Interest (%)	2.4	7.5	6.7	5.2	5.8	4.2	7.3	3.9	3.3	6.8
Maturity (years)	28.4	12.8	14.6	13.7	24.8	21.5	16.8	22.7	29.1	20.2
Grace period (years)	4.8	4.3	4.1	5.9	6.4	6.2	4.1	5.7	8.3	5.4
Grant element (%)	53.4	17.5	16.8	29.3	31.9	40.5	14.3	41.4	52.4	20.2
Private creditors										
Interest (%)	0.0	11.8	0.0	0.0	9.8	9.0	0.0	0.0	0.0	8.4
Maturity (years)	0.0	11.3	0.0	0.0	9.1	8.6	0.0	0.0	0.0	9.5
Grace period (years)	0.0	3.4	0.0	0.0	4.6	2.9	0.0	0.0	0.0	2.0
Grant element (%)	0.0	-3.9	0.0	0.0	-0.2	2.9	0.0	0.0	0.0	5.8
Memorandum items										
Commitments	20	519	197	137	204	124	130	101	202	155
Official creditors	20	342	197	137	199	102	130	101	202	149
Private creditors	0	176	0	0	5	22	0	0	0	6

10. CONTRACTUAL OBLIGATIONS ON OUTSTANDING LONG-TERM DEBT

	1996	1997	1998	1999	2000	2001	2002	2003	2004	2005
TOTAL										
Disbursements	158	134	87	51	26	11	6	3	3	2
Principal	235	222	194	166	243	255	259	254	257	244
Interest	180	173	164	156	148	135	120	105	91	77
Official creditors										
Disbursements	152	130	85	50	26	11	6	3	3	2
Principal	194	186	158	142	226	238	243	238	241	229
Interest	138	134	128	122	116	104	90	77	64	51
Bilateral creditors										
Disbursements	46	42	26	17	9	4	2	0	0	0
Principal	112	101	82	70	153	159	167	165	167	158
Interest	83	80	76	74	71	63	54	44	35	26
Multilateral creditors										
Disbursements	106	88	59	33	16	6	4	2	3	2
Principal	82	85	77	72	74	80	76	73	74	71
Interest	56	54	52	48	45	41	37	32	29	25
Private creditors										
Disbursements	6	4	2	1	0	0	0	0	0	0
Principal	41	36	36	24	17	17	16	16	16	15
Interest	42	39	36	34	32	31	30	29	28	27
Commercial banks										
Disbursements	6	4	2	1	0	0	0	0	0	0
Principal	9	10	9	9	2	2	1	1	1	0
Interest	3	2	2	1	1	0	0	0	0	0
Other private										
Disbursements	0	0	0	0	0	0	0	0	0	0
Principal	32	26	27	15	15	15	15	15	15	15
Interest	39	37	35	33	32	31	30	29	28	27

ECUADOR

(US$ million, unless otherwise indicated)

	1970	1980	1988	1989	1990	1991	1992	1993	1994	1995
1. SUMMARY DEBT DATA										
TOTAL DEBT STOCKS (EDT)	..	5,997	10,745	11,318	12,109	12,468	12,280	14,150	15,034	13,957
Long-term debt (LDOD)	242	4,422	9,147	9,585	10,030	10,094	9,931	10,215	10,748	12,472
Public and publicly guaranteed	193	3,300	9,028	9,427	9,867	9,951	9,831	9,974	10,523	12,032
Private nonguaranteed	49	1,122	119	158	164	143	100	241	224	440
Use of IMF credit	14	0	405	325	265	182	100	71	198	174
Short-term debt	..	1,575	1,194	1,407	1,814	2,192	2,249	3,864	4,088	1,312
of which interest arrears on LDOD	..	0	800	1,071	1,522	1,892	2,045	2,330	2,337	13
Official creditors	..	0	11	1	10	89	21	88	3	8
Private creditors	..	0	788	1,071	1,513	1,804	2,024	2,242	2,335	5
Memo: principal arrears on LDOD	..	1	320	546	1,097	1,809	2,207	2,875	3,396	11
Official creditors	..	0	13	5	6	116	15	45	5	9
Private creditors	..	1	307	541	1,091	1,693	2,192	2,830	3,392	2
Memo: export credits	..	..	1,603	1,916	2,090	2,194	1,832	1,892	1,822	1,719
TOTAL DEBT FLOWS										
Disbursements	58	1,283	865	894	638	546	352	666	666	1,049
Long-term debt	48	1,283	788	874	606	521	352	666	524	1,049
IMF purchases	10	0	78	20	32	25	0	0	142	0
Principal repayments	33	535	686	535	611	602	561	517	509	750
Long-term debt	26	535	549	446	496	497	483	488	487	721
IMF repurchases	7	0	138	89	115	105	77	29	21	29
Net flows on debt	25	748	181	341	-1	-48	-306	1,479	375	-152
of which short-term debt	..	..	2	-18	-28	8	-97	1,330	218	-451
Interest payments (INT)	..	473	372	494	474	504	420	404	492	666
Long-term debt	10	365	281	411	416	457	376	302	401	575
IMF charges	0	0	32	31	30	20	11	7	3	10
Short-term debt	..	108	59	53	28	27	33	95	88	81
Net transfers on debt	..	275	-191	-153	-475	-552	-726	1,076	-117	-818
Total debt service paid (TDS)	..	1,008	1,059	1,029	1,084	1,106	981	921	1,000	1,416
Long-term debt	36	900	830	857	911	954	859	790	888	1,296
IMF repurchases and charges	7	0	169	119	145	125	89	36	25	39
Short-term debt (interest only)	..	108	59	53	28	27	33	95	88	81
2. AGGREGATE NET RESOURCE FLOWS AND NET TRANSFERS (LONG-TERM)										
NET RESOURCE FLOWS	113	825	349	548	289	230	129	679	617	867
Net flow of long-term debt (ex. IMF)	21	748	239	428	110	24	-132	178	37	328
Foreign direct investment (net)	89	70	80	80	126	160	178	469	531	470
Portfolio equity flows	0	0	0	0	0	0	0	0	4	1
Grants (excluding technical coop.)	3	7	30	40	53	46	83	32	46	69
Memo: technical coop. grants	8	28	60	58	67	77	81	89	96	122
NET TRANSFERS	84	349	-62	17	-251	-355	-377	231	67	140
Interest on long-term debt	10	365	281	411	416	457	376	302	401	575
Profit remittances on FDI	19	111	130	120	125	128	130	147	150	152
3. MAJOR ECONOMIC AGGREGATES										
Gross national product (GNP)	1,642	11,152	9,326	9,093	9,867	11,049	12,049	13,732	15,327	16,597
Exports of goods & services (XGS)	..	2,975	2,659	2,890	3,277	3,438	3,660	3,742	4,641	5,298
of which workers remittances	..	0	0	0	0	0	0	0	0	0
Imports of goods & services (MGS)	..	3,647	3,439	3,703	3,750	4,255	3,995	4,554	5,466	6,351
International reserves (RES)	76	1,257	568	707	1,009	1,081	1,016	1,542	2,003	1,788
Current account balance	..	-642	-683	-716	-366	-707	-215	-682	-680	-822
4. DEBT INDICATORS										
EDT / XGS (%)	..	201.6	404.1	391.6	369.5	362.7	335.5	378.1	323.9	263.4
EDT / GNP (%)	..	53.8	115.2	124.5	122.7	112.8	101.9	103.0	98.1	84.1
TDS / XGS (%)	..	33.9	39.8	35.6	33.1	32.2	26.8	24.6	21.6	26.7
INT / XGS (%)	..	15.9	14.0	17.1	14.5	14.7	11.5	10.8	10.6	12.6
INT / GNP (%)	..	4.2	4.0	5.4	4.8	4.6	3.5	2.9	3.2	4.0
RES / EDT (%)	..	21.0	5.3	6.2	8.3	8.7	8.3	10.9	13.3	12.8
RES / MGS (months)	..	4.1	2.0	2.3	3.2	3.0	3.1	4.1	4.4	3.4
Short-term / EDT (%)	..	26.3	11.1	12.4	15.0	17.6	18.3	27.3	27.2	9.4
Concessional / EDT (%)	..	5.0	7.6	7.6	7.5	8.3	10.9	10.6	11.4	13.6
Multilateral / EDT (%)	..	5.4	18.1	17.4	17.6	17.9	18.3	16.8	17.2	21.4

ECUADOR

(US$ million, unless otherwise indicated)

	1970	1980	1988	1989	1990	1991	1992	1993	1994	1995
5. LONG-TERM DEBT										
DEBT OUTSTANDING (LDOD)	**242**	**4,422**	**9,147**	**9,585**	**10,030**	**10,094**	**9,931**	**10,215**	**10,748**	**12,472**
Public and publicly guaranteed	**193**	**3,300**	**9,028**	**9,427**	**9,867**	**9,951**	**9,831**	**9,974**	**10,523**	**12,032**
Official creditors	133	1,325	3,472	3,739	4,065	4,211	4,399	4,570	4,932	5,252
Multilateral	51	323	1,943	1,965	2,127	2,233	2,253	2,371	2,580	2,991
Concessional	47	114	412	435	451	490	513	588	624	720
Bilateral	83	1,002	1,529	1,774	1,938	1,978	2,146	2,199	2,352	2,260
Concessional	75	188	409	422	455	539	828	914	1,091	1,182
Private creditors	60	1,976	5,556	5,689	5,802	5,740	5,432	5,405	5,592	6,780
Bonds	3	55	0	0	0	0	0	0	191	5,999
Commercial banks	4	1,697	4,842	4,847	4,885	4,908	4,763	4,831	4,959	492
Other private	53	223	714	841	917	832	669	574	442	289
Private nonguaranteed	**49**	**1,122**	**119**	**158**	**164**	**143**	**100**	**241**	**224**	**440**
Bonds	0	0	0	0	0	0	0	0	0	10
Commercial banks	49	1,122	119	158	164	143	100	241	224	430
Memo:										
IBRD	34	109	756	761	816	816	783	759	830	1,082
IDA	6	36	33	32	32	31	30	29	28	27
DISBURSEMENTS	**48**	**1,283**	**788**	**874**	**606**	**521**	**352**	**666**	**524**	**1,049**
Public and publicly guaranteed	**41**	**968**	**731**	**810**	**575**	**519**	**352**	**500**	**524**	**839**
Official creditors	17	348	501	453	329	364	321	359	377	724
Multilateral	5	91	340	226	227	246	218	269	310	582
Concessional	4	11	31	32	24	50	35	90	57	115
Bilateral	12	257	160	227	101	119	103	90	67	142
Concessional	9	4	101	38	31	76	97	74	66	128
Private creditors	25	620	230	357	247	155	30	142	147	115
Bonds	0	0	0	0	0	0	0	0	0	0
Commercial banks	2	497	96	99	39	77	16	136	131	114
Other private	22	122	134	258	207	78	14	6	16	1
Private nonguaranteed	**7**	**315**	**57**	**63**	**30**	**1**	**0**	**166**	**0**	**210**
Bonds	0	0	0	0	0	0	0	0	0	10
Commercial banks	7	315	57	63	30	1	0	166	0	200
Memo:										
IBRD	2	34	175	75	47	60	63	52	112	319
IDA	2	0	0	0	0	0	0	0	0	0
PRINCIPAL REPAYMENTS	**26**	**535**	**549**	**446**	**496**	**497**	**483**	**488**	**487**	**721**
Public and publicly guaranteed	**16**	**272**	**537**	**422**	**471**	**474**	**441**	**463**	**471**	**711**
Official creditors	7	125	223	267	276	262	250	277	310	486
Multilateral	3	16	156	156	164	162	155	193	225	236
Concessional	3	2	6	8	8	11	13	17	22	23
Bilateral	4	108	67	111	112	100	95	85	85	251
Concessional	3	8	2	3	1	3	10	16	18	49
Private creditors	8	147	314	155	195	212	192	186	160	225
Bonds	0	14	0	0	0	0	0	0	0	10
Commercial banks	3	110	211	36	27	50	76	86	62	60
Other private	6	23	103	119	167	163	116	100	99	155
Private nonguaranteed	**11**	**263**	**12**	**25**	**25**	**22**	**42**	**25**	**17**	**10**
Bonds	0	0	0	0	0	0	0	0	0	0
Commercial banks	11	263	12	25	25	22	42	25	17	10
Memo:										
IBRD	2	10	50	45	42	78	74	93	94	98
IDA	0	0	1	1	1	1	1	1	1	1
NET FLOWS ON DEBT	**21**	**748**	**239**	**428**	**110**	**24**	**-132**	**178**	**37**	**328**
Public and publicly guaranteed	**26**	**696**	**194**	**389**	**105**	**45**	**-90**	**37**	**54**	**128**
Official creditors	9	224	278	186	53	102	72	82	67	238
Multilateral	1	75	184	70	64	83	63	77	85	347
Concessional	1	9	25	24	16	38	22	74	35	92
Bilateral	8	149	94	116	-11	19	9	5	-18	-109
Concessional	6	-4	99	35	30	73	87	59	49	79
Private creditors	16	473	-84	203	52	-57	-161	-44	-14	-110
Bonds	0	-14	0	0	0	0	0	0	0	-10
Commercial banks	0	387	-115	64	12	27	-59	50	69	54
Other private	17	99	31	139	40	-85	-102	-94	-83	-154
Private nonguaranteed	**-4**	**52**	**45**	**39**	**5**	**-21**	**-42**	**141**	**-17**	**200**
Bonds	0	0	0	0	0	0	0	0	0	10
Commercial banks	-4	52	45	39	5	-21	-42	141	-17	190
Memo:										
IBRD	0	24	125	31	5	-18	-11	-41	18	221
IDA	2	0	-1	-1	-1	-1	-1	-1	-1	-1

ECUADOR

(US$ million, unless otherwise indicated)

	1970	1980	1988	1989	1990	1991	1992	1993	1994	1995
INTEREST PAYMENTS (LINT)	**10**	**365**	**281**	**411**	**416**	**457**	**376**	**302**	**401**	**575**
Public and publicly guaranteed	**7**	**288**	**280**	**399**	**404**	**453**	**371**	**299**	**399**	**573**
Official creditors	4	89	178	219	212	225	242	226	252	327
Multilateral	3	19	141	152	140	159	151	159	157	170
Concessional	2	3	7	7	8	9	10	11	13	14
Bilateral	2	71	37	67	72	66	91	67	94	157
Concessional	1	5	4	14	7	9	21	23	30	48
Private creditors	2	199	102	180	192	228	130	73	148	246
Bonds	0	6	0	0	0	0	0	0	0	147
Commercial banks	1	184	53	122	132	173	87	34	121	58
Other private	2	8	49	58	60	55	43	39	27	41
Private nonguaranteed	**3**	**78**	**2**	**12**	**12**	**4**	**5**	**2**	**2**	**1**
Bonds	0	0	0	0	0	0	0	0	0	0
Commercial banks	3	78	2	12	12	4	5	2	2	1
Memo:										
IBRD	2	9	56	70	62	72	63	67	59	69
IDA	0	0	0	0	0	0	0	0	0	0
NET TRANSFERS ON DEBT	**11**	**383**	**-42**	**17**	**-306**	**-433**	**-508**	**-124**	**-364**	**-247**
Public and publicly guaranteed	**19**	**408**	**-86**	**-10**	**-299**	**-408**	**-461**	**-262**	**-345**	**-446**
Official creditors	5	134	100	-33	-160	-123	-170	-145	-184	-89
Multilateral	-1	56	43	-82	-77	-76	-88	-82	-72	177
Concessional	-1	7	18	17	8	29	13	63	23	79
Bilateral	6	78	57	49	-83	-47	-82	-63	-112	-267
Concessional	5	-9	95	22	23	63	66	36	19	31
Private creditors	14	274	-186	23	-140	-285	-291	-117	-161	-356
Bonds	0	-20	0	0	0	0	0	0	0	-157
Commercial banks	-1	203	-168	-58	-120	-146	-146	16	-52	-4
Other private	15	91	-18	81	-20	-139	-145	-133	-110	-196
Private nonguaranteed	**-8**	**-26**	**44**	**27**	**-7**	**-25**	**-47**	**138**	**-18**	**199**
Bonds	0	0	0	0	0	0	0	0	0	10
Commercial banks	-8	-26	44	27	-7	-25	-47	138	-18	189
Memo:										
IBRD	-2	16	68	-39	-56	-90	-74	-108	-41	152
IDA	2	0	-1	-1	-1	-1	-1	-1	-1	-1
DEBT SERVICE (LTDS)	**36**	**900**	**830**	**857**	**911**	**954**	**859**	**790**	**888**	**1,296**
Public and publicly guaranteed	**22**	**559**	**817**	**820**	**875**	**927**	**812**	**762**	**870**	**1,285**
Official creditors	12	214	401	486	488	487	491	504	562	813
Multilateral	6	35	297	308	304	322	306	352	383	405
Concessional	6	5	13	15	16	21	22	28	35	37
Bilateral	6	179	103	178	184	165	186	152	179	408
Concessional	4	13	6	16	8	13	31	39	47	98
Private creditors	11	346	416	335	386	440	321	259	308	471
Bonds	0	20	0	0	0	0	0	0	0	157
Commercial banks	3	294	264	157	159	223	163	120	182	118
Other private	8	31	152	177	227	218	159	139	126	197
Private nonguaranteed	**14**	**341**	**13**	**36**	**37**	**26**	**47**	**27**	**18**	**11**
Bonds	0	0	0	0	0	0	0	0	0	0
Commercial banks	14	341	13	36	37	26	47	27	18	11
Memo:										
IBRD	4	19	106	114	103	150	137	160	153	167
IDA	0	0	1	1	1	1	1	1	1	1
UNDISBURSED DEBT	**142**	**1,039**	**1,952**	**1,640**	**1,648**	**1,620**	**1,938**	**1,698**	**2,018**	**2,252**
Official creditors	60	695	1,578	1,485	1,535	1,534	1,715	1,445	1,809	1,758
Private creditors	82	345	374	155	114	86	223	253	208	494
Memorandum items										
Concessional LDOD	122	302	821	856	907	1,029	1,341	1,502	1,715	1,902
Variable rate LDOD	49	2,766	6,131	6,163	6,246	6,161	6,051	6,202	6,626	6,515
Public sector LDOD	193	3,300	9,028	9,427	9,867	9,951	9,831	9,974	10,523	12,032
Private sector LDOD	49	1,122	119	158	164	143	100	241	224	440

6. CURRENCY COMPOSITION OF LONG-TERM DEBT (PERCENT)

	1970	1980	1988	1989	1990	1991	1992	1993	1994	1995
Deutsche mark	4.7	1.7	2.4	2.6	2.8	2.8	2.6	2.4	2.5	1.1
French franc	2.0	0.0	1.1	1.2	1.5	1.9	2.4	2.3	2.6	2.3
Japanese yen	0.0	2.7	6.6	6.6	6.9	7.2	7.9	8.8	9.6	5.0
Pound sterling	0.8	1.1	1.5	1.4	1.6	1.5	1.3	1.3	1.3	0.6
Swiss franc	0.2	0.7	0.5	0.4	0.5	0.5	0.5	0.4	0.2	0.0
U.S.dollars	71.4	64.2	55.4	56.1	54.5	53.6	53.5	53.4	53.5	70.5
Multiple currency	19.8	28.1	30.2	29.3	29.7	30.1	29.7	29.3	28.2	19.7
Special drawing rights	0.0	0.0	0.0	0.0	0.0	0.0	0.0	0.0	0.0	0.0
All other currencies	1.2	1.4	2.3	2.3	2.4	2.4	2.2	2.0	2.1	0.7

ECUADOR

(US$ million, unless otherwise indicated)

	1970	1980	1988	1989	1990	1991	1992	1993	1994	1995
7. DEBT RESTRUCTURINGS										
Total amount rescheduled	0	0	945	726	249	0	362	37	533	5,818
Debt stock rescheduled	0	0	44	40	16	0	0	0	0	3,350
Principal rescheduled	0	0	773	595	152	0	210	8	329	0
Official	0	0	225	96	110	0	151	8	278	0
Private	0	0	548	498	42	0	60	0	51	0
Interest rescheduled	0	0	128	80	81	0	143	6	128	1,757
Official	0	0	115	64	61	0	117	6	115	0
Private	0	0	13	16	19	0	26	0	13	1,757
Debt forgiven	..	..	0	0	1	0	2	0	0	0
Memo: interest forgiven	..	..	0	0	0	0	0	0	0	0
Debt stock reduction	0	0	259	31	45	20	50	0	10	1,183
of which debt buyback	0	0	0	0	0	0	0	0	0	0
8. DEBT STOCK-FLOW RECONCILIATION										
Total change in debt stocks	..	..	..	572	792	359	-188	1,871	884	-1,077
Net flows on debt	..	..	..	341	-1	-48	-306	1,479	375	-152
Net change in interest arrears	..	..	..	272	451	370	153	285	7	-2,325
Interest capitalized	..	..	..	80	81	0	143	6	128	1,757
Debt forgiveness or reduction	..	..	..	-31	-46	-20	-52	0	-10	-1,183
Cross-currency valuation	..	..	..	-104	213	42	-112	55	243	26
Residual	..	..	..	15	94	14	-15	45	142	800
9. AVERAGE TERMS OF NEW COMMITMENTS										
ALL CREDITORS										
Interest (%)	6.2	10.7	5.9	7.4	6.4	5.8	6.9	5.4	6.0	6.4
Maturity (years)	20.0	14.1	18.3	13.1	17.4	18.0	18.6	13.8	20.7	15.8
Grace period (years)	3.9	3.8	4.9	3.3	4.2	4.9	4.9	3.8	5.4	5.5
Grant element (%)	24.0	-0.9	26.5	15.1	24.2	22.9	18.9	23.7	27.2	21.9
Official creditors										
Interest (%)	4.3	8.6	5.4	6.5	5.2	6.3	6.7	5.4	5.9	5.5
Maturity (years)	35.7	20.5	23.1	14.6	22.2	21.3	21.4	19.3	21.9	18.2
Grace period (years)	7.9	4.3	6.8	4.2	6.0	5.9	5.5	5.2	5.8	6.8
Grant element (%)	48.8	11.2	34.7	20.7	35.2	24.9	21.5	29.4	29.0	29.3
Private creditors										
Interest (%)	7.3	12.7	6.9	9.9	8.6	3.7	7.4	5.3	6.8	8.2
Maturity (years)	10.2	7.9	9.0	9.2	8.7	6.4	9.8	8.4	10.6	11.2
Grace period (years)	1.3	3.2	1.2	1.0	1.0	1.5	3.0	2.4	2.5	3.1
Grant element (%)	8.4	-12.7	10.5	-0.6	4.0	15.8	10.6	18.3	13.5	7.8
Memorandum items										
Commitments	78	1,148	468	565	643	602	766	312	924	1,165
Official creditors	30	564	310	416	415	471	583	153	820	764
Private creditors	48	584	158	149	228	131	183	159	104	402

10. CONTRACTUAL OBLIGATIONS ON OUTSTANDING LONG-TERM DEBT

	1996	1997	1998	1999	2000	2001	2002	2003	2004	2005
TOTAL										
Disbursements	958	558	338	204	100	55	30	6	2	0
Principal	858	876	755	626	630	583	556	540	516	567
Interest	684	750	727	697	660	622	586	549	514	481
Official creditors										
Disbursements	682	414	281	189	100	55	30	6	2	0
Principal	533	490	477	462	476	451	430	439	419	393
Interest	346	335	316	294	270	245	218	190	163	137
Bilateral creditors										
Disbursements	234	125	77	43	23	14	7	2	0	0
Principal	257	213	212	183	183	152	131	167	167	168
Interest	137	124	110	98	87	79	72	64	54	44
Multilateral creditors										
Disbursements	448	289	205	146	76	41	23	4	2	0
Principal	276	277	265	279	294	299	299	272	252	225
Interest	209	211	206	197	183	166	147	127	109	93
Private creditors										
Disbursements	277	145	57	15	0	0	0	0	0	0
Principal	325	387	278	164	154	132	126	102	97	173
Interest	338	415	411	402	390	378	368	359	351	345
Commercial banks										
Disbursements	277	145	57	15	0	0	0	0	0	0
Principal	100	93	118	119	120	104	91	66	63	53
Interest	49	51	55	51	42	33	25	18	13	8
Other private										
Disbursements	0	0	0	0	0	0	0	0	0	0
Principal	224	293	160	45	34	28	35	35	35	120
Interest	289	364	356	351	348	345	343	341	338	337

EGYPT

(US$ million, unless otherwise indicated)

	1970	1980	1988	1989	1990	1991	1992	1993	1994	1995
1. SUMMARY DEBT DATA										
TOTAL DEBT STOCKS (EDT)	..	**19,131**	**46,441**	**45,963**	**33,402**	**33,033**	**31,575**	**31,110**	**33,039**	**34,116**
Long-term debt (LDOD)	**1,351**	**14,693**	**39,381**	**37,918**	**28,828**	**29,806**	**28,857**	**28,905**	**30,913**	**31,638**
Public and publicly guaranteed	1,351	14,428	37,771	36,358	27,349	28,956	28,257	28,405	30,538	31,325
Private nonguaranteed	0	265	1,610	1,560	1,479	850	600	500	375	313
Use of IMF credit	**49**	**411**	**190**	**161**	**125**	**127**	**202**	**202**	**193**	**103**
Short-term debt	..	**4,027**	**6,871**	**7,884**	**4,450**	**3,099**	**2,516**	**2,003**	**1,933**	**2,375**
of which interest arrears on LDOD	..	383	2,471	3,370	1,438	1	1	1	3	7
Official creditors	..	383	2,277	2,965	873	1	1	1	1	4
Private creditors	..	0	194	405	565	1	1	1	2	3
Memo: principal arrears on LDOD	..	74	5,861	5,106	3,507	5	5	11	43	195
Official creditors	..	74	5,153	3,748	1,775	0	0	6	13	151
Private creditors	..	0	708	1,358	1,733	5	5	5	30	44
Memo: export credits	..	..	21,026	20,748	14,578	11,823	11,110	10,544	10,778	12,456
TOTAL DEBT FLOWS										
Disbursements	**188**	**2,743**	**2,662**	**2,128**	**2,010**	**2,039**	**1,518**	**1,261**	**1,074**	**504**
Long-term debt	170	2,680	2,662	2,128	2,010	1,956	1,395	1,261	1,074	504
IMF purchases	18	63	0	0	0	82	123	0	0	0
Principal repayments	**234**	**446**	**1,249**	**1,496**	**1,746**	**1,725**	**1,487**	**975**	**930**	**995**
Long-term debt	225	343	1,191	1,473	1,698	1,644	1,446	975	909	900
IMF repurchases	9	103	59	24	47	80	41	0	22	95
Net flows on debt	**-46**	**2,297**	**1,343**	**746**	**-1,237**	**400**	**-552**	**-227**	**72**	**-53**
of which short-term debt	..	..	-69	114	-1,502	86	-583	-513	-72	438
Interest payments (INT)	..	**790**	**1,233**	**1,447**	**1,364**	**892**	**1,229**	**1,225**	**1,308**	**1,400**
Long-term debt	37	350	917	1,134	1,048	661	1,047	1,050	1,167	1,259
IMF charges	0	18	10	13	15	11	14	12	10	9
Short-term debt	..	422	305	300	301	220	168	164	130	132
Net transfers on debt	..	**1,508**	**111**	**-701**	**-2,602**	**-492**	**-1,781**	**-1,452**	**-1,236**	**-1,453**
Total debt service paid (TDS)	..	**1,235**	**2,482**	**2,943**	**3,110**	**2,616**	**2,717**	**2,200**	**2,238**	**2,395**
Long-term debt	261	693	2,108	2,606	2,747	2,305	2,493	2,024	2,076	2,159
IMF repurchases and charges	9	121	69	37	62	92	55	12	32	105
Short-term debt (interest only)	..	422	305	300	301	220	168	164	130	132
2. AGGREGATE NET RESOURCE FLOWS AND NET TRANSFERS (LONG-TERM)										
NET RESOURCE FLOWS	**99**	**3,051**	**3,105**	**2,361**	**5,247**	**3,892**	**2,836**	**1,662**	**2,622**	**1,210**
Net flow of long-term debt (ex. IMF)	-54	2,337	1,471	656	312	312	-51	286	165	-396
Foreign direct investment (net)	0	548	1,190	1,250	734	253	459	493	1,256	598
Portfolio equity flows	0	0	0	0	0	0	0	0	10	2
Grants (excluding technical coop.)	153	165	444	455	4,201	3,327	2,428	883	1,192	1,006
Memo: technical coop. grants	14	156	597	712	813	758	828	981	599	750
NET TRANSFERS	**62**	**2,686**	**2,164**	**1,202**	**4,185**	**3,224**	**1,775**	**600**	**1,435**	**-72**
Interest on long-term debt	37	350	917	1,134	1,048	661	1,047	1,050	1,167	1,259
Profit remittances on FDI	0	15	24	25	14	7	14	13	20	23
3. MAJOR ECONOMIC AGGREGATES										
Gross national product (GNP)	7,618	21,453	30,818	33,469	34,330	32,309	35,316	39,160	42,298	46,525
Exports of goods & services (XGS)	991	9,212	11,196	12,482	13,670	15,323	17,740	16,167	15,585	16,397
of which workers remittances	29	2,696	3,384	3,532	3,743	3,751	5,478	4,960	5,073	5,060
Imports of goods & services (MGS)	1,447	9,745	12,525	13,662	15,398	15,437	15,042	15,959	16,121	17,354
International reserves (RES)	165	2,480	2,261	2,495	3,620	6,185	11,620	13,854	14,413	17,122
Current account balance	-452	-438	-1,329	-1,180	-1,728	-114	2,698	209	-536	-957
4. DEBT INDICATORS										
EDT / XGS (%)	..	207.7	414.8	368.2	244.3	215.6	178.0	192.4	212.0	208.1
EDT / GNP (%)	..	89.2	150.7	137.3	97.3	102.2	89.4	79.4	78.1	73.3
TDS / XGS (%)	..	13.4	22.2	23.6	22.7	17.1	15.3	13.6	14.4	14.6
INT / XGS (%)	..	8.6	11.0	11.6	10.0	5.8	6.9	7.6	8.4	8.5
INT / GNP (%)	..	3.7	4.0	4.3	4.0	2.8	3.5	3.1	3.1	3.0
RES / EDT (%)	..	13.0	4.9	5.4	10.8	18.7	36.8	44.5	43.6	50.2
RES / MGS (months)	1.4	3.1	2.2	2.2	2.8	4.8	9.3	10.4	10.7	11.8
Short-term / EDT (%)	..	21.1	14.8	17.2	13.3	9.4	8.0	6.4	5.9	7.0
Concessional / EDT (%)	..	42.5	31.1	32.0	37.5	50.9	54.8	58.4	59.8	60.2
Multilateral / EDT (%)	..	13.7	10.5	10.8	10.6	10.2	10.9	12.2	12.6	12.4

EGYPT

(US$ million, unless otherwise indicated)

	1970	1980	1988	1989	1990	1991	1992	1993	1994	1995
5. LONG-TERM DEBT										
DEBT OUTSTANDING (LDOD)	**1,351**	**14,693**	**39,381**	**37,918**	**28,828**	**29,806**	**28,857**	**28,905**	**30,913**	**31,638**
Public and publicly guaranteed	**1,351**	**14,428**	**37,771**	**36,358**	**27,349**	**28,956**	**28,257**	**28,405**	**30,538**	**31,325**
Official creditors	1,189	12,623	32,226	30,493	21,165	24,955	25,180	26,042	28,428	29,605
Multilateral	22	2,625	4,894	4,976	3,547	3,374	3,430	3,789	4,161	4,229
Concessional	0	1,901	2,780	2,847	1,454	1,393	1,414	1,556	1,734	1,906
Bilateral	1,167	9,997	27,332	25,517	17,618	21,581	21,750	22,252	24,268	25,376
Concessional	864	6,231	11,659	11,849	11,079	15,415	15,876	16,607	18,017	18,643
Private creditors	162	1,805	5,545	5,865	6,184	4,001	3,076	2,363	2,110	1,720
Bonds	0	132	52	1	0	0	0	0	0	0
Commercial banks	36	257	402	472	624	852	713	575	553	516
Other private	126	1,416	5,092	5,392	5,560	3,150	2,363	1,788	1,557	1,204
Private nonguaranteed	**0**	**265**	**1,610**	**1,560**	**1,479**	**850**	**600**	**500**	**375**	**313**
Bonds	0	0	0	0	0	0	0	0	0	0
Commercial banks	0	265	1,610	1,560	1,479	850	600	500	375	313
Memo:										
IBRD	22	421	1,515	1,448	1,480	1,382	1,381	1,357	1,411	1,320
IDA	0	307	900	905	921	915	904	912	961	1,035
DISBURSEMENTS	**170**	**2,680**	**2,662**	**2,128**	**2,010**	**1,956**	**1,395**	**1,261**	**1,074**	**504**
Public and publicly guaranteed	**170**	**2,554**	**2,482**	**1,986**	**1,959**	**1,917**	**1,375**	**1,241**	**1,014**	**504**
Official creditors	137	1,904	1,280	1,046	1,237	1,282	1,006	1,092	812	469
Multilateral	0	242	252	307	287	224	519	653	487	282
Concessional	0	63	27	90	92	48	128	177	189	199
Bilateral	137	1,662	1,028	739	950	1,058	487	438	325	187
Concessional	53	1,011	735	384	664	915	412	427	311	177
Private creditors	33	650	1,202	940	722	635	369	149	202	34
Bonds	0	30	0	0	0	0	0	0	0	0
Commercial banks	0	8	155	90	170	251	47	25	77	31
Other private	33	613	1,047	851	552	384	322	124	125	3
Private nonguaranteed	**0**	**126**	**180**	**142**	**51**	**39**	**20**	**20**	**60**	**0**
Bonds	0	0	0	0	0	0	0	0	0	0
Commercial banks	0	126	180	142	51	39	20	20	60	0
Memo:										
IBRD	0	169	110	105	92	100	237	144	149	42
IDA	0	41	21	13	8	3	8	19	50	83
PRINCIPAL REPAYMENTS	**225**	**343**	**1,191**	**1,473**	**1,698**	**1,644**	**1,446**	**975**	**909**	**900**
Public and publicly guaranteed	**225**	**297**	**1,044**	**1,281**	**1,566**	**1,455**	**1,176**	**855**	**724**	**838**
Official creditors	162	151	498	649	889	763	521	400	386	560
Multilateral	6	18	177	186	285	398	340	295	299	327
Concessional	0	0	15	16	63	110	73	34	36	43
Bilateral	156	134	321	463	604	365	181	105	88	233
Concessional	92	119	112	147	216	48	37	32	43	121
Private creditors	63	145	546	632	677	693	655	455	338	278
Bonds	0	4	1	51	1	0	0	0	0	0
Commercial banks	0	65	11	19	34	86	179	167	119	74
Other private	63	76	534	561	643	607	476	288	218	205
Private nonguaranteed	**0**	**46**	**147**	**192**	**132**	**189**	**270**	**120**	**185**	**62**
Bonds	0	0	0	0	0	0	0	0	0	0
Commercial banks	0	46	147	192	132	189	270	120	185	62
Memo:										
IBRD	6	7	138	139	176	213	187	189	191	198
IDA	0	0	4	5	7	11	11	12	12	14
NET FLOWS ON DEBT	**-54**	**2,337**	**1,471**	**656**	**312**	**312**	**-51**	**286**	**165**	**-396**
Public and publicly guaranteed	**-54**	**2,257**	**1,438**	**706**	**393**	**462**	**199**	**386**	**290**	**-334**
Official creditors	-24	1,753	782	397	348	520	485	692	426	-90
Multilateral	-6	224	75	121	2	-174	179	359	189	-44
Concessional	0	62	12	74	29	-62	56	143	153	156
Bilateral	-19	1,529	707	276	346	694	306	333	237	-46
Concessional	-39	892	623	236	449	867	375	395	268	56
Private creditors	-30	505	656	309	45	-58	-286	-306	-135	-244
Bonds	0	26	-1	-51	-1	0	0	0	0	0
Commercial banks	0	-58	144	70	136	165	-132	-142	-42	-43
Other private	-30	537	513	289	-91	-222	-154	-163	-93	-202
Private nonguaranteed	**0**	**80**	**33**	**-50**	**-81**	**-150**	**-250**	**-100**	**-125**	**-62**
Bonds	0	0	0	0	0	0	0	0	0	0
Commercial banks	0	80	33	-50	-81	-150	-250	-100	-125	-62
Memo:										
IBRD	-6	162	-28	-34	-84	-113	50	-45	-42	-156
IDA	0	41	17	8	1	-7	-3	8	38	69

EGYPT

(US$ million, unless otherwise indicated)

	1970	1980	1988	1989	1990	1991	1992	1993	1994	1995
INTEREST PAYMENTS (LINT)	**37**	**350**	**917**	**1,134**	**1,048**	**661**	**1,047**	**1,050**	**1,167**	**1,259**
Public and publicly guaranteed	**37**	**327**	**797**	**990**	**923**	**591**	**1,006**	**1,008**	**1,132**	**1,235**
Official creditors	30	221	654	803	731	404	856	882	1,030	1,129
Multilateral	2	40	188	156	189	216	188	201	222	236
Concessional	0	7	15	17	19	20	20	23	27	33
Bilateral	28	181	467	648	543	188	668	681	809	893
Concessional	18	146	116	189	194	65	376	401	448	545
Private creditors	7	106	143	187	192	188	150	125	102	106
Bonds	0	11	4	5	0	0	0	0	0	0
Commercial banks	0	36	26	40	45	57	48	32	31	40
Other private	7	59	112	143	146	130	102	93	72	66
Private nonguaranteed	**0**	**23**	**120**	**143**	**125**	**69**	**41**	**42**	**35**	**24**
Bonds	0	0	0	0	0	0	0	0	0	0
Commercial banks	0	23	120	143	125	69	41	42	35	24
Memo:										
IBRD	2	29	153	111	138	144	115	115	114	114
IDA	0	2	6	7	7	8	7	7	7	7
NET TRANSFERS ON DEBT	**-91**	**1,988**	**554**	**-478**	**-737**	**-348**	**-1,098**	**-763**	**-1,002**	**-1,655**
Public and publicly guaranteed	**-91**	**1,931**	**641**	**-285**	**-530**	**-129**	**-807**	**-621**	**-842**	**-1,569**
Official creditors	-54	1,532	128	-406	-384	116	-371	-191	-605	-1,219
Multilateral	-7	184	-113	-34	-187	-390	-9	157	-33	-280
Concessional	0	55	-2	57	10	-82	35	120	126	123
Bilateral	-47	1,348	240	-372	-196	506	-362	-348	-572	-939
Concessional	-57	746	507	48	255	802	-2	-6	-180	-489
Private creditors	-37	399	513	121	-147	-245	-436	-431	-237	-350
Bonds	0	15	-5	-56	-1	0	0	0	0	0
Commercial banks	0	-94	118	30	91	108	-180	-174	-73	-82
Other private	-37	478	401	146	-237	-353	-256	-256	-165	-268
Private nonguaranteed	**0**	**57**	**-87**	**-193**	**-206**	**-219**	**-291**	**-142**	**-160**	**-86**
Bonds	0	0	0	0	0	0	0	0	0	0
Commercial banks	0	57	-87	-193	-206	-219	-291	-142	-160	-86
Memo:										
IBRD	-7	133	-180	-145	-222	-257	-65	-160	-157	-270
IDA	0	39	11	1	-6	-15	-10	1	31	62
DEBT SERVICE (LTDS)	**261**	**693**	**2,108**	**2,606**	**2,747**	**2,305**	**2,493**	**2,024**	**2,076**	**2,159**
Public and publicly guaranteed	**261**	**624**	**1,840**	**2,271**	**2,489**	**2,047**	**2,182**	**1,862**	**1,856**	**2,073**
Official creditors	192	372	1,152	1,452	1,621	1,166	1,377	1,282	1,417	1,688
Multilateral	7	58	365	342	474	614	529	496	520	562
Concessional	0	8	29	33	82	130	93	57	63	76
Bilateral	184	315	787	1,110	1,147	552	848	786	896	1,126
Concessional	110	265	228	336	410	113	413	433	491	666
Private creditors	70	251	688	819	869	880	805	580	440	384
Bonds	0	15	5	56	1	0	0	0	0	0
Commercial banks	0	101	37	59	79	143	227	199	150	113
Other private	70	135	646	704	789	737	578	381	290	271
Private nonguaranteed	**0**	**69**	**267**	**335**	**257**	**258**	**311**	**162**	**220**	**86**
Bonds	0	0	0	0	0	0	0	0	0	0
Commercial banks	0	69	267	335	257	258	311	162	220	86
Memo:										
IBRD	7	36	291	250	314	356	302	304	306	312
IDA	0	3	10	12	14	18	18	19	19	21
UNDISBURSED DEBT	**315**	**4,999**	**4,909**	**5,177**	**4,656**	**5,002**	**4,934**	**4,110**	**3,511**	**2,947**
Official creditors	282	4,162	3,343	3,245	3,419	4,297	4,479	3,759	3,340	2,819
Private creditors	33	837	1,565	1,933	1,237	705	455	351	171	128
Memorandum items										
Concessional LDOD	864	8,131	14,439	14,696	12,533	16,808	17,290	18,163	19,751	20,549
Variable rate LDOD	0	663	4,614	4,968	4,877	2,563	1,971	1,719	1,673	1,560
Public sector LDOD	1,351	14,427	37,763	36,351	27,322	28,938	28,238	28,388	30,523	31,314
Private sector LDOD	0	266	1,617	1,567	1,506	868	618	517	390	324

6. CURRENCY COMPOSITION OF LONG-TERM DEBT (PERCENT)

	1970	1980	1988	1989	1990	1991	1992	1993	1994	1995
Deutsche mark	10.1	4.8	7.1	8.3	12.4	11.1	11.1	10.5	11.2	12.0
French franc	0.9	5.6	7.3	8.1	13.8	18.9	19.2	18.2	18.9	19.8
Japanese yen	0.0	4.0	6.2	5.7	8.2	10.8	11.4	12.9	13.7	12.8
Pound sterling	2.9	1.2	1.6	1.7	2.5	2.6	2.2	2.1	2.0	2.0
Swiss franc	2.4	1.3	1.9	1.9	3.0	2.6	2.4	2.3	2.4	2.6
U.S.dollars	23.0	73.0	63.8	61.2	41.9	37.6	37.5	37.3	34.4	33.5
Multiple currency	1.6	3.3	5.8	6.1	8.9	8.0	8.2	8.7	8.6	8.0
Special drawing rights	0.0	0.0	0.4	0.5	0.6	0.2	0.0	0.0	0.0	0.1
All other currencies	59.0	6.7	5.9	6.5	8.6	8.2	8.1	8.0	8.7	9.2

EGYPT

(US$ million, unless otherwise indicated)

	1970	1980	1988	1989	1990	1991	1992	1993	1994	1995
7. DEBT RESTRUCTURINGS										
Total amount rescheduled	0	0	1,261	0	0	17,010	699	555	448	404
Debt stock rescheduled	0	0	0	0	0	11,523	0	0	0	0
Principal rescheduled	0	0	636	0	0	3,663	545	420	351	281
Official	0	0	228	0	0	1,785	130	106	88	57
Private	0	0	408	0	0	1,878	415	315	263	224
Interest rescheduled	0	0	499	0	0	1,651	154	107	85	53
Official	0	0	357	0	0	1,054	36	25	25	11
Private	0	0	143	0	0	597	118	83	60	42
Debt forgiven	..	..	0	2,705	10,576	192	45	31	27	22
Memo: interest forgiven	..	..	0	0	2,481	72	144	142	80	4
Debt stock reduction	0	0	0	0	0	406	0	0	0	0
of which debt buyback	0	0	0	0	0	0	0	0	0	0
8. DEBT STOCK-FLOW RECONCILIATION										
Total change in debt stocks	..	..	..	-478	-12,561	-369	-1,458	-465	1,929	1,078
Net flows on debt	..	..	..	746	-1,237	400	-552	-227	72	-53
Net change in interest arrears	..	..	..	900	-1,933	-1,436	0	0	1	5
Interest capitalized	..	..	..	0	0	1,651	154	107	85	53
Debt forgiveness or reduction	..	..	..	-2,705	-10,576	-598	-45	-31	-27	-22
Cross-currency valuation	..	..	..	-78	1,763	34	-952	-282	1,873	1,036
Residual	..	..	..	660	-578	-420	-62	-33	-76	59
9. AVERAGE TERMS OF NEW COMMITMENTS										
ALL CREDITORS										
Interest (%)	5.2	5.0	6.2	7.2	5.3	4.6	4.0	2.5	2.2	2.4
Maturity (years)	14.2	26.6	18.2	15.0	25.5	23.0	25.6	28.3	32.9	25.3
Grace period (years)	7.8	6.6	5.5	4.2	6.9	6.8	7.0	6.7	8.3	7.0
Grant element (%)	26.5	38.9	27.3	19.7	36.0	40.1	45.2	57.1	63.6	54.9
Official creditors										
Interest (%)	5.2	3.3	5.2	4.5	4.7	4.4	4.0	2.2	2.1	2.4
Maturity (years)	14.9	36.4	23.8	22.2	28.2	24.1	26.1	30.0	33.4	25.6
Grace period (years)	8.2	8.9	6.9	6.7	7.6	7.1	7.1	7.0	8.5	7.0
Grant element (%)	27.5	56.9	37.6	40.4	41.7	42.4	45.7	60.6	64.7	55.6
Private creditors										
Interest (%)	5.9	7.9	8.3	9.5	8.4	7.0	4.0	6.2	7.0	6.5
Maturity (years)	4.7	9.5	6.4	9.0	11.5	9.3	20.6	6.8	11.8	4.3
Grace period (years)	1.5	2.5	2.6	2.1	3.4	2.1	6.7	2.5	0.1	2.4
Grant element (%)	10.6	7.7	6.0	2.2	6.9	10.3	40.4	12.3	13.0	7.7
Memorandum items										
Commitments	306	2,176	2,708	2,401	1,228	2,830	1,716	842	326	100
Official creditors	288	1,378	1,830	1,100	1,027	2,620	1,550	780	318	99
Private creditors	18	798	878	1,301	201	210	166	62	8	1

10. CONTRACTUAL OBLIGATIONS ON OUTSTANDING LONG-TERM DEBT

	1996	1997	1998	1999	2000	2001	2002	2003	2004	2005
TOTAL										
Disbursements	975	748	470	286	162	104	60	44	30	22
Principal	1,083	1,101	1,111	1,243	1,136	1,125	1,159	1,178	1,244	1,364
Interest	1,342	1,301	1,269	1,214	1,152	1,101	1,049	996	943	889
Official creditors										
Disbursements	900	718	460	285	161	104	60	44	30	22
Principal	703	760	805	920	1,035	1,073	1,119	1,141	1,217	1,346
Interest	1,233	1,216	1,206	1,173	1,131	1,086	1,038	987	937	884
Bilateral creditors										
Disbursements	329	259	154	91	47	25	10	4	0	0
Principal	306	362	434	539	685	739	799	836	927	1,072
Interest	1,007	1,001	1,003	986	964	937	906	872	835	796
Multilateral creditors										
Disbursements	570	459	306	194	114	79	51	40	30	22
Principal	398	398	371	381	350	334	320	306	290	274
Interest	226	215	203	187	167	149	132	116	102	88
Private creditors										
Disbursements	75	30	10	2	0	0	0	0	0	0
Principal	380	341	306	323	101	52	39	36	27	18
Interest	109	85	63	42	21	15	12	9	7	5
Commercial banks										
Disbursements	37	17	5	1	0	0	0	0	0	0
Principal	109	111	111	110	46	23	22	20	14	7
Interest	37	30	23	15	9	6	4	3	1	1
Other private										
Disbursements	39	14	6	1	0	0	0	0	0	0
Principal	271	231	195	213	55	29	18	16	14	11
Interest	72	55	40	27	13	9	7	6	5	5

EL SALVADOR

(US$ million, unless otherwise indicated)

1. SUMMARY DEBT DATA

	1970	1980	1988	1989	1990	1991	1992	1993	1994	1995
TOTAL DEBT STOCKS (EDT)	**..**	**911**	**1,994**	**2,078**	**2,147**	**2,180**	**2,261**	**2,012**	**2,188**	**2,583**
Long-term debt (LDOD)	**176**	**659**	**1,740**	**1,865**	**1,938**	**2,078**	**2,159**	**1,905**	**2,002**	**2,060**
Public and publicly guaranteed	88	499	1,685	1,826	1,912	2,057	2,147	1,897	1,994	2,055
Private nonguaranteed	88	161	55	39	26	21	12	8	8	5
Use of IMF credit	**7**	**32**	**11**	**5**	**0**	**0**	**0**	**0**	**0**	**0**
Short-term debt	**..**	**220**	**243**	**208**	**209**	**102**	**102**	**107**	**185**	**523**
of which interest arrears on LDOD	..	0	9	23	6	6	14	5	0	0
Official creditors	..	0	9	21	6	6	13	5	0	0
Private creditors	..	0	0	1	0	0	1	0	0	0
Memo: principal arrears on LDOD	..	0	11	31	7	10	18	3	0	0
Official creditors	..	0	11	29	7	10	18	3	0	0
Private creditors	..	0	0	2	0	0	0	0	0	0
Memo: export credits	..	..	279	231	236	248	197	282	337	367
TOTAL DEBT FLOWS										
Disbursements	**31**	**149**	**144**	**237**	**109**	**276**	**247**	**467**	**293**	**189**
Long-term debt	31	110	144	237	109	276	247	467	293	189
IMF purchases	0	40	0	0	0	0	0	0	0	0
Principal repayments	**27**	**35**	**124**	**102**	**124**	**167**	**149**	**170**	**242**	**158**
Long-term debt	22	35	114	97	119	167	149	170	242	158
IMF repurchases	5	0	11	5	5	0	0	0	0	0
Net flows on debt	**4**	**114**	**45**	**86**	**3**	**2**	**91**	**309**	**135**	**368**
of which short-term debt	..	..	25	-49	18	-107	-7	13	83	337
Interest payments (INT)	**..**	**61**	**78**	**69**	**84**	**81**	**84**	**122**	**99**	**123**
Long-term debt	9	36	72	61	75	72	80	117	91	101
IMF charges	0	0	0	0	0	0	0	0	0	0
Short-term debt	..	25	6	8	9	10	4	5	8	22
Net transfers on debt	**..**	**53**	**-34**	**17**	**-81**	**-80**	**7**	**187**	**36**	**245**
Total debt service paid (TDS)	**..**	**96**	**203**	**171**	**209**	**248**	**233**	**293**	**341**	**281**
Long-term debt	31	71	186	158	194	239	229	288	333	259
IMF repurchases and charges	5	0	11	5	5	0	0	0	0	0
Short-term debt (interest only)	..	25	6	8	9	10	4	5	8	22

2. AGGREGATE NET RESOURCE FLOWS AND NET TRANSFERS (LONG-TERM)

	1970	1980	1988	1989	1990	1991	1992	1993	1994	1995
NET RESOURCE FLOWS	**14**	**111**	**294**	**352**	**152**	**254**	**336**	**923**	**158**	**170**
Net flow of long-term debt (ex. IMF)	9	74	30	140	-10	109	98	296	51	31
Foreign direct investment (net)	4	6	17	13	2	25	15	16	20	38
Portfolio equity flows	0	0	0	0	0	0	0	0	0	0
Grants (excluding technical coop.)	1	31	247	199	160	120	223	611	87	101
Memo: technical coop. grants	6	9	108	138	127	121	165	173	194	140
NET TRANSFERS	**-2**	**34**	**185**	**253**	**49**	**146**	**230**	**781**	**43**	**43**
Interest on long-term debt	9	36	72	61	75	72	80	117	91	101
Profit remittances on FDI	7	41	37	38	28	36	26	25	24	26

3. MAJOR ECONOMIC AGGREGATES

	1970	1980	1988	1989	1990	1991	1992	1993	1994	1995
Gross national product (GNP)	1,123	3,490	4,069	4,251	4,705	5,211	5,904	6,939	8,124	9,569
Exports of goods & services (XGS)	..	1,282	1,157	1,163	1,360	1,395	1,694	1,958	2,642	3,164
of which workers remittances	..	11	194	228	358	467	687	789	967	1,061
Imports of goods & services (MGS)	..	1,289	1,438	1,740	1,785	1,765	2,054	2,291	2,982	3,562
International reserves (RES)	64	382	354	454	596	453	579	720	829	940
Current account balance	..	34	-129	-370	-261	-212	-195	-118	-18	-70

4. DEBT INDICATORS

	1970	1980	1988	1989	1990	1991	1992	1993	1994	1995
EDT / XGS (%)	..	71.1	172.3	178.7	157.8	156.3	133.5	102.8	82.8	81.6
EDT / GNP (%)	..	26.1	49.0	48.9	45.6	41.8	38.3	29.0	26.9	27.0
TDS / XGS (%)	..	7.5	17.5	14.7	15.3	17.8	13.7	14.9	12.9	8.9
INT / XGS (%)	..	4.7	6.8	5.9	6.2	5.8	5.0	6.2	3.7	3.9
INT / GNP (%)	..	1.7	1.9	1.6	1.8	1.6	1.4	1.8	1.2	1.3
RES / EDT (%)	..	41.9	17.8	21.9	27.7	20.8	25.6	35.8	37.9	36.4
RES / MGS (months)	..	3.6	3.0	3.1	4.0	3.1	3.4	3.8	3.3	3.2
Short-term / EDT (%)	..	24.1	12.2	10.0	9.7	4.7	4.5	5.3	8.5	20.2
Concessional / EDT (%)	..	26.0	51.6	56.1	57.3	59.3	58.8	51.7	50.3	43.7
Multilateral / EDT (%)	..	28.3	36.3	37.3	36.5	38.3	40.7	52.4	57.2	52.4

EL SALVADOR

(US$ million, unless otherwise indicated)

	1970	1980	1988	1989	1990	1991	1992	1993	1994	1995
5. LONG-TERM DEBT										
DEBT OUTSTANDING (LDOD)	**176**	**659**	**1,740**	**1,865**	**1,938**	**2,078**	**2,159**	**1,905**	**2,002**	**2,060**
Public and publicly guaranteed	**88**	**499**	**1,685**	**1,826**	**1,912**	**2,057**	**2,147**	**1,897**	**1,994**	**2,055**
Official creditors	70	487	1,596	1,678	1,744	1,870	1,966	1,713	1,868	1,954
Multilateral	41	258	724	775	784	835	921	1,055	1,252	1,353
Concessional	34	153	353	416	433	453	491	551	621	638
Bilateral	30	229	871	903	960	1,034	1,045	658	617	601
Concessional	29	84	676	750	797	839	839	489	480	491
Private creditors	17	12	89	148	168	187	181	185	126	101
Bonds	3	0	0	0	0	0	0	0	0	0
Commercial banks	14	8	68	111	127	151	135	146	94	74
Other private	0	4	21	37	41	36	46	38	32	27
Private nonguaranteed	**88**	**161**	**55**	**39**	**26**	**21**	**12**	**8**	**8**	**5**
Bonds	0	0	0	0	0	0	0	0	0	0
Commercial banks	88	161	55	39	26	21	12	8	8	5
Memo:										
IBRD	25	87	155	142	140	189	182	220	290	307
IDA	8	27	24	24	23	23	22	22	21	20
DISBURSEMENTS	**31**	**110**	**144**	**237**	**109**	**276**	**247**	**467**	**293**	**189**
Public and publicly guaranteed	**8**	**110**	**144**	**237**	**109**	**276**	**247**	**467**	**289**	**189**
Official creditors	6	105	126	171	79	186	233	435	271	183
Multilateral	5	36	54	78	44	98	151	191	268	160
Concessional	3	17	23	68	33	32	53	72	81	32
Bilateral	2	69	72	93	35	87	83	245	3	24
Concessional	2	20	59	83	20	43	23	218	2	23
Private creditors	1	5	18	65	30	90	13	31	19	5
Bonds	0	0	0	0	0	0	0	0	0	0
Commercial banks	1	3	11	50	25	90	0	31	19	5
Other private	0	2	7	15	5	0	13	1	0	0
Private nonguaranteed	**24**	**0**	**0**	**0**	**0**	**0**	**0**	**0**	**4**	**0**
Bonds	0	0	0	0	0	0	0	0	0	0
Commercial banks	24	0	0	0	0	0	0	0	4	0
Memo:										
IBRD	1	10	13	1	3	56	11	51	70	26
IDA	0	3	0	0	0	0	0	0	0	0
PRINCIPAL REPAYMENTS	**22**	**35**	**114**	**97**	**119**	**167**	**149**	**170**	**242**	**158**
Public and publicly guaranteed	**6**	**17**	**99**	**81**	**105**	**162**	**139**	**167**	**238**	**155**
Official creditors	3	8	82	73	94	93	121	140	159	123
Multilateral	3	5	32	33	56	52	59	62	106	76
Concessional	2	3	8	6	13	12	15	12	15	16
Bilateral	0	3	50	40	38	41	62	79	53	47
Concessional	0	1	7	7	9	12	15	24	19	19
Private creditors	3	10	17	8	11	69	19	27	79	32
Bonds	0	0	0	0	0	0	0	0	0	0
Commercial banks	3	2	14	7	9	66	16	20	71	26
Other private	0	8	3	1	2	3	3	7	8	6
Private nonguaranteed	**16**	**18**	**15**	**16**	**14**	**5**	**9**	**4**	**4**	**3**
Bonds	0	0	0	0	0	0	0	0	0	0
Commercial banks	16	18	15	16	14	5	9	4	4	3
Memo:										
IBRD	2	3	11	9	15	12	13	17	19	21
IDA	0	0	1	0	1	1	1	1	1	1
NET FLOWS ON DEBT	**9**	**74**	**30**	**140**	**-10**	**109**	**98**	**296**	**51**	**31**
Public and publicly guaranteed	**2**	**92**	**45**	**156**	**4**	**114**	**107**	**300**	**51**	**34**
Official creditors	3	97	44	98	-15	92	113	295	111	61
Multilateral	2	31	22	46	-12	46	91	129	161	83
Concessional	2	14	15	62	21	20	38	59	65	16
Bilateral	2	66	22	53	-3	46	21	166	-50	-23
Concessional	2	18	52	76	11	31	8	195	-18	5
Private creditors	-2	-5	1	58	19	21	-5	5	-60	-26
Bonds	0	0	0	0	0	0	0	0	0	0
Commercial banks	-2	1	-3	43	16	24	-16	11	-52	-20
Other private	0	-6	4	14	3	-3	11	-7	-8	-6
Private nonguaranteed	**8**	**-18**	**-15**	**-16**	**-14**	**-5**	**-9**	**-4**	**0**	**-3**
Bonds	0	0	0	0	0	0	0	0	0	0
Commercial banks	8	-18	-15	-16	-14	-5	-9	-4	0	-3
Memo:										
IBRD	-1	8	3	-9	-13	44	-1	34	52	5
IDA	0	3	-1	0	-1	-1	-1	-1	-1	-1

EL SALVADOR

(US$ million, unless otherwise indicated)

	1970	1980	1988	1989	1990	1991	1992	1993	1994	1995
INTEREST PAYMENTS (LINT)	**9**	**36**	**72**	**61**	**75**	**72**	**80**	**117**	**91**	**101**
Public and publicly guaranteed	**4**	**25**	**67**	**57**	**72**	**69**	**79**	**117**	**91**	**101**
Official creditors	2	22	59	50	63	56	69	107	82	92
Multilateral	2	11	33	31	50	38	42	45	56	62
Concessional	2	3	6	5	11	9	11	10	11	12
Bilateral	0	11	26	19	13	18	27	62	26	31
Concessional	0	2	10	13	9	6	14	46	14	16
Private creditors	1	2	8	6	10	13	10	10	8	9
Bonds	0	0	0	0	0	0	0	0	0	0
Commercial banks	1	1	6	4	8	11	8	7	6	7
Other private	0	1	2	2	2	2	2	2	2	2
Private nonguaranteed	**6**	**11**	**6**	**4**	**3**	**2**	**1**	**0**	**0**	**0**
Bonds	0	0	0	0	0	0	0	0	0	0
Commercial banks	6	11	6	4	3	2	1	0	0	0
Memo:										
IBRD	1	7	12	10	14	11	14	15	17	22
IDA	0	0	0	0	0	0	0	0	0	0
NET TRANSFERS ON DEBT	**0**	**39**	**-42**	**79**	**-85**	**37**	**18**	**179**	**-40**	**-70**
Public and publicly guaranteed	**-2**	**68**	**-22**	**99**	**-68**	**44**	**28**	**183**	**-39**	**-67**
Official creditors	1	75	-15	48	-78	36	44	188	29	-32
Multilateral	0	20	-11	15	-62	8	50	84	105	22
Concessional	0	11	9	56	10	11	27	49	55	3
Bilateral	1	55	-4	33	-16	28	-6	104	-76	-54
Concessional	2	16	42	63	2	24	-7	148	-32	-12
Private creditors	-3	-7	-7	51	10	8	-16	-5	-69	-35
Bonds	0	0	0	0	0	0	0	0	0	0
Commercial banks	-3	0	-9	39	8	13	-24	4	-59	-27
Other private	0	-7	2	12	2	-5	8	-9	-10	-8
Private nonguaranteed	**2**	**-29**	**-20**	**-20**	**-17**	**-7**	**-11**	**-4**	**0**	**-4**
Bonds	0	0	0	0	0	0	0	0	0	0
Commercial banks	2	-29	-20	-20	-17	-7	-11	-4	0	-4
Memo:										
IBRD	-2	0	-9	-19	-27	33	-15	19	35	-17
IDA	0	3	-1	0	-1	-1	-1	-1	-1	-1
DEBT SERVICE (LTDS)	**31**	**71**	**186**	**158**	**194**	**239**	**229**	**288**	**333**	**259**
Public and publicly guaranteed	**9**	**42**	**166**	**137**	**177**	**232**	**219**	**284**	**329**	**256**
Official creditors	5	30	141	123	157	150	190	248	242	215
Multilateral	5	16	65	63	106	91	101	107	163	138
Concessional	3	6	14	11	24	21	25	22	26	28
Bilateral	1	14	76	60	51	59	89	141	79	77
Concessional	0	3	17	20	18	18	29	70	33	35
Private creditors	4	12	25	14	21	82	29	36	87	40
Bonds	0	0	0	0	0	0	0	0	0	0
Commercial banks	4	3	20	11	17	77	24	27	77	32
Other private	0	9	5	3	4	5	5	10	10	8
Private nonguaranteed	**22**	**29**	**20**	**20**	**17**	**7**	**11**	**4**	**4**	**4**
Bonds	0	0	0	0	0	0	0	0	0	0
Commercial banks	22	29	20	20	17	7	11	4	4	4
Memo:										
IBRD	4	10	22	20	29	23	27	32	36	43
IDA	0	0	1	0	1	1	1	1	1	1
UNDISBURSED DEBT	**38**	**421**	**497**	**304**	**322**	**514**	**700**	**817**	**698**	**1,324**
Official creditors	38	397	475	298	320	512	665	793	693	1,262
Private creditors	0	24	22	7	2	2	35	24	5	62
Memorandum items										
Concessional LDOD	63	236	1,029	1,166	1,230	1,292	1,330	1,039	1,101	1,128
Variable rate LDOD	88	181	134	182	192	292	289	337	359	405
Public sector LDOD	88	496	1,676	1,817	1,904	2,049	2,140	1,890	1,987	2,049
Private sector LDOD	88	163	64	48	34	29	19	15	15	11

6. CURRENCY COMPOSITION OF LONG-TERM DEBT (PERCENT)

	1970	1980	1988	1989	1990	1991	1992	1993	1994	1995
Deutsche mark	0.0	0.2	2.2	3.0	3.8	3.5	3.2	3.6	3.9	4.1
French franc	0.0	5.5	1.6	2.3	3.3	3.1	2.8	2.5	2.4	2.4
Japanese yen	0.0	3.6	0.3	1.1	1.3	1.2	1.0	1.0	0.8	1.8
Pound sterling	0.0	0.3	0.0	0.0	0.0	0.0	0.0	0.0	0.0	0.0
Swiss franc	0.0	0.0	0.0	0.0	0.0	0.0	0.0	0.0	0.0	0.0
U.S.dollars	65.2	37.8	56.8	57.2	56.6	57.1	59.3	52.4	50.9	50.2
Multiple currency	31.1	32.6	35.8	34.8	33.6	33.6	32.5	39.5	41.0	40.6
Special drawing rights	0.0	0.0	0.0	0.0	0.0	0.0	0.0	0.0	0.2	0.3
All other currencies	3.6	20.1	3.4	1.6	1.4	1.5	1.2	1.0	0.7	0.6

EL SALVADOR

(US$ million, unless otherwise indicated)

	1970	1980	1988	1989	1990	1991	1992	1993	1994	1995
7. DEBT RESTRUCTURINGS										
Total amount rescheduled	0	0	0	17	86	49	0	156	0	0
Debt stock rescheduled	0	0	0	0	0	0	0	156	0	0
Principal rescheduled	0	0	0	4	42	22	0	0	0	0
Official	0	0	0	4	40	21	0	0	0	0
Private	0	0	0	0	2	1	0	0	0	0
Interest rescheduled	0	0	0	4	43	15	0	0	0	0
Official	0	0	0	4	40	14	0	0	0	0
Private	0	0	0	0	3	1	0	0	0	0
Debt forgiven	..	..	0	0	0	0	0	500	0	0
Memo: interest forgiven	..	..	0	0	0	0	0	0	0	0
Debt stock reduction	0	0	0	0	0	0	0	47	0	0
of which debt buyback	0	0	0	0	0	0	0	0	0	0
8. DEBT STOCK-FLOW RECONCILIATION										
Total change in debt stocks	..	..	..	84	69	34	81	-250	176	395
Net flows on debt	..	..	..	86	3	2	91	309	135	368
Net change in interest arrears	..	..	..	13	-17	0	7	-8	-5	0
Interest capitalized	..	..	..	4	43	15	0	0	0	0
Debt forgiveness or reduction	..	..	..	0	0	0	0	-546	0	0
Cross-currency valuation	..	..	..	-14	26	-1	-21	-7	29	15
Residual	..	..	..	-5	13	18	4	4	17	12
9. AVERAGE TERMS OF NEW COMMITMENTS										
ALL CREDITORS										
Interest (%)	4.7	4.2	2.9	8.0	4.6	6.4	6.1	5.0	3.8	6.6
Maturity (years)	23.4	27.6	36.1	11.3	29.8	17.3	20.4	22.3	24.2	22.5
Grace period (years)	6.0	8.4	9.2	5.6	7.2	4.9	5.3	4.8	7.6	5.2
Grant element (%)	37.6	45.8	60.1	12.8	45.5	22.6	24.4	30.8	45.9	22.1
Official creditors										
Interest (%)	4.4	3.3	2.8	5.3	3.2	6.2	6.1	5.0	3.8	6.5
Maturity (years)	25.0	28.4	37.2	20.8	35.6	20.4	22.2	22.8	24.2	21.9
Grace period (years)	6.5	8.9	9.5	6.4	8.8	5.1	5.7	4.9	7.6	5.1
Grant element (%)	40.7	53.5	62.0	32.3	56.6	25.7	26.3	31.3	45.9	22.6
Private creditors										
Interest (%)	7.5	11.7	7.0	9.8	10.4	7.1	6.8	4.1	0.0	7.1
Maturity (years)	7.2	20.7	8.0	5.0	5.0	4.2	5.4	7.2	0.0	29.9
Grace period (years)	0.7	4.3	1.0	5.0	0.5	4.2	1.9	0.8	0.0	6.9
Grant element (%)	6.9	-17.3	9.5	0.0	-1.4	9.6	8.1	17.6	0.0	16.6
Memorandum items										
Commitments	12	225	300	83	131	470	439	624	161	820
Official creditors	11	200	290	33	106	380	393	604	161	758
Private creditors	1	25	11	50	25	90	46	20	0	62

10. CONTRACTUAL OBLIGATIONS ON OUTSTANDING LONG-TERM DEBT

	1996	1997	1998	1999	2000	2001	2002	2003	2004	2005
TOTAL										
Disbursements	300	363	257	181	114	64	30	7	6	2
Principal	187	143	150	149	148	182	177	179	165	156
Interest	108	121	128	131	129	124	116	106	96	88
Official creditors										
Disbursements	276	340	246	177	113	64	30	7	6	2
Principal	121	126	133	136	141	180	175	179	164	154
Interest	101	115	123	126	125	120	112	103	93	85
Bilateral creditors										
Disbursements	47	57	38	25	15	10	5	2	2	0
Principal	35	27	27	29	32	36	38	44	35	35
Interest	23	23	24	24	23	21	20	18	16	15
Multilateral creditors										
Disbursements	229	283	208	152	98	54	25	5	4	2
Principal	86	98	106	107	109	144	138	135	129	119
Interest	78	92	99	102	103	99	92	85	77	70
Private creditors										
Disbursements	24	23	11	4	1	0	0	0	0	0
Principal	66	17	17	13	7	2	1	1	1	2
Interest	7	6	5	5	4	4	3	3	3	3
Commercial banks										
Disbursements	10	7	3	1	0	0	0	0	0	0
Principal	56	12	12	9	3	2	1	0	0	0
Interest	4	2	2	1	0	0	0	0	0	0
Other private										
Disbursements	14	16	8	3	1	0	0	0	0	0
Principal	10	5	5	4	4	1	1	1	1	2
Interest	3	4	4	4	4	3	3	3	3	3

EQUATORIAL GUINEA

(US$ million, unless otherwise indicated)

	1970	1980	1988	1989	1990	1991	1992	1993	1994	1995
1. SUMMARY DEBT DATA										
TOTAL DEBT STOCKS (EDT)	..	**75.6**	**210.6**	**229.1**	**241.1**	**253.8**	**255.3**	**264.1**	**287.6**	**293.0**
Long-term debt (LDOD)	**5.0**	**52.5**	**184.5**	**205.4**	**209.2**	**215.5**	**214.4**	**214.8**	**219.3**	**229.6**
Public and publicly guaranteed	5.0	52.5	184.5	205.4	209.2	215.5	214.4	214.8	219.3	229.6
Private nonguaranteed	0.0	0.0	0.0	0.0	0.0	0.0	0.0	0.0	0.0	0.0
Use of IMF credit	**0.0**	**16.1**	**14.3**	**8.8**	**5.8**	**13.2**	**12.6**	**16.4**	**19.6**	**18.9**
Short-term debt	..	**7.0**	**11.9**	**14.9**	**26.0**	**25.1**	**28.3**	**32.9**	**48.6**	**44.6**
of which interest arrears on LDOD	..	0.0	9.4	12.5	19.7	24.9	28.0	32.6	37.6	42.6
Official creditors	..	0.0	8.9	11.1	17.3	21.8	24.5	28.4	32.7	37.1
Private creditors	..	0.0	0.6	1.3	2.3	3.1	3.5	4.2	4.9	5.4
Memo: principal arrears on LDOD	..	5.6	20.2	20.8	28.4	44.2	54.6	56.1	71.9	94.3
Official creditors	..	5.6	15.4	17.5	24.4	37.3	45.8	47.7	59.8	77.7
Private creditors	..	0.0	4.8	3.3	4.0	6.9	8.8	8.4	12.1	16.7
Memo: export credits	..	..	36.0	38.0	37.0	33.0	63.0	84.0	103.0	73.0
TOTAL DEBT FLOWS										
Disbursements	**0.0**	**37.6**	**26.5**	**19.1**	**9.9**	**16.4**	**14.5**	**13.4**	**6.6**	**2.2**
Long-term debt	0.0	19.6	21.5	19.1	9.9	8.8	14.5	9.6	4.0	2.2
IMF purchases	0.0	18.0	4.9	0.0	0.0	7.6	0.0	3.9	2.6	0.0
Principal repayments	**0.0**	**1.7**	**2.7**	**5.0**	**4.2**	**2.3**	**2.0**	**0.5**	**0.7**	**1.3**
Long-term debt	0.0	1.7	1.1	0.0	0.6	1.7	2.0	0.5	0.1	0.2
IMF repurchases	0.0	0.0	1.6	5.0	3.6	0.6	0.0	0.0	0.5	1.1
Net flows on debt	**0.0**	**35.9**	**22.1**	**14.1**	**9.8**	**8.0**	**12.5**	**12.9**	**16.7**	**-8.1**
of which short-term debt	..	..	-1.6	0.0	4.0	-6.1	0.0	0.0	10.8	-9.0
Interest payments (INT)	..	**0.8**	**2.5**	**0.9**	**0.9**	**1.7**	**1.1**	**0.7**	**1.4**	**0.8**
Long-term debt	0.0	0.1	1.8	0.2	0.5	1.6	1.0	0.6	0.8	0.4
IMF charges	0.0	0.2	0.4	0.5	0.2	0.1	0.1	0.1	0.0	0.1
Short-term debt	..	0.6	0.3	0.2	0.2	0.0	0.0	0.0	0.5	0.3
Net transfers on debt	..	**35.0**	**19.7**	**13.2**	**8.8**	**6.3**	**11.4**	**12.2**	**15.4**	**-8.9**
Total debt service paid (TDS)	..	**2.6**	**5.2**	**5.9**	**5.1**	**4.0**	**3.1**	**1.2**	**2.0**	**2.1**
Long-term debt	0.0	1.8	2.9	0.2	1.1	3.3	3.0	1.1	0.9	0.6
IMF repurchases and charges	0.0	0.2	2.0	5.5	3.8	0.6	0.1	0.1	0.6	1.2
Short-term debt (interest only)	..	0.6	0.3	0.2	0.2	0.0	0.0	0.0	0.5	0.3
2. AGGREGATE NET RESOURCE FLOWS AND NET TRANSFERS (LONG-TERM)										
NET RESOURCE FLOWS	**0.0**	**19.2**	**36.0**	**46.1**	**62.9**	**59.1**	**55.4**	**46.7**	**40.8**	**18.0**
Net flow of long-term debt (ex. IMF)	0.0	17.8	20.4	19.1	9.4	7.1	12.5	9.1	3.8	2.0
Foreign direct investment (net)	0.0	0.0	0.0	-0.3	10.0	42.0	20.0	23.0	26.0	1.0
Portfolio equity flows	0.0	0.0	0.0	0.0	0.0	0.0	0.0	0.0	0.0	0.0
Grants (excluding technical coop.)	0.0	1.4	15.6	27.3	43.5	10.0	22.9	14.6	11.0	15.0
Memo: technical coop. grants	0.0	1.9	10.1	12.4	14.0	34.1	24.0	21.3	13.6	17.5
NET TRANSFERS	**-0.6**	**19.2**	**34.2**	**45.9**	**62.4**	**57.5**	**54.4**	**46.0**	**40.1**	**17.7**
Interest on long-term debt	0.0	0.1	1.8	0.2	0.5	1.6	1.0	0.6	0.8	0.4
Profit remittances on FDI	0.6	0.0	0.0	0.0	0.0	0.0	0.0	0.0	0.0	0.0
3. MAJOR ECONOMIC AGGREGATES										
Gross national product (GNP)	66.9	..	121.5	106.6	126.4	124.8	148.5	148.1	112.0	149.9
Exports of goods & services (XGS)	..	..	50.5	38.6	42.3	42.0	55.2	56.0	66.8	85.2
of which workers remittances	..	..	0.0	0.0	0.0	0.0	0.0	0.0	0.0	0.0
Imports of goods & services (MGS)	..	..	113.1	83.4	99.2	127.7	102.2	102.4	77.9	190.1
International reserves (RES)	..	..	5.5	0.8	0.7	9.5	13.4	0.5	0.4	..
Current account balance	..	..	-20.6	-21.0	-19.0	-103.2	..	..	..	..
4. DEBT INDICATORS										
EDT / XGS (%)	..	..	417.0	593.5	569.9	604.2	462.5	471.6	430.5	343.9
EDT / GNP (%)	..	..	173.3	214.9	190.7	203.3	171.9	178.3	256.8	195.5
TDS / XGS (%)	..	..	10.3	15.2	12.1	9.5	5.6	2.2	3.0	2.5
INT / XGS (%)	..	..	4.9	2.3	2.2	4.0	2.0	1.3	2.0	0.9
INT / GNP (%)	..	..	2.0	0.8	0.7	1.3	0.8	0.5	1.2	0.5
RES / EDT (%)	..	..	2.6	0.3	0.3	3.7	5.2	0.2	0.1	..
RES / MGS (months)	..	..	0.6	0.1	0.1	0.9	1.6	0.1	0.1	..
Short-term / EDT (%)	..	9.3	5.6	6.5	10.8	9.9	11.1	12.4	16.9	15.2
Concessional / EDT (%)	..	41.7	49.4	55.6	51.3	51.9	54.2	55.0	51.7	52.9
Multilateral / EDT (%)	..	3.6	22.3	25.8	27.9	28.1	31.4	33.8	33.7	34.6

EQUATORIAL GUINEA

(US$ million, unless otherwise indicated)

	1970	1980	1988	1989	1990	1991	1992	1993	1994	1995
5. LONG-TERM DEBT										
DEBT OUTSTANDING (LDOD)	**5.0**	**52.5**	**184.5**	**205.4**	**209.2**	**215.5**	**214.4**	**214.8**	**219.3**	**229.6**
Public and publicly guaranteed	**5.0**	**52.5**	**184.5**	**205.4**	**209.2**	**215.5**	**214.4**	**214.8**	**219.3**	**229.6**
Official creditors	5.0	45.3	166.6	189.6	191.5	198.0	198.4	199.9	203.6	212.8
Multilateral	0.0	2.7	46.9	59.0	67.4	71.4	80.2	89.1	96.8	101.4
Concessional	0.0	2.0	39.0	51.1	58.2	63.4	74.1	83.6	91.7	96.1
Bilateral	5.0	42.6	119.7	130.5	124.1	126.7	118.2	110.7	106.8	111.5
Concessional	0.0	29.5	65.1	76.3	65.5	68.2	64.3	61.6	56.9	59.1
Private creditors	0.0	7.2	17.8	15.8	17.8	17.4	16.0	15.0	15.7	16.8
Bonds	0.0	0.0	0.0	0.0	0.0	0.0	0.0	0.0	0.0	0.0
Commercial banks	0.0	0.0	0.0	0.0	0.0	0.0	0.0	0.0	0.0	0.0
Other private	0.0	7.2	17.8	15.8	17.8	17.4	16.0	15.0	15.7	16.8
Private nonguaranteed	**0.0**	**0.0**	**0.0**	**0.0**	**0.0**	**0.0**	**0.0**	**0.0**	**0.0**	**0.0**
Bonds	0.0	0.0	0.0	0.0	0.0	0.0	0.0	0.0	0.0	0.0
Commercial banks	0.0	0.0	0.0	0.0	0.0	0.0	0.0	0.0	0.0	0.0
Memo:										
IBRD	0.0	0.0	0.0	0.0	0.0	0.0	0.0	0.0	0.0	0.0
IDA	0.0	0.0	25.4	32.8	37.6	40.4	41.2	45.3	49.9	53.1
DISBURSEMENTS	**0.0**	**19.6**	**21.5**	**19.1**	**9.9**	**8.8**	**14.5**	**9.6**	**4.0**	**2.2**
Public and publicly guaranteed	**0.0**	**19.6**	**21.5**	**19.1**	**9.9**	**8.8**	**14.5**	**9.6**	**4.0**	**2.2**
Official creditors	0.0	14.8	21.4	19.1	9.9	8.8	14.5	9.6	4.0	2.2
Multilateral	0.0	1.7	11.4	12.4	3.7	5.2	14.3	9.6	4.0	2.2
Concessional	0.0	1.0	9.9	12.3	3.1	5.2	14.3	9.6	4.0	2.2
Bilateral	0.0	13.1	10.1	6.6	6.3	3.6	0.2	0.0	0.0	0.0
Concessional	0.0	3.3	10.1	6.6	6.3	3.6	0.2	0.0	0.0	0.0
Private creditors	0.0	4.8	0.1	0.0	0.0	0.0	0.0	0.0	0.0	0.0
Bonds	0.0	0.0	0.0	0.0	0.0	0.0	0.0	0.0	0.0	0.0
Commercial banks	0.0	0.0	0.0	0.0	0.0	0.0	0.0	0.0	0.0	0.0
Other private	0.0	4.8	0.1	0.0	0.0	0.0	0.0	0.0	0.0	0.0
Private nonguaranteed	**0.0**	**0.0**	**0.0**	**0.0**	**0.0**	**0.0**	**0.0**	**0.0**	**0.0**	**0.0**
Bonds	0.0	0.0	0.0	0.0	0.0	0.0	0.0	0.0	0.0	0.0
Commercial banks	0.0	0.0	0.0	0.0	0.0	0.0	0.0	0.0	0.0	0.0
Memo:										
IBRD	0.0	0.0	0.0	0.0	0.0	0.0	0.0	0.0	0.0	0.0
IDA	0.0	0.0	6.9	7.8	2.0	2.4	2.5	4.0	2.4	2.2
PRINCIPAL REPAYMENTS	**0.0**	**1.7**	**1.1**	**0.0**	**0.6**	**1.7**	**2.0**	**0.5**	**0.1**	**0.2**
Public and publicly guaranteed	**0.0**	**1.7**	**1.1**	**0.0**	**0.6**	**1.7**	**2.0**	**0.5**	**0.1**	**0.2**
Official creditors	0.0	1.4	0.6	0.0	0.6	1.7	1.9	0.5	0.1	0.2
Multilateral	0.0	0.0	0.6	0.0	0.5	1.7	1.9	0.5	0.1	0.2
Concessional	0.0	0.0	0.3	0.0	0.5	0.5	0.3	0.0	0.1	0.2
Bilateral	0.0	1.4	0.0	0.0	0.1	0.0	0.0	0.0	0.0	0.0
Concessional	0.0	0.0	0.0	0.0	0.0	0.0	0.0	0.0	0.0	0.0
Private creditors	0.0	0.3	0.5	0.0	0.0	0.1	0.0	0.0	0.0	0.0
Bonds	0.0	0.0	0.0	0.0	0.0	0.0	0.0	0.0	0.0	0.0
Commercial banks	0.0	0.0	0.0	0.0	0.0	0.0	0.0	0.0	0.0	0.0
Other private	0.0	0.3	0.5	0.0	0.0	0.1	0.0	0.0	0.0	0.0
Private nonguaranteed	**0.0**	**0.0**	**0.0**	**0.0**	**0.0**	**0.0**	**0.0**	**0.0**	**0.0**	**0.0**
Bonds	0.0	0.0	0.0	0.0	0.0	0.0	0.0	0.0	0.0	0.0
Commercial banks	0.0	0.0	0.0	0.0	0.0	0.0	0.0	0.0	0.0	0.0
Memo:										
IBRD	0.0	0.0	0.0	0.0	0.0	0.0	0.0	0.0	0.0	0.0
IDA	0.0	0.0	0.0	0.0	0.0	0.0	0.0	0.0	0.1	0.2
NET FLOWS ON DEBT	**0.0**	**17.8**	**20.4**	**19.1**	**9.4**	**7.1**	**12.5**	**9.1**	**3.8**	**2.0**
Public and publicly guaranteed	**0.0**	**17.8**	**20.4**	**19.1**	**9.4**	**7.1**	**12.5**	**9.1**	**3.8**	**2.0**
Official creditors	0.0	13.4	20.8	19.1	9.4	7.1	12.5	9.1	3.8	2.0
Multilateral	0.0	1.7	10.7	12.4	3.2	3.6	12.3	9.1	3.8	2.0
Concessional	0.0	1.0	9.6	12.3	2.6	4.8	13.9	9.6	3.8	2.0
Bilateral	0.0	11.7	10.1	6.6	6.2	3.6	0.2	0.0	0.0	0.0
Concessional	0.0	3.3	10.1	6.6	6.3	3.6	0.2	0.0	0.0	0.0
Private creditors	0.0	4.5	-0.4	0.0	0.0	-0.1	0.0	0.0	0.0	0.0
Bonds	0.0	0.0	0.0	0.0	0.0	0.0	0.0	0.0	0.0	0.0
Commercial banks	0.0	0.0	0.0	0.0	0.0	0.0	0.0	0.0	0.0	0.0
Other private	0.0	4.5	-0.4	0.0	0.0	-0.1	0.0	0.0	0.0	0.0
Private nonguaranteed	**0.0**	**0.0**	**0.0**	**0.0**	**0.0**	**0.0**	**0.0**	**0.0**	**0.0**	**0.0**
Bonds	0.0	0.0	0.0	0.0	0.0	0.0	0.0	0.0	0.0	0.0
Commercial banks	0.0	0.0	0.0	0.0	0.0	0.0	0.0	0.0	0.0	0.0
Memo:										
IBRD	0.0	0.0	0.0	0.0	0.0	0.0	0.0	0.0	0.0	0.0
IDA	0.0	0.0	6.9	7.8	2.0	2.4	2.5	4.0	2.4	2.0

EQUATORIAL GUINEA

(US$ million, unless otherwise indicated)

	1970	1980	1988	1989	1990	1991	1992	1993	1994	1995
INTEREST PAYMENTS (LINT)	**0.0**	**0.1**	**1.8**	**0.2**	**0.5**	**1.6**	**1.0**	**0.6**	**0.8**	**0.4**
Public and publicly guaranteed	**0.0**	**0.1**	**1.8**	**0.2**	**0.5**	**1.6**	**1.0**	**0.6**	**0.8**	**0.4**
Official creditors	0.0	0.1	1.3	0.2	0.5	1.6	1.0	0.6	0.8	0.4
Multilateral	0.0	0.0	0.8	0.2	0.3	1.3	1.0	0.6	0.8	0.4
Concessional	0.0	0.0	0.3	0.2	0.3	0.7	0.4	0.3	0.5	0.4
Bilateral	0.0	0.1	0.5	0.0	0.1	0.2	0.1	0.0	0.0	0.0
Concessional	0.0	0.1	0.2	0.0	0.1	0.2	0.1	0.0	0.0	0.0
Private creditors	0.0	0.0	0.4	0.0	0.0	0.0	0.0	0.0	0.0	0.0
Bonds	0.0	0.0	0.0	0.0	0.0	0.0	0.0	0.0	0.0	0.0
Commercial banks	0.0	0.0	0.0	0.0	0.0	0.0	0.0	0.0	0.0	0.0
Other private	0.0	0.0	0.4	0.0	0.0	0.0	0.0	0.0	0.0	0.0
Private nonguaranteed	**0.0**	**0.0**	**0.0**	**0.0**	**0.0**	**0.0**	**0.0**	**0.0**	**0.0**	**0.0**
Bonds	0.0	0.0	0.0	0.0	0.0	0.0	0.0	0.0	0.0	0.0
Commercial banks	0.0	0.0	0.0	0.0	0.0	0.0	0.0	0.0	0.0	0.0
Memo:										
IBRD	0.0	0.0	0.0	0.0	0.0	0.0	0.0	0.0	0.0	0.0
IDA	0.0	0.0	0.2	0.2	0.2	0.3	0.3	0.3	0.4	0.4
NET TRANSFERS ON DEBT	**0.0**	**17.8**	**18.6**	**18.9**	**8.9**	**5.5**	**11.5**	**8.4**	**3.1**	**1.7**
Public and publicly guaranteed	**0.0**	**17.8**	**18.6**	**18.9**	**8.9**	**5.5**	**11.5**	**8.4**	**3.1**	**1.7**
Official creditors	0.0	13.3	19.5	18.9	8.9	5.6	11.5	8.4	3.1	1.7
Multilateral	0.0	1.7	9.9	12.2	2.9	2.2	11.3	8.4	3.1	1.7
Concessional	0.0	1.0	9.2	12.1	2.3	4.1	13.5	9.3	3.4	1.7
Bilateral	0.0	11.6	9.5	6.6	6.0	3.3	0.1	0.0	0.0	0.0
Concessional	0.0	3.2	9.9	6.6	6.1	3.3	0.1	0.0	0.0	0.0
Private creditors	0.0	4.4	-0.9	0.0	0.0	-0.1	0.0	0.0	0.0	0.0
Bonds	0.0	0.0	0.0	0.0	0.0	0.0	0.0	0.0	0.0	0.0
Commercial banks	0.0	0.0	0.0	0.0	0.0	0.0	0.0	0.0	0.0	0.0
Other private	0.0	4.4	-0.9	0.0	0.0	-0.1	0.0	0.0	0.0	0.0
Private nonguaranteed	**0.0**	**0.0**	**0.0**	**0.0**	**0.0**	**0.0**	**0.0**	**0.0**	**0.0**	**0.0**
Bonds	0.0	0.0	0.0	0.0	0.0	0.0	0.0	0.0	0.0	0.0
Commercial banks	0.0	0.0	0.0	0.0	0.0	0.0	0.0	0.0	0.0	0.0
Memo:										
IBRD	0.0	0.0	0.0	0.0	0.0	0.0	0.0	0.0	0.0	0.0
IDA	0.0	0.0	6.6	7.6	1.8	2.1	2.2	3.7	2.0	1.7
DEBT SERVICE (LTDS)	**0.0**	**1.8**	**2.9**	**0.2**	**1.1**	**3.3**	**3.0**	**1.1**	**0.9**	**0.6**
Public and publicly guaranteed	**0.0**	**1.8**	**2.9**	**0.2**	**1.1**	**3.3**	**3.0**	**1.1**	**0.9**	**0.6**
Official creditors	0.0	1.5	2.0	0.2	1.1	3.3	3.0	1.1	0.9	0.6
Multilateral	0.0	0.0	1.4	0.2	0.8	3.0	2.9	1.1	0.9	0.6
Concessional	0.0	0.0	0.6	0.2	0.8	1.2	0.7	0.3	0.6	0.6
Bilateral	0.0	1.5	0.5	0.0	0.3	0.2	0.1	0.0	0.0	0.0
Concessional	0.0	0.1	0.2	0.0	0.1	0.2	0.1	0.0	0.0	0.0
Private creditors	0.0	0.4	1.0	0.0	0.0	0.1	0.0	0.0	0.0	0.0
Bonds	0.0	0.0	0.0	0.0	0.0	0.0	0.0	0.0	0.0	0.0
Commercial banks	0.0	0.0	0.0	0.0	0.0	0.0	0.0	0.0	0.0	0.0
Other private	0.0	0.4	1.0	0.0	0.0	0.1	0.0	0.0	0.0	0.0
Private nonguaranteed	**0.0**	**0.0**	**0.0**	**0.0**	**0.0**	**0.0**	**0.0**	**0.0**	**0.0**	**0.0**
Bonds	0.0	0.0	0.0	0.0	0.0	0.0	0.0	0.0	0.0	0.0
Commercial banks	0.0	0.0	0.0	0.0	0.0	0.0	0.0	0.0	0.0	0.0
Memo:										
IBRD	0.0	0.0	0.0	0.0	0.0	0.0	0.0	0.0	0.0	0.0
IDA	0.0	0.0	0.2	0.2	0.2	0.3	0.3	0.3	0.5	0.6
UNDISBURSED DEBT	**0.0**	**70.6**	**77.1**	**59.0**	**64.9**	**71.3**	**66.8**	**56.8**	**44.4**	**43.0**
Official creditors	0.0	67.6	77.1	59.0	64.9	71.3	66.8	56.8	44.4	43.0
Private creditors	0.0	3.0	0.0	0.0	0.0	0.0	0.0	0.0	0.0	0.0
Memorandum items										
Concessional LDOD	0.0	31.5	104.1	127.4	123.7	131.6	138.4	145.2	148.5	155.1
Variable rate LDOD	0.0	0.0	4.8	4.9	5.1	5.1	5.0	4.9	4.2	4.2
Public sector LDOD	5.0	46.9	184.5	205.4	209.2	215.5	214.4	214.8	219.3	229.6
Private sector LDOD	0.0	5.6	0.0	0.0	0.0	0.0	0.0	0.0	0.0	0.0

6. CURRENCY COMPOSITION OF LONG-TERM DEBT (PERCENT)

	1970	1980	1988	1989	1990	1991	1992	1993	1994	1995
Deutsche mark	0.0	0.0	4.1	5.3	5.9	5.7	5.4	5.0	5.5	5.7
French franc	0.0	0.0	10.8	13.2	7.0	7.8	7.5	7.0	7.6	7.9
Japanese yen	0.0	0.0	0.0	0.0	0.0	0.0	0.0	0.0	0.0	0.0
Pound sterling	0.0	0.0	0.0	0.0	0.0	0.0	0.0	0.0	0.0	0.0
Swiss franc	0.0	0.0	0.0	0.0	0.0	0.0	0.0	0.0	0.0	0.0
U.S.dollars	0.0	16.4	34.4	36.1	37.9	37.7	38.1	39.8	41.1	40.7
Multiple currency	0.0	0.0	5.0	4.9	5.6	5.9	11.0	13.8	15.0	14.6
Special drawing rights	0.0	0.0	0.0	0.0	0.0	0.0	0.0	0.0	0.0	0.0
All other currencies	100.0	83.5	45.5	40.5	43.6	42.9	38.1	34.4	30.8	31.1

EQUATORIAL GUINEA

(US$ million, unless otherwise indicated)

	1970	*1980*	*1988*	*1989*	*1990*	*1991*	*1992*	*1993*	*1994*	*1995*
7. DEBT RESTRUCTURINGS										
Total amount rescheduled	0.0	0.0	1.2	12.1	0.0	0.0	0.0	0.0	0.0	0.0
Debt stock rescheduled	0.0	0.0	0.0	0.0	0.0	0.0	0.0	0.0	0.0	0.0
Principal rescheduled	0.0	0.0	1.1	7.1	0.0	0.0	0.0	0.0	0.0	0.0
Official	0.0	0.0	0.0	4.7	0.0	0.0	0.0	0.0	0.0	0.0
Private	0.0	0.0	1.1	2.4	0.0	0.0	0.0	0.0	0.0	0.0
Interest rescheduled	0.0	0.0	0.1	4.5	0.0	0.0	0.0	0.0	0.0	0.0
Official	0.0	0.0	0.0	4.2	0.0	0.0	0.0	0.0	0.0	0.0
Private	0.0	0.0	0.1	0.2	0.0	0.0	0.0	0.0	0.0	0.0
Debt forgiven	..	..	1.3	0.0	18.5	0.0	0.0	0.0	0.0	0.0
Memo: interest forgiven	..	..	0.1	0.0	0.0	0.0	0.0	0.0	0.0	0.0
Debt stock reduction	0.0	0.0	0.0	0.0	0.0	0.0	0.0	0.0	0.0	0.0
of which debt buyback	0.0	0.0	0.0	0.0	0.0	0.0	0.0	0.0	0.0	0.0
8. DEBT STOCK-FLOW RECONCILIATION										
Total change in debt stocks	..	..	..	18.5	12.0	12.7	1.5	8.8	23.5	5.5
Net flows on debt	..	..	..	14.1	9.8	8.0	12.5	12.9	16.7	-8.1
Net change in interest arrears	..	..	..	3.0	7.2	5.2	3.2	4.6	5.0	4.9
Interest capitalized	..	..	..	4.5	0.0	0.0	0.0	0.0	0.0	0.0
Debt forgiveness or reduction	..	..	..	0.0	-18.5	0.0	0.0	0.0	0.0	0.0
Cross-currency valuation	..	..	..	2.8	11.8	-0.9	-8.8	-7.7	4.8	6.7
Residual	..	..	..	-5.9	1.7	0.4	-5.3	-1.0	-3.0	1.9
9. AVERAGE TERMS OF NEW COMMITMENTS										
ALL CREDITORS										
Interest (%)	0.0	6.5	2.4	4.1	0.9	0.1	0.8	0.7	0.7	0.0
Maturity (years)	0.0	14.2	19.1	13.2	38.2	19.9	40.0	39.0	20.2	0.0
Grace period (years)	0.0	3.4	2.8	5.5	10.1	10.2	10.2	19.5	10.2	0.0
Grant element (%)	0.0	21.0	45.5	31.6	77.5	74.2	80.6	85.7	69.6	0.0
Official creditors										
Interest (%)	0.0	6.5	2.4	4.1	0.9	0.1	0.8	0.7	0.7	0.0
Maturity (years)	0.0	14.2	19.3	13.2	38.2	19.9	40.0	39.0	20.2	0.0
Grace period (years)	0.0	3.4	2.9	5.5	10.1	10.2	10.2	19.5	10.2	0.0
Grant element (%)	0.0	21.0	45.9	31.6	77.5	74.2	80.6	85.7	69.6	0.0
Private creditors										
Interest (%)	0.0	0.0	0.0	0.0	0.0	0.0	0.0	0.0	0.0	0.0
Maturity (years)	0.0	0.0	4.4	0.0	0.0	0.0	0.0	0.0	0.0	0.0
Grace period (years)	0.0	0.0	0.9	0.0	0.0	0.0	0.0	0.0	0.0	0.0
Grant element (%)	0.0	0.0	22.0	0.0	0.0	0.0	0.0	0.0	0.0	0.0
Memorandum items										
Commitments	0.0	27.2	5.0	3.1	18.1	16.5	19.6	9.0	6.6	0.0
Official creditors	0.0	27.2	4.9	3.1	18.1	16.5	19.6	9.0	6.6	0.0
Private creditors	0.0	0.0	0.1	0.0	0.0	0.0	0.0	0.0	0.0	0.0

10. CONTRACTUAL OBLIGATIONS ON OUTSTANDING LONG-TERM DEBT

	1996	*1997*	*1998*	*1999*	*2000*	*2001*	*2002*	*2003*	*2004*	*2005*
TOTAL										
Disbursements	7.9	10.4	7.2	4.7	3.6	2.6	2.0	0.8	0.4	0.2
Principal	5.1	5.8	6.4	6.5	5.6	5.9	6.6	5.6	5.6	5.2
Interest	2.2	2.1	2.0	1.9	1.7	1.5	1.3	1.1	1.1	1.0
Official creditors										
Disbursements	7.9	10.4	7.2	4.7	3.6	2.6	2.0	0.8	0.4	0.2
Principal	5.0	5.8	6.4	6.5	5.6	5.9	6.6	5.6	5.6	5.2
Interest	2.2	2.1	2.0	1.9	1.7	1.5	1.3	1.1	1.1	1.0
Bilateral creditors										
Disbursements	1.4	2.1	1.6	1.3	1.0	0.7	0.5	0.5	0.4	0.2
Principal	3.2	3.7	4.3	4.4	3.6	3.8	4.1	2.8	2.6	1.8
Interest	1.1	1.0	0.9	0.8	0.6	0.5	0.3	0.2	0.2	0.2
Multilateral creditors										
Disbursements	6.5	8.3	5.6	3.4	2.6	1.9	1.5	0.4	0.0	0.0
Principal	1.8	2.1	2.1	2.1	2.0	2.1	2.6	2.8	3.1	3.3
Interest	1.1	1.1	1.1	1.1	1.0	1.0	1.0	0.9	0.9	0.8
Private creditors										
Disbursements	0.0	0.0	0.0	0.0	0.0	0.0	0.0	0.0	0.0	0.0
Principal	0.1	0.0	0.0	0.0	0.0	0.0	0.0	0.0	0.0	0.0
Interest	0.0	0.0	0.0	0.0	0.0	0.0	0.0	0.0	0.0	0.0
Commercial banks										
Disbursements	0.0	0.0	0.0	0.0	0.0	0.0	0.0	0.0	0.0	0.0
Principal	0.0	0.0	0.0	0.0	0.0	0.0	0.0	0.0	0.0	0.0
Interest	0.0	0.0	0.0	0.0	0.0	0.0	0.0	0.0	0.0	0.0
Other private										
Disbursements	0.0	0.0	0.0	0.0	0.0	0.0	0.0	0.0	0.0	0.0
Principal	0.1	0.0	0.0	0.0	0.0	0.0	0.0	0.0	0.0	0.0
Interest	0.0	0.0	0.0	0.0	0.0	0.0	0.0	0.0	0.0	0.0

ESTONIA

(US$ million, unless otherwise indicated)

1. SUMMARY DEBT DATA

	1970	*1980*	*1988*	*1989*	*1990*	*1991*	*1992*	*1993*	*1994*	*1995*
TOTAL DEBT STOCKS (EDT)	..	..	..	..	..	..	**58.4**	**153.9**	**186.0**	**308.8**
Long-term debt (LDOD)	..	..	..	..	..	..	**47.8**	**96.1**	**117.0**	**187.2**
Public and publicly guaranteed	..	..	..	..	..	..	33.8	84.9	108.6	181.7
Private nonguaranteed	0.0	0.0	0.0	0.0	0.0	0.0	14.0	11.2	8.4	5.6
Use of IMF credit	**0.0**	**0.0**	**0.0**	**0.0**	**0.0**	**0.0**	**10.7**	**57.5**	**61.1**	**91.9**
Short-term debt	..	..	..	..	..	..	**0.0**	**0.3**	**8.0**	**29.7**
of which interest arrears on LDOD	..	..	..	..	..	..	0.0	0.0	0.0	0.0
Official creditors	..	..	..	..	..	..	0.0	0.0	0.0	0.0
Private creditors	..	..	..	..	..	..	0.0	0.0	0.0	0.0
Memo: principal arrears on LDOD	..	..	..	..	..	..	0.0	0.0	0.0	0.0
Official creditors	..	..	..	..	..	..	0.0	0.0	0.0	0.0
Private creditors	..	..	..	..	..	..	0.0	0.0	0.0	0.0
Memo: export credits	..	..	0.0	0.0	0.0	0.0	0.0	23.0	48.0	58.0
TOTAL DEBT FLOWS										
Disbursements	..	..	..	..	..	..	**46.9**	**110.2**	**31.1**	**103.3**
Long-term debt	..	..	..	..	..	..	35.9	62.5	31.1	71.6
IMF purchases	0.0	0.0	0.0	0.0	0.0	0.0	10.9	47.6	0.0	31.7
Principal repayments	..	..	..	..	..	..	**2.5**	**12.7**	**15.6**	**6.8**
Long-term debt	..	..	..	..	..	..	2.5	12.7	15.6	5.3
IMF repurchases	0.0	0.0	0.0	0.0	0.0	0.0	0.0	0.0	0.0	1.5
Net flows on debt	..	..	..	..	..	..	**44.3**	**97.8**	**23.2**	**118.2**
of which short-term debt	..	..	..	..	..	..	0.0	0.3	7.7	21.7
Interest payments (INT)	..	..	..	..	..	..	**1.3**	**5.7**	**10.8**	**14.5**
Long-term debt	..	..	..	..	..	..	1.2	4.6	7.2	8.6
IMF charges	0.0	0.0	0.0	0.0	0.0	0.0	0.1	1.1	3.1	4.7
Short-term debt	..	..	..	..	..	..	0.0	0.0	0.5	1.1
Net transfers on debt	..	..	..	..	..	..	**43.1**	**92.0**	**12.4**	**103.8**
Total debt service paid (TDS)	..	..	..	..	..	..	**3.8**	**18.4**	**26.4**	**21.3**
Long-term debt	..	..	..	..	..	..	3.7	17.3	22.8	13.9
IMF repurchases and charges	0.0	0.0	0.0	0.0	0.0	0.0	0.1	1.1	3.1	6.2
Short-term debt (interest only)	..	..	..	..	..	..	0.0	0.0	0.5	1.1

2. AGGREGATE NET RESOURCE FLOWS AND NET TRANSFERS (LONG-TERM)

	1970	*1980*	*1988*	*1989*	*1990*	*1991*	*1992*	*1993*	*1994*	*1995*
NET RESOURCE FLOWS	..	..	..	..	..	..	**186.4**	**236.9**	**257.2**	**291.2**
Net flow of long-term debt (ex. IMF)	..	..	..	..	..	..	33.4	49.8	15.5	66.3
Foreign direct investment (net)	..	..	..	..	..	..	82.0	162.0	214.0	201.0
Portfolio equity flows	..	..	..	..	..	..	0.0	0.0	9.8	7.0
Grants (excluding technical coop.)	..	..	..	..	..	..	71.0	25.1	17.9	16.9
Memo: technical coop. grants	..	..	..	..	..	..	23.3	17.3	22.6	37.0
NET TRANSFERS	..	..	..	..	..	..	**185.3**	**232.3**	**250.0**	**282.6**
Interest on long-term debt	..	..	..	..	..	..	1.2	4.6	7.2	8.6
Profit remittances on FDI	..	..	..	..	..	..	0.0	0.0	0.0	0.0

3. MAJOR ECONOMIC AGGREGATES

	1970	*1980*	*1988*	*1989*	*1990*	*1991*	*1992*	*1993*	*1994*	*1995*
Gross national product (GNP)	..	..	..	..	..	..	3,774.9	3,628.8	3,844.0	4,604.3
Exports of goods & services (XGS)	..	..	..	..	..	..	664.3	1,173.2	1,880.1	2,801.4
of which workers remittances	..	..	..	..	..	..	0.0	0.0	0.1	0.0
Imports of goods & services (MGS)	..	..	..	..	..	..	725.2	1,255.1	2,165.4	3,112.1
International reserves (RES)	..	..	..	..	..	..	197.5	389.3	446.4	583.0
Current account balance	..	..	..	..	..	..	36.1	23.3	-170.8	-184.4

4. DEBT INDICATORS

	1970	*1980*	*1988*	*1989*	*1990*	*1991*	*1992*	*1993*	*1994*	*1995*
EDT / XGS (%)	..	..	..	..	..	..	8.8	13.1	9.9	11.0
EDT / GNP (%)	..	..	..	..	..	..	1.5	4.2	4.8	6.7
TDS / XGS (%)	..	..	..	..	..	..	0.6	1.6	1.4	0.8
INT / XGS (%)	..	..	..	..	..	..	0.2	0.5	0.6	0.5
INT / GNP (%)	..	..	..	..	..	..	0.0	0.2	0.3	0.3
RES / EDT (%)	..	..	..	..	..	..	338.1	253.0	239.9	188.8
RES / MGS (months)	..	..	..	..	..	..	3.3	3.7	2.5	2.2
Short-term / EDT (%)	..	..	..	..	..	..	0.0	0.2	4.3	9.6
Concessional / EDT (%)	..	..	..	..	..	..	17.1	23.7	26.0	17.7
Multilateral / EDT (%)	..	..	..	..	..	..	1.8	29.4	35.2	42.2

ESTONIA

(US$ million, unless otherwise indicated)

	1970	1980	1988	1989	1990	1991	1992	1993	1994	1995
5. LONG-TERM DEBT										
DEBT OUTSTANDING (LDOD)	..	..	..	..	..	..	**47.8**	**96.1**	**117.0**	**187.2**
Public and publicly guaranteed	..	..	..	..	..	..	**33.8**	**84.9**	**108.6**	**181.7**
Official creditors	..	..	..	..	..	..	11.0	59.3	92.0	162.9
Multilateral	..	..	..	..	..	..	1.1	45.3	65.5	130.4
Concessional	..	..	..	..	..	..	0.0	22.4	24.6	26.3
Bilateral	..	..	..	..	..	..	10.0	14.0	26.4	32.5
Concessional	..	..	..	..	..	..	10.0	14.0	23.8	28.4
Private creditors	..	..	..	..	..	..	22.7	25.5	16.6	18.7
Bonds	..	..	..	..	..	..	0.0	0.0	0.0	0.0
Commercial banks	..	..	..	..	..	..	0.0	0.0	0.0	2.1
Other private	..	..	..	..	..	..	22.7	25.5	16.6	16.6
Private nonguaranteed	**0.0**	**0.0**	**0.0**	**0.0**	**0.0**	**0.0**	**14.0**	**11.2**	**8.4**	**5.6**
Bonds	..	..	..	..	..	..	0.0	0.0	0.0	0.0
Commercial banks	..	..	..	..	..	..	14.0	11.2	8.4	5.6
Memo:										
IBRD	0.0	0.0	0.0	0.0	0.0	0.0	1.1	19.8	31.0	49.8
IDA	0.0	0.0	0.0	0.0	0.0	0.0	0.0	0.0	0.0	0.0
DISBURSEMENTS	..	..	..	..	..	..	**35.9**	**62.5**	**31.1**	**71.6**
Public and publicly guaranteed	..	..	..	..	..	..	**34.0**	**62.5**	**31.1**	**71.6**
Official creditors	..	..	..	..	..	..	11.0	49.7	28.2	67.4
Multilateral	..	..	..	..	..	..	1.1	45.6	15.8	61.5
Concessional	..	..	..	..	..	..	0.0	23.4	0.0	0.0
Bilateral	..	..	..	..	..	..	10.0	4.1	12.4	6.0
Concessional	..	..	..	..	..	..	10.0	4.1	9.8	4.6
Private creditors	..	..	..	..	..	..	23.0	12.8	2.9	4.2
Bonds	..	..	..	..	..	..	0.0	0.0	0.0	0.0
Commercial banks	..	..	..	..	..	..	0.0	0.0	0.0	2.1
Other private	..	..	..	..	..	..	23.0	12.8	2.9	2.1
Private nonguaranteed	**0.0**	**0.0**	**0.0**	**0.0**	**0.0**	**0.0**	**1.9**	**0.0**	**0.0**	**0.0**
Bonds	..	..	..	..	..	..	0.0	0.0	0.0	0.0
Commercial banks	..	..	..	..	..	..	1.9	0.0	0.0	0.0
Memo:										
IBRD	0.0	0.0	0.0	0.0	0.0	0.0	1.1	18.9	9.7	18.0
IDA	0.0	0.0	0.0	0.0	0.0	0.0	0.0	0.0	0.0	0.0
PRINCIPAL REPAYMENTS	..	..	..	..	..	..	**2.5**	**12.7**	**15.6**	**5.3**
Public and publicly guaranteed	..	..	..	..	..	..	**0.0**	**9.9**	**12.8**	**2.5**
Official creditors	..	..	..	..	..	..	0.0	0.0	0.0	0.0
Multilateral	..	..	..	..	..	..	0.0	0.0	0.0	0.0
Concessional	..	..	..	..	..	..	0.0	0.0	0.0	0.0
Bilateral	..	..	..	..	..	..	0.0	0.0	0.0	0.0
Concessional	..	..	..	..	..	..	0.0	0.0	0.0	0.0
Private creditors	..	..	..	..	..	..	0.0	9.9	12.8	2.5
Bonds	..	..	..	..	..	..	0.0	0.0	0.0	0.0
Commercial banks	..	..	..	..	..	..	0.0	0.0	0.0	0.0
Other private	..	..	..	..	..	..	0.0	9.9	12.8	2.5
Private nonguaranteed	**0.0**	**0.0**	**0.0**	**0.0**	**0.0**	**0.0**	**2.5**	**2.8**	**2.8**	**2.8**
Bonds	..	..	..	..	..	..	0.0	0.0	0.0	0.0
Commercial banks	..	..	..	..	..	..	2.5	2.8	2.8	2.8
Memo:										
IBRD	0.0	0.0	0.0	0.0	0.0	0.0	0.0	0.0	0.0	0.0
IDA	0.0	0.0	0.0	0.0	0.0	0.0	0.0	0.0	0.0	0.0
NET FLOWS ON DEBT	..	..	..	..	..	..	**33.4**	**49.8**	**15.5**	**66.3**
Public and publicly guaranteed	..	..	..	..	..	..	**34.0**	**52.6**	**18.3**	**69.1**
Official creditors	..	..	..	..	..	..	11.0	49.7	28.2	67.4
Multilateral	..	..	..	..	..	..	1.1	45.6	15.8	61.5
Concessional	..	..	..	..	..	..	0.0	23.4	0.0	0.0
Bilateral	..	..	..	..	..	..	10.0	4.0	12.4	6.0
Concessional	..	..	..	..	..	..	10.0	4.1	9.8	4.6
Private creditors	..	..	..	..	..	..	23.0	3.0	-9.9	1.6
Bonds	..	..	..	..	..	..	0.0	0.0	0.0	0.0
Commercial banks	..	..	..	..	..	..	0.0	0.0	0.0	2.1
Other private	..	..	..	..	..	..	23.0	3.0	-9.9	-0.5
Private nonguaranteed	**0.0**	**0.0**	**0.0**	**0.0**	**0.0**	**0.0**	**-0.6**	**-2.8**	**-2.8**	**-2.8**
Bonds	..	..	..	..	..	..	0.0	0.0	0.0	0.0
Commercial banks	..	..	..	..	..	..	-0.6	-2.8	-2.8	-2.8
Memo:										
IBRD	0.0	0.0	0.0	0.0	0.0	0.0	1.1	18.9	9.7	18.0
IDA	0.0	0.0	0.0	0.0	0.0	0.0	0.0	0.0	0.0	0.0

ESTONIA

(US$ million, unless otherwise indicated)

	1970	1980	1988	1989	1990	1991	1992	1993	1994	1995
INTEREST PAYMENTS (LINT)	..	..	..	..	..	..	**1.2**	**4.6**	**7.2**	**8.6**
Public and publicly guaranteed	..	..	..	..	..	..	**0.0**	**3.6**	**6.5**	**8.0**
Official creditors	..	..	..	..	..	..	0.0	1.9	4.0	6.8
Multilateral	..	..	..	..	..	..	0.0	1.7	3.3	5.6
Concessional	..	..	..	..	..	..	0.0	1.1	1.3	1.7
Bilateral	..	..	..	..	..	..	0.0	0.2	0.6	1.1
Concessional	..	..	..	..	..	..	0.0	0.2	0.5	0.9
Private creditors	..	..	..	..	..	..	0.0	1.7	2.5	1.2
Bonds	..	..	..	..	..	..	0.0	0.0	0.0	0.0
Commercial banks	..	..	..	..	..	..	0.0	0.0	0.0	0.1
Other private	..	..	..	..	..	..	0.0	1.7	2.5	1.1
Private nonguaranteed	**0.0**	**0.0**	**0.0**	**0.0**	**0.0**	**0.0**	**1.1**	**1.0**	**0.8**	**0.6**
Bonds	..	..	..	..	..	..	0.0	0.0	0.0	0.0
Commercial banks	..	..	..	..	..	..	1.1	1.0	0.8	0.6
Memo:										
IBRD	0.0	0.0	0.0	0.0	0.0	0.0	0.0	0.4	1.7	2.5
IDA	0.0	0.0	0.0	0.0	0.0	0.0	0.0	0.0	0.0	0.0
NET TRANSFERS ON DEBT	..	..	..	..	..	..	**32.3**	**45.2**	**8.3**	**57.7**
Public and publicly guaranteed	..	..	..	..	..	..	**34.0**	**49.0**	**11.9**	**61.1**
Official creditors	..	..	..	..	..	..	11.0	47.8	24.3	60.7
Multilateral	..	..	..	..	..	..	1.1	43.9	12.5	55.8
Concessional	..	..	..	..	..	..	0.0	22.4	-1.3	-1.7
Bilateral	..	..	..	..	..	..	10.0	3.8	11.8	4.8
Concessional	..	..	..	..	..	..	10.0	3.9	9.3	3.7
Private creditors	..	..	..	..	..	..	22.9	1.3	-12.4	0.4
Bonds	..	..	..	..	..	..	0.0	0.0	0.0	0.0
Commercial banks	..	..	..	..	..	..	0.0	0.0	0.0	2.0
Other private	..	..	..	..	..	..	22.9	1.3	-12.4	-1.6
Private nonguaranteed	**0.0**	**0.0**	**0.0**	**0.0**	**0.0**	**0.0**	**-1.7**	**-3.8**	**-3.6**	**-3.4**
Bonds	..	..	..	..	..	..	0.0	0.0	0.0	0.0
Commercial banks	..	..	..	..	..	..	-1.7	-3.8	-3.6	-3.4
Memo:										
IBRD	0.0	0.0	0.0	0.0	0.0	0.0	1.1	18.5	8.0	15.5
IDA	0.0	0.0	0.0	0.0	0.0	0.0	0.0	0.0	0.0	0.0
DEBT SERVICE (LTDS)	..	..	..	..	..	..	**3.7**	**17.3**	**22.8**	**13.9**
Public and publicly guaranteed	..	..	..	..	..	..	**0.0**	**13.5**	**19.2**	**10.5**
Official creditors	..	..	..	..	..	..	0.0	1.9	4.0	6.8
Multilateral	..	..	..	..	..	..	0.0	1.7	3.3	5.6
Concessional	..	..	..	..	..	..	0.0	1.1	1.3	1.7
Bilateral	..	..	..	..	..	..	0.0	0.2	0.6	1.1
Concessional	..	..	..	..	..	..	0.0	0.2	0.5	0.9
Private creditors	..	..	..	..	..	..	0.0	11.6	15.3	3.8
Bonds	..	..	..	..	..	..	0.0	0.0	0.0	0.0
Commercial banks	..	..	..	..	..	..	0.0	0.0	0.0	0.1
Other private	..	..	..	..	..	..	0.0	11.6	15.3	3.6
Private nonguaranteed	**0.0**	**0.0**	**0.0**	**0.0**	**0.0**	**0.0**	**3.7**	**3.8**	**3.6**	**3.4**
Bonds	..	..	..	..	..	..	0.0	0.0	0.0	0.0
Commercial banks	..	..	..	..	..	..	3.7	3.8	3.6	3.4
Memo:										
IBRD	0.0	0.0	0.0	0.0	0.0	0.0	0.0	0.4	1.7	2.5
IDA	0.0	0.0	0.0	0.0	0.0	0.0	0.0	0.0	0.0	0.0
UNDISBURSED DEBT	..	..	..	..	..	..	**82.7**	**74.0**	**154.8**	**105.7**
Official creditors	..	..	..	..	..	..	74.5	66.8	149.6	104.4
Private creditors	..	..	..	..	..	..	8.2	7.2	5.2	1.3
Memorandum items										
Concessional LDOD	..	..	..	..	..	..	10.0	36.4	48.4	54.7
Variable rate LDOD	..	..	..	..	..	..	16.4	64.1	95.3	159.4
Public sector LDOD	..	..	..	..	..	..	33.8	84.9	108.6	181.7
Private sector LDOD	..	..	..	..	..	..	14.0	11.2	8.4	5.6

6. CURRENCY COMPOSITION OF LONG-TERM DEBT (PERCENT)

	1970	1980	1988	1989	1990	1991	1992	1993	1994	1995
Deutsche mark	..	..	..	..	..	..	0.0	3.7	9.1	12.9
French franc	..	..	..	..	..	..	0.0	0.0	0.0	0.0
Japanese yen	..	..	..	..	..	..	0.0	0.0	0.0	0.0
Pound sterling	..	..	..	..	..	..	0.0	0.0	0.0	0.0
Swiss franc	..	..	..	..	..	..	0.0	0.0	0.0	0.0
U.S.dollars	..	..	..	..	..	..	92.7	42.4	32.7	24.0
Multiple currency	..	..	..	..	..	..	3.3	23.3	28.6	27.4
Special drawing rights	..	..	..	..	..	..	0.0	0.0	0.0	0.0
All other currencies	..	..	..	..	..	..	4.1	30.5	29.6	35.7

ESTONIA

(US$ million, unless otherwise indicated)

	1970	1980	1988	1989	1990	1991	1992	1993	1994	1995
7. DEBT RESTRUCTURINGS										
Total amount rescheduled	0.0	0.0	0.0	0.0	0.0	0.0	0.0	0.0	0.0	0.0
Debt stock rescheduled	0.0	0.0	0.0	0.0	0.0	0.0	0.0	0.0	0.0	0.0
Principal rescheduled	0.0	0.0	0.0	0.0	0.0	0.0	0.0	0.0	0.0	0.0
Official	0.0	0.0	0.0	0.0	0.0	0.0	0.0	0.0	0.0	0.0
Private	0.0	0.0	0.0	0.0	0.0	0.0	0.0	0.0	0.0	0.0
Interest rescheduled	0.0	0.0	0.0	0.0	0.0	0.0	0.0	0.0	0.0	0.0
Official	0.0	0.0	0.0	0.0	0.0	0.0	0.0	0.0	0.0	0.0
Private	0.0	0.0	0.0	0.0	0.0	0.0	0.0	0.0	0.0	0.0
Debt forgiven	..	..	0.0	0.0	0.0	0.0	0.0	0.0	0.0	0.0
Memo: interest forgiven	..	..	0.0	0.0	0.0	0.0	0.0	0.0	0.0	0.0
Debt stock reduction	0.0	0.0	0.0	0.0	0.0	0.0	0.0	0.0	0.0	0.0
of which debt buyback	0.0	0.0	0.0	0.0	0.0	0.0	0.0	0.0	0.0	0.0
8. DEBT STOCK-FLOW RECONCILIATION										
Total change in debt stocks	..	..	..	..	..	..	58.0	95.5	32.2	122.7
Net flows on debt	..	..	..	..	..	..	44.3	97.8	23.2	118.2
Net change in interest arrears	..	..	..	..	..	..	0.0	0.0	0.0	0.0
Interest capitalized	..	..	..	..	..	..	0.0	0.0	0.0	0.0
Debt forgiveness or reduction	..	..	..	..	..	..	0.0	0.0	0.0	0.0
Cross-currency valuation	..	..	..	..	..	..	-0.4	-2.8	7.1	7.5
Residual	..	..	..	..	..	..	14.0	0.5	1.8	-3.0
9. AVERAGE TERMS OF NEW COMMITMENTS										
ALL CREDITORS										
Interest (%)	..	..	..	..	..	..	8.3	4.4	7.7	7.1
Maturity (years)	..	..	..	..	..	..	11.1	9.8	14.8	15.0
Grace period (years)	..	..	..	..	..	..	3.7	6.4	5.6	5.5
Grant element (%)	..	..	..	..	..	..	11.8	29.2	12.7	16.4
Official creditors										
Interest (%)	..	..	..	..	..	..	6.9	4.0	7.7	7.1
Maturity (years)	..	..	..	..	..	..	13.5	10.4	14.8	15.0
Grace period (years)	..	..	..	..	..	..	4.7	6.2	5.6	5.5
Grant element (%)	..	..	..	..	..	..	17.3	31.9	12.7	16.4
Private creditors										
Interest (%)	..	..	..	..	..	..	11.9	6.0	0.0	0.0
Maturity (years)	..	..	..	..	..	..	4.9	7.4	0.0	0.0
Grace period (years)	..	..	..	..	..	..	1.0	7.3	0.0	0.0
Grant element (%)	..	..	..	..	..	..	-2.7	19.9	0.0	0.0
Memorandum items										
Commitments	..	..	..	..	..	..	119.8	57.4	105.6	20.0
Official creditors	..	..	..	..	..	..	87.2	44.8	105.6	20.0
Private creditors	..	..	..	..	..	..	32.6	12.6	0.0	0.0

10. CONTRACTUAL OBLIGATIONS ON OUTSTANDING LONG-TERM DEBT

	1996	1997	1998	1999	2000	2001	2002	2003	2004	2005
TOTAL										
Disbursements	31.6	25.2	15.5	10.5	8.7	5.0	3.0	2.4	2.1	1.7
Principal	11.0	10.9	13.0	14.5	61.5	28.2	28.6	21.6	18.2	18.2
Interest	13.2	15.2	15.5	15.4	13.6	11.0	9.3	7.7	6.5	5.4
Official creditors										
Disbursements	30.3	25.2	15.5	10.5	8.7	5.0	3.0	2.4	2.1	1.7
Principal	6.8	6.8	11.8	13.3	49.1	25.9	28.1	21.6	18.2	18.2
Interest	11.5	13.8	14.4	14.3	13.0	10.9	9.3	7.7	6.5	5.4
Bilateral creditors										
Disbursements	4.5	3.2	1.6	0.8	0.4	0.1	0.1	0.0	0.0	0.0
Principal	0.0	0.0	1.8	2.3	2.8	4.4	6.6	3.5	3.5	3.5
Interest	1.3	1.5	1.6	1.5	1.4	1.2	1.1	1.0	0.8	0.7
Multilateral creditors										
Disbursements	25.8	22.0	13.9	9.7	8.4	4.9	2.9	2.4	2.1	1.7
Principal	6.8	6.8	9.9	11.0	46.3	21.5	21.5	18.1	14.7	14.7
Interest	10.2	12.3	12.8	12.8	11.6	9.6	8.2	6.7	5.7	4.7
Private creditors										
Disbursements	1.3	0.0	0.0	0.0	0.0	0.0	0.0	0.0	0.0	0.0
Principal	4.1	4.1	1.2	1.2	12.4	2.3	0.4	0.0	0.0	0.0
Interest	1.7	1.4	1.1	1.0	0.6	0.1	0.0	0.0	0.0	0.0
Commercial banks										
Disbursements	0.0	0.0	0.0	0.0	0.0	0.0	0.0	0.0	0.0	0.0
Principal	0.0	0.0	0.0	0.0	0.7	1.4	0.0	0.0	0.0	0.0
Interest	0.1	0.1	0.1	0.1	0.1	0.1	0.0	0.0	0.0	0.0
Other private										
Disbursements	1.3	0.0	0.0	0.0	0.0	0.0	0.0	0.0	0.0	0.0
Principal	4.1	4.1	1.2	1.2	11.7	0.9	0.4	0.0	0.0	0.0
Interest	1.5	1.3	1.0	0.9	0.5	0.1	0.0	0.0	0.0	0.0

ETHIOPIA

(US$ million, unless otherwise indicated)

	1970	1980	1988	1989	1990	1991	1992	1993	1994	1995
1. SUMMARY DEBT DATA										
TOTAL DEBT STOCKS (EDT)	..	**824**	**3,274**	**3,489**	**3,809**	**4,198**	**4,343**	**4,661**	**5,001**	**5,221**
Long-term debt (LDOD)	**169**	**688**	**3,085**	**3,347**	**3,657**	**4,005**	**4,167**	**4,459**	**4,754**	**4,958**
Public and publicly guaranteed	169	688	3,085	3,347	3,657	4,005	4,167	4,459	4,754	4,958
Private nonguaranteed	0	0	0	0	0	0	0	0	0	0
Use of IMF credit	**0**	**79**	**55**	**30**	**6**	**0**	**19**	**49**	**72**	**74**
Short-term debt	..	**57**	**134**	**112**	**145**	**193**	**157**	**154**	**175**	**190**
of which interest arrears on LDOD	..	1	2	16	43	83	97	123	144	166
Official creditors	..	0	1	15	39	75	92	115	133	156
Private creditors	..	0	1	1	3	8	5	8	11	11
Memo: principal arrears on LDOD	..	1	14	53	236	493	595	652	902	1,027
Official creditors	..	0	8	40	196	405	547	590	821	962
Private creditors	..	1	6	13	40	88	48	63	81	65
Memo: export credits	..	..	372	323	311	292	214	206	245	254
TOTAL DEBT FLOWS										
Disbursements	**28**	**119**	**572**	**493**	**360**	**431**	**342**	**407**	**274**	**237**
Long-term debt	28	110	572	493	360	431	322	378	253	237
IMF purchases	0	9	0	0	0	0	20	30	20	0
Principal repayments	**15**	**17**	**214**	**219**	**177**	**92**	**62**	**66**	**68**	**92**
Long-term debt	15	17	197	196	152	86	62	66	68	92
IMF repurchases	0	0	17	23	25	6	0	0	0	0
Net flows on debt	**13**	**102**	**396**	**238**	**190**	**346**	**229**	**312**	**206**	**138**
of which short-term debt	..	..	38	-36	7	7	-50	-29	0	-8
Interest payments (INT)	..	**28**	**96**	**85**	**59**	**45**	**47**	**29**	**44**	**63**
Long-term debt	6	17	84	73	49	38	42	24	40	61
IMF charges	0	2	4	4	2	0	0	0	0	0
Short-term debt	..	9	8	8	8	7	5	5	4	1
Net transfers on debt	..	**75**	**300**	**153**	**131**	**301**	**182**	**283**	**162**	**75**
Total debt service paid (TDS)	..	**45**	**309**	**304**	**236**	**138**	**109**	**95**	**112**	**155**
Long-term debt	21	34	280	269	201	124	104	90	107	153
IMF repurchases and charges	0	2	21	27	27	6	0	0	0	0
Short-term debt (interest only)	..	9	8	8	8	7	5	5	4	1
2. AGGREGATE NET RESOURCE FLOWS AND NET TRANSFERS (LONG-TERM)										
NET RESOURCE FLOWS	**23**	**218**	**955**	**680**	**824**	**1,128**	**1,152**	**880**	**830**	**627**
Net flow of long-term debt (ex. IMF)	13	93	375	297	208	345	259	312	186	145
Foreign direct investment (net)	4	0	2	0	12	1	6	6	7	7
Portfolio equity flows	0	0	0	0	0	0	0	0	0	0
Grants (excluding technical coop.)	6	125	578	383	604	781	886	562	638	475
Memo: technical coop. grants	20	44	197	234	254	206	190	171	126	167
NET TRANSFERS	**10**	**201**	**871**	**606**	**776**	**1,089**	**1,110**	**856**	**791**	**566**
Interest on long-term debt	6	17	84	73	49	38	42	24	40	61
Profit remittances on FDI	6	0	0	0	0	0	0	0	0	0
3. MAJOR ECONOMIC AGGREGATES										
Gross national product (GNP)	..	..	7,663	8,069	8,567	9,499	5,163	6,004	4,607	5,227
Exports of goods & services (XGS)	185	612	770	947	850	748	775	761	810	1,139
of which workers remittances	0	22	122	189	174	201	316	248	247	312
Imports of goods & services (MGS)	226	797	1,328	1,290	1,141	1,304	1,165	1,344	1,189	1,400
International reserves (RES)	72	262	150	123	55	106	270	500	588	815
Current account balance	-32	-126	-374	-135	-131	-266	41	-183	-93	..
4. DEBT INDICATORS										
EDT / XGS (%)	..	134.5	425.1	368.4	448.1	561.3	560.6	612.4	617.2	458.2
EDT / GNP (%)	..	..	42.7	43.2	44.5	44.2	84.1	77.6	108.5	99.9
TDS / XGS (%)	..	7.3	40.2	32.1	27.8	18.4	14.1	12.5	13.8	13.6
INT / XGS (%)	..	4.5	12.4	9.0	6.9	6.1	6.1	3.9	5.4	5.5
INT / GNP (%)	..	..	1.2	1.1	0.7	0.5	0.9	0.5	1.0	1.2
RES / EDT (%)	..	31.8	4.6	3.5	1.4	2.5	6.2	10.7	11.7	15.6
RES / MGS (months)	3.8	4.0	1.4	1.1	0.6	1.0	2.8	4.5	5.9	7.0
Short-term / EDT (%)	..	6.9	4.1	3.2	3.8	4.6	3.6	3.3	3.5	3.6
Concessional / EDT (%)	..	71.3	74.1	76.0	77.4	73.3	74.9	76.9	77.9	79.0
Multilateral / EDT (%)	..	41.2	29.5	30.9	33.3	33.0	34.6	39.5	43.0	45.3

ETHIOPIA

(US$ million, unless otherwise indicated)

	1970	1980	1988	1989	1990	1991	1992	1993	1994	1995
5. LONG-TERM DEBT										
DEBT OUTSTANDING (LDOD)	**169**	**688**	**3,085**	**3,347**	**3,657**	**4,005**	**4,167**	**4,459**	**4,754**	**4,958**
Public and publicly guaranteed	**169**	**688**	**3,085**	**3,347**	**3,657**	**4,005**	**4,167**	**4,459**	**4,754**	**4,958**
Official creditors	140	638	2,592	2,938	3,287	3,426	3,608	3,957	4,296	4,558
Multilateral	70	340	967	1,078	1,268	1,387	1,503	1,840	2,150	2,366
Concessional	66	306	909	1,006	1,187	1,291	1,398	1,726	2,025	2,220
Bilateral	70	299	1,624	1,860	2,019	2,040	2,105	2,117	2,147	2,193
Concessional	70	281	1,517	1,646	1,762	1,786	1,857	1,857	1,873	1,908
Private creditors	29	49	493	409	370	579	559	502	457	400
Bonds	0	0	0	0	0	0	0	0	0	0
Commercial banks	0	10	195	160	116	100	99	97	81	63
Other private	29	39	298	249	254	479	460	405	377	336
Private nonguaranteed	**0**	**0**	**0**	**0**	**0**	**0**	**0**	**0**	**0**	**0**
Bonds	0	0	0	0	0	0	0	0	0	0
Commercial banks	0	0	0	0	0	0	0	0	0	0
Memo:										
IBRD	47	56	42	31	27	20	12	7	4	0
IDA	23	249	658	718	824	883	964	1,189	1,391	1,494
DISBURSEMENTS	**28**	**110**	**572**	**493**	**360**	**431**	**322**	**378**	**253**	**237**
Public and publicly guaranteed	**28**	**110**	**572**	**493**	**360**	**431**	**322**	**378**	**253**	**237**
Official creditors	25	77	425	464	310	170	209	367	250	237
Multilateral	8	36	131	138	139	133	187	367	250	214
Concessional	5	34	128	116	128	111	162	346	236	183
Bilateral	17	41	294	326	171	37	22	1	0	23
Concessional	17	37	259	198	114	36	18	0	0	23
Private creditors	2	33	147	29	51	261	113	10	4	0
Bonds	0	0	0	0	0	0	0	0	0	0
Commercial banks	0	2	65	0	0	0	0	0	0	0
Other private	2	31	82	29	51	261	113	10	4	0
Private nonguaranteed	**0**	**0**	**0**	**0**	**0**	**0**	**0**	**0**	**0**	**0**
Bonds	0	0	0	0	0	0	0	0	0	0
Commercial banks	0	0	0	0	0	0	0	0	0	0
Memo:										
IBRD	6	0	0	0	0	0	0	0	0	0
IDA	3	28	75	70	74	59	112	232	166	89
PRINCIPAL REPAYMENTS	**15**	**17**	**197**	**196**	**152**	**86**	**62**	**66**	**68**	**92**
Public and publicly guaranteed	**15**	**17**	**197**	**196**	**152**	**86**	**62**	**66**	**68**	**92**
Official creditors	6	11	117	90	46	38	29	29	31	43
Multilateral	3	4	19	18	16	24	23	23	28	39
Concessional	3	3	12	11	9	15	13	12	18	26
Bilateral	3	6	98	72	30	14	6	6	3	3
Concessional	3	6	68	51	13	9	4	4	1	3
Private creditors	9	7	80	106	107	48	33	37	36	49
Bonds	0	0	0	0	0	0	0	0	0	0
Commercial banks	0	3	16	36	45	9	1	3	16	17
Other private	9	4	64	70	62	39	32	34	20	32
Private nonguaranteed	**0**	**0**	**0**	**0**	**0**	**0**	**0**	**0**	**0**	**0**
Bonds	0	0	0	0	0	0	0	0	0	0
Commercial banks	0	0	0	0	0	0	0	0	0	0
Memo:										
IBRD	3	4	10	10	7	7	7	6	4	4
IDA	0	0	4	4	4	5	6	8	10	12
NET FLOWS ON DEBT	**13**	**93**	**375**	**297**	**208**	**345**	**259**	**312**	**186**	**145**
Public and publicly guaranteed	**13**	**93**	**375**	**297**	**208**	**345**	**259**	**312**	**186**	**145**
Official creditors	20	67	308	373	264	132	180	339	219	194
Multilateral	5	32	113	120	123	109	163	344	222	175
Concessional	2	31	116	106	119	97	149	334	218	157
Bilateral	14	35	195	253	141	23	16	-5	-3	19
Concessional	14	30	191	147	101	26	14	-4	-1	20
Private creditors	-7	26	67	-76	-56	213	80	-27	-33	-49
Bonds	0	0	0	0	0	0	0	0	0	0
Commercial banks	0	-1	49	-36	-45	-9	-1	-3	-16	-17
Other private	-7	27	18	-41	-11	222	81	-24	-17	-32
Private nonguaranteed	**0**	**0**	**0**	**0**	**0**	**0**	**0**	**0**	**0**	**0**
Bonds	0	0	0	0	0	0	0	0	0	0
Commercial banks	0	0	0	0	0	0	0	0	0	0
Memo:										
IBRD	3	-4	-10	-10	-7	-7	-7	-6	-4	-4
IDA	3	28	71	66	69	53	106	225	156	77

ETHIOPIA

(US$ million, unless otherwise indicated)

	1970	1980	1988	1989	1990	1991	1992	1993	1994	1995
INTEREST PAYMENTS (LINT)	**6**	**17**	**84**	**73**	**49**	**38**	**42**	**24**	**40**	**61**
Public and publicly guaranteed	**6**	**17**	**84**	**73**	**49**	**38**	**42**	**24**	**40**	**61**
Official creditors	5	15	50	42	25	22	20	21	31	32
Multilateral	3	8	13	16	13	17	19	20	25	24
Concessional	3	4	9	9	10	11	11	11	14	16
Bilateral	2	6	37	27	11	5	1	1	6	9
Concessional	2	5	32	23	9	4	1	1	3	6
Private creditors	2	2	33	31	24	16	22	3	9	29
Bonds	0	0	0	0	0	0	0	0	0	0
Commercial banks	0	2	15	16	11	6	5	2	2	7
Other private	2	1	18	16	13	10	18	1	7	22
Private nonguaranteed	**0**	**0**	**0**	**0**	**0**	**0**	**0**	**0**	**0**	**0**
Bonds	0	0	0	0	0	0	0	0	0	0
Commercial banks	0	0	0	0	0	0	0	0	0	0
Memo:										
IBRD	3	7	3	3	2	2	1	1	0	0
IDA	0	2	6	5	6	6	7	7	10	11
NET TRANSFERS ON DEBT	**7**	**76**	**291**	**224**	**160**	**307**	**217**	**288**	**146**	**84**
Public and publicly guaranteed	**7**	**76**	**291**	**224**	**160**	**307**	**217**	**288**	**146**	**84**
Official creditors	15	52	258	331	240	110	160	318	188	162
Multilateral	3	23	100	104	110	91	145	324	197	152
Concessional	-1	26	107	97	109	86	139	324	204	141
Bilateral	12	29	158	227	130	18	15	-6	-9	11
Concessional	12	25	159	125	92	23	13	-5	-4	14
Private creditors	-8	24	33	-107	-80	197	57	-30	-42	-78
Bonds	0	0	0	0	0	0	0	0	0	0
Commercial banks	0	-2	34	-51	-56	-14	-6	-5	-18	-24
Other private	-8	26	-1	-56	-24	212	63	-25	-23	-54
Private nonguaranteed	**0**	**0**	**0**	**0**	**0**	**0**	**0**	**0**	**0**	**0**
Bonds	0	0	0	0	0	0	0	0	0	0
Commercial banks	0	0	0	0	0	0	0	0	0	0
Memo:										
IBRD	0	-10	-12	-13	-9	-9	-8	-7	-4	-4
IDA	3	26	65	61	64	47	99	217	147	66
DEBT SERVICE (LTDS)	**21**	**34**	**280**	**269**	**201**	**124**	**104**	**90**	**107**	**153**
Public and publicly guaranteed	**21**	**34**	**280**	**269**	**201**	**124**	**104**	**90**	**107**	**153**
Official creditors	11	25	167	133	70	60	49	49	62	75
Multilateral	6	13	32	34	29	42	42	42	53	63
Concessional	5	7	21	20	19	25	23	22	32	42
Bilateral	5	13	136	99	41	19	7	7	10	12
Concessional	5	11	100	74	22	13	4	5	4	9
Private creditors	11	9	113	137	131	64	56	40	45	78
Bonds	0	0	0	0	0	0	0	0	0	0
Commercial banks	0	4	31	51	56	14	6	5	18	24
Other private	11	5	82	86	75	50	50	35	27	54
Private nonguaranteed	**0**	**0**	**0**	**0**	**0**	**0**	**0**	**0**	**0**	**0**
Bonds	0	0	0	0	0	0	0	0	0	0
Commercial banks	0	0	0	0	0	0	0	0	0	0
Memo:										
IBRD	6	10	12	13	9	9	8	7	4	4
IDA	0	2	10	9	10	11	13	15	19	23
UNDISBURSED DEBT	**108**	**436**	**1,456**	**1,646**	**1,979**	**1,457**	**1,178**	**1,430**	**1,305**	**1,167**
Official creditors	105	383	1,322	1,507	1,542	1,281	1,148	1,411	1,290	1,160
Private creditors	4	54	135	138	436	176	30	19	15	8
Memorandum items										
Concessional LDOD	136	587	2,426	2,652	2,949	3,078	3,255	3,583	3,898	4,127
Variable rate LDOD	0	10	189	159	114	105	104	101	84	65
Public sector LDOD	161	685	3,082	3,345	3,656	4,004	4,167	4,459	4,753	4,958
Private sector LDOD	8	3	3	2	1	1	1	0	0	0

6. CURRENCY COMPOSITION OF LONG-TERM DEBT (PERCENT)

	1970	1980	1988	1989	1990	1991	1992	1993	1994	1995
Deutsche mark	2.7	8.1	3.8	3.9	2.3	2.6	2.0	2.1	2.4	2.4
French franc	0.0	0.0	0.3	0.3	0.4	0.2	0.1	0.2	0.1	0.1
Japanese yen	0.0	2.5	2.2	1.5	1.1	1.0	0.8	1.0	1.1	1.0
Pound sterling	2.1	2.3	1.1	0.7	0.6	0.5	0.4	0.3	0.3	0.4
Swiss franc	0.2	0.1	0.4	0.3	0.2	0.2	0.1	0.2	0.2	0.2
U.S.dollars	41.8	64.5	56.2	57.7	55.9	57.4	59.4	59.3	58.9	57.5
Multiple currency	28.1	14.7	9.2	9.2	10.1	10.3	10.9	12.7	13.9	15.5
Special drawing rights	0.0	0.0	0.6	0.5	0.5	0.5	0.4	0.4	0.4	0.4
All other currencies	25.0	7.8	26.2	26.0	28.8	27.5	25.9	23.9	22.9	22.3

ETHIOPIA

(US$ million, unless otherwise indicated)

	1970	1980	1988	1989	1990	1991	1992	1993	1994	1995
7. DEBT RESTRUCTURINGS										
Total amount rescheduled	0	0	0	0	0	0	134	66	47	28
Debt stock rescheduled	0	0	0	0	0	0	0	0	0	0
Principal rescheduled	0	0	0	0	0	0	106	47	33	22
Official	0	0	0	0	0	0	38	25	19	13
Private	0	0	0	0	0	0	68	22	14	9
Interest rescheduled	0	0	0	0	0	0	27	16	11	6
Official	0	0	0	0	0	0	15	9	5	3
Private	0	0	0	0	0	0	12	7	5	3
Debt forgiven	..	..	0	0	67	6	44	13	15	6
Memo: interest forgiven	..	..	0	0	0	0	7	2	3	1
Debt stock reduction	0	0	0	0	0	0	0	0	0	0
of which debt buyback	0	0	0	0	0	0	0	0	0	0
8. DEBT STOCK-FLOW RECONCILIATION										
Total change in debt stocks	..	..	..	215	320	390	145	318	340	220
Net flows on debt	..	..	..	238	190	346	229	312	206	138
Net change in interest arrears	..	..	..	14	27	40	14	26	21	22
Interest capitalized	..	..	..	0	0	0	27	16	11	6
Debt forgiveness or reduction	..	..	..	0	-67	-6	-44	-13	-15	-6
Cross-currency valuation	..	..	..	-10	126	-6	-41	-21	40	24
Residual	..	..	..	-27	44	16	-40	-2	77	37
9. AVERAGE TERMS OF NEW COMMITMENTS										
ALL CREDITORS										
Interest (%)	4.4	3.6	3.1	3.3	6.6	4.7	1.0	1.6	0.9	0.7
Maturity (years)	31.8	18.1	22.5	21.8	21.8	20.3	40.1	40.7	42.6	39.4
Grace period (years)	6.6	3.8	6.4	6.0	2.9	6.0	9.8	9.2	9.7	9.9
Grant element (%)	43.3	38.4	49.2	42.8	23.7	36.0	73.7	72.8	73.9	80.2
Official creditors										
Interest (%)	4.2	2.4	1.7	3.1	1.9	4.5	1.0	1.6	0.9	0.7
Maturity (years)	37.7	22.5	25.6	22.4	32.9	21.4	40.7	40.7	42.6	39.4
Grace period (years)	7.9	4.5	7.4	6.2	6.6	6.3	9.9	9.2	9.7	9.9
Grant element (%)	49.6	49.2	60.2	44.3	59.0	38.3	74.1	72.8	73.9	80.2
Private creditors										
Interest (%)	4.9	6.3	8.4	6.9	9.8	7.8	0.0	0.0	0.0	0.0
Maturity (years)	8.9	8.3	11.0	8.8	14.1	5.7	12.4	0.0	0.0	0.0
Grace period (years)	1.7	2.1	2.9	1.9	0.4	1.6	4.9	0.0	0.0	0.0
Grant element (%)	18.9	14.3	6.7	11.1	-0.4	5.6	55.2	0.0	0.0	0.0
Memorandum items										
Commitments	21	194	555	740	580	102	248	656	173	142
Official creditors	17	134	440	708	236	95	242	656	173	142
Private creditors	4	60	115	32	345	7	5	0	0	0

10. CONTRACTUAL OBLIGATIONS ON OUTSTANDING LONG-TERM DEBT	1996	1997	1998	1999	2000	2001	2002	2003	2004	2005
TOTAL										
Disbursements	402	320	195	125	69	29	13	1	1	0
Principal	307	278	240	219	193	161	161	158	155	134
Interest	91	86	80	74	68	62	56	51	45	40
Official creditors										
Disbursements	398	317	194	125	69	29	13	1	1	0
Principal	233	213	194	186	167	138	140	137	134	123
Interest	63	63	62	60	56	53	50	46	42	39
Bilateral creditors										
Disbursements	12	10	6	4	3	1	1	1	1	0
Principal	183	159	132	118	96	65	57	50	44	31
Interest	29	25	21	18	16	14	13	12	11	10
Multilateral creditors										
Disbursements	386	308	188	121	66	27	13	1	0	0
Principal	50	54	62	69	71	73	83	86	90	93
Interest	34	39	41	42	41	39	37	34	32	29
Private creditors										
Disbursements	4	3	1	0	0	0	0	0	0	0
Principal	74	65	46	33	26	23	21	21	21	11
Interest	28	23	18	14	11	9	7	5	3	1
Commercial banks										
Disbursements	0	0	0	0	0	0	0	0	0	0
Principal	26	26	12	0	0	0	0	0	0	0
Interest	4	2	1	0	0	0	0	0	0	0
Other private										
Disbursements	4	3	1	0	0	0	0	0	0	0
Principal	48	39	34	33	26	23	21	21	21	11
Interest	24	20	17	14	11	9	7	5	3	1

FIJI

(US$ million, unless otherwise indicated)

	1970	1980	1988	1989	1990	1991	1992	1993	1994	1995
1. SUMMARY DEBT DATA										
TOTAL DEBT STOCKS (EDT)	..	**281.2**	**471.9**	**414.2**	**412.7**	**360.4**	**338.7**	**330.3**	**285.7**	**252.8**
Long-term debt (LDOD)	**11.7**	**244.9**	**436.6**	**399.4**	**400.7**	**349.0**	**308.2**	**283.6**	**269.7**	**237.9**
Public and publicly guaranteed	11.7	180.0	335.6	301.6	306.0	270.6	226.9	199.6	182.2	169.9
Private nonguaranteed	0.0	64.9	101.0	97.8	94.7	78.4	81.3	84.0	87.5	68.0
Use of IMF credit	**0.0**	**0.0**	**4.0**	**0.8**	**0.0**	**0.0**	**0.0**	**0.0**	**0.0**	**0.0**
Short-term debt	..	**36.3**	**31.4**	**14.0**	**12.0**	**11.4**	**30.5**	**46.7**	**16.0**	**14.9**
of which interest arrears on LDOD	..	0.3	0.0	0.0	0.0	0.0	0.0	0.0	0.0	0.1
Official creditors	..	0.3	0.0	0.0	0.0	0.0	0.0	0.0	0.0	0.1
Private creditors	..	0.0	0.0	0.0	0.0	0.0	0.0	0.0	0.0	0.0
Memo: principal arrears on LDOD	..	0.0	0.0	0.0	0.0	0.0	0.1	0.2	3.7	3.2
Official creditors	..	0.0	0.0	0.0	0.0	0.0	0.1	0.2	3.7	3.2
Private creditors	..	0.0	0.0	0.0	0.0	0.0	0.0	0.0	0.0	0.0
Memo: export credits	..	..	56.0	136.0	61.0	42.0	39.0	24.0	28.0	28.0
TOTAL DEBT FLOWS										
Disbursements	**2.3**	**78.2**	**46.9**	**27.8**	**33.5**	**34.4**	**36.8**	**32.6**	**41.4**	**15.2**
Long-term debt	2.3	78.2	46.9	27.8	33.5	34.4	36.8	32.6	41.4	15.2
IMF purchases	0.0	0.0	0.0	0.0	0.0	0.0	0.0	0.0	0.0	0.0
Principal repayments	**1.6**	**19.7**	**39.1**	**58.1**	**73.0**	**73.2**	**59.8**	**56.8**	**70.5**	**51.3**
Long-term debt	1.6	11.2	36.7	55.0	72.2	73.2	59.8	56.8	70.5	51.3
IMF repurchases	0.0	8.5	2.4	3.0	0.8	0.0	0.0	0.0	0.0	0.0
Net flows on debt	**0.7**	**58.6**	**17.6**	**-47.7**	**-41.5**	**-39.4**	**-4.0**	**-7.9**	**-59.8**	**-37.2**
of which short-term debt	..	..	9.9	-17.4	-2.0	-0.6	19.1	16.2	-30.7	-1.1
Interest payments (INT)	..	**16.2**	**28.2**	**33.2**	**32.9**	**29.7**	**24.1**	**21.4**	**21.0**	**16.0**
Long-term debt	1.1	9.5	24.9	31.9	31.4	28.5	22.8	19.5	19.1	15.0
IMF charges	0.0	0.3	0.4	0.2	0.0	0.0	0.0	0.0	0.0	0.0
Short-term debt	..	6.3	3.0	1.0	1.5	1.2	1.3	1.9	1.9	0.9
Net transfers on debt	..	**42.4**	**-10.6**	**-80.8**	**-74.4**	**-69.1**	**-28.1**	**-29.4**	**-80.8**	**-53.2**
Total debt service paid (TDS)	..	**35.8**	**67.3**	**91.3**	**105.9**	**102.9**	**83.9**	**78.2**	**91.5**	**67.3**
Long-term debt	2.7	20.7	61.6	86.9	103.5	101.7	82.6	76.2	89.6	66.4
IMF repurchases and charges	0.0	8.8	2.7	3.3	0.8	0.0	0.0	0.0	0.0	0.0
Short-term debt (interest only)	..	6.3	3.0	1.0	1.5	1.2	1.3	1.9	1.9	0.9
2. AGGREGATE NET RESOURCE FLOWS AND NET TRANSFERS (LONG-TERM)										
NET RESOURCE FLOWS	**11.2**	**118.6**	**61.4**	**-4.8**	**55.6**	**-13.6**	**52.3**	**28.4**	**46.8**	**51.1**
Net flow of long-term debt (ex. IMF)	0.7	67.1	10.1	-27.2	-38.7	-38.8	-23.1	-24.1	-29.1	-36.1
Foreign direct investment (net)	6.4	36.4	32.0	8.0	80.0	15.0	50.0	29.0	65.0	67.0
Portfolio equity flows	0.0	0.0	0.0	0.0	0.0	0.0	0.0	0.0	0.0	0.0
Grants (excluding technical coop.)	4.1	15.1	19.3	14.4	14.3	10.2	25.4	23.5	10.9	20.2
Memo: technical coop. grants	2.9	17.0	36.6	28.8	36.6	34.9	40.3	36.9	34.1	30.7
NET TRANSFERS	**-1.4**	**78.7**	**2.5**	**-88.3**	**-15.6**	**-85.7**	**-24.9**	**-53.3**	**-40.3**	**-30.0**
Interest on long-term debt	1.1	9.5	24.9	31.9	31.4	28.5	22.8	19.5	19.1	15.0
Profit remittances on FDI	11.5	30.4	34.1	51.6	39.9	43.6	54.4	62.2	68.0	66.0
3. MAJOR ECONOMIC AGGREGATES										
Gross national product (GNP)	210.8	1,186.2	1,072.3	1,206.6	1,345.8	1,472.9	1,579.4	1,608.5	1,683.1	1,805.1
Exports of goods & services (XGS)	..	597.1	663.8	834.6	933.5	920.2	932.8	1,000.1	1,053.8	1,141.5
of which workers remittances	..	0.0	0.0	0.0	0.0	0.0	0.0	0.0	0.0	0.0
Imports of goods & services (MGS)	..	656.6	633.9	790.3	961.6	903.8	910.6	1,029.2	1,192.5	1,251.8
International reserves (RES)	27.4	174.1	233.7	211.9	261.1	271.7	317.1	269.8	273.5	349.3
Current account balance	..	-17.5	70.6	77.3	-9.7	52.5	59.4	13.0	-59.4	0.1
4. DEBT INDICATORS										
EDT / XGS (%)	..	47.1	71.1	49.6	44.2	39.2	36.3	33.0	27.1	22.1
EDT / GNP (%)	..	23.7	44.0	34.3	30.7	24.5	21.4	20.5	17.0	14.0
TDS / XGS (%)	..	6.0	10.1	10.9	11.3	11.2	9.0	7.8	8.7	5.9
INT / XGS (%)	..	2.7	4.2	4.0	3.5	3.2	2.6	2.1	2.0	1.4
INT / GNP (%)	..	1.4	2.6	2.7	2.4	2.0	1.5	1.3	1.2	0.9
RES / EDT (%)	..	61.9	49.5	51.2	63.3	75.4	93.6	81.7	95.7	138.2
RES / MGS (months)	..	3.2	4.4	3.2	3.3	3.6	4.2	3.1	2.8	3.3
Short-term / EDT (%)	..	12.9	6.6	3.4	2.9	3.2	9.0	14.1	5.6	5.9
Concessional / EDT (%)	..	11.1	8.8	9.6	10.9	13.8	15.0	15.8	20.3	23.5
Multilateral / EDT (%)	..	23.2	42.2	46.2	49.0	56.2	54.4	50.2	56.1	59.8

FIJI

(US$ million, unless otherwise indicated)

5. LONG-TERM DEBT

	1970	1980	1988	1989	1990	1991	1992	1993	1994	1995
DEBT OUTSTANDING (LDOD)	**11.7**	**244.9**	**436.6**	**399.4**	**400.7**	**349.0**	**308.2**	**283.6**	**269.7**	**237.9**
Public and publicly guaranteed	**11.7**	**180.0**	**335.6**	**301.6**	**306.0**	**270.6**	**226.9**	**199.6**	**182.2**	**169.9**
Official creditors	8.2	123.7	281.4	263.6	279.1	253.5	221.2	196.7	180.7	169.3
Multilateral	0.0	65.1	199.4	191.3	202.0	202.5	184.2	165.7	160.3	151.2
Concessional	0.0	9.6	26.5	26.0	29.6	34.6	38.6	40.5	47.8	50.1
Bilateral	8.2	58.6	82.1	72.3	77.1	51.0	37.0	31.0	20.4	18.1
Concessional	1.7	21.5	15.0	13.5	15.2	15.1	12.0	11.7	10.3	9.3
Private creditors	3.5	56.3	54.1	38.1	26.9	17.2	5.7	2.9	1.5	0.6
Bonds	3.5	2.5	0.0	0.0	0.0	0.0	0.0	0.0	0.0	0.0
Commercial banks	0.0	41.0	27.0	16.5	12.1	6.1	1.7	0.7	0.6	0.4
Other private	0.0	12.8	27.2	21.6	14.7	11.0	4.0	2.2	0.9	0.1
Private nonguaranteed	**0.0**	**64.9**	**101.0**	**97.8**	**94.7**	**78.4**	**81.3**	**84.0**	**87.5**	**68.0**
Bonds	0.0	0.0	0.0	0.0	0.0	0.0	0.0	0.0	0.0	0.0
Commercial banks	0.0	64.9	101.0	97.8	94.7	78.4	81.3	84.0	87.5	68.0
Memo:										
IBRD	0.0	33.5	71.9	66.2	67.8	65.1	53.2	43.6	39.6	35.3
IDA	0.0	0.0	0.0	0.0	0.0	0.0	0.0	0.0	0.0	0.0
DISBURSEMENTS	**2.3**	**78.2**	**46.9**	**27.8**	**33.5**	**34.4**	**36.8**	**32.6**	**41.4**	**15.2**
Public and publicly guaranteed	**2.3**	**78.2**	**46.9**	**15.0**	**19.3**	**22.4**	**16.6**	**11.1**	**16.9**	**15.2**
Official creditors	2.3	43.4	33.1	13.9	18.6	22.4	16.5	11.1	16.9	15.2
Multilateral	0.0	23.2	33.1	8.5	13.2	21.2	16.5	10.2	16.9	15.2
Concessional	0.0	6.7	2.1	0.5	2.1	7.2	10.0	7.1	5.3	3.1
Bilateral	2.3	20.2	0.0	5.4	5.3	1.2	0.0	1.0	0.0	0.0
Concessional	2.3	0.0	0.0	1.1	1.0	1.2	0.0	1.0	0.0	0.0
Private creditors	0.0	34.8	13.7	1.1	0.7	0.0	0.0	0.0	0.0	0.0
Bonds	0.0	0.0	0.0	0.0	0.0	0.0	0.0	0.0	0.0	0.0
Commercial banks	0.0	31.0	0.0	1.1	0.6	0.0	0.0	0.0	0.0	0.0
Other private	0.0	3.8	13.7	0.0	0.1	0.0	0.0	0.0	0.0	0.0
Private nonguaranteed	**0.0**	**0.0**	**0.0**	**12.8**	**14.2**	**12.0**	**20.2**	**21.5**	**24.5**	**0.0**
Bonds	0.0	0.0	0.0	0.0	0.0	0.0	0.0	0.0	0.0	0.0
Commercial banks	0.0	0.0	0.0	12.8	14.2	12.0	20.2	21.5	24.5	0.0
Memo:										
IBRD	0.0	5.7	7.7	5.6	5.1	7.9	2.2	1.5	5.8	5.6
IDA	0.0	0.0	0.0	0.0	0.0	0.0	0.0	0.0	0.0	0.0
PRINCIPAL REPAYMENTS	**1.6**	**11.2**	**36.7**	**55.0**	**72.2**	**73.2**	**59.8**	**56.8**	**70.5**	**51.3**
Public and publicly guaranteed	**1.6**	**11.2**	**36.7**	**39.0**	**54.7**	**56.9**	**42.1**	**38.0**	**51.4**	**31.8**
Official creditors	0.7	4.2	23.3	23.1	41.5	47.5	32.0	35.1	49.8	30.9
Multilateral	0.0	1.0	15.7	15.8	33.8	22.0	25.1	29.0	38.5	28.2
Concessional	0.0	0.0	1.3	1.4	2.2	2.0	2.3	2.4	2.1	3.2
Bilateral	0.7	3.2	7.6	7.3	7.7	25.5	6.9	6.2	11.2	2.7
Concessional	0.6	1.4	0.9	0.8	0.8	0.9	1.1	1.0	1.1	1.4
Private creditors	0.9	7.0	13.4	15.9	13.2	9.4	10.2	2.8	1.6	1.0
Bonds	0.9	1.6	0.1	0.0	0.0	0.0	0.0	0.0	0.0	0.0
Commercial banks	0.0	0.0	11.3	11.2	5.7	5.9	3.5	0.9	0.2	0.2
Other private	0.0	5.3	2.1	4.7	7.5	3.5	6.7	1.9	1.4	0.7
Private nonguaranteed	**0.0**	**0.0**	**0.0**	**16.0**	**17.5**	**16.3**	**17.7**	**18.8**	**19.1**	**19.5**
Bonds	0.0	0.0	0.0	0.0	0.0	0.0	0.0	0.0	0.0	0.0
Commercial banks	0.0	0.0	0.0	16.0	17.5	16.3	17.7	18.8	19.1	19.5
Memo:										
IBRD	0.0	0.7	9.2	9.2	9.1	11.3	12.0	12.2	12.9	11.5
IDA	0.0	0.0	0.0	0.0	0.0	0.0	0.0	0.0	0.0	0.0
NET FLOWS ON DEBT	**0.7**	**67.1**	**10.1**	**-27.2**	**-38.7**	**-38.8**	**-23.1**	**-24.1**	**-29.1**	**-36.1**
Public and publicly guaranteed	**0.7**	**67.1**	**10.1**	**-24.0**	**-35.4**	**-34.5**	**-25.6**	**-26.8**	**-34.5**	**-16.6**
Official creditors	1.6	39.2	9.8	-9.2	-22.9	-25.1	-15.4	-24.0	-32.9	-15.7
Multilateral	0.0	22.2	17.5	-7.3	-20.5	-0.8	-8.5	-18.8	-21.6	-13.0
Concessional	0.0	6.7	0.8	-0.9	-0.1	5.1	7.7	4.8	3.2	0.0
Bilateral	1.6	17.0	-7.6	-1.9	-2.4	-24.3	-6.9	-5.2	-11.2	-2.7
Concessional	1.7	-1.4	-0.9	0.3	0.1	0.3	-1.1	0.0	-1.1	-1.4
Private creditors	-0.9	27.9	0.3	-14.8	-12.5	-9.4	-10.1	-2.8	-1.6	-1.0
Bonds	-0.9	-1.6	-0.1	0.0	0.0	0.0	0.0	0.0	0.0	0.0
Commercial banks	0.0	31.0	-11.3	-10.1	-5.1	-5.9	-3.4	-0.9	-0.2	-0.2
Other private	0.0	-1.5	11.6	-4.7	-7.3	-3.5	-6.7	-1.9	-1.4	-0.7
Private nonguaranteed	**0.0**	**0.0**	**0.0**	**-3.2**	**-3.3**	**-4.3**	**2.5**	**2.7**	**5.4**	**-19.5**
Bonds	0.0	0.0	0.0	0.0	0.0	0.0	0.0	0.0	0.0	0.0
Commercial banks	0.0	0.0	0.0	-3.2	-3.3	-4.3	2.5	2.7	5.4	-19.5
Memo:										
IBRD	0.0	5.0	-1.5	-3.6	-4.0	-3.4	-9.7	-10.7	-7.0	-5.9
IDA	0.0	0.0	0.0	0.0	0.0	0.0	0.0	0.0	0.0	0.0

FIJI

(US$ million, unless otherwise indicated)

	1970	1980	1988	1989	1990	1991	1992	1993	1994	1995
INTEREST PAYMENTS (LINT)	**1.1**	**9.5**	**24.9**	**31.9**	**31.4**	**28.5**	**22.8**	**19.5**	**19.1**	**15.0**
Public and publicly guaranteed	**1.1**	**9.5**	**24.9**	**24.1**	**24.0**	**21.7**	**17.2**	**14.8**	**13.7**	**10.7**
Official creditors	0.6	6.1	21.2	19.7	21.4	19.5	16.7	14.5	13.5	10.6
Multilateral	0.0	3.4	13.5	12.9	15.0	13.0	13.2	12.0	11.4	9.4
Concessional	0.0	0.1	0.6	0.5	0.6	0.6	1.0	1.3	1.5	1.7
Bilateral	0.6	2.7	7.7	6.8	6.3	6.4	3.5	2.5	2.1	1.1
Concessional	0.1	0.8	0.5	0.5	0.3	0.5	0.5	0.4	0.4	0.3
Private creditors	0.5	3.5	3.7	4.4	2.6	2.2	0.6	0.3	0.2	0.1
Bonds	0.5	0.3	0.0	0.0	0.0	0.0	0.0	0.0	0.0	0.0
Commercial banks	0.0	2.1	2.7	2.4	1.1	1.5	0.3	0.1	0.1	0.1
Other private	0.0	1.1	1.0	2.0	1.5	0.7	0.3	0.2	0.1	0.0
Private nonguaranteed	**0.0**	**0.0**	**0.0**	**7.8**	**7.4**	**6.8**	**5.6**	**4.7**	**5.5**	**4.4**
Bonds	0.0	0.0	0.0	0.0	0.0	0.0	0.0	0.0	0.0	0.0
Commercial banks	0.0	0.0	0.0	7.8	7.4	6.8	5.6	4.7	5.5	4.4
Memo:										
IBRD	0.0	2.7	6.2	5.5	5.6	5.3	4.8	4.0	3.4	3.0
IDA	0.0	0.0	0.0	0.0	0.0	0.0	0.0	0.0	0.0	0.0
NET TRANSFERS ON DEBT	**-0.4**	**57.6**	**-14.7**	**-59.1**	**-70.0**	**-67.3**	**-45.9**	**-43.6**	**-48.2**	**-51.2**
Public and publicly guaranteed	**-0.4**	**57.6**	**-14.7**	**-48.1**	**-59.3**	**-56.2**	**-42.8**	**-41.6**	**-48.1**	**-27.3**
Official creditors	0.9	33.1	-11.3	-28.9	-44.3	-44.6	-32.1	-38.5	-46.4	-26.3
Multilateral	0.0	18.9	4.0	-20.3	-35.5	-13.9	-21.7	-30.8	-33.0	-22.5
Concessional	0.0	6.6	0.2	-1.4	-0.7	4.5	6.8	3.4	1.7	-1.8
Bilateral	0.9	14.3	-15.3	-8.6	-8.7	-30.7	-10.4	-7.7	-13.3	-3.8
Concessional	1.6	-2.2	-1.5	-0.2	-0.2	-0.2	-1.6	-0.4	-1.5	-1.7
Private creditors	-1.4	24.4	-3.4	-19.2	-15.1	-11.6	-10.7	-3.1	-1.8	-1.0
Bonds	-1.4	-1.9	-0.1	0.0	0.0	0.0	0.0	0.0	0.0	0.0
Commercial banks	0.0	28.9	-13.9	-12.5	-6.2	-7.3	-3.7	-1.0	-0.2	-0.3
Other private	0.0	-2.5	10.6	-6.7	-8.9	-4.3	-7.0	-2.0	-1.5	-0.8
Private nonguaranteed	**0.0**	**0.0**	**0.0**	**-11.0**	**-10.7**	**-11.1**	**-3.1**	**-2.0**	**-0.1**	**-23.9**
Bonds	0.0	0.0	0.0	0.0	0.0	0.0	0.0	0.0	0.0	0.0
Commercial banks	0.0	0.0	0.0	-11.0	-10.7	-11.1	-3.1	-2.0	-0.1	-23.9
Memo:										
IBRD	0.0	2.3	-7.7	-9.1	-9.6	-8.7	-14.6	-14.7	-10.5	-8.9
IDA	0.0	0.0	0.0	0.0	0.0	0.0	0.0	0.0	0.0	0.0
DEBT SERVICE (LTDS)	**2.7**	**20.7**	**61.6**	**86.9**	**103.5**	**101.7**	**82.6**	**76.2**	**89.6**	**66.4**
Public and publicly guaranteed	**2.7**	**20.7**	**61.6**	**63.1**	**78.6**	**78.6**	**59.3**	**52.8**	**65.0**	**42.5**
Official creditors	1.4	10.3	44.5	42.8	62.8	67.0	48.6	49.7	63.3	41.5
Multilateral	0.0	4.4	29.2	28.8	48.8	35.1	38.2	41.0	49.9	37.7
Concessional	0.0	0.1	1.9	1.9	2.8	2.7	3.2	3.7	3.6	4.9
Bilateral	1.4	5.9	15.3	14.1	14.0	31.9	10.4	8.6	13.3	3.8
Concessional	0.7	2.2	1.5	1.3	1.2	1.5	1.6	1.4	1.5	1.7
Private creditors	1.4	10.4	17.1	20.3	15.8	11.6	10.7	3.1	1.8	1.0
Bonds	1.4	1.9	0.1	0.0	0.0	0.0	0.0	0.0	0.0	0.0
Commercial banks	0.0	2.1	13.9	13.6	6.8	7.3	3.7	1.0	0.2	0.3
Other private	0.0	6.4	3.1	6.7	9.0	4.3	7.0	2.0	1.5	0.8
Private nonguaranteed	**0.0**	**0.0**	**0.0**	**23.8**	**24.9**	**23.1**	**23.3**	**23.5**	**24.6**	**23.9**
Bonds	0.0	0.0	0.0	0.0	0.0	0.0	0.0	0.0	0.0	0.0
Commercial banks	0.0	0.0	0.0	23.8	24.9	23.1	23.3	23.5	24.6	23.9
Memo:										
IBRD	0.0	3.3	15.4	14.7	14.7	16.6	16.8	16.2	16.3	14.5
IDA	0.0	0.0	0.0	0.0	0.0	0.0	0.0	0.0	0.0	0.0
UNDISBURSED DEBT	**1.4**	**120.8**	**45.3**	**69.3**	**81.2**	**64.9**	**45.1**	**66.2**	**48.8**	**37.5**
Official creditors	1.2	120.8	41.8	66.8	80.6	64.3	45.1	66.2	48.8	37.5
Private creditors	0.2	0.0	3.5	2.5	0.6	0.6	0.0	0.0	0.0	0.0
Memorandum items										
Concessional LDOD	1.7	31.1	41.4	39.6	44.8	49.7	50.6	52.2	58.1	59.4
Variable rate LDOD	0.0	105.9	136.7	126.1	124.0	108.6	107.4	110.7	125.1	113.9
Public sector LDOD	11.7	180.0	335.6	301.6	306.0	270.6	226.9	199.6	182.2	169.9
Private sector LDOD	0.0	64.9	101.0	97.8	94.7	78.4	81.3	84.0	87.5	68.0
6. CURRENCY COMPOSITION OF LONG-TERM DEBT (PERCENT)										
Deutsche mark	0.0	0.0	0.0	0.0	0.0	0.0	0.0	0.0	0.0	0.0
French franc	0.0	0.0	0.0	0.8	1.4	1.7	1.7	1.7	1.9	2.1
Japanese yen	0.0	0.0	0.1	0.1	0.0	0.0	0.0	0.0	0.0	0.0
Pound sterling	34.3	24.7	14.9	14.4	16.4	14.9	12.2	11.3	7.0	6.2
Swiss franc	0.0	0.0	0.0	0.0	0.0	0.0	0.0	0.0	0.0	0.0
U.S.dollars	14.6	26.1	12.3	9.5	5.2	3.5	0.6	1.0	0.9	0.8
Multiple currency	0.0	36.2	52.8	56.3	58.9	67.8	74.7	77.2	82.1	83.4
Special drawing rights	0.0	0.0	0.0	0.0	0.0	0.0	0.0	0.0	0.0	0.0
All other currencies	51.4	13.1	19.9	19.0	18.0	12.1	10.8	8.9	8.2	7.5

FIJI

(US$ million, unless otherwise indicated)

	1970	1980	1988	1989	1990	1991	1992	1993	1994	1995
7. DEBT RESTRUCTURINGS										
Total amount rescheduled	0.0	0.0	0.0	0.0	0.0	0.0	0.0	0.0	0.0	0.0
Debt stock rescheduled	0.0	0.0	0.0	0.0	0.0	0.0	0.0	0.0	0.0	0.0
Principal rescheduled	0.0	0.0	0.0	0.0	0.0	0.0	0.0	0.0	0.0	0.0
Official	0.0	0.0	0.0	0.0	0.0	0.0	0.0	0.0	0.0	0.0
Private	0.0	0.0	0.0	0.0	0.0	0.0	0.0	0.0	0.0	0.0
Interest rescheduled	0.0	0.0	0.0	0.0	0.0	0.0	0.0	0.0	0.0	0.0
Official	0.0	0.0	0.0	0.0	0.0	0.0	0.0	0.0	0.0	0.0
Private	0.0	0.0	0.0	0.0	0.0	0.0	0.0	0.0	0.0	0.0
Debt forgiven	..	..	0.0	0.0	0.0	0.0	0.0	0.0	0.0	0.0
Memo: interest forgiven	..	..	0.0	0.0	0.0	0.0	0.0	0.0	0.0	0.0
Debt stock reduction	0.0	0.0	0.0	0.0	0.0	0.0	0.0	0.0	0.0	0.0
of which debt buyback	0.0	0.0	0.0	0.0	0.0	0.0	0.0	0.0	0.0	0.0
8. DEBT STOCK-FLOW RECONCILIATION										
Total change in debt stocks	..	..	..	-57.7	-1.5	-52.3	-21.7	-8.4	-44.6	-32.8
Net flows on debt	..	..	..	-47.7	-41.5	-39.4	-4.0	-7.9	-59.8	-37.2
Net change in interest arrears	..	..	..	0.0	0.0	0.0	0.0	0.0	0.0	0.1
Interest capitalized	..	..	..	0.0	0.0	0.0	0.0	0.0	0.0	0.0
Debt forgiveness or reduction	..	..	..	0.0	0.0	0.0	0.0	0.0	0.0	0.0
Cross-currency valuation	..	..	..	-17.1	25.2	-5.6	-24.1	-7.0	5.7	1.5
Residual	..	..	..	7.1	14.7	-7.2	6.3	6.5	9.5	2.8
9. AVERAGE TERMS OF NEW COMMITMENTS										
ALL CREDITORS										
Interest (%)	3.1	8.1	6.5	6.2	6.6	2.9	0.0	6.9	0.0	4.5
Maturity (years)	17.7	14.4	15.5	14.6	24.7	11.9	0.0	20.5	0.0	12.0
Grace period (years)	5.2	3.7	3.4	4.2	5.1	3.6	0.0	4.6	0.0	4.5
Grant element (%)	43.6	9.5	17.5	20.5	22.9	36.0	0.0	19.6	0.0	28.8
Official creditors										
Interest (%)	3.0	7.9	6.8	6.2	6.6	2.9	0.0	6.9	0.0	4.5
Maturity (years)	18.5	14.7	17.7	14.6	24.8	11.9	0.0	20.5	0.0	12.0
Grace period (years)	5.5	3.7	4.0	4.2	5.1	3.6	0.0	4.6	0.0	4.5
Grant element (%)	45.6	10.6	19.2	20.5	22.9	36.0	0.0	19.6	0.0	28.8
Private creditors										
Interest (%)	5.5	10.2	5.7	0.0	8.8	0.0	0.0	0.0	0.0	0.0
Maturity (years)	5.2	10.0	7.9	0.0	10.4	0.0	0.0	0.0	0.0	0.0
Grace period (years)	0.7	3.3	1.1	0.0	6.2	0.0	0.0	0.0	0.0	0.0
Grant element (%)	10.5	-4.3	11.6	0.0	3.5	0.0	0.0	0.0	0.0	0.0
Memorandum items										
Commitments	3.7	89.1	77.4	37.2	30.0	6.7	0.0	33.0	0.0	10.5
Official creditors	3.5	82.6	60.0	37.2	29.8	6.7	0.0	33.0	0.0	10.5
Private creditors	0.2	6.5	17.4	0.0	0.1	0.0	0.0	0.0	0.0	0.0

10. CONTRACTUAL OBLIGATIONS ON OUTSTANDING LONG-TERM DEBT

	1996	1997	1998	1999	2000	2001	2002	2003	2004	2005
TOTAL										
Disbursements	10.1	10.3	6.5	4.2	2.9	1.9	1.1	0.7	0.0	0.0
Principal	33.9	26.9	25.6	24.4	23.8	21.9	21.0	18.5	11.5	7.8
Interest	13.4	12.5	11.0	9.7	8.2	7.1	6.1	5.1	4.2	3.5
Official creditors										
Disbursements	10.1	10.3	6.5	4.2	2.9	1.9	1.1	0.7	0.0	0.0
Principal	18.2	15.4	16.6	16.9	18.1	15.8	15.5	13.5	9.0	7.8
Interest	9.9	9.5	9.0	8.2	7.4	6.4	5.6	4.7	4.0	3.5
Bilateral creditors										
Disbursements	0.0	0.0	0.0	0.0	0.0	0.0	0.0	0.0	0.0	0.0
Principal	2.6	2.2	2.5	2.5	2.3	1.0	1.0	1.0	0.4	0.2
Interest	1.0	0.8	0.7	0.5	0.4	0.2	0.2	0.1	0.1	0.1
Multilateral creditors										
Disbursements	10.1	10.3	6.5	4.2	2.9	1.9	1.1	0.7	0.0	0.0
Principal	15.6	13.2	14.2	14.4	15.8	14.8	14.5	12.4	8.6	7.6
Interest	8.9	8.7	8.3	7.7	7.0	6.2	5.4	4.6	3.9	3.4
Private creditors										
Disbursements	0.0	0.0	0.0	0.0	0.0	0.0	0.0	0.0	0.0	0.0
Principal	15.7	11.5	9.0	7.5	5.6	6.1	5.5	5.0	2.5	0.0
Interest	3.6	3.0	2.0	1.5	0.8	0.7	0.5	0.4	0.2	0.0
Commercial banks										
Disbursements	0.0	0.0	0.0	0.0	0.0	0.0	0.0	0.0	0.0	0.0
Principal	0.2	0.2	0.0	0.0	0.0	0.0	0.0	0.0	0.0	0.0
Interest	0.0	0.0	0.0	0.0	0.0	0.0	0.0	0.0	0.0	0.0
Other private										
Disbursements	0.0	0.0	0.0	0.0	0.0	0.0	0.0	0.0	0.0	0.0
Principal	15.5	11.3	9.0	7.5	5.6	6.1	5.5	5.0	2.5	0.0
Interest	3.5	3.0	2.0	1.5	0.8	0.7	0.5	0.4	0.2	0.0

GABON

(US$ million, unless otherwise indicated)

	1970	1980	1988	1989	1990	1991	1992	1993	1994	1995
1. SUMMARY DEBT DATA										
TOTAL DEBT STOCKS (EDT)	..	1,514	2,845	3,351	3,984	4,223	3,851	3,861	3,986	4,492
Long-term debt (LDOD)	91	1,272	2,301	2,611	3,151	3,225	3,049	2,933	3,509	4,099
Public and publicly guaranteed	91	1,272	2,301	2,611	3,151	3,225	3,049	2,933	3,509	4,099
Private nonguaranteed	0	0	0	0	0	0	0	0	0	0
Use of IMF credit	0	15	133	135	140	121	81	45	90	97
Short-term debt	..	228	411	605	693	878	722	883	387	297
of which interest arrears on LDOD	..	0	9	43	131	278	286	450	51	9
Official creditors	..	0	9	36	111	220	211	361	36	9
Private creditors	..	0	0	7	20	58	75	90	15	0
Memo: principal arrears on LDOD	..	0	2	29	82	261	423	650	110	28
Official creditors	..	0	1	2	17	82	144	279	47	2
Private creditors	..	0	1	27	65	179	279	371	63	26
Memo: export credits	..	..	1,643	1,608	1,917	2,140	2,134	2,050	2,194	2,476
TOTAL DEBT FLOWS										
Disbursements	26	171	349	158	186	162	108	93	188	355
Long-term debt	26	171	274	153	178	157	108	93	125	298
IMF purchases	0	0	76	5	9	6	0	0	64	57
Principal repayments	9	279	33	22	40	114	137	71	119	216
Long-term debt	9	279	33	22	26	89	100	35	96	165
IMF repurchases	0	0	0	0	15	25	36	36	23	52
Net flows on debt	17	-109	313	296	146	87	-193	19	-27	90
of which short-term debt	..	..	-3	160	0	38	-164	-3	-97	-49
Interest payments (INT)	..	153	101	124	136	196	296	86	149	226
Long-term debt	3	119	64	70	78	136	238	35	103	203
IMF charges	0	1	4	9	13	12	9	6	3	5
Short-term debt	..	33	32	45	45	48	50	45	43	17
Net transfers on debt	..	-262	213	172	11	-109	-489	-67	-176	-136
Total debt service paid (TDS)	..	432	133	146	176	309	433	157	268	442
Long-term debt	12	398	97	92	104	225	338	70	198	368
IMF repurchases and charges	0	1	4	9	27	36	45	42	26	57
Short-term debt (interest only)	..	33	32	45	45	48	50	45	43	17
2. AGGREGATE NET RESOURCE FLOWS AND NET TRANSFERS (LONG-TERM)										
NET RESOURCE FLOWS	26	-73	397	136	256	41	164	9	72	170
Net flow of long-term debt (ex. IMF)	17	-109	241	131	152	68	8	58	29	133
Foreign direct investment (net)	-1	32	133	-31	74	-55	127	-114	-103	-50
Portfolio equity flows	0	0	0	0	0	0	0	0	0	0
Grants (excluding technical coop.)	10	4	23	35	30	28	29	65	147	87
Memo: technical coop. grants	7	37	38	32	36	34	49	50	44	47
NET TRANSFERS	15	-465	301	117	61	-236	-230	-227	-250	-234
Interest on long-term debt	3	119	64	70	78	136	238	35	103	203
Profit remittances on FDI	8	273	32	-52	116	141	156	200	220	200
3. MAJOR ECONOMIC AGGREGATES										
Gross national product (GNP)	305	3,861	3,553	3,891	4,859	4,885	4,853	4,784	3,241	3,694
Exports of goods & services (XGS)	..	2,434	1,424	1,934	2,750	2,580	2,654	2,670	2,581	2,802
of which workers remittances	..	0	0	0	0	0	0	0	0	0
Imports of goods & services (MGS)	..	1,926	1,895	2,000	2,448	2,385	2,680	2,526	2,138	2,264
International reserves (RES)	15	115	73	40	279	332	75	6	180	153
Current account balance	..	384	-616	-192	168	75	-168	-49	320	324
4. DEBT INDICATORS										
EDT / XGS (%)	..	62.2	199.8	173.2	144.9	163.7	145.1	144.6	154.5	160.3
EDT / GNP (%)	..	39.2	80.1	86.1	82.0	86.5	79.4	80.7	123.0	121.6
TDS / XGS (%)	..	17.7	9.4	7.5	6.4	12.0	16.3	5.9	10.4	15.8
INT / XGS (%)	..	6.3	7.1	6.4	4.9	7.6	11.2	3.2	5.8	8.1
INT / GNP (%)	..	4.0	2.8	3.2	2.8	4.0	6.1	1.8	4.6	6.1
RES / EDT (%)	..	7.6	2.6	1.2	7.0	7.9	2.0	0.1	4.5	3.4
RES / MGS (months)	..	0.7	0.5	0.2	1.4	1.7	0.3	0.0	1.0	0.8
Short-term / EDT (%)	..	15.1	14.5	18.1	17.4	20.8	18.7	22.9	9.7	6.6
Concessional / EDT (%)	..	8.3	10.0	9.1	10.7	11.7	11.7	10.7	14.2	21.9
Multilateral / EDT (%)	..	2.7	6.0	7.1	8.0	8.2	9.3	10.6	11.5	14.8

GABON

(US$ million, unless otherwise indicated)

	1970	1980	1988	1989	1990	1991	1992	1993	1994	1995
5. LONG-TERM DEBT										
DEBT OUTSTANDING (LDOD)	**91**	**1,272**	**2,301**	**2,611**	**3,151**	**3,225**	**3,049**	**2,933**	**3,509**	**4,099**
Public and publicly guaranteed	**91**	**1,272**	**2,301**	**2,611**	**3,151**	**3,225**	**3,049**	**2,933**	**3,509**	**4,099**
Official creditors	67	316	1,423	1,843	2,435	2,548	2,423	2,337	3,242	3,900
Multilateral	31	40	171	239	317	347	358	408	458	663
Concessional	12	23	29	29	35	32	30	29	30	113
Bilateral	36	276	1,252	1,604	2,118	2,201	2,065	1,929	2,784	3,237
Concessional	35	103	256	277	393	461	423	384	536	871
Private creditors	24	955	878	768	716	676	626	596	268	199
Bonds	8	2	0	0	0	0	0	0	0	0
Commercial banks	0	721	177	176	182	176	163	161	175	148
Other private	16	232	701	593	535	500	462	435	92	51
Private nonguaranteed	**0**	**0**	**0**	**0**	**0**	**0**	**0**	**0**	**0**	**0**
Bonds	0	0	0	0	0	0	0	0	0	0
Commercial banks	0	0	0	0	0	0	0	0	0	0
Memo:										
IBRD	29	19	20	56	69	81	82	86	114	110
IDA	0	0	0	0	0	0	0	0	0	0
DISBURSEMENTS	**26**	**171**	**274**	**153**	**178**	**157**	**108**	**93**	**125**	**298**
Public and publicly guaranteed	**26**	**171**	**274**	**153**	**178**	**157**	**108**	**93**	**125**	**298**
Official creditors	13	36	141	122	141	141	108	90	123	298
Multilateral	4	2	28	81	67	44	43	66	69	226
Concessional	1	0	0	1	4	1	2	0	2	83
Bilateral	9	33	113	42	74	97	65	24	54	72
Concessional	9	16	41	15	63	70	8	19	52	62
Private creditors	13	135	133	31	37	16	0	3	2	0
Bonds	4	0	0	0	0	0	0	0	0	0
Commercial banks	0	95	60	0	0	0	0	0	0	0
Other private	9	40	73	31	37	16	0	3	2	0
Private nonguaranteed	**0**	**0**	**0**	**0**	**0**	**0**	**0**	**0**	**0**	**0**
Bonds	0	0	0	0	0	0	0	0	0	0
Commercial banks	0	0	0	0	0	0	0	0	0	0
Memo:										
IBRD	3	0	9	38	10	11	8	8	33	4
IDA	0	0	0	0	0	0	0	0	0	0
PRINCIPAL REPAYMENTS	**9**	**279**	**33**	**22**	**26**	**89**	**100**	**35**	**96**	**165**
Public and publicly guaranteed	**9**	**279**	**33**	**22**	**26**	**89**	**100**	**35**	**96**	**165**
Official creditors	6	19	18	17	18	41	84	31	63	90
Multilateral	4	3	12	13	13	16	16	15	36	43
Concessional	1	2	2	2	2	2	2	1	3	2
Bilateral	2	17	6	4	5	25	68	16	27	48
Concessional	2	4	3	1	0	6	22	7	5	10
Private creditors	4	260	15	5	8	48	17	4	33	75
Bonds	0	1	0	0	0	0	0	0	0	0
Commercial banks	0	185	11	4	3	5	12	0	3	26
Other private	3	74	4	1	5	42	5	4	30	49
Private nonguaranteed	**0**	**0**	**0**	**0**	**0**	**0**	**0**	**0**	**0**	**0**
Bonds	0	0	0	0	0	0	0	0	0	0
Commercial banks	0	0	0	0	0	0	0	0	0	0
Memo:										
IBRD	3	2	2	1	1	1	4	5	10	12
IDA	0	0	0	0	0	0	0	0	0	0
NET FLOWS ON DEBT	**17**	**-109**	**241**	**131**	**152**	**68**	**8**	**58**	**29**	**133**
Public and publicly guaranteed	**17**	**-109**	**241**	**131**	**152**	**68**	**8**	**58**	**29**	**133**
Official creditors	7	16	123	105	123	100	25	60	60	208
Multilateral	0	0	15	68	53	28	28	51	32	183
Concessional	1	-2	-2	-1	2	-2	0	0	-1	82
Bilateral	7	17	107	37	70	72	-3	8	27	24
Concessional	7	13	38	13	63	65	-14	12	47	52
Private creditors	9	-125	118	26	29	-32	-17	-2	-31	-75
Bonds	4	-1	0	0	0	0	0	0	0	0
Commercial banks	0	-91	49	-3	-3	-5	-12	0	-3	-26
Other private	6	-34	69	29	32	-26	-5	-2	-28	-49
Private nonguaranteed	**0**	**0**	**0**	**0**	**0**	**0**	**0**	**0**	**0**	**0**
Bonds	0	0	0	0	0	0	0	0	0	0
Commercial banks	0	0	0	0	0	0	0	0	0	0
Memo:										
IBRD	-1	-2	8	37	9	9	3	3	23	-8
IDA	0	0	0	0	0	0	0	0	0	0

GABON

(US$ million, unless otherwise indicated)

	1970	1980	1988	1989	1990	1991	1992	1993	1994	1995
INTEREST PAYMENTS (LINT)	**3**	**119**	**64**	**70**	**78**	**136**	**238**	**35**	**103**	**203**
Public and publicly guaranteed	**3**	**119**	**64**	**70**	**78**	**136**	**238**	**35**	**103**	**203**
Official creditors	2	19	44	55	68	85	201	30	74	160
Multilateral	1	2	13	14	21	23	26	17	37	26
Concessional	1	1	1	1	1	1	0	0	1	1
Bilateral	1	17	31	41	47	62	176	13	37	133
Concessional	1	3	2	3	2	9	19	4	14	39
Private creditors	1	100	20	15	11	51	36	6	29	44
Bonds	0	0	0	0	0	0	0	0	0	0
Commercial banks	0	81	16	14	5	23	34	6	16	27
Other private	0	19	4	2	6	28	3	0	13	17
Private nonguaranteed	**0**	**0**	**0**	**0**	**0**	**0**	**0**	**0**	**0**	**0**
Bonds	0	0	0	0	0	0	0	0	0	0
Commercial banks	0	0	0	0	0	0	0	0	0	0
Memo:										
IBRD	1	2	1	2	5	5	7	4	8	8
IDA	0	0	0	0	0	0	0	0	0	0
NET TRANSFERS ON DEBT	**14**	**-227**	**177**	**61**	**74**	**-68**	**-230**	**23**	**-74**	**-71**
Public and publicly guaranteed	**14**	**-227**	**177**	**61**	**74**	**-68**	**-230**	**23**	**-74**	**-71**
Official creditors	5	-3	78	50	55	14	-177	30	-14	48
Multilateral	-1	-2	3	54	33	5	2	34	-5	157
Concessional	0	-2	-3	-1	2	-3	0	0	-2	80
Bilateral	6	-1	76	-4	23	9	-179	-5	-10	-109
Concessional	7	10	36	11	62	56	-33	8	33	13
Private creditors	9	-224	98	11	18	-82	-53	-7	-60	-119
Bonds	3	-1	0	0	0	0	0	0	0	0
Commercial banks	0	-171	33	-17	-8	-28	-46	-6	-18	-53
Other private	6	-53	65	27	26	-54	-8	-2	-41	-66
Private nonguaranteed	**0**	**0**	**0**	**0**	**0**	**0**	**0**	**0**	**0**	**0**
Bonds	0	0	0	0	0	0	0	0	0	0
Commercial banks	0	0	0	0	0	0	0	0	0	0
Memo:										
IBRD	-2	-3	7	35	4	4	-3	-1	15	-16
IDA	0	0	0	0	0	0	0	0	0	0
DEBT SERVICE (LTDS)	**12**	**398**	**97**	**92**	**104**	**225**	**338**	**70**	**198**	**368**
Public and publicly guaranteed	**12**	**398**	**97**	**92**	**104**	**225**	**338**	**70**	**198**	**368**
Official creditors	8	39	62	72	85	127	285	60	137	250
Multilateral	5	4	25	26	34	39	41	31	74	69
Concessional	1	2	3	2	3	3	2	1	4	3
Bilateral	3	34	37	45	51	88	244	29	64	181
Concessional	3	6	5	4	2	14	41	12	19	49
Private creditors	4	359	35	20	19	98	53	10	61	119
Bonds	1	1	0	0	0	0	0	0	0	0
Commercial banks	0	266	27	17	8	28	46	6	18	53
Other private	4	93	8	3	11	70	8	4	43	66
Private nonguaranteed	**0**	**0**	**0**	**0**	**0**	**0**	**0**	**0**	**0**	**0**
Bonds	0	0	0	0	0	0	0	0	0	0
Commercial banks	0	0	0	0	0	0	0	0	0	0
Memo:										
IBRD	5	4	3	4	6	6	11	8	18	20
IDA	0	0	0	0	0	0	0	0	0	0
UNDISBURSED DEBT	**34**	**164**	**467**	**440**	**269**	**253**	**209**	**461**	**629**	**494**
Official creditors	15	133	361	362	252	253	204	460	629	494
Private creditors	19	31	106	78	17	0	5	2	0	0
Memorandum items										
Concessional LDOD	47	125	286	306	427	493	452	412	565	983
Variable rate LDOD	0	500	271	342	416	437	428	426	676	797
Public sector LDOD	65	1,246	2,299	2,609	3,149	3,223	3,047	2,933	3,509	4,099
Private sector LDOD	26	26	2	2	2	2	2	0	0	0

6. CURRENCY COMPOSITION OF LONG-TERM DEBT (PERCENT)

	1970	1980	1988	1989	1990	1991	1992	1993	1994	1995
Deutsche mark	4.8	4.8	7.9	9.7	8.4	8.2	8.1	7.9	8.6	8.1
French franc	43.3	39.0	54.3	53.0	54.8	53.9	53.2	50.7	49.4	45.3
Japanese yen	0.0	1.5	1.0	0.8	0.7	0.7	0.8	0.9	1.0	0.9
Pound sterling	0.0	0.8	6.0	4.2	5.3	4.9	4.2	4.3	4.6	4.0
Swiss franc	0.0	0.5	0.4	0.3	0.3	0.3	0.3	0.3	0.7	0.7
U.S.dollars	7.6	42.7	12.7	12.7	10.3	11.0	12.0	12.5	13.3	11.0
Multiple currency	32.3	1.5	2.5	3.4	3.7	4.7	5.6	7.7	8.4	8.5
Special drawing rights	0.0	0.0	0.0	0.0	0.0	0.0	0.0	0.0	0.0	0.2
All other currencies	12.0	9.2	15.3	15.8	16.5	16.2	15.9	15.7	13.9	21.3

GABON

(US$ million, unless otherwise indicated)

	1970	1980	1988	1989	1990	1991	1992	1993	1994	1995
7. DEBT RESTRUCTURINGS										
Total amount rescheduled	0	0	333	287	271	78	26	2	1,403	431
Debt stock rescheduled	0	0	0	0	0	0	0	0	74	0
Principal rescheduled	0	0	222	174	188	50	23	0	766	253
Official	0	0	30	29	32	0	0	0	397	249
Private	0	0	192	145	156	50	23	0	369	4
Interest rescheduled	0	0	102	82	77	0	0	2	449	70
Official	0	0	30	27	27	0	0	2	376	69
Private	0	0	72	55	50	0	0	0	73	1
Debt forgiven	..	..	0	4	0	0	0	29	240	40
Memo: interest forgiven	..	..	0	0	0	0	0	0	0	0
Debt stock reduction	0	0	0	0	0	0	0	0	0	1
of which debt buyback	0	0	0	0	0	0	0	0	0	0
8. DEBT STOCK-FLOW RECONCILIATION										
Total change in debt stocks	..	..	..	506	634	239	-372	10	125	506
Net flows on debt	..	..	..	296	146	87	-193	19	-27	90
Net change in interest arrears	..	..	..	34	88	147	8	164	-399	-42
Interest capitalized	..	..	..	82	77	0	0	2	449	70
Debt forgiveness or reduction	..	..	..	-4	0	0	0	-29	-240	-41
Cross-currency valuation	..	..	..	69	359	-25	-167	-134	272	251
Residual	..	..	..	29	-36	31	-21	-12	70	179
9. AVERAGE TERMS OF NEW COMMITMENTS										
ALL CREDITORS										
Interest (%)	5.1	11.2	7.9	7.3	7.8	5.3	8.1	8.2	5.7	5.5
Maturity (years)	10.7	11.5	14.5	15.4	17.5	16.5	12.8	19.9	23.3	24.1
Grace period (years)	1.5	3.4	5.1	4.9	4.5	5.6	6.8	6.2	5.2	5.7
Grant element (%)	19.2	-5.2	11.8	16.1	12.4	29.1	10.9	10.1	26.9	29.6
Official creditors										
Interest (%)	4.0	7.4	7.6	6.9	7.5	5.3	7.9	8.2	5.7	5.5
Maturity (years)	17.3	14.8	16.2	16.6	18.9	16.5	13.3	19.9	23.3	24.1
Grace period (years)	3.6	4.9	5.7	5.4	5.3	5.6	7.2	6.2	5.2	5.7
Grant element (%)	34.4	15.0	14.0	19.1	14.8	29.1	11.8	10.1	26.9	29.6
Private creditors										
Interest (%)	5.2	13.0	9.0	9.8	9.0	0.0	11.0	0.0	0.0	0.0
Maturity (years)	9.9	9.8	8.0	8.3	11.7	0.0	5.2	0.0	0.0	0.0
Grace period (years)	1.2	2.6	3.0	1.6	1.3	0.0	1.2	0.0	0.0	0.0
Grant element (%)	17.4	-15.2	3.3	-1.6	3.3	0.0	-2.5	0.0	0.0	0.0
Memorandum items										
Commitments	33	196	268	157	48	176	76	358	276	167
Official creditors	4	65	212	134	38	176	71	358	276	167
Private creditors	29	131	57	23	10	0	5	0	0	0

10. CONTRACTUAL OBLIGATIONS ON OUTSTANDING LONG-TERM DEBT

	1996	1997	1998	1999	2000	2001	2002	2003	2004	2005
TOTAL										
Disbursements	142	124	87	57	37	26	15	4	2	1
Principal	123	205	254	343	403	309	312	327	328	328
Interest	251	271	277	281	258	231	211	190	169	147
Official creditors										
Disbursements	142	124	87	57	37	26	15	4	2	1
Principal	104	182	234	324	384	290	294	310	319	327
Interest	239	261	269	274	252	227	208	188	168	146
Bilateral creditors										
Disbursements	51	34	19	10	5	3	2	1	1	1
Principal	65	142	193	275	316	217	225	242	255	265
Interest	192	211	217	221	201	179	165	149	133	116
Multilateral creditors										
Disbursements	90	90	68	47	32	23	14	3	1	0
Principal	39	40	40	49	68	73	69	68	65	63
Interest	47	51	52	53	51	48	44	39	35	30
Private creditors										
Disbursements	0	0	0	0	0	0	0	0	0	0
Principal	20	22	20	19	19	19	18	17	9	1
Interest	12	10	8	7	6	4	3	2	1	1
Commercial banks										
Disbursements	0	0	0	0	0	0	0	0	0	0
Principal	1	17	17	17	17	17	16	16	8	0
Interest	8	8	7	6	5	3	2	1	0	0
Other private										
Disbursements	0	0	0	0	0	0	0	0	0	0
Principal	19	6	4	2	2	2	2	1	1	1
Interest	3	2	2	1	1	1	1	1	1	1

GAMBIA, THE

(US$ million, unless otherwise indicated)

	1970	1980	1988	1989	1990	1991	1992	1993	1994	1995
1. SUMMARY DEBT DATA										
TOTAL DEBT STOCKS (EDT)	**..**	**136.8**	**325.1**	**337.9**	**369.3**	**383.2**	**403.4**	**425.4**	**421.3**	**425.6**
Long-term debt (LDOD)	**5.1**	**97.3**	**276.9**	**289.2**	**308.6**	**322.4**	**346.2**	**349.6**	**366.3**	**383.7**
Public and publicly guaranteed	5.1	97.3	276.9	289.2	308.6	322.4	346.2	349.6	366.3	383.7
Private nonguaranteed	0.0	0.0	0.0	0.0	0.0	0.0	0.0	0.0	0.0	0.0
Use of IMF credit	**0.0**	**16.2**	**34.6**	**37.7**	**44.9**	**40.2**	**35.6**	**33.2**	**31.3**	**25.8**
Short-term debt	**..**	**23.3**	**13.6**	**11.1**	**15.7**	**20.5**	**21.6**	**42.6**	**23.7**	**16.1**
of which interest arrears on LDOD	..	0.3	2.6	4.1	0.6	0.5	0.6	0.6	0.7	..
Official creditors	..	0.2	2.3	1.6	0.6	0.5	0.6	0.6	0.7	..
Private creditors	..	0.1	0.3	2.5	0.0	0.0	0.0	0.0	0.0	..
Memo: principal arrears on LDOD	..	0.0	7.2	6.9	0.9	1.7	1.7	3.9	5.6	..
Official creditors	..	0.0	5.6	2.8	0.9	1.7	1.7	3.9	5.6	..
Private creditors	..	0.0	1.6	4.1	0.0	0.0	0.0	0.0	0.1	
Memo: export credits	..	..	58.0	40.0	32.0	41.0	41.0	38.0	38.0	30.0
TOTAL DEBT FLOWS										
Disbursements	**0.8**	**55.7**	**26.5**	**37.6**	**32.8**	**30.7**	**55.3**	**25.3**	**22.2**	**19.8**
Long-term debt	0.8	51.2	22.0	28.9	23.5	29.4	55.3	25.3	22.2	19.8
IMF purchases	0.0	4.4	4.6	8.8	9.3	1.3	0.0	0.0	0.0	0.0
Principal repayments	**0.1**	**0.4**	**14.8**	**16.4**	**25.5**	**23.0**	**21.8**	**21.2**	**24.1**	**20.1**
Long-term debt	0.1	0.4	8.9	11.5	20.2	17.0	18.7	18.8	20.2	13.8
IMF repurchases	0.0	0.0	5.9	5.0	5.3	6.0	3.1	2.4	3.9	6.2
Net flows on debt	**0.7**	**55.3**	**11.8**	**17.2**	**15.4**	**12.5**	**34.5**	**25.1**	**-20.9**	**-9.1**
of which short-term debt	..	..	0.0	-4.0	8.1	4.9	1.0	21.0	-19.0	-8.8
Interest payments (INT)	**..**	**3.8**	**8.2**	**7.1**	**12.2**	**8.0**	**7.8**	**7.2**	**7.6**	**5.2**
Long-term debt	0.0	0.4	5.1	4.7	10.2	6.5	6.7	6.0	5.8	4.2
IMF charges	0.0	0.5	1.5	1.5	1.3	0.7	0.3	0.2	0.2	0.2
Short-term debt	..	2.9	1.5	0.8	0.8	0.9	0.9	1.0	1.6	0.9
Net transfers on debt	**..**	**51.5**	**3.6**	**10.1**	**3.2**	**4.5**	**26.7**	**17.9**	**-28.5**	**-14.4**
Total debt service paid (TDS)	**..**	**4.1**	**22.9**	**23.5**	**37.7**	**31.1**	**29.6**	**28.4**	**31.7**	**25.3**
Long-term debt	0.1	0.8	14.0	16.2	30.3	23.5	25.3	24.9	26.0	18.0
IMF repurchases and charges	0.0	0.5	7.4	6.5	6.7	6.7	3.4	2.6	4.1	6.4
Short-term debt (interest only)	..	2.9	1.5	0.8	0.8	0.9	0.9	1.0	1.6	0.9
2. AGGREGATE NET RESOURCE FLOWS AND NET TRANSFERS (LONG-TERM)										
NET RESOURCE FLOWS	**1.0**	**77.9**	**62.5**	**80.1**	**48.1**	**66.2**	**86.6**	**62.0**	**49.6**	**33.5**
Net flow of long-term debt (ex. IMF)	0.7	50.9	13.1	17.4	3.4	12.4	36.7	6.5	2.0	5.9
Foreign direct investment (net)	0.1	0.0	1.2	14.8	0.0	10.0	6.0	11.0	10.0	10.0
Portfolio equity flows	0.0	0.0	0.0	0.0	0.0	0.0	0.0	0.0	0.0	0.0
Grants (excluding technical coop.)	0.2	27.0	48.2	47.9	44.7	43.8	43.9	44.5	37.6	17.6
Memo: technical coop. grants	0.6	12.5	27.6	23.7	25.1	26.8	29.5	27.2	25.1	23.4
NET TRANSFERS	**0.8**	**75.7**	**57.9**	**75.4**	**37.9**	**59.7**	**79.9**	**56.0**	**43.8**	**29.4**
Interest on long-term debt	0.0	0.4	5.1	4.7	10.2	6.5	6.7	6.0	5.8	4.2
Profit remittances on FDI	0.2	1.8	-0.6	0.0	0.0	0.0	0.0	0.0	0.0	0.0
3. MAJOR ECONOMIC AGGREGATES										
Gross national product (GNP)	53.7	222.5	252.4	264.2	318.6	317.2	360.2	354.1	357.4	..
Exports of goods & services (XGS)	..	66.2	146.7	167.9	169.7	227.2	232.7	242.4	220.3	181.0
of which workers remittances	..	0.0	0.0	0.0	0.0	0.0	0.0	0.0	0.0	0.0
Imports of goods & services (MGS)	..	181.5	167.3	191.8	205.4	268.5	252.0	294.1	253.8	241.4
International reserves (RES)	8.1	5.7	19.1	20.6	55.4	67.6	94.0	..	98.0	106.2
Current account balance	..	-86.9	26.5	15.0	21.6	13.2	37.2	-5.3	8.2	-8.2
4. DEBT INDICATORS										
EDT / XGS (%)	..	206.6	221.6	201.3	217.6	168.6	173.3	175.5	191.2	235.1
EDT / GNP (%)	..	61.5	128.8	127.9	115.9	120.8	112.0	120.1	117.9	..
TDS / XGS (%)	..	6.2	15.6	14.0	22.2	13.7	12.7	11.7	14.4	14.0
INT / XGS (%)	..	5.7	5.6	4.2	7.2	3.5	3.4	3.0	3.5	2.9
INT / GNP (%)	..	1.7	3.2	2.7	3.8	2.5	2.2	2.0	2.1	..
RES / EDT (%)	..	4.2	5.9	6.1	15.0	17.6	23.3	..	23.3	25.0
RES / MGS (months)	..	0.4	1.4	1.3	3.2	3.0	4.5	..	4.6	5.3
Short-term / EDT (%)	..	17.0	4.2	3.3	4.3	5.4	5.3	10.0	5.6	3.8
Concessional / EDT (%)	..	49.9	65.9	67.3	68.3	71.6	76.2	75.6	82.5	87.2
Multilateral / EDT (%)	..	29.9	49.1	52.6	55.0	56.2	62.9	64.1	71.6	76.0

GAMBIA, THE

(US$ million, unless otherwise indicated)

	1970	1980	1988	1989	1990	1991	1992	1993	1994	1995
5. LONG-TERM DEBT										
DEBT OUTSTANDING (LDOD)	**5.1**	**97.3**	**276.9**	**289.2**	**308.6**	**322.4**	**346.2**	**349.6**	**366.3**	**383.7**
Public and publicly guaranteed	**5.1**	**97.3**	**276.9**	**289.2**	**308.6**	**322.4**	**346.2**	**349.6**	**366.3**	**383.7**
Official creditors	5.1	73.4	250.9	263.7	290.3	308.8	337.1	344.8	365.8	383.4
Multilateral	0.0	40.9	159.6	177.8	203.3	215.4	253.8	272.7	301.7	323.3
Concessional	0.0	35.8	141.8	160.4	185.2	199.3	238.5	259.9	290.2	313.9
Bilateral	5.1	32.5	91.3	86.0	87.1	93.4	83.3	72.0	64.1	60.1
Concessional	4.9	32.5	72.4	66.9	66.8	74.9	69.0	61.7	57.2	57.1
Private creditors	0.0	23.9	26.0	25.4	18.3	13.7	9.1	4.8	0.5	0.2
Bonds	0.0	0.0	0.0	0.0	0.0	0.0	0.0	0.0	0.0	0.0
Commercial banks	0.0	7.4	19.0	19.0	16.0	12.0	8.0	4.0	0.0	0.0
Other private	0.0	16.5	7.0	6.4	2.3	1.7	1.1	0.8	0.5	0.2
Private nonguaranteed	**0.0**	**0.0**	**0.0**	**0.0**	**0.0**	**0.0**	**0.0**	**0.0**	**0.0**	**0.0**
Bonds	0.0	0.0	0.0	0.0	0.0	0.0	0.0	0.0	0.0	0.0
Commercial banks	0.0	0.0	0.0	0.0	0.0	0.0	0.0	0.0	0.0	0.0
Memo:										
IBRD	0.0	0.0	0.0	0.0	0.0	0.0	0.0	0.0	0.0	0.0
IDA	0.0	15.9	72.0	86.6	101.6	108.4	126.0	133.7	147.8	161.6
DISBURSEMENTS	**0.8**	**51.2**	**22.0**	**28.9**	**23.5**	**29.4**	**55.3**	**25.3**	**22.2**	**19.8**
Public and publicly guaranteed	**0.8**	**51.2**	**22.0**	**28.9**	**23.5**	**29.4**	**55.3**	**25.3**	**22.2**	**19.8**
Official creditors	0.8	29.6	22.0	28.9	23.5	29.4	55.3	25.3	22.2	19.8
Multilateral	0.0	18.3	12.7	25.3	17.7	16.3	52.4	25.2	20.3	19.8
Concessional	0.0	16.2	12.7	24.3	16.6	16.2	50.7	25.1	20.3	19.7
Bilateral	0.8	11.3	9.3	3.5	5.8	13.1	3.0	0.1	1.9	0.0
Concessional	0.8	11.3	9.3	3.5	5.8	13.1	3.0	0.1	1.9	0.0
Private creditors	0.0	21.7	0.0	0.0	0.0	0.0	0.0	0.0	0.0	0.0
Bonds	0.0	0.0	0.0	0.0	0.0	0.0	0.0	0.0	0.0	0.0
Commercial banks	0.0	7.0	0.0	0.0	0.0	0.0	0.0	0.0	0.0	0.0
Other private	0.0	14.7	0.0	0.0	0.0	0.0	0.0	0.0	0.0	0.0
Private nonguaranteed	**0.0**	**0.0**	**0.0**	**0.0**	**0.0**	**0.0**	**0.0**	**0.0**	**0.0**	**0.0**
Bonds	0.0	0.0	0.0	0.0	0.0	0.0	0.0	0.0	0.0	0.0
Commercial banks	0.0	0.0	0.0	0.0	0.0	0.0	0.0	0.0	0.0	0.0
Memo:										
IBRD	0.0	0.0	0.0	0.0	0.0	0.0	0.0	0.0	0.0	0.0
IDA	0.0	5.2	5.1	15.5	9.8	6.5	21.9	7.8	9.2	11.6
PRINCIPAL REPAYMENTS	**0.1**	**0.4**	**8.9**	**11.5**	**20.2**	**17.0**	**18.7**	**18.8**	**20.2**	**13.8**
Public and publicly guaranteed	**0.1**	**0.4**	**8.9**	**11.5**	**20.2**	**17.0**	**18.7**	**18.8**	**20.2**	**13.8**
Official creditors	0.1	0.0	8.2	11.0	12.7	12.5	14.2	14.5	15.9	13.5
Multilateral	0.0	0.0	5.7	5.2	4.7	5.7	5.2	5.4	5.8	6.3
Concessional	0.0	0.0	4.0	4.0	2.9	3.6	3.2	2.9	3.7	3.8
Bilateral	0.1	0.0	2.5	5.7	7.9	6.8	9.1	9.1	10.0	7.2
Concessional	0.1	0.0	2.5	5.7	7.9	5.3	5.4	5.5	6.1	3.0
Private creditors	0.0	0.3	0.7	0.5	7.5	4.5	4.5	4.3	4.3	0.4
Bonds	0.0	0.0	0.0	0.0	0.0	0.0	0.0	0.0	0.0	0.0
Commercial banks	0.0	0.1	0.1	0.0	3.0	4.0	4.0	4.0	4.0	0.0
Other private	0.0	0.3	0.5	0.5	4.5	0.5	0.5	0.3	0.3	0.4
Private nonguaranteed	**0.0**	**0.0**	**0.0**	**0.0**	**0.0**	**0.0**	**0.0**	**0.0**	**0.0**	**0.0**
Bonds	0.0	0.0	0.0	0.0	0.0	0.0	0.0	0.0	0.0	0.0
Commercial banks	0.0	0.0	0.0	0.0	0.0	0.0	0.0	0.0	0.0	0.0
Memo:										
IBRD	0.0	0.0	0.0	0.0	0.0	0.0	0.0	0.0	0.0	0.0
IDA	0.0	0.0	0.2	0.3	0.3	0.4	0.4	0.5	0.6	0.8
NET FLOWS ON DEBT	**0.7**	**50.9**	**13.1**	**17.4**	**3.4**	**12.4**	**36.7**	**6.5**	**2.0**	**5.9**
Public and publicly guaranteed	**0.7**	**50.9**	**13.1**	**17.4**	**3.4**	**12.4**	**36.7**	**6.5**	**2.0**	**5.9**
Official creditors	0.7	29.5	13.7	17.9	10.9	16.9	41.1	10.8	6.3	6.3
Multilateral	0.0	18.2	7.0	20.1	13.0	10.6	47.2	19.8	14.4	13.4
Concessional	0.0	16.1	8.6	20.4	13.7	12.5	47.5	22.2	16.6	16.0
Bilateral	0.7	11.3	6.8	-2.2	-2.1	6.3	-6.1	-9.0	-8.1	-7.2
Concessional	0.7	11.3	6.8	-2.2	-2.1	7.8	-2.4	-5.3	-4.2	-3.0
Private creditors	0.0	21.3	-0.7	-0.5	-7.5	-4.5	-4.5	-4.3	-4.3	-0.4
Bonds	0.0	0.0	0.0	0.0	0.0	0.0	0.0	0.0	0.0	0.0
Commercial banks	0.0	6.9	-0.1	0.0	-3.0	-4.0	-4.0	-4.0	-4.0	0.0
Other private	0.0	14.4	-0.5	-0.5	-4.5	-0.5	-0.5	-0.3	-0.3	-0.4
Private nonguaranteed	**0.0**	**0.0**	**0.0**	**0.0**	**0.0**	**0.0**	**0.0**	**0.0**	**0.0**	**0.0**
Bonds	0.0	0.0	0.0	0.0	0.0	0.0	0.0	0.0	0.0	0.0
Commercial banks	0.0	0.0	0.0	0.0	0.0	0.0	0.0	0.0	0.0	0.0
Memo:										
IBRD	0.0	0.0	0.0	0.0	0.0	0.0	0.0	0.0	0.0	0.0
IDA	0.0	5.2	4.9	15.3	9.5	6.1	21.4	7.3	8.6	10.9

GAMBIA, THE

(US$ million, unless otherwise indicated)

	1970	1980	1988	1989	1990	1991	1992	1993	1994	1995
INTEREST PAYMENTS (LINT)	**0.0**	**0.4**	**5.1**	**4.7**	**10.2**	**6.5**	**6.7**	**6.0**	**5.8**	**4.2**
Public and publicly guaranteed	**0.0**	**0.4**	**5.1**	**4.7**	**10.2**	**6.5**	**6.7**	**6.0**	**5.8**	**4.2**
Official creditors	0.0	0.4	4.9	4.5	5.5	5.0	5.9	5.6	5.6	4.1
Multilateral	0.0	0.4	3.3	2.6	2.9	2.9	3.3	3.3	3.5	3.2
Concessional	0.0	0.2	1.7	1.4	1.6	1.6	2.0	2.3	2.6	2.3
Bilateral	0.0	0.0	1.6	1.9	2.6	2.1	2.7	2.3	2.1	0.9
Concessional	0.0	0.0	1.6	1.9	2.6	1.6	1.5	1.4	1.3	0.4
Private creditors	0.0	0.0	0.2	0.2	4.7	1.5	0.8	0.4	0.2	0.0
Bonds	0.0	0.0	0.0	0.0	0.0	0.0	0.0	0.0	0.0	0.0
Commercial banks	0.0	0.0	0.0	0.0	3.8	1.3	0.7	0.4	0.2	0.0
Other private	0.0	0.0	0.2	0.2	0.9	0.1	0.1	0.1	0.0	0.0
Private nonguaranteed	**0.0**	**0.0**	**0.0**	**0.0**	**0.0**	**0.0**	**0.0**	**0.0**	**0.0**	**0.0**
Bonds	0.0	0.0	0.0	0.0	0.0	0.0	0.0	0.0	0.0	0.0
Commercial banks	0.0	0.0	0.0	0.0	0.0	0.0	0.0	0.0	0.0	0.0
Memo:										
IBRD	0.0	0.0	0.0	0.0	0.0	0.0	0.0	0.0	0.0	0.0
IDA	0.0	0.1	0.7	0.5	0.7	0.7	0.8	0.9	1.1	1.2
NET TRANSFERS ON DEBT	**0.7**	**50.5**	**7.9**	**12.7**	**-6.8**	**5.9**	**30.0**	**0.5**	**-3.8**	**1.8**
Public and publicly guaranteed	**0.7**	**50.5**	**7.9**	**12.7**	**-6.8**	**5.9**	**30.0**	**0.5**	**-3.8**	**1.8**
Official creditors	0.7	29.2	8.8	13.4	5.4	11.9	35.2	5.2	0.8	2.2
Multilateral	0.0	17.9	3.7	17.5	10.1	7.7	44.0	16.5	10.9	10.2
Concessional	0.0	15.9	6.9	19.0	12.2	10.9	45.4	19.9	13.9	13.7
Bilateral	0.7	11.3	5.2	-4.1	-4.7	4.2	-8.7	-11.3	-10.2	-8.1
Concessional	0.7	11.3	5.2	-4.1	-4.7	6.3	-3.9	-6.7	-5.5	-3.5
Private creditors	0.0	21.3	-0.9	-0.7	-12.1	-6.0	-5.2	-4.7	-4.6	-0.4
Bonds	0.0	0.0	0.0	0.0	0.0	0.0	0.0	0.0	0.0	0.0
Commercial banks	0.0	6.9	-0.2	0.0	-6.8	-5.3	-4.7	-4.4	-4.2	0.0
Other private	0.0	14.4	-0.8	-0.7	-5.4	-0.7	-0.6	-0.4	-0.4	-0.4
Private nonguaranteed	**0.0**	**0.0**	**0.0**	**0.0**	**0.0**	**0.0**	**0.0**	**0.0**	**0.0**	**0.0**
Bonds	0.0	0.0	0.0	0.0	0.0	0.0	0.0	0.0	0.0	0.0
Commercial banks	0.0	0.0	0.0	0.0	0.0	0.0	0.0	0.0	0.0	0.0
Memo:										
IBRD	0.0	0.0	0.0	0.0	0.0	0.0	0.0	0.0	0.0	0.0
IDA	0.0	5.1	4.2	14.7	8.8	5.4	20.6	6.3	7.5	9.7
DEBT SERVICE (LTDS)	**0.1**	**0.8**	**14.0**	**16.2**	**30.3**	**23.5**	**25.3**	**24.9**	**26.0**	**18.0**
Public and publicly guaranteed	**0.1**	**0.8**	**14.0**	**16.2**	**30.3**	**23.5**	**25.3**	**24.9**	**26.0**	**18.0**
Official creditors	0.1	0.4	13.1	15.5	18.2	17.5	20.1	20.1	21.4	17.6
Multilateral	0.0	0.4	9.0	7.8	7.7	8.6	8.4	8.7	9.4	9.6
Concessional	0.0	0.2	5.7	5.4	4.4	5.2	5.3	5.2	6.3	6.0
Bilateral	0.1	0.0	4.1	7.7	10.5	8.9	11.7	11.4	12.1	8.1
Concessional	0.1	0.0	4.1	7.7	10.5	6.8	6.9	6.8	7.4	3.5
Private creditors	0.0	0.4	0.9	0.7	12.1	6.0	5.2	4.7	4.6	0.4
Bonds	0.0	0.0	0.0	0.0	0.0	0.0	0.0	0.0	0.0	0.0
Commercial banks	0.0	0.1	0.2	0.0	6.8	5.3	4.7	4.4	4.2	0.0
Other private	0.0	0.3	0.8	0.7	5.4	0.7	0.6	0.4	0.4	0.4
Private nonguaranteed	**0.0**	**0.0**	**0.0**	**0.0**	**0.0**	**0.0**	**0.0**	**0.0**	**0.0**	**0.0**
Bonds	0.0	0.0	0.0	0.0	0.0	0.0	0.0	0.0	0.0	0.0
Commercial banks	0.0	0.0	0.0	0.0	0.0	0.0	0.0	0.0	0.0	0.0
Memo:										
IBRD	0.0	0.0	0.0	0.0	0.0	0.0	0.0	0.0	0.0	0.0
IDA	0.0	0.1	0.8	0.8	1.0	1.1	1.3	1.4	1.7	1.9
UNDISBURSED DEBT	**5.5**	**106.3**	**116.6**	**158.8**	**176.9**	**152.2**	**112.1**	**87.8**	**104.6**	**90.5**
Official creditors	5.5	87.7	116.6	158.8	176.9	152.2	112.1	87.8	104.6	90.5
Private creditors	0.0	18.6	0.0	0.0	0.0	0.0	0.0	0.0	0.0	0.0
Memorandum items										
Concessional LDOD	4.9	68.3	214.2	227.3	252.1	274.2	307.6	321.6	347.5	371.0
Variable rate LDOD	0.0	7.6	20.6	20.6	17.6	13.6	9.5	5.3	0.9	0.6
Public sector LDOD	5.1	94.0	274.8	287.3	306.8	321.0	345.2	348.8	365.8	383.5
Private sector LDOD	0.0	3.4	2.2	1.8	1.8	1.4	1.0	0.7	0.5	0.2
6. CURRENCY COMPOSITION OF LONG-TERM DEBT (PERCENT)										
Deutsche mark	0.0	1.8	2.1	1.9	1.8	1.5	1.1	0.7	0.5	0.3
French franc	0.0	1.4	8.0	7.8	7.7	6.8	5.4	4.3	3.8	3.7
Japanese yen	0.0	0.0	0.0	0.0	0.0	0.0	0.0	0.0	0.0	0.0
Pound sterling	100.0	16.3	9.7	9.2	8.5	8.0	7.3	7.2	6.7	6.3
Swiss franc	0.0	0.5	1.4	1.2	1.3	1.1	0.7	0.5	0.4	0.2
U.S.dollars	0.0	32.4	35.4	38.8	39.1	38.3	38.8	39.4	40.5	41.7
Multiple currency	0.0	7.0	19.1	18.8	19.8	18.8	21.9	23.2	25.2	25.3
Special drawing rights	0.0	0.0	0.0	0.0	0.0	0.0	0.0	0.0	0.0	0.0
All other currencies	0.0	40.6	24.3	22.2	21.8	25.5	24.8	24.7	22.9	22.6

GAMBIA, THE

(US$ million, unless otherwise indicated)

	1970	1980	1988	1989	1990	1991	1992	1993	1994	1995
7. DEBT RESTRUCTURINGS										
Total amount rescheduled	0.0	0.0	19.0	0.0	0.0	0.0	0.0	0.0	0.0	0.0
Debt stock rescheduled	0.0	0.0	16.1	0.0	0.0	0.0	0.0	0.0	0.0	0.0
Principal rescheduled	0.0	0.0	2.5	0.0	0.0	0.0	0.0	0.0	0.0	0.0
Official	0.0	0.0	0.0	0.0	0.0	0.0	0.0	0.0	0.0	0.0
Private	0.0	0.0	2.5	0.0	0.0	0.0	0.0	0.0	0.0	0.0
Interest rescheduled	0.0	0.0	0.0	0.0	0.0	0.0	0.0	0.0	0.0	0.0
Official	0.0	0.0	0.0	0.0	0.0	0.0	0.0	0.0	0.0	0.0
Private	0.0	0.0	0.0	0.0	0.0	0.0	0.0	0.0	0.0	0.0
Debt forgiven	..	..	0.0	0.3	0.0	0.0	0.0	0.0	0.0	0.0
Memo: interest forgiven	..	..	0.0	0.0	0.0	0.0	0.0	0.0	0.0	0.0
Debt stock reduction	0.0	0.0	0.0	0.0	0.0	0.0	0.0	0.0	0.0	0.0
of which debt buyback	0.0	0.0	0.0	0.0	0.0	0.0	0.0	0.0	0.0	0.0
8. DEBT STOCK-FLOW RECONCILIATION										
Total change in debt stocks	..	..	..	12.8	31.4	13.9	20.2	22.0	-4.1	4.3
Net flows on debt	..	..	..	17.2	15.4	12.5	34.5	25.1	-20.9	-9.1
Net change in interest arrears	..	..	..	1.5	-3.5	-0.1	0.1	0.0	0.1	1.3
Interest capitalized	..	..	..	0.0	0.0	0.0	0.0	0.0	0.0	0.0
Debt forgiveness or reduction	..	..	..	-0.3	0.0	0.0	0.0	0.0	0.0	0.0
Cross-currency valuation	..	..	..	-5.3	11.5	-1.7	-10.5	-3.6	5.8	4.6
Residual	..	..	..	-0.3	7.9	3.2	-3.9	0.5	11.0	7.5
9. AVERAGE TERMS OF NEW COMMITMENTS										
ALL CREDITORS										
Interest (%)	0.7	3.9	1.6	1.1	0.8	2.0	0.8	0.7	0.8	0.2
Maturity (years)	49.7	16.3	33.1	37.7	35.1	20.0	49.8	39.6	45.6	34.9
Grace period (years)	10.4	4.9	7.6	9.6	10.0	6.0	10.3	10.1	10.2	10.7
Grant element (%)	83.3	37.3	61.2	72.3	76.6	54.6	82.9	80.4	82.0	83.5
Official creditors										
Interest (%)	0.7	1.7	1.6	1.1	0.8	2.0	0.8	0.7	0.8	0.2
Maturity (years)	49.7	18.8	33.1	37.7	35.1	20.0	49.8	39.6	45.6	34.9
Grace period (years)	10.4	5.8	7.6	9.6	10.0	6.0	10.3	10.1	10.2	10.7
Grant element (%)	83.3	52.8	61.2	72.3	76.6	54.6	82.9	80.4	82.0	83.5
Private creditors										
Interest (%)	0.0	7.5	0.0	0.0	0.0	0.0	0.0	0.0	0.0	0.0
Maturity (years)	0.0	12.2	0.0	0.0	0.0	0.0	0.0	0.0	0.0	0.0
Grace period (years)	0.0	3.4	0.0	0.0	0.0	0.0	0.0	0.0	0.0	0.0
Grant element (%)	0.0	11.3	0.0	0.0	0.0	0.0	0.0	0.0	0.0	0.0
Memorandum items										
Commitments	2.1	72.9	38.1	71.8	37.9	5.3	20.5	12.3	36.8	7.0
Official creditors	2.1	45.7	38.1	71.8	37.9	5.3	20.5	12.3	36.8	7.0
Private creditors	0.0	27.3	0.0	0.0	0.0	0.0	0.0	0.0	0.0	0.0

10. CONTRACTUAL OBLIGATIONS ON OUTSTANDING LONG-TERM DEBT

	1996	1997	1998	1999	2000	2001	2002	2003	2004	2005
TOTAL										
Disbursements	29.9	22.3	15.1	11.2	7.1	2.2	0.8	0.5	0.3	0.0
Principal	17.5	14.9	14.4	14.3	13.2	13.1	12.8	11.3	11.2	11.2
Interest	4.9	4.6	4.3	4.1	3.8	3.6	3.4	3.2	3.1	2.9
Official creditors										
Disbursements	29.9	22.3	15.1	11.2	7.1	2.2	0.8	0.5	0.3	0.0
Principal	17.3	14.9	14.4	14.3	13.2	13.1	12.8	11.3	11.2	11.2
Interest	4.9	4.6	4.3	4.1	3.8	3.6	3.4	3.2	3.1	2.9
Bilateral creditors										
Disbursements	2.2	1.7	1.3	1.0	0.7	0.5	0.5	0.4	0.2	0.0
Principal	8.9	6.2	5.6	5.0	3.8	3.7	3.4	2.1	2.1	1.8
Interest	1.3	1.0	0.9	0.7	0.6	0.6	0.6	0.5	0.5	0.5
Multilateral creditors										
Disbursements	27.7	20.6	13.8	10.2	6.4	1.7	0.3	0.1	0.1	0.0
Principal	8.4	8.7	8.8	9.2	9.4	9.4	9.4	9.2	9.1	9.4
Interest	3.6	3.6	3.5	3.3	3.2	3.0	2.8	2.7	2.6	2.5
Private creditors										
Disbursements	0.0	0.0	0.0	0.0	0.0	0.0	0.0	0.0	0.0	0.0
Principal	0.2	0.0	0.0	0.0	0.0	0.0	0.0	0.0	0.0	0.0
Interest	0.0	0.0	0.0	0.0	0.0	0.0	0.0	0.0	0.0	0.0
Commercial banks										
Disbursements	0.0	0.0	0.0	0.0	0.0	0.0	0.0	0.0	0.0	0.0
Principal	0.0	0.0	0.0	0.0	0.0	0.0	0.0	0.0	0.0	0.0
Interest	0.0	0.0	0.0	0.0	0.0	0.0	0.0	0.0	0.0	0.0
Other private										
Disbursements	0.0	0.0	0.0	0.0	0.0	0.0	0.0	0.0	0.0	0.0
Principal	0.2	0.0	0.0	0.0	0.0	0.0	0.0	0.0	0.0	0.0
Interest	0.0	0.0	0.0	0.0	0.0	0.0	0.0	0.0	0.0	0.0

GEORGIA

(US$ million, unless otherwise indicated)

1. SUMMARY DEBT DATA

	1970	1980	1988	1989	1990	1991	1992	1993	1994	1995
TOTAL DEBT STOCKS (EDT)	..	..	..	..	..	..	**79**	**559**	**1,411**	**1,189**
Long-term debt (LDOD)	..	..	..	..	..	..	**79**	**559**	**885**	**988**
Public and publicly guaranteed	..	..	..	..	..	..	79	559	885	988
Private nonguaranteed	0	0	0	0	0	0	0	0	0	0
Use of IMF credit	**0**	**0**	**0**	**0**	**0**	**0**	**0**	**0**	**41**	**116**
Short-term debt	..	..	..	..	..	..	**0**	**0**	**485**	**86**
of which interest arrears on LDOD	..	..	..	..	..	..	0	0	15	62
Official creditors	..	..	..	..	..	..	0	0	15	54
Private creditors	..	..	..	..	..	..	0	0	0	8
Memo: principal arrears on LDOD	..	..	..	..	..	..	1	0	43	212
Official creditors	..	..	..	..	..	..	0	0	42	203
Private creditors	..	..	..	..	..	..	1	0	1	9
Memo: export credits	..	..	0	0	0	0	48	78	89	106
TOTAL DEBT FLOWS										
Disbursements	..	..	..	..	..	..	**21**	**124**	**140**	**161**
Long-term debt	..	..	..	..	..	..	21	124	101	85
IMF purchases	0	0	0	0	0	0	0	0	40	76
Principal repayments	..	..	..	..	..	..	**0**	**5**	**1**	**0**
Long-term debt	..	..	..	..	..	..	0	5	1	0
IMF repurchases	0	0	0	0	0	0	0	0	0	0
Net flows on debt	..	..	..	..	..	..	**21**	**120**	**609**	**-285**
of which short-term debt	..	..	..	..	..	..	0	0	470	-446
Interest payments (INT)	..	..	..	..	..	..	**0**	**8**	**5**	**20**
Long-term debt	..	..	..	..	..	..	0	8	5	17
IMF charges	0	0	0	0	0	0	0	0	0	3
Short-term debt	..	..	..	..	..	..	0	0	0	0
Net transfers on debt	..	..	..	..	..	..	**21**	**112**	**605**	**-305**
Total debt service paid (TDS)	..	..	..	..	..	..	**0**	**13**	**6**	**20**
Long-term debt	..	..	..	..	..	..	0	13	6	17
IMF repurchases and charges	0	0	0	0	0	0	0	0	0	3
Short-term debt (interest only)	..	..	..	..	..	..	0	0	0	0

2. AGGREGATE NET RESOURCE FLOWS AND NET TRANSFERS (LONG-TERM)

	1970	1980	1988	1989	1990	1991	1992	1993	1994	1995
NET RESOURCE FLOWS	..	..	..	..	..	..	**26**	**214**	**272**	**169**
Net flow of long-term debt (ex. IMF)	..	..	..	..	..	..	21	120	100	85
Foreign direct investment (net)	..	..	..	..	..	..	0	0	0	0
Portfolio equity flows	..	..	..	..	..	..	0	0	0	0
Grants (excluding technical coop.)	..	..	..	..	..	..	5	95	172	84
Memo: technical coop. grants	..	..	..	..	..	..	0	6	3	37
NET TRANSFERS	..	..	..	..	..	..	**26**	**206**	**267**	**152**
Interest on long-term debt	..	..	..	..	..	..	0	8	5	17
Profit remittances on FDI	..	..	..	..	..	..	0	0	0	0

3. MAJOR ECONOMIC AGGREGATES

	1970	1980	1988	1989	1990	1991	1992	1993	1994	1995
Gross national product (GNP)	..	..	..	..	..	..	3,541	2,770	2,347	2,303
Exports of goods & services (XGS)	..	..	..	..	..	..	..	..	..	..
of which workers remittances	..	..	..	..	..	..	..	..	..	..
Imports of goods & services (MGS)	..	..	..	..	..	..	..	..	..	..
International reserves (RES)	..	..	..	..	..	..	..	..	43	94
Current account balance	..	..	..	..	..	..	..	..	..	..

4. DEBT INDICATORS

	1970	1980	1988	1989	1990	1991	1992	1993	1994	1995
EDT / XGS (%)	..	..	..	..	..	..	..	..	..	..
EDT / GNP (%)	..	..	..	..	..	..	2.2	20.2	60.1	51.6
TDS / XGS (%)	..	..	..	..	..	..	..	..	..	..
INT / XGS (%)	..	..	..	..	..	..	..	..	..	..
INT / GNP (%)	..	..	..	..	..	..	0.0	0.3	0.2	0.9
RES / EDT (%)	..	..	..	..	..	..	..	..	3.1	7.9
RES / MGS (months)	..	..	..	..	..	..	..	..	..	..
Short-term / EDT (%)	..	..	..	..	..	..	0.0	0.0	34.4	7.2
Concessional / EDT (%)	..	..	..	..	..	..	0.0	0.0	0.1	7.1
Multilateral / EDT (%)	..	..	..	..	..	..	0.0	17.2	10.0	19.7

GEORGIA

(US$ million, unless otherwise indicated)

	1970	1980	1988	1989	1990	1991	1992	1993	1994	1995
5. LONG-TERM DEBT										
DEBT OUTSTANDING (LDOD)	..	..	..	..	..	..	**79**	**559**	**885**	**988**
Public and publicly guaranteed	..	..	..	..	..	..	**79**	**559**	**885**	**988**
Official creditors	..	..	..	..	..	..	0	489	786	880
Multilateral	..	..	..	..	..	..	0	96	141	234
Concessional	..	..	..	..	..	..	0	0	1	84
Bilateral	..	..	..	..	..	..	0	393	645	646
Concessional	..	..	..	..	..	..	0	0	0	0
Private creditors	..	..	..	..	..	..	79	70	98	108
Bonds	..	..	..	..	..	..	0	0	0	0
Commercial banks	..	..	..	..	..	..	1	1	0	0
Other private	..	..	..	..	..	..	78	69	98	108
Private nonguaranteed	**0**	**0**	**0**	**0**	**0**	**0**	**0**	**0**	**0**	**0**
Bonds	..	..	..	..	..	..	0	0	0	0
Commercial banks	..	..	..	..	..	..	0	0	0	0
Memo:										
IBRD	0	0	0	0	0	0	0	0	0	0
IDA	0	0	0	0	0	0	0	0	1	84
DISBURSEMENTS	..	..	..	..	..	..	**21**	**124**	**101**	**85**
Public and publicly guaranteed	..	..	..	..	..	..	**21**	**124**	**101**	**85**
Official creditors	..	..	..	..	..	..	0	124	94	85
Multilateral	..	..	..	..	..	..	0	101	34	85
Concessional	..	..	..	..	..	..	0	0	1	85
Bilateral	..	..	..	..	..	..	0	24	60	0
Concessional	..	..	..	..	..	..	0	0	0	0
Private creditors	..	..	..	..	..	..	21	0	7	0
Bonds	..	..	..	..	..	..	0	0	0	0
Commercial banks	..	..	..	..	..	..	1	0	0	0
Other private	..	..	..	..	..	..	21	0	7	0
Private nonguaranteed	**0**	**0**	**0**	**0**	**0**	**0**	**0**	**0**	**0**	**0**
Bonds	..	..	..	..	..	..	0	0	0	0
Commercial banks	..	..	..	..	..	..	0	0	0	0
Memo:										
IBRD	0	0	0	0	0	0	0	0	0	0
IDA	0	0	0	0	0	0	0	0	1	85
PRINCIPAL REPAYMENTS	..	..	..	..	..	..	**0**	**5**	**1**	**0**
Public and publicly guaranteed	..	..	..	..	..	..	**0**	**5**	**1**	**0**
Official creditors	..	..	..	..	..	..	0	0	0	0
Multilateral	..	..	..	..	..	..	0	0	0	0
Concessional	..	..	..	..	..	..	0	0	0	0
Bilateral	..	..	..	..	..	..	0	0	0	0
Concessional	..	..	..	..	..	..	0	0	0	0
Private creditors	..	..	..	..	..	..	0	5	1	0
Bonds	..	..	..	..	..	..	0	0	0	0
Commercial banks	..	..	..	..	..	..	0	0	1	0
Other private	..	..	..	..	..	..	0	5	0	0
Private nonguaranteed	**0**	**0**	**0**	**0**	**0**	**0**	**0**	**0**	**0**	**0**
Bonds	..	..	..	..	..	..	0	0	0	0
Commercial banks	..	..	..	..	..	..	0	0	0	0
Memo:										
IBRD	0	0	0	0	0	0	0	0	0	0
IDA	0	0	0	0	0	0	0	0	0	0
NET FLOWS ON DEBT	..	..	..	..	..	..	**21**	**120**	**100**	**85**
Public and publicly guaranteed	..	..	..	..	..	..	**21**	**120**	**100**	**85**
Official creditors	..	..	..	..	..	..	0	124	94	85
Multilateral	..	..	..	..	..	..	0	101	34	85
Concessional	..	..	..	..	..	..	0	0	1	85
Bilateral	..	..	..	..	..	..	0	24	60	0
Concessional	..	..	..	..	..	..	0	0	0	0
Private creditors	..	..	..	..	..	..	21	-5	6	0
Bonds	..	..	..	..	..	..	0	0	0	0
Commercial banks	..	..	..	..	..	..	1	0	-1	0
Other private	..	..	..	..	..	..	21	-5	7	0
Private nonguaranteed	**0**	**0**	**0**	**0**	**0**	**0**	**0**	**0**	**0**	**0**
Bonds	..	..	..	..	..	..	0	0	0	0
Commercial banks	..	..	..	..	..	..	0	0	0	0
Memo:										
IBRD	0	0	0	0	0	0	0	0	0	0
IDA	0	0	0	0	0	0	0	0	1	85

GEORGIA

(US$ million, unless otherwise indicated)

	1970	1980	1988	1989	1990	1991	1992	1993	1994	1995
INTEREST PAYMENTS (LINT)	..	..	..	..	..	..	**0**	**8**	**5**	**17**
Public and publicly guaranteed	..	..	..	..	..	..	**0**	**8**	**5**	**17**
Official creditors	..	..	..	..	..	..	0	5	5	17
Multilateral	..	..	..	..	..	..	0	5	5	0
Concessional	..	..	..	..	..	..	0	0	0	0
Bilateral	..	..	..	..	..	..	0	0	0	17
Concessional	..	..	..	..	..	..	0	0	0	0
Private creditors	..	..	..	..	..	..	0	4	0	0
Bonds	..	..	..	..	..	..	0	0	0	0
Commercial banks	..	..	..	..	..	..	0	0	0	0
Other private	..	..	..	..	..	..	0	4	0	0
Private nonguaranteed	**0**	**0**	**0**	**0**	**0**	**0**	**0**	**0**	**0**	**0**
Bonds	..	..	..	..	..	..	0	0	0	0
Commercial banks	..	..	..	..	..	..	0	0	0	0
Memo:										
IBRD	0	0	0	0	0	0	0	0	0	0
IDA	0	0	0	0	0	0	0	0	0	0
NET TRANSFERS ON DEBT	..	..	..	..	..	..	**21**	**112**	**95**	**68**
Public and publicly guaranteed	..	..	..	..	..	..	**21**	**112**	**95**	**68**
Official creditors	..	..	..	..	..	..	0	120	89	68
Multilateral	..	..	..	..	..	..	0	96	30	85
Concessional	..	..	..	..	..	..	0	0	1	85
Bilateral	..	..	..	..	..	..	0	24	60	-17
Concessional	..	..	..	..	..	..	0	0	0	0
Private creditors	..	..	..	..	..	..	21	-8	6	0
Bonds	..	..	..	..	..	..	0	0	0	0
Commercial banks	..	..	..	..	..	..	1	0	-1	0
Other private	..	..	..	..	..	..	21	-8	7	0
Private nonguaranteed	**0**	**0**	**0**	**0**	**0**	**0**	**0**	**0**	**0**	**0**
Bonds	..	..	..	..	..	..	0	0	0	0
Commercial banks	..	..	..	..	..	..	0	0	0	0
Memo:										
IBRD	0	0	0	0	0	0	0	0	0	0
IDA	0	0	0	0	0	0	0	0	1	85
DEBT SERVICE (LTDS)	..	..	..	..	..	..	**0**	**13**	**6**	**17**
Public and publicly guaranteed	..	..	..	..	..	..	**0**	**13**	**6**	**17**
Official creditors	..	..	..	..	..	..	0	5	5	17
Multilateral	..	..	..	..	..	..	0	5	5	0
Concessional	..	..	..	..	..	..	0	0	0	0
Bilateral	..	..	..	..	..	..	0	0	0	17
Concessional	..	..	..	..	..	..	0	0	0	0
Private creditors	..	..	..	..	..	..	0	8	1	0
Bonds	..	..	..	..	..	..	0	0	0	0
Commercial banks	..	..	..	..	..	..	0	0	1	0
Other private	..	..	..	..	..	..	0	8	0	0
Private nonguaranteed	**0**	**0**	**0**	**0**	**0**	**0**	**0**	**0**	**0**	**0**
Bonds	..	..	..	..	..	..	0	0	0	0
Commercial banks	..	..	..	..	..	..	0	0	0	0
Memo:										
IBRD	0	0	0	0	0	0	0	0	0	0
IDA	0	0	0	0	0	0	0	0	0	0
UNDISBURSED DEBT	..	..	..	..	..	..	**85**	**38**	**50**	**44**
Official creditors	..	..	..	..	..	..	85	38	50	44
Private creditors	..	..	..	..	..	..	0	0	0	0
Memorandum items										
Concessional LDOD	..	..	..	..	..	..	0	0	1	84
Variable rate LDOD	..	..	..	..	..	..	1	490	388	398
Public sector LDOD	..	..	..	..	..	..	79	559	885	988
Private sector LDOD	..	..	..	..	..	..	0	0	0	0

6. CURRENCY COMPOSITION OF LONG-TERM DEBT (PERCENT)

	1970	1980	1988	1989	1990	1991	1992	1993	1994	1995
Deutsche mark	..	..	..	..	..	..	0.0	0.0	0.8	0.8
French franc	..	..	..	..	..	..	0.0	0.0	0.0	0.0
Japanese yen	..	..	..	..	..	..	0.0	0.0	0.0	0.0
Pound sterling	..	..	..	..	..	..	0.0	0.0	0.0	0.0
Swiss franc	..	..	..	..	..	..	0.0	0.0	0.4	0.5
U.S.dollars	..	..	..	..	..	..	1.1	70.5	72.6	73.5
Multiple currency	..	..	..	..	..	..	0.0	0.0	0.0	0.0
Special drawing rights	..	..	..	..	..	..	0.0	0.0	0.0	0.0
All other currencies	..	..	..	..	..	..	98.8	29.5	26.2	25.3

GEORGIA

(US$ million, unless otherwise indicated)

	1970	1980	1988	1989	1990	1991	1992	1993	1994	1995
7. DEBT RESTRUCTURINGS										
Total amount rescheduled	0	0	0	0	0	0	0	369	412	0
Debt stock rescheduled	0	0	0	0	0	0	0	0	201	0
Principal rescheduled	0	0	0	0	0	0	0	0	3	0
Official	0	0	0	0	0	0	0	0	0	0
Private	0	0	0	0	0	0	0	0	3	0
Interest rescheduled	0	0	0	0	0	0	0	0	5	0
Official	0	0	0	0	0	0	0	0	0	0
Private	0	0	0	0	0	0	0	0	5	0
Debt forgiven	..	..	0	0	0	0	0	0	0	0
Memo: interest forgiven	..	..	0	0	0	0	0	0	0	0
Debt stock reduction	0	0	0	0	0	0	0	0	0	0
of which debt buyback	0	0	0	0	0	0	0	0	0	0
8. DEBT STOCK-FLOW RECONCILIATION										
Total change in debt stocks	..	..	..	..	..	..	79	480	852	-221
Net flows on debt	..	..	..	..	..	..	21	120	609	-285
Net change in interest arrears	..	..	..	..	..	..	0	0	15	47
Interest capitalized	..	..	..	..	..	..	0	0	5	0
Debt forgiveness or reduction	..	..	..	..	..	..	0	0	0	0
Cross-currency valuation	..	..	..	..	..	..	-5	-12	24	22
Residual	..	..	..	..	..	..	62	372	198	-4
9. AVERAGE TERMS OF NEW COMMITMENTS										
ALL CREDITORS										
Interest (%)	..	..	..	..	..	..	4.1	4.0	4.1	0.8
Maturity (years)	..	..	..	..	..	..	3.2	3.4	14.8	34.9
Grace period (years)	..	..	..	..	..	..	3.2	2.7	4.2	10.4
Grant element (%)	..	..	..	..	..	..	15.3	14.9	34.4	79.0
Official creditors										
Interest (%)	..	..	..	..	..	..	4.1	4.0	3.9	0.8
Maturity (years)	..	..	..	..	..	..	3.2	3.4	15.1	34.9
Grace period (years)	..	..	..	..	..	..	3.2	2.7	4.3	10.4
Grant element (%)	..	..	..	..	..	..	15.4	14.9	36.1	79.0
Private creditors										
Interest (%)	..	..	..	..	..	..	4.6	0.0	8.0	0.0
Maturity (years)	..	..	..	..	..	..	1.6	0.0	9.8	0.0
Grace period (years)	..	..	..	..	..	..	1.6	0.0	1.8	0.0
Grant element (%)	..	..	..	..	..	..	7.5	0.0	7.6	0.0
Memorandum items										
Commitments	..	..	..	..	..	..	92	77	113	75
Official creditors	..	..	..	..	..	..	91	77	106	75
Private creditors	..	..	..	..	..	..	1	0	7	0

10. CONTRACTUAL OBLIGATIONS ON OUTSTANDING LONG-TERM DEBT

	1996	1997	1998	1999	2000	2001	2002	2003	2004	2005
TOTAL										
Disbursements	12	12	9	5	2	2	1	0	0	0
Principal	97	172	98	96	89	87	28	9	8	10
Interest	34	28	19	15	11	7	4	3	3	2
Official creditors										
Disbursements	12	12	9	5	2	2	1	0	0	0
Principal	85	160	87	84	82	80	21	2	2	3
Interest	28	22	14	10	7	4	1	1	1	1
Bilateral creditors										
Disbursements	1	2	1	1	0	0	0	0	0	0
Principal	72	116	85	83	81	79	20	0	0	0
Interest	24	18	13	9	6	3	0	0	0	0
Multilateral creditors										
Disbursements	11	11	8	5	2	1	1	0	0	0
Principal	13	45	2	2	2	2	2	2	2	3
Interest	4	4	1	1	1	1	1	1	1	1
Private creditors										
Disbursements	0	0	0	0	0	0	0	0	0	0
Principal	11	11	11	11	7	7	7	7	6	6
Interest	7	6	5	4	4	3	3	2	2	1
Commercial banks										
Disbursements	0	0	0	0	0	0	0	0	0	0
Principal	0	0	0	0	0	0	0	0	0	0
Interest	0	0	0	0	0	0	0	0	0	0
Other private										
Disbursements	0	0	0	0	0	0	0	0	0	0
Principal	11	11	11	11	7	7	7	7	6	6
Interest	7	6	5	4	4	3	3	2	2	1

GHANA

(US$ million, unless otherwise indicated)

	1970	1980	1988	1989	1990	1991	1992	1993	1994	1995
1. SUMMARY DEBT DATA										
TOTAL DEBT STOCKS (EDT)	..	**1,398**	**3,128**	**3,397**	**3,873**	**4,371**	**4,499**	**4,882**	**5,463**	**5,874**
Long-term debt (LDOD)	**520**	**1,162**	**2,287**	**2,455**	**2,808**	**3,144**	**3,345**	**3,669**	**4,180**	**4,595**
Public and publicly guaranteed	510	1,152	2,255	2,422	2,775	3,110	3,310	3,632	4,148	4,568
Private nonguaranteed	10	10	32	33	33	34	35	37	32	27
Use of IMF credit	**46**	**105**	**762**	**737**	**745**	**834**	**740**	**738**	**700**	**649**
Short-term debt	..	**131**	**78**	**205**	**320**	**394**	**414**	**476**	**583**	**631**
of which interest arrears on LDOD	..	5	23	39	56	37	41	56	60	37
Official creditors	..	4	19	31	45	18	19	26	23	31
Private creditors	..	1	4	8	11	18	22	30	38	6
Memo: principal arrears on LDOD	..	5	55	74	77	76	81	107	97	100
Official creditors	..	3	41	44	50	39	43	66	54	54
Private creditors	..	2	14	29	27	37	38	41	43	46
Memo: export credits	..	..	267	311	411	396	384	332	449	612
TOTAL DEBT FLOWS										
Disbursements	**44**	**249**	**639**	**574**	**502**	**659**	**487**	**517**	**457**	**551**
Long-term debt	42	220	422	397	436	499	487	451	457	509
IMF purchases	2	29	217	177	65	159	0	66	0	42
Principal repayments	**39**	**106**	**418**	**338**	**262**	**190**	**200**	**190**	**248**	**273**
Long-term debt	14	77	142	155	145	113	137	124	166	166
IMF repurchases	25	29	277	183	117	78	64	66	83	108
Net flows on debt	**5**	**143**	**177**	**346**	**338**	**561**	**303**	**374**	**312**	**348**
of which short-term debt	..	..	-44	110	98	92	16	47	103	71
Interest payments (INT)	..	**53**	**128**	**117**	**108**	**112**	**121**	**120**	**119**	**97**
Long-term debt	12	31	72	63	59	66	81	84	82	59
IMF charges	0	4	47	43	37	29	20	14	11	10
Short-term debt	..	18	9	10	12	17	19	22	26	28
Net transfers on debt	..	**90**	**49**	**230**	**230**	**449**	**182**	**254**	**193**	**251**
Total debt service paid (TDS)	..	**159**	**546**	**455**	**370**	**302**	**321**	**310**	**367**	**370**
Long-term debt	26	108	213	218	204	179	218	208	248	224
IMF repurchases and charges	25	33	324	226	154	107	84	81	93	117
Short-term debt (interest only)	..	18	9	10	12	17	19	22	26	28
2. AGGREGATE NET RESOURCE FLOWS AND NET TRANSFERS (LONG-TERM)										
NET RESOURCE FLOWS	**101**	**181**	**456**	**466**	**755**	**877**	**591**	**675**	**1,300**	**1,078**
Net flow of long-term debt (ex. IMF)	28	143	281	242	291	387	351	328	291	343
Foreign direct investment (net)	68	16	5	15	15	20	23	125	233	230
Portfolio equity flows	0	0	0	0	0	0	0	0	557	267
Grants (excluding technical coop.)	6	23	171	208	449	470	218	222	218	238
Memo: technical coop. grants	15	42	60	59	62	82	103	98	88	108
NET TRANSFERS	**77**	**135**	**379**	**396**	**689**	**803**	**501**	**582**	**1,207**	**999**
Interest on long-term debt	12	31	72	63	59	66	81	84	82	59
Profit remittances on FDI	12	15	6	7	7	8	9	9	10	20
3. MAJOR ECONOMIC AGGREGATES										
Gross national product (GNP)	2,170	4,426	5,064	5,131	6,114	6,878	6,778	5,972	6,422	6,179
Exports of goods & services (XGS)	..	1,214	965	895	990	1,114	1,123	1,230	1,402	1,603
of which workers remittances	..	1	6	6	6	6	7	10	16	18
Imports of goods & services (MGS)	..	1,264	1,393	1,410	1,624	1,782	1,962	2,296	2,123	2,248
International reserves (RES)	43	330	310	436	309	644	412	517	689	804
Current account balance	..	30	-65	-98	-224	-251	-375	-558	-264	-399
4. DEBT INDICATORS										
EDT / XGS (%)	..	115.2	324.2	379.5	391.3	392.4	400.8	396.9	389.7	366.5
EDT / GNP (%)	..	31.6	61.8	66.2	63.3	63.6	66.4	81.7	85.1	95.1
TDS / XGS (%)	..	13.1	56.6	50.8	37.4	27.1	28.6	25.2	26.2	23.1
INT / XGS (%)	..	4.4	13.3	13.0	10.9	10.1	10.8	9.8	8.5	6.0
INT / GNP (%)	..	1.2	2.5	2.3	1.8	1.6	1.8	2.0	1.9	1.6
RES / EDT (%)	..	23.6	9.9	12.8	8.0	14.7	9.1	10.6	12.6	13.7
RES / MGS (months)	..	3.1	2.7	3.7	2.3	4.3	2.5	2.7	3.9	4.3
Short-term / EDT (%)	..	9.4	2.5	6.0	8.3	9.0	9.2	9.7	10.7	10.7
Concessional / EDT (%)	..	58.3	53.1	54.9	56.0	56.0	58.7	60.6	62.6	64.9
Multilateral / EDT (%)	..	19.9	42.1	43.5	47.5	47.6	48.9	49.3	49.5	50.8

GHANA

(US$ million, unless otherwise indicated)

	1970	1980	1988	1989	1990	1991	1992	1993	1994	1995
5. LONG-TERM DEBT										
DEBT OUTSTANDING (LDOD)	**520**	**1,162**	**2,287**	**2,455**	**2,808**	**3,144**	**3,345**	**3,669**	**4,180**	**4,595**
Public and publicly guaranteed	**510**	**1,152**	**2,255**	**2,422**	**2,775**	**3,110**	**3,310**	**3,632**	**4,148**	**4,568**
Official creditors	332	1,031	1,958	2,186	2,551	2,825	3,013	3,323	3,768	4,143
Multilateral	53	279	1,316	1,479	1,838	2,083	2,200	2,407	2,706	2,984
Concessional	53	182	1,092	1,246	1,558	1,795	1,924	2,141	2,444	2,738
Bilateral	279	752	643	707	713	742	813	916	1,062	1,159
Concessional	236	633	570	618	611	653	716	818	974	1,073
Private creditors	178	121	297	236	224	285	297	308	380	425
Bonds	0	0	0	0	0	0	0	0	0	0
Commercial banks	12	0	63	17	10	6	5	5	28	86
Other private	166	121	234	219	214	279	292	303	352	339
Private nonguaranteed	**10**	**10**	**32**	**33**	**33**	**34**	**35**	**37**	**32**	**27**
Bonds	0	0	0	0	0	0	0	0	0	0
Commercial banks	10	10	32	33	33	34	35	37	32	27
Memo:										
IBRD	43	114	128	114	113	103	87	77	70	59
IDA	11	99	876	1,030	1,310	1,522	1,631	1,838	2,094	2,375
DISBURSEMENTS	**42**	**220**	**422**	**397**	**436**	**499**	**487**	**451**	**457**	**509**
Public and publicly guaranteed	**42**	**220**	**413**	**388**	**428**	**490**	**480**	**444**	**457**	**509**
Official creditors	39	220	356	353	377	417	385	375	340	418
Multilateral	4	50	254	209	273	265	248	260	219	282
Concessional	4	26	233	176	224	233	217	245	204	268
Bilateral	35	170	102	144	105	152	137	115	121	135
Concessional	35	93	93	125	95	147	110	108	121	135
Private creditors	3	0	57	35	51	73	96	70	117	92
Bonds	0	0	0	0	0	0	0	0	0	0
Commercial banks	0	0	0	0	9	0	3	3	23	60
Other private	3	0	57	35	42	73	92	67	94	31
Private nonguaranteed	**0**	**0**	**9**	**9**	**8**	**9**	**7**	**7**	**0**	**0**
Bonds	0	0	0	0	0	0	0	0	0	0
Commercial banks	0	0	9	9	8	9	7	7	0	0
Memo:										
IBRD	0	25	0	0	0	0	0	0	0	0
IDA	4	5	205	168	201	199	170	205	178	242
PRINCIPAL REPAYMENTS	**14**	**77**	**142**	**155**	**145**	**113**	**137**	**124**	**166**	**166**
Public and publicly guaranteed	**14**	**77**	**135**	**147**	**137**	**105**	**131**	**119**	**161**	**161**
Official creditors	9	35	58	49	66	65	79	72	100	103
Multilateral	2	4	23	26	31	41	47	45	52	67
Concessional	2	3	7	7	10	13	15	19	19	28
Bilateral	8	31	35	24	35	24	32	27	48	36
Concessional	7	14	31	21	33	20	23	22	42	34
Private creditors	5	42	77	97	71	40	52	47	61	58
Bonds	0	0	0	0	0	0	0	0	0	0
Commercial banks	0	22	38	47	17	4	4	2	1	1
Other private	5	20	39	51	55	36	48	45	60	57
Private nonguaranteed	**0**	**0**	**7**	**8**	**8**	**8**	**6**	**5**	**5**	**5**
Bonds	0	0	0	0	0	0	0	0	0	0
Commercial banks	0	0	7	8	8	8	6	5	5	5
Memo:										
IBRD	2	3	11	9	10	12	12	13	13	15
IDA	0	0	1	1	2	3	3	4	6	8
NET FLOWS ON DEBT	**28**	**143**	**281**	**242**	**291**	**387**	**351**	**328**	**291**	**343**
Public and publicly guaranteed	**28**	**143**	**278**	**241**	**291**	**386**	**350**	**326**	**296**	**348**
Official creditors	29	185	298	304	311	352	306	303	240	315
Multilateral	3	47	230	184	242	225	201	215	167	216
Concessional	3	23	226	169	214	220	202	227	185	240
Bilateral	27	138	68	120	69	128	105	88	73	99
Concessional	28	79	62	104	62	128	87	86	80	101
Private creditors	-2	-42	-20	-62	-20	34	44	23	56	34
Bonds	0	0	0	0	0	0	0	0	0	0
Commercial banks	0	-22	-38	-47	-8	-4	0	1	22	59
Other private	-2	-20	19	-16	-13	37	44	22	34	-25
Private nonguaranteed	**0**	**0**	**2**	**1**	**0**	**1**	**1**	**2**	**-5**	**-5**
Bonds	0	0	0	0	0	0	0	0	0	0
Commercial banks	0	0	2	1	0	1	1	2	-5	-5
Memo:										
IBRD	-1	21	-11	-9	-10	-12	-12	-13	-13	-15
IDA	4	5	204	167	199	197	168	202	172	234

GHANA

(US$ million, unless otherwise indicated)

	1970	1980	1988	1989	1990	1991	1992	1993	1994	1995
INTEREST PAYMENTS (LINT)	**12**	**31**	**72**	**63**	**59**	**66**	**81**	**84**	**82**	**59**
Public and publicly guaranteed	**12**	**31**	**70**	**61**	**57**	**63**	**79**	**82**	**80**	**57**
Official creditors	7	24	48	45	45	52	62	67	61	51
Multilateral	3	10	30	31	30	37	42	41	35	40
Concessional	3	4	10	10	12	14	17	17	18	20
Bilateral	4	14	18	14	15	15	21	27	26	11
Concessional	4	10	16	12	13	13	17	23	23	10
Private creditors	5	7	21	16	12	11	17	14	19	7
Bonds	0	0	0	0	0	0	0	0	0	0
Commercial banks	0	2	7	5	2	1	1	0	0	0
Other private	5	4	14	11	11	10	16	14	19	6
Private nonguaranteed	**0**	**0**	**2**	**2**	**2**	**3**	**2**	**3**	**2**	**2**
Bonds	0	0	0	0	0	0	0	0	0	0
Commercial banks	0	0	2	2	2	3	2	3	2	2
Memo:										
IBRD	3	8	13	10	9	9	9	7	6	6
IDA	0	1	7	7	8	10	11	13	14	17
NET TRANSFERS ON DEBT	**16**	**112**	**209**	**179**	**232**	**321**	**269**	**244**	**209**	**285**
Public and publicly guaranteed	**16**	**112**	**209**	**181**	**234**	**323**	**271**	**244**	**216**	**291**
Official creditors	22	161	250	259	267	300	244	236	179	264
Multilateral	0	37	200	153	212	187	160	174	132	176
Concessional	0	19	216	159	202	206	186	210	167	220
Bilateral	22	124	50	106	54	113	84	62	47	88
Concessional	24	69	46	92	49	115	70	63	57	91
Private creditors	-7	-48	-41	-79	-32	22	27	8	37	27
Bonds	0	0	0	0	0	0	0	0	0	0
Commercial banks	0	-24	-45	-52	-9	-4	-1	1	22	59
Other private	-7	-25	4	-27	-23	27	28	7	15	-32
Private nonguaranteed	**0**	**0**	**0**	**-1**	**-2**	**-2**	**-1**	**-1**	**-7**	**-7**
Bonds	0	0	0	0	0	0	0	0	0	0
Commercial banks	0	0	0	-1	-2	-2	-1	-1	-7	-7
Memo:										
IBRD	-4	13	-24	-19	-20	-21	-21	-20	-20	-21
IDA	4	4	197	160	191	187	156	189	157	218
DEBT SERVICE (LTDS)	**26**	**108**	**213**	**218**	**204**	**179**	**218**	**208**	**248**	**224**
Public and publicly guaranteed	**26**	**108**	**204**	**208**	**194**	**168**	**209**	**200**	**241**	**218**
Official creditors	16	59	106	94	111	117	141	139	161	153
Multilateral	4	14	53	57	61	78	88	86	87	107
Concessional	4	7	17	18	22	27	32	36	37	47
Bilateral	12	46	53	37	50	39	53	54	74	47
Concessional	11	24	48	33	46	32	40	45	64	44
Private creditors	10	48	98	114	83	51	69	61	80	64
Bonds	0	0	0	0	0	0	0	0	0	0
Commercial banks	0	24	45	52	18	4	5	2	1	1
Other private	10	25	53	62	65	47	64	59	79	63
Private nonguaranteed	**0**	**0**	**9**	**10**	**10**	**11**	**8**	**8**	**7**	**7**
Bonds	0	0	0	0	0	0	0	0	0	0
Commercial banks	0	0	9	10	10	11	8	8	7	7
Memo:										
IBRD	4	11	24	19	20	21	21	20	20	21
IDA	0	1	8	8	10	12	14	17	21	25
UNDISBURSED DEBT	**76**	**431**	**1,116**	**1,307**	**1,674**	**1,545**	**1,700**	**1,729**	**1,802**	**2,040**
Official creditors	76	431	1,068	1,255	1,565	1,433	1,561	1,574	1,585	1,722
Private creditors	0	0	48	52	109	111	139	155	216	318
Memorandum items										
Concessional LDOD	289	815	1,662	1,864	2,168	2,448	2,640	2,959	3,418	3,811
Variable rate LDOD	10	10	115	67	51	77	68	65	58	57
Public sector LDOD	510	1,125	2,255	2,422	2,775	3,110	3,310	3,632	4,148	4,568
Private sector LDOD	10	38	32	33	33	34	35	37	32	27

6. CURRENCY COMPOSITION OF LONG-TERM DEBT (PERCENT)

	1970	1980	1988	1989	1990	1991	1992	1993	1994	1995
Deutsche mark	12.3	12.9	3.1	3.6	3.9	4.2	4.1	4.1	4.3	4.0
French franc	2.7	1.9	2.2	2.7	2.2	2.5	3.0	2.5	2.5	2.2
Japanese yen	0.0	0.1	4.2	5.4	6.7	9.1	10.1	11.4	13.2	13.8
Pound sterling	28.3	11.8	4.1	2.9	2.8	3.4	4.1	4.1	4.6	5.0
Swiss franc	0.0	0.0	0.0	0.0	0.4	0.2	0.2	0.0	0.0	0.0
U.S.dollars	22.5	38.7	59.3	58.0	58.8	56.3	55.8	56.8	55.0	56.3
Multiple currency	8.4	10.8	6.2	5.2	4.6	3.8	3.1	2.8	2.3	1.9
Special drawing rights	0.0	0.0	0.6	0.6	0.6	0.6	0.7	0.7	0.7	0.7
All other currencies	25.8	23.7	20.3	21.5	20.0	19.8	19.0	17.7	17.4	16.2

GHANA

(US$ million, unless otherwise indicated)

	1970	1980	1988	1989	1990	1991	1992	1993	1994	1995
7. DEBT RESTRUCTURINGS										
Total amount rescheduled	0	0	3	0	0	40	0	0	0	0
Debt stock rescheduled	0	0	0	0	0	0	0	0	0	0
Principal rescheduled	0	0	3	0	0	14	0	0	0	0
Official	0	0	3	0	0	14	0	0	0	0
Private	0	0	0	0	0	0	0	0	0	0
Interest rescheduled	0	0	0	0	0	27	0	0	0	0
Official	0	0	0	0	0	27	0	0	0	0
Private	0	0	0	0	0	0	0	0	0	0
Debt forgiven	..	..	16	44	102	116	0	0	12	1
Memo: interest forgiven	..	..	2	1	0	1	0	0	1	0
Debt stock reduction	0	0	204	0	0	0	0	0	0	0
of which debt buyback	0	0	0	0	0	0	0	0	0	0
8. DEBT STOCK-FLOW RECONCILIATION										
Total change in debt stocks	..	..	..	269	476	499	128	384	581	411
Net flows on debt	..	..	..	346	338	561	303	374	312	348
Net change in interest arrears	..	..	..	16	17	-19	5	14	5	-23
Interest capitalized	..	..	..	0	0	27	0	0	0	0
Debt forgiveness or reduction	..	..	..	-44	-102	-116	0	0	-12	-1
Cross-currency valuation	..	..	..	-27	109	9	-88	3	159	31
Residual	..	..	..	-22	115	37	-92	-7	117	56
9. AVERAGE TERMS OF NEW COMMITMENTS										
ALL CREDITORS										
Interest (%)	2.0	1.4	1.2	3.3	3.0	3.1	1.8	3.1	4.1	2.8
Maturity (years)	36.7	43.7	31.2	29.9	32.1	31.1	32.9	30.3	26.9	28.5
Grace period (years)	9.7	9.7	9.2	8.4	8.4	7.9	8.0	7.6	7.4	7.5
Grant element (%)	66.8	74.1	70.2	54.2	58.1	55.9	63.7	54.5	46.0	55.6
Official creditors										
Interest (%)	1.8	1.4	1.0	3.0	2.1	1.6	1.1	2.2	1.9	1.4
Maturity (years)	38.6	43.7	32.0	31.5	35.9	37.2	37.1	34.2	35.8	36.2
Grace period (years)	10.2	9.7	9.5	8.8	9.4	9.4	9.1	8.6	9.9	9.7
Grant element (%)	70.2	74.1	72.7	57.6	67.3	69.8	73.9	65.2	69.2	72.6
Private creditors										
Interest (%)	5.3	0.0	7.1	7.8	8.1	8.5	5.2	6.9	7.5	6.5
Maturity (years)	8.4	0.0	9.9	6.4	11.0	8.9	15.2	15.2	13.3	8.4
Grace period (years)	1.4	0.0	2.5	1.5	2.8	2.2	3.2	3.7	3.6	1.7
Grant element (%)	16.3	0.0	8.1	5.0	6.1	5.5	19.8	12.0	10.5	11.9
Memorandum items										
Commitments	51	170	512	636	676	362	720	496	421	709
Official creditors	48	170	492	595	573	284	583	396	254	511
Private creditors	3	0	20	41	102	78	136	100	167	198

10. CONTRACTUAL OBLIGATIONS ON OUTSTANDING LONG-TERM DEBT

	1996	1997	1998	1999	2000	2001	2002	2003	2004	2005
TOTAL										
Disbursements	708	591	367	205	98	34	17	3	1	0
Principal	208	204	225	235	240	218	217	213	206	202
Interest	116	121	120	115	107	98	89	81	73	66
Official creditors										
Disbursements	549	496	328	195	95	34	17	3	1	0
Principal	126	121	144	159	167	158	163	167	173	179
Interest	79	82	83	82	79	74	70	66	61	56
Bilateral creditors										
Disbursements	134	136	84	49	28	13	6	0	0	0
Principal	54	55	73	83	84	75	73	73	76	78
Interest	32	33	33	33	31	29	27	24	22	20
Multilateral creditors										
Disbursements	415	360	244	146	68	21	10	3	1	0
Principal	71	66	70	76	83	82	90	94	98	101
Interest	47	48	50	49	48	46	43	41	39	36
Private creditors										
Disbursements	159	95	39	11	3	0	0	0	0	0
Principal	82	83	82	76	72	60	54	46	33	23
Interest	38	40	37	33	28	23	19	16	13	10
Commercial banks										
Disbursements	79	41	14	5	0	0	0	0	0	0
Principal	19	32	34	33	33	24	18	15	11	6
Interest	9	11	10	9	7	5	3	2	1	1
Other private										
Disbursements	80	54	25	6	3	0	0	0	0	0
Principal	64	51	48	44	40	36	36	32	22	17
Interest	29	29	27	24	22	19	16	14	11	10

GRENADA

(US$ million, unless otherwise indicated)

	1970	1980	1988	1989	1990	1991	1992	1993	1994	1995
1. SUMMARY DEBT DATA										
TOTAL DEBT STOCKS (EDT)	..	**16.1**	**79.8**	**81.9**	**102.5**	**113.1**	**105.3**	**135.5**	**115.5**	**112.8**
Long-term debt (LDOD)	**7.6**	**12.3**	**69.3**	**71.1**	**89.9**	**99.7**	**94.1**	**92.5**	**100.1**	**98.4**
Public and publicly guaranteed	7.6	12.3	69.3	71.1	89.9	99.7	94.1	92.5	100.1	98.4
Private nonguaranteed	0.0	0.0	0.0	0.0	0.0	0.0	0.0	0.0	0.0	0.0
Use of IMF credit	**0.0**	**2.8**	**1.1**	**0.5**	**0.0**	**0.0**	**0.0**	**0.0**	**0.0**	**0.0**
Short-term debt	..	**1.0**	**9.3**	**10.4**	**12.6**	**13.4**	**11.3**	**43.0**	**15.4**	**14.4**
of which interest arrears on LDOD	..	0.0	3.3	4.4	6.6	7.4	6.2	6.2	6.4	6.4
Official creditors	..	0.0	3.2	4.2	6.3	7.3	6.0	6.0	6.2	6.1
Private creditors	..	0.0	0.1	0.2	0.2	0.1	0.2	0.2	0.2	0.2
Memo: principal arrears on LDOD	..	0.0	6.9	10.1	15.4	16.7	17.5	17.8	18.7	19.0
Official creditors	..	0.0	6.9	9.6	14.4	15.7	16.6	16.9	17.8	18.4
Private creditors	..	0.0	0.1	0.6	1.0	1.1	0.9	0.9	1.0	0.5
Memo: export credits	..	..	15.0	22.0	23.0	22.0	19.0	25.0	28.0	14.0
TOTAL DEBT FLOWS										
Disbursements	**3.0**	**1.7**	**8.2**	**6.2**	**14.6**	**15.5**	**7.6**	**4.5**	**10.7**	**3.3**
Long-term debt	3.0	1.0	8.2	6.2	14.6	15.5	7.6	4.5	10.7	3.3
IMF purchases	0.0	0.7	0.0	0.0	0.0	0.0	0.0	0.0	0.0	0.0
Principal repayments	**0.0**	**1.6**	**3.8**	**1.7**	**1.7**	**2.0**	**3.8**	**5.2**	**5.2**	**4.8**
Long-term debt	0.0	0.9	3.0	1.0	1.2	2.0	3.8	5.2	5.2	4.8
IMF repurchases	0.0	0.7	0.8	0.6	0.5	0.0	0.0	0.0	0.0	0.0
Net flows on debt	**3.0**	**0.1**	**10.4**	**4.5**	**12.9**	**13.5**	**2.8**	**31.0**	**-22.3**	**-2.5**
of which short-term debt	..	..	6.0	0.0	0.0	0.0	-0.9	31.7	-27.8	-1.0
Interest payments (INT)	..	**0.7**	**2.7**	**1.6**	**1.5**	**1.5**	**1.9**	**2.8**	**2.9**	**2.1**
Long-term debt	0.1	0.5	2.4	1.2	1.1	1.1	1.6	1.5	1.5	1.6
IMF charges	0.0	0.1	0.1	0.1	0.0	0.0	0.0	0.0	0.0	0.0
Short-term debt	..	0.2	0.3	0.4	0.4	0.4	0.4	1.3	1.4	0.5
Net transfers on debt	..	**-0.6**	**7.7**	**2.9**	**11.4**	**12.0**	**0.9**	**28.2**	**-25.2**	**-4.5**
Total debt service paid (TDS)	..	**2.3**	**6.5**	**3.2**	**3.2**	**3.4**	**5.7**	**7.9**	**8.1**	**6.8**
Long-term debt	0.1	1.3	5.4	2.2	2.3	3.1	5.4	6.7	6.7	6.3
IMF repurchases and charges	0.0	0.8	0.9	0.7	0.5	0.0	0.0	0.0	0.0	0.0
Short-term debt (interest only)	..	0.2	0.3	0.4	0.4	0.4	0.4	1.3	1.4	0.5
2. AGGREGATE NET RESOURCE FLOWS AND NET TRANSFERS (LONG-TERM)										
NET RESOURCE FLOWS	**3.0**	**1.1**	**29.1**	**21.2**	**30.6**	**37.0**	**30.8**	**21.6**	**35.8**	**29.9**
Net flow of long-term debt (ex. IMF)	3.0	0.1	5.2	5.1	13.4	13.5	3.7	-0.7	5.5	-1.5
Foreign direct investment (net)	0.0	0.0	15.0	10.5	13.0	15.0	23.0	20.0	19.0	24.0
Portfolio equity flows	0.0	0.0	0.0	0.0	0.0	0.0	0.0	0.0	0.0	0.0
Grants (excluding technical coop.)	0.0	1.0	8.9	5.6	4.2	8.5	4.1	2.3	11.3	7.4
Memo: technical coop. grants	0.0	0.7	3.1	2.4	2.9	3.8	3.9	3.9	3.4	3.8
NET TRANSFERS	**2.8**	**0.5**	**22.6**	**14.2**	**21.1**	**30.1**	**23.1**	**14.1**	**27.3**	**19.4**
Interest on long-term debt	0.1	0.5	2.4	1.2	1.1	1.1	1.6	1.5	1.5	1.6
Profit remittances on FDI	0.0	0.2	4.1	5.9	8.4	5.8	6.2	6.0	7.0	9.0
3. MAJOR ECONOMIC AGGREGATES										
Gross national product (GNP)	..	78.7	158.2	177.5	211.2	236.1	237.6	239.4	250.3	267.3
Exports of goods & services (XGS)	..	39.1	100.5	96.2	105.5	111.9	112.6	123.2	..	..
of which workers remittances	..	0.0	11.6	8.4	9.9	10.9	10.7	10.1	..	..
Imports of goods & services (MGS)	..	63.1	128.9	140.6	153.2	158.9	147.0	170.3	..	..
International reserves (RES)	5.3	12.9	16.9	15.4	17.6	17.5	25.9	26.9	31.2	36.7
Current account balance	..	0.2	-27.8	-36.3	-46.2	-46.6	-33.1	-43.5	..	..
4. DEBT INDICATORS										
EDT / XGS (%)	..	41.1	79.4	85.2	97.1	101.1	93.5	110.0	..	..
EDT / GNP (%)	..	20.4	50.4	46.2	48.5	47.9	44.3	56.6	46.2	42.2
TDS / XGS (%)	..	5.9	6.5	3.4	3.0	3.1	5.1	6.5	..	..
INT / XGS (%)	..	1.9	2.7	1.6	1.5	1.3	1.7	2.3	..	..
INT / GNP (%)	..	0.9	1.7	0.9	0.7	0.6	0.8	1.2	1.1	0.8
RES / EDT (%)	..	80.3	21.2	18.8	17.2	15.5	24.6	19.9	27.0	32.5
RES / MGS (months)	..	2.5	1.6	1.3	1.4	1.3	2.1	1.9	..	..
Short-term / EDT (%)	..	6.2	11.6	12.7	12.3	11.9	10.7	31.7	13.3	12.8
Concessional / EDT (%)	..	51.9	67.9	69.9	61.7	54.7	58.2	45.5	58.6	58.3
Multilateral / EDT (%)	..	32.1	41.8	43.5	37.5	35.0	41.0	30.6	39.0	40.6

GRENADA

(US$ million, unless otherwise indicated)

	1970	1980	1988	1989	1990	1991	1992	1993	1994	1995
5. LONG-TERM DEBT										
DEBT OUTSTANDING (LDOD)	**7.6**	**12.3**	**69.3**	**71.1**	**89.9**	**99.7**	**94.1**	**92.5**	**100.1**	**98.4**
Public and publicly guaranteed	**7.6**	**12.3**	**69.3**	**71.1**	**89.9**	**99.7**	**94.1**	**92.5**	**100.1**	**98.4**
Official creditors	2.5	9.7	67.6	69.4	87.6	85.8	82.9	82.7	91.1	91.1
Multilateral	0.0	5.2	33.3	35.7	38.4	39.6	43.2	41.4	45.1	45.8
Concessional	0.0	4.2	32.7	35.1	37.8	39.1	42.4	41.0	44.2	42.8
Bilateral	2.5	4.6	34.3	33.7	49.2	46.2	39.7	41.2	46.0	45.3
Concessional	2.4	4.2	21.4	22.2	25.4	22.8	18.9	20.7	23.5	22.9
Private creditors	5.1	2.6	1.7	1.8	2.3	13.9	11.2	9.8	9.0	7.3
Bonds	5.1	2.1	0.0	0.0	0.0	0.0	0.0	0.0	0.0	0.0
Commercial banks	0.0	0.0	0.8	0.7	0.7	0.6	0.5	0.6	0.6	0.4
Other private	0.0	0.5	0.9	1.0	1.6	13.3	10.7	9.2	8.5	6.9
Private nonguaranteed	**0.0**	**0.0**	**0.0**	**0.0**	**0.0**	**0.0**	**0.0**	**0.0**	**0.0**	**0.0**
Bonds	0.0	0.0	0.0	0.0	0.0	0.0	0.0	0.0	0.0	0.0
Commercial banks	0.0	0.0	0.0	0.0	0.0	0.0	0.0	0.0	0.0	0.0
Memo:										
IBRD	0.0	0.0	0.0	0.0	0.0	0.0	0.0	0.0	0.0	0.0
IDA	0.0	0.0	3.6	4.2	5.5	7.1	6.8	6.9	7.2	7.3
DISBURSEMENTS	**3.0**	**1.0**	**8.2**	**6.2**	**14.6**	**15.5**	**7.6**	**4.5**	**10.7**	**3.3**
Public and publicly guaranteed	**3.0**	**1.0**	**8.2**	**6.2**	**14.6**	**15.5**	**7.6**	**4.5**	**10.7**	**3.3**
Official creditors	0.1	1.0	8.2	6.0	14.1	4.2	6.3	4.4	10.7	3.3
Multilateral	0.0	1.0	4.0	3.3	2.8	2.8	6.1	1.6	5.6	2.8
Concessional	0.0	0.0	4.0	3.3	2.8	2.8	5.8	1.4	5.2	0.7
Bilateral	0.1	0.0	4.2	2.7	11.3	1.3	0.3	2.8	5.1	0.5
Concessional	0.0	0.0	4.2	2.7	1.0	1.3	0.3	2.8	3.8	0.5
Private creditors	2.8	0.0	0.0	0.1	0.5	11.3	1.2	0.1	0.0	0.0
Bonds	2.8	0.0	0.0	0.0	0.0	0.0	0.0	0.0	0.0	0.0
Commercial banks	0.0	0.0	0.0	0.0	0.0	0.0	0.0	0.1	0.0	0.0
Other private	0.0	0.0	0.0	0.1	0.5	11.3	1.2	0.0	0.0	0.0
Private nonguaranteed	**0.0**	**0.0**	**0.0**	**0.0**	**0.0**	**0.0**	**0.0**	**0.0**	**0.0**	**0.0**
Bonds	0.0	0.0	0.0	0.0	0.0	0.0	0.0	0.0	0.0	0.0
Commercial banks	0.0	0.0	0.0	0.0	0.0	0.0	0.0	0.0	0.0	0.0
Memo:										
IBRD	0.0	0.0	0.0	0.0	0.0	0.0	0.0	0.0	0.0	0.0
IDA	0.0	0.0	0.5	0.6	1.0	1.5	0.0	0.0	0.0	0.0
PRINCIPAL REPAYMENTS	**0.0**	**0.9**	**3.0**	**1.0**	**1.2**	**2.0**	**3.8**	**5.2**	**5.2**	**4.8**
Public and publicly guaranteed	**0.0**	**0.9**	**3.0**	**1.0**	**1.2**	**2.0**	**3.8**	**5.2**	**5.2**	**4.8**
Official creditors	0.0	0.3	2.1	1.0	1.0	1.7	2.4	3.9	3.9	3.1
Multilateral	0.0	0.0	1.9	0.9	1.0	1.7	1.9	3.2	2.5	2.5
Concessional	0.0	0.0	1.6	0.9	0.9	1.6	1.9	2.7	2.5	2.5
Bilateral	0.0	0.3	0.2	0.1	0.1	0.1	0.5	0.7	1.4	0.6
Concessional	0.0	0.2	0.2	0.1	0.0	0.0	0.3	0.7	1.4	0.6
Private creditors	0.0	0.6	0.9	0.1	0.2	0.2	1.4	1.2	1.3	1.7
Bonds	0.0	0.6	0.0	0.0	0.0	0.0	0.0	0.0	0.0	0.0
Commercial banks	0.0	0.0	0.2	0.1	0.1	0.1	0.0	0.0	0.0	0.2
Other private	0.0	0.0	0.7	0.0	0.1	0.1	1.4	1.2	1.3	1.5
Private nonguaranteed	**0.0**	**0.0**	**0.0**	**0.0**	**0.0**	**0.0**	**0.0**	**0.0**	**0.0**	**0.0**
Bonds	0.0	0.0	0.0	0.0	0.0	0.0	0.0	0.0	0.0	0.0
Commercial banks	0.0	0.0	0.0	0.0	0.0	0.0	0.0	0.0	0.0	0.0
Memo:										
IBRD	0.0	0.0	0.0	0.0	0.0	0.0	0.0	0.0	0.0	0.0
IDA	0.0	0.0	0.0	0.0	0.0	0.0	0.0	0.0	0.0	0.1
NET FLOWS ON DEBT	**3.0**	**0.1**	**5.2**	**5.1**	**13.4**	**13.5**	**3.7**	**-0.7**	**5.5**	**-1.5**
Public and publicly guaranteed	**3.0**	**0.1**	**5.2**	**5.1**	**13.4**	**13.5**	**3.7**	**-0.7**	**5.5**	**-1.5**
Official creditors	0.1	0.7	6.1	5.1	13.1	2.4	4.0	0.4	6.8	0.2
Multilateral	0.0	1.0	2.1	2.4	1.9	1.1	4.2	-1.7	3.1	0.4
Concessional	0.0	0.0	2.4	2.4	1.9	1.2	3.9	-1.4	2.7	-1.7
Bilateral	0.1	-0.3	4.1	2.6	11.2	1.3	-0.2	2.1	3.7	-0.1
Concessional	0.0	-0.2	4.1	2.6	1.0	1.3	0.0	2.1	2.4	-0.1
Private creditors	2.8	-0.6	-0.9	0.0	0.3	11.1	-0.2	-1.1	-1.3	-1.7
Bonds	2.8	-0.6	0.0	0.0	0.0	0.0	0.0	0.0	0.0	0.0
Commercial banks	0.0	0.0	-0.2	-0.1	-0.1	-0.1	0.0	0.1	0.0	-0.2
Other private	0.0	0.0	-0.7	0.1	0.4	11.2	-0.2	-1.2	-1.3	-1.5
Private nonguaranteed	**0.0**	**0.0**	**0.0**	**0.0**	**0.0**	**0.0**	**0.0**	**0.0**	**0.0**	**0.0**
Bonds	0.0	0.0	0.0	0.0	0.0	0.0	0.0	0.0	0.0	0.0
Commercial banks	0.0	0.0	0.0	0.0	0.0	0.0	0.0	0.0	0.0	0.0
Memo:										
IBRD	0.0	0.0	0.0	0.0	0.0	0.0	0.0	0.0	0.0	0.0
IDA	0.0	0.0	0.5	0.6	1.0	1.5	0.0	0.0	0.0	-0.1

GRENADA

(US$ million, unless otherwise indicated)

	1970	1980	1988	1989	1990	1991	1992	1993	1994	1995
INTEREST PAYMENTS (LINT)	**0.1**	**0.5**	**2.4**	**1.2**	**1.1**	**1.1**	**1.6**	**1.5**	**1.5**	**1.6**
Public and publicly guaranteed	**0.1**	**0.5**	**2.4**	**1.2**	**1.1**	**1.1**	**1.6**	**1.5**	**1.5**	**1.6**
Official creditors	0.0	0.3	2.1	1.0	1.0	0.9	1.5	1.5	1.5	1.4
Multilateral	0.0	0.2	1.1	0.8	1.0	0.7	1.0	1.3	1.2	1.2
Concessional	0.0	0.2	1.0	0.8	1.0	0.7	1.0	1.2	1.2	1.1
Bilateral	0.0	0.1	1.0	0.1	0.0	0.2	0.6	0.2	0.2	0.2
Concessional	0.0	0.0	0.0	0.0	0.0	0.0	0.0	0.0	0.0	0.2
Private creditors	0.1	0.2	0.3	0.2	0.2	0.2	0.1	0.1	0.0	0.2
Bonds	0.1	0.2	0.0	0.0	0.0	0.0	0.0	0.0	0.0	0.0
Commercial banks	0.0	0.0	0.2	0.2	0.2	0.1	0.0	0.0	0.0	0.0
Other private	0.0	0.0	0.1	0.0	0.0	0.1	0.0	0.0	0.0	0.1
Private nonguaranteed	**0.0**	**0.0**	**0.0**	**0.0**	**0.0**	**0.0**	**0.0**	**0.0**	**0.0**	**0.0**
Bonds	0.0	0.0	0.0	0.0	0.0	0.0	0.0	0.0	0.0	0.0
Commercial banks	0.0	0.0	0.0	0.0	0.0	0.0	0.0	0.0	0.0	0.0
Memo:										
IBRD	0.0	0.0	0.0	0.0	0.0	0.0	0.0	0.0	0.0	0.0
IDA	0.0	0.0	0.0	0.0	0.0	0.0	0.1	0.1	0.1	0.1
NET TRANSFERS ON DEBT	**2.8**	**-0.3**	**2.8**	**4.0**	**12.3**	**12.4**	**2.2**	**-2.2**	**4.0**	**-3.0**
Public and publicly guaranteed	**2.8**	**-0.3**	**2.8**	**4.0**	**12.3**	**12.4**	**2.2**	**-2.2**	**4.0**	**-3.0**
Official creditors	0.1	0.4	4.0	4.1	12.1	1.5	2.5	-1.1	5.3	-1.2
Multilateral	0.0	0.8	1.0	1.6	0.9	0.4	3.2	-2.9	1.8	-0.8
Concessional	0.0	-0.2	1.4	1.6	0.9	0.4	2.9	-2.6	1.5	-2.8
Bilateral	0.1	-0.4	3.0	2.5	11.2	1.1	-0.8	1.9	3.5	-0.3
Concessional	0.0	-0.2	4.1	2.6	1.0	1.3	0.0	2.1	2.3	-0.3
Private creditors	2.7	-0.7	-1.2	-0.2	0.2	10.9	-0.3	-1.2	-1.3	-1.9
Bonds	2.7	-0.7	0.0	0.0	0.0	0.0	0.0	0.0	0.0	0.0
Commercial banks	0.0	0.0	-0.4	-0.3	-0.3	-0.2	-0.1	0.1	-0.1	-0.2
Other private	0.0	0.0	-0.7	0.1	0.4	11.1	-0.2	-1.2	-1.3	-1.7
Private nonguaranteed	**0.0**	**0.0**	**0.0**	**0.0**	**0.0**	**0.0**	**0.0**	**0.0**	**0.0**	**0.0**
Bonds	0.0	0.0	0.0	0.0	0.0	0.0	0.0	0.0	0.0	0.0
Commercial banks	0.0	0.0	0.0	0.0	0.0	0.0	0.0	0.0	0.0	0.0
Memo:										
IBRD	0.0	0.0	0.0	0.0	0.0	0.0	0.0	0.0	0.0	0.0
IDA	0.0	0.0	0.5	0.6	0.9	1.5	0.0	-0.1	-0.1	-0.1
DEBT SERVICE (LTDS)	**0.1**	**1.3**	**5.4**	**2.2**	**2.3**	**3.1**	**5.4**	**6.7**	**6.7**	**6.3**
Public and publicly guaranteed	**0.1**	**1.3**	**5.4**	**2.2**	**2.3**	**3.1**	**5.4**	**6.7**	**6.7**	**6.3**
Official creditors	0.0	0.6	4.2	1.9	2.0	2.6	3.9	5.4	5.4	4.4
Multilateral	0.0	0.2	3.0	1.7	1.9	2.4	2.8	4.5	3.7	3.6
Concessional	0.0	0.2	2.6	1.7	1.9	2.3	2.8	4.0	3.7	3.6
Bilateral	0.0	0.4	1.2	0.2	0.1	0.2	1.1	0.9	1.7	0.8
Concessional	0.0	0.2	0.2	0.1	0.0	0.0	0.3	0.7	1.4	0.8
Private creditors	0.1	0.7	1.2	0.3	0.3	0.4	1.5	1.3	1.3	1.9
Bonds	0.1	0.7	0.0	0.0	0.0	0.0	0.0	0.0	0.0	0.0
Commercial banks	0.0	0.0	0.4	0.3	0.3	0.2	0.1	0.0	0.1	0.2
Other private	0.0	0.0	0.7	0.0	0.1	0.3	1.4	1.2	1.3	1.7
Private nonguaranteed	**0.0**	**0.0**	**0.0**	**0.0**	**0.0**	**0.0**	**0.0**	**0.0**	**0.0**	**0.0**
Bonds	0.0	0.0	0.0	0.0	0.0	0.0	0.0	0.0	0.0	0.0
Commercial banks	0.0	0.0	0.0	0.0	0.0	0.0	0.0	0.0	0.0	0.0
Memo:										
IBRD	0.0	0.0	0.0	0.0	0.0	0.0	0.0	0.0	0.0	0.0
IDA	0.0	0.0	0.0	0.0	0.0	0.0	0.1	0.1	0.1	0.1
UNDISBURSED DEBT	**1.0**	**7.3**	**19.6**	**13.8**	**12.9**	**18.2**	**16.6**	**14.5**	**16.1**	**12.7**
Official creditors	1.0	7.3	19.6	13.4	12.9	16.9	16.6	14.5	16.1	12.7
Private creditors	0.0	0.0	0.0	0.4	0.0	1.3	0.0	0.0	0.0	0.0
Memorandum items										
Concessional LDOD	2.4	8.3	54.1	57.3	63.2	61.8	61.3	61.6	67.7	65.7
Variable rate LDOD	0.0	0.0	12.8	11.3	13.4	12.9	10.5	10.4	10.9	10.6
Public sector LDOD	7.6	12.3	69.3	71.1	89.9	99.7	94.1	92.5	100.1	98.4
Private sector LDOD	0.0	0.0	0.0	0.0	0.0	0.0	0.0	0.0	0.0	0.0

6. CURRENCY COMPOSITION OF LONG-TERM DEBT (PERCENT)

	1970	1980	1988	1989	1990	1991	1992	1993	1994	1995
Deutsche mark	0.0	0.0	0.0	0.0	0.0	0.0	0.0	0.0	0.0	0.0
French franc	0.0	0.0	0.0	0.0	0.0	0.0	0.0	0.5	1.7	2.0
Japanese yen	0.0	0.0	0.0	0.0	0.0	0.0	0.0	0.0	0.0	0.0
Pound sterling	100.0	48.0	32.5	31.5	31.4	40.6	34.4	34.7	31.6	30.0
Swiss franc	0.0	0.0	0.0	0.0	0.0	0.0	0.0	0.0	0.0	0.0
U.S.dollars	0.0	46.4	57.1	59.3	61.1	52.8	59.3	58.8	61.6	63.6
Multiple currency	0.0	0.0	0.0	0.0	0.0	0.0	0.0	0.0	0.0	0.0
Special drawing rights	0.0	0.0	2.9	2.8	2.3	2.2	2.2	2.3	1.8	1.4
All other currencies	0.0	5.7	7.5	6.3	5.2	4.5	4.0	3.7	3.5	2.9

GRENADA

(US$ million, unless otherwise indicated)

	1970	1980	1988	1989	1990	1991	1992	1993	1994	1995
7. DEBT RESTRUCTURINGS										
Total amount rescheduled	0.0	0.0	0.0	0.0	0.0	0.0	0.0	0.0	0.0	0.0
Debt stock rescheduled	0.0	0.0	0.0	0.0	0.0	0.0	0.0	0.0	0.0	0.0
Principal rescheduled	0.0	0.0	0.0	0.0	0.0	0.0	0.0	0.0	0.0	0.0
Official	0.0	0.0	0.0	0.0	0.0	0.0	0.0	0.0	0.0	0.0
Private	0.0	0.0	0.0	0.0	0.0	0.0	0.0	0.0	0.0	0.0
Interest rescheduled	0.0	0.0	0.0	0.0	0.0	0.0	0.0	0.0	0.0	0.0
Official	0.0	0.0	0.0	0.0	0.0	0.0	0.0	0.0	0.0	0.0
Private	0.0	0.0	0.0	0.0	0.0	0.0	0.0	0.0	0.0	0.0
Debt forgiven	..	..	0.0	0.0	0.0	3.6	0.8	0.0	0.0	0.6
Memo: interest forgiven	..	..	0.0	0.0	0.0	0.0	0.0	0.0	0.0	0.0
Debt stock reduction	0.0	0.0	0.0	0.0	0.0	0.0	0.0	0.0	0.0	0.0
of which debt buyback	0.0	0.0	0.0	0.0	0.0	0.0	0.0	0.0	0.0	0.0
8. DEBT STOCK-FLOW RECONCILIATION										
Total change in debt stocks	..	..	..	2.2	20.5	10.6	-7.8	30.1	-19.9	-2.7
Net flows on debt	..	..	..	4.5	12.9	13.5	2.8	31.0	-22.3	-2.5
Net change in interest arrears	..	..	..	1.1	2.2	0.9	-1.3	0.0	0.2	0.0
Interest capitalized	..	..	..	0.0	0.0	0.0	0.0	0.0	0.0	0.0
Debt forgiveness or reduction	..	..	..	0.0	0.0	-3.6	-0.8	0.0	0.0	-0.6
Cross-currency valuation	..	..	..	-2.8	6.1	-1.4	-6.7	-0.9	2.0	0.1
Residual	..	..	..	-0.6	-0.7	1.2	-1.8	0.0	0.1	0.3
9. AVERAGE TERMS OF NEW COMMITMENTS										
ALL CREDITORS										
Interest (%)	7.4	1.6	2.5	5.1	4.8	1.1	2.9	3.9	4.8	0.0
Maturity (years)	12.7	14.4	18.6	16.5	11.2	23.2	31.8	22.1	17.0	0.0
Grace period (years)	12.7	4.6	9.4	2.4	2.1	4.2	8.7	1.3	4.0	0.0
Grant element (%)	17.0	43.8	54.0	27.8	22.9	51.9	57.7	37.0	31.1	0.0
Official creditors										
Interest (%)	0.0	1.6	2.5	4.0	4.8	2.7	2.9	3.8	4.8	0.0
Maturity (years)	29.5	14.4	18.6	21.0	11.2	37.6	31.8	22.8	17.0	0.0
Grace period (years)	29.5	4.6	9.4	3.0	2.1	9.8	8.7	1.3	4.0	0.0
Grant element (%)	94.0	43.8	54.0	37.7	22.9	62.4	57.7	38.4	31.1	0.0
Private creditors										
Interest (%)	7.5	0.0	0.0	7.5	0.0	0.0	0.0	8.3	0.0	0.0
Maturity (years)	12.5	0.0	0.0	7.0	0.0	13.4	0.0	3.6	0.0	0.0
Grace period (years)	12.5	0.0	0.0	1.0	0.0	0.4	0.0	0.1	0.0	0.0
Grant element (%)	16.1	0.0	0.0	7.1	0.0	44.7	0.0	3.4	0.0	0.0
Memorandum items										
Commitments	2.8	7.3	5.5	1.7	11.9	21.1	7.5	2.6	13.5	0.0
Official creditors	0.0	7.3	5.5	1.2	11.9	8.5	7.5	2.5	13.5	0.0
Private creditors	2.8	0.0	0.0	0.6	0.0	12.6	0.0	0.1	0.0	0.0

10. CONTRACTUAL OBLIGATIONS ON OUTSTANDING LONG-TERM DEBT

	1996	1997	1998	1999	2000	2001	2002	2003	2004	2005
TOTAL										
Disbursements	4.7	3.5	2.2	1.3	0.6	0.3	0.2	0.0	0.0	0.0
Principal	6.1	6.6	7.5	7.4	6.4	5.4	5.3	5.1	4.7	4.2
Interest	2.2	2.1	1.9	1.8	1.5	1.4	1.2	1.1	0.9	0.8
Official creditors										
Disbursements	4.7	3.5	2.2	1.3	0.6	0.3	0.2	0.0	0.0	0.0
Principal	5.3	5.9	6.8	6.7	5.7	4.7	4.6	4.4	4.0	3.9
Interest	2.1	2.1	1.9	1.7	1.5	1.3	1.2	1.1	0.9	0.8
Bilateral creditors										
Disbursements	3.9	2.5	1.6	1.0	0.5	0.2	0.2	0.0	0.0	0.0
Principal	3.2	3.3	3.9	3.9	2.9	1.7	1.7	1.7	1.7	1.7
Interest	0.9	0.8	0.8	0.7	0.5	0.5	0.4	0.4	0.3	0.3
Multilateral creditors										
Disbursements	0.8	1.0	0.6	0.2	0.1	0.1	0.0	0.0	0.0	0.0
Principal	2.2	2.5	2.9	2.8	2.8	3.0	2.9	2.6	2.3	2.2
Interest	1.2	1.2	1.1	1.1	1.0	0.9	0.8	0.7	0.6	0.5
Private creditors										
Disbursements	0.0	0.0	0.0	0.0	0.0	0.0	0.0	0.0	0.0	0.0
Principal	0.8	0.7	0.7	0.7	0.7	0.7	0.7	0.7	0.7	0.3
Interest	0.0	0.0	0.0	0.0	0.0	0.0	0.0	0.0	0.0	0.0
Commercial banks										
Disbursements	0.0	0.0	0.0	0.0	0.0	0.0	0.0	0.0	0.0	0.0
Principal	0.1	0.0	0.0	0.0	0.0	0.0	0.0	0.0	0.0	0.0
Interest	0.0	0.0	0.0	0.0	0.0	0.0	0.0	0.0	0.0	0.0
Other private										
Disbursements	0.0	0.0	0.0	0.0	0.0	0.0	0.0	0.0	0.0	0.0
Principal	0.7	0.7	0.7	0.7	0.7	0.7	0.7	0.7	0.7	0.2
Interest	0.0	0.0	0.0	0.0	0.0	0.0	0.0	0.0	0.0	0.0

GUATEMALA

(US$ million, unless otherwise indicated)

1. SUMMARY DEBT DATA

	1970	*1980*	*1988*	*1989*	*1990*	*1991*	*1992*	*1993*	*1994*	*1995*
TOTAL DEBT STOCKS (EDT)	**..**	**1,166**	**2,636**	**2,633**	**2,840**	**2,825**	**2,742**	**2,886**	**3,109**	**3,275**
Long-term debt (LDOD)	**120**	**831**	**2,252**	**2,240**	**2,368**	**2,362**	**2,240**	**2,416**	**2,622**	**2,635**
Public and publicly guaranteed	106	549	2,139	2,117	2,241	2,235	2,099	2,233	2,461	2,493
Private nonguaranteed	14	282	113	123	127	127	141	183	161	142
Use of IMF credit	**0**	**0**	**88**	**73**	**67**	**64**	**31**	**0**	**0**	**0**
Short-term debt	**..**	**335**	**296**	**320**	**406**	**399**	**471**	**470**	**487**	**640**
of which interest arrears on LDOD	..	0	97	117	199	192	195	29	48	48
Official creditors	..	0	94	114	192	183	186	23	37	36
Private creditors	..	0	2	3	7	9	8	6	11	12
Memo: principal arrears on LDOD	..	0	260	264	306	355	317	242	295	291
Official creditors	..	0	129	159	203	242	207	123	164	160
Private creditors	..	0	131	104	102	114	110	120	131	131
Memo: export credits	..	..	468	426	545	570	486	400	418	421
TOTAL DEBT FLOWS										
Disbursements	**43**	**170**	**272**	**174**	**165**	**166**	**221**	**145**	**310**	**183**
Long-term debt	43	170	212	174	165	166	221	145	310	183
IMF purchases	0	0	60	0	0	0	0	0	0	0
Principal repayments	**30**	**78**	**247**	**172**	**102**	**157**	**346**	**190**	**167**	**194**
Long-term debt	22	78	219	159	90	155	315	159	167	194
IMF repurchases	8	0	28	13	12	3	32	31	0	0
Net flows on debt	**13**	**92**	**25**	**13**	**67**	**8**	**-56**	**120**	**141**	**142**
of which short-term debt	..	..	1	11	4	0	69	165	-2	153
Interest payments (INT)	**..**	**67**	**126**	**132**	**111**	**132**	**171**	**112**	**116**	**148**
Long-term debt	7	60	111	111	87	112	158	93	93	116
IMF charges	0	0	4	7	7	6	4	1	0	0
Short-term debt	..	8	11	14	16	14	9	18	23	32
Net transfers on debt	**..**	**25**	**-101**	**-119**	**-43**	**-123**	**-227**	**8**	**26**	**-6**
Total debt service paid (TDS)	**..**	**145**	**373**	**304**	**212**	**289**	**517**	**302**	**283**	**342**
Long-term debt	29	137	330	270	177	267	473	252	260	310
IMF repurchases and charges	8	0	32	20	19	8	35	32	0	0
Short-term debt (interest only)	..	8	11	14	16	14	9	18	23	32

2. AGGREGATE NET RESOURCE FLOWS AND NET TRANSFERS (LONG-TERM)

	1970	*1980*	*1988*	*1989*	*1990*	*1991*	*1992*	*1993*	*1994*	*1995*
NET RESOURCE FLOWS	**53**	**217**	**441**	**218**	**192**	**174**	**96**	**213**	**298**	**169**
Net flow of long-term debt (ex. IMF)	21	92	-8	14	75	11	-94	-14	143	-11
Foreign direct investment (net)	29	111	330	76	48	91	94	143	65	75
Portfolio equity flows	0	0	0	0	0	0	0	0	0	0
Grants (excluding technical coop.)	2	14	119	127	69	72	95	83	89	105
Memo: technical coop. grants	9	18	55	68	90	88	86	95	73	98
NET TRANSFERS	**16**	**114**	**300**	**62**	**68**	**18**	**-99**	**75**	**160**	**-2**
Interest on long-term debt	7	60	111	111	87	112	158	93	93	116
Profit remittances on FDI	30	44	29	44	37	44	36	44	45	55

3. MAJOR ECONOMIC AGGREGATES

	1970	*1980*	*1988*	*1989*	*1990*	*1991*	*1992*	*1993*	*1994*	*1995*
Gross national product (GNP)	1,866	7,834	7,665	8,231	7,455	9,232	10,286	11,248	12,966	14,708
Exports of goods & services (XGS)	..	1,834	1,343	1,523	1,695	1,892	2,154	2,290	2,574	3,225
of which workers remittances	..	0	43	69	107	139	187	205	263	358
Imports of goods & services (MGS)	..	2,107	1,939	2,072	2,028	2,196	3,063	3,150	3,385	3,933
International reserves (RES)	79	753	416	524	362	881	806	950	943	783
Current account balance	..	-163	-414	-367	-233	-184	-706	-702	-625	-572

4. DEBT INDICATORS

	1970	*1980*	*1988*	*1989*	*1990*	*1991*	*1992*	*1993*	*1994*	*1995*
EDT / XGS (%)	..	63.6	196.2	172.9	167.6	149.3	127.3	126.0	120.8	101.5
EDT / GNP (%)	..	14.9	34.4	32.0	38.1	30.6	26.7	25.7	24.0	22.3
TDS / XGS (%)	..	7.9	27.8	19.9	12.5	15.3	24.0	13.2	11.0	10.6
INT / XGS (%)	..	3.7	9.4	8.7	6.5	7.0	8.0	4.9	4.5	4.6
INT / GNP (%)	..	0.9	1.6	1.6	1.5	1.4	1.7	1.0	0.9	1.0
RES / EDT (%)	..	64.6	15.8	19.9	12.7	31.2	29.4	32.9	30.3	23.9
RES / MGS (months)	..	4.3	2.6	3.0	2.1	4.8	3.2	3.6	3.3	2.4
Short-term / EDT (%)	..	28.7	11.2	12.2	14.3	14.1	17.2	16.3	15.7	19.5
Concessional / EDT (%)	..	21.6	21.9	23.6	24.4	27.5	28.5	39.9	39.2	38.2
Multilateral / EDT (%)	..	30.0	33.8	34.4	34.8	33.6	32.3	29.0	30.6	28.8

GUATEMALA

(US$ million, unless otherwise indicated)

	1970	1980	1988	1989	1990	1991	1992	1993	1994	1995
5. LONG-TERM DEBT										
DEBT OUTSTANDING (LDOD)	**120**	**831**	**2,252**	**2,240**	**2,368**	**2,362**	**2,240**	**2,416**	**2,622**	**2,635**
Public and publicly guaranteed	**106**	**549**	**2,139**	**2,117**	**2,241**	**2,235**	**2,099**	**2,233**	**2,461**	**2,493**
Official creditors	54	534	1,707	1,711	1,838	1,842	1,734	1,898	2,057	2,057
Multilateral	33	350	892	906	988	950	886	836	953	943
Concessional	27	156	294	315	329	332	322	320	350	358
Bilateral	21	183	815	805	850	892	848	1,062	1,104	1,115
Concessional	21	96	284	306	364	446	460	831	869	892
Private creditors	52	15	432	407	404	393	365	335	404	436
Bonds	14	0	229	200	190	176	158	144	220	265
Commercial banks	36	14	179	169	162	165	164	149	143	132
Other private	3	1	25	37	52	53	43	42	42	39
Private nonguaranteed	**14**	**282**	**113**	**123**	**127**	**127**	**141**	**183**	**161**	**142**
Bonds	0	0	0	0	0	0	0	0	0	0
Commercial banks	14	282	113	123	127	127	141	183	161	142
Memo:										
IBRD	14	144	280	261	293	279	213	178	177	158
IDA	0	0	0	0	0	0	0	0	0	0
DISBURSEMENTS	**43**	**170**	**212**	**174**	**165**	**166**	**221**	**145**	**310**	**183**
Public and publicly guaranteed	**37**	**138**	**212**	**161**	**158**	**163**	**191**	**84**	**310**	**183**
Official creditors	12	125	201	117	130	144	154	70	206	121
Multilateral	9	77	105	85	68	70	95	29	149	57
Concessional	8	31	29	32	20	18	13	11	40	19
Bilateral	2	48	96	32	62	75	59	41	56	64
Concessional	2	23	53	28	57	74	26	17	35	45
Private creditors	26	13	10	44	28	18	37	13	105	62
Bonds	0	0	0	0	0	0	2	0	89	59
Commercial banks	25	13	2	21	14	16	32	7	10	2
Other private	0	0	9	22	14	2	3	6	6	1
Private nonguaranteed	**6**	**32**	**0**	**13**	**7**	**3**	**30**	**62**	**0**	**0**
Bonds	0	0	0	0	0	0	0	0	0	0
Commercial banks	6	32	0	13	7	3	30	62	0	0
Memo:										
IBRD	4	39	7	14	17	4	49	1	29	13
IDA	0	0	0	0	0	0	0	0	0	0
PRINCIPAL REPAYMENTS	**22**	**78**	**219**	**159**	**90**	**155**	**315**	**159**	**167**	**194**
Public and publicly guaranteed	**20**	**15**	**216**	**156**	**87**	**152**	**299**	**139**	**145**	**175**
Official creditors	5	12	101	106	49	123	243	101	107	143
Multilateral	3	12	63	58	28	109	145	83	82	86
Concessional	2	3	9	10	6	14	23	13	14	12
Bilateral	2	1	39	48	21	14	98	18	26	57
Concessional	2	1	2	4	2	5	9	13	8	25
Private creditors	16	3	115	51	38	29	56	38	37	33
Bonds	8	0	69	8	11	14	20	14	14	14
Commercial banks	6	1	26	33	23	13	34	22	15	13
Other private	1	2	20	10	4	2	2	2	8	6
Private nonguaranteed	**2**	**62**	**3**	**3**	**3**	**3**	**16**	**20**	**22**	**19**
Bonds	0	0	0	0	0	0	0	0	0	0
Commercial banks	2	62	3	3	3	3	16	20	22	19
Memo:										
IBRD	2	4	29	27	5	21	107	40	44	40
IDA	0	0	0	0	0	0	0	0	0	0
NET FLOWS ON DEBT	**21**	**92**	**-8**	**14**	**75**	**11**	**-94**	**-14**	**143**	**-11**
Public and publicly guaranteed	**17**	**122**	**-4**	**5**	**71**	**11**	**-108**	**-55**	**166**	**8**
Official creditors	7	113	100	12	81	22	-89	-31	98	-21
Multilateral	6	65	43	27	41	-39	-50	-54	68	-29
Concessional	6	29	19	21	14	4	-10	-2	26	7
Bilateral	1	47	58	-16	41	61	-39	24	31	7
Concessional	1	23	51	24	55	70	17	4	26	20
Private creditors	10	10	-105	-7	-10	-10	-19	-24	67	29
Bonds	-8	0	-69	-8	-11	-14	-18	-14	75	46
Commercial banks	19	11	-24	-11	-9	3	-2	-15	-6	-11
Other private	-1	-2	-11	13	10	0	1	4	-2	-5
Private nonguaranteed	**4**	**-30**	**-3**	**10**	**4**	**0**	**14**	**42**	**-22**	**-19**
Bonds	0	0	0	0	0	0	0	0	0	0
Commercial banks	4	-30	-3	10	4	0	14	42	-22	-19
Memo:										
IBRD	2	35	-22	-13	11	-17	-58	-39	-15	-26
IDA	0	0	0	0	0	0	0	0	0	0

GUATEMALA

(US$ million, unless otherwise indicated)

	1970	1980	1988	1989	1990	1991	1992	1993	1994	1995
INTEREST PAYMENTS (LINT)	**7**	**60**	**111**	**111**	**87**	**112**	**158**	**93**	**93**	**116**
Public and publicly guaranteed	**6**	**30**	**106**	**106**	**77**	**102**	**150**	**86**	**87**	**110**
Official creditors	3	29	76	73	52	78	129	67	69	83
Multilateral	2	20	56	56	33	58	90	52	49	49
Concessional	1	4	7	6	4	8	9	7	7	7
Bilateral	1	9	20	17	19	19	39	15	20	34
Concessional	1	3	4	6	3	9	9	12	14	25
Private creditors	4	0	30	33	26	25	22	20	18	27
Bonds	1	0	9	16	18	18	16	15	13	23
Commercial banks	2	0	17	15	5	5	4	3	2	2
Other private	0	0	3	2	3	1	1	2	3	2
Private nonguaranteed	**1**	**30**	**6**	**6**	**10**	**10**	**8**	**7**	**6**	**5**
Bonds	0	0	0	0	0	0	0	0	0	0
Commercial banks	1	30	6	6	10	10	8	7	6	5
Memo:										
IBRD	1	11	23	21	4	9	53	16	16	14
IDA	0	0	0	0	0	0	0	0	0	0
NET TRANSFERS ON DEBT	**14**	**33**	**-119**	**-97**	**-12**	**-101**	**-252**	**-107**	**50**	**-127**
Public and publicly guaranteed	**11**	**93**	**-110**	**-101**	**-6**	**-91**	**-258**	**-142**	**79**	**-102**
Official creditors	4	83	24	-61	29	-56	-218	-97	29	-105
Multilateral	5	45	-13	-28	8	-98	-139	-106	19	-78
Concessional	4	25	13	15	11	-5	-19	-9	19	0
Bilateral	0	38	37	-33	22	42	-78	9	11	-27
Concessional	0	19	47	19	52	61	8	-8	12	-5
Private creditors	6	10	-134	-39	-36	-35	-41	-44	49	2
Bonds	-10	0	-78	-24	-28	-32	-34	-29	62	23
Commercial banks	17	11	-42	-26	-15	-2	-6	-18	-8	-14
Other private	-1	-2	-15	11	7	-1	0	3	-5	-7
Private nonguaranteed	**3**	**-60**	**-9**	**4**	**-6**	**-10**	**7**	**35**	**-28**	**-24**
Bonds	0	0	0	0	0	0	0	0	0	0
Commercial banks	3	-60	-9	4	-6	-10	7	35	-28	-24
Memo:										
IBRD	1	24	-45	-34	8	-26	-111	-55	-31	-41
IDA	0	0	0	0	0	0	0	0	0	0
DEBT SERVICE (LTDS)	**29**	**137**	**330**	**270**	**177**	**267**	**473**	**252**	**260**	**310**
Public and publicly guaranteed	**26**	**45**	**322**	**262**	**164**	**254**	**449**	**225**	**232**	**286**
Official creditors	7	42	177	179	101	200	372	168	176	226
Multilateral	4	32	119	114	61	167	234	135	131	135
Concessional	3	7	16	16	10	22	32	20	21	19
Bilateral	3	10	59	65	40	33	138	33	46	91
Concessional	3	4	6	10	5	13	18	25	22	49
Private creditors	19	3	144	83	64	54	77	58	55	60
Bonds	10	0	78	24	28	32	36	29	27	36
Commercial banks	8	2	43	47	29	18	38	25	17	15
Other private	1	2	23	12	7	3	3	4	11	9
Private nonguaranteed	**3**	**92**	**9**	**9**	**13**	**13**	**24**	**27**	**28**	**24**
Bonds	0	0	0	0	0	0	0	0	0	0
Commercial banks	3	92	9	9	13	13	24	27	28	24
Memo:										
IBRD	3	15	52	48	9	31	160	56	60	54
IDA	0	0	0	0	0	0	0	0	0	0
UNDISBURSED DEBT	**70**	**501**	**861**	**789**	**769**	**657**	**790**	**739**	**494**	**299**
Official creditors	59	501	829	754	716	608	610	572	432	298
Private creditors	10	0	32	35	52	50	180	166	63	1
Memorandum items										
Concessional LDOD	49	252	577	622	693	778	782	1,151	1,219	1,250
Variable rate LDOD	25	296	439	403	409	408	449	469	616	667
Public sector LDOD	106	549	2,136	2,114	2,238	2,232	2,097	2,233	2,461	2,493
Private sector LDOD	15	282	116	126	130	130	144	183	161	142

6. CURRENCY COMPOSITION OF LONG-TERM DEBT (PERCENT)

	1970	1980	1988	1989	1990	1991	1992	1993	1994	1995
Deutsche mark	0.0	0.0	0.8	0.8	1.8	2.3	2.4	1.9	2.1	2.6
French franc	0.0	0.0	1.1	0.9	1.0	1.0	1.0	0.9	0.8	0.7
Japanese yen	0.0	0.0	0.0	0.0	0.0	2.1	2.2	2.4	2.4	2.3
Pound sterling	0.0	0.0	0.0	0.0	0.0	0.0	0.0	0.0	0.0	0.0
Swiss franc	0.0	0.0	0.0	0.0	0.0	0.0	0.2	0.4	0.5	0.5
U.S.dollars	76.2	17.3	53.1	53.6	51.6	52.4	53.5	58.7	58.5	59.4
Multiple currency	23.8	82.6	44.7	44.5	45.5	41.9	40.3	35.6	35.6	34.3
Special drawing rights	0.0	0.0	0.0	0.0	0.0	0.0	0.1	0.1	0.2	0.2
All other currencies	0.0	0.1	0.3	0.2	0.2	0.3	0.3	0.1	0.1	0.0

GUATEMALA

(US$ million, unless otherwise indicated)

	1970	1980	1988	1989	1990	1991	1992	1993	1994	1995
7. DEBT RESTRUCTURINGS										
Total amount rescheduled	0	0	237	39	30	0	0	375	0	0
Debt stock rescheduled	0	0	236	39	8	0	0	0	0	0
Principal rescheduled	0	0	0	0	13	0	0	191	0	0
Official	0	0	0	0	13	0	0	186	0	0
Private	0	0	0	0	0	0	0	5	0	0
Interest rescheduled	0	0	0	0	7	0	0	176	0	0
Official	0	0	0	0	7	0	0	173	0	0
Private	0	0	0	0	0	0	0	3	0	0
Debt forgiven	..	..	0	0	0	0	0	0	0	0
Memo: interest forgiven	..	..	0	0	0	0	0	0	0	0
Debt stock reduction	0	0	152	20	0	0	0	0	0	0
of which debt buyback	0	0	0	0	0	0	0	0	0	0
8. DEBT STOCK-FLOW RECONCILIATION										
Total change in debt stocks	..	..	..	-3	207	-15	-83	144	223	165
Net flows on debt	..	..	..	13	67	8	-56	120	141	142
Net change in interest arrears	..	..	..	21	82	-7	2	-165	19	-1
Interest capitalized	..	..	..	0	7	0	0	176	0	0
Debt forgiveness or reduction	..	..	..	-20	0	0	0	0	0	0
Cross-currency valuation	..	..	..	-12	30	-1	-47	-6	18	0
Residual	..	..	..	-3	22	-16	17	18	45	24
9. AVERAGE TERMS OF NEW COMMITMENTS										
ALL CREDITORS										
Interest (%)	5.5	7.9	5.5	8.3	5.9	3.7	7.5	5.2	5.3	1.8
Maturity (years)	25.8	15.5	19.5	12.4	17.8	18.3	16.7	22.9	26.3	39.9
Grace period (years)	6.3	3.9	5.5	2.6	4.8	2.6	5.2	5.9	7.0	10.4
Grant element (%)	36.0	10.9	29.9	10.8	27.7	35.6	14.5	32.9	36.2	71.8
Official creditors										
Interest (%)	2.9	7.7	5.5	7.7	4.8	3.7	6.4	5.4	5.3	1.8
Maturity (years)	39.4	15.8	19.7	15.8	22.6	20.8	20.8	24.7	26.3	39.9
Grace period (years)	10.6	3.9	5.6	3.3	6.3	3.0	5.5	6.4	7.0	10.4
Grant element (%)	61.0	11.8	30.4	14.8	36.8	39.3	23.9	34.8	36.2	71.8
Private creditors										
Interest (%)	8.5	10.9	10.7	9.3	8.8	3.5	8.7	3.7	0.0	0.0
Maturity (years)	9.7	8.8	5.5	6.4	4.0	5.1	12.3	3.3	0.0	0.0
Grace period (years)	1.2	3.8	0.0	1.5	0.5	0.4	4.8	0.3	0.0	0.0
Grant element (%)	6.6	-5.3	-2.3	3.8	1.7	15.8	4.5	11.4	0.0	0.0
Memorandum items										
Commitments	50	247	402	128	146	98	348	120	134	0
Official creditors	27	234	396	82	108	83	179	110	134	0
Private creditors	23	13	6	46	38	16	168	10	0	0

10. CONTRACTUAL OBLIGATIONS ON OUTSTANDING LONG-TERM DEBT

	1996	1997	1998	1999	2000	2001	2002	2003	2004	2005
TOTAL										
Disbursements	133	62	43	30	18	8	4	2	1	0
Principal	225	210	184	172	158	153	179	160	120	119
Interest	116	104	92	82	72	63	54	46	40	35
Official creditors										
Disbursements	132	62	43	30	18	8	4	2	1	0
Principal	154	147	130	122	112	104	99	128	120	119
Interest	88	80	73	66	60	55	50	44	40	35
Bilateral creditors										
Disbursements	48	28	14	7	2	1	0	0	0	0
Principal	57	55	53	50	47	41	39	75	72	71
Interest	33	31	29	28	26	24	23	21	19	16
Multilateral creditors										
Disbursements	85	34	29	23	16	6	3	2	1	0
Principal	97	92	77	72	65	62	61	53	48	48
Interest	55	49	44	39	35	31	27	24	21	19
Private creditors										
Disbursements	1	0	0	0	0	0	0	0	0	0
Principal	72	63	54	50	46	50	80	33	0	0
Interest	28	23	19	15	12	8	5	2	0	0
Commercial banks										
Disbursements	0	0	0	0	0	0	0	0	0	0
Principal	12	6	3	3	0	0	0	0	0	0
Interest	1	1	0	0	0	0	0	0	0	0
Other private										
Disbursements	1	0	0	0	0	0	0	0	0	0
Principal	60	57	52	48	46	50	80	33	0	0
Interest	26	23	19	15	12	8	5	2	0	0

GUINEA

(US$ million, unless otherwise indicated)

	1970	1980	1988	1989	1990	1991	1992	1993	1994	1995
1. SUMMARY DEBT DATA										
TOTAL DEBT STOCKS (EDT)	..	1,134	2,266	2,175	2,476	2,622	2,648	2,848	3,108	3,242
Long-term debt (LDOD)	320	1,019	2,042	1,968	2,253	2,399	2,462	2,659	2,884	2,975
Public and publicly guaranteed	320	1,019	2,042	1,968	2,253	2,399	2,462	2,659	2,884	2,975
Private nonguaranteed	0	0	0	0	0	0	0	0	0	0
Use of IMF credit	3	35	49	61	52	55	64	60	71	94
Short-term debt	..	80	176	146	172	168	122	128	152	173
of which interest arrears on LDOD	..	29	79	29	55	77	48	68	100	94
Official creditors	..	23	69	21	49	70	40	58	90	84
Private creditors	..	5	9	8	6	7	8	9	10	11
Memo: principal arrears on LDOD	..	105	225	194	190	226	220	342	460	376
Official creditors	..	89	190	173	164	197	180	290	401	319
Private creditors	..	15	35	20	26	29	40	52	59	58
Memo: export credits	..	..	268	375	352	341	239	157	176	200
TOTAL DEBT FLOWS										
Disbursements	98	129	290	278	196	241	210	286	182	211
Long-term debt	94	121	274	256	196	229	198	286	169	180
IMF purchases	4	8	16	22	0	12	12	0	12	31
Principal repayments	11	76	92	78	110	93	50	44	56	134
Long-term debt	11	75	87	69	96	84	49	41	50	126
IMF repurchases	0	1	5	9	14	9	1	3	6	9
Net flows on debt	87	54	197	220	86	122	143	228	118	104
of which short-term debt	..	..	0	20	0	-26	-17	-14	-9	27
Interest payments (INT)	..	33	35	38	59	43	37	40	43	47
Long-term debt	4	23	30	32	53	39	33	37	40	42
IMF charges	0	1	2	2	2	1	0	0	0	0
Short-term debt	..	9	4	4	4	4	4	3	3	5
Net transfers on debt	..	20	162	182	27	79	106	188	74	57
Total debt service paid (TDS)	..	109	128	116	169	136	87	84	99	181
Long-term debt	15	98	117	101	149	123	82	78	90	167
IMF repurchases and charges	0	2	7	11	16	10	1	4	6	9
Short-term debt (interest only)	..	9	4	4	4	4	4	3	3	5
2. AGGREGATE NET RESOURCE FLOWS AND NET TRANSFERS (LONG-TERM)										
NET RESOURCE FLOWS	85	106	269	329	212	338	390	414	312	325
Net flow of long-term debt (ex. IMF)	83	47	187	186	100	145	149	245	120	55
Foreign direct investment (net)	0	34	16	12	18	39	20	3	30	35
Portfolio equity flows	0	0	0	0	0	0	0	0	0	0
Grants (excluding technical coop.)	2	25	66	130	94	154	222	166	162	235
Memo: technical coop. grants	4	19	42	43	63	74	77	84	66	73
NET TRANSFERS	80	43	195	226	98	208	298	351	231	273
Interest on long-term debt	4	23	30	32	53	39	33	37	40	42
Profit remittances on FDI	0	40	44	71	61	91	60	26	40	10
3. MAJOR ECONOMIC AGGREGATES										
Gross national product (GNP)	..	..	2,207	2,227	2,606	2,803	2,829	3,055	3,277	3,553
Exports of goods & services (XGS)	..	..	602	708	841	847	685	757	676	715
of which workers remittances	..	..	0	0	0	0	0	0	0	0
Imports of goods & services (MGS)	..	..	884	970	1,115	1,224	1,080	1,010	1,131	1,090
International reserves (RES)	..	..	..	..	..	80	87	132	88	87
Current account balance	..	..	-222	-180	-203	-289	-263	-57	-248	-197
4. DEBT INDICATORS										
EDT / XGS (%)	..	..	376.1	307.2	294.4	309.5	386.7	376.2	460.0	453.4
EDT / GNP (%)	..	..	102.7	97.7	95.0	93.5	93.6	93.2	94.8	91.2
TDS / XGS (%)	..	..	21.2	16.4	20.0	16.1	12.7	11.1	14.6	25.3
INT / XGS (%)	..	..	5.8	5.4	7.0	5.1	5.3	5.3	6.4	6.5
INT / GNP (%)	..	..	1.6	1.7	2.3	1.5	1.3	1.3	1.3	1.3
RES / EDT (%)	..	..	..	..	..	3.1	3.3	4.6	2.8	2.7
RES / MGS (months)	..	..	..	..	..	0.8	1.0	1.6	0.9	1.0
Short-term / EDT (%)	..	7.0	7.7	6.7	6.9	6.4	4.6	4.5	4.9	5.3
Concessional / EDT (%)	..	59.8	65.9	64.4	67.8	70.2	76.4	77.7	77.2	78.8
Multilateral / EDT (%)	..	11.5	21.3	26.0	27.4	31.2	34.5	39.2	41.9	45.2

GUINEA

(US$ million, unless otherwise indicated)

	1970	1980	1988	1989	1990	1991	1992	1993	1994	1995
5. LONG-TERM DEBT										
DEBT OUTSTANDING (LDOD)	**320**	**1,019**	**2,042**	**1,968**	**2,253**	**2,399**	**2,462**	**2,659**	**2,884**	**2,975**
Public and publicly guaranteed	**320**	**1,019**	**2,042**	**1,968**	**2,253**	**2,399**	**2,462**	**2,659**	**2,884**	**2,975**
Official creditors	279	860	1,899	1,847	2,145	2,301	2,359	2,555	2,787	2,892
Multilateral	20	130	482	565	678	818	913	1,118	1,304	1,466
Concessional	0	63	401	487	605	755	844	1,021	1,175	1,313
Bilateral	259	731	1,418	1,282	1,467	1,484	1,446	1,437	1,483	1,427
Concessional	246	615	1,092	914	1,073	1,087	1,179	1,191	1,223	1,241
Private creditors	40	159	142	121	108	98	103	104	98	82
Bonds	0	0	0	0	0	0	0	0	0	0
Commercial banks	0	9	33	30	24	24	24	23	24	25
Other private	40	150	109	91	84	74	80	81	74	57
Private nonguaranteed	**0**	**0**	**0**	**0**	**0**	**0**	**0**	**0**	**0**	**0**
Bonds	0	0	0	0	0	0	0	0	0	0
Commercial banks	0	0	0	0	0	0	0	0	0	0
Memo:										
IBRD	20	55	47	37	28	15	0	0	0	0
IDA	0	32	257	317	392	479	548	681	773	847
DISBURSEMENTS	**94**	**121**	**274**	**256**	**196**	**229**	**198**	**286**	**169**	**180**
Public and publicly guaranteed	**94**	**121**	**274**	**256**	**196**	**229**	**198**	**286**	**169**	**180**
Official creditors	83	64	237	256	196	229	198	275	169	180
Multilateral	15	34	85	107	90	153	160	237	139	173
Concessional	0	32	83	95	85	145	131	203	107	142
Bilateral	68	30	152	149	106	76	38	38	30	8
Concessional	57	24	150	147	105	72	38	38	30	8
Private creditors	10	57	38	0	0	0	0	11	0	0
Bonds	0	0	0	0	0	0	0	0	0	0
Commercial banks	0	4	0	0	0	0	0	0	0	0
Other private	10	53	38	0	0	0	0	11	0	0
Private nonguaranteed	**0**	**0**	**0**	**0**	**0**	**0**	**0**	**0**	**0**	**0**
Bonds	0	0	0	0	0	0	0	0	0	0
Commercial banks	0	0	0	0	0	0	0	0	0	0
Memo:										
IBRD	15	0	0	0	0	0	0	0	0	0
IDA	0	10	48	64	52	83	88	134	63	59
PRINCIPAL REPAYMENTS	**11**	**75**	**87**	**69**	**96**	**84**	**49**	**41**	**50**	**126**
Public and publicly guaranteed	**11**	**75**	**87**	**69**	**96**	**84**	**49**	**41**	**50**	**126**
Official creditors	6	63	69	56	77	74	41	33	40	111
Multilateral	0	14	23	20	21	23	29	14	15	41
Concessional	0	0	6	5	6	6	8	8	8	33
Bilateral	6	50	46	36	56	51	13	19	25	69
Concessional	6	44	36	34	48	46	11	8	20	58
Private creditors	5	11	18	13	19	10	8	8	9	15
Bonds	0	0	0	0	0	0	0	0	0	0
Commercial banks	0	0	10	3	7	0	0	0	0	0
Other private	5	11	9	10	11	10	8	8	9	15
Private nonguaranteed	**0**	**0**	**0**	**0**	**0**	**0**	**0**	**0**	**0**	**0**
Bonds	0	0	0	0	0	0	0	0	0	0
Commercial banks	0	0	0	0	0	0	0	0	0	0
Memo:										
IBRD	0	3	12	11	12	12	15	0	0	0
IDA	0	0	0	1	1	1	1	1	2	2
NET FLOWS ON DEBT	**83**	**47**	**187**	**186**	**100**	**145**	**149**	**245**	**120**	**55**
Public and publicly guaranteed	**83**	**47**	**187**	**186**	**100**	**145**	**149**	**245**	**120**	**55**
Official creditors	77	1	168	200	119	155	157	242	129	70
Multilateral	15	20	62	87	68	131	131	223	124	132
Concessional	0	32	76	90	79	140	123	195	99	109
Bilateral	62	-19	106	113	51	24	26	19	5	-62
Concessional	51	-19	115	113	57	26	26	30	10	-51
Private creditors	6	46	19	-13	-19	-10	-8	3	-9	-15
Bonds	0	0	0	0	0	0	0	0	0	0
Commercial banks	0	4	-10	-3	-7	0	0	0	0	0
Other private	6	43	29	-10	-11	-10	-8	3	-9	-15
Private nonguaranteed	**0**	**0**	**0**	**0**	**0**	**0**	**0**	**0**	**0**	**0**
Bonds	0	0	0	0	0	0	0	0	0	0
Commercial banks	0	0	0	0	0	0	0	0	0	0
Memo:										
IBRD	15	-3	-12	-11	-12	-12	-15	0	0	0
IDA	0	10	48	63	51	82	87	132	61	57

GUINEA

(US$ million, unless otherwise indicated)

	1970	1980	1988	1989	1990	1991	1992	1993	1994	1995
INTEREST PAYMENTS (LINT)	**4**	**23**	**30**	**32**	**53**	**39**	**33**	**37**	**40**	**42**
Public and publicly guaranteed	**4**	**23**	**30**	**32**	**53**	**39**	**33**	**37**	**40**	**42**
Official creditors	3	21	25	29	47	39	33	36	39	41
Multilateral	1	8	9	15	12	9	17	15	16	15
Concessional	0	0	4	6	5	5	9	9	11	11
Bilateral	2	13	16	14	35	30	16	22	23	26
Concessional	2	12	9	10	23	22	11	15	17	18
Private creditors	1	2	5	3	6	1	0	1	2	1
Bonds	0	0	0	0	0	0	0	0	0	0
Commercial banks	0	0	4	3	6	0	0	0	0	0
Other private	1	2	1	1	1	1	0	1	2	1
Private nonguaranteed	**0**	**0**	**0**	**0**	**0**	**0**	**0**	**0**	**0**	**0**
Bonds	0	0	0	0	0	0	0	0	0	0
Commercial banks	0	0	0	0	0	0	0	0	0	0
Memo:										
IBRD	1	6	4	3	2	2	1	0	0	0
IDA	0	0	2	2	2	3	4	4	6	6
NET TRANSFERS ON DEBT	**79**	**24**	**157**	**154**	**47**	**106**	**116**	**208**	**79**	**13**
Public and publicly guaranteed	**79**	**24**	**157**	**154**	**47**	**106**	**116**	**208**	**79**	**13**
Official creditors	74	-20	143	171	72	117	124	206	90	29
Multilateral	14	12	53	72	57	122	115	209	108	117
Concessional	0	31	72	84	74	135	114	185	88	98
Bilateral	60	-32	90	99	15	-5	10	-3	-18	-88
Concessional	49	-31	106	103	34	4	16	15	-8	-68
Private creditors	5	44	14	-17	-25	-11	-8	2	-11	-16
Bonds	0	0	0	0	0	0	0	0	0	0
Commercial banks	0	3	-14	-6	-13	0	0	0	0	0
Other private	5	40	28	-10	-12	-11	-8	2	-11	-16
Private nonguaranteed	**0**	**0**	**0**	**0**	**0**	**0**	**0**	**0**	**0**	**0**
Bonds	0	0	0	0	0	0	0	0	0	0
Commercial banks	0	0	0	0	0	0	0	0	0	0
Memo:										
IBRD	14	-9	-16	-14	-14	-14	-15	0	0	0
IDA	0	10	46	61	49	79	83	128	55	51
DEBT SERVICE (LTDS)	**15**	**98**	**117**	**101**	**149**	**123**	**82**	**78**	**90**	**167**
Public and publicly guaranteed	**15**	**98**	**117**	**101**	**149**	**123**	**82**	**78**	**90**	**167**
Official creditors	9	84	94	85	124	112	74	69	79	151
Multilateral	1	22	32	34	33	31	45	28	31	56
Concessional	0	0	10	11	11	10	17	18	19	44
Bilateral	8	63	62	50	91	81	29	41	48	95
Concessional	8	55	44	44	71	67	22	22	37	76
Private creditors	6	14	23	17	25	11	8	9	11	16
Bonds	0	0	0	0	0	0	0	0	0	0
Commercial banks	0	1	14	6	13	0	0	0	0	0
Other private	6	13	9	10	12	11	8	9	11	16
Private nonguaranteed	**0**	**0**	**0**	**0**	**0**	**0**	**0**	**0**	**0**	**0**
Bonds	0	0	0	0	0	0	0	0	0	0
Commercial banks	0	0	0	0	0	0	0	0	0	0
Memo:										
IBRD	1	9	16	14	14	14	15	0	0	0
IDA	0	0	2	3	3	4	5	6	8	8
UNDISBURSED DEBT	**196**	**527**	**994**	**932**	**1,184**	**1,050**	**1,000**	**753**	**619**	**666**
Official creditors	173	412	993	932	1,184	1,050	1,000	753	619	623
Private creditors	24	115	1	0	0	0	0	0	0	44
Memorandum items										
Concessional LDOD	246	678	1,492	1,401	1,679	1,842	2,023	2,212	2,399	2,553
Variable rate LDOD	0	3	158	163	173	172	98	93	100	33
Public sector LDOD	320	1,019	2,042	1,968	2,253	2,399	2,462	2,659	2,884	2,975
Private sector LDOD	0	0	0	0	0	0	0	0	0	0

6. CURRENCY COMPOSITION OF LONG-TERM DEBT (PERCENT)

	1970	1980	1988	1989	1990	1991	1992	1993	1994	1995
Deutsche mark	7.1	5.1	1.9	1.2	1.3	1.1	1.0	0.8	0.8	0.8
French franc	5.1	11.3	18.4	13.2	14.9	15.0	13.7	11.9	11.8	9.6
Japanese yen	0.0	0.1	2.2	2.3	2.2	2.3	2.3	2.9	3.8	3.6
Pound sterling	4.0	4.1	1.7	1.7	1.8	1.5	1.2	1.0	1.0	0.9
Swiss franc	0.0	0.8	0.6	0.6	0.6	0.5	0.5	0.4	0.5	0.3
U.S.dollars	16.0	28.2	33.1	34.7	33.1	36.6	39.5	42.7	43.6	48.1
Multiple currency	6.4	5.5	6.5	7.2	7.6	7.3	7.3	7.5	7.9	8.0
Special drawing rights	0.0	0.0	0.5	0.6	0.6	0.9	0.9	1.0	1.0	1.3
All other currencies	61.4	44.9	35.1	38.4	38.0	34.9	33.7	31.7	29.7	27.4

GUINEA

(US$ million, unless otherwise indicated)

	1970	1980	1988	1989	1990	1991	1992	1993	1994	1995
7. DEBT RESTRUCTURINGS										
Total amount rescheduled	0	0	28	127	110	29	156	0	0	115
Debt stock rescheduled	0	0	1	0	0	0	0	0	0	0
Principal rescheduled	0	0	16	66	71	27	110	0	0	94
Official	0	0	0	38	71	20	107	0	0	93
Private	0	0	16	29	0	7	3	0	0	2
Interest rescheduled	0	0	5	57	0	2	45	0	0	16
Official	0	0	0	52	0	0	45	0	0	15
Private	0	0	5	5	0	2	0	0	0	0
Debt forgiven	..	..	0	289	2	8	48	1	1	53
Memo: interest forgiven	..	..	0	20	0	3	13	0	0	8
Debt stock reduction	0	0	0	0	0	0	0	0	0	0
of which debt buyback	0	0	0	0	0	0	0	0	0	0
8. DEBT STOCK-FLOW RECONCILIATION										
Total change in debt stocks	..	..	..	-91	302	146	26	200	260	134
Net flows on debt	..	..	..	220	86	122	143	228	118	104
Net change in interest arrears	..	..	..	-50	26	22	-29	20	33	-6
Interest capitalized	..	..	..	57	0	2	45	0	0	16
Debt forgiveness or reduction	..	..	..	-289	-2	-8	-48	-1	-1	-53
Cross-currency valuation	..	..	..	-9	106	-12	-60	-26	66	39
Residual	..	..	..	-19	86	20	-26	-21	45	35
9. AVERAGE TERMS OF NEW COMMITMENTS										
ALL CREDITORS										
Interest (%)	2.9	4.6	1.0	1.8	2.6	2.6	3.0	2.9	1.3	2.1
Maturity (years)	12.9	19.3	31.5	33.1	30.4	24.5	31.5	30.7	32.7	20.7
Grace period (years)	5.2	5.6	8.3	9.6	8.2	5.5	8.3	7.5	8.7	5.4
Grant element (%)	40.1	36.2	68.1	67.7	59.5	50.7	55.2	56.9	70.2	48.5
Official creditors										
Interest (%)	0.9	3.4	1.1	1.8	2.6	2.6	3.0	2.0	1.3	1.9
Maturity (years)	15.0	22.8	35.0	33.1	30.4	24.5	31.5	35.3	32.7	26.2
Grace period (years)	7.0	6.6	9.5	9.6	8.2	5.5	8.3	8.8	8.7	7.1
Grant element (%)	55.5	46.5	73.5	67.7	59.5	50.7	55.2	65.9	70.2	60.6
Private creditors										
Interest (%)	6.2	7.9	0.0	0.0	0.0	0.0	0.0	8.0	0.0	2.7
Maturity (years)	9.5	9.8	7.6	0.0	0.0	0.0	0.0	3.2	0.0	3.5
Grace period (years)	2.5	3.0	0.6	0.0	0.0	0.0	0.0	0.2	0.0	0.1
Grant element (%)	15.6	8.0	30.8	0.0	0.0	0.0	0.0	3.5	0.0	10.8
Memorandum items										
Commitments	68	269	292	265	487	100	197	76	75	179
Official creditors	42	197	255	265	487	100	197	65	75	135
Private creditors	26	72	37	0	0	0	0	11	0	44

10. CONTRACTUAL OBLIGATIONS ON OUTSTANDING LONG-TERM DEBT

	1996	1997	1998	1999	2000	2001	2002	2003	2004	2005
TOTAL										
Disbursements	200	199	121	70	36	20	10	4	2	0
Principal	167	162	129	137	134	130	128	124	123	112
Interest	62	61	60	57	57	52	48	44	40	37
Official creditors										
Disbursements	183	179	117	69	35	20	10	4	2	0
Principal	143	140	120	128	131	130	128	124	123	112
Interest	60	60	59	57	57	52	48	44	40	37
Bilateral creditors										
Disbursements	13	16	10	7	4	2	1	1	0	0
Principal	107	97	72	75	69	67	62	57	56	44
Interest	33	30	28	26	27	24	21	19	18	16
Multilateral creditors										
Disbursements	170	163	107	62	31	18	9	3	2	0
Principal	37	43	48	53	62	63	65	67	67	68
Interest	28	30	31	31	30	28	27	25	22	20
Private creditors										
Disbursements	18	20	4	1	1	0	0	0	0	0
Principal	24	22	9	9	3	0	0	0	0	0
Interest	1	1	1	0	0	0	0	0	0	0
Commercial banks										
Disbursements	0	0	0	0	0	0	0	0	0	0
Principal	0	0	0	0	0	0	0	0	0	0
Interest	0	0	0	0	0	0	0	0	0	0
Other private										
Disbursements	18	20	4	1	1	0	0	0	0	0
Principal	24	22	9	9	3	0	0	0	0	0
Interest	1	1	1	0	0	0	0	0	0	0

GUINEA-BISSAU

(US$ million, unless otherwise indicated)

1. SUMMARY DEBT DATA

	1970	1980	1988	1989	1990	1991	1992	1993	1994	1995
TOTAL DEBT STOCKS (EDT)	..	144.5	557.8	604.9	712.1	764.2	773.9	802.4	858.7	894.0
Long-term debt (LDOD)	0.0	138.0	513.2	559.8	649.5	693.8	705.8	728.8	776.7	848.6
Public and publicly guaranteed	0.0	138.0	513.2	559.8	649.5	693.8	705.8	728.8	776.7	848.6
Private nonguaranteed	0.0	0.0	0.0	0.0	0.0	0.0	0.0	0.0	0.0	0.0
Use of IMF credit	0.0	1.4	3.0	4.9	5.3	5.4	5.2	4.7	4.6	5.9
Short-term debt	..	5.1	41.6	40.2	57.3	65.1	62.9	68.9	77.5	39.5
of which interest arrears on LDOD	..	1.1	20.6	25.1	30.7	43.0	55.1	64.2	70.5	33.6
Official creditors	..	1.1	17.3	20.3	28.4	38.7	49.7	58.3	63.5	33.6
Private creditors	..	0.0	3.4	4.8	2.4	4.3	5.4	5.9	7.0	0.0
Memo: principal arrears on LDOD	..	4.5	42.6	61.6	75.3	103.0	137.0	171.1	189.2	147.1
Official creditors	..	2.7	37.6	54.6	69.4	91.8	120.7	151.2	161.2	147.1
Private creditors	..	1.8	5.0	7.0	5.9	11.2	16.3	19.9	28.0	0.0
Memo: export credits	..	..	62.0	72.0	98.0	117.0	124.0	76.0	80.0	104.0
TOTAL DEBT FLOWS										
Disbursements	0.0	79.5	47.7	45.5	36.6	45.4	42.1	23.5	23.7	24.5
Long-term debt	0.0	79.5	47.7	42.6	36.6	45.4	42.1	23.5	23.7	22.1
IMF purchases	0.0	0.0	0.0	2.9	0.0	0.0	0.0	0.0	0.0	2.4
Principal repayments	0.0	3.0	3.9	6.2	2.6	3.9	5.3	2.8	5.8	10.0
Long-term debt	0.0	3.0	2.6	5.3	2.6	3.9	5.3	2.4	5.3	8.9
IMF repurchases	0.0	0.0	1.3	0.9	0.0	0.0	0.0	0.4	0.4	1.1
Net flows on debt	0.0	76.5	43.9	33.3	45.4	37.1	22.6	17.6	20.3	13.5
of which short-term debt	..	0.0	0.0	-6.0	11.5	-4.5	-14.2	-3.1	2.3	-1.0
Interest payments (INT)	..	1.6	5.7	5.5	6.2	4.3	3.6	2.3	4.1	6.0
Long-term debt	0.0	1.1	3.5	3.9	3.6	2.9	3.2	2.1	3.9	5.6
IMF charges	0.0	0.1	0.1	0.1	0.0	0.0	0.0	0.0	0.0	0.0
Short-term debt	..	0.5	2.1	1.5	2.7	1.3	0.4	0.2	0.3	0.4
Net transfers on debt	..	74.9	38.2	27.8	39.2	32.8	19.0	15.3	16.1	7.5
Total debt service paid (TDS)	..	4.6	9.6	11.7	8.9	8.1	9.0	5.1	9.9	16.1
Long-term debt	0.0	4.1	6.1	9.2	6.2	6.8	8.6	4.5	9.2	14.5
IMF repurchases and charges	0.0	0.1	1.4	1.0	0.0	0.0	0.0	0.4	0.4	1.2
Short-term debt (interest only)	..	0.5	2.1	1.5	2.7	1.3	0.4	0.2	0.3	0.4

2. AGGREGATE NET RESOURCE FLOWS AND NET TRANSFERS (LONG-TERM)

	1970	1980	1988	1989	1990	1991	1992	1993	1994	1995
NET RESOURCE FLOWS	0.0	113.1	79.8	102.3	98.4	91.8	64.3	52.7	68.8	65.4
Net flow of long-term debt (ex. IMF)	0.0	76.5	45.1	37.3	33.9	41.6	36.8	21.1	18.4	13.3
Foreign direct investment (net)	0.0	0.0	1.0	1.0	2.0	0.0	0.0	0.0	1.0	1.0
Portfolio equity flows	0.0	0.0	0.0	0.0	0.0	0.0	0.0	0.0	0.0	0.0
Grants (excluding technical coop.)	0.0	36.6	33.7	64.0	62.5	50.2	27.5	31.6	49.4	51.1
Memo: technical coop. grants	0.1	12.0	33.4	25.3	22.6	32.0	51.0	50.7	44.8	49.8
NET TRANSFERS	0.0	112.1	76.4	98.4	94.9	88.9	61.1	50.7	64.9	59.7
Interest on long-term debt	0.0	1.1	3.5	3.9	3.6	2.9	3.2	2.1	3.9	5.6
Profit remittances on FDI	0.0	0.0	0.0	0.0	0.0	0.0	0.0	0.0	0.0	0.0

3. MAJOR ECONOMIC AGGREGATES

	1970	1980	1988	1989	1990	1991	1992	1993	1994	1995
Gross national product (GNP)	78.7	104.8	153.8	194.6	248.6	233.8	222.7	236.9	238.5	252.8
Exports of goods & services (XGS)	..	..	17.4	15.4	20.3	20.4	18.0	36.6	57.1	47.7
of which workers remittances	..	..	1.5	1.2	1.0	0.0	0.0	0.0	0.0	0.0
Imports of goods & services (MGS)	..	..	95.9	117.9	103.5	114.7	125.4	103.4	104.2	110.9
International reserves (RES)	..	..	16.0	20.8	18.2	14.6	17.8	14.2	18.4	20.3
Current account balance	..	..	-68.4	-92.8	-60.4	-79.0	-108.0	-68.5	-48.2	-61.9

4. DEBT INDICATORS

	1970	1980	1988	1989	1990	1991	1992	1993	1994	1995
EDT / XGS (%)	..	..	3,205.8	3,927.9	3,508.0	3,746.2	4,299.2	2,192.4	1,503.9	1,874.3
EDT / GNP (%)	..	137.8	362.7	310.8	286.5	326.9	347.5	338.7	360.1	353.7
TDS / XGS (%)	..	..	54.9	76.0	43.7	39.8	49.8	14.1	17.4	33.7
INT / XGS (%)	..	..	32.8	35.6	30.7	20.9	20.3	6.4	7.3	12.7
INT / GNP (%)	..	1.6	3.7	2.8	2.5	1.8	1.6	1.0	1.7	2.4
RES / EDT (%)	..	..	2.9	3.4	2.6	1.9	2.3	1.8	2.1	2.3
RES / MGS (months)	..	..	2.0	2.1	2.1	1.5	1.7	1.6	2.1	2.2
Short-term / EDT (%)	..	3.5	7.5	6.6	8.0	8.5	8.1	8.6	9.0	4.4
Concessional / EDT (%)	..	66.9	64.2	67.8	70.2	70.6	72.0	72.7	74.9	85.5
Multilateral / EDT (%)	..	20.1	35.4	36.7	37.8	41.2	42.0	42.5	42.6	56.1

GUINEA-BISSAU

(US$ million, unless otherwise indicated)

	1970	1980	1988	1989	1990	1991	1992	1993	1994	1995
5. LONG-TERM DEBT										
DEBT OUTSTANDING (LDOD)	**0.0**	**138.0**	**513.2**	**559.8**	**649.5**	**693.8**	**705.8**	**728.8**	**776.7**	**848.6**
Public and publicly guaranteed	**0.0**	**138.0**	**513.2**	**559.8**	**649.5**	**693.8**	**705.8**	**728.8**	**776.7**	**848.6**
Official creditors	0.0	101.8	467.5	523.7	616.6	662.2	676.1	699.4	744.2	846.1
Multilateral	0.0	29.0	197.6	221.9	269.1	314.7	325.2	340.9	365.9	501.7
Concessional	0.0	29.0	177.3	202.9	250.1	294.4	305.8	321.4	346.4	485.7
Bilateral	0.0	72.7	269.9	301.8	347.5	347.4	351.0	358.5	378.3	344.4
Concessional	0.0	67.6	180.9	207.1	250.0	244.9	251.1	261.7	296.9	278.5
Private creditors	0.0	36.2	45.7	36.1	32.9	31.6	29.7	29.4	32.4	2.5
Bonds	0.0	0.0	0.0	0.0	0.0	0.0	0.0	0.0	0.0	0.0
Commercial banks	0.0	2.1	1.1	1.0	0.9	0.9	0.7	0.6	0.6	0.4
Other private	0.0	34.0	44.6	35.1	32.0	30.8	29.0	28.8	31.9	2.0
Private nonguaranteed	**0.0**	**0.0**	**0.0**	**0.0**	**0.0**	**0.0**	**0.0**	**0.0**	**0.0**	**0.0**
Bonds	0.0	0.0	0.0	0.0	0.0	0.0	0.0	0.0	0.0	0.0
Commercial banks	0.0	0.0	0.0	0.0	0.0	0.0	0.0	0.0	0.0	0.0
Memo:										
IBRD	0.0	0.0	0.0	0.0	0.0	0.0	0.0	0.0	0.0	0.0
IDA	0.0	4.7	100.1	120.1	145.5	160.3	164.7	178.4	197.3	209.9
DISBURSEMENTS	**0.0**	**79.5**	**47.7**	**42.6**	**36.6**	**45.4**	**42.1**	**23.5**	**23.7**	**22.1**
Public and publicly guaranteed	**0.0**	**79.5**	**47.7**	**42.6**	**36.6**	**45.4**	**42.1**	**23.5**	**23.7**	**22.1**
Official creditors	0.0	59.0	47.7	42.6	36.6	45.4	42.1	21.9	23.7	22.1
Multilateral	0.0	24.3	35.0	30.2	30.9	42.0	25.0	17.4	12.7	18.5
Concessional	0.0	24.3	33.9	30.1	30.9	42.0	24.4	17.4	12.3	18.5
Bilateral	0.0	34.7	12.8	12.4	5.7	3.5	17.1	4.5	11.0	3.6
Concessional	0.0	34.2	12.8	12.4	5.7	3.5	16.9	4.5	11.0	3.6
Private creditors	0.0	20.5	0.0	0.0	0.0	0.0	0.0	1.7	0.0	0.0
Bonds	0.0	0.0	0.0	0.0	0.0	0.0	0.0	0.0	0.0	0.0
Commercial banks	0.0	0.0	0.0	0.0	0.0	0.0	0.0	0.0	0.0	0.0
Other private	0.0	20.5	0.0	0.0	0.0	0.0	0.0	1.7	0.0	0.0
Private nonguaranteed	**0.0**	**0.0**	**0.0**	**0.0**	**0.0**	**0.0**	**0.0**	**0.0**	**0.0**	**0.0**
Bonds	0.0	0.0	0.0	0.0	0.0	0.0	0.0	0.0	0.0	0.0
Commercial banks	0.0	0.0	0.0	0.0	0.0	0.0	0.0	0.0	0.0	0.0
Memo:										
IBRD	0.0	0.0	0.0	0.0	0.0	0.0	0.0	0.0	0.0	0.0
IDA	0.0	4.2	17.6	21.7	15.5	13.6	10.7	13.6	11.1	8.8
PRINCIPAL REPAYMENTS	**0.0**	**3.0**	**2.6**	**5.3**	**2.6**	**3.9**	**5.3**	**2.4**	**5.3**	**8.9**
Public and publicly guaranteed	**0.0**	**3.0**	**2.6**	**5.3**	**2.6**	**3.9**	**5.3**	**2.4**	**5.3**	**8.9**
Official creditors	0.0	0.2	2.6	5.2	2.6	3.8	5.1	2.2	5.1	8.9
Multilateral	0.0	0.0	1.4	2.8	1.5	1.7	2.3	0.7	2.7	7.6
Concessional	0.0	0.0	0.3	1.7	0.6	0.8	1.1	0.7	1.9	3.8
Bilateral	0.0	0.2	1.2	2.4	1.1	2.1	2.8	1.5	2.4	1.2
Concessional	0.0	0.0	1.1	1.8	0.3	0.6	1.8	1.5	2.4	1.2
Private creditors	0.0	2.8	0.0	0.1	0.1	0.1	0.2	0.2	0.2	0.0
Bonds	0.0	0.0	0.0	0.0	0.0	0.0	0.0	0.0	0.0	0.0
Commercial banks	0.0	0.4	0.0	0.1	0.1	0.1	0.2	0.1	0.0	0.0
Other private	0.0	2.4	0.0	0.0	0.0	0.0	0.0	0.1	0.2	0.0
Private nonguaranteed	**0.0**	**0.0**	**0.0**	**0.0**	**0.0**	**0.0**	**0.0**	**0.0**	**0.0**	**0.0**
Bonds	0.0	0.0	0.0	0.0	0.0	0.0	0.0	0.0	0.0	0.0
Commercial banks	0.0	0.0	0.0	0.0	0.0	0.0	0.0	0.0	0.0	0.0
Memo:										
IBRD	0.0	0.0	0.0	0.0	0.0	0.0	0.0	0.0	0.0	0.0
IDA	0.0	0.0	0.0	0.1	0.1	0.2	0.1	0.4	0.6	0.9
NET FLOWS ON DEBT	**0.0**	**76.5**	**45.1**	**37.3**	**33.9**	**41.6**	**36.8**	**21.1**	**18.4**	**13.3**
Public and publicly guaranteed	**0.0**	**76.5**	**45.1**	**37.3**	**33.9**	**41.6**	**36.8**	**21.1**	**18.4**	**13.3**
Official creditors	0.0	58.8	45.1	37.4	34.0	41.7	37.0	19.7	18.6	13.3
Multilateral	0.0	24.3	33.6	27.4	29.4	40.3	22.7	16.6	10.0	10.9
Concessional	0.0	24.3	33.6	28.4	30.3	41.2	23.3	16.6	10.5	14.7
Bilateral	0.0	34.5	11.6	10.0	4.6	1.4	14.3	3.0	8.6	2.4
Concessional	0.0	34.2	11.7	10.6	5.4	2.9	15.1	3.0	8.7	2.4
Private creditors	0.0	17.8	0.0	-0.1	-0.1	-0.1	-0.2	1.5	-0.2	0.0
Bonds	0.0	0.0	0.0	0.0	0.0	0.0	0.0	0.0	0.0	0.0
Commercial banks	0.0	-0.4	0.0	-0.1	-0.1	-0.1	-0.2	-0.1	0.0	0.0
Other private	0.0	18.1	0.0	0.0	0.0	0.0	0.0	1.6	-0.2	0.0
Private nonguaranteed	**0.0**	**0.0**	**0.0**	**0.0**	**0.0**	**0.0**	**0.0**	**0.0**	**0.0**	**0.0**
Bonds	0.0	0.0	0.0	0.0	0.0	0.0	0.0	0.0	0.0	0.0
Commercial banks	0.0	0.0	0.0	0.0	0.0	0.0	0.0	0.0	0.0	0.0
Memo:										
IBRD	0.0	0.0	0.0	0.0	0.0	0.0	0.0	0.0	0.0	0.0
IDA	0.0	4.2	17.6	21.6	15.4	13.5	10.6	13.1	10.4	7.9

GUINEA-BISSAU

(US$ million, unless otherwise indicated)

	1970	1980	1988	1989	1990	1991	1992	1993	1994	1995
INTEREST PAYMENTS (LINT)	**0.0**	**1.1**	**3.5**	**3.9**	**3.6**	**2.9**	**3.2**	**2.1**	**3.9**	**5.6**
Public and publicly guaranteed	**0.0**	**1.1**	**3.5**	**3.9**	**3.6**	**2.9**	**3.2**	**2.1**	**3.9**	**5.6**
Official creditors	0.0	0.3	3.5	3.8	3.3	2.8	3.2	2.1	3.9	5.6
Multilateral	0.0	0.0	2.2	3.0	2.6	2.3	2.6	1.8	3.0	4.3
Concessional	0.0	0.0	1.0	2.0	1.8	1.6	1.5	1.7	1.8	3.3
Bilateral	0.0	0.2	1.3	0.8	0.7	0.5	0.6	0.3	0.9	1.3
Concessional	0.0	0.2	0.4	0.6	0.3	0.1	0.3	0.3	0.8	0.3
Private creditors	0.0	0.8	0.0	0.1	0.3	0.1	0.0	0.0	0.0	0.0
Bonds	0.0	0.0	0.0	0.0	0.0	0.0	0.0	0.0	0.0	0.0
Commercial banks	0.0	0.1	0.0	0.1	0.1	0.1	0.0	0.0	0.0	0.0
Other private	0.0	0.7	0.0	0.0	0.2	0.0	0.0	0.0	0.0	0.0
Private nonguaranteed	**0.0**	**0.0**	**0.0**	**0.0**	**0.0**	**0.0**	**0.0**	**0.0**	**0.0**	**0.0**
Bonds	0.0	0.0	0.0	0.0	0.0	0.0	0.0	0.0	0.0	0.0
Commercial banks	0.0	0.0	0.0	0.0	0.0	0.0	0.0	0.0	0.0	0.0
Memo:										
IBRD	0.0	0.0	0.0	0.0	0.0	0.0	0.0	0.0	0.0	0.0
IDA	0.0	0.0	0.7	0.8	1.1	1.0	1.0	1.4	1.4	1.6
NET TRANSFERS ON DEBT	**0.0**	**75.5**	**41.7**	**33.4**	**30.4**	**38.7**	**33.6**	**19.1**	**14.5**	**7.6**
Public and publicly guaranteed	**0.0**	**75.5**	**41.7**	**33.4**	**30.4**	**38.7**	**33.6**	**19.1**	**14.5**	**7.6**
Official creditors	0.0	58.5	41.7	33.6	30.7	38.8	33.8	17.6	14.7	7.6
Multilateral	0.0	24.3	31.4	24.4	26.8	37.9	20.1	14.9	7.0	6.6
Concessional	0.0	24.3	32.6	26.4	28.5	39.5	21.7	14.9	8.7	11.4
Bilateral	0.0	34.2	10.3	9.2	3.9	0.9	13.7	2.7	7.7	1.1
Concessional	0.0	34.0	11.2	10.0	5.1	2.8	14.8	2.7	7.8	2.0
Private creditors	0.0	16.9	0.0	-0.2	-0.3	-0.1	-0.2	1.5	-0.2	0.0
Bonds	0.0	0.0	0.0	0.0	0.0	0.0	0.0	0.0	0.0	0.0
Commercial banks	0.0	-0.5	0.0	-0.2	-0.2	-0.1	-0.2	-0.1	0.0	0.0
Other private	0.0	17.4	0.0	0.0	-0.2	0.0	0.0	1.6	-0.2	0.0
Private nonguaranteed	**0.0**	**0.0**	**0.0**	**0.0**	**0.0**	**0.0**	**0.0**	**0.0**	**0.0**	**0.0**
Bonds	0.0	0.0	0.0	0.0	0.0	0.0	0.0	0.0	0.0	0.0
Commercial banks	0.0	0.0	0.0	0.0	0.0	0.0	0.0	0.0	0.0	0.0
Memo:										
IBRD	0.0	0.0	0.0	0.0	0.0	0.0	0.0	0.0	0.0	0.0
IDA	0.0	4.2	16.9	20.9	14.2	12.5	9.6	11.7	9.1	6.3
DEBT SERVICE (LTDS)	**0.0**	**4.1**	**6.1**	**9.2**	**6.2**	**6.8**	**8.6**	**4.5**	**9.2**	**14.5**
Public and publicly guaranteed	**0.0**	**4.1**	**6.1**	**9.2**	**6.2**	**6.8**	**8.6**	**4.5**	**9.2**	**14.5**
Official creditors	0.0	0.5	6.1	9.1	5.8	6.6	8.3	4.3	9.0	14.5
Multilateral	0.0	0.0	3.6	5.8	4.0	4.0	4.9	2.5	5.7	12.0
Concessional	0.0	0.0	1.3	3.7	2.3	2.4	2.6	2.4	3.7	7.1
Bilateral	0.0	0.4	2.5	3.2	1.8	2.6	3.4	1.8	3.3	2.5
Concessional	0.0	0.2	1.5	2.5	0.5	0.7	2.1	1.8	3.2	1.6
Private creditors	0.0	3.6	0.0	0.2	0.3	0.1	0.2	0.2	0.2	0.0
Bonds	0.0	0.0	0.0	0.0	0.0	0.0	0.0	0.0	0.0	0.0
Commercial banks	0.0	0.5	0.0	0.2	0.2	0.1	0.2	0.1	0.0	0.0
Other private	0.0	3.1	0.0	0.0	0.2	0.0	0.0	0.1	0.2	0.0
Private nonguaranteed	**0.0**	**0.0**	**0.0**	**0.0**	**0.0**	**0.0**	**0.0**	**0.0**	**0.0**	**0.0**
Bonds	0.0	0.0	0.0	0.0	0.0	0.0	0.0	0.0	0.0	0.0
Commercial banks	0.0	0.0	0.0	0.0	0.0	0.0	0.0	0.0	0.0	0.0
Memo:										
IBRD	0.0	0.0	0.0	0.0	0.0	0.0	0.0	0.0	0.0	0.0
IDA	0.0	0.0	0.7	0.8	1.2	1.2	1.1	1.8	2.0	2.5
UNDISBURSED DEBT	**0.0**	**102.6**	**163.1**	**212.5**	**287.1**	**244.1**	**180.7**	**167.5**	**150.0**	**128.9**
Official creditors	0.0	96.6	155.1	204.5	278.7	244.1	180.7	167.5	150.0	128.9
Private creditors	0.0	6.0	8.0	8.0	8.3	0.0	0.0	0.0	0.0	0.0
Memorandum items										
Concessional LDOD	0.0	96.6	358.2	410.1	500.1	539.3	556.9	583.2	643.3	764.2
Variable rate LDOD	0.0	2.1	34.0	34.2	38.0	37.8	34.5	43.1	46.2	26.4
Public sector LDOD	0.0	138.0	513.2	559.8	649.5	693.8	705.8	728.8	776.7	848.6
Private sector LDOD	0.0	0.0	0.0	0.0	0.0	0.0	0.0	0.0	0.0	0.0

6. CURRENCY COMPOSITION OF LONG-TERM DEBT (PERCENT)

	1970	1980	1988	1989	1990	1991	1992	1993	1994	1995
Deutsche mark	0.0	0.0	0.5	0.5	0.5	0.4	0.4	0.4	0.4	0.4
French franc	0.0	14.3	2.9	3.0	2.8	2.6	2.4	2.1	2.2	2.2
Japanese yen	0.0	0.0	0.0	0.0	0.0	0.0	0.0	0.0	0.0	0.0
Pound sterling	0.0	0.0	0.0	0.0	0.0	0.0	0.0	0.0	0.0	0.0
Swiss franc	0.0	2.7	9.6	10.5	12.8	11.5	10.5	10.3	10.9	5.5
U.S.dollars	0.0	27.7	32.0	33.5	32.0	33.0	35.5	38.4	39.0	50.6
Multiple currency	0.0	3.4	26.5	25.3	26.2	27.4	27.1	26.5	25.8	24.4
Special drawing rights	0.0	0.0	0.0	0.0	0.0	0.0	0.0	0.0	0.0	0.0
All other currencies	0.0	52.0	28.5	27.2	25.7	25.1	24.1	22.4	21.8	17.0

GUINEA-BISSAU

(US$ million, unless otherwise indicated)

	1970	1980	1988	1989	1990	1991	1992	1993	1994	1995
7. DEBT RESTRUCTURINGS										
Total amount rescheduled	0.0	0.0	34.9	29.6	27.1	11.2	1.1	16.1	25.0	133.8
Debt stock rescheduled	0.0	0.0	0.0	0.0	0.0	0.0	0.0	0.9	0.0	0.0
Principal rescheduled	0.0	0.0	23.9	10.2	12.6	7.1	0.9	2.6	23.3	85.1
Official	0.0	0.0	17.1	3.7	4.2	7.1	0.9	1.2	23.3	53.8
Private	0.0	0.0	6.9	6.5	8.4	0.0	0.0	1.4	0.0	31.3
Interest rescheduled	0.0	0.0	0.5	8.4	10.1	1.9	0.2	0.9	0.3	40.7
Official	0.0	0.0	0.5	3.4	5.3	1.9	0.2	0.5	0.3	32.9
Private	0.0	0.0	0.0	5.0	4.9	0.0	0.0	0.3	0.0	7.8
Debt forgiven	..	..	4.1	1.9	0.6	0.0	0.0	0.0	0.0	12.7
Memo: interest forgiven	..	..	0.0	0.4	0.8	0.0	0.0	0.0	8.4	7.9
Debt stock reduction	0.0	0.0	0.0	0.0	0.0	0.0	0.0	0.0	0.0	0.0
of which debt buyback	0.0	0.0	0.0	0.0	0.0	0.0	0.0	0.0	0.0	0.0
8. DEBT STOCK-FLOW RECONCILIATION										
Total change in debt stocks	..	..	..	47.1	107.2	52.1	9.6	28.6	56.3	35.3
Net flows on debt	..	..	..	33.3	45.4	37.1	22.6	17.6	20.3	13.5
Net change in interest arrears	..	..	..	4.5	5.6	12.3	12.0	9.1	6.3	-36.9
Interest capitalized	..	..	..	8.4	10.1	1.9	0.2	0.9	0.3	40.7
Debt forgiveness or reduction	..	..	..	-1.9	-0.6	0.0	0.0	0.0	0.0	-12.7
Cross-currency valuation	..	..	..	-4.8	31.6	-4.6	-13.1	-8.6	17.2	10.3
Residual	..	..	..	7.5	15.1	5.4	-12.1	9.6	12.2	20.4
9. AVERAGE TERMS OF NEW COMMITMENTS										
ALL CREDITORS										
Interest (%)	0.0	2.2	1.1	0.9	2.2	1.0	1.4	0.6	0.0	0.9
Maturity (years)	0.0	15.4	36.2	32.1	25.2	36.8	36.4	35.1	0.0	37.7
Grace period (years)	0.0	4.3	8.3	9.4	10.4	9.0	8.7	8.6	0.0	9.7
Grant element (%)	0.0	43.5	72.2	74.0	60.4	75.1	73.0	74.0	0.0	77.5
Official creditors										
Interest (%)	0.0	2.1	1.1	0.9	2.2	1.0	1.4	0.8	0.0	0.9
Maturity (years)	0.0	15.5	36.2	32.1	25.2	36.8	36.4	39.8	0.0	37.7
Grace period (years)	0.0	4.4	8.3	9.4	10.4	9.0	8.7	10.3	0.0	9.7
Grant element (%)	0.0	44.2	72.2	74.0	60.4	75.1	73.0	80.6	0.0	77.5
Private creditors										
Interest (%)	0.0	7.4	0.0	0.0	0.0	0.0	0.0	0.0	0.0	0.0
Maturity (years)	0.0	3.8	0.0	0.0	0.0	0.0	0.0	11.0	0.0	0.0
Grace period (years)	0.0	1.2	0.0	0.0	0.0	0.0	0.0	0.0	0.0	0.0
Grant element (%)	0.0	5.1	0.0	0.0	0.0	0.0	0.0	39.5	0.0	0.0
Memorandum items										
Commitments	0.0	77.7	27.7	97.7	97.9	17.8	11.3	10.5	0.0	25.3
Official creditors	0.0	76.4	27.7	97.7	97.9	17.8	11.3	8.8	0.0	25.3
Private creditors	0.0	1.3	0.0	0.0	0.0	0.0	0.0	1.7	0.0	0.0

10. CONTRACTUAL OBLIGATIONS ON OUTSTANDING LONG-TERM DEBT

	1996	1997	1998	1999	2000	2001	2002	2003	2004	2005
TOTAL										
Disbursements	34.2	26.3	19.3	13.3	5.8	1.0	0.4	0.2	0.0	0.0
Principal	25.4	18.0	25.0	28.5	30.1	31.6	32.3	32.3	30.3	26.7
Interest	15.1	15.3	19.0	18.2	17.3	16.4	15.4	14.3	13.3	12.5
Official creditors										
Disbursements	34.2	26.3	19.3	13.3	5.8	1.0	0.4	0.2	0.0	0.0
Principal	25.4	18.0	24.8	28.3	29.9	31.4	32.0	32.2	30.1	26.5
Interest	15.1	15.3	18.8	18.0	17.2	16.3	15.3	14.2	13.3	12.5
Bilateral creditors										
Disbursements	0.9	0.6	0.3	0.1	0.1	0.1	0.1	0.1	0.0	0.0
Principal	15.5	9.4	15.4	16.7	16.1	14.4	15.9	16.2	13.6	11.5
Interest	4.9	4.8	8.3	7.7	6.9	6.2	5.5	4.8	4.0	3.4
Multilateral creditors										
Disbursements	33.4	25.8	19.0	13.2	5.7	0.9	0.4	0.1	0.0	0.0
Principal	9.9	8.6	9.3	11.5	13.8	17.0	16.2	15.9	16.5	15.0
Interest	10.1	10.5	10.5	10.4	10.2	10.0	9.7	9.5	9.3	9.1
Private creditors										
Disbursements	0.0	0.0	0.0	0.0	0.0	0.0	0.0	0.0	0.0	0.0
Principal	0.0	0.0	0.3	0.2	0.2	0.2	0.2	0.1	0.1	0.1
Interest	0.0	0.0	0.2	0.2	0.1	0.1	0.1	0.1	0.1	0.0
Commercial banks										
Disbursements	0.0	0.0	0.0	0.0	0.0	0.0	0.0	0.0	0.0	0.0
Principal	0.0	0.0	0.1	0.1	0.1	0.1	0.1	0.0	0.0	0.0
Interest	0.0	0.0	0.0	0.0	0.0	0.0	0.0	0.0	0.0	0.0
Other private										
Disbursements	0.0	0.0	0.0	0.0	0.0	0.0	0.0	0.0	0.0	0.0
Principal	0.0	0.0	0.2	0.1	0.1	0.1	0.1	0.1	0.1	0.1
Interest	0.0	0.0	0.2	0.1	0.1	0.1	0.1	0.1	0.1	0.0

GUYANA

(US$ million, unless otherwise indicated)

	1970	1980	1988	1989	1990	1991	1992	1993	1994	1995
1. SUMMARY DEBT DATA										
TOTAL DEBT STOCKS (EDT)	..	811	1,866	1,633	1,945	1,960	1,897	1,954	2,038	2,105
Long-term debt (LDOD)	83	607	995	1,261	1,757	1,760	1,673	1,732	1,787	1,782
Public and publicly guaranteed	83	607	995	1,261	1,757	1,760	1,673	1,732	1,787	1,782
Private nonguaranteed	0	0	0	0	0	0	0	0	0	0
Use of IMF credit	0	86	110	106	113	149	168	177	179	172
Short-term debt	..	118	761	266	75	50	56	46	72	151
of which interest arrears on LDOD	..	8	110	100	63	49	52	37	63	135
Official creditors	..	5	75	83	40	26	40	23	49	115
Private creditors	..	3	35	17	23	23	12	14	14	19
Memo: principal arrears on LDOD	..	37	333	300	169	142	76	79	85	99
Official creditors	..	34	184	211	89	64	64	66	70	85
Private creditors	..	3	149	89	80	78	12	13	15	14
Memo: export credits	..	..	58	147	257	271	237	235	236	93
TOTAL DEBT FLOWS										
Disbursements	14	169	37	53	264	137	84	81	47	59
Long-term debt	14	115	37	53	160	100	59	69	34	45
IMF purchases	0	55	0	0	104	38	25	12	13	14
Principal repayments	2	58	12	30	175	49	53	51	61	74
Long-term debt	2	43	12	29	69	46	53	48	39	51
IMF repurchases	0	16	0	1	107	3	0	3	22	24
Net flows on debt	12	111	121	-266	256	83	33	36	-14	-8
of which short-term debt	..	..	95	-290	167	-5	2	5	0	7
Interest payments (INT)	..	31	55	59	120	53	49	42	37	35
Long-term debt	3	27	11	15	73	47	43	36	32	31
IMF charges	0	4	0	3	40	5	6	5	4	3
Short-term debt	..	1	43	41	7	1	0	0	1	1
Net transfers on debt	..	80	66	-325	135	30	-16	-6	-51	-43
Total debt service paid (TDS)	..	89	66	88	295	102	102	92	97	109
Long-term debt	6	69	23	43	142	93	96	83	71	82
IMF repurchases and charges	0	19	0	4	146	9	6	9	26	27
Short-term debt (interest only)	..	1	43	41	7	1	0	0	1	1
2. AGGREGATE NET RESOURCE FLOWS AND NET TRANSFERS (LONG-TERM)										
NET RESOURCE FLOWS	22	76	39	51	165	212	48	82	31	19
Net flow of long-term debt (ex. IMF)	12	72	25	25	91	54	6	22	-5	-5
Foreign direct investment (net)	9	1	0	0	0	0	0	0	3	3
Portfolio equity flows	0	0	0	0	0	0	0	0	0	0
Grants (excluding technical coop.)	2	4	14	26	74	158	42	61	32	21
Memo: technical coop. grants	3	8	6	7	9	12	13	12	13	18
NET TRANSFERS	5	50	28	36	92	164	5	47	-2	-13
Interest on long-term debt	3	27	11	15	73	47	43	36	32	31
Profit remittances on FDI	14	0	0	0	0	0	0	0	0	0
3. MAJOR ECONOMIC AGGREGATES										
Gross national product (GNP)	247	550	319	257	275	214	264	373	465	558
Exports of goods & services (XGS)	..	411	..	..	..	..	493	536	593	641
of which workers remittances	..	0	..	..	..	..	0	0	0	0
Imports of goods & services (MGS)	..	538	..	..	..	..	684	739	780	838
International reserves (RES)	20	13	4	13	29	124	188	248	247	269
Current account balance	..	-129	..	..	..	..	-139	-140	-125	-135
4. DEBT INDICATORS										
EDT / XGS (%)	..	197.4	..	..	..	..	385.1	364.7	343.8	328.1
EDT / GNP (%)	..	147.3	584.8	636.2	707.7	918.0	719.8	524.6	438.2	377.2
TDS / XGS (%)	..	21.6	..	..	..	..	20.7	17.2	16.4	17.0
INT / XGS (%)	..	7.5	..	..	..	..	10.0	7.7	6.2	5.4
INT / GNP (%)	..	5.6	17.1	22.9	43.8	24.8	18.6	11.1	7.9	6.3
RES / EDT (%)	..	1.6	0.2	0.8	1.5	6.3	9.9	12.7	12.1	12.8
RES / MGS (months)	..	0.3	..	..	..	..	3.3	4.0	3.8	3.8
Short-term / EDT (%)	..	14.5	40.8	16.3	3.9	2.6	2.9	2.4	3.6	7.2
Concessional / EDT (%)	..	28.7	25.0	42.3	58.3	57.7	60.1	62.2	63.0	62.3
Multilateral / EDT (%)	..	13.9	19.2	22.6	24.0	27.0	28.3	29.4	29.9	30.4

GUYANA

(US$ million, unless otherwise indicated)

	1970	1980	1988	1989	1990	1991	1992	1993	1994	1995
5. LONG-TERM DEBT										
DEBT OUTSTANDING (LDOD)	**83**	**607**	**995**	**1,261**	**1,757**	**1,760**	**1,673**	**1,732**	**1,787**	**1,782**
Public and publicly guaranteed	**83**	**607**	**995**	**1,261**	**1,757**	**1,760**	**1,673**	**1,732**	**1,787**	**1,782**
Official creditors	66	379	767	1,092	1,610	1,625	1,594	1,661	1,716	1,720
Multilateral	1	112	357	369	468	529	536	574	609	639
Concessional	0	73	193	195	305	366	386	437	476	517
Bilateral	66	267	409	723	1,142	1,096	1,058	1,086	1,107	1,081
Concessional	40	160	273	496	831	765	753	780	809	794
Private creditors	17	228	228	170	148	135	79	71	71	62
Bonds	17	15	7	1	0	0	0	0	0	0
Commercial banks	0	100	109	96	80	80	12	13	15	13
Other private	0	113	112	73	68	55	66	58	57	49
Private nonguaranteed	**0**	**0**	**0**	**0**	**0**	**0**	**0**	**0**	**0**	**0**
Bonds	0	0	0	0	0	0	0	0	0	0
Commercial banks	0	0	0	0	0	0	0	0	0	0
Memo:										
IBRD	0	36	89	85	59	55	46	41	39	35
IDA	0	18	36	35	93	134	134	163	182	203
DISBURSEMENTS	**14**	**115**	**37**	**53**	**160**	**100**	**59**	**69**	**34**	**45**
Public and publicly guaranteed	**14**	**115**	**37**	**53**	**160**	**100**	**59**	**69**	**34**	**45**
Official creditors	14	84	20	38	153	100	58	69	34	45
Multilateral	1	35	13	24	123	73	42	62	33	41
Concessional	0	29	3	9	110	65	39	62	33	41
Bilateral	13	50	6	14	31	26	16	7	1	4
Concessional	6	21	6	8	19	13	13	1	0	3
Private creditors	0	31	17	16	6	0	1	0	0	0
Bonds	0	0	0	0	0	0	0	0	0	0
Commercial banks	0	21	0	0	0	0	0	0	0	0
Other private	0	9	17	16	6	0	1	0	0	0
Private nonguaranteed	**0**	**0**	**0**	**0**	**0**	**0**	**0**	**0**	**0**	**0**
Bonds	0	0	0	0	0	0	0	0	0	0
Commercial banks	0	0	0	0	0	0	0	0	0	0
Memo:										
IBRD	0	2	0	0	0	0	0	0	0	0
IDA	0	2	0	0	54	40	4	30	12	18
PRINCIPAL REPAYMENTS	**2**	**43**	**12**	**29**	**69**	**46**	**53**	**48**	**39**	**51**
Public and publicly guaranteed	**2**	**43**	**12**	**29**	**69**	**46**	**53**	**48**	**39**	**51**
Official creditors	1	18	4	6	46	33	34	40	35	40
Multilateral	0	1	2	5	42	17	20	23	22	24
Concessional	0	0	1	3	8	6	9	7	7	8
Bilateral	1	17	2	1	4	17	14	17	13	16
Concessional	1	9	0	0	0	0	0	6	3	5
Private creditors	1	25	8	23	22	13	19	7	4	10
Bonds	0	0	0	6	1	0	0	0	0	0
Commercial banks	1	11	0	0	8	0	10	0	0	2
Other private	0	14	8	17	14	13	9	7	4	8
Private nonguaranteed	**0**	**0**	**0**	**0**	**0**	**0**	**0**	**0**	**0**	**0**
Bonds	0	0	0	0	0	0	0	0	0	0
Commercial banks	0	0	0	0	0	0	0	0	0	0
Memo:										
IBRD	0	1	0	1	31	6	7	6	5	6
IDA	0	0	0	0	0	0	0	1	1	1
NET FLOWS ON DEBT	**12**	**72**	**25**	**25**	**91**	**54**	**6**	**22**	**-5**	**-5**
Public and publicly guaranteed	**12**	**72**	**25**	**25**	**91**	**54**	**6**	**22**	**-5**	**-5**
Official creditors	13	66	16	32	107	67	25	29	-1	5
Multilateral	1	34	11	19	80	57	22	39	11	17
Concessional	0	29	2	7	102	59	30	55	26	33
Bilateral	12	33	4	13	27	10	2	-10	-12	-12
Concessional	5	12	6	8	19	13	13	-6	-3	-2
Private creditors	-1	6	10	-7	-16	-13	-19	-7	-4	-10
Bonds	0	0	0	-6	-1	0	0	0	0	0
Commercial banks	-1	10	0	0	-8	0	-10	0	0	-2
Other private	0	-4	10	-1	-8	-13	-9	-7	-4	-8
Private nonguaranteed	**0**	**0**	**0**	**0**	**0**	**0**	**0**	**0**	**0**	**0**
Bonds	0	0	0	0	0	0	0	0	0	0
Commercial banks	0	0	0	0	0	0	0	0	0	0
Memo:										
IBRD	0	1	0	-1	-31	-6	-7	-6	-5	-6
IDA	0	2	0	0	54	40	4	29	12	17

(US$ million, unless otherwise indicated)

	1970	1980	1988	1989	1990	1991	1992	1993	1994	1995
INTEREST PAYMENTS (LINT)	**3**	**27**	**11**	**15**	**73**	**47**	**43**	**36**	**32**	**31**
Public and publicly guaranteed	**3**	**27**	**11**	**15**	**73**	**47**	**43**	**36**	**32**	**31**
Official creditors	3	11	9	9	64	45	42	35	29	30
Multilateral	0	4	8	9	58	21	19	19	18	18
Concessional	0	1	2	3	10	5	6	6	6	7
Bilateral	3	7	1	0	6	24	23	17	11	12
Concessional	1	4	0	0	3	8	14	12	8	8
Private creditors	1	15	2	6	9	3	2	1	3	2
Bonds	1	1	0	1	0	0	0	0	0	0
Commercial banks	0	9	0	0	5	0	0	0	0	1
Other private	0	5	2	4	4	3	2	1	3	1
Private nonguaranteed	**0**	**0**	**0**	**0**	**0**	**0**	**0**	**0**	**0**	**0**
Bonds	0	0	0	0	0	0	0	0	0	0
Commercial banks	0	0	0	0	0	0	0	0	0	0
Memo:										
IBRD	0	3	0	1	31	6	4	4	3	3
IDA	0	0	0	0	0	1	1	1	1	1
NET TRANSFERS ON DEBT	**8**	**45**	**14**	**10**	**18**	**7**	**-37**	**-14**	**-37**	**-37**
Public and publicly guaranteed	**8**	**45**	**14**	**10**	**18**	**7**	**-37**	**-14**	**-37**	**-37**
Official creditors	10	55	7	23	43	22	-17	-6	-30	-25
Multilateral	1	30	3	10	23	36	3	20	-7	-1
Concessional	0	28	0	4	93	53	24	49	20	26
Bilateral	9	25	4	12	20	-14	-20	-26	-23	-24
Concessional	4	8	6	8	17	5	-2	-18	-11	-11
Private creditors	-2	-9	7	-13	-26	-15	-20	-8	-7	-12
Bonds	-1	-1	0	-7	-1	0	0	0	0	0
Commercial banks	-1	1	0	0	-12	0	-10	0	0	-3
Other private	0	-10	7	-6	-12	-15	-10	-8	-7	-9
Private nonguaranteed	**0**	**0**	**0**	**0**	**0**	**0**	**0**	**0**	**0**	**0**
Bonds	0	0	0	0	0	0	0	0	0	0
Commercial banks	0	0	0	0	0	0	0	0	0	0
Memo:										
IBRD	0	-2	0	-2	-62	-11	-11	-10	-9	-9
IDA	0	2	0	-1	54	39	3	28	11	16
DEBT SERVICE (LTDS)	**6**	**69**	**23**	**43**	**142**	**93**	**96**	**83**	**71**	**82**
Public and publicly guaranteed	**6**	**69**	**23**	**43**	**142**	**93**	**96**	**83**	**71**	**82**
Official creditors	4	29	13	15	110	78	75	75	64	70
Multilateral	0	5	10	13	100	37	39	42	40	42
Concessional	0	1	3	5	17	12	15	13	13	15
Bilateral	4	24	3	2	11	41	36	34	24	28
Concessional	2	13	0	0	3	8	14	19	11	14
Private creditors	2	40	10	28	32	15	21	8	7	12
Bonds	1	1	0	7	1	0	0	0	0	0
Commercial banks	1	20	0	0	12	0	10	0	0	3
Other private	0	19	10	21	18	15	11	8	7	9
Private nonguaranteed	**0**	**0**	**0**	**0**	**0**	**0**	**0**	**0**	**0**	**0**
Bonds	0	0	0	0	0	0	0	0	0	0
Commercial banks	0	0	0	0	0	0	0	0	0	0
Memo:										
IBRD	0	4	0	2	62	11	11	10	9	9
IDA	0	0	0	1	1	1	1	2	2	2
UNDISBURSED DEBT	**53**	**223**	**129**	**163**	**272**	**213**	**232**	**242**	**274**	**255**
Official creditors	53	207	123	143	268	213	232	242	274	246
Private creditors	0	16	5	21	4	0	0	0	0	9
Memorandum items										
Concessional LDOD	40	233	467	691	1,135	1,131	1,139	1,216	1,285	1,311
Variable rate LDOD	0	124	135	209	235	259	177	181	215	195
Public sector LDOD	83	607	995	1,261	1,757	1,760	1,673	1,732	1,787	1,782
Private sector LDOD	0	0	0	0	0	0	0	0	0	0

6. CURRENCY COMPOSITION OF LONG-TERM DEBT (PERCENT)

	1970	1980	1988	1989	1990	1991	1992	1993	1994	1995
Deutsche mark	0.0	0.9	0.3	1.3	2.2	2.0	2.5	2.3	2.6	2.5
French franc	0.0	0.1	0.0	0.0	0.0	0.1	0.1	0.1	0.1	0.1
Japanese yen	0.0	0.0	0.5	0.5	0.3	0.2	0.2	0.2	0.2	0.2
Pound sterling	68.9	21.7	11.3	11.1	10.5	10.7	9.4	9.1	9.7	9.3
Swiss franc	0.0	0.0	0.1	0.1	0.1	0.1	0.1	0.1	0.1	0.1
U.S.dollars	24.7	58.3	54.1	59.1	67.7	66.1	65.0	65.6	64.5	64.5
Multiple currency	0.4	10.1	25.8	21.5	14.9	14.8	16.3	16.1	16.1	16.2
Special drawing rights	0.0	0.0	0.1	0.2	0.1	0.2	0.2	0.2	0.2	0.2
All other currencies	6.0	9.0	7.9	6.3	4.2	5.8	6.3	6.4	6.6	6.8

GUYANA

(US$ million, unless otherwise indicated)

	1970	1980	1988	1989	1990	1991	1992	1993	1994	1995
7. DEBT RESTRUCTURINGS										
Total amount rescheduled	0	0	12	393	474	90	41	53	49	1
Debt stock rescheduled	0	0	0	217	320	33	1	0	0	0
Principal rescheduled	0	0	5	111	89	26	16	1	14	1
Official	0	0	0	62	89	23	7	1	14	0
Private	0	0	5	49	0	3	9	0	0	0
Interest rescheduled	0	0	7	51	38	27	16	51	16	0
Official	0	0	0	30	38	27	16	51	16	0
Private	0	0	7	21	0	1	0	0	0	0
Debt forgiven	..	..	18	2	31	89	24	7	11	0
Memo: interest forgiven	..	..	0	0	1	1	0	2	3	0
Debt stock reduction	0	0	0	0	0	0	76	0	0	0
of which debt buyback	0	0	0	0	0	0	10	0	0	0
8. DEBT STOCK-FLOW RECONCILIATION										
Total change in debt stocks	..	..	..	-233	312	15	-63	58	84	67
Net flows on debt	..	..	..	-266	256	83	33	36	-14	-8
Net change in interest arrears	..	..	..	-9	-37	-14	3	-15	26	71
Interest capitalized	..	..	..	51	38	27	16	51	16	0
Debt forgiveness or reduction	..	..	..	-2	-31	-89	-90	-7	-11	0
Cross-currency valuation	..	..	..	-18	47	-9	-45	-13	24	9
Residual	..	..	..	11	40	16	19	5	42	-5
9. AVERAGE TERMS OF NEW COMMITMENTS										
ALL CREDITORS										
Interest (%)	6.0	10.5	8.5	6.0	1.3	3.1	1.7	1.5	1.6	3.0
Maturity (years)	25.3	8.1	6.8	20.5	39.7	34.0	37.4	34.3	39.7	37.2
Grace period (years)	9.7	2.4	1.4	5.2	9.9	11.6	9.9	9.8	10.6	10.0
Grant element (%)	32.4	2.9	4.7	30.8	74.9	58.1	70.4	71.0	73.0	60.5
Official creditors										
Interest (%)	6.0	9.2	7.0	3.9	1.3	3.1	1.7	1.5	1.6	1.5
Maturity (years)	25.3	9.5	4.8	27.3	39.7	34.0	37.6	34.3	39.7	38.8
Grace period (years)	9.7	3.2	0.8	6.9	9.9	11.6	9.9	9.8	10.6	10.5
Grant element (%)	32.4	11.2	6.5	46.7	74.9	58.1	71.0	71.0	73.0	73.4
Private creditors										
Interest (%)	0.0	12.3	9.3	10.1	0.0	0.0	8.0	0.0	0.0	8.8
Maturity (years)	0.0	6.2	7.8	6.5	0.0	0.0	13.9	0.0	0.0	31.0
Grace period (years)	0.0	1.3	1.7	1.8	0.0	0.0	13.9	0.0	0.0	8.0
Grant element (%)	0.0	-8.9	3.8	-1.8	0.0	0.0	14.7	0.0	0.0	9.6
Memorandum items										
Commitments	20	96	17	93	281	54	83	98	64	45
Official creditors	20	56	6	63	281	54	82	98	64	36
Private creditors	0	39	11	31	0	0	1	0	0	9

10. CONTRACTUAL OBLIGATIONS ON OUTSTANDING LONG-TERM DEBT

	1996	1997	1998	1999	2000	2001	2002	2003	2004	2005
TOTAL										
Disbursements	81	71	51	29	14	4	2	1	1	0
Principal	51	45	44	56	100	125	123	126	127	126
Interest	70	68	66	64	61	56	50	44	39	33
Official creditors										
Disbursements	77	69	50	28	14	4	2	1	1	0
Principal	41	41	39	55	100	125	123	126	126	126
Interest	67	65	63	62	58	53	48	42	37	31
Bilateral creditors										
Disbursements	2	2	2	1	1	1	0	0	0	0
Principal	19	19	18	36	77	98	97	97	97	97
Interest	50	49	48	47	44	39	35	30	25	20
Multilateral creditors										
Disbursements	74	66	48	27	14	4	2	1	1	0
Principal	22	22	22	20	22	27	26	28	29	29
Interest	17	16	15	15	14	14	13	12	11	11
Private creditors										
Disbursements	4	3	1	1	0	0	0	0	0	0
Principal	10	4	4	1	1	0	0	1	1	1
Interest	3	3	3	2	2	2	2	2	2	2
Commercial banks										
Disbursements	4	3	1	1	0	0	0	0	0	0
Principal	3	3	3	0	0	0	0	0	0	0
Interest	1	1	1	1	1	1	1	1	1	1
Other private										
Disbursements	0	0	0	0	0	0	0	0	0	0
Principal	7	1	1	0	0	0	0	0	0	0
Interest	2	2	2	1	1	1	1	1	1	1

HAITI

(US$ million, unless otherwise indicated)

	1970	*1980*	*1988*	*1989*	*1990*	*1991*	*1992*	*1993*	*1994*	*1995*
1. SUMMARY DEBT DATA										
TOTAL DEBT STOCKS (EDT)	..	**302.4**	**820.0**	**806.2**	**888.9**	**758.4**	**785.1**	**803.0**	**716.9**	**806.8**
Long-term debt (LDOD)	**39.9**	**242.3**	**685.1**	**688.0**	**750.6**	**620.7**	**638.0**	**648.0**	**634.9**	**751.8**
Public and publicly guaranteed	39.9	242.3	685.1	688.0	750.6	620.7	638.0	648.0	634.9	751.8
Private nonguaranteed	0.0	0.0	0.0	0.0	0.0	0.0	0.0	0.0	0.0	0.0
Use of IMF credit	**2.9**	**46.2**	**47.4**	**41.3**	**37.6**	**32.6**	**35.1**	**33.8**	**35.0**	**28.7**
Short-term debt	..	**14.0**	**87.5**	**76.8**	**100.7**	**105.1**	**112.1**	**121.2**	**47.0**	**26.3**
of which interest arrears on LDOD	..	0.0	16.5	15.8	23.7	14.1	21.1	30.2	34.0	0.7
Official creditors	..	0.0	5.4	7.3	13.6	2.7	8.8	14.8	18.3	0.7
Private creditors	..	0.0	11.1	8.5	10.2	11.4	12.2	15.4	15.7	0.0
Memo: principal arrears on LDOD	..	0.0	36.5	30.7	42.7	44.4	58.9	103.6	121.4	1.3
Official creditors	..	0.0	6.3	7.8	13.7	9.5	18.0	36.7	54.5	1.3
Private creditors	..	0.0	30.1	23.0	29.0	35.0	41.0	67.0	67.0	0.0
Memo: export credits	..	..	117.0	113.0	117.0	107.0	83.0	69.0	70.0	83.0
TOTAL DEBT FLOWS										
Disbursements	**4.3**	**76.6**	**50.5**	**45.7**	**43.6**	**40.2**	**0.6**	**0.0**	**0.0**	**128.3**
Long-term debt	4.3	47.1	50.5	31.4	38.4	40.2	0.6	0.0	0.0	103.5
IMF purchases	0.0	29.5	0.0	14.3	5.2	0.0	0.0	0.0	0.0	24.8
Principal repayments	**3.4**	**18.2**	**41.7**	**35.4**	**18.1**	**10.6**	**0.4**	**0.4**	**0.5**	**62.4**
Long-term debt	3.4	15.3	15.1	15.3	5.8	6.2	0.4	0.4	0.5	30.4
IMF repurchases	0.0	2.9	26.6	20.1	12.3	4.4	0.0	0.0	0.0	32.0
Net flows on debt	**1.0**	**58.4**	**0.8**	**0.3**	**41.6**	**43.6**	**0.2**	**-0.4**	**-78.5**	**78.5**
of which short-term debt	..	..	-8.0	-10.0	16.0	14.0	0.0	0.0	-78.0	12.6
Interest payments (INT)	..	**7.6**	**17.3**	**17.1**	**14.8**	**16.1**	**4.9**	**4.5**	**0.8**	**31.9**
Long-term debt	0.4	5.1	8.1	9.2	5.6	6.2	0.4	0.0	0.0	24.9
IMF charges	0.0	0.6	3.2	2.6	2.6	2.2	0.0	0.0	0.0	5.5
Short-term debt	..	1.9	6.0	5.2	6.5	7.7	4.5	4.5	0.8	1.5
Net transfers on debt	..	**50.9**	**-16.5**	**-16.7**	**26.7**	**27.5**	**-4.7**	**-5.0**	**-79.3**	**46.6**
Total debt service paid (TDS)	..	**25.7**	**59.0**	**52.4**	**32.9**	**26.7**	**5.4**	**5.0**	**1.3**	**94.3**
Long-term debt	3.8	20.4	23.2	24.6	11.5	12.4	0.8	0.4	0.5	55.3
IMF repurchases and charges	0.0	3.5	29.8	22.7	14.9	6.5	0.0	0.0	0.0	37.5
Short-term debt (interest only)	..	1.9	6.0	5.2	6.5	7.7	4.5	4.5	0.8	1.5
2. AGGREGATE NET RESOURCE FLOWS AND NET TRANSFERS (LONG-TERM)										
NET RESOURCE FLOWS	**6.1**	**75.1**	**97.7**	**127.5**	**105.3**	**225.7**	**68.2**	**79.6**	**599.0**	**586.8**
Net flow of long-term debt (ex. IMF)	1.0	31.8	35.5	16.1	32.6	34.0	0.2	-0.4	-0.5	73.1
Foreign direct investment (net)	2.8	13.0	10.1	9.4	8.0	14.0	8.0	8.0	2.0	2.0
Portfolio equity flows	0.0	0.0	0.0	0.0	0.0	0.0	0.0	0.0	0.0	0.0
Grants (excluding technical coop.)	2.3	30.3	52.1	102.0	64.7	177.7	60.0	72.0	597.5	511.7
Memo: technical coop. grants	3.6	32.1	58.1	66.2	70.0	68.2	41.0	51.4	58.0	113.8
NET TRANSFERS	**2.4**	**59.1**	**78.8**	**110.6**	**91.2**	**211.4**	**59.8**	**72.6**	**594.0**	**555.9**
Interest on long-term debt	0.4	5.1	8.1	9.2	5.6	6.2	0.4	0.0	0.0	24.9
Profit remittances on FDI	3.2	11.0	10.7	7.6	8.4	8.1	8.0	7.0	5.0	6.0
3. MAJOR ECONOMIC AGGREGATES										
Gross national product (GNP)	390.8	1,445.9	2,194.2	2,487.6	2,954.0	3,247.5	1,880.2	1,566.2	1,611.3	2,026.0
Exports of goods & services (XGS)	..	415.2	405.2	364.2	324.9	261.6	115.1	119.4	64.1	208.6
of which workers remittances	..	106.4	124.1	122.8	..	..	..	..	..	..
Imports of goods & services (MGS)	..	498.4	514.3	478.3	539.7	551.9	262.2	309.4	216.3	780.4
International reserves (RES)	4.3	26.7	20.4	19.8	10.2	23.7	..	..	30.9	105.8
Current account balance	..	-101.1	-40.4	-62.7	-21.9	-56.1	7.9	-16.6	4.0	-66.6
4. DEBT INDICATORS										
EDT / XGS (%)	..	72.8	202.4	221.3	273.6	289.9	682.1	672.5	1,118.3	386.8
EDT / GNP (%)	..	20.9	37.4	32.4	30.1	23.4	41.8	51.3	44.5	39.8
TDS / XGS (%)	..	6.2	14.6	14.4	10.1	10.2	4.7	4.2	2.0	45.2
INT / XGS (%)	..	1.8	4.3	4.7	4.6	6.1	4.3	3.8	1.2	15.3
INT / GNP (%)	..	0.5	0.8	0.7	0.5	0.5	0.3	0.3	0.0	1.6
RES / EDT (%)	..	8.8	2.5	2.5	1.1	3.1	..	..	4.3	13.1
RES / MGS (months)	..	0.6	0.5	0.5	0.2	0.5	..	..	1.7	1.6
Short-term / EDT (%)	..	4.6	10.7	9.5	11.3	13.9	14.3	15.1	6.6	3.3
Concessional / EDT (%)	..	70.7	75.4	78.9	78.6	75.3	74.9	72.0	78.9	93.0
Multilateral / EDT (%)	..	43.8	52.7	55.8	55.0	67.0	66.5	64.2	73.0	75.7

HAITI

(US$ million, unless otherwise indicated)

	1970	1980	1988	1989	1990	1991	1992	1993	1994	1995
5. LONG-TERM DEBT										
DEBT OUTSTANDING (LDOD)	**39.9**	**242.3**	**685.1**	**688.0**	**750.6**	**620.7**	**638.0**	**648.0**	**634.9**	**751.8**
Public and publicly guaranteed	**39.9**	**242.3**	**685.1**	**688.0**	**750.6**	**620.7**	**638.0**	**648.0**	**634.9**	**751.8**
Official creditors	29.2	218.8	625.0	641.1	703.6	573.7	591.0	581.0	567.9	751.8
Multilateral	0.3	132.4	432.2	449.5	489.1	508.0	521.9	515.3	523.6	610.4
Concessional	0.3	132.4	432.2	449.5	489.1	508.0	521.9	515.3	523.6	610.4
Bilateral	28.9	86.4	192.8	191.6	214.6	65.7	69.1	65.7	44.3	141.4
Concessional	28.9	81.4	185.9	186.4	209.8	63.1	66.5	63.1	41.7	139.6
Private creditors	10.7	23.5	60.1	47.0	47.0	47.0	47.0	67.0	67.0	0.0
Bonds	4.0	0.0	0.0	0.0	0.0	0.0	0.0	0.0	0.0	0.0
Commercial banks	0.0	7.6	48.2	47.0	47.0	47.0	47.0	67.0	67.0	0.0
Other private	6.7	15.9	12.0	0.0	0.0	0.0	0.0	0.0	0.0	0.0
Private nonguaranteed	**0.0**	**0.0**	**0.0**	**0.0**	**0.0**	**0.0**	**0.0**	**0.0**	**0.0**	**0.0**
Bonds	0.0	0.0	0.0	0.0	0.0	0.0	0.0	0.0	0.0	0.0
Commercial banks	0.0	0.0	0.0	0.0	0.0	0.0	0.0	0.0	0.0	0.0
Memo:										
IBRD	0.0	0.0	0.0	0.0	0.0	0.0	0.0	0.0	0.0	0.0
IDA	0.3	66.3	285.3	293.8	323.6	329.8	343.5	337.3	346.2	389.4
DISBURSEMENTS	**4.3**	**47.1**	**50.5**	**31.4**	**38.4**	**40.2**	**0.6**	**0.0**	**0.0**	**103.5**
Public and publicly guaranteed	**4.3**	**47.1**	**50.5**	**31.4**	**38.4**	**40.2**	**0.6**	**0.0**	**0.0**	**103.5**
Official creditors	0.1	32.4	50.5	31.4	38.4	40.2	0.6	0.0	0.0	103.5
Multilateral	0.0	21.2	32.8	24.0	27.3	28.3	0.6	0.0	0.0	102.7
Concessional	0.0	21.2	32.8	24.0	27.3	28.3	0.6	0.0	0.0	102.7
Bilateral	0.1	11.2	17.8	7.5	11.1	11.9	0.0	0.0	0.0	0.7
Concessional	0.1	7.0	17.8	7.5	11.1	11.9	0.0	0.0	0.0	0.7
Private creditors	4.2	14.7	0.0	0.0	0.0	0.0	0.0	0.0	0.0	0.0
Bonds	0.0	0.0	0.0	0.0	0.0	0.0	0.0	0.0	0.0	0.0
Commercial banks	0.0	5.2	0.0	0.0	0.0	0.0	0.0	0.0	0.0	0.0
Other private	4.2	9.5	0.0	0.0	0.0	0.0	0.0	0.0	0.0	0.0
Private nonguaranteed	**0.0**	**0.0**	**0.0**	**0.0**	**0.0**	**0.0**	**0.0**	**0.0**	**0.0**	**0.0**
Bonds	0.0	0.0	0.0	0.0	0.0	0.0	0.0	0.0	0.0	0.0
Commercial banks	0.0	0.0	0.0	0.0	0.0	0.0	0.0	0.0	0.0	0.0
Memo:										
IBRD	0.0	0.0	0.0	0.0	0.0	0.0	0.0	0.0	0.0	0.0
IDA	0.0	13.1	22.3	11.3	13.6	11.5	0.0	0.0	0.0	49.1
PRINCIPAL REPAYMENTS	**3.4**	**15.3**	**15.1**	**15.3**	**5.8**	**6.2**	**0.4**	**0.4**	**0.5**	**30.4**
Public and publicly guaranteed	**3.4**	**15.3**	**15.1**	**15.3**	**5.8**	**6.2**	**0.4**	**0.4**	**0.5**	**30.4**
Official creditors	0.9	7.9	13.9	14.1	5.8	6.2	0.4	0.4	0.5	30.4
Multilateral	0.0	0.0	3.5	5.0	4.9	5.4	0.4	0.4	0.5	29.3
Concessional	0.0	0.0	3.5	5.0	4.9	5.4	0.4	0.4	0.5	29.3
Bilateral	0.9	7.9	10.4	9.2	0.9	0.8	0.0	0.0	0.0	1.1
Concessional	0.9	7.7	8.4	7.4	0.5	0.5	0.0	0.0	0.0	0.6
Private creditors	2.5	7.3	1.2	1.2	0.0	0.0	0.0	0.0	0.0	0.0
Bonds	0.0	0.0	0.0	0.0	0.0	0.0	0.0	0.0	0.0	0.0
Commercial banks	0.0	0.5	0.0	1.2	0.0	0.0	0.0	0.0	0.0	0.0
Other private	2.5	6.8	1.2	0.0	0.0	0.0	0.0	0.0	0.0	0.0
Private nonguaranteed	**0.0**	**0.0**	**0.0**	**0.0**	**0.0**	**0.0**	**0.0**	**0.0**	**0.0**	**0.0**
Bonds	0.0	0.0	0.0	0.0	0.0	0.0	0.0	0.0	0.0	0.0
Commercial banks	0.0	0.0	0.0	0.0	0.0	0.0	0.0	0.0	0.0	0.0
Memo:										
IBRD	0.0	0.0	0.0	0.0	0.0	0.0	0.0	0.0	0.0	0.0
IDA	0.0	0.0	0.8	1.1	1.0	1.3	0.0	0.0	0.0	9.7
NET FLOWS ON DEBT	**1.0**	**31.8**	**35.5**	**16.1**	**32.6**	**34.0**	**0.2**	**-0.4**	**-0.5**	**73.1**
Public and publicly guaranteed	**1.0**	**31.8**	**35.5**	**16.1**	**32.6**	**34.0**	**0.2**	**-0.4**	**-0.5**	**73.1**
Official creditors	-0.7	24.5	36.6	17.3	32.6	34.0	0.2	-0.4	-0.5	73.1
Multilateral	0.0	21.2	29.3	19.0	22.4	22.9	0.2	-0.4	-0.5	73.5
Concessional	0.0	21.2	29.3	19.0	22.4	22.9	0.2	-0.4	-0.5	73.5
Bilateral	-0.7	3.3	7.4	-1.7	10.2	11.1	0.0	0.0	0.0	-0.4
Concessional	-0.7	-0.7	9.3	0.1	10.6	11.4	0.0	0.0	0.0	0.2
Private creditors	1.7	7.4	-1.2	-1.2	0.0	0.0	0.0	0.0	0.0	0.0
Bonds	0.0	0.0	0.0	0.0	0.0	0.0	0.0	0.0	0.0	0.0
Commercial banks	0.0	4.7	0.0	-1.2	0.0	0.0	0.0	0.0	0.0	0.0
Other private	1.7	2.7	-1.2	0.0	0.0	0.0	0.0	0.0	0.0	0.0
Private nonguaranteed	**0.0**	**0.0**	**0.0**	**0.0**	**0.0**	**0.0**	**0.0**	**0.0**	**0.0**	**0.0**
Bonds	0.0	0.0	0.0	0.0	0.0	0.0	0.0	0.0	0.0	0.0
Commercial banks	0.0	0.0	0.0	0.0	0.0	0.0	0.0	0.0	0.0	0.0
Memo:										
IBRD	0.0	0.0	0.0	0.0	0.0	0.0	0.0	0.0	0.0	0.0
IDA	0.0	13.1	21.6	10.2	12.6	10.2	0.0	0.0	0.0	39.3

HAITI

(US$ million, unless otherwise indicated)

	1970	1980	1988	1989	1990	1991	1992	1993	1994	1995
INTEREST PAYMENTS (LINT)	**0.4**	**5.1**	**8.1**	**9.2**	**5.6**	**6.2**	**0.4**	**0.0**	**0.0**	**24.9**
Public and publicly guaranteed	**0.4**	**5.1**	**8.1**	**9.2**	**5.6**	**6.2**	**0.4**	**0.0**	**0.0**	**24.9**
Official creditors	0.2	3.1	7.7	9.1	5.6	6.2	0.4	0.0	0.0	24.9
Multilateral	0.0	1.2	4.8	5.2	5.0	5.4	0.4	0.0	0.0	23.6
Concessional	0.0	1.2	4.8	5.2	5.0	5.4	0.4	0.0	0.0	23.6
Bilateral	0.2	1.9	3.0	3.9	0.6	0.7	0.0	0.0	0.0	1.3
Concessional	0.2	1.8	2.7	3.5	0.4	0.5	0.0	0.0	0.0	0.6
Private creditors	0.2	2.0	0.4	0.1	0.0	0.0	0.0	0.0	0.0	0.0
Bonds	0.0	0.0	0.0	0.0	0.0	0.0	0.0	0.0	0.0	0.0
Commercial banks	0.0	1.0	0.0	0.1	0.0	0.0	0.0	0.0	0.0	0.0
Other private	0.2	1.0	0.4	0.0	0.0	0.0	0.0	0.0	0.0	0.0
Private nonguaranteed	**0.0**	**0.0**	**0.0**	**0.0**	**0.0**	**0.0**	**0.0**	**0.0**	**0.0**	**0.0**
Bonds	0.0	0.0	0.0	0.0	0.0	0.0	0.0	0.0	0.0	0.0
Commercial banks	0.0	0.0	0.0	0.0	0.0	0.0	0.0	0.0	0.0	0.0
Memo:										
IBRD	0.0	0.0	0.0	0.0	0.0	0.0	0.0	0.0	0.0	0.0
IDA	0.0	0.4	2.3	2.4	2.1	2.7	0.0	0.0	0.0	10.4
NET TRANSFERS ON DEBT	**0.5**	**26.8**	**27.3**	**6.8**	**26.9**	**27.8**	**-0.2**	**-0.4**	**-0.5**	**48.2**
Public and publicly guaranteed	**0.5**	**26.8**	**27.3**	**6.8**	**26.9**	**27.8**	**-0.2**	**-0.4**	**-0.5**	**48.2**
Official creditors	-0.9	21.3	28.9	8.2	26.9	27.8	-0.2	-0.4	-0.5	48.2
Multilateral	0.0	20.0	24.5	13.8	17.4	17.4	-0.2	-0.4	-0.5	49.9
Concessional	0.0	20.0	24.5	13.8	17.4	17.4	-0.2	-0.4	-0.5	49.9
Bilateral	-0.9	1.3	4.4	-5.6	9.6	10.4	0.0	0.0	0.0	-1.7
Concessional	-0.9	-2.5	6.6	-3.4	10.2	10.9	0.0	0.0	0.0	-0.4
Private creditors	1.4	5.4	-1.5	-1.3	0.0	0.0	0.0	0.0	0.0	0.0
Bonds	0.0	0.0	0.0	0.0	0.0	0.0	0.0	0.0	0.0	0.0
Commercial banks	0.0	3.7	0.0	-1.3	0.0	0.0	0.0	0.0	0.0	0.0
Other private	1.4	1.7	-1.5	0.0	0.0	0.0	0.0	0.0	0.0	0.0
Private nonguaranteed	**0.0**	**0.0**	**0.0**	**0.0**	**0.0**	**0.0**	**0.0**	**0.0**	**0.0**	**0.0**
Bonds	0.0	0.0	0.0	0.0	0.0	0.0	0.0	0.0	0.0	0.0
Commercial banks	0.0	0.0	0.0	0.0	0.0	0.0	0.0	0.0	0.0	0.0
Memo:										
IBRD	0.0	0.0	0.0	0.0	0.0	0.0	0.0	0.0	0.0	0.0
IDA	0.0	12.7	19.3	7.8	10.5	7.5	0.0	0.0	0.0	29.0
DEBT SERVICE (LTDS)	**3.8**	**20.4**	**23.2**	**24.6**	**11.5**	**12.4**	**0.8**	**0.4**	**0.5**	**55.3**
Public and publicly guaranteed	**3.8**	**20.4**	**23.2**	**24.6**	**11.5**	**12.4**	**0.8**	**0.4**	**0.5**	**55.3**
Official creditors	1.1	11.1	21.6	23.2	11.5	12.4	0.8	0.4	0.5	55.3
Multilateral	0.0	1.2	8.3	10.2	9.9	10.9	0.8	0.4	0.5	52.8
Concessional	0.0	1.2	8.3	10.2	9.9	10.9	0.8	0.4	0.5	52.8
Bilateral	1.0	9.9	13.4	13.1	1.5	1.5	0.0	0.0	0.0	2.5
Concessional	1.0	9.5	11.1	10.9	0.9	1.0	0.0	0.0	0.0	1.1
Private creditors	2.8	9.3	1.5	1.3	0.0	0.0	0.0	0.0	0.0	0.0
Bonds	0.0	0.0	0.0	0.0	0.0	0.0	0.0	0.0	0.0	0.0
Commercial banks	0.0	1.5	0.0	1.3	0.0	0.0	0.0	0.0	0.0	0.0
Other private	2.8	7.8	1.5	0.0	0.0	0.0	0.0	0.0	0.0	0.0
Private nonguaranteed	**0.0**	**0.0**	**0.0**	**0.0**	**0.0**	**0.0**	**0.0**	**0.0**	**0.0**	**0.0**
Bonds	0.0	0.0	0.0	0.0	0.0	0.0	0.0	0.0	0.0	0.0
Commercial banks	0.0	0.0	0.0	0.0	0.0	0.0	0.0	0.0	0.0	0.0
Memo:										
IBRD	0.0	0.0	0.0	0.0	0.0	0.0	0.0	0.0	0.0	0.0
IDA	0.0	0.4	3.0	3.5	3.1	4.0	0.0	0.0	0.0	20.1
UNDISBURSED DEBT	**4.9**	**144.7**	**189.4**	**189.4**	**266.5**	**265.2**	**274.8**	**261.0**	**266.5**	**392.4**
Official creditors	0.0	127.6	189.4	189.4	266.5	265.2	274.8	261.0	266.5	392.4
Private creditors	4.9	17.1	0.0	0.0	0.0	0.0	0.0	0.0	0.0	0.0
Memorandum items										
Concessional LDOD	29.2	213.8	618.0	635.9	698.9	571.1	588.4	578.4	565.3	750.0
Variable rate LDOD	0.0	7.6	8.7	6.8	6.8	5.0	5.0	5.0	5.0	0.0
Public sector LDOD	39.9	234.9	682.1	688.0	750.6	620.7	638.0	648.0	634.9	751.8
Private sector LDOD	0.0	7.4	3.0	0.0	0.0	0.0	0.0	0.0	0.0	0.0

6. CURRENCY COMPOSITION OF LONG-TERM DEBT (PERCENT)

	1970	1980	1988	1989	1990	1991	1992	1993	1994	1995
Deutsche mark	0.0	5.0	0.0	0.0	0.0	0.0	0.0	0.0	0.0	0.0
French franc	0.0	3.1	7.6	8.2	10.6	2.9	3.3	2.8	3.0	2.6
Japanese yen	0.0	0.0	0.0	0.0	0.0	0.0	0.0	0.0	0.0	0.0
Pound sterling	0.0	0.0	0.0	0.0	0.0	0.0	0.0	0.0	0.0	0.0
Swiss franc	0.0	0.0	0.0	0.0	0.0	0.0	0.0	0.0	0.0	0.0
U.S.dollars	99.9	79.1	74.0	72.4	70.4	71.9	72.0	73.0	72.2	77.2
Multiple currency	0.0	12.9	18.4	19.4	19.0	25.2	24.7	24.3	24.8	20.2
Special drawing rights	0.0	0.0	0.0	0.0	0.0	0.0	0.0	0.0	0.0	0.0
All other currencies	0.0	0.0	0.0	0.0	0.0	0.0	0.0	0.0	0.0	0.0

HAITI

(US$ million, unless otherwise indicated)

	1970	1980	1988	1989	1990	1991	1992	1993	1994	1995
7. DEBT RESTRUCTURINGS										
Total amount rescheduled	0.0	0.0	0.0	0.0	0.0	0.0	0.0	0.0	0.0	108.3
Debt stock rescheduled	0.0	0.0	0.0	0.0	0.0	0.0	0.0	0.0	0.0	0.0
Principal rescheduled	0.0	0.0	0.0	0.0	0.0	0.0	0.0	0.0	0.0	71.0
Official	0.0	0.0	0.0	0.0	0.0	0.0	0.0	0.0	0.0	4.0
Private	0.0	0.0	0.0	0.0	0.0	0.0	0.0	0.0	0.0	67.0
Interest rescheduled	0.0	0.0	0.0	0.0	0.0	0.0	0.0	0.0	0.0	17.1
Official	0.0	0.0	0.0	0.0	0.0	0.0	0.0	0.0	0.0	1.4
Private	0.0	0.0	0.0	0.0	0.0	0.0	0.0	0.0	0.0	15.7
Debt forgiven	..	..	0.0	0.0	0.0	155.7	0.0	0.0	22.8	8.2
Memo: interest forgiven	..	..	0.0	0.0	0.0	16.6	0.0	0.0	0.0	2.9
Debt stock reduction	0.0	0.0	0.0	0.0	0.0	0.0	0.0	0.0	0.0	0.0
of which debt buyback	0.0	0.0	0.0	0.0	0.0	0.0	0.0	0.0	0.0	0.0
8. DEBT STOCK-FLOW RECONCILIATION										
Total change in debt stocks	..	..	..	-13.9	82.8	-130.5	26.7	17.8	-86.1	89.9
Net flows on debt	..	..	..	0.3	41.6	43.6	0.2	-0.4	-78.5	78.5
Net change in interest arrears	..	..	..	-0.7	8.0	-9.6	6.9	9.1	3.8	-33.3
Interest capitalized	..	..	..	0.0	0.0	0.0	0.0	0.0	0.0	17.1
Debt forgiveness or reduction	..	..	..	0.0	0.0	-155.7	0.0	0.0	-22.8	-8.2
Cross-currency valuation	..	..	..	2.6	10.2	-0.2	-1.3	-1.2	2.0	1.8
Residual	..	..	..	-16.0	23.0	-8.6	20.9	10.3	9.3	34.0
9. AVERAGE TERMS OF NEW COMMITMENTS										
ALL CREDITORS										
Interest (%)	4.8	5.2	0.0	1.4	1.4	1.3	0.0	0.0	0.0	1.2
Maturity (years)	9.5	19.6	0.0	34.7	38.8	39.5	0.0	0.0	0.0	39.9
Grace period (years)	1.0	6.3	0.0	9.2	10.5	10.3	0.0	0.0	0.0	10.4
Grant element (%)	16.0	32.6	0.0	71.7	74.8	75.4	0.0	0.0	0.0	76.6
Official creditors										
Interest (%)	3.4	2.8	0.0	1.4	1.4	1.3	0.0	0.0	0.0	1.2
Maturity (years)	43.0	29.8	0.0	34.7	38.8	39.5	0.0	0.0	0.0	39.9
Grace period (years)	7.3	10.3	0.0	9.2	10.5	10.3	0.0	0.0	0.0	10.4
Grant element (%)	55.8	54.5	0.0	71.7	74.8	75.4	0.0	0.0	0.0	76.6
Private creditors										
Interest (%)	4.8	8.2	0.0	0.0	0.0	0.0	0.0	0.0	0.0	0.0
Maturity (years)	8.6	7.0	0.0	0.0	0.0	0.0	0.0	0.0	0.0	0.0
Grace period (years)	0.9	1.4	0.0	0.0	0.0	0.0	0.0	0.0	0.0	0.0
Grant element (%)	14.9	5.2	0.0	0.0	0.0	0.0	0.0	0.0	0.0	0.0
Memorandum items										
Commitments	5.4	51.3	0.0	60.1	103.8	51.9	0.0	0.0	0.0	253.6
Official creditors	0.1	28.5	0.0	60.1	103.8	51.9	0.0	0.0	0.0	253.6
Private creditors	5.3	22.9	0.0	0.0	0.0	0.0	0.0	0.0	0.0	0.0

10. CONTRACTUAL OBLIGATIONS ON OUTSTANDING LONG-TERM DEBT

	1996	1997	1998	1999	2000	2001	2002	2003	2004	2005
TOTAL										
Disbursements	106.6	92.4	73.3	57.4	35.9	16.9	9.4	0.6	0.0	0.0
Principal	13.3	16.2	17.6	18.4	20.9	23.6	24.6	24.6	25.3	27.5
Interest	10.5	14.1	14.7	14.8	14.8	14.6	14.4	14.1	13.9	14.1
Official creditors										
Disbursements	106.6	92.4	73.3	57.4	35.9	16.9	9.4	0.6	0.0	0.0
Principal	13.3	16.2	17.6	18.4	20.9	23.6	24.6	24.6	25.3	27.5
Interest	10.5	14.1	14.7	14.8	14.8	14.6	14.4	14.1	13.9	14.1
Bilateral creditors										
Disbursements	6.4	4.2	2.7	1.5	0.7	0.3	0.1	0.0	0.0	0.0
Principal	0.9	1.5	1.5	1.6	3.0	4.0	4.0	4.1	4.2	3.8
Interest	2.9	5.6	5.6	5.5	5.5	5.4	5.2	5.1	5.0	4.8
Multilateral creditors										
Disbursements	100.2	88.1	70.6	56.0	35.2	16.5	9.3	0.6	0.0	0.0
Principal	12.5	14.6	16.1	16.8	17.8	19.7	20.6	20.5	21.1	23.8
Interest	7.7	8.6	9.1	9.3	9.3	9.2	9.2	9.0	9.0	9.2
Private creditors										
Disbursements	0.0	0.0	0.0	0.0	0.0	0.0	0.0	0.0	0.0	0.0
Principal	0.0	0.0	0.0	0.0	0.0	0.0	0.0	0.0	0.0	0.0
Interest	0.0	0.0	0.0	0.0	0.0	0.0	0.0	0.0	0.0	0.0
Commercial banks										
Disbursements	0.0	0.0	0.0	0.0	0.0	0.0	0.0	0.0	0.0	0.0
Principal	0.0	0.0	0.0	0.0	0.0	0.0	0.0	0.0	0.0	0.0
Interest	0.0	0.0	0.0	0.0	0.0	0.0	0.0	0.0	0.0	0.0
Other private										
Disbursements	0.0	0.0	0.0	0.0	0.0	0.0	0.0	0.0	0.0	0.0
Principal	0.0	0.0	0.0	0.0	0.0	0.0	0.0	0.0	0.0	0.0
Interest	0.0	0.0	0.0	0.0	0.0	0.0	0.0	0.0	0.0	0.0

HONDURAS

(US$ million, unless otherwise indicated)

	1970	1980	1988	1989	1990	1991	1992	1993	1994	1995
1. SUMMARY DEBT DATA										
TOTAL DEBT STOCKS (EDT)	**..**	**1,473**	**3,308**	**3,386**	**3,724**	**3,396**	**3,614**	**4,077**	**4,434**	**4,567**
Long-term debt (LDOD)	**111**	**1,168**	**2,859**	**2,951**	**3,492**	**3,171**	**3,322**	**3,740**	**4,000**	**4,093**
Public and publicly guaranteed	91	976	2,758	2,867	3,426	3,096	3,232	3,651	3,900	3,979
Private nonguaranteed	19	191	101	84	66	75	90	88	100	114
Use of IMF credit	**0**	**33**	**37**	**35**	**32**	**34**	**112**	**118**	**109**	**99**
Short-term debt	**..**	**272**	**412**	**400**	**199**	**192**	**180**	**219**	**325**	**375**
of which interest arrears on LDOD	..	0	137	172	89	75	55	92	68	56
Official creditors	..	0	41	62	34	37	30	36	40	28
Private creditors	..	0	96	110	55	38	25	56	28	28
Memo: principal arrears on LDOD	..	3	341	354	190	138	109	167	150	142
Official creditors	..	1	63	114	63	49	54	74	70	56
Private creditors	..	2	278	241	128	89	55	93	80	87
Memo: export credits	..	..	302	279	338	326	416	423	487	533
TOTAL DEBT FLOWS										
Disbursements	**45**	**375**	**309**	**199**	**461**	**274**	**489**	**584**	**352**	**379**
Long-term debt	39	346	309	199	432	271	408	574	352	348
IMF purchases	6	29	0	0	29	3	81	10	0	31
Principal repayments	**6**	**87**	**211**	**70**	**211**	**147**	**203**	**210**	**254**	**336**
Long-term debt	6	87	175	70	177	145	203	207	238	293
IMF repurchases	0	0	36	0	35	2	0	3	16	44
Net flows on debt	**38**	**288**	**73**	**81**	**133**	**134**	**294**	**375**	**228**	**105**
of which short-term debt	..	..	-25	-48	-117	7	8	2	130	62
Interest payments (INT)	**..**	**120**	**158**	**72**	**178**	**160**	**174**	**151**	**178**	**217**
Long-term debt	4	83	129	49	157	147	162	140	163	195
IMF charges	0	1	4	0	6	3	6	6	5	5
Short-term debt	..	36	25	23	15	10	6	4	10	18
Net transfers on debt	**..**	**168**	**-85**	**9**	**-45**	**-26**	**120**	**225**	**50**	**-112**
Total debt service paid (TDS)	**..**	**207**	**369**	**142**	**389**	**307**	**377**	**361**	**433**	**553**
Long-term debt	10	170	303	119	333	293	365	347	402	487
IMF repurchases and charges	0	1	41	1	41	5	6	9	21	48
Short-term debt (interest only)	..	36	25	23	15	10	6	4	10	18
2. AGGREGATE NET RESOURCE FLOWS AND NET TRANSFERS (LONG-TERM)										
NET RESOURCE FLOWS	**41**	**284**	**335**	**251**	**511**	**727**	**415**	**488**	**232**	**228**
Net flow of long-term debt (ex. IMF)	32	259	135	129	256	126	205	367	114	56
Foreign direct investment (net)	8	6	48	51	44	52	48	27	35	50
Portfolio equity flows	0	0	0	0	0	0	0	0	0	0
Grants (excluding technical coop.)	0	20	152	71	211	549	162	93	83	122
Memo: technical coop. grants	6	18	78	90	96	79	88	93	59	96
NET TRANSFERS	**17**	**124**	**134**	**127**	**282**	**508**	**179**	**257**	**-27**	**-57**
Interest on long-term debt	4	83	129	49	157	147	162	140	163	195
Profit remittances on FDI	20	78	73	75	72	72	74	90	95	90
3. MAJOR ECONOMIC AGGREGATES										
Gross national product (GNP)	700	2,429	3,787	3,302	2,773	2,787	3,081	3,249	3,147	3,664
Exports of goods & services (XGS)	..	968	1,048	1,085	1,053	1,055	1,103	1,300	1,453	1,787
of which workers remittances	..	0	0	0	0	0	0	60	85	120
Imports of goods & services (MGS)	..	1,306	1,394	1,448	1,384	1,425	1,577	1,713	1,900	2,111
International reserves (RES)	20	159	57	28	47	112	205	106	179	270
Current account balance	..	-317	-181	-206	-228	-258	-351	-309	-343	-201
4. DEBT INDICATORS										
EDT / XGS (%)	..	152.2	315.7	312.0	353.5	321.8	327.8	313.5	305.2	255.5
EDT / GNP (%)	..	60.6	87.3	102.5	134.3	121.9	117.3	125.5	140.9	124.6
TDS / XGS (%)	..	21.4	35.2	13.1	36.9	29.1	34.2	27.7	29.8	31.0
INT / XGS (%)	..	12.4	15.1	6.6	16.9	15.2	15.8	11.6	12.3	12.2
INT / GNP (%)	..	4.9	4.2	2.2	6.4	5.7	5.6	4.6	5.7	5.9
RES / EDT (%)	..	10.8	1.7	0.8	1.3	3.3	5.7	2.6	4.0	5.9
RES / MGS (months)	..	1.5	0.5	0.2	0.4	0.9	1.6	0.7	1.1	1.5
Short-term / EDT (%)	..	18.5	12.5	11.8	5.3	5.7	5.0	5.4	7.3	8.2
Concessional / EDT (%)	..	23.4	35.3	35.8	37.6	32.7	37.7	39.7	42.3	44.2
Multilateral / EDT (%)	..	31.1	41.2	43.8	42.5	48.8	49.8	47.9	46.5	47.2

HONDURAS

(US$ million, unless otherwise indicated)

	1970	1980	1988	1989	1990	1991	1992	1993	1994	1995
5. LONG-TERM DEBT										
DEBT OUTSTANDING (LDOD)	**111**	**1,168**	**2,859**	**2,951**	**3,492**	**3,171**	**3,322**	**3,740**	**4,000**	**4,093**
Public and publicly guaranteed	**91**	**976**	**2,758**	**2,867**	**3,426**	**3,096**	**3,232**	**3,651**	**3,900**	**3,979**
Official creditors	88	697	2,269	2,406	2,987	2,750	2,971	3,273	3,561	3,647
Multilateral	63	459	1,361	1,484	1,581	1,658	1,801	1,952	2,062	2,162
Concessional	54	225	499	510	544	596	722	822	927	1,040
Bilateral	24	238	908	923	1,406	1,092	1,170	1,321	1,498	1,485
Concessional	24	120	669	702	857	515	642	796	947	978
Private creditors	4	280	489	461	439	346	261	378	339	333
Bonds	0	0	0	0	0	0	0	152	152	139
Commercial banks	0	205	285	229	205	152	105	106	98	115
Other private	4	75	204	232	234	194	156	121	89	79
Private nonguaranteed	**19**	**191**	**101**	**84**	**66**	**75**	**90**	**88**	**100**	**114**
Bonds	0	0	0	0	0	0	0	0	0	0
Commercial banks	19	191	101	84	66	75	90	88	100	114
Memo:										
IBRD	30	152	538	528	558	551	489	479	469	443
IDA	15	64	79	79	77	126	182	236	307	386
DISBURSEMENTS	**39**	**346**	**309**	**199**	**432**	**271**	**408**	**574**	**352**	**348**
Public and publicly guaranteed	**29**	**265**	**292**	**179**	**425**	**248**	**378**	**559**	**320**	**296**
Official creditors	29	151	278	144	368	238	377	389	317	270
Multilateral	21	113	129	61	190	152	291	269	195	218
Concessional	16	39	33	15	54	67	151	120	119	132
Bilateral	7	38	149	84	179	86	86	121	122	51
Concessional	7	12	79	56	88	53	48	92	84	45
Private creditors	0	114	14	35	56	10	1	169	3	26
Bonds	0	0	0	0	0	0	0	152	0	0
Commercial banks	0	59	4	3	23	2	1	17	3	26
Other private	0	55	10	32	34	8	0	0	0	1
Private nonguaranteed	**10**	**81**	**17**	**20**	**8**	**23**	**29**	**16**	**32**	**52**
Bonds	0	0	0	0	0	0	0	0	0	0
Commercial banks	10	81	17	20	8	23	29	16	32	52
Memo:										
IBRD	10	24	53	2	82	30	3	26	5	7
IDA	2	18	0	0	0	48	60	55	64	78
PRINCIPAL REPAYMENTS	**6**	**87**	**175**	**70**	**177**	**145**	**203**	**207**	**238**	**293**
Public and publicly guaranteed	**3**	**39**	**149**	**62**	**151**	**131**	**189**	**189**	**218**	**254**
Official creditors	2	23	131	58	143	117	153	164	199	229
Multilateral	2	20	66	18	137	94	121	118	158	158
Concessional	1	3	13	5	21	18	23	20	25	23
Bilateral	0	2	65	40	6	23	33	46	41	70
Concessional	0	1	11	7	2	3	2	6	11	10
Private creditors	1	16	18	4	8	14	36	26	19	25
Bonds	0	0	0	0	0	0	0	0	0	13
Commercial banks	0	14	8	0	4	8	26	15	12	6
Other private	1	3	10	4	4	6	10	11	7	6
Private nonguaranteed	**3**	**48**	**26**	**8**	**25**	**15**	**14**	**18**	**20**	**39**
Bonds	0	0	0	0	0	0	0	0	0	0
Commercial banks	3	48	26	8	25	15	14	18	20	39
Memo:										
IBRD	1	4	36	0	94	44	46	46	51	58
IDA	0	0	1	0	2	1	1	1	2	2
NET FLOWS ON DEBT	**32**	**259**	**135**	**129**	**256**	**126**	**205**	**367**	**114**	**56**
Public and publicly guaranteed	**26**	**226**	**143**	**117**	**274**	**117**	**189**	**369**	**102**	**42**
Official creditors	27	128	147	86	225	121	224	226	118	41
Multilateral	20	92	63	43	53	58	171	151	37	60
Concessional	15	36	20	10	33	49	128	100	95	109
Bilateral	7	36	84	43	173	64	53	74	81	-19
Concessional	7	11	69	49	86	51	46	85	73	35
Private creditors	-1	98	-4	31	48	-4	-35	144	-16	1
Bonds	0	0	0	0	0	0	0	152	0	-13
Commercial banks	0	46	-4	3	19	-6	-25	2	-9	20
Other private	-1	52	0	28	30	2	-10	-11	-7	-5
Private nonguaranteed	**7**	**33**	**-9**	**12**	**-18**	**9**	**15**	**-2**	**12**	**14**
Bonds	0	0	0	0	0	0	0	0	0	0
Commercial banks	7	33	-9	12	-18	9	15	-2	12	14
Memo:										
IBRD	9	20	17	2	-12	-14	-43	-20	-46	-51
IDA	2	18	-1	0	-2	47	59	54	62	76

HONDURAS

(US$ million, unless otherwise indicated)

	1970	*1980*	*1988*	*1989*	*1990*	*1991*	*1992*	*1993*	*1994*	*1995*
INTEREST PAYMENTS (LINT)	**4**	**83**	**129**	**49**	**157**	**147**	**162**	**140**	**163**	**195**
Public and publicly guaranteed	**3**	**58**	**122**	**46**	**156**	**143**	**160**	**140**	**161**	**190**
Official creditors	2	31	110	40	150	124	143	126	149	172
Multilateral	2	24	85	23	141	91	108	97	104	104
Concessional	2	5	11	4	12	11	13	12	14	14
Bilateral	0	7	24	17	8	33	35	30	44	68
Concessional	0	2	12	9	1	3	7	9	13	20
Private creditors	0	27	12	5	6	19	17	14	13	19
Bonds	0	0	0	0	0	0	0	0	5	7
Commercial banks	0	26	6	2	5	17	14	10	3	7
Other private	0	1	7	3	1	2	3	3	5	5
Private nonguaranteed	**1**	**25**	**7**	**3**	**1**	**4**	**2**	**0**	**2**	**5**
Bonds	0	0	0	0	0	0	0	0	0	0
Commercial banks	1	25	7	3	1	4	2	0	2	5
Memo:										
IBRD	1	12	44	1	96	44	43	39	38	38
IDA	0	0	1	0	1	1	1	1	2	3
NET TRANSFERS ON DEBT	**29**	**176**	**6**	**80**	**99**	**-21**	**43**	**227**	**-49**	**-139**
Public and publicly guaranteed	**23**	**168**	**21**	**71**	**118**	**-26**	**29**	**229**	**-59**	**-148**
Official creditors	25	97	38	46	76	-3	81	99	-30	-131
Multilateral	18	68	-22	20	-89	-34	63	54	-67	-44
Concessional	13	31	10	6	20	38	115	88	81	94
Bilateral	7	29	60	26	164	31	18	45	37	-87
Concessional	7	9	57	40	85	48	39	76	60	14
Private creditors	-2	71	-16	25	42	-23	-52	130	-29	-17
Bonds	0	0	0	0	0	0	0	152	-5	-21
Commercial banks	0	20	-9	1	14	-23	-39	-8	-12	13
Other private	-2	51	-7	25	29	0	-13	-14	-12	-10
Private nonguaranteed	**6**	**8**	**-15**	**9**	**-19**	**4**	**14**	**-2**	**10**	**9**
Bonds	0	0	0	0	0	0	0	0	0	0
Commercial banks	6	8	-15	9	-19	4	14	-2	10	9
Memo:										
IBRD	8	8	-27	1	-108	-58	-85	-59	-85	-89
IDA	2	17	-2	0	-4	46	58	52	60	73
DEBT SERVICE (LTDS)	**10**	**170**	**303**	**119**	**333**	**293**	**365**	**347**	**402**	**487**
Public and publicly guaranteed	**6**	**97**	**271**	**108**	**307**	**274**	**349**	**329**	**379**	**444**
Official creditors	4	54	240	98	293	241	296	290	348	400
Multilateral	4	45	151	41	278	186	229	214	262	262
Concessional	3	9	24	10	34	29	36	32	39	37
Bilateral	0	9	89	57	15	55	68	76	86	138
Concessional	0	3	22	16	3	5	9	15	24	31
Private creditors	2	44	30	9	14	33	53	39	32	44
Bonds	0	0	0	0	0	0	0	0	5	21
Commercial banks	0	39	13	2	9	25	39	25	15	13
Other private	2	4	17	7	5	8	13	14	12	10
Private nonguaranteed	**4**	**73**	**33**	**11**	**27**	**19**	**16**	**18**	**22**	**44**
Bonds	0	0	0	0	0	0	0	0	0	0
Commercial banks	4	73	33	11	27	19	16	18	22	44
Memo:										
IBRD	2	17	80	1	191	88	89	85	90	96
IDA	0	1	2	0	4	2	2	3	3	4
UNDISBURSED DEBT	**54**	**729**	**666**	**626**	**666**	**671**	**885**	**906**	**741**	**775**
Official creditors	54	716	640	603	655	667	882	878	715	763
Private creditors	0	13	26	24	10	4	3	29	26	12
Memorandum items										
Concessional LDOD	78	345	1,168	1,213	1,401	1,110	1,363	1,617	1,874	2,018
Variable rate LDOD	19	400	620	617	753	748	728	774	784	768
Public sector LDOD	91	841	2,626	2,739	3,319	3,020	3,180	3,619	3,875	3,946
Private sector LDOD	19	327	233	213	173	150	142	120	125	147

6. CURRENCY COMPOSITION OF LONG-TERM DEBT (PERCENT)

	1970	*1980*	*1988*	*1989*	*1990*	*1991*	*1992*	*1993*	*1994*	*1995*
Deutsche mark	0.0	0.0	1.7	2.3	2.6	3.2	3.0	2.9	3.2	3.4
French franc	0.5	0.4	2.3	2.5	3.1	3.4	3.1	2.7	2.7	2.6
Japanese yen	0.0	0.0	6.7	6.1	8.4	9.7	9.5	9.7	10.5	9.8
Pound sterling	0.0	0.0	1.1	0.8	0.9	1.0	0.8	0.7	0.7	0.6
Swiss franc	0.0	0.0	1.6	1.5	2.1	1.8	1.4	1.3	1.4	1.5
U.S.dollars	66.7	62.9	44.1	46.2	45.2	39.5	43.7	46.2	44.9	45.8
Multiple currency	32.8	25.4	39.5	38.2	34.4	37.9	35.4	33.0	32.5	31.8
Special drawing rights	0.0	0.0	0.0	0.0	0.0	0.0	0.0	0.0	0.0	0.0
All other currencies	21.0	11.5	3.1	2.4	3.2	3.5	3.2	3.5	4.3	4.5

HONDURAS

(US$ million, unless otherwise indicated)

	1970	1980	1988	1989	1990	1991	1992	1993	1994	1995
7. DEBT RESTRUCTURINGS										
Total amount rescheduled	0	0	0	101	310	88	133	83	43	25
Debt stock rescheduled	0	0	0	0	0	0	0	0	0	0
Principal rescheduled	0	0	0	13	153	64	99	50	29	17
Official	0	0	0	13	71	24	68	23	12	8
Private	0	0	0	0	83	40	31	27	17	9
Interest rescheduled	0	0	0	10	140	23	34	32	14	8
Official	0	0	0	10	79	11	21	23	8	4
Private	0	0	0	0	62	12	13	9	6	4
Debt forgiven	..	..	0	0	10	442	8	3	20	10
Memo: interest forgiven	..	..	0	6	11	0	2	1	0	0
Debt stock reduction	0	0	10	57	41	48	20	0	0	0
of which debt buyback	0	0	0	0	0	0	0	0	0	0
8. DEBT STOCK-FLOW RECONCILIATION										
Total change in debt stocks	..	..	..	78	337	-327	218	462	357	133
Net flows on debt	..	..	..	81	133	134	294	375	228	105
Net change in interest arrears	..	..	..	35	-83	-14	-20	37	-24	-12
Interest capitalized	..	..	..	10	140	23	34	32	14	8
Debt forgiveness or reduction	..	..	..	-57	-51	-490	-29	-3	-20	-10
Cross-currency valuation	..	..	..	-37	91	8	-63	14	113	30
Residual	..	..	..	46	108	12	2	8	47	12
9. AVERAGE TERMS OF NEW COMMITMENTS										
ALL CREDITORS										
Interest (%)	4.1	6.8	7.1	6.0	6.5	4.0	4.3	3.8	5.6	2.4
Maturity (years)	29.6	23.9	18.7	16.6	21.3	24.1	24.6	23.7	19.4	30.4
Grace period (years)	6.8	6.7	4.4	3.6	5.9	6.7	6.7	8.7	5.2	7.2
Grant element (%)	45.5	26.9	17.7	21.7	26.6	45.4	41.5	45.9	29.7	57.6
Official creditors										
Interest (%)	4.1	5.9	7.1	6.1	6.1	4.0	4.3	2.8	5.6	2.2
Maturity (years)	29.6	25.5	19.0	19.1	22.7	24.5	24.6	28.8	19.4	30.4
Grace period (years)	6.8	7.1	4.5	4.3	6.5	6.8	6.7	7.1	5.2	7.4
Grant element (%)	45.5	31.6	18.1	22.9	29.4	46.2	41.5	54.5	29.7	59.1
Private creditors										
Interest (%)	0.0	16.0	8.0	5.3	9.9	7.8	5.6	5.8	0.0	7.5
Maturity (years)	0.0	6.7	13.5	7.6	7.1	5.0	2.0	13.8	0.0	29.8
Grace period (years)	0.0	2.5	2.9	0.8	0.6	1.5	2.0	11.9	0.0	2.3
Grant element (%)	0.0	-22.3	9.4	17.2	-0.8	5.4	7.4	29.0	0.0	16.6
Memorandum items										
Commitments	23	495	303	150	452	302	609	582	144	335
Official creditors	23	452	289	118	410	296	609	385	144	322
Private creditors	0	43	14	32	42	6	0	197	0	12

10. CONTRACTUAL OBLIGATIONS ON OUTSTANDING LONG-TERM DEBT

	1996	1997	1998	1999	2000	2001	2002	2003	2004	2005
TOTAL										
Disbursements	245	224	130	82	50	26	13	3	2	1
Principal	273	297	279	273	260	232	229	222	216	267
Interest	198	190	176	161	144	129	115	102	90	76
Official creditors										
Disbursements	238	220	128	81	50	26	13	3	2	1
Principal	250	273	254	250	240	214	212	205	200	189
Interest	173	167	155	141	126	113	101	89	78	67
Bilateral creditors										
Disbursements	56	52	31	18	11	5	3	2	2	1
Principal	85	87	83	87	98	91	90	90	93	87
Interest	66	63	60	56	51	46	41	37	32	28
Multilateral creditors										
Disbursements	182	168	97	64	39	21	11	1	0	0
Principal	165	186	171	163	143	123	123	115	107	102
Interest	107	103	95	85	75	67	59	52	45	39
Private creditors										
Disbursements	6	4	1	1	0	0	0	0	0	0
Principal	24	24	25	23	20	18	17	17	16	78
Interest	24	23	21	19	18	16	15	13	12	9
Commercial banks										
Disbursements	6	4	1	1	0	0	0	0	0	0
Principal	5	7	9	9	8	7	6	6	6	6
Interest	7	7	6	5	5	4	4	3	3	2
Other private										
Disbursements	0	0	0	0	0	0	0	0	0	0
Principal	19	17	16	14	12	11	11	11	10	73
Interest	18	16	15	14	13	12	11	10	9	7

HUNGARY

(US$ million, unless otherwise indicated)

	1970	1980	1988	1989	1990	1991	1992	1993	1994	1995
1. SUMMARY DEBT DATA										
TOTAL DEBT STOCKS (EDT)	..	**9,764**	**19,609**	**20,397**	**21,277**	**22,624**	**21,975**	**24,250**	**28,083**	**31,248**
Long-term debt (LDOD)	..	**6,416**	**15,612**	**16,634**	**18,006**	**19,188**	**18,485**	**21,014**	**24,545**	**27,660**
Public and publicly guaranteed	..	6,416	15,612	16,634	18,006	18,931	17,843	19,796	22,157	23,572
Private nonguaranteed	0	0	0	0	0	257	642	1,218	2,388	4,089
Use of IMF credit	**0**	**0**	**634**	**456**	**330**	**1,259**	**1,204**	**1,231**	**1,141**	**385**
Short-term debt	..	**3,347**	**3,363**	**3,307**	**2,941**	**2,177**	**2,286**	**2,005**	**2,397**	**3,203**
of which interest arrears on LDOD	..	0	0	0	0	0	0	0	0	0
Official creditors	..	0	0	0	0	0	0	0	0	0
Private creditors	..	0	0	0	0	0	0	0	0	0
Memo: principal arrears on LDOD	..	0	0	0	0	0	0	0	0	37
Official creditors	..	0	0	0	0	0	0	0	0	0
Private creditors	..	0	0	0	0	0	0	0	0	36
Memo: export credits	..	..	1,538	1,321	1,424	1,743	1,937	2,025	2,252	2,171
TOTAL DEBT FLOWS										
Disbursements	..	**1,552**	**2,779**	**3,156**	**2,516**	**3,818**	**2,879**	**5,325**	**5,087**	**6,718**
Long-term debt	..	1,552	2,557	3,092	2,343	2,855	2,712	5,246	5,087	6,718
IMF purchases	0	0	222	64	173	963	167	79	0	0
Principal repayments	..	**824**	**2,206**	**1,965**	**2,547**	**2,339**	**3,115**	**2,898**	**3,915**	**4,910**
Long-term debt	..	824	1,851	1,742	2,217	2,263	2,942	2,848	3,751	4,117
IMF repurchases	0	0	355	223	330	76	173	51	164	793
Net flows on debt	..	**728**	**834**	**1,134**	**-397**	**716**	**-127**	**2,146**	**1,564**	**2,613**
of which short-term debt	..	..	260	-57	-366	-763	109	-281	392	806
Interest payments (INT)	..	**1,099**	**1,307**	**1,605**	**1,683**	**1,658**	**1,850**	**1,516**	**1,731**	**2,111**
Long-term debt	..	636	1,123	1,479	1,533	1,437	1,614	1,343	1,501	1,877
IMF charges	0	0	52	50	35	68	91	71	63	60
Short-term debt	..	463	132	77	115	153	145	102	166	174
Net transfers on debt	..	**-371**	**-473**	**-471**	**-2,080**	**-942**	**-1,977**	**630**	**-167**	**503**
Total debt service paid (TDS)	..	**1,923**	**3,513**	**3,570**	**4,230**	**3,997**	**4,965**	**4,414**	**5,646**	**7,021**
Long-term debt	..	1,460	2,974	3,221	3,751	3,700	4,556	4,191	5,252	5,994
IMF repurchases and charges	0	0	407	273	364	144	264	122	228	853
Short-term debt (interest only)	..	463	132	77	115	153	145	102	166	174
2. AGGREGATE NET RESOURCE FLOWS AND NET TRANSFERS (LONG-TERM)										
NET RESOURCE FLOWS	..	**728**	**706**	**1,350**	**280**	**2,194**	**1,398**	**4,847**	**2,960**	**7,628**
Net flow of long-term debt (ex. IMF)	0	728	706	1,350	126	592	-230	2,398	1,337	2,600
Foreign direct investment (net)	0	0	0	0	0	1,462	1,479	2,350	1,144	4,519
Portfolio equity flows	..	0	0	0	150	0	34	13	340	483
Grants (excluding technical coop.)	0	0	0	0	4	140	115	85	139	26
Memo: technical coop. grants	0	0	0	0	0	39	104	79	61	158
NET TRANSFERS	..	**92**	**-417**	**-129**	**-1,291**	**714**	**-267**	**3,437**	**1,369**	**5,642**
Interest on long-term debt	..	636	1,123	1,479	1,533	1,437	1,614	1,343	1,501	1,877
Profit remittances on FDI	0	0	0	0	37	43	51	66	90	110
3. MAJOR ECONOMIC AGGREGATES										
Gross national product (GNP)	..	21,774	27,477	27,774	31,641	31,985	35,608	37,294	39,976	42,924
Exports of goods & services (XGS)	..	..	11,276	12,015	12,315	12,535	13,926	11,419	11,441	17,939
of which workers remittances	..	..	0	0	0	0	0	0	0	6
Imports of goods & services (MGS)	..	..	11,965	12,733	12,724	12,999	14,432	16,415	16,404	21,528
International reserves (RES)	..	..	2,121	1,846	1,186	4,028	4,462	6,816	6,853	12,095
Current account balance	..	..	-572	-588	379	403	352	-4,263	-4,054	-2,535
4. DEBT INDICATORS										
EDT / XGS (%)	..	..	173.9	169.8	172.8	180.5	157.8	212.4	245.5	174.2
EDT / GNP (%)	..	44.8	71.4	73.4	67.2	70.7	61.7	65.0	70.2	72.8
TDS / XGS (%)	..	..	31.2	29.7	34.3	31.9	35.7	38.7	49.3	39.1
INT / XGS (%)	..	..	11.6	13.4	13.7	13.2	13.3	13.3	15.1	11.8
INT / GNP (%)	..	5.0	4.8	5.8	5.3	5.2	5.2	4.1	4.3	4.9
RES / EDT (%)	..	..	10.8	9.1	5.6	17.8	20.3	28.1	24.4	38.7
RES / MGS (months)	..	..	2.1	1.7	1.1	3.7	3.7	5.0	5.0	6.7
Short-term / EDT (%)	..	34.3	17.1	16.2	13.8	9.6	10.4	8.3	8.5	10.3
Concessional / EDT (%)	..	5.6	0.4	0.4	0.4	0.4	0.5	0.8	1.2	1.7
Multilateral / EDT (%)	..	0.0	8.6	9.0	12.0	14.7	14.7	13.3	12.3	10.5

HUNGARY

(US$ million, unless otherwise indicated)

	1970	1980	1988	1989	1990	1991	1992	1993	1994	1995
5. LONG-TERM DEBT										
DEBT OUTSTANDING (LDOD)	..	**6,416**	**15,612**	**16,634**	**18,006**	**19,188**	**18,485**	**21,014**	**24,545**	**27,660**
Public and publicly guaranteed	..	**6,416**	**15,612**	**16,634**	**18,006**	**18,931**	**17,843**	**19,796**	**22,157**	**23,572**
Official creditors	..	542	1,760	1,994	2,715	3,857	3,835	3,906	4,288	4,182
Multilateral	..	0	1,679	1,842	2,555	3,337	3,226	3,219	3,465	3,282
Concessional	..	0	66	58	62	66	64	91	130	178
Bilateral	..	542	81	152	160	520	609	688	823	900
Concessional	..	542	10	18	19	15	51	98	202	368
Private creditors	..	5,874	13,852	14,640	15,292	15,075	14,009	15,889	17,869	19,389
Bonds	..	25	2,530	3,384	4,657	6,009	6,780	10,087	13,456	15,755
Commercial banks	..	5,523	9,913	10,249	9,647	8,134	6,419	5,131	3,934	3,314
Other private	..	326	1,409	1,007	988	932	809	671	479	321
Private nonguaranteed	**0**	**0**	**0**	**0**	**0**	**257**	**642**	**1,218**	**2,388**	**4,089**
Bonds	..	0	0	0	0	0	0	0	0	0
Commercial banks	..	0	0	0	0	257	642	1,218	2,388	4,089
Memo:										
IBRD	0	0	1,147	1,275	1,513	1,819	1,968	2,095	2,208	2,218
IDA	0	0	0	0	0	0	0	0	0	0
DISBURSEMENTS	..	**1,552**	**2,557**	**3,092**	**2,343**	**2,855**	**2,712**	**5,246**	**5,087**	**6,718**
Public and publicly guaranteed	..	**1,552**	**2,557**	**3,092**	**2,343**	**2,855**	**2,222**	**4,425**	**3,673**	**3,980**
Official creditors	..	187	590	365	728	1,195	457	427	330	558
Multilateral	..	0	578	274	714	848	342	364	234	386
Concessional	..	0	0	0	0	0	13	23	27	77
Bilateral	..	187	12	91	15	347	115	63	96	173
Concessional	..	187	6	9	3	1	41	47	94	173
Private creditors	..	1,365	1,967	2,727	1,615	1,660	1,765	3,998	3,343	3,422
Bonds	..	0	823	952	940	1,234	1,499	3,802	2,835	3,103
Commercial banks	..	1,240	1,029	1,716	575	360	195	147	503	313
Other private	..	125	115	59	99	66	71	49	6	7
Private nonguaranteed	**0**	**0**	**0**	**0**	**0**	**0**	**490**	**821**	**1,414**	**2,737**
Bonds	..	0	0	0	0	0	0	0	0	0
Commercial banks	..	0	0	0	0	0	490	821	1,414	2,737
Memo:										
IBRD	0	0	290	229	268	397	317	229	168	188
IDA	0	0	0	0	0	0	0	0	0	0
PRINCIPAL REPAYMENTS	..	**824**	**1,851**	**1,742**	**2,217**	**2,263**	**2,942**	**2,848**	**3,751**	**4,117**
Public and publicly guaranteed	..	**824**	**1,851**	**1,742**	**2,217**	**2,263**	**2,769**	**2,562**	**3,143**	**3,081**
Official creditors	..	55	237	94	145	152	333	377	272	797
Multilateral	..	0	57	73	125	138	310	342	227	715
Concessional	..	0	0	0	0	0	14	0	0	33
Bilateral	..	55	179	22	19	14	23	35	45	82
Concessional	..	55	157	0	0	5	5	5	5	0
Private creditors	..	769	1,614	1,647	2,073	2,111	2,435	2,186	2,871	2,283
Bonds	..	0	38	20	19	68	522	504	579	1,009
Commercial banks	..	652	1,133	1,447	1,895	1,918	1,747	1,501	2,059	1,088
Other private	..	117	443	180	159	125	166	180	233	186
Private nonguaranteed	**0**	**0**	**0**	**0**	**0**	**0**	**174**	**285**	**608**	**1,036**
Bonds	..	0	0	0	0	0	0	0	0	0
Commercial banks	..	0	0	0	0	0	174	285	608	1,036
Memo:										
IBRD	0	0	56	65	108	135	124	144	196	251
IDA	0	0	0	0	0	0	0	0	0	0
NET FLOWS ON DEBT	..	**728**	**706**	**1,350**	**126**	**592**	**-230**	**2,398**	**1,337**	**2,600**
Public and publicly guaranteed	..	**728**	**706**	**1,350**	**126**	**592**	**-547**	**1,862**	**530**	**900**
Official creditors	..	132	353	270	584	1,043	124	50	57	-239
Multilateral	..	0	520	202	589	710	31	22	6	-330
Concessional	..	0	0	0	0	0	-1	23	27	44
Bilateral	..	132	-167	69	-5	333	92	27	51	91
Concessional	..	132	-151	9	2	-4	36	43	89	173
Private creditors	..	596	353	1,080	-458	-451	-670	1,813	473	1,139
Bonds	..	0	786	932	921	1,166	977	3,297	2,255	2,094
Commercial banks	..	588	-104	269	-1,320	-1,558	-1,553	-1,354	-1,556	-776
Other private	..	8	-329	-122	-59	-59	-95	-131	-227	-180
Private nonguaranteed	**0**	**0**	**0**	**0**	**0**	**0**	**317**	**536**	**807**	**1,701**
Bonds	..	0	0	0	0	0	0	0	0	0
Commercial banks	..	0	0	0	0	0	317	536	807	1,701
Memo:										
IBRD	0	0	234	164	161	262	193	85	-28	-63
IDA	0	0	0	0	0	0	0	0	0	0

HUNGARY

(US$ million, unless otherwise indicated)

	1970	1980	1988	1989	1990	1991	1992	1993	1994	1995
INTEREST PAYMENTS (LINT)	..	**636**	**1,123**	**1,479**	**1,533**	**1,437**	**1,614**	**1,343**	**1,501**	**1,877**
Public and publicly guaranteed	..	**636**	**1,123**	**1,479**	**1,533**	**1,437**	**1,585**	**1,311**	**1,449**	**1,710**
Official creditors	..	12	127	145	187	251	299	277	281	305
Multilateral	..	0	95	138	178	228	262	234	234	244
Concessional	..	0	3	3	4	5	5	5	5	9
Bilateral	..	12	32	7	9	23	37	43	47	61
Concessional	..	12	24	1	1	1	1	2	4	13
Private creditors	..	624	997	1,334	1,346	1,186	1,286	1,034	1,168	1,405
Bonds	..	3	139	175	242	332	490	572	878	1,129
Commercial banks	..	583	694	1,050	1,034	789	739	416	262	242
Other private	..	38	163	110	70	66	56	47	28	34
Private nonguaranteed	**0**	**0**	**0**	**0**	**0**	**0**	**29**	**32**	**52**	**166**
Bonds	..	0	0	0	0	0	0	0	0	0
Commercial banks	..	0	0	0	0	0	29	32	52	166
Memo:										
IBRD	0	0	77	93	106	126	139	147	157	160
IDA	0	0	0	0	0	0	0	0	0	0
NET TRANSFERS ON DEBT	..	**92**	**-417**	**-129**	**-1,407**	**-845**	**-1,844**	**1,055**	**-165**	**724**
Public and publicly guaranteed	..	**92**	**-417**	**-129**	**-1,407**	**-845**	**-2,132**	**551**	**-919**	**-811**
Official creditors	..	120	227	126	396	792	-176	-227	-224	-544
Multilateral	..	0	425	63	410	483	-231	-212	-228	-574
Concessional	..	0	-3	-3	-4	-5	-6	18	22	35
Bilateral	..	120	-199	62	-14	310	55	-15	4	30
Concessional	..	120	-175	8	1	-4	35	40	85	160
Private creditors	..	-28	-644	-255	-1,804	-1,637	-1,956	778	-695	-267
Bonds	..	-3	646	758	679	834	487	2,726	1,377	964
Commercial banks	..	5	-798	-781	-2,354	-2,347	-2,292	-1,769	-1,818	-1,017
Other private	..	-30	-492	-232	-129	-125	-152	-178	-255	-214
Private nonguaranteed	**0**	**0**	**0**	**0**	**0**	**0**	**288**	**504**	**754**	**1,534**
Bonds	..	0	0	0	0	0	0	0	0	0
Commercial banks	..	0	0	0	0	0	288	504	754	1,534
Memo:										
IBRD	0	0	157	71	54	136	54	-62	-185	-223
IDA	0	0	0	0	0	0	0	0	0	0
DEBT SERVICE (LTDS)	..	**1,460**	**2,974**	**3,221**	**3,751**	**3,700**	**4,556**	**4,191**	**5,252**	**5,994**
Public and publicly guaranteed	..	**1,460**	**2,974**	**3,221**	**3,751**	**3,700**	**4,353**	**3,873**	**4,592**	**4,791**
Official creditors	..	67	363	239	332	403	633	653	553	1,102
Multilateral	..	0	152	211	304	366	573	576	462	959
Concessional	..	0	3	3	4	5	19	5	5	42
Bilateral	..	67	211	28	29	37	60	78	92	143
Concessional	..	67	181	2	1	5	6	7	9	13
Private creditors	..	1,393	2,611	2,981	3,418	3,297	3,721	3,220	4,039	3,689
Bonds	..	3	177	194	261	400	1,012	1,076	1,458	2,138
Commercial banks	..	1,236	1,827	2,497	2,930	2,707	2,486	1,917	2,321	1,330
Other private	..	155	607	290	228	190	222	227	261	220
Private nonguaranteed	**0**	**0**	**0**	**0**	**0**	**0**	**203**	**318**	**660**	**1,203**
Bonds	..	0	0	0	0	0	0	0	0	0
Commercial banks	..	0	0	0	0	0	203	318	660	1,203
Memo:										
IBRD	0	0	133	158	214	261	264	292	353	411
IDA	0	0	0	0	0	0	0	0	0	0
UNDISBURSED DEBT	..	**930**	**1,200**	**1,536**	**2,874**	**2,738**	**2,587**	**3,079**	**2,206**	**2,170**
Official creditors	..	141	709	767	1,979	1,862	1,869	2,031	1,928	1,504
Private creditors	..	789	491	769	895	876	718	1,048	277	666
Memorandum items										
Concessional LDOD	..	542	76	76	81	81	115	189	331	546
Variable rate LDOD	..	2,553	9,917	10,708	10,893	10,944	9,705	9,194	10,180	11,034
Public sector LDOD	..	6,416	15,612	16,634	18,006	18,931	17,843	19,796	22,157	23,572
Private sector LDOD	..	0	0	0	0	257	642	1,218	2,388	4,089
6. CURRENCY COMPOSITION OF LONG-TERM DEBT (PERCENT)										
Deutsche mark	..	0.0	19.8	23.1	26.2	25.9	27.5	27.3	29.8	29.8
French franc	..	0.0	0.1	0.1	0.1	0.1	0.1	0.9	0.9	0.8
Japanese yen	..	2.9	28.7	26.0	25.3	28.3	29.9	32.7	31.9	35.1
Pound sterling	..	0.0	0.1	0.0	0.3	0.1	0.0	0.8	0.7	0.6
Swiss franc	..	0.0	4.2	3.8	3.9	2.3	1.6	1.8	1.9	2.6
U.S.dollars	..	1.8	20.6	20.8	18.5	15.5	14.0	13.3	11.2	10.5
Multiple currency	..	95.3	22.5	21.3	17.8	16.9	16.8	14.1	13.5	12.2
Special drawing rights	..	0.0	0.0	0.0	0.0	0.0	0.0	0.0	0.0	0.0
All other currencies	..	0.0	3.9	4.9	8.0	10.9	10.1	9.0	10.1	8.4

HUNGARY

(US$ million, unless otherwise indicated)

	1970	1980	1988	1989	1990	1991	1992	1993	1994	1995
7. DEBT RESTRUCTURINGS										
Total amount rescheduled	0	0	0	0	0	0	0	0	0	0
Debt stock rescheduled	0	0	0	0	0	0	0	0	0	0
Principal rescheduled	0	0	0	0	0	0	0	0	0	0
Official	0	0	0	0	0	0	0	0	0	0
Private	0	0	0	0	0	0	0	0	0	0
Interest rescheduled	0	0	0	0	0	0	0	0	0	0
Official	0	0	0	0	0	0	0	0	0	0
Private	0	0	0	0	0	0	0	0	0	0
Debt forgiven	..	..	0	0	0	0	0	0	0	0
Memo: interest forgiven	..	..	0	0	0	0	0	0	0	0
Debt stock reduction	0	0	0	0	0	0	0	0	0	0
of which debt buyback	0	0	0	0	0	0	0	0	0	0
8. DEBT STOCK-FLOW RECONCILIATION										
Total change in debt stocks	..	..	..	787	880	1,348	-649	2,275	3,833	3,165
Net flows on debt	..	..	..	1,134	-397	716	-127	2,146	1,564	2,613
Net change in interest arrears	..	..	..	0	0	0	0	0	0	0
Interest capitalized	..	..	..	0	0	0	0	0	0	0
Debt forgiveness or reduction	..	..	..	0	0	0	0	0	0	0
Cross-currency valuation	..	..	..	-350	1,330	306	-534	275	2,253	728
Residual	..	..	..	2	-53	326	12	-146	16	-176
9. AVERAGE TERMS OF NEW COMMITMENTS										
ALL CREDITORS										
Interest (%)	..	9.8	7.3	8.9	9.0	8.4	8.2	7.5	7.6	6.2
Maturity (years)	..	13.2	9.9	9.2	9.8	9.7	9.5	9.1	7.2	10.3
Grace period (years)	..	3.0	6.3	4.9	5.1	5.8	6.8	7.7	6.5	9.6
Grant element (%)	..	-0.5	13.5	6.1	4.7	9.0	9.1	12.9	10.6	23.2
Official creditors										
Interest (%)	..	2.5	7.9	7.5	8.6	6.9	6.8	6.5	7.4	4.7
Maturity (years)	..	15.2	14.0	14.6	12.0	13.1	15.4	15.1	10.3	13.6
Grace period (years)	..	1.2	6.8	5.5	5.2	5.3	5.3	5.5	3.9	3.4
Grant element (%)	..	37.5	11.8	14.2	7.1	16.2	18.2	20.2	11.1	27.4
Private creditors										
Interest (%)	..	10.3	7.1	9.1	9.4	9.3	8.7	7.7	7.6	6.3
Maturity (years)	..	13.0	8.3	8.4	7.2	7.5	7.6	8.0	7.0	10.1
Grace period (years)	..	3.2	6.1	4.8	5.0	6.2	7.2	8.0	6.6	10.1
Grant element (%)	..	-3.1	14.2	5.0	2.0	4.3	6.2	11.6	10.6	22.9
Memorandum items										
Commitments	..	1,225	2,247	3,466	3,549	2,786	2,190	5,137	2,963	4,032
Official creditors	..	80	630	423	1,891	1,091	537	741	150	284
Private creditors	..	1,145	1,617	3,043	1,658	1,696	1,653	4,396	2,813	3,748

10. CONTRACTUAL OBLIGATIONS ON OUTSTANDING LONG-TERM DEBT

	1996	1997	1998	1999	2000	2001	2002	2003	2004	2005
TOTAL										
Disbursements	1,049	562	278	114	64	42	29	13	12	8
Principal	3,660	3,319	3,952	4,303	3,685	2,230	1,576	1,588	1,707	1,222
Interest	1,725	1,588	1,408	1,205	914	660	496	422	297	197
Official creditors										
Disbursements	621	345	264	107	64	42	29	13	12	8
Principal	581	585	772	738	597	461	435	421	326	270
Interest	296	282	259	217	174	143	116	90	65	46
Bilateral creditors										
Disbursements	185	106	55	19	7	2	1	0	0	0
Principal	98	106	132	109	116	119	119	119	100	86
Interest	45	46	44	40	36	31	26	21	16	12
Multilateral creditors										
Disbursements	436	239	209	88	57	39	28	13	12	8
Principal	483	479	640	629	480	342	316	302	226	183
Interest	251	236	214	177	138	112	90	69	49	34
Private creditors										
Disbursements	428	217	14	6	0	0	0	0	0	0
Principal	3,079	2,734	3,180	3,564	3,089	1,770	1,141	1,168	1,381	953
Interest	1,429	1,306	1,150	988	740	517	380	332	232	152
Commercial banks										
Disbursements	28	19	8	4	0	0	0	0	0	0
Principal	936	702	415	548	362	25	21	8	6	6
Interest	196	150	107	81	38	22	21	20	19	19
Other private										
Disbursements	400	198	7	3	0	0	0	0	0	0
Principal	2,144	2,032	2,765	3,016	2,727	1,745	1,120	1,160	1,375	947
Interest	1,233	1,156	1,043	908	702	495	360	313	212	133

INDIA

(US$ million, unless otherwise indicated)

	1970	1980	1988	1989	1990	1991	1992	1993	1994	1995
1. SUMMARY DEBT DATA										
TOTAL DEBT STOCKS (EDT)	..	**20,581**	**60,627**	**75,557**	**83,862**	**85,516**	**90,120**	**93,968**	**101,501**	**93,766**
Long-term debt (LDOD)	**7,936**	**18,333**	**51,696**	**66,490**	**72,696**	**74,995**	**78,981**	**85,302**	**92,925**	**86,343**
Public and publicly guaranteed	7,836	17,997	50,223	64,939	71,208	73,450	77,776	83,532	86,499	79,725
Private nonguaranteed	100	336	1,473	1,551	1,488	1,545	1,205	1,770	6,427	6,618
Use of IMF credit	**0**	**977**	**2,573**	**1,566**	**2,623**	**3,451**	**4,799**	**5,041**	**4,312**	**2,374**
Short-term debt	..	**1,271**	**6,358**	**7,501**	**8,544**	**7,070**	**6,340**	**3,626**	**4,264**	**5,049**
of which interest arrears on LDOD	..	0	0	0	0	0	0	0	0	0
Official creditors	..	0	0	0	0	0	0	0	0	0
Private creditors	..	0	0	0	0	0	0	0	0	0
Memo: principal arrears on LDOD	..	0	0	0	0	0	0	0	0	0
Official creditors	..	0	0	0	0	0	0	0	0	0
Private creditors	..	0	0	0	0	0	0	0	0	0
Memo: export credits	..	..	4,023	4,968	5,998	6,416	6,541	6,782	8,041	8,045
TOTAL DEBT FLOWS										
Disbursements	**908**	**3,473**	**10,330**	**7,317**	**8,352**	**8,449**	**8,817**	**8,570**	**6,800**	**6,689**
Long-term debt	908	2,450	10,330	7,317	6,598	7,216	7,193	8,247	6,800	6,689
IMF purchases	0	1,023	0	0	1,754	1,233	1,624	323	0	0
Principal repayments	**519**	**765**	**3,160**	**2,974**	**3,395**	**3,363**	**3,641**	**4,162**	**6,003**	**8,499**
Long-term debt	314	755	1,949	1,966	2,670	2,903	3,307	4,027	4,829	6,780
IMF repurchases	205	9	1,210	1,008	726	460	334	134	1,174	1,719
Net flows on debt	**389**	**2,708**	**7,856**	**5,486**	**6,000**	**3,612**	**4,445**	**1,694**	**1,435**	**-1,025**
of which short-term debt	..	..	685	1,143	1,043	-1,474	-730	-2,714	638	785
Interest payments (INT)	..	**642**	**2,799**	**4,068**	**4,828**	**4,572**	**4,118**	**4,200**	**4,255**	**4,624**
Long-term debt	193	503	2,128	3,314	3,795	3,542	3,448	3,561	3,715	4,057
IMF charges	0	4	233	184	134	203	271	271	228	182
Short-term debt	..	134	437	570	899	826	399	367	312	385
Net transfers on debt	..	**2,066**	**5,057**	**1,418**	**1,172**	**-960**	**328**	**-2,505**	**-2,819**	**-5,649**
Total debt service paid (TDS)	..	**1,407**	**5,958**	**7,042**	**8,223**	**7,934**	**7,759**	**8,361**	**10,257**	**13,123**
Long-term debt	507	1,259	4,078	5,280	6,465	6,445	6,755	7,589	8,543	10,838
IMF repurchases and charges	205	14	1,444	1,192	859	663	605	405	1,402	1,901
Short-term debt (interest only)	..	134	437	570	899	826	399	367	312	385
2. AGGREGATE NET RESOURCE FLOWS AND NET TRANSFERS (LONG-TERM)										
NET RESOURCE FLOWS	**787**	**2,422**	**9,228**	**6,469**	**4,708**	**5,019**	**4,859**	**6,818**	**7,932**	**3,282**
Net flow of long-term debt (ex. IMF)	594	1,695	8,381	5,351	3,928	4,313	3,886	4,219	1,971	-91
Foreign direct investment (net)	46	79	91	252	162	141	151	273	620	1,300
Portfolio equity flows	0	0	56	168	105	0	241	1,840	4,729	1,517
Grants (excluding technical coop.)	147	649	700	698	512	565	581	485	612	556
Memo: technical coop. grants	46	151	338	413	341	338	436	387	388	439
NET TRANSFERS	**595**	**1,919**	**7,099**	**3,155**	**913**	**1,477**	**1,411**	**3,257**	**4,217**	**-776**
Interest on long-term debt	193	503	2,128	3,314	3,795	3,542	3,448	3,561	3,715	4,057
Profit remittances on FDI	0	0	0	0	0	0	0	0	0	0
3. MAJOR ECONOMIC AGGREGATES										
Gross national product (GNP)	57,307	172,758	281,096	277,936	301,708	266,808	267,564	257,906	296,757	331,941
Exports of goods & services (XGS)	2,220	15,134	20,835	23,782	26,196	27,059	26,824	32,332	39,995	46,600
of which workers remittances	80	2,786	2,225	2,186	1,947	2,540	2,506	3,080	4,976	4,416
Imports of goods & services (MGS)	2,814	18,105	29,873	31,798	36,458	29,941	30,981	33,761	43,692	53,097
International reserves (RES)	1,023	12,010	9,186	8,048	5,637	7,616	9,539	14,675	24,221	22,865
Current account balance	-591	-2,897	-8,609	-7,946	-10,140	-1,639	-3,890	-684	-2,473	-5,414
4. DEBT INDICATORS										
EDT / XGS (%)	..	136.0	291.0	317.7	320.1	316.0	336.0	290.6	253.8	201.2
EDT / GNP (%)	..	11.9	21.6	27.2	27.8	32.1	33.7	36.4	34.2	28.2
TDS / XGS (%)	..	9.3	28.6	29.6	31.4	29.3	28.9	25.9	25.6	28.2
INT / XGS (%)	..	4.2	13.4	17.1	18.4	16.9	15.4	13.0	10.6	9.9
INT / GNP (%)	..	0.4	1.0	1.5	1.6	1.7	1.5	1.6	1.4	1.4
RES / EDT (%)	..	58.4	15.2	10.7	6.7	8.9	10.6	15.6	23.9	24.4
RES / MGS (months)	4.4	8.0	3.7	3.0	1.9	3.1	3.7	5.2	6.7	5.2
Short-term / EDT (%)	..	6.2	10.5	9.9	10.2	8.3	7.0	3.9	4.2	5.4
Concessional / EDT (%)	..	75.1	40.9	47.2	46.4	45.2	45.7	45.8	46.3	46.5
Multilateral / EDT (%)	..	29.5	29.8	26.0	26.0	28.0	29.0	29.6	31.0	32.0

INDIA

(US$ million, unless otherwise indicated)

	1970	1980	1988	1989	1990	1991	1992	1993	1994	1995
5. LONG-TERM DEBT										
DEBT OUTSTANDING (LDOD)	**7,936**	**18,333**	**51,696**	**66,490**	**72,696**	**74,995**	**78,981**	**85,302**	**92,925**	**86,343**
Public and publicly guaranteed	**7,836**	**17,997**	**50,223**	**64,939**	**71,208**	**73,450**	**77,776**	**83,532**	**86,499**	**79,725**
Official creditors	7,506	16,336	31,191	43,609	48,353	49,420	52,974	55,858	61,885	57,083
Multilateral	1,562	6,070	18,061	19,664	21,768	23,964	26,130	27,826	31,475	29,986
Concessional	1,473	5,400	12,519	13,003	13,839	14,765	15,977	16,659	18,424	18,179
Bilateral	5,945	10,266	13,130	23,945	26,584	25,457	26,844	28,032	30,410	27,097
Concessional	5,450	10,053	12,248	22,650	25,111	23,866	25,208	26,385	28,609	25,397
Private creditors	330	1,661	19,032	21,330	22,855	24,030	24,803	27,674	24,613	22,642
Bonds	2	2	1,846	2,479	2,707	4,169	4,088	3,903	3,853	3,279
Commercial banks	45	1,498	12,938	14,727	16,145	16,018	16,954	18,586	14,439	13,526
Other private	283	161	4,248	4,125	4,003	3,843	3,760	5,185	6,321	5,837
Private nonguaranteed	**100**	**336**	**1,473**	**1,551**	**1,488**	**1,545**	**1,205**	**1,770**	**6,427**	**6,618**
Bonds	0	0	0	0	0	0	0	794	1,158	1,020
Commercial banks	100	336	1,473	1,551	1,488	1,545	1,205	976	5,268	5,598
Memo:										
IBRD	496	827	5,590	6,615	7,685	8,459	9,067	9,870	11,120	9,849
IDA	1,065	5,142	12,019	12,521	13,312	14,203	15,339	15,978	17,666	17,499
DISBURSEMENTS	**908**	**2,450**	**10,330**	**7,317**	**6,598**	**7,216**	**7,193**	**8,247**	**6,800**	**6,689**
Public and publicly guaranteed	**883**	**2,165**	**10,155**	**7,077**	**6,384**	**6,907**	**6,940**	**7,187**	**5,933**	**5,510**
Official creditors	842	1,492	3,635	3,559	3,570	4,367	4,170	3,661	3,305	2,932
Multilateral	101	863	2,625	2,105	2,211	2,758	2,424	2,084	2,221	1,894
Concessional	83	712	796	581	818	1,022	1,280	719	1,003	759
Bilateral	741	629	1,010	1,453	1,360	1,610	1,746	1,577	1,083	1,038
Concessional	687	571	846	962	1,130	1,424	1,628	1,404	903	808
Private creditors	41	673	6,520	3,519	2,814	2,540	2,769	3,526	2,629	2,578
Bonds	0	0	679	705	427	1,619	0	0	0	0
Commercial banks	16	639	3,361	2,623	1,983	509	2,129	1,504	845	1,258
Other private	25	34	2,480	190	404	413	640	2,021	1,784	1,320
Private nonguaranteed	**25**	**285**	**175**	**240**	**214**	**309**	**254**	**1,060**	**867**	**1,179**
Bonds	0	0	0	0	0	0	0	794	367	520
Commercial banks	25	285	175	240	214	309	254	266	500	659
Memo:										
IBRD	41	174	1,717	1,445	1,219	1,231	852	1,216	741	589
IDA	60	652	755	566	762	953	1,186	669	966	729
PRINCIPAL REPAYMENTS	**314**	**755**	**1,949**	**1,966**	**2,670**	**2,903**	**3,307**	**4,027**	**4,829**	**6,780**
Public and publicly guaranteed	**289**	**664**	**1,670**	**1,644**	**2,351**	**2,630**	**3,001**	**3,532**	**4,705**	**6,624**
Official creditors	236	587	991	1,117	1,226	1,466	1,610	1,892	2,412	3,799
Multilateral	40	86	397	467	609	703	838	1,000	1,103	1,515
Concessional	30	44	113	126	151	180	184	206	227	267
Bilateral	196	500	594	651	618	763	772	892	1,309	2,283
Concessional	137	473	531	520	562	673	695	751	1,139	2,093
Private creditors	53	78	679	527	1,125	1,164	1,391	1,641	2,294	2,826
Bonds	0	0	14	27	280	239	206	338	381	310
Commercial banks	10	34	367	223	269	320	469	650	992	1,681
Other private	43	44	298	277	577	605	717	653	920	835
Private nonguaranteed	**25**	**91**	**280**	**322**	**318**	**273**	**306**	**495**	**123**	**156**
Bonds	0	0	0	0	0	0	0	0	0	0
Commercial banks	25	91	280	322	318	273	306	495	123	156
Memo:										
IBRD	40	71	303	352	472	527	634	758	827	943
IDA	0	15	81	98	114	141	155	174	194	226
NET FLOWS ON DEBT	**594**	**1,695**	**8,381**	**5,351**	**3,928**	**4,313**	**3,886**	**4,219**	**1,971**	**-91**
Public and publicly guaranteed	**594**	**1,501**	**8,485**	**5,433**	**4,033**	**4,277**	**3,938**	**3,654**	**1,228**	**-1,114**
Official creditors	606	906	2,644	2,441	2,344	2,901	2,560	1,770	893	-867
Multilateral	61	777	2,228	1,639	1,602	2,054	1,587	1,084	1,118	379
Concessional	53	668	683	455	667	841	1,096	513	776	492
Bilateral	545	129	416	803	742	847	974	685	-225	-1,245
Concessional	550	98	315	442	567	751	933	653	-235	-1,285
Private creditors	-12	595	5,841	2,992	1,689	1,376	1,378	1,885	335	-248
Bonds	0	0	665	678	147	1,380	-206	-338	-381	-310
Commercial banks	6	605	2,995	2,400	1,715	188	1,660	855	-148	-423
Other private	-18	-10	2,181	-87	-173	-192	-77	1,368	864	485
Private nonguaranteed	**0**	**194**	**-104**	**-82**	**-104**	**36**	**-53**	**565**	**744**	**1,023**
Bonds	0	0	0	0	0	0	0	794	367	520
Commercial banks	0	194	-104	-82	-104	36	-53	-229	376	503
Memo:										
IBRD	1	103	1,414	1,094	747	703	219	458	-86	-354
IDA	60	637	675	468	648	812	1,030	495	773	503

INDIA

(US$ million, unless otherwise indicated)

	1970	1980	1988	1989	1990	1991	1992	1993	1994	1995
INTEREST PAYMENTS (LINT)	**193**	**503**	**2,128**	**3,314**	**3,795**	**3,542**	**3,448**	**3,561**	**3,715**	**4,057**
Public and publicly guaranteed	**187**	**473**	**2,002**	**3,174**	**3,660**	**3,416**	**3,325**	**3,422**	**3,324**	**3,526**
Official creditors	164	348	941	1,352	1,493	1,510	1,629	1,684	1,826	1,889
Multilateral	34	101	581	640	738	796	899	943	1,014	1,059
Concessional	29	47	112	103	110	117	126	138	147	160
Bilateral	130	247	360	712	755	714	730	741	812	830
Concessional	105	234	294	621	638	605	625	634	695	699
Private creditors	22	125	1,061	1,822	2,167	1,906	1,695	1,738	1,498	1,636
Bonds	0	0	108	147	187	200	234	342	214	195
Commercial banks	3	113	788	1,520	1,755	1,430	1,201	1,142	874	985
Other private	19	12	165	156	226	277	260	254	411	457
Private nonguaranteed	**6**	**30**	**127**	**140**	**135**	**126**	**123**	**139**	**391**	**531**
Bonds	0	0	0	0	0	0	0	1	20	56
Commercial banks	6	30	127	140	135	126	123	138	371	475
Memo:										
IBRD	27	66	474	529	615	643	709	721	768	770
IDA	7	35	98	90	97	101	109	114	121	131
NET TRANSFERS ON DEBT	**401**	**1,191**	**6,253**	**2,037**	**133**	**771**	**438**	**658**	**-1,743**	**-4,149**
Public and publicly guaranteed	**407**	**1,027**	**6,484**	**2,259**	**373**	**861**	**614**	**232**	**-2,096**	**-4,640**
Official creditors	441	557	1,703	1,090	851	1,391	931	85	-933	-2,756
Multilateral	26	676	1,647	999	864	1,259	688	141	104	-681
Concessional	24	621	571	352	558	725	970	376	629	332
Bilateral	415	-118	56	91	-13	133	244	-56	-1,037	-2,075
Concessional	446	-136	20	-179	-71	146	309	19	-930	-1,984
Private creditors	-34	470	4,781	1,170	-479	-530	-317	147	-1,163	-1,884
Bonds	0	0	557	532	-40	1,180	-440	-680	-595	-505
Commercial banks	3	492	2,207	880	-40	-1,241	460	-287	-1,021	-1,407
Other private	-37	-22	2,017	-242	-399	-469	-337	1,114	453	29
Private nonguaranteed	**-6**	**164**	**-231**	**-222**	**-239**	**-90**	**-176**	**426**	**353**	**492**
Bonds	0	0	0	0	0	0	0	793	347	464
Commercial banks	-6	164	-231	-222	-239	-90	-176	-368	6	28
Memo:										
IBRD	-26	37	940	564	132	61	-490	-263	-853	-1,124
IDA	52	602	576	378	551	711	922	381	651	372
DEBT SERVICE (LTDS)	**507**	**1,259**	**4,078**	**5,280**	**6,465**	**6,445**	**6,755**	**7,589**	**8,543**	**10,838**
Public and publicly guaranteed	**476**	**1,138**	**3,671**	**4,818**	**6,011**	**6,047**	**6,326**	**6,955**	**8,029**	**10,150**
Official creditors	400	935	1,932	2,469	2,719	2,976	3,239	3,576	4,237	5,688
Multilateral	74	187	978	1,106	1,347	1,499	1,736	1,943	2,117	2,574
Concessional	59	91	225	229	260	297	310	343	374	427
Bilateral	326	748	954	1,363	1,372	1,477	1,503	1,633	2,120	3,114
Concessional	242	706	825	1,141	1,200	1,278	1,319	1,385	1,833	2,792
Private creditors	75	203	1,739	2,349	3,293	3,070	3,087	3,379	3,792	4,462
Bonds	0	0	122	174	467	439	440	680	595	505
Commercial banks	12	147	1,154	1,743	2,023	1,750	1,669	1,792	1,866	2,665
Other private	63	56	463	432	803	882	977	907	1,331	1,292
Private nonguaranteed	**31**	**121**	**406**	**462**	**453**	**399**	**429**	**634**	**514**	**688**
Bonds	0	0	0	0	0	0	0	1	20	56
Commercial banks	31	121	406	462	453	399	429	633	494	631
Memo:										
IBRD	67	137	777	881	1,087	1,170	1,342	1,479	1,595	1,714
IDA	7	50	179	188	211	242	264	289	315	357
UNDISBURSED DEBT	**1,664**	**7,825**	**19,205**	**23,079**	**24,725**	**24,483**	**22,114**	**21,928**	**20,762**	**17,705**
Official creditors	1,502	6,928	18,661	21,827	22,389	22,221	18,991	17,678	18,184	16,456
Private creditors	162	898	544	1,252	2,335	2,262	3,124	4,249	2,578	1,248
Memorandum items										
Concessional LDOD	6,924	15,453	24,766	35,653	38,950	38,630	41,185	43,043	47,033	43,576
Variable rate LDOD	100	790	9,190	11,015	12,180	13,380	13,906	15,684	21,571	21,047
Public sector LDOD	7,512	17,583	49,652	64,367	70,670	72,926	77,259	83,009	85,970	79,266
Private sector LDOD	425	750	2,044	2,123	2,026	2,069	1,723	2,293	6,955	7,077

6. CURRENCY COMPOSITION OF LONG-TERM DEBT (PERCENT)

	1970	1980	1988	1989	1990	1991	1992	1993	1994	1995
Deutsche mark	9.7	10.0	7.0	6.2	6.0	6.4	6.4	5.8	6.7	6.5
French franc	1.3	2.3	2.0	1.8	1.7	2.0	2.0	1.8	2.0	2.1
Japanese yen	5.2	6.7	11.0	8.5	9.6	10.8	12.0	13.6	15.4	13.7
Pound sterling	24.7	26.8	9.1	6.9	6.2	6.2	5.5	4.9	4.6	4.8
Swiss franc	0.4	0.1	0.8	0.8	0.7	0.7	0.7	0.7	0.9	0.9
U.S.dollars	41.3	39.3	54.1	61.5	60.5	57.3	56.1	56.0	51.4	53.3
Multiple currency	6.3	6.4	11.0	10.1	10.9	12.4	13.1	13.5	15.3	14.9
Special drawing rights	0.0	0.0	0.0	0.0	0.3	0.3	0.3	0.2	0.2	0.2
All other currencies	11.1	8.4	5.0	4.3	4.0	4.0	4.0	3.3	3.4	3.5

INDIA

(US$ million, unless otherwise indicated)

	1970	1980	1988	1989	1990	1991	1992	1993	1994	1995
7. DEBT RESTRUCTURINGS										
Total amount rescheduled	0	0	0	0	0	0	0	0	0	0
Debt stock rescheduled	0	0	0	0	0	0	0	0	0	0
Principal rescheduled	0	0	0	0	0	0	0	0	0	0
Official	0	0	0	0	0	0	0	0	0	0
Private	0	0	0	0	0	0	0	0	0	0
Interest rescheduled	0	0	0	0	0	0	0	0	0	0
Official	0	0	0	0	0	0	0	0	0	0
Private	0	0	0	0	0	0	0	0	0	0
Debt forgiven	..	..	0	0	0	0	0	0	0	0
Memo: interest forgiven	..	..	0	0	0	0	0	0	0	0
Debt stock reduction	0	0	0	0	0	0	0	0	0	0
of which debt buyback	0	0	0	0	0	0	0	0	0	0
8. DEBT STOCK-FLOW RECONCILIATION										
Total change in debt stocks	..	..	..	14,930	8,305	1,654	4,604	3,849	7,533	-7,735
Net flows on debt	..	..	..	5,486	6,000	3,612	4,445	1,694	1,435	-1,025
Net change in interest arrears	..	..	..	0	0	0	0	0	0	0
Interest capitalized	..	..	..	0	0	0	0	0	0	0
Debt forgiveness or reduction	..	..	..	0	0	0	0	0	0	0
Cross-currency valuation	..	..	..	-276	1,239	797	1,162	1,376	6,044	-3,782
Residual	..	..	..	9,720	1,067	-2,755	-1,004	779	54	-2,928
9. AVERAGE TERMS OF NEW COMMITMENTS										
ALL CREDITORS										
Interest (%)	2.5	5.6	6.2	5.8	5.2	5.8	5.0	6.1	3.6	4.1
Maturity (years)	34.1	32.5	18.0	19.3	22.4	20.2	23.3	18.0	24.2	18.7
Grace period (years)	8.2	7.4	6.4	6.4	7.8	6.8	6.8	5.1	7.8	6.5
Grant element (%)	60.8	42.9	24.1	28.7	35.8	31.5	36.3	25.9	46.8	38.0
Official creditors										
Interest (%)	2.2	2.5	5.4	4.5	3.8	4.2	3.5	3.9	3.4	4.6
Maturity (years)	35.5	40.7	24.7	22.9	28.8	25.7	29.6	26.6	27.7	23.9
Grace period (years)	8.5	8.6	6.6	5.7	8.4	7.4	6.7	7.6	8.7	6.7
Grant element (%)	63.7	65.0	34.2	38.4	50.1	44.3	51.4	47.1	53.0	40.7
Private creditors										
Interest (%)	6.3	14.0	7.0	8.1	6.7	9.5	7.2	7.7	5.0	3.1
Maturity (years)	12.9	10.7	12.0	12.8	15.3	7.7	14.1	11.3	7.1	7.9
Grace period (years)	4.5	4.0	6.2	7.6	7.1	5.3	6.9	3.3	3.1	6.0
Grant element (%)	19.1	-15.5	15.1	10.9	20.0	2.6	14.5	9.5	16.0	32.6
Memorandum items										
Commitments	954	5,158	11,985	11,930	8,220	7,946	8,914	8,264	4,740	3,965
Official creditors	892	3,745	5,619	7,707	4,318	5,509	5,261	3,596	3,951	2,673
Private creditors	62	1,413	6,366	4,223	3,903	2,437	3,653	4,667	789	1,293

10. CONTRACTUAL OBLIGATIONS ON OUTSTANDING LONG-TERM DEBT

	1996	1997	1998	1999	2000	2001	2002	2003	2004	2005
TOTAL										
Disbursements	5,826	4,608	3,076	1,944	1,154	526	293	129	84	65
Principal	7,756	5,795	5,700	5,815	5,288	4,737	5,809	4,435	4,067	3,915
Interest	3,914	3,592	3,398	3,169	2,937	2,681	2,449	2,189	2,002	1,841
Official creditors										
Disbursements	4,996	4,298	2,974	1,939	1,153	526	293	129	84	65
Principal	2,911	3,118	3,210	3,280	3,292	3,360	3,419	3,428	3,386	3,293
Interest	1,880	1,891	1,850	1,771	1,676	1,544	1,410	1,275	1,139	1,010
Bilateral creditors										
Disbursements	1,827	1,579	934	541	276	135	59	7	2	0
Principal	1,556	1,618	1,580	1,565	1,468	1,502	1,589	1,574	1,561	1,508
Interest	767	761	733	695	659	607	563	515	468	423
Multilateral creditors										
Disbursements	3,169	2,719	2,040	1,398	877	391	234	122	82	65
Principal	1,355	1,500	1,631	1,715	1,824	1,858	1,830	1,853	1,825	1,785
Interest	1,113	1,130	1,117	1,076	1,018	937	847	759	671	587
Private creditors										
Disbursements	830	310	102	5	1	0	0	0	0	0
Principal	4,845	2,677	2,490	2,535	1,996	1,377	2,390	1,007	681	622
Interest	2,034	1,702	1,547	1,398	1,261	1,138	1,039	914	864	831
Commercial banks										
Disbursements	155	60	17	0	0	0	0	0	0	0
Principal	1,201	990	701	645	446	356	1,247	135	125	114
Interest	913	855	806	768	733	715	678	627	620	614
Other private										
Disbursements	675	251	85	5	1	0	0	0	0	0
Principal	3,644	1,687	1,789	1,890	1,549	1,021	1,143	872	556	508
Interest	1,121	847	741	630	528	423	361	287	244	217

INDONESIA

(US$ million, unless otherwise indicated)

	1970	1980	1988	1989	1990	1991	1992	1993	1994	1995
1. SUMMARY DEBT DATA										
TOTAL DEBT STOCKS (EDT)	..	**20,938**	**54,079**	**59,402**	**69,872**	**79,548**	**88,004**	**89,148**	**96,543**	**107,831**
Long-term debt (LDOD)	**2,948**	**18,163**	**46,729**	**50,818**	**58,242**	**65,067**	**69,947**	**71,161**	**79,434**	**85,481**
Public and publicly guaranteed	2,487	15,021	41,183	44,262	47,982	51,891	53,666	57,132	63,891	65,347
Private nonguaranteed	461	3,142	5,545	6,556	10,261	13,176	16,281	14,029	15,543	20,134
Use of IMF credit	**139**	**0**	**623**	**608**	**494**	**166**	**0**	**0**	**0**	**0**
Short-term debt	..	**2,775**	**6,727**	**7,975**	**11,135**	**14,315**	**18,057**	**17,987**	**17,109**	**22,350**
of which interest arrears on LDOD	..	0	0	0	0	0	0	0	0	0
Official creditors	..	0	0	0	0	0	0	0	0	0
Private creditors	..	0	0	0	0	0	0	0	0	0
Memo: principal arrears on LDOD	..	0	74	71	1	1	1	1	0	0
Official creditors	..	0	73	71	1	1	1	1	0	0
Private creditors	..	0	1	0	0	0	0	0	0	0
Memo: export credits	..	..	8,349	8,364	10,032	11,535	13,656	15,125	17,722	20,215
TOTAL DEBT FLOWS										
Disbursements	**674**	**3,246**	**8,180**	**9,009**	**10,024**	**11,758**	**13,558**	**8,064**	**12,538**	**13,728**
Long-term debt	636	3,246	8,180	9,009	10,024	11,758	13,558	8,064	12,538	13,728
IMF purchases	38	0	0	0	0	0	0	0	0	0
Principal repayments	**123**	**1,633**	**5,297**	**5,994**	**5,969**	**6,858**	**7,944**	**9,144**	**8,955**	**10,199**
Long-term debt	120	1,633	5,241	5,994	5,812	6,541	7,781	9,144	8,955	10,199
IMF repurchases	3	0	56	0	157	317	163	0	0	0
Net flows on debt	**551**	**1,613**	**3,250**	**4,263**	**7,216**	**8,080**	**9,356**	**-1,149**	**2,704**	**8,770**
of which short-term debt	..	..	367	1,248	3,160	3,180	3,742	-70	-878	5,241
Interest payments (INT)	..	**1,452**	**3,345**	**3,839**	**3,978**	**4,618**	**4,513**	**4,952**	**5,316**	**6,220**
Long-term debt	46	1,182	2,955	3,348	3,413	3,770	3,771	4,112	4,174	4,935
IMF charges	0	0	41	51	59	31	5	0	0	0
Short-term debt	..	270	349	440	506	816	737	840	1,142	1,284
Net transfers on debt	..	**161**	**-96**	**424**	**3,238**	**3,462**	**4,843**	**-6,101**	**-2,612**	**2,551**
Total debt service paid (TDS)	..	**3,084**	**8,642**	**9,833**	**9,946**	**11,475**	**12,457**	**14,095**	**14,272**	**16,419**
Long-term debt	165	2,814	8,195	9,342	9,224	10,311	11,552	13,255	13,130	15,134
IMF repurchases and charges	3	0	98	51	216	348	168	0	0	0
Short-term debt (interest only)	..	270	349	440	506	816	737	840	1,142	1,284
2. AGGREGATE NET RESOURCE FLOWS AND NET TRANSFERS (LONG-TERM)										
NET RESOURCE FLOWS	**686**	**1,902**	**3,716**	**4,110**	**5,901**	**6,961**	**7,970**	**3,596**	**9,581**	**12,999**
Net flow of long-term debt (ex. IMF)	517	1,613	2,939	3,015	4,213	5,217	5,777	-1,079	3,582	3,529
Foreign direct investment (net)	83	180	576	682	1,093	1,482	1,777	2,004	2,109	4,348
Portfolio equity flows	0	0	0	199	312	0	119	2,452	3,672	4,873
Grants (excluding technical coop.)	87	109	201	214	283	263	298	219	218	249
Memo: technical coop. grants	26	187	348	373	407	451	437	430	447	496
NET TRANSFERS	**513**	**-2,514**	**-557**	**-1,032**	**296**	**873**	**1,576**	**-3,093**	**2,606**	**5,064**
Interest on long-term debt	46	1,182	2,955	3,348	3,413	3,770	3,771	4,112	4,174	4,935
Profit remittances on FDI	128	3,234	1,318	1,794	2,192	2,318	2,623	2,577	2,800	3,000
3. MAJOR ECONOMIC AGGREGATES										
Gross national product (GNP)	9,698	74,806	84,682	96,894	109,209	122,573	132,938	151,992	168,892	189,370
Exports of goods & services (XGS)	..	..	21,469	25,578	29,870	33,504	38,234	41,940	46,517	53,134
of which workers remittances	..	..	99	167	166	130	229	346	449	629
Imports of goods & services (MGS)	..	..	23,021	26,858	33,110	37,896	41,356	44,237	49,479	60,367
International reserves (RES)	160	6,803	6,322	6,699	8,657	10,358	11,482	12,474	13,321	14,908
Current account balance	..	..	-1,397	-1,108	-2,988	-4,260	-2,780	-2,106	-2,792	-7,023
4. DEBT INDICATORS										
EDT / XGS (%)	..	..	251.9	232.2	233.9	237.4	230.2	212.6	207.5	202.9
EDT / GNP (%)	..	28.0	63.9	61.3	64.0	64.9	66.2	58.7	57.2	56.9
TDS / XGS (%)	..	..	40.3	38.4	33.3	34.3	32.6	33.6	30.7	30.9
INT / XGS (%)	..	..	15.6	15.0	13.3	13.8	11.8	11.8	11.4	11.7
INT / GNP (%)	..	1.9	4.0	4.0	3.6	3.8	3.4	3.3	3.1	3.3
RES / EDT (%)	..	32.5	11.7	11.3	12.4	13.0	13.0	14.0	13.8	13.8
RES / MGS (months)	..	..	3.3	3.0	3.1	3.3	3.3	3.4	3.2	3.0
Short-term / EDT (%)	..	13.3	12.4	13.4	15.9	18.0	20.5	20.2	17.7	20.7
Concessional / EDT (%)	..	36.4	27.8	26.7	26.7	26.8	25.6	28.1	30.1	27.1
Multilateral / EDT (%)	..	8.8	19.9	20.0	20.4	20.1	18.7	20.0	19.8	18.6

INDONESIA

(US$ million, unless otherwise indicated)

	1970	1980	1988	1989	1990	1991	1992	1993	1994	1995
5. LONG-TERM DEBT										
DEBT OUTSTANDING (LDOD)	**2,948**	**18,163**	**46,729**	**50,818**	**58,242**	**65,067**	**69,947**	**71,161**	**79,434**	**85,481**
Public and publicly guaranteed	**2,487**	**15,021**	**41,183**	**44,262**	**47,982**	**51,891**	**53,666**	**57,132**	**63,891**	**65,347**
Official creditors	2,205	9,563	26,378	28,103	33,007	37,589	40,070	44,282	49,976	51,231
Multilateral	6	1,834	10,741	11,904	14,285	15,996	16,424	17,822	19,163	20,010
Concessional	6	661	1,180	1,298	1,600	1,895	2,103	2,419	2,827	2,987
Bilateral	2,199	7,729	15,637	16,198	18,722	21,593	23,646	26,460	30,813	31,221
Concessional	1,981	6,961	13,868	14,570	17,088	19,388	20,415	22,654	26,208	26,275
Private creditors	282	5,458	14,805	16,159	14,975	14,303	13,596	12,850	13,915	14,116
Bonds	0	199	944	763	696	680	580	99	99	704
Commercial banks	1	2,431	6,724	9,593	8,606	8,290	8,076	7,631	7,354	6,569
Other private	281	2,828	7,138	5,803	5,673	5,332	4,940	5,120	6,463	6,844
Private nonguaranteed	**461**	**3,142**	**5,545**	**6,556**	**10,261**	**13,176**	**16,281**	**14,029**	**15,543**	**20,134**
Bonds	0	0	0	0	120	515	751	1,233	1,750	3,420
Commercial banks	461	3,142	5,545	6,556	10,141	12,661	15,530	12,796	13,794	16,714
Memo:										
IBRD	0	1,040	8,003	8,542	9,542	10,597	10,640	11,283	12,008	12,503
IDA	5	566	861	854	842	829	814	796	776	756
DISBURSEMENTS	**636**	**3,246**	**8,180**	**9,009**	**10,024**	**11,758**	**13,558**	**8,064**	**12,538**	**13,728**
Public and publicly guaranteed	**441**	**2,551**	**6,387**	**6,942**	**5,009**	**6,944**	**7,855**	**6,869**	**7,618**	**6,765**
Official creditors	376	1,130	4,180	4,276	3,969	5,103	5,087	4,470	4,906	4,239
Multilateral	4	431	2,200	1,964	1,794	2,082	1,649	1,872	1,853	1,776
Concessional	4	48	114	137	239	288	266	298	292	251
Bilateral	372	698	1,981	2,312	2,175	3,021	3,438	2,598	3,053	2,463
Concessional	372	592	1,488	2,143	1,979	2,206	2,050	1,753	2,254	1,913
Private creditors	66	1,421	2,207	2,666	1,041	1,841	2,767	2,400	2,711	2,526
Bonds	0	45	171	0	0	0	0	0	0	605
Commercial banks	0	1,013	1,375	2,222	487	1,109	1,723	1,128	760	865
Other private	66	363	661	444	554	732	1,044	1,272	1,952	1,057
Private nonguaranteed	**195**	**695**	**1,793**	**2,067**	**5,015**	**4,814**	**5,703**	**1,195**	**4,920**	**6,963**
Bonds	0	0	0	0	120	393	244	485	495	1,763
Commercial banks	195	695	1,793	2,067	4,895	4,421	5,460	710	4,425	5,200
Memo:										
IBRD	0	331	1,648	1,256	987	1,398	1,003	1,195	1,184	1,045
IDA	3	42	1	1	0	0	0	0	0	0
PRINCIPAL REPAYMENTS	**120**	**1,633**	**5,241**	**5,994**	**5,812**	**6,541**	**7,781**	**9,144**	**8,955**	**10,199**
Public and publicly guaranteed	**59**	**940**	**4,422**	**4,938**	**4,588**	**4,642**	**5,183**	**5,697**	**5,550**	**5,717**
Official creditors	22	324	1,304	1,341	1,586	1,777	1,992	2,143	3,291	3,138
Multilateral	0	38	500	555	677	765	872	1,008	1,888	1,289
Concessional	0	4	14	17	24	30	37	45	57	70
Bilateral	22	286	805	786	909	1,012	1,120	1,135	1,403	1,849
Concessional	19	184	530	516	611	721	816	767	1,035	1,270
Private creditors	37	616	3,118	3,597	3,001	2,865	3,191	3,554	2,259	2,579
Bonds	0	5	330	176	94	12	88	477	0	0
Commercial banks	1	190	1,488	2,094	1,718	1,674	1,912	1,946	1,188	1,678
Other private	37	421	1,301	1,327	1,190	1,178	1,191	1,131	1,071	901
Private nonguaranteed	**61**	**693**	**818**	**1,056**	**1,224**	**1,899**	**2,598**	**3,447**	**3,405**	**4,483**
Bonds	0	0	0	0	0	0	0	0	0	120
Commercial banks	61	693	818	1,056	1,224	1,899	2,598	3,447	3,405	4,363
Memo:										
IBRD	0	31	429	473	551	608	677	765	1,240	955
IDA	0	1	6	8	11	13	15	18	20	20
NET FLOWS ON DEBT	**517**	**1,613**	**2,939**	**3,015**	**4,213**	**5,217**	**5,777**	**-1,079**	**3,582**	**3,529**
Public and publicly guaranteed	**383**	**1,611**	**1,965**	**2,004**	**422**	**2,302**	**2,671**	**1,173**	**2,067**	**1,048**
Official creditors	354	806	2,876	2,935	2,382	3,326	3,095	2,327	1,615	1,101
Multilateral	4	393	1,700	1,409	1,117	1,317	777	864	-35	487
Concessional	4	44	99	120	215	258	229	253	234	182
Bilateral	350	413	1,176	1,526	1,265	2,009	2,318	1,463	1,650	614
Concessional	353	409	958	1,627	1,368	1,484	1,234	986	1,219	643
Private creditors	28	805	-912	-931	-1,961	-1,024	-424	-1,154	452	-53
Bonds	0	40	-158	-176	-94	-12	-88	-477	0	605
Commercial banks	0	823	-114	128	-1,231	-565	-189	-818	-429	-813
Other private	29	-58	-640	-883	-636	-446	-147	141	881	155
Private nonguaranteed	**134**	**2**	**974**	**1,011**	**3,791**	**2,915**	**3,105**	**-2,252**	**1,515**	**2,481**
Bonds	0	0	0	0	120	393	244	485	495	1,643
Commercial banks	134	2	974	1,011	3,671	2,522	2,862	-2,737	1,020	838
Memo:										
IBRD	0	301	1,219	783	436	790	327	430	-56	90
IDA	3	40	-5	-7	-11	-13	-15	-18	-20	-20

INDONESIA

(US$ million, unless otherwise indicated)

	1970	1980	1988	1989	1990	1991	1992	1993	1994	1995
INTEREST PAYMENTS (LINT)	**46**	**1,182**	**2,955**	**3,348**	**3,413**	**3,770**	**3,771**	**4,112**	**4,174**	**4,935**
Public and publicly guaranteed	**25**	**824**	**2,526**	**2,779**	**2,808**	**2,941**	**2,994**	**3,233**	**3,248**	**3,774**
Official creditors	20	312	1,300	1,383	1,585	1,796	2,024	2,259	2,484	2,668
Multilateral	0	107	773	831	990	1,113	1,202	1,273	1,395	1,404
Concessional	0	7	15	17	29	40	58	77	93	111
Bilateral	20	205	527	552	595	683	822	986	1,089	1,265
Concessional	18	130	369	395	451	539	617	708	777	875
Private creditors	5	512	1,226	1,396	1,223	1,145	970	974	764	1,106
Bonds	0	14	89	72	62	50	38	28	5	6
Commercial banks	0	268	527	806	699	673	532	561	372	656
Other private	5	230	609	517	462	422	401	385	387	444
Private nonguaranteed	**21**	**358**	**429**	**570**	**605**	**829**	**777**	**879**	**926**	**1,161**
Bonds	0	0	0	0	0	13	32	41	91	139
Commercial banks	21	358	429	570	605	816	745	838	835	1,022
Memo:										
IBRD	0	89	634	661	731	804	838	855	916	921
IDA	0	4	7	6	6	6	6	6	6	6
NET TRANSFERS ON DEBT	**471**	**431**	**-16**	**-333**	**800**	**1,447**	**2,006**	**-5,191**	**-592**	**-1,406**
Public and publicly guaranteed	**358**	**787**	**-561**	**-775**	**-2,386**	**-639**	**-323**	**-2,060**	**-1,181**	**-2,725**
Official creditors	334	494	1,576	1,552	798	1,530	1,071	68	-869	-1,567
Multilateral	4	286	927	579	128	204	-425	-410	-1,430	-917
Concessional	4	37	84	103	186	218	170	176	141	70
Bilateral	330	207	649	974	670	1,325	1,496	477	561	-650
Concessional	335	278	589	1,232	917	945	617	277	443	-231
Private creditors	24	294	-2,137	-2,327	-3,184	-2,169	-1,394	-2,128	-312	-1,159
Bonds	0	26	-248	-249	-156	-62	-126	-504	-5	599
Commercial banks	0	555	-641	-679	-1,930	-1,239	-721	-1,380	-801	-1,469
Other private	24	-288	-1,249	-1,400	-1,098	-868	-548	-244	494	-288
Private nonguaranteed	**113**	**-356**	**546**	**442**	**3,186**	**2,086**	**2,328**	**-3,131**	**589**	**1,319**
Bonds	0	0	0	0	120	381	211	444	404	1,504
Commercial banks	113	-356	546	442	3,066	1,705	2,117	-3,575	185	-185
Memo:										
IBRD	0	212	585	123	-294	-14	-512	-424	-972	-831
IDA	3	36	-11	-14	-18	-20	-22	-24	-26	-26
DEBT SERVICE (LTDS)	**165**	**2,814**	**8,195**	**9,342**	**9,224**	**10,311**	**11,552**	**13,255**	**13,130**	**15,134**
Public and publicly guaranteed	**83**	**1,763**	**6,948**	**7,716**	**7,395**	**7,583**	**8,177**	**8,930**	**8,799**	**9,491**
Official creditors	42	636	2,605	2,724	3,171	3,573	4,016	4,402	5,775	5,806
Multilateral	0	145	1,273	1,386	1,667	1,878	2,074	2,282	3,283	2,692
Concessional	0	11	29	34	52	70	95	122	151	181
Bilateral	42	491	1,332	1,338	1,504	1,695	1,942	2,120	2,492	3,113
Concessional	37	314	899	911	1,062	1,261	1,433	1,476	1,812	2,144
Private creditors	42	1,127	4,344	4,993	4,225	4,010	4,161	4,528	3,024	3,685
Bonds	0	19	419	249	156	62	126	504	5	6
Commercial banks	1	458	2,015	2,900	2,417	2,348	2,444	2,508	1,561	2,334
Other private	41	651	1,910	1,844	1,652	1,600	1,592	1,516	1,458	1,345
Private nonguaranteed	**82**	**1,051**	**1,247**	**1,626**	**1,829**	**2,728**	**3,375**	**4,326**	**4,331**	**5,644**
Bonds	0	0	0	0	0	13	32	41	91	259
Commercial banks	82	1,051	1,247	1,626	1,829	2,716	3,342	4,285	4,240	5,385
Memo:										
IBRD	0	120	1,063	1,134	1,282	1,412	1,515	1,620	2,156	1,875
IDA	0	5	13	15	18	20	22	24	26	26
UNDISBURSED DEBT	**499**	**9,483**	**18,866**	**18,513**	**20,169**	**20,373**	**19,045**	**20,386**	**21,138**	**24,885**
Official creditors	482	7,060	12,398	13,043	14,225	15,600	14,681	15,468	16,452	19,127
Private creditors	16	2,422	6,468	5,470	5,944	4,773	4,364	4,919	4,687	5,757
Memorandum items										
Concessional LDOD	1,987	7,622	15,047	15,868	18,688	21,284	22,517	25,073	29,035	29,263
Variable rate LDOD	461	5,574	17,323	22,151	25,978	30,230	33,664	32,247	35,272	41,095
Public sector LDOD	2,485	15,021	41,183	44,262	47,982	51,891	53,666	57,132	63,891	65,347
Private sector LDOD	463	3,142	5,545	6,556	10,261	13,176	16,281	14,029	15,543	20,134

6. CURRENCY COMPOSITION OF LONG-TERM DEBT (PERCENT)

	1970	1980	1988	1989	1990	1991	1992	1993	1994	1995
Deutsche mark	3.9	7.8	5.5	5.2	5.0	4.9	4.7	4.1	4.8	4.9
French franc	4.5	4.0	2.9	2.8	3.4	3.6	3.7	3.3	3.3	3.7
Japanese yen	11.5	20.0	39.9	34.4	34.6	35.7	36.4	37.6	38.0	35.4
Pound sterling	2.2	0.8	1.9	1.5	1.4	1.2	1.0	0.9	0.9	0.8
Swiss franc	0.9	0.7	0.7	0.4	0.4	0.4	0.4	0.5	0.7	0.7
U.S.dollars	36.1	43.5	18.5	24.6	20.9	19.4	19.9	19.9	20.0	21.5
Multiple currency	0.0	8.6	23.8	24.6	27.3	28.0	27.6	28.1	26.7	27.2
Special drawing rights	0.0	0.0	0.1	0.0	0.0	0.0	0.0	0.0	0.0	0.0
All other currencies	40.9	14.7	6.8	6.4	7.0	6.7	6.3	5.6	5.5	5.7

INDONESIA

(US$ million, unless otherwise indicated)

	1970	1980	1988	1989	1990	1991	1992	1993	1994	1995
7. DEBT RESTRUCTURINGS										
Total amount rescheduled	0	0	0	0	0	0	0	0	0	0
Debt stock rescheduled	0	0	0	0	0	0	0	0	0	0
Principal rescheduled	0	0	0	0	0	0	0	0	0	0
Official	0	0	0	0	0	0	0	0	0	0
Private	0	0	0	0	0	0	0	0	0	0
Interest rescheduled	0	0	0	0	0	0	0	0	0	0
Official	0	0	0	0	0	0	0	0	0	0
Private	0	0	0	0	0	0	0	0	0	0
Debt forgiven	..	..	0	0	0	0	0	0	0	0
Memo: interest forgiven	..	..	0	0	0	0	0	0	0	0
Debt stock reduction	0	0	0	0	0	0	0	0	0	0
of which debt buyback	0	0	0	0	0	0	0	0	0	0
8. DEBT STOCK-FLOW RECONCILIATION										
Total change in debt stocks	..	..	..	5,323	10,470	9,676	8,456	1,144	7,396	11,288
Net flows on debt	..	..	..	4,263	7,216	8,080	9,356	-1,149	2,704	8,770
Net change in interest arrears	..	..	..	0	0	0	0	0	0	0
Interest capitalized	..	..	..	0	0	0	0	0	0	0
Debt forgiveness or reduction	..	..	..	0	0	0	0	0	0	0
Cross-currency valuation	..	..	..	-2,377	3,266	1,821	-1,150	2,742	5,684	296
Residual	..	..	..	3,437	-12	-224	250	-449	-992	2,222
9. AVERAGE TERMS OF NEW COMMITMENTS										
ALL CREDITORS										
Interest (%)	2.6	8.1	5.3	6.1	6.1	6.2	5.8	5.4	5.2	5.3
Maturity (years)	34.1	19.5	20.7	20.7	21.1	19.6	19.5	19.5	19.9	17.4
Grace period (years)	9.0	5.6	6.8	6.4	6.0	5.6	5.3	5.2	5.6	5.1
Grant element (%)	59.8	17.6	33.6	27.8	28.0	25.4	26.7	29.1	31.1	29.0
Official creditors										
Interest (%)	2.4	5.4	4.8	5.5	5.7	6.2	5.2	4.9	4.9	4.7
Maturity (years)	35.9	25.2	23.4	23.2	22.8	21.5	21.8	23.3	23.0	20.4
Grace period (years)	9.5	7.2	7.5	7.0	6.5	6.1	6.3	6.6	6.5	5.9
Grant element (%)	62.9	36.2	38.5	32.8	31.9	27.4	33.2	36.9	36.2	34.9
Private creditors										
Interest (%)	6.0	12.0	6.9	7.6	7.5	6.3	7.1	6.2	6.0	6.5
Maturity (years)	8.1	11.3	11.3	13.2	14.5	14.7	15.0	13.6	12.0	11.4
Grace period (years)	2.0	3.3	4.4	4.8	4.4	4.1	3.2	3.0	3.4	3.7
Grant element (%)	14.1	-9.2	16.3	12.7	13.7	20.3	14.0	17.3	18.3	17.3
Memorandum items										
Commitments	520	4,277	6,087	7,513	6,691	8,811	7,879	8,135	7,808	11,147
Official creditors	487	2,524	4,730	5,637	5,282	6,321	5,186	4,921	5,591	7,417
Private creditors	33	1,753	1,357	1,875	1,409	2,490	2,693	3,214	2,217	3,730

10. CONTRACTUAL OBLIGATIONS ON OUTSTANDING LONG-TERM DEBT

	1996	1997	1998	1999	2000	2001	2002	2003	2004	2005
TOTAL										
Disbursements	8,085	6,198	3,939	2,469	1,457	811	478	175	79	5
Principal	13,115	10,395	10,285	8,852	8,142	6,736	5,625	5,004	4,566	4,760
Interest	5,123	4,848	4,496	3,913	3,486	2,849	2,340	2,030	1,766	1,530
Official creditors										
Disbursements	5,575	4,785	3,358	2,309	1,430	811	478	175	79	5
Principal	3,539	3,792	4,036	4,219	4,255	4,501	4,399	4,195	3,827	3,576
Interest	2,730	2,741	2,680	2,538	2,410	2,211	1,986	1,758	1,542	1,350
Bilateral creditors										
Disbursements	3,522	2,865	1,727	985	506	263	118	30	2	1
Principal	2,006	2,156	2,239	2,330	2,257	2,500	2,472	2,293	2,090	1,990
Interest	1,244	1,249	1,207	1,112	1,060	965	856	750	660	583
Multilateral creditors										
Disbursements	2,052	1,920	1,631	1,324	924	548	360	145	77	5
Principal	1,533	1,636	1,797	1,889	1,998	2,001	1,927	1,902	1,738	1,586
Interest	1,486	1,492	1,473	1,427	1,351	1,245	1,130	1,007	882	767
Private creditors										
Disbursements	2,510	1,413	580	160	28	0	0	0	0	0
Principal	9,576	6,603	6,249	4,633	3,887	2,235	1,225	809	738	1,184
Interest	2,393	2,108	1,815	1,375	1,076	639	354	273	224	180
Commercial banks										
Disbursements	985	597	239	71	0	0	0	0	0	0
Principal	2,338	1,358	1,289	1,078	827	520	304	220	216	214
Interest	750	571	425	290	144	93	64	46	31	17
Other private										
Disbursements	1,526	816	341	89	28	0	0	0	0	0
Principal	7,238	5,245	4,960	3,555	3,060	1,716	921	589	522	971
Interest	1,644	1,537	1,390	1,085	932	546	290	227	193	163

IRAN, ISLAMIC REPUBLIC OF

(US$ million, unless otherwise indicated)

	1970	1980	1988	1989	1990	1991	1992	1993	1994	1995
1. SUMMARY DEBT DATA										
TOTAL DEBT STOCKS (EDT)	..	**4,500**	**5,831**	**6,519**	**9,021**	**11,330**	**16,033**	**23,362**	**22,712**	**21,935**
Long-term debt (LDOD)	..	**4,500**	**2,055**	**1,862**	**1,797**	**2,065**	**1,730**	**5,759**	**16,005**	**17,392**
Public and publicly guaranteed	..	4,500	2,055	1,862	1,797	2,065	1,730	5,759	15,613	17,078
Private nonguaranteed	0	0	0	0	0	0	0	0	392	314
Use of IMF credit	**0**	**0**	**0**	**0**	**0**	**0**	**0**	**0**	**0**	**0**
Short-term debt	..	**0**	**3,776**	**4,657**	**7,224**	**9,266**	**14,304**	**17,604**	**6,707**	**4,543**
of which interest arrears on LDOD	..	0	453	455	456	451	4	4	7	7
Official creditors	..	0	6	6	6	0	0	0	2	..
Private creditors	..	0	448	449	449	450	4	4	5	..
Memo: principal arrears on LDOD	..	1	1,507	1,513	1,517	1,493	37	37	50	..
Official creditors	..	1	25	27	29	2	0	0	0	..
Private creditors	..	0	1,482	1,486	1,488	1,492	37	37	50	..
Memo: export credits	..	..	3,016	3,824	7,826	8,764	8,677	9,112	9,711	9,869
TOTAL DEBT FLOWS										
Disbursements	..	**264**	**157**	**0**	**139**	**438**	**1,359**	**1,623**	**1,990**	..
Long-term debt	..	264	157	0	139	438	1,359	1,623	1,990	..
IMF purchases	0	0	0	0	0	0	0	0	0	..
Principal repayments	..	**527**	**335**	**124**	**225**	**184**	**193**	**389**	**3,313**	..
Long-term debt	..	527	335	124	225	184	193	389	3,313	..
IMF repurchases	0	0	0	0	0	0	0	0	0	..
Net flows on debt	..	**-263**	**-268**	**756**	**2,480**	**2,301**	**6,651**	**7,334**	**-1,323**	..
of which short-term debt	..	..	-90	880	2,566	2,047	5,485	6,100	0	..
Interest payments (INT)	..	**431**	**291**	**333**	**430**	**619**	**878**	**1,407**	**1,001**	..
Long-term debt	..	431	62	44	28	41	93	175	369	..
IMF charges	0	0	0	0	0	0	0	0	0	..
Short-term debt	..	0	229	289	402	578	785	1,232	632	..
Net transfers on debt	..	**-694**	**-559**	**423**	**2,050**	**1,682**	**5,773**	**5,927**	**-2,324**	..
Total debt service paid (TDS)	..	**959**	**625**	**457**	**655**	**803**	**1,071**	**1,796**	**4,314**	..
Long-term debt	..	959	396	168	253	225	286	564	3,682	..
IMF repurchases and charges	0	0	0	0	0	0	0	0	0	..
Short-term debt (interest only)	..	0	229	289	402	578	785	1,232	632	..
2. AGGREGATE NET RESOURCE FLOWS AND NET TRANSFERS (LONG-TERM)										
NET RESOURCE FLOWS	..	**-262**	**-110**	**-133**	**-371**	**363**	**1,051**	**1,229**	**-1,265**	..
Net flow of long-term debt (ex. IMF)	0	-263	-178	-124	-86	254	1,166	1,234	-1,323	..
Foreign direct investment (net)	28	0	61	-19	-362	23	-170	-50	2	17
Portfolio equity flows	..	0	0	0	0	0	0	0	0	0
Grants (excluding technical coop.)	1	1	7	10	76	86	55	45	56	41
Memo: technical coop. grants	12	19	83	88	99	150	110	114	93	107
NET TRANSFERS	..	**-1,091**	**-254**	**-281**	**-477**	**236**	**801**	**1,054**	**-1,635**	..
Interest on long-term debt	..	431	62	44	28	41	93	175	369	..
Profit remittances on FDI	816	398	82	104	78	85	157	0	0	0
3. MAJOR ECONOMIC AGGREGATES										
Gross national product (GNP)	..	93,270	125,466	123,200	119,290	120,835	109,400	..	..	..
Exports of goods & services (XGS)	..	14,073	11,176	13,879	20,197	19,542	20,714	19,315	20,014	19,140
of which workers remittances	..	0	0	0	0	0	0	0	0	0
Imports of goods & services (MGS)	..	16,509	13,045	16,570	22,370	30,990	29,214	25,030	16,435	16,725
International reserves (RES)	217	12,783	..	..	..	..	..	..	..	..
Current account balance	..	-2,438	-1,869	-191	327	-9,448	-6,504	-4,215	4,777	3,516
4. DEBT INDICATORS										
EDT / XGS (%)	..	32.0	52.2	47.0	44.7	58.0	77.4	121.0	113.5	114.6
EDT / GNP (%)	..	4.8	4.6	5.3	7.6	9.4	14.7	..	..	..
TDS / XGS (%)	..	6.8	5.6	3.3	3.2	4.1	5.2	9.3	21.6	..
INT / XGS (%)	..	3.1	2.6	2.4	2.1	3.2	4.2	7.3	5.0	..
INT / GNP (%)	..	0.5	0.2	0.3	0.4	0.5	0.8	..	..	..
RES / EDT (%)	..	284.0	..	..	..	..	..	..	..	..
RES / MGS (months)	..	9.3	..	..	..	..	..	..	..	..
Short-term / EDT (%)	..	0.0	64.8	71.4	80.1	81.8	89.2	75.4	29.5	20.7
Concessional / EDT (%)	..	7.4	3.3	1.9	1.3	0.6	0.4	0.2	0.7	..
Multilateral / EDT (%)	..	13.8	3.5	2.2	1.3	0.7	0.9	0.9	1.3	..

IRAN, ISLAMIC REPUBLIC OF

(US$ million, unless otherwise indicated)

	1970	1980	1988	1989	1990	1991	1992	1993	1994	1995
5. LONG-TERM DEBT										
DEBT OUTSTANDING (LDOD)	..	**4,500**	**2,055**	**1,862**	**1,797**	**2,065**	**1,730**	**5,759**	**16,005**	**17,392**
Public and publicly guaranteed	..	**4,500**	**2,055**	**1,862**	**1,797**	**2,065**	**1,730**	**5,759**	**15,613**	**17,078**
Official creditors	..	903	413	262	225	140	197	3,095	11,492	..
Multilateral	..	622	202	143	116	76	138	211	302	..
Concessional	..	68	11	7	3	2	0	0	0	..
Bilateral	..	282	211	119	110	65	59	2,884	11,190	..
Concessional	..	264	181	119	110	65	58	47	162	..
Private creditors	..	3,597	1,642	1,600	1,572	1,924	1,533	2,664	4,122	..
Bonds	..	0	0	0	0	0	0	0	0	..
Commercial banks	..	1,055	1,055	1,055	1,055	1,055	0	6	5	..
Other private	..	2,542	587	545	517	869	1,533	2,658	4,116	..
Private nonguaranteed	**0**	**0**	**0**	**0**	**0**	**0**	**0**	**0**	**392**	**314**
Bonds	..	0	0	0	0	0	0	0	0	0
Commercial banks	..	0	0	0	0	0	0	0	392	314
Memo:										
IBRD	0	622	202	143	86	46	133	190	260	316
IDA	0	0	0	0	0	0	0	0	0	0
DISBURSEMENTS	..	**264**	**157**	**0**	**139**	**438**	**1,359**	**1,623**	**1,990**	..
Public and publicly guaranteed	..	**264**	**157**	**0**	**139**	**438**	**1,359**	**1,623**	**1,598**	..
Official creditors	..	4	1	0	30	0	120	160	285	..
Multilateral	..	4	0	0	30	0	119	74	80	..
Concessional	..	0	0	0	0	0	0	0	0	..
Bilateral	..	0	1	0	0	0	1	86	204	..
Concessional	..	0	1	0	0	0	0	50	127	..
Private creditors	..	261	156	0	109	438	1,239	1,463	1,313	..
Bonds	..	0	0	0	0	0	0	0	0	..
Commercial banks	..	0	0	0	0	0	0	6	0	..
Other private	..	261	156	0	109	438	1,239	1,457	1,313	..
Private nonguaranteed	**0**	**0**	**0**	**0**	**0**	**0**	**0**	**0**	**392**	0
Bonds	..	0	0	0	0	0	0	0	0	0
Commercial banks	..	0	0	0	0	0	0	0	392	0
Memo:										
IBRD	0	4	0	0	0	0	114	58	48	85
IDA	0	0	0	0	0	0	0	0	0	0
PRINCIPAL REPAYMENTS	..	**527**	**335**	**124**	**225**	**184**	**193**	**389**	**3,313**	..
Public and publicly guaranteed	..	**527**	**335**	**124**	**225**	**184**	**193**	**389**	**3,313**	..
Official creditors	..	89	89	105	86	90	71	74	2,838	..
Multilateral	..	70	85	61	67	40	56	7	19	..
Concessional	..	8	5	5	4	2	2	0	0	..
Bilateral	..	19	4	44	18	49	15	67	2,819	..
Concessional	..	9	4	44	18	49	15	67	19	..
Private creditors	..	439	245	19	139	94	121	315	474	..
Bonds	..	0	0	0	0	0	0	0	0	..
Commercial banks	..	45	1	0	0	0	0	0	2	..
Other private	..	394	244	19	139	94	121	315	472	..
Private nonguaranteed	**0**	**0**	**0**	**0**	**0**	**0**	**0**	**0**	**0**	**0**
Bonds	..	0	0	0	0	0	0	0	0	0
Commercial banks	..	0	0	0	0	0	0	0	0	0
Memo:										
IBRD	0	70	85	61	67	40	26	7	8	6
IDA	0	0	0	0	0	0	0	0	0	0
NET FLOWS ON DEBT	..	**-263**	**-178**	**-124**	**-86**	**254**	**1,166**	**1,234**	**-1,323**	..
Public and publicly guaranteed	..	**-263**	**-178**	**-124**	**-86**	**254**	**1,166**	**1,234**	**-1,715**	..
Official creditors	..	-85	-88	-105	-56	-90	49	85	-2,554	..
Multilateral	..	-66	-85	-61	-37	-40	63	67	61	..
Concessional	..	-8	-5	-5	-4	-2	-2	0	0	..
Bilateral	..	-19	-3	-44	-18	-49	-14	19	-2,615	..
Concessional	..	-9	-3	-44	-18	-49	-15	-18	108	..
Private creditors	..	-178	-90	-19	-30	344	1,118	1,148	839	..
Bonds	..	0	0	0	0	0	0	0	0	..
Commercial banks	..	-45	-1	0	0	0	0	6	-2	..
Other private	..	-133	-89	-18	-30	344	1,118	1,142	841	..
Private nonguaranteed	**0**	**0**	**0**	**0**	**0**	**0**	**0**	**0**	**392**	**0**
Bonds	..	0	0	0	0	0	0	0	0	0
Commercial banks	..	0	0	0	0	0	0	0	392	0
Memo:										
IBRD	0	-66	-85	-61	-67	-40	88	51	40	79
IDA	0	0	0	0	0	0	0	0	0	0

IRAN, ISLAMIC REPUBLIC OF

(US$ million, unless otherwise indicated)

	1970	1980	1988	1989	1990	1991	1992	1993	1994	1995
INTEREST PAYMENTS (LINT)	..	**431**	**62**	**44**	**28**	**41**	**93**	**175**	**369**	..
Public and publicly guaranteed	..	**431**	**62**	**44**	**28**	**41**	**93**	**175**	**369**	..
Official creditors	..	65	21	43	14	20	12	30	121	..
Multilateral	..	49	20	13	10	8	9	12	19	..
Concessional	..	5	1	1	0	0	0	0	0	..
Bilateral	..	16	1	29	4	12	3	17	102	..
Concessional	..	14	1	29	4	12	3	5	3	..
Private creditors	..	366	41	1	14	21	81	145	249	..
Bonds	..	0	0	0	0	0	0	0	0	..
Commercial banks	..	153	0	0	0	0	0	0	0	..
Other private	..	213	41	1	14	21	81	145	248	..
Private nonguaranteed	**0**	**0**	**0**	**0**	**0**	**0**	**0**	**0**	**0**	**0**
Bonds	..	0	0	0	0	0	0	0	0	0
Commercial banks	..	0	0	0	0	0	0	0	0	0
Memo:										
IBRD	0	49	20	13	10	5	6	12	16	19
IDA	0	0	0	0	0	0	0	0	0	0
NET TRANSFERS ON DEBT	..	**-694**	**-239**	**-168**	**-114**	**213**	**1,073**	**1,059**	**-1,693**	..
Public and publicly guaranteed	..	**-694**	**-239**	**-168**	**-114**	**213**	**1,073**	**1,059**	**-2,085**	..
Official creditors	..	-150	-109	-148	-69	-110	37	56	-2,675	..
Multilateral	..	-116	-105	-74	-47	-48	54	55	43	..
Concessional	..	-13	-6	-6	-4	-2	-2	0	0	..
Bilateral	..	-35	-4	-73	-22	-62	-18	1	-2,717	..
Concessional	..	-24	-4	-73	-22	-62	-19	-23	104	..
Private creditors	..	-544	-130	-20	-45	323	1,037	1,003	590	..
Bonds	..	0	0	0	0	0	0	0	0	..
Commercial banks	..	-198	-1	0	0	0	0	6	-2	..
Other private	..	-346	-130	-20	-45	323	1,037	997	593	..
Private nonguaranteed	**0**	**0**	**0**	**0**	**0**	**0**	**0**	**0**	**392**	**0**
Bonds	..	0	0	0	0	0	0	0	0	0
Commercial banks	..	0	0	0	0	0	0	0	392	0
Memo:										
IBRD	0	-116	-105	-74	-77	-46	82	39	24	61
IDA	0	0	0	0	0	0	0	0	0	0
DEBT SERVICE (LTDS)	..	**959**	**396**	**168**	**253**	**225**	**286**	**564**	**3,682**	..
Public and publicly guaranteed	..	**959**	**396**	**168**	**253**	**225**	**286**	**564**	**3,682**	..
Official creditors	..	154	110	148	99	110	83	104	2,959	..
Multilateral	..	119	105	74	77	48	65	19	38	..
Concessional	..	13	6	6	4	2	2	0	0	..
Bilateral	..	35	5	73	22	62	19	85	2,922	..
Concessional	..	24	5	73	22	62	19	73	23	..
Private creditors	..	805	286	20	154	115	202	460	723	..
Bonds	..	0	0	0	0	0	0	0	0	..
Commercial banks	..	198	1	0	0	0	0	0	2	..
Other private	..	607	285	20	154	115	202	460	721	..
Private nonguaranteed	**0**	**0**	**0**	**0**	**0**	**0**	**0**	**0**	**0**	**0**
Bonds	..	0	0	0	0	0	0	0	0	0
Commercial banks	..	0	0	0	0	0	0	0	0	0
Memo:										
IBRD	0	119	105	74	77	46	32	19	24	24
IDA	0	0	0	0	0	0	0	0	0	0
UNDISBURSED DEBT	..	**1,173**	**244**	**497**	**1,512**	**3,750**	**5,709**	**4,560**	**3,205**	**1,862**
Official creditors	..	63	0	0	250	286	2,004	2,396	1,598	1,075
Private creditors	..	1,109	244	497	1,262	3,464	3,706	2,164	1,607	787
Memorandum items										
Concessional LDOD	..	332	192	126	113	67	58	47	162	445
Variable rate LDOD	..	1,706	1,273	1,273	1,273	1,669	1,409	5,245	15,344	16,759
Public sector LDOD	..	4,500	2,055	1,862	1,797	2,065	1,730	5,757	15,588	16,994
Private sector LDOD	..	0	0	0	0	0	0	2	417	398

6. CURRENCY COMPOSITION OF LONG-TERM DEBT (PERCENT)

	1970	1980	1988	1989	1990	1991	1992	1993	1994	1995
Deutsche mark	..	15.5	0.2	0.1	0.0	19.2	71.3	31.3	17.9	13.8
French franc	..	8.8	0.9	0.7	0.7	0.6	0.9	2.2	2.2	2.3
Japanese yen	..	9.0	10.4	4.9	4.2	3.1	9.0	7.2	4.3	4.4
Pound sterling	..	0.9	0.0	0.0	0.0	0.0	0.0	0.0	0.0	0.0
Swiss franc	..	0.0	0.0	0.0	0.0	0.0	2.3	1.6	0.8	0.5
U.S.dollars	..	43.4	77.5	85.5	88.6	73.4	2.5	50.8	70.7	75.1
Multiple currency	..	13.8	9.8	7.7	6.4	3.7	7.7	3.3	1.7	1.9
Special drawing rights	..	0.0	0.0	0.0	0.0	0.0	0.0	0.0	0.0	0.0
All other currencies	..	8.6	1.2	1.1	0.1	0.0	6.4	3.6	2.4	2.0

IRAN, ISLAMIC REPUBLIC OF

(US$ million, unless otherwise indicated)

	1970	1980	1988	1989	1990	1991	1992	1993	1994	1995
7. DEBT RESTRUCTURINGS										
Total amount rescheduled	0	0	0	0	0	0	0	2,800	10,900	..
Debt stock rescheduled	0	0	0	0	0	0	0	2,800	10,900	..
Principal rescheduled	0	0	0	0	0	0	0	0	0	..
Official	0	0	0	0	0	0	0	0	0	..
Private	0	0	0	0	0	0	0	0	0	..
Interest rescheduled	0	0	0	0	0	0	0	0	0	..
Official	0	0	0	0	0	0	0	0	0	..
Private	0	0	0	0	0	0	0	0	0	..
Debt forgiven	..	..	0	48	0	0	0	0	0	..
Memo: interest forgiven	..	..	0	0	0	0	0	0	0	..
Debt stock reduction	0	0	0	0	0	0	0	0	0	..
of which debt buyback	0	0	0	0	0	0	0	0	0	..
8. DEBT STOCK-FLOW RECONCILIATION										
Total change in debt stocks	..	..	..	688	2,502	2,310	4,703	7,329	-650	..
Net flows on debt	..	..	..	756	2,480	2,301	6,651	7,334	-1,323	..
Net change in interest arrears	..	..	..	2	1	-5	-447	0	3	..
Interest capitalized	..	..	..	0	0	0	0	0	0	..
Debt forgiveness or reduction	..	..	..	-48	0	0	0	0	0	..
Cross-currency valuation	..	..	..	-30	-9	9	38	-13	886	..
Residual	..	..	..	9	30	4	-1,539	8	-216	..
9. AVERAGE TERMS OF NEW COMMITMENTS										
ALL CREDITORS										
Interest (%)	..	0.0	11.8	8.6	8.5	7.3	5.4	4.5	6.3	..
Maturity (years)	..	0.0	9.4	9.6	9.2	7.5	9.1	19.7	6.3	..
Grace period (years)	..	0.0	2.4	2.5	4.0	3.1	3.4	2.4	1.8	..
Grant element (%)	..	0.0	-9.6	4.9	5.7	9.8	19.6	31.9	11.1	..
Official creditors										..
Interest (%)	..	0.0	0.0	0.0	7.8	11.6	4.9	4.5	0.0	..
Maturity (years)	..	0.0	0.0	0.0	13.5	7.5	10.3	21.3	0.0	..
Grace period (years)	..	0.0	0.0	0.0	5.0	3.2	3.7	2.5	0.0	..
Grant element (%)	..	0.0	0.0	0.0	11.7	-2.5	23.1	33.6	0.0	..
Private creditors										..
Interest (%)	..	0.0	11.8	8.6	8.7	7.3	6.0	4.3	6.3	..
Maturity (years)	..	0.0	9.4	9.6	7.9	7.5	7.5	6.1	6.3	..
Grace period (years)	..	0.0	2.4	2.5	3.7	3.1	3.0	1.7	1.8	..
Grant element (%)	..	0.0	-9.6	4.9	4.0	10.0	15.0	17.0	11.1	..
Memorandum items										
Commitments	..	0	61	233	1,241	2,599	3,214	615	309	..
Official creditors	..	0	0	0	280	36	1,844	552	0	..
Private creditors	..	0	61	233	961	2,563	1,371	64	309	..

10. CONTRACTUAL OBLIGATIONS ON OUTSTANDING LONG-TERM DEBT

	1996	1997	1998	1999	2000	2001	2002	2003	2004	2005
TOTAL										
Disbursements	871	406	217	118	91	56	36	32	19	17
Principal	2,321	3,567	3,935	3,728	3,409	1,379	123	121	121	92
Interest	827	848	652	446	251	97	41	35	28	24
Official creditors										
Disbursements	313	230	164	118	91	56	36	32	19	17
Principal	995	2,370	2,988	3,007	3,005	1,300	93	92	92	92
Interest	594	676	540	384	225	88	36	32	28	24
Bilateral creditors										
Disbursements	237	144	85	37	18	4	0	0	0	0
Principal	962	2,332	2,925	2,925	2,925	1,221	16	16	16	16
Interest	566	645	507	350	193	57	8	7	7	6
Multilateral creditors										
Disbursements	76	85	79	81	73	52	36	32	19	17
Principal	33	38	63	82	81	79	78	77	77	77
Interest	28	31	33	34	33	31	28	25	22	18
Private creditors										
Disbursements	558	176	53	0	0	0	0	0	0	0
Principal	1,326	1,197	947	721	404	79	30	29	29	0
Interest	233	172	112	62	26	9	5	2	0	0
Commercial banks										
Disbursements	0	0	0	0	0	0	0	0	0	0
Principal	1	1	1	1	0	0	0	0	0	0
Interest	0	0	0	0	0	0	0	0	0	0
Other private										
Disbursements	557	176	53	0	0	0	0	0	0	0
Principal	1,324	1,196	946	720	403	79	30	29	29	0
Interest	233	172	112	62	26	9	5	2	0	0

JAMAICA

(US$ million, unless otherwise indicated)

	1970	1980	1988	1989	1990	1991	1992	1993	1994	1995
1. SUMMARY DEBT DATA										
TOTAL DEBT STOCKS (EDT)	..	**1,913**	**4,553**	**4,560**	**4,671**	**4,410**	**4,263**	**4,111**	**4,316**	**4,270**
Long-term debt (LDOD)	**982**	**1,505**	**3,774**	**3,785**	**3,968**	**3,737**	**3,594**	**3,487**	**3,516**	**3,537**
Public and publicly guaranteed	160	1,430	3,723	3,743	3,934	3,709	3,567	3,459	3,438	3,409
Private nonguaranteed	822	75	51	42	34	28	28	28	78	128
Use of IMF credit	**0**	**309**	**483**	**383**	**357**	**391**	**357**	**335**	**318**	**240**
Short-term debt	..	**98**	**295**	**391**	**347**	**281**	**311**	**289**	**483**	**493**
of which interest arrears on LDOD	..	0	62	124	125	127	135	135	107	103
Official creditors	..	0	48	96	87	87	92	100	92	88
Private creditors	..	0	15	29	37	40	43	35	15	15
Memo: principal arrears on LDOD	..	27	131	188	157	218	215	257	192	189
Official creditors	..	8	93	130	84	126	143	176	156	153
Private creditors	..	19	38	59	73	92	72	80	36	37
Memo: export credits	..	..	547	568	651	679	547	526	527	533
TOTAL DEBT FLOWS										
Disbursements	**184**	**363**	**380**	**390**	**340**	**570**	**419**	**276**	**210**	**312**
Long-term debt	180	363	321	309	284	451	360	225	161	301
IMF purchases	4	0	59	82	56	119	59	51	49	11
Principal repayments	**170**	**121**	**485**	**412**	**401**	**480**	**499**	**338**	**381**	**440**
Long-term debt	170	102	265	245	290	392	420	266	293	344
IMF repurchases	0	19	219	168	112	88	79	72	87	96
Net flows on debt	**13**	**242**	**-71**	**12**	**-106**	**23**	**-58**	**-84**	**52**	**-114**
of which short-term debt	..	..	34	34	-45	-68	22	-22	222	14
Interest payments (INT)	..	**159**	**251**	**230**	**260**	**240**	**212**	**204**	**216**	**233**
Long-term debt	64	121	193	173	202	192	167	167	185	193
IMF charges	0	23	42	37	34	31	29	24	17	17
Short-term debt	..	15	17	20	24	17	16	12	14	24
Net transfers on debt	..	**83**	**-322**	**-218**	**-366**	**-217**	**-270**	**-288**	**-164**	**-347**
Total debt service paid (TDS)	..	**280**	**736**	**643**	**662**	**720**	**711**	**542**	**597**	**673**
Long-term debt	234	223	458	418	492	583	588	433	478	537
IMF repurchases and charges	0	42	261	205	145	119	108	97	105	112
Short-term debt (interest only)	..	15	17	20	24	17	16	12	14	24
2. AGGREGATE NET RESOURCE FLOWS AND NET TRANSFERS (LONG-TERM)										
NET RESOURCE FLOWS	**174**	**301**	**130**	**244**	**249**	**474**	**139**	**280**	**75**	**188**
Net flow of long-term debt (ex. IMF)	10	261	56	64	-6	59	-60	-40	-133	-43
Foreign direct investment (net)	162	28	-12	57	138	133	142	78	117	167
Portfolio equity flows	0	0	0	0	0	0	0	0	0	0
Grants (excluding technical coop.)	3	13	87	123	117	282	57	242	91	63
Memo: technical coop. grants	5	17	35	38	35	42	40	42	42	52
NET TRANSFERS	**6**	**66**	**-172**	**-38**	**-142**	**110**	**-85**	**108**	**-134**	**-37**
Interest on long-term debt	64	121	193	173	202	192	167	167	185	193
Profit remittances on FDI	105	114	110	109	189	172	57	5	24	31
3. MAJOR ECONOMIC AGGREGATES										
Gross national product (GNP)	1,344	2,451	3,438	3,802	3,734	3,198	2,994	3,951	3,923	3,165
Exports of goods & services (XGS)	..	1,472	1,848	2,125	2,461	2,384	2,453	2,670	3,260	3,770
of which workers remittances	..	51	76	116	136	136	158	187	332	443
Imports of goods & services (MGS)	..	1,678	2,246	2,794	2,928	2,757	2,624	3,057	3,369	4,107
International reserves (RES)	139	105	147	108	168	106	324	417	736	681
Current account balance	..	-136	47	-283	-312	-240	29	-184	17	-245
4. DEBT INDICATORS										
EDT / XGS (%)	..	129.9	246.4	214.6	189.8	185.0	173.8	153.9	132.4	113.2
EDT / GNP (%)	..	78.0	132.4	119.9	125.1	137.9	142.4	104.0	110.0	134.9
TDS / XGS (%)	..	19.0	39.8	30.2	26.9	30.2	29.0	20.3	18.3	17.9
INT / XGS (%)	..	10.8	13.6	10.8	10.6	10.1	8.6	7.6	6.6	6.2
INT / GNP (%)	..	6.5	7.3	6.1	7.0	7.5	7.1	5.2	5.5	7.4
RES / EDT (%)	..	5.5	3.2	2.4	3.6	2.4	7.6	10.1	17.0	16.0
RES / MGS (months)	..	0.8	0.8	0.5	0.7	0.5	1.5	1.6	2.6	2.0
Short-term / EDT (%)	..	5.1	6.5	8.6	7.4	6.4	7.3	7.0	11.2	11.5
Concessional / EDT (%)	..	20.8	27.8	28.5	30.5	28.9	31.0	30.0	30.6	32.7
Multilateral / EDT (%)	..	14.9	23.8	23.9	25.0	26.8	26.2	28.0	27.4	28.5

JAMAICA

(US$ million, unless otherwise indicated)

	1970	1980	1988	1989	1990	1991	1992	1993	1994	1995
5. LONG-TERM DEBT										
DEBT OUTSTANDING (LDOD)	**982**	**1,505**	**3,774**	**3,785**	**3,968**	**3,737**	**3,594**	**3,487**	**3,516**	**3,537**
Public and publicly guaranteed	**160**	**1,430**	**3,723**	**3,743**	**3,934**	**3,709**	**3,567**	**3,459**	**3,438**	**3,409**
Official creditors	59	920	3,105	3,156	3,406	3,268	3,155	3,054	3,092	3,093
Multilateral	30	284	1,083	1,092	1,168	1,181	1,117	1,153	1,183	1,216
Concessional	10	89	190	194	200	193	178	173	177	188
Bilateral	29	636	2,022	2,064	2,239	2,087	2,038	1,901	1,909	1,877
Concessional	19	310	1,074	1,104	1,223	1,083	1,143	1,059	1,144	1,209
Private creditors	101	510	619	587	528	441	411	405	346	316
Bonds	83	19	0	0	0	0	0	0	13	25
Commercial banks	17	384	358	323	298	278	254	281	265	227
Other private	0	108	261	265	230	164	158	124	68	65
Private nonguaranteed	**822**	**75**	**51**	**42**	**34**	**28**	**28**	**28**	**78**	**128**
Bonds	0	0	0	0	0	0	0	0	55	55
Commercial banks	822	75	51	42	34	28	28	28	23	73
Memo:										
IBRD	30	176	671	650	672	664	594	607	595	595
IDA	0	0	0	0	0	0	0	0	0	0
DISBURSEMENTS	**180**	**363**	**321**	**309**	**284**	**451**	**360**	**225**	**161**	**301**
Public and publicly guaranteed	**15**	**338**	**321**	**309**	**284**	**451**	**355**	**219**	**106**	**246**
Official creditors	14	317	250	234	246	437	298	178	83	196
Multilateral	7	93	93	113	102	130	122	151	67	122
Concessional	6	34	12	10	10	2	2	7	14	21
Bilateral	7	224	158	121	144	307	177	27	16	74
Concessional	2	84	75	60	103	161	40	3	10	42
Private creditors	1	21	71	75	39	14	56	41	23	50
Bonds	0	0	0	0	0	0	0	0	13	13
Commercial banks	1	4	0	0	0	6	0	40	10	35
Other private	0	17	71	75	39	8	56	1	0	3
Private nonguaranteed	**165**	**25**	**0**	**0**	**0**	**0**	**6**	**6**	**55**	**55**
Bonds	0	0	0	0	0	0	0	0	55	0
Commercial banks	165	25	0	0	0	0	6	6	0	55
Memo:										
IBRD	7	55	55	52	35	43	27	77	22	61
IDA	0	0	0	0	0	0	0	0	0	0
PRINCIPAL REPAYMENTS	**170**	**102**	**265**	**245**	**290**	**392**	**420**	**266**	**293**	**344**
Public and publicly guaranteed	**6**	**92**	**258**	**236**	**282**	**386**	**414**	**260**	**288**	**339**
Official creditors	2	37	166	159	205	315	347	217	222	260
Multilateral	1	11	75	82	100	129	156	124	123	129
Concessional	0	1	7	6	9	9	13	10	14	14
Bilateral	1	26	91	77	105	186	190	94	99	130
Concessional	1	2	8	6	19	21	23	22	30	30
Private creditors	4	55	92	77	76	71	68	42	66	80
Bonds	2	9	0	0	0	0	0	0	0	0
Commercial banks	2	16	11	10	1	1	10	11	10	73
Other private	0	31	81	67	75	70	58	32	56	6
Private nonguaranteed	**164**	**10**	**7**	**9**	**8**	**6**	**6**	**6**	**5**	**5**
Bonds	0	0	0	0	0	0	0	0	0	0
Commercial banks	164	10	7	9	8	6	6	6	5	5
Memo:										
IBRD	1	6	53	54	62	62	78	73	76	85
IDA	0	0	0	0	0	0	0	0	0	0
NET FLOWS ON DEBT	**10**	**261**	**56**	**64**	**-6**	**59**	**-60**	**-40**	**-133**	**-43**
Public and publicly guaranteed	**9**	**246**	**63**	**73**	**3**	**65**	**-60**	**-41**	**-182**	**-93**
Official creditors	12	280	85	75	41	122	-48	-39	-139	-64
Multilateral	6	82	18	31	2	1	-35	28	-56	-7
Concessional	6	33	4	4	0	-7	-11	-2	0	7
Bilateral	6	198	67	44	39	121	-14	-67	-83	-56
Concessional	1	82	67	55	84	140	17	-19	-20	12
Private creditors	-3	-34	-22	-2	-38	-57	-12	-2	-43	-29
Bonds	-2	-9	0	0	0	0	0	0	13	13
Commercial banks	-1	-12	-11	-10	-1	5	-10	29	0	-38
Other private	0	-13	-11	8	-37	-62	-2	-31	-56	-4
Private nonguaranteed	**1**	**15**	**-7**	**-9**	**-8**	**-6**	**0**	**0**	**50**	**50**
Bonds	0	0	0	0	0	0	0	0	55	0
Commercial banks	1	15	-7	-9	-8	-6	0	0	-5	50
Memo:										
IBRD	6	50	2	-2	-26	-19	-51	4	-54	-24
IDA	0	0	0	0	0	0	0	0	0	0

JAMAICA

(US$ million, unless otherwise indicated)

	1970	1980	1988	1989	1990	1991	1992	1993	1994	1995
INTEREST PAYMENTS (LINT)	**64**	**121**	**193**	**173**	**202**	**192**	**167**	**167**	**185**	**193**
Public and publicly guaranteed	**9**	**115**	**189**	**170**	**200**	**189**	**165**	**165**	**182**	**182**
Official creditors	2	45	141	120	164	158	145	151	147	159
Multilateral	1	17	84	78	86	91	93	84	85	84
Concessional	0	3	5	5	6	5	5	5	4	4
Bilateral	1	29	57	42	79	67	52	67	63	76
Concessional	1	10	12	10	16	22	13	28	24	33
Private creditors	7	69	47	50	35	31	21	14	35	23
Bonds	6	2	0	0	0	0	0	0	0	2
Commercial banks	1	55	32	34	20	20	13	11	13	19
Other private	0	13	16	16	15	11	7	4	22	2
Private nonguaranteed	**54**	**7**	**4**	**3**	**3**	**3**	**2**	**2**	**3**	**11**
Bonds	0	0	0	0	0	0	0	0	1	5
Commercial banks	54	7	4	3	3	3	2	2	2	6
Memo:										
IBRD	1	13	61	55	58	59	59	49	49	47
IDA	0	0	0	0	0	0	0	0	0	0
NET TRANSFERS ON DEBT	**-54**	**140**	**-137**	**-109**	**-208**	**-133**	**-227**	**-208**	**-317**	**-236**
Public and publicly guaranteed	**-1**	**132**	**-126**	**-97**	**-197**	**-124**	**-225**	**-206**	**-365**	**-275**
Official creditors	9	235	-57	-45	-124	-37	-193	-190	-286	-223
Multilateral	5	66	-67	-47	-84	-91	-127	-56	-141	-91
Concessional	5	30	-1	-1	-6	-12	-16	-7	-5	3
Bilateral	4	169	10	2	-40	54	-66	-134	-146	-132
Concessional	0	72	55	45	68	118	4	-47	-44	-22
Private creditors	-10	-103	-69	-52	-73	-88	-32	-16	-78	-52
Bonds	-7	-10	0	0	0	0	0	0	13	11
Commercial banks	-3	-66	-42	-44	-22	-15	-23	19	-14	-57
Other private	0	-26	-26	-8	-51	-73	-9	-35	-77	-6
Private nonguaranteed	**-53**	**8**	**-11**	**-12**	**-11**	**-9**	**-2**	**-2**	**47**	**39**
Bonds	0	0	0	0	0	0	0	0	54	-5
Commercial banks	-53	8	-11	-12	-11	-9	-2	-2	-7	44
Memo:										
IBRD	5	37	-59	-57	-85	-78	-110	-45	-102	-71
IDA	0	0	0	0	0	0	0	0	0	0
DEBT SERVICE (LTDS)	**234**	**223**	**458**	**418**	**492**	**583**	**588**	**433**	**478**	**537**
Public and publicly guaranteed	**15**	**206**	**447**	**406**	**481**	**575**	**580**	**425**	**470**	**522**
Official creditors	4	82	307	279	370	473	491	368	370	419
Multilateral	2	27	159	160	186	220	249	208	208	213
Concessional	0	3	12	11	15	14	18	15	19	18
Bilateral	2	55	148	119	184	253	242	161	162	206
Concessional	2	12	20	15	35	42	36	51	53	63
Private creditors	11	124	140	127	112	102	88	57	101	103
Bonds	7	10	0	0	0	0	0	0	0	2
Commercial banks	4	70	42	44	22	21	23	21	24	92
Other private	0	44	97	83	90	81	65	36	77	9
Private nonguaranteed	**218**	**17**	**11**	**12**	**11**	**9**	**8**	**8**	**8**	**16**
Bonds	0	0	0	0	0	0	0	0	1	5
Commercial banks	218	17	11	12	11	9	8	8	7	11
Memo:										
IBRD	2	18	114	109	120	121	137	123	124	132
IDA	0	0	0	0	0	0	0	0	0	0
UNDISBURSED DEBT	**38**	**325**	**579**	**530**	**558**	**588**	**552**	**612**	**572**	**443**
Official creditors	38	314	570	520	549	585	550	601	559	443
Private creditors	0	11	9	9	9	3	2	11	13	0
Memorandum items										
Concessional LDOD	29	399	1,264	1,298	1,423	1,275	1,321	1,232	1,321	1,397
Variable rate LDOD	822	344	1,094	1,031	1,023	979	890	967	1,014	1,002
Public sector LDOD	158	1,384	3,720	3,741	3,934	3,709	3,567	3,459	3,438	3,409
Private sector LDOD	824	122	54	45	34	28	28	28	78	128

6. CURRENCY COMPOSITION OF LONG-TERM DEBT (PERCENT)

	1970	1980	1988	1989	1990	1991	1992	1993	1994	1995
Deutsche mark	0.0	0.7	1.6	1.7	2.0	2.7	2.8	2.8	3.0	3.4
French franc	0.0	1.1	0.6	0.6	0.7	0.8	0.8	0.9	1.0	1.0
Japanese yen	0.0	0.7	3.4	3.5	4.9	6.6	6.9	7.8	8.6	9.1
Pound sterling	47.7	8.5	5.0	5.0	5.6	5.4	4.2	4.2	4.4	4.2
Swiss franc	0.0	0.3	0.0	0.0	0.0	0.0	0.0	0.0	0.0	0.0
U.S.dollars	27.6	58.5	52.3	52.3	49.3	46.8	50.2	49.0	47.2	46.2
Multiple currency	18.7	17.1	27.2	27.3	27.8	29.5	27.8	28.6	28.6	28.5
Special drawing rights	0.0	0.0	0.0	0.0	0.0	0.0	0.0	0.0	0.0	0.1
All other currencies	6.1	13.2	9.9	9.6	9.7	8.1	7.3	6.8	7.2	7.5

JAMAICA

(US$ million, unless otherwise indicated)

	1970	1980	1988	1989	1990	1991	1992	1993	1994	1995
7. DEBT RESTRUCTURINGS										
Total amount rescheduled	0	0	66	100	469	107	131	149	106	105
Debt stock rescheduled	0	0	0	0	314	0	0	40	0	0
Principal rescheduled	0	0	38	59	99	73	96	84	76	88
Official	0	0	34	56	96	70	93	82	74	87
Private	0	0	4	3	3	3	3	2	1	1
Interest rescheduled	0	0	20	18	55	34	36	24	30	17
Official	0	0	19	17	54	34	35	24	30	16
Private	0	0	1	1	1	1	0	0	0	0
Debt forgiven	..	..	0	0	0	298	7	100	6	0
Memo: interest forgiven	..	..	0	0	1	11	4	3	3	0
Debt stock reduction	0	0	9	25	24	44	14	2	16	0
of which debt buyback	0	0	0	0	0	0	0	0	0	0
8. DEBT STOCK-FLOW RECONCILIATION										
Total change in debt stocks	..	..	..	8	111	-261	-147	-152	206	-47
Net flows on debt	..	..	..	12	-106	23	-58	-84	52	-114
Net change in interest arrears	..	..	..	62	0	2	9	-1	-28	-4
Interest capitalized	..	..	..	18	55	34	36	24	30	17
Debt forgiveness or reduction	..	..	..	-25	-25	-341	-21	-102	-21	0
Cross-currency valuation	..	..	..	-61	131	1	-97	-5	99	15
Residual	..	..	..	2	55	20	-15	16	74	40
9. AVERAGE TERMS OF NEW COMMITMENTS										
ALL CREDITORS										
Interest (%)	6.0	7.2	6.3	7.9	8.0	6.8	7.8	6.8	5.3	6.7
Maturity (years)	16.0	13.7	18.2	16.0	16.6	19.5	19.4	17.7	14.4	14.8
Grace period (years)	3.2	4.6	4.7	3.6	3.8	4.6	4.1	4.4	5.3	3.2
Grant element (%)	21.7	21.5	27.6	16.4	10.8	18.7	12.6	15.5	26.2	17.3
Official creditors										
Interest (%)	6.0	6.5	5.4	6.8	7.9	6.8	7.8	7.3	5.2	6.2
Maturity (years)	16.0	14.6	20.3	21.0	18.7	19.8	21.0	21.0	17.7	19.5
Grace period (years)	3.2	5.0	5.4	4.7	4.2	4.6	4.9	5.0	5.4	4.0
Grant element (%)	21.7	24.0	33.1	23.2	12.3	19.0	13.5	17.2	30.2	22.6
Private creditors										
Interest (%)	0.0	13.0	11.0	11.1	8.7	8.9	8.0	4.5	5.8	7.9
Maturity (years)	0.0	5.7	6.6	2.4	1.9	4.5	11.7	1.6	6.0	1.9
Grace period (years)	0.0	1.3	0.8	0.5	0.4	0.4	0.2	1.6	5.0	1.2
Grant element (%)	0.0	0.2	-3.3	-2.0	0.5	1.9	8.5	7.7	15.9	3.2
Memorandum items										
Commitments	24	245	394	295	318	490	324	292	89	139
Official creditors	24	219	334	215	279	481	269	242	64	101
Private creditors	0	26	60	79	39	8	55	50	25	38

10. CONTRACTUAL OBLIGATIONS ON OUTSTANDING LONG-TERM DEBT

	1996	1997	1998	1999	2000	2001	2002	2003	2004	2005
TOTAL										
Disbursements	129	105	78	58	38	17	9	5	4	0
Principal	383	344	334	325	336	230	208	194	192	170
Interest	203	184	166	148	128	111	98	86	74	64
Official creditors										
Disbursements	129	105	78	58	38	17	9	5	4	0
Principal	313	308	297	280	236	198	176	162	167	170
Interest	174	160	146	130	116	104	93	83	74	64
Bilateral creditors										
Disbursements	19	7	2	1	0	0	0	0	0	0
Principal	168	162	152	135	111	85	84	71	80	92
Interest	85	75	66	58	51	46	43	39	36	31
Multilateral creditors										
Disbursements	110	98	76	57	38	17	9	5	4	0
Principal	146	147	145	145	126	113	92	91	88	78
Interest	89	85	79	72	65	57	50	44	38	32
Private creditors										
Disbursements	0	0	0	0	0	0	0	0	0	0
Principal	70	36	36	45	100	32	32	32	25	0
Interest	29	23	21	18	12	7	5	3	1	0
Commercial banks										
Disbursements	0	0	0	0	0	0	0	0	0	0
Principal	58	22	22	22	22	22	22	22	16	0
Interest	15	11	9	8	6	5	3	2	1	0
Other private										
Disbursements	0	0	0	0	0	0	0	0	0	0
Principal	12	14	14	23	78	10	10	10	9	0
Interest	14	13	12	10	6	2	2	1	0	0

JORDAN

(US$ million, unless otherwise indicated)

	1970	1980	1988	1989	1990	1991	1992	1993	1994	1995
1. SUMMARY DEBT DATA										
TOTAL DEBT STOCKS (EDT)	..	**1,971**	**5,759**	**7,162**	**8,184**	**9,553**	**7,819**	**7,501**	**7,606**	**7,944**
Long-term debt (LDOD)	**120**	**1,486**	**5,380**	**6,261**	**7,050**	**7,461**	**6,924**	**6,663**	**6,781**	**6,904**
Public and publicly guaranteed	120	1,486	5,380	6,261	7,050	7,461	6,924	6,663	6,781	6,904
Private nonguaranteed	0	0	0	0	0	0	0	0	0	0
Use of IMF credit	**0**	**0**	**48**	**97**	**94**	**95**	**112**	**81**	**144**	**252**
Short-term debt	..	**485**	**331**	**805**	**1,040**	**1,997**	**784**	**757**	**681**	**789**
of which interest arrears on LDOD	..	5	15	40	110	219	144	53	60	71
Official creditors	..	5	6	6	34	48	49	47	56	67
Private creditors	..	0	9	34	77	171	95	7	4	4
Memo: principal arrears on LDOD	..	22	51	288	549	960	856	149	184	221
Official creditors	..	22	27	33	54	117	120	149	183	220
Private creditors	..	0	24	255	495	843	736	1	1	1
Memo: export credits	..	..	1,340	1,695	2,366	2,180	1,956	1,901	2,363	2,783
TOTAL DEBT FLOWS										
Disbursements	**15**	**369**	**1,024**	**1,184**	**693**	**661**	**463**	**261**	**307**	**719**
Long-term debt	15	369	1,024	1,099	693	661	431	245	213	604
IMF purchases	0	0	0	85	0	0	31	16	94	115
Principal repayments	**3**	**104**	**634**	**300**	**253**	**341**	**388**	**348**	**321**	**339**
Long-term debt	3	104	605	264	243	341	378	302	284	331
IMF repurchases	0	0	29	37	10	0	10	46	37	8
Net flows on debt	**12**	**266**	**-614**	**1,333**	**606**	**1,168**	**-1,063**	**-23**	**-98**	**477**
of which short-term debt	..	..	-1,004	449	165	848	-1,138	64	-84	97
Interest payments (INT)	..	**107**	**407**	**294**	**374**	**399**	**325**	**255**	**245**	**271**
Long-term debt	2	79	304	240	307	283	278	206	200	218
IMF charges	0	0	4	4	9	8	8	6	5	10
Short-term debt	..	28	99	50	58	109	39	43	40	43
Net transfers on debt	..	**159**	**-1,021**	**1,039**	**232**	**769**	**-1,388**	**-278**	**-342**	**206**
Total debt service paid (TDS)	..	**210**	**1,040**	**594**	**627**	**741**	**712**	**603**	**566**	**610**
Long-term debt	5	182	908	503	550	624	655	507	484	549
IMF repurchases and charges	0	0	33	41	19	8	18	53	42	18
Short-term debt (interest only)	..	28	99	50	58	109	39	43	40	43
2. AGGREGATE NET RESOURCE FLOWS AND NET TRANSFERS (LONG-TERM)										
NET RESOURCE FLOWS	**53**	**1,427**	**803**	**1,050**	**1,161**	**691**	**206**	**-18**	**238**	**546**
Net flow of long-term debt (ex. IMF)	12	266	419	836	450	320	54	-57	-71	273
Foreign direct investment (net)	0	34	24	-1	38	-12	41	-34	3	43
Portfolio equity flows	0	0	0	0	0	0	0	0	0	11
Grants (excluding technical coop.)	41	1,127	359	216	672	383	112	73	306	219
Memo: technical coop. grants	31	25	83	70	68	62	123	130	132	161
NET TRANSFERS	**51**	**1,348**	**499**	**811**	**854**	**408**	**-71**	**-224**	**38**	**328**
Interest on long-term debt	2	79	304	240	307	283	278	206	200	218
Profit remittances on FDI	1	0	0	0	0	0	0	0	0	0
3. MAJOR ECONOMIC AGGREGATES										
Gross national product (GNP)	..	..	5,744	3,746	3,617	3,825	4,802	5,193	5,686	6,296
Exports of goods & services (XGS)	124	2,496	3,365	3,013	2,958	3,045	3,579	3,961	4,152	4,850
of which workers remittances	0	715	894	623	380	450	800	1,040	1,093	1,244
Imports of goods & services (MGS)	254	3,318	4,112	3,657	4,039	3,857	4,740	4,908	4,612	5,199
International reserves (RES)	258	1,745	414	771	1,139	1,105	1,030	1,946	1,997	2,280
Current account balance	-130	-942	-838	-705	-1,147	-876	-1,089	-990	-551	-476
4. DEBT INDICATORS										
EDT / XGS (%)	..	79.0	171.1	237.7	276.7	313.7	218.5	189.4	183.2	163.8
EDT / GNP (%)	..	..	100.3	191.2	226.3	249.7	162.8	144.5	133.8	126.2
TDS / XGS (%)	..	8.4	30.9	19.7	21.2	24.3	19.9	15.2	13.6	12.6
INT / XGS (%)	..	4.3	12.1	9.8	12.6	13.1	9.1	6.4	5.9	5.6
INT / GNP (%)	..	..	7.1	7.8	10.3	10.4	6.8	4.9	4.3	4.3
RES / EDT (%)	..	88.5	7.2	10.8	13.9	11.6	13.2	25.9	26.3	28.7
RES / MGS (months)	12.2	6.3	1.2	2.5	3.4	3.4	2.6	4.8	5.2	5.3
Short-term / EDT (%)	..	24.6	5.7	11.2	12.7	20.9	10.0	10.1	8.9	9.9
Concessional / EDT (%)	..	41.6	34.6	31.2	31.4	31.3	34.7	38.8	39.8	42.2
Multilateral / EDT (%)	..	8.0	13.0	11.0	10.8	9.2	11.4	12.7	13.3	14.9

JORDAN

(US$ million, unless otherwise indicated)

	1970	1980	1988	1989	1990	1991	1992	1993	1994	1995
5. LONG-TERM DEBT										
DEBT OUTSTANDING (LDOD)	**120**	**1,486**	**5,380**	**6,261**	**7,050**	**7,461**	**6,924**	**6,663**	**6,781**	**6,904**
Public and publicly guaranteed	**120**	**1,486**	**5,380**	**6,261**	**7,050**	**7,461**	**6,924**	**6,663**	**6,781**	**6,904**
Official creditors	109	1,210	2,685	3,063	3,611	4,155	4,000	4,223	4,568	4,979
Multilateral	9	159	750	787	887	879	895	953	1,009	1,187
Concessional	9	113	202	224	234	251	233	246	254	296
Bilateral	100	1,052	1,935	2,276	2,723	3,276	3,106	3,270	3,559	3,793
Concessional	100	707	1,793	2,007	2,334	2,734	2,476	2,661	2,777	3,055
Private creditors	10	276	2,695	3,197	3,439	3,306	2,924	2,440	2,214	1,925
Bonds	0	0	238	263	263	208	191	768	768	801
Commercial banks	0	206	1,413	1,566	1,604	1,576	1,509	587	465	337
Other private	10	70	1,045	1,368	1,572	1,523	1,224	1,085	981	786
Private nonguaranteed	**0**	**0**	**0**	**0**	**0**	**0**	**0**	**0**	**0**	**0**
Bonds	0	0	0	0	0	0	0	0	0	0
Commercial banks	0	0	0	0	0	0	0	0	0	0
Memo:										
IBRD	0	26	414	412	516	511	569	592	635	736
IDA	9	76	79	78	77	76	75	73	71	69
DISBURSEMENTS	**15**	**369**	**1,024**	**1,099**	**693**	**661**	**431**	**245**	**213**	**604**
Public and publicly guaranteed	**15**	**369**	**1,024**	**1,099**	**693**	**661**	**431**	**245**	**213**	**604**
Official creditors	10	326	283	443	379	596	374	205	213	604
Multilateral	0	54	119	128	143	79	143	148	102	269
Concessional	0	18	18	33	14	33	10	33	23	61
Bilateral	10	272	165	315	236	517	231	57	111	335
Concessional	10	106	155	271	225	514	230	57	111	321
Private creditors	5	44	741	657	315	66	57	41	0	0
Bonds	0	0	0	26	0	0	0	15	0	0
Commercial banks	0	15	513	246	73	1	0	0	0	0
Other private	5	29	227	385	241	65	57	26	0	0
Private nonguaranteed	**0**	**0**	**0**	**0**	**0**	**0**	**0**	**0**	**0**	**0**
Bonds	0	0	0	0	0	0	0	0	0	0
Commercial banks	0	0	0	0	0	0	0	0	0	0
Memo:										
IBRD	0	22	66	52	123	40	128	69	58	158
IDA	0	9	0	0	0	0	0	0	0	0
PRINCIPAL REPAYMENTS	**3**	**104**	**605**	**264**	**243**	**341**	**378**	**302**	**284**	**331**
Public and publicly guaranteed	**3**	**104**	**605**	**264**	**243**	**341**	**378**	**302**	**284**	**331**
Official creditors	2	54	327	124	144	180	188	154	103	133
Multilateral	0	1	75	76	96	96	94	95	98	118
Concessional	0	1	11	11	14	17	18	18	21	23
Bilateral	2	53	252	48	48	84	95	58	5	15
Concessional	2	23	84	46	33	77	8	6	2	11
Private creditors	0	50	278	140	99	162	189	148	181	197
Bonds	0	0	0	0	0	56	4	0	0	0
Commercial banks	0	46	181	93	69	31	90	86	131	135
Other private	0	4	96	46	30	75	96	63	50	63
Private nonguaranteed	**0**	**0**	**0**	**0**	**0**	**0**	**0**	**0**	**0**	**0**
Bonds	0	0	0	0	0	0	0	0	0	0
Commercial banks	0	0	0	0	0	0	0	0	0	0
Memo:										
IBRD	0	0	42	42	52	55	54	57	57	77
IDA	0	0	1	1	1	1	1	2	2	2
NET FLOWS ON DEBT	**12**	**266**	**419**	**836**	**450**	**320**	**54**	**-57**	**-71**	**273**
Public and publicly guaranteed	**12**	**266**	**419**	**836**	**450**	**320**	**54**	**-57**	**-71**	**273**
Official creditors	8	272	-44	319	235	416	186	51	110	471
Multilateral	0	52	44	51	47	-17	49	53	4	150
Concessional	0	17	7	22	1	16	-7	16	2	38
Bilateral	7	220	-87	268	188	433	137	-1	106	320
Concessional	7	83	72	225	193	437	222	51	109	310
Private creditors	4	-6	463	517	216	-96	-132	-108	-181	-197
Bonds	0	0	0	26	0	-56	-4	15	0	0
Commercial banks	0	-31	332	153	4	-30	-90	-86	-131	-135
Other private	4	25	131	339	211	-10	-39	-37	-50	-63
Private nonguaranteed	**0**	**0**	**0**	**0**	**0**	**0**	**0**	**0**	**0**	**0**
Bonds	0	0	0	0	0	0	0	0	0	0
Commercial banks	0	0	0	0	0	0	0	0	0	0
Memo:										
IBRD	0	22	24	10	71	-15	74	12	2	81
IDA	0	9	-1	-1	-1	-1	-1	-2	-2	-2

JORDAN

(US$ million, unless otherwise indicated)

	1970	1980	1988	1989	1990	1991	1992	1993	1994	1995
INTEREST PAYMENTS (LINT)	**2**	**79**	**304**	**240**	**307**	**283**	**278**	**206**	**200**	**218**
Public and publicly guaranteed	**2**	**79**	**304**	**240**	**307**	**283**	**278**	**206**	**200**	**218**
Official creditors	1	43	152	87	123	155	124	126	110	128
Multilateral	0	5	49	47	54	57	55	57	60	64
Concessional	0	3	6	6	8	7	7	6	7	8
Bilateral	1	38	102	40	69	97	69	69	50	65
Concessional	1	13	55	30	57	55	23	38	28	45
Private creditors	1	36	152	153	184	128	154	80	90	90
Bonds	0	0	1	0	15	34	4	2	31	41
Commercial banks	0	32	85	116	67	28	80	40	34	32
Other private	1	4	67	37	103	67	69	37	25	17
Private nonguaranteed	**0**	**0**	**0**	**0**	**0**	**0**	**0**	**0**	**0**	**0**
Bonds	0	0	0	0	0	0	0	0	0	0
Commercial banks	0	0	0	0	0	0	0	0	0	0
Memo:										
IBRD	0	1	36	33	37	42	41	43	46	48
IDA	0	1	1	1	1	1	1	1	1	1
NET TRANSFERS ON DEBT	**10**	**187**	**116**	**596**	**143**	**38**	**-224**	**-262**	**-271**	**55**
Public and publicly guaranteed	**10**	**187**	**116**	**596**	**143**	**38**	**-224**	**-262**	**-271**	**55**
Official creditors	6	229	-195	232	112	261	62	-75	0	342
Multilateral	0	47	-5	5	-7	-75	-6	-4	-56	86
Concessional	0	14	1	17	-7	9	-14	9	-5	30
Bilateral	6	182	-190	227	119	336	68	-71	56	256
Concessional	6	71	17	195	136	383	199	13	82	265
Private creditors	4	-42	311	364	31	-224	-286	-187	-271	-287
Bonds	0	0	-1	26	-15	-89	-8	13	-31	-41
Commercial banks	0	-63	247	37	-63	-58	-170	-126	-166	-166
Other private	4	20	64	301	109	-77	-108	-75	-74	-80
Private nonguaranteed	**0**	**0**	**0**	**0**	**0**	**0**	**0**	**0**	**0**	**0**
Bonds	0	0	0	0	0	0	0	0	0	0
Commercial banks	0	0	0	0	0	0	0	0	0	0
Memo:										
IBRD	0	22	-12	-23	33	-57	33	-31	-44	33
IDA	0	8	-2	-2	-2	-2	-2	-2	-2	-3
DEBT SERVICE (LTDS)	**5**	**182**	**908**	**503**	**550**	**624**	**655**	**507**	**484**	**549**
Public and publicly guaranteed	**5**	**182**	**908**	**503**	**550**	**624**	**655**	**507**	**484**	**549**
Official creditors	4	97	478	211	267	334	312	279	213	262
Multilateral	0	6	124	123	150	154	149	152	158	182
Concessional	0	4	17	17	22	24	24	24	29	31
Bilateral	4	90	355	88	117	181	163	128	55	79
Concessional	4	36	138	77	90	131	31	44	30	55
Private creditors	1	86	430	292	283	290	343	228	271	287
Bonds	0	0	1	0	15	89	8	2	31	41
Commercial banks	0	78	266	209	136	58	170	126	166	166
Other private	1	8	163	84	133	142	165	100	74	80
Private nonguaranteed	**0**	**0**	**0**	**0**	**0**	**0**	**0**	**0**	**0**	**0**
Bonds	0	0	0	0	0	0	0	0	0	0
Commercial banks	0	0	0	0	0	0	0	0	0	0
Memo:										
IBRD	0	1	78	75	89	97	94	101	102	125
IDA	0	1	2	2	2	2	2	2	2	3
UNDISBURSED DEBT	**74**	**1,354**	**2,124**	**1,510**	**1,454**	**1,301**	**1,004**	**1,027**	**1,214**	**1,273**
Official creditors	62	1,136	947	846	1,103	988	709	763	1,214	1,273
Private creditors	12	217	1,177	663	351	313	295	263	0	0
Memorandum items										
Concessional LDOD	109	819	1,995	2,231	2,568	2,986	2,709	2,907	3,031	3,351
Variable rate LDOD	0	200	1,788	2,112	2,501	2,465	2,292	1,938	1,916	2,035
Public sector LDOD	118	1,485	5,380	6,261	7,050	7,461	6,924	6,663	6,781	6,904
Private sector LDOD	1	1	0	0	0	0	0	0	0	0

6. CURRENCY COMPOSITION OF LONG-TERM DEBT (PERCENT)

	1970	1980	1988	1989	1990	1991	1992	1993	1994	1995
Deutsche mark	8.7	10.6	6.4	7.4	7.9	7.6	8.3	7.3	7.8	7.6
French franc	2.7	2.0	2.0	2.9	3.5	3.5	7.9	7.6	9.0	9.9
Japanese yen	0.0	1.1	4.4	3.6	5.9	12.2	15.7	18.6	21.9	24.4
Pound sterling	32.5	6.4	7.6	7.5	8.0	7.4	7.6	7.2	6.8	6.8
Swiss franc	0.0	0.0	0.4	0.7	0.8	0.7	0.7	0.4	0.5	0.5
U.S.dollars	31.0	59.6	46.9	47.2	44.3	42.6	39.7	39.4	33.9	28.3
Multiple currency	0.0	4.4	8.8	7.6	8.4	8.0	9.5	10.2	10.7	12.0
Special drawing rights	0.0	0.0	0.0	0.8	2.8	7.4	0.2	0.1	0.3	0.5
All other currencies	25.2	16.0	23.4	22.5	18.3	10.6	10.4	9.0	9.1	9.9

JORDAN

(US$ million, unless otherwise indicated)

	1970	1980	1988	1989	1990	1991	1992	1993	1994	1995
7. DEBT RESTRUCTURINGS										
Total amount rescheduled	0	0	223	334	350	0	588	1,055	344	353
Debt stock rescheduled	0	0	131	19	0	0	0	193	0	0
Principal rescheduled	0	0	12	194	350	0	433	722	208	256
Official	0	0	12	79	193	0	112	88	95	115
Private	0	0	0	115	157	0	322	634	112	141
Interest rescheduled	0	0	0	103	0	0	145	249	119	97
Official	0	0	0	35	0	0	41	33	66	53
Private	0	0	0	69	0	0	104	215	52	45
Debt forgiven	..	..	0	0	0	0	0	184	297	334
Memo: interest forgiven	..	..	0	0	0	0	0	0	0	0
Debt stock reduction	0	0	0	0	0	0	530	97	0	0
of which debt buyback	0	0	0	0	0	0	0	0	0	0
8. DEBT STOCK-FLOW RECONCILIATION										
Total change in debt stocks	..	..	..	1,403	1,023	1,369	-1,734	-318	105	338
Net flows on debt	..	..	..	1,333	606	1,168	-1,063	-23	-98	477
Net change in interest arrears	..	..	..	24	71	109	-76	-90	7	11
Interest capitalized	..	..	..	103	0	0	145	249	119	97
Debt forgiveness or reduction	..	..	..	0	0	0	-530	-281	-297	-334
Cross-currency valuation	..	..	..	-83	372	39	-233	62	377	73
Residual	..	..	..	24	-26	53	22	-234	-2	13
9. AVERAGE TERMS OF NEW COMMITMENTS										
ALL CREDITORS										
Interest (%)	3.7	7.3	7.5	6.0	4.6	2.1	4.1	6.3	4.8	3.9
Maturity (years)	23.5	15.4	12.6	19.4	19.9	27.1	18.4	19.2	22.2	20.5
Grace period (years)	5.0	4.0	3.7	5.7	6.5	8.8	5.8	5.4	6.7	6.4
Grant element (%)	42.6	16.5	12.5	28.1	38.5	63.2	37.7	22.9	36.9	40.7
Official creditors										
Interest (%)	2.6	7.3	6.3	4.7	4.0	1.8	2.8	6.4	4.8	3.9
Maturity (years)	31.4	16.0	15.3	22.3	21.8	28.5	22.2	19.7	22.2	20.5
Grace period (years)	6.4	4.3	4.6	6.7	7.3	9.3	7.0	5.5	6.7	6.4
Grant element (%)	56.7	17.2	20.5	37.2	43.9	66.7	50.0	23.1	36.9	40.7
Private creditors										
Interest (%)	6.2	7.2	7.9	9.4	8.9	6.2	6.9	5.0	0.0	0.0
Maturity (years)	5.5	11.5	11.7	11.3	7.0	7.0	10.3	15.7	0.0	0.0
Grace period (years)	1.9	2.4	3.4	3.1	1.0	1.2	3.3	4.7	0.0	0.0
Grant element (%)	10.4	12.0	9.7	2.8	2.8	11.5	11.4	21.4	0.0	0.0
Memorandum items										
Commitments	36	759	885	601	739	556	180	301	638	650
Official creditors	25	653	226	443	642	520	123	260	638	650
Private creditors	11	106	658	158	97	36	57	41	0	0

10. CONTRACTUAL OBLIGATIONS ON OUTSTANDING LONG-TERM DEBT

	1996	1997	1998	1999	2000	2001	2002	2003	2004	2005
TOTAL										
Disbursements	372	301	203	136	83	50	30	15	9	3
Principal	389	433	413	450	421	481	455	449	440	435
Interest	287	311	312	316	295	274	250	228	205	183
Official creditors										
Disbursements	372	301	203	136	83	50	30	15	9	3
Principal	186	248	280	340	347	416	394	390	380	377
Interest	195	220	222	234	218	202	183	164	145	127
Bilateral creditors										
Disbursements	166	124	74	43	20	10	4	1	0	0
Principal	60	124	153	203	208	273	264	268	269	275
Interest	114	135	139	155	144	134	122	110	98	86
Multilateral creditors										
Disbursements	206	177	130	93	63	40	26	14	9	3
Principal	127	124	127	138	139	143	130	122	111	102
Interest	81	85	83	79	74	68	61	54	47	41
Private creditors										
Disbursements	0	0	0	0	0	0	0	0	0	0
Principal	202	185	134	110	74	65	61	59	60	58
Interest	91	92	89	82	76	72	68	64	60	56
Commercial banks										
Disbursements	0	0	0	0	0	0	0	0	0	0
Principal	159	84	38	38	19	0	0	0	0	0
Interest	22	13	8	4	1	0	0	0	0	0
Other private										
Disbursements	0	0	0	0	0	0	0	0	0	0
Principal	44	101	95	72	55	65	61	59	60	58
Interest	70	79	82	78	76	72	68	64	60	56

KAZAKSTAN

(US$ million, unless otherwise indicated)

	1970	1980	1988	1989	1990	1991	1992	1993	1994	1995
1. SUMMARY DEBT DATA										
TOTAL DEBT STOCKS (EDT)	..	..	..	..	..	..	**35**	**1,724**	**2,670**	**3,712**
Long-term debt (LDOD)	..	..	..	..	..	..	**26**	**1,617**	**2,149**	**2,899**
Public and publicly guaranteed	..	..	..	..	..	..	26	1,617	2,107	2,833
Private nonguaranteed	0	0	0	0	0	0	0	0	41	65
Use of IMF credit	**0**	**0**	**0**	**0**	**0**	**0**	**0**	**85**	**289**	**432**
Short-term debt	..	..	..	..	..	..	**9**	**22**	**232**	**381**
of which interest arrears on LDOD	..	..	..	..	..	..	0	22	105	162
Official creditors	..	..	..	..	..	..	0	1	80	162
Private creditors	..	..	..	..	..	..	0	21	25	0
Memo: principal arrears on LDOD	..	..	..	..	..	..	0	0	0	0
Official creditors	..	..	..	..	..	..	0	0	0	0
Private creditors	..	..	..	..	..	..	0	0	0	0
Memo: export credits	..	..	0	0	0	0	91	330	773	893
TOTAL DEBT FLOWS										
Disbursements	..	..	..	..	..	..	**27**	**424**	**689**	**951**
Long-term debt	..	..	..	..	..	..	27	337	494	810
IMF purchases	0	0	0	0	0	0	0	86	195	141
Principal repayments	..	..	..	..	..	..	**0**	**0**	**20**	**104**
Long-term debt	..	..	..	..	..	..	0	0	20	104
IMF repurchases	0	0	0	0	0	0	0	0	0	0
Net flows on debt	..	..	..	..	..	..	**36**	**414**	**796**	**939**
of which short-term debt	..	..	..	..	..	..	9	-9	127	93
Interest payments (INT)	..	..	..	..	..	..	**0**	**9**	**45**	**139**
Long-term debt	..	..	..	..	..	..	0	8	31	111
IMF charges	0	0	0	0	0	0	0	1	9	18
Short-term debt	..	..	..	..	..	..	0	1	5	10
Net transfers on debt	..	..	..	..	..	..	**36**	**405**	**752**	**800**
Total debt service paid (TDS)	..	..	..	..	..	..	**0**	**10**	**65**	**243**
Long-term debt	..	..	..	..	..	..	0	8	51	215
IMF repurchases and charges	0	0	0	0	0	0	0	1	9	18
Short-term debt (interest only)	..	..	..	..	..	..	0	1	5	10
2. AGGREGATE NET RESOURCE FLOWS AND NET TRANSFERS (LONG-TERM)										
NET RESOURCE FLOWS	..	..	..	..	..	..	**129**	**498**	**686**	**1,000**
Net flow of long-term debt (ex. IMF)	..	..	..	..	..	..	27	337	475	705
Foreign direct investment (net)	..	..	..	..	..	..	100	150	185	284
Portfolio equity flows	..	..	..	..	..	..	0	0	0	0
Grants (excluding technical coop.)	..	..	..	..	..	..	3	11	26	10
Memo: technical coop. grants	..	..	..	..	..	..	6	3	17	47
NET TRANSFERS	..	..	..	..	..	..	**129**	**490**	**655**	**889**
Interest on long-term debt	..	..	..	..	..	..	0	8	31	111
Profit remittances on FDI	..	..	..	..	..	..	0	0	0	0
3. MAJOR ECONOMIC AGGREGATES										
Gross national product (GNP)	..	..	..	..	..	..	28,756	27,069	16,701	15,771
Exports of goods & services (XGS)	..	..	..	..	..	..	5,758	4,249	3,841	6,110
of which workers remittances	..	..	..	..	..	..	0	0	0	0
Imports of goods & services (MGS)	..	..	..	..	..	..	6,037	5,019	5,112	7,079
International reserves (RES)	..	..	..	..	..	..	..	711	1,216	1,660
Current account balance	..	..	..	..	..	..	-111	-716	-1,174	-910
4. DEBT INDICATORS										
EDT / XGS (%)	..	..	..	..	..	..	0.6	40.6	69.5	60.8
EDT / GNP (%)	..	..	..	..	..	..	0.1	6.4	16.0	23.5
TDS / XGS (%)	..	..	..	..	..	..	0.0	0.2	1.7	4.0
INT / XGS (%)	..	..	..	..	..	..	0.0	0.2	1.2	2.3
INT / GNP (%)	..	..	..	..	..	..	0.0	0.0	0.3	0.9
RES / EDT (%)	..	..	..	..	..	..	..	41.3	45.6	44.7
RES / MGS (months)	..	..	..	..	..	..	..	1.7	2.9	2.8
Short-term / EDT (%)	..	..	..	..	..	..	26.4	1.3	8.7	10.3
Concessional / EDT (%)	..	..	..	..	..	..	0.0	0.0	0.1	4.0
Multilateral / EDT (%)	..	..	..	..	..	..	0.0	1.5	8.1	10.6

KAZAKSTAN

(US$ million, unless otherwise indicated)

	1970	*1980*	*1988*	*1989*	*1990*	*1991*	*1992*	*1993*	*1994*	*1995*
5. LONG-TERM DEBT										
DEBT OUTSTANDING (LDOD)	..	..	..	..	..	..	**26**	**1,617**	**2,149**	**2,899**
Public and publicly guaranteed	..	..	..	..	..	..	**26**	**1,617**	**2,107**	**2,833**
Official creditors	..	..	..	..	..	..	10	1,419	1,777	2,288
Multilateral	..	..	..	..	..	..	0	26	217	392
Concessional	..	..	..	..	..	..	0	0	0	40
Bilateral	..	..	..	..	..	..	10	1,393	1,560	1,897
Concessional	..	..	..	..	..	..	0	0	2	109
Private creditors	..	..	..	..	..	..	16	198	330	545
Bonds	..	..	..	..	..	..	0	0	0	0
Commercial banks	..	..	..	..	..	..	0	0	0	0
Other private	..	..	..	..	..	..	16	198	330	545
Private nonguaranteed	**0**	**0**	**0**	**0**	**0**	**0**	**0**	**0**	**41**	**65**
Bonds	..	..	..	..	..	..	0	0	0	0
Commercial banks	..	..	..	..	..	..	0	0	41	65
Memo:										
IBRD	0	0	0	0	0	0	0	0	187	295
IDA	0	0	0	0	0	0	0	0	0	0
DISBURSEMENTS	..	..	..	..	..	..	**27**	**337**	**494**	**810**
Public and publicly guaranteed	..	..	..	..	..	..	**27**	**337**	**474**	**778**
Official creditors	..	..	..	..	..	..	10	166	341	518
Multilateral	..	..	..	..	..	..	0	27	184	171
Concessional	..	..	..	..	..	..	0	0	0	40
Bilateral	..	..	..	..	..	..	10	139	157	347
Concessional	..	..	..	..	..	..	0	0	2	108
Private creditors	..	..	..	..	..	..	17	171	133	259
Bonds	..	..	..	..	..	..	0	0	0	0
Commercial banks	..	..	..	..	..	..	0	0	0	0
Other private	..	..	..	..	..	..	17	171	133	259
Private nonguaranteed	**0**	**0**	**0**	**0**	**0**	**0**	**0**	**0**	**20**	**32**
Bonds	..	..	..	..	..	..	0	0	0	0
Commercial banks	..	..	..	..	..	..	0	0	20	32
Memo:										
IBRD	0	0	0	0	0	0	0	0	182	107
IDA	0	0	0	0	0	0	0	0	0	0
PRINCIPAL REPAYMENTS	..	..	..	..	..	..	**0**	**0**	**20**	**104**
Public and publicly guaranteed	..	..	..	..	..	..	**0**	**0**	**15**	**96**
Official creditors	..	..	..	..	..	..	0	0	9	29
Multilateral	..	..	..	..	..	..	0	0	0	0
Concessional	..	..	..	..	..	..	0	0	0	0
Bilateral	..	..	..	..	..	..	0	0	9	29
Concessional	..	..	..	..	..	..	0	0	0	0
Private creditors	..	..	..	..	..	..	0	0	6	67
Bonds	..	..	..	..	..	..	0	0	0	0
Commercial banks	..	..	..	..	..	..	0	0	0	0
Other private	..	..	..	..	..	..	0	0	6	67
Private nonguaranteed	**0**	**0**	**0**	**0**	**0**	**0**	**0**	**0**	**5**	**8**
Bonds	..	..	..	..	..	..	0	0	0	0
Commercial banks	..	..	..	..	..	..	0	0	5	8
Memo:										
IBRD	0	0	0	0	0	0	0	0	0	0
IDA	0	0	0	0	0	0	0	0	0	0
NET FLOWS ON DEBT	..	..	..	..	..	..	**27**	**337**	**475**	**705**
Public and publicly guaranteed	..	..	..	..	..	..	**27**	**337**	**460**	**681**
Official creditors	..	..	..	..	..	..	10	166	332	489
Multilateral	..	..	..	..	..	..	0	27	184	171
Concessional	..	..	..	..	..	..	0	0	0	40
Bilateral	..	..	..	..	..	..	10	139	148	318
Concessional	..	..	..	..	..	..	0	0	2	108
Private creditors	..	..	..	..	..	..	17	171	127	192
Bonds	..	..	..	..	..	..	0	0	0	0
Commercial banks	..	..	..	..	..	..	0	0	0	0
Other private	..	..	..	..	..	..	17	171	127	192
Private nonguaranteed	**0**	**0**	**0**	**0**	**0**	**0**	**0**	**0**	**15**	**24**
Bonds	..	..	..	..	..	..	0	0	0	0
Commercial banks	..	..	..	..	..	..	0	0	15	24
Memo:										
IBRD	0	0	0	0	0	0	0	0	182	107
IDA	0	0	0	0	0	0	0	0	0	0

KAZAKSTAN

(US$ million, unless otherwise indicated)

	1970	1980	1988	1989	1990	1991	1992	1993	1994	1995
INTEREST PAYMENTS (LINT)	..	..	..	..	..	..	**0**	**8**	**31**	**111**
Public and publicly guaranteed	..	..	..	..	..	..	**0**	**8**	**29**	**105**
Official creditors	..	..	..	..	..	..	0	4	15	59
Multilateral	..	..	..	..	..	..	0	0	7	15
Concessional	..	..	..	..	..	..	0	0	0	1
Bilateral	..	..	..	..	..	..	0	4	8	44
Concessional	..	..	..	..	..	..	0	0	0	2
Private creditors	..	..	..	..	..	..	0	4	14	46
Bonds	..	..	..	..	..	..	0	0	0	0
Commercial banks	..	..	..	..	..	..	0	0	0	0
Other private	..	..	..	..	..	..	0	4	14	46
Private nonguaranteed	**0**	**0**	**0**	**0**	**0**	**0**	**0**	**0**	**3**	**6**
Bonds	..	..	..	..	..	..	0	0	0	0
Commercial banks	..	..	..	..	..	..	0	0	3	6
Memo:										
IBRD	0	0	0	0	0	0	0	0	7	14
IDA	0	0	0	0	0	0	0	0	0	0
NET TRANSFERS ON DEBT	..	..	..	..	..	..	**27**	**329**	**443**	**594**
Public and publicly guaranteed	..	..	..	..	..	..	**27**	**329**	**431**	**576**
Official creditors	..	..	..	..	..	..	10	162	318	430
Multilateral	..	..	..	..	..	..	0	27	177	156
Concessional	..	..	..	..	..	..	0	0	0	39
Bilateral	..	..	..	..	..	..	10	135	140	274
Concessional	..	..	..	..	..	..	0	0	2	106
Private creditors	..	..	..	..	..	..	16	167	113	146
Bonds	..	..	..	..	..	..	0	0	0	0
Commercial banks	..	..	..	..	..	..	0	0	0	0
Other private	..	..	..	..	..	..	16	167	113	146
Private nonguaranteed	**0**	**0**	**0**	**0**	**0**	**0**	**0**	**0**	**13**	**18**
Bonds	..	..	..	..	..	..	0	0	0	0
Commercial banks	..	..	..	..	..	..	0	0	13	18
Memo:										
IBRD	0	0	0	0	0	0	0	0	175	93
IDA	0	0	0	0	0	0	0	0	0	0
DEBT SERVICE (LTDS)	..	..	..	..	..	..	**0**	**8**	**51**	**215**
Public and publicly guaranteed	..	..	..	..	..	..	**0**	**8**	**43**	**202**
Official creditors	..	..	..	..	..	..	0	4	24	89
Multilateral	..	..	..	..	..	..	0	0	7	15
Concessional	..	..	..	..	..	..	0	0	0	1
Bilateral	..	..	..	..	..	..	0	4	17	73
Concessional	..	..	..	..	..	..	0	0	0	2
Private creditors	..	..	..	..	..	..	0	4	20	113
Bonds	..	..	..	..	..	..	0	0	0	0
Commercial banks	..	..	..	..	..	..	0	0	0	0
Other private	..	..	..	..	..	..	0	4	20	113
Private nonguaranteed	**0**	**0**	**0**	**0**	**0**	**0**	**0**	**0**	**8**	**14**
Bonds	..	..	..	..	..	..	0	0	0	0
Commercial banks	..	..	..	..	..	..	0	0	8	14
Memo:										
IBRD	0	0	0	0	0	0	0	0	7	14
IDA	0	0	0	0	0	0	0	0	0	0
UNDISBURSED DEBT	..	..	..	..	..	..	**374**	**780**	**756**	**885**
Official creditors	..	..	..	..	..	..	274	476	503	803
Private creditors	..	..	..	..	..	..	100	304	252	83
Memorandum items										
Concessional LDOD	..	..	..	..	..	..	0	0	2	149
Variable rate LDOD	..	..	..	..	..	..	26	1,596	2,072	2,462
Public sector LDOD	..	..	..	..	..	..	26	1,617	2,107	2,833
Private sector LDOD	..	..	..	..	..	..	0	0	41	65

6. CURRENCY COMPOSITION OF LONG-TERM DEBT (PERCENT)

	1970	1980	1988	1989	1990	1991	1992	1993	1994	1995
Deutsche mark	..	..	..	..	..	..	100.0	18.8	23.9	20.8
French franc	..	..	..	..	..	..	0.0	0.0	0.5	0.3
Japanese yen	..	..	..	..	..	..	0.0	0.0	0.0	7.7
Pound sterling	..	..	..	..	..	..	0.0	0.0	0.0	0.0
Swiss franc	..	..	..	..	..	..	0.0	0.0	0.2	0.0
U.S.dollars	..	..	..	..	..	..	0.0	1.8	4.5	9.1
Multiple currency	..	..	..	..	..	..	0.0	0.0	8.9	11.8
Special drawing rights	..	..	..	..	..	..	0.0	0.0	0.0	0.0
All other currencies	..	..	..	..	..	..	0.0	79.4	62.1	50.2

KAZAKSTAN

(US$ million, unless otherwise indicated)

	1970	1980	1988	1989	1990	1991	1992	1993	1994	1995
7. DEBT RESTRUCTURINGS										
Total amount rescheduled	0	0	0	0	0	0	0	1,250	0	0
Debt stock rescheduled	0	0	0	0	0	0	0	0	0	0
Principal rescheduled	0	0	0	0	0	0	0	0	0	0
Official	0	0	0	0	0	0	0	0	0	0
Private	0	0	0	0	0	0	0	0	0	0
Interest rescheduled	0	0	0	0	0	0	0	0	0	0
Official	0	0	0	0	0	0	0	0	0	0
Private	0	0	0	0	0	0	0	0	0	0
Debt forgiven	..	..	0	0	0	0	0	0	0	0
Memo: interest forgiven	..	..	0	0	0	0	0	0	0	0
Debt stock reduction	0	0	0	0	0	0	0	0	0	0
of which debt buyback	0	0	0	0	0	0	0	0	0	0
8. DEBT STOCK-FLOW RECONCILIATION										
Total change in debt stocks	..	..	..	..	..	..	35	1,689	946	1,042
Net flows on debt	..	..	..	..	..	..	36	414	796	939
Net change in interest arrears	..	..	..	..	..	..	0	22	84	56
Interest capitalized	..	..	..	..	..	..	0	0	0	0
Debt forgiveness or reduction	..	..	..	..	..	..	0	0	0	0
Cross-currency valuation	..	..	..	..	..	..	-2	-873	-757	-219
Residual	..	..	..	..	..	..	1	2,126	823	266
9. AVERAGE TERMS OF NEW COMMITMENTS										
ALL CREDITORS										
Interest (%)	..	..	..	..	..	..	8.0	6.5	5.6	5.6
Maturity (years)	..	..	..	..	..	..	10.2	10.3	12.6	13.4
Grace period (years)	..	..	..	..	..	..	4.0	3.4	5.4	4.0
Grant element (%)	..	..	..	..	..	..	7.1	13.0	22.2	22.0
Official creditors										
Interest (%)	..	..	..	..	..	..	8.4	7.2	5.5	5.5
Maturity (years)	..	..	..	..	..	..	10.9	13.1	13.3	14.6
Grace period (years)	..	..	..	..	..	..	4.4	4.5	5.8	4.3
Grant element (%)	..	..	..	..	..	..	5.0	12.1	23.6	23.7
Private creditors										
Interest (%)	..	..	..	..	..	..	7.1	5.9	6.4	6.4
Maturity (years)	..	..	..	..	..	..	8.6	7.6	6.5	5.8
Grace period (years)	..	..	..	..	..	..	2.9	2.4	1.7	2.2
Grant element (%)	..	..	..	..	..	..	12.5	13.9	10.7	10.1
Memorandum items										
Commitments	..	..	..	..	..	..	414	791	391	1,035
Official creditors	..	..	..	..	..	..	295	383	351	902
Private creditors	..	..	..	..	..	..	120	408	40	134

10. CONTRACTUAL OBLIGATIONS ON OUTSTANDING LONG-TERM DEBT

	1996	1997	1998	1999	2000	2001	2002	2003	2004	2005
TOTAL										
Disbursements	398	218	100	65	36	26	18	11	9	6
Principal	270	532	548	569	526	230	206	160	144	91
Interest	184	171	143	119	88	68	58	49	41	34
Official creditors										
Disbursements	349	194	93	62	36	26	18	11	9	6
Principal	161	388	430	463	446	173	167	136	129	91
Interest	152	144	124	105	78	63	55	47	41	34
Bilateral creditors										
Disbursements	217	145	44	20	8	4	1	0	0	0
Principal	128	388	430	433	414	118	112	81	74	36
Interest	118	106	83	62	36	22	17	12	9	6
Multilateral creditors										
Disbursements	133	49	49	42	28	22	16	11	9	6
Principal	33	0	0	30	32	55	55	55	55	56
Interest	34	38	41	43	42	41	38	35	32	28
Private creditors										
Disbursements	49	24	7	3	0	0	0	0	0	0
Principal	110	144	118	107	80	58	39	24	15	0
Interest	32	28	20	14	10	6	3	1	1	0
Commercial banks										
Disbursements	0	0	0	0	0	0	0	0	0	0
Principal	0	0	0	0	0	0	0	0	0	0
Interest	0	0	0	0	0	0	0	0	0	0
Other private										
Disbursements	49	24	7	3	0	0	0	0	0	0
Principal	110	144	118	107	80	58	39	24	15	0
Interest	32	28	20	14	10	6	3	1	1	0

KENYA

(US$ million, unless otherwise indicated)

	1970	*1980*	*1988*	*1989*	*1990*	*1991*	*1992*	*1993*	*1994*	*1995*
1. SUMMARY DEBT DATA										
TOTAL DEBT STOCKS (EDT)	**..**	**3,383**	**5,781**	**5,862**	**7,056**	**7,455**	**6,907**	**7,118**	**7,160**	**7,381**
Long-term debt (LDOD)	**409**	**2,489**	**4,792**	**4,836**	**5,640**	**6,254**	**5,736**	**5,852**	**6,077**	**6,372**
Public and publicly guaranteed	321	2,052	4,144	4,166	4,760	5,267	5,157	5,252	5,547	5,927
Private nonguaranteed	88	437	648	670	880	987	579	600	530	445
Use of IMF credit	**0**	**254**	**455**	**415**	**482**	**493**	**393**	**363**	**405**	**374**
Short-term debt	**..**	**640**	**534**	**610**	**934**	**708**	**777**	**903**	**678**	**636**
of which interest arrears on LDOD	..	2	40	65	95	141	189	242	82	34
Official creditors	..	2	29	37	49	59	62	59	19	24
Private creditors	..	0	11	27	46	82	127	183	63	9
Memo: principal arrears on LDOD	..	3	26	49	72	155	263	409	7	28
Official creditors	..	0	10	19	22	41	72	96	7	20
Private creditors	..	3	16	30	50	114	192	314	0	8
Memo: export credits	..	..	1,316	1,453	1,540	1,831	1,720	1,636	1,690	1,457
TOTAL DEBT FLOWS										
Disbursements	**78**	**713**	**898**	**944**	**802**	**950**	**502**	**436**	**257**	**695**
Long-term debt	78	619	722	840	666	902	502	404	225	695
IMF purchases	0	94	176	103	136	48	0	32	32	0
Principal repayments	**33**	**205**	**423**	**425**	**454**	**396**	**407**	**363**	**546**	**508**
Long-term debt	29	195	322	293	348	356	324	301	532	469
IMF repurchases	4	9	101	132	106	40	83	62	14	39
Net flows on debt	**45**	**509**	**405**	**571**	**642**	**281**	**117**	**146**	**-354**	**193**
of which short-term debt	..	..	-70	52	294	-273	21	73	-65	6
Interest payments (INT)	**..**	**229**	**312**	**280**	**331**	**318**	**259**	**264**	**328**	**258**
Long-term debt	17	163	238	198	228	246	200	207	289	220
IMF charges	0	8	28	31	26	18	10	4	2	2
Short-term debt	..	58	46	51	78	55	49	53	38	36
Net transfers on debt	**..**	**280**	**93**	**290**	**311**	**-38**	**-142**	**-118**	**-682**	**-64**
Total debt service paid (TDS)	**..**	**434**	**735**	**705**	**785**	**715**	**665**	**627**	**874**	**765**
Long-term debt	46	359	560	491	576	602	524	508	820	688
IMF repurchases and charges	4	17	129	163	131	58	93	66	16	41
Short-term debt (interest only)	..	58	46	51	78	55	49	53	38	36

	1970	*1980*	*1988*	*1989*	*1990*	*1991*	*1992*	*1993*	*1994*	*1995*
2. AGGREGATE NET RESOURCE FLOWS AND NET TRANSFERS (LONG-TERM)										
NET RESOURCE FLOWS	**67**	**623**	**789**	**988**	**1,351**	**983**	**563**	**397**	**8**	**500**
Net flow of long-term debt (ex. IMF)	49	424	400	547	317	545	178	103	-307	226
Foreign direct investment (net)	14	79	0	62	57	19	6	2	4	32
Portfolio equity flows	0	0	0	0	0	0	0	0	0	0
Grants (excluding technical coop.)	4	121	389	379	977	418	378	292	311	242
Memo: technical coop. grants	27	128	178	175	208	223	282	260	193	222
NET TRANSFERS	**0**	**310**	**461**	**691**	**991**	**678**	**237**	**73**	**-380**	**186**
Interest on long-term debt	17	163	238	198	228	246	200	207	289	220
Profit remittances on FDI	49	150	90	100	132	59	126	117	100	95

	1970	*1980*	*1988*	*1989*	*1990*	*1991*	*1992*	*1993*	*1994*	*1995*
3. MAJOR ECONOMIC AGGREGATES										
Gross national product (GNP)	1,545	7,039	8,158	7,996	8,089	7,586	7,563	5,102	6,486	7,557
Exports of goods & services (XGS)	..	2,061	1,892	1,935	2,233	2,206	2,152	2,329	2,675	2,974
of which workers remittances	..	0	0	0	0	0	0	0	0	0
Imports of goods & services (MGS)	..	3,095	2,698	2,897	3,128	2,765	2,532	2,471	2,848	3,874
International reserves (RES)	220	539	297	317	236	145	80	437	588	384
Current account balance	..	-878	-472	-591	-527	-213	-180	71	98	-400

	1970	*1980*	*1988*	*1989*	*1990*	*1991*	*1992*	*1993*	*1994*	*1995*
4. DEBT INDICATORS										
EDT / XGS (%)	..	164.1	305.6	303.0	315.9	338.0	320.9	305.6	267.7	248.2
EDT / GNP (%)	..	48.1	70.9	73.3	87.2	98.3	91.3	139.5	110.4	97.7
TDS / XGS (%)	..	21.0	38.9	36.4	35.2	32.4	30.9	26.9	32.7	25.7
INT / XGS (%)	..	11.1	16.5	14.5	14.8	14.4	12.0	11.3	12.3	8.7
INT / GNP (%)	..	3.3	3.8	3.5	4.1	4.2	3.4	5.2	5.1	3.4
RES / EDT (%)	..	15.9	5.1	5.4	3.3	1.9	1.2	6.1	8.2	5.2
RES / MGS (months)	..	2.1	1.3	1.3	0.9	0.6	0.4	2.1	2.5	1.2
Short-term / EDT (%)	..	18.9	9.2	10.4	13.2	9.5	11.2	12.7	9.5	8.6
Concessional / EDT (%)	..	20.9	36.1	34.9	35.3	37.9	42.0	44.7	48.5	53.8
Multilateral / EDT (%)	..	18.6	33.1	36.7	35.2	35.0	36.3	36.6	38.5	39.5

KENYA

(US$ million, unless otherwise indicated)

5. LONG-TERM DEBT

	1970	1980	1988	1989	1990	1991	1992	1993	1994	1995
DEBT OUTSTANDING (LDOD)	**409**	**2,489**	**4,792**	**4,836**	**5,640**	**6,254**	**5,736**	**5,852**	**6,077**	**6,372**
Public and publicly guaranteed	**321**	**2,052**	**4,144**	**4,166**	**4,760**	**5,267**	**5,157**	**5,252**	**5,547**	**5,927**
Official creditors	237	1,203	3,448	3,319	3,737	4,001	3,982	4,166	4,801	5,207
Multilateral	38	630	1,912	2,152	2,487	2,609	2,507	2,608	2,755	2,913
Concessional	35	293	860	1,129	1,479	1,684	1,721	1,923	2,129	2,342
Bilateral	199	572	1,536	1,167	1,250	1,392	1,475	1,557	2,046	2,294
Concessional	138	414	1,228	919	1,014	1,143	1,178	1,259	1,343	1,630
Private creditors	84	849	696	847	1,023	1,266	1,176	1,087	746	719
Bonds	71	10	0	0	0	0	0	0	0	0
Commercial banks	1	394	673	777	899	1,118	1,014	946	664	616
Other private	12	445	23	71	124	148	162	141	83	103
Private nonguaranteed	**88**	**437**	**648**	**670**	**880**	**987**	**579**	**600**	**530**	**445**
Bonds	0	0	0	0	0	0	0	0	0	0
Commercial banks	88	437	648	670	880	987	579	600	530	445
Memo:										
IBRD	6	308	973	889	872	783	656	566	501	435
IDA	32	220	673	893	1,185	1,370	1,411	1,631	1,789	1,977
DISBURSEMENTS	**78**	**619**	**722**	**840**	**666**	**902**	**502**	**404**	**225**	**695**
Public and publicly guaranteed	**37**	**532**	**526**	**820**	**611**	**842**	**442**	**339**	**225**	**695**
Official creditors	36	232	387	538	430	462	327	317	219	566
Multilateral	10	153	202	366	295	228	130	238	160	221
Concessional	7	97	158	283	284	207	119	236	148	194
Bilateral	26	79	186	173	135	234	197	80	59	345
Concessional	20	66	146	108	134	190	122	65	37	345
Private creditors	1	300	138	282	181	380	115	22	6	130
Bonds	0	0	0	0	0	0	0	0	0	0
Commercial banks	0	215	125	230	118	334	68	17	5	69
Other private	1	85	13	52	63	45	47	5	0	60
Private nonguaranteed	**41**	**87**	**196**	**20**	**55**	**60**	**60**	**65**	**0**	**0**
Bonds	0	0	0	0	0	0	0	0	0	0
Commercial banks	41	87	196	20	55	60	60	65	0	0
Memo:										
IBRD	3	45	25	18	4	0	1	0	0	0
IDA	7	72	136	227	235	178	91	226	97	159
PRINCIPAL REPAYMENTS	**29**	**195**	**322**	**293**	**348**	**356**	**324**	**301**	**532**	**469**
Public and publicly guaranteed	**17**	**108**	**257**	**259**	**311**	**316**	**264**	**251**	**462**	**469**
Official creditors	6	31	149	154	179	189	174	178	250	265
Multilateral	1	13	98	99	126	127	133	140	150	150
Concessional	0	2	11	12	17	16	19	28	29	32
Bilateral	5	17	51	55	53	62	40	38	100	116
Concessional	3	5	22	27	25	32	24	24	50	46
Private creditors	12	77	108	105	132	127	91	73	211	204
Bonds	10	0	0	0	0	0	0	0	0	0
Commercial banks	0	25	91	98	112	108	75	53	164	161
Other private	1	53	17	7	20	20	16	20	48	43
Private nonguaranteed	**12**	**88**	**65**	**34**	**37**	**40**	**60**	**50**	**70**	**0**
Bonds	0	0	0	0	0	0	0	0	0	0
Commercial banks	12	88	65	34	37	40	60	50	70	0
Memo:										
IBRD	1	11	77	76	95	97	98	100	106	100
IDA	0	1	3	3	4	5	6	7	8	9
NET FLOWS ON DEBT	**49**	**424**	**400**	**547**	**317**	**545**	**178**	**103**	**-307**	**226**
Public and publicly guaranteed	**20**	**424**	**269**	**561**	**300**	**525**	**178**	**88**	**-237**	**226**
Official creditors	30	202	239	384	251	273	154	140	-31	300
Multilateral	9	140	104	267	168	101	-3	98	10	71
Concessional	7	95	147	271	267	191	100	208	118	162
Bilateral	21	62	135	118	83	171	157	42	-41	230
Concessional	17	61	123	82	109	158	99	41	-13	299
Private creditors	-10	223	30	177	49	253	25	-52	-206	-74
Bonds	-10	0	0	0	0	0	0	0	0	0
Commercial banks	0	190	34	132	6	227	-7	-37	-158	-92
Other private	0	33	-4	45	43	26	31	-15	-48	18
Private nonguaranteed	**30**	**-1**	**131**	**-14**	**18**	**20**	**0**	**15**	**-70**	**0**
Bonds	0	0	0	0	0	0	0	0	0	0
Commercial banks	30	-1	131	-14	18	20	0	15	-70	0
Memo:										
IBRD	2	35	-52	-58	-92	-96	-97	-100	-106	-100
IDA	7	71	133	224	230	173	85	219	89	150

KENYA

(US$ million, unless otherwise indicated)

	1970	*1980*	*1988*	*1989*	*1990*	*1991*	*1992*	*1993*	*1994*	*1995*
INTEREST PAYMENTS (LINT)	**17**	**163**	**238**	**198**	**228**	**246**	**200**	**207**	**289**	**220**
Public and publicly guaranteed	**13**	**124**	**193**	**165**	**191**	**201**	**144**	**153**	**243**	**220**
Official creditors	8	54	148	124	134	154	111	126	160	166
Multilateral	1	36	105	91	100	93	85	84	80	77
Concessional	0	3	10	9	13	17	19	18	22	22
Bilateral	8	18	43	33	34	61	26	42	80	88
Concessional	4	7	24	15	14	43	17	26	31	42
Private creditors	5	70	45	42	57	47	32	27	82	54
Bonds	4	1	0	0	0	0	0	0	0	0
Commercial banks	0	30	44	42	51	41	27	21	68	48
Other private	1	39	1	0	6	6	6	6	14	7
Private nonguaranteed	**4**	**39**	**45**	**33**	**38**	**45**	**56**	**54**	**46**	**0**
Bonds	0	0	0	0	0	0	0	0	0	0
Commercial banks	4	39	45	33	38	45	56	54	46	0
Memo:										
IBRD	0	31	88	74	78	68	61	55	49	44
IDA	0	1	5	5	7	9	10	11	13	14
NET TRANSFERS ON DEBT	**32**	**260**	**162**	**349**	**89**	**299**	**-21**	**-104**	**-596**	**7**
Public and publicly guaranteed	**7**	**300**	**76**	**396**	**109**	**324**	**35**	**-65**	**-480**	**7**
Official creditors	21	148	91	261	117	118	42	14	-192	135
Multilateral	8	104	-1	176	68	8	-88	14	-71	-7
Concessional	7	92	137	262	254	174	81	190	96	141
Bilateral	13	44	92	85	49	110	131	0	-121	141
Concessional	13	53	100	67	95	115	82	15	-44	257
Private creditors	-15	152	-15	135	-8	206	-8	-79	-288	-128
Bonds	-14	-1	0	0	0	0	0	0	0	0
Commercial banks	0	160	-10	91	-45	187	-34	-57	-226	-139
Other private	-1	-6	-5	45	37	20	26	-22	-62	11
Private nonguaranteed	**25**	**-40**	**86**	**-47**	**-20**	**-25**	**-56**	**-39**	**-116**	**0**
Bonds	0	0	0	0	0	0	0	0	0	0
Commercial banks	25	-40	86	-47	-20	-25	-56	-39	-116	0
Memo:										
IBRD	2	3	-140	-132	-169	-165	-158	-156	-155	-144
IDA	7	70	128	219	223	164	75	208	76	135
DEBT SERVICE (LTDS)	**46**	**359**	**560**	**491**	**576**	**602**	**524**	**508**	**820**	**688**
Public and publicly guaranteed	**30**	**232**	**450**	**424**	**502**	**517**	**408**	**404**	**704**	**688**
Official creditors	14	84	297	278	313	343	285	304	410	431
Multilateral	2	49	203	189	226	220	219	224	230	227
Concessional	1	5	21	21	30	33	38	45	52	53
Bilateral	13	35	94	88	86	123	66	79	180	204
Concessional	7	13	46	42	39	75	41	50	81	88
Private creditors	16	148	153	147	189	174	123	101	294	258
Bonds	14	1	0	0	0	0	0	0	0	0
Commercial banks	0	55	135	139	163	148	101	74	232	208
Other private	2	91	18	7	26	26	22	27	62	49
Private nonguaranteed	**16**	**127**	**110**	**67**	**75**	**85**	**116**	**104**	**116**	**0**
Bonds	0	0	0	0	0	0	0	0	0	0
Commercial banks	16	127	110	67	75	85	116	104	116	0
Memo:										
IBRD	1	42	165	150	173	165	159	156	155	144
IDA	0	2	8	8	11	14	16	19	21	24
UNDISBURSED DEBT	**119**	**1,332**	**1,417**	**1,579**	**1,942**	**1,954**	**1,644**	**1,530**	**1,506**	**1,219**
Official creditors	119	1,239	1,110	1,301	1,587	1,652	1,457	1,368	1,341	1,014
Private creditors	0	92	306	278	355	302	188	161	165	205
Memorandum items										
Concessional LDOD	173	707	2,088	2,048	2,493	2,827	2,899	3,182	3,472	3,971
Variable rate LDOD	88	690	837	878	1,090	1,180	748	747	875	775
Public sector LDOD	321	2,052	4,144	4,166	4,760	5,267	5,157	5,252	5,547	5,927
Private sector LDOD	88	437	648	670	880	987	579	600	530	445

6. CURRENCY COMPOSITION OF LONG-TERM DEBT (PERCENT)

	1970	*1980*	*1988*	*1989*	*1990*	*1991*	*1992*	*1993*	*1994*	*1995*
Deutsche mark	6.0	9.8	8.6	1.8	1.7	1.6	1.6	1.6	1.9	2.6
French franc	0.0	9.0	6.7	5.2	6.2	5.7	5.6	5.0	6.9	6.2
Japanese yen	0.2	4.6	8.2	8.4	9.1	12.1	13.4	15.2	16.2	18.5
Pound sterling	76.4	14.4	7.5	8.4	8.6	6.9	5.6	5.0	4.5	3.7
Swiss franc	0.0	2.3	3.7	3.6	3.4	7.7	6.9	6.4	4.4	3.8
U.S.dollars	15.7	35.8	25.3	30.7	30.9	30.1	32.0	35.4	35.3	36.4
Multiple currency	1.2	14.9	28.5	27.1	24.4	21.2	19.1	17.1	15.3	13.4
Special drawing rights	0.0	0.0	0.3	0.3	0.3	0.3	0.3	0.3	0.4	0.4
All other currencies	0.5	9.2	11.3	14.5	15.5	14.4	15.5	14.1	15.2	14.8

KENYA

(US$ million, unless otherwise indicated)

	1970	1980	1988	1989	1990	1991	1992	1993	1994	1995
7. DEBT RESTRUCTURINGS										
Total amount rescheduled	0	0	0	0	0	0	0	0	517	0
Debt stock rescheduled	0	0	0	0	0	0	0	0	0	0
Principal rescheduled	0	0	0	0	0	0	0	0	352	0
Official	0	0	0	0	0	0	0	0	74	0
Private	0	0	0	0	0	0	0	0	278	0
Interest rescheduled	0	0	0	0	0	0	0	0	163	0
Official	0	0	0	0	0	0	0	0	45	0
Private	0	0	0	0	0	0	0	0	118	0
Debt forgiven	..	..	13	433	84	66	30	0	0	0
Memo: interest forgiven	..	..	0	3	13	0	0	0	0	0
Debt stock reduction	0	0	0	0	0	0	0	0	0	0
of which debt buyback	0	0	0	0	0	0	0	0	0	0
8. DEBT STOCK-FLOW RECONCILIATION										
Total change in debt stocks	..	..	..	81	1,194	399	-548	212	42	221
Net flows on debt	..	..	..	571	642	281	117	146	-354	193
Net change in interest arrears	..	..	..	24	30	46	48	53	-160	-49
Interest capitalized	..	..	..	0	0	0	0	0	163	0
Debt forgiveness or reduction	..	..	..	-433	-84	-66	-30	0	0	0
Cross-currency valuation	..	..	..	-121	385	-18	-244	-8	312	100
Residual	..	..	..	40	221	155	-439	21	80	-24
9. AVERAGE TERMS OF NEW COMMITMENTS										
ALL CREDITORS										
Interest (%)	2.5	3.5	4.0	3.4	4.1	4.4	0.9	2.3	2.0	4.8
Maturity (years)	37.3	31.3	22.8	27.3	25.5	26.2	34.2	31.8	30.1	22.7
Grace period (years)	7.9	8.0	7.0	7.6	7.5	6.1	8.3	8.8	6.8	5.7
Grant element (%)	62.6	53.3	44.8	52.5	46.0	44.2	71.1	63.6	62.0	38.6
Official creditors										
Interest (%)	2.4	3.5	2.1	2.2	3.0	2.1	0.7	2.3	2.0	2.1
Maturity (years)	37.9	31.5	28.2	32.8	29.9	34.9	39.0	31.8	30.1	35.4
Grace period (years)	8.0	8.1	9.3	9.2	8.4	8.9	9.3	8.8	6.8	9.9
Grant element (%)	63.7	53.7	63.3	65.3	57.7	66.6	79.6	63.6	62.0	66.7
Private creditors										
Interest (%)	7.0	8.0	7.7	7.4	7.4	8.1	1.8	0.0	0.0	8.2
Maturity (years)	11.2	5.9	12.3	9.4	13.2	12.2	2.7	0.0	0.0	6.3
Grace period (years)	1.7	-0.6	2.4	2.6	4.9	1.7	1.7	0.0	0.0	0.5
Grant element (%)	12.4	5.2	9.3	10.4	13.5	8.2	15.1	0.0	0.0	2.4
Memorandum items										
Commitments	50	518	640	1,125	825	869	227	212	98	382
Official creditors	49	514	421	863	606	536	197	212	98	215
Private creditors	1	4	219	262	219	334	30	0	0	167

10. CONTRACTUAL OBLIGATIONS ON OUTSTANDING LONG-TERM DEBT

	1996	1997	1998	1999	2000	2001	2002	2003	2004	2005
TOTAL										
Disbursements	540	312	175	93	38	13	7	0	0	0
Principal	528	470	458	513	500	498	347	298	206	193
Interest	248	226	200	173	145	115	88	69	59	53
Official creditors										
Disbursements	431	249	152	82	38	13	7	0	0	0
Principal	269	281	300	356	344	351	214	206	181	182
Interest	156	146	133	117	98	81	67	60	54	50
Bilateral creditors										
Disbursements	188	120	66	36	18	8	4	0	0	0
Principal	123	138	162	218	230	253	123	120	103	105
Interest	87	85	80	73	62	51	41	36	32	30
Multilateral creditors										
Disbursements	242	129	87	46	21	5	3	0	0	0
Principal	146	143	137	138	114	98	91	86	78	77
Interest	69	62	53	44	36	30	26	24	22	20
Private creditors										
Disbursements	109	63	23	11	0	0	0	0	0	0
Principal	259	188	158	158	157	146	133	92	26	11
Interest	92	80	68	56	46	33	21	10	5	3
Commercial banks										
Disbursements	105	58	22	10	0	0	0	0	0	0
Principal	169	120	100	84	85	77	72	41	19	9
Interest	49	44	37	31	25	18	12	6	4	3
Other private										
Disbursements	4	5	1	0	0	0	0	0	0	0
Principal	91	69	59	74	72	70	61	51	6	3
Interest	42	36	30	25	22	15	9	3	1	0

KYRGYZ REPUBLIC

(US$ million, unless otherwise indicated)

	1970	1980	1988	1989	1990	1991	1992	1993	1994	1995
1. SUMMARY DEBT DATA										
TOTAL DEBT STOCKS (EDT)	..	..	..	..	..	..	**0.5**	**294.3**	**449.7**	**610.2**
Long-term debt (LDOD)	..	..	..	..	..	..	**0.5**	**234.0**	**359.2**	**474.3**
Public and publicly guaranteed	..	..	..	..	..	..	0.5	234.0	359.2	474.3
Private nonguaranteed	0.0	0.0	0.0	0.0	0.0	0.0	0.0	0.0	0.0	0.0
Use of IMF credit	**0.0**	**0.0**	**0.0**	**0.0**	**0.0**	**0.0**	**0.0**	**60.2**	**77.8**	**124.3**
Short-term debt	..	..	..	..	..	..	**0.0**	**0.0**	**12.6**	**11.6**
of which interest arrears on LDOD	..	..	..	..	..	..	0.0	0.0	12.6	9.4
Official creditors	..	..	..	..	..	..	0.0	0.0	12.6	9.4
Private creditors	..	..	..	..	..	..	0.0	0.0	0.0	0.0
Memo: principal arrears on LDOD	..	..	..	..	..	..	0.0	0.0	9.8	5.3
Official creditors	..	..	..	..	..	..	0.0	0.0	9.8	5.3
Private creditors	..	..	..	..	..	..	0.0	0.0	0.0	0.0
Memo: export credits	..	..	0.0	0.0	0.0	0.0	0.0	0.0	0.0	15.0
TOTAL DEBT FLOWS										
Disbursements	..	..	..	..	..	..	**0.5**	**140.3**	**132.7**	**200.6**
Long-term debt	..	..	..	..	..	..	0.5	79.1	119.2	154.6
IMF purchases	0.0	0.0	0.0	0.0	0.0	0.0	0.0	61.2	13.5	46.0
Principal repayments	..	..	..	..	..	..	**0.0**	**0.0**	**0.0**	**36.3**
Long-term debt	..	..	..	..	..	..	0.0	0.0	0.0	36.3
IMF repurchases	0.0	0.0	0.0	0.0	0.0	0.0	0.0	0.0	0.0	0.0
Net flows on debt	..	..	..	..	..	..	**0.5**	**140.3**	**132.7**	**166.4**
of which short-term debt	..	..	..	..	..	..	0.0	0.0	0.0	2.2
Interest payments (INT)	..	..	..	..	..	..	**0.0**	**1.4**	**16.4**	**23.5**
Long-term debt	..	..	..	..	..	..	0.0	0.4	13.1	19.7
IMF charges	0.0	0.0	0.0	0.0	0.0	0.0	0.0	1.1	3.3	3.7
Short-term debt	..	..	..	..	..	..	0.0	0.0	0.0	0.1
Net transfers on debt	..	..	..	..	..	..	**0.5**	**138.9**	**116.4**	**142.9**
Total debt service paid (TDS)	..	..	..	..	..	..	**0.0**	**1.4**	**16.4**	**59.9**
Long-term debt	..	..	..	..	..	..	0.0	0.4	13.1	56.1
IMF repurchases and charges	0.0	0.0	0.0	0.0	0.0	0.0	0.0	1.1	3.3	3.7
Short-term debt (interest only)	..	..	..	..	..	..	0.0	0.0	0.0	0.1
2. AGGREGATE NET RESOURCE FLOWS AND NET TRANSFERS (LONG-TERM)										
NET RESOURCE FLOWS	..	..	..	..	..	..	**0.7**	**142.4**	**201.4**	**186.5**
Net flow of long-term debt (ex. IMF)	..	..	..	..	..	..	0.5	79.1	119.2	118.2
Foreign direct investment (net)	..	..	..	..	..	..	0.0	0.0	10.0	15.0
Portfolio equity flows	..	..	..	..	..	..	0.0	0.0	0.0	0.0
Grants (excluding technical coop.)	..	..	..	..	..	..	0.2	63.3	72.2	53.3
Memo: technical coop. grants	..	..	..	..	..	..	1.8	7.4	10.3	27.3
NET TRANSFERS	..	..	..	..	..	..	**0.7**	**142.0**	**188.3**	**166.8**
Interest on long-term debt	..	..	..	..	..	..	0.0	0.4	13.1	19.7
Profit remittances on FDI	..	..	..	..	..	..	0.0	0.0	0.0	0.0
3. MAJOR ECONOMIC AGGREGATES										
Gross national product (GNP)	..	..	..	..	..	..	4,691.8	4,106.6	2,842.0	3,027.9
Exports of goods & services (XGS)	..	..	..	..	..	..	..	..	..	..
of which workers remittances	..	..	..	..	..	..	..	..	..	..
Imports of goods & services (MGS)	..	..	..	..	..	..	..	..	..	..
International reserves (RES)	..	..	..	..	..	..	..	31.0	53.9	98.7
Current account balance	..	..	..	..	..	..	..	..	..	..
4. DEBT INDICATORS										
EDT / XGS (%)	..	..	..	..	..	..	..	..	..	..
EDT / GNP (%)	..	..	..	..	..	..	0.0	7.2	15.8	20.2
TDS / XGS (%)	..	..	..	..	..	..	..	..	..	..
INT / XGS (%)	..	..	..	..	..	..	..	..	..	..
INT / GNP (%)	..	..	..	..	..	..	0.0	0.0	0.6	0.8
RES / EDT (%)	..	..	..	..	..	..	..	10.5	12.0	16.2
RES / MGS (months)	..	..	..	..	..	..	..	..	..	..
Short-term / EDT (%)	..	..	..	..	..	..	0.0	0.0	2.8	1.9
Concessional / EDT (%)	..	..	..	..	..	..	100.0	50.0	53.2	61.4
Multilateral / EDT (%)	..	..	..	..	..	..	0.0	16.5	19.8	29.9

KYRGYZ REPUBLIC

(US$ million, unless otherwise indicated)

	1970	1980	1988	1989	1990	1991	1992	1993	1994	1995
5. LONG-TERM DEBT										
DEBT OUTSTANDING (LDOD)	..	..	..	..	..	..	**0.5**	**234.0**	**359.2**	**474.3**
Public and publicly guaranteed	..	..	..	..	..	..	**0.5**	**234.0**	**359.2**	**474.3**
Official creditors	..	..	..	..	..	..	0.5	234.0	359.2	474.3
Multilateral	..	..	..	..	..	..	0.0	48.6	88.9	182.6
Concessional	..	..	..	..	..	..	0.0	22.6	60.4	173.6
Bilateral	..	..	..	..	..	..	0.5	185.4	270.3	291.7
Concessional	..	..	..	..	..	..	0.5	124.6	178.7	201.2
Private creditors	..	..	..	..	..	..	0.0	0.0	0.0	0.0
Bonds	..	..	..	..	..	..	0.0	0.0	0.0	0.0
Commercial banks	..	..	..	..	..	..	0.0	0.0	0.0	0.0
Other private	..	..	..	..	..	..	0.0	0.0	0.0	0.0
Private nonguaranteed	**0.0**	**0.0**	**0.0**	**0.0**	**0.0**	**0.0**	**0.0**	**0.0**	**0.0**	**0.0**
Bonds	..	..	..	..	..	..	0.0	0.0	0.0	0.0
Commercial banks	..	..	..	..	..	..	0.0	0.0	0.0	0.0
Memo:										
IBRD	0.0	0.0	0.0	0.0	0.0	0.0	0.0	0.0	0.0	0.0
IDA	0.0	0.0	0.0	0.0	0.0	0.0	0.0	22.6	60.4	141.2
DISBURSEMENTS	..	..	..	..	..	..	**0.5**	**79.1**	**119.2**	**154.6**
Public and publicly guaranteed	..	..	..	..	..	..	**0.5**	**79.1**	**119.2**	**154.6**
Official creditors	..	..	..	..	..	..	0.5	79.1	119.2	154.6
Multilateral	..	..	..	..	..	..	0.0	50.1	35.7	124.2
Concessional	..	..	..	..	..	..	0.0	22.8	35.7	115.3
Bilateral	..	..	..	..	..	..	0.5	29.0	83.5	30.3
Concessional	..	..	..	..	..	..	0.5	12.3	52.8	25.6
Private creditors	..	..	..	..	..	..	0.0	0.0	0.0	0.0
Bonds	..	..	..	..	..	..	0.0	0.0	0.0	0.0
Commercial banks	..	..	..	..	..	..	0.0	0.0	0.0	0.0
Other private	..	..	..	..	..	..	0.0	0.0	0.0	0.0
Private nonguaranteed	**0.0**	**0.0**	**0.0**	**0.0**	**0.0**	**0.0**	**0.0**	**0.0**	**0.0**	**0.0**
Bonds	..	..	..	..	..	..	0.0	0.0	0.0	0.0
Commercial banks	..	..	..	..	..	..	0.0	0.0	0.0	0.0
Memo:										
IBRD	0.0	0.0	0.0	0.0	0.0	0.0	0.0	0.0	0.0	0.0
IDA	0.0	0.0	0.0	0.0	0.0	0.0	0.0	22.8	35.7	81.3
PRINCIPAL REPAYMENTS	..	..	..	..	..	..	**0.0**	**0.0**	**0.0**	**36.3**
Public and publicly guaranteed	..	..	..	..	..	..	**0.0**	**0.0**	**0.0**	**36.3**
Official creditors	..	..	..	..	..	..	0.0	0.0	0.0	36.3
Multilateral	..	..	..	..	..	..	0.0	0.0	0.0	30.4
Concessional	..	..	..	..	..	..	0.0	0.0	0.0	0.0
Bilateral	..	..	..	..	..	..	0.0	0.0	0.0	5.9
Concessional	..	..	..	..	..	..	0.0	0.0	0.0	0.2
Private creditors	..	..	..	..	..	..	0.0	0.0	0.0	0.0
Bonds	..	..	..	..	..	..	0.0	0.0	0.0	0.0
Commercial banks	..	..	..	..	..	..	0.0	0.0	0.0	0.0
Other private	..	..	..	..	..	..	0.0	0.0	0.0	0.0
Private nonguaranteed	**0.0**	**0.0**	**0.0**	**0.0**	**0.0**	**0.0**	**0.0**	**0.0**	**0.0**	**0.0**
Bonds	..	..	..	..	..	..	0.0	0.0	0.0	0.0
Commercial banks	..	..	..	..	..	..	0.0	0.0	0.0	0.0
Memo:										
IBRD	0.0	0.0	0.0	0.0	0.0	0.0	0.0	0.0	0.0	0.0
IDA	0.0	0.0	0.0	0.0	0.0	0.0	0.0	0.0	0.0	0.0
NET FLOWS ON DEBT	..	..	..	..	..	..	**0.5**	**79.1**	**119.2**	**118.2**
Public and publicly guaranteed	..	..	..	..	..	..	**0.5**	**79.1**	**119.2**	**118.2**
Official creditors	..	..	..	..	..	..	0.5	79.1	119.2	118.2
Multilateral	..	..	..	..	..	..	0.0	50.1	35.7	93.8
Concessional	..	..	..	..	..	..	0.0	22.8	35.7	115.3
Bilateral	..	..	..	..	..	..	0.5	29.0	83.5	24.4
Concessional	..	..	..	..	..	..	0.5	12.3	52.8	25.4
Private creditors	..	..	..	..	..	..	0.0	0.0	0.0	0.0
Bonds	..	..	..	..	..	..	0.0	0.0	0.0	0.0
Commercial banks	..	..	..	..	..	..	0.0	0.0	0.0	0.0
Other private	..	..	..	..	..	..	0.0	0.0	0.0	0.0
Private nonguaranteed	**0.0**	**0.0**	**0.0**	**0.0**	**0.0**	**0.0**	**0.0**	**0.0**	**0.0**	**0.0**
Bonds	..	..	..	..	..	..	0.0	0.0	0.0	0.0
Commercial banks	..	..	..	..	..	..	0.0	0.0	0.0	0.0
Memo:										
IBRD	0.0	0.0	0.0	0.0	0.0	0.0	0.0	0.0	0.0	0.0
IDA	0.0	0.0	0.0	0.0	0.0	0.0	0.0	22.8	35.7	81.3

KYRGYZ REPUBLIC

(US$ million, unless otherwise indicated)

	1970	1980	1988	1989	1990	1991	1992	1993	1994	1995
INTEREST PAYMENTS (LINT)	..	..	..	..	..	..	**0.0**	**0.4**	**13.1**	**19.7**
Public and publicly guaranteed	..	..	..	..	..	..	**0.0**	**0.4**	**13.1**	**19.7**
Official creditors	..	..	..	..	..	..	0.0	0.4	13.1	19.7
Multilateral	..	..	..	..	..	..	0.0	0.3	5.1	2.7
Concessional	..	..	..	..	..	..	0.0	0.0	0.2	0.7
Bilateral	..	..	..	..	..	..	0.0	0.0	8.0	17.1
Concessional	..	..	..	..	..	..	0.0	0.0	1.7	11.0
Private creditors	..	..	..	..	..	..	0.0	0.0	0.0	0.0
Bonds	..	..	..	..	..	..	0.0	0.0	0.0	0.0
Commercial banks	..	..	..	..	..	..	0.0	0.0	0.0	0.0
Other private	..	..	..	..	..	..	0.0	0.0	0.0	0.0
Private nonguaranteed	**0.0**	**0.0**	**0.0**	**0.0**	**0.0**	**0.0**	**0.0**	**0.0**	**0.0**	**0.0**
Bonds	..	..	..	..	..	..	0.0	0.0	0.0	0.0
Commercial banks	..	..	..	..	..	..	0.0	0.0	0.0	0.0
Memo:										
IBRD	0.0	0.0	0.0	0.0	0.0	0.0	0.0	0.0	0.0	0.0
IDA	0.0	0.0	0.0	0.0	0.0	0.0	0.0	0.0	0.2	0.6
NET TRANSFERS ON DEBT	..	..	..	..	..	..	**0.5**	**78.7**	**106.1**	**98.5**
Public and publicly guaranteed	..	..	..	..	..	..	**0.5**	**78.7**	**106.1**	**98.5**
Official creditors	..	..	..	..	..	..	0.5	78.7	106.1	98.5
Multilateral	..	..	..	..	..	..	0.0	49.7	30.6	91.2
Concessional	..	..	..	..	..	..	0.0	22.8	35.5	114.6
Bilateral	..	..	..	..	..	..	0.5	29.0	75.5	7.3
Concessional	..	..	..	..	..	..	0.5	12.3	51.1	14.4
Private creditors	..	..	..	..	..	..	0.0	0.0	0.0	0.0
Bonds	..	..	..	..	..	..	0.0	0.0	0.0	0.0
Commercial banks	..	..	..	..	..	..	0.0	0.0	0.0	0.0
Other private	..	..	..	..	..	..	0.0	0.0	0.0	0.0
Private nonguaranteed	**0.0**	**0.0**	**0.0**	**0.0**	**0.0**	**0.0**	**0.0**	**0.0**	**0.0**	**0.0**
Bonds	..	..	..	..	..	..	0.0	0.0	0.0	0.0
Commercial banks	..	..	..	..	..	..	0.0	0.0	0.0	0.0
Memo:										
IBRD	0.0	0.0	0.0	0.0	0.0	0.0	0.0	0.0	0.0	0.0
IDA	0.0	0.0	0.0	0.0	0.0	0.0	0.0	22.8	35.5	80.7
DEBT SERVICE (LTDS)	..	..	..	..	..	..	**0.0**	**0.4**	**13.1**	**56.1**
Public and publicly guaranteed	..	..	..	..	..	..	**0.0**	**0.4**	**13.1**	**56.1**
Official creditors	..	..	..	..	..	..	0.0	0.4	13.1	56.1
Multilateral	..	..	..	..	..	..	0.0	0.3	5.1	33.1
Concessional	..	..	..	..	..	..	0.0	0.0	0.2	0.7
Bilateral	..	..	..	..	..	..	0.0	0.0	8.0	23.0
Concessional	..	..	..	..	..	..	0.0	0.0	1.7	11.2
Private creditors	..	..	..	..	..	..	0.0	0.0	0.0	0.0
Bonds	..	..	..	..	..	..	0.0	0.0	0.0	0.0
Commercial banks	..	..	..	..	..	..	0.0	0.0	0.0	0.0
Other private	..	..	..	..	..	..	0.0	0.0	0.0	0.0
Private nonguaranteed	**0.0**	**0.0**	**0.0**	**0.0**	**0.0**	**0.0**	**0.0**	**0.0**	**0.0**	**0.0**
Bonds	..	..	..	..	..	..	0.0	0.0	0.0	0.0
Commercial banks	..	..	..	..	..	..	0.0	0.0	0.0	0.0
Memo:										
IBRD	0.0	0.0	0.0	0.0	0.0	0.0	0.0	0.0	0.0	0.0
IDA	0.0	0.0	0.0	0.0	0.0	0.0	0.0	0.0	0.2	0.6
UNDISBURSED DEBT	..	..	..	..	..	..	**29.9**	**173.2**	**251.9**	**265.6**
Official creditors	..	..	..	..	..	..	29.9	173.2	251.9	265.6
Private creditors	..	..	..	..	..	..	0.0	0.0	0.0	0.0
Memorandum items										
Concessional LDOD	..	..	..	..	..	..	0.5	147.2	239.0	374.8
Variable rate LDOD	..	..	..	..	..	..	0.0	207.0	231.5	206.2
Public sector LDOD	..	..	..	..	..	..	0.5	234.0	359.2	474.3
Private sector LDOD	..	..	..	..	..	..	0.0	0.0	0.0	0.0

6. CURRENCY COMPOSITION OF LONG-TERM DEBT (PERCENT)

	1970	1980	1988	1989	1990	1991	1992	1993	1994	1995
Deutsche mark	..	..	..	..	..	..	0.0	0.0	0.7	2.6
French franc	..	..	..	..	..	..	0.0	0.0	0.0	0.0
Japanese yen	..	..	..	..	..	..	0.0	0.0	13.9	14.2
Pound sterling	..	..	..	..	..	..	0.0	0.0	0.0	0.0
Swiss franc	..	..	..	..	..	..	100.0	0.2	0.5	0.4
U.S.dollars	..	..	..	..	..	..	0.0	40.9	45.7	52.4
Multiple currency	..	..	..	..	..	..	0.0	0.0	0.0	6.8
Special drawing rights	..	..	..	..	..	..	0.0	0.0	0.0	0.0
All other currencies	..	..	..	..	..	..	0.0	58.9	39.1	23.6

KYRGYZ REPUBLIC

(US$ million, unless otherwise indicated)

	1970	1980	1988	1989	1990	1991	1992	1993	1994	1995
7. DEBT RESTRUCTURINGS										
Total amount rescheduled	0.0	0.0	0.0	0.0	0.0	0.0	0.0	155.9	0.0	0.0
Debt stock rescheduled	0.0	0.0	0.0	0.0	0.0	0.0	0.0	0.0	0.0	0.0
Principal rescheduled	0.0	0.0	0.0	0.0	0.0	0.0	0.0	0.0	0.0	0.0
Official	0.0	0.0	0.0	0.0	0.0	0.0	0.0	0.0	0.0	0.0
Private	0.0	0.0	0.0	0.0	0.0	0.0	0.0	0.0	0.0	0.0
Interest rescheduled	0.0	0.0	0.0	0.0	0.0	0.0	0.0	0.0	0.0	0.0
Official	0.0	0.0	0.0	0.0	0.0	0.0	0.0	0.0	0.0	0.0
Private	0.0	0.0	0.0	0.0	0.0	0.0	0.0	0.0	0.0	0.0
Debt forgiven	..	..	0.0	0.0	0.0	0.0	0.0	0.0	0.0	0.0
Memo: interest forgiven	..	..	0.0	0.0	0.0	0.0	0.0	0.0	0.0	0.0
Debt stock reduction	0.0	0.0	0.0	0.0	0.0	0.0	0.0	0.0	0.0	0.0
of which debt buyback	0.0	0.0	0.0	0.0	0.0	0.0	0.0	0.0	0.0	0.0
8. DEBT STOCK-FLOW RECONCILIATION										
Total change in debt stocks	..	..	..	..	..	..	..	293.8	155.4	160.5
Net flows on debt	..	..	..	..	..	..	..	140.3	132.7	166.4
Net change in interest arrears	..	..	..	..	..	..	..	0.0	12.6	-3.3
Interest capitalized	..	..	..	..	..	..	..	0.0	0.0	0.0
Debt forgiveness or reduction	..	..	..	..	..	..	..	0.0	0.0	0.0
Cross-currency valuation	..	..	..	..	..	..	..	-78.0	-63.1	-25.1
Residual	..	..	..	..	..	..	..	231.4	73.1	22.4
9. AVERAGE TERMS OF NEW COMMITMENTS										
ALL CREDITORS										
Interest (%)	..	..	..	..	..	..	3.4	4.5	1.6	3.9
Maturity (years)	..	..	..	..	..	..	4.1	21.8	34.3	28.8
Grace period (years)	..	..	..	..	..	..	3.9	7.0	10.0	8.1
Grant element (%)	..	..	..	..	..	..	20.7	38.8	71.2	48.4
Official creditors										
Interest (%)	..	..	..	..	..	..	3.4	4.5	1.6	3.9
Maturity (years)	..	..	..	..	..	..	4.1	21.8	34.3	28.8
Grace period (years)	..	..	..	..	..	..	3.9	7.0	10.0	8.1
Grant element (%)	..	..	..	..	..	..	20.7	38.8	71.2	48.4
Private creditors										
Interest (%)	..	..	..	..	..	..	0.0	0.0	0.0	0.0
Maturity (years)	..	..	..	..	..	..	0.0	0.0	0.0	0.0
Grace period (years)	..	..	..	..	..	..	0.0	0.0	0.0	0.0
Grant element (%)	..	..	..	..	..	..	0.0	0.0	0.0	0.0
Memorandum items										
Commitments	..	..	..	..	..	..	32.5	223.8	188.0	163.7
Official creditors	..	..	..	..	..	..	32.5	223.8	188.0	163.7
Private creditors	..	..	..	..	..	..	0.0	0.0	0.0	0.0

10. CONTRACTUAL OBLIGATIONS ON OUTSTANDING LONG-TERM DEBT

	1996	1997	1998	1999	2000	2001	2002	2003	2004	2005
TOTAL										
Disbursements	89.4	70.2	41.8	28.5	17.0	10.7	6.6	1.3	0.1	0.0
Principal	42.5	42.7	48.0	41.3	40.1	32.0	32.0	9.1	11.9	16.0
Interest	21.1	21.3	19.6	18.5	16.0	13.6	11.5	10.3	9.8	9.2
Official creditors										
Disbursements	89.4	70.2	41.8	28.5	17.0	10.7	6.6	1.3	0.1	0.0
Principal	42.5	42.7	48.0	41.3	40.1	32.0	32.0	9.1	11.9	16.0
Interest	21.1	21.3	19.6	18.5	16.0	13.6	11.5	10.3	9.8	9.2
Bilateral creditors										
Disbursements	43.8	24.9	9.7	3.9	2.4	0.1	0.0	0.0	0.0	0.0
Principal	42.5	42.5	47.9	36.3	34.7	26.5	26.5	3.0	3.9	5.1
Interest	17.8	16.5	13.9	12.2	9.8	7.5	5.7	4.8	4.7	4.5
Multilateral creditors										
Disbursements	45.6	45.3	32.1	24.6	14.7	10.6	6.6	1.3	0.1	0.0
Principal	0.0	0.1	0.1	5.0	5.5	5.5	5.5	6.1	8.0	11.0
Interest	3.4	4.9	5.7	6.2	6.2	6.0	5.8	5.5	5.1	4.7
Private creditors										
Disbursements	0.0	0.0	0.0	0.0	0.0	0.0	0.0	0.0	0.0	0.0
Principal	0.0	0.0	0.0	0.0	0.0	0.0	0.0	0.0	0.0	0.0
Interest	0.0	0.0	0.0	0.0	0.0	0.0	0.0	0.0	0.0	0.0
Commercial banks										
Disbursements	0.0	0.0	0.0	0.0	0.0	0.0	0.0	0.0	0.0	0.0
Principal	0.0	0.0	0.0	0.0	0.0	0.0	0.0	0.0	0.0	0.0
Interest	0.0	0.0	0.0	0.0	0.0	0.0	0.0	0.0	0.0	0.0
Other private										
Disbursements	0.0	0.0	0.0	0.0	0.0	0.0	0.0	0.0	0.0	0.0
Principal	0.0	0.0	0.0	0.0	0.0	0.0	0.0	0.0	0.0	0.0
Interest	0.0	0.0	0.0	0.0	0.0	0.0	0.0	0.0	0.0	0.0

LAO PEOPLE'S DEMOCRATIC REPUBLIC

(US$ million, unless otherwise indicated)

	1970	1980	1988	1989	1990	1991	1992	1993	1994	1995
1. SUMMARY DEBT DATA										
TOTAL DEBT STOCKS (EDT)	**..**	**350**	**1,330**	**1,473**	**1,768**	**1,875**	**1,917**	**1,985**	**2,080**	**2,165**
Long-term debt (LDOD)	**8**	**333**	**1,323**	**1,463**	**1,758**	**1,850**	**1,887**	**1,948**	**2,022**	**2,091**
Public and publicly guaranteed	8	333	1,323	1,463	1,758	1,850	1,887	1,948	2,022	2,091
Private nonguaranteed	0	0	0	0	0	0	0	0	0	0
Use of IMF credit	**0**	**16**	**3**	**8**	**8**	**21**	**28**	**36**	**47**	**64**
Short-term debt	**..**	**1**	**5**	**1**	**2**	**4**	**2**	**1**	**11**	**10**
of which interest arrears on LDOD	..	1	0	0	0	0	0	0	0	0
Official creditors	..	1	0	0	0	0	0	0	0	0
Private creditors	..	1	0	0	0	0	0	0	0	0
Memo: principal arrears on LDOD	..	4	1	0	1	1	0	0	0	0
Official creditors	..	1	1	0	1	1	0	0	0	0
Private creditors	..	4	0	0	0	0	0	0	0	0
Memo: export credits	..	..	7	3	3	2	2	2	5	3
TOTAL DEBT FLOWS										
Disbursements	**6**	**60**	**194**	**192**	**152**	**118**	**63**	**86**	**66**	**110**
Long-term debt	6	55	194	185	152	106	55	78	58	92
IMF purchases	0	4	0	8	0	12	8	8	8	18
Principal repayments	**1**	**1**	**8**	**15**	**6**	**5**	**6**	**24**	**15**	**19**
Long-term debt	1	1	5	13	6	5	6	24	15	18
IMF repurchases	0	0	3	2	1	0	0	0	0	2
Net flows on debt	**4**	**59**	**191**	**173**	**147**	**115**	**55**	**61**	**62**	**90**
of which short-term debt	..	..	5	-4	1	2	-2	-1	10	-1
Interest payments (INT)	**..**	**1**	**3**	**3**	**3**	**3**	**4**	**5**	**5**	**7**
Long-term debt	0	1	2	3	3	3	4	5	5	6
IMF charges	0	0	0	0	0	0	0	0	0	0
Short-term debt	..	0	0	0	0	0	0	0	0	1
Net transfers on debt	**..**	**57**	**188**	**171**	**144**	**111**	**51**	**56**	**56**	**83**
Total debt service paid (TDS)	**..**	**3**	**11**	**18**	**9**	**9**	**10**	**29**	**20**	**26**
Long-term debt	2	2	7	16	8	8	9	28	20	23
IMF repurchases and charges	0	0	3	2	1	0	0	0	0	2
Short-term debt (interest only)	..	0	0	0	0	0	0	0	0	1
2. AGGREGATE NET RESOURCE FLOWS AND NET TRANSFERS (LONG-TERM)										
NET RESOURCE FLOWS	**33**	**70**	**232**	**216**	**199**	**162**	**116**	**242**	**200**	**292**
Net flow of long-term debt (ex. IMF)	4	54	190	172	146	101	49	54	43	75
Foreign direct investment (net)	0	0	2	4	6	7	8	120	59	88
Portfolio equity flows	0	0	0	0	0	0	0	0	0	0
Grants (excluding technical coop.)	28	16	41	40	47	54	59	69	98	130
Memo: technical coop. grants	40	14	24	34	32	38	49	58	59	79
NET TRANSFERS	**32**	**69**	**230**	**213**	**196**	**159**	**112**	**238**	**195**	**286**
Interest on long-term debt	0	1	2	3	3	3	4	5	5	6
Profit remittances on FDI	0	0	0	0	0	0	0	0	0	0
3. MAJOR ECONOMIC AGGREGATES										
Gross national product (GNP)	..	..	597	730	868	1,027	1,179	1,325	1,543	1,734
Exports of goods & services (XGS)	..	..	76	87	105	138	200	336	394	453
of which workers remittances	..	..	0	0	0	0	0	0	0	0
Imports of goods & services (MGS)	..	..	179	223	215	250	309	500	634	673
International reserves (RES)	..	..	..	8	8	35	46	70	68	99
Current account balance	..	..	-103	-137	-111	-115	-111	-166	-243	-224
4. DEBT INDICATORS										
EDT / XGS (%)	..	..	1,750.2	1,700.4	1,690.3	1,361.4	960.4	591.3	527.5	478.3
EDT / GNP (%)	..	..	222.8	201.9	203.7	182.6	162.6	149.8	134.8	124.9
TDS / XGS (%)	..	..	14.1	20.4	8.7	6.3	4.8	8.5	5.1	5.8
INT / XGS (%)	..	..	3.3	3.2	2.9	2.5	2.1	1.4	1.3	1.5
INT / GNP (%)	..	..	0.4	0.4	0.4	0.3	0.4	0.4	0.3	0.4
RES / EDT (%)	..	..	..	0.6	0.5	1.9	2.4	3.5	3.2	4.6
RES / MGS (months)	..	..	..	0.4	0.5	1.7	1.8	1.7	1.3	1.8
Short-term / EDT (%)	..	0.4	0.4	0.1	0.1	0.2	0.1	0.1	0.5	0.5
Concessional / EDT (%)	..	93.3	99.0	99.0	99.1	98.4	98.2	97.9	97.0	96.4
Multilateral / EDT (%)	..	5.9	8.7	12.3	15.1	17.4	19.1	22.5	25.4	28.7

LAO PEOPLE'S DEMOCRATIC REPUBLIC

(US$ million, unless otherwise indicated)

	1970	1980	1988	1989	1990	1991	1992	1993	1994	1995
5. LONG-TERM DEBT										
DEBT OUTSTANDING (LDOD)	**8**	**333**	**1,323**	**1,463**	**1,758**	**1,850**	**1,887**	**1,948**	**2,022**	**2,091**
Public and publicly guaranteed	**8**	**333**	**1,323**	**1,463**	**1,758**	**1,850**	**1,887**	**1,948**	**2,022**	**2,091**
Official creditors	8	327	1,317	1,458	1,752	1,844	1,882	1,944	2,018	2,088
Multilateral	0	21	116	181	267	326	366	447	529	621
Concessional	0	21	116	181	267	326	366	447	529	621
Bilateral	8	306	1,201	1,277	1,485	1,518	1,516	1,498	1,489	1,467
Concessional	8	306	1,201	1,277	1,485	1,518	1,516	1,498	1,489	1,466
Private creditors	1	6	6	5	6	5	4	4	4	4
Bonds	0	0	0	0	0	0	0	0	0	0
Commercial banks	0	0	0	0	0	0	0	0	0	0
Other private	1	6	6	5	6	5	4	4	4	4
Private nonguaranteed	**0**	**0**	**0**	**0**	**0**	**0**	**0**	**0**	**0**	**0**
Bonds	0	0	0	0	0	0	0	0	0	0
Commercial banks	0	0	0	0	0	0	0	0	0	0
Memo:										
IBRD	0	0	0	0	0	0	0	0	0	0
IDA	0	6	57	92	131	147	180	217	253	285
DISBURSEMENTS	**6**	**55**	**194**	**185**	**152**	**106**	**55**	**78**	**58**	**92**
Public and publicly guaranteed	**6**	**55**	**194**	**185**	**152**	**106**	**55**	**78**	**58**	**92**
Official creditors	6	55	194	185	152	106	55	78	58	92
Multilateral	0	7	21	68	78	44	55	78	58	92
Concessional	0	7	21	68	78	44	55	78	58	92
Bilateral	6	48	174	117	74	62	0	0	0	0
Concessional	6	48	174	117	74	62	0	0	0	0
Private creditors	0	0	0	0	0	0	0	0	0	0
Bonds	0	0	0	0	0	0	0	0	0	0
Commercial banks	0	0	0	0	0	0	0	0	0	0
Other private	0	0	0	0	0	0	0	0	0	0
Private nonguaranteed	**0**	**0**	**0**	**0**	**0**	**0**	**0**	**0**	**0**	**0**
Bonds	0	0	0	0	0	0	0	0	0	0
Commercial banks	0	0	0	0	0	0	0	0	0	0
Memo:										
IBRD	0	0	0	0	0	0	0	0	0	0
IDA	0	5	10	35	32	15	38	38	27	28
PRINCIPAL REPAYMENTS	**1**	**1**	**5**	**13**	**6**	**5**	**6**	**24**	**15**	**18**
Public and publicly guaranteed	**1**	**1**	**5**	**13**	**6**	**5**	**6**	**24**	**15**	**18**
Official creditors	1	1	5	13	5	5	5	23	15	17
Multilateral	0	0	1	2	3	3	3	3	3	4
Concessional	0	0	1	2	3	3	3	3	3	4
Bilateral	1	1	3	11	2	2	2	20	11	13
Concessional	1	1	3	11	2	2	2	20	11	13
Private creditors	0	0	0	0	1	1	0	0	0	0
Bonds	0	0	0	0	0	0	0	0	0	0
Commercial banks	0	0	0	0	0	0	0	0	0	0
Other private	0	0	0	0	1	1	0	0	0	0
Private nonguaranteed	**0**	**0**	**0**	**0**	**0**	**0**	**0**	**0**	**0**	**0**
Bonds	0	0	0	0	0	0	0	0	0	0
Commercial banks	0	0	0	0	0	0	0	0	0	0
Memo:										
IBRD	0	0	0	0	0	0	0	0	0	0
IDA	0	0	0	0	0	0	1	1	1	1
NET FLOWS ON DEBT	**4**	**54**	**190**	**172**	**146**	**101**	**49**	**54**	**43**	**75**
Public and publicly guaranteed	**4**	**54**	**190**	**172**	**146**	**101**	**49**	**54**	**43**	**75**
Official creditors	5	54	190	172	147	101	49	54	44	75
Multilateral	0	7	20	66	75	41	51	74	55	88
Concessional	0	7	20	66	75	41	51	74	55	88
Bilateral	5	47	170	106	72	61	-2	-20	-11	-13
Concessional	5	47	170	106	72	61	-2	-20	-11	-13
Private creditors	0	0	0	0	-1	-1	0	0	0	0
Bonds	0	0	0	0	0	0	0	0	0	0
Commercial banks	0	0	0	0	0	0	0	0	0	0
Other private	0	0	0	0	-1	-1	0	0	0	0
Private nonguaranteed	**0**	**0**	**0**	**0**	**0**	**0**	**0**	**0**	**0**	**0**
Bonds	0	0	0	0	0	0	0	0	0	0
Commercial banks	0	0	0	0	0	0	0	0	0	0
Memo:										
IBRD	0	0	0	0	0	0	0	0	0	0
IDA	0	5	10	35	32	15	38	37	26	27

LAO PEOPLE'S DEMOCRATIC REPUBLIC

(US$ million, unless otherwise indicated)

	1970	1980	1988	1989	1990	1991	1992	1993	1994	1995
INTEREST PAYMENTS (LINT)	**0**	**1**	**2**	**3**	**3**	**3**	**4**	**5**	**5**	**6**
Public and publicly guaranteed	**0**	**1**	**2**	**3**	**3**	**3**	**4**	**5**	**5**	**6**
Official creditors	0	1	2	2	3	3	4	4	5	6
Multilateral	0	0	1	1	2	2	3	4	4	5
Concessional	0	0	1	1	2	2	3	4	4	5
Bilateral	0	1	1	1	1	1	1	1	1	1
Concessional	0	1	1	1	1	1	1	1	1	1
Private creditors	0	0	0	0	0	0	0	0	0	0
Bonds	0	0	0	0	0	0	0	0	0	0
Commercial banks	0	0	0	0	0	0	0	0	0	0
Other private	0	0	0	0	0	0	0	0	0	0
Private nonguaranteed	**0**	**0**	**0**	**0**	**0**	**0**	**0**	**0**	**0**	**0**
Bonds	0	0	0	0	0	0	0	0	0	0
Commercial banks	0	0	0	0	0	0	0	0	0	0
Memo:										
IBRD	0	0	0	0	0	0	0	0	0	0
IDA	0	0	1	1	1	1	1	1	2	2
NET TRANSFERS ON DEBT	**4**	**53**	**188**	**169**	**144**	**98**	**45**	**49**	**38**	**69**
Public and publicly guaranteed	**4**	**53**	**188**	**169**	**144**	**98**	**45**	**49**	**38**	**69**
Official creditors	4	53	188	170	144	98	46	50	39	69
Multilateral	0	7	18	65	73	38	48	70	51	83
Concessional	0	7	18	65	73	38	48	70	51	83
Bilateral	4	46	169	105	71	60	-3	-20	-12	-14
Concessional	4	46	169	105	71	60	-3	-20	-12	-14
Private creditors	0	0	0	-1	-1	-1	-1	-1	-1	-1
Bonds	0	0	0	0	0	0	0	0	0	0
Commercial banks	0	0	0	0	0	0	0	0	0	0
Other private	0	0	0	-1	-1	-1	-1	-1	-1	-1
Private nonguaranteed	**0**	**0**	**0**	**0**	**0**	**0**	**0**	**0**	**0**	**0**
Bonds	0	0	0	0	0	0	0	0	0	0
Commercial banks	0	0	0	0	0	0	0	0	0	0
Memo:										
IBRD	0	0	0	0	0	0	0	0	0	0
IDA	0	5	10	35	32	14	37	36	25	25
DEBT SERVICE (LTDS)	**2**	**2**	**7**	**16**	**8**	**8**	**9**	**28**	**20**	**23**
Public and publicly guaranteed	**2**	**2**	**7**	**16**	**8**	**8**	**9**	**28**	**20**	**23**
Official creditors	1	2	7	15	8	8	9	28	19	23
Multilateral	0	0	3	3	5	5	6	7	7	9
Concessional	0	0	3	3	5	5	6	7	7	9
Bilateral	1	2	4	12	3	2	3	20	12	14
Concessional	1	2	4	12	3	2	3	20	12	14
Private creditors	0	0	0	1	1	1	1	1	1	1
Bonds	0	0	0	0	0	0	0	0	0	0
Commercial banks	0	0	0	0	0	0	0	0	0	0
Other private	0	0	0	1	1	1	1	1	1	1
Private nonguaranteed	**0**	**0**	**0**	**0**	**0**	**0**	**0**	**0**	**0**	**0**
Bonds	0	0	0	0	0	0	0	0	0	0
Commercial banks	0	0	0	0	0	0	0	0	0	0
Memo:										
IBRD	0	0	0	0	0	0	0	0	0	0
IDA	0	0	1	1	1	1	2	2	2	3
UNDISBURSED DEBT	**10**	**254**	**270**	**232**	**221**	**328**	**319**	**327**	**458**	**484**
Official creditors	9	254	270	232	221	328	319	327	458	484
Private creditors	1	0	0	0	0	0	0	0	0	0
Memorandum items										
Concessional LDOD	8	327	1,317	1,458	1,752	1,844	1,882	1,944	2,018	2,086
Variable rate LDOD	0	0	0	0	0	0	0	0	0	0
Public sector LDOD	8	333	1,323	1,463	1,758	1,850	1,887	1,948	2,022	2,091
Private sector LDOD	0	0	0	0	0	0	0	0	0	0

6. CURRENCY COMPOSITION OF LONG-TERM DEBT (PERCENT)

	1970	1980	1988	1989	1990	1991	1992	1993	1994	1995
Deutsche mark	76.7	10.3	2.2	2.0	1.8	0.0	0.0	0.0	0.0	0.1
French franc	13.2	4.3	0.4	0.4	0.3	0.3	0.2	0.2	0.2	0.2
Japanese yen	0.0	7.7	2.5	1.8	1.5	1.4	1.3	1.3	1.3	1.1
Pound sterling	0.0	0.0	0.0	0.0	0.0	0.0	0.0	0.0	0.0	0.0
Swiss franc	0.0	0.0	0.0	0.0	0.0	0.0	0.0	0.0	0.0	0.0
U.S.dollars	9.6	3.6	4.1	6.0	7.1	7.7	9.2	10.7	12.0	13.1
Multiple currency	0.0	2.9	3.4	5.2	7.1	9.1	9.4	11.4	13.1	15.5
Special drawing rights	0.0	0.0	1.3	1.2	1.1	1.0	1.0	0.9	1.1	1.2
All other currencies	0.0	71.1	86.1	83.4	81.1	80.5	78.9	75.5	72.2	68.9

LAO PEOPLE'S DEMOCRATIC REPUBLIC

(US$ million, unless otherwise indicated)

	1970	1980	1988	1989	1990	1991	1992	1993	1994	1995
7. DEBT RESTRUCTURINGS										
Total amount rescheduled	0	0	6	0	0	1,262	0	0	0	0
Debt stock rescheduled	0	0	0	0	0	1,262	0	0	0	0
Principal rescheduled	0	0	5	0	0	0	0	0	0	0
Official	0	0	0	0	0	0	0	0	0	0
Private	0	0	5	0	0	0	0	0	0	0
Interest rescheduled	0	0	1	0	0	0	0	0	0	0
Official	0	0	0	0	0	0	0	0	0	0
Private	0	0	1	0	0	0	0	0	0	0
Debt forgiven	..	..	9	0	0	29	0	0	0	0
Memo: interest forgiven	..	..	2	0	0	0	0	0	0	0
Debt stock reduction	0	0	0	0	0	0	0	0	0	0
of which debt buyback	0	0	0	0	0	0	0	0	0	0
8. DEBT STOCK-FLOW RECONCILIATION										
Total change in debt stocks	..	..	..	142	296	107	42	69	95	85
Net flows on debt	..	..	..	173	147	115	55	61	62	90
Net change in interest arrears	..	..	..	0	0	0	0	0	0	0
Interest capitalized	..	..	..	0	0	0	0	0	0	0
Debt forgiveness or reduction	..	..	..	0	0	-29	0	0	0	0
Cross-currency valuation	..	..	..	-2	157	2	-1	3	5	0
Residual	..	..	..	-29	-8	19	-12	5	28	-5
9. AVERAGE TERMS OF NEW COMMITMENTS										
ALL CREDITORS										
Interest (%)	3.0	0.2	0.2	0.4	0.9	0.6	0.9	0.9	0.5	2.5
Maturity (years)	28.2	33.0	35.0	34.6	39.9	36.9	39.8	39.4	39.7	37.1
Grace period (years)	4.4	25.6	23.6	20.1	10.0	15.8	10.2	9.9	10.2	9.7
Grant element (%)	51.0	91.1	90.4	86.9	79.0	83.8	79.6	78.5	82.5	62.0
Official creditors										
Interest (%)	2.5	0.2	0.2	0.4	0.9	0.6	0.9	0.9	0.5	2.5
Maturity (years)	30.8	33.0	35.0	34.6	39.9	36.9	39.8	39.4	39.7	37.1
Grace period (years)	4.2	25.6	23.6	20.1	10.0	15.8	10.2	9.9	10.2	9.7
Grant element (%)	55.8	91.1	90.4	86.9	79.0	83.8	79.6	78.5	82.5	62.0
Private creditors										
Interest (%)	6.3	0.0	0.0	0.0	0.0	0.0	0.0	0.0	0.0	0.0
Maturity (years)	10.1	0.0	0.0	0.0	0.0	0.0	0.0	0.0	0.0	0.0
Grace period (years)	5.6	0.0	0.0	0.0	0.0	0.0	0.0	0.0	0.0	0.0
Grant element (%)	18.2	0.0	0.0	0.0	0.0	0.0	0.0	0.0	0.0	0.0
Memorandum items										
Commitments	12	96	119	153	125	213	64	84	171	110
Official creditors	11	96	119	153	125	213	64	84	171	110
Private creditors	2	0	0	0	0	0	0	0	0	0

10. CONTRACTUAL OBLIGATIONS ON OUTSTANDING LONG-TERM DEBT

	1996	1997	1998	1999	2000	2001	2002	2003	2004	2005
TOTAL										
Disbursements	101	110	90	65	45	26	16	4	0	0
Principal	17	17	19	20	24	25	27	30	32	109
Interest	7	8	8	9	9	9	9	9	9	9
Official creditors										
Disbursements	101	110	90	65	45	26	16	4	0	0
Principal	17	17	18	20	24	24	27	30	32	109
Interest	7	8	8	9	9	9	9	9	9	9
Bilateral creditors										
Disbursements	0	0	0	0	0	0	0	0	0	0
Principal	14	14	14	14	14	13	13	13	12	87
Interest	1	0	0	0	0	0	0	0	0	0
Multilateral creditors										
Disbursements	101	110	90	65	45	26	16	4	0	0
Principal	3	3	5	6	10	12	14	17	20	23
Interest	6	7	8	8	9	9	9	9	9	9
Private creditors										
Disbursements	0	0	0	0	0	0	0	0	0	0
Principal	1	1	1	1	1	1	1	1	0	0
Interest	0	0	0	0	0	0	0	0	0	0
Commercial banks										
Disbursements	0	0	0	0	0	0	0	0	0	0
Principal	0	0	0	0	0	0	0	0	0	0
Interest	0	0	0	0	0	0	0	0	0	0
Other private										
Disbursements	0	0	0	0	0	0	0	0	0	0
Principal	1	1	1	1	1	1	1	1	0	0
Interest	0	0	0	0	0	0	0	0	0	0

LATVIA

(US$ million, unless otherwise indicated)

	1970	1980	1988	1989	1990	1991	1992	1993	1994	1995
1. SUMMARY DEBT DATA										
TOTAL DEBT STOCKS (EDT)	..	..	..	..	..	..	**64.6**	**235.8**	**373.8**	**461.7**
Long-term debt (LDOD)	..	..	..	..	..	..	**30.0**	**123.6**	**207.5**	**270.2**
Public and publicly guaranteed	..	..	..	..	..	..	30.0	123.6	207.5	270.2
Private nonguaranteed	0.0	0.0	0.0	0.0	0.0	0.0	0.0	0.0	0.0	0.0
Use of IMF credit	**0.0**	**0.0**	**0.0**	**0.0**	**0.0**	**0.0**	**34.6**	**106.8**	**160.3**	**160.4**
Short-term debt	..	..	..	..	..	..	**0.0**	**5.4**	**6.0**	**31.2**
of which interest arrears on LDOD	..	..	..	..	..	..	0.0	0.0	0.0	0.0
Official creditors	..	..	..	..	..	..	0.0	0.0	0.0	0.0
Private creditors	..	..	..	..	..	..	0.0	0.0	0.0	0.0
Memo: principal arrears on LDOD	..	..	..	..	..	..	0.0	1.9	0.0	0.0
Official creditors	..	..	..	..	..	..	0.0	1.9	0.0	0.0
Private creditors	..	..	..	..	..	..	0.0	0.0	0.0	0.0
Memo: export credits	..	..	0.0	0.0	0.0	0.0	13.0	41.0	92.0	122.0
TOTAL DEBT FLOWS										
Disbursements	..	..	..	..	..	..	**66.6**	**174.9**	**130.0**	**73.8**
Long-term debt	..	..	..	..	..	..	31.2	101.5	84.2	73.8
IMF purchases	0.0	0.0	0.0	0.0	0.0	0.0	35.4	73.5	45.9	0.0
Principal repayments	..	..	..	..	..	..	**0.0**	**4.4**	**9.5**	**9.5**
Long-term debt	..	..	..	..	..	..	0.0	4.4	9.5	6.6
IMF repurchases	0.0	0.0	0.0	0.0	0.0	0.0	0.0	0.0	0.0	2.9
Net flows on debt	..	..	..	..	..	..	**66.6**	**175.8**	**121.2**	**89.6**
of which short-term debt	..	..	..	..	..	..	0.0	5.3	0.7	25.2
Interest payments (INT)	..	..	..	..	..	..	**0.2**	**6.6**	**16.0**	**24.3**
Long-term debt	..	..	..	..	..	..	0.2	3.8	9.5	14.2
IMF charges	0.0	0.0	0.0	0.0	0.0	0.0	0.0	2.7	6.2	9.0
Short-term debt	..	..	..	..	..	..	0.0	0.1	0.3	1.1
Net transfers on debt	..	..	..	..	..	..	**66.4**	**169.2**	**105.2**	**65.2**
Total debt service paid (TDS)	..	..	..	..	..	..	**0.2**	**11.0**	**25.6**	**33.8**
Long-term debt	..	..	..	..	..	..	0.2	8.2	19.0	20.8
IMF repurchases and charges	0.0	0.0	0.0	0.0	0.0	0.0	0.0	2.7	6.2	11.8
Short-term debt (interest only)	..	..	..	..	..	..	0.0	0.1	0.3	1.1
2. AGGREGATE NET RESOURCE FLOWS AND NET TRANSFERS (LONG-TERM)										
NET RESOURCE FLOWS	..	..	..	..	..	..	**113.4**	**160.6**	**309.7**	**268.5**
Net flow of long-term debt (ex. IMF)	..	..	..	..	..	..	31.2	97.0	74.6	67.2
Foreign direct investment (net)	..	..	..	..	..	..	29.0	45.0	214.0	180.0
Portfolio equity flows	..	..	..	..	..	..	0.0	0.0	0.0	0.0
Grants (excluding technical coop.)	..	..	..	..	..	..	53.2	18.6	21.1	21.3
Memo: technical coop. grants	..	..	..	..	..	..	18.1	14.9	28.0	37.6
NET TRANSFERS	..	..	..	..	..	..	**113.1**	**156.9**	**300.2**	**254.3**
Interest on long-term debt	..	..	..	..	..	..	0.2	3.8	9.5	14.2
Profit remittances on FDI	..	..	..	..	..	..	0.0	0.0	0.0	0.0
3. MAJOR ECONOMIC AGGREGATES										
Gross national product (GNP)	..	..	..	..	..	..	6,794.9	5,661.2	5,849.7	6,046.7
Exports of goods & services (XGS)	..	..	..	..	..	..	1,092.9	1,605.1	1,729.7	2,151.1
of which workers remittances	..	..	..	..	..	..	0.0	0.0	0.0	0.0
Imports of goods & services (MGS)	..	..	..	..	..	..	997.6	1,266.1	1,661.2	2,245.7
International reserves (RES)	..	..	..	..	..	..	..	526.4	640.7	602.1
Current account balance	..	..	..	..	..	..	191.4	416.8	201.2	-27.1
4. DEBT INDICATORS										
EDT / XGS (%)	..	..	..	..	..	..	5.9	14.7	21.6	21.5
EDT / GNP (%)	..	..	..	..	..	..	1.0	4.2	6.4	7.6
TDS / XGS (%)	..	..	..	..	..	..	0.0	0.7	1.5	1.6
INT / XGS (%)	..	..	..	..	..	..	0.0	0.4	0.9	1.1
INT / GNP (%)	..	..	..	..	..	..	0.0	0.1	0.3	0.4
RES / EDT (%)	..	..	..	..	..	..	..	223.2	171.4	130.4
RES / MGS (months)	..	..	..	..	..	..	..	5.0	4.6	3.2
Short-term / EDT (%)	..	..	..	..	..	..	0.0	2.3	1.6	6.8
Concessional / EDT (%)	..	..	..	..	..	..	14.4	33.6	30.3	26.3
Multilateral / EDT (%)	..	..	..	..	..	..	0.0	28.3	30.7	30.3

LATVIA

(US$ million, unless otherwise indicated)

	1970	1980	1988	1989	1990	1991	1992	1993	1994	1995
5. LONG-TERM DEBT										
DEBT OUTSTANDING (LDOD)	..	..	..	..	..	..	**30.0**	**123.6**	**207.5**	**270.2**
Public and publicly guaranteed	..	..	..	..	..	..	**30.0**	**123.6**	**207.5**	**270.2**
Official creditors	..	..	..	..	..	..	17.2	107.0	173.7	200.9
Multilateral	..	..	..	..	..	..	0.0	66.8	114.8	139.7
Concessional	..	..	..	..	..	..	0.0	44.8	54.4	62.5
Bilateral	..	..	..	..	..	..	17.2	40.2	58.9	61.2
Concessional	..	..	..	..	..	..	9.3	34.5	58.9	58.9
Private creditors	..	..	..	..	..	..	12.8	16.6	33.8	69.2
Bonds	..	..	..	..	..	..	0.0	0.0	0.0	38.9
Commercial banks	..	..	..	..	..	..	2.5	0.0	0.0	0.0
Other private	..	..	..	..	..	..	10.3	16.6	33.8	30.3
Private nonguaranteed	**0.0**	**0.0**	**0.0**	**0.0**	**0.0**	**0.0**	**0.0**	**0.0**	**0.0**	**0.0**
Bonds	..	..	..	..	..	..	0.0	0.0	0.0	0.0
Commercial banks	..	..	..	..	..	..	0.0	0.0	0.0	0.0
Memo:										
IBRD	0.0	0.0	0.0	0.0	0.0	0.0	0.0	20.9	44.8	54.9
IDA	0.0	0.0	0.0	0.0	0.0	0.0	0.0	0.0	0.0	0.0
DISBURSEMENTS	..	..	..	..	..	..	**31.2**	**101.5**	**84.2**	**73.8**
Public and publicly guaranteed	..	..	..	..	..	..	**31.2**	**101.5**	**84.2**	**73.8**
Official creditors	..	..	..	..	..	..	17.6	94.5	65.4	26.4
Multilateral	..	..	..	..	..	..	0.0	69.3	41.6	23.2
Concessional	..	..	..	..	..	..	0.0	46.9	5.2	4.7
Bilateral	..	..	..	..	..	..	17.6	25.2	23.8	3.2
Concessional	..	..	..	..	..	..	9.3	25.2	23.8	0.8
Private creditors	..	..	..	..	..	..	13.6	7.0	18.8	47.5
Bonds	..	..	..	..	..	..	0.0	0.0	0.0	42.8
Commercial banks	..	..	..	..	..	..	2.5	0.0	0.0	0.0
Other private	..	..	..	..	..	..	11.1	7.0	18.8	4.7
Private nonguaranteed	**0.0**	**0.0**	**0.0**	**0.0**	**0.0**	**0.0**	**0.0**	**0.0**	**0.0**	**0.0**
Bonds	..	..	..	..	..	..	0.0	0.0	0.0	0.0
Commercial banks	..	..	..	..	..	..	0.0	0.0	0.0	0.0
Memo:										
IBRD	0.0	0.0	0.0	0.0	0.0	0.0	0.0	21.3	22.0	8.7
IDA	0.0	0.0	0.0	0.0	0.0	0.0	0.0	0.0	0.0	0.0
PRINCIPAL REPAYMENTS	..	..	..	..	..	..	**0.0**	**4.4**	**9.5**	**6.6**
Public and publicly guaranteed	..	..	..	..	..	..	**0.0**	**4.4**	**9.5**	**6.6**
Official creditors	..	..	..	..	..	..	0.0	1.9	5.5	3.3
Multilateral	..	..	..	..	..	..	0.0	0.0	0.0	3.3
Concessional	..	..	..	..	..	..	0.0	0.0	0.0	0.0
Bilateral	..	..	..	..	..	..	0.0	1.9	5.5	0.0
Concessional	..	..	..	..	..	..	0.0	0.0	0.0	0.0
Private creditors	..	..	..	..	..	..	0.0	2.5	4.0	3.3
Bonds	..	..	..	..	..	..	0.0	0.0	0.0	0.0
Commercial banks	..	..	..	..	..	..	0.0	2.5	0.0	0.0
Other private	..	..	..	..	..	..	0.0	0.0	4.0	3.3
Private nonguaranteed	**0.0**	**0.0**	**0.0**	**0.0**	**0.0**	**0.0**	**0.0**	**0.0**	**0.0**	**0.0**
Bonds	..	..	..	..	..	..	0.0	0.0	0.0	0.0
Commercial banks	..	..	..	..	..	..	0.0	0.0	0.0	0.0
Memo:										
IBRD	0.0	0.0	0.0	0.0	0.0	0.0	0.0	0.0	0.0	0.0
IDA	0.0	0.0	0.0	0.0	0.0	0.0	0.0	0.0	0.0	0.0
NET FLOWS ON DEBT	..	..	..	..	..	..	**31.2**	**97.0**	**74.6**	**67.2**
Public and publicly guaranteed	..	..	..	..	..	..	**31.2**	**97.0**	**74.6**	**67.2**
Official creditors	..	..	..	..	..	..	17.6	92.5	59.9	23.1
Multilateral	..	..	..	..	..	..	0.0	69.3	41.6	19.9
Concessional	..	..	..	..	..	..	0.0	46.9	5.2	4.7
Bilateral	..	..	..	..	..	..	17.6	23.3	18.3	3.2
Concessional	..	..	..	..	..	..	9.3	25.2	23.8	0.8
Private creditors	..	..	..	..	..	..	13.6	4.5	14.7	44.2
Bonds	..	..	..	..	..	..	0.0	0.0	0.0	42.8
Commercial banks	..	..	..	..	..	..	2.5	-2.5	0.0	0.0
Other private	..	..	..	..	..	..	11.1	7.0	14.7	1.4
Private nonguaranteed	**0.0**	**0.0**	**0.0**	**0.0**	**0.0**	**0.0**	**0.0**	**0.0**	**0.0**	**0.0**
Bonds	..	..	..	..	..	..	0.0	0.0	0.0	0.0
Commercial banks	..	..	..	..	..	..	0.0	0.0	0.0	0.0
Memo:										
IBRD	0.0	0.0	0.0	0.0	0.0	0.0	0.0	21.3	22.0	8.7
IDA	0.0	0.0	0.0	0.0	0.0	0.0	0.0	0.0	0.0	0.0

LATVIA

(US$ million, unless otherwise indicated)

	1970	*1980*	*1988*	*1989*	*1990*	*1991*	*1992*	*1993*	*1994*	*1995*
INTEREST PAYMENTS (LINT)	..	..	..	..	..	..	**0.2**	**3.8**	**9.5**	**14.2**
Public and publicly guaranteed	..	..	..	..	..	..	**0.2**	**3.8**	**9.5**	**14.2**
Official creditors	..	..	..	..	..	..	0.1	3.2	8.6	12.8
Multilateral	..	..	..	..	..	..	0.0	2.6	6.3	9.1
Concessional	..	..	..	..	..	..	0.0	2.1	3.5	3.9
Bilateral	..	..	..	..	..	..	0.1	0.5	2.2	3.7
Concessional	..	..	..	..	..	..	0.0	0.2	1.7	3.6
Private creditors	..	..	..	..	..	..	0.2	0.6	1.0	1.4
Bonds	..	..	..	..	..	..	0.0	0.0	0.0	0.0
Commercial banks	..	..	..	..	..	..	0.2	0.0	0.0	0.0
Other private	..	..	..	..	..	..	0.0	0.6	1.0	1.4
Private nonguaranteed	**0.0**	**0.0**	**0.0**	**0.0**	**0.0**	**0.0**	**0.0**	**0.0**	**0.0**	**0.0**
Bonds	..	..	..	..	..	..	0.0	0.0	0.0	0.0
Commercial banks	..	..	..	..	..	..	0.0	0.0	0.0	0.0
Memo:										
IBRD	0.0	0.0	0.0	0.0	0.0	0.0	0.0	0.3	2.0	3.5
IDA	0.0	0.0	0.0	0.0	0.0	0.0	0.0	0.0	0.0	0.0
NET TRANSFERS ON DEBT	..	..	..	..	..	..	**30.9**	**93.3**	**65.1**	**53.0**
Public and publicly guaranteed	..	..	..	..	..	..	**30.9**	**93.3**	**65.1**	**53.0**
Official creditors	..	..	..	..	..	..	17.5	89.4	51.4	10.3
Multilateral	..	..	..	..	..	..	0.0	66.7	35.3	10.8
Concessional	..	..	..	..	..	..	0.0	44.8	1.7	0.8
Bilateral	..	..	..	..	..	..	17.5	22.7	16.1	-0.5
Concessional	..	..	..	..	..	..	9.3	25.0	22.1	-2.8
Private creditors	..	..	..	..	..	..	13.4	3.9	13.8	42.7
Bonds	..	..	..	..	..	..	0.0	0.0	0.0	42.8
Commercial banks	..	..	..	..	..	..	2.3	-2.5	0.0	0.0
Other private	..	..	..	..	..	..	11.1	6.5	13.8	0.0
Private nonguaranteed	**0.0**	**0.0**	**0.0**	**0.0**	**0.0**	**0.0**	**0.0**	**0.0**	**0.0**	**0.0**
Bonds	..	..	..	..	..	..	0.0	0.0	0.0	0.0
Commercial banks	..	..	..	..	..	..	0.0	0.0	0.0	0.0
Memo:										
IBRD	0.0	0.0	0.0	0.0	0.0	0.0	0.0	21.0	20.0	5.2
IDA	0.0	0.0	0.0	0.0	0.0	0.0	0.0	0.0	0.0	0.0
DEBT SERVICE (LTDS)	..	..	..	..	..	..	**0.2**	**8.2**	**19.0**	**20.8**
Public and publicly guaranteed	..	..	..	..	..	..	**0.2**	**8.2**	**19.0**	**20.8**
Official creditors	..	..	..	..	..	..	0.1	5.1	14.0	16.1
Multilateral	..	..	..	..	..	..	0.0	2.6	6.3	12.4
Concessional	..	..	..	..	..	..	0.0	2.1	3.5	3.9
Bilateral	..	..	..	..	..	..	0.1	2.5	7.7	3.7
Concessional	..	..	..	..	..	..	0.0	0.2	1.7	3.6
Private creditors	..	..	..	..	..	..	0.2	3.1	5.0	4.8
Bonds	..	..	..	..	..	..	0.0	0.0	0.0	0.0
Commercial banks	..	..	..	..	..	..	0.2	2.5	0.0	0.0
Other private	..	..	..	..	..	..	0.0	0.6	5.0	4.8
Private nonguaranteed	**0.0**	**0.0**	**0.0**	**0.0**	**0.0**	**0.0**	**0.0**	**0.0**	**0.0**	**0.0**
Bonds	..	..	..	..	..	..	0.0	0.0	0.0	0.0
Commercial banks	..	..	..	..	..	..	0.0	0.0	0.0	0.0
Memo:										
IBRD	0.0	0.0	0.0	0.0	0.0	0.0	0.0	0.3	2.0	3.5
IDA	0.0	0.0	0.0	0.0	0.0	0.0	0.0	0.0	0.0	0.0
UNDISBURSED DEBT	..	..	..	..	..	..	**95.0**	**173.6**	**183.8**	**223.4**
Official creditors	..	..	..	..	..	..	84.6	159.0	176.3	207.2
Private creditors	..	..	..	..	..	..	10.4	14.6	7.5	16.3
Memorandum items										
Concessional LDOD	..	..	..	..	..	..	9.3	79.3	113.3	121.4
Variable rate LDOD	..	..	..	..	..	..	15.7	110.2	153.2	173.1
Public sector LDOD	..	..	..	..	..	..	30.0	122.7	196.0	250.7
Private sector LDOD	..	..	..	..	..	..	0.0	0.9	11.5	19.4

6. CURRENCY COMPOSITION OF LONG-TERM DEBT (PERCENT)

	1970	1980	1988	1989	1990	1991	1992	1993	1994	1995
Deutsche mark	..	..	..	..	..	..	8.0	3.7	3.6	8.6
French franc	..	..	..	..	..	..	0.0	0.0	0.0	0.0
Japanese yen	..	..	..	..	..	..	0.0	0.0	15.6	26.3
Pound sterling	..	..	..	..	..	..	0.0	0.0	0.0	0.0
Swiss franc	..	..	..	..	..	..	0.0	0.0	0.0	0.0
U.S.dollars	..	..	..	..	..	..	52.4	67.7	54.8	44.8
Multiple currency	..	..	..	..	..	..	0.0	16.9	21.6	20.3
Special drawing rights	..	..	..	..	..	..	0.0	0.0	0.0	0.0
All other currencies	..	..	..	..	..	..	39.4	11.6	4.4	0.1

LATVIA

(US$ million, unless otherwise indicated)

	1970	1980	1988	1989	1990	1991	1992	1993	1994	1995
7. DEBT RESTRUCTURINGS										
Total amount rescheduled	0.0	0.0	0.0	0.0	0.0	0.0	0.0	0.0	0.0	0.0
Debt stock rescheduled	0.0	0.0	0.0	0.0	0.0	0.0	0.0	0.0	0.0	0.0
Principal rescheduled	0.0	0.0	0.0	0.0	0.0	0.0	0.0	0.0	0.0	0.0
Official	0.0	0.0	0.0	0.0	0.0	0.0	0.0	0.0	0.0	0.0
Private	0.0	0.0	0.0	0.0	0.0	0.0	0.0	0.0	0.0	0.0
Interest rescheduled	0.0	0.0	0.0	0.0	0.0	0.0	0.0	0.0	0.0	0.0
Official	0.0	0.0	0.0	0.0	0.0	0.0	0.0	0.0	0.0	0.0
Private	0.0	0.0	0.0	0.0	0.0	0.0	0.0	0.0	0.0	0.0
Debt forgiven	..	..	0.0	0.0	0.0	0.0	0.0	0.0	0.0	0.0
Memo: interest forgiven	..	..	0.0	0.0	0.0	0.0	0.0	0.0	0.0	0.0
Debt stock reduction	0.0	0.0	0.0	0.0	0.0	0.0	0.0	0.0	0.0	0.0
of which debt buyback	0.0	0.0	0.0	0.0	0.0	0.0	0.0	0.0	0.0	0.0
8. DEBT STOCK-FLOW RECONCILIATION										
Total change in debt stocks	..	..	..	..	..	..	65.0	171.2	138.0	88.0
Net flows on debt	..	..	..	..	..	..	66.6	175.8	121.2	89.6
Net change in interest arrears	..	..	..	..	..	..	0.0	0.0	0.0	0.0
Interest capitalized	..	..	..	..	..	..	0.0	0.0	0.0	0.0
Debt forgiveness or reduction	..	..	..	..	..	..	0.0	0.0	0.0	0.0
Cross-currency valuation	..	..	..	..	..	..	-1.7	-1.7	8.6	1.1
Residual	..	..	..	..	..	..	0.0	-2.9	8.2	-2.7
9. AVERAGE TERMS OF NEW COMMITMENTS										
ALL CREDITORS										
Interest (%)	..	..	..	..	..	..	6.0	4.2	6.9	5.2
Maturity (years)	..	..	..	..	..	..	13.7	9.5	14.7	8.9
Grace period (years)	..	..	..	..	..	..	4.0	5.8	4.2	3.2
Grant element (%)	..	..	..	..	..	..	19.5	29.2	16.5	19.0
Official creditors										
Interest (%)	..	..	..	..	..	..	6.2	4.1	6.9	5.3
Maturity (years)	..	..	..	..	..	..	14.6	9.8	16.3	14.1
Grace period (years)	..	..	..	..	..	..	4.3	6.1	4.7	4.1
Grant element (%)	..	..	..	..	..	..	19.5	30.3	18.3	25.3
Private creditors										
Interest (%)	..	..	..	..	..	..	5.0	5.8	7.6	5.0
Maturity (years)	..	..	..	..	..	..	8.1	6.3	3.3	3.6
Grace period (years)	..	..	..	..	..	..	2.4	2.0	0.6	2.2
Grant element (%)	..	..	..	..	..	..	19.2	13.3	3.6	12.4
Memorandum items										
Commitments	..	..	..	..	..	..	120.3	184.5	82.7	114.3
Official creditors	..	..	..	..	..	..	102.7	172.4	72.5	58.4
Private creditors	..	..	..	..	..	..	17.6	12.1	10.2	56.0

10. CONTRACTUAL OBLIGATIONS ON OUTSTANDING LONG-TERM DEBT

	1996	1997	1998	1999	2000	2001	2002	2003	2004	2005
TOTAL										
Disbursements	77.3	58.0	34.3	21.2	13.6	7.2	5.3	3.8	2.0	0.7
Principal	18.6	53.6	24.6	28.4	158.0	26.8	32.3	19.6	19.6	19.6
Interest	19.1	22.4	21.4	21.1	17.1	11.3	10.0	8.3	7.3	6.3
Official creditors										
Disbursements	69.7	52.5	32.1	20.4	13.5	7.2	5.3	3.8	2.0	0.7
Principal	6.8	6.8	17.5	21.5	152.8	24.1	30.4	18.8	18.8	18.8
Interest	15.9	18.5	20.0	20.2	16.7	11.1	9.9	8.3	7.3	6.3
Bilateral creditors										
Disbursements	29.6	17.6	6.7	2.7	0.5	0.3	0.1	0.0	0.0	0.0
Principal	0.5	0.5	5.5	8.6	31.0	6.8	13.1	6.8	6.8	6.8
Interest	4.2	5.1	5.5	5.4	5.0	3.2	2.9	2.2	1.9	1.6
Multilateral creditors										
Disbursements	40.1	34.9	25.4	17.7	13.0	6.9	5.2	3.8	2.0	0.7
Principal	6.3	6.3	11.9	12.9	121.8	17.4	17.4	12.0	12.0	12.0
Interest	11.7	13.4	14.6	14.9	11.7	7.9	7.0	6.1	5.4	4.7
Private creditors										
Disbursements	7.6	5.5	2.2	0.8	0.1	0.0	0.0	0.0	0.0	0.0
Principal	11.8	46.8	7.1	6.9	5.2	2.6	1.9	0.8	0.8	0.8
Interest	3.2	3.9	1.3	0.9	0.4	0.2	0.1	0.0	0.0	0.0
Commercial banks										
Disbursements	0.0	0.0	0.0	0.0	0.0	0.0	0.0	0.0	0.0	0.0
Principal	0.0	0.0	0.0	0.0	0.0	0.0	0.0	0.0	0.0	0.0
Interest	0.0	0.0	0.0	0.0	0.0	0.0	0.0	0.0	0.0	0.0
Other private										
Disbursements	7.6	5.5	2.2	0.8	0.1	0.0	0.0	0.0	0.0	0.0
Principal	11.8	46.8	7.1	6.9	5.2	2.6	1.9	0.8	0.8	0.8
Interest	3.2	3.9	1.3	0.9	0.4	0.2	0.1	0.0	0.0	0.0

LEBANON

(US$ million, unless otherwise indicated)

	1970	1980	1988	1989	1990	1991	1992	1993	1994	1995
1. SUMMARY DEBT DATA										
TOTAL DEBT STOCKS (EDT)	..	**510**	**985**	**1,023**	**1,779**	**1,554**	**1,806**	**1,345**	**1,718**	**2,966**
Long-term debt (LDOD)	**64**	**216**	**372**	**354**	**358**	**336**	**301**	**368**	**378**	**1,601**
Public and publicly guaranteed	64	216	372	354	358	336	301	368	378	1,551
Private nonguaranteed	0	0	0	0	0	0	0	0	0	50
Use of IMF credit	**0**	**0**	**0**	**0**	**0**	**0**	**0**	**0**	**0**	**0**
Short-term debt	..	**294**	**614**	**669**	**1,421**	**1,218**	**1,505**	**977**	**1,340**	**1,365**
of which interest arrears on LDOD	..	0	21	29	39	42	22	18	11	10
Official creditors	..	0	7	12	16	12	4	2	1	0
Private creditors	..	0	13	18	23	30	18	16	10	10
Memo: principal arrears on LDOD	..	0	76	101	132	141	56	54	49	41
Official creditors	..	0	9	18	28	17	9	10	12	0
Private creditors	..	0	66	83	104	125	47	44	37	41
Memo: export credits	..	..	208	228	345	356	336	309	428	376
TOTAL DEBT FLOWS										
Disbursements	**12**	**120**	**22**	**7**	**12**	**12**	**6**	**55**	**81**	**1,307**
Long-term debt	12	120	22	7	12	12	6	55	81	1,307
IMF purchases	0	0	0	0	0	0	0	0	0	0
Principal repayments	**2**	**7**	**34**	**29**	**27**	**33**	**40**	**45**	**96**	**104**
Long-term debt	2	7	34	29	27	33	40	45	96	104
IMF repurchases	0	0	0	0	0	0	0	0	0	0
Net flows on debt	**10**	**112**	**40**	**25**	**726**	**-227**	**274**	**-514**	**355**	**1,230**
of which short-term debt	..	..	52	47	742	-206	308	-524	370	26
Interest payments (INT)	..	**45**	**60**	**63**	**72**	**80**	**98**	**90**	**89**	**141**
Long-term debt	1	6	17	11	11	15	25	23	26	74
IMF charges	0	0	0	0	0	0	0	0	0	0
Short-term debt	..	39	43	52	61	66	73	67	63	67
Net transfers on debt	..	**67**	**-21**	**-38**	**654**	**-307**	**176**	**-605**	**266**	**1,089**
Total debt service paid (TDS)	..	**53**	**95**	**92**	**99**	**113**	**138**	**135**	**185**	**245**
Long-term debt	4	13	52	40	39	47	65	68	122	178
IMF repurchases and charges	0	0	0	0	0	0	0	0	0	0
Short-term debt (interest only)	..	39	43	52	61	66	73	67	63	67
2. AGGREGATE NET RESOURCE FLOWS AND NET TRANSFERS (LONG-TERM)										
NET RESOURCE FLOWS	**12**	**311**	**61**	**49**	**203**	**86**	**11**	**60**	**89**	**1,317**
Net flow of long-term debt (ex. IMF)	10	112	-12	-22	-16	-20	-34	10	-15	1,204
Foreign direct investment (net)	0	0	0	2	6	2	4	6	7	35
Portfolio equity flows	0	0	0	0	0	0	0	0	1	34
Grants (excluding technical coop.)	2	199	74	69	213	105	41	43	96	44
Memo: technical coop. grants	9	19	55	44	39	34	90	84	99	96
NET TRANSFERS	**11**	**305**	**44**	**39**	**192**	**72**	**-14**	**36**	**63**	**1,243**
Interest on long-term debt	1	6	17	11	11	15	25	23	26	74
Profit remittances on FDI	0	0	0	0	0	0	0	0	0	0
3. MAJOR ECONOMIC AGGREGATES										
Gross national product (GNP)	..	..	..	3,443	3,533	4,908	5,866	7,769	9,572	11,646
Exports of goods & services (XGS)	..	..	..	1,758	1,560	1,256	1,205	1,324	1,532	1,942
of which workers remittances	..	..	..	480	280	180	200	300	320	350
Imports of goods & services (MGS)	..	..	..	2,543	2,911	4,191	4,258	4,741	5,476	6,642
International reserves (RES)	405	7,025	4,761	4,636	4,210	4,536	4,570	5,863	7,419	8,100
Current account balance	..	..	..	-785	-1,351	-2,935	-3,053	-3,417	-3,944	-5,051
4. DEBT INDICATORS										
EDT / XGS (%)	..	..	..	58.2	114.0	123.8	149.9	101.5	112.2	152.7
EDT / GNP (%)	..	..	..	29.7	50.4	31.7	30.8	17.3	18.0	25.5
TDS / XGS (%)	..	..	..	5.2	6.4	9.0	11.4	10.2	12.1	12.6
INT / XGS (%)	..	..	..	3.6	4.6	6.4	8.1	6.8	5.8	7.3
INT / GNP (%)	..	..	..	1.8	2.0	1.6	1.7	1.2	0.9	1.2
RES / EDT (%)	..	1,376.6	483.2	453.0	236.7	291.9	253.0	436.0	431.8	273.1
RES / MGS (months)	..	..	..	21.9	17.4	13.0	12.9	14.8	16.3	14.6
Short-term / EDT (%)	..	57.6	62.3	65.4	79.9	78.4	83.4	72.6	78.0	46.0
Concessional / EDT (%)	..	14.5	9.5	9.7	6.2	6.7	4.9	7.2	7.8	9.2
Multilateral / EDT (%)	..	15.2	9.2	8.3	4.8	4.1	2.6	5.9	7.2	6.7

LEBANON

(US$ million, unless otherwise indicated)

5. LONG-TERM DEBT

	1970	1980	1988	1989	1990	1991	1992	1993	1994	1995
DEBT OUTSTANDING (LDOD)	**64**	**216**	**372**	**354**	**358**	**336**	**301**	**368**	**378**	**1,601**
Public and publicly guaranteed	**64**	**216**	**372**	**354**	**358**	**336**	**301**	**368**	**378**	**1,551**
Official creditors	64	146	220	199	188	161	212	289	295	428
Multilateral	18	78	90	85	85	64	48	79	125	198
Concessional	18	21	30	30	30	22	17	24	45	63
Bilateral	46	68	130	113	104	97	165	210	170	230
Concessional	31	53	63	70	81	82	71	72	89	209
Private creditors	0	71	152	156	169	176	88	79	83	1,123
Bonds	0	0	0	0	0	0	0	0	0	700
Commercial banks	0	70	0	0	0	0	0	27	26	359
Other private	0	1	152	156	169	176	88	52	58	64
Private nonguaranteed	**0**	**0**	**0**	**0**	**0**	**0**	**0**	**0**	**0**	**50**
Bonds	0	0	0	0	0	0	0	0	0	50
Commercial banks	0	0	0	0	0	0	0	0	0	0
Memo:										
IBRD	18	27	38	37	34	29	23	39	64	113
IDA	0	0	0	0	0	0	0	0	0	0
DISBURSEMENTS	**12**	**120**	**22**	**7**	**12**	**12**	**6**	**55**	**81**	**1,307**
Public and publicly guaranteed	**12**	**120**	**22**	**7**	**12**	**12**	**6**	**55**	**81**	**1,257**
Official creditors	12	50	7	5	5	6	3	52	69	213
Multilateral	0	17	0	0	0	0	0	42	52	80
Concessional	0	5	0	0	0	0	0	10	24	21
Bilateral	12	33	7	5	5	6	3	10	17	133
Concessional	6	18	7	5	5	6	3	10	17	125
Private creditors	0	70	15	2	6	6	3	3	11	1,044
Bonds	0	0	0	0	0	0	0	0	0	700
Commercial banks	0	70	0	0	0	0	0	0	8	340
Other private	0	0	15	2	6	6	3	3	4	4
Private nonguaranteed	**0**	**0**	**0**	**0**	**0**	**0**	**0**	**0**	**0**	**50**
Bonds	0	0	0	0	0	0	0	0	0	50
Commercial banks	0	0	0	0	0	0	0	0	0	0
Memo:										
IBRD	0	8	0	0	0	0	0	22	27	51
IDA	0	0	0	0	0	0	0	0	0	0
PRINCIPAL REPAYMENTS	**2**	**7**	**34**	**29**	**27**	**33**	**40**	**45**	**96**	**104**
Public and publicly guaranteed	**2**	**7**	**34**	**29**	**27**	**33**	**40**	**45**	**96**	**104**
Official creditors	2	7	34	29	27	33	33	37	83	93
Multilateral	1	3	9	4	7	20	13	10	10	10
Concessional	1	2	0	0	0	8	4	3	3	3
Bilateral	1	4	25	24	21	13	19	27	73	83
Concessional	1	4	1	1	1	5	11	4	6	10
Private creditors	0	0	0	0	0	0	7	8	13	11
Bonds	0	0	0	0	0	0	0	0	0	0
Commercial banks	0	0	0	0	0	0	0	0	12	9
Other private	0	0	0	0	0	0	7	8	2	2
Private nonguaranteed	**0**	**0**	**0**	**0**	**0**	**0**	**0**	**0**	**0**	**0**
Bonds	0	0	0	0	0	0	0	0	0	0
Commercial banks	0	0	0	0	0	0	0	0	0	0
Memo:										
IBRD	1	3	6	2	7	4	5	5	4	4
IDA	0	0	0	0	0	0	0	0	0	0
NET FLOWS ON DEBT	**10**	**112**	**-12**	**-22**	**-16**	**-20**	**-34**	**10**	**-15**	**1,204**
Public and publicly guaranteed	**10**	**112**	**-12**	**-22**	**-16**	**-20**	**-34**	**10**	**-15**	**1,154**
Official creditors	10	43	-27	-23	-22	-27	-29	15	-13	120
Multilateral	-1	14	-9	-4	-6	-20	-13	33	42	70
Concessional	-1	3	0	0	0	-8	-4	7	21	18
Bilateral	11	29	-18	-19	-16	-6	-16	-17	-55	50
Concessional	5	14	5	4	4	2	-7	5	12	115
Private creditors	0	70	15	2	6	6	-5	-5	-2	1,033
Bonds	0	0	0	0	0	0	0	0	0	700
Commercial banks	0	70	0	0	0	0	0	0	-4	331
Other private	0	0	15	2	6	6	-5	-5	2	2
Private nonguaranteed	**0**	**0**	**0**	**0**	**0**	**0**	**0**	**0**	**0**	**50**
Bonds	0	0	0	0	0	0	0	0	0	50
Commercial banks	0	0	0	0	0	0	0	0	0	0
Memo:										
IBRD	-1	5	-6	-2	-7	-4	-5	17	23	47
IDA	0	0	0	0	0	0	0	0	0	0

LEBANON

(US$ million, unless otherwise indicated)

	1970	1980	1988	1989	1990	1991	1992	1993	1994	1995
INTEREST PAYMENTS (LINT)	**1**	**6**	**17**	**11**	**11**	**15**	**25**	**23**	**26**	**74**
Public and publicly guaranteed	**1**	**6**	**17**	**11**	**11**	**15**	**25**	**23**	**26**	**74**
Official creditors	1	6	16	9	9	15	19	18	21	19
Multilateral	1	4	5	1	4	10	12	3	7	11
Concessional	1	1	0	0	0	4	2	1	2	3
Bilateral	0	2	10	8	5	5	7	15	14	8
Concessional	0	2	1	0	0	3	5	2	2	3
Private creditors	0	0	2	2	2	0	6	5	5	55
Bonds	0	0	0	0	0	0	0	0	0	41
Commercial banks	0	0	0	0	0	0	0	0	3	12
Other private	0	0	2	2	2	0	6	5	2	3
Private nonguaranteed	**0**	**0**	**0**	**0**	**0**	**0**	**0**	**0**	**0**	**0**
Bonds	0	0	0	0	0	0	0	0	0	0
Commercial banks	0	0	0	0	0	0	0	0	0	0
Memo:										
IBRD	1	2	5	1	4	2	2	2	4	7
IDA	0	0	0	0	0	0	0	0	0	0
NET TRANSFERS ON DEBT	**9**	**106**	**-30**	**-33**	**-27**	**-35**	**-59**	**-13**	**-41**	**1,130**
Public and publicly guaranteed	**9**	**106**	**-30**	**-33**	**-27**	**-35**	**-59**	**-13**	**-41**	**1,080**
Official creditors	9	37	-43	-33	-31	-41	-48	-3	-34	101
Multilateral	-2	10	-14	-6	-11	-30	-25	29	35	59
Concessional	-2	2	0	0	0	-13	-6	6	18	15
Bilateral	11	27	-29	-27	-21	-12	-23	-32	-69	42
Concessional	5	12	5	4	4	-2	-12	4	10	112
Private creditors	0	69	13	0	5	6	-11	-10	-7	978
Bonds	0	0	0	0	0	0	0	0	0	660
Commercial banks	0	70	0	0	0	0	0	0	-7	319
Other private	0	0	13	0	5	6	-11	-10	0	0
Private nonguaranteed	**0**	**0**	**0**	**0**	**0**	**0**	**0**	**0**	**0**	**50**
Bonds	0	0	0	0	0	0	0	0	0	50
Commercial banks	0	0	0	0	0	0	0	0	0	0
Memo:										
IBRD	-2	3	-11	-3	-11	-7	-7	16	19	40
IDA	0	0	0	0	0	0	0	0	0	0
DEBT SERVICE (LTDS)	**4**	**13**	**52**	**40**	**39**	**47**	**65**	**68**	**122**	**178**
Public and publicly guaranteed	**4**	**13**	**52**	**40**	**39**	**47**	**65**	**68**	**122**	**178**
Official creditors	4	13	50	38	37	47	51	55	103	112
Multilateral	2	7	14	6	11	30	25	13	17	21
Concessional	2	3	0	0	0	13	6	4	5	6
Bilateral	1	6	35	32	26	18	27	42	86	91
Concessional	1	6	2	1	1	8	16	6	8	13
Private creditors	0	1	2	2	2	0	13	13	18	66
Bonds	0	0	0	0	0	0	0	0	0	41
Commercial banks	0	0	0	0	0	0	0	0	15	21
Other private	0	0	2	2	2	0	13	13	4	4
Private nonguaranteed	**0**	**0**	**0**	**0**	**0**	**0**	**0**	**0**	**0**	**0**
Bonds	0	0	0	0	0	0	0	0	0	0
Commercial banks	0	0	0	0	0	0	0	0	0	0
Memo:										
IBRD	2	5	11	3	11	7	7	6	8	11
IDA	0	0	0	0	0	0	0	0	0	0
UNDISBURSED DEBT	**1**	**401**	**126**	**120**	**116**	**189**	**226**	**500**	**1,022**	**1,091**
Official creditors	1	164	88	82	79	159	201	475	606	773
Private creditors	0	237	38	38	37	30	25	25	416	319
Memorandum items										
Concessional LDOD	49	74	94	100	111	104	88	96	134	272
Variable rate LDOD	0	70	0	0	0	0	0	22	51	164
Public sector LDOD	64	216	372	354	358	336	301	368	378	1,551
Private sector LDOD	0	0	0	0	0	0	0	0	0	50

6. CURRENCY COMPOSITION OF LONG-TERM DEBT (PERCENT)

	1970	1980	1988	1989	1990	1991	1992	1993	1994	1995
Deutsche mark	0.0	0.7	4.3	4.7	5.3	4.6	3.9	2.6	2.5	1.1
French franc	22.0	6.0	21.2	25.3	31.7	35.2	64.1	62.0	48.3	8.2
Japanese yen	0.0	0.0	0.5	0.5	0.5	0.4	0.3	0.2	0.2	0.0
Pound sterling	0.0	0.0	0.7	0.6	0.8	0.5	0.3	0.5	0.4	0.1
Swiss franc	0.0	0.0	0.4	0.4	0.5	0.2	0.1	0.1	0.1	0.0
U.S.dollars	44.7	53.7	51.6	47.3	40.9	41.5	17.5	13.8	12.5	69.2
Multiple currency	0.0	18.4	10.4	10.3	9.4	8.7	7.6	10.7	17.2	7.4
Special drawing rights	0.0	0.0	0.0	0.0	0.0	0.0	0.0	0.0	0.0	0.0
All other currencies	33.3	21.2	10.9	10.8	10.9	8.9	6.2	10.2	18.9	14.0

LEBANON

(US$ million, unless otherwise indicated)

	1970	1980	1988	1989	1990	1991	1992	1993	1994	1995
7. DEBT RESTRUCTURINGS										
Total amount rescheduled	0	0	0	0	0	0	0	0	0	0
Debt stock rescheduled	0	0	0	0	0	0	0	0	0	0
Principal rescheduled	0	0	0	0	0	0	0	0	0	0
Official	0	0	0	0	0	0	0	0	0	0
Private	0	0	0	0	0	0	0	0	0	0
Interest rescheduled	0	0	0	0	0	0	0	0	0	0
Official	0	0	0	0	0	0	0	0	0	0
Private	0	0	0	0	0	0	0	0	0	0
Debt forgiven	..	..	0	0	0	0	0	0	0	0
Memo: interest forgiven	..	..	0	0	0	0	0	0	0	0
Debt stock reduction	0	0	0	0	0	0	0	0	0	0
of which debt buyback	0	0	0	0	0	0	0	0	0	0
8. DEBT STOCK-FLOW RECONCILIATION										
Total change in debt stocks	..	..	..	38	756	-225	252	-461	374	1,248
Net flows on debt	..	..	..	25	726	-227	274	-514	355	1,230
Net change in interest arrears	..	..	..	9	10	3	-20	-4	-7	-1
Interest capitalized	..	..	..	0	0	0	0	0	0	0
Debt forgiveness or reduction	..	..	..	0	0	0	0	0	0	0
Cross-currency valuation	..	..	..	4	21	-3	-16	-18	22	23
Residual	..	..	..	1	-1	2	15	75	3	-4
9. AVERAGE TERMS OF NEW COMMITMENTS										
ALL CREDITORS										
Interest (%)	2.9	3.0	6.3	0.0	0.0	3.8	3.4	5.7	8.4	8.0
Maturity (years)	20.4	12.4	23.4	0.0	0.0	19.4	21.3	19.0	8.6	10.4
Grace period (years)	1.4	2.6	7.2	0.0	0.0	4.1	5.1	5.2	3.7	4.2
Grant element (%)	42.0	34.3	30.8	0.0	0.0	39.1	43.6	28.1	11.1	10.2
Official creditors										
Interest (%)	2.9	2.7	2.3	0.0	0.0	3.8	3.4	5.7	4.9	5.6
Maturity (years)	20.4	15.1	34.1	0.0	0.0	19.4	21.3	19.1	20.1	18.6
Grace period (years)	1.4	3.9	12.1	0.0	0.0	4.1	5.1	5.2	5.2	3.8
Grant element (%)	42.0	42.2	66.7	0.0	0.0	39.1	43.6	28.5	34.6	26.7
Private creditors										
Interest (%)	0.0	3.0	9.8	0.0	0.0	0.0	0.0	10.1	10.1	9.0
Maturity (years)	0.0	11.9	14.2	0.0	0.0	0.0	0.0	11.3	3.0	7.2
Grace period (years)	0.0	2.4	3.0	0.0	0.0	0.0	0.0	1.8	3.0	4.3
Grant element (%)	0.0	32.9	-0.1	0.0	0.0	0.0	0.0	-1.6	-0.3	3.7
Memorandum items										
Commitments	7	92	45	0	0	115	88	332	594	1,324
Official creditors	7	14	21	0	0	115	88	328	194	373
Private creditors	0	78	24	0	0	0	0	4	400	951

10. CONTRACTUAL OBLIGATIONS ON OUTSTANDING LONG-TERM DEBT

	1996	1997	1998	1999	2000	2001	2002	2003	2004	2005
TOTAL										
Disbursements	314	286	179	116	71	46	32	22	16	10
Principal	38	446	84	121	723	120	116	165	114	114
Interest	129	159	129	130	125	65	60	51	43	36
Official creditors										
Disbursements	151	186	139	100	71	46	32	22	16	10
Principal	25	34	41	67	75	79	78	78	77	77
Interest	25	31	39	42	43	41	39	37	34	30
Bilateral creditors										
Disbursements	66	59	37	20	11	6	2	1	0	0
Principal	11	13	18	27	28	26	25	25	24	25
Interest	9	10	13	13	12	11	10	9	9	8
Multilateral creditors										
Disbursements	85	128	102	79	61	40	29	22	16	10
Principal	14	21	23	40	47	53	53	53	53	53
Interest	16	21	26	29	30	30	29	27	25	23
Private creditors										
Disbursements	164	100	40	16	0	0	0	0	0	0
Principal	14	412	43	55	648	41	38	87	37	37
Interest	104	128	90	87	83	24	20	15	9	6
Commercial banks										
Disbursements	158	99	40	16	0	0	0	0	0	0
Principal	8	11	41	52	346	39	36	36	36	36
Interest	31	53	56	53	49	18	14	11	8	5
Other private										
Disbursements	5	1	0	0	0	0	0	0	0	0
Principal	6	401	2	2	302	2	2	51	1	1
Interest	73	75	34	34	34	6	6	4	1	1

LESOTHO

(US$ million, unless otherwise indicated)

	1970	1980	1988	1989	1990	1991	1992	1993	1994	1995
1. SUMMARY DEBT DATA										
TOTAL DEBT STOCKS (EDT)	..	**71.9**	**287.1**	**327.8**	**394.8**	**446.2**	**492.5**	**529.6**	**601.7**	**659.0**
Long-term debt (LDOD)	**8.1**	**57.7**	**276.0**	**315.6**	**376.9**	**424.3**	**462.6**	**489.4**	**553.7**	**611.0**
Public and publicly guaranteed	8.1	57.7	276.0	315.6	376.9	424.3	462.6	489.4	553.7	611.0
Private nonguaranteed	0.0	0.0	0.0	0.0	0.0	0.0	0.0	0.0	0.0	0.0
Use of IMF credit	**0.0**	**6.2**	**5.0**	**10.1**	**15.1**	**18.4**	**24.9**	**34.2**	**40.3**	**38.4**
Short-term debt	..	**8.0**	**6.0**	**2.0**	**2.8**	**3.5**	**5.0**	**6.0**	**7.7**	**9.7**
of which interest arrears on LDOD	..	0.0	0.0	0.0	0.8	0.5	1.0	2.0	3.7	5.7
Official creditors	..	0.0	0.0	0.0	0.5	0.1	0.3	0.8	1.8	3.6
Private creditors	..	0.0	0.0	0.0	0.3	0.4	0.7	1.2	1.8	2.1
Memo: principal arrears on LDOD	..	0.0	0.0	0.0	3.6	6.0	7.6	10.1	14.1	14.6
Official creditors	..	0.0	0.0	0.0	2.0	3.1	4.3	6.4	9.3	9.4
Private creditors	..	0.0	0.0	0.0	1.6	2.9	3.3	3.7	4.9	5.2
Memo: export credits	..	..	30.0	35.0	115.0	50.0	139.0	145.0	246.0	385.0
TOTAL DEBT FLOWS										
Disbursements	**1.0**	**15.0**	**56.6**	**59.8**	**61.6**	**65.0**	**85.7**	**70.0**	**59.5**	**63.7**
Long-term debt	0.4	13.3	52.6	54.0	57.5	61.9	78.3	60.5	54.1	63.7
IMF purchases	0.6	1.7	4.1	5.8	4.1	3.1	7.4	9.5	5.4	0.0
Principal repayments	**0.3**	**3.4**	**16.8**	**14.7**	**15.0**	**16.2**	**20.4**	**20.5**	**18.5**	**24.7**
Long-term debt	0.3	3.4	15.7	14.0	14.8	16.1	20.4	20.5	16.9	21.9
IMF repurchases	0.0	0.0	1.1	0.7	0.2	0.0	0.0	0.0	1.5	2.7
Net flows on debt	**0.6**	**11.6**	**41.8**	**41.1**	**46.6**	**49.8**	**66.4**	**49.5**	**41.0**	**39.0**
of which short-term debt	..	..	2.0	-4.0	0.0	1.0	1.0	0.0	0.0	0.0
Interest payments (INT)	..	**2.1**	**7.6**	**7.7**	**8.3**	**10.3**	**13.9**	**12.3**	**11.0**	**15.4**
Long-term debt	0.2	1.5	7.1	7.4	8.0	10.0	13.5	11.8	10.7	15.0
IMF charges	0.0	0.0	0.0	0.0	0.1	0.1	0.1	0.2	0.1	0.2
Short-term debt	..	0.6	0.4	0.3	0.2	0.2	0.3	0.3	0.2	0.2
Net transfers on debt	..	**9.5**	**34.3**	**33.5**	**38.3**	**39.6**	**52.5**	**37.2**	**30.1**	**23.5**
Total debt service paid (TDS)	..	**5.5**	**24.4**	**22.3**	**23.3**	**26.4**	**34.3**	**32.8**	**29.4**	**40.1**
Long-term debt	0.5	4.8	22.8	21.4	22.8	26.1	33.9	32.3	27.6	37.0
IMF repurchases and charges	0.0	0.0	1.1	0.7	0.3	0.1	0.1	0.2	1.6	3.0
Short-term debt (interest only)	..	0.6	0.4	0.3	0.2	0.2	0.3	0.3	0.2	0.2
2. AGGREGATE NET RESOURCE FLOWS AND NET TRANSFERS (LONG-TERM)										
NET RESOURCE FLOWS	**7.6**	**66.4**	**99.2**	**101.3**	**119.6**	**108.3**	**124.7**	**122.2**	**102.1**	**123.3**
Net flow of long-term debt (ex. IMF)	0.1	9.9	36.9	40.1	42.7	45.8	57.9	40.0	37.1	41.7
Foreign direct investment (net)	0.0	4.5	21.0	13.4	17.0	8.0	3.0	15.0	19.0	23.0
Portfolio equity flows	0.0	0.0	0.0	0.0	0.0	0.0	0.0	0.0	0.0	0.0
Grants (excluding technical coop.)	7.5	52.0	41.3	47.8	59.9	54.5	63.8	67.2	46.0	58.6
Memo: technical coop. grants	2.5	31.9	49.6	46.9	45.4	43.1	46.0	39.8	36.2	37.3
NET TRANSFERS	**7.4**	**59.0**	**83.5**	**81.3**	**98.9**	**87.0**	**88.0**	**93.9**	**74.5**	**93.3**
Interest on long-term debt	0.2	1.5	7.1	7.4	8.0	10.0	13.5	11.8	10.7	15.0
Profit remittances on FDI	0.0	6.0	8.5	12.6	12.7	11.3	23.2	16.5	17.0	15.0
3. MAJOR ECONOMIC AGGREGATES										
Gross national product (GNP)	104.7	630.8	816.5	849.1	1,042.2	1,080.4	1,216.7	1,233.5	1,310.0	1,478.6
Exports of goods & services (XGS)	..	363.5	480.7	479.3	555.0	584.8	646.8	615.4	550.8	605.7
of which workers remittances	..	0.0	0.0	0.0	0.0	0.0	0.0	0.0	0.0	0.0
Imports of goods & services (MGS)	..	482.4	643.4	683.8	775.9	907.9	1,048.0	961.3	913.8	1,019.8
International reserves (RES)	..	50.3	56.3	49.0	72.4	115.0	157.5	252.7	372.6	456.7
Current account balance	..	56.3	-24.6	10.4	65.0	83.1	37.6	29.3	108.1	-695.1
4. DEBT INDICATORS										
EDT / XGS (%)	..	19.8	59.7	68.4	71.1	76.3	76.1	86.1	109.2	108.8
EDT / GNP (%)	..	11.4	35.2	38.6	37.9	41.3	40.5	42.9	45.9	44.6
TDS / XGS (%)	..	1.5	5.1	4.7	4.2	4.5	5.3	5.3	5.3	6.6
INT / XGS (%)	..	0.6	1.6	1.6	1.5	1.8	2.1	2.0	2.0	2.5
INT / GNP (%)	..	0.3	0.9	0.9	0.8	1.0	1.1	1.0	0.8	1.0
RES / EDT (%)	..	69.9	19.6	14.9	18.3	25.8	32.0	47.7	61.9	69.3
RES / MGS (months)	..	1.3	1.1	0.9	1.1	1.5	1.8	3.2	4.9	5.4
Short-term / EDT (%)	..	11.1	2.1	0.6	0.7	0.8	1.0	1.1	1.3	1.5
Concessional / EDT (%)	..	61.6	72.0	74.3	75.2	76.0	75.8	72.5	72.4	71.0
Multilateral / EDT (%)	..	56.0	75.7	75.3	73.7	69.4	66.4	67.7	70.1	69.6

LESOTHO

(US$ million, unless otherwise indicated)

	1970	1980	1988	1989	1990	1991	1992	1993	1994	1995
5. LONG-TERM DEBT										
DEBT OUTSTANDING (LDOD)	**8.1**	**57.7**	**276.0**	**315.6**	**376.9**	**424.3**	**462.6**	**489.4**	**553.7**	**611.0**
Public and publicly guaranteed	**8.1**	**57.7**	**276.0**	**315.6**	**376.9**	**424.3**	**462.6**	**489.4**	**553.7**	**611.0**
Official creditors	7.6	46.4	247.0	283.5	343.3	389.4	434.4	468.1	536.4	582.9
Multilateral	4.1	40.3	217.3	246.9	291.0	309.6	326.8	358.3	422.0	458.9
Concessional	4.1	40.3	188.9	217.5	257.4	279.5	297.2	306.8	349.9	376.4
Bilateral	3.5	6.1	29.7	36.6	52.3	79.8	107.7	109.8	114.4	124.0
Concessional	3.0	4.1	17.8	26.0	39.3	59.5	76.3	77.2	85.7	91.6
Private creditors	0.5	11.4	29.0	32.1	33.7	34.9	28.1	21.3	17.3	28.0
Bonds	0.0	0.0	0.0	0.0	0.0	0.0	0.0	0.0	0.0	0.0
Commercial banks	0.0	2.0	0.1	3.6	6.0	6.1	5.7	4.1	2.8	14.9
Other private	0.5	9.4	29.0	28.5	27.7	28.8	22.4	17.2	14.5	13.2
Private nonguaranteed	**0.0**	**0.0**	**0.0**	**0.0**	**0.0**	**0.0**	**0.0**	**0.0**	**0.0**	**0.0**
Bonds	0.0	0.0	0.0	0.0	0.0	0.0	0.0	0.0	0.0	0.0
Commercial banks	0.0	0.0	0.0	0.0	0.0	0.0	0.0	0.0	0.0	0.0
Memo:										
IBRD	0.0	0.0	0.0	0.0	0.0	0.0	4.5	26.0	41.7	54.0
IDA	4.1	24.1	86.8	98.8	111.7	120.7	127.1	133.6	143.0	152.8
DISBURSEMENTS	**0.4**	**13.3**	**52.6**	**54.0**	**57.5**	**61.9**	**78.3**	**60.5**	**54.1**	**63.7**
Public and publicly guaranteed	**0.4**	**13.3**	**52.6**	**54.0**	**57.5**	**61.9**	**78.3**	**60.5**	**54.1**	**63.7**
Official creditors	0.2	8.0	37.6	46.5	51.0	55.7	76.4	60.2	54.1	50.3
Multilateral	0.0	6.5	24.6	36.7	32.0	23.6	35.9	43.9	47.8	40.2
Concessional	0.0	6.5	21.8	32.8	28.3	23.5	31.3	19.0	30.9	26.9
Bilateral	0.2	1.5	13.0	9.8	19.0	32.1	40.5	16.3	6.3	10.1
Concessional	0.2	0.9	6.1	9.0	15.3	20.8	22.5	8.6	6.1	3.7
Private creditors	0.2	5.3	15.0	7.6	6.5	6.3	1.9	0.3	0.0	13.4
Bonds	0.0	0.0	0.0	0.0	0.0	0.0	0.0	0.0	0.0	0.0
Commercial banks	0.0	2.0	0.0	3.5	3.0	1.4	1.9	0.3	0.0	13.4
Other private	0.2	3.3	15.0	4.0	3.5	4.9	0.0	0.0	0.0	0.0
Private nonguaranteed	**0.0**	**0.0**	**0.0**	**0.0**	**0.0**	**0.0**	**0.0**	**0.0**	**0.0**	**0.0**
Bonds	0.0	0.0	0.0	0.0	0.0	0.0	0.0	0.0	0.0	0.0
Commercial banks	0.0	0.0	0.0	0.0	0.0	0.0	0.0	0.0	0.0	0.0
Memo:										
IBRD	0.0	0.0	0.0	0.0	0.0	0.0	4.6	21.8	13.7	11.2
IDA	0.0	3.8	7.3	12.9	9.2	9.0	9.9	7.0	6.3	8.8
PRINCIPAL REPAYMENTS	**0.3**	**3.4**	**15.7**	**14.0**	**14.8**	**16.1**	**20.4**	**20.5**	**16.9**	**21.9**
Public and publicly guaranteed	**0.3**	**3.4**	**15.7**	**14.0**	**14.8**	**16.1**	**20.4**	**20.5**	**16.9**	**21.9**
Official creditors	0.3	0.4	11.3	8.3	8.3	11.3	13.4	14.8	11.5	17.8
Multilateral	0.0	0.2	5.0	5.7	5.4	6.4	7.2	6.7	7.6	14.1
Concessional	0.0	0.2	2.8	3.3	3.2	2.9	3.3	4.3	4.5	9.4
Bilateral	0.3	0.2	6.2	2.6	2.9	4.9	6.2	8.0	3.9	3.7
Concessional	0.2	0.2	0.7	0.8	0.9	1.3	1.8	4.5	1.1	1.7
Private creditors	0.0	3.0	4.5	5.6	6.5	4.8	7.0	5.7	5.4	4.1
Bonds	0.0	0.0	0.0	0.0	0.0	0.0	0.0	0.0	0.0	0.0
Commercial banks	0.0	0.0	0.0	0.0	0.6	1.1	2.0	1.7	1.2	1.5
Other private	0.0	3.0	4.4	5.6	5.9	3.7	5.0	4.0	4.2	2.6
Private nonguaranteed	**0.0**	**0.0**	**0.0**	**0.0**	**0.0**	**0.0**	**0.0**	**0.0**	**0.0**	**0.0**
Bonds	0.0	0.0	0.0	0.0	0.0	0.0	0.0	0.0	0.0	0.0
Commercial banks	0.0	0.0	0.0	0.0	0.0	0.0	0.0	0.0	0.0	0.0
Memo:										
IBRD	0.0	0.0	0.0	0.0	0.0	0.0	0.0	0.0	0.0	0.0
IDA	0.0	0.0	0.4	0.5	0.6	0.7	0.8	0.8	1.1	1.3
NET FLOWS ON DEBT	**0.1**	**9.9**	**36.9**	**40.1**	**42.7**	**45.8**	**57.9**	**40.0**	**37.1**	**41.7**
Public and publicly guaranteed	**0.1**	**9.9**	**36.9**	**40.1**	**42.7**	**45.8**	**57.9**	**40.0**	**37.1**	**41.7**
Official creditors	-0.1	7.6	26.4	38.1	42.7	44.3	63.0	45.4	42.6	32.5
Multilateral	0.0	6.4	19.6	30.9	26.6	17.2	28.7	37.2	40.2	26.1
Concessional	0.0	6.4	19.0	29.5	25.0	20.7	27.9	14.7	26.4	17.6
Bilateral	-0.1	1.3	6.8	7.2	16.1	27.1	34.4	8.2	2.3	6.4
Concessional	0.0	0.7	5.4	8.2	14.4	19.5	20.7	4.1	5.0	2.0
Private creditors	0.1	2.3	10.5	1.9	0.0	1.4	-5.1	-5.4	-5.4	9.2
Bonds	0.0	0.0	0.0	0.0	0.0	0.0	0.0	0.0	0.0	0.0
Commercial banks	0.0	2.0	0.0	3.5	2.4	0.3	-0.1	-1.4	-1.2	11.9
Other private	0.1	0.3	10.5	-1.6	-2.5	1.2	-5.0	-4.0	-4.2	-2.6
Private nonguaranteed	**0.0**	**0.0**	**0.0**	**0.0**	**0.0**	**0.0**	**0.0**	**0.0**	**0.0**	**0.0**
Bonds	0.0	0.0	0.0	0.0	0.0	0.0	0.0	0.0	0.0	0.0
Commercial banks	0.0	0.0	0.0	0.0	0.0	0.0	0.0	0.0	0.0	0.0
Memo:										
IBRD	0.0	0.0	0.0	0.0	0.0	0.0	4.6	21.8	13.7	11.2
IDA	0.0	3.8	6.9	12.4	8.6	8.3	9.2	6.2	5.2	7.4

LESOTHO

(US$ million, unless otherwise indicated)

	1970	1980	1988	1989	1990	1991	1992	1993	1994	1995
INTEREST PAYMENTS (LINT)	**0.2**	**1.5**	**7.1**	**7.4**	**8.0**	**10.0**	**13.5**	**11.8**	**10.7**	**15.0**
Public and publicly guaranteed	**0.2**	**1.5**	**7.1**	**7.4**	**8.0**	**10.0**	**13.5**	**11.8**	**10.7**	**15.0**
Official creditors	0.2	0.6	5.5	5.7	6.1	8.7	12.1	10.6	10.1	12.2
Multilateral	0.0	0.4	4.6	4.6	4.7	5.9	6.6	5.6	6.5	8.6
Concessional	0.0	0.3	1.9	1.8	2.3	2.0	3.9	2.6	2.4	3.2
Bilateral	0.2	0.2	0.9	1.1	1.4	2.9	5.5	5.0	3.5	3.5
Concessional	0.1	0.0	0.3	0.4	0.6	1.6	2.5	2.1	1.3	1.5
Private creditors	0.0	0.9	1.7	1.7	1.9	1.2	1.4	1.2	0.6	2.9
Bonds	0.0	0.0	0.0	0.0	0.0	0.0	0.0	0.0	0.0	0.0
Commercial banks	0.0	0.3	0.0	0.0	0.3	0.2	0.4	0.4	0.2	2.6
Other private	0.0	0.6	1.6	1.7	1.6	1.0	1.0	0.8	0.4	0.3
Private nonguaranteed	**0.0**	**0.0**	**0.0**	**0.0**	**0.0**	**0.0**	**0.0**	**0.0**	**0.0**	**0.0**
Bonds	0.0	0.0	0.0	0.0	0.0	0.0	0.0	0.0	0.0	0.0
Commercial banks	0.0	0.0	0.0	0.0	0.0	0.0	0.0	0.0	0.0	0.0
Memo:										
IBRD	0.0	0.0	0.0	0.0	0.0	0.0	0.3	1.1	2.5	3.5
IDA	0.0	0.2	0.8	0.7	0.8	0.8	0.9	1.0	1.0	1.1
NET TRANSFERS ON DEBT	**-0.1**	**8.5**	**29.7**	**32.7**	**34.7**	**35.8**	**44.4**	**28.2**	**26.5**	**26.7**
Public and publicly guaranteed	**-0.1**	**8.5**	**29.7**	**32.7**	**34.7**	**35.8**	**44.4**	**28.2**	**26.5**	**26.7**
Official creditors	-0.2	7.1	20.9	32.4	36.7	35.6	50.9	34.8	32.5	20.3
Multilateral	0.0	6.0	15.0	26.3	21.9	11.4	22.1	31.6	33.7	17.5
Concessional	0.0	6.1	17.1	27.6	22.8	18.6	24.0	12.1	24.0	14.4
Bilateral	-0.2	1.1	5.9	6.1	14.8	24.3	28.9	3.3	-1.2	2.9
Concessional	-0.1	0.7	5.1	7.8	13.8	17.9	18.2	2.1	3.7	0.6
Private creditors	0.1	1.4	8.9	0.3	-2.0	0.2	-6.5	-6.6	-6.0	6.4
Bonds	0.0	0.0	0.0	0.0	0.0	0.0	0.0	0.0	0.0	0.0
Commercial banks	0.0	1.8	0.0	3.5	2.2	0.1	-0.6	-1.8	-1.4	9.3
Other private	0.1	-0.3	8.9	-3.2	-4.1	0.1	-5.9	-4.9	-4.6	-2.9
Private nonguaranteed	**0.0**	**0.0**	**0.0**	**0.0**	**0.0**	**0.0**	**0.0**	**0.0**	**0.0**	**0.0**
Bonds	0.0	0.0	0.0	0.0	0.0	0.0	0.0	0.0	0.0	0.0
Commercial banks	0.0	0.0	0.0	0.0	0.0	0.0	0.0	0.0	0.0	0.0
Memo:										
IBRD	0.0	0.0	0.0	0.0	0.0	0.0	4.3	20.7	11.3	7.7
IDA	0.0	3.6	6.1	11.7	7.9	7.4	8.3	5.2	4.2	6.3
DEBT SERVICE (LTDS)	**0.5**	**4.8**	**22.8**	**21.4**	**22.8**	**26.1**	**33.9**	**32.3**	**27.6**	**37.0**
Public and publicly guaranteed	**0.5**	**4.8**	**22.8**	**21.4**	**22.8**	**26.1**	**33.9**	**32.3**	**27.6**	**37.0**
Official creditors	0.4	1.0	16.7	14.1	14.4	20.0	25.4	25.4	21.6	30.0
Multilateral	0.0	0.5	9.6	10.4	10.2	12.2	13.8	12.4	14.2	22.7
Concessional	0.0	0.4	4.7	5.2	5.5	4.9	7.2	6.9	6.9	12.5
Bilateral	0.4	0.4	7.1	3.7	4.2	7.8	11.6	13.0	7.4	7.2
Concessional	0.3	0.3	1.0	1.2	1.5	2.9	4.3	6.6	2.4	3.1
Private creditors	0.1	3.9	6.1	7.3	8.5	6.1	8.4	7.0	6.0	7.0
Bonds	0.0	0.0	0.0	0.0	0.0	0.0	0.0	0.0	0.0	0.0
Commercial banks	0.0	0.3	0.0	0.0	0.9	1.3	2.5	2.1	1.4	4.1
Other private	0.1	3.6	6.1	7.3	7.6	4.7	6.0	4.9	4.6	2.9
Private nonguaranteed	**0.0**	**0.0**	**0.0**	**0.0**	**0.0**	**0.0**	**0.0**	**0.0**	**0.0**	**0.0**
Bonds	0.0	0.0	0.0	0.0	0.0	0.0	0.0	0.0	0.0	0.0
Commercial banks	0.0	0.0	0.0	0.0	0.0	0.0	0.0	0.0	0.0	0.0
Memo:										
IBRD	0.0	0.0	0.0	0.0	0.0	0.0	0.3	1.1	2.5	3.5
IDA	0.0	0.2	1.2	1.2	1.4	1.5	1.7	1.8	2.2	2.5
UNDISBURSED DEBT	**0.8**	**118.0**	**350.8**	**323.0**	**314.9**	**431.9**	**515.9**	**515.9**	**505.7**	**455.4**
Official creditors	0.1	110.0	338.9	313.7	312.2	428.3	394.4	391.5	358.0	322.9
Private creditors	0.7	8.0	12.0	9.4	2.7	3.6	121.5	124.5	147.7	132.6
Memorandum items										
Concessional LDOD	7.1	44.3	206.7	243.5	296.7	339.0	373.5	384.1	435.6	468.0
Variable rate LDOD	0.0	2.0	0.1	0.0	0.0	0.1	4.7	26.0	41.7	54.0
Public sector LDOD	8.1	55.7	274.7	314.5	375.7	423.1	461.7	488.5	552.9	610.2
Private sector LDOD	0.0	2.0	1.3	1.1	1.2	1.1	0.9	0.9	0.8	0.7

6. CURRENCY COMPOSITION OF LONG-TERM DEBT (PERCENT)

	1970	1980	1988	1989	1990	1991	1992	1993	1994	1995
Deutsche mark	0.0	0.0	0.8	0.6	0.4	0.2	0.1	0.0	0.0	0.0
French franc	0.0	0.0	2.7	4.9	7.6	9.9	10.3	9.1	8.7	8.5
Japanese yen	0.0	0.0	0.0	0.0	0.0	0.0	0.0	0.0	0.0	0.0
Pound sterling	43.1	16.5	2.6	2.1	1.7	1.5	1.3	1.2	1.0	0.9
Swiss franc	0.0	0.0	0.0	0.0	0.0	0.0	0.0	0.0	0.0	0.0
U.S.dollars	50.5	46.4	24.5	26.9	24.9	24.5	24.7	24.5	23.0	21.9
Multiple currency	0.0	7.1	7.3	6.7	5.7	6.2	8.2	13.3	15.3	18.8
Special drawing rights	0.0	0.0	11.0	10.3	9.9	9.1	8.7	8.4	7.9	7.3
All other currencies	6.2	30.1	51.0	48.6	49.9	48.6	46.8	43.5	44.1	42.7

LESOTHO

(US$ million, unless otherwise indicated)

	1970	1980	1988	1989	1990	1991	1992	1993	1994	1995
7. DEBT RESTRUCTURINGS										
Total amount rescheduled	0.0	0.0	0.0	0.0	0.0	0.0	0.0	0.0	0.0	0.0
Debt stock rescheduled	0.0	0.0	0.0	0.0	0.0	0.0	0.0	0.0	0.0	0.0
Principal rescheduled	0.0	0.0	0.0	0.0	0.0	0.0	0.0	0.0	0.0	0.0
Official	0.0	0.0	0.0	0.0	0.0	0.0	0.0	0.0	0.0	0.0
Private	0.0	0.0	0.0	0.0	0.0	0.0	0.0	0.0	0.0	0.0
Interest rescheduled	0.0	0.0	0.0	0.0	0.0	0.0	0.0	0.0	0.0	0.0
Official	0.0	0.0	0.0	0.0	0.0	0.0	0.0	0.0	0.0	0.0
Private	0.0	0.0	0.0	0.0	0.0	0.0	0.0	0.0	0.0	0.0
Debt forgiven	..	..	1.1	0.0	3.7	0.0	0.0	4.9	0.0	0.0
Memo: interest forgiven	..	..	0.0	0.0	0.0	0.0	0.0	0.0	0.0	0.0
Debt stock reduction	0.0	0.0	0.0	0.0	0.0	0.0	0.0	0.0	0.0	0.0
of which debt buyback	0.0	0.0	0.0	0.0	0.0	0.0	0.0	0.0	0.0	0.0
8. DEBT STOCK-FLOW RECONCILIATION										
Total change in debt stocks	..	..	..	40.7	67.0	51.4	46.3	37.1	72.1	57.3
Net flows on debt	..	..	..	41.1	46.6	49.8	66.4	49.5	41.0	39.0
Net change in interest arrears	..	..	..	0.0	0.8	-0.3	0.5	1.0	1.7	2.0
Interest capitalized	..	..	..	0.0	0.0	0.0	0.0	0.0	0.0	0.0
Debt forgiveness or reduction	..	..	..	0.0	-3.7	0.0	0.0	-4.9	0.0	0.0
Cross-currency valuation	..	..	..	-1.9	23.8	-1.4	-18.3	-9.4	23.0	13.0
Residual	..	..	..	1.4	-0.5	3.2	-2.2	0.9	6.4	3.4
9. AVERAGE TERMS OF NEW COMMITMENTS										
ALL CREDITORS										
Interest (%)	5.0	5.9	4.5	2.7	1.2	5.8	13.7	4.0	4.9	5.6
Maturity (years)	18.1	24.3	25.3	28.2	24.1	24.9	12.2	30.8	17.0	29.2
Grace period (years)	1.9	5.7	5.3	8.9	5.8	7.1	3.6	9.7	6.4	6.4
Grant element (%)	31.9	37.3	40.1	59.3	64.2	33.3	-2.5	44.8	38.8	37.2
Official creditors										
Interest (%)	0.0	3.0	4.3	1.7	0.9	5.6	5.4	1.8	1.0	5.6
Maturity (years)	25.0	29.8	26.2	31.4	24.9	25.5	30.3	32.8	22.0	29.2
Grace period (years)	5.5	6.7	5.5	10.1	6.0	7.3	6.1	6.9	9.2	6.4
Grant element (%)	72.7	52.7	41.7	68.4	66.9	34.8	38.1	63.5	66.0	37.2
Private creditors										
Interest (%)	7.5	15.8	8.0	8.4	8.4	10.3	17.5	13.9	9.2	0.0
Maturity (years)	14.6	5.5	5.6	9.6	5.9	11.7	4.0	22.0	11.5	0.0
Grace period (years)	0.1	2.2	1.8	2.1	1.8	1.9	2.5	22.0	3.2	0.0
Grant element (%)	10.9	-14.9	5.0	5.9	4.3	1.6	-21.0	-37.1	8.6	0.0
Memorandum items										
Commitments	0.4	58.5	204.7	34.7	46.0	183.3	186.8	86.9	58.2	23.0
Official creditors	0.2	45.2	195.5	29.6	44.0	175.1	58.4	70.7	30.7	23.0
Private creditors	0.3	13.3	9.2	5.1	2.0	8.2	128.4	16.2	27.5	0.0

10. CONTRACTUAL OBLIGATIONS ON OUTSTANDING LONG-TERM DEBT

	1996	1997	1998	1999	2000	2001	2002	2003	2004	2005
TOTAL										
Disbursements	213.8	96.5	59.1	37.3	22.6	14.6	10.0	1.4	0.1	0.0
Principal	129.2	34.8	42.8	40.0	40.4	40.6	41.7	41.0	40.7	42.3
Interest	29.4	23.2	23.4	22.4	21.1	19.6	18.1	16.3	14.5	12.8
Official creditors										
Disbursements	93.8	86.7	56.9	36.9	22.6	14.6	10.0	1.4	0.1	0.0
Principal	23.3	31.5	39.5	36.6	37.1	37.3	38.4	37.9	37.6	39.3
Interest	16.8	18.9	19.1	18.3	17.3	16.0	14.8	13.2	11.7	10.2
Bilateral creditors										
Disbursements	31.3	23.8	13.0	5.2	2.6	0.4	0.1	0.0	0.0	0.0
Principal	11.7	13.7	14.5	10.9	10.8	11.1	11.5	11.5	11.0	10.8
Interest	6.1	7.2	7.3	6.8	6.4	5.9	5.3	4.8	4.2	3.7
Multilateral creditors										
Disbursements	62.5	62.9	43.9	31.7	20.0	14.1	9.9	1.4	0.1	0.0
Principal	11.6	17.8	24.9	25.7	26.3	26.2	26.8	26.4	26.6	28.6
Interest	10.8	11.7	11.8	11.5	10.9	10.2	9.4	8.5	7.5	6.5
Private creditors										
Disbursements	120.0	9.8	2.3	0.4	0.0	0.0	0.0	0.0	0.0	0.0
Principal	105.8	3.3	3.4	3.3	3.3	3.3	3.3	3.1	3.1	2.9
Interest	12.5	4.3	4.3	4.1	3.8	3.6	3.3	3.1	2.8	2.6
Commercial banks										
Disbursements	119.0	9.4	2.3	0.4	0.0	0.0	0.0	0.0	0.0	0.0
Principal	104.2	2.5	2.6	2.6	2.6	2.6	2.6	2.6	2.6	2.6
Interest	11.9	3.7	3.8	3.6	3.4	3.2	3.0	2.8	2.6	2.4
Other private										
Disbursements	1.1	0.4	0.0	0.0	0.0	0.0	0.0	0.0	0.0	0.0
Principal	1.6	0.9	0.7	0.7	0.7	0.7	0.7	0.5	0.5	0.3
Interest	0.6	0.6	0.5	0.5	0.4	0.3	0.3	0.2	0.2	0.2

LIBERIA

(US$ million, unless otherwise indicated)

	1970	1980	1988	1989	1990	1991	1992	1993	1994	1995
1. SUMMARY DEBT DATA										
TOTAL DEBT STOCKS (EDT)	**..**	**686**	**1,656**	**1,685**	**1,849**	**1,954**	**1,923**	**1,957**	**2,056**	**2,127**
Long-term debt (LDOD)	**158**	**516**	**1,077**	**1,064**	**1,116**	**1,106**	**1,081**	**1,102**	**1,137**	**1,161**
Public and publicly guaranteed	158	516	1,077	1,064	1,116	1,106	1,081	1,102	1,137	1,161
Private nonguaranteed	0	0	0	0	0	0	0	0	0	0
Use of IMF credit	**4**	**89**	**309**	**299**	**322**	**324**	**312**	**311**	**330**	**336**
Short-term debt	**..**	**81**	**271**	**322**	**411**	**523**	**530**	**544**	**589**	**630**
of which interest arrears on LDOD	..	2	216	267	355	469	477	500	545	586
Official creditors	..	1	142	186	251	342	329	349	390	431
Private creditors	..	1	74	81	104	127	148	151	155	155
Memo: principal arrears on LDOD	..	3	500	595	722	781	798	823	924	967
Official creditors	..	2	327	408	530	586	603	623	715	760
Private creditors	..	1	174	187	192	196	195	200	208	208
Memo: export credits	..	..	298	180	203	207	286	77	481	114
TOTAL DEBT FLOWS										
Disbursements	**9**	**109**	**15**	**0**	**0**	**2**	**0**	**33**	**0**	**0**
Long-term debt	7	76	15	0	0	2	0	33	0	0
IMF purchases	2	34	0	0	0	0	0	0	0	0
Principal repayments	**17**	**18**	**12**	**5**	**2**	**15**	**0**	**13**	**15**	**0**
Long-term debt	11	15	11	2	1	15	0	13	14	0
IMF repurchases	5	3	1	3	1	0	0	0	1	0
Net flows on debt	**-7**	**91**	**8**	**-4**	**-1**	**-15**	**-1**	**10**	**-14**	**0**
of which short-term debt	..	..	5	0	1	-2	-1	-10	1	0
Interest payments (INT)	**..**	**35**	**12**	**1**	**1**	**2**	**1**	**9**	**0**	**2**
Long-term debt	6	23	8	1	1	1	0	8	0	0
IMF charges	0	2	0	0	0	1	1	1	0	2
Short-term debt	..	11	4	0	0	0	0	0	0	0
Net transfers on debt	**..**	**56**	**-4**	**-5**	**-2**	**-17**	**-1**	**1**	**-14**	**-2**
Total debt service paid (TDS)	**..**	**54**	**25**	**6**	**3**	**17**	**1**	**22**	**15**	**2**
Long-term debt	18	38	19	3	2	17	0	21	14	0
IMF repurchases and charges	5	5	2	3	1	1	1	1	1	2
Short-term debt (interest only)	..	11	4	0	0	0	0	0	0	0
2. AGGREGATE NET RESOURCE FLOWS AND NET TRANSFERS (LONG-TERM)										
NET RESOURCE FLOWS	**-3**	**83**	**27**	**26**	**59**	**134**	**96**	**120**	**40**	**107**
Net flow of long-term debt (ex. IMF)	-4	61	4	-1	-1	-13	0	20	-14	0
Foreign direct investment (net)	0	0	0	0	0	0	0	0	0	0
Portfolio equity flows	0	0	0	0	0	0	0	0	0	0
Grants (excluding technical coop.)	1	23	23	27	60	147	96	100	53	107
Memo: technical coop. grants	8	24	39	36	21	12	24	24	12	17
NET TRANSFERS	**-9**	**61**	**19**	**25**	**59**	**133**	**96**	**112**	**40**	**107**
Interest on long-term debt	6	23	8	1	1	1	0	8	0	0
Profit remittances on FDI	0	0	0	0	0	0	0	0	0	0
3. MAJOR ECONOMIC AGGREGATES										
Gross national product (GNP)	402	1,093	..	..	..	..	..	..	..	..
Exports of goods & services (XGS)	..	614	..	..	..	..	..	..	..	..
of which workers remittances	..	0	..	..	..	..	..	..	..	..
Imports of goods & services (MGS)	..	575	..	..	..	..	..	..	..	..
International reserves (RES)	..	6	0	8	..	1	1	2	5	..
Current account balance	..	46	..	..	..	..	..	..	..	..
4. DEBT INDICATORS										
EDT / XGS (%)	..	111.8	..	..	..	..	..	..	..	..
EDT / GNP (%)	..	62.7	..	..	..	..	..	..	..	..
TDS / XGS (%)	..	8.7	..	..	..	..	..	..	..	..
INT / XGS (%)	..	5.8	..	..	..	..	..	..	..	..
INT / GNP (%)	..	3.2	..	..	..	..	..	..	..	..
RES / EDT (%)	..	0.8	0.0	0.5	..	0.1	0.1	0.1	0.2	..
RES / MGS (months)	..	0.1	..	..	..	..	..	..	..	..
Short-term / EDT (%)	..	11.8	16.4	19.1	22.2	26.8	27.6	27.8	28.7	29.6
Concessional / EDT (%)	..	31.4	34.0	33.4	31.9	29.7	29.6	30.4	30.0	29.6
Multilateral / EDT (%)	..	19.1	25.0	24.1	23.4	21.6	21.2	22.0	21.4	21.3

LIBERIA

(US$ million, unless otherwise indicated)

	1970	1980	1988	1989	1990	1991	1992	1993	1994	1995
5. LONG-TERM DEBT										
DEBT OUTSTANDING (LDOD)	**158**	**516**	**1,077**	**1,064**	**1,116**	**1,106**	**1,081**	**1,102**	**1,137**	**1,161**
Public and publicly guaranteed	**158**	**516**	**1,077**	**1,064**	**1,116**	**1,106**	**1,081**	**1,102**	**1,137**	**1,161**
Official creditors	124	359	883	876	924	911	886	902	929	954
Multilateral	8	131	414	406	433	421	407	430	439	453
Concessional	4	37	173	171	179	171	167	200	206	209
Bilateral	116	229	469	471	491	490	479	472	490	501
Concessional	110	179	391	393	410	409	401	395	411	421
Private creditors	34	156	193	188	192	196	195	200	208	208
Bonds	0	0	0	0	0	0	0	0	0	0
Commercial banks	0	129	175	169	172	175	176	181	189	187
Other private	34	28	19	19	20	20	19	19	20	21
Private nonguaranteed	**0**	**0**	**0**	**0**	**0**	**0**	**0**	**0**	**0**	**0**
Bonds	0	0	0	0	0	0	0	0	0	0
Commercial banks	0	0	0	0	0	0	0	0	0	0
Memo:										
IBRD	7	69	134	131	143	144	139	141	151	161
IDA	0	23	102	101	105	106	103	104	107	108
DISBURSEMENTS	**7**	**76**	**15**	**0**	**0**	**2**	**0**	**33**	**0**	**0**
Public and publicly guaranteed	**7**	**76**	**15**	**0**	**0**	**2**	**0**	**33**	**0**	**0**
Official creditors	7	65	15	0	0	2	0	33	0	0
Multilateral	2	33	15	0	0	2	0	33	0	0
Concessional	0	9	3	0	0	2	0	33	0	0
Bilateral	5	32	0	0	0	0	0	0	0	0
Concessional	4	30	0	0	0	0	0	0	0	0
Private creditors	0	11	0	0	0	0	0	0	0	0
Bonds	0	0	0	0	0	0	0	0	0	0
Commercial banks	0	6	0	0	0	0	0	0	0	0
Other private	0	5	0	0	0	0	0	0	0	0
Private nonguaranteed	**0**	**0**	**0**	**0**	**0**	**0**	**0**	**0**	**0**	**0**
Bonds	0	0	0	0	0	0	0	0	0	0
Commercial banks	0	0	0	0	0	0	0	0	0	0
Memo:										
IBRD	2	17	0	0	0	0	0	0	0	0
IDA	0	5	1	0	0	0	0	0	0	0
PRINCIPAL REPAYMENTS	**11**	**15**	**11**	**2**	**1**	**15**	**0**	**13**	**14**	**0**
Public and publicly guaranteed	**11**	**15**	**11**	**2**	**1**	**15**	**0**	**13**	**14**	**0**
Official creditors	5	4	11	2	1	15	0	13	14	0
Multilateral	0	2	2	1	1	15	0	13	14	0
Concessional	0	0	0	0	0	11	0	0	1	0
Bilateral	5	1	9	1	0	0	0	0	0	0
Concessional	5	1	4	1	0	0	0	0	0	0
Private creditors	7	12	0	0	0	0	0	0	0	0
Bonds	0	0	0	0	0	0	0	0	0	0
Commercial banks	0	3	0	0	0	0	0	0	0	0
Other private	7	9	0	0	0	0	0	0	0	0
Private nonguaranteed	**0**	**0**	**0**	**0**	**0**	**0**	**0**	**0**	**0**	**0**
Bonds	0	0	0	0	0	0	0	0	0	0
Commercial banks	0	0	0	0	0	0	0	0	0	0
Memo:										
IBRD	0	2	0	0	0	0	0	0	0	0
IDA	0	0	0	0	0	0	0	0	0	0
NET FLOWS ON DEBT	**-4**	**61**	**4**	**-1**	**-1**	**-13**	**0**	**20**	**-14**	**0**
Public and publicly guaranteed	**-4**	**61**	**4**	**-1**	**-1**	**-13**	**0**	**20**	**-14**	**0**
Official creditors	3	61	4	-1	-1	-13	0	20	-14	0
Multilateral	2	31	14	-1	-1	-13	0	20	-14	0
Concessional	0	9	3	0	0	-8	0	33	-1	0
Bilateral	0	30	-9	-1	0	0	0	0	0	0
Concessional	-1	29	-4	-1	0	0	0	0	0	0
Private creditors	-7	0	0	0	0	0	0	0	0	0
Bonds	0	0	0	0	0	0	0	0	0	0
Commercial banks	0	3	0	0	0	0	0	0	0	0
Other private	-7	-3	0	0	0	0	0	0	0	0
Private nonguaranteed	**0**	**0**	**0**	**0**	**0**	**0**	**0**	**0**	**0**	**0**
Bonds	0	0	0	0	0	0	0	0	0	0
Commercial banks	0	0	0	0	0	0	0	0	0	0
Memo:										
IBRD	2	16	0	0	0	0	0	0	0	0
IDA	0	5	1	0	0	0	0	0	0	0

LIBERIA

(US$ million, unless otherwise indicated)

	1970	1980	1988	1989	1990	1991	1992	1993	1994	1995
INTEREST PAYMENTS (LINT)	**6**	**23**	**8**	**1**	**1**	**1**	**0**	**8**	**0**	**0**
Public and publicly guaranteed	**6**	**23**	**8**	**1**	**1**	**1**	**0**	**8**	**0**	**0**
Official creditors	3	7	8	1	1	1	0	8	0	0
Multilateral	0	5	3	1	1	1	0	8	0	0
Concessional	0	0	0	0	0	1	0	0	0	0
Bilateral	3	2	6	0	0	0	0	0	0	0
Concessional	2	2	3	0	0	0	0	0	0	0
Private creditors	3	16	0	0	0	0	0	0	0	0
Bonds	0	0	0	0	0	0	0	0	0	0
Commercial banks	0	14	0	0	0	0	0	0	0	0
Other private	3	2	0	0	0	0	0	0	0	0
Private nonguaranteed	**0**	**0**	**0**	**0**	**0**	**0**	**0**	**0**	**0**	**0**
Bonds	0	0	0	0	0	0	0	0	0	0
Commercial banks	0	0	0	0	0	0	0	0	0	0
Memo:										
IBRD	0	4	0	0	0	0	0	0	0	0
IDA	0	0	0	0	0	0	0	0	0	0
NET TRANSFERS ON DEBT	**-10**	**38**	**-4**	**-3**	**-2**	**-14**	**0**	**12**	**-14**	**0**
Public and publicly guaranteed	**-10**	**38**	**-4**	**-3**	**-2**	**-14**	**0**	**12**	**-14**	**0**
Official creditors	-1	54	-4	-3	-2	-14	0	12	-14	0
Multilateral	2	25	11	-2	-2	-14	0	12	-14	0
Concessional	0	8	3	0	0	-9	0	33	-1	0
Bilateral	-2	29	-15	-1	0	0	0	0	0	0
Concessional	-3	28	-7	-1	0	0	0	0	0	0
Private creditors	-10	-16	0	0	0	0	0	0	0	0
Bonds	0	0	0	0	0	0	0	0	0	0
Commercial banks	0	-11	0	0	0	0	0	0	0	0
Other private	-10	-5	0	0	0	0	0	0	0	0
Private nonguaranteed	**0**	**0**	**0**	**0**	**0**	**0**	**0**	**0**	**0**	**0**
Bonds	0	0	0	0	0	0	0	0	0	0
Commercial banks	0	0	0	0	0	0	0	0	0	0
Memo:										
IBRD	1	12	0	0	0	0	0	0	0	0
IDA	0	5	0	0	0	0	0	0	0	0
DEBT SERVICE (LTDS)	**18**	**38**	**19**	**3**	**2**	**17**	**0**	**21**	**14**	**0**
Public and publicly guaranteed	**18**	**38**	**19**	**3**	**2**	**17**	**0**	**21**	**14**	**0**
Official creditors	8	11	19	3	2	17	0	21	14	0
Multilateral	0	8	4	2	2	17	0	21	14	0
Concessional	0	1	0	0	0	11	0	0	1	0
Bilateral	8	3	15	1	0	0	0	0	0	0
Concessional	7	3	7	1	0	0	0	0	0	0
Private creditors	10	27	0	0	0	0	0	0	0	0
Bonds	0	0	0	0	0	0	0	0	0	0
Commercial banks	0	17	0	0	0	0	0	0	0	0
Other private	10	11	0	0	0	0	0	0	0	0
Private nonguaranteed	**0**	**0**	**0**	**0**	**0**	**0**	**0**	**0**	**0**	**0**
Bonds	0	0	0	0	0	0	0	0	0	0
Commercial banks	0	0	0	0	0	0	0	0	0	0
Memo:										
IBRD	0	6	0	0	0	0	0	0	0	0
IDA	0	0	0	0	0	0	0	0	0	0
UNDISBURSED DEBT	**20**	**228**	**88**	**55**	**84**	**80**	**74**	**40**	**36**	**18**
Official creditors	18	220	88	55	84	80	74	40	36	18
Private creditors	2	8	0	0	0	0	0	0	0	0
Memorandum items										
Concessional LDOD	114	216	563	564	590	581	568	595	617	630
Variable rate LDOD	0	100	123	123	123	123	123	123	123	123
Public sector LDOD	158	514	1,077	1,064	1,116	1,106	1,081	1,102	1,137	1,161
Private sector LDOD	0	1	0	0	0	0	0	0	0	0

6. CURRENCY COMPOSITION OF LONG-TERM DEBT (PERCENT)

	1970	1980	1988	1989	1990	1991	1992	1993	1994	1995
Deutsche mark	12.7	9.2	9.6	10.2	11.1	11.0	10.6	9.7	10.5	11.1
French franc	0.0	0.0	0.9	1.0	1.1	1.1	1.0	0.9	1.0	1.1
Japanese yen	0.0	7.6	6.8	6.0	6.1	6.6	6.8	7.4	8.1	7.7
Pound sterling	0.3	1.5	1.3	1.3	1.2	1.2	1.2	1.2	1.2	1.2
Swiss franc	0.0	0.0	0.0	0.0	0.0	0.0	0.0	0.0	0.0	0.0
U.S.dollars	82.1	62.6	52.8	53.2	51.2	51.6	52.6	51.6	50.3	49.4
Multiple currency	4.9	17.4	22.4	22.0	22.7	21.8	21.4	20.1	20.8	21.4
Special drawing rights	0.0	0.0	1.4	1.4	1.5	1.5	1.5	1.4	1.5	1.5
All other currencies	0.0	1.7	4.8	4.9	5.2	5.2	4.9	7.5	6.6	6.8

LIBERIA

(US$ million, unless otherwise indicated)

	1970	1980	1988	1989	1990	1991	1992	1993	1994	1995
7. DEBT RESTRUCTURINGS										
Total amount rescheduled	0	..	0	0	0	0	0	0	0	0
Debt stock rescheduled	0	..	0	0	0	0	0	0	0	0
Principal rescheduled	0	..	0	0	0	0	0	0	0	0
Official	0	..	0	0	0	0	0	0	0	0
Private	0	..	0	0	0	0	0	0	0	0
Interest rescheduled	0	..	0	0	0	0	0	0	0	0
Official	0	..	0	0	0	0	0	0	0	0
Private	0	..	0	0	0	0	0	0	0	0
Debt forgiven	..	..	0	0	0	1	0	0	0	0
Memo: interest forgiven	..	..	0	0	0	0	0	0	0	0
Debt stock reduction	0	..	0	0	0	0	0	0	0	0
of which debt buyback	0	..	0	0	0	0	0	0	0	0
8. DEBT STOCK-FLOW RECONCILIATION										
Total change in debt stocks	..	..	..	29	164	105	-31	34	99	71
Net flows on debt	..	..	..	-4	-1	-15	-1	10	-14	0
Net change in interest arrears	..	..	..	52	87	115	7	24	45	41
Interest capitalized	..	..	..	0	0	0	0	0	0	0
Debt forgiveness or reduction	..	..	..	0	0	-1	0	0	0	0
Cross-currency valuation	..	..	..	-7	46	4	-20	2	44	22
Residual	..	..	..	-11	32	2	-18	-1	24	8
9. AVERAGE TERMS OF NEW COMMITMENTS										
ALL CREDITORS										
Interest (%)	6.6	7.3	0.0	0.0	4.0	0.0	0.0	0.0	0.0	0.0
Maturity (years)	18.7	18.8	0.0	0.0	23.2	0.0	0.0	0.0	0.0	0.0
Grace period (years)	4.5	4.5	0.0	0.0	5.1	0.0	0.0	0.0	0.0	0.0
Grant element (%)	20.7	25.1	0.0	0.0	41.6	0.0	0.0	0.0	0.0	0.0
Official creditors										
Interest (%)	6.4	5.3	0.0	0.0	4.0	0.0	0.0	0.0	0.0	0.0
Maturity (years)	20.9	23.1	0.0	0.0	23.2	0.0	0.0	0.0	0.0	0.0
Grace period (years)	5.1	5.5	0.0	0.0	5.1	0.0	0.0	0.0	0.0	0.0
Grant element (%)	23.6	35.5	0.0	0.0	41.6	0.0	0.0	0.0	0.0	0.0
Private creditors										
Interest (%)	7.9	12.6	0.0	0.0	0.0	0.0	0.0	0.0	0.0	0.0
Maturity (years)	8.1	7.3	0.0	0.0	0.0	0.0	0.0	0.0	0.0	0.0
Grace period (years)	1.5	1.6	0.0	0.0	0.0	0.0	0.0	0.0	0.0	0.0
Grant element (%)	6.6	-3.1	0.0	0.0	0.0	0.0	0.0	0.0	0.0	0.0
Memorandum items										
Commitments	12	40	0	0	32	0	0	0	0	0
Official creditors	10	30	0	0	32	0	0	0	0	0
Private creditors	2	11	0	0	0	0	0	0	0	0

10. CONTRACTUAL OBLIGATIONS ON OUTSTANDING LONG-TERM DEBT

	1996	1997	1998	1999	2000	2001	2002	2003	2004	2005
TOTAL										
Disbursements	0	0	0	0	0	0	0	0	0	0
Principal	62	59	47	38	35	23	21	21	20	18
Interest	17	14	11	9	7	6	5	4	4	3
Official creditors										
Disbursements	0	0	0	0	0	0	0	0	0	0
Principal	62	59	47	38	35	23	21	21	20	18
Interest	17	14	11	9	7	6	5	4	4	3
Bilateral creditors										
Disbursements	0	0	0	0	0	0	0	0	0	0
Principal	19	19	18	17	16	15	15	15	14	12
Interest	5	5	5	4	4	3	3	3	2	2
Multilateral creditors										
Disbursements	0	0	0	0	0	0	0	0	0	0
Principal	43	40	29	21	19	8	7	6	6	6
Interest	12	9	6	5	3	2	2	2	2	2
Private creditors										
Disbursements	0	0	0	0	0	0	0	0	0	0
Principal	0	0	0	0	0	0	0	0	0	0
Interest	0	0	0	0	0	0	0	0	0	0
Commercial banks										
Disbursements	0	0	0	0	0	0	0	0	0	0
Principal	0	0	0	0	0	0	0	0	0	0
Interest	0	0	0	0	0	0	0	0	0	0
Other private										
Disbursements	0	0	0	0	0	0	0	0	0	0
Principal	0	0	0	0	0	0	0	0	0	0
Interest	0	0	0	0	0	0	0	0	0	0

LITHUANIA

(US$ million, unless otherwise indicated)

	1970	1980	1988	1989	1990	1991	1992	1993	1994	1995
1. SUMMARY DEBT DATA										
TOTAL DEBT STOCKS (EDT)	..	..	..	..	..	..	**55.5**	**330.4**	**493.9**	**802.3**
Long-term debt (LDOD)	..	..	..	..	..	..	**27.4**	**202.8**	**268.5**	**491.3**
Public and publicly guaranteed	..	..	..	..	..	..	27.4	202.8	268.5	491.3
Private nonguaranteed	0.0	0.0	0.0	0.0	0.0	0.0	0.0	0.0	0.0	0.0
Use of IMF credit	**0.0**	**0.0**	**0.0**	**0.0**	**0.0**	**0.0**	**23.7**	**120.8**	**196.4**	**261.5**
Short-term debt	..	..	..	..	..	..	**4.5**	**6.8**	**29.0**	**49.4**
of which interest arrears on LDOD	..	..	..	..	..	..	0.0	0.0	0.0	0.0
Official creditors	..	..	..	..	..	..	0.0	0.0	0.0	0.0
Private creditors	..	..	..	..	..	..	0.0	0.0	0.0	0.0
Memo: principal arrears on LDOD	..	..	..	..	..	..	0.0	0.0	0.0	0.0
Official creditors	..	..	..	..	..	..	0.0	0.0	0.0	0.0
Private creditors	..	..	..	..	..	..	0.0	0.0	0.0	0.0
Memo: export credits	..	..	0.0	0.0	0.0	0.0	4.0	6.0	97.0	126.0
TOTAL DEBT FLOWS										
Disbursements	..	..	..	..	..	..	**33.8**	**281.7**	**155.1**	**290.0**
Long-term debt	..	..	..	..	..	..	9.5	183.0	88.4	227.2
IMF purchases	0.0	0.0	0.0	0.0	0.0	0.0	24.3	98.8	66.7	62.8
Principal repayments	..	..	..	..	..	..	**2.9**	**3.3**	**36.1**	**12.6**
Long-term debt	..	..	..	..	..	..	2.9	3.3	36.1	12.6
IMF repurchases	0.0	0.0	0.0	0.0	0.0	0.0	0.0	0.0	0.0	0.0
Net flows on debt	..	..	..	..	..	..	**35.5**	**280.8**	**141.2**	**297.8**
of which short-term debt	..	..	..	..	..	..	4.5	2.4	22.2	20.4
Interest payments (INT)	..	..	..	..	..	..	**1.1**	**4.0**	**32.7**	**31.2**
Long-term debt	..	..	..	..	..	..	1.1	1.2	23.3	17.3
IMF charges	0.0	0.0	0.0	0.0	0.0	0.0	0.0	2.5	7.6	11.5
Short-term debt	..	..	..	..	..	..	0.0	0.3	1.8	2.4
Net transfers on debt	..	..	..	..	..	..	**34.3**	**276.8**	**108.5**	**266.6**
Total debt service paid (TDS)	..	..	..	..	..	..	**4.0**	**7.3**	**68.7**	**43.8**
Long-term debt	..	..	..	..	..	..	4.0	4.5	59.4	29.9
IMF repurchases and charges	0.0	0.0	0.0	0.0	0.0	0.0	0.0	2.5	7.6	11.5
Short-term debt (interest only)	..	..	..	..	..	..	0.0	0.3	1.8	2.4
2. AGGREGATE NET RESOURCE FLOWS AND NET TRANSFERS (LONG-TERM)										
NET RESOURCE FLOWS	..	..	..	..	..	..	**85.0**	**211.0**	**110.3**	**306.9**
Net flow of long-term debt (ex. IMF)	..	..	..	..	..	..	6.7	179.7	52.3	214.6
Foreign direct investment (net)	..	..	..	..	..	..	10.0	12.0	31.0	73.0
Portfolio equity flows	..	..	..	..	..	..	0.0	0.0	0.0	4.3
Grants (excluding technical coop.)	..	..	..	..	..	..	68.3	19.3	27.0	15.0
Memo: technical coop. grants	..	..	..	..	..	..	16.4	18.9	28.3	116.9
NET TRANSFERS	..	..	..	..	..	..	**83.8**	**209.8**	**87.0**	**289.5**
Interest on long-term debt	..	..	..	..	..	..	1.1	1.2	23.3	17.3
Profit remittances on FDI	..	..	..	..	..	..	0.0	0.0	0.0	0.0
3. MAJOR ECONOMIC AGGREGATES										
Gross national product (GNP)	..	..	..	..	..	..	12,154.8	7,661.6	7,536.3	7,976.3
Exports of goods & services (XGS)	..	..	..	..	..	..	..	2,236.1	2,373.3	3,243.3
of which workers remittances	..	..	..	..	..	..	..	0.0	0.7	1.1
Imports of goods & services (MGS)	..	..	..	..	..	..	..	2,437.6	2,623.3	3,965.9
International reserves (RES)	..	..	..	..	..	..	107.3	423.0	596.7	829.0
Current account balance	..	..	..	..	..	..	..	-85.7	-94.0	-614.4
4. DEBT INDICATORS										
EDT / XGS (%)	..	..	..	..	..	..	..	14.8	20.8	24.7
EDT / GNP (%)	..	..	..	..	..	..	0.5	4.3	6.6	10.1
TDS / XGS (%)	..	..	..	..	..	..	..	0.3	2.9	1.4
INT / XGS (%)	..	..	..	..	..	..	..	0.2	1.4	1.0
INT / GNP (%)	..	..	..	..	..	..	0.0	0.1	0.4	0.4
RES / EDT (%)	..	..	..	..	..	..	193.2	128.0	120.8	103.3
RES / MGS (months)	..	..	..	..	..	..	..	2.1	2.7	2.5
Short-term / EDT (%)	..	..	..	..	..	..	8.0	2.1	5.9	6.2
Concessional / EDT (%)	..	..	..	..	..	..	17.1	10.2	15.7	12.8
Multilateral / EDT (%)	..	..	..	..	..	..	0.0	30.2	24.1	20.7

LITHUANIA

(US$ million, unless otherwise indicated)

5. LONG-TERM DEBT

	1970	1980	1988	1989	1990	1991	1992	1993	1994	1995
DEBT OUTSTANDING (LDOD)	..	..	..	..	..	..	**27.4**	**202.8**	**268.5**	**491.3**
Public and publicly guaranteed	..	..	..	..	..	..	**27.4**	**202.8**	**268.5**	**491.3**
Official creditors	..	..	..	..	..	..	9.5	136.4	214.9	318.4
Multilateral	..	..	..	..	..	..	0.0	99.8	119.2	165.7
Concessional	..	..	..	..	..	..	0.0	0.0	0.0	0.0
Bilateral	..	..	..	..	..	..	9.5	36.6	95.7	152.6
Concessional	..	..	..	..	..	..	9.5	33.6	77.7	103.0
Private creditors	..	..	..	..	..	..	17.9	66.4	53.6	173.0
Bonds	..	..	..	..	..	..	0.0	0.0	0.0	60.0
Commercial banks	..	..	..	..	..	..	0.0	0.0	0.0	0.0
Other private	..	..	..	..	..	..	17.9	66.4	53.6	113.0
Private nonguaranteed	**0.0**	**0.0**	**0.0**	**0.0**	**0.0**	**0.0**	**0.0**	**0.0**	**0.0**	**0.0**
Bonds	..	..	..	..	..	..	0.0	0.0	0.0	0.0
Commercial banks	..	..	..	..	..	..	0.0	0.0	0.0	0.0
Memo:										
IBRD	0.0	0.0	0.0	0.0	0.0	0.0	0.0	41.6	48.9	61.8
IDA	0.0	0.0	0.0	0.0	0.0	0.0	0.0	0.0	0.0	0.0
DISBURSEMENTS	..	..	..	..	..	..	**9.5**	**183.0**	**88.4**	**227.2**
Public and publicly guaranteed	..	..	..	..	..	..	**9.5**	**183.0**	**88.4**	**227.2**
Official creditors	..	..	..	..	..	..	9.5	130.4	69.0	101.8
Multilateral	..	..	..	..	..	..	0.0	103.2	10.6	41.1
Concessional	..	..	..	..	..	..	0.0	0.0	0.0	0.0
Bilateral	..	..	..	..	..	..	9.5	27.2	58.4	60.7
Concessional	..	..	..	..	..	..	9.5	24.1	43.3	27.7
Private creditors	..	..	..	..	..	..	0.0	52.6	19.3	125.4
Bonds	..	..	..	..	..	..	0.0	0.0	0.0	60.0
Commercial banks	..	..	..	..	..	..	0.0	0.0	0.0	0.0
Other private	..	..	..	..	..	..	0.0	52.6	19.3	65.4
Private nonguaranteed	**0.0**	**0.0**	**0.0**	**0.0**	**0.0**	**0.0**	**0.0**	**0.0**	**0.0**	**0.0**
Bonds	..	..	..	..	..	..	0.0	0.0	0.0	0.0
Commercial banks	..	..	..	..	..	..	0.0	0.0	0.0	0.0
Memo:										
IBRD	0.0	0.0	0.0	0.0	0.0	0.0	0.0	42.4	4.2	12.1
IDA	0.0	0.0	0.0	0.0	0.0	0.0	0.0	0.0	0.0	0.0
PRINCIPAL REPAYMENTS	..	..	..	..	..	..	**2.9**	**3.3**	**36.1**	**12.6**
Public and publicly guaranteed	..	..	..	..	..	..	**2.9**	**3.3**	**36.1**	**12.6**
Official creditors	..	..	..	..	..	..	0.0	0.0	1.0	3.6
Multilateral	..	..	..	..	..	..	0.0	0.0	0.0	0.0
Concessional	..	..	..	..	..	..	0.0	0.0	0.0	0.0
Bilateral	..	..	..	..	..	..	0.0	0.0	1.0	3.6
Concessional	..	..	..	..	..	..	0.0	0.0	0.0	0.6
Private creditors	..	..	..	..	..	..	2.9	3.3	35.1	9.0
Bonds	..	..	..	..	..	..	0.0	0.0	0.0	0.0
Commercial banks	..	..	..	..	..	..	0.0	0.0	0.0	0.0
Other private	..	..	..	..	..	..	2.9	3.3	35.1	9.0
Private nonguaranteed	**0.0**	**0.0**	**0.0**	**0.0**	**0.0**	**0.0**	**0.0**	**0.0**	**0.0**	**0.0**
Bonds	..	..	..	..	..	..	0.0	0.0	0.0	0.0
Commercial banks	..	..	..	..	..	..	0.0	0.0	0.0	0.0
Memo:										
IBRD	0.0	0.0	0.0	0.0	0.0	0.0	0.0	0.0	0.0	0.0
IDA	0.0	0.0	0.0	0.0	0.0	0.0	0.0	0.0	0.0	0.0
NET FLOWS ON DEBT	..	..	..	..	..	..	**6.7**	**179.7**	**52.3**	**214.6**
Public and publicly guaranteed	..	..	..	..	..	..	**6.7**	**179.7**	**52.3**	**214.6**
Official creditors	..	..	..	..	..	..	9.5	130.4	68.1	98.2
Multilateral	..	..	..	..	..	..	0.0	103.2	10.6	41.1
Concessional	..	..	..	..	..	..	0.0	0.0	0.0	0.0
Bilateral	..	..	..	..	..	..	9.5	27.2	57.5	57.1
Concessional	..	..	..	..	..	..	9.5	24.1	43.3	27.1
Private creditors	..	..	..	..	..	..	-2.9	49.2	-15.8	116.4
Bonds	..	..	..	..	..	..	0.0	0.0	0.0	60.0
Commercial banks	..	..	..	..	..	..	0.0	0.0	0.0	0.0
Other private	..	..	..	..	..	..	-2.9	49.2	-15.8	56.4
Private nonguaranteed	**0.0**	**0.0**	**0.0**	**0.0**	**0.0**	**0.0**	**0.0**	**0.0**	**0.0**	**0.0**
Bonds	..	..	..	..	..	..	0.0	0.0	0.0	0.0
Commercial banks	..	..	..	..	..	..	0.0	0.0	0.0	0.0
Memo:										
IBRD	0.0	0.0	0.0	0.0	0.0	0.0	0.0	42.4	4.2	12.1
IDA	0.0	0.0	0.0	0.0	0.0	0.0	0.0	0.0	0.0	0.0

LITHUANIA

(US$ million, unless otherwise indicated)

	1970	1980	1988	1989	1990	1991	1992	1993	1994	1995
INTEREST PAYMENTS (LINT)	..	..	..	..	..	..	**1.1**	**1.2**	**23.3**	**17.3**
Public and publicly guaranteed	..	..	..	..	..	..	**1.1**	**1.2**	**23.3**	**17.3**
Official creditors	..	..	..	..	..	..	0.0	0.5	8.8	13.3
Multilateral	..	..	..	..	..	..	0.0	0.3	7.8	9.4
Concessional	..	..	..	..	..	..	0.0	0.0	0.0	0.0
Bilateral	..	..	..	..	..	..	0.0	0.2	1.0	3.9
Concessional	..	..	..	..	..	..	0.0	0.2	0.7	2.7
Private creditors	..	..	..	..	..	..	1.1	0.7	14.5	4.0
Bonds	..	..	..	..	..	..	0.0	0.0	0.0	0.0
Commercial banks	..	..	..	..	..	..	0.0	0.0	0.0	0.0
Other private	..	..	..	..	..	..	1.1	0.7	14.5	4.0
Private nonguaranteed	**0.0**	**0.0**	**0.0**	**0.0**	**0.0**	**0.0**	**0.0**	**0.0**	**0.0**	**0.0**
Bonds	..	..	..	..	..	..	0.0	0.0	0.0	0.0
Commercial banks	..	..	..	..	..	..	0.0	0.0	0.0	0.0
Memo:										
IBRD	0.0	0.0	0.0	0.0	0.0	0.0	0.0	0.3	3.2	3.6
IDA	0.0	0.0	0.0	0.0	0.0	0.0	0.0	0.0	0.0	0.0
NET TRANSFERS ON DEBT	..	..	..	..	..	..	**5.5**	**178.5**	**29.0**	**197.2**
Public and publicly guaranteed	..	..	..	..	..	..	**5.5**	**178.5**	**29.0**	**197.2**
Official creditors	..	..	..	..	..	..	9.5	129.9	59.3	84.8
Multilateral	..	..	..	..	..	..	0.0	102.9	2.8	31.7
Concessional	..	..	..	..	..	..	0.0	0.0	0.0	0.0
Bilateral	..	..	..	..	..	..	9.5	27.0	56.5	53.2
Concessional	..	..	..	..	..	..	9.5	23.9	42.7	24.3
Private creditors	..	..	..	..	..	..	-4.0	48.6	-30.3	112.4
Bonds	..	..	..	..	..	..	0.0	0.0	0.0	60.0
Commercial banks	..	..	..	..	..	..	0.0	0.0	0.0	0.0
Other private	..	..	..	..	..	..	-4.0	48.6	-30.3	52.4
Private nonguaranteed	**0.0**	**0.0**	**0.0**	**0.0**	**0.0**	**0.0**	**0.0**	**0.0**	**0.0**	**0.0**
Bonds	..	..	..	..	..	..	0.0	0.0	0.0	0.0
Commercial banks	..	..	..	..	..	..	0.0	0.0	0.0	0.0
Memo:										
IBRD	0.0	0.0	0.0	0.0	0.0	0.0	0.0	42.1	1.0	8.5
IDA	0.0	0.0	0.0	0.0	0.0	0.0	0.0	0.0	0.0	0.0
DEBT SERVICE (LTDS)	..	..	..	..	..	..	**4.0**	**4.5**	**59.4**	**29.9**
Public and publicly guaranteed	..	..	..	..	..	..	**4.0**	**4.5**	**59.4**	**29.9**
Official creditors	..	..	..	..	..	..	0.0	0.5	9.8	17.0
Multilateral	..	..	..	..	..	..	0.0	0.3	7.8	9.4
Concessional	..	..	..	..	..	..	0.0	0.0	0.0	0.0
Bilateral	..	..	..	..	..	..	0.0	0.2	2.0	7.5
Concessional	..	..	..	..	..	..	0.0	0.2	0.7	3.4
Private creditors	..	..	..	..	..	..	4.0	4.0	49.6	13.0
Bonds	..	..	..	..	..	..	0.0	0.0	0.0	0.0
Commercial banks	..	..	..	..	..	..	0.0	0.0	0.0	0.0
Other private	..	..	..	..	..	..	4.0	4.0	49.6	13.0
Private nonguaranteed	**0.0**	**0.0**	**0.0**	**0.0**	**0.0**	**0.0**	**0.0**	**0.0**	**0.0**	**0.0**
Bonds	..	..	..	..	..	..	0.0	0.0	0.0	0.0
Commercial banks	..	..	..	..	..	..	0.0	0.0	0.0	0.0
Memo:										
IBRD	0.0	0.0	0.0	0.0	0.0	0.0	0.0	0.3	3.2	3.6
IDA	0.0	0.0	0.0	0.0	0.0	0.0	0.0	0.0	0.0	0.0
UNDISBURSED DEBT	..	..	..	..	..	..	**135.4**	**143.4**	**203.7**	**339.0**
Official creditors	..	..	..	..	..	..	104.8	119.4	142.1	224.0
Private creditors	..	..	..	..	..	..	30.6	24.0	61.6	115.0
Memorandum items										
Concessional LDOD	..	..	..	..	..	..	9.5	33.6	77.7	103.0
Variable rate LDOD	..	..	..	..	..	..	17.9	102.1	128.1	216.1
Public sector LDOD	..	..	..	..	..	..	27.4	202.8	264.1	478.9
Private sector LDOD	..	..	..	..	..	..	0.0	0.0	4.4	12.4

6. CURRENCY COMPOSITION OF LONG-TERM DEBT (PERCENT)

	1970	1980	1988	1989	1990	1991	1992	1993	1994	1995
Deutsche mark	..	..	..	..	..	..	0.0	6.0	12.1	15.0
French franc	..	..	..	..	..	..	0.0	0.0	0.0	0.0
Japanese yen	..	..	..	..	..	..	0.0	0.0	12.8	8.5
Pound sterling	..	..	..	..	..	..	0.0	0.0	0.0	0.0
Swiss franc	..	..	..	..	..	..	65.4	7.3	5.1	2.8
U.S.dollars	..	..	..	..	..	..	34.7	38.6	27.2	42.5
Multiple currency	..	..	..	..	..	..	0.0	20.5	18.2	12.6
Special drawing rights	..	..	..	..	..	..	0.0	0.0	0.0	0.0
All other currencies	..	..	..	..	..	..	0.0	27.6	24.6	18.6

LITHUANIA

(US$ million, unless otherwise indicated)

	1970	1980	1988	1989	1990	1991	1992	1993	1994	1995
7. DEBT RESTRUCTURINGS										
Total amount rescheduled	0.0	0.0	0.0	0.0	0.0	0.0	0.0	0.0	0.0	0.0
Debt stock rescheduled	0.0	0.0	0.0	0.0	0.0	0.0	0.0	0.0	0.0	0.0
Principal rescheduled	0.0	0.0	0.0	0.0	0.0	0.0	0.0	0.0	0.0	0.0
Official	0.0	0.0	0.0	0.0	0.0	0.0	0.0	0.0	0.0	0.0
Private	0.0	0.0	0.0	0.0	0.0	0.0	0.0	0.0	0.0	0.0
Interest rescheduled	0.0	0.0	0.0	0.0	0.0	0.0	0.0	0.0	0.0	0.0
Official	0.0	0.0	0.0	0.0	0.0	0.0	0.0	0.0	0.0	0.0
Private	0.0	0.0	0.0	0.0	0.0	0.0	0.0	0.0	0.0	0.0
Debt forgiven	..	..	0.0	0.0	0.0	0.0	0.0	0.0	0.0	0.0
Memo: interest forgiven	..	..	0.0	0.0	0.0	0.0	0.0	0.0	0.0	0.0
Debt stock reduction	0.0	0.0	0.0	0.0	0.0	0.0	0.0	0.0	0.0	0.0
of which debt buyback	0.0	0.0	0.0	0.0	0.0	0.0	0.0	0.0	0.0	0.0
8. DEBT STOCK-FLOW RECONCILIATION										
Total change in debt stocks	..	..	..	..	..	..	33.0	274.9	163.5	308.3
Net flows on debt	..	..	..	..	..	..	35.5	280.8	141.2	297.8
Net change in interest arrears	..	..	..	..	..	..	0.0	0.0	0.0	0.0
Interest capitalized	..	..	..	..	..	..	0.0	0.0	0.0	0.0
Debt forgiveness or reduction	..	..	..	..	..	..	0.0	0.0	0.0	0.0
Cross-currency valuation	..	..	..	..	..	..	-1.2	-6.0	19.2	14.2
Residual	..	..	..	..	..	..	-1.0	0.1	3.1	-3.6
9. AVERAGE TERMS OF NEW COMMITMENTS										
ALL CREDITORS										
Interest (%)	..	..	..	..	..	..	7.2	5.7	4.8	7.1
Maturity (years)	..	..	..	..	..	..	14.6	11.4	13.0	10.3
Grace period (years)	..	..	..	..	..	..	4.1	5.1	3.8	2.5
Grant element (%)	..	..	..	..	..	..	15.4	22.5	26.1	14.6
Official creditors										
Interest (%)	..	..	..	..	..	..	7.4	5.4	5.1	6.2
Maturity (years)	..	..	..	..	..	..	15.7	14.1	14.9	14.4
Grace period (years)	..	..	..	..	..	..	4.3	6.3	4.9	3.6
Grant element (%)	..	..	..	..	..	..	15.2	28.0	27.7	22.6
Private creditors										
Interest (%)	..	..	..	..	..	..	6.5	6.5	4.3	8.1
Maturity (years)	..	..	..	..	..	..	10.6	2.8	10.1	6.1
Grace period (years)	..	..	..	..	..	..	3.1	1.2	2.0	1.4
Grant element (%)	..	..	..	..	..	..	16.0	4.5	23.8	6.4
Memorandum items										
Commitments	..	..	..	..	..	..	145.9	193.9	141.9	359.8
Official creditors	..	..	..	..	..	..	115.2	147.8	85.9	181.4
Private creditors	..	..	..	..	..	..	30.6	46.1	56.0	178.4

10. CONTRACTUAL OBLIGATIONS ON OUTSTANDING LONG-TERM DEBT

	1996	1997	1998	1999	2000	2001	2002	2003	2004	2005
TOTAL										
Disbursements	121.2	97.0	55.0	26.1	16.0	10.0	6.0	4.3	2.5	0.9
Principal	74.7	110.7	66.9	63.0	122.5	55.3	57.2	44.8	39.3	56.2
Interest	30.8	33.7	31.1	28.6	25.6	18.5	15.9	12.7	10.4	7.8
Official creditors										
Disbursements	55.2	64.0	41.6	24.0	15.5	10.0	6.0	4.3	2.5	0.9
Principal	18.3	29.2	36.7	37.2	100.9	37.9	43.5	31.1	28.0	46.8
Interest	17.5	20.5	22.2	21.5	20.1	14.4	12.8	10.3	8.8	6.8
Bilateral creditors										
Disbursements	26.9	27.0	15.3	5.2	1.9	0.6	0.0	0.0	0.0	0.0
Principal	10.9	15.9	20.8	19.2	16.2	18.5	24.0	14.9	14.9	13.1
Interest	4.8	6.9	8.1	7.5	6.5	5.9	5.2	3.7	2.9	2.2
Multilateral creditors										
Disbursements	28.3	37.0	26.3	18.9	13.5	9.4	6.0	4.3	2.5	0.9
Principal	7.4	13.3	15.8	18.0	84.8	19.4	19.4	16.3	13.1	33.7
Interest	12.7	13.5	14.1	14.0	13.6	8.4	7.6	6.6	5.9	4.6
Private creditors										
Disbursements	66.0	33.0	13.4	2.0	0.6	0.0	0.0	0.0	0.0	0.0
Principal	56.4	81.6	30.2	25.8	21.6	17.4	13.7	13.7	11.3	9.4
Interest	13.3	13.3	8.9	7.1	5.5	4.1	3.1	2.4	1.6	1.0
Commercial banks										
Disbursements	0.0	0.0	0.0	0.0	0.0	0.0	0.0	0.0	0.0	0.0
Principal	0.0	0.0	0.0	0.0	0.0	0.0	0.0	0.0	0.0	0.0
Interest	0.0	0.0	0.0	0.0	0.0	0.0	0.0	0.0	0.0	0.0
Other private										
Disbursements	66.0	33.0	13.4	2.0	0.6	0.0	0.0	0.0	0.0	0.0
Principal	56.4	81.6	30.2	25.8	21.6	17.4	13.7	13.7	11.3	9.4
Interest	13.3	13.3	8.9	7.1	5.5	5.2	3.1	2.4	1.6	1.0

MACEDONIA, FYR

(US$ million, unless otherwise indicated)

	1970	1980	1988	1989	1990	1991	1992	1993	1994	1995
1. SUMMARY DEBT DATA										
TOTAL DEBT STOCKS (EDT)	..	..	..	..	..	..	..	**972**	**1,034**	**1,21[illegible]**
Long-term debt (LDOD)	..	..	..	..	..	..	..	**844**	**858**	**1,06[illegible]**
Public and publicly guaranteed	..	..	..	..	..	..	..	635	640	77[illegible]
Private nonguaranteed	0	0	0	0	0	0	0	210	218	28[illegible]
Use of IMF credit	**0**	**0**	**0**	**0**	**0**	**0**	**0**	**4**	**21**	**5[illegible]**
Short-term debt	..	..	..	..	..	..	..	**124**	**156**	**9[illegible]**
of which interest arrears on LDOD	..	..	..	..	..	..	..	108	138	9[illegible]
Official creditors	..	..	..	..	..	..	..	20	30	2[illegible]
Private creditors	..	..	..	..	..	..	..	89	108	6[illegible]
Memo: principal arrears on LDOD	..	..	..	..	..	..	..	301	315	19[illegible]
Official creditors	..	..	..	..	..	..	..	217	190	2[illegible]
Private creditors	..	..	..	..	..	..	..	84	126	16[illegible]
Memo: export credits	..	..	0	0	0	0	10	33	90	11[illegible]
TOTAL DEBT FLOWS										
Disbursements	..	..	..	..	..	..	..	**1**	**104**	**11[illegible]**
Long-term debt	..	..	..	..	..	..	..	1	86	7[illegible]
IMF purchases	0	0	0	0	0	0	0	0	18	3[illegible]
Principal repayments	..	..	..	..	..	..	..	**12**	**121**	**2[illegible]**
Long-term debt	..	..	..	..	..	..	..	5	119	1[illegible]
IMF repurchases	0	0	0	0	0	0	0	7	2	[illegible]
Net flows on debt	..	..	..	..	..	..	..	**5**	**-15**	**7[illegible]**
of which short-term debt	..	..	..	..	..	..	..	16	2	-1[illegible]
Interest payments (INT)	..	..	..	..	..	..	..	**4**	**35**	**1[illegible]**
Long-term debt	..	..	..	..	..	..	..	3	33	[illegible]
IMF charges	0	0	0	0	0	0	0	1	1	[illegible]
Short-term debt	..	..	..	..	..	..	..	1	1	[illegible]
Net transfers on debt	..	..	..	..	..	..	..	**0**	**-50**	**6[illegible]**
Total debt service paid (TDS)	..	..	..	..	..	..	..	**16**	**156**	**3[illegible]**
Long-term debt	..	..	..	..	..	..	..	8	152	2[illegible]
IMF repurchases and charges	0	0	0	0	0	0	0	7	3	[illegible]
Short-term debt (interest only)	..	..	..	..	..	..	..	1	1	[illegible]
2. AGGREGATE NET RESOURCE FLOWS AND NET TRANSFERS (LONG-TERM)										
NET RESOURCE FLOWS	..	..	..	..	..	..	..	**-5**	**-33**	**5[illegible]**
Net flow of long-term debt (ex. IMF)	..	..	..	..	..	..	..	-5	-33	5[illegible]
Foreign direct investment (net)	..	..	..	..	..	..	..	0	0	[illegible]
Portfolio equity flows	..	..	..	..	..	..	..	0	0	[illegible]
Grants (excluding technical coop.)	..	..	..	..	..	..	..	0	0	[illegible]
Memo: technical coop. grants	..	..	..	..	..	..	..	0	0	[illegible]
NET TRANSFERS	..	..	..	..	..	..	..	**-7**	**-67**	**4[illegible]**
Interest on long-term debt	..	..	..	..	..	..	..	3	33	[illegible]
Profit remittances on FDI	..	..	..	..	..	..	..	0	0	[illegible]
3. MAJOR ECONOMIC AGGREGATES										
Gross national product (GNP)	..	..	..	..	..	..	..	1,655	1,849	1,84[illegible]
Exports of goods & services (XGS)	..	..	..	..	..	..	..	..	1,321	1,51[illegible]
of which workers remittances	..	..	..	..	..	..	..	..	0	[illegible]
Imports of goods & services (MGS)	..	..	..	..	..	..	..	..	1,752	1,95[illegible]
International reserves (RES)	..	..	..	..	..	..	..	105	166	27[illegible]
Current account balance	..	..	..	..	..	..	..	..	-207	-25[illegible]
4. DEBT INDICATORS										
EDT / XGS (%)	..	..	..	..	..	..	..	..	78.3	79.[illegible]
EDT / GNP (%)	..	..	..	..	..	..	..	58.7	55.9	65.[illegible]
TDS / XGS (%)	..	..	..	..	..	..	..	..	11.8	2.[illegible]
INT / XGS (%)	..	..	..	..	..	..	..	..	2.7	0.[illegible]
INT / GNP (%)	..	..	..	..	..	..	..	0.3	1.9	0.[illegible]
RES / EDT (%)	..	..	..	..	..	..	..	10.8	16.1	22.[illegible]
RES / MGS (months)	..	..	..	..	..	..	..	..	1.1	1.[illegible]
Short-term / EDT (%)	..	..	..	..	..	..	..	12.8	15.1	7.[illegible]
Concessional / EDT (%)	..	..	..	..	..	..	..	0.9	4.9	27.[illegible]
Multilateral / EDT (%)	..	..	..	..	..	..	..	23.3	21.7	24.[illegible]

MACEDONIA, FYR

(US$ million, unless otherwise indicated)

	1970	1980	1988	1989	1990	1991	1992	1993	1994	1995
5. LONG-TERM DEBT										
DEBT OUTSTANDING (LDOD)	..	..	..	..	..	..	..	**844**	**858**	**1,062**
Public and publicly guaranteed	..	..	..	..	..	..	..	**635**	**640**	**773**
Official creditors	..	..	..	..	..	..	..	451	450	618
Multilateral	..	..	..	..	..	..	..	226	224	291
Concessional	..	..	..	..	..	..	..	0	42	84
Bilateral	..	..	..	..	..	..	..	225	226	327
Concessional	..	..	..	..	..	..	..	9	9	247
Private creditors	..	..	..	..	..	..	..	183	190	155
Bonds	..	..	..	..	..	..	..	0	0	0
Commercial banks	..	..	..	..	..	..	..	104	107	86
Other private	..	..	..	..	..	..	..	80	82	68
Private nonguaranteed	**0**	**0**	**0**	**0**	**0**	**0**	**0**	**210**	**218**	**289**
Bonds	..	..	..	..	..	..	..	0	0	0
Commercial banks	..	..	..	..	..	..	..	210	218	289
Memo:										
IBRD	0	0	0	0	0	0	0	151	93	97
IDA	0	0	0	0	0	0	0	0	42	84
DISBURSEMENTS	..	..	..	..	..	..	..	**1**	**86**	**77**
Public and publicly guaranteed	..	..	..	..	..	..	..	**1**	**86**	**77**
Official creditors	..	..	..	..	..	..	..	1	86	77
Multilateral	..	..	..	..	..	..	..	1	86	77
Concessional	..	..	..	..	..	..	..	0	40	42
Bilateral	..	..	..	..	..	..	..	0	0	0
Concessional	..	..	..	..	..	..	..	0	0	0
Private creditors	..	..	..	..	..	..	..	0	0	0
Bonds	..	..	..	..	..	..	..	0	0	0
Commercial banks	..	..	..	..	..	..	..	0	0	0
Other private	..	..	..	..	..	..	..	0	0	0
Private nonguaranteed	**0**	**0**	**0**	**0**	**0**	**0**	**0**	**0**	**0**	**0**
Bonds	..	..	..	..	..	..	..	0	0	0
Commercial banks	..	..	..	..	..	..	..	0	0	0
Memo:										
IBRD	0	0	0	0	0	0	0	1	40	20
IDA	0	0	0	0	0	0	0	0	40	42
PRINCIPAL REPAYMENTS	..	..	..	..	..	..	..	**5**	**119**	**19**
Public and publicly guaranteed	..	..	..	..	..	..	..	**5**	**104**	**19**
Official creditors	..	..	..	..	..	..	..	5	104	19
Multilateral	..	..	..	..	..	..	..	5	104	19
Concessional	..	..	..	..	..	..	..	0	0	0
Bilateral	..	..	..	..	..	..	..	0	0	0
Concessional	..	..	..	..	..	..	..	0	0	0
Private creditors	..	..	..	..	..	..	..	0	0	0
Bonds	..	..	..	..	..	..	..	0	0	0
Commercial banks	..	..	..	..	..	..	..	0	0	0
Other private	..	..	..	..	..	..	..	0	0	0
Private nonguaranteed	**0**	**0**	**0**	**0**	**0**	**0**	**0**	**0**	**15**	**0**
Bonds	..	..	..	..	..	..	..	0	0	0
Commercial banks	..	..	..	..	..	..	..	0	15	0
Memo:										
IBRD	0	0	0	0	0	0	0	5	104	19
IDA	0	0	0	0	0	0	0	0	0	0
NET FLOWS ON DEBT	..	..	..	..	..	..	..	**-5**	**-33**	**58**
Public and publicly guaranteed	..	..	..	..	..	..	..	**-5**	**-18**	**58**
Official creditors	..	..	..	..	..	..	..	-4	-18	58
Multilateral	..	..	..	..	..	..	..	-4	-18	58
Concessional	..	..	..	..	..	..	..	0	40	42
Bilateral	..	..	..	..	..	..	..	0	0	0
Concessional	..	..	..	..	..	..	..	0	0	0
Private creditors	..	..	..	..	..	..	..	0	0	0
Bonds	..	..	..	..	..	..	..	0	0	0
Commercial banks	..	..	..	..	..	..	..	0	0	0
Other private	..	..	..	..	..	..	..	0	0	0
Private nonguaranteed	**0**	**0**	**0**	**0**	**0**	**0**	**0**	**0**	**-15**	**0**
Bonds	..	..	..	..	..	..	..	0	0	0
Commercial banks	..	..	..	..	..	..	..	0	-15	0
Memo:										
IBRD	0	0	0	0	0	0	0	-4	-64	1
IDA	0	0	0	0	0	0	0	0	40	42

MACEDONIA, FYR

(US$ million, unless otherwise indicated)

	1970	*1980*	*1988*	*1989*	*1990*	*1991*	*1992*	*1993*	*1994*	*1995*
INTEREST PAYMENTS (LINT)	..	..	..	..	..	..	..	**3**	**33**	**9**
Public and publicly guaranteed	..	..	..	..	..	..	..	**3**	**33**	**9**
Official creditors	..	..	..	..	..	..	..	3	33	9
Multilateral	..	..	..	..	..	..	..	3	33	9
Concessional	..	..	..	..	..	..	..	0	0	0
Bilateral	..	..	..	..	..	..	..	0	0	0
Concessional	..	..	..	..	..	..	..	0	0	0
Private creditors	..	..	..	..	..	..	..	0	0	0
Bonds	..	..	..	..	..	..	..	0	0	0
Commercial banks	..	..	..	..	..	..	..	0	0	0
Other private	..	..	..	..	..	..	..	0	0	0
Private nonguaranteed	**0**	**0**	**0**	**0**	**0**	**0**	**0**	**0**	**0**	**0**
Bonds	..	..	..	..	..	..	..	0	0	0
Commercial banks	..	..	..	..	..	..	..	0	0	0
Memo:										
IBRD	0	0	0	0	0	0	0	3	32	8
IDA	0	0	0	0	0	0	0	0	0	0
NET TRANSFERS ON DEBT	..	..	..	..	..	..	..	**-7**	**-67**	**49**
Public and publicly guaranteed	..	..	..	..	..	..	..	**-7**	**-52**	**49**
Official creditors	..	..	..	..	..	..	..	-7	-52	49
Multilateral	..	..	..	..	..	..	..	-7	-52	49
Concessional	..	..	..	..	..	..	..	0	40	41
Bilateral	..	..	..	..	..	..	..	0	0	0
Concessional	..	..	..	..	..	..	..	0	0	0
Private creditors	..	..	..	..	..	..	..	0	0	0
Bonds	..	..	..	..	..	..	..	0	0	0
Commercial banks	..	..	..	..	..	..	..	0	0	0
Other private	..	..	..	..	..	..	..	0	0	0
Private nonguaranteed	**0**	**0**	**0**	**0**	**0**	**0**	**0**	**0**	**-15**	**0**
Bonds	..	..	..	..	..	..	..	0	0	0
Commercial banks	..	..	..	..	..	..	..	0	-15	0
Memo:										
IBRD	0	0	0	0	0	0	0	-7	-96	-7
IDA	0	0	0	0	0	0	0	0	40	41
DEBT SERVICE (LTDS)	..	..	..	..	..	..	..	**8**	**152**	**28**
Public and publicly guaranteed	..	..	..	..	..	..	..	**8**	**137**	**28**
Official creditors	..	..	..	..	..	..	..	8	137	28
Multilateral	..	..	..	..	..	..	..	8	137	28
Concessional	..	..	..	..	..	..	..	0	0	0
Bilateral	..	..	..	..	..	..	..	0	0	0
Concessional	..	..	..	..	..	..	..	0	0	0
Private creditors	..	..	..	..	..	..	..	0	0	0
Bonds	..	..	..	..	..	..	..	0	0	0
Commercial banks	..	..	..	..	..	..	..	0	0	0
Other private	..	..	..	..	..	..	..	0	0	0
Private nonguaranteed	**0**	**0**	**0**	**0**	**0**	**0**	**0**	**0**	**15**	**0**
Bonds	..	..	..	..	..	..	..	0	0	0
Commercial banks	..	..	..	..	..	..	..	0	15	0
Memo:										
IBRD	0	0	0	0	0	0	0	8	136	27
IDA	0	0	0	0	0	0	0	0	0	0
UNDISBURSED DEBT	..	..	..	..	..	..	..	**29**	**46**	**154**
Official creditors	..	..	..	..	..	..	..	29	46	154
Private creditors	..	..	..	..	..	..	..	0	0	0
Memorandum items										
Concessional LDOD	..	..	..	..	..	..	..	9	51	331
Variable rate LDOD	..	..	..	..	..	..	..	459	509	548
Public sector LDOD	..	..	..	..	..	..	..	628	635	769
Private sector LDOD	..	..	..	..	..	..	..	217	222	293
6. CURRENCY COMPOSITION OF LONG-TERM DEBT (PERCENT)										
Deutsche mark	..	..	..	..	..	..	..	4.9	6.3	5.9
French franc	..	..	..	..	..	..	..	0.6	0.6	0.5
Japanese yen	..	..	..	..	..	..	..	6.7	7.5	5.3
Pound sterling	..	..	..	..	..	..	..	1.4	1.5	0.9
Swiss franc	..	..	..	..	..	..	..	0.9	1.0	0.9
U.S.dollars	..	..	..	..	..	..	..	53.0	59.2	66.0
Multiple currency	..	..	..	..	..	..	..	32.3	23.7	20.5
Special drawing rights	..	..	..	..	..	..	..	0.1	0.1	0.1
All other currencies	..	..	..	..	..	..	..	0.1	0.1	0.1

MACEDONIA, FYR

(US$ million, unless otherwise indicated)

	1970	1980	1988	1989	1990	1991	1992	1993	1994	1995
7. DEBT RESTRUCTURINGS										
Total amount rescheduled	0	0	0	0	0	0	0	0	0	288
Debt stock rescheduled	0	0	0	0	0	0	0	0	0	0
Principal rescheduled	0	0	0	0	0	0	0	0	0	224
Official	0	0	0	0	0	0	0	0	0	188
Private	0	0	0	0	0	0	0	0	0	36
Interest rescheduled	0	0	0	0	0	0	0	0	0	65
Official	0	0	0	0	0	0	0	0	0	13
Private	0	0	0	0	0	0	0	0	0	52
Debt forgiven	..	..	0	0	0	0	0	0	0	0
Memo: interest forgiven	..	..	0	0	0	0	0	0	0	0
Debt stock reduction	0	0	0	0	0	0	0	0	0	0
of which debt buyback	0	0	0	0	0	0	0	0	0	0
8. DEBT STOCK-FLOW RECONCILIATION										
Total change in debt stocks	..	..	..	..	..	..	..	972	62	179
Net flows on debt	..	..	..	..	..	..	..	5	-15	77
Net change in interest arrears	..	..	..	..	..	..	..	108	30	-44
Interest capitalized	..	..	..	..	..	..	..	0	0	65
Debt forgiveness or reduction	..	..	..	..	..	..	..	0	0	0
Cross-currency valuation	..	..	..	..	..	..	..	52	-15	2
Residual	..	..	..	..	..	..	..	808	62	80
9. AVERAGE TERMS OF NEW COMMITMENTS										
ALL CREDITORS										
Interest (%)	..	..	..	..	..	..	..	6.8	4.3	3.6
Maturity (years)	..	..	..	..	..	..	..	15.6	25.0	24.0
Grace period (years)	..	..	..	..	..	..	..	3.6	6.9	7.0
Grant element (%)	..	..	..	..	..	..	..	17.3	43.6	48.5
Official creditors										
Interest (%)	..	..	..	..	..	..	..	6.8	4.3	3.6
Maturity (years)	..	..	..	..	..	..	..	15.6	25.0	24.0
Grace period (years)	..	..	..	..	..	..	..	3.6	6.9	7.0
Grant element (%)	..	..	..	..	..	..	..	17.3	43.6	48.5
Private creditors										
Interest (%)	..	..	..	..	..	..	..	0.0	0.0	0.0
Maturity (years)	..	..	..	..	..	..	..	0.0	0.0	0.0
Grace period (years)	..	..	..	..	..	..	..	0.0	0.0	0.0
Grant element (%)	..	..	..	..	..	..	..	0.0	0.0	0.0
Memorandum items										
Commitments	..	..	..	..	..	..	..	28	102	187
Official creditors	..	..	..	..	..	..	..	28	102	187
Private creditors	..	..	..	..	..	..	..	0	0	0

10. CONTRACTUAL OBLIGATIONS ON OUTSTANDING LONG-TERM DEBT

	1996	1997	1998	1999	2000	2001	2002	2003	2004	2005
TOTAL										
Disbursements	53	52	31	11	5	2	0	0	0	0
Principal	61	59	69	58	63	65	66	69	68	63
Interest	48	50	46	43	39	35	31	27	22	18
Official creditors										
Disbursements	53	52	31	11	5	2	0	0	0	0
Principal	27	24	39	36	41	43	44	48	47	42
Interest	30	30	29	27	25	23	21	18	16	14
Bilateral creditors										
Disbursements	1	2	2	1	1	0	0	0	0	0
Principal	4	7	12	13	16	18	24	29	29	29
Interest	14	14	13	13	12	12	11	10	9	8
Multilateral creditors										
Disbursements	51	50	30	10	4	2	0	0	0	0
Principal	23	18	27	24	25	25	20	19	17	13
Interest	16	16	16	15	13	12	10	9	7	6
Private creditors										
Disbursements	0	0	0	0	0	0	0	0	0	0
Principal	34	34	30	22	22	21	21	21	21	21
Interest	18	19	17	16	14	12	10	8	6	5
Commercial banks										
Disbursements	0	0	0	0	0	0	0	0	0	0
Principal	4	8	8	8	8	8	8	8	8	8
Interest	3	5	5	4	4	3	3	2	1	1
Other private										
Disbursements	0	0	0	0	0	0	0	0	0	0
Principal	30	27	23	14	14	14	14	14	14	14
Interest	15	14	12	11	10	9	8	6	5	4

MADAGASCAR

(US$ million, unless otherwise indicated)

	1970	1980	1988	1989	1990	1991	1992	1993	1994	1995
1. SUMMARY DEBT DATA										
TOTAL DEBT STOCKS (EDT)	..	**1,241**	**3,669**	**3,444**	**3,720**	**3,916**	**3,931**	**3,818**	**4,117**	**4,302**
Long-term debt (LDOD)	**485**	**911**	**3,320**	**3,156**	**3,353**	**3,535**	**3,489**	**3,343**	**3,548**	**3,691**
Public and publicly guaranteed	485	911	3,320	3,156	3,353	3,535	3,489	3,343	3,548	3,691
Private nonguaranteed	0	0	0	0	0	0	0	0	0	0
Use of IMF credit	**0**	**87**	**190**	**165**	**144**	**127**	**106**	**92**	**86**	**73**
Short-term debt	..	**244**	**159**	**123**	**223**	**254**	**337**	**384**	**483**	**538**
of which interest arrears on LDOD	..	6	144	107	124	169	262	319	435	482
Official creditors	..	2	125	92	113	157	248	303	413	461
Private creditors	..	4	19	15	11	11	14	16	22	22
Memo: principal arrears on LDOD	..	10	194	184	261	379	589	742	984	1,193
Official creditors	..	4	172	172	249	361	562	709	945	1,148
Private creditors	..	5	22	12	12	18	27	32	39	45
Memo: export credits	..	..	662	696	795	777	844	730	725	837
TOTAL DEBT FLOWS										
Disbursements	**54**	**437**	**247**	**255**	**228**	**217**	**122**	**118**	**78**	**84**
Long-term debt	54	367	237	222	210	200	122	118	78	84
IMF purchases	0	70	11	33	17	18	0	0	0	0
Principal repayments	**46**	**49**	**133**	**128**	**113**	**84**	**59**	**49**	**42**	**43**
Long-term debt	46	47	87	75	62	50	43	35	30	28
IMF repurchases	0	2	46	53	51	34	16	14	12	15
Net flows on debt	**8**	**388**	**59**	**129**	**198**	**119**	**53**	**59**	**19**	**48**
of which short-term debt	..	..	-55	1	83	-14	-10	-10	-17	7
Interest payments (INT)	..	**57**	**87**	**117**	**101**	**79**	**40**	**30**	**21**	**27**
Long-term debt	16	27	73	101	85	68	34	25	18	23
IMF charges	0	1	13	12	10	6	3	2	1	1
Short-term debt	..	29	1	4	7	5	3	3	2	3
Net transfers on debt	..	**331**	**-28**	**12**	**96**	**40**	**13**	**29**	**-3**	**21**
Total debt service paid (TDS)	..	**105**	**220**	**245**	**215**	**163**	**99**	**79**	**63**	**70**
Long-term debt	62	74	160	176	147	117	76	60	48	52
IMF repurchases and charges	0	3	59	65	61	40	19	16	13	15
Short-term debt (interest only)	..	29	1	4	7	5	3	3	2	3

	1970	1980	1988	1989	1990	1991	1992	1993	1994	1995
2. AGGREGATE NET RESOURCE FLOWS AND NET TRANSFERS (LONG-TERM)										
NET RESOURCE FLOWS	**39**	**349**	**276**	**303**	**518**	**424**	**303**	**295**	**222**	**230**
Net flow of long-term debt (ex. IMF)	8	320	150	148	148	150	79	83	48	55
Foreign direct investment (net)	10	-1	3	13	22	14	21	15	6	10
Portfolio equity flows	0	0	0	0	0	0	0	0	0	0
Grants (excluding technical coop.)	20	30	123	143	348	260	203	198	168	164
Memo: technical coop. grants	21	51	69	65	85	82	88	100	105	126
NET TRANSFERS	**17**	**321**	**202**	**201**	**432**	**355**	**268**	**269**	**201**	**204**
Interest on long-term debt	16	27	73	101	85	68	34	25	18	23
Profit remittances on FDI	5	1	1	1	1	2	1	1	2	2

	1970	1980	1988	1989	1990	1991	1992	1993	1994	1995
3. MAJOR ECONOMIC AGGREGATES										
Gross national product (GNP)	1,075	3,996	2,263	2,309	2,933	2,483	2,853	3,224	2,828	3,037
Exports of goods & services (XGS)	..	519	419	480	490	497	518	536	669	765
of which workers remittances	..	0	3	8	5	9	12	12	11	9
Imports of goods & services (MGS)	..	1,121	761	757	985	845	884	970	1,032	1,161
International reserves (RES)	37	9	224	245	92	89	..	..	72	109
Current account balance	..	-556	-150	-84	-265	-230	-198	-258	-277	-276

	1970	1980	1988	1989	1990	1991	1992	1993	1994	1995
4. DEBT INDICATORS										
EDT / XGS (%)	..	239.3	874.8	717.7	759.3	788.5	758.4	712.0	615.3	562.2
EDT / GNP (%)	..	31.1	162.1	149.1	126.8	157.7	137.8	118.4	145.6	141.7
TDS / XGS (%)	..	20.3	52.4	50.9	43.9	32.7	19.1	14.7	9.5	9.2
INT / XGS (%)	..	10.9	20.7	24.4	20.7	15.8	7.7	5.6	3.2	3.6
INT / GNP (%)	..	1.4	3.8	5.1	3.5	3.2	1.4	0.9	0.8	0.9
RES / EDT (%)	..	0.7	6.1	7.1	2.5	2.3	..	..	1.7	2.5
RES / MGS (months)	..	0.1	3.5	3.9	1.1	1.3	..	..	0.8	1.1
Short-term / EDT (%)	..	19.6	4.3	3.6	6.0	6.5	8.6	10.0	11.7	12.5
Concessional / EDT (%)	..	38.8	41.9	45.7	48.9	52.1	52.3	53.6	53.5	53.9
Multilateral / EDT (%)	..	14.7	26.4	30.3	33.2	35.5	35.7	38.5	38.7	39.2

MADAGASCAR

(US$ million, unless otherwise indicated)

	1970	1980	1988	1989	1990	1991	1992	1993	1994	1995
5. LONG-TERM DEBT										
DEBT OUTSTANDING (LDOD)	**485**	**911**	**3,320**	**3,156**	**3,353**	**3,535**	**3,489**	**3,343**	**3,548**	**3,691**
Public and publicly guaranteed	**485**	**911**	**3,320**	**3,156**	**3,353**	**3,535**	**3,489**	**3,343**	**3,548**	**3,691**
Official creditors	484	573	3,113	2,998	3,220	3,416	3,382	3,261	3,467	3,614
Multilateral	42	182	967	1,044	1,234	1,390	1,403	1,471	1,591	1,686
Concessional	12	162	885	961	1,147	1,304	1,323	1,392	1,512	1,609
Bilateral	443	390	2,146	1,953	1,986	2,026	1,979	1,789	1,876	1,928
Concessional	442	320	653	614	673	738	735	655	693	710
Private creditors	1	338	207	159	133	119	107	82	81	77
Bonds	0	0	0	0	0	0	0	0	0	0
Commercial banks	0	134	71	53	42	38	33	30	30	29
Other private	1	204	135	106	91	81	74	52	51	48
Private nonguaranteed	**0**	**0**	**0**	**0**	**0**	**0**	**0**	**0**	**0**	**0**
Bonds	0	0	0	0	0	0	0	0	0	0
Commercial banks	0	0	0	0	0	0	0	0	0	0
Memo:										
IBRD	2	30	30	27	26	23	20	17	14	12
IDA	10	122	607	670	770	881	887	932	1,021	1,110
DISBURSEMENTS	**54**	**367**	**237**	**222**	**210**	**200**	**122**	**118**	**78**	**84**
Public and publicly guaranteed	**54**	**367**	**237**	**222**	**210**	**200**	**122**	**118**	**78**	**84**
Official creditors	54	212	223	222	210	199	121	117	77	83
Multilateral	6	42	145	112	134	166	83	91	70	78
Concessional	6	40	133	103	132	160	79	84	67	78
Bilateral	48	170	78	111	76	33	39	26	7	5
Concessional	48	115	71	107	75	32	37	26	6	4
Private creditors	0	155	14	0	0	1	1	1	0	1
Bonds	0	0	0	0	0	0	0	0	0	0
Commercial banks	0	62	5	0	0	0	0	0	0	0
Other private	0	93	9	0	0	1	1	1	0	1
Private nonguaranteed	**0**	**0**	**0**	**0**	**0**	**0**	**0**	**0**	**0**	**0**
Bonds	0	0	0	0	0	0	0	0	0	0
Commercial banks	0	0	0	0	0	0	0	0	0	0
Memo:										
IBRD	1	2	0	0	0	0	0	0	0	0
IDA	5	25	81	73	64	106	37	47	60	76
PRINCIPAL REPAYMENTS	**46**	**47**	**87**	**75**	**62**	**50**	**43**	**35**	**30**	**28**
Public and publicly guaranteed	**46**	**47**	**87**	**75**	**62**	**50**	**43**	**35**	**30**	**28**
Official creditors	45	24	58	58	46	37	32	27	25	22
Multilateral	3	1	16	17	19	20	20	22	21	18
Concessional	0	1	11	11	13	14	13	14	13	13
Bilateral	42	23	42	41	27	18	13	5	4	4
Concessional	42	22	10	8	9	2	12	3	4	1
Private creditors	1	23	28	17	16	12	11	8	5	7
Bonds	0	0	0	0	0	0	0	0	0	0
Commercial banks	0	12	18	11	11	4	5	2	1	2
Other private	1	12	10	6	6	8	6	7	4	4
Private nonguaranteed	**0**	**0**	**0**	**0**	**0**	**0**	**0**	**0**	**0**	**0**
Bonds	0	0	0	0	0	0	0	0	0	0
Commercial banks	0	0	0	0	0	0	0	0	0	0
Memo:										
IBRD	0	0	2	3	3	3	3	3	3	4
IDA	0	0	2	2	3	3	4	5	6	7
NET FLOWS ON DEBT	**8**	**320**	**150**	**148**	**148**	**150**	**79**	**83**	**48**	**55**
Public and publicly guaranteed	**8**	**320**	**150**	**148**	**148**	**150**	**79**	**83**	**48**	**55**
Official creditors	9	188	164	164	164	161	89	91	52	61
Multilateral	3	41	129	95	116	146	63	69	49	60
Concessional	6	39	122	93	119	146	67	70	54	65
Bilateral	6	147	35	70	48	15	26	21	3	1
Concessional	6	93	61	99	66	30	25	23	2	4
Private creditors	-1	132	-15	-17	-16	-11	-10	-8	-4	-6
Bonds	0	0	0	0	0	0	0	0	0	0
Commercial banks	0	50	-14	-11	-10	-4	-5	-2	-1	-2
Other private	-1	82	-1	-6	-6	-7	-6	-6	-4	-4
Private nonguaranteed	**0**	**0**	**0**	**0**	**0**	**0**	**0**	**0**	**0**	**0**
Bonds	0	0	0	0	0	0	0	0	0	0
Commercial banks	0	0	0	0	0	0	0	0	0	0
Memo:										
IBRD	1	1	-2	-3	-3	-3	-3	-3	-3	-4
IDA	5	25	79	70	61	103	33	42	54	69

MADAGASCAR

(US$ million, unless otherwise indicated)

	1970	1980	1988	1989	1990	1991	1992	1993	1994	1995
INTEREST PAYMENTS (LINT)	**16**	**27**	**73**	**101**	**85**	**68**	**34**	**25**	**18**	**23**
Public and publicly guaranteed	**16**	**27**	**73**	**101**	**85**	**68**	**34**	**25**	**18**	**23**
Official creditors	16	8	55	85	71	59	30	24	18	20
Multilateral	1	4	16	17	18	18	18	21	14	11
Concessional	0	2	8	8	9	10	11	13	11	10
Bilateral	15	4	39	69	54	41	12	4	3	8
Concessional	15	4	8	7	11	10	10	3	3	2
Private creditors	0	19	18	16	13	9	3	1	1	4
Bonds	0	0	0	0	0	0	0	0	0	0
Commercial banks	0	9	13	13	10	6	2	0	0	3
Other private	0	10	5	3	3	3	2	1	1	1
Private nonguaranteed	**0**	**0**	**0**	**0**	**0**	**0**	**0**	**0**	**0**	**0**
Bonds	0	0	0	0	0	0	0	0	0	0
Commercial banks	0	0	0	0	0	0	0	0	0	0
Memo:										
IBRD	0	2	2	2	2	2	2	1	1	1
IDA	0	1	5	5	5	6	7	7	7	8
NET TRANSFERS ON DEBT	**-8**	**293**	**77**	**46**	**63**	**83**	**45**	**58**	**29**	**32**
Public and publicly guaranteed	**-8**	**293**	**77**	**46**	**63**	**83**	**45**	**58**	**29**	**32**
Official creditors	-7	180	109	79	93	102	59	66	34	41
Multilateral	2	37	113	78	98	128	45	49	35	49
Concessional	6	37	113	85	110	137	56	57	43	55
Bilateral	-9	143	-4	1	-5	-26	14	18	0	-7
Concessional	-9	89	53	92	55	20	15	20	-1	1
Private creditors	-1	113	-33	-33	-29	-20	-13	-9	-5	-9
Bonds	0	0	0	0	0	0	0	0	0	0
Commercial banks	0	42	-27	-25	-21	-10	-6	-2	-1	-5
Other private	-1	72	-6	-8	-9	-10	-7	-7	-4	-4
Private nonguaranteed	**0**	**0**	**0**	**0**	**0**	**0**	**0**	**0**	**0**	**0**
Bonds	0	0	0	0	0	0	0	0	0	0
Commercial banks	0	0	0	0	0	0	0	0	0	0
Memo:										
IBRD	1	-1	-4	-5	-5	-5	-4	-4	-5	-5
IDA	5	24	74	66	56	97	26	35	46	62
DEBT SERVICE (LTDS)	**62**	**74**	**160**	**176**	**147**	**117**	**76**	**60**	**48**	**52**
Public and publicly guaranteed	**62**	**74**	**160**	**176**	**147**	**117**	**76**	**60**	**48**	**52**
Official creditors	61	32	114	143	118	96	63	51	43	42
Multilateral	4	4	32	34	37	38	38	42	36	29
Concessional	0	3	19	19	21	23	23	27	24	22
Bilateral	57	27	81	109	81	58	25	9	7	12
Concessional	57	26	18	15	20	12	22	6	7	3
Private creditors	1	42	46	33	29	21	14	9	5	10
Bonds	0	0	0	0	0	0	0	0	0	0
Commercial banks	0	20	31	25	21	10	6	2	1	5
Other private	1	22	15	8	9	11	8	7	4	5
Private nonguaranteed	**0**	**0**	**0**	**0**	**0**	**0**	**0**	**0**	**0**	**0**
Bonds	0	0	0	0	0	0	0	0	0	0
Commercial banks	0	0	0	0	0	0	0	0	0	0
Memo:										
IBRD	0	3	4	5	5	5	4	4	5	5
IDA	0	1	7	7	8	9	10	12	13	15
UNDISBURSED DEBT	**186**	**713**	**886**	**834**	**910**	**788**	**708**	**642**	**638**	**638**
Official creditors	177	491	885	833	910	786	707	640	636	637
Private creditors	10	222	1	0	0	2	1	2	2	2
Memorandum items										
Concessional LDOD	453	482	1,538	1,575	1,820	2,041	2,058	2,048	2,205	2,320
Variable rate LDOD	0	74	300	319	348	344	322	267	281	294
Public sector LDOD	483	897	3,259	3,117	3,279	3,445	3,380	3,236	3,433	3,569
Private sector LDOD	2	14	61	40	74	91	109	107	115	122

6. CURRENCY COMPOSITION OF LONG-TERM DEBT (PERCENT)

	1970	1980	1988	1989	1990	1991	1992	1993	1994	1995
Deutsche mark	2.3	5.1	5.1	3.0	3.2	3.1	3.0	3.0	3.1	3.2
French franc	88.3	12.8	21.8	18.0	15.5	15.3	15.0	11.2	11.7	12.3
Japanese yen	0.0	7.4	7.3	7.3	7.3	7.3	7.3	8.3	8.7	8.0
Pound sterling	0.0	0.1	0.1	0.1	0.1	0.1	0.1	0.1	0.1	0.1
Swiss franc	0.0	0.3	1.2	1.1	1.3	1.1	1.0	1.0	1.0	1.1
U.S.dollars	9.1	53.6	39.4	41.9	42.0	42.8	43.2	44.5	44.3	44.8
Multiple currency	0.3	4.0	6.6	7.5	8.6	8.7	9.2	10.4	10.4	10.1
Special drawing rights	0.0	0.0	2.8	2.9	3.1	3.0	3.0	3.1	3.1	3.0
All other currencies	0.0	16.8	15.7	18.0	19.0	18.7	18.2	18.4	17.6	17.3

MADAGASCAR

(US$ million, unless otherwise indicated)

	1970	1980	1988	1989	1990	1991	1992	1993	1994	1995
7. DEBT RESTRUCTURINGS										
Total amount rescheduled	0	0	147	177	88	81	0	0	0	0
Debt stock rescheduled	0	0	0	0	0	0	0	0	0	0
Principal rescheduled	0	0	69	99	65	54	0	0	0	0
Official	0	0	41	76	52	50	0	0	0	0
Private	0	0	29	22	13	4	0	0	0	0
Interest rescheduled	0	0	16	43	16	16	0	0	0	0
Official	0	0	11	39	15	16	0	0	0	0
Private	0	0	5	4	1	0	0	0	0	0
Debt forgiven	..	..	19	349	185	3	9	210	0	0
Memo: interest forgiven	..	..	1	3	0	0	0	18	0	0
Debt stock reduction	0	0	7	0	0	0	0	0	0	0
of which debt buyback	0	0	0	0	0	0	0	0	0	0
8. DEBT STOCK-FLOW RECONCILIATION										
Total change in debt stocks	..	..	..	-225	275	196	16	-113	298	185
Net flows on debt	..	..	..	129	198	119	53	59	19	48
Net change in interest arrears	..	..	..	-37	17	45	93	57	117	47
Interest capitalized	..	..	..	43	16	16	0	0	0	0
Debt forgiveness or reduction	..	..	..	-349	-185	-3	-9	-210	0	0
Cross-currency valuation	..	..	..	-8	173	6	-73	-16	123	68
Residual	..	..	..	-2	58	13	-48	-4	41	22
9. AVERAGE TERMS OF NEW COMMITMENTS										
ALL CREDITORS										
Interest (%)	2.3	5.8	2.4	1.8	1.4	1.5	1.4	0.9	0.9	1.0
Maturity (years)	39.0	18.6	31.8	33.8	36.2	34.8	36.7	39.9	37.8	36.9
Grace period (years)	9.2	4.6	8.8	10.8	9.7	9.1	9.0	9.4	9.7	9.6
Grant element (%)	65.4	27.6	62.0	69.3	73.1	70.6	70.9	78.5	76.9	75.7
Official creditors										
Interest (%)	1.4	4.1	2.1	1.8	1.4	1.3	1.4	0.8	0.9	1.0
Maturity (years)	44.6	26.8	32.6	33.8	36.2	35.6	36.7	40.1	37.8	36.9
Grace period (years)	10.4	6.0	9.0	10.8	9.7	9.3	9.0	9.5	9.7	9.6
Grant element (%)	75.3	43.3	64.1	69.3	73.1	72.5	70.9	78.9	76.9	75.7
Private creditors										
Interest (%)	6.5	7.5	8.5	0.0	0.0	7.8	0.0	2.8	0.0	0.0
Maturity (years)	10.5	10.1	10.6	0.0	0.0	8.4	0.0	25.4	0.0	0.0
Grace period (years)	2.8	3.2	2.6	0.0	0.0	2.9	0.0	5.9	0.0	0.0
Grant element (%)	14.8	11.3	4.3	0.0	0.0	8.3	0.0	53.1	0.0	0.0
Memorandum items										
Commitments	22	460	378	210	211	82	90	121	78	80
Official creditors	19	235	365	210	211	80	90	119	78	80
Private creditors	4	225	14	0	0	3	0	2	0	0

10. CONTRACTUAL OBLIGATIONS ON OUTSTANDING LONG-TERM DEBT

	1996	1997	1998	1999	2000	2001	2002	2003	2004	2005
TOTAL										
Disbursements	199	180	125	74	33	14	9	3	1	0
Principal	168	129	116	127	130	129	120	106	90	74
Interest	60	53	50	46	42	37	33	28	26	24
Official creditors										
Disbursements	198	180	125	74	33	14	9	3	1	0
Principal	161	123	111	123	126	126	118	105	89	74
Interest	58	52	49	45	41	37	33	28	25	24
Bilateral creditors										
Disbursements	26	21	12	7	4	2	1	1	1	0
Principal	119	76	64	72	74	72	65	52	39	25
Interest	38	32	29	26	23	19	17	13	11	10
Multilateral creditors										
Disbursements	172	159	113	67	29	11	8	2	1	0
Principal	42	47	47	51	52	54	54	53	51	48
Interest	20	20	20	19	18	17	16	15	14	14
Private creditors										
Disbursements	1	1	0	0	0	0	0	0	0	0
Principal	8	6	4	4	4	4	2	1	1	1
Interest	2	2	1	1	1	0	0	0	0	0
Commercial banks										
Disbursements	0	0	0	0	0	0	0	0	0	0
Principal	3	3	3	3	3	3	1	0	0	0
Interest	1	1	1	1	1	0	0	0	0	0
Other private										
Disbursements	1	1	0	0	0	0	0	0	0	0
Principal	4	3	1	1	1	1	1	1	1	1
Interest	1	0	0	0	0	0	0	0	0	0

MALAWI

(US$ million, unless otherwise indicated)

1. SUMMARY DEBT DATA

	1970	*1980*	*1988*	*1989*	*1990*	*1991*	*1992*	*1993*	*1994*	*1995*
TOTAL DEBT STOCKS (EDT)	**..**	**821**	**1,361**	**1,419**	**1,579**	**1,670**	**1,697**	**1,812**	**2,009**	**2,140**
Long-term debt (LDOD)	**122**	**625**	**1,205**	**1,270**	**1,402**	**1,524**	**1,555**	**1,714**	**1,883**	**1,978**
Public and publicly guaranteed	122	625	1,202	1,266	1,399	1,522	1,555	1,714	1,883	1,978
Private nonguaranteed	0	0	3	4	3	3	0	0	0	0
Use of IMF credit	**0**	**80**	**106**	**101**	**115**	**115**	**92**	**86**	**112**	**116**
Short-term debt	**..**	**116**	**50**	**49**	**62**	**31**	**50**	**12**	**14**	**47**
of which interest arrears on LDOD	..	3	6	10	10	3	3	3	4	4
Official creditors	..	2	5	7	7	2	2	2	2	2
Private creditors	..	1	2	2	3	1	1	2	2	3
Memo: principal arrears on LDOD	..	1	13	19	22	4	4	6	12	11
Official creditors	..	1	10	15	15	4	3	4	9	7
Private creditors	..	0	3	5	7	1	1	2	3	4
Memo: export credits	..	..	94	95	94	87	97	88	98	103
TOTAL DEBT FLOWS										
Disbursements	**41**	**190**	**142**	**146**	**158**	**190**	**141**	**189**	**138**	**129**
Long-term debt	40	153	117	122	132	170	141	189	112	118
IMF purchases	1	37	25	24	25	20	0	0	26	12
Principal repayments	**3**	**35**	**65**	**56**	**65**	**82**	**69**	**47**	**46**	**68**
Long-term debt	3	33	35	30	45	61	50	41	40	59
IMF repurchases	0	1	30	27	19	21	19	6	6	10
Net flows on debt	**38**	**156**	**32**	**85**	**106**	**84**	**90**	**104**	**93**	**93**
of which short-term debt	..	..	-45	-5	13	-24	19	-38	1	32
Interest payments (INT)	**..**	**53**	**41**	**40**	**43**	**49**	**36**	**28**	**25**	**40**
Long-term debt	4	35	29	29	33	41	30	26	24	36
IMF charges	0	2	8	7	6	5	2	1	1	1
Short-term debt	..	16	5	5	4	4	4	1	1	3
Net transfers on debt	**..**	**103**	**-9**	**45**	**63**	**35**	**54**	**76**	**68**	**53**
Total debt service paid (TDS)	**..**	**87**	**106**	**96**	**108**	**131**	**105**	**75**	**71**	**108**
Long-term debt	6	68	63	58	78	102	80	68	64	94
IMF repurchases and charges	0	3	38	33	25	25	21	7	6	11
Short-term debt (interest only)	..	16	5	5	4	4	4	1	1	3

2. AGGREGATE NET RESOURCE FLOWS AND NET TRANSFERS (LONG-TERM)

	1970	*1980*	*1988*	*1989*	*1990*	*1991*	*1992*	*1993*	*1994*	*1995*
NET RESOURCE FLOWS	**52**	**178**	**253**	**283**	**314**	**351**	**426**	**350**	**303**	**319**
Net flow of long-term debt (ex. IMF)	37	120	82	93	87	109	90	148	72	59
Foreign direct investment (net)	9	10	0	0	0	0	0	0	1	1
Portfolio equity flows	0	0	0	0	0	0	0	0	0	0
Grants (excluding technical coop.)	7	49	171	191	227	242	335	203	231	259
Memo: technical coop. grants	9	36	101	116	113	145	103	110	67	89
NET TRANSFERS	**41**	**135**	**215**	**255**	**281**	**311**	**395**	**324**	**279**	**284**
Interest on long-term debt	4	35	29	29	33	41	30	26	24	36
Profit remittances on FDI	8	9	9	0	0	0	0	0	0	0

3. MAJOR ECONOMIC AGGREGATES

	1970	*1980*	*1988*	*1989*	*1990*	*1991*	*1992*	*1993*	*1994*	*1995*
Gross national product (GNP)	283	1,138	1,281	1,472	1,815	2,131	1,819	1,962	1,244	1,284
Exports of goods & services (XGS)	..	315	342	310	452	521	435	350	387	428
of which workers remittances	..	0	0	0	0	0	0	0	0	0
Imports of goods & services (MGS)	..	638	544	522	627	847	820	608	960	929
International reserves (RES)	29	76	151	106	142	158	44	62	48	115
Current account balance	..	-260	-72	-38	-76	-209	-268	-102	-274	-232

4. DEBT INDICATORS

	1970	*1980*	*1988*	*1989*	*1990*	*1991*	*1992*	*1993*	*1994*	*1995*
EDT / XGS (%)	..	260.8	398.4	457.9	348.9	320.3	390.3	518.4	519.7	499.6
EDT / GNP (%)	..	72.1	106.3	96.4	87.0	78.3	93.3	92.4	161.5	166.8
TDS / XGS (%)	..	27.7	30.9	31.0	23.9	25.2	24.2	21.4	18.3	25.3
INT / XGS (%)	..	16.7	11.9	12.9	9.6	9.4	8.2	8.0	6.5	9.3
INT / GNP (%)	..	4.6	3.2	2.7	2.4	2.3	2.0	1.4	2.0	3.1
RES / EDT (%)	..	9.3	11.1	7.4	9.0	9.4	2.6	3.4	2.4	5.4
RES / MGS (months)	..	1.4	3.3	2.4	2.7	2.2	0.6	1.2	0.6	1.5
Short-term / EDT (%)	..	14.1	3.7	3.4	3.9	1.8	2.9	0.7	0.7	2.2
Concessional / EDT (%)	..	33.8	66.7	69.1	70.8	76.7	80.1	85.1	85.5	86.4
Multilateral / EDT (%)	..	26.7	62.3	64.4	68.2	71.8	74.7	79.1	78.9	78.8

MALAWI

(US$ million, unless otherwise indicated)

	1970	*1980*	*1988*	*1989*	*1990*	*1991*	*1992*	*1993*	*1994*	*1995*
5. LONG-TERM DEBT										
DEBT OUTSTANDING (LDOD)	**122**	**625**	**1,205**	**1,270**	**1,402**	**1,524**	**1,555**	**1,714**	**1,883**	**1,978**
Public and publicly guaranteed	**122**	**625**	**1,202**	**1,266**	**1,399**	**1,522**	**1,555**	**1,714**	**1,883**	**1,978**
Official creditors	103	433	1,149	1,206	1,338	1,471	1,515	1,683	1,855	1,964
Multilateral	17	219	847	914	1,076	1,199	1,267	1,433	1,584	1,686
Concessional	17	176	705	784	947	1,078	1,161	1,337	1,491	1,606
Bilateral	86	214	302	291	261	272	248	251	271	277
Concessional	49	102	203	197	171	204	198	206	226	243
Private creditors	20	192	53	60	62	51	40	31	28	14
Bonds	16	2	0	0	0	0	0	0	0	0
Commercial banks	1	153	39	39	38	38	29	20	12	1
Other private	3	38	13	22	24	13	11	10	16	13
Private nonguaranteed	**0**	**0**	**3**	**4**	**3**	**3**	**0**	**0**	**0**	**0**
Bonds	0	0	0	0	0	0	0	0	0	0
Commercial banks	0	0	3	4	3	3	0	0	0	0
Memo:										
IBRD	0	26	99	91	91	85	74	67	65	55
IDA	17	131	555	625	764	866	919	1,062	1,160	1,251
DISBURSEMENTS	**40**	**153**	**117**	**122**	**132**	**170**	**141**	**189**	**112**	**118**
Public and publicly guaranteed	**40**	**153**	**108**	**121**	**132**	**170**	**141**	**189**	**112**	**118**
Official creditors	37	105	104	111	131	170	138	187	105	118
Multilateral	10	49	89	94	115	132	134	187	104	93
Concessional	10	39	79	91	110	128	131	185	100	93
Bilateral	27	56	15	17	16	38	4	0	1	25
Concessional	7	18	14	8	16	38	4	0	1	25
Private creditors	3	48	4	10	2	0	2	1	7	0
Bonds	0	0	0	0	0	0	0	0	0	0
Commercial banks	0	39	4	0	0	0	0	0	0	0
Other private	3	9	0	10	2	0	2	1	7	0
Private nonguaranteed	**0**	**0**	**9**	**1**	**0**	**0**	**0**	**0**	**0**	**0**
Bonds	0	0	0	0	0	0	0	0	0	0
Commercial banks	0	0	9	1	0	0	0	0	0	0
Memo:										
IBRD	0	8	8	2	2	1	0	0	0	0
IDA	10	15	65	79	99	98	86	146	59	73
PRINCIPAL REPAYMENTS	**3**	**33**	**35**	**30**	**45**	**61**	**50**	**41**	**40**	**59**
Public and publicly guaranteed	**3**	**33**	**29**	**29**	**44**	**61**	**48**	**41**	**40**	**59**
Official creditors	2	6	26	27	41	52	36	31	29	44
Multilateral	0	2	15	16	19	19	21	21	22	28
Concessional	0	1	4	4	5	6	6	8	10	12
Bilateral	2	4	11	11	22	33	16	10	7	16
Concessional	1	1	0	2	5	13	7	5	3	6
Private creditors	1	28	4	2	3	10	11	10	11	15
Bonds	1	1	0	0	0	0	0	0	0	0
Commercial banks	0	21	0	1	1	0	9	9	8	11
Other private	0	6	3	2	3	10	3	1	2	4
Private nonguaranteed	**0**	**0**	**6**	**1**	**1**	**0**	**3**	**0**	**0**	**0**
Bonds	0	0	0	0	0	0	0	0	0	0
Commercial banks	0	0	6	1	1	0	3	0	0	0
Memo:										
IBRD	0	0	6	7	8	8	9	9	7	12
IDA	0	1	2	2	3	3	4	4	6	7
NET FLOWS ON DEBT	**37**	**120**	**82**	**93**	**87**	**109**	**90**	**148**	**72**	**59**
Public and publicly guaranteed	**37**	**120**	**79**	**92**	**88**	**109**	**93**	**148**	**72**	**59**
Official creditors	35	100	78	85	90	118	102	156	76	74
Multilateral	10	48	74	79	96	113	114	167	81	65
Concessional	10	38	75	87	106	122	125	178	90	81
Bilateral	25	52	4	6	-6	6	-12	-10	-6	9
Concessional	6	17	14	6	11	26	-2	-5	-2	18
Private creditors	2	20	1	7	-2	-10	-9	-9	-4	-15
Bonds	-1	-1	0	0	0	0	0	0	0	0
Commercial banks	0	18	4	-1	-1	0	-9	-9	-8	-11
Other private	3	4	-3	8	-1	-10	0	0	5	-4
Private nonguaranteed	**0**	**0**	**3**	**1**	**-1**	**0**	**-3**	**0**	**0**	**0**
Bonds	0	0	0	0	0	0	0	0	0	0
Commercial banks	0	0	3	1	-1	0	-3	0	0	0
Memo:										
IBRD	0	8	2	-5	-6	-7	-9	-9	-7	-12
IDA	10	14	63	77	96	95	82	142	53	66

MALAWI

(US$ million, unless otherwise indicated)

	1970	1980	1988	1989	1990	1991	1992	1993	1994	1995
INTEREST PAYMENTS (LINT)	**4**	**35**	**29**	**29**	**33**	**41**	**30**	**26**	**24**	**36**
Public and publicly guaranteed	**4**	**35**	**28**	**28**	**33**	**41**	**30**	**26**	**24**	**36**
Official creditors	2	9	25	24	28	34	27	25	23	34
Multilateral	0	3	18	18	18	19	19	18	18	24
Concessional	0	2	6	6	7	9	9	10	11	14
Bilateral	2	6	6	6	10	15	8	7	5	10
Concessional	1	2	1	2	3	7	4	4	3	6
Private creditors	1	25	4	5	5	6	3	1	1	2
Bonds	1	0	0	0	0	0	0	0	0	0
Commercial banks	0	22	3	4	4	3	2	1	1	1
Other private	0	2	1	0	1	3	1	1	0	1
Private nonguaranteed	**0**	**0**	**0**	**0**	**0**	**0**	**0**	**0**	**0**	**0**
Bonds	0	0	0	0	0	0	0	0	0	0
Commercial banks	0	0	0	0	0	0	0	0	0	0
Memo:										
IBRD	0	1	9	8	8	8	7	6	4	7
IDA	0	1	4	4	5	6	6	8	8	9
NET TRANSFERS ON DEBT	**33**	**86**	**54**	**64**	**54**	**68**	**60**	**121**	**48**	**23**
Public and publicly guaranteed	**33**	**86**	**51**	**64**	**56**	**68**	**63**	**121**	**48**	**23**
Official creditors	33	90	54	61	62	84	75	131	52	40
Multilateral	10	45	56	61	78	94	95	148	63	41
Concessional	10	37	69	81	99	114	116	168	79	68
Bilateral	23	46	-2	1	-16	-10	-20	-17	-11	-1
Concessional	6	14	13	4	8	19	-6	-9	-5	12
Private creditors	0	-5	-3	3	-7	-16	-12	-10	-5	-17
Bonds	-2	-1	0	0	0	0	0	0	0	0
Commercial banks	0	-5	1	-5	-4	-3	-11	-10	-9	-12
Other private	2	1	-4	8	-3	-13	-1	-1	5	-5
Private nonguaranteed	**0**	**0**	**3**	**0**	**-2**	**0**	**-3**	**0**	**0**	**0**
Bonds	0	0	0	0	0	0	0	0	0	0
Commercial banks	0	0	3	0	-2	0	-3	0	0	0
Memo:										
IBRD	0	6	-7	-13	-13	-14	-16	-15	-11	-19
IDA	10	13	59	73	91	90	76	134	45	57
DEBT SERVICE (LTDS)	**6**	**68**	**63**	**58**	**78**	**102**	**80**	**68**	**64**	**94**
Public and publicly guaranteed	**6**	**68**	**57**	**57**	**77**	**102**	**78**	**68**	**64**	**94**
Official creditors	4	15	50	50	69	86	64	56	53	78
Multilateral	0	5	33	34	37	38	39	39	40	52
Concessional	0	3	10	10	11	14	15	18	21	25
Bilateral	4	10	17	16	32	48	24	17	12	26
Concessional	1	4	2	5	8	19	11	9	6	13
Private creditors	3	53	7	7	8	16	14	11	11	17
Bonds	2	1	0	0	0	0	0	0	0	0
Commercial banks	0	44	3	5	4	3	11	10	9	12
Other private	1	8	4	2	4	13	3	2	2	5
Private nonguaranteed	**0**	**0**	**6**	**1**	**2**	**0**	**3**	**0**	**0**	**0**
Bonds	0	0	0	0	0	0	0	0	0	0
Commercial banks	0	0	6	1	2	0	3	0	0	0
Memo:										
IBRD	0	1	16	15	16	16	16	15	11	19
IDA	0	2	6	6	8	9	10	12	14	16
UNDISBURSED DEBT	**38**	**162**	**429**	**404**	**550**	**582**	**635**	**565**	**550**	**529**
Official creditors	38	152	417	402	543	574	630	558	550	529
Private creditors	0	10	13	2	7	8	6	7	0	0
Memorandum items										
Concessional LDOD	66	278	908	981	1,118	1,282	1,358	1,543	1,717	1,849
Variable rate LDOD	0	145	49	51	51	52	39	30	21	10
Public sector LDOD	122	576	1,198	1,262	1,397	1,520	1,553	1,713	1,882	1,976
Private sector LDOD	0	49	7	7	5	5	2	1	1	1

6. CURRENCY COMPOSITION OF LONG-TERM DEBT (PERCENT)

	1970	1980	1988	1989	1990	1991	1992	1993	1994	1995
Deutsche mark	4.6	2.5	0.7	0.6	0.7	0.3	0.2	0.2	0.1	0.1
French franc	0.0	1.2	2.7	2.7	1.8	1.6	1.6	1.3	1.3	1.3
Japanese yen	0.0	4.1	10.0	8.8	9.0	10.1	9.7	9.7	9.8	8.9
Pound sterling	61.7	17.7	20.0	19.2	18.0	15.1	13.3	11.7	10.8	10.0
Swiss franc	0.0	0.0	0.0	0.0	0.0	0.0	0.0	0.0	0.0	0.0
U.S.dollars	14.3	47.2	38.8	42.3	46.2	49.1	49.3	47.7	47.5	48.6
Multiple currency	0.0	12.6	23.8	22.1	21.6	21.1	21.5	20.8	21.7	21.2
Special drawing rights	0.0	0.0	0.0	0.0	0.0	0.0	2.0	6.8	6.8	6.9
All other currencies	19.4	14.7	4.1	4.2	2.6	2.5	2.3	1.9	2.0	3.1

MALAWI

(US$ million, unless otherwise indicated)

	1970	1980	1988	1989	1990	1991	1992	1993	1994	1995
7. DEBT RESTRUCTURINGS										
Total amount rescheduled	0	0	69	10	0	0	0	0	0	0
Debt stock rescheduled	0	0	36	0	0	0	0	0	0	0
Principal rescheduled	0	0	16	4	0	0	0	0	0	0
Official	0	0	14	4	0	0	0	0	0	0
Private	0	0	2	0	0	0	0	0	0	0
Interest rescheduled	0	0	5	1	0	0	0	0	0	0
Official	0	0	4	1	0	0	0	0	0	0
Private	0	0	0	0	0	0	0	0	0	0
Debt forgiven	..	..	0	0	51	2	0	0	0	0
Memo: interest forgiven	..	..	0	0	0	0	0	0	0	0
Debt stock reduction	0	0	0	0	0	0	0	0	0	0
of which debt buyback	0	0	0	0	0	0	0	0	0	0
8. DEBT STOCK-FLOW RECONCILIATION										
Total change in debt stocks	..	..	..	58	160	91	27	116	197	131
Net flows on debt	..	..	..	85	106	84	90	104	93	93
Net change in interest arrears	..	..	..	3	1	-7	0	0	1	1
Interest capitalized	..	..	..	1	0	0	0	0	0	0
Debt forgiveness or reduction	..	..	..	0	-51	-2	0	0	0	0
Cross-currency valuation	..	..	..	-43	70	3	-49	10	50	1
Residual	..	..	..	12	35	14	-15	2	53	37
9. AVERAGE TERMS OF NEW COMMITMENTS										
ALL CREDITORS										
Interest (%)	3.8	6.0	1.2	1.2	1.2	2.1	0.8	1.5	0.8	0.7
Maturity (years)	29.4	23.5	38.5	36.8	35.6	39.2	39.6	36.5	38.3	39.3
Grace period (years)	6.0	5.9	9.3	9.1	9.7	9.8	10.1	9.0	8.8	9.8
Grant element (%)	47.1	32.4	72.5	74.4	74.9	69.2	80.5	72.5	78.7	80.0
Official creditors										
Interest (%)	3.1	4.0	0.9	1.2	1.0	2.1	0.8	1.3	0.8	0.7
Maturity (years)	35.3	28.5	39.6	36.8	36.2	39.5	39.6	37.6	38.3	39.3
Grace period (years)	7.6	6.9	9.6	9.1	9.9	9.8	10.1	9.3	8.8	9.8
Grant element (%)	56.9	44.9	74.8	74.4	76.7	69.6	80.5	74.9	78.7	80.0
Private creditors										
Interest (%)	6.5	13.2	8.0	0.0	8.6	8.3	0.0	9.0	0.0	0.0
Maturity (years)	8.4	5.7	6.9	0.0	9.6	5.0	0.0	4.4	0.0	0.0
Grace period (years)	0.3	2.6	-0.1	0.0	0.9	0.5	0.0	0.9	0.0	0.0
Grant element (%)	12.0	-12.3	5.1	0.0	4.4	3.3	0.0	1.7	0.0	0.0
Memorandum items										
Commitments	14	130	137	124	241	200	220	151	67	100
Official creditors	11	102	132	124	235	198	220	146	67	100
Private creditors	3	28	4	0	6	1	0	5	0	0

10. CONTRACTUAL OBLIGATIONS ON OUTSTANDING LONG-TERM DEBT

	1996	1997	1998	1999	2000	2001	2002	2003	2004	2005
TOTAL										
Disbursements	172	136	102	69	38	6	3	0	0	0
Principal	46	48	48	52	59	61	61	65	66	67
Interest	28	27	26	25	24	22	20	19	18	17
Official creditors										
Disbursements	172	136	102	69	38	6	3	0	0	0
Principal	43	45	46	50	59	61	61	65	66	66
Interest	27	26	25	24	24	22	20	19	18	17
Bilateral creditors										
Disbursements	0	1	2	2	2	1	1	0	0	0
Principal	13	14	13	15	19	19	19	17	18	16
Interest	6	5	5	5	5	4	4	3	3	2
Multilateral creditors										
Disbursements	171	135	101	67	36	5	2	0	0	0
Principal	30	32	33	35	40	41	42	48	49	51
Interest	21	21	20	20	19	18	17	16	15	15
Private creditors										
Disbursements	0	0	0	0	0	0	0	0	0	0
Principal	3	3	2	1	1	0	0	0	0	0
Interest	1	1	0	0	0	0	0	0	0	0
Commercial banks										
Disbursements	0	0	0	0	0	0	0	0	0	0
Principal	0	0	0	0	0	0	0	0	0	0
Interest	0	0	0	0	0	0	0	0	0	0
Other private										
Disbursements	0	0	0	0	0	0	0	0	0	0
Principal	3	3	2	1	1	0	0	0	0	0
Interest	1	1	0	0	0	0	0	0	0	0

MALAYSIA

(US$ million, unless otherwise indicated)

	1970	1980	1988	1989	1990	1991	1992	1993	1994	1995
1. SUMMARY DEBT DATA										
TOTAL DEBT STOCKS (EDT)	..	**6,611**	**18,567**	**16,278**	**16,421**	**18,155**	**20,024**	**26,148**	**29,537**	**34,352**
Long-term debt (LDOD)	**440**	**5,256**	**16,972**	**14,005**	**14,514**	**16,081**	**16,385**	**19,197**	**23,348**	**27,078**
Public and publicly guaranteed	390	4,008	14,632	12,628	12,684	13,614	12,377	13,460	13,650	15,857
Private nonguaranteed	50	1,248	2,340	1,377	1,830	2,467	4,008	5,737	9,698	11,220
Use of IMF credit	**0**	**0**	**0**	**0**	**0**	**0**	**0**	**0**	**0**	**0**
Short-term debt	..	**1,355**	**1,595**	**2,273**	**1,906**	**2,074**	**3,639**	**6,951**	**6,189**	**7,274**
of which interest arrears on LDOD	..	0	0	0	0	0	0	0	0	0
Official creditors	..	0	0	0	0	0	0	0	0	0
Private creditors	..	0	0	0	0	0	0	0	0	0
Memo: principal arrears on LDOD	..	0	0	0	0	0	0	0	15	0
Official creditors	..	0	0	0	0	0	0	0	3	0
Private creditors	..	0	0	0	0	0	0	0	12	0
Memo: export credits	..	..	1,402	1,204	1,395	1,638	2,541	2,316	3,445	4,032
TOTAL DEBT FLOWS										
Disbursements	**58**	**1,456**	**1,506**	**1,713**	**1,884**	**2,209**	**3,563**	**5,582**	**8,063**	**8,688**
Long-term debt	58	1,456	1,506	1,713	1,884	2,209	3,563	5,582	8,063	8,688
IMF purchases	0	0	0	0	0	0	0	0	0	0
Principal repayments	**57**	**345**	**4,422**	**3,016**	**2,342**	**1,841**	**3,154**	**3,420**	**4,700**	**4,942**
Long-term debt	57	345	4,422	3,016	2,342	1,841	3,154	3,420	4,700	4,942
IMF repurchases	0	0	0	0	0	0	0	0	0	0
Net flows on debt	**1**	**1,111**	**-3,666**	**-625**	**-824**	**537**	**1,975**	**5,473**	**2,600**	**4,831**
of which short-term debt	..	..	-750	678	-367	168	1,565	3,312	-762	1,085
Interest payments (INT)	..	**589**	**1,635**	**1,322**	**1,166**	**1,159**	**1,107**	**1,173**	**1,427**	**1,591**
Long-term debt	25	338	1,461	1,123	997	971	932	889	1,033	1,187
IMF charges	0	0	0	0	0	0	0	0	0	0
Short-term debt	..	251	174	199	169	188	176	284	394	404
Net transfers on debt	..	**522**	**-5,301**	**-1,947**	**-1,990**	**-622**	**867**	**4,300**	**1,173**	**3,240**
Total debt service paid (TDS)	..	**934**	**6,057**	**4,338**	**3,508**	**3,000**	**4,261**	**4,594**	**6,127**	**6,532**
Long-term debt	82	683	5,883	4,139	3,339	2,811	4,086	4,310	5,733	6,129
IMF repurchases and charges	0	0	0	0	0	0	0	0	0	0
Short-term debt (interest only)	..	251	174	199	169	188	176	284	394	404
2. AGGREGATE NET RESOURCE FLOWS AND NET TRANSFERS (LONG-TERM)										
NET RESOURCE FLOWS	**99**	**2,052**	**-2,177**	**583**	**2,210**	**4,412**	**6,026**	**10,927**	**9,066**	**11,856**
Net flow of long-term debt (ex. IMF)	1	1,111	-2,916	-1,303	-457	369	409	2,162	3,362	3,746
Foreign direct investment (net)	94	934	719	1,668	2,333	3,998	5,183	5,006	4,348	5,800
Portfolio equity flows	0	0	0	195	293	0	385	3,700	1,320	2,299
Grants (excluding technical coop.)	4	6	19	23	42	46	49	59	36	11
Memo: technical coop. grants	13	54	123	110	125	128	122	124	116	127
NET TRANSFERS	**-93**	**524**	**-4,967**	**-2,170**	**-713**	**1,167**	**2,382**	**7,052**	**4,784**	**6,669**
Interest on long-term debt	25	338	1,461	1,123	997	971	932	889	1,033	1,187
Profit remittances on FDI	166	1,190	1,329	1,630	1,926	2,275	2,713	2,985	3,250	4,000
3. MAJOR ECONOMIC AGGREGATES										
Gross national product (GNP)	4,089	23,607	32,754	35,693	40,902	44,573	54,460	59,641	67,204	80,585
Exports of goods & services (XGS)	..	14,837	24,449	28,818	34,514	39,512	46,421	53,451	65,795	84,212
of which workers remittances	..	0	0	0	0	0	0	0	0	0
Imports of goods & services (MGS)	..	15,101	22,790	28,641	35,486	43,783	48,760	56,469	70,106	92,440
International reserves (RES)	668	5,755	7,491	8,733	10,659	11,717	18,024	28,183	26,339	24,699
Current account balance	..	-266	1,867	315	-870	-4,183	-2,167	-2,809	-4,148	-1,644
4. DEBT INDICATORS										
EDT / XGS (%)	..	44.6	75.9	56.5	47.6	45.9	43.1	48.9	44.9	40.8
EDT / GNP (%)	..	28.0	56.7	45.6	40.1	40.7	36.8	43.8	44.0	42.6
TDS / XGS (%)	..	6.3	24.8	15.1	10.2	7.6	9.2	8.6	9.3	7.8
INT / XGS (%)	..	4.0	6.7	4.6	3.4	2.9	2.4	2.2	2.2	1.9
INT / GNP (%)	..	2.5	5.0	3.7	2.9	2.6	2.0	2.0	2.1	2.0
RES / EDT (%)	..	87.1	40.3	53.7	64.9	64.5	90.0	107.8	89.2	71.9
RES / MGS (months)	..	4.6	3.9	3.7	3.6	3.2	4.4	6.0	4.5	3.2
Short-term / EDT (%)	..	20.5	8.6	14.0	11.6	11.4	18.2	26.6	21.0	21.2
Concessional / EDT (%)	..	10.1	10.5	10.9	13.7	14.0	13.0	10.7	11.0	9.1
Multilateral / EDT (%)	..	11.3	7.9	9.0	11.0	10.7	9.3	6.2	5.8	4.8

MALAYSIA

(US$ million, unless otherwise indicated)

	1970	1980	1988	1989	1990	1991	1992	1993	1994	1995
5. LONG-TERM DEBT										
DEBT OUTSTANDING (LDOD)	**440**	**5,256**	**16,972**	**14,005**	**14,514**	**16,081**	**16,385**	**19,197**	**23,348**	**27,078**
Public and publicly guaranteed	**390**	**4,008**	**14,632**	**12,628**	**12,684**	**13,614**	**12,377**	**13,460**	**13,650**	**15,857**
Official creditors	265	1,444	3,814	3,367	4,188	4,598	4,514	4,470	5,082	4,976
Multilateral	141	745	1,472	1,461	1,812	1,942	1,861	1,626	1,721	1,645
Concessional	133	101	39	29	20	15	10	7	3	3
Bilateral	124	699	2,343	1,905	2,375	2,656	2,652	2,843	3,361	3,331
Concessional	94	565	1,915	1,743	2,222	2,531	2,590	2,796	3,260	3,136
Private creditors	125	2,564	10,818	9,261	8,496	9,016	7,863	8,991	8,568	10,881
Bonds	111	278	5,383	5,111	5,182	5,333	4,095	4,185	3,939	5,381
Commercial banks	0	1,397	3,549	2,786	2,290	2,213	2,064	3,035	3,458	4,370
Other private	14	889	1,886	1,364	1,025	1,470	1,704	1,771	1,171	1,131
Private nonguaranteed	**50**	**1,248**	**2,340**	**1,377**	**1,830**	**2,467**	**4,008**	**5,737**	**9,698**	**11,220**
Bonds	0	0	0	0	0	0	0	0	1,885	2,715
Commercial banks	50	1,248	2,340	1,377	1,830	2,467	4,008	5,737	7,813	8,505
Memo:										
IBRD	141	504	998	983	1,103	1,149	1,072	1,083	1,118	1,059
IDA	0	0	0	0	0	0	0	0	0	0
DISBURSEMENTS	**58**	**1,456**	**1,506**	**1,713**	**1,884**	**2,209**	**3,563**	**5,582**	**8,063**	**8,688**
Public and publicly guaranteed	**45**	**1,015**	**891**	**1,038**	**999**	**1,089**	**1,413**	**3,072**	**3,643**	**4,485**
Official creditors	39	211	331	361	735	617	440	336	818	516
Multilateral	22	119	169	199	273	306	224	217	198	135
Concessional	14	0	2	1	2	1	1	1	0	0
Bilateral	18	93	162	163	462	312	216	119	620	381
Concessional	16	78	150	160	458	295	202	119	552	282
Private creditors	6	804	561	677	264	472	973	2,736	2,825	3,969
Bonds	0	0	360	418	200	190	0	951	460	1,750
Commercial banks	0	510	164	193	60	16	0	1,050	1,493	1,565
Other private	6	294	37	66	4	266	973	735	871	655
Private nonguaranteed	**12**	**441**	**615**	**675**	**885**	**1,120**	**2,150**	**2,510**	**4,420**	**4,202**
Bonds	0	0	0	0	0	0	0	0	1,885	830
Commercial banks	12	441	615	675	885	1,120	2,150	2,510	2,535	3,372
Memo:										
IBRD	21	80	127	148	205	187	148	159	144	88
IDA	0	0	0	0	0	0	0	0	0	0
PRINCIPAL REPAYMENTS	**57**	**345**	**4,422**	**3,016**	**2,342**	**1,841**	**3,154**	**3,420**	**4,700**	**4,942**
Public and publicly guaranteed	**47**	**127**	**3,537**	**2,424**	**1,871**	**1,357**	**2,574**	**2,625**	**3,256**	**2,262**
Official creditors	16	79	826	540	367	408	470	738	681	596
Multilateral	5	34	173	179	216	217	257	536	241	260
Concessional	5	12	16	10	13	6	6	4	4	1
Bilateral	11	45	654	361	150	191	213	201	440	336
Concessional	4	17	119	121	124	145	140	185	421	329
Private creditors	32	48	2,711	1,884	1,505	949	2,104	1,887	2,575	1,666
Bonds	30	11	800	571	412	48	1,144	911	914	340
Commercial banks	0	17	1,437	785	664	161	135	185	1,240	678
Other private	2	20	474	528	428	741	825	792	422	648
Private nonguaranteed	**9**	**218**	**885**	**592**	**470**	**483**	**580**	**795**	**1,444**	**2,680**
Bonds	0	0	0	0	0	0	0	0	0	0
Commercial banks	9	218	885	592	470	483	580	795	1,444	2,680
Memo:										
IBRD	5	26	144	132	164	163	191	172	185	194
IDA	0	0	0	0	0	0	0	0	0	0
NET FLOWS ON DEBT	**1**	**1,111**	**-2,916**	**-1,303**	**-457**	**369**	**409**	**2,162**	**3,362**	**3,746**
Public and publicly guaranteed	**-2**	**889**	**-2,646**	**-1,386**	**-872**	**-268**	**-1,161**	**447**	**386**	**2,223**
Official creditors	23	133	-496	-178	369	209	-30	-401	137	-80
Multilateral	17	85	-4	20	57	89	-33	-320	-44	-124
Concessional	9	-12	-14	-9	-11	-5	-5	-3	-4	-1
Bilateral	7	48	-492	-199	312	120	3	-82	181	45
Concessional	12	61	31	38	334	150	62	-66	132	-48
Private creditors	-25	756	-2,150	-1,207	-1,241	-477	-1,131	848	249	2,303
Bonds	-30	-11	-440	-153	-212	143	-1,144	40	-454	1,410
Commercial banks	0	493	-1,273	-591	-604	-145	-135	865	254	887
Other private	5	274	-437	-463	-424	-475	148	-57	449	6
Private nonguaranteed	**3**	**223**	**-270**	**83**	**415**	**637**	**1,570**	**1,715**	**2,976**	**1,522**
Bonds	0	0	0	0	0	0	0	0	1,885	830
Commercial banks	3	223	-270	83	415	637	1,570	1,715	1,091	692
Memo:										
IBRD	16	54	-17	15	41	24	-43	-13	-41	-106
IDA	0	0	0	0	0	0	0	0	0	0

MALAYSIA

(US$ million, unless otherwise indicated)

	1970	1980	1988	1989	1990	1991	1992	1993	1994	1995
INTEREST PAYMENTS (LINT)	**25**	**338**	**1,461**	**1,123**	**997**	**971**	**932**	**889**	**1,033**	**1,187**
Public and publicly guaranteed	**22**	**250**	**1,182**	**1,035**	**956**	**927**	**880**	**761**	**766**	**781**
Official creditors	13	86	274	216	232	248	260	268	254	276
Multilateral	8	60	128	121	145	147	154	151	127	129
Concessional	8	10	3	2	2	1	1	0	0	0
Bilateral	5	26	145	95	87	102	105	117	127	147
Concessional	3	19	81	76	75	91	96	113	124	139
Private creditors	9	163	908	819	724	678	620	494	512	505
Bonds	8	18	422	422	414	358	285	251	244	240
Commercial banks	0	108	308	255	199	162	153	149	171	178
Other private	1	37	178	143	111	158	182	93	98	87
Private nonguaranteed	**3**	**88**	**279**	**88**	**41**	**44**	**52**	**128**	**267**	**406**
Bonds	0	0	0	0	0	0	0	0	16	75
Commercial banks	3	88	279	88	41	44	52	128	252	331
Memo:										
IBRD	8	39	87	78	86	86	87	83	83	83
IDA	0	0	0	0	0	0	0	0	0	0
NET TRANSFERS ON DEBT	**-25**	**774**	**-4,377**	**-2,426**	**-1,454**	**-602**	**-523**	**1,272**	**2,330**	**2,559**
Public and publicly guaranteed	**-24**	**639**	**-3,828**	**-2,421**	**-1,828**	**-1,195**	**-2,041**	**-314**	**-379**	**1,442**
Official creditors	10	46	-769	-394	137	-39	-289	-669	-117	-355
Multilateral	9	25	-132	-101	-88	-58	-187	-471	-170	-253
Concessional	1	-22	-17	-11	-13	-6	-6	-4	-5	-1
Bilateral	1	22	-637	-293	224	19	-102	-199	53	-102
Concessional	9	42	-50	-38	259	60	-34	-179	7	-186
Private creditors	-34	593	-3,059	-2,027	-1,965	-1,155	-1,751	355	-263	1,798
Bonds	-38	-29	-862	-575	-627	-215	-1,429	-211	-697	1,170
Commercial banks	0	384	-1,581	-846	-803	-307	-288	715	83	708
Other private	4	237	-616	-606	-535	-633	-34	-150	352	-81
Private nonguaranteed	**0**	**135**	**-549**	**-5**	**374**	**593**	**1,518**	**1,587**	**2,709**	**1,117**
Bonds	0	0	0	0	0	0	0	0	1,870	755
Commercial banks	0	135	-549	-5	374	593	1,518	1,587	839	362
Memo:										
IBRD	9	15	-104	-63	-46	-62	-130	-96	-124	-189
IDA	0	0	0	0	0	0	0	0	0	0
DEBT SERVICE (LTDS)	**82**	**683**	**5,883**	**4,139**	**3,339**	**2,811**	**4,086**	**4,310**	**5,733**	**6,129**
Public and publicly guaranteed	**70**	**376**	**4,719**	**3,459**	**2,827**	**2,284**	**3,454**	**3,386**	**4,022**	**3,043**
Official creditors	29	165	1,100	756	599	657	730	1,005	934	871
Multilateral	13	94	301	300	361	364	411	688	368	388
Concessional	13	22	19	13	15	7	7	4	5	1
Bilateral	16	71	799	456	238	293	318	318	567	483
Concessional	7	37	200	197	199	235	236	299	545	468
Private creditors	40	211	3,619	2,703	2,229	1,627	2,724	2,381	3,087	2,172
Bonds	38	29	1,222	993	827	406	1,429	1,162	1,157	580
Commercial banks	0	126	1,746	1,039	863	323	288	334	1,410	857
Other private	2	57	652	672	539	899	1,007	885	520	735
Private nonguaranteed	**13**	**307**	**1,164**	**680**	**511**	**527**	**632**	**923**	**1,711**	**3,086**
Bonds	0	0	0	0	0	0	0	0	16	75
Commercial banks	13	307	1,164	680	511	527	632	923	1,696	3,011
Memo:										
IBRD	13	65	231	211	251	249	278	255	268	277
IDA	0	0	0	0	0	0	0	0	0	0
UNDISBURSED DEBT	**201**	**1,761**	**2,616**	**2,179**	**2,068**	**1,865**	**1,971**	**3,158**	**2,672**	**1,432**
Official creditors	181	1,404	2,265	1,987	1,795	1,262	1,580	1,932	1,833	1,380
Private creditors	20	357	351	192	274	603	391	1,226	839	53
Memorandum items										
Concessional LDOD	228	666	1,955	1,772	2,243	2,546	2,600	2,804	3,264	3,138
Variable rate LDOD	50	2,665	8,805	7,011	7,363	8,001	8,454	9,934	13,786	15,505
Public sector LDOD	390	4,008	14,632	12,628	12,684	13,614	12,377	13,460	13,650	15,857
Private sector LDOD	50	1,248	2,340	1,377	1,830	2,467	4,008	5,737	9,698	11,220

6. CURRENCY COMPOSITION OF LONG-TERM DEBT (PERCENT)

	1970	1980	1988	1989	1990	1991	1992	1993	1994	1995
Deutsche mark	6.9	3.3	9.1	11.2	11.7	10.0	4.0	3.0	2.4	1.1
French franc	0.0	13.0	3.3	3.1	2.6	1.5	1.1	0.8	0.7	0.5
Japanese yen	2.2	19.0	36.4	33.9	33.4	33.2	35.4	38.2	41.4	31.7
Pound sterling	37.8	3.6	1.5	1.4	1.5	2.5	3.0	3.4	2.5	1.0
Swiss franc	0.0	2.3	3.6	3.7	4.0	3.4	3.2	3.1	4.1	4.2
U.S.dollars	14.0	36.7	33.7	32.6	30.7	28.9	29.3	30.9	31.0	45.1
Multiple currency	36.3	21.0	9.8	11.2	13.7	18.6	22.8	20.0	17.4	16.1
Special drawing rights	0.0	0.0	0.0	0.0	0.0	0.0	0.0	0.0	0.0	0.0
All other currencies	2.8	1.2	2.7	2.8	2.5	1.9	1.2	0.6	0.5	0.4

MALAYSIA

(US$ million, unless otherwise indicated)

	1970	1980	1988	1989	1990	1991	1992	1993	1994	1995
7. DEBT RESTRUCTURINGS										
Total amount rescheduled	0	0	0	0	0	0	0	0	0	0
Debt stock rescheduled	0	0	0	0	0	0	0	0	0	0
Principal rescheduled	0	0	0	0	0	0	0	0	0	0
Official	0	0	0	0	0	0	0	0	0	0
Private	0	0	0	0	0	0	0	0	0	0
Interest rescheduled	0	0	0	0	0	0	0	0	0	0
Official	0	0	0	0	0	0	0	0	0	0
Private	0	0	0	0	0	0	0	0	0	0
Debt forgiven	..	..	0	0	0	0	0	0	0	0
Memo: interest forgiven	..	..	0	0	0	0	0	0	0	0
Debt stock reduction	0	0	0	0	0	0	0	0	0	0
of which debt buyback	0	0	0	0	0	0	0	0	0	0
8. DEBT STOCK-FLOW RECONCILIATION										
Total change in debt stocks	..	..	..	-2,289	143	1,735	1,869	6,124	3,389	4,814
Net flows on debt	..	..	..	-625	-824	537	1,975	5,473	2,600	4,831
Net change in interest arrears	..	..	..	0	0	0	0	0	0	0
Interest capitalized	..	..	..	0	0	0	0	0	0	0
Debt forgiveness or reduction	..	..	..	0	0	0	0	0	0	0
Cross-currency valuation	..	..	..	-565	848	333	-261	817	1,563	-80
Residual	..	..	..	-1,100	119	865	156	-166	-774	64
9. AVERAGE TERMS OF NEW COMMITMENTS										
ALL CREDITORS										
Interest (%)	6.1	11.2	5.2	7.6	5.9	7.4	5.8	5.3	5.7	6.3
Maturity (years)	18.7	13.8	17.5	12.1	18.5	13.3	20.9	10.8	14.6	16.6
Grace period (years)	4.8	5.4	6.7	7.2	6.9	6.5	4.0	4.5	3.4	10.3
Grant element (%)	22.7	-6.6	31.4	14.8	29.2	14.5	27.3	21.9	21.3	22.0
Official creditors										
Interest (%)	6.4	6.7	4.9	7.0	4.0	6.8	4.7	5.3	7.5	6.9
Maturity (years)	21.0	18.3	21.7	19.3	22.9	15.2	21.9	13.2	24.8	25.1
Grace period (years)	5.7	5.0	5.4	6.6	6.6	4.0	6.1	3.7	3.6	5.6
Grant element (%)	24.0	20.9	35.0	19.9	44.2	17.5	37.7	22.7	15.9	21.4
Private creditors										
Interest (%)	5.1	14.1	5.7	7.9	9.5	7.6	7.0	5.3	5.2	6.3
Maturity (years)	8.8	10.9	10.7	8.2	10.5	12.9	19.9	10.4	12.0	16.4
Grace period (years)	1.3	5.7	8.7	7.5	7.2	7.0	1.9	4.7	3.4	10.4
Grant element (%)	17.3	-23.9	25.5	12.0	2.1	13.9	17.0	21.7	22.6	22.0
Memorandum items										
Commitments	84	1,423	1,434	832	901	872	1,680	4,227	3,104	3,249
Official creditors	68	550	879	288	579	138	840	638	625	72
Private creditors	16	873	555	544	322	734	840	3,589	2,479	3,177

10. CONTRACTUAL OBLIGATIONS ON OUTSTANDING LONG-TERM DEBT

	1996	1997	1998	1999	2000	2001	2002	2003	2004	2005
TOTAL										
Disbursements	414	337	249	164	115	78	50	19	1	0
Principal	1,556	2,117	2,400	2,201	2,509	1,768	1,172	2,872	3,173	3,614
Interest	1,212	1,237	1,138	1,033	943	823	754	660	545	419
Official creditors										
Disbursements	366	334	248	164	115	78	50	19	1	0
Principal	445	483	485	482	448	422	410	380	365	329
Interest	270	260	247	229	210	192	174	154	135	116
Bilateral creditors										
Disbursements	239	196	135	85	52	36	24	13	0	0
Principal	208	258	263	293	278	267	265	243	243	208
Interest	142	141	137	130	121	112	103	93	83	73
Multilateral creditors										
Disbursements	127	138	114	79	62	43	26	6	1	0
Principal	236	226	222	189	171	155	145	137	122	121
Interest	128	119	110	99	89	80	71	61	52	43
Private creditors										
Disbursements	48	3	1	0	0	0	0	0	0	0
Principal	1,112	1,634	1,915	1,719	2,061	1,346	762	2,492	2,808	3,285
Interest	942	977	891	804	733	631	580	506	411	303
Commercial banks										
Disbursements	10	0	0	0	0	0	0	0	0	0
Principal	365	640	593	583	555	485	364	303	165	121
Interest	217	203	164	130	98	69	44	26	13	8
Other private										
Disbursements	38	3	1	0	0	0	0	0	0	0
Principal	746	994	1,322	1,136	1,505	861	398	2,189	2,643	3,165
Interest	725	774	727	674	635	562	536	480	397	296

MALDIVES

(US$ million, unless otherwise indicated)

	1970	1980	1988	1989	1990	1991	1992	1993	1994	1995
1. SUMMARY DEBT DATA										
TOTAL DEBT STOCKS (EDT)	..	**25.8**	**71.4**	**66.8**	**78.0**	**81.2**	**94.9**	**112.3**	**123.5**	**154.9**
Long-term debt (LDOD)	..	**24.8**	**59.4**	**54.4**	**64.0**	**78.0**	**90.5**	**109.3**	**122.5**	**151.9**
Public and publicly guaranteed	..	24.8	59.4	54.4	64.0	78.0	90.5	109.3	122.5	151.9
Private nonguaranteed	0.0	0.0	0.0	0.0	0.0	0.0	0.0	0.0	0.0	0.0
Use of IMF credit	**0.0**	**0.0**	**0.0**	**0.0**	**0.0**	**0.0**	**0.0**	**0.0**	**0.0**	**0.0**
Short-term debt	..	**1.0**	**12.0**	**12.4**	**14.0**	**3.2**	**4.4**	**3.0**	**1.0**	**2.9**
of which interest arrears on LDOD	..	0.0	0.0	0.0	0.0	0.0	0.0	0.0	0.0	0.0
Official creditors	..	0.0	0.0	0.0	0.0	0.0	0.0	0.0	0.0	0.0
Private creditors	..	0.0	0.0	0.0	0.0	0.0	0.0	0.0	0.0	0.0
Memo: principal arrears on LDOD	..	0.0	0.0	0.0	0.0	0.0	0.0	0.0	0.0	0.0
Official creditors	..	0.0	0.0	0.0	0.0	0.0	0.0	0.0	0.0	0.0
Private creditors	..	0.0	0.0	0.0	0.0	0.0	0.0	0.0	0.0	0.0
Memo: export credits	..	..	1.0	1.0	8.0	7.0	6.0	12.0	29.0	26.0
TOTAL DEBT FLOWS										
Disbursements	..	**17.9**	**6.3**	**3.3**	**13.0**	**16.8**	**20.8**	**25.0**	**15.4**	**34.7**
Long-term debt	..	17.9	6.3	3.3	13.0	16.8	20.8	25.0	15.4	34.7
IMF purchases	0.0	0.0	0.0	0.0	0.0	0.0	0.0	0.0	0.0	0.0
Principal repayments	..	**0.0**	**6.9**	**7.4**	**6.0**	**5.4**	**5.2**	**5.7**	**6.4**	**7.1**
Long-term debt	..	0.0	6.9	7.4	6.0	5.4	5.2	5.7	6.4	7.1
IMF repurchases	0.0	0.0	0.0	0.0	0.0	0.0	0.0	0.0	0.0	0.0
Net flows on debt	..	**17.9**	**0.4**	**-3.7**	**8.6**	**0.6**	**16.8**	**17.9**	**7.0**	**29.5**
of which short-term debt	..	..	1.0	0.4	1.6	-10.8	1.2	-1.4	-2.0	1.9
Interest payments (INT)	..	**0.5**	**2.8**	**2.3**	**2.8**	**2.1**	**1.9**	**2.7**	**3.1**	**3.7**
Long-term debt	..	0.3	1.7	1.3	1.3	1.4	1.5	2.4	3.0	3.6
IMF charges	0.0	0.0	0.0	0.0	0.0	0.0	0.0	0.0	0.0	0.0
Short-term debt	..	0.3	1.1	1.1	1.5	0.7	0.3	0.3	0.1	0.2
Net transfers on debt	..	**17.4**	**-2.5**	**-6.0**	**5.8**	**-1.5**	**14.9**	**15.2**	**3.9**	**25.8**
Total debt service paid (TDS)	..	**0.5**	**9.7**	**9.7**	**8.8**	**7.5**	**7.1**	**8.4**	**9.5**	**10.8**
Long-term debt	..	0.3	8.6	8.6	7.3	6.8	6.8	8.1	9.3	10.7
IMF repurchases and charges	0.0	0.0	0.0	0.0	0.0	0.0	0.0	0.0	0.0	0.0
Short-term debt (interest only)	..	0.3	1.1	1.1	1.5	0.7	0.3	0.3	0.1	0.2
2. AGGREGATE NET RESOURCE FLOWS AND NET TRANSFERS (LONG-TERM)										
NET RESOURCE FLOWS	..	**19.1**	**20.2**	**18.6**	**24.3**	**29.4**	**34.7**	**42.0**	**32.4**	**60.2**
Net flow of long-term debt (ex. IMF)	0.0	17.9	-0.6	-4.1	7.0	11.4	15.6	19.3	9.0	27.6
Foreign direct investment (net)	0.0	0.0	1.2	4.4	6.0	7.0	7.0	7.0	8.0	9.0
Portfolio equity flows	..	0.0	0.0	0.0	0.0	0.0	0.0	0.0	0.0	0.0
Grants (excluding technical coop.)	0.1	1.2	19.6	18.3	11.3	11.0	12.1	15.7	15.4	23.6
Memo: technical coop. grants	0.2	2.5	6.2	10.1	6.3	11.5	11.5	9.8	8.4	10.1
NET TRANSFERS	..	**17.3**	**10.7**	**5.3**	**9.1**	**12.4**	**16.4**	**22.0**	**10.4**	**38.6**
Interest on long-term debt	..	0.3	1.7	1.3	1.3	1.4	1.5	2.4	3.0	3.6
Profit remittances on FDI	0.0	1.5	7.8	12.1	13.9	15.6	16.8	17.6	19.0	18.0
3. MAJOR ECONOMIC AGGREGATES										
Gross national product (GNP)	..	..	97.7	114.5	131.1	149.6	174.9	198.3	220.6	251.5
Exports of goods & services (XGS)	..	65.2	129.9	153.9	182.5	188.1	222.2	219.5	129.9	151.6
of which workers remittances	..	0.0	0.0	0.0	0.0	0.0	0.0	0.0	0.0	0.0
Imports of goods & services (MGS)	..	89.8	127.5	156.5	177.7	202.6	237.3	257.1	261.1	311.0
International reserves (RES)	..	1.0	21.7	24.8	24.5	23.7	28.4	26.4	36.9	53.7
Current account balance	..	-22.2	8.9	10.6	8.6	-9.0	-19.7	-162.9	-153.4	-186.0
4. DEBT INDICATORS										
EDT / XGS (%)	..	39.5	54.9	43.4	42.7	43.2	42.7	51.2	95.1	102.2
EDT / GNP (%)	..	..	73.0	58.3	59.5	54.3	54.3	56.7	56.0	61.6
TDS / XGS (%)	..	0.8	7.5	6.3	4.8	4.0	3.2	3.8	7.3	7.1
INT / XGS (%)	..	0.8	2.2	1.5	1.5	1.1	0.8	1.2	2.4	2.5
INT / GNP (%)	..	..	2.9	2.0	2.1	1.4	1.1	1.3	1.4	1.5
RES / EDT (%)	..	3.9	30.4	37.1	31.4	29.2	29.9	23.5	29.9	34.7
RES / MGS (months)	..	0.1	2.0	1.9	1.7	1.4	1.4	1.2	1.7	2.1
Short-term / EDT (%)	..	3.9	16.8	18.6	18.0	3.9	4.6	2.7	0.8	1.9
Concessional / EDT (%)	..	96.1	75.0	78.0	71.0	87.5	86.1	75.5	79.6	81.6
Multilateral / EDT (%)	..	13.6	39.1	42.5	41.7	55.1	58.5	53.8	58.8	58.8

MALDIVES

(US$ million, unless otherwise indicated)

	1970	1980	1988	1989	1990	1991	1992	1993	1994	1995
5. LONG-TERM DEBT										
DEBT OUTSTANDING (LDOD)	..	**24.8**	**59.4**	**54.4**	**64.0**	**78.0**	**90.5**	**109.3**	**122.5**	**151.9**
Public and publicly guaranteed	..	**24.8**	**59.4**	**54.4**	**64.0**	**78.0**	**90.5**	**109.3**	**122.5**	**151.9**
Official creditors	..	24.8	53.5	52.1	60.2	75.1	84.8	102.1	115.1	142.6
Multilateral	..	3.5	27.9	28.4	32.5	44.8	55.6	60.4	72.6	91.1
Concessional	..	3.5	27.9	28.4	32.5	44.8	55.6	60.4	72.6	91.1
Bilateral	..	21.3	25.6	23.6	27.6	30.3	29.3	41.7	42.5	51.5
Concessional	..	21.3	25.6	23.6	22.8	26.3	26.2	24.5	25.7	35.3
Private creditors	..	0.0	5.9	2.3	3.8	3.0	5.7	7.2	7.4	9.4
Bonds	..	0.0	0.0	0.0	0.0	0.0	0.0	0.0	0.0	0.0
Commercial banks	..	0.0	4.4	1.5	0.0	0.0	1.1	1.0	1.8	4.7
Other private	..	0.0	1.5	0.8	3.8	2.9	4.6	6.2	5.6	4.7
Private nonguaranteed	**0.0**	**0.0**	**0.0**	**0.0**	**0.0**	**0.0**	**0.0**	**0.0**	**0.0**	**0.0**
Bonds	..	0.0	0.0	0.0	0.0	0.0	0.0	0.0	0.0	0.0
Commercial banks	..	0.0	0.0	0.0	0.0	0.0	0.0	0.0	0.0	0.0
Memo:										
IBRD	0.0	0.0	0.0	0.0	0.0	0.0	0.0	0.0	0.0	0.0
IDA	0.0	1.6	7.4	8.3	10.0	14.5	21.8	24.9	31.6	36.1
DISBURSEMENTS	..	**17.9**	**6.3**	**3.3**	**13.0**	**16.8**	**20.8**	**25.0**	**15.4**	**34.7**
Public and publicly guaranteed	..	**17.9**	**6.3**	**3.3**	**13.0**	**16.8**	**20.8**	**25.0**	**15.4**	**34.7**
Official creditors	..	17.9	5.0	3.3	9.6	16.8	17.3	21.9	14.0	30.9
Multilateral	..	2.6	2.9	2.3	3.6	11.0	13.8	6.2	9.9	18.7
Concessional	..	2.6	2.9	2.3	3.6	11.0	13.8	6.2	9.9	18.7
Bilateral	..	15.3	2.1	1.0	5.9	5.8	3.5	15.7	4.1	12.2
Concessional	..	15.3	2.1	1.0	1.1	5.8	3.5	0.7	4.1	12.2
Private creditors	..	0.0	1.3	0.0	3.5	0.0	3.6	3.1	1.4	3.8
Bonds	..	0.0	0.0	0.0	0.0	0.0	0.0	0.0	0.0	0.0
Commercial banks	..	0.0	1.3	0.0	0.0	0.0	1.1	0.1	1.2	3.5
Other private	..	0.0	0.0	0.0	3.5	0.0	2.5	3.0	0.2	0.3
Private nonguaranteed	**0.0**	**0.0**	**0.0**	**0.0**	**0.0**	**0.0**	**0.0**	**0.0**	**0.0**	**0.0**
Bonds	..	0.0	0.0	0.0	0.0	0.0	0.0	0.0	0.0	0.0
Commercial banks	..	0.0	0.0	0.0	0.0	0.0	0.0	0.0	0.0	0.0
Memo:										
IBRD	0.0	0.0	0.0	0.0	0.0	0.0	0.0	0.0	0.0	0.0
IDA	0.0	1.6	0.6	1.0	1.2	4.3	8.1	3.0	5.6	3.9
PRINCIPAL REPAYMENTS	..	**0.0**	**6.9**	**7.4**	**6.0**	**5.4**	**5.2**	**5.7**	**6.4**	**7.1**
Public and publicly guaranteed	..	**0.0**	**6.9**	**7.4**	**6.0**	**5.4**	**5.2**	**5.7**	**6.4**	**7.1**
Official creditors	..	0.0	3.7	3.9	3.7	4.7	4.6	4.5	4.6	4.8
Multilateral	..	0.0	1.1	1.4	1.5	1.4	1.3	1.2	1.3	1.4
Concessional	..	0.0	1.1	1.4	1.5	1.4	1.3	1.2	1.3	1.4
Bilateral	..	0.0	2.6	2.5	2.2	3.3	3.3	3.3	3.3	3.4
Concessional	..	0.0	2.6	2.5	1.9	2.7	2.6	2.6	2.6	2.7
Private creditors	..	0.0	3.2	3.5	2.3	0.7	0.6	1.2	1.8	2.3
Bonds	..	0.0	0.0	0.0	0.0	0.0	0.0	0.0	0.0	0.0
Commercial banks	..	0.0	2.6	2.9	1.5	0.0	0.0	0.3	0.4	0.6
Other private	..	0.0	0.6	0.6	0.9	0.7	0.6	1.0	1.4	1.7
Private nonguaranteed	**0.0**	**0.0**	**0.0**	**0.0**	**0.0**	**0.0**	**0.0**	**0.0**	**0.0**	**0.0**
Bonds	..	0.0	0.0	0.0	0.0	0.0	0.0	0.0	0.0	0.0
Commercial banks	..	0.0	0.0	0.0	0.0	0.0	0.0	0.0	0.0	0.0
Memo:										
IBRD	0.0	0.0	0.0	0.0	0.0	0.0	0.0	0.0	0.0	0.0
IDA	0.0	0.0	0.0	0.0	0.0	0.0	0.0	0.1	0.1	0.1
NET FLOWS ON DEBT	..	**17.9**	**-0.6**	**-4.1**	**7.0**	**11.4**	**15.6**	**19.3**	**9.0**	**27.6**
Public and publicly guaranteed	..	**17.9**	**-0.6**	**-4.1**	**7.0**	**11.4**	**15.6**	**19.3**	**9.0**	**27.6**
Official creditors	..	17.9	1.3	-0.6	5.9	12.1	12.6	17.4	9.4	26.1
Multilateral	..	2.6	1.8	0.9	2.2	9.7	12.5	5.0	8.6	17.3
Concessional	..	2.6	1.8	0.9	2.2	9.7	12.5	5.0	8.6	17.3
Bilateral	..	15.3	-0.5	-1.5	3.7	2.5	0.2	12.4	0.8	8.7
Concessional	..	15.3	-0.5	-1.5	-0.8	3.1	0.9	-1.9	1.5	9.5
Private creditors	..	0.0	-2.0	-3.5	1.1	-0.7	3.0	1.9	-0.4	1.6
Bonds	..	0.0	0.0	0.0	0.0	0.0	0.0	0.0	0.0	0.0
Commercial banks	..	0.0	-1.4	-2.9	-1.5	0.0	1.1	-0.2	0.8	2.9
Other private	..	0.0	-0.6	-0.6	2.6	-0.7	1.9	2.0	-1.2	-1.3
Private nonguaranteed	**0.0**	**0.0**	**0.0**	**0.0**	**0.0**	**0.0**	**0.0**	**0.0**	**0.0**	**0.0**
Bonds	..	0.0	0.0	0.0	0.0	0.0	0.0	0.0	0.0	0.0
Commercial banks	..	0.0	0.0	0.0	0.0	0.0	0.0	0.0	0.0	0.0
Memo:										
IBRD	0.0	0.0	0.0	0.0	0.0	0.0	0.0	0.0	0.0	0.0
IDA	0.0	1.6	0.6	1.0	1.2	4.3	8.1	3.0	5.5	3.8

MALDIVES

(US$ million, unless otherwise indicated)

	1970	1980	1988	1989	1990	1991	1992	1993	1994	1995
INTEREST PAYMENTS (LINT)	..	**0.3**	**1.7**	**1.3**	**1.3**	**1.4**	**1.5**	**2.4**	**3.0**	**3.6**
Public and publicly guaranteed	..	**0.3**	**1.7**	**1.3**	**1.3**	**1.4**	**1.5**	**2.4**	**3.0**	**3.6**
Official creditors	..	0.3	0.8	0.7	0.8	1.1	1.1	1.8	2.3	2.7
Multilateral	..	0.0	0.4	0.3	0.3	0.3	0.4	0.8	0.9	1.0
Concessional	..	0.0	0.4	0.3	0.3	0.3	0.4	0.8	0.9	1.0
Bilateral	..	0.3	0.5	0.4	0.5	0.8	0.7	1.0	1.3	1.7
Concessional	..	0.3	0.5	0.4	0.3	0.4	0.4	0.4	0.4	0.4
Private creditors	..	0.0	0.9	0.5	0.5	0.3	0.4	0.6	0.7	0.8
Bonds	..	0.0	0.0	0.0	0.0	0.0	0.0	0.0	0.0	0.0
Commercial banks	..	0.0	0.7	0.4	0.1	0.0	0.0	0.0	0.1	0.3
Other private	..	0.0	0.2	0.1	0.4	0.3	0.4	0.5	0.6	0.5
Private nonguaranteed	**0.0**	**0.0**	**0.0**	**0.0**	**0.0**	**0.0**	**0.0**	**0.0**	**0.0**	**0.0**
Bonds	..	0.0	0.0	0.0	0.0	0.0	0.0	0.0	0.0	0.0
Commercial banks	..	0.0	0.0	0.0	0.0	0.0	0.0	0.0	0.0	0.0
Memo:										
IBRD	0.0	0.0	0.0	0.0	0.0	0.0	0.0	0.0	0.0	0.0
IDA	0.0	0.0	0.1	0.1	0.1	0.1	0.1	0.2	0.2	0.3
NET TRANSFERS ON DEBT	..	**17.6**	**-2.3**	**-5.3**	**5.7**	**10.0**	**14.1**	**16.9**	**6.0**	**24.0**
Public and publicly guaranteed	..	**17.6**	**-2.3**	**-5.3**	**5.7**	**10.0**	**14.1**	**16.9**	**6.0**	**24.0**
Official creditors	..	17.6	0.5	-1.3	5.0	11.0	11.5	15.6	7.2	23.3
Multilateral	..	2.6	1.5	0.6	1.8	9.4	12.1	4.2	7.7	16.3
Concessional	..	2.6	1.5	0.6	1.8	9.4	12.1	4.2	7.7	16.3
Bilateral	..	15.0	-1.0	-1.9	3.2	1.7	-0.5	11.4	-0.5	7.0
Concessional	..	15.0	-1.0	-1.9	-1.1	2.7	0.5	-2.3	1.1	9.1
Private creditors	..	0.0	-2.8	-4.0	0.6	-1.0	2.6	1.3	-1.1	0.7
Bonds	..	0.0	0.0	0.0	0.0	0.0	0.0	0.0	0.0	0.0
Commercial banks	..	0.0	-2.0	-3.3	-1.6	0.0	1.1	-0.2	0.7	2.6
Other private	..	0.0	-0.8	-0.7	2.2	-1.0	1.5	1.5	-1.8	-1.8
Private nonguaranteed	**0.0**	**0.0**	**0.0**	**0.0**	**0.0**	**0.0**	**0.0**	**0.0**	**0.0**	**0.0**
Bonds	..	0.0	0.0	0.0	0.0	0.0	0.0	0.0	0.0	0.0
Commercial banks	..	0.0	0.0	0.0	0.0	0.0	0.0	0.0	0.0	0.0
Memo:										
IBRD	0.0	0.0	0.0	0.0	0.0	0.0	0.0	0.0	0.0	0.0
IDA	0.0	1.6	0.6	0.9	1.1	4.2	8.0	2.8	5.3	3.5
DEBT SERVICE (LTDS)	..	**0.3**	**8.6**	**8.6**	**7.3**	**6.8**	**6.8**	**8.1**	**9.3**	**10.7**
Public and publicly guaranteed	..	**0.3**	**8.6**	**8.6**	**7.3**	**6.8**	**6.8**	**8.1**	**9.3**	**10.7**
Official creditors	..	0.3	4.5	4.6	4.5	5.8	5.8	6.3	6.8	7.6
Multilateral	..	0.0	1.5	1.7	1.8	1.7	1.7	2.0	2.2	2.4
Concessional	..	0.0	1.5	1.7	1.8	1.7	1.7	2.0	2.2	2.4
Bilateral	..	0.3	3.0	2.9	2.7	4.1	4.0	4.3	4.6	5.1
Concessional	..	0.3	3.0	2.9	2.2	3.1	3.0	3.0	3.0	3.1
Private creditors	..	0.0	4.1	4.0	2.8	1.0	1.0	1.8	2.5	3.1
Bonds	..	0.0	0.0	0.0	0.0	0.0	0.0	0.0	0.0	0.0
Commercial banks	..	0.0	3.3	3.3	1.6	0.0	0.0	0.3	0.5	0.9
Other private	..	0.0	0.8	0.7	1.2	1.0	1.0	1.5	2.0	2.2
Private nonguaranteed	**0.0**	**0.0**	**0.0**	**0.0**	**0.0**	**0.0**	**0.0**	**0.0**	**0.0**	**0.0**
Bonds	..	0.0	0.0	0.0	0.0	0.0	0.0	0.0	0.0	0.0
Commercial banks	..	0.0	0.0	0.0	0.0	0.0	0.0	0.0	0.0	0.0
Memo:										
IBRD	0.0	0.0	0.0	0.0	0.0	0.0	0.0	0.0	0.0	0.0
IDA	0.0	0.0	0.1	0.1	0.1	0.1	0.1	0.2	0.3	0.4
UNDISBURSED DEBT	..	**21.0**	**26.0**	**46.0**	**51.3**	**36.6**	**70.5**	**67.7**	**63.9**	**59.0**
Official creditors	..	19.1	24.5	41.3	49.6	30.0	67.3	67.7	59.5	54.8
Private creditors	..	1.9	1.6	4.7	1.7	6.5	3.2	0.0	4.3	4.2
Memorandum items										
Concessional LDOD	..	24.8	53.5	52.1	55.4	71.1	81.8	84.9	98.3	126.4
Variable rate LDOD	..	0.0	4.4	1.5	0.0	0.0	1.1	16.0	16.1	16.4
Public sector LDOD	..	24.8	59.4	54.4	64.0	78.0	90.5	109.3	122.5	151.9
Private sector LDOD	..	0.0	0.0	0.0	0.0	0.0	0.0	0.0	0.0	0.0

6. CURRENCY COMPOSITION OF LONG-TERM DEBT (PERCENT)

	1970	1980	1988	1989	1990	1991	1992	1993	1994	1995
Deutsche mark	..	0.0	1.2	0.7	13.0	8.8	6.0	5.5	4.1	2.3
French franc	..	0.0	0.0	0.0	0.0	0.0	0.0	0.0	0.0	0.0
Japanese yen	..	0.0	0.0	0.0	0.0	0.0	0.0	0.0	0.0	0.0
Pound sterling	..	0.0	1.0	0.7	0.3	0.0	0.0	0.0	0.0	0.0
Swiss franc	..	0.0	0.0	0.0	0.0	0.0	0.0	0.0	0.0	0.0
U.S.dollars	..	14.1	31.5	30.1	25.5	28.4	35.0	46.2	49.8	51.3
Multiple currency	..	0.0	7.7	9.7	12.4	19.1	20.3	18.8	19.3	20.3
Special drawing rights	..	0.0	0.0	0.0	0.0	0.0	0.0	0.0	0.0	0.7
All other currencies	..	86.0	58.5	58.5	48.8	43.6	38.6	29.5	26.9	25.3

MALDIVES

(US$ million, unless otherwise indicated)

	1970	1980	1988	1989	1990	1991	1992	1993	1994	1995
7. DEBT RESTRUCTURINGS										
Total amount rescheduled	0.0	0.0	0.0	0.0	0.0	0.0	0.0	0.0	0.0	0.0
Debt stock rescheduled	0.0	0.0	0.0	0.0	0.0	0.0	0.0	0.0	0.0	0.0
Principal rescheduled	0.0	0.0	0.0	0.0	0.0	0.0	0.0	0.0	0.0	0.0
Official	0.0	0.0	0.0	0.0	0.0	0.0	0.0	0.0	0.0	0.0
Private	0.0	0.0	0.0	0.0	0.0	0.0	0.0	0.0	0.0	0.0
Interest rescheduled	0.0	0.0	0.0	0.0	0.0	0.0	0.0	0.0	0.0	0.0
Official	0.0	0.0	0.0	0.0	0.0	0.0	0.0	0.0	0.0	0.0
Private	0.0	0.0	0.0	0.0	0.0	0.0	0.0	0.0	0.0	0.0
Debt forgiven	..	..	0.0	0.0	0.0	0.0	0.0	0.0	0.0	0.0
Memo: interest forgiven	..	..	0.0	0.0	0.0	0.0	0.0	0.0	0.0	0.0
Debt stock reduction	0.0	0.0	0.0	0.0	0.0	0.0	0.0	0.0	0.0	0.0
of which debt buyback	0.0	0.0	0.0	0.0	0.0	0.0	0.0	0.0	0.0	0.0
8. DEBT STOCK-FLOW RECONCILIATION										
Total change in debt stocks	..	..	..	-4.6	11.2	3.3	13.7	17.5	11.2	31.3
Net flows on debt	..	..	..	-3.7	8.6	0.6	16.8	17.9	7.0	29.5
Net change in interest arrears	..	..	..	0.0	0.0	0.0	0.0	0.0	0.0	0.0
Interest capitalized	..	..	..	0.0	0.0	0.0	0.0	0.0	0.0	0.0
Debt forgiveness or reduction	..	..	..	0.0	0.0	0.0	0.0	0.0	0.0	0.0
Cross-currency valuation	..	..	..	-0.7	2.1	-0.1	-1.8	-0.3	1.1	0.7
Residual	..	..	..	-0.2	0.5	2.8	-1.3	-0.1	3.1	1.1
9. AVERAGE TERMS OF NEW COMMITMENTS										
ALL CREDITORS										
Interest (%)	..	2.9	7.2	3.5	0.8	9.9	1.5	3.4	4.8	3.1
Maturity (years)	..	14.7	11.6	27.8	37.2	6.8	27.0	17.7	14.0	31.1
Grace period (years)	..	4.4	3.0	6.8	9.2	1.2	6.9	6.8	3.7	9.1
Grant element (%)	..	41.2	17.0	53.0	77.2	-0.3	62.7	41.2	30.9	56.4
Official creditors										
Interest (%)	..	2.5	3.0	2.6	0.8	0.0	1.3	3.4	2.1	2.4
Maturity (years)	..	15.5	16.4	30.7	37.2	0.0	27.8	17.7	19.8	34.6
Grace period (years)	..	4.6	4.9	7.7	9.2	0.0	7.1	6.8	5.6	10.1
Grant element (%)	..	44.2	42.8	60.6	77.2	0.0	64.7	41.2	52.7	63.4
Private creditors										
Interest (%)	..	7.5	10.2	9.4	0.0	9.9	6.3	0.0	7.5	7.9
Maturity (years)	..	6.6	8.1	7.5	0.0	6.8	4.7	0.0	8.0	6.0
Grace period (years)	..	1.1	1.7	0.5	0.0	1.2	0.8	0.0	1.7	1.7
Grant element (%)	..	6.9	-1.3	1.2	0.0	-0.3	7.3	0.0	8.6	6.3
Memorandum items										
Commitments	..	22.1	4.8	23.1	15.5	4.5	57.4	23.8	11.6	29.5
Official creditors	..	20.3	2.0	20.2	15.5	0.0	55.3	23.8	5.8	25.9
Private creditors	..	1.8	2.8	3.0	0.0	4.5	2.1	0.0	5.7	3.6

10. CONTRACTUAL OBLIGATIONS ON OUTSTANDING LONG-TERM DEBT

	1996	1997	1998	1999	2000	2001	2002	2003	2004	2005
TOTAL										
Disbursements	15.6	16.7	11.2	7.2	4.1	2.5	1.2	0.2	0.2	0.0
Principal	8.9	8.9	22.8	7.5	7.2	6.6	6.2	6.3	6.5	6.7
Interest	4.0	4.0	3.4	2.7	2.5	2.4	2.2	2.1	2.0	1.9
Official creditors										
Disbursements	13.2	15.5	10.7	7.1	4.1	2.5	1.2	0.2	0.2	0.0
Principal	5.7	6.0	20.7	5.7	5.8	5.3	5.7	6.1	6.3	6.7
Interest	3.1	3.3	2.9	2.4	2.3	2.3	2.2	2.1	2.0	1.9
Bilateral creditors										
Disbursements	3.5	2.5	1.4	0.8	0.5	0.3	0.1	0.1	0.1	0.0
Principal	4.3	4.5	18.9	3.4	3.2	2.7	2.6	2.6	2.7	2.7
Interest	1.8	1.7	1.2	0.6	0.5	0.5	0.4	0.4	0.4	0.3
Multilateral creditors										
Disbursements	9.7	13.0	9.3	6.3	3.6	2.2	1.1	0.2	0.2	0.0
Principal	1.4	1.5	1.9	2.3	2.7	2.6	3.2	3.5	3.6	4.0
Interest	1.3	1.5	1.7	1.8	1.8	1.8	1.7	1.7	1.6	1.6
Private creditors										
Disbursements	2.4	1.2	0.4	0.2	0.0	0.0	0.0	0.0	0.0	0.0
Principal	3.2	2.9	2.1	1.8	1.3	1.3	0.5	0.2	0.2	0.0
Interest	0.8	0.7	0.5	0.4	0.2	0.1	0.0	0.0	0.0	0.0
Commercial banks										
Disbursements	2.0	1.0	0.4	0.2	0.0	0.0	0.0	0.0	0.0	0.0
Principal	1.1	1.2	1.4	1.4	1.1	1.1	0.5	0.2	0.2	0.0
Interest	0.4	0.5	0.4	0.3	0.2	0.1	0.0	0.0	0.0	0.0
Other private										
Disbursements	0.4	0.1	0.1	0.0	0.0	0.0	0.0	0.0	0.0	0.0
Principal	2.1	1.8	0.7	0.4	0.2	0.2	0.0	0.0	0.0	0.0
Interest	0.4	0.2	0.1	0.0	0.0	0.0	0.0	0.0	0.0	0.0

MALI

(US$ million, unless otherwise indicated)

	1970	1980	1988	1989	1990	1991	1992	1993	1994	1995
1. SUMMARY DEBT DATA										
TOTAL DEBT STOCKS (EDT)	..	**732**	**2,040**	**2,159**	**2,502**	**2,618**	**2,623**	**2,656**	**2,796**	**3,066**
Long-term debt (LDOD)	**238**	**669**	**1,912**	**2,058**	**2,369**	**2,477**	**2,494**	**2,515**	**2,638**	**2,840**
Public and publicly guaranteed	238	669	1,912	2,058	2,369	2,477	2,494	2,515	2,638	2,840
Private nonguaranteed	0	0	0	0	0	0	0	0	0	0
Use of IMF credit	**9**	**39**	**74**	**55**	**69**	**60**	**65**	**71**	**108**	**147**
Short-term debt	..	**24**	**54**	**47**	**63**	**81**	**64**	**70**	**50**	**79**
of which interest arrears on LDOD	..	1	4	2	10	31	34	42	30	35
Official creditors	..	1	4	2	10	30	34	41	30	35
Private creditors	..	0	0	0	0	1	0	1	0	0
Memo: principal arrears on LDOD	..	75	19	8	68	188	263	337	382	453
Official creditors	..	73	18	8	68	187	263	336	382	453
Private creditors	..	2	2	0	0	1	0	1	0	0
Memo: export credits	..	..	86	94	86	87	83	75	60	84
TOTAL DEBT FLOWS										
Disbursements	**24**	**109**	**157**	**186**	**183**	**117**	**139**	**72**	**163**	**219**
Long-term debt	23	95	140	180	155	117	124	58	121	174
IMF purchases	2	14	17	7	28	0	14	14	42	45
Principal repayments	**4**	**9**	**54**	**45**	**41**	**17**	**28**	**29**	**88**	**55**
Long-term debt	0	6	30	22	23	8	21	21	78	48
IMF repurchases	4	3	24	23	18	9	7	9	10	7
Net flows on debt	**20**	**100**	**97**	**136**	**150**	**97**	**91**	**62**	**66**	**187**
of which short-term debt	..	..	-6	-5	8	-3	-20	19	-9	24
Interest payments (INT)	..	**7**	**24**	**22**	**24**	**14**	**17**	**13**	**39**	**25**
Long-term debt	0	3	15	14	17	8	12	10	38	23
IMF charges	0	1	5	4	4	3	2	1	1	1
Short-term debt	..	3	4	4	3	3	2	2	1	2
Net transfers on debt	..	**93**	**73**	**114**	**126**	**83**	**74**	**49**	**27**	**162**
Total debt service paid (TDS)	..	**16**	**79**	**67**	**65**	**31**	**44**	**43**	**127**	**80**
Long-term debt	1	9	46	36	40	16	34	31	116	71
IMF repurchases and charges	4	4	29	27	22	12	8	10	10	7
Short-term debt (interest only)	..	3	4	4	3	3	2	2	1	2
2. AGGREGATE NET RESOURCE FLOWS AND NET TRANSFERS (LONG-TERM)										
NET RESOURCE FLOWS	**34**	**195**	**300**	**368**	**326**	**322**	**298**	**193**	**308**	**334**
Net flow of long-term debt (ex. IMF)	23	89	110	157	133	109	103	38	42	126
Foreign direct investment (net)	0	2	1	15	-7	4	-8	-20	45	1
Portfolio equity flows	0	0	0	0	0	0	0	0	0	0
Grants (excluding technical coop.)	12	104	190	195	201	208	203	175	221	208
Memo: technical coop. grants	8	77	92	88	99	122	130	133	113	134
NET TRANSFERS	**32**	**192**	**285**	**346**	**286**	**291**	**272**	**170**	**256**	**297**
Interest on long-term debt	0	3	15	14	17	8	12	10	38	23
Profit remittances on FDI	2	0	0	8	24	23	14	13	14	15
3. MAJOR ECONOMIC AGGREGATES										
Gross national product (GNP)	333	1,612	1,953	2,024	2,442	2,393	2,818	2,652	1,832	2,324
Exports of goods & services (XGS)	..	322	434	444	562	565	565	576	486	656
of which workers remittances	..	59	94	99	125	128	142	134	94	108
Imports of goods & services (MGS)	..	537	731	693	889	859	934	873	787	985
International reserves (RES)	1	26	44	123	198	326	314	340	229	330
Current account balance	..	-130	-234	-191	-250	-176	-253	-213	-164	47
4. DEBT INDICATORS										
EDT / XGS (%)	..	227.3	470.4	486.2	444.9	463.3	464.0	461.3	575.3	467.1
EDT / GNP (%)	..	45.4	104.4	106.7	102.4	109.4	93.1	100.2	152.6	131.9
TDS / XGS (%)	..	5.1	18.1	15.1	11.5	5.4	7.8	7.4	26.2	12.2
INT / XGS (%)	..	2.3	5.6	4.9	4.2	2.4	2.9	2.3	8.1	3.8
INT / GNP (%)	..	0.5	1.2	1.1	1.0	0.6	0.6	0.5	2.1	1.1
RES / EDT (%)	..	3.5	2.1	5.7	7.9	12.5	12.0	12.8	8.2	10.8
RES / MGS (months)	..	0.6	0.7	2.1	2.7	4.6	4.0	4.7	3.5	4.0
Short-term / EDT (%)	..	3.3	2.7	2.2	2.5	3.1	2.4	2.6	1.8	2.6
Concessional / EDT (%)	..	84.7	89.7	91.2	91.2	91.4	92.4	91.6	92.1	90.8
Multilateral / EDT (%)	..	23.7	34.2	35.9	37.3	39.9	41.5	42.4	44.5	45.2

MALI

(US$ million, unless otherwise indicated)

	1970	1980	1988	1989	1990	1991	1992	1993	1994	1995
5. LONG-TERM DEBT										
DEBT OUTSTANDING (LDOD)	**238**	**669**	**1,912**	**2,058**	**2,369**	**2,477**	**2,494**	**2,515**	**2,638**	**2,840**
Public and publicly guaranteed	**238**	**669**	**1,912**	**2,058**	**2,369**	**2,477**	**2,494**	**2,515**	**2,638**	**2,840**
Official creditors	232	634	1,888	2,036	2,351	2,463	2,489	2,513	2,635	2,837
Multilateral	6	173	697	774	933	1,044	1,088	1,126	1,243	1,387
Concessional	6	166	681	760	919	1,030	1,075	1,110	1,230	1,376
Bilateral	226	460	1,191	1,262	1,419	1,419	1,402	1,387	1,392	1,451
Concessional	226	454	1,149	1,210	1,361	1,362	1,348	1,324	1,345	1,408
Private creditors	6	36	25	21	18	14	5	3	2	2
Bonds	0	0	0	0	0	0	0	0	0	0
Commercial banks	1	11	2	2	2	2	2	2	2	2
Other private	5	25	22	19	16	12	3	1	0	0
Private nonguaranteed	**0**	**0**	**0**	**0**	**0**	**0**	**0**	**0**	**0**	**0**
Bonds	0	0	0	0	0	0	0	0	0	0
Commercial banks	0	0	0	0	0	0	0	0	0	0
Memo:										
IBRD	0	0	0	0	0	0	0	0	0	0
IDA	6	121	390	432	498	569	611	656	770	863
DISBURSEMENTS	**23**	**95**	**140**	**180**	**155**	**117**	**124**	**58**	**121**	**174**
Public and publicly guaranteed	**23**	**95**	**140**	**180**	**155**	**117**	**124**	**58**	**121**	**174**
Official creditors	23	85	140	180	155	117	124	58	121	174
Multilateral	1	35	103	97	123	110	93	58	116	141
Concessional	1	32	97	97	123	109	93	58	116	141
Bilateral	22	50	37	82	32	7	31	0	5	33
Concessional	22	45	32	75	31	6	31	0	5	33
Private creditors	0	10	0	0	0	0	0	0	0	0
Bonds	0	0	0	0	0	0	0	0	0	0
Commercial banks	0	5	0	0	0	0	0	0	0	0
Other private	0	5	0	0	0	0	0	0	0	0
Private nonguaranteed	**0**	**0**	**0**	**0**	**0**	**0**	**0**	**0**	**0**	**0**
Bonds	0	0	0	0	0	0	0	0	0	0
Commercial banks	0	0	0	0	0	0	0	0	0	0
Memo:										
IBRD	0	0	0	0	0	0	0	0	0	0
IDA	1	19	61	48	44	69	62	47	93	86
PRINCIPAL REPAYMENTS	**0**	**6**	**30**	**22**	**23**	**8**	**21**	**21**	**78**	**48**
Public and publicly guaranteed	**0**	**6**	**30**	**22**	**23**	**8**	**21**	**21**	**78**	**48**
Official creditors	0	4	28	21	22	7	19	21	78	48
Multilateral	0	0	18	13	15	7	13	17	37	21
Concessional	0	0	17	12	14	6	12	14	33	19
Bilateral	0	4	10	8	7	0	6	4	41	27
Concessional	0	3	10	7	6	0	5	4	25	22
Private creditors	0	2	2	1	1	1	3	0	1	0
Bonds	0	0	0	0	0	0	0	0	0	0
Commercial banks	0	1	0	0	0	0	0	0	0	0
Other private	0	1	2	1	1	1	3	0	1	0
Private nonguaranteed	**0**	**0**	**0**	**0**	**0**	**0**	**0**	**0**	**0**	**0**
Bonds	0	0	0	0	0	0	0	0	0	0
Commercial banks	0	0	0	0	0	0	0	0	0	0
Memo:										
IBRD	0	0	0	0	0	0	0	0	0	0
IDA	0	0	2	2	2	2	3	4	6	6
NET FLOWS ON DEBT	**23**	**89**	**110**	**157**	**133**	**109**	**103**	**38**	**42**	**126**
Public and publicly guaranteed	**23**	**89**	**110**	**157**	**133**	**109**	**103**	**38**	**42**	**126**
Official creditors	23	81	112	158	134	110	106	38	43	126
Multilateral	1	35	84	84	108	103	80	41	79	120
Concessional	1	32	80	85	110	104	81	44	83	123
Bilateral	21	46	28	74	26	7	26	-4	-36	6
Concessional	21	42	23	68	24	6	26	-4	-20	11
Private creditors	0	8	-2	-1	-1	-1	-3	0	-1	0
Bonds	0	0	0	0	0	0	0	0	0	0
Commercial banks	0	4	0	0	0	0	0	0	0	0
Other private	0	4	-2	-1	-1	-1	-3	0	-1	0
Private nonguaranteed	**0**	**0**	**0**	**0**	**0**	**0**	**0**	**0**	**0**	**0**
Bonds	0	0	0	0	0	0	0	0	0	0
Commercial banks	0	0	0	0	0	0	0	0	0	0
Memo:										
IBRD	0	0	0	0	0	0	0	0	0	0
IDA	1	19	59	46	42	67	59	43	87	80

MALI

(US$ million, unless otherwise indicated)

	1970	1980	1988	1989	1990	1991	1992	1993	1994	1995
INTEREST PAYMENTS (LINT)	**0**	**3**	**15**	**14**	**17**	**8**	**12**	**10**	**38**	**23**
Public and publicly guaranteed	**0**	**3**	**15**	**14**	**17**	**8**	**12**	**10**	**38**	**23**
Official creditors	0	2	15	14	16	8	12	10	37	23
Multilateral	0	1	9	8	10	7	9	9	15	11
Concessional	0	1	8	7	9	6	8	8	14	10
Bilateral	0	1	6	6	7	1	4	2	22	12
Concessional	0	1	6	5	6	0	3	2	18	12
Private creditors	0	1	0	0	1	0	0	0	1	0
Bonds	0	0	0	0	0	0	0	0	0	0
Commercial banks	0	1	0	0	0	0	0	0	1	0
Other private	0	0	0	0	1	0	0	0	0	0
Private nonguaranteed	**0**	**0**	**0**	**0**	**0**	**0**	**0**	**0**	**0**	**0**
Bonds	0	0	0	0	0	0	0	0	0	0
Commercial banks	0	0	0	0	0	0	0	0	0	0
Memo:										
IBRD	0	0	0	0	0	0	0	0	0	0
IDA	0	1	4	3	3	3	4	5	6	6
NET TRANSFERS ON DEBT	**22**	**86**	**94**	**144**	**116**	**101**	**91**	**27**	**4**	**103**
Public and publicly guaranteed	**22**	**86**	**94**	**144**	**116**	**101**	**91**	**27**	**4**	**103**
Official creditors	22	79	97	145	117	102	94	27	6	103
Multilateral	1	34	75	76	99	96	72	33	64	110
Concessional	1	31	72	78	101	97	73	36	68	113
Bilateral	21	45	22	68	19	6	22	-5	-58	-7
Concessional	21	41	18	63	18	6	23	-5	-38	-1
Private creditors	0	7	-3	-1	-2	-1	-3	0	-1	0
Bonds	0	0	0	0	0	0	0	0	0	0
Commercial banks	0	3	-1	0	0	0	0	0	-1	0
Other private	0	4	-2	-1	-2	-1	-3	0	-1	0
Private nonguaranteed	**0**	**0**	**0**	**0**	**0**	**0**	**0**	**0**	**0**	**0**
Bonds	0	0	0	0	0	0	0	0	0	0
Commercial banks	0	0	0	0	0	0	0	0	0	0
Memo:										
IBRD	0	0	0	0	0	0	0	0	0	0
IDA	1	18	56	43	38	63	54	39	82	73
DEBT SERVICE (LTDS)	**1**	**9**	**46**	**36**	**40**	**16**	**34**	**31**	**116**	**71**
Public and publicly guaranteed	**1**	**9**	**46**	**36**	**40**	**16**	**34**	**31**	**116**	**71**
Official creditors	1	6	43	35	38	15	31	31	115	71
Multilateral	0	2	27	21	25	14	22	25	52	32
Concessional	0	1	25	19	22	12	20	22	47	29
Bilateral	1	5	16	14	13	1	9	5	63	39
Concessional	1	4	15	13	13	0	8	5	43	34
Private creditors	0	3	3	1	2	1	3	0	1	0
Bonds	0	0	0	0	0	0	0	0	0	0
Commercial banks	0	2	1	0	0	0	0	0	1	0
Other private	0	1	2	1	2	1	3	0	1	0
Private nonguaranteed	**0**	**0**	**0**	**0**	**0**	**0**	**0**	**0**	**0**	**0**
Bonds	0	0	0	0	0	0	0	0	0	0
Commercial banks	0	0	0	0	0	0	0	0	0	0
Memo:										
IBRD	0	0	0	0	0	0	0	0	0	0
IDA	0	1	5	5	5	5	7	8	12	12
UNDISBURSED DEBT	**54**	**368**	**550**	**643**	**639**	**705**	**704**	**668**	**685**	**686**
Official creditors	50	361	550	643	639	705	704	668	685	686
Private creditors	4	7	0	0	0	0	0	0	0	0
Memorandum items										
Concessional LDOD	232	620	1,831	1,970	2,280	2,392	2,424	2,433	2,575	2,784
Variable rate LDOD	0	0	6	8	8	8	2	2	2	2
Public sector LDOD	238	669	1,904	2,052	2,363	2,471	2,488	2,510	2,632	2,834
Private sector LDOD	0	0	8	6	6	6	6	5	6	6

6. CURRENCY COMPOSITION OF LONG-TERM DEBT (PERCENT)

	1970	1980	1988	1989	1990	1991	1992	1993	1994	1995
Deutsche mark	2.8	0.9	0.3	0.2	0.2	0.1	0.1	0.1	0.1	0.1
French franc	16.9	21.6	34.0	36.8	35.8	34.2	31.6	29.4	29.1	28.0
Japanese yen	0.0	0.0	0.3	0.3	0.2	0.3	0.3	0.3	0.3	0.9
Pound sterling	37.5	11.4	3.0	2.5	2.6	2.4	1.9	1.9	1.8	1.7
Swiss franc	5.9	5.5	2.4	2.2	2.2	2.0	1.9	1.8	2.0	2.1
U.S.dollars	4.9	11.5	14.7	14.4	14.6	17.0	19.7	22.3	24.8	26.1
Multiple currency	0.3	6.5	13.1	13.8	15.7	16.4	16.3	16.6	17.4	18.4
Special drawing rights	0.0	0.0	0.0	0.0	0.0	0.0	0.0	0.0	0.0	0.0
All other currencies	31.5	42.4	32.3	29.9	28.6	27.6	28.2	27.6	24.5	22.8

MALI

(US$ million, unless otherwise indicated)

	1970	1980	1988	1989	1990	1991	1992	1993	1994	1995
7. DEBT RESTRUCTURINGS										
Total amount rescheduled	0	0	59	28	12	11	38	57	15	12
Debt stock rescheduled	0	0	19	0	0	0	0	0	0	0
Principal rescheduled	0	0	22	19	7	7	21	45	10	9
Official	0	0	2	15	4	4	15	23	10	9
Private	0	0	20	4	3	3	6	22	0	0
Interest rescheduled	0	0	18	8	5	3	10	12	5	3
Official	0	0	8	7	4	2	9	10	5	3
Private	0	0	10	1	1	1	1	1	0	0
Debt forgiven	..	..	30	7	2	1	13	9	10	8
Memo: interest forgiven	..	..	3	1	2	1	6	4	3	2
Debt stock reduction	0	0	0	0	0	0	0	0	0	0
of which debt buyback	0	0	0	0	0	0	0	0	0	0
8. DEBT STOCK-FLOW RECONCILIATION										
Total change in debt stocks	..	..	..	119	343	116	6	33	140	270
Net flows on debt	..	..	..	136	150	97	91	62	66	187
Net change in interest arrears	..	..	..	-3	8	21	3	7	-12	5
Interest capitalized	..	..	..	8	5	3	10	12	5	3
Debt forgiveness or reduction	..	..	..	-7	-2	-1	-13	-9	-10	-8
Cross-currency valuation	..	..	..	15	177	-15	-67	-52	78	83
Residual	..	..	..	-31	4	11	-17	13	12	-1
9. AVERAGE TERMS OF NEW COMMITMENTS										
ALL CREDITORS										
Interest (%)	1.1	2.2	1.2	1.0	1.1	0.9	2.1	0.9	0.8	1.5
Maturity (years)	25.0	23.0	39.0	32.4	31.3	40.1	30.2	40.6	39.5	30.7
Grace period (years)	9.5	5.5	9.4	9.1	9.3	9.4	8.3	9.8	10.0	8.8
Grant element (%)	68.2	50.6	75.3	71.9	71.5	77.9	61.2	80.0	80.3	68.6
Official creditors										
Interest (%)	0.3	1.8	1.2	1.0	1.1	0.9	2.1	0.9	0.8	1.5
Maturity (years)	27.4	23.9	39.0	32.4	31.3	40.1	30.2	40.6	39.5	30.7
Grace period (years)	10.6	5.6	9.4	9.1	9.3	9.4	8.3	9.8	10.0	8.8
Grant element (%)	76.4	53.3	75.3	71.9	71.5	77.9	61.2	80.0	80.3	68.6
Private creditors										
Interest (%)	6.7	9.9	0.0	0.0	0.0	0.0	0.0	0.0	0.0	0.0
Maturity (years)	8.5	6.3	0.0	0.0	0.0	0.0	0.0	0.0	0.0	0.0
Grace period (years)	1.6	2.2	0.0	0.0	0.0	0.0	0.0	0.0	0.0	0.0
Grant element (%)	11.5	-0.4	0.0	0.0	0.0	0.0	0.0	0.0	0.0	0.0
Memorandum items										
Commitments	34	145	173	285	115	180	151	63	120	163
Official creditors	30	138	173	285	115	180	151	63	120	163
Private creditors	4	7	0	0	0	0	0	0	0	0

10. CONTRACTUAL OBLIGATIONS ON OUTSTANDING LONG-TERM DEBT

	1996	1997	1998	1999	2000	2001	2002	2003	2004	2005
TOTAL										
Disbursements	203	188	120	71	44	24	13	3	2	0
Principal	146	122	97	104	100	102	98	95	95	95
Interest	35	35	35	34	32	31	29	27	26	24
Official creditors										
Disbursements	203	188	120	71	44	24	13	3	2	0
Principal	146	122	97	104	100	101	98	95	95	95
Interest	35	35	35	34	32	31	29	27	26	24
Bilateral creditors										
Disbursements	64	53	32	18	9	4	2	0	0	0
Principal	112	85	59	63	58	58	54	50	49	45
Interest	22	21	20	19	17	16	15	14	13	12
Multilateral creditors										
Disbursements	139	135	88	53	36	20	11	2	2	0
Principal	34	37	38	40	41	44	44	45	46	49
Interest	13	14	15	15	15	15	14	14	13	12
Private creditors										
Disbursements	0	0	0	0	0	0	0	0	0	0
Principal	0	0	0	0	0	0	0	0	0	0
Interest	0	0	0	0	0	0	0	0	0	0
Commercial banks										
Disbursements	0	0	0	0	0	0	0	0	0	0
Principal	0	0	0	0	0	0	0	0	0	0
Interest	0	0	0	0	0	0	0	0	0	0
Other private										
Disbursements	0	0	0	0	0	0	0	0	0	0
Principal	0	0	0	0	0	0	0	0	0	0
Interest	0	0	0	0	0	0	0	0	0	0

MALTA

(US$ million, unless otherwise indicated)

	1970	1980	1988	1989	1990	1991	1992	1993	1994	1995
1. SUMMARY DEBT DATA										
TOTAL DEBT STOCKS (EDT)	..	**108.2**	**369.9**	**409.5**	**600.6**	**616.4**	**603.3**	**746.1**	**806.6**	**954.9**
Long-term debt (LDOD)	**25.0**	**86.2**	**84.9**	**78.5**	**124.6**	**146.4**	**129.4**	**127.9**	**157.6**	**152.5**
Public and publicly guaranteed	25.0	86.2	84.9	78.5	124.6	146.4	129.4	127.9	157.6	152.5
Private nonguaranteed	0.0	0.0	0.0	0.0	0.0	0.0	0.0	0.0	0.0	0.0
Use of IMF credit	**0.0**	**0.0**	**0.0**	**0.0**	**0.0**	**0.0**	**0.0**	**0.0**	**0.0**	**0.0**
Short-term debt	..	**22.0**	**285.0**	**331.0**	**476.0**	**470.0**	**473.9**	**618.2**	**649.0**	**802.4**
of which interest arrears on LDOD	..	0.0	0.0	0.0	0.0	0.0	0.0	0.0	0.0	0.0
Official creditors	..	0.0	0.0	0.0	0.0	0.0	0.0	0.0	0.0	0.0
Private creditors	..	0.0	0.0	0.0	0.0	0.0	0.0	0.0	0.0	0.0
Memo: principal arrears on LDOD	..	0.0	0.0	0.0	0.0	5.8	0.9	0.0	0.0	0.0
Official creditors	..	0.0	0.0	0.0	0.0	5.8	0.9	0.0	0.0	0.0
Private creditors	..	0.0	0.0	0.0	0.0	0.0	0.0	0.0	0.0	0.0
Memo: export credits	..	..	48.0	44.0	70.0	103.0	119.0	170.0	181.0	197.0
TOTAL DEBT FLOWS										
Disbursements	**0.0**	**6.7**	**14.6**	**1.5**	**46.4**	**28.2**	**2.8**	**8.0**	**35.6**	**25.3**
Long-term debt	0.0	6.7	14.6	1.5	46.4	28.2	2.8	8.0	35.6	25.3
IMF purchases	0.0	0.0	0.0	0.0	0.0	0.0	0.0	0.0	0.0	0.0
Principal repayments	**0.7**	**1.8**	**7.3**	**7.3**	**6.6**	**7.6**	**15.4**	**8.9**	**12.2**	**32.4**
Long-term debt	0.7	1.8	7.3	7.3	6.6	7.6	15.4	8.9	12.2	32.4
IMF repurchases	0.0	0.0	0.0	0.0	0.0	0.0	0.0	0.0	0.0	0.0
Net flows on debt	**-0.7**	**4.9**	**110.0**	**40.2**	**184.8**	**14.7**	**-8.7**	**143.4**	**54.3**	**146.4**
of which short-term debt	..	..	102.7	46.0	145.0	-6.0	3.9	144.3	30.8	153.4
Interest payments (INT)	..	**5.2**	**21.1**	**27.9**	**39.4**	**37.2**	**37.9**	**31.1**	**33.9**	**42.2**
Long-term debt	1.7	1.3	2.0	2.0	2.3	4.2	4.8	5.0	5.0	5.9
IMF charges	0.0	0.0	0.0	0.0	0.0	0.0	0.0	0.0	0.0	0.0
Short-term debt	..	3.9	19.1	25.9	37.1	33.0	33.1	26.2	28.9	36.3
Net transfers on debt	..	**-0.3**	**88.9**	**12.4**	**145.4**	**-22.5**	**-46.5**	**112.3**	**20.3**	**104.2**
Total debt service paid (TDS)	..	**7.0**	**28.4**	**35.2**	**46.0**	**44.7**	**53.2**	**40.0**	**46.1**	**74.6**
Long-term debt	2.4	3.1	9.3	9.3	8.9	11.7	20.1	13.8	17.2	38.3
IMF repurchases and charges	0.0	0.0	0.0	0.0	0.0	0.0	0.0	0.0	0.0	0.0
Short-term debt (interest only)	..	3.9	19.1	25.9	37.1	33.0	33.1	26.2	28.9	36.3
2. AGGREGATE NET RESOURCE FLOWS AND NET TRANSFERS (LONG-TERM)										
NET RESOURCE FLOWS	**29.9**	**42.6**	**48.1**	**47.0**	**87.5**	**103.1**	**36.1**	**75.3**	**167.1**	**103.5**
Net flow of long-term debt (ex. IMF)	-0.7	4.9	7.3	-5.8	39.8	20.7	-12.6	-0.9	23.5	-7.0
Foreign direct investment (net)	11.6	26.6	40.8	51.7	46.0	77.0	40.0	56.0	120.0	98.0
Portfolio equity flows	0.0	0.0	0.0	0.0	0.0	0.0	0.0	0.0	0.0	0.0
Grants (excluding technical coop.)	19.0	11.1	0.0	1.1	1.7	5.4	8.7	20.2	23.6	12.5
Memo: technical coop. grants	0.8	2.7	2.7	3.1	3.9	2.7	2.4	5.8	1.4	1.8
NET TRANSFERS	**21.7**	**-3.3**	**13.5**	**5.8**	**52.8**	**66.5**	**-0.9**	**35.3**	**124.0**	**62.6**
Interest on long-term debt	1.7	1.3	2.0	2.0	2.3	4.2	4.8	5.0	5.0	5.9
Profit remittances on FDI	6.5	44.6	32.6	39.3	32.4	32.4	32.3	35.0	38.0	35.0
3. MAJOR ECONOMIC AGGREGATES										
Gross national product (GNP)	245.0	1,223.2	1,918.6	2,025.6	2,485.6	2,650.0	2,868.6	2,557.1	..	..
Exports of goods & services (XGS)	..	1,194.2	1,616.7	1,766.8	2,235.2	2,402.0	2,730.0	2,519.9	2,770.6	3,197.9
of which workers remittances	..	22.3	26.9	40.5	37.2	15.5	3.0	1.3	5.3	6.6
Imports of goods & services (MGS)	..	1,185.2	1,688.0	1,834.2	2,326.6	2,496.2	2,786.3	2,644.7	2,995.6	3,646.9
International reserves (RES)	158.6	1,246.0	1,555.9	1,445.8	1,492.2	1,374.7	1,308.3	1,401.7	1,890.0	1,620.3
Current account balance	..	38.8	61.1	-9.5	-41.1	5.9	34.5	-65.2	-136.2	-405.6
4. DEBT INDICATORS										
EDT / XGS (%)	..	9.1	22.9	23.2	26.9	25.7	22.1	29.6	29.1	29.9
EDT / GNP (%)	..	8.8	19.3	20.2	24.2	23.3	21.0	29.2	..	..
TDS / XGS (%)	..	0.6	1.8	2.0	2.1	1.9	1.9	1.6	1.7	2.3
INT / XGS (%)	..	0.4	1.3	1.6	1.8	1.5	1.4	1.2	1.2	1.3
INT / GNP (%)	..	0.4	1.1	1.4	1.6	1.4	1.3	1.2	..	..
RES / EDT (%)	..	1,151.1	420.7	353.1	248.4	223.0	216.8	187.9	234.3	169.7
RES / MGS (months)	..	12.6	11.1	9.5	7.7	6.6	5.6	6.4	7.6	5.3
Short-term / EDT (%)	..	20.3	77.1	80.8	79.3	76.2	78.5	82.9	80.5	84.0
Concessional / EDT (%)	..	74.8	22.7	18.9	18.0	18.1	15.8	12.7	14.4	12.0
Multilateral / EDT (%)	..	5.8	1.7	1.7	3.9	6.8	6.9	5.5	7.0	3.6

MALTA

(US$ million, unless otherwise indicated)

	1970	1980	1988	1989	1990	1991	1992	1993	1994	1995
5. LONG-TERM DEBT										
DEBT OUTSTANDING (LDOD)	**25.0**	**86.2**	**84.9**	**78.5**	**124.6**	**146.4**	**129.4**	**127.9**	**157.6**	**152.5**
Public and publicly guaranteed	**25.0**	**86.2**	**84.9**	**78.5**	**124.6**	**146.4**	**129.4**	**127.9**	**157.6**	**152.5**
Official creditors	25.0	85.3	84.9	78.5	124.6	146.4	129.4	127.9	157.6	132.4
Multilateral	4.6	6.3	6.2	7.1	23.2	42.2	41.9	40.8	56.6	34.8
Concessional	4.6	6.3	6.2	6.4	7.1	7.4	8.1	7.3	15.0	16.7
Bilateral	20.4	79.0	78.6	71.4	101.4	104.2	87.5	87.1	101.0	97.6
Concessional	7.2	74.7	77.7	70.9	101.1	104.0	87.5	87.1	101.0	97.6
Private creditors	0.0	1.0	0.0	0.0	0.0	0.0	0.0	0.0	0.0	20.1
Bonds	0.0	0.0	0.0	0.0	0.0	0.0	0.0	0.0	0.0	0.0
Commercial banks	0.0	1.0	0.0	0.0	0.0	0.0	0.0	0.0	0.0	20.1
Other private	0.0	0.0	0.0	0.0	0.0	0.0	0.0	0.0	0.0	0.0
Private nonguaranteed	**0.0**	**0.0**	**0.0**	**0.0**	**0.0**	**0.0**	**0.0**	**0.0**	**0.0**	**0.0**
Bonds	0.0	0.0	0.0	0.0	0.0	0.0	0.0	0.0	0.0	0.0
Commercial banks	0.0	0.0	0.0	0.0	0.0	0.0	0.0	0.0	0.0	0.0
Memo:										
IBRD	4.6	0.3	0.0	0.0	0.0	0.0	0.0	0.0	0.0	0.0
IDA	0.0	0.0	0.0	0.0	0.0	0.0	0.0	0.0	0.0	0.0
DISBURSEMENTS	**0.0**	**6.7**	**14.6**	**1.5**	**46.4**	**28.2**	**2.8**	**8.0**	**35.6**	**25.3**
Public and publicly guaranteed	**0.0**	**6.7**	**14.6**	**1.5**	**46.4**	**28.2**	**2.8**	**8.0**	**35.6**	**25.3**
Official creditors	0.0	6.7	14.6	1.5	46.4	28.2	2.8	8.0	35.6	1.7
Multilateral	0.0	2.2	14.6	1.2	14.2	17.4	2.8	0.0	13.7	0.8
Concessional	0.0	2.2	0.0	0.5	0.0	0.6	1.7	0.0	6.9	0.8
Bilateral	0.0	4.5	0.0	0.3	32.2	10.9	0.0	8.0	21.9	0.9
Concessional	0.0	4.5	0.0	0.3	32.2	10.9	0.0	8.0	21.9	0.9
Private creditors	0.0	0.0	0.0	0.0	0.0	0.0	0.0	0.0	0.0	23.6
Bonds	0.0	0.0	0.0	0.0	0.0	0.0	0.0	0.0	0.0	0.0
Commercial banks	0.0	0.0	0.0	0.0	0.0	0.0	0.0	0.0	0.0	23.6
Other private	0.0	0.0	0.0	0.0	0.0	0.0	0.0	0.0	0.0	0.0
Private nonguaranteed	**0.0**	**0.0**	**0.0**	**0.0**	**0.0**	**0.0**	**0.0**	**0.0**	**0.0**	**0.0**
Bonds	0.0	0.0	0.0	0.0	0.0	0.0	0.0	0.0	0.0	0.0
Commercial banks	0.0	0.0	0.0	0.0	0.0	0.0	0.0	0.0	0.0	0.0
Memo:										
IBRD	0.0	0.0	0.0	0.0	0.0	0.0	0.0	0.0	0.0	0.0
IDA	0.0	0.0	0.0	0.0	0.0	0.0	0.0	0.0	0.0	0.0
PRINCIPAL REPAYMENTS	**0.7**	**1.8**	**7.3**	**7.3**	**6.6**	**7.6**	**15.4**	**8.9**	**12.2**	**32.4**
Public and publicly guaranteed	**0.7**	**1.8**	**7.3**	**7.3**	**6.6**	**7.6**	**15.4**	**8.9**	**12.2**	**32.4**
Official creditors	0.7	1.6	7.3	7.3	6.6	7.6	15.4	8.9	12.2	30.9
Multilateral	0.3	0.4	0.7	0.5	0.2	0.2	0.9	2.1	2.7	24.8
Concessional	0.3	0.4	0.7	0.5	0.2	0.2	0.2	0.2	0.2	0.2
Bilateral	0.4	1.2	6.6	6.8	6.4	7.4	14.5	6.8	9.4	6.1
Concessional	0.1	0.9	6.2	6.5	6.1	7.2	14.4	6.8	9.4	6.1
Private creditors	0.0	0.2	0.0	0.0	0.0	0.0	0.0	0.0	0.0	1.5
Bonds	0.0	0.0	0.0	0.0	0.0	0.0	0.0	0.0	0.0	0.0
Commercial banks	0.0	0.2	0.0	0.0	0.0	0.0	0.0	0.0	0.0	1.5
Other private	0.0	0.0	0.0	0.0	0.0	0.0	0.0	0.0	0.0	0.0
Private nonguaranteed	**0.0**	**0.0**	**0.0**	**0.0**	**0.0**	**0.0**	**0.0**	**0.0**	**0.0**	**0.0**
Bonds	0.0	0.0	0.0	0.0	0.0	0.0	0.0	0.0	0.0	0.0
Commercial banks	0.0	0.0	0.0	0.0	0.0	0.0	0.0	0.0	0.0	0.0
Memo:										
IBRD	0.3	0.4	0.0	0.0	0.0	0.0	0.0	0.0	0.0	0.0
IDA	0.0	0.0	0.0	0.0	0.0	0.0	0.0	0.0	0.0	0.0
NET FLOWS ON DEBT	**-0.7**	**4.9**	**7.3**	**-5.8**	**39.8**	**20.7**	**-12.6**	**-0.9**	**23.5**	**-7.0**
Public and publicly guaranteed	**-0.7**	**4.9**	**7.3**	**-5.8**	**39.8**	**20.7**	**-12.6**	**-0.9**	**23.5**	**-7.0**
Official creditors	-0.7	5.0	7.3	-5.8	39.8	20.7	-12.6	-0.9	23.5	-29.2
Multilateral	-0.3	1.7	13.8	0.7	14.1	17.2	1.9	-2.1	11.0	-23.9
Concessional	-0.3	1.7	-0.7	0.1	-0.2	0.4	1.5	-0.2	6.8	0.6
Bilateral	-0.4	3.3	-6.6	-6.5	25.8	3.5	-14.5	1.2	12.5	-5.2
Concessional	-0.1	3.6	-6.2	-6.1	26.0	3.7	-14.4	1.2	12.5	-5.2
Private creditors	0.0	-0.2	0.0	0.0	0.0	0.0	0.0	0.0	0.0	22.2
Bonds	0.0	0.0	0.0	0.0	0.0	0.0	0.0	0.0	0.0	0.0
Commercial banks	0.0	-0.2	0.0	0.0	0.0	0.0	0.0	0.0	0.0	22.2
Other private	0.0	0.0	0.0	0.0	0.0	0.0	0.0	0.0	0.0	0.0
Private nonguaranteed	**0.0**	**0.0**	**0.0**	**0.0**	**0.0**	**0.0**	**0.0**	**0.0**	**0.0**	**0.0**
Bonds	0.0	0.0	0.0	0.0	0.0	0.0	0.0	0.0	0.0	0.0
Commercial banks	0.0	0.0	0.0	0.0	0.0	0.0	0.0	0.0	0.0	0.0
Memo:										
IBRD	-0.3	-0.4	0.0	0.0	0.0	0.0	0.0	0.0	0.0	0.0
IDA	0.0	0.0	0.0	0.0	0.0	0.0	0.0	0.0	0.0	0.0

MALTA

(US$ million, unless otherwise indicated)

	1970	1980	1988	1989	1990	1991	1992	1993	1994	1995
INTEREST PAYMENTS (LINT)	**1.7**	**1.3**	**2.0**	**2.0**	**2.3**	**4.2**	**4.8**	**5.0**	**5.0**	**5.9**
Public and publicly guaranteed	**1.7**	**1.3**	**2.0**	**2.0**	**2.3**	**4.2**	**4.8**	**5.0**	**5.0**	**5.9**
Official creditors	1.7	1.2	2.0	2.0	2.3	4.2	4.8	5.0	5.0	5.5
Multilateral	0.3	0.2	0.1	0.1	0.1	1.7	2.2	2.6	2.6	2.7
Concessional	0.3	0.2	0.1	0.1	0.1	0.1	0.1	0.1	0.1	0.4
Bilateral	1.5	1.1	1.9	1.9	2.2	2.5	2.5	2.3	2.4	2.7
Concessional	0.4	0.8	1.8	1.8	2.2	2.5	2.5	2.3	2.4	2.7
Private creditors	0.0	0.0	0.0	0.0	0.0	0.0	0.0	0.0	0.0	0.4
Bonds	0.0	0.0	0.0	0.0	0.0	0.0	0.0	0.0	0.0	0.0
Commercial banks	0.0	0.0	0.0	0.0	0.0	0.0	0.0	0.0	0.0	0.4
Other private	0.0	0.0	0.0	0.0	0.0	0.0	0.0	0.0	0.0	0.0
Private nonguaranteed	**0.0**	**0.0**	**0.0**	**0.0**	**0.0**	**0.0**	**0.0**	**0.0**	**0.0**	**0.0**
Bonds	0.0	0.0	0.0	0.0	0.0	0.0	0.0	0.0	0.0	0.0
Commercial banks	0.0	0.0	0.0	0.0	0.0	0.0	0.0	0.0	0.0	0.0
Memo:										
IBRD	0.3	0.0	0.0	0.0	0.0	0.0	0.0	0.0	0.0	0.0
IDA	0.0	0.0	0.0	0.0	0.0	0.0	0.0	0.0	0.0	0.0
NET TRANSFERS ON DEBT	**-2.4**	**3.6**	**5.3**	**-7.7**	**37.5**	**16.5**	**-17.3**	**-5.9**	**18.4**	**-12.9**
Public and publicly guaranteed	**-2.4**	**3.6**	**5.3**	**-7.7**	**37.5**	**16.5**	**-17.3**	**-5.9**	**18.4**	**-12.9**
Official creditors	-2.4	3.8	5.3	-7.7	37.5	16.5	-17.3	-5.9	18.4	-34.7
Multilateral	-0.6	1.6	13.8	0.7	14.0	15.6	-0.3	-4.7	8.4	-26.7
Concessional	-0.6	1.6	-0.8	0.0	-0.3	0.3	1.4	-0.3	6.7	0.2
Bilateral	-1.9	2.2	-8.5	-8.4	23.5	0.9	-17.0	-1.2	10.1	-8.0
Concessional	-0.5	2.8	-8.0	-8.0	23.8	1.2	-16.9	-1.2	10.1	-8.0
Private creditors	0.0	-0.2	0.0	0.0	0.0	0.0	0.0	0.0	0.0	21.7
Bonds	0.0	0.0	0.0	0.0	0.0	0.0	0.0	0.0	0.0	0.0
Commercial banks	0.0	-0.2	0.0	0.0	0.0	0.0	0.0	0.0	0.0	21.7
Other private	0.0	0.0	0.0	0.0	0.0	0.0	0.0	0.0	0.0	0.0
Private nonguaranteed	**0.0**	**0.0**	**0.0**	**0.0**	**0.0**	**0.0**	**0.0**	**0.0**	**0.0**	**0.0**
Bonds	0.0	0.0	0.0	0.0	0.0	0.0	0.0	0.0	0.0	0.0
Commercial banks	0.0	0.0	0.0	0.0	0.0	0.0	0.0	0.0	0.0	0.0
Memo:										
IBRD	-0.6	-0.5	0.0	0.0	0.0	0.0	0.0	0.0	0.0	0.0
IDA	0.0	0.0	0.0	0.0	0.0	0.0	0.0	0.0	0.0	0.0
DEBT SERVICE (LTDS)	**2.4**	**3.1**	**9.3**	**9.3**	**8.9**	**11.7**	**20.1**	**13.8**	**17.2**	**38.3**
Public and publicly guaranteed	**2.4**	**3.1**	**9.3**	**9.3**	**8.9**	**11.7**	**20.1**	**13.8**	**17.2**	**38.3**
Official creditors	2.4	2.9	9.3	9.3	8.9	11.7	20.1	13.8	17.2	36.4
Multilateral	0.6	0.6	0.8	0.5	0.3	1.8	3.1	4.7	5.4	27.5
Concessional	0.6	0.6	0.8	0.5	0.3	0.2	0.3	0.3	0.3	0.6
Bilateral	1.9	2.3	8.5	8.7	8.6	9.9	17.0	9.1	11.8	8.9
Concessional	0.5	1.7	8.0	8.3	8.4	9.7	16.9	9.1	11.8	8.9
Private creditors	0.0	0.2	0.0	0.0	0.0	0.0	0.0	0.0	0.0	1.9
Bonds	0.0	0.0	0.0	0.0	0.0	0.0	0.0	0.0	0.0	0.0
Commercial banks	0.0	0.2	0.0	0.0	0.0	0.0	0.0	0.0	0.0	1.9
Other private	0.0	0.0	0.0	0.0	0.0	0.0	0.0	0.0	0.0	0.0
Private nonguaranteed	**0.0**	**0.0**	**0.0**	**0.0**	**0.0**	**0.0**	**0.0**	**0.0**	**0.0**	**0.0**
Bonds	0.0	0.0	0.0	0.0	0.0	0.0	0.0	0.0	0.0	0.0
Commercial banks	0.0	0.0	0.0	0.0	0.0	0.0	0.0	0.0	0.0	0.0
Memo:										
IBRD	0.6	0.5	0.0	0.0	0.0	0.0	0.0	0.0	0.0	0.0
IDA	0.0	0.0	0.0	0.0	0.0	0.0	0.0	0.0	0.0	0.0
UNDISBURSED DEBT	**6.7**	**37.0**	**36.3**	**64.9**	**33.3**	**3.9**	**0.9**	**29.6**	**2.5**	**0.9**
Official creditors	6.7	37.0	36.3	64.9	33.3	3.9	0.9	29.6	2.5	0.9
Private creditors	0.0	0.0	0.0	0.0	0.0	0.0	0.0	0.0	0.0	0.0
Memorandum items										
Concessional LDOD	11.8	81.0	83.9	77.3	108.2	111.4	95.6	94.4	116.0	114.3
Variable rate LDOD	0.0	0.0	0.0	0.0	0.0	0.0	0.0	0.0	0.0	0.0
Public sector LDOD	25.0	86.2	84.9	78.5	124.6	146.4	129.4	127.9	157.6	152.5
Private sector LDOD	0.0	0.0	0.0	0.0	0.0	0.0	0.0	0.0	0.0	0.0

6. CURRENCY COMPOSITION OF LONG-TERM DEBT (PERCENT)

	1970	1980	1988	1989	1990	1991	1992	1993	1994	1995
Deutsche mark	0.0	23.2	18.0	19.2	12.9	11.1	11.0	9.7	8.1	8.0
French franc	0.0	3.4	1.2	1.1	0.6	0.5	0.4	0.2	0.1	0.1
Japanese yen	0.0	0.0	0.0	0.0	9.2	13.3	14.8	15.6	13.2	16.3
Pound sterling	62.5	6.6	1.2	0.6	1.2	1.6	1.5	1.5	1.2	1.1
Swiss franc	0.0	4.5	0.5	0.0	0.0	4.3	4.3	4.1	3.4	0.0
U.S.dollars	0.0	10.8	23.8	23.3	33.9	31.9	34.7	33.8	30.8	30.9
Multiple currency	18.4	0.3	0.0	0.9	2.8	2.4	2.9	2.7	2.2	1.9
Special drawing rights	0.0	0.0	0.0	0.0	0.0	0.0	0.0	0.0	0.0	0.0
All other currencies	19.2	51.1	55.5	54.7	39.4	35.0	30.3	32.4	41.0	41.6

MALTA

(US$ million, unless otherwise indicated)

	1970	1980	1988	1989	1990	1991	1992	1993	1994	1995
7. DEBT RESTRUCTURINGS										
Total amount rescheduled	0.0	0.0	0.0	0.0	0.0	0.0	0.0	0.0	0.0	0.0
Debt stock rescheduled	0.0	0.0	0.0	0.0	0.0	0.0	0.0	0.0	0.0	0.0
Principal rescheduled	0.0	0.0	0.0	0.0	0.0	0.0	0.0	0.0	0.0	0.0
Official	0.0	0.0	0.0	0.0	0.0	0.0	0.0	0.0	0.0	0.0
Private	0.0	0.0	0.0	0.0	0.0	0.0	0.0	0.0	0.0	0.0
Interest rescheduled	0.0	0.0	0.0	0.0	0.0	0.0	0.0	0.0	0.0	0.0
Official	0.0	0.0	0.0	0.0	0.0	0.0	0.0	0.0	0.0	0.0
Private	0.0	0.0	0.0	0.0	0.0	0.0	0.0	0.0	0.0	0.0
Debt forgiven	..	..	0.0	0.0	0.0	0.0	0.0	0.0	0.0	0.0
Memo: interest forgiven	..	..	0.0	0.0	0.0	0.0	0.0	0.0	0.0	0.0
Debt stock reduction	0.0	0.0	0.0	0.0	0.0	0.0	0.0	0.0	0.0	0.0
of which debt buyback	0.0	0.0	0.0	0.0	0.0	0.0	0.0	0.0	0.0	0.0
8. DEBT STOCK-FLOW RECONCILIATION										
Total change in debt stocks	..	..	..	39.7	191.1	15.8	-13.1	142.8	60.5	148.3
Net flows on debt	..	..	..	40.2	184.8	14.7	-8.7	143.4	54.3	146.4
Net change in interest arrears	..	..	..	0.0	0.0	0.0	0.0	0.0	0.0	0.0
Interest capitalized	..	..	..	0.0	0.0	0.0	0.0	0.0	0.0	0.0
Debt forgiveness or reduction	..	..	..	0.0	0.0	0.0	0.0	0.0	0.0	0.0
Cross-currency valuation	..	..	..	0.9	4.3	0.7	-2.5	-0.3	7.8	2.3
Residual	..	..	..	-1.5	2.0	0.4	-1.9	-0.3	-1.6	-0.4
9. AVERAGE TERMS OF NEW COMMITMENTS										
ALL CREDITORS										
Interest (%)	9.1	0.0	7.0	2.5	7.5	0.0	0.0	2.9	8.4	3.7
Maturity (years)	25.6	22.0	14.9	20.0	14.9	0.0	0.0	19.4	12.0	8.0
Grace period (years)	1.6	11.5	4.4	6.5	3.4	0.0	0.0	5.4	6.0	0.5
Grant element (%)	5.7	78.8	16.8	51.8	13.3	0.0	0.0	47.8	7.9	19.8
Official creditors										
Interest (%)	9.1	0.0	7.0	2.5	7.5	0.0	0.0	2.9	8.4	0.0
Maturity (years)	25.6	22.0	14.9	20.0	14.9	0.0	0.0	19.4	12.0	0.0
Grace period (years)	1.6	11.5	4.4	6.5	3.4	0.0	0.0	5.4	6.0	0.0
Grant element (%)	5.7	78.8	16.8	51.8	13.3	0.0	0.0	47.8	7.9	0.0
Private creditors										
Interest (%)	0.0	0.0	0.0	0.0	0.0	0.0	0.0	0.0	0.0	3.7
Maturity (years)	0.0	0.0	0.0	0.0	0.0	0.0	0.0	0.0	0.0	8.0
Grace period (years)	0.0	0.0	0.0	0.0	0.0	0.0	0.0	0.0	0.0	0.5
Grant element (%)	0.0	0.0	0.0	0.0	0.0	0.0	0.0	0.0	0.0	19.8
Memorandum items										
Commitments	7.6	3.7	21.5	32.2	12.5	0.0	0.0	38.9	6.8	23.6
Official creditors	7.6	3.7	21.5	32.2	12.5	0.0	0.0	38.9	6.8	0.0
Private creditors	0.0	0.0	0.0	0.0	0.0	0.0	0.0	0.0	0.0	23.6

10. CONTRACTUAL OBLIGATIONS ON OUTSTANDING LONG-TERM DEBT

	1996	1997	1998	1999	2000	2001	2002	2003	2004	2005
TOTAL										
Disbursements	0.2	0.1	0.0	0.0	0.0	0.0	0.0	0.0	0.0	0.0
Principal	12.2	11.6	10.9	10.8	13.1	13.8	13.5	11.0	9.7	8.9
Interest	4.2	3.8	3.4	3.1	2.7	2.3	1.8	1.4	1.1	0.7
Official creditors										
Disbursements	0.2	0.1	0.0	0.0	0.0	0.0	0.0	0.0	0.0	0.0
Principal	9.5	8.9	8.2	8.1	10.4	11.1	10.9	9.7	9.7	8.9
Interest	3.5	3.2	2.9	2.7	2.4	2.1	1.7	1.4	1.1	0.7
Bilateral creditors										
Disbursements	0.0	0.0	0.0	0.0	0.0	0.0	0.0	0.0	0.0	0.0
Principal	8.4	7.8	6.5	6.0	7.7	7.7	7.4	6.1	5.9	5.9
Interest	1.6	1.4	1.2	1.1	0.9	0.8	0.6	0.5	0.5	0.4
Multilateral creditors										
Disbursements	0.2	0.1	0.0	0.0	0.0	0.0	0.0	0.0	0.0	0.0
Principal	1.1	1.1	1.7	2.2	2.8	3.4	3.5	3.6	3.7	3.0
Interest	1.8	1.8	1.7	1.6	1.5	1.3	1.1	0.8	0.6	0.4
Private creditors										
Disbursements	0.0	0.0	0.0	0.0	0.0	0.0	0.0	0.0	0.0	0.0
Principal	2.7	2.7	2.7	2.7	2.7	2.7	2.7	1.4	0.0	0.0
Interest	0.7	0.6	0.5	0.4	0.3	0.2	0.1	0.0	0.0	0.0
Commercial banks										
Disbursements	0.0	0.0	0.0	0.0	0.0	0.0	0.0	0.0	0.0	0.0
Principal	2.7	2.7	2.7	2.7	2.7	2.7	2.7	1.4	0.0	0.0
Interest	0.7	0.6	0.5	0.4	0.3	0.2	0.1	0.0	0.0	0.0
Other private										
Disbursements	0.0	0.0	0.0	0.0	0.0	0.0	0.0	0.0	0.0	0.0
Principal	0.0	0.0	0.0	0.0	0.0	0.0	0.0	0.0	0.0	0.0
Interest	0.0	0.0	0.0	0.0	0.0	0.0	0.0	0.0	0.0	0.0

MAURITANIA

(US$ million, unless otherwise indicated)

	1970	1980	1988	1989	1990	1991	1992	1993	1994	1995
1. SUMMARY DEBT DATA										
TOTAL DEBT STOCKS (EDT)	..	**843**	**2,082**	**2,004**	**2,141**	**2,233**	**2,134**	**2,174**	**2,329**	**2,467**
Long-term debt (LDOD)	**26**	**717**	**1,831**	**1,764**	**1,826**	**1,857**	**1,863**	**1,932**	**2,086**	**2,184**
Public and publicly guaranteed	26	717	1,831	1,764	1,826	1,857	1,863	1,932	2,086	2,184
Private nonguaranteed	0	0	0	0	0	0	0	0	0	0
Use of IMF credit	**0**	**62**	**71**	**69**	**70**	**57**	**58**	**63**	**86**	**100**
Short-term debt	..	**65**	**180**	**171**	**245**	**320**	**213**	**178**	**157**	**184**
of which interest arrears on LDOD	..	10	52	50	71	96	121	98	81	94
Official creditors	..	9	49	46	64	84	108	97	79	92
Private creditors	..	1	4	4	7	11	14	2	2	2
Memo: principal arrears on LDOD	..	44	99	140	175	259	410	289	290	285
Official creditors	..	24	81	129	154	222	358	285	285	280
Private creditors	..	21	18	11	21	37	52	4	5	5
Memo: export credits	..	..	180	179	230	217	196	187	154	171
TOTAL DEBT FLOWS										
Disbursements	**5**	**156**	**154**	**99**	**148**	**71**	**145**	**169**	**163**	**133**
Long-term debt	5	126	148	88	137	71	133	157	139	111
IMF purchases	0	30	5	11	12	0	12	12	24	22
Principal repayments	**3**	**26**	**89**	**66**	**103**	**62**	**61**	**82**	**64**	**78**
Long-term debt	3	17	80	55	87	48	53	76	58	69
IMF repurchases	0	9	9	11	16	13	8	6	6	9
Net flows on debt	**1**	**130**	**102**	**27**	**98**	**60**	**-49**	**75**	**96**	**69**
of which short-term debt	..	..	37	-6	53	51	-133	-12	-4	14
Interest payments (INT)	..	**22**	**44**	**38**	**47**	**36**	**26**	**47**	**42**	**38**
Long-term debt	0	13	33	25	35	25	20	42	38	32
IMF charges	0	2	3	4	3	2	1	0	0	1
Short-term debt	..	7	9	8	9	10	6	4	4	5
Net transfers on debt	..	**108**	**57**	**-11**	**50**	**24**	**-74**	**28**	**54**	**31**
Total debt service paid (TDS)	..	**48**	**134**	**104**	**150**	**98**	**87**	**129**	**106**	**116**
Long-term debt	4	30	112	80	122	74	72	118	95	101
IMF repurchases and charges	0	11	13	15	19	15	9	7	6	10
Short-term debt (interest only)	..	7	9	8	9	10	6	4	4	5
2. AGGREGATE NET RESOURCE FLOWS AND NET TRANSFERS (LONG-TERM)										
NET RESOURCE FLOWS	**5**	**198**	**156**	**192**	**134**	**139**	**195**	**270**	**210**	**181**
Net flow of long-term debt (ex. IMF)	1	109	69	33	49	23	81	81	82	43
Foreign direct investment (net)	1	27	2	4	7	2	8	16	2	3
Portfolio equity flows	0	0	0	0	0	0	0	0	0	0
Grants (excluding technical coop.)	3	61	86	155	78	114	106	173	127	135
Memo: technical coop. grants	4	29	48	47	53	48	54	57	46	51
NET TRANSFERS	**-8**	**162**	**90**	**154**	**98**	**114**	**174**	**225**	**169**	**146**
Interest on long-term debt	0	13	33	25	35	25	20	42	38	32
Profit remittances on FDI	13	23	34	13	1	1	2	3	3	3
3. MAJOR ECONOMIC AGGREGATES										
Gross national product (GNP)	196	672	886	921	961	1,069	1,124	875	973	1,014
Exports of goods & services (XGS)	..	275	486	492	488	481	478	428	432	538
of which workers remittances	..	6	9	5	14	12	50	2	5	5
Imports of goods & services (MGS)	..	493	656	601	570	585	670	683	581	636
International reserves (RES)	3	146	60	87	59	72	65	49	44	90
Current account balance	..	-134	-96	-19	-10	-30	-118	-174	-70	-27
4. DEBT INDICATORS										
EDT / XGS (%)	..	306.1	428.1	407.5	438.6	464.6	446.3	508.5	539.7	458.5
EDT / GNP (%)	..	125.5	235.1	217.6	222.9	208.9	189.8	248.4	239.4	243.3
TDS / XGS (%)	..	17.3	27.5	21.1	30.8	20.4	18.1	30.1	24.4	21.5
INT / XGS (%)	..	7.9	9.1	7.6	9.7	7.6	5.4	10.9	9.7	7.1
INT / GNP (%)	..	3.2	5.0	4.1	4.9	3.4	2.3	5.3	4.3	3.7
RES / EDT (%)	..	17.4	2.9	4.3	2.7	3.2	3.0	2.3	1.9	3.6
RES / MGS (months)	..	3.6	1.1	1.7	1.2	1.5	1.2	0.9	0.9	1.7
Short-term / EDT (%)	..	7.7	8.6	8.6	11.4	14.3	10.0	8.2	6.7	7.4
Concessional / EDT (%)	..	60.9	62.1	63.2	61.9	61.8	65.2	72.6	74.5	74.6
Multilateral / EDT (%)	..	14.8	26.0	28.4	30.6	30.3	33.3	33.3	35.9	36.8

MAURITANIA

(US$ million, unless otherwise indicated)

	1970	1980	1988	1989	1990	1991	1992	1993	1994	1995
5. LONG-TERM DEBT										
DEBT OUTSTANDING (LDOD)	**26**	**717**	**1,831**	**1,764**	**1,826**	**1,857**	**1,863**	**1,932**	**2,086**	**2,184**
Public and publicly guaranteed	**26**	**717**	**1,831**	**1,764**	**1,826**	**1,857**	**1,863**	**1,932**	**2,086**	**2,184**
Official creditors	18	586	1,710	1,671	1,730	1,763	1,775	1,913	2,078	2,175
Multilateral	6	125	541	570	654	678	711	725	837	908
Concessional	6	106	374	423	510	550	571	601	706	779
Bilateral	13	462	1,169	1,101	1,075	1,085	1,064	1,189	1,241	1,267
Concessional	8	407	918	844	816	830	821	977	1,029	1,060
Private creditors	8	131	122	93	97	94	88	19	9	8
Bonds	0	0	0	0	0	0	0	0	0	0
Commercial banks	0	16	6	0	0	0	0	0	0	0
Other private	8	115	116	93	97	94	88	19	9	8
Private nonguaranteed	**0**	**0**	**0**	**0**	**0**	**0**	**0**	**0**	**0**	**0**
Bonds	0	0	0	0	0	0	0	0	0	0
Commercial banks	0	0	0	0	0	0	0	0	0	0
Memo:										
IBRD	0	0	74	61	54	43	30	19	13	11
IDA	5	38	151	160	210	224	229	256	301	336
DISBURSEMENTS	**5**	**126**	**148**	**88**	**137**	**71**	**133**	**157**	**139**	**111**
Public and publicly guaranteed	**5**	**126**	**148**	**88**	**137**	**71**	**133**	**157**	**139**	**111**
Official creditors	4	113	147	86	136	71	133	157	139	111
Multilateral	2	27	103	68	112	54	110	87	117	88
Concessional	2	12	68	66	76	50	68	71	96	79
Bilateral	2	86	44	19	24	17	24	70	22	23
Concessional	2	84	44	19	24	17	24	70	22	23
Private creditors	1	14	2	2	0	0	0	0	0	0
Bonds	0	0	0	0	0	0	0	0	0	0
Commercial banks	0	0	0	0	0	0	0	0	0	0
Other private	1	14	2	2	0	0	0	0	0	0
Private nonguaranteed	**0**	**0**	**0**	**0**	**0**	**0**	**0**	**0**	**0**	**0**
Bonds	0	0	0	0	0	0	0	0	0	0
Commercial banks	0	0	0	0	0	0	0	0	0	0
Memo:										
IBRD	0	0	0	0	0	0	0	0	0	0
IDA	2	4	30	12	39	14	13	28	35	31
PRINCIPAL REPAYMENTS	**3**	**17**	**80**	**55**	**87**	**48**	**53**	**76**	**58**	**69**
Public and publicly guaranteed	**3**	**17**	**80**	**55**	**87**	**48**	**53**	**76**	**58**	**69**
Official creditors	1	4	79	49	86	46	51	76	58	69
Multilateral	0	2	54	28	66	37	44	59	42	35
Concessional	0	1	15	12	15	15	20	26	20	21
Bilateral	1	2	25	20	20	9	7	16	16	34
Concessional	1	2	22	13	15	6	6	16	16	19
Private creditors	2	13	1	6	1	2	2	0	0	0
Bonds	0	0	0	0	0	0	0	0	0	0
Commercial banks	0	5	0	6	0	0	0	0	0	0
Other private	2	9	1	1	1	2	2	0	0	0
Private nonguaranteed	**0**	**0**	**0**	**0**	**0**	**0**	**0**	**0**	**0**	**0**
Bonds	0	0	0	0	0	0	0	0	0	0
Commercial banks	0	0	0	0	0	0	0	0	0	0
Memo:										
IBRD	0	0	9	10	11	11	12	13	8	2
IDA	0	0	1	1	1	1	1	1	1	2
NET FLOWS ON DEBT	**1**	**109**	**69**	**33**	**49**	**23**	**81**	**81**	**82**	**43**
Public and publicly guaranteed	**1**	**109**	**69**	**33**	**49**	**23**	**81**	**81**	**82**	**43**
Official creditors	3	109	68	38	51	25	83	81	82	43
Multilateral	2	25	48	39	46	17	67	28	76	53
Concessional	2	12	53	54	61	34	48	45	77	58
Bilateral	1	84	20	-2	5	8	16	53	6	-10
Concessional	1	82	23	5	10	12	18	53	6	4
Private creditors	-2	0	1	-5	-1	-2	-2	0	0	0
Bonds	0	0	0	0	0	0	0	0	0	0
Commercial banks	0	-5	0	-6	0	0	0	0	0	0
Other private	-2	5	1	1	-1	-2	-2	0	0	0
Private nonguaranteed	**0**	**0**	**0**	**0**	**0**	**0**	**0**	**0**	**0**	**0**
Bonds	0	0	0	0	0	0	0	0	0	0
Commercial banks	0	0	0	0	0	0	0	0	0	0
Memo:										
IBRD	0	0	-9	-10	-11	-11	-12	-13	-8	-2
IDA	2	4	29	11	38	13	12	27	33	29

MAURITANIA

(US$ million, unless otherwise indicated)

	1970	1980	1988	1989	1990	1991	1992	1993	1994	1995
INTEREST PAYMENTS (LINT)	**0**	**13**	**33**	**25**	**35**	**25**	**20**	**42**	**38**	**32**
Public and publicly guaranteed	**0**	**13**	**33**	**25**	**35**	**25**	**20**	**42**	**38**	**32**
Official creditors	0	9	31	25	34	25	19	42	38	32
Multilateral	0	3	21	16	20	14	14	27	23	15
Concessional	0	2	6	7	7	7	7	11	14	10
Bilateral	0	6	10	9	14	11	6	16	15	17
Concessional	0	5	5	6	6	6	4	10	10	10
Private creditors	0	4	1	1	1	1	0	0	0	0
Bonds	0	0	0	0	0	0	0	0	0	0
Commercial banks	0	2	0	0	0	0	0	0	0	0
Other private	0	2	1	0	1	1	0	0	0	0
Private nonguaranteed	**0**	**0**	**0**	**0**	**0**	**0**	**0**	**0**	**0**	**0**
Bonds	0	0	0	0	0	0	0	0	0	0
Commercial banks	0	0	0	0	0	0	0	0	0	0
Memo:										
IBRD	0	0	7	5	5	4	3	2	1	1
IDA	0	0	1	1	1	2	2	2	2	2
NET TRANSFERS ON DEBT	**1**	**97**	**36**	**8**	**14**	**-2**	**61**	**39**	**44**	**10**
Public and publicly guaranteed	**1**	**97**	**36**	**8**	**14**	**-2**	**61**	**39**	**44**	**10**
Official creditors	3	100	37	13	16	1	64	39	44	11
Multilateral	2	23	27	23	26	4	53	1	53	38
Concessional	2	9	47	47	54	28	41	34	63	48
Bilateral	0	78	10	-10	-9	-3	11	38	-9	-28
Concessional	1	78	17	-1	4	6	14	43	-4	-6
Private creditors	-2	-4	-1	-5	-2	-3	-3	0	0	0
Bonds	0	0	0	0	0	0	0	0	0	0
Commercial banks	0	-7	0	-6	0	0	0	0	0	0
Other private	-2	3	-1	0	-2	-3	-3	0	0	0
Private nonguaranteed	**0**	**0**	**0**	**0**	**0**	**0**	**0**	**0**	**0**	**0**
Bonds	0	0	0	0	0	0	0	0	0	0
Commercial banks	0	0	0	0	0	0	0	0	0	0
Memo:										
IBRD	0	0	-16	-15	-16	-15	-15	-15	-9	-3
IDA	2	4	28	10	37	11	11	25	31	26
DEBT SERVICE (LTDS)	**4**	**30**	**112**	**80**	**122**	**74**	**72**	**118**	**95**	**101**
Public and publicly guaranteed	**4**	**30**	**112**	**80**	**122**	**74**	**72**	**118**	**95**	**101**
Official creditors	1	13	110	73	120	71	70	118	95	101
Multilateral	0	5	75	44	87	50	57	86	65	50
Concessional	0	3	21	19	22	22	27	37	33	31
Bilateral	1	8	35	29	34	20	13	32	31	51
Concessional	1	7	27	19	20	12	10	26	26	29
Private creditors	2	17	2	7	2	3	3	0	0	0
Bonds	0	0	0	0	0	0	0	0	0	0
Commercial banks	0	7	0	6	0	0	0	0	0	0
Other private	2	10	2	1	2	3	3	0	0	0
Private nonguaranteed	**0**	**0**	**0**	**0**	**0**	**0**	**0**	**0**	**0**	**0**
Bonds	0	0	0	0	0	0	0	0	0	0
Commercial banks	0	0	0	0	0	0	0	0	0	0
Memo:										
IBRD	0	0	16	15	16	15	15	15	9	3
IDA	0	1	2	2	2	3	3	3	3	4
UNDISBURSED DEBT	**16**	**683**	**541**	**555**	**577**	**575**	**481**	**479**	**408**	**370**
Official creditors	11	654	525	540	572	575	481	479	408	370
Private creditors	5	29	16	15	5	0	0	0	0	0
Memorandum items										
Concessional LDOD	14	513	1,292	1,268	1,326	1,380	1,392	1,577	1,735	1,839
Variable rate LDOD	0	17	162	157	163	160	153	165	164	175
Public sector LDOD	26	717	1,831	1,764	1,826	1,857	1,863	1,932	2,086	2,184
Private sector LDOD	0	0	0	0	0	0	0	0	0	0

6. CURRENCY COMPOSITION OF LONG-TERM DEBT (PERCENT)

	1970	1980	1988	1989	1990	1991	1992	1993	1994	1995
Deutsche mark	0.0	3.1	3.6	0.4	0.5	0.4	0.4	0.3	0.3	0.3
French franc	49.0	7.6	7.7	7.5	5.4	5.8	6.4	6.4	7.1	7.8
Japanese yen	0.0	0.0	1.5	1.3	1.2	1.2	1.2	3.3	3.3	3.0
Pound sterling	0.0	0.2	0.5	0.5	0.6	0.6	0.5	0.6	0.6	0.6
Swiss franc	0.0	0.3	0.0	0.0	0.0	0.0	0.0	0.0	0.0	0.0
U.S.dollars	23.6	42.9	33.6	34.1	35.8	35.8	35.5	36.8	38.3	37.9
Multiple currency	2.7	2.9	5.2	4.6	4.1	3.7	3.2	2.4	2.0	1.8
Special drawing rights	0.0	0.0	1.8	1.9	2.1	2.1	2.0	2.0	2.1	2.3
All other currencies	24.3	43.0	46.1	49.6	50.3	50.4	50.9	48.1	46.3	46.3

MAURITANIA

(US$ million, unless otherwise indicated)

	1970	1980	1988	1989	1990	1991	1992	1993	1994	1995
7. DEBT RESTRUCTURINGS										
Total amount rescheduled	0	0	16	63	12	0	0	203	91	67
Debt stock rescheduled	0	0	0	0	0	0	0	0	0	0
Principal rescheduled	0	0	13	41	7	0	0	155	57	46
Official	0	0	2	20	5	0	0	98	48	45
Private	0	0	10	21	3	0	0	58	9	1
Interest rescheduled	0	0	3	16	5	0	0	43	24	21
Official	0	0	1	11	4	0	0	29	24	21
Private	0	0	2	5	1	0	0	13	0	0
Debt forgiven	..	..	0	89	61	0	0	23	6	13
Memo: interest forgiven	..	..	0	4	1	0	0	10	1	2
Debt stock reduction	0	0	0	0	0	0	4	0	0	0
of which debt buyback	0	0	0	0	0	0	0	0	0	0
8. DEBT STOCK-FLOW RECONCILIATION										
Total change in debt stocks	..	..	..	-77	137	92	-100	40	156	138
Net flows on debt	..	..	..	27	98	60	-49	75	96	69
Net change in interest arrears	..	..	..	-2	21	25	26	-23	-17	13
Interest capitalized	..	..	..	16	5	0	0	43	24	21
Debt forgiveness or reduction	..	..	..	-89	-61	0	-4	-23	-6	-13
Cross-currency valuation	..	..	..	-23	55	-7	-58	-18	46	44
Residual	..	..	..	-6	19	14	-15	-13	13	5
9. AVERAGE TERMS OF NEW COMMITMENTS										
ALL CREDITORS										
Interest (%)	6.0	3.6	1.6	2.9	3.1	2.0	1.5	1.9	2.0	0.9
Maturity (years)	10.6	20.0	32.4	26.6	29.7	24.9	31.7	28.4	26.7	35.5
Grace period (years)	2.9	6.9	9.1	7.5	8.4	8.5	8.0	7.4	8.6	9.9
Grant element (%)	18.9	44.5	66.8	53.4	56.1	60.2	66.9	61.8	61.3	77.1
Official creditors										
Interest (%)	3.2	2.7	1.6	2.9	3.1	2.0	1.5	1.9	2.0	0.9
Maturity (years)	20.8	21.8	32.4	26.6	29.7	24.9	31.7	28.4	26.7	35.5
Grace period (years)	5.4	7.7	9.1	7.5	8.4	8.5	8.0	7.4	8.6	9.9
Grant element (%)	44.4	51.6	66.8	53.4	56.1	60.2	66.9	61.8	61.3	77.1
Private creditors										
Interest (%)	6.7	7.7	0.0	0.0	0.0	0.0	0.0	0.0	0.0	0.0
Maturity (years)	8.3	11.4	0.0	0.0	0.0	0.0	0.0	0.0	0.0	0.0
Grace period (years)	2.4	2.9	0.0	0.0	0.0	0.0	0.0	0.0	0.0	0.0
Grant element (%)	13.2	10.0	0.0	0.0	0.0	0.0	0.0	0.0	0.0	0.0
Memorandum items										
Commitments	7	211	141	149	216	85	74	182	65	112
Official creditors	1	175	141	149	216	85	74	182	65	112
Private creditors	6	36	0	0	0	0	0	0	0	0

10. CONTRACTUAL OBLIGATIONS ON OUTSTANDING LONG-TERM DEBT

	1996	1997	1998	1999	2000	2001	2002	2003	2004	2005
TOTAL										
Disbursements	100	92	64	41	23	12	6	2	1	0
Principal	104	107	117	110	108	102	94	91	79	82
Interest	34	36	48	44	42	39	36	33	30	28
Official creditors										
Disbursements	100	92	64	41	23	12	6	2	1	0
Principal	103	106	116	110	108	102	94	91	79	82
Interest	34	36	47	44	42	39	36	33	30	28
Bilateral creditors										
Disbursements	16	15	10	6	4	2	1	0	0	0
Principal	49	53	68	62	57	56	52	52	41	42
Interest	13	17	30	28	27	25	24	22	21	20
Multilateral creditors										
Disbursements	85	76	55	35	20	10	6	1	1	0
Principal	53	54	48	48	51	46	42	39	39	40
Interest	21	19	18	16	15	13	12	11	9	8
Private creditors										
Disbursements	0	0	0	0	0	0	0	0	0	0
Principal	1	1	1	0	0	0	0	0	0	0
Interest	0	0	0	0	0	0	0	0	0	0
Commercial banks										
Disbursements	0	0	0	0	0	0	0	0	0	0
Principal	0	0	0	0	0	0	0	0	0	0
Interest	0	0	0	0	0	0	0	0	0	0
Other private										
Disbursements	0	0	0	0	0	0	0	0	0	0
Principal	1	1	1	0	0	0	0	0	0	0
Interest	0	0	0	0	0	0	0	0	0	0

MAURITIUS

(US$ million, unless otherwise indicated)

	1970	*1980*	*1988*	*1989*	*1990*	*1991*	*1992*	*1993*	*1994*	*1995*
1. SUMMARY DEBT DATA										
TOTAL DEBT STOCKS (EDT)	..	**467**	**880**	**855**	**995**	**1,058**	**1,070**	**1,030**	**1,411**	**1,801**
Long-term debt (LDOD)	**32**	**318**	**729**	**760**	**920**	**1,002**	**959**	**916**	**1,119**	**1,449**
Public and publicly guaranteed	32	294	663	654	772	830	764	749	873	1,182
Private nonguaranteed	0	24	66	106	148	172	195	167	245	267
Use of IMF credit	**0**	**102**	**103**	**63**	**22**	**0**	**0**	**0**	**0**	**0**
Short-term debt	..	**47**	**48**	**32**	**53**	**56**	**111**	**114**	**292**	**351**
of which interest arrears on LDOD	..	0	0	0	3	6	5	8	9	11
Official creditors	..	0	0	0	2	4	4	6	6	8
Private creditors	..	0	0	0	1	2	1	2	4	3
Memo: principal arrears on LDOD	..	2	0	0	5	12	14	24	20	33
Official creditors	..	2	0	0	4	8	9	16	12	19
Private creditors	..	0	0	0	1	3	4	8	9	15
Memo: export credits	..	..	115	124	201	198	166	141	207	227
TOTAL DEBT FLOWS										
Disbursements	**2**	**143**	**243**	**106**	**162**	**173**	**127**	**98**	**183**	**411**
Long-term debt	2	97	243	106	162	173	127	98	183	411
IMF purchases	0	46	0	0	0	0	0	0	0	0
Principal repayments	**5**	**19**	**146**	**90**	**104**	**113**	**124**	**75**	**96**	**143**
Long-term debt	1	19	105	53	60	92	124	75	96	143
IMF repurchases	4	0	41	37	44	21	0	0	0	0
Net flows on debt	**-3**	**124**	**112**	**-1**	**77**	**60**	**59**	**23**	**264**	**326**
of which short-term debt	..	..	15	-16	18	0	56	0	177	58
Interest payments (INT)	..	**34**	**57**	**55**	**52**	**58**	**60**	**48**	**54**	**73**
Long-term debt	2	23	43	43	42	51	57	45	44	57
IMF charges	0	3	10	8	5	2	0	0	0	0
Short-term debt	..	8	3	4	5	5	3	4	10	16
Net transfers on debt	..	**90**	**56**	**-56**	**25**	**2**	**-1**	**-26**	**210**	**253**
Total debt service paid (TDS)	..	**52**	**202**	**145**	**155**	**171**	**184**	**124**	**150**	**216**
Long-term debt	3	41	148	96	102	143	181	120	140	200
IMF repurchases and charges	4	3	51	45	49	23	0	0	0	0
Short-term debt (interest only)	..	8	3	4	5	5	3	4	10	16

	1970	*1980*	*1988*	*1989*	*1990*	*1991*	*1992*	*1993*	*1994*	*1995*
2. AGGREGATE NET RESOURCE FLOWS AND NET TRANSFERS (LONG-TERM)										
NET RESOURCE FLOWS	**5**	**93**	**178**	**108**	**168**	**115**	**30**	**70**	**129**	**309**
Net flow of long-term debt (ex. IMF)	1	79	138	53	103	81	3	23	87	268
Foreign direct investment (net)	2	1	24	36	41	19	15	15	19	15
Portfolio equity flows	0	0	0	0	0	0	0	17	10	4
Grants (excluding technical coop.)	3	13	16	20	25	15	12	15	12	22
Memo: technical coop. grants	1	11	17	19	20	21	21	18	21	25
NET TRANSFERS	**3**	**69**	**119**	**48**	**104**	**44**	**-49**	**6**	**63**	**232**
Interest on long-term debt	2	23	43	43	42	51	57	45	44	57
Profit remittances on FDI	1	1	16	17	22	21	22	20	22	20

	1970	*1980*	*1988*	*1989*	*1990*	*1991*	*1992*	*1993*	*1994*	*1995*
3. MAJOR ECONOMIC AGGREGATES										
Gross national product (GNP)	222	1,124	2,026	2,088	2,536	2,744	3,091	3,113	3,405	3,920
Exports of goods & services (XGS)	..	579	1,406	1,449	1,778	1,864	2,003	1,971	2,041	2,402
of which workers remittances	..	0	0	0	0	0	0	0	0	0
Imports of goods & services (MGS)	..	718	1,556	1,629	1,995	1,965	2,097	2,164	2,377	2,525
International reserves (RES)	46	113	463	542	761	915	841	781	771	887
Current account balance	..	-117	-56	-104	-119	-18	0	-92	-232	-22

	1970	*1980*	*1988*	*1989*	*1990*	*1991*	*1992*	*1993*	*1994*	*1995*
4. DEBT INDICATORS										
EDT / XGS (%)	..	80.8	62.6	59.0	55.9	56.7	53.4	52.3	69.1	75.0
EDT / GNP (%)	..	41.6	43.4	40.9	39.2	38.6	34.6	33.1	41.4	45.9
TDS / XGS (%)	..	9.0	14.4	10.0	8.7	9.2	9.2	6.3	7.3	9.0
INT / XGS (%)	..	5.8	4.0	3.8	2.9	3.1	3.0	2.5	2.7	3.0
INT / GNP (%)	..	3.0	2.8	2.6	2.0	2.1	1.9	1.6	1.6	1.8
RES / EDT (%)	..	24.1	52.6	63.5	76.5	86.5	78.6	75.9	54.7	49.3
RES / MGS (months)	..	1.9	3.6	4.0	4.6	5.6	4.8	4.3	3.9	4.2
Short-term / EDT (%)	..	10.1	5.5	3.8	5.3	5.3	10.4	11.0	20.7	19.5
Concessional / EDT (%)	..	15.6	29.1	32.7	37.9	40.1	38.5	39.6	31.4	26.1
Multilateral / EDT (%)	..	16.6	34.0	33.9	31.4	29.2	25.9	26.8	19.4	15.0

MAURITIUS

(US$ million, unless otherwise indicated)

	1970	1980	1988	1989	1990	1991	1992	1993	1994	1995
5. LONG-TERM DEBT										
DEBT OUTSTANDING (LDOD)	**32**	**318**	**729**	**760**	**920**	**1,002**	**959**	**916**	**1,119**	**1,449**
Public and publicly guaranteed	**32**	**294**	**663**	**654**	**772**	**830**	**764**	**749**	**873**	**1,182**
Official creditors	21	154	546	546	658	707	647	635	664	682
Multilateral	6	78	299	290	312	309	277	276	274	270
Concessional	6	34	67	76	92	92	85	86	88	91
Bilateral	16	76	247	256	345	398	370	359	390	413
Concessional	6	39	188	204	285	332	327	321	355	379
Private creditors	10	141	117	108	115	123	117	114	210	500
Bonds	9	0	0	0	0	0	0	0	0	150
Commercial banks	2	138	27	23	106	108	101	98	188	325
Other private	0	3	90	85	9	15	16	17	21	25
Private nonguaranteed	**0**	**24**	**66**	**106**	**148**	**172**	**195**	**167**	**245**	**267**
Bonds	0	0	0	0	0	0	0	0	0	0
Commercial banks	0	24	66	106	148	172	195	167	245	267
Memo:										
IBRD	6	35	190	175	176	167	151	149	147	140
IDA	0	20	19	19	19	19	18	18	17	17
DISBURSEMENTS	**2**	**97**	**243**	**106**	**162**	**173**	**127**	**98**	**183**	**411**
Public and publicly guaranteed	**2**	**93**	**218**	**58**	**105**	**117**	**87**	**70**	**142**	**355**
Official creditors	2	36	123	58	97	97	64	59	36	41
Multilateral	0	18	59	20	23	21	16	29	14	18
Concessional	0	5	11	10	13	3	4	10	3	5
Bilateral	2	18	64	38	74	76	48	30	23	23
Concessional	1	13	37	31	66	63	47	26	23	19
Private creditors	0	56	95	0	8	20	23	12	106	314
Bonds	0	0	0	0	0	0	0	0	0	150
Commercial banks	0	56	5	0	0	14	17	9	102	159
Other private	0	0	91	0	7	6	6	2	4	6
Private nonguaranteed	**0**	**4**	**25**	**48**	**57**	**56**	**40**	**28**	**41**	**56**
Bonds	0	0	0	0	0	0	0	0	0	0
Commercial banks	0	4	25	48	57	56	40	28	41	56
Memo:										
IBRD	0	7	29	8	6	7	9	16	10	11
IDA	0	1	0	0	0	0	0	0	0	0
PRINCIPAL REPAYMENTS	**1**	**19**	**105**	**53**	**60**	**92**	**124**	**75**	**96**	**143**
Public and publicly guaranteed	**1**	**15**	**101**	**48**	**44**	**61**	**108**	**62**	**68**	**83**
Official creditors	1	5	37	40	39	49	84	51	54	58
Multilateral	0	2	22	22	22	27	36	30	33	33
Concessional	0	1	3	3	3	4	6	5	7	5
Bilateral	0	3	15	18	17	21	48	21	21	25
Concessional	0	2	10	13	12	16	27	14	15	19
Private creditors	1	10	64	7	4	12	25	11	14	25
Bonds	0	0	0	0	0	0	0	0	0	0
Commercial banks	1	8	59	2	4	12	24	10	13	22
Other private	0	1	5	5	0	0	1	0	1	3
Private nonguaranteed	**0**	**4**	**4**	**5**	**16**	**31**	**16**	**14**	**27**	**60**
Bonds	0	0	0	0	0	0	0	0	0	0
Commercial banks	0	4	4	5	16	31	16	14	27	60
Memo:										
IBRD	0	2	16	15	16	19	22	21	22	23
IDA	0	0	0	0	0	0	0	1	1	1
NET FLOWS ON DEBT	**1**	**79**	**138**	**53**	**103**	**81**	**3**	**23**	**87**	**268**
Public and publicly guaranteed	**1**	**78**	**117**	**10**	**61**	**56**	**-22**	**9**	**74**	**272**
Official creditors	2	31	86	17	58	48	-20	8	-18	-17
Multilateral	0	16	37	-2	1	-7	-20	-1	-20	-15
Concessional	0	5	8	8	10	0	-2	5	-4	-1
Bilateral	2	15	49	19	57	55	-1	9	2	-2
Concessional	0	11	27	18	54	47	20	12	7	0
Private creditors	-1	47	32	-7	3	8	-2	1	92	289
Bonds	0	0	0	0	0	0	0	0	0	150
Commercial banks	-1	48	-55	-2	-4	3	-6	-1	89	137
Other private	0	-1	86	-5	7	6	5	2	3	3
Private nonguaranteed	**0**	**0**	**21**	**42**	**41**	**25**	**25**	**14**	**13**	**-4**
Bonds	0	0	0	0	0	0	0	0	0	0
Commercial banks	0	0	21	42	41	25	25	14	13	-4
Memo:										
IBRD	0	5	13	-7	-10	-13	-12	-6	-12	-13
IDA	0	1	0	0	0	0	0	-1	-1	-1

MAURITIUS

(US$ million, unless otherwise indicated)

	1970	1980	1988	1989	1990	1991	1992	1993	1994	1995
INTEREST PAYMENTS (LINT)	**2**	**23**	**43**	**43**	**42**	**51**	**57**	**45**	**44**	**57**
Public and publicly guaranteed	**2**	**20**	**42**	**40**	**37**	**46**	**51**	**41**	**40**	**51**
Official creditors	1	7	32	30	33	35	40	34	34	35
Multilateral	0	4	20	19	19	20	20	17	17	16
Concessional	0	1	2	2	2	3	3	2	2	3
Bilateral	1	3	12	11	13	15	20	17	17	19
Concessional	0	1	8	7	9	10	14	14	15	16
Private creditors	1	13	10	10	4	11	11	7	6	16
Bonds	1	0	0	0	0	0	0	0	0	0
Commercial banks	0	13	7	3	4	11	11	7	6	15
Other private	0	0	3	7	0	0	0	0	0	1
Private nonguaranteed	**0**	**3**	**1**	**3**	**6**	**5**	**6**	**4**	**4**	**6**
Bonds	0	0	0	0	0	0	0	0	0	0
Commercial banks	0	3	1	3	6	5	6	4	4	6
Memo:										
IBRD	0	3	15	14	14	13	12	11	11	11
IDA	0	0	0	0	0	0	0	0	0	0
NET TRANSFERS ON DEBT	**-1**	**56**	**95**	**9**	**60**	**30**	**-54**	**-22**	**43**	**211**
Public and publicly guaranteed	**-1**	**58**	**75**	**-30**	**25**	**10**	**-73**	**-32**	**34**	**221**
Official creditors	1	24	54	-13	25	13	-60	-26	-52	-52
Multilateral	-1	12	17	-21	-19	-27	-40	-18	-36	-31
Concessional	-1	4	6	6	8	-3	-5	3	-6	-3
Bilateral	1	12	37	9	44	40	-20	-8	-16	-21
Concessional	0	11	19	11	45	38	5	-2	-7	-17
Private creditors	-2	34	21	-17	-1	-3	-13	-6	86	273
Bonds	-1	0	0	0	0	0	0	0	0	150
Commercial banks	-1	35	-62	-5	-8	-9	-17	-8	84	122
Other private	0	-1	83	-13	7	6	5	2	2	2
Private nonguaranteed	**0**	**-2**	**20**	**39**	**35**	**20**	**19**	**10**	**9**	**-10**
Bonds	0	0	0	0	0	0	0	0	0	0
Commercial banks	0	-2	20	39	35	20	19	10	9	-10
Memo:										
IBRD	-1	2	-2	-22	-24	-26	-25	-17	-23	-24
IDA	0	1	0	0	0	0	-1	-1	-1	-1
DEBT SERVICE (LTDS)	**3**	**41**	**148**	**96**	**102**	**143**	**181**	**120**	**140**	**206**
Public and publicly guaranteed	**3**	**35**	**143**	**88**	**80**	**107**	**159**	**102**	**108**	**134**
Official creditors	2	12	69	71	72	84	123	85	88	93
Multilateral	1	7	42	41	42	47	56	47	50	49
Concessional	1	1	4	5	5	7	9	7	9	8
Bilateral	1	6	27	29	30	36	68	37	38	4
Concessional	0	2	18	20	20	25	42	28	30	36
Private creditors	2	22	74	17	8	23	36	18	20	41
Bonds	1	0	0	0	0	0	0	0	0	0
Commercial banks	1	21	67	5	8	23	35	17	19	37
Other private	0	1	8	13	0	0	1	0	1	4
Private nonguaranteed	**0**	**7**	**5**	**9**	**22**	**36**	**21**	**18**	**31**	**66**
Bonds	0	0	0	0	0	0	0	0	0	0
Commercial banks	0	7	5	9	22	36	21	18	31	66
Memo:										
IBRD	1	4	31	29	30	32	34	32	33	34
IDA	0	0	0	0	0	0	1	1	1	[illegible]
UNDISBURSED DEBT	**15**	**175**	**192**	**202**	**249**	**263**	**249**	**257**	**308**	**497**
Official creditors	15	172	190	183	236	232	230	226	276	394
Private creditors	0	3	2	19	13	31	19	31	33	103
Memorandum items										
Concessional LDOD	11	73	256	280	377	424	412	407	443	46
Variable rate LDOD	2	150	190	231	281	321	342	323	495	809
Public sector LDOD	32	294	657	654	772	830	764	749	873	1,182
Private sector LDOD	0	24	72	106	148	172	195	167	245	267

6. CURRENCY COMPOSITION OF LONG-TERM DEBT (PERCENT)

	1970	1980	1988	1989	1990	1991	1992	1993	1994	1995
Deutsche mark	0.0	0.0	3.0	3.1	6.3	5.5	5.2	4.7	4.1	3.0
French franc	0.0	14.2	17.7	20.5	23.3	28.5	30.8	29.3	27.0	22.2
Japanese yen	0.0	0.0	0.2	1.0	1.0	1.3	1.8	2.5	2.3	1.7
Pound sterling	82.2	18.4	10.5	9.4	8.6	7.3	3.5	3.3	2.6	1.8
Swiss franc	0.0	0.0	0.6	0.6	0.5	0.4	0.4	0.3	0.3	0.2
U.S.dollars	0.0	46.1	20.2	18.6	15.4	15.2	15.8	15.3	23.8	42.4
Multiple currency	17.6	13.3	29.6	28.5	24.9	22.4	22.0	22.2	19.0	13.7
Special drawing rights	0.0	0.0	0.0	0.0	0.0	0.0	0.0	0.0	0.0	0.0
All other currencies	0.0	8.1	18.3	18.3	20.0	19.5	20.5	22.5	20.9	15.1

MAURITIUS

(US$ million, unless otherwise indicated)

	1970	1980	1988	1989	1990	1991	1992	1993	1994	1995
7. DEBT RESTRUCTURINGS										
Total amount rescheduled	0	0	0	0	0	0	0	0	0	0
Debt stock rescheduled	0	0	0	0	0	0	0	0	0	0
Principal rescheduled	0	0	0	0	0	0	0	0	0	0
Official	0	0	0	0	0	0	0	0	0	0
Private	0	0	0	0	0	0	0	0	0	0
Interest rescheduled	0	0	0	0	0	0	0	0	0	0
Official	0	0	0	0	0	0	0	0	0	0
Private	0	0	0	0	0	0	0	0	0	0
Debt forgiven	..	..	0	3	0	0	0	0	0	0
Memo: interest forgiven	..	..	0	0	0	0	0	0	0	0
Debt stock reduction	0	0	0	0	0	0	0	0	0	0
of which debt buyback	0	0	0	0	0	0	0	0	0	0
8. DEBT STOCK-FLOW RECONCILIATION										
Total change in debt stocks	..	..	..	-25	140	63	12	-40	381	390
Net flows on debt	..	..	..	-1	77	60	59	23	264	326
Net change in interest arrears	..	..	..	0	3	3	-1	3	1	2
Interest capitalized	..	..	..	0	0	0	0	0	0	0
Debt forgiveness or reduction	..	..	..	-3	0	0	0	0	0	0
Cross-currency valuation	..	..	..	-14	73	-9	-51	-32	59	39
Residual	..	..	..	-8	-13	10	5	-34	57	24
9. AVERAGE TERMS OF NEW COMMITMENTS										
ALL CREDITORS										
Interest (%)	0.0	10.6	7.7	5.0	6.0	5.9	5.0	4.8	5.4	5.9
Maturity (years)	24.2	13.6	15.0	16.3	17.9	17.9	18.0	14.9	16.0	9.6
Grace period (years)	1.7	4.2	3.0	6.3	6.3	6.2	4.7	4.3	3.3	4.9
Grant element (%)	64.6	7.3	14.1	30.5	26.7	26.3	30.1	29.1	26.5	19.4
Official creditors										
Interest (%)	0.0	5.2	6.4	4.6	6.0	5.5	4.8	4.5	4.0	5.2
Maturity (years)	24.2	19.6	18.0	17.1	17.9	18.8	19.3	17.0	20.3	17.5
Grace period (years)	1.7	5.4	6.0	7.0	6.3	7.8	5.1	4.9	6.3	6.3
Grant element (%)	64.6	30.6	24.3	33.7	26.7	30.6	32.2	33.5	41.2	31.0
Private creditors										
Interest (%)	0.0	18.4	9.0	7.0	0.0	7.0	5.9	5.6	6.8	6.3
Maturity (years)	0.0	5.0	12.3	12.0	0.0	15.7	9.3	8.9	11.9	6.1
Grace period (years)	0.0	2.5	0.3	2.5	0.0	2.0	2.1	2.4	0.4	4.3
Grant element (%)	0.0	-26.5	4.5	13.6	0.0	14.9	15.8	16.5	12.7	14.3
Memorandum items										
Commitments	14	111	176	104	137	136	90	90	210	559
Official creditors	14	66	85	87	137	99	79	67	102	170
Private creditors	0	45	91	17	0	38	12	23	108	389

10. CONTRACTUAL OBLIGATIONS ON OUTSTANDING LONG-TERM DEBT

	1996	1997	1998	1999	2000	2001	2002	2003	2004	2005
TOTAL										
Disbursements	134	133	88	55	37	23	14	7	5	3
Principal	120	128	133	135	428	124	124	121	106	81
Interest	81	83	80	76	66	46	41	35	30	24
Official creditors										
Disbursements	75	105	75	52	35	23	14	7	5	3
Principal	70	75	72	69	69	70	71	68	64	61
Interest	37	38	37	35	33	30	27	24	21	18
Bilateral creditors										
Disbursements	47	45	28	16	8	4	2	0	0	0
Principal	38	39	35	33	33	35	37	35	35	35
Interest	20	21	20	19	18	16	15	13	11	10
Multilateral creditors										
Disbursements	28	59	48	37	27	19	12	7	4	3
Principal	32	35	37	37	36	35	34	33	29	27
Interest	17	17	17	16	15	14	12	11	10	8
Private creditors										
Disbursements	59	28	12	3	1	0	0	0	0	0
Principal	50	53	62	66	359	55	53	53	42	19
Interest	44	45	43	41	33	16	14	11	9	6
Commercial banks										
Disbursements	40	10	4	0	0	0	0	0	0	0
Principal	18	19	25	24	169	16	17	17	17	11
Interest	26	27	26	25	23	12	10	9	7	5
Other private										
Disbursements	18	18	9	3	1	0	0	0	0	0
Principal	32	35	37	42	190	38	36	36	25	8
Interest	18	18	17	16	10	4	3	3	2	1

MEXICO

(US$ million, unless otherwise indicated)

	1970	1980	1988	1989	1990	1991	1992	1993	1994	1995
1. SUMMARY DEBT DATA										
TOTAL DEBT STOCKS (EDT)	..	**57,378**	**99,216**	**93,841**	**104,442**	**114,068**	**112,265**	**131,572**	**139,955**	**165,743**
Long-term debt (LDOD)	**5,967**	**41,215**	**86,532**	**80,088**	**81,809**	**85,445**	**81,780**	**90,528**	**96,772**	**112,614**
Public and publicly guaranteed	3,197	33,915	80,601	76,117	75,974	77,825	71,105	74,989	79,284	94,027
Private nonguaranteed	2,770	7,300	5,931	3,971	5,835	7,620	10,675	15,539	17,489	18,587
Use of IMF credit	**0**	**0**	**4,805**	**5,091**	**6,551**	**6,766**	**5,950**	**4,787**	**3,860**	**15,828**
Short-term debt	..	**16,163**	**7,879**	**8,662**	**16,082**	**21,857**	**24,535**	**36,257**	**39,323**	**37,300**
of which interest arrears on LDOD	..	0	0	0	0	0	0	0	0	0
Official creditors	..	0	0	0	0	0	0	0	0	0
Private creditors	..	0	0	0	0	0	0	0	0	0
Memo: principal arrears on LDOD	..	0	1	4	0	0	0	0	0	0
Official creditors	..	0	1	1	0	0	0	0	0	0
Private creditors	..	0	0	3	0	0	0	0	0	0
Memo: export credits	..	..	11,052	11,152	15,583	18,826	22,644	24,968	26,921	24,713
TOTAL DEBT FLOWS										
Disbursements	**1,375**	**11,581**	**5,181**	**5,182**	**14,229**	**9,701**	**12,761**	**17,436**	**16,130**	**40,503**
Long-term debt	1,375	11,581	4,710	3,974	12,045	8,425	12,432	17,436	16,130	27,215
IMF purchases	0	0	471	1,209	2,184	1,276	328	0	0	13,288
Principal repayments	**1,017**	**4,894**	**6,761**	**6,253**	**4,012**	**5,359**	**13,275**	**16,117**	**12,706**	**12,430**
Long-term debt	1,017	4,760	6,198	5,433	2,821	4,254	12,379	14,942	11,501	11,286
IMF repurchases	0	134	563	820	1,191	1,105	896	1,175	1,204	1,144
Net flows on debt	**358**	**6,686**	**499**	**-288**	**17,637**	**10,117**	**2,164**	**13,041**	**6,489**	**26,051**
of which short-term debt	..	..	2,079	783	7,420	5,775	2,678	11,722	3,065	-2,022
Interest payments (INT)	..	**6,068**	**8,712**	**9,310**	**7,304**	**8,186**	**7,538**	**8,101**	**9,237**	**11,127**
Long-term debt	283	4,580	7,543	7,916	5,800	6,223	5,875	5,854	6,556	7,971
IMF charges	0	4	339	398	522	541	503	426	233	545
Short-term debt	..	1,484	830	997	982	1,423	1,160	1,822	2,448	2,611
Net transfers on debt	..	**618**	**-8,214**	**-9,598**	**10,333**	**1,931**	**-5,374**	**4,940**	**-2,748**	**14,924**
Total debt service paid (TDS)	..	**10,962**	**15,473**	**15,563**	**11,316**	**13,545**	**20,813**	**24,218**	**21,943**	**23,556**
Long-term debt	1,301	9,340	13,741	13,349	8,621	10,477	18,254	20,795	18,057	19,256
IMF repurchases and charges	0	138	903	1,218	1,712	1,646	1,399	1,601	1,437	1,689
Short-term debt (interest only)	..	1,484	830	997	982	1,423	1,160	1,822	2,448	2,611
2. AGGREGATE NET RESOURCE FLOWS AND NET TRANSFERS (LONG-TERM)										
NET RESOURCE FLOWS	**689**	**8,991**	**1,183**	**1,615**	**12,390**	**13,363**	**9,825**	**21,233**	**20,168**	**23,443**
Net flow of long-term debt (ex. IMF)	358	6,821	-1,488	-1,459	9,224	4,171	54	2,494	4,628	15,929
Foreign direct investment (net)	323	2,156	2,594	3,037	2,549	4,742	4,393	4,389	10,972	6,963
Portfolio equity flows	0	0	0	0	563	4,404	5,365	14,297	4,521	520
Grants (excluding technical coop.)	8	14	76	37	54	46	14	53	47	31
Memo: technical coop. grants	6	44	69	66	81	90	113	117	110	127
NET TRANSFERS	**46**	**3,043**	**-7,443**	**-7,553**	**5,276**	**4,649**	**1,638**	**13,034**	**11,212**	**12,972**
Interest on long-term debt	283	4,580	7,543	7,916	5,800	6,223	5,875	5,854	6,556	7,971
Profit remittances on FDI	359	1,368	1,083	1,252	1,314	2,492	2,312	2,346	2,400	2,500
3. MAJOR ECONOMIC AGGREGATES										
Gross national product (GNP)	37,867	188,322	165,965	199,949	238,432	282,230	324,740	356,199	364,102	237,090
Exports of goods & services (XGS)	..	24,685	41,722	47,752	54,570	57,493	61,330	67,428	78,244	97,201
of which workers remittances	..	698	1,897	2,213	2,492	2,414	3,070	3,332	3,694	3,672
Imports of goods & services (MGS)	..	35,243	44,454	53,907	63,504	72,713	86,087	91,136	107,980	98,145
International reserves (RES)	756	4,175	6,327	6,740	10,217	18,052	19,171	25,299	6,441	17,046
Current account balance	..	-10,422	-2,374	-5,825	-7,451	-14,888	-24,442	-23,400	-29,418	-654
4. DEBT INDICATORS										
EDT / XGS (%)	..	232.4	237.8	196.5	191.4	198.4	183.1	195.1	178.9	170.5
EDT / GNP (%)	..	30.5	59.8	46.9	43.8	40.4	34.6	36.9	38.4	69.9
TDS / XGS (%)	..	44.4	37.1	32.6	20.7	23.6	33.9	35.9	28.0	24.2
INT / XGS (%)	..	24.6	20.9	19.5	13.4	14.2	12.3	12.0	11.8	11.4
INT / GNP (%)	..	3.2	5.2	4.7	3.1	2.9	2.3	2.3	2.5	4.7
RES / EDT (%)	..	7.3	6.4	7.2	9.8	15.8	17.1	19.2	4.6	10.3
RES / MGS (months)	..	1.4	1.7	1.5	1.9	3.0	2.7	3.3	0.7	2.1
Short-term / EDT (%)	..	28.2	7.9	9.2	15.4	19.2	21.9	27.6	28.1	22.5
Concessional / EDT (%)	..	0.9	0.5	0.5	1.0	1.0	1.1	1.1	1.2	0.9
Multilateral / EDT (%)	..	5.6	10.4	11.5	13.7	13.6	13.8	12.2	12.2	11.2

MEXICO

(US$ million, unless otherwise indicated)

	1970	1980	1988	1989	1990	1991	1992	1993	1994	1995
5. LONG-TERM DEBT										
DEBT OUTSTANDING (LDOD)	**5,967**	**41,215**	**86,532**	**80,088**	**81,809**	**85,445**	**81,780**	**90,528**	**96,772**	**112,614**
Public and publicly guaranteed	**3,197**	**33,915**	**80,601**	**76,117**	**75,974**	**77,825**	**71,105**	**74,989**	**79,284**	**94,027**
Official creditors	1,150	4,481	16,082	16,796	22,763	25,092	25,239	26,094	27,466	38,432
Multilateral	749	3,189	10,333	10,753	14,303	15,475	15,537	16,077	17,075	18,642
Concessional	505	376	100	88	72	58	45	35	26	19
Bilateral	401	1,291	5,749	6,044	8,461	9,617	9,702	10,017	10,391	19,790
Concessional	123	120	386	367	932	1,082	1,200	1,362	1,628	1,549
Private creditors	2,047	29,434	64,520	59,321	53,211	52,733	45,866	48,896	51,818	55,595
Bonds	386	3,100	4,203	3,743	40,100	40,660	35,018	37,616	41,045	45,195
Commercial banks	1,267	25,637	54,047	49,429	6,631	6,457	5,898	6,639	6,957	6,524
Other private	394	698	6,269	6,149	6,480	5,617	4,951	4,640	3,816	3,876
Private nonguaranteed	**2,770**	**7,300**	**5,931**	**3,971**	**5,835**	**7,620**	**10,675**	**15,539**	**17,489**	**18,587**
Bonds	0	0	0	0	150	703	3,310	9,127	12,767	13,026
Commercial banks	2,770	7,300	5,931	3,971	5,685	6,917	7,365	6,412	4,722	5,562
Memo:										
IBRD	582	2,063	7,427	7,821	11,030	11,928	11,966	12,322	13,038	13,823
IDA	0	0	0	0	0	0	0	0	0	0
DISBURSEMENTS	**1,375**	**11,581**	**4,710**	**3,974**	**12,045**	**8,425**	**12,432**	**17,436**	**16,130**	**27,215**
Public and publicly guaranteed	**772**	**9,131**	**4,507**	**2,904**	**9,985**	**6,031**	**7,319**	**8,426**	**8,691**	**19,836**
Official creditors	229	1,081	2,260	2,141	5,467	2,827	2,900	2,813	2,120	13,424
Multilateral	161	642	1,631	1,618	3,647	2,114	1,749	1,483	1,281	2,669
Concessional	54	10	4	4	0	3	0	0	0	0
Bilateral	68	439	629	523	1,821	713	1,151	1,329	839	10,756
Concessional	9	17	23	13	641	113	164	175	125	7
Private creditors	543	8,050	2,247	763	4,518	3,204	4,419	5,614	6,571	6,412
Bonds	0	236	0	0	975	1,324	1,157	3,750	4,388	5,522
Commercial banks	432	7,625	1,240	47	2,554	823	2,025	593	1,200	55
Other private	111	189	1,007	715	990	1,057	1,237	1,271	982	835
Private nonguaranteed	**603**	**2,450**	**203**	**1,070**	**2,060**	**2,394**	**5,113**	**9,010**	**7,439**	**7,379**
Bonds	0	0	0	0	150	553	2,766	5,861	3,657	843
Commercial banks	603	2,450	203	1,070	1,910	1,841	2,347	3,149	3,782	6,535
Memo:										
IBRD	98	422	1,347	1,297	3,326	1,581	1,352	1,098	943	1,732
IDA	0	0	0	0	0	0	0	0	0	0
PRINCIPAL REPAYMENTS	**1,017**	**4,760**	**6,198**	**5,433**	**2,821**	**4,254**	**12,379**	**14,942**	**11,501**	**11,286**
Public and publicly guaranteed	**476**	**4,010**	**3,280**	**2,403**	**2,625**	**3,645**	**10,321**	**5,958**	**6,585**	**5,892**
Official creditors	88	286	1,263	1,204	1,286	1,479	2,281	2,790	2,719	3,081
Multilateral	32	141	881	890	1,037	1,211	1,259	1,276	1,423	1,714
Concessional	26	49	21	17	16	17	12	10	8	8
Bilateral	56	145	382	314	249	268	1,022	1,514	1,296	1,367
Concessional	9	12	13	9	0	1	35	91	17	96
Private creditors	388	3,724	2,017	1,199	1,339	2,166	8,040	3,168	3,866	2,810
Bonds	16	123	1,130	259	464	84	4,592	650	1,113	1,434
Commercial banks	266	3,445	429	287	185	694	1,756	799	743	487
Other private	106	156	458	653	690	1,388	1,692	1,719	2,010	889
Private nonguaranteed	**542**	**750**	**2,918**	**3,030**	**196**	**609**	**2,058**	**8,983**	**4,917**	**5,394**
Bonds	0	0	0	0	0	0	150	25	50	610
Commercial banks	542	750	2,918	3,030	196	609	1,908	8,958	4,867	4,784
Memo:										
IBRD	23	89	673	677	801	954	981	991	1,065	1,411
IDA	0	0	0	0	0	0	0	0	0	0
NET FLOWS ON DEBT	**358**	**6,821**	**-1,488**	**-1,459**	**9,224**	**4,171**	**54**	**2,494**	**4,628**	**15,929**
Public and publicly guaranteed	**297**	**5,121**	**1,227**	**501**	**7,360**	**2,386**	**-3,001**	**2,468**	**2,106**	**13,944**
Official creditors	141	795	997	937	4,181	1,348	619	23	-599	10,343
Multilateral	129	501	750	728	2,610	903	490	207	-142	955
Concessional	28	-39	-18	-12	-16	-14	-12	-10	-8	-8
Bilateral	12	294	247	209	1,571	445	129	-185	-457	9,388
Concessional	0	5	10	4	641	112	129	84	108	-89
Private creditors	155	4,326	231	-436	3,179	1,038	-3,621	2,445	2,705	3,601
Bonds	-16	112	-1,130	-259	511	1,240	-3,435	3,099	3,275	4,088
Commercial banks	166	4,180	811	-240	2,369	129	269	-206	457	-433
Other private	5	33	550	63	300	-331	-455	-448	-1,027	-54
Private nonguaranteed	**61**	**1,700**	**-2,715**	**-1,960**	**1,864**	**1,785**	**3,055**	**27**	**2,523**	**1,985**
Bonds	0	0	0	0	150	553	2,616	5,836	3,608	233
Commercial banks	61	1,700	-2,715	-1,960	1,714	1,232	439	-5,809	-1,085	1,752
Memo:										
IBRD	76	333	674	620	2,524	628	371	107	-123	321
IDA	0	0	0	0	0	0	0	0	0	0

MEXICO

(US$ million, unless otherwise indicated)

	1970	1980	1988	1989	1990	1991	1992	1993	1994	1995
INTEREST PAYMENTS (LINT)	**283**	**4,580**	**7,543**	**7,916**	**5,800**	**6,223**	**5,875**	**5,854**	**6,556**	**7,971**
Public and publicly guaranteed	**216**	**3,880**	**6,632**	**7,088**	**5,218**	**5,613**	**5,043**	**4,708**	**5,197**	**6,247**
Official creditors	60	314	1,128	1,123	1,378	1,677	1,891	1,919	1,994	2,666
Multilateral	39	236	832	809	1,005	1,126	1,176	1,196	1,232	1,291
Concessional	27	22	4	4	3	3	2	2	1	1
Bilateral	21	78	295	314	373	551	716	723	762	1,374
Concessional	4	5	13	5	8	40	49	49	51	69
Private creditors	156	3,566	5,504	5,965	3,841	3,935	3,152	2,789	3,204	3,582
Bonds	27	252	410	457	1,112	3,084	2,527	2,206	2,611	2,852
Commercial banks	106	3,261	4,623	4,957	2,198	487	297	312	352	407
Other private	24	52	471	551	531	364	328	271	241	322
Private nonguaranteed	**67**	**700**	**911**	**828**	**582**	**610**	**832**	**1,146**	**1,358**	**1,723**
Bonds	0	0	0	0	0	28	64	353	826	1,054
Commercial banks	67	700	911	828	582	582	768	793	533	670
Memo:										
IBRD	31	166	574	567	751	861	892	905	924	961
IDA	0	0	0	0	0	0	0	0	0	0
NET TRANSFERS ON DEBT	**75**	**2,241**	**-9,031**	**-9,375**	**3,424**	**-2,051**	**-5,822**	**-3,359**	**-1,928**	**7,958**
Public and publicly guaranteed	**81**	**1,241**	**-5,405**	**-6,587**	**2,142**	**-3,226**	**-8,045**	**-2,240**	**-3,092**	**7,697**
Official creditors	81	481	-131	-186	2,803	-329	-1,272	-1,896	-2,593	7,677
Multilateral	90	264	-83	-80	1,605	-223	-685	-988	-1,373	-336
Concessional	1	-61	-22	-16	-19	-17	-15	-12	-10	-9
Bilateral	-9	216	-49	-106	1,198	-106	-587	-908	-1,220	8,014
Concessional	-4	0	-2	-2	633	72	80	35	57	-158
Private creditors	-1	760	-5,273	-6,401	-661	-2,897	-6,773	-344	-499	20
Bonds	-42	-140	-1,540	-716	-601	-1,844	-5,962	894	664	1,236
Commercial banks	60	919	-3,812	-5,197	171	-358	-28	-518	106	-840
Other private	-18	-19	78	-488	-231	-695	-783	-719	-1,269	-376
Private nonguaranteed	**-6**	**1,000**	**-3,626**	**-2,788**	**1,282**	**1,175**	**2,223**	**-1,119**	**1,164**	**261**
Bonds	0	0	0	0	150	525	2,552	5,482	2,782	-821
Commercial banks	-6	1,000	-3,626	-2,788	1,132	650	-329	-6,602	-1,618	1,082
Memo:										
IBRD	45	167	101	52	1,773	-234	-522	-797	-1,046	-641
IDA	0	0	0	0	0	0	0	0	0	0
DEBT SERVICE (LTDS)	**1,301**	**9,340**	**13,741**	**13,349**	**8,621**	**10,477**	**18,254**	**20,795**	**18,057**	**19,256**
Public and publicly guaranteed	**692**	**7,890**	**9,912**	**9,491**	**7,843**	**9,258**	**15,364**	**10,666**	**11,782**	**12,139**
Official creditors	148	601	2,391	2,327	2,664	3,156	4,172	4,709	4,713	5,747
Multilateral	71	378	1,714	1,699	2,042	2,337	2,434	2,472	2,654	3,005
Concessional	52	71	25	20	19	20	15	12	10	9
Bilateral	77	223	678	628	622	819	1,738	2,237	2,059	2,742
Concessional	14	16	25	14	9	41	84	140	68	165
Private creditors	544	7,289	7,521	7,164	5,179	6,101	11,192	5,957	7,070	6,392
Bonds	42	376	1,540	716	1,576	3,169	7,118	2,856	3,724	4,286
Commercial banks	372	6,706	5,052	5,244	2,383	1,180	2,053	1,111	1,095	895
Other private	130	208	929	1,204	1,221	1,752	2,020	1,990	2,251	1,211
Private nonguaranteed	**609**	**1,450**	**3,829**	**3,858**	**778**	**1,219**	**2,890**	**10,129**	**6,275**	**7,117**
Bonds	0	0	0	0	0	28	214	378	876	1,664
Commercial banks	609	1,450	3,829	3,858	778	1,191	2,676	9,751	5,399	5,453
Memo:										
IBRD	54	255	1,246	1,245	1,553	1,815	1,874	1,895	1,989	2,372
IDA	0	0	0	0	0	0	0	0	0	0
UNDISBURSED DEBT	**557**	**4,817**	**8,141**	**6,563**	**8,437**	**11,405**	**11,370**	**13,382**	**15,113**	**15,140**
Official creditors	439	2,976	5,772	5,297	5,379	7,772	8,127	6,929	8,234	8,368
Private creditors	118	1,841	2,369	1,266	3,058	3,634	3,243	6,453	6,879	6,772
Memorandum items										
Concessional LDOD	627	495	486	455	1,004	1,139	1,245	1,397	1,655	1,567
Variable rate LDOD	2,951	31,271	69,892	64,375	40,382	40,014	39,514	45,660	49,077	64,265
Public sector LDOD	3,165	33,249	80,298	75,917	75,595	77,440	70,600	74,509	78,830	93,596
Private sector LDOD	2,801	7,966	6,235	4,171	6,214	8,005	11,180	16,019	17,942	19,018

6. CURRENCY COMPOSITION OF LONG-TERM DEBT (PERCENT)

	1970	1980	1988	1989	1990	1991	1992	1993	1994	1995
Deutsche mark	11.2	4.3	3.3	4.2	3.7	3.9	4.1	3.7	3.8	3.0
French franc	7.7	1.2	2.3	3.3	3.8	3.8	3.6	3.1	3.1	2.8
Japanese yen	0.5	1.4	9.4	10.6	6.3	7.2	8.2	8.8	9.1	6.7
Pound sterling	1.1	0.5	3.3	3.5	1.4	1.5	1.2	0.9	0.9	0.7
Swiss franc	3.4	2.0	0.8	0.8	0.6	0.6	0.4	0.4	0.4	0.4
U.S.dollars	51.2	78.7	64.3	58.9	64.3	61.8	59.2	60.6	60.4	66.8
Multiple currency	21.9	9.9	13.1	14.5	18.6	19.7	21.6	20.9	20.8	18.3
Special drawing rights	0.0	0.0	0.0	0.0	0.0	0.0	0.0	0.0	0.0	0.0
All other currencies	2.9	2.0	3.4	4.2	1.2	1.5	1.6	1.5	1.5	1.3

MEXICO

(US$ million, unless otherwise indicated)

	1970	1980	1988	1989	1990	1991	1992	1993	1994	1995
7. DEBT RESTRUCTURINGS										
Total amount rescheduled	0	0	2,926	519	36,950	1,332	327	0	0	0
Debt stock rescheduled	0	0	2,557	0	36,160	627	0	0	0	0
Principal rescheduled	0	0	219	358	570	544	234	0	0	0
Official	0	0	96	207	391	305	169	0	0	0
Private	0	0	122	151	179	239	65	0	0	0
Interest rescheduled	0	0	0	127	204	161	76	0	0	0
Official	0	0	0	94	137	89	45	0	0	0
Private	0	0	0	33	67	72	31	0	0	0
Debt forgiven	..	..	0	0	0	0	0	0	0	0
Memo: interest forgiven	..	..	0	0	0	0	0	0	0	0
Debt stock reduction	0	0	4,036	2,546	8,145	526	7,426	936	299	306
of which debt buyback	0	0	0	0	0	0	5,086	562	51	13
8. DEBT STOCK-FLOW RECONCILIATION										
Total change in debt stocks	..	..	..	-5,375	10,602	9,625	-1,803	19,308	8,383	25,788
Net flows on debt	..	..	..	-288	17,637	10,117	2,164	13,041	6,489	26,051
Net change in interest arrears	..	..	..	0	0	0	0	0	0	0
Interest capitalized	..	..	..	127	204	161	76	0	0	0
Debt forgiveness or reduction	..	..	..	-2,546	-8,145	-526	-2,340	-374	-248	-293
Cross-currency valuation	..	..	..	-1,368	2,143	389	-1,254	406	2,675	593
Residual	..	..	..	-1,301	-1,238	-516	-448	6,235	-534	-563
9. AVERAGE TERMS OF NEW COMMITMENTS										
ALL CREDITORS										
Interest (%)	8.1	11.3	8.0	8.2	8.6	8.0	7.3	6.7	5.7	8.5
Maturity (years)	11.6	9.9	13.2	14.7	13.0	12.5	10.8	10.3	7.6	7.5
Grace period (years)	3.4	4.3	3.0	4.2	5.1	4.1	3.4	4.6	3.6	2.9
Grant element (%)	9.9	-5.7	10.4	9.9	7.1	10.3	9.7	14.4	13.8	5.9
Official creditors										
Interest (%)	6.7	8.0	7.6	7.8	7.9	7.3	7.4	6.9	7.0	9.2
Maturity (years)	18.5	15.3	15.3	16.7	15.5	15.6	14.9	11.5	13.7	9.1
Grace period (years)	4.0	3.3	3.7	5.2	4.5	4.6	3.9	3.4	4.3	2.8
Grant element (%)	19.4	10.1	12.9	12.6	11.5	14.4	12.7	14.3	15.1	5.0
Private creditors										
Interest (%)	8.9	12.6	9.2	9.7	9.2	9.0	7.2	6.7	5.1	6.8
Maturity (years)	7.1	7.7	7.2	7.4	10.8	8.2	7.5	10.0	4.8	3.9
Grace period (years)	3.1	4.7	0.9	0.7	5.5	3.4	3.0	4.9	3.3	3.0
Grant element (%)	3.6	-12.0	3.0	0.4	3.3	4.6	7.3	14.4	13.1	7.9
Memorandum items										
Commitments	858	7,632	2,615	3,408	12,762	9,045	7,624	11,667	10,693	21,341
Official creditors	338	2,187	1,939	2,663	5,918	5,217	3,357	2,054	3,391	14,919
Private creditors	520	5,445	675	745	6,845	3,828	4,267	9,613	7,302	6,422

10. CONTRACTUAL OBLIGATIONS ON OUTSTANDING LONG-TERM DEBT

	1996	1997	1998	1999	2000	2001	2002	2003	2004	2005
TOTAL										
Disbursements	9,338	2,406	1,408	852	511	303	185	87	35	14
Principal	15,304	14,978	16,773	12,562	10,189	5,022	4,446	3,463	4,128	2,278
Interest	8,497	7,697	6,589	5,347	4,445	3,823	3,458	3,128	2,850	2,621
Official creditors										
Disbursements	3,425	1,797	1,198	812	511	303	185	87	35	14
Principal	4,163	5,319	7,366	7,975	4,095	2,871	2,442	2,167	2,013	1,895
Interest	3,201	2,972	2,532	1,931	1,442	1,188	999	839	692	553
Bilateral creditors										
Disbursements	1,163	400	153	46	23	16	0	0	0	0
Principal	2,354	3,416	5,401	5,848	1,891	763	492	401	329	251
Interest	1,729	1,533	1,159	649	280	160	107	78	52	32
Multilateral creditors										
Disbursements	2,262	1,397	1,044	766	488	287	185	87	35	14
Principal	1,809	1,903	1,965	2,127	2,204	2,109	1,950	1,766	1,684	1,644
Interest	1,472	1,439	1,373	1,282	1,162	1,027	892	762	640	521
Private creditors										
Disbursements	5,913	608	211	40	0	0	0	0	0	0
Principal	11,142	9,659	9,407	4,586	6,095	2,151	2,004	1,297	2,115	383
Interest	5,296	4,725	4,057	3,416	3,004	2,635	2,459	2,289	2,158	2,067
Commercial banks										
Disbursements	226	92	41	0	0	0	0	0	0	0
Principal	1,804	934	744	596	432	431	431	431	431	257
Interest	417	342	279	228	190	160	131	101	72	44
Other private										
Disbursements	5,688	516	170	40	0	0	0	0	0	0
Principal	9,337	8,725	8,664	3,990	5,662	1,720	1,574	866	1,684	127
Interest	4,880	4,383	3,778	3,188	2,814	2,475	2,329	2,187	2,086	2,023

MOLDOVA

(US$ million, unless otherwise indicated)

	1970	1980	1988	1989	1990	1991	1992	1993	1994	1995
1. SUMMARY DEBT DATA										
TOTAL DEBT STOCKS (EDT)	..	..	..	..	..	..	**38.5**	**284.5**	**503.9**	**690.9**
Long-term debt (LDOD)	..	..	..	..	..	..	**38.5**	**197.1**	**331.7**	**454.6**
Public and publicly guaranteed	..	..	..	..	..	..	38.5	197.1	331.7	454.6
Private nonguaranteed	0.0	0.0	0.0	0.0	0.0	0.0	0.0	0.0	0.0	0.0
Use of IMF credit	**0.0**	**0.0**	**0.0**	**0.0**	**0.0**	**0.0**	**0.0**	**86.5**	**164.2**	**230.2**
Short-term debt	..	..	..	..	..	..	**0.0**	**0.9**	**8.1**	**6.1**
of which interest arrears on LDOD	..	..	..	..	..	..	0.0	0.9	7.1	5.1
Official creditors	..	..	..	..	..	..	0.0	0.9	7.1	5.1
Private creditors	..	..	..	..	..	..	0.0	0.0	0.0	0.0
Memo: principal arrears on LDOD	..	..	..	..	..	..	0.0	5.0	17.8	42.7
Official creditors	..	..	..	..	..	..	0.0	5.0	17.8	42.7
Private creditors	..	..	..	..	..	..	0.0	0.0	0.0	0.0
Memo: export credits	..	..	0.0	0.0	0.0	0.0	0.0	0.0	0.0	8.0
TOTAL DEBT FLOWS										
Disbursements	..	..	..	..	..	..	**35.1**	**167.3**	**206.9**	**227.2**
Long-term debt	..	..	..	..	..	..	35.1	79.3	136.0	162.8
IMF purchases	0.0	0.0	0.0	0.0	0.0	0.0	0.0	88.0	70.8	64.3
Principal repayments	..	..	..	..	..	..	**5.0**	**0.8**	**6.4**	**39.4**
Long-term debt	..	..	..	..	..	..	5.0	0.8	6.4	39.4
IMF repurchases	0.0	0.0	0.0	0.0	0.0	0.0	0.0	0.0	0.0	0.0
Net flows on debt	..	..	..	..	..	..	**30.1**	**166.6**	**201.4**	**187.8**
of which short-term debt	..	..	..	..	..	..	0.0	0.0	1.0	0.0
Interest payments (INT)	..	..	..	..	..	..	**0.0**	**1.2**	**8.6**	**29.9**
Long-term debt	..	..	..	..	..	..	0.0	0.3	3.6	19.8
IMF charges	0.0	0.0	0.0	0.0	0.0	0.0	0.0	1.0	5.0	10.1
Short-term debt	..	..	..	..	..	..	0.0	0.0	0.0	0.0
Net transfers on debt	..	..	..	..	..	..	**30.1**	**165.3**	**192.8**	**157.8**
Total debt service paid (TDS)	..	..	..	..	..	..	**5.0**	**2.0**	**15.0**	**69.3**
Long-term debt	..	..	..	..	..	..	5.0	1.0	10.0	59.2
IMF repurchases and charges	0.0	0.0	0.0	0.0	0.0	0.0	0.0	1.0	5.0	10.1
Short-term debt (interest only)	..	..	..	..	..	..	0.0	0.0	0.0	0.0
2. AGGREGATE NET RESOURCE FLOWS AND NET TRANSFERS (LONG-TERM)										
NET RESOURCE FLOWS	..	..	..	..	..	..	**47.8**	**110.6**	**174.0**	**196.9**
Net flow of long-term debt (ex. IMF)	..	..	..	..	..	..	30.1	78.6	129.6	123.4
Foreign direct investment (net)	..	..	..	..	..	..	17.0	14.0	12.0	64.0
Portfolio equity flows	..	..	..	..	..	..	0.0	0.0	0.0	0.0
Grants (excluding technical coop.)	..	..	..	..	..	..	0.7	18.0	32.4	9.5
Memo: technical coop. grants	..	..	..	..	..	..	0.0	0.4	1.6	20.8
NET TRANSFERS	..	..	..	..	..	..	**47.8**	**110.3**	**170.4**	**177.1**
Interest on long-term debt	..	..	..	..	..	..	0.0	0.3	3.6	19.8
Profit remittances on FDI	..	..	..	..	..	..	0.0	0.0	0.0	0.0
3. MAJOR ECONOMIC AGGREGATES										
Gross national product (GNP)	..	..	..	..	..	..	5,375.0	5,202.9	3,727.8	3,874.0
Exports of goods & services (XGS)	..	..	..	..	..	..	..	..	662.1	864.7
of which workers remittances	..	..	..	..	..	..	..	..	0.0	0.0
Imports of goods & services (MGS)	..	..	..	..	..	..	..	..	777.4	999.0
International reserves (RES)	..	..	..	..	..	..	2.5	76.3	179.9	239.8
Current account balance	..	..	..	..	..	..	..	..	-82.0	-94.7
4. DEBT INDICATORS										
EDT / XGS (%)	..	..	..	..	..	..	..	..	76.1	79.9
EDT / GNP (%)	..	..	..	..	..	..	0.7	5.5	13.5	17.8
TDS / XGS (%)	..	..	..	..	..	..	..	..	2.3	8.0
INT / XGS (%)	..	..	..	..	..	..	..	..	1.3	3.5
INT / GNP (%)	..	..	..	..	..	..	0.0	0.0	0.2	0.8
RES / EDT (%)	..	..	..	..	..	..	6.5	26.8	35.7	34.7
RES / MGS (months)	..	..	..	..	..	..	..	..	2.8	2.9
Short-term / EDT (%)	..	..	..	..	..	..	0.0	0.3	1.6	0.9
Concessional / EDT (%)	..	..	..	..	..	..	25.6	9.5	15.9	24.1
Multilateral / EDT (%)	..	..	..	..	..	..	59.4	19.7	32.3	31.3

MOLDOVA

(US$ million, unless otherwise indicated)

	1970	1980	1988	1989	1990	1991	1992	1993	1994	1995
5. LONG-TERM DEBT										
DEBT OUTSTANDING (LDOD)	..	..	..	..	..	..	**38.5**	**197.1**	**331.7**	**454.6**
Public and publicly guaranteed	..	..	..	..	..	..	**38.5**	**197.1**	**331.7**	**454.6**
Official creditors	..	..	..	..	..	..	38.5	197.1	331.7	439.6
Multilateral	..	..	..	..	..	..	22.9	56.2	162.6	216.5
Concessional	..	..	..	..	..	..	0.0	0.0	30.8	59.1
Bilateral	..	..	..	..	..	..	15.6	140.9	169.1	223.1
Concessional	..	..	..	..	..	..	9.9	27.0	49.4	107.5
Private creditors	..	..	..	..	..	..	0.0	0.0	0.0	15.0
Bonds	..	..	..	..	..	..	0.0	0.0	0.0	0.0
Commercial banks	..	..	..	..	..	..	0.0	0.0	0.0	0.0
Other private	..	..	..	..	..	..	0.0	0.0	0.0	15.0
Private nonguaranteed	**0.0**	**0.0**	**0.0**	**0.0**	**0.0**	**0.0**	**0.0**	**0.0**	**0.0**	**0.0**
Bonds	..	..	..	..	..	..	0.0	0.0	0.0	0.0
Commercial banks	..	..	..	..	..	..	0.0	0.0	0.0	0.0
Memo:										
IBRD	0.0	0.0	0.0	0.0	0.0	0.0	0.0	28.1	98.8	152.4
IDA	0.0	0.0	0.0	0.0	0.0	0.0	0.0	0.0	0.0	0.0
DISBURSEMENTS	..	..	..	..	..	..	**35.1**	**79.3**	**136.0**	**162.8**
Public and publicly guaranteed	..	..	..	..	..	..	**35.1**	**79.3**	**136.0**	**162.8**
Official creditors	..	..	..	..	..	..	35.1	79.3	136.0	147.8
Multilateral	..	..	..	..	..	..	24.5	35.8	98.9	81.4
Concessional	..	..	..	..	..	..	0.0	0.0	29.7	26.2
Bilateral	..	..	..	..	..	..	10.6	43.5	37.1	66.4
Concessional	..	..	..	..	..	..	9.9	23.5	24.9	66.4
Private creditors	..	..	..	..	..	..	0.0	0.0	0.0	15.0
Bonds	..	..	..	..	..	..	0.0	0.0	0.0	0.0
Commercial banks	..	..	..	..	..	..	0.0	0.0	0.0	0.0
Other private	..	..	..	..	..	..	0.0	0.0	0.0	15.0
Private nonguaranteed	**0.0**	**0.0**	**0.0**	**0.0**	**0.0**	**0.0**	**0.0**	**0.0**	**0.0**	**0.0**
Bonds	..	..	..	..	..	..	0.0	0.0	0.0	0.0
Commercial banks	..	..	..	..	..	..	0.0	0.0	0.0	0.0
Memo:										
IBRD	0.0	0.0	0.0	0.0	0.0	0.0	0.0	28.6	67.1	50.2
IDA	0.0	0.0	0.0	0.0	0.0	0.0	0.0	0.0	0.0	0.0
PRINCIPAL REPAYMENTS	..	..	..	..	..	..	**5.0**	**0.8**	**6.4**	**39.4**
Public and publicly guaranteed	..	..	..	..	..	..	**5.0**	**0.8**	**6.4**	**39.4**
Official creditors	..	..	..	..	..	..	5.0	0.8	6.4	39.4
Multilateral	..	..	..	..	..	..	0.0	0.0	0.0	35.3
Concessional	..	..	..	..	..	..	0.0	0.0	0.0	0.0
Bilateral	..	..	..	..	..	..	5.0	0.8	6.4	4.1
Concessional	..	..	..	..	..	..	0.0	0.0	0.0	0.0
Private creditors	..	..	..	..	..	..	0.0	0.0	0.0	0.0
Bonds	..	..	..	..	..	..	0.0	0.0	0.0	0.0
Commercial banks	..	..	..	..	..	..	0.0	0.0	0.0	0.0
Other private	..	..	..	..	..	..	0.0	0.0	0.0	0.0
Private nonguaranteed	**0.0**	**0.0**	**0.0**	**0.0**	**0.0**	**0.0**	**0.0**	**0.0**	**0.0**	**0.0**
Bonds	..	..	..	..	..	..	0.0	0.0	0.0	0.0
Commercial banks	..	..	..	..	..	..	0.0	0.0	0.0	0.0
Memo:										
IBRD	0.0	0.0	0.0	0.0	0.0	0.0	0.0	0.0	0.0	0.0
IDA	0.0	0.0	0.0	0.0	0.0	0.0	0.0	0.0	0.0	0.0
NET FLOWS ON DEBT	..	..	..	..	..	..	**30.1**	**78.6**	**129.6**	**123.4**
Public and publicly guaranteed	..	..	..	..	..	..	**30.1**	**78.6**	**129.6**	**123.4**
Official creditors	..	..	..	..	..	..	30.1	78.6	129.6	108.4
Multilateral	..	..	..	..	..	..	24.5	35.8	98.9	46.1
Concessional	..	..	..	..	..	..	0.0	0.0	29.7	26.2
Bilateral	..	..	..	..	..	..	5.6	42.8	30.7	62.3
Concessional	..	..	..	..	..	..	9.9	23.5	24.9	66.4
Private creditors	..	..	..	..	..	..	0.0	0.0	0.0	15.0
Bonds	..	..	..	..	..	..	0.0	0.0	0.0	0.0
Commercial banks	..	..	..	..	..	..	0.0	0.0	0.0	0.0
Other private	..	..	..	..	..	..	0.0	0.0	0.0	15.0
Private nonguaranteed	**0.0**	**0.0**	**0.0**	**0.0**	**0.0**	**0.0**	**0.0**	**0.0**	**0.0**	**0.0**
Bonds	..	..	..	..	..	..	0.0	0.0	0.0	0.0
Commercial banks	..	..	..	..	..	..	0.0	0.0	0.0	0.0
Memo:										
IBRD	0.0	0.0	0.0	0.0	0.0	0.0	0.0	28.6	67.1	50.2
IDA	0.0	0.0	0.0	0.0	0.0	0.0	0.0	0.0	0.0	0.0

MOLDOVA

(US$ million, unless otherwise indicated)

	1970	1980	1988	1989	1990	1991	1992	1993	1994	1995
INTEREST PAYMENTS (LINT)	..	..	..	..	..	..	**0.0**	**0.3**	**3.6**	**19.8**
Public and publicly guaranteed	..	..	..	..	..	..	**0.0**	**0.3**	**3.6**	**19.8**
Official creditors	..	..	..	..	..	..	0.0	0.3	3.6	19.8
Multilateral	..	..	..	..	..	..	0.0	0.3	3.6	11.7
Concessional	..	..	..	..	..	..	0.0	0.0	0.0	2.0
Bilateral	..	..	..	..	..	..	0.0	0.0	0.0	8.1
Concessional	..	..	..	..	..	..	0.0	0.0	0.0	2.3
Private creditors	..	..	..	..	..	..	0.0	0.0	0.0	0.0
Bonds	..	..	..	..	..	..	0.0	0.0	0.0	0.0
Commercial banks	..	..	..	..	..	..	0.0	0.0	0.0	0.0
Other private	..	..	..	..	..	..	0.0	0.0	0.0	0.0
Private nonguaranteed	**0.0**	**0.0**	**0.0**	**0.0**	**0.0**	**0.0**	**0.0**	**0.0**	**0.0**	**0.0**
Bonds	..	..	..	..	..	..	0.0	0.0	0.0	0.0
Commercial banks	..	..	..	..	..	..	0.0	0.0	0.0	0.0
Memo:										
IBRD	0.0	0.0	0.0	0.0	0.0	0.0	0.0	0.3	3.6	7.8
IDA	0.0	0.0	0.0	0.0	0.0	0.0	0.0	0.0	0.0	0.0
NET TRANSFERS ON DEBT	..	..	..	..	..	..	**30.1**	**78.3**	**126.0**	**103.6**
Public and publicly guaranteed	..	..	..	..	..	..	**30.1**	**78.3**	**126.0**	**103.6**
Official creditors	..	..	..	..	..	..	30.1	78.3	126.0	88.6
Multilateral	..	..	..	..	..	..	24.5	35.5	95.3	34.4
Concessional	..	..	..	..	..	..	0.0	0.0	29.7	24.1
Bilateral	..	..	..	..	..	..	5.6	42.8	30.7	54.2
Concessional	..	..	..	..	..	..	9.9	23.5	24.9	64.1
Private creditors	..	..	..	..	..	..	0.0	0.0	0.0	15.0
Bonds	..	..	..	..	..	..	0.0	0.0	0.0	0.0
Commercial banks	..	..	..	..	..	..	0.0	0.0	0.0	0.0
Other private	..	..	..	..	..	..	0.0	0.0	0.0	15.0
Private nonguaranteed	**0.0**	**0.0**	**0.0**	**0.0**	**0.0**	**0.0**	**0.0**	**0.0**	**0.0**	**0.0**
Bonds	..	..	..	..	..	..	0.0	0.0	0.0	0.0
Commercial banks	..	..	..	..	..	..	0.0	0.0	0.0	0.0
Memo:										
IBRD	0.0	0.0	0.0	0.0	0.0	0.0	0.0	28.3	63.5	42.3
IDA	0.0	0.0	0.0	0.0	0.0	0.0	0.0	0.0	0.0	0.0
DEBT SERVICE (LTDS)	..	..	..	..	..	..	**5.0**	**1.0**	**10.0**	**59.2**
Public and publicly guaranteed	..	..	..	..	..	..	**5.0**	**1.0**	**10.0**	**59.2**
Official creditors	..	..	..	..	..	..	5.0	1.0	10.0	59.2
Multilateral	..	..	..	..	..	..	0.0	0.3	3.6	47.0
Concessional	..	..	..	..	..	..	0.0	0.0	0.0	2.0
Bilateral	..	..	..	..	..	..	5.0	0.8	6.4	12.2
Concessional	..	..	..	..	..	..	0.0	0.0	0.0	2.3
Private creditors	..	..	..	..	..	..	0.0	0.0	0.0	0.0
Bonds	..	..	..	..	..	..	0.0	0.0	0.0	0.0
Commercial banks	..	..	..	..	..	..	0.0	0.0	0.0	0.0
Other private	..	..	..	..	..	..	0.0	0.0	0.0	0.0
Private nonguaranteed	**0.0**	**0.0**	**0.0**	**0.0**	**0.0**	**0.0**	**0.0**	**0.0**	**0.0**	**0.0**
Bonds	..	..	..	..	..	..	0.0	0.0	0.0	0.0
Commercial banks	..	..	..	..	..	..	0.0	0.0	0.0	0.0
Memo:										
IBRD	0.0	0.0	0.0	0.0	0.0	0.0	0.0	0.3	3.6	7.8
IDA	0.0	0.0	0.0	0.0	0.0	0.0	0.0	0.0	0.0	0.0
UNDISBURSED DEBT	..	..	..	..	..	..	**15.1**	**80.4**	**159.8**	**146.7**
Official creditors	..	..	..	..	..	..	15.1	80.4	159.8	136.3
Private creditors	..	..	..	..	..	..	0.0	0.0	0.0	10.5
Memorandum items										
Concessional LDOD	..	..	..	..	..	..	9.9	27.0	80.2	166.6
Variable rate LDOD	..	..	..	..	..	..	22.9	165.1	278.5	390.0
Public sector LDOD	..	..	..	..	..	..	38.5	197.1	331.7	454.6
Private sector LDOD	..	..	..	..	..	..	0.0	0.0	0.0	0.0

6. CURRENCY COMPOSITION OF LONG-TERM DEBT (PERCENT)

	1970	1980	1988	1989	1990	1991	1992	1993	1994	1995
Deutsche mark	..	..	..	..	..	..	0.0	0.0	0.0	0.9
French franc	..	..	..	..	..	..	0.0	0.0	0.0	0.0
Japanese yen	..	..	..	..	..	..	0.0	0.0	0.0	11.4
Pound sterling	..	..	..	..	..	..	0.0	0.0	0.0	0.0
Swiss franc	..	..	..	..	..	..	0.0	0.0	0.0	0.0
U.S.dollars	..	..	..	..	..	..	40.5	22.4	21.3	20.2
Multiple currency	..	..	..	..	..	..	0.0	14.3	29.8	33.5
Special drawing rights	..	..	..	..	..	..	0.0	0.0	0.0	0.0
All other currencies	..	..	..	..	..	..	59.5	63.3	49.0	34.0

MOLDOVA

(US$ million, unless otherwise indicated)

	1970	1980	1988	1989	1990	1991	1992	1993	1994	1995
7. DEBT RESTRUCTURINGS										
Total amount rescheduled	0.0	0.0	0.0	0.0	0.0	0.0	0.0	88.9	0.0	0.0
Debt stock rescheduled	0.0	0.0	0.0	0.0	0.0	0.0	0.0	0.0	0.0	0.0
Principal rescheduled	0.0	0.0	0.0	0.0	0.0	0.0	0.0	0.0	0.0	0.0
Official	0.0	0.0	0.0	0.0	0.0	0.0	0.0	0.0	0.0	0.0
Private	0.0	0.0	0.0	0.0	0.0	0.0	0.0	0.0	0.0	0.0
Interest rescheduled	0.0	0.0	0.0	0.0	0.0	0.0	0.0	0.0	0.0	0.0
Official	0.0	0.0	0.0	0.0	0.0	0.0	0.0	0.0	0.0	0.0
Private	0.0	0.0	0.0	0.0	0.0	0.0	0.0	0.0	0.0	0.0
Debt forgiven	..	..	0.0	0.0	0.0	0.0	0.0	0.0	0.0	0.0
Memo: interest forgiven	..	..	0.0	0.0	0.0	0.0	0.0	0.0	0.0	0.0
Debt stock reduction	0.0	0.0	0.0	0.0	0.0	0.0	0.0	0.0	0.0	0.0
of which debt buyback	0.0	0.0	0.0	0.0	0.0	0.0	0.0	0.0	0.0	0.0
8. DEBT STOCK-FLOW RECONCILIATION										
Total change in debt stocks	..	..	..	..	..	..	29.0	246.0	219.4	187.0
Net flows on debt	..	..	..	..	..	..	30.1	166.6	201.4	187.8
Net change in interest arrears	..	..	..	..	..	..	0.0	0.9	6.2	-1.9
Interest capitalized	..	..	..	..	..	..	0.0	0.0	0.0	0.0
Debt forgiveness or reduction	..	..	..	..	..	..	0.0	0.0	0.0	0.0
Cross-currency valuation	..	..	..	..	..	..	-2.2	-68.1	-50.5	-15.2
Residual	..	..	..	..	..	..	1.0	146.7	62.3	16.3
9. AVERAGE TERMS OF NEW COMMITMENTS										
ALL CREDITORS										
Interest (%)	..	..	..	..	..	..	3.5	5.2	5.6	6.6
Maturity (years)	..	..	..	..	..	..	7.7	15.0	17.1	11.7
Grace period (years)	..	..	..	..	..	..	3.9	4.4	5.4	4.8
Grant element (%)	..	..	..	..	..	..	23.6	22.7	28.2	17.2
Official creditors										
Interest (%)	..	..	..	..	..	..	3.5	5.2	5.6	6.5
Maturity (years)	..	..	..	..	..	..	7.7	15.0	17.1	13.4
Grace period (years)	..	..	..	..	..	..	3.9	4.4	5.4	5.5
Grant element (%)	..	..	..	..	..	..	23.6	22.7	28.2	19.6
Private creditors										
Interest (%)	..	..	..	..	..	..	0.0	0.0	0.0	6.9
Maturity (years)	..	..	..	..	..	..	0.0	0.0	0.0	3.4
Grace period (years)	..	..	..	..	..	..	0.0	0.0	0.0	1.3
Grant element (%)	..	..	..	..	..	..	0.0	0.0	0.0	5.6
Memorandum items										
Commitments	..	..	..	..	..	..	50.9	151.4	215.0	144.3
Official creditors	..	..	..	..	..	..	50.9	151.4	215.0	118.8
Private creditors	..	..	..	..	..	..	0.0	0.0	0.0	25.5

10. CONTRACTUAL OBLIGATIONS ON OUTSTANDING LONG-TERM DEBT

	1996	1997	1998	1999	2000	2001	2002	2003	2004	2005
TOTAL										
Disbursements	35.9	47.1	28.6	15.0	7.6	4.9	2.4	2.4	1.8	0.9
Principal	37.0	53.8	18.2	22.6	41.5	42.1	41.4	41.0	38.4	51.8
Interest	24.7	25.2	24.6	24.4	23.6	22.0	19.3	16.8	14.4	12.3
Official creditors										
Disbursements	32.0	43.2	26.8	14.4	7.4	4.9	2.4	2.4	1.8	0.9
Principal	35.1	36.6	16.1	20.4	39.3	42.1	41.4	41.0	38.4	51.8
Interest	23.5	24.1	24.2	24.1	23.4	22.0	19.3	16.8	14.4	12.3
Bilateral creditors										
Disbursements	2.8	2.8	1.5	0.6	0.2	0.1	0.0	0.0	0.0	0.0
Principal	35.1	33.0	9.7	5.5	6.5	7.3	6.6	6.6	6.6	6.6
Interest	6.3	4.4	3.0	2.4	2.4	3.0	2.4	2.2	2.1	1.9
Multilateral creditors										
Disbursements	29.2	40.4	25.2	13.8	7.2	4.9	2.4	2.4	1.8	0.9
Principal	0.0	3.6	6.4	14.9	32.8	34.8	34.8	34.4	31.8	45.2
Interest	17.2	19.7	21.3	21.7	21.0	19.0	16.8	14.5	12.3	10.4
Private creditors										
Disbursements	3.9	3.9	1.8	0.6	0.2	0.0	0.0	0.0	0.0	0.0
Principal	1.9	17.1	2.1	2.1	2.1	0.0	0.0	0.0	0.0	0.0
Interest	1.1	1.1	0.4	0.3	0.1	0.0	0.0	0.0	0.0	0.0
Commercial banks										
Disbursements	0.0	0.0	0.0	0.0	0.0	0.0	0.0	0.0	0.0	0.0
Principal	0.0	0.0	0.0	0.0	0.0	0.0	0.0	0.0	0.0	0.0
Interest	0.0	0.0	0.0	0.0	0.0	0.0	0.0	0.0	0.0	0.0
Other private										
Disbursements	3.9	3.9	1.8	0.6	0.2	0.0	0.0	0.0	0.0	0.0
Principal	1.9	17.1	2.1	2.1	2.1	0.0	0.0	0.0	0.0	0.0
Interest	1.1	1.1	0.4	0.3	0.1	0.0	0.0	0.0	0.0	0.0

MONGOLIA

(US$ million, unless otherwise indicated)

1. SUMMARY DEBT DATA

	1970	*1980*	*1988*	*1989*	*1990*	*1991*	*1992*	*1993*	*1994*	*1995*
TOTAL DEBT STOCKS (EDT)	..	..	..	..	..	..	**350.2**	**373.6**	**447.2**	**512.4**
Long-term debt (LDOD)	..	..	..	..	..	..	**272.2**	**328.3**	**386.5**	**451.7**
Public and publicly guaranteed	..	..	..	..	..	..	272.2	328.3	386.5	451.7
Private nonguaranteed	0.0	0.0	0.0	0.0	0.0	0.0	0.0	0.0	0.0	0.0
Use of IMF credit	**0.0**	**0.0**	**0.0**	**0.0**	**0.0**	**16.1**	**18.9**	**31.6**	**55.3**	**47.0**
Short-term debt	..	..	..	..	..	..	**59.2**	**13.7**	**5.5**	**13.7**
of which interest arrears on LDOD	..	..	..	..	..	..	1.7	1.6	2.5	2.5
Official creditors	..	..	..	..	..	..	0.0	1.2	2.1	2.0
Private creditors	..	..	..	..	..	..	1.6	0.4	0.4	0.5
Memo: principal arrears on LDOD	..	..	..	..	..	..	6.0	17.5	16.0	3.9
Official creditors	..	..	..	..	..	..	0.8	1.9	13.5	0.0
Private creditors	..	..	..	..	..	..	5.3	15.6	2.6	3.9
Memo: export credits	..	..	0.0	4.0	56.0	71.0	62.0	60.0	63.0	51.0
TOTAL DEBT FLOWS										
Disbursements	..	..	..	..	..	..	**161.1**	**71.1**	**86.5**	**95.0**
Long-term debt	..	..	..	..	..	..	157.6	58.2	65.3	95.0
IMF purchases	0.0	0.0	0.0	0.0	0.0	15.4	3.5	13.0	21.3	0.0
Principal repayments	..	..	..	..	..	..	**56.1**	**10.3**	**29.2**	**37.2**
Long-term debt	..	..	..	..	..	..	56.1	10.3	29.2	27.7
IMF repurchases	0.0	0.0	0.0	0.0	0.0	0.0	0.0	0.0	0.0	9.5
Net flows on debt	..	..	..	..	..	..	**162.4**	**15.6**	**48.1**	**66.1**
of which short-term debt	..	..	..	..	..	..	57.5	-45.3	-9.2	8.2
Interest payments (INT)	..	..	..	..	..	..	**11.5**	**9.6**	**9.5**	**9.6**
Long-term debt	..	..	..	..	..	..	9.5	6.2	7.9	8.0
IMF charges	0.0	0.0	0.0	0.0	0.0	0.1	1.3	1.2	1.1	1.1
Short-term debt	..	..	..	..	..	..	0.7	2.3	0.5	0.4
Net transfers on debt	..	..	..	..	..	..	**151.0**	**6.0**	**38.6**	**56.5**
Total debt service paid (TDS)	..	..	..	..	..	..	**67.6**	**19.9**	**38.7**	**46.7**
Long-term debt	..	..	..	..	..	..	65.7	16.4	37.2	35.7
IMF repurchases and charges	0.0	0.0	0.0	0.0	0.0	0.1	1.3	1.2	1.1	10.6
Short-term debt (interest only)	..	..	..	..	..	..	0.7	2.3	0.5	0.4

2. AGGREGATE NET RESOURCE FLOWS AND NET TRANSFERS (LONG-TERM)

	1970	*1980*	*1988*	*1989*	*1990*	*1991*	*1992*	*1993*	*1994*	*1995*
NET RESOURCE FLOWS	..	..	..	..	..	..	**146.0**	**89.1**	**107.9**	**151.4**
Net flow of long-term debt (ex. IMF)	0.0	0.0	0.0	0.0	0.0	0.0	101.4	47.9	36.0	67.3
Foreign direct investment (net)	0.0	0.0	0.0	0.0	0.0	2.0	8.0	8.0	10.0	10.0
Portfolio equity flows	..	..	..	..	..	..	0.0	0.0	0.0	0.0
Grants (excluding technical coop.)	0.0	0.0	0.0	0.4	1.3	26.9	36.6	33.2	61.9	74.1
Memo: technical coop. grants	0.0	0.0	3.0	5.9	11.8	18.2	21.6	37.6	54.4	58.0
NET TRANSFERS	..	..	..	..	..	..	**136.5**	**83.0**	**100.0**	**143.4**
Interest on long-term debt	..	..	..	..	..	..	9.5	6.2	7.9	8.0
Profit remittances on FDI	0.0	0.0	0.0	0.0	0.0	0.0	0.0	0.0	0.0	0.0

3. MAJOR ECONOMIC AGGREGATES

	1970	*1980*	*1988*	*1989*	*1990*	*1991*	*1992*	*1993*	*1994*	*1995*
Gross national product (GNP)	..	..	..	..	..	..	734.1	620.3	667.0	832.9
Exports of goods & services (XGS)	..	..	..	..	..	..	390.8	392.6	415.6	511.3
of which workers remittances	..	..	..	..	..	..	0.0	0.0	0.0	0.0
Imports of goods & services (MGS)	..	..	..	..	..	..	481.7	432.4	447.0	549.5
International reserves (RES)	..	..	..	..	..	..	22.8	66.0	94.2	157.5
Current account balance	..	..	..	..	..	..	-55.7	31.1	46.4	38.9

4. DEBT INDICATORS

	1970	*1980*	*1988*	*1989*	*1990*	*1991*	*1992*	*1993*	*1994*	*1995*
EDT / XGS (%)	..	..	..	..	..	..	89.6	95.2	107.6	100.2
EDT / GNP (%)	..	..	..	..	..	..	47.7	60.2	67.1	61.5
TDS / XGS (%)	..	..	..	..	..	..	17.3	5.1	9.3	9.1
INT / XGS (%)	..	..	..	..	..	..	2.9	2.4	2.3	1.9
INT / GNP (%)	..	..	..	..	..	..	1.6	1.5	1.4	1.1
RES / EDT (%)	..	..	..	..	..	..	6.5	17.7	21.1	30.7
RES / MGS (months)	..	..	..	..	..	..	0.6	1.8	2.5	3.4
Short-term / EDT (%)	..	..	..	..	..	..	16.9	3.7	1.2	2.7
Concessional / EDT (%)	..	..	..	..	..	..	42.9	52.6	58.3	67.4
Multilateral / EDT (%)	..	..	..	..	..	..	16.1	19.1	25.3	33.2

MONGOLIA

(US$ million, unless otherwise indicated)

	1970	1980	1988	1989	1990	1991	1992	1993	1994	1995
5. LONG-TERM DEBT										
DEBT OUTSTANDING (LDOD)	..	..	..	..	..	..	**272.2**	**328.3**	**386.5**	**451.7**
Public and publicly guaranteed	..	..	..	..	..	..	**272.2**	**328.3**	**386.5**	**451.7**
Official creditors	..	..	..	..	..	..	163.0	225.0	297.3	373.7
Multilateral	..	..	..	..	..	..	56.4	71.5	113.1	169.9
Concessional	..	..	..	..	..	..	53.4	68.5	113.1	169.9
Bilateral	..	..	..	..	..	..	106.6	153.5	184.2	203.9
Concessional	..	..	..	..	..	..	97.0	128.0	147.5	175.5
Private creditors	..	..	..	..	..	..	109.2	103.3	89.2	78.0
Bonds	..	..	..	..	..	..	0.0	0.0	0.0	0.0
Commercial banks	..	..	..	..	..	..	19.7	19.6	19.6	14.6
Other private	..	..	..	..	..	..	89.6	83.7	69.7	63.4
Private nonguaranteed	**0.0**	**0.0**	**0.0**	**0.0**	**0.0**	**0.0**	**0.0**	**0.0**	**0.0**	**0.0**
Bonds	..	..	..	..	..	..	0.0	0.0	0.0	0.0
Commercial banks	..	..	..	..	..	..	0.0	0.0	0.0	0.0
Memo:										
IBRD	0.0	0.0	0.0	0.0	0.0	0.0	0.0	0.0	0.0	0.0
IDA	0.0	0.0	0.0	0.0	0.0	0.0	27.4	30.1	49.2	58.7
DISBURSEMENTS	..	..	..	..	..	..	**157.6**	**58.2**	**65.3**	**95.0**
Public and publicly guaranteed	..	..	..	..	..	..	**157.6**	**58.2**	**65.3**	**95.0**
Official creditors	..	..	..	..	..	..	75.0	58.2	62.7	89.4
Multilateral	..	..	..	..	..	..	44.3	14.7	38.9	58.3
Concessional	..	..	..	..	..	..	43.4	14.7	38.9	58.3
Bilateral	..	..	..	..	..	..	30.7	43.5	23.8	31.2
Concessional	..	..	..	..	..	..	21.2	27.5	10.6	31.2
Private creditors	..	..	..	..	..	..	82.5	0.0	2.6	5.6
Bonds	..	..	..	..	..	..	0.0	0.0	0.0	0.0
Commercial banks	..	..	..	..	..	..	58.2	0.0	1.7	0.1
Other private	..	..	..	..	..	..	24.3	0.0	0.9	5.5
Private nonguaranteed	**0.0**	**0.0**	**0.0**	**0.0**	**0.0**	**0.0**	**0.0**	**0.0**	**0.0**	**0.0**
Bonds	..	..	..	..	..	..	0.0	0.0	0.0	0.0
Commercial banks	..	..	..	..	..	..	0.0	0.0	0.0	0.0
Memo:										
IBRD	0.0	0.0	0.0	0.0	0.0	0.0	0.0	0.0	0.0	0.0
IDA	0.0	0.0	0.0	0.0	0.0	0.0	27.4	3.4	17.4	8.4
PRINCIPAL REPAYMENTS	..	..	..	..	..	..	**56.1**	**10.3**	**29.2**	**27.7**
Public and publicly guaranteed	..	..	..	..	..	..	**56.1**	**10.3**	**29.2**	**27.7**
Official creditors	..	..	..	..	..	..	0.0	0.0	5.0	8.4
Multilateral	..	..	..	..	..	..	0.0	0.0	3.0	0.0
Concessional	..	..	..	..	..	..	0.0	0.0	0.0	0.0
Bilateral	..	..	..	..	..	..	0.0	0.0	2.0	8.4
Concessional	..	..	..	..	..	..	0.0	0.0	0.0	0.1
Private creditors	..	..	..	..	..	..	56.1	10.3	24.2	19.2
Bonds	..	..	..	..	..	..	0.0	0.0	0.0	0.0
Commercial banks	..	..	..	..	..	..	40.2	0.0	2.0	5.2
Other private	..	..	..	..	..	..	15.9	10.3	22.2	14.0
Private nonguaranteed	**0.0**	**0.0**	**0.0**	**0.0**	**0.0**	**0.0**	**0.0**	**0.0**	**0.0**	**0.0**
Bonds	..	..	..	..	..	..	0.0	0.0	0.0	0.0
Commercial banks	..	..	..	..	..	..	0.0	0.0	0.0	0.0
Memo:										
IBRD	0.0	0.0	0.0	0.0	0.0	0.0	0.0	0.0	0.0	0.0
IDA	0.0	0.0	0.0	0.0	0.0	0.0	0.0	0.0	0.0	0.0
NET FLOWS ON DEBT	..	..	..	..	..	..	**101.4**	**47.9**	**36.0**	**67.3**
Public and publicly guaranteed	..	..	..	..	..	..	**101.4**	**47.9**	**36.0**	**67.3**
Official creditors	..	..	..	..	..	..	75.0	58.2	57.7	81.0
Multilateral	..	..	..	..	..	..	44.3	14.7	35.9	58.3
Concessional	..	..	..	..	..	..	43.4	14.7	38.9	58.3
Bilateral	..	..	..	..	..	..	30.7	43.5	21.8	22.7
Concessional	..	..	..	..	..	..	21.2	27.5	10.6	31.0
Private creditors	..	..	..	..	..	..	26.4	-10.3	-21.7	-13.7
Bonds	..	..	..	..	..	..	0.0	0.0	0.0	0.0
Commercial banks	..	..	..	..	..	..	18.0	0.0	-0.3	-5.2
Other private	..	..	..	..	..	..	8.4	-10.3	-21.4	-8.5
Private nonguaranteed	**0.0**	**0.0**	**0.0**	**0.0**	**0.0**	**0.0**	**0.0**	**0.0**	**0.0**	**0.0**
Bonds	..	..	..	..	..	..	0.0	0.0	0.0	0.0
Commercial banks	..	..	..	..	..	..	0.0	0.0	0.0	0.0
Memo:										
IBRD	0.0	0.0	0.0	0.0	0.0	0.0	0.0	0.0	0.0	0.0
IDA	0.0	0.0	0.0	0.0	0.0	0.0	27.4	3.4	17.4	8.4

MONGOLIA

(US$ million, unless otherwise indicated)

	1970	1980	1988	1989	1990	1991	1992	1993	1994	1995
INTEREST PAYMENTS (LINT)	..	..	..	..	..	..	**9.5**	**6.2**	**7.9**	**8.0**
Public and publicly guaranteed	..	..	..	..	..	..	**9.5**	**6.2**	**7.9**	**8.0**
Official creditors	..	..	..	..	..	..	0.7	1.1	2.8	4.1
Multilateral	..	..	..	..	..	..	0.3	0.5	1.0	1.1
Concessional	..	..	..	..	..	..	0.2	0.5	0.8	1.1
Bilateral	..	..	..	..	..	..	0.3	0.6	1.8	3.0
Concessional	..	..	..	..	..	..	0.3	0.6	0.8	2.1
Private creditors	..	..	..	..	..	..	8.8	5.0	5.1	3.9
Bonds	..	..	..	..	..	..	0.0	0.0	0.0	0.0
Commercial banks	..	..	..	..	..	..	4.7	0.6	1.4	1.0
Other private	..	..	..	..	..	..	4.1	4.4	3.7	3.0
Private nonguaranteed	**0.0**	**0.0**	**0.0**	**0.0**	**0.0**	**0.0**	**0.0**	**0.0**	**0.0**	**0.0**
Bonds	..	..	..	..	..	..	0.0	0.0	0.0	0.0
Commercial banks	..	..	..	..	..	..	0.0	0.0	0.0	0.0
Memo:										
IBRD	0.0	0.0	0.0	0.0	0.0	0.0	0.0	0.0	0.0	0.0
IDA	0.0	0.0	0.0	0.0	0.0	0.0	0.1	0.2	0.3	0.4
NET TRANSFERS ON DEBT	..	..	..	..	..	..	**91.9**	**41.8**	**28.1**	**59.3**
Public and publicly guaranteed	..	..	..	..	..	..	**91.9**	**41.8**	**28.1**	**59.3**
Official creditors	..	..	..	..	..	..	74.4	57.1	54.9	76.9
Multilateral	..	..	..	..	..	..	44.0	14.2	34.9	57.1
Concessional	..	..	..	..	..	..	43.2	14.2	38.1	57.1
Bilateral	..	..	..	..	..	..	30.4	42.9	20.0	19.8
Concessional	..	..	..	..	..	..	20.9	26.9	9.7	29.0
Private creditors	..	..	..	..	..	..	17.5	-15.3	-26.8	-17.6
Bonds	..	..	..	..	..	..	0.0	0.0	0.0	0.0
Commercial banks	..	..	..	..	..	..	13.3	-0.6	-1.7	-6.2
Other private	..	..	..	..	..	..	4.2	-14.7	-25.1	-11.4
Private nonguaranteed	**0.0**	**0.0**	**0.0**	**0.0**	**0.0**	**0.0**	**0.0**	**0.0**	**0.0**	**0.0**
Bonds	..	..	..	..	..	..	0.0	0.0	0.0	0.0
Commercial banks	..	..	..	..	..	..	0.0	0.0	0.0	0.0
Memo:										
IBRD	0.0	0.0	0.0	0.0	0.0	0.0	0.0	0.0	0.0	0.0
IDA	0.0	0.0	0.0	0.0	0.0	0.0	27.3	3.2	17.1	8.0
DEBT SERVICE (LTDS)	..	..	..	..	..	..	**65.7**	**16.4**	**37.2**	**35.7**
Public and publicly guaranteed	..	..	..	..	..	..	**65.7**	**16.4**	**37.2**	**35.7**
Official creditors	..	..	..	..	..	..	0.7	1.1	7.8	12.5
Multilateral	..	..	..	..	..	..	0.3	0.5	4.0	1.1
Concessional	..	..	..	..	..	..	0.2	0.5	0.8	1.1
Bilateral	..	..	..	..	..	..	0.3	0.6	3.8	11.4
Concessional	..	..	..	..	..	..	0.3	0.6	0.8	2.2
Private creditors	..	..	..	..	..	..	65.0	15.3	29.3	23.2
Bonds	..	..	..	..	..	..	0.0	0.0	0.0	0.0
Commercial banks	..	..	..	..	..	..	44.9	0.6	3.4	6.2
Other private	..	..	..	..	..	..	20.1	14.7	25.9	17.0
Private nonguaranteed	**0.0**	**0.0**	**0.0**	**0.0**	**0.0**	**0.0**	**0.0**	**0.0**	**0.0**	**0.0**
Bonds	..	..	..	..	..	..	0.0	0.0	0.0	0.0
Commercial banks	..	..	..	..	..	..	0.0	0.0	0.0	0.0
Memo:										
IBRD	0.0	0.0	0.0	0.0	0.0	0.0	0.0	0.0	0.0	0.0
IDA	0.0	0.0	0.0	0.0	0.0	0.0	0.1	0.2	0.3	0.4
UNDISBURSED DEBT	..	..	..	..	..	..	**75.7**	**173.9**	**180.3**	**325.6**
Official creditors	..	..	..	..	..	..	60.4	156.9	165.8	316.7
Private creditors	..	..	..	..	..	..	15.3	17.0	14.5	8.9
Memorandum items										
Concessional LDOD	..	..	..	..	..	..	150.4	196.5	260.5	345.3
Variable rate LDOD	..	..	..	..	..	..	35.0	30.6	16.0	12.0
Public sector LDOD	..	..	..	..	..	..	255.9	312.7	370.4	429.9
Private sector LDOD	..	..	..	..	..	..	16.3	15.5	16.0	21.9
6. CURRENCY COMPOSITION OF LONG-TERM DEBT (PERCENT)										
Deutsche mark	..	..	..	..	..	..	3.2	3.5	4.1	5.4
French franc	..	..	..	..	..	..	0.0	0.0	0.0	0.0
Japanese yen	..	..	..	..	..	..	30.9	33.9	30.2	27.7
Pound sterling	..	..	..	..	..	..	0.0	0.0	0.0	0.0
Swiss franc	..	..	..	..	..	..	3.3	2.7	2.8	2.3
U.S.dollars	..	..	..	..	..	..	48.7	44.3	42.9	36.9
Multiple currency	..	..	..	..	..	..	9.6	12.3	16.9	24.9
Special drawing rights	..	..	..	..	..	..	0.0	0.0	0.0	0.0
All other currencies	..	..	..	..	..	..	4.3	3.4	3.1	2.8

MONGOLIA

(US$ million, unless otherwise indicated)

	1970	1980	1988	1989	1990	1991	1992	1993	1994	1995
7. DEBT RESTRUCTURINGS										
Total amount rescheduled	0.0	0.0	0.0	0.0	0.0	0.0	0.0	0.0	0.0	0.0
Debt stock rescheduled	0.0	0.0	0.0	0.0	0.0	0.0	0.0	0.0	0.0	0.0
Principal rescheduled	0.0	0.0	0.0	0.0	0.0	0.0	0.0	0.0	0.0	0.0
Official	0.0	0.0	0.0	0.0	0.0	0.0	0.0	0.0	0.0	0.0
Private	0.0	0.0	0.0	0.0	0.0	0.0	0.0	0.0	0.0	0.0
Interest rescheduled	0.0	0.0	0.0	0.0	0.0	0.0	0.0	0.0	0.0	0.0
Official	0.0	0.0	0.0	0.0	0.0	0.0	0.0	0.0	0.0	0.0
Private	0.0	0.0	0.0	0.0	0.0	0.0	0.0	0.0	0.0	0.0
Debt forgiven	..	..	0.0	0.0	0.0	0.0	0.0	0.1	0.0	0.0
Memo: interest forgiven	..	..	0.0	0.0	0.0	0.0	0.0	0.0	0.0	0.0
Debt stock reduction	0.0	0.0	0.0	0.0	0.0	0.0	0.0	0.0	0.0	0.0
of which debt buyback	0.0	0.0	0.0	0.0	0.0	0.0	0.0	0.0	0.0	0.0
8. DEBT STOCK-FLOW RECONCILIATION										
Total change in debt stocks	..	..	..	0.0	0.0	0.0	162.4	23.4	73.6	65.2
Net flows on debt	..	..	..	0.0	0.0	0.0	162.4	15.6	48.1	66.1
Net change in interest arrears	..	..	..	0.0	0.0	0.0	2.0	-0.1	0.9	0.0
Interest capitalized	..	..	..	0.0	0.0	0.0	0.0	0.0	0.0	0.0
Debt forgiveness or reduction	..	..	..	0.0	0.0	0.0	0.0	-0.1	0.0	0.0
Cross-currency valuation	..	..	..	0.0	0.0	0.0	-1.5	11.2	18.5	0.9
Residual	..	..	..	0.0	0.0	0.0	-0.5	-3.2	6.1	-1.8
9. AVERAGE TERMS OF NEW COMMITMENTS										
ALL CREDITORS										
Interest (%)	..	..	..	..	..	..	5.4	1.1	0.9	2.2
Maturity (years)	..	..	..	..	..	..	8.5	34.9	39.8	35.2
Grace period (years)	..	..	..	..	..	..	3.4	9.8	10.4	10.1
Grant element (%)	..	..	..	..	..	..	21.3	75.3	79.7	65.0
Official creditors										
Interest (%)	..	..	..	..	..	..	2.2	1.0	0.9	2.2
Maturity (years)	..	..	..	..	..	..	12.3	35.2	39.8	35.2
Grace period (years)	..	..	..	..	..	..	4.9	9.9	10.4	10.1
Grant element (%)	..	..	..	..	..	..	37.3	75.7	79.7	65.0
Private creditors										
Interest (%)	..	..	..	..	..	..	7.6	3.4	0.0	0.0
Maturity (years)	..	..	..	..	..	..	5.9	14.5	0.0	0.0
Grace period (years)	..	..	..	..	..	..	2.4	3.0	0.0	0.0
Grant element (%)	..	..	..	..	..	..	10.4	35.4	0.0	0.0
Memorandum items										
Commitments	..	..	..	..	..	..	135.9	157.0	64.7	244.1
Official creditors	..	..	..	..	..	..	54.8	155.2	64.7	244.1
Private creditors	..	..	..	..	..	..	81.1	1.8	0.0	0.0

10. CONTRACTUAL OBLIGATIONS ON OUTSTANDING LONG-TERM DEBT

	1996	1997	1998	1999	2000	2001	2002	2003	2004	2005
TOTAL										
Disbursements	74.9	80.4	61.8	42.7	29.3	18.4	12.1	2.9	0.2	0.0
Principal	39.9	37.7	22.8	9.2	9.2	10.3	14.6	16.1	16.5	21.7
Interest	9.1	8.6	8.0	7.6	7.8	7.8	7.8	7.5	7.2	8.1
Official creditors										
Disbursements	69.0	78.5	60.8	42.7	29.3	18.4	12.1	2.9	0.2	0.0
Principal	18.7	18.7	4.5	4.8	4.8	6.0	10.3	11.8	14.8	20.8
Interest	5.1	5.6	6.2	6.6	7.0	7.2	7.3	7.2	7.0	8.0
Bilateral creditors										
Disbursements	37.1	35.1	23.2	14.4	7.7	3.7	2.2	0.4	0.2	0.0
Principal	18.7	18.7	4.5	4.8	4.8	6.0	8.9	10.1	11.0	14.5
Interest	3.2	3.0	3.0	3.0	3.0	2.9	2.8	2.7	2.5	2.3
Multilateral creditors										
Disbursements	31.9	43.4	37.6	28.3	21.6	14.6	10.0	2.6	0.0	0.0
Principal	0.0	0.0	0.0	0.0	0.0	0.0	1.4	1.7	3.8	6.2
Interest	1.8	2.6	3.2	3.6	4.0	4.3	4.5	4.5	4.5	5.7
Private creditors										
Disbursements	5.9	1.9	1.0	0.0	0.0	0.0	0.0	0.0	0.0	0.0
Principal	21.2	19.0	18.3	4.3	4.3	4.3	4.3	4.3	1.7	0.9
Interest	4.0	3.0	1.9	1.0	0.8	0.6	0.5	0.3	0.1	0.0
Commercial banks										
Disbursements	0.0	0.0	0.0	0.0	0.0	0.0	0.0	0.0	0.0	0.0
Principal	4.6	4.1	4.1	0.1	0.1	0.1	0.1	0.1	0.1	0.1
Interest	1.1	0.7	0.3	0.0	0.0	0.0	0.0	0.0	0.0	0.0
Other private										
Disbursements	5.9	1.9	1.0	0.0	0.0	0.0	0.0	0.0	0.0	0.0
Principal	16.7	14.9	14.2	4.2	4.2	4.2	4.2	4.2	1.5	0.8
Interest	2.9	2.3	1.6	1.1	1.0	0.7	0.4	0.3	0.1	0.0

MOROCCO

(US$ million, unless otherwise indicated)

	1970	1980	1988	1989	1990	1991	1992	1993	1994	1995
1. SUMMARY DEBT DATA										
TOTAL DEBT STOCKS (EDT)	..	**9,247**	**20,716**	**21,753**	**23,527**	**21,139**	**21,273**	**20,687**	**21,587**	**22,147**
Long-term debt (LDOD)	**886**	**8,013**	**19,446**	**20,689**	**22,431**	**20,187**	**20,505**	**20,071**	**21,065**	**21,678**
Public and publicly guaranteed	871	7,863	19,246	20,489	22,231	19,987	20,301	19,892	20,806	21,347
Private nonguaranteed	15	150	200	200	200	200	204	179	259	331
Use of IMF credit	**28**	**457**	**957**	**850**	**750**	**574**	**439**	**285**	**148**	**52**
Short-term debt	..	**778**	**314**	**214**	**346**	**377**	**329**	**332**	**375**	**418**
of which interest arrears on LDOD	..	3	114	75	121	168	40	30	22	18
Official creditors	..	3	114	75	121	145	31	30	19	17
Private creditors	..	0	0	0	0	23	9	0	3	0
Memo: principal arrears on LDOD	..	3	78	750	661	482	78	71	57	61
Official creditors	..	3	78	332	661	422	78	71	48	60
Private creditors	..	0	0	418	0	61	0	0	9	1
Memo: export credits	..	..	5,653	7,066	8,416	8,878	8,056	7,777	8,445	8,316
TOTAL DEBT FLOWS										
Disbursements	**196**	**2,262**	**1,425**	**1,682**	**1,659**	**1,549**	**1,930**	**1,943**	**1,761**	**1,913**
Long-term debt	186	1,985	1,277	1,502	1,594	1,549	1,904	1,943	1,761	1,913
IMF purchases	10	278	148	180	65	0	26	0	0	0
Principal repayments	**54**	**678**	**794**	**886**	**938**	**1,231**	**1,530**	**2,003**	**2,025**	**2,164**
Long-term debt	40	591	541	624	711	1,059	1,388	1,847	1,873	2,064
IMF repurchases	14	88	253	262	228	172	142	156	152	101
Net flows on debt	**142**	**1,584**	**801**	**735**	**806**	**303**	**480**	**-47**	**-213**	**-205**
of which short-term debt	..	..	170	-61	86	-16	80	13	51	47
Interest payments (INT)	..	**768**	**995**	**1,190**	**893**	**1,142**	**2,338**	**1,292**	**1,313**	**1,377**
Long-term debt	26	651	854	1,110	801	1,061	2,279	1,243	1,282	1,346
IMF charges	0	12	69	68	72	63	43	31	13	7
Short-term debt	..	105	73	13	20	18	15	18	18	24
Net transfers on debt	..	**817**	**-194**	**-456**	**-87**	**-840**	**-1,858**	**-1,339**	**-1,526**	**-1,582**
Total debt service paid (TDS)	..	**1,446**	**1,789**	**2,077**	**1,831**	**2,373**	**3,868**	**3,295**	**3,338**	**3,541**
Long-term debt	66	1,241	1,395	1,734	1,512	2,120	3,667	3,089	3,156	3,410
IMF repurchases and charges	14	100	321	330	300	235	186	187	165	107
Short-term debt (interest only)	..	105	73	13	20	18	15	18	18	24
2. AGGREGATE NET RESOURCE FLOWS AND NET TRANSFERS (LONG-TERM)										
NET RESOURCE FLOWS	**190**	**1,559**	**929**	**1,146**	**1,528**	**1,370**	**1,121**	**896**	**781**	**388**
Net flow of long-term debt (ex. IMF)	146	1,394	736	878	883	490	516	96	-112	-151
Foreign direct investment (net)	20	89	85	167	165	317	422	491	551	290
Portfolio equity flows	0	0	0	0	0	0	0	0	63	150
Grants (excluding technical coop.)	24	75	108	101	480	563	182	309	279	100
Memo: technical coop. grants	29	123	150	153	184	192	199	204	202	267
NET TRANSFERS	**145**	**860**	**14**	**-20**	**657**	**214**	**-1,330**	**-450**	**-611**	**-1,088**
Interest on long-term debt	26	651	854	1,110	801	1,061	2,279	1,243	1,282	1,346
Profit remittances on FDI	20	49	61	56	69	95	171	103	110	130
3. MAJOR ECONOMIC AGGREGATES										
Gross national product (GNP)	3,911	18,223	21,161	21,688	24,839	26,721	27,315	25,640	29,178	31,203
Exports of goods & services (XGS)	..	4,324	6,709	6,349	8,328	8,901	9,597	9,169	9,606	11,022
of which workers remittances	..	1,054	1,303	1,337	2,006	1,990	2,171	1,959	1,827	1,904
Imports of goods & services (MGS)	..	5,807	6,545	7,423	8,853	9,599	10,392	10,026	10,772	12,900
International reserves (RES)	142	814	836	771	2,338	3,349	3,819	3,930	4,622	3,874
Current account balance	..	-1,407	473	-787	-196	-413	-433	-521	-720	-1,521
4. DEBT INDICATORS										
EDT / XGS (%)	..	213.9	308.8	342.6	282.5	237.5	221.7	225.6	224.7	200.9
EDT / GNP (%)	..	50.7	97.9	100.3	94.7	79.1	77.9	80.7	74.0	71.0
TDS / XGS (%)	..	33.4	26.7	32.7	22.0	26.7	40.3	35.9	34.7	32.1
INT / XGS (%)	..	17.7	14.8	18.7	10.7	12.8	24.4	14.1	13.7	12.5
INT / GNP (%)	..	4.2	4.7	5.5	3.6	4.3	8.6	5.0	4.5	4.4
RES / EDT (%)	..	8.8	4.0	3.5	9.9	15.8	18.0	19.0	21.4	17.5
RES / MGS (months)	..	1.7	1.5	1.2	3.2	4.2	4.4	4.7	5.1	3.6
Short-term / EDT (%)	..	8.4	1.5	1.0	1.5	1.8	1.5	1.6	1.7	1.9
Concessional / EDT (%)	..	29.4	30.8	30.2	29.8	20.6	21.2	21.9	22.6	23.8
Multilateral / EDT (%)	..	7.8	17.4	18.0	20.0	24.7	25.4	27.9	29.2	30.8

MOROCCO

(US$ million, unless otherwise indicated)

	1970	1980	1988	1989	1990	1991	1992	1993	1994	1995
5. LONG-TERM DEBT										
DEBT OUTSTANDING (LDOD)	**886**	**8,013**	**19,446**	**20,689**	**22,431**	**20,187**	**20,505**	**20,071**	**21,065**	**21,678**
Public and publicly guaranteed	**871**	**7,863**	**19,246**	**20,489**	**22,231**	**19,987**	**20,301**	**19,892**	**20,806**	**21,347**
Official creditors	742	3,522	13,285	14,443	16,403	14,390	15,030	14,910	15,573	15,935
Multilateral	59	723	3,602	3,912	4,701	5,222	5,398	5,767	6,312	6,830
Concessional	27	90	381	389	445	489	442	484	561	827
Bilateral	683	2,799	9,683	10,531	11,702	9,168	9,632	9,143	9,261	9,105
Concessional	620	2,633	6,006	6,181	6,558	3,871	4,068	4,054	4,327	4,449
Private creditors	129	4,341	5,960	6,046	5,828	5,597	5,271	4,982	5,233	5,412
Bonds	32	173	12	7	0	0	0	0	0	0
Commercial banks	0	2,343	3,413	3,572	3,394	3,344	3,253	3,242	3,417	3,461
Other private	98	1,825	2,535	2,467	2,434	2,253	2,018	1,740	1,817	1,951
Private nonguaranteed	**15**	**150**	**200**	**200**	**200**	**200**	**204**	**179**	**259**	**331**
Bonds	0	0	0	0	0	0	0	0	0	0
Commercial banks	15	150	200	200	200	200	204	179	259	331
Memo:										
IBRD	56	539	2,574	2,686	3,099	3,295	3,408	3,559	3,746	3,966
IDA	3	39	41	40	39	38	37	36	35	33
DISBURSEMENTS	**186**	**1,985**	**1,277**	**1,502**	**1,594**	**1,549**	**1,904**	**1,943**	**1,761**	**1,913**
Public and publicly guaranteed	**179**	**1,910**	**1,269**	**1,494**	**1,586**	**1,541**	**1,892**	**1,810**	**1,681**	**1,838**
Official creditors	145	867	819	1,070	1,178	1,175	1,373	1,302	1,017	1,256
Multilateral	16	109	563	663	783	773	858	759	657	962
Concessional	4	22	32	28	45	59	113	75	98	290
Bilateral	130	758	256	407	395	402	516	543	360	295
Concessional	90	709	206	191	260	227	353	368	300	194
Private creditors	34	1,042	450	425	408	367	519	508	665	581
Bonds	0	7	0	0	0	0	0	0	0	0
Commercial banks	0	482	24	161	47	80	50	140	266	142
Other private	34	554	426	264	361	286	470	368	399	439
Private nonguaranteed	**8**	**75**	**8**	**8**	**8**	**8**	**12**	**133**	**80**	**75**
Bonds	0	0	0	0	0	0	0	0	0	0
Commercial banks	8	75	8	8	8	8	12	133	80	75
Memo:										
IBRD	14	64	415	364	426	357	477	377	246	426
IDA	2	1	0	0	0	0	0	0	0	0
PRINCIPAL REPAYMENTS	**40**	**591**	**541**	**624**	**711**	**1,059**	**1,388**	**1,847**	**1,873**	**2,064**
Public and publicly guaranteed	**38**	**566**	**533**	**616**	**703**	**1,051**	**1,380**	**1,816**	**1,872**	**2,061**
Official creditors	25	116	376	424	480	595	855	1,143	1,329	1,540
Multilateral	5	39	279	277	297	338	486	433	479	641
Concessional	1	2	18	17	14	19	133	29	31	30
Bilateral	20	77	97	148	183	257	369	710	851	899
Concessional	15	62	54	43	47	51	58	264	297	250
Private creditors	13	450	157	192	223	456	525	673	543	521
Bonds	3	9	11	6	0	0	0	0	0	0
Commercial banks	0	295	24	6	40	129	138	148	98	104
Other private	10	147	122	180	183	327	387	525	445	417
Private nonguaranteed	**3**	**25**	**8**	**8**	**8**	**8**	**8**	**31**	**1**	**3**
Bonds	0	0	0	0	0	0	0	0	0	0
Commercial banks	3	25	8	8	8	8	8	31	1	3
Memo:										
IBRD	5	29	188	181	202	229	269	293	301	349
IDA	0	0	1	1	1	1	1	1	1	1
NET FLOWS ON DEBT	**146**	**1,394**	**736**	**878**	**883**	**490**	**516**	**96**	**-112**	**-151**
Public and publicly guaranteed	**141**	**1,344**	**736**	**878**	**883**	**490**	**512**	**-6**	**-191**	**-223**
Official creditors	120	752	443	645	698	580	518	160	-313	-284
Multilateral	11	70	284	386	486	434	371	327	178	321
Concessional	3	20	14	11	31	40	-20	46	67	259
Bilateral	109	681	159	259	212	146	147	-167	-491	-604
Concessional	75	647	151	148	213	176	295	104	3	-56
Private creditors	21	592	293	233	185	-90	-6	-165	122	60
Bonds	-3	-2	-11	-6	0	0	0	0	0	0
Commercial banks	0	188	0	155	7	-49	-89	-8	168	38
Other private	24	407	304	84	178	-41	83	-157	-46	22
Private nonguaranteed	**5**	**50**	**0**	**0**	**0**	**0**	**4**	**102**	**79**	**72**
Bonds	0	0	0	0	0	0	0	0	0	0
Commercial banks	5	50	0	0	0	0	4	102	79	72
Memo:										
IBRD	9	35	227	183	224	128	208	84	-55	78
IDA	2	1	-1	-1	-1	-1	-1	-1	-1	-1

MOROCCO

(US$ million, unless otherwise indicated)

	1970	1980	1988	1989	1990	1991	1992	1993	1994	1995
INTEREST PAYMENTS (LINT)	**26**	**651**	**854**	**1,110**	**801**	**1,061**	**2,279**	**1,243**	**1,282**	**1,346**
Public and publicly guaranteed	**25**	**639**	**849**	**1,105**	**796**	**1,056**	**2,272**	**1,240**	**1,282**	**1,344**
Official creditors	19	135	471	630	604	725	779	915	967	930
Multilateral	4	56	255	273	308	353	381	406	429	467
Concessional	1	3	7	14	9	13	19	17	19	25
Bilateral	15	79	215	357	295	371	398	509	538	463
Concessional	13	69	39	63	56	56	63	124	127	126
Private creditors	6	504	379	476	192	332	1,494	326	315	415
Bonds	2	15	1	1	0	0	0	0	0	0
Commercial banks	0	364	260	335	43	170	1,328	152	158	258
Other private	4	125	117	140	149	162	165	174	158	157
Private nonguaranteed	**1**	**11**	**5**	**5**	**5**	**5**	**7**	**2**	**1**	**2**
Bonds	0	0	0	0	0	0	0	0	0	0
Commercial banks	1	11	5	5	5	5	7	2	1	2
Memo:										
IBRD	4	49	198	200	226	242	249	259	271	282
IDA	0	0	0	0	0	0	0	0	0	0
NET TRANSFERS ON DEBT	**121**	**743**	**-118**	**-232**	**82**	**-571**	**-1,763**	**-1,147**	**-1,394**	**-1,497**
Public and publicly guaranteed	**116**	**705**	**-113**	**-227**	**87**	**-566**	**-1,760**	**-1,246**	**-1,473**	**-1,568**
Official creditors	102	617	-27	15	94	-145	-261	-755	-1,280	-1,213
Multilateral	7	14	29	113	178	81	-10	-79	-251	-146
Concessional	2	18	7	-3	22	27	-39	29	48	235
Bilateral	95	602	-56	-98	-84	-226	-251	-676	-1,029	-1,067
Concessional	62	578	113	85	157	120	232	-20	-124	-182
Private creditors	15	88	-86	-242	-8	-421	-1,499	-491	-193	-354
Bonds	-5	-17	-12	-6	0	0	0	0	0	0
Commercial banks	0	-177	-260	-180	-36	-219	-1,417	-161	10	-220
Other private	20	282	187	-56	29	-203	-83	-330	-203	-135
Private nonguaranteed	**4**	**39**	**-5**	**-5**	**-5**	**-5**	**-3**	**99**	**79**	**70**
Bonds	0	0	0	0	0	0	0	0	0	0
Commercial banks	4	39	-5	-5	-5	-5	-3	99	79	70
Memo:										
IBRD	5	-14	30	-17	-2	-114	-41	-175	-326	-205
IDA	2	0	-1	-1	-1	-1	-1	-2	-2	-2
DEBT SERVICE (LTDS)	**66**	**1,241**	**1,395**	**1,734**	**1,512**	**2,120**	**3,667**	**3,089**	**3,156**	**3,410**
Public and publicly guaranteed	**62**	**1,205**	**1,382**	**1,721**	**1,499**	**2,107**	**3,652**	**3,056**	**3,154**	**3,405**
Official creditors	44	251	846	1,054	1,083	1,320	1,634	2,058	2,296	2,470
Multilateral	9	95	535	549	605	692	868	838	908	1,108
Concessional	2	5	25	31	23	32	152	46	50	55
Bilateral	35	156	312	505	479	628	766	1,219	1,388	1,362
Concessional	28	131	93	105	103	106	121	388	424	376
Private creditors	19	954	536	667	416	788	2,019	999	858	936
Bonds	5	23	12	6	0	0	0	0	0	0
Commercial banks	0	659	284	341	83	299	1,467	300	255	362
Other private	14	272	239	320	332	489	552	698	603	574
Private nonguaranteed	**3**	**36**	**13**	**13**	**13**	**13**	**15**	**33**	**2**	**5**
Bonds	0	0	0	0	0	0	0	0	0	0
Commercial banks	3	36	13	13	13	13	15	33	2	5
Memo:										
IBRD	9	78	386	381	428	471	518	552	572	630
IDA	0	1	1	1	1	1	1	2	2	2
UNDISBURSED DEBT	**242**	**2,291**	**3,077**	**3,244**	**3,981**	**4,847**	**4,649**	**4,998**	**4,981**	**5,032**
Official creditors	221	1,966	2,858	2,974	3,373	4,033	3,824	4,067	4,138	4,534
Private creditors	21	325	219	270	608	814	825	931	844	498
Memorandum items										
Concessional LDOD	646	2,723	6,387	6,570	7,003	4,359	4,510	4,537	4,888	5,276
Variable rate LDOD	15	2,626	6,930	7,783	8,155	8,206	8,477	8,552	8,842	9,180
Public sector LDOD	864	7,808	19,172	20,426	22,181	19,948	20,218	19,763	20,661	21,201
Private sector LDOD	23	204	274	263	250	240	287	308	404	476

6. CURRENCY COMPOSITION OF LONG-TERM DEBT (PERCENT)

	1970	1980	1988	1989	1990	1991	1992	1993	1994	1995
Deutsche mark	11.7	3.9	5.6	5.5	5.6	6.7	7.0	7.7	8.1	8.3
French franc	29.5	22.1	20.9	19.6	21.6	23.0	21.4	19.6	19.6	19.3
Japanese yen	0.0	1.9	2.8	2.2	2.3	3.1	3.8	4.2	4.3	3.9
Pound sterling	0.0	0.4	0.2	0.1	0.1	0.1	0.1	0.1	0.1	0.1
Swiss franc	0.1	0.3	0.4	0.2	0.2	0.2	0.1	0.1	0.1	0.1
U.S.dollars	40.9	54.2	45.8	45.8	41.8	32.8	32.9	32.3	30.0	28.4
Multiple currency	6.8	7.0	14.7	15.1	16.4	20.3	21.2	23.2	24.3	24.8
Special drawing rights	0.0	0.2	0.1	0.1	0.1	0.1	0.1	0.1	0.1	0.1
All other currencies	11.0	9.9	9.6	11.3	12.0	13.8	13.4	12.7	13.4	15.0

MOROCCO

(US$ million, unless otherwise indicated)

	1970	1980	1988	1989	1990	1991	1992	1993	1994	1995
7. DEBT RESTRUCTURINGS										
Total amount rescheduled	0	0	3,323	730	4,089	247	1,321	0	0	0
Debt stock rescheduled	0	0	595	0	2,732	0	0	0	0	0
Principal rescheduled	0	0	2,303	462	591	186	750	0	0	0
Official	0	0	1,549	254	403	74	557	0	0	0
Private	0	0	754	208	189	112	194	0	0	0
Interest rescheduled	0	0	392	258	219	54	203	0	0	0
Official	0	0	279	173	152	26	143	0	0	0
Private	0	0	113	84	67	29	60	0	0	0
Debt forgiven	..	..	0	0	31	2,875	0	0	0	0
Memo: interest forgiven	..	..	0	0	0	97	0	0	0	0
Debt stock reduction	0	0	0	0	0	0	0	0	0	0
of which debt buyback	0	0	0	0	0	0	0	0	0	0
8. DEBT STOCK-FLOW RECONCILIATION										
Total change in debt stocks	..	..	..	1,037	1,774	-2,388	134	-585	900	560
Net flows on debt	..	..	..	735	806	303	480	-47	-213	-205
Net change in interest arrears	..	..	..	-39	46	47	-128	-10	-8	-4
Interest capitalized	..	..	..	258	219	54	203	0	0	0
Debt forgiveness or reduction	..	..	..	0	-31	-2,875	0	0	0	0
Cross-currency valuation	..	..	..	85	1,170	-12	-755	-409	1,045	692
Residual	..	..	..	-2	-436	95	334	-119	76	77
9. AVERAGE TERMS OF NEW COMMITMENTS										
ALL CREDITORS										
Interest (%)	4.5	8.1	7.4	7.4	6.8	6.7	7.6	6.9	4.9	4.7
Maturity (years)	21.1	15.4	21.3	16.8	20.0	19.0	13.9	18.7	16.3	18.7
Grace period (years)	3.5	5.1	4.6	4.3	6.2	5.6	4.2	4.9	4.2	5.3
Grant element (%)	32.3	14.8	16.6	16.5	23.8	22.3	10.7	18.1	29.6	30.7
Official creditors										
Interest (%)	4.0	4.1	6.7	6.8	5.5	6.2	8.1	7.0	4.2	4.4
Maturity (years)	25.1	19.8	27.2	19.9	24.1	21.6	15.9	21.8	19.0	19.8
Grace period (years)	4.1	6.4	6.0	5.5	8.1	6.5	5.1	6.3	5.9	5.9
Grant element (%)	38.5	39.8	22.6	21.5	35.0	27.6	10.7	20.8	37.6	33.2
Private creditors										
Interest (%)	6.1	12.2	8.8	9.0	9.8	8.4	6.5	6.8	6.2	7.1
Maturity (years)	8.6	10.7	8.2	8.3	11.2	11.0	9.2	10.6	11.5	10.0
Grace period (years)	1.6	3.7	1.5	1.0	2.2	2.6	2.3	1.5	1.2	0.6
Grant element (%)	13.7	-11.2	3.1	2.9	-0.4	5.6	10.9	11.2	15.1	10.1
Memorandum items										
Commitments	200	1,876	1,400	1,795	2,205	2,396	1,934	2,327	1,468	1,824
Official creditors	151	955	968	1,313	1,505	1,827	1,345	1,673	950	1,629
Private creditors	50	920	432	482	700	569	589	654	518	195

10. CONTRACTUAL OBLIGATIONS ON OUTSTANDING LONG-TERM DEBT

	1996	1997	1998	1999	2000	2001	2002	2003	2004	2005
TOTAL										
Disbursements	1,574	1,308	836	521	315	176	114	51	32	11
Principal	2,323	2,267	2,075	2,146	1,977	1,990	1,911	1,661	1,431	1,329
Interest	1,423	1,342	1,240	1,126	1,005	884	759	636	537	445
Official creditors										
Disbursements	1,264	1,178	790	508	314	176	114	51	32	11
Principal	1,361	1,402	1,251	1,366	1,261	1,322	1,292	1,288	1,269	1,247
Interest	1,021	994	948	890	822	751	669	588	507	426
Bilateral creditors										
Disbursements	385	354	223	130	70	35	21	12	3	0
Principal	737	748	513	564	476	626	637	657	652	645
Interest	513	480	445	416	386	356	315	275	236	196
Multilateral creditors										
Disbursements	879	824	568	378	244	141	93	39	29	11
Principal	624	654	738	801	786	695	655	631	617	602
Interest	508	514	502	474	437	395	354	313	271	229
Private creditors										
Disbursements	310	130	45	13	1	0	0	0	0	0
Principal	963	865	824	780	716	668	619	373	162	82
Interest	402	348	292	237	183	133	89	49	30	19
Commercial banks										
Disbursements	27	19	7	3	0	0	0	0	0	0
Principal	490	477	463	453	447	435	416	211	22	20
Interest	223	192	161	131	101	72	43	16	8	7
Other private										
Disbursements	283	111	38	9	1	0	0	0	0	0
Principal	473	388	361	328	269	234	204	162	140	62
Interest	179	156	131	105	81	61	46	32	22	12

MOZAMBIQUE

(US$ million, unless otherwise indicated)

	1970	1980	1988	1989	1990	1991	1992	1993	1994	1995
1. SUMMARY DEBT DATA										
TOTAL DEBT STOCKS (EDT)	..	..	**4,148**	**4,354**	**4,665**	**4,725**	**5,138**	**5,209**	**5,651**	**5,781**
Long-term debt (LDOD)	..	..	**3,776**	**3,865**	**4,249**	**4,364**	**4,728**	**4,859**	**5,253**	**5,299**
Public and publicly guaranteed	..	..	3,758	3,854	4,230	4,348	4,711	4,841	5,239	5,251
Private nonguaranteed	0	0	18	11	19	16	17	18	14	48
Use of IMF credit	**0**	**0**	**41**	**56**	**74**	**118**	**175**	**189**	**212**	**202**
Short-term debt	..	..	**332**	**433**	**342**	**244**	**235**	**161**	**186**	**281**
of which interest arrears on LDOD	..	..	200	267	204	163	150	145	168	251
Official creditors	..	..	90	119	73	98	133	142	164	246
Private creditors	..	..	110	148	131	65	17	3	5	5
Memo: principal arrears on LDOD	..	..	641	788	723	743	676	776	879	1,091
Official creditors	..	..	357	427	371	496	610	726	865	1,078
Private creditors	..	..	284	361	352	247	66	50	15	13
Memo: export credits	..	..	927	1,085	986	732	840	1,050	1,156	998
TOTAL DEBT FLOWS										
Disbursements	..	..	**207**	**234**	**242**	**158**	**265**	**201**	**282**	**271**
Long-term debt	..	..	183	219	230	116	201	180	261	271
IMF purchases	0	0	25	16	12	42	64	21	21	0
Principal repayments	..	..	**33**	**34**	**40**	**41**	**34**	**43**	**78**	**90**
Long-term debt	..	..	33	34	40	41	32	37	68	76
IMF repurchases	0	0	0	0	0	0	2	6	11	14
Net flows on debt	..	..	**182**	**234**	**174**	**61**	**235**	**89**	**206**	**192**
of which short-term debt	..	..	8	34	-28	-57	4	-69	2	11
Interest payments (INT)	..	..	**39**	**48**	**38**	**42**	**48**	**78**	**56**	**83**
Long-term debt	..	..	30	36	23	34	43	74	54	80
IMF charges	0	0	0	0	0	1	0	1	1	1
Short-term debt	..	..	9	12	15	7	5	3	1	1
Net transfers on debt	..	..	**143**	**186**	**136**	**19**	**188**	**11**	**150**	**109**
Total debt service paid (TDS)	..	..	**72**	**82**	**78**	**82**	**82**	**121**	**134**	**173**
Long-term debt	..	..	63	70	63	74	75	112	122	156
IMF repurchases and charges	0	0	0	0	0	1	2	7	12	16
Short-term debt (interest only)	..	..	9	12	15	7	5	3	1	1
2. AGGREGATE NET RESOURCE FLOWS AND NET TRANSFERS (LONG-TERM)										
NET RESOURCE FLOWS	..	..	**717**	**761**	**950**	**965**	**919**	**809**	**864**	**1,001**
Net flow of long-term debt (ex. IMF)	0	0	150	184	190	76	169	142	194	195
Foreign direct investment (net)	0	0	5	3	9	23	25	30	33	36
Portfolio equity flows	..	..	0	0	0	0	0	0	0	0
Grants (excluding technical coop.)	0	76	563	573	751	866	726	637	638	770
Memo: technical coop. grants	0	38	92	99	96	139	203	233	270	274
NET TRANSFERS	..	..	**687**	**725**	**927**	**931**	**877**	**735**	**808**	**920**
Interest on long-term debt	..	..	30	36	23	34	43	74	54	80
Profit remittances on FDI	0	0	0	0	0	0	0	0	2	0
3. MAJOR ECONOMIC AGGREGATES										
Gross national product (GNP)	..	2,022	1,042	1,114	1,228	1,224	1,044	1,229	1,219	1,303
Exports of goods & services (XGS)	..	452	260	272	300	365	359	368	402	485
of which workers remittances	..	0	0	0	0	0	0	0	0	0
Imports of goods & services (MGS)	..	875	995	1,119	1,164	1,211	1,224	1,321	1,403	1,172
International reserves (RES)	..	..	174	204	232	240	385	372	428	..
Current account balance	..	-367	-359	-460	-415	-344	-350	-450	-500	-200
4. DEBT INDICATORS										
EDT / XGS (%)	..	..	1,598.0	1,603.7	1,555.9	1,294.2	1,433.1	1,415.1	1,406.4	1,192.5
EDT / GNP (%)	..	..	398.3	391.0	380.0	386.2	492.0	423.8	463.5	443.6
TDS / XGS (%)	..	..	27.9	30.3	26.0	22.5	22.8	33.0	33.4	35.7
INT / XGS (%)	..	..	15.1	17.7	12.7	11.4	13.4	21.2	13.9	17.1
INT / GNP (%)	..	..	3.8	4.3	3.1	3.4	4.6	6.3	4.6	6.4
RES / EDT (%)	..	..	4.2	4.7	5.0	5.1	7.5	7.1	7.6	..
RES / MGS (months)	..	..	2.1	2.2	2.4	2.4	3.8	3.4	3.7	..
Short-term / EDT (%)	..	..	8.0	9.9	7.3	5.2	4.6	3.1	3.3	4.9
Concessional / EDT (%)	..	..	53.5	52.5	46.0	51.5	51.9	55.4	58.7	52.6
Multilateral / EDT (%)	..	..	6.9	8.2	10.1	11.7	13.2	15.6	19.3	22.7

MOZAMBIQUE

(US$ million, unless otherwise indicated)

	1970	1980	1988	1989	1990	1991	1992	1993	1994	1995
5. LONG-TERM DEBT										
DEBT OUTSTANDING (LDOD)	..	..	**3,776**	**3,865**	**4,249**	**4,364**	**4,728**	**4,859**	**5,253**	**5,299**
Public and publicly guaranteed	..	..	**3,758**	**3,854**	**4,230**	**4,348**	**4,711**	**4,841**	**5,239**	**5,251**
Official creditors	..	..	3,070	3,143	3,574	3,868	4,497	4,692	5,142	5,197
Multilateral	..	..	286	356	473	554	678	814	1,089	1,315
Concessional	..	..	236	304	416	488	610	738	1,013	1,239
Bilateral	..	..	2,784	2,787	3,101	3,314	3,819	3,878	4,053	3,882
Concessional	..	..	1,985	1,984	1,732	1,944	2,055	2,149	2,304	1,804
Private creditors	..	..	688	712	656	479	214	150	97	55
Bonds	..	..	0	0	0	0	0	0	0	0
Commercial banks	..	..	147	147	147	20	9	10	8	7
Other private	..	..	542	565	509	460	206	140	89	47
Private nonguaranteed	**0**	**0**	**18**	**11**	**19**	**16**	**17**	**18**	**14**	**48**
Bonds	..	..	0	0	0	0	0	0	0	0
Commercial banks	..	..	18	11	19	16	17	18	14	48
Memo:										
IBRD	0	0	0	0	0	0	0	0	0	0
IDA	0	0	127	176	268	328	417	512	714	890
DISBURSEMENTS	..	..	**183**	**219**	**230**	**116**	**201**	**180**	**261**	**271**
Public and publicly guaranteed	..	..	**172**	**215**	**210**	**116**	**197**	**176**	**258**	**235**
Official creditors	..	..	169	187	186	111	197	172	258	235
Multilateral	..	..	60	80	94	83	159	148	243	215
Concessional	..	..	55	74	88	71	149	135	240	211
Bilateral	..	..	109	106	91	28	38	25	15	19
Concessional	..	..	102	88	91	28	38	25	15	19
Private creditors	..	..	4	28	24	6	0	4	1	0
Bonds	..	..	0	0	0	0	0	0	0	0
Commercial banks	..	..	0	4	0	0	0	3	0	0
Other private	..	..	4	24	24	6	0	1	1	0
Private nonguaranteed	**0**	**0**	**11**	**4**	**20**	**0**	**4**	**4**	**3**	**36**
Bonds	..	..	0	0	0	0	0	0	0	0
Commercial banks	..	..	11	4	20	0	4	4	3	36
Memo:										
IBRD	0	0	0	0	0	0	0	0	0	0
IDA	0	0	44	51	74	56	106	93	176	160
PRINCIPAL REPAYMENTS	..	..	**33**	**34**	**40**	**41**	**32**	**37**	**68**	**76**
Public and publicly guaranteed	..	..	**23**	**24**	**28**	**37**	**29**	**34**	**65**	**73**
Official creditors	..	..	15	16	22	19	26	27	62	67
Multilateral	..	..	7	8	8	7	9	11	12	13
Concessional	..	..	3	3	3	3	4	6	5	6
Bilateral	..	..	8	8	13	12	16	16	51	55
Concessional	..	..	3	4	5	7	8	7	11	26
Private creditors	..	..	9	8	7	18	4	7	2	5
Bonds	..	..	0	0	0	0	0	0	0	0
Commercial banks	..	..	4	3	3	15	2	0	1	0
Other private	..	..	5	5	3	4	1	7	2	5
Private nonguaranteed	**0**	**0**	**10**	**11**	**12**	**3**	**3**	**3**	**3**	**3**
Bonds	..	..	0	0	0	0	0	0	0	0
Commercial banks	..	..	10	11	12	3	3	3	3	3
Memo:										
IBRD	0	0	0	0	0	0	0	0	0	0
IDA	0	0	0	0	0	0	0	0	0	0
NET FLOWS ON DEBT	..	..	**150**	**184**	**190**	**76**	**169**	**142**	**194**	**195**
Public and publicly guaranteed	..	..	**149**	**191**	**181**	**79**	**168**	**142**	**193**	**162**
Official creditors	..	..	154	171	164	92	171	145	195	168
Multilateral	..	..	53	73	86	76	149	137	231	203
Concessional	..	..	52	71	84	68	144	129	234	204
Bilateral	..	..	101	98	78	16	22	8	-36	-35
Concessional	..	..	99	84	86	21	30	18	3	-6
Private creditors	..	..	-5	20	17	-13	-4	-3	-2	-5
Bonds	..	..	0	0	0	0	0	0	0	0
Commercial banks	..	..	-4	1	-3	-15	-2	3	-1	0
Other private	..	..	-1	19	21	2	-1	-6	-1	-5
Private nonguaranteed	**0**	**0**	**1**	**-7**	**8**	**-3**	**1**	**1**	**0**	**33**
Bonds	..	..	0	0	0	0	0	0	0	0
Commercial banks	..	..	1	-7	8	-3	1	1	0	33
Memo:										
IBRD	0	0	0	0	0	0	0	0	0	0
IDA	0	0	44	51	74	56	106	93	176	160

MOZAMBIQUE

(US$ million, unless otherwise indicated)

	1970	1980	1988	1989	1990	1991	1992	1993	1994	1995
INTEREST PAYMENTS (LINT)	..	..	**30**	**36**	**23**	**34**	**43**	**74**	**54**	**80**
Public and publicly guaranteed	..	..	**30**	**36**	**23**	**34**	**43**	**74**	**54**	**79**
Official creditors	..	..	23	30	17	28	37	70	52	76
Multilateral	..	..	6	7	7	8	10	10	12	13
Concessional	..	..	3	3	3	4	4	5	7	7
Bilateral	..	..	17	23	10	20	28	60	40	64
Concessional	..	..	8	9	6	9	13	25	11	18
Private creditors	..	..	7	6	6	5	5	4	1	3
Bonds	..	..	0	0	0	0	0	0	0	0
Commercial banks	..	..	3	1	1	1	0	0	0	0
Other private	..	..	4	5	5	5	5	4	1	3
Private nonguaranteed	**0**	**0**	**0**	**0**	**0**	**0**	**0**	**0**	**0**	**1**
Bonds	..	..	0	0	0	0	0	0	0	0
Commercial banks	..	..	0	0	0	0	0	0	0	1
Memo:										
IBRD	0	0	0	0	0	0	0	0	0	0
IDA	0	0	1	1	1	2	3	3	4	6
NET TRANSFERS ON DEBT	..	..	**119**	**148**	**167**	**42**	**126**	**68**	**140**	**115**
Public and publicly guaranteed	..	..	**119**	**155**	**159**	**46**	**125**	**68**	**140**	**83**
Official creditors	..	..	131	141	148	64	134	75	143	91
Multilateral	..	..	47	66	79	68	140	126	219	190
Concessional	..	..	50	69	81	64	140	124	228	197
Bilateral	..	..	84	75	68	-5	-6	-52	-76	-99
Concessional	..	..	91	75	80	11	17	-8	-7	-24
Private creditors	..	..	-12	15	11	-18	-9	-7	-3	-8
Bonds	..	..	0	0	0	0	0	0	0	0
Commercial banks	..	..	-7	0	-5	-15	-3	3	-1	0
Other private	..	..	-5	15	16	-3	-6	-10	-3	-8
Private nonguaranteed	**0**	**0**	**1**	**-7**	**8**	**-4**	**1**	**0**	**0**	**32**
Bonds	..	..	0	0	0	0	0	0	0	0
Commercial banks	..	..	1	-7	8	-4	1	0	0	32
Memo:										
IBRD	0	0	0	0	0	0	0	0	0	0
IDA	0	0	43	50	73	54	103	90	172	154
DEBT SERVICE (LTDS)	..	..	**63**	**70**	**63**	**74**	**75**	**112**	**122**	**156**
Public and publicly guaranteed	..	..	**53**	**59**	**51**	**71**	**72**	**108**	**119**	**152**
Official creditors	..	..	38	46	38	47	63	97	115	144
Multilateral	..	..	13	15	15	15	19	21	24	26
Concessional	..	..	5	6	7	7	9	11	12	14
Bilateral	..	..	25	31	23	33	44	76	91	118
Concessional	..	..	11	14	11	16	22	32	22	43
Private creditors	..	..	16	13	13	24	9	11	4	8
Bonds	..	..	0	0	0	0	0	0	0	0
Commercial banks	..	..	7	4	5	15	3	0	1	0
Other private	..	..	9	9	8	9	6	11	3	8
Private nonguaranteed	**0**	**0**	**10**	**11**	**12**	**4**	**3**	**3**	**3**	**5**
Bonds	..	..	0	0	0	0	0	0	0	0
Commercial banks	..	..	10	11	12	4	3	3	3	5
Memo:										
IBRD	0	0	0	0	0	0	0	0	0	0
IDA	0	0	1	1	1	2	3	3	4	6
UNDISBURSED DEBT	..	..	**694**	**824**	**828**	**739**	**956**	**961**	**1,290**	**1,225**
Official creditors	..	..	633	785	815	737	954	960	1,290	1,225
Private creditors	..	..	62	39	13	2	2	1	0	0
Memorandum items										
Concessional LDOD	..	..	2,221	2,288	2,148	2,433	2,665	2,887	3,317	3,043
Variable rate LDOD	..	..	216	211	236	228	657	625	585	583
Public sector LDOD	..	..	3,758	3,854	4,230	4,347	4,711	4,841	5,238	5,251
Private sector LDOD	..	..	18	11	20	16	17	18	14	48

6. CURRENCY COMPOSITION OF LONG-TERM DEBT (PERCENT)

	1970	1980	1988	1989	1990	1991	1992	1993	1994	1995
Deutsche mark	..	..	4.7	5.0	5.0	5.3	4.7	4.8	5.5	4.6
French franc	..	..	11.7	13.6	12.1	11.2	9.5	8.7	9.4	10.0
Japanese yen	..	..	1.9	1.6	1.6	1.7	1.6	1.7	1.7	1.6
Pound sterling	..	..	2.1	1.8	2.4	2.7	2.2	2.2	2.1	2.0
Swiss franc	..	..	0.0	0.0	0.0	0.0	0.0	0.0	0.0	0.0
U.S.dollars	..	..	62.1	59.9	52.7	52.9	58.3	60.0	60.5	60.3
Multiple currency	..	..	3.5	3.8	4.7	5.6	6.5	6.9	7.8	8.6
Special drawing rights	..	..	1.4	1.5	1.4	1.4	1.2	1.2	1.2	1.2
All other currencies	..	..	12.8	12.9	20.1	19.1	16.0	14.5	11.9	11.6

MOZAMBIQUE

(US$ million, unless otherwise indicated)

	1970	1980	1988	1989	1990	1991	1992	1993	1994	1995
7. DEBT RESTRUCTURINGS										
Total amount rescheduled	0	0	148	0	385	202	672	173	200	63
Debt stock rescheduled	0	0	0	0	0	0	8	0	0	0
Principal rescheduled	0	0	95	0	225	93	283	76	73	20
Official	0	0	24	0	134	51	51	41	66	18
Private	0	0	71	0	92	43	232	35	7	2
Interest rescheduled	0	0	51	0	160	49	86	60	64	24
Official	0	0	25	0	125	39	35	43	63	24
Private	0	0	26	0	35	10	51	17	1	0
Debt forgiven	..	..	0	0	210	58	19	27	56	298
Memo: interest forgiven	..	..	0	0	14	72	4	6	7	12
Debt stock reduction	0	0	0	0	0	118	0	3	0	0
of which debt buyback	0	0	0	0	0	12	0	0	0	0
8. DEBT STOCK-FLOW RECONCILIATION										
Total change in debt stocks	..	..	..	206	311	61	413	71	442	130
Net flows on debt	..	..	..	234	174	61	235	89	206	192
Net change in interest arrears	..	..	..	67	-63	-41	-13	-5	24	83
Interest capitalized	..	..	..	0	160	49	86	60	64	24
Debt forgiveness or reduction	..	..	..	0	-210	-165	-19	-30	-56	-298
Cross-currency valuation	..	..	..	8	209	-15	-92	-66	114	74
Residual	..	..	..	-104	41	172	216	23	91	55
9. AVERAGE TERMS OF NEW COMMITMENTS										
ALL CREDITORS										
Interest (%)	..	..	2.5	1.2	1.4	2.0	0.8	1.0	0.8	0.9
Maturity (years)	..	..	31.3	37.8	35.0	32.3	41.7	37.9	35.0	35.8
Grace period (years)	..	..	7.5	9.7	9.2	9.1	10.1	9.2	9.9	9.0
Grant element (%)	..	..	59.8	74.7	71.8	65.3	79.9	76.1	76.8	74.8
Official creditors										
Interest (%)	..	..	2.5	1.1	1.3	2.0	0.8	0.8	0.8	0.9
Maturity (years)	..	..	31.4	39.0	35.2	32.3	41.7	38.5	35.0	35.8
Grace period (years)	..	..	7.5	10.0	9.2	9.1	10.1	9.4	9.9	9.0
Grant element (%)	..	..	59.9	76.7	72.3	65.3	79.9	77.4	76.8	74.8
Private creditors										
Interest (%)	..	..	9.0	4.2	9.0	0.0	0.0	7.0	0.0	0.0
Maturity (years)	..	..	2.3	9.9	4.9	0.0	0.0	11.5	0.0	0.0
Grace period (years)	..	..	0.8	2.6	2.9	0.0	0.0	2.4	0.0	0.0
Grant element (%)	..	..	1.0	27.0	2.4	0.0	0.0	16.3	0.0	0.0
Memorandum items										
Commitments	..	..	302	359	177	87	456	187	570	156
Official creditors	..	..	302	344	176	87	456	183	570	156
Private creditors	..	..	1	14	1	0	0	4	0	0

10. CONTRACTUAL OBLIGATIONS ON OUTSTANDING LONG-TERM DEBT

	1996	1997	1998	1999	2000	2001	2002	2003	2004	2005
TOTAL										
Disbursements	333	335	244	162	85	37	24	6	2	0
Principal	200	205	220	203	339	330	341	342	309	273
Interest	147	144	142	135	125	109	93	76	60	47
Official creditors										
Disbursements	333	335	244	162	85	37	24	6	2	0
Principal	186	191	213	196	332	323	334	336	303	267
Interest	143	141	139	133	123	108	92	75	59	46
Bilateral creditors										
Disbursements	13	10	6	4	3	2	2	1	1	0
Principal	166	168	187	165	299	290	290	293	251	207
Interest	125	120	117	110	100	85	70	55	39	28
Multilateral creditors										
Disbursements	320	325	238	157	82	35	22	4	1	0
Principal	20	22	27	30	34	34	44	43	52	60
Interest	18	21	23	23	23	23	22	21	20	19
Private creditors										
Disbursements	0	0	0	0	0	0	0	0	0	0
Principal	13	14	7	7	7	7	7	6	6	6
Interest	4	3	3	2	2	2	1	1	1	1
Commercial banks										
Disbursements	0	0	0	0	0	0	0	0	0	0
Principal	0	0	0	0	0	0	0	0	0	0
Interest	0	0	0	0	0	0	0	0	0	0
Other private										
Disbursements	0	0	0	0	0	0	0	0	0	0
Principal	13	14	7	7	7	7	7	6	6	6
Interest	4	3	2	2	2	2	1	1	1	1

MYANMAR

(US$ million, unless otherwise indicated)

	1970	1980	1988	1989	1990	1991	1992	1993	1994	1995
1. SUMMARY DEBT DATA										
TOTAL DEBT STOCKS (EDT)	**..**	**1,500**	**4,432**	**4,191**	**4,695**	**4,875**	**5,355**	**5,757**	**6,555**	**5,771**
Long-term debt (LDOD)	**106**	**1,390**	**4,238**	**4,065**	**4,466**	**4,580**	**5,003**	**5,394**	**6,154**	**5,378**
Public and publicly guaranteed	106	1,390	4,238	4,065	4,466	4,580	5,003	5,394	6,154	5,378
Private nonguaranteed	0	0	0	0	0	0	0	0	0	0
Use of IMF credit	**17**	**106**	**8**	**2**	**0**	**0**	**0**	**0**	**0**	**0**
Short-term debt	**..**	**4**	**186**	**125**	**229**	**295**	**352**	**362**	**401**	**393**
of which interest arrears on LDOD	..	0	90	110	200	248	340	354	380	352
Official creditors	..	0	70	93	168	203	286	299	312	285
Private creditors	..	0	21	17	32	45	54	55	68	67
Memo: principal arrears on LDOD	..	0	167	221	377	561	787	1,045	1,431	1,359
Official creditors	..	0	108	181	291	430	617	841	1,178	1,100
Private creditors	..	0	58	40	85	130	170	203	252	259
Memo: export credits	..	..	283	302	282	292	398	405	488	600
TOTAL DEBT FLOWS										
Disbursements	**22**	**282**	**287**	**215**	**122**	**59**	**78**	**72**	**59**	**86**
Long-term debt	22	269	287	215	122	59	78	72	59	86
IMF purchases	0	14	0	0	0	0	0	0	0	0
Principal repayments	**20**	**89**	**85**	**121**	**46**	**29**	**26**	**22**	**42**	**180**
Long-term debt	20	66	65	116	44	29	26	22	42	180
IMF repurchases	0	23	21	6	2	0	0	0	0	0
Net flows on debt	**2**	**193**	**218**	**11**	**91**	**49**	**17**	**46**	**30**	**-74**
of which short-term debt	..	..	16	-82	15	18	-35	-4	13	20
Interest payments (INT)	**..**	**52**	**42**	**71**	**15**	**51**	**28**	**89**	**121**	**70**
Long-term debt	3	45	39	69	13	49	26	89	120	68
IMF charges	0	4	0	0	0	0	0	0	0	0
Short-term debt	..	3	3	1	2	2	2	1	1	2
Net transfers on debt	**..**	**141**	**175**	**-59**	**76**	**-2**	**-11**	**-43**	**-91**	**-144**
Total debt service paid (TDS)	**..**	**141**	**128**	**192**	**60**	**80**	**54**	**111**	**163**	**250**
Long-term debt	23	112	104	185	57	78	52	111	162	248
IMF repurchases and charges	0	26	21	6	2	0	0	0	0	0
Short-term debt (interest only)	..	3	3	1	2	2	2	1	1	2
2. AGGREGATE NET RESOURCE FLOWS AND NET TRANSFERS (LONG-TERM)										
NET RESOURCE FLOWS	**16**	**269**	**319**	**158**	**120**	**86**	**94**	**97**	**167**	**95**
Net flow of long-term debt (ex. IMF)	2	202	222	99	78	30	52	50	17	-95
Foreign direct investment (net)	0	0	0	8	5	0	3	4	4	10
Portfolio equity flows	0	0	0	0	0	0	0	0	29	16
Grants (excluding technical coop.)	15	66	97	51	37	56	39	43	117	164
Memo: technical coop. grants	6	31	55	32	35	39	31	30	30	45
NET TRANSFERS	**13**	**223**	**280**	**88**	**107**	**37**	**68**	**8**	**47**	**27**
Interest on long-term debt	3	45	39	69	13	49	26	89	120	68
Profit remittances on FDI	0	0	0	0	0	0	0	0	0	0
3. MAJOR ECONOMIC AGGREGATES										
Gross national product (GNP)	..	..	..	..	..	..	..	..	..	..
Exports of goods & services (XGS)	129	556	372	564	668	610	865	943	1,125	..
of which workers remittances	0	0	0	0	0	0	0	0	0	..
Imports of goods & services (MGS)	211	869	585	696	1,270	1,037	1,262	1,508	1,776	..
International reserves (RES)	98	409	181	364	410	347	364	401	518	651
Current account balance	-81	-307	-246	-78	-526	-344	-275	-292	-339	..
4. DEBT INDICATORS										
EDT / XGS (%)	..	270.0	1,191.0	742.5	703.2	798.8	618.9	610.6	582.7	..
EDT / GNP (%)	..	..	..	..	..	..	..	..	..	..
TDS / XGS (%)	..	25.4	34.3	34.0	9.0	13.1	6.2	11.8	14.5	..
INT / XGS (%)	..	9.4	11.3	12.5	2.2	8.4	3.2	9.5	10.8	..
INT / GNP (%)	..	..	..	..	..	..	..	..	..	..
RES / EDT (%)	..	27.2	4.1	8.7	8.7	7.1	6.8	7.0	7.9	11.3
RES / MGS (months)	5.6	5.6	3.7	6.3	3.9	4.0	3.5	3.2	3.5	..
Short-term / EDT (%)	..	0.3	4.2	3.0	4.9	6.1	6.6	6.3	6.1	6.8
Concessional / EDT (%)	..	72.7	86.3	88.6	87.6	86.5	86.5	86.6	86.6	84.7
Multilateral / EDT (%)	..	18.7	22.2	25.2	26.3	25.8	24.4	23.4	22.2	23.1

MYANMAR

(US$ million, unless otherwise indicated)

	1970	1980	1988	1989	1990	1991	1992	1993	1994	1995
5. LONG-TERM DEBT										
DEBT OUTSTANDING (LDOD)	**106**	**1,390**	**4,238**	**4,065**	**4,466**	**4,580**	**5,003**	**5,394**	**6,154**	**5,378**
Public and publicly guaranteed	**106**	**1,390**	**4,238**	**4,065**	**4,466**	**4,580**	**5,003**	**5,394**	**6,154**	**5,378**
Official creditors	72	1,109	3,924	3,811	4,216	4,327	4,747	5,105	5,820	5,011
Multilateral	15	280	984	1,057	1,234	1,258	1,306	1,348	1,458	1,331
Concessional	7	274	980	1,053	1,228	1,254	1,301	1,343	1,454	1,328
Bilateral	57	829	2,939	2,753	2,982	3,068	3,441	3,758	4,362	3,680
Concessional	56	817	2,843	2,659	2,884	2,965	3,330	3,642	4,225	3,558
Private creditors	34	281	314	254	250	253	256	289	334	367
Bonds	0	0	0	0	0	0	0	0	0	0
Commercial banks	0	51	4	0	0	0	0	0	0	0
Other private	34	231	310	254	250	253	256	289	334	367
Private nonguaranteed	**0**	**0**	**0**	**0**	**0**	**0**	**0**	**0**	**0**	**0**
Bonds	0	0	0	0	0	0	0	0	0	0
Commercial banks	0	0	0	0	0	0	0	0	0	0
Memo:										
IBRD	15	0	0	0	0	0	0	0	0	0
IDA	0	146	594	653	716	749	765	766	818	777
DISBURSEMENTS	**22**	**269**	**287**	**215**	**122**	**59**	**78**	**72**	**59**	**86**
Public and publicly guaranteed	**22**	**269**	**287**	**215**	**122**	**59**	**78**	**72**	**59**	**86**
Official creditors	3	199	282	205	119	59	74	37	31	17
Multilateral	0	38	108	82	68	38	21	14	12	0
Concessional	0	38	107	82	68	38	21	14	12	0
Bilateral	3	161	175	123	51	21	53	23	19	16
Concessional	2	160	168	123	51	21	53	23	19	16
Private creditors	19	70	5	9	3	0	4	35	28	69
Bonds	0	0	0	0	0	0	0	0	0	0
Commercial banks	0	15	0	0	0	0	0	0	0	0
Other private	19	55	5	9	3	0	4	35	28	69
Private nonguaranteed	**0**	**0**	**0**	**0**	**0**	**0**	**0**	**0**	**0**	**0**
Bonds	0	0	0	0	0	0	0	0	0	0
Commercial banks	0	0	0	0	0	0	0	0	0	0
Memo:										
IBRD	0	0	0	0	0	0	0	0	0	0
IDA	0	23	60	59	57	31	15	0	7	0
PRINCIPAL REPAYMENTS	**20**	**66**	**65**	**116**	**44**	**29**	**26**	**22**	**42**	**180**
Public and publicly guaranteed	**20**	**66**	**65**	**116**	**44**	**29**	**26**	**22**	**42**	**180**
Official creditors	8	26	29	40	33	27	22	20	24	147
Multilateral	2	0	10	13	15	16	19	18	23	25
Concessional	1	0	10	12	14	15	19	17	22	24
Bilateral	5	25	19	27	18	11	2	3	1	122
Concessional	5	18	18	27	18	11	2	3	1	122
Private creditors	12	41	36	76	11	2	5	2	18	34
Bonds	0	0	0	0	0	0	0	0	0	0
Commercial banks	0	13	6	4	0	0	0	0	0	0
Other private	12	28	31	72	11	2	5	2	18	34
Private nonguaranteed	**0**	**0**	**0**	**0**	**0**	**0**	**0**	**0**	**0**	**0**
Bonds	0	0	0	0	0	0	0	0	0	0
Commercial banks	0	0	0	0	0	0	0	0	0	0
Memo:										
IBRD	2	0	0	0	0	0	0	0	0	0
IDA	0	0	2	2	4	4	5	4	9	10
NET FLOWS ON DEBT	**2**	**202**	**222**	**99**	**78**	**30**	**52**	**50**	**17**	**-95**
Public and publicly guaranteed	**2**	**202**	**222**	**99**	**78**	**30**	**52**	**50**	**17**	**-95**
Official creditors	-5	173	253	166	86	33	53	17	7	-130
Multilateral	-2	38	98	70	53	22	2	-3	-10	-24
Concessional	-1	38	98	70	54	23	2	-3	-10	-24
Bilateral	-3	135	156	96	33	11	51	21	18	-106
Concessional	-2	142	150	96	33	11	51	21	18	-106
Private creditors	7	29	-31	-67	-8	-2	-1	33	10	36
Bonds	0	0	0	0	0	0	0	0	0	0
Commercial banks	0	2	-6	-4	0	0	0	0	0	0
Other private	7	27	-25	-63	-8	-2	-1	33	10	36
Private nonguaranteed	**0**	**0**	**0**	**0**	**0**	**0**	**0**	**0**	**0**	**0**
Bonds	0	0	0	0	0	0	0	0	0	0
Commercial banks	0	0	0	0	0	0	0	0	0	0
Memo:										
IBRD	-2	0	0	0	0	0	0	0	0	0
IDA	0	23	58	57	53	27	10	-4	-2	-10

MYANMAR

(US$ million, unless otherwise indicated)

	1970	1980	1988	1989	1990	1991	1992	1993	1994	1995
INTEREST PAYMENTS (LINT)	**3**	**45**	**39**	**69**	**13**	**49**	**26**	**89**	**120**	**68**
Public and publicly guaranteed	**3**	**45**	**39**	**69**	**13**	**49**	**26**	**89**	**120**	**68**
Official creditors	2	21	30	44	11	49	25	85	119	66
Multilateral	1	3	9	9	10	11	11	8	12	13
Concessional	0	2	9	9	10	11	11	8	12	12
Bilateral	1	19	21	35	1	38	13	76	107	53
Concessional	1	17	21	35	1	38	13	76	107	50
Private creditors	1	24	9	26	2	0	1	4	1	2
Bonds	0	0	0	0	0	0	0	0	0	0
Commercial banks	0	8	0	1	0	0	0	0	0	0
Other private	1	16	9	25	2	0	1	4	1	2
Private nonguaranteed	**0**	**0**	**0**	**0**	**0**	**0**	**0**	**0**	**0**	**0**
Bonds	0	0	0	0	0	0	0	0	0	0
Commercial banks	0	0	0	0	0	0	0	0	0	0
Memo:										
IBRD	1	0	0	0	0	0	0	0	0	0
IDA	0	1	5	5	5	6	6	2	6	6
NET TRANSFERS ON DEBT	**-1**	**157**	**183**	**30**	**65**	**-18**	**26**	**-39**	**-104**	**-162**
Public and publicly guaranteed	**-1**	**157**	**183**	**30**	**65**	**-18**	**26**	**-39**	**-104**	**-162**
Official creditors	-7	152	223	122	76	-16	28	-67	-112	-196
Multilateral	-3	36	89	61	43	11	-10	-12	-23	-37
Concessional	-2	36	89	61	44	12	-9	-11	-22	-36
Bilateral	-4	117	135	62	33	-27	38	-56	-89	-159
Concessional	-3	125	130	62	33	-27	38	-56	-89	-156
Private creditors	6	5	-40	-93	-10	-3	-2	29	8	33
Bonds	0	0	0	0	0	0	0	0	0	0
Commercial banks	0	-6	-6	-5	0	0	0	0	0	0
Other private	6	11	-34	-88	-10	-3	-2	29	8	33
Private nonguaranteed	**0**	**0**	**0**	**0**	**0**	**0**	**0**	**0**	**0**	**0**
Bonds	0	0	0	0	0	0	0	0	0	0
Commercial banks	0	0	0	0	0	0	0	0	0	0
Memo:										
IBRD	-3	0	0	0	0	0	0	0	0	0
IDA	0	22	53	52	48	22	4	-6	-8	-16
DEBT SERVICE (LTDS)	**23**	**112**	**104**	**185**	**57**	**78**	**52**	**111**	**162**	**248**
Public and publicly guaranteed	**23**	**112**	**104**	**185**	**57**	**78**	**52**	**111**	**162**	**248**
Official creditors	10	47	59	83	44	75	46	105	143	212
Multilateral	3	3	19	22	25	27	31	26	35	37
Concessional	2	2	18	21	24	26	30	25	34	36
Bilateral	6	44	40	62	19	48	16	79	108	175
Concessional	6	35	39	61	19	48	16	79	108	172
Private creditors	13	65	45	102	13	3	6	6	20	36
Bonds	0	0	0	0	0	0	0	0	0	0
Commercial banks	0	21	6	5	0	0	0	0	0	0
Other private	13	44	39	97	13	3	6	6	20	36
Private nonguaranteed	**0**	**0**	**0**	**0**	**0**	**0**	**0**	**0**	**0**	**0**
Bonds	0	0	0	0	0	0	0	0	0	0
Commercial banks	0	0	0	0	0	0	0	0	0	0
Memo:										
IBRD	3	0	0	0	0	0	0	0	0	[illegible]
IDA	0	1	7	7	9	10	11	6	15	16
UNDISBURSED DEBT	**106**	**1,282**	**1,344**	**1,016**	**906**	**890**	**870**	**901**	**940**	**849**
Official creditors	74	1,072	1,333	1,013	882	866	804	827	863	760
Private creditors	32	211	11	3	24	24	66	74	76	89
Memorandum items										
Concessional LDOD	63	1,090	3,823	3,712	4,112	4,218	4,632	4,985	5,679	4,886
Variable rate LDOD	0	70	5	0	0	0	0	0	0	[illegible]
Public sector LDOD	106	1,390	4,238	4,065	4,466	4,580	5,003	5,394	6,154	5,378
Private sector LDOD	0	0	0	0	0	0	0	0	0	0

6. CURRENCY COMPOSITION OF LONG-TERM DEBT (PERCENT)

	1970	1980	1988	1989	1990	1991	1992	1993	1994	1995
Deutsche mark	15.4	11.6	11.6	13.8	12.4	12.7	11.8	10.6	11.2	12.0
French franc	0.0	2.6	2.6	3.1	3.0	1.5	1.4	1.2	1.2	1.4
Japanese yen	0.0	42.8	50.9	45.3	46.8	48.7	52.2	55.0	55.9	52.3
Pound sterling	31.2	4.3	2.1	1.9	1.7	1.7	1.3	1.2	1.2	1.3
Swiss franc	0.0	0.2	0.1	0.0	0.0	0.0	0.0	0.0	0.0	0.0
U.S.dollars	21.7	23.3	22.4	24.8	24.3	24.1	22.5	21.7	20.3	22.6
Multiple currency	14.0	7.7	5.9	6.3	7.6	7.4	7.3	7.2	7.1	7.0
Special drawing rights	0.0	0.0	0.0	0.0	0.0	0.0	0.0	0.0	0.0	0.0
All other currencies	17.7	7.5	4.5	4.7	4.1	4.1	3.6	3.0	3.2	3.5

MYANMAR

(US$ million, unless otherwise indicated)

	1970	1980	1988	1989	1990	1991	1992	1993	1994	1995
7. DEBT RESTRUCTURINGS										
Total amount rescheduled	0	0	0	0	0	0	0	0	0	0
Debt stock rescheduled	0	0	0	0	0	0	0	0	0	0
Principal rescheduled	0	0	0	0	0	0	0	0	0	0
Official	0	0	0	0	0	0	0	0	0	0
Private	0	0	0	0	0	0	0	0	0	0
Interest rescheduled	0	0	0	0	0	0	0	0	0	0
Official	0	0	0	0	0	0	0	0	0	0
Private	0	0	0	0	0	0	0	0	0	0
Debt forgiven	..	..	0	0	0	72	0	0	0	0
Memo: interest forgiven	..	..	0	0	0	5	0	0	0	0
Debt stock reduction	0	0	0	0	0	0	0	0	0	0
of which debt buyback	0	0	0	0	0	0	0	0	0	0
8. DEBT STOCK-FLOW RECONCILIATION										
Total change in debt stocks	..	..	..	-241	504	180	480	402	799	-785
Net flows on debt	..	..	..	11	91	49	17	46	30	-74
Net change in interest arrears	..	..	..	20	90	48	92	14	26	-29
Interest capitalized	..	..	..	0	0	0	0	0	0	0
Debt forgiveness or reduction	..	..	..	0	0	-72	0	0	0	0
Cross-currency valuation	..	..	..	-207	231	162	379	344	725	-501
Residual	..	..	..	-66	92	-7	-8	-2	17	-181
9. AVERAGE TERMS OF NEW COMMITMENTS										
ALL CREDITORS										
Interest (%)	4.1	3.5	0.0	0.0	2.7	0.0	1.5	2.3	0.5	1.4
Maturity (years)	16.2	29.0	0.0	20.0	13.7	19.2	7.8	6.2	7.5	14.4
Grace period (years)	4.5	7.3	0.0	8.0	3.4	10.2	1.5	1.0	2.1	8.7
Grant element (%)	33.6	52.2	0.0	72.1	39.3	74.4	29.6	22.7	25.6	39.1
Official creditors										
Interest (%)	2.9	1.6	0.0	0.0	1.5	0.0	0.0	0.0	2.5	2.8
Maturity (years)	26.1	37.0	0.0	20.0	16.7	19.2	0.0	0.0	24.6	33.0
Grace period (years)	7.3	9.5	0.0	8.0	5.2	10.2	0.0	0.0	7.1	24.4
Grant element (%)	53.4	71.0	0.0	72.1	53.3	74.4	0.0	0.0	55.9	62.6
Private creditors										
Interest (%)	5.3	8.0	0.0	0.0	3.5	0.0	1.5	2.3	0.0	0.8
Maturity (years)	6.3	10.4	0.0	0.0	11.6	0.0	7.8	6.2	3.4	6.4
Grace period (years)	1.8	2.2	0.0	0.0	2.1	0.0	1.5	1.0	0.9	1.8
Grant element (%)	13.9	8.5	0.0	0.0	29.4	0.0	29.6	22.7	18.4	28.8
Memorandum items										
Commitments	48	605	0	13	42	9	45	43	37	118
Official creditors	24	423	0	13	17	9	0	0	7	36
Private creditors	24	182	0	0	24	0	45	43	30	82

10. CONTRACTUAL OBLIGATIONS ON OUTSTANDING LONG-TERM DEBT

	1996	1997	1998	1999	2000	2001	2002	2003	2004	2005
TOTAL										
Disbursements	54	55	36	20	14	10	7	3	1	1
Principal	267	263	238	233	225	219	191	194	195	192
Interest	70	65	60	55	51	47	43	39	35	31
Official creditors										
Disbursements	28	31	25	17	12	10	7	3	1	1
Principal	228	220	215	211	203	205	188	192	194	191
Interest	68	63	58	54	50	46	42	38	35	31
Bilateral creditors										
Disbursements	17	15	11	6	4	3	2	2	1	1
Principal	193	183	176	173	163	163	145	145	145	142
Interest	56	51	47	43	40	36	32	29	25	22
Multilateral creditors										
Disbursements	11	16	14	11	8	7	5	1	0	0
Principal	35	37	38	38	40	42	44	47	49	49
Interest	12	12	11	11	11	10	10	10	9	9
Private creditors										
Disbursements	26	24	11	3	2	0	0	0	0	0
Principal	38	43	23	22	22	14	3	2	1	1
Interest	3	2	2	1	1	1	1	1	0	0
Commercial banks										
Disbursements	0	0	0	0	0	0	0	0	0	0
Principal	0	0	0	0	0	0	0	0	0	0
Interest	0	0	0	0	0	0	0	0	0	0
Other private										
Disbursements	26	24	11	3	2	0	0	0	0	0
Principal	38	43	23	22	22	14	3	2	1	1
Interest	3	2	2	1	1	1	1	1	0	0

NEPAL

(US$ million, unless otherwise indicated)

	1970	1980	1988	1989	1990	1991	1992	1993	1994	1995
1. SUMMARY DEBT DATA										
TOTAL DEBT STOCKS (EDT)	..	**205**	**1,178**	**1,368**	**1,640**	**1,771**	**1,802**	**2,004**	**2,320**	**2,398**
Long-term debt (LDOD)	**3**	**156**	**1,100**	**1,295**	**1,572**	**1,707**	**1,753**	**1,934**	**2,202**	**2,328**
Public and publicly guaranteed	3	156	1,100	1,295	1,572	1,707	1,753	1,934	2,202	2,328
Private nonguaranteed	0	0	0	0	0	0	0	0	0	0
Use of IMF credit	**0**	**42**	**53**	**52**	**44**	**39**	**44**	**49**	**55**	**48**
Short-term debt	..	**7**	**26**	**21**	**24**	**25**	**6**	**21**	**63**	**23**
of which interest arrears on LDOD	..	0	3	4	4	4	4	3	2	2
Official creditors	..	0	3	4	4	4	4	3	2	2
Private creditors	..	0	0	0	0	0	0	0	0	0
Memo: principal arrears on LDOD	..	0	3	4	6	6	8	6	3	4
Official creditors	..	0	3	4	6	6	8	6	3	3
Private creditors	..	0	0	0	0	0	0	0	0	1
Memo: export credits	..	..	99	119	109	108	86	75	82	46
TOTAL DEBT FLOWS										
Disbursements	**1**	**69**	**218**	**244**	**173**	**158**	**140**	**195**	**203**	**162**
Long-term debt	1	50	203	234	173	158	132	187	195	162
IMF purchases	0	18	15	10	0	0	8	8	8	0
Principal repayments	**2**	**3**	**25**	**34**	**42**	**37**	**39**	**43**	**50**	**61**
Long-term debt	2	2	22	25	29	31	38	41	44	54
IMF repurchases	0	1	3	9	13	5	1	2	6	8
Net flows on debt	**-2**	**66**	**197**	**204**	**134**	**122**	**82**	**169**	**196**	**60**
of which short-term debt	..	..	4	-6	2	1	-19	16	43	-40
Interest payments (INT)	..	**5**	**24**	**29**	**29**	**30**	**29**	**28**	**33**	**33**
Long-term debt	0	2	20	26	26	27	28	27	30	30
IMF charges	0	1	2	2	2	1	0	0	0	0
Short-term debt	..	2	2	2	2	3	1	1	2	2
Net transfers on debt	..	**61**	**173**	**175**	**105**	**92**	**53**	**140**	**164**	**27**
Total debt service paid (TDS)	..	**8**	**49**	**63**	**71**	**67**	**68**	**71**	**82**	**94**
Long-term debt	2	4	42	51	55	58	66	68	74	84
IMF repurchases and charges	0	1	5	11	14	6	1	2	6	8
Short-term debt (interest only)	..	2	2	2	2	3	1	1	2	2
2. AGGREGATE NET RESOURCE FLOWS AND NET TRANSFERS (LONG-TERM)										
NET RESOURCE FLOWS	**7**	**127**	**339**	**380**	**293**	**270**	**256**	**299**	**329**	**287**
Net flow of long-term debt (ex. IMF)	-2	48	181	209	144	126	94	147	151	108
Foreign direct investment (net)	0	0	1	1	6	2	4	6	7	8
Portfolio equity flows	0	0	0	0	0	0	0	0	0	0
Grants (excluding technical coop.)	9	79	157	170	143	142	158	146	171	171
Memo: technical coop. grants	8	50	100	102	109	117	127	146	143	143
NET TRANSFERS	**7**	**125**	**319**	**354**	**267**	**244**	**228**	**271**	**299**	**257**
Interest on long-term debt	0	2	20	26	26	27	28	27	30	30
Profit remittances on FDI	0	0	0	0	0	0	0	0	0	0
3. MAJOR ECONOMIC AGGREGATES										
Gross national product (GNP)	866	1,958	3,535	3,554	3,678	3,770	3,564	3,840	4,111	4,497
Exports of goods & services (XGS)	71	239	488	471	463	529	651	775	1,074	1,211
of which workers remittances	0	0	77	64	61	65	54	66	70	101
Imports of goods & services (MGS)	96	368	758	763	766	868	933	1,081	1,320	1,592
International reserves (RES)	94	272	283	273	354	451	518	700	752	646
Current account balance	..	-93	-269	-298	-305	-344	-275	-296	-240	-375
4. DEBT INDICATORS										
EDT / XGS (%)	..	85.4	241.4	290.7	354.1	334.8	276.9	258.7	216.0	198.[illegible]
EDT / GNP (%)	..	10.4	33.3	38.5	44.6	47.0	50.6	52.2	56.4	53.[illegible]
TDS / XGS (%)	..	3.3	10.0	13.4	15.3	12.6	10.5	9.2	7.7	7.[illegible]
INT / XGS (%)	..	2.1	4.9	6.2	6.3	5.7	4.5	3.7	3.0	2.[illegible]
INT / GNP (%)	..	0.3	0.7	0.8	0.8	0.8	0.8	0.7	0.8	0.[illegible]
RES / EDT (%)	..	133.0	24.0	19.9	21.6	25.5	28.8	34.9	32.4	26.[illegible]
RES / MGS (months)	11.8	8.9	4.5	4.3	5.5	6.2	6.7	7.8	6.8	4.[illegible]
Short-term / EDT (%)	..	3.4	2.2	1.5	1.5	1.4	0.3	1.0	2.7	0.[illegible]
Concessional / EDT (%)	..	75.7	81.6	85.1	88.6	90.5	92.3	92.8	92.2	94.[illegible]
Multilateral / EDT (%)	..	62.0	69.4	73.7	77.3	78.6	80.4	79.2	77.8	81.[illegible]

NEPAL

(US$ million, unless otherwise indicated)

	1970	1980	1988	1989	1990	1991	1992	1993	1994	1995
5. LONG-TERM DEBT										
DEBT OUTSTANDING (LDOD)	**3**	**156**	**1,100**	**1,295**	**1,572**	**1,707**	**1,753**	**1,934**	**2,202**	**2,328**
Public and publicly guaranteed	**3**	**156**	**1,100**	**1,295**	**1,572**	**1,707**	**1,753**	**1,934**	**2,202**	**2,328**
Official creditors	2	156	969	1,174	1,463	1,611	1,670	1,864	2,141	2,276
Multilateral	0	127	818	1,008	1,268	1,392	1,449	1,588	1,805	1,950
Concessional	0	126	810	1,000	1,259	1,383	1,442	1,583	1,802	1,947
Bilateral	2	29	152	166	194	220	221	276	337	326
Concessional	2	29	152	166	194	220	221	276	337	326
Private creditors	1	0	131	121	109	96	83	70	61	51
Bonds	0	0	0	0	0	0	0	0	0	0
Commercial banks	0	0	0	0	0	0	0	0	0	0
Other private	1	0	131	121	109	96	83	70	61	51
Private nonguaranteed	**0**	**0**	**0**	**0**	**0**	**0**	**0**	**0**	**0**	**0**
Bonds	0	0	0	0	0	0	0	0	0	0
Commercial banks	0	0	0	0	0	0	0	0	0	0
Memo:										
IBRD	0	0	0	0	0	0	0	0	0	0
IDA	0	76	466	572	668	719	765	832	932	1,023
DISBURSEMENTS	**1**	**50**	**203**	**234**	**173**	**158**	**132**	**187**	**195**	**162**
Public and publicly guaranteed	**1**	**50**	**203**	**234**	**173**	**158**	**132**	**187**	**195**	**162**
Official creditors	1	50	144	229	172	157	131	187	195	162
Multilateral	0	36	132	199	150	124	118	136	153	148
Concessional	0	36	132	199	150	124	118	136	153	148
Bilateral	0	14	12	30	22	33	14	51	42	13
Concessional	0	14	12	30	22	33	14	51	42	13
Private creditors	0	0	59	5	1	0	1	0	0	0
Bonds	0	0	0	0	0	0	0	0	0	0
Commercial banks	0	0	0	0	0	0	0	0	0	0
Other private	0	0	59	5	1	0	1	0	0	0
Private nonguaranteed	**0**	**0**	**0**	**0**	**0**	**0**	**0**	**0**	**0**	**0**
Bonds	0	0	0	0	0	0	0	0	0	0
Commercial banks	0	0	0	0	0	0	0	0	0	0
Memo:										
IBRD	0	0	0	0	0	0	0	0	0	0
IDA	0	25	82	109	70	49	71	69	76	81
PRINCIPAL REPAYMENTS	**2**	**2**	**22**	**25**	**29**	**31**	**38**	**41**	**44**	**54**
Public and publicly guaranteed	**2**	**2**	**22**	**25**	**29**	**31**	**38**	**41**	**44**	**54**
Official creditors	2	2	9	10	13	19	25	28	34	43
Multilateral	0	2	6	7	10	13	17	17	23	24
Concessional	0	2	6	7	10	12	15	15	20	24
Bilateral	2	0	3	3	3	6	8	11	11	19
Concessional	1	0	3	3	3	6	8	11	11	19
Private creditors	0	0	13	15	16	13	13	12	10	10
Bonds	0	0	0	0	0	0	0	0	0	0
Commercial banks	0	0	0	0	0	0	0	0	0	0
Other private	0	0	13	15	16	13	13	12	10	10
Private nonguaranteed	**0**	**0**	**0**	**0**	**0**	**0**	**0**	**0**	**0**	**0**
Bonds	0	0	0	0	0	0	0	0	0	0
Commercial banks	0	0	0	0	0	0	0	0	0	0
Memo:										
IBRD	0	0	0	0	0	0	0	0	0	0
IDA	0	0	2	2	2	3	3	4	5	7
NET FLOWS ON DEBT	**-2**	**48**	**181**	**209**	**144**	**126**	**94**	**147**	**151**	**108**
Public and publicly guaranteed	**-2**	**48**	**181**	**209**	**144**	**126**	**94**	**147**	**151**	**108**
Official creditors	-2	48	135	219	159	139	107	159	161	118
Multilateral	0	35	126	191	140	111	101	119	130	124
Concessional	0	35	126	191	140	112	103	121	133	124
Bilateral	-2	14	10	28	19	27	6	39	31	-6
Concessional	0	14	10	28	19	27	6	39	31	-6
Private creditors	0	0	46	-10	-15	-12	-12	-12	-10	-10
Bonds	0	0	0	0	0	0	0	0	0	0
Commercial banks	0	0	0	0	0	0	0	0	0	0
Other private	0	0	46	-10	-15	-12	-12	-12	-10	-10
Private nonguaranteed	**0**	**0**	**0**	**0**	**0**	**0**	**0**	**0**	**0**	**0**
Bonds	0	0	0	0	0	0	0	0	0	0
Commercial banks	0	0	0	0	0	0	0	0	0	0
Memo:										
IBRD	0	0	0	0	0	0	0	0	0	0
IDA	0	25	81	107	68	46	68	66	70	74

NEPAL

(US$ million, unless otherwise indicated)

	1970	1980	1988	1989	1990	1991	1992	1993	1994	1995
INTEREST PAYMENTS (LINT)	**0**	**2**	**20**	**26**	**26**	**27**	**28**	**27**	**30**	**30**
Public and publicly guaranteed	**0**	**2**	**20**	**26**	**26**	**27**	**28**	**27**	**30**	**30**
Official creditors	0	2	12	13	14	17	19	20	24	25
Multilateral	0	1	9	9	10	11	14	14	17	17
Concessional	0	1	9	9	10	11	13	13	16	17
Bilateral	0	1	2	4	4	5	5	6	8	7
Concessional	0	1	2	4	4	5	5	6	8	7
Private creditors	0	0	9	13	12	10	10	8	6	6
Bonds	0	0	0	0	0	0	0	0	0	0
Commercial banks	0	0	0	0	0	0	0	0	0	0
Other private	0	0	9	13	12	10	10	8	6	6
Private nonguaranteed	**0**	**0**	**0**	**0**	**0**	**0**	**0**	**0**	**0**	**0**
Bonds	0	0	0	0	0	0	0	0	0	0
Commercial banks	0	0	0	0	0	0	0	0	0	0
Memo:										
IBRD	0	0	0	0	0	0	0	0	0	0
IDA	0	0	5	4	5	5	6	6	7	7
NET TRANSFERS ON DEBT	**-2**	**46**	**161**	**183**	**118**	**100**	**66**	**119**	**120**	**78**
Public and publicly guaranteed	**-2**	**46**	**161**	**183**	**118**	**100**	**66**	**119**	**120**	**78**
Official creditors	-2	46	124	206	145	122	88	139	137	94
Multilateral	0	33	117	182	130	100	88	105	113	107
Concessional	0	34	117	182	130	101	90	108	117	107
Bilateral	-2	13	7	24	15	22	1	33	23	-13
Concessional	0	13	7	24	15	22	1	33	23	-14
Private creditors	0	0	37	-23	-27	-23	-22	-19	-16	-16
Bonds	0	0	0	0	0	0	0	0	0	0
Commercial banks	0	0	0	0	0	0	0	0	0	0
Other private	0	0	37	-23	-27	-23	-22	-19	-16	-16
Private nonguaranteed	**0**	**0**	**0**	**0**	**0**	**0**	**0**	**0**	**0**	**0**
Bonds	0	0	0	0	0	0	0	0	0	0
Commercial banks	0	0	0	0	0	0	0	0	0	0
Memo:										
IBRD	0	0	0	0	0	0	0	0	0	0
IDA	0	25	76	104	63	41	62	60	64	67
DEBT SERVICE (LTDS)	**2**	**4**	**42**	**51**	**55**	**58**	**66**	**68**	**74**	**84**
Public and publicly guaranteed	**2**	**4**	**42**	**51**	**55**	**58**	**66**	**68**	**74**	**84**
Official creditors	2	4	21	23	27	35	43	48	58	68
Multilateral	0	3	16	17	20	24	30	31	39	41
Concessional	0	3	16	17	20	23	28	28	36	41
Bilateral	2	1	5	6	7	11	13	17	19	27
Concessional	1	1	5	6	7	11	13	17	19	27
Private creditors	0	0	21	28	27	23	23	20	16	16
Bonds	0	0	0	0	0	0	0	0	0	0
Commercial banks	0	0	0	0	0	0	0	0	0	0
Other private	0	0	21	28	27	23	23	20	16	16
Private nonguaranteed	**0**	**0**	**0**	**0**	**0**	**0**	**0**	**0**	**0**	**0**
Bonds	0	0	0	0	0	0	0	0	0	0
Commercial banks	0	0	0	0	0	0	0	0	0	0
Memo:										
IBRD	0	0	0	0	0	0	0	0	0	0
IDA	0	1	6	6	7	8	9	10	12	14
UNDISBURSED DEBT	**26**	**366**	**1,198**	**1,220**	**1,318**	**1,217**	**1,229**	**1,035**	**984**	**781**
Official creditors	26	366	1,189	1,216	1,314	1,213	1,226	1,033	982	779
Private creditors	0	0	9	4	4	3	3	2	2	2
Memorandum items										
Concessional LDOD	2	155	961	1,165	1,453	1,603	1,663	1,859	2,139	2,273
Variable rate LDOD	0	0	4	2	0	0	0	0	0	0
Public sector LDOD	3	156	1,093	1,289	1,566	1,704	1,751	1,933	2,202	2,327
Private sector LDOD	0	0	7	6	5	4	2	1	1	1
6. CURRENCY COMPOSITION OF LONG-TERM DEBT (PERCENT)										
Deutsche mark	21.4	0.0	1.0	0.9	0.9	0.7	0.6	0.4	0.3	0.3
French franc	0.0	0.3	1.4	1.7	2.0	1.3	1.0	0.9	1.6	1.5
Japanese yen	0.0	7.9	9.8	8.9	8.4	9.9	9.6	11.7	12.3	11.2
Pound sterling	50.0	0.1	0.3	0.2	0.2	0.2	0.1	0.1	0.1	0.1
Swiss franc	0.0	0.0	0.0	0.0	0.0	0.0	0.0	0.0	0.0	0.0
U.S.dollars	7.1	49.5	54.4	53.6	49.6	48.1	48.8	46.9	44.4	44.0
Multiple currency	3.6	31.2	25.9	28.0	32.6	34.4	34.5	35.2	36.1	36.2
Special drawing rights	0.0	0.0	2.4	2.5	2.7	2.5	2.3	2.4	3.2	5.0
All other currencies	17.9	11.0	4.8	4.2	3.6	3.0	3.0	2.3	1.9	1.7

NEPAL

(US$ million, unless otherwise indicated)

	1970	1980	1988	1989	1990	1991	1992	1993	1994	1995
7. DEBT RESTRUCTURINGS										
Total amount rescheduled	0	0	0	0	0	0	0	0	0	0
Debt stock rescheduled	0	0	0	0	0	0	0	0	0	0
Principal rescheduled	0	0	0	0	0	0	0	0	0	0
Official	0	0	0	0	0	0	0	0	0	0
Private	0	0	0	0	0	0	0	0	0	0
Interest rescheduled	0	0	0	0	0	0	0	0	0	0
Official	0	0	0	0	0	0	0	0	0	0
Private	0	0	0	0	0	0	0	0	0	0
Debt forgiven	..	..	0	0	0	13	2	0	0	0
Memo: interest forgiven	..	..	0	0	0	0	0	0	0	0
Debt stock reduction	0	0	0	0	0	0	0	0	0	0
of which debt buyback	0	0	0	0	0	0	0	0	0	0
8. DEBT STOCK-FLOW RECONCILIATION										
Total change in debt stocks	..	..	..	190	272	131	31	202	316	79
Net flows on debt	..	..	..	204	134	122	82	169	196	60
Net change in interest arrears	..	..	..	1	1	0	-1	-1	-1	0
Interest capitalized	..	..	..	0	0	0	0	0	0	0
Debt forgiveness or reduction	..	..	..	0	0	-13	-2	0	0	0
Cross-currency valuation	..	..	..	-14	22	12	-6	23	44	-1
Residual	..	..	..	-1	116	10	-43	11	77	19
9. AVERAGE TERMS OF NEW COMMITMENTS										
ALL CREDITORS										
Interest (%)	2.8	0.8	1.0	1.0	0.9	1.0	0.9	1.0	0.8	4.1
Maturity (years)	26.9	45.9	38.8	38.5	39.3	38.3	39.7	39.7	39.6	39.1
Grace period (years)	6.2	10.1	9.9	10.0	10.3	9.7	10.2	10.2	10.1	9.8
Grant element (%)	53.1	81.2	77.2	77.8	78.9	77.8	79.5	78.5	80.4	50.0
Official creditors										
Interest (%)	2.8	0.8	1.0	1.0	0.9	1.0	0.9	1.0	0.8	4.1
Maturity (years)	26.9	45.9	38.8	38.5	39.3	38.3	39.7	39.7	39.6	39.1
Grace period (years)	6.2	10.1	9.9	10.0	10.3	9.7	10.2	10.2	10.1	9.8
Grant element (%)	53.1	81.2	77.2	77.8	78.9	77.8	79.5	78.5	80.4	50.0
Private creditors										
Interest (%)	0.0	0.0	0.0	9.8	0.0	0.0	0.0	0.0	0.0	0.0
Maturity (years)	0.0	0.0	0.0	10.5	0.0	0.0	0.0	0.0	0.0	0.0
Grace period (years)	0.0	0.0	0.0	4.0	0.0	0.0	0.0	0.0	0.0	0.0
Grant element (%)	0.0	0.0	0.0	-0.4	0.0	0.0	0.0	0.0	0.0	0.0
Memorandum items										
Commitments	17	92	234	343	220	68	303	57	101	52
Official creditors	17	92	234	343	220	68	303	57	101	52
Private creditors	0	0	0	0	0	0	0	0	0	0

10. CONTRACTUAL OBLIGATIONS ON OUTSTANDING LONG-TERM DEBT

	1996	1997	1998	1999	2000	2001	2002	2003	2004	2005
TOTAL										
Disbursements	272	207	144	90	43	15	9	2	0	0
Principal	54	59	59	67	69	66	72	76	79	86
Interest	30	30	30	30	28	28	27	26	25	24
Official creditors										
Disbursements	270	206	144	90	43	15	9	2	0	0
Principal	39	46	50	58	63	66	72	76	79	86
Interest	25	27	28	28	28	28	27	26	25	24
Bilateral creditors										
Disbursements	51	29	16	10	3	1	0	0	0	0
Principal	14	18	22	23	23	24	24	24	24	24
Interest	7	7	7	7	6	6	5	5	4	4
Multilateral creditors										
Disbursements	219	177	128	81	40	14	8	2	0	0
Principal	25	28	28	35	40	42	48	51	55	62
Interest	19	20	21	22	22	22	22	21	21	21
Private creditors										
Disbursements	2	1	0	0	0	0	0	0	0	0
Principal	15	14	10	9	5	0	0	0	0	0
Interest	5	4	2	1	0	0	0	0	0	0
Commercial banks										
Disbursements	0	0	0	0	0	0	0	0	0	0
Principal	0	0	0	0	0	0	0	0	0	0
Interest	0	0	0	0	0	0	0	0	0	0
Other private										
Disbursements	2	1	0	0	0	0	0	0	0	0
Principal	15	14	10	9	5	0	0	0	0	0
Interest	5	4	2	1	0	0	0	0	0	0

NICARAGUA

(US$ million, unless otherwise indicated)

	1970	1980	1988	1989	1990	1991	1992	1993	1994	1995
1. SUMMARY DEBT DATA										
TOTAL DEBT STOCKS (EDT)	..	**2,192**	**8,741**	**9,743**	**10,692**	**10,563**	**11,033**	**10,448**	**11,010**	**9,287**
Long-term debt (LDOD)	**147**	**1,671**	**7,020**	**7,660**	**8,245**	**8,714**	**8,937**	**8,695**	**9,013**	**7,937**
Public and publicly guaranteed	147	1,671	7,020	7,660	8,245	8,714	8,937	8,695	9,013	7,937
Private nonguaranteed	0	0	0	0	0	0	0	0	0	0
Use of IMF credit	**8**	**49**	**0**	**0**	**0**	**24**	**23**	**23**	**51**	**39**
Short-term debt	..	**472**	**1,721**	**2,082**	**2,447**	**1,825**	**2,073**	**1,730**	**1,947**	**1,311**
of which interest arrears on LDOD	..	12	1,056	1,364	1,713	1,268	1,395	1,417	1,763	1,215
Official creditors	..	11	594	845	1,124	660	754	774	1,102	1,208
Private creditors	..	2	462	519	589	607	641	643	661	7
Memo: principal arrears on LDOD	..	32	1,393	1,922	2,504	2,457	3,020	3,119	3,986	2,786
Official creditors	..	28	909	1,286	1,615	1,503	2,013	2,108	2,965	2,764
Private creditors	..	4	484	636	889	954	1,008	1,011	1,021	22
Memo: export credits	..	..	552	565	643	544	497	488	631	698
TOTAL DEBT FLOWS										
Disbursements	**54**	**276**	**427**	**590**	**469**	**342**	**283**	**99**	**334**	**228**
Long-term debt	44	276	427	590	469	319	283	99	305	228
IMF purchases	10	0	0	0	0	23	0	0	29	0
Principal repayments	**29**	**46**	**9**	**7**	**4**	**329**	**42**	**52**	**96**	**195**
Long-term debt	16	45	9	7	4	329	42	52	93	182
IMF repurchases	13	1	0	0	0	0	0	0	3	13
Net flows on debt	**24**	**230**	**438**	**636**	**480**	**-3**	**362**	**-318**	**110**	**-55**
of which short-term debt	..	..	20	53	16	-16	121	-365	-129	-88
Interest payments (INT)	..	**69**	**12**	**5**	**11**	**201**	**62**	**64**	**100**	**87**
Long-term debt	7	42	8	3	5	196	34	51	91	78
IMF charges	0	3	0	0	0	0	2	1	1	1
Short-term debt	..	25	4	2	6	5	27	13	7	8
Net transfers on debt	..	**161**	**427**	**632**	**469**	**-204**	**300**	**-382**	**10**	**-142**
Total debt service paid (TDS)	..	**115**	**20**	**11**	**16**	**530**	**104**	**116**	**195**	**282**
Long-term debt	23	86	17	9	10	525	75	103	184	260
IMF repurchases and charges	13	3	0	0	0	0	2	1	4	14
Short-term debt (interest only)	..	25	4	2	6	5	27	13	7	8
2. AGGREGATE NET RESOURCE FLOWS AND NET TRANSFERS (LONG-TERM)										
NET RESOURCE FLOWS	**43**	**279**	**557**	**756**	**705**	**785**	**627**	**294**	**434**	**524**
Net flow of long-term debt (ex. IMF)	28	231	418	583	464	-10	241	47	213	46
Foreign direct investment (net)	15	0	0	0	0	0	15	39	40	70
Portfolio equity flows	0	0	0	0	0	0	0	0	0	0
Grants (excluding technical coop.)	0	48	138	173	241	795	371	207	181	408
Memo: technical coop. grants	4	19	56	53	75	121	149	122	135	144
NET TRANSFERS	**13**	**217**	**549**	**754**	**700**	**590**	**581**	**233**	**331**	**435**
Interest on long-term debt	7	42	8	3	5	196	34	51	91	78
Profit remittances on FDI	23	21	0	0	0	0	12	10	12	11
3. MAJOR ECONOMIC AGGREGATES										
Gross national product (GNP)	755	2,020	2,914	809	989	1,293	1,351	1,401	1,306	1,575
Exports of goods & services (XGS)	..	514	275	348	404	348	327	398	489	730
of which workers remittances	..	0	0	0	0	0	10	25	30	75
Imports of goods & services (MGS)	..	1,049	1,121	878	911	1,197	1,421	1,251	1,429	1,436
International reserves (RES)	49	75	166	164	166	170	289	59	146	142
Current account balance	..	-411	-715	-362	-305	-5	-834	-644	-729	-706
4. DEBT INDICATORS										
EDT / XGS (%)	..	426.5	3,176.2	2,803.6	2,646.4	3,035.4	3,376.2	2,627.8	2,250.2	1,272.7
EDT / GNP (%)	..	108.5	300.0	1,205.0	1,081.0	816.7	816.6	745.8	843.3	589.7
TDS / XGS (%)	..	22.3	7.4	3.2	3.9	152.3	31.8	29.3	39.9	38.7
INT / XGS (%)	..	13.4	4.2	1.4	2.8	57.7	19.1	16.2	20.4	12.0
INT / GNP (%)	..	3.4	0.4	0.6	1.2	15.5	4.6	4.6	7.6	5.5
RES / EDT (%)	..	3.4	1.9	1.7	1.5	1.6	2.6	0.6	1.3	1.5
RES / MGS (months)	..	0.9	1.8	2.2	2.2	1.7	2.4	0.6	1.2	1.2
Short-term / EDT (%)	..	21.5	19.7	21.4	22.9	17.3	18.8	16.6	17.7	14.1
Concessional / EDT (%)	..	21.8	28.5	29.4	29.6	29.8	30.0	29.3	29.5	35.2
Multilateral / EDT (%)	..	19.2	10.5	9.5	9.1	9.4	10.2	11.1	12.4	16.0

NICARAGUA

(US$ million, unless otherwise indicated)

	1970	1980	1988	1989	1990	1991	1992	1993	1994	1995
5. LONG-TERM DEBT										
DEBT OUTSTANDING (LDOD)	**147**	**1,671**	**7,020**	**7,660**	**8,245**	**8,714**	**8,937**	**8,695**	**9,013**	**7,937**
Public and publicly guaranteed	**147**	**1,671**	**7,020**	**7,660**	**8,245**	**8,714**	**8,937**	**8,695**	**9,013**	**7,937**
Official creditors	102	907	5,616	6,244	6,805	6,698	6,936	6,690	7,012	6,968
Multilateral	48	421	918	928	977	988	1,124	1,158	1,363	1,489
Concessional	26	205	356	356	357	464	575	587	681	775
Bilateral	53	486	4,698	5,316	5,828	5,710	5,812	5,532	5,649	5,479
Concessional	49	274	2,132	2,510	2,805	2,680	2,733	2,476	2,564	2,491
Private creditors	45	764	1,404	1,416	1,440	2,016	2,001	2,005	2,001	969
Bonds	0	0	0	0	0	524	524	524	524	524
Commercial banks	38	746	1,305	1,305	1,306	1,397	1,395	1,393	1,394	388
Other private	8	18	99	112	134	95	83	88	83	57
Private nonguaranteed	**0**	**0**	**0**	**0**	**0**	**0**	**0**	**0**	**0**	**0**
Bonds	0	0	0	0	0	0	0	0	0	0
Commercial banks	0	0	0	0	0	0	0	0	0	0
Memo:										
IBRD	27	93	227	221	239	124	104	87	76	65
IDA	3	43	60	60	60	113	182	196	254	276
DISBURSEMENTS	**44**	**276**	**427**	**590**	**469**	**319**	**283**	**99**	**305**	**228**
Public and publicly guaranteed	**44**	**276**	**427**	**590**	**469**	**319**	**283**	**99**	**305**	**228**
Official creditors	32	276	421	575	445	319	281	98	305	209
Multilateral	11	90	13	4	7	155	161	70	248	163
Concessional	4	73	0	0	0	132	126	22	124	112
Bilateral	21	186	408	572	438	164	120	29	57	46
Concessional	19	108	204	371	262	66	96	9	36	32
Private creditors	12	0	6	15	24	0	2	1	1	20
Bonds	0	0	0	0	0	0	0	0	0	0
Commercial banks	12	0	4	0	0	0	2	1	1	20
Other private	0	0	3	15	24	0	0	0	0	0
Private nonguaranteed	**0**	**0**	**0**	**0**	**0**	**0**	**0**	**0**	**0**	**0**
Bonds	0	0	0	0	0	0	0	0	0	0
Commercial banks	0	0	0	0	0	0	0	0	0	0
Memo:										
IBRD	6	12	0	0	0	0	0	0	0	0
IDA	0	19	0	0	0	54	74	15	52	18
PRINCIPAL REPAYMENTS	**16**	**45**	**9**	**7**	**4**	**329**	**42**	**52**	**93**	**182**
Public and publicly guaranteed	**16**	**45**	**9**	**7**	**4**	**329**	**42**	**52**	**93**	**182**
Official creditors	4	19	5	3	1	326	38	48	86	86
Multilateral	3	14	3	0	1	157	31	37	67	47
Concessional	1	2	0	0	0	28	10	10	36	21
Bilateral	1	5	2	3	1	169	7	10	18	38
Concessional	0	2	0	2	0	52	0	1	0	1
Private creditors	13	26	4	3	3	3	4	5	7	96
Bonds	0	0	0	0	0	0	0	0	0	0
Commercial banks	11	20	1	1	0	0	0	0	0	92
Other private	2	6	3	2	3	3	4	5	7	4
Private nonguaranteed	**0**	**0**	**0**	**0**	**0**	**0**	**0**	**0**	**0**	**0**
Bonds	0	0	0	0	0	0	0	0	0	0
Commercial banks	0	0	0	0	0	0	0	0	0	0
Memo:										
IBRD	2	4	0	0	1	111	16	20	18	15
IDA	0	0	0	0	0	3	1	1	1	1
NET FLOWS ON DEBT	**28**	**231**	**418**	**583**	**464**	**-10**	**241**	**47**	**213**	**46**
Public and publicly guaranteed	**28**	**231**	**418**	**583**	**464**	**-10**	**241**	**47**	**213**	**46**
Official creditors	28	257	416	572	444	-7	243	51	219	123
Multilateral	9	76	9	4	6	-2	130	32	180	116
Concessional	2	70	0	0	0	104	116	12	88	92
Bilateral	20	181	406	569	437	-5	113	19	39	7
Concessional	18	106	204	369	262	14	96	8	36	31
Private creditors	-1	-26	3	11	21	-3	-2	-3	-6	-77
Bonds	0	0	0	0	0	0	0	0	0	0
Commercial banks	1	-20	3	-1	0	0	2	1	0	-73
Other private	-2	-6	0	12	21	-3	-4	-5	-7	-4
Private nonguaranteed	**0**	**0**	**0**	**0**	**0**	**0**	**0**	**0**	**0**	**0**
Bonds	0	0	0	0	0	0	0	0	0	0
Commercial banks	0	0	0	0	0	0	0	0	0	0
Memo:										
IBRD	4	8	0	0	-1	-111	-16	-20	-18	-15
IDA	0	19	0	0	0	51	73	14	51	17

NICARAGUA

(US$ million, unless otherwise indicated)

	1970	1980	1988	1989	1990	1991	1992	1993	1994	1995
INTEREST PAYMENTS (LINT)	**7**	**42**	**8**	**3**	**5**	**196**	**34**	**51**	**91**	**78**
Public and publicly guaranteed	**7**	**42**	**8**	**3**	**5**	**196**	**34**	**51**	**91**	**78**
Official creditors	3	38	7	2	4	195	33	50	90	76
Multilateral	2	29	5	0	1	184	22	26	55	33
Concessional	1	7	0	0	0	22	6	7	26	11
Bilateral	1	9	2	1	3	10	11	24	35	43
Concessional	1	3	1	1	0	0	3	8	16	19
Private creditors	4	4	1	1	1	1	1	1	1	2
Bonds	0	0	0	0	0	0	0	0	0	0
Commercial banks	3	0	0	0	0	0	0	0	0	1
Other private	0	4	1	1	1	1	1	1	1	1
Private nonguaranteed	**0**	**0**	**0**	**0**	**0**	**0**	**0**	**0**	**0**	**0**
Bonds	0	0	0	0	0	0	0	0	0	0
Commercial banks	0	0	0	0	0	0	0	0	0	0
Memo:										
IBRD	2	11	0	0	1	137	10	10	8	6
IDA	0	0	0	0	0	3	1	1	2	2
NET TRANSFERS ON DEBT	**21**	**190**	**411**	**581**	**459**	**-206**	**208**	**-3**	**122**	**-32**
Public and publicly guaranteed	**21**	**190**	**411**	**581**	**459**	**-206**	**208**	**-3**	**122**	**-32**
Official creditors	25	220	409	571	440	-202	210	1	130	47
Multilateral	7	47	5	3	5	-186	109	7	126	83
Concessional	1	63	0	0	0	82	111	5	62	80
Bilateral	19	173	404	568	435	-15	102	-6	4	-36
Concessional	18	103	202	368	262	14	93	-1	20	12
Private creditors	-5	-30	2	10	19	-4	-3	-4	-8	-79
Bonds	0	0	0	0	0	0	0	0	0	0
Commercial banks	-2	-20	3	-1	0	0	2	1	0	-74
Other private	-2	-10	-1	12	20	-4	-4	-5	-8	-5
Private nonguaranteed	**0**	**0**	**0**	**0**	**0**	**0**	**0**	**0**	**0**	**0**
Bonds	0	0	0	0	0	0	0	0	0	0
Commercial banks	0	0	0	0	0	0	0	0	0	0
Memo:										
IBRD	3	-3	0	0	-2	-248	-26	-29	-25	-21
IDA	0	19	0	0	0	47	72	12	49	16
DEBT SERVICE (LTDS)	**23**	**86**	**17**	**9**	**10**	**525**	**75**	**103**	**184**	**260**
Public and publicly guaranteed	**23**	**86**	**17**	**9**	**10**	**525**	**75**	**103**	**184**	**260**
Official creditors	7	56	12	5	5	521	71	97	176	162
Multilateral	5	43	8	0	2	341	52	63	122	81
Concessional	2	10	0	0	0	49	15	16	62	32
Bilateral	2	13	4	4	3	179	18	34	53	81
Concessional	1	5	1	3	0	52	3	9	16	21
Private creditors	16	30	5	4	4	4	4	6	8	98
Bonds	0	0	0	0	0	0	0	0	0	0
Commercial banks	14	20	1	1	0	0	0	0	0	93
Other private	3	10	4	3	4	4	4	5	8	5
Private nonguaranteed	**0**	**0**	**0**	**0**	**0**	**0**	**0**	**0**	**0**	**0**
Bonds	0	0	0	0	0	0	0	0	0	0
Commercial banks	0	0	0	0	0	0	0	0	0	0
Memo:										
IBRD	3	15	0	0	1	248	26	29	25	21
IDA	0	0	0	0	0	6	1	3	3	3
UNDISBURSED DEBT	**62**	**449**	**1,109**	**707**	**573**	**722**	**716**	**842**	**1,029**	**1,035**
Official creditors	52	418	1,081	692	562	714	710	837	1,005	1,011
Private creditors	9	30	28	16	11	8	6	5	24	24
Memorandum items										
Concessional LDOD	75	478	2,487	2,866	3,162	3,144	3,309	3,064	3,245	3,266
Variable rate LDOD	0	796	1,792	1,832	1,869	2,049	2,134	2,157	2,235	1,347
Public sector LDOD	138	1,656	7,020	7,660	8,245	8,714	8,937	8,695	9,013	7,937
Private sector LDOD	9	15	0	0	0	0	0	0	0	0

6. CURRENCY COMPOSITION OF LONG-TERM DEBT (PERCENT)

	1970	1980	1988	1989	1990	1991	1992	1993	1994	1995
Deutsche mark	4.0	2.9	1.1	1.0	1.3	1.9	1.9	1.9	2.1	5.9
French franc	0.0	0.0	1.3	1.3	1.3	1.6	1.6	1.6	1.6	2.5
Japanese yen	0.0	0.2	0.1	0.1	0.1	0.5	0.9	1.1	1.4	1.5
Pound sterling	1.6	0.2	0.0	0.0	0.0	0.0	0.0	0.0	0.0	0.0
Swiss franc	0.0	0.0	0.0	0.0	0.0	0.0	0.0	0.0	0.0	0.0
U.S.dollars	66.4	72.5	81.9	83.0	82.5	83.9	83.5	83.5	82.4	75.3
Multiple currency	28.1	20.9	11.5	10.6	10.4	9.1	9.4	9.5	9.3	11.2
Special drawing rights	0.0	0.0	0.0	0.0	0.0	0.0	0.0	0.0	0.0	0.0
All other currencies	0.0	3.4	4.1	4.0	4.3	3.0	2.5	2.4	3.2	3.7

NICARAGUA

(US$ million, unless otherwise indicated)

	1970	1980	1988	1989	1990	1991	1992	1993	1994	1995
7. DEBT RESTRUCTURINGS										
Total amount rescheduled	0	..	500	54	30	1,898	102	117	15	335
Debt stock rescheduled	0	..	200	0	0	644	0	2	0	0
Principal rescheduled	0	..	121	0	0	698	65	73	3	151
Official	0	..	115	0	0	655	54	71	3	129
Private	0	..	6	0	0	43	11	2	0	23
Interest rescheduled	0	..	178	54	30	518	36	29	3	35
Official	0	..	166	54	30	496	31	28	3	30
Private	0	..	12	0	0	22	6	1	0	5
Debt forgiven	..	..	0	0	0	228	6	1	7	430
Memo: interest forgiven	..	..	0	0	0	205	1	0	0	722
Debt stock reduction	0	..	0	0	0	159	0	0	9	1,200
of which debt buyback	0	..	0	0	0	159	0	0	0	89
8. DEBT STOCK-FLOW RECONCILIATION										
Total change in debt stocks	..	..	..	1,002	949	-129	470	-585	562	-1,723
Net flows on debt	..	..	..	636	480	-3	362	-318	110	-55
Net change in interest arrears	..	..	..	308	349	-445	127	22	346	-548
Interest capitalized	..	..	..	54	30	518	36	29	3	35
Debt forgiveness or reduction	..	..	..	0	0	-228	-6	-1	-15	-1,541
Cross-currency valuation	..	..	..	6	87	-44	-48	-28	65	67
Residual	..	..	..	-3	4	73	-2	-290	55	318
9. AVERAGE TERMS OF NEW COMMITMENTS										
ALL CREDITORS										
Interest (%)	7.1	4.0	4.3	4.7	5.1	2.8	4.7	4.7	3.1	2.7
Maturity (years)	17.9	25.3	9.6	14.2	10.0	28.9	22.6	25.2	31.0	31.0
Grace period (years)	3.9	6.7	1.8	1.3	2.1	8.1	6.0	6.0	8.2	8.2
Grant element (%)	18.9	44.1	22.1	24.9	19.1	56.2	37.5	40.5	55.9	58.9
Official creditors										
Interest (%)	5.8	3.9	4.2	4.7	4.9	2.8	4.7	4.7	3.0	2.3
Maturity (years)	27.8	26.4	9.5	14.3	10.3	29.0	22.6	25.2	31.9	32.9
Grace period (years)	6.5	7.0	1.8	1.3	2.2	8.1	6.0	6.0	8.5	8.7
Grant element (%)	32.7	45.5	22.5	25.2	20.1	56.3	37.5	40.5	57.6	63.1
Private creditors										
Interest (%)	8.6	4.3	9.8	11.5	9.4	2.9	0.0	0.0	6.0	7.4
Maturity (years)	7.0	9.2	13.0	3.0	4.9	24.2	0.0	0.0	7.5	8.2
Grace period (years)	1.0	2.1	1.0	0.5	0.4	4.2	0.0	0.0	1.9	1.0
Grant element (%)	3.7	22.7	-0.2	-2.8	0.9	49.1	0.0	0.0	13.2	8.1
Memorandum items										
Commitments	23	434	775	188	338	483	282	256	497	313
Official creditors	12	408	764	186	320	480	282	256	478	289
Private creditors	11	27	11	2	18	4	0	0	20	24

10. CONTRACTUAL OBLIGATIONS ON OUTSTANDING LONG-TERM DEBT

	1996	1997	1998	1999	2000	2001	2002	2003	2004	2005
TOTAL										
Disbursements	240	207	134	85	45	23	12	1	0	0
Principal	489	595	417	371	311	268	285	248	118	138
Interest	195	199	222	199	177	157	140	122	108	104
Official creditors										
Disbursements	228	199	131	83	45	23	12	1	0	0
Principal	349	459	401	357	298	258	276	241	112	112
Interest	157	171	185	163	141	122	105	88	74	71
Bilateral creditors										
Disbursements	80	55	32	17	4	2	1	0	0	0
Principal	274	379	307	264	203	164	174	150	66	65
Interest	96	110	128	111	95	82	71	60	51	48
Multilateral creditors										
Disbursements	148	144	99	66	41	21	11	1	0	0
Principal	75	80	94	93	96	94	102	91	45	47
Interest	61	60	57	52	46	40	34	28	23	23
Private creditors										
Disbursements	12	8	3	1	0	0	0	0	0	0
Principal	140	136	16	13	13	10	9	7	7	26
Interest	38	28	37	36	36	35	35	34	34	33
Commercial banks										
Disbursements	12	8	3	1	0	0	0	0	0	0
Principal	138	132	12	12	11	9	8	7	6	25
Interest	22	12	5	5	4	3	3	3	3	2
Other private										
Disbursements	0	0	0	0	0	0	0	0	0	0
Principal	3	3	4	2	2	2	1	1	1	1
Interest	16	16	32	32	32	32	32	32	32	32

NIGER

(US$ million, unless otherwise indicated)

	1970	1980	1988	1989	1990	1991	1992	1993	1994	1995
1. SUMMARY DEBT DATA										
TOTAL DEBT STOCKS (EDT)	..	**863**	**1,742**	**1,564**	**1,793**	**1,565**	**1,580**	**1,614**	**1,566**	**1,633**
Long-term debt (LDOD)	**32**	**687**	**1,542**	**1,372**	**1,555**	**1,434**	**1,432**	**1,456**	**1,466**	**1,509**
Public and publicly guaranteed	32	383	1,286	1,113	1,294	1,209	1,227	1,275	1,309	1,376
Private nonguaranteed	0	305	256	259	261	225	205	181	157	133
Use of IMF credit	**0**	**16**	**95**	**85**	**85**	**73**	**61**	**52**	**61**	**52**
Short-term debt	..	**159**	**105**	**107**	**153**	**58**	**87**	**106**	**39**	**72**
of which interest arrears on LDOD	..	0	3	23	31	21	49	78	24	54
Official creditors	..	0	3	14	16	21	48	77	24	54
Private creditors	..	0	0	9	16	0	0	0	0	0
Memo: principal arrears on LDOD	..	1	17	44	80	40	89	119	40	76
Official creditors	..	1	17	24	39	40	88	118	40	76
Private creditors	..	0	0	20	41	0	0	1	0	0
Memo: export credits	..	..	408	348	398	364	324	313	369	459
TOTAL DEBT FLOWS										
Disbursements	**12**	**290**	**189**	**156**	**148**	**40**	**83**	**103**	**86**	**27**
Long-term debt	12	281	178	145	139	40	83	103	71	27
IMF purchases	0	10	11	11	9	0	0	0	16	0
Principal repayments	**2**	**58**	**89**	**74**	**63**	**75**	**36**	**66**	**48**	**42**
Long-term debt	2	58	56	56	47	63	27	56	38	32
IMF repurchases	0	0	33	18	16	11	10	10	10	10
Net flows on debt	**11**	**233**	**128**	**64**	**123**	**-121**	**48**	**28**	**25**	**-12**
of which short-term debt	..	..	28	-18	38	-86	2	-9	-14	4
Interest payments (INT)	..	**84**	**86**	**48**	**36**	**33**	**17**	**25**	**19**	**16**
Long-term debt	1	65	74	35	23	21	13	23	16	13
IMF charges	0	0	5	4	4	3	2	1	1	1
Short-term debt	..	19	7	9	9	10	2	2	2	1
Net transfers on debt	..	**149**	**42**	**16**	**87**	**-154**	**31**	**3**	**5**	**-27**
Total debt service paid (TDS)	..	**141**	**175**	**122**	**99**	**108**	**53**	**91**	**67**	**58**
Long-term debt	2	122	130	91	71	84	40	79	55	46
IMF repurchases and charges	0	0	38	23	19	14	11	10	11	11
Short-term debt (interest only)	..	19	7	9	9	10	2	2	2	1
2. AGGREGATE NET RESOURCE FLOWS AND NET TRANSFERS (LONG-TERM)										
NET RESOURCE FLOWS	**26**	**324**	**282**	**258**	**316**	**225**	**263**	**247**	**289**	**161**
Net flow of long-term debt (ex. IMF)	11	223	121	90	92	-24	56	47	32	-6
Foreign direct investment (net)	1	49	-1	0	-1	1	0	1	1	1
Portfolio equity flows	0	0	0	0	0	0	0	0	0	0
Grants (excluding technical coop.)	15	51	162	169	226	247	207	198	255	165
Memo: technical coop. grants	11	62	99	87	102	113	135	127	103	111
NET TRANSFERS	**23**	**248**	**208**	**223**	**293**	**204**	**250**	**224**	**272**	**148**
Interest on long-term debt	1	65	74	35	23	21	13	23	16	13
Profit remittances on FDI	2	11	0	0	0	0	0	0	0	0
3. MAJOR ECONOMIC AGGREGATES										
Gross national product (GNP)	638	2,499	2,218	2,133	2,425	2,289	2,314	2,187	1,507	1,791
Exports of goods & services (XGS)	..	650	429	378	386	354	331	301	270	286
of which workers remittances	..	6	10	10	12	12	13	12	10	8
Imports of goods & services (MGS)	..	1,016	611	571	594	469	452	420	429	458
International reserves (RES)	19	132	237	217	227	207	229	196	115	99
Current account balance	..	-277	-83	-111	-109	-25	-45	-29	-78	-80
4. DEBT INDICATORS										
EDT / XGS (%)	..	132.8	406.0	413.4	464.1	442.1	478.0	537.0	579.9	571.7
EDT / GNP (%)	..	34.5	78.5	73.3	74.0	68.4	68.3	73.8	104.0	91.2
TDS / XGS (%)	..	21.7	40.8	32.3	25.5	30.4	16.1	30.3	24.9	20.2
INT / XGS (%)	..	12.9	20.0	12.7	9.3	9.4	5.1	8.4	7.1	5.4
INT / GNP (%)	..	3.3	3.9	2.3	1.5	1.4	0.7	1.2	1.3	0.9
RES / EDT (%)	..	15.3	13.6	13.9	12.6	13.2	14.5	12.2	7.3	6.1
RES / MGS (months)	..	1.6	4.6	4.6	4.6	5.3	6.1	5.6	3.2	2.6
Short-term / EDT (%)	..	18.5	6.0	6.8	8.6	3.7	5.5	6.6	2.5	4.4
Concessional / EDT (%)	..	18.0	44.8	44.4	45.8	53.5	56.0	59.5	64.2	64.1
Multilateral / EDT (%)	..	16.5	31.7	38.0	39.0	46.8	45.7	46.5	52.8	53.2

NIGER

(US$ million, unless otherwise indicated)

	1970	1980	1988	1989	1990	1991	1992	1993	1994	1995
5. LONG-TERM DEBT										
DEBT OUTSTANDING (LDOD)	**32**	**687**	**1,542**	**1,372**	**1,555**	**1,434**	**1,432**	**1,456**	**1,466**	**1,509**
Public and publicly guaranteed	**32**	**383**	**1,286**	**1,113**	**1,294**	**1,209**	**1,227**	**1,275**	**1,309**	**1,376**
Official creditors	31	255	1,187	1,010	1,179	1,208	1,226	1,274	1,309	1,376
Multilateral	4	143	552	595	700	732	722	751	827	869
Concessional	4	114	502	547	651	679	673	721	807	849
Bilateral	27	112	636	416	479	476	504	523	482	507
Concessional	25	42	278	147	171	159	212	240	198	198
Private creditors	1	128	99	103	115	1	1	1	0	0
Bonds	0	0	0	0	0	0	0	0	0	0
Commercial banks	0	68	89	101	114	1	1	1	0	0
Other private	0	60	10	2	1	0	0	0	0	0
Private nonguaranteed	**0**	**305**	**256**	**259**	**261**	**225**	**205**	**181**	**157**	**133**
Bonds	0	0	0	0	0	0	0	0	0	0
Commercial banks	0	305	256	259	261	225	205	181	157	133
Memo:										
IBRD	0	0	0	0	0	0	0	0	0	0
IDA	4	66	348	383	461	479	483	504	565	598
DISBURSEMENTS	**12**	**281**	**178**	**145**	**139**	**40**	**83**	**103**	**71**	**27**
Public and publicly guaranteed	**12**	**167**	**150**	**105**	**96**	**40**	**83**	**103**	**71**	**27**
Official creditors	12	91	150	97	90	40	83	103	71	27
Multilateral	2	60	109	58	70	24	24	59	64	26
Concessional	2	47	106	56	69	24	24	59	63	26
Bilateral	10	31	41	39	21	15	58	44	7	0
Concessional	10	11	38	38	21	15	58	33	4	0
Private creditors	0	76	0	9	5	0	0	0	0	0
Bonds	0	0	0	0	0	0	0	0	0	0
Commercial banks	0	56	0	9	5	0	0	0	0	0
Other private	0	20	0	0	0	0	0	0	0	0
Private nonguaranteed	**0**	**113**	**28**	**40**	**43**	**0**	**0**	**0**	**0**	**0**
Bonds	0	0	0	0	0	0	0	0	0	0
Commercial banks	0	113	28	40	43	0	0	0	0	0
Memo:										
IBRD	0	0	0	0	0	0	0	0	0	0
IDA	2	18	85	40	55	17	21	21	44	24
PRINCIPAL REPAYMENTS	**2**	**58**	**56**	**56**	**47**	**63**	**27**	**56**	**38**	**32**
Public and publicly guaranteed	**2**	**23**	**30**	**19**	**10**	**27**	**7**	**32**	**15**	**8**
Official creditors	1	17	21	17	9	8	7	32	15	8
Multilateral	0	15	13	9	7	6	6	30	14	7
Concessional	0	14	5	4	3	4	4	11	8	7
Bilateral	1	3	8	8	2	2	1	2	1	1
Concessional	1	2	5	2	2	2	0	1	0	1
Private creditors	1	5	9	1	2	19	0	0	0	0
Bonds	0	0	0	0	0	0	0	0	0	0
Commercial banks	0	1	8	0	0	19	0	0	0	0
Other private	1	4	2	1	2	0	0	0	0	0
Private nonguaranteed	**0**	**35**	**26**	**37**	**37**	**36**	**20**	**24**	**24**	**24**
Bonds	0	0	0	0	0	0	0	0	0	0
Commercial banks	0	35	26	37	37	36	20	24	24	24
Memo:										
IBRD	0	0	0	0	0	0	0	0	0	0
IDA	0	0	1	1	1	2	2	2	3	3
NET FLOWS ON DEBT	**11**	**223**	**121**	**90**	**92**	**-24**	**56**	**47**	**32**	**-6**
Public and publicly guaranteed	**11**	**144**	**120**	**87**	**86**	**12**	**76**	**71**	**56**	**18**
Official creditors	11	74	129	79	82	32	76	71	56	18
Multilateral	2	46	96	49	63	18	18	29	50	19
Concessional	2	33	101	52	66	21	20	48	54	20
Bilateral	9	28	33	30	19	14	58	42	6	-1
Concessional	9	10	33	36	19	14	58	32	4	0
Private creditors	-1	71	-9	7	4	-19	0	0	0	0
Bonds	0	0	0	0	0	0	0	0	0	0
Commercial banks	0	55	-8	9	5	-19	0	0	0	0
Other private	-1	16	-2	-1	-2	0	0	0	0	0
Private nonguaranteed	**0**	**79**	**2**	**3**	**6**	**-36**	**-20**	**-24**	**-24**	**-24**
Bonds	0	0	0	0	0	0	0	0	0	0
Commercial banks	0	79	2	3	6	-36	-20	-24	-24	-24
Memo:										
IBRD	0	0	0	0	0	0	0	0	0	0
IDA	2	18	84	39	54	16	19	19	42	21

NIGER

(US$ million, unless otherwise indicated)

	1970	1980	1988	1989	1990	1991	1992	1993	1994	1995
INTEREST PAYMENTS (LINT)	**1**	**65**	**74**	**35**	**23**	**21**	**13**	**23**	**16**	**13**
Public and publicly guaranteed	**1**	**16**	**54**	**14**	**7**	**11**	**5**	**16**	**10**	**8**
Official creditors	1	7	43	14	7	11	5	16	10	8
Multilateral	0	3	10	7	6	5	5	14	7	7
Concessional	0	2	6	4	4	4	4	7	6	7
Bilateral	1	5	32	8	1	6	0	2	3	1
Concessional	1	1	5	3	1	1	0	2	2	1
Private creditors	0	9	11	0	0	0	0	0	0	0
Bonds	0	0	0	0	0	0	0	0	0	0
Commercial banks	0	6	10	0	0	0	0	0	0	0
Other private	0	3	1	0	0	0	0	0	0	0
Private nonguaranteed	**0**	**49**	**20**	**21**	**16**	**10**	**8**	**7**	**6**	**6**
Bonds	0	0	0	0	0	0	0	0	0	0
Commercial banks	0	49	20	21	16	10	8	7	6	6
Memo:										
IBRD	0	0	0	0	0	0	0	0	0	0
IDA	0	0	3	2	3	4	4	3	5	5
NET TRANSFERS ON DEBT	**10**	**158**	**47**	**54**	**68**	**-45**	**43**	**24**	**16**	**-19**
Public and publicly guaranteed	**10**	**128**	**66**	**72**	**78**	**1**	**71**	**55**	**46**	**11**
Official creditors	11	66	87	65	75	21	71	55	46	11
Multilateral	2	43	86	42	57	13	13	16	43	12
Concessional	2	32	95	48	62	16	16	41	49	13
Bilateral	8	23	1	23	18	8	57	40	3	-2
Concessional	8	9	28	33	18	13	58	31	2	-1
Private creditors	-1	62	-21	7	4	-19	0	0	0	0
Bonds	0	0	0	0	0	0	0	0	0	0
Commercial banks	0	49	-18	9	5	-19	0	0	0	0
Other private	-1	14	-3	-2	-2	0	0	0	0	0
Private nonguaranteed	**0**	**30**	**-19**	**-18**	**-10**	**-46**	**-28**	**-31**	**-30**	**-29**
Bonds	0	0	0	0	0	0	0	0	0	0
Commercial banks	0	30	-19	-18	-10	-46	-28	-31	-30	-29
Memo:										
IBRD	0	0	0	0	0	0	0	0	0	0
IDA	2	18	81	37	51	12	15	16	37	16
DEBT SERVICE (LTDS)	**2**	**122**	**130**	**91**	**71**	**84**	**40**	**79**	**55**	**46**
Public and publicly guaranteed	**2**	**39**	**84**	**33**	**17**	**38**	**12**	**48**	**25**	**16**
Official creditors	2	25	64	32	16	19	12	48	25	16
Multilateral	0	17	24	16	12	11	11	44	21	14
Concessional	0	16	11	8	7	8	8	18	14	13
Bilateral	2	8	40	16	3	8	1	4	4	2
Concessional	1	3	10	5	3	2	1	3	2	2
Private creditors	1	14	21	2	2	19	0	0	0	0
Bonds	0	0	0	0	0	0	0	0	0	0
Commercial banks	0	7	18	0	0	19	0	0	0	0
Other private	1	7	3	2	2	0	0	0	0	0
Private nonguaranteed	**0**	**83**	**46**	**58**	**53**	**46**	**28**	**31**	**30**	**29**
Bonds	0	0	0	0	0	0	0	0	0	0
Commercial banks	0	83	46	58	53	46	28	31	30	29
Memo:										
IBRD	0	0	0	0	0	0	0	0	0	0
IDA	0	1	4	4	4	5	6	5	7	8
UNDISBURSED DEBT	**41**	**413**	**425**	**389**	**373**	**354**	**341**	**328**	**331**	**290**
Official creditors	24	277	425	384	373	354	341	328	331	290
Private creditors	17	136	1	5	0	0	0	0	0	0
Memorandum items										
Concessional LDOD	29	156	780	694	822	838	885	961	1,006	1,046
Variable rate LDOD	0	387	351	366	382	232	211	187	169	145
Public sector LDOD	25	372	1,283	1,110	1,291	1,208	1,226	1,275	1,309	1,376
Private sector LDOD	7	316	260	262	264	227	206	182	157	133

6. CURRENCY COMPOSITION OF LONG-TERM DEBT (PERCENT)

	1970	1980	1988	1989	1990	1991	1992	1993	1994	1995
Deutsche mark	12.0	0.0	0.0	0.0	0.0	0.6	0.5	0.5	0.5	0.5
French franc	67.5	53.8	53.5	43.3	42.4	42.1	39.7	37.6	35.0	37.9
Japanese yen	0.0	0.0	0.0	0.5	1.2	3.5	4.1	4.2	4.6	4.3
Pound sterling	0.0	0.0	0.9	0.7	0.7	0.9	0.7	0.7	1.1	1.0
Swiss franc	0.0	0.0	0.0	0.0	0.0	0.7	0.7	0.3	0.2	0.3
U.S.dollars	6.9	30.2	24.9	30.5	31.2	32.6	36.1	37.0	38.7	36.4
Multiple currency	0.0	2.1	0.6	0.6	0.5	0.5	0.4	0.1	0.0	0.0
Special drawing rights	0.0	0.0	0.7	1.6	2.5	2.6	2.5	2.8	3.1	3.1
All other currencies	13.6	13.9	19.3	22.7	21.4	16.5	15.2	17.0	16.8	16.5

NIGER

(US$ million, unless otherwise indicated)

	1970	1980	1988	1989	1990	1991	1992	1993	1994	1995
7. DEBT RESTRUCTURINGS										
Total amount rescheduled	0	0	48	19	29	27	0	15	119	45
Debt stock rescheduled	0	0	0	0	0	0	0	0	0	0
Principal rescheduled	0	0	41	12	12	17	0	7	76	38
Official	0	0	12	6	12	17	0	7	75	38
Private	0	0	29	6	0	0	0	0	1	0
Interest rescheduled	0	0	7	6	16	11	0	5	42	3
Official	0	0	6	6	16	11	0	5	42	3
Private	0	0	1	0	0	0	0	0	0	0
Debt forgiven	..	..	0	254	0	26	10	13	109	0
Memo: interest forgiven	..	..	0	0	0	18	0	1	37	0
Debt stock reduction	0	0	0	0	0	107	0	0	0	0
of which debt buyback	0	0	0	0	0	19	0	0	0	0
8. DEBT STOCK-FLOW RECONCILIATION										
Total change in debt stocks	..	..	..	-178	229	-228	15	34	-48	67
Net flows on debt	..	..	..	64	123	-121	48	28	25	-12
Net change in interest arrears	..	..	..	20	8	-10	27	29	-54	30
Interest capitalized	..	..	..	6	16	11	0	5	42	3
Debt forgiveness or reduction	..	..	..	-254	0	-114	-10	-13	-109	0
Cross-currency valuation	..	..	..	18	113	-5	-51	-39	64	62
Residual	..	..	..	-32	-31	11	1	24	-15	-15
9. AVERAGE TERMS OF NEW COMMITMENTS										
ALL CREDITORS										
Interest (%)	1.2	7.4	1.4	3.2	2.2	1.1	3.1	2.2	1.0	0.7
Maturity (years)	39.7	18.3	31.3	28.8	32.8	33.8	23.8	28.3	35.2	36.0
Grace period (years)	8.2	4.7	8.9	8.4	8.7	8.6	7.8	7.6	9.0	9.2
Grant element (%)	72.5	18.7	69.6	54.1	63.9	72.9	50.8	59.2	73.7	76.1
Official creditors										
Interest (%)	0.6	5.4	1.4	2.1	2.2	1.1	3.1	2.2	1.0	0.7
Maturity (years)	44.7	26.2	31.3	30.4	32.8	33.8	23.8	28.3	35.2	36.0
Grace period (years)	9.1	6.8	8.9	9.4	8.7	8.6	7.8	7.6	9.0	9.2
Grant element (%)	80.9	35.3	69.6	62.5	63.9	72.9	50.8	59.2	73.7	76.1
Private creditors										
Interest (%)	4.5	9.8	0.0	12.2	0.0	0.0	0.0	0.0	0.0	0.0
Maturity (years)	13.6	8.8	0.0	16.0	0.0	0.0	0.0	0.0	0.0	0.0
Grace period (years)	3.6	2.2	0.0	0.3	0.0	0.0	0.0	0.0	0.0	0.0
Grant element (%)	29.1	-1.0	0.0	-12.3	0.0	0.0	0.0	0.0	0.0	0.0
Memorandum items										
Commitments	19	341	159	126	64	33	94	97	89	8
Official creditors	16	185	159	111	64	33	94	97	89	8
Private creditors	3	156	0	14	0	0	0	0	0	0

10. CONTRACTUAL OBLIGATIONS ON OUTSTANDING LONG-TERM DEBT

	1996	1997	1998	1999	2000	2001	2002	2003	2004	2005
TOTAL										
Disbursements	68	61	42	27	14	6	4	2	1	0
Principal	68	54	73	79	93	81	68	66	63	50
Interest	40	37	35	34	31	28	25	23	20	18
Official creditors										
Disbursements	68	61	42	27	14	6	4	2	1	0
Principal	44	40	49	55	69	67	63	61	63	50
Interest	35	34	34	32	31	28	25	23	20	18
Bilateral creditors										
Disbursements	18	18	12	8	5	3	2	2	1	0
Principal	24	20	28	33	46	47	42	41	40	26
Interest	27	26	26	25	23	21	18	16	13	11
Multilateral creditors										
Disbursements	50	43	30	20	9	3	2	1	0	0
Principal	20	20	21	23	23	20	20	21	23	25
Interest	8	8	8	8	8	7	7	7	7	6
Private creditors										
Disbursements	0	0	0	0	0	0	0	0	0	0
Principal	24	14	24	24	24	15	5	5	0	0
Interest	5	3	2	1	1	0	0	0	0	0
Commercial banks										
Disbursements	0	0	0	0	0	0	0	0	0	0
Principal	0	0	0	0	0	0	0	0	0	0
Interest	0	0	0	0	0	0	0	0	0	0
Other private										
Disbursements	0	0	0	0	0	0	0	0	0	0
Principal	24	14	24	24	24	15	5	5	0	0
Interest	5	3	2	1	1	0	0	0	0	0

NIGERIA

(US$ million, unless otherwise indicated)

1. SUMMARY DEBT DATA

	1970	1980	1988	1989	1990	1991	1992	1993	1994	1995
TOTAL DEBT STOCKS (EDT)	**..**	**8,921**	**29,621**	**30,122**	**33,440**	**33,527**	**29,019**	**30,699**	**33,519**	**35,005**
Long-term debt (LDOD)	**567**	**5,368**	**28,074**	**29,657**	**31,936**	**32,668**	**26,809**	**26,742**	**28,479**	**29,002**
Public and publicly guaranteed	452	4,271	27,537	29,251	31,546	32,325	26,478	26,421	28,168	28,701
Private nonguaranteed	115	1,097	537	406	391	343	331	321	311	301
Use of IMF credit	**0**	**0**	**0**	**0**	**0**	**0**	**0**	**0**	**0**	**0**
Short-term debt	**..**	**3,553**	**1,547**	**465**	**1,504**	**859**	**2,210**	**3,957**	**5,040**	**6,003**
of which interest arrears on LDOD	..	0	887	221	1,040	482	1,197	2,438	4,033	5,070
Official creditors	..	0	414	64	465	180	1,021	2,065	3,361	4,278
Private creditors	..	0	473	157	575	302	176	374	672	791
Memo: principal arrears on LDOD	..	0	2,955	313	1,091	531	1,841	3,866	6,250	8,801
Official creditors	..	0	380	99	194	133	1,333	2,723	4,410	6,598
Private creditors	..	0	2,575	214	897	398	508	1,144	1,840	2,202
Memo: export credits	..	..	14,504	20,029	20,116	20,935	17,598	17,299	19,012	17,459
TOTAL DEBT FLOWS										
Disbursements	**81**	**1,753**	**914**	**1,588**	**927**	**787**	**535**	**544**	**599**	**433**
Long-term debt	81	1,753	914	1,588	927	787	535	544	599	433
IMF purchases	0	0	0	0	0	0	0	0	0	0
Principal repayments	**68**	**242**	**692**	**607**	**1,180**	**862**	**1,878**	**579**	**746**	**809**
Long-term debt	68	242	692	607	1,180	862	1,878	579	746	809
IMF repurchases	0	0	0	0	0	0	0	0	0	0
Net flows on debt	**13**	**1,510**	**1,637**	**566**	**-34**	**-162**	**-708**	**472**	**-660**	**-450**
of which short-term debt	..	..	1,415	-415	219	-86	635	507	-512	-73
Interest payments (INT)	**..**	**909**	**1,518**	**1,511**	**2,156**	**2,082**	**1,871**	**912**	**1,125**	**762**
Long-term debt	28	529	1,478	1,480	2,124	2,054	1,831	862	1,075	706
IMF charges	0	0	0	0	0	0	0	0	0	0
Short-term debt	..	379	40	31	32	28	40	50	50	56
Net transfers on debt	**..**	**602**	**118**	**-945**	**-2,190**	**-2,244**	**-2,579**	**-440**	**-1,785**	**-1,212**
Total debt service paid (TDS)	**..**	**1,151**	**2,210**	**2,118**	**3,336**	**2,945**	**3,749**	**1,491**	**1,872**	**1,571**
Long-term debt	96	772	2,170	2,087	3,304	2,917	3,709	1,441	1,822	1,515
IMF repurchases and charges	0	0	0	0	0	0	0	0	0	0
Short-term debt (interest only)	..	379	40	31	32	28	40	50	50	56

2. AGGREGATE NET RESOURCE FLOWS AND NET TRANSFERS (LONG-TERM)

	1970	1980	1988	1989	1990	1991	1992	1993	1994	1995
NET RESOURCE FLOWS	**259**	**773**	**634**	**2,991**	**460**	**767**	**-330**	**1,363**	**1,871**	**312**
Net flow of long-term debt (ex. IMF)	13	1,510	222	981	-253	-76	-1,343	-35	-148	-376
Foreign direct investment (net)	205	-740	377	1,882	588	712	897	1,345	1,959	650
Portfolio equity flows	0	0	0	0	0	0	0	0	17	6
Grants (excluding technical coop.)	40	3	36	128	125	131	116	53	43	32
Memo: technical coop. grants	36	47	66	71	95	96	99	98	78	79
NET TRANSFERS	**-207**	**-1,354**	**-1,180**	**1,415**	**-1,799**	**-1,473**	**-2,277**	**351**	**631**	**-539**
Interest on long-term debt	28	529	1,478	1,480	2,124	2,054	1,831	862	1,075	706
Profit remittances on FDI	438	1,598	336	97	135	186	116	150	165	145

3. MAJOR ECONOMIC AGGREGATES

	1970	1980	1988	1989	1990	1991	1992	1993	1994	1995
Gross national product (GNP)	12,081	88,610	29,110	27,855	29,138	29,730	27,102	26,088	30,345	24,912
Exports of goods & services (XGS)	..	27,772	7,282	8,586	14,772	13,417	13,056	11,924	10,429	12,754
of which workers remittances	..	13	2	10	10	66	57	793	550	657
Imports of goods & services (MGS)	..	22,005	7,564	7,612	9,858	12,893	11,485	12,723	12,504	13,287
International reserves (RES)	224	10,640	933	2,041	4,129	4,678	1,196	1,641	1,649	1,709
Current account balance	..	5,178	-297	1,090	4,988	1,203	2,268	-780	-2,128	-510

4. DEBT INDICATORS

	1970	1980	1988	1989	1990	1991	1992	1993	1994	1995
EDT / XGS (%)	..	32.1	406.8	350.8	226.4	249.9	222.3	257.5	321.4	274.5
EDT / GNP (%)	..	10.1	101.8	108.1	114.8	112.8	107.1	117.7	110.5	140.5
TDS / XGS (%)	..	4.1	30.4	24.7	22.6	21.9	28.7	12.5	17.9	12.3
INT / XGS (%)	..	3.3	20.9	17.6	14.6	15.5	14.3	7.6	10.8	6.0
INT / GNP (%)	..	1.0	5.2	5.4	7.4	7.0	6.9	3.5	3.7	3.1
RES / EDT (%)	..	119.3	3.1	6.8	12.3	14.0	4.1	5.3	4.9	4.9
RES / MGS (months)	..	5.8	1.5	3.2	5.0	4.4	1.2	1.5	1.6	1.5
Short-term / EDT (%)	..	39.8	5.2	1.5	4.5	2.6	7.6	12.9	15.0	17.1
Concessional / EDT (%)	..	6.0	1.8	1.7	1.8	3.1	3.6	3.8	4.0	4.1
Multilateral / EDT (%)	..	6.4	9.6	10.5	11.2	12.0	14.1	14.1	14.3	14.1

NIGERIA

(US$ million, unless otherwise indicated)

	1970	1980	1988	1989	1990	1991	1992	1993	1994	1995
5. LONG-TERM DEBT										
DEBT OUTSTANDING (LDOD)	**567**	**5,368**	**28,074**	**29,657**	**31,936**	**32,668**	**26,809**	**26,742**	**28,479**	**29,002**
Public and publicly guaranteed	**452**	**4,271**	**27,537**	**29,251**	**31,546**	**32,325**	**26,478**	**26,421**	**28,168**	**28,701**
Official creditors	358	992	10,771	14,681	17,011	19,153	18,328	18,247	19,812	20,493
Multilateral	182	571	2,849	3,173	3,733	4,011	4,088	4,339	4,807	4,944
Concessional	169	131	118	112	115	154	174	216	296	392
Bilateral	175	422	7,922	11,508	13,278	15,143	14,241	13,908	15,005	15,549
Concessional	111	401	408	412	485	889	868	938	1,051	1,038
Private creditors	94	3,279	16,766	14,570	14,535	13,172	8,150	8,173	8,355	8,208
Bonds	10	0	0	0	0	0	2,051	2,051	2,051	2,051
Commercial banks	18	2,634	6,238	6,022	5,714	5,590	0	0	0	0
Other private	66	645	10,528	8,548	8,821	7,582	6,099	6,122	6,304	6,157
Private nonguaranteed	**115**	**1,097**	**537**	**406**	**391**	**343**	**331**	**321**	**311**	**301**
Bonds	0	0	0	0	0	0	0	0	0	0
Commercial banks	115	1,097	537	406	391	343	331	321	311	301
Memo:										
IBRD	165	517	2,728	2,907	3,284	3,297	3,174	3,188	3,286	3,221
IDA	17	38	31	30	36	59	80	116	181	268
DISBURSEMENTS	**81**	**1,753**	**914**	**1,588**	**927**	**787**	**535**	**544**	**599**	**433**
Public and publicly guaranteed	**56**	**1,187**	**831**	**1,490**	**927**	**787**	**531**	**544**	**599**	**433**
Official creditors	45	122	413	758	642	594	531	544	599	433
Multilateral	14	73	265	606	542	501	531	529	599	433
Concessional	5	0	2	0	10	44	36	53	77	99
Bilateral	31	49	148	152	100	92	0	15	0	0
Concessional	29	49	9	91	100	9	0	15	0	0
Private creditors	11	1,065	418	732	285	193	0	0	0	0
Bonds	0	0	0	0	0	0	0	0	0	0
Commercial banks	3	492	23	27	0	0	0	0	0	0
Other private	8	573	395	705	285	193	0	0	0	0
Private nonguaranteed	**25**	**565**	**83**	**99**	**0**	**0**	**4**	**0**	**0**	**0**
Bonds	0	0	0	0	0	0	0	0	0	0
Commercial banks	25	565	83	99	0	0	4	0	0	0
Memo:										
IBRD	13	63	244	450	384	232	272	264	258	189
IDA	1	0	0	0	7	23	24	38	60	86
PRINCIPAL REPAYMENTS	**68**	**242**	**692**	**607**	**1,180**	**862**	**1,878**	**579**	**746**	**809**
Public and publicly guaranteed	**38**	**65**	**602**	**594**	**1,165**	**815**	**1,866**	**569**	**736**	**799**
Official creditors	16	45	341	298	776	551	333	490	655	606
Multilateral	5	25	207	213	247	291	316	329	431	470
Concessional	5	7	5	8	13	7	9	8	8	10
Bilateral	11	20	133	84	530	260	17	161	225	136
Concessional	4	14	6	0	6	1	0	161	225	136
Private creditors	22	20	262	296	388	264	1,534	79	81	193
Bonds	0	0	0	0	0	0	0	0	0	0
Commercial banks	0	1	160	156	388	54	1,335	0	0	0
Other private	22	19	101	140	0	210	199	79	81	193
Private nonguaranteed	**30**	**177**	**90**	**14**	**15**	**47**	**12**	**10**	**10**	**10**
Bonds	0	0	0	0	0	0	0	0	0	0
Commercial banks	30	177	90	14	15	47	12	10	10	10
Memo:										
IBRD	5	24	194	199	241	275	294	309	384	392
IDA	0	0	1	1	1	1	1	1	1	1
NET FLOWS ON DEBT	**13**	**1,510**	**222**	**981**	**-253**	**-76**	**-1,343**	**-35**	**-148**	**-376**
Public and publicly guaranteed	**18**	**1,122**	**229**	**896**	**-238**	**-28**	**-1,335**	**-25**	**-138**	**-366**
Official creditors	29	77	72	460	-134	42	198	54	-57	-173
Multilateral	10	48	57	393	296	210	215	200	168	-37
Concessional	0	-7	-3	-8	-3	36	27	45	69	89
Bilateral	20	29	15	68	-430	-168	-17	-146	-225	-136
Concessional	25	35	3	91	95	8	0	-146	-225	-136
Private creditors	-11	1,046	157	436	-103	-70	-1,534	-79	-81	-193
Bonds	0	0	0	0	0	0	0	0	0	0
Commercial banks	3	491	-137	-129	-388	-54	-1,335	0	0	0
Other private	-14	555	294	565	285	-17	-199	-79	-81	-193
Private nonguaranteed	**-5**	**388**	**-7**	**85**	**-15**	**-47**	**-8**	**-10**	**-10**	**-10**
Bonds	0	0	0	0	0	0	0	0	0	0
Commercial banks	-5	388	-7	85	-15	-47	-8	-10	-10	-10
Memo:										
IBRD	8	38	50	252	144	-43	-21	-45	-126	-202
IDA	1	0	-1	-1	6	22	23	37	59	85

NIGERIA

(US$ million, unless otherwise indicated)

	1970	1980	1988	1989	1990	1991	1992	1993	1994	1995
INTEREST PAYMENTS (LINT)	**28**	**529**	**1,478**	**1,480**	**2,124**	**2,054**	**1,831**	**862**	**1,075**	**706**
Public and publicly guaranteed	**20**	**438**	**1,452**	**1,470**	**2,120**	**2,041**	**1,828**	**860**	**1,073**	**687**
Official creditors	16	63	717	582	1,301	1,250	827	570	773	460
Multilateral	9	46	240	219	262	355	322	315	337	323
Concessional	9	8	5	5	5	7	5	4	4	5
Bilateral	7	17	477	363	1,038	895	505	256	436	136
Concessional	3	8	0	5	312	33	360	256	436	136
Private creditors	4	375	735	888	820	792	1,001	290	301	228
Bonds	0	0	0	0	0	0	0	113	127	161
Commercial banks	1	352	484	545	378	421	563	0	0	0
Other private	3	24	251	343	442	371	438	177	174	67
Private nonguaranteed	**8**	**91**	**26**	**10**	**3**	**13**	**3**	**2**	**2**	**19**
Bonds	0	0	0	0	0	0	0	0	0	0
Commercial banks	8	91	26	10	3	13	3	2	2	19
Memo:										
IBRD	9	45	235	212	243	312	266	265	265	266
IDA	0	0	0	0	0	0	0	1	1	2
NET TRANSFERS ON DEBT	**-15**	**981**	**-1,257**	**-499**	**-2,376**	**-2,130**	**-3,174**	**-897**	**-1,223**	**-1,083**
Public and publicly guaranteed	**-2**	**684**	**-1,224**	**-574**	**-2,358**	**-2,069**	**-3,164**	**-885**	**-1,211**	**-1,054**
Official creditors	14	14	-645	-122	-1,435	-1,207	-629	-516	-830	-633
Multilateral	1	2	-183	174	33	-144	-108	-115	-169	-361
Concessional	-9	-15	-8	-13	-8	29	23	41	64	84
Bilateral	13	12	-463	-296	-1,468	-1,063	-521	-401	-661	-272
Concessional	22	27	3	87	-217	-25	-360	-401	-661	-272
Private creditors	-15	670	-578	-452	-923	-862	-2,535	-369	-382	-421
Bonds	0	0	0	0	0	0	0	-113	-127	-161
Commercial banks	2	140	-621	-674	-766	-475	-1,897	0	0	0
Other private	-17	531	43	222	-157	-387	-637	-256	-255	-260
Private nonguaranteed	**-13**	**297**	**-33**	**75**	**-18**	**-60**	**-11**	**-12**	**-12**	**-29**
Bonds	0	0	0	0	0	0	0	0	0	0
Commercial banks	-13	297	-33	75	-18	-60	-11	-12	-12	-29
Memo:										
IBRD	-1	-6	-185	39	-100	-354	-287	-310	-390	-468
IDA	1	-1	-1	-1	6	21	23	36	58	83
DEBT SERVICE (LTDS)	**96**	**772**	**2,170**	**2,087**	**3,304**	**2,917**	**3,709**	**1,441**	**1,822**	**1,515**
Public and publicly guaranteed	**58**	**503**	**2,055**	**2,063**	**3,285**	**2,856**	**3,695**	**1,429**	**1,810**	**1,486**
Official creditors	32	108	1,058	880	2,077	1,801	1,160	1,060	1,428	1,065
Multilateral	14	71	447	432	509	645	638	644	767	793
Concessional	13	15	10	13	18	15	14	12	13	15
Bilateral	18	37	611	448	1,568	1,156	521	416	661	272
Concessional	7	22	6	5	317	34	360	416	661	272
Private creditors	26	395	997	1,184	1,208	1,055	2,535	369	382	421
Bonds	0	0	0	0	0	0	0	113	127	161
Commercial banks	1	352	645	701	766	475	1,897	0	0	0
Other private	25	43	352	483	442	581	637	256	255	260
Private nonguaranteed	**38**	**269**	**116**	**23**	**18**	**60**	**15**	**12**	**12**	**29**
Bonds	0	0	0	0	0	0	0	0	0	0
Commercial banks	38	269	116	23	18	60	15	12	12	29
Memo:										
IBRD	14	69	429	411	484	587	559	574	649	657
IDA	0	1	1	1	1	2	2	2	2	3
UNDISBURSED DEBT	**185**	**3,714**	**3,702**	**3,734**	**5,246**	**5,597**	**5,639**	**5,204**	**4,940**	**4,335**
Official creditors	167	1,112	2,487	3,033	3,968	4,474	4,709	4,157	3,786	3,183
Private creditors	18	2,602	1,215	701	1,278	1,124	930	1,047	1,154	1,152
Memorandum items										
Concessional LDOD	280	531	526	524	600	1,043	1,042	1,154	1,347	1,430
Variable rate LDOD	127	4,001	11,101	10,853	11,044	10,681	5,108	5,198	5,511	5,632
Public sector LDOD	450	4,271	27,537	29,251	31,546	32,325	26,473	26,390	28,127	28,638
Private sector LDOD	117	1,097	537	406	391	344	337	352	352	364

6. CURRENCY COMPOSITION OF LONG-TERM DEBT (PERCENT)

	1970	1980	1988	1989	1990	1991	1992	1993	1994	1995
Deutsche mark	9.0	23.5	11.8	12.2	14.8	14.6	13.6	12.8	13.4	14.2
French franc	0.0	0.9	5.5	8.7	9.0	10.4	10.9	10.2	10.6	11.3
Japanese yen	0.8	2.0	8.1	8.1	8.2	9.4	11.3	12.6	13.3	12.7
Pound sterling	30.4	2.7	11.2	10.8	11.8	12.3	10.4	10.2	10.1	9.8
Swiss franc	0.3	0.4	1.3	1.1	0.7	0.7	0.5	0.5	0.5	0.6
U.S.dollars	9.9	55.0	41.3	43.7	38.8	35.5	32.7	32.6	30.4	29.5
Multiple currency	38.5	12.1	16.4	9.9	10.4	10.2	12.0	12.1	11.7	11.3
Special drawing rights	0.0	0.0	0.0	0.0	0.0	0.0	0.0	0.0	0.0	0.0
All other currencies	11.2	3.4	4.5	5.6	6.3	7.0	8.6	9.0	10.0	10.7

NIGERIA

(US$ million, unless otherwise indicated)

	1970	1980	1988	1989	1990	1991	1992	1993	1994	1995
7. DEBT RESTRUCTURINGS										
Total amount rescheduled	0	0	4,852	9,843	1,480	2,615	2,497	0	0	0
Debt stock rescheduled	0	0	1,654	5,697	0	0	2,051	0	0	0
Principal rescheduled	0	0	20	2,879	1,280	1,731	327	0	0	0
Official	0	0	20	684	1,090	589	277	0	0	0
Private	0	0	0	2,194	191	1,142	51	0	0	0
Interest rescheduled	0	0	10	1,206	169	834	60	0	0	0
Official	0	0	10	569	149	568	49	0	0	0
Private	0	0	0	637	21	266	11	0	0	0
Debt forgiven	..	..	0	31	0	14	0	0	0	0
Memo: interest forgiven	..	..	0	1	0	0	0	0	0	0
Debt stock reduction	0	0	40	247	286	113	3,532	30	30	0
of which debt buyback	0	0	0	0	0	0	1,335	0	0	0
8. DEBT STOCK-FLOW RECONCILIATION										
Total change in debt stocks	..	..	..	501	3,318	87	-4,508	1,681	2,819	1,487
Net flows on debt	..	..	..	566	-34	-162	-708	472	-660	-450
Net change in interest arrears	..	..	..	-667	820	-559	716	1,241	1,594	1,037
Interest capitalized	..	..	..	1,206	169	834	60	0	0	0
Debt forgiveness or reduction	..	..	..	-279	-286	-127	-2,197	-30	-30	0
Cross-currency valuation	..	..	..	-421	2,406	-30	-1,227	-192	1,779	716
Residual	..	..	..	95	243	131	-1,151	190	136	184
9. AVERAGE TERMS OF NEW COMMITMENTS										
ALL CREDITORS										
Interest (%)	6.0	10.5	7.6	7.0	6.5	6.1	4.6	3.7	7.7	0.0
Maturity (years)	14.0	10.9	15.8	18.8	19.1	21.7	23.1	24.5	26.5	0.0
Grace period (years)	3.9	3.5	4.5	5.1	5.3	5.9	7.3	6.8	5.5	0.0
Grant element (%)	21.3	-2.2	13.1	20.2	23.6	27.8	40.2	48.4	16.0	0.0
Official creditors										
Interest (%)	5.9	8.2	7.3	6.5	5.8	6.1	4.6	2.8	7.7	0.0
Maturity (years)	15.4	16.1	19.0	21.4	22.5	22.2	23.1	27.6	26.5	0.0
Grace period (years)	4.3	3.9	5.1	5.8	6.2	6.0	7.3	7.7	5.5	0.0
Grant element (%)	23.2	9.2	16.4	24.7	31.1	28.7	40.2	58.1	16.0	0.0
Private creditors										
Interest (%)	6.5	11.4	8.3	8.7	7.9	7.3	0.0	7.3	0.0	0.0
Maturity (years)	6.5	8.9	9.6	9.7	13.1	12.1	0.0	13.5	0.0	0.0
Grace period (years)	1.9	3.4	3.5	2.7	3.7	2.6	0.0	3.8	0.0	0.0
Grant element (%)	11.0	-6.6	6.6	4.2	10.4	12.3	0.0	14.0	0.0	0.0
Memorandum items										
Commitments	65	1,904	1,434	1,828	2,216	1,362	1,101	288	472	0
Official creditors	55	525	949	1,427	1,415	1,292	1,101	225	472	0
Private creditors	10	1,380	485	401	801	70	0	63	0	0

10. CONTRACTUAL OBLIGATIONS ON OUTSTANDING LONG-TERM DEBT

	1996	1997	1998	1999	2000	2001	2002	2003	2004	2005
TOTAL										
Disbursements	581	579	424	297	176	90	45	18	3	1
Principal	3,379	2,783	2,377	2,333	834	756	1,093	1,089	1,051	1,011
Interest	1,289	1,016	853	694	596	555	514	455	394	332
Official creditors										
Disbursements	581	579	424	297	176	90	45	18	3	1
Principal	2,841	2,285	1,926	1,918	574	496	835	834	816	805
Interest	955	770	634	496	416	381	346	294	238	183
Bilateral creditors										
Disbursements	14	8	3	1	0	0	0	0	0	0
Principal	2,314	1,715	1,366	1,375	48	38	424	424	413	413
Interest	596	425	305	193	142	140	134	109	81	53
Multilateral creditors										
Disbursements	567	571	420	296	176	90	45	18	3	1
Principal	527	570	560	542	526	459	410	410	404	392
Interest	359	346	328	303	273	241	212	185	158	130
Private creditors										
Disbursements	0	0	0	0	0	0	0	0	0	0
Principal	538	497	451	415	260	260	258	256	235	206
Interest	334	246	220	198	180	174	168	162	156	149
Commercial banks										
Disbursements	0	0	0	0	0	0	0	0	0	0
Principal	0	0	0	0	0	0	0	0	0	0
Interest	0	0	0	0	0	0	0	0	0	0
Other private										
Disbursements	0	0	0	0	0	0	0	0	0	0
Principal	538	497	451	415	260	260	258	256	235	206
Interest	334	246	220	198	180	174	168	162	156	149

OMAN

(US$ million, unless otherwise indicated)

	1970	1980	1988	1989	1990	1991	1992	1993	1994	1995
1. SUMMARY DEBT DATA										
TOTAL DEBT STOCKS (EDT)	..	**599**	**2,932**	**2,969**	**2,736**	**2,901**	**2,855**	**2,657**	**3,087**	**3,107**
Long-term debt (LDOD)	..	**436**	**2,481**	**2,620**	**2,400**	**2,474**	**2,340**	**2,315**	**2,610**	**2,566**
Public and publicly guaranteed	..	436	2,481	2,620	2,400	2,474	2,340	2,315	2,608	2,563
Private nonguaranteed	0	0	0	0	0	0	0	0	3	3
Use of IMF credit	**0**	**0**	**0**	**0**	**0**	**0**	**0**	**0**	**0**	**0**
Short-term debt	..	**163**	**452**	**348**	**335**	**427**	**515**	**342**	**477**	**541**
of which interest arrears on LDOD	..	0	0	0	1	0	0	0	0	2
Official creditors	..	0	0	0	1	0	0	0	0	2
Private creditors	..	0	0	0	0	0	0	0	0	0
Memo: principal arrears on LDOD	..	0	0	38	3	0	0	0	0	85
Official creditors	..	0	0	0	3	0	0	0	0	29
Private creditors	..	0	0	38	0	0	0	0	0	56
Memo: export credits	..	..	850	435	561	574	590	726	827	941
TOTAL DEBT FLOWS										
Disbursements	..	**98**	**409**	**558**	**125**	**441**	**253**	**366**	**601**	**248**
Long-term debt	..	98	409	558	125	441	253	366	601	248
IMF purchases	0	0	0	0	0	0	0	0	0	0
Principal repayments	..	**179**	**348**	**375**	**536**	**385**	**340**	**425**	**376**	**282**
Long-term debt	..	179	348	375	536	385	340	425	376	282
IMF repurchases	0	0	0	0	0	0	0	0	0	0
Net flows on debt	..	**-81**	**108**	**80**	**-425**	**149**	**0**	**-231**	**360**	**29**
of which short-term debt	..	..	47	-104	-14	93	87	-173	135	62
Interest payments (INT)	..	**70**	**227**	**259**	**203**	**195**	**189**	**181**	**174**	**204**
Long-term debt	..	44	187	225	178	167	153	158	149	184
IMF charges	0	0	0	0	0	0	0	0	0	0
Short-term debt	..	26	40	34	25	27	36	24	25	21
Net transfers on debt	..	**-151**	**-120**	**-179**	**-627**	**-46**	**-189**	**-413**	**186**	**-176**
Total debt service paid (TDS)	..	**249**	**575**	**634**	**739**	**580**	**529**	**606**	**550**	**486**
Long-term debt	..	223	535	600	714	552	493	583	525	466
IMF repurchases and charges	0	0	0	0	0	0	0	0	0	0
Short-term debt (interest only)	..	26	40	34	25	27	36	24	25	21
2. AGGREGATE NET RESOURCE FLOWS AND NET TRANSFERS (LONG-TERM)										
NET RESOURCE FLOWS	..	**174**	**153**	**299**	**-213**	**206**	**-1**	**77**	**452**	**136**
Net flow of long-term debt (ex. IMF)	0	-81	61	184	-411	57	-88	-59	225	-34
Foreign direct investment (net)	0	98	92	112	141	149	87	99	130	150
Portfolio equity flows	..	0	0	0	0	0	0	0	26	5
Grants (excluding technical coop.)	0	157	0	3	57	0	0	36	70	15
Memo: technical coop. grants	0	4	14	15	18	17	22	16	22	17
NET TRANSFERS	..	**-155**	**-388**	**-272**	**-780**	**-368**	**-592**	**-539**	**-163**	**-498**
Interest on long-term debt	..	44	187	225	178	167	153	158	149	184
Profit remittances on FDI	0	286	354	345	390	407	439	458	465	450
3. MAJOR ECONOMIC AGGREGATES										
Gross national product (GNP)	213	5,338	6,549	7,351	9,445	9,088	9,820	9,565	9,360	10,531
Exports of goods & services (XGS)	..	3,887	3,652	4,504	5,990	5,331	5,935	5,839	5,852	6,442
of which workers remittances	..	35	39	39	39	39	39	39	39	39
Imports of goods & services (MGS)	..	2,650	3,202	3,384	3,971	4,663	5,292	5,626	5,283	5,671
International reserves (RES)	13	705	1,173	1,470	1,784	1,765	2,080	1,021	1,090	1,251
Current account balance	..	942	-310	305	1,106	-245	-592	-1,191	-984	-980
4. DEBT INDICATORS										
EDT / XGS (%)	..	15.4	80.3	65.9	45.7	54.4	48.1	45.5	52.8	48.2
EDT / GNP (%)	..	11.2	44.8	40.4	29.0	31.9	29.1	27.8	33.0	29.5
TDS / XGS (%)	..	6.4	15.8	14.1	12.3	10.9	8.9	10.4	9.4	7.5
INT / XGS (%)	..	1.8	6.2	5.8	3.4	3.7	3.2	3.1	3.0	3.2
INT / GNP (%)	..	1.3	3.5	3.5	2.1	2.1	1.9	1.9	1.9	1.9
RES / EDT (%)	..	117.7	40.0	49.5	65.2	60.9	72.8	38.4	35.3	40.3
RES / MGS (months)	..	3.2	4.4	5.2	5.4	4.5	4.7	2.2	2.5	2.6
Short-term / EDT (%)	..	27.2	15.4	11.7	12.3	14.7	18.0	12.9	15.5	17.4
Concessional / EDT (%)	..	43.6	8.2	8.1	8.9	9.7	14.0	18.3	16.9	16.9
Multilateral / EDT (%)	..	5.8	4.6	4.4	4.7	4.9	5.9	6.2	5.2	5.7

OMAN

(US$ million, unless otherwise indicated)

	1970	1980	1988	1989	1990	1991	1992	1993	1994	1995
5. LONG-TERM DEBT										
DEBT OUTSTANDING (LDOD)	..	**436**	**2,481**	**2,620**	**2,400**	**2,474**	**2,340**	**2,315**	**2,610**	**2,566**
Public and publicly guaranteed	..	**436**	**2,481**	**2,620**	**2,400**	**2,474**	**2,340**	**2,315**	**2,608**	**2,563**
Official creditors	..	349	330	332	327	379	500	579	601	591
Multilateral	..	35	134	130	129	143	167	164	162	178
Concessional	..	6	45	44	49	49	71	73	88	117
Bilateral	..	314	195	202	198	235	333	416	439	413
Concessional	..	255	195	196	194	231	330	414	434	408
Private creditors	..	87	2,151	2,289	2,073	2,095	1,840	1,736	2,007	1,972
Bonds	..	0	0	0	0	0	0	0	0	0
Commercial banks	..	0	1,653	1,926	1,721	1,812	1,578	1,312	1,521	1,470
Other private	..	87	498	363	353	283	262	424	486	502
Private nonguaranteed	**0**	**0**	**0**	**0**	**0**	**0**	**0**	**0**	**3**	**3**
Bonds	..	0	0	0	0	0	0	0	0	0
Commercial banks	..	0	0	0	0	0	0	0	3	3
Memo:										
IBRD	0	14	58	54	52	53	52	46	33	25
IDA	0	0	0	0	0	0	0	0	0	0
DISBURSEMENTS	..	**98**	**409**	**558**	**125**	**441**	**253**	**366**	**601**	**248**
Public and publicly guaranteed	..	**98**	**409**	**558**	**125**	**441**	**253**	**366**	**601**	**248**
Official creditors	..	45	29	58	34	97	184	108	58	42
Multilateral	..	13	25	23	22	42	60	21	21	37
Concessional	..	6	14	6	12	9	32	10	20	37
Bilateral	..	32	4	35	13	54	124	88	37	5
Concessional	..	7	4	29	13	53	124	88	32	5
Private creditors	..	52	380	501	91	345	69	258	543	206
Bonds	..	0	0	0	0	0	0	0	0	0
Commercial banks	..	0	317	500	0	300	0	51	431	132
Other private	..	52	63	1	91	45	69	207	112	74
Private nonguaranteed	**0**	**0**	**0**	**0**	**0**	**0**	**0**	**0**	**0**	**0**
Bonds	..	0	0	0	0	0	0	0	0	0
Commercial banks	..	0	0	0	0	0	0	0	0	0
Memo:										
IBRD	0	6	11	12	10	13	15	6	0	0
IDA	0	0	0	0	0	0	0	0	0	0
PRINCIPAL REPAYMENTS	..	**179**	**348**	**375**	**536**	**385**	**340**	**425**	**376**	**282**
Public and publicly guaranteed	..	**179**	**348**	**375**	**536**	**385**	**340**	**425**	**376**	**282**
Official creditors	..	62	56	49	46	54	52	49	71	48
Multilateral	..	3	24	24	30	30	29	26	30	23
Concessional	..	0	7	6	10	10	8	8	9	10
Bilateral	..	60	32	25	16	24	23	23	41	25
Concessional	..	9	32	25	15	22	22	22	40	24
Private creditors	..	117	292	326	491	331	288	376	304	234
Bonds	..	0	0	0	0	0	0	0	0	0
Commercial banks	..	32	85	202	370	220	234	335	242	178
Other private	..	85	207	125	120	111	54	41	62	56
Private nonguaranteed	**0**	**0**	**0**	**0**	**0**	**0**	**0**	**0**	**0**	**0**
Bonds	..	0	0	0	0	0	0	0	0	0
Commercial banks	..	0	0	0	0	0	0	0	0	0
Memo:										
IBRD	0	1	12	13	16	13	14	13	17	9
IDA	0	0	0	0	0	0	0	0	0	0
NET FLOWS ON DEBT	..	**-81**	**61**	**184**	**-411**	**57**	**-88**	**-59**	**225**	**-34**
Public and publicly guaranteed	..	**-81**	**61**	**184**	**-411**	**57**	**-88**	**-59**	**225**	**-34**
Official creditors	..	-17	-27	9	-12	43	131	59	-13	-6
Multilateral	..	11	1	0	-9	12	31	-6	-9	14
Concessional	..	6	7	-1	2	-1	24	2	11	27
Bilateral	..	-27	-28	10	-3	30	101	65	-4	-19
Concessional	..	-1	-28	5	-2	31	102	66	-8	-19
Private creditors	..	-65	88	174	-400	14	-219	-118	238	-28
Bonds	..	0	0	0	0	0	0	0	0	0
Commercial banks	..	-32	232	298	-370	81	-234	-284	189	-46
Other private	..	-33	-144	-124	-30	-67	15	166	50	18
Private nonguaranteed	**0**	**0**	**0**	**0**	**0**	**0**	**0**	**0**	**0**	**0**
Bonds	..	0	0	0	0	0	0	0	0	0
Commercial banks	..	0	0	0	0	0	0	0	0	0
Memo:										
IBRD	0	5	-1	-2	-6	0	1	-8	-16	-9
IDA	0	0	0	0	0	0	0	0	0	0

OMAN

(US$ million, unless otherwise indicated)

	1970	1980	1988	1989	1990	1991	1992	1993	1994	1995
INTEREST PAYMENTS (LINT)	..	**44**	**187**	**225**	**178**	**167**	**153**	**158**	**149**	**184**
Public and publicly guaranteed	..	**44**	**187**	**225**	**178**	**167**	**153**	**158**	**149**	**184**
Official creditors	..	14	17	16	14	16	18	22	24	29
Multilateral	..	2	8	7	6	6	7	6	6	11
Concessional	..	0	0	0	0	0	0	0	0	6
Bilateral	..	12	9	9	8	9	11	16	18	18
Concessional	..	1	9	8	8	9	11	16	18	18
Private creditors	..	30	171	209	164	152	135	136	125	155
Bonds	..	0	0	0	0	0	0	0	0	0
Commercial banks	..	3	114	169	133	122	108	104	91	109
Other private	..	28	56	40	31	30	27	32	34	46
Private nonguaranteed	**0**	**0**	**0**	**0**	**0**	**0**	**0**	**0**	**0**	**0**
Bonds	..	0	0	0	0	0	0	0	0	0
Commercial banks	..	0	0	0	0	0	0	0	0	0
Memo:										
IBRD	0	1	6	5	5	4	4	4	4	2
IDA	0	0	0	0	0	0	0	0	0	0
NET TRANSFERS ON DEBT	..	**-125**	**-126**	**-42**	**-589**	**-111**	**-240**	**-217**	**76**	**-218**
Public and publicly guaranteed	..	**-125**	**-126**	**-42**	**-589**	**-111**	**-240**	**-217**	**76**	**-217**
Official creditors	..	-30	-44	-7	-26	27	114	37	-38	-34
Multilateral	..	9	-7	-8	-15	6	24	-12	-15	3
Concessional	..	6	7	-1	2	-1	24	2	11	21
Bilateral	..	-39	-37	1	-11	21	90	49	-23	-37
Concessional	..	-2	-37	-4	-10	22	91	50	-26	-36
Private creditors	..	-95	-82	-35	-563	-138	-354	-254	114	-183
Bonds	..	0	0	0	0	0	0	0	0	0
Commercial banks	..	-35	118	129	-503	-42	-342	-389	98	-155
Other private	..	-60	-200	-165	-60	-96	-12	135	15	-29
Private nonguaranteed	**0**	**0**	**0**	**0**	**0**	**0**	**0**	**0**	**0**	**0**
Bonds	..	0	0	0	0	0	0	0	0	0
Commercial banks	..	0	0	0	0	0	0	0	0	0
Memo:										
IBRD	0	4	-7	-7	-11	-4	-3	-12	-20	-11
IDA	0	0	0	0	0	0	0	0	0	0
DEBT SERVICE (LTDS)	..	**223**	**535**	**600**	**714**	**552**	**493**	**583**	**525**	**466**
Public and publicly guaranteed	..	**223**	**535**	**600**	**714**	**552**	**493**	**583**	**525**	**465**
Official creditors	..	76	73	64	60	70	70	71	96	76
Multilateral	..	5	32	31	37	36	36	33	36	34
Concessional	..	0	7	6	10	10	8	8	9	16
Bilateral	..	71	41	33	23	33	34	39	60	43
Concessional	..	9	41	33	23	31	33	37	58	41
Private creditors	..	147	462	536	654	483	423	512	429	389
Bonds	..	0	0	0	0	0	0	0	0	0
Commercial banks	..	35	199	371	503	342	342	440	333	287
Other private	..	113	263	165	151	141	81	72	96	102
Private nonguaranteed	**0**	**0**	**0**	**0**	**0**	**0**	**0**	**0**	**0**	**1**
Bonds	..	0	0	0	0	0	0	0	0	0
Commercial banks	..	0	0	0	0	0	0	0	0	1
Memo:										
IBRD	0	2	18	18	20	18	18	17	20	11
IDA	0	0	0	0	0	0	0	0	0	0
UNDISBURSED DEBT	..	**499**	**691**	**792**	**897**	**753**	**568**	**464**	**490**	**475**
Official creditors	..	176	294	446	454	386	232	114	137	328
Private creditors	..	323	398	346	443	367	336	350	353	148
Memorandum items										
Concessional LDOD	..	261	241	240	243	280	401	487	522	525
Variable rate LDOD	..	0	991	1,420	1,386	1,548	1,397	1,160	1,363	1,329
Public sector LDOD	..	436	2,481	2,620	2,400	2,474	2,340	2,315	2,608	2,563
Private sector LDOD	..	0	0	0	0	0	0	0	3	3

6. CURRENCY COMPOSITION OF LONG-TERM DEBT (PERCENT)

	1970	1980	1988	1989	1990	1991	1992	1993	1994	1995
Deutsche mark	..	0.0	0.0	0.0	0.0	0.0	0.0	0.0	0.0	0.0
French franc	..	7.5	0.0	0.0	0.5	0.4	0.3	0.2	0.0	0.0
Japanese yen	..	0.0	6.4	6.0	7.3	9.2	13.2	17.2	16.1	15.6
Pound sterling	..	8.8	6.2	4.3	5.5	6.3	6.6	9.4	10.2	9.9
Swiss franc	..	0.0	0.0	0.0	0.0	0.0	0.0	0.0	0.0	0.0
U.S.dollars	..	16.8	75.0	78.8	75.5	72.9	66.9	60.7	62.1	62.9
Multiple currency	..	3.1	2.3	2.1	2.2	2.1	2.2	2.0	1.2	1.0
Special drawing rights	..	0.0	0.0	0.0	0.0	0.0	0.0	0.0	0.0	0.0
All other currencies	..	63.7	10.0	8.8	9.1	9.1	10.8	10.5	10.3	10.7

OMAN

(US$ million, unless otherwise indicated)

	1970	1980	1988	1989	1990	1991	1992	1993	1994	1995
7. DEBT RESTRUCTURINGS										
Total amount rescheduled	0	0	0	0	0	0	0	0	0	0
Debt stock rescheduled	0	0	0	0	0	0	0	0	0	0
Principal rescheduled	0	0	0	0	0	0	0	0	0	0
Official	0	0	0	0	0	0	0	0	0	0
Private	0	0	0	0	0	0	0	0	0	0
Interest rescheduled	0	0	0	0	0	0	0	0	0	0
Official	0	0	0	0	0	0	0	0	0	0
Private	0	0	0	0	0	0	0	0	0	0
Debt forgiven	..	..	0	0	0	0	0	0	0	0
Memo: interest forgiven	..	..	0	0	0	0	0	0	0	0
Debt stock reduction	0	0	0	0	0	0	0	0	0	0
of which debt buyback	0	0	0	0	0	0	0	0	0	0
8. DEBT STOCK-FLOW RECONCILIATION										
Total change in debt stocks	..	..	..	36	-233	165	-46	-198	430	20
Net flows on debt	..	..	..	80	-425	149	0	-231	360	29
Net change in interest arrears	..	..	..	0	1	-1	0	0	0	2
Interest capitalized	..	..	..	0	0	0	0	0	0	0
Debt forgiveness or reduction	..	..	..	0	0	0	0	0	0	0
Cross-currency valuation	..	..	..	-40	46	12	-42	43	70	-12
Residual	..	..	..	-3	145	5	-3	-10	0	2
9. AVERAGE TERMS OF NEW COMMITMENTS										
ALL CREDITORS										
Interest (%)	..	7.9	7.6	7.9	7.5	5.5	5.0	5.5	4.7	4.5
Maturity (years)	..	9.4	9.8	11.2	13.8	6.9	11.6	11.8	8.8	16.8
Grace period (years)	..	3.2	6.2	4.3	4.0	4.9	2.7	3.8	3.2	3.5
Grant element (%)	..	9.1	13.4	12.1	12.8	18.5	23.4	22.6	21.9	32.4
Official creditors										
Interest (%)	..	10.0	6.1	4.0	1.9	3.9	2.9	0.0	3.3	4.5
Maturity (years)	..	10.5	23.4	18.3	16.7	16.0	16.5	0.0	16.7	16.8
Grace period (years)	..	2.9	6.7	5.1	4.5	4.0	3.9	0.0	3.5	3.5
Grant element (%)	..	2.9	26.9	37.5	45.1	30.8	39.3	0.0	37.0	32.4
Private creditors										
Interest (%)	..	7.5	7.8	9.7	8.0	5.8	6.6	5.5	5.0	0.0
Maturity (years)	..	9.2	8.3	8.0	13.5	5.1	7.9	11.8	7.6	0.0
Grace period (years)	..	3.3	6.1	4.0	4.0	5.1	1.7	3.8	3.2	0.0
Grant element (%)	..	10.3	11.9	0.5	9.9	16.0	11.1	22.6	19.6	0.0
Memorandum items										
Commitments	..	454	297	728	412	362	144	275	622	240
Official creditors	..	76	30	228	34	62	63	0	80	240
Private creditors	..	379	267	500	379	300	81	275	542	0

10. CONTRACTUAL OBLIGATIONS ON OUTSTANDING LONG-TERM DEBT

	1996	1997	1998	1999	2000	2001	2002	2003	2004	2005
TOTAL										
Disbursements	190	133	67	40	22	13	6	4	1	0
Principal	632	361	498	392	164	158	159	151	132	72
Interest	152	121	103	72	55	46	37	28	19	13
Official creditors										
Disbursements	79	98	64	40	22	13	6	4	1	0
Principal	71	76	80	75	68	62	63	58	56	46
Interest	24	26	26	25	23	21	19	17	14	12
Bilateral creditors										
Disbursements	44	52	35	23	13	7	4	3	0	0
Principal	47	42	45	45	37	37	38	38	37	37
Interest	18	17	17	16	15	14	13	11	10	8
Multilateral creditors										
Disbursements	35	47	30	17	9	6	2	1	1	0
Principal	24	33	35	30	30	25	24	19	19	8
Interest	7	9	9	9	8	7	7	6	5	4
Private creditors										
Disbursements	111	34	2	0	0	0	0	0	0	0
Principal	562	286	418	317	96	96	96	93	76	27
Interest	128	95	77	47	32	25	18	12	5	1
Commercial banks										
Disbursements	53	15	0	0	0	0	0	0	0	0
Principal	511	211	343	247	32	32	32	32	32	16
Interest	90	59	46	21	11	9	7	5	3	1
Other private										
Disbursements	58	19	2	0	0	0	0	0	0	0
Principal	50	75	75	69	64	64	64	61	44	11
Interest	38	36	31	26	21	16	12	7	3	0

PAKISTAN

(US$ million, unless otherwise indicated)

	1970	1980	1988	1989	1990	1991	1992	1993	1994	1995
1. SUMMARY DEBT DATA										
TOTAL DEBT STOCKS (EDT)	..	**9,930**	**16,985**	**18,348**	**20,663**	**23,363**	**24,911**	**24,518**	**27,342**	**30,152**
Long-term debt (LDOD)	**3,073**	**8,519**	**14,002**	**14,644**	**16,643**	**18,162**	**19,390**	**21,450**	**23,847**	**25,305**
Public and publicly guaranteed	3,068	8,501	13,909	14,507	16,506	17,737	18,556	20,393	22,669	23,711
Private nonguaranteed	5	18	93	138	138	425	834	1,057	1,178	1,593
Use of IMF credit	**45**	**674**	**554**	**933**	**836**	**1,068**	**1,127**	**1,122**	**1,557**	**1,613**
Short-term debt	..	**737**	**2,429**	**2,771**	**3,185**	**4,134**	**4,394**	**1,946**	**1,938**	**3,235**
of which interest arrears on LDOD	..	0	0	1	1	1	0	0	0	0
Official creditors	..	0	0	1	1	1	0	0	0	0
Private creditors	..	0	0	0	0	0	0	0	0	0
Memo: principal arrears on LDOD	..	0	0	19	15	9	0	0	0	0
Official creditors	..	0	0	18	15	9	0	0	0	0
Private creditors	..	0	0	0	0	0	0	0	0	0
Memo: export credits	..	..	1,850	1,790	2,343	2,419	2,576	2,665	3,330	5,222
TOTAL DEBT FLOWS										
Disbursements	**492**	**1,371**	**1,639**	**2,373**	**1,766**	**2,308**	**2,923**	**3,215**	**4,045**	**3,161**
Long-term debt	492	1,063	1,639	1,778	1,766	1,992	2,923	3,092	3,613	2,959
IMF purchases	0	308	0	595	0	315	0	123	432	202
Principal repayments	**143**	**492**	**1,159**	**1,075**	**1,087**	**1,095**	**1,452**	**1,522**	**2,482**	**1,948**
Long-term debt	115	353	848	860	916	996	1,286	1,394	2,416	1,774
IMF repurchases	28	139	311	216	172	99	166	128	66	174
Net flows on debt	**348**	**879**	**629**	**1,639**	**1,093**	**2,162**	**1,732**	**-754**	**1,555**	**2,510**
of which short-term debt	..	..	149	341	414	949	261	-2,448	-8	1,297
Interest payments (INT)	..	**378**	**674**	**766**	**839**	**866**	**888**	**866**	**999**	**1,197**
Long-term debt	78	248	435	455	521	595	662	750	855	950
IMF charges	0	27	26	54	54	36	36	36	34	44
Short-term debt	..	103	212	258	264	236	190	80	109	203
Net transfers on debt	..	**501**	**-45**	**873**	**254**	**1,296**	**844**	**-1,620**	**556**	**1,313**
Total debt service paid (TDS)	..	**870**	**1,833**	**1,841**	**1,926**	**1,961**	**2,340**	**2,387**	**3,481**	**3,145**
Long-term debt	193	601	1,283	1,314	1,437	1,591	1,948	2,144	3,271	2,724
IMF repurchases and charges	28	166	337	270	226	134	202	163	100	219
Short-term debt (interest only)	..	103	212	258	264	236	190	80	109	203
2. AGGREGATE NET RESOURCE FLOWS AND NET TRANSFERS (LONG-TERM)										
NET RESOURCE FLOWS	**453**	**1,256**	**1,400**	**1,509**	**1,419**	**1,755**	**2,421**	**2,430**	**3,150**	**2,511**
Net flow of long-term debt (ex. IMF)	377	710	791	918	851	996	1,637	1,699	1,197	1,186
Foreign direct investment (net)	23	63	186	210	244	257	335	346	419	409
Portfolio equity flows	0	0	0	0	0	23	139	185	1,335	729
Grants (excluding technical coop.)	53	482	424	381	324	479	310	201	199	188
Memo: technical coop. grants	24	120	269	305	319	317	320	273	181	181
NET TRANSFERS	**369**	**1,002**	**909**	**1,009**	**844**	**1,118**	**1,704**	**1,618**	**2,225**	**1,461**
Interest on long-term debt	78	248	435	455	521	595	662	750	855	950
Profit remittances on FDI	6	6	56	45	53	42	54	62	70	100
3. MAJOR ECONOMIC AGGREGATES										
Gross national product (GNP)	10,028	23,409	40,131	41,635	41,733	46,694	49,389	52,195	52,241	60,932
Exports of goods & services (XGS)	891	4,758	7,345	7,612	8,266	9,380	9,810	9,972	9,849	11,692
of which workers remittances	86	1,748	2,013	1,897	1,942	1,848	1,468	1,562	1,446	1,866
Imports of goods & services (MGS)	1,591	6,042	9,270	9,749	10,425	11,805	12,802	14,425	12,758	14,625
International reserves (RES)	195	1,568	1,193	1,302	1,046	1,220	1,524	1,995	3,716	2,528
Current account balance	-705	-1,137	-1,682	-1,934	-1,891	-2,171	-1,346	-3,688	-1,965	-2,402
4. DEBT INDICATORS										
EDT / XGS (%)	..	208.7	231.2	241.0	250.0	249.1	253.9	245.9	277.6	257.9
EDT / GNP (%)	..	42.4	42.3	44.1	49.5	50.0	50.4	47.0	52.3	49.5
TDS / XGS (%)	..	18.3	25.0	24.2	23.3	20.9	23.8	23.9	35.3	26.9
INT / XGS (%)	..	7.9	9.2	10.1	10.2	9.2	9.0	8.7	10.1	10.2
INT / GNP (%)	..	1.6	1.7	1.8	2.0	1.9	1.8	1.7	1.9	2.0
RES / EDT (%)	..	15.8	7.0	7.1	5.1	5.2	6.1	8.1	13.6	8.4
RES / MGS (months)	1.5	3.1	1.5	1.6	1.2	1.2	1.4	1.7	3.5	2.1
Short-term / EDT (%)	..	7.4	14.3	15.1	15.4	17.7	17.6	7.9	7.1	10.7
Concessional / EDT (%)	..	72.9	65.4	60.5	58.7	54.4	51.2	54.7	55.7	53.9
Multilateral / EDT (%)	..	15.4	27.3	30.0	33.4	34.6	35.1	40.4	41.9	40.5

PAKISTAN

(US$ million, unless otherwise indicated)

	1970	1980	1988	1989	1990	1991	1992	1993	1994	1995
5. LONG-TERM DEBT										
DEBT OUTSTANDING (LDOD)	**3,073**	**8,519**	**14,002**	**14,644**	**16,643**	**18,162**	**19,390**	**21,450**	**23,847**	**25,305**
Public and publicly guaranteed	**3,068**	**8,501**	**13,909**	**14,507**	**16,506**	**17,737**	**18,556**	**20,393**	**22,669**	**23,711**
Official creditors	2,782	7,952	13,091	13,747	15,791	17,108	17,733	19,094	21,509	22,644
Multilateral	614	1,532	4,641	5,502	6,894	8,078	8,749	9,906	11,468	12,204
Concessional	473	1,089	2,995	3,254	3,932	4,455	4,696	5,236	6,298	6,913
Bilateral	2,168	6,420	8,450	8,245	8,897	9,031	8,983	9,189	10,041	10,440
Concessional	1,907	6,153	8,117	7,846	8,207	8,258	8,065	8,177	8,931	9,353
Private creditors	285	550	818	760	714	628	823	1,299	1,160	1,067
Bonds	0	0	0	0	0	0	0	0	150	150
Commercial banks	6	123	482	484	404	323	467	873	424	344
Other private	280	427	336	276	311	306	356	425	587	573
Private nonguaranteed	**5**	**18**	**93**	**138**	**138**	**425**	**834**	**1,057**	**1,178**	**1,593**
Bonds	0	0	0	0	0	0	0	0	45	45
Commercial banks	5	18	93	138	138	425	834	1,057	1,133	1,548
Memo:										
IBRD	330	330	1,108	1,428	1,816	2,181	2,384	2,624	2,934	3,082
IDA	280	821	1,842	1,915	2,106	2,311	2,457	2,683	3,054	3,321
DISBURSEMENTS	**492**	**1,063**	**1,639**	**1,778**	**1,766**	**1,992**	**2,923**	**3,092**	**3,613**	**2,959**
Public and publicly guaranteed	**489**	**1,054**	**1,573**	**1,701**	**1,728**	**1,840**	**2,384**	**2,697**	**3,182**	**2,204**
Official creditors	420	797	1,532	1,578	1,648	1,775	1,955	2,050	2,701	2,118
Multilateral	94	161	772	1,078	984	1,272	1,174	1,337	1,484	1,148
Concessional	33	109	251	331	366	499	427	512	817	634
Bilateral	326	636	761	500	664	504	781	713	1,217	970
Concessional	274	544	609	371	336	263	356	312	841	815
Private creditors	69	257	41	123	80	65	429	647	481	86
Bonds	0	0	0	0	0	0	0	0	150	0
Commercial banks	0	101	20	103	9	29	318	530	134	44
Other private	69	156	21	20	72	35	111	118	197	42
Private nonguaranteed	**3**	**9**	**67**	**77**	**39**	**152**	**540**	**395**	**431**	**755**
Bonds	0	0	0	0	0	0	0	0	45	0
Commercial banks	3	9	67	77	39	152	540	395	386	755
Memo:										
IBRD	66	16	342	410	356	413	387	349	314	271
IDA	24	74	113	105	138	210	226	249	321	254
PRINCIPAL REPAYMENTS	**115**	**353**	**848**	**860**	**916**	**996**	**1,286**	**1,394**	**2,416**	**1,774**
Public and publicly guaranteed	**114**	**346**	**819**	**827**	**877**	**927**	**1,155**	**1,222**	**2,151**	**1,434**
Official creditors	69	254	586	647	735	777	937	1,061	1,515	1,237
Multilateral	22	41	147	175	307	262	298	417	634	555
Concessional	16	16	48	53	58	56	60	66	70	80
Bilateral	47	213	439	473	428	514	639	645	880	683
Concessional	22	177	328	396	368	351	386	362	565	463
Private creditors	46	92	233	180	143	150	218	161	636	197
Bonds	0	0	0	0	0	0	0	0	0	0
Commercial banks	1	10	177	101	89	111	168	120	585	127
Other private	44	82	57	78	53	39	50	41	51	70
Private nonguaranteed	**1**	**7**	**29**	**33**	**39**	**70**	**131**	**171**	**265**	**340**
Bonds	0	0	0	0	0	0	0	0	0	0
Commercial banks	1	7	29	33	39	70	131	171	265	340
Memo:										
IBRD	22	26	66	66	73	102	126	155	180	219
IDA	0	4	14	16	19	21	23	26	30	35
NET FLOWS ON DEBT	**377**	**710**	**791**	**918**	**851**	**996**	**1,637**	**1,699**	**1,197**	**1,186**
Public and publicly guaranteed	**375**	**708**	**753**	**874**	**851**	**914**	**1,228**	**1,475**	**1,031**	**770**
Official creditors	351	544	946	931	913	999	1,017	989	1,187	881
Multilateral	72	120	624	904	677	1,009	876	920	850	594
Concessional	17	93	203	278	308	443	366	446	747	554
Bilateral	279	424	322	27	236	-11	142	68	337	287
Concessional	252	367	281	-26	-32	-88	-30	-50	276	351
Private creditors	24	164	-193	-57	-63	-85	211	486	-155	-111
Bonds	0	0	0	0	0	0	0	0	150	0
Commercial banks	-1	90	-157	2	-81	-81	150	409	-451	-83
Other private	25	74	-36	-58	18	-4	61	77	146	-28
Private nonguaranteed	**2**	**2**	**38**	**44**	**0**	**83**	**409**	**223**	**166**	**416**
Bonds	0	0	0	0	0	0	0	0	45	0
Commercial banks	2	2	38	44	0	83	409	223	121	416
Memo:										
IBRD	44	-10	276	344	283	311	260	194	134	52
IDA	23	70	99	89	119	189	202	223	291	218

PAKISTAN

(US$ million, unless otherwise indicated)

	1970	1980	1988	1989	1990	1991	1992	1993	1994	1995
INTEREST PAYMENTS (LINT)	**78**	**248**	**435**	**455**	**521**	**595**	**662**	**750**	**855**	**950**
Public and publicly guaranteed	**77**	**247**	**428**	**445**	**511**	**576**	**623**	**684**	**764**	**820**
Official creditors	64	203	364	387	456	529	578	641	692	755
Multilateral	21	61	161	190	247	288	330	377	423	445
Concessional	14	20	33	30	34	36	41	45	52	60
Bilateral	43	143	204	197	209	242	248	263	269	309
Concessional	29	128	181	170	178	190	189	192	201	255
Private creditors	14	44	63	58	55	47	46	44	73	65
Bonds	0	0	0	0	0	0	0	0	0	9
Commercial banks	0	9	44	39	38	33	28	25	45	31
Other private	13	34	19	19	17	14	18	19	27	26
Private nonguaranteed	**0**	**2**	**8**	**10**	**11**	**19**	**39**	**66**	**91**	**130**
Bonds	0	0	0	0	0	0	0	0	1	2
Commercial banks	0	2	8	10	11	19	39	66	90	128
Memo:										
IBRD	19	33	86	99	126	152	170	187	203	217
IDA	2	6	17	14	15	16	18	19	21	24
NET TRANSFERS ON DEBT	**299**	**462**	**356**	**464**	**329**	**401**	**975**	**949**	**342**	**235**
Public and publicly guaranteed	**298**	**461**	**326**	**429**	**340**	**337**	**605**	**791**	**267**	**-50**
Official creditors	287	341	582	544	457	469	440	348	495	126
Multilateral	51	60	464	713	430	721	546	543	427	149
Concessional	4	73	170	249	274	407	325	401	696	494
Bilateral	236	281	118	-169	27	-252	-106	-195	68	-22
Concessional	223	238	100	-196	-210	-277	-218	-242	75	96
Private creditors	10	121	-256	-115	-117	-132	165	443	-228	-176
Bonds	0	0	0	0	0	0	0	0	150	-9
Commercial banks	-1	81	-201	-38	-119	-114	122	384	-497	-114
Other private	12	40	-55	-77	2	-18	43	58	119	-54
Private nonguaranteed	**2**	**1**	**30**	**34**	**-11**	**64**	**370**	**158**	**75**	**285**
Bonds	0	0	0	0	0	0	0	0	44	-2
Commercial banks	2	1	30	34	-11	64	370	158	31	287
Memo:										
IBRD	25	-43	190	245	157	160	90	7	-69	-165
IDA	21	64	82	75	104	173	185	204	270	194
DEBT SERVICE (LTDS)	**193**	**601**	**1,283**	**1,314**	**1,437**	**1,591**	**1,948**	**2,144**	**3,271**	**2,724**
Public and publicly guaranteed	**192**	**593**	**1,247**	**1,272**	**1,388**	**1,503**	**1,779**	**1,907**	**2,915**	**2,254**
Official creditors	133	457	950	1,034	1,191	1,306	1,515	1,702	2,207	1,992
Multilateral	43	102	308	365	554	550	628	794	1,057	1,000
Concessional	30	36	81	82	92	92	102	111	121	140
Bilateral	90	355	643	669	636	756	887	908	1,150	992
Concessional	51	305	509	566	546	540	575	554	766	718
Private creditors	59	136	297	238	197	197	264	205	708	262
Bonds	0	0	0	0	0	0	0	0	0	9
Commercial banks	1	19	221	141	127	143	196	145	631	158
Other private	58	116	76	97	70	53	68	59	78	96
Private nonguaranteed	**1**	**8**	**37**	**43**	**49**	**89**	**170**	**237**	**356**	**470**
Bonds	0	0	0	0	0	0	0	0	1	2
Commercial banks	1	8	37	43	49	89	170	237	355	468
Memo:										
IBRD	41	59	151	165	199	254	296	343	383	436
IDA	2	10	31	30	34	37	41	45	51	59
UNDISBURSED DEBT	**1,517**	**2,705**	**7,131**	**7,607**	**9,153**	**8,982**	**9,131**	**9,599**	**9,742**	**8,615**
Official creditors	1,319	2,559	6,967	7,393	8,922	8,655	8,629	9,084	9,341	8,349
Private creditors	198	145	164	215	231	327	502	515	401	265
Memorandum items										
Concessional LDOD	2,381	7,242	11,111	11,101	12,139	12,712	12,761	13,412	15,229	16,267
Variable rate LDOD	5	129	1,298	1,696	2,232	2,881	4,013	5,243	5,427	6,020
Public sector LDOD	2,953	8,431	13,733	14,377	16,374	17,614	18,450	20,304	22,581	23,627
Private sector LDOD	120	88	269	268	269	548	940	1,147	1,266	1,678

6. CURRENCY COMPOSITION OF LONG-TERM DEBT (PERCENT)

	1970	1980	1988	1989	1990	1991	1992	1993	1994	1995
Deutsche mark	9.3	9.1	9.1	9.9	10.2	9.7	8.8	7.3	7.9	8.1
French franc	1.6	3.2	2.0	1.9	1.8	1.7	1.7	1.6	2.5	2.8
Japanese yen	6.0	8.4	15.6	13.9	13.6	14.0	13.9	14.1	15.6	15.2
Pound sterling	16.1	3.7	2.0	1.7	1.5	1.3	1.2	1.0	0.9	0.8
Swiss franc	0.7	0.4	0.3	0.2	0.3	0.2	0.3	0.2	0.3	0.3
U.S.dollars	46.2	53.8	40.7	38.9	35.7	33.5	33.9	35.1	31.1	31.1
Multiple currency	13.5	9.6	17.0	21.3	26.2	29.7	30.9	32.2	34.5	34.8
Special drawing rights	0.0	0.0	3.3	3.2	3.1	3.0	2.9	2.8	2.9	3.0
All other currencies	6.6	11.7	10.1	8.9	7.6	6.9	6.6	5.7	4.3	4.0

PAKISTAN

(US$ million, unless otherwise indicated)

	1970	1980	1988	1989	1990	1991	1992	1993	1994	1995
7. DEBT RESTRUCTURINGS										
Total amount rescheduled	0	0	0	0	0	0	0	0	0	0
Debt stock rescheduled	0	0	0	0	0	0	0	0	0	0
Principal rescheduled	0	0	0	0	0	0	0	0	0	0
Official	0	0	0	0	0	0	0	0	0	0
Private	0	0	0	0	0	0	0	0	0	0
Interest rescheduled	0	0	0	0	0	0	0	0	0	0
Official	0	0	0	0	0	0	0	0	0	0
Private	0	0	0	0	0	0	0	0	0	0
Debt forgiven	..	..	2	0	0	0	0	0	0	0
Memo: interest forgiven	..	..	0	0	0	0	0	0	0	0
Debt stock reduction	0	0	0	0	0	0	0	0	0	0
of which debt buyback	0	0	0	0	0	0	0	0	0	0
8. DEBT STOCK-FLOW RECONCILIATION										
Total change in debt stocks	..	..	..	1,363	2,315	2,700	1,548	-394	2,825	2,810
Net flows on debt	..	..	..	1,639	1,093	2,162	1,732	-754	1,555	2,510
Net change in interest arrears	..	..	..	1	0	0	-1	0	0	0
Interest capitalized	..	..	..	0	0	0	0	0	0	0
Debt forgiveness or reduction	..	..	..	0	0	0	0	0	0	0
Cross-currency valuation	..	..	..	-227	679	189	-344	205	984	238
Residual	..	..	..	-49	544	349	161	156	286	62
9. AVERAGE TERMS OF NEW COMMITMENTS										
ALL CREDITORS										
Interest (%)	2.8	4.4	5.3	5.0	5.3	5.7	4.4	3.6	4.2	4.1
Maturity (years)	31.6	30.1	23.7	23.6	22.5	20.4	18.7	20.2	23.3	21.5
Grace period (years)	11.9	6.6	6.2	6.6	6.1	5.4	6.6	5.7	6.6	6.5
Grant element (%)	59.2	47.9	36.7	39.3	34.9	31.5	36.6	40.9	42.3	39.5
Official creditors										
Interest (%)	2.3	2.5	5.2	4.7	5.2	5.5	4.1	3.0	3.7	4.0
Maturity (years)	35.1	35.4	23.9	24.8	22.9	21.5	21.9	24.4	25.2	22.1
Grace period (years)	13.6	8.2	6.3	6.8	6.2	5.7	7.7	6.9	7.0	6.7
Grant element (%)	66.3	62.2	37.2	42.1	35.7	33.6	42.7	49.9	46.6	40.7
Private creditors										
Interest (%)	5.7	11.3	7.7	9.3	8.8	7.6	5.5	5.6	8.4	5.6
Maturity (years)	11.1	10.8	12.9	7.9	10.6	9.4	6.7	4.3	7.8	9.4
Grace period (years)	1.9	0.8	3.3	3.1	4.8	2.6	2.6	1.2	2.9	2.0
Grant element (%)	17.5	-4.0	10.8	2.7	5.0	8.7	14.0	6.8	5.8	18.4
Memorandum items										
Commitments	949	1,115	2,187	2,434	2,972	1,893	2,861	3,289	3,390	1,604
Official creditors	811	874	2,146	2,262	2,890	1,730	2,254	2,606	3,034	1,523
Private creditors	139	242	41	173	82	163	606	683	357	81

10. CONTRACTUAL OBLIGATIONS ON OUTSTANDING LONG-TERM DEBT

	1996	1997	1998	1999	2000	2001	2002	2003	2004	2005
TOTAL										
Disbursements	2,863	2,238	1,482	942	562	283	160	54	23	9
Principal	2,024	1,834	1,811	1,969	1,719	1,642	1,474	1,447	1,426	1,380
Interest	1,050	990	929	857	770	694	625	561	500	441
Official creditors										
Disbursements	2,723	2,156	1,450	931	561	283	160	54	23	9
Principal	1,398	1,318	1,321	1,383	1,425	1,445	1,416	1,410	1,392	1,353
Interest	846	837	815	776	726	671	611	551	492	436
Bilateral creditors										
Disbursements	1,162	827	481	263	125	57	23	3	2	1
Principal	752	712	693	708	695	677	653	653	635	629
Interest	335	332	321	302	280	259	238	219	199	181
Multilateral creditors										
Disbursements	1,561	1,329	970	668	436	226	137	51	21	8
Principal	646	606	628	675	730	767	763	756	757	725
Interest	511	505	494	474	446	411	373	333	293	255
Private creditors										
Disbursements	140	82	31	11	1	0	0	0	0	0
Principal	627	516	490	586	294	197	58	37	34	27
Interest	203	152	114	81	44	24	14	10	8	5
Commercial banks										
Disbursements	43	27	11	4	0	0	0	0	0	0
Principal	133	65	50	43	44	38	21	7	7	7
Interest	24	17	14	11	8	5	3	2	2	1
Other private										
Disbursements	97	55	20	7	1	0	0	0	0	0
Principal	494	451	440	544	249	159	37	30	28	21
Interest	180	135	99	70	36	19	11	8	6	4

PANAMA

(US$ million, unless otherwise indicated)

	1970	1980	1988	1989	1990	1991	1992	1993	1994	1995
1. SUMMARY DEBT DATA										
TOTAL DEBT STOCKS (EDT)	..	**2,975**	**6,066**	**6,318**	**6,679**	**6,733**	**6,486**	**6,958**	**7,121**	**7,180**
Long-term debt (LDOD)	**194**	**2,271**	**4,005**	**3,935**	**3,988**	**3,918**	**3,771**	**3,799**	**3,923**	**3,905**
Public and publicly guaranteed	194	2,271	4,005	3,935	3,988	3,918	3,771	3,799	3,923	3,905
Private nonguaranteed	0	0	0	0	0	0	0	0	0	0
Use of IMF credit	**0**	**23**	**328**	**320**	**272**	**216**	**110**	**113**	**133**	**111**
Short-term debt	..	**681**	**1,733**	**2,063**	**2,418**	**2,599**	**2,605**	**3,046**	**3,065**	**3,165**
of which interest arrears on LDOD	..	1	333	663	1,018	1,199	1,205	1,595	1,600	1,652
Official creditors	..	0	90	163	266	216	64	167	192	225
Private creditors	..	1	243	500	753	983	1,141	1,427	1,408	1,427
Memo: principal arrears on LDOD	..	0	1,261	1,723	2,116	2,215	1,972	2,163	2,035	2,127
Official creditors	..	0	214	336	554	588	112	175	198	204
Private creditors	..	0	1,047	1,387	1,562	1,627	1,861	1,989	1,838	1,923
Memo: export credits	..	..	137	200	204	193	264	73	461	27
TOTAL DEBT FLOWS										
Disbursements	**67**	**404**	**65**	**33**	**6**	**5**	**268**	**38**	**54**	**113**
Long-term debt	67	404	65	33	6	5	168	25	40	99
IMF purchases	0	0	0	0	0	0	101	14	14	13
Principal repayments	**25**	**232**	**15**	**8**	**121**	**129**	**603**	**146**	**165**	**171**
Long-term debt	24	215	15	8	51	73	402	136	163	132
IMF repurchases	2	17	0	1	71	56	201	10	1	39
Net flows on debt	**42**	**172**	**209**	**24**	**-115**	**-124**	**-334**	**-56**	**-97**	**-11**
of which short-term debt	..	..	160	0	0	0	0	51	14	48
Interest payments (INT)	..	**256**	**13**	**5**	**224**	**207**	**364**	**136**	**220**	**202**
Long-term debt	7	252	13	5	91	108	231	80	140	101
IMF charges	0	3	0	0	16	14	79	7	6	7
Short-term debt	..	2	0	0	117	85	55	50	74	94
Net transfers on debt	..	**-84**	**197**	**19**	**-339**	**-331**	**-698**	**-192**	**-317**	**-212**
Total debt service paid (TDS)	..	**488**	**28**	**13**	**345**	**336**	**966**	**282**	**385**	**373**
Long-term debt	31	466	28	13	141	182	633	215	303	233
IMF repurchases and charges	2	20	0	1	87	69	279	17	8	46
Short-term debt (interest only)	..	2	0	0	117	85	55	50	74	94
2. AGGREGATE NET RESOURCE FLOWS AND NET TRANSFERS (LONG-TERM)										
NET RESOURCE FLOWS	**76**	**149**	**4**	**65**	**213**	**47**	**133**	**100**	**211**	**221**
Net flow of long-term debt (ex. IMF)	44	189	50	25	-45	-69	-234	-111	-124	-33
Foreign direct investment (net)	33	-47	-52	37	132	41	139	156	200	220
Portfolio equity flows	0	0	0	0	0	0	88	0	115	20
Grants (excluding technical coop.)	..	6	6	4	126	75	141	55	20	13
Memo: technical coop. grants	8	9	15	15	-16	38	34	46	37	54
NET TRANSFERS	**50**	**-174**	**-42**	**63**	**80**	**-112**	**-173**	**-12**	**31**	**77**
Interest on long-term debt	7	252	13	5	91	108	231	80	140	101
Profit remittances on FDI	19	72	33	-3	42	51	76	33	40	43
3. MAJOR ECONOMIC AGGREGATES										
Gross national product (GNP)	1,034	3,637	4,563	4,246	4,595	5,562	5,539	6,156	6,627	7,083
Exports of goods & services (XGS)	..	7,931	4,764	5,490	5,941	6,701	7,874	8,309	8,814	9,614
of which workers remittances	..	2	19	14	18	14	13	17	17	19
Imports of goods & services (MGS)	..	8,599	4,517	6,464	6,454	7,687	8,965	9,137	9,536	10,046
International reserves (RES)	16	117	72	119	344	499	504	597	704	782
Current account balance	..	-578	353	-890	-253	-713	-710	-574	-519	-367
4. DEBT INDICATORS										
EDT / XGS (%)	..	37.5	127.3	115.1	112.4	100.5	82.4	83.7	80.8	74.7
EDT / GNP (%)	..	81.8	132.9	148.8	145.3	121.0	117.1	113.0	107.5	101.4
TDS / XGS (%)	..	6.2	0.6	0.2	5.8	5.0	12.3	3.4	4.4	3.9
INT / XGS (%)	..	3.2	0.3	0.1	3.8	3.1	4.6	1.6	2.5	2.1
INT / GNP (%)	..	7.0	0.3	0.1	4.9	3.7	6.6	2.2	3.3	2.8
RES / EDT (%)	..	3.9	1.2	1.9	5.1	7.4	7.8	8.6	9.9	10.9
RES / MGS (months)	..	0.2	0.2	0.2	0.6	0.8	0.7	0.8	0.9	0.9
Short-term / EDT (%)	..	22.9	28.6	32.7	36.2	38.6	40.2	43.8	43.0	44.1
Concessional / EDT (%)	..	9.0	6.5	6.2	5.9	6.2	7.0	6.4	6.2	6.0
Multilateral / EDT (%)	..	11.0	16.8	15.8	15.3	14.2	10.7	9.0	8.2	8.5

PANAMA

(US$ million, unless otherwise indicated)

	1970	1980	1988	1989	1990	1991	1992	1993	1994	1995
5. LONG-TERM DEBT										
DEBT OUTSTANDING (LDOD)	**194**	**2,271**	**4,005**	**3,935**	**3,988**	**3,918**	**3,771**	**3,799**	**3,923**	**3,905**
Public and publicly guaranteed	**194**	**2,271**	**4,005**	**3,935**	**3,988**	**3,918**	**3,771**	**3,799**	**3,923**	**3,905**
Official creditors	93	595	1,534	1,478	1,504	1,537	1,314	1,307	1,257	1,258
Multilateral	38	327	1,017	997	1,021	956	694	625	583	612
Concessional	33	131	201	201	202	186	155	154	152	150
Bilateral	55	268	516	480	483	581	620	682	674	647
Concessional	49	138	192	193	194	229	299	294	292	281
Private creditors	101	1,676	2,472	2,458	2,484	2,382	2,457	2,492	2,666	2,647
Bonds	29	395	257	251	260	175	267	260	3	3
Commercial banks	6	1,161	2,090	2,081	2,102	2,127	2,124	2,160	2,599	2,593
Other private	66	120	125	125	123	80	67	72	65	51
Private nonguaranteed	**0**	**0**	**0**	**0**	**0**	**0**	**0**	**0**	**0**	**0**
Bonds	0	0	0	0	0	0	0	0	0	0
Commercial banks	0	0	0	0	0	0	0	0	0	0
Memo:										
IBRD	7	133	478	465	462	417	288	241	206	175
IDA	0	0	0	0	0	0	0	0	0	0
DISBURSEMENTS	**67**	**404**	**65**	**33**	**6**	**5**	**168**	**25**	**40**	**99**
Public and publicly guaranteed	**67**	**404**	**65**	**33**	**6**	**5**	**168**	**25**	**40**	**99**
Official creditors	15	95	32	7	6	4	165	24	15	95
Multilateral	6	68	8	1	0	0	113	16	15	93
Concessional	6	23	1	0	0	0	3	7	7	7
Bilateral	9	27	24	6	6	4	52	8	0	2
Concessional	8	10	1	1	0	0	51	2	0	0
Private creditors	52	309	33	26	0	0	2	1	25	5
Bonds	0	25	0	0	0	0	0	0	0	0
Commercial banks	0	272	22	24	0	0	2	1	25	5
Other private	52	13	11	2	0	0	0	0	0	0
Private nonguaranteed	**0**	**0**	**0**	**0**	**0**	**0**	**0**	**0**	**0**	**0**
Bonds	0	0	0	0	0	0	0	0	0	0
Commercial banks	0	0	0	0	0	0	0	0	0	0
Memo:										
IBRD	0	20	4	0	0	0	60	0	2	3
IDA	0	0	0	0	0	0	0	0	0	0
PRINCIPAL REPAYMENTS	**24**	**215**	**15**	**8**	**51**	**73**	**402**	**136**	**163**	**132**
Public and publicly guaranteed	**24**	**215**	**15**	**8**	**51**	**73**	**402**	**136**	**163**	**132**
Official creditors	5	18	5	4	45	61	393	122	108	115
Multilateral	2	9	4	0	43	60	363	93	92	84
Concessional	1	4	1	0	0	8	34	8	10	10
Bilateral	3	9	1	4	2	1	30	29	16	31
Concessional	2	2	0	0	0	0	7	13	9	10
Private creditors	19	197	10	3	6	13	9	14	56	17
Bonds	1	9	8	2	2	2	2	1	1	1
Commercial banks	2	165	1	1	1	2	0	2	47	3
Other private	16	23	1	1	3	9	8	10	8	13
Private nonguaranteed	**0**	**0**	**0**	**0**	**0**	**0**	**0**	**0**	**0**	**0**
Bonds	0	0	0	0	0	0	0	0	0	0
Commercial banks	0	0	0	0	0	0	0	0	0	0
Memo:										
IBRD	1	6	3	0	41	49	178	54	54	43
IDA	0	0	0	0	0	0	0	0	0	0
NET FLOWS ON DEBT	**44**	**189**	**50**	**25**	**-45**	**-69**	**-234**	**-111**	**-124**	**-33**
Public and publicly guaranteed	**44**	**189**	**50**	**25**	**-45**	**-69**	**-234**	**-111**	**-124**	**-33**
Official creditors	11	77	27	2	-39	-57	-227	-98	-93	-21
Multilateral	5	59	4	1	-43	-60	-249	-77	-77	9
Concessional	5	20	0	0	0	-8	-31	-1	-2	-4
Bilateral	6	18	23	2	4	3	22	-21	-16	-29
Concessional	6	8	1	1	0	0	44	-11	-9	-10
Private creditors	33	112	23	23	-5	-12	-7	-13	-31	-12
Bonds	-1	16	-8	-2	-2	-2	-2	-1	-1	-1
Commercial banks	-2	107	21	23	-1	-2	2	-2	-23	1
Other private	36	-10	10	1	-3	-9	-8	-10	-8	-13
Private nonguaranteed	**0**	**0**	**0**	**0**	**0**	**0**	**0**	**0**	**0**	**0**
Bonds	0	0	0	0	0	0	0	0	0	0
Commercial banks	0	0	0	0	0	0	0	0	0	0
Memo:										
IBRD	-1	15	1	0	-41	-49	-118	-54	-52	-40
IDA	0	0	0	0	0	0	0	0	0	0

PANAMA

(US$ million, unless otherwise indicated)

	1970	1980	1988	1989	1990	1991	1992	1993	1994	1995
INTEREST PAYMENTS (LINT)	**7**	**252**	**13**	**5**	**91**	**108**	**231**	**80**	**140**	**101**
Public and publicly guaranteed	**7**	**252**	**13**	**5**	**91**	**108**	**231**	**80**	**140**	**101**
Official creditors	3	35	4	1	88	102	220	73	63	59
Multilateral	1	20	4	1	85	99	172	47	44	39
Concessional	1	3	1	0	9	6	5	4	4	4
Bilateral	1	15	0	1	2	3	48	25	19	20
Concessional	1	4	0	0	0	0	15	17	10	11
Private creditors	4	217	9	4	3	6	11	7	77	42
Bonds	1	40	3	1	0	0	0	1	38	1
Commercial banks	0	168	5	2	0	2	8	3	34	36
Other private	3	9	1	1	3	4	3	3	5	5
Private nonguaranteed	**0**	**0**	**0**	**0**	**0**	**0**	**0**	**0**	**0**	**0**
Bonds	0	0	0	0	0	0	0	0	0	0
Commercial banks	0	0	0	0	0	0	0	0	0	0
Memo:										
IBRD	0	12	2	0	27	36	121	21	18	15
IDA	0	0	0	0	0	0	0	0	0	0
NET TRANSFERS ON DEBT	**37**	**-63**	**37**	**20**	**-135**	**-177**	**-465**	**-191**	**-263**	**-134**
Public and publicly guaranteed	**37**	**-63**	**37**	**20**	**-135**	**-177**	**-465**	**-191**	**-263**	**-134**
Official creditors	8	42	22	1	-127	-159	-447	-171	-156	-79
Multilateral	3	39	0	0	-128	-159	-421	-124	-121	-30
Concessional	4	17	-1	0	-9	-14	-36	-5	-6	-8
Bilateral	5	4	22	1	1	0	-26	-46	-35	-49
Concessional	5	4	1	1	0	0	29	-28	-20	-20
Private creditors	29	-105	15	19	-9	-18	-18	-20	-108	-55
Bonds	-2	-24	-11	-2	-2	-2	-2	-2	-38	-1
Commercial banks	-3	-61	16	21	-1	-3	-6	-5	-57	-35
Other private	33	-20	10	0	-6	-13	-11	-14	-13	-18
Private nonguaranteed	**0**	**0**	**0**	**0**	**0**	**0**	**0**	**0**	**0**	**0**
Bonds	0	0	0	0	0	0	0	0	0	0
Commercial banks	0	0	0	0	0	0	0	0	0	0
Memo:										
IBRD	-1	3	-1	0	-68	-85	-239	-75	-70	-55
IDA	0	0	0	0	0	0	0	0	0	0
DEBT SERVICE (LTDS)	**31**	**466**	**28**	**13**	**141**	**182**	**633**	**215**	**303**	**233**
Public and publicly guaranteed	**31**	**466**	**28**	**13**	**141**	**182**	**633**	**215**	**303**	**233**
Official creditors	7	52	9	6	133	163	612	194	171	174
Multilateral	3	29	8	1	128	159	535	140	136	123
Concessional	2	7	1	0	9	14	39	12	14	14
Bilateral	5	23	2	5	4	4	78	54	35	51
Concessional	3	6	0	0	0	0	22	30	20	20
Private creditors	23	414	19	7	9	19	20	21	133	59
Bonds	2	49	11	2	2	2	2	2	38	1
Commercial banks	3	333	6	3	1	4	8	6	81	40
Other private	19	32	1	2	6	13	11	14	13	18
Private nonguaranteed	**0**	**0**	**0**	**0**	**0**	**0**	**0**	**0**	**0**	**0**
Bonds	0	0	0	0	0	0	0	0	0	0
Commercial banks	0	0	0	0	0	0	0	0	0	0
Memo:										
IBRD	1	17	5	0	68	85	299	76	72	58
IDA	0	0	0	0	0	0	0	0	0	0
UNDISBURSED DEBT	**97**	**595**	**304**	**229**	**222**	**161**	**343**	**582**	**573**	**529**
Official creditors	92	522	270	221	214	153	338	557	573	529
Private creditors	5	73	35	8	8	8	6	25	0	0
Memorandum items										
Concessional LDOD	82	269	393	394	396	415	454	448	444	430
Variable rate LDOD	0	1,197	2,309	2,308	2,318	2,415	2,378	2,386	2,671	2,653
Public sector LDOD	194	2,271	4,005	3,935	3,988	3,918	3,771	3,799	3,923	3,905
Private sector LDOD	0	0	0	0	0	0	0	0	0	0

6. CURRENCY COMPOSITION OF LONG-TERM DEBT (PERCENT)

	1970	1980	1988	1989	1990	1991	1992	1993	1994	1995
Deutsche mark	0.0	0.0	0.0	0.0	0.0	0.0	0.0	0.0	0.0	0.0
French franc	0.0	0.0	0.1	0.1	0.1	0.1	0.1	0.1	0.1	0.2
Japanese yen	0.0	9.6	9.7	9.0	9.4	8.1	12.3	10.8	10.3	10.0
Pound sterling	0.0	0.0	0.6	0.6	0.7	0.7	0.6	0.5	0.5	0.4
Swiss franc	0.3	0.0	0.1	0.1	0.1	0.1	0.1	0.1	0.1	0.1
U.S.dollars	94.5	70.8	62.2	64.1	63.1	65.4	67.0	68.6	71.2	71.5
Multiple currency	5.2	11.7	23.7	23.6	23.9	22.8	17.5	15.6	14.1	14.1
Special drawing rights	0.0	0.0	0.5	0.5	0.4	0.4	0.3	0.3	0.2	0.2
All other currencies	0.0	7.8	3.1	2.0	2.1	2.3	2.0	3.9	3.4	3.4

PANAMA

(US$ million, unless otherwise indicated)

	1970	1980	1988	1989	1990	1991	1992	1993	1994	1995
7. DEBT RESTRUCTURINGS										
Total amount rescheduled	0	0	0	0	0	174	28	58	422	0
Debt stock rescheduled	0	0	0	0	0	7	0	0	0	0
Principal rescheduled	0	0	0	0	0	105	4	36	260	0
Official	0	0	0	0	0	63	0	3	0	0
Private	0	0	0	0	0	42	3	34	260	0
Interest rescheduled	0	0	0	0	0	63	24	16	161	0
Official	0	0	0	0	0	45	2	0	0	0
Private	0	0	0	0	0	18	22	16	161	0
Debt forgiven	..	..	1	0	0	0	3	0	0	0
Memo: interest forgiven	..	..	0	0	0	0	0	0	0	0
Debt stock reduction	0	0	0	0	0	0	0	0	0	0
of which debt buyback	0	0	0	0	0	0	0	0	0	0
8. DEBT STOCK-FLOW RECONCILIATION										
Total change in debt stocks	..	..	..	252	361	55	-247	472	163	59
Net flows on debt	..	..	..	24	-115	-124	-334	-56	-97	-11
Net change in interest arrears	..	..	..	330	355	181	6	390	6	52
Interest capitalized	..	..	..	0	0	63	24	16	161	0
Debt forgiveness or reduction	..	..	..	0	0	0	-3	0	0	0
Cross-currency valuation	..	..	..	-75	63	8	-81	6	16	-54
Residual	..	..	..	-28	57	-73	141	118	77	72
9. AVERAGE TERMS OF NEW COMMITMENTS										
ALL CREDITORS										
Interest (%)	6.9	11.3	9.4	6.5	5.0	0.0	6.4	7.7	7.3	6.9
Maturity (years)	15.0	11.4	3.1	15.2	8.3	0.0	20.4	20.6	17.2	20.1
Grace period (years)	4.0	4.5	1.1	5.2	4.8	0.0	5.9	4.6	5.7	4.2
Grant element (%)	17.0	-4.2	0.6	20.2	22.6	0.0	24.3	13.5	16.6	19.0
Official creditors										
Interest (%)	5.9	6.3	0.0	6.5	5.0	0.0	6.4	7.9	7.3	6.9
Maturity (years)	24.4	15.4	0.0	15.2	8.3	0.0	20.4	20.9	17.2	21.2
Grace period (years)	6.1	5.3	0.0	5.2	4.8	0.0	5.9	4.7	5.7	4.5
Grant element (%)	28.0	21.2	0.0	20.2	22.6	0.0	24.3	12.3	16.6	20.0
Private creditors										
Interest (%)	7.9	15.2	9.4	0.0	0.0	0.0	0.0	5.0	0.0	7.4
Maturity (years)	4.3	8.3	3.1	0.0	0.0	0.0	0.0	16.2	0.0	6.7
Grace period (years)	1.6	4.0	1.1	0.0	0.0	0.0	0.0	4.2	0.0	0.3
Grant element (%)	4.5	-24.0	0.6	0.0	0.0	0.0	0.0	29.2	0.0	6.9
Memorandum items										
Commitments	111	534	20	6	4	0	351	274	60	61
Official creditors	59	233	0	6	4	0	351	254	60	57
Private creditors	52	300	20	0	0	0	0	20	0	5

10. CONTRACTUAL OBLIGATIONS ON OUTSTANDING LONG-TERM DEBT

	1996	1997	1998	1999	2000	2001	2002	2003	2004	2005
TOTAL										
Disbursements	194	120	85	58	34	16	11	6	4	3
Principal	268	298	223	223	214	208	129	86	81	80
Interest	114	105	95	84	73	61	49	43	38	33
Official creditors										
Disbursements	194	120	85	58	34	16	11	6	4	3
Principal	108	141	145	144	135	129	83	80	76	74
Interest	70	72	69	64	58	51	44	40	35	31
Bilateral creditors										
Disbursements	28	18	10	5	1	1	0	0	0	0
Principal	29	62	62	66	59	53	16	15	13	12
Interest	22	20	17	14	10	7	5	5	4	4
Multilateral creditors										
Disbursements	166	102	74	53	32	15	11	6	4	3
Principal	78	79	83	78	77	76	67	65	63	62
Interest	48	51	52	50	48	44	39	35	31	27
Private creditors										
Disbursements	0	0	0	0	0	0	0	0	0	0
Principal	161	157	78	79	79	79	46	6	5	5
Interest	44	33	26	21	15	10	5	3	3	2
Commercial banks										
Disbursements	0	0	0	0	0	0	0	0	0	0
Principal	152	150	72	73	73	73	40	5	4	4
Interest	41	30	23	18	13	9	4	2	2	2
Other private										
Disbursements	0	0	0	0	0	0	0	0	0	0
Principal	9	6	6	6	6	6	6	1	1	1
Interest	4	3	3	2	2	1	1	1	1	0

PAPUA NEW GUINEA

(US$ million, unless otherwise indicated)

	1970	*1980*	*1988*	*1989*	*1990*	*1991*	*1992*	*1993*	*1994*	*1995*
1. SUMMARY DEBT DATA										
TOTAL DEBT STOCKS (EDT)	**..**	**719**	**2,250**	**2,306**	**2,576**	**2,742**	**3,748**	**3,232**	**2,696**	**2,431**
Long-term debt (LDOD)	**209**	**624**	**2,109**	**2,138**	**2,443**	**2,563**	**3,277**	**2,924**	**2,582**	**2,303**
Public and publicly guaranteed	36	486	1,253	1,314	1,505	1,599	1,551	1,579	1,636	1,614
Private nonguaranteed	173	139	856	824	938	964	1,726	1,344	946	689
Use of IMF credit	**0**	**31**	**6**	**3**	**61**	**61**	**59**	**44**	**16**	**50**
Short-term debt	**..**	**64**	**135**	**165**	**72**	**117**	**412**	**264**	**99**	**78**
of which interest arrears on LDOD	..	0	0	0	0	0	0	0	0	0
Official creditors	..	0	0	0	0	0	0	0	0	0
Private creditors	..	0	0	0	0	0	0	0	0	0
Memo: principal arrears on LDOD	..	0	0	0	0	0	0	0	0	0
Official creditors	..	0	0	0	0	0	0	0	0	0
Private creditors	..	0	0	0	0	0	0	0	0	0
Memo: export credits	..	..	297	214	223	375	610	556	554	352
TOTAL DEBT FLOWS										
Disbursements	**154**	**150**	**400**	**551**	**678**	**441**	**1,081**	**248**	**426**	**307**
Long-term debt	154	135	400	551	620	441	1,081	248	426	256
IMF purchases	0	15	0	0	58	0	0	0	0	51
Principal repayments	**20**	**78**	**321**	**346**	**391**	**358**	**479**	**681**	**731**	**513**
Long-term debt	20	72	316	343	388	358	479	666	701	497
IMF repurchases	0	7	5	3	3	0	0	15	31	16
Net flows on debt	**134**	**72**	**109**	**235**	**193**	**128**	**897**	**-581**	**-470**	**-227**
of which short-term debt	..	..	30	30	-93	46	295	-148	-165	-21
Interest payments (INT)	**..**	**72**	**177**	**170**	**162**	**145**	**181**	**166**	**154**	**113**
Long-term debt	10	52	165	158	156	133	160	140	142	107
IMF charges	0	1	0	0	0	6	4	3	2	1
Short-term debt	..	19	13	12	6	7	16	22	11	5
Net transfers on debt	**..**	**0**	**-69**	**65**	**32**	**-17**	**716**	**-747**	**-624**	**-341**
Total debt service paid (TDS)	**..**	**150**	**498**	**516**	**553**	**504**	**660**	**847**	**886**	**626**
Long-term debt	30	123	480	501	544	491	640	806	842	604
IMF repurchases and charges	0	7	5	3	3	6	4	18	32	17
Short-term debt (interest only)	..	19	13	12	6	7	16	22	11	5
2. AGGREGATE NET RESOURCE FLOWS AND NET TRANSFERS (LONG-TERM)										
NET RESOURCE FLOWS	**278**	**418**	**545**	**680**	**690**	**555**	**1,203**	**-203**	**-46**	**931**
Net flow of long-term debt (ex. IMF)	134	64	84	208	231	83	602	-418	-274	-240
Foreign direct investment (net)	0	76	154	203	155	203	294	-2	-5	453
Portfolio equity flows	0	0	0	0	0	0	0	0	0	450
Grants (excluding technical coop.)	144	279	307	268	304	269	307	217	234	268
Memo: technical coop. grants	1	13	41	44	46	57	61	69	75	91
NET TRANSFERS	**268**	**163**	**136**	**313**	**534**	**422**	**932**	**-458**	**-317**	**688**
Interest on long-term debt	10	52	165	158	156	133	160	140	142	107
Profit remittances on FDI	0	204	244	210	0	0	110	115	130	136
3. MAJOR ECONOMIC AGGREGATES										
Gross national product (GNP)	626	2,488	3,517	3,308	3,098	3,664	3,905	4,743	5,101	4,559
Exports of goods & services (XGS)	..	1,089	1,716	1,573	1,488	1,856	2,337	2,945	2,909	3,014
of which workers remittances	..	0	0	0	0	0	0	0	0	0
Imports of goods & services (MGS)	..	1,561	2,146	2,015	1,719	2,267	2,434	2,342	2,356	2,415
International reserves (RES)	..	458	419	410	427	345	260	166	120	267
Current account balance	..	-289	-296	-313	-76	-157	95	646	569	674
4. DEBT INDICATORS										
EDT / XGS (%)	..	66.0	131.1	146.5	173.2	147.7	160.4	109.7	92.7	80.6
EDT / GNP (%)	..	28.9	64.0	69.7	83.1	74.8	96.0	68.1	52.9	53.3
TDS / XGS (%)	..	13.8	29.0	32.8	37.2	27.1	28.2	28.7	30.4	20.8
INT / XGS (%)	..	6.6	10.3	10.8	10.9	7.8	7.7	5.6	5.3	3.8
INT / GNP (%)	..	2.9	5.0	5.1	5.2	4.0	4.6	3.5	3.0	2.5
RES / EDT (%)	..	63.7	18.6	17.8	16.6	12.6	6.9	5.1	4.5	11.0
RES / MGS (months)	..	3.5	2.3	2.4	3.0	1.8	1.3	0.9	0.6	1.3
Short-term / EDT (%)	..	8.9	6.0	7.1	2.8	4.3	11.0	8.2	3.7	3.2
Concessional / EDT (%)	..	12.2	19.7	19.9	23.9	25.7	18.8	24.2	31.7	37.1
Multilateral / EDT (%)	..	21.2	22.8	23.7	29.3	31.7	22.3	26.1	33.8	38.3

PAPUA NEW GUINEA

(US$ million, unless otherwise indicated)

	1970	1980	1988	1989	1990	1991	1992	1993	1994	1995
5. LONG-TERM DEBT										
DEBT OUTSTANDING (LDOD)	**209**	**624**	**2,109**	**2,138**	**2,443**	**2,563**	**3,277**	**2,924**	**2,582**	**2,303**
Public and publicly guaranteed	**36**	**486**	**1,253**	**1,314**	**1,505**	**1,599**	**1,551**	**1,579**	**1,636**	**1,614**
Official creditors	4	184	720	792	1,056	1,213	1,206	1,282	1,378	1,460
Multilateral	2	152	512	547	755	869	835	844	912	930
Concessional	1	81	288	304	422	478	455	457	499	507
Bilateral	2	32	208	245	300	344	370	437	466	530
Concessional	0	7	154	154	193	228	250	327	355	396
Private creditors	32	302	533	522	449	386	346	298	259	154
Bonds	0	85	75	35	37	36	32	31	30	0
Commercial banks	32	211	427	461	366	298	259	205	180	120
Other private	0	6	32	26	46	52	54	61	48	34
Private nonguaranteed	**173**	**139**	**856**	**824**	**938**	**964**	**1,726**	**1,344**	**946**	**689**
Bonds	0	0	0	0	0	0	0	0	0	0
Commercial banks	173	139	856	824	938	964	1,726	1,344	946	689
Memo:										
IBRD	1	55	162	172	235	275	264	266	281	299
IDA	1	55	114	113	115	114	111	109	109	108
DISBURSEMENTS	**154**	**135**	**400**	**551**	**620**	**441**	**1,081**	**248**	**426**	**256**
Public and publicly guaranteed	**43**	**120**	**183**	**266**	**276**	**213**	**109**	**132**	**170**	**185**
Official creditors	5	41	87	134	231	183	89	112	78	173
Multilateral	2	36	70	70	180	137	40	52	65	55
Concessional	1	23	20	18	101	65	18	29	41	19
Bilateral	4	4	17	64	51	46	49	59	13	117
Concessional	0	4	12	16	28	24	26	58	3	66
Private creditors	37	80	97	132	45	31	19	21	92	12
Bonds	0	0	37	0	0	0	0	0	0	0
Commercial banks	37	75	60	130	20	13	6	0	92	12
Other private	0	5	0	2	25	18	14	21	0	0
Private nonguaranteed	**111**	**15**	**217**	**285**	**343**	**228**	**973**	**116**	**256**	**72**
Bonds	0	0	0	0	0	0	0	0	0	0
Commercial banks	111	15	217	285	343	228	973	116	256	72
Memo:										
IBRD	1	2	36	41	64	49	18	21	21	34
IDA	1	13	0	0	0	0	0	0	0	0
PRINCIPAL REPAYMENTS	**20**	**72**	**316**	**343**	**388**	**358**	**479**	**666**	**701**	**497**
Public and publicly guaranteed	**0**	**32**	**226**	**160**	**184**	**155**	**119**	**169**	**242**	**208**
Official creditors	0	6	50	38	48	53	63	84	93	88
Multilateral	0	3	44	33	35	38	47	64	67	47
Concessional	0	1	30	3	17	20	23	35	36	12
Bilateral	0	3	6	6	13	16	17	20	27	41
Concessional	0	1	0	0	2	2	2	4	11	12
Private creditors	0	25	176	122	136	102	56	85	148	120
Bonds	0	8	77	33	0	4	4	5	5	32
Commercial banks	0	17	92	82	129	87	41	66	129	74
Other private	0	1	7	7	7	12	11	15	14	14
Private nonguaranteed	**20**	**40**	**90**	**183**	**204**	**203**	**360**	**497**	**459**	**289**
Bonds	0	0	0	0	0	0	0	0	0	0
Commercial banks	20	40	90	183	204	203	360	497	459	289
Memo:										
IBRD	0	2	12	27	14	15	20	23	24	27
IDA	0	0	1	1	1	1	2	2	2	2
NET FLOWS ON DEBT	**134**	**64**	**84**	**208**	**231**	**83**	**602**	**-418**	**-274**	**-240**
Public and publicly guaranteed	**43**	**89**	**-43**	**106**	**92**	**58**	**-11**	**-37**	**-72**	**-23**
Official creditors	5	34	37	96	183	129	26	28	-15	84
Multilateral	2	33	26	38	145	99	-6	-12	-1	8
Concessional	1	22	-10	15	84	45	-5	-6	6	7
Bilateral	4	1	11	58	38	30	32	40	-13	76
Concessional	0	4	12	16	26	23	24	54	-8	54
Private creditors	37	55	-79	10	-91	-72	-36	-65	-57	-108
Bonds	0	-8	-41	-33	0	-4	-4	-5	-5	-32
Commercial banks	37	58	-32	48	-109	-74	-36	-66	-38	-62
Other private	0	4	-7	-5	18	6	3	6	-14	-14
Private nonguaranteed	**91**	**-25**	**127**	**102**	**139**	**25**	**612**	**-381**	**-203**	**-217**
Bonds	0	0	0	0	0	0	0	0	0	0
Commercial banks	91	-25	127	102	139	25	612	-381	-203	-217
Memo:										
IBRD	1	0	24	14	50	34	-2	-3	-4	7
IDA	1	13	0	-1	-1	-1	-2	-2	-2	-2

PAPUA NEW GUINEA

(US$ million, unless otherwise indicated)

	1970	1980	1988	1989	1990	1991	1992	1993	1994	1995
INTEREST PAYMENTS (LINT)	**10**	**52**	**165**	**158**	**156**	**133**	**160**	**140**	**142**	**107**
Public and publicly guaranteed	**1**	**30**	**85**	**72**	**86**	**78**	**77**	**81**	**77**	**79**
Official creditors	0	7	37	32	40	46	52	57	56	61
Multilateral	0	6	20	22	27	32	37	38	38	43
Concessional	0	1	3	3	5	6	7	7	7	8
Bilateral	0	2	17	10	13	14	15	19	18	18
Concessional	0	0	12	5	5	5	8	9	11	12
Private creditors	1	23	48	40	46	32	25	24	21	17
Bonds	0	7	9	4	3	3	3	3	3	2
Commercial banks	1	15	37	34	41	26	19	17	14	11
Other private	0	0	2	3	2	3	4	5	4	4
Private nonguaranteed	**8**	**22**	**79**	**86**	**70**	**55**	**84**	**59**	**65**	**29**
Bonds	0	0	0	0	0	0	0	0	0	0
Commercial banks	8	22	79	86	70	55	84	59	65	29
Memo:										
IBRD	0	4	12	13	15	18	20	20	20	22
IDA	0	0	1	1	1	1	1	1	1	1
NET TRANSFERS ON DEBT	**124**	**12**	**-80**	**50**	**75**	**-50**	**441**	**-558**	**-416**	**-348**
Public and publicly guaranteed	**41**	**59**	**-128**	**34**	**6**	**-20**	**-88**	**-118**	**-148**	**-102**
Official creditors	5	27	0	64	143	83	-26	-29	-70	23
Multilateral	2	28	6	16	118	67	-43	-50	-39	-35
Concessional	1	21	-13	12	78	39	-12	-13	-1	0
Bilateral	4	-1	-6	48	25	16	17	21	-31	58
Concessional	0	4	0	11	21	17	16	45	-19	42
Private creditors	36	32	-128	-30	-137	-103	-62	-89	-78	-125
Bonds	0	-15	-49	-36	-3	-7	-7	-7	-8	-35
Commercial banks	36	43	-69	15	-150	-99	-55	-83	-52	-72
Other private	0	4	-9	-8	16	3	-1	1	-18	-18
Private nonguaranteed	**83**	**-47**	**47**	**16**	**69**	**-30**	**529**	**-440**	**-268**	**-246**
Bonds	0	0	0	0	0	0	0	0	0	0
Commercial banks	83	-47	47	16	69	-30	529	-440	-268	-246
Memo:										
IBRD	1	-4	12	1	35	17	-22	-23	-24	-15
IDA	1	12	-1	-2	-2	-2	-2	-3	-3	-3
DEBT SERVICE (LTDS)	**30**	**123**	**480**	**501**	**544**	**491**	**640**	**806**	**842**	**604**
Public and publicly guaranteed	**1**	**61**	**311**	**231**	**270**	**233**	**196**	**250**	**318**	**286**
Official creditors	0	14	87	70	88	99	115	141	149	150
Multilateral	0	9	64	54	62	70	83	102	104	90
Concessional	0	2	33	6	22	26	30	42	43	19
Bilateral	0	5	23	16	26	30	32	39	45	59
Concessional	0	1	12	5	7	7	9	13	22	24
Private creditors	1	48	224	162	182	134	81	110	169	137
Bonds	0	15	86	36	3	7	7	7	8	35
Commercial banks	1	32	129	115	170	112	60	83	143	84
Other private	0	1	9	10	9	15	14	20	18	18
Private nonguaranteed	**29**	**62**	**169**	**269**	**274**	**258**	**444**	**556**	**524**	**318**
Bonds	0	0	0	0	0	0	0	0	0	0
Commercial banks	29	62	169	269	274	258	444	556	524	318
Memo:										
IBRD	0	6	24	40	28	33	40	44	45	49
IDA	0	0	2	2	2	2	2	3	3	3
UNDISBURSED DEBT	**41**	**181**	**568**	**535**	**510**	**560**	**605**	**661**	**629**	**548**
Official creditors	41	151	521	481	476	514	579	598	557	487
Private creditors	0	30	46	54	34	46	27	63	73	61
Memorandum items										
Concessional LDOD	1	88	442	458	615	706	705	784	854	902
Variable rate LDOD	173	271	1,252	1,194	1,339	1,343	2,075	1,661	1,337	1,050
Public sector LDOD	36	463	1,228	1,293	1,483	1,579	1,538	1,570	1,629	1,614
Private sector LDOD	173	162	881	845	960	984	1,739	1,354	952	690
6. CURRENCY COMPOSITION OF LONG-TERM DEBT (PERCENT)										
Deutsche mark	0.0	5.2	1.9	1.9	1.8	1.7	1.7	1.6	1.6	1.7
French franc	0.0	0.0	0.3	0.3	0.2	0.2	0.2	0.1	0.1	0.1
Japanese yen	0.0	4.4	18.7	20.3	20.5	23.0	26.2	30.4	26.1	24.7
Pound sterling	0.0	2.7	2.1	1.7	2.2	1.8	1.3	1.0	0.8	0.6
Swiss franc	0.0	5.8	7.3	4.2	1.5	1.5	1.4	0.0	0.0	0.0
U.S.dollars	2.8	35.0	28.6	31.9	27.1	22.8	21.4	19.1	21.4	19.1
Multiple currency	2.2	27.4	30.9	30.2	37.8	41.7	42.4	43.3	46.5	47.2
Special drawing rights	0.0	0.0	0.1	0.1	0.3	0.4	0.4	0.4	0.5	0.5
All other currencies	95.1	19.6	10.0	9.4	8.5	6.8	5.1	4.1	3.1	6.1

PAPUA NEW GUINEA

(US$ million, unless otherwise indicated)

	1970	1980	1988	1989	1990	1991	1992	1993	1994	1995
7. DEBT RESTRUCTURINGS										
Total amount rescheduled	0	0	0	0	0	0	0	0	0	0
Debt stock rescheduled	0	0	0	0	0	0	0	0	0	0
Principal rescheduled	0	0	0	0	0	0	0	0	0	0
Official	0	0	0	0	0	0	0	0	0	0
Private	0	0	0	0	0	0	0	0	0	0
Interest rescheduled	0	0	0	0	0	0	0	0	0	0
Official	0	0	0	0	0	0	0	0	0	0
Private	0	0	0	0	0	0	0	0	0	0
Debt forgiven	..	..	90	0	0	0	0	0	0	0
Memo: interest forgiven	..	..	0	0	0	0	0	0	0	0
Debt stock reduction	0	0	0	0	0	0	0	0	0	0
of which debt buyback	0	0	0	0	0	0	0	0	0	0
8. DEBT STOCK-FLOW RECONCILIATION										
Total change in debt stocks	..	..	..	56	270	166	1,007	-517	-535	-266
Net flows on debt	..	..	..	235	193	128	897	-581	-470	-227
Net change in interest arrears	..	..	..	0	0	0	0	0	0	0
Interest capitalized	..	..	..	0	0	0	0	0	0	0
Debt forgiveness or reduction	..	..	..	0	0	0	0	0	0	0
Cross-currency valuation	..	..	..	-80	105	50	-48	129	137	-14
Residual	..	..	..	-99	-28	-12	158	-64	-203	-24
9. AVERAGE TERMS OF NEW COMMITMENTS										
ALL CREDITORS										
Interest (%)	6.4	11.2	5.6	6.3	6.1	4.4	2.9	4.8	6.2	6.3
Maturity (years)	21.7	17.7	15.6	14.4	16.0	24.7	28.8	19.6	6.9	12.8
Grace period (years)	8.1	4.8	4.7	4.6	4.7	7.6	9.0	4.6	1.3	4.2
Grant element (%)	25.4	1.1	25.8	23.9	22.0	43.1	57.4	31.3	10.2	21.3
Official creditors										
Interest (%)	5.4	5.8	3.9	4.2	5.7	3.7	2.9	5.8	6.2	6.3
Maturity (years)	20.9	29.1	22.7	24.3	16.9	27.9	28.8	23.6	18.1	12.8
Grace period (years)	5.2	6.9	6.7	6.6	4.9	8.9	9.0	6.0	4.4	4.2
Grant element (%)	30.5	34.9	43.5	43.4	24.4	50.3	57.4	31.3	23.0	21.3
Private creditors										
Interest (%)	7.7	15.5	7.6	8.2	9.1	7.9	0.0	3.1	6.2	0.0
Maturity (years)	22.9	8.8	7.1	5.6	8.4	8.8	0.0	12.3	4.9	0.0
Grace period (years)	12.3	3.1	2.3	2.9	2.5	0.6	0.0	1.9	0.7	0.0
Grant element (%)	18.0	-25.1	4.9	6.6	2.7	7.0	0.0	31.2	7.8	0.0
Memorandum items										
Commitments	91	184	288	265	232	257	170	163	120	116
Official creditors	53	80	156	124	207	215	170	106	19	116
Private creditors	37	103	132	140	25	42	0	57	102	0

10. CONTRACTUAL OBLIGATIONS ON OUTSTANDING LONG-TERM DEBT

	1996	1997	1998	1999	2000	2001	2002	2003	2004	2005
TOTAL										
Disbursements	188	130	87	64	30	17	7	2	1	0
Principal	399	327	261	144	131	136	123	116	134	102
Interest	105	97	80	67	60	53	46	39	35	30
Official creditors										
Disbursements	152	113	80	62	30	17	7	2	1	0
Principal	113	103	127	94	90	99	95	94	92	84
Interest	58	62	59	53	50	46	41	37	33	29
Bilateral creditors										
Disbursements	74	47	34	26	8	8	1	1	1	0
Principal	60	48	68	31	26	36	34	38	38	38
Interest	18	22	20	16	16	15	13	12	11	10
Multilateral creditors										
Disbursements	79	66	47	37	21	9	6	2	0	0
Principal	54	56	59	63	64	64	60	56	54	46
Interest	40	41	39	37	34	31	28	24	21	19
Private creditors										
Disbursements	36	17	7	1	0	0	0	0	0	0
Principal	285	223	134	50	42	36	28	22	43	18
Interest	47	35	20	14	10	7	4	2	2	1
Commercial banks										
Disbursements	32	15	7	1	0	0	0	0	0	0
Principal	48	45	13	13	13	10	7	7	7	2
Interest	9	7	4	4	3	2	2	1	1	1
Other private										
Disbursements	5	2	0	0	0	0	0	0	0	0
Principal	238	179	122	37	29	27	21	15	36	17
Interest	38	29	16	10	8	5	3	1	1	1

PARAGUAY

(US$ million, unless otherwise indicated)

1. SUMMARY DEBT DATA

	1970	1980	1988	1989	1990	1991	1992	1993	1994	1995
TOTAL DEBT STOCKS (EDT)	..	**955**	**2,352**	**2,383**	**2,106**	**2,067**	**1,634**	**1,597**	**1,985**	**2,288**
Long-term debt (LDOD)	**112**	**780**	**2,121**	**2,123**	**1,733**	**1,706**	**1,386**	**1,308**	**1,377**	**1,504**
Public and publicly guaranteed	112	630	2,093	2,095	1,714	1,685	1,365	1,283	1,359	1,488
Private nonguaranteed	0	151	28	27	19	20	21	26	18	17
Use of IMF credit	**0**	**0**	**0**	**0**	**0**	**0**	**0**	**0**	**0**	**0**
Short-term debt	..	**174**	**230**	**261**	**373**	**361**	**248**	**289**	**608**	**783**
of which interest arrears on LDOD	..	0	92	78	115	120	30	28	28	7
Official creditors	..	0	9	18	31	41	14	17	18	4
Private creditors	..	0	83	60	84	79	17	11	10	4
Memo: principal arrears on LDOD	..	2	134	226	321	333	101	95	76	68
Official creditors	..	0	15	42	66	96	26	33	19	17
Private creditors	..	1	119	185	255	236	74	62	58	51
Memo: export credits	..	..	386	518	501	617	307	213	211	203
TOTAL DEBT FLOWS										
Disbursements	**14**	**206**	**142**	**202**	**77**	**135**	**128**	**99**	**148**	**264**
Long-term debt	14	206	142	202	77	135	128	99	148	264
IMF purchases	0	0	0	0	0	0	0	0	0	0
Principal repayments	**7**	**79**	**183**	**77**	**235**	**151**	**380**	**197**	**160**	**155**
Long-term debt	7	79	183	77	235	151	380	197	160	155
IMF repurchases	0	0	0	0	0	0	0	0	0	0
Net flows on debt	**7**	**127**	**-104**	**170**	**-83**	**-33**	**-275**	**-56**	**308**	**305**
of which short-term debt	..	..	-63	45	75	-17	-23	43	319	196
Interest payments (INT)	..	**66**	**133**	**74**	**90**	**107**	**246**	**88**	**96**	**129**
Long-term debt	4	45	113	65	77	92	232	80	74	87
IMF charges	0	0	0	0	0	0	0	0	0	0
Short-term debt	..	22	20	10	13	15	15	9	22	42
Net transfers on debt	..	**61**	**-238**	**95**	**-173**	**-139**	**-521**	**-144**	**212**	**176**
Total debt service paid (TDS)	..	**145**	**316**	**152**	**325**	**258**	**626**	**286**	**256**	**284**
Long-term debt	11	124	296	142	312	243	612	277	234	242
IMF repurchases and charges	0	0	0	0	0	0	0	0	0	0
Short-term debt (interest only)	..	22	20	10	13	15	15	9	22	42

2. AGGREGATE NET RESOURCE FLOWS AND NET TRANSFERS (LONG-TERM)

	1970	1980	1988	1989	1990	1991	1992	1993	1994	1995
NET RESOURCE FLOWS	**12**	**168**	**-18**	**151**	**-75**	**88**	**-72**	**34**	**187**	**343**
Net flow of long-term debt (ex. IMF)	7	127	-41	125	-158	-16	-252	-98	-12	109
Foreign direct investment (net)	4	32	8	13	76	84	137	111	180	200
Portfolio equity flows	0	0	0	0	0	0	0	0	0	0
Grants (excluding technical coop.)	1	10	15	14	7	19	43	21	19	34
Memo: technical coop. grants	7	21	37	35	40	47	65	68	64	73
NET TRANSFERS	**4**	**70**	**-131**	**87**	**-174**	**-26**	**-325**	**-71**	**83**	**221**
Interest on long-term debt	4	45	113	65	77	92	232	80	74	87
Profit remittances on FDI	5	54	0	0	22	22	22	25	30	35

3. MAJOR ECONOMIC AGGREGATES

	1970	1980	1988	1989	1990	1991	1992	1993	1994	1995
Gross national product (GNP)	585	4,621	3,941	4,451	5,381	6,335	6,461	6,899	7,867	7,784
Exports of goods & services (XGS)	90	781	1,490	1,662	1,682	1,808	1,750	2,658	3,316	4,256
of which workers remittances	0	0	0	0	0	0	0	0	0	0
Imports of goods & services (MGS)	111	1,399	1,610	1,435	2,233	2,556	2,800	3,583	4,420	5,771
International reserves (RES)	18	783	338	447	675	975	573	645	1,030	1,040
Current account balance	-19	-618	-84	251	-496	-675	-978	-825	-1,073	-1,473

4. DEBT INDICATORS

	1970	1980	1988	1989	1990	1991	1992	1993	1994	1995
EDT / XGS (%)	..	122.2	157.8	143.4	125.2	114.3	93.4	60.1	59.9	53.8
EDT / GNP (%)	..	20.7	59.7	53.5	39.1	32.6	25.3	23.2	25.2	29.4
TDS / XGS (%)	..	18.6	21.2	9.1	19.3	14.2	35.8	10.7	7.7	6.7
INT / XGS (%)	..	8.5	8.9	4.5	5.4	5.9	14.1	3.3	2.9	3.0
INT / GNP (%)	..	1.4	3.4	1.7	1.7	1.7	3.8	1.3	1.2	1.7
RES / EDT (%)	..	82.0	14.4	18.7	32.1	47.1	35.1	40.4	51.9	45.5
RES / MGS (months)	1.9	6.7	2.5	3.7	3.6	4.6	2.5	2.2	2.8	2.2
Short-term / EDT (%)	..	18.2	9.8	10.9	17.7	17.5	15.2	18.1	30.6	34.2
Concessional / EDT (%)	..	31.9	24.0	23.3	27.5	32.3	41.7	44.3	38.5	38.5
Multilateral / EDT (%)	..	20.2	33.1	30.8	34.9	35.0	42.5	43.1	35.9	34.0

PARAGUAY

(US$ million, unless otherwise indicated)

	1970	1980	1988	1989	1990	1991	1992	1993	1994	1995
5. LONG-TERM DEBT										
DEBT OUTSTANDING (LDOD)	**112**	**780**	**2,121**	**2,123**	**1,733**	**1,706**	**1,386**	**1,308**	**1,377**	**1,504**
Public and publicly guaranteed	**112**	**630**	**2,093**	**2,095**	**1,714**	**1,685**	**1,365**	**1,283**	**1,359**	**1,488**
Official creditors	83	409	1,256	1,611	1,203	1,271	1,154	1,137	1,237	1,384
Multilateral	45	193	778	734	734	722	695	688	712	778
Concessional	42	109	233	234	236	249	270	287	291	328
Bilateral	38	216	478	877	469	548	460	449	525	606
Concessional	29	195	332	321	343	419	412	420	474	554
Private creditors	30	221	837	485	511	415	211	146	122	103
Bonds	0	0	0	0	0	0	0	0	0	0
Commercial banks	2	105	629	270	263	202	87	55	46	37
Other private	28	116	209	215	248	213	124	91	77	66
Private nonguaranteed	**0**	**151**	**28**	**27**	**19**	**20**	**21**	**26**	**18**	**17**
Bonds	0	0	0	0	0	0	0	0	0	0
Commercial banks	0	151	28	27	19	20	21	26	18	17
Memo:										
IBRD	6	80	315	282	279	252	213	185	162	154
IDA	18	45	43	42	41	40	39	38	37	36
DISBURSEMENTS	**14**	**206**	**142**	**202**	**77**	**135**	**128**	**99**	**148**	**264**
Public and publicly guaranteed	**14**	**158**	**142**	**202**	**77**	**130**	**123**	**87**	**148**	**264**
Official creditors	7	55	90	160	49	116	95	75	142	264
Multilateral	4	40	49	34	30	44	55	57	73	129
Concessional	4	8	18	9	7	20	29	26	13	49
Bilateral	4	15	40	126	19	72	40	18	70	135
Concessional	3	11	38	120	18	72	29	11	47	131
Private creditors	7	103	52	42	27	14	28	12	6	0
Bonds	0	0	0	0	0	0	0	0	0	0
Commercial banks	2	33	37	1	2	0	2	3	3	0
Other private	5	69	15	41	25	14	27	9	2	0
Private nonguaranteed	**0**	**48**	**0**	**0**	**0**	**6**	**5**	**12**	**0**	**1**
Bonds	0	0	0	0	0	0	0	0	0	0
Commercial banks	0	48	0	0	0	6	5	12	0	1
Memo:										
IBRD	2	30	18	16	16	9	10	8	7	26
IDA	2	3	0	0	0	0	0	0	0	0
PRINCIPAL REPAYMENTS	**7**	**79**	**183**	**77**	**235**	**151**	**380**	**197**	**160**	**155**
Public and publicly guaranteed	**7**	**44**	**183**	**76**	**226**	**144**	**376**	**191**	**152**	**154**
Official creditors	3	17	97	69	199	77	184	124	112	128
Multilateral	1	4	56	60	62	67	68	72	76	77
Concessional	1	2	7	7	6	8	8	9	11	11
Bilateral	3	13	41	9	137	10	116	52	37	51
Concessional	1	9	15	9	21	10	31	26	33	44
Private creditors	4	27	86	7	27	67	192	67	40	26
Bonds	0	0	0	0	0	0	0	0	0	0
Commercial banks	0	17	44	1	10	31	90	32	15	10
Other private	3	10	42	6	18	36	102	36	25	16
Private nonguaranteed	**0**	**36**	**1**	**1**	**9**	**7**	**4**	**6**	**8**	**1**
Bonds	0	0	0	0	0	0	0	0	0	0
Commercial banks	0	36	1	1	9	7	4	6	8	1
Memo:										
IBRD	0	2	43	38	40	40	42	42	43	41
IDA	0	0	1	1	1	1	1	1	1	1
NET FLOWS ON DEBT	**7**	**127**	**-41**	**125**	**-158**	**-16**	**-252**	**-98**	**-12**	**109**
Public and publicly guaranteed	**7**	**114**	**-41**	**126**	**-149**	**-15**	**-252**	**-104**	**-4**	**110**
Official creditors	4	38	-7	90	-149	38	-89	-49	30	136
Multilateral	3	36	-7	-26	-31	-23	-13	-15	-3	52
Concessional	3	6	12	2	1	13	21	17	3	37
Bilateral	1	2	-1	117	-118	62	-76	-34	33	83
Concessional	2	2	23	111	-3	62	-2	-15	14	88
Private creditors	3	76	-34	35	0	-53	-164	-55	-34	-26
Bonds	0	0	0	0	0	0	0	0	0	0
Commercial banks	2	16	-6	0	-7	-31	-89	-28	-11	-10
Other private	2	60	-27	35	8	-22	-75	-27	-23	-16
Private nonguaranteed	**0**	**13**	**-1**	**-1**	**-9**	**-1**	**1**	**6**	**-7**	**-1**
Bonds	0	0	0	0	0	0	0	0	0	0
Commercial banks	0	13	-1	-1	-9	-1	1	6	-7	-1
Memo:										
IBRD	1	29	-25	-22	-24	-31	-32	-34	-36	-16
IDA	2	3	-1	-1	-1	-1	-1	-1	-1	-1

PARAGUAY

(US$ million, unless otherwise indicated)

	1970	1980	1988	1989	1990	1991	1992	1993	1994	1995
INTEREST PAYMENTS (LINT)	**4**	**45**	**113**	**65**	**77**	**92**	**232**	**80**	**74**	**87**
Public and publicly guaranteed	**4**	**35**	**113**	**65**	**77**	**92**	**231**	**79**	**74**	**87**
Official creditors	3	17	69	55	57	54	113	58	62	72
Multilateral	1	10	51	46	47	45	42	41	42	41
Concessional	1	2	4	5	4	5	5	5	6	7
Bilateral	1	7	18	9	11	9	71	17	21	30
Concessional	1	5	8	7	10	9	20	16	19	22
Private creditors	1	18	44	10	20	38	118	21	12	16
Bonds	0	0	0	0	0	0	0	0	0	0
Commercial banks	0	12	19	3	2	16	66	9	3	2
Other private	1	7	25	7	18	21	53	12	9	14
Private nonguaranteed	**0**	**9**	**0**	**0**	**0**	**0**	**0**	**1**	**0**	**0**
Bonds	0	0	0	0	0	0	0	0	0	0
Commercial banks	0	9	0	0	0	0	0	1	0	0
Memo:										
IBRD	0	6	30	26	25	23	21	19	16	15
IDA	0	0	0	0	0	0	0	0	0	0
NET TRANSFERS ON DEBT	**4**	**82**	**-154**	**60**	**-236**	**-108**	**-483**	**-178**	**-86**	**22**
Public and publicly guaranteed	**4**	**79**	**-154**	**61**	**-226**	**-107**	**-484**	**-183**	**-78**	**23**
Official creditors	1	22	-76	35	-207	-16	-202	-107	-32	64
Multilateral	2	26	-57	-72	-78	-68	-55	-56	-45	11
Concessional	2	4	8	-3	-4	8	16	12	-4	31
Bilateral	0	-5	-19	107	-128	52	-147	-51	12	53
Concessional	2	-4	15	104	-13	52	-23	-31	-5	65
Private creditors	3	57	-78	26	-20	-91	-282	-76	-46	-41
Bonds	0	0	0	0	0	0	0	0	0	0
Commercial banks	2	4	-26	-3	-10	-48	-154	-37	-14	-11
Other private	1	53	-52	28	-10	-43	-128	-39	-32	-30
Private nonguaranteed	**0**	**4**	**-1**	**-1**	**-9**	**-1**	**0**	**5**	**-7**	**-1**
Bonds	0	0	0	0	0	0	0	0	0	0
Commercial banks	0	4	-1	-1	-9	-1	0	5	-7	-1
Memo:										
IBRD	1	23	-55	-47	-49	-55	-52	-53	-52	-30
IDA	2	2	-1	-1	-1	-1	-1	-1	-1	-2
DEBT SERVICE (LTDS)	**11**	**124**	**296**	**142**	**312**	**243**	**612**	**277**	**234**	**242**
Public and publicly guaranteed	**11**	**79**	**296**	**141**	**303**	**236**	**607**	**270**	**226**	**241**
Official creditors	6	34	166	125	256	131	297	182	175	200
Multilateral	2	14	107	106	109	112	110	113	117	118
Concessional	2	4	11	12	10	13	13	15	17	18
Bilateral	4	20	59	18	147	20	187	69	58	82
Concessional	2	15	23	16	30	20	51	42	52	66
Private creditors	5	45	130	16	47	105	310	88	52	41
Bonds	0	0	0	0	0	0	0	0	0	0
Commercial banks	0	29	63	4	12	48	156	40	17	11
Other private	4	16	67	13	35	57	155	48	34	30
Private nonguaranteed	**0**	**45**	**1**	**1**	**9**	**7**	**4**	**7**	**8**	**1**
Bonds	0	0	0	0	0	0	0	0	0	0
Commercial banks	0	45	1	1	9	7	4	7	8	1
Memo:										
IBRD	1	7	73	63	65	64	62	61	59	56
IDA	0	1	1	1	1	1	1	1	1	2
UNDISBURSED DEBT	**47**	**567**	**672**	**500**	**561**	**373**	**724**	**814**	**1,028**	**1,114**
Official creditors	41	423	518	378	454	332	709	808	1,028	1,113
Private creditors	5	145	155	121	107	40	15	6	1	1
Memorandum items										
Concessional LDOD	71	304	565	555	579	668	681	707	765	882
Variable rate LDOD	0	213	310	744	287	208	142	124	123	172
Public sector LDOD	110	628	2,093	2,095	1,714	1,685	1,365	1,283	1,359	1,488
Private sector LDOD	2	152	28	27	19	20	21	26	18	17

6. CURRENCY COMPOSITION OF LONG-TERM DEBT (PERCENT)

	1970	1980	1988	1989	1990	1991	1992	1993	1994	1995
Deutsche mark	11.4	9.4	6.0	7.8	11.4	10.3	10.8	10.0	10.1	9.3
French franc	0.0	0.3	6.9	7.6	10.5	10.6	6.4	4.5	3.6	2.7
Japanese yen	0.0	5.0	7.8	11.9	15.6	17.4	19.2	20.9	23.9	25.6
Pound sterling	0.3	0.6	1.6	1.4	2.0	1.8	0.5	0.4	0.3	0.3
Swiss franc	0.0	0.1	0.2	0.2	0.3	0.1	0.1	0.1	0.1	0.1
U.S.dollars	66.4	56.2	40.3	36.1	17.3	17.4	18.2	19.9	22.2	27.3
Multiple currency	19.7	22.9	33.2	31.0	37.8	37.1	42.6	43.1	38.8	33.8
Special drawing rights	0.0	0.0	0.8	0.7	0.8	0.7	0.8	0.8	0.8	0.7
All other currencies	2.2	10.9	3.3	3.4	4.2	4.5	1.4	0.2	0.2	0.2

PARAGUAY

(US$ million, unless otherwise indicated)

	1970	1980	1988	1989	1990	1991	1992	1993	1994	1995
7. DEBT RESTRUCTURINGS										
Total amount rescheduled	0	0	0	436	0	0	0	0	0	0
Debt stock rescheduled	0	0	0	406	0	0	0	0	0	0
Principal rescheduled	0	0	0	0	0	0	0	0	0	0
Official	0	0	0	0	0	0	0	0	0	0
Private	0	0	0	0	0	0	0	0	0	0
Interest rescheduled	0	0	0	30	0	0	0	0	0	0
Official	0	0	0	1	0	0	0	0	0	0
Private	0	0	0	29	0	0	0	0	0	0
Debt forgiven	..	..	0	108	16	38	28	2	0	0
Memo: interest forgiven	..	..	0	0	0	0	0	0	0	0
Debt stock reduction	0	0	0	0	436	0	2	0	0	0
of which debt buyback	0	0	0	0	111	0	0	0	0	0
8. DEBT STOCK-FLOW RECONCILIATION										
Total change in debt stocks	..	..	..	32	-278	-39	-433	-37	388	303
Net flows on debt	..	..	..	170	-83	-33	-275	-56	308	305
Net change in interest arrears	..	..	..	-15	38	5	-90	-2	0	-21
Interest capitalized	..	..	..	30	0	0	0	0	0	0
Debt forgiveness or reduction	..	..	..	-108	-340	-38	-30	-2	0	0
Cross-currency valuation	..	..	..	-35	688	11	-37	12	62	-4
Residual	..	..	..	-10	-579	16	-1	11	18	23
9. AVERAGE TERMS OF NEW COMMITMENTS										
ALL CREDITORS										
Interest (%)	5.7	7.0	5.7	5.2	3.5	0.0	7.3	4.9	5.1	5.5
Maturity (years)	24.9	24.2	21.5	16.9	34.4	0.0	21.9	27.1	21.6	19.3
Grace period (years)	5.5	6.6	5.5	2.2	10.1	0.0	5.6	6.9	7.1	5.6
Grant element (%)	33.1	25.2	31.1	29.7	53.9	0.0	18.6	38.3	34.7	28.7
Official creditors										
Interest (%)	4.9	5.4	3.0	4.0	3.5	0.0	7.3	4.8	5.1	5.5
Maturity (years)	28.5	27.9	35.0	20.0	34.4	0.0	22.1	27.5	21.6	19.3
Grace period (years)	6.3	7.2	8.6	2.5	10.1	0.0	5.7	7.0	7.1	5.6
Grant element (%)	39.0	36.9	58.5	36.3	53.9	0.0	18.8	38.9	34.7	28.7
Private creditors										
Interest (%)	10.1	13.0	7.8	11.0	0.0	0.0	9.8	8.3	0.0	0.0
Maturity (years)	5.3	10.5	10.8	2.2	0.0	0.0	3.7	8.1	0.0	0.0
Grace period (years)	1.4	4.6	3.1	0.7	0.0	0.0	0.7	3.3	0.0	0.0
Grant element (%)	-0.2	-18.2	9.5	-1.7	0.0	0.0	0.4	6.3	0.0	0.0
Memorandum items										
Commitments	14	99	217	60	117	0	483	174	338	352
Official creditors	12	78	96	50	117	0	478	171	338	352
Private creditors	2	21	121	10	0	0	5	3	0	0

10. CONTRACTUAL OBLIGATIONS ON OUTSTANDING LONG-TERM DEBT

	1996	1997	1998	1999	2000	2001	2002	2003	2004	2005
TOTAL										
Disbursements	268	278	205	150	92	50	31	17	13	9
Principal	158	143	152	151	150	149	139	134	133	128
Interest	83	89	92	92	88	83	76	70	63	57
Official creditors										
Disbursements	268	278	205	150	92	50	31	17	13	9
Principal	127	130	138	145	147	145	139	134	133	128
Interest	78	86	90	91	88	83	76	70	63	57
Bilateral creditors										
Disbursements	89	84	52	32	17	9	4	0	0	0
Principal	52	50	50	46	54	56	51	47	50	49
Interest	26	27	26	25	23	21	19	17	15	13
Multilateral creditors										
Disbursements	178	194	154	118	75	41	27	16	13	9
Principal	75	79	88	99	92	90	88	86	83	79
Interest	52	59	64	66	65	62	57	53	48	43
Private creditors										
Disbursements	1	0	0	0	0	0	0	0	0	0
Principal	31	14	14	6	3	4	0	0	0	0
Interest	4	2	1	1	0	0	0	0	0	0
Commercial banks										
Disbursements	0	0	0	0	0	0	0	0	0	0
Principal	7	1	1	1	1	0	0	0	0	0
Interest	1	0	0	0	0	0	0	0	0	0
Other private										
Disbursements	1	0	0	0	0	0	0	0	0	0
Principal	24	13	12	5	2	3	0	0	0	0
Interest	4	2	1	0	0	0	0	0	0	0

PERU

(US$ million, unless otherwise indicated)

	1970	1980	1988	1989	1990	1991	1992	1993	1994	1995
1. SUMMARY DEBT DATA										
TOTAL DEBT STOCKS (EDT)	..	**9,386**	**18,240**	**18,577**	**20,064**	**20,713**	**20,335**	**23,571**	**26,526**	**30,831**
Long-term debt (LDOD)	**2,655**	**6,828**	**12,718**	**12,995**	**13,959**	**15,657**	**15,805**	**16,947**	**18,852**	**20,199**
Public and publicly guaranteed	856	6,218	12,332	12,611	13,629	15,439	15,577	16,383	17,679	18,929
Private nonguaranteed	1,799	610	386	384	330	218	228	564	1,173	1,270
Use of IMF credit	**10**	**474**	**801**	**758**	**755**	**706**	**631**	**883**	**938**	**955**
Short-term debt	..	**2,084**	**4,721**	**4,824**	**5,350**	**4,350**	**3,899**	**5,742**	**6,736**	**9,677**
of which interest arrears on LDOD	..	0	2,972	3,273	3,733	2,431	1,793	4,090	4,450	4,602
Official creditors	..	0	1,036	1,150	1,386	594	481	252	210	207
Private creditors	..	0	1,936	2,124	2,347	1,837	1,313	3,838	4,239	4,395
Memo: principal arrears on LDOD	..	0	6,021	6,948	8,345	5,641	4,739	4,088	4,148	4,147
Official creditors	..	0	2,251	2,552	3,215	1,754	1,675	1,023	1,017	999
Private creditors	..	0	3,770	4,396	5,130	3,887	3,064	3,065	3,131	3,147
Memo: export credits	..	..	4,683	4,700	4,632	6,782	6,266	6,471	6,863	7,424
TOTAL DEBT FLOWS										
Disbursements	**405**	**1,452**	**295**	**338**	**291**	**533**	**699**	**2,723**	**1,223**	**862**
Long-term debt	387	1,308	295	338	291	533	699	1,826	1,223	862
IMF purchases	18	145	0	0	0	0	0	897	0	0
Principal repayments	**360**	**1,187**	**129**	**168**	**229**	**627**	**539**	**1,620**	**600**	**519**
Long-term debt	333	1,019	129	145	166	579	490	980	600	519
IMF repurchases	27	168	0	24	63	48	49	641	0	0
Net flows on debt	**45**	**265**	**560**	**-29**	**128**	**208**	**347**	**649**	**1,257**	**3,132**
of which short-term debt	..	..	393	-198	66	302	187	-454	634	2,789
Interest payments (INT)	..	**964**	**219**	**238**	**246**	**524**	**464**	**1,138**	**542**	**663**
Long-term debt	162	670	119	151	91	370	313	778	392	479
IMF charges	0	35	1	14	74	23	51	266	47	0
Short-term debt	..	259	99	73	82	132	101	94	102	184
Net transfers on debt	..	**-699**	**341**	**-267**	**-118**	**-316**	**-117**	**-489**	**715**	**2,469**
Total debt service paid (TDS)	..	**2,151**	**347**	**406**	**475**	**1,152**	**1,003**	**2,758**	**1,142**	**1,182**
Long-term debt	495	1,689	248	296	257	949	803	1,758	993	998
IMF repurchases and charges	27	202	1	38	137	71	100	906	47	0
Short-term debt (interest only)	..	259	99	73	82	132	101	94	102	184
2. AGGREGATE NET RESOURCE FLOWS AND NET TRANSFERS (LONG-TERM)										
NET RESOURCE FLOWS	**2**	**347**	**312**	**373**	**346**	**199**	**583**	**2,978**	**4,685**	**4,119**
Net flow of long-term debt (ex. IMF)	54	289	167	193	126	-46	209	846	623	343
Foreign direct investment (net)	-70	27	26	59	41	-7	136	670	2,860	1,895
Portfolio equity flows	0	0	0	0	0	0	0	1,226	977	1,611
Grants (excluding technical coop.)	18	31	119	121	180	251	238	236	226	271
Memo: technical coop. grants	13	64	126	111	128	126	116	134	180	189
NET TRANSFERS	**-233**	**-580**	**154**	**203**	**245**	**-205**	**214**	**2,139**	**4,213**	**3,541**
Interest on long-term debt	162	670	119	151	91	370	313	778	392	479
Profit remittances on FDI	73	256	39	18	10	34	56	61	80	99
3. MAJOR ECONOMIC AGGREGATES										
Gross national product (GNP)	7,118	19,700	15,846	24,588	31,822	28,826	40,790	39,250	49,038	56,938
Exports of goods & services (XGS)	..	4,832	3,686	4,564	4,479	4,686	4,978	4,911	6,416	7,717
of which workers remittances	..	0	0	0	122	186	244	276	366	334
Imports of goods & services (MGS)	..	5,080	5,505	4,980	5,739	6,279	7,087	7,274	9,195	12,097
International reserves (RES)	339	2,804	1,213	1,597	1,891	3,090	3,456	3,918	7,420	8,653
Current account balance	..	-101	-1,657	-240	-1,066	-1,368	-1,922	-2,170	-2,544	-4,223
4. DEBT INDICATORS										
EDT / XGS (%)	..	194.2	494.9	407.0	447.9	442.0	408.5	480.0	413.4	399.5
EDT / GNP (%)	..	47.6	115.1	75.6	63.1	71.9	49.9	60.1	54.1	54.1
TDS / XGS (%)	..	44.5	9.4	8.9	10.6	24.6	20.2	56.2	17.8	15.3
INT / XGS (%)	..	19.9	5.9	5.2	5.5	11.2	9.3	23.2	8.4	8.6
INT / GNP (%)	..	4.9	1.4	1.0	0.8	1.8	1.1	2.9	1.1	1.2
RES / EDT (%)	..	29.9	6.7	8.6	9.4	14.9	17.0	16.6	28.0	28.1
RES / MGS (months)	..	6.6	2.6	3.8	4.0	5.9	5.9	6.5	9.7	8.6
Short-term / EDT (%)	..	22.2	25.9	26.0	26.7	21.0	19.2	24.4	25.4	31.4
Concessional / EDT (%)	..	15.1	9.1	9.2	9.6	15.9	17.9	16.8	16.4	14.9
Multilateral / EDT (%)	..	5.5	11.2	10.9	11.0	9.1	10.2	11.6	12.0	12.1

PERU

(US$ million, unless otherwise indicated)

	1970	1980	1988	1989	1990	1991	1992	1993	1994	1995
5. LONG-TERM DEBT										
DEBT OUTSTANDING (LDOD)	**2,655**	**6,828**	**12,718**	**12,995**	**13,959**	**15,657**	**15,805**	**16,947**	**18,852**	**20,199**
Public and publicly guaranteed	**856**	**6,218**	**12,332**	**12,611**	**13,629**	**15,439**	**15,577**	**16,383**	**17,679**	**18,929**
Official creditors	373	3,123	6,199	6,102	6,589	9,898	11,108	11,845	13,029	14,172
Multilateral	148	514	2,048	2,029	2,199	1,884	2,081	2,743	3,187	3,718
Concessional	111	98	249	253	269	241	226	169	163	179
Bilateral	225	2,610	4,151	4,073	4,390	8,013	9,026	9,102	9,842	10,455
Concessional	112	1,318	1,413	1,460	1,653	3,058	3,423	3,780	4,183	4,418
Private creditors	483	3,095	6,133	6,509	7,040	5,541	4,469	4,538	4,650	4,756
Bonds	22	2	1	1	1	1	0	0	0	0
Commercial banks	148	1,694	2,970	3,073	3,159	3,147	3,120	3,075	3,056	3,040
Other private	314	1,399	3,162	3,435	3,881	2,394	1,349	1,463	1,593	1,717
Private nonguaranteed	**1,799**	**610**	**386**	**384**	**330**	**218**	**228**	**564**	**1,173**	**1,270**
Bonds	0	0	0	0	0	0	0	0	60	60
Commercial banks	1,799	610	386	384	330	218	228	564	1,113	1,210
Memo:										
IBRD	125	359	1,103	1,085	1,188	1,100	956	1,369	1,554	1,729
IDA	0	0	0	0	0	0	0	0	0	0
DISBURSEMENTS	**387**	**1,308**	**295**	**338**	**291**	**533**	**699**	**1,826**	**1,223**	**862**
Public and publicly guaranteed	**148**	**1,248**	**295**	**338**	**291**	**533**	**631**	**1,516**	**613**	**725**
Official creditors	59	664	235	231	189	451	617	1,484	609	720
Multilateral	18	209	89	37	38	39	473	1,312	500	631
Concessional	10	12	6	7	10	6	11	20	5	37
Bilateral	41	455	146	195	150	411	144	172	109	89
Concessional	8	232	29	84	94	379	138	152	79	26
Private creditors	88	584	60	106	103	83	14	32	4	5
Bonds	0	0	0	0	0	0	0	0	0	0
Commercial banks	3	248	2	58	69	64	3	0	0	0
Other private	85	336	58	48	34	19	11	32	4	5
Private nonguaranteed	**240**	**60**	**0**	**0**	**0**	**0**	**68**	**310**	**610**	**137**
Bonds	0	0	0	0	0	0	0	0	60	0
Commercial banks	240	60	0	0	0	0	68	310	550	137
Memo:										
IBRD	10	140	2	0	0	0	0	975	171	203
IDA	0	0	0	0	0	0	0	0	0	0
PRINCIPAL REPAYMENTS	**333**	**1,019**	**129**	**145**	**166**	**579**	**490**	**980**	**600**	**519**
Public and publicly guaranteed	**100**	**959**	**128**	**143**	**112**	**504**	**432**	**933**	**559**	**479**
Official creditors	23	281	96	114	81	431	311	816	447	403
Multilateral	11	24	27	22	24	359	214	662	195	201
Concessional	5	8	4	4	3	35	22	76	14	22
Bilateral	12	257	69	93	57	72	96	154	252	202
Concessional	3	48	10	11	6	6	15	18	132	56
Private creditors	77	678	32	28	31	72	122	117	113	76
Bonds	7	0	0	0	0	0	1	0	0	0
Commercial banks	25	445	13	14	9	26	44	37	37	28
Other private	46	233	19	14	22	46	76	80	76	48
Private nonguaranteed	**233**	**60**	**1**	**2**	**54**	**76**	**58**	**47**	**41**	**40**
Bonds	0	0	0	0	0	0	0	0	0	0
Commercial banks	233	60	1	2	54	76	58	47	41	40
Memo:										
IBRD	8	15	0	0	0	94	94	574	80	86
IDA	0	0	0	0	0	0	0	0	0	0
NET FLOWS ON DEBT	**54**	**289**	**167**	**193**	**126**	**-46**	**209**	**846**	**623**	**343**
Public and publicly guaranteed	**48**	**289**	**168**	**195**	**180**	**30**	**199**	**583**	**54**	**246**
Official creditors	36	383	139	117	108	19	306	668	162	317
Multilateral	7	185	62	15	14	-320	259	650	305	429
Concessional	5	4	2	3	7	-29	-11	-56	-8	14
Bilateral	29	198	78	102	94	339	47	18	-143	-113
Concessional	5	184	18	73	89	373	123	134	-54	-29
Private creditors	11	-94	28	78	72	11	-107	-85	-109	-71
Bonds	-7	0	0	0	0	0	-1	0	0	0
Commercial banks	-22	-197	-11	44	60	38	-41	-37	-37	-28
Other private	40	103	40	34	12	-28	-65	-48	-72	-43
Private nonguaranteed	**7**	**0**	**-1**	**-2**	**-54**	**-76**	**10**	**263**	**569**	**97**
Bonds	0	0	0	0	0	0	0	0	60	0
Commercial banks	7	0	-1	-2	-54	-76	10	263	509	97
Memo:										
IBRD	2	125	2	0	0	-94	-94	401	91	116
IDA	0	0	0	0	0	0	0	0	0	0

PERU

(US$ million, unless otherwise indicated)

	1970	1980	1988	1989	1990	1991	1992	1993	1994	1995
INTEREST PAYMENTS (LINT)	**162**	**670**	**119**	**151**	**91**	**370**	**313**	**778**	**392**	**479**
Public and publicly guaranteed	**43**	**547**	**92**	**124**	**66**	**351**	**299**	**762**	**370**	**413**
Official creditors	17	152	79	109	51	332	258	720	319	393
Multilateral	8	33	38	44	27	300	190	574	212	245
Concessional	6	7	3	2	3	17	11	31	6	7
Bilateral	9	118	41	65	24	31	68	146	108	149
Concessional	3	27	16	16	7	13	28	47	68	73
Private creditors	26	395	13	16	16	19	41	43	51	20
Bonds	1	0	0	0	0	0	0	0	0	0
Commercial banks	12	273	5	4	8	8	17	15	13	10
Other private	13	122	8	12	7	11	23	28	38	10
Private nonguaranteed	**119**	**124**	**27**	**27**	**25**	**19**	**14**	**16**	**22**	**66**
Bonds	0	0	0	0	0	0	0	0	1	6
Commercial banks	119	124	27	27	25	19	14	16	21	60
Memo:										
IBRD	7	24	2	0	0	83	100	483	109	118
IDA	0	0	0	0	0	0	0	0	0	0
NET TRANSFERS ON DEBT	**-108**	**-382**	**48**	**42**	**35**	**-415**	**-104**	**68**	**230**	**-137**
Public and publicly guaranteed	**4**	**-258**	**76**	**71**	**114**	**-321**	**-100**	**-179**	**-317**	**-167**
Official creditors	20	231	60	8	57	-312	48	-52	-157	-76
Multilateral	-1	152	24	-29	-13	-620	69	76	93	185
Concessional	-1	-2	-1	2	4	-46	-22	-87	-14	7
Bilateral	21	80	36	37	70	308	-21	-128	-250	-261
Concessional	3	157	3	57	81	360	95	87	-122	-102
Private creditors	-15	-490	15	63	56	-8	-148	-128	-160	-91
Bonds	-8	-1	0	0	0	0	-1	0	0	0
Commercial banks	-34	-470	-16	40	52	31	-59	-52	-50	-38
Other private	27	-19	31	23	5	-39	-88	-76	-110	-53
Private nonguaranteed	**-112**	**-124**	**-28**	**-29**	**-79**	**-95**	**-4**	**247**	**547**	**31**
Bonds	0	0	0	0	0	0	0	0	59	-6
Commercial banks	-112	-124	-28	-29	-79	-95	-4	247	488	37
Memo:										
IBRD	-5	101	0	0	0	-178	-194	-82	-18	-2
IDA	0	0	0	0	0	0	0	0	0	0
DEBT SERVICE (LTDS)	**495**	**1,689**	**248**	**296**	**257**	**949**	**803**	**1,758**	**993**	**998**
Public and publicly guaranteed	**144**	**1,506**	**220**	**267**	**178**	**854**	**731**	**1,695**	**930**	**892**
Official creditors	40	433	175	223	131	763	569	1,535	766	796
Multilateral	19	58	65	65	51	660	404	1,236	406	446
Concessional	11	14	7	5	6	52	33	107	20	29
Bilateral	21	375	110	158	81	103	165	299	359	350
Concessional	5	75	26	27	13	19	43	65	200	128
Private creditors	104	1,073	45	44	46	91	162	160	164	96
Bonds	8	1	0	0	0	0	1	0	0	0
Commercial banks	37	718	18	18	17	33	62	52	50	38
Other private	59	355	27	26	29	58	100	108	114	58
Private nonguaranteed	**352**	**184**	**28**	**29**	**79**	**95**	**72**	**63**	**63**	**106**
Bonds	0	0	0	0	0	0	0	0	1	6
Commercial banks	352	184	28	29	79	95	72	63	62	100
Memo:										
IBRD	15	39	2	0	0	178	194	1,057	189	205
IDA	0	0	0	0	0	0	0	0	0	0
UNDISBURSED DEBT	**238**	**2,397**	**2,330**	**2,258**	**1,511**	**1,509**	**2,084**	**1,136**	**1,610**	**1,739**
Official creditors	166	1,126	1,014	1,058	865	1,033	2,057	1,129	1,592	1,727
Private creditors	72	1,272	1,316	1,200	646	476	27	7	18	12
Memorandum items										
Concessional LDOD	223	1,415	1,662	1,713	1,922	3,299	3,648	3,948	4,346	4,597
Variable rate LDOD	1,799	2,130	4,608	4,565	4,626	6,438	7,079	8,115	9,220	9,952
Public sector LDOD	840	6,200	12,291	12,571	13,583	15,429	15,570	16,377	17,673	18,923
Private sector LDOD	1,816	628	427	424	376	228	235	570	1,179	1,276

6. CURRENCY COMPOSITION OF LONG-TERM DEBT (PERCENT)

	1970	1980	1988	1989	1990	1991	1992	1993	1994	1995
Deutsche mark	13.9	6.6	4.5	4.7	5.0	4.6	4.5	4.1	4.4	4.4
French franc	1.1	4.2	8.7	9.0	9.3	10.2	9.4	8.6	9.1	9.7
Japanese yen	0.0	10.9	7.4	6.4	6.3	9.8	10.4	12.7	14.3	14.6
Pound sterling	0.9	2.0	0.9	0.8	0.9	1.4	1.1	1.1	1.2	1.2
Swiss franc	0.1	1.4	1.5	1.4	1.5	1.4	1.3	1.2	1.2	1.2
U.S.dollars	59.0	44.1	48.2	49.7	48.0	43.7	47.2	46.1	43.6	41.9
Multiple currency	17.0	7.5	15.6	15.1	15.1	11.5	10.0	12.1	12.5	13.2
Special drawing rights	0.0	0.0	0.0	0.0	0.0	0.0	0.0	0.0	0.1	0.1
All other currencies	8.0	23.5	13.2	13.0	13.7	17.4	16.2	14.0	13.7	13.6

PERU

(US$ million, unless otherwise indicated)

	1970	1980	1988	1989	1990	1991	1992	1993	1994	1995
7. DEBT RESTRUCTURINGS										
Total amount rescheduled	0	..	0	9	0	5,016	1,584	632	712	919
Debt stock rescheduled	0	..	0	2	0	0	0	0	0	0
Principal rescheduled	0	..	0	3	0	3,497	1,093	230	277	301
Official	0	..	0	3	0	1,534	148	179	230	277
Private	0	..	0	0	0	1,963	945	51	48	24
Interest rescheduled	0	..	0	3	0	1,519	490	401	419	505
Official	0	..	0	3	0	736	71	387	398	439
Private	0	..	0	0	0	783	419	14	22	66
Debt forgiven	..	..	0	0	0	2	48	0	0	0
Memo: interest forgiven	..	..	0	0	0	1	24	0	0	0
Debt stock reduction	0	..	0	0	0	0	0	0	0	0
of which debt buyback	0	..	0	0	0	0	0	0	0	0
8. DEBT STOCK-FLOW RECONCILIATION										
Total change in debt stocks	..	..	..	338	1,486	649	-378	3,236	2,955	4,306
Net flows on debt	..	..	..	-29	128	208	347	649	1,257	3,132
Net change in interest arrears	..	..	..	301	460	-1,302	-638	2,297	360	152
Interest capitalized	..	..	..	3	0	1,519	490	401	419	505
Debt forgiveness or reduction	..	..	..	0	0	-2	-48	0	0	0
Cross-currency valuation	..	..	..	-12	716	33	-490	-261	891	381
Residual	..	..	..	74	182	193	-39	151	28	135
9. AVERAGE TERMS OF NEW COMMITMENTS										
ALL CREDITORS										
Interest (%)	7.4	9.4	6.7	5.4	6.7	5.6	7.2	6.5	6.9	6.1
Maturity (years)	13.3	12.2	11.3	14.8	8.5	24.7	20.1	21.0	18.4	17.6
Grace period (years)	4.3	3.5	4.0	4.8	2.1	7.6	5.6	5.2	4.5	4.7
Grant element (%)	11.8	5.5	17.0	29.0	13.1	33.7	17.8	21.9	18.7	24.0
Official creditors										
Interest (%)	7.2	7.5	5.3	5.0	7.1	5.6	7.2	6.5	6.9	6.1
Maturity (years)	13.8	15.3	11.5	13.8	9.1	24.7	20.1	21.3	18.5	17.6
Grace period (years)	4.5	4.3	4.0	6.0	2.4	7.6	5.6	5.2	4.5	4.7
Grant element (%)	12.6	18.6	25.3	32.0	14.0	33.7	17.8	22.2	18.8	24.0
Private creditors										
Interest (%)	8.7	10.7	8.1	6.7	5.5	0.0	0.0	7.5	7.7	0.0
Maturity (years)	9.2	10.3	11.0	18.1	6.7	0.0	0.0	6.5	7.3	0.0
Grace period (years)	2.0	3.0	4.1	1.0	1.3	0.0	0.0	2.0	2.3	0.0
Grant element (%)	4.8	-3.2	8.7	19.2	10.5	0.0	0.0	7.6	7.5	0.0
Memorandum items										
Commitments	125	1,614	458	610	179	849	1,801	714	1,081	932
Official creditors	112	643	229	468	137	849	1,801	703	1,065	932
Private creditors	13	971	229	142	43	0	0	12	16	0

10. CONTRACTUAL OBLIGATIONS ON OUTSTANDING LONG-TERM DEBT

	1996	1997	1998	1999	2000	2001	2002	2003	2004	2005
TOTAL										
Disbursements	518	349	273	213	146	84	63	37	31	25
Principal	777	955	783	670	1,000	1,297	1,280	1,373	1,367	1,359
Interest	1,009	976	927	893	862	791	730	644	555	466
Official creditors										
Disbursements	513	345	271	212	146	84	63	37	31	25
Principal	660	720	674	565	878	1,172	1,157	1,253	1,247	1,248
Interest	886	869	838	807	782	715	635	553	469	384
Bilateral creditors										
Disbursements	74	88	57	36	20	10	5	1	0	0
Principal	469	483	365	208	499	813	823	946	942	965
Interest	590	568	542	525	517	473	414	354	288	224
Multilateral creditors										
Disbursements	439	257	214	177	125	75	58	37	31	25
Principal	191	236	309	356	379	359	334	306	305	283
Interest	296	301	295	282	265	242	221	200	180	161
Private creditors										
Disbursements	5	4	2	1	0	0	0	0	0	0
Principal	117	235	109	105	122	126	123	120	120	110
Interest	123	108	89	86	80	76	95	91	86	82
Commercial banks										
Disbursements	0	0	0	0	0	0	0	0	0	0
Principal	26	24	24	22	11	0	2	2	2	2
Interest	12	10	8	7	5	5	5	4	4	4
Other private										
Disbursements	5	4	2	1	0	0	0	0	0	0
Principal	91	211	86	83	111	126	121	118	118	108
Interest	111	97	81	80	75	72	91	86	82	78

PHILIPPINES

(US$ million, unless otherwise indicated)

	1970	1980	1988	1989	1990	1991	1992	1993	1994	1995
1. SUMMARY DEBT DATA										
TOTAL DEBT STOCKS (EDT)	..	**17,417**	**29,009**	**28,720**	**30,615**	**32,448**	**32,998**	**35,928**	**39,996**	**39,445**
Long-term debt (LDOD)	**1,544**	**8,817**	**24,050**	**23,590**	**25,277**	**26,419**	**26,641**	**29,683**	**33,216**	**33,438**
Public and publicly guaranteed	625	6,363	22,440	22,401	24,076	25,057	25,611	27,474	30,271	29,908
Private nonguaranteed	919	2,454	1,611	1,189	1,201	1,362	1,030	2,210	2,945	3,531
Use of IMF credit	**69**	**1,044**	**1,094**	**1,177**	**912**	**1,086**	**1,100**	**1,210**	**1,064**	**728**
Short-term debt	..	**7,556**	**3,865**	**3,953**	**4,426**	**4,943**	**5,256**	**5,035**	**5,716**	**5,279**
of which interest arrears on LDOD	..	0	104	3	51	116	0	0	0	0
Official creditors	..	0	66	3	5	27	0	0	0	0
Private creditors	..	0	39	1	47	89	0	0	0	0
Memo: principal arrears on LDOD	..	1	235	21	180	225	6	0	0	0
Official creditors	..	0	80	19	13	11	0	0	0	0
Private creditors	..	1	155	3	167	214	6	0	0	0
Memo: export credits	..	..	4,147	4,101	4,366	5,124	5,907	7,616	8,466	9,017
TOTAL DEBT FLOWS										
Disbursements	**444**	**2,300**	**1,351**	**1,789**	**2,516**	**2,586**	**2,976**	**4,427**	**4,263**	**3,157**
Long-term debt	416	1,854	1,257	1,486	2,516	2,129	2,763	4,250	4,211	3,157
IMF purchases	28	446	94	302	0	457	213	177	52	0
Principal repayments	**262**	**686**	**1,399**	**1,084**	**1,818**	**1,774**	**2,791**	**2,767**	**2,520**	**3,002**
Long-term debt	260	541	1,203	888	1,473	1,479	2,637	2,702	2,249	2,639
IMF repurchases	3	145	196	196	345	295	155	64	270	363
Net flows on debt	**182**	**1,614**	**-79**	**894**	**1,123**	**1,264**	**614**	**1,439**	**2,425**	**-281**
of which short-term debt	..	..	-31	189	425	452	429	-221	681	-437
Interest payments (INT)	..	**1,496**	**1,998**	**2,161**	**1,772**	**1,625**	**1,511**	**2,141**	**2,117**	**2,327**
Long-term debt	44	579	1,583	1,676	1,573	1,457	1,335	1,759	1,651	1,921
IMF charges	0	42	74	84	99	95	82	73	62	55
Short-term debt	..	875	341	402	100	73	94	309	403	351
Net transfers on debt	..	**118**	**-2,077**	**-1,268**	**-649**	**-360**	**-897**	**-701**	**308**	**-2,608**
Total debt service paid (TDS)	..	**2,183**	**3,397**	**3,245**	**3,590**	**3,398**	**4,302**	**4,907**	**4,637**	**5,328**
Long-term debt	304	1,120	2,786	2,563	3,046	2,935	3,971	4,461	3,901	4,560
IMF repurchases and charges	3	187	270	280	444	390	237	137	333	417
Short-term debt (interest only)	..	875	341	402	100	73	94	309	403	351
2. AGGREGATE NET RESOURCE FLOWS AND NET TRANSFERS (LONG-TERM)										
NET RESOURCE FLOWS	**155**	**1,266**	**1,209**	**1,794**	**1,935**	**1,488**	**895**	**4,501**	**5,244**	**4,234**
Net flow of long-term debt (ex. IMF)	157	1,313	54	599	1,043	651	127	1,548	1,962	519
Foreign direct investment (net)	-25	-106	936	563	530	544	228	1,238	1,591	1,478
Portfolio equity flows	0	0	0	253	0	0	333	1,445	1,407	1,961
Grants (excluding technical coop.)	23	59	219	380	362	293	208	270	284	276
Memo: technical coop. grants	16	64	184	190	244	332	468	451	329	382
NET TRANSFERS	**87**	**489**	**-569**	**-176**	**51**	**-272**	**-844**	**2,373**	**3,197**	**1,912**
Interest on long-term debt	44	579	1,583	1,676	1,573	1,457	1,335	1,759	1,651	1,921
Profit remittances on FDI	24	198	195	295	311	303	405	369	395	400
3. MAJOR ECONOMIC AGGREGATES										
Gross national product (GNP)	6,576	32,436	37,527	42,126	44,549	46,039	54,336	55,361	65,785	76,566
Exports of goods & services (XGS)	..	8,202	11,054	12,767	13,290	14,792	17,636	19,183	24,476	32,399
of which workers remittances	..	205	388	360	262	329	315	311	443	586
Imports of goods & services (MGS)	..	10,348	11,831	14,693	16,437	16,324	19,137	22,554	27,809	35,479
International reserves (RES)	255	3,978	2,169	2,398	2,036	4,436	5,336	5,934	7,126	7,757
Current account balance	..	-1,917	-390	-1,456	-2,695	-1,034	-1,000	-2,983	-2,840	-2,855
4. DEBT INDICATORS										
EDT / XGS (%)	..	212.4	262.4	225.0	230.4	219.4	187.1	187.3	163.4	121.7
EDT / GNP (%)	..	53.7	77.3	68.2	68.7	70.5	60.7	64.9	60.8	51.5
TDS / XGS (%)	..	26.6	30.7	25.4	27.0	23.0	24.4	25.6	18.9	16.4
INT / XGS (%)	..	18.2	18.1	16.9	13.3	11.0	8.6	11.2	8.6	7.2
INT / GNP (%)	..	4.6	5.3	5.1	4.0	3.5	2.8	3.9	3.2	3.0
RES / EDT (%)	..	22.8	7.5	8.4	6.7	13.7	16.2	16.5	17.8	19.7
RES / MGS (months)	..	4.6	2.2	2.0	1.5	3.3	3.3	3.2	3.1	2.6
Short-term / EDT (%)	..	43.4	13.3	13.8	14.5	15.2	15.9	14.0	14.3	13.4
Concessional / EDT (%)	..	6.7	18.5	19.3	22.7	24.6	27.0	29.0	28.8	28.8
Multilateral / EDT (%)	..	7.5	16.5	17.3	20.5	20.5	20.9	21.3	20.9	21.5

PHILIPPINES

(US$ million, unless otherwise indicated)

	1970	1980	1988	1989	1990	1991	1992	1993	1994	1995
5. LONG-TERM DEBT										
DEBT OUTSTANDING (LDOD)	**1,544**	**8,817**	**24,050**	**23,590**	**25,277**	**26,419**	**26,641**	**29,683**	**33,216**	**33,438**
Public and publicly guaranteed	**625**	**6,363**	**22,440**	**22,401**	**24,076**	**25,057**	**25,611**	**27,474**	**30,271**	**29,908**
Official creditors	272	2,636	11,726	12,657	15,405	17,313	19,084	21,183	22,974	22,292
Multilateral	120	1,310	4,774	4,982	6,273	6,668	6,908	7,645	8,348	8,488
Concessional	75	279	821	880	1,308	1,488	1,592	1,780	1,967	1,978
Bilateral	152	1,326	6,952	7,675	9,132	10,645	12,176	13,539	14,626	13,804
Concessional	68	894	4,561	4,663	5,647	6,505	7,329	8,639	9,553	9,387
Private creditors	353	3,727	10,714	9,745	8,671	7,744	6,527	6,291	7,297	7,615
Bonds	11	888	626	422	825	956	4,232	4,720	4,915	5,099
Commercial banks	267	2,256	8,373	8,038	6,658	5,814	1,315	624	569	587
Other private	75	583	1,716	1,284	1,188	975	980	947	1,813	1,929
Private nonguaranteed	**919**	**2,454**	**1,611**	**1,189**	**1,201**	**1,362**	**1,030**	**2,210**	**2,945**	**3,531**
Bonds	0	0	0	0	0	0	20	270	1,062	1,925
Commercial banks	919	2,454	1,611	1,189	1,201	1,362	1,010	1,939	1,883	1,606
Memo:										
IBRD	119	926	3,408	3,492	3,943	4,073	4,179	4,598	4,855	5,002
IDA	0	34	102	102	101	135	166	167	174	183
DISBURSEMENTS	**416**	**1,854**	**1,257**	**1,486**	**2,516**	**2,129**	**2,763**	**4,250**	**4,211**	**3,157**
Public and publicly guaranteed	**141**	**1,382**	**1,257**	**1,367**	**2,225**	**1,869**	**2,490**	**3,285**	**3,225**	**2,133**
Official creditors	74	461	1,089	1,244	1,373	1,423	2,155	2,287	1,801	1,339
Multilateral	17	321	424	654	854	658	845	965	612	620
Concessional	6	61	75	90	159	184	181	157	90	86
Bilateral	57	140	665	591	519	765	1,310	1,322	1,189	718
Concessional	15	102	661	389	458	401	908	931	761	616
Private creditors	66	920	167	123	852	446	334	998	1,425	795
Bonds	0	96	0	0	575	263	0	765	365	278
Commercial banks	50	657	8	0	167	44	45	57	35	102
Other private	17	167	159	123	110	139	290	176	1,025	415
Private nonguaranteed	**276**	**472**	**0**	**119**	**291**	**261**	**274**	**966**	**985**	**1,024**
Bonds	0	0	0	0	0	0	20	251	785	864
Commercial banks	276	472	0	119	291	261	254	714	201	161
Memo:										
IBRD	16	229	259	463	506	353	544	671	300	393
IDA	0	2	3	1	0	33	34	2	5	10
PRINCIPAL REPAYMENTS	**260**	**541**	**1,203**	**888**	**1,473**	**1,479**	**2,637**	**2,702**	**2,249**	**2,639**
Public and publicly guaranteed	**74**	**221**	**1,103**	**681**	**1,411**	**1,367**	**2,494**	**2,581**	**2,103**	**2,489**
Official creditors	15	95	386	370	439	633	691	1,334	1,588	1,986
Multilateral	5	45	347	332	388	409	438	470	520	653
Concessional	3	9	29	31	40	43	47	52	62	75
Bilateral	10	49	40	38	51	224	253	865	1,069	1,334
Concessional	3	24	17	21	21	54	74	354	404	561
Private creditors	59	126	717	311	972	734	1,803	1,247	515	503
Bonds	1	16	220	171	180	138	72	283	178	82
Commercial banks	39	44	459	81	743	536	1,584	762	108	92
Other private	19	67	39	59	49	59	147	202	229	329
Private nonguaranteed	**186**	**320**	**100**	**207**	**62**	**112**	**143**	**121**	**146**	**150**
Bonds	0	0	0	0	0	0	0	0	0	0
Commercial banks	186	320	100	207	62	112	143	121	146	150
Memo:										
IBRD	5	33	283	268	301	309	323	338	358	413
IDA	0	0	1	1	1	1	1	2	2	2
NET FLOWS ON DEBT	**157**	**1,313**	**54**	**599**	**1,043**	**651**	**127**	**1,548**	**1,962**	**519**
Public and publicly guaranteed	**67**	**1,161**	**154**	**686**	**814**	**502**	**-4**	**704**	**1,122**	**-356**
Official creditors	60	367	703	874	934	790	1,464	952	213	-648
Multilateral	12	276	77	322	466	249	407	495	92	-32
Concessional	3	52	47	59	119	142	134	105	28	12
Bilateral	48	91	626	552	468	541	1,057	458	120	-615
Concessional	12	78	644	368	437	347	834	577	358	55
Private creditors	7	794	-550	-188	-120	-288	-1,468	-249	909	292
Bonds	-1	80	-220	-171	395	124	-72	483	187	196
Commercial banks	11	614	-450	-81	-576	-492	-1,540	-705	-74	9
Other private	-3	100	121	64	61	80	143	-26	796	86
Private nonguaranteed	**90**	**152**	**-100**	**-88**	**229**	**149**	**131**	**844**	**839**	**874**
Bonds	0	0	0	0	0	0	20	251	785	864
Commercial banks	90	152	-100	-88	229	149	111	593	55	11
Memo:										
IBRD	11	195	-24	195	206	44	221	333	-58	-21
IDA	0	2	3	1	-1	32	33	1	3	8

PHILIPPINES

(US$ million, unless otherwise indicated)

	1970	1980	1988	1989	1990	1991	1992	1993	1994	1995
INTEREST PAYMENTS (LINT)	**44**	**579**	**1,583**	**1,676**	**1,573**	**1,457**	**1,335**	**1,759**	**1,651**	**1,921**
Public and publicly guaranteed	**26**	**375**	**1,460**	**1,542**	**1,486**	**1,391**	**1,295**	**1,661**	**1,518**	**1,770**
Official creditors	11	140	576	608	749	763	843	1,108	1,150	1,296
Multilateral	7	100	388	381	444	479	495	526	565	605
Concessional	5	18	49	57	72	77	83	90	94	100
Bilateral	4	40	188	228	305	284	348	581	586	691
Concessional	2	21	70	92	125	124	147	274	271	359
Private creditors	15	235	884	934	737	628	451	554	368	474
Bonds	1	36	67	49	31	72	78	213	278	307
Commercial banks	11	165	769	845	671	521	342	280	33	48
Other private	3	34	49	40	35	35	32	60	58	119
Private nonguaranteed	**19**	**204**	**123**	**134**	**87**	**66**	**40**	**98**	**133**	**152**
Bonds	0	0	0	0	0	0	0	1	20	82
Commercial banks	19	204	123	134	87	66	40	97	113	70
Memo:										
IBRD	7	73	289	268	296	314	316	331	359	377
IDA	0	0	1	1	1	1	1	1	1	1
NET TRANSFERS ON DEBT	**113**	**733**	**-1,529**	**-1,077**	**-530**	**-806**	**-1,208**	**-211**	**310**	**-1,403**
Public and publicly guaranteed	**41**	**785**	**-1,306**	**-856**	**-672**	**-889**	**-1,299**	**-957**	**-396**	**-2,125**
Official creditors	49	227	127	266	185	27	621	-155	-938	-1,943
Multilateral	5	176	-311	-59	22	-230	-88	-32	-472	-637
Concessional	-2	34	-2	3	47	65	51	15	-66	-88
Bilateral	43	51	438	325	163	257	709	-124	-465	-1,306
Concessional	9	57	574	276	312	223	687	303	87	-304
Private creditors	-7	559	-1,434	-1,121	-857	-917	-1,920	-802	541	-182
Bonds	-2	44	-287	-220	364	53	-149	269	-91	-111
Commercial banks	0	448	-1,219	-926	-1,247	-1,013	-1,882	-985	-106	-39
Other private	-6	66	72	24	25	44	111	-87	739	-33
Private nonguaranteed	**71**	**-52**	**-223**	**-221**	**142**	**83**	**91**	**746**	**706**	**723**
Bonds	0	0	0	0	0	0	20	250	764	782
Commercial banks	71	-52	-223	-221	142	83	71	496	-58	-59
Memo:										
IBRD	4	123	-313	-73	-90	-270	-95	2	-417	-397
IDA	0	1	2	0	-2	31	32	-1	2	7
DEBT SERVICE (LTDS)	**304**	**1,120**	**2,786**	**2,563**	**3,046**	**2,935**	**3,971**	**4,461**	**3,901**	**4,560**
Public and publicly guaranteed	**100**	**596**	**2,563**	**2,223**	**2,897**	**2,758**	**3,788**	**4,242**	**3,622**	**4,259**
Official creditors	26	235	962	979	1,188	1,396	1,534	2,442	2,738	3,282
Multilateral	12	145	735	713	832	888	933	996	1,084	1,258
Concessional	8	26	78	87	112	120	130	142	156	174
Bilateral	14	90	227	266	356	508	601	1,446	1,654	2,024
Concessional	6	45	87	113	146	178	221	628	675	920
Private creditors	74	362	1,601	1,244	1,709	1,362	2,254	1,800	883	977
Bonds	2	52	287	220	211	210	149	496	456	389
Commercial banks	50	209	1,227	926	1,414	1,057	1,927	1,042	141	140
Other private	22	101	87	99	85	95	178	263	287	448
Private nonguaranteed	**204**	**524**	**223**	**340**	**149**	**177**	**183**	**219**	**279**	**302**
Bonds	0	0	0	0	0	0	0	1	20	82
Commercial banks	204	524	223	340	149	177	183	218	259	220
Memo:										
IBRD	12	106	572	536	597	622	640	669	717	790
IDA	0	0	1	2	2	2	2	3	3	3
UNDISBURSED DEBT	**193**	**4,365**	**4,415**	**5,221**	**6,590**	**7,857**	**7,483**	**7,764**	**6,654**	**7,691**
Official creditors	176	3,246	4,007	4,854	6,171	7,450	7,102	6,878	6,255	6,759
Private creditors	16	1,119	408	367	419	407	380	886	399	932
Memorandum items										
Concessional LDOD	143	1,173	5,381	5,543	6,955	7,993	8,921	10,419	11,520	11,366
Variable rate LDOD	924	4,399	10,516	10,514	10,732	10,763	8,566	9,859	12,145	13,116
Public sector LDOD	624	6,363	22,013	21,984	23,703	24,797	25,410	27,308	30,127	29,839
Private sector LDOD	920	2,454	2,037	1,606	1,573	1,622	1,231	2,375	3,090	3,600

6. CURRENCY COMPOSITION OF LONG-TERM DEBT (PERCENT)

	1970	1980	1988	1989	1990	1991	1992	1993	1994	1995
Deutsche mark	12.0	2.0	1.4	1.6	1.5	1.6	1.5	1.4	1.4	1.5
French franc	0.2	2.2	1.2	1.4	1.5	1.1	0.9	0.8	0.8	0.8
Japanese yen	2.7	21.9	32.2	30.8	31.1	34.3	34.7	38.3	38.7	36.9
Pound sterling	0.0	0.2	0.7	0.8	1.0	1.0	0.3	0.3	0.3	0.2
Swiss franc	3.1	0.5	0.6	0.4	0.5	0.3	0.3	0.4	0.4	0.4
U.S.dollars	62.1	51.6	40.8	40.5	36.2	32.9	33.9	30.4	30.3	31.5
Multiple currency	19.2	19.0	19.3	20.1	23.6	24.0	24.3	25.2	24.9	25.4
Special drawing rights	0.0	0.0	0.0	0.0	0.0	0.0	0.1	0.2	0.3	0.4
All other currencies	0.7	2.6	3.7	4.3	4.6	4.8	4.1	3.2	3.0	2.8

PHILIPPINES

(US$ million, unless otherwise indicated)

	1970	1980	1988	1989	1990	1991	1992	1993	1994	1995
7. DEBT RESTRUCTURINGS										
Total amount rescheduled	0	0	1,963	1,968	1,068	1,067	4,408	282	0	0
Debt stock rescheduled	0	0	0	0	0	0	2,253	0	0	0
Principal rescheduled	0	0	1,859	1,657	882	910	748	216	0	0
Official	0	0	112	236	196	313	503	191	0	0
Private	0	0	1,747	1,422	686	597	245	25	0	0
Interest rescheduled	0	0	92	311	186	156	235	66	0	0
Official	0	0	59	180	117	119	199	62	0	0
Private	0	0	33	131	69	37	37	4	0	0
Debt forgiven	..	..	0	0	0	0	0	0	0	0
Memo: interest forgiven	..	..	0	0	0	0	0	0	0	0
Debt stock reduction	0	0	808	493	1,803	245	2,259	0	0	0
of which debt buyback	0	0	0	0	721	94	1,175	0	0	0
8. DEBT STOCK-FLOW RECONCILIATION										
Total change in debt stocks	..	..	..	-290	1,895	1,834	550	2,931	4,068	-551
Net flows on debt	..	..	..	894	1,123	1,264	614	1,439	2,425	-281
Net change in interest arrears	..	..	..	-101	48	65	-116	0	0	0
Interest capitalized	..	..	..	311	186	156	235	66	0	0
Debt forgiveness or reduction	..	..	..	-493	-1,082	-151	-1,085	0	0	0
Cross-currency valuation	..	..	..	-1,024	1,036	649	-329	1,193	2,028	-194
Residual	..	..	..	124	584	-150	1,230	233	-385	-76
9. AVERAGE TERMS OF NEW COMMITMENTS										
ALL CREDITORS										
Interest (%)	7.3	9.9	5.1	5.5	6.3	5.1	5.7	5.2	5.3	5.1
Maturity (years)	11.4	16.7	22.4	20.1	21.9	22.9	18.6	15.8	16.0	21.8
Grace period (years)	2.1	5.3	7.0	5.9	7.3	6.6	4.6	5.2	5.6	6.5
Grant element (%)	12.4	4.0	35.7	30.4	27.2	35.7	25.8	27.1	26.4	34.2
Official creditors										
Interest (%)	6.7	6.9	4.6	5.5	5.3	4.6	5.8	4.9	5.3	4.4
Maturity (years)	14.3	21.6	24.3	20.4	24.4	25.4	20.0	23.3	23.9	26.9
Grace period (years)	2.2	6.2	7.2	5.9	7.3	7.3	5.0	6.6	7.2	7.9
Grant element (%)	16.0	22.1	39.8	30.5	35.4	40.9	27.0	36.2	35.0	43.6
Private creditors										
Interest (%)	8.1	13.5	8.0	5.7	9.2	7.3	5.4	5.6	5.3	6.3
Maturity (years)	6.7	10.8	10.7	12.8	15.0	11.3	10.5	6.2	8.3	13.7
Grace period (years)	1.9	4.1	5.5	6.1	7.4	3.6	1.9	3.4	4.1	4.2
Grant element (%)	6.4	-17.6	9.9	26.8	4.0	12.5	18.6	15.5	18.0	19.4
Memorandum items										
Commitments	171	2,143	2,450	2,584	3,520	3,147	2,372	3,435	1,845	3,430
Official creditors	107	1,164	2,113	2,489	2,603	2,579	2,033	1,924	910	2,092
Private creditors	64	979	337	95	917	568	339	1,512	935	1,338

10. CONTRACTUAL OBLIGATIONS ON OUTSTANDING LONG-TERM DEBT

	1996	1997	1998	1999	2000	2001	2002	2003	2004	2005
TOTAL										
Disbursements	2,431	2,053	1,314	853	502	292	169	40	26	12
Principal	2,938	3,045	2,885	2,553	3,219	2,427	2,591	2,168	2,337	2,144
Interest	1,924	1,847	1,733	1,598	1,463	1,298	1,164	1,020	901	792
Official creditors										
Disbursements	1,949	1,757	1,201	814	501	292	169	40	26	12
Principal	1,926	2,115	1,788	1,792	1,743	1,676	1,696	1,619	1,517	1,453
Interest	1,162	1,121	1,058	994	917	837	756	672	592	521
Bilateral creditors										
Disbursements	1,252	1,077	641	375	187	93	39	1	1	0
Principal	1,192	1,334	987	1,000	972	935	962	938	887	860
Interest	586	561	523	491	450	412	373	335	297	263
Multilateral creditors										
Disbursements	697	680	560	438	313	199	129	39	25	12
Principal	734	780	801	793	770	741	734	681	630	593
Interest	576	560	536	503	466	425	383	337	295	258
Private creditors										
Disbursements	481	297	113	40	1	0	0	0	0	0
Principal	1,012	931	1,097	761	1,476	752	895	549	820	691
Interest	762	727	674	604	546	460	408	348	309	271
Commercial banks										
Disbursements	26	13	5	1	0	0	0	0	0	0
Principal	65	62	71	63	161	56	53	48	42	10
Interest	41	38	34	29	21	13	9	6	3	0
Other private										
Disbursements	455	284	108	39	1	0	0	0	0	0
Principal	947	868	1,026	697	1,315	696	842	502	778	681
Interest	721	689	641	575	525	447	399	343	306	271

POLAND

(US$ million, unless otherwise indicated)

	1970	1980	1988	1989	1990	1991	1992	1993	1994	1995
1. SUMMARY DEBT DATA										
TOTAL DEBT STOCKS (EDT)	..	..	**42,103**	**43,096**	**49,366**	**53,421**	**48,495**	**45,176**	**42,553**	**42,291**
Long-term debt (LDOD)	..	..	**33,627**	**34,519**	**39,263**	**45,001**	**43,142**	**41,837**	**40,367**	**42,086**
Public and publicly guaranteed	..	..	33,627	34,519	39,263	44,867	42,741	41,297	39,503	41,073
Private nonguaranteed	0	0	0	0	0	135	401	541	864	1,012
Use of IMF credit	**0**	**0**	**0**	**0**	**509**	**853**	**820**	**684**	**1,341**	**0**
Short-term debt	..	..	**8,476**	**8,577**	**9,595**	**7,566**	**4,532**	**2,656**	**845**	**206**
of which interest arrears on LDOD	..	..	7,100	7,330	8,316	6,218	3,281	1,513	139	136
Official creditors	..	..	5,567	6,100	6,568	3,650	1,868	124	139	136
Private creditors	..	..	1,533	1,230	1,747	2,567	1,413	1,390	0	0
Memo: principal arrears on LDOD	..	..	7,002	4,986	5,672	4,974	2,828	580	585	625
Official creditors	..	..	3,171	3,285	4,284	3,789	2,274	429	578	619
Private creditors	..	..	3,831	1,701	1,388	1,185	554	152	7	5
Memo: export credits	..	..	20,533	24,328	28,076	33,020	18,159	15,104	15,560	14,764
TOTAL DEBT FLOWS										
Disbursements	..	..	**578**	**273**	**1,025**	**1,191**	**819**	**751**	**2,429**	**1,279**
Long-term debt	..	..	578	273	540	864	819	751	1,512	1,279
IMF purchases	0	0	0	0	485	327	0	0	917	0
Principal repayments	..	..	**833**	**674**	**635**	**366**	**540**	**669**	**1,897**	**2,279**
Long-term debt	..	..	833	674	635	366	540	531	1,583	885
IMF repurchases	0	0	0	0	0	0	0	138	314	1,394
Net flows on debt	..	..	**-394**	**-531**	**423**	**893**	**183**	**-27**	**96**	**-1,637**
of which short-term debt	..	..	-139	-129	33	69	-97	-109	-436	-637
Interest payments (INT)	..	..	**930**	**867**	**332**	**603**	**929**	**1,026**	**1,208**	**1,790**
Long-term debt	..	..	828	761	203	436	760	869	1,123	1,719
IMF charges	0	0	0	0	23	57	62	47	48	47
Short-term debt	..	..	103	106	105	110	108	110	37	24
Net transfers on debt	..	..	**-1,324**	**-1,398**	**92**	**290**	**-747**	**-1,053**	**-1,112**	**-3,426**
Total debt service paid (TDS)	..	..	**1,763**	**1,542**	**966**	**969**	**1,469**	**1,695**	**3,104**	**4,069**
Long-term debt	..	..	1,661	1,436	838	803	1,299	1,399	2,705	2,604
IMF repurchases and charges	0	0	0	0	23	57	62	185	362	1,440
Short-term debt (interest only)	..	..	103	106	105	110	108	110	37	24
2. AGGREGATE NET RESOURCE FLOWS AND NET TRANSFERS (LONG-TERM)										
NET RESOURCE FLOWS	..	..	**-240**	**-391**	**21**	**3,239**	**2,077**	**3,247**	**3,497**	**8,375**
Net flow of long-term debt (ex. IMF)	0	0	-255	-402	-95	497	279	220	-71	394
Foreign direct investment (net)	0	10	15	11	89	291	678	1,715	1,875	3,659
Portfolio equity flows	..	..	0	0	0	0	0	400	5	921
Grants (excluding technical coop.)	0	0	0	0	27	2,451	1,119	912	1,688	3,402
Memo: technical coop. grants	0	0	0	0	0	70	196	119	101	335
NET TRANSFERS	..	..	**-1,068**	**-1,152**	**-201**	**2,753**	**1,163**	**2,179**	**2,174**	**6,432**
Interest on long-term debt	..	..	828	761	203	436	760	869	1,123	1,719
Profit remittances on FDI	0	0	0	0	20	50	154	199	200	225
3. MAJOR ECONOMIC AGGREGATES										
Gross national product (GNP)	..	54,705	65,821	79,027	55,620	73,582	82,672	84,561	91,233	117,057
Exports of goods & services (XGS)	..	16,200	16,589	16,480	19,640	18,653	19,430	18,362	22,247	33,215
of which workers remittances	..	0	0	0	0	0	0	0	58	46
Imports of goods & services (MGS)	..	20,338	18,387	19,498	19,084	21,567	23,000	24,910	25,898	36,929
International reserves (RES)	..	574	2,249	2,504	4,674	3,800	4,257	4,277	6,023	14,957
Current account balance	..	-3,417	-107	-1,409	3,067	-2,146	-3,104	-5,788	-2,590	-4,245
4. DEBT INDICATORS										
EDT / XGS (%)	..	..	253.8	261.5	251.4	286.4	249.6	246.0	191.3	127.3
EDT / GNP (%)	..	..	64.0	54.5	88.8	72.6	58.7	53.4	46.6	36.1
TDS / XGS (%)	..	..	10.6	9.4	4.9	5.2	7.6	9.2	14.0	12.2
INT / XGS (%)	..	..	5.6	5.3	1.7	3.2	4.8	5.6	5.4	5.4
INT / GNP (%)	..	..	1.4	1.1	0.6	0.8	1.1	1.2	1.3	1.5
RES / EDT (%)	..	..	5.3	5.8	9.5	7.1	8.8	9.5	14.2	35.4
RES / MGS (months)	..	0.3	1.5	1.5	2.9	2.1	2.2	2.1	2.8	4.9
Short-term / EDT (%)	..	..	20.1	19.9	19.4	14.2	9.3	5.9	2.0	0.5
Concessional / EDT (%)	..	..	10.6	8.1	7.7	6.9	26.8	27.8	25.4	26.2
Multilateral / EDT (%)	..	..	1.8	1.2	1.1	1.6	2.4	3.3	4.6	4.9

POLAND

(US$ million, unless otherwise indicated)

	1970	1980	1988	1989	1990	1991	1992	1993	1994	1995
5. LONG-TERM DEBT										
DEBT OUTSTANDING (LDOD)	..	..	**33,627**	**34,519**	**39,263**	**45,001**	**43,142**	**41,837**	**40,367**	**42,086**
Public and publicly guaranteed	..	..	**33,627**	**34,519**	**39,263**	**44,867**	**42,741**	**41,297**	**39,503**	**41,073**
Official creditors	..	..	21,890	23,591	27,919	33,867	32,819	32,446	31,040	32,232
Multilateral	..	..	749	496	524	878	1,167	1,471	1,957	2,067
Concessional	..	..	0	0	0	0	0	0	0	0
Bilateral	..	..	21,141	23,095	27,395	32,989	31,652	30,975	29,083	30,165
Concessional	..	..	4,449	3,494	3,822	3,711	12,976	12,555	10,797	11,097
Private creditors	..	..	11,737	10,929	11,344	11,000	9,922	8,850	8,463	8,841
Bonds	..	..	0	0	0	0	0	0	7,860	8,110
Commercial banks	..	..	9,160	8,964	9,760	9,715	9,108	8,640	362	556
Other private	..	..	2,577	1,964	1,584	1,285	814	211	241	175
Private nonguaranteed	**0**	**0**	**0**	**0**	**0**	**135**	**401**	**541**	**864**	**1,012**
Bonds	..	..	0	0	0	0	0	0	0	0
Commercial banks	..	..	0	0	0	135	401	541	864	1,012
Memo:										
IBRD	0	0	0	0	55	417	743	1,073	1,818	2,067
IDA	0	0	0	0	0	0	0	0	0	0
DISBURSEMENTS	..	..	**578**	**273**	**540**	**864**	**819**	**751**	**1,512**	**1,279**
Public and publicly guaranteed	..	..	**578**	**273**	**540**	**864**	**773**	**566**	**1,015**	**856**
Official creditors	..	..	86	39	70	403	412	330	712	248
Multilateral	..	..	67	15	56	349	343	317	672	210
Concessional	..	..	0	0	0	0	0	0	0	0
Bilateral	..	..	19	24	14	53	69	12	40	38
Concessional	..	..	10	14	10	27	4	0	16	7
Private creditors	..	..	492	234	470	461	361	237	303	608
Bonds	..	..	0	0	0	0	0	0	138	250
Commercial banks	..	..	405	139	300	233	220	168	72	353
Other private	..	..	87	95	171	229	141	69	93	5
Private nonguaranteed	**0**	**0**	**0**	**0**	**0**	**0**	**46**	**185**	**497**	**423**
Bonds	..	..	0	0	0	0	0	0	0	0
Commercial banks	..	..	0	0	0	0	46	185	497	423
Memo:										
IBRD	0	0	0	0	54	349	343	317	672	210
IDA	0	0	0	0	0	0	0	0	0	0
PRINCIPAL REPAYMENTS	..	..	**833**	**674**	**635**	**366**	**540**	**531**	**1,583**	**885**
Public and publicly guaranteed	..	..	**833**	**674**	**635**	**366**	**494**	**485**	**1,409**	**611**
Official creditors	..	..	490	292	147	150	178	153	147	332
Multilateral	..	..	228	149	46	5	29	20	0	158
Concessional	..	..	0	0	0	0	0	0	0	0
Bilateral	..	..	262	143	101	144	149	133	147	174
Concessional	..	..	21	18	43	102	54	112	48	44
Private creditors	..	..	343	383	488	217	316	332	1,262	279
Bonds	..	..	3	0	0	0	0	0	0	0
Commercial banks	..	..	275	310	400	134	177	172	1,179	192
Other private	..	..	64	72	88	83	139	161	83	87
Private nonguaranteed	**0**	**0**	**0**	**0**	**0**	**0**	**46**	**46**	**174**	**275**
Bonds	..	..	0	0	0	0	0	0	0	0
Commercial banks	..	..	0	0	0	0	46	46	174	275
Memo:										
IBRD	0	0	0	0	0	0	0	0	0	19
IDA	0	0	0	0	0	0	0	0	0	0
NET FLOWS ON DEBT	..	..	**-255**	**-402**	**-95**	**497**	**279**	**220**	**-71**	**394**
Public and publicly guaranteed	..	..	**-255**	**-402**	**-95**	**497**	**280**	**81**	**-394**	**245**
Official creditors	..	..	-404	-253	-77	253	234	176	565	-84
Multilateral	..	..	-161	-134	10	344	314	297	672	52
Concessional	..	..	0	0	0	0	0	0	0	0
Bilateral	..	..	-243	-119	-87	-91	-80	-120	-107	-136
Concessional	..	..	-11	-4	-33	-75	-51	-112	-33	-37
Private creditors	..	..	149	-149	-18	244	45	-95	-959	329
Bonds	..	..	-3	0	0	0	0	0	138	250
Commercial banks	..	..	130	-172	-100	98	43	-3	-1,107	161
Other private	..	..	22	23	83	146	2	-92	10	-82
Private nonguaranteed	**0**	**0**	**0**	**0**	**0**	**0**	**0**	**139**	**323**	**148**
Bonds	..	..	0	0	0	0	0	0	0	0
Commercial banks	..	..	0	0	0	0	0	139	323	148
Memo:										
IBRD	0	0	0	0	54	349	343	317	672	191
IDA	0	0	0	0	0	0	0	0	0	0

POLAND

(US$ million, unless otherwise indicated)

	1970	1980	1988	1989	1990	1991	1992	1993	1994	1995
INTEREST PAYMENTS (LINT)	..	..	**828**	**761**	**203**	**436**	**760**	**869**	**1,123**	**1,719**
Public and publicly guaranteed	..	..	**828**	**761**	**203**	**436**	**751**	**832**	**1,075**	**1,663**
Official creditors	..	..	253	138	113	233	643	718	736	1,216
Multilateral	..	..	62	50	31	24	37	71	152	148
Concessional	..	..	0	0	0	0	0	0	0	0
Bilateral	..	..	191	88	82	209	606	647	584	1,068
Concessional	..	..	95	48	56	11	167	339	338	478
Private creditors	..	..	575	623	90	204	109	114	339	447
Bonds	..	..	0	0	0	0	0	0	0	386
Commercial banks	..	..	565	613	74	173	71	85	318	47
Other private	..	..	10	10	15	30	38	29	21	14
Private nonguaranteed	**0**	**0**	**0**	**0**	**0**	**0**	**8**	**37**	**48**	**56**
Bonds	..	..	0	0	0	0	0	0	0	0
Commercial banks	..	..	0	0	0	0	8	37	48	56
Memo:										
IBRD	0	0	0	0	1	8	33	64	88	133
IDA	0	0	0	0	0	0	0	0	0	0
NET TRANSFERS ON DEBT	..	..	**-1,083**	**-1,163**	**-298**	**61**	**-480**	**-648**	**-1,194**	**-1,325**
Public and publicly guaranteed	..	..	**-1,083**	**-1,163**	**-298**	**61**	**-472**	**-751**	**-1,469**	**-1,418**
Official creditors	..	..	-657	-391	-190	20	-408	-542	-171	-1,300
Multilateral	..	..	-222	-184	-22	320	277	226	520	-96
Concessional	..	..	0	0	0	0	0	0	0	0
Bilateral	..	..	-434	-206	-169	-300	-686	-768	-691	-1,204
Concessional	..	..	-106	-51	-90	-87	-218	-450	-371	-515
Private creditors	..	..	-426	-772	-107	41	-63	-209	-1,298	-118
Bonds	..	..	-3	0	0	0	0	0	138	-136
Commercial banks	..	..	-435	-784	-175	-75	-28	-88	-1,425	114
Other private	..	..	13	12	67	116	-36	-121	-11	-96
Private nonguaranteed	**0**	**0**	**0**	**0**	**0**	**0**	**-9**	**102**	**275**	**93**
Bonds	..	..	0	0	0	0	0	0	0	0
Commercial banks	..	..	0	0	0	0	-9	102	275	93
Memo:										
IBRD	0	0	0	0	54	341	310	253	585	58
IDA	0	0	0	0	0	0	0	0	0	0
DEBT SERVICE (LTDS)	..	..	**1,661**	**1,436**	**838**	**803**	**1,299**	**1,399**	**2,705**	**2,604**
Public and publicly guaranteed	..	..	**1,661**	**1,436**	**838**	**803**	**1,245**	**1,317**	**2,484**	**2,274**
Official creditors	..	..	743	430	260	383	820	871	883	1,548
Multilateral	..	..	290	199	77	29	66	91	152	306
Concessional	..	..	0	0	0	0	0	0	0	0
Bilateral	..	..	453	230	183	353	755	780	731	1,241
Concessional	..	..	115	65	100	114	221	450	387	522
Private creditors	..	..	918	1,006	578	420	425	446	1,601	726
Bonds	..	..	3	0	0	0	0	0	0	386
Commercial banks	..	..	840	923	474	308	248	256	1,497	239
Other private	..	..	74	83	103	113	177	190	104	102
Private nonguaranteed	**0**	**0**	**0**	**0**	**0**	**0**	**54**	**82**	**221**	**331**
Bonds	..	..	0	0	0	0	0	0	0	0
Commercial banks	..	..	0	0	0	0	54	82	221	331
Memo:										
IBRD	0	0	0	0	1	8	33	64	88	152
IDA	0	0	0	0	0	0	0	0	0	0
UNDISBURSED DEBT	..	..	**1,055**	**939**	**1,967**	**2,754**	**2,429**	**2,958**	**2,246**	**1,731**
Official creditors	..	..	281	100	1,138	1,907	1,835	2,609	2,082	1,622
Private creditors	..	..	774	839	829	848	594	348	164	109
Memorandum items										
Concessional LDOD	..	..	4,449	3,494	3,822	3,711	12,976	12,555	10,797	11,097
Variable rate LDOD	..	..	21,241	22,241	26,112	30,756	28,144	28,628	24,013	25,387
Public sector LDOD	..	..	33,627	34,519	39,261	44,816	42,695	41,268	39,488	41,071
Private sector LDOD	..	..	0	0	2	186	447	569	879	1,015

6. CURRENCY COMPOSITION OF LONG-TERM DEBT (PERCENT)

	1970	1980	1988	1989	1990	1991	1992	1993	1994	1995
Deutsche mark	..	..	20.9	23.9	23.3	23.2	21.2	19.2	10.1	10.2
French franc	..	..	7.6	8.5	11.0	11.9	11.9	11.7	12.7	13.1
Japanese yen	..	..	2.9	3.0	2.9	3.1	3.0	3.8	3.9	3.6
Pound sterling	..	..	3.1	3.0	3.8	3.2	2.7	3.8	2.6	2.5
Swiss franc	..	..	10.0	8.5	9.2	8.1	5.2	5.3	0.0	0.0
U.S.dollars	..	..	35.2	34.1	32.2	30.9	35.9	35.8	47.0	45.9
Multiple currency	..	..	0.0	0.0	0.1	0.9	1.7	2.6	4.6	5.0
Special drawing rights	..	..	0.0	0.0	0.0	0.0	0.0	0.0	0.0	0.0
All other currencies	..	..	20.2	18.9	17.5	18.5	18.4	17.8	19.0	19.6

POLAND

(US$ million, unless otherwise indicated)

	1970	1980	1988	1989	1990	1991	1992	1993	1994	1995
7. DEBT RESTRUCTURINGS										
Total amount rescheduled	0	0	370	10,902	3,559	8,975	28,236	8,076	7,723	0
Debt stock rescheduled	0	0	0	6,821	0	29	22,488	2,259	3,307	0
Principal rescheduled	0	0	354	2,266	1,391	4,329	3,270	3,772	325	0
Official	0	0	10	989	746	3,923	2,709	3,419	0	0
Private	0	0	344	1,277	645	406	562	353	325	0
Interest rescheduled	0	0	10	1,815	2,168	4,617	2,477	2,045	1,838	0
Official	0	0	10	1,660	1,998	4,517	1,843	1,948	0	0
Private	0	0	0	155	170	100	635	98	1,838	0
Debt forgiven	..	..	0	0	233	7	1,001	653	3,791	0
Memo: interest forgiven	..	..	0	0	61	0	0	0	0	0
Debt stock reduction	0	0	0	0	284	0	1,092	1,674	4,809	0
of which debt buyback	0	0	0	0	0	0	0	0	956	0
8. DEBT STOCK-FLOW RECONCILIATION										
Total change in debt stocks	..	..	..	993	6,270	4,054	-4,926	-3,318	-2,623	-262
Net flows on debt	..	..	..	-531	423	893	183	-27	96	-1,637
Net change in interest arrears	..	..	..	230	986	-2,098	-2,937	-1,767	-1,375	-3
Interest capitalized	..	..	..	1,815	2,168	4,617	2,477	2,045	1,838	0
Debt forgiveness or reduction	..	..	..	0	-517	-7	-2,093	-2,327	-7,643	0
Cross-currency valuation	..	..	..	-201	3,386	-305	-1,780	-1,149	1,845	1,471
Residual	..	..	..	-321	-176	955	-776	-94	2,616	-94
9. AVERAGE TERMS OF NEW COMMITMENTS										
ALL CREDITORS										
Interest (%)	..	..	6.6	9.3	8.0	8.0	7.0	7.3	6.8	7.8
Maturity (years)	..	..	7.1	6.1	14.3	13.4	13.9	15.6	14.1	2.9
Grace period (years)	..	..	3.2	2.6	4.9	4.3	3.6	4.6	6.3	2.8
Grant element (%)	..	..	11.0	2.0	10.7	10.2	14.2	14.7	17.8	5.0
Official creditors										
Interest (%)	..	..	6.7	7.2	7.8	7.6	7.4	7.4	6.9	0.0
Maturity (years)	..	..	5.4	6.1	16.8	16.7	16.9	16.3	14.8	0.0
Grace period (years)	..	..	2.4	2.5	5.4	5.3	4.3	4.8	5.1	0.0
Grant element (%)	..	..	5.6	9.8	13.1	14.2	15.2	15.1	17.0	0.0
Private creditors										
Interest (%)	..	..	6.6	9.3	8.5	8.8	6.3	6.7	6.7	7.8
Maturity (years)	..	..	7.3	6.1	7.3	6.3	7.5	6.8	13.1	2.9
Grace period (years)	..	..	3.2	2.6	3.6	2.0	1.9	2.5	8.3	2.8
Grant element (%)	..	..	11.5	1.9	3.9	1.4	12.1	10.3	19.1	5.0
Memorandum items										
Commitments	..	..	1,114	300	1,518	1,721	610	1,201	462	558
Official creditors	..	..	106	5	1,111	1,181	414	1,109	289	0
Private creditors	..	..	1,008	296	407	540	196	92	173	558

10. CONTRACTUAL OBLIGATIONS ON OUTSTANDING LONG-TERM DEBT

	1996	1997	1998	1999	2000	2001	2002	2003	2004	2005
TOTAL										
Disbursements	615	379	228	149	111	71	54	34	9	2
Principal	1,221	948	1,000	1,080	1,559	1,734	2,224	2,632	3,132	3,744
Interest	1,941	1,924	1,902	1,902	1,882	1,811	1,732	1,652	1,526	1,367
Official creditors										
Disbursements	585	379	228	149	111	71	54	34	9	2
Principal	550	743	808	965	1,145	1,503	1,969	2,464	2,921	3,516
Interest	1,480	1,483	1,469	1,442	1,404	1,353	1,280	1,183	1,062	914
Bilateral creditors										
Disbursements	30	31	17	7	3	1	0	0	0	0
Principal	407	538	566	685	854	1,204	1,671	2,165	2,622	3,217
Interest	1,301	1,289	1,274	1,254	1,228	1,192	1,137	1,059	957	831
Multilateral creditors										
Disbursements	555	349	212	142	108	70	54	34	9	2
Principal	143	205	243	280	291	299	299	299	299	299
Interest	179	194	196	188	176	160	143	124	104	83
Private creditors										
Disbursements	30	0	0	0	0	0	0	0	0	0
Principal	671	205	192	115	414	232	254	168	211	228
Interest	461	441	433	460	478	458	452	469	464	453
Commercial banks										
Disbursements	5	0	0	0	0	0	0	0	0	0
Principal	382	39	34	31	23	21	16	10	0	0
Interest	30	14	11	8	5	4	2	0	0	0
Other private										
Disbursements	25	0	0	0	0	0	0	0	0	0
Principal	289	166	158	83	391	210	238	158	211	228
Interest	431	836	422	452	472	455	450	469	464	453

ROMANIA

(US$ million, unless otherwise indicated)

	1970	1980	1988	1989	1990	1991	1992	1993	1994	1995
1. SUMMARY DEBT DATA										
TOTAL DEBT STOCKS (EDT)	..	**9,762**	**2,960**	**1,087**	**1,140**	**2,131**	**3,240**	**4,239**	**5,528**	**6,653**
Long-term debt (LDOD)	..	**7,131**	**2,117**	**199**	**230**	**334**	**1,447**	**2,316**	**3,238**	**4,312**
Public and publicly guaranteed	..	7,131	2,117	199	223	218	1,287	2,070	2,920	3,896
Private nonguaranteed	0	0	0	0	7	116	160	246	318	416
Use of IMF credit	**0**	**328**	**144**	**0**	**0**	**809**	**1,033**	**1,031**	**1,323**	**1,038**
Short-term debt	..	**2,303**	**700**	**888**	**910**	**988**	**761**	**892**	**966**	**1,303**
of which interest arrears on LDOD	..	0	0	0	0	0	0	0	0	0
Official creditors	..	0	0	0	0	0	0	0	0	0
Private creditors	..	0	0	0	0	0	0	0	0	0
Memo: principal arrears on LDOD	..	0	0	0	0	0	0	0	0	0
Official creditors	..	0	0	0	0	0	0	0	0	0
Private creditors	..	0	0	0	0	0	0	0	0	0
Memo: export credits	..	..	655	182	188	695	616	1,149	1,539	1,804
TOTAL DEBT FLOWS										
Disbursements	..	**2,955**	**52**	**26**	**27**	**902**	**1,706**	**1,048**	**1,344**	**1,325**
Long-term debt	..	2,797	52	26	27	128	1,229	1,048	993	1,268
IMF purchases	0	158	0	0	0	774	477	0	351	57
Principal repayments	..	**928**	**3,777**	**1,783**	**4**	**13**	**300**	**148**	**387**	**675**
Long-term debt	..	824	3,440	1,646	4	13	84	148	259	303
IMF repurchases	0	104	337	137	0	0	216	0	128	373
Net flows on debt	..	**2,027**	**-3,755**	**-1,569**	**45**	**967**	**1,179**	**1,031**	**1,031**	**986**
of which short-term debt	..	..	-30	188	22	78	-227	131	74	337
Interest payments (INT)	..	**601**	**363**	**158**	**14**	**107**	**162**	**205**	**232**	**292**
Long-term debt	..	332	322	84	0	2	42	123	129	176
IMF charges	0	20	32	2	0	29	62	61	63	69
Short-term debt	..	249	9	72	14	75	57	21	40	47
Net transfers on debt	..	**1,426**	**-4,118**	**-1,727**	**30**	**860**	**1,018**	**826**	**799**	**695**
Total debt service paid (TDS)	..	**1,529**	**4,140**	**1,941**	**18**	**120**	**462**	**353**	**619**	**967**
Long-term debt	..	1,156	3,762	1,730	4	16	126	271	388	479
IMF repurchases and charges	0	124	369	139	0	29	279	61	191	442
Short-term debt (interest only)	..	249	9	72	14	75	57	21	40	47
2. AGGREGATE NET RESOURCE FLOWS AND NET TRANSFERS (LONG-TERM)										
NET RESOURCE FLOWS	..	**1,973**	**-3,388**	**-1,620**	**26**	**423**	**1,422**	**1,093**	**1,173**	**1,415**
Net flow of long-term debt (ex. IMF)	0	1,973	-3,388	-1,620	23	114	1,146	900	734	965
Foreign direct investment (net)	0	0	0	0	0	40	77	94	341	419
Portfolio equity flows	..	0	0	0	0	0	0	0	1	1
Grants (excluding technical coop.)	0	0	0	0	3	268	199	99	96	30
Memo: technical coop. grants	0	0	0	0	0	46	45	57	42	151
NET TRANSFERS	..	**1,641**	**-3,710**	**-1,704**	**25**	**421**	**1,379**	**966**	**1,037**	**1,239**
Interest on long-term debt	..	332	322	84	0	2	42	123	129	176
Profit remittances on FDI	0	0	0	0	0	0	0	4	6	0
3. MAJOR ECONOMIC AGGREGATES										
Gross national product (GNP)	..	..	40,293	41,513	38,401	28,867	24,994	26,229	29,955	34,180
Exports of goods & services (XGS)	..	12,160	12,415	11,502	6,555	5,050	5,077	5,754	7,315	9,098
of which workers remittances	..	0	0	0	0	0	0	0	4	4
Imports of goods & services (MGS)	..	14,580	8,493	8,988	9,915	6,280	6,648	7,142	8,022	10,799
International reserves (RES)	..	2,511	1,375	2,731	1,374	1,489	1,595	1,921	3,092	2,624
Current account balance	..	-2,420	3,922	2,514	-3,254	-1,012	-1,506	-1,231	-455	-1,342
4. DEBT INDICATORS										
EDT / XGS (%)	..	80.3	23.8	9.4	17.4	42.2	63.8	73.7	75.6	73.1
EDT / GNP (%)	..	..	7.3	2.6	3.0	7.4	13.0	16.2	18.5	19.5
TDS / XGS (%)	..	12.6	33.3	16.9	0.3	2.4	9.1	6.1	8.5	10.6
INT / XGS (%)	..	4.9	2.9	1.4	0.2	2.1	3.2	3.6	3.2	3.2
INT / GNP (%)	..	..	0.9	0.4	0.0	0.4	0.6	0.8	0.8	0.9
RES / EDT (%)	..	25.7	46.4	251.2	120.5	69.9	49.2	45.3	55.9	39.4
RES / MGS (months)	..	2.1	1.9	3.6	1.7	2.8	2.9	3.2	4.6	2.9
Short-term / EDT (%)	..	23.6	23.6	81.7	79.8	46.4	23.5	21.0	17.5	19.6
Concessional / EDT (%)	..	1.8	6.9	18.3	19.2	9.7	7.4	1.8	2.7	6.5
Multilateral / EDT (%)	..	8.3	25.7	0.0	0.0	0.2	24.4	23.2	23.8	25.5

ROMANIA

(US$ million, unless otherwise indicated)

	1970	1980	1988	1989	1990	1991	1992	1993	1994	1995
5. LONG-TERM DEBT										
DEBT OUTSTANDING (LDOD)	..	**7,131**	**2,117**	**199**	**230**	**334**	**1,447**	**2,316**	**3,238**	**4,312**
Public and publicly guaranteed	..	**7,131**	**2,117**	**199**	**223**	**218**	**1,287**	**2,070**	**2,920**	**3,896**
Official creditors	..	2,468	1,427	199	218	210	1,187	1,580	2,213	2,995
Multilateral	..	807	762	0	0	3	789	982	1,315	1,695
Concessional	..	0	0	0	0	0	0	7	7	7
Bilateral	..	1,661	666	199	218	206	398	598	898	1,300
Concessional	..	174	205	199	218	206	241	68	142	424
Private creditors	..	4,663	690	0	5	9	100	491	707	901
Bonds	..	0	0	0	0	0	0	0	0	0
Commercial banks	..	4,222	558	0	0	0	0	148	210	314
Other private	..	441	132	0	5	9	100	343	498	587
Private nonguaranteed	**0**	**0**	**0**	**0**	**7**	**116**	**160**	**246**	**318**	**416**
Bonds	..	0	0	0	0	0	0	0	0	0
Commercial banks	..	0	0	0	7	116	160	246	318	416
Memo:										
IBRD	0	807	762	0	0	3	210	403	695	844
IDA	0	0	0	0	0	0	0	0	0	0
DISBURSEMENTS	..	**2,797**	**52**	**26**	**27**	**128**	**1,229**	**1,048**	**993**	**1,268**
Public and publicly guaranteed	..	**2,797**	**52**	**26**	**24**	**19**	**1,160**	**883**	**921**	**1,085**
Official creditors	..	954	52	26	19	3	1,054	792	678	831
Multilateral	..	239	0	0	0	3	826	770	338	328
Concessional	..	0	0	0	0	0	0	7	0	0
Bilateral	..	715	52	26	19	0	227	22	340	503
Concessional	..	0	0	0	19	0	66	0	65	286
Private creditors	..	1,843	0	0	5	15	107	91	243	254
Bonds	..	0	0	0	0	0	0	0	0	0
Commercial banks	..	1,402	0	0	0	0	0	4	64	117
Other private	..	441	0	0	5	15	107	87	179	137
Private nonguaranteed	**0**	**0**	**0**	**0**	**3**	**109**	**69**	**165**	**72**	**183**
Bonds	..	0	0	0	0	0	0	0	0	0
Commercial banks	..	0	0	0	3	109	69	165	72	183
Memo:										
IBRD	0	239	0	0	0	3	211	189	263	129
IDA	0	0	0	0	0	0	0	0	0	0
PRINCIPAL REPAYMENTS	..	**824**	**3,440**	**1,646**	**4**	**13**	**84**	**148**	**259**	**303**
Public and publicly guaranteed	..	**824**	**3,440**	**1,646**	**0**	**13**	**59**	**69**	**259**	**217**
Official creditors	..	341	1,554	1,215	0	0	48	46	213	133
Multilateral	..	22	1,066	727	0	0	0	6	148	14
Concessional	..	0	0	0	0	0	0	0	0	0
Bilateral	..	319	488	487	0	0	48	40	65	118
Concessional	..	0	0	0	0	0	48	40	1	0
Private creditors	..	483	1,886	432	0	13	11	23	46	85
Bonds	..	0	0	0	0	0	0	0	0	0
Commercial banks	..	483	1,333	300	0	0	0	0	7	19
Other private	..	0	554	132	0	13	11	23	39	65
Private nonguaranteed	**0**	**0**	**0**	**0**	**4**	**0**	**25**	**79**	**0**	**86**
Bonds	..	0	0	0	0	0	0	0	0	0
Commercial banks	..	0	0	0	4	0	25	79	0	86
Memo:										
IBRD	0	22	1,066	727	0	0	0	0	0	0
IDA	0	0	0	0	0	0	0	0	0	0
NET FLOWS ON DEBT	..	**1,973**	**-3,388**	**-1,620**	**23**	**114**	**1,146**	**900**	**734**	**965**
Public and publicly guaranteed	..	**1,973**	**-3,388**	**-1,620**	**24**	**5**	**1,102**	**814**	**662**	**868**
Official creditors	..	613	-1,502	-1,189	19	3	1,006	746	466	698
Multilateral	..	217	-1,066	-727	0	3	826	764	191	313
Concessional	..	0	0	0	0	0	0	7	0	0
Bilateral	..	396	-436	-461	19	0	179	-18	275	385
Concessional	..	0	0	0	19	0	18	-40	65	286
Private creditors	..	1,360	-1,886	-432	5	2	96	68	196	169
Bonds	..	0	0	0	0	0	0	0	0	0
Commercial banks	..	919	-1,333	-300	0	0	0	4	57	97
Other private	..	441	-554	-132	5	2	96	64	140	72
Private nonguaranteed	**0**	**0**	**0**	**0**	**-1**	**109**	**44**	**86**	**72**	**98**
Bonds	..	0	0	0	0	0	0	0	0	0
Commercial banks	..	0	0	0	-1	109	44	86	72	98
Memo:										
IBRD	0	217	-1,066	-727	0	3	211	189	263	129
IDA	0	0	0	0	0	0	0	0	0	0

ROMANIA

(US$ million, unless otherwise indicated)

	1970	1980	1988	1989	1990	1991	1992	1993	1994	1995
INTEREST PAYMENTS (LINT)	..	**332**	**322**	**84**	**0**	**2**	**42**	**123**	**129**	**176**
Public and publicly guaranteed	..	**332**	**322**	**84**	**0**	**2**	**34**	**115**	**129**	**176**
Official creditors	..	118	213	64	0	0	31	104	100	124
Multilateral	..	59	139	29	0	0	25	87	68	70
Concessional	..	0	0	0	0	0	0	0	1	0
Bilateral	..	59	74	36	0	0	6	17	33	54
Concessional	..	0	0	0	0	0	2	3	4	7
Private creditors	..	214	109	20	0	2	3	12	29	52
Bonds	..	0	0	0	0	0	0	0	0	0
Commercial banks	..	173	86	8	0	0	0	0	8	9
Other private	..	42	23	11	0	2	3	11	21	43
Private nonguaranteed	**0**	**0**	**0**	**0**	**0**	**0**	**8**	**8**	**0**	**0**
Bonds	..	0	0	0	0	0	0	0	0	0
Commercial banks	..	0	0	0	0	0	8	8	0	0
Memo:										
IBRD	0	59	139	29	0	0	2	19	32	53
IDA	0	0	0	0	0	0	0	0	0	0
NET TRANSFERS ON DEBT	..	**1,641**	**-3,710**	**-1,704**	**22**	**112**	**1,103**	**777**	**605**	**789**
Public and publicly guaranteed	..	**1,641**	**-3,710**	**-1,704**	**24**	**4**	**1,067**	**699**	**533**	**692**
Official creditors	..	495	-1,715	-1,253	19	3	974	643	366	575
Multilateral	..	158	-1,205	-756	0	3	801	678	123	243
Concessional	..	0	0	0	0	0	0	7	0	0
Bilateral	..	337	-510	-497	19	0	173	-35	243	331
Concessional	..	0	0	0	19	0	16	-44	61	279
Private creditors	..	1,146	-1,995	-451	5	1	93	56	168	117
Bonds	..	0	0	0	0	0	0	0	0	0
Commercial banks	..	747	-1,418	-308	0	0	0	4	49	88
Other private	..	399	-577	-143	5	1	93	52	118	29
Private nonguaranteed	**0**	**0**	**0**	**0**	**-1**	**109**	**36**	**78**	**72**	**97**
Bonds	..	0	0	0	0	0	0	0	0	0
Commercial banks	..	0	0	0	-1	109	36	78	72	97
Memo:										
IBRD	0	158	-1,205	-756	0	3	209	169	230	76
IDA	0	0	0	0	0	0	0	0	0	0
DEBT SERVICE (LTDS)	..	**1,156**	**3,762**	**1,730**	**4**	**16**	**126**	**271**	**388**	**479**
Public and publicly guaranteed	..	**1,156**	**3,762**	**1,730**	**0**	**15**	**93**	**184**	**388**	**393**
Official creditors	..	459	1,767	1,279	0	0	79	149	313	256
Multilateral	..	81	1,205	756	0	0	25	92	216	85
Concessional	..	0	0	0	0	0	0	0	1	0
Bilateral	..	378	562	523	0	0	54	57	97	172
Concessional	..	0	0	0	0	0	51	44	4	8
Private creditors	..	698	1,995	451	0	15	14	35	75	137
Bonds	..	0	0	0	0	0	0	0	0	0
Commercial banks	..	656	1,418	308	0	0	0	0	15	29
Other private	..	42	577	143	0	15	14	35	61	108
Private nonguaranteed	**0**	**0**	**0**	**0**	**4**	**1**	**33**	**87**	**0**	**86**
Bonds	..	0	0	0	0	0	0	0	0	0
Commercial banks	..	0	0	0	4	1	33	87	0	86
Memo:										
IBRD	0	81	1,205	756	0	0	2	19	32	53
IDA	0	0	0	0	0	0	0	0	0	0
UNDISBURSED DEBT	..	**1,865**	**136**	**0**	**113**	**1,673**	**3,599**	**1,889**	**1,950**	**2,328**
Official creditors	..	1,347	136	0	0	1,223	2,299	1,463	1,489	1,870
Private creditors	..	518	0	0	113	451	1,300	426	462	458
Memorandum items										
Concessional LDOD	..	174	205	199	218	206	241	76	149	432
Variable rate LDOD	..	4,222	561	0	7	121	1,084	912	1,417	1,758
Public sector LDOD	..	7,131	2,117	199	223	218	1,287	2,070	2,920	3,896
Private sector LDOD	..	0	0	0	7	116	160	246	318	416

6. CURRENCY COMPOSITION OF LONG-TERM DEBT (PERCENT)

	1970	1980	1988	1989	1990	1991	1992	1993	1994	1995
Deutsche mark	..	2.1	0.0	0.0	0.0	0.0	0.0	3.6	4.3	11.0
French franc	..	0.0	0.0	0.0	0.8	3.0	3.1	4.0	5.0	5.0
Japanese yen	..	0.0	0.0	0.0	0.0	0.0	0.0	3.0	3.7	2.8
Pound sterling	..	0.0	0.0	0.0	0.0	0.0	0.0	0.0	0.0	0.0
Swiss franc	..	2.6	9.7	100.0	89.5	85.9	12.1	5.9	4.0	1.8
U.S.dollars	..	83.8	32.3	0.0	9.8	9.6	15.6	35.4	36.4	35.2
Multiple currency	..	11.5	58.0	0.0	0.0	1.5	19.5	19.5	23.8	21.7
Special drawing rights	..	0.0	0.0	0.0	0.0	0.0	0.0	0.0	0.0	0.0
All other currencies	..	0.0	0.0	0.0	0.0	0.0	49.7	28.6	22.7	22.6

ROMANIA

(US$ million, unless otherwise indicated)

	1970	1980	1988	1989	1990	1991	1992	1993	1994	1995
7. DEBT RESTRUCTURINGS										
Total amount rescheduled	0	0	0	0	0	0	0	0	0	0
Debt stock rescheduled	0	0	0	0	0	0	0	0	0	0
Principal rescheduled	0	0	0	0	0	0	0	0	0	0
Official	0	0	0	0	0	0	0	0	0	0
Private	0	0	0	0	0	0	0	0	0	0
Interest rescheduled	0	0	0	0	0	0	0	0	0	0
Official	0	0	0	0	0	0	0	0	0	0
Private	0	0	0	0	0	0	0	0	0	0
Debt forgiven	..	..	0	0	0	0	0	0	0	0
Memo: interest forgiven	..	..	0	0	0	0	0	0	0	0
Debt stock reduction	0	0	0	0	0	0	0	0	0	0
of which debt buyback	0	0	0	0	0	0	0	0	0	0
8. DEBT STOCK-FLOW RECONCILIATION										
Total change in debt stocks	..	..	..	-1,874	53	992	1,109	999	1,288	1,125
Net flows on debt	..	..	..	-1,569	45	967	1,179	1,031	1,031	986
Net change in interest arrears	..	..	..	0	0	0	0	0	0	0
Interest capitalized	..	..	..	0	0	0	0	0	0	0
Debt forgiveness or reduction	..	..	..	0	0	0	0	0	0	0
Cross-currency valuation	..	..	..	-212	40	-13	-91	-55	161	150
Residual	..	..	..	-92	-32	38	21	24	97	-11
9. AVERAGE TERMS OF NEW COMMITMENTS										
ALL CREDITORS										
Interest (%)	..	14.1	0.0	0.0	7.6	7.6	7.2	6.1	6.6	6.2
Maturity (years)	..	8.5	0.0	0.0	10.7	9.7	13.0	12.5	12.2	11.9
Grace period (years)	..	3.5	0.0	0.0	4.5	4.4	4.4	3.9	3.8	3.9
Grant element (%)	..	-16.0	0.0	0.0	13.2	9.2	13.7	20.1	14.6	18.0
Official creditors										
Interest (%)	..	8.0	0.0	0.0	2.7	7.3	6.6	5.8	6.3	6.0
Maturity (years)	..	14.9	0.0	0.0	25.5	9.0	14.1	14.6	13.4	13.2
Grace period (years)	..	3.4	0.0	0.0	10.0	4.4	4.9	4.7	4.4	4.3
Grant element (%)	..	10.0	0.0	0.0	57.3	10.8	17.8	24.2	16.2	20.0
Private creditors										
Interest (%)	..	15.0	0.0	0.0	8.4	9.0	8.6	6.6	7.2	7.0
Maturity (years)	..	7.5	0.0	0.0	8.2	11.9	10.7	8.9	9.3	6.0
Grace period (years)	..	3.6	0.0	0.0	3.6	4.4	3.2	2.5	2.1	2.1
Grant element (%)	..	-19.8	0.0	0.0	5.8	3.6	5.2	13.1	10.7	8.6
Memorandum items										
Commitments	..	1,886	0	0	132	1,507	3,103	689	974	1,417
Official creditors	..	240	0	0	19	1,167	2,100	437	694	1,171
Private creditors	..	1,646	0	0	113	340	1,003	253	280	246

10. CONTRACTUAL OBLIGATIONS ON OUTSTANDING LONG-TERM DEBT

	1996	1997	1998	1999	2000	2001	2002	2003	2004	2005
TOTAL										
Disbursements	656	615	407	248	162	111	64	37	22	6
Principal	419	567	867	766	685	580	593	442	407	296
Interest	326	337	317	282	233	198	167	131	104	79
Official creditors										
Disbursements	419	475	347	232	158	111	64	37	22	6
Principal	206	260	633	520	471	362	442	362	343	267
Interest	242	253	247	222	186	165	146	118	96	76
Bilateral creditors										
Disbursements	153	94	49	11	4	2	0	0	0	0
Principal	171	176	248	193	150	129	136	128	121	56
Interest	78	72	65	56	46	37	29	21	13	7
Multilateral creditors										
Disbursements	266	381	299	221	153	109	64	37	22	6
Principal	35	84	385	326	322	233	306	233	222	211
Interest	164	182	182	167	140	128	117	97	83	69
Private creditors										
Disbursements	237	140	59	16	5	0	0	0	0	0
Principal	213	307	234	246	214	218	152	80	64	29
Interest	84	84	70	60	47	33	21	13	7	3
Commercial banks										
Disbursements	95	50	18	6	0	0	0	0	0	0
Principal	38	129	60	59	54	50	43	22	18	8
Interest	21	25	19	17	13	9	6	3	2	1
Other private										
Disbursements	142	91	42	11	5	0	0	0	0	0
Principal	175	178	174	188	160	168	109	58	46	22
Interest	63	59	51	43	34	24	15	10	6	2

RUSSIAN FEDERATION

(US$ million, unless otherwise indicated)

1. SUMMARY DEBT DATA

	1970	1980	1988	1989	1990	1991	1992	1993	1994	1995
TOTAL DEBT STOCKS (EDT)	..	..	**42,188**	**53,942**	**59,817**	**67,590**	**78,992**	**112,940**	**121,921**	**120,461**
Long-term debt (LDOD)	..	..	**30,988**	**35,742**	**48,017**	**54,973**	**64,891**	**102,158**	**107,748**	**100,279**
Public and publicly guaranteed	..	..	30,988	35,742	48,017	54,973	64,891	102,158	107,748	100,279
Private nonguaranteed	0	0	0	0	0	0	0	0	0	0
Use of IMF credit	**0**	**0**	**0**	**0**	**0**	**0**	**989**	**2,469**	**4,198**	**9,617**
Short-term debt	..	..	**11,200**	**18,200**	**11,800**	**12,618**	**13,112**	**8,314**	**9,976**	**10,564**
of which interest arrears on LDOD	..	..	0	500	4,500	4,818	4,412	2,914	5,276	6,214
Official creditors	..	..	0	0	0	0	518	703	1,203	1,704
Private creditors	..	..	0	500	4,500	4,818	3,895	2,211	4,072	4,510
Memo: principal arrears on LDOD	..	..	0	0	0	158	6,615	7,093	14,181	23,762
Official creditors	..	..	0	0	0	8	334	455	1,109	4,726
Private creditors	..	..	0	0	0	149	6,281	6,638	13,073	19,036
Memo: export credits	..	..	11,440	12,060	15,056	22,218	24,184	17,976	36,331	43,997
TOTAL DEBT FLOWS										
Disbursements	..	..	**8,583**	**10,071**	**16,978**	**13,393**	**13,612**	**6,492**	**3,872**	**7,784**
Long-term debt	..	..	8,583	10,071	16,978	13,393	12,600	4,986	2,328	2,331
IMF purchases	0	0	0	0	0	0	1,013	1,506	1,544	5,453
Principal repayments	..	..	**5,412**	**5,501**	**7,942**	**9,392**	**948**	**1,558**	**2,283**	**3,275**
Long-term debt	..	..	5,412	5,501	7,942	9,392	948	1,558	2,283	3,275
IMF repurchases	0	0	0	0	0	0	0	0	0	0
Net flows on debt	..	..	**5,771**	**11,069**	**-1,363**	**4,501**	**13,565**	**4,334**	**1,089**	**4,619**
of which short-term debt	..	..	2,600	6,500	-10,400	500	900	-600	-500	110
Interest payments (INT)	..	..	**2,846**	**3,605**	**3,884**	**4,103**	**357**	**775**	**1,392**	**3,028**
Long-term debt	..	..	1,995	2,104	2,642	3,044	357	683	1,217	2,733
IMF charges	0	0	0	0	0	0	0	78	175	294
Short-term debt	..	..	850	1,501	1,242	1,058	0	14	0	0
Net transfers on debt	..	..	**2,926**	**7,465**	**-5,247**	**398**	**13,207**	**3,558**	**-303**	**1,591**
Total debt service paid (TDS)	..	..	**8,257**	**9,106**	**11,826**	**13,495**	**1,305**	**2,333**	**3,674**	**6,303**
Long-term debt	..	..	7,407	7,605	10,584	12,437	1,305	2,241	3,499	6,009
IMF repurchases and charges	0	0	0	0	0	0	0	78	175	294
Short-term debt (interest only)	..	..	850	1,501	1,242	1,058	0	14	0	0

2. AGGREGATE NET RESOURCE FLOWS AND NET TRANSFERS (LONG-TERM)

	1970	1980	1988	1989	1990	1991	1992	1993	1994	1995
NET RESOURCE FLOWS	..	..	**3,171**	**4,569**	**9,637**	**6,582**	**15,219**	**6,625**	**2,259**	**2,121**
Net flow of long-term debt (ex. IMF)	..	..	3,171	4,569	9,037	4,001	11,652	3,428	45	-944
Foreign direct investment (net)	..	..	0	0	0	0	700	700	637	2,017
Portfolio equity flows	..	..	0	0	0	0	0	0	271	141
Grants (excluding technical coop.)	..	..	0	0	600	2,581	2,867	2,497	1,306	908
Memo: technical coop. grants	..	..	0	0	0	19	133	303	242	527
NET TRANSFERS	..	..	**1,176**	**2,466**	**6,995**	**3,537**	**14,862**	**5,942**	**1,042**	**-612**
Interest on long-term debt	..	..	1,995	2,104	2,642	3,044	357	683	1,217	2,733
Profit remittances on FDI	..	..	0	0	0	0	0	0	0	0

3. MAJOR ECONOMIC AGGREGATES

	1970	1980	1988	1989	1990	1991	1992	1993	1994	1995
Gross national product (GNP)	..	..	556,478	600,042	577,888	540,623	424,705	383,491	323,543	320,297
Exports of goods & services (XGS)	..	..	..	..	81,000	54,300	54,783	65,785	77,800	95,100
of which workers remittances	..	..	..	..	0	0	0	0	0	0
Imports of goods & services (MGS)	..	..	..	..	76,900	49,600	54,315	63,110	67,600	85,800
International reserves (RES)	..	..	..	..	..	..	..	9,818	7,206	18,024
Current account balance	..	..	..	..	4,100	4,700	468	2,675	10,105	9,604

4. DEBT INDICATORS

	1970	1980	1988	1989	1990	1991	1992	1993	1994	1995
EDT / XGS (%)	..	..	..	..	73.8	124.5	144.2	171.7	156.7	126.7
EDT / GNP (%)	..	..	7.6	9.0	10.4	12.5	18.6	29.5	37.7	37.6
TDS / XGS (%)	..	..	..	..	14.6	24.9	2.4	3.5	4.7	6.6
INT / XGS (%)	..	..	..	..	4.8	7.6	0.7	1.2	1.8	3.2
INT / GNP (%)	..	..	0.5	0.6	0.7	0.8	0.1	0.2	0.4	0.9
RES / EDT (%)	..	..	..	..	..	..	..	8.7	5.9	15.0
RES / MGS (months)	..	..	..	..	..	..	..	1.9	1.3	2.5
Short-term / EDT (%)	..	..	26.5	33.7	19.7	18.7	16.6	7.4	8.2	8.8
Concessional / EDT (%)	..	..	0.0	0.0	0.0	1.0	1.9	30.3	27.1	18.4
Multilateral / EDT (%)	..	..	0.4	0.4	0.7	0.6	0.7	1.2	1.3	1.7

RUSSIAN FEDERATION

(US$ million, unless otherwise indicated)

	1970	1980	1988	1989	1990	1991	1992	1993	1994	1995
5. LONG-TERM DEBT										
DEBT OUTSTANDING (LDOD)	..	..	**30,988**	**35,742**	**48,017**	**54,973**	**64,891**	**102,158**	**107,748**	**100,279**
Public and publicly guaranteed	..	..	**30,988**	**35,742**	**48,017**	**54,973**	**64,891**	**102,158**	**107,748**	**100,279**
Official creditors	..	..	2,123	2,443	6,305	9,954	11,547	55,149	62,782	56,765
Multilateral	..	..	188	214	439	413	538	1,373	1,600	2,069
Concessional	..	..	0	0	0	0	180	213	227	165
Bilateral	..	..	1,935	2,229	5,866	9,541	11,009	53,776	61,183	54,696
Concessional	..	..	0	0	0	660	1,315	33,985	32,852	21,953
Private creditors	..	..	28,865	33,299	41,712	45,018	53,344	47,009	44,966	43,514
Bonds	..	..	347	1,370	1,891	1,863	1,740	1,626	1,776	1,115
Commercial banks	..	..	15,329	17,950	18,590	16,952	17,786	15,076	15,406	15,882
Other private	..	..	13,189	13,980	21,231	26,204	33,818	30,307	27,785	26,517
Private nonguaranteed	**0**	**0**	**0**	**0**	**0**	**0**	**0**	**0**	**0**	**0**
Bonds	..	..	0	0	0	0	0	0	0	0
Commercial banks	..	..	0	0	0	0	0	0	0	0
Memo:										
IBRD	0	0	0	0	0	0	0	367	684	1,524
IDA	0	0	0	0	0	0	0	0	0	0
DISBURSEMENTS	..	..	**8,583**	**10,071**	**16,978**	**13,393**	**12,600**	**4,986**	**2,328**	**2,331**
Public and publicly guaranteed	..	..	**8,583**	**10,071**	**16,978**	**13,393**	**12,600**	**4,986**	**2,328**	**2,331**
Official creditors	..	..	640	422	3,652	3,966	1,997	1,204	926	983
Multilateral	..	..	94	21	201	3	181	1,006	392	856
Concessional	..	..	0	0	0	0	180	180	161	105
Bilateral	..	..	546	401	3,451	3,963	1,816	198	534	127
Concessional	..	..	0	0	0	605	296	0	158	22
Private creditors	..	..	7,943	9,649	13,326	9,428	10,603	3,782	1,402	1,348
Bonds	..	..	354	914	310	0	0	0	0	0
Commercial banks	..	..	4,827	3,920	506	580	1,601	102	0	0
Other private	..	..	2,763	4,815	12,509	8,847	9,002	3,680	1,402	1,348
Private nonguaranteed	**0**	**0**	**0**	**0**	**0**	**0**	**0**	**0**	**0**	**0**
Bonds	..	..	0	0	0	0	0	0	0	0
Commercial banks	..	..	0	0	0	0	0	0	0	0
Memo:										
IBRD	0	0	0	0	0	0	1	371	283	824
IDA	0	0	0	0	0	0	0	0	0	0
PRINCIPAL REPAYMENTS	..	..	**5,412**	**5,501**	**7,942**	**9,392**	**948**	**1,558**	**2,283**	**3,275**
Public and publicly guaranteed	..	..	**5,412**	**5,501**	**7,942**	**9,392**	**948**	**1,558**	**2,283**	**3,275**
Official creditors	..	..	84	148	220	189	153	166	267	885
Multilateral	..	..	0	0	7	21	33	147	222	427
Concessional	..	..	0	0	0	0	0	147	147	166
Bilateral	..	..	84	148	213	168	120	19	45	458
Concessional	..	..	0	0	0	0	0	0	0	0
Private creditors	..	..	5,327	5,353	7,722	9,204	795	1,392	2,015	2,391
Bonds	..	..	0	0	0	0	0	0	34	810
Commercial banks	..	..	2,802	3,497	4,182	3,623	234	490	70	0
Other private	..	..	2,525	1,857	3,540	5,581	561	902	1,911	1,581
Private nonguaranteed	**0**	**0**	**0**	**0**	**0**	**0**	**0**	**0**	**0**	**0**
Bonds	..	..	0	0	0	0	0	0	0	0
Commercial banks	..	..	0	0	0	0	0	0	0	0
Memo:										
IBRD	0	0	0	0	0	0	0	0	0	0
IDA	0	0	0	0	0	0	0	0	0	0
NET FLOWS ON DEBT	..	..	**3,171**	**4,569**	**9,037**	**4,001**	**11,652**	**3,428**	**45**	**-944**
Public and publicly guaranteed	..	..	**3,171**	**4,569**	**9,037**	**4,001**	**11,652**	**3,428**	**45**	**-944**
Official creditors	..	..	556	274	3,433	3,777	1,844	1,038	658	98
Multilateral	..	..	94	21	194	-18	148	858	169	429
Concessional	..	..	0	0	0	0	180	33	14	-61
Bilateral	..	..	462	253	3,239	3,795	1,695	180	489	-331
Concessional	..	..	0	0	0	605	296	0	158	22
Private creditors	..	..	2,616	4,295	5,604	224	9,809	2,390	-613	-1,043
Bonds	..	..	354	914	310	0	0	0	-34	-810
Commercial banks	..	..	2,024	423	-3,676	-3,042	1,367	-388	-70	0
Other private	..	..	238	2,958	8,969	3,266	8,441	2,778	-509	-232
Private nonguaranteed	**0**	**0**	**0**	**0**	**0**	**0**	**0**	**0**	**0**	**0**
Bonds	..	..	0	0	0	0	0	0	0	0
Commercial banks	..	..	0	0	0	0	0	0	0	0
Memo:										
IBRD	0	0	0	0	0	0	1	371	283	824
IDA	0	0	0	0	0	0	0	0	0	0

RUSSIAN FEDERATION

(US$ million, unless otherwise indicated)

	1970	1980	1988	1989	1990	1991	1992	1993	1994	1995
INTEREST PAYMENTS (LINT)	..	..	**1,995**	**2,104**	**2,642**	**3,044**	**357**	**683**	**1,217**	**2,733**
Public and publicly guaranteed	..	..	**1,995**	**2,104**	**2,642**	**3,044**	**357**	**683**	**1,217**	**2,733**
Official creditors	..	..	76	102	132	309	59	67	501	1,389
Multilateral	..	..	7	14	17	25	7	41	106	135
Concessional	..	..	0	0	0	0	0	5	11	24
Bilateral	..	..	69	88	114	284	52	26	394	1,254
Concessional	..	..	0	0	0	0	9	5	53	198
Private creditors	..	..	1,919	2,002	2,511	2,735	298	616	716	1,344
Bonds	..	..	0	20	96	122	132	118	121	140
Commercial banks	..	..	1,025	1,219	1,478	1,302	136	318	1	597
Other private	..	..	895	763	936	1,311	30	180	594	607
Private nonguaranteed	**0**	**0**	**0**	**0**	**0**	**0**	**0**	**0**	**0**	**0**
Bonds	..	..	0	0	0	0	0	0	0	0
Commercial banks	..	..	0	0	0	0	0	0	0	0
Memo:										
IBRD	0	0	0	0	0	0	0	12	38	57
IDA	0	0	0	0	0	0	0	0	0	0
NET TRANSFERS ON DEBT	..	..	**1,176**	**2,466**	**6,395**	**957**	**11,295**	**2,745**	**-1,172**	**-3,678**
Public and publicly guaranteed	..	..	**1,176**	**2,466**	**6,395**	**957**	**11,295**	**2,745**	**-1,172**	**-3,678**
Official creditors	..	..	480	172	3,301	3,468	1,784	971	158	-1,291
Multilateral	..	..	87	8	177	-43	141	817	63	294
Concessional	..	..	0	0	0	0	180	27	4	-85
Bilateral	..	..	393	165	3,125	3,511	1,643	154	95	-1,585
Concessional	..	..	0	0	0	605	287	-5	105	-176
Private creditors	..	..	697	2,293	3,093	-2,511	9,510	1,774	-1,329	-2,387
Bonds	..	..	354	894	214	-122	-132	-118	-155	-951
Commercial banks	..	..	1,000	-796	-5,154	-4,344	1,231	-705	-71	-597
Other private	..	..	-657	2,195	8,033	1,956	8,411	2,598	-1,104	-839
Private nonguaranteed	**0**	**0**	**0**	**0**	**0**	**0**	**0**	**0**	**0**	**0**
Bonds	..	..	0	0	0	0	0	0	0	0
Commercial banks	..	..	0	0	0	0	0	0	0	0
Memo:										
IBRD	0	0	0	0	0	0	1	360	245	767
IDA	0	0	0	0	0	0	0	0	0	0
DEBT SERVICE (LTDS)	..	..	**7,407**	**7,605**	**10,584**	**12,437**	**1,305**	**2,241**	**3,499**	**6,009**
Public and publicly guaranteed	..	..	**7,407**	**7,605**	**10,584**	**12,437**	**1,305**	**2,241**	**3,499**	**6,009**
Official creditors	..	..	160	250	351	498	212	233	768	2,274
Multilateral	..	..	7	14	24	46	40	188	328	562
Concessional	..	..	0	0	0	0	0	153	158	190
Bilateral	..	..	153	236	327	452	173	45	440	1,712
Concessional	..	..	0	0	0	0	9	5	53	198
Private creditors	..	..	7,247	7,355	10,233	11,939	1,093	2,008	2,731	3,735
Bonds	..	..	0	20	96	122	132	118	155	951
Commercial banks	..	..	3,827	4,716	5,660	4,925	370	807	71	597
Other private	..	..	3,420	2,619	4,477	6,892	592	1,082	2,506	2,188
Private nonguaranteed	**0**	**0**	**0**	**0**	**0**	**0**	**0**	**0**	**0**	**0**
Bonds	..	..	0	0	0	0	0	0	0	0
Commercial banks	..	..	0	0	0	0	0	0	0	0
Memo:										
IBRD	0	0	0	0	0	0	0	12	38	57
IDA	0	0	0	0	0	0	0	0	0	0
UNDISBURSED DEBT	..	..	**114**	**292**	**1,301**	**6,125**	**8,287**	**8,501**	**8,398**	**8,961**
Official creditors	..	..	35	15	62	1,876	2,730	2,807	3,274	3,838
Private creditors	..	..	79	277	1,240	4,250	5,557	5,694	5,124	5,123
Memorandum items										
Concessional LDOD	..	..	0	0	0	660	1,495	34,198	33,079	22,118
Variable rate LDOD	..	..	9,783	11,772	17,749	26,329	36,475	49,137	48,748	49,179
Public sector LDOD	..	..	30,988	35,742	48,017	54,973	64,891	102,158	107,748	100,279
Private sector LDOD	..	..	0	0	0	0	0	0	0	0

6. CURRENCY COMPOSITION OF LONG-TERM DEBT (PERCENT)

	1970	1980	1988	1989	1990	1991	1992	1993	1994	1995
Deutsche mark	..	..	22.0	28.9	34.1	38.9	39.2	24.2	24.0	24.9
French franc	..	..	6.2	5.7	6.1	4.5	4.4	1.6	1.2	1.4
Japanese yen	..	..	3.6	3.8	2.9	2.7	2.4	1.7	1.8	1.9
Pound sterling	..	..	4.6	3.1	2.3	1.8	1.2	1.0	0.8	0.8
Swiss franc	..	..	8.0	7.8	6.4	4.8	3.7	2.2	2.4	2.9
U.S.dollars	..	..	42.8	33.6	33.6	34.5	38.3	62.6	63.6	61.7
Multiple currency	..	..	0.0	0.0	0.0	0.0	0.0	0.4	0.6	1.5
Special drawing rights	..	..	0.0	0.0	0.0	0.0	0.0	0.0	0.0	0.0
All other currencies	..	..	12.7	17.1	14.6	12.9	10.9	6.2	5.5	4.9

RUSSIAN FEDERATION

(US$ million, unless otherwise indicated)

	1970	1980	1988	1989	1990	1991	1992	1993	1994	1995
7. DEBT RESTRUCTURINGS										
Total amount rescheduled	0	0	0	0	0	0	0	14,498	7,799	6,400
Debt stock rescheduled	0	0	0	0	0	0	0	0	0	0
Principal rescheduled	0	0	0	0	0	0	0	9,227	5,312	5,299
Official	0	0	0	0	0	0	0	275	337	2,069
Private	0	0	0	0	0	0	0	8,953	4,975	3,230
Interest rescheduled	0	0	0	0	0	0	0	4,334	2,234	1,101
Official	0	0	0	0	0	0	0	394	754	543
Private	0	0	0	0	0	0	0	3,941	1,479	558
Debt forgiven	..	..	0	0	0	0	0	0	0	0
Memo: interest forgiven	..	..	0	0	0	0	0	0	0	0
Debt stock reduction	0	0	0	0	0	0	0	0	0	0
of which debt buyback	0	0	0	0	0	0	0	0	0	0
8. DEBT STOCK-FLOW RECONCILIATION										
Total change in debt stocks	..	..	..	11,754	5,875	7,773	11,402	33,949	8,981	-1,461
Net flows on debt	..	..	..	11,069	-1,363	4,501	13,565	4,334	1,089	4,619
Net change in interest arrears	..	..	..	500	4,000	318	-405	-1,499	2,362	938
Interest capitalized	..	..	..	0	0	0	0	4,334	2,234	1,101
Debt forgiveness or reduction	..	..	..	0	0	0	0	0	0	0
Cross-currency valuation	..	..	..	455	4,408	-501	-2,685	-2,052	4,345	2,859
Residual	..	..	..	-271	-1,170	3,455	927	28,831	-1,050	-10,978
9. AVERAGE TERMS OF NEW COMMITMENTS										
ALL CREDITORS										
Interest (%)	..	..	8.0	8.4	8.3	7.1	6.0	4.3	6.4	7.2
Maturity (years)	..	..	9.8	7.9	21.1	10.3	7.5	6.8	13.1	13.6
Grace period (years)	..	..	3.9	3.2	6.0	3.4	2.1	2.1	4.3	3.8
Grant element (%)	..	..	7.7	5.8	8.5	10.5	12.5	17.1	16.4	14.0
Official creditors										
Interest (%)	..	..	7.6	7.4	8.4	5.7	5.0	4.6	7.0	7.1
Maturity (years)	..	..	10.2	6.1	11.5	7.6	10.4	13.4	16.0	16.0
Grace period (years)	..	..	3.0	1.5	6.0	3.1	3.7	4.2	5.1	5.1
Grant element (%)	..	..	9.2	7.4	7.8	16.5	20.6	28.3	17.1	16.7
Private creditors										
Interest (%)	..	..	8.0	8.4	8.3	7.8	6.3	4.2	4.7	7.4
Maturity (years)	..	..	9.8	7.9	23.6	11.6	6.8	4.9	5.6	9.9
Grace period (years)	..	..	4.0	3.2	6.1	3.5	1.7	1.5	2.2	1.7
Grant element (%)	..	..	7.5	5.7	8.7	7.6	10.5	13.8	14.7	9.9
Memorandum items										
Commitments	..	..	8,694	10,448	17,932	18,211	14,981	5,752	2,632	3,003
Official creditors	..	..	675	402	3,694	5,988	2,869	1,303	1,890	1,811
Private creditors	..	..	8,019	10,046	14,237	12,223	12,113	4,449	742	1,191

10. CONTRACTUAL OBLIGATIONS ON OUTSTANDING LONG-TERM DEBT

	1996	1997	1998	1999	2000	2001	2002	2003	2004	2005
TOTAL										
Disbursements	4,195	2,066	1,052	485	327	242	174	152	126	86
Principal	17,913	11,747	10,429	8,617	12,717	4,591	4,072	3,309	2,098	1,899
Interest	4,402	3,590	2,873	2,226	1,751	1,394	1,121	901	727	603
Official creditors										
Disbursements	851	785	654	409	306	242	174	152	126	86
Principal	6,668	5,328	5,151	6,297	11,423	3,770	3,720	3,059	1,921	1,727
Interest	2,608	2,407	2,098	1,777	1,448	1,178	956	761	604	492
Bilateral creditors										
Disbursements	221	28	12	0	0	0	0	0	0	0
Principal	6,464	5,114	4,994	6,035	11,039	3,341	3,292	2,632	1,495	1,300
Interest	2,434	2,199	1,858	1,517	1,188	928	723	546	410	321
Multilateral creditors										
Disbursements	630	757	642	409	306	242	174	152	126	86
Principal	204	214	158	262	385	429	428	427	427	427
Interest	174	208	240	259	261	250	233	214	194	171
Private creditors										
Disbursements	3,344	1,281	399	76	21	0	0	0	0	0
Principal	11,245	6,420	5,277	2,320	1,293	821	352	250	177	172
Interest	1,794	1,183	775	449	302	216	165	141	123	111
Commercial banks										
Disbursements	187	24	4	0	0	0	0	0	0	0
Principal	2,341	1,026	503	299	115	69	27	14	0	0
Interest	243	121	60	31	15	7	3	1	0	0
Other private										
Disbursements	3,157	1,257	394	76	21	0	0	0	0	0
Principal	8,905	5,394	4,774	2,021	1,178	752	325	237	177	172
Interest	1,552	1,125	715	419	288	209	163	140	123	111

RWANDA

(US$ million, unless otherwise indicated)

	1970	*1980*	*1988*	*1989*	*1990*	*1991*	*1992*	*1993*	*1994*	*1995*
1. SUMMARY DEBT DATA										
TOTAL DEBT STOCKS (EDT)	..	**190**	**655**	**623**	**711**	**808**	**849**	**890**	**931**	**1,008**
Long-term debt (LDOD)	**2**	**150**	**609**	**578**	**664**	**745**	**782**	**819**	**885**	**949**
Public and publicly guaranteed	2	150	609	578	664	745	782	819	885	949
Private nonguaranteed	0	0	0	0	0	0	0	0	0	0
Use of IMF credit	**3**	**14**	**4**	**1**	**0**	**13**	**12**	**12**	**13**	**26**
Short-term debt	..	**26**	**42**	**44**	**47**	**50**	**55**	**59**	**33**	**33**
of which interest arrears on LDOD	..	0	1	1	2	3	5	9	15	18
Official creditors	..	0	1	1	2	3	5	9	15	18
Private creditors	..	0	0	0	0	0	0	0	0	0
Memo: principal arrears on LDOD	..	0	5	6	8	9	14	24	40	47
Official creditors	..	0	5	6	8	9	14	23	39	45
Private creditors	..	0	0	0	0	0	0	1	2	2
Memo: export credits	..	..	30	27	41	41	34	21	23	30
TOTAL DEBT FLOWS										
Disbursements	**0**	**34**	**85**	**64**	**62**	**101**	**77**	**48**	**20**	**68**
Long-term debt	0	27	85	64	62	89	77	48	20	54
IMF purchases	0	6	0	0	0	12	0	0	0	14
Principal repayments	**1**	**3**	**12**	**17**	**10**	**13**	**12**	**10**	**1**	**11**
Long-term debt	0	3	9	14	10	13	12	10	1	11
IMF repurchases	1	0	3	3	1	0	0	0	0	0
Net flows on debt	**-1**	**31**	**75**	**51**	**54**	**90**	**67**	**38**	**-12**	**53**
of which short-term debt	..	..	2	3	2	2	2	0	-31	-4
Interest payments (INT)	..	**5**	**11**	**12**	**11**	**12**	**13**	**10**	**3**	**9**
Long-term debt	0	2	8	8	6	7	7	4	2	8
IMF charges	0	0	0	0	0	0	0	0	0	0
Short-term debt	..	3	3	5	5	6	6	6	1	1
Net transfers on debt	..	**26**	**64**	**38**	**42**	**78**	**54**	**28**	**-15**	**44**
Total debt service paid (TDS)	..	**8**	**23**	**29**	**22**	**25**	**25**	**20**	**3**	**20**
Long-term debt	0	4	17	21	16	20	18	14	3	19
IMF repurchases and charges	1	0	3	3	1	0	0	0	0	0
Short-term debt (interest only)	..	3	3	5	5	6	6	6	1	1
2. AGGREGATE NET RESOURCE FLOWS AND NET TRANSFERS (LONG-TERM)										
NET RESOURCE FLOWS	**10**	**109**	**197**	**162**	**205**	**250**	**256**	**255**	**617**	**608**
Net flow of long-term debt (ex. IMF)	0	25	76	50	53	76	65	38	19	43
Foreign direct investment (net)	0	16	21	16	8	5	2	3	1	1
Portfolio equity flows	0	0	0	0	0	0	0	0	0	0
Grants (excluding technical coop.)	10	68	101	96	145	169	190	214	597	565
Memo: technical coop. grants	12	55	88	82	92	98	96	90	107	107
NET TRANSFERS	**10**	**98**	**178**	**145**	**193**	**238**	**247**	**247**	**614**	**600**
Interest on long-term debt	0	2	8	8	6	7	7	4	2	8
Profit remittances on FDI	0	9	11	9	6	5	3	4	2	0
3. MAJOR ECONOMIC AGGREGATES										
Gross national product (GNP)	220	1,163	2,394	2,413	2,579	1,902	2,025	1,955	746	1,131
Exports of goods & services (XGS)	..	184	176	158	150	143	118	180	86	153
of which workers remittances	..	1	1	1	1	1	0	3	0	0
Imports of goods & services (MGS)	..	335	444	396	380	357	386	405	475	324
International reserves (RES)	8	187	118	70	44	110	79	48	32	126
Current account balance	..	-48	-145	-123	-108	-34	-154	-207	-348	-156
4. DEBT INDICATORS										
EDT / XGS (%)	..	103.5	372.3	394.4	474.1	566.1	717.1	493.4	1,080.9	657.3
EDT / GNP (%)	..	16.3	27.3	25.8	27.6	42.5	41.9	45.5	124.8	89.1
TDS / XGS (%)	..	4.1	12.9	18.4	14.4	17.7	20.7	11.3	4.0	12.9
INT / XGS (%)	..	2.7	6.3	7.8	7.5	8.6	10.9	5.8	3.0	5.5
INT / GNP (%)	..	0.4	0.5	0.5	0.4	0.6	0.6	0.5	0.3	0.7
RES / EDT (%)	..	98.3	18.1	11.3	6.2	13.6	9.3	5.3	3.4	12.5
RES / MGS (months)	..	6.7	3.2	2.1	1.4	3.7	2.4	1.4	0.8	4.7
Short-term / EDT (%)	..	13.7	6.3	7.1	6.6	6.2	6.4	6.6	3.6	3.3
Concessional / EDT (%)	..	74.4	91.7	91.8	92.6	91.7	91.8	91.7	94.8	93.3
Multilateral / EDT (%)	..	47.8	66.7	76.8	76.2	75.9	76.2	77.1	80.8	80.4

RWANDA

(US$ million, unless otherwise indicated)

	1970	1980	1988	1989	1990	1991	1992	1993	1994	1995
5. LONG-TERM DEBT										
DEBT OUTSTANDING (LDOD)	**2**	**150**	**609**	**578**	**664**	**745**	**782**	**819**	**885**	**949**
Public and publicly guaranteed	**2**	**150**	**609**	**578**	**664**	**745**	**782**	**819**	**885**	**949**
Official creditors	2	143	602	573	660	743	781	818	883	947
Multilateral	0	91	436	478	542	613	647	686	752	810
Concessional	0	91	435	477	541	612	646	686	752	809
Bilateral	1	52	166	95	118	130	134	132	131	137
Concessional	1	51	166	95	117	129	133	131	130	130
Private creditors	0	8	7	5	4	3	2	1	2	2
Bonds	0	0	0	0	0	0	0	0	0	0
Commercial banks	0	0	0	0	0	0	0	0	0	0
Other private	0	8	7	5	4	3	2	1	2	2
Private nonguaranteed	**0**	**0**	**0**	**0**	**0**	**0**	**0**	**0**	**0**	**0**
Bonds	0	0	0	0	0	0	0	0	0	0
Commercial banks	0	0	0	0	0	0	0	0	0	0
Memo:										
IBRD	0	0	0	0	0	0	0	0	0	0
IDA	0	58	274	302	340	390	408	446	474	512
DISBURSEMENTS	**0**	**27**	**85**	**64**	**62**	**89**	**77**	**48**	**20**	**54**
Public and publicly guaranteed	**0**	**27**	**85**	**64**	**62**	**89**	**77**	**48**	**20**	**54**
Official creditors	0	27	85	64	62	89	77	48	20	54
Multilateral	0	21	63	52	37	72	62	48	20	54
Concessional	0	20	63	52	37	72	61	48	20	54
Bilateral	0	7	22	12	25	17	15	0	0	0
Concessional	0	7	22	12	25	17	15	0	0	0
Private creditors	0	0	0	0	0	0	0	0	0	0
Bonds	0	0	0	0	0	0	0	0	0	0
Commercial banks	0	0	0	0	0	0	0	0	0	0
Other private	0	0	0	0	0	0	0	0	0	0
Private nonguaranteed	**0**	**0**	**0**	**0**	**0**	**0**	**0**	**0**	**0**	**0**
Bonds	0	0	0	0	0	0	0	0	0	0
Commercial banks	0	0	0	0	0	0	0	0	0	0
Memo:										
IBRD	0	0	0	0	0	0	0	0	0	0
IDA	0	10	31	32	22	48	32	39	12	35
PRINCIPAL REPAYMENTS	**0**	**3**	**9**	**14**	**10**	**13**	**12**	**10**	**1**	**11**
Public and publicly guaranteed	**0**	**3**	**9**	**14**	**10**	**13**	**12**	**10**	**1**	**11**
Official creditors	0	0	6	11	8	12	11	10	1	11
Multilateral	0	0	3	6	5	6	6	10	1	11
Concessional	0	0	3	5	5	6	6	10	1	11
Bilateral	0	0	3	6	3	6	5	0	0	0
Concessional	0	0	3	6	3	6	5	0	0	0
Private creditors	0	2	3	3	2	1	1	0	0	0
Bonds	0	0	0	0	0	0	0	0	0	0
Commercial banks	0	0	0	0	0	0	0	0	0	0
Other private	0	2	3	3	2	1	1	0	0	0
Private nonguaranteed	**0**	**0**	**0**	**0**	**0**	**0**	**0**	**0**	**0**	**0**
Bonds	0	0	0	0	0	0	0	0	0	0
Commercial banks	0	0	0	0	0	0	0	0	0	0
Memo:										
IBRD	0	0	0	0	0	0	0	0	0	0
IDA	0	0	1	1	1	2	2	3	1	6
NET FLOWS ON DEBT	**0**	**25**	**76**	**50**	**53**	**76**	**65**	**38**	**19**	**43**
Public and publicly guaranteed	**0**	**25**	**76**	**50**	**53**	**76**	**65**	**38**	**19**	**43**
Official creditors	0	27	79	53	54	77	66	38	19	43
Multilateral	0	20	60	47	32	66	56	38	19	43
Concessional	0	20	60	47	32	67	56	38	19	43
Bilateral	0	7	19	6	22	11	10	0	0	0
Concessional	0	7	19	6	22	11	10	0	0	0
Private creditors	0	-2	-3	-3	-2	-1	-1	0	0	0
Bonds	0	0	0	0	0	0	0	0	0	0
Commercial banks	0	0	0	0	0	0	0	0	0	0
Other private	0	-2	-3	-3	-2	-1	-1	0	0	0
Private nonguaranteed	**0**	**0**	**0**	**0**	**0**	**0**	**0**	**0**	**0**	**0**
Bonds	0	0	0	0	0	0	0	0	0	0
Commercial banks	0	0	0	0	0	0	0	0	0	0
Memo:										
IBRD	0	0	0	0	0	0	0	0	0	0
IDA	0	10	30	31	21	47	30	37	11	29

RWANDA

(US$ million, unless otherwise indicated)

	1970	*1980*	*1988*	*1989*	*1990*	*1991*	*1992*	*1993*	*1994*	*1995*
INTEREST PAYMENTS (LINT)	**0**	**2**	**8**	**8**	**6**	**7**	**7**	**4**	**2**	**8**
Public and publicly guaranteed	**0**	**2**	**8**	**8**	**6**	**7**	**7**	**4**	**2**	**8**
Official creditors	0	1	8	7	6	7	7	4	2	8
Multilateral	0	1	4	5	4	4	5	4	2	8
Concessional	0	1	4	5	4	4	5	4	2	8
Bilateral	0	1	4	2	2	2	1	0	0	0
Concessional	0	0	4	2	1	2	1	0	0	0
Private creditors	0	0	1	0	0	0	0	0	0	0
Bonds	0	0	0	0	0	0	0	0	0	0
Commercial banks	0	0	0	0	0	0	0	0	0	0
Other private	0	0	1	0	0	0	0	0	0	0
Private nonguaranteed	**0**	**0**	**0**	**0**	**0**	**0**	**0**	**0**	**0**	**0**
Bonds	0	0	0	0	0	0	0	0	0	0
Commercial banks	0	0	0	0	0	0	0	0	0	0
Memo:										
IBRD	0	0	0	0	0	0	0	0	0	0
IDA	0	0	3	2	2	2	3	3	1	7
NET TRANSFERS ON DEBT	**0**	**23**	**68**	**43**	**46**	**70**	**58**	**34**	**18**	**35**
Public and publicly guaranteed	**0**	**23**	**68**	**43**	**46**	**70**	**58**	**34**	**18**	**35**
Official creditors	0	26	71	46	49	71	59	34	18	35
Multilateral	0	20	56	42	28	62	50	34	18	35
Concessional	0	19	57	42	28	62	51	34	18	35
Bilateral	0	6	15	4	21	9	9	0	0	0
Concessional	0	6	15	4	20	9	9	0	0	0
Private creditors	0	-3	-3	-3	-2	-1	-1	0	0	0
Bonds	0	0	0	0	0	0	0	0	0	0
Commercial banks	0	0	0	0	0	0	0	0	0	0
Other private	0	-3	-3	-3	-2	-1	-1	0	0	0
Private nonguaranteed	**0**	**0**	**0**	**0**	**0**	**0**	**0**	**0**	**0**	**0**
Bonds	0	0	0	0	0	0	0	0	0	0
Commercial banks	0	0	0	0	0	0	0	0	0	0
Memo:										
IBRD	0	0	0	0	0	0	0	0	0	0
IDA	0	10	28	29	18	44	27	33	11	22
DEBT SERVICE (LTDS)	**0**	**4**	**17**	**21**	**16**	**20**	**18**	**14**	**3**	**19**
Public and publicly guaranteed	**0**	**4**	**17**	**21**	**16**	**20**	**18**	**14**	**3**	**19**
Official creditors	0	2	14	19	14	18	17	14	3	19
Multilateral	0	1	7	11	9	10	11	14	3	19
Concessional	0	1	6	10	9	10	11	14	2	19
Bilateral	0	1	7	8	5	8	6	0	0	0
Concessional	0	0	7	8	4	8	6	0	0	0
Private creditors	0	3	3	3	2	1	1	0	0	0
Bonds	0	0	0	0	0	0	0	0	0	0
Commercial banks	0	0	0	0	0	0	0	0	0	0
Other private	0	3	3	3	2	1	1	0	0	0
Private nonguaranteed	**0**	**0**	**0**	**0**	**0**	**0**	**0**	**0**	**0**	**0**
Bonds	0	0	0	0	0	0	0	0	0	0
Commercial banks	0	0	0	0	0	0	0	0	0	0
Memo:										
IBRD	0	0	0	0	0	0	0	0	0	0
IDA	0	1	3	3	3	4	5	6	1	12
UNDISBURSED DEBT	**10**	**110**	**354**	**424**	**464**	**563**	**515**	**511**	**468**	**427**
Official creditors	10	110	348	419	458	556	508	511	468	427
Private creditors	0	0	7	6	6	7	7	0	0	0
Memorandum items										
Concessional LDOD	2	141	601	572	658	741	780	817	882	940
Variable rate LDOD	0	0	0	0	0	0	0	0	0	0
Public sector LDOD	2	150	609	578	664	745	782	819	885	949
Private sector LDOD	0	0	0	0	0	0	0	0	0	0

6. CURRENCY COMPOSITION OF LONG-TERM DEBT (PERCENT)

	1970	*1980*	*1988*	*1989*	*1990*	*1991*	*1992*	*1993*	*1994*	*1995*
Deutsche mark	46.2	0.7	0.4	0.1	0.0	0.0	0.0	0.0	0.0	0.0
French franc	0.0	7.3	12.1	2.7	3.9	5.0	6.2	5.6	5.5	7.4
Japanese yen	0.0	4.5	1.8	1.6	1.5	1.4	1.3	1.4	1.4	1.3
Pound sterling	0.0	0.0	0.0	0.0	0.0	0.0	0.0	0.0	0.0	0.0
Swiss franc	0.0	0.0	0.0	0.0	0.0	0.0	0.0	0.0	0.0	0.0
U.S.dollars	10.3	48.0	32.4	38.0	38.7	42.3	43.9	46.6	45.8	46.5
Multiple currency	0.0	5.9	14.4	15.8	15.0	13.4	13.3	12.7	12.3	11.6
Special drawing rights	0.0	0.0	5.8	6.3	6.2	5.5	5.1	4.8	4.7	4.5
All other currencies	41.0	33.5	33.1	35.5	34.8	32.4	30.2	28.8	30.2	28.8

RWANDA

(US$ million, unless otherwise indicated)

	1970	1980	1988	1989	1990	1991	1992	1993	1994	1995
7. DEBT RESTRUCTURINGS										
Total amount rescheduled	0	0	0	0	0	0	0	0	0	6
Debt stock rescheduled	0	0	0	0	0	0	0	0	0	0
Principal rescheduled	0	0	0	0	0	0	0	0	0	5
Official	0	0	0	0	0	0	0	0	0	5
Private	0	0	0	0	0	0	0	0	0	0
Interest rescheduled	0	0	0	0	0	0	0	0	0	2
Official	0	0	0	0	0	0	0	0	0	2
Private	0	0	0	0	0	0	0	0	0	0
Debt forgiven	..	..	0	66	0	0	0	0	0	0
Memo: interest forgiven	..	..	0	0	0	0	0	0	0	0
Debt stock reduction	0	0	0	0	0	0	0	0	0	0
of which debt buyback	0	0	0	0	0	0	0	0	0	0
8. DEBT STOCK-FLOW RECONCILIATION										
Total change in debt stocks	..	..	..	-32	88	97	41	41	41	77
Net flows on debt	..	..	..	51	54	90	67	38	-12	53
Net change in interest arrears	..	..	..	0	1	1	3	4	6	3
Interest capitalized	..	..	..	0	0	0	0	0	0	2
Debt forgiveness or reduction	..	..	..	-66	0	0	0	0	0	0
Cross-currency valuation	..	..	..	-7	22	0	-15	-5	21	14
Residual	..	..	..	-9	12	6	-13	3	27	6
9. AVERAGE TERMS OF NEW COMMITMENTS										
ALL CREDITORS										
Interest (%)	0.8	1.5	1.7	1.7	1.4	0.8	1.1	0.6	0.0	0.7
Maturity (years)	50.0	39.4	34.5	34.7	33.9	41.9	42.1	32.1	0.0	39.7
Grace period (years)	10.5	8.7	8.4	8.8	9.0	10.7	9.5	10.1	0.0	10.3
Grant element (%)	83.4	70.1	67.4	68.8	71.3	81.2	76.3	77.2	0.0	80.6
Official creditors										
Interest (%)	0.8	1.5	1.3	1.7	1.4	0.8	1.1	0.6	0.0	0.7
Maturity (years)	50.0	39.4	37.4	34.7	33.9	41.9	42.1	32.1	0.0	39.7
Grace period (years)	10.5	8.7	9.2	8.8	9.0	10.7	9.5	10.1	0.0	10.3
Grant element (%)	83.4	70.1	73.1	68.8	71.3	81.2	76.3	77.2	0.0	80.6
Private creditors										
Interest (%)	0.0	0.0	5.5	0.0	0.0	0.0	0.0	0.0	0.0	0.0
Maturity (years)	0.0	0.0	5.2	0.0	0.0	0.0	0.0	0.0	0.0	0.0
Grace period (years)	0.0	0.0	0.7	0.0	0.0	0.0	0.0	0.0	0.0	0.0
Grant element (%)	0.0	0.0	10.3	0.0	0.0	0.0	0.0	0.0	0.0	0.0
Memorandum items										
Commitments	9	48	71	141	72	181	56	61	0	50
Official creditors	9	48	65	141	72	181	56	61	0	50
Private creditors	0	0	7	0	0	0	0	0	0	0

10. CONTRACTUAL OBLIGATIONS ON OUTSTANDING LONG-TERM DEBT

	1996	1997	1998	1999	2000	2001	2002	2003	2004	2005
TOTAL										
Disbursements	68	60	42	25	11	3	2	0	0	0
Principal	24	25	26	27	28	28	29	31	32	32
Interest	9	9	9	9	9	9	8	8	8	7
Official creditors										
Disbursements	68	60	42	25	11	3	2	0	0	0
Principal	24	25	26	27	28	28	29	31	32	32
Interest	9	9	9	9	9	9	8	8	8	7
Bilateral creditors										
Disbursements	0	0	0	0	0	0	0	0	0	0
Principal	8	9	10	10	10	8	8	8	8	7
Interest	2	2	2	2	2	1	1	1	1	1
Multilateral creditors										
Disbursements	68	60	42	25	11	3	2	0	0	0
Principal	16	16	16	17	18	20	20	23	24	25
Interest	7	7	7	7	7	7	7	7	7	6
Private creditors										
Disbursements	0	0	0	0	0	0	0	0	0	0
Principal	0	0	0	0	0	0	0	0	0	0
Interest	0	0	0	0	0	0	0	0	0	0
Commercial banks										
Disbursements	0	0	0	0	0	0	0	0	0	0
Principal	0	0	0	0	0	0	0	0	0	0
Interest	0	0	0	0	0	0	0	0	0	0
Other private										
Disbursements	0	0	0	0	0	0	0	0	0	0
Principal	0	0	0	0	0	0	0	0	0	0
Interest	0	0	0	0	0	0	0	0	0	0

SAO TOME AND PRINCIPE

(US$ million, unless otherwise indicated)

	1970	1980	1988	1989	1990	1991	1992	1993	1994	1995
1. SUMMARY DEBT DATA										
TOTAL DEBT STOCKS (EDT)	..	**23.5**	**109.3**	**136.1**	**152.9**	**198.0**	**216.9**	**238.6**	**253.9**	**277.3**
Long-term debt (LDOD)	..	**23.5**	**100.9**	**114.9**	**135.6**	**180.4**	**195.6**	**210.4**	**230.9**	**260.8**
Public and publicly guaranteed	..	23.5	100.9	114.9	135.6	180.4	195.6	210.4	230.9	260.8
Private nonguaranteed	0.0	0.0	0.0	0.0	0.0	0.0	0.0	0.0	0.0	0.0
Use of IMF credit	**0.0**	**0.0**	**0.0**	**1.1**	**1.1**	**1.1**	**1.1**	**1.1**	**1.1**	**0.8**
Short-term debt	..	**0.0**	**8.4**	**20.1**	**16.1**	**16.5**	**20.2**	**27.1**	**22.0**	**15.6**
of which interest arrears on LDOD	..	0.0	4.9	6.4	7.7	9.1	9.9	15.9	16.0	8.6
Official creditors	..	0.0	4.6	6.2	7.5	8.8	9.6	15.6	15.6	8.6
Private creditors	..	0.0	0.2	0.2	0.2	0.2	0.3	0.3	0.3	0.0
Memo: principal arrears on LDOD	..	0.0	10.0	16.1	22.6	28.2	30.1	36.2	42.4	31.5
Official creditors	..	0.0	9.0	15.1	21.5	27.0	28.9	35.0	41.2	31.4
Private creditors	..	0.0	1.0	1.0	1.1	1.2	1.2	1.2	1.2	0.1
Memo: export credits	..	..	17.0	18.0	18.0	17.0	17.0	16.0	16.0	33.0
TOTAL DEBT FLOWS										
Disbursements	..	**9.9**	**12.0**	**18.9**	**16.7**	**43.6**	**21.7**	**15.8**	**15.2**	**12.3**
Long-term debt	..	9.9	12.0	17.9	16.7	43.6	21.7	15.8	15.2	12.3
IMF purchases	0.0	0.0	0.0	1.0	0.0	0.0	0.0	0.0	0.0	0.0
Principal repayments	..	**0.9**	**1.3**	**1.5**	**1.1**	**0.8**	**1.3**	**0.8**	**1.3**	**0.9**
Long-term debt	..	0.9	1.3	1.5	1.1	0.8	1.3	0.8	1.2	0.6
IMF repurchases	0.0	0.0	0.0	0.0	0.0	0.0	0.0	0.0	0.1	0.2
Net flows on debt	..	**9.0**	**10.8**	**27.6**	**10.3**	**41.8**	**23.2**	**15.9**	**8.7**	**12.5**
of which short-term debt	..	..	0.0	10.2	-5.3	-1.0	2.8	0.9	-5.2	1.0
Interest payments (INT)	..	**0.3**	**1.2**	**3.4**	**1.7**	**1.1**	**1.2**	**1.8**	**1.5**	**1.2**
Long-term debt	..	0.2	0.9	2.6	1.2	0.7	0.9	1.0	1.2	0.9
IMF charges	0.0	0.0	0.0	0.0	0.0	0.0	0.0	0.0	0.0	0.0
Short-term debt	..	0.1	0.3	0.8	0.5	0.3	0.4	0.8	0.3	0.3
Net transfers on debt	..	**8.7**	**9.6**	**24.2**	**8.5**	**40.7**	**22.0**	**14.1**	**7.2**	**11.3**
Total debt service paid (TDS)	..	**1.2**	**2.4**	**4.9**	**2.8**	**1.9**	**2.5**	**2.7**	**2.7**	**2.1**
Long-term debt	..	1.1	2.1	4.1	2.3	1.6	2.2	1.8	2.3	1.5
IMF repurchases and charges	0.0	0.0	0.0	0.0	0.0	0.0	0.0	0.0	0.1	0.2
Short-term debt (interest only)	..	0.1	0.3	0.8	0.5	0.3	0.4	0.8	0.3	0.3
2. AGGREGATE NET RESOURCE FLOWS AND NET TRANSFERS (LONG-TERM)										
NET RESOURCE FLOWS	..	**11.5**	**19.1**	**35.4**	**43.5**	**61.7**	**43.3**	**34.8**	**36.7**	**30.0**
Net flow of long-term debt (ex. IMF)	0.0	9.0	10.8	16.4	15.6	42.8	20.4	15.0	14.0	11.7
Foreign direct investment (net)	0.0	0.0	0.0	0.0	0.0	0.0	0.0	0.0	0.0	0.0
Portfolio equity flows	..	0.0	0.0	0.0	0.0	0.0	0.0	0.0	0.0	0.0
Grants (excluding technical coop.)	0.0	2.5	8.3	19.0	27.9	18.9	22.9	19.8	22.7	18.3
Memo: technical coop. grants	0.0	1.3	6.1	7.5	7.2	11.4	16.3	16.3	13.7	21.5
NET TRANSFERS	..	**11.3**	**18.2**	**32.8**	**42.3**	**61.0**	**42.5**	**33.8**	**35.5**	**29.1**
Interest on long-term debt	..	0.2	0.9	2.6	1.2	0.7	0.9	1.0	1.2	0.9
Profit remittances on FDI	0.0	0.0	0.0	0.0	0.0	0.0	0.0	0.0	0.0	0.0
3. MAJOR ECONOMIC AGGREGATES										
Gross national product (GNP)	19.7	45.8	48.3	45.7	49.0	47.3	40.4	42.1	44.1	40.0
Exports of goods & services (XGS)	..	23.3	11.5	9.6	7.7	9.9	9.5	11.0	11.3	12.8
of which workers remittances	..	0.8	0.0	0.1	0.1	0.1	0.1	0.1	0.1	0.1
Imports of goods & services (MGS)	..	22.0	23.1	22.2	22.8	24.4	22.0	23.1	22.4	23.0
International reserves (RES)	..	..	..	..	..	..	..	..	..	..
Current account balance	..	0.7	-10.8	-11.4	-12.0	-14.0	-12.0	-12.0	-11.0	-10.0
4. DEBT INDICATORS										
EDT / XGS (%)	..	100.7	950.2	1,417.2	1,985.2	2,000.5	2,283.2	2,168.8	2,247.1	2,166.3
EDT / GNP (%)	..	51.2	226.2	297.7	312.0	418.7	536.9	566.7	575.8	693.2
TDS / XGS (%)	..	5.0	21.0	51.3	36.9	19.3	26.6	24.1	24.2	16.2
INT / XGS (%)	..	1.1	10.1	35.5	22.2	11.0	12.8	16.5	12.9	9.5
INT / GNP (%)	..	0.6	2.4	7.5	3.5	2.3	3.0	4.3	3.3	3.0
RES / EDT (%)	..	..	..	..	..	..	..	..	..	..
RES / MGS (months)	..	..	..	..	..	..	..	..	..	..
Short-term / EDT (%)	..	0.0	7.7	14.8	10.5	8.3	9.3	11.4	8.7	5.6
Concessional / EDT (%)	..	83.6	69.9	67.1	73.6	79.6	79.9	78.9	82.5	91.2
Multilateral / EDT (%)	..	45.0	38.5	42.1	49.2	59.9	61.5	61.0	65.9	65.7

SAO TOME AND PRINCIPE

(US$ million, unless otherwise indicated)

5. LONG-TERM DEBT

	1970	1980	1988	1989	1990	1991	1992	1993	1994	1995
DEBT OUTSTANDING (LDOD)	..	**23.5**	**100.9**	**114.9**	**135.6**	**180.4**	**195.6**	**210.4**	**230.9**	**260.8**
Public and publicly guaranteed	..	**23.5**	**100.9**	**114.9**	**135.6**	**180.4**	**195.6**	**210.4**	**230.9**	**260.8**
Official creditors	..	23.1	99.1	113.6	134.4	179.2	194.4	209.1	229.6	260.7
Multilateral	..	10.6	42.0	57.2	75.2	118.6	133.5	145.5	167.3	182.2
Concessional	..	10.6	41.0	56.1	74.0	117.3	132.2	144.6	167.0	181.9
Bilateral	..	12.6	57.1	56.3	59.2	60.6	60.9	63.6	62.3	78.5
Concessional	..	9.1	35.4	35.2	38.6	40.3	41.0	43.7	42.4	70.9
Private creditors	..	0.3	1.8	1.4	1.2	1.2	1.2	1.2	1.2	0.1
Bonds	..	0.0	0.0	0.0	0.0	0.0	0.0	0.0	0.0	0.0
Commercial banks	..	0.0	0.0	0.0	0.0	0.0	0.0	0.0	0.0	0.0
Other private	..	0.3	1.8	1.4	1.2	1.2	1.2	1.2	1.2	0.1
Private nonguaranteed	**0.0**	**0.0**	**0.0**	**0.0**	**0.0**	**0.0**	**0.0**	**0.0**	**0.0**	**0.0**
Bonds	..	0.0	0.0	0.0	0.0	0.0	0.0	0.0	0.0	0.0
Commercial banks	..	0.0	0.0	0.0	0.0	0.0	0.0	0.0	0.0	0.0
Memo:										
IBRD	0.0	0.0	0.0	0.0	0.0	0.0	0.0	0.0	0.0	0.0
IDA	0.0	0.0	10.1	16.8	23.9	29.4	33.6	38.3	46.9	53.6
DISBURSEMENTS	..	**9.9**	**12.0**	**17.9**	**16.7**	**43.6**	**21.7**	**15.8**	**15.2**	**12.3**
Public and publicly guaranteed	..	**9.9**	**12.0**	**17.9**	**16.7**	**43.6**	**21.7**	**15.8**	**15.2**	**12.3**
Official creditors	..	9.9	12.0	17.9	16.7	43.6	21.7	15.8	15.2	12.3
Multilateral	..	6.5	12.0	16.0	14.0	41.7	20.1	12.4	14.7	12.3
Concessional	..	6.5	12.0	15.9	13.9	41.6	20.1	12.4	14.7	12.3
Bilateral	..	3.4	0.0	1.9	2.7	1.9	1.6	3.4	0.5	0.0
Concessional	..	1.4	0.0	1.9	2.7	1.9	1.6	3.4	0.5	0.0
Private creditors	..	0.0	0.0	0.0	0.0	0.0	0.0	0.0	0.0	0.0
Bonds	..	0.0	0.0	0.0	0.0	0.0	0.0	0.0	0.0	0.0
Commercial banks	..	0.0	0.0	0.0	0.0	0.0	0.0	0.0	0.0	0.0
Other private	..	0.0	0.0	0.0	0.0	0.0	0.0	0.0	0.0	0.0
Private nonguaranteed	**0.0**	**0.0**	**0.0**	**0.0**	**0.0**	**0.0**	**0.0**	**0.0**	**0.0**	**0.0**
Bonds	..	0.0	0.0	0.0	0.0	0.0	0.0	0.0	0.0	0.0
Commercial banks	..	0.0	0.0	0.0	0.0	0.0	0.0	0.0	0.0	0.0
Memo:										
IBRD	0.0	0.0	0.0	0.0	0.0	0.0	0.0	0.0	0.0	0.0
IDA	0.0	0.0	7.1	6.8	5.4	5.2	5.5	4.6	6.5	5.6
PRINCIPAL REPAYMENTS	..	**0.9**	**1.3**	**1.5**	**1.1**	**0.8**	**1.3**	**0.8**	**1.2**	**0.6**
Public and publicly guaranteed	..	**0.9**	**1.3**	**1.5**	**1.1**	**0.8**	**1.3**	**0.8**	**1.2**	**0.6**
Official creditors	..	0.9	1.3	1.1	1.0	0.8	1.3	0.8	1.2	0.6
Multilateral	..	0.0	0.8	0.5	0.4	0.5	1.0	0.8	1.2	0.6
Concessional	..	0.0	0.8	0.5	0.4	0.5	0.9	0.5	0.6	0.6
Bilateral	..	0.9	0.4	0.6	0.6	0.3	0.3	0.0	0.0	0.0
Concessional	..	0.2	0.0	0.0	0.0	0.0	0.0	0.0	0.0	0.0
Private creditors	..	0.0	0.0	0.4	0.1	0.0	0.0	0.0	0.0	0.0
Bonds	..	0.0	0.0	0.0	0.0	0.0	0.0	0.0	0.0	0.0
Commercial banks	..	0.0	0.0	0.0	0.0	0.0	0.0	0.0	0.0	0.0
Other private	..	0.0	0.0	0.4	0.1	0.0	0.0	0.0	0.0	0.0
Private nonguaranteed	**0.0**	**0.0**	**0.0**	**0.0**	**0.0**	**0.0**	**0.0**	**0.0**	**0.0**	**0.0**
Bonds	..	0.0	0.0	0.0	0.0	0.0	0.0	0.0	0.0	0.0
Commercial banks	..	0.0	0.0	0.0	0.0	0.0	0.0	0.0	0.0	0.0
Memo:										
IBRD	0.0	0.0	0.0	0.0	0.0	0.0	0.0	0.0	0.0	0.0
IDA	0.0	0.0	0.0	0.0	0.0	0.0	0.0	0.0	0.0	0.1
NET FLOWS ON DEBT	..	**9.0**	**10.8**	**16.4**	**15.6**	**42.8**	**20.4**	**15.0**	**14.0**	**11.7**
Public and publicly guaranteed	..	**9.0**	**10.8**	**16.4**	**15.6**	**42.8**	**20.4**	**15.0**	**14.0**	**11.7**
Official creditors	..	9.0	10.8	16.8	15.7	42.8	20.4	15.0	14.0	11.7
Multilateral	..	6.5	11.2	15.4	13.5	41.2	19.2	11.6	13.5	11.7
Concessional	..	6.5	11.2	15.3	13.4	41.1	19.3	11.9	14.1	11.7
Bilateral	..	2.5	-0.4	1.4	2.2	1.6	1.2	3.4	0.5	0.0
Concessional	..	1.2	0.0	1.9	2.7	1.9	1.6	3.4	0.5	0.0
Private creditors	..	0.0	0.0	-0.4	-0.1	0.0	0.0	0.0	0.0	0.0
Bonds	..	0.0	0.0	0.0	0.0	0.0	0.0	0.0	0.0	0.0
Commercial banks	..	0.0	0.0	0.0	0.0	0.0	0.0	0.0	0.0	0.0
Other private	..	0.0	0.0	-0.4	-0.1	0.0	0.0	0.0	0.0	0.0
Private nonguaranteed	**0.0**	**0.0**	**0.0**	**0.0**	**0.0**	**0.0**	**0.0**	**0.0**	**0.0**	**0.0**
Bonds	..	0.0	0.0	0.0	0.0	0.0	0.0	0.0	0.0	0.0
Commercial banks	..	0.0	0.0	0.0	0.0	0.0	0.0	0.0	0.0	0.0
Memo:										
IBRD	0.0	0.0	0.0	0.0	0.0	0.0	0.0	0.0	0.0	0.0
IDA	0.0	0.0	7.1	6.8	5.4	5.2	5.5	4.6	6.5	5.6

SAO TOME AND PRINCIPE

(US$ million, unless otherwise indicated)

	1970	1980	1988	1989	1990	1991	1992	1993	1994	1995
INTEREST PAYMENTS (LINT)	..	**0.2**	**0.9**	**2.6**	**1.2**	**0.7**	**0.9**	**1.0**	**1.2**	**0.9**
Public and publicly guaranteed	..	**0.2**	**0.9**	**2.6**	**1.2**	**0.7**	**0.9**	**1.0**	**1.2**	**0.9**
Official creditors	..	0.2	0.9	2.5	1.1	0.7	0.9	1.0	1.2	0.9
Multilateral	..	0.0	0.3	0.2	0.3	0.6	0.7	0.9	1.0	0.7
Concessional	..	0.0	0.3	0.2	0.3	0.6	0.7	0.8	1.0	0.7
Bilateral	..	0.2	0.6	2.3	0.9	0.2	0.2	0.1	0.1	0.1
Concessional	..	0.0	0.4	0.1	0.1	0.1	0.1	0.1	0.1	0.1
Private creditors	..	0.0	0.0	0.1	0.1	0.0	0.0	0.0	0.0	0.0
Bonds	..	0.0	0.0	0.0	0.0	0.0	0.0	0.0	0.0	0.0
Commercial banks	..	0.0	0.0	0.0	0.0	0.0	0.0	0.0	0.0	0.0
Other private	..	0.0	0.0	0.1	0.1	0.0	0.0	0.0	0.0	0.0
Private nonguaranteed	**0.0**	**0.0**	**0.0**	**0.0**	**0.0**	**0.0**	**0.0**	**0.0**	**0.0**	**0.0**
Bonds	..	0.0	0.0	0.0	0.0	0.0	0.0	0.0	0.0	0.0
Commercial banks	..	0.0	0.0	0.0	0.0	0.0	0.0	0.0	0.0	0.0
Memo:										
IBRD	0.0	0.0	0.0	0.0	0.0	0.0	0.0	0.0	0.0	0.0
IDA	0.0	0.0	0.1	0.0	0.1	0.3	0.2	0.3	0.3	0.3
NET TRANSFERS ON DEBT	..	**8.8**	**9.9**	**13.8**	**14.4**	**42.1**	**19.6**	**14.0**	**12.8**	**10.8**
Public and publicly guaranteed	..	**8.8**	**9.9**	**13.8**	**14.4**	**42.1**	**19.6**	**14.0**	**12.8**	**10.8**
Official creditors	..	8.8	9.9	14.3	14.5	42.1	19.6	14.0	12.8	10.8
Multilateral	..	6.5	10.9	15.2	13.2	40.6	18.5	10.7	12.5	11.0
Concessional	..	6.5	10.9	15.1	13.1	40.5	18.6	11.0	13.1	11.0
Bilateral	..	2.4	-1.0	-1.0	1.3	1.4	1.1	3.3	0.3	-0.1
Concessional	..	1.2	-0.4	1.9	2.7	1.8	1.5	3.3	0.3	-0.1
Private creditors	..	0.0	0.0	-0.5	-0.2	0.0	0.0	0.0	0.0	0.0
Bonds	..	0.0	0.0	0.0	0.0	0.0	0.0	0.0	0.0	0.0
Commercial banks	..	0.0	0.0	0.0	0.0	0.0	0.0	0.0	0.0	0.0
Other private	..	0.0	0.0	-0.5	-0.2	0.0	0.0	0.0	0.0	0.0
Private nonguaranteed	**0.0**	**0.0**	**0.0**	**0.0**	**0.0**	**0.0**	**0.0**	**0.0**	**0.0**	**0.0**
Bonds	..	0.0	0.0	0.0	0.0	0.0	0.0	0.0	0.0	0.0
Commercial banks	..	0.0	0.0	0.0	0.0	0.0	0.0	0.0	0.0	0.0
Memo:										
IBRD	0.0	0.0	0.0	0.0	0.0	0.0	0.0	0.0	0.0	0.0
IDA	0.0	0.0	7.0	6.8	5.3	4.9	5.2	4.4	6.2	5.2
DEBT SERVICE (LTDS)	..	**1.1**	**2.1**	**4.1**	**2.3**	**1.6**	**2.2**	**1.8**	**2.3**	**1.5**
Public and publicly guaranteed	..	**1.1**	**2.1**	**4.1**	**2.3**	**1.6**	**2.2**	**1.8**	**2.3**	**1.5**
Official creditors	..	1.1	2.1	3.6	2.2	1.6	2.2	1.8	2.3	1.5
Multilateral	..	0.0	1.1	0.8	0.7	1.1	1.7	1.7	2.2	1.3
Concessional	..	0.0	1.1	0.8	0.7	1.1	1.6	1.4	1.6	1.3
Bilateral	..	1.1	1.0	2.9	1.4	0.5	0.5	0.1	0.1	0.1
Concessional	..	0.2	0.4	0.1	0.1	0.1	0.1	0.1	0.1	0.1
Private creditors	..	0.0	0.0	0.5	0.2	0.0	0.0	0.0	0.0	0.0
Bonds	..	0.0	0.0	0.0	0.0	0.0	0.0	0.0	0.0	0.0
Commercial banks	..	0.0	0.0	0.0	0.0	0.0	0.0	0.0	0.0	0.0
Other private	..	0.0	0.0	0.5	0.2	0.0	0.0	0.0	0.0	0.0
Private nonguaranteed	**0.0**	**0.0**	**0.0**	**0.0**	**0.0**	**0.0**	**0.0**	**0.0**	**0.0**	**0.0**
Bonds	..	0.0	0.0	0.0	0.0	0.0	0.0	0.0	0.0	0.0
Commercial banks	..	0.0	0.0	0.0	0.0	0.0	0.0	0.0	0.0	0.0
Memo:										
IBRD	0.0	0.0	0.0	0.0	0.0	0.0	0.0	0.0	0.0	0.0
IDA	0.0	0.0	0.1	0.0	0.1	0.3	0.2	0.3	0.3	0.4
UNDISBURSED DEBT	..	**32.1**	**71.5**	**67.1**	**100.2**	**74.6**	**86.9**	**68.1**	**65.8**	**54.9**
Official creditors	..	32.1	71.5	67.1	100.2	74.6	86.9	68.1	65.8	54.9
Private creditors	..	0.0	0.0	0.0	0.0	0.0	0.0	0.0	0.0	0.0
Memorandum items										
Concessional LDOD	..	19.6	76.4	91.3	112.6	157.6	173.2	188.3	209.4	252.8
Variable rate LDOD	..	0.0	0.0	0.0	0.0	0.0	0.0	0.0	0.0	0.0
Public sector LDOD	..	23.5	100.9	114.9	135.6	180.4	195.6	210.4	230.9	260.8
Private sector LDOD	..	0.0	0.0	0.0	0.0	0.0	0.0	0.0	0.0	0.0

6. CURRENCY COMPOSITION OF LONG-TERM DEBT (PERCENT)

	1970	1980	1988	1989	1990	1991	1992	1993	1994	1995
Deutsche mark	..	0.0	0.0	0.0	0.0	0.0	0.0	0.0	0.0	0.0
French franc	..	0.0	0.0	1.8	3.9	3.9	4.0	3.9	3.9	3.8
Japanese yen	..	0.0	0.0	0.0	0.0	0.0	0.0	0.0	0.0	0.0
Pound sterling	..	0.0	0.0	0.0	0.0	0.0	0.0	0.0	0.0	0.0
Swiss franc	..	0.0	0.0	0.0	0.0	0.0	0.0	0.0	0.0	0.0
U.S.dollars	..	63.1	50.9	44.6	39.4	32.0	31.4	31.5	31.4	35.5
Multiple currency	..	0.0	29.7	38.6	43.9	54.4	55.7	55.7	57.3	54.2
Special drawing rights	..	0.0	0.0	0.0	0.0	0.0	0.0	0.0	0.0	0.0
All other currencies	..	37.1	19.4	15.0	12.9	9.6	8.8	8.9	7.3	6.6

SAO TOME AND PRINCIPE

(US$ million, unless otherwise indicated)

	1970	1980	1988	1989	1990	1991	1992	1993	1994	1995
7. DEBT RESTRUCTURINGS										
Total amount rescheduled	0.0	0.0	0.0	0.0	0.0	0.0	4.3	0.0	0.0	29.5
Debt stock rescheduled	0.0	0.0	0.0	0.0	0.0	0.0	0.0	0.0	0.0	0.0
Principal rescheduled	0.0	0.0	0.0	0.0	0.0	0.0	3.8	0.0	0.0	15.5
Official	0.0	0.0	0.0	0.0	0.0	0.0	3.8	0.0	0.0	14.4
Private	0.0	0.0	0.0	0.0	0.0	0.0	0.0	0.0	0.0	1.1
Interest rescheduled	0.0	0.0	0.0	0.0	0.0	0.0	0.4	0.0	0.0	8.5
Official	0.0	0.0	0.0	0.0	0.0	0.0	0.4	0.0	0.0	8.1
Private	0.0	0.0	0.0	0.0	0.0	0.0	0.0	0.0	0.0	0.3
Debt forgiven	..	..	0.0	0.0	0.0	0.0	0.0	0.0	0.0	0.0
Memo: interest forgiven	..	..	0.0	0.0	0.0	0.0	0.0	0.0	0.0	0.0
Debt stock reduction	0.0	0.0	0.0	0.0	0.0	0.0	0.0	0.0	0.0	0.0
of which debt buyback	0.0	0.0	0.0	0.0	0.0	0.0	0.0	0.0	0.0	0.0
8. DEBT STOCK-FLOW RECONCILIATION										
Total change in debt stocks	..	..	..	26.8	16.8	45.2	18.9	21.7	15.3	23.4
Net flows on debt	..	..	..	27.6	10.3	41.8	23.2	15.9	8.7	12.5
Net change in interest arrears	..	..	..	1.6	1.3	1.4	0.9	6.0	0.1	-7.3
Interest capitalized	..	..	..	0.0	0.0	0.0	0.4	0.0	0.0	8.5
Debt forgiveness or reduction	..	..	..	0.0	0.0	0.0	0.0	0.0	0.0	0.0
Cross-currency valuation	..	..	..	-1.5	1.1	-0.3	-0.9	-0.7	-0.6	1.1
Residual	..	..	..	-0.9	4.2	2.3	-4.8	0.5	7.2	8.7
9. AVERAGE TERMS OF NEW COMMITMENTS										
ALL CREDITORS										
Interest (%)	..	4.0	1.4	2.6	0.8	0.8	0.8	3.0	0.7	0.0
Maturity (years)	..	11.1	33.7	26.4	38.2	49.4	37.9	20.0	20.4	0.0
Grace period (years)	..	4.4	10.2	7.4	10.2	9.9	9.5	10.0	10.4	0.0
Grant element (%)	..	31.5	72.3	55.9	77.7	82.7	77.7	52.5	70.2	0.0
Official creditors										
Interest (%)	..	4.0	1.4	2.6	0.8	0.8	0.8	3.0	0.7	0.0
Maturity (years)	..	11.1	33.7	26.4	38.2	49.4	37.9	20.0	20.4	0.0
Grace period (years)	..	4.4	10.2	7.4	10.2	9.9	9.5	10.0	10.4	0.0
Grant element (%)	..	31.5	72.3	55.9	77.7	82.7	77.7	52.5	70.2	0.0
Private creditors										
Interest (%)	..	0.0	0.0	0.0	0.0	0.0	0.0	0.0	0.0	0.0
Maturity (years)	..	0.0	0.0	0.0	0.0	0.0	0.0	0.0	0.0	0.0
Grace period (years)	..	0.0	0.0	0.0	0.0	0.0	0.0	0.0	0.0	0.0
Grant element (%)	..	0.0	0.0	0.0	0.0	0.0	0.0	0.0	0.0	0.0
Memorandum items										
Commitments	..	8.2	9.0	15.2	43.8	18.9	36.0	1.1	12.2	0.0
Official creditors	..	8.2	9.0	15.2	43.8	18.9	36.0	1.1	12.2	0.0
Private creditors	..	0.0	0.0	0.0	0.0	0.0	0.0	0.0	0.0	0.0

10. CONTRACTUAL OBLIGATIONS ON OUTSTANDING LONG-TERM DEBT

	1996	1997	1998	1999	2000	2001	2002	2003	2004	2005
TOTAL										
Disbursements	15.3	15.7	10.3	5.6	3.7	2.1	1.5	0.5	0.2	0.0
Principal	5.4	5.7	5.1	5.1	5.3	5.8	8.5	8.5	8.6	8.0
Interest	2.8	2.9	2.9	2.9	2.9	2.8	2.7	2.6	2.4	2.3
Official creditors										
Disbursements	15.3	15.7	10.3	5.6	3.7	2.1	1.5	0.5	0.2	0.0
Principal	5.4	5.7	5.1	5.1	5.3	5.8	8.5	8.5	8.6	8.0
Interest	2.8	2.9	2.9	2.9	2.9	2.8	2.7	2.6	2.4	2.3
Bilateral creditors										
Disbursements	0.4	0.4	0.3	0.2	0.1	0.1	0.0	0.0	0.0	0.0
Principal	2.5	2.5	1.6	1.4	1.4	1.1	3.1	3.1	3.1	3.1
Interest	1.3	1.2	1.2	1.1	1.1	1.1	1.1	1.0	0.9	0.8
Multilateral creditors										
Disbursements	14.9	15.4	10.0	5.3	3.5	2.0	1.5	0.4	0.2	0.0
Principal	2.9	3.2	3.5	3.7	3.9	4.6	5.4	5.4	5.5	4.9
Interest	1.5	1.6	1.7	1.7	1.7	1.7	1.7	1.6	1.5	1.5
Private creditors										
Disbursements	0.0	0.0	0.0	0.0	0.0	0.0	0.0	0.0	0.0	0.0
Principal	0.0	0.0	0.0	0.0	0.0	0.0	0.0	0.0	0.0	0.0
Interest	0.0	0.0	0.0	0.0	0.0	0.0	0.0	0.0	0.0	0.0
Commercial banks										
Disbursements	0.0	0.0	0.0	0.0	0.0	0.0	0.0	0.0	0.0	0.0
Principal	0.0	0.0	0.0	0.0	0.0	0.0	0.0	0.0	0.0	0.0
Interest	0.0	0.0	0.0	0.0	0.0	0.0	0.0	0.0	0.0	0.0
Other private										
Disbursements	0.0	0.0	0.0	0.0	0.0	0.0	0.0	0.0	0.0	0.0
Principal	0.0	0.0	0.0	0.0	0.0	0.0	0.0	0.0	0.0	0.0
Interest	0.0	0.0	0.0	0.0	0.0	0.0	0.0	0.0	0.0	0.0

SENEGAL

(US$ million, unless otherwise indicated)

	1970	1980	1988	1989	1990	1991	1992	1993	1994	1995
1. SUMMARY DEBT DATA										
TOTAL DEBT STOCKS (EDT)	..	**1,473**	**3,886**	**3,269**	**3,731**	**3,554**	**3,634**	**3,766**	**3,659**	**3,845**
Long-term debt (LDOD)	**145**	**1,114**	**3,287**	**2,693**	**2,999**	**2,921**	**3,011**	**3,059**	**3,096**	**3,235**
Public and publicly guaranteed	115	1,105	3,253	2,659	2,939	2,863	2,961	3,009	3,049	3,191
Private nonguaranteed	31	9	34	33	60	58	50	50	48	44
Use of IMF credit	**0**	**140**	**318**	**316**	**314**	**327**	**271**	**244**	**300**	**347**
Short-term debt	..	**219**	**281**	**261**	**418**	**305**	**352**	**462**	**262**	**263**
of which interest arrears on LDOD	..	0	3	11	0	0	50	163	39	13
Official creditors	..	0	3	10	0	0	48	118	30	7
Private creditors	..	0	0	1	0	0	2	45	10	6
Memo: principal arrears on LDOD	..	0	2	7	0	29	92	207	227	68
Official creditors	..	0	2	6	0	1	62	153	155	12
Private creditors	..	0	0	1	0	29	30	53	72	56
Memo: export credits	..	..	719	795	812	759	775	569	455	656
TOTAL DEBT FLOWS										
Disbursements	**20**	**395**	**340**	**440**	**251**	**228**	**316**	**150**	**199**	**247**
Long-term debt	20	327	283	375	222	169	316	150	131	164
IMF purchases	0	68	57	66	29	58	0	0	68	83
Principal repayments	**9**	**165**	**229**	**192**	**197**	**191**	**143**	**80**	**151**	**223**
Long-term debt	9	156	165	132	141	144	98	52	122	141
IMF repurchases	0	8	64	61	55	47	44	27	29	81
Net flows on debt	**11**	**230**	**70**	**220**	**222**	**-76**	**170**	**67**	**-28**	**52**
of which short-term debt	..	..	-41	-28	167	-112	-3	-3	-76	28
Interest payments (INT)	..	**95**	**160**	**189**	**128**	**124**	**67**	**41**	**72**	**74**
Long-term debt	2	67	119	149	84	92	47	23	55	57
IMF charges	0	3	18	16	15	10	6	3	3	3
Short-term debt	..	24	23	24	29	21	15	15	14	14
Net transfers on debt	..	**135**	**-90**	**30**	**94**	**-200**	**103**	**27**	**-100**	**-22**
Total debt service paid (TDS)	..	**260**	**389**	**382**	**325**	**315**	**210**	**120**	**223**	**296**
Long-term debt	12	224	284	281	225	236	145	75	177	198
IMF repurchases and charges	0	12	83	77	70	58	50	30	31	84
Short-term debt (interest only)	..	24	23	24	29	21	15	15	14	14
2. AGGREGATE NET RESOURCE FLOWS AND NET TRANSFERS (LONG-TERM)										
NET RESOURCE FLOWS	**32**	**263**	**333**	**513**	**691**	**365**	**570**	**396**	**553**	**394**
Net flow of long-term debt (ex. IMF)	11	171	118	243	81	26	218	97	9	23
Foreign direct investment (net)	5	15	14	0	57	-8	21	-1	67	1
Portfolio equity flows	0	0	0	0	0	0	0	0	0	0
Grants (excluding technical coop.)	16	78	200	270	553	347	331	299	476	371
Memo: technical coop. grants	21	122	131	132	180	172	201	180	165	189
NET TRANSFERS	**15**	**161**	**185**	**336**	**574**	**234**	**481**	**336**	**460**	**297**
Interest on long-term debt	2	67	119	149	84	92	47	23	55	57
Profit remittances on FDI	15	34	29	28	33	39	42	37	38	40
3. MAJOR ECONOMIC AGGREGATES										
Gross national product (GNP)	844	2,916	4,728	4,452	5,467	5,302	5,893	5,411	3,711	4,672
Exports of goods & services (XGS)	..	905	1,247	1,336	1,585	1,494	1,544	1,424	1,478	1,715
of which workers remittances	..	75	77	55	91	105	120	117	73	84
Imports of goods & services (MGS)	..	1,337	1,708	1,745	1,970	1,909	2,039	1,889	1,567	1,777
International reserves (RES)	22	25	22	31	22	24	22	15	191	283
Current account balance	..	-387	-261	-198	-181	-226	-298	-302	222	-97
4. DEBT INDICATORS										
EDT / XGS (%)	..	162.7	311.6	244.7	235.3	237.8	235.4	264.4	247.6	224.3
EDT / GNP (%)	..	50.5	82.2	73.4	68.2	67.0	61.7	69.6	98.6	82.3
TDS / XGS (%)	..	28.7	31.2	28.6	20.5	21.1	13.6	8.4	15.1	17.3
INT / XGS (%)	..	10.5	12.8	14.2	8.1	8.3	4.3	2.9	4.9	4.3
INT / GNP (%)	..	3.3	3.4	4.3	2.3	2.3	1.1	0.8	1.9	1.6
RES / EDT (%)	..	1.7	0.6	0.9	0.6	0.7	0.6	0.4	5.2	7.4
RES / MGS (months)	..	0.2	0.2	0.2	0.1	0.1	0.1	0.1	1.5	1.9
Short-term / EDT (%)	..	14.9	7.2	8.0	11.2	8.6	9.7	12.3	7.2	6.8
Concessional / EDT (%)	..	27.9	52.5	53.3	53.1	54.9	57.7	56.5	62.0	62.9
Multilateral / EDT (%)	..	17.8	30.0	36.6	36.5	40.0	43.3	44.0	47.9	48.4

SENEGAL

(US$ million, unless otherwise indicated)

	1970	1980	1988	1989	1990	1991	1992	1993	1994	1995
5. LONG-TERM DEBT										
DEBT OUTSTANDING (LDOD)	**145**	**1,114**	**3,287**	**2,693**	**2,999**	**2,921**	**3,011**	**3,059**	**3,096**	**3,235**
Public and publicly guaranteed	**115**	**1,105**	**3,253**	**2,659**	**2,939**	**2,863**	**2,961**	**3,009**	**3,049**	**3,191**
Official creditors	100	652	3,017	2,458	2,758	2,719	2,848	2,903	2,942	3,107
Multilateral	13	263	1,167	1,196	1,363	1,422	1,572	1,657	1,754	1,861
Concessional	9	190	963	994	1,164	1,227	1,350	1,386	1,492	1,616
Bilateral	87	390	1,850	1,263	1,395	1,297	1,276	1,246	1,188	1,246
Concessional	78	221	1,078	749	816	724	746	742	777	803
Private creditors	14	452	237	201	181	144	113	106	106	84
Bonds	0	4	0	0	0	0	0	0	0	0
Commercial banks	0	129	92	86	85	77	70	67	66	66
Other private	14	319	145	115	96	67	43	40	40	18
Private nonguaranteed	**31**	**9**	**34**	**33**	**60**	**58**	**50**	**50**	**48**	**44**
Bonds	0	0	0	0	0	0	0	0	0	0
Commercial banks	31	9	34	33	60	58	50	50	48	44
Memo:										
IBRD	2	57	106	94	88	76	62	52	44	35
IDA	9	100	552	592	747	800	873	918	1,005	1,126
DISBURSEMENTS	**20**	**327**	**283**	**375**	**222**	**169**	**316**	**150**	**131**	**164**
Public and publicly guaranteed	**19**	**327**	**275**	**367**	**207**	**160**	**310**	**148**	**131**	**163**
Official creditors	12	186	269	366	207	158	308	148	131	163
Multilateral	5	93	122	91	135	113	251	142	115	149
Concessional	4	68	110	70	127	90	196	75	82	142
Bilateral	7	94	147	276	72	45	57	7	16	14
Concessional	7	50	146	276	72	42	57	7	15	14
Private creditors	8	141	6	0	0	2	3	0	0	0
Bonds	0	0	0	0	0	0	0	0	0	0
Commercial banks	0	23	1	0	0	0	0	0	0	0
Other private	8	118	5	0	0	2	3	0	0	0
Private nonguaranteed	**1**	**0**	**8**	**8**	**15**	**10**	**6**	**1**	**1**	**1**
Bonds	0	0	0	0	0	0	0	0	0	0
Commercial banks	1	0	8	8	15	10	6	1	1	1
Memo:										
IBRD	1	18	0	0	0	0	0	0	0	0
IDA	4	12	66	50	117	51	103	46	54	107
PRINCIPAL REPAYMENTS	**9**	**156**	**165**	**132**	**141**	**144**	**98**	**52**	**122**	**141**
Public and publicly guaranteed	**7**	**152**	**157**	**124**	**130**	**132**	**87**	**50**	**115**	**136**
Official creditors	6	19	101	73	111	99	59	48	112	115
Multilateral	0	3	45	48	58	61	41	46	103	86
Concessional	0	1	25	27	30	33	24	31	61	54
Bilateral	6	16	56	25	53	38	19	2	9	29
Concessional	5	7	10	14	25	13	11	0	8	12
Private creditors	0	133	56	51	19	33	27	2	3	21
Bonds	0	1	0	0	0	0	0	0	0	0
Commercial banks	0	58	31	28	5	7	5	2	3	3
Other private	0	74	25	23	14	26	23	0	0	19
Private nonguaranteed	**3**	**4**	**8**	**8**	**12**	**11**	**12**	**2**	**7**	**5**
Bonds	0	0	0	0	0	0	0	0	0	0
Commercial banks	3	4	8	8	12	11	12	2	7	5
Memo:										
IBRD	0	2	10	10	13	13	11	11	11	12
IDA	0	0	2	2	3	3	3	4	5	6
NET FLOWS ON DEBT	**11**	**171**	**118**	**243**	**81**	**26**	**218**	**97**	**9**	**23**
Public and publicly guaranteed	**13**	**175**	**118**	**243**	**77**	**28**	**224**	**98**	**15**	**27**
Official creditors	6	167	168	294	96	60	248	100	19	48
Multilateral	5	90	77	42	77	52	210	96	12	63
Concessional	4	68	85	43	97	57	173	44	21	88
Bilateral	1	77	91	251	19	7	38	4	7	-15
Concessional	2	43	136	262	47	29	45	6	7	2
Private creditors	7	8	-50	-51	-19	-32	-25	-2	-3	-21
Bonds	0	-1	0	0	0	0	0	0	0	0
Commercial banks	0	-35	-30	-28	-5	-7	-5	-2	-3	-3
Other private	7	43	-20	-23	-14	-25	-20	0	0	-19
Private nonguaranteed	**-2**	**-4**	**0**	**0**	**4**	**-2**	**-6**	**-1**	**-6**	**-4**
Bonds	0	0	0	0	0	0	0	0	0	0
Commercial banks	-2	-4	0	0	4	-2	-6	-1	-6	-4
Memo:										
IBRD	1	16	-10	-10	-13	-13	-11	-11	-11	-12
IDA	4	12	64	48	114	48	100	42	49	101

SENEGAL

(US$ million, unless otherwise indicated)

	1970	1980	1988	1989	1990	1991	1992	1993	1994	1995
INTEREST PAYMENTS (LINT)	**2**	**67**	**119**	**149**	**84**	**92**	**47**	**23**	**55**	**57**
Public and publicly guaranteed	**2**	**67**	**115**	**148**	**82**	**89**	**44**	**21**	**53**	**56**
Official creditors	2	22	94	127	71	74	39	20	53	53
Multilateral	0	6	27	37	26	31	20	15	46	38
Concessional	0	2	9	12	10	12	8	7	19	16
Bilateral	2	15	67	90	45	44	19	6	7	15
Concessional	2	6	22	63	20	19	12	1	7	6
Private creditors	0	45	21	21	10	15	6	0	0	3
Bonds	0	0	0	0	0	0	0	0	0	0
Commercial banks	0	23	12	11	5	8	1	0	0	0
Other private	0	22	10	10	5	6	5	0	0	3
Private nonguaranteed	**0**	**0**	**3**	**1**	**3**	**3**	**3**	**2**	**2**	**1**
Bonds	0	0	0	0	0	0	0	0	0	0
Commercial banks	0	0	3	1	3	3	3	2	2	1
Memo:										
IBRD	0	4	9	8	6	9	6	5	4	4
IDA	0	1	5	4	4	6	6	6	8	8
NET TRANSFERS ON DEBT	**8**	**103**	**-1**	**94**	**-3**	**-67**	**171**	**75**	**-46**	**-34**
Public and publicly guaranteed	**10**	**108**	**3**	**95**	**-4**	**-61**	**179**	**78**	**-38**	**-29**
Official creditors	3	146	74	167	25	-15	210	80	-34	-5
Multilateral	4	84	49	5	51	22	191	81	-35	25
Concessional	4	66	76	31	87	45	164	37	2	72
Bilateral	-1	62	24	161	-26	-37	19	-1	0	-29
Concessional	1	37	114	199	27	10	34	6	1	-5
Private creditors	7	-38	-71	-72	-29	-47	-30	-2	-4	-25
Bonds	0	-1	0	0	0	0	0	0	0	0
Commercial banks	0	-58	-42	-39	-10	-16	-6	-2	-3	-3
Other private	7	21	-29	-33	-19	-31	-25	0	0	-22
Private nonguaranteed	**-2**	**-5**	**-3**	**-1**	**1**	**-5**	**-9**	**-3**	**-8**	**-5**
Bonds	0	0	0	0	0	0	0	0	0	0
Commercial banks	-2	-5	-3	-1	1	-5	-9	-3	-8	-5
Memo:										
IBRD	1	12	-19	-18	-19	-21	-17	-16	-15	-16
IDA	4	11	59	44	110	42	94	36	41	93
DEBT SERVICE (LTDS)	**12**	**224**	**284**	**281**	**225**	**236**	**145**	**75**	**177**	**198**
Public and publicly guaranteed	**9**	**219**	**272**	**272**	**211**	**221**	**131**	**71**	**169**	**192**
Official creditors	9	41	195	200	182	173	98	69	165	167
Multilateral	0	9	72	85	84	92	60	60	149	124
Concessional	0	3	34	38	39	45	32	38	80	70
Bilateral	8	32	123	115	98	81	38	8	15	43
Concessional	6	13	32	77	45	32	23	1	14	19
Private creditors	1	178	77	72	29	48	33	2	4	25
Bonds	0	1	0	0	0	0	0	0	0	0
Commercial banks	0	81	43	39	10	16	6	2	3	3
Other private	1	96	35	33	19	32	27	0	0	22
Private nonguaranteed	**3**	**5**	**11**	**10**	**14**	**15**	**15**	**4**	**9**	**6**
Bonds	0	0	0	0	0	0	0	0	0	0
Commercial banks	3	5	11	10	14	15	15	4	9	6
Memo:										
IBRD	0	6	19	18	19	21	17	16	15	16
IDA	0	1	6	6	7	9	9	10	13	14
UNDISBURSED DEBT	**42**	**605**	**891**	**788**	**949**	**1,081**	**966**	**850**	**731**	**842**
Official creditors	37	564	886	783	940	1,074	961	847	728	834
Private creditors	5	41	5	5	9	8	5	3	3	8
Memorandum items										
Concessional LDOD	87	411	2,041	1,743	1,981	1,951	2,096	2,128	2,269	2,419
Variable rate LDOD	31	141	113	108	140	135	167	227	425	482
Public sector LDOD	112	1,078	3,224	2,627	2,901	2,825	2,926	2,976	3,020	3,160
Private sector LDOD	33	35	63	66	97	96	85	83	77	76

6. CURRENCY COMPOSITION OF LONG-TERM DEBT (PERCENT)

	1970	1980	1988	1989	1990	1991	1992	1993	1994	1995
Deutsche mark	23.5	4.6	5.9	1.0	1.3	1.2	1.0	0.9	1.0	1.0
French franc	26.9	39.3	33.2	24.7	25.8	26.4	24.5	22.8	15.3	15.6
Japanese yen	0.0	0.0	0.4	1.6	1.5	2.5	3.1	3.4	3.7	3.5
Pound sterling	0.0	0.8	0.3	0.2	0.2	0.1	0.1	0.1	0.1	0.1
Swiss franc	0.0	0.3	0.8	0.9	1.0	0.7	0.6	0.6	0.6	0.6
U.S.dollars	1.7	23.0	25.4	32.5	32.8	30.6	32.0	33.0	39.9	42.1
Multiple currency	1.9	6.7	8.2	9.5	8.6	9.6	11.6	13.3	14.8	13.9
Special drawing rights	0.0	0.0	0.2	0.2	0.4	0.4	0.4	0.4	0.5	0.6
All other currencies	46.0	25.5	25.7	29.4	28.3	28.5	26.8	25.6	24.2	22.7

SENEGAL

(US$ million, unless otherwise indicated)

	1970	1980	1988	1989	1990	1991	1992	1993	1994	1995
7. DEBT RESTRUCTURINGS										
Total amount rescheduled	0	0	111	166	111	73	33	0	212	224
Debt stock rescheduled	0	0	0	9	0	0	0	0	0	0
Principal rescheduled	0	0	68	95	76	42	24	0	89	173
Official	0	0	57	79	58	41	23	0	87	166
Private	0	0	11	15	18	1	1	0	2	7
Interest rescheduled	0	0	40	63	27	19	9	0	83	49
Official	0	0	36	57	23	19	9	0	83	48
Private	0	0	4	6	4	0	0	0	0	1
Debt forgiven	..	..	0	862	18	138	6	0	217	12
Memo: interest forgiven	..	..	0	15	0	8	3	0	28	5
Debt stock reduction	0	0	0	0	0	0	0	0	0	0
of which debt buyback	0	0	0	0	0	0	0	0	0	0
8. DEBT STOCK-FLOW RECONCILIATION										
Total change in debt stocks	..	..	..	-617	461	-177	81	132	-107	187
Net flows on debt	..	..	..	220	222	-76	170	67	-28	52
Net change in interest arrears	..	..	..	8	-11	0	50	113	-124	-26
Interest capitalized	..	..	..	63	27	19	9	0	83	49
Debt forgiveness or reduction	..	..	..	-862	-18	-138	-6	0	-217	-12
Cross-currency valuation	..	..	..	13	176	-11	-102	-59	82	68
Residual	..	..	..	-57	64	29	-41	11	97	56
9. AVERAGE TERMS OF NEW COMMITMENTS										
ALL CREDITORS										
Interest (%)	3.9	5.9	1.8	1.5	1.9	3.7	1.7	1.5	0.8	1.1
Maturity (years)	23.1	20.0	31.6	31.5	33.3	28.6	33.4	30.7	34.6	38.4
Grace period (years)	6.8	5.7	8.8	9.4	8.7	7.2	8.6	8.0	8.6	9.5
Grant element (%)	43.8	30.3	66.4	69.4	66.1	49.2	67.5	66.9	73.8	76.4
Official creditors										
Interest (%)	2.3	5.4	1.8	1.5	1.9	3.7	1.7	1.5	0.8	1.0
Maturity (years)	30.5	21.3	31.7	31.5	33.6	28.6	33.4	30.7	34.6	38.6
Grace period (years)	8.8	6.0	8.9	9.4	8.7	7.2	8.6	8.0	8.6	9.5
Grant element (%)	59.6	33.8	66.6	69.4	66.8	49.2	67.5	66.9	73.8	76.6
Private creditors										
Interest (%)	7.5	10.8	11.1	0.0	8.3	0.0	0.0	0.0	0.0	2.0
Maturity (years)	5.8	8.3	5.5	0.0	10.1	0.0	0.0	0.0	0.0	29.5
Grace period (years)	2.2	2.5	1.5	0.0	2.6	0.0	0.0	0.0	0.0	10.0
Grant element (%)	6.8	-0.7	-4.0	0.0	6.6	0.0	0.0	0.0	0.0	65.5
Memorandum items										
Commitments	7	470	322	349	366	295	247	76	40	290
Official creditors	5	421	321	349	361	295	247	76	40	283
Private creditors	2	49	1	0	4	0	0	0	0	7

10. CONTRACTUAL OBLIGATIONS ON OUTSTANDING LONG-TERM DEBT

	1996	1997	1998	1999	2000	2001	2002	2003	2004	2005
TOTAL										
Disbursements	272	228	143	86	45	19	10	5	2	0
Principal	134	138	145	150	178	173	177	173	161	154
Interest	80	90	101	96	90	82	74	66	59	53
Official creditors										
Disbursements	268	225	142	86	45	19	10	5	2	0
Principal	122	126	134	139	173	168	172	168	156	153
Interest	77	88	99	95	89	81	74	66	59	52
Bilateral creditors										
Disbursements	65	55	35	21	11	6	3	2	0	0
Principal	43	53	61	67	99	98	100	99	87	82
Interest	40	51	64	61	58	52	47	41	36	31
Multilateral creditors										
Disbursements	203	170	107	65	34	13	6	3	2	0
Principal	79	73	73	72	74	70	72	69	69	71
Interest	37	37	35	33	31	29	27	25	23	21
Private creditors										
Disbursements	4	2	1	0	0	0	0	0	0	0
Principal	12	11	11	11	5	5	5	5	5	1
Interest	3	2	2	1	1	1	1	0	0	0
Commercial banks										
Disbursements	3	2	1	0	0	0	0	0	0	0
Principal	6	6	6	6	0	0	0	0	0	0
Interest	2	1	1	0	0	0	0	0	0	0
Other private										
Disbursements	1	0	0	0	0	0	0	0	0	0
Principal	6	5	5	5	5	5	5	5	5	1
Interest	1	1	1	1	1	1	1	0	0	0

SEYCHELLES

(US$ million, unless otherwise indicated)

	1970	1980	1988	1989	1990	1991	1992	1993	1994	1995
1. SUMMARY DEBT DATA										
TOTAL DEBT STOCKS (EDT)	..	**84.1**	**167.6**	**166.4**	**195.0**	**198.2**	**180.3**	**162.9**	**169.9**	**164.4**
Long-term debt (LDOD)	**0.0**	**25.1**	**131.3**	**130.7**	**149.0**	**151.0**	**146.5**	**137.9**	**146.8**	**151.1**
Public and publicly guaranteed	0.0	25.1	131.3	130.7	149.0	151.0	146.5	137.9	146.8	151.1
Private nonguaranteed	0.0	0.0	0.0	0.0	0.0	0.0	0.0	0.0	0.0	0.0
Use of IMF credit	**0.0**	**0.0**	**0.0**	**0.0**	**0.0**	**0.0**	**0.0**	**0.0**	**0.0**	**0.0**
Short-term debt	..	**59.0**	**36.3**	**35.7**	**46.0**	**47.2**	**33.8**	**25.1**	**23.1**	**13.3**
of which interest arrears on LDOD	..	0.0	1.3	1.1	1.2	1.3	1.4	1.6	2.1	2.3
Official creditors	..	0.0	1.3	1.1	0.6	0.5	0.4	0.5	0.7	0.6
Private creditors	..	0.0	0.1	0.0	0.7	0.8	1.0	1.1	1.4	1.7
Memo: principal arrears on LDOD	..	0.0	10.1	9.9	12.9	17.9	18.0	16.1	18.7	21.1
Official creditors	..	0.0	7.0	8.3	10.8	9.7	9.7	7.2	7.9	7.9
Private creditors	..	0.0	3.0	1.6	2.1	8.1	8.3	8.9	10.8	13.2
Memo: export credits	..	..	39.0	33.0	45.0	192.0	179.0	174.0	42.0	40.0
TOTAL DEBT FLOWS										
Disbursements	**0.0**	**11.7**	**12.0**	**14.4**	**15.7**	**17.1**	**18.1**	**8.0**	**10.9**	**10.8**
Long-term debt	0.0	11.7	12.0	14.4	15.7	17.1	18.1	8.0	10.9	10.8
IMF purchases	0.0	0.0	0.0	0.0	0.0	0.0	0.0	0.0	0.0	0.0
Principal repayments	**0.0**	**0.1**	**9.3**	**13.1**	**12.5**	**13.9**	**12.6**	**11.5**	**12.2**	**13.7**
Long-term debt	0.0	0.1	9.3	13.1	12.5	13.9	12.6	11.5	12.2	13.7
IMF repurchases	0.0	0.0	0.0	0.0	0.0	0.0	0.0	0.0	0.0	0.0
Net flows on debt	**0.0**	**11.7**	**2.7**	**0.9**	**13.5**	**4.3**	**-8.0**	**-12.4**	**-3.7**	**-12.9**
of which short-term debt	..	..	0.0	-0.4	10.2	1.1	-13.5	-8.9	-2.5	-10.0
Interest payments (INT)	..	**37.1**	**8.2**	**10.7**	**10.7**	**9.3**	**7.2**	**6.8**	**6.3**	**7.1**
Long-term debt	0.0	0.2	7.0	6.3	7.1	6.1	5.6	5.8	5.5	6.3
IMF charges	0.0	0.0	0.0	0.0	0.0	0.0	0.0	0.0	0.0	0.0
Short-term debt	..	36.9	1.2	4.4	3.6	3.3	1.6	1.0	0.8	0.8
Net transfers on debt	..	**-25.5**	**-5.6**	**-9.8**	**2.7**	**-5.0**	**-15.2**	**-19.2**	**-10.0**	**-19.9**
Total debt service paid (TDS)	..	**37.2**	**17.5**	**23.8**	**23.2**	**23.3**	**19.9**	**18.4**	**18.4**	**20.7**
Long-term debt	0.0	0.3	16.3	19.4	19.6	20.0	18.3	17.3	17.7	19.9
IMF repurchases and charges	0.0	0.0	0.0	0.0	0.0	0.0	0.0	0.0	0.0	0.0
Short-term debt (interest only)	..	36.9	1.2	4.4	3.6	3.3	1.6	1.0	0.8	0.8
2. AGGREGATE NET RESOURCE FLOWS AND NET TRANSFERS (LONG-TERM)										
NET RESOURCE FLOWS	**3.1**	**26.8**	**31.1**	**31.1**	**34.9**	**31.5**	**43.2**	**26.6**	**55.9**	**44.3**
Net flow of long-term debt (ex. IMF)	0.0	11.7	2.7	1.3	3.3	3.2	5.5	-3.5	-1.2	-2.9
Foreign direct investment (net)	0.0	9.5	23.2	22.9	20.0	20.0	29.0	19.0	50.0	40.0
Portfolio equity flows	0.0	0.0	0.0	0.0	0.0	0.0	0.0	0.0	0.0	0.0
Grants (excluding technical coop.)	3.1	5.6	5.2	6.9	11.6	8.3	8.7	11.1	7.1	7.2
Memo: technical coop. grants	0.6	7.8	9.5	9.2	10.3	10.0	12.2	9.7	7.8	8.8
NET TRANSFERS	**3.1**	**18.9**	**12.2**	**14.4**	**13.4**	**13.9**	**27.3**	**8.8**	**37.9**	**25.1**
Interest on long-term debt	0.0	0.2	7.0	6.3	7.1	6.1	5.6	5.8	5.5	6.3
Profit remittances on FDI	0.0	7.6	11.8	10.4	14.3	11.5	10.3	12.0	12.5	13.0
3. MAJOR ECONOMIC AGGREGATES										
Gross national product (GNP)	18.4	142.0	266.4	293.5	353.6	359.0	427.6	462.3	471.3	479.0
Exports of goods & services (XGS)	..	102.8	184.8	186.4	240.5	228.8	257.8	278.6	268.4	291.9
of which workers remittances	..	0.0	0.0	3.9	7.1	6.9	10.4	8.8	6.0	5.9
Imports of goods & services (MGS)	..	131.4	237.1	234.6	264.6	246.5	271.5	325.3	285.1	327.5
International reserves (RES)	..	18.4	8.7	12.1	16.6	27.7	31.3	35.7	30.2	27.1
Current account balance	..	-15.6	-28.4	-39.7	-13.0	-8.2	-6.9	-38.8	-14.7	-33.1
4. DEBT INDICATORS										
EDT / XGS (%)	..	81.8	90.7	89.3	81.1	86.6	69.9	58.5	63.3	56.3
EDT / GNP (%)	..	59.2	62.9	56.7	55.2	55.2	42.2	35.2	36.1	34.3
TDS / XGS (%)	..	36.2	9.5	12.7	9.7	10.2	7.7	6.6	6.9	7.1
INT / XGS (%)	..	36.1	4.5	5.7	4.5	4.1	2.8	2.4	2.3	2.4
INT / GNP (%)	..	26.2	3.1	3.6	3.0	2.6	1.7	1.5	1.3	1.5
RES / EDT (%)	..	21.9	5.2	7.3	8.5	14.0	17.4	21.9	17.8	16.5
RES / MGS (months)	..	1.7	0.4	0.6	0.8	1.3	1.4	1.3	1.3	1.0
Short-term / EDT (%)	..	70.1	21.7	21.4	23.6	23.8	18.7	15.4	13.6	8.1
Concessional / EDT (%)	..	22.4	44.6	46.9	47.9	49.9	52.2	53.4	52.6	54.3
Multilateral / EDT (%)	..	5.4	23.3	25.6	23.9	23.5	27.3	30.9	34.2	38.2

SEYCHELLES

(US$ million, unless otherwise indicated)

	1970	1980	1988	1989	1990	1991	1992	1993	1994	1995
5. LONG-TERM DEBT										
DEBT OUTSTANDING (LDOD)	**0.0**	**25.1**	**131.3**	**130.7**	**149.0**	**151.0**	**146.5**	**137.9**	**146.8**	**151.1**
Public and publicly guaranteed	**0.0**	**25.1**	**131.3**	**130.7**	**149.0**	**151.0**	**146.5**	**137.9**	**146.8**	**151.1**
Official creditors	0.0	25.1	101.5	104.0	120.8	124.8	121.6	116.2	125.0	129.0
Multilateral	0.0	4.5	39.0	42.5	46.7	46.6	49.2	50.3	58.1	62.8
Concessional	0.0	2.5	17.9	21.4	24.2	25.2	25.9	25.1	26.3	26.7
Bilateral	0.0	20.6	62.5	61.5	74.2	78.2	72.4	65.8	66.9	66.2
Concessional	0.0	16.3	56.9	56.7	69.3	73.7	68.2	61.9	63.1	62.5
Private creditors	0.0	0.0	29.8	26.7	28.2	26.2	25.0	21.7	21.8	22.1
Bonds	0.0	0.0	0.0	0.0	0.0	0.0	0.0	0.0	0.0	0.0
Commercial banks	0.0	0.0	25.0	22.8	23.8	22.2	21.1	18.4	19.3	20.4
Other private	0.0	0.0	4.8	3.9	4.4	4.0	3.9	3.3	2.5	1.7
Private nonguaranteed	**0.0**	**0.0**	**0.0**	**0.0**	**0.0**	**0.0**	**0.0**	**0.0**	**0.0**	**0.0**
Bonds	0.0	0.0	0.0	0.0	0.0	0.0	0.0	0.0	0.0	0.0
Commercial banks	0.0	0.0	0.0	0.0	0.0	0.0	0.0	0.0	0.0	0.0
Memo:										
IBRD	0.0	0.0	4.9	4.6	5.8	5.5	4.7	4.2	4.8	5.4
IDA	0.0	0.0	0.0	0.0	0.0	0.0	0.0	0.0	0.0	0.0
DISBURSEMENTS	**0.0**	**11.7**	**12.0**	**14.4**	**15.7**	**17.1**	**18.1**	**8.0**	**10.9**	**10.8**
Public and publicly guaranteed	**0.0**	**11.7**	**12.0**	**14.4**	**15.7**	**17.1**	**18.1**	**8.0**	**10.9**	**10.8**
Official creditors	0.0	11.7	7.7	9.3	9.9	11.7	13.4	7.6	9.5	9.0
Multilateral	0.0	3.5	3.8	6.8	3.4	2.6	8.8	6.5	8.6	8.3
Concessional	0.0	1.6	1.3	4.1	1.2	1.5	3.2	1.5	1.1	1.3
Bilateral	0.0	8.2	3.9	2.5	6.4	9.1	4.7	1.1	0.9	0.7
Concessional	0.0	4.5	3.9	2.5	6.4	8.7	4.3	1.1	0.9	0.7
Private creditors	0.0	0.0	4.3	5.1	5.9	5.4	4.7	0.4	1.5	1.8
Bonds	0.0	0.0	0.0	0.0	0.0	0.0	0.0	0.0	0.0	0.0
Commercial banks	0.0	0.0	3.5	4.6	4.4	4.2	3.8	0.1	1.5	1.8
Other private	0.0	0.0	0.8	0.5	1.5	1.2	0.9	0.3	0.0	0.0
Private nonguaranteed	**0.0**	**0.0**	**0.0**	**0.0**	**0.0**	**0.0**	**0.0**	**0.0**	**0.0**	**0.0**
Bonds	0.0	0.0	0.0	0.0	0.0	0.0	0.0	0.0	0.0	0.0
Commercial banks	0.0	0.0	0.0	0.0	0.0	0.0	0.0	0.0	0.0	0.0
Memo:										
IBRD	0.0	0.0	0.7	0.5	1.4	0.3	0.0	0.0	0.9	1.3
IDA	0.0	0.0	0.0	0.0	0.0	0.0	0.0	0.0	0.0	0.0
PRINCIPAL REPAYMENTS	**0.0**	**0.1**	**9.3**	**13.1**	**12.5**	**13.9**	**12.6**	**11.5**	**12.2**	**13.7**
Public and publicly guaranteed	**0.0**	**0.1**	**9.3**	**13.1**	**12.5**	**13.9**	**12.6**	**11.5**	**12.2**	**13.7**
Official creditors	0.0	0.1	2.1	4.8	4.7	7.3	8.0	8.5	8.7	9.9
Multilateral	0.0	0.0	1.3	2.6	2.9	2.9	4.1	4.4	4.1	4.8
Concessional	0.0	0.0	0.1	0.4	0.3	0.6	1.2	1.2	1.4	1.5
Bilateral	0.0	0.1	0.8	2.2	1.8	4.4	3.9	4.2	4.6	5.1
Concessional	0.0	0.1	0.6	1.6	1.7	3.7	3.2	4.1	4.5	5.0
Private creditors	0.0	0.0	7.2	8.3	7.8	6.6	4.6	3.0	3.5	3.7
Bonds	0.0	0.0	0.0	0.0	0.0	0.0	0.0	0.0	0.0	0.0
Commercial banks	0.0	0.0	5.5	6.9	6.6	5.1	3.7	2.1	2.6	2.8
Other private	0.0	0.0	1.7	1.4	1.2	1.5	0.9	0.9	0.9	1.0
Private nonguaranteed	**0.0**	**0.0**	**0.0**	**0.0**	**0.0**	**0.0**	**0.0**	**0.0**	**0.0**	**0.0**
Bonds	0.0	0.0	0.0	0.0	0.0	0.0	0.0	0.0	0.0	0.0
Commercial banks	0.0	0.0	0.0	0.0	0.0	0.0	0.0	0.0	0.0	0.0
Memo:										
IBRD	0.0	0.0	0.0	0.6	0.6	0.7	0.6	0.7	0.7	0.8
IDA	0.0	0.0	0.0	0.0	0.0	0.0	0.0	0.0	0.0	0.0
NET FLOWS ON DEBT	**0.0**	**11.7**	**2.7**	**1.3**	**3.3**	**3.2**	**5.5**	**-3.5**	**-1.2**	**-2.9**
Public and publicly guaranteed	**0.0**	**11.7**	**2.7**	**1.3**	**3.3**	**3.2**	**5.5**	**-3.5**	**-1.2**	**-2.9**
Official creditors	0.0	11.7	5.6	4.5	5.2	4.4	5.4	-0.9	0.8	-0.9
Multilateral	0.0	3.5	2.5	4.2	0.6	-0.3	4.6	2.1	4.5	3.5
Concessional	0.0	1.6	1.2	3.7	0.9	0.9	2.0	0.3	-0.4	-0.2
Bilateral	0.0	8.2	3.1	0.3	4.6	4.7	0.8	-3.0	-3.7	-4.4
Concessional	0.0	4.5	3.3	0.9	4.7	5.0	1.0	-2.9	-3.6	-4.3
Private creditors	0.0	0.0	-2.9	-3.2	-1.9	-1.2	0.1	-2.6	-2.0	-1.9
Bonds	0.0	0.0	0.0	0.0	0.0	0.0	0.0	0.0	0.0	0.0
Commercial banks	0.0	0.0	-2.0	-2.3	-2.2	-0.9	0.1	-2.1	-1.1	-1.0
Other private	0.0	0.0	-0.9	-0.9	0.3	-0.3	0.0	-0.5	-0.9	-1.0
Private nonguaranteed	**0.0**	**0.0**	**0.0**	**0.0**	**0.0**	**0.0**	**0.0**	**0.0**	**0.0**	**0.0**
Bonds	0.0	0.0	0.0	0.0	0.0	0.0	0.0	0.0	0.0	0.0
Commercial banks	0.0	0.0	0.0	0.0	0.0	0.0	0.0	0.0	0.0	0.0
Memo:										
IBRD	0.0	0.0	0.7	-0.1	0.8	-0.4	-0.7	-0.6	0.2	0.5
IDA	0.0	0.0	0.0	0.0	0.0	0.0	0.0	0.0	0.0	0.0

SEYCHELLES

(US$ million, unless otherwise indicated)

	1970	1980	1988	1989	1990	1991	1992	1993	1994	1995
INTEREST PAYMENTS (LINT)	**0.0**	**0.2**	**7.0**	**6.3**	**7.1**	**6.1**	**5.6**	**5.8**	**5.5**	**6.3**
Public and publicly guaranteed	**0.0**	**0.2**	**7.0**	**6.3**	**7.1**	**6.1**	**5.6**	**5.8**	**5.5**	**6.3**
Official creditors	0.0	0.2	4.3	4.2	4.8	4.7	4.7	4.9	4.7	5.6
Multilateral	0.0	0.2	2.7	2.5	2.7	2.0	2.7	3.0	2.9	3.7
Concessional	0.0	0.0	0.5	0.5	0.5	0.5	0.7	0.7	0.6	0.7
Bilateral	0.0	0.1	1.6	1.7	2.1	2.7	2.0	1.9	1.8	1.8
Concessional	0.0	0.0	1.5	1.6	2.0	2.6	1.9	1.9	1.8	1.8
Private creditors	0.0	0.0	2.7	2.1	2.3	1.4	0.9	0.9	0.8	0.7
Bonds	0.0	0.0	0.0	0.0	0.0	0.0	0.0	0.0	0.0	0.0
Commercial banks	0.0	0.0	2.1	1.7	2.1	1.1	0.7	0.7	0.6	0.6
Other private	0.0	0.0	0.7	0.5	0.2	0.3	0.2	0.2	0.2	0.1
Private nonguaranteed	**0.0**	**0.0**	**0.0**	**0.0**	**0.0**	**0.0**	**0.0**	**0.0**	**0.0**	**0.0**
Bonds	0.0	0.0	0.0	0.0	0.0	0.0	0.0	0.0	0.0	0.0
Commercial banks	0.0	0.0	0.0	0.0	0.0	0.0	0.0	0.0	0.0	0.0
Memo:										
IBRD	0.0	0.0	0.5	0.4	0.4	0.4	0.4	0.3	0.3	0.4
IDA	0.0	0.0	0.0	0.0	0.0	0.0	0.0	0.0	0.0	0.0
NET TRANSFERS ON DEBT	**0.0**	**11.4**	**-4.4**	**-5.0**	**-3.9**	**-2.9**	**-0.1**	**-9.3**	**-6.7**	**-9.1**
Public and publicly guaranteed	**0.0**	**11.4**	**-4.4**	**-5.0**	**-3.9**	**-2.9**	**-0.1**	**-9.3**	**-6.7**	**-9.1**
Official creditors	0.0	11.4	1.3	0.3	0.4	-0.2	0.7	-5.8	-3.9	-6.5
Multilateral	0.0	3.3	-0.2	1.7	-2.1	-2.3	1.9	-0.9	1.6	-0.3
Concessional	0.0	1.6	0.7	3.2	0.4	0.5	1.3	-0.4	-1.0	-0.9
Bilateral	0.0	8.1	1.5	-1.4	2.5	2.0	-1.2	-4.9	-5.5	-6.2
Concessional	0.0	4.4	1.7	-0.6	2.7	2.4	-0.9	-4.8	-5.4	-6.1
Private creditors	0.0	0.0	-5.6	-5.3	-4.3	-2.6	-0.9	-3.5	-2.8	-2.6
Bonds	0.0	0.0	0.0	0.0	0.0	0.0	0.0	0.0	0.0	0.0
Commercial banks	0.0	0.0	-4.0	-4.0	-4.3	-2.0	-0.6	-2.8	-1.8	-1.6
Other private	0.0	0.0	-1.6	-1.3	0.0	-0.6	-0.2	-0.7	-1.1	-1.1
Private nonguaranteed	**0.0**	**0.0**	**0.0**	**0.0**	**0.0**	**0.0**	**0.0**	**0.0**	**0.0**	**0.0**
Bonds	0.0	0.0	0.0	0.0	0.0	0.0	0.0	0.0	0.0	0.0
Commercial banks	0.0	0.0	0.0	0.0	0.0	0.0	0.0	0.0	0.0	0.0
Memo:										
IBRD	0.0	0.0	0.2	-0.4	0.4	-0.8	-1.1	-1.0	-0.1	0.1
IDA	0.0	0.0	0.0	0.0	0.0	0.0	0.0	0.0	0.0	0.0
DEBT SERVICE (LTDS)	**0.0**	**0.3**	**16.3**	**19.4**	**19.6**	**20.0**	**18.3**	**17.3**	**17.7**	**19.9**
Public and publicly guaranteed	**0.0**	**0.3**	**16.3**	**19.4**	**19.6**	**20.0**	**18.3**	**17.3**	**17.7**	**19.9**
Official creditors	0.0	0.3	6.4	9.0	9.5	12.0	12.7	13.4	13.4	15.5
Multilateral	0.0	0.2	4.0	5.1	5.5	4.9	6.8	7.4	7.0	8.6
Concessional	0.0	0.0	0.6	0.9	0.8	1.1	1.9	1.9	2.1	2.2
Bilateral	0.0	0.1	2.4	3.9	3.9	7.1	5.9	6.1	6.4	6.9
Concessional	0.0	0.1	2.2	3.1	3.7	6.3	5.1	5.9	6.3	6.8
Private creditors	0.0	0.0	9.9	10.4	10.2	8.0	5.6	3.9	4.3	4.4
Bonds	0.0	0.0	0.0	0.0	0.0	0.0	0.0	0.0	0.0	0.0
Commercial banks	0.0	0.0	7.6	8.6	8.7	6.2	4.4	2.8	3.2	3.4
Other private	0.0	0.0	2.4	1.8	1.5	1.8	1.1	1.1	1.1	1.1
Private nonguaranteed	**0.0**	**0.0**	**0.0**	**0.0**	**0.0**	**0.0**	**0.0**	**0.0**	**0.0**	**0.0**
Bonds	0.0	0.0	0.0	0.0	0.0	0.0	0.0	0.0	0.0	0.0
Commercial banks	0.0	0.0	0.0	0.0	0.0	0.0	0.0	0.0	0.0	0.0
Memo:										
IBRD	0.0	0.0	0.5	1.0	1.0	1.1	1.0	1.0	1.0	1.1
IDA	0.0	0.0	0.0	0.0	0.0	0.0	0.0	0.0	0.0	0.0
UNDISBURSED DEBT	**0.0**	**23.9**	**53.1**	**61.4**	**64.3**	**74.9**	**57.0**	**46.0**	**36.0**	**27.7**
Official creditors	0.0	23.4	45.7	47.8	54.6	60.1	48.6	41.9	32.9	26.1
Private creditors	0.0	0.6	7.4	13.6	9.8	14.8	8.3	4.1	3.1	1.5
Memorandum items										
Concessional LDOD	0.0	18.8	74.8	78.1	93.4	98.9	94.1	87.0	89.4	89.3
Variable rate LDOD	0.0	0.0	5.9	6.3	9.8	10.3	8.9	7.2	6.5	6.0
Public sector LDOD	0.0	25.1	131.3	130.7	149.0	151.0	146.5	137.9	146.8	151.1
Private sector LDOD	0.0	0.0	0.0	0.0	0.0	0.0	0.0	0.0	0.0	0.0

6. CURRENCY COMPOSITION OF LONG-TERM DEBT (PERCENT)

	1970	1980	1988	1989	1990	1991	1992	1993	1994	1995
Deutsche mark	0.0	8.0	3.0	3.7	3.7	4.0	4.0	3.7	3.6	3.6
French franc	0.0	2.8	19.3	20.3	22.5	22.2	22.3	20.8	20.0	19.1
Japanese yen	0.0	0.0	0.0	0.0	0.0	0.0	0.0	0.0	0.0	0.0
Pound sterling	0.0	68.0	16.3	14.1	14.6	12.7	9.7	9.5	8.9	7.9
Swiss franc	0.0	0.0	7.4	8.9	9.2	8.9	8.5	8.6	8.9	9.5
U.S.dollars	0.0	8.4	12.6	10.9	10.5	9.7	9.5	9.0	7.2	5.8
Multiple currency	0.0	12.7	22.1	23.5	23.0	22.4	24.6	26.9	30.6	32.4
Special drawing rights	0.0	0.0	0.0	0.0	0.0	0.0	0.0	0.0	0.1	0.4
All other currencies	0.0	0.0	19.3	18.5	16.6	20.2	21.6	21.5	20.8	21.3

SEYCHELLES

(US$ million, unless otherwise indicated)

	1970	1980	1988	1989	1990	1991	1992	1993	1994	1995
7. DEBT RESTRUCTURINGS										
Total amount rescheduled	0.0	0.0	0.0	0.0	0.0	0.0	0.0	0.0	0.0	0.0
Debt stock rescheduled	0.0	0.0	0.0	0.0	0.0	0.0	0.0	0.0	0.0	0.0
Principal rescheduled	0.0	0.0	0.0	0.0	0.0	0.0	0.0	0.0	0.0	0.0
Official	0.0	0.0	0.0	0.0	0.0	0.0	0.0	0.0	0.0	0.0
Private	0.0	0.0	0.0	0.0	0.0	0.0	0.0	0.0	0.0	0.0
Interest rescheduled	0.0	0.0	0.0	0.0	0.0	0.0	0.0	0.0	0.0	0.0
Official	0.0	0.0	0.0	0.0	0.0	0.0	0.0	0.0	0.0	0.0
Private	0.0	0.0	0.0	0.0	0.0	0.0	0.0	0.0	0.0	0.0
Debt forgiven	..	..	0.0	0.0	0.0	0.0	0.0	0.0	0.0	0.0
Memo: interest forgiven	..	..	0.0	0.0	0.0	0.0	0.0	0.0	0.0	0.0
Debt stock reduction	0.0	0.0	0.0	0.0	0.0	0.0	0.0	0.0	0.0	0.0
of which debt buyback	0.0	0.0	0.0	0.0	0.0	0.0	0.0	0.0	0.0	0.0
8. DEBT STOCK-FLOW RECONCILIATION										
Total change in debt stocks	..	..	..	-1.2	28.6	3.2	-17.9	-17.3	7.0	-5.5
Net flows on debt	..	..	..	0.9	13.5	4.3	-8.0	-12.4	-3.7	-12.9
Net change in interest arrears	..	..	..	-0.3	0.2	0.1	0.1	0.2	0.5	0.2
Interest capitalized	..	..	..	0.0	0.0	0.0	0.0	0.0	0.0	0.0
Debt forgiveness or reduction	..	..	..	0.0	0.0	0.0	0.0	0.0	0.0	0.0
Cross-currency valuation	..	..	..	-1.2	14.8	-2.0	-7.9	-4.0	8.7	6.6
Residual	..	..	..	-0.6	0.2	0.8	-2.1	-1.1	1.5	0.5
9. AVERAGE TERMS OF NEW COMMITMENTS										
ALL CREDITORS										
Interest (%)	0.0	6.6	6.4	6.7	4.4	7.6	8.1	7.6	0.0	8.0
Maturity (years)	15.0	15.6	10.8	16.2	21.3	26.3	35.0	15.1	0.0	35.0
Grace period (years)	1.0	5.1	3.3	5.5	7.7	3.6	5.0	5.6	0.0	5.0
Grant element (%)	49.3	20.2	20.1	21.3	43.9	13.7	13.9	13.7	0.0	13.9
Official creditors										
Interest (%)	0.0	6.6	4.8	5.2	3.6	8.1	8.1	7.6	0.0	8.0
Maturity (years)	15.0	15.7	16.1	21.4	23.6	36.0	35.0	15.1	0.0	35.0
Grace period (years)	1.0	5.1	4.4	7.4	8.5	6.0	5.0	5.6	0.0	5.0
Grant element (%)	49.3	20.3	30.7	33.8	49.5	14.2	13.9	13.7	0.0	13.9
Private creditors										
Interest (%)	0.0	7.2	9.2	9.2	11.5	6.7	0.0	0.0	0.0	0.0
Maturity (years)	0.0	5.0	1.2	8.0	3.0	9.0	0.0	0.0	0.0	0.0
Grace period (years)	0.0	0.5	1.2	2.5	0.9	-0.7	0.0	0.0	0.0	0.0
Grant element (%)	0.0	5.8	0.8	1.8	-1.6	12.8	0.0	0.0	0.0	0.0
Memorandum items										
Commitments	0.1	11.4	2.9	29.7	14.0	27.6	5.6	4.5	0.0	1.5
Official creditors	0.1	11.4	1.8	18.2	12.4	17.7	5.6	4.5	0.0	1.5
Private creditors	0.0	0.1	1.0	11.6	1.5	9.9	0.0	0.0	0.0	0.0

10. CONTRACTUAL OBLIGATIONS ON OUTSTANDING LONG-TERM DEBT

	1996	1997	1998	1999	2000	2001	2002	2003	2004	2005
TOTAL										
Disbursements	13.5	7.9	4.0	1.6	0.4	0.2	0.1	0.0	0.0	0.0
Principal	14.1	12.4	12.0	11.1	10.5	9.5	8.5	7.8	7.3	6.4
Interest	6.5	6.6	6.3	5.8	5.3	4.8	4.4	4.0	3.7	3.3
Official creditors										
Disbursements	12.5	7.5	3.9	1.6	0.4	0.2	0.1	0.0	0.0	0.0
Principal	10.0	10.0	10.4	10.6	10.0	9.0	8.0	7.4	7.3	6.4
Interest	6.0	6.3	6.1	5.7	5.2	4.8	4.4	4.0	3.7	3.3
Bilateral creditors										
Disbursements	0.4	0.2	0.0	0.0	0.0	0.0	0.0	0.0	0.0	0.0
Principal	5.8	5.4	5.4	5.1	4.9	4.9	4.0	3.4	3.3	2.9
Interest	1.7	1.6	1.4	1.2	1.0	0.9	0.8	0.6	0.5	0.4
Multilateral creditors										
Disbursements	12.1	7.3	3.9	1.6	0.4	0.2	0.1	0.0	0.0	0.0
Principal	4.2	4.6	5.0	5.4	5.1	4.1	4.0	4.0	4.0	3.5
Interest	4.3	4.7	4.8	4.6	4.2	3.9	3.7	3.4	3.1	2.9
Private creditors										
Disbursements	1.0	0.4	0.1	0.0	0.0	0.0	0.0	0.0	0.0	0.0
Principal	4.1	2.3	1.6	0.6	0.5	0.5	0.5	0.4	0.0	0.0
Interest	0.5	0.3	0.2	0.1	0.0	0.0	0.0	0.0	0.0	0.0
Commercial banks										
Disbursements	1.0	0.4	0.1	0.0	0.0	0.0	0.0	0.0	0.0	0.0
Principal	3.1	1.6	1.6	0.6	0.5	0.5	0.5	0.4	0.0	0.0
Interest	0.4	0.3	0.2	0.1	0.0	0.0	0.0	0.0	0.0	0.0
Other private										
Disbursements	0.0	0.0	0.0	0.0	0.0	0.0	0.0	0.0	0.0	0.0
Principal	1.0	0.7	0.0	0.0	0.0	0.0	0.0	0.0	0.0	0.0
Interest	0.1	0.0	0.0	0.0	0.0	0.0	0.0	0.0	0.0	0.0

SIERRA LEONE

(US$ million, unless otherwise indicated)

	1970	1980	1988	1989	1990	1991	1992	1993	1994	1995
1. SUMMARY DEBT DATA										
TOTAL DEBT STOCKS (EDT)	..	**435**	**1,054**	**1,088**	**1,206**	**1,303**	**1,313**	**1,452**	**1,532**	**1,226**
Long-term debt (LDOD)	**61**	**323**	**568**	**573**	**652**	**704**	**745**	**820**	**888**	**968**
Public and publicly guaranteed	61	323	568	573	652	704	745	820	888	968
Private nonguaranteed	0	0	0	0	0	0	0	0	0	0
Use of IMF credit	**0**	**59**	**109**	**105**	**108**	**101**	**92**	**84**	**146**	**165**
Short-term debt	..	**53**	**377**	**411**	**446**	**498**	**476**	**548**	**498**	**94**
of which interest arrears on LDOD	..	7	57	78	114	153	55	52	15	7
Official creditors	..	4	42	60	88	121	46	48	10	7
Private creditors	..	4	15	18	25	31	9	4	4	0
Memo: principal arrears on LDOD	..	18	176	213	256	279	137	124	49	29
Official creditors	..	6	124	153	182	195	112	105	30	25
Private creditors	..	12	52	60	74	84	26	19	19	4
Memo: export credits	..	..	107	116	166	166	144	159	144	131
TOTAL DEBT FLOWS										
Disbursements	**8**	**106**	**32**	**17**	**46**	**53**	**48**	**92**	**209**	**124**
Long-term debt	8	86	32	17	46	53	48	92	72	105
IMF purchases	0	21	0	0	0	0	0	0	137	20
Principal repayments	**16**	**49**	**8**	**3**	**7**	**9**	**17**	**13**	**93**	**62**
Long-term debt	11	32	7	1	2	1	11	5	13	58
IMF repurchases	5	17	1	2	5	8	5	8	81	4
Net flows on debt	**-8**	**58**	**19**	**27**	**38**	**57**	**108**	**154**	**102**	**-147**
of which short-term debt	..	..	-5	13	-1	13	76	75	-13	-210
Interest payments (INT)	..	**16**	**8**	**2**	**9**	**5**	**18**	**19**	**65**	**21**
Long-term debt	3	8	3	1	3	1	11	13	22	18
IMF charges	0	2	0	0	0	1	3	2	38	1
Short-term debt	..	6	5	1	5	4	5	4	5	2
Net transfers on debt	..	**42**	**11**	**26**	**30**	**52**	**89**	**135**	**38**	**-168**
Total debt service paid (TDS)	..	**64**	**16**	**5**	**16**	**14**	**35**	**31**	**158**	**83**
Long-term debt	13	39	10	2	6	3	22	18	35	76
IMF repurchases and charges	5	19	1	2	5	8	9	10	119	4
Short-term debt (interest only)	..	6	5	1	5	4	5	4	5	2
2. AGGREGATE NET RESOURCE FLOWS AND NET TRANSFERS (LONG-TERM)										
NET RESOURCE FLOWS	**7**	**59**	**57**	**90**	**106**	**90**	**76**	**224**	**128**	**135**
Net flow of long-term debt (ex. IMF)	-3	54	25	16	44	52	37	87	59	47
Foreign direct investment (net)	8	-19	-23	22	32	8	-6	-7	-4	1
Portfolio equity flows	0	0	0	0	0	0	0	0	0	0
Grants (excluding technical coop.)	1	24	55	51	30	30	45	144	72	87
Memo: technical coop. grants	5	21	33	29	30	28	28	30	27	25
NET TRANSFERS	**0**	**47**	**66**	**59**	**52**	**79**	**64**	**209**	**102**	**114**
Interest on long-term debt	3	8	3	1	3	1	11	13	22	18
Profit remittances on FDI	5	5	-12	30	51	10	1	2	3	2
3. MAJOR ECONOMIC AGGREGATES										
Gross national product (GNP)	415	1,136	1,210	1,094	785	709	584	681	769	768
Exports of goods & services (XGS)	..	276	157	178	210	225	204	175	167	105
of which workers remittances	..	0	0	0	0	0	0	0	0	0
Imports of goods & services (MGS)	..	494	177	245	287	220	217	209	214	226
International reserves (RES)	39	31	7	4	5	10	21	33	50	52
Current account balance	..	-165	-3	-60	-69	15	-6	-10	-35	-113
4. DEBT INDICATORS										
EDT / XGS (%)	..	157.7	672.9	611.3	573.2	578.6	642.9	827.7	916.9	1,163.5
EDT / GNP (%)	..	38.3	87.1	99.5	153.6	183.8	224.8	213.1	199.3	159.7
TDS / XGS (%)	..	23.2	9.9	2.6	7.5	6.3	17.1	17.9	94.7	78.5
INT / XGS (%)	..	5.6	5.0	1.0	4.1	2.4	9.0	10.6	38.9	20.1
INT / GNP (%)	..	1.4	0.6	0.2	1.1	0.8	3.2	2.7	8.4	2.8
RES / EDT (%)	..	7.0	0.7	0.3	0.4	0.7	1.6	2.3	3.2	4.2
RES / MGS (months)	..	0.7	0.5	0.2	0.2	0.5	1.1	1.9	2.8	2.7
Short-term / EDT (%)	..	12.2	35.8	37.7	37.0	38.2	36.2	37.8	32.5	7.6
Concessional / EDT (%)	..	32.8	30.9	29.4	29.7	31.9	35.1	38.4	41.3	61.9
Multilateral / EDT (%)	..	14.2	16.1	15.8	15.1	14.3	15.6	18.2	21.7	34.3

SIERRA LEONE

(US$ million, unless otherwise indicated)

	1970	1980	1988	1989	1990	1991	1992	1993	1994	1995
5. LONG-TERM DEBT										
DEBT OUTSTANDING (LDOD)	**61**	**323**	**568**	**573**	**652**	**704**	**745**	**820**	**888**	**968**
Public and publicly guaranteed	**61**	**323**	**568**	**573**	**652**	**704**	**745**	**820**	**888**	**968**
Official creditors	34	212	486	492	557	611	714	798	868	964
Multilateral	6	62	170	172	182	187	205	264	332	420
Concessional	3	40	157	160	170	175	201	261	329	417
Bilateral	28	150	316	320	376	424	509	534	535	544
Concessional	14	103	169	161	188	240	260	297	305	341
Private creditors	27	111	82	81	95	93	32	22	21	4
Bonds	0	0	0	0	0	0	0	0	0	0
Commercial banks	3	20	17	17	17	17	17	17	17	0
Other private	24	91	65	64	78	76	15	5	4	4
Private nonguaranteed	**0**	**0**	**0**	**0**	**0**	**0**	**0**	**0**	**0**	**0**
Bonds	0	0	0	0	0	0	0	0	0	0
Commercial banks	0	0	0	0	0	0	0	0	0	0
Memo:										
IBRD	6	13	10	10	11	10	4	3	3	3
IDA	0	29	78	78	81	81	108	143	186	231
DISBURSEMENTS	**8**	**86**	**32**	**17**	**46**	**53**	**48**	**92**	**72**	**105**
Public and publicly guaranteed	**8**	**86**	**32**	**17**	**46**	**53**	**48**	**92**	**72**	**105**
Official creditors	4	44	32	17	42	53	48	92	72	105
Multilateral	3	9	19	5	1	6	36	64	58	91
Concessional	0	5	19	5	1	6	36	64	58	91
Bilateral	1	35	13	13	41	47	12	28	14	13
Concessional	1	30	13	1	41	47	12	28	14	13
Private creditors	4	42	0	0	4	0	0	0	0	0
Bonds	0	0	0	0	0	0	0	0	0	0
Commercial banks	0	0	0	0	0	0	0	0	0	0
Other private	4	42	0	0	4	0	0	0	0	0
Private nonguaranteed	**0**	**0**	**0**	**0**	**0**	**0**	**0**	**0**	**0**	**0**
Bonds	0	0	0	0	0	0	0	0	0	0
Commercial banks	0	0	0	0	0	0	0	0	0	0
Memo:										
IBRD	3	2	0	0	0	0	0	0	0	0
IDA	0	2	1	0	0	0	32	36	38	44
PRINCIPAL REPAYMENTS	**11**	**32**	**7**	**1**	**2**	**1**	**11**	**5**	**13**	**58**
Public and publicly guaranteed	**11**	**32**	**7**	**1**	**2**	**1**	**11**	**5**	**13**	**58**
Official creditors	1	3	6	0	2	1	11	5	13	29
Multilateral	0	1	5	0	2	1	11	3	4	4
Concessional	0	0	0	0	0	1	4	2	3	3
Bilateral	1	2	1	0	0	0	1	2	9	25
Concessional	0	0	0	0	0	0	1	0	1	4
Private creditors	10	29	1	1	0	0	0	0	0	29
Bonds	5	0	0	0	0	0	0	0	0	0
Commercial banks	1	3	0	0	0	0	0	0	0	29
Other private	4	27	1	1	0	0	0	0	0	0
Private nonguaranteed	**0**	**0**	**0**	**0**	**0**	**0**	**0**	**0**	**0**	**0**
Bonds	0	0	0	0	0	0	0	0	0	0
Commercial banks	0	0	0	0	0	0	0	0	0	0
Memo:										
IBRD	0	1	0	0	0	0	6	0	0	1
IDA	0	0	0	0	0	0	3	1	1	2
NET FLOWS ON DEBT	**-3**	**54**	**25**	**16**	**44**	**52**	**37**	**87**	**59**	**47**
Public and publicly guaranteed	**-3**	**54**	**25**	**16**	**44**	**52**	**37**	**87**	**59**	**47**
Official creditors	3	42	26	17	40	52	37	87	59	76
Multilateral	3	8	14	4	-1	4	25	61	54	88
Concessional	0	5	19	5	1	5	32	62	55	88
Bilateral	1	34	12	13	41	47	12	26	5	-12
Concessional	1	29	13	1	41	47	12	28	12	9
Private creditors	-6	12	-1	-1	4	0	0	0	0	-29
Bonds	-5	0	0	0	0	0	0	0	0	0
Commercial banks	-1	-3	0	0	0	0	0	0	0	-29
Other private	-1	15	-1	-1	4	0	0	0	0	0
Private nonguaranteed	**0**	**0**	**0**	**0**	**0**	**0**	**0**	**0**	**0**	**0**
Bonds	0	0	0	0	0	0	0	0	0	0
Commercial banks	0	0	0	0	0	0	0	0	0	0
Memo:										
IBRD	3	2	0	0	0	0	-6	0	0	-1
IDA	0	2	1	0	0	0	29	35	37	42

SIERRA LEONE

(US$ million, unless otherwise indicated)

	1970	1980	1988	1989	1990	1991	1992	1993	1994	1995
INTEREST PAYMENTS (LINT)	**3**	**8**	**3**	**1**	**3**	**1**	**11**	**13**	**22**	**18**
Public and publicly guaranteed	**3**	**8**	**3**	**1**	**3**	**1**	**11**	**13**	**22**	**18**
Official creditors	1	2	3	1	3	1	11	13	22	18
Multilateral	0	1	3	0	2	1	8	2	2	3
Concessional	0	0	0	0	1	1	4	2	2	2
Bilateral	1	1	0	0	1	0	3	11	20	16
Concessional	0	0	0	0	1	0	3	1	2	2
Private creditors	1	5	0	0	0	0	0	0	0	0
Bonds	0	0	0	0	0	0	0	0	0	0
Commercial banks	0	1	0	0	0	0	0	0	0	0
Other private	1	4	0	0	0	0	0	0	0	0
Private nonguaranteed	**0**	**0**	**0**	**0**	**0**	**0**	**0**	**0**	**0**	**0**
Bonds	0	0	0	0	0	0	0	0	0	0
Commercial banks	0	0	0	0	0	0	0	0	0	0
Memo:										
IBRD	0	1	0	0	0	1	4	0	0	0
IDA	0	0	0	0	0	0	4	1	1	2
NET TRANSFERS ON DEBT	**-5**	**46**	**22**	**16**	**41**	**50**	**27**	**74**	**37**	**28**
Public and publicly guaranteed	**-5**	**46**	**22**	**16**	**41**	**50**	**27**	**74**	**37**	**28**
Official creditors	2	39	23	17	37	50	27	74	37	58
Multilateral	3	7	12	4	-3	3	17	59	52	85
Concessional	0	5	19	5	0	4	27	60	53	86
Bilateral	-1	33	11	13	40	47	9	15	-15	-28
Concessional	1	29	12	1	40	47	9	27	11	7
Private creditors	-7	7	-1	-1	4	0	0	0	0	-29
Bonds	-5	0	0	0	0	0	0	0	0	0
Commercial banks	-1	-4	0	0	0	0	0	0	0	-29
Other private	-1	11	-1	-1	4	0	0	0	0	0
Private nonguaranteed	**0**	**0**	**0**	**0**	**0**	**0**	**0**	**0**	**0**	**0**
Bonds	0	0	0	0	0	0	0	0	0	0
Commercial banks	0	0	0	0	0	0	0	0	0	0
Memo:										
IBRD	2	1	0	-1	0	-1	-10	-1	-1	-1
IDA	0	2	1	0	0	-1	26	34	36	41
DEBT SERVICE (LTDS)	**13**	**39**	**10**	**2**	**6**	**3**	**22**	**18**	**35**	**76**
Public and publicly guaranteed	**13**	**39**	**10**	**2**	**6**	**3**	**22**	**18**	**35**	**76**
Official creditors	2	5	9	1	6	3	22	18	35	47
Multilateral	0	2	7	1	4	3	19	5	6	6
Concessional	0	1	1	0	1	1	9	4	5	5
Bilateral	2	3	1	0	1	0	3	13	29	41
Concessional	1	1	0	0	1	0	3	1	3	6
Private creditors	11	35	1	1	0	0	0	0	0	29
Bonds	5	0	0	0	0	0	0	0	0	0
Commercial banks	1	4	0	0	0	0	0	0	0	29
Other private	5	31	1	1	0	0	0	0	0	0
Private nonguaranteed	**0**	**0**	**0**	**0**	**0**	**0**	**0**	**0**	**0**	**0**
Bonds	0	0	0	0	0	0	0	0	0	0
Commercial banks	0	0	0	0	0	0	0	0	0	0
Memo:										
IBRD	0	1	0	1	0	1	10	1	1	1
IDA	0	0	0	0	0	1	6	2	2	3
UNDISBURSED DEBT	**25**	**115**	**137**	**237**	**233**	**217**	**328**	**357**	**331**	**286**
Official creditors	22	94	137	237	233	217	328	357	331	286
Private creditors	2	22	0	0	0	0	0	0	0	0
Memorandum items										
Concessional LDOD	17	143	326	320	358	415	460	557	633	759
Variable rate LDOD	6	0	7	7	8	8	9	6	12	12
Public sector LDOD	61	323	568	573	652	704	745	820	888	968
Private sector LDOD	0	0	0	0	0	0	0	0	0	0

6. CURRENCY COMPOSITION OF LONG-TERM DEBT (PERCENT)

	1970	1980	1988	1989	1990	1991	1992	1993	1994	1995
Deutsche mark	10.9	17.4	4.9	5.1	5.1	4.6	3.2	2.3	2.2	1.7
French franc	19.1	3.0	5.5	5.7	5.6	5.2	4.2	3.8	2.8	2.3
Japanese yen	0.0	5.3	8.4	7.3	6.9	6.8	6.0	5.4	5.2	4.2
Pound sterling	38.9	11.5	2.4	2.1	2.2	2.0	1.4	0.8	0.6	0.7
Swiss franc	0.8	11.8	8.2	7.3	7.7	6.8	4.0	3.1	3.1	2.9
U.S.dollars	16.9	26.2	31.1	31.5	29.4	27.2	40.7	44.2	43.1	41.3
Multiple currency	10.3	4.4	5.7	5.6	5.0	5.1	4.6	6.8	8.5	10.8
Special drawing rights	0.0	0.0	10.9	10.8	10.3	9.6	8.6	8.7	9.5	9.6
All other currencies	2.9	20.4	23.0	24.5	27.8	32.7	27.3	25.0	25.0	26.4

SIERRA LEONE

(US$ million, unless otherwise indicated)

	1970	1980	1988	1989	1990	1991	1992	1993	1994	1995
7. DEBT RESTRUCTURINGS										
Total amount rescheduled	0	..	0	0	0	0	204	43	30	32
Debt stock rescheduled	0	..	0	0	0	0	0	0	0	0
Principal rescheduled	0	..	0	0	0	0	127	31	23	26
Official	0	..	0	0	0	0	73	21	22	26
Private	0	..	0	0	0	0	54	10	1	0
Interest rescheduled	0	..	0	0	0	0	77	12	7	5
Official	0	..	0	0	0	0	57	7	7	5
Private	0	..	0	0	0	0	20	5	0	0
Debt forgiven	..	..	0	0	0	0	27	7	24	7
Memo: interest forgiven	..	..	0	0	0	0	13	2	2	119
Debt stock reduction	0	..	0	0	0	0	0	0	0	231
of which debt buyback	0	..	0	0	0	0	0	0	0	29
8. DEBT STOCK-FLOW RECONCILIATION										
Total change in debt stocks	..	..	..	34	118	96	10	139	80	-306
Net flows on debt	..	..	..	27	38	57	108	154	102	-147
Net change in interest arrears	..	..	..	21	36	39	-98	-3	-38	-7
Interest capitalized	..	..	..	0	0	0	77	12	7	5
Debt forgiveness or reduction	..	..	..	0	0	0	-27	-7	-24	-208
Cross-currency valuation	..	..	..	-6	48	-3	-36	-16	26	19
Residual	..	..	..	-8	-5	4	-13	-1	7	32
9. AVERAGE TERMS OF NEW COMMITMENTS										
ALL CREDITORS										
Interest (%)	2.9	5.2	2.5	2.4	2.4	0.7	1.0	0.7	1.5	0.9
Maturity (years)	26.7	25.8	40.1	21.0	28.3	48.3	39.3	38.9	32.4	32.2
Grace period (years)	5.6	6.5	9.9	11.2	9.0	10.3	9.4	10.2	8.8	7.8
Grant element (%)	49.9	34.5	64.0	60.2	61.0	82.2	76.2	80.2	68.0	67.8
Official creditors										
Interest (%)	2.1	4.5	2.5	2.4	1.4	0.7	1.0	0.7	1.5	0.9
Maturity (years)	33.0	30.6	40.1	21.0	32.0	48.3	39.3	38.9	32.4	32.2
Grace period (years)	6.8	8.4	9.9	11.2	10.2	10.3	9.4	10.2	8.8	7.8
Grant element (%)	61.6	42.4	64.0	60.2	69.8	82.2	76.2	80.2	68.0	67.8
Private creditors										
Interest (%)	5.4	7.0	0.0	0.0	9.1	0.0	0.0	0.0	0.0	0.0
Maturity (years)	6.7	12.8	0.0	0.0	3.0	0.0	0.0	0.0	0.0	0.0
Grace period (years)	1.7	1.3	0.0	0.0	1.0	0.0	0.0	0.0	0.0	0.0
Grant element (%)	12.7	12.5	0.0	0.0	1.2	0.0	0.0	0.0	0.0	0.0
Memorandum items										
Commitments	25	70	12	123	31	46	181	137	35	50
Official creditors	19	51	12	123	27	46	181	137	35	50
Private creditors	6	19	0	0	4	0	0	0	0	0

10. CONTRACTUAL OBLIGATIONS ON OUTSTANDING LONG-TERM DEBT

	1996	1997	1998	1999	2000	2001	2002	2003	2004	2005
TOTAL										
Disbursements	84	82	55	32	18	9	5	1	0	0
Principal	87	66	24	23	26	33	39	42	45	45
Interest	24	20	18	18	18	17	16	16	15	14
Official creditors										
Disbursements	84	82	55	32	18	9	5	1	0	0
Principal	87	66	24	23	26	33	39	42	45	45
Interest	24	20	18	18	18	17	16	16	15	14
Bilateral creditors										
Disbursements	6	5	2	1	1	0	0	0	0	0
Principal	80	57	13	11	14	21	26	27	26	26
Interest	20	16	13	13	13	12	11	11	10	9
Multilateral creditors										
Disbursements	78	77	53	31	18	9	4	1	0	0
Principal	7	8	11	12	12	11	12	16	19	20
Interest	4	5	5	5	5	5	5	5	5	5
Private creditors										
Disbursements	0	0	0	0	0	0	0	0	0	0
Principal	0	0	0	0	0	0	0	0	0	0
Interest	0	0	0	0	0	0	0	0	0	0
Commercial banks										
Disbursements	0	0	0	0	0	0	0	0	0	0
Principal	0	0	0	0	0	0	0	0	0	0
Interest	0	0	0	0	0	0	0	0	0	0
Other private										
Disbursements	0	0	0	0	0	0	0	0	0	0
Principal	0	0	0	0	0	0	0	0	0	0
Interest	0	0	0	0	0	0	0	0	0	0

SLOVAK REPUBLIC

(US$ million, unless otherwise indicated)

1. SUMMARY DEBT DATA

	1970	*1980*	*1988*	*1989*	*1990*	*1991*	*1992*	*1993*	*1994*	*1995*
TOTAL DEBT STOCKS (EDT)	..	..	**1,718**	**1,816**	**2,008**	**2,655**	**2,846**	**3,331**	**4,800**	**5,827**
Long-term debt (LDOD)	..	..	**1,147**	**1,222**	**1,505**	**1,764**	**1,810**	**2,060**	**2,922**	**3,656**
Public and publicly guaranteed	..	..	1,147	1,222	1,505	1,764	1,810	2,059	2,909	3,570
Private nonguaranteed	0	0	0	0	0	0	0	1	13	85
Use of IMF credit	**0**	**0**	**0**	**0**	**0**	**399**	**469**	**557**	**642**	**457**
Short-term debt	..	..	**571**	**594**	**503**	**492**	**567**	**715**	**1,236**	**1,714**
of which interest arrears on LDOD	..	..	0	0	0	0	0	0	0	0
Official creditors	..	..	0	0	0	0	0	0	0	0
Private creditors	..	..	0	0	0	0	0	0	0	0
Memo: principal arrears on LDOD	..	..	0	0	0	0	0	1	2	2
Official creditors	..	..	0	0	0	0	0	0	0	0
Private creditors	..	..	0	0	0	0	0	1	2	2
Memo: export credits	..	..	533	518	834	1,132	770	748	1,397	1,527
TOTAL DEBT FLOWS										
Disbursements	..	..	**477**	**325**	**436**	**881**	**412**	**950**	**1,090**	**1,214**
Long-term debt	..	..	477	325	436	499	310	861	952	1,214
IMF purchases	0	0	0	0	0	382	102	90	138	0
Principal repayments	..	..	**331**	**365**	**171**	**248**	**364**	**434**	**542**	**813**
Long-term debt	..	..	331	365	171	248	349	434	453	613
IMF repurchases	0	0	0	0	0	0	15	0	89	201
Net flows on debt	..	..	**201**	**-17**	**173**	**622**	**123**	**664**	**1,069**	**878**
of which short-term debt	..	..	54	23	-91	-11	75	148	521	478
Interest payments (INT)	..	..	**132**	**134**	**147**	**155**	**196**	**212**	**250**	**270**
Long-term debt	..	..	90	97	84	106	120	153	134	133
IMF charges	0	0	0	0	0	16	32	32	30	32
Short-term debt	..	..	42	37	63	33	44	27	85	105
Net transfers on debt	..	..	**69**	**-151**	**26**	**467**	**-73**	**452**	**820**	**608**
Total debt service paid (TDS)	..	..	**463**	**500**	**318**	**402**	**560**	**646**	**791**	**1,083**
Long-term debt	..	..	421	462	256	354	469	587	588	746
IMF repurchases and charges	0	0	0	0	0	16	47	32	119	233
Short-term debt (interest only)	..	..	42	37	63	33	44	27	85	105

2. AGGREGATE NET RESOURCE FLOWS AND NET TRANSFERS (LONG-TERM)

	1970	*1980*	*1988*	*1989*	*1990*	*1991*	*1992*	*1993*	*1994*	*1995*
NET RESOURCE FLOWS	..	..	**147**	**-40**	**264**	**278**	**-14**	**652**	**762**	**855**
Net flow of long-term debt (ex. IMF)	0	0	147	-40	264	251	-39	426	499	601
Foreign direct investment (net)	0	0	0	0	0	0	0	199	203	183
Portfolio equity flows	..	..	0	0	0	0	0	0	0	60
Grants (excluding technical coop.)	0	0	0	0	0	27	26	27	61	12
Memo: technical coop. grants	0	0	0	0	0	11	38	23	18	68
NET TRANSFERS	..	..	**56**	**-137**	**180**	**172**	**-133**	**500**	**628**	**722**
Interest on long-term debt	..	..	90	97	84	106	120	153	134	133
Profit remittances on FDI	0	0	0	0	0	0	0	0	0	0

3. MAJOR ECONOMIC AGGREGATES

	1970	*1980*	*1988*	*1989*	*1990*	*1991*	*1992*	*1993*	*1994*	*1995*
Gross national product (GNP)	..	..	17,862	17,655	15,496	10,811	11,711	11,898	13,731	17,377
Exports of goods & services (XGS)	..	..	..	..	..	..	..	7,576	9,160	11,188
of which workers remittances	..	..	..	..	..	..	..	0	0	0
Imports of goods & services (MGS)	..	..	..	..	..	..	..	8,254	8,509	10,639
International reserves (RES)	..	..	..	..	..	..	..	920	2,186	3,863
Current account balance	..	..	..	..	..	..	..	-580	719	635

4. DEBT INDICATORS

	1970	*1980*	*1988*	*1989*	*1990*	*1991*	*1992*	*1993*	*1994*	*1995*
EDT / XGS (%)	..	..	..	..	..	..	..	44.0	52.4	52.1
EDT / GNP (%)	..	..	9.6	10.3	13.0	24.6	24.3	28.0	35.0	33.5
TDS / XGS (%)	..	..	..	..	..	..	..	8.5	8.6	9.7
INT / XGS (%)	..	..	..	..	..	..	..	2.8	2.7	2.4
INT / GNP (%)	..	..	0.7	0.8	0.9	1.4	1.7	1.8	1.8	1.6
RES / EDT (%)	..	..	..	..	..	..	..	27.6	45.5	66.3
RES / MGS (months)	..	..	..	..	..	..	..	1.3	3.1	4.4
Short-term / EDT (%)	..	..	33.2	32.7	25.0	18.5	19.9	21.5	25.8	29.4
Concessional / EDT (%)	..	..	4.7	4.4	4.1	7.2	11.8	6.1	10.6	15.3
Multilateral / EDT (%)	..	..	5.2	4.9	4.4	9.0	11.7	10.7	10.6	16.3

SLOVAK REPUBLIC

(US$ million, unless otherwise indicated)

	1970	1980	1988	1989	1990	1991	1992	1993	1994	1995
5. LONG-TERM DEBT										
DEBT OUTSTANDING (LDOD)	..	..	**1,147**	**1,222**	**1,505**	**1,764**	**1,810**	**2,060**	**2,922**	**3,656**
Public and publicly guaranteed	..	..	**1,147**	**1,222**	**1,505**	**1,764**	**1,810**	**2,059**	**2,909**	**3,570**
Official creditors	..	..	136	128	126	284	458	396	870	1,333
Multilateral	..	..	89	89	89	239	334	355	507	950
Concessional	..	..	80	80	82	165	222	204	215	577
Bilateral	..	..	47	38	36	45	124	41	363	382
Concessional	..	..	0	0	0	27	113	0	293	315
Private creditors	..	..	1,011	1,095	1,380	1,480	1,352	1,662	2,039	2,238
Bonds	..	..	0	0	0	73	73	348	552	552
Commercial banks	..	..	587	660	866	894	790	708	596	508
Other private	..	..	424	435	514	513	489	607	891	1,179
Private nonguaranteed	**0**	**0**	**0**	**0**	**0**	**0**	**0**	**1**	**13**	**85**
Bonds	..	..	0	0	0	0	0	0	0	0
Commercial banks	..	..	0	0	0	0	0	1	13	85
Memo:										
IBRD	0	0	0	0	0	70	110	151	247	263
IDA	0	0	0	0	0	0	0	0	0	0
DISBURSEMENTS	..	..	**477**	**325**	**436**	**499**	**310**	**861**	**952**	**1,214**
Public and publicly guaranteed	..	..	**477**	**325**	**436**	**499**	**310**	**860**	**939**	**1,146**
Official creditors	..	..	6	3	8	171	216	89	231	254
Multilateral	..	..	2	0	2	143	126	44	170	205
Concessional	..	..	0	0	2	77	82	4	39	132
Bilateral	..	..	4	3	6	27	91	45	61	49
Concessional	..	..	0	0	0	27	86	9	26	45
Private creditors	..	..	472	323	428	328	93	771	709	892
Bonds	..	..	0	0	0	73	0	275	267	0
Commercial banks	..	..	202	202	209	48	23	212	113	56
Other private	..	..	270	120	218	207	70	285	329	836
Private nonguaranteed	**0**	**0**	**0**	**0**	**0**	**0**	**0**	**1**	**12**	**68**
Bonds	..	..	0	0	0	0	0	0	0	0
Commercial banks	..	..	0	0	0	0	0	1	12	68
Memo:										
IBRD	0	0	0	0	0	67	44	40	86	8
IDA	0	0	0	0	0	0	0	0	0	0
PRINCIPAL REPAYMENTS	..	..	**331**	**365**	**171**	**248**	**349**	**434**	**453**	**613**
Public and publicly guaranteed	..	..	**331**	**365**	**171**	**248**	**349**	**434**	**453**	**609**
Official creditors	..	..	11	16	22	20	26	16	19	63
Multilateral	..	..	0	4	3	3	14	12	11	52
Concessional	..	..	0	4	0	0	11	11	11	52
Bilateral	..	..	11	12	19	17	11	4	8	11
Concessional	..	..	0	0	0	0	0	0	0	0
Private creditors	..	..	320	350	150	228	324	418	434	547
Bonds	..	..	0	0	0	0	0	0	63	0
Commercial banks	..	..	145	128	14	25	105	200	156	191
Other private	..	..	174	222	136	203	218	218	215	355
Private nonguaranteed	**0**	**0**	**0**	**0**	**0**	**0**	**0**	**0**	**0**	**3**
Bonds	..	..	0	0	0	0	0	0	0	0
Commercial banks	..	..	0	0	0	0	0	0	0	3
Memo:										
IBRD	0	0	0	0	0	0	0	0	0	0
IDA	0	0	0	0	0	0	0	0	0	0
NET FLOWS ON DEBT	..	..	**147**	**-40**	**264**	**251**	**-39**	**426**	**499**	**601**
Public and publicly guaranteed	..	..	**147**	**-40**	**264**	**251**	**-39**	**426**	**486**	**536**
Official creditors	..	..	-6	-13	-14	151	191	73	212	191
Multilateral	..	..	2	-4	0	141	111	32	159	153
Concessional	..	..	0	-4	2	77	72	-6	28	80
Bilateral	..	..	-7	-9	-13	10	80	41	53	38
Concessional	..	..	0	0	0	27	86	9	26	45
Private creditors	..	..	152	-27	278	101	-230	353	274	345
Bonds	..	..	0	0	0	73	0	275	204	0
Commercial banks	..	..	56	74	195	23	-82	12	-44	-136
Other private	..	..	96	-101	83	5	-148	67	115	481
Private nonguaranteed	**0**	**0**	**0**	**0**	**0**	**0**	**0**	**1**	**12**	**65**
Bonds	..	..	0	0	0	0	0	0	0	0
Commercial banks	..	..	0	0	0	0	0	1	12	65
Memo:										
IBRD	0	0	0	0	0	67	44	40	86	8
IDA	0	0	0	0	0	0	0	0	0	0

SLOVAK REPUBLIC

(US$ million, unless otherwise indicated)

	1970	1980	1988	1989	1990	1991	1992	1993	1994	1995
INTEREST PAYMENTS (LINT)	..	..	**90**	**97**	**84**	**106**	**120**	**153**	**134**	**133**
Public and publicly guaranteed	..	..	**90**	**97**	**84**	**106**	**120**	**153**	**134**	**133**
Official creditors	..	..	11	12	12	9	27	19	29	40
Multilateral	..	..	7	9	9	7	23	17	24	34
Concessional	..	..	6	8	8	6	17	8	12	11
Bilateral	..	..	4	3	3	2	4	1	4	7
Concessional	..	..	0	0	0	0	3	0	0	2
Private creditors	..	..	80	85	72	97	93	134	106	92
Bonds	..	..	0	0	0	0	7	12	7	39
Commercial banks	..	..	46	43	46	63	54	79	86	20
Other private	..	..	34	41	27	34	32	43	13	34
Private nonguaranteed	**0**	**0**	**0**	**0**	**0**	**0**	**0**	**0**	**0**	**1**
Bonds	..	..	0	0	0	0	0	0	0	0
Commercial banks	..	..	0	0	0	0	0	0	0	1
Memo:										
IBRD	0	0	0	0	0	0	5	9	12	17
IDA	0	0	0	0	0	0	0	0	0	0
NET TRANSFERS ON DEBT	..	..	**56**	**-137**	**180**	**145**	**-159**	**274**	**364**	**468**
Public and publicly guaranteed	..	..	**56**	**-137**	**180**	**145**	**-159**	**273**	**352**	**404**
Official creditors	..	..	-16	-25	-26	141	164	54	184	150
Multilateral	..	..	-5	-13	-9	134	89	15	135	119
Concessional	..	..	-6	-12	-6	70	54	-15	16	69
Bilateral	..	..	-11	-12	-17	8	75	39	49	31
Concessional	..	..	0	0	0	27	83	9	26	43
Private creditors	..	..	72	-112	206	4	-323	219	169	253
Bonds	..	..	0	0	0	73	-7	263	197	-39
Commercial banks	..	..	11	31	150	-40	-136	-68	-130	-156
Other private	..	..	62	-143	56	-29	-180	24	102	448
Private nonguaranteed	**0**	**0**	**0**	**0**	**0**	**0**	**0**	**1**	**12**	**64**
Bonds	..	..	0	0	0	0	0	0	0	0
Commercial banks	..	..	0	0	0	0	0	1	12	64
Memo:										
IBRD	0	0	0	0	0	67	39	31	74	-9
IDA	0	0	0	0	0	0	0	0	0	0
DEBT SERVICE (LTDS)	..	..	**421**	**462**	**256**	**354**	**469**	**587**	**588**	**746**
Public and publicly guaranteed	..	..	**421**	**462**	**256**	**354**	**469**	**587**	**587**	**742**
Official creditors	..	..	22	28	34	29	52	34	47	103
Multilateral	..	..	7	13	11	9	37	29	35	85
Concessional	..	..	6	12	8	6	28	19	23	62
Bilateral	..	..	15	15	22	20	15	5	12	18
Concessional	..	..	0	0	0	0	3	0	0	2
Private creditors	..	..	399	435	222	325	416	552	540	639
Bonds	..	..	0	0	0	0	7	12	70	39
Commercial banks	..	..	191	172	59	88	159	280	243	211
Other private	..	..	208	263	162	236	251	261	228	389
Private nonguaranteed	**0**	**0**	**0**	**0**	**0**	**0**	**0**	**0**	**1**	**4**
Bonds	..	..	0	0	0	0	0	0	0	0
Commercial banks	..	..	0	0	0	0	0	0	1	4
Memo:										
IBRD	0	0	0	0	0	0	5	9	12	17
IDA	0	0	0	0	0	0	0	0	0	0
UNDISBURSED DEBT	..	..	**437**	**640**	**211**	**277**	**127**	**335**	**337**	**303**
Official creditors	..	..	28	29	0	167	88	269	282	136
Private creditors	..	..	409	611	211	110	40	66	55	167
Memorandum items										
Concessional LDOD	..	..	80	80	82	192	336	204	508	892
Variable rate LDOD	..	..	357	245	182	226	206	226	414	961
Public sector LDOD	..	..	1,147	1,222	1,505	1,761	1,792	2,045	2,852	3,449
Private sector LDOD	..	..	0	0	0	3	18	15	70	207

6. CURRENCY COMPOSITION OF LONG-TERM DEBT (PERCENT)

	1970	1980	1988	1989	1990	1991	1992	1993	1994	1995
Deutsche mark	..	..	18.3	18.6	39.2	33.0	22.7	13.7	11.3	3.6
French franc	..	..	0.5	1.2	4.7	6.4	5.7	4.2	3.2	2.9
Japanese yen	..	..	5.2	4.2	3.7	3.4	1.2	0.8	0.8	1.2
Pound sterling	..	..	0.2	0.2	0.5	0.2	0.1	0.0	0.2	0.1
Swiss franc	..	..	3.6	3.9	5.1	3.4	1.9	1.0	0.3	0.1
U.S.dollars	..	..	23.1	38.7	35.5	33.2	30.7	25.6	21.7	18.3
Multiple currency	..	..	45.5	29.1	5.6	15.5	34.6	53.2	60.5	71.0
Special drawing rights	..	..	0.0	0.0	0.0	0.0	0.0	0.0	0.0	0.0
All other currencies	..	..	3.6	4.1	5.6	4.9	3.1	1.6	2.1	2.7

SLOVAK REPUBLIC

(US$ million, unless otherwise indicated)

	1970	1980	1988	1989	1990	1991	1992	1993	1994	1995
7. DEBT RESTRUCTURINGS										
Total amount rescheduled	0	0	0	0	0	0	0	0	0	0
Debt stock rescheduled	0	0	0	0	0	0	0	0	0	0
Principal rescheduled	0	0	0	0	0	0	0	0	0	0
Official	0	0	0	0	0	0	0	0	0	0
Private	0	0	0	0	0	0	0	0	0	0
Interest rescheduled	0	0	0	0	0	0	0	0	0	0
Official	0	0	0	0	0	0	0	0	0	0
Private	0	0	0	0	0	0	0	0	0	0
Debt forgiven	..	..	0	0	0	0	0	0	0	0
Memo: interest forgiven	..	..	0	0	0	0	0	0	0	0
Debt stock reduction	0	0	0	0	0	0	0	0	0	0
of which debt buyback	0	0	0	0	0	0	0	0	0	0
8. DEBT STOCK-FLOW RECONCILIATION										
Total change in debt stocks	..	..	..	98	192	647	190	486	1,469	1,026
Net flows on debt	..	..	..	-17	173	622	123	664	1,069	878
Net change in interest arrears	..	..	..	0	0	0	0	0	0	0
Interest capitalized	..	..	..	0	0	0	0	0	0	0
Debt forgiveness or reduction	..	..	..	0	0	0	0	0	-1	0
Cross-currency valuation	..	..	..	6	119	-6	-41	-24	68	37
Residual	..	..	..	110	-101	31	109	-155	332	112
9. AVERAGE TERMS OF NEW COMMITMENTS										
ALL CREDITORS										
Interest (%)	..	..	6.5	4.9	7.8	5.5	3.8	8.7	7.8	6.5
Maturity (years)	..	..	7.2	8.7	5.4	11.5	15.7	12.3	10.7	9.7
Grace period (years)	..	..	2.7	2.8	3.6	3.4	4.1	7.3	5.9	5.8
Grant element (%)	..	..	13.0	21.2	6.2	22.2	36.7	1.5	6.5	16.1
Official creditors										
Interest (%)	..	..	5.8	6.5	3.4	4.3	3.7	4.8	5.9	2.1
Maturity (years)	..	..	6.6	5.1	19.1	16.7	17.3	15.3	12.1	12.1
Grace period (years)	..	..	1.9	0.7	5.3	4.5	4.4	4.7	3.1	4.6
Grant element (%)	..	..	13.4	7.7	46.1	33.5	39.8	30.7	17.7	42.0
Private creditors										
Interest (%)	..	..	6.5	4.9	7.8	7.3	4.3	10.7	8.7	7.1
Maturity (years)	..	..	7.2	8.7	5.3	4.3	7.5	10.8	10.0	9.3
Grace period (years)	..	..	2.7	2.8	3.5	1.8	2.5	8.7	7.4	5.9
Grant element (%)	..	..	13.0	21.3	5.9	6.5	20.6	-13.8	0.8	12.4
Memorandum items										
Commitments	..	..	426	468	265	579	166	807	816	311
Official creditors	..	..	10	3	2	337	139	278	275	39
Private creditors	..	..	415	465	263	242	27	528	541	272

10. CONTRACTUAL OBLIGATIONS ON OUTSTANDING LONG-TERM DEBT

	1996	1997	1998	1999	2000	2001	2002	2003	2004	2005
TOTAL										
Disbursements	113	98	41	25	14	9	3	1	0	0
Principal	428	480	948	412	445	277	274	261	125	98
Interest	213	212	185	124	100	72	55	38	22	15
Official creditors										
Disbursements	37	37	25	17	11	7	1	1	0	0
Principal	55	120	136	145	150	148	145	136	125	98
Interest	57	76	70	63	55	46	38	29	22	15
Bilateral creditors										
Disbursements	2	0	0	0	0	0	0	0	0	0
Principal	17	44	47	47	46	44	41	36	36	9
Interest	14	20	18	15	12	9	7	5	3	1
Multilateral creditors										
Disbursements	36	37	25	17	11	7	1	1	0	0
Principal	39	76	89	98	104	104	104	101	89	89
Interest	43	55	52	48	43	37	31	25	19	14
Private creditors										
Disbursements	75	61	15	9	3	2	2	0	0	0
Principal	373	360	812	267	294	129	129	124	0	0
Interest	156	137	115	61	45	26	17	9	0	0
Commercial banks										
Disbursements	40	27	10	5	0	0	0	0	0	0
Principal	97	115	106	105	166	1	0	0	0	0
Interest	33	29	23	17	11	0	0	0	0	0
Other private										
Disbursements	35	34	5	4	3	2	2	0	0	0
Principal	276	245	706	162	129	128	128	124	0	0
Interest	123	107	93	44	34	26	17	8	0	0

SLOVENIA

(US$ million, unless otherwise indicated)

	1970	1980	1988	1989	1990	1991	1992	1993	1994	1995
1. SUMMARY DEBT DATA										
TOTAL DEBT STOCKS (EDT)	..	..	..	..	..	..	..	**1,909**	**2,632**	**3,489**
Long-term debt (LDOD)	..	..	..	..	..	..	..	**1,772**	**2,148**	**2,966**
Public and publicly guaranteed	..	..	..	..	..	..	..	1,256	1,358	1,491
Private nonguaranteed	0	0	0	0	0	0	0	517	791	1,475
Use of IMF credit	**0**	**0**	**0**	**0**	**0**	**0**	**0**	**12**	**7**	**4**
Short-term debt	..	..	..	..	..	..	..	**125**	**477**	**520**
of which interest arrears on LDOD	..	..	..	..	..	..	..	8	36	62
Official creditors	..	..	..	..	..	..	..	2	3	4
Private creditors	..	..	..	..	..	..	..	6	32	59
Memo: principal arrears on LDOD	..	..	..	..	..	..	..	102	140	146
Official creditors	..	..	..	..	..	..	..	82	88	60
Private creditors	..	..	..	..	..	..	..	20	52	87
Memo: export credits	..	..	0	0	0	28	143	204	581	553
TOTAL DEBT FLOWS										
Disbursements	..	..	..	..	..	..	..	**324**	**543**	**1,131**
Long-term debt	..	..	..	..	..	..	..	324	543	1,131
IMF purchases	0	0	0	0	0	0	0	0	0	0
Principal repayments	..	..	..	..	..	..	..	**281**	**314**	**532**
Long-term debt	..	..	..	..	..	..	..	257	308	529
IMF repurchases	0	0	0	0	0	0	0	24	5	3
Net flows on debt	..	..	..	..	..	..	..	**160**	**553**	**615**
of which short-term debt	..	..	..	..	..	..	..	117	324	16
Interest payments (INT)	..	..	..	..	..	..	..	**144**	**125**	**191**
Long-term debt	..	..	..	..	..	..	..	129	105	158
IMF charges	0	0	0	0	0	0	0	2	1	0
Short-term debt	..	..	..	..	..	..	..	13	20	32
Net transfers on debt	..	..	..	..	..	..	..	**17**	**428**	**424**
Total debt service paid (TDS)	..	..	..	..	..	..	..	**425**	**439**	**723**
Long-term debt	..	..	..	..	..	..	..	386	413	687
IMF repurchases and charges	0	0	0	0	0	0	0	26	6	4
Short-term debt (interest only)	..	..	..	..	..	..	..	13	20	32
2. AGGREGATE NET RESOURCE FLOWS AND NET TRANSFERS (LONG-TERM)										
NET RESOURCE FLOWS	..	..	..	..	..	..	..	**180**	**362**	**778**
Net flow of long-term debt (ex. IMF)	..	..	..	..	..	..	..	67	234	602
Foreign direct investment (net)	..	..	..	..	..	..	..	113	128	176
Portfolio equity flows	..	..	..	..	..	..	..	0	0	0
Grants (excluding technical coop.)	..	..	..	..	..	..	..	0	0	0
Memo: technical coop. grants	..	..	..	..	..	..	..	0	0	0
NET TRANSFERS	..	..	..	..	..	..	..	**52**	**258**	**620**
Interest on long-term debt	..	..	..	..	..	..	..	129	105	158
Profit remittances on FDI	..	..	..	..	..	..	..	0	0	0
3. MAJOR ECONOMIC AGGREGATES										
Gross national product (GNP)	..	..	..	..	..	..	..	12,622	14,428	18,680
Exports of goods & services (XGS)	..	..	..	..	..	..	..	7,635	8,716	10,487
of which workers remittances	..	..	..	..	..	..	..	44	56	53
Imports of goods & services (MGS)	..	..	..	..	..	..	..	7,423	8,246	10,420
International reserves (RES)	..	..	..	..	..	..	..	788	1,499	1,821
Current account balance	..	..	..	..	..	..	..	188	457	42
4. DEBT INDICATORS										
EDT / XGS (%)	..	..	..	..	..	..	..	25.0	30.2	33.3
EDT / GNP (%)	..	..	..	..	..	..	..	15.1	18.2	18.7
TDS / XGS (%)	..	..	..	..	..	..	..	5.6	5.0	6.9
INT / XGS (%)	..	..	..	..	..	..	..	1.9	1.4	1.8
INT / GNP (%)	..	..	..	..	..	..	..	1.1	0.9	1.0
RES / EDT (%)	..	..	..	..	..	..	..	41.3	57.0	52.2
RES / MGS (months)	..	..	..	..	..	..	..	1.3	2.2	2.1
Short-term / EDT (%)	..	..	..	..	..	..	..	6.5	18.1	14.9
Concessional / EDT (%)	..	..	..	..	..	..	..	1.3	1.4	1.2
Multilateral / EDT (%)	..	..	..	..	..	..	..	24.3	18.8	15.4

SLOVENIA

(US$ million, unless otherwise indicated)

	1970	1980	1988	1989	1990	1991	1992	1993	1994	1995
5. LONG-TERM DEBT										
DEBT OUTSTANDING (LDOD)	..	..	..	..	..	..	..	**1,772**	**2,148**	**2,966**
Public and publicly guaranteed	..	..	..	..	..	..	..	**1,256**	**1,358**	**1,491**
Official creditors	..	..	..	..	..	..	..	722	745	727
Multilateral	..	..	..	..	..	..	..	463	494	536
Concessional	..	..	..	..	..	..	..	18	29	32
Bilateral	..	..	..	..	..	..	..	259	250	190
Concessional	..	..	..	..	..	..	..	6	7	9
Private creditors	..	..	..	..	..	..	..	534	613	764
Bonds	..	..	..	..	..	..	..	0	0	0
Commercial banks	..	..	..	..	..	..	..	497	578	731
Other private	..	..	..	..	..	..	..	37	35	33
Private nonguaranteed	**0**	**0**	**0**	**0**	**0**	**0**	**0**	**517**	**791**	**1,475**
Bonds	..	..	..	..	..	..	..	0	0	0
Commercial banks	..	..	..	..	..	..	..	517	791	1,475
Memo:										
IBRD	0	0	0	0	0	0	0	151	165	187
IDA	0	0	0	0	0	0	0	0	0	0
DISBURSEMENTS	..	..	..	..	..	..	..	**324**	**543**	**1,131**
Public and publicly guaranteed	..	..	..	..	..	..	..	**137**	**159**	**305**
Official creditors	..	..	..	..	..	..	..	40	84	114
Multilateral	..	..	..	..	..	..	..	20	72	99
Concessional	..	..	..	..	..	..	..	1	9	10
Bilateral	..	..	..	..	..	..	..	20	11	15
Concessional	..	..	..	..	..	..	..	5	1	1
Private creditors	..	..	..	..	..	..	..	97	75	192
Bonds	..	..	..	..	..	..	..	0	0	0
Commercial banks	..	..	..	..	..	..	..	97	75	192
Other private	..	..	..	..	..	..	..	0	0	0
Private nonguaranteed	**0**	**0**	**0**	**0**	**0**	**0**	**0**	**187**	**384**	**826**
Bonds	..	..	..	..	..	..	..	0	0	0
Commercial banks	..	..	..	..	..	..	..	187	384	826
Memo:										
IBRD	0	0	0	0	0	0	0	0	40	45
IDA	0	0	0	0	0	0	0	0	0	0
PRINCIPAL REPAYMENTS	..	..	..	..	..	..	..	**257**	**308**	**529**
Public and publicly guaranteed	..	..	..	..	..	..	..	**104**	**146**	**220**
Official creditors	..	..	..	..	..	..	..	100	116	173
Multilateral	..	..	..	..	..	..	..	68	83	88
Concessional	..	..	..	..	..	..	..	2	2	9
Bilateral	..	..	..	..	..	..	..	32	33	86
Concessional	..	..	..	..	..	..	..	0	0	0
Private creditors	..	..	..	..	..	..	..	5	30	47
Bonds	..	..	..	..	..	..	..	0	0	0
Commercial banks	..	..	..	..	..	..	..	0	25	42
Other private	..	..	..	..	..	..	..	4	5	5
Private nonguaranteed	**0**	**0**	**0**	**0**	**0**	**0**	**0**	**153**	**162**	**309**
Bonds	..	..	..	..	..	..	..	0	0	0
Commercial banks	..	..	..	..	..	..	..	153	162	309
Memo:										
IBRD	0	0	0	0	0	0	0	25	36	31
IDA	0	0	0	0	0	0	0	0	0	0
NET FLOWS ON DEBT	..	..	..	..	..	..	..	**67**	**234**	**602**
Public and publicly guaranteed	..	..	..	..	..	..	..	**33**	**13**	**86**
Official creditors	..	..	..	..	..	..	..	-60	-32	-59
Multilateral	..	..	..	..	..	..	..	-48	-10	12
Concessional	..	..	..	..	..	..	..	-1	8	1
Bilateral	..	..	..	..	..	..	..	-12	-22	-71
Concessional	..	..	..	..	..	..	..	5	1	1
Private creditors	..	..	..	..	..	..	..	93	45	145
Bonds	..	..	..	..	..	..	..	0	0	0
Commercial banks	..	..	..	..	..	..	..	97	50	150
Other private	..	..	..	..	..	..	..	-4	-5	-5
Private nonguaranteed	**0**	**0**	**0**	**0**	**0**	**0**	**0**	**34**	**222**	**517**
Bonds	..	..	..	..	..	..	..	0	0	0
Commercial banks	..	..	..	..	..	..	..	34	222	517
Memo:										
IBRD	0	0	0	0	0	0	0	-25	4	14
IDA	0	0	0	0	0	0	0	0	0	0

SLOVENIA

(US$ million, unless otherwise indicated)

	1970	1980	1988	1989	1990	1991	1992	1993	1994	1995
INTEREST PAYMENTS (LINT)	..	..	..	..	..	..	..	**129**	**105**	**158**
Public and publicly guaranteed	..	..	..	..	..	..	..	**83**	**61**	**76**
Official creditors	..	..	..	..	..	..	..	61	52	61
Multilateral	..	..	..	..	..	..	..	47	40	42
Concessional	..	..	..	..	..	..	..	1	2	2
Bilateral	..	..	..	..	..	..	..	14	12	20
Concessional	..	..	..	..	..	..	..	0	0	0
Private creditors	..	..	..	..	..	..	..	22	10	15
Bonds	..	..	..	..	..	..	..	0	0	0
Commercial banks	..	..	..	..	..	..	..	20	8	14
Other private	..	..	..	..	..	..	..	2	1	1
Private nonguaranteed	**0**	**0**	**0**	**0**	**0**	**0**	**0**	**46**	**44**	**82**
Bonds	..	..	..	..	..	..	..	0	0	0
Commercial banks	..	..	..	..	..	..	..	46	44	82
Memo:										
IBRD	0	0	0	0	0	0	0	13	12	11
IDA	0	0	0	0	0	0	0	0	0	0
NET TRANSFERS ON DEBT	..	..	..	..	..	..	..	**-61**	**130**	**444**
Public and publicly guaranteed	..	..	..	..	..	..	..	**-50**	**-48**	**9**
Official creditors	..	..	..	..	..	..	..	-120	-84	-120
Multilateral	..	..	..	..	..	..	..	-95	-50	-30
Concessional	..	..	..	..	..	..	..	-2	6	-1
Bilateral	..	..	..	..	..	..	..	-25	-34	-90
Concessional	..	..	..	..	..	..	..	5	1	1
Private creditors	..	..	..	..	..	..	..	71	36	130
Bonds	..	..	..	..	..	..	..	0	0	0
Commercial banks	..	..	..	..	..	..	..	77	42	135
Other private	..	..	..	..	..	..	..	-6	-6	-6
Private nonguaranteed	**0**	**0**	**0**	**0**	**0**	**0**	**0**	**-12**	**178**	**435**
Bonds	..	..	..	..	..	..	..	0	0	0
Commercial banks	..	..	..	..	..	..	..	-12	178	435
Memo:										
IBRD	0	0	0	0	0	0	0	-38	-7	3
IDA	0	0	0	0	0	0	0	0	0	0
DEBT SERVICE (LTDS)	..	..	..	..	..	..	..	**386**	**413**	**687**
Public and publicly guaranteed	..	..	..	..	..	..	..	**187**	**207**	**296**
Official creditors	..	..	..	..	..	..	..	161	167	234
Multilateral	..	..	..	..	..	..	..	115	123	129
Concessional	..	..	..	..	..	..	..	3	3	11
Bilateral	..	..	..	..	..	..	..	45	45	105
Concessional	..	..	..	..	..	..	..	0	0	0
Private creditors	..	..	..	..	..	..	..	26	40	62
Bonds	..	..	..	..	..	..	..	0	0	0
Commercial banks	..	..	..	..	..	..	..	21	34	56
Other private	..	..	..	..	..	..	..	6	6	6
Private nonguaranteed	**0**	**0**	**0**	**0**	**0**	**0**	**0**	**199**	**206**	**391**
Bonds	..	..	..	..	..	..	..	0	0	0
Commercial banks	..	..	..	..	..	..	..	199	206	391
Memo:										
IBRD	0	0	0	0	0	0	0	38	47	42
IDA	0	0	0	0	0	0	0	0	0	0
UNDISBURSED DEBT	..	..	..	..	..	..	..	**313**	**404**	**285**
Official creditors	..	..	..	..	..	..	..	263	365	266
Private creditors	..	..	..	..	..	..	..	50	39	19
Memorandum items										
Concessional LDOD	..	..	..	..	..	..	..	25	36	42
Variable rate LDOD	..	..	..	..	..	..	..	1,342	1,746	2,624
Public sector LDOD	..	..	..	..	..	..	..	1,176	1,297	1,452
Private sector LDOD	..	..	..	..	..	..	..	596	852	1,514

6. CURRENCY COMPOSITION OF LONG-TERM DEBT (PERCENT)

	1970	1980	1988	1989	1990	1991	1992	1993	1994	1995
Deutsche mark	..	..	..	..	..	..	..	15.5	14.1	14.7
French franc	..	..	..	..	..	..	..	3.7	3.4	3.0
Japanese yen	..	..	..	..	..	..	..	10.5	10.9	9.4
Pound sterling	..	..	..	..	..	..	..	0.9	0.9	0.8
Swiss franc	..	..	..	..	..	..	..	3.1	2.8	2.5
U.S.dollars	..	..	..	..	..	..	..	32.8	34.5	36.2
Multiple currency	..	..	..	..	..	..	..	12.0	12.2	12.5
Special drawing rights	..	..	..	..	..	..	..	0.0	0.0	0.0
All other currencies	..	..	..	..	..	..	..	21.3	21.4	20.9

SLOVENIA

(US$ million, unless otherwise indicated)

	1970	1980	1988	1989	1990	1991	1992	1993	1994	1995
7. DEBT RESTRUCTURINGS										
Total amount rescheduled	0	0	0	0	0	0	0	0	0	0
Debt stock rescheduled	0	0	0	0	0	0	0	0	0	0
Principal rescheduled	0	0	0	0	0	0	0	0	0	0
Official	0	0	0	0	0	0	0	0	0	0
Private	0	0	0	0	0	0	0	0	0	0
Interest rescheduled	0	0	0	0	0	0	0	0	0	0
Official	0	0	0	0	0	0	0	0	0	0
Private	0	0	0	0	0	0	0	0	0	0
Debt forgiven	..	..	0	0	0	0	0	0	0	0
Memo: interest forgiven	..	..	0	0	0	0	0	0	0	0
Debt stock reduction	0	0	0	0	0	0	0	0	0	0
of which debt buyback	0	0	0	0	0	0	0	0	0	0
8. DEBT STOCK-FLOW RECONCILIATION										
Total change in debt stocks	..	..	..	..	..	..	..	1,909	723	857
Net flows on debt	..	..	..	..	..	..	..	160	553	615
Net change in interest arrears	..	..	..	..	..	..	..	8	28	27
Interest capitalized	..	..	..	..	..	..	..	0	0	0
Debt forgiveness or reduction	..	..	..	..	..	..	..	0	0	0
Cross-currency valuation	..	..	..	..	..	..	..	-13	129	92
Residual	..	..	..	..	..	..	..	1,754	13	123
9. AVERAGE TERMS OF NEW COMMITMENTS										
ALL CREDITORS										
Interest (%)	..	..	..	..	..	..	..	6.2	7.3	4.4
Maturity (years)	..	..	..	..	..	..	..	10.4	12.2	7.0
Grace period (years)	..	..	..	..	..	..	..	3.1	1.8	3.8
Grant element (%)	..	..	..	..	..	..	..	14.9	12.5	22.8
Official creditors										
Interest (%)	..	..	..	..	..	..	..	6.2	6.8	0.0
Maturity (years)	..	..	..	..	..	..	..	14.3	15.1	0.0
Grace period (years)	..	..	..	..	..	..	..	4.4	2.3	0.0
Grant element (%)	..	..	..	..	..	..	..	19.5	16.4	0.0
Private creditors										
Interest (%)	..	..	..	..	..	..	..	6.2	8.5	4.4
Maturity (years)	..	..	..	..	..	..	..	3.7	5.0	7.0
Grace period (years)	..	..	..	..	..	..	..	0.9	0.5	3.8
Grant element (%)	..	..	..	..	..	..	..	7.0	2.9	22.8
Memorandum items										
Commitments	..	..	..	..	..	..	..	352	261	172
Official creditors	..	..	..	..	..	..	..	222	186	0
Private creditors	..	..	..	..	..	..	..	130	75	172

10. CONTRACTUAL OBLIGATIONS ON OUTSTANDING LONG-TERM DEBT

	1996	1997	1998	1999	2000	2001	2002	2003	2004	2005
TOTAL										
Disbursements	109	81	44	23	13	6	3	1	0	0
Principal	578	432	376	308	297	313	197	127	108	94
Interest	212	169	137	111	91	73	62	43	29	26
Official creditors										
Disbursements	102	74	40	22	13	6	3	1	0	0
Principal	111	104	95	70	77	73	66	63	51	40
Interest	57	53	48	42	39	34	29	24	19	16
Bilateral creditors										
Disbursements	1	0	0	0	0	0	0	0	0	0
Principal	42	35	35	5	3	3	0	1	1	1
Interest	9	6	3	1	1	0	0	0	0	0
Multilateral creditors										
Disbursements	102	74	40	22	13	6	3	1	0	0
Principal	69	69	60	65	73	70	65	62	50	39
Interest	49	47	45	41	39	33	28	24	19	15
Private creditors										
Disbursements	7	7	4	1	1	0	0	0	0	0
Principal	467	328	281	238	220	240	132	64	58	54
Interest	155	115	89	69	52	39	34	19	10	11
Commercial banks										
Disbursements	0	0	0	0	0	0	0	0	0	0
Principal	95	79	65	59	51	92	92	33	33	33
Interest	42	37	32	27	24	20	14	8	6	4
Other private										
Disbursements	7	7	4	1	1	0	0	0	0	0
Principal	373	249	216	180	169	148	39	32	25	21
Interest	112	79	58	42	28	19	20	11	4	7

SOLOMON ISLANDS

(US$ million, unless otherwise indicated)

	1970	1980	1988	1989	1990	1991	1992	1993	1994	1995
1. SUMMARY DEBT DATA										
TOTAL DEBT STOCKS (EDT)	..	**19.4**	**103.7**	**100.0**	**120.5**	**129.5**	**94.3**	**150.5**	**154.9**	**157.5**
Long-term debt (LDOD)	..	**17.4**	**100.4**	**98.5**	**103.2**	**98.4**	**92.5**	**144.4**	**152.9**	**147.8**
Public and publicly guaranteed	..	17.4	100.4	98.5	103.2	98.4	92.5	94.3	98.4	99.0
Private nonguaranteed	0.0	0.0	0.0	0.0	0.0	0.0	0.0	50.1	54.5	48.8
Use of IMF credit	**0.0**	**0.0**	**1.7**	**1.4**	**0.7**	**0.0**	**0.0**	**0.0**	**0.0**	**0.0**
Short-term debt	..	**2.0**	**1.6**	**0.0**	**16.6**	**31.0**	**1.8**	**6.1**	**2.0**	**9.7**
of which interest arrears on LDOD	..	0.0	0.0	0.0	0.1	0.0	0.2	0.0	0.0	8.4
Official creditors	..	0.0	0.0	0.0	0.1	0.0	0.1	0.0	0.0	0.5
Private creditors	..	0.0	0.0	0.0	0.0	0.0	0.1	0.0	0.0	8.0
Memo: principal arrears on LDOD	..	0.0	0.0	0.0	0.2	0.0	0.5	0.0	1.2	11.4
Official creditors	..	0.0	0.0	0.0	0.2	0.0	0.3	0.0	0.0	1.5
Private creditors	..	0.0	0.0	0.0	0.0	0.0	0.2	0.0	1.2	9.9
Memo: export credits	..	..	32.0	28.0	29.0	69.0	65.0	64.0	62.0	65.0
TOTAL DEBT FLOWS										
Disbursements	..	**4.0**	**12.7**	**7.2**	**5.2**	**3.3**	**4.9**	**8.0**	**10.4**	**10.5**
Long-term debt	..	4.0	12.7	7.2	5.2	3.3	4.9	8.0	10.4	10.5
IMF purchases	0.0	0.0	0.0	0.0	0.0	0.0	0.0	0.0	0.0	0.0
Principal repayments	..	**0.0**	**3.4**	**5.9**	**7.9**	**9.2**	**5.2**	**7.1**	**12.5**	**6.5**
Long-term debt	..	0.0	3.0	5.7	7.0	8.6	5.2	7.1	12.5	6.5
IMF repurchases	0.0	0.0	0.4	0.2	0.8	0.6	0.0	0.0	0.0	0.0
Net flows on debt	..	**3.9**	**9.5**	**-0.3**	**13.8**	**8.6**	**-29.7**	**5.4**	**-6.3**	**3.2**
of which short-term debt	..	..	0.2	-1.6	16.5	14.5	-29.4	4.5	-4.1	-0.8
Interest payments (INT)	..	**0.3**	**3.8**	**3.8**	**3.7**	**4.2**	**2.4**	**2.8**	**3.3**	**1.6**
Long-term debt	..	0.0	3.5	3.6	3.1	2.7	1.5	2.6	3.1	1.5
IMF charges	0.0	0.0	0.1	0.1	0.1	0.0	0.0	0.0	0.0	0.0
Short-term debt	..	0.3	0.1	0.1	0.5	1.4	0.9	0.2	0.2	0.1
Net transfers on debt	..	**3.7**	**5.7**	**-4.1**	**10.1**	**4.4**	**-32.1**	**2.6**	**-9.6**	**1.6**
Total debt service paid (TDS)	..	**0.3**	**7.2**	**9.7**	**11.6**	**13.4**	**7.6**	**10.0**	**15.9**	**8.1**
Long-term debt	..	0.0	6.5	9.3	10.1	11.3	6.7	9.7	15.6	8.0
IMF repurchases and charges	0.0	0.0	0.5	0.3	1.0	0.7	0.0	0.0	0.0	0.0
Short-term debt (interest only)	..	0.3	0.1	0.1	0.5	1.4	0.9	0.2	0.2	0.1
2. AGGREGATE NET RESOURCE FLOWS AND NET TRANSFERS (LONG-TERM)										
NET RESOURCE FLOWS	..	**27.3**	**32.8**	**30.4**	**28.4**	**24.3**	**34.3**	**25.9**	**32.4**	**40.3**
Net flow of long-term debt (ex. IMF)	0.0	3.9	9.7	1.5	-1.8	-5.2	-0.3	0.9	-2.2	4.0
Foreign direct investment (net)	0.0	2.4	1.7	11.6	10.0	15.0	14.0	15.0	17.0	17.0
Portfolio equity flows	..	0.0	0.0	0.0	0.0	0.0	0.0	0.0	0.0	0.0
Grants (excluding technical coop.)	5.0	21.0	21.4	17.3	20.2	14.5	20.6	10.0	17.6	19.3
Memo: technical coop. grants	2.9	11.5	20.4	19.6	19.5	18.5	20.0	21.3	25.5	26.0
NET TRANSFERS	..	**12.4**	**23.9**	**20.9**	**23.3**	**17.7**	**28.8**	**18.3**	**23.3**	**33.8**
Interest on long-term debt	..	0.0	3.5	3.6	3.1	2.7	1.5	2.6	3.1	1.5
Profit remittances on FDI	0.0	14.9	5.3	5.9	2.0	3.8	4.0	5.0	6.0	5.0
3. MAJOR ECONOMIC AGGREGATES										
Gross national product (GNP)	..	107.9	212.1	227.8	207.3	230.4	258.7	264.1	304.3	350.3
Exports of goods & services (XGS)	..	85.0	107.5	105.1	97.8	116.4	139.4	227.4	255.1	..
of which workers remittances	..	0.0	0.0	0.0	0.0	0.0	0.0	0.0	0.0	..
Imports of goods & services (MGS)	..	117.0	183.0	181.3	163.6	190.6	182.8	208.1	236.1	..
International reserves (RES)	..	29.6	39.6	26.2	17.6	8.5	23.5	20.1	17.4	15.9
Current account balance	..	-12.2	-37.7	-33.2	-27.8	-35.8	13.1	24.4	20.1	..
4. DEBT INDICATORS										
EDT / XGS (%)	..	22.8	96.4	95.1	123.2	111.2	67.6	66.2	60.7	..
EDT / GNP (%)	..	18.0	48.9	43.9	58.1	56.2	36.4	57.0	50.9	44.9
TDS / XGS (%)	..	0.4	6.7	9.2	11.8	11.5	5.5	4.4	6.2	..
INT / XGS (%)	..	0.3	3.5	3.6	3.8	3.6	1.7	1.2	1.3	..
INT / GNP (%)	..	0.3	1.8	1.7	1.8	1.8	0.9	1.1	1.1	0.4
RES / EDT (%)	..	152.6	38.2	26.2	14.6	6.6	24.9	13.4	11.2	10.1
RES / MGS (months)	..	3.0	2.6	1.7	1.3	0.5	1.5	1.2	0.9	..
Short-term / EDT (%)	..	10.3	1.6	0.0	13.8	24.0	1.9	4.1	1.3	6.1
Concessional / EDT (%)	..	89.7	63.4	68.6	64.1	59.8	77.9	50.4	53.6	54.7
Multilateral / EDT (%)	..	36.7	46.4	53.4	51.0	49.3	66.9	44.6	48.3	49.7

SOLOMON ISLANDS

(US$ million, unless otherwise indicated)

	1970	1980	1988	1989	1990	1991	1992	1993	1994	1995
5. LONG-TERM DEBT										
DEBT OUTSTANDING (LDOD)	..	**17.4**	**100.4**	**98.5**	**103.2**	**98.4**	**92.5**	**144.4**	**152.9**	**147.8**
Public and publicly guaranteed	..	**17.4**	**100.4**	**98.5**	**103.2**	**98.4**	**92.5**	**94.3**	**98.4**	**99.0**
Official creditors	..	17.4	82.0	81.7	89.1	87.6	83.2	84.7	91.2	93.8
Multilateral	..	7.1	48.1	53.4	61.5	63.8	63.1	67.1	74.8	78.2
Concessional	..	7.1	48.1	53.4	61.5	63.8	63.1	67.1	74.8	78.2
Bilateral	..	10.3	33.9	28.3	27.7	23.8	20.1	17.6	16.4	15.6
Concessional	..	10.3	17.6	15.2	15.8	13.7	10.4	8.7	8.2	8.0
Private creditors	..	0.0	18.4	16.8	14.1	10.8	9.3	9.5	7.2	5.2
Bonds	..	0.0	0.0	0.0	0.0	0.0	0.0	0.0	0.0	0.0
Commercial banks	..	0.0	15.0	13.6	10.9	8.2	5.5	2.7	0.0	0.0
Other private	..	0.0	3.4	3.2	3.2	2.7	3.9	6.8	7.2	5.2
Private nonguaranteed	**0.0**	**0.0**	**0.0**	**0.0**	**0.0**	**0.0**	**0.0**	**50.1**	**54.5**	**48.8**
Bonds	..	0.0	0.0	0.0	0.0	0.0	0.0	0.0	0.0	0.0
Commercial banks	..	0.0	0.0	0.0	0.0	0.0	0.0	50.1	54.5	48.8
Memo:										
IBRD	0.0	0.0	0.0	0.0	0.0	0.0	0.0	0.0	0.0	0.0
IDA	0.0	0.0	10.8	12.8	16.6	18.7	18.4	19.6	22.4	25.9
DISBURSEMENTS	..	**4.0**	**12.7**	**7.2**	**5.2**	**3.3**	**4.9**	**8.0**	**10.4**	**10.5**
Public and publicly guaranteed	..	**4.0**	**12.7**	**7.2**	**5.2**	**3.3**	**4.9**	**8.0**	**2.8**	**7.8**
Official creditors	..	4.0	12.7	7.2	5.2	3.3	3.4	4.5	2.8	3.5
Multilateral	..	4.0	7.7	6.6	5.2	3.3	3.4	4.5	2.8	3.5
Concessional	..	4.0	7.7	6.6	5.2	3.3	3.4	4.5	2.8	3.5
Bilateral	..	0.0	4.9	0.6	0.0	0.0	0.0	0.0	0.0	0.0
Concessional	..	0.0	0.5	0.6	0.0	0.0	0.0	0.0	0.0	0.0
Private creditors	..	0.0	0.0	0.0	0.0	0.0	1.5	3.5	0.0	4.2
Bonds	..	0.0	0.0	0.0	0.0	0.0	0.0	0.0	0.0	0.0
Commercial banks	..	0.0	0.0	0.0	0.0	0.0	0.0	0.0	0.0	0.0
Other private	..	0.0	0.0	0.0	0.0	0.0	1.5	3.5	0.0	4.2
Private nonguaranteed	**0.0**	**0.0**	**0.0**	**0.0**	**0.0**	**0.0**	**0.0**	**0.0**	**7.6**	**2.8**
Bonds	..	0.0	0.0	0.0	0.0	0.0	0.0	0.0	0.0	0.0
Commercial banks	..	0.0	0.0	0.0	0.0	0.0	0.0	0.0	7.6	2.8
Memo:										
IBRD	0.0	0.0	0.0	0.0	0.0	0.0	0.0	0.0	0.0	0.0
IDA	0.0	0.0	1.3	2.3	2.5	1.9	0.5	1.2	1.8	3.2
PRINCIPAL REPAYMENTS	..	**0.0**	**3.0**	**5.7**	**7.0**	**8.6**	**5.2**	**7.1**	**12.5**	**6.5**
Public and publicly guaranteed	..	**0.0**	**3.0**	**5.7**	**7.0**	**8.6**	**5.2**	**7.1**	**6.0**	**1.8**
Official creditors	..	0.0	2.6	3.9	3.9	5.4	2.2	3.8	2.9	1.3
Multilateral	..	0.0	0.6	0.5	0.5	1.7	0.7	0.9	0.9	0.6
Concessional	..	0.0	0.6	0.5	0.5	1.7	0.7	0.9	0.9	0.6
Bilateral	..	0.0	2.1	3.5	3.4	3.8	1.5	2.9	2.0	0.7
Concessional	..	0.0	0.9	1.5	1.4	1.8	1.4	1.6	0.8	0.2
Private creditors	..	0.0	0.4	1.7	3.1	3.1	2.9	3.3	3.1	0.5
Bonds	..	0.0	0.0	0.0	0.0	0.0	0.0	0.0	0.0	0.0
Commercial banks	..	0.0	0.0	1.4	2.7	2.7	2.7	2.7	2.7	0.0
Other private	..	0.0	0.4	0.4	0.4	0.4	0.2	0.6	0.4	0.5
Private nonguaranteed	**0.0**	**0.0**	**0.0**	**0.0**	**0.0**	**0.0**	**0.0**	**0.0**	**6.5**	**4.7**
Bonds	..	0.0	0.0	0.0	0.0	0.0	0.0	0.0	0.0	0.0
Commercial banks	..	0.0	0.0	0.0	0.0	0.0	0.0	0.0	6.5	4.7
Memo:										
IBRD	0.0	0.0	0.0	0.0	0.0	0.0	0.0	0.0	0.0	0.0
IDA	0.0	0.0	0.0	0.0	0.0	0.0	0.0	0.1	0.1	0.1
NET FLOWS ON DEBT	..	**3.9**	**9.7**	**1.5**	**-1.8**	**-5.2**	**-0.3**	**0.9**	**-2.2**	**4.0**
Public and publicly guaranteed	..	**3.9**	**9.7**	**1.5**	**-1.8**	**-5.2**	**-0.3**	**0.9**	**-3.2**	**6.0**
Official creditors	..	3.9	10.0	3.2	1.3	-2.1	1.1	0.7	-0.1	2.2
Multilateral	..	4.0	7.2	6.1	4.7	1.7	2.6	3.6	1.9	2.9
Concessional	..	4.0	7.2	6.1	4.7	1.7	2.6	3.6	1.9	2.9
Bilateral	..	0.0	2.9	-2.8	-3.4	-3.8	-1.5	-2.9	-2.0	-0.7
Concessional	..	0.0	-0.5	-0.9	-1.4	-1.8	-1.4	-1.6	-0.8	-0.2
Private creditors	..	0.0	-0.4	-1.7	-3.1	-3.1	-1.4	0.2	-3.1	3.8
Bonds	..	0.0	0.0	0.0	0.0	0.0	0.0	0.0	0.0	0.0
Commercial banks	..	0.0	0.0	-1.4	-2.7	-2.7	-2.7	-2.7	-2.7	0.0
Other private	..	0.0	-0.4	-0.4	-0.4	-0.4	1.3	2.9	-0.4	3.8
Private nonguaranteed	**0.0**	**0.0**	**0.0**	**0.0**	**0.0**	**0.0**	**0.0**	**0.0**	**1.1**	**-2.0**
Bonds	..	0.0	0.0	0.0	0.0	0.0	0.0	0.0	0.0	0.0
Commercial banks	..	0.0	0.0	0.0	0.0	0.0	0.0	0.0	1.1	-2.0
Memo:										
IBRD	0.0	0.0	0.0	0.0	0.0	0.0	0.0	0.0	0.0	0.0
IDA	0.0	0.0	1.3	2.3	2.5	1.9	0.5	1.1	1.7	3.1

SOLOMON ISLANDS

(US$ million, unless otherwise indicated)

	1970	1980	1988	1989	1990	1991	1992	1993	1994	1995
INTEREST PAYMENTS (LINT)	..	**0.0**	**3.5**	**3.6**	**3.1**	**2.7**	**1.5**	**2.6**	**3.1**	**1.5**
Public and publicly guaranteed	..	**0.0**	**3.5**	**3.6**	**3.1**	**2.7**	**1.5**	**2.6**	**2.1**	**0.9**
Official creditors	..	0.0	1.9	1.8	1.6	1.7	1.0	1.8	1.5	0.8
Multilateral	..	0.0	0.5	0.5	0.6	0.6	0.6	0.7	0.7	0.5
Concessional	..	0.0	0.5	0.5	0.6	0.6	0.6	0.7	0.7	0.5
Bilateral	..	0.0	1.4	1.3	1.0	1.1	0.4	1.2	0.8	0.3
Concessional	..	0.0	0.2	0.2	0.0	0.2	0.1	0.2	0.1	0.0
Private creditors	..	0.0	1.6	1.8	1.5	1.1	0.5	0.8	0.6	0.1
Bonds	..	0.0	0.0	0.0	0.0	0.0	0.0	0.0	0.0	0.0
Commercial banks	..	0.0	1.3	1.5	1.2	0.8	0.4	0.2	0.1	0.0
Other private	..	0.0	0.3	0.3	0.3	0.2	0.1	0.5	0.5	0.1
Private nonguaranteed	**0.0**	**0.0**	**0.0**	**0.0**	**0.0**	**0.0**	**0.0**	**0.0**	**1.0**	**0.6**
Bonds	..	0.0	0.0	0.0	0.0	0.0	0.0	0.0	0.0	0.0
Commercial banks	..	0.0	0.0	0.0	0.0	0.0	0.0	0.0	1.0	0.6
Memo:										
IBRD	0.0	0.0	0.0	0.0	0.0	0.0	0.0	0.0	0.0	0.0
IDA	0.0	0.0	0.1	0.1	0.1	0.1	0.1	0.2	0.1	0.2
NET TRANSFERS ON DEBT	..	**3.9**	**6.1**	**-2.1**	**-4.9**	**-8.0**	**-1.8**	**-1.7**	**-5.3**	**2.5**
Public and publicly guaranteed	..	**3.9**	**6.1**	**-2.1**	**-4.9**	**-8.0**	**-1.8**	**-1.7**	**-5.3**	**5.1**
Official creditors	..	3.9	8.2	1.4	-0.3	-3.8	0.1	-1.1	-1.6	1.4
Multilateral	..	3.9	6.7	5.6	4.1	1.1	2.0	2.9	1.2	2.4
Concessional	..	3.9	6.7	5.6	4.1	1.1	2.0	2.9	1.2	2.4
Bilateral	..	0.0	1.5	-4.1	-4.4	-4.9	-2.0	-4.0	-2.8	-1.0
Concessional	..	0.0	-0.7	-1.1	-1.4	-2.0	-1.5	-1.8	-0.9	-0.2
Private creditors	..	0.0	-2.0	-3.5	-4.7	-4.2	-1.9	-0.6	-3.7	3.7
Bonds	..	0.0	0.0	0.0	0.0	0.0	0.0	0.0	0.0	0.0
Commercial banks	..	0.0	-1.3	-2.9	-3.9	-3.5	-3.1	-2.9	-2.8	0.0
Other private	..	0.0	-0.7	-0.6	-0.7	-0.6	1.2	2.4	-0.9	3.7
Private nonguaranteed	**0.0**	**0.0**	**0.0**	**0.0**	**0.0**	**0.0**	**0.0**	**0.0**	**0.0**	**-2.5**
Bonds	..	0.0	0.0	0.0	0.0	0.0	0.0	0.0	0.0	0.0
Commercial banks	..	0.0	0.0	0.0	0.0	0.0	0.0	0.0	0.0	-2.5
Memo:										
IBRD	0.0	0.0	0.0	0.0	0.0	0.0	0.0	0.0	0.0	0.0
IDA	0.0	0.0	1.2	2.2	2.4	1.8	0.4	0.9	1.6	3.0
DEBT SERVICE (LTDS)	..	**0.0**	**6.5**	**9.3**	**10.1**	**11.3**	**6.7**	**9.7**	**15.6**	**8.0**
Public and publicly guaranteed	..	**0.0**	**6.5**	**9.3**	**10.1**	**11.3**	**6.7**	**9.7**	**8.1**	**2.7**
Official creditors	..	0.0	4.5	5.8	5.5	7.1	3.3	5.7	4.4	2.1
Multilateral	..	0.0	1.0	1.0	1.1	2.2	1.3	1.6	1.6	1.1
Concessional	..	0.0	1.0	1.0	1.1	2.2	1.3	1.6	1.6	1.1
Bilateral	..	0.0	3.5	4.8	4.4	4.9	2.0	4.0	2.8	1.0
Concessional	..	0.0	1.1	1.7	1.4	2.0	1.5	1.8	0.9	0.2
Private creditors	..	0.0	2.0	3.5	4.7	4.2	3.4	4.1	3.7	0.6
Bonds	..	0.0	0.0	0.0	0.0	0.0	0.0	0.0	0.0	0.0
Commercial banks	..	0.0	1.3	2.9	3.9	3.5	3.1	2.9	2.8	0.0
Other private	..	0.0	0.7	0.6	0.7	0.6	0.3	1.2	0.9	0.6
Private nonguaranteed	**0.0**	**0.0**	**0.0**	**0.0**	**0.0**	**0.0**	**0.0**	**0.0**	**7.5**	**5.3**
Bonds	..	0.0	0.0	0.0	0.0	0.0	0.0	0.0	0.0	0.0
Commercial banks	..	0.0	0.0	0.0	0.0	0.0	0.0	0.0	7.5	5.3
Memo:										
IBRD	0.0	0.0	0.0	0.0	0.0	0.0	0.0	0.0	0.0	0.0
IDA	0.0	0.0	0.1	0.1	0.1	0.1	0.2	0.3	0.3	0.3
UNDISBURSED DEBT	..	**12.9**	**42.3**	**33.4**	**25.4**	**26.5**	**11.3**	**20.8**	**18.5**	**15.7**
Official creditors	..	12.9	27.3	18.4	10.4	11.5	8.1	20.8	18.5	15.7
Private creditors	..	0.0	15.0	15.0	15.0	15.0	3.1	0.0	0.0	0.0
Memorandum items										
Concessional LDOD	..	17.4	65.7	68.6	77.2	77.4	73.5	75.8	83.0	86.2
Variable rate LDOD	..	0.0	15.0	13.6	10.9	8.2	5.5	52.9	54.5	48.8
Public sector LDOD	..	17.4	100.4	98.5	103.2	98.4	92.5	94.3	98.4	99.0
Private sector LDOD	..	0.0	0.0	0.0	0.0	0.0	0.0	50.1	54.5	48.8

6. CURRENCY COMPOSITION OF LONG-TERM DEBT (PERCENT)

	1970	1980	1988	1989	1990	1991	1992	1993	1994	1995
Deutsche mark	..	0.0	3.4	3.2	3.1	2.7	2.5	1.7	1.3	0.9
French franc	..	0.0	0.0	0.0	0.0	0.0	0.0	0.0	0.0	0.0
Japanese yen	..	0.0	7.2	5.6	4.7	4.4	6.4	10.2	10.3	3.8
Pound sterling	..	59.2	14.9	12.8	13.1	11.8	8.9	7.1	6.5	6.5
Swiss franc	..	0.0	0.0	0.0	0.0	0.0	0.0	0.0	0.0	0.0
U.S.dollars	..	40.8	51.8	53.1	52.0	53.2	52.0	49.0	48.0	54.6
Multiple currency	..	0.0	3.3	6.0	7.3	7.1	8.6	11.7	12.8	12.7
Special drawing rights	..	0.0	6.2	6.2	6.3	6.9	7.2	7.8	8.5	8.4
All other currencies	..	0.0	13.3	13.2	13.5	14.0	14.3	12.6	12.6	13.0

SOLOMON ISLANDS

(US$ million, unless otherwise indicated)

	1970	1980	1988	1989	1990	1991	1992	1993	1994	1995
7. DEBT RESTRUCTURINGS										
Total amount rescheduled	0.0	0.0	0.0	0.0	0.0	0.0	8.1	0.0	0.0	0.0
Debt stock rescheduled	0.0	0.0	0.0	0.0	0.0	0.0	8.1	0.0	0.0	0.0
Principal rescheduled	0.0	0.0	0.0	0.0	0.0	0.0	0.0	0.0	0.0	0.0
Official	0.0	0.0	0.0	0.0	0.0	0.0	0.0	0.0	0.0	0.0
Private	0.0	0.0	0.0	0.0	0.0	0.0	0.0	0.0	0.0	0.0
Interest rescheduled	0.0	0.0	0.0	0.0	0.0	0.0	0.0	0.0	0.0	0.0
Official	0.0	0.0	0.0	0.0	0.0	0.0	0.0	0.0	0.0	0.0
Private	0.0	0.0	0.0	0.0	0.0	0.0	0.0	0.0	0.0	0.0
Debt forgiven	..	..	0.0	0.0	0.0	0.0	0.0	0.0	0.0	6.3
Memo: interest forgiven	..	..	0.0	0.0	0.0	0.0	0.0	0.0	0.0	0.0
Debt stock reduction	0.0	0.0	0.0	0.0	0.0	0.0	0.0	0.0	0.0	0.0
of which debt buyback	0.0	0.0	0.0	0.0	0.0	0.0	0.0	0.0	0.0	0.0
8. DEBT STOCK-FLOW RECONCILIATION										
Total change in debt stocks	..	..	..	-3.7	20.5	9.0	-35.2	56.2	4.4	2.5
Net flows on debt	..	..	..	-0.3	13.8	8.6	-29.7	5.4	-6.3	3.2
Net change in interest arrears	..	..	..	0.0	0.1	-0.1	0.2	-0.2	0.0	8.4
Interest capitalized	..	..	..	0.0	0.0	0.0	0.0	0.0	0.0	0.0
Debt forgiveness or reduction	..	..	..	0.0	0.0	0.0	0.0	0.0	0.0	-6.3
Cross-currency valuation	..	..	..	-2.1	5.3	-0.2	-3.1	0.4	5.2	1.2
Residual	..	..	..	-1.3	1.3	0.6	-2.6	50.7	5.5	-4.0
9. AVERAGE TERMS OF NEW COMMITMENTS										
ALL CREDITORS										
Interest (%)	..	1.0	0.0	0.0	2.2	1.0	4.2	0.8	0.0	7.8
Maturity (years)	..	39.8	0.0	0.0	17.7	41.6	18.4	39.5	0.0	10.2
Grace period (years)	..	10.3	0.0	0.0	11.5	9.6	5.0	10.0	0.0	0.7
Grant element (%)	..	78.4	0.0	0.0	56.9	78.4	36.2	80.2	0.0	7.6
Official creditors										
Interest (%)	..	1.0	0.0	0.0	2.2	1.0	1.0	0.8	0.0	0.0
Maturity (years)	..	39.8	0.0	0.0	17.7	41.6	39.7	39.5	0.0	0.0
Grace period (years)	..	10.3	0.0	0.0	11.5	9.6	10.2	10.0	0.0	0.0
Grant element (%)	..	78.4	0.0	0.0	56.9	78.4	78.3	80.2	0.0	0.0
Private creditors										
Interest (%)	..	0.0	0.0	0.0	0.0	0.0	6.0	0.0	0.0	7.8
Maturity (years)	..	0.0	0.0	0.0	0.0	0.0	6.5	0.0	0.0	10.2
Grace period (years)	..	0.0	0.0	0.0	0.0	0.0	2.0	0.0	0.0	0.7
Grant element (%)	..	0.0	0.0	0.0	0.0	0.0	12.6	0.0	0.0	7.6
Memorandum items										
Commitments	..	8.3	0.0	0.0	2.5	6.3	7.2	17.4	0.0	4.2
Official creditors	..	8.3	0.0	0.0	2.5	6.3	2.6	17.4	0.0	0.0
Private creditors	..	0.0	0.0	0.0	0.0	0.0	4.6	0.0	0.0	4.2

10. CONTRACTUAL OBLIGATIONS ON OUTSTANDING LONG-TERM DEBT

	1996	1997	1998	1999	2000	2001	2002	2003	2004	2005
TOTAL										
Disbursements	5.4	4.5	3.3	1.9	0.4	0.1	0.0	0.0	0.0	0.0
Principal	15.6	13.4	11.6	10.4	6.2	5.2	4.2	4.1	3.6	3.5
Interest	3.1	3.2	2.5	1.9	1.4	1.2	1.0	0.9	0.8	0.7
Official creditors										
Disbursements	5.4	4.5	3.3	1.9	0.4	0.1	0.0	0.0	0.0	0.0
Principal	3.3	3.6	3.7	3.6	3.7	3.9	2.9	2.7	3.1	3.2
Interest	1.3	1.3	1.2	1.1	1.0	0.9	0.8	0.7	0.7	0.7
Bilateral creditors										
Disbursements	0.0	0.0	0.0	0.0	0.0	0.0	0.0	0.0	0.0	0.0
Principal	1.9	1.9	1.9	1.9	1.9	2.0	0.7	0.4	0.4	0.4
Interest	0.5	0.4	0.4	0.3	0.2	0.1	0.0	0.0	0.0	0.0
Multilateral creditors										
Disbursements	5.4	4.5	3.3	1.9	0.4	0.1	0.0	0.0	0.0	0.0
Principal	1.3	1.6	1.8	1.7	1.7	1.9	2.1	2.3	2.7	2.8
Interest	0.8	0.8	0.8	0.8	0.8	0.8	0.7	0.7	0.7	0.7
Private creditors										
Disbursements	0.0	0.0	0.0	0.0	0.0	0.0	0.0	0.0	0.0	0.0
Principal	12.3	9.9	7.9	6.7	2.6	1.3	1.3	1.3	0.5	0.3
Interest	1.8	1.9	1.3	0.8	0.5	0.4	0.3	0.2	0.1	0.0
Commercial banks										
Disbursements	0.0	0.0	0.0	0.0	0.0	0.0	0.0	0.0	0.0	0.0
Principal	0.0	0.0	0.0	0.0	0.0	0.0	0.0	0.0	0.0	0.0
Interest	0.0	0.0	0.0	0.0	0.0	0.0	0.0	0.0	0.0	0.0
Other private										
Disbursements	0.0	0.0	0.0	0.0	0.0	0.0	0.0	0.0	0.0	0.0
Principal	12.3	9.9	7.9	6.7	2.6	1.3	1.3	1.3	0.5	0.3
Interest	1.8	1.9	1.3	0.8	0.5	0.4	0.3	0.2	0.1	0.0

SOMALIA

(US$ million, unless otherwise indicated)

	1970	1980	1988	1989	1990	1991	1992	1993	1994	1995
1. SUMMARY DEBT DATA										
TOTAL DEBT STOCKS (EDT)	**..**	**660**	**2,086**	**2,159**	**2,370**	**2,449**	**2,447**	**2,501**	**2,616**	**2,678**
Long-term debt (LDOD)	**77**	**595**	**1,779**	**1,813**	**1,926**	**1,945**	**1,898**	**1,897**	**1,935**	**1,961**
Public and publicly guaranteed	77	595	1,779	1,813	1,926	1,945	1,898	1,897	1,935	1,961
Private nonguaranteed	0	0	0	0	0	0	0	0	0	0
Use of IMF credit	**0**	**18**	**166**	**150**	**159**	**160**	**154**	**154**	**164**	**167**
Short-term debt	**..**	**47**	**141**	**196**	**285**	**344**	**395**	**450**	**518**	**551**
of which interest arrears on LDOD	..	8	129	183	255	313	364	419	487	520
Official creditors	..	8	129	181	249	305	354	406	471	503
Private creditors	..	0	0	3	5	8	11	13	16	17
Memo: principal arrears on LDOD	..	14	428	515	674	785	843	930	1,032	1,135
Official creditors	..	13	427	503	646	750	809	896	997	1,098
Private creditors	..	0	1	12	28	35	35	34	36	37
Memo: export credits	..	..	259	335	357	361	297	280	292	298
TOTAL DEBT FLOWS										
Disbursements	**4**	**135**	**64**	**71**	**46**	**13**	**0**	**0**	**0**	**0**
Long-term debt	4	114	64	71	46	13	0	0	0	0
IMF purchases	0	22	0	0	0	0	0	0	0	0
Principal repayments	**2**	**11**	**2**	**18**	**5**	**0**	**0**	**0**	**0**	**0**
Long-term debt	1	7	1	7	3	0	0	0	0	0
IMF repurchases	2	4	1	11	3	0	0	0	0	0
Net flows on debt	**2**	**125**	**48**	**53**	**58**	**13**	**0**	**0**	**0**	**0**
of which short-term debt	..	..	-13	0	18	0	0	0	0	0
Interest payments (INT)	**..**	**2**	**3**	**14**	**5**	**0**	**0**	**0**	**0**	**1**
Long-term debt	0	2	3	10	4	0	0	0	0	0
IMF charges	0	0	0	3	1	0	0	0	0	1
Short-term debt	..	0	1	0	0	0	0	0	0	0
Net transfers on debt	**..**	**122**	**45**	**39**	**53**	**12**	**0**	**0**	**0**	**-1**
Total debt service paid (TDS)	**..**	**13**	**5**	**32**	**11**	**0**	**0**	**0**	**0**	**1**
Long-term debt	1	9	4	17	7	0	0	0	0	0
IMF repurchases and charges	2	4	1	15	4	0	0	0	0	1
Short-term debt (interest only)	..	0	1	0	0	0	0	0	0	0
2. AGGREGATE NET RESOURCE FLOWS AND NET TRANSFERS (LONG-TERM)										
NET RESOURCE FLOWS	**17**	**380**	**296**	**279**	**372**	**154**	**609**	**806**	**494**	**150**
Net flow of long-term debt (ex. IMF)	4	106	63	64	43	13	0	0	0	0
Foreign direct investment (net)	5	0	-43	-41	6	0	3	2	1	1
Portfolio equity flows	0	0	0	0	0	0	0	0	0	0
Grants (excluding technical coop.)	9	274	276	255	323	142	606	804	493	149
Memo: technical coop. grants	11	93	119	126	95	41	52	86	47	45
NET TRANSFERS	**16**	**378**	**293**	**269**	**368**	**154**	**609**	**806**	**494**	**150**
Interest on long-term debt	0	2	3	10	4	0	0	0	0	0
Profit remittances on FDI	0	0	0	0	0	0	0	0	0	0
3. MAJOR ECONOMIC AGGREGATES										
Gross national product (GNP)	323	603	978	1,015	835	..	..	..	..	..
Exports of goods & services (XGS)	..	262	58	68	..	..	..	..	..	..
of which workers remittances	..	57	0	0	..	..	..	..	..	..
Imports of goods & services (MGS)	..	541	381	553	..	..	..	..	..	..
International reserves (RES)	21	26	23	23	..	..	..	..	..	..
Current account balance	..	-136	-99	-157	..	..	..	..	..	..
4. DEBT INDICATORS										
EDT / XGS (%)	..	252.0	3,572.1	3,189.4	..	..	..	..	..	..
EDT / GNP (%)	..	109.5	213.4	212.8	283.9	..	..	..	..	..
TDS / XGS (%)	..	4.9	9.2	47.6	..	..	..	..	..	..
INT / XGS (%)	..	0.9	5.7	20.4	..	..	..	..	..	..
INT / GNP (%)	..	0.4	0.3	1.4	0.6	..	..	..	..	..
RES / EDT (%)	..	3.9	1.1	1.1	..	..	..	..	..	..
RES / MGS (months)	..	0.6	0.7	0.5	..	..	..	..	..	..
Short-term / EDT (%)	..	7.1	6.8	9.1	12.0	14.0	16.1	18.0	19.8	20.6
Concessional / EDT (%)	..	83.2	68.3	67.7	65.9	64.6	63.2	62.0	60.4	59.8
Multilateral / EDT (%)	..	24.1	29.8	31.3	31.8	31.5	30.5	29.9	29.6	29.4

SOMALIA

(US$ million, unless otherwise indicated)

	1970	1980	1988	1989	1990	1991	1992	1993	1994	1995
5. LONG-TERM DEBT										
DEBT OUTSTANDING (LDOD)	**77**	**595**	**1,779**	**1,813**	**1,926**	**1,945**	**1,898**	**1,897**	**1,935**	**1,961**
Public and publicly guaranteed	**77**	**595**	**1,779**	**1,813**	**1,926**	**1,945**	**1,898**	**1,897**	**1,935**	**1,961**
Official creditors	75	568	1,745	1,779	1,889	1,909	1,863	1,863	1,899	1,924
Multilateral	7	159	622	675	754	772	746	748	774	786
Concessional	7	150	607	663	741	759	734	736	761	773
Bilateral	68	408	1,123	1,104	1,136	1,137	1,117	1,114	1,125	1,138
Concessional	63	400	817	798	822	824	812	815	820	828
Private creditors	2	28	35	35	37	36	35	34	36	37
Bonds	0	0	0	0	0	0	0	0	0	0
Commercial banks	2	0	0	0	0	0	0	0	0	0
Other private	0	28	35	35	37	36	35	34	36	37
Private nonguaranteed	**0**	**0**	**0**	**0**	**0**	**0**	**0**	**0**	**0**	**0**
Bonds	0	0	0	0	0	0	0	0	0	0
Commercial banks	0	0	0	0	0	0	0	0	0	0
Memo:										
IBRD	0	0	0	0	0	0	0	0	0	0
IDA	7	72	318	366	419	421	410	411	425	432
DISBURSEMENTS	**4**	**114**	**64**	**71**	**46**	**13**	**0**	**0**	**0**	**0**
Public and publicly guaranteed	**4**	**114**	**64**	**71**	**46**	**13**	**0**	**0**	**0**	**0**
Official creditors	4	87	64	71	46	13	0	0	0	0
Multilateral	0	36	36	69	46	13	0	0	0	0
Concessional	0	25	36	69	46	13	0	0	0	0
Bilateral	4	50	28	2	0	0	0	0	0	0
Concessional	4	49	28	2	0	0	0	0	0	0
Private creditors	0	27	0	0	0	0	0	0	0	0
Bonds	0	0	0	0	0	0	0	0	0	0
Commercial banks	0	0	0	0	0	0	0	0	0	0
Other private	0	27	0	0	0	0	0	0	0	0
Private nonguaranteed	**0**	**0**	**0**	**0**	**0**	**0**	**0**	**0**	**0**	**0**
Bonds	0	0	0	0	0	0	0	0	0	0
Commercial banks	0	0	0	0	0	0	0	0	0	0
Memo:										
IBRD	0	0	0	0	0	0	0	0	0	0
IDA	0	10	29	55	35	1	0	0	0	0
PRINCIPAL REPAYMENTS	**1**	**7**	**1**	**7**	**3**	**0**	**0**	**0**	**0**	**0**
Public and publicly guaranteed	**1**	**7**	**1**	**7**	**3**	**0**	**0**	**0**	**0**	**0**
Official creditors	0	7	1	7	3	0	0	0	0	0
Multilateral	0	5	1	4	3	0	0	0	0	0
Concessional	0	0	1	3	2	0	0	0	0	0
Bilateral	0	2	0	3	0	0	0	0	0	0
Concessional	0	2	0	0	0	0	0	0	0	0
Private creditors	1	0	0	0	0	0	0	0	0	0
Bonds	0	0	0	0	0	0	0	0	0	0
Commercial banks	1	0	0	0	0	0	0	0	0	0
Other private	0	0	0	0	0	0	0	0	0	0
Private nonguaranteed	**0**	**0**	**0**	**0**	**0**	**0**	**0**	**0**	**0**	**0**
Bonds	0	0	0	0	0	0	0	0	0	0
Commercial banks	0	0	0	0	0	0	0	0	0	0
Memo:										
IBRD	0	0	0	0	0	0	0	0	0	0
IDA	0	0	1	1	2	0	0	0	0	0
NET FLOWS ON DEBT	**4**	**106**	**63**	**64**	**43**	**13**	**0**	**0**	**0**	**0**
Public and publicly guaranteed	**4**	**106**	**63**	**64**	**43**	**13**	**0**	**0**	**0**	**0**
Official creditors	4	80	63	64	43	13	0	0	0	0
Multilateral	0	31	35	65	43	13	0	0	0	0
Concessional	0	25	35	67	43	13	0	0	0	0
Bilateral	4	49	28	0	0	0	0	0	0	0
Concessional	4	47	28	2	0	0	0	0	0	0
Private creditors	-1	27	0	0	0	0	0	0	0	0
Bonds	0	0	0	0	0	0	0	0	0	0
Commercial banks	-1	0	0	0	0	0	0	0	0	0
Other private	0	27	0	0	0	0	0	0	0	0
Private nonguaranteed	**0**	**0**	**0**	**0**	**0**	**0**	**0**	**0**	**0**	**0**
Bonds	0	0	0	0	0	0	0	0	0	0
Commercial banks	0	0	0	0	0	0	0	0	0	0
Memo:										
IBRD	0	0	0	0	0	0	0	0	0	0
IDA	0	10	28	54	32	1	0	0	0	0

SOMALIA

(US$ million, unless otherwise indicated)

	1970	1980	1988	1989	1990	1991	1992	1993	1994	1995
INTEREST PAYMENTS (LINT)	**0**	**2**	**3**	**10**	**4**	**0**	**0**	**0**	**0**	**0**
Public and publicly guaranteed	**0**	**2**	**3**	**10**	**4**	**0**	**0**	**0**	**0**	**0**
Official creditors	0	2	3	10	4	0	0	0	0	0
Multilateral	0	1	3	4	4	0	0	0	0	0
Concessional	0	1	3	3	4	0	0	0	0	0
Bilateral	0	1	0	6	0	0	0	0	0	0
Concessional	0	1	0	1	0	0	0	0	0	0
Private creditors	0	0	0	0	0	0	0	0	0	0
Bonds	0	0	0	0	0	0	0	0	0	0
Commercial banks	0	0	0	0	0	0	0	0	0	0
Other private	0	0	0	0	0	0	0	0	0	0
Private nonguaranteed	**0**	**0**	**0**	**0**	**0**	**0**	**0**	**0**	**0**	**0**
Bonds	0	0	0	0	0	0	0	0	0	0
Commercial banks	0	0	0	0	0	0	0	0	0	0
Memo:										
IBRD	0	0	0	0	0	0	0	0	0	0
IDA	0	1	3	2	3	0	0	0	0	0
NET TRANSFERS ON DEBT	**3**	**104**	**60**	**54**	**39**	**12**	**0**	**0**	**0**	**0**
Public and publicly guaranteed	**3**	**104**	**60**	**54**	**39**	**12**	**0**	**0**	**0**	**0**
Official creditors	4	78	60	54	39	12	0	0	0	0
Multilateral	0	31	32	61	39	12	0	0	0	0
Concessional	0	25	32	63	40	12	0	0	0	0
Bilateral	4	47	28	-7	0	0	0	0	0	0
Concessional	4	46	28	2	0	0	0	0	0	0
Private creditors	-1	27	0	0	0	0	0	0	0	0
Bonds	0	0	0	0	0	0	0	0	0	0
Commercial banks	-1	0	0	0	0	0	0	0	0	0
Other private	0	27	0	0	0	0	0	0	0	0
Private nonguaranteed	**0**	**0**	**0**	**0**	**0**	**0**	**0**	**0**	**0**	**0**
Bonds	0	0	0	0	0	0	0	0	0	0
Commercial banks	0	0	0	0	0	0	0	0	0	0
Memo:										
IBRD	0	0	0	0	0	0	0	0	0	0
IDA	0	9	26	51	29	0	0	0	0	0
DEBT SERVICE (LTDS)	**1**	**9**	**4**	**17**	**7**	**0**	**0**	**0**	**0**	**0**
Public and publicly guaranteed	**1**	**9**	**4**	**17**	**7**	**0**	**0**	**0**	**0**	**0**
Official creditors	0	9	4	17	7	0	0	0	0	0
Multilateral	0	6	4	8	7	0	0	0	0	0
Concessional	0	1	4	6	6	0	0	0	0	0
Bilateral	0	3	0	9	0	0	0	0	0	0
Concessional	0	3	0	1	0	0	0	0	0	0
Private creditors	1	0	0	0	0	0	0	0	0	0
Bonds	0	0	0	0	0	0	0	0	0	0
Commercial banks	1	0	0	0	0	0	0	0	0	0
Other private	0	0	0	0	0	0	0	0	0	0
Private nonguaranteed	**0**	**0**	**0**	**0**	**0**	**0**	**0**	**0**	**0**	**0**
Bonds	0	0	0	0	0	0	0	0	0	0
Commercial banks	0	0	0	0	0	0	0	0	0	0
Memo:										
IBRD	0	0	0	0	0	0	0	0	0	0
IDA	0	1	4	4	6	0	0	0	0	0
UNDISBURSED DEBT	**67**	**565**	**409**	**443**	**497**	**456**	**437**	**437**	**452**	**314**
Official creditors	67	494	409	443	497	456	437	437	452	314
Private creditors	0	70	0	0	0	0	0	0	0	0
Memorandum items										
Concessional LDOD	70	549	1,424	1,461	1,562	1,582	1,545	1,551	1,581	1,601
Variable rate LDOD	0	0	20	20	20	20	20	20	20	20
Public sector LDOD	77	568	1,779	1,813	1,926	1,945	1,898	1,897	1,935	1,961
Private sector LDOD	0	28	0	0	0	0	0	0	0	0

6. CURRENCY COMPOSITION OF LONG-TERM DEBT (PERCENT)

	1970	1980	1988	1989	1990	1991	1992	1993	1994	1995
Deutsche mark	18.6	0.0	0.0	0.0	0.0	0.0	0.0	0.0	0.0	0.0
French franc	0.0	0.0	4.3	4.4	4.7	4.6	4.5	4.2	4.5	4.8
Japanese yen	0.0	0.0	2.7	2.4	2.4	2.6	2.6	2.9	3.2	3.1
Pound sterling	0.0	0.4	0.2	0.1	0.2	0.2	0.1	0.1	0.1	0.1
Swiss franc	0.0	0.0	0.0	0.0	0.0	0.0	0.0	0.0	0.0	0.0
U.S.dollars	24.6	34.1	49.1	50.7	50.5	50.1	50.7	50.8	50.5	50.2
Multiple currency	47.9	16.7	7.1	6.8	7.2	7.1	7.1	7.0	7.2	7.4
Special drawing rights	0.0	0.0	1.3	1.3	1.3	1.3	1.3	1.3	1.3	1.3
All other currencies	9.1	48.8	35.4	34.3	33.7	34.3	33.7	33.6	33.1	33.0

SOMALIA

(US$ million, unless otherwise indicated)

	1970	1980	1988	1989	1990	1991	1992	1993	1994	1995
7. DEBT RESTRUCTURINGS										
Total amount rescheduled	0	0	45	0	0	0	0	0	0	0
Debt stock rescheduled	0	0	0	0	0	0	0	0	0	0
Principal rescheduled	0	0	24	0	0	0	0	0	0	0
Official	0	0	14	0	0	0	0	0	0	0
Private	0	0	11	0	0	0	0	0	0	0
Interest rescheduled	0	0	20	0	0	0	0	0	0	0
Official	0	0	16	0	0	0	0	0	0	0
Private	0	0	4	0	0	0	0	0	0	0
Debt forgiven	..	..	0	0	0	0	0	0	0	0
Memo: interest forgiven	..	..	0	0	0	0	0	0	0	0
Debt stock reduction	0	0	0	0	0	0	0	0	0	0
of which debt buyback	0	0	0	0	0	0	0	0	0	0
8. DEBT STOCK-FLOW RECONCILIATION										
Total change in debt stocks	..	..	..	73	211	79	-3	54	116	62
Net flows on debt	..	..	..	53	58	13	0	0	0	0
Net change in interest arrears	..	..	..	54	71	59	51	55	68	33
Interest capitalized	..	..	..	0	0	0	0	0	0	0
Debt forgiveness or reduction	..	..	..	0	0	0	0	0	0	0
Cross-currency valuation	..	..	..	-18	38	2	-31	0	25	13
Residual	..	..	..	-16	44	6	-23	-1	23	16
9. AVERAGE TERMS OF NEW COMMITMENTS										
ALL CREDITORS										
Interest (%)	0.0	3.3	2.5	0.8	0.8	0.0	0.0	0.0	0.0	0.0
Maturity (years)	20.3	24.6	28.4	39.6	42.2	0.0	0.0	0.0	0.0	0.0
Grace period (years)	15.6	5.9	6.7	10.4	10.6	0.0	0.0	0.0	0.0	0.0
Grant element (%)	79.7	44.3	57.4	80.5	81.1	0.0	0.0	0.0	0.0	0.0
Official creditors										
Interest (%)	0.0	3.0	2.5	0.8	0.8	0.0	0.0	0.0	0.0	0.0
Maturity (years)	20.3	26.1	28.4	39.6	42.2	0.0	0.0	0.0	0.0	0.0
Grace period (years)	15.6	6.2	6.7	10.4	10.6	0.0	0.0	0.0	0.0	0.0
Grant element (%)	79.7	47.0	57.4	80.5	81.1	0.0	0.0	0.0	0.0	0.0
Private creditors										
Interest (%)	0.0	7.0	0.0	0.0	0.0	0.0	0.0	0.0	0.0	0.0
Maturity (years)	0.0	6.3	0.0	0.0	0.0	0.0	0.0	0.0	0.0	0.0
Grace period (years)	0.0	2.0	0.0	0.0	0.0	0.0	0.0	0.0	0.0	0.0
Grant element (%)	0.0	9.1	0.0	0.0	0.0	0.0	0.0	0.0	0.0	0.0
Memorandum items										
Commitments	22	188	24	128	72	0	0	0	0	0
Official creditors	22	174	24	128	72	0	0	0	0	0
Private creditors	0	14	0	0	0	0	0	0	0	0

10. CONTRACTUAL OBLIGATIONS ON OUTSTANDING LONG-TERM DEBT

	1996	1997	1998	1999	2000	2001	2002	2003	2004	2005
TOTAL										
Disbursements	24	25	17	11	7	2	1	0	0	0
Principal	64	65	52	51	48	42	38	35	32	31
Interest	19	16	15	14	13	11	10	10	9	8
Official creditors										
Disbursements	24	25	17	11	7	2	1	0	0	0
Principal	64	65	52	51	48	42	38	35	32	31
Interest	19	16	15	14	13	11	10	10	9	8
Bilateral creditors										
Disbursements	3	2	2	1	1	0	0	0	0	0
Principal	41	38	24	23	22	19	16	15	15	14
Interest	13	11	9	8	7	7	6	6	5	5
Multilateral creditors										
Disbursements	21	22	15	10	6	2	1	0	0	0
Principal	23	27	27	27	26	23	22	20	17	17
Interest	6	6	6	5	5	5	4	4	4	4
Private creditors										
Disbursements	0	0	0	0	0	0	0	0	0	0
Principal	0	0	0	0	0	0	0	0	0	0
Interest	0	0	0	0	0	0	0	0	0	0
Commercial banks										
Disbursements	0	0	0	0	0	0	0	0	0	0
Principal	0	0	0	0	0	0	0	0	0	0
Interest	0	0	0	0	0	0	0	0	0	0
Other private										
Disbursements	0	0	0	0	0	0	0	0	0	0
Principal	0	0	0	0	0	0	0	0	0	0
Interest	0	0	0	0	0	0	0	0	0	0

SRI LANKA

(US$ million, unless otherwise indicated)

	1970	1980	1988	1989	1990	1991	1992	1993	1994	1995
1. SUMMARY DEBT DATA										
TOTAL DEBT STOCKS (EDT)	..	**1,841**	**5,207**	**5,182**	**5,864**	**6,580**	**6,457**	**6,854**	**7,891**	**8,230**
Long-term debt (LDOD)	**317**	**1,231**	**4,267**	**4,415**	**5,049**	**5,770**	**5,743**	**6,072**	**6,735**	**7,099**
Public and publicly guaranteed	317	1,227	4,154	4,283	4,947	5,671	5,643	5,982	6,653	7,010
Private nonguaranteed	0	3	113	132	102	99	99	90	83	90
Use of IMF credit	**79**	**391**	**359**	**366**	**410**	**401**	**464**	**516**	**617**	**595**
Short-term debt	..	**220**	**581**	**401**	**405**	**410**	**250**	**266**	**538**	**535**
of which interest arrears on LDOD	..	0	4	7	11	15	19	25	32	35
Official creditors	..	0	0	0	0	0	0	0	0	0
Private creditors	..	0	4	7	11	15	19	25	32	35
Memo: principal arrears on LDOD	..	0	0	0	0	0	4	8	9	39
Official creditors	..	0	0	0	0	0	0	0	0	3
Private creditors	..	0	0	0	0	0	4	8	9	36
Memo: export credits	..	..	577	539	566	507	470	550	755	892
TOTAL DEBT FLOWS										
Disbursements	**75**	**344**	**607**	**531**	**545**	**839**	**539**	**504**	**551**	**548**
Long-term debt	66	272	400	445	485	763	381	426	471	548
IMF purchases	10	72	206	86	61	77	158	78	80	0
Principal repayments	**57**	**94**	**318**	**266**	**214**	**252**	**329**	**253**	**245**	**250**
Long-term debt	30	51	208	195	167	165	252	228	232	216
IMF repurchases	27	43	109	71	47	88	77	25	13	34
Net flows on debt	**19**	**250**	**593**	**82**	**331**	**587**	**47**	**261**	**571**	**293**
of which short-term debt	..	..	304	-183	0	0	-164	11	265	-6
Interest payments (INT)	..	**85**	**170**	**156**	**170**	**166**	**154**	**142**	**147**	**160**
Long-term debt	12	33	125	112	122	128	134	130	128	132
IMF charges	0	17	19	22	21	16	8	3	3	3
Short-term debt	..	36	26	22	27	22	13	9	17	24
Net transfers on debt	..	**164**	**423**	**-74**	**161**	**421**	**-107**	**119**	**424**	**133**
Total debt service paid (TDS)	..	**179**	**487**	**422**	**384**	**418**	**482**	**395**	**392**	**409**
Long-term debt	42	84	333	306	289	293	386	358	360	348
IMF repurchases and charges	27	59	128	94	69	104	84	28	16	37
Short-term debt (interest only)	..	36	26	22	27	22	13	9	17	24
2. AGGREGATE NET RESOURCE FLOWS AND NET TRANSFERS (LONG-TERM)										
NET RESOURCE FLOWS	**51**	**425**	**433**	**465**	**582**	**819**	**394**	**590**	**677**	**631**
Net flow of long-term debt (ex. IMF)	36	221	192	250	318	598	129	198	239	333
Foreign direct investment (net)	0	43	46	20	43	48	123	195	166	63
Portfolio equity flows	0	0	0	0	0	0	0	0	112	61
Grants (excluding technical coop.)	15	161	195	195	221	173	142	197	160	174
Memo: technical coop. grants	7	57	107	100	105	132	131	115	98	115
NET TRANSFERS	**31**	**377**	**288**	**332**	**435**	**671**	**227**	**427**	**509**	**465**
Interest on long-term debt	12	33	125	112	122	128	134	130	128	132
Profit remittances on FDI	8	15	20	21	25	20	33	33	40	34
3. MAJOR ECONOMIC AGGREGATES										
Gross national product (GNP)	2,259	3,997	6,962	6,937	7,973	8,822	9,527	10,219	11,552	12,777
Exports of goods & services (XGS)	..	1,492	2,243	2,267	2,787	3,047	3,539	4,164	4,732	5,866
of which workers remittances	..	152	358	358	401	442	548	632	715	754
Imports of goods & services (MGS)	..	2,269	2,805	2,842	3,225	3,803	4,086	4,636	5,567	5,950
International reserves (RES)	43	283	248	269	447	724	980	1,686	2,046	2,088
Current account balance	..	-657	-395	-414	-298	-595	-451	-382	-441	-159
4. DEBT INDICATORS										
EDT / XGS (%)	..	123.4	232.2	228.5	210.4	216.0	182.5	164.6	166.8	140.3
EDT / GNP (%)	..	46.1	74.8	74.7	73.5	74.6	67.8	67.1	68.3	64.4
TDS / XGS (%)	..	12.0	21.7	18.6	13.8	13.7	13.6	9.5	8.3	7.0
INT / XGS (%)	..	5.7	7.6	6.9	6.1	5.4	4.3	3.4	3.1	2.7
INT / GNP (%)	..	2.1	2.4	2.2	2.1	1.9	1.6	1.4	1.3	1.2
RES / EDT (%)	..	15.3	4.8	5.2	7.6	11.0	15.2	24.6	25.9	25.4
RES / MGS (months)	..	1.5	1.1	1.1	1.7	2.3	2.9	4.4	4.4	4.2
Short-term / EDT (%)	..	11.9	11.2	7.7	6.9	6.2	3.9	3.9	6.8	6.5
Concessional / EDT (%)	..	56.2	65.8	69.6	71.9	73.8	76.5	78.1	76.6	77.5
Multilateral / EDT (%)	..	11.7	21.9	24.3	27.7	30.1	32.5	34.5	33.7	34.7

SRI LANKA

(US$ million, unless otherwise indicated)

	1970	1980	1988	1989	1990	1991	1992	1993	1994	1995
5. LONG-TERM DEBT										
DEBT OUTSTANDING (LDOD)	**317**	**1,231**	**4,267**	**4,415**	**5,049**	**5,770**	**5,743**	**6,072**	**6,735**	**7,099**
Public and publicly guaranteed	**317**	**1,227**	**4,154**	**4,283**	**4,947**	**5,671**	**5,643**	**5,982**	**6,653**	**7,010**
Official creditors	253	1,087	3,538	3,739	4,349	5,030	5,061	5,461	6,149	6,485
Multilateral	29	216	1,142	1,257	1,623	1,983	2,100	2,363	2,656	2,858
Concessional	25	181	1,053	1,169	1,536	1,903	2,031	2,302	2,600	2,806
Bilateral	224	872	2,396	2,483	2,727	3,047	2,961	3,098	3,492	3,627
Concessional	186	854	2,373	2,437	2,681	2,953	2,908	3,048	3,441	3,575
Private creditors	64	140	616	544	598	641	582	521	504	525
Bonds	12	0	0	0	0	0	0	0	0	0
Commercial banks	3	57	264	208	253	294	272	244	264	303
Other private	49	83	352	336	345	347	310	277	240	222
Private nonguaranteed	**0**	**3**	**113**	**132**	**102**	**99**	**99**	**90**	**83**	**90**
Bonds	0	0	0	0	0	0	0	0	0	0
Commercial banks	0	3	113	132	102	99	99	90	83	90
Memo:										
IBRD	26	31	83	82	82	75	65	58	54	49
IDA	1	98	658	702	864	1,058	1,095	1,222	1,339	1,463
DISBURSEMENTS	**66**	**272**	**400**	**445**	**485**	**763**	**381**	**426**	**471**	**548**
Public and publicly guaranteed	**66**	**269**	**400**	**445**	**485**	**763**	**381**	**426**	**471**	**548**
Official creditors	55	174	350	373	396	662	309	396	420	460
Multilateral	4	32	131	141	234	341	209	258	172	197
Concessional	1	31	124	134	233	341	209	258	172	197
Bilateral	52	142	219	232	162	322	100	137	248	263
Concessional	40	141	217	202	162	273	100	137	246	260
Private creditors	11	96	51	72	89	101	72	30	51	88
Bonds	0	0	0	0	0	0	0	0	0	0
Commercial banks	0	57	25	34	54	69	48	16	51	77
Other private	11	39	26	38	35	32	24	15	0	11
Private nonguaranteed	**0**	**2**	**0**	**0**	**0**	**0**	**0**	**0**	**0**	**0**
Bonds	0	0	0	0	0	0	0	0	0	0
Commercial banks	0	2	0	0	0	0	0	0	0	0
Memo:										
IBRD	1	0	7	7	1	0	0	0	0	0
IDA	1	20	56	53	127	187	74	130	78	106
PRINCIPAL REPAYMENTS	**30**	**51**	**208**	**195**	**167**	**165**	**252**	**228**	**232**	**216**
Public and publicly guaranteed	**30**	**51**	**202**	**193**	**165**	**161**	**249**	**224**	**229**	**216**
Official creditors	16	39	65	75	89	100	147	125	131	143
Multilateral	2	5	14	15	21	22	25	27	26	26
Concessional	2	2	9	9	13	14	17	18	18	19
Bilateral	14	34	50	60	68	78	121	97	105	117
Concessional	6	28	49	55	64	75	85	92	101	115
Private creditors	14	12	138	119	76	61	102	99	98	73
Bonds	3	0	0	0	0	0	0	0	0	0
Commercial banks	1	0	85	81	29	25	48	40	38	42
Other private	10	12	53	38	47	36	54	59	60	31
Private nonguaranteed	**0**	**0**	**6**	**2**	**2**	**3**	**3**	**4**	**3**	**0**
Bonds	0	0	0	0	0	0	0	0	0	0
Commercial banks	0	0	6	2	2	3	3	4	3	0
Memo:										
IBRD	2	2	5	5	7	8	8	9	8	7
IDA	0	0	1	2	3	5	6	6	7	8
NET FLOWS ON DEBT	**36**	**221**	**192**	**250**	**318**	**598**	**129**	**198**	**239**	**333**
Public and publicly guaranteed	**36**	**219**	**198**	**252**	**320**	**602**	**132**	**202**	**242**	**333**
Official creditors	40	135	285	298	307	562	163	271	288	317
Multilateral	2	27	117	126	214	318	184	231	146	171
Concessional	-1	29	116	125	220	326	192	240	154	178
Bilateral	38	108	168	173	94	244	-21	40	142	146
Concessional	34	113	168	147	98	198	15	45	145	144
Private creditors	-4	84	-87	-47	13	39	-30	-69	-46	16
Bonds	-3	0	0	0	0	0	0	0	0	0
Commercial banks	-1	57	-60	-47	24	43	0	-25	13	35
Other private	1	27	-27	1	-12	-4	-31	-44	-59	-19
Private nonguaranteed	**0**	**2**	**-6**	**-2**	**-2**	**-3**	**-3**	**-4**	**-3**	**0**
Bonds	0	0	0	0	0	0	0	0	0	0
Commercial banks	0	2	-6	-2	-2	-3	-3	-4	-3	0
Memo:										
IBRD	-1	-2	2	2	-6	-8	-8	-9	-8	-7
IDA	1	20	55	51	124	182	68	123	71	98

SRI LANKA

(US$ million, unless otherwise indicated)

	1970	1980	1988	1989	1990	1991	1992	1993	1994	1995
INTEREST PAYMENTS (LINT)	**12**	**33**	**125**	**112**	**122**	**128**	**134**	**130**	**128**	**132**
Public and publicly guaranteed	**12**	**33**	**123**	**111**	**120**	**126**	**132**	**129**	**127**	**132**
Official creditors	8	25	70	73	77	86	94	100	104	109
Multilateral	3	5	21	19	19	21	23	25	26	29
Concessional	2	2	12	11	11	14	17	19	21	24
Bilateral	6	20	49	54	58	65	71	75	77	81
Concessional	3	19	49	53	55	62	67	71	77	81
Private creditors	4	8	53	38	43	41	38	29	23	23
Bonds	1	0	0	0	0	0	0	0	0	0
Commercial banks	0	0	24	21	16	20	20	15	14	18
Other private	3	8	29	18	27	21	18	14	10	5
Private nonguaranteed	**0**	**0**	**2**	**1**	**2**	**2**	**2**	**1**	**1**	**0**
Bonds	0	0	0	0	0	0	0	0	0	0
Commercial banks	0	0	2	1	2	2	2	1	1	0
Memo:										
IBRD	3	3	8	7	8	7	7	6	5	5
IDA	0	1	6	5	6	7	8	9	10	11
NET TRANSFERS ON DEBT	**24**	**188**	**67**	**139**	**196**	**470**	**-5**	**68**	**111**	**200**
Public and publicly guaranteed	**24**	**186**	**75**	**141**	**200**	**475**	**0**	**73**	**115**	**201**
Official creditors	32	110	216	226	230	477	69	171	185	208
Multilateral	-1	22	96	107	195	297	161	206	120	142
Concessional	-2	27	104	114	209	313	176	222	133	154
Bilateral	33	87	120	119	35	179	-92	-35	65	65
Concessional	31	94	120	94	43	136	-53	-26	69	64
Private creditors	-8	76	-140	-85	-30	-1	-69	-98	-70	-7
Bonds	-4	0	0	0	0	0	0	0	0	0
Commercial banks	-1	57	-84	-68	8	24	-20	-40	-1	17
Other private	-2	19	-56	-17	-38	-25	-49	-58	-69	-24
Private nonguaranteed	**0**	**2**	**-8**	**-2**	**-4**	**-6**	**-5**	**-5**	**-4**	**0**
Bonds	0	0	0	0	0	0	0	0	0	0
Commercial banks	0	2	-8	-2	-4	-6	-5	-5	-4	0
Memo:										
IBRD	-3	-5	-7	-6	-13	-15	-15	-15	-13	-12
IDA	1	19	49	46	118	176	60	115	61	88
DEBT SERVICE (LTDS)	**42**	**84**	**333**	**306**	**289**	**293**	**386**	**358**	**360**	**348**
Public and publicly guaranteed	**42**	**84**	**325**	**304**	**285**	**287**	**381**	**353**	**356**	**348**
Official creditors	24	64	134	147	166	186	241	224	235	252
Multilateral	4	10	35	34	39	43	49	52	52	54
Concessional	3	5	21	21	24	28	33	37	39	43
Bilateral	19	54	99	113	126	142	192	172	183	198
Concessional	9	47	98	108	119	137	153	163	178	196
Private creditors	18	20	191	157	119	102	140	128	121	95
Bonds	4	0	0	0	0	0	0	0	0	0
Commercial banks	1	0	109	102	46	45	68	55	52	60
Other private	13	20	82	55	74	57	72	73	69	35
Private nonguaranteed	**0**	**0**	**8**	**2**	**4**	**6**	**5**	**5**	**4**	**0**
Bonds	0	0	0	0	0	0	0	0	0	0
Commercial banks	0	0	8	2	4	6	5	5	4	0
Memo:										
IBRD	4	5	14	12	14	15	15	15	13	12
IDA	0	1	7	7	8	11	14	15	16	19
UNDISBURSED DEBT	**215**	**1,147**	**2,070**	**1,770**	**2,169**	**2,315**	**2,333**	**2,513**	**2,781**	**2,518**
Official creditors	196	899	1,950	1,634	2,070	2,216	2,255	2,429	2,650	2,476
Private creditors	19	248	120	135	99	99	77	84	130	41
Memorandum items										
Concessional LDOD	211	1,035	3,426	3,606	4,217	4,856	4,940	5,350	6,041	6,381
Variable rate LDOD	0	85	299	288	256	314	323	311	297	308
Public sector LDOD	311	1,219	4,055	4,196	4,855	5,572	5,544	5,871	6,529	6,889
Private sector LDOD	5	11	212	219	194	198	199	201	206	210

6. CURRENCY COMPOSITION OF LONG-TERM DEBT (PERCENT)

	1970	1980	1988	1989	1990	1991	1992	1993	1994	1995
Deutsche mark	13.8	11.2	10.9	12.0	12.0	10.3	9.5	8.1	8.0	8.0
French franc	3.6	2.7	3.0	3.1	3.2	2.7	2.7	2.3	2.2	2.2
Japanese yen	6.4	15.0	24.3	23.1	22.7	25.1	25.4	27.5	29.8	29.3
Pound sterling	28.8	2.3	2.7	2.8	3.2	3.1	2.2	1.7	1.3	1.4
Swiss franc	0.3	2.4	0.6	0.6	0.9	0.8	0.6	0.5	0.5	0.5
U.S.dollars	19.7	37.0	38.4	37.5	36.2	36.2	36.9	36.5	34.5	34.9
Multiple currency	14.3	8.5	9.9	11.3	13.9	15.1	16.6	18.0	18.8	19.0
Special drawing rights	0.0	0.0	0.5	0.5	0.5	0.5	0.5	0.5	0.5	0.5
All other currencies	13.2	21.0	9.8	9.0	7.5	6.2	5.5	4.8	4.4	4.3

SRI LANKA

(US$ million, unless otherwise indicated)

	1970	1980	1988	1989	1990	1991	1992	1993	1994	1995
7. DEBT RESTRUCTURINGS										
Total amount rescheduled	0	0	0	0	0	0	0	0	0	0
Debt stock rescheduled	0	0	0	0	0	0	0	0	0	0
Principal rescheduled	0	0	0	0	0	0	0	0	0	0
Official	0	0	0	0	0	0	0	0	0	0
Private	0	0	0	0	0	0	0	0	0	0
Interest rescheduled	0	0	0	0	0	0	0	0	0	0
Official	0	0	0	0	0	0	0	0	0	0
Private	0	0	0	0	0	0	0	0	0	0
Debt forgiven	..	..	0	0	0	0	0	0	0	7
Memo: interest forgiven	..	..	0	0	0	0	0	0	0	0
Debt stock reduction	0	0	0	0	0	0	0	0	0	0
of which debt buyback	0	0	0	0	0	0	0	0	0	0
8. DEBT STOCK-FLOW RECONCILIATION										
Total change in debt stocks	..	..	..	-26	682	716	-123	397	1,037	339
Net flows on debt	..	..	..	82	331	587	47	261	571	293
Net change in interest arrears	..	..	..	3	4	5	4	6	7	3
Interest capitalized	..	..	..	0	0	0	0	0	0	0
Debt forgiveness or reduction	..	..	..	0	0	0	0	0	0	-7
Cross-currency valuation	..	..	..	-113	243	86	-93	135	339	16
Residual	..	..	..	3	104	39	-81	-5	119	34
9. AVERAGE TERMS OF NEW COMMITMENTS										
ALL CREDITORS										
Interest (%)	3.0	3.9	2.1	4.0	1.8	2.4	2.5	2.4	2.7	2.4
Maturity (years)	27.1	30.5	34.8	27.7	34.7	30.7	29.9	30.6	27.1	32.9
Grace period (years)	4.9	7.7	9.7	6.9	9.5	8.3	9.0	8.9	8.4	9.9
Grant element (%)	47.9	50.4	67.2	49.8	69.3	60.9	60.3	60.8	56.2	62.6
Official creditors										
Interest (%)	2.9	1.3	1.7	1.2	1.4	1.8	2.1	1.9	2.2	2.4
Maturity (years)	27.9	40.9	36.1	38.7	36.2	34.6	31.9	33.1	30.6	32.9
Grace period (years)	5.1	9.9	10.1	10.0	10.0	9.4	9.8	9.6	9.5	9.9
Grant element (%)	49.2	75.1	70.7	75.4	73.0	68.8	65.1	67.0	63.4	62.6
Private creditors										
Interest (%)	5.9	8.7	8.4	9.0	8.5	6.6	5.6	6.9	5.6	0.0
Maturity (years)	7.4	11.9	14.4	7.5	8.5	4.9	13.5	8.7	8.2	0.0
Grace period (years)	1.4	3.8	4.2	1.1	0.8	1.4	2.1	2.3	2.6	0.0
Grant element (%)	12.6	5.8	8.1	2.7	4.3	7.7	21.2	7.2	17.4	0.0
Memorandum items										
Commitments	81	752	879	272	837	913	489	622	585	404
Official creditors	78	484	829	176	791	794	435	558	494	404
Private creditors	3	268	50	96	46	119	54	64	91	0

10. CONTRACTUAL OBLIGATIONS ON OUTSTANDING LONG-TERM DEBT

	1996	1997	1998	1999	2000	2001	2002	2003	2004	2005
TOTAL										
Disbursements	846	698	458	272	148	57	26	4	1	1
Principal	347	299	298	294	270	290	305	313	326	340
Interest	162	160	157	152	145	139	132	124	117	113
Official creditors										
Disbursements	817	690	455	271	148	57	26	4	1	1
Principal	191	196	213	224	238	261	283	291	309	323
Interest	127	134	137	138	135	131	125	119	113	110
Bilateral creditors										
Disbursements	514	449	279	163	92	42	19	2	1	1
Principal	154	155	168	177	184	194	207	214	227	238
Interest	96	102	105	105	103	99	95	90	84	81
Multilateral creditors										
Disbursements	303	241	175	108	55	15	7	2	0	0
Principal	37	40	45	47	53	67	76	78	82	86
Interest	31	32	33	33	32	32	31	30	29	30
Private creditors										
Disbursements	29	8	4	1	0	0	0	0	0	0
Principal	156	104	85	71	32	29	22	22	18	17
Interest	35	26	20	14	10	8	7	5	4	3
Commercial banks										
Disbursements	18	3	2	0	0	0	0	0	0	0
Principal	62	52	35	24	22	19	12	12	11	11
Interest	19	16	12	10	8	7	6	5	4	3
Other private										
Disbursements	12	4	2	1	0	0	0	0	0	0
Principal	95	51	50	47	10	10	10	9	7	6
Interest	16	11	7	4	2	1	1	1	1	0

ST. KITTS AND NEVIS

(US$ million, unless otherwise indicated)

	1970	1980	1988	1989	1990	1991	1992	1993	1994	1995
1. SUMMARY DEBT DATA										
TOTAL DEBT STOCKS (EDT)	..	..	**26.6**	**36.6**	**45.2**	**49.8**	**51.4**	**53.7**	**58.1**	**56.3**
Long-term debt (LDOD)	..	..	**26.6**	**36.5**	**44.2**	**48.6**	**47.4**	**49.7**	**55.1**	**53.6**
Public and publicly guaranteed	..	..	26.6	36.5	44.2	48.6	47.4	49.7	55.1	53.6
Private nonguaranteed	0.0	0.0	0.0	0.0	0.0	0.0	0.0	0.0	0.0	0.0
Use of IMF credit	**0.0**	**0.0**	**0.0**	**0.0**	**0.0**	**0.0**	**0.0**	**0.0**	**0.0**	**0.0**
Short-term debt	..	..	**0.0**	**0.2**	**1.0**	**1.1**	**4.0**	**4.0**	**3.0**	**2.7**
of which interest arrears on LDOD	..	..	0.0	0.2	0.0	0.0	0.9	0.9	1.0	1.2
Official creditors	..	..	0.0	0.2	0.0	0.0	0.9	0.8	1.0	1.2
Private creditors	..	..	0.0	0.0	0.0	0.0	0.0	0.0	0.0	0.0
Memo: principal arrears on LDOD	..	..	0.0	0.0	0.0	0.0	0.3	0.3	0.7	0.7
Official creditors	..	..	0.0	0.0	0.0	0.0	0.3	0.3	0.6	0.3
Private creditors	..	..	0.0	0.0	0.0	0.0	0.0	0.0	0.1	0.4
Memo: export credits	..	..	16.0	26.0	30.0	39.0	26.0	23.0	26.0	30.0
TOTAL DEBT FLOWS										
Disbursements	..	..	**7.0**	**11.1**	**7.3**	**6.8**	**3.7**	**6.5**	**8.2**	**5.4**
Long-term debt	..	..	7.0	11.1	7.3	6.8	3.7	6.5	8.2	5.4
IMF purchases	0.0	0.0	0.0	0.0	0.0	0.0	0.0	0.0	0.0	0.0
Principal repayments	..	..	**0.9**	**1.0**	**1.5**	**2.1**	**2.5**	**3.4**	**3.7**	**4.9**
Long-term debt	..	..	0.9	1.0	1.5	2.1	2.5	3.4	3.7	4.9
IMF repurchases	0.0	0.0	0.0	0.0	0.0	0.0	0.0	0.0	0.0	0.0
Net flows on debt	..	..	**6.1**	**10.1**	**6.8**	**4.8**	**3.2**	**3.1**	**3.4**	**-0.1**
of which short-term debt	..	..	0.0	0.0	1.0	0.1	2.0	0.0	-1.1	-0.6
Interest payments (INT)	..	..	**0.7**	**0.8**	**1.5**	**1.4**	**1.2**	**1.5**	**1.9**	**2.0**
Long-term debt	..	..	0.7	0.8	1.4	1.3	1.0	1.3	1.7	1.9
IMF charges	0.0	0.0	0.0	0.0	0.0	0.0	0.0	0.0	0.0	0.0
Short-term debt	..	..	0.0	0.0	0.1	0.1	0.2	0.2	0.1	0.1
Net transfers on debt	..	..	**5.5**	**9.3**	**5.3**	**3.4**	**2.0**	**1.6**	**1.6**	**-2.1**
Total debt service paid (TDS)	..	..	**1.5**	**1.8**	**3.0**	**3.5**	**3.7**	**4.9**	**5.6**	**6.9**
Long-term debt	..	..	1.5	1.8	2.9	3.4	3.5	4.7	5.4	6.8
IMF repurchases and charges	0.0	0.0	0.0	0.0	0.0	0.0	0.0	0.0	0.0	0.0
Short-term debt (interest only)	..	..	0.0	0.0	0.1	0.1	0.2	0.2	0.1	0.1
2. AGGREGATE NET RESOURCE FLOWS AND NET TRANSFERS (LONG-TERM)										
NET RESOURCE FLOWS	..	..	**27.9**	**53.5**	**56.8**	**27.9**	**15.2**	**17.3**	**19.9**	**21.3**
Net flow of long-term debt (ex. IMF)	0.0	0.0	6.1	10.1	5.8	4.7	1.2	3.1	4.5	0.5
Foreign direct investment (net)	0.0	1.0	13.1	40.8	49.0	21.0	13.0	14.0	15.0	20.0
Portfolio equity flows	..	..	0.0	0.0	0.0	0.0	0.0	0.0	0.0	0.0
Grants (excluding technical coop.)	0.0	2.3	8.7	2.6	2.0	2.2	1.0	0.2	0.4	0.8
Memo: technical coop. grants	0.0	1.1	1.4	1.6	2.3	1.6	2.1	6.3	4.0	2.3
NET TRANSFERS	..	..	**20.6**	**44.8**	**50.4**	**19.6**	**3.6**	**7.4**	**9.2**	**10.9**
Interest on long-term debt	..	..	0.7	0.8	1.4	1.3	1.0	1.3	1.7	1.9
Profit remittances on FDI	0.0	0.0	6.7	7.9	5.0	7.0	10.5	8.5	9.0	8.5
3. MAJOR ECONOMIC AGGREGATES										
Gross national product (GNP)	..	46.5	122.6	137.1	151.9	157.7	170.9	185.9	193.9	208.7
Exports of goods & services (XGS)	..	33.7	90.4	99.9	102.9	113.0	127.9	131.4	138.1	..
of which workers remittances	..	0.8	10.7	17.1	17.2	13.4	13.3	13.6	14.1	..
Imports of goods & services (MGS)	..	48.6	115.5	132.1	140.1	142.3	138.4	155.8	160.0	..
International reserves (RES)	..	..	10.3	16.4	16.3	16.6	26.2	29.4	31.8	33.5
Current account balance	..	-2.7	-27.5	-38.4	-47.0	-34.9	-15.8	-30.1	-26.0	..
4. DEBT INDICATORS										
EDT / XGS (%)	..	..	29.4	36.7	43.9	44.0	40.2	40.8	42.1	..
EDT / GNP (%)	..	..	21.7	26.7	29.8	31.6	30.1	28.9	30.0	27.0
TDS / XGS (%)	..	..	1.7	1.9	2.9	3.1	2.9	3.7	4.0	..
INT / XGS (%)	..	..	0.7	0.8	1.5	1.2	0.9	1.1	1.4	..
INT / GNP (%)	..	..	0.5	0.6	1.0	0.9	0.7	0.8	1.0	0.9
RES / EDT (%)	..	..	38.7	44.8	36.0	33.4	51.0	54.8	54.8	59.5
RES / MGS (months)	..	..	1.1	1.5	1.4	1.4	2.3	2.3	2.4	..
Short-term / EDT (%)	..	..	0.0	0.4	2.3	2.3	7.8	7.4	5.2	4.7
Concessional / EDT (%)	..	..	94.2	83.5	85.4	81.6	76.5	76.2	72.1	78.1
Multilateral / EDT (%)	..	..	59.5	47.4	44.2	42.8	42.0	46.8	46.2	52.1

ST. KITTS AND NEVIS

(US$ million, unless otherwise indicated)

	1970	1980	1988	1989	1990	1991	1992	1993	1994	1995
5. LONG-TERM DEBT										
DEBT OUTSTANDING (LDOD)	..	..	**26.6**	**36.5**	**44.2**	**48.6**	**47.4**	**49.7**	**55.1**	**53.6**
Public and publicly guaranteed	..	..	**26.6**	**36.5**	**44.2**	**48.6**	**47.4**	**49.7**	**55.1**	**53.6**
Official creditors	..	..	26.6	33.5	41.4	44.6	43.2	45.3	48.4	48.2
Multilateral	..	..	15.8	17.4	20.0	21.3	21.6	25.1	26.9	29.3
Concessional	..	..	15.0	16.5	19.1	20.3	20.4	22.9	23.9	26.3
Bilateral	..	..	10.8	16.2	21.5	23.3	21.6	20.2	21.5	18.8
Concessional	..	..	10.1	14.1	19.5	20.4	18.9	18.0	18.0	17.7
Private creditors	..	..	0.0	3.0	2.7	4.0	4.2	4.4	6.7	5.5
Bonds	..	..	0.0	0.0	0.0	0.0	0.0	0.0	0.0	0.0
Commercial banks	..	..	0.0	0.0	0.0	0.0	0.0	0.0	0.0	0.0
Other private	..	..	0.0	3.0	2.7	4.0	4.2	4.4	6.7	5.5
Private nonguaranteed	**0.0**	**0.0**	**0.0**	**0.0**	**0.0**	**0.0**	**0.0**	**0.0**	**0.0**	**0.0**
Bonds	..	..	0.0	0.0	0.0	0.0	0.0	0.0	0.0	0.0
Commercial banks	..	..	0.0	0.0	0.0	0.0	0.0	0.0	0.0	0.0
Memo:										
IBRD	0.0	0.0	0.0	0.0	0.0	0.0	0.2	0.2	0.8	1.1
IDA	0.0	0.0	0.0	0.0	0.0	0.0	0.6	1.4	1.6	1.6
DISBURSEMENTS	..	..	**7.0**	**11.1**	**7.3**	**6.8**	**3.7**	**6.5**	**8.2**	**5.4**
Public and publicly guaranteed	..	..	**7.0**	**11.1**	**7.3**	**6.8**	**3.7**	**6.5**	**8.2**	**5.4**
Official creditors	..	..	7.0	8.1	7.3	4.9	2.4	5.2	4.9	5.0
Multilateral	..	..	1.8	2.2	2.4	2.5	2.4	5.2	2.6	3.7
Concessional	..	..	1.7	2.1	2.4	2.1	2.1	4.0	1.7	3.4
Bilateral	..	..	5.2	6.0	4.9	2.4	0.0	0.0	2.3	1.3
Concessional	..	..	5.2	4.5	4.9	1.2	0.0	0.0	0.2	1.3
Private creditors	..	..	0.0	3.0	0.0	1.9	1.3	1.3	3.3	0.4
Bonds	..	..	0.0	0.0	0.0	0.0	0.0	0.0	0.0	0.0
Commercial banks	..	..	0.0	0.0	0.0	0.0	0.0	0.0	0.0	0.0
Other private	..	..	0.0	3.0	0.0	1.9	1.3	1.3	3.3	0.4
Private nonguaranteed	**0.0**	**0.0**	**0.0**	**0.0**	**0.0**	**0.0**	**0.0**	**0.0**	**0.0**	**0.0**
Bonds	..	..	0.0	0.0	0.0	0.0	0.0	0.0	0.0	0.0
Commercial banks	..	..	0.0	0.0	0.0	0.0	0.0	0.0	0.0	0.0
Memo:										
IBRD	0.0	0.0	0.0	0.0	0.0	0.0	0.2	0.0	0.6	0.3
IDA	0.0	0.0	0.0	0.0	0.0	0.0	0.6	0.9	0.1	0.0
PRINCIPAL REPAYMENTS	..	..	**0.9**	**1.0**	**1.5**	**2.1**	**2.5**	**3.4**	**3.7**	**4.9**
Public and publicly guaranteed	..	..	**0.9**	**1.0**	**1.5**	**2.1**	**2.5**	**3.4**	**3.7**	**4.9**
Official creditors	..	..	0.9	1.0	1.1	1.5	1.6	2.4	2.7	3.4
Multilateral	..	..	0.6	0.6	0.7	1.0	1.2	1.2	1.4	1.5
Concessional	..	..	0.5	0.6	0.6	0.9	1.1	1.0	1.2	1.2
Bilateral	..	..	0.3	0.4	0.3	0.4	0.4	1.2	1.2	1.9
Concessional	..	..	0.2	0.2	0.2	0.2	0.1	0.7	0.5	1.6
Private creditors	..	..	0.0	0.0	0.4	0.6	1.0	1.0	1.0	1.5
Bonds	..	..	0.0	0.0	0.0	0.0	0.0	0.0	0.0	0.0
Commercial banks	..	..	0.0	0.0	0.0	0.0	0.0	0.0	0.0	0.0
Other private	..	..	0.0	0.0	0.4	0.6	1.0	1.0	1.0	1.5
Private nonguaranteed	**0.0**	**0.0**	**0.0**	**0.0**	**0.0**	**0.0**	**0.0**	**0.0**	**0.0**	**0.0**
Bonds	..	..	0.0	0.0	0.0	0.0	0.0	0.0	0.0	0.0
Commercial banks	..	..	0.0	0.0	0.0	0.0	0.0	0.0	0.0	0.0
Memo:										
IBRD	0.0	0.0	0.0	0.0	0.0	0.0	0.0	0.0	0.0	0.0
IDA	0.0	0.0	0.0	0.0	0.0	0.0	0.0	0.0	0.0	0.0
NET FLOWS ON DEBT	..	..	**6.1**	**10.1**	**5.8**	**4.7**	**1.2**	**3.1**	**4.5**	**0.5**
Public and publicly guaranteed	..	..	**6.1**	**10.1**	**5.8**	**4.7**	**1.2**	**3.1**	**4.5**	**0.5**
Official creditors	..	..	6.1	7.1	6.2	3.4	0.8	2.8	2.3	1.5
Multilateral	..	..	1.2	1.5	1.7	1.4	1.2	4.0	1.2	2.2
Concessional	..	..	1.2	1.5	1.7	1.2	1.0	3.0	0.5	2.1
Bilateral	..	..	4.9	5.6	4.6	2.0	-0.4	-1.2	1.1	-0.7
Concessional	..	..	5.0	4.2	4.7	0.9	-0.1	-0.7	-0.3	-0.3
Private creditors	..	..	0.0	3.0	-0.4	1.3	0.4	0.2	2.3	-1.0
Bonds	..	..	0.0	0.0	0.0	0.0	0.0	0.0	0.0	0.0
Commercial banks	..	..	0.0	0.0	0.0	0.0	0.0	0.0	0.0	0.0
Other private	..	..	0.0	3.0	-0.4	1.3	0.4	0.2	2.3	-1.0
Private nonguaranteed	**0.0**	**0.0**	**0.0**	**0.0**	**0.0**	**0.0**	**0.0**	**0.0**	**0.0**	**0.0**
Bonds	..	..	0.0	0.0	0.0	0.0	0.0	0.0	0.0	0.0
Commercial banks	..	..	0.0	0.0	0.0	0.0	0.0	0.0	0.0	0.0
Memo:										
IBRD	0.0	0.0	0.0	0.0	0.0	0.0	0.2	0.0	0.6	0.3
IDA	0.0	0.0	0.0	0.0	0.0	0.0	0.6	0.9	0.1	0.0

ST. KITTS AND NEVIS

(US$ million, unless otherwise indicated)

	1970	1980	1988	1989	1990	1991	1992	1993	1994	1995
INTEREST PAYMENTS (LINT)	..	..	**0.7**	**0.8**	**1.4**	**1.3**	**1.0**	**1.3**	**1.7**	**1.9**
Public and publicly guaranteed	..	..	**0.7**	**0.8**	**1.4**	**1.3**	**1.0**	**1.3**	**1.7**	**1.9**
Official creditors	..	..	0.7	0.8	1.4	1.2	0.9	1.2	1.5	1.5
Multilateral	..	..	0.5	0.6	0.7	0.7	0.5	0.8	0.9	1.0
Concessional	..	..	0.5	0.5	0.6	0.6	0.4	0.6	0.7	0.7
Bilateral	..	..	0.1	0.3	0.7	0.5	0.4	0.5	0.6	0.5
Concessional	..	..	0.1	0.2	0.6	0.4	0.3	0.3	0.4	0.4
Private creditors	..	..	0.0	0.0	0.0	0.1	0.1	0.1	0.2	0.4
Bonds	..	..	0.0	0.0	0.0	0.0	0.0	0.0	0.0	0.0
Commercial banks	..	..	0.0	0.0	0.0	0.0	0.0	0.0	0.0	0.0
Other private	..	..	0.0	0.0	0.0	0.1	0.1	0.1	0.2	0.4
Private nonguaranteed	**0.0**	**0.0**	**0.0**	**0.0**	**0.0**	**0.0**	**0.0**	**0.0**	**0.0**	**0.0**
Bonds	..	..	0.0	0.0	0.0	0.0	0.0	0.0	0.0	0.0
Commercial banks	..	..	0.0	0.0	0.0	0.0	0.0	0.0	0.0	0.0
Memo:										
IBRD	0.0	0.0	0.0	0.0	0.0	0.0	0.0	0.0	0.0	0.1
IDA	0.0	0.0	0.0	0.0	0.0	0.0	0.0	0.0	0.0	0.0
NET TRANSFERS ON DEBT	..	..	**5.5**	**9.3**	**4.4**	**3.4**	**0.1**	**1.7**	**2.8**	**-1.4**
Public and publicly guaranteed	..	..	**5.5**	**9.3**	**4.4**	**3.4**	**0.1**	**1.7**	**2.8**	**-1.4**
Official creditors	..	..	5.5	6.3	4.8	2.2	-0.1	1.6	0.8	0.1
Multilateral	..	..	0.7	1.0	1.0	0.7	0.7	3.3	0.3	1.3
Concessional	..	..	0.8	1.0	1.1	0.6	0.6	2.3	-0.3	1.4
Bilateral	..	..	4.8	5.3	3.8	1.5	-0.8	-1.7	0.5	-1.2
Concessional	..	..	4.9	4.0	4.1	0.5	-0.4	-1.0	-0.7	-0.7
Private creditors	..	..	0.0	3.0	-0.5	1.2	0.3	0.1	2.0	-1.4
Bonds	..	..	0.0	0.0	0.0	0.0	0.0	0.0	0.0	0.0
Commercial banks	..	..	0.0	0.0	0.0	0.0	0.0	0.0	0.0	0.0
Other private	..	..	0.0	3.0	-0.5	1.2	0.3	0.1	2.0	-1.4
Private nonguaranteed	**0.0**	**0.0**	**0.0**	**0.0**	**0.0**	**0.0**	**0.0**	**0.0**	**0.0**	**0.0**
Bonds	..	..	0.0	0.0	0.0	0.0	0.0	0.0	0.0	0.0
Commercial banks	..	..	0.0	0.0	0.0	0.0	0.0	0.0	0.0	0.0
Memo:										
IBRD	0.0	0.0	0.0	0.0	0.0	0.0	0.2	0.0	0.6	0.3
IDA	0.0	0.0	0.0	0.0	0.0	0.0	0.6	0.8	0.1	0.0
DEBT SERVICE (LTDS)	..	..	**1.5**	**1.8**	**2.9**	**3.4**	**3.5**	**4.7**	**5.4**	**6.8**
Public and publicly guaranteed	..	..	**1.5**	**1.8**	**2.9**	**3.4**	**3.5**	**4.7**	**5.4**	**6.8**
Official creditors	..	..	1.5	1.8	2.4	2.7	2.5	3.6	4.2	4.9
Multilateral	..	..	1.1	1.2	1.4	1.7	1.7	2.0	2.3	2.4
Concessional	..	..	0.9	1.1	1.2	1.6	1.5	1.7	2.0	2.0
Bilateral	..	..	0.4	0.6	1.0	1.0	0.8	1.7	1.8	2.4
Concessional	..	..	0.3	0.5	0.8	0.6	0.4	1.0	0.9	2.0
Private creditors	..	..	0.0	0.0	0.5	0.7	1.1	1.1	1.3	1.9
Bonds	..	..	0.0	0.0	0.0	0.0	0.0	0.0	0.0	0.0
Commercial banks	..	..	0.0	0.0	0.0	0.0	0.0	0.0	0.0	0.0
Other private	..	..	0.0	0.0	0.5	0.7	1.1	1.1	1.3	1.9
Private nonguaranteed	**0.0**	**0.0**	**0.0**	**0.0**	**0.0**	**0.0**	**0.0**	**0.0**	**0.0**	**0.0**
Bonds	..	..	0.0	0.0	0.0	0.0	0.0	0.0	0.0	0.0
Commercial banks	..	..	0.0	0.0	0.0	0.0	0.0	0.0	0.0	0.0
Memo:										
IBRD	0.0	0.0	0.0	0.0	0.0	0.0	0.0	0.0	0.0	0.1
IDA	0.0	0.0	0.0	0.0	0.0	0.0	0.0	0.0	0.0	0.0
UNDISBURSED DEBT	..	..	**14.7**	**16.0**	**15.3**	**28.6**	**35.1**	**42.4**	**38.2**	**41.8**
Official creditors	..	..	14.7	16.0	14.3	28.6	33.9	42.4	37.8	41.8
Private creditors	..	..	0.0	0.0	1.1	0.0	1.3	0.0	0.4	0.0
Memorandum items										
Concessional LDOD	..	..	25.1	30.6	38.6	40.6	39.3	40.9	41.9	43.9
Variable rate LDOD	..	..	0.0	0.0	0.0	0.7	0.9	0.8	1.3	1.5
Public sector LDOD	..	..	24.4	32.9	40.7	45.4	44.4	47.5	53.4	52.4
Private sector LDOD	..	..	2.2	3.6	3.4	3.2	3.0	2.2	1.7	1.3

6. CURRENCY COMPOSITION OF LONG-TERM DEBT (PERCENT)

	1970	1980	1988	1989	1990	1991	1992	1993	1994	1995
Deutsche mark	..	..	0.0	0.0	0.0	0.0	0.0	0.0	0.0	0.0
French franc	..	..	0.0	0.0	0.0	0.0	0.0	0.0	0.0	0.0
Japanese yen	..	..	0.0	0.0	0.0	0.0	0.0	0.0	0.0	0.0
Pound sterling	..	..	5.3	10.4	16.3	16.7	13.1	11.3	9.8	7.3
Swiss franc	..	..	0.0	0.0	0.0	0.0	0.0	0.0	0.0	0.0
U.S.dollars	..	..	32.7	40.8	37.8	39.9	43.7	46.5	51.6	51.3
Multiple currency	..	..	48.5	38.1	35.5	34.8	35.9	36.2	33.1	34.1
Special drawing rights	..	..	0.0	0.0	0.0	0.0	0.0	0.0	0.0	0.0
All other currencies	..	..	13.2	11.0	10.2	8.6	7.4	6.0	5.4	7.5

ST. KITTS AND NEVIS

(US$ million, unless otherwise indicated)

	1970	1980	1988	1989	1990	1991	1992	1993	1994	1995
7. DEBT RESTRUCTURINGS										
Total amount rescheduled	0.0	0.0	0.0	0.0	0.0	0.0	0.0	0.0	0.0	0.0
Debt stock rescheduled	0.0	0.0	0.0	0.0	0.0	0.0	0.0	0.0	0.0	0.0
Principal rescheduled	0.0	0.0	0.0	0.0	0.0	0.0	0.0	0.0	0.0	0.0
Official	0.0	0.0	0.0	0.0	0.0	0.0	0.0	0.0	0.0	0.0
Private	0.0	0.0	0.0	0.0	0.0	0.0	0.0	0.0	0.0	0.0
Interest rescheduled	0.0	0.0	0.0	0.0	0.0	0.0	0.0	0.0	0.0	0.0
Official	0.0	0.0	0.0	0.0	0.0	0.0	0.0	0.0	0.0	0.0
Private	0.0	0.0	0.0	0.0	0.0	0.0	0.0	0.0	0.0	0.0
Debt forgiven	..	..	0.0	0.0	0.0	0.0	0.0	0.0	0.0	0.0
Memo: interest forgiven	..	..	0.0	0.0	0.0	0.0	0.0	0.0	0.0	0.0
Debt stock reduction	0.0	0.0	0.0	0.0	0.0	0.0	0.0	0.0	0.0	0.0
of which debt buyback	0.0	0.0	0.0	0.0	0.0	0.0	0.0	0.0	0.0	0.0
8. DEBT STOCK-FLOW RECONCILIATION										
Total change in debt stocks	..	..	..	10.0	8.6	4.6	1.6	2.3	4.4	-1.8
Net flows on debt	..	..	..	10.1	6.8	4.8	3.2	3.1	3.4	-0.1
Net change in interest arrears	..	..	..	0.1	-0.1	0.0	0.9	-0.1	0.2	0.2
Interest capitalized	..	..	..	0.0	0.0	0.0	0.0	0.0	0.0	0.0
Debt forgiveness or reduction	..	..	..	0.0	0.0	0.0	0.0	0.0	0.0	0.0
Cross-currency valuation	..	..	..	-0.3	2.1	-0.3	-1.5	-0.3	0.6	0.2
Residual	..	..	..	0.1	-0.2	0.1	-0.9	-0.4	0.2	-2.1
9. AVERAGE TERMS OF NEW COMMITMENTS										
ALL CREDITORS										
Interest (%)	..	..	1.9	0.9	4.0	4.3	2.9	3.8	5.7	3.9
Maturity (years)	..	..	28.0	14.8	31.7	19.0	25.6	21.9	6.1	17.6
Grace period (years)	..	..	7.6	4.3	7.5	5.4	7.9	6.0	1.6	4.8
Grant element (%)	..	..	62.7	51.2	41.5	38.2	53.1	43.7	13.0	38.5
Official creditors										
Interest (%)	..	..	1.9	0.8	4.5	4.0	2.0	3.8	2.0	3.9
Maturity (years)	..	..	28.0	17.5	38.0	19.7	31.7	21.9	10.9	17.6
Grace period (years)	..	..	7.6	5.4	9.0	5.6	9.8	6.0	3.4	4.8
Grant element (%)	..	..	62.7	60.1	46.1	39.9	65.8	43.7	38.3	38.5
Private creditors										
Interest (%)	..	..	0.0	1.5	2.0	9.5	5.9	0.0	5.8	0.0
Maturity (years)	..	..	0.0	5.9	5.8	4.3	6.0	0.0	6.0	0.0
Grace period (years)	..	..	0.0	0.8	1.3	0.3	1.6	0.0	1.5	0.0
Grant element (%)	..	..	0.0	22.1	22.5	0.4	11.8	0.0	12.3	0.0
Memorandum items										
Commitments	..	..	5.1	12.7	5.5	20.3	11.0	13.7	3.8	10.3
Official creditors	..	..	5.1	9.7	4.4	19.4	8.4	13.7	0.1	10.3
Private creditors	..	..	0.0	3.0	1.1	0.9	2.6	0.0	3.8	0.0

10. CONTRACTUAL OBLIGATIONS ON OUTSTANDING LONG-TERM DEBT

	1996	1997	1998	1999	2000	2001	2002	2003	2004	2005
TOTAL										
Disbursements	12.2	10.9	7.3	4.8	3.0	1.7	1.1	0.5	0.3	0.1
Principal	3.8	3.9	4.6	5.9	4.9	5.3	5.1	5.3	5.2	5.1
Interest	2.1	2.3	2.3	2.3	2.2	2.1	1.9	1.8	1.6	1.4
Official creditors										
Disbursements	12.2	10.9	7.3	4.8	3.0	1.7	1.1	0.5	0.3	0.1
Principal	2.3	2.7	3.5	4.8	4.9	5.3	5.1	5.3	5.2	5.1
Interest	1.8	2.1	2.2	2.2	2.2	2.1	1.9	1.8	1.6	1.4
Bilateral creditors										
Disbursements	5.5	3.8	2.5	1.4	0.8	0.4	0.2	0.0	0.0	0.0
Principal	1.1	1.0	1.6	2.5	2.4	2.4	2.2	2.3	2.2	2.2
Interest	0.7	0.8	0.9	0.9	0.8	0.8	0.7	0.7	0.6	0.5
Multilateral creditors										
Disbursements	6.6	7.1	4.9	3.4	2.2	1.3	0.9	0.5	0.3	0.1
Principal	1.2	1.6	1.8	2.3	2.5	3.0	2.8	3.0	3.0	2.9
Interest	1.1	1.2	1.3	1.3	1.3	1.3	1.2	1.1	1.0	0.9
Private creditors										
Disbursements	0.0	0.0	0.0	0.0	0.0	0.0	0.0	0.0	0.0	0.0
Principal	1.5	1.3	1.2	1.0	0.1	0.0	0.0	0.0	0.0	0.0
Interest	0.3	0.2	0.1	0.1	0.0	0.0	0.0	0.0	0.0	0.0
Commercial banks										
Disbursements	0.0	0.0	0.0	0.0	0.0	0.0	0.0	0.0	0.0	0.0
Principal	0.0	0.0	0.0	0.0	0.0	0.0	0.0	0.0	0.0	0.0
Interest	0.0	0.0	0.0	0.0	0.0	0.0	0.0	0.0	0.0	0.0
Other private										
Disbursements	0.0	0.0	0.0	0.0	0.0	0.0	0.0	0.0	0.0	0.0
Principal	1.5	1.3	1.2	1.0	0.1	0.0	0.0	0.0	0.0	0.0
Interest	0.3	0.2	0.1	0.1	0.0	0.0	0.0	0.0	0.0	0.0

ST. LUCIA

(US$ million, unless otherwise indicated)

	1970	1980	1988	1989	1990	1991	1992	1993	1994	1995
1. SUMMARY DEBT DATA										
TOTAL DEBT STOCKS (EDT)	..	..	**57.5**	**65.7**	**79.6**	**82.3**	**98.0**	**100.6**	**113.3**	**128.0**
Long-term debt (LDOD)	..	..	**52.8**	**61.6**	**72.6**	**76.1**	**89.8**	**96.2**	**103.3**	**111.0**
Public and publicly guaranteed	..	..	52.8	61.6	72.6	76.1	89.8	96.2	103.3	111.0
Private nonguaranteed	0.0	0.0	0.0	0.0	0.0	0.0	0.0	0.0	0.0	0.0
Use of IMF credit	**0.0**	**0.0**	**0.0**	**0.0**	**0.0**	**0.0**	**0.0**	**0.0**	**0.0**	**0.0**
Short-term debt	..	..	**4.7**	**4.1**	**7.0**	**6.2**	**8.2**	**4.4**	**10.0**	**17.0**
of which interest arrears on LDOD	..	..	0.0	0.1	0.8	0.0	0.0	0.0	0.0	0.1
Official creditors	..	..	0.0	0.1	0.8	0.0	0.0	0.0	0.0	0.1
Private creditors	..	..	0.0	0.0	0.0	0.0	0.0	0.0	0.0	0.0
Memo: principal arrears on LDOD	..	..	0.1	0.1	0.1	0.2	0.3	0.5	0.2	0.1
Official creditors	..	..	0.1	0.1	0.1	0.2	0.3	0.5	0.2	0.1
Private creditors	..	..	0.0	0.0	0.0	0.0	0.0	0.0	0.0	0.0
Memo: export credits	..	..	21.0	27.0	40.0	39.0	33.0	31.0	31.0	30.0
TOTAL DEBT FLOWS										
Disbursements	..	..	**13.2**	**13.9**	**8.1**	**10.0**	**28.0**	**15.3**	**8.9**	**11.5**
Long-term debt	..	..	13.2	13.9	8.1	10.0	28.0	15.3	8.9	11.5
IMF purchases	0.0	0.0	0.0	0.0	0.0	0.0	0.0	0.0	0.0	0.0
Principal repayments	..	..	**1.3**	**2.4**	**3.2**	**5.9**	**7.2**	**6.1**	**5.7**	**6.3**
Long-term debt	..	..	1.3	2.4	3.2	5.9	7.2	6.1	5.7	6.3
IMF repurchases	0.0	0.0	0.0	0.0	0.0	0.0	0.0	0.0	0.0	0.0
Net flows on debt	..	..	**11.8**	**10.9**	**7.1**	**4.1**	**22.7**	**5.5**	**8.7**	**12.2**
of which short-term debt	..	..	-0.1	-0.6	2.2	0.0	1.9	-3.8	5.6	6.9
Interest payments (INT)	..	..	**2.2**	**2.9**	**3.2**	**4.3**	**4.4**	**5.1**	**5.0**	**5.7**
Long-term debt	..	..	1.8	2.5	2.8	3.8	4.2	4.9	4.5	4.7
IMF charges	0.0	0.0	0.0	0.0	0.0	0.0	0.0	0.0	0.0	0.0
Short-term debt	..	..	0.4	0.4	0.3	0.5	0.3	0.2	0.5	0.9
Net transfers on debt	..	..	**9.6**	**8.0**	**4.0**	**-0.3**	**18.3**	**0.3**	**3.7**	**6.5**
Total debt service paid (TDS)	..	..	**3.5**	**5.3**	**6.4**	**10.3**	**11.6**	**11.2**	**10.8**	**11.9**
Long-term debt	..	..	3.1	4.9	6.0	9.8	11.3	11.0	10.3	11.0
IMF repurchases and charges	0.0	0.0	0.0	0.0	0.0	0.0	0.0	0.0	0.0	0.0
Short-term debt (interest only)	..	..	0.4	0.4	0.3	0.5	0.3	0.2	0.5	0.9
2. AGGREGATE NET RESOURCE FLOWS AND NET TRANSFERS (LONG-TERM)										
NET RESOURCE FLOWS	..	..	**36.3**	**44.3**	**53.0**	**69.5**	**66.9**	**57.6**	**52.9**	**110.5**
Net flow of long-term debt (ex. IMF)	0.0	0.0	11.9	11.5	4.9	4.1	20.8	9.3	3.1	5.3
Foreign direct investment (net)	0.0	30.9	16.4	26.6	45.0	58.0	41.0	34.0	32.0	63.0
Portfolio equity flows	..	..	0.0	0.0	0.0	0.0	0.0	0.0	0.0	0.0
Grants (excluding technical coop.)	0.0	5.8	8.0	6.2	3.1	7.4	5.1	14.3	17.8	42.2
Memo: technical coop. grants	0.0	1.6	3.2	3.3	3.5	5.0	3.9	4.3	7.2	4.8
NET TRANSFERS	..	..	**19.8**	**28.3**	**23.7**	**36.5**	**33.7**	**19.6**	**14.4**	**72.7**
Interest on long-term debt	..	..	1.8	2.5	2.8	3.8	4.2	4.9	4.5	4.7
Profit remittances on FDI	0.0	0.0	14.7	13.5	26.5	29.1	29.1	33.0	34.0	33.0
3. MAJOR ECONOMIC AGGREGATES										
Gross national product (GNP)	..	100.0	316.0	361.9	370.9	397.9	447.7	464.4	481.7	525.0
Exports of goods & services (XGS)	..	87.5	258.6	270.6	301.2	306.3	343.7	346.2	344.8	376.1
of which workers remittances	..	0.0	12.7	12.3	13.7	15.6	16.1	13.6	14.0	0.0
Imports of goods & services (MGS)	..	135.4	271.4	328.7	340.6	376.2	391.4	383.0	407.9	434.9
International reserves (RES)	..	8.3	32.7	38.2	44.6	48.8	55.5	60.0	57.8	63.1
Current account balance	..	-33.3	-18.0	-63.3	-45.5	-72.1	-54.8	-41.2	-65.0	-51.2
4. DEBT INDICATORS										
EDT / XGS (%)	..	..	22.2	24.3	26.4	26.9	28.5	29.1	32.9	34.0
EDT / GNP (%)	..	..	18.2	18.1	21.5	20.7	21.9	21.7	23.5	24.4
TDS / XGS (%)	..	..	1.4	2.0	2.1	3.4	3.4	3.2	3.1	3.2
INT / XGS (%)	..	..	0.9	1.1	1.0	1.4	1.3	1.5	1.5	1.5
INT / GNP (%)	..	..	0.7	0.8	0.9	1.1	1.0	1.1	1.0	1.1
RES / EDT (%)	..	..	56.9	58.2	56.0	59.3	56.6	59.6	51.0	49.3
RES / MGS (months)	..	0.7	1.4	1.4	1.6	1.6	1.7	1.9	1.7	1.7
Short-term / EDT (%)	..	..	8.1	6.2	8.8	7.5	8.3	4.3	8.8	13.3
Concessional / EDT (%)	..	..	51.7	53.3	50.4	56.8	62.4	66.6	63.9	63.2
Multilateral / EDT (%)	..	..	53.3	55.2	53.6	59.2	60.6	65.9	62.7	61.5

ST. LUCIA

(US$ million, unless otherwise indicated)

	1970	1980	1988	1989	1990	1991	1992	1993	1994	1995
5. LONG-TERM DEBT										
DEBT OUTSTANDING (LDOD)	..	..	**52.8**	**61.6**	**72.6**	**76.1**	**89.8**	**96.2**	**103.3**	**111.0**
Public and publicly guaranteed	..	..	**52.8**	**61.6**	**72.6**	**76.1**	**89.8**	**96.2**	**103.3**	**111.0**
Official creditors	..	..	49.1	58.7	70.0	74.6	89.2	96.2	103.3	110.9
Multilateral	..	..	30.6	36.2	42.7	48.8	59.3	66.3	71.0	78.7
Concessional	..	..	28.7	34.4	39.7	45.0	51.1	54.3	56.8	63.2
Bilateral	..	..	18.5	22.4	27.3	25.8	29.9	29.9	32.3	32.2
Concessional	..	..	1.0	0.6	0.4	1.8	10.0	12.7	15.6	17.7
Private creditors	..	..	3.7	2.9	2.6	1.6	0.6	0.1	0.1	0.0
Bonds	..	..	0.0	0.0	0.0	0.0	0.0	0.0	0.0	0.0
Commercial banks	..	..	3.7	2.9	2.6	1.6	0.6	0.1	0.1	0.0
Other private	..	..	0.0	0.0	0.0	0.0	0.0	0.0	0.0	0.0
Private nonguaranteed	**0.0**	**0.0**	**0.0**	**0.0**	**0.0**	**0.0**	**0.0**	**0.0**	**0.0**	**0.0**
Bonds	..	..	0.0	0.0	0.0	0.0	0.0	0.0	0.0	0.0
Commercial banks	..	..	0.0	0.0	0.0	0.0	0.0	0.0	0.0	0.0
Memo:										
IBRD	0.0	0.0	0.0	0.0	0.0	0.0	0.0	0.4	1.5	2.1
IDA	0.0	0.0	0.0	0.0	0.0	0.6	4.4	5.3	5.7	7.9
DISBURSEMENTS	..	..	**13.2**	**13.9**	**8.1**	**10.0**	**28.0**	**15.3**	**8.9**	**11.5**
Public and publicly guaranteed	..	..	**13.2**	**13.9**	**8.1**	**10.0**	**28.0**	**15.3**	**8.9**	**11.5**
Official creditors	..	..	13.2	13.6	8.1	10.0	28.0	15.3	8.9	11.5
Multilateral	..	..	6.1	7.3	7.0	8.6	15.8	11.7	6.7	10.8
Concessional	..	..	6.1	7.2	5.6	7.6	11.1	7.6	4.0	9.3
Bilateral	..	..	7.1	6.3	1.1	1.4	12.1	3.6	2.2	0.8
Concessional	..	..	0.0	0.0	0.2	1.4	9.1	3.6	1.7	0.8
Private creditors	..	..	0.0	0.4	0.0	0.0	0.0	0.0	0.0	0.0
Bonds	..	..	0.0	0.0	0.0	0.0	0.0	0.0	0.0	0.0
Commercial banks	..	..	0.0	0.4	0.0	0.0	0.0	0.0	0.0	0.0
Other private	..	..	0.0	0.0	0.0	0.0	0.0	0.0	0.0	0.0
Private nonguaranteed	**0.0**	**0.0**	**0.0**	**0.0**	**0.0**	**0.0**	**0.0**	**0.0**	**0.0**	**0.0**
Bonds	..	..	0.0	0.0	0.0	0.0	0.0	0.0	0.0	0.0
Commercial banks	..	..	0.0	0.0	0.0	0.0	0.0	0.0	0.0	0.0
Memo:										
IBRD	0.0	0.0	0.0	0.0	0.0	0.0	0.0	0.5	1.0	0.7
IDA	0.0	0.0	0.0	0.0	0.0	0.6	4.0	0.8	0.2	2.1
PRINCIPAL REPAYMENTS	..	..	**1.3**	**2.4**	**3.2**	**5.9**	**7.2**	**6.1**	**5.7**	**6.3**
Public and publicly guaranteed	..	..	**1.3**	**2.4**	**3.2**	**5.9**	**7.2**	**6.1**	**5.7**	**6.3**
Official creditors	..	..	1.3	1.7	2.4	5.0	6.4	5.5	5.7	6.3
Multilateral	..	..	1.2	1.6	2.4	2.9	3.1	3.4	3.7	4.1
Concessional	..	..	1.1	1.4	2.1	2.7	2.9	3.2	3.5	3.9
Bilateral	..	..	0.1	0.0	0.0	2.1	3.3	2.1	2.1	2.1
Concessional	..	..	0.1	0.0	0.0	0.0	0.5	0.1	0.1	0.1
Private creditors	..	..	0.0	0.7	0.8	0.9	0.8	0.5	0.0	0.0
Bonds	..	..	0.0	0.0	0.0	0.0	0.0	0.0	0.0	0.0
Commercial banks	..	..	0.0	0.7	0.8	0.9	0.8	0.5	0.0	0.0
Other private	..	..	0.0	0.0	0.0	0.0	0.0	0.0	0.0	0.0
Private nonguaranteed	**0.0**	**0.0**	**0.0**	**0.0**	**0.0**	**0.0**	**0.0**	**0.0**	**0.0**	**0.0**
Bonds	..	..	0.0	0.0	0.0	0.0	0.0	0.0	0.0	0.0
Commercial banks	..	..	0.0	0.0	0.0	0.0	0.0	0.0	0.0	0.0
Memo:										
IBRD	0.0	0.0	0.0	0.0	0.0	0.0	0.0	0.0	0.0	0.1
IDA	0.0	0.0	0.0	0.0	0.0	0.0	0.0	0.0	0.0	0.0
NET FLOWS ON DEBT	..	..	**11.9**	**11.5**	**4.9**	**4.1**	**20.8**	**9.3**	**3.1**	**5.3**
Public and publicly guaranteed	..	..	**11.9**	**11.5**	**4.9**	**4.1**	**20.8**	**9.3**	**3.1**	**5.3**
Official creditors	..	..	12.0	11.9	5.7	5.0	21.6	9.8	3.1	5.3
Multilateral	..	..	4.9	5.6	4.6	5.7	12.7	8.3	3.0	6.6
Concessional	..	..	5.0	5.8	3.5	4.9	8.2	4.4	0.5	5.4
Bilateral	..	..	7.0	6.3	1.1	-0.7	8.9	1.5	0.1	-1.4
Concessional	..	..	-0.1	0.0	0.2	1.4	8.6	3.5	1.6	0.7
Private creditors	..	..	0.0	-0.4	-0.8	-0.9	-0.8	-0.5	0.0	0.0
Bonds	..	..	0.0	0.0	0.0	0.0	0.0	0.0	0.0	0.0
Commercial banks	..	..	0.0	-0.4	-0.8	-0.9	-0.8	-0.5	0.0	0.0
Other private	..	..	0.0	0.0	0.0	0.0	0.0	0.0	0.0	0.0
Private nonguaranteed	**0.0**	**0.0**	**0.0**	**0.0**	**0.0**	**0.0**	**0.0**	**0.0**	**0.0**	**0.0**
Bonds	..	..	0.0	0.0	0.0	0.0	0.0	0.0	0.0	0.0
Commercial banks	..	..	0.0	0.0	0.0	0.0	0.0	0.0	0.0	0.0
Memo:										
IBRD	0.0	0.0	0.0	0.0	0.0	0.0	0.0	0.5	1.0	0.6
IDA	0.0	0.0	0.0	0.0	0.0	0.6	4.0	0.8	0.2	2.1

ST. LUCIA

(US$ million, unless otherwise indicated)

	1970	1980	1988	1989	1990	1991	1992	1993	1994	1995
INTEREST PAYMENTS (LINT)	**..**	**..**	**1.8**	**2.5**	**2.8**	**3.8**	**4.2**	**4.9**	**4.5**	**4.7**
Public and publicly guaranteed	**..**	**..**	**1.8**	**2.5**	**2.8**	**3.8**	**4.2**	**4.9**	**4.5**	**4.7**
Official creditors	..	..	1.5	2.3	2.6	3.7	4.1	4.9	4.5	4.7
Multilateral	..	..	1.1	1.3	1.8	1.9	2.1	2.6	2.8	2.9
Concessional	..	..	0.9	1.1	1.5	1.6	1.5	1.7	1.8	1.9
Bilateral	..	..	0.4	1.0	0.8	1.7	1.9	2.3	1.7	1.8
Concessional	..	..	0.0	0.0	0.0	0.0	0.6	1.0	0.8	0.9
Private creditors	..	..	0.3	0.2	0.2	0.2	0.1	0.0	0.0	0.0
Bonds	..	..	0.0	0.0	0.0	0.0	0.0	0.0	0.0	0.0
Commercial banks	..	..	0.3	0.2	0.2	0.2	0.1	0.0	0.0	0.0
Other private	..	..	0.0	0.0	0.0	0.0	0.0	0.0	0.0	0.0
Private nonguaranteed	**0.0**	**0.0**	**0.0**	**0.0**	**0.0**	**0.0**	**0.0**	**0.0**	**0.0**	**0.0**
Bonds	..	..	0.0	0.0	0.0	0.0	0.0	0.0	0.0	0.0
Commercial banks	..	..	0.0	0.0	0.0	0.0	0.0	0.0	0.0	0.0
Memo:										
IBRD	0.0	0.0	0.0	0.0	0.0	0.0	0.0	0.0	0.0	0.1
IDA	0.0	0.0	0.0	0.0	0.0	0.0	0.0	0.0	0.0	0.0
NET TRANSFERS ON DEBT	**..**	**..**	**10.1**	**9.0**	**2.1**	**0.2**	**16.7**	**4.3**	**-1.4**	**0.5**
Public and publicly guaranteed	**..**	**..**	**10.1**	**9.0**	**2.1**	**0.2**	**16.7**	**4.3**	**-1.4**	**0.5**
Official creditors	..	..	10.4	9.6	3.1	1.3	17.5	4.9	-1.4	0.5
Multilateral	..	..	3.8	4.3	2.8	3.8	10.6	5.7	0.2	3.7
Concessional	..	..	4.1	4.7	1.9	3.3	6.7	2.8	-1.2	3.5
Bilateral	..	..	6.6	5.3	0.3	-2.4	6.9	-0.8	-1.6	-3.2
Concessional	..	..	-0.1	0.0	0.2	1.4	7.9	2.6	0.8	-0.3
Private creditors	..	..	-0.3	-0.6	-1.0	-1.1	-0.9	-0.6	0.0	0.0
Bonds	..	..	0.0	0.0	0.0	0.0	0.0	0.0	0.0	0.0
Commercial banks	..	..	-0.3	-0.6	-1.0	-1.1	-0.9	-0.6	0.0	0.0
Other private	..	..	0.0	0.0	0.0	0.0	0.0	0.0	0.0	0.0
Private nonguaranteed	**0.0**	**0.0**	**0.0**	**0.0**	**0.0**	**0.0**	**0.0**	**0.0**	**0.0**	**0.0**
Bonds	..	..	0.0	0.0	0.0	0.0	0.0	0.0	0.0	0.0
Commercial banks	..	..	0.0	0.0	0.0	0.0	0.0	0.0	0.0	0.0
Memo:										
IBRD	0.0	0.0	0.0	0.0	0.0	0.0	0.0	0.5	1.0	0.4
IDA	0.0	0.0	0.0	0.0	0.0	0.6	3.9	0.8	0.1	2.0
DEBT SERVICE (LTDS)	**..**	**..**	**3.1**	**4.9**	**6.0**	**9.8**	**11.3**	**11.0**	**10.3**	**11.0**
Public and publicly guaranteed	**..**	**..**	**3.1**	**4.9**	**6.0**	**9.8**	**11.3**	**11.0**	**10.3**	**11.0**
Official creditors	..	..	2.8	4.0	5.0	8.7	10.5	10.4	10.3	11.0
Multilateral	..	..	2.3	2.9	4.2	4.8	5.3	6.0	6.4	7.1
Concessional	..	..	2.0	2.5	3.6	4.3	4.4	4.8	5.2	5.8
Bilateral	..	..	0.5	1.0	0.8	3.8	5.2	4.4	3.8	3.9
Concessional	..	..	0.1	0.0	0.0	0.0	1.1	1.0	0.9	1.0
Private creditors	..	..	0.3	1.0	1.0	1.1	0.9	0.6	0.0	0.0
Bonds	..	..	0.0	0.0	0.0	0.0	0.0	0.0	0.0	0.0
Commercial banks	..	..	0.3	1.0	1.0	1.1	0.9	0.6	0.0	0.0
Other private	..	..	0.0	0.0	0.0	0.0	0.0	0.0	0.0	0.0
Private nonguaranteed	**0.0**	**0.0**	**0.0**	**0.0**	**0.0**	**0.0**	**0.0**	**0.0**	**0.0**	**0.0**
Bonds	..	..	0.0	0.0	0.0	0.0	0.0	0.0	0.0	0.0
Commercial banks	..	..	0.0	0.0	0.0	0.0	0.0	0.0	0.0	0.0
Memo:										
IBRD	0.0	0.0	0.0	0.0	0.0	0.0	0.0	0.0	0.0	0.2
IDA	0.0	0.0	0.0	0.0	0.0	0.0	0.0	0.0	0.0	0.0
UNDISBURSED DEBT	**..**	**..**	**38.6**	**24.4**	**54.0**	**66.7**	**43.7**	**34.6**	**33.5**	**59.5**
Official creditors	..	..	38.2	24.4	54.0	66.7	43.7	34.6	33.5	59.5
Private creditors	..	..	0.4	0.0	0.0	0.0	0.0	0.0	0.0	0.0
Memorandum items										
Concessional LDOD	..	..	29.7	35.0	40.1	46.8	61.1	67.0	72.5	80.9
Variable rate LDOD	..	..	0.0	0.0	0.0	0.0	0.0	0.4	1.5	2.1
Public sector LDOD	..	..	52.8	61.6	72.6	76.1	89.8	96.2	103.3	111.0
Private sector LDOD	..	..	0.0	0.0	0.0	0.0	0.0	0.0	0.0	0.0
6. CURRENCY COMPOSITION OF LONG-TERM DEBT (PERCENT)										
Deutsche mark	..	..	6.1	5.7	5.9	5.5	4.1	3.2	3.0	2.7
French franc	..	..	0.0	0.0	0.3	1.7	11.0	13.1	15.1	15.9
Japanese yen	..	..	3.2	3.7	4.0	4.5	3.6	3.3	3.1	2.4
Pound sterling	..	..	39.0	39.1	39.9	32.7	22.0	18.5	16.5	13.6
Swiss franc	..	..	0.8	0.8	1.1	1.1	0.8	0.6	0.6	0.5
U.S.dollars	..	..	31.3	32.3	32.6	36.4	45.3	51.1	50.5	53.4
Multiple currency	..	..	0.0	0.0	0.0	0.0	0.0	0.4	1.8	3.2
Special drawing rights	..	..	1.3	1.0	0.8	0.7	0.4	1.1	1.8	1.8
All other currencies	..	..	18.4	17.4	15.3	17.5	12.8	8.4	7.5	6.3

ST. LUCIA

(US$ million, unless otherwise indicated)

	1970	1980	1988	1989	1990	1991	1992	1993	1994	1995
7. DEBT RESTRUCTURINGS										
Total amount rescheduled	0.0	0.0	0.0	0.0	0.0	0.0	0.0	0.0	0.0	0.0
Debt stock rescheduled	0.0	0.0	0.0	0.0	0.0	0.0	0.0	0.0	0.0	0.0
Principal rescheduled	0.0	0.0	0.0	0.0	0.0	0.0	0.0	0.0	0.0	0.0
Official	0.0	0.0	0.0	0.0	0.0	0.0	0.0	0.0	0.0	0.0
Private	0.0	0.0	0.0	0.0	0.0	0.0	0.0	0.0	0.0	0.0
Interest rescheduled	0.0	0.0	0.0	0.0	0.0	0.0	0.0	0.0	0.0	0.0
Official	0.0	0.0	0.0	0.0	0.0	0.0	0.0	0.0	0.0	0.0
Private	0.0	0.0	0.0	0.0	0.0	0.0	0.0	0.0	0.0	0.0
Debt forgiven	..	..	0.0	0.0	0.4	0.0	0.0	0.6	0.2	0.0
Memo: interest forgiven	..	..	0.0	0.0	0.0	0.0	0.0	0.0	0.0	0.0
Debt stock reduction	0.0	0.0	0.0	0.0	0.0	0.0	0.0	0.0	0.0	0.0
of which debt buyback	0.0	0.0	0.0	0.0	0.0	0.0	0.0	0.0	0.0	0.0
8. DEBT STOCK-FLOW RECONCILIATION										
Total change in debt stocks	..	..	..	8.2	14.0	2.7	15.6	2.6	12.8	14.6
Net flows on debt	..	..	..	10.9	7.1	4.1	22.7	5.5	8.7	12.2
Net change in interest arrears	..	..	..	0.1	0.8	-0.8	0.0	0.0	0.0	0.1
Interest capitalized	..	..	..	0.0	0.0	0.0	0.0	0.0	0.0	0.0
Debt forgiveness or reduction	..	..	..	0.0	-0.4	0.0	0.0	-0.6	-0.2	0.0
Cross-currency valuation	..	..	..	-2.9	7.6	-0.6	-5.8	-1.8	4.0	2.3
Residual	..	..	..	0.1	-1.1	0.0	-1.3	-0.4	0.2	0.1
9. AVERAGE TERMS OF NEW COMMITMENTS										
ALL CREDITORS										
Interest (%)	..	..	4.8	4.0	4.3	5.4	3.6	3.6	4.1	4.9
Maturity (years)	..	..	23.6	13.4	24.1	23.4	31.1	20.0	19.8	26.8
Grace period (years)	..	..	5.9	3.9	8.3	6.8	8.2	5.5	4.1	7.6
Grant element (%)	..	..	36.5	32.0	42.8	33.3	52.0	42.5	36.9	38.4
Official creditors										
Interest (%)	..	..	4.8	4.0	4.3	5.4	3.6	3.6	4.1	4.9
Maturity (years)	..	..	23.6	13.4	24.1	23.4	31.1	20.0	19.8	26.8
Grace period (years)	..	..	5.9	3.9	8.3	6.8	8.2	5.5	4.1	7.6
Grant element (%)	..	..	36.5	32.0	42.8	33.3	52.0	42.5	36.9	38.4
Private creditors										
Interest (%)	..	..	0.0	0.0	0.0	0.0	0.0	0.0	0.0	0.0
Maturity (years)	..	..	0.0	0.0	0.0	0.0	0.0	0.0	0.0	0.0
Grace period (years)	..	..	0.0	0.0	0.0	0.0	0.0	0.0	0.0	0.0
Grant element (%)	..	..	0.0	0.0	0.0	0.0	0.0	0.0	0.0	0.0
Memorandum items										
Commitments	..	..	6.5	1.3	34.9	23.0	7.0	8.1	6.9	41.4
Official creditors	..	..	6.5	1.3	34.9	23.0	7.0	8.1	6.9	41.4
Private creditors	..	..	0.0	0.0	0.0	0.0	0.0	0.0	0.0	0.0

10. CONTRACTUAL OBLIGATIONS ON OUTSTANDING LONG-TERM DEBT

	1996	1997	1998	1999	2000	2001	2002	2003	2004	2005
TOTAL										
Disbursements	17.7	16.2	10.4	6.3	3.6	2.4	1.2	0.7	0.6	0.3
Principal	7.2	7.7	9.5	10.6	11.4	10.8	9.5	9.3	9.2	8.8
Interest	5.5	6.0	6.2	5.9	5.5	5.0	4.5	4.1	3.7	3.2
Official creditors										
Disbursements	17.7	16.2	10.4	6.3	3.6	2.4	1.2	0.7	0.6	0.3
Principal	7.2	7.7	9.5	10.5	11.4	10.8	9.5	9.3	9.2	8.8
Interest	5.5	6.0	6.2	5.9	5.5	5.0	4.5	4.1	3.7	3.2
Bilateral creditors										
Disbursements	4.4	2.0	1.1	0.3	0.1	0.0	0.0	0.0	0.0	0.0
Principal	2.5	2.4	3.7	4.4	4.5	2.7	2.7	2.6	2.6	2.6
Interest	2.2	2.1	2.0	1.7	1.4	1.2	1.0	0.9	0.7	0.6
Multilateral creditors										
Disbursements	13.4	14.2	9.3	6.0	3.5	2.3	1.2	0.7	0.6	0.3
Principal	4.8	5.3	5.9	6.1	6.9	8.0	6.7	6.7	6.6	6.1
Interest	3.3	3.9	4.2	4.2	4.1	3.8	3.5	3.2	3.0	2.7
Private creditors										
Disbursements	0.0	0.0	0.0	0.0	0.0	0.0	0.0	0.0	0.0	0.0
Principal	0.0	0.0	0.0	0.0	0.0	0.0	0.0	0.0	0.0	0.0
Interest	0.0	0.0	0.0	0.0	0.0	0.0	0.0	0.0	0.0	0.0
Commercial banks										
Disbursements	0.0	0.0	0.0	0.0	0.0	0.0	0.0	0.0	0.0	0.0
Principal	0.0	0.0	0.0	0.0	0.0	0.0	0.0	0.0	0.0	0.0
Interest	0.0	0.0	0.0	0.0	0.0	0.0	0.0	0.0	0.0	0.0
Other private										
Disbursements	0.0	0.0	0.0	0.0	0.0	0.0	0.0	0.0	0.0	0.0
Principal	0.0	0.0	0.0	0.0	0.0	0.0	0.0	0.0	0.0	0.0
Interest	0.0	0.0	0.0	0.0	0.0	0.0	0.0	0.0	0.0	0.0

ST. VINCENT AND THE GRENADINES

(US$ million, unless otherwise indicated)

1. SUMMARY DEBT DATA

	1970	1980	1988	1989	1990	1991	1992	1993	1994	1995
TOTAL DEBT STOCKS (EDT)	..	**10.6**	**46.4**	**51.0**	**59.1**	**64.8**	**72.3**	**97.3**	**140.9**	**205.6**
Long-term debt (LDOD)	**0.7**	**10.3**	**43.3**	**49.3**	**57.0**	**62.7**	**70.5**	**73.3**	**86.6**	**85.7**
Public and publicly guaranteed	0.7	10.3	43.3	49.3	57.0	62.7	70.5	73.3	86.6	85.7
Private nonguaranteed	0.0	0.0	0.0	0.0	0.0	0.0	0.0	0.0	0.0	0.0
Use of IMF credit	**0.0**	**0.3**	**0.0**	**0.0**	**0.0**	**0.0**	**0.0**	**0.0**	**0.0**	**0.0**
Short-term debt	..	**0.0**	**3.1**	**1.7**	**2.1**	**2.1**	**1.8**	**24.0**	**54.3**	**119.8**
of which interest arrears on LDOD	..	0.0	0.1	0.1	0.1	0.2	0.3	0.3	0.3	0.6
Official creditors	..	0.0	0.1	0.1	0.1	0.2	0.3	0.3	0.3	0.6
Private creditors	..	0.0	0.0	0.0	0.0	0.0	0.0	0.0	0.0	0.0
Memo: principal arrears on LDOD	..	0.0	0.0	0.1	0.1	0.1	0.3	0.4	0.9	2.1
Official creditors	..	0.0	0.0	0.1	0.1	0.1	0.3	0.4	0.9	1.9
Private creditors	..	0.0	0.0	0.0	0.0	0.0	0.0	0.0	0.0	0.2
Memo: export credits	..	..	2.0	2.0	2.0	2.0	2.0	3.0	3.0	4.0
TOTAL DEBT FLOWS										
Disbursements	**0.2**	**3.5**	**9.0**	**8.0**	**7.0**	**8.2**	**8.0**	**9.1**	**15.6**	**2.0**
Long-term debt	0.2	3.0	9.0	8.0	7.0	8.2	8.0	9.1	15.6	2.0
IMF purchases	0.0	0.5	0.0	0.0	0.0	0.0	0.0	0.0	0.0	0.0
Principal repayments	**0.0**	**0.1**	**1.9**	**1.8**	**2.2**	**2.8**	**3.6**	**5.4**	**4.5**	**4.0**
Long-term debt	0.0	0.1	1.9	1.8	2.2	2.8	3.6	5.4	4.5	4.0
IMF repurchases	0.0	0.0	0.0	0.0	0.0	0.0	0.0	0.0	0.0	0.0
Net flows on debt	**0.2**	**3.4**	**7.0**	**4.9**	**5.1**	**5.3**	**4.0**	**25.9**	**41.4**	**63.4**
of which short-term debt	..	..	0.0	-1.3	0.4	-0.1	-0.4	22.2	30.3	65.3
Interest payments (INT)	..	**0.3**	**1.5**	**1.7**	**1.8**	**1.9**	**2.0**	**2.8**	**3.9**	**6.2**
Long-term debt	0.0	0.3	1.3	1.5	1.7	1.7	1.9	2.1	2.3	2.5
IMF charges	0.0	0.0	0.0	0.0	0.0	0.0	0.0	0.0	0.0	0.0
Short-term debt	..	0.0	0.2	0.2	0.2	0.2	0.1	0.7	1.7	3.7
Net transfers on debt	..	**3.1**	**5.5**	**3.2**	**3.3**	**3.5**	**2.0**	**23.1**	**37.5**	**57.1**
Total debt service paid (TDS)	..	**0.4**	**3.5**	**3.5**	**4.1**	**4.7**	**5.6**	**8.2**	**8.4**	**10.2**
Long-term debt	0.0	0.4	3.2	3.3	3.9	4.5	5.5	7.5	6.7	6.5
IMF repurchases and charges	0.0	0.0	0.0	0.0	0.0	0.0	0.0	0.0	0.0	0.0
Short-term debt (interest only)	..	0.0	0.2	0.2	0.2	0.2	0.1	0.7	1.7	3.7

2. AGGREGATE NET RESOURCE FLOWS AND NET TRANSFERS (LONG-TERM)

	1970	1980	1988	1989	1990	1991	1992	1993	1994	1995
NET RESOURCE FLOWS	**0.2**	**8.8**	**20.6**	**21.6**	**16.1**	**17.7**	**31.7**	**37.4**	**64.9**	**74.4**
Net flow of long-term debt (ex. IMF)	0.2	2.9	7.0	6.2	4.7	5.4	4.4	3.7	11.1	-1.9
Foreign direct investment (net)	0.0	1.1	9.5	10.6	8.0	9.0	19.0	31.0	51.0	31.0
Portfolio equity flows	0.0	0.0	0.0	0.0	0.0	0.0	0.0	0.0	0.0	0.0
Grants (excluding technical coop.)	0.0	4.8	4.1	4.8	3.4	3.3	8.3	2.7	2.8	45.3
Memo: technical coop. grants	0.0	1.0	3.2	2.5	2.5	3.7	2.4	3.9	2.3	2.9
NET TRANSFERS	**0.1**	**8.5**	**11.4**	**11.8**	**1.2**	**3.8**	**20.6**	**24.3**	**50.7**	**58.9**
Interest on long-term debt	0.0	0.3	1.3	1.5	1.7	1.7	1.9	2.1	2.3	2.5
Profit remittances on FDI	0.0	0.0	7.9	8.3	13.2	12.2	9.2	11.0	12.0	13.0

3. MAJOR ECONOMIC AGGREGATES

	1970	1980	1988	1989	1990	1991	1992	1993	1994	1995
Gross national product (GNP)	18.5	56.8	150.9	163.7	182.9	198.3	223.7	229.0	229.1	246.1
Exports of goods & services (XGS)	..	39.6	141.3	133.1	148.7	132.2	147.2	123.2	114.1	144.0
of which workers remittances	..	0.0	12.3	13.0	13.9	13.7	13.9	14.5	16.7	14.8
Imports of goods & services (MGS)	..	65.0	152.0	158.1	171.3	169.7	164.6	162.3	172.0	173.1
International reserves (RES)	..	7.3	21.8	22.8	26.5	22.7	33.4	31.5	31.3	29.8
Current account balance	..	-9.3	-16.8	-29.7	-26.9	-44.0	-25.9	-47.5	-61.3	-36.0

4. DEBT INDICATORS

	1970	1980	1988	1989	1990	1991	1992	1993	1994	1995
EDT / XGS (%)	..	26.8	32.8	38.3	39.8	49.0	49.1	79.0	123.5	142.8
EDT / GNP (%)	..	18.7	30.7	31.2	32.3	32.7	32.3	42.5	61.5	83.5
TDS / XGS (%)	..	1.1	2.4	2.7	2.7	3.5	3.8	6.6	7.4	7.1
INT / XGS (%)	..	0.7	1.1	1.3	1.2	1.4	1.3	2.3	3.4	4.3
INT / GNP (%)	..	0.5	1.0	1.1	1.0	1.0	0.9	1.2	1.7	2.5
RES / EDT (%)	..	68.7	47.0	44.7	44.8	35.0	46.2	32.4	22.2	14.5
RES / MGS (months)	..	1.3	1.7	1.7	1.9	1.6	2.4	2.3	2.2	2.1
Short-term / EDT (%)	..	0.0	6.6	3.4	3.6	3.2	2.5	24.7	38.5	58.3
Concessional / EDT (%)	..	56.9	86.2	91.1	91.0	92.4	93.2	72.1	55.2	37.7
Multilateral / EDT (%)	..	58.4	74.7	78.4	80.4	81.0	71.6	52.7	39.9	26.7

ST. VINCENT AND THE GRENADINES

(US$ million, unless otherwise indicated)

	1970	1980	1988	1989	1990	1991	1992	1993	1994	1995
5. LONG-TERM DEBT										
DEBT OUTSTANDING (LDOD)	**0.7**	**10.3**	**43.3**	**49.3**	**57.0**	**62.7**	**70.5**	**73.3**	**86.6**	**85.7**
Public and publicly guaranteed	**0.7**	**10.3**	**43.3**	**49.3**	**57.0**	**62.7**	**70.5**	**73.3**	**86.6**	**85.7**
Official creditors	0.0	9.4	43.3	49.2	57.0	62.7	70.5	73.3	81.9	80.9
Multilateral	0.0	6.2	34.7	40.0	47.5	52.5	51.7	51.3	56.2	54.9
Concessional	0.0	5.1	32.1	37.7	45.3	50.5	49.1	48.5	53.5	52.5
Bilateral	0.0	3.2	8.6	9.3	9.5	10.2	18.7	22.1	25.7	26.1
Concessional	0.0	1.0	7.9	8.7	8.5	9.4	18.3	21.8	24.3	25.0
Private creditors	0.7	0.9	0.0	0.0	0.0	0.0	0.0	0.0	4.7	4.8
Bonds	0.7	0.8	0.0	0.0	0.0	0.0	0.0	0.0	0.0	0.0
Commercial banks	0.0	0.0	0.0	0.0	0.0	0.0	0.0	0.0	4.7	4.8
Other private	0.0	0.1	0.0	0.0	0.0	0.0	0.0	0.0	0.0	0.0
Private nonguaranteed	**0.0**	**0.0**	**0.0**	**0.0**	**0.0**	**0.0**	**0.0**	**0.0**	**0.0**	**0.0**
Bonds	0.0	0.0	0.0	0.0	0.0	0.0	0.0	0.0	0.0	0.0
Commercial banks	0.0	0.0	0.0	0.0	0.0	0.0	0.0	0.0	0.0	0.0
Memo:										
IBRD	0.0	0.0	0.0	0.0	0.0	0.0	0.2	0.4	0.5	0.4
IDA	0.0	0.0	3.6	4.9	6.2	7.9	7.6	7.6	8.0	8.1
DISBURSEMENTS	**0.2**	**3.0**	**9.0**	**8.0**	**7.0**	**8.2**	**8.0**	**9.1**	**15.6**	**2.0**
Public and publicly guaranteed	**0.2**	**3.0**	**9.0**	**8.0**	**7.0**	**8.2**	**8.0**	**9.1**	**15.6**	**2.0**
Official creditors	0.0	2.9	9.0	8.0	7.0	8.2	8.0	9.1	10.8	2.0
Multilateral	0.0	2.8	6.9	7.2	6.3	7.2	3.9	5.0	6.6	1.1
Concessional	0.0	1.9	6.9	7.2	6.3	7.2	3.1	4.6	6.3	1.0
Bilateral	0.0	0.1	2.1	0.9	0.6	1.0	4.1	4.1	4.3	0.9
Concessional	0.0	0.0	2.1	0.9	0.6	1.0	4.1	4.1	2.8	0.9
Private creditors	0.2	0.1	0.0	0.0	0.0	0.0	0.0	0.0	4.7	0.1
Bonds	0.2	0.0	0.0	0.0	0.0	0.0	0.0	0.0	0.0	0.0
Commercial banks	0.0	0.0	0.0	0.0	0.0	0.0	0.0	0.0	4.7	0.1
Other private	0.0	0.1	0.0	0.0	0.0	0.0	0.0	0.0	0.0	0.0
Private nonguaranteed	**0.0**	**0.0**	**0.0**	**0.0**	**0.0**	**0.0**	**0.0**	**0.0**	**0.0**	**0.0**
Bonds	0.0	0.0	0.0	0.0	0.0	0.0	0.0	0.0	0.0	0.0
Commercial banks	0.0	0.0	0.0	0.0	0.0	0.0	0.0	0.0	0.0	0.0
Memo:										
IBRD	0.0	0.0	0.0	0.0	0.0	0.0	0.1	0.3	0.0	0.0
IDA	0.0	0.0	0.7	1.4	0.9	1.6	0.0	0.0	0.0	0.0
PRINCIPAL REPAYMENTS	**0.0**	**0.1**	**1.9**	**1.8**	**2.2**	**2.8**	**3.6**	**5.4**	**4.5**	**4.0**
Public and publicly guaranteed	**0.0**	**0.1**	**1.9**	**1.8**	**2.2**	**2.8**	**3.6**	**5.4**	**4.5**	**4.0**
Official creditors	0.0	0.1	1.7	1.8	2.2	2.8	3.6	5.4	4.5	4.0
Multilateral	0.0	0.1	1.5	1.6	2.0	2.5	3.0	4.8	3.3	3.1
Concessional	0.0	0.1	1.3	1.4	1.8	2.3	2.7	4.6	2.9	2.7
Bilateral	0.0	0.0	0.2	0.2	0.2	0.3	0.7	0.6	1.2	0.8
Concessional	0.0	0.0	0.1	0.1	0.1	0.1	0.5	0.4	0.8	0.4
Private creditors	0.0	0.0	0.3	0.0	0.0	0.0	0.0	0.0	0.0	0.0
Bonds	0.0	0.0	0.2	0.0	0.0	0.0	0.0	0.0	0.0	0.0
Commercial banks	0.0	0.0	0.0	0.0	0.0	0.0	0.0	0.0	0.0	0.0
Other private	0.0	0.0	0.1	0.0	0.0	0.0	0.0	0.0	0.0	0.0
Private nonguaranteed	**0.0**	**0.0**	**0.0**	**0.0**	**0.0**	**0.0**	**0.0**	**0.0**	**0.0**	**0.0**
Bonds	0.0	0.0	0.0	0.0	0.0	0.0	0.0	0.0	0.0	0.0
Commercial banks	0.0	0.0	0.0	0.0	0.0	0.0	0.0	0.0	0.0	0.0
Memo:										
IBRD	0.0	0.0	0.0	0.0	0.0	0.0	0.0	0.0	0.1	0.1
IDA	0.0	0.0	0.0	0.0	0.0	0.0	0.0	0.0	0.0	0.1
NET FLOWS ON DEBT	**0.2**	**2.9**	**7.0**	**6.2**	**4.7**	**5.4**	**4.4**	**3.7**	**11.1**	**-1.9**
Public and publicly guaranteed	**0.2**	**2.9**	**7.0**	**6.2**	**4.7**	**5.4**	**4.4**	**3.7**	**11.1**	**-1.9**
Official creditors	0.0	2.8	7.3	6.2	4.7	5.4	4.4	3.7	6.4	-2.0
Multilateral	0.0	2.7	5.4	5.5	4.3	4.7	1.0	0.2	3.3	-2.0
Concessional	0.0	1.7	5.6	5.7	4.5	4.8	0.4	0.1	3.5	-1.6
Bilateral	0.0	0.1	1.9	0.7	0.4	0.8	3.4	3.5	3.0	0.0
Concessional	0.0	0.0	2.0	0.8	0.6	1.0	3.6	3.7	2.0	0.4
Private creditors	0.2	0.1	-0.3	0.0	0.0	0.0	0.0	0.0	4.7	0.1
Bonds	0.2	0.0	-0.2	0.0	0.0	0.0	0.0	0.0	0.0	0.0
Commercial banks	0.0	0.0	0.0	0.0	0.0	0.0	0.0	0.0	4.7	0.1
Other private	0.0	0.1	-0.1	0.0	0.0	0.0	0.0	0.0	0.0	0.0
Private nonguaranteed	**0.0**	**0.0**	**0.0**	**0.0**	**0.0**	**0.0**	**0.0**	**0.0**	**0.0**	**0.0**
Bonds	0.0	0.0	0.0	0.0	0.0	0.0	0.0	0.0	0.0	0.0
Commercial banks	0.0	0.0	0.0	0.0	0.0	0.0	0.0	0.0	0.0	0.0
Memo:										
IBRD	0.0	0.0	0.0	0.0	0.0	0.0	0.1	0.3	0.0	-0.1
IDA	0.0	0.0	0.7	1.4	0.9	1.6	0.0	0.0	0.0	-0.1

ST. VINCENT AND THE GRENADINES

(US$ million, unless otherwise indicated)

	1970	1980	1988	1989	1990	1991	1992	1993	1994	1995
INTEREST PAYMENTS (LINT)	**0.0**	**0.3**	**1.3**	**1.5**	**1.7**	**1.7**	**1.9**	**2.1**	**2.3**	**2.5**
Public and publicly guaranteed	**0.0**	**0.3**	**1.3**	**1.5**	**1.7**	**1.7**	**1.9**	**2.1**	**2.3**	**2.5**
Official creditors	0.0	0.2	1.3	1.5	1.7	1.7	1.9	2.1	2.3	2.2
Multilateral	0.0	0.2	1.1	1.2	1.4	1.5	1.6	1.7	1.7	1.5
Concessional	0.0	0.1	0.9	1.0	1.1	1.3	1.4	1.4	1.4	1.3
Bilateral	0.0	0.0	0.1	0.3	0.3	0.3	0.3	0.4	0.6	0.7
Concessional	0.0	0.0	0.1	0.2	0.2	0.2	0.2	0.4	0.5	0.6
Private creditors	0.0	0.1	0.0	0.0	0.0	0.0	0.0	0.0	0.0	0.3
Bonds	0.0	0.1	0.0	0.0	0.0	0.0	0.0	0.0	0.0	0.0
Commercial banks	0.0	0.0	0.0	0.0	0.0	0.0	0.0	0.0	0.0	0.3
Other private	0.0	0.0	0.0	0.0	0.0	0.0	0.0	0.0	0.0	0.0
Private nonguaranteed	**0.0**	**0.0**	**0.0**	**0.0**	**0.0**	**0.0**	**0.0**	**0.0**	**0.0**	**0.0**
Bonds	0.0	0.0	0.0	0.0	0.0	0.0	0.0	0.0	0.0	0.0
Commercial banks	0.0	0.0	0.0	0.0	0.0	0.0	0.0	0.0	0.0	0.0
Memo:										
IBRD	0.0	0.0	0.0	0.0	0.0	0.0	0.0	0.0	0.0	0.0
IDA	0.0	0.0	0.0	0.0	0.0	0.0	0.1	0.1	0.1	0.1
NET TRANSFERS ON DEBT	**0.1**	**2.6**	**5.7**	**4.7**	**3.0**	**3.7**	**2.5**	**1.6**	**8.9**	**-4.4**
Public and publicly guaranteed	**0.1**	**2.6**	**5.7**	**4.7**	**3.0**	**3.7**	**2.5**	**1.6**	**8.9**	**-4.4**
Official creditors	0.0	2.5	6.0	4.7	3.0	3.7	2.5	1.7	4.1	-4.2
Multilateral	0.0	2.5	4.3	4.3	2.9	3.2	-0.6	-1.4	1.6	-3.6
Concessional	0.0	1.6	4.8	4.7	3.4	3.6	-1.0	-1.4	2.0	-3.0
Bilateral	0.0	0.1	1.7	0.4	0.1	0.5	3.1	3.1	2.5	-0.7
Concessional	0.0	0.0	1.9	0.6	0.4	0.8	3.3	3.3	1.5	-0.1
Private creditors	0.1	0.1	-0.3	0.0	0.0	0.0	0.0	0.0	4.7	-0.2
Bonds	0.1	-0.1	-0.2	0.0	0.0	0.0	0.0	0.0	0.0	0.0
Commercial banks	0.0	0.0	0.0	0.0	0.0	0.0	0.0	0.0	4.7	-0.2
Other private	0.0	0.1	-0.1	0.0	0.0	0.0	0.0	0.0	0.0	0.0
Private nonguaranteed	**0.0**	**0.0**	**0.0**	**0.0**	**0.0**	**0.0**	**0.0**	**0.0**	**0.0**	**0.0**
Bonds	0.0	0.0	0.0	0.0	0.0	0.0	0.0	0.0	0.0	0.0
Commercial banks	0.0	0.0	0.0	0.0	0.0	0.0	0.0	0.0	0.0	0.0
Memo:										
IBRD	0.0	0.0	0.0	0.0	0.0	0.0	0.1	0.3	-0.1	-0.1
IDA	0.0	0.0	0.6	1.4	0.8	1.5	0.0	-0.1	-0.1	-0.1
DEBT SERVICE (LTDS)	**0.0**	**0.4**	**3.2**	**3.3**	**3.9**	**4.5**	**5.5**	**7.5**	**6.7**	**6.5**
Public and publicly guaranteed	**0.0**	**0.4**	**3.2**	**3.3**	**3.9**	**4.5**	**5.5**	**7.5**	**6.7**	**6.5**
Official creditors	0.0	0.4	2.9	3.3	3.9	4.5	5.5	7.4	6.7	6.2
Multilateral	0.0	0.4	2.6	2.9	3.4	4.0	4.5	6.4	5.0	4.7
Concessional	0.0	0.3	2.2	2.4	2.9	3.6	4.1	6.0	4.3	4.0
Bilateral	0.0	0.0	0.3	0.4	0.5	0.5	1.0	1.0	1.8	1.5
Concessional	0.0	0.0	0.1	0.3	0.2	0.2	0.8	0.8	1.3	1.0
Private creditors	0.0	0.1	0.3	0.0	0.0	0.0	0.0	0.0	0.0	0.3
Bonds	0.0	0.1	0.2	0.0	0.0	0.0	0.0	0.0	0.0	0.0
Commercial banks	0.0	0.0	0.0	0.0	0.0	0.0	0.0	0.0	0.0	0.3
Other private	0.0	0.0	0.1	0.0	0.0	0.0	0.0	0.0	0.0	0.0
Private nonguaranteed	**0.0**	**0.0**	**0.0**	**0.0**	**0.0**	**0.0**	**0.0**	**0.0**	**0.0**	**0.0**
Bonds	0.0	0.0	0.0	0.0	0.0	0.0	0.0	0.0	0.0	0.0
Commercial banks	0.0	0.0	0.0	0.0	0.0	0.0	0.0	0.0	0.0	0.0
Memo:										
IBRD	0.0	0.0	0.0	0.0	0.0	0.0	0.0	0.0	0.1	0.2
IDA	0.0	0.0	0.0	0.0	0.0	0.0	0.1	0.1	0.1	0.1
UNDISBURSED DEBT	**0.0**	**11.0**	**30.3**	**26.2**	**24.8**	**29.4**	**30.7**	**38.2**	**30.9**	**39.9**
Official creditors	0.0	9.8	30.3	26.2	24.8	29.4	30.7	35.8	30.9	39.9
Private creditors	0.0	1.2	0.0	0.0	0.0	0.0	0.0	2.4	0.1	0.0
Memorandum items										
Concessional LDOD	0.0	6.1	40.0	46.4	53.8	59.9	67.4	70.2	77.7	77.5
Variable rate LDOD	0.0	0.0	0.0	0.0	0.0	0.1	0.9	1.3	1.4	1.2
Public sector LDOD	0.7	10.3	43.3	49.3	57.0	62.7	70.5	73.3	86.6	85.7
Private sector LDOD	0.0	0.0	0.0	0.0	0.0	0.0	0.0	0.0	0.0	0.0

6. CURRENCY COMPOSITION OF LONG-TERM DEBT (PERCENT)

	1970	1980	1988	1989	1990	1991	1992	1993	1994	1995
Deutsche mark	0.0	0.0	0.2	0.2	0.7	0.8	0.7	0.7	0.6	0.6
French franc	0.0	0.0	0.0	0.0	0.2	0.2	0.6	3.1	3.8	4.3
Japanese yen	0.0	0.0	0.2	0.2	0.2	0.2	0.1	0.1	0.1	0.1
Pound sterling	0.0	36.8	4.8	3.2	4.7	3.5	8.9	7.5	5.9	5.6
Swiss franc	0.0	0.0	0.0	0.0	0.2	2.1	1.7	1.5	1.4	1.5
U.S.dollars	0.0	21.3	61.6	67.4	66.1	64.7	64.4	66.0	68.0	68.3
Multiple currency	0.0	11.6	15.2	12.6	10.2	8.5	6.8	6.3	5.7	4.9
Special drawing rights	0.0	0.0	2.8	3.0	3.7	3.2	3.0	3.3	3.0	3.4
All other currencies	100.0	31.0	15.0	13.6	13.9	16.9	13.6	11.6	11.7	11.3

ST. VINCENT AND THE GRENADINES

(US$ million, unless otherwise indicated)

	1970	1980	1988	1989	1990	1991	1992	1993	1994	1995
7. DEBT RESTRUCTURINGS										
Total amount rescheduled	0.0	0.0	0.0	0.0	0.0	0.0	0.0	0.0	0.0	0.0
Debt stock rescheduled	0.0	0.0	0.0	0.0	0.0	0.0	0.0	0.0	0.0	0.0
Principal rescheduled	0.0	0.0	0.0	0.0	0.0	0.0	0.0	0.0	0.0	0.0
Official	0.0	0.0	0.0	0.0	0.0	0.0	0.0	0.0	0.0	0.0
Private	0.0	0.0	0.0	0.0	0.0	0.0	0.0	0.0	0.0	0.0
Interest rescheduled	0.0	0.0	0.0	0.0	0.0	0.0	0.0	0.0	0.0	0.0
Official	0.0	0.0	0.0	0.0	0.0	0.0	0.0	0.0	0.0	0.0
Private	0.0	0.0	0.0	0.0	0.0	0.0	0.0	0.0	0.0	0.0
Debt forgiven	..	..	0.0	0.0	0.8	0.0	0.0	0.0	0.0	0.0
Memo: interest forgiven	..	..	0.0	0.0	0.0	0.0	0.0	0.0	0.0	0.0
Debt stock reduction	0.0	0.0	0.0	0.0	0.0	0.0	0.0	0.0	0.0	0.0
of which debt buyback	0.0	0.0	0.0	0.0	0.0	0.0	0.0	0.0	0.0	0.0
8. DEBT STOCK-FLOW RECONCILIATION										
Total change in debt stocks	..	..	..	4.6	8.1	5.7	7.5	25.1	43.6	64.6
Net flows on debt	..	..	..	4.9	5.1	5.3	4.0	25.9	41.4	63.4
Net change in interest arrears	..	..	..	0.0	0.0	0.1	0.1	0.1	0.0	0.2
Interest capitalized	..	..	..	0.0	0.0	0.0	0.0	0.0	0.0	0.0
Debt forgiveness or reduction	..	..	..	0.0	-0.8	0.0	0.0	0.0	0.0	0.0
Cross-currency valuation	..	..	..	-0.1	1.6	-0.2	-2.3	-0.9	1.9	1.3
Residual	..	..	..	-0.2	2.2	0.5	5.7	0.0	0.2	-0.3
9. AVERAGE TERMS OF NEW COMMITMENTS										
ALL CREDITORS										
Interest (%)	7.5	5.3	2.3	4.1	4.0	3.3	2.5	4.3	1.4	3.5
Maturity (years)	13.5	15.4	27.1	27.1	21.0	19.2	18.0	19.5	16.0	20.8
Grace period (years)	13.5	5.1	7.2	6.4	4.8	5.8	7.3	5.6	3.3	4.4
Grant element (%)	18.1	29.0	58.3	45.4	39.7	44.4	51.0	39.8	45.6	42.5
Official creditors										
Interest (%)	0.0	4.0	2.3	4.1	4.0	3.3	2.5	3.4	2.0	3.5
Maturity (years)	0.0	20.1	27.1	27.1	21.0	19.2	18.0	21.3	20.0	20.8
Grace period (years)	0.0	7.6	7.2	6.4	4.8	5.8	7.3	6.1	4.0	4.4
Grant element (%)	0.0	41.7	58.3	45.4	39.7	44.4	51.0	46.4	51.6	42.5
Private creditors										
Interest (%)	7.5	7.5	0.0	0.0	0.0	0.0	0.0	9.7	0.0	0.0
Maturity (years)	13.5	7.3	0.0	0.0	0.0	0.0	0.0	8.5	6.2	0.0
Grace period (years)	13.5	0.8	0.0	0.0	0.0	0.0	0.0	3.0	1.7	0.0
Grant element (%)	18.1	7.2	0.0	0.0	0.0	0.0	0.0	0.0	30.5	0.0
Memorandum items										
Commitments	0.2	3.6	10.6	4.1	2.5	13.0	7.3	16.9	8.3	11.5
Official creditors	0.0	2.3	10.6	4.1	2.5	13.0	7.3	14.5	5.9	11.5
Private creditors	0.2	1.3	0.0	0.0	0.0	0.0	0.0	2.4	2.4	0.0

10. CONTRACTUAL OBLIGATIONS ON OUTSTANDING LONG-TERM DEBT

	1996	1997	1998	1999	2000	2001	2002	2003	2004	2005
TOTAL										
Disbursements	5.7	9.9	7.7	5.8	4.1	2.7	1.8	0.8	0.1	0.1
Principal	5.7	6.3	7.6	7.3	7.4	6.7	6.5	6.9	7.0	6.9
Interest	2.5	2.6	2.6	2.4	2.3	2.1	2.0	1.8	1.6	1.4
Official creditors										
Disbursements	5.7	9.9	7.7	5.8	4.1	2.7	1.8	0.8	0.1	0.1
Principal	5.0	5.4	6.7	6.4	6.7	6.3	6.3	6.9	7.0	6.9
Interest	2.3	2.4	2.4	2.3	2.2	2.1	2.0	1.8	1.6	1.4
Bilateral creditors										
Disbursements	3.3	4.2	2.9	2.0	1.2	0.6	0.3	0.2	0.0	0.0
Principal	1.7	1.8	2.4	2.1	2.3	2.3	2.4	2.4	2.4	2.4
Interest	0.8	0.8	0.8	0.8	0.7	0.7	0.6	0.6	0.5	0.5
Multilateral creditors										
Disbursements	2.4	5.8	4.8	3.8	3.0	2.1	1.5	0.6	0.1	0.1
Principal	3.3	3.6	4.3	4.3	4.4	4.0	3.9	4.5	4.6	4.5
Interest	1.6	1.6	1.6	1.5	1.5	1.4	1.3	1.2	1.1	0.9
Private creditors										
Disbursements	0.0	0.0	0.0	0.0	0.0	0.0	0.0	0.0	0.0	0.0
Principal	0.7	0.9	0.9	0.9	0.6	0.4	0.2	0.0	0.0	0.0
Interest	0.2	0.2	0.2	0.1	0.1	0.0	0.0	0.0	0.0	0.0
Commercial banks										
Disbursements	0.0	0.0	0.0	0.0	0.0	0.0	0.0	0.0	0.0	0.0
Principal	0.7	0.9	0.9	0.9	0.6	0.4	0.2	0.0	0.0	0.0
Interest	0.2	0.2	0.2	0.1	0.1	0.0	0.0	0.0	0.0	0.0
Other private										
Disbursements	0.0	0.0	0.0	0.0	0.0	0.0	0.0	0.0	0.0	0.0
Principal	0.0	0.0	0.0	0.0	0.0	0.0	0.0	0.0	0.0	0.0
Interest	0.0	0.0	0.0	0.0	0.0	0.0	0.0	0.0	0.0	0.0

SUDAN

(US$ million, unless otherwise indicated)

	1970	1980	1988	1989	1990	1991	1992	1993	1994	1995
1. SUMMARY DEBT DATA										
TOTAL DEBT STOCKS (EDT)	**..**	**5,177**	**11,531**	**13,359**	**14,762**	**15,227**	**15,450**	**15,837**	**16,918**	**17,623**
Long-term debt (LDOD)	**298**	**4,147**	**8,377**	**8,965**	**9,651**	**9,716**	**9,480**	**9,490**	**9,896**	**10,275**
Public and publicly guaranteed	298	3,822	8,003	8,469	9,155	9,220	8,984	8,994	9,400	9,779
Private nonguaranteed	0	325	374	496	496	496	496	496	496	496
Use of IMF credit	**31**	**431**	**905**	**884**	**956**	**961**	**924**	**923**	**980**	**960**
Short-term debt	**..**	**599**	**2,249**	**3,511**	**4,155**	**4,550**	**5,047**	**5,424**	**6,042**	**6,388**
of which interest arrears on LDOD	..	63	1,822	3,061	3,705	4,100	4,419	4,796	5,414	5,757
Official creditors	..	33	1,621	2,776	3,244	3,578	3,813	4,100	4,550	4,768
Private creditors	..	30	201	284	461	522	606	697	863	989
Memo: principal arrears on LDOD	..	551	3,284	4,763	5,704	6,298	6,417	6,599	7,155	7,642
Official creditors	..	108	2,615	3,713	3,893	4,327	4,445	4,650	5,024	5,287
Private creditors	..	444	669	1,049	1,811	1,971	1,972	1,949	2,131	2,355
Memo: export credits	..	..	2,418	2,683	2,972	2,996	2,625	2,996	2,959	2,757
TOTAL DEBT FLOWS										
Disbursements	**53**	**921**	**382**	**237**	**185**	**128**	**108**	**101**	**12**	**51**
Long-term debt	53	711	382	237	185	128	108	101	12	51
IMF purchases	0	210	0	0	0	0	0	0	0	0
Principal repayments	**30**	**131**	**58**	**45**	**16**	**12**	**14**	**9**	**3**	**54**
Long-term debt	22	53	58	45	15	12	14	9	3	15
IMF repurchases	8	78	0	0	1	0	0	0	0	39
Net flows on debt	**22**	**790**	**346**	**214**	**169**	**116**	**272**	**91**	**9**	**0**
of which short-term debt	..	..	22	23	0	0	178	0	0	3
Interest payments (INT)	**..**	**133**	**121**	**50**	**34**	**10**	**13**	**11**	**1**	**15**
Long-term debt	12	49	20	11	9	10	11	8	0	3
IMF charges	0	14	1	14	0	0	2	3	0	13
Short-term debt	..	70	100	25	25	0	0	0	0	0
Net transfers on debt	**..**	**657**	**225**	**164**	**135**	**106**	**259**	**80**	**9**	**-16**
Total debt service paid (TDS)	**..**	**264**	**179**	**96**	**50**	**22**	**27**	**20**	**3**	**69**
Long-term debt	34	102	78	57	23	22	25	17	3	17
IMF repurchases and charges	8	92	1	14	1	0	2	3	0	52
Short-term debt (interest only)	..	70	100	25	25	0	0	0	0	0
2. AGGREGATE NET RESOURCE FLOWS AND NET TRANSFERS (LONG-TERM)										
NET RESOURCE FLOWS	**33**	**1,046**	**839**	**606**	**603**	**666**	**409**	**344**	**372**	**184**
Net flow of long-term debt (ex. IMF)	31	658	324	191	171	116	94	91	9	36
Foreign direct investment (net)	0	0	0	4	0	0	0	0	0	0
Portfolio equity flows	0	0	0	0	0	0	0	0	0	0
Grants (excluding technical coop.)	3	388	515	412	433	549	315	252	363	147
Memo: technical coop. grants	6	103	156	208	189	184	124	114	87	76
NET TRANSFERS	**17**	**997**	**819**	**595**	**595**	**656**	**398**	**336**	**372**	**181**
Interest on long-term debt	12	49	20	11	9	10	11	8	0	3
Profit remittances on FDI	4	0	0	0	0	0	0	0	0	0
3. MAJOR ECONOMIC AGGREGATES										
Gross national product (GNP)	2,012	6,690	9,892	10,380	8,732	7,176	5,896	..	..	..
Exports of goods & services (XGS)	325	1,034	1,106	1,050	841	472	485	504	663	..
of which workers remittances	0	209	445	297	188	62	96	101	54	..
Imports of goods & services (MGS)	367	1,682	2,105	2,269	2,058	2,416	2,180	1,995	2,209	..
International reserves (RES)	22	49	12	16	11	8	28	37	78	..
Current account balance	-42	-564	-630	-920	-875	-1,722	-1,353	-1,299	-1,457	..
4. DEBT INDICATORS										
EDT / XGS (%)	..	500.7	1,042.7	1,272.0	1,755.3	3,226.0	3,183.6	3,142.8	2,550.1	..
EDT / GNP (%)	..	77.4	116.6	128.7	169.1	212.2	262.1	..	..	..
TDS / XGS (%)	..	25.5	16.2	9.1	5.9	4.7	5.5	4.0	0.5	..
INT / XGS (%)	..	12.8	10.9	4.8	4.0	2.1	2.6	2.2	0.1	..
INT / GNP (%)	..	2.0	1.2	0.5	0.4	0.1	0.2	..	..	..
RES / EDT (%)	..	0.9	0.1	0.1	0.1	0.0	0.2	0.2	0.5	..
RES / MGS (months)	0.7	0.3	0.1	0.1	0.1	0.0	0.2	0.2	0.4	..
Short-term / EDT (%)	..	11.6	19.5	26.3	28.1	29.9	32.7	34.3	35.7	36.2
Concessional / EDT (%)	..	34.3	34.3	31.6	30.3	30.3	29.8	29.5	28.3	27.5
Multilateral / EDT (%)	..	12.2	11.9	11.1	11.7	12.2	12.2	12.4	12.2	12.1

SUDAN

(US$ million, unless otherwise indicated)

	1970	1980	1988	1989	1990	1991	1992	1993	1994	1995
5. LONG-TERM DEBT										
DEBT OUTSTANDING (LDOD)	**298**	**4,147**	**8,377**	**8,965**	**9,651**	**9,716**	**9,480**	**9,490**	**9,896**	**10,275**
Public and publicly guaranteed	**298**	**3,822**	**8,003**	**8,469**	**9,155**	**9,220**	**8,984**	**8,994**	**9,400**	**9,779**
Official creditors	260	3,293	6,573	7,077	7,500	7,637	7,508	7,541	7,765	7,920
Multilateral	104	634	1,374	1,480	1,723	1,855	1,889	1,959	2,064	2,133
Concessional	93	415	1,250	1,342	1,568	1,701	1,728	1,794	1,886	1,934
Bilateral	157	2,659	5,198	5,597	5,777	5,782	5,618	5,582	5,701	5,787
Concessional	127	1,361	2,709	2,880	2,903	2,913	2,878	2,883	2,895	2,910
Private creditors	38	529	1,430	1,392	1,655	1,583	1,476	1,453	1,635	1,859
Bonds	1	0	0	0	0	0	0	0	0	0
Commercial banks	27	298	1,426	1,388	1,651	1,579	1,472	1,449	1,631	1,855
Other private	9	231	4	4	4	4	4	4	4	4
Private nonguaranteed	**0**	**325**	**374**	**496**	**496**	**496**	**496**	**496**	**496**	**496**
Bonds	0	0	0	0	0	0	0	0	0	0
Commercial banks	0	325	374	496	496	496	496	496	496	496
Memo:										
IBRD	91	46	37	28	19	15	9	6	6	6
IDA	12	190	796	871	1,028	1,105	1,133	1,205	1,251	1,272
DISBURSEMENTS	**53**	**711**	**382**	**237**	**185**	**128**	**108**	**101**	**12**	**51**
Public and publicly guaranteed	**53**	**711**	**382**	**237**	**185**	**128**	**108**	**101**	**12**	**51**
Official creditors	50	566	382	237	185	128	108	101	12	51
Multilateral	15	189	202	150	185	128	108	101	12	51
Concessional	15	81	200	133	180	128	93	95	10	27
Bilateral	35	377	181	87	0	0	0	0	0	0
Concessional	15	190	93	87	0	0	0	0	0	0
Private creditors	2	145	0	0	0	0	0	0	0	0
Bonds	0	0	0	0	0	0	0	0	0	0
Commercial banks	0	108	0	0	0	0	0	0	0	0
Other private	2	37	0	0	0	0	0	0	0	0
Private nonguaranteed	**0**	**0**	**0**	**0**	**0**	**0**	**0**	**0**	**0**	**0**
Bonds	0	0	0	0	0	0	0	0	0	0
Commercial banks	0	0	0	0	0	0	0	0	0	0
Memo:										
IBRD	15	1	0	0	0	0	0	0	0	0
IDA	0	37	123	85	121	76	61	74	8	0
PRINCIPAL REPAYMENTS	**22**	**53**	**58**	**45**	**15**	**12**	**14**	**9**	**3**	**15**
Public and publicly guaranteed	**22**	**53**	**58**	**45**	**15**	**12**	**14**	**9**	**3**	**15**
Official creditors	17	46	58	45	15	12	14	9	3	15
Multilateral	4	15	24	28	15	12	14	9	3	15
Concessional	3	7	22	27	14	11	13	9	3	9
Bilateral	13	32	34	18	0	0	0	0	0	0
Concessional	5	11	28	17	0	0	0	0	0	0
Private creditors	5	7	0	0	0	0	0	0	0	0
Bonds	1	0	0	0	0	0	0	0	0	0
Commercial banks	3	4	0	0	0	0	0	0	0	0
Other private	1	3	0	0	0	0	0	0	0	0
Private nonguaranteed	**0**	**0**	**0**	**0**	**0**	**0**	**0**	**0**	**0**	**0**
Bonds	0	0	0	0	0	0	0	0	0	0
Commercial banks	0	0	0	0	0	0	0	0	0	0
Memo:										
IBRD	4	4	8	8	10	5	5	3	0	0
IDA	0	0	3	3	4	6	6	4	0	0
NET FLOWS ON DEBT	**31**	**658**	**324**	**191**	**171**	**116**	**94**	**91**	**9**	**36**
Public and publicly guaranteed	**31**	**658**	**324**	**191**	**171**	**116**	**94**	**91**	**9**	**36**
Official creditors	33	520	324	191	171	116	94	91	9	36
Multilateral	11	174	177	122	171	116	94	91	9	36
Concessional	12	75	178	106	166	118	80	87	7	18
Bilateral	23	346	147	69	0	0	0	0	0	0
Concessional	10	179	65	70	0	0	0	0	0	0
Private creditors	-3	138	0	0	0	0	0	0	0	0
Bonds	-1	0	0	0	0	0	0	0	0	0
Commercial banks	-3	104	0	0	0	0	0	0	0	0
Other private	1	33	0	0	0	0	0	0	0	0
Private nonguaranteed	**0**	**0**	**0**	**0**	**0**	**0**	**0**	**0**	**0**	**0**
Bonds	0	0	0	0	0	0	0	0	0	0
Commercial banks	0	0	0	0	0	0	0	0	0	0
Memo:										
IBRD	11	-3	-8	-8	-10	-5	-5	-3	0	0
IDA	0	37	120	81	117	71	55	70	8	0

SUDAN

(US$ million, unless otherwise indicated)

	1970	1980	1988	1989	1990	1991	1992	1993	1994	1995
INTEREST PAYMENTS (LINT)	**12**	**49**	**20**	**11**	**9**	**10**	**11**	**8**	**0**	**3**
Public and publicly guaranteed	**12**	**49**	**20**	**11**	**9**	**10**	**11**	**8**	**0**	**3**
Official creditors	10	44	20	11	9	10	11	8	0	3
Multilateral	5	8	15	10	9	10	11	8	0	3
Concessional	4	6	13	9	8	10	11	7	0	1
Bilateral	5	35	5	1	0	0	0	0	0	0
Concessional	3	26	5	1	0	0	0	0	0	0
Private creditors	2	5	0	0	0	0	0	0	0	0
Bonds	0	0	0	0	0	0	0	0	0	0
Commercial banks	2	2	0	0	0	0	0	0	0	0
Other private	0	3	0	0	0	0	0	0	0	0
Private nonguaranteed	**0**	**0**	**0**	**0**	**0**	**0**	**0**	**0**	**0**	**0**
Bonds	0	0	0	0	0	0	0	0	0	0
Commercial banks	0	0	0	0	0	0	0	0	0	0
Memo:										
IBRD	5	4	3	2	2	1	1	0	0	0
IDA	0	1	7	6	6	8	8	6	0	0
NET TRANSFERS ON DEBT	**18**	**609**	**304**	**180**	**162**	**106**	**83**	**84**	**9**	**34**
Public and publicly guaranteed	**18**	**609**	**304**	**180**	**162**	**106**	**83**	**84**	**9**	**34**
Official creditors	23	476	304	180	162	106	83	84	9	34
Multilateral	6	166	162	112	162	106	83	84	9	34
Concessional	7	69	165	97	158	108	69	80	7	17
Bilateral	18	310	141	68	0	0	0	0	0	0
Concessional	6	153	60	69	0	0	0	0	0	0
Private creditors	-5	133	0	0	0	0	0	0	0	0
Bonds	-1	0	0	0	0	0	0	0	0	0
Commercial banks	-5	102	0	0	0	0	0	0	0	0
Other private	1	31	0	0	0	0	0	0	0	0
Private nonguaranteed	**0**	**0**	**0**	**0**	**0**	**0**	**0**	**0**	**0**	**0**
Bonds	0	0	0	0	0	0	0	0	0	0
Commercial banks	0	0	0	0	0	0	0	0	0	0
Memo:										
IBRD	6	-7	-11	-10	-11	-6	-6	-4	0	0
IDA	0	35	114	76	110	62	47	64	8	0
DEBT SERVICE (LTDS)	**34**	**102**	**78**	**57**	**23**	**22**	**25**	**17**	**3**	**17**
Public and publicly guaranteed	**34**	**102**	**78**	**57**	**23**	**22**	**25**	**17**	**3**	**17**
Official creditors	27	90	78	57	23	22	25	17	3	17
Multilateral	9	23	39	38	23	22	25	17	3	17
Concessional	8	12	35	36	22	20	24	15	3	10
Bilateral	18	67	39	19	0	0	0	0	0	0
Concessional	9	37	33	18	0	0	0	0	0	0
Private creditors	7	12	0	0	0	0	0	0	0	0
Bonds	1	0	0	0	0	0	0	0	0	0
Commercial banks	5	6	0	0	0	0	0	0	0	0
Other private	1	6	0	0	0	0	0	0	0	0
Private nonguaranteed	**0**	**0**	**0**	**0**	**0**	**0**	**0**	**0**	**0**	**0**
Bonds	0	0	0	0	0	0	0	0	0	0
Commercial banks	0	0	0	0	0	0	0	0	0	0
Memo:										
IBRD	9	8	11	10	11	6	6	4	0	0
IDA	0	1	9	9	10	14	14	10	0	0
UNDISBURSED DEBT	**126**	**1,310**	**1,438**	**1,378**	**1,284**	**1,028**	**908**	**801**	**678**	**634**
Official creditors	122	1,167	1,438	1,378	1,284	1,028	908	801	678	634
Private creditors	5	143	0	0	0	0	0	0	0	0
Memorandum items										
Concessional LDOD	220	1,776	3,959	4,221	4,471	4,614	4,606	4,677	4,781	4,844
Variable rate LDOD	0	408	1,610	1,699	1,927	1,865	1,772	1,752	1,909	2,103
Public sector LDOD	298	3,820	8,003	8,469	9,155	9,220	8,984	8,994	9,400	9,779
Private sector LDOD	0	327	374	496	496	496	496	496	496	496

6. CURRENCY COMPOSITION OF LONG-TERM DEBT (PERCENT)

	1970	1980	1988	1989	1990	1991	1992	1993	1994	1995
Deutsche mark	6.9	0.5	1.0	0.9	1.0	1.0	0.9	0.9	0.9	1.0
French franc	0.0	2.3	3.3	3.2	3.4	3.3	3.2	3.0	3.2	3.3
Japanese yen	0.0	2.0	2.9	2.4	2.3	2.5	2.6	2.9	3.1	2.9
Pound sterling	15.4	7.0	4.6	4.0	4.3	4.1	3.6	3.5	3.5	3.4
Swiss franc	0.0	0.6	18.4	16.9	18.6	17.7	16.9	16.6	17.9	19.6
U.S.dollars	12.4	54.4	47.7	50.0	48.1	48.6	50.2	50.9	49.3	47.6
Multiple currency	30.6	2.0	1.5	1.3	1.2	1.2	1.4	1.4	1.4	1.5
Special drawing rights	0.0	0.0	0.5	0.5	0.5	0.5	0.5	0.5	0.5	0.5
All other currencies	34.6	31.1	20.3	20.7	20.6	21.1	20.8	20.4	20.3	20.3

SUDAN

(US$ million, unless otherwise indicated)

	1970	1980	1988	1989	1990	1991	1992	1993	1994	1995
7. DEBT RESTRUCTURINGS										
Total amount rescheduled	0	..	30	0	0	0	0	0	0	0
Debt stock rescheduled	0	..	0	0	0	0	0	0	0	0
Principal rescheduled	0	..	24	0	0	0	0	0	0	0
Official	0	..	24	0	0	0	0	0	0	0
Private	0	..	0	0	0	0	0	0	0	0
Interest rescheduled	0	..	6	0	0	0	0	0	0	0
Official	0	..	6	0	0	0	0	0	0	0
Private	0	..	0	0	0	0	0	0	0	0
Debt forgiven	..	..	5	1	0	0	0	0	0	0
Memo: interest forgiven	..	..	0	0	0	0	0	0	0	0
Debt stock reduction	0	..	0	0	0	0	0	0	0	0
of which debt buyback	0	..	0	0	0	0	0	0	0	0
8. DEBT STOCK-FLOW RECONCILIATION										
Total change in debt stocks	..	..	..	1,828	1,403	465	224	386	1,081	706
Net flows on debt	..	..	..	214	169	116	272	91	9	0
Net change in interest arrears	..	..	..	1,238	645	395	319	377	618	344
Interest capitalized	..	..	..	0	0	0	0	0	0	0
Debt forgiveness or reduction	..	..	..	-1	0	0	0	0	0	0
Cross-currency valuation	..	..	..	-117	597	-86	-306	-58	398	380
Residual	..	..	..	493	-8	39	-62	-24	57	-18
9. AVERAGE TERMS OF NEW COMMITMENTS										
ALL CREDITORS										
Interest (%)	1.8	5.7	1.9	1.1	0.7	3.8	8.0	0.0	0.0	0.0
Maturity (years)	17.1	17.9	34.4	38.3	40.5	37.8	32.5	0.0	0.0	0.0
Grace period (years)	8.7	4.6	8.3	9.9	10.5	8.4	4.0	0.0	0.0	0.0
Grant element (%)	54.5	30.1	62.6	75.8	81.0	52.7	13.4	0.0	0.0	0.0
Official creditors										
Interest (%)	1.5	3.7	1.9	1.1	0.7	3.8	8.0	0.0	0.0	0.0
Maturity (years)	17.7	22.7	34.4	38.3	40.5	37.8	32.5	0.0	0.0	0.0
Grace period (years)	9.1	5.9	8.3	9.9	10.5	8.4	4.0	0.0	0.0	0.0
Grant element (%)	57.1	40.7	62.6	75.8	81.0	52.7	13.4	0.0	0.0	0.0
Private creditors										
Interest (%)	5.6	12.0	0.0	0.0	0.0	0.0	0.0	0.0	0.0	0.0
Maturity (years)	9.2	2.9	0.0	0.0	0.0	0.0	0.0	0.0	0.0	0.0
Grace period (years)	3.6	0.4	0.0	0.0	0.0	0.0	0.0	0.0	0.0	0.0
Grant element (%)	17.5	-3.4	0.0	0.0	0.0	0.0	0.0	0.0	0.0	0.0
Memorandum items										
Commitments	98	905	483	216	35	61	39	0	0	0
Official creditors	91	687	483	216	35	61	39	0	0	0
Private creditors	7	218	0	0	0	0	0	0	0	0

10. CONTRACTUAL OBLIGATIONS ON OUTSTANDING LONG-TERM DEBT

	1996	1997	1998	1999	2000	2001	2002	2003	2004	2005
TOTAL										
Disbursements	49	37	21	11	5	2	1	0	0	0
Principal	273	255	246	192	147	101	98	98	95	91
Interest	110	96	83	69	61	56	52	49	46	44
Official creditors										
Disbursements	49	37	21	11	5	2	1	0	0	0
Principal	273	255	246	192	147	101	98	98	95	91
Interest	110	96	83	69	61	56	52	49	46	44
Bilateral creditors										
Disbursements	4	3	0	0	0	0	0	0	0	0
Principal	217	200	191	143	96	45	45	44	43	41
Interest	88	75	63	50	41	37	35	33	31	29
Multilateral creditors										
Disbursements	45	34	21	11	5	2	1	0	0	0
Principal	55	55	55	49	52	56	53	54	52	51
Interest	22	21	21	20	19	18	17	16	15	14
Private creditors										
Disbursements	0	0	0	0	0	0	0	0	0	0
Principal	0	0	0	0	0	0	0	0	0	0
Interest	0	0	0	0	0	0	0	0	0	0
Commercial banks										
Disbursements	0	0	0	0	0	0	0	0	0	0
Principal	0	0	0	0	0	0	0	0	0	0
Interest	0	0	0	0	0	0	0	0	0	0
Other private										
Disbursements	0	0	0	0	0	0	0	0	0	0
Principal	0	0	0	0	0	0	0	0	0	0
Interest	0	0	0	0	0	0	0	0	0	0

SWAZILAND

(US$ million, unless otherwise indicated)

	1970	1980	1988	1989	1990	1991	1992	1993	1994	1995
1. SUMMARY DEBT DATA										
TOTAL DEBT STOCKS (EDT)	..	**209.5**	**263.9**	**269.2**	**261.7**	**261.1**	**237.9**	**223.9**	**237.4**	**251.4**
Long-term debt (LDOD)	**37.0**	**188.8**	**254.4**	**247.5**	**257.1**	**256.2**	**231.3**	**216.1**	**227.7**	**236.8**
Public and publicly guaranteed	37.0	188.8	254.4	247.5	257.1	256.2	231.3	216.1	227.7	236.8
Private nonguaranteed	0.0	0.0	0.0	0.0	0.0	0.0	0.0	0.0	0.0	0.0
Use of IMF credit	**0.0**	**5.7**	**1.6**	**0.4**	**0.0**	**0.0**	**0.0**	**0.0**	**0.0**	**0.0**
Short-term debt	..	**15.0**	**7.9**	**21.3**	**4.6**	**4.9**	**6.6**	**7.8**	**9.7**	**14.6**
of which interest arrears on LDOD	..	0.0	0.1	0.1	0.1	0.9	1.8	2.2	3.3	3.9
Official creditors	..	0.0	0.1	0.1	0.1	0.9	1.7	2.2	3.3	3.9
Private creditors	..	0.0	0.0	0.0	0.0	0.0	0.0	0.0	0.0	0.0
Memo: principal arrears on LDOD	..	0.0	0.2	0.0	0.5	2.4	4.9	5.3	6.2	6.4
Official creditors	..	0.0	0.2	0.0	0.5	2.3	4.5	4.3	5.7	6.2
Private creditors	..	0.0	0.0	0.0	0.0	0.2	0.3	0.9	0.5	0.3
Memo: export credits	..	..	40.0	29.0	28.0	28.0	20.0	18.0	18.0	14.0
TOTAL DEBT FLOWS										
Disbursements	**4.6**	**31.2**	**13.0**	**16.0**	**22.7**	**22.7**	**7.1**	**7.9**	**16.6**	**16.2**
Long-term debt	3.5	28.5	13.0	16.0	22.7	22.7	7.1	7.9	16.6	16.2
IMF purchases	1.1	2.7	0.0	0.0	0.0	0.0	0.0	0.0	0.0	0.0
Principal repayments	**2.5**	**7.5**	**25.1**	**21.2**	**35.8**	**21.0**	**17.0**	**16.3**	**19.2**	**16.5**
Long-term debt	1.5	7.5	20.9	20.1	35.5	21.0	17.0	16.3	19.2	16.5
IMF repurchases	1.0	0.0	4.2	1.1	0.3	0.0	0.0	0.0	0.0	0.0
Net flows on debt	**2.1**	**23.6**	**-21.2**	**8.2**	**-29.8**	**1.3**	**-9.1**	**-7.6**	**-1.8**	**4.0**
of which short-term debt	..	..	-9.2	13.4	-16.7	-0.4	0.8	0.8	0.8	4.3
Interest payments (INT)	..	**10.6**	**14.1**	**13.0**	**10.7**	**9.1**	**8.4**	**7.4**	**6.8**	**6.1**
Long-term debt	1.9	9.0	13.1	11.3	10.2	8.9	8.1	7.1	6.6	5.7
IMF charges	0.0	0.0	0.1	0.0	0.0	0.0	0.0	0.0	0.0	0.0
Short-term debt	..	1.6	0.9	1.6	0.4	0.3	0.3	0.3	0.2	0.4
Net transfers on debt	..	**13.0**	**-35.4**	**-4.7**	**-40.5**	**-7.9**	**-17.5**	**-15.0**	**-8.6**	**-2.1**
Total debt service paid (TDS)	..	**18.1**	**39.2**	**34.2**	**46.5**	**30.2**	**25.4**	**23.7**	**26.0**	**22.6**
Long-term debt	3.4	16.5	34.0	31.4	45.8	29.8	25.1	23.5	25.7	22.2
IMF repurchases and charges	1.0	0.0	4.3	1.2	0.3	0.0	0.0	0.0	0.0	0.0
Short-term debt (interest only)	..	1.6	0.9	1.6	0.4	0.3	0.3	0.3	0.2	0.4
2. AGGREGATE NET RESOURCE FLOWS AND NET TRANSFERS (LONG-TERM)										
NET RESOURCE FLOWS	**5.3**	**59.3**	**54.1**	**83.0**	**46.3**	**97.6**	**96.9**	**70.3**	**96.4**	**74.0**
Net flow of long-term debt (ex. IMF)	2.0	21.0	-7.8	-4.0	-12.8	1.7	-9.9	-8.4	-2.6	-0.3
Foreign direct investment (net)	0.0	26.5	54.2	75.1	39.0	79.0	81.0	60.0	81.0	58.0
Portfolio equity flows	0.0	0.0	0.0	0.0	0.0	0.0	0.0	0.0	0.0	0.0
Grants (excluding technical coop.)	3.3	11.8	7.7	11.9	20.1	16.9	25.8	18.7	18.0	16.3
Memo: technical coop. grants	1.9	22.4	29.4	26.5	28.5	33.1	30.3	31.5	23.6	28.0
NET TRANSFERS	**3.4**	**23.1**	**-16.6**	**-69.4**	**-72.0**	**-8.0**	**-5.5**	**-32.9**	**-10.1**	**-34.7**
Interest on long-term debt	1.9	9.0	13.1	11.3	10.2	8.9	8.1	7.1	6.6	5.7
Profit remittances on FDI	0.0	27.2	57.6	141.0	108.1	96.8	94.3	96.0	100.0	103.0
3. MAJOR ECONOMIC AGGREGATES										
Gross national product (GNP)	111.2	540.3	712.4	667.0	895.6	914.5	986.3	918.0	963.2	1,048.0
Exports of goods & services (XGS)	..	450.7	651.1	707.6	825.5	860.6	920.3	913.9	980.4	1,038.4
of which workers remittances	..	0.0	0.0	0.0	0.0	0.0	0.0	0.0	0.0	0.0
Imports of goods & services (MGS)	..	659.2	658.2	777.7	855.7	930.6	1,020.6	1,053.9	1,110.1	1,187.4
International reserves (RES)	..	158.7	140.0	180.6	216.5	171.9	309.1	264.3	297.0	298.2
Current account balance	..	-129.7	65.7	17.2	65.9	28.3	23.4	-41.3	-41.4	-51.1
4. DEBT INDICATORS										
EDT / XGS (%)	..	46.5	40.5	38.0	31.7	30.3	25.8	24.5	24.2	24.2
EDT / GNP (%)	..	38.8	37.0	40.4	29.2	28.6	24.1	24.4	24.6	24.0
TDS / XGS (%)	..	4.0	6.0	4.8	5.6	3.5	2.8	2.6	2.6	2.2
INT / XGS (%)	..	2.4	2.2	1.8	1.3	1.1	0.9	0.8	0.7	0.6
INT / GNP (%)	..	2.0	2.0	1.9	1.2	1.0	0.9	0.8	0.7	0.6
RES / EDT (%)	..	75.8	53.1	67.1	82.7	65.8	130.0	118.1	125.1	118.6
RES / MGS (months)	..	2.9	2.6	2.8	3.0	2.2	3.6	3.0	3.2	3.0
Short-term / EDT (%)	..	7.2	3.0	7.9	1.7	1.9	2.8	3.5	4.1	5.8
Concessional / EDT (%)	..	47.6	51.2	52.9	64.6	67.2	69.2	69.4	74.1	74.2
Multilateral / EDT (%)	..	29.5	49.9	47.4	45.7	45.8	47.4	49.1	50.3	49.1

SWAZILAND

(US$ million, unless otherwise indicated)

	1970	1980	1988	1989	1990	1991	1992	1993	1994	1995
5. LONG-TERM DEBT										
DEBT OUTSTANDING (LDOD)	**37.0**	**188.8**	**254.4**	**247.5**	**257.1**	**256.2**	**231.3**	**216.1**	**227.7**	**236.8**
Public and publicly guaranteed	**37.0**	**188.8**	**254.4**	**247.5**	**257.1**	**256.2**	**231.3**	**216.1**	**227.7**	**236.8**
Official creditors	20.9	164.6	244.3	239.0	250.3	251.0	227.7	214.1	227.1	236.6
Multilateral	8.9	61.8	131.6	127.6	119.7	119.5	112.7	109.9	119.4	123.5
Concessional	6.2	30.7	39.9	44.5	50.9	54.3	57.0	56.8	72.5	76.4
Bilateral	12.0	102.8	112.7	111.4	130.6	131.5	115.0	104.2	107.7	113.1
Concessional	9.4	69.1	95.3	97.9	118.1	121.0	107.6	98.6	103.3	110.0
Private creditors	16.1	24.2	10.1	8.5	6.8	5.2	3.6	2.0	0.5	0.3
Bonds	0.0	0.0	0.0	0.0	0.0	0.0	0.0	0.0	0.0	0.0
Commercial banks	14.8	23.8	0.4	0.2	0.0	0.0	0.0	0.0	0.0	0.0
Other private	1.3	0.4	9.6	8.3	6.8	5.2	3.6	2.0	0.5	0.3
Private nonguaranteed	**0.0**	**0.0**	**0.0**	**0.0**	**0.0**	**0.0**	**0.0**	**0.0**	**0.0**	**0.0**
Bonds	0.0	0.0	0.0	0.0	0.0	0.0	0.0	0.0	0.0	0.0
Commercial banks	0.0	0.0	0.0	0.0	0.0	0.0	0.0	0.0	0.0	0.0
Memo:										
IBRD	6.1	17.7	58.7	53.3	36.9	33.3	27.6	23.5	20.9	19.2
IDA	2.8	7.5	7.1	6.9	6.8	6.6	6.5	6.3	6.2	5.9
DISBURSEMENTS	**3.5**	**28.5**	**13.0**	**16.0**	**22.7**	**22.7**	**7.1**	**7.9**	**16.6**	**16.2**
Public and publicly guaranteed	**3.5**	**28.5**	**13.0**	**16.0**	**22.7**	**22.7**	**7.1**	**7.9**	**16.6**	**16.2**
Official creditors	3.5	28.5	12.9	16.0	22.7	22.7	7.1	7.9	16.6	16.2
Multilateral	0.4	15.4	7.4	9.0	9.1	10.9	7.0	7.2	13.5	7.8
Concessional	0.0	8.4	4.7	6.3	3.6	6.6	6.0	2.1	12.8	3.4
Bilateral	3.1	13.1	5.5	7.0	13.6	11.8	0.1	0.7	3.1	8.4
Concessional	3.1	8.2	4.3	5.8	12.6	11.5	0.1	0.7	3.1	8.4
Private creditors	0.0	0.0	0.1	0.0	0.0	0.0	0.0	0.0	0.0	0.0
Bonds	0.0	0.0	0.0	0.0	0.0	0.0	0.0	0.0	0.0	0.0
Commercial banks	0.0	0.0	0.0	0.0	0.0	0.0	0.0	0.0	0.0	0.0
Other private	0.0	0.0	0.1	0.0	0.0	0.0	0.0	0.0	0.0	0.0
Private nonguaranteed	**0.0**	**0.0**	**0.0**	**0.0**	**0.0**	**0.0**	**0.0**	**0.0**	**0.0**	**0.0**
Bonds	0.0	0.0	0.0	0.0	0.0	0.0	0.0	0.0	0.0	0.0
Commercial banks	0.0	0.0	0.0	0.0	0.0	0.0	0.0	0.0	0.0	0.0
Memo:										
IBRD	0.4	2.1	1.4	0.5	1.0	0.2	0.0	0.0	0.0	0.0
IDA	0.0	0.3	0.0	0.0	0.0	0.0	0.0	0.0	0.0	0.0
PRINCIPAL REPAYMENTS	**1.5**	**7.5**	**20.9**	**20.1**	**35.5**	**21.0**	**17.0**	**16.3**	**19.2**	**16.5**
Public and publicly guaranteed	**1.5**	**7.5**	**20.9**	**20.1**	**35.5**	**21.0**	**17.0**	**16.3**	**19.2**	**16.5**
Official creditors	0.5	4.9	19.0	18.5	33.6	19.4	15.4	14.8	17.6	16.2
Multilateral	0.2	1.2	12.2	11.4	26.5	11.5	7.8	8.3	11.5	8.2
Concessional	0.2	0.4	2.7	1.6	0.9	3.4	0.4	0.9	1.0	1.6
Bilateral	0.3	3.7	6.8	7.0	7.1	7.9	7.7	6.5	6.1	8.0
Concessional	0.2	1.2	2.9	3.3	4.3	6.3	5.9	5.1	5.0	6.7
Private creditors	1.0	2.6	1.8	1.6	1.9	1.5	1.6	1.5	1.5	0.3
Bonds	0.0	0.0	0.0	0.0	0.0	0.0	0.0	0.0	0.0	0.0
Commercial banks	0.9	2.5	0.2	0.2	0.2	0.0	0.0	0.0	0.0	0.0
Other private	0.1	0.1	1.6	1.4	1.7	1.5	1.6	1.5	1.5	0.3
Private nonguaranteed	**0.0**	**0.0**	**0.0**	**0.0**	**0.0**	**0.0**	**0.0**	**0.0**	**0.0**	**0.0**
Bonds	0.0	0.0	0.0	0.0	0.0	0.0	0.0	0.0	0.0	0.0
Commercial banks	0.0	0.0	0.0	0.0	0.0	0.0	0.0	0.0	0.0	0.0
Memo:										
IBRD	0.2	0.7	4.9	4.9	20.4	4.0	4.0	4.1	4.4	3.5
IDA	0.0	0.0	0.2	0.2	0.2	0.2	0.1	0.2	0.2	0.3
NET FLOWS ON DEBT	**2.0**	**21.0**	**-7.8**	**-4.0**	**-12.8**	**1.7**	**-9.9**	**-8.4**	**-2.6**	**-0.3**
Public and publicly guaranteed	**2.0**	**21.0**	**-7.8**	**-4.0**	**-12.8**	**1.7**	**-9.9**	**-8.4**	**-2.6**	**-0.3**
Official creditors	3.0	23.6	-6.1	-2.5	-10.8	3.3	-8.3	-6.9	-1.0	0.0
Multilateral	0.2	14.3	-4.7	-2.4	-17.4	-0.6	-0.8	-1.1	2.0	-0.4
Concessional	-0.2	8.0	1.9	4.7	2.7	3.2	5.6	1.2	11.8	1.8
Bilateral	2.8	9.4	-1.4	-0.1	6.5	3.8	-7.6	-5.8	-3.0	0.4
Concessional	2.9	7.0	1.4	2.5	8.3	5.2	-5.8	-4.4	-1.9	1.7
Private creditors	-1.0	-2.6	-1.7	-1.6	-1.9	-1.5	-1.6	-1.5	-1.5	-0.3
Bonds	0.0	0.0	0.0	0.0	0.0	0.0	0.0	0.0	0.0	0.0
Commercial banks	-0.9	-2.5	-0.2	-0.2	-0.2	0.0	0.0	0.0	0.0	0.0
Other private	-0.1	-0.1	-1.5	-1.4	-1.7	-1.5	-1.6	-1.5	-1.5	-0.3
Private nonguaranteed	**0.0**	**0.0**	**0.0**	**0.0**	**0.0**	**0.0**	**0.0**	**0.0**	**0.0**	**0.0**
Bonds	0.0	0.0	0.0	0.0	0.0	0.0	0.0	0.0	0.0	0.0
Commercial banks	0.0	0.0	0.0	0.0	0.0	0.0	0.0	0.0	0.0	0.0
Memo:										
IBRD	0.2	1.3	-3.5	-4.4	-19.4	-3.8	-4.0	-4.1	-4.4	-3.5
IDA	0.0	0.3	-0.2	-0.2	-0.2	-0.2	-0.1	-0.2	-0.2	-0.3

SWAZILAND

(US$ million, unless otherwise indicated)

	1970	1980	1988	1989	1990	1991	1992	1993	1994	1995
INTEREST PAYMENTS (LINT)	**1.9**	**9.0**	**13.1**	**11.3**	**10.2**	**8.9**	**8.1**	**7.1**	**6.6**	**5.7**
Public and publicly guaranteed	**1.9**	**9.0**	**13.1**	**11.3**	**10.2**	**8.9**	**8.1**	**7.1**	**6.6**	**5.7**
Official creditors	0.8	7.1	11.9	10.4	9.4	8.4	7.7	6.7	6.4	5.6
Multilateral	0.4	3.1	8.6	7.5	6.5	5.0	4.6	4.3	4.0	3.2
Concessional	0.2	0.6	0.6	0.5	0.6	0.5	0.2	0.4	0.4	0.4
Bilateral	0.4	3.9	3.3	2.9	2.9	3.4	3.1	2.5	2.4	2.4
Concessional	0.2	0.7	1.6	1.4	1.6	2.4	2.2	1.9	2.0	2.0
Private creditors	1.1	2.0	1.2	1.0	0.8	0.5	0.5	0.4	0.2	0.1
Bonds	0.0	0.0	0.0	0.0	0.0	0.0	0.0	0.0	0.0	0.0
Commercial banks	1.1	1.9	0.1	0.1	0.0	0.0	0.0	0.0	0.0	0.0
Other private	0.1	0.0	1.1	0.9	0.8	0.5	0.5	0.4	0.2	0.1
Private nonguaranteed	**0.0**	**0.0**	**0.0**	**0.0**	**0.0**	**0.0**	**0.0**	**0.0**	**0.0**	**0.0**
Bonds	0.0	0.0	0.0	0.0	0.0	0.0	0.0	0.0	0.0	0.0
Commercial banks	0.0	0.0	0.0	0.0	0.0	0.0	0.0	0.0	0.0	0.0
Memo:										
IBRD	0.4	1.8	5.2	4.6	3.6	2.7	2.4	2.1	1.8	1.2
IDA	0.0	0.1	0.1	0.1	0.1	0.1	0.0	0.1	0.0	0.0
NET TRANSFERS ON DEBT	**0.1**	**12.0**	**-20.9**	**-15.4**	**-23.0**	**-7.1**	**-18.0**	**-15.6**	**-9.1**	**-6.0**
Public and publicly guaranteed	**0.1**	**12.0**	**-20.9**	**-15.4**	**-23.0**	**-7.1**	**-18.0**	**-15.6**	**-9.1**	**-6.0**
Official creditors	2.2	16.6	-18.1	-12.8	-20.3	-5.1	-16.0	-13.6	-7.4	-5.6
Multilateral	-0.2	11.1	-13.4	-9.9	-23.9	-5.6	-5.3	-5.4	-2.0	-3.6
Concessional	-0.4	7.4	1.3	4.2	2.1	2.7	5.5	0.7	11.4	1.4
Bilateral	2.4	5.4	-4.7	-3.0	3.6	0.5	-10.7	-8.2	-5.4	-2.0
Concessional	2.7	6.3	-0.2	1.1	6.7	2.8	-8.0	-6.3	-3.9	-0.4
Private creditors	-2.1	-4.6	-2.9	-2.6	-2.7	-2.0	-2.0	-1.9	-1.7	-0.4
Bonds	0.0	0.0	0.0	0.0	0.0	0.0	0.0	0.0	0.0	0.0
Commercial banks	-2.0	-4.4	-0.3	-0.3	-0.2	0.0	0.0	0.0	0.0	0.0
Other private	-0.1	-0.2	-2.6	-2.3	-2.5	-2.0	-2.0	-1.9	-1.7	-0.4
Private nonguaranteed	**0.0**	**0.0**	**0.0**	**0.0**	**0.0**	**0.0**	**0.0**	**0.0**	**0.0**	**0.0**
Bonds	0.0	0.0	0.0	0.0	0.0	0.0	0.0	0.0	0.0	0.0
Commercial banks	0.0	0.0	0.0	0.0	0.0	0.0	0.0	0.0	0.0	0.0
Memo:										
IBRD	-0.2	-0.4	-8.7	-9.0	-23.0	-6.5	-6.4	-6.2	-6.3	-4.8
IDA	0.0	0.2	-0.2	-0.2	-0.2	-0.2	-0.2	-0.2	-0.2	-0.3
DEBT SERVICE (LTDS)	**3.4**	**16.5**	**34.0**	**31.4**	**45.8**	**29.8**	**25.1**	**23.5**	**25.7**	**22.2**
Public and publicly guaranteed	**3.4**	**16.5**	**34.0**	**31.4**	**45.8**	**29.8**	**25.1**	**23.5**	**25.7**	**22.2**
Official creditors	1.3	11.9	31.0	28.9	43.0	27.8	23.1	21.5	24.1	21.8
Multilateral	0.6	4.3	20.8	18.9	33.1	16.5	12.3	12.6	15.5	11.4
Concessional	0.4	1.0	3.4	2.1	1.5	3.9	0.6	1.3	1.4	2.0
Bilateral	0.7	7.6	10.2	9.9	9.9	11.3	10.8	8.9	8.5	10.4
Concessional	0.4	1.8	4.5	4.7	5.9	8.7	8.1	7.0	7.0	8.7
Private creditors	2.1	4.6	3.0	2.6	2.7	2.0	2.0	1.9	1.7	0.4
Bonds	0.0	0.0	0.0	0.0	0.0	0.0	0.0	0.0	0.0	0.0
Commercial banks	2.0	4.4	0.3	0.3	0.2	0.0	0.0	0.0	0.0	0.0
Other private	0.1	0.2	2.7	2.3	2.5	2.0	2.0	1.9	1.7	0.4
Private nonguaranteed	**0.0**	**0.0**	**0.0**	**0.0**	**0.0**	**0.0**	**0.0**	**0.0**	**0.0**	**0.0**
Bonds	0.0	0.0	0.0	0.0	0.0	0.0	0.0	0.0	0.0	0.0
Commercial banks	0.0	0.0	0.0	0.0	0.0	0.0	0.0	0.0	0.0	0.0
Memo:										
IBRD	0.5	2.5	10.0	9.5	24.1	6.7	6.4	6.2	6.3	4.8
IDA	0.0	0.1	0.2	0.2	0.2	0.2	0.2	0.2	0.2	0.3
UNDISBURSED DEBT	**0.0**	**64.8**	**70.6**	**77.8**	**76.7**	**68.1**	**65.6**	**128.0**	**135.4**	**151.5**
Official creditors	0.0	64.8	70.6	77.8	76.7	68.1	65.6	128.0	135.4	151.5
Private creditors	0.0	0.0	0.0	0.0	0.0	0.0	0.0	0.0	0.0	0.0
Memorandum items										
Concessional LDOD	15.6	99.8	135.2	142.4	169.0	175.4	164.6	155.4	175.8	186.4
Variable rate LDOD	0.0	23.8	7.3	7.3	8.1	7.7	6.8	6.2	5.9	5.3
Public sector LDOD	37.0	188.8	254.4	247.5	257.1	256.2	231.3	216.1	227.7	236.8
Private sector LDOD	0.0	0.0	0.0	0.0	0.0	0.0	0.0	0.0	0.0	0.0

6. CURRENCY COMPOSITION OF LONG-TERM DEBT (PERCENT)

	1970	1980	1988	1989	1990	1991	1992	1993	1994	1995
Deutsche mark	0.0	12.7	14.6	15.7	17.3	16.4	16.1	15.5	16.2	18.9
French franc	0.0	0.0	1.3	1.5	1.5	1.4	1.3	1.3	1.2	1.1
Japanese yen	0.0	0.0	0.0	0.0	0.0	0.0	0.0	0.0	0.0	0.0
Pound sterling	38.1	20.4	11.3	9.4	10.1	9.2	7.3	6.7	5.8	5.1
Swiss franc	0.0	12.6	0.0	0.0	0.0	0.0	0.0	0.0	0.0	0.0
U.S.dollars	7.6	11.4	13.6	13.4	14.8	17.6	18.5	18.8	16.9	15.8
Multiple currency	16.5	17.0	39.7	38.5	32.7	31.3	32.7	34.2	36.2	36.4
Special drawing rights	0.0	0.0	1.1	1.7	2.1	2.4	2.5	2.5	2.5	2.4
All other currencies	37.8	26.0	18.4	19.8	21.5	21.8	21.5	21.0	21.1	20.2

SWAZILAND

(US$ million, unless otherwise indicated)

	1970	1980	1988	1989	1990	1991	1992	1993	1994	1995
7. DEBT RESTRUCTURINGS										
Total amount rescheduled	0.0	0.0	0.0	0.0	0.0	0.0	0.0	0.0	0.0	0.0
Debt stock rescheduled	0.0	0.0	0.0	0.0	0.0	0.0	0.0	0.0	0.0	0.0
Principal rescheduled	0.0	0.0	0.0	0.0	0.0	0.0	0.0	0.0	0.0	0.0
Official	0.0	0.0	0.0	0.0	0.0	0.0	0.0	0.0	0.0	0.0
Private	0.0	0.0	0.0	0.0	0.0	0.0	0.0	0.0	0.0	0.0
Interest rescheduled	0.0	0.0	0.0	0.0	0.0	0.0	0.0	0.0	0.0	0.0
Official	0.0	0.0	0.0	0.0	0.0	0.0	0.0	0.0	0.0	0.0
Private	0.0	0.0	0.0	0.0	0.0	0.0	0.0	0.0	0.0	0.0
Debt forgiven	..	..	0.0	0.0	0.0	0.0	0.0	0.0	0.0	0.0
Memo: interest forgiven	..	..	0.0	0.0	0.0	0.0	0.0	0.0	0.0	0.0
Debt stock reduction	0.0	0.0	0.0	0.0	0.0	0.0	0.0	0.0	0.0	0.0
of which debt buyback	0.0	0.0	0.0	0.0	0.0	0.0	0.0	0.0	0.0	0.0
8. DEBT STOCK-FLOW RECONCILIATION										
Total change in debt stocks	..	..	..	5.3	-7.5	-0.6	-23.2	-14.0	13.5	14.0
Net flows on debt	..	..	..	8.2	-29.8	1.3	-9.1	-7.6	-1.8	4.0
Net change in interest arrears	..	..	..	0.0	0.0	0.8	0.9	0.4	1.1	0.6
Interest capitalized	..	..	..	0.0	0.0	0.0	0.0	0.0	0.0	0.0
Debt forgiveness or reduction	..	..	..	0.0	0.0	0.0	0.0	0.0	0.0	0.0
Cross-currency valuation	..	..	..	-2.4	16.0	-3.7	-12.7	-7.4	10.2	7.9
Residual	..	..	..	-0.5	6.4	1.0	-2.3	0.6	3.9	1.5
9. AVERAGE TERMS OF NEW COMMITMENTS										
ALL CREDITORS										
Interest (%)	0.0	7.2	0.7	2.1	5.0	2.7	8.0	6.4	0.7	7.1
Maturity (years)	25.5	22.5	49.7	35.7	15.0	29.2	17.7	22.6	40.0	19.5
Grace period (years)	7.7	6.3	10.2	8.5	8.0	6.9	3.7	4.6	9.6	5.0
Grant element (%)	76.8	20.1	70.1	63.1	32.1	55.3	10.7	25.7	80.1	18.1
Official creditors										
Interest (%)	0.0	7.2	0.7	2.1	5.0	2.7	8.0	6.4	0.7	7.1
Maturity (years)	25.5	22.5	49.7	35.7	15.0	29.2	17.7	22.6	40.0	19.5
Grace period (years)	7.7	6.3	10.2	8.5	8.0	6.9	3.7	4.6	9.6	5.0
Grant element (%)	76.8	20.1	70.1	63.1	32.1	55.3	10.7	25.7	80.1	18.1
Private creditors										
Interest (%)	0.0	0.0	0.0	0.0	0.0	0.0	0.0	0.0	0.0	0.0
Maturity (years)	0.0	0.0	0.0	0.0	0.0	0.0	0.0	0.0	0.0	0.0
Grace period (years)	0.0	0.0	0.0	0.0	0.0	0.0	0.0	0.0	0.0	0.0
Grant element (%)	0.0	0.0	0.0	0.0	0.0	0.0	0.0	0.0	0.0	0.0
Memorandum items										
Commitments	3.1	16.9	6.4	24.5	15.0	24.1	8.5	75.4	16.1	29.0
Official creditors	3.1	16.9	6.4	24.5	15.0	24.1	8.5	75.4	16.1	29.0
Private creditors	0.0	0.0	0.0	0.0	0.0	0.0	0.0	0.0	0.0	0.0

10. CONTRACTUAL OBLIGATIONS ON OUTSTANDING LONG-TERM DEBT

	1996	1997	1998	1999	2000	2001	2002	2003	2004	2005
TOTAL										
Disbursements	31.3	30.4	27.1	22.0	17.2	8.4	5.0	2.6	2.5	1.9
Principal	23.7	22.9	20.9	21.3	20.5	21.4	20.5	18.6	18.7	18.7
Interest	7.8	8.1	8.5	8.8	8.9	8.5	7.8	7.1	6.5	5.8
Official creditors										
Disbursements	31.3	30.4	27.1	22.0	17.2	8.4	5.0	2.6	2.5	1.9
Principal	23.7	22.9	20.9	21.3	20.5	21.4	20.5	18.6	18.7	18.7
Interest	7.8	8.1	8.5	8.8	8.9	8.5	7.8	7.1	6.5	5.8
Bilateral creditors										
Disbursements	9.5	5.9	3.6	2.3	1.7	1.2	0.8	0.0	0.0	0.0
Principal	8.5	8.3	9.2	10.0	9.6	9.4	8.9	8.3	8.2	8.2
Interest	2.6	2.6	2.5	2.4	2.2	2.0	1.8	1.5	1.3	1.1
Multilateral creditors										
Disbursements	21.8	24.5	23.5	19.7	15.5	7.2	4.1	2.6	2.5	1.9
Principal	15.2	14.7	11.8	11.3	10.9	12.0	11.6	10.3	10.5	10.5
Interest	5.2	5.5	5.9	6.4	6.8	6.5	6.0	5.5	5.2	4.7
Private creditors										
Disbursements	0.0	0.0	0.0	0.0	0.0	0.0	0.0	0.0	0.0	0.0
Principal	0.0	0.0	0.0	0.0	0.0	0.0	0.0	0.0	0.0	0.0
Interest	0.0	0.0	0.0	0.0	0.0	0.0	0.0	0.0	0.0	0.0
Commercial banks										
Disbursements	0.0	0.0	0.0	0.0	0.0	0.0	0.0	0.0	0.0	0.0
Principal	0.0	0.0	0.0	0.0	0.0	0.0	0.0	0.0	0.0	0.0
Interest	0.0	0.0	0.0	0.0	0.0	0.0	0.0	0.0	0.0	0.0
Other private										
Disbursements	0.0	0.0	0.0	0.0	0.0	0.0	0.0	0.0	0.0	0.0
Principal	0.0	0.0	0.0	0.0	0.0	0.0	0.0	0.0	0.0	0.0
Interest	0.0	0.0	0.0	0.0	0.0	0.0	0.0	0.0	0.0	0.0

SYRIAN ARAB REPUBLIC

(US$ million, unless otherwise indicated)

	1970	1980	1988	1989	1990	1991	1992	1993	1994	1995
1. SUMMARY DEBT DATA										
TOTAL DEBT STOCKS (EDT)	..	3,552	16,544	17,389	17,068	18,942	19,017	19,976	20,558	21,318
Long-term debt (LDOD)	233	2,921	15,095	15,693	14,917	16,353	15,913	16,235	16,540	16,757
Public and publicly guaranteed	233	2,921	15,095	15,693	14,917	16,353	15,913	16,235	16,540	16,757
Private nonguaranteed	0	0	0	0	0	0	0	0	0	0
Use of IMF credit	10	0	0	0	0	0	0	0	0	0
Short-term debt	..	631	1,449	1,696	2,151	2,589	3,104	3,741	4,018	4,562
of which interest arrears on LDOD	..	0	151	213	460	688	912	1,149	1,400	1,633
Official creditors	..	0	123	175	407	622	833	1,045	1,281	1,502
Private creditors	..	0	29	38	53	66	78	104	119	131
Memo: principal arrears on LDOD	..	0	832	579	864	1,712	2,588	3,512	4,563	5,654
Official creditors	..	0	674	368	580	1,350	2,125	2,887	3,824	4,831
Private creditors	..	0	157	211	284	362	463	626	739	823
Memo: export credits	..	..	480	423	360	360	391	665	701	692
TOTAL DEBT FLOWS										
Disbursements	63	1,147	1,131	1,431	196	1,535	193	223	265	242
Long-term debt	60	1,147	1,131	1,431	196	1,535	193	223	265	242
IMF purchases	3	0	0	0	0	0	0	0	0	0
Principal repayments	31	225	272	798	1,137	338	139	102	129	92
Long-term debt	31	225	272	798	1,137	338	139	102	129	92
IMF repurchases	0	0	0	0	0	0	0	0	0	0
Net flows on debt	32	922	927	818	-733	1,408	345	522	163	460
of which short-term debt	..	..	68	185	208	210	291	400	26	311
Interest payments (INT)	..	157	122	129	135	139	166	182	269	201
Long-term debt	6	77	54	58	54	46	68	72	100	63
IMF charges	0	0	0	0	0	0	0	0	0	0
Short-term debt	..	80	68	71	82	93	98	110	169	139
Net transfers on debt	..	765	805	689	-869	1,269	179	340	-107	259
Total debt service paid (TDS)	..	382	394	927	1,273	476	305	283	398	293
Long-term debt	37	302	326	856	1,191	383	207	174	229	155
IMF repurchases and charges	0	0	0	0	0	0	0	0	0	0
Short-term debt (interest only)	..	80	68	71	82	93	98	110	169	139
2. AGGREGATE NET RESOURCE FLOWS AND NET TRANSFERS (LONG-TERM)										
NET RESOURCE FLOWS	41	2,573	1,005	731	-250	1,469	148	344	398	285
Net flow of long-term debt (ex. IMF)	29	922	859	633	-941	1,198	54	122	137	149
Foreign direct investment (net)	0	0	121	74	71	62	67	176	143	65
Portfolio equity flows	0	0	0	0	0	0	0	0	0	0
Grants (excluding technical coop.)	11	1,651	26	24	621	209	26	46	118	70
Memo: technical coop. grants	8	26	28	25	32	33	69	62	63	83
NET TRANSFERS	35	2,496	951	674	-303	1,423	80	272	298	222
Interest on long-term debt	6	77	54	58	54	46	68	72	100	63
Profit remittances on FDI	0	0	0	0	0	0	0	0	0	0
3. MAJOR ECONOMIC AGGREGATES										
Gross national product (GNP)	2,138	13,074	10,138	9,130	11,522	11,955	12,340	12,729	14,117	15,810
Exports of goods & services (XGS)	..	3,341	2,397	4,358	5,460	4,917	4,999	5,240	5,649	6,329
of which workers remittances	..	774	360	430	385	350	550	426	370	400
Imports of goods & services (MGS)	..	4,610	3,084	3,358	3,786	4,452	5,257	5,793	7,079	6,406
International reserves (RES)	57	828	535	..	..	..	..	..	..	..
Current account balance	..	251	-151	1,222	1,762	699	55	-493	-922	440
4. DEBT INDICATORS										
EDT / XGS (%)	..	106.3	690.2	399.1	312.6	385.2	380.4	381.2	363.9	336.8
EDT / GNP (%)	..	27.2	163.2	190.5	148.1	158.4	154.1	156.9	145.6	134.8
TDS / XGS (%)	..	11.4	16.4	21.3	23.3	9.7	6.1	5.4	7.0	4.6
INT / XGS (%)	..	4.7	5.1	3.0	2.5	2.8	3.3	3.5	4.8	3.2
INT / GNP (%)	..	1.2	1.2	1.4	1.2	1.2	1.3	1.4	1.9	1.3
RES / EDT (%)	..	23.3	3.2	..	..	..	..	..	..	..
RES / MGS (months)	..	2.2	2.1	..	..	..	..	..	..	..
Short-term / EDT (%)	..	17.8	8.8	9.8	12.6	13.7	16.3	18.7	19.5	21.4
Concessional / EDT (%)	..	52.0	80.5	80.1	76.9	77.2	75.4	72.8	72.4	70.8
Multilateral / EDT (%)	..	8.8	4.9	4.7	5.1	4.5	4.4	4.2	4.5	4.8

SYRIAN ARAB REPUBLIC

(US$ million, unless otherwise indicated)

	1970	1980	1988	1989	1990	1991	1992	1993	1994	1995
5. LONG-TERM DEBT										
DEBT OUTSTANDING (LDOD)	**233**	**2,921**	**15,095**	**15,693**	**14,917**	**16,353**	**15,913**	**16,235**	**16,540**	**16,757**
Public and publicly guaranteed	**233**	**2,921**	**15,095**	**15,693**	**14,917**	**16,353**	**15,913**	**16,235**	**16,540**	**16,757**
Official creditors	59	2,165	13,889	14,513	13,744	15,238	14,875	15,058	15,370	15,601
Multilateral	4	311	809	813	877	860	834	835	918	1,031
Concessional	4	95	230	236	251	240	289	320	425	526
Bilateral	55	1,854	13,080	13,700	12,868	14,378	14,041	14,223	14,452	14,570
Concessional	35	1,753	13,080	13,700	12,868	14,376	14,041	14,222	14,450	14,568
Private creditors	174	756	1,206	1,181	1,173	1,115	1,039	1,177	1,170	1,156
Bonds	0	0	0	0	0	0	0	0	0	0
Commercial banks	0	0	0	0	0	0	0	0	0	0
Other private	174	756	1,206	1,181	1,173	1,115	1,039	1,177	1,170	1,156
Private nonguaranteed	**0**	**0**	**0**	**0**	**0**	**0**	**0**	**0**	**0**	**0**
Bonds	0	0	0	0	0	0	0	0	0	0
Commercial banks	0	0	0	0	0	0	0	0	0	0
Memo:										
IBRD	0	215	440	434	479	485	433	419	405	428
IDA	4	42	46	46	44	44	44	44	44	44
DISBURSEMENTS	**60**	**1,147**	**1,131**	**1,431**	**196**	**1,535**	**193**	**223**	**265**	**242**
Public and publicly guaranteed	**60**	**1,147**	**1,131**	**1,431**	**196**	**1,535**	**193**	**223**	**265**	**242**
Official creditors	9	972	934	1,330	159	1,515	190	223	265	242
Multilateral	3	64	95	36	30	7	79	47	123	123
Concessional	3	7	34	17	20	2	77	47	122	122
Bilateral	6	907	839	1,294	128	1,508	111	176	142	118
Concessional	5	900	839	1,294	128	1,508	111	174	142	118
Private creditors	51	176	197	101	37	21	3	1	0	0
Bonds	0	0	0	0	0	0	0	0	0	0
Commercial banks	0	0	0	0	0	0	0	0	0	0
Other private	51	176	197	101	37	21	3	1	0	0
Private nonguaranteed	**0**	**0**	**0**	**0**	**0**	**0**	**0**	**0**	**0**	**0**
Bonds	0	0	0	0	0	0	0	0	0	0
Commercial banks	0	0	0	0	0	0	0	0	0	0
Memo:										
IBRD	0	60	0	0	0	0	0	0	0	0
IDA	3	2	0	0	0	0	0	0	0	0
PRINCIPAL REPAYMENTS	**31**	**225**	**272**	**798**	**1,137**	**338**	**139**	**102**	**129**	**92**
Public and publicly guaranteed	**31**	**225**	**272**	**798**	**1,137**	**338**	**139**	**102**	**129**	**92**
Official creditors	10	92	163	687	1,048	259	83	73	103	70
Multilateral	0	4	14	21	32	31	61	52	85	53
Concessional	0	1	7	10	15	14	15	18	23	25
Bilateral	10	88	149	666	1,016	228	22	21	17	17
Concessional	5	31	140	666	1,016	227	20	21	17	17
Private creditors	21	133	109	112	90	79	56	29	26	22
Bonds	0	0	0	0	0	0	0	0	0	0
Commercial banks	0	0	0	0	0	0	0	0	0	0
Other private	21	133	109	112	90	79	56	29	26	22
Private nonguaranteed	**0**	**0**	**0**	**0**	**0**	**0**	**0**	**0**	**0**	**0**
Bonds	0	0	0	0	0	0	0	0	0	0
Commercial banks	0	0	0	0	0	0	0	0	0	0
Memo:										
IBRD	0	3	1	0	1	0	29	19	49	13
IDA	0	0	0	0	2	0	0	0	0	0
NET FLOWS ON DEBT	**29**	**922**	**859**	**633**	**-941**	**1,198**	**54**	**122**	**137**	**149**
Public and publicly guaranteed	**29**	**922**	**859**	**633**	**-941**	**1,198**	**54**	**122**	**137**	**149**
Official creditors	-1	880	771	643	-889	1,256	107	150	163	172
Multilateral	3	60	81	15	-2	-24	18	-5	38	71
Concessional	3	6	28	8	5	-12	62	28	99	97
Bilateral	-3	820	690	628	-887	1,280	89	155	125	101
Concessional	0	869	699	628	-887	1,281	91	153	125	101
Private creditors	30	42	88	-10	-53	-58	-53	-28	-26	-22
Bonds	0	0	0	0	0	0	0	0	0	0
Commercial banks	0	0	0	0	0	0	0	0	0	0
Other private	30	42	88	-10	-53	-58	-53	-28	-26	-22
Private nonguaranteed	**0**	**0**	**0**	**0**	**0**	**0**	**0**	**0**	**0**	**0**
Bonds	0	0	0	0	0	0	0	0	0	0
Commercial banks	0	0	0	0	0	0	0	0	0	0
Memo:										
IBRD	0	57	-1	0	-1	0	-29	-19	-49	-13
IDA	3	2	0	0	-2	0	0	0	0	0

SYRIAN ARAB REPUBLIC

(US$ million, unless otherwise indicated)

	1970	1980	1988	1989	1990	1991	1992	1993	1994	1995
INTEREST PAYMENTS (LINT)	**6**	**77**	**54**	**58**	**54**	**46**	**68**	**72**	**100**	**63**
Public and publicly guaranteed	**6**	**77**	**54**	**58**	**54**	**46**	**68**	**72**	**100**	**63**
Official creditors	2	46	28	33	36	32	61	67	96	60
Multilateral	0	20	12	15	17	15	41	36	80	40
Concessional	0	1	6	6	6	6	6	9	15	21
Bilateral	2	26	16	19	19	17	20	31	16	20
Concessional	1	18	16	19	19	17	20	31	16	20
Private creditors	4	31	26	24	17	13	8	5	4	3
Bonds	0	0	0	0	0	0	0	0	0	0
Commercial banks	0	0	0	0	0	0	0	0	0	0
Other private	4	31	26	24	17	13	8	5	4	3
Private nonguaranteed	**0**	**0**	**0**	**0**	**0**	**0**	**0**	**0**	**0**	**0**
Bonds	0	0	0	0	0	0	0	0	0	0
Commercial banks	0	0	0	0	0	0	0	0	0	0
Memo:										
IBRD	0	18	2	0	1	0	27	20	59	12
IDA	0	0	0	0	1	0	0	0	0	0
NET TRANSFERS ON DEBT	**23**	**845**	**805**	**575**	**-995**	**1,152**	**-14**	**50**	**36**	**87**
Public and publicly guaranteed	**23**	**845**	**805**	**575**	**-995**	**1,152**	**-14**	**50**	**36**	**87**
Official creditors	-2	834	743	610	-925	1,223	47	83	66	112
Multilateral	3	40	69	0	-19	-39	-23	-41	-42	31
Concessional	3	5	22	2	-2	-18	56	19	84	76
Bilateral	-5	794	674	609	-907	1,262	69	124	109	81
Concessional	-1	851	683	609	-907	1,263	71	122	109	81
Private creditors	26	11	62	-35	-70	-72	-60	-33	-30	-25
Bonds	0	0	0	0	0	0	0	0	0	0
Commercial banks	0	0	0	0	0	0	0	0	0	0
Other private	26	11	62	-35	-70	-72	-60	-33	-30	-25
Private nonguaranteed	**0**	**0**	**0**	**0**	**0**	**0**	**0**	**0**	**0**	**0**
Bonds	0	0	0	0	0	0	0	0	0	0
Commercial banks	0	0	0	0	0	0	0	0	0	0
Memo:										
IBRD	0	39	-3	0	-2	0	-56	-39	-107	-25
IDA	3	1	0	0	-2	0	0	0	0	0
DEBT SERVICE (LTDS)	**37**	**302**	**326**	**856**	**1,191**	**383**	**207**	**174**	**229**	**155**
Public and publicly guaranteed	**37**	**302**	**326**	**856**	**1,191**	**383**	**207**	**174**	**229**	**155**
Official creditors	11	138	191	720	1,084	291	143	140	199	130
Multilateral	0	24	26	36	49	46	101	89	166	92
Concessional	0	2	13	16	22	20	21	28	38	47
Bilateral	11	114	165	684	1,035	245	42	52	33	38
Concessional	6	49	156	684	1,035	244	40	52	33	38
Private creditors	25	165	135	136	107	92	64	34	30	25
Bonds	0	0	0	0	0	0	0	0	0	0
Commercial banks	0	0	0	0	0	0	0	0	0	0
Other private	25	165	135	136	107	92	64	34	30	25
Private nonguaranteed	**0**	**0**	**0**	**0**	**0**	**0**	**0**	**0**	**0**	**0**
Bonds	0	0	0	0	0	0	0	0	0	0
Commercial banks	0	0	0	0	0	0	0	0	0	0
Memo:										
IBRD	0	21	3	0	2	0	56	39	107	25
IDA	0	0	0	0	2	0	0	0	0	0
UNDISBURSED DEBT	**110**	**1,971**	**1,014**	**531**	**712**	**1,210**	**1,226**	**1,377**	**1,167**	**917**
Official creditors	11	1,388	837	468	673	1,193	1,213	1,369	1,157	907
Private creditors	99	583	177	64	39	17	13	8	9	10
Memorandum items										
Concessional LDOD	39	1,848	13,310	13,935	13,119	14,616	14,330	14,542	14,875	15,094
Variable rate LDOD	0	0	0	0	0	0	0	0	0	0
Public sector LDOD	233	2,921	15,094	15,693	14,917	16,353	15,913	16,235	16,540	16,756
Private sector LDOD	0	0	0	0	0	0	0	0	0	0

6. CURRENCY COMPOSITION OF LONG-TERM DEBT (PERCENT)

	1970	1980	1988	1989	1990	1991	1992	1993	1994	1995
Deutsche mark	1.7	1.5	1.5	1.6	2.1	2.2	2.2	2.1	2.3	2.4
French franc	7.0	3.6	0.6	0.6	0.8	0.7	0.7	0.7	0.7	0.8
Japanese yen	0.0	0.3	1.3	1.4	1.9	2.8	2.9	3.5	3.8	3.5
Pound sterling	4.0	0.2	0.7	0.6	0.8	0.6	0.4	0.8	0.8	0.7
Swiss franc	4.1	0.8	0.0	0.0	0.0	0.0	0.0	0.0	0.0	0.0
U.S.dollars	31.2	70.0	88.2	88.4	86.4	86.4	86.8	85.1	83.5	82.4
Multiple currency	0.0	8.0	3.1	2.9	3.4	3.1	2.8	2.7	2.5	2.7
Special drawing rights	0.0	0.0	0.0	0.0	0.0	0.0	0.0	0.0	0.0	0.0
All other currencies	52.0	15.7	4.6	4.5	4.8	4.2	4.1	5.1	6.4	7.5

SYRIAN ARAB REPUBLIC

(US$ million, unless otherwise indicated)

	1970	1980	1988	1989	1990	1991	1992	1993	1994	1995
7. DEBT RESTRUCTURINGS										
Total amount rescheduled	0	0	0	0	0	3	0	0	0	0
Debt stock rescheduled	0	0	0	0	0	0	0	0	0	0
Principal rescheduled	0	0	0	0	0	3	0	0	0	0
Official	0	0	0	0	0	0	0	0	0	0
Private	0	0	0	0	0	3	0	0	0	0
Interest rescheduled	0	0	0	0	0	0	0	0	0	0
Official	0	0	0	0	0	0	0	0	0	0
Private	0	0	0	0	0	0	0	0	0	0
Debt forgiven	..	..	0	0	0	0	398	0	0	0
Memo: interest forgiven	..	..	0	0	0	0	6	0	0	0
Debt stock reduction	0	0	0	0	0	0	0	0	0	0
of which debt buyback	0	0	0	0	0	0	0	0	0	0
8. DEBT STOCK-FLOW RECONCILIATION										
Total change in debt stocks	..	..	..	845	-321	1,874	75	959	582	760
Net flows on debt	..	..	..	818	-733	1,408	345	522	163	460
Net change in interest arrears	..	..	..	62	247	228	224	238	251	233
Interest capitalized	..	..	..	0	0	0	0	0	0	0
Debt forgiveness or reduction	..	..	..	0	0	0	-398	0	0	0
Cross-currency valuation	..	..	..	-36	185	29	-99	35	164	64
Residual	..	..	..	1	-20	209	2	166	5	3
9. AVERAGE TERMS OF NEW COMMITMENTS										
ALL CREDITORS										
Interest (%)	4.2	2.5	2.4	2.0	3.7	2.4	4.2	3.8	0.0	0.0
Maturity (years)	8.7	22.4	24.1	25.8	22.7	25.3	22.0	21.7	0.0	0.0
Grace period (years)	2.4	4.3	4.2	4.0	6.1	5.0	6.0	5.1	0.0	0.0
Grant element (%)	24.1	50.7	52.5	56.4	43.6	54.6	40.0	41.6	0.0	0.0
Official creditors										
Interest (%)	2.7	2.0	2.3	2.0	3.8	2.4	4.2	3.8	0.0	0.0
Maturity (years)	8.7	25.1	25.4	26.0	23.0	25.3	22.0	21.7	0.0	0.0
Grace period (years)	3.0	4.2	4.2	4.0	6.2	5.0	6.0	5.1	0.0	0.0
Grant element (%)	30.4	55.8	54.8	56.8	43.9	54.6	40.0	41.6	0.0	0.0
Private creditors										
Interest (%)	4.4	4.1	4.3	2.8	3.0	2.0	0.0	0.0	0.0	0.0
Maturity (years)	8.7	12.6	8.3	12.9	12.8	15.6	0.0	0.0	0.0	0.0
Grace period (years)	2.4	4.4	3.2	2.3	3.6	6.1	0.0	0.0	0.0	0.0
Grant element (%)	23.4	32.2	23.5	33.6	36.3	50.1	0.0	0.0	0.0	0.0
Memorandum items										
Commitments	14	1,169	926	1,211	344	1,996	262	345	0	0
Official creditors	2	918	856	1,193	334	1,996	262	345	0	0
Private creditors	13	251	69	18	10	1	0	0	0	0

10. CONTRACTUAL OBLIGATIONS ON OUTSTANDING LONG-TERM DEBT

	1996	1997	1998	1999	2000	2001	2002	2003	2004	2005
TOTAL										
Disbursements	188	122	68	36	20	7	0	0	0	0
Principal	1,145	1,106	1,111	977	962	922	913	901	892	871
Interest	280	257	233	208	183	158	136	113	91	70
Official creditors										
Disbursements	182	120	67	36	20	7	0	0	0	0
Principal	1,045	1,028	1,053	943	934	912	905	894	885	866
Interest	270	249	228	204	180	157	135	113	91	70
Bilateral creditors										
Disbursements	93	58	32	16	7	2	0	0	0	0
Principal	926	934	957	847	846	847	848	837	835	828
Interest	219	203	186	168	149	131	112	93	74	55
Multilateral creditors										
Disbursements	89	61	35	21	13	4	0	0	0	0
Principal	120	95	96	96	88	65	58	57	50	38
Interest	51	46	41	36	31	26	23	20	17	14
Private creditors										
Disbursements	6	3	1	0	0	0	0	0	0	0
Principal	100	78	59	34	28	10	8	7	7	6
Interest	10	7	5	4	3	2	1	1	1	1
Commercial banks										
Disbursements	0	0	0	0	0	0	0	0	0	0
Principal	0	0	0	0	0	0	0	0	0	0
Interest	0	0	0	0	0	0	0	0	0	0
Other private										
Disbursements	6	3	1	0	0	0	0	0	0	0
Principal	100	78	59	34	28	10	8	7	7	6
Interest	10	7	5	4	3	2	1	1	1	1

TAJIKISTAN

(US$ million, unless otherwise indicated)

	1970	1980	1988	1989	1990	1991	1992	1993	1994	1995
1. SUMMARY DEBT DATA										
TOTAL DEBT STOCKS (EDT)	..	..	..	..	..	..	9.7	382.4	594.3	665.4
Long-term debt (LDOD)	..	..	..	..	..	..	9.7	382.1	570.3	612.4
Public and publicly guaranteed	..	..	..	..	..	..	9.7	382.1	570.3	612.4
Private nonguaranteed	0.0	0.0	0.0	0.0	0.0	0.0	0.0	0.0	0.0	0.0
Use of IMF credit	0.0	0.0	0.0	0.0	0.0	0.0	0.0	0.0	0.0	0.0
Short-term debt	..	..	..	..	..	..	0.0	0.3	24.0	53.0
of which interest arrears on LDOD	..	..	..	..	..	..	0.0	0.3	24.0	53.0
Official creditors	..	..	..	..	..	..	0.0	0.3	24.0	53.0
Private creditors	..	..	..	..	..	..	0.0	0.0	0.0	0.0
Memo: principal arrears on LDOD	..	..	..	..	..	..	0.0	0.0	60.3	146.0
Official creditors	..	..	..	..	..	..	0.0	0.0	60.3	146.0
Private creditors	..	..	..	..	..	..	0.0	0.0	0.0	0.0
Memo: export credits	..	..	0.0	0.0	0.0	0.0	0.0	0.0	0.0	0.0
TOTAL DEBT FLOWS										
Disbursements	..	..	..	..	..	..	9.7	78.3	182.1	37.5
Long-term debt	..	..	..	..	..	..	9.7	78.3	182.1	37.5
IMF purchases	0.0	0.0	0.0	0.0	0.0	0.0	0.0	0.0	0.0	0.0
Principal repayments	..	..	..	..	..	..	0.0	0.0	0.0	0.0
Long-term debt	..	..	..	..	..	..	0.0	0.0	0.0	0.0
IMF repurchases	0.0	0.0	0.0	0.0	0.0	0.0	0.0	0.0	0.0	0.0
Net flows on debt	..	..	..	..	..	..	9.7	78.3	182.1	37.5
of which short-term debt	..	..	..	..	..	..	0.0	0.0	0.0	0.0
Interest payments (INT)	..	..	..	..	..	..	0.0	1.2	0.4	0.0
Long-term debt	..	..	..	..	..	..	0.0	1.2	0.4	0.0
IMF charges	0.0	0.0	0.0	0.0	0.0	0.0	0.0	0.0	0.0	0.0
Short-term debt	..	..	..	..	..	..	0.0	0.0	0.0	0.0
Net transfers on debt	..	..	..	..	..	..	9.7	77.1	181.7	37.5
Total debt service paid (TDS)	..	..	..	..	..	..	0.0	1.2	0.4	0.0
Long-term debt	..	..	..	..	..	..	0.0	1.2	0.4	0.0
IMF repurchases and charges	0.0	0.0	0.0	0.0	0.0	0.0	0.0	0.0	0.0	0.0
Short-term debt (interest only)	..	..	..	..	..	..	0.0	0.0	0.0	0.0
2. AGGREGATE NET RESOURCE FLOWS AND NET TRANSFERS (LONG-TERM)										
NET RESOURCE FLOWS	..	..	..	..	..	..	9.9	88.9	254.8	106.0
Net flow of long-term debt (ex. IMF)	..	..	..	..	..	..	9.7	78.3	182.1	37.5
Foreign direct investment (net)	..	..	..	..	..	..	0.0	0.0	10.0	15.0
Portfolio equity flows	..	..	..	..	..	..	0.0	0.0	0.0	0.0
Grants (excluding technical coop.)	..	..	..	..	..	..	0.2	10.6	62.7	53.5
Memo: technical coop. grants	..	..	..	..	..	..	0.4	1.0	4.0	11.2
NET TRANSFERS	..	..	..	..	..	..	9.9	87.7	254.4	106.0
Interest on long-term debt	..	..	..	..	..	..	0.0	1.2	0.4	0.0
Profit remittances on FDI	..	..	..	..	..	..	0.0	0.0	0.0	0.0
3. MAJOR ECONOMIC AGGREGATES										
Gross national product (GNP)	..	..	..	..	..	..	2,983.8	2,932.9	2,168.2	1,901.7
Exports of goods & services (XGS)	..	..	..	..	..	..	..	456.0	559.0	657.0
of which workers remittances	..	..	..	..	..	..	..	0.0	0.0	0.0
Imports of goods & services (MGS)	..	..	..	..	..	..	..	690.0	754.0	669.9
International reserves (RES)	..	..	..	..	..	..	..	..	..	..
Current account balance	..	..	..	..	..	..	..	-209.0	-170.0	12.1
4. DEBT INDICATORS										
EDT / XGS (%)	..	..	..	..	..	..	..	83.9	106.3	101.3
EDT / GNP (%)	..	..	..	..	..	..	0.3	13.0	27.4	35.0
TDS / XGS (%)	..	..	..	..	..	..	..	0.3	0.1	0.0
INT / XGS (%)	..	..	..	..	..	..	..	0.3	0.1	0.0
INT / GNP (%)	..	..	..	..	..	..	0.0	0.0	0.0	0.0
RES / EDT (%)	..	..	..	..	..	..	..	..	..	..
RES / MGS (months)	..	..	..	..	..	..	..	..	..	..
Short-term / EDT (%)	..	..	..	..	..	..	0.0	0.1	4.0	8.0
Concessional / EDT (%)	..	..	..	..	..	..	100.0	6.1	4.0	3.7
Multilateral / EDT (%)	..	..	..	..	..	..	0.0	16.1	11.4	10.9

TAJIKISTAN

(US$ million, unless otherwise indicated)

	1970	1980	1988	1989	1990	1991	1992	1993	1994	1995
5. LONG-TERM DEBT										
DEBT OUTSTANDING (LDOD)	..	..	..	..	..	..	**9.7**	**382.1**	**570.3**	**612.4**
Public and publicly guaranteed	..	..	..	..	..	..	**9.7**	**382.1**	**570.3**	**612.4**
Official creditors	..	..	..	..	..	..	9.7	382.1	570.3	612.4
Multilateral	..	..	..	..	..	..	0.0	61.6	67.7	72.3
Concessional	..	..	..	..	..	..	0.0	0.0	0.0	0.0
Bilateral	..	..	..	..	..	..	9.7	320.5	502.6	540.1
Concessional	..	..	..	..	..	..	9.7	23.5	23.5	24.5
Private creditors	..	..	..	..	..	..	0.0	0.0	0.0	0.0
Bonds	..	..	..	..	..	..	0.0	0.0	0.0	0.0
Commercial banks	..	..	..	..	..	..	0.0	0.0	0.0	0.0
Other private	..	..	..	..	..	..	0.0	0.0	0.0	0.0
Private nonguaranteed	**0.0**	**0.0**	**0.0**	**0.0**	**0.0**	**0.0**	**0.0**	**0.0**	**0.0**	**0.0**
Bonds	..	..	..	..	..	..	0.0	0.0	0.0	0.0
Commercial banks	..	..	..	..	..	..	0.0	0.0	0.0	0.0
Memo:										
IBRD	0.0	0.0	0.0	0.0	0.0	0.0	0.0	0.0	0.0	0.0
IDA	0.0	0.0	0.0	0.0	0.0	0.0	0.0	0.0	0.0	0.0
DISBURSEMENTS	..	..	..	..	..	..	**9.7**	**78.3**	**182.1**	**37.5**
Public and publicly guaranteed	..	..	..	..	..	..	**9.7**	**78.3**	**182.1**	**37.5**
Official creditors	..	..	..	..	..	..	9.7	78.3	182.1	37.5
Multilateral	..	..	..	..	..	..	0.0	64.5	0.0	0.0
Concessional	..	..	..	..	..	..	0.0	0.0	0.0	0.0
Bilateral	..	..	..	..	..	..	9.7	13.8	182.1	37.5
Concessional	..	..	..	..	..	..	9.7	13.8	0.0	1.0
Private creditors	..	..	..	..	..	..	0.0	0.0	0.0	0.0
Bonds	..	..	..	..	..	..	0.0	0.0	0.0	0.0
Commercial banks	..	..	..	..	..	..	0.0	0.0	0.0	0.0
Other private	..	..	..	..	..	..	0.0	0.0	0.0	0.0
Private nonguaranteed	**0.0**	**0.0**	**0.0**	**0.0**	**0.0**	**0.0**	**0.0**	**0.0**	**0.0**	**0.0**
Bonds	..	..	..	..	..	..	0.0	0.0	0.0	0.0
Commercial banks	..	..	..	..	..	..	0.0	0.0	0.0	0.0
Memo:										
IBRD	0.0	0.0	0.0	0.0	0.0	0.0	0.0	0.0	0.0	0.0
IDA	0.0	0.0	0.0	0.0	0.0	0.0	0.0	0.0	0.0	0.0
PRINCIPAL REPAYMENTS	..	..	..	..	..	..	**0.0**	**0.0**	**0.0**	**0.0**
Public and publicly guaranteed	..	..	..	..	..	..	**0.0**	**0.0**	**0.0**	**0.0**
Official creditors	..	..	..	..	..	..	0.0	0.0	0.0	0.0
Multilateral	..	..	..	..	..	..	0.0	0.0	0.0	0.0
Concessional	..	..	..	..	..	..	0.0	0.0	0.0	0.0
Bilateral	..	..	..	..	..	..	0.0	0.0	0.0	0.0
Concessional	..	..	..	..	..	..	0.0	0.0	0.0	0.0
Private creditors	..	..	..	..	..	..	0.0	0.0	0.0	0.0
Bonds	..	..	..	..	..	..	0.0	0.0	0.0	0.0
Commercial banks	..	..	..	..	..	..	0.0	0.0	0.0	0.0
Other private	..	..	..	..	..	..	0.0	0.0	0.0	0.0
Private nonguaranteed	**0.0**	**0.0**	**0.0**	**0.0**	**0.0**	**0.0**	**0.0**	**0.0**	**0.0**	**0.0**
Bonds	..	..	..	..	..	..	0.0	0.0	0.0	0.0
Commercial banks	..	..	..	..	..	..	0.0	0.0	0.0	0.0
Memo:										
IBRD	0.0	0.0	0.0	0.0	0.0	0.0	0.0	0.0	0.0	0.0
IDA	0.0	0.0	0.0	0.0	0.0	0.0	0.0	0.0	0.0	0.0
NET FLOWS ON DEBT	..	..	..	..	..	..	**9.7**	**78.3**	**182.1**	**37.5**
Public and publicly guaranteed	..	..	..	..	..	..	**9.7**	**78.3**	**182.1**	**37.5**
Official creditors	..	..	..	..	..	..	9.7	78.3	182.1	37.5
Multilateral	..	..	..	..	..	..	0.0	64.5	0.0	0.0
Concessional	..	..	..	..	..	..	0.0	0.0	0.0	0.0
Bilateral	..	..	..	..	..	..	9.7	13.8	182.1	37.5
Concessional	..	..	..	..	..	..	9.7	13.8	0.0	1.0
Private creditors	..	..	..	..	..	..	0.0	0.0	0.0	0.0
Bonds	..	..	..	..	..	..	0.0	0.0	0.0	0.0
Commercial banks	..	..	..	..	..	..	0.0	0.0	0.0	0.0
Other private	..	..	..	..	..	..	0.0	0.0	0.0	0.0
Private nonguaranteed	**0.0**	**0.0**	**0.0**	**0.0**	**0.0**	**0.0**	**0.0**	**0.0**	**0.0**	**0.0**
Bonds	..	..	..	..	..	..	0.0	0.0	0.0	0.0
Commercial banks	..	..	..	..	..	..	0.0	0.0	0.0	0.0
Memo:										
IBRD	0.0	0.0	0.0	0.0	0.0	0.0	0.0	0.0	0.0	0.0
IDA	0.0	0.0	0.0	0.0	0.0	0.0	0.0	0.0	0.0	0.0

TAJIKISTAN

(US$ million, unless otherwise indicated)

	1970	1980	1988	1989	1990	1991	1992	1993	1994	1995
INTEREST PAYMENTS (LINT)	..	..	..	..	..	..	**0.0**	**1.2**	**0.4**	**0.0**
Public and publicly guaranteed	..	..	..	..	..	..	**0.0**	**1.2**	**0.4**	**0.0**
Official creditors	..	..	..	..	..	..	0.0	1.2	0.4	0.0
Multilateral	..	..	..	..	..	..	0.0	1.2	0.0	0.0
Concessional	..	..	..	..	..	..	0.0	0.0	0.0	0.0
Bilateral	..	..	..	..	..	..	0.0	0.0	0.4	0.0
Concessional	..	..	..	..	..	..	0.0	0.0	0.4	0.0
Private creditors	..	..	..	..	..	..	0.0	0.0	0.0	0.0
Bonds	..	..	..	..	..	..	0.0	0.0	0.0	0.0
Commercial banks	..	..	..	..	..	..	0.0	0.0	0.0	0.0
Other private	..	..	..	..	..	..	0.0	0.0	0.0	0.0
Private nonguaranteed	**0.0**	**0.0**	**0.0**	**0.0**	**0.0**	**0.0**	**0.0**	**0.0**	**0.0**	**0.0**
Bonds	..	..	..	..	..	..	0.0	0.0	0.0	0.0
Commercial banks	..	..	..	..	..	..	0.0	0.0	0.0	0.0
Memo:										
IBRD	0.0	0.0	0.0	0.0	0.0	0.0	0.0	0.0	0.0	0.0
IDA	0.0	0.0	0.0	0.0	0.0	0.0	0.0	0.0	0.0	0.0
NET TRANSFERS ON DEBT	..	..	..	..	..	..	**9.7**	**77.1**	**181.7**	**37.5**
Public and publicly guaranteed	..	..	..	..	..	..	**9.7**	**77.1**	**181.7**	**37.5**
Official creditors	..	..	..	..	..	..	9.7	77.1	181.7	37.5
Multilateral	..	..	..	..	..	..	0.0	63.3	0.0	0.0
Concessional	..	..	..	..	..	..	0.0	0.0	0.0	0.0
Bilateral	..	..	..	..	..	..	9.7	13.8	181.7	37.5
Concessional	..	..	..	..	..	..	9.7	13.8	-0.4	1.0
Private creditors	..	..	..	..	..	..	0.0	0.0	0.0	0.0
Bonds	..	..	..	..	..	..	0.0	0.0	0.0	0.0
Commercial banks	..	..	..	..	..	..	0.0	0.0	0.0	0.0
Other private	..	..	..	..	..	..	0.0	0.0	0.0	0.0
Private nonguaranteed	**0.0**	**0.0**	**0.0**	**0.0**	**0.0**	**0.0**	**0.0**	**0.0**	**0.0**	**0.0**
Bonds	..	..	..	..	..	..	0.0	0.0	0.0	0.0
Commercial banks	..	..	..	..	..	..	0.0	0.0	0.0	0.0
Memo:										
IBRD	0.0	0.0	0.0	0.0	0.0	0.0	0.0	0.0	0.0	0.0
IDA	0.0	0.0	0.0	0.0	0.0	0.0	0.0	0.0	0.0	0.0
DEBT SERVICE (LTDS)	..	..	..	..	..	..	**0.0**	**1.2**	**0.4**	**0.0**
Public and publicly guaranteed	..	..	..	..	..	..	**0.0**	**1.2**	**0.4**	**0.0**
Official creditors	..	..	..	..	..	..	0.0	1.2	0.4	0.0
Multilateral	..	..	..	..	..	..	0.0	1.2	0.0	0.0
Concessional	..	..	..	..	..	..	0.0	0.0	0.0	0.0
Bilateral	..	..	..	..	..	..	0.0	0.0	0.4	0.0
Concessional	..	..	..	..	..	..	0.0	0.0	0.4	0.0
Private creditors	..	..	..	..	..	..	0.0	0.0	0.0	0.0
Bonds	..	..	..	..	..	..	0.0	0.0	0.0	0.0
Commercial banks	..	..	..	..	..	..	0.0	0.0	0.0	0.0
Other private	..	..	..	..	..	..	0.0	0.0	0.0	0.0
Private nonguaranteed	**0.0**	**0.0**	**0.0**	**0.0**	**0.0**	**0.0**	**0.0**	**0.0**	**0.0**	**0.0**
Bonds	..	..	..	..	..	..	0.0	0.0	0.0	0.0
Commercial banks	..	..	..	..	..	..	0.0	0.0	0.0	0.0
Memo:										
IBRD	0.0	0.0	0.0	0.0	0.0	0.0	0.0	0.0	0.0	0.0
IDA	0.0	0.0	0.0	0.0	0.0	0.0	0.0	0.0	0.0	0.0
UNDISBURSED DEBT	..	..	..	..	..	..	**72.9**	**32.0**	**48.5**	**49.0**
Official creditors	..	..	..	..	..	..	72.9	32.0	48.5	49.0
Private creditors	..	..	..	..	..	..	0.0	0.0	0.0	0.0
Memorandum items										
Concessional LDOD	..	..	..	..	..	..	9.7	23.5	23.5	24.5
Variable rate LDOD	..	..	..	..	..	..	0.0	358.6	541.8	576.9
Public sector LDOD	..	..	..	..	..	..	9.7	382.1	570.3	612.4
Private sector LDOD	..	..	..	..	..	..	0.0	0.0	0.0	0.0

6. CURRENCY COMPOSITION OF LONG-TERM DEBT (PERCENT)

	1970	1980	1988	1989	1990	1991	1992	1993	1994	1995
Deutsche mark	..	..	..	..	..	..	0.0	0.0	0.0	0.0
French franc	..	..	..	..	..	..	0.0	0.0	0.0	0.0
Japanese yen	..	..	..	..	..	..	0.0	0.0	0.0	0.0
Pound sterling	..	..	..	..	..	..	0.0	0.0	0.0	0.0
Swiss franc	..	..	..	..	..	..	0.0	0.0	0.0	0.0
U.S.dollars	..	..	..	..	..	..	100.0	79.2	85.0	85.3
Multiple currency	..	..	..	..	..	..	0.0	0.0	0.0	0.0
Special drawing rights	..	..	..	..	..	..	0.0	0.0	0.0	0.0
All other currencies	..	..	..	..	..	..	0.0	20.8	15.0	14.7

TAJIKISTAN

(US$ million, unless otherwise indicated)

	1970	1980	1988	1989	1990	1991	1992	1993	1994	1995
7. DEBT RESTRUCTURINGS										
Total amount rescheduled	0.0	0.0	0.0	0.0	0.0	0.0	0.0	297.0	0.0	0.0
Debt stock rescheduled	0.0	0.0	0.0	0.0	0.0	0.0	0.0	0.0	0.0	0.0
Principal rescheduled	0.0	0.0	0.0	0.0	0.0	0.0	0.0	0.0	0.0	0.0
Official	0.0	0.0	0.0	0.0	0.0	0.0	0.0	0.0	0.0	0.0
Private	0.0	0.0	0.0	0.0	0.0	0.0	0.0	0.0	0.0	0.0
Interest rescheduled	0.0	0.0	0.0	0.0	0.0	0.0	0.0	0.0	0.0	0.0
Official	0.0	0.0	0.0	0.0	0.0	0.0	0.0	0.0	0.0	0.0
Private	0.0	0.0	0.0	0.0	0.0	0.0	0.0	0.0	0.0	0.0
Debt forgiven	..	..	0.0	0.0	0.0	0.0	0.0	0.0	0.0	0.0
Memo: interest forgiven	..	..	0.0	0.0	0.0	0.0	0.0	0.0	0.0	0.0
Debt stock reduction	0.0	0.0	0.0	0.0	0.0	0.0	0.0	0.0	0.0	0.0
of which debt buyback	0.0	0.0	0.0	0.0	0.0	0.0	0.0	0.0	0.0	0.0
8. DEBT STOCK-FLOW RECONCILIATION										
Total change in debt stocks	..	..	..	..	..	..	9.7	372.7	211.9	71.1
Net flows on debt	..	..	..	..	..	..	9.7	78.3	182.1	37.5
Net change in interest arrears	..	..	..	..	..	..	0.0	0.3	23.7	29.0
Interest capitalized	..	..	..	..	..	..	0.0	0.0	0.0	0.0
Debt forgiveness or reduction	..	..	..	..	..	..	0.0	0.0	0.0	0.0
Cross-currency valuation	..	..	..	..	..	..	0.0	-16.7	-4.8	1.1
Residual	..	..	..	..	..	..	0.0	310.8	10.9	3.5
9. AVERAGE TERMS OF NEW COMMITMENTS										
ALL CREDITORS										
Interest (%)	..	..	..	..	..	..	4.1	2.7	7.3	8.1
Maturity (years)	..	..	..	..	..	..	11.3	20.3	7.2	3.9
Grace period (years)	..	..	..	..	..	..	4.1	5.5	2.1	0.9
Grant element (%)	..	..	..	..	..	..	25.8	47.4	9.6	3.4
Official creditors										
Interest (%)	..	..	..	..	..	..	4.1	2.7	7.3	8.1
Maturity (years)	..	..	..	..	..	..	11.3	20.3	7.2	3.9
Grace period (years)	..	..	..	..	..	..	4.1	5.5	2.1	0.9
Grant element (%)	..	..	..	..	..	..	25.8	47.4	9.6	3.4
Private creditors										
Interest (%)	..	..	..	..	..	..	0.0	0.0	0.0	0.0
Maturity (years)	..	..	..	..	..	..	0.0	0.0	0.0	0.0
Grace period (years)	..	..	..	..	..	..	0.0	0.0	0.0	0.0
Grant element (%)	..	..	..	..	..	..	0.0	0.0	0.0	0.0
Memorandum items										
Commitments	..	..	..	..	..	..	87.3	39.5	198.6	38.0
Official creditors	..	..	..	..	..	..	87.3	39.5	198.6	38.0
Private creditors	..	..	..	..	..	..	0.0	0.0	0.0	0.0

10. CONTRACTUAL OBLIGATIONS ON OUTSTANDING LONG-TERM DEBT

	1996	1997	1998	1999	2000	2001	2002	2003	2004	2005
TOTAL										
Disbursements	28.3	13.3	5.8	1.3	0.2	0.2	0.0	0.0	0.0	0.0
Principal	134.6	134.6	105.8	36.3	33.3	33.8	4.6	1.8	1.2	1.2
Interest	28.8	21.0	12.3	7.1	4.9	2.8	0.7	0.5	0.4	0.4
Official creditors										
Disbursements	28.3	13.3	5.8	1.3	0.2	0.2	0.0	0.0	0.0	0.0
Principal	134.6	134.6	105.8	36.3	33.3	33.8	4.6	1.8	1.2	1.2
Interest	28.8	21.0	12.3	7.1	4.9	2.8	0.7	0.5	0.4	0.4
Bilateral creditors										
Disbursements	28.3	13.3	5.8	1.3	0.2	0.2	0.0	0.0	0.0	0.0
Principal	110.5	110.5	105.8	36.3	33.3	33.8	4.6	1.8	1.2	1.2
Interest	26.2	19.9	12.3	7.1	4.9	2.8	0.7	0.5	0.4	0.4
Multilateral creditors										
Disbursements	0.0	0.0	0.0	0.0	0.0	0.0	0.0	0.0	0.0	0.0
Principal	24.1	24.1	0.0	0.0	0.0	0.0	0.0	0.0	0.0	0.0
Interest	2.6	1.1	0.0	0.0	0.0	0.0	0.0	0.0	0.0	0.0
Private creditors										
Disbursements	0.0	0.0	0.0	0.0	0.0	0.0	0.0	0.0	0.0	0.0
Principal	0.0	0.0	0.0	0.0	0.0	0.0	0.0	0.0	0.0	0.0
Interest	0.0	0.0	0.0	0.0	0.0	0.0	0.0	0.0	0.0	0.0
Commercial banks										
Disbursements	0.0	0.0	0.0	0.0	0.0	0.0	0.0	0.0	0.0	0.0
Principal	0.0	0.0	0.0	0.0	0.0	0.0	0.0	0.0	0.0	0.0
Interest	0.0	0.0	0.0	0.0	0.0	0.0	0.0	0.0	0.0	0.0
Other private										
Disbursements	0.0	0.0	0.0	0.0	0.0	0.0	0.0	0.0	0.0	0.0
Principal	0.0	0.0	0.0	0.0	0.0	0.0	0.0	0.0	0.0	0.0
Interest	0.0	0.0	0.0	0.0	0.0	0.0	0.0	0.0	0.0	0.0

TANZANIA

(US$ million, unless otherwise indicated)

	1970	*1980*	*1988*	*1989*	*1990*	*1991*	*1992*	*1993*	*1994*	*1995*
1. SUMMARY DEBT DATA										
TOTAL DEBT STOCKS (EDT)	..	**2,460**	**5,878**	**5,733**	**6,286**	**6,400**	**6,495**	**6,655**	**7,095**	**7,333**
Long-term debt (LDOD)	**188**	**1,970**	**5,120**	**5,161**	**5,625**	**5,646**	**5,672**	**5,671**	**5,977**	**6,129**
Public and publicly guaranteed	173	1,886	5,107	5,149	5,613	5,635	5,661	5,659	5,965	6,086
Private nonguaranteed	15	84	13	13	12	12	12	12	12	44
Use of IMF credit	**0**	**171**	**141**	**129**	**140**	**143**	**221**	**215**	**212**	**197**
Short-term debt	..	**319**	**616**	**444**	**521**	**611**	**602**	**769**	**906**	**1,007**
of which interest arrears on LDOD	..	16	266	343	405	528	517	708	825	948
Official creditors	..	12	170	234	280	388	427	568	666	775
Private creditors	..	3	96	110	125	140	90	140	159	173
Memo: principal arrears on LDOD	..	50	586	712	818	966	1,016	1,134	1,293	1,572
Official creditors	..	43	480	560	629	729	811	905	1,039	1,263
Private creditors	..	7	105	152	189	238	205	228	254	309
Memo: export credits	..	..	850	767	1,278	1,142	1,137	1,103	894	866
TOTAL DEBT FLOWS										
Disbursements	**57**	**433**	**416**	**227**	**334**	**309**	**481**	**241**	**270**	**259**
Long-term debt	57	366	372	227	305	280	391	241	270	259
IMF purchases	0	66	43	0	29	29	90	0	0	0
Principal repayments	**4**	**81**	**83**	**114**	**116**	**143**	**167**	**106**	**111**	**132**
Long-term debt	4	49	74	105	88	116	162	100	96	113
IMF repurchases	0	33	9	9	28	27	6	6	15	20
Net flows on debt	**52**	**352**	**382**	**-136**	**233**	**134**	**316**	**111**	**178**	**106**
of which short-term debt	..	0	50	-250	16	-33	2	-24	20	-22
Interest payments (INT)	..	**80**	**76**	**61**	**62**	**63**	**62**	**116**	**69**	**86**
Long-term debt	3	48	50	48	47	55	56	112	63	81
IMF charges	0	7	4	5	6	3	1	1	1	1
Short-term debt	..	26	22	7	9	5	5	4	5	4
Net transfers on debt	..	**271**	**306**	**-197**	**171**	**71**	**254**	**-5**	**109**	**20**
Total debt service paid (TDS)	..	**161**	**159**	**175**	**178**	**205**	**229**	**222**	**180**	**218**
Long-term debt	7	96	124	153	135	171	218	211	159	194
IMF repurchases and charges	0	39	13	15	34	29	7	7	16	21
Short-term debt (interest only)	..	26	22	7	9	5	5	4	5	4
2. AGGREGATE NET RESOURCE FLOWS AND NET TRANSFERS (LONG-TERM)										
NET RESOURCE FLOWS	**59**	**803**	**902**	**665**	**894**	**869**	**938**	**947**	**788**	**747**
Net flow of long-term debt (ex. IMF)	52	318	299	123	217	164	229	141	174	147
Foreign direct investment (net)	0	0	4	6	0	0	12	20	50	150
Portfolio equity flows	0	0	0	0	0	0	0	0	0	0
Grants (excluding technical coop.)	6	485	600	536	677	705	697	786	565	451
Memo: technical coop. grants	21	173	210	202	209	209	237	239	212	267
NET TRANSFERS	**56**	**756**	**833**	**584**	**821**	**789**	**852**	**801**	**689**	**629**
Interest on long-term debt	3	48	50	48	47	55	56	112	63	81
Profit remittances on FDI	0	0	19	32	25	25	30	35	36	37
3. MAJOR ECONOMIC AGGREGATES										
Gross national product (GNP)	..	..	3,320	3,783	3,668	3,995	3,902	3,535	3,243	3,536
Exports of goods & services (XGS)	..	762	507	538	544	513	576	779	961	1,253
of which workers remittances	..	0	0	0	0	0	0	0	0	0
Imports of goods & services (MGS)	..	1,412	1,504	1,525	1,665	1,723	1,887	2,055	2,002	2,236
International reserves (RES)	65	20	78	54	193	204	327	203	332	270
Current account balance	..	-522	-376	-335	-559	-738	-704	-770	-681	-629
4. DEBT INDICATORS										
EDT / XGS (%)	..	323.0	1,159.1	1,066.1	1,154.9	1,247.1	1,127.0	854.5	738.5	585.2
EDT / GNP (%)	..	..	177.1	151.5	171.4	160.2	166.5	188.2	218.8	207.4
TDS / XGS (%)	..	21.1	31.4	32.5	32.7	40.0	39.7	28.5	18.7	17.4
INT / XGS (%)	..	10.5	15.0	11.3	11.3	12.2	10.7	14.9	7.2	6.8
INT / GNP (%)	..	..	2.3	1.6	1.7	1.6	1.6	3.3	2.1	2.4
RES / EDT (%)	..	0.8	1.3	0.9	3.1	3.2	5.0	3.1	4.7	3.7
RES / MGS (months)	..	0.2	0.6	0.4	1.4	1.4	2.1	1.2	2.0	1.5
Short-term / EDT (%)	..	13.0	10.5	7.7	8.3	9.5	9.3	11.6	12.8	13.7
Concessional / EDT (%)	..	53.7	53.3	54.6	54.4	55.1	58.2	59.6	60.5	60.5
Multilateral / EDT (%)	..	23.0	28.3	30.4	31.7	33.9	35.6	36.6	37.6	39.1

TANZANIA

(US$ million, unless otherwise indicated)

	1970	*1980*	*1988*	*1989*	*1990*	*1991*	*1992*	*1993*	*1994*	*1995*
5. LONG-TERM DEBT										
DEBT OUTSTANDING (LDOD)	**188**	**1,970**	**5,120**	**5,161**	**5,625**	**5,646**	**5,672**	**5,671**	**5,977**	**6,129**
Public and publicly guaranteed	**173**	**1,886**	**5,107**	**5,149**	**5,613**	**5,635**	**5,661**	**5,659**	**5,965**	**6,086**
Official creditors	168	1,629	4,638	4,665	5,140	5,182	5,288	5,281	5,581	5,716
Multilateral	38	565	1,665	1,742	1,996	2,172	2,311	2,434	2,667	2,868
Concessional	35	350	1,347	1,446	1,696	1,904	2,076	2,222	2,479	2,713
Bilateral	129	1,064	2,973	2,922	3,145	3,009	2,977	2,847	2,914	2,848
Concessional	129	972	1,786	1,686	1,724	1,621	1,701	1,746	1,814	1,725
Private creditors	6	257	469	484	473	453	373	379	384	370
Bonds	0	0	0	0	0	0	0	0	0	0
Commercial banks	0	31	61	59	68	60	46	43	57	58
Other private	6	227	408	425	405	393	326	336	327	311
Private nonguaranteed	**15**	**84**	**13**	**13**	**12**	**12**	**12**	**12**	**12**	**44**
Bonds	0	0	0	0	0	0	0	0	0	0
Commercial banks	15	84	13	13	12	12	12	12	12	44
Memo:										
IBRD	4	198	279	252	243	208	171	140	114	87
IDA	35	242	914	1,016	1,250	1,434	1,618	1,759	1,998	2,182
DISBURSEMENTS	**57**	**366**	**372**	**227**	**305**	**280**	**391**	**241**	**270**	**259**
Public and publicly guaranteed	**49**	**335**	**372**	**227**	**305**	**280**	**391**	**241**	**270**	**258**
Official creditors	43	244	337	192	288	276	350	195	248	255
Multilateral	11	122	279	132	205	227	256	175	211	221
Concessional	9	75	271	123	195	222	254	166	208	219
Bilateral	33	123	58	60	83	50	93	20	37	34
Concessional	32	95	55	34	53	41	87	13	18	28
Private creditors	6	91	36	35	17	4	41	45	21	3
Bonds	0	0	0	0	0	0	0	0	0	0
Commercial banks	0	9	2	1	3	2	2	7	12	0
Other private	6	82	34	34	13	2	39	39	9	3
Private nonguaranteed	**8**	**31**	**0**	**0**	**0**	**0**	**0**	**0**	**0**	**1**
Bonds	0	0	0	0	0	0	0	0	0	0
Commercial banks	8	31	0	0	0	0	0	0	0	1
Memo:										
IBRD	1	34	3	0	0	0	0	0	0	0
IDA	9	35	135	115	187	181	235	146	183	160
PRINCIPAL REPAYMENTS	**4**	**49**	**74**	**105**	**88**	**116**	**162**	**100**	**96**	**113**
Public and publicly guaranteed	**2**	**32**	**74**	**105**	**88**	**116**	**162**	**100**	**96**	**107**
Official creditors	2	26	65	96	76	103	83	89	83	96
Multilateral	0	8	36	37	44	64	51	52	64	72
Concessional	0	1	8	11	17	26	20	19	33	30
Bilateral	2	18	29	59	33	39	32	37	18	24
Concessional	2	18	23	55	24	17	18	27	11	16
Private creditors	0	6	9	9	12	13	79	10	13	12
Bonds	0	0	0	0	0	0	0	0	0	0
Commercial banks	0	1	1	1	1	3	8	9	1	1
Other private	0	6	8	9	11	10	71	2	13	11
Private nonguaranteed	**3**	**16**	**0**	**0**	**0**	**0**	**0**	**0**	**0**	**5**
Bonds	0	0	0	0	0	0	0	0	0	0
Commercial banks	3	16	0	0	0	0	0	0	0	5
Memo:										
IBRD	0	5	24	23	26	36	31	33	33	34
IDA	0	1	4	5	6	7	8	9	11	12
NET FLOWS ON DEBT	**52**	**318**	**299**	**123**	**217**	**164**	**229**	**141**	**174**	**147**
Public and publicly guaranteed	**47**	**303**	**299**	**123**	**217**	**164**	**229**	**141**	**174**	**151**
Official creditors	42	218	272	96	212	174	267	106	166	159
Multilateral	11	114	243	96	161	163	206	123	147	149
Concessional	9	75	263	112	178	196	235	146	175	190
Bilateral	31	104	29	0	50	11	61	-17	19	10
Concessional	30	77	32	-21	29	23	69	-14	7	12
Private creditors	6	85	27	26	5	-10	-38	35	8	-9
Bonds	0	0	0	0	0	0	0	0	0	0
Commercial banks	0	9	1	0	3	-2	-6	-2	12	0
Other private	6	76	26	26	2	-8	-33	37	-4	-8
Private nonguaranteed	**5**	**15**	**0**	**0**	**0**	**0**	**0**	**0**	**0**	**-4**
Bonds	0	0	0	0	0	0	0	0	0	0
Commercial banks	5	15	0	0	0	0	0	0	0	-4
Memo:										
IBRD	1	29	-21	-23	-26	-36	-31	-33	-33	-34
IDA	9	34	131	110	181	174	226	137	172	148

TANZANIA

(US$ million, unless otherwise indicated)

	1970	1980	1988	1989	1990	1991	1992	1993	1994	1995
INTEREST PAYMENTS (LINT)	**3**	**48**	**50**	**48**	**47**	**55**	**56**	**112**	**63**	**81**
Public and publicly guaranteed	**2**	**41**	**50**	**48**	**47**	**55**	**56**	**112**	**63**	**80**
Official creditors	2	34	46	44	44	51	51	106	63	79
Multilateral	0	18	30	27	27	34	33	33	33	58
Concessional	0	4	10	10	11	16	16	18	19	20
Bilateral	2	16	16	17	17	18	18	73	30	21
Concessional	2	14	11	9	11	11	9	42	13	13
Private creditors	0	7	4	4	3	4	5	6	0	1
Bonds	0	0	0	0	0	0	0	0	0	0
Commercial banks	0	1	1	1	0	1	3	4	0	0
Other private	0	6	4	4	3	2	2	2	0	1
Private nonguaranteed	**1**	**7**	**0**	**0**	**0**	**0**	**0**	**0**	**0**	**1**
Bonds	0	0	0	0	0	0	0	0	0	0
Commercial banks	1	7	0	0	0	0	0	0	0	1
Memo:										
IBRD	0	15	22	19	17	20	15	12	10	9
IDA	0	2	7	7	8	10	10	14	14	16
NET TRANSFERS ON DEBT	**49**	**270**	**249**	**74**	**169**	**109**	**173**	**30**	**110**	**66**
Public and publicly guaranteed	**45**	**262**	**249**	**74**	**169**	**109**	**173**	**30**	**110**	**71**
Official creditors	40	184	226	52	168	122	216	0	103	80
Multilateral	10	96	213	69	134	129	173	90	114	91
Concessional	9	71	253	102	167	180	219	129	156	170
Bilateral	29	89	13	-17	33	-7	44	-90	-11	-11
Concessional	29	64	20	-30	18	12	60	-55	-6	-1
Private creditors	6	78	23	22	2	-13	-43	29	8	-9
Bonds	0	0	0	0	0	0	0	0	0	0
Commercial banks	0	8	1	0	3	-3	-9	-6	11	0
Other private	6	70	22	22	-1	-10	-34	35	-4	-9
Private nonguaranteed	**4**	**9**	**0**	**0**	**0**	**0**	**0**	**0**	**0**	**-5**
Bonds	0	0	0	0	0	0	0	0	0	0
Commercial banks	4	9	0	0	0	0	0	0	0	-5
Memo:										
IBRD	1	14	-43	-42	-44	-56	-45	-45	-42	-43
IDA	9	33	125	103	172	164	216	123	158	132
DEBT SERVICE (LTDS)	**7**	**96**	**124**	**153**	**135**	**171**	**218**	**211**	**159**	**194**
Public and publicly guaranteed	**4**	**73**	**124**	**153**	**135**	**171**	**218**	**211**	**159**	**187**
Official creditors	4	60	111	140	120	154	134	195	146	175
Multilateral	0	26	66	63	71	98	84	85	98	130
Concessional	0	5	18	21	28	42	36	37	52	49
Bilateral	4	34	45	77	50	56	50	110	48	45
Concessional	4	32	34	64	34	28	28	68	24	29
Private creditors	0	13	13	13	15	17	84	16	14	13
Bonds	0	0	0	0	0	0	0	0	0	0
Commercial banks	0	2	1	1	1	5	11	12	1	1
Other private	0	12	12	12	14	12	73	4	13	12
Private nonguaranteed	**3**	**23**	**0**	**0**	**0**	**0**	**0**	**0**	**0**	**6**
Bonds	0	0	0	0	0	0	0	0	0	0
Commercial banks	3	23	0	0	0	0	0	0	0	6
Memo:										
IBRD	0	20	46	42	44	56	45	45	42	43
IDA	0	2	11	12	14	17	19	23	25	28
UNDISBURSED DEBT	**315**	**1,165**	**787**	**678**	**1,138**	**1,403**	**1,230**	**1,500**	**1,521**	**1,333**
Official creditors	311	1,088	749	664	1,133	1,384	1,204	1,471	1,500	1,315
Private creditors	4	77	38	14	5	19	26	29	21	19
Memorandum items										
Concessional LDOD	163	1,322	3,133	3,132	3,420	3,525	3,778	3,967	4,293	4,438
Variable rate LDOD	15	89	354	352	471	460	523	484	485	524
Public sector LDOD	173	1,854	5,064	5,101	5,548	5,567	5,586	5,567	5,842	5,949
Private sector LDOD	15	116	57	60	77	79	87	104	135	181
6. CURRENCY COMPOSITION OF LONG-TERM DEBT (PERCENT)										
Deutsche mark	3.2	2.3	3.3	3.5	3.9	3.8	4.4	3.9	3.9	3.0
French franc	0.0	3.5	3.9	3.5	3.7	3.7	3.6	2.8	2.7	2.9
Japanese yen	0.0	12.0	8.5	7.0	6.6	6.9	8.9	10.0	10.6	10.0
Pound sterling	24.1	8.7	11.1	11.5	12.5	12.4	11.7	11.4	11.1	10.9
Swiss franc	0.0	0.6	0.6	0.5	0.6	0.5	0.6	0.2	0.2	0.3
U.S.dollars	15.1	22.2	34.6	37.3	36.4	38.3	37.4	38.6	39.4	41.2
Multiple currency	2.1	11.3	7.2	6.6	6.2	5.7	5.1	4.5	4.0	3.9
Special drawing rights	0.0	0.2	1.4	1.4	1.3	2.3	3.1	4.3	5.1	5.2
All other currencies	55.5	39.3	29.4	28.8	28.8	26.5	25.1	24.3	22.9	22.6

TANZANIA

(US$ million, unless otherwise indicated)

	1970	1980	1988	1989	1990	1991	1992	1993	1994	1995
7. DEBT RESTRUCTURINGS										
Total amount rescheduled	0	0	254	76	174	17	358	67	8	0
Debt stock rescheduled	0	0	0	0	0	0	0	0	0	0
Principal rescheduled	0	0	77	15	59	13	224	34	5	0
Official	0	0	40	9	35	11	198	23	5	0
Private	0	0	37	6	24	2	26	11	0	0
Interest rescheduled	0	0	116	51	89	2	107	15	1	0
Official	0	0	107	45	84	2	105	13	1	0
Private	0	0	9	6	5	0	2	2	0	0
Debt forgiven	..	..	7	41	124	130	128	157	87	135
Memo: interest forgiven	..	..	9	5	10	37	32	39	14	0
Debt stock reduction	0	0	0	0	0	0	0	0	0	0
of which debt buyback	0	0	0	0	0	0	0	0	0	0
8. DEBT STOCK-FLOW RECONCILIATION										
Total change in debt stocks	..	..	..	-144	553	114	95	159	441	238
Net flows on debt	..	..	..	-136	233	134	316	111	178	106
Net change in interest arrears	..	..	..	77	62	122	-11	191	117	122
Interest capitalized	..	..	..	51	89	2	107	15	1	0
Debt forgiveness or reduction	..	..	..	-41	-124	-130	-128	-157	-87	-135
Cross-currency valuation	..	..	..	-127	378	-29	-248	-28	207	54
Residual	..	..	..	32	-86	15	59	28	24	91
9. AVERAGE TERMS OF NEW COMMITMENTS										
ALL CREDITORS										
Interest (%)	1.4	4.1	2.9	3.8	1.2	1.4	1.1	1.9	1.1	0.8
Maturity (years)	41.0	22.9	28.4	30.7	34.7	38.4	33.2	35.7	35.2	35.4
Grace period (years)	22.5	7.5	7.7	7.4	9.2	10.7	6.9	8.7	9.4	8.7
Grant element (%)	81.0	42.9	56.1	51.6	71.8	74.1	64.3	68.0	74.0	74.7
Official creditors										
Interest (%)	1.4	3.6	1.4	3.7	1.1	1.1	1.2	1.4	1.0	0.8
Maturity (years)	41.0	24.2	33.9	32.1	35.1	39.4	39.3	38.6	36.9	35.4
Grace period (years)	22.5	8.0	9.2	7.8	9.3	10.9	8.3	9.2	9.9	8.8
Grant element (%)	81.0	46.8	70.0	54.1	72.4	76.7	74.0	73.4	77.6	74.8
Private creditors										
Interest (%)	0.0	7.5	7.9	5.6	3.1	10.7	0.4	5.8	4.2	11.8
Maturity (years)	0.0	11.7	9.9	5.1	12.3	10.6	3.6	7.6	6.1	10.6
Grace period (years)	0.0	3.2	2.8	1.4	6.3	4.5	0.5	3.3	0.7	2.6
Grant element (%)	0.0	10.4	8.7	8.1	43.2	-4.1	17.7	16.9	15.7	-9.7
Memorandum items										
Commitments	271	742	437	214	703	527	283	516	226	154
Official creditors	271	663	338	202	689	510	234	467	213	154
Private creditors	0	79	99	12	13	17	49	49	13	0

10. CONTRACTUAL OBLIGATIONS ON OUTSTANDING LONG-TERM DEBT

	1996	1997	1998	1999	2000	2001	2002	2003	2004	2005
TOTAL										
Disbursements	361	367	265	166	89	42	33	9	2	1
Principal	336	255	198	190	204	206	194	173	166	164
Interest	116	99	91	84	77	69	62	56	51	48
Official creditors										
Disbursements	350	362	263	166	89	42	33	9	2	1
Principal	304	231	180	178	193	197	189	170	164	161
Interest	109	94	88	82	76	68	61	55	51	47
Bilateral creditors										
Disbursements	55	52	31	19	11	7	4	3	2	1
Principal	236	170	116	116	124	124	113	90	78	74
Interest	77	63	57	52	46	40	34	28	25	22
Multilateral creditors										
Disbursements	295	310	232	147	78	36	29	6	0	0
Principal	68	61	65	62	70	72	76	80	86	88
Interest	32	31	31	30	30	29	28	27	26	25
Private creditors										
Disbursements	11	5	2	0	0	0	0	0	0	0
Principal	32	25	18	13	11	10	5	3	2	2
Interest	6	5	4	2	2	1	1	1	0	0
Commercial banks										
Disbursements	11	5	2	0	0	0	0	0	0	0
Principal	4	6	7	5	4	3	3	3	2	2
Interest	2	2	1	1	1	1	1	1	0	0
Other private										
Disbursements	0	0	0	0	0	0	0	0	0	0
Principal	28	18	11	8	7	6	2	0	0	0
Interest	5	3	2	2	1	0	0	0	0	0

THAILAND

(US$ million, unless otherwise indicated)

1. SUMMARY DEBT DATA

	1970	1980	1988	1989	1990	1991	1992	1993	1994	1995
TOTAL DEBT STOCKS (EDT)	..	**8,297**	**21,717**	**23,496**	**28,088**	**37,705**	**41,812**	**42,697**	**48,095**	**56,789**
Long-term debt (LDOD)	**726**	**5,646**	**16,255**	**17,111**	**19,765**	**25,213**	**27,085**	**29,312**	**34,058**	**38,476**
Public and publicly guaranteed	324	3,943	13,239	12,472	12,454	13,242	13,310	14,726	17,120	17,231
Private nonguaranteed	402	1,703	3,016	4,640	7,311	11,971	13,775	14,585	16,938	21,245
Use of IMF credit	**0**	**348**	**662**	**273**	**1**	**0**	**0**	**0**	**0**	**0**
Short-term debt	..	**2,303**	**4,800**	**6,112**	**8,322**	**12,492**	**14,727**	**13,385**	**14,037**	**18,312**
of which interest arrears on LDOD	..	0	0	0	0	0	0	0	0	0
Official creditors	..	0	0	0	0	0	0	0	0	0
Private creditors	..	0	0	0	0	0	0	0	0	0
Memo: principal arrears on LDOD	..	0	0	0	0	0	0	0	0	0
Official creditors	..	0	0	0	0	0	0	0	0	0
Private creditors	..	0	0	0	0	0	0	0	0	0
Memo: export credits	..	..	2,058	2,563	3,106	3,194	4,145	5,226	7,613	9,265
TOTAL DEBT FLOWS										
Disbursements	**220**	**2,648**	**2,714**	**4,084**	**4,588**	**5,352**	**5,094**	**6,750**	**9,649**	**10,133**
Long-term debt	220	2,604	2,714	4,084	4,588	5,352	5,094	6,750	9,649	10,133
IMF purchases	0	45	0	0	0	0	0	0	0	0
Principal repayments	**131**	**804**	**2,845**	**2,769**	**3,265**	**2,262**	**3,198**	**4,270**	**5,359**	**4,702**
Long-term debt	131	782	2,585	2,404	2,984	2,261	3,198	4,270	5,359	4,702
IMF repurchases	0	22	260	365	281	1	0	0	0	0
Net flows on debt	**90**	**1,845**	**2,005**	**2,627**	**3,534**	**7,260**	**4,132**	**1,138**	**4,942**	**9,707**
of which short-term debt	..	0	2,136	1,312	2,210	4,170	2,235	-1,342	652	4,275
Interest payments (INT)	..	**814**	**1,544**	**1,628**	**2,031**	**2,649**	**2,707**	**2,543**	**2,542**	**2,831**
Long-term debt	33	473	1,126	1,090	1,360	1,774	1,872	1,818	1,835	1,996
IMF charges	0	13	58	47	21	0	0	0	0	0
Short-term debt	..	328	360	491	650	875	834	725	708	835
Net transfers on debt	..	**1,031**	**461**	**999**	**1,503**	**4,612**	**1,425**	**-1,405**	**2,400**	**6,876**
Total debt service paid (TDS)	..	**1,617**	**4,389**	**4,397**	**5,296**	**4,910**	**5,904**	**6,813**	**7,901**	**7,533**
Long-term debt	164	1,254	3,711	3,495	4,344	4,035	5,070	6,088	7,194	6,698
IMF repurchases and charges	0	35	318	412	302	1	0	0	0	0
Short-term debt (interest only)	..	328	360	491	650	875	834	725	708	835

2. AGGREGATE NET RESOURCE FLOWS AND NET TRANSFERS (LONG-TERM)

	1970	1980	1988	1989	1990	1991	1992	1993	1994	1995
NET RESOURCE FLOWS	**139**	**2,087**	**1,816**	**5,061**	**4,690**	**5,300**	**4,175**	**7,500**	**5,223**	**9,753**
Net flow of long-term debt (ex. IMF)	90	1,822	129	1,680	1,605	3,091	1,897	2,479	4,290	5,432
Foreign direct investment (net)	43	190	1,105	1,776	2,444	2,014	2,113	1,804	1,366	2,068
Portfolio equity flows	0	0	487	1,426	449	41	4	3,117	-538	2,154
Grants (excluding technical coop.)	6	75	95	179	193	154	161	100	105	99
Memo: technical coop. grants	48	103	233	272	231	257	257	266	245	270
NET TRANSFERS	**87**	**1,576**	**475**	**3,641**	**3,019**	**3,470**	**1,953**	**5,263**	**2,924**	**7,276**
Interest on long-term debt	33	473	1,126	1,090	1,360	1,774	1,872	1,818	1,835	1,996
Profit remittances on FDI	19	38	215	329	312	56	350	420	465	480

3. MAJOR ECONOMIC AGGREGATES

	1970	1980	1988	1989	1990	1991	1992	1993	1994	1995
Gross national product (GNP)	7,096	32,091	60,687	71,329	84,573	96,677	109,083	122,252	139,921	162,686
Exports of goods & services (XGS)	..	8,575	21,725	26,880	31,289	37,759	42,920	49,597	58,680	74,093
of which workers remittances	..	0	0	0	0	0	0	0	0	0
Imports of goods & services (MGS)	..	10,861	23,616	29,624	38,783	45,591	49,869	56,710	67,893	88,134
International reserves (RES)	911	3,026	7,112	10,508	14,258	18,393	21,183	25,439	30,280	36,939
Current account balance	..	-2,076	-1,654	-2,498	-7,281	-7,572	-6,355	-7,047	-8,420	-13,554

4. DEBT INDICATORS

	1970	1980	1988	1989	1990	1991	1992	1993	1994	1995
EDT / XGS (%)	..	96.8	100.0	87.4	89.8	99.9	97.4	86.1	82.0	76.6
EDT / GNP (%)	..	25.9	35.8	32.9	33.2	39.0	38.3	34.9	34.4	34.9
TDS / XGS (%)	..	18.9	20.2	16.4	16.9	13.0	13.8	13.7	13.5	10.2
INT / XGS (%)	..	9.5	7.1	6.1	6.5	7.0	6.3	5.1	4.3	3.8
INT / GNP (%)	..	2.5	2.5	2.3	2.4	2.7	2.5	2.1	1.8	1.7
RES / EDT (%)	..	36.5	32.8	44.7	50.8	48.8	50.7	59.6	63.0	65.0
RES / MGS (months)	..	3.3	3.6	4.3	4.4	4.8	5.1	5.4	5.4	5.0
Short-term / EDT (%)	..	27.8	22.1	26.0	29.6	33.1	35.2	31.3	29.2	32.2
Concessional / EDT (%)	..	10.9	16.9	15.5	15.3	12.9	12.1	13.9	14.1	12.7
Multilateral / EDT (%)	..	12.0	16.8	14.2	13.2	9.4	7.0	7.1	6.5	5.6

THAILAND

(US$ million, unless otherwise indicated)

	1970	*1980*	*1988*	*1989*	*1990*	*1991*	*1992*	*1993*	*1994*	*1995*
5. LONG-TERM DEBT										
DEBT OUTSTANDING (LDOD)	**726**	**5,646**	**16,255**	**17,111**	**19,765**	**25,213**	**27,085**	**29,312**	**34,058**	**38,476**
Public and publicly guaranteed	**324**	**3,943**	**13,239**	**12,472**	**12,454**	**13,242**	**13,310**	**14,726**	**17,120**	**17,231**
Official creditors	291	2,167	7,755	7,317	8,172	8,608	8,209	9,360	10,626	11,029
Multilateral	164	992	3,646	3,327	3,721	3,544	2,925	3,040	3,121	3,208
Concessional	146	116	295	281	311	336	351	387	411	426
Bilateral	127	1,174	4,110	3,991	4,451	5,064	5,284	6,320	7,506	7,820
Concessional	93	786	3,366	3,364	3,994	4,517	4,711	5,539	6,382	6,787
Private creditors	33	1,777	5,484	5,154	4,282	4,634	5,101	5,367	6,494	6,202
Bonds	0	148	480	551	516	412	683	794	1,643	1,588
Commercial banks	3	1,340	3,631	3,280	2,170	2,408	2,519	2,654	3,026	3,160
Other private	30	289	1,373	1,323	1,596	1,814	1,899	1,919	1,825	1,455
Private nonguaranteed	**402**	**1,703**	**3,016**	**4,640**	**7,311**	**11,971**	**13,775**	**14,585**	**16,938**	**21,245**
Bonds	0	0	0	33	40	56	310	2,031	5,223	7,375
Commercial banks	402	1,703	3,016	4,607	7,272	11,915	13,465	12,554	11,715	13,871
Memo:										
IBRD	159	671	2,616	2,271	2,421	2,420	1,898	1,925	1,782	1,805
IDA	0	32	111	110	109	108	106	105	103	102
DISBURSEMENTS	**220**	**2,604**	**2,714**	**4,084**	**4,588**	**5,352**	**5,094**	**6,750**	**9,649**	**10,133**
Public and publicly guaranteed	**51**	**1,315**	**1,694**	**1,559**	**1,296**	**1,487**	**1,612**	**2,104**	**2,998**	**2,137**
Official creditors	38	620	690	789	788	780	745	1,190	1,183	1,417
Multilateral	21	236	201	246	263	260	283	334	331	358
Concessional	13	10	6	3	23	31	34	43	19	31
Bilateral	18	385	488	542	525	520	462	856	852	1,059
Concessional	11	178	365	459	472	392	372	587	487	1,043
Private creditors	13	695	1,005	771	508	707	866	914	1,815	720
Bonds	0	44	251	84	0	0	300	244	866	142
Commercial banks	0	607	547	414	110	387	321	588	935	572
Other private	13	44	206	273	398	320	246	83	14	5
Private nonguaranteed	**169**	**1,288**	**1,020**	**2,525**	**3,292**	**3,865**	**3,483**	**4,646**	**6,651**	**7,996**
Bonds	0	0	0	31	0	17	259	1,723	3,165	2,080
Commercial banks	169	1,288	1,020	2,494	3,292	3,848	3,223	2,923	3,486	5,916
Memo:										
IBRD	19	145	110	163	174	162	177	169	128	146
IDA	0	5	1	0	0	0	0	0	0	0
PRINCIPAL REPAYMENTS	**131**	**782**	**2,585**	**2,404**	**2,984**	**2,261**	**3,198**	**4,270**	**5,359**	**4,702**
Public and publicly guaranteed	**23**	**172**	**1,745**	**1,521**	**2,393**	**1,121**	**1,390**	**1,438**	**1,851**	**1,931**
Official creditors	17	73	1,017	746	788	667	1,034	590	847	907
Multilateral	9	35	681	466	439	486	819	304	499	360
Concessional	8	13	13	14	16	11	12	13	16	16
Bilateral	8	38	336	281	349	181	216	286	348	546
Concessional	5	13	91	93	102	142	173	228	282	440
Private creditors	6	99	728	775	1,605	454	355	848	1,004	1,024
Bonds	0	0	209	6	87	95	11	132	49	199
Commercial banks	0	52	391	541	1,324	188	190	545	697	444
Other private	6	47	128	228	194	171	154	172	259	381
Private nonguaranteed	**107**	**610**	**841**	**883**	**591**	**1,140**	**1,808**	**2,833**	**3,508**	**2,771**
Bonds	0	0	0	0	0	0	0	0	0	0
Commercial banks	107	610	841	883	591	1,140	1,808	2,833	3,508	2,771
Memo:										
IBRD	9	26	603	409	207	209	645	189	415	201
IDA	0	0	1	1	1	1	1	1	2	2
NET FLOWS ON DEBT	**90**	**1,822**	**129**	**1,680**	**1,605**	**3,091**	**1,897**	**2,479**	**4,290**	**5,432**
Public and publicly guaranteed	**28**	**1,143**	**-50**	**38**	**-1,097**	**367**	**222**	**666**	**1,147**	**206**
Official creditors	21	547	-327	43	0	114	-289	600	336	511
Multilateral	12	200	-480	-219	-176	-225	-536	30	-168	-2
Concessional	5	-3	-8	-11	7	20	22	29	4	14
Bilateral	10	347	153	262	176	339	247	570	504	513
Concessional	6	165	274	367	370	250	199	359	205	603
Private creditors	7	597	277	-4	-1,097	253	511	66	811	-305
Bonds	0	44	42	78	-87	-95	289	112	817	-57
Commercial banks	0	556	156	-128	-1,214	199	131	44	238	129
Other private	7	-3	78	45	204	149	92	-89	-244	-376
Private nonguaranteed	**62**	**678**	**179**	**1,642**	**2,702**	**2,725**	**1,675**	**1,813**	**3,143**	**5,225**
Bonds	0	0	0	31	0	17	259	1,723	3,165	2,080
Commercial banks	62	678	179	1,610	2,702	2,707	1,416	90	-21	3,145
Memo:										
IBRD	10	120	-493	-246	-34	-47	-469	-20	-287	-56
IDA	0	4	0	-1	-1	-1	-1	-1	-2	-2

THAILAND

(US$ million, unless otherwise indicated)

	1970	1980	1988	1989	1990	1991	1992	1993	1994	1995
INTEREST PAYMENTS (LINT)	**33**	**473**	**1,126**	**1,090**	**1,360**	**1,774**	**1,872**	**1,818**	**1,835**	**1,996**
Public and publicly guaranteed	**16**	**269**	**911**	**858**	**879**	**705**	**702**	**718**	**779**	**890**
Official creditors	14	117	521	444	440	439	427	443	475	510
Multilateral	9	76	346	280	284	278	240	225	218	219
Concessional	8	7	8	8	7	10	11	12	14	17
Bilateral	5	42	175	164	156	161	188	218	257	291
Concessional	3	19	98	102	109	127	151	174	203	220
Private creditors	2	152	390	414	439	266	275	275	304	379
Bonds	0	9	31	31	34	30	34	44	40	94
Commercial banks	0	117	260	264	230	135	137	128	150	198
Other private	2	26	99	119	175	102	105	103	113	88
Private nonguaranteed	**17**	**204**	**215**	**233**	**481**	**1,069**	**1,170**	**1,100**	**1,056**	**1,107**
Bonds	0	0	0	0	2	3	2	11	69	255
Commercial banks	17	204	215	233	479	1,067	1,168	1,088	987	852
Memo:										
IBRD	9	53	271	204	189	186	169	158	144	135
IDA	0	0	1	1	1	1	1	1	1	1
NET TRANSFERS ON DEBT	**57**	**1,349**	**-997**	**590**	**245**	**1,317**	**25**	**662**	**2,456**	**3,435**
Public and publicly guaranteed	**12**	**875**	**-961**	**-819**	**-1,976**	**-339**	**-480**	**-52**	**368**	**-683**
Official creditors	7	430	-848	-401	-441	-325	-716	157	-139	1
Multilateral	2	125	-826	-499	-460	-503	-775	-196	-386	-221
Concessional	-3	-10	-16	-19	-1	10	10	17	-11	-2
Bilateral	5	305	-22	98	20	178	59	353	247	222
Concessional	3	146	175	265	261	123	48	185	3	383
Private creditors	5	445	-113	-418	-1,536	-14	236	-209	507	-684
Bonds	0	35	11	47	-121	-124	255	68	777	-151
Commercial banks	-1	439	-104	-392	-1,444	64	-6	-84	88	-69
Other private	5	-29	-20	-73	29	47	-13	-192	-357	-464
Private nonguaranteed	**45**	**475**	**-36**	**1,409**	**2,221**	**1,656**	**505**	**713**	**2,087**	**4,119**
Bonds	0	0	0	31	-2	15	257	1,712	3,096	1,826
Commercial banks	45	475	-36	1,378	2,223	1,641	248	-998	-1,009	2,293
Memo:										
IBRD	1	66	-764	-450	-222	-233	-638	-178	-431	-191
IDA	0	4	-1	-2	-2	-2	-2	-2	-3	-3
DEBT SERVICE (LTDS)	**164**	**1,254**	**3,711**	**3,495**	**4,344**	**4,035**	**5,070**	**6,088**	**7,194**	**6,698**
Public and publicly guaranteed	**39**	**441**	**2,656**	**2,379**	**3,272**	**1,826**	**2,092**	**2,156**	**2,630**	**2,820**
Official creditors	31	191	1,538	1,190	1,228	1,106	1,462	1,033	1,322	1,417
Multilateral	18	111	1,027	745	723	764	1,058	529	717	579
Concessional	16	20	22	22	24	21	24	25	30	33
Bilateral	13	80	511	445	506	342	403	504	605	838
Concessional	8	32	190	194	212	269	324	402	484	660
Private creditors	8	250	1,118	1,189	2,044	720	630	1,123	1,308	1,403
Bonds	0	9	240	37	121	124	45	175	89	293
Commercial banks	1	168	651	805	1,554	324	327	673	847	642
Other private	7	73	227	347	369	273	259	275	372	469
Private nonguaranteed	**124**	**814**	**1,056**	**1,116**	**1,071**	**2,210**	**2,978**	**3,932**	**4,564**	**3,878**
Bonds	0	0	0	0	2	3	2	11	69	255
Commercial banks	124	814	1,056	1,116	1,070	2,207	2,976	3,921	4,495	3,623
Memo:										
IBRD	18	79	874	613	396	395	815	347	559	336
IDA	0	1	1	2	2	2	2	2	3	3
UNDISBURSED DEBT	**156**	**3,023**	**3,521**	**3,072**	**3,625**	**3,269**	**4,747**	**6,564**	**7,700**	**7,418**
Official creditors	145	2,652	3,241	2,370	2,854	2,691	3,325	5,162	6,576	5,607
Private creditors	11	371	281	702	772	579	1,421	1,402	1,124	1,811
Memorandum items										
Concessional LDOD	239	902	3,660	3,645	4,305	4,853	5,063	5,927	6,793	7,213
Variable rate LDOD	402	2,903	7,240	8,553	10,171	14,926	16,471	17,280	19,536	24,164
Public sector LDOD	312	3,943	13,239	12,472	12,454	13,242	13,310	14,726	17,120	17,231
Private sector LDOD	414	1,703	3,016	4,640	7,311	11,971	13,775	14,585	16,938	21,245

6. CURRENCY COMPOSITION OF LONG-TERM DEBT (PERCENT)

	1970	1980	1988	1989	1990	1991	1992	1993	1994	1995
Deutsche mark	17.6	4.7	2.9	3.1	3.6	3.7	3.8	2.3	2.2	2.3
French franc	0.0	1.8	0.8	1.0	1.0	1.0	1.3	1.2	1.1	1.1
Japanese yen	6.0	25.3	44.0	41.4	43.2	45.6	47.2	50.1	49.7	48.1
Pound sterling	2.4	0.2	0.5	0.3	0.4	0.4	0.3	0.2	0.2	0.2
Swiss franc	0.0	0.1	3.2	3.3	3.9	3.1	2.7	2.3	1.5	0.5
U.S.dollars	21.6	41.0	19.7	22.9	17.0	19.1	22.9	22.6	25.9	26.6
Multiple currency	50.7	24.3	26.0	25.1	28.3	25.0	19.8	19.8	18.2	19.9
Special drawing rights	0.0	0.0	0.2	0.2	0.2	0.2	0.2	0.2	0.2	0.1
All other currencies	1.7	2.6	2.6	2.6	2.3	2.0	1.7	1.3	1.0	1.1

THAILAND

(US$ million, unless otherwise indicated)

	1970	1980	1988	1989	1990	1991	1992	1993	1994	1995
7. DEBT RESTRUCTURINGS										
Total amount rescheduled	0	0	0	0	0	0	0	0	0	0
Debt stock rescheduled	0	0	0	0	0	0	0	0	0	0
Principal rescheduled	0	0	0	0	0	0	0	0	0	0
Official	0	0	0	0	0	0	0	0	0	0
Private	0	0	0	0	0	0	0	0	0	0
Interest rescheduled	0	0	0	0	0	0	0	0	0	0
Official	0	0	0	0	0	0	0	0	0	0
Private	0	0	0	0	0	0	0	0	0	0
Debt forgiven	..	..	2	0	0	7	0	0	0	0
Memo: interest forgiven	..	..	0	0	0	0	0	0	0	0
Debt stock reduction	0	0	0	0	0	0	0	0	0	0
of which debt buyback	0	0	0	0	0	0	0	0	0	0
8. DEBT STOCK-FLOW RECONCILIATION										
Total change in debt stocks	..	..	..	1,779	4,592	9,617	4,107	885	5,398	8,693
Net flows on debt	..	..	..	2,627	3,534	7,260	4,132	1,138	4,942	9,707
Net change in interest arrears	..	..	..	0	0	0	0	0	0	0
Interest capitalized	..	..	..	0	0	0	0	0	0	0
Debt forgiveness or reduction	..	..	..	0	0	-7	0	0	0	0
Cross-currency valuation	..	..	..	-1,120	1,146	901	-402	1,785	2,496	-447
Residual	..	..	..	271	-88	1,463	377	-2,038	-2,040	-567
9. AVERAGE TERMS OF NEW COMMITMENTS										
ALL CREDITORS										
Interest (%)	6.8	9.5	5.5	7.4	4.8	5.0	6.6	4.7	4.7	5.5
Maturity (years)	19.2	16.8	16.9	12.9	22.1	19.0	18.9	19.7	16.8	15.1
Grace period (years)	4.3	5.3	5.8	4.8	7.2	4.7	5.7	5.3	4.9	5.5
Grant element (%)	19.6	6.6	28.8	13.1	38.2	33.4	19.7	35.4	31.6	27.9
Official creditors										
Interest (%)	6.8	7.1	4.4	6.1	4.4	3.5	6.0	4.1	4.2	3.8
Maturity (years)	19.6	21.4	25.0	23.3	25.6	24.7	20.5	22.4	20.2	23.5
Grace period (years)	4.4	5.9	7.9	6.4	7.8	6.8	5.6	5.8	5.2	6.6
Grant element (%)	19.7	20.6	42.9	28.1	43.3	48.0	27.0	41.6	38.1	45.5
Private creditors										
Interest (%)	6.0	13.8	6.6	7.9	5.8	7.1	7.1	6.5	5.5	6.7
Maturity (years)	11.5	8.7	8.3	8.9	14.7	10.7	17.5	11.1	12.0	9.0
Grace period (years)	3.0	4.1	3.7	4.1	5.9	1.5	5.9	3.7	4.6	4.8
Grant element (%)	18.6	-18.3	13.7	7.3	27.5	12.1	13.2	15.6	22.3	15.0
Memorandum items										
Commitments	106	1,877	2,163	1,682	1,755	1,256	3,210	3,702	3,746	2,277
Official creditors	100	1,199	1,117	467	1,196	745	1,499	2,815	2,194	963
Private creditors	6	678	1,046	1,214	560	511	1,711	887	1,551	1,314

10. CONTRACTUAL OBLIGATIONS ON OUTSTANDING LONG-TERM DEBT

	1996	1997	1998	1999	2000	2001	2002	2003	2004	2005
TOTAL										
Disbursements	2,527	1,980	1,149	674	341	180	91	18	8	0
Principal	4,231	4,312	4,357	4,432	3,613	3,481	2,721	3,784	2,792	2,677
Interest	2,145	2,015	1,783	1,548	1,300	1,099	917	782	594	471
Official creditors										
Disbursements	1,796	1,565	1,000	610	340	180	91	18	8	0
Principal	684	726	853	837	911	924	956	959	912	882
Interest	549	567	566	546	518	483	446	405	364	325
Bilateral creditors										
Disbursements	1,501	1,276	768	432	220	105	44	0	0	0
Principal	382	395	474	508	614	667	707	705	683	664
Interest	315	338	347	343	330	310	287	262	237	213
Multilateral creditors										
Disbursements	295	289	232	178	119	75	47	18	8	0
Principal	302	331	378	329	297	257	250	254	229	218
Interest	233	228	219	204	188	173	159	143	127	112
Private creditors										
Disbursements	731	415	150	65	1	0	0	0	0	0
Principal	3,547	3,587	3,505	3,595	2,702	2,557	1,765	2,825	1,881	1,795
Interest	1,597	1,448	1,217	1,002	782	616	470	377	230	146
Commercial banks										
Disbursements	502	266	73	33	1	0	0	0	0	0
Principal	255	260	364	573	495	360	351	323	339	344
Interest	227	230	219	198	156	126	103	81	61	36
Other private										
Disbursements	230	149	76	32	0	0	0	0	0	0
Principal	3,292	3,326	3,141	3,022	2,207	2,196	1,414	2,502	1,542	1,451
Interest	1,370	1,218	998	804	626	490	368	297	169	110

TOGO

(US$ million, unless otherwise indicated)

	1970	1980	1988	1989	1990	1991	1992	1993	1994	1995
1. SUMMARY DEBT DATA										
TOTAL DEBT STOCKS (EDT)	..	**1,052**	**1,227**	**1,184**	**1,286**	**1,354**	**1,352**	**1,291**	**1,458**	**1,486**
Long-term debt (LDOD)	**40**	**899**	**1,063**	**945**	**1,086**	**1,142**	**1,134**	**1,125**	**1,231**	**1,297**
Public and publicly guaranteed	40	899	1,063	945	1,086	1,142	1,134	1,125	1,231	1,297
Private nonguaranteed	0	0	0	0	0	0	0	0	0	0
Use of IMF credit	**0**	**33**	**78**	**75**	**87**	**79**	**77**	**69**	**82**	**105**
Short-term debt	..	**120**	**86**	**164**	**113**	**133**	**141**	**97**	**145**	**85**
of which interest arrears on LDOD	..	15	0	0	1	16	32	51	85	27
Official creditors	..	7	0	0	1	11	24	41	73	13
Private creditors	..	9	0	0	0	5	8	10	12	14
Memo: principal arrears on LDOD	..	34	4	2	3	5	21	54	112	68
Official creditors	..	14	1	0	2	4	11	33	78	21
Private creditors	..	19	3	1	1	1	10	21	34	47
Memo: export credits	..	..	384	339	351	339	341	274	283	285
TOTAL DEBT FLOWS										
Disbursements	**5**	**122**	**137**	**84**	**104**	**67**	**55**	**17**	**55**	**59**
Long-term debt	5	100	113	61	83	67	44	17	40	26
IMF purchases	0	22	24	23	21	0	11	0	16	33
Principal repayments	**2**	**19**	**52**	**49**	**43**	**28**	**20**	**15**	**14**	**19**
Long-term debt	2	19	25	25	27	20	10	6	7	8
IMF repurchases	0	0	27	24	16	8	10	8	7	11
Net flows on debt	**3**	**104**	**95**	**113**	**10**	**44**	**27**	**-60**	**55**	**38**
of which short-term debt	..	..	10	78	-51	5	-8	-62	13	-2
Interest payments (INT)	..	**34**	**79**	**43**	**43**	**27**	**17**	**13**	**10**	**12**
Long-term debt	1	19	69	33	33	20	11	8	6	8
IMF charges	0	0	5	5	4	3	2	1	0	1
Short-term debt	..	14	6	6	6	5	5	4	4	3
Net transfers on debt	..	**70**	**16**	**70**	**-34**	**17**	**10**	**-73**	**45**	**26**
Total debt service paid (TDS)	..	**52**	**132**	**91**	**86**	**55**	**37**	**28**	**24**	**30**
Long-term debt	2	38	94	57	60	39	20	14	13	15
IMF repurchases and charges	0	0	32	28	20	11	12	10	7	12
Short-term debt (interest only)	..	14	6	6	6	5	5	4	4	3
2. AGGREGATE NET RESOURCE FLOWS AND NET TRANSFERS (LONG-TERM)										
NET RESOURCE FLOWS	**11**	**139**	**158**	**116**	**176**	**128**	**141**	**66**	**106**	**138**
Net flow of long-term debt (ex. IMF)	3	82	88	36	56	47	34	10	33	18
Foreign direct investment (net)	1	42	13	7	0	0	0	0	0	0
Portfolio equity flows	0	0	0	0	0	0	0	0	0	0
Grants (excluding technical coop.)	7	15	57	72	120	81	107	55	73	120
Memo: technical coop. grants	7	29	51	47	61	58	54	38	23	32
NET TRANSFERS	**5**	**119**	**83**	**74**	**130**	**96**	**117**	**49**	**94**	**125**
Interest on long-term debt	1	19	69	33	33	20	11	8	6	8
Profit remittances on FDI	6	0	7	10	12	12	14	9	6	5
3. MAJOR ECONOMIC AGGREGATES										
Gross national product (GNP)	248	1,097	1,331	1,314	1,605	1,573	1,611	1,244	912	1,227
Exports of goods & services (XGS)	..	580	583	587	723	690	452	233	251	320
of which workers remittances	..	10	21	23	27	29	16	9	10	12
Imports of goods & services (MGS)	..	752	775	730	912	835	680	442	341	452
International reserves (RES)	35	85	237	290	358	369	277	161	99	135
Current account balance	..	-95	-87	-51	-100	-70	-156	-178	-69	-141
4. DEBT INDICATORS										
EDT / XGS (%)	..	181.3	210.6	201.8	178.0	196.4	299.1	555.3	581.6	464.5
EDT / GNP (%)	..	95.9	92.2	90.2	80.1	86.1	83.9	103.8	159.9	121.2
TDS / XGS (%)	..	9.0	22.6	15.6	11.9	8.0	8.2	11.9	9.5	9.5
INT / XGS (%)	..	5.8	13.6	7.3	6.0	3.9	3.8	5.5	4.0	3.6
INT / GNP (%)	..	3.1	6.0	3.3	2.7	1.7	1.1	1.0	1.1	1.0
RES / EDT (%)	..	8.1	19.3	24.5	27.8	27.3	20.5	12.5	6.8	9.1
RES / MGS (months)	..	1.4	3.7	4.8	4.7	5.3	4.9	4.4	3.5	3.6
Short-term / EDT (%)	..	11.4	7.0	13.8	8.8	9.8	10.4	7.5	9.9	5.7
Concessional / EDT (%)	..	24.2	47.8	46.9	55.5	57.7	59.9	63.5	62.2	63.5
Multilateral / EDT (%)	..	11.3	38.3	42.2	43.9	45.2	45.8	48.4	47.0	48.4

TOGO

(US$ million, unless otherwise indicated)

	1970	1980	1988	1989	1990	1991	1992	1993	1994	1995
5. LONG-TERM DEBT										
DEBT OUTSTANDING (LDOD)	**40**	**899**	**1,063**	**945**	**1,086**	**1,142**	**1,134**	**1,125**	**1,231**	**1,297**
Public and publicly guaranteed	**40**	**899**	**1,063**	**945**	**1,086**	**1,142**	**1,134**	**1,125**	**1,231**	**1,297**
Official creditors	32	484	1,011	895	1,034	1,091	1,084	1,076	1,180	1,244
Multilateral	2	119	470	500	565	611	618	626	685	719
Concessional	2	99	415	455	526	582	594	604	667	702
Bilateral	30	365	541	395	470	480	465	450	495	524
Concessional	30	155	171	101	188	200	215	215	238	241
Private creditors	8	415	52	50	52	52	51	50	51	53
Bonds	0	0	0	0	0	0	0	0	0	0
Commercial banks	0	96	49	49	51	50	49	48	50	52
Other private	8	319	3	1	1	1	1	1	1	1
Private nonguaranteed	**0**	**0**	**0**	**0**	**0**	**0**	**0**	**0**	**0**	**0**
Bonds	0	0	0	0	0	0	0	0	0	0
Commercial banks	0	0	0	0	0	0	0	0	0	0
Memo:										
IBRD	0	4	18	12	5	0	0	0	0	0
IDA	2	43	306	340	393	444	460	469	513	541
DISBURSEMENTS	**5**	**100**	**113**	**61**	**83**	**67**	**44**	**17**	**40**	**26**
Public and publicly guaranteed	**5**	**100**	**113**	**61**	**83**	**67**	**44**	**17**	**40**	**26**
Official creditors	4	50	113	61	83	67	44	17	40	26
Multilateral	1	38	64	52	45	58	38	16	39	26
Concessional	1	33	56	50	44	58	38	16	39	26
Bilateral	3	12	49	9	38	9	6	1	1	0
Concessional	3	5	49	9	38	9	6	1	1	0
Private creditors	0	50	0	0	0	0	0	0	0	0
Bonds	0	0	0	0	0	0	0	0	0	0
Commercial banks	0	2	0	0	0	0	0	0	0	0
Other private	0	47	0	0	0	0	0	0	0	0
Private nonguaranteed	**0**	**0**	**0**	**0**	**0**	**0**	**0**	**0**	**0**	**0**
Bonds	0	0	0	0	0	0	0	0	0	0
Commercial banks	0	0	0	0	0	0	0	0	0	0
Memo:										
IBRD	0	0	0	0	0	0	0	0	0	0
IDA	1	13	49	39	31	48	32	9	28	20
PRINCIPAL REPAYMENTS	**2**	**19**	**25**	**25**	**27**	**20**	**10**	**6**	**7**	**8**
Public and publicly guaranteed	**2**	**19**	**25**	**25**	**27**	**20**	**10**	**6**	**7**	**8**
Official creditors	1	10	23	23	27	20	10	6	7	8
Multilateral	0	0	13	18	17	15	8	6	7	7
Concessional	0	0	4	6	6	5	4	4	4	6
Bilateral	1	9	10	5	10	4	2	0	0	1
Concessional	1	1	4	3	1	4	2	0	0	1
Private creditors	1	9	2	2	0	0	0	0	0	0
Bonds	0	0	0	0	0	0	0	0	0	0
Commercial banks	0	4	2	0	0	0	0	0	0	0
Other private	1	4	0	2	0	0	0	0	0	0
Private nonguaranteed	**0**	**0**	**0**	**0**	**0**	**0**	**0**	**0**	**0**	**0**
Bonds	0	0	0	0	0	0	0	0	0	0
Commercial banks	0	0	0	0	0	0	0	0	0	0
Memo:										
IBRD	0	0	7	7	8	6	0	0	0	0
IDA	0	0	1	1	1	1	1	2	3	3
NET FLOWS ON DEBT	**3**	**82**	**88**	**36**	**56**	**47**	**34**	**10**	**33**	**18**
Public and publicly guaranteed	**3**	**82**	**88**	**36**	**56**	**47**	**34**	**10**	**33**	**18**
Official creditors	3	41	90	38	56	47	34	10	33	18
Multilateral	1	38	52	34	28	42	30	9	32	19
Concessional	1	33	53	44	38	52	34	12	35	19
Bilateral	2	3	38	4	28	5	4	1	1	-1
Concessional	2	4	44	6	37	6	4	1	1	-1
Private creditors	-1	41	-2	-2	0	0	0	0	0	0
Bonds	0	0	0	0	0	0	0	0	0	0
Commercial banks	0	-2	-2	0	0	0	0	0	0	0
Other private	-1	43	0	-2	0	0	0	0	0	0
Private nonguaranteed	**0**	**0**	**0**	**0**	**0**	**0**	**0**	**0**	**0**	**0**
Bonds	0	0	0	0	0	0	0	0	0	0
Commercial banks	0	0	0	0	0	0	0	0	0	0
Memo:										
IBRD	0	0	-7	-7	-8	-6	0	0	0	0
IDA	1	13	49	38	30	47	31	7	25	17

TOGO

(US$ million, unless otherwise indicated)

	1970	1980	1988	1989	1990	1991	1992	1993	1994	1995
INTEREST PAYMENTS (LINT)	**1**	**19**	**69**	**33**	**33**	**20**	**11**	**8**	**6**	**8**
Public and publicly guaranteed	**1**	**19**	**69**	**33**	**33**	**20**	**11**	**8**	**6**	**8**
Official creditors	1	12	62	27	28	20	11	8	6	8
Multilateral	0	2	11	9	8	7	7	7	6	5
Concessional	0	1	5	4	4	5	5	5	5	4
Bilateral	1	9	52	19	21	12	4	1	0	3
Concessional	1	0	5	2	4	4	2	1	0	1
Private creditors	0	8	6	5	5	0	0	0	0	0
Bonds	0	0	0	0	0	0	0	0	0	0
Commercial banks	0	8	6	5	5	0	0	0	0	0
Other private	0	0	0	0	0	0	0	0	0	0
Private nonguaranteed	**0**	**0**	**0**	**0**	**0**	**0**	**0**	**0**	**0**	**0**
Bonds	0	0	0	0	0	0	0	0	0	0
Commercial banks	0	0	0	0	0	0	0	0	0	0
Memo:										
IBRD	0	0	2	1	1	0	0	0	0	0
IDA	0	0	3	2	3	3	3	4	4	4
NET TRANSFERS ON DEBT	**2**	**62**	**19**	**4**	**22**	**28**	**24**	**3**	**27**	**10**
Public and publicly guaranteed	**2**	**62**	**19**	**4**	**22**	**28**	**24**	**3**	**27**	**10**
Official creditors	3	29	27	11	28	28	24	3	27	10
Multilateral	1	36	41	25	20	35	23	3	26	14
Concessional	1	32	48	40	34	48	29	7	30	15
Bilateral	2	-7	-14	-14	7	-7	0	0	1	-4
Concessional	2	3	39	4	33	2	2	0	1	-2
Private creditors	-1	33	-8	-7	-5	0	0	0	0	0
Bonds	0	0	0	0	0	0	0	0	0	0
Commercial banks	0	-10	-8	-5	-5	0	0	0	0	0
Other private	-1	43	0	-2	0	0	0	0	0	0
Private nonguaranteed	**0**	**0**	**0**	**0**	**0**	**0**	**0**	**0**	**0**	**0**
Bonds	0	0	0	0	0	0	0	0	0	0
Commercial banks	0	0	0	0	0	0	0	0	0	0
Memo:										
IBRD	0	0	-9	-8	-9	-6	0	0	0	0
IDA	1	12	46	36	28	44	29	3	21	14
DEBT SERVICE (LTDS)	**2**	**38**	**94**	**57**	**60**	**39**	**20**	**14**	**13**	**15**
Public and publicly guaranteed	**2**	**38**	**94**	**57**	**60**	**39**	**20**	**14**	**13**	**15**
Official creditors	2	21	86	50	55	39	20	14	13	15
Multilateral	0	3	24	27	25	23	15	13	13	12
Concessional	0	1	9	10	10	10	9	9	9	11
Bilateral	2	19	62	23	31	17	5	1	0	4
Concessional	2	2	9	5	5	7	4	1	0	2
Private creditors	1	16	8	7	5	0	0	0	0	0
Bonds	0	0	0	0	0	0	0	0	0	0
Commercial banks	0	12	8	5	5	0	0	0	0	0
Other private	1	5	0	2	0	0	0	0	0	0
Private nonguaranteed	**0**	**0**	**0**	**0**	**0**	**0**	**0**	**0**	**0**	**0**
Bonds	0	0	0	0	0	0	0	0	0	0
Commercial banks	0	0	0	0	0	0	0	0	0	0
Memo:										
IBRD	0	0	9	8	9	6	0	0	0	0
IDA	0	0	3	3	4	4	4	6	7	6
UNDISBURSED DEBT	**7**	**156**	**220**	**249**	**277**	**213**	**208**	**190**	**138**	**156**
Official creditors	6	153	220	249	277	213	208	190	138	156
Private creditors	1	3	0	0	0	0	0	0	0	0
Memorandum items										
Concessional LDOD	31	255	586	556	714	782	810	820	906	944
Variable rate LDOD	0	108	37	37	37	37	37	37	37	135
Public sector LDOD	36	898	1,063	945	1,086	1,142	1,134	1,125	1,231	1,297
Private sector LDOD	3	1	0	0	0	0	0	0	0	0

6. CURRENCY COMPOSITION OF LONG-TERM DEBT (PERCENT)

	1970	1980	1988	1989	1990	1991	1992	1993	1994	1995
Deutsche mark	62.4	17.5	2.0	2.2	1.9	1.9	1.9	1.9	1.9	1.9
French franc	7.8	24.1	25.0	12.4	12.8	13.4	13.2	12.8	13.0	9.0
Japanese yen	0.0	0.0	1.9	1.8	3.0	3.1	3.1	3.5	3.6	3.3
Pound sterling	0.0	5.8	1.9	1.8	1.9	1.9	1.7	1.7	1.6	1.7
Swiss franc	0.0	10.2	8.7	9.4	10.6	9.3	9.1	9.3	9.5	11.9
U.S.dollars	15.3	19.8	37.4	46.1	44.5	46.5	47.6	48.1	47.4	47.5
Multiple currency	0.0	2.3	6.6	7.6	7.5	6.8	6.9	6.9	7.3	7.4
Special drawing rights	0.0	0.0	0.4	0.7	1.0	0.9	0.9	1.1	1.0	1.0
All other currencies	14.6	20.2	16.0	18.0	16.7	16.2	15.5	14.8	14.7	16.4

TOGO

(US$ million, unless otherwise indicated)

	1970	1980	1988	1989	1990	1991	1992	1993	1994	1995
7. DEBT RESTRUCTURINGS										
Total amount rescheduled	0	..	171	57	81	31	40	12	0	141
Debt stock rescheduled	0	..	0	0	0	0	0	0	0	1
Principal rescheduled	0	..	168	48	66	21	26	11	0	63
Official	0	..	113	48	66	20	26	11	0	63
Private	0	..	55	0	0	0	0	0	0	0
Interest rescheduled	0	..	3	9	14	6	10	1	0	63
Official	0	..	2	9	14	5	10	1	0	63
Private	0	..	0	0	0	0	0	0	0	0
Debt forgiven	..	..	4	153	18	2	3	1	0	85
Memo: interest forgiven	..	..	0	16	0	1	3	0	0	22
Debt stock reduction	0	..	0	0	0	0	0	0	0	0
of which debt buyback	0	..	0	0	0	0	0	0	0	0
8. DEBT STOCK-FLOW RECONCILIATION										
Total change in debt stocks	..	..	..	-43	102	68	-3	-60	166	29
Net flows on debt	..	..	..	113	10	44	27	-60	55	38
Net change in interest arrears	..	..	..	0	1	15	16	19	34	-58
Interest capitalized	..	..	..	9	14	6	10	1	0	63
Debt forgiveness or reduction	..	..	..	-153	-18	-2	-3	-1	0	-85
Cross-currency valuation	..	..	..	-1	71	-6	-34	-18	56	48
Residual	..	..	..	-11	25	13	-19	-1	21	23
9. AVERAGE TERMS OF NEW COMMITMENTS										
ALL CREDITORS										
Interest (%)	4.6	4.0	1.9	1.5	0.8	0.7	0.8	0.0	0.0	0.7
Maturity (years)	16.8	24.5	33.2	35.5	41.4	39.7	49.0	0.0	0.0	39.3
Grace period (years)	4.4	7.4	8.4	8.7	11.7	10.2	27.1	0.0	0.0	9.8
Grant element (%)	32.8	46.5	66.1	67.8	81.0	80.5	89.1	0.0	0.0	80.0
Official creditors										
Interest (%)	3.5	3.2	1.9	1.5	0.8	0.7	0.8	0.0	0.0	0.7
Maturity (years)	21.3	26.7	33.2	35.5	41.4	39.7	49.0	0.0	0.0	39.3
Grace period (years)	5.4	8.0	8.4	8.7	11.7	10.2	27.1	0.0	0.0	9.8
Grant element (%)	42.6	52.6	66.1	67.8	81.0	80.5	89.1	0.0	0.0	80.0
Private creditors										
Interest (%)	7.6	10.1	0.0	0.0	0.0	0.0	0.0	0.0	0.0	0.0
Maturity (years)	4.2	6.9	0.0	0.0	0.0	0.0	0.0	0.0	0.0	0.0
Grace period (years)	1.6	2.7	0.0	0.0	0.0	0.0	0.0	0.0	0.0	0.0
Grant element (%)	5.5	-1.3	0.0	0.0	0.0	0.0	0.0	0.0	0.0	0.0
Memorandum items										
Commitments	3	97	164	104	105	14	54	0	0	63
Official creditors	2	86	164	104	105	14	54	0	0	63
Private creditors	1	11	0	0	0	0	0	0	0	0

10. CONTRACTUAL OBLIGATIONS ON OUTSTANDING LONG-TERM DEBT

	1996	1997	1998	1999	2000	2001	2002	2003	2004	2005
TOTAL										
Disbursements	45	38	24	16	10	3	2	0	0	0
Principal	26	26	36	47	49	51	51	50	48	36
Interest	22	30	39	37	35	33	31	28	26	24
Official creditors										
Disbursements	45	38	24	16	10	3	2	0	0	0
Principal	20	26	36	47	49	51	51	50	48	36
Interest	22	30	39	37	35	33	31	28	26	24
Bilateral creditors										
Disbursements	0	0	0	0	0	0	0	0	0	0
Principal	7	14	22	32	34	34	34	33	29	16
Interest	15	23	32	30	29	26	24	22	20	19
Multilateral creditors										
Disbursements	45	38	24	16	10	3	2	0	0	0
Principal	12	12	14	15	16	17	17	17	19	20
Interest	7	7	7	7	7	6	6	6	6	5
Private creditors										
Disbursements	0	0	0	0	0	0	0	0	0	0
Principal	6	0	0	0	0	0	0	0	0	0
Interest	0	0	0	0	0	0	0	0	0	0
Commercial banks										
Disbursements	0	0	0	0	0	0	0	0	0	0
Principal	6	0	0	0	0	0	0	0	0	0
Interest	0	0	0	0	0	0	0	0	0	0
Other private										
Disbursements	0	0	0	0	0	0	0	0	0	0
Principal	0	0	0	0	0	0	0	0	0	0
Interest	0	0	0	0	0	0	0	0	0	0

TONGA

(US$ million, unless otherwise indicated)

	1970	1980	1988	1989	1990	1991	1992	1993	1994	1995
1. SUMMARY DEBT DATA										
TOTAL DEBT STOCKS (EDT)	..	..	**37.6**	**39.1**	**53.7**	**45.0**	**43.5**	**44.2**	**64.4**	**70.1**
Long-term debt (LDOD)	..	..	**37.0**	**38.1**	**44.5**	**44.2**	**42.6**	**43.7**	**63.4**	**68.7**
Public and publicly guaranteed	..	..	37.0	38.1	44.5	44.2	42.6	43.7	63.4	68.7
Private nonguaranteed	0.0	0.0	0.0	0.0	0.0	0.0	0.0	0.0	0.0	0.0
Use of IMF credit	**0.0**	**0.0**	**0.0**	**0.0**	**0.0**	**0.0**	**0.0**	**0.0**	**0.0**	**0.0**
Short-term debt	..	..	**0.6**	**1.1**	**9.2**	**0.8**	**0.8**	**0.6**	**1.0**	**1.3**
of which interest arrears on LDOD	..	..	0.0	0.0	0.0	0.0	0.0	0.0	0.0	0.0
Official creditors	..	..	0.0	0.0	0.0	0.0	0.0	0.0	0.0	0.0
Private creditors	..	..	0.0	0.0	0.0	0.0	0.0	0.0	0.0	0.0
Memo: principal arrears on LDOD	..	..	0.0	0.0	0.0	0.0	0.0	0.0	0.0	0.0
Official creditors	..	..	0.0	0.0	0.0	0.0	0.0	0.0	0.0	0.0
Private creditors	..	..	0.0	0.0	0.0	0.0	0.0	0.0	0.0	0.0
Memo: export credits	..	..	2.0	2.0	1.0	1.0	1.0	1.0	8.0	8.0
TOTAL DEBT FLOWS										
Disbursements	..	..	**4.8**	**1.6**	**3.3**	**2.0**	**2.2**	**3.3**	**7.7**	**6.2**
Long-term debt	..	..	4.8	1.6	3.3	2.0	2.2	3.3	7.7	6.2
IMF purchases	0.0	0.0	0.0	0.0	0.0	0.0	0.0	0.0	0.0	0.0
Principal repayments	..	..	**0.8**	**0.8**	**1.0**	**1.1**	**1.0**	**1.2**	**2.1**	**2.4**
Long-term debt	..	..	0.8	0.8	1.0	1.1	1.0	1.2	2.1	2.4
IMF repurchases	0.0	0.0	0.0	0.0	0.0	0.0	0.0	0.0	0.0	0.0
Net flows on debt	..	..	**4.1**	**1.3**	**10.4**	**-7.6**	**1.3**	**1.9**	**6.0**	**4.1**
of which short-term debt	..	..	0.1	0.5	8.2	-8.5	0.1	-0.3	0.4	0.3
Interest payments (INT)	..	..	**0.5**	**0.5**	**0.9**	**0.5**	**0.6**	**0.6**	**0.6**	**0.8**
Long-term debt	..	..	0.4	0.5	0.5	0.5	0.5	0.5	0.6	0.7
IMF charges	0.0	0.0	0.0	0.0	0.0	0.0	0.0	0.0	0.0	0.0
Short-term debt	..	..	0.1	0.1	0.4	0.1	0.0	0.1	0.1	0.1
Net transfers on debt	..	..	**3.6**	**0.8**	**9.5**	**-8.2**	**0.7**	**1.3**	**5.3**	**3.3**
Total debt service paid (TDS)	..	..	**1.3**	**1.3**	**1.9**	**1.7**	**1.6**	**1.7**	**2.7**	**3.2**
Long-term debt	..	..	1.2	1.2	1.5	1.6	1.6	1.7	2.7	3.1
IMF repurchases and charges	0.0	0.0	0.0	0.0	0.0	0.0	0.0	0.0	0.0	0.0
Short-term debt (interest only)	..	..	0.1	0.1	0.4	0.1	0.0	0.1	0.1	0.1
2. AGGREGATE NET RESOURCE FLOWS AND NET TRANSFERS (LONG-TERM)										
NET RESOURCE FLOWS	..	..	**13.5**	**13.1**	**19.1**	**7.9**	**11.2**	**19.3**	**22.8**	**24.1**
Net flow of long-term debt (ex. IMF)	0.0	0.0	4.0	0.8	2.2	0.9	1.2	2.2	5.6	3.8
Foreign direct investment (net)	0.0	0.0	0.1	0.1	0.0	0.0	1.0	2.0	2.0	2.0
Portfolio equity flows	..	..	0.0	0.0	0.0	0.0	0.0	0.0	0.0	0.0
Grants (excluding technical coop.)	1.0	6.9	9.4	12.2	16.9	7.0	9.0	15.1	15.2	18.3
Memo: technical coop. grants	0.3	4.9	7.5	11.2	10.9	10.7	13.8	14.4	14.0	16.3
NET TRANSFERS	..	..	**13.1**	**12.0**	**18.6**	**7.4**	**10.2**	**18.7**	**22.2**	**23.4**
Interest on long-term debt	..	..	0.4	0.5	0.5	0.5	0.5	0.5	0.6	0.7
Profit remittances on FDI	0.0	0.2	0.0	0.7	0.0	0.0	0.5	0.0	0.0	0.0
3. MAJOR ECONOMIC AGGREGATES										
Gross national product (GNP)	..	..	97.1	114.4	117.3	139.2	143.5	145.2	159.1	171.9
Exports of goods & services (XGS)	..	19.0	46.5	54.4	66.5	55.2	53.3	56.8	59.5	..
of which workers remittances	..	0.0	15.7	14.0	23.0	17.8	20.1	18.8	19.0	..
Imports of goods & services (MGS)	..	39.6	75.6	71.9	75.0	73.0	74.8	80.0	95.3	..
International reserves (RES)	..	13.8	30.5	24.9	31.3	32.3	31.8	37.1	35.5	28.7
Current account balance	..	-6.8	-12.7	7.4	5.8	-0.1	-0.5	-6.0	-20.4	..
4. DEBT INDICATORS										
EDT / XGS (%)	..	..	80.8	71.9	80.7	81.5	81.6	77.9	108.2	..
EDT / GNP (%)	..	..	38.7	34.2	45.8	32.3	30.3	30.5	40.5	40.8
TDS / XGS (%)	..	..	2.8	2.4	2.9	3.0	3.0	3.0	4.6	..
INT / XGS (%)	..	..	1.0	1.0	1.3	1.0	1.1	1.0	1.1	..
INT / GNP (%)	..	..	0.5	0.5	0.8	0.4	0.4	0.4	0.4	0.3
RES / EDT (%)	..	..	81.2	63.6	58.3	71.8	73.1	83.9	55.1	41.[illegible]
RES / MGS (months)	..	4.2	4.8	4.2	5.0	5.3	5.1	5.6	4.5	..
Short-term / EDT (%)	..	..	1.6	2.7	17.2	1.7	2.0	1.3	1.6	1.9
Concessional / EDT (%)	..	..	94.7	94.4	81.0	96.6	96.8	97.8	82.3	83.[illegible]
Multilateral / EDT (%)	..	..	46.0	47.2	42.4	52.3	55.4	60.8	56.1	59.[illegible]

TONGA

(US$ million, unless otherwise indicated)

	1970	1980	1988	1989	1990	1991	1992	1993	1994	1995
5. LONG-TERM DEBT										
DEBT OUTSTANDING (LDOD)	..	..	**37.0**	**38.1**	**44.5**	**44.2**	**42.6**	**43.7**	**63.4**	**68.7**
Public and publicly guaranteed	..	..	**37.0**	**38.1**	**44.5**	**44.2**	**42.6**	**43.7**	**63.4**	**68.7**
Official creditors	..	..	37.0	38.1	44.5	44.2	42.6	43.7	53.3	58.5
Multilateral	..	..	17.3	18.5	22.7	23.5	24.1	26.9	36.1	41.7
Concessional	..	..	17.3	18.5	22.7	23.5	24.1	26.9	36.1	41.7
Bilateral	..	..	19.7	19.6	21.7	20.7	18.5	16.8	17.2	16.8
Concessional	..	..	18.3	18.5	20.8	19.9	18.0	16.4	16.9	16.8
Private creditors	..	..	0.0	0.0	0.0	0.0	0.0	0.0	10.1	10.2
Bonds	..	..	0.0	0.0	0.0	0.0	0.0	0.0	0.0	0.0
Commercial banks	..	..	0.0	0.0	0.0	0.0	0.0	0.0	0.0	0.0
Other private	..	..	0.0	0.0	0.0	0.0	0.0	0.0	10.1	10.2
Private nonguaranteed	**0.0**	**0.0**	**0.0**	**0.0**	**0.0**	**0.0**	**0.0**	**0.0**	**0.0**	**0.0**
Bonds	..	..	0.0	0.0	0.0	0.0	0.0	0.0	0.0	0.0
Commercial banks	..	..	0.0	0.0	0.0	0.0	0.0	0.0	0.0	0.0
Memo:										
IBRD	0.0	0.0	0.0	0.0	0.0	0.0	0.0	0.0	0.0	0.0
IDA	0.0	0.0	1.5	1.5	2.6	3.2	3.2	3.4	4.4	4.8
DISBURSEMENTS	..	..	**4.8**	**1.6**	**3.3**	**2.0**	**2.2**	**3.3**	**7.7**	**6.2**
Public and publicly guaranteed	..	..	**4.8**	**1.6**	**3.3**	**2.0**	**2.2**	**3.3**	**7.7**	**6.2**
Official creditors	..	..	4.8	1.6	3.3	2.0	2.2	3.3	7.7	6.2
Multilateral	..	..	4.0	1.6	3.3	2.0	2.2	3.3	7.7	6.2
Concessional	..	..	4.0	1.6	3.3	2.0	2.2	3.3	7.7	6.2
Bilateral	..	..	0.8	0.0	0.0	0.0	0.0	0.0	0.0	0.0
Concessional	..	..	0.0	0.0	0.0	0.0	0.0	0.0	0.0	0.0
Private creditors	..	..	0.0	0.0	0.0	0.0	0.0	0.0	0.0	0.0
Bonds	..	..	0.0	0.0	0.0	0.0	0.0	0.0	0.0	0.0
Commercial banks	..	..	0.0	0.0	0.0	0.0	0.0	0.0	0.0	0.0
Other private	..	..	0.0	0.0	0.0	0.0	0.0	0.0	0.0	0.0
Private nonguaranteed	**0.0**	**0.0**	**0.0**	**0.0**	**0.0**	**0.0**	**0.0**	**0.0**	**0.0**	**0.0**
Bonds	..	..	0.0	0.0	0.0	0.0	0.0	0.0	0.0	0.0
Commercial banks	..	..	0.0	0.0	0.0	0.0	0.0	0.0	0.0	0.0
Memo:										
IBRD	0.0	0.0	0.0	0.0	0.0	0.0	0.0	0.0	0.0	0.0
IDA	0.0	0.0	1.5	0.0	1.0	0.6	0.1	0.2	0.8	0.2
PRINCIPAL REPAYMENTS	..	..	**0.8**	**0.8**	**1.0**	**1.1**	**1.0**	**1.2**	**2.1**	**2.4**
Public and publicly guaranteed	..	..	**0.8**	**0.8**	**1.0**	**1.1**	**1.0**	**1.2**	**2.1**	**2.4**
Official creditors	..	..	0.8	0.8	1.0	1.1	1.0	1.2	2.1	2.4
Multilateral	..	..	0.3	0.4	0.5	0.5	0.4	0.5	0.7	0.8
Concessional	..	..	0.3	0.4	0.5	0.5	0.4	0.5	0.7	0.8
Bilateral	..	..	0.5	0.4	0.5	0.6	0.6	0.7	1.4	1.7
Concessional	..	..	0.3	0.2	0.4	0.5	0.5	0.5	1.2	1.4
Private creditors	..	..	0.0	0.0	0.0	0.0	0.0	0.0	0.0	0.0
Bonds	..	..	0.0	0.0	0.0	0.0	0.0	0.0	0.0	0.0
Commercial banks	..	..	0.0	0.0	0.0	0.0	0.0	0.0	0.0	0.0
Other private	..	..	0.0	0.0	0.0	0.0	0.0	0.0	0.0	0.0
Private nonguaranteed	**0.0**	**0.0**	**0.0**	**0.0**	**0.0**	**0.0**	**0.0**	**0.0**	**0.0**	**0.0**
Bonds	..	..	0.0	0.0	0.0	0.0	0.0	0.0	0.0	0.0
Commercial banks	..	..	0.0	0.0	0.0	0.0	0.0	0.0	0.0	0.0
Memo:										
IBRD	0.0	0.0	0.0	0.0	0.0	0.0	0.0	0.0	0.0	0.0
IDA	0.0	0.0	0.0	0.0	0.0	0.0	0.0	0.0	0.0	0.0
NET FLOWS ON DEBT	..	..	**4.0**	**0.8**	**2.2**	**0.9**	**1.2**	**2.2**	**5.6**	**3.8**
Public and publicly guaranteed	..	..	**4.0**	**0.8**	**2.2**	**0.9**	**1.2**	**2.2**	**5.6**	**3.8**
Official creditors	..	..	4.0	0.8	2.2	0.9	1.2	2.2	5.6	3.8
Multilateral	..	..	3.7	1.2	2.8	1.5	1.8	2.8	7.0	5.4
Concessional	..	..	3.7	1.2	2.8	1.5	1.8	2.8	7.0	5.4
Bilateral	..	..	0.2	-0.4	-0.5	-0.6	-0.6	-0.7	-1.4	-1.7
Concessional	..	..	-0.3	-0.2	-0.4	-0.5	-0.5	-0.5	-1.2	-1.4
Private creditors	..	..	0.0	0.0	0.0	0.0	0.0	0.0	0.0	0.0
Bonds	..	..	0.0	0.0	0.0	0.0	0.0	0.0	0.0	0.0
Commercial banks	..	..	0.0	0.0	0.0	0.0	0.0	0.0	0.0	0.0
Other private	..	..	0.0	0.0	0.0	0.0	0.0	0.0	0.0	0.0
Private nonguaranteed	**0.0**	**0.0**	**0.0**	**0.0**	**0.0**	**0.0**	**0.0**	**0.0**	**0.0**	**0.0**
Bonds	..	..	0.0	0.0	0.0	0.0	0.0	0.0	0.0	0.0
Commercial banks	..	..	0.0	0.0	0.0	0.0	0.0	0.0	0.0	0.0
Memo:										
IBRD	0.0	0.0	0.0	0.0	0.0	0.0	0.0	0.0	0.0	0.0
IDA	0.0	0.0	1.5	0.0	1.0	0.6	0.1	0.2	0.8	0.2

TONGA

(US$ million, unless otherwise indicated)

	1970	1980	1988	1989	1990	1991	1992	1993	1994	1995
INTEREST PAYMENTS (LINT)	..	..	**0.4**	**0.5**	**0.5**	**0.5**	**0.5**	**0.5**	**0.6**	**0.7**
Public and publicly guaranteed	..	..	**0.4**	**0.5**	**0.5**	**0.5**	**0.5**	**0.5**	**0.6**	**0.7**
Official creditors	..	..	0.4	0.5	0.5	0.5	0.5	0.5	0.6	0.7
Multilateral	..	..	0.2	0.2	0.2	0.2	0.3	0.3	0.4	0.5
Concessional	..	..	0.2	0.2	0.2	0.2	0.3	0.3	0.4	0.5
Bilateral	..	..	0.2	0.2	0.3	0.2	0.2	0.2	0.2	0.2
Concessional	..	..	0.2	0.1	0.2	0.2	0.2	0.2	0.2	0.2
Private creditors	..	..	0.0	0.0	0.0	0.0	0.0	0.0	0.0	0.0
Bonds	..	..	0.0	0.0	0.0	0.0	0.0	0.0	0.0	0.0
Commercial banks	..	..	0.0	0.0	0.0	0.0	0.0	0.0	0.0	0.0
Other private	..	..	0.0	0.0	0.0	0.0	0.0	0.0	0.0	0.0
Private nonguaranteed	**0.0**	**0.0**	**0.0**	**0.0**	**0.0**	**0.0**	**0.0**	**0.0**	**0.0**	**0.0**
Bonds	..	..	0.0	0.0	0.0	0.0	0.0	0.0	0.0	0.0
Commercial banks	..	..	0.0	0.0	0.0	0.0	0.0	0.0	0.0	0.0
Memo:										
IBRD	0.0	0.0	0.0	0.0	0.0	0.0	0.0	0.0	0.0	0.0
IDA	0.0	0.0	0.0	0.0	0.0	0.0	0.0	0.0	0.0	0.0
NET TRANSFERS ON DEBT	..	..	**3.6**	**0.4**	**1.7**	**0.4**	**0.7**	**1.6**	**5.0**	**3.1**
Public and publicly guaranteed	..	..	**3.6**	**0.4**	**1.7**	**0.4**	**0.7**	**1.6**	**5.0**	**3.1**
Official creditors	..	..	3.6	0.4	1.7	0.4	0.7	1.6	5.0	3.1
Multilateral	..	..	3.6	1.0	2.5	1.2	1.5	2.5	6.6	4.9
Concessional	..	..	3.6	1.0	2.5	1.2	1.5	2.5	6.6	4.9
Bilateral	..	..	0.0	-0.6	-0.8	-0.9	-0.9	-0.9	-1.6	-1.9
Concessional	..	..	-0.4	-0.4	-0.5	-0.6	-0.7	-0.7	-1.4	-1.5
Private creditors	..	..	0.0	0.0	0.0	0.0	0.0	0.0	0.0	0.0
Bonds	..	..	0.0	0.0	0.0	0.0	0.0	0.0	0.0	0.0
Commercial banks	..	..	0.0	0.0	0.0	0.0	0.0	0.0	0.0	0.0
Other private	..	..	0.0	0.0	0.0	0.0	0.0	0.0	0.0	0.0
Private nonguaranteed	**0.0**	**0.0**	**0.0**	**0.0**	**0.0**	**0.0**	**0.0**	**0.0**	**0.0**	**0.0**
Bonds	..	..	0.0	0.0	0.0	0.0	0.0	0.0	0.0	0.0
Commercial banks	..	..	0.0	0.0	0.0	0.0	0.0	0.0	0.0	0.0
Memo:										
IBRD	0.0	0.0	0.0	0.0	0.0	0.0	0.0	0.0	0.0	0.0
IDA	0.0	0.0	1.5	0.0	1.0	0.5	0.1	0.2	0.8	0.2
DEBT SERVICE (LTDS)	..	..	**1.2**	**1.2**	**1.5**	**1.6**	**1.6**	**1.7**	**2.7**	**3.1**
Public and publicly guaranteed	..	..	**1.2**	**1.2**	**1.5**	**1.6**	**1.6**	**1.7**	**2.7**	**3.1**
Official creditors	..	..	1.2	1.2	1.5	1.6	1.6	1.7	2.7	3.1
Multilateral	..	..	0.5	0.6	0.7	0.7	0.7	0.8	1.1	1.3
Concessional	..	..	0.5	0.6	0.7	0.7	0.7	0.8	1.1	1.3
Bilateral	..	..	0.8	0.6	0.8	0.9	0.9	0.9	1.6	1.9
Concessional	..	..	0.4	0.4	0.5	0.6	0.7	0.7	1.4	1.5
Private creditors	..	..	0.0	0.0	0.0	0.0	0.0	0.0	0.0	0.0
Bonds	..	..	0.0	0.0	0.0	0.0	0.0	0.0	0.0	0.0
Commercial banks	..	..	0.0	0.0	0.0	0.0	0.0	0.0	0.0	0.0
Other private	..	..	0.0	0.0	0.0	0.0	0.0	0.0	0.0	0.0
Private nonguaranteed	**0.0**	**0.0**	**0.0**	**0.0**	**0.0**	**0.0**	**0.0**	**0.0**	**0.0**	**0.0**
Bonds	..	..	0.0	0.0	0.0	0.0	0.0	0.0	0.0	0.0
Commercial banks	..	..	0.0	0.0	0.0	0.0	0.0	0.0	0.0	0.0
Memo:										
IBRD	0.0	0.0	0.0	0.0	0.0	0.0	0.0	0.0	0.0	0.0
IDA	0.0	0.0	0.0	0.0	0.0	0.0	0.0	0.0	0.0	0.0
UNDISBURSED DEBT	..	..	**8.2**	**14.4**	**18.0**	**23.1**	**19.9**	**20.2**	**15.2**	**19.9**
Official creditors	..	..	8.2	14.4	18.0	23.1	19.9	20.2	13.7	18.3
Private creditors	..	..	0.0	0.0	0.0	0.0	0.0	0.0	1.6	1.6
Memorandum items										
Concessional LDOD	..	..	35.6	36.9	43.5	43.5	42.1	43.3	53.0	58.5
Variable rate LDOD	..	..	0.0	0.0	0.0	0.0	0.0	0.0	0.0	0.0
Public sector LDOD	..	..	37.0	38.1	44.5	44.2	42.6	43.7	63.4	68.7
Private sector LDOD	..	..	0.0	0.0	0.0	0.0	0.0	0.0	0.0	0.0

6. CURRENCY COMPOSITION OF LONG-TERM DEBT (PERCENT)

	1970	1980	1988	1989	1990	1991	1992	1993	1994	1995
Deutsche mark	..	..	41.4	42.3	40.7	39.8	38.2	34.3	24.8	23.0
French franc	..	..	0.0	0.0	0.0	0.0	0.0	0.0	0.0	0.0
Japanese yen	..	..	0.0	0.0	0.0	0.0	0.0	0.0	0.0	0.0
Pound sterling	..	..	8.1	6.3	5.8	5.2	3.8	3.2	1.9	1.5
Swiss franc	..	..	0.0	0.0	0.0	0.0	0.0	0.0	0.0	0.0
U.S.dollars	..	..	1.1	0.5	1.1	2.3	2.6	2.7	3.5	3.5
Multiple currency	..	..	41.4	43.3	45.4	46.6	49.7	55.2	65.3	67.7
Special drawing rights	..	..	0.0	0.0	0.0	0.0	0.0	0.0	1.6	2.2
All other currencies	..	..	8.1	7.6	6.7	6.3	5.6	4.6	3.0	2.2

TONGA

(US$ million, unless otherwise indicated)

	1970	1980	1988	1989	1990	1991	1992	1993	1994	1995
7. DEBT RESTRUCTURINGS										
Total amount rescheduled	0.0	0.0	0.0	0.0	0.0	0.0	0.0	0.0	0.0	0.0
Debt stock rescheduled	0.0	0.0	0.0	0.0	0.0	0.0	0.0	0.0	0.0	0.0
Principal rescheduled	0.0	0.0	0.0	0.0	0.0	0.0	0.0	0.0	0.0	0.0
Official	0.0	0.0	0.0	0.0	0.0	0.0	0.0	0.0	0.0	0.0
Private	0.0	0.0	0.0	0.0	0.0	0.0	0.0	0.0	0.0	0.0
Interest rescheduled	0.0	0.0	0.0	0.0	0.0	0.0	0.0	0.0	0.0	0.0
Official	0.0	0.0	0.0	0.0	0.0	0.0	0.0	0.0	0.0	0.0
Private	0.0	0.0	0.0	0.0	0.0	0.0	0.0	0.0	0.0	0.0
Debt forgiven	..	..	0.0	0.0	0.0	0.0	0.0	0.0	0.0	0.0
Memo: interest forgiven	..	..	0.0	0.0	0.0	0.0	0.0	0.0	0.0	0.0
Debt stock reduction	0.0	0.0	0.0	0.0	0.0	0.0	0.0	0.0	0.0	0.0
of which debt buyback	0.0	0.0	0.0	0.0	0.0	0.0	0.0	0.0	0.0	0.0
8. DEBT STOCK-FLOW RECONCILIATION										
Total change in debt stocks	..	..	..	1.6	14.5	-8.7	-1.5	0.8	20.2	5.7
Net flows on debt	..	..	..	1.3	10.4	-7.6	1.3	1.9	6.0	4.1
Net change in interest arrears	..	..	..	0.0	0.0	0.0	0.0	0.0	0.0	0.0
Interest capitalized	..	..	..	0.0	0.0	0.0	0.0	0.0	0.0	0.0
Debt forgiveness or reduction	..	..	..	0.0	0.0	0.0	0.0	0.0	0.0	0.0
Cross-currency valuation	..	..	..	0.5	3.3	-0.4	-1.5	-1.1	2.1	1.4
Residual	..	..	..	-0.3	0.8	-0.6	-1.3	0.0	12.1	0.2
9. AVERAGE TERMS OF NEW COMMITMENTS										
ALL CREDITORS										
Interest (%)	..	..	1.0	2.2	0.9	1.0	0.0	1.6	0.0	4.4
Maturity (years)	..	..	43.4	31.2	39.7	39.3	0.0	39.1	0.0	39.0
Grace period (years)	..	..	10.0	8.7	10.2	9.8	0.0	8.5	0.0	9.5
Grant element (%)	..	..	79.1	62.9	79.5	77.9	0.0	68.6	0.0	47.6
Official creditors										
Interest (%)	..	..	1.0	2.2	0.9	1.0	0.0	1.6	0.0	4.4
Maturity (years)	..	..	43.4	31.2	39.7	39.3	0.0	39.1	0.0	39.0
Grace period (years)	..	..	10.0	8.7	10.2	9.8	0.0	8.5	0.0	9.5
Grant element (%)	..	..	79.1	62.9	79.5	77.9	0.0	68.6	0.0	47.6
Private creditors										
Interest (%)	..	..	0.0	0.0	0.0	0.0	0.0	0.0	0.0	0.0
Maturity (years)	..	..	0.0	0.0	0.0	0.0	0.0	0.0	0.0	0.0
Grace period (years)	..	..	0.0	0.0	0.0	0.0	0.0	0.0	0.0	0.0
Grant element (%)	..	..	0.0	0.0	0.0	0.0	0.0	0.0	0.0	0.0
Memorandum items										
Commitments	..	..	5.9	7.6	5.7	7.3	0.0	4.2	0.0	10.5
Official creditors	..	..	5.9	7.6	5.7	7.3	0.0	4.2	0.0	10.5
Private creditors	..	..	0.0	0.0	0.0	0.0	0.0	0.0	0.0	0.0

10. CONTRACTUAL OBLIGATIONS ON OUTSTANDING LONG-TERM DEBT

	1996	1997	1998	1999	2000	2001	2002	2003	2004	2005
TOTAL										
Disbursements	6.5	4.7	3.1	2.6	1.9	0.8	0.3	0.1	0.0	0.0
Principal	4.7	4.7	5.0	4.9	5.1	2.9	2.5	2.3	2.6	2.8
Interest	1.4	1.4	1.2	1.1	1.0	0.8	0.8	0.7	0.7	1.1
Official creditors										
Disbursements	5.4	4.2	3.1	2.6	1.9	0.8	0.3	0.1	0.0	0.0
Principal	2.3	2.3	2.6	2.5	2.7	2.9	2.5	2.3	2.6	2.8
Interest	0.8	0.8	0.8	0.8	0.8	0.8	0.8	0.7	0.7	1.1
Bilateral creditors										
Disbursements	0.0	0.0	0.0	0.0	0.0	0.0	0.0	0.0	0.0	0.0
Principal	1.4	1.3	1.3	1.3	1.3	1.3	1.1	1.1	1.1	1.1
Interest	0.2	0.1	0.1	0.1	0.1	0.1	0.1	0.1	0.1	0.1
Multilateral creditors										
Disbursements	5.4	4.2	3.1	2.6	1.9	0.8	0.3	0.1	0.0	0.0
Principal	1.0	1.0	1.2	1.2	1.5	1.7	1.4	1.2	1.5	1.6
Interest	0.6	0.7	0.7	0.7	0.7	0.7	0.7	0.7	0.7	1.0
Private creditors										
Disbursements	1.1	0.5	0.0	0.0	0.0	0.0	0.0	0.0	0.0	0.0
Principal	2.4	2.4	2.4	2.4	2.4	0.0	0.0	0.0	0.0	0.0
Interest	0.7	0.6	0.4	0.3	0.1	0.0	0.0	0.0	0.0	0.0
Commercial banks										
Disbursements	0.0	0.0	0.0	0.0	0.0	0.0	0.0	0.0	0.0	0.0
Principal	0.0	0.0	0.0	0.0	0.0	0.0	0.0	0.0	0.0	0.0
Interest	0.0	0.0	0.0	0.0	0.0	0.0	0.0	0.0	0.0	0.0
Other private										
Disbursements	1.1	0.5	0.0	0.0	0.0	0.0	0.0	0.0	0.0	0.0
Principal	2.4	2.4	2.4	2.4	2.4	0.0	0.0	0.0	0.0	0.0
Interest	0.7	0.6	0.4	0.3	0.1	0.0	0.0	0.0	0.0	0.0

TRINIDAD AND TOBAGO

(US$ million, unless otherwise indicated)

1. SUMMARY DEBT DATA

	1970	1980	1988	1989	1990	1991	1992	1993	1994	1995
TOTAL DEBT STOCKS (EDT)	..	**829**	**2,102**	**2,138**	**2,512**	**2,488**	**2,375**	**2,131**	**2,221**	**2,556**
Long-term debt (LDOD)	**101**	**713**	**1,857**	**1,806**	**2,055**	**1,976**	**1,896**	**1,848**	**1,805**	**1,849**
Public and publicly guaranteed	101	713	1,857	1,806	1,782	1,750	1,710	1,698	1,687	1,759
Private nonguaranteed	0	0	0	0	273	226	186	150	118	90
Use of IMF credit	**0**	**0**	**115**	**205**	**329**	**385**	**282**	**155**	**91**	**50**
Short-term debt	..	**116**	**131**	**127**	**127**	**127**	**197**	**128**	**325**	**656**
of which interest arrears on LDOD	..	0	4	0	0	0	0	0	2	7
Official creditors	..	0	0	0	0	0	0	0	2	3
Private creditors	..	0	3	0	0	0	0	0	0	5
Memo: principal arrears on LDOD	..	0	128	7	37	78	57	58	76	86
Official creditors	..	0	37	6	7	18	9	11	14	10
Private creditors	..	0	90	1	31	60	48	47	62	76
Memo: export credits	..	..	553	521	591	598	601	663	676	701
TOTAL DEBT FLOWS										
Disbursements	**12**	**363**	**382**	**200**	**188**	**152**	**289**	**258**	**195**	**227**
Long-term debt	8	363	268	110	85	101	289	258	195	227
IMF purchases	5	0	114	91	103	51	0	0	0	0
Principal repayments	**14**	**176**	**183**	**67**	**233**	**215**	**396**	**481**	**398**	**250**
Long-term debt	10	176	183	67	233	215	307	352	326	206
IMF repurchases	4	0	0	0	0	0	90	129	72	44
Net flows on debt	**-2**	**187**	**160**	**133**	**-45**	**-63**	**-38**	**-292**	**-7**	**303**
of which short-term debt	..	..	-39	0	0	0	70	-70	196	326
Interest payments (INT)	..	**54**	**161**	**180**	**216**	**213**	**180**	**139**	**145**	**181**
Long-term debt	6	50	146	151	177	169	143	113	122	152
IMF charges	0	0	0	13	24	29	26	16	7	4
Short-term debt	..	4	15	15	15	15	11	10	16	25
Net transfers on debt	..	**133**	**-1**	**-47**	**-262**	**-276**	**-218**	**-432**	**-152**	**122**
Total debt service paid (TDS)	..	**230**	**344**	**247**	**449**	**428**	**576**	**620**	**542**	**431**
Long-term debt	16	226	329	219	410	384	449	465	447	358
IMF repurchases and charges	4	0	0	13	24	29	116	146	79	48
Short-term debt (interest only)	..	4	15	15	15	15	11	10	16	25

2. AGGREGATE NET RESOURCE FLOWS AND NET TRANSFERS (LONG-TERM)

	1970	1980	1988	1989	1990	1991	1992	1993	1994	1995
NET RESOURCE FLOWS	**81**	**372**	**153**	**198**	**-26**	**56**	**168**	**290**	**394**	**330**
Net flow of long-term debt (ex. IMF)	-3	187	85	43	-148	-115	-18	-94	-131	21
Foreign direct investment (net)	83	185	63	149	109	169	178	379	516	299
Portfolio equity flows	0	0	0	0	0	0	0	0	0	0
Grants (excluding technical coop.)	1	1	5	6	13	2	8	5	9	10
Memo: technical coop. grants	1	4	5	4	5	5	6	6	5	6
NET TRANSFERS	**16**	**-157**	**-124**	**-130**	**-401**	**-349**	**-225**	**-63**	**22**	**-85**
Interest on long-term debt	6	50	146	151	177	169	143	113	122	152
Profit remittances on FDI	59	479	131	176	197	236	251	240	250	263

3. MAJOR ECONOMIC AGGREGATES

	1970	1980	1988	1989	1990	1991	1992	1993	1994	1995
Gross national product (GNP)	757	5,925	4,185	3,938	4,673	4,869	4,995	4,345	4,378	4,772
Exports of goods & services (XGS)	..	3,373	1,763	1,867	2,331	2,233	2,180	1,912	2,187	2,906
of which workers remittances	..	1	2	3	3	5	6	18	26	30
Imports of goods & services (MGS)	..	2,972	1,840	1,895	1,863	2,235	2,035	1,785	1,943	2,577
International reserves (RES)	43	2,813	149	268	513	358	190	228	373	379
Current account balance	..	357	-89	-39	459	-5	139	113	218	294

4. DEBT INDICATORS

	1970	1980	1988	1989	1990	1991	1992	1993	1994	1995
EDT / XGS (%)	..	24.6	119.2	114.5	107.7	111.4	109.0	111.5	101.6	87.9
EDT / GNP (%)	..	14.0	50.2	54.3	53.7	51.1	47.6	49.1	50.7	53.6
TDS / XGS (%)	..	6.8	19.5	13.2	19.3	19.2	26.4	32.4	24.8	14.8
INT / XGS (%)	..	1.6	9.1	9.6	9.3	9.5	8.3	7.3	6.6	6.2
INT / GNP (%)	..	0.9	3.8	4.6	4.6	4.4	3.6	3.2	3.3	3.8
RES / EDT (%)	..	339.4	7.1	12.5	20.4	14.4	8.0	10.7	16.8	14.8
RES / MGS (months)	..	11.4	1.0	1.7	3.3	1.9	1.1	1.5	2.3	1.8
Short-term / EDT (%)	..	14.0	6.2	5.9	5.1	5.1	8.3	6.0	14.6	25.7
Concessional / EDT (%)	..	4.7	3.7	3.3	2.6	2.3	2.2	2.3	2.5	2.7
Multilateral / EDT (%)	..	8.6	3.2	3.2	4.1	6.3	8.7	13.9	18.1	20.7

TRINIDAD AND TOBAGO

(US$ million, unless otherwise indicated)

	1970	1980	1988	1989	1990	1991	1992	1993	1994	1995
5. LONG-TERM DEBT										
DEBT OUTSTANDING (LDOD)	**101**	**713**	**1,857**	**1,806**	**2,055**	**1,976**	**1,896**	**1,848**	**1,805**	**1,849**
Public and publicly guaranteed	**101**	**713**	**1,857**	**1,806**	**1,782**	**1,750**	**1,710**	**1,698**	**1,687**	**1,759**
Official creditors	45	263	355	515	634	707	756	799	879	951
Multilateral	23	71	67	69	103	158	208	296	402	529
Concessional	22	30	21	17	17	14	17	19	28	44
Bilateral	22	192	289	446	532	550	549	503	478	421
Concessional	6	8	57	54	48	43	35	29	27	24
Private creditors	56	450	1,502	1,291	1,147	1,043	954	900	808	808
Bonds	36	53	441	366	335	304	304	343	303	400
Commercial banks	15	348	747	682	624	619	555	505	482	404
Other private	4	50	314	244	188	120	95	51	24	4
Private nonguaranteed	**0**	**0**	**0**	**0**	**273**	**226**	**186**	**150**	**118**	**90**
Bonds	0	0	0	0	0	0	0	0	0	0
Commercial banks	0	0	0	0	273	226	186	150	118	90
Memo:										
IBRD	23	57	32	26	41	38	35	57	61	72
IDA	0	0	0	0	0	0	0	0	0	0
DISBURSEMENTS	**8**	**363**	**268**	**110**	**85**	**101**	**289**	**258**	**195**	**227**
Public and publicly guaranteed	**8**	**363**	**268**	**110**	**85**	**101**	**289**	**258**	**195**	**227**
Official creditors	5	125	26	45	43	66	131	105	94	130
Multilateral	3	11	10	14	39	64	69	94	92	128
Concessional	3	4	1	2	3	1	7	5	8	19
Bilateral	2	114	16	31	4	2	62	11	2	2
Concessional	2	0	0	0	0	0	0	0	0	0
Private creditors	3	238	242	65	42	34	158	153	101	97
Bonds	0	0	137	0	0	0	100	123	80	97
Commercial banks	3	197	81	7	0	3	10	13	17	0
Other private	0	41	24	58	42	32	48	18	4	0
Private nonguaranteed	**0**	**0**	**0**	**0**	**0**	**0**	**0**	**0**	**0**	**0**
Bonds	0	0	0	0	0	0	0	0	0	0
Commercial banks	0	0	0	0	0	0	0	0	0	0
Memo:										
IBRD	3	4	0	0	20	2	5	26	3	15
IDA	0	0	0	0	0	0	0	0	0	0
PRINCIPAL REPAYMENTS	**10**	**176**	**183**	**67**	**233**	**215**	**307**	**352**	**326**	**206**
Public and publicly guaranteed	**10**	**176**	**183**	**67**	**189**	**168**	**266**	**316**	**293**	**179**
Official creditors	3	11	52	11	14	42	68	64	57	81
Multilateral	1	6	11	11	10	12	13	10	11	14
Concessional	1	3	5	5	3	4	4	3	1	3
Bilateral	3	5	42	0	3	30	55	53	47	67
Concessional	0	0	2	0	0	4	5	5	5	6
Private creditors	7	165	131	56	176	127	198	253	236	98
Bonds	5	7	12	22	52	52	99	108	132	0
Commercial banks	1	150	94	17	99	19	27	83	72	79
Other private	0	7	26	17	25	56	72	62	31	20
Private nonguaranteed	**0**	**0**	**0**	**0**	**44**	**47**	**41**	**36**	**32**	**27**
Bonds	0	0	0	0	0	0	0	0	0	0
Commercial banks	0	0	0	0	44	47	41	36	32	27
Memo:										
IBRD	1	6	6	6	7	6	7	5	2	6
IDA	0	0	0	0	0	0	0	0	0	0
NET FLOWS ON DEBT	**-3**	**187**	**85**	**43**	**-148**	**-115**	**-18**	**-94**	**-131**	**21**
Public and publicly guaranteed	**-3**	**187**	**85**	**43**	**-105**	**-68**	**23**	**-58**	**-98**	**48**
Official creditors	1	114	-26	34	30	25	63	41	37	49
Multilateral	2	5	0	3	29	53	57	84	81	114
Concessional	2	1	-4	-3	-1	-3	3	2	7	16
Bilateral	-1	109	-26	31	1	-28	7	-42	-45	-65
Concessional	2	0	-2	0	0	-4	-5	-5	-5	-6
Private creditors	-4	73	111	9	-134	-93	-40	-99	-135	-1
Bonds	-5	-7	125	-22	-52	-52	1	14	-52	97
Commercial banks	2	47	-13	-10	-99	-16	-17	-70	-55	-79
Other private	0	34	-1	41	17	-24	-24	-44	-28	-20
Private nonguaranteed	**0**	**0**	**0**	**0**	**-44**	**-47**	**-41**	**-36**	**-32**	**-27**
Bonds	0	0	0	0	0	0	0	0	0	0
Commercial banks	0	0	0	0	-44	-47	-41	-36	-32	-27
Memo:										
IBRD	2	-1	-6	-6	13	-4	-2	21	0	9
IDA	0	0	0	0	0	0	0	0	0	0

TRINIDAD AND TOBAGO

(US$ million, unless otherwise indicated)

	1970	1980	1988	1989	1990	1991	1992	1993	1994	1995
INTEREST PAYMENTS (LINT)	**6**	**50**	**146**	**151**	**177**	**169**	**143**	**113**	**122**	**152**
Public and publicly guaranteed	**6**	**50**	**146**	**151**	**151**	**147**	**125**	**104**	**113**	**145**
Official creditors	3	16	30	29	51	56	57	53	56	66
Multilateral	1	5	5	5	6	9	12	18	23	30
Concessional	1	2	1	1	1	1	1	1	1	2
Bilateral	1	11	26	24	45	47	45	35	33	35
Concessional	0	0	2	2	2	2	2	1	1	1
Private creditors	4	35	116	122	101	91	68	51	58	79
Bonds	2	5	29	28	25	22	20	14	31	42
Commercial banks	1	25	63	62	55	58	42	33	24	37
Other private	0	5	24	32	21	12	7	4	2	1
Private nonguaranteed	**0**	**0**	**0**	**0**	**26**	**22**	**18**	**9**	**8**	**7**
Bonds	0	0	0	0	0	0	0	0	0	0
Commercial banks	0	0	0	0	26	22	18	9	8	7
Memo:										
IBRD	1	5	3	2	2	3	3	4	4	5
IDA	0	0	0	0	0	0	0	0	0	0
NET TRANSFERS ON DEBT	**-9**	**137**	**-61**	**-109**	**-326**	**-284**	**-161**	**-207**	**-252**	**-131**
Public and publicly guaranteed	**-9**	**137**	**-61**	**-109**	**-256**	**-215**	**-102**	**-162**	**-212**	**-97**
Official creditors	-1	98	-56	5	-21	-31	6	-12	-19	-17
Multilateral	1	0	-5	-2	23	44	45	65	58	83
Concessional	0	-1	-5	-4	-2	-5	2	1	7	14
Bilateral	-2	98	-51	6	-44	-75	-39	-77	-77	-100
Concessional	1	0	-4	-2	-2	-5	-7	-6	-6	-7
Private creditors	-7	39	-5	-113	-235	-184	-109	-150	-193	-80
Bonds	-7	-12	96	-50	-77	-74	-18	1	-83	56
Commercial banks	1	22	-76	-73	-154	-74	-59	-103	-79	-115
Other private	-1	29	-25	9	-4	-36	-31	-48	-30	-21
Private nonguaranteed	**0**	**0**	**0**	**0**	**-70**	**-69**	**-58**	**-45**	**-41**	**-34**
Bonds	0	0	0	0	0	0	0	0	0	0
Commercial banks	0	0	0	0	-70	-69	-58	-45	-41	-34
Memo:										
IBRD	1	-6	-9	-8	11	-7	-4	17	-4	5
IDA	0	0	0	0	0	0	0	0	0	0
DEBT SERVICE (LTDS)	**16**	**226**	**329**	**219**	**410**	**384**	**449**	**465**	**447**	**358**
Public and publicly guaranteed	**16**	**226**	**329**	**219**	**340**	**316**	**391**	**420**	**407**	**324**
Official creditors	6	27	82	40	64	97	125	117	113	146
Multilateral	2	11	15	16	16	21	24	29	34	44
Concessional	2	5	6	6	4	5	5	4	1	5
Bilateral	4	16	67	24	48	77	101	88	79	102
Concessional	0	0	4	2	2	5	7	6	6	7
Private creditors	10	199	247	178	276	218	266	303	293	178
Bonds	7	12	41	50	77	74	118	122	163	42
Commercial banks	2	175	157	80	154	76	69	116	96	115
Other private	1	12	49	48	46	67	79	66	34	21
Private nonguaranteed	**0**	**0**	**0**	**0**	**70**	**69**	**58**	**45**	**41**	**34**
Bonds	0	0	0	0	0	0	0	0	0	0
Commercial banks	0	0	0	0	70	69	58	45	41	34
Memo:										
IBRD	2	10	9	8	9	9	9	9	7	10
IDA	0	0	0	0	0	0	0	0	0	0
UNDISBURSED DEBT	**21**	**280**	**195**	**230**	**327**	**592**	**498**	**493**	**468**	**247**
Official creditors	21	201	166	179	244	540	447	445	371	247
Private creditors	0	79	30	51	83	52	51	48	97	0
Memorandum items										
Concessional LDOD	28	39	78	71	65	57	52	48	55	68
Variable rate LDOD	0	227	739	837	1,202	1,185	1,158	1,111	1,095	1,043
Public sector LDOD	101	713	1,857	1,806	1,782	1,750	1,710	1,698	1,687	1,759
Private sector LDOD	0	0	0	0	273	226	186	150	118	90

6. CURRENCY COMPOSITION OF LONG-TERM DEBT (PERCENT)

	1970	1980	1988	1989	1990	1991	1992	1993	1994	1995
Deutsche mark	0.0	5.6	7.2	6.8	6.8	5.8	4.3	3.4	3.4	3.0
French franc	0.0	0.1	3.3	3.6	4.1	3.5	3.0	2.7	2.9	2.6
Japanese yen	0.0	18.4	40.2	34.6	34.8	34.1	31.4	26.5	21.2	18.3
Pound sterling	33.4	0.2	4.9	2.8	3.4	3.4	2.8	2.8	2.8	2.8
Swiss franc	0.0	4.3	4.0	4.0	0.0	0.0	0.1	0.2	0.2	0.2
U.S.dollars	37.7	61.3	37.0	43.9	44.9	44.1	46.6	47.8	46.8	45.5
Multiple currency	23.1	8.3	2.4	2.6	4.1	6.4	9.4	14.6	20.7	26.3
Special drawing rights	0.0	0.0	0.0	0.0	0.0	0.0	0.0	0.0	0.0	0.0
All other currencies	5.9	1.8	1.0	1.7	1.8	2.7	2.3	2.0	2.0	1.3

TRINIDAD AND TOBAGO

(US$ million, unless otherwise indicated)

	1970	1980	1988	1989	1990	1991	1992	1993	1994	1995
7. DEBT RESTRUCTURINGS										
Total amount rescheduled	0	0	0	405	262	126	54	0	0	0
Debt stock rescheduled	0	0	0	0	0	0	0	0	0	0
Principal rescheduled	0	0	0	405	262	126	54	0	0	0
Official	0	0	0	95	56	2	0	0	0	0
Private	0	0	0	311	206	124	54	0	0	0
Interest rescheduled	0	0	0	0	0	0	0	0	0	0
Official	0	0	0	0	0	0	0	0	0	0
Private	0	0	0	0	0	0	0	0	0	0
Debt forgiven	..	..	0	0	7	0	0	0	0	0
Memo: interest forgiven	..	..	0	0	0	0	0	0	0	0
Debt stock reduction	0	0	0	0	0	0	32	10	0	7
of which debt buyback	0	0	0	0	0	0	0	0	0	0
8. DEBT STOCK-FLOW RECONCILIATION										
Total change in debt stocks	..	..	..	36	374	-24	-113	-244	90	335
Net flows on debt	..	..	..	133	-45	-63	-38	-292	-7	303
Net change in interest arrears	..	..	..	-3	0	0	0	0	1	6
Interest capitalized	..	..	..	0	0	0	0	0	0	0
Debt forgiveness or reduction	..	..	..	0	-7	0	-32	-10	0	-7
Cross-currency valuation	..	..	..	-76	98	43	-25	45	70	2
Residual	..	..	..	-18	329	-3	-19	13	26	32
9. AVERAGE TERMS OF NEW COMMITMENTS										
ALL CREDITORS										
Interest (%)	7.5	10.4	8.9	9.1	8.0	7.5	8.6	8.8	10.8	7.3
Maturity (years)	9.8	8.7	6.9	9.0	14.9	18.8	6.4	13.1	10.5	16.8
Grace period (years)	1.2	3.7	2.7	2.3	4.6	4.8	3.7	6.0	9.1	3.6
Grant element (%)	10.5	-2.6	3.8	5.2	10.7	15.0	2.6	7.9	-5.2	14.8
Official creditors										
Interest (%)	3.0	7.6	10.2	7.6	7.9	7.5	7.9	7.4	7.2	7.3
Maturity (years)	29.6	9.5	10.5	18.2	18.1	18.9	14.7	20.9	15.0	16.8
Grace period (years)	7.1	2.3	3.0	4.6	5.4	4.9	4.9	5.2	5.4	3.6
Grant element (%)	54.6	9.1	-1.1	14.2	12.0	15.1	11.5	16.3	15.8	14.8
Private creditors										
Interest (%)	8.0	10.6	8.6	10.0	8.1	7.5	8.8	9.8	11.4	0.0
Maturity (years)	7.5	8.6	6.1	3.4	9.8	4.5	4.4	6.7	9.7	0.0
Grace period (years)	0.5	3.9	2.6	0.9	3.3	1.4	3.4	6.7	9.7	0.0
Grant element (%)	5.5	-3.6	4.9	-0.4	8.6	5.6	0.5	1.0	-9.0	0.0
Memorandum items										
Commitments	3	211	205	153	187	364	204	273	177	15
Official creditors	0	17	37	58	115	361	38	123	27	15
Private creditors	3	194	168	95	73	4	166	150	150	0

10. CONTRACTUAL OBLIGATIONS ON OUTSTANDING LONG-TERM DEBT

	1996	1997	1998	1999	2000	2001	2002	2003	2004	2005
TOTAL										
Disbursements	96	66	39	24	12	5	3	1	0	0
Principal	248	374	217	213	289	66	65	65	65	52
Interest	140	127	98	85	72	51	47	42	37	33
Official creditors										
Disbursements	96	66	39	24	12	5	3	1	0	0
Principal	132	137	136	138	96	61	60	60	60	52
Interest	72	67	60	52	44	38	34	30	25	21
Bilateral creditors										
Disbursements	0	0	0	0	0	0	0	0	0	0
Principal	88	88	88	84	39	6	5	5	5	5
Interest	29	23	16	10	4	2	2	1	1	1
Multilateral creditors										
Disbursements	96	66	39	24	12	5	3	1	0	0
Principal	44	49	49	54	57	55	55	55	55	47
Interest	43	44	44	42	39	36	32	28	24	21
Private creditors										
Disbursements	0	0	0	0	0	0	0	0	0	0
Principal	117	237	80	75	193	5	5	5	5	0
Interest	68	60	38	33	29	13	13	12	12	12
Commercial banks										
Disbursements	0	0	0	0	0	0	0	0	0	0
Principal	66	63	61	61	61	5	5	5	5	0
Interest	19	15	11	8	4	1	1	1	0	0
Other private										
Disbursements	0	0	0	0	0	0	0	0	0	0
Principal	51	174	20	14	133	0	0	0	0	0
Interest	49	45	27	25	24	12	12	12	12	12

TUNISIA

(US$ million, unless otherwise indicated)

	1970	1980	1988	1989	1990	1991	1992	1993	1994	1995
1. SUMMARY DEBT DATA										
TOTAL DEBT STOCKS (EDT)	..	**3,527**	**6,799**	**6,974**	**7,691**	**8,250**	**8,542**	**8,682**	**9,348**	**9,938**
Long-term debt (LDOD)	**541**	**3,390**	**6,188**	**6,328**	**6,880**	**7,322**	**7,409**	**7,608**	**8,206**	**9,007**
Public and publicly guaranteed	541	3,210	5,953	6,103	6,662	7,109	7,201	7,405	8,008	8,814
Private nonguaranteed	0	180	235	225	218	213	208	203	198	193
Use of IMF credit	**13**	**0**	**277**	**270**	**176**	**258**	**290**	**285**	**303**	**293**
Short-term debt	..	**136**	**335**	**376**	**634**	**670**	**843**	**789**	**839**	**638**
of which interest arrears on LDOD	..	0	0	0	0	10	2	0	0	3
Official creditors	..	0	0	0	0	9	2	0	0	3
Private creditors	..	0	0	0	0	1	0	0	0	0
Memo: principal arrears on LDOD	..	6	0	1	15	59	9	2	15	30
Official creditors	..	6	0	0	8	28	7	2	15	29
Private creditors	..	0	0	1	7	31	2	0	0	1
Memo: export credits	..	..	1,454	1,321	1,547	1,471	1,381	1,526	1,921	3,525
TOTAL DEBT FLOWS										
Disbursements	**96**	**611**	**915**	**860**	**1,018**	**1,358**	**1,286**	**1,104**	**1,076**	**1,518**
Long-term debt	89	611	895	860	1,018	1,145	1,213	1,104	1,076	1,518
IMF purchases	8	0	20	0	0	213	73	0	0	0
Principal repayments	**54**	**290**	**650**	**673**	**984**	**930**	**889**	**847**	**926**	**948**
Long-term debt	47	258	650	673	873	794	859	842	926	933
IMF repurchases	7	31	0	0	111	136	29	5	0	16
Net flows on debt	**42**	**321**	**345**	**228**	**293**	**454**	**577**	**205**	**200**	**366**
of which short-term debt	..	..	80	41	259	26	180	-51	50	-205
Interest payments (INT)	..	**255**	**409**	**427**	**448**	**440**	**454**	**503**	**530**	**542**
Long-term debt	18	228	374	378	394	384	398	419	463	487
IMF charges	0	1	17	23	23	18	19	17	15	17
Short-term debt	..	26	18	27	30	39	37	67	52	38
Net transfers on debt	..	**66**	**-63**	**-199**	**-155**	**14**	**123**	**-298**	**-331**	**-176**
Total debt service paid (TDS)	..	**545**	**1,058**	**1,101**	**1,432**	**1,370**	**1,343**	**1,350**	**1,456**	**1,490**
Long-term debt	65	486	1,023	1,051	1,267	1,178	1,258	1,261	1,389	1,420
IMF repurchases and charges	7	33	17	23	135	153	49	22	15	32
Short-term debt (interest only)	..	26	18	27	30	39	37	67	52	38
2. AGGREGATE NET RESOURCE FLOWS AND NET TRANSFERS (LONG-TERM)										
NET RESOURCE FLOWS	**100**	**612**	**430**	**354**	**395**	**577**	**1,020**	**927**	**665**	**907**
Net flow of long-term debt (ex. IMF)	42	352	245	187	145	351	353	262	150	586
Foreign direct investment (net)	16	235	61	79	76	126	526	562	432	264
Portfolio equity flows	0	0	0	0	0	0	0	0	0	0
Grants (excluding technical coop.)	43	26	124	88	174	100	140	103	83	58
Memo: technical coop. grants	27	74	84	83	101	91	99	104	85	123
NET TRANSFERS	**62**	**232**	**-45**	**-128**	**-145**	**-76**	**341**	**271**	**-38**	**175**
Interest on long-term debt	18	228	374	378	394	384	398	419	463	487
Profit remittances on FDI	20	153	100	104	146	268	280	237	240	245
3. MAJOR ECONOMIC AGGREGATES										
Gross national product (GNP)	1,379	8,484	9,627	9,561	11,817	12,568	15,074	14,152	15,231	17,331
Exports of goods & services (XGS)	..	3,675	4,798	4,896	5,851	5,687	6,645	6,305	7,610	8,778
of which workers remittances	..	319	498	450	551	525	531	446	629	680
Imports of goods & services (MGS)	..	4,119	4,759	5,372	6,591	6,345	7,882	7,795	8,319	9,646
International reserves (RES)	60	700	976	1,037	867	866	924	938	1,544	1,689
Current account balance	..	-353	210	-218	-463	-469	-1,104	-1,323	-539	-737
4. DEBT INDICATORS										
EDT / XGS (%)	..	96.0	141.7	142.4	131.4	145.1	128.5	137.7	122.8	113.2
EDT / GNP (%)	..	41.6	70.6	72.9	65.1	65.6	56.7	61.3	61.4	57.3
TDS / XGS (%)	..	14.8	22.1	22.5	24.5	24.1	20.2	21.4	19.1	17.0
INT / XGS (%)	..	6.9	8.5	8.7	7.6	7.7	6.8	8.0	7.0	6.2
INT / GNP (%)	..	3.0	4.2	4.5	3.8	3.5	3.0	3.6	3.5	3.1
RES / EDT (%)	..	19.9	14.4	14.9	11.3	10.5	10.8	10.8	16.5	17.0
RES / MGS (months)	..	2.0	2.5	2.3	1.6	1.6	1.4	1.4	2.2	2.1
Short-term / EDT (%)	..	3.9	4.9	5.4	8.2	8.1	9.9	9.1	9.0	6.4
Concessional / EDT (%)	..	39.9	35.6	36.2	36.3	35.2	34.3	34.0	33.7	33.7
Multilateral / EDT (%)	..	12.3	23.1	26.1	29.0	32.8	32.4	35.6	37.3	37.2

TUNISIA

(US$ million, unless otherwise indicated)

5. LONG-TERM DEBT

	1970	1980	1988	1989	1990	1991	1992	1993	1994	1995
DEBT OUTSTANDING (LDOD)	**541**	**3,390**	**6,188**	**6,328**	**6,880**	**7,322**	**7,409**	**7,608**	**8,206**	**9,007**
Public and publicly guaranteed	**541**	**3,210**	**5,953**	**6,103**	**6,662**	**7,109**	**7,201**	**7,405**	**8,008**	**8,814**
Official creditors	364	1,961	4,269	4,559	5,229	5,836	5,907	6,238	6,892	7,200
Multilateral	44	433	1,572	1,819	2,229	2,707	2,769	3,094	3,485	3,695
Concessional	29	95	224	248	324	361	357	355	385	424
Bilateral	321	1,529	2,698	2,740	3,000	3,128	3,138	3,143	3,407	3,505
Concessional	317	1,311	2,196	2,273	2,469	2,539	2,572	2,599	2,763	2,926
Private creditors	177	1,249	1,684	1,543	1,434	1,273	1,294	1,167	1,117	1,614
Bonds	2	6	60	60	0	0	0	0	0	535
Commercial banks	0	493	440	357	343	310	488	548	626	663
Other private	175	750	1,184	1,126	1,091	963	806	619	491	416
Private nonguaranteed	**0**	**180**	**235**	**225**	**218**	**213**	**208**	**203**	**198**	**193**
Bonds	0	0	0	0	0	0	0	0	0	0
Commercial banks	0	180	235	225	218	213	208	203	198	193
Memo:										
IBRD	26	269	1,019	1,154	1,347	1,552	1,470	1,595	1,715	1,717
IDA	16	68	62	61	59	58	56	54	52	50
DISBURSEMENTS	**89**	**611**	**895**	**860**	**1,018**	**1,145**	**1,213**	**1,104**	**1,076**	**1,518**
Public and publicly guaranteed	**89**	**558**	**841**	**830**	**988**	**1,115**	**1,183**	**1,074**	**1,046**	**1,488**
Official creditors	54	323	542	652	699	901	756	830	877	745
Multilateral	13	82	318	414	430	593	402	566	482	467
Concessional	6	8	44	31	66	54	36	27	37	60
Bilateral	41	242	223	238	269	308	354	264	395	278
Concessional	40	197	197	200	177	197	273	215	258	252
Private creditors	34	235	299	178	289	214	426	244	169	743
Bonds	0	0	0	0	0	0	0	0	0	588
Commercial banks	0	51	5	0	91	96	292	216	159	102
Other private	34	184	294	178	198	118	135	28	10	52
Private nonguaranteed	**0**	**53**	**54**	**30**	**30**	**30**	**30**	**30**	**30**	**30**
Bonds	0	0	0	0	0	0	0	0	0	0
Commercial banks	0	53	54	30	30	30	30	30	30	30
Memo:										
IBRD	9	51	173	259	213	297	111	248	189	138
IDA	3	1	0	0	0	0	0	0	0	0
PRINCIPAL REPAYMENTS	**47**	**258**	**650**	**673**	**873**	**794**	**859**	**842**	**926**	**933**
Public and publicly guaranteed	**47**	**216**	**605**	**633**	**836**	**759**	**824**	**807**	**891**	**898**
Official creditors	14	72	333	323	356	381	465	467	605	646
Multilateral	1	20	150	142	168	191	233	250	285	363
Concessional	0	2	7	6	8	13	19	21	23	32
Bilateral	13	52	183	181	188	190	232	218	320	283
Concessional	11	40	122	130	134	126	137	134	245	188
Private creditors	33	144	272	310	480	378	360	340	286	251
Bonds	0	5	0	0	60	0	0	0	0	0
Commercial banks	0	24	67	84	113	134	103	141	112	102
Other private	33	114	205	227	307	245	257	199	174	150
Private nonguaranteed	**0**	**43**	**45**	**40**	**37**	**35**	**35**	**35**	**35**	**35**
Bonds	0	0	0	0	0	0	0	0	0	0
Commercial banks	0	43	45	40	37	35	35	35	35	35
Memo:										
IBRD	1	15	111	103	111	125	147	147	173	203
IDA	0	0	1	1	2	2	2	2	2	2
NET FLOWS ON DEBT	**42**	**352**	**245**	**187**	**145**	**351**	**353**	**262**	**150**	**586**
Public and publicly guaranteed	**42**	**342**	**236**	**197**	**152**	**356**	**358**	**267**	**155**	**591**
Official creditors	40	251	209	329	343	520	292	363	272	99
Multilateral	12	61	169	272	262	402	170	316	197	104
Concessional	5	6	37	25	58	41	17	6	14	28
Bilateral	29	190	40	57	81	118	122	47	75	-5
Concessional	30	156	75	70	44	71	136	81	12	64
Private creditors	1	92	27	-132	-191	-164	67	-96	-117	492
Bonds	0	-5	0	0	-60	0	0	0	0	588
Commercial banks	0	27	-62	-83	-22	-38	189	76	47	1
Other private	1	70	90	-49	-109	-127	-123	-172	-164	-98
Private nonguaranteed	**0**	**10**	**9**	**-10**	**-7**	**-5**	**-5**	**-5**	**-5**	**-5**
Bonds	0	0	0	0	0	0	0	0	0	0
Commercial banks	0	10	9	-10	-7	-5	-5	-5	-5	-5
Memo:										
IBRD	8	36	62	156	102	172	-37	101	15	-65
IDA	3	1	-1	-1	-2	-2	-2	-2	-2	-2

TUNISIA

(US$ million, unless otherwise indicated)

	1970	*1980*	*1988*	*1989*	*1990*	*1991*	*1992*	*1993*	*1994*	*1995*
INTEREST PAYMENTS (LINT)	**18**	**228**	**374**	**378**	**394**	**384**	**398**	**419**	**463**	**487**
Public and publicly guaranteed	**18**	**212**	**363**	**367**	**384**	**371**	**390**	**412**	**456**	**480**
Official creditors	8	74	221	222	247	261	288	308	363	369
Multilateral	2	28	119	120	148	169	191	208	231	251
Concessional	1	2	6	6	9	12	13	13	15	14
Bilateral	7	46	103	102	99	92	97	100	132	118
Concessional	6	29	64	68	66	62	66	67	95	79
Private creditors	10	138	142	146	138	110	102	103	93	111
Bonds	0	1	5	6	5	0	0	0	0	14
Commercial banks	0	69	42	46	35	24	30	39	44	56
Other private	10	68	95	93	97	86	72	65	48	40
Private nonguaranteed	**0**	**16**	**11**	**11**	**10**	**13**	**8**	**7**	**7**	**8**
Bonds	0	0	0	0	0	0	0	0	0	0
Commercial banks	0	16	11	11	10	13	8	7	7	8
Memo:										
IBRD	1	23	89	87	103	111	119	117	124	129
IDA	0	1	1	1	1	0	0	0	0	0
NET TRANSFERS ON DEBT	**23**	**125**	**-129**	**-191**	**-249**	**-33**	**-45**	**-157**	**-313**	**99**
Public and publicly guaranteed	**23**	**131**	**-127**	**-170**	**-232**	**-15**	**-32**	**-145**	**-301**	**111**
Official creditors	32	177	-13	107	96	259	3	55	-91	-270
Multilateral	10	33	50	153	114	233	-21	108	-34	-147
Concessional	5	3	31	18	48	29	5	-7	-1	14
Bilateral	22	144	-63	-45	-18	26	25	-54	-57	-123
Concessional	23	127	11	2	-23	9	71	14	-82	-15
Private creditors	-9	-46	-114	-277	-328	-274	-35	-200	-209	381
Bonds	0	-6	-5	-6	-65	0	0	0	0	574
Commercial banks	0	-43	-104	-130	-57	-62	160	37	3	-55
Other private	-9	3	-5	-142	-206	-213	-195	-236	-212	-138
Private nonguaranteed	**0**	**-6**	**-2**	**-21**	**-17**	**-18**	**-13**	**-12**	**-12**	**-13**
Bonds	0	0	0	0	0	0	0	0	0	0
Commercial banks	0	-6	-2	-21	-17	-18	-13	-12	-12	-13
Memo:										
IBRD	7	14	-26	69	-1	62	-156	-16	-109	-194
IDA	3	0	-2	-2	-2	-2	-2	-3	-3	-3
DEBT SERVICE (LTDS)	**65**	**486**	**1,023**	**1,051**	**1,267**	**1,178**	**1,258**	**1,261**	**1,389**	**1,420**
Public and publicly guaranteed	**65**	**428**	**967**	**1,000**	**1,220**	**1,131**	**1,215**	**1,219**	**1,346**	**1,377**
Official creditors	22	146	554	545	603	642	753	776	968	1,015
Multilateral	3	48	269	261	316	360	423	458	516	614
Concessional	1	5	13	13	17	25	31	34	38	46
Bilateral	20	98	286	284	287	282	330	318	452	401
Concessional	17	70	187	198	200	188	202	201	340	267
Private creditors	43	281	413	456	618	488	462	443	378	362
Bonds	0	6	5	6	65	0	0	0	0	14
Commercial banks	0	94	109	130	148	158	132	179	156	158
Other private	43	182	299	320	404	330	329	264	222	190
Private nonguaranteed	**0**	**58**	**56**	**51**	**47**	**48**	**43**	**42**	**42**	**43**
Bonds	0	0	0	0	0	0	0	0	0	0
Commercial banks	0	58	56	51	47	48	43	42	42	43
Memo:										
IBRD	3	37	199	190	214	236	267	264	297	332
IDA	0	1	2	2	2	2	2	3	3	3
UNDISBURSED DEBT	**319**	**2,050**	**3,606**	**3,979**	**3,857**	**3,976**	**3,805**	**3,940**	**3,384**	**3,869**
Official creditors	270	1,578	2,998	3,267	3,114	3,238	3,061	3,369	2,960	3,250
Private creditors	50	472	608	712	743	738	744	571	424	619
Memorandum items										
Concessional LDOD	346	1,405	2,420	2,522	2,793	2,900	2,929	2,954	3,147	3,350
Variable rate LDOD	0	680	1,285	1,461	1,557	1,723	1,743	1,984	2,211	2,270
Public sector LDOD	528	3,120	5,953	6,103	6,662	7,109	7,190	7,396	8,001	8,807
Private sector LDOD	13	270	235	225	218	213	219	212	206	200
6. CURRENCY COMPOSITION OF LONG-TERM DEBT (PERCENT)										
Deutsche mark	8.7	10.8	10.7	10.8	11.0	10.3	9.7	8.5	8.0	7.3
French franc	23.4	21.1	12.9	12.7	13.6	14.2	13.5	13.1	14.7	14.5
Japanese yen	0.0	1.7	10.5	8.9	8.6	8.5	7.8	8.3	9.4	13.9
Pound sterling	0.8	0.2	0.1	0.1	0.1	0.1	0.1	0.0	0.0	0.0
Swiss franc	0.1	0.9	0.6	0.6	0.6	0.4	0.2	0.2	0.2	0.2
U.S.dollars	37.8	33.4	27.1	26.1	21.8	18.9	20.8	19.3	16.3	14.0
Multiple currency	5.5	8.4	19.1	21.2	22.7	23.9	23.6	25.9	27.0	25.4
Special drawing rights	0.0	0.0	0.3	0.3	0.3	0.3	0.3	0.2	0.2	0.2
All other currencies	23.7	23.6	18.7	19.5	21.3	23.5	24.1	24.5	24.2	24.5

(US$ million, unless otherwise indicated)

	1970	1980	1988	1989	1990	1991	1992	1993	1994	1995
7. DEBT RESTRUCTURINGS										
Total amount rescheduled	0	0	0	0	0	0	0	0	0	0
Debt stock rescheduled	0	0	0	0	0	0	0	0	0	0
Principal rescheduled	0	0	0	0	0	0	0	0	0	0
Official	0	0	0	0	0	0	0	0	0	0
Private	0	0	0	0	0	0	0	0	0	0
Interest rescheduled	0	0	0	0	0	0	0	0	0	0
Official	0	0	0	0	0	0	0	0	0	0
Private	0	0	0	0	0	0	0	0	0	0
Debt forgiven	..	..	0	6	7	13	1	0	1	0
Memo: interest forgiven	..	..	0	0	0	0	0	0	0	0
Debt stock reduction	0	0	0	0	0	0	0	0	0	0
of which debt buyback	0	0	0	0	0	0	0	0	0	0
8. DEBT STOCK-FLOW RECONCILIATION										
Total change in debt stocks	..	..	..	175	717	559	292	140	667	590
Net flows on debt	..	..	..	228	293	454	577	205	200	366
Net change in interest arrears	..	..	..	0	0	10	-8	-2	0	3
Interest capitalized	..	..	..	0	0	0	0	0	0	0
Debt forgiveness or reduction	..	..	..	-6	-7	-13	-1	0	-1	0
Cross-currency valuation	..	..	..	-45	436	30	-282	-79	456	220
Residual	..	..	..	-3	-5	78	6	16	12	1
9. AVERAGE TERMS OF NEW COMMITMENTS										
ALL CREDITORS										
Interest (%)	3.5	6.7	4.6	7.2	6.8	6.6	7.1	6.1	7.8	6.3
Maturity (years)	27.4	18.1	18.8	15.5	13.9	15.7	13.1	17.9	22.4	17.3
Grace period (years)	6.4	5.4	5.5	4.4	3.7	4.5	3.6	5.1	5.2	4.8
Grant element (%)	47.9	23.4	37.1	17.9	18.2	19.4	13.3	24.2	13.7	20.3
Official creditors										
Interest (%)	2.7	5.6	3.7	6.5	5.8	6.3	6.2	6.1	7.7	6.8
Maturity (years)	32.0	20.9	21.4	17.8	17.9	17.0	14.6	18.7	23.0	25.0
Grace period (years)	7.6	6.5	6.2	5.3	5.0	5.0	4.6	5.3	5.5	4.5
Grant element (%)	57.2	31.0	44.6	23.2	26.6	22.1	20.2	25.1	14.3	21.4
Private creditors										
Interest (%)	6.3	9.6	9.0	9.4	8.1	8.0	8.3	6.1	9.1	5.9
Maturity (years)	11.0	10.7	7.1	8.4	8.4	9.8	11.2	10.5	10.3	8.8
Grace period (years)	1.9	2.4	2.3	1.6	1.9	1.8	2.2	3.0	0.8	5.1
Grant element (%)	15.1	2.8	2.8	1.3	6.6	7.1	4.2	16.1	2.7	19.1
Memorandum items										
Commitments	144	777	1,674	1,348	801	1,377	1,280	1,468	810	1,947
Official creditors	112	567	1,374	1,019	462	1,128	727	1,315	773	1,022
Private creditors	32	210	300	329	339	250	553	153	37	925

10. CONTRACTUAL OBLIGATIONS ON OUTSTANDING LONG-TERM DEBT

	1996	1997	1998	1999	2000	2001	2002	2003	2004	2005
TOTAL										
Disbursements	1,122	983	650	421	247	145	71	42	28	17
Principal	1,051	1,012	966	995	1,349	923	856	808	745	808
Interest	529	508	485	497	449	393	345	299	255	214
Official creditors										
Disbursements	886	843	585	396	238	141	69	42	28	17
Principal	740	769	764	797	785	774	760	729	671	595
Interest	401	396	378	397	371	337	300	261	224	189
Bilateral creditors										
Disbursements	402	322	187	103	50	26	9	2	1	0
Principal	374	373	337	338	325	313	311	295	281	255
Interest	131	125	118	116	105	94	85	75	65	56
Multilateral creditors										
Disbursements	484	521	398	293	187	115	60	40	26	17
Principal	366	396	427	460	460	462	449	435	390	340
Interest	270	270	260	281	266	243	215	187	159	134
Private creditors										
Disbursements	237	141	65	25	9	4	2	1	0	0
Principal	311	243	203	198	564	148	95	79	74	212
Interest	128	113	107	100	78	56	45	37	31	25
Commercial banks										
Disbursements	116	48	19	9	0	0	0	0	0	0
Principal	163	131	92	86	84	75	60	44	40	33
Interest	62	55	49	42	35	27	20	15	11	7
Other private										
Disbursements	120	92	46	16	9	4	2	1	0	0
Principal	148	111	111	111	481	73	36	34	34	180
Interest	66	58	58	58	43	29	25	22	20	18

TURKEY

(US$ million, unless otherwise indicated)

	1970	*1980*	*1988*	*1989*	*1990*	*1991*	*1992*	*1993*	*1994*	*1995*
1. SUMMARY DEBT DATA										
TOTAL DEBT STOCKS (EDT)	**..**	**19,131**	**40,814**	**41,447**	**49,238**	**50,747**	**56,451**	**68,800**	**66,391**	**73,592**
Long-term debt (LDOD)	**1,888**	**15,575**	**34,098**	**35,654**	**39,738**	**41,630**	**43,791**	**50,267**	**54,737**	**57,207**
Public and publicly guaranteed	1,846	15,040	33,563	34,859	38,684	39,703	40,360	44,259	48,579	50,128
Private nonguaranteed	42	535	535	795	1,054	1,928	3,431	6,008	6,159	7,079
Use of IMF credit	**74**	**1,054**	**299**	**48**	**0**	**0**	**0**	**0**	**344**	**685**
Short-term debt	**..**	**2,502**	**6,417**	**5,745**	**9,500**	**9,117**	**12,660**	**18,533**	**11,310**	**15,701**
of which interest arrears on LDOD	..	12	0	0	0	0	0	0	0	0
Official creditors	..	12	0	0	0	0	0	0	0	0
Private creditors	..	0	0	0	0	0	0	0	0	0
Memo: principal arrears on LDOD	..	23	0	0	0	0	0	0	0	0
Official creditors	..	21	0	0	0	0	0	0	0	0
Private creditors	..	1	0	0	0	0	0	0	0	0
Memo: export credits	..	..	9,182	9,107	11,519	11,138	11,475	11,280	12,850	13,121
TOTAL DEBT FLOWS										
Disbursements	**407**	**3,115**	**7,360**	**4,897**	**5,177**	**5,624**	**8,444**	**10,307**	**5,940**	**6,670**
Long-term debt	332	2,475	7,360	4,897	5,177	5,624	8,444	10,307	5,603	6,328
IMF purchases	75	640	0	0	0	0	0	0	337	341
Principal repayments	**158**	**750**	**4,331**	**4,009**	**3,997**	**4,870**	**5,326**	**4,648**	**6,285**	**7,033**
Long-term debt	131	595	3,900	3,771	3,947	4,870	5,326	4,648	6,285	7,033
IMF repurchases	27	155	431	238	49	0	0	0	0	0
Net flows on debt	**249**	**2,365**	**1,823**	**216**	**4,936**	**371**	**6,660**	**11,532**	**-7,568**	**4,028**
of which short-term debt	..	..	-1,206	-672	3,755	-383	3,543	5,873	-7,223	4,391
Interest payments (INT)	**..**	**858**	**3,180**	**3,071**	**3,397**	**3,383**	**3,760**	**4,034**	**3,991**	**4,443**
Long-term debt	44	507	2,446	2,653	2,877	2,882	3,190	3,184	3,211	3,477
IMF charges	0	51	55	11	4	0	0	0	4	24
Short-term debt	..	299	679	407	517	501	570	850	776	942
Net transfers on debt	**..**	**1,508**	**-1,357**	**-2,856**	**1,538**	**-3,012**	**2,900**	**7,499**	**-11,559**	**-416**
Total debt service paid (TDS)	**..**	**1,607**	**7,511**	**7,080**	**7,394**	**8,253**	**9,086**	**8,682**	**10,276**	**11,476**
Long-term debt	176	1,102	6,346	6,424	6,824	7,752	8,516	7,832	9,497	10,510
IMF repurchases and charges	27	206	486	250	53	0	0	0	4	24
Short-term debt (interest only)	..	299	679	407	517	501	570	850	776	942
2. AGGREGATE NET RESOURCE FLOWS AND NET TRANSFERS (LONG-TERM)										
NET RESOURCE FLOWS	**300**	**2,083**	**3,863**	**1,940**	**2,753**	**2,769**	**4,233**	**7,286**	**1,293**	**1,249**
Net flow of long-term debt (ex. IMF)	201	1,880	3,460	1,126	1,230	754	3,117	5,659	-683	-705
Foreign direct investment (net)	58	18	354	663	684	810	844	636	608	885
Portfolio equity flows	0	0	0	56	35	0	0	534	1,059	630
Grants (excluding technical coop.)	41	185	49	95	804	1,205	272	457	309	439
Memo: technical coop. grants	14	38	107	111	149	159	179	176	176	200
NET TRANSFERS	**222**	**1,545**	**1,329**	**-817**	**-285**	**-281**	**624**	**3,683**	**-2,348**	**-2,668**
Interest on long-term debt	44	507	2,446	2,653	2,877	2,882	3,190	3,184	3,211	3,477
Profit remittances on FDI	34	31	88	104	161	168	420	419	430	440
3. MAJOR ECONOMIC AGGREGATES										
Gross national product (GNP)	18,071	69,742	90,818	108,579	152,255	152,066	160,585	181,829	131,313	166,740
Exports of goods & services (XGS)	..	5,743	19,731	21,918	25,205	25,793	28,318	30,317	32,708	41,396
of which workers remittances	..	2,071	1,776	3,040	3,246	2,819	3,008	2,919	2,627	3,327
Imports of goods & services (MGS)	..	9,251	18,518	21,475	29,077	27,823	30,343	37,599	30,542	44,904
International reserves (RES)	440	3,298	3,912	6,298	7,626	6,616	7,508	7,846	8,633	13,891
Current account balance	..	-3,408	1,596	938	-2,625	250	-974	-6,433	2,631	-2,339
4. DEBT INDICATORS										
EDT / XGS (%)	..	333.1	206.9	189.1	195.3	196.7	199.3	226.9	203.0	177.8
EDT / GNP (%)	..	27.4	44.9	38.2	32.3	33.4	35.2	37.8	50.6	44.1
TDS / XGS (%)	..	28.0	38.1	32.3	29.3	32.0	32.1	28.6	31.4	27.7
INT / XGS (%)	..	14.9	16.1	14.0	13.5	13.1	13.3	13.3	12.2	10.7
INT / GNP (%)	..	1.2	3.5	2.8	2.2	2.2	2.3	2.2	3.0	2.7
RES / EDT (%)	..	17.2	9.6	15.2	15.5	13.0	13.3	11.4	13.0	18.9
RES / MGS (months)	..	4.3	2.5	3.5	3.1	2.9	3.0	2.5	3.4	3.7
Short-term / EDT (%)	..	13.1	15.7	13.9	19.3	18.0	22.4	26.9	17.0	21.3
Concessional / EDT (%)	..	23.0	17.0	16.4	16.2	16.2	13.6	10.8	12.1	10.7
Multilateral / EDT (%)	..	11.2	21.6	20.8	19.6	20.0	17.0	13.5	14.0	12.2

TURKEY

(US$ million, unless otherwise indicated)

	1970	1980	1988	1989	1990	1991	1992	1993	1994	1995
5. LONG-TERM DEBT										
DEBT OUTSTANDING (LDOD)	**1,888**	**15,575**	**34,098**	**35,654**	**39,738**	**41,630**	**43,791**	**50,267**	**54,737**	**57,207**
Public and publicly guaranteed	**1,846**	**15,040**	**33,563**	**34,859**	**38,684**	**39,703**	**40,360**	**44,259**	**48,579**	**50,128**
Official creditors	1,766	9,636	17,354	16,509	18,120	18,772	17,577	17,034	17,809	17,281
Multilateral	383	2,149	8,810	8,627	9,627	10,156	9,587	9,321	9,293	8,962
Concessional	247	738	1,257	1,235	1,370	1,548	1,416	1,381	1,506	1,535
Bilateral	1,383	7,487	8,544	7,882	8,493	8,616	7,990	7,713	8,516	8,319
Concessional	1,328	3,661	5,662	5,562	6,595	6,691	6,259	6,053	6,535	6,372
Private creditors	81	5,405	16,209	18,350	20,564	20,931	22,784	27,225	30,770	32,847
Bonds	20	64	2,741	4,209	4,976	5,522	8,081	11,956	13,223	13,836
Commercial banks	8	4,112	11,417	11,975	13,296	12,090	11,679	11,816	13,631	15,257
Other private	53	1,229	2,051	2,166	2,292	3,319	3,023	3,453	3,916	3,754
Private nonguaranteed	**42**	**535**	**535**	**795**	**1,054**	**1,928**	**3,431**	**6,008**	**6,159**	**7,079**
Bonds	0	0	0	16	16	16	66	50	149	149
Commercial banks	42	535	535	779	1,038	1,912	3,365	5,958	6,009	6,929
Memo:										
IBRD	54	1,158	6,130	5,869	6,272	6,179	5,564	5,285	5,195	4,939
IDA	83	189	166	162	157	153	148	142	136	130
DISBURSEMENTS	**332**	**2,475**	**7,360**	**4,897**	**5,177**	**5,624**	**8,444**	**10,307**	**5,603**	**6,328**
Public and publicly guaranteed	**331**	**2,400**	**7,199**	**4,465**	**4,634**	**5,314**	**6,214**	**7,069**	**4,239**	**4,551**
Official creditors	310	1,618	2,190	1,247	2,133	2,287	1,339	1,144	1,235	796
Multilateral	126	476	1,147	710	1,083	1,217	881	745	473	469
Concessional	33	32	192	50	18	219	19	82	45	8
Bilateral	185	1,142	1,043	537	1,050	1,070	458	398	763	326
Concessional	177	801	581	324	894	441	197	163	355	109
Private creditors	21	782	5,009	3,218	2,502	3,027	4,875	5,925	3,004	3,756
Bonds	0	0	2,551	1,447	644	577	3,043	3,909	898	2,332
Commercial banks	0	600	1,846	1,208	1,334	568	1,170	892	1,276	968
Other private	21	182	612	563	524	1,881	663	1,124	830	455
Private nonguaranteed	**1**	**75**	**161**	**432**	**543**	**310**	**2,230**	**3,239**	**1,364**	**1,777**
Bonds	0	0	0	16	0	0	50	0	99	0
Commercial banks	1	75	161	416	543	310	2,180	3,239	1,264	1,777
Memo:										
IBRD	18	313	832	419	627	453	286	354	343	422
IDA	7	0	0	0	0	0	0	0	0	0
PRINCIPAL REPAYMENTS	**131**	**595**	**3,900**	**3,771**	**3,947**	**4,870**	**5,326**	**4,648**	**6,285**	**7,033**
Public and publicly guaranteed	**128**	**566**	**3,762**	**3,503**	**3,664**	**4,241**	**4,600**	**3,987**	**4,785**	**6,000**
Official creditors	95	379	1,700	1,802	1,920	1,851	1,854	1,870	1,853	1,986
Multilateral	70	66	568	648	825	848	1,048	1,137	1,180	1,226
Concessional	25	9	28	56	45	33	46	76	57	82
Bilateral	24	314	1,132	1,154	1,094	1,003	807	732	673	759
Concessional	18	77	295	391	364	391	413	388	433	465
Private creditors	34	186	2,062	1,701	1,745	2,390	2,746	2,117	2,932	4,014
Bonds	0	1	0	1	47	91	389	103	539	1,716
Commercial banks	1	154	1,587	1,276	1,210	1,294	1,471	1,316	1,836	1,596
Other private	32	31	475	424	488	1,005	886	698	558	702
Private nonguaranteed	**3**	**29**	**138**	**268**	**283**	**630**	**726**	**662**	**1,500**	**1,033**
Bonds	0	0	0	0	0	0	0	16	0	0
Commercial banks	3	29	138	268	283	630	726	646	1,500	1,033
Memo:										
IBRD	3	45	472	501	620	669	728	748	800	882
IDA	0	1	4	5	4	4	5	6	6	6
NET FLOWS ON DEBT	**201**	**1,880**	**3,460**	**1,126**	**1,230**	**754**	**3,117**	**5,659**	**-683**	**-705**
Public and publicly guaranteed	**203**	**1,834**	**3,437**	**963**	**970**	**1,073**	**1,614**	**3,082**	**-546**	**-1,449**
Official creditors	216	1,239	491	-555	213	436	-515	-726	-618	-1,190
Multilateral	55	410	580	62	258	369	-166	-392	-707	-757
Concessional	9	23	164	-5	-27	186	-26	6	-12	-73
Bilateral	160	828	-89	-617	-45	67	-349	-334	90	-433
Concessional	158	724	285	-67	530	50	-216	-225	-78	-357
Private creditors	-13	596	2,947	1,517	757	637	2,129	3,808	71	-259
Bonds	0	-1	2,551	1,447	597	487	2,654	3,806	360	616
Commercial banks	-1	446	258	-68	124	-726	-302	-424	-560	-628
Other private	-11	151	137	139	36	876	-223	426	272	-247
Private nonguaranteed	**-2**	**46**	**23**	**163**	**260**	**-319**	**1,504**	**2,577**	**-136**	**744**
Bonds	0	0	0	16	0	0	50	-16	99	0
Commercial banks	-2	46	23	147	260	-319	1,454	2,593	-236	744
Memo:										
IBRD	15	268	360	-82	6	-215	-442	-394	-457	-460
IDA	7	-1	-4	-5	-4	-4	-5	-6	-6	-6

TURKEY

(US$ million, unless otherwise indicated)

	1970	1980	1988	1989	1990	1991	1992	1993	1994	1995
INTEREST PAYMENTS (LINT)	**44**	**507**	**2,446**	**2,653**	**2,877**	**2,882**	**3,190**	**3,184**	**3,211**	**3,477**
Public and publicly guaranteed	**42**	**487**	**2,386**	**2,593**	**2,816**	**2,735**	**2,865**	**3,004**	**2,887**	**3,138**
Official creditors	37	211	1,129	1,156	1,043	1,029	1,058	1,115	979	976
Multilateral	11	128	691	654	688	689	713	693	668	655
Concessional	7	20	50	46	44	45	55	48	50	53
Bilateral	26	84	439	502	355	340	345	422	311	321
Concessional	25	33	195	267	172	190	216	303	204	204
Private creditors	5	276	1,257	1,437	1,772	1,706	1,808	1,889	1,908	2,162
Bonds	1	4	31	237	383	424	533	741	993	1,087
Commercial banks	1	250	1,053	1,020	1,204	1,035	984	892	662	777
Other private	3	21	172	180	185	248	291	256	254	298
Private nonguaranteed	**2**	**20**	**60**	**60**	**61**	**146**	**325**	**179**	**324**	**339**
Bonds	0	0	0	0	1	1	2	2	2	13
Commercial banks	2	20	60	60	60	145	323	177	322	326
Memo:										
IBRD	3	88	536	509	512	506	479	436	418	396
IDA	1	1	2	1	1	1	1	1	1	1
NET TRANSFERS ON DEBT	**156**	**1,373**	**1,014**	**-1,527**	**-1,647**	**-2,128**	**-73**	**2,476**	**-3,894**	**-4,182**
Public and publicly guaranteed	**161**	**1,347**	**1,051**	**-1,630**	**-1,845**	**-1,662**	**-1,251**	**78**	**-3,433**	**-4,587**
Official creditors	178	1,027	-639	-1,711	-830	-593	-1,573	-1,841	-1,596	-2,166
Multilateral	44	283	-111	-592	-431	-320	-879	-1,085	-1,375	-1,412
Concessional	2	3	114	-51	-71	141	-81	-42	-62	-127
Bilateral	134	744	-527	-1,119	-400	-273	-694	-756	-221	-754
Concessional	134	691	91	-334	357	-140	-432	-528	-283	-560
Private creditors	-18	320	1,690	81	-1,015	-1,069	321	1,919	-1,837	-2,421
Bonds	-1	-5	2,520	1,210	214	63	2,121	3,065	-634	-471
Commercial banks	-2	196	-795	-1,088	-1,080	-1,760	-1,286	-1,316	-1,221	-1,405
Other private	-15	130	-35	-41	-149	628	-514	170	18	-544
Private nonguaranteed	**-5**	**26**	**-37**	**103**	**199**	**-466**	**1,179**	**2,398**	**-461**	**405**
Bonds	0	0	0	16	-1	-1	48	-18	98	-13
Commercial banks	-5	26	-37	87	200	-464	1,131	2,416	-558	418
Memo:										
IBRD	12	179	-175	-591	-505	-721	-921	-829	-875	-856
IDA	7	-2	-5	-6	-5	-6	-6	-7	-7	-7
DEBT SERVICE (LTDS)	**176**	**1,102**	**6,346**	**6,424**	**6,824**	**7,752**	**8,516**	**7,832**	**9,497**	**10,510**
Public and publicly guaranteed	**170**	**1,053**	**6,148**	**6,095**	**6,480**	**6,976**	**7,465**	**6,991**	**7,672**	**9,138**
Official creditors	132	591	2,829	2,958	2,963	2,880	2,912	2,985	2,832	2,962
Multilateral	81	193	1,258	1,302	1,514	1,537	1,760	1,830	1,848	1,882
Concessional	31	30	78	101	89	77	100	124	107	135
Bilateral	51	398	1,570	1,656	1,449	1,343	1,152	1,154	984	1,081
Concessional	43	110	490	659	537	581	628	691	638	669
Private creditors	38	462	3,319	3,138	3,517	4,096	4,554	4,006	4,841	6,176
Bonds	1	5	31	238	430	514	922	845	1,532	2,804
Commercial banks	2	405	2,641	2,296	2,414	2,329	2,455	2,208	2,497	2,373
Other private	35	52	648	604	673	1,253	1,177	954	812	1,000
Private nonguaranteed	**6**	**49**	**198**	**328**	**344**	**776**	**1,051**	**841**	**1,824**	**1,372**
Bonds	0	0	0	0	1	1	2	18	2	13
Commercial banks	6	49	198	328	343	774	1,049	823	1,822	1,359
Memo:										
IBRD	6	133	1,007	1,010	1,132	1,175	1,207	1,183	1,218	1,278
IDA	1	3	5	6	5	6	6	7	7	7
UNDISBURSED DEBT	**857**	**3,706**	**8,078**	**8,428**	**8,755**	**8,397**	**8,531**	**9,194**	**8,294**	**8,078**
Official creditors	753	2,938	5,150	5,288	4,853	5,074	5,375	5,468	4,564	3,768
Private creditors	104	768	2,928	3,139	3,902	3,323	3,157	3,726	3,729	4,310
Memorandum items										
Concessional LDOD	1,575	4,399	6,919	6,797	7,964	8,239	7,675	7,434	8,041	7,907
Variable rate LDOD	58	4,122	11,211	11,680	13,469	14,900	15,327	18,402	18,744	19,228
Public sector LDOD	1,839	14,956	33,303	34,569	38,384	39,386	39,826	43,734	48,214	49,942
Private sector LDOD	50	620	795	1,085	1,354	2,245	3,965	6,533	6,524	7,265

6. CURRENCY COMPOSITION OF LONG-TERM DEBT (PERCENT)

	1970	1980	1988	1989	1990	1991	1992	1993	1994	1995
Deutsche mark	17.6	17.0	16.1	16.5	17.5	18.6	17.1	17.2	17.5	16.6
French franc	3.2	5.6	1.8	1.7	1.7	1.7	1.9	1.6	1.6	1.6
Japanese yen	0.0	4.0	12.6	11.2	12.2	15.5	18.7	21.5	23.2	23.4
Pound sterling	6.0	3.8	0.8	0.6	0.8	0.8	0.6	1.0	1.0	0.9
Swiss franc	1.6	8.6	4.9	4.6	5.3	4.5	3.8	3.3	3.0	2.9
U.S.dollars	49.3	43.5	38.9	41.3	39.8	35.9	36.3	36.7	36.6	38.4
Multiple currency	9.1	8.1	19.8	19.5	19.0	19.2	17.5	15.6	14.3	13.4
Special drawing rights	0.0	0.0	0.0	0.0	0.0	0.0	0.0	0.0	0.0	0.0
All other currencies	13.2	9.4	5.1	4.5	3.9	3.8	4.0	3.0	2.9	2.8

TURKEY

(US$ million, unless otherwise indicated)

	1970	1980	1988	1989	1990	1991	1992	1993	1994	1995
7. DEBT RESTRUCTURINGS										
Total amount rescheduled	0	..	0	0	0	0	0	0	0	0
Debt stock rescheduled	0	..	0	0	0	0	0	0	0	0
Principal rescheduled	0	..	0	0	0	0	0	0	0	0
Official	0	..	0	0	0	0	0	0	0	0
Private	0	..	0	0	0	0	0	0	0	0
Interest rescheduled	0	..	0	0	0	0	0	0	0	0
Official	0	..	0	0	0	0	0	0	0	0
Private	0	..	0	0	0	0	0	0	0	0
Debt forgiven	..	..	0	2	0	0	0	9	0	0
Memo: interest forgiven	..	..	0	0	0	0	0	0	0	0
Debt stock reduction	0	..	0	0	0	0	0	0	0	0
of which debt buyback	0	..	0	0	0	0	0	0	0	0
8. DEBT STOCK-FLOW RECONCILIATION										
Total change in debt stocks	..	..	..	633	7,791	1,510	5,704	12,349	-2,409	7,201
Net flows on debt	..	..	..	216	4,936	371	6,660	11,532	-7,568	4,028
Net change in interest arrears	..	..	..	0	0	0	0	0	0	0
Interest capitalized	..	..	..	0	0	0	0	0	0	0
Debt forgiveness or reduction	..	..	..	-2	0	0	0	-9	0	0
Cross-currency valuation	..	..	..	-476	2,232	221	-1,128	446	3,316	752
Residual	..	..	..	895	623	917	172	380	1,844	2,422
9. AVERAGE TERMS OF NEW COMMITMENTS										
ALL CREDITORS										
Interest (%)	3.6	8.3	7.7	7.8	8.4	7.5	7.3	5.9	6.2	6.1
Maturity (years)	19.0	16.4	14.2	12.3	10.2	13.7	8.4	10.0	10.4	5.5
Grace period (years)	4.8	5.0	6.9	5.0	4.6	5.0	4.8	5.7	4.7	3.0
Grant element (%)	37.5	17.4	11.8	12.1	9.1	13.5	11.4	20.1	18.5	12.3
Official creditors										
Interest (%)	3.4	7.1	6.4	5.7	6.7	6.7	7.0	4.6	6.0	5.5
Maturity (years)	19.6	18.3	16.0	18.2	17.0	17.6	14.3	20.3	13.7	17.7
Grace period (years)	4.9	5.7	6.0	6.4	7.3	6.9	6.1	6.6	4.8	5.7
Grant element (%)	39.1	22.9	21.2	29.1	23.1	20.5	17.2	38.0	22.2	27.3
Private creditors										
Interest (%)	5.5	14.4	8.3	8.6	9.4	8.3	7.4	6.2	6.3	6.2
Maturity (years)	13.7	7.4	13.3	9.7	6.5	9.9	6.3	7.8	9.5	4.6
Grace period (years)	3.1	1.9	7.3	4.4	3.2	3.2	4.3	5.5	4.7	2.8
Grant element (%)	22.7	-9.6	7.1	4.9	1.5	6.7	9.3	16.1	17.3	11.1
Memorandum items										
Commitments	489	2,925	6,183	4,976	4,628	5,427	6,763	8,032	3,800	4,519
Official creditors	440	2,426	2,065	1,485	1,624	2,690	1,805	1,460	890	318
Private creditors	49	499	4,118	3,491	3,004	2,737	4,958	6,572	2,910	4,201

10. CONTRACTUAL OBLIGATIONS ON OUTSTANDING LONG-TERM DEBT

	1996	1997	1998	1999	2000	2001	2002	2003	2004	2005
TOTAL										
Disbursements	3,850	2,084	1,019	474	238	158	96	71	46	31
Principal	7,309	6,856	8,757	5,948	5,109	4,707	2,960	3,439	2,090	1,812
Interest	3,292	2,980	2,619	2,119	1,755	1,516	1,252	1,103	901	798
Official creditors										
Disbursements	1,284	890	586	375	230	158	96	71	46	31
Principal	2,187	2,059	1,997	1,856	1,916	2,471	1,270	1,111	932	820
Interest	916	830	736	642	543	450	317	258	210	170
Bilateral creditors										
Disbursements	855	511	275	126	55	34	6	0	0	0
Principal	871	792	825	740	725	663	639	576	538	497
Interest	303	282	255	224	196	170	148	126	108	91
Multilateral creditors										
Disbursements	430	379	311	249	175	125	90	71	46	31
Principal	1,315	1,267	1,172	1,115	1,190	1,809	631	535	394	324
Interest	614	547	481	418	347	280	169	132	102	79
Private creditors										
Disbursements	2,566	1,194	433	100	9	0	0	0	0	0
Principal	5,122	4,797	6,760	4,093	3,194	2,236	1,690	2,328	1,158	991
Interest	2,375	2,150	1,883	1,477	1,212	1,066	935	845	691	628
Commercial banks										
Disbursements	1,544	782	260	66	0	0	0	0	0	0
Principal	1,571	1,417	1,280	887	619	463	363	291	223	182
Interest	852	817	747	679	624	582	550	525	505	490
Other private										
Disbursements	1,022	412	173	34	9	0	0	0	0	0
Principal	3,552	3,380	5,480	3,206	2,575	1,773	1,326	2,037	935	810
Interest	1,524	1,333	1,137	798	588	483	386	321	185	138

TURKMENISTAN

(US$ million, unless otherwise indicated)

1. SUMMARY DEBT DATA

	1970	1980	1988	1989	1990	1991	1992	1993	1994	1995
TOTAL DEBT STOCKS (EDT)	..	..	..	..	..	..	..	**276.4**	**427.0**	**392.5**
Long-term debt (LDOD)	..	..	..	..	..	..	..	**276.4**	**342.3**	**374.7**
Public and publicly guaranteed	..	..	..	..	..	..	..	276.4	342.3	374.7
Private nonguaranteed	0.0	0.0	0.0	0.0	0.0	0.0	0.0	0.0	0.0	0.0
Use of IMF credit	**0.0**	**0.0**	**0.0**	**0.0**	**0.0**	**0.0**	**0.0**	**0.0**	**0.0**	**0.0**
Short-term debt	..	..	..	..	..	..	..	**0.0**	**84.7**	**17.8**
of which interest arrears on LDOD	..	..	..	..	..	..	..	0.0	4.7	9.8
Official creditors	..	..	..	..	..	..	..	0.0	4.2	4.9
Private creditors	..	..	..	..	..	..	..	0.0	0.5	4.9
Memo: principal arrears on LDOD	..	..	..	..	..	..	..	0.0	33.7	132.8
Official creditors	..	..	..	..	..	..	..	0.0	15.7	114.8
Private creditors	..	..	..	..	..	..	..	0.0	18.0	18.0
Memo: export credits	..	..	0.0	0.0	0.0	0.0	0.0	0.0	121.0	101.0
TOTAL DEBT FLOWS										
Disbursements	..	..	..	..	..	..	..	**239.7**	**133.1**	**102.5**
Long-term debt	..	..	..	..	..	..	..	239.7	133.1	102.5
IMF purchases	0.0	0.0	0.0	0.0	0.0	0.0	0.0	0.0	0.0	0.0
Principal repayments	..	..	..	..	..	..	..	**8.7**	**71.6**	**75.5**
Long-term debt	..	..	..	..	..	..	..	8.7	71.6	75.5
IMF repurchases	0.0	0.0	0.0	0.0	0.0	0.0	0.0	0.0	0.0	0.0
Net flows on debt	..	..	..	..	..	..	..	**231.1**	**141.5**	**-45.0**
of which short-term debt	..	..	..	..	..	..	..	0.0	80.0	-72.0
Interest payments (INT)	..	..	..	..	..	..	..	**1.7**	**27.9**	**24.0**
Long-term debt	..	..	..	..	..	..	..	1.7	26.1	22.0
IMF charges	0.0	0.0	0.0	0.0	0.0	0.0	0.0	0.0	0.0	0.0
Short-term debt	..	..	..	..	..	..	..	0.0	1.8	2.0
Net transfers on debt	..	..	..	..	..	..	..	**229.4**	**113.6**	**-69.0**
Total debt service paid (TDS)	..	..	..	..	..	..	..	**10.4**	**99.5**	**99.5**
Long-term debt	..	..	..	..	..	..	..	10.4	97.7	97.4
IMF repurchases and charges	0.0	0.0	0.0	0.0	0.0	0.0	0.0	0.0	0.0	0.0
Short-term debt (interest only)	..	..	..	..	..	..	..	0.0	1.8	2.0

2. AGGREGATE NET RESOURCE FLOWS AND NET TRANSFERS (LONG-TERM)

	1970	1980	1988	1989	1990	1991	1992	1993	1994	1995
NET RESOURCE FLOWS	..	..	..	..	..	..	..	**246.1**	**72.7**	**28.1**
Net flow of long-term debt (ex. IMF)	..	..	..	..	..	..	..	231.1	61.5	27.0
Foreign direct investment (net)	..	..	..	..	..	..	..	0.0	0.0	0.0
Portfolio equity flows	..	..	..	..	..	..	..	0.0	0.0	0.0
Grants (excluding technical coop.)	..	..	..	..	..	..	..	15.0	11.2	1.1
Memo: technical coop. grants	..	..	..	..	..	..	..	0.6	2.8	11.1
NET TRANSFERS	..	..	..	..	..	..	..	**244.4**	**46.6**	**6.1**
Interest on long-term debt	..	..	..	..	..	..	..	1.7	26.1	22.0
Profit remittances on FDI	..	..	..	..	..	..	..	0.0	0.0	0.0

3. MAJOR ECONOMIC AGGREGATES

	1970	1980	1988	1989	1990	1991	1992	1993	1994	1995
Gross national product (GNP)	..	..	..	..	..	..	..	5,707.8	4,393.6	3,918.9
Exports of goods & services (XGS)	..	..	..	..	..	..	..	..	..	..
of which workers remittances	..	..	..	..	..	..	..	..	..	..
Imports of goods & services (MGS)	..	..	..	..	..	..	..	..	..	..
International reserves (RES)	..	..	..	..	..	..	..	..	..	..
Current account balance	..	..	..	..	..	..	..	..	..	..

4. DEBT INDICATORS

	1970	1980	1988	1989	1990	1991	1992	1993	1994	1995
EDT / XGS (%)	..	..	..	..	..	..	..	..	..	..
EDT / GNP (%)	..	..	..	..	..	..	..	4.8	9.7	10.0
TDS / XGS (%)	..	..	..	..	..	..	..	..	..	..
INT / XGS (%)	..	..	..	..	..	..	..	..	..	..
INT / GNP (%)	..	..	..	..	..	..	..	0.0	0.6	0.6
RES / EDT (%)	..	..	..	..	..	..	..	..	..	..
RES / MGS (months)	..	..	..	..	..	..	..	..	..	..
Short-term / EDT (%)	..	..	..	..	..	..	..	0.0	19.8	4.5
Concessional / EDT (%)	..	..	..	..	..	..	..	3.2	4.6	5.1
Multilateral / EDT (%)	..	..	..	..	..	..	..	9.1	12.6	14.8

TURKMENISTAN

(US$ million, unless otherwise indicated)

5. LONG-TERM DEBT

	1970	1980	1988	1989	1990	1991	1992	1993	1994	1995
DEBT OUTSTANDING (LDOD)	..	..	..	..	..	..	..	**276.4**	**342.3**	**374.7**
Public and publicly guaranteed	..	..	..	..	..	..	..	**276.4**	**342.3**	**374.7**
Official creditors	..	..	..	..	..	..	..	147.9	202.5	213.8
Multilateral	..	..	..	..	..	..	..	25.2	53.6	58.2
Concessional	..	..	..	..	..	..	..	0.0	0.0	0.0
Bilateral	..	..	..	..	..	..	..	122.7	148.9	155.5
Concessional	..	..	..	..	..	..	..	9.0	19.8	19.9
Private creditors	..	..	..	..	..	..	..	128.6	139.8	160.9
Bonds	..	..	..	..	..	..	..	0.0	0.0	0.0
Commercial banks	..	..	..	..	..	..	..	0.0	0.0	24.9
Other private	..	..	..	..	..	..	..	128.6	139.8	136.1
Private nonguaranteed	**0.0**	**0.0**	**0.0**	**0.0**	**0.0**	**0.0**	**0.0**	**0.0**	**0.0**	**0.0**
Bonds	..	..	..	..	..	..	..	0.0	0.0	0.0
Commercial banks	..	..	..	..	..	..	..	0.0	0.0	0.0
Memo:										
IBRD	0.0	0.0	0.0	0.0	0.0	0.0	0.0	0.0	0.0	0.9
IDA	0.0	0.0	0.0	0.0	0.0	0.0	0.0	0.0	0.0	0.0
DISBURSEMENTS	..	..	..	..	..	..	..	**239.7**	**133.1**	**102.5**
Public and publicly guaranteed	..	..	..	..	..	..	..	**239.7**	**133.1**	**102.5**
Official creditors	..	..	..	..	..	..	..	149.1	69.9	27.6
Multilateral	..	..	..	..	..	..	..	26.4	25.1	1.0
Concessional	..	..	..	..	..	..	..	0.0	0.0	0.0
Bilateral	..	..	..	..	..	..	..	122.7	44.8	26.6
Concessional	..	..	..	..	..	..	..	9.0	10.9	0.1
Private creditors	..	..	..	..	..	..	..	90.7	63.2	74.9
Bonds	..	..	..	..	..	..	..	0.0	0.0	0.0
Commercial banks	..	..	..	..	..	..	..	0.0	0.0	24.9
Other private	..	..	..	..	..	..	..	90.7	63.2	50.0
Private nonguaranteed	**0.0**	**0.0**	**0.0**	**0.0**	**0.0**	**0.0**	**0.0**	**0.0**	**0.0**	**0.0**
Bonds	..	..	..	..	..	..	..	0.0	0.0	0.0
Commercial banks	..	..	..	..	..	..	..	0.0	0.0	0.0
Memo:										
IBRD	0.0	0.0	0.0	0.0	0.0	0.0	0.0	0.0	0.0	1.0
IDA	0.0	0.0	0.0	0.0	0.0	0.0	0.0	0.0	0.0	0.0
PRINCIPAL REPAYMENTS	..	..	..	..	..	..	..	**8.7**	**71.6**	**75.5**
Public and publicly guaranteed	..	..	..	..	..	..	..	**8.7**	**71.6**	**75.5**
Official creditors	..	..	..	..	..	..	..	0.0	18.6	20.0
Multilateral	..	..	..	..	..	..	..	0.0	0.0	0.0
Concessional	..	..	..	..	..	..	..	0.0	0.0	0.0
Bilateral	..	..	..	..	..	..	..	0.0	18.6	20.0
Concessional	..	..	..	..	..	..	..	0.0	0.0	0.0
Private creditors	..	..	..	..	..	..	..	8.7	53.0	55.5
Bonds	..	..	..	..	..	..	..	0.0	0.0	0.0
Commercial banks	..	..	..	..	..	..	..	0.0	0.0	0.0
Other private	..	..	..	..	..	..	..	8.7	53.0	55.5
Private nonguaranteed	**0.0**	**0.0**	**0.0**	**0.0**	**0.0**	**0.0**	**0.0**	**0.0**	**0.0**	**0.0**
Bonds	..	..	..	..	..	..	..	0.0	0.0	0.0
Commercial banks	..	..	..	..	..	..	..	0.0	0.0	0.0
Memo:										
IBRD	0.0	0.0	0.0	0.0	0.0	0.0	0.0	0.0	0.0	0.0
IDA	0.0	0.0	0.0	0.0	0.0	0.0	0.0	0.0	0.0	0.0
NET FLOWS ON DEBT	..	..	..	..	..	..	..	**231.1**	**61.5**	**27.0**
Public and publicly guaranteed	..	..	..	..	..	..	..	**231.1**	**61.5**	**27.0**
Official creditors	..	..	..	..	..	..	..	149.1	51.3	7.6
Multilateral	..	..	..	..	..	..	..	26.4	25.1	1.0
Concessional	..	..	..	..	..	..	..	0.0	0.0	0.0
Bilateral	..	..	..	..	..	..	..	122.7	26.2	6.6
Concessional	..	..	..	..	..	..	..	9.0	10.9	0.1
Private creditors	..	..	..	..	..	..	..	82.0	10.2	19.4
Bonds	..	..	..	..	..	..	..	0.0	0.0	0.0
Commercial banks	..	..	..	..	..	..	..	0.0	0.0	24.9
Other private	..	..	..	..	..	..	..	82.0	10.2	-5.5
Private nonguaranteed	**0.0**	**0.0**	**0.0**	**0.0**	**0.0**	**0.0**	**0.0**	**0.0**	**0.0**	**0.0**
Bonds	..	..	..	..	..	..	..	0.0	0.0	0.0
Commercial banks	..	..	..	..	..	..	..	0.0	0.0	0.0
Memo:										
IBRD	0.0	0.0	0.0	0.0	0.0	0.0	0.0	0.0	0.0	1.0
IDA	0.0	0.0	0.0	0.0	0.0	0.0	0.0	0.0	0.0	0.0

TURKMENISTAN

(US$ million, unless otherwise indicated)

	1970	1980	1988	1989	1990	1991	1992	1993	1994	1995
INTEREST PAYMENTS (LINT)	..	..	..	..	..	..	..	**1.7**	**26.1**	**22.0**
Public and publicly guaranteed	..	..	..	..	..	..	..	**1.7**	**26.1**	**22.0**
Official creditors	..	..	..	..	..	..	..	0.7	18.3	11.6
Multilateral	..	..	..	..	..	..	..	0.3	6.8	1.9
Concessional	..	..	..	..	..	..	..	0.0	0.0	0.0
Bilateral	..	..	..	..	..	..	..	0.3	11.5	9.7
Concessional	..	..	..	..	..	..	..	0.0	0.2	0.5
Private creditors	..	..	..	..	..	..	..	1.0	7.8	10.3
Bonds	..	..	..	..	..	..	..	0.0	0.0	0.0
Commercial banks	..	..	..	..	..	..	..	0.0	0.0	0.2
Other private	..	..	..	..	..	..	..	1.0	7.8	10.2
Private nonguaranteed	**0.0**	**0.0**	**0.0**	**0.0**	**0.0**	**0.0**	**0.0**	**0.0**	**0.0**	**0.0**
Bonds	..	..	..	..	..	..	..	0.0	0.0	0.0
Commercial banks	..	..	..	..	..	..	..	0.0	0.0	0.0
Memo:										
IBRD	0.0	0.0	0.0	0.0	0.0	0.0	0.0	0.0	0.0	0.1
IDA	0.0	0.0	0.0	0.0	0.0	0.0	0.0	0.0	0.0	0.0
NET TRANSFERS ON DEBT	..	..	..	..	..	..	..	**229.4**	**35.4**	**5.0**
Public and publicly guaranteed	..	..	..	..	..	..	..	**229.4**	**35.4**	**5.0**
Official creditors	..	..	..	..	..	..	..	148.4	33.0	-4.0
Multilateral	..	..	..	..	..	..	..	26.0	18.2	-0.9
Concessional	..	..	..	..	..	..	..	0.0	0.0	0.0
Bilateral	..	..	..	..	..	..	..	122.4	14.7	-3.1
Concessional	..	..	..	..	..	..	..	9.0	10.7	-0.4
Private creditors	..	..	..	..	..	..	..	81.0	2.4	9.1
Bonds	..	..	..	..	..	..	..	0.0	0.0	0.0
Commercial banks	..	..	..	..	..	..	..	0.0	0.0	24.7
Other private	..	..	..	..	..	..	..	81.0	2.4	-15.6
Private nonguaranteed	**0.0**	**0.0**	**0.0**	**0.0**	**0.0**	**0.0**	**0.0**	**0.0**	**0.0**	**0.0**
Bonds	..	..	..	..	..	..	..	0.0	0.0	0.0
Commercial banks	..	..	..	..	..	..	..	0.0	0.0	0.0
Memo:										
IBRD	0.0	0.0	0.0	0.0	0.0	0.0	0.0	0.0	0.0	0.9
IDA	0.0	0.0	0.0	0.0	0.0	0.0	0.0	0.0	0.0	0.0
DEBT SERVICE (LTDS)	..	..	..	..	..	..	..	**10.4**	**97.7**	**97.4**
Public and publicly guaranteed	..	..	..	..	..	..	..	**10.4**	**97.7**	**97.4**
Official creditors	..	..	..	..	..	..	..	0.7	36.9	31.6
Multilateral	..	..	..	..	..	..	..	0.3	6.8	1.9
Concessional	..	..	..	..	..	..	..	0.0	0.0	0.0
Bilateral	..	..	..	..	..	..	..	0.3	30.1	29.7
Concessional	..	..	..	..	..	..	..	0.0	0.2	0.5
Private creditors	..	..	..	..	..	..	..	9.7	60.8	65.8
Bonds	..	..	..	..	..	..	..	0.0	0.0	0.0
Commercial banks	..	..	..	..	..	..	..	0.0	0.0	0.2
Other private	..	..	..	..	..	..	..	9.7	60.8	65.6
Private nonguaranteed	**0.0**	**0.0**	**0.0**	**0.0**	**0.0**	**0.0**	**0.0**	**0.0**	**0.0**	**0.0**
Bonds	..	..	..	..	..	..	..	0.0	0.0	0.0
Commercial banks	..	..	..	..	..	..	..	0.0	0.0	0.0
Memo:										
IBRD	0.0	0.0	0.0	0.0	0.0	0.0	0.0	0.0	0.0	0.1
IDA	0.0	0.0	0.0	0.0	0.0	0.0	0.0	0.0	0.0	0.0
UNDISBURSED DEBT	..	..	..	..	..	..	..	**71.2**	**65.6**	**226.4**
Official creditors	..	..	..	..	..	..	..	44.1	57.0	46.1
Private creditors	..	..	..	..	..	..	..	27.0	8.7	180.3
Memorandum items										
Concessional LDOD	..	..	..	..	..	..	..	9.0	19.8	19.9
Variable rate LDOD	..	..	..	..	..	..	..	267.5	286.0	285.7
Public sector LDOD	..	..	..	..	..	..	..	276.4	342.3	374.7
Private sector LDOD	..	..	..	..	..	..	..	0.0	0.0	0.0

6. CURRENCY COMPOSITION OF LONG-TERM DEBT (PERCENT)

	1970	1980	1988	1989	1990	1991	1992	1993	1994	1995
Deutsche mark	..	..	..	..	..	..	..	0.0	6.1	11.3
French franc	..	..	..	..	..	..	..	0.0	0.0	0.0
Japanese yen	..	..	..	..	..	..	..	0.0	0.0	0.0
Pound sterling	..	..	..	..	..	..	..	0.0	0.0	0.0
Swiss franc	..	..	..	..	..	..	..	0.0	0.0	0.0
U.S.dollars	..	..	..	..	..	..	..	90.9	77.9	72.7
Multiple currency	..	..	..	..	..	..	..	0.0	0.0	0.2
Special drawing rights	..	..	..	..	..	..	..	0.0	0.0	0.0
All other currencies	..	..	..	..	..	..	..	9.1	16.0	15.7

TURKMENISTAN

(US$ million, unless otherwise indicated)

	1970	1980	1988	1989	1990	1991	1992	1993	1994	1995
7. DEBT RESTRUCTURINGS										
Total amount rescheduled	0.0	0.0	0.0	0.0	0.0	0.0	0.0	0.0	0.0	0.0
Debt stock rescheduled	0.0	0.0	0.0	0.0	0.0	0.0	0.0	0.0	0.0	0.0
Principal rescheduled	0.0	0.0	0.0	0.0	0.0	0.0	0.0	0.0	0.0	0.0
Official	0.0	0.0	0.0	0.0	0.0	0.0	0.0	0.0	0.0	0.0
Private	0.0	0.0	0.0	0.0	0.0	0.0	0.0	0.0	0.0	0.0
Interest rescheduled	0.0	0.0	0.0	0.0	0.0	0.0	0.0	0.0	0.0	0.0
Official	0.0	0.0	0.0	0.0	0.0	0.0	0.0	0.0	0.0	0.0
Private	0.0	0.0	0.0	0.0	0.0	0.0	0.0	0.0	0.0	0.0
Debt forgiven	..	..	0.0	0.0	0.0	0.0	0.0	0.0	0.0	0.0
Memo: interest forgiven	..	..	0.0	0.0	0.0	0.0	0.0	0.0	0.0	0.0
Debt stock reduction	0.0	0.0	0.0	0.0	0.0	0.0	0.0	0.0	0.0	0.0
of which debt buyback	0.0	0.0	0.0	0.0	0.0	0.0	0.0	0.0	0.0	0.0
8. DEBT STOCK-FLOW RECONCILIATION										
Total change in debt stocks	..	..	..	..	..	..	..	230.0	150.6	-34.5
Net flows on debt	..	..	..	..	..	..	..	231.1	141.5	-45.0
Net change in interest arrears	..	..	..	..	..	..	..	0.0	4.7	5.0
Interest capitalized	..	..	..	..	..	..	..	0.0	0.0	0.0
Debt forgiveness or reduction	..	..	..	..	..	..	..	0.0	0.0	0.0
Cross-currency valuation	..	..	..	..	..	..	..	-1.9	7.8	7.5
Residual	..	..	..	..	..	..	..	1.0	-3.5	-2.1
9. AVERAGE TERMS OF NEW COMMITMENTS										
ALL CREDITORS										
Interest (%)	..	..	..	..	..	..	..	3.8	6.0	6.6
Maturity (years)	..	..	..	..	..	..	..	6.6	10.4	7.4
Grace period (years)	..	..	..	..	..	..	..	3.0	3.1	1.8
Grant element (%)	..	..	..	..	..	..	..	18.6	16.1	10.7
Official creditors										
Interest (%)	..	..	..	..	..	..	..	3.4	5.8	4.9
Maturity (years)	..	..	..	..	..	..	..	18.4	13.3	2.4
Grace period (years)	..	..	..	..	..	..	..	5.6	4.2	0.7
Grant element (%)	..	..	..	..	..	..	..	36.9	20.3	7.0
Private creditors										
Interest (%)	..	..	..	..	..	..	..	3.9	6.3	6.7
Maturity (years)	..	..	..	..	..	..	..	3.0	5.2	7.7
Grace period (years)	..	..	..	..	..	..	..	2.2	1.0	1.9
Grant element (%)	..	..	..	..	..	..	..	12.9	8.4	10.9
Memorandum items										
Commitments	..	..	..	..	..	..	..	101.9	127.3	261.6
Official creditors	..	..	..	..	..	..	..	24.2	82.6	15.1
Private creditors	..	..	..	..	..	..	..	77.7	44.7	246.5

10. CONTRACTUAL OBLIGATIONS ON OUTSTANDING LONG-TERM DEBT

	1996	1997	1998	1999	2000	2001	2002	2003	2004	2005
TOTAL										
Disbursements	105.5	69.7	29.3	12.2	3.3	2.3	2.0	1.0	1.0	0.2
Principal	91.0	85.5	71.0	43.3	38.9	29.6	21.1	13.8	13.8	12.9
Interest	18.3	16.6	15.2	12.4	10.0	7.7	6.0	4.9	4.1	3.2
Official creditors										
Disbursements	15.1	10.1	6.8	4.3	3.3	2.3	2.0	1.0	1.0	0.2
Principal	39.2	25.4	15.1	5.9	7.5	3.6	4.0	4.4	4.4	3.5
Interest	5.8	4.0	3.2	2.8	2.6	2.4	2.3	2.1	1.9	1.6
Bilateral creditors										
Disbursements	12.1	6.8	2.8	0.3	0.0	0.0	0.0	0.0	0.0	0.0
Principal	39.2	25.4	15.1	5.9	5.9	1.9	2.3	2.8	2.8	1.8
Interest	5.5	3.5	2.4	1.7	1.4	1.1	0.9	0.8	0.6	0.5
Multilateral creditors										
Disbursements	3.0	3.3	4.0	4.0	3.3	2.3	2.0	1.0	1.0	0.2
Principal	0.0	0.0	0.0	0.0	1.7	1.7	1.7	1.7	1.7	1.7
Interest	0.3	0.5	0.8	1.1	1.3	1.3	1.3	1.3	1.2	1.1
Private creditors										
Disbursements	90.4	59.6	22.4	7.9	0.0	0.0	0.0	0.0	0.0	0.0
Principal	51.8	60.1	55.9	37.5	31.4	26.0	17.1	9.4	9.4	9.4
Interest	12.6	12.5	12.0	9.5	7.3	5.3	3.8	2.8	2.2	1.6
Commercial banks										
Disbursements	70.7	46.4	16.6	7.7	0.0	0.0	0.0	0.0	0.0	0.0
Principal	5.4	10.3	22.0	22.0	22.0	22.0	17.1	9.4	9.4	9.4
Interest	4.1	6.5	8.8	8.0	6.6	5.2	3.8	2.8	2.2	1.6
Other private										
Disbursements	19.6	13.2	5.8	0.2	0.0	0.0	0.0	0.0	0.0	0.0
Principal	46.3	49.8	34.0	15.5	9.4	4.1	0.0	0.0	0.0	0.0
Interest	8.5	6.1	3.2	1.5	0.7	0.1	0.0	0.0	0.0	0.0

UGANDA

(US$ million, unless otherwise indicated)

	1970	1980	1988	1989	1990	1991	1992	1993	1994	1995
1. SUMMARY DEBT DATA										
TOTAL DEBT STOCKS (EDT)	..	**689**	**1,923**	**2,177**	**2,583**	**2,777**	**2,928**	**3,029**	**3,369**	**3,564**
Long-term debt (LDOD)	**152**	**537**	**1,593**	**1,847**	**2,161**	**2,283**	**2,433**	**2,599**	**2,867**	**3,054**
Public and publicly guaranteed	152	537	1,593	1,847	2,161	2,283	2,433	2,599	2,867	3,054
Private nonguaranteed	0	0	0	0	0	0	0	0	0	0
Use of IMF credit	**0**	**89**	**252**	**225**	**282**	**330**	**344**	**334**	**383**	**417**
Short-term debt	..	**63**	**78**	**106**	**140**	**164**	**150**	**96**	**118**	**93**
of which interest arrears on LDOD	..	19	38	55	83	102	81	71	80	59
Official creditors	..	10	15	22	32	51	43	50	67	47
Private creditors	..	9	23	33	51	51	39	22	13	12
Memo: principal arrears on LDOD	..	82	98	135	215	300	268	196	207	211
Official creditors	..	30	37	52	94	148	130	134	144	150
Private creditors	..	52	61	83	122	152	138	62	63	61
Memo: export credits	..	..	224	293	270	271	305	293	272	270
TOTAL DEBT FLOWS										
Disbursements	**26**	**161**	**241**	**362**	**382**	**264**	**311**	**408**	**322**	**287**
Long-term debt	26	83	167	311	301	186	255	408	270	231
IMF purchases	0	78	74	51	81	78	56	0	53	56
Principal repayments	**5**	**45**	**158**	**141**	**111**	**102**	**80**	**119**	**112**	**99**
Long-term debt	5	32	78	71	66	68	51	109	88	70
IMF repurchases	0	13	81	70	45	34	29	10	25	29
Net flows on debt	**22**	**116**	**91**	**232**	**277**	**167**	**239**	**244**	**224**	**185**
of which short-term debt	..	..	8	10	6	5	7	-45	14	-4
Interest payments (INT)	..	**12**	**43**	**46**	**37**	**46**	**34**	**37**	**38**	**38**
Long-term debt	5	4	24	25	19	33	26	33	34	34
IMF charges	0	3	16	16	13	8	3	2	2	2
Short-term debt	..	5	3	4	5	5	5	3	3	2
Net transfers on debt	..	**104**	**48**	**186**	**241**	**121**	**204**	**206**	**185**	**146**
Total debt service paid (TDS)	..	**57**	**202**	**186**	**147**	**148**	**114**	**157**	**151**	**137**
Long-term debt	9	36	102	96	85	102	77	142	122	104
IMF repurchases and charges	0	16	97	86	58	42	32	12	26	31
Short-term debt (interest only)	..	5	3	4	5	5	5	3	3	2
2. AGGREGATE NET RESOURCE FLOWS AND NET TRANSFERS (LONG-TERM)										
NET RESOURCE FLOWS	**28**	**113**	**281**	**388**	**492**	**433**	**544**	**613**	**589**	**682**
Net flow of long-term debt (ex. IMF)	22	51	90	240	234	118	204	298	182	161
Foreign direct investment (net)	4	0	5	-2	0	1	3	55	88	121
Portfolio equity flows	0	0	0	0	0	0	0	0	0	0
Grants (excluding technical coop.)	2	62	187	150	257	314	336	260	319	399
Memo: technical coop. grants	14	21	76	88	94	107	122	124	125	148
NET TRANSFERS	**10**	**109**	**257**	**362**	**473**	**399**	**518**	**568**	**542**	**635**
Interest on long-term debt	5	4	24	25	19	33	26	33	34	34
Profit remittances on FDI	13	0	0	0	0	0	0	13	13	12
3. MAJOR ECONOMIC AGGREGATES										
Gross national product (GNP)	..	1,262	6,452	5,186	4,227	3,263	2,769	3,172	3,920	5,597
Exports of goods & services (XGS)	297	331	324	304	246	202	199	242	344	642
of which workers remittances	0	0	0	0	0	0	0	0	0	0
Imports of goods & services (MGS)	271	450	739	779	753	732	672	752	965	1,440
International reserves (RES)	57	3	49	14	44	59	94	146	321	459
Current account balance	20	-83	-295	-361	-429	-449	-338	-381	-309	-428
4. DEBT INDICATORS										
EDT / XGS (%)	..	208.1	593.6	716.1	1,050.0	1,374.9	1,471.1	1,251.5	979.2	555.1
EDT / GNP (%)	..	54.6	29.8	42.0	61.1	85.1	105.7	95.5	85.9	63.7
TDS / XGS (%)	..	17.3	62.2	61.3	59.9	73.3	57.3	64.7	43.8	21.3
INT / XGS (%)	..	3.7	13.4	15.0	14.9	22.8	17.2	15.4	11.1	6.0
INT / GNP (%)	..	1.0	0.7	0.9	0.9	1.4	1.2	1.2	1.0	0.7
RES / EDT (%)	..	0.4	2.6	0.6	1.7	2.1	3.2	4.8	9.5	12.9
RES / MGS (months)	2.5	0.1	0.8	0.2	0.7	1.0	1.7	2.3	4.0	3.8
Short-term / EDT (%)	..	9.1	4.1	4.8	5.4	5.9	5.1	3.2	3.5	2.6
Concessional / EDT (%)	..	37.0	47.2	53.5	56.7	59.0	62.1	70.9	73.4	78.1
Multilateral / EDT (%)	..	11.5	45.6	45.1	49.2	51.3	53.3	57.0	59.7	61.8

UGANDA

(US$ million, unless otherwise indicated)

	1970	1980	1988	1989	1990	1991	1992	1993	1994	1995
5. LONG-TERM DEBT										
DEBT OUTSTANDING (LDOD)	**152**	**537**	**1,593**	**1,847**	**2,161**	**2,283**	**2,433**	**2,599**	**2,867**	**3,054**
Public and publicly guaranteed	**152**	**537**	**1,593**	**1,847**	**2,161**	**2,283**	**2,433**	**2,599**	**2,867**	**3,054**
Official creditors	127	293	1,246	1,512	1,826	1,983	2,173	2,485	2,774	2,970
Multilateral	19	79	876	983	1,270	1,425	1,561	1,727	2,010	2,202
Concessional	19	64	733	855	1,142	1,309	1,450	1,624	1,933	2,147
Bilateral	108	214	370	529	556	557	612	758	764	768
Concessional	95	191	175	311	322	330	368	523	542	635
Private creditors	25	244	347	335	335	301	260	115	93	84
Bonds	10	0	4	4	4	4	4	4	4	4
Commercial banks	14	23	79	97	89	73	68	40	27	21
Other private	1	221	265	234	242	224	189	71	62	59
Private nonguaranteed	**0**	**0**	**0**	**0**	**0**	**0**	**0**	**0**	**0**	**0**
Bonds	0	0	0	0	0	0	0	0	0	0
Commercial banks	0	0	0	0	0	0	0	0	0	0
Memo:										
IBRD	6	1	44	37	34	30	21	16	11	0
IDA	13	46	585	673	935	1,080	1,188	1,327	1,604	1,792
DISBURSEMENTS	**26**	**83**	**167**	**311**	**301**	**186**	**255**	**408**	**270**	**231**
Public and publicly guaranteed	**26**	**83**	**167**	**311**	**301**	**186**	**255**	**408**	**270**	**231**
Official creditors	19	18	134	270	262	180	250	390	270	231
Multilateral	6	7	115	143	227	165	218	201	250	210
Concessional	5	2	111	137	223	162	203	185	249	201
Bilateral	14	11	19	126	36	16	32	189	20	22
Concessional	14	11	7	102	23	14	27	150	20	21
Private creditors	7	65	33	41	38	5	6	18	0	0
Bonds	0	0	0	0	0	0	0	0	0	0
Commercial banks	6	17	19	39	5	1	2	9	0	0
Other private	2	49	14	2	34	4	4	9	0	0
Private nonguaranteed	**0**	**0**	**0**	**0**	**0**	**0**	**0**	**0**	**0**	**0**
Bonds	0	0	0	0	0	0	0	0	0	0
Commercial banks	0	0	0	0	0	0	0	0	0	0
Memo:										
IBRD	0	0	0	0	0	0	0	0	0	0
IDA	5	1	74	98	206	137	156	139	222	160
PRINCIPAL REPAYMENTS	**5**	**32**	**78**	**71**	**66**	**68**	**51**	**109**	**88**	**70**
Public and publicly guaranteed	**5**	**32**	**78**	**71**	**66**	**68**	**51**	**109**	**88**	**70**
Official creditors	4	11	44	35	44	38	37	77	72	61
Multilateral	1	1	20	23	19	21	23	37	52	50
Concessional	0	1	6	6	6	7	8	12	20	21
Bilateral	3	10	24	12	25	17	13	40	21	11
Concessional	3	2	1	1	4	6	3	6	4	4
Private creditors	1	21	34	36	22	30	14	32	16	10
Bonds	0	0	0	0	0	0	0	0	0	0
Commercial banks	1	0	2	14	14	15	5	11	6	7
Other private	0	21	33	21	8	15	9	22	10	3
Private nonguaranteed	**0**	**0**	**0**	**0**	**0**	**0**	**0**	**0**	**0**	**0**
Bonds	0	0	0	0	0	0	0	0	0	0
Commercial banks	0	0	0	0	0	0	0	0	0	0
Memo:										
IBRD	0	1	3	5	5	5	8	7	6	12
IDA	0	0	1	1	2	2	3	4	7	8
NET FLOWS ON DEBT	**22**	**51**	**90**	**240**	**234**	**118**	**204**	**298**	**182**	**161**
Public and publicly guaranteed	**22**	**51**	**90**	**240**	**234**	**118**	**204**	**298**	**182**	**161**
Official creditors	16	7	90	234	218	143	213	312	198	171
Multilateral	5	5	95	120	208	143	195	164	198	160
Concessional	5	1	104	132	217	154	195	173	229	180
Bilateral	11	1	-5	114	11	-1	18	148	-1	11
Concessional	11	9	6	101	20	8	24	144	16	17
Private creditors	6	44	-1	5	16	-25	-8	-14	-16	-10
Bonds	0	0	0	0	0	0	0	0	0	0
Commercial banks	5	17	18	25	-10	-14	-3	-2	-6	-7
Other private	2	28	-19	-20	26	-11	-5	-13	-10	-3
Private nonguaranteed	**0**	**0**	**0**	**0**	**0**	**0**	**0**	**0**	**0**	**0**
Bonds	0	0	0	0	0	0	0	0	0	0
Commercial banks	0	0	0	0	0	0	0	0	0	0
Memo:										
IBRD	0	-1	-3	-5	-5	-5	-8	-7	-6	-12
IDA	5	1	73	97	205	134	153	135	215	152

UGANDA

(US$ million, unless otherwise indicated)

	1970	1980	1988	1989	1990	1991	1992	1993	1994	1995
INTEREST PAYMENTS (LINT)	**5**	**4**	**24**	**25**	**19**	**33**	**26**	**33**	**34**	**34**
Public and publicly guaranteed	**5**	**4**	**24**	**25**	**19**	**33**	**26**	**33**	**34**	**34**
Official creditors	3	2	21	22	18	26	21	30	33	33
Multilateral	0	1	17	18	13	18	17	20	25	23
Concessional	0	1	6	6	6	10	10	11	14	18
Bilateral	3	1	3	3	5	9	4	9	8	10
Concessional	2	1	1	1	1	1	1	2	5	7
Private creditors	2	1	4	4	1	7	5	3	1	2
Bonds	1	0	0	0	0	0	0	0	0	0
Commercial banks	1	0	1	1	1	3	3	2	1	2
Other private	0	1	3	3	1	4	2	1	0	0
Private nonguaranteed	**0**	**0**	**0**	**0**	**0**	**0**	**0**	**0**	**0**	**0**
Bonds	0	0	0	0	0	0	0	0	0	0
Commercial banks	0	0	0	0	0	0	0	0	0	0
Memo:										
IBRD	0	0	3	3	2	2	2	1	1	1
IDA	0	0	5	4	5	8	8	9	11	13
NET TRANSFERS ON DEBT	**17**	**47**	**65**	**214**	**216**	**84**	**178**	**266**	**148**	**127**
Public and publicly guaranteed	**17**	**47**	**65**	**214**	**216**	**84**	**178**	**266**	**148**	**127**
Official creditors	13	4	70	213	201	116	192	283	165	139
Multilateral	5	4	78	102	195	126	178	144	174	138
Concessional	5	0	98	126	211	145	186	162	215	163
Bilateral	8	0	-8	111	6	-9	14	139	-9	1
Concessional	9	9	5	100	19	8	23	142	11	11
Private creditors	5	43	-4	1	15	-32	-13	-17	-17	-11
Bonds	-1	0	0	0	0	0	0	0	0	0
Commercial banks	4	17	18	24	-10	-17	-6	-3	-7	-8
Other private	2	26	-22	-23	25	-15	-7	-14	-10	-3
Private nonguaranteed	**0**	**0**	**0**	**0**	**0**	**0**	**0**	**0**	**0**	**0**
Bonds	0	0	0	0	0	0	0	0	0	0
Commercial banks	0	0	0	0	0	0	0	0	0	0
Memo:										
IBRD	-1	-1	-6	-8	-6	-7	-10	-8	-7	-12
IDA	5	0	68	93	200	126	145	126	205	139
DEBT SERVICE (LTDS)	**9**	**36**	**102**	**96**	**85**	**102**	**77**	**142**	**122**	**104**
Public and publicly guaranteed	**9**	**36**	**102**	**96**	**85**	**102**	**77**	**142**	**122**	**104**
Official creditors	7	14	64	57	62	64	58	107	105	93
Multilateral	1	3	37	42	32	39	40	57	76	72
Concessional	1	2	13	12	12	17	18	23	34	38
Bilateral	6	11	27	15	30	25	18	50	29	21
Concessional	4	3	2	2	5	7	4	8	9	10
Private creditors	3	22	38	39	23	37	19	35	17	11
Bonds	1	0	0	0	0	0	0	0	0	0
Commercial banks	2	0	2	15	15	18	7	12	7	8
Other private	0	22	36	24	9	19	11	23	10	3
Private nonguaranteed	**0**	**0**	**0**	**0**	**0**	**0**	**0**	**0**	**0**	**0**
Bonds	0	0	0	0	0	0	0	0	0	0
Commercial banks	0	0	0	0	0	0	0	0	0	0
Memo:										
IBRD	1	1	6	8	6	7	10	8	7	12
IDA	0	1	6	5	7	10	11	13	17	21
UNDISBURSED DEBT	**47**	**162**	**623**	**669**	**844**	**1,027**	**1,252**	**1,169**	**1,250**	**1,079**
Official creditors	44	143	611	631	821	1,006	1,232	1,151	1,232	1,061
Private creditors	3	19	12	38	23	22	20	18	18	18
Memorandum items										
Concessional LDOD	114	255	908	1,166	1,464	1,638	1,818	2,148	2,474	2,782
Variable rate LDOD	4	7	35	52	49	47	39	96	88	78
Public sector LDOD	151	533	1,589	1,844	2,158	2,280	2,430	2,592	2,863	3,048
Private sector LDOD	1	4	3	3	3	3	3	7	4	6

6. CURRENCY COMPOSITION OF LONG-TERM DEBT (PERCENT)

	1970	1980	1988	1989	1990	1991	1992	1993	1994	1995
Deutsche mark	6.5	8.3	0.7	0.7	0.7	0.4	0.4	0.4	0.2	0.0
French franc	0.2	6.3	3.2	3.4	3.5	3.4	2.1	1.4	1.4	0.3
Japanese yen	0.3	0.7	0.6	0.4	0.3	0.3	0.3	1.1	1.3	1.2
Pound sterling	73.3	20.4	8.3	6.8	6.7	6.1	4.4	3.4	3.1	2.0
Swiss franc	0.0	9.9	0.5	0.1	0.0	0.0	0.0	0.3	0.0	0.0
U.S.dollars	6.9	43.8	47.6	51.5	53.4	54.7	59.5	63.0	63.6	67.0
Multiple currency	4.1	2.3	26.2	23.1	21.8	20.9	18.6	16.8	15.3	13.7
Special drawing rights	0.0	0.1	2.7	2.3	2.4	2.4	2.8	3.7	4.8	5.8
All other currencies	8.8	8.3	10.1	11.8	11.3	11.7	11.8	10.0	10.2	9.9

UGANDA

(US$ million, unless otherwise indicated)

	1970	1980	1988	1989	1990	1991	1992	1993	1994	1995
7. DEBT RESTRUCTURINGS										
Total amount rescheduled	0	0	23	60	18	9	100	38	0	168
Debt stock rescheduled	0	0	0	0	0	0	0	0	0	141
Principal rescheduled	0	0	13	18	4	4	55	24	0	0
Official	0	0	7	10	4	4	31	11	0	0
Private	0	0	6	8	0	0	24	13	0	0
Interest rescheduled	0	0	9	11	1	3	38	10	0	29
Official	0	0	8	8	1	3	24	9	0	29
Private	0	0	1	3	0	0	14	1	0	0
Debt forgiven	..	..	41	0	51	1	14	16	7	0
Memo: interest forgiven	..	..	0	0	1	1	2	19	0	1
Debt stock reduction	0	0	0	0	0	0	0	139	0	42
of which debt buyback	0	0	0	0	0	0	0	17	0	0
8. DEBT STOCK-FLOW RECONCILIATION										
Total change in debt stocks	..	..	..	254	406	194	150	101	340	195
Net flows on debt	..	..	..	232	277	167	239	244	224	185
Net change in interest arrears	..	..	..	17	28	19	-20	-10	9	-21
Interest capitalized	..	..	..	11	1	3	38	10	0	29
Debt forgiveness or reduction	..	..	..	0	-51	-1	-14	-138	-7	-42
Cross-currency valuation	..	..	..	-20	64	-13	-43	-10	34	6
Residual	..	..	..	15	86	19	-49	5	80	38
9. AVERAGE TERMS OF NEW COMMITMENTS										
ALL CREDITORS										
Interest (%)	3.9	4.9	1.8	2.2	1.0	2.3	1.5	1.6	0.9	0.8
Maturity (years)	28.4	26.2	36.8	19.5	33.2	34.4	34.5	31.6	38.4	39.6
Grace period (years)	6.7	5.9	8.8	6.3	9.1	9.2	8.9	10.9	10.1	10.1
Grant element (%)	46.3	40.0	68.8	46.3	68.7	63.3	68.5	66.8	78.5	80.4
Official creditors										
Interest (%)	3.2	2.7	1.2	2.3	1.1	2.3	1.5	1.7	0.9	0.8
Maturity (years)	33.8	38.2	40.3	23.2	36.6	34.9	34.8	32.9	38.4	39.6
Grace period (years)	8.1	8.2	9.7	7.6	10.0	9.3	8.9	11.4	10.1	10.1
Grant element (%)	55.5	61.9	75.8	53.8	75.0	64.2	69.0	69.2	78.5	80.4
Private creditors										
Interest (%)	6.9	8.2	8.0	1.8	0.5	9.0	0.0	0.0	0.0	0.0
Maturity (years)	5.3	7.8	4.2	2.6	1.3	1.6	1.1	1.9	0.0	0.0
Grace period (years)	0.7	2.4	1.1	0.5	0.8	0.1	1.1	0.6	0.0	0.0
Grant element (%)	7.2	6.4	4.6	11.4	8.8	0.8	9.5	11.9	0.0	0.0
Memorandum items										
Commitments	12	199	317	377	452	362	520	413	299	94
Official creditors	10	120	286	310	409	357	516	395	299	94
Private creditors	2	78	31	67	43	5	4	18	0	0

10. CONTRACTUAL OBLIGATIONS ON OUTSTANDING LONG-TERM DEBT

	1996	1997	1998	1999	2000	2001	2002	2003	2004	2005
TOTAL										
Disbursements	265	269	204	138	72	33	19	2	0	0
Principal	71	66	75	74	85	90	97	98	103	95
Interest	42	43	43	42	46	43	40	37	35	33
Official creditors										
Disbursements	264	269	204	138	72	33	19	2	0	0
Principal	64	63	73	73	83	89	96	97	102	94
Interest	41	42	43	42	45	43	40	37	35	33
Bilateral creditors										
Disbursements	17	13	9	5	2	1	0	0	0	0
Principal	31	31	42	38	43	41	41	34	29	18
Interest	19	18	17	16	19	17	15	13	11	10
Multilateral creditors										
Disbursements	248	256	195	133	70	33	19	2	0	0
Principal	33	33	31	35	40	48	55	63	73	77
Interest	22	24	25	26	27	26	25	24	23	22
Private creditors										
Disbursements	0	0	0	0	0	0	0	0	0	0
Principal	7	3	2	1	1	1	1	1	1	1
Interest	1	0	0	0	0	0	0	0	0	0
Commercial banks										
Disbursements	0	0	0	0	0	0	0	0	0	0
Principal	6	1	1	1	1	1	1	1	1	1
Interest	0	0	0	0	0	0	0	0	0	0
Other private										
Disbursements	0	0	0	0	0	0	0	0	0	0
Principal	1	1	1	0	0	0	0	0	0	0
Interest	0	0	0	0	0	0	0	0	0	0

UKRAINE

(US$ million, unless otherwise indicated)

	1970	1980	1988	1989	1990	1991	1992	1993	1994	1995
1. SUMMARY DEBT DATA										
TOTAL DEBT STOCKS (EDT)	..	..	..	..	..	..	**551**	**3,713**	**5,439**	**8,434**
Long-term debt (LDOD)	..	..	..	..	..	..	**458**	**3,552**	**4,657**	**6,669**
Public and publicly guaranteed	..	..	..	..	..	..	454	3,540	4,612	6,585
Private nonguaranteed	0	0	0	0	0	0	4	12	45	84
Use of IMF credit	**0**	**0**	**0**	**0**	**0**	**0**	**0**	**0**	**364**	**1,542**
Short-term debt	..	..	..	..	..	..	**93**	**161**	**417**	**223**
of which interest arrears on LDOD	..	..	..	..	..	..	0	29	205	35
Official creditors	..	..	..	..	..	..	0	29	191	5
Private creditors	..	..	..	..	..	..	0	0	14	30
Memo: principal arrears on LDOD	..	..	..	..	..	..	2	2	602	88
Official creditors	..	..	..	..	..	..	0	0	541	17
Private creditors	..	..	..	..	..	..	2	2	61	71
Memo: export credits	..	..	0	0	0	0	223	932	399	1,193
TOTAL DEBT FLOWS										
Disbursements	..	..	..	..	..	..	**469**	**740**	**882**	**1,997**
Long-term debt	..	..	..	..	..	..	469	740	525	801
IMF purchases	0	0	0	0	0	0	0	0	357	1,196
Principal repayments	..	..	..	..	..	..	**0**	**140**	**219**	**421**
Long-term debt	..	..	..	..	..	..	0	140	219	421
IMF repurchases	0	0	0	0	0	0	0	0	0	0
Net flows on debt	..	..	..	..	..	..	**561**	**639**	**744**	**1,552**
of which short-term debt	..	..	..	..	..	..	93	38	81	-24
Interest payments (INT)	..	..	..	..	..	..	**12**	**62**	**81**	**501**
Long-term debt	..	..	..	..	..	..	8	55	74	447
IMF charges	0	0	0	0	0	0	0	0	0	42
Short-term debt	..	..	..	..	..	..	4	7	7	12
Net transfers on debt	..	..	..	..	..	..	**550**	**577**	**662**	**1,051**
Total debt service paid (TDS)	..	..	..	..	..	..	**12**	**202**	**300**	**922**
Long-term debt	..	..	..	..	..	..	8	195	293	868
IMF repurchases and charges	0	0	0	0	0	0	0	0	0	42
Short-term debt (interest only)	..	..	..	..	..	..	4	7	7	12
2. AGGREGATE NET RESOURCE FLOWS AND NET TRANSFERS (LONG-TERM)										
NET RESOURCE FLOWS	..	..	..	..	..	..	**1,193**	**917**	**683**	**710**
Net flow of long-term debt (ex. IMF)	..	..	..	..	..	..	469	600	306	380
Foreign direct investment (net)	..	..	..	..	..	..	200	200	159	267
Portfolio equity flows	..	..	..	..	..	..	0	0	0	0
Grants (excluding technical coop.)	..	..	..	..	..	..	525	117	218	63
Memo: technical coop. grants	..	..	..	..	..	..	33	61	52	120
NET TRANSFERS	..	..	..	..	..	..	**1,186**	**862**	**609**	**263**
Interest on long-term debt	..	..	..	..	..	..	8	55	74	447
Profit remittances on FDI	..	..	..	..	..	..	0	0	0	0
3. MAJOR ECONOMIC AGGREGATES										
Gross national product (GNP)	..	..	..	..	..	..	154,974	127,113	89,804	78,963
Exports of goods & services (XGS)	..	..	..	..	..	..	..	..	16,697	17,337
of which workers remittances	..	..	..	..	..	..	..	..	0	0
Imports of goods & services (MGS)	..	..	..	..	..	..	..	..	18,407	18,961
International reserves (RES)	..	..	..	..	..	..	469	166	665	1,069
Current account balance	..	..	..	..	..	..	..	..	-1,163	-1,152
4. DEBT INDICATORS										
EDT / XGS (%)	..	..	..	..	..	..	..	..	32.6	48.6
EDT / GNP (%)	..	..	..	..	..	..	0.4	2.9	6.1	10.7
TDS / XGS (%)	..	..	..	..	..	..	..	..	1.8	5.3
INT / XGS (%)	..	..	..	..	..	..	..	..	0.5	2.9
INT / GNP (%)	..	..	..	..	..	..	0.0	0.0	0.1	0.6
RES / EDT (%)	..	..	..	..	..	..	85.1	4.5	12.2	12.7
RES / MGS (months)	..	..	..	..	..	..	..	..	0.4	0.7
Short-term / EDT (%)	..	..	..	..	..	..	16.9	4.3	7.7	2.6
Concessional / EDT (%)	..	..	..	..	..	..	0.0	0.5	0.7	0.8
Multilateral / EDT (%)	..	..	..	..	..	..	10.7	3.7	4.1	7.3

UKRAINE

(US$ million, unless otherwise indicated)

	1970	1980	1988	1989	1990	1991	1992	1993	1994	1995
5. LONG-TERM DEBT										
DEBT OUTSTANDING (LDOD)	..	..	..	..	..	..	**458**	**3,552**	**4,657**	**6,669**
Public and publicly guaranteed	..	..	..	..	..	..	**454**	**3,540**	**4,612**	**6,585**
Official creditors	..	..	..	..	..	..	95	2,922	3,758	4,322
Multilateral	..	..	..	..	..	..	59	139	225	619
Concessional	..	..	..	..	..	..	0	0	0	0
Bilateral	..	..	..	..	..	..	36	2,784	3,533	3,702
Concessional	..	..	..	..	..	..	0	20	40	64
Private creditors	..	..	..	..	..	..	358	618	854	2,263
Bonds	..	..	..	..	..	..	0	0	0	1,400
Commercial banks	..	..	..	..	..	..	0	118	124	130
Other private	..	..	..	..	..	..	358	500	731	733
Private nonguaranteed	**0**	**0**	**0**	**0**	**0**	**0**	**4**	**12**	**45**	**84**
Bonds	..	..	..	..	..	..	0	0	0	0
Commercial banks	..	..	..	..	..	..	4	12	45	84
Memo:										
IBRD	0	0	0	0	0	0	0	0	102	491
IDA	0	0	0	0	0	0	0	0	0	0
DISBURSEMENTS	..	..	..	..	..	..	**469**	**740**	**525**	**801**
Public and publicly guaranteed	..	..	..	..	..	..	**464**	**700**	**431**	**732**
Official creditors	..	..	..	..	..	..	100	319	152	550
Multilateral	..	..	..	..	..	..	63	88	113	525
Concessional	..	..	..	..	..	..	0	0	0	0
Bilateral	..	..	..	..	..	..	36	231	39	25
Concessional	..	..	..	..	..	..	0	20	20	25
Private creditors	..	..	..	..	..	..	365	380	279	182
Bonds	..	..	..	..	..	..	0	0	0	0
Commercial banks	..	..	..	..	..	..	0	123	0	0
Other private	..	..	..	..	..	..	365	257	279	182
Private nonguaranteed	**0**	**0**	**0**	**0**	**0**	**0**	**4**	**41**	**94**	**69**
Bonds	..	..	..	..	..	..	0	0	0	0
Commercial banks	..	..	..	..	..	..	4	41	94	69
Memo:										
IBRD	0	0	0	0	0	0	0	0	102	401
IDA	0	0	0	0	0	0	0	0	0	0
PRINCIPAL REPAYMENTS	..	..	..	..	..	..	**0**	**140**	**219**	**421**
Public and publicly guaranteed	..	..	..	..	..	..	**0**	**107**	**158**	**381**
Official creditors	..	..	..	..	..	..	0	12	54	150
Multilateral	..	..	..	..	..	..	0	0	39	127
Concessional	..	..	..	..	..	..	0	0	0	0
Bilateral	..	..	..	..	..	..	0	12	15	23
Concessional	..	..	..	..	..	..	0	0	0	0
Private creditors	..	..	..	..	..	..	0	95	104	231
Bonds	..	..	..	..	..	..	0	0	0	0
Commercial banks	..	..	..	..	..	..	0	0	6	3
Other private	..	..	..	..	..	..	0	95	98	228
Private nonguaranteed	**0**	**0**	**0**	**0**	**0**	**0**	**0**	**33**	**60**	**40**
Bonds	..	..	..	..	..	..	0	0	0	0
Commercial banks	..	..	..	..	..	..	0	33	60	40
Memo:										
IBRD	0	0	0	0	0	0	0	0	0	0
IDA	0	0	0	0	0	0	0	0	0	0
NET FLOWS ON DEBT	..	..	..	..	..	..	**469**	**600**	**306**	**380**
Public and publicly guaranteed	..	..	..	..	..	..	**464**	**592**	**273**	**351**
Official creditors	..	..	..	..	..	..	100	307	98	400
Multilateral	..	..	..	..	..	..	63	88	73	398
Concessional	..	..	..	..	..	..	0	0	0	0
Bilateral	..	..	..	..	..	..	36	219	25	2
Concessional	..	..	..	..	..	..	0	20	20	25
Private creditors	..	..	..	..	..	..	365	285	175	-49
Bonds	..	..	..	..	..	..	0	0	0	0
Commercial banks	..	..	..	..	..	..	0	123	-6	-3
Other private	..	..	..	..	..	..	365	162	181	-46
Private nonguaranteed	**0**	**0**	**0**	**0**	**0**	**0**	**4**	**8**	**33**	**29**
Bonds	..	..	..	..	..	..	0	0	0	0
Commercial banks	..	..	..	..	..	..	4	8	33	29
Memo:										
IBRD	0	0	0	0	0	0	0	0	102	401
IDA	0	0	0	0	0	0	0	0	0	0

UKRAINE

(US$ million, unless otherwise indicated)

	1970	1980	1988	1989	1990	1991	1992	1993	1994	1995
INTEREST PAYMENTS (LINT)	..	..	..	..	..	..	**8**	**55**	**74**	**447**
Public and publicly guaranteed	..	..	..	..	..	..	**7**	**53**	**69**	**440**
Official creditors	..	..	..	..	..	..	2	12	13	306
Multilateral	..	..	..	..	..	..	0	9	10	13
Concessional	..	..	..	..	..	..	0	0	0	0
Bilateral	..	..	..	..	..	..	2	3	3	293
Concessional	..	..	..	..	..	..	0	0	1	1
Private creditors	..	..	..	..	..	..	5	41	56	134
Bonds	..	..	..	..	..	..	0	0	0	87
Commercial banks	..	..	..	..	..	..	0	5	12	4
Other private	..	..	..	..	..	..	5	37	45	44
Private nonguaranteed	**0**	**0**	**0**	**0**	**0**	**0**	**0**	**2**	**5**	**7**
Bonds	..	..	..	..	..	..	0	0	0	0
Commercial banks	..	..	..	..	..	..	0	2	5	7
Memo:										
IBRD	0	0	0	0	0	0	0	0	0	8
IDA	0	0	0	0	0	0	0	0	0	0
NET TRANSFERS ON DEBT	..	..	..	..	..	..	**461**	**545**	**232**	**-67**
Public and publicly guaranteed	..	..	..	..	..	..	**457**	**539**	**204**	**-89**
Official creditors	..	..	..	..	..	..	97	295	86	94
Multilateral	..	..	..	..	..	..	63	79	64	384
Concessional	..	..	..	..	..	..	0	0	0	0
Bilateral	..	..	..	..	..	..	34	216	22	-291
Concessional	..	..	..	..	..	..	0	20	19	24
Private creditors	..	..	..	..	..	..	360	244	119	-183
Bonds	..	..	..	..	..	..	0	0	0	-87
Commercial banks	..	..	..	..	..	..	0	119	-18	-6
Other private	..	..	..	..	..	..	360	126	136	-90
Private nonguaranteed	**0**	**0**	**0**	**0**	**0**	**0**	**4**	**6**	**28**	**22**
Bonds	..	..	..	..	..	..	0	0	0	0
Commercial banks	..	..	..	..	..	..	4	6	28	22
Memo:										
IBRD	0	0	0	0	0	0	0	0	102	393
IDA	0	0	0	0	0	0	0	0	0	0
DEBT SERVICE (LTDS)	..	..	..	..	..	..	**8**	**195**	**293**	**868**
Public and publicly guaranteed	..	..	..	..	..	..	**7**	**161**	**227**	**821**
Official creditors	..	..	..	..	..	..	2	24	67	456
Multilateral	..	..	..	..	..	..	0	9	49	141
Concessional	..	..	..	..	..	..	0	0	0	0
Bilateral	..	..	..	..	..	..	2	15	18	316
Concessional	..	..	..	..	..	..	0	0	1	1
Private creditors	..	..	..	..	..	..	5	136	161	365
Bonds	..	..	..	..	..	..	0	0	0	87
Commercial banks	..	..	..	..	..	..	0	5	18	6
Other private	..	..	..	..	..	..	5	132	143	272
Private nonguaranteed	**0**	**0**	**0**	**0**	**0**	**0**	**0**	**35**	**66**	**47**
Bonds	..	..	..	..	..	..	0	0	0	0
Commercial banks	..	..	..	..	..	..	0	35	66	47
Memo:										
IBRD	0	0	0	0	0	0	0	0	0	8
IDA	0	0	0	0	0	0	0	0	0	0
UNDISBURSED DEBT	..	..	..	..	..	..	**867**	**483**	**901**	**565**
Official creditors	..	..	..	..	..	..	126	83	574	281
Private creditors	..	..	..	..	..	..	742	401	328	284
Memorandum items										
Concessional LDOD	..	..	..	..	..	..	0	20	40	64
Variable rate LDOD	..	..	..	..	..	..	420	3,423	4,487	5,088
Public sector LDOD	..	..	..	..	..	..	454	3,540	4,612	6,585
Private sector LDOD	..	..	..	..	..	..	4	12	45	84

6. CURRENCY COMPOSITION OF LONG-TERM DEBT (PERCENT)

	1970	1980	1988	1989	1990	1991	1992	1993	1994	1995
Deutsche mark	..	..	..	..	..	..	40.0	11.4	14.4	11.3
French franc	..	..	..	..	..	..	0.0	0.0	0.1	0.4
Japanese yen	..	..	..	..	..	..	0.0	0.0	0.0	0.0
Pound sterling	..	..	..	..	..	..	0.0	0.0	0.0	0.0
Swiss franc	..	..	..	..	..	..	0.0	0.0	0.0	0.0
U.S.dollars	..	..	..	..	..	..	47.0	5.3	3.9	40.3
Multiple currency	..	..	..	..	..	..	0.0	5.8	22.3	19.5
Special drawing rights	..	..	..	..	..	..	0.0	0.0	0.0	0.0
All other currencies	..	..	..	..	..	..	13.1	77.5	59.3	28.5

UKRAINE

(US$ million, unless otherwise indicated)

	1970	1980	1988	1989	1990	1991	1992	1993	1994	1995
7. DEBT RESTRUCTURINGS										
Total amount rescheduled	0	0	0	0	0	0	0	2,528	723	2,535
Debt stock rescheduled	0	0	0	0	0	0	0	0	0	0
Principal rescheduled	0	0	0	0	0	0	0	0	0	969
Official	0	0	0	0	0	0	0	0	0	969
Private	0	0	0	0	0	0	0	0	0	0
Interest rescheduled	0	0	0	0	0	0	0	0	0	166
Official	0	0	0	0	0	0	0	0	0	166
Private	0	0	0	0	0	0	0	0	0	0
Debt forgiven	..	..	0	0	0	0	0	0	0	0
Memo: interest forgiven	..	..	0	0	0	0	0	0	0	0
Debt stock reduction	0	0	0	0	0	0	0	0	0	0
of which debt buyback	0	0	0	0	0	0	0	0	0	0
8. DEBT STOCK-FLOW RECONCILIATION										
Total change in debt stocks	..	..	..	..	..	..	551	3,162	1,726	2,995
Net flows on debt	..	..	..	..	..	..	561	639	744	1,552
Net change in interest arrears	..	..	..	..	..	..	0	29	176	-170
Interest capitalized	..	..	..	..	..	..	0	0	0	166
Debt forgiveness or reduction	..	..	..	..	..	..	0	0	0	0
Cross-currency valuation	..	..	..	..	..	..	-17	-1,770	-1,563	-308
Residual	..	..	..	..	..	..	6	4,264	2,369	1,756
9. AVERAGE TERMS OF NEW COMMITMENTS										
ALL CREDITORS										
Interest (%)	..	..	..	..	..	..	6.5	6.4	6.6	6.6
Maturity (years)	..	..	..	..	..	..	6.2	6.8	13.7	11.3
Grace period (years)	..	..	..	..	..	..	2.2	2.5	4.6	4.3
Grant element (%)	..	..	..	..	..	..	7.8	11.0	16.6	16.2
Official creditors										
Interest (%)	..	..	..	..	..	..	4.7	5.0	7.2	6.6
Maturity (years)	..	..	..	..	..	..	3.6	6.9	15.8	13.9
Grace period (years)	..	..	..	..	..	..	1.2	2.6	5.3	5.7
Grant element (%)	..	..	..	..	..	..	9.7	15.4	16.5	19.4
Private creditors										
Interest (%)	..	..	..	..	..	..	6.9	7.7	5.0	6.5
Maturity (years)	..	..	..	..	..	..	6.8	6.8	7.0	6.8
Grace period (years)	..	..	..	..	..	..	2.4	2.4	2.3	2.1
Grant element (%)	..	..	..	..	..	..	7.5	7.1	17.0	11.0
Memorandum items										
Commitments	..	..	..	..	..	..	1,361	594	839	412
Official creditors	..	..	..	..	..	..	233	281	642	257
Private creditors	..	..	..	..	..	..	1,128	313	197	155

10. CONTRACTUAL OBLIGATIONS ON OUTSTANDING LONG-TERM DEBT

	1996	1997	1998	1999	2000	2001	2002	2003	2004	2005
TOTAL										
Disbursements	187	145	83	48	37	22	18	14	10	2
Principal	716	970	1,029	921	584	607	443	396	369	344
Interest	449	407	346	279	231	192	155	127	101	74
Official creditors										
Disbursements	63	47	39	35	31	22	18	14	10	2
Principal	524	700	707	606	294	346	204	204	204	204
Interest	290	253	208	160	131	110	90	77	64	50
Bilateral creditors										
Disbursements	1	0	0	0	0	0	0	0	0	0
Principal	523	699	698	587	250	252	110	110	110	110
Interest	245	204	156	107	77	58	43	35	28	20
Multilateral creditors										
Disbursements	62	47	39	35	31	22	18	14	10	2
Principal	1	1	9	19	44	94	94	94	94	94
Interest	46	49	52	54	54	52	47	42	36	30
Private creditors										
Disbursements	124	98	44	13	6	0	0	0	0	0
Principal	192	269	323	315	290	260	239	192	165	140
Interest	159	154	139	119	100	82	65	50	37	24
Commercial banks										
Disbursements	0	0	0	0	0	0	0	0	0	0
Principal	22	22	22	11	0	0	0	0	0	0
Interest	6	5	3	1	0	0	0	0	0	0
Other private										
Disbursements	124	98	44	13	6	0	0	0	0	0
Principal	171	248	301	304	290	260	239	192	165	140
Interest	153	150	136	118	100	82	65	50	37	24

URUGUAY

(US$ million, unless otherwise indicated)

	1970	1980	1988	1989	1990	1991	1992	1993	1994	1995
1. SUMMARY DEBT DATA										
TOTAL DEBT STOCKS (EDT)	..	**1,660**	**3,821**	**4,449**	**4,415**	**4,189**	**4,569**	**4,846**	**5,070**	**5,307**
Long-term debt (LDOD)	**298**	**1,338**	**3,037**	**3,113**	**3,114**	**2,926**	**3,172**	**3,434**	**3,807**	**3,950**
Public and publicly guaranteed	269	1,127	2,951	3,008	3,045	2,897	3,138	3,367	3,745	3,823
Private nonguaranteed	29	211	86	105	69	29	35	67	62	127
Use of IMF credit	**18**	**0**	**309**	**202**	**101**	**58**	**52**	**38**	**30**	**21**
Short-term debt	..	**322**	**475**	**1,134**	**1,201**	**1,205**	**1,344**	**1,374**	**1,233**	**1,336**
of which interest arrears on LDOD	..	0	0	0	0	0	0	0	0	0
Official creditors	..	0	0	0	0	0	0	0	0	0
Private creditors	..	0	0	0	0	0	0	0	0	0
Memo: principal arrears on LDOD	..	0	0	0	0	0	0	0	0	0
Official creditors	..	0	0	0	0	0	0	0	0	0
Private creditors	..	0	0	0	0	0	0	0	0	0
Memo: export credits	..	..	105	118	183	197	184	226	249	312
TOTAL DEBT FLOWS										
Disbursements	**91**	**356**	**283**	**295**	**358**	**512**	**553**	**566**	**498**	**573**
Long-term debt	50	356	283	295	346	512	530	566	498	573
IMF purchases	40	0	0	0	12	0	23	0	0	0
Principal repayments	**80**	**130**	**376**	**291**	**559**	**551**	**262**	**324**	**231**	**486**
Long-term debt	51	130	313	193	434	509	236	309	221	476
IMF repurchases	28	0	63	98	124	42	26	14	11	10
Net flows on debt	**11**	**226**	**-254**	**664**	**-134**	**-34**	**430**	**273**	**126**	**191**
of which short-term debt	..	..	-161	659	66	5	139	30	-141	104
Interest payments (INT)	..	**169**	**354**	**369**	**428**	**255**	**262**	**263**	**304**	**379**
Long-term debt	17	121	267	274	319	174	206	211	237	298
IMF charges	0	0	25	22	16	9	5	4	2	2
Short-term debt	..	48	62	72	93	72	51	48	65	80
Net transfers on debt	..	**57**	**-608**	**295**	**-563**	**-289**	**168**	**10**	**-178**	**-188**
Total debt service paid (TDS)	..	**299**	**729**	**660**	**987**	**806**	**524**	**586**	**535**	**865**
Long-term debt	69	251	580	468	753	683	442	521	458	774
IMF repurchases and charges	28	0	88	120	141	50	31	18	13	11
Short-term debt (interest only)	..	48	62	72	93	72	51	48	65	80
2. AGGREGATE NET RESOURCE FLOWS AND NET TRANSFERS (LONG-TERM)										
NET RESOURCE FLOWS	**0**	**516**	**35**	**109**	**-78**	**10**	**307**	**376**	**466**	**241**
Net flow of long-term debt (ex. IMF)	-1	226	-30	102	-89	3	294	257	277	97
Foreign direct investment (net)	0	290	47	0	0	0	1	102	155	124
Portfolio equity flows	0	0	0	0	0	0	0	0	25	4
Grants (excluding technical coop.)	1	1	17	7	11	7	12	18	9	15
Memo: technical coop. grants	3	9	20	23	26	26	35	41	44	49
NET TRANSFERS	**-19**	**395**	**-251**	**-165**	**-396**	**-164**	**101**	**165**	**229**	**-57**
Interest on long-term debt	17	121	267	274	319	174	206	211	237	298
Profit remittances on FDI	2	0	19	0	0	0	0	0	0	0
3. MAJOR ECONOMIC AGGREGATES										
Gross national product (GNP)	2,287	9,753	7,270	7,644	8,034	9,804	11,657	13,263	15,337	16,380
Exports of goods & services (XGS)	..	1,594	1,868	2,236	2,417	2,436	2,857	3,010	3,531	3,679
of which workers remittances	..	0	0	0	0	0	0	0	0	0
Imports of goods & services (MGS)	..	2,312	1,867	2,110	2,239	2,433	2,894	3,307	4,010	4,069
International reserves (RES)	186	2,401	1,602	1,548	1,446	1,136	1,185	1,423	1,622	1,813
Current account balance	..	-709	22	134	186	42	-9	-244	-438	-358
4. DEBT INDICATORS										
EDT / XGS (%)	..	104.1	204.6	199.0	182.7	172.0	159.9	161.0	143.6	144.3
EDT / GNP (%)	..	17.0	52.6	58.2	55.0	42.7	39.2	36.5	33.1	32.4
TDS / XGS (%)	..	18.8	39.1	29.5	40.8	33.1	18.3	19.5	15.2	23.5
INT / XGS (%)	..	10.6	18.9	16.5	17.7	10.5	9.2	8.7	8.6	10.3
INT / GNP (%)	..	1.7	4.9	4.8	5.3	2.6	2.2	2.0	2.0	2.3
RES / EDT (%)	..	144.7	41.9	34.8	32.7	27.1	25.9	29.4	32.0	34.2
RES / MGS (months)	..	12.5	10.3	8.8	7.7	5.6	4.9	5.2	4.9	5.3
Short-term / EDT (%)	..	19.4	12.4	25.5	27.2	28.8	29.4	28.4	24.3	25.2
Concessional / EDT (%)	..	5.2	1.7	2.2	2.3	2.5	2.6	3.1	4.2	4.6
Multilateral / EDT (%)	..	11.0	14.8	14.1	15.8	20.5	21.3	22.5	24.0	23.7

URUGUAY

(US$ million, unless otherwise indicated)

	1970	1980	1988	1989	1990	1991	1992	1993	1994	1995
5. LONG-TERM DEBT										
DEBT OUTSTANDING (LDOD)	**298**	**1,338**	**3,037**	**3,113**	**3,114**	**2,926**	**3,172**	**3,434**	**3,807**	**3,950**
Public and publicly guaranteed	**269**	**1,127**	**2,951**	**3,008**	**3,045**	**2,897**	**3,138**	**3,367**	**3,745**	**3,823**
Official creditors	126	333	657	740	895	1,053	1,172	1,331	1,539	1,597
Multilateral	62	182	565	626	699	859	973	1,091	1,217	1,259
Concessional	53	23	18	20	22	27	31	31	33	48
Bilateral	64	151	92	114	196	193	199	240	322	338
Concessional	55	64	47	76	78	79	89	121	177	196
Private creditors	143	794	2,294	2,268	2,150	1,845	1,966	2,036	2,206	2,226
Bonds	45	263	491	581	567	1,471	1,647	1,758	1,966	1,963
Commercial banks	82	502	1,791	1,678	1,576	364	311	270	234	256
Other private	16	30	12	9	8	9	8	8	6	8
Private nonguaranteed	**29**	**211**	**86**	**105**	**69**	**29**	**35**	**67**	**62**	**127**
Bonds	0	0	0	0	0	0	0	40	40	110
Commercial banks	29	211	86	105	69	29	35	27	22	18
Memo:										
IBRD	49	72	298	328	359	407	521	522	539	513
IDA	0	0	0	0	0	0	0	0	0	0
DISBURSEMENTS	**50**	**356**	**283**	**295**	**346**	**512**	**530**	**566**	**498**	**573**
Public and publicly guaranteed	**37**	**293**	**283**	**295**	**346**	**512**	**524**	**526**	**498**	**504**
Official creditors	20	58	100	120	174	215	226	247	219	135
Multilateral	7	25	98	119	90	212	211	189	148	103
Concessional	3	4	2	3	3	6	4	1	4	16
Bilateral	13	34	2	2	85	4	15	59	71	32
Concessional	6	3	1	2	3	4	13	56	53	25
Private creditors	18	235	183	175	172	297	298	279	280	368
Bonds	7	0	181	172	164	180	290	270	271	266
Commercial banks	10	230	0	1	4	112	6	5	9	102
Other private	1	4	2	3	4	6	2	4	0	1
Private nonguaranteed	**13**	**63**	**0**	**0**	**0**	**0**	**6**	**40**	**0**	**70**
Bonds	0	0	0	0	0	0	0	40	0	70
Commercial banks	13	63	0	0	0	0	6	0	0	0
Memo:										
IBRD	2	4	58	68	51	81	174	41	37	32
IDA	0	0	0	0	0	0	0	0	0	0
PRINCIPAL REPAYMENTS	**51**	**130**	**313**	**193**	**434**	**509**	**236**	**309**	**221**	**476**
Public and publicly guaranteed	**47**	**93**	**255**	**157**	**398**	**469**	**236**	**302**	**216**	**471**
Official creditors	11	22	52	58	71	75	79	93	99	126
Multilateral	8	9	45	48	61	62	70	81	93	117
Concessional	6	2	1	1	1	1	1	1	2	2
Bilateral	3	12	7	10	10	13	9	11	7	9
Concessional	3	3	3	2	2	3	3	7	1	3
Private creditors	36	72	203	99	328	394	157	209	117	345
Bonds	9	6	127	80	180	67	94	159	70	274
Commercial banks	21	59	69	14	143	323	59	46	45	69
Other private	6	6	7	6	5	4	4	4	2	3
Private nonguaranteed	**4**	**37**	**58**	**36**	**36**	**40**	**0**	**8**	**5**	**5**
Bonds	0	0	0	0	0	0	0	0	0	0
Commercial banks	4	37	58	36	36	40	0	8	5	5
Memo:										
IBRD	6	6	34	32	43	42	45	49	56	78
IDA	0	0	0	0	0	0	0	0	0	0
NET FLOWS ON DEBT	**-1**	**226**	**-30**	**102**	**-89**	**3**	**294**	**257**	**277**	**97**
Public and publicly guaranteed	**-10**	**200**	**28**	**138**	**-53**	**44**	**288**	**224**	**282**	**32**
Official creditors	9	37	48	62	104	141	147	155	120	9
Multilateral	-1	15	53	71	29	150	140	107	55	-14
Concessional	-3	1	1	2	2	6	4	0	3	14
Bilateral	9	21	-6	-9	75	-9	6	47	65	23
Concessional	2	0	-3	-1	1	1	10	49	52	23
Private creditors	-19	163	-20	76	-156	-97	142	70	163	23
Bonds	-2	-6	54	91	-16	113	196	111	201	-7
Commercial banks	-11	171	-69	-13	-139	-211	-53	-41	-36	33
Other private	-5	-2	-5	-3	-1	1	-2	0	-2	-2
Private nonguaranteed	**9**	**26**	**-58**	**-36**	**-36**	**-40**	**6**	**32**	**-5**	**65**
Bonds	0	0	0	0	0	0	0	40	0	70
Commercial banks	9	26	-58	-36	-36	-40	6	-8	-5	-5
Memo:										
IBRD	-4	-2	23	36	8	39	130	-9	-19	-46
IDA	0	0	0	0	0	0	0	0	0	0

URUGUAY

(US$ million, unless otherwise indicated)

	1970	1980	1988	1989	1990	1991	1992	1993	1994	1995
INTEREST PAYMENTS (LINT)	**17**	**121**	**267**	**274**	**319**	**174**	**206**	**211**	**237**	**298**
Public and publicly guaranteed	**16**	**105**	**257**	**273**	**312**	**170**	**204**	**209**	**232**	**293**
Official creditors	4	23	50	51	61	61	68	83	96	125
Multilateral	3	16	45	46	54	56	64	79	85	91
Concessional	2	1	0	0	1	1	1	2	1	1
Bilateral	1	7	6	5	7	5	4	4	11	34
Concessional	1	2	1	1	2	2	2	2	3	25
Private creditors	12	82	207	222	252	109	136	126	136	169
Bonds	3	30	41	54	61	80	116	106	118	151
Commercial banks	7	50	165	167	190	28	19	19	17	17
Other private	1	2	1	1	1	1	1	1	0	0
Private nonguaranteed	**2**	**17**	**10**	**1**	**6**	**4**	**3**	**3**	**5**	**5**
Bonds	0	0	0	0	0	0	0	1	3	3
Commercial banks	2	17	10	1	6	4	3	2	2	1
Memo:										
IBRD	2	7	25	23	28	28	31	38	39	40
IDA	0	0	0	0	0	0	0	0	0	0
NET TRANSFERS ON DEBT	**-19**	**105**	**-297**	**-172**	**-407**	**-171**	**88**	**45**	**41**	**-200**
Public and publicly guaranteed	**-26**	**95**	**-229**	**-135**	**-365**	**-127**	**84**	**16**	**50**	**-261**
Official creditors	4	14	-3	11	43	79	79	72	23	-116
Multilateral	-4	0	9	25	-25	94	77	29	-30	-105
Concessional	-5	0	1	1	1	5	3	-2	2	13
Bilateral	8	14	-11	-13	68	-14	2	43	54	-11
Concessional	1	-2	-4	-2	-1	-1	9	47	49	-2
Private creditors	-30	81	-227	-146	-408	-206	6	-56	27	-145
Bonds	-5	-36	13	37	-77	33	79	5	82	-158
Commercial banks	-18	121	-234	-180	-329	-239	-71	-60	-53	15
Other private	-6	-4	-6	-4	-2	1	-2	0	-2	-2
Private nonguaranteed	**7**	**10**	**-68**	**-37**	**-42**	**-44**	**4**	**30**	**-10**	**61**
Bonds	0	0	0	0	0	0	0	39	-3	67
Commercial banks	7	10	-68	-37	-42	-44	4	-10	-6	-6
Memo:										
IBRD	-6	-9	-1	14	-19	11	99	-47	-58	-86
IDA	0	0	0	0	0	0	0	0	0	0
DEBT SERVICE (LTDS)	**69**	**251**	**580**	**468**	**753**	**683**	**442**	**521**	**458**	**774**
Public and publicly guaranteed	**63**	**198**	**512**	**430**	**711**	**639**	**440**	**510**	**448**	**764**
Official creditors	16	44	102	109	132	136	147	176	195	251
Multilateral	11	25	89	94	115	118	134	160	178	208
Concessional	8	3	1	1	1	1	1	3	2	3
Bilateral	5	19	13	15	17	18	13	15	18	43
Concessional	4	5	5	3	4	4	4	8	5	27
Private creditors	48	153	410	321	579	503	292	335	253	514
Bonds	12	36	168	134	241	147	210	265	189	425
Commercial banks	28	109	234	181	333	351	78	66	62	86
Other private	8	8	8	6	5	5	4	4	2	3
Private nonguaranteed	**6**	**54**	**68**	**37**	**42**	**44**	**3**	**11**	**10**	**9**
Bonds	0	0	0	0	0	0	0	1	3	3
Commercial banks	6	54	68	37	42	44	3	10	6	6
Memo:										
IBRD	9	13	59	54	70	70	75	88	95	117
IDA	0	0	0	0	0	0	0	0	0	0
UNDISBURSED DEBT	**87**	**519**	**547**	**802**	**735**	**673**	**838**	**737**	**741**	**542**
Official creditors	79	326	480	770	675	562	751	657	595	467
Private creditors	8	193	67	32	61	111	87	80	147	74
Memorandum items										
Concessional LDOD	107	86	64	96	100	106	119	152	211	244
Variable rate LDOD	31	474	2,202	2,280	2,286	1,623	1,812	1,909	2,049	2,014
Public sector LDOD	269	1,123	2,946	3,004	3,042	2,895	3,136	3,366	3,745	3,820
Private sector LDOD	29	215	91	109	72	31	37	68	62	130
6. CURRENCY COMPOSITION OF LONG-TERM DEBT (PERCENT)										
Deutsche mark	2.3	0.3	2.5	1.8	1.7	0.2	0.2	0.2	0.1	6.4
French franc	0.0	3.6	0.3	0.2	0.3	0.4	0.5	0.5	0.7	0.7
Japanese yen	0.0	1.1	1.9	2.1	5.1	4.0	3.7	4.4	4.5	6.4
Pound sterling	4.9	0.2	3.5	3.0	3.6	3.7	2.8	2.5	2.4	1.9
Swiss franc	8.0	0.0	1.3	1.3	1.5	0.0	0.0	0.0	0.0	0.0
U.S.dollars	62.9	77.9	71.3	70.7	64.9	62.7	62.5	60.8	61.2	53.8
Multiple currency	20.0	14.7	18.7	20.4	22.5	29.0	30.4	31.7	31.0	30.8
Special drawing rights	0.0	0.0	0.0	0.0	0.0	0.0	0.0	0.0	0.0	0.0
All other currencies	2.0	2.2	0.5	0.5	0.4	0.0	0.0	0.0	0.0	0.0

URUGUAY

(US$ million, unless otherwise indicated)

	1970	1980	1988	1989	1990	1991	1992	1993	1994	1995
7. DEBT RESTRUCTURINGS										
Total amount rescheduled	0	0	1,512	30	0	785	0	0	0	0
Debt stock rescheduled	0	0	1,503	0	0	759	0	0	0	0
Principal rescheduled	0	0	2	0	0	0	0	0	0	0
Official	0	0	0	0	0	0	0	0	0	0
Private	0	0	2	0	0	0	0	0	0	0
Interest rescheduled	0	0	0	0	0	0	0	0	0	0
Official	0	0	0	0	0	0	0	0	0	0
Private	0	0	0	0	0	0	0	0	0	0
Debt forgiven	..	..	4	0	0	0	0	16	0	0
Memo: interest forgiven	..	..	0	0	0	0	0	0	0	0
Debt stock reduction	0	0	144	50	0	506	0	0	0	0
of which debt buyback	0	0	0	0	0	284	0	0	0	0
8. DEBT STOCK-FLOW RECONCILIATION										
Total change in debt stocks	..	..	..	628	-34	-226	380	278	224	238
Net flows on debt	..	..	..	664	-134	-34	430	273	126	191
Net change in interest arrears	..	..	..	0	0	0	0	0	0	0
Interest capitalized	..	..	..	0	0	0	0	0	0	0
Debt forgiveness or reduction	..	..	..	-50	0	-223	0	-16	0	0
Cross-currency valuation	..	..	..	-27	67	6	-44	14	54	20
Residual	..	..	..	41	34	25	-6	6	45	26
9. AVERAGE TERMS OF NEW COMMITMENTS										
ALL CREDITORS										
Interest (%)	7.9	10.1	9.5	7.8	9.1	7.8	6.5	5.9	6.4	7.8
Maturity (years)	11.8	14.3	11.7	13.5	12.9	13.9	15.7	12.3	10.8	6.5
Grace period (years)	3.0	5.9	2.4	4.8	2.4	3.6	3.9	3.1	3.6	4.2
Grant element (%)	10.3	0.9	3.1	13.3	5.1	10.5	18.8	18.6	15.9	8.4
Official creditors										
Interest (%)	7.1	7.9	8.2	7.0	7.8	8.0	6.7	5.6	5.5	7.1
Maturity (years)	16.0	18.8	20.9	15.8	20.2	20.9	21.1	19.9	18.9	15.3
Grace period (years)	3.7	8.0	6.0	6.0	5.0	5.5	5.2	4.1	4.5	5.2
Grant element (%)	15.3	13.3	11.3	18.4	12.9	12.0	22.0	25.2	27.8	16.8
Private creditors										
Interest (%)	9.5	13.0	10.1	9.9	9.8	7.6	6.2	6.1	6.8	7.9
Maturity (years)	3.9	8.4	7.9	7.8	8.7	10.4	7.4	8.1	7.0	6.0
Grace period (years)	1.6	3.2	0.9	1.7	1.0	2.6	1.8	2.5	3.2	4.1
Grant element (%)	1.1	-15.4	-0.4	0.7	0.6	9.7	13.8	15.0	10.3	7.9
Memorandum items										
Commitments	71	347	293	584	339	522	694	422	504	333
Official creditors	46	197	87	417	124	172	419	151	161	17
Private creditors	25	150	206	167	215	350	275	272	343	315

10. CONTRACTUAL OBLIGATIONS ON OUTSTANDING LONG-TERM DEBT

	1996	1997	1998	1999	2000	2001	2002	2003	2004	2005
TOTAL										
Disbursements	166	131	95	62	35	20	14	9	6	4
Principal	451	450	499	341	611	379	259	235	193	149
Interest	276	254	228	202	182	133	111	94	79	67
Official creditors										
Disbursements	131	108	84	58	34	19	14	9	6	4
Principal	151	173	179	179	166	160	155	148	124	94
Interest	113	110	103	95	85	75	65	55	46	39
Bilateral creditors										
Disbursements	5	2	1	1	0	0	0	0	0	0
Principal	28	28	28	28	28	28	29	29	15	14
Interest	12	11	10	9	7	6	5	3	3	2
Multilateral creditors										
Disbursements	127	106	83	57	34	19	14	9	6	4
Principal	123	146	152	152	138	132	126	119	109	80
Interest	101	99	93	86	78	69	60	52	44	36
Private creditors										
Disbursements	34	23	11	4	1	1	0	0	0	0
Principal	301	277	320	162	446	220	105	87	69	55
Interest	163	144	125	107	97	58	46	39	33	29
Commercial banks										
Disbursements	26	23	11	4	1	1	0	0	0	0
Principal	44	27	29	21	121	20	17	15	15	11
Interest	21	20	19	17	16	5	4	3	2	1
Other private										
Disbursements	8	0	0	0	0	0	0	0	0	0
Principal	257	251	291	141	325	199	88	72	55	44
Interest	142	125	106	91	81	53	42	36	32	28

UZBEKISTAN

(US$ million, unless otherwise indicated)

1. SUMMARY DEBT DATA

	1970	1980	1988	1989	1990	1991	1992	1993	1994	1995
TOTAL DEBT STOCKS (EDT)	..	..	..	..	..	..	**60**	**1,032**	**1,194**	**1,630**
Long-term debt (LDOD)	..	..	..	..	..	..	**60**	**940**	**903**	**1,260**
Public and publicly guaranteed	..	..	..	..	..	..	60	940	903	1,260
Private nonguaranteed	0	0	0	0	0	0	0	0	0	0
Use of IMF credit	**0**	**0**	**0**	**0**	**0**	**0**	**0**	**0**	**0**	**158**
Short-term debt	..	..	..	..	..	..	**0**	**92**	**291**	**212**
of which interest arrears on LDOD	..	..	..	..	..	..	0	0	0	0
Official creditors	..	..	..	..	..	..	0	0	0	0
Private creditors	..	..	..	..	..	..	0	0	0	0
Memo: principal arrears on LDOD	..	..	..	..	..	..	0	0	0	0
Official creditors	..	..	..	..	..	..	0	0	0	0
Private creditors	..	..	..	..	..	..	0	0	0	0
Memo: export credits	..	..	0	0	0	0	0	94	67	359
TOTAL DEBT FLOWS										
Disbursements	..	..	..	..	..	..	**65**	**623**	**57**	**671**
Long-term debt	..	..	..	..	..	..	65	623	57	510
IMF purchases	0	0	0	0	0	0	0	0	0	161
Principal repayments	..	..	..	..	..	..	**4**	**16**	**97**	**150**
Long-term debt	..	..	..	..	..	..	4	16	97	150
IMF repurchases	0	0	0	0	0	0	0	0	0	0
Net flows on debt	..	..	..	..	..	..	**61**	**699**	**160**	**442**
of which short-term debt	..	..	..	..	..	..	0	92	199	-79
Interest payments (INT)	..	..	..	..	..	..	**1**	**4**	**31**	**74**
Long-term debt	..	..	..	..	..	..	1	4	25	58
IMF charges	0	0	0	0	0	0	0	0	0	3
Short-term debt	..	..	..	..	..	..	0	0	6	13
Net transfers on debt	..	..	..	..	..	..	**60**	**695**	**129**	**368**
Total debt service paid (TDS)	..	..	..	..	..	..	**5**	**20**	**128**	**224**
Long-term debt	..	..	..	..	..	..	5	20	122	208
IMF repurchases and charges	0	0	0	0	0	0	0	0	0	3
Short-term debt (interest only)	..	..	..	..	..	..	0	0	6	13

2. AGGREGATE NET RESOURCE FLOWS AND NET TRANSFERS (LONG-TERM)

	1970	1980	1988	1989	1990	1991	1992	1993	1994	1995
NET RESOURCE FLOWS	..	..	..	..	..	..	**101**	**655**	**28**	**488**
Net flow of long-term debt (ex. IMF)	..	..	..	..	..	..	61	607	-39	360
Foreign direct investment (net)	..	..	..	..	..	..	40	45	50	115
Portfolio equity flows	..	..	..	..	..	..	0	0	0	0
Grants (excluding technical coop.)	..	..	..	..	..	..	0	4	18	13
Memo: technical coop. grants	..	..	..	..	..	..	1	4	10	25
NET TRANSFERS	..	..	..	..	..	..	**100**	**651**	**3**	**430**
Interest on long-term debt	..	..	..	..	..	..	1	4	25	58
Profit remittances on FDI	..	..	..	..	..	..	0	0	0	0

3. MAJOR ECONOMIC AGGREGATES

	1970	1980	1988	1989	1990	1991	1992	1993	1994	1995
Gross national product (GNP)	..	..	..	..	..	..	20,327	22,017	19,153	21,590
Exports of goods & services (XGS)	..	..	..	..	..	..	..	2,850	3,561	4,618
of which workers remittances	..	..	..	..	..	..	..	0	0	0
Imports of goods & services (MGS)	..	..	..	..	..	..	1,866	3,254	3,569	4,895
International reserves (RES)	..	..	..	..	..	..	..	850	1,269	1,695
Current account balance	..	..	..	..	..	..	-369	-404	-8	-300

4. DEBT INDICATORS

	1970	1980	1988	1989	1990	1991	1992	1993	1994	1995
EDT / XGS (%)	..	..	..	..	..	..	..	36.2	33.5	35.3
EDT / GNP (%)	..	..	..	..	..	..	0.3	4.7	6.2	7.5
TDS / XGS (%)	..	..	..	..	..	..	..	0.7	3.6	4.8
INT / XGS (%)	..	..	..	..	..	..	..	0.1	0.9	1.6
INT / GNP (%)	..	..	..	..	..	..	0.0	0.0	0.2	0.3
RES / EDT (%)	..	..	..	..	..	..	..	82.4	106.3	104.0
RES / MGS (months)	..	..	..	..	..	..	..	3.1	4.3	4.2
Short-term / EDT (%)	..	..	..	..	..	..	0.0	8.9	24.4	13.0
Concessional / EDT (%)	..	..	..	..	..	..	0.0	13.9	12.0	10.8
Multilateral / EDT (%)	..	..	..	..	..	..	0.0	0.0	0.4	15.1

UZBEKISTAN

(US$ million, unless otherwise indicated)

	1970	1980	1988	1989	1990	1991	1992	1993	1994	1995
5. LONG-TERM DEBT										
DEBT OUTSTANDING (LDOD)	..	..	..	..	..	..	**60**	**940**	**903**	**1,260**
Public and publicly guaranteed	..	..	..	..	..	..	**60**	**940**	**903**	**1,260**
Official creditors	..	..	..	..	..	..	60	789	751	988
Multilateral	..	..	..	..	..	..	0	0	5	246
Concessional	..	..	..	..	..	..	0	0	0	0
Bilateral	..	..	..	..	..	..	60	789	746	743
Concessional	..	..	..	..	..	..	0	143	143	177
Private creditors	..	..	..	..	..	..	0	151	152	272
Bonds	..	..	..	..	..	..	0	0	0	0
Commercial banks	..	..	..	..	..	..	0	0	0	0
Other private	..	..	..	..	..	..	0	151	152	272
Private nonguaranteed	**0**	**0**	**0**	**0**	**0**	**0**	**0**	**0**	**0**	**0**
Bonds	..	..	..	..	..	..	0	0	0	0
Commercial banks	..	..	..	..	..	..	0	0	0	0
Memo:										
IBRD	0	0	0	0	0	0	0	0	1	157
IDA	0	0	0	0	0	0	0	0	0	0
DISBURSEMENTS	..	..	..	..	..	..	**65**	**623**	**57**	**510**
Public and publicly guaranteed	..	..	..	..	..	..	**65**	**623**	**57**	**510**
Official creditors	..	..	..	..	..	..	65	469	43	360
Multilateral	..	..	..	..	..	..	0	0	5	246
Concessional	..	..	..	..	..	..	0	0	0	0
Bilateral	..	..	..	..	..	..	65	469	37	115
Concessional	..	..	..	..	..	..	0	143	0	34
Private creditors	..	..	..	..	..	..	0	154	15	150
Bonds	..	..	..	..	..	..	0	0	0	0
Commercial banks	..	..	..	..	..	..	0	0	0	0
Other private	..	..	..	..	..	..	0	154	15	150
Private nonguaranteed	**0**	**0**	**0**	**0**	**0**	**0**	**0**	**0**	**0**	**0**
Bonds	..	..	..	..	..	..	0	0	0	0
Commercial banks	..	..	..	..	..	..	0	0	0	0
Memo:										
IBRD	0	0	0	0	0	0	0	0	1	162
IDA	0	0	0	0	0	0	0	0	0	0
PRINCIPAL REPAYMENTS	..	..	..	..	..	..	**4**	**16**	**97**	**150**
Public and publicly guaranteed	..	..	..	..	..	..	**4**	**16**	**97**	**150**
Official creditors	..	..	..	..	..	..	4	14	83	120
Multilateral	..	..	..	..	..	..	0	0	0	0
Concessional	..	..	..	..	..	..	0	0	0	0
Bilateral	..	..	..	..	..	..	4	14	83	120
Concessional	..	..	..	..	..	..	0	0	0	0
Private creditors	..	..	..	..	..	..	0	3	14	30
Bonds	..	..	..	..	..	..	0	0	0	0
Commercial banks	..	..	..	..	..	..	0	0	0	0
Other private	..	..	..	..	..	..	0	3	14	30
Private nonguaranteed	**0**	**0**	**0**	**0**	**0**	**0**	**0**	**0**	**0**	**0**
Bonds	..	..	..	..	..	..	0	0	0	0
Commercial banks	..	..	..	..	..	..	0	0	0	0
Memo:										
IBRD	0	0	0	0	0	0	0	0	0	0
IDA	0	0	0	0	0	0	0	0	0	0
NET FLOWS ON DEBT	..	..	..	..	..	..	**61**	**607**	**-39**	**360**
Public and publicly guaranteed	..	..	..	..	..	..	**61**	**607**	**-39**	**360**
Official creditors	..	..	..	..	..	..	61	456	-40	241
Multilateral	..	..	..	..	..	..	0	0	5	246
Concessional	..	..	..	..	..	..	0	0	0	0
Bilateral	..	..	..	..	..	..	61	456	-45	-5
Concessional	..	..	..	..	..	..	0	143	0	34
Private creditors	..	..	..	..	..	..	0	151	1	120
Bonds	..	..	..	..	..	..	0	0	0	0
Commercial banks	..	..	..	..	..	..	0	0	0	0
Other private	..	..	..	..	..	..	0	151	1	120
Private nonguaranteed	**0**	**0**	**0**	**0**	**0**	**0**	**0**	**0**	**0**	**0**
Bonds	..	..	..	..	..	..	0	0	0	0
Commercial banks	..	..	..	..	..	..	0	0	0	0
Memo:										
IBRD	0	0	0	0	0	0	0	0	1	162
IDA	0	0	0	0	0	0	0	0	0	0

UZBEKISTAN

(US$ million, unless otherwise indicated)

	1970	1980	1988	1989	1990	1991	1992	1993	1994	1995
INTEREST PAYMENTS (LINT)	..	..	..	..	..	..	**1**	**4**	**25**	**58**
Public and publicly guaranteed	..	..	..	..	..	..	**1**	**4**	**25**	**58**
Official creditors	..	..	..	..	..	..	1	4	22	52
Multilateral	..	..	..	..	..	..	0	0	0	4
Concessional	..	..	..	..	..	..	0	0	0	0
Bilateral	..	..	..	..	..	..	1	4	22	47
Concessional	..	..	..	..	..	..	0	0	0	0
Private creditors	..	..	..	..	..	..	0	0	3	6
Bonds	..	..	..	..	..	..	0	0	0	0
Commercial banks	..	..	..	..	..	..	0	0	0	0
Other private	..	..	..	..	..	..	0	0	3	6
Private nonguaranteed	**0**	**0**	**0**	**0**	**0**	**0**	**0**	**0**	**0**	**0**
Bonds	..	..	..	..	..	..	0	0	0	0
Commercial banks	..	..	..	..	..	..	0	0	0	0
Memo:										
IBRD	0	0	0	0	0	0	0	0	0	2
IDA	0	0	0	0	0	0	0	0	0	0
NET TRANSFERS ON DEBT	..	..	..	..	..	..	**60**	**603**	**-64**	**303**
Public and publicly guaranteed	..	..	..	..	..	..	**60**	**603**	**-64**	**303**
Official creditors	..	..	..	..	..	..	60	452	-62	189
Multilateral	..	..	..	..	..	..	0	0	5	242
Concessional	..	..	..	..	..	..	0	0	0	0
Bilateral	..	..	..	..	..	..	60	452	-67	-52
Concessional	..	..	..	..	..	..	0	143	0	33
Private creditors	..	..	..	..	..	..	0	151	-2	113
Bonds	..	..	..	..	..	..	0	0	0	0
Commercial banks	..	..	..	..	..	..	0	0	0	0
Other private	..	..	..	..	..	..	0	151	-2	113
Private nonguaranteed	**0**	**0**	**0**	**0**	**0**	**0**	**0**	**0**	**0**	**0**
Bonds	..	..	..	..	..	..	0	0	0	0
Commercial banks	..	..	..	..	..	..	0	0	0	0
Memo:										
IBRD	0	0	0	0	0	0	0	0	1	161
IDA	0	0	0	0	0	0	0	0	0	0
DEBT SERVICE (LTDS)	..	..	..	..	..	..	**5**	**20**	**122**	**208**
Public and publicly guaranteed	..	..	..	..	..	..	**5**	**20**	**122**	**208**
Official creditors	..	..	..	..	..	..	5	18	105	171
Multilateral	..	..	..	..	..	..	0	0	0	4
Concessional	..	..	..	..	..	..	0	0	0	0
Bilateral	..	..	..	..	..	..	5	18	104	167
Concessional	..	..	..	..	..	..	0	0	0	0
Private creditors	..	..	..	..	..	..	0	3	17	37
Bonds	..	..	..	..	..	..	0	0	0	0
Commercial banks	..	..	..	..	..	..	0	0	0	0
Other private	..	..	..	..	..	..	0	3	17	37
Private nonguaranteed	**0**	**0**	**0**	**0**	**0**	**0**	**0**	**0**	**0**	**0**
Bonds	..	..	..	..	..	..	0	0	0	0
Commercial banks	..	..	..	..	..	..	0	0	0	0
Memo:										
IBRD	0	0	0	0	0	0	0	0	0	2
IDA	0	0	0	0	0	0	0	0	0	0
UNDISBURSED DEBT	..	..	..	..	..	..	**482**	**423**	**591**	**792**
Official creditors	..	..	..	..	..	..	443	423	551	602
Private creditors	..	..	..	..	..	..	39	0	40	190
Memorandum items										
Concessional LDOD	..	..	..	..	..	..	0	143	143	177
Variable rate LDOD	..	..	..	..	..	..	27	759	729	856
Public sector LDOD	..	..	..	..	..	..	33	917	889	1,254
Private sector LDOD	..	..	..	..	..	..	27	22	14	6

6. CURRENCY COMPOSITION OF LONG-TERM DEBT (PERCENT)

	1970	1980	1988	1989	1990	1991	1992	1993	1994	1995
Deutsche mark	..	..	..	..	..	..	45.2	2.4	1.5	12.1
French franc	..	..	..	..	..	..	0.0	0.0	0.0	3.4
Japanese yen	..	..	..	..	..	..	0.0	0.0	0.0	0.0
Pound sterling	..	..	..	..	..	..	0.0	0.0	0.0	0.0
Swiss franc	..	..	..	..	..	..	9.4	0.6	0.5	0.2
U.S.dollars	..	..	..	..	..	..	45.4	97.1	97.9	65.7
Multiple currency	..	..	..	..	..	..	0.0	0.0	0.1	12.5
Special drawing rights	..	..	..	..	..	..	0.0	0.0	0.0	0.0
All other currencies	..	..	..	..	..	..	0.0	0.0	0.0	6.2

UZBEKISTAN

(US$ million, unless otherwise indicated)

	1970	1980	1988	1989	1990	1991	1992	1993	1994	1995
7. DEBT RESTRUCTURINGS										
Total amount rescheduled	0	0	0	0	0	0	0	275	0	0
Debt stock rescheduled	0	0	0	0	0	0	0	0	0	0
Principal rescheduled	0	0	0	0	0	0	0	0	0	0
Official	0	0	0	0	0	0	0	0	0	0
Private	0	0	0	0	0	0	0	0	0	0
Interest rescheduled	0	0	0	0	0	0	0	0	0	0
Official	0	0	0	0	0	0	0	0	0	0
Private	0	0	0	0	0	0	0	0	0	0
Debt forgiven	..	..	0	0	0	0	0	0	0	0
Memo: interest forgiven	..	..	0	0	0	0	0	0	0	0
Debt stock reduction	0	0	0	0	0	0	0	0	0	0
of which debt buyback	0	0	0	0	0	0	0	0	0	0
8. DEBT STOCK-FLOW RECONCILIATION										
Total change in debt stocks	..	..	..	..	..	..	60	972	162	436
Net flows on debt	..	..	..	..	..	..	61	699	160	442
Net change in interest arrears	..	..	..	..	..	..	0	0	0	0
Interest capitalized	..	..	..	..	..	..	0	0	0	0
Debt forgiveness or reduction	..	..	..	..	..	..	0	0	0	0
Cross-currency valuation	..	..	..	..	..	..	-2	-2	2	16
Residual	..	..	..	..	..	..	1	275	1	-22
9. AVERAGE TERMS OF NEW COMMITMENTS										
ALL CREDITORS										
Interest (%)	..	..	..	..	..	..	5.8	4.4	6.8	6.2
Maturity (years)	..	..	..	..	..	..	4.2	9.6	6.8	14.0
Grace period (years)	..	..	..	..	..	..	1.7	2.4	1.7	3.7
Grant element (%)	..	..	..	..	..	..	9.9	22.4	10.4	19.0
Official creditors										
Interest (%)	..	..	..	..	..	..	5.9	3.9	6.7	6.4
Maturity (years)	..	..	..	..	..	..	4.1	9.1	7.7	18.0
Grace period (years)	..	..	..	..	..	..	1.7	2.7	2.0	4.6
Grant element (%)	..	..	..	..	..	..	9.5	25.2	12.1	22.1
Private creditors										
Interest (%)	..	..	..	..	..	..	4.4	6.3	7.1	5.9
Maturity (years)	..	..	..	..	..	..	5.5	11.7	3.8	8.6
Grace period (years)	..	..	..	..	..	..	0.9	1.1	1.0	2.4
Grant element (%)	..	..	..	..	..	..	14.8	11.4	5.1	14.7
Memorandum items										
Commitments	..	..	..	..	..	..	547	564	217	696
Official creditors	..	..	..	..	..	..	508	449	165	400
Private creditors	..	..	..	..	..	..	39	115	53	296

10. CONTRACTUAL OBLIGATIONS ON OUTSTANDING LONG-TERM DEBT

	1996	1997	1998	1999	2000	2001	2002	2003	2004	2005
TOTAL										
Disbursements	454	159	83	38	21	12	8	6	6	5
Principal	558	262	232	225	211	112	92	61	42	40
Interest	103	72	62	51	40	30	25	20	17	14
Official creditors										
Disbursements	343	107	61	34	21	12	8	6	6	5
Principal	494	196	158	159	145	81	66	38	24	23
Interest	79	49	42	36	29	22	18	15	14	12
Bilateral creditors										
Disbursements	314	84	43	20	7	2	0	0	0	0
Principal	448	150	150	150	129	57	43	15	8	7
Interest	59	31	26	19	12	6	4	2	1	1
Multilateral creditors										
Disbursements	29	23	18	15	15	10	8	6	6	5
Principal	46	46	8	9	16	24	24	24	16	16
Interest	19	17	16	16	17	16	15	14	12	12
Private creditors										
Disbursements	112	52	22	4	0	0	0	0	0	0
Principal	64	66	74	67	66	31	26	23	18	16
Interest	24	23	20	16	12	8	6	4	3	2
Commercial banks										
Disbursements	0	0	0	0	0	0	0	0	0	0
Principal	0	0	0	0	0	0	0	0	0	0
Interest	0	0	0	0	0	0	0	0	0	0
Other private										
Disbursements	112	52	22	4	0	0	0	0	0	0
Principal	64	66	74	67	66	31	26	23	18	16
Interest	24	23	20	16	12	8	6	4	3	2

VANUATU

(US$ million, unless otherwise indicated)

	1970	1980	1988	1989	1990	1991	1992	1993	1994	1995
1. SUMMARY DEBT DATA										
TOTAL DEBT STOCKS (EDT)	..	**4.1**	**26.8**	**30.3**	**40.2**	**39.3**	**40.4**	**42.4**	**46.5**	**48.2**
Long-term debt (LDOD)	..	**4.1**	**15.3**	**20.8**	**30.6**	**38.1**	**39.6**	**39.4**	**41.5**	**43.2**
Public and publicly guaranteed	..	4.1	15.3	20.8	30.6	38.1	39.6	39.4	41.5	43.2
Private nonguaranteed	0.0	0.0	0.0	0.0	0.0	0.0	0.0	0.0	0.0	0.0
Use of IMF credit	**0.0**	**0.0**	**0.0**	**0.0**	**0.0**	**0.0**	**0.0**	**0.0**	**0.0**	**0.0**
Short-term debt	..	**0.0**	**11.5**	**9.5**	**9.6**	**1.2**	**0.8**	**3.0**	**5.0**	**5.0**
of which interest arrears on LDOD	..	0.0	0.0	0.0	0.0	0.0	0.0	0.0	0.0	0.0
Official creditors	..	0.0	0.0	0.0	0.0	0.0	0.0	0.0	0.0	0.0
Private creditors	..	0.0	0.0	0.0	0.0	0.0	0.0	0.0	0.0	0.0
Memo: principal arrears on LDOD	..	0.0	0.0	0.0	0.0	0.0	0.0	0.0	0.0	0.0
Official creditors	..	0.0	0.0	0.0	0.0	0.0	0.0	0.0	0.0	0.0
Private creditors	..	0.0	0.0	0.0	0.0	0.0	0.0	0.0	0.0	0.0
Memo: export credits	..	..	23.0	21.0	23.0	20.0	20.0	17.0	15.0	14.0
TOTAL DEBT FLOWS										
Disbursements	..	**0.0**	**3.5**	**5.8**	**8.7**	**14.5**	**4.5**	**1.1**	**1.8**	**1.6**
Long-term debt	..	0.0	3.5	5.8	8.7	14.5	4.5	1.1	1.8	1.6
IMF purchases	0.0	0.0	0.0	0.0	0.0	0.0	0.0	0.0	0.0	0.0
Principal repayments	..	**0.4**	**0.7**	**0.6**	**1.0**	**0.8**	**0.9**	**0.9**	**1.0**	**0.9**
Long-term debt	..	0.4	0.7	0.6	1.0	0.8	0.9	0.9	1.0	0.9
IMF repurchases	0.0	0.0	0.0	0.0	0.0	0.0	0.0	0.0	0.0	0.0
Net flows on debt	..	**-0.4**	**4.3**	**3.2**	**7.8**	**5.3**	**3.2**	**2.4**	**2.8**	**0.7**
of which short-term debt	..	..	1.5	-2.0	0.1	-8.4	-0.4	2.2	2.0	0.0
Interest payments (INT)	..	**0.2**	**1.7**	**1.4**	**1.5**	**0.8**	**0.6**	**0.7**	**0.9**	**1.0**
Long-term debt	..	0.2	0.6	0.7	0.7	0.4	0.6	0.5	0.7	0.7
IMF charges	0.0	0.0	0.0	0.0	0.0	0.0	0.0	0.0	0.0	0.0
Short-term debt	..	0.0	1.1	0.7	0.7	0.4	0.1	0.1	0.2	0.3
Net transfers on debt	..	**-0.6**	**2.6**	**1.8**	**6.4**	**4.5**	**2.6**	**1.8**	**1.9**	**-0.3**
Total debt service paid (TDS)	..	**0.6**	**2.4**	**2.0**	**2.4**	**1.6**	**1.5**	**1.5**	**1.9**	**1.9**
Long-term debt	..	0.6	1.3	1.3	1.7	1.2	1.4	1.4	1.6	1.6
IMF repurchases and charges	0.0	0.0	0.0	0.0	0.0	0.0	0.0	0.0	0.0	0.0
Short-term debt (interest only)	..	0.0	1.1	0.7	0.7	0.4	0.1	0.1	0.2	0.3
2. AGGREGATE NET RESOURCE FLOWS AND NET TRANSFERS (LONG-TERM)										
NET RESOURCE FLOWS	..	**19.3**	**33.3**	**30.1**	**42.7**	**56.3**	**40.1**	**37.5**	**44.1**	**54.2**
Net flow of long-term debt (ex. IMF)	0.0	-0.4	2.8	5.2	7.7	13.7	3.6	0.2	0.8	0.7
Foreign direct investment (net)	0.0	0.0	10.8	9.2	13.0	25.0	26.0	26.0	30.0	31.0
Portfolio equity flows	..	0.0	0.0	0.0	0.0	0.0	0.0	0.0	0.0	0.0
Grants (excluding technical coop.)	2.3	19.7	19.7	15.7	22.0	17.6	10.5	11.3	13.3	22.5
Memo: technical coop. grants	0.6	24.6	17.4	17.9	22.3	23.4	26.0	23.4	27.7	21.7
NET TRANSFERS	..	**19.1**	**17.4**	**17.5**	**26.8**	**26.8**	**9.3**	**6.6**	**10.5**	**19.5**
Interest on long-term debt	..	0.2	0.6	0.7	0.7	0.4	0.6	0.5	0.7	0.7
Profit remittances on FDI	0.0	0.0	15.3	12.0	15.2	29.1	30.2	30.4	33.0	34.0
3. MAJOR ECONOMIC AGGREGATES										
Gross national product (GNP)	..	95.9	139.6	145.7	163.3	172.7	174.6	170.7	188.1	213.2
Exports of goods & services (XGS)	..	..	85.7	84.0	112.7	112.8	112.1	106.2	119.0	129.1
of which workers remittances	..	..	7.0	6.5	6.9	7.0	6.8	4.9	5.8	6.1
Imports of goods & services (MGS)	..	..	116.7	106.2	136.5	150.1	141.1	138.2	155.5	164.5
International reserves (RES)	..	..	40.7	35.1	37.7	39.8	42.5	45.6	43.6	..
Current account balance	..	..	-15.2	-12.3	-6.2	-13.7	-13.1	-14.9	-19.8	-18.3
4. DEBT INDICATORS										
EDT / XGS (%)	..	..	31.2	36.1	35.7	34.9	36.1	39.9	39.1	37.3
EDT / GNP (%)	..	4.3	19.2	20.8	24.6	22.8	23.2	24.8	24.7	22.6
TDS / XGS (%)	..	..	2.8	2.3	2.1	1.4	1.3	1.4	1.6	1.5
INT / XGS (%)	..	..	1.9	1.6	1.3	0.7	0.6	0.6	0.8	0.8
INT / GNP (%)	..	0.3	1.2	0.9	0.9	0.5	0.4	0.4	0.5	0.5
RES / EDT (%)	..	..	152.0	115.8	93.7	101.2	105.1	107.6	93.7	..
RES / MGS (months)	..	..	4.2	4.0	3.3	3.2	3.6	4.0	3.4	..
Short-term / EDT (%)	..	0.0	42.9	31.3	23.9	3.2	2.1	7.1	10.7	10.4
Concessional / EDT (%)	..	78.3	47.8	59.9	70.0	91.2	93.2	89.1	86.3	87.3
Multilateral / EDT (%)	..	0.0	28.0	41.8	41.6	64.7	66.9	65.2	65.8	66.1

VANUATU

(US$ million, unless otherwise indicated)

	1970	1980	1988	1989	1990	1991	1992	1993	1994	1995
5. LONG-TERM DEBT										
DEBT OUTSTANDING (LDOD)	..	**4.1**	**15.3**	**20.8**	**30.6**	**38.1**	**39.6**	**39.4**	**41.5**	**43.2**
Public and publicly guaranteed	..	**4.1**	**15.3**	**20.8**	**30.6**	**38.1**	**39.6**	**39.4**	**41.5**	**43.2**
Official creditors	..	3.9	13.5	19.1	29.1	36.8	38.6	38.6	40.9	42.8
Multilateral	..	0.0	7.5	12.7	16.7	25.4	27.1	27.6	30.6	31.9
Concessional	..	0.0	6.9	11.9	15.9	24.5	26.2	26.9	29.9	31.2
Bilateral	..	3.9	6.0	6.5	12.4	11.4	11.6	11.0	10.3	10.9
Concessional	..	3.2	5.9	6.3	12.3	11.3	11.5	10.9	10.2	10.9
Private creditors	..	0.2	1.7	1.7	1.5	1.3	1.0	0.8	0.6	0.4
Bonds	..	0.0	0.0	0.0	0.0	0.0	0.0	0.0	0.0	0.0
Commercial banks	..	0.0	0.0	0.0	0.0	0.0	0.0	0.0	0.0	0.0
Other private	..	0.2	1.7	1.7	1.5	1.3	1.0	0.8	0.6	0.4
Private nonguaranteed	**0.0**	**0.0**	**0.0**	**0.0**	**0.0**	**0.0**	**0.0**	**0.0**	**0.0**	**0.0**
Bonds	..	0.0	0.0	0.0	0.0	0.0	0.0	0.0	0.0	0.0
Commercial banks	..	0.0	0.0	0.0	0.0	0.0	0.0	0.0	0.0	0.0
Memo:										
IBRD	0.0	0.0	0.0	0.0	0.0	0.0	0.0	0.0	0.0	0.0
IDA	0.0	0.0	1.8	2.9	4.0	8.6	11.1	11.4	12.5	13.2
DISBURSEMENTS	..	**0.0**	**3.5**	**5.8**	**8.7**	**14.5**	**4.5**	**1.1**	**1.8**	**1.6**
Public and publicly guaranteed	..	**0.0**	**3.5**	**5.8**	**8.7**	**14.5**	**4.5**	**1.1**	**1.8**	**1.6**
Official creditors	..	0.0	3.0	5.6	8.7	14.5	4.5	1.1	1.8	1.6
Multilateral	..	0.0	1.9	5.2	3.4	9.3	3.5	1.0	1.6	1.4
Concessional	..	0.0	1.5	5.0	3.3	9.3	3.5	1.0	1.6	1.4
Bilateral	..	0.0	1.1	0.4	5.3	5.1	1.0	0.1	0.2	0.2
Concessional	..	0.0	1.1	0.4	5.3	5.1	1.0	0.1	0.2	0.2
Private creditors	..	0.0	0.4	0.2	0.0	0.0	0.0	0.0	0.0	0.0
Bonds	..	0.0	0.0	0.0	0.0	0.0	0.0	0.0	0.0	0.0
Commercial banks	..	0.0	0.0	0.0	0.0	0.0	0.0	0.0	0.0	0.0
Other private	..	0.0	0.4	0.2	0.0	0.0	0.0	0.0	0.0	0.0
Private nonguaranteed	**0.0**	**0.0**	**0.0**	**0.0**	**0.0**	**0.0**	**0.0**	**0.0**	**0.0**	**0.0**
Bonds	..	0.0	0.0	0.0	0.0	0.0	0.0	0.0	0.0	0.0
Commercial banks	..	0.0	0.0	0.0	0.0	0.0	0.0	0.0	0.0	0.0
Memo:										
IBRD	0.0	0.0	0.0	0.0	0.0	0.0	0.0	0.0	0.0	0.0
IDA	0.0	0.0	0.4	1.2	0.8	4.3	3.0	0.3	0.5	0.4
PRINCIPAL REPAYMENTS	..	**0.4**	**0.7**	**0.6**	**1.0**	**0.8**	**0.9**	**0.9**	**1.0**	**0.9**
Public and publicly guaranteed	..	**0.4**	**0.7**	**0.6**	**1.0**	**0.8**	**0.9**	**0.9**	**1.0**	**0.9**
Official creditors	..	0.3	0.4	0.4	0.8	0.6	0.7	0.7	0.8	0.7
Multilateral	..	0.0	0.2	0.1	0.5	0.5	0.6	0.5	0.5	0.4
Concessional	..	0.0	0.2	0.1	0.5	0.5	0.5	0.5	0.4	0.4
Bilateral	..	0.3	0.3	0.2	0.2	0.0	0.1	0.1	0.3	0.3
Concessional	..	0.3	0.3	0.2	0.2	0.0	0.1	0.1	0.3	0.3
Private creditors	..	0.0	0.3	0.2	0.2	0.2	0.2	0.2	0.2	0.2
Bonds	..	0.0	0.0	0.0	0.0	0.0	0.0	0.0	0.0	0.0
Commercial banks	..	0.0	0.1	0.0	0.0	0.0	0.0	0.0	0.0	0.0
Other private	..	0.0	0.2	0.2	0.2	0.2	0.2	0.2	0.2	0.2
Private nonguaranteed	**0.0**	**0.0**	**0.0**	**0.0**	**0.0**	**0.0**	**0.0**	**0.0**	**0.0**	**0.0**
Bonds	..	0.0	0.0	0.0	0.0	0.0	0.0	0.0	0.0	0.0
Commercial banks	..	0.0	0.0	0.0	0.0	0.0	0.0	0.0	0.0	0.0
Memo:										
IBRD	0.0	0.0	0.0	0.0	0.0	0.0	0.0	0.0	0.0	0.0
IDA	0.0	0.0	0.0	0.0	0.0	0.0	0.0	0.0	0.0	0.0
NET FLOWS ON DEBT	..	**-0.4**	**2.8**	**5.2**	**7.7**	**13.7**	**3.6**	**0.2**	**0.8**	**0.7**
Public and publicly guaranteed	..	**-0.4**	**2.8**	**5.2**	**7.7**	**13.7**	**3.6**	**0.2**	**0.8**	**0.7**
Official creditors	..	-0.3	2.6	5.2	8.0	13.9	3.8	0.4	1.0	0.9
Multilateral	..	0.0	1.7	5.1	2.8	8.8	2.9	0.5	1.1	1.0
Concessional	..	0.0	1.3	4.8	2.8	8.8	3.0	0.6	1.1	1.0
Bilateral	..	-0.3	0.8	0.1	5.1	5.1	0.9	-0.1	-0.1	-0.1
Concessional	..	-0.3	0.9	0.2	5.2	5.1	0.9	-0.1	0.0	-0.1
Private creditors	..	0.0	0.2	0.0	-0.2	-0.2	-0.2	-0.2	-0.2	-0.2
Bonds	..	0.0	0.0	0.0	0.0	0.0	0.0	0.0	0.0	0.0
Commercial banks	..	0.0	-0.1	0.0	0.0	0.0	0.0	0.0	0.0	0.0
Other private	..	0.0	0.3	0.0	-0.2	-0.2	-0.2	-0.2	-0.2	-0.2
Private nonguaranteed	**0.0**	**0.0**	**0.0**	**0.0**	**0.0**	**0.0**	**0.0**	**0.0**	**0.0**	**0.0**
Bonds	..	0.0	0.0	0.0	0.0	0.0	0.0	0.0	0.0	0.0
Commercial banks	0.0	0.0	0.0	0.0	0.0	0.0	0.0	0.0	0.0	0.0
Memo:										
IBRD	0.0	0.0	0.0	0.0	0.0	0.0	0.0	0.0	0.0	0.0
IDA	0.0	0.0	0.4	1.2	0.8	4.3	3.0	0.3	0.5	0.4

VANUATU

(US$ million, unless otherwise indicated)

	1970	1980	1988	1989	1990	1991	1992	1993	1994	1995
INTEREST PAYMENTS (LINT)	..	**0.2**	**0.6**	**0.7**	**0.7**	**0.4**	**0.6**	**0.5**	**0.7**	**0.7**
Public and publicly guaranteed	..	**0.2**	**0.6**	**0.7**	**0.7**	**0.4**	**0.6**	**0.5**	**0.7**	**0.7**
Official creditors	..	0.2	0.4	0.5	0.6	0.3	0.5	0.5	0.6	0.6
Multilateral	..	0.0	0.2	0.2	0.2	0.3	0.3	0.3	0.3	0.3
Concessional	..	0.0	0.1	0.2	0.2	0.2	0.3	0.3	0.3	0.3
Bilateral	..	0.2	0.3	0.3	0.3	0.0	0.1	0.1	0.3	0.3
Concessional	..	0.2	0.3	0.3	0.3	0.0	0.1	0.1	0.3	0.3
Private creditors	..	0.0	0.2	0.2	0.2	0.1	0.1	0.1	0.0	0.0
Bonds	..	0.0	0.0	0.0	0.0	0.0	0.0	0.0	0.0	0.0
Commercial banks	..	0.0	0.0	0.0	0.0	0.0	0.0	0.0	0.0	0.0
Other private	..	0.0	0.1	0.2	0.2	0.1	0.1	0.1	0.0	0.0
Private nonguaranteed	**0.0**	**0.0**	**0.0**	**0.0**	**0.0**	**0.0**	**0.0**	**0.0**	**0.0**	**0.0**
Bonds	..	0.0	0.0	0.0	0.0	0.0	0.0	0.0	0.0	0.0
Commercial banks	..	0.0	0.0	0.0	0.0	0.0	0.0	0.0	0.0	0.0
Memo:										
IBRD	0.0	0.0	0.0	0.0	0.0	0.0	0.0	0.0	0.0	0.0
IDA	0.0	0.0	0.0	0.0	0.0	0.0	0.1	0.1	0.1	0.1
NET TRANSFERS ON DEBT	..	**-0.6**	**2.2**	**4.6**	**7.0**	**13.3**	**3.0**	**-0.3**	**0.2**	**0.0**
Public and publicly guaranteed	..	**-0.6**	**2.2**	**4.6**	**7.0**	**13.3**	**3.0**	**-0.3**	**0.2**	**0.0**
Official creditors	..	-0.6	2.2	4.7	7.4	13.6	3.3	0.0	0.4	0.2
Multilateral	..	0.0	1.6	4.8	2.6	8.5	2.6	0.2	0.7	0.6
Concessional	..	0.0	1.2	4.7	2.6	8.6	2.7	0.3	0.9	0.7
Bilateral	..	-0.6	0.6	-0.1	4.8	5.1	0.7	-0.2	-0.3	-0.4
Concessional	..	-0.4	0.6	-0.1	4.8	5.1	0.7	-0.2	-0.3	-0.4
Private creditors	..	0.0	0.0	-0.2	-0.4	-0.3	-0.3	-0.3	-0.3	-0.2
Bonds	..	0.0	0.0	0.0	0.0	0.0	0.0	0.0	0.0	0.0
Commercial banks	..	0.0	-0.1	0.0	0.0	0.0	0.0	0.0	0.0	0.0
Other private	..	0.0	0.1	-0.2	-0.4	-0.3	-0.3	-0.3	-0.3	-0.2
Private nonguaranteed	**0.0**	**0.0**	**0.0**	**0.0**	**0.0**	**0.0**	**0.0**	**0.0**	**0.0**	**0.0**
Bonds	..	0.0	0.0	0.0	0.0	0.0	0.0	0.0	0.0	0.0
Commercial banks	..	0.0	0.0	0.0	0.0	0.0	0.0	0.0	0.0	0.0
Memo:										
IBRD	0.0	0.0	0.0	0.0	0.0	0.0	0.0	0.0	0.0	0.0
IDA	0.0	0.0	0.4	1.1	0.8	4.3	2.9	0.2	0.4	0.3
DEBT SERVICE (LTDS)	..	**0.6**	**1.3**	**1.3**	**1.7**	**1.2**	**1.4**	**1.4**	**1.6**	**1.6**
Public and publicly guaranteed	..	**0.6**	**1.3**	**1.3**	**1.7**	**1.2**	**1.4**	**1.4**	**1.6**	**1.6**
Official creditors	..	0.6	0.9	0.9	1.3	0.9	1.1	1.1	1.4	1.4
Multilateral	..	0.0	0.3	0.4	0.8	0.8	0.9	0.9	0.8	0.8
Concessional	..	0.0	0.3	0.3	0.7	0.7	0.8	0.7	0.7	0.7
Bilateral	..	0.6	0.5	0.5	0.5	0.1	0.3	0.3	0.6	0.6
Concessional	..	0.4	0.5	0.5	0.5	0.0	0.2	0.3	0.5	0.6
Private creditors	..	0.0	0.4	0.4	0.4	0.3	0.3	0.3	0.3	0.2
Bonds	..	0.0	0.0	0.0	0.0	0.0	0.0	0.0	0.0	0.0
Commercial banks	..	0.0	0.1	0.0	0.0	0.0	0.0	0.0	0.0	0.0
Other private	..	0.0	0.3	0.4	0.4	0.3	0.3	0.3	0.3	0.2
Private nonguaranteed	**0.0**	**0.0**	**0.0**	**0.0**	**0.0**	**0.0**	**0.0**	**0.0**	**0.0**	**0.0**
Bonds	..	0.0	0.0	0.0	0.0	0.0	0.0	0.0	0.0	0.0
Commercial banks	..	0.0	0.0	0.0	0.0	0.0	0.0	0.0	0.0	0.0
Memo:										
IBRD	0.0	0.0	0.0	0.0	0.0	0.0	0.0	0.0	0.0	0.0
IDA	0.0	0.0	0.0	0.0	0.0	0.0	0.1	0.1	0.1	0.1
UNDISBURSED DEBT	..	**0.0**	**21.9**	**28.9**	**18.1**	**12.1**	**12.5**	**11.4**	**9.8**	**8.4**
Official creditors	..	0.0	21.7	28.9	18.1	12.1	12.5	11.4	9.8	8.4
Private creditors	..	0.0	0.2	0.0	0.0	0.0	0.0	0.0	0.0	0.0
Memorandum items										
Concessional LDOD	..	3.2	12.8	18.2	28.2	35.9	37.7	37.7	40.1	42.1
Variable rate LDOD	..	0.0	1.1	0.9	0.8	0.7	0.6	0.5	0.5	0.4
Public sector LDOD	..	4.1	15.3	20.8	30.6	38.1	39.6	39.4	41.5	43.2
Private sector LDOD	..	0.0	0.0	0.0	0.0	0.0	0.0	0.0	0.0	0.0

6. CURRENCY COMPOSITION OF LONG-TERM DEBT (PERCENT)

	1970	1980	1988	1989	1990	1991	1992	1993	1994	1995
Deutsche mark	..	0.0	0.0	0.0	0.0	0.0	0.0	0.0	0.0	0.0
French franc	..	82.5	38.0	30.3	33.3	17.9	18.2	17.0	17.6	18.1
Japanese yen	..	0.0	0.0	0.0	0.0	0.0	0.0	0.0	0.0	0.0
Pound sterling	..	14.6	1.3	1.0	0.7	0.3	0.3	0.3	0.2	0.0
Swiss franc	..	0.0	0.0	0.0	0.0	0.0	0.0	0.0	0.0	0.0
U.S.dollars	..	0.0	24.9	25.9	20.9	33.9	38.4	39.1	40.0	39.3
Multiple currency	..	0.0	19.6	28.3	28.7	29.7	28.0	30.0	33.2	33.8
Special drawing rights	..	0.0	0.0	0.0	0.0	0.0	0.0	0.0	0.0	0.0
All other currencies	..	4.9	15.7	14.9	16.3	18.1	15.1	13.7	9.4	8.6

VANUATU

(US$ million, unless otherwise indicated)

	1970	1980	1988	1989	1990	1991	1992	1993	1994	1995
7. DEBT RESTRUCTURINGS										
Total amount rescheduled	0.0	0.0	0.0	0.0	0.0	0.0	0.0	0.0	0.0	0.0
Debt stock rescheduled	0.0	0.0	0.0	0.0	0.0	0.0	0.0	0.0	0.0	0.0
Principal rescheduled	0.0	0.0	0.0	0.0	0.0	0.0	0.0	0.0	0.0	0.0
Official	0.0	0.0	0.0	0.0	0.0	0.0	0.0	0.0	0.0	0.0
Private	0.0	0.0	0.0	0.0	0.0	0.0	0.0	0.0	0.0	0.0
Interest rescheduled	0.0	0.0	0.0	0.0	0.0	0.0	0.0	0.0	0.0	0.0
Official	0.0	0.0	0.0	0.0	0.0	0.0	0.0	0.0	0.0	0.0
Private	0.0	0.0	0.0	0.0	0.0	0.0	0.0	0.0	0.0	0.0
Debt forgiven	..	..	0.0	0.0	0.0	5.6	0.0	0.0	0.0	0.0
Memo: interest forgiven	..	..	0.0	0.0	0.0	0.0	0.0	0.0	0.0	0.0
Debt stock reduction	0.0	0.0	0.0	0.0	0.0	0.0	0.0	0.0	0.0	0.0
of which debt buyback	0.0	0.0	0.0	0.0	0.0	0.0	0.0	0.0	0.0	0.0
8. DEBT STOCK-FLOW RECONCILIATION										
Total change in debt stocks	..	..	..	3.5	9.9	-0.9	1.1	1.9	4.1	1.7
Net flows on debt	..	..	..	3.2	7.8	5.3	3.2	2.4	2.8	0.7
Net change in interest arrears	..	..	..	0.0	0.0	0.0	0.0	0.0	0.0	0.0
Interest capitalized	..	..	..	0.0	0.0	0.0	0.0	0.0	0.0	0.0
Debt forgiveness or reduction	..	..	..	0.0	0.0	-5.6	0.0	0.0	0.0	0.0
Cross-currency valuation	..	..	..	0.3	1.6	-0.3	-0.9	-0.6	-0.1	0.8
Residual	..	..	..	0.0	0.5	-0.3	-1.2	0.1	1.4	0.2
9. AVERAGE TERMS OF NEW COMMITMENTS										
ALL CREDITORS										
Interest (%)	..	0.0	1.0	1.2	0.0	2.1	1.0	0.0	0.0	0.0
Maturity (years)	..	0.0	39.6	35.9	0.0	37.6	39.5	0.0	0.0	0.0
Grace period (years)	..	0.0	10.1	10.4	0.0	8.6	10.0	0.0	0.0	0.0
Grant element (%)	..	0.0	78.2	75.4	0.0	67.1	78.1	0.0	0.0	0.0
Official creditors										
Interest (%)	..	0.0	1.0	1.2	0.0	2.1	1.0	0.0	0.0	0.0
Maturity (years)	..	0.0	39.6	35.9	0.0	37.6	39.5	0.0	0.0	0.0
Grace period (years)	..	0.0	10.1	10.4	0.0	8.6	10.0	0.0	0.0	0.0
Grant element (%)	..	0.0	78.2	75.4	0.0	67.1	78.1	0.0	0.0	0.0
Private creditors										
Interest (%)	..	0.0	0.0	0.0	0.0	0.0	0.0	0.0	0.0	0.0
Maturity (years)	..	0.0	0.0	0.0	0.0	0.0	0.0	0.0	0.0	0.0
Grace period (years)	..	0.0	0.0	0.0	0.0	0.0	0.0	0.0	0.0	0.0
Grant element (%)	..	0.0	0.0	0.0	0.0	0.0	0.0	0.0	0.0	0.0
Memorandum items										
Commitments	..	0.0	6.0	13.6	0.0	9.5	5.2	0.0	0.0	0.0
Official creditors	..	0.0	6.0	13.6	0.0	9.5	5.2	0.0	0.0	0.0
Private creditors	..	0.0	0.0	0.0	0.0	0.0	0.0	0.0	0.0	0.0

10. CONTRACTUAL OBLIGATIONS ON OUTSTANDING LONG-TERM DEBT

	1996	1997	1998	1999	2000	2001	2002	2003	2004	2005
TOTAL										
Disbursements	3.4	2.7	1.4	0.6	0.2	0.0	0.0	0.0	0.0	0.0
Principal	1.0	0.9	0.7	0.8	1.1	1.1	1.2	1.2	1.3	1.3
Interest	0.7	0.7	0.7	0.6	0.6	0.6	0.6	0.6	0.5	0.5
Official creditors										
Disbursements	3.4	2.7	1.4	0.6	0.2	0.0	0.0	0.0	0.0	0.0
Principal	0.8	0.8	0.6	0.7	1.1	1.1	1.2	1.2	1.3	1.3
Interest	0.7	0.7	0.6	0.6	0.6	0.6	0.6	0.6	0.5	0.5
Bilateral creditors										
Disbursements	0.2	0.1	0.0	0.0	0.0	0.0	0.0	0.0	0.0	0.0
Principal	0.3	0.3	0.3	0.3	0.6	0.6	0.5	0.5	0.5	0.5
Interest	0.3	0.3	0.3	0.3	0.3	0.3	0.2	0.2	0.2	0.2
Multilateral creditors										
Disbursements	3.3	2.6	1.4	0.6	0.2	0.0	0.0	0.0	0.0	0.0
Principal	0.5	0.6	0.4	0.5	0.5	0.6	0.7	0.7	0.8	0.8
Interest	0.4	0.4	0.4	0.4	0.4	0.4	0.3	0.3	0.3	0.3
Private creditors										
Disbursements	0.0	0.0	0.0	0.0	0.0	0.0	0.0	0.0	0.0	0.0
Principal	0.1	0.1	0.1	0.1	0.0	0.0	0.0	0.0	0.0	0.0
Interest	0.0	0.0	0.0	0.0	0.0	0.0	0.0	0.0	0.0	0.0
Commercial banks										
Disbursements	0.0	0.0	0.0	0.0	0.0	0.0	0.0	0.0	0.0	0.0
Principal	0.0	0.0	0.0	0.0	0.0	0.0	0.0	0.0	0.0	0.0
Interest	0.0	0.0	0.0	0.0	0.0	0.0	0.0	0.0	0.0	0.0
Other private										
Disbursements	0.0	0.0	0.0	0.0	0.0	0.0	0.0	0.0	0.0	0.0
Principal	0.1	0.1	0.1	0.1	0.0	0.0	0.0	0.0	0.0	0.0
Interest	0.0	0.0	0.0	0.0	0.0	0.0	0.0	0.0	0.0	0.0

VENEZUELA

(US$ million, unless otherwise indicated)

	1970	*1980*	*1988*	*1989*	*1990*	*1991*	*1992*	*1993*	*1994*	*1995*
1. SUMMARY DEBT DATA										
TOTAL DEBT STOCKS (EDT)	**..**	**29,344**	**34,738**	**32,377**	**33,170**	**34,122**	**37,848**	**37,539**	**36,853**	**35,842**
Long-term debt (LDOD)	**954**	**13,795**	**29,464**	**29,089**	**28,159**	**28,589**	**29,628**	**30,177**	**30,478**	**30,508**
Public and publicly guaranteed	718	10,614	25,181	25,166	24,509	24,939	25,830	26,855	28,042	28,494
Private nonguaranteed	236	3,181	4,283	3,923	3,650	3,650	3,798	3,322	2,436	2,013
Use of IMF credit	**0**	**0**	**0**	**998**	**3,012**	**3,249**	**2,946**	**2,680**	**2,643**	**2,239**
Short-term debt	**..**	**15,550**	**5,274**	**2,290**	**2,000**	**2,284**	**5,275**	**4,682**	**3,732**	**3,096**
of which interest arrears on LDOD	..	15	3	6	0	0	147	189	293	305
Official creditors	..	0	0	0	0	0	13	10	25	25
Private creditors	..	15	3	6	0	0	134	179	268	280
Memo: principal arrears on LDOD	..	37	27	44	0	0	472	834	1,249	1,301
Official creditors	..	0	1	1	0	0	31	66	144	144
Private creditors	..	37	26	43	0	0	441	768	1,105	1,157
Memo: export credits	..	..	2,296	2,141	2,386	4,073	5,548	6,491	7,759	7,435
TOTAL DEBT FLOWS										
Disbursements	**282**	**4,761**	**1,727**	**2,241**	**4,069**	**2,091**	**2,572**	**2,137**	**1,045**	**1,712**
Long-term debt	282	4,761	1,727	1,267	2,226	1,774	2,572	2,137	1,045	1,712
IMF purchases	0	0	0	974	1,843	317	0	0	0	0
Principal repayments	**67**	**2,972**	**2,429**	**745**	**1,747**	**897**	**1,194**	**1,783**	**1,573**	**2,464**
Long-term debt	67	2,972	2,429	745	1,747	791	1,013	1,515	1,372	2,003
IMF repurchases	0	0	0	0	0	106	181	268	201	462
Net flows on debt	**215**	**1,789**	**489**	**-1,491**	**2,037**	**1,478**	**4,222**	**-281**	**-1,582**	**-1,401**
of which short-term debt	..	..	1,190	-2,987	-284	284	2,844	-635	-1,054	-648
Interest payments (INT)	**..**	**3,065**	**3,123**	**3,086**	**3,242**	**2,425**	**2,137**	**2,162**	**2,118**	**2,403**
Long-term debt	53	1,475	2,665	2,452	2,993	1,980	1,626	1,768	1,771	2,067
IMF charges	0	0	0	35	37	232	229	174	141	142
Short-term debt	..	1,590	458	600	212	212	282	220	206	193
Net transfers on debt	**..**	**-1,276**	**-2,634**	**-4,577**	**-1,205**	**-947**	**2,084**	**-2,443**	**-3,700**	**-3,804**
Total debt service paid (TDS)	**..**	**6,037**	**5,552**	**3,831**	**4,990**	**3,321**	**3,331**	**3,945**	**3,691**	**4,867**
Long-term debt	120	4,447	5,094	3,196	4,741	2,772	2,639	3,283	3,143	4,070
IMF repurchases and charges	0	0	0	35	37	338	410	442	342	604
Short-term debt (interest only)	..	1,590	458	600	212	212	282	220	206	193

	1970	*1980*	*1988*	*1989*	*1990*	*1991*	*1992*	*1993*	*1994*	*1995*
2. AGGREGATE NET RESOURCE FLOWS AND NET TRANSFERS (LONG-TERM)										
NET RESOURCE FLOWS	**192**	**1,844**	**-608**	**749**	**934**	**3,006**	**2,338**	**1,062**	**533**	**634**
Net flow of long-term debt (ex. IMF)	215	1,789	-702	523	478	983	1,559	622	-327	-291
Foreign direct investment (net)	-23	55	89	213	451	1,916	629	372	813	900
Portfolio equity flows	0	0	0	10	0	100	146	59	42	7
Grants (excluding technical coop.)	0	0	4	3	5	7	5	9	6	18
Memo: technical coop. grants	6	19	19	21	27	28	40	41	32	40
NET TRANSFERS	**-429**	**47**	**-3,483**	**-1,928**	**-2,283**	**798**	**205**	**-1,280**	**-1,837**	**-2,053**
Interest on long-term debt	53	1,475	2,665	2,452	2,993	1,980	1,626	1,768	1,771	2,067
Profit remittances on FDI	568	322	210	225	224	228	507	574	600	620

	1970	*1980*	*1988*	*1989*	*1990*	*1991*	*1992*	*1993*	*1994*	*1995*
3. MAJOR ECONOMIC AGGREGATES										
Gross national product (GNP)	12,872	69,706	58,510	41,753	47,143	52,450	58,617	58,265	56,389	73,184
Exports of goods & services (XGS)	2,833	22,232	12,705	15,570	21,464	18,556	17,121	17,718	19,305	22,406
of which workers remittances	0	0	0	0	0	0	0	0	0	0
Imports of goods & services (MGS)	2,845	17,065	18,367	13,226	12,883	16,456	20,496	19,343	16,681	20,262
International reserves (RES)	1,047	13,360	7,793	8,702	12,733	14,719	13,381	13,693	12,459	10,715
Current account balance	-104	4,728	-5,809	2,161	8,279	1,736	-3,749	-1,993	2,541	2,255

	1970	*1980*	*1988*	*1989*	*1990*	*1991*	*1992*	*1993*	*1994*	*1995*
4. DEBT INDICATORS										
EDT / XGS (%)	..	132.0	273.4	207.9	154.5	183.9	221.1	211.9	190.9	160.0
EDT / GNP (%)	..	42.1	59.4	77.5	70.4	65.1	64.6	64.4	65.4	49.0
TDS / XGS (%)	..	27.2	43.7	24.6	23.2	17.9	19.5	22.3	19.1	21.7
INT / XGS (%)	..	13.8	24.6	19.8	15.1	13.1	12.5	12.2	11.0	10.7
INT / GNP (%)	..	4.4	5.3	7.4	6.9	4.6	3.6	3.7	3.8	3.3
RES / EDT (%)	..	45.5	22.4	26.9	38.4	43.1	35.4	36.5	33.8	29.9
RES / MGS (months)	4.4	9.4	5.1	7.9	11.9	10.7	7.8	8.5	9.0	6.3
Short-term / EDT (%)	..	53.0	15.2	7.1	6.0	6.7	13.9	12.5	10.1	8.6
Concessional / EDT (%)	..	0.4	0.1	0.2	0.3	0.2	0.2	0.2	0.3	0.3
Multilateral / EDT (%)	..	0.7	0.9	1.7	4.9	6.5	7.2	7.7	8.5	9.2

VENEZUELA

(US$ million, unless otherwise indicated)

	1970	1980	1988	1989	1990	1991	1992	1993	1994	1995
5. LONG-TERM DEBT										
DEBT OUTSTANDING (LDOD)	**954**	**13,795**	**29,464**	**29,089**	**28,159**	**28,589**	**29,628**	**30,177**	**30,478**	**30,508**
Public and publicly guaranteed	**718**	**10,614**	**25,181**	**25,166**	**24,509**	**24,939**	**25,830**	**26,855**	**28,042**	**28,494**
Official creditors	366	571	505	817	1,954	2,878	3,599	3,823	4,544	4,763
Multilateral	244	216	297	560	1,639	2,210	2,728	2,884	3,133	3,300
Concessional	190	101	18	15	12	9	8	7	8	10
Bilateral	122	355	209	257	315	668	871	938	1,411	1,463
Concessional	81	8	0	49	73	72	67	64	86	96
Private creditors	352	10,043	24,676	24,350	22,554	22,060	22,231	23,033	23,498	23,732
Bonds	37	1,261	1,422	1,486	19,644	19,778	20,099	20,998	21,061	20,885
Commercial banks	237	8,159	20,973	20,375	364	148	202	289	585	1,158
Other private	78	623	2,281	2,489	2,547	2,134	1,930	1,745	1,853	1,689
Private nonguaranteed	**236**	**3,181**	**4,283**	**3,923**	**3,650**	**3,650**	**3,798**	**3,322**	**2,436**	**2,013**
Bonds	0	0	0	0	0	0	174	264	114	114
Commercial banks	236	3,181	4,283	3,923	3,650	3,650	3,624	3,058	2,322	1,899
Memo:										
IBRD	217	133	4	119	974	1,340	1,479	1,529	1,653	1,639
IDA	0	0	0	0	0	0	0	0	0	0
DISBURSEMENTS	**282**	**4,761**	**1,727**	**1,267**	**2,226**	**1,774**	**2,572**	**2,137**	**1,045**	**1,712**
Public and publicly guaranteed	**216**	**2,870**	**1,727**	**1,267**	**2,226**	**1,601**	**1,714**	**1,877**	**1,045**	**1,632**
Official creditors	30	88	182	401	1,112	911	839	177	508	532
Multilateral	21	3	178	273	1,035	541	597	126	103	267
Concessional	11	2	0	0	0	0	0	1	2	4
Bilateral	10	85	4	128	77	370	242	51	405	265
Concessional	0	0	0	45	15	0	0	2	19	16
Private creditors	186	2,782	1,545	866	1,114	690	875	1,700	537	1,100
Bonds	0	276	357	263	599	502	757	1,500	0	349
Commercial banks	140	2,362	67	141	26	51	82	123	304	586
Other private	46	144	1,122	463	488	136	36	77	233	165
Private nonguaranteed	**67**	**1,891**	**0**	**0**	**0**	**173**	**858**	**260**	**0**	**80**
Bonds	0	0	0	0	0	0	174	90	0	0
Commercial banks	67	1,891	0	0	0	173	684	170	0	80
Memo:										
IBRD	15	1	0	115	840	330	177	20	20	47
IDA	0	0	0	0	0	0	0	0	0	0
PRINCIPAL REPAYMENTS	**67**	**2,972**	**2,429**	**745**	**1,747**	**791**	**1,013**	**1,515**	**1,372**	**2,003**
Public and publicly guaranteed	**42**	**1,737**	**1,239**	**585**	**1,574**	**618**	**303**	**779**	**486**	**1,500**
Official creditors	26	68	93	47	50	50	52	81	102	386
Multilateral	13	33	36	10	8	10	17	33	65	202
Concessional	9	17	3	3	3	2	1	1	1	1
Bilateral	13	35	57	37	42	40	35	48	37	184
Concessional	4	6	0	0	0	0	1	0	4	12
Private creditors	16	1,668	1,146	537	1,525	568	251	698	384	1,114
Bonds	1	13	249	165	254	12	53	466	145	677
Commercial banks	5	1,324	524	86	706	47	23	27	32	46
Other private	10	331	373	286	565	509	176	206	207	391
Private nonguaranteed	**25**	**1,235**	**1,190**	**160**	**173**	**173**	**710**	**736**	**886**	**503**
Bonds	0	0	0	0	0	0	0	0	150	0
Commercial banks	25	1,235	1,190	160	173	173	710	736	736	503
Memo:										
IBRD	10	23	7	4	0	0	0	0	0	116
IDA	0	0	0	0	0	0	0	0	0	0
NET FLOWS ON DEBT	**215**	**1,789**	**-702**	**523**	**478**	**983**	**1,559**	**622**	**-327**	**-291**
Public and publicly guaranteed	**174**	**1,133**	**489**	**683**	**651**	**983**	**1,411**	**1,098**	**559**	**132**
Official creditors	4	20	89	354	1,062	861	787	96	406	147
Multilateral	8	-30	142	264	1,027	531	580	92	38	65
Concessional	2	-15	-3	-3	-3	-2	-1	-1	0	2
Bilateral	-4	50	-53	91	35	330	207	3	368	81
Concessional	-4	-6	0	45	15	0	-1	2	15	4
Private creditors	169	1,114	399	328	-411	122	624	1,002	153	-15
Bonds	-1	263	108	97	345	490	704	1,035	-145	-328
Commercial banks	134	1,038	-457	54	-680	5	59	96	272	540
Other private	36	-187	749	177	-77	-373	-140	-129	27	-227
Private nonguaranteed	**41**	**656**	**-1,190**	**-160**	**-173**	**0**	**148**	**-476**	**-886**	**-423**
Bonds	0	0	0	0	0	0	174	90	-150	0
Commercial banks	41	656	-1,190	-160	-173	0	-26	-566	-736	-423
Memo:										
IBRD	6	-22	-7	111	840	330	177	20	20	-69
IDA	0	0	0	0	0	0	0	0	0	0

VENEZUELA

(US$ million, unless otherwise indicated)

	1970	1980	1988	1989	1990	1991	1992	1993	1994	1995
INTEREST PAYMENTS (LINT)	**53**	**1,475**	**2,665**	**2,452**	**2,993**	**1,980**	**1,626**	**1,768**	**1,771**	**2,067**
Public and publicly guaranteed	**40**	**1,218**	**2,033**	**1,988**	**2,593**	**1,580**	**1,526**	**1,521**	**1,639**	**1,957**
Official creditors	20	36	37	46	71	142	228	268	274	301
Multilateral	15	18	23	33	59	124	187	212	234	231
Concessional	11	7	1	1	0	0	0	0	0	0
Bilateral	5	18	14	13	13	18	41	56	40	70
Concessional	3	1	0	0	0	0	1	1	2	3
Private creditors	20	1,183	1,996	1,941	2,522	1,438	1,298	1,253	1,365	1,655
Bonds	3	61	78	161	135	1,260	1,255	1,179	1,307	1,518
Commercial banks	16	1,052	1,790	1,628	2,198	19	6	6	19	65
Other private	2	70	128	153	188	159	37	68	40	73
Private nonguaranteed	**13**	**257**	**632**	**464**	**400**	**400**	**100**	**246**	**132**	**111**
Bonds	0	0	0	0	0	0	2	14	20	10
Commercial banks	13	257	632	464	400	400	98	232	112	101
Memo:										
IBRD	13	12	1	0	19	62	106	111	115	120
IDA	0	0	0	0	0	0	0	0	0	0
NET TRANSFERS ON DEBT	**162**	**314**	**-3,366**	**-1,929**	**-2,515**	**-998**	**-68**	**-1,146**	**-2,097**	**-2,359**
Public and publicly guaranteed	**134**	**-85**	**-1,544**	**-1,305**	**-1,942**	**-598**	**-115**	**-424**	**-1,080**	**-1,825**
Official creditors	-16	-16	53	308	991	718	559	-173	132	-155
Multilateral	-7	-48	120	231	968	407	393	-120	-196	-166
Concessional	-9	-22	-4	-4	-4	-3	-2	-1	0	2
Bilateral	-9	32	-67	77	23	312	166	-53	328	11
Concessional	-6	-6	0	45	15	0	-2	1	13	2
Private creditors	150	-69	-1,597	-1,613	-2,933	-1,316	-674	-251	-1,212	-1,670
Bonds	-4	202	30	-63	210	-770	-550	-145	-1,452	-1,846
Commercial banks	119	-15	-2,248	-1,574	-2,878	-15	53	90	253	475
Other private	35	-256	621	24	-265	-532	-176	-196	-13	-299
Private nonguaranteed	**28**	**399**	**-1,822**	**-624**	**-573**	**-400**	**48**	**-722**	**-1,018**	**-534**
Bonds	0	0	0	0	0	0	172	76	-170	-10
Commercial banks	28	399	-1,822	-624	-573	-400	-124	-798	-848	-524
Memo:										
IBRD	-7	-35	-7	111	821	268	71	-91	-95	-189
IDA	0	0	0	0	0	0	0	0	0	0
DEBT SERVICE (LTDS)	**120**	**4,447**	**5,094**	**3,196**	**4,741**	**2,772**	**2,639**	**3,283**	**3,143**	**4,070**
Public and publicly guaranteed	**82**	**2,955**	**3,272**	**2,572**	**4,168**	**2,198**	**1,829**	**2,301**	**2,125**	**3,456**
Official creditors	46	104	129	94	121	192	280	349	376	687
Multilateral	28	51	58	43	67	134	204	246	299	433
Concessional	20	24	4	4	4	3	2	2	2	2
Bilateral	18	53	71	51	55	58	76	104	77	254
Concessional	6	6	0	0	0	0	2	1	6	14
Private creditors	36	2,851	3,143	2,479	4,046	2,006	1,549	1,951	1,750	2,769
Bonds	4	74	328	326	389	1,272	1,308	1,645	1,452	2,195
Commercial banks	21	2,377	2,314	1,714	2,905	66	29	33	51	110
Other private	11	401	501	438	753	668	213	273	246	464
Private nonguaranteed	**38**	**1,492**	**1,822**	**624**	**573**	**573**	**810**	**982**	**1,018**	**614**
Bonds	0	0	0	0	0	0	2	14	170	10
Commercial banks	38	1,492	1,822	624	573	573	808	968	848	604
Memo:										
IBRD	23	35	7	4	19	62	106	111	115	235
IDA	0	0	0	0	0	0	0	0	0	0
UNDISBURSED DEBT	**196**	**364**	**2,289**	**2,534**	**2,986**	**3,275**	**3,395**	**4,557**	**4,175**	**3,075**
Official creditors	106	101	975	1,373	1,628	2,099	2,240	3,692	3,608	2,854
Private creditors	90	263	1,314	1,160	1,357	1,175	1,155	865	567	220
Memorandum items										
Concessional LDOD	271	109	18	64	84	81	75	71	94	107
Variable rate LDOD	255	11,224	26,659	25,994	17,448	17,912	18,592	17,997	17,768	17,837
Public sector LDOD	682	10,277	25,180	25,166	24,508	24,938	25,523	26,110	27,280	27,920
Private sector LDOD	272	3,518	4,284	3,924	3,650	3,650	4,104	4,067	3,198	2,588

6. CURRENCY COMPOSITION OF LONG-TERM DEBT (PERCENT)

	1970	1980	1988	1989	1990	1991	1992	1993	1994	1995
Deutsche mark	5.2	7.8	2.8	3.3	6.9	6.3	5.7	6.5	6.9	9.6
French franc	1.5	1.9	3.6	3.7	4.1	3.3	2.7	2.3	2.6	2.6
Japanese yen	0.0	4.9	1.5	1.1	0.6	2.0	2.8	2.6	4.0	4.2
Pound sterling	0.1	0.0	0.0	0.0	1.5	1.6	1.3	1.3	1.3	1.2
Swiss franc	4.6	0.0	0.1	0.1	0.9	0.7	0.6	0.6	0.7	0.7
U.S.dollars	54.3	82.8	90.7	89.4	78.2	76.2	75.6	75.1	72.1	68.5
Multiple currency	32.0	2.3	0.9	2.0	6.5	8.7	10.4	10.6	11.1	11.5
Special drawing rights	0.0	0.0	0.0	0.0	0.0	0.0	0.0	0.0	0.0	0.0
All other currencies	2.3	0.3	0.3	0.2	1.3	1.2	0.9	1.1	1.4	1.7

VENEZUELA

(US$ million, unless otherwise indicated)

	1970	1980	1988	1989	1990	1991	1992	1993	1994	1995
7. DEBT RESTRUCTURINGS										
Total amount rescheduled	0	0	400	0	17,659	0	0	0	0	0
Debt stock rescheduled	0	0	400	0	17,630	0	0	0	0	0
Principal rescheduled	0	0	0	0	0	0	0	0	0	0
Official	0	0	0	0	0	0	0	0	0	0
Private	0	0	0	0	0	0	0	0	0	0
Interest rescheduled	0	0	0	0	0	0	0	0	0	0
Official	0	0	0	0	0	0	0	0	0	0
Private	0	0	0	0	0	0	0	0	0	0
Debt forgiven	..	..	0	0	0	0	0	0	0	0
Memo: interest forgiven	..	..	0	0	0	0	0	0	0	0
Debt stock reduction	0	0	47	656	2,361	565	204	18	0	0
of which debt buyback	0	0	0	0	634	0	0	0	0	0
8. DEBT STOCK-FLOW RECONCILIATION										
Total change in debt stocks	..	..	..	-2,361	793	951	3,727	-309	-687	-1,011
Net flows on debt	..	..	..	-1,491	2,037	1,478	4,222	-281	-1,582	-1,401
Net change in interest arrears	..	..	..	3	-6	0	147	43	103	12
Interest capitalized	..	..	..	0	0	0	0	0	0	0
Debt forgiveness or reduction	..	..	..	-656	-1,727	-565	-204	-18	0	0
Cross-currency valuation	..	..	..	64	625	13	-333	-103	657	365
Residual	..	..	..	-281	-136	25	-105	50	135	13
9. AVERAGE TERMS OF NEW COMMITMENTS										
ALL CREDITORS										
Interest (%)	7.6	12.1	8.4	8.5	8.2	8.4	8.1	7.5	7.0	7.4
Maturity (years)	8.3	7.7	7.2	11.9	14.5	14.0	12.4	12.8	14.1	8.1
Grace period (years)	1.9	3.1	2.9	4.7	5.6	4.1	5.5	5.2	3.6	3.8
Grant element (%)	9.5	-8.5	4.8	7.7	9.4	8.2	10.4	13.1	15.1	10.3
Official creditors										
Interest (%)	8.0	8.3	8.0	7.3	7.9	8.0	7.1	6.9	6.9	6.8
Maturity (years)	17.8	12.4	14.5	14.7	15.6	15.5	17.3	19.0	15.9	17.8
Grace period (years)	2.9	2.7	4.2	5.2	4.9	3.8	5.2	6.5	4.3	5.3
Grant element (%)	9.4	7.1	10.3	14.3	11.5	10.5	17.1	19.8	17.1	19.6
Private creditors										
Interest (%)	7.5	12.3	8.5	9.6	8.5	9.3	9.2	8.2	7.4	7.7
Maturity (years)	6.8	7.5	5.3	9.0	13.6	10.0	6.8	5.9	9.0	3.2
Grace period (years)	1.7	3.1	2.5	4.1	6.1	4.8	5.8	3.8	1.4	3.0
Grant element (%)	9.6	-9.3	3.4	0.9	7.8	2.2	2.8	5.6	9.0	5.6
Memorandum items										
Commitments	188	2,769	2,566	1,635	3,209	1,850	1,884	2,969	757	1,103
Official creditors	25	133	532	826	1,362	1,343	1,001	1,576	566	368
Private creditors	163	2,636	2,034	809	1,847	507	883	1,393	191	735

10. CONTRACTUAL OBLIGATIONS ON OUTSTANDING LONG-TERM DEBT

	1996	1997	1998	1999	2000	2001	2002	2003	2004	2005
TOTAL										
Disbursements	769	641	515	399	296	192	130	65	42	25
Principal	1,925	1,914	2,962	2,017	2,207	2,046	2,229	1,946	1,853	1,502
Interest	1,947	1,916	1,807	1,627	1,516	1,380	1,255	1,107	983	873
Official creditors										
Disbursements	590	608	508	399	296	192	130	65	42	25
Principal	488	538	620	636	639	689	681	614	599	452
Interest	324	335	333	320	300	272	238	200	163	126
Bilateral creditors										
Disbursements	134	56	28	9	2	2	0	0	0	0
Principal	192	193	210	198	179	171	162	96	81	56
Interest	56	52	45	36	28	21	14	8	5	2
Multilateral creditors										
Disbursements	456	552	479	390	294	190	130	65	42	25
Principal	296	345	410	438	460	519	519	519	519	396
Interest	268	282	288	284	272	252	224	191	157	124
Private creditors										
Disbursements	179	33	8	0	0	0	0	0	0	0
Principal	1,437	1,375	2,342	1,380	1,568	1,357	1,549	1,332	1,254	1,050
Interest	1,624	1,582	1,475	1,307	1,216	1,108	1,018	907	821	747
Commercial banks										
Disbursements	77	3	0	0	0	0	0	0	0	0
Principal	54	90	451	101	98	98	90	80	70	50
Interest	89	87	80	53	44	36	27	20	13	7
Other private										
Disbursements	102	30	8	0	0	0	0	0	0	0
Principal	1,383	1,286	1,891	1,279	1,470	1,259	1,459	1,252	1,184	1,000
Interest	1,534	1,495	1,395	1,254	1,172	1,072	990	888	808	740

VIETNAM

(US$ million, unless otherwise indicated)

	1970	1980	1988	1989	1990	1991	1992	1993	1994	1995
1. SUMMARY DEBT DATA										
TOTAL DEBT STOCKS (EDT)	..	..	..	19,498	22,253	22,435	23,891	24,856	25,571	26,495
Long-term debt (LDOD)	..	..	..	18,461	20,775	20,813	21,524	22,342	22,704	22,962
Public and publicly guaranteed	..	..	..	18,461	20,775	20,813	21,524	22,342	22,704	22,962
Private nonguaranteed	0	0	0	0	0	0	0	0	0	0
Use of IMF credit	0	0	120	108	112	102	98	100	282	377
Short-term debt	..	..	..	930	1,366	1,520	2,269	2,414	2,584	3,156
of which interest arrears on LDOD	..	..	..	676	1,116	1,344	1,649	1,810	2,130	2,385
Official creditors	..	..	..	523	903	1,124	1,424	1,438	1,738	1,973
Private creditors	..	..	..	153	213	220	226	372	392	413
Memo: principal arrears on LDOD	..	..	..	1,096	1,314	3,118	5,517	5,492	7,222	9,292
Official creditors	..	..	..	593	710	2,497	4,924	5,121	6,821	8,745
Private creditors	..	..	..	504	603	621	593	371	402	547
Memo: export credits	..	..	346	385	431	430	506	475	530	544
TOTAL DEBT FLOWS										
Disbursements	..	..	..	119	58	90	695	615	588	540
Long-term debt	..	..	..	119	58	90	695	514	415	448
IMF purchases	0	0	0	0	0	0	0	101	173	92
Principal repayments	..	..	..	190	129	161	347	374	266	217
Long-term debt	..	..	..	181	124	151	347	274	266	217
IMF repurchases	0	0	0	9	5	10	0	100	0	0
Net flows on debt	..	..	..	183	-75	-144	792	225	172	639
of which short-term debt	..	..	..	254	-4	-74	444	-16	-150	317
Interest payments (INT)	..	..	..	89	73	47	64	126	127	169
Long-term debt	..	..	..	63	49	32	44	69	88	111
IMF charges	0	0	0	0	0	1	1	31	7	12
Short-term debt	..	..	..	26	23	15	19	26	32	46
Net transfers on debt	..	..	..	94	-148	-192	728	99	45	471
Total debt service paid (TDS)	..	..	..	279	202	208	411	500	393	386
Long-term debt	..	..	..	244	174	183	391	343	354	328
IMF repurchases and charges	0	0	0	9	5	10	1	131	7	12
Short-term debt (interest only)	..	..	..	26	23	15	19	26	32	46
2. AGGREGATE NET RESOURCE FLOWS AND NET TRANSFERS (LONG-TERM)										
NET RESOURCE FLOWS	..	..	..	-14	45	107	485	496	981	881
Net flow of long-term debt (ex. IMF)	0	0	0	-62	-66	-61	348	240	149	231
Foreign direct investment (net)	0	0	8	4	16	32	24	25	100	150
Portfolio equity flows	..	..	..	0	0	10	0	87	283	155
Grants (excluding technical coop.)	216	131	79	44	96	126	113	145	449	345
Memo: technical coop. grants	130	58	71	78	99	109	157	157	195	231
NET TRANSFERS	..	..	..	-77	-4	75	441	427	893	770
Interest on long-term debt	..	..	..	63	49	32	44	69	88	111
Profit remittances on FDI	0	0	0	0	0	0	0	0	0	0
3. MAJOR ECONOMIC AGGREGATES										
Gross national product (GNP)	..	..	..	..	..	9,613	9,867	12,834	15,532	20,351
Exports of goods & services (XGS)	..	..	..	..	1,953	2,534	3,241	3,788	5,372	6,691
of which workers remittances	..	..	..	..	0	0	0	0	0	0
Imports of goods & services (MGS)	..	..	..	..	2,350	2,757	3,373	4,813	6,963	9,480
International reserves (RES)	48	..	..	..	..	..	..	7	16	..
Current account balance	..	..	-672	-586	-260	-133	-9	-761	-1,205	-1,869
4. DEBT INDICATORS										
EDT / XGS (%)	..	..	..	..	1,139.4	885.4	737.1	656.2	476.0	396.0
EDT / GNP (%)	..	..	..	..	..	233.4	242.1	193.7	164.6	130.2
TDS / XGS (%)	..	..	..	..	10.3	8.2	12.7	13.2	7.3	5.8
INT / XGS (%)	..	..	..	..	3.7	1.9	2.0	3.3	2.4	2.5
INT / GNP (%)	..	..	..	..	..	0.5	0.6	1.0	0.8	0.8
RES / EDT (%)	..	..	..	..	..	..	..	0.0	0.1	..
RES / MGS (months)	..	..	..	..	..	..	..	0.0	0.0	..
Short-term / EDT (%)	..	..	..	4.8	6.1	6.8	9.5	9.7	10.1	11.9
Concessional / EDT (%)	..	..	..	87.4	86.6	86.0	81.5	83.1	81.9	80.5
Multilateral / EDT (%)	..	..	..	0.6	0.5	0.6	0.6	0.4	0.9	1.2

VIETNAM

(US$ million, unless otherwise indicated)

	1970	1980	1988	1989	1990	1991	1992	1993	1994	1995
5. LONG-TERM DEBT										
DEBT OUTSTANDING (LDOD)	..	..	..	**18,461**	**20,775**	**20,813**	**21,524**	**22,342**	**22,704**	**22,962**
Public and publicly guaranteed	..	..	..	**18,461**	**20,775**	**20,813**	**21,524**	**22,342**	**22,704**	**22,962**
Official creditors	..	..	..	17,439	19,670	19,649	20,261	21,347	21,760	22,066
Multilateral	..	..	..	119	122	138	138	100	225	318
Concessional	..	..	..	96	96	112	109	100	225	318
Bilateral	..	..	..	17,320	19,548	19,512	20,123	21,247	21,535	21,747
Concessional	..	..	..	16,953	19,176	19,177	19,364	20,547	20,728	21,007
Private creditors	..	..	..	1,022	1,105	1,164	1,263	996	944	896
Bonds	..	..	..	0	0	0	0	0	0	0
Commercial banks	..	..	..	30	34	34	29	52	103	118
Other private	..	..	..	993	1,071	1,130	1,234	943	841	778
Private nonguaranteed	**0**	**0**	**0**	**0**	**0**	**0**	**0**	**0**	**0**	**0**
Bonds	..	..	..	0	0	0	0	0	0	0
Commercial banks	..	..	..	0	0	0	0	0	0	0
Memo:										
IBRD	0	0	0	0	0	0	0	0	0	0
IDA	0	2	60	59	59	58	57	57	181	231
DISBURSEMENTS	..	..	..	**119**	**58**	**90**	**695**	**514**	**415**	**448**
Public and publicly guaranteed	..	..	..	**119**	**58**	**90**	**695**	**514**	**415**	**448**
Official creditors	..	..	..	119	56	30	522	474	365	429
Multilateral	..	..	..	0	4	16	3	0	129	97
Concessional	..	..	..	0	0	16	0	0	129	97
Bilateral	..	..	..	119	52	14	519	474	236	332
Concessional	..	..	..	30	51	10	512	458	131	311
Private creditors	..	..	..	0	2	60	173	40	50	19
Bonds	..	..	..	0	0	0	0	0	0	0
Commercial banks	..	..	..	0	0	0	0	30	50	14
Other private	..	..	..	0	2	60	173	10	0	5
Private nonguaranteed	**0**	**0**	**0**	**0**	**0**	**0**	**0**	**0**	**0**	**0**
Bonds	..	..	..	0	0	0	0	0	0	0
Commercial banks	..	..	..	0	0	0	0	0	0	0
Memo:										
IBRD	0	0	0	0	0	0	0	0	0	0
IDA	0	1	0	0	0	0	0	0	126	47
PRINCIPAL REPAYMENTS	..	..	..	**181**	**124**	**151**	**347**	**274**	**266**	**217**
Public and publicly guaranteed	..	..	..	**181**	**124**	**151**	**347**	**274**	**266**	**217**
Official creditors	..	..	..	178	124	141	314	227	101	131
Multilateral	..	..	..	2	2	2	2	40	6	6
Concessional	..	..	..	2	2	2	2	11	6	6
Bilateral	..	..	..	176	122	139	312	187	96	125
Concessional	..	..	..	75	112	137	301	146	96	42
Private creditors	..	..	..	3	0	10	33	47	165	86
Bonds	..	..	..	0	0	0	0	0	0	0
Commercial banks	..	..	..	0	0	0	0	0	0	1
Other private	..	..	..	3	0	10	33	47	165	86
Private nonguaranteed	**0**	**0**	**0**	**0**	**0**	**0**	**0**	**0**	**0**	**0**
Bonds	..	..	..	0	0	0	0	0	0	0
Commercial banks	..	..	..	0	0	0	0	0	0	0
Memo:										
IBRD	0	0	0	0	0	0	0	0	0	0
IDA	0	0	0	1	1	1	1	1	1	1
NET FLOWS ON DEBT	..	..	..	**-62**	**-66**	**-61**	**348**	**240**	**149**	**231**
Public and publicly guaranteed	..	..	..	**-62**	**-66**	**-61**	**348**	**240**	**149**	**231**
Official creditors	..	..	..	-59	-68	-111	208	246	264	298
Multilateral	..	..	..	-2	2	14	1	-40	123	91
Concessional	..	..	..	-2	-2	14	-2	-11	123	91
Bilateral	..	..	..	-57	-70	-125	208	286	140	207
Concessional	..	..	..	-45	-62	-127	211	312	36	269
Private creditors	..	..	..	-3	2	50	140	-7	-115	-67
Bonds	..	..	..	0	0	0	0	0	0	0
Commercial banks	..	..	..	0	0	0	0	30	50	14
Other private	..	..	..	-3	2	50	140	-37	-165	-81
Private nonguaranteed	**0**	**0**	**0**	**0**	**0**	**0**	**0**	**0**	**0**	**0**
Bonds	..	..	..	0	0	0	0	0	0	0
Commercial banks	..	..	..	0	0	0	0	0	0	0
Memo:										
IBRD	0	0	0	0	0	0	0	0	0	0
IDA	0	1	0	-1	-1	-1	-1	-1	125	46

VIETNAM

(US$ million, unless otherwise indicated)

	1970	1980	1988	1989	1990	1991	1992	1993	1994	1995
INTEREST PAYMENTS (LINT)	..	..	..	**63**	**49**	**32**	**44**	**69**	**88**	**111**
Public and publicly guaranteed	..	..	..	**63**	**49**	**32**	**44**	**69**	**88**	**111**
Official creditors	..	..	..	32	28	17	30	55	69	103
Multilateral	..	..	..	2	2	2	2	8	2	3
Concessional	..	..	..	0	0	1	1	6	2	3
Bilateral	..	..	..	30	26	15	27	47	67	100
Concessional	..	..	..	5	9	6	14	43	64	88
Private creditors	..	..	..	31	22	15	14	14	20	8
Bonds	..	..	..	0	0	0	0	0	0	0
Commercial banks	..	..	..	1	0	0	0	0	1	2
Other private	..	..	..	30	22	15	14	14	18	7
Private nonguaranteed	**0**	**0**	**0**	**0**	**0**	**0**	**0**	**0**	**0**	**0**
Bonds	..	..	..	0	0	0	0	0	0	0
Commercial banks	..	..	..	0	0	0	0	0	0	0
Memo:										
IBRD	0	0	0	0	0	0	0	0	0	0
IDA	0	0	0	0	0	0	0	0	1	2
NET TRANSFERS ON DEBT	..	..	..	**-125**	**-116**	**-93**	**304**	**170**	**60**	**120**
Public and publicly guaranteed	..	..	..	**-125**	**-116**	**-93**	**304**	**170**	**60**	**120**
Official creditors	..	..	..	-91	-96	-128	179	192	195	196
Multilateral	..	..	..	-4	0	11	-2	-48	122	88
Concessional	..	..	..	-2	-3	13	-3	-17	122	88
Bilateral	..	..	..	-87	-96	-140	180	239	73	107
Concessional	..	..	..	-50	-70	-132	197	270	-29	181
Private creditors	..	..	..	-34	-20	35	126	-21	-135	-76
Bonds	..	..	..	0	0	0	0	0	0	0
Commercial banks	..	..	..	-1	0	0	0	30	48	12
Other private	..	..	..	-33	-20	35	126	-51	-183	-88
Private nonguaranteed	**0**	**0**	**0**	**0**	**0**	**0**	**0**	**0**	**0**	**0**
Bonds	..	..	..	0	0	0	0	0	0	0
Commercial banks	..	..	..	0	0	0	0	0	0	0
Memo:										
IBRD	0	0	0	0	0	0	0	0	0	0
IDA	0	1	0	-1	-1	-1	-1	-1	125	45
DEBT SERVICE (LTDS)	..	..	..	**244**	**174**	**183**	**391**	**343**	**354**	**328**
Public and publicly guaranteed	..	..	..	**244**	**174**	**183**	**391**	**343**	**354**	**328**
Official creditors	..	..	..	210	152	158	344	282	170	233
Multilateral	..	..	..	4	4	5	5	48	7	8
Concessional	..	..	..	2	3	3	3	17	7	8
Bilateral	..	..	..	206	148	154	339	234	163	225
Concessional	..	..	..	81	121	142	315	188	160	130
Private creditors	..	..	..	34	22	25	47	61	185	95
Bonds	..	..	..	0	0	0	0	0	0	0
Commercial banks	..	..	..	1	0	0	0	0	2	2
Other private	..	..	..	33	22	25	47	61	183	93
Private nonguaranteed	**0**	**0**	**0**	**0**	**0**	**0**	**0**	**0**	**0**	**0**
Bonds	..	..	..	0	0	0	0	0	0	0
Commercial banks	..	..	..	0	0	0	0	0	0	0
Memo:										
IBRD	0	0	0	0	0	0	0	0	0	0
IDA	0	0	0	1	1	1	1	1	1	2
UNDISBURSED DEBT	..	..	..	**80**	**130**	**675**	**574**	**580**	**2,492**	**2,706**
Official creditors	..	..	..	20	64	579	574	580	2,302	2,535
Private creditors	..	..	..	60	66	96	0	0	190	171
Memorandum items										
Concessional LDOD	..	..	..	17,049	19,272	19,289	19,474	20,647	20,953	21,326
Variable rate LDOD	..	..	..	529	583	643	674	653	679	700
Public sector LDOD	..	..	..	18,461	20,775	20,813	21,524	22,342	22,704	22,962
Private sector LDOD	..	..	..	0	0	0	0	0	0	0

6. CURRENCY COMPOSITION OF LONG-TERM DEBT (PERCENT)

	1970	1980	1988	1989	1990	1991	1992	1993	1994	1995
Deutsche mark	..	..	..	1.8	1.8	1.8	1.6	1.7	1.9	2.0
French franc	..	..	..	1.0	1.0	1.0	0.9	1.2	1.3	1.4
Japanese yen	..	..	..	2.3	2.1	2.5	4.8	5.0	5.5	5.9
Pound sterling	..	..	..	0.2	0.2	0.2	0.1	0.2	0.2	0.2
Swiss franc	..	..	..	0.0	0.0	0.0	0.0	0.0	0.0	0.2
U.S.dollars	..	..	..	4.8	4.2	4.1	4.2	4.2	4.6	4.9
Multiple currency	..	..	..	2.0	1.8	1.8	1.8	1.4	1.4	1.4
Special drawing rights	..	..	..	0.0	0.0	0.0	0.0	0.0	0.0	0.0
All other currencies	..	..	..	88.0	88.9	88.5	86.6	86.3	85.2	84.1

VIETNAM

(US$ million, unless otherwise indicated)

	1970	1980	1988	1989	1990	1991	1992	1993	1994	1995
7. DEBT RESTRUCTURINGS										
Total amount rescheduled	0	0	0	0	0	0	0	796	0	0
Debt stock rescheduled	0	0	0	0	0	0	0	258	0	0
Principal rescheduled	0	0	0	0	0	0	0	317	0	0
Official	0	0	0	0	0	0	0	88	0	0
Private	0	0	0	0	0	0	0	229	0	0
Interest rescheduled	0	0	0	0	0	0	0	166	0	0
Official	0	0	0	0	0	0	0	57	0	0
Private	0	0	0	0	0	0	0	109	0	0
Debt forgiven	..	..	0	0	0	0	0	37	0	0
Memo: interest forgiven	..	..	0	0	0	0	0	20	0	0
Debt stock reduction	0	0	0	0	0	0	0	0	0	0
of which debt buyback	0	0	0	0	0	0	0	0	0	0
8. DEBT STOCK-FLOW RECONCILIATION										
Total change in debt stocks	..	..	..	..	2,755	182	1,456	965	715	925
Net flows on debt	..	..	..	..	-75	-144	792	225	172	639
Net change in interest arrears	..	..	..	..	440	228	305	161	320	255
Interest capitalized	..	..	..	..	0	0	0	166	0	0
Debt forgiveness or reduction	..	..	..	..	0	0	0	-37	0	0
Cross-currency valuation	..	..	..	..	125	-2	-56	51	255	49
Residual	..	..	..	..	2,265	101	415	398	-33	-19
9. AVERAGE TERMS OF NEW COMMITMENTS										
ALL CREDITORS										
Interest (%)	..	..	..	5.0	2.2	1.3	1.3	2.1	1.9	3.5
Maturity (years)	..	..	..	10.0	14.1	5.0	24.2	31.3	29.9	34.4
Grace period (years)	..	..	..	4.0	6.2	2.7	6.5	8.1	8.0	8.5
Grant element (%)	..	..	..	23.3	43.0	20.8	61.9	61.7	65.5	54.4
Official creditors										
Interest (%)	..	..	..	5.0	2.3	0.7	1.0	2.0	1.3	3.5
Maturity (years)	..	..	..	10.0	14.3	5.2	26.0	32.0	32.3	34.4
Grace period (years)	..	..	..	4.0	6.3	3.0	7.0	8.4	8.6	8.5
Grant element (%)	..	..	..	23.3	43.6	22.3	66.5	63.3	71.3	54.4
Private creditors										
Interest (%)	..	..	..	0.0	0.0	5.0	4.6	3.2	6.3	0.0
Maturity (years)	..	..	..	0.0	2.5	3.5	3.0	23.2	10.4	0.0
Grace period (years)	..	..	..	0.0	1.0	1.3	0.5	4.1	3.2	0.0
Grant element (%)	..	..	..	0.0	15.2	12.2	8.0	41.5	17.4	0.0
Memorandum items										
Commitments	..	..	..	95	99	614	1,019	549	2,258	668
Official creditors	..	..	..	95	97	525	939	509	2,019	668
Private creditors	..	..	..	0	2	89	80	40	240	0

10. CONTRACTUAL OBLIGATIONS ON OUTSTANDING LONG-TERM DEBT

	1996	1997	1998	1999	2000	2001	2002	2003	2004	2005
TOTAL										
Disbursements	775	716	497	332	208	111	59	8	0	0
Principal	2,005	2,005	2,015	1,978	2,001	1,112	220	257	288	299
Interest	314	282	245	203	160	113	98	93	86	87
Official creditors										
Disbursements	662	678	484	327	208	111	59	8	0	0
Principal	1,899	1,915	1,911	1,913	1,976	1,097	205	242	274	285
Interest	297	266	232	194	152	107	93	88	83	84
Bilateral creditors										
Disbursements	477	423	265	156	81	40	17	0	0	0
Principal	1,894	1,909	1,906	1,908	1,970	1,093	202	239	257	256
Interest	291	258	222	183	141	95	81	76	71	65
Multilateral creditors										
Disbursements	185	255	219	170	127	71	42	7	0	0
Principal	6	6	5	5	6	4	3	3	17	28
Interest	7	8	10	11	12	12	12	12	12	19
Private creditors										
Disbursements	113	38	14	6	0	0	0	0	0	0
Principal	106	90	104	65	25	15	15	15	14	14
Interest	17	16	14	10	8	6	5	5	4	3
Commercial banks										
Disbursements	107	37	13	6	0	0	0	0	0	0
Principal	17	34	47	29	13	13	13	13	13	13
Interest	10	12	10	7	6	5	5	4	3	3
Other private										
Disbursements	6	2	1	0	0	0	0	0	0	0
Principal	89	56	57	35	12	2	2	2	1	1
Interest	7	4	3	3	2	1	1	1	0	0

WESTERN SAMOA

(US$ million, unless otherwise indicated)

	1970	1980	1988	1989	1990	1991	1992	1993	1994	1995
1. SUMMARY DEBT DATA										
TOTAL DEBT STOCKS (EDT)	**..**	**60.2**	**76.0**	**73.6**	**92.0**	**140.7**	**117.9**	**193.8**	**154.4**	**161.9**
Long-term debt (LDOD)	**2.7**	**53.4**	**71.1**	**71.9**	**91.0**	**113.4**	**117.8**	**140.4**	**154.2**	**159.6**
Public and publicly guaranteed	2.7	53.4	71.1	71.9	91.0	113.4	117.8	140.4	154.2	159.6
Private nonguaranteed	0.0	0.0	0.0	0.0	0.0	0.0	0.0	0.0	0.0	0.0
Use of IMF credit	**0.0**	**5.8**	**3.8**	**1.6**	**0.8**	**0.2**	**0.0**	**0.0**	**0.0**	**0.0**
Short-term debt	**..**	**1.0**	**1.0**	**0.2**	**0.1**	**27.1**	**0.1**	**53.4**	**0.2**	**2.3**
of which interest arrears on LDOD	..	0.0	0.0	0.1	0.0	0.0	0.0	0.1	0.0	0.0
Official creditors	..	0.0	0.0	0.1	0.0	0.0	0.0	0.1	0.0	0.0
Private creditors	..	0.0	0.0	0.0	0.0	0.0	0.0	0.0	0.0	0.0
Memo: principal arrears on LDOD	..	0.0	0.0	0.1	0.0	0.0	0.0	0.2	0.0	0.0
Official creditors	..	0.0	0.0	0.1	0.0	0.0	0.0	0.2	0.0	0.0
Private creditors	..	0.0	0.0	0.0	0.0	0.0	0.0	0.0	0.0	0.0
Memo: export credits	..	..	6.0	5.0	2.0	1.0	1.0	0.0	0.0	0.0
TOTAL DEBT FLOWS										
Disbursements	**2.4**	**11.2**	**4.2**	**5.0**	**15.3**	**24.1**	**12.2**	**24.0**	**9.7**	**6.7**
Long-term debt	2.4	10.5	4.2	5.0	15.3	24.1	12.2	24.0	9.7	6.7
IMF purchases	0.0	0.7	0.0	0.0	0.0	0.0	0.0	0.0	0.0	0.0
Principal repayments	**0.1**	**2.8**	**6.8**	**5.4**	**4.1**	**3.5**	**3.5**	**2.8**	**3.6**	**2.9**
Long-term debt	0.1	2.3	2.9	3.3	3.3	2.9	3.3	2.8	3.6	2.9
IMF repurchases	0.0	0.5	4.0	2.1	0.9	0.6	0.2	0.0	0.0	0.0
Net flows on debt	**2.3**	**8.4**	**-2.6**	**-1.3**	**11.3**	**47.5**	**-18.2**	**74.3**	**-47.0**	**5.8**
of which short-term debt	..	..	0.0	-0.9	0.1	26.9	-26.9	53.1	-53.1	2.1
Interest payments (INT)	**..**	**2.7**	**1.8**	**1.4**	**1.3**	**2.0**	**1.3**	**2.6**	**2.8**	**1.6**
Long-term debt	0.0	2.3	1.3	1.1	1.2	1.2	1.3	1.3	1.4	1.6
IMF charges	0.0	0.2	0.4	0.2	0.1	0.1	0.0	0.0	0.0	0.0
Short-term debt	..	0.2	0.1	0.0	0.0	0.7	0.0	1.3	1.3	0.1
Net transfers on debt	**..**	**5.7**	**-4.4**	**-2.7**	**10.0**	**45.5**	**-19.5**	**71.7**	**-49.8**	**4.2**
Total debt service paid (TDS)	**..**	**5.5**	**8.6**	**6.8**	**5.5**	**5.5**	**4.8**	**5.4**	**6.4**	**4.6**
Long-term debt	0.1	4.6	4.2	4.4	4.5	4.1	4.6	4.1	5.1	4.5
IMF repurchases and charges	0.0	0.7	4.3	2.3	1.0	0.7	0.2	0.0	0.0	0.0
Short-term debt (interest only)	..	0.2	0.1	0.0	0.0	0.7	0.0	1.3	1.3	0.1
2. AGGREGATE NET RESOURCE FLOWS AND NET TRANSFERS (LONG-TERM)										
NET RESOURCE FLOWS	**2.3**	**17.1**	**19.6**	**17.7**	**39.3**	**46.7**	**35.6**	**48.2**	**34.8**	**27.5**
Net flow of long-term debt (ex. IMF)	2.3	8.2	1.3	1.7	12.1	21.1	8.9	21.2	6.1	3.7
Foreign direct investment (net)	0.0	0.0	0.0	0.0	7.0	3.0	5.0	5.0	3.0	3.0
Portfolio equity flows	0.0	0.0	0.0	0.0	0.0	0.0	0.0	0.0	0.0	0.0
Grants (excluding technical coop.)	0.0	8.9	18.3	16.0	20.2	22.6	21.7	22.0	25.7	20.8
Memo: technical coop. grants	0.9	9.6	10.6	12.2	13.9	11.5	17.4	16.9	17.6	17.0
NET TRANSFERS	**2.3**	**14.8**	**17.9**	**15.7**	**38.1**	**45.6**	**34.3**	**46.9**	**33.3**	**26.0**
Interest on long-term debt	0.0	2.3	1.3	1.1	1.2	1.2	1.3	1.3	1.4	1.6
Profit remittances on FDI	0.0	0.0	0.4	0.9	0.0	0.0	0.0	0.0	0.0	0.0
3. MAJOR ECONOMIC AGGREGATES										
Gross national product (GNP)	..	..	143.1	140.8	150.9	149.1	151.5	154.6	173.2	196.6
Exports of goods & services (XGS)	..	44.4	82.6	89.1	93.9	78.5	87.7	77.8	87.2	108.1
of which workers remittances	..	18.7	37.7	40.9	42.8	34.1	39.1	31.3	36.5	39.4
Imports of goods & services (MGS)	..	74.3	86.9	88.2	96.3	114.7	135.9	130.0	101.7	119.2
International reserves (RES)	5.2	2.8	49.2	55.1	69.1	67.8	61.2	50.7	50.8	55.3
Current account balance	..	-12.9	8.0	12.8	7.3	-28.7	-52.5	-38.7	5.8	9.8
4. DEBT INDICATORS										
EDT / XGS (%)	..	135.6	92.0	82.6	97.9	179.3	134.4	249.1	177.1	149.7
EDT / GNP (%)	..	..	53.1	52.3	60.9	94.4	77.8	125.3	89.2	82.3
TDS / XGS (%)	..	12.3	10.4	7.6	5.8	7.0	5.5	6.9	7.3	4.2
INT / XGS (%)	..	6.0	2.1	1.5	1.4	2.6	1.5	3.4	3.2	1.5
INT / GNP (%)	..	..	1.2	1.0	0.9	1.3	0.9	1.7	1.6	0.8
RES / EDT (%)	..	4.7	64.8	74.8	75.1	48.2	51.9	26.2	32.9	34.2
RES / MGS (months)	..	0.5	6.8	7.5	8.6	7.1	5.4	4.7	6.0	5.6
Short-term / EDT (%)	..	1.7	1.3	0.2	0.2	19.2	0.1	27.5	0.1	1.4
Concessional / EDT (%)	..	56.2	86.9	92.2	95.5	78.9	98.7	72.1	99.9	98.6
Multilateral / EDT (%)	..	54.2	78.3	83.2	88.2	74.1	93.3	64.8	92.8	91.9

WESTERN SAMOA

(US$ million, unless otherwise indicated)

	1970	1980	1988	1989	1990	1991	1992	1993	1994	1995
5. LONG-TERM DEBT										
DEBT OUTSTANDING (LDOD)	**2.7**	**53.4**	**71.1**	**71.9**	**91.0**	**113.4**	**117.8**	**140.4**	**154.2**	**159.6**
Public and publicly guaranteed	**2.7**	**53.4**	**71.1**	**71.9**	**91.0**	**113.4**	**117.8**	**140.4**	**154.2**	**159.6**
Official creditors	2.4	45.1	69.3	70.5	89.6	112.2	117.0	139.9	154.2	159.6
Multilateral	2.4	32.6	59.5	61.3	81.1	104.2	110.1	125.6	143.3	148.7
Concessional	2.4	32.6	59.5	61.3	81.1	104.2	110.1	125.6	143.3	148.7
Bilateral	0.0	12.5	9.8	9.2	8.5	7.9	6.9	14.2	11.0	10.9
Concessional	0.0	1.2	6.5	6.6	6.7	6.8	6.3	14.0	11.0	10.9
Private creditors	0.3	8.3	1.8	1.4	1.4	1.2	0.8	0.6	0.0	0.0
Bonds	0.0	4.5	1.4	1.4	1.4	1.2	0.8	0.6	0.0	0.0
Commercial banks	0.0	1.9	0.0	0.0	0.0	0.0	0.0	0.0	0.0	0.0
Other private	0.3	1.9	0.4	0.0	0.0	0.0	0.0	0.0	0.0	0.0
Private nonguaranteed	**0.0**	**0.0**	**0.0**	**0.0**	**0.0**	**0.0**	**0.0**	**0.0**	**0.0**	**0.0**
Bonds	0.0	0.0	0.0	0.0	0.0	0.0	0.0	0.0	0.0	0.0
Commercial banks	0.0	0.0	0.0	0.0	0.0	0.0	0.0	0.0	0.0	0.0
Memo:										
IBRD	0.0	0.0	0.0	0.0	0.0	0.0	0.0	0.0	0.0	0.0
IDA	0.0	6.3	13.5	14.4	18.3	25.2	31.8	40.2	43.3	44.7
DISBURSEMENTS	**2.4**	**10.5**	**4.2**	**5.0**	**15.3**	**24.1**	**12.2**	**24.0**	**9.7**	**6.7**
Public and publicly guaranteed	**2.4**	**10.5**	**4.2**	**5.0**	**15.3**	**24.1**	**12.2**	**24.0**	**9.7**	**6.7**
Official creditors	2.4	10.5	4.2	5.0	15.3	24.1	12.2	24.0	9.7	6.7
Multilateral	2.4	10.5	3.1	4.0	15.0	23.8	12.2	15.9	9.5	6.6
Concessional	2.4	10.5	3.1	4.0	15.0	23.8	12.2	15.9	9.5	6.6
Bilateral	0.0	0.0	1.1	1.0	0.4	0.3	0.0	8.1	0.2	0.1
Concessional	0.0	0.0	1.1	1.0	0.4	0.3	0.0	8.1	0.2	0.1
Private creditors	0.0	0.0	0.0	0.0	0.0	0.0	0.0	0.0	0.0	0.0
Bonds	0.0	0.0	0.0	0.0	0.0	0.0	0.0	0.0	0.0	0.0
Commercial banks	0.0	0.0	0.0	0.0	0.0	0.0	0.0	0.0	0.0	0.0
Other private	0.0	0.0	0.0	0.0	0.0	0.0	0.0	0.0	0.0	0.0
Private nonguaranteed	**0.0**	**0.0**	**0.0**	**0.0**	**0.0**	**0.0**	**0.0**	**0.0**	**0.0**	**0.0**
Bonds	0.0	0.0	0.0	0.0	0.0	0.0	0.0	0.0	0.0	0.0
Commercial banks	0.0	0.0	0.0	0.0	0.0	0.0	0.0	0.0	0.0	0.0
Memo:										
IBRD	0.0	0.0	0.0	0.0	0.0	0.0	0.0	0.0	0.0	0.0
IDA	0.0	2.0	1.0	1.0	3.5	6.7	7.4	8.6	1.7	0.7
PRINCIPAL REPAYMENTS	**0.1**	**2.3**	**2.9**	**3.3**	**3.3**	**2.9**	**3.3**	**2.8**	**3.6**	**2.9**
Public and publicly guaranteed	**0.1**	**2.3**	**2.9**	**3.3**	**3.3**	**2.9**	**3.3**	**2.8**	**3.6**	**2.9**
Official creditors	0.0	0.5	2.5	2.9	3.3	2.9	2.8	2.5	3.0	2.9
Multilateral	0.0	0.3	1.6	1.8	2.2	2.2	2.0	1.7	2.5	2.6
Concessional	0.0	0.3	1.6	1.8	2.2	2.2	2.0	1.7	2.5	2.6
Bilateral	0.0	0.1	0.8	1.1	1.0	0.7	0.8	0.7	0.5	0.3
Concessional	0.0	0.0	0.0	0.3	0.0	0.2	0.3	0.3	0.3	0.3
Private creditors	0.1	1.8	0.4	0.4	0.0	0.0	0.4	0.3	0.6	0.0
Bonds	0.0	0.0	0.0	0.0	0.0	0.0	0.4	0.3	0.6	0.0
Commercial banks	0.0	0.6	0.0	0.0	0.0	0.0	0.0	0.0	0.0	0.0
Other private	0.1	1.2	0.4	0.4	0.0	0.0	0.0	0.0	0.0	0.0
Private nonguaranteed	**0.0**	**0.0**	**0.0**	**0.0**	**0.0**	**0.0**	**0.0**	**0.0**	**0.0**	**0.0**
Bonds	0.0	0.0	0.0	0.0	0.0	0.0	0.0	0.0	0.0	0.0
Commercial banks	0.0	0.0	0.0	0.0	0.0	0.0	0.0	0.0	0.0	0.0
Memo:										
IBRD	0.0	0.0	0.0	0.0	0.0	0.0	0.0	0.0	0.0	0.0
IDA	0.0	0.0	0.0	0.0	0.1	0.1	0.1	0.1	0.1	0.2
NET FLOWS ON DEBT	**2.3**	**8.2**	**1.3**	**1.7**	**12.1**	**21.1**	**8.9**	**21.2**	**6.1**	**3.7**
Public and publicly guaranteed	**2.3**	**8.2**	**1.3**	**1.7**	**12.1**	**21.1**	**8.9**	**21.2**	**6.1**	**3.7**
Official creditors	2.4	10.0	1.7	2.1	12.1	21.1	9.4	21.5	6.7	3.7
Multilateral	2.4	10.2	1.5	2.2	12.8	21.6	10.2	14.1	6.9	4.0
Concessional	2.4	10.2	1.5	2.2	12.8	21.6	10.2	14.1	6.9	4.0
Bilateral	0.0	-0.1	0.2	-0.1	-0.7	-0.5	-0.8	7.4	-0.3	-0.2
Concessional	0.0	0.0	1.1	0.7	0.3	0.1	-0.3	7.8	-0.1	-0.2
Private creditors	-0.1	-1.8	-0.4	-0.4	0.0	0.0	-0.4	-0.3	-0.6	0.0
Bonds	0.0	0.0	0.0	0.0	0.0	0.0	-0.4	-0.3	-0.6	0.0
Commercial banks	0.0	-0.6	0.0	0.0	0.0	0.0	0.0	0.0	0.0	0.0
Other private	-0.1	-1.2	-0.4	-0.4	0.0	0.0	0.0	0.0	0.0	0.0
Private nonguaranteed	**0.0**	**0.0**	**0.0**	**0.0**	**0.0**	**0.0**	**0.0**	**0.0**	**0.0**	**0.0**
Bonds	0.0	0.0	0.0	0.0	0.0	0.0	0.0	0.0	0.0	0.0
Commercial banks	0.0	0.0	0.0	0.0	0.0	0.0	0.0	0.0	0.0	0.0
Memo:										
IBRD	0.0	0.0	0.0	0.0	0.0	0.0	0.0	0.0	0.0	0.0
IDA	0.0	2.0	1.0	1.0	3.4	6.6	7.3	8.5	1.6	0.5

WESTERN SAMOA

(US$ million, unless otherwise indicated)

	1970	1980	1988	1989	1990	1991	1992	1993	1994	1995
INTEREST PAYMENTS (LINT)	**0.0**	**2.3**	**1.3**	**1.1**	**1.2**	**1.2**	**1.3**	**1.3**	**1.4**	**1.6**
Public and publicly guaranteed	**0.0**	**2.3**	**1.3**	**1.1**	**1.2**	**1.2**	**1.3**	**1.3**	**1.4**	**1.6**
Official creditors	0.0	1.4	1.1	1.0	1.1	1.1	1.2	1.3	1.4	1.6
Multilateral	0.0	0.3	0.7	0.6	0.7	0.9	1.0	1.1	1.3	1.5
Concessional	0.0	0.3	0.7	0.6	0.7	0.9	1.0	1.1	1.3	1.5
Bilateral	0.0	1.1	0.5	0.3	0.4	0.2	0.2	0.2	0.1	0.1
Concessional	0.0	0.1	0.1	0.1	0.1	0.1	0.1	0.1	0.1	0.1
Private creditors	0.0	0.9	0.2	0.1	0.1	0.1	0.1	0.0	0.0	0.0
Bonds	0.0	0.3	0.1	0.1	0.1	0.1	0.1	0.0	0.0	0.0
Commercial banks	0.0	0.4	0.0	0.0	0.0	0.0	0.0	0.0	0.0	0.0
Other private	0.0	0.2	0.1	0.0	0.0	0.0	0.0	0.0	0.0	0.0
Private nonguaranteed	**0.0**	**0.0**	**0.0**	**0.0**	**0.0**	**0.0**	**0.0**	**0.0**	**0.0**	**0.0**
Bonds	0.0	0.0	0.0	0.0	0.0	0.0	0.0	0.0	0.0	0.0
Commercial banks	0.0	0.0	0.0	0.0	0.0	0.0	0.0	0.0	0.0	0.0
Memo:										
IBRD	0.0	0.0	0.0	0.0	0.0	0.0	0.0	0.0	0.0	0.0
IDA	0.0	0.0	0.1	0.1	0.1	0.1	0.2	0.3	0.3	0.3
NET TRANSFERS ON DEBT	**2.3**	**5.9**	**0.0**	**0.6**	**10.9**	**20.0**	**7.6**	**19.9**	**4.6**	**2.2**
Public and publicly guaranteed	**2.3**	**5.9**	**0.0**	**0.6**	**10.9**	**20.0**	**7.6**	**19.9**	**4.6**	**2.2**
Official creditors	2.4	8.6	0.6	1.1	11.0	20.0	8.1	20.2	5.3	2.2
Multilateral	2.4	9.9	0.8	1.5	12.0	20.7	9.1	13.0	5.7	2.5
Concessional	2.4	9.9	0.8	1.5	12.0	20.7	9.1	13.0	5.7	2.5
Bilateral	0.0	-1.3	-0.2	-0.4	-1.1	-0.7	-1.0	7.2	-0.4	-0.3
Concessional	0.0	-0.1	1.0	0.6	0.2	0.0	-0.4	7.7	-0.2	-0.3
Private creditors	-0.1	-2.7	-0.6	-0.5	-0.1	-0.1	-0.5	-0.3	-0.6	0.0
Bonds	0.0	-0.3	-0.1	-0.1	-0.1	-0.1	-0.5	-0.3	-0.6	0.0
Commercial banks	0.0	-1.0	0.0	0.0	0.0	0.0	0.0	0.0	0.0	0.0
Other private	-0.1	-1.4	-0.5	-0.4	0.0	0.0	0.0	0.0	0.0	0.0
Private nonguaranteed	**0.0**	**0.0**	**0.0**	**0.0**	**0.0**	**0.0**	**0.0**	**0.0**	**0.0**	**0.0**
Bonds	0.0	0.0	0.0	0.0	0.0	0.0	0.0	0.0	0.0	0.0
Commercial banks	0.0	0.0	0.0	0.0	0.0	0.0	0.0	0.0	0.0	0.0
Memo:										
IBRD	0.0	0.0	0.0	0.0	0.0	0.0	0.0	0.0	0.0	0.0
IDA	0.0	2.0	0.8	0.9	3.3	6.5	7.1	8.3	1.3	0.2
DEBT SERVICE (LTDS)	**0.1**	**4.6**	**4.2**	**4.4**	**4.5**	**4.1**	**4.6**	**4.1**	**5.1**	**4.5**
Public and publicly guaranteed	**0.1**	**4.6**	**4.2**	**4.4**	**4.5**	**4.1**	**4.6**	**4.1**	**5.1**	**4.5**
Official creditors	0.0	1.9	3.6	3.9	4.4	4.0	4.1	3.8	4.4	4.5
Multilateral	0.0	0.6	2.3	2.5	3.0	3.1	3.1	2.9	3.8	4.1
Concessional	0.0	0.6	2.3	2.5	3.0	3.1	3.1	2.9	3.8	4.1
Bilateral	0.0	1.3	1.3	1.4	1.4	1.0	1.0	0.9	0.6	0.4
Concessional	0.0	0.1	0.1	0.4	0.1	0.3	0.4	0.4	0.4	0.4
Private creditors	0.1	2.7	0.6	0.5	0.1	0.1	0.5	0.3	0.6	0.0
Bonds	0.0	0.3	0.1	0.1	0.1	0.1	0.5	0.3	0.6	0.0
Commercial banks	0.0	1.0	0.0	0.0	0.0	0.0	0.0	0.0	0.0	0.0
Other private	0.1	1.4	0.5	0.4	0.0	0.0	0.0	0.0	0.0	0.0
Private nonguaranteed	**0.0**	**0.0**	**0.0**	**0.0**	**0.0**	**0.0**	**0.0**	**0.0**	**0.0**	**0.0**
Bonds	0.0	0.0	0.0	0.0	0.0	0.0	0.0	0.0	0.0	0.0
Commercial banks	0.0	0.0	0.0	0.0	0.0	0.0	0.0	0.0	0.0	0.0
Memo:										
IBRD	0.0	0.0	0.0	0.0	0.0	0.0	0.0	0.0	0.0	0.0
IDA	0.0	0.0	0.2	0.1	0.2	0.3	0.3	0.4	0.4	0.5
UNDISBURSED DEBT	**0.3**	**24.9**	**34.7**	**56.8**	**56.7**	**36.1**	**35.4**	**23.8**	**14.9**	**7.9**
Official creditors	0.3	24.9	34.7	56.8	56.7	36.1	35.4	23.8	14.9	7.9
Private creditors	0.0	0.0	0.0	0.0	0.0	0.0	0.0	0.0	0.0	0.0
Memorandum items										
Concessional LDOD	2.4	33.9	66.0	67.9	87.8	111.0	116.4	139.7	154.2	159.6
Variable rate LDOD	0.0	1.8	0.4	0.0	0.0	0.0	0.0	0.0	0.0	0.0
Public sector LDOD	2.7	53.4	71.1	71.9	91.0	113.4	117.8	140.4	154.2	159.6
Private sector LDOD	0.0	0.0	0.0	0.0	0.0	0.0	0.0	0.0	0.0	0.0

6. CURRENCY COMPOSITION OF LONG-TERM DEBT (PERCENT)

	1970	1980	1988	1989	1990	1991	1992	1993	1994	1995
Deutsche mark	0.0	12.0	3.2	2.6	1.8	0.9	0.5	0.1	0.0	0.0
French franc	0.0	0.0	0.0	0.0	0.1	0.4	0.3	0.3	0.3	0.3
Japanese yen	0.0	0.6	0.0	0.0	0.0	0.0	0.0	0.0	0.0	0.0
Pound sterling	0.0	0.0	0.0	0.0	0.0	0.0	0.0	0.0	0.0	0.0
Swiss franc	0.0	0.0	0.0	0.0	0.0	0.0	0.0	0.0	0.0	0.0
U.S.dollars	100.0	53.7	45.0	42.7	38.6	36.0	39.0	38.6	37.8	36.7
Multiple currency	0.0	12.7	33.6	35.9	43.9	48.8	48.0	44.7	48.4	46.7
Special drawing rights	0.0	0.0	1.4	1.4	1.3	1.1	1.0	1.1	1.9	5.1
All other currencies	0.0	21.2	16.7	17.4	14.4	12.8	11.2	15.1	11.7	11.3

WESTERN SAMOA

(US$ million, unless otherwise indicated)

	1970	1980	1988	1989	1990	1991	1992	1993	1994	1995
7. DEBT RESTRUCTURINGS										
Total amount rescheduled	0.0	0.0	0.0	0.0	0.0	0.0	0.0	0.0	0.0	0.0
Debt stock rescheduled	0.0	0.0	0.0	0.0	0.0	0.0	0.0	0.0	0.0	0.0
Principal rescheduled	0.0	0.0	0.0	0.0	0.0	0.0	0.0	0.0	0.0	0.0
Official	0.0	0.0	0.0	0.0	0.0	0.0	0.0	0.0	0.0	0.0
Private	0.0	0.0	0.0	0.0	0.0	0.0	0.0	0.0	0.0	0.0
Interest rescheduled	0.0	0.0	0.0	0.0	0.0	0.0	0.0	0.0	0.0	0.0
Official	0.0	0.0	0.0	0.0	0.0	0.0	0.0	0.0	0.0	0.0
Private	0.0	0.0	0.0	0.0	0.0	0.0	0.0	0.0	0.0	0.0
Debt forgiven	..	..	0.0	0.0	0.0	0.0	0.0	0.0	0.0	0.0
Memo: interest forgiven	..	..	0.0	0.0	0.0	0.0	0.0	0.0	0.0	0.0
Debt stock reduction	0.0	0.0	0.0	0.0	0.0	0.0	0.0	0.0	0.0	0.0
of which debt buyback	0.0	0.0	0.0	0.0	0.0	0.0	0.0	0.0	0.0	0.0
8. DEBT STOCK-FLOW RECONCILIATION										
Total change in debt stocks	..	..	..	-2.3	18.3	48.8	-22.8	75.9	-39.4	7.5
Net flows on debt	..	..	..	-1.3	11.3	47.5	-18.2	74.3	-47.0	5.8
Net change in interest arrears	..	..	..	0.0	-0.1	0.0	0.0	0.1	-0.1	0.0
Interest capitalized	..	..	..	0.0	0.0	0.0	0.0	0.0	0.0	0.0
Debt forgiveness or reduction	..	..	..	0.0	0.0	0.0	0.0	0.0	0.0	0.0
Cross-currency valuation	..	..	..	-0.4	0.8	-0.3	-0.9	-0.6	-1.2	0.8
Residual	..	..	..	-0.7	6.3	1.6	-3.7	2.1	8.9	0.8
9. AVERAGE TERMS OF NEW COMMITMENTS										
ALL CREDITORS										
Interest (%)	4.7	0.4	1.9	0.9	0.8	1.6	0.5	0.8	0.0	0.0
Maturity (years)	20.0	40.2	22.0	37.9	39.7	32.1	29.2	38.9	0.0	0.0
Grace period (years)	6.0	20.6	8.1	10.3	10.2	7.4	10.4	8.2	0.0	0.0
Grant element (%)	36.4	86.2	58.3	78.0	80.5	67.0	77.0	77.8	0.0	0.0
Official creditors										
Interest (%)	4.7	0.4	1.9	0.9	0.8	1.6	0.5	0.8	0.0	0.0
Maturity (years)	20.0	40.2	22.0	37.9	39.7	32.1	29.2	38.9	0.0	0.0
Grace period (years)	6.0	20.6	8.1	10.3	10.2	7.4	10.4	8.2	0.0	0.0
Grant element (%)	36.4	86.2	58.3	78.0	80.5	67.0	77.0	77.8	0.0	0.0
Private creditors										
Interest (%)	0.0	0.0	0.0	0.0	0.0	0.0	0.0	0.0	0.0	0.0
Maturity (years)	0.0	0.0	0.0	0.0	0.0	0.0	0.0	0.0	0.0	0.0
Grace period (years)	0.0	0.0	0.0	0.0	0.0	0.0	0.0	0.0	0.0	0.0
Grant element (%)	0.0	0.0	0.0	0.0	0.0	0.0	0.0	0.0	0.0	0.0
Memorandum items										
Commitments	0.6	12.2	4.8	37.4	15.3	5.0	13.2	10.0	0.0	0.0
Official creditors	0.6	12.2	4.8	37.4	15.3	5.0	13.2	10.0	0.0	0.0
Private creditors	0.0	0.0	0.0	0.0	0.0	0.0	0.0	0.0	0.0	0.0

10. CONTRACTUAL OBLIGATIONS ON OUTSTANDING LONG-TERM DEBT

	1996	1997	1998	1999	2000	2001	2002	2003	2004	2005
TOTAL										
Disbursements	3.5	2.6	1.3	0.5	0.1	0.0	0.0	0.0	0.0	0.0
Principal	3.2	3.7	3.3	3.7	4.8	5.0	4.8	4.9	5.0	5.1
Interest	1.6	1.5	1.5	1.5	1.4	1.4	1.3	1.3	1.2	1.2
Official creditors										
Disbursements	3.5	2.6	1.3	0.5	0.1	0.0	0.0	0.0	0.0	0.0
Principal	3.2	3.7	3.3	3.7	4.8	5.0	4.8	4.9	5.0	5.1
Interest	1.6	1.5	1.5	1.5	1.4	1.4	1.3	1.3	1.2	1.2
Bilateral creditors										
Disbursements	0.0	0.0	0.0	0.0	0.0	0.0	0.0	0.0	0.0	0.0
Principal	0.4	0.4	0.4	0.6	0.9	0.9	0.9	0.9	0.9	0.9
Interest	0.1	0.1	0.1	0.1	0.0	0.0	0.0	0.0	0.0	0.0
Multilateral creditors										
Disbursements	3.5	2.6	1.3	0.5	0.1	0.0	0.0	0.0	0.0	0.0
Principal	2.9	3.3	2.9	3.1	3.8	4.1	3.9	4.0	4.1	4.2
Interest	1.5	1.5	1.4	1.4	1.4	1.3	1.3	1.2	1.2	1.1
Private creditors										
Disbursements	0.0	0.0	0.0	0.0	0.0	0.0	0.0	0.0	0.0	0.0
Principal	0.0	0.0	0.0	0.0	0.0	0.0	0.0	0.0	0.0	0.0
Interest	0.0	0.0	0.0	0.0	0.0	0.0	0.0	0.0	0.0	0.0
Commercial banks										
Disbursements	0.0	0.0	0.0	0.0	0.0	0.0	0.0	0.0	0.0	0.0
Principal	0.0	0.0	0.0	0.0	0.0	0.0	0.0	0.0	0.0	0.0
Interest	0.0	0.0	0.0	0.0	0.0	0.0	0.0	0.0	0.0	0.0
Other private										
Disbursements	0.0	0.0	0.0	0.0	0.0	0.0	0.0	0.0	0.0	0.0
Principal	0.0	0.0	0.0	0.0	0.0	0.0	0.0	0.0	0.0	0.0
Interest	0.0	0.0	0.0	0.0	0.0	0.0	0.0	0.0	0.0	0.0

YEMEN, REPUBLIC OF

(US$ million, unless otherwise indicated)

	1970	1980	1988	1989	1990	1991	1992	1993	1994	1995
1. SUMMARY DEBT DATA										
TOTAL DEBT STOCKS (EDT)	..	**1,684**	**5,246**	**5,593**	**6,345**	**6,473**	**6,571**	**5,923**	**6,121**	**6,212**
Long-term debt (LDOD)	..	**1,453**	**4,394**	**4,643**	**5,154**	**5,256**	**5,253**	**5,341**	**5,460**	**5,528**
Public and publicly guaranteed	..	1,453	4,394	4,643	5,154	5,256	5,253	5,341	5,460	5,528
Private nonguaranteed	0	0	0	0	0	0	0	0	0	0
Use of IMF credit	**0**	**48**	**6**	**1**	**0**	**0**	**0**	**0**	**0**	**0**
Short-term debt	..	**183**	**846**	**948**	**1,191**	**1,218**	**1,318**	**582**	**662**	**684**
of which interest arrears on LDOD	..	1	70	109	191	218	318	387	429	468
Official creditors	..	0	53	81	130	156	218	264	287	311
Private creditors	..	0	18	29	61	62	100	123	142	156
Memo: principal arrears on LDOD	..	7	457	566	839	1,076	1,565	1,922	2,162	2,389
Official creditors	..	3	212	254	377	485	822	1,054	1,182	1,310
Private creditors	..	4	246	311	463	591	744	869	980	1,079
Memo: export credits	..	..	375	326	338	301	246	157	118	127
TOTAL DEBT FLOWS										
Disbursements	..	**576**	**566**	**525**	**305**	**211**	**148**	**136**	**119**	**119**
Long-term debt	..	566	566	525	305	211	148	136	119	119
IMF purchases	0	10	0	0	0	0	0	0	0	0
Principal repayments	..	**36**	**194**	**158**	**81**	**118**	**83**	**78**	**58**	**66**
Long-term debt	..	25	186	154	80	117	83	78	58	66
IMF repurchases	0	11	8	4	1	0	0	0	0	0
Net flows on debt	..	**540**	**690**	**430**	**386**	**94**	**66**	**-747**	**99**	**36**
of which short-term debt	..	..	318	63	161	0	0	-805	38	-17
Interest payments (INT)	..	**37**	**116**	**104**	**88**	**84**	**51**	**42**	**48**	**37**
Long-term debt	..	10	69	54	28	34	21	21	23	26
IMF charges	0	2	0	0	0	0	0	0	0	0
Short-term debt	..	25	47	50	60	50	30	21	25	11
Net transfers on debt	..	**503**	**574**	**326**	**297**	**10**	**15**	**-788**	**51**	**-1**
Total debt service paid (TDS)	..	**73**	**310**	**262**	**169**	**201**	**133**	**120**	**106**	**102**
Long-term debt	..	35	255	207	108	151	103	99	81	91
IMF repurchases and charges	0	13	8	4	1	0	0	0	0	0
Short-term debt (interest only)	..	25	47	50	60	50	30	21	25	11
2. AGGREGATE NET RESOURCE FLOWS AND NET TRANSFERS (LONG-TERM)										
NET RESOURCE FLOWS	..	**944**	**498**	**507**	**333**	**756**	**882**	**1,071**	**160**	**145**
Net flow of long-term debt (ex. IMF)	6	542	380	371	226	94	66	58	61	53
Foreign direct investment (net)	0	34	0	0	-131	583	719	903	17	0
Portfolio equity flows	..	0	0	0	0	0	0	0	0	0
Grants (excluding technical coop.)	10	368	118	136	238	79	98	109	82	92
Memo: technical coop. grants	5	62	115	105	108	95	96	84	59	67
NET TRANSFERS	..	**934**	**429**	**453**	**304**	**723**	**862**	**1,050**	**137**	**120**
Interest on long-term debt	..	10	69	54	28	34	21	21	23	26
Profit remittances on FDI	0	0	0	0	0	0	0	0	0	0
3. MAJOR ECONOMIC AGGREGATES										
Gross national product (GNP)	..	..	..	..	6,338	4,343	3,657	3,155	3,735	4,002
Exports of goods & services (XGS)	..	..	..	..	3,079	2,464	2,353	2,432	3,056	3,234
of which workers remittances	..	..	..	..	1,498	998	1,018	1,039	1,059	1,080
Imports of goods & services (MGS)	..	..	..	..	2,661	3,281	3,457	3,681	2,745	3,075
International reserves (RES)	..	..	..	..	442	697	337	165	274	638
Current account balance	..	..	..	..	393	-862	-1,130	-1,275	296	146
4. DEBT INDICATORS										
EDT / XGS (%)	..	..	..	..	206.1	262.7	279.3	243.6	200.3	192.1
EDT / GNP (%)	..	..	..	..	100.1	149.1	179.7	187.7	163.9	155.2
TDS / XGS (%)	..	..	..	..	5.5	8.2	5.7	4.9	3.5	3.2
INT / XGS (%)	..	..	..	..	2.9	3.4	2.1	1.7	1.6	1.1
INT / GNP (%)	..	..	..	..	1.4	1.9	1.4	1.3	1.3	0.9
RES / EDT (%)	..	..	..	..	7.0	10.8	5.1	2.8	4.5	10.3
RES / MGS (months)	..	..	..	..	2.0	2.5	1.2	0.5	1.2	2.5
Short-term / EDT (%)	..	10.8	16.1	17.0	18.8	18.8	20.1	9.8	10.8	11.0
Concessional / EDT (%)	..	72.0	53.0	52.2	50.7	50.8	50.2	57.0	56.7	56.8
Multilateral / EDT (%)	..	14.9	17.5	17.3	16.2	16.2	16.1	18.7	19.7	20.6

YEMEN, REPUBLIC OF

(US$ million, unless otherwise indicated)

	1970	1980	1988	1989	1990	1991	1992	1993	1994	1995
5. LONG-TERM DEBT										
DEBT OUTSTANDING (LDOD)	..	**1,453**	**4,394**	**4,643**	**5,154**	**5,256**	**5,253**	**5,341**	**5,460**	**5,528**
Public and publicly guaranteed	..	**1,453**	**4,394**	**4,643**	**5,154**	**5,256**	**5,253**	**5,341**	**5,460**	**5,528**
Official creditors	..	1,238	3,225	3,273	3,496	3,547	3,545	3,626	3,740	3,811
Multilateral	..	252	918	970	1,025	1,046	1,056	1,108	1,206	1,278
Concessional	..	252	867	922	989	1,031	1,051	1,103	1,183	1,239
Bilateral	..	986	2,307	2,303	2,470	2,501	2,490	2,518	2,534	2,532
Concessional	..	962	1,912	1,999	2,225	2,255	2,244	2,272	2,288	2,287
Private creditors	..	216	1,169	1,371	1,658	1,708	1,708	1,716	1,720	1,718
Bonds	..	0	0	0	0	0	0	0	0	0
Commercial banks	..	0	103	80	80	80	80	80	80	80
Other private	..	216	1,067	1,291	1,578	1,628	1,628	1,636	1,640	1,638
Private nonguaranteed	**0**	**0**	**0**	**0**	**0**	**0**	**0**	**0**	**0**	**0**
Bonds	..	0	0	0	0	0	0	0	0	0
Commercial banks	..	0	0	0	0	0	0	0	0	0
Memo:										
IBRD	0	0	0	0	0	0	0	0	0	0
IDA	0	137	510	546	602	651	684	726	780	828
DISBURSEMENTS	..	**566**	**566**	**525**	**305**	**211**	**148**	**136**	**119**	**119**
Public and publicly guaranteed	..	**566**	**566**	**525**	**305**	**211**	**148**	**136**	**119**	**119**
Official creditors	..	501	177	211	139	133	138	127	118	119
Multilateral	..	65	125	92	56	80	91	92	113	110
Concessional	..	65	88	91	55	79	90	91	95	88
Bilateral	..	437	52	119	84	53	47	35	6	9
Concessional	..	426	52	119	84	53	47	35	6	9
Private creditors	..	65	390	314	166	78	10	10	0	0
Bonds	..	0	0	0	0	0	0	0	0	0
Commercial banks	..	0	82	38	0	0	0	0	0	0
Other private	..	65	308	276	166	78	10	10	0	0
Private nonguaranteed	**0**	**0**	**0**	**0**	**0**	**0**	**0**	**0**	**0**	**0**
Bonds	..	0	0	0	0	0	0	0	0	0
Commercial banks	..	0	0	0	0	0	0	0	0	0
Memo:										
IBRD	0	0	0	0	0	0	0	0	0	0
IDA	0	28	49	44	27	49	53	46	37	42
PRINCIPAL REPAYMENTS	..	**25**	**186**	**154**	**80**	**117**	**83**	**78**	**58**	**66**
Public and publicly guaranteed	..	**25**	**186**	**154**	**80**	**117**	**83**	**78**	**58**	**66**
Official creditors	..	23	125	67	74	86	79	78	52	64
Multilateral	..	3	67	26	41	69	49	44	44	54
Concessional	..	3	28	22	26	47	37	44	44	48
Bilateral	..	20	58	41	34	17	30	34	8	10
Concessional	..	16	56	41	34	17	30	34	8	10
Private creditors	..	2	61	86	5	31	4	0	5	2
Bonds	..	0	0	0	0	0	0	0	0	0
Commercial banks	..	0	25	61	0	0	0	0	0	0
Other private	..	2	36	26	5	31	4	0	5	2
Private nonguaranteed	**0**	**0**	**0**	**0**	**0**	**0**	**0**	**0**	**0**	**0**
Bonds	..	0	0	0	0	0	0	0	0	0
Commercial banks	..	0	0	0	0	0	0	0	0	0
Memo:										
IBRD	0	0	0	0	0	0	0	0	0	0
IDA	0	0	2	2	2	3	4	6	7	8
NET FLOWS ON DEBT	..	**542**	**380**	**371**	**226**	**94**	**66**	**58**	**61**	**53**
Public and publicly guaranteed	..	**542**	**380**	**371**	**226**	**94**	**66**	**58**	**61**	**53**
Official creditors	..	479	52	143	65	47	59	48	66	55
Multilateral	..	62	58	66	15	11	43	48	68	56
Concessional	..	62	60	69	29	32	53	47	51	40
Bilateral	..	416	-6	77	50	36	17	1	-2	-1
Concessional	..	410	-5	78	50	36	17	1	-2	-1
Private creditors	..	63	329	228	161	47	6	10	-5	-2
Bonds	..	0	0	0	0	0	0	0	0	0
Commercial banks	..	0	57	-23	0	0	0	0	0	0
Other private	..	63	272	251	161	47	6	10	-5	-2
Private nonguaranteed	**0**	**0**	**0**	**0**	**0**	**0**	**0**	**0**	**0**	**0**
Bonds	..	0	0	0	0	0	0	0	0	0
Commercial banks	0	0	0	0	0	0	0	0	0	0
Memo:										
IBRD	0	0	0	0	0	0	0	0	0	0
IDA	0	28	48	41	25	45	49	41	30	34

YEMEN, REPUBLIC OF

(US$ million, unless otherwise indicated)

	1970	1980	1988	1989	1990	1991	1992	1993	1994	1995
INTEREST PAYMENTS (LINT)	..	**10**	**69**	**54**	**28**	**34**	**21**	**21**	**23**	**26**
Public and publicly guaranteed	..	**10**	**69**	**54**	**28**	**34**	**21**	**21**	**23**	**26**
Official creditors	..	9	59	36	23	29	20	20	20	25
Multilateral	..	5	17	13	14	21	15	15	16	18
Concessional	..	5	15	11	12	20	15	15	16	17
Bilateral	..	4	42	24	9	8	5	5	3	7
Concessional	..	4	30	22	9	8	5	5	3	7
Private creditors	..	1	10	17	5	4	0	0	3	1
Bonds	..	0	0	0	0	0	0	0	0	0
Commercial banks	..	0	2	13	0	0	0	0	0	0
Other private	..	1	8	4	5	4	0	0	3	1
Private nonguaranteed	**0**	**0**	**0**	**0**	**0**	**0**	**0**	**0**	**0**	**0**
Bonds	..	0	0	0	0	0	0	0	0	0
Commercial banks	..	0	0	0	0	0	0	0	0	0
Memo:										
IBRD	0	0	0	0	0	0	0	0	0	0
IDA	0	1	5	4	4	5	5	5	6	6
NET TRANSFERS ON DEBT	..	**531**	**311**	**318**	**198**	**61**	**45**	**38**	**38**	**28**
Public and publicly guaranteed	..	**531**	**311**	**318**	**198**	**61**	**45**	**38**	**38**	**28**
Official creditors	..	469	-8	107	42	18	39	28	47	30
Multilateral	..	57	40	53	1	-10	28	33	52	38
Concessional	..	57	45	58	17	12	39	32	35	23
Bilateral	..	412	-48	54	41	28	11	-5	-5	-8
Concessional	..	405	-34	56	41	28	11	-5	-5	-8
Private creditors	..	62	319	211	156	43	6	10	-8	-2
Bonds	..	0	0	0	0	0	0	0	0	0
Commercial banks	..	0	55	-35	0	0	0	0	0	0
Other private	..	62	264	246	156	43	6	10	-8	-2
Private nonguaranteed	**0**	**0**	**0**	**0**	**0**	**0**	**0**	**0**	**0**	**0**
Bonds	..	0	0	0	0	0	0	0	0	0
Commercial banks	..	0	0	0	0	0	0	0	0	0
Memo:										
IBRD	0	0	0	0	0	0	0	0	0	0
IDA	0	27	43	38	22	41	44	36	24	28
DEBT SERVICE (LTDS)	..	**35**	**255**	**207**	**108**	**151**	**103**	**99**	**81**	**91**
Public and publicly guaranteed	..	**35**	**255**	**207**	**108**	**151**	**103**	**99**	**81**	**91**
Official creditors	..	32	184	104	98	115	99	99	72	89
Multilateral	..	7	84	39	55	90	64	59	61	71
Concessional	..	7	43	33	38	66	52	59	60	65
Bilateral	..	24	100	65	43	25	35	39	11	17
Concessional	..	21	86	63	43	25	35	39	11	17
Private creditors	..	3	71	104	10	35	4	0	9	2
Bonds	..	0	0	0	0	0	0	0	0	0
Commercial banks	..	0	27	74	0	0	0	0	0	0
Other private	..	3	44	30	10	35	4	0	9	2
Private nonguaranteed	**0**	**0**	**0**	**0**	**0**	**0**	**0**	**0**	**0**	**0**
Bonds	..	0	0	0	0	0	0	0	0	0
Commercial banks	..	0	0	0	0	0	0	0	0	0
Memo:										
IBRD	0	0	0	0	0	0	0	0	0	0
IDA	0	1	6	6	6	8	9	11	13	14
UNDISBURSED DEBT	..	**1,589**	**2,233**	**1,796**	**1,655**	**1,095**	**993**	**886**	**809**	**726**
Official creditors	..	1,252	1,258	1,142	1,205	1,088	978	885	809	726
Private creditors	..	336	975	654	450	7	15	2	0	0
Memorandum items										
Concessional LDOD	..	1,214	2,778	2,922	3,214	3,287	3,295	3,375	3,471	3,526
Variable rate LDOD	..	0	103	80	80	80	80	80	80	80
Public sector LDOD	..	1,453	4,394	4,643	5,154	5,256	5,253	5,341	5,460	5,528
Private sector LDOD	..	0	0	0	0	0	0	0	0	0

6. CURRENCY COMPOSITION OF LONG-TERM DEBT (PERCENT)

	1970	1980	1988	1989	1990	1991	1992	1993	1994	1995
Deutsche mark	..	0.0	0.0	0.0	0.0	0.0	0.0	0.0	0.0	0.0
French franc	..	1.5	0.7	0.6	0.8	0.6	1.2	1.4	1.4	1.5
Japanese yen	..	0.6	2.9	3.5	4.4	5.2	5.2	6.0	6.5	6.1
Pound sterling	..	3.2	0.8	0.7	0.7	0.7	0.6	0.5	0.6	0.6
Swiss franc	..	2.8	0.3	0.3	0.3	0.3	0.3	0.3	0.3	0.3
U.S.dollars	..	22.4	22.7	21.4	20.2	20.6	20.7	20.5	20.8	21.2
Multiple currency	..	0.1	1.8	1.7	1.6	1.6	1.6	1.5	1.5	1.4
Special drawing rights	..	0.0	2.3	2.4	2.5	2.5	2.4	2.5	2.7	2.8
All other currencies	..	69.5	68.4	69.4	69.5	68.6	68.0	67.2	66.2	66.0

YEMEN, REPUBLIC OF

(US$ million, unless otherwise indicated)

	1970	1980	1988	1989	1990	1991	1992	1993	1994	1995
7. DEBT RESTRUCTURINGS										
Total amount rescheduled	0	0	103	158	98	0	0	0	0	0
Debt stock rescheduled	0	0	0	0	0	0	0	0	0	0
Principal rescheduled	0	0	104	158	98	0	0	0	0	0
Official	0	0	104	158	98	0	0	0	0	0
Private	0	0	0	0	0	0	0	0	0	0
Interest rescheduled	0	0	0	0	0	0	0	0	0	0
Official	0	0	0	0	0	0	0	0	0	0
Private	0	0	0	0	0	0	0	0	0	0
Debt forgiven	..	..	2	0	0	15	0	0	0	0
Memo: interest forgiven	..	..	0	0	0	0	0	0	0	0
Debt stock reduction	0	0	0	0	0	0	0	0	0	0
of which debt buyback	0	0	0	0	0	0	0	0	0	0
8. DEBT STOCK-FLOW RECONCILIATION										
Total change in debt stocks	..	..	..	347	752	128	98	-648	199	91
Net flows on debt	..	..	..	430	386	94	66	-747	99	36
Net change in interest arrears	..	..	..	39	81	27	100	69	42	39
Interest capitalized	..	..	..	0	0	0	0	0	0	0
Debt forgiveness or reduction	..	..	..	0	0	-15	0	0	0	0
Cross-currency valuation	..	..	..	-60	313	16	-50	34	58	5
Residual	..	..	..	-62	-29	7	-18	-4	0	10
9. AVERAGE TERMS OF NEW COMMITMENTS										
ALL CREDITORS										
Interest (%)	..	2.7	3.6	2.2	1.8	1.0	2.1	0.9	1.9	5.1
Maturity (years)	..	26.9	23.3	28.5	28.6	36.5	30.1	31.6	27.6	10.8
Grace period (years)	..	5.8	6.1	7.9	7.2	9.4	8.4	9.3	7.3	3.3
Grant element (%)	..	51.8	47.0	60.6	61.3	75.5	63.3	73.8	57.6	21.4
Official creditors										
Interest (%)	..	2.4	2.3	1.7	1.8	0.9	1.2	0.9	1.9	5.1
Maturity (years)	..	28.2	26.2	31.6	28.6	37.1	34.6	31.6	27.6	10.8
Grace period (years)	..	6.0	8.4	8.9	7.2	9.6	9.7	9.3	7.3	3.3
Grant element (%)	..	54.1	58.4	67.6	61.3	76.8	74.1	73.8	57.6	21.4
Private creditors										
Interest (%)	..	4.4	4.5	6.0	0.0	6.0	6.0	0.0	0.0	0.0
Maturity (years)	..	18.9	21.2	7.3	0.0	7.3	11.5	0.0	0.0	0.0
Grace period (years)	..	4.9	4.5	1.3	0.0	1.3	3.0	0.0	0.0	0.0
Grant element (%)	..	37.6	38.8	12.4	0.0	12.4	18.6	0.0	0.0	0.0
Memorandum items										
Commitments	..	553	1,140	178	201	155	98	49	49	80
Official creditors	..	476	480	155	201	152	79	49	49	80
Private creditors	..	77	661	23	0	3	19	0	0	0

10. CONTRACTUAL OBLIGATIONS ON OUTSTANDING LONG-TERM DEBT

	1996	1997	1998	1999	2000	2001	2002	2003	2004	2005
TOTAL										
Disbursements	249	204	127	79	39	14	6	2	1	0
Principal	289	270	289	281	274	187	179	166	158	133
Interest	62	59	54	48	42	36	32	29	26	24
Official creditors										
Disbursements	249	204	127	79	39	14	6	2	1	0
Principal	202	197	216	208	201	150	143	134	128	122
Interest	48	47	44	40	35	30	27	25	22	20
Bilateral creditors										
Disbursements	69	72	43	23	12	7	3	1	1	0
Principal	133	129	133	126	120	92	87	81	75	71
Interest	25	23	21	18	16	13	12	10	9	8
Multilateral creditors										
Disbursements	180	132	84	56	27	7	3	1	1	0
Principal	70	67	83	82	81	58	56	53	53	51
Interest	23	24	23	21	19	17	16	14	13	12
Private creditors										
Disbursements	0	0	0	0	0	0	0	0	0	0
Principal	87	73	73	73	73	37	36	33	30	11
Interest	14	12	11	9	7	6	5	4	4	4
Commercial banks										
Disbursements	0	0	0	0	0	0	0	0	0	0
Principal	0	0	0	0	0	0	0	0	0	0
Interest	0	0	0	0	0	0	0	0	0	0
Other private										
Disbursements	0	0	0	0	0	0	0	0	0	0
Principal	87	73	73	73	73	37	36	33	30	11
Interest	14	12	11	9	7	6	5	4	4	4

FORMER YUGOSLAVIA

(US$ million, unless otherwise indicated)

	1970	1980	1988	1989	1990	1991	1992	1993	1994	1995
1. SUMMARY DEBT DATA										
TOTAL DEBT STOCKS (EDT)	..	**18,486**	**21,176**	**19,072**	**17,837**	**16,472**	**16,483**	**12,709**	**13,035**	**13,839**
Long-term debt (LDOD)	**2,053**	**15,586**	**18,745**	**17,591**	**16,846**	**15,872**	**15,195**	**10,990**	**11,270**	**11,484**
Public and publicly guaranteed	1,199	4,581	14,053	14,110	12,986	11,641	11,117	8,231	8,511	8,725
Private nonguaranteed	854	11,005	4,692	3,481	3,860	4,231	4,078	2,759	2,759	2,759
Use of IMF credit	**0**	**760**	**1,310**	**686**	**467**	**307**	**196**	**78**	**83**	**85**
Short-term debt	..	**2,140**	**1,121**	**795**	**524**	**293**	**1,092**	**1,641**	**1,682**	**2,271**
of which interest arrears on LDOD	..	0	0	0	0	0	90	616	1,059	1,528
Official creditors	..	0	0	0	0	0	79	197	322	443
Private creditors	..	0	0	0	0	0	11	419	737	1,085
Memo: principal arrears on LDOD	..	0	3	7	298	637	989	1,965	4,030	5,329
Official creditors	..	0	3	7	298	629	983	1,279	1,824	2,595
Private creditors	..	0	0	0	0	8	7	687	2,206	2,735
Memo: export credits	..	..	5,019	5,242	5,521	5,054	3,894	4,262	4,118	4,818
TOTAL DEBT FLOWS										
Disbursements	**645**	**5,029**	**1,196**	**1,283**	**1,590**	**771**	**580**	**0**	**0**	**0**
Long-term debt	645	4,589	1,032	1,283	1,501	771	580	0	0	0
IMF purchases	0	441	165	0	89	0	0	0	0	0
Principal repayments	**420**	**2,450**	**1,854**	**2,398**	**3,079**	**2,545**	**1,066**	**12**	**0**	**0**
Long-term debt	375	2,381	1,243	1,820	2,726	2,390	964	12	0	0
IMF repurchases	45	70	611	579	353	155	102	0	0	0
Net flows on debt	**225**	**2,579**	**-837**	**-1,442**	**-1,760**	**-2,006**	**223**	**10**	**-402**	**120**
of which short-term debt	..	..	-179	-326	-271	-231	710	23	-402	120
Interest payments (INT)	..	**1,286**	**1,893**	**1,410**	**1,704**	**1,288**	**833**	**3**	**0**	**0**
Long-term debt	104	1,077	1,614	1,219	1,583	1,222	773	2	0	0
IMF charges	0	32	139	105	66	41	21	1	0	0
Short-term debt	..	177	140	86	55	25	39	0	0	0
Net transfers on debt	..	**1,293**	**-2,729**	**-2,851**	**-3,464**	**-3,294**	**-609**	**7**	**-402**	**120**
Total debt service paid (TDS)	..	**3,736**	**3,746**	**3,808**	**4,783**	**3,833**	**1,899**	**15**	**0**	**0**
Long-term debt	479	3,458	2,857	3,038	4,309	3,613	1,738	14	0	0
IMF repurchases and charges	45	101	750	684	419	196	123	1	0	0
Short-term debt (interest only)	..	177	140	86	55	25	39	0	0	0
2. AGGREGATE NET RESOURCE FLOWS AND NET TRANSFERS (LONG-TERM)										
NET RESOURCE FLOWS	**277**	**2,208**	**-186**	**-522**	**-1,151**	**-1,435**	**812**	**2,029**	**1,559**	**1,412**
Net flow of long-term debt (ex. IMF)	270	2,208	-211	-537	-1,225	-1,620	-384	-12	0	0
Foreign direct investment (net)	0	0	22	9	67	119	93	80	0	0
Portfolio equity flows	0	0	0	0	0	0	0	0	0	0
Grants (excluding technical coop.)	7	0	3	7	7	66	1,103	1,961	1,559	1,412
Memo: technical coop. grants	3	7	27	27	35	45	359	611	98	171
NET TRANSFERS	**173**	**1,131**	**-1,800**	**-1,740**	**-2,734**	**-2,657**	**39**	**2,027**	**1,559**	**1,412**
Interest on long-term debt	104	1,077	1,614	1,219	1,583	1,222	773	2	0	0
Profit remittances on FDI	0	0	0	0	0	0	0	0	0	0
3. MAJOR ECONOMIC AGGREGATES										
Gross national product (GNP)	13,688	72,282	59,968	76,825	87,356	..	..	..	..	..
Exports of goods & services (XGS)	..	..	..	..	..	..	..	..	..	..
of which workers remittances	..	..	..	..	..	..	..	..	..	..
Imports of goods & services (MGS)	..	..	..	..	..	..	..	..	..	..
International reserves (RES)	143	2,478	3,074	4,899	6,208	3,360	..	..	..	..
Current account balance	..	-2,317	2,487	2,427	-2,364	-1,161	..	..	..	..
4. DEBT INDICATORS										
EDT / XGS (%)	..	..	..	..	..	..	..	..	..	..
EDT / GNP (%)	..	25.6	35.3	24.8	20.4	..	..	..	..	..
TDS / XGS (%)	..	..	..	..	..	..	..	..	..	..
INT / XGS (%)	..	..	..	..	..	..	..	..	..	..
INT / GNP (%)	..	1.8	3.2	1.8	2.0	..	..	..	..	..
RES / EDT (%)	..	13.4	14.5	25.7	34.8	20.4	..	..	..	..
RES / MGS (months)	..	..	..	..	..	..	..	..	..	..
Short-term / EDT (%)	..	11.6	5.3	4.2	2.9	1.8	6.6	12.9	12.9	16.4
Concessional / EDT (%)	..	7.9	4.6	5.0	5.6	4.3	4.1	2.6	2.7	2.7
Multilateral / EDT (%)	..	7.6	14.1	15.6	17.3	16.9	15.5	9.3	9.7	9.5

FORMER YUGOSLAVIA

(US$ million, unless otherwise indicated)

	1970	1980	1988	1989	1990	1991	1992	1993	1994	1995
5. LONG-TERM DEBT										
DEBT OUTSTANDING (LDOD)	**2,053**	**15,586**	**18,745**	**17,591**	**16,846**	**15,872**	**15,195**	**10,990**	**11,270**	**11,484**
Public and publicly guaranteed	**1,199**	**4,581**	**14,053**	**14,110**	**12,986**	**11,641**	**11,117**	**8,231**	**8,511**	**8,725**
Official creditors	858	3,600	6,688	7,299	7,539	6,785	6,286	4,103	4,377	4,588
Multilateral	251	1,408	2,987	2,983	3,093	2,784	2,553	1,176	1,259	1,311
Concessional	219	137	58	38	25	16	10	11	12	12
Bilateral	606	2,192	3,701	4,316	4,446	4,001	3,733	2,927	3,118	3,277
Concessional	387	1,328	909	906	967	699	658	316	344	366
Private creditors	341	981	7,365	6,811	5,447	4,855	4,831	4,128	4,134	4,137
Bonds	21	10	0	0	0	0	0	0	0	0
Commercial banks	2	808	7,264	6,682	5,325	4,735	4,725	4,121	4,127	4,130
Other private	318	163	101	128	122	121	106	7	7	7
Private nonguaranteed	**854**	**11,005**	**4,692**	**3,481**	**3,860**	**4,231**	**4,078**	**2,759**	**2,759**	**2,759**
Bonds	0	0	0	0	0	0	0	0	0	0
Commercial banks	854	11,005	4,692	3,481	3,860	4,231	4,078	2,759	2,759	2,759
Memo:										
IBRD	244	1,359	2,720	2,395	2,433	2,149	1,978	1,126	1,204	1,252
IDA	0	0	0	0	0	0	0	0	0	0
DISBURSEMENTS	**645**	**4,589**	**1,032**	**1,283**	**1,501**	**771**	**580**	**0**	**0**	**0**
Public and publicly guaranteed	**179**	**1,366**	**566**	**446**	**286**	**105**	**86**	**0**	**0**	**0**
Official creditors	139	644	259	446	286	105	86	0	0	0
Multilateral	37	308	207	423	276	100	86	0	0	0
Concessional	18	0	0	0	0	0	0	0	0	0
Bilateral	102	336	52	22	10	5	0	0	0	0
Concessional	64	77	16	16	8	2	0	0	0	0
Private creditors	40	721	307	0	0	0	0	0	0	0
Bonds	0	0	0	0	0	0	0	0	0	0
Commercial banks	0	686	307	0	0	0	0	0	0	0
Other private	40	36	0	0	0	0	0	0	0	0
Private nonguaranteed	**465**	**3,223**	**466**	**837**	**1,215**	**666**	**494**	**0**	**0**	**0**
Bonds	0	0	0	0	0	0	0	0	0	0
Commercial banks	465	3,223	466	837	1,215	666	494	0	0	0
Memo:										
IBRD	37	281	151	121	269	100	51	0	0	0
IDA	0	0	0	0	0	0	0	0	0	0
PRINCIPAL REPAYMENTS	**375**	**2,381**	**1,243**	**1,820**	**2,726**	**2,390**	**964**	**12**	**0**	**0**
Public and publicly guaranteed	**170**	**368**	**800**	**1,149**	**1,516**	**1,351**	**317**	**12**	**0**	**0**
Official creditors	88	272	640	565	607	845	317	12	0	0
Multilateral	11	67	473	376	421	428	187	12	0	0
Concessional	10	14	25	19	15	9	5	0	0	0
Bilateral	78	206	167	189	186	416	131	0	0	0
Concessional	22	65	78	41	26	259	3	0	0	0
Private creditors	82	96	160	584	909	507	0	0	0	0
Bonds	2	2	0	0	0	0	0	0	0	0
Commercial banks	1	39	79	559	891	507	0	0	0	0
Other private	80	55	81	24	18	0	0	0	0	0
Private nonguaranteed	**204**	**2,012**	**443**	**671**	**1,210**	**1,039**	**647**	**0**	**0**	**0**
Bonds	0	0	0	0	0	0	0	0	0	0
Commercial banks	204	2,012	443	671	1,210	1,039	647	0	0	0
Memo:										
IBRD	10	66	463	365	405	415	155	12	0	0
IDA	0	0	0	0	0	0	0	0	0	0
NET FLOWS ON DEBT	**270**	**2,208**	**-211**	**-537**	**-1,225**	**-1,620**	**-384**	**-12**	**0**	**0**
Public and publicly guaranteed	**9**	**998**	**-234**	**-703**	**-1,230**	**-1,247**	**-231**	**-12**	**0**	**0**
Official creditors	51	372	-381	-119	-321	-740	-231	-12	0	0
Multilateral	27	242	-266	47	-145	-329	-101	-12	0	0
Concessional	9	-14	-25	-19	-15	-9	-5	0	0	0
Bilateral	24	131	-116	-166	-176	-411	-131	0	0	0
Concessional	42	12	-61	-24	-18	-257	-3	0	0	0
Private creditors	-42	625	147	-584	-909	-507	0	0	0	0
Bonds	-2	-2	0	0	0	0	0	0	0	0
Commercial banks	-1	647	228	-559	-891	-507	0	0	0	0
Other private	-40	-19	-81	-24	-18	0	0	0	0	0
Private nonguaranteed	**261**	**1,211**	**23**	**166**	**5**	**-373**	**-153**	**0**	**0**	**0**
Bonds	0	0	0	0	0	0	0	0	0	0
Commercial banks	261	1,211	23	166	5	-373	-153	0	0	0
Memo:										
IBRD	27	216	-312	-244	-136	-316	-103	-12	0	0
IDA	0	0	0	0	0	0	0	0	0	0

FORMER YUGOSLAVIA

(US$ million, unless otherwise indicated)

	1970	1980	1988	1989	1990	1991	1992	1993	1994	1995
INTEREST PAYMENTS (LINT)	**104**	**1,077**	**1,614**	**1,219**	**1,583**	**1,222**	**773**	**2**	**0**	**0**
Public and publicly guaranteed	**73**	**249**	**1,113**	**980**	**1,203**	**987**	**469**	**2**	**0**	**0**
Official creditors	37	215	401	411	731	469	240	2	0	0
Multilateral	14	111	317	231	252	242	133	2	0	0
Concessional	12	13	5	3	2	1	1	0	0	0
Bilateral	23	103	84	179	479	226	106	0	0	0
Concessional	10	39	9	19	17	21	9	0	0	0
Private creditors	36	34	712	569	472	519	230	0	0	0
Bonds	0	0	0	0	0	0	0	0	0	0
Commercial banks	0	17	620	563	454	501	225	0	0	0
Other private	35	17	91	7	19	18	5	0	0	0
Private nonguaranteed	**32**	**829**	**501**	**239**	**380**	**235**	**304**	**0**	**0**	**0**
Bonds	0	0	0	0	0	0	0	0	0	0
Commercial banks	32	829	501	239	380	235	304	0	0	0
Memo:										
IBRD	13	110	282	205	191	185	69	2	0	0
IDA	0	0	0	0	0	0	0	0	0	0
NET TRANSFERS ON DEBT	**166**	**1,131**	**-1,825**	**-1,756**	**-2,809**	**-2,842**	**-1,158**	**-14**	**0**	**0**
Public and publicly guaranteed	**-64**	**749**	**-1,347**	**-1,683**	**-2,434**	**-2,234**	**-701**	**-14**	**0**	**0**
Official creditors	14	158	-782	-530	-1,052	-1,209	-471	-14	0	0
Multilateral	13	130	-583	-184	-397	-571	-234	-14	0	0
Concessional	-3	-27	-30	-22	-17	-11	-5	0	0	0
Bilateral	1	27	-199	-346	-656	-638	-237	0	0	0
Concessional	32	-27	-70	-43	-35	-278	-12	0	0	0
Private creditors	-78	591	-565	-1,153	-1,381	-1,026	-230	0	0	0
Bonds	-2	-2	0	0	0	0	0	0	0	0
Commercial banks	-1	630	-393	-1,122	-1,345	-1,008	-225	0	0	0
Other private	-75	-36	-172	-31	-36	-18	-5	0	0	0
Private nonguaranteed	**230**	**382**	**-478**	**-73**	**-375**	**-608**	**-457**	**0**	**0**	**0**
Bonds	0	0	0	0	0	0	0	0	0	0
Commercial banks	230	382	-478	-73	-375	-608	-457	0	0	0
Memo:										
IBRD	14	106	-594	-449	-327	-500	-172	-14	0	0
IDA	0	0	0	0	0	0	0	0	0	0
DEBT SERVICE (LTDS)	**479**	**3,458**	**2,857**	**3,038**	**4,309**	**3,613**	**1,738**	**14**	**0**	**0**
Public and publicly guaranteed	**243**	**617**	**1,913**	**2,128**	**2,719**	**2,339**	**787**	**14**	**0**	**0**
Official creditors	125	487	1,041	975	1,338	1,313	557	14	0	0
Multilateral	24	178	790	608	673	670	320	14	0	0
Concessional	22	27	30	22	17	11	5	0	0	0
Bilateral	101	309	251	368	665	643	237	0	0	0
Concessional	33	103	87	60	43	280	12	0	0	0
Private creditors	118	130	872	1,153	1,381	1,026	230	0	0	0
Bonds	2	2	0	0	0	0	0	0	0	0
Commercial banks	1	56	700	1,122	1,345	1,008	225	0	0	0
Other private	115	72	172	31	36	18	5	0	0	0
Private nonguaranteed	**236**	**2,841**	**944**	**910**	**1,590**	**1,274**	**951**	**0**	**0**	**0**
Bonds	0	0	0	0	0	0	0	0	0	0
Commercial banks	236	2,841	944	910	1,590	1,274	951	0	0	0
Memo:										
IBRD	23	175	745	570	596	600	224	14	0	0
IDA	0	0	0	0	0	0	0	0	0	0
UNDISBURSED DEBT	**550**	**1,218**	**1,220**	**448**	**973**	**1,443**	**714**	**200**	**208**	**222**
Official creditors	462	1,205	1,220	448	973	1,443	714	200	208	222
Private creditors	87	13	0	0	0	0	0	0	0	0
Memorandum items										
Concessional LDOD	605	1,465	967	944	992	715	669	326	355	378
Variable rate LDOD	893	12,100	13,847	12,734	12,016	11,914	11,626	8,857	8,945	9,020
Public sector LDOD	980	3,826	13,797	13,609	12,485	11,180	10,700	8,142	8,418	8,629
Private sector LDOD	1,073	11,759	4,948	3,981	4,361	4,691	4,495	2,848	2,852	2,854

6. CURRENCY COMPOSITION OF LONG-TERM DEBT (PERCENT)

	1970	1980	1988	1989	1990	1991	1992	1993	1994	1995
Deutsche mark	13.9	13.3	6.7	6.9	8.4	9.1	8.9	6.9	7.5	7.9
French franc	2.0	0.0	2.8	3.8	4.4	4.6	4.3	5.5	5.8	6.2
Japanese yen	0.3	0.7	1.0	0.9	1.0	1.1	1.1	1.7	1.8	1.7
Pound sterling	3.6	0.1	0.2	0.3	0.4	0.5	0.4	0.5	0.5	0.5
Swiss franc	1.1	0.1	1.3	1.4	1.7	1.8	1.7	2.3	2.5	2.8
U.S.dollars	36.5	52.3	15.8	16.7	17.3	14.8	15.3	16.4	15.8	15.4
Multiple currency	24.8	30.7	66.6	61.2	56.3	56.8	57.9	60.7	59.6	58.7
Special drawing rights	0.0	0.0	0.0	0.0	0.0	0.0	0.0	0.0	0.0	0.0
All other currencies	17.8	2.8	5.6	8.8	10.5	11.2	10.3	6.0	6.4	6.7

FORMER YUGOSLAVIA

(US$ million, unless otherwise indicated)

	1970	1980	1988	1989	1990	1991	1992	1993	1994	1995
7. DEBT RESTRUCTURINGS										
Total amount rescheduled	0	0	7,562	1,367	0	0	0	0	0	0
Debt stock rescheduled	0	0	6,427	0	0	0	0	0	0	0
Principal rescheduled	0	0	996	1,248	0	0	0	0	0	0
Official	0	0	274	160	0	0	0	0	0	0
Private	0	0	721	1,089	0	0	0	0	0	0
Interest rescheduled	0	0	141	119	0	0	0	0	0	0
Official	0	0	134	117	0	0	0	0	0	0
Private	0	0	8	2	0	0	0	0	0	0
Debt forgiven	..	..	0	0	0	0	0	0	0	0
Memo: interest forgiven	..	..	0	0	0	0	0	0	0	0
Debt stock reduction	0	0	128	619	1,496	554	0	0	0	0
of which debt buyback	0	0	64	365	883	327	0	0	0	0
8. DEBT STOCK-FLOW RECONCILIATION										
Total change in debt stocks	..	..	..	-2,105	-1,235	-1,365	11	-3,774	326	804
Net flows on debt	..	..	..	-1,442	-1,760	-2,006	223	10	-402	120
Net change in interest arrears	..	..	..	0	0	0	90	526	443	469
Interest capitalized	..	..	..	119	0	0	0	0	0	0
Debt forgiveness or reduction	..	..	..	-254	-613	-227	0	0	0	0
Cross-currency valuation	..	..	..	-28	829	-151	-526	-336	482	369
Residual	..	..	..	-500	310	1,019	224	-3,974	-198	-153
9. AVERAGE TERMS OF NEW COMMITMENTS										
ALL CREDITORS										
Interest (%)	7.0	15.1	9.3	9.3	8.2	7.8	0.0	0.0	0.0	0.0
Maturity (years)	17.2	8.5	11.8	19.2	16.2	14.4	0.0	0.0	0.0	0.0
Grace period (years)	6.1	3.1	4.5	4.8	5.2	4.9	0.0	0.0	0.0	0.0
Grant element (%)	17.9	-19.3	2.7	3.3	9.9	11.8	0.0	0.0	0.0	0.0
Official creditors										
Interest (%)	7.0	12.0	9.1	9.3	8.2	7.8	0.0	0.0	0.0	0.0
Maturity (years)	18.8	10.8	17.8	19.2	16.2	14.4	0.0	0.0	0.0	0.0
Grace period (years)	6.9	3.3	4.0	4.8	5.2	4.9	0.0	0.0	0.0	0.0
Grant element (%)	19.3	-7.4	3.6	3.3	9.9	11.8	0.0	0.0	0.0	0.0
Private creditors										
Interest (%)	7.0	17.0	9.6	0.0	0.0	0.0	0.0	0.0	0.0	0.0
Maturity (years)	13.1	7.1	5.0	0.0	0.0	0.0	0.0	0.0	0.0	0.0
Grace period (years)	4.1	3.0	5.0	0.0	0.0	0.0	0.0	0.0	0.0	0.0
Grant element (%)	14.2	-26.8	1.7	0.0	0.0	0.0	0.0	0.0	0.0	0.0
Memorandum items										
Commitments	199	1,187	653	74	830	595	0	0	0	0
Official creditors	143	461	346	74	830	595	0	0	0	0
Private creditors	56	726	307	0	0	0	0	0	0	0

10. CONTRACTUAL OBLIGATIONS ON OUTSTANDING LONG-TERM DEBT

	1996	1997	1998	1999	2000	2001	2002	2003	2004	2005
TOTAL										
Disbursements	0	0	0	0	0	0	0	0	0	0
Principal	1,190	955	942	502	467	453	426	351	319	310
Interest	431	345	273	211	176	143	112	82	55	33
Official creditors										
Disbursements	0	0	0	0	0	0	0	0	0	0
Principal	718	523	519	85	63	49	35	27	22	13
Interest	142	93	53	21	15	11	7	5	4	2
Bilateral creditors										
Disbursements	0	0	0	0	0	0	0	0	0	0
Principal	374	284	284	9	9	9	9	5	0	0
Interest	54	32	15	1	1	1	0	0	0	0
Multilateral creditors										
Disbursements	0	0	0	0	0	0	0	0	0	0
Principal	343	239	236	76	54	40	26	22	22	13
Interest	89	60	38	20	14	10	7	5	4	2
Private creditors										
Disbursements	0	0	0	0	0	0	0	0	0	0
Principal	473	433	423	418	404	404	391	324	297	297
Interest	288	253	221	191	161	132	104	77	51	31
Commercial banks										
Disbursements	0	0	0	0	0	0	0	0	0	0
Principal	297	297	297	297	297	297	297	297	297	297
Interest	209	189	169	149	130	110	90	71	51	31
Other private										
Disbursements	0	0	0	0	0	0	0	0	0	0
Principal	175	135	126	120	107	107	94	27	0	0
Interest	80	64	51	41	32	22	14	6	0	0

ZAIRE

(US$ million, unless otherwise indicated)

1. SUMMARY DEBT DATA

	1970	*1980*	*1988*	*1989*	*1990*	*1991*	*1992*	*1993*	*1994*	*1995*
TOTAL DEBT STOCKS (EDT)	**..**	**4,770**	**8,562**	**9,239**	**10,270**	**10,826**	**10,964**	**11,270**	**12,322**	**13,137**
Long-term debt (LDOD)	**311**	**4,071**	**6,941**	**7,966**	**9,006**	**9,271**	**8,948**	**8,769**	**9,281**	**9,621**
Public and publicly guaranteed	311	4,071	6,941	7,966	9,006	9,271	8,948	8,769	9,281	9,621
Private nonguaranteed	0	0	0	0	0	0	0	0	0	0
Use of IMF credit	**0**	**373**	**786**	**628**	**521**	**473**	**454**	**454**	**478**	**485**
Short-term debt	**..**	**326**	**835**	**645**	**743**	**1,083**	**1,562**	**2,047**	**2,564**	**3,031**
of which interest arrears on LDOD	..	30	340	140	265	692	1,253	1,792	2,445	2,849
Official creditors	..	21	236	48	166	585	1,058	1,512	2,127	2,523
Private creditors	..	8	104	92	99	108	195	280	318	326
Memo: principal arrears on LDOD	..	37	873	725	1,049	1,762	2,089	2,450	3,080	4,555
Official creditors	..	13	428	149	375	1,035	1,359	1,713	2,299	3,738
Private creditors	..	23	445	576	674	727	730	737	781	817
Memo: export credits	..	..	3,912	4,309	4,604	4,672	4,061	4,360	4,315	4,339
TOTAL DEBT FLOWS										
Disbursements	**32**	**603**	**410**	**659**	**316**	**304**	**83**	**58**	**1**	**0**
Long-term debt	32	463	410	451	316	304	83	58	1	0
IMF purchases	0	140	0	208	0	0	0	0	0	0
Principal repayments	**28**	**277**	**211**	**441**	**200**	**91**	**29**	**4**	**5**	**1**
Long-term debt	28	192	80	98	49	41	29	4	0	0
IMF repurchases	0	85	131	344	152	49	0	0	4	1
Net flows on debt	**3**	**326**	**232**	**228**	**89**	**125**	**-28**	**0**	**-140**	**61**
of which short-term debt	..	..	32	11	-27	-88	-81	-54	-136	63
Interest payments (INT)	**..**	**265**	**181**	**168**	**148**	**87**	**48**	**23**	**11**	**24**
Long-term debt	9	205	97	94	89	56	27	7	0	0
IMF charges	0	15	50	48	38	11	9	3	1	16
Short-term debt	..	45	34	26	21	20	13	13	9	8
Net transfers on debt	**..**	**61**	**50**	**61**	**-59**	**38**	**-76**	**-23**	**-151**	**38**
Total debt service paid (TDS)	**..**	**542**	**392**	**609**	**348**	**177**	**77**	**28**	**16**	**25**
Long-term debt	37	397	177	192	137	98	56	12	1	0
IMF repurchases and charges	0	101	181	391	190	60	9	3	6	18
Short-term debt (interest only)	..	45	34	26	21	20	13	13	9	8

2. AGGREGATE NET RESOURCE FLOWS AND NET TRANSFERS (LONG-TERM)

	1970	*1980*	*1988*	*1989*	*1990*	*1991*	*1992*	*1993*	*1994*	*1995*
NET RESOURCE FLOWS	**42**	**368**	**454**	**562**	**629**	**752**	**164**	**129**	**222**	**161**
Net flow of long-term debt (ex. IMF)	3	271	330	353	267	263	54	53	1	0
Foreign direct investment (net)	0	0	-4	-6	-12	15	1	1	1	1
Portfolio equity flows	0	0	0	0	0	0	0	0	0	0
Grants (excluding technical coop.)	38	96	128	215	374	474	109	75	220	160
Memo: technical coop. grants	42	168	189	150	147	110	87	57	39	55
NET TRANSFERS	**3**	**36**	**406**	**522**	**532**	**696**	**74**	**72**	**182**	**111**
Interest on long-term debt	9	205	97	94	89	56	27	7	0	0
Profit remittances on FDI	30	128	-50	-54	8	0	63	50	40	50

3. MAJOR ECONOMIC AGGREGATES

	1970	*1980*	*1988*	*1989*	*1990*	*1991*	*1992*	*1993*	*1994*	*1995*
Gross national product (GNP)	4,721	13,895	8,331	8,258	8,173	6,663	6,619	5,571	5,302	5,147
Exports of goods & services (XGS)	..	..	2,364	2,366	2,310	..	..	..	..	..
of which workers remittances	..	..	0	0	0	..	..	..	..	..
Imports of goods & services (MGS)	..	..	3,103	3,143	3,087	..	..	..	..	..
International reserves (RES)	189	380	372	282	261	193	166	55	131	..
Current account balance	..	..	-580	-610	519	..	..	..	..	..

4. DEBT INDICATORS

	1970	*1980*	*1988*	*1989*	*1990*	*1991*	*1992*	*1993*	*1994*	*1995*
EDT / XGS (%)	..	..	362.2	390.5	444.6	..	..	..	..	..
EDT / GNP (%)	..	34.3	102.8	111.9	125.7	162.5	165.6	202.3	232.4	255.2
TDS / XGS (%)	..	..	16.6	25.7	15.1	..	..	..	..	..
INT / XGS (%)	..	..	7.7	7.1	6.4	..	..	..	..	..
INT / GNP (%)	..	1.9	2.2	2.0	1.8	1.3	0.7	0.4	0.2	0.5
RES / EDT (%)	..	8.0	4.3	3.0	2.5	1.8	1.5	0.5	1.1	..
RES / MGS (months)	..	..	1.4	1.1	1.0	..	..	..	..	..
Short-term / EDT (%)	..	6.8	9.7	7.0	7.2	10.0	14.2	18.2	20.8	23.1
Concessional / EDT (%)	..	18.1	23.7	28.5	30.6	30.2	29.3	28.6	27.7	26.8
Multilateral / EDT (%)	..	6.7	16.3	17.4	18.8	20.4	19.8	19.6	18.9	18.1

ZAIRE

(US$ million, unless otherwise indicated)

	1970	1980	1988	1989	1990	1991	1992	1993	1994	1995
5. LONG-TERM DEBT										
DEBT OUTSTANDING (LDOD)	**311**	**4,071**	**6,941**	**7,966**	**9,006**	**9,271**	**8,948**	**8,769**	**9,281**	**9,621**
Public and publicly guaranteed	**311**	**4,071**	**6,941**	**7,966**	**9,006**	**9,271**	**8,948**	**8,769**	**9,281**	**9,621**
Official creditors	222	2,609	6,095	7,088	8,117	8,399	8,096	7,933	8,420	8,744
Multilateral	6	322	1,399	1,608	1,929	2,205	2,174	2,211	2,326	2,382
Concessional	5	195	1,087	1,240	1,455	1,552	1,559	1,598	1,674	1,715
Bilateral	216	2,287	4,695	5,480	6,189	6,194	5,921	5,722	6,095	6,362
Concessional	216	667	945	1,395	1,689	1,717	1,654	1,624	1,735	1,804
Private creditors	90	1,462	847	878	889	872	852	836	860	878
Bonds	4	7	4	4	5	5	4	4	5	5
Commercial banks	0	553	518	520	524	519	516	511	518	523
Other private	85	902	324	354	360	348	332	321	337	350
Private nonguaranteed	**0**	**0**	**0**	**0**	**0**	**0**	**0**	**0**	**0**	**0**
Bonds	0	0	0	0	0	0	0	0	0	0
Commercial banks	0	0	0	0	0	0	0	0	0	0
Memo:										
IBRD	5	87	37	30	49	87	81	83	88	92
IDA	1	159	837	962	1,113	1,183	1,194	1,243	1,294	1,321
DISBURSEMENTS	**32**	**463**	**410**	**451**	**316**	**304**	**83**	**58**	**1**	**0**
Public and publicly guaranteed	**32**	**463**	**410**	**451**	**316**	**304**	**83**	**58**	**1**	**0**
Official creditors	13	201	404	392	313	304	83	58	1	0
Multilateral	1	69	279	260	222	283	83	58	1	0
Concessional	1	27	178	169	125	95	75	58	1	0
Bilateral	12	132	125	132	91	21	0	0	0	0
Concessional	12	105	109	126	88	21	0	0	0	0
Private creditors	19	263	6	59	3	0	0	0	0	0
Bonds	0	0	0	0	0	0	0	0	0	0
Commercial banks	0	92	3	13	0	0	0	0	0	0
Other private	19	171	3	46	3	0	0	0	0	0
Private nonguaranteed	**0**	**0**	**0**	**0**	**0**	**0**	**0**	**0**	**0**	**0**
Bonds	0	0	0	0	0	0	0	0	0	0
Commercial banks	0	0	0	0	0	0	0	0	0	0
Memo:										
IBRD	0	23	10	17	21	48	7	0	0	0
IDA	1	20	125	138	89	66	54	48	1	0
PRINCIPAL REPAYMENTS	**28**	**192**	**80**	**98**	**49**	**41**	**29**	**4**	**0**	**0**
Public and publicly guaranteed	**28**	**192**	**80**	**98**	**49**	**41**	**29**	**4**	**0**	**0**
Official creditors	6	102	57	63	34	28	24	4	0	0
Multilateral	1	12	36	36	28	27	23	4	0	0
Concessional	1	0	4	6	4	5	5	4	0	0
Bilateral	5	90	21	27	6	1	1	0	0	0
Concessional	4	2	6	3	5	0	0	0	0	0
Private creditors	23	90	23	35	15	13	5	0	0	0
Bonds	0	0	0	0	0	0	0	0	0	0
Commercial banks	0	36	14	14	5	4	0	0	0	0
Other private	22	53	9	21	10	10	5	0	0	0
Private nonguaranteed	**0**	**0**	**0**	**0**	**0**	**0**	**0**	**0**	**0**	**0**
Bonds	0	0	0	0	0	0	0	0	0	0
Commercial banks	0	0	0	0	0	0	0	0	0	0
Memo:										
IBRD	1	6	18	21	5	14	10	0	0	0
IDA	0	0	2	2	2	3	5	3	0	0
NET FLOWS ON DEBT	**3**	**271**	**330**	**353**	**267**	**263**	**54**	**53**	**1**	**0**
Public and publicly guaranteed	**3**	**271**	**330**	**353**	**267**	**263**	**54**	**53**	**1**	**0**
Official creditors	7	98	346	329	279	276	58	53	1	0
Multilateral	-1	56	243	224	194	256	59	53	1	0
Concessional	0	27	174	163	121	90	70	53	1	0
Bilateral	7	42	104	105	85	20	-1	0	0	0
Concessional	8	102	104	123	84	21	0	0	0	0
Private creditors	-4	173	-17	25	-12	-13	-5	0	0	0
Bonds	0	0	0	0	0	0	0	0	0	0
Commercial banks	0	56	-11	-1	-5	-4	0	0	0	0
Other private	-4	117	-6	25	-7	-10	-5	0	0	0
Private nonguaranteed	**0**	**0**	**0**	**0**	**0**	**0**	**0**	**0**	**0**	**0**
Bonds	0	0	0	0	0	0	0	0	0	0
Commercial banks	0	0	0	0	0	0	0	0	0	0
Memo:										
IBRD	-1	17	-8	-4	16	34	-3	0	0	0
IDA	1	20	123	136	87	63	49	45	1	0

ZAIRE

(US$ million, unless otherwise indicated)

	1970	1980	1988	1989	1990	1991	1992	1993	1994	1995
INTEREST PAYMENTS (LINT)	**9**	**205**	**97**	**94**	**89**	**56**	**27**	**7**	**0**	**0**
Public and publicly guaranteed	**9**	**205**	**97**	**94**	**89**	**56**	**27**	**7**	**0**	**0**
Official creditors	5	105	84	60	76	50	26	7	0	0
Multilateral	0	11	35	29	40	43	26	7	0	0
Concessional	0	2	9	7	11	10	12	7	0	0
Bilateral	5	94	48	31	36	7	0	0	0	0
Concessional	5	45	5	8	8	5	0	0	0	0
Private creditors	4	99	14	34	12	7	1	0	0	0
Bonds	0	1	0	1	0	0	0	0	0	0
Commercial banks	0	69	7	27	6	2	0	0	0	0
Other private	4	30	7	6	6	4	1	0	0	0
Private nonguaranteed	**0**	**0**	**0**	**0**	**0**	**0**	**0**	**0**	**0**	**0**
Bonds	0	0	0	0	0	0	0	0	0	0
Commercial banks	0	0	0	0	0	0	0	0	0	0
Memo:										
IBRD	0	8	4	3	1	6	7	1	0	0
IDA	0	1	8	6	7	8	9	5	0	0
NET TRANSFERS ON DEBT	**-6**	**67**	**232**	**260**	**179**	**207**	**27**	**46**	**1**	**0**
Public and publicly guaranteed	**-6**	**67**	**232**	**260**	**179**	**207**	**27**	**46**	**1**	**0**
Official creditors	2	-7	263	269	203	226	32	46	1	0
Multilateral	-1	45	207	195	154	213	34	46	1	0
Concessional	-1	25	165	156	111	80	58	47	1	0
Bilateral	3	-52	56	74	49	13	-1	0	0	0
Concessional	3	57	98	115	76	17	0	0	0	0
Private creditors	-7	74	-31	-9	-24	-20	-5	0	0	0
Bonds	0	-1	-1	-1	-1	-1	0	0	0	0
Commercial banks	0	-14	-18	-28	-11	-6	0	0	0	0
Other private	-7	88	-12	19	-13	-14	-5	0	0	0
Private nonguaranteed	**0**	**0**	**0**	**0**	**0**	**0**	**0**	**0**	**0**	**0**
Bonds	0	0	0	0	0	0	0	0	0	0
Commercial banks	0	0	0	0	0	0	0	0	0	0
Memo:										
IBRD	-2	9	-12	-8	14	28	-9	-1	0	0
IDA	1	19	116	129	80	54	41	41	1	0
DEBT SERVICE (LTDS)	**37**	**397**	**177**	**192**	**137**	**98**	**56**	**12**	**1**	**0**
Public and publicly guaranteed	**37**	**397**	**177**	**192**	**137**	**98**	**56**	**12**	**1**	**0**
Official creditors	11	208	141	123	110	78	50	12	1	0
Multilateral	2	24	72	65	68	70	49	12	1	0
Concessional	1	2	13	13	15	16	17	11	1	0
Bilateral	10	184	69	58	42	8	1	0	0	0
Concessional	9	48	11	11	13	5	0	0	0	0
Private creditors	26	189	37	69	27	20	5	0	0	0
Bonds	0	1	1	1	1	1	0	0	0	0
Commercial banks	0	105	21	41	11	6	0	0	0	0
Other private	26	83	15	27	16	14	5	0	0	0
Private nonguaranteed	**0**	**0**	**0**	**0**	**0**	**0**	**0**	**0**	**0**	**0**
Bonds	0	0	0	0	0	0	0	0	0	0
Commercial banks	0	0	0	0	0	0	0	0	0	0
Memo:										
IBRD	2	14	22	24	6	20	16	1	0	0
IDA	0	1	9	9	9	11	13	8	0	0
UNDISBURSED DEBT	**288**	**818**	**1,617**	**1,779**	**1,659**	**1,395**	**1,209**	**1,050**	**943**	**962**
Official creditors	52	743	1,471	1,704	1,595	1,340	1,158	1,002	891	906
Private creditors	236	75	146	75	65	55	52	48	52	57
Memorandum items										
Concessional LDOD	221	862	2,032	2,635	3,144	3,269	3,214	3,222	3,409	3,519
Variable rate LDOD	0	508	440	1,051	1,369	1,403	1,359	1,327	1,372	1,406
Public sector LDOD	311	4,071	6,941	7,966	9,006	9,257	8,934	8,755	9,266	9,606
Private sector LDOD	0	0	0	0	0	14	14	14	15	15

6. CURRENCY COMPOSITION OF LONG-TERM DEBT (PERCENT)

	1970	1980	1988	1989	1990	1991	1992	1993	1994	1995
Deutsche mark	2.2	5.9	5.7	6.4	6.9	6.6	6.5	6.2	6.5	6.8
French franc	3.8	13.6	14.4	15.3	16.4	16.0	15.6	14.9	15.5	16.3
Japanese yen	0.0	1.5	3.8	3.1	3.0	3.1	3.3	3.7	3.9	3.7
Pound sterling	2.4	4.1	1.8	1.1	1.2	1.1	0.9	0.9	0.9	0.9
Swiss franc	0.0	0.4	0.2	0.2	0.2	0.2	0.2	0.2	0.2	0.3
U.S.dollars	41.5	42.2	44.5	44.4	41.4	40.9	42.5	43.9	42.1	40.9
Multiple currency	1.6	2.1	2.0	2.4	3.2	4.0	4.1	4.2	4.3	4.2
Special drawing rights	0.0	0.0	0.2	0.2	0.2	0.4	0.4	0.4	0.4	0.4
All other currencies	48.5	30.3	27.3	26.8	27.5	27.6	26.6	25.6	26.2	26.7

ZAIRE

(US$ million, unless otherwise indicated)

	1970	1980	1988	1989	1990	1991	1992	1993	1994	1995
7. DEBT RESTRUCTURINGS										
Total amount rescheduled	0	..	239	1,275	446	0	0	0	0	0
Debt stock rescheduled	0	..	0	0	0	0	0	0	0	0
Principal rescheduled	0	..	92	556	259	0	0	0	0	0
Official	0	..	82	507	252	0	0	0	0	0
Private	0	..	10	49	7	0	0	0	0	0
Interest rescheduled	0	..	89	419	131	0	0	0	0	0
Official	0	..	85	413	129	0	0	0	0	0
Private	0	..	4	6	2	0	0	0	0	0
Debt forgiven	..	..	324	122	9	0	0	0	0	0
Memo: interest forgiven	..	..	0	41	15	0	0	0	0	0
Debt stock reduction	0	..	0	0	0	0	0	0	0	0
of which debt buyback	0	..	0	0	0	0	0	0	0	0
8. DEBT STOCK-FLOW RECONCILIATION										
Total change in debt stocks	..	..	..	677	1,031	556	137	307	1,052	815
Net flows on debt	..	..	..	228	89	125	-28	0	-140	61
Net change in interest arrears	..	..	..	-200	125	428	560	539	653	404
Interest capitalized	..	..	..	419	131	0	0	0	0	0
Debt forgiveness or reduction	..	..	..	-122	-9	0	0	0	0	0
Cross-currency valuation	..	..	..	80	598	-18	-296	-209	489	338
Residual	..	..	..	273	98	21	-99	-23	50	11
9. AVERAGE TERMS OF NEW COMMITMENTS										
ALL CREDITORS										
Interest (%)	6.5	5.1	3.9	4.0	5.8	2.5	12.0	0.0	0.0	2.5
Maturity (years)	12.5	22.7	27.5	29.0	23.4	34.5	7.3	0.0	0.0	19.9
Grace period (years)	3.6	6.3	8.4	8.4	6.0	8.7	0.3	0.0	0.0	4.4
Grant element (%)	18.3	39.4	48.3	48.1	30.8	67.5	-6.8	0.0	0.0	48.7
Official creditors										
Interest (%)	2.6	2.8	3.6	4.0	5.8	2.5	12.0	0.0	0.0	2.5
Maturity (years)	32.6	28.9	28.5	29.0	23.4	34.5	7.3	0.0	0.0	19.9
Grace period (years)	8.5	8.5	8.7	8.4	6.0	8.7	0.3	0.0	0.0	4.4
Grant element (%)	59.8	57.2	50.9	48.1	30.8	67.5	-6.8	0.0	0.0	48.7
Private creditors										
Interest (%)	6.9	9.8	7.2	0.0	0.0	0.0	0.0	0.0	0.0	0.0
Maturity (years)	10.1	9.5	16.2	0.0	0.0	0.0	0.0	0.0	0.0	0.0
Grace period (years)	3.0	1.6	4.9	0.0	0.0	0.0	0.0	0.0	0.0	0.0
Grant element (%)	13.3	1.6	19.6	0.0	0.0	0.0	0.0	0.0	0.0	0.0
Memorandum items										
Commitments	258	438	483	708	109	92	4	0	0	14
Official creditors	27	298	443	708	109	92	4	0	0	14
Private creditors	231	140	40	0	0	0	0	0	0	0

10. CONTRACTUAL OBLIGATIONS ON OUTSTANDING LONG-TERM DEBT

	1996	1997	1998	1999	2000	2001	2002	2003	2004	2005
TOTAL										
Disbursements	6	6	4	2	1	1	0	0	0	0
Principal	334	328	381	368	347	333	313	209	213	207
Interest	231	210	191	169	149	129	111	96	86	76
Official creditors										
Disbursements	6	6	4	2	1	1	0	0	0	0
Principal	314	311	365	364	347	332	313	209	213	207
Interest	228	209	190	169	149	129	111	96	86	76
Bilateral creditors										
Disbursements	2	4	3	2	1	1	0	0	0	0
Principal	221	216	269	271	252	252	248	145	149	149
Interest	178	163	149	133	117	102	86	74	66	58
Multilateral creditors										
Disbursements	4	2	1	0	0	0	0	0	0	0
Principal	93	95	96	93	95	81	65	64	64	58
Interest	51	46	41	36	32	27	24	22	20	18
Private creditors										
Disbursements	0	0	0	0	0	0	0	0	0	0
Principal	20	17	16	3	0	1	1	1	1	1
Interest	2	2	1	0	0	0	0	0	0	0
Commercial banks										
Disbursements	0	0	0	0	0	0	0	0	0	0
Principal	0	0	0	0	0	0	0	0	0	0
Interest	0	0	0	0	0	0	0	0	0	0
Other private										
Disbursements	0	0	0	0	0	0	0	0	0	0
Principal	20	17	16	3	0	1	1	1	1	1
Interest	2	2	1	0	0	0	0	0	0	0

ZAMBIA

(US$ million, unless otherwise indicated)

1. SUMMARY DEBT DATA

	1970	1980	1988	1989	1990	1991	1992	1993	1994	1995
TOTAL DEBT STOCKS (EDT)	..	3,261	6,863	6,729	7,265	7,335	7,001	6,819	6,611	6,853
Long-term debt (LDOD)	654	2,227	4,460	4,252	4,882	5,050	4,799	4,722	4,911	5,091
Public and publicly guaranteed	624	2,141	4,460	4,252	4,880	5,046	4,785	4,708	4,897	5,078
Private nonguaranteed	30	87	0	0	2	4	14	13	14	14
Use of IMF credit	0	447	940	900	949	918	847	777	805	1,239
Short-term debt	..	586	1,463	1,577	1,435	1,367	1,356	1,320	896	523
of which interest arrears on LDOD	..	6	508	737	760	637	643	608	555	285
Official creditors	..	3	438	662	692	561	562	527	530	259
Private creditors	..	3	70	75	68	76	81	81	25	26
Memo: principal arrears on LDOD	..	33	1,193	1,496	1,516	1,467	1,455	1,437	1,426	727
Official creditors	..	21	1,000	1,268	1,411	1,351	1,349	1,316	1,359	651
Private creditors	..	13	193	228	104	116	106	121	67	76
Memo: export credits	..	..	900	1,143	1,123	1,095	894	979	1,175	1,066
TOTAL DEBT FLOWS										
Disbursements	363	693	244	213	165	384	293	290	249	2,550
Long-term debt	363	603	244	213	165	384	293	290	249	296
IMF purchases	0	90	0	0	0	0	0	0	0	2,253
Principal repayments	45	269	112	130	126	292	184	213	215	2,067
Long-term debt	41	212	112	112	101	258	148	143	194	242
IMF repurchases	4	57	0	18	25	34	37	70	21	1,825
Net flows on debt	318	424	285	-33	-100	147	92	77	34	379
of which short-term debt	..	..	153	-115	-139	55	-17	-1	0	-104
Interest payments (INT)	..	142	79	76	77	307	169	156	159	550
Long-term debt	31	116	78	76	72	238	98	95	117	129
IMF charges	0	26	1	0	2	66	69	60	41	419
Short-term debt	..	0	0	0	3	3	1	1	2	1
Net transfers on debt	..	282	207	-109	-177	-160	-77	-79	-125	-170
Total debt service paid (TDS)	..	411	191	206	203	599	353	369	374	2,616
Long-term debt	72	328	190	188	173	496	246	239	311	371
IMF repurchases and charges	4	84	1	18	27	100	106	129	62	2,244
Short-term debt (interest only)	..	0	0	0	3	3	1	1	2	1

2. AGGREGATE NET RESOURCE FLOWS AND NET TRANSFERS (LONG-TERM)

	1970	1980	1988	1989	1990	1991	1992	1993	1994	1995
NET RESOURCE FLOWS	26	524	467	458	930	586	838	680	471	482
Net flow of long-term debt (ex. IMF)	321	391	132	100	64	127	146	147	55	55
Foreign direct investment (net)	-297	62	93	164	203	34	50	55	60	66
Portfolio equity flows	0	0	0	0	0	0	0	0	0	0
Grants (excluding technical coop.)	2	71	242	194	663	426	642	478	355	362
Memo: technical coop. grants	13	87	121	127	129	129	144	165	135	165
NET TRANSFERS	-65	324	283	344	743	320	699	540	306	303
Interest on long-term debt	31	116	78	76	72	238	98	95	117	129
Profit remittances on FDI	60	84	106	38	115	28	40	45	48	50

3. MAJOR ECONOMIC AGGREGATES

	1970	1980	1988	1989	1990	1991	1992	1993	1994	1995
Gross national product (GNP)	1,742	3,594	3,318	3,588	3,008	2,993	2,859	3,347	3,218	3,581
Exports of goods & services (XGS)	..	1,625	1,251	1,427	1,362	1,189	1,222	1,071	1,202	1,296
of which workers remittances	..	0	0	0	0	0	0	0	0	0
Imports of goods & services (MGS)	..	1,987	1,580	1,726	2,336	1,811	2,115	1,660	1,750	2,150
International reserves (RES)	515	206	139	123	201	192	..	192	260	315
Current account balance	..	-516	-293	-219	-594	-306	-630	-320	-308	-550

4. DEBT INDICATORS

	1970	1980	1988	1989	1990	1991	1992	1993	1994	1995
EDT / XGS (%)	..	200.7	548.7	471.7	533.5	616.9	572.9	636.7	549.9	528.7
EDT / GNP (%)	..	90.7	206.8	187.6	241.5	245.1	244.9	203.7	205.5	191.3
TDS / XGS (%)	..	25.3	15.2	14.5	14.9	50.4	28.9	34.4	31.1	201.9
INT / XGS (%)	..	8.7	6.3	5.3	5.6	25.8	13.8	14.6	13.3	42.4
INT / GNP (%)	..	3.9	2.4	2.1	2.5	10.2	5.9	4.7	5.0	15.3
RES / EDT (%)	..	6.3	2.0	1.8	2.8	2.6	..	2.8	3.9	4.6
RES / MGS (months)	..	1.2	1.1	0.9	1.0	1.3	..	1.4	1.8	1.8
Short-term / EDT (%)	..	18.0	21.3	23.4	19.7	18.6	19.4	19.4	13.6	7.6
Concessional / EDT (%)	..	25.4	26.6	24.0	31.7	37.2	38.2	41.9	48.7	50.7
Multilateral / EDT (%)	..	12.2	17.6	18.4	19.5	20.6	22.7	25.9	30.1	31.9

ZAMBIA

(US$ million, unless otherwise indicated)

	1970	1980	1988	1989	1990	1991	1992	1993	1994	1995
5. LONG-TERM DEBT										
DEBT OUTSTANDING (LDOD)	**654**	**2,227**	**4,460**	**4,252**	**4,882**	**5,050**	**4,799**	**4,722**	**4,911**	**5,091**
Public and publicly guaranteed	**624**	**2,141**	**4,460**	**4,252**	**4,880**	**5,046**	**4,785**	**4,708**	**4,897**	**5,078**
Official creditors	120	1,501	3,861	3,654	4,406	4,632	4,422	4,388	4,703	4,917
Multilateral	61	397	1,205	1,239	1,418	1,514	1,589	1,764	1,987	2,186
Concessional	39	49	494	526	613	888	1,044	1,272	1,538	1,792
Bilateral	59	1,105	2,655	2,415	2,988	3,118	2,832	2,624	2,716	2,731
Concessional	51	778	1,331	1,092	1,688	1,840	1,631	1,584	1,679	1,681
Private creditors	503	639	599	599	474	414	363	320	194	160
Bonds	55	3	0	0	0	0	0	0	0	0
Commercial banks	0	77	70	70	70	73	73	73	7	13
Other private	449	560	529	529	404	341	290	247	187	148
Private nonguaranteed	**30**	**87**	**0**	**0**	**2**	**4**	**14**	**13**	**14**	**14**
Bonds	0	0	0	0	0	0	0	0	0	0
Commercial banks	30	87	0	0	2	4	14	13	14	14
Memo:										
IBRD	61	346	508	501	539	373	289	240	201	163
IDA	0	2	254	253	274	493	643	817	1,043	1,270
DISBURSEMENTS	**363**	**603**	**244**	**213**	**165**	**384**	**293**	**290**	**249**	**296**
Public and publicly guaranteed	**351**	**597**	**244**	**213**	**163**	**382**	**283**	**289**	**247**	**295**
Official creditors	22	314	202	120	117	338	261	279	240	277
Multilateral	6	60	84	56	106	284	248	276	225	277
Concessional	1	10	41	35	41	278	215	252	210	240
Bilateral	16	254	118	65	11	54	13	4	16	0
Concessional	16	237	82	43	9	21	9	4	2	0
Private creditors	330	282	42	92	46	45	23	10	7	18
Bonds	0	0	0	0	0	0	0	0	0	0
Commercial banks	0	9	0	0	0	3	0	0	7	8
Other private	330	273	42	92	46	42	23	10	0	10
Private nonguaranteed	**11**	**6**	**0**	**0**	**2**	**2**	**10**	**1**	**2**	**1**
Bonds	0	0	0	0	0	0	0	0	0	0
Commercial banks	11	6	0	0	2	2	10	1	2	1
Memo:										
IBRD	6	28	1	0	0	0	0	0	0	0
IDA	0	2	6	4	3	210	174	174	186	209
PRINCIPAL REPAYMENTS	**41**	**212**	**112**	**112**	**101**	**258**	**148**	**143**	**194**	**242**
Public and publicly guaranteed	**35**	**181**	**112**	**112**	**101**	**258**	**148**	**141**	**192**	**241**
Official creditors	6	37	37	30	44	204	102	92	119	186
Multilateral	4	18	21	12	39	200	99	87	101	126
Concessional	4	4	1	1	5	14	10	10	13	18
Bilateral	2	18	17	18	6	4	3	6	18	60
Concessional	1	3	6	2	0	0	0	4	12	35
Private creditors	29	144	75	82	57	54	46	49	73	54
Bonds	7	3	0	0	0	0	0	0	0	0
Commercial banks	0	4	0	0	0	0	0	0	8	2
Other private	22	137	75	82	57	54	46	49	66	52
Private nonguaranteed	**6**	**31**	**0**	**0**	**0**	**0**	**0**	**2**	**2**	**1**
Bonds	0	0	0	0	0	0	0	0	0	0
Commercial banks	6	31	0	0	0	0	0	2	2	1
Memo:										
IBRD	4	18	1	0	5	168	71	51	55	50
IDA	0	0	0	0	0	1	1	1	1	2
NET FLOWS ON DEBT	**321**	**391**	**132**	**100**	**64**	**127**	**146**	**147**	**55**	**55**
Public and publicly guaranteed	**316**	**416**	**132**	**100**	**62**	**125**	**136**	**148**	**55**	**55**
Official creditors	16	278	165	90	73	134	159	187	122	91
Multilateral	1	42	63	44	67	84	149	189	124	151
Concessional	-3	5	40	34	36	263	206	242	197	222
Bilateral	15	236	102	47	6	49	10	-2	-2	-60
Concessional	15	234	77	41	9	21	9	-1	-10	-35
Private creditors	300	138	-33	10	-11	-9	-24	-39	-67	-36
Bonds	-7	-3	0	0	0	0	0	0	0	0
Commercial banks	0	5	0	0	0	3	0	0	-1	6
Other private	307	136	-33	10	-11	-12	-24	-39	-66	-42
Private nonguaranteed	**5**	**-25**	**0**	**0**	**2**	**2**	**10**	**-1**	**0**	**0**
Bonds	0	0	0	0	0	0	0	0	0	0
Commercial banks	5	-25	0	0	2	2	10	-1	0	0
Memo:										
IBRD	1	10	0	0	-5	-168	-71	-51	-55	-50
IDA	0	2	6	4	3	209	173	173	185	207

ZAMBIA

(US$ million, unless otherwise indicated)

	1970	1980	1988	1989	1990	1991	1992	1993	1994	1995
INTEREST PAYMENTS (LINT)	**31**	**116**	**78**	**76**	**72**	**238**	**98**	**95**	**117**	**129**
Public and publicly guaranteed	**29**	**106**	**78**	**76**	**72**	**238**	**98**	**95**	**117**	**129**
Official creditors	6	53	43	45	43	219	79	80	106	113
Multilateral	4	33	23	16	33	216	68	58	61	63
Concessional	2	2	6	4	4	20	12	16	16	19
Bilateral	2	20	19	29	10	3	11	22	44	50
Concessional	2	13	7	4	9	0	8	10	24	20
Private creditors	23	53	35	31	29	20	20	15	11	16
Bonds	3	1	0	0	0	0	0	0	0	0
Commercial banks	0	12	0	0	0	0	0	0	0	1
Other private	20	40	35	31	29	20	20	15	11	15
Private nonguaranteed	**2**	**10**	**0**	**0**	**0**	**0**	**0**	**0**	**0**	**0**
Bonds	0	0	0	0	0	0	0	0	0	0
Commercial banks	2	10	0	0	0	0	0	0	0	0
Memo:										
IBRD	4	31	0	0	1	177	36	21	21	15
IDA	0	0	0	0	0	10	6	5	6	9
NET TRANSFERS ON DEBT	**291**	**275**	**54**	**24**	**-8**	**-112**	**48**	**52**	**-62**	**-74**
Public and publicly guaranteed	**287**	**310**	**54**	**24**	**-10**	**-114**	**37**	**53**	**-62**	**-74**
Official creditors	10	224	122	46	30	-85	80	106	16	-23
Multilateral	-2	9	40	27	34	-131	81	130	62	88
Concessional	-5	3	34	30	33	244	194	226	181	203
Bilateral	12	216	82	18	-4	47	-1	-24	-46	-111
Concessional	13	221	69	37	1	21	1	-11	-34	-55
Private creditors	278	85	-68	-21	-40	-29	-43	-54	-78	-52
Bonds	-10	-4	0	0	0	0	0	0	0	0
Commercial banks	0	-6	0	0	0	3	0	0	-1	6
Other private	288	96	-68	-21	-40	-32	-43	-54	-77	-57
Private nonguaranteed	**3**	**-35**	**0**	**0**	**2**	**2**	**10**	**-1**	**0**	**0**
Bonds	0	0	0	0	0	0	0	0	0	0
Commercial banks	3	-35	0	0	2	2	10	-1	0	0
Memo:										
IBRD	-2	-21	0	0	-5	-344	-107	-72	-76	-65
IDA	0	2	5	4	3	199	168	168	179	198
DEBT SERVICE (LTDS)	**72**	**328**	**190**	**188**	**173**	**496**	**246**	**239**	**311**	**371**
Public and publicly guaranteed	**64**	**287**	**190**	**188**	**173**	**496**	**246**	**236**	**309**	**369**
Official creditors	12	90	80	75	88	423	180	173	224	300
Multilateral	8	51	44	28	72	416	167	145	162	189
Concessional	6	6	7	5	8	34	22	26	29	37
Bilateral	4	39	36	46	16	7	14	27	62	111
Concessional	3	16	13	6	9	0	8	15	36	55
Private creditors	52	197	110	113	85	73	66	64	85	70
Bonds	10	4	0	0	0	0	0	0	0	0
Commercial banks	0	16	0	0	0	0	0	0	8	3
Other private	42	177	110	113	85	73	66	64	77	67
Private nonguaranteed	**8**	**41**	**0**	**0**	**0**	**0**	**0**	**2**	**2**	**1**
Bonds	0	0	0	0	0	0	0	0	0	0
Commercial banks	8	41	0	0	0	0	0	2	2	1
Memo:										
IBRD	8	48	1	0	5	344	107	72	76	65
IDA	0	0	0	0	0	10	6	6	8	11
UNDISBURSED DEBT	**309**	**884**	**677**	**626**	**689**	**573**	**620**	**528**	**572**	**577**
Official creditors	291	686	653	576	610	545	603	528	563	576
Private creditors	18	198	24	49	79	28	17	0	9	0
Memorandum items										
Concessional LDOD	90	827	1,825	1,618	2,301	2,728	2,676	2,856	3,217	3,473
Variable rate LDOD	30	280	603	555	521	549	520	497	449	454
Public sector LDOD	624	2,124	4,459	4,252	4,879	5,046	4,784	4,708	4,897	5,077
Private sector LDOD	30	104	0	0	3	5	14	13	14	14

6. CURRENCY COMPOSITION OF LONG-TERM DEBT (PERCENT)

	1970	1980	1988	1989	1990	1991	1992	1993	1994	1995
Deutsche mark	0.4	9.4	13.0	9.5	13.8	13.8	11.9	10.1	11.0	11.3
French franc	0.9	3.2	3.1	3.4	2.8	3.2	3.2	3.0	3.1	3.3
Japanese yen	0.0	4.8	9.3	8.7	9.3	9.3	9.5	10.1	9.8	9.1
Pound sterling	17.7	11.1	8.2	7.4	9.8	10.2	8.6	7.4	7.5	7.0
Swiss franc	0.0	0.0	0.5	0.5	0.5	0.5	0.5	0.6	0.1	0.1
U.S.dollars	53.7	20.1	28.9	31.3	26.8	29.8	34.2	38.8	41.0	43.4
Multiple currency	9.8	16.6	15.2	15.8	16.4	13.1	12.5	12.0	11.3	10.7
Special drawing rights	0.0	0.0	0.7	1.0	1.0	0.9	1.0	0.0	0.0	0.0
All other currencies	17.4	34.9	21.1	22.5	19.6	19.2	18.5	17.9	16.3	15.2

ZAMBIA

(US$ million, unless otherwise indicated)

	1970	1980	1988	1989	1990	1991	1992	1993	1994	1995
7. DEBT RESTRUCTURINGS										
Total amount rescheduled	0	0	22	0	879	268	269	192	146	35
Debt stock rescheduled	0	0	0	0	38	36	0	0	0	0
Principal rescheduled	0	0	22	0	498	131	118	110	75	0
Official	0	0	0	0	342	100	101	105	74	0
Private	0	0	22	0	156	31	17	5	0	0
Interest rescheduled	0	0	0	0	333	64	121	81	68	0
Official	0	0	0	0	299	53	120	80	67	0
Private	0	0	0	0	34	11	1	1	1	0
Debt forgiven	..	..	0	188	114	76	294	282	84	8
Memo: interest forgiven	..	..	0	1	22	13	14	31	67	1
Debt stock reduction	0	0	0	0	26	0	0	0	446	2
of which debt buyback	0	0	0	0	0	0	0	0	8	0
8. DEBT STOCK-FLOW RECONCILIATION										
Total change in debt stocks	..	..	..	-134	536	70	-334	-182	-207	241
Net flows on debt	..	..	..	-33	-100	147	92	77	34	379
Net change in interest arrears	..	..	..	229	23	-123	6	-35	-53	-270
Interest capitalized	..	..	..	0	333	64	121	81	68	0
Debt forgiveness or reduction	..	..	..	-188	-140	-76	-294	-282	-522	-10
Cross-currency valuation	..	..	..	-80	353	-49	-202	-31	150	57
Residual	..	..	..	-62	68	106	-58	8	116	84
9. AVERAGE TERMS OF NEW COMMITMENTS										
ALL CREDITORS										
Interest (%)	4.2	6.7	5.3	7.3	8.1	1.1	1.3	1.3	1.3	1.1
Maturity (years)	26.7	18.8	16.8	18.7	12.6	39.2	39.3	39.8	36.1	38.5
Grace period (years)	9.1	4.5	5.6	4.1	4.9	9.9	9.6	9.8	9.3	9.8
Grant element (%)	43.5	22.3	32.6	21.9	13.0	76.0	72.6	74.6	73.1	77.7
Official creditors										
Interest (%)	1.4	3.8	3.8	1.6	6.3	1.0	1.2	1.3	1.0	0.8
Maturity (years)	46.0	29.2	20.4	39.1	16.0	39.5	40.4	39.8	37.8	39.6
Grace period (years)	19.2	8.5	7.4	8.4	7.0	10.0	9.9	9.8	9.7	10.1
Grant element (%)	80.7	48.5	44.1	61.0	23.3	76.7	74.5	74.6	76.7	80.4
Private creditors										
Interest (%)	6.6	8.8	8.3	11.0	11.0	8.8	3.5	0.0	6.0	10.0
Maturity (years)	10.4	11.0	9.2	5.5	6.9	6.0	2.6	0.0	4.8	8.3
Grace period (years)	0.5	1.4	1.9	1.4	1.4	0.5	0.3	0.0	1.9	2.8
Grant element (%)	12.1	2.6	8.5	-3.4	-4.1	2.6	8.1	0.0	10.4	-1.0
Memorandum items										
Commitments	557	645	95	203	192	324	387	243	282	303
Official creditors	255	277	64	80	120	321	376	243	267	293
Private creditors	302	368	31	123	72	3	11	0	15	10

10. CONTRACTUAL OBLIGATIONS ON OUTSTANDING LONG-TERM DEBT	1996	1997	1998	1999	2000	2001	2002	2003	2004	2005
TOTAL										
Disbursements	169	158	105	70	38	19	12	1	0	0
Principal	240	171	146	216	268	264	249	233	219	164
Interest	162	150	141	133	120	107	94	81	71	61
Official creditors										
Disbursements	168	158	105	70	38	19	12	1	0	0
Principal	198	141	129	212	266	263	248	232	219	164
Interest	156	147	140	133	120	107	94	81	71	61
Bilateral creditors										
Disbursements	1	2	1	1	1	1	0	0	0	0
Principal	96	53	47	146	206	199	199	177	159	104
Interest	104	100	98	96	86	75	65	55	46	39
Multilateral creditors										
Disbursements	167	156	104	69	37	18	11	1	0	0
Principal	101	88	83	66	60	64	49	55	60	59
Interest	52	46	42	38	34	31	28	26	25	23
Private creditors										
Disbursements	0	0	0	0	0	0	0	0	0	0
Principal	42	31	16	4	2	2	1	1	0	0
Interest	6	3	1	0	0	0	0	0	0	0
Commercial banks										
Disbursements	0	0	0	0	0	0	0	0	0	0
Principal	4	4	4	2	0	0	0	0	0	0
Interest	1	1	0	0	0	0	0	0	0	0
Other private										
Disbursements	0	0	0	0	0	0	0	0	0	0
Principal	38	27	13	2	2	2	1	1	0	0
Interest	5	2	1	0	0	0	0	0	0	0

ZIMBABWE

(US$ million, unless otherwise indicated)

	1970	*1980*	*1988*	*1989*	*1990*	*1991*	*1992*	*1993*	*1994*	*1995*
1. SUMMARY DEBT DATA										
TOTAL DEBT STOCKS (EDT)	..	**786**	**2,668**	**2,791**	**3,247**	**3,436**	**4,006**	**4,210**	**4,411**	**4,885**
Long-term debt (LDOD)	**229**	**696**	**2,297**	**2,352**	**2,649**	**2,876**	**3,084**	**3,329**	**3,539**	**3,741**
Public and publicly guaranteed	229	696	2,228	2,276	2,464	2,612	2,788	3,023	3,296	3,360
Private nonguaranteed	0	0	69	76	185	264	296	306	243	381
Use of IMF credit	**0**	**0**	**70**	**29**	**7**	**0**	**216**	**282**	**376**	**461**
Short-term debt	..	**90**	**301**	**410**	**591**	**561**	**706**	**600**	**496**	**684**
of which interest arrears on LDOD	..	0	1	1	0	0	0	0	0	1
Official creditors	..	0	1	1	0	0	0	0	0	1
Private creditors	..	0	0	0	0	0	0	0	0	0
Memo: principal arrears on LDOD	..	0	0	1	0	0	0	2	15	55
Official creditors	..	0	0	1	0	0	0	2	15	33
Private creditors	..	0	0	0	0	0	0	0	0	23
Memo: export credits	..	..	534	615	660	652	935	795	808	718
TOTAL DEBT FLOWS										
Disbursements	**0**	**132**	**276**	**357**	**424**	**498**	**985**	**776**	**477**	**574**
Long-term debt	0	132	276	357	424	498	764	709	402	494
IMF purchases	0	0	0	0	0	0	221	67	75	80
Principal repayments	**5**	**40**	**356**	**264**	**270**	**266**	**391**	**409**	**380**	**410**
Long-term debt	5	40	277	225	247	260	391	409	380	410
IMF repurchases	0	0	78	38	24	7	0	0	0	0
Net flows on debt	**-5**	**93**	**-40**	**202**	**335**	**201**	**740**	**261**	**-7**	**350**
of which short-term debt	..	..	40	109	181	-30	146	-106	-104	187
Interest payments (INT)	..	**26**	**178**	**175**	**201**	**195**	**207**	**211**	**228**	**240**
Long-term debt	5	10	147	138	149	147	157	168	190	192
IMF charges	0	0	9	5	2	0	6	10	10	13
Short-term debt	..	15	22	33	49	48	45	33	28	35
Net transfers on debt	..	**67**	**-218**	**27**	**134**	**7**	**532**	**50**	**-235**	**110**
Total debt service paid (TDS)	..	**65**	**533**	**439**	**471**	**461**	**599**	**620**	**608**	**651**
Long-term debt	9	50	424	363	396	406	548	577	570	602
IMF repurchases and charges	0	0	87	43	26	7	6	10	10	13
Short-term debt (interest only)	..	15	22	33	49	48	45	33	28	35
2. AGGREGATE NET RESOURCE FLOWS AND NET TRANSFERS (LONG-TERM)										
NET RESOURCE FLOWS	**-5**	**221**	**112**	**250**	**364**	**457**	**723**	**479**	**371**	**450**
Net flow of long-term debt (ex. IMF)	-5	93	-2	131	177	238	373	300	22	84
Foreign direct investment (net)	0	2	-18	-10	-12	3	15	28	35	40
Portfolio equity flows	0	0	0	0	0	0	0	0	50	18
Grants (excluding technical coop.)	0	127	131	128	199	216	336	151	264	307
Memo: technical coop. grants	1	70	93	97	104	114	191	158	117	133
NET TRANSFERS	**-9**	**133**	**-97**	**42**	**122**	**239**	**493**	**250**	**110**	**183**
Interest on long-term debt	5	10	147	138	149	147	157	168	190	192
Profit remittances on FDI	0	78	62	70	92	71	74	61	70	75
3. MAJOR ECONOMIC AGGREGATES										
Gross national product (GNP)	1,481	5,281	6,071	6,298	6,549	6,257	5,109	5,267	5,484	6,190
Exports of goods & services (XGS)	..	1,724	1,873	1,961	2,035	1,993	1,859	2,016	2,372	..
of which workers remittances	..	9	0	0	0	0	0	0	0	..
Imports of goods & services (MGS)	..	1,895	1,809	2,012	2,287	2,551	2,745	2,338	2,836	..
International reserves (RES)	59	419	341	274	295	295	405	628	585	888
Current account balance	..	-149	125	17	-140	-457	-604	-116	-425	..
4. DEBT INDICATORS										
EDT / XGS (%)	..	45.6	142.5	142.3	159.5	172.4	215.5	208.8	186.0	..
EDT / GNP (%)	..	14.9	43.9	44.3	49.6	54.9	78.4	79.9	80.4	78.9
TDS / XGS (%)	..	3.8	28.5	22.4	23.1	23.1	32.2	30.7	25.6	..
INT / XGS (%)	..	1.5	9.5	8.9	9.9	9.8	11.2	10.5	9.6	..
INT / GNP (%)	..	0.5	2.9	2.8	3.1	3.1	4.1	4.0	4.2	3.9
RES / EDT (%)	..	53.4	12.8	9.8	9.1	8.6	10.1	14.9	13.3	18.2
RES / MGS (months)	..	2.7	2.3	1.6	1.5	1.4	1.8	3.2	2.5	..
Short-term / EDT (%)	..	11.5	11.3	14.7	18.2	16.3	17.6	14.2	11.2	14.0
Concessional / EDT (%)	..	2.3	28.3	29.2	29.0	29.3	27.4	29.0	33.1	32.5
Multilateral / EDT (%)	..	0.4	20.1	20.4	19.6	21.2	24.1	31.1	34.3	33.1

ZIMBABWE

(US$ million, unless otherwise indicated)

	1970	1980	1988	1989	1990	1991	1992	1993	1994	1995
5. LONG-TERM DEBT										
DEBT OUTSTANDING (LDOD)	**229**	**696**	**2,297**	**2,352**	**2,649**	**2,876**	**3,084**	**3,329**	**3,539**	**3,741**
Public and publicly guaranteed	**229**	**696**	**2,228**	**2,276**	**2,464**	**2,612**	**2,788**	**3,023**	**3,296**	**3,360**
Official creditors	85	101	1,268	1,330	1,508	1,643	1,894	2,299	2,638	2,786
Multilateral	41	3	536	569	637	730	966	1,311	1,513	1,616
Concessional	41	3	121	144	164	182	255	329	475	550
Bilateral	44	98	732	761	871	913	927	988	1,125	1,170
Concessional	44	15	633	672	778	824	843	892	984	1,037
Private creditors	145	595	959	946	956	969	894	724	658	574
Bonds	145	592	426	356	293	263	210	180	150	120
Commercial banks	0	3	143	199	192	150	194	98	83	96
Other private	0	0	390	392	472	556	490	446	425	358
Private nonguaranteed	**0**	**0**	**69**	**76**	**185**	**264**	**296**	**306**	**243**	**381**
Bonds	0	0	0	0	0	0	0	0	0	0
Commercial banks	0	0	69	76	185	264	296	306	243	381
Memo:										
IBRD	41	3	347	353	381	410	442	528	556	560
IDA	0	0	61	62	67	68	138	200	313	336
DISBURSEMENTS	**0**	**132**	**276**	**357**	**424**	**498**	**764**	**709**	**402**	**494**
Public and publicly guaranteed	**0**	**132**	**246**	**327**	**297**	**385**	**678**	**619**	**369**	**265**
Official creditors	0	77	160	142	158	214	438	551	300	214
Multilateral	0	0	78	81	72	124	321	414	183	146
Concessional	0	0	31	26	11	21	93	88	131	75
Bilateral	0	77	82	61	86	90	117	137	118	68
Concessional	0	1	72	52	76	83	105	111	65	57
Private creditors	0	55	87	185	139	171	241	68	68	51
Bonds	0	52	0	0	0	0	0	0	0	0
Commercial banks	0	3	68	94	17	12	159	13	28	36
Other private	0	0	19	91	122	160	81	55	40	15
Private nonguaranteed	**0**	**0**	**29**	**29**	**127**	**112**	**86**	**90**	**33**	**229**
Bonds	0	0	0	0	0	0	0	0	0	0
Commercial banks	0	0	29	29	127	112	86	90	33	229
Memo:										
IBRD	0	0	22	47	40	52	76	114	33	32
IDA	0	0	6	3	0	0	75	63	102	15
PRINCIPAL REPAYMENTS	**5**	**40**	**277**	**225**	**247**	**260**	**391**	**409**	**380**	**410**
Public and publicly guaranteed	**5**	**40**	**266**	**213**	**229**	**227**	**337**	**329**	**284**	**319**
Official creditors	5	5	52	64	78	74	83	104	126	171
Multilateral	4	3	24	37	46	44	49	63	73	94
Concessional	4	3	4	4	4	4	6	8	9	16
Bilateral	1	2	28	26	32	30	34	41	53	76
Concessional	1	2	10	12	17	21	28	28	40	57
Private creditors	0	34	215	149	151	152	255	225	157	149
Bonds	0	19	57	43	30	27	52	30	30	30
Commercial banks	0	0	77	28	45	49	108	108	47	26
Other private	0	16	81	78	76	77	95	88	80	92
Private nonguaranteed	**0**	**0**	**11**	**13**	**18**	**33**	**54**	**80**	**96**	**91**
Bonds	0	0	0	0	0	0	0	0	0	0
Commercial banks	0	0	11	13	18	33	54	80	96	91
Memo:										
IBRD	4	3	17	30	33	33	33	36	41	48
IDA	0	0	0	0	0	0	0	1	1	1
NET FLOWS ON DEBT	**-5**	**93**	**-2**	**131**	**177**	**238**	**373**	**300**	**22**	**84**
Public and publicly guaranteed	**-5**	**93**	**-20**	**115**	**69**	**159**	**341**	**290**	**85**	**-54**
Official creditors	-5	72	108	79	80	140	355	448	174	43
Multilateral	-4	-3	54	44	26	80	272	352	109	52
Concessional	-4	-3	26	22	7	16	87	80	122	59
Bilateral	-1	75	54	35	54	60	83	96	65	-9
Concessional	-1	-1	62	40	59	62	77	82	25	0
Private creditors	0	21	-128	36	-12	19	-14	-158	-89	-97
Bonds	0	34	-57	-43	-30	-27	-52	-30	-30	-30
Commercial banks	0	3	-9	67	-28	-37	52	-95	-19	10
Other private	0	-16	-62	13	47	83	-14	-33	-40	-77
Private nonguaranteed	**0**	**0**	**19**	**16**	**109**	**79**	**32**	**10**	**-63**	**138**
Bonds	0	0	0	0	0	0	0	0	0	0
Commercial banks	0	0	19	16	109	79	32	10	-63	138
Memo:										
IBRD	-4	-3	5	17	7	19	43	78	-8	-16
IDA	0	0	6	3	0	0	75	62	101	15

ZIMBABWE

(US$ million, unless otherwise indicated)

	1970	1980	1988	1989	1990	1991	1992	1993	1994	1995
INTEREST PAYMENTS (LINT)	**5**	**10**	**147**	**138**	**149**	**147**	**157**	**168**	**190**	**192**
Public and publicly guaranteed	**5**	**10**	**142**	**132**	**141**	**132**	**133**	**147**	**157**	**166**
Official creditors	4	2	69	60	67	66	76	97	112	120
Multilateral	2	0	46	39	43	44	53	77	85	90
Concessional	2	0	2	3	3	3	4	6	6	9
Bilateral	2	1	23	21	24	22	23	20	27	31
Concessional	2	1	14	13	15	15	16	15	19	21
Private creditors	0	9	73	72	74	67	57	50	46	45
Bonds	0	7	13	15	13	11	10	8	7	6
Commercial banks	0	0	21	22	28	18	15	12	5	7
Other private	0	1	39	35	33	38	33	30	34	32
Private nonguaranteed	**0**	**0**	**5**	**6**	**9**	**15**	**24**	**22**	**33**	**26**
Bonds	0	0	0	0	0	0	0	0	0	0
Commercial banks	0	0	5	6	9	15	24	22	33	26
Memo:										
IBRD	2	0	37	31	33	33	35	39	44	46
IDA	0	0	1	0	1	1	1	1	2	3
NET TRANSFERS ON DEBT	**-9**	**82**	**-148**	**-6**	**28**	**91**	**216**	**132**	**-168**	**-108**
Public and publicly guaranteed	**-9**	**82**	**-162**	**-17**	**-72**	**27**	**208**	**143**	**-72**	**-220**
Official creditors	-9	71	39	18	13	74	279	351	62	-77
Multilateral	-6	-3	9	4	-17	36	219	275	25	-38
Concessional	-6	-3	24	19	5	14	83	75	116	50
Bilateral	-3	74	31	14	30	38	60	76	38	-39
Concessional	-3	-2	48	27	43	48	60	67	6	-20
Private creditors	-1	12	-201	-36	-85	-48	-71	-207	-135	-143
Bonds	-1	26	-70	-59	-43	-38	-61	-38	-37	-36
Commercial banks	0	3	-30	45	-56	-55	37	-107	-24	2
Other private	0	-17	-101	-22	13	45	-47	-63	-74	-109
Private nonguaranteed	**0**	**0**	**14**	**11**	**100**	**65**	**8**	**-12**	**-96**	**112**
Bonds	0	0	0	0	0	0	0	0	0	0
Commercial banks	0	0	14	11	100	65	8	-12	-96	112
Memo:										
IBRD	-6	-3	-33	-14	-26	-14	7	39	-52	-62
IDA	0	0	5	2	-1	-1	74	61	99	12
DEBT SERVICE (LTDS)	**9**	**50**	**424**	**363**	**396**	**406**	**548**	**577**	**570**	**602**
Public and publicly guaranteed	**9**	**50**	**409**	**345**	**370**	**359**	**470**	**476**	**441**	**485**
Official creditors	9	7	121	124	145	140	159	201	238	291
Multilateral	6	3	70	77	89	88	101	139	158	184
Concessional	6	3	7	7	7	7	10	14	15	25
Bilateral	3	4	51	47	56	52	57	62	80	107
Concessional	3	3	24	26	33	36	44	43	59	78
Private creditors	1	43	288	221	225	219	312	275	203	194
Bonds	1	26	70	59	43	38	61	38	37	36
Commercial banks	0	0	98	49	73	67	122	120	52	34
Other private	0	17	120	113	109	114	128	117	114	125
Private nonguaranteed	**0**	**0**	**16**	**18**	**27**	**47**	**78**	**102**	**129**	**117**
Bonds	0	0	0	0	0	0	0	0	0	0
Commercial banks	0	0	16	18	27	47	78	102	129	117
Memo:										
IBRD	6	3	54	61	67	66	68	75	84	94
IDA	0	0	1	0	1	1	1	2	3	3
UNDISBURSED DEBT	**0**	**86**	**949**	**829**	**1,035**	**1,577**	**1,484**	**1,375**	**1,395**	**1,174**
Official creditors	0	60	669	635	934	1,257	1,404	1,273	1,284	1,111
Private creditors	0	26	280	194	102	320	80	102	111	64
Memorandum items										
Concessional LDOD	85	18	755	815	942	1,006	1,098	1,220	1,459	1,587
Variable rate LDOD	0	3	500	576	699	770	889	890	817	955
Public sector LDOD	229	696	2,226	2,274	2,463	2,610	2,787	3,022	3,296	3,360
Private sector LDOD	0	0	71	78	186	265	297	307	244	381
6. CURRENCY COMPOSITION OF LONG-TERM DEBT (PERCENT)										
Deutsche mark	0.0	0.1	10.4	10.5	11.7	11.4	10.6	9.6	10.2	10.8
French franc	0.0	0.0	6.3	6.5	7.2	7.3	6.0	5.1	4.7	5.0
Japanese yen	0.0	0.0	2.1	1.8	2.1	2.6	2.7	3.2	3.4	3.2
Pound sterling	76.2	40.3	15.4	13.0	14.0	14.7	9.7	8.3	8.0	6.7
Swiss franc	0.0	0.0	0.9	0.9	1.2	0.9	0.8	0.8	0.8	0.9
U.S.dollars	0.3	0.4	32.0	33.5	30.3	27.8	30.8	26.7	26.5	24.6
Multiple currency	20.2	59.2	18.2	18.2	18.4	20.1	24.2	28.2	27.2	27.1
Special drawing rights	0.0	0.0	0.0	0.0	0.0	0.1	0.1	0.2	0.3	0.4
All other currencies	3.4	0.0	14.7	15.6	15.1	15.1	15.0	18.1	19.0	21.3

ZIMBABWE

(US$ million, unless otherwise indicated)

	1970	1980	1988	1989	1990	1991	1992	1993	1994	1995
7. DEBT RESTRUCTURINGS										
Total amount rescheduled	0	0	0	0	0	0	0	0	0	0
Debt stock rescheduled	0	0	0	0	0	0	0	0	0	0
Principal rescheduled	0	0	0	0	0	0	0	0	0	0
Official	0	0	0	0	0	0	0	0	0	0
Private	0	0	0	0	0	0	0	0	0	0
Interest rescheduled	0	0	0	0	0	0	0	0	0	0
Official	0	0	0	0	0	0	0	0	0	0
Private	0	0	0	0	0	0	0	0	0	0
Debt forgiven	..	..	0	0	24	8	1	0	0	0
Memo: interest forgiven	..	..	0	0	0	0	0	0	0	0
Debt stock reduction	0	0	0	0	0	0	0	0	0	0
of which debt buyback	0	0	0	0	0	0	0	0	0	0
8. DEBT STOCK-FLOW RECONCILIATION										
Total change in debt stocks	..	..	..	123	456	190	570	204	201	474
Net flows on debt	..	..	..	202	335	201	740	261	-7	350
Net change in interest arrears	..	..	..	1	-1	0	0	0	0	1
Interest capitalized	..	..	..	0	0	0	0	0	0	0
Debt forgiveness or reduction	..	..	..	0	-24	-8	-1	0	0	0
Cross-currency valuation	..	..	..	-42	206	-26	-156	-68	182	115
Residual	..	..	..	-38	-61	22	-13	11	26	8
9. AVERAGE TERMS OF NEW COMMITMENTS										
ALL CREDITORS										
Interest (%)	0.0	7.1	6.4	7.1	6.7	6.0	4.5	3.2	5.9	5.9
Maturity (years)	0.0	15.2	17.6	15.4	16.8	14.1	24.5	25.9	17.5	7.8
Grace period (years)	0.0	5.5	4.5	3.7	4.4	3.8	6.4	8.0	4.8	3.4
Grant element (%)	0.0	25.8	23.6	19.1	20.3	21.2	40.7	52.8	23.7	15.2
Official creditors										
Interest (%)	0.0	4.9	5.2	3.5	6.5	5.1	4.5	2.6	5.9	5.9
Maturity (years)	0.0	16.8	21.0	23.9	17.3	19.8	24.8	29.0	20.1	7.8
Grace period (years)	0.0	5.7	5.4	7.8	4.6	5.6	6.5	9.1	5.7	3.4
Grant element (%)	0.0	35.6	32.3	48.2	21.4	31.7	41.3	59.8	26.3	15.2
Private creditors										
Interest (%)	0.0	17.2	9.7	9.0	8.4	7.3	6.8	6.4	6.0	0.0
Maturity (years)	0.0	7.8	8.5	10.9	9.4	6.3	11.1	9.3	8.3	0.0
Grace period (years)	0.0	4.5	2.3	1.5	1.5	1.2	2.4	2.3	1.7	0.0
Grant element (%)	0.0	-18.7	0.3	3.6	5.2	6.4	14.0	15.8	14.8	0.0
Memorandum items										
Commitments	0	171	299	350	438	930	674	591	334	39
Official creditors	0	140	218	122	408	542	658	497	261	39
Private creditors	0	31	81	229	30	388	17	94	74	0

10. CONTRACTUAL OBLIGATIONS ON OUTSTANDING LONG-TERM DEBT

	1996	1997	1998	1999	2000	2001	2002	2003	2004	2005
TOTAL										
Disbursements	426	336	181	105	66	35	19	3	1	0
Principal	458	433	415	406	349	283	248	218	199	188
Interest	189	176	186	145	125	104	89	77	67	58
Official creditors										
Disbursements	385	319	176	104	66	35	19	3	1	0
Principal	212	225	239	248	257	241	227	199	187	182
Interest	129	132	127	119	108	96	85	74	65	57
Bilateral creditors										
Disbursements	79	80	48	29	16	8	4	0	0	0
Principal	70	72	76	76	78	79	77	69	73	73
Interest	32	32	31	29	28	26	24	22	20	19
Multilateral creditors										
Disbursements	306	240	128	75	50	28	15	3	1	0
Principal	142	153	163	172	179	162	149	130	115	109
Interest	97	100	96	89	81	71	61	52	45	39
Private creditors										
Disbursements	41	17	5	1	0	0	0	0	0	0
Principal	246	209	175	158	92	42	22	19	12	6
Interest	61	44	59	27	17	7	4	3	2	1
Commercial banks										
Disbursements	29	12	4	0	0	0	0	0	0	0
Principal	31	27	19	17	11	8	7	7	6	5
Interest	8	6	5	4	3	2	2	1	1	0
Other private										
Disbursements	12	5	1	1	0	0	0	0	0	0
Principal	215	182	156	142	81	34	15	13	6	1
Interest	53	38	54	23	15	5	3	2	1	1

Country notes

Albania

Data source. Data on long-term public and publicly guaranteed debt as of 1995 are based on reports provided by the country. Short-term debt data are from the BIS semiannual series on international bank lending and short-term export credits from the OECD.

Rescheduling. Albania concluded a rescheduling agreement with official creditors outside of formal Paris Club auspices in December 1993 and a debt buyback operation in 1995.

Algeria

Data source. Data on long-term public and publicly guaranteed debt as of 1995 are based on reports provided by the country. Short-term debt data are also as reported by the country.

Rescheduling. Projected debt service is based on contractual obligations on debt outstanding at the end of 1995. It includes the effect of the Paris Club agreement signed in June 1994 and the commercial bank agreement signed in July 1995.

Angola

Data source. Data on long-term public and publicly guaranteed debt for 1995 are based on reports provided by the country. Short-term debt data are from the BIS semiannual series on international bank lending and short-term export credits from the OECD, supplemented by World Bank staff estimates.

Rescheduling. In 1987 Angola concluded an informal agreement with Paris Club creditors that was signed in July 1989. In addition, two major reschedulings with the former Soviet Union and other Eastern Bloc countries took place in 1987 and 1989. Debt owed to Brazil and Portugal was also rescheduled in 1987 and 1989 and again in 1994 with Portugal and Spain.

Argentina

Data source. Data on long-term public and publicly guaranteed, private nonguaranteed, and short-term debt for 1995 and data revisions for 1993 are based on reports provided by the country.

The increase in debt outstanding in 1989 is mostly due to the conversion of austral-denominated time deposits and government domestic debt into dollar-denominated bonds (BONEX 89).

Rescheduling. In March 1993 Argentina concluded a debt and debt service reduction exchanging its commercial bank debt to either par or discount bonds for a total face value of $17 billion. Interest arrears were also swapped into bonds at par with a face value of $8.2 billion, after a down payment of $910 million. These operations enabled Argentina to reduce its stock of debt by $3.3 billion in 1993. Through buybacks, debt was reduced by $399 million in 1994, and $863 million in 1995.

Other. The residual in debt stock-flow reconciliation is due to data revisions introduced in 1993.

Armenia

Data source. Data on long-term public and publicly guaranteed debt for 1995 are preliminary, based on partial reports provided by the country. Short-term debt data are from the BIS semiannual series on international bank lending and short-term export credits from the OECD.

Rescheduling. In 1993, $30.8 million of technical credits were rescheduled with the Russian Federation.

Azerbaijan

Data source. Data on long-term public and publicly guaranteed debt for 1995 are preliminary, based on partial reports provided by the country. Short-term debt data are from the BIS semiannual series on international bank lending and short-term export credits from the OECD.

Rescheduling. In 1993, $36 million of technical credits were rescheduled with the Russian Federation.

Bangladesh

Data source. Data on long-term public and publicly guaranteed debt for 1995 are based on reports provided by the country. Short-term debt data are from the BIS semiannual series on international bank lending and short-term export credits from the OECD.

Other. Public debt stock was revised back to 1987.

Barbados

Data source. Data on long-term public and publicly guaranteed debt for 1995 are based on reports provided by the country. Short-term debt data are from the BIS semiannual series on international bank lending and short-term export credits from the OECD.

Belarus

Data source. Data on long-term public and publicly guaranteed debt for 1995 are based on reports provided by the country. Short-term debt data are from the BIS semiannual series on international bank lending and short-term export credits from the OECD.

Rescheduling. In 1993, $385 million of technical credits were rescheduled with the Russian Federation.

Belize

Data source. Data on long-term public and publicly guaranteed debt for 1995 are based on reports provided by the country. Long-term private nonguaranteed debt data are World Bank staff estimates. Short-term debt data are from the BIS semiannual series on international bank lending and short-term export credits from the OECD.

Other. The increase in debt outstanding in 1995 is due mostly to data revisions introduced through transfers during the year. This is reflected as part of the residual in the debt stock-flow reconciliation.

Benin

Data source. Data on long-term public and publicly guaranteed debt for 1995 are based on reports provided by the country and augmented by World Bank staff estimates. Short-term debt data are from the BIS semiannual series on international bank lending and short-term export credits from the OECD.

Rescheduling. Projected debt service is based on contractual obligations on debt outstanding at the end of 1995. It includes the effect of the Paris Club agreement signed in December 1991 and the Paris Club agreement on enhanced Toronto terms signed in June 1993 and covering 1994–95.

Bhutan

Data source. Data on long-term public and publicly guaranteed debt for 1995 are based on reports provided by the country. They exclude rupee debt owed to India. Short-term debt data are from the BIS semiannual series on international bank lending and short-term export credits from the OECD.

Bolivia

Data source. Data on long-term public and publicly guaranteed and private nonguaranteed debt for 1995 are based on reports provided by the country. Short-term debt data are from the BIS semiannual series on international bank lending and short-term export credits from the OECD.

Rescheduling. Projected debt service is based on contractual obligations on debt outstanding at the end of 1995. It includes the effect of the March 1995 Paris Club agreement, but does not include the effect of the December 1995 Paris Club agreement.

Debt reduction. The continuation of the debt buyback scheme arranged with commercial banks retired $20 million in 1992 and $171 million under the IDA Debt Reduction Facility in 1993. For 1992 Belgium, Romania, and the United Kingdom forgave $13 million. Principal repayments during 1988-92 include $57 million cash payments in connection with buybacks: 1988, $33.5 million; 1989, $15.9 million; 1990, $3.7 million; 1991, $2.1 million; and 1992, $2.2 million.

Bosnia and Herzegovina

Data source. Data on long-term public and publicly guaranteed debt for 1995 include only IBRD. Other long-term obligations are included under Yugoslavia (former). Short-term debt data are from the BIS semiannual series on international bank lending and short-term export credits from the OECD.

Botswana

Data source. Data on long-term public and publicly guaranteed debt for 1995 are based on reports provided by the country. Short-term debt data are from the BIS semiannual series on international bank lending and short-term export credits from the OECD.

Brazil

Data source. Data on long-term public and publicly guaranteed, private nonguaranteed, and short-term debt for 1995 and data revisions for 1986-94 are preliminary, based on partial reports provided by the country.

Rescheduling. From 1983 onward, the increase in long-term public and publicly guaranteed debt is due to the transfer of liabilities from private nonguaranteed and short-term debt as a result of Paris Club and commercial bank restructuring. In 1992 an agreement was reached with Paris Club creditors to reschedule $6.2 billion, of which $5.1 billion corresponded to rescheduling of arrears and debt service due in 1992. Brazil also rescheduled $7.1 billion of interest in arrears with commercial banks. Interest payments for 1992 include a $836 million cash payment on the interest arrears.

Debt reduction. Debt owed to commercial banks at the end of 1994 was reduced by $4.1 billion as a result of the April 1994 Brady accord.

Bulgaria

Data source. Data on long-term public and publicly guaranteed debt for 1995 are based on reports provided by the country. Short-term debt data are from the BIS semiannual series on international bank lending and short-term export credits from the OECD.

Rescheduling. Projected debt service is based on contractual obligations on debt outstanding at the end of 1995. It includes the effect of the Paris Club agreements signed in 1991, 1992, and 1994. Commercial bank creditors agreed to restructure $8.3 billion of external public debt in July 1994.

Burkina Faso

Data source. Data on long-term public and publicly guaranteed debt for 1995 are based on reports provided by the country. Short-term debt data are from the BIS semiannual series on international bank lending and short-term export credits from the OECD.

Rescheduling. Projected debt service is based on contractual obligations on debt outstanding at the end of 1995. It includes the effect of the Paris Club agreement signed in March 1991 and the Paris Club agreement on enhanced Toronto terms signed in May 1993.

Burundi

Data source. Data on long-term public and publicly guaranteed debt for 1995 are based on reports provided by the country. Short-term debt data are from the BIS semiannual series on international bank lending and short-term export credits from the OECD.

Rescheduling. Projected debt service is based on contractual obligations on debt outstanding at the end of 1995. It includes the effect of the cancellation of all concessional debt owed to Belgium, France, Korea and Russia. In 1989 Burundi rescheduled $13.3 million of debt owed to China.

Cambodia

Data source. Data on long-term public and publicly guaranteed and short-term debt for 1995 are preliminary, based on partial reports provided by the country and World Bank staff estimates. Debt data include both convertible and non-covertible currency debt.

Rescheduling. Projected debt service is based on contractual obligations on debt outstanding at the end of 1995. It includes the effect of the Paris Club agreement on Naples terms signed in January 1995.

Cameroon

Data source. Data on long-term and publicly guaranteed debt for 1995 are based on reports provided by the country. Long-term private nonguaranteed debt data are World Bank staff estimates. Short-term debt data are from the BIS semiannual series on international bank lending and short-term export credits from the OECD.

Rescheduling. Projected debt service is based on contractual obligations on debt outstanding at the end of 1995. It includes the effect of the Paris Club agreements signed in January 1992 and November 1995.

Cape Verde

Data source. Data on long-term public and publicly guaranteed debt for 1995 are based on reports provided by the country. Short-term debt data are from the BIS semiannual series on international bank lending and short-term export credits from the OECD.

Rescheduling. In 1987, $8.4 million of long-term debt owed to Portugal was rescheduled.

Central African Republic

Data source. Data on long-term public and publicly guaranteed debt for 1995 are based on reports provided by the country. Short-term debt data are from the BIS semiannual series on international bank lending and short-term export credits from the OECD.

Rescheduling. Projected debt service is based on contractual obligations on debt outstanding at the end of 1995. It includes the effect of the Paris Club agreements signed in 1988, 1990, and 1994.

Chad

Data source. Data on long-term public and publicly guaranteed debt for 1995 are based on reports provided by the country and World Bank staff estimates. Short-term debt data are from the BIS semiannual series on international bank lending and short-term export credits from the OECD.

Rescheduling. Projected debt service is based on contractual obligations on debt outstanding at the end of 1995. It includes the effect of the debt relief agreement signed in 1989, concluded outside the Paris Club. In addition, it includes the effect of the 1995 Paris Club agreement. The reporting of the loans covered by this agreement remains partial including the February 1995 Paris Club.

Chile

Data source. Data on long-term public and publicly guaranteed, private nonguaranteed debt for 1995 are based on reports provided by the country. Short-term debt data for 1990–95 are from the BIS semiannual series on international bank lending and short-term export credits from the OECD.

Rescheduling. Projected debt service is based on contractual obligations on debt outstanding at the end of 1995. It includes the effect of a 1990 agreement with commercial banks under which repayment of principal was not made during 1991-94. The data also reflect the forgiveness of $15 million and the rescheduling of $132 million under the Enterprise for the Americas Initiative.

Debt reduction. By end-1993 reduction of debt owed to commercial banks through various debt conversion programs reached $8.7 billion. In 1985, it was $96 million; 1986, $411 million; 1987, $1.1 billion; 1988, $2.5 billion; 1989, $2.5 billion; 1990, $1.1 billion; 1991, $496 million; 1992, $279 million; and 1993, $264 million. Also, 1988 principal repayments include a $164 million cash payment in connection with a buyback.

China

Data source. Data on long-term public and publicly guaranteed debt for 1995 are based on aggregate reports provided by the country and World Bank staff estimates. Short-term debt data for 1990-1995 are from the BIS semiannual series on international bank lending and short-term export credits from the OECD.

Colombia

Data source. Data on long-term public and publicly guaranteed debt for 1995 are based on reports provided by the country. Data on private non-guaranteed debt are World Bank staff estimates. Short-term debt data are from the BIS semiannual series on international bank lending and short-term export credits from the OECD.

Rescheduling. Data reflect the 1993 Enterprise for the Americas Initiative (EAI) operations. After an agreement signed in 1992, about $349 million of debt owed to the US Agency for International Development was rescheduled as follows: $35 million was forgiven, $272 million was rescheduled, and $41.6 million was swapped (EAI local fund).

Debt reduction. In addition to the $41.6 million of EAI debt swap, the Canadian International Development Agency, as part of the Canadian Initiative, signed an agreement converting $12.2 million of debt owed to Canada to local currency in 1993.

Comoros

Data source. Data on long-term public and publicly guaranteed debt for 1995 are based on reports provided by the country. Short-term debt data are from the BIS semiannual series on international bank lending and short-term export credits from the OECD.

Debt reduction. France wrote off all outstanding debt in 1994.

Congo

Data source. Data on long-term public and publicly guaranteed debt for 1995 are based on reports provided by the government. Short-term debt data are from the BIS semiannual series on international bank lending and short-term export credits from the OECD.

Rescheduling. Projected debt service is based on contractual obligations on debt outstanding at the end of 1995. It includes the effect of the Paris Club agreements of 1986, 1990, and 1994, but excludes the effect of the 1988 agreement with commercial banks because it was not implemented. In 1986, in addition to Paris Club, the government rescheduled with Eastern Bloc creditors. Under the 1986 Brazzaville Club agreement, $23 million was rescheduled.

Costa Rica

Data source. Data on long-term public and publicly guaranteed debt for 1995 are based on reports provided by the country. Long-term private non-guaranteed debt data are World Bank staff estimates. Short-term debt data are from the BIS semiannual series on international bank lending and short-term export credits from the OECD.

Rescheduling. Projected debt service is based on contractual obligations on debt outstanding at the end of 1995. It includes the effect of the Paris Club agreement signed in July 1991, the two rescheduling agreements signed in 1992 with Japan ($23 million) and the United States ($4 million), and the Paris Club agreement signed in June 1993.

Côte d'Ivoire

Data source. Data on long-term public and publicly guaranteed debt for 1995 are based on reports provided by the country. Long-term private nonguaranteed debt data are World Bank staff estimates. Short-term debt data are from the BIS semiannual series on international bank lending and short-term export credits from the OECD and from the Caisse Autonome d'Amortissement's estimate of penalty and late charges on long-term debt. They also include World Bank staff estimates on the balance of the operations account.

Rescheduling. Projected debt service is based on contractual obligations on debt outstanding at the end of 1995. It includes the effect of all Paris Club agreements beginning in 1984 and the commercial bank agreements of 1985–86.

Croatia

Data source. Data on long-term public and publicly guaranteed and private nonguaranteed debt for 1995 are based on reports provided by the country. Short-term debt data are from the BIS semiannual series on international bank lending and short-term export credits from the OECD.

Other. Croatia became a member of the World Bank in 1993. Debt data as of end-1995 includes the effect of the Paris Club agreement signed in March 1995. Projections exclude the effects of the March 1996 commercial bank agreement.

Czech Republic

Data source. Data on long-term public and publicly guaranteed, private nonguaranteed, and short-term debt for 1995 are preliminary, based on partial reports provided by the country, and include only convertible currency debt.

Other. The Czech Republic became a member of the World Bank in 1993. Data for 1985–92 are based on preliminary information on the succession of the former Czechoslovakia (effective January 1, 1993).

Djibouti

Data source. Data on long-term public and publicly guaranteed debt for 1995 are estimates based on the original terms of the loans. Short-term debt data are from the BIS semiannual series on international bank lending and short-term export credits from the OECD.

Debt reduction. At the end of 1989 France wrote off all outstanding and disbursed debt.

Dominica

Data source. Data on long-term public and publicly guaranteed debt for 1995 are based on reports provided by the country. Short-term debt data are from the BIS semiannual series on international bank lending and short-term export credits from the OECD.

Debt reduction. As part of its Caribbean initiative, Canada forgave all its official development assistance loans, about $1.7 million, in 1990.

Dominican Republic

Data source. Data on long-term public and publicly guaranteed debt for 1995 are based on reports provided by the country. Private nonguaranteed debt data are World Bank staff estimates. Short-term debt data are from the BIS semiannual series on international bank lending and short-term export credits from the OECD.

Rescheduling. Projected debt service is based on contractual obligations on debt outstanding at the end of 1995. It includes the effect of the Paris Club agreement signed in November 1991 rescheduling $843 million, and of the 1994 DDSR agreement to restructure $1.2 billion owed to commercial banks.

Ecuador

Data source. Data on long-term public and publicly guaranteed debt for 1995 are based on reports provided by the country. Private nonguaranteed debt are World Bank staff estimates. Short-term debt data are from the BIS semiannual series on international bank lending and short-term export credits from the OECD.

Rescheduling. Projected debt service is based on contractual obligations on debt outstanding at the end of 1995. It includes the effect of the Paris Club agreement on Houston terms signed in June 1994 and of the 1995 DDSR operation.

Debt reduction. Between 1987 and 1992 a debt conversion program enabled the country to reduce its stock of debt by $539 million. Debt reduction resulting from the 1995 DDSR operations amounts to $1.2 billion.

Egypt

Data source. Data on long-term public and publicly guaranteed debt for 1995 and revised data for 1991-93 are based on reports provided by the country. Data on private nonguaranteed debt are World Bank staff estimates. Short-term debt data are from the BIS semiannual series on international bank lending and short-term export credits from OECD.

Rescheduling. Projected debt service is based on contractual obligations on debt outstanding at the end of 1995. It includes the effects of the Paris Club agreement signed in May 1991.

El Salvador

Data source. Data on long-term public and publicly guaranteed debt for 1995 are based on reports provided by the country. Long-term private non-guaranteed debt are World Bank staff estimates. Short-term debt data are from the BIS semiannual series on international bank lending and short-term export credits from the OECD.

Rescheduling. Projected debt service is based on contractual obligations on debt outstanding at the end of 1995. It includes the effect of the Paris Club agreement signed in September 1990. It also includes the effect of the 1993 Enterprise for the Americas Initiative (EAI) operations signed on 1992. As a result of these operations, about $256 million of debt owed to the U.S. Agency for International Development (USAID) and $400 million of PL480 loans were rescheduled. Of the USAID loans, $179 million was forgiven, $61.4 million was rescheduled, and $15.6 million was converted into local currency (EAI local fund). Of the PL480 loans $320 million was forgiven, $54.4 million was rescheduled, and $25.6 million (EAI local fund) was converted into local currency.

Debt reduction. In addition to the $41 million of EAI debt swap, the Canadian International Development Agency, as part of the Canadian Initiative, signed an agreement in June 1993 converting about $6 million to local currency.

Equatorial Guinea

Data source. Data on long-term public and publicly guaranteed debt for 1995 are estimates based on the original terms of the loans. Short-term debt data are from the BIS semiannual series on international bank lending and short-term export credits from the OECD.

Rescheduling. Projected debt service is based on contractual obligations on debt outstanding at the end of 1995. It does not include the effect of the Paris Club agreement of April 1992 because Italy and Spain have not signed the agreement.

Estonia

Data source. Data on long-term public and publicly guaranteed and private nonguaranteed debt for 1995 are based on reports provided by the country. Short-term debt data are from the BIS semiannual series on international bank lending and short-term export credits from the OECD.

Ethiopia

Data source. Data on long-term public and publicly guaranteed debt for 1995 are based on reports provided by the country. Short-term debt data are from the BIS semiannual series on international bank lending and short-term export credits from the OECD. The data include debt contracted from commercial sources for military expenditures. Debt data include Eritrea.

Fiji

Data source. Data on long-term public and publicly guaranteed debt for 1995 are based on reports provided by the country. Long-term private nonguaranteed debt data are World Bank staff estimates. Short-term debt data are from the BIS semiannual series on international bank lending and short-term export credits from the OECD.

Gabon

Data source. Data on long-term public and publicly guaranteed debt for 1995 are based on reports provided by the country. Short-term debt data are from the BIS semiannual series on international bank lending and short-term export credits from the OECD.

Rescheduling. Projected debt service is based on contractual obligations on debt outstanding at the end of 1995. It includes the effect of the Paris Club agreements signed in April 1994 and December 1995. Projections exclude the effect of a Paris Club agreement signed in October 1991. According to Caisse Autonome d'Amortissement, the agreement was canceled because of difficulties in meeting certain conditions requested by one of the creditor countries.

Gambia, The

Data source. Data on long-term public and publicly guaranteed debt for 1995 are projections of the 1994 reported data. Short-term debt data are from the BIS semiannual series on international bank lending and short-term export credits from the OECD.

Rescheduling. Projected debt service is based on contractual obligations on debt outstanding at the end of 1995. It includes the effect of the Paris Club agreement from September 1986 and the commercial bank rescheduling of 1988 amounting to $19 million, converting $9 million of short-term debt to long-term debt.

Other. Data on principal (and interest) arrears are not available due to incomplete reporting from the country.

Georgia

Data source. Data on long-term public and publicly guaranteed debt for 1995 are based on the reports provided by the country. Short-term debt data are from the BIS semiannual series on international bank lending and short-term export credits from the OECD.

Rescheduling. In 1993 a total of $366 million of technical credits were rescheduled with Armenia ($10.6 million), Azerbaijan ($2.1 million), Kazakstan ($17.9 million), the Russian Federation ($135.0 million), and Turkmenistan ($200.8 million).

Ghana

Data source. Data on long-term public and publicly guaranteed debt for 1995 are based on reports provided by the country. Long-term private nonguaranteed debt data are World Bank staff estimates. Short-term debt data are from the BIS semiannual series on international bank lending and short-term export credits from the OECD.

Rescheduling. Short-term debt of the Bank of Ghana amounting to $42 million was rescheduled into long-term debt in 1987. In 1991 the Netherlands rescheduled all payment arrears.

Grenada

Data source. Data on public and publicly guaranteed debt for 1995 are based on reports provided by the country. Short-term debt data are from the BIS semiannual series on international bank lending and short-term export credits from the OECD.

Guatemala

Data source. Data on long-term public and publicly guaranteed debt for 1995 are preliminary, based on the partial report provided by the country. Long-term private non-guaranteed debt data are World Bank staff estimates. Short-term debt data are from the BIS semiannual series on international bank lending and short-term export credits from the OECD.

Rescheduling. Projected debt service is based on contractual obligations on debt outstanding at the end of 1995. It includes the effect of the Paris Club agreement on Houston terms signed in March 1993. About $440 million of arrears were rescheduled of which $195 million were principal and $179 million were interest arrears.

Debt reduction. The reduction in long-term public debt of $152 million in 1988 and $20 million in 1989 was the result of a debt-equity operation in local currency in connection with the rescheduling of the 1984 stabilization bonds.

Guinea

Data source. Data on long-term public and publicly guaranteed debt for 1995 are preliminary, based on partial reports provided by the country. Short-term debt data are from the BIS semiannual series on international bank lending and short-term export credits from the OECD.

Rescheduling. Projected debt service is based on contractual obligations on debt outstanding at the end of 1995. It includes the effects of the Paris Club agreements of 1986, 1989, 1992, and 1995 and the commercial bank rescheduling agreement of April 1988.

Guinea-Bissau

Data source. Data on long-term public and publicly guaranteed debt for 1995 are preliminary, based on partial reports provided by the country. Short-term debt data are from the BIS semiannual series on international bank lending and short-term export credits from the OECD.

Rescheduling. Projected debt service is based on contractual obligations on debt outstanding at the end of 1995. It includes the effects of the Paris Club agreements signed in October 1987 and October 1989.

Guyana

Data source. Data on long-term public and publicly guaranteed debt for 1995 are based on reports provided by the country. Long-term private non-guaranteed debt data are World Bank staff estimates. Short-term debt data are from the BIS semiannual series on international bank lending and short-term export credits from the OECD.

Rescheduling. Projected debt service is based on contractual obligations on debt outstanding at the end of 1995. It includes the effect of the Paris Club agreement on enhanced Toronto Terms signed in May 1993.

Debt reduction. For 1991 the debt outstanding reflects debt forgiveness of $87 million from the United States. For 1992 Brazil and the United Kingdom forgave $11 million of bilateral debt, and Guyana paid $9.9 million to buy back $76 million of debt owed to commercial banks. This operation was funded by a grant from the International Development Association Debt Reduction Facility.

Haiti

Data source. Data on long-term public and publicly guaranteed debt as of end-September 1995 are preliminary, based on partial reports provided by the country. Short-term debt data are from the BIS semiannual series on international bank lending and short-term export credits from the OECD.

The government cleared a total of $81.5 million of arrears to the Inter-American Development Bank, IDA, and the IMF in December 1994 and arrears to the International Fund for Agricultural Development, OPEC Fund, and bilateral donors, either through bilateral agreements or in the context of the May 1995 Paris Club meeting.

Rescheduling. Projected debt service includes the effect of the March 1995 Paris Club agreement.

Honduras

Data source. Data on long-term public and publicly guaranteed and private non-guaranteed debt for 1995 are based on reports provided by the country. Short-term debt data are from the BIS semiannual series on international bank lending and short-term export credits from the OECD.

Rescheduling. Projected debt service is based on contractual obligations on debt outstanding at the end of 1995. It includes the effect of the Paris Club agreement signed in October 1992. In addition, in 1992 the government rescheduled $57 million owed to Mexico.

Debt reduction. For 1991, the debt data reflect the forgiveness of $425 million by the United States, $11 million by Switzerland, and $7 million by the Netherlands.

Hungary

Data source. Data on long-term public and publicly guaranteed, private non-guaranteed, and short-term debt for 1995 are based on reports provided by the country.

India

Data source. Data relate to year ending in March (latest data is for the year ending in March 1996). Details on long-term public and publicly guaranteed, private non-guaranteed and short-term debt as at the end of March 1996 are based on reports provided by the country.

Nonresident deposits. Data include nonresident Indian deposits for March 1980 to March 1996. These deposits amounted to $14.70 billion and $14.35 billion at the end of March 1995 and 1996, respectively. From March 1989 to March 1994, these deposits are broken into long-term and short-term deposits. From 1995 onwards, long-term deposits are further broken down into publicly guaranteed and private nonguaranteed deposits.

Military debt. Data have been revised from March 1990 to include military debt.

Indonesia

Data source. Data on long-term public and publicly guaranteed and private nonguaranteed debt for 1995 are preliminary based on reports provided by the country. Short-term debt data are from the Bank of Indonesia and World Bank staff estimates.

Other. The residual in debt stock-flow reconciliation is due to data revisions introduced in 1989.

Iran, Islamic Republic of

Data source. Data on long-term public and publicly guaranteed and private non-guaranteed debt for 1995 are not reported. Short-term debt data are based on data published by the country.

Rescheduling. Iran rescheduled an estimated $13.7 billion of short-term debt into long-term debt in 1993–94: $2.8 billion in 1993 (which was repaid in the same year) and $10.9 billion in 1994.

Jamaica

Data source. Data on long-term public and publicly guaranteed debt for 1995 are preliminary, based on the partial report provided by the country. Long-term private non-guaranteed debt data are World Bank staff estimates. Short-term debt data are from the BIS semiannual series on international bank lending and short-term export credits from the OECD.

Rescheduling. Projected debt service are based on contractual obligations on debt outstanding at the end of 1995. It includes the effect of the Paris Club agreement on Houston terms signed in January 1993. Total amount rescheduled during 1993-94 was $255 million, with rescheduled principal of $160 million and interest of $54 million.

Debt reduction. In March 1991, the Canadian International Development Agency (CIDA) forgave $90 million of official development assistant debt. The Netherlands Investment Bank forgave a total of $28 million consisting of arrears of principal and interest as well as payments falling due in 1991–94. As part of a debt waiver agreement signed in 1991, the United Kingdom forgave principal and interest due from June 1991 to June 1992 amounting to $13.3 million. In addition, the stock of debt owed to commercial banks was reduced during 1991–94 by $75 million with continuation of debt-equity swap programs. Finally, as part of the Enterprise for the Americas Initiative (EAI), about $134 million of debt owed to U.S. Agency for International Development was rescheduled of which $94 million was the amount of forgiveness in 1993.

Jordan

Data source. Data on long-term public and publicly guaranteed debt for 1995 are based on reports provided by the country. Short-term debt data have been revised from 1989 onwards based on the BIS semiannual series on international bank lending and short-term export credits from the OECD.

Rescheduling. Projected debt service is based on contractual obligations at the end of 1995. It reflects the effect of the agreements signed with the Paris Club in July 1989, February 1992, and June 1994, other bilateral rescheduling arrangements, and the London Club agreement of December 1993.

Kazakstan

Data source. Data on long-term public and publicly guaranteed debt for 1995 are based on reports provided by the country. Short-term debt data are from the BIS semiannual series on international bank lending and short-term export credits from the OECD.

Rescheduling. In 1993, $1.3 billion of technical credits were rescheduled with the Russian Federation.

Kenya

Data source. Data on long-term public and publicly guaranteed debt for 1995 are based on reports provided by the country. Long-term private nonguaranteed debt for 1995 are based on World Bank staff estimates. Short-term debt data are from the BIS semiannual series on international bank lending and short-term export credits from the OECD.

Rescheduling. Projected debt service is based on contractual obligations on debt outstanding at the end of 1995. It includes the effect of the Paris Club agreement signed in January 1994 rescheduling all arrears accumulated as of December 1993.

Kyrgyz Republic

Data source. Data on long-term public and publicly guaranteed debt for 1995 are based on reports provided by the country. Short-term debt data are from the BIS semiannual series on international bank lending and short-term export credits from the OECD.

Rescheduling. In 1993 a total of $125.8 million of technical credits were rescheduled with Kazakstan ($31.5 million), the Russian Federation ($81.0 million), and Uzbekistan ($13.3 million).

Lao People's Democratic Republic

Data source. Data on long-term public and publicly guaranteed debt for 1995 are preliminary, based on partial reports provided by the country and include both convertible and nonconvertible currency obligations. Short-term debt data are from the BIS semiannual series on international bank lending and short-term export credits from the OECD.

Rescheduling. Projected debt service is based on contractual obligations on debt outstanding at the end of 1995. It includes the effects of bilateral debt restructuring agreements of 1988 and 1991.

Latvia

Data source. Data on long-term public and publicly guaranteed debt for 1995 are based on preliminary reports provided by the country. Short-term debt data are from the BIS semiannual series on international bank lending and short-term export credits from the OECD.

Lebanon

Data source. Data on long-term public and publicly guaranteed debt for 1995 are based on reports provided by the country. Short-term debt data are from the BIS semiannual series on international bank lending and short-term export credits from the OECD.

Lesotho

Data source. Data on long-term public and publicly guaranteed debt for 1995 are based on reports provided by the country. Short-term debt data are World Bank staff estimates.

Liberia

Data source. Data on long-term public and publicly guaranteed debt for 1995 are estimates based on the original terms of the loans, augmented by creditor source information. Short-term debt data are from the BIS semiannual series on international bank lending and short-term export credits from the OECD.

Lithuania

Data source. Data on long-term public and publicly guaranteed debt for 1995 are based on reports provided by the country. Short-term debt data are from the BIS semiannual series on international bank lending and short-term export credits from the OECD.

Macedonia, FYR

Data source. Data on long-term public and publicly guaranteed and private nonguaranteed debt for 1995 are based on reports provided by the country. Short-term debt data are from the BIS semiannual series on international bank lending and short-term export credits from the OECD.

Other. The former Yugoslav Republic of Macedonia became a member of the World Bank in 1993. Debt outstanding as of end-1993 reflect only loans used directly by Macedonian beneficiaries. Projected debt service includes the effects of the 1995 Paris Club agreement.

Madagascar

Data source. Data on long-term public and publicly guaranteed debt for 1995 are based on reports provided by the country. Short-term debt data are from the BIS semiannual series on international bank lending and short-term export credits from the OECD.

Rescheduling. Projected debt service is based on contractual obligations on debt outstanding at the end of 1995. It includes the effect of all Paris Club agreements signed during 1981–90 and commercial bank rescheduling arrangements.

Malawi

Data source. Data on long-term public and publicly guaranteed debt for 1995 are preliminary, based on partial reports provided by the country. Long-term private nonguaranteed debt data are World Bank staff estimates. Short-term debt data are from the BIS semiannual series on international bank lending and short-term export credits from the OECD.

Rescheduling. Projected debt service is based on contractual obligations on debt outstanding at the end of 1995. It includes the effect of the Paris Club agreement signed in April 1988. The agreement to reschedule debt owed to the Commonwealth Development Corporation has not been implemented; as a result there are both principal and interest arrears due to the corporation.

Malaysia

Data source. Data on long-term public and publicly guaranteed and private nonguaranteed debt for 1995 are preliminary, based on partial reports provided by the country. Short-term debt data are from the BIS semiannual series on international bank lending and short-term export credits from the OECD.

Other. Principal repayments during 1985–95 include prepayments of $2.2 billion in 1985; $1.5 billion in 1987; and $1.7 billion in 1988.

Maldives

Data source. Data on long-term public and publicly guaranteed debt for 1995 are based on reports provided by the country. Short-term debt data are from the BIS semiannual series on international bank lending and short-term export credits from the OECD.

Mali

Data source. Data on long-term public and publicly guaranteed debt for 1995 are preliminary, based on partial reports provided by the country and augmented by World Bank staff estimates. Short-term debt data are from the BIS semiannual series on international bank lending and short-term export credits from the OECD.

Rescheduling. Projected debt service is based on contractual obligations of debt outstanding at the end of 1995. It includes the effect of the Paris Club agreements of 1988, 1989, and 1992. The reporting of the loans covered by these agreements remains partial.

Debt reduction. The reductions in the stock of debt were $3.4 million at the end of 1988, $1.2 million in 1989, $2.0 million in 1990, and $13.3 million in 1992. These were write-offs in connection with Paris Club agreements within the enhanced Toronto terms framework.

Malta

Data source. Data on long-term public and publicly guaranteed debt for 1995 are based on reports provided by the country. Short-term debt data are from the BIS semiannual series on international bank lending and short-term export credits from the OECD.

Mauritania

Data source. Data on long-term public and publicly guaranteed debt for 1995 are based on reports provided by the country and World Bank staff estimates. Short-term debt data are from the BIS semiannual series on international bank lending and short-term export credits from the OECD.

Rescheduling. Projected debt service is based on contractual obligations on debt outstanding at the end of 1995. It reflects the effect of the Paris Club agreements of 1989, 1993, and 1995. The reporting of the loans covered by these agreement remains partial. There have also been bilateral rescheduling arrangements with Algeria, Brazil, Iraq, Kuwait, Qatar, and Saudi Arabia.

Mauritius

Data source. Data on long-term public and publicly guaranteed and private nonguaranteed debt for 1995 are based on reports provided by the country. Short-term debt data are from the BIS semiannual series on international bank lending and short-term export credits from the OECD.

Mexico

Data source. Data on long-term public and publicly guaranteed, private nonguaranteed, and short-term debt for 1995 are based on reports provided by the country. Data revision on short-term and public nonguaranteed debt were provided by the country.

Rescheduling. Projected debt service is based on contractual obligations on debt outstanding at the end of 1995. It includes the effect of all agreements concluded to date, including the effect of the issuance of zero-coupon bonds and the swap operations. In 1992, $327 million was rescheduled as a result of the 1989 Paris Club agreement. In 1993 a number of public borrowers, including the government, swapped liabilities to meet the ceiling on borrowings.

Debt reduction. The decline in private nonguaranteed debt in 1988 is due primarily to prepayment and swaps operations. The debt reduction in 1989 of $2.5 billion comprised debt-equity swaps of $800 million and buybacks of $1.7 billion. In 1990 swaps amounted to $846 million, and debt reduction from discount bonds to $7.3 billion. The debt conversion program continued in 1991 and amounted to $1.1 billion, including privatization of $431 million and debt equity swaps of $95 million. In 1992, $7.5 billion was bought back for $5.2 billion, which is shown under principal repayments. Also, $137 million was converted from foreign debt to equity. The increase in 1995 long-term debt includes the stock transfer of the "Tesobonos."

Moldova

Data source. Data on long-term public and publicly guaranteed debt for 1995 are based on reports provided by the country. Short-term debt data are from the BIS semiannual series on international bank lending and short-term export credits from the OECD

Rescheduling. In 1993, $89 million of technical credits were rescheduled with the Russian Federation.

Mongolia

Data source. Data on long-term public and publicly guaranteed debt for 1995 are based on reports provided by the country. Short-term debt data are from the BIS semiannual series on international bank lending and short-term export credits from the OECD. Data exclude military debt of about 10.6 billion rubles owed to the Russian Federation.

Morocco

Data source. Data on long-term public and publicly guaranteed and private nonguaranteed debt for 1995 are preliminary based on partial reports provided by the country and World Bank staff estimates. Data on short-term debt are based on reports by the country and World Bank staff estimates. Major revisions to the database, especially on short-term debt and arrears were based on information provided by the authorities. The arrears are mostly late payments to creditor countries.

Rescheduling. Projected debt service is based on contractual obligations on debt outstanding at the end of 1995. It includes the effect of the Paris Club agreement signed in February 1992.

Mozambique

Data source. Data on long-term public and publicly guaranteed debt for 1995 are based on reports provided by the country. Private nonguaranteed debt data are World Bank staff estimates. Short-term debt data are from the BIS semiannual series on international bank lending and short-term export credits from the OECD.

Rescheduling. Projected debt service is based on contractual obligations on debt outstanding at the end of 1995. It does not include the effect of the Paris Club agreement signed in November 1996.

Debt reduction. Debt reduction in 1990 amounted to $231 million and in 1991 to $237 million. In 1991 there was a debt buyback, at a discount of 90 percent, of $124 million under the IDA Debt Reduction Facility.

Myanmar

Data source. Data on long-term public and publicly guaranteed debt for 1995 are based on reports provided by the country. Short-term debt data are from the BIS semiannual series on international bank lending and short-term export credits from the OECD.

Nepal

Data source. Data on long-term public and publicly guaranteed debt for 1995 are based on reports provided by the country. Short-term debt data are from the BIS semiannual series on international bank lending and short-term export credits from the OECD.

Nicaragua

Data source. Data on long-term public and publicly guaranteed debt for 1995 are preliminary, based on partial reports provided by the country. Short-term debt data are from the BIS semiannual series on international bank lending and short-term export credits from the OECD.

Rescheduling. Projected debt service is based on contractual obligations on debt outstanding at the end of 1995. It includes the effect of agreements reached with Mexico ($950 million) and Venezuela ($159 million) in 1991, with Brazil in 1992 ($66 million), and with Argentina ($76 million) and Cuba ($7 million) in 1993, and the 1995 Paris Club agreement.

Debt reduction. In 1995, debt reduction was $1.2 billion using the IDA Debt Reduction Facility.

Niger

Data source. Data on long-term public and publicly guaranteed debt for 1995 are based on reports provided by the country. Long term private nonguaranteed debt data are World Bank staff estimates. Short-term debt data are from the BIS semiannual series on international bank lending and short-term export credits from the OECD.

Debt reduction. In 1991 Niger bought back $107 million of debt at a discount of 82 percent under the IDA Debt Reduction Facility.

Nigeria

Data source. Data on long-term public and private nonguaranteed debt for 1995 are estimates based on the original terms of the loans and World Bank staff estimates. Short-term debt data are from the BIS semiannual series on international bank lending and short-term export credits from the OECD.

Rescheduling. Projected debt service is based on contractual obligations on debt outstanding at the end of 1995. It includes the effect of all Paris Club and London Club agreements signed as well as those signed with other bilateral creditors.

Debt reduction. Debt reduction in 1988 was $40 million and in 1989, $247 million, all of it due to debt-equity swaps. In 1990 the debt reduction was $286 million, $48 million of which was due to debt forgiveness and $238 million to debt-equity swaps. In 1991 debt reduction was $243 million, of which $134 million represented a buyback, $95 million was debt-equity swaps, and $14 million was debt forgiveness. In 1992 there was a $1.3 billion buyback.

Other. The Central Bank of Nigeria reported a large cancellation of promissory notes in 1992 that led to a reduction of about $1.1 billion in the stock of notes outstanding. This reduction, classified under private suppliers' credits, is not recorded as part of the DDSR accounts and therefore is included in the residual imbalance during 1992.

Oman

Data source. Data on long-term public and publicly guaranteed debt for 1995 are based on reports provided by the country. Short-term debt data are from the BIS semiannual series on international bank lending and short-term export credits from the OECD.

Pakistan

Data source. Data on long-term public and publicly guaranteed and private non-guaranteed debt for 1995 are based on reports provided by the country. Short-term debt data are from the BIS semiannual series on international bank lending and short-term export credits from the OECD, and exclude foreign currency deposits in local banks made by nonresident individuals.

Panama

Data source. Data on long-term public and publicly guaranteed debt for 1995 are based on reports provided by the country. Short-term debt data are World Bank staff estimates.

Rescheduling. Projected debt service is based on contractual obligations on debt outstanding at the end of 1995. It includes the effect of the Paris Club agreement signed in November 1990, effective in 1991, after completion of a standby agreement with the IMF. Total rescheduled principal and interest were $109 million and $87 million, respectively. It also includes the effect of the rescheduling of $422 million of the outstanding amount on bonds. Principal and interest arrears rescheduled were $261 million and $161 million, respectively. Projected debt service does not include the effect of the May 1996 agreement with commercial banks.

Papua New Guinea

Data source. Data on long-term public and publicly guaranteed and private nonguaranteed debt for 1995 are based on reports provided by the country. Short-term debt data are from the BIS semiannual series on international bank lending and short-term export credits from the OECD.

Paraguay

Data source. Data on long-term public and publicly guaranteed and private nonguaranteed debt for 1995 are based on reports provided by the country. Short-term debt data are from the BIS semiannual series on international bank lending and short-term export credits from the OECD.

Rescheduling. In 1988, Paraguay signed a bilateral rescheduling agreement with the Central Bank of Brazil for the total amount of $436 million due to the Central Bank of Brazil with the option of buying it back. In 1990 Paraguay exercised this option, enabling the country to retire the entire amount at one-fourth of its face value.

Peru

Data source. Data on long-term public and publicly guaranteed debt for 1995 are based on reports provided by the country. Long-term private nonguaranteed debt data are World Bank staff estimates. Short-term debt data are also as reported by the country.

Rescheduling. Projected debt service is based on contractual obligations on debt outstanding at the end of 1995. It includes the effect of the Paris Club agreement signed in May 1993. Total amount rescheduled reached about $1.3 billion, including $632 million and $711 million of debt service payments due in 1993 and 1994, respectively, and does not include the effects of the Paris Club rescheduling signed in July 1996.

Philippines

Data source. Data on long-term public and publicly guaranteed, private nonguaranteed, and short-term debt for 1995 are based on reports provided by the country, augmented by World Bank staff estimates.

Rescheduling. Projected debt service is based on contractual obligations on debt outstanding as of December 1995. It includes the effect of the Paris Club agreement signed in June 1991. The Paris Club agreement signed in July 1994 was not implemented because the Philippines decided to meet Paris Club debt service due.

Debt reduction. Cash buyback of $1.3 billion at the price of 52 cents per dollar (equivalent to $656 million) was implemented in May 1992 as well as the DDSR $4.4 billion multioption package of July 1992.

Poland

Data source. Data on long-term public and publicly guaranteed, private nonguaranteed, and short-term debt for 1995 are based on reports by the country, and include both convertible and nonconvertible debt.

Rescheduling. Projected debt service is based on contractual obligations on debt outstanding at the end of 1995. It includes the effect of the Paris Club agreement signed in April 1991, which provided for about 50 percent cancellation of the stock of debt or an equivalent reduction in scheduled debt service on a net present value basis. It also includes the effect of the DDSR operation with commercial banks that was concluded in October 1994. The 1994 DDSR agreement restructured $14.3 billion of debt.

Romania

Data source. Data on long-term public and publicly guaranteed, private nonguaranteed, and short-term debt for 1995 are based on reports provided by the country. Major revisions to the database were based on information provided by the authorities.

Russian Federation

Data source. Data on long-term public and publicly guaranteed and short-term debt for 1995 are preliminary, based on aggregate data provided by the country. Data prior to 1992 are for the former Soviet Union. Beginning in 1993, the database has been revised to incude obligations to former COMECON and other countries in the form of trade related credits amounting to $16.6 billion as of the end of 1995.

Rescheduling. Projected debt service is based on contractual obligations on debt outstanding at the end of 1995. It includes the effect of the Paris Club agreement signed in June 1995. It does not include the effects of the rescheduling agreements signed with the Paris Club in July 1996 and with commercial banks in November 1996.

Rwanda

Data source. Data on long-term public and publicly guaranteed debt for 1995 are estimates based on the original terms of the loans. Short-term debt data are from the BIS semiannual series on international bank lending and short-term export credits from the OECD.

Rescheduling. Projected debt service is based on contractual obligations on debt outstanding at the end of 1995. It includes the effect of bilateral rescheduling of loans from Kuwait in 1995.

São Tomé and Principe

Data source. Data on long-term public and publicly guaranteed debt for 1995 are based on reports provided by the country. Short-term debt data are from the BIS semiannual series on international bank lending and short-term export credits from the OECD.

Rescheduling: In 1995, $23.9 million were rescheduled with Portugal.

Senegal

Data source. Data on long-term public and publicly guaranteed debt and private nonguaranteed debt for 1995 are based on reports provided by the country. Short-term debt data are from the BIS semiannual series on international bank lending and short-term export credits from the OECD.

Rescheduling. Projected debt service is based on contractual obligations on debt outstanding at the end of 1995. It includes the effect of the Paris Club agreement signed in April 1995.

Seychelles

Data source. Data on long-term public and publicly guaranteed debt for 1995 are estimates based on the original terms of the loans. Short-term debt data are from the BIS semiannual series on international bank lending and short-term export credits from the OECD.

Sierra Leone

Data source. Data on long-term public and publicly guaranteed debt for 1995 are based on reports provided by the country. Long-term private nonguaranteed debt data are World Bank staff estimates. Short-term debt data are from the BIS semiannual series on international bank lending and short-term export credits from the OECD.

Rescheduling. Projected debt service is based on contractual obligations on debt outstanding at the end of 1995. It includes the effect of Paris Club agreements signed in November 1986, November 1992, and July 1994. It also includes the effect of a DDSR operation with commercial banks that was concluded in August 1995.

Debt reduction. The debt reduction in 1987–89 amounts to $229 million of debt-equity swaps. Principal repayments in 1991 include a $284 million cash payment in connection with a debt buy back, which retired $506 million of debt outstanding. Debt data also reflect the forgiveness of $16 million by the United States in 1993.

Slovak Republic

Data source. Data on long-term public and publicly guaranteed, private nonguaranteed, and short-term debt for 1995 are preliminary, based on partial reports provided by the country and include only convertible-currency debt.

Other. The Slovak Republic became a member of the World Bank in 1993. Data for 1985–92 are based on preliminary information on the succession of the former Czechoslovakia (effective January 1, 1993).

Slovenia

Data source. Data on long-term public and publicly guaranteed and private nonguaranteed debt for 1995 are based on reports provided by the country. Short-term debt data are from the BIS semiannual series on international bank lending and short-term export credits from the OECD.

Other. Slovenia became a member of the World Bank in 1993. Debt data as of the end of 1995 reflect only loans used directly by Slovenian beneficiaries. The division of the federal debt (approximately $2.6 billion, excluding obligations to the IMF) is subject to negotiations on the succession of the former Yugoslavia.

By a decision of the IMF Executive Board, Slovenia was declared a successor state to a percentage share of the assets and liabilities of the former Yugoslavia. At the time of succession, total liabilities were SDR 51.0 million, of which SDR 25.5 million was disbursed.

Solomon Islands

Data source. Data on long-term public and publicly guaranteed debt for 1995 are based on reports provided by the country. Short-term debt data are from the BIS semiannual series on international bank lending and short-term export credits from the OECD.

Rescheduling. Projected debt service is based on contractual obligations on debt outstanding at the end of 1995. It includes the effects of a bilateral debt restructuring agreement signed in 1992.

Somalia

Data source. Data on long-term public and publicly guaranteed debt for 1995 are estimates based on the original terms of the loans and augmented by creditor source information. Short-term debt data are World Bank staff estimates.

Rescheduling. Projected debt service is based on contractual obligations on debt outstanding at the end of 1995. It includes the effect of the Paris Club agreements of 1985 and 1987.

Debt reduction. Debt outstanding at end-1991 reflects debt forgiveness of $101 million by the United Arab Emirates in 1983 and $32.4 million by the Arab Fund in 1987.

Sri Lanka

Data source. Data on long-term public and publicly guaranteed and private nonguaranteed debt for 1995 are based on reports provided by the country. Short-term debt data are from the BIS semiannual series on international bank lending and short-term export credits from the OECD.

St. Kitts and Nevis

Data source. Data on long-term public and publicly guaranteed debt for 1995 are based on reports provided by the country. Short-term debt data are from the BIS semiannual series on international bank lending and short-term export credits from the OECD.

St. Lucia

Data source. Data on long-term public and publicly guaranteed debt for 1995 are based on reports provided by the country. Short-term debt data are from the BIS semiannual series on international bank lending and short-term export credits from the OECD.

Debt reduction. As part of its Caribbean Initiative, Canada forgave all official development assistance loans, about $0.4 million, in 1991.

St. Vincent and the Grenadines

Data source. Data on long-term public and publicly guaranteed debt for 1995 are based on reports provided by the country. Short-term debt data are from the BIS semiannual series on international bank lending and short-term export credits from the OECD.

Debt reduction. As part of its Caribbean Initiative, Canada forgave all official development assistance loans, about $0.8 million, in 1990.

Sudan

Data source. Data on long-term public and publicly guaranteed and private nonguaranteed debt for 1995 are estimates based on the original terms of the loans and augmented by creditor source information. Short-term debt data are from the BIS semiannual series on international bank lending and short-term export credits from the OECD.

Rescheduling. Projected debt service is based on contractual obligations on debt outstanding at the end of 1995. It includes the effect of all London and Paris Club agreements concluded since 1979 as well as various bilateral rescheduling arrangements. These include agreements with centrally planned economies in 1981 and 1985–86 and with OPEC countries in 1987–88. In 1985 the former Soviet Union rescheduled $28.5 million of long-term debt, and in 1986 Poland and the former Yugoslavia each rescheduled $20.1 million of long-term debt. In 1987 the United Arab Emirates rescheduled 19 million dirhams of principal and interest arrears and wrote off 88 million dirhams of outstanding debt. In 1988 Saudi Arabia rescheduled 65 million riyals of principal and interest arrears and wrote off 79 million riyals.

Swaziland

Data source. Data on long-term public and publicly guaranteed debt for 1995 are preliminary, based on partial reports provided by the country. Short-term debt data are from the BIS semiannual series on international bank lending and short-term export credits from the OECD.

Syrian Arab Republic

Data source. Data on long-term public and publicly guaranteed debt for 1995 are estimates based on the original terms of the loans and include only civilian debt. Data on noncivilian debt, which is substantial and owed mainly to Eastern European countries, are estimates using creditor source information. Short-term debt are World Bank staff estimates.

Tajikistan

Data source. Data on long-term public and publicly guaranteed debt for 1995 are estimates based on creditor source information. Short-term debt data are from the BIS semiannual series on international bank lending and short-term export credits from the OECD.

Rescheduling. In 1993, $18 million of technical credits were rescheduled with Kazakstan.

Tanzania

Data source. Data on long-term public and publicly guaranteed debt for 1995 are based on reports provided by the country. Long-term private nonguaranteed debt data are World Bank staff estimates. Short-term debt data are from the BIS semiannual series on international bank lending and short-term export credits from the OECD.

Rescheduling. Projected debt service is based on contractual obligations on debt outstanding at the end of 1995. It includes the effects of all signed Paris Club agreements until the end of 1995.

Thailand

Data source. Data on long-term public and publicly guaranteed and private nonguaranteed debt for 1995 are based on preliminary reports provided by the country. Short-term debt data are World Bank staff estimates and exclude Bangkok International Banking Facility (BIBF) commercial bank transactions.

Prepayments. Principal repayments include the following prepayments to commercial bank creditors: 1985, $390 million; 1986, $670 million; 1987, $300 million; 1988, $974 million; 1989, $551 million; 1990, $486 million; 1993, $763 million; 1994, $1147 million; and 1995, $558 million.

Togo

Data source. Data on long-term public and publicly guaranteed debt for 1995 are based on reports provided by the country. Short-term debt data are from the BIS semiannual series on international bank lending and short-term export credits from the OECD.

Rescheduling. Projected debt service is based on contractual obligations on debt outstanding at the end of 1995. It includes the effect of all signed Paris Club agreements and commercial bank arrangements until the end of 1995.

Tonga

Data source. Data on long-term public and publicly guaranteed debt for 1995 are based on reports provided by the country. Short-term debt data are from the BIS semiannual series on international bank lending and short-term export credits from the OECD.

Trinidad and Tobago

Data source. Data on long-term public and publicly guaranteed debt for 1995 are based on reports provided by the country. Long-term private nonguarantee debt data are World Bank staff estimates. Short-term debt data are from the BIS semiannual series on international bank lending and short-term export credits from the OECD.

Rescheduling. In 1989 an agreement was reached with commercial banks to reschedule $702 million in two tranches over four years, of which $54 million refer to principal payments in 1992.

Debt reduction. In 1993 the reduction in long-term debt amounted to $40 million because of a debt conversion to local currency that was part of the 1989 commercial bank agreement. In 1991, $7 million was forgiven; in 1992, $30 million; and in 1993, $10 million.

Tunisia

Data source. Data on long-term public and publicly guaranteed debt for 1995 are preliminary, based on partial reports provided by the country and World Bank staff estimates. Private nonguaranteed debt are World Bank staff estimates. Short-term debt data are from the BIS semiannual series on international bank lending and short-term export credits from the OECD.

Turkey

Data source. Data on long-term public and publicly guaranteed, private nonguaranteed, and short-term debt for 1995 are based on reports provided by the country.

Nonresident deposits. Long-term debt data include nonresident deposits made under the Dresdner Bank scheme, amounting to $6.3 billion at end-1990, $5.7 billion at end-1991, $5.8 billion at end-1992, $6.3 billion at end-1993, $8.3 billion at end-1994, and $10.4 billion at end-1995.

Turkmenistan

Data source. Data on long-term public and publicly guaranteed debt for 1995 are based on reports provided by the country. Short-term debt data are from the BIS semiannual series on international bank lending and short-term export credits from the OECD.

Uganda

Data source. Data on long-term public and publicly guaranteed debt for 1995 are based on reports provided by the country and World Bank staff estimates. Short-term debt data are from the BIS semiannual series on international bank lending and short-term export credits from the OECD.

Rescheduling. Projected debt service is based on contractual obligations on debt outstanding at the end of 1995. It includes the effect of the Paris Club agreement signed in February 1995.

Debt reduction. In 1993 Uganda bought back $149 million of debt at a discount of 88 percent under the IDA Debt Reduction Facility.

Ukraine

Data source. Data on long-term public and publicly guaranteed and private nonguaranteed debt for 1995 are based on reports provided by the country. Short-term debt data are from the BIS semiannual series on international bank lending and short-term export credits from the OECD.

Rescheduling. A total of $2,528 million of technical credits were rescheduled under agreements with Moldova in 1993 and the Russian Federation in 1993 and 1995.

Uruguay

Data source. Data on long-term public and publicly guaranteed and private non-guaranteed debt for 1995 are based on reports provided by the country. Short-term debt data are World Bank staff estimates.

Rescheduling. Projected debt service are based on contractual obligations on debt outstanding at the end of 1995. It includes the effect of the commercial bank rescheduling of 1988, and the DDSR of 1991.

Debt reduction. The debt reductions in 1987-89 amount to $229 million of debt-equity swaps. Principal repayments in 1991 include a $284 million cash payment in connection with a debt buy back, which retired $506 million of debt outstanding. Debt data also reflect forgiveness of $16 million by the United States in 1993.

Uzbekistan

Data source. Data on long-term public and publicly guaranteed debt for 1995 are based on reports provided by the country. Short-term debt data are from the BIS semiannual series on international bank lending and short-term export credits from the OECD.

Rescheduling. In 1993 a total of $321 million of trade credits were rescheduled with Kazakstan ($46.4 million) and the Russian Federation ($275.0 million).

Vanuatu

Data source. Data on long-term public and publicly guaranteed debt for 1995 are as reported by the country. Short-term debt data are from the BIS semiannual series on international bank lending and short-term export credits from the OECD.

Venezuela

Data source. Data on long-term public and publicly guaranteed debt for 1995 are preliminary, based on partial reports provided by the country. Long-term private nonguaranteed debt data are World Bank staff estimates. Short-term debt data are from the BIS semiannual series on international bank lending and short-term export credits from the OECD.

Rescheduling. Data reflect the 1990 DDSR with commercial banks. The operation converted $18.3 billion into bonds and $1.4 billion into short-term notes. In addition, Venezuela obtained $1.2 billion of new money, of which $600 million was disbursed in 1990, $295 million in 1991, and $296 million in 1992.

Debt reduction. Principal repayments for 1990 include $634 million of cash payment to buy back debt outstanding under the commercial bank debt restructuring agreement. Total reduction in debt outstanding to commercial banks through various programs at the end of 1993 reached $3.9 billion. The reduction was $47 million in 1988, $656 million in 1989, $2.4 billion in 1990, $565 million in 1991, $204 million in 1992, and $18 million in 1993.

Vietnam

Data source. Data on long-term public and publicly guaranteed and short-term debt for 1995 are preliminary, based on partial reports provided by the country and World Bank staff estimates. Debt data include convertible and nonconvertible currency debt. Of this, the transferable ruble obligations comprised about 11.5 billion Rubles (including interest arrears) at the end of 1995.

Debt rescheduling. Projected debt service is based on contractual obligations and existing terms on debt outstanding at the end of 1995. It includes the effect of the Paris Club agreement signed in December 1993.

Western Samoa

Data source. Data on long-term public and publicly guaranteed debt for 1995 are based on reports provided by the country. Short-term debt data are from the BIS semiannual series on international bank lending and short-term export credits from the OECD.

Yemen, Republic of

Data source. Data on long-term public and publicly guaranteed debt for 1995 are based on reports provided by the country. Short-term debt data are from the BIS semiannual series on international bank lending and short-term export credits from the OECD.

Yugoslavia, former

Data source. Data on long-term public and publicly guaranteed and private nonguaranteed debt for 1995 are estimates and reflect borrowings by the former Yugoslavia that are not yet allocated to the various republics. Short-term data are from the BIS semiannual series on international bank lending and short-term export credits from the OECD.

Debt reduction. The debt reduction of 1988–91 consisted of buybacks of $128 million in 1988, $610 million in 1989, $1.5 billion in 1990, and $554 million in 1991.

Other. In 1992 Yugoslavia split into several republics; information on debt outstanding by the various republics is shown in the country tables for Croatia, Macedonia FYR, and Slovenia. External debt obligations, excluding IBRD, IMF, and short-term, of Bosnia and Herzegovina are included under Yugoslavia, former.

Zaire

Data source. Data on long-term public and publicly guaranteed debt for 1995 are estimates based on the original terms of the loans. Short-term debt data are from the BIS semiannual series on international bank lending and short-term export credits from the OECD.

Rescheduling. Projected debt service is based on contractual obligations on debt outstanding at the end of 1995. It includes the effect of the back-to-back agreements with the Paris Club since 1976, a London Club rescheduling agreement in 1980, and a Kinshasa Club rescheduling agreement, covering uninsured commercial and suppliers credits, in 1984.

Debt reduction. Debt outstanding was reduced by $29 million in 1989 and $9 million in 1990 as a result of debt forgiveness.

Zambia

Data source. Data on long-term public and publicly guaranteed, private nonguaranteed, and short-term debt for 1995 are preliminary, based on partial non-standard reports provided by the country.

Rescheduling. Projected debt service is based on contractual obligations on debt outstanding at the end of 1995. It includes the effects of the Paris Club agreements of 1986, 1989, and 1992.

Debt reduction. Debt outstanding was reduced by $11.4 million in 1990, $14.8 million in 1991, and $45.3 million in 1992 as a result of debt forgiveness. In 1994 Zambia bought back $181 million of debt at a discount of 89 percent under the IDA Debt Reduction Facility.

Zimbabwe

Data source. Data on long-term public and private nonguaranteed debt for 1995 are based on reports provided by the country. Short-term debt data are from the BIS semiannual series on international bank lending and short-term export credits from the OECD.

Order Form

CUSTOMERS IN THE UNITED STATES

Complete this coupon and return to:

The World Bank
Box 7247-8619
Philadelphia, PA 19170-8619
USA.

To have your order shipped faster, charge by credit card by calling (202) 473-1155 or send this competed order coupon by facsimile by dialing (202) 522-2627.

CUSTOMERS OUTSIDE THE UNITED STATES

Contact your local Bank publications distributor for information on prices in local currency and payment terms. If no distributor is listed for your country, use this order form and return it to the U.S. address. Orders that are sent to the U.S. address from countries with distributors will be returned to the customer.

Quantity	Title	Stock #	Price	Total price

Subtotal cost US$ ________

Shipping and handling* US$ ________

Total US$ ________

* SHIPPING AND HANDLING charges are $5.00 per order. If a purchase order is used, actual shipping will be charged. For air mail delivery outside the United Sates, add $8.00 for one item plus $6.00 for each additional item.

CHECK METHOD OF PAYMENT

❑ Enclosed is my check payable to the World Bank.

❑ Charge my ❑ VISA ❑ MasterCard ❑ American Express

Credit card account number

Expiration Date

Signature (required to validate all orders)

❑ Bill me. (Institutional customers only. Purchase order must be included.)

PLEASE PRINT CLEARLY

Name ________

Address ________

____

City ________ State ________ Postal code ________

Country ________ Telephone ________

Distributors of World Bank Publications

Prices and credit terms vary from country to country. Consult your local distributor before placing an order.

ARGENTINA
Oficina del Libro Internacional
Av. Cordoba 1877
1120 Buenos Aires
Tel: (54 1) 815-8354
Fax: (54 1) 815-8156

AUSTRALIA, FIJI, PAPUA NEW GUINEA, SOLOMON ISLANDS, VANUATU, AND WESTERN SAMOA
D.A. Information Services
648 Whitehorse Road
Mitcham 3132
Victoria
Tel: (61) 3 9210 7777
Fax: (61) 3 9210 7788
E-mail: service@dadirect.com.au
URL: http://www .dadirect.com.au

AUSTRIA
Gerold and Co.
Weihburggasse 26
A-1011 Wien
Tel: (43 1) 512-47-31-0
Fax: (43 1) 512-47-31-29
URL: http://www .gerold.co/at.online

BANGLADESH
Micro Industries Development Assistance Society (MIDAS)
House 5, Road 16
Dhanmondi R/Area
Dhaka 1209
Tel: (880 2) 326427
Fax: (880 2) 811188

BELGIUM
Jean De Lannoy
Av. du Roi 202
1060 Brussels
Tel: (32 2) 538-5169
Fax: (32 2) 538-0841

BRAZIL
Publicacões Tecnicas Internacionais Ltda.
Rua Peixoto Gomide, 209
01409 Sao Paulo, SP.
Tel: (55 11) 259-6644
Fax: (55 11) 258-6990
E-mail: postmaster@pti.uol.br
URL: http://www .uol.br

CANADA
Renouf Publishing Co. Ltd.
5369 Canotek Road
Ottawa, Ontario K1J 9J3
Tel: (613) 745-2665
Fax: (613) 745-7660
E-mail: renouf@fox.nstn.ca
URL: http:// www .fox.nstn.ca/~renouf

CHINA
China Financial & Economic Publishing House
8, Da Fo Si Dong Jie
Beijing
Tel: (86 10) 6333-8257
Fax: (86 10) 6401-7365

COLOMBIA
Infoenlace Ltda.
Carrera 6 No. 51-21
Apartado Aereo 34270
Santafé de Bogotá, D.C.
Tel: (57 1) 285-2798
Fax: (57 1) 285-2798

CYPRUS
Center for Applied Research
Cyprus College
6, Diogenes Street, Engomi
P.O. Box 2006
Nicosia
Tel: (357 2) 44-1730
Fax: (357 2) 46-2051

CZECH REPUBLIC
National Information Center
prodejna, Konviktska 5
CS – 113 57 Prague 1
Tel: (42 2) 2422-9433
Fax: (42 2) 2422-1484
URL: http://www .nis.cz/

DENMARK
SamfundsLitteratur
Rosenoerns Allé 11
DK-1970 Frederiksberg C
Tel: (45 31) 351942
Fax: (45 31) 357822

EGYPT, ARAB REPUBLIC OF
Al Ahram Distribution Agency
Al Galaa Street
Cairo
Tel: (20 2) 578-6083
Fax: (20 2) 578-6833

The Middle East Observer
41, Sherif Street
Cairo
Tel: (20 2) 393-9732
Fax: (20 2) 393-9732

FINLAND
Akateeminen Kirjakauppa
P.O. Box 128
FIN-00101 Helsinki
Tel: (358 0) 12141
Fax: (358 0) 121-4441
URL: http://booknet.cultnet.fi/aka/

FRANCE
World Bank Publications
66, avenue d'Iéna
75116 Paris
Tel: (33 1) 40-69-30-56/57
Fax: (33 1) 40-69-30-68

GERMANY
UNO-Verlag
Poppelsdorfer Allee 55
53115 Bonn
Tel: (49 228) 212940
Fax: (49 228) 217492

GREECE
Papasotiriou S.A.
35, Stoumara Str.
106 82 Athens
Tel: (30 1) 364-1826
Fax: (30 1) 364-8254

HAITI
Culture Diffusion
5, Rue Capois
C.P. 257
Port-au-Prince
Tel: (509 1) 3 9260

HONG KONG, MACAO
Asia 2000 Ltd.
Sales & Circulation Department
Seabird House, unit 1101-02
22-28 Wyndham Street, Central
Hong Kong
Tel: (852) 2530-1409
Fax: (852) 2526-1107
E-mail: sales@asia2000.com.hk
URL: http://www .asia2000.com.hk

INDIA
Allied Publishers Ltd.
751 Mount Road
Madras - 600 002
Tel: (91 44) 852-3938
Fax: (91 44) 852-0649

INDONESIA
Pt. Indira Limited
Jalan Borobudur 20
P.O. Box 181
Jakarta 10320
Tel: (62 21) 390-4290
Fax: (62 21) 421-4289

IRAN
Ketab Sara Co. Publishers
Khaled Eslamboli Ave.,
6th Street
Kusheh Delafrooz No. 8
P.O. Box 15745-733
Tehran
Tel: (98 21) 8717819; 8716104
Fax: (98 21) 8712479
E-mail: ketab-sara@neda.net.ir

Kowkab Publishers
P.O. Box 19575-511
Tehran
Tel: (98 21) 258-3723
Fax: (98 21) 258-3723

IRELAND
Government Supplies Agency
Oifig an tSoláthair
4-5 Harcourt Road
Dublin 2
Tel: (353 1) 661-3111
Fax: (353 1) 475-2670

ISRAEL
Yozmot Literature Ltd.
P.O. Box 56055
3 Yohanan Hasandlar Street
Tel Aviv 61560
Tel: (972 3) 5285-397
Fax: (972 3) 5285-397

R.O.Y. International
PO Box 13056
Tel Aviv 61130
Tel: (972 3) 5461423
Fax: (972 3) 5461442
E-mail: royil@netvision.net.il

Palestinian Authority/Middle East
Index Information Services
P.O.B. 19502 Jerusalem
Tel: (972 2) 6271219
Fax: (972 2) 6271634

ITALY
Licosa Commissionaria Sansoni SPA
Via Duca Di Calabria, 1/1
Casella Postale 552
50125 Firenze
Tel: (55) 645-415
Fax: (55) 641-257
E-mail: licosa@ftbcc.it
Url: http://www .ftbcc.it/licosa

JAMAICA
Ian Randle Publishers Ltd.
206 Old Hope Road
Kingston 6
Tel: 809-927-2085
Fax: 809-977-0243
E-mail: irpl@colis.com

JAPAN
Eastern Book Service
3-13 Hongo 3-chome, Bunkyo-ku
Tokyo 113
Tel: (81 3) 3818-0861
Fax: (81 3) 3818-0864
E-mail: svt-ebs@ppp.bekkoame.or .jp
URL: http://www .bekkoame.or.jp/~svt-ebs

KENYA
Africa Book Service (E.A.) Ltd.
Quaran House, Mfangano Street
P.O. Box 45245
Nairobi
Tel: (254 2) 223 641
Fax: (254 2) 330 272

KOREA, REPUBLIC OF
Daejon Trading Co. Ltd.
P.O. Box 34, Youida
706 Seoun Bldg
44-6 Youido-Dong, Yeongchengpo-Ku
Seoul
Tel: (82 2) 785-1631/4
Fax: (82 2) 784-0315

MALAYSIA
University of Malaya Cooperative Bookshop, Limited
P.O. Box 1127
Jalan Pantai Baru
59700 Kuala Lumpur
Tel: (60 3) 756-5000
Fax: (60 3) 755-4424

MEXICO
INFOTEC
Av. San Fernando No. 37
Col. Toriello Guerra
14050 Mexico, D.F.
Tel: (52 5) 624-2800
Fax: (52 5) 624-2822
E-mail: infotec@rtn.net.mx
URL: http://rtn.net.mx

NEPAL
Everest Media International Services (P.) Ltd.
GPO Box 5443
Kathmandu
Tel: (977 1) 472 152
Fax: (977 1) 224 431

NETHERLANDS
De Lindeboom/InOr-Publikaties
P.O. Box 202
7480 AE Haaksbergen
Tel: (31 53) 574-0004
Fax: (31 53) 572-9296
E-mail: lindeboo@worldonline.nl
URL: http://www .worldonline.nl~lindeboo

NEW ZEALAND
EBSCO NZ Ltd.
Private Mail Bag 99914
New Market
Auckland
Tel: (64 9) 524-8119
Fax: (64 9) 524-8067

NIGERIA
University Press Limited
Three Crowns Building Jericho
Private Mail Bag 5095
Ibadan
Tel: (234 22) 41-1356
Fax: (234 22) 41-2056

NORWAY
NIC Info A/S
Book Department
P.O. Box 6125 Etterstad
N-0602 Oslo 6
Tel: (47 22) 57-3300
Fax: (47 22) 68-1901

PAKISTAN
Mirza Book Agency
65, Shahrah-e-Quaid-e-Azam
Lahore 54000
Tel: (92 42) 735 3601
Fax: (92 42) 758 5283

Oxford University Press
5 Bangalore Town
Sharae Faisal
PO Box 13033
Karachi-75350
Tel: (92 21) 446307
Fax: (92 21) 4547640
E-mail: oup@oup.khi.erum.com.pk

Pak Book Corporation
Aziz Chambers 21
Queen's Road
Lahore
Tel: (92 42) 636 3222; 636 0885
Fax: (92 42) 636 2328
E-mail: pbc@brain.net.pk

PERU
Editorial Desarrollo SA
Apartado 3824
Lima 1
Tel: (51 14) 285380
Fax: (51 14) 286628

PHILIPPINES
International Booksource Center Inc.
1127-A Antipolo St.
Barangay, Venezuela
Makati City
Tel: (63 2) 896 6501; 6505; 6507
Fax: (63 2) 896 1741

POLAND
International Publishing Service
Ul. Piekna 31/37
00-677 Warzawa
Tel: (48 2) 628-6089
Fax: (48 2) 621-7255
E-mail: books%ips@ikp.atm.com.pl
URL: http://www .ipscg.waw.pl/ips/export/

PORTUGAL
Livraria Portugal
Apartado 2681
Rua Do Carmo 70-74
1200 Lisbon
Tel: (1) 347-4982
Fax: (1) 347-0264

ROMANIA
Compani De Librarii Bucuresti S.A.
Str. Lipscani no. 26, sector 3
Bucharest
Tel: (40 1) 613 9645
Fax: (40 1) 312 4000

RUSSIAN FEDERATION
Isdatelstvo <Ves Mir>
9a, Lolpachniy Pereulok
Moscow 101831
Tel: (7 095) 917 87 49
Fax: (7 095) 917 92 59

SINGAPORE, TAIWAN, MYANMAR, BRUNEI
Asahgate Publishing Asia Pacific Pte. Ltd.
41 Kallang Pudding Road #04-03
Golden Wheel Building
Singapore 349316
Tel: (65) 741-5166
Fax: (65) 742-9356
E-mail: ashgate@asianconnect.com

SLOVENIA
Gospodarski Vestnik Publishing Group
Dunajska cesta 5
1000 Ljubljana
Tel: (386 61) 133 83 47; 132 12 30
Fax: (386 61) 133 80 30
E-mail: belicd@gvestnik.si

SOUTH AFRICA, BOTSWANA
For single titles:
Oxford University Press Southern Africa
P.O. Box 1141
Cape Town 8000
Tel: (27 21) 45-7266
Fax: (27 21) 45-7265

For subscription orders:
International Subscription Service
P.O. Box 41095
Craighall
Johannesburg 2024
Tel: (27 11) 880-1448
Fax: (27 11) 880-6248
E-mail: iss@is.co.za

SPAIN
Mundi-Prensa Libros, S.A.
Castello 37
28001 Madrid
Tel: (34 1) 431-3399
Fax: (34 1) 575-3998
E-mail: libreria@mundiprensa.es
URL: http://www .mundiprensa.es/

Mundi-Prensa Barcelona
Consell de Cent, 391
08009 Barcelona
Tel: (34 3) 488-3492
Fax: (34 3) 487-7659

SRI LANKA, THE MALDIVES
Lake House Bookshop
100, Sir Chittampalam Gardiner Mawatha
Colombo 2
Tel: (94 1) 32105
Fax: (94 1) 432104

SWEDEN
Wennergren-Williams AB
P. O. Box 1305
S-171 25 Solna
Tel: (46 8) 705-97-50
Fax: (46 8) 27-00-71
E-mail: mail@wwi.se

SWITZERLAND
Librairie Payot
Service Institutionnel
Côtes-de-Montbenon 30
1002 Lausanne
Tel: (41 21) 341-3229
Fax: (41 21) 341-3235

ADECO Van Diermen Editions Techniques
Ch. de Lacuez 41
CH1807 Blonay
Tel: (41 21) 943 2673
Fax: (41 21) 943 3605

TANZANIA
Oxford University Press
Maktaba Street
PO Box 5299
Dar es Salaam
Tel: (255 51) 29209
Fax: (255 51) 46822

THAILAND
Central Books Distribution
306 Silom Road
Bangkok 10500
Tel: (66 2) 235-5400
Fax: (66 2) 237-8321

TRINIDAD & TOBAGO, AND THE CARRIBBEAN
Systematics Studies Unit
9 Watts Street
Curepe
Trinidad, West Indies
Tel: (809) 662-5654
Fax: (809) 662-5654
E-mail: tobe@trinidad.net

UGANDA
Gustro Ltd.
PO Box 9997
Madhvani Building
Plot 16/4 Jinja Rd.
Kampala
Tel: (256 41) 254 763
Fax: (256 41) 251 468

UNITED KINGDOM
Microinfo Ltd.
P.O. Box 3
Alton, Hampshire GU34 2PG
England
Tel: (44 1420) 86848
Fax: (44 1420) 89889
E-mail: wbank@ukminfo.demon.co.uk
URL: http://www .microinfo.co.uk

VENEZUELA
Tecni-Ciencia Libros, S.A.
Centro Cuidad Comercial Tamanco
Nivel C2
Caracas
Tel: (58 2) 959 5547; 5035; 0016
Fax: (58 2) 959 5636

ZAMBIA
University Bookshop
University of Zambia
Great East Road Campus
P.O. Box 32379
Lusaka
Tel: (260 1) 252 576
Fax: (260 1) 253 952

ZIMBABWE
Longman Zimbabwe (Pte.)Ltd.
Tourle Road, Ardbennie
P.O. Box ST125
Southerton
Harare
Tel: (263 4) 6216617
Fax: (263 4) 621670